cific person and the person's full name is included in the title, then the park is listed alphabetically in the main body of text according to the person's first name. For example, the Lyndon B. Johnson National Historical Park is listed alphabetically under "Lyndon," not "Johnson."

③ **Address**. The mailing address of the park (which may differ from the park's actual location) is listed here. A few parks that are staffed seasonally may include addresses of the administering regional office of the National Park Service.

④ **Web address**. The official web address is provided as available. Web addresses are also included for the administering agencies listed at the beginning of most sections.

⑤ **Phone, fax, and toll free number**. In most cases, phone and fax numbers listed are for the park units themselves. In some cases, the numbers may refer to the administering regional office. The toll free numbers are usually for campground reservations.

⑥ **Size**. If a park includes an adjoining preserve, then separate acreage figures are provided for each unit. If the reporting park unit provides separate land and water acreage, then both figures are included. For some western states, the park elevation has also been included (in feet above sea level).

⑦ **History/established date and chronology**. Information presented here includes the date the park was authorized, designated, proclaimed, and/or established. It also may include information pertaining to changes in park title or administering agency, as well as any special designations assigned to the park unit, such as Biosphere Reserve, World Heritage Site, etc.

⑧ **Location.** Includes basic information on a park's location, including a listing of major access roads (if any) or other means of transportation needed to reach park (i.e., plane, ferry, private boat, etc.).

⑨ **Facilities**. Provides information on campsites, lodging and cabin rentals, picnic areas and shelters, nature and interpretive trails, boat ramps, equipment rentals, concession areas, visitor centers, exhibits, etc. Campsites may be for recreational vehicles, tents, or both. Most are available on a first-come, first-served basis, but reservations may be required/recommended for some areas. If no camping facilities are listed in the entry, the park is considered a "day-use only" facility.

If a wheelchair icon (&) is listed parenthetically after a specific facility, it means that this facility is accessible to people in wheelchairs. A double-wheelchair icon (& &) at the end of the facilities section indicates that one or more of the facilities at the site provides disabled access. (We recommend that you call the park you are planning to visit in order to check the level of accessibility. Disabled-accessible facilities are being added every year.)

⑩ **Activities**. Describes opportunities for recreational activities at the park, such as camping, fishing, swimming, boating, hiking, horseback riding, hunting, winter sports, cultural programs, guided tours, etc. For the purposes of this directory, "picnicking" is not listed as an activity. Information relating to picnicking is, however, included in the "Facilities" section.

⑪ **Special features**. Included here are unique or outstanding characteristics of the park, including special scenic or natural features, historical or cultural attractions, etc.

Parks
DIRECTORY
of the United States
5th Edition

Parks
DIRECTORY
of the United States
5th Edition

A Guide to More Than 5,270 National and State Parks, Historic Sites, Battlefields, Monuments, Forests, Preserves, Memorials, Seashores, Trails, Heritage Areas, Scenic Byways, Marine Sanctuaries, Wildlife Refuges, Urban Parks, and Other Designated Recreation Areas in the United States Administered by National, State, and Municipal Park Agencies. Also Includes Canadian National Parks.

Darren L. Smith,
Kay Gill, *Editors*

615 Griswold Street • Detroit, MI 48226

Omnigraphics, Inc.

Darren L. Smith, *Managing Editor*
Patricia H. Cook, *Editor*
Sue Lynch, *Verification Assistant*

* * *

Peter E. Ruffner, *Publisher*
Frederick G. Ruffner, Jr., *Chairman*
Matthew P. Barbour, *Senior Vice President*
Kay Gill, *Vice President—Directories*

* * *

David P. Bianco, *Marketing Director*
Elizabeth Collins, *Research and Permissions Coordinator*
Kevin Hayes, *Operations Manager*
Barry Puckett, *Librarian*
Cherry Stockdale, *Permissions Assistant*
Allison A. Beckett, Mary Butler, and Linda Strand, *Research Staff*

Shirley Amore, Martha Johns, Kirk Kauffman,
and Johnny Lawrence, *Administrative Staff*

ISBN-13 978- 0-7808-0932-1
Printed in the United States of America

Omnigraphics, Inc.
615 Griswold Street • Detroit, MI 48226
Phone Orders: 800-234-1340 • Fax Orders: 800-875-1340
Mail Orders: P.O. Box 625 • Holmes, PA 19043
www.omnigraphics.com

Table of Contents

Introduction

Objective of the Work

The *Parks Directory of the United States* is a one-stop comprehensive reference source on parks, forests, wildlife refuges, and recreation areas administered by the National Park Service, the U.S. Forest Service, the U.S. Fish and Wildlife Service, the National Oceanic and Atmospheric Administration, the Federal Highway Administration, state and municipal park agencies, and Parks Canada.

The *Directory* provides brief descriptive information on each unit, including facilities, activities, and special features, as well as important contact information (including mailing address, phone, fax, and web addresses) to enable users to contact individual parks, park agencies, and their regional offices in order to obtain information quickly and easily. The *Directory* is especially useful in its coverage of the lesser-known areas located away from principal highways, which contain significant scenic and cultural resources of comparable quality to the more "famous" parks.

Visitors who are planning trips are encouraged to contact individual parks, forests, and wildlife refuges, or the national, state, or regional offices listed at the beginning of each section. They can provide literature or answer specific questions on entrance fee requirements, vehicle limitations, camping availability, and reservation information. Most of the individual listings throughout the *Directory* include web sites, which are excellent sources of information. Visitors centers located at the parks, forests, and refuges themselves are also a valuable source of information on attractions, facilities, and activities available on the premises and in nearby areas.

New Features

Expanded Coverage. The scope of the *Parks Directory of the United States* has been expanded with this edition to include two new sections: 1) National Scenic Byways, covering 155 "All-American" Roads and National Scenic Byways; and 2) Urban Parks, featuring 200 major parks covering 63 cities.

Entry Enhancements. More than 5,200 web addresses are now included to provide users with additional access to detailed information on each park.

Index Enhancements. The Special Features Index has been expanded to include more than 500 new citations that provide users with additional geographic and historical references that are described in the text portion of the park listings.

Definition of Terms

The *Parks Directory of the United States* provides descriptive information on 390 national parks and 24 affiliated areas, 155 national forests and 22 national grasslands, 450 national wildlife refuges, 24 national trails, 14 national marine sanctuaries, 27 national heritage programs, 155 national scenic byways, 3,410 state parks, and 200 urban parks covering all 50 states, Puerto Rico, Guam, American Samoa, and the Virgin Islands. Included also are 44 Canadian national parks and national park reserves, as well as more than 300 park- and conservation-related organizations and agencies.

The diversity of the areas listed in the *Directory* is reflected in the variety of titles given to them. Within the National Park System alone there are 20 separate designations used to classify the 390 park units. These include:

International Historic Site. 1
National Battlefields. 11
National Battlefield Parks 3
National Battlefield Sites 1
National Historic Sites 78
National Historical Parks 42
National Lakeshores. 4
National Memorials 28
National Military Parks 9
National Monuments 74
National Parks. 58
National Parkways 4
National Preserves 18
National Recreation Areas 18
National Reserves. 2
National Rivers. 5
National Scenic Trails. 3
National Seashores 10
National Wild and Scenic Rivers 10
Parks (Other). 11

—————
390

The 3,410 parks administered by state park agencies also include a variety of designations. In some states the park agency has under its control forests, fish and wildlife areas, historical parks, and other related facilities. In other states only state parks are under the state park system. This directory includes listings of those areas under the jurisdiction of each state park agency. Thus some states show fish and wildlife and forest lands, as well as historic sites, while other states do not show them, as they would be found under a separate agency of that state's government.

Park Nomenclature

The general classification system used by the U.S. Department of the Interior is a helpful guide to understanding the categories of both national and state parks described in this directory:

A **national or state park** contains a variety of resources and encompasses large land or water areas to help provide adequate protection of the resources.

A **national or state monument** is intended to preserve at least one significant resource at the national or state level. It is usually smaller than a park and lacks a park's diversity of attractions.

National and state preserves were established primarily for the protection of certain resources, though safeguards are less stringent than at parks. Activities such as hunting and fishing or the extraction of minerals and fuels may be permitted if they do not jeopardize the natural values.

Originally **national and state recreation areas** were units surrounding reservoirs impounded by dams built by other federal or state agencies. The concept of recreational areas has grown to encompass other lands and waters set aside for recreational use by acts of Congress and state legislatures and now includes major areas in urban centers.

Preserving shoreline areas and offshore islands, the **lakeshores** and **seashores** focus on the preservation of natural values while at the same time providing water-oriented recreation. Other areas set aside for the protection of shorelines and coastal areas, as well as for recreational use, include **state beaches**, **state marine parks**, and **state underwater parks**.

Although best known for their great scenic parks, more than half the areas of the National Park System and a great many parks in the state systems preserve places and commemorate persons, events, and activities important in national or state history. These range from archeological sites associated with prehistoric Indian civilizations to sites related to the lives of modern Americans. In recent years, the title **national or state historical site** has been commonly applied in authorizing the addition of such areas to the national and state park systems.

A wide variety of titles—**military park**, **battlefield park**, **battlefield site**, and **battlefield** — have been used for areas associated with American military history, but other areas such as **monuments** and **historical parks** may also include features associated with military history. Historical parks are usually areas of greater physical extent and complexity than historic sites.

The term **memorial** is most often used for areas that are primarily commemorative. However, these need not be sites or structures historically associated with their subjects. For example, the home of Abraham Lincoln in Springfield, Illinois, is a national historic site, but the Lincoln Memorial in the District of Columbia is a national memorial.

Other less common classification categories include **trails**, **parkways**, **rivers**, and **wild and scenic rivers** at the national level, and **conservation areas** and **conservation parks**, **waysides**, **fish and wildlife areas**, **archeological sites**, **geological sites**, **reserves**, **wildernesses**, **reservations**, **vehicular recreation areas**, **gardens** and **arboreta**, and some **forests**, at the state level.

Other public land and water areas described in this directory fall under the jurisdiction of other federal government agencies. The USDA Forest Service manages **national forests** as public land designated by Congress to provide "sustained yields" of renewable resources, such as water, wood, recreation, forage, wilderness, and wildlife. The Forest Service also manages **national grasslands**, revegetated areas that provide for soil and water conservation as well as the protection of important wildlife habitat.

The U.S. Fish and Wildlife Service maintains a system of **national wildlife refuges,** which are unique and highly diverse lands and waters managed for the conservation and enhancement of fish and wildlife and their habitats. Marine areas identified for their biodiversity, ecological integrity, and cultural legacy are designated as **national marine sanctuaries** through NOAA's National Marine Sanctuary Program. Congress has designated **national heritage areas**, which are regions in which entire communities live and work, and in which residents, businesses, and local governments have come together to conserve special landscapes and their own heritage.

The Federal Highway Administration maintains the National Scenic Byways Program, a grass-roots collaborative effort established to help recognize, preserve, and enhance selected roads throughout the United States. The U.S. Secretary of Transportation recognizes certain roads as **All-American Roads** or **National Scenic Byways** based on one of more archeological, cultural, historic, natural, recreational and scenic qualities.

Parks Canada is the government agency responsible for managing a system of Canadian national parks, national historic sites, and other heritage places. Currently there are 44 **national parks** and **national park reserves** in Canada, located in every province and territory.

Arrangement and Content of Entries

The main body of *Parks Directory of the United States* is divided into eleven main sections:

1. The **National Parks** section includes descriptive listings of 390 park units and 24 affiliated areas. Arrangement is alphabetical by park name, with the affiliated areas listed at the end of the section. Entries include the name, address, phone number, fax number, and web site for each park, its location, acreage, established date, facilities, activities, and special features. (See sample National Parks entry on inside front cover of book.)

2. The **Canadian National Parks** section features 44 national parks and national park reserves in Canada, located in every province and territory. Arrangement is alphabetical by park name. Entries include the name, address, phone number, fax number, and web site for each park, its location, acreage, established date, facilities, activities, and special features.

3. The **National Forests and Grasslands** section has descriptive listings of 155 forests and 22 grasslands and is arranged alphabetically by unit name, with the forests listed first, followed by the grasslands. Entries include the name, address, phone number, fax number, and web site for each forest, its acreage, location, facilities, activities, and special features.

4. The **National Wildlife Refuges** section provides descriptive listings of 450 wildlife refuges and is arranged alphabetically by refuge name. Entries include the name, address, phone number, fax number, and web site for each wildlife refuge, its location, habitat, facilities, activities, access, primary wildlife, and special features.

5. The **National Trails** section includes 24 national scenic and historic trails and is arranged alphabetically by trail name. Entries include the name of the trail, the address, web site, phone and fax number for each administering agency, and the trail's length, established date, and description.

6. The **National Marine Sanctuaries** section provides information on the National Marine Sanctuaries Program and the 14 designated sanctuaries. The section is arranged alphabetically by sanctuary name, and entries include the year designated, location, description, facilities, activities, habitat, common species, and environmental issues.

7. The **National Heritage Areas** section provides information on the National Heritage Areas Program and includes descriptive listings of 27 national heritage areas. It is arranged alphabetically by heritage area name, and entries include the name, address, phone number, fax number, and web site for each national heritage area, along with its location and special features.

8. The **National Scenic Byways** section provides information on the National Scenic Byways Program and includes descriptive listings of 155 national scenic byways and "All-American" roads. It is arranged alphabetically by state and then by byway name within each state. Entries

include the name of the byway, the address, phone number and web site of the affiliated agency, along with the year designated, type of byway, location, description, start/endpoints, and approximate drive time.

9. The **State Parks** section includes descriptive listings of 3,410 park units. Arrangement is by state and then alphabetical by park name within each state. The address and phone number of each state park division are listed at the beginning of each state section. Entries include the name, address, phone number, fax number, and web site for each park, its acreage, location, facilities, activities, special features, and special events.

10. The **Urban Parks** section has descriptive listings of 200 major urban parks and is arranged alphabetically by city and then by park name within each city. Entries include the name, address, phone number, and web site for each park, along with its acreage, location, facilities, activities, and special features.

11. The **Park- and Conservation-Related Organizations** section provides descriptions of 300+ associations and agencies that are concerned with the conservation, protection, and recreational usage of parklands in the United States and Canada. Entries are arranged alphabetically by organization name.

The editors have endeavored to present the information in this directory in the most consistent and standardized manner possible. However, with the number of different types of units described, the specific categories of information vary slightly from section to section. For example, in the national wildlife refuge section, it is important to provide information on access and primary wildlife; in the national trails section, trail length is more relevant than acreage, and so on.

Though categories of information may vary slightly from section to section, the format is generally consistent within each section. The one exception to this is that the classification of campsites varies considerably from state to state due to the fact that each state park agency has established its own set of criteria for classifying campgrounds. For example, state park campsites in Indiana are designated as Class AA, A, B, and C, based on the types of facilities available, while in Pennsylvania they are classified as A, B, and A/B. In Michigan, campsites are defined as modern, semi-modern, and rustic; in Louisiana, as improved and unimproved; in Washington, as utility and standard. Other states designate campsites "with hookups" or "without hookups," "developed" or "primitive," "family," "group" or "youth," etc. Because of this diversity, no attempt has been made to change or standardize the terminology used by each state agency with regard to its campsites. In cases where specific terminology is used in the text to describe a state's campsite, a "key to campsite classification" is provided at the beginning of that section.

Following the main body of listings are four separate indexes: Classification Index, Special Features Index, Geographic Index, and Master Index. Refer to page 10 for detailed information on each index.

Maps

Two types of maps are included in this Directory: 1) a 12-page section of color maps (beginning on page 15) that graphically depicts all the U.S. National Parks, National Forests, National Wildlife Refuges, National Trails, Marine Sanctuaries, as well as the Canadian National Parks; and 2) the State Parks section (beginning on page 273), which includes maps for the 50 states, each pinpointing the various state park units described there. An alphabetical list of parks and corresponding map grids are included with each state's map.

Acknowledgments

The editors are grateful to thank the National Park Service, the U.S. Forest Service, the U.S. Fish and Wildlife Service, Parks Canada, the National Oceanic and Atmospheric Administration, the Federal Highway Administration as well as all the state and municipal park agencies and other conservation organizations that have supplied information needed to produce this directory.

Comments and suggestions are welcome. Please send to:

Editor
Parks Directory of the United States
Omnigraphics, Inc.
615 Griswold Street
Detroit, MI 48226
800-234-1340
www.omnigraphics.com
or e-mail to: parks-editorial@omnigraphics.com

Explanation of Indexes

The *Parks Directory of the United States* features four separate indexes:

1) **Classification Index.** An alphabetical index of all parks, subdivided by type of park (i.e. national park, state park, recreation area, historical monument, etc.). A table explaining the classification system used in this index is provided on page 949.

2) **Special Features Index.** An alphabetical list of geographic and historical references described in the text portion of the park listings, such as references to a particular battle, a fort, a historical personage, a mountain peak, etc.

3) **Geographic Index.** A state-by-state list of all the parks, forests, refuges, historic sites, and other properties, agencies, and organizations covered in the main body of the directory. Canadian national parks are arranged alphabetically by province and appear at the end of the U.S. state listings.

4) The **Master Index.** An alphabetical list of all the parks described in the directory.

In all four indexes, reference is to *entry number* rather than to page number.

Several national parks, forests, and trails are located in more than one state. In the Geographic Index, these multi-state listings are identified by a star (★) and separate listings are included under each state. For example, the Appalachian National Scenic Trail, which extends from Maine to Georgia, is listed in the Geographic Index under 14 different states. In the Classification and Master indexes, the two-letter state code listed parenthetically after an entry corresponds to the state that encompasses the largest portion of the park unit, or, in the case of a trail, the two-letter state code corresponds to the primary non-profit organization that serves as a partner in the development and maintenance of the trail. For example, Yellowstone National Park has portions in Idaho and Montana, but most of the park is located in Wyoming so it would be listed with (WY). In the case of the Appalachian Trail, the main office of the Appalachian Trail Conference is located in West Virginia, and therefore the index citation for the Appalachian National Scenic Trail would be (WV).

If a national or state park unit has multiple designations, then separate listings are provided for each in the Classification Index. For example, Lake Clark National Park and Preserve is listed as both a park and a preserve.

If two park units are listed as a single entry in the main body of text, separate listings are provided in the indexes. For example, the following index citations are given for Forestville/Mystery Cave State Park in Minnesota:

Parks named to commemorate individuals are generally indexed under both first and last names if both names appear in the title. For example: Richard B. Russell State Park in Georgia would include the following index citations:

In the Special Features Index, references are presented alphabetically by state and then by the entry number applicable for each state:

How to Order Park Entrance Passes

New Interagency Program

In January of 2007 the National Parks Pass was replaced by a new Interagency Annual Pass that combines several previously available federal recreation passes. The new pass, named "America the Beautiful – National Parks and Federal Recreational Lands Pass," covers recreation opportunities on public lands managed by five federal agencies: National Park Service, Fish and Wildlife Service, Bureau of Land Management, Bureau of Reclamation, and U.S. Forest Service.

Features of the new Interagency Pass:

- Costs $80 and is valid for one full year from month of purchase.

- Provides entrance or access to pass holder and accompanying passengers in a single, private, non-commercial vehicle at Federally operated recreation sites across the country.

- Covers the pass holder and three accompanying adults age 16 and older at sites where per person entrance fees are charged. No entry fees are charged for children 15 and under.

- May require photo identification to verify ownership.

- Passes are non-refundable, non-transferable, and cannot be replaced if lost or stolen.

The Annual Interagency Pass does not cover concessions or other use fees such as parking, campgrounds, shuttles, boat launches, or interpretive tours. Since fees vary widely across the thousands of federal recreation sites, it is recommended that those interested in obtaining a pass contact specific sites directly to find out exactly what is or is not covered.

One hundred percent of the revenue derived from passes sold at federal recreation sites will directly benefit the selling agency, and no less than 80 percent of the revenue will remain at the site where the pass was sold.

The Interagency Annual Pass can be purchased: 1) at federal recreation sites that charge entrance and standard amenity fees; 2) online through the government's federal lands recreation web portal at www.recreation.gov or at store.usgs.gov/pass; or 3) by calling 1-888-275-8747, ext 1. It is expected that the Annual Pass also will be available through some third-party partners.

The new Interagency Annual Pass replaces the National Parks Pass, Golden Eagle, and National Parks Pass with Golden Eagle Hologram. National Parks Passes purchased in 2006 will expire 12 months from the date of first use.

Other Interagency Passes

Three other passes in the new interagency program include:

- a $10 lifetime Senior Pass for U.S. citizens 62 or over;

- a free lifetime Access Pass for citizens with permanent disabilities; and

- a free annual Volunteer Pass for volunteers acquiring 500 hours of service on a cumulative basis.

The Senior Pass replaces the Golden Age Passport and still remains $10.00. The Access Pass replaces the Golden Access Pass and still remains free to individuals with documented proof of permanent disability. All old Golden Age and Golden Access passes remain valid for lifetime — there is no need to obtain a replacement Senior or Access Pass. The new Senior and Access Passes can be obtained with proper documentation at Federal recreation sites that charge an Entrance or Standard Amenity Fee. To locate the nearest recreation site, visit www.recreation.gov. It's a good idea to call ahead before visiting the site to be sure there is an inventory on hand.

Canadian Park Passes

Parks Canada offers three different passes that allow visitors to explore many of the natural and historic areas of Canada: 1) the annual **National Parks of Canada Pass** permits unlimited access into 27 of Canada's national parks; 2) an annual **National Historic Sites of Canada Pass** provides entry into 78 of Canada's national historic sites; and 3) the **Discovery Package** includes passes for both the national parks and the national historic sites of Canada, giving visitors access to Parks Canada's extensive national system. All three passes are good for a period of 12 months from the month of purchase.

Passes are non-transferable and are valid for entry only and not for other Parks Canada services or facilities. They are available at different price levels for individuals, seniors, youth (ages 6-16), and families/groups, and may be purchased at participating national parks and historic sites. For further information, contact Parks Canada by phone at 888-773-8888 (toll-free for North America) or by e-mail at information@pc.gc.ca.

Job Opportunities at the National Parks

The National Park Service (NPS) offers many professional, volunteer, and trade opportunities across the country. From parks to regional offices, the Park Service employs more than 20,000 individuals (permanent and temporary) and receives additional support from 90,000 volunteers.

In order to be eligible for consideration for employment with NPS, a person must be a United States citizen. Certain jobs may also have age and physical qualifications; generally, applicants must be at least 18 years of age. The National Park Service fills all positions in accordance with U.S. Office of Personnel Management (OPM) regulations. Normally, a person seeking an initial appointment to a permanent position must gain eligibility on an appropriate OPM register.

For current information on job openings, pay scales, and application requirements, visit the Office of Personnel Management's USAJOBS site at www.usajobs.opm.gov; or contact the OPM by mail or by telephone:

United States Office of Personnel Management:
1900 E Street, NW
Washington, DC 20415
(202) 606-1800
1-800-336-4562
www.opm.gov

Specific information on application requirements and job openings in different areas of the country is available from NPS regional offices. A complete list of the regional offices, with full contact information, is provided on page 27 of this directory. Information on current volunteer/permanent positions can be obtained directly from national parks offices (see pages 27-98 for a complete list of parks).

How Jobs Are Filled

Federal agencies, including the National Park Service, fill jobs in several ways. Not all jobs are open to external applicants. Agencies can: promote an employee; hire an employee who wants to transfer from another agency; reinstate a former Federal employee; or request the names of applicants from an OPM register.

National Park Service Employment Information General Resource Bulletins provide general information on employment opportunities for permanent, seasonal, and student jobs, along with instructions on how to prepare an application for Federal Government employment and other helpful information for job seekers. Further information is available on the web at www.nps.gov/personnel/general-resource-bulletins/general_bulletins.htm.

Additional information on National Park Service jobs, including a career guide, is available online at www.nps.gov/personnel. For information on the NPS Seasonal Employment Program, or to apply online, go to www.sep.nps.gov; or call 877-554-4550.

Your Application

For those pursuing a Federal Government position for the first time, the best source of information is the job announcement, which explains what the job duties are, what experience or education is necessary to qualify, the pay, and where to send an application. Help is also available at USAJOBS, the Federal Government's one-stop source for Federal jobs and employment information, at www.usajobs.opm.gov; or call 1-478-757-3000 or TDD 1-478-744-2299.

Internships

Internships are administered at the park level or in various NPS centers and offices. There is no centralized list of available internships. For internships in a park, contact the park directly by telephone or mail. For internships dealing with cultural resources, such as history, archeology, curation and museums, or historic architecture, visit the National Council for Preservation Education at PreserveNet for more information. They can be reached by e-mail at preservenet@cornell.edu or online at www.preservenet.cornell.edu/employ.html.

The Student Conservation Association (SCA) is a nonprofit educational organization that operates three volunteer programs:

1. In the Resource Assistant Program, young adults serve in areas administered by National Park Service, Bureau of Land Management, and other federal, state, local, and private entities. Resource Assistants serve as volunteer seasonal staff, working side by side with other professional staff. They are not paid, but receive funds to cover travel, a stipend for food and housing, and a uniform allowance.

2. In the High School Program, crews consisting of 6-10 volunteers and their leaders perform conservation maintenance tasks. Leaders are experienced in all aspects of outdoor living and conservation work. Some 2,600 high school students and young adults are placed each year, and most groups are co-educational.

3. The Conservation Career Development Program fosters conservation career opportunities for minority youth through service, counseling, and educational grants.

For further information, contact the Student Conservation Association at: 1800 N. Kent St., Arlington, VA 22209. They can be reached by phone at 703-524-2441 or online at http://www.thesca.org.

Information on Job Opportunities at Other Federal Land Agencies

USDA Forest Service
202-205-8333
www.fs.fed.us/fsjobs/
E-mail: fsjobs@fs.fed.us
(see page 115 of this directory for further information)

US Fish & Wildlife Service
202-452-5125
www.fws.gov/jobs/
(see page 143 of this directory for further information)

Bureau of Land Management
202-452-5125
www.blm.gov/careers/

Parks Canada
819-997-0055
www.pc.gc.ca/agen/empl/index_e.asp
(see page 103 of this directory for further information)

National Maps
Table of Contents

US National Parks

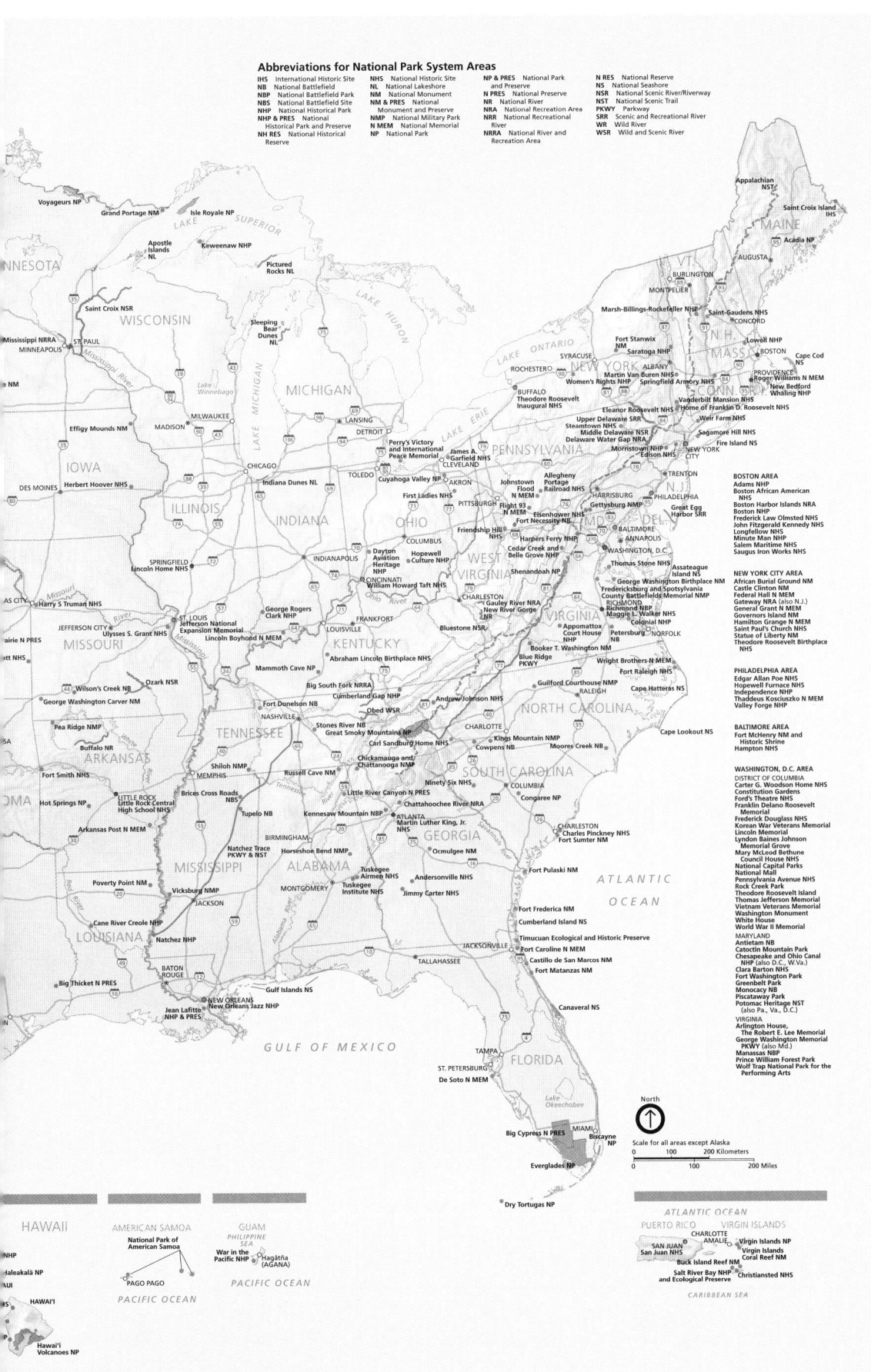

Abbreviations for National Park System Areas

IHS	International Historic Site	NHS	National Historic Site	NP & PRES	National Park and Preserve	N RES	National Reserve
NB	National Battlefield	NL	National Lakeshore			NS	National Seashore
NBP	National Battlefield Park	NM	National Monument	N PRES	National Preserve	NSR	National Scenic River/Riverway
NBS	National Battlefield Site	NM & PRES	National Monument and Preserve	NR	National River	NST	National Scenic Trail
NHP	National Historical Park			NRA	National Recreation Area	PKWY	Parkway
NHP & PRES	National Historical Park and Preserve	NMP	National Military Park	NRR	National Recreational River	SRR	Scenic and Recreational River
NH RES	National Historical Reserve	N MEM	National Memorial	NRRA	National River and Recreation Area	WR	Wild River
		NP	National Park			WSR	Wild and Scenic River

BOSTON AREA
Adams NHP
Boston African American NHS
Boston Harbor Islands NRA
Boston NHP
Frederick Law Olmsted NHS
John Fitzgerald Kennedy NHS
Longfellow NHS
Minute Man NHP
Salem Maritime NHS
Saugus Iron Works NHS

NEW YORK CITY AREA
African Burial Ground NM
Castle Clinton NM
Federal Hall N MEM
Gateway NRA (also N.J.)
General Grant N MEM
Governors Island NM
Hamilton Grange NHS
Saint Paul's Church NHS
Statue of Liberty NM
Theodore Roosevelt Birthplace NHS

PHILADELPHIA AREA
Edgar Allan Poe NHS
Hopewell Furnace NHS
Independence NHP
Thaddeus Kosciuszko N MEM
Valley Forge NHP

BALTIMORE AREA
Fort McHenry NM and Historic Shrine
Hampton NHS

WASHINGTON, D.C. AREA
DISTRICT OF COLUMBIA
Carter G. Woodson Home NHS
Constitution Gardens
Ford's Theatre NHS
Franklin Delano Roosevelt Memorial
Frederick Douglass NHS
Korean War Veterans Memorial
Lincoln Memorial
Lyndon Baines Johnson Memorial Grove
Mary McLeod Bethune Council House NHS
National Capital Parks
National Mall
Pennsylvania Avenue NHS
Rock Creek Park
Theodore Roosevelt Island
Thomas Jefferson Memorial
Vietnam Veterans Memorial
Washington Monument
White House
World War II Memorial
MARYLAND
Antietam NB
Catoctin Mountain Park
Chesapeake and Ohio Canal NHP (also D.C., W.Va.)
Clara Barton NHS
Fort Washington Park
Greenbelt Park
Monocacy NB
Piscataway Park
Potomac Heritage NST (also Pa., Va., D.C.)
VIRGINIA
Arlington House, The Robert E. Lee Memorial
George Washington Memorial PKWY (also Md.)
Manassas NBP
Prince William Forest Park
Wolf Trap National Park for the Performing Arts

North

Scale for all areas except Alaska
0   100   200 Kilometers
0   100   200 Miles

Canadian National Parks

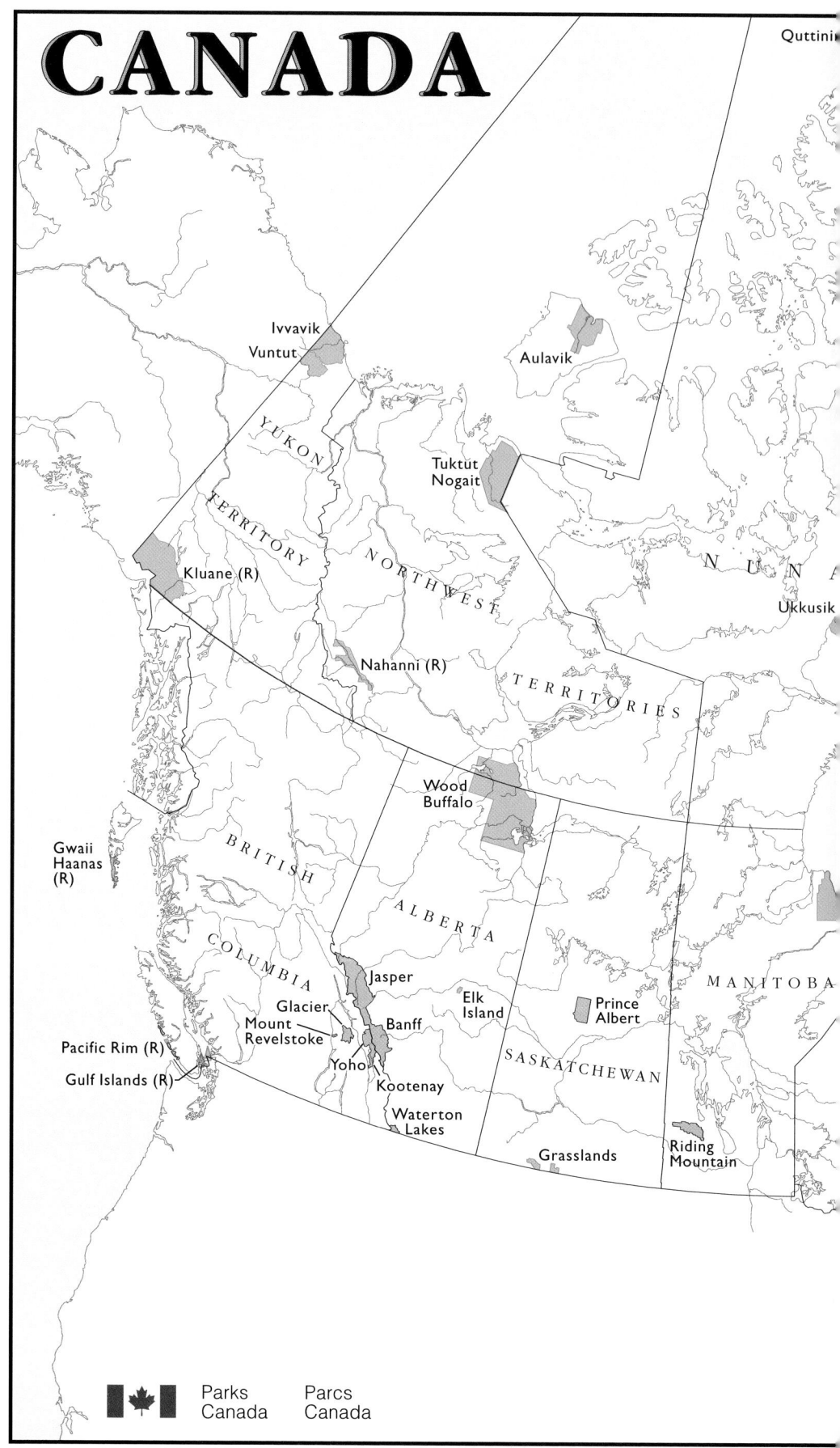

NATIONAL PARKS AND NATIONAL PARK RESERVES OF CANADA

NATIONAL MARINE CONSERVATION AREAS

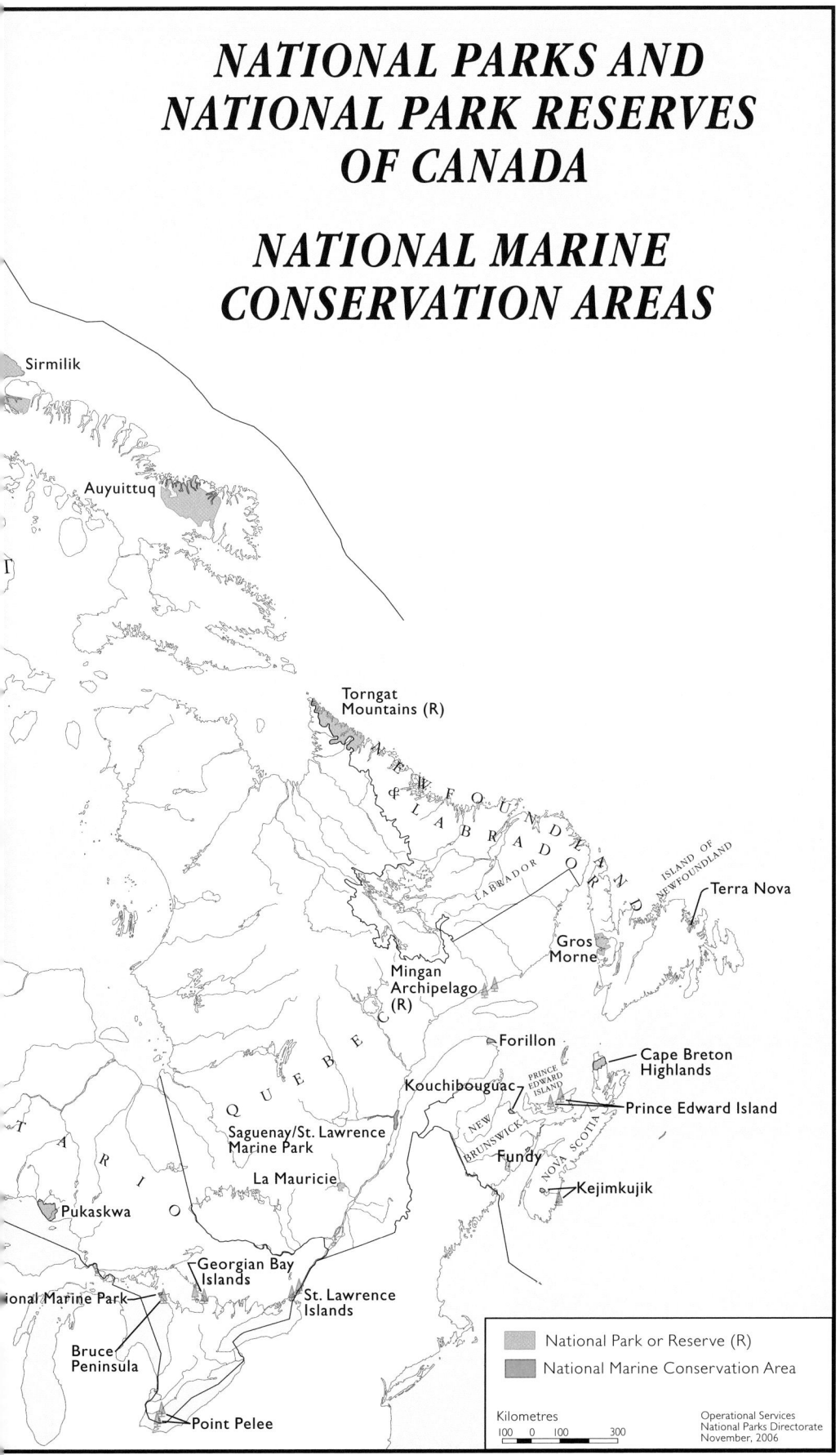

Sirmilik

Auyuittuq

Torngat Mountains (R)

NEWFOUNDLAND & LABRADOR

LABRADOR

ISLAND OF NEWFOUNDLAND

Terra Nova

Gros Morne

Mingan Archipelago (R)

QUEBEC

Forillon

Cape Breton Highlands

Kouchibouguac

PRINCE EDWARD ISLAND

Prince Edward Island

NEW BRUNSWICK

NOVA SCOTIA

Saguenay/St. Lawrence Marine Park

Fundy

La Mauricie

Kejimkujik

ONTARIO

Pukaskwa

Georgian Bay Islands

St. Lawrence Islands

ional Marine Park

Bruce Peninsula

Point Pelee

National Park or Reserve (R)

National Marine Conservation Area

Kilometres
100 0 100   300

Operational Services
National Parks Directorate
November, 2006

National Forests and Grasslands

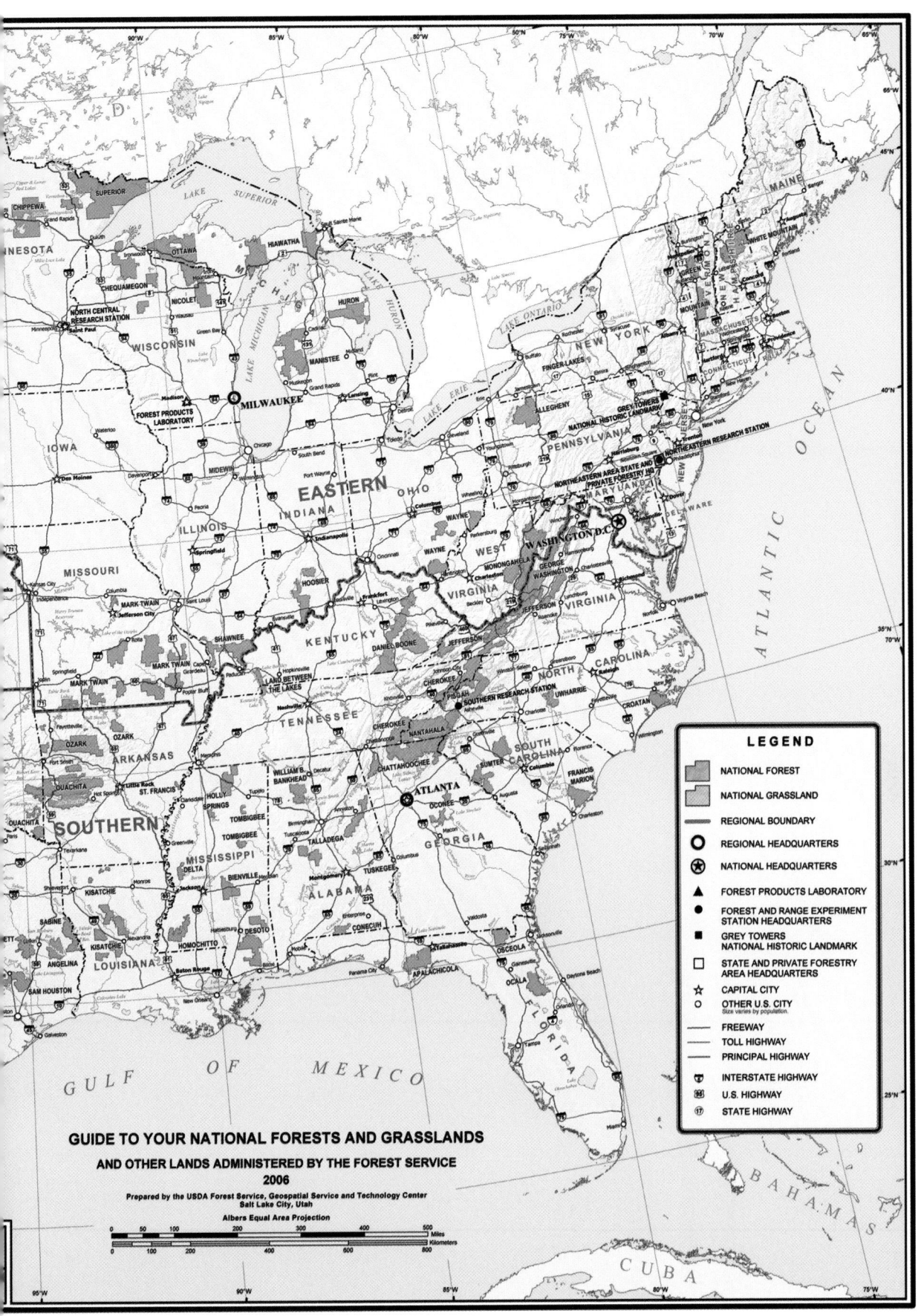

GUIDE TO YOUR NATIONAL FORESTS AND GRASSLANDS

AND OTHER LANDS ADMINISTERED BY THE FOREST SERVICE

2006

Prepared by the USDA Forest Service, Geospatial Service and Technology Center
Salt Lake City, Utah

Albers Equal Area Projection

LEGEND

	NATIONAL FOREST
	NATIONAL GRASSLAND
	REGIONAL BOUNDARY
◎	REGIONAL HEADQUARTERS
⊛	NATIONAL HEADQUARTERS
▲	FOREST PRODUCTS LABORATORY
●	FOREST AND RANGE EXPERIMENT STATION HEADQUARTERS
■	GREY TOWERS NATIONAL HISTORIC LANDMARK
□	STATE AND PRIVATE FORESTRY AREA HEADQUARTERS
☆	CAPITAL CITY
○	OTHER U.S. CITY Size varies by population.
—	FREEWAY
—	TOLL HIGHWAY
—	PRINCIPAL HIGHWAY
	INTERSTATE HIGHWAY
	U.S. HIGHWAY
	STATE HIGHWAY

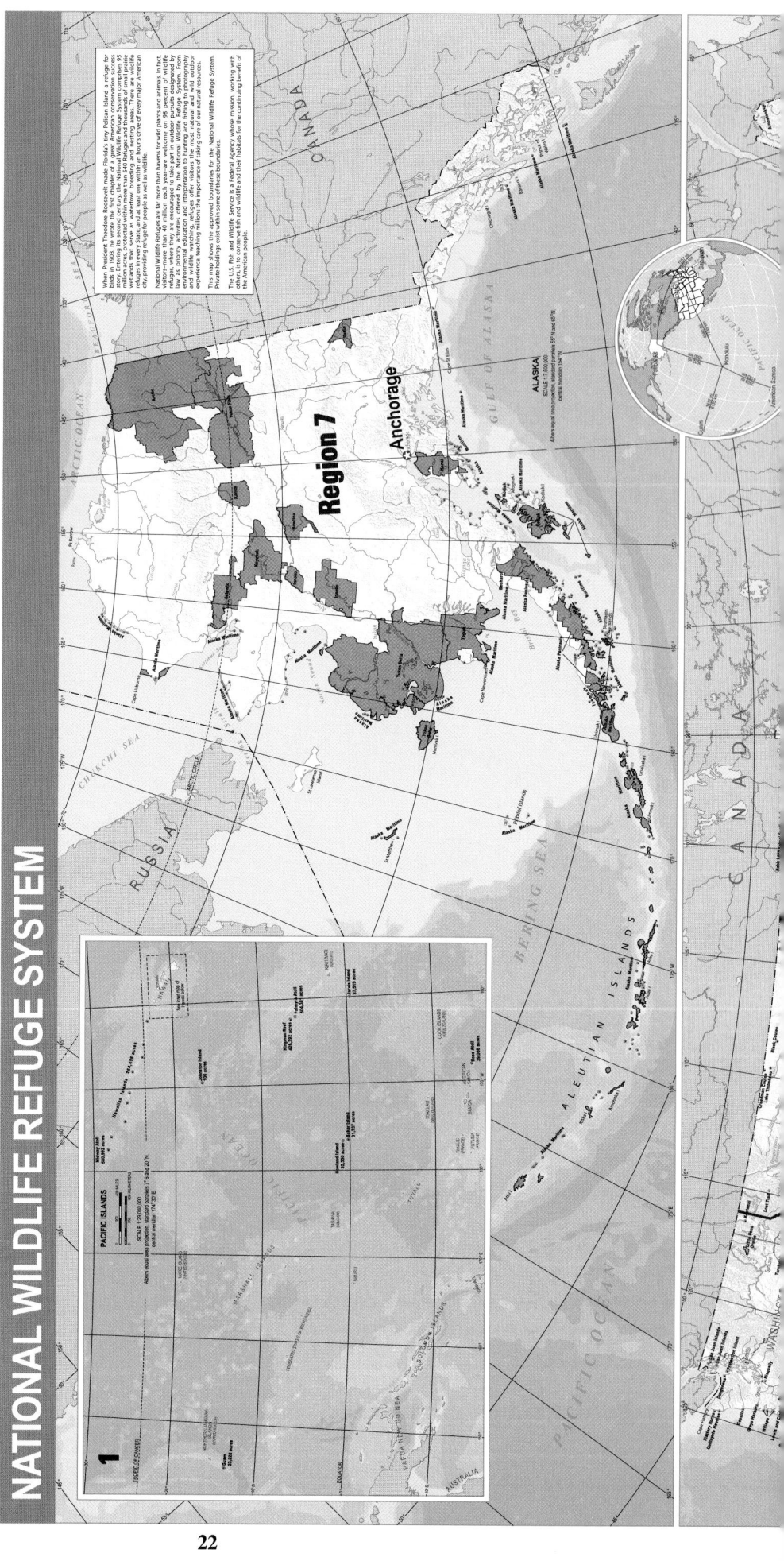

NATIONAL WILDLIFE REFUGE SYSTEM

When President Theodore Roosevelt made Florida's tiny Pelican Island a refuge for birds in 1903, he wrote the first chapter of a great American conservation success story. Entering its second century, the National Wildlife Refuge System comprises 95 million acres, contained within more than 540 Refuges and thousands of small prairie wetlands that serve as waterfowl breeding and nesting areas. There are wildlife refuge in every State, and at least one within an hour's drive of every major American city, providing refuge for people as well as wildlife.

National Wildlife Refuges are far more than havens for wild plants and animals. In fact, visitors–more than 40 million each year–are welcome on 98 percent of wildlife refuges, where they are encouraged to take part in outdoor pursuits designated by law as priority activities offered by the National Wildlife Refuge System. From environmental education and interpretation to hunting and fishing to photography and wildlife watching, refuges offer visitors the most natural and wild outdoor experience, teaching millions within some of these boundaries.

This map shows the approved boundaries for the National Wildlife Refuge System. Private holdings exist within some of these boundaries.

The U.S. Fish and Wildlife Service is a Federal Agency whose mission, working with others, is to conserve fish and wildlife and their habitats for the continuing benefit of the American people.

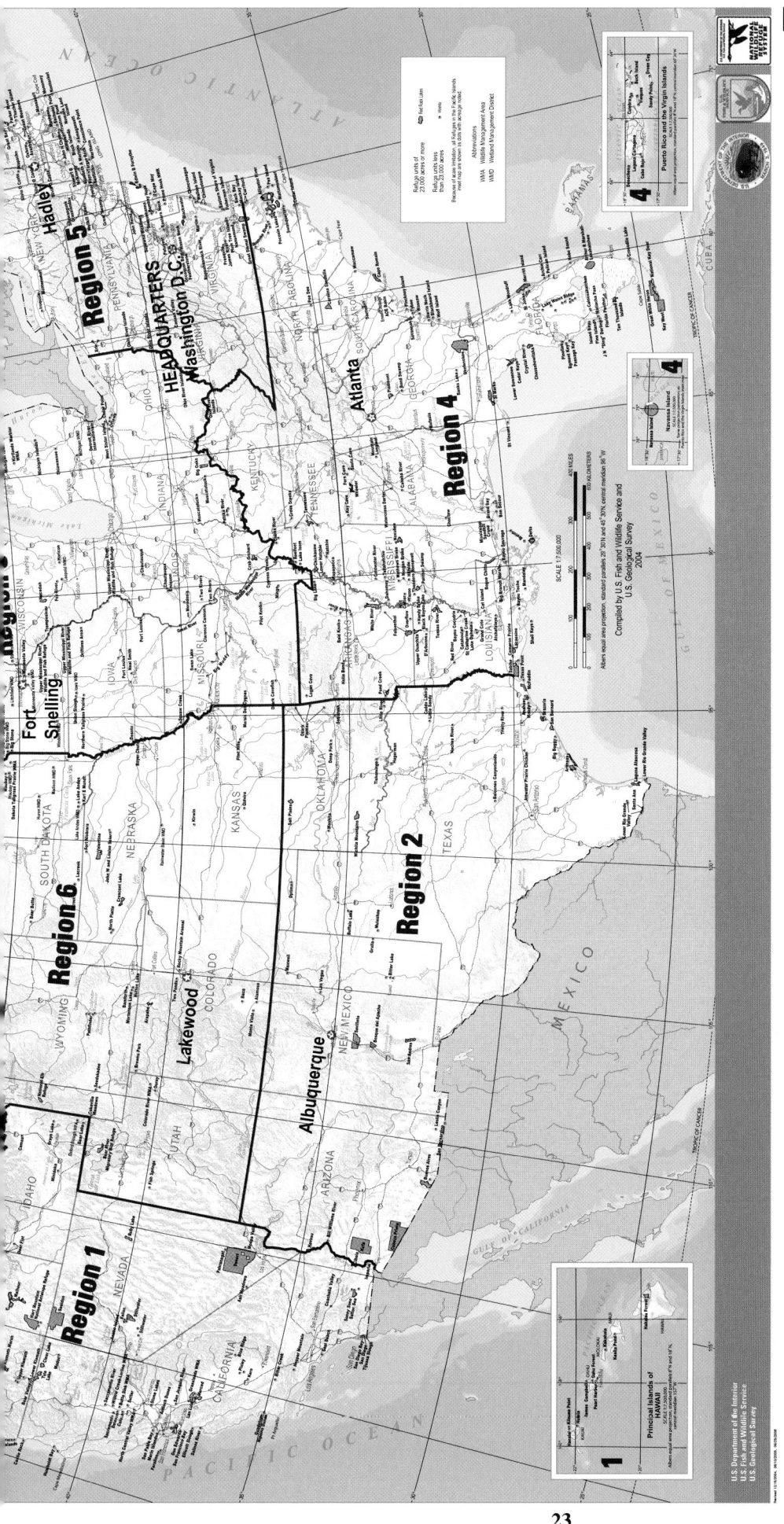

National Wildlife Refuges

23

National Trails

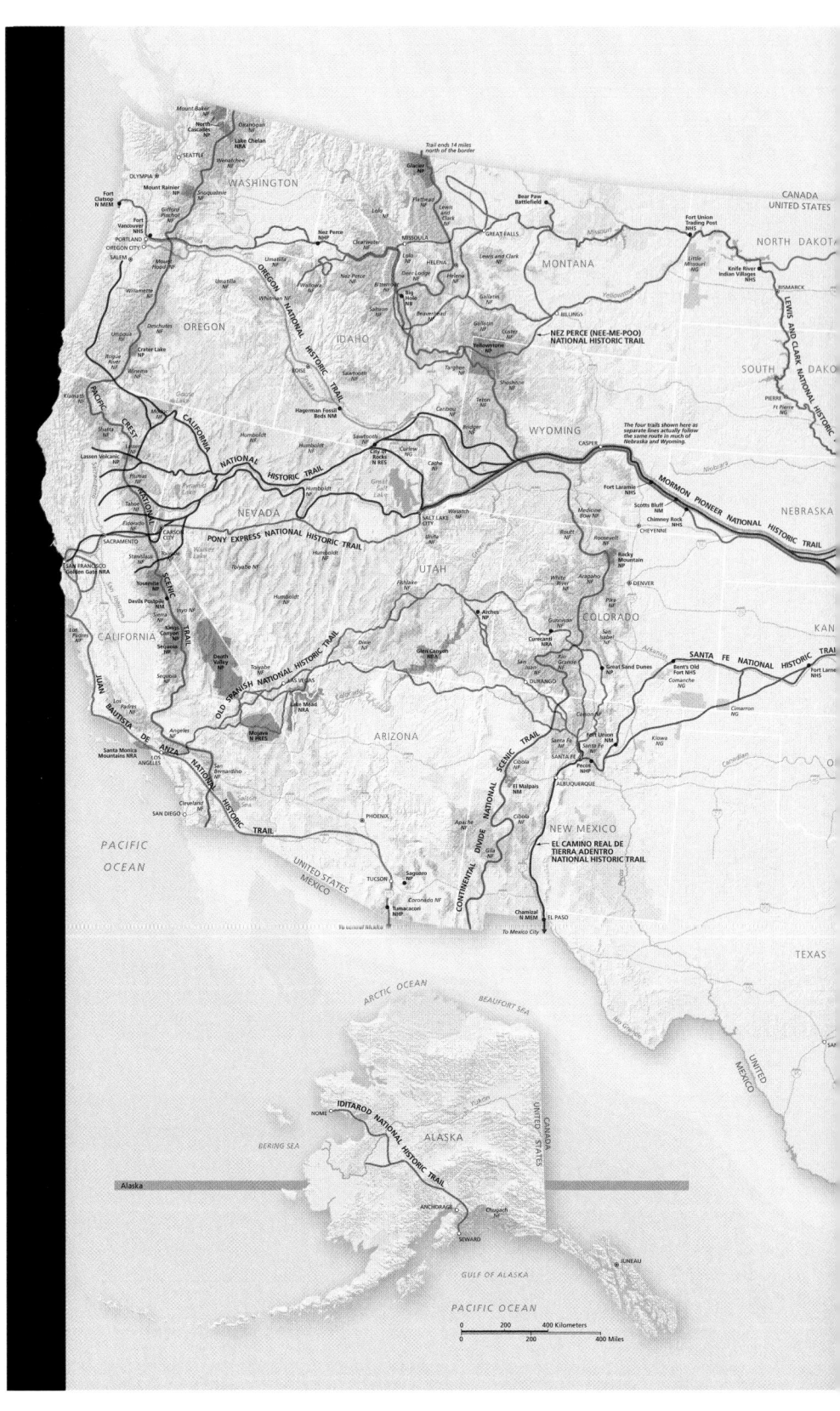

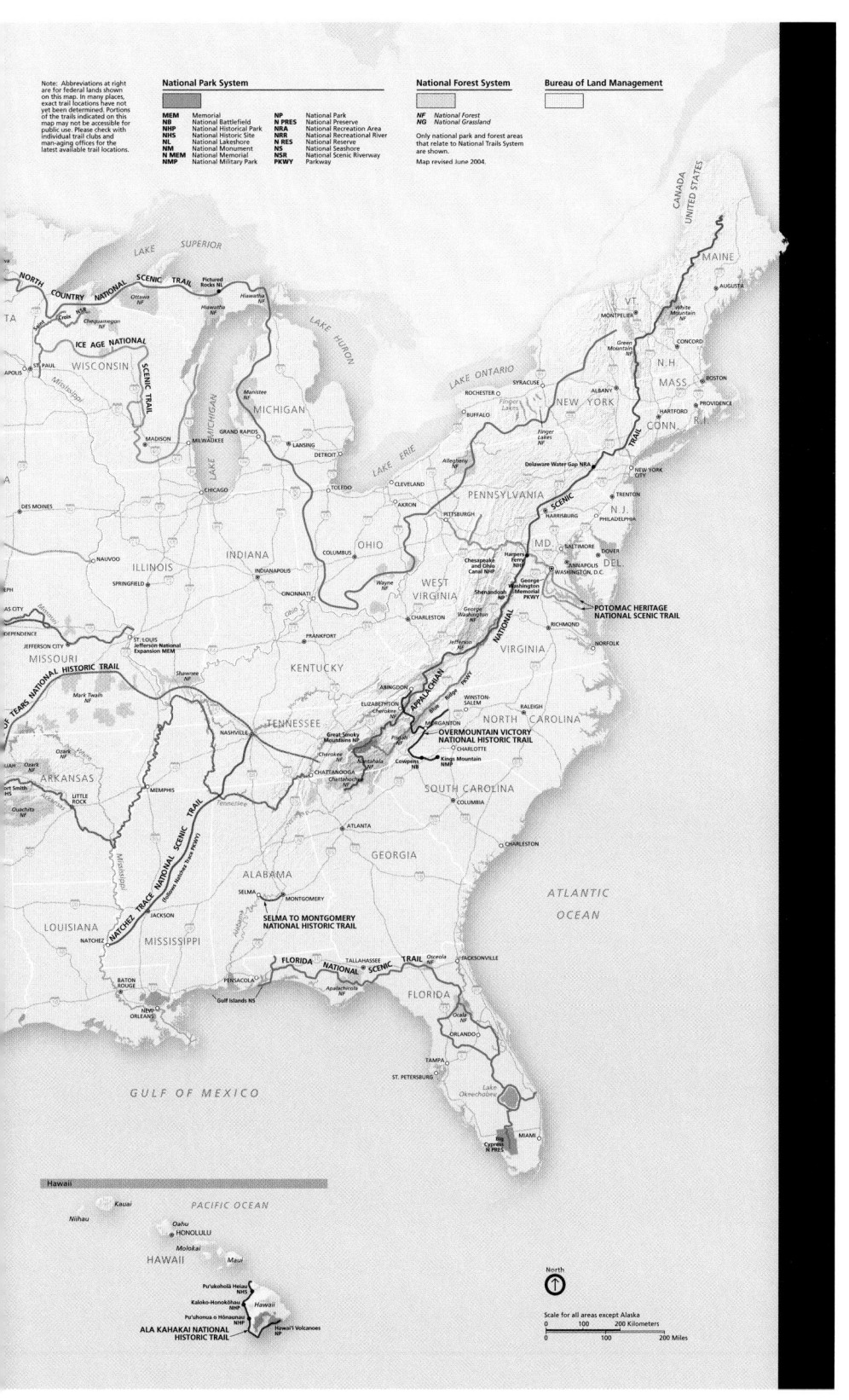

National Marine Sanctuaries

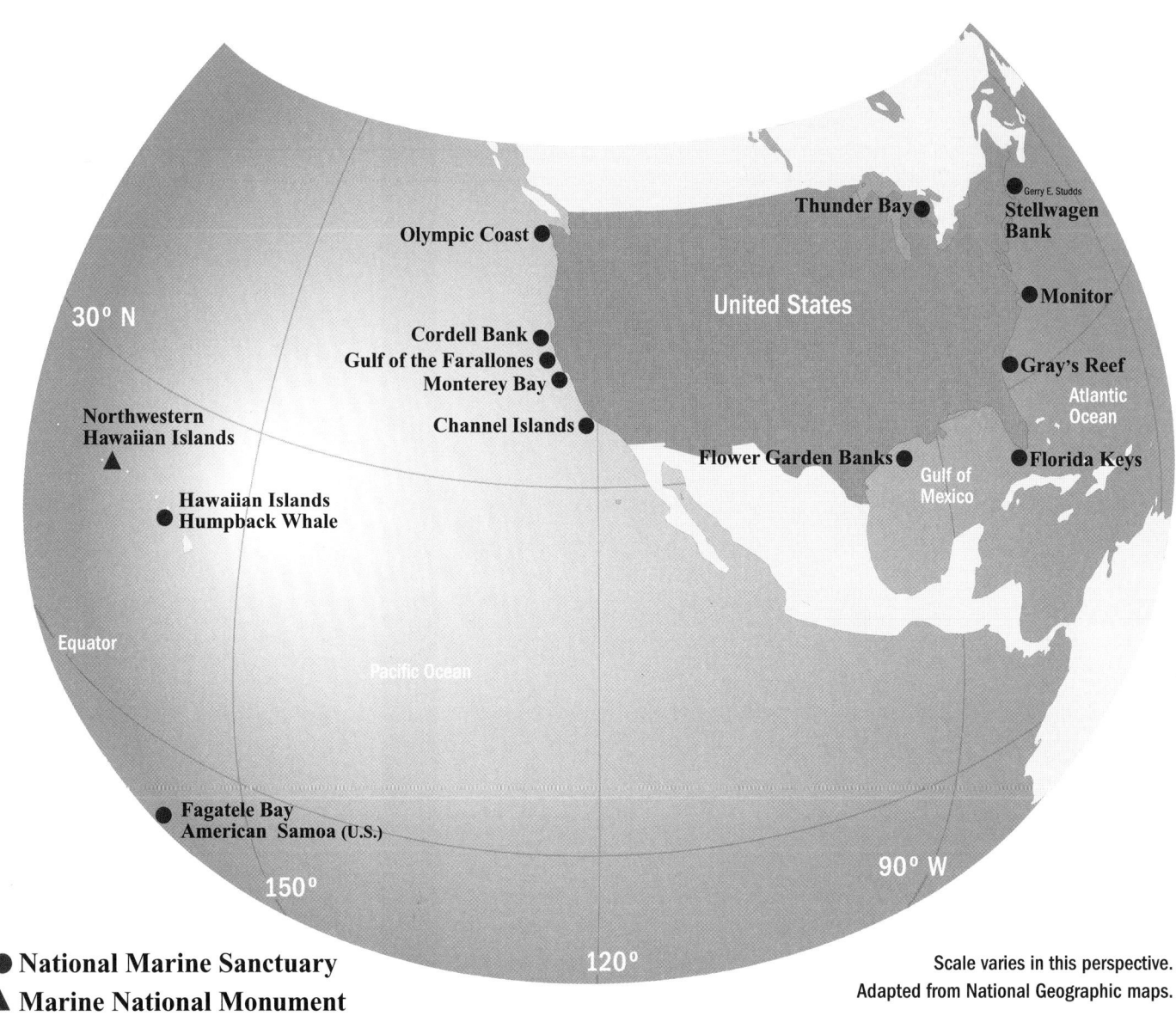

● National Marine Sanctuary
▲ Marine National Monument

Scale varies in this perspective.
Adapted from National Geographic maps.

1. US NATIONAL PARKS

★1★ NATIONAL PARK SERVICE (NPS)
1849 'C' St, NW
Washington, DC 20240
202-208-6843 - Phone
202-219-0910 - Fax
Web: www.nps.gov

National Park Service Reservation Center
800-365-CAMP (2267) - Campground reservations
800-436-PARK (7275) - Yosemite National Park Reservations
800-967-CAVE (2283) - Tour Reservations
800-388-2733 - Customer Service
301-722-1257 - From outside the US or Canada
888-530-9796 - TDD
Web: reservations.nps.gov

The National Park Service was established by Congress in 1916 to protect the nation's natural, historical, and cultural resources and to ''provide for the enjoyment of the same in such manner and by such means as will leave them unimpaired for the enjoyment of future generations.''

NPS manages 390 properties that can be grouped into 19 primary designations, including national parks, historic sites, historical parks, monuments, memorials, battlefields, seashores, lakeshores, recreation areas, and preserves. These properties are located in 49 states and in American Trust territories.

This section provides information on the individual units that comprise the National Park System. Following the park listings, a subsection entitled ''Affiliated Areas'' provides information on a variety of locations that preserve significant properties outside the National Park System, but that still draw technical or financial aid from NPS. For additional information about specific recreational opportunities in the parks you plan to visit, write or call the park of your choice or visit its web site.

Regional Offices:

Alaska Region
240 W 5th Ave, Suite 114
Anchorage, AK 99501
907-644-3510 - Phone
907-644-3804 - Fax
(Alaska)

Intermountain Region
12795 W Alameda Pkwy
Lakewood, CO 80228
303-969-2500 - Phone
303-969-2785 - Fax
(Arizona, Colorado, Montana, New Mexico, Oklahoma, Texas, Utah, Wyoming)

Midwest Region
601 Riverfront Drive
Omaha, NE 68102
402-661-1524 - Phone
402-661-1737 - Fax
(Arkansas, Illinois, Indiana, Iowa, Kansas, Michigan, Minnesota, Missouri, Nebraska, North Dakota, Ohio, South Dakota, Wisconsin)

National Capital Region
1100 Ohio Dr SW
Washington, DC 20242
202-619-7000 - Phone
202-619-7302 - Fax
Web: www.nps.gov/ncro
(Metropolitan area of Washington, DC, with some units in Maryland, Virginia, and West Virginia)

Northeast Region
US Customs House
200 Chestnut St, 3rd Fl
Philadelphia, PA 19106
215-597-7013 - Phone
215-597-0815 - Fax
(Connecticut, Delaware, Maine, Maryland, Massachusetts, New Hampshire, New Jersey, New York, Pennsylvania, Rhode Island, Vermont, Virginia, West Virginia)

Pacific West Region
One Jackson Center
1111 Jackson St, Suite 700
Oakland, CA 94607
510-817-1300 - Phone
510-419-0197 - Fax
Web: www.nps.gov/pwro
(American Samoa, California, Guam, Hawaii, Idaho, Nevada, Oregon, Washington)

Southeast Region
100 Alabama St SW, 1924 Bldg
Atlanta, GA 30303
404-562-3100 - Phone
404-562-3263 - Fax
(Alabama, Florida, Georgia, Kentucky, Louisiana, Mississippi, North Carolina, Puerto Rico, South Carolina, Tennessee, U.S. Virgin Islands)

See pages 16-17 for map of U.S. National Parks.

★2★ ABRAHAM LINCOLN BIRTHPLACE NATIONAL HISTORIC SITE

2995 Lincoln Farm Rd
Hodgenville, KY 42748
Web: www.nps.gov/abli/
Phone: 270-358-3137; **Fax:** 270-358-3874
Size: 345 acres. **History:** Established as Abraham Lincoln National Park on July 17, 1916; changed to a national historical park on August 11, 1939; redesignated and renamed on September 8, 1959. **Location:** 3 miles south of Hodgenville, Kentucky, on US 31E and KY 61. **Facilities:** Picnic area (&), rest rooms (&), visitor center (&), museum/exhibit, boardwalk and hiking trails. Open year round. **Activities:** Hiking, educational programs. **Special Features:** An early 19th-century Kentucky cabin, symbolic of the one in which Lincoln was born, is preserved in a memorial building at the site of his birth. The Boyhood Home Unit at Knob Creek Farm was home to Lincoln from the time he was two until he was seven years old.

★3★ ACADIA NATIONAL PARK

PO Box 177
Eagle Lake Rd
Bar Harbor, ME 04609
Web: www.nps.gov/acad/
Phone: 207-288-3338; **Fax:** 207-288-8813; **Toll Free:** 800-365-2267
Size: 47,390 acres. **History:** Proclaimed Sieur de Monts National Monument on July 8, 1916; established as Lafayette National Park on February 26, 1919, and renamed Acadia National Park on January 19, 1929. **Location:** Approximately six hours north of Boston by car. From Boston take I-95 north to Augusta, Maine; from Augusta take Route 3 east to Ellsworth and on to Mount Desert Island or take I-95 north to Bangor, Maine; from Bangor take Route 1A east to Ellsworth; from Ellsworth take Route 3 to Mount Desert Island. **Facilities:** Campgrounds (&), picnic areas (&), rest rooms (&), carriage roads (45 miles), hiking trails (125+ miles), boat rental, boat ramp, visitor centers, nature center, historical museum. Entrance fee required. **Activities:** Camping, hiking, bicycling, horseback riding, mountain climbing, swimming, boating, fishing, snowmobiling, cross-country skiing, showshoeing, wildlife viewing, interpretive programs. **Special Features:** Acadia was the first national park established east of the Mississippi River. The sea here joins the rugged coastline of Mount Desert Island (highest elevation on the eastern seaboard), picturesque Schoodic Peninsula on the mainland, and the spectacular cliffs of Isle au Haut. Visitors can drive the 27-mile Park Loop Road which includes views of some of the most dramatic scenery along the eastern seaboard.

★4★ ADAMS NATIONAL HISTORICAL PARK

135 Adams St
Quincy, MA 02169
Web: www.nps.gov/adam/
Phone: 617-773-1177; **Fax:** 617-472-7562
Size: 24 acres. **History:** Designated as Adams Mansion National Historic Site on December 9, 1946; changed to Adams National Historic Site on November 26, 1952; redesignated Adams National Historical Park on November 2, 1998. **Location:** In the City of Quincy, Massachusetts, approximately ten miles south of Boston. All tours begin at the Visitor Center which is located at 1250 Hancock Street in the Presidents Place Galleria. **Facilities:** Museum/exhibit. Entrance fee required. A free trolley bus provides regularly scheduled shuttle service between the park visitor center and the historic homes. **Activities:** Regularly scheduled tours of the historic homes (mid-April - mid-November), family-oriented special events program (throughout the year), and annual lecture series (last week in June). **Special Features:** The site includes 11 historic structures detailing the lives of five generations of the Adams family (1720 to 1927), including two US Presidents and First Ladies, three US Ministers, historians, writers and family members. The main historic features include: John Adams Birthplace, where John Adams, the 2nd US President was born (1735), and the John Quincy Adams Birthplace, where his son, John Quincy Adams, 6th US President was born (1767); the "Old House," home to four generations of the Adams family; and the United First Parish Church, where both Presidents and the First Ladies are entombed in the Adams family crypt.

★5★ AFRICAN BURIAL GROUND NATIONAL MONUMENT

Office of Public Education and Interpretation
290 Broadway
New York, NY 19106
Web: www.africanburialground.gov
Phone: 212-637-2039
Size: 0.35 acres. **History:** In 1991, the remains of more than 400 17th and 18th century Africans were discovered during pre-construction work for a federal building in New York City. Site is part of a seven-acre National Historic Landmark established on April 19, 1993. Designated a National Monument on February 27, 2006. **Location:** In Lower Manhattan, at the corners of Duane and Elk streets, adjacent to the Ted Weiss Federal Building at 290 Broadway. **Activities:** Memorial Site is open for public visitation Monday through Friday. Plans are underway to build the African Burial Ground Interpretive Center. When completed in 2008, the Center will provide opportunities to learn about the free and enslaved Africans who lived and worked in Manhattan and were interred in the 17th and 18th century African Burial Ground. Development of the Memorial and the Interpretive Center will be carried out through interagency collaboration between the National Park Service and the General Services Administration, working in conjunction with the public for partnership and ideas. **Special Features:** From the 1690s to the 1790s, the African Burial Ground served as the final resting place of enslaved and free Africans in New York City, New York. It contains the remains of those interred, as well as the archeological resources and artifacts associated with their burials.

★6★ AGATE FOSSIL BEDS NATIONAL MONUMENT

301 River Rd
Harrison, NE 69346
Web: www.nps.gov/agfo/
Phone: 308-668-2211; **Fax:** 308-668-2318
Size: 3,055 acres. **History:** Authorized on June 5, 1965. **Location:** On the Niobrara River, 22 miles from Harrison, in northwestern Nebraska. **Facilities:** Picnic area, rest rooms (&), visitor

See pages 16-17 for map of U.S. National Parks.

center, museum/exhibit, self-guided trails. Entrance fee required. **Activities:** Hiking, fishing, ranger-led walks. **Special Features:** Park was originally part of Captain James Cook's Agate Springs Ranch. The renowned quarries contain numerous, well preserved Miocene mammal fossils and represent an important chapter in the evolution of mammals. The park's museum collection also includes more than 500 Plains Indian artifacts from the Cook Collection.

★7★ ALAGNAK WILD RIVER

#1 King Salmon Mall
PO Box 245
King Salmon, AK 99613
Web: www.nps.gov/alag/
Phone: 907-246-3305; **Fax:** 907-246-2116
Size: 30,665 acres. Length: 69 miles. **History:** Authorized on December 2, 1980. **Location:** Located 290 miles southwest of Anchorage, the Alagnak River flows from Kukaklek Lake in Katmai National Park & Preserve, situated in the Aleutian Range in southern Alaska. The area is inaccessible by road; charter flights are available from Anchorage and King Salmon or access is via power boat from any of the villages along the river. **Facilities:** Visitor center at King Salmon. **Activities:** Rafting (both scenic and whitewater), fishing, wildlife viewing, primitive camping. **Special Features:** Meandering west towards Bristol Bay and the Bering Sea, the Alagnak traverses the beautiful Alaska Peninsula, providing an outstanding opportunity to experience the unique wilderness, wildlife, and cultural heritage of southwest Alaska. Its popularity among anglers around the world has also made it one of the most popular fishing destinations in the region.

★8★ ALIBATES FLINT QUARRIES NATIONAL MONUMENT

PO Box 1460
Fritch, TX 79036
Web: www.nps.gov/alfl/
Phone: 806-857-3151; **Fax:** 806-857-2319
Size: 1,371 acres. **History:** Authorized as Alibates Flint Quarries and Texas Panhandle Pueblo Culture National Monument on August 21, 1965; redesignated November 10, 1978. **Location:** On the Texas Panhandle, 30 miles north of Amarillo and just southwest of Fritch, off TX 136. Adjoins Lake Meredith National Recreation Area (see separate entry for description). **Facilities:** Contact station. **Activities:** Ranger-guided tours of the flint quarries. **Special Features:** For more than 10,000 years, pre-Columbian Indians dug agatized dolomite from quarries here to make projectile points, knives, scrapers, and other tools. The 736 largely unexcavated quarry pits located within the park reflect a long story of continuous excavation and use. Due to its unique colors and its ability to be chipped (or knapped) into sharp cutting edges, Alibates flint was highly prized and traded extensively throughout much of North America.

★9★ ALLEGHENY PORTAGE RAILROAD NATIONAL HISTORIC SITE

110 Federal Park Rd
Gallitzin, PA 16641
Web: www.nps.gov/alpo/
Phone: 814-886-6150; **Fax:** 814-884-0206

Size: 1,284 acres. **History:** Authorized on August 31, 1964. **Location:** On US 22, Gallitzin Exit, 12 miles west of Altoona in southwestern Pennsylvania. **Facilities:** Picnic area, rest rooms, visitor center, museum/exhibit, self- guided tour/trail (& &). Entrance fee required. **Activities:** Guided tour, hiking. **Special Features:** Site preserves traces of the first railroad crossing of the Allegheny Mountains. Built between 1831-1834, the inclined plane railroad permitted transportation of passengers and freight over the mountains from 1834-1854, providing a critical link in the Pennsylvania Mainline Canal system and an important role in opening the interior of the United States to trade and settlement.

★10★ AMISTAD NATIONAL RECREATION AREA

4121 Hwy 90 West
Del Rio, TX 78840
Web: www.nps.gov/amis/
Phone: 830-775-7491; **Fax:** 830-778-9248
Size: 58,500 acres. **History:** Administered under cooperative agreement with the International Boundary and Water Commission as Amistad Recreation Area, November 11, 1965; authorized as a national recreation area November 28, 1990. **Location:** In southwest Texas, west of San Antonio between Del Rio and Langtry. Accessible via US 90 from the east and west and US 277/377 from the north and south. **Facilities:** Primitive campgrounds (&), picnic area, rest rooms (&), groceries, restaurant/snacks, boat rental, boat ramp, self-guided tour/trail. **Activities:** Camping, hiking, horseback riding, swimming, boating, fishing, hunting, water-skiing, scuba diving, interpretive programs. **Special Features:** Amistad is an international recreation area on the United States-Mexico border. The Amistad Reservoir on the Rio Grande includes 850 miles of lake shoreline, of which 540 are in Texas. Boating and water sports highlight activities in the U.S. section of the reservoir. In addition, the area is rich in archeology and rock art, and contains a wide variety of plant and animal life.

★11★ ANDERSONVILLE NATIONAL HISTORIC SITE

496 Cemetery Rd
Andersonville, GA 31711
Web: www.nps.gov/ande/
Phone: 229-924-0343; **Fax:** 229-928-9640
Size: 515 acres. **History:** Authorized on October 16, 1970. **Location:** 10 miles north of Americus, Georgia, on GA 49. **Facilities:** Picnic area, rest rooms (&), visitor center (&), museum/exhibit, self-guided tour/trail, primitive campsite (available at no charge to educational and scout groups). **Activities:** Guided tour, audio driving tour. **Special Features:** Andersonville, or Camp Sumter as it was officially known, was one of the largest of many Confederate military prisons established during the Civil War. During the 14 months of its existence (1864-1865), more than 45,000 Union soldiers were confined here, of which nearly 13,000 died from disease, poor sanitation, malnutrition, overcrowding, or exposure to the elements. Today, Andersonville is the only park in the National Park System to serve as a memorial to all American prisoners of war throughout the nation's history. The park also features the National Prisoners of War Museum and Andersonville National Cemetery.

See pages 16-17 for map of U.S. National Parks.

★12★ ANDREW JOHNSON NATIONAL HISTORIC SITE

121 Monument Ave
Greeneville, TN 37743
Web: www.nps.gov/anjo/
Phone: 423-638-3551; **Fax:** 423-638-9194
Size: 16.7 acres. **History:** Authorized as a national monument on August 29, 1935; redesignated as a national historic site on December 11, 1963. **Location:** On the corner of College and Depot streets in Greeneville, Tennessee. From I-81S take Exit 36 to Rt. 172 south to Greeneville. From I-81N take Exit 23 to Rt. 11E north to Greeneville. **Facilities:** Rest rooms (&), visitor center (&), museum/exhibit (&), self-guided tour/trail. Entrance fee required. **Activities:** Guided tours. **Special Features:** This site includes two homes and the tailor shop of the 17th President, who served from 1865 to 1869, and the Andrew Johnson National Cemetery, where the President is buried.

★13★ ANIAKCHAK NATIONAL MONUMENT & PRESERVE

#1 King Salmon Mall
PO Box 245
King Salmon, AK 99613
Web: www.nps.gov/ania/
Phone: 907-246-3305; **Fax:** 907-246-2116
Size: 137,176 acres (monument) and 464,117 acres (preserve). **History:** Proclaimed as Aniakchak National Monument on December 1, 1978; established as a national monument and preserve on December 2, 1980. **Location:** 450 miles south of Anchorage on the roadless Alaska Peninsula. Air charters fly from King Salmon to Meshik Lake, Surprise Lake, or Aniakchak, Amber, or Kujulik bays on the Pacific Ocean. King Salmon has daily commercial air service from Anchorage. **Facilities:** None. **Activities:** Hiking, rafting, fishing, hunting, primitive camping. **Special Features:** The 2,500-foot-deep Aniakchak Caldera, covering some 30 square miles, is one of the great dry calderas in the world. Located in the volcanically active Aleutian Mountains, the Aniakchak formed during a massive eruption 3,500 years ago and last erupted in 1931. The crater includes lava flows, cinder cones, and explosion pits, as well as Surprise Lake, source of the Aniakchak River, which cascades through a 1,500-foot gash in the crater wall.

★14★ ANTIETAM NATIONAL BATTLEFIELD

PO Box 158
Sharpsburg, MD 21782
Web: www.nps.gov/anti/
Phone: 301-432-5124; **Fax:** 301-432-4590
Size: 3,255 acres. **History:** Established as a national battlefield site on August 30, 1890; transferred from War Department on August 10, 1933. Entrance fee required. **Location:** North and east of Sharpsburg, Maryland, along MD 34 and 65. Both routes intersect either US 40 or 40A and I-70. Visitor center is north of Sharpsburg on MD 65. **Facilities:** Campground (10 sites; &), rest rooms (&), bicycle trail, visitor center (&), museum/exhibit, self-guided tour/trail. **Activities:** Auto touring (8.5 miles), camping, hiking, bicycling, fishing, interpretive programs (during the summer season). **Special Features:** General Robert E. Lee's first invasion of the North was ended on this battlefield on

September 17, 1862. The battle claimed more than 23,000 men killed, wounded, and missing in a single day — more than on any other day of the Civil War — and led to Lincoln's issuance of the Emancipation Proclamation. The Pry House Field Hospital Museum is located in the historic Pry House, which served as Union Commander General George B. McClellan's headquarters during the battle. Antietam (Sharpsburg) National Cemetery (5,032 interments; 1,836 unidentified) adjoins the park.

★15★ APOSTLE ISLANDS NATIONAL LAKESHORE

415 Washington Ave
Bayfield, WI 54814
Web: www.nps.gov/apis/
Phone: 715-779-3397; **Fax:** 715-779-3049
Size: 69,372 acres. **History:** Established on September 26, 1970. Gaylord Nelson Wilderness Area added on December 4, 2004. **Location:** The headquarters visitor center is one block off WI 13 in Bayfield, Wisconsin. The visitor center and fishery exhibit at Little Sand Bay is accessible by road, 13 miles north of Bayfield. Meyers Road, off WI 13, 5 miles east of Cornucopia, offers lake access and a trailhead. Most other facilities are accessible only by water. **Facilities:** Campgrounds, picnic area, rest rooms (&), visitor centers (&), museum/exhibit, trails. **Activities:** Camping, hiking, swimming, boating, sea kayaking, scuba diving, fishing, hunting, excursion boat trips (late May - mid-October), cross-country skiing, interpretive programs (seasonal). **Special Features:** Wisconsin's northernmost landscape juts out into Lake Superior as the scenic archipelago known as the Apostle Islands. The 21 picturesque islands and an 12-mile mainland unit of adjacent Bayfield Peninsula along the south shore of Lake Superior together include more than 154 miles of shoreline. Features include pristine stretches of sand beach, sea caves, remnant old-growth forests, and the largest collection of lighthouses anywhere in the National Park System.

APPALACHIAN NATIONAL SCENIC TRAIL

(See separate listing in National Trails section.)

★16★ APPOMATTOX COURT HOUSE NATIONAL HISTORICAL PARK

Hwy 24
PO Box 218
Appomattox, VA 24522
Web: www.nps.gov/apco/
Phone: 434-352-8987; **Fax:** 434-352-8330
Size: 1,774 acres. **History:** Authorized as Appomattox Battlefield Site on June 18, 1930; designated a national historical park on April 15, 1954. **Location:** In south-central Virginia, 92 miles west of Richmond and 18 miles east of Lynchburg. It is on VA 24, 3 miles northeast of the town of Appomattox, which sits astride US 460. **Facilities:** Picnic area, rest rooms (&), visitor center (&), museum/exhibit, self-guided tour/trail. Entrance fee required. **Activities:** Self-guided walking tours, and living history and ranger talks (summer). **Special Features:** Here on April 9, 1865, General Robert E. Lee surrendered the Confederacy's largest field army to Lieutenant General Ulysses S. Grant. The site includes the McLean home (surrender site), the village of Appomattox Court House, and the home and burial place of

See pages 16-17 for map of U.S. National Parks.

Joel Sweeney - the popularizer of the modern five string banjo. There are twenty seven original 19th-century structures on the site.

★17★ ARCHES NATIONAL PARK

PO Box 907
Moab, UT 84532
Web: www.nps.gov/arch/
Phone: 435-719-2100; **Fax:** 435-719-2305
Size: 76,519 acres. **History:** Proclaimed as a national monument on April 12, 1929; established as a national park on November 12, 1971. **Location:** In southeast Utah, 5 miles north of Moab along Highway 191. **Facilities:** Campground (&), group campsites, picnic area, rest rooms (&), visitor center (&), museum/exhibit, self-guided tour/trail. Entrance fee required. **Activities:** Camping, hiking, bicycling, auto touring, interpretive programs (March-October). **Special Features:** Highlighted by a striking environment of contrasting colors, landforms and textures, park preserves more than 2,000 natural sandstone arches, in addition to a variety of unique geological resources and formations including balanced rocks, fins, and pinnacles.

★18★ ARKANSAS POST NATIONAL MEMORIAL

1741 Old Post Rd
Gillett, AR 72055
Web: www.nps.gov/arpo/
Phone: 870-548-2207; **Fax:** 870-548-2431
Size: 758 acres. **History:** Named a state park in 1929; transferred to federal control and designated a national memorial in 1964. **Location:** On AR 169, 7 miles south of Gillett via US 165, and 20 miles northeast of Dumas via US 165. **Facilities:** Picnic area, rest rooms (&), bicycle trail, visitor center (&), museum/exhibit, self-guided tour/trail. **Activities:** Hiking, bicycling, fishing, guided tours, musket and cannon demonstrations. **Special Features:** The park commemorates the first permanent French settlement in the Lower Mississippi Valley, founded in 1686. Often called the ''Birthplace of Arkansas,'' the post was the site of French and Spanish forts and trading stations, the scene of a skirmish in the wake of the Revolutionary War, a territorial capital, a thriving river port, and a battleground during the Civil War.

★19★ ARLINGTON HOUSE-ROBERT E LEE MEMORIAL

George Washington Memorial Pkwy
Turkey Run Park
McLean, VA 22101
Web: www.nps.gov/arho/
Phone: 703-235-1530
Size: 28 acres. **History:** Lee Mansion restoration authorized on March 4, 1925; transferred from War Department on August 10, 1933; designated as Custis-Lee Mansion by Congress on June 29, 1955; restoration of historic name on June 30, 1972. **Location:** Overlooks the Potomac River and Washington, DC. Accessible by shuttle bus or by a 10-minute walk from the Arlington National Cemetery Visitor Center/parking area. Access from Washington is via the Memorial Bridge. Access from Virginia is from the George Washington Memorial Parkway.

Facilities: Rest rooms (&), visitor center, museum/exhibit. **Activities:** Self-guided tours, guided tours (by appointment). **Special Features:** This antebellum home of the Custis and Lee families was home to Robert E. Lee for 30 years (1831-1861). It was built by George Washington Parke Custis and his slaves between 1802 and 1818.

★20★ ASSATEAGUE ISLAND NATIONAL SEASHORE

7206 National Seashore Ln
Berlin, MD 21811
Web: www.nps.gov/asis/
Phone: 410-641-1441
Size: 39,727 acres. **History:** Authorized on September 21, 1965. **Location:** Assateague Island is a barrier island situated on the Maryland/Virginia border. There are two entrances to Assateague Island National Seashore. The north entrance is at the end of Route 611, 8 miles south of Ocean City, MD; the south entrance is at the end of Route 175, 2 miles from Chincoteague, VA. **Facilities:** Oceanside and bayside campgrounds (&), group campsites, picnic area, rest rooms (&), off-road vehicle trail, bathhouse, visitor centers (&), museum/exhibit, aquarium, self-guided tour/trail. Entrance fee required. **Activities:** Camping, hiking, swimming, boating, kayaking and canoeing, fishing, clamming and crabbing, bird-watching, hunting, off-road vehicle use, interpretive programs (seasonally). **Special Features:** This 37-mile barrier island, with sandy beach, migratory waterfowl, and wild ponies, consists of three major public areas: Assateague Island National Seashore, managed by the National Park Service; Chincoteague National Wildlife Refuge (see separate entry in national wildlife refuges section), administered by the US Fish and Wildlife Service; and Assateague State Park (see separate entry in Maryland state park section), managed by the Maryland Department of Natural Resources.

★21★ AZTEC RUINS NATIONAL MONUMENT

84 County Rd 2900
Aztec, NM 87410
Web: www.nps.gov/azru/
Phone: 505-334-6174; **Fax:** 505-334-6372
Size: 318 acres. **History:** Proclaimed on January 24, 1923. **Location:** On Ruins Road about 3/4 mile north of US 516, just outside the town of Aztec, New Mexico. **Facilities:** Picnic area (&), visitor center (&), museum/exhibit, self-guided tour/trail. Entrance fee required. **Activities:** Self-guided walk, guided programs (seasonally). **Special Features:** Ruins of this large 12th-century Pueblo Indian community have been partially excavated. Contrary to the name, these structures were not built by the Aztecs of central Mexico, but centuries earlier. Aztec West stands three-stories high and once had as many as 500 rooms including a ceremonial ''great kiva'' over 40-feet in diameter.

★22★ BADLANDS NATIONAL PARK

25216 Ben Reifel Rd
PO Box 6
Interior, SD 57750
Web: www.nps.gov/badl/
Phone: 605-433-5361; **Fax:** 605-433-5404

See pages 16-17 for map of U.S. National Parks.

Size: 242,756 acres. **History:** Authorized as Badlands National Monument on March 4, 1929; redesignated on November 10, 1978. **Location:** In southwestern South Dakota. From eastbound I-90, take Exit 110 near the community of Wall and go south 7 miles to the Pinnacles entrance of the park. From westbound I-90, take Exit 131 and go south 11 miles to the Northeast entrance to the park. From Hwy 44, travel north to town of Interior, and then take Hwy 377 for 2 miles to the Interior entrance to the park. **Facilities:** Lodge (open mid-April - mid-October), campgrounds, picnic area, restaurant, 2 visitor centers (&), museum/exhibit, self-guided tour/trail (&). Entrance fee required. **Activities:** Camping, hiking, bicycling, interpetive programs and field trips, wildlife viewing. **Special Features:** Carved by erosion, this scenic landscape contains the world's richest Oligocene epoch fossil beds, dating 37-28 million years old. This land of sharply eroded buttes, pinnacles, and spires, also includes the largest, protected mixed grass prairie in the United States which supports bison, bighorn sheep, deer, and antelope. The Sage Creek Wilderness is the site of the reintroduction of the black-footed ferret, and the Stronghold Unit is co-managed with the Oglala Sioux Tribe and includes the sites of 1890's Ghost Dances.

★23★ **BANDELIER NATIONAL MONUMENT**
15 Entrance Rd
Los Alamos, NM 87544
Web: www.nps.gov/band/
Phone: 505-672-0343; **Fax:** 505-672-9607
Size: 33,677 acres. **History:** Proclaimed on February 11, 1916; transferred from Forest Service on February 25, 1932. Wilderness designated on October 20, 1976. **Location:** 48 miles (by road) northwest of Santa Fe, New Mexico. From Santa Fe, travel north on 285/84 to Pojoaque, then west on NM 502 and south on NM 4. From Albuquerque take I-25 north to NM 44 to NM 4. **Facilities:** Campgrounds (&), picnic area, rest rooms (&), visitor center (&), gift shop (&), snack bar (&), museum/exhibit, self-guided tour/trail. Entrance fee required. **Activities:** Camping, hiking, wildlife viewing, ranger-guided walks, evening programs and crafts demonstrations (summer months). **Special Features:** Several thousand ancestral Pueblo dwellings are found among the pink mesas and sheer-walled canyons of the Pajarito Plateau. The best-known archeological sites, in Frijoles Canyon near the park visitor center, were inhabited from the 1100s into the mid-1500s, and earlier groups had used the area for thousands of years.

★24★ **BENT'S OLD FORT NATIONAL HISTORIC SITE**
35110 Hwy 194 E
La Junta, CO 81050
Web: www.nps.gov/beol/
Phone: 719-383-5010; **Fax:** 719-383-2129
Size: 799 acres. **History:** Authorized on June 3, 1960. **Location:** 8 miles east of La Junta, Colorado, and 15 miles west of Las Animas on CO 194. From La Junta on US 50, take Hwy 109 north 1 mile to Highway 194, then 6 miles east; from Las Animas on US 50, take Highway 194 west 13 miles. **Facilities:** Picnic area, rest rooms (&), museum/exhibit, self-guided tour/trail. Entrance fee required. **Activities:** Guided and self-guided tours. **Special Features:** An Anglo-American outpost on the Southern Plains, the fort was an Indian trading center and a center of civilization on the Santa Fe Trail. During the war with Mexico in 1846, the fort became a staging area for Colonel Stephen Watts Kearny's "Army of the West". Disasters and disease caused the fort's abandonment in 1849. Today's fort is a reconstruction of the original fort (built in 1833).

★25★ **BERING LAND BRIDGE NATIONAL PRESERVE**
PO Box 220
Nome, AK 99762
Web: www.nps.gov/bela/
Phone: 907-443-2522; **Fax:** 907-443-6139
Size: 2,697,393 acres. **History:** Proclaimed as Bering Land Bridge National Monument on December 1, 1978; established as a national preserve on December 2, 1980. **Location:** On the northern Seward Peninsula in northwestern Alaska. Western boundary lies 42 miles from the Bering Strait and the United States-Russia fishing boundary. There are no roads that lead directly into the preserve, and summer access is usually by bush planes and small boats. Winter access is mostly by small planes on skis, by snowmachine, or by dog sleds. **Facilities:** Bunkhouse-style cabin (sleeps 15-20). **Activities:** Camping, hiking, fishing, coastal boating, bird-watching, wildlife viewing, hunting, snowmobiling, cross-country skiing. **Special Features:** Preserve is a remnant of the land bridge that once connected Asia with North America more than 13,000 years ago. Paleontological and archeological resources abound, and large populations of migratory birds nest here. Ash explosion craters and lava flows, rare in the Arctic, are also present. The preserve and surrounding areas include native villages, offering opportunities to observe and learn about traditional subsistence lifestyles and historic reindeer herding.

★26★ **BIG BEND NATIONAL PARK**
PO Box 129
Big Bend National Park, TX 79834
Web: www.nps.gov/bibe/
Phone: 432-477-2251; **Fax:** 432-477-1175
Size: 801,163 acres. **History:** Authorized on June 20, 1935; established on June 12, 1944. Designated a Biosphere Reserve in 1976. **Location:** Situated on the boundary with Mexico along the Rio Grande; park headquarters is 70 miles south of Marathon, TX and 108 miles from Alpine, TX via Hwy 118. Three paved roads lead to the park: US 385 from Marathon to the north entrance; SR 118 from Alpine to the west entrance; and Ranch Road 170 from Presidio to Study Butte, and then SR 118 to the west entrance. **Facilities:** Lodge (&), campgrounds (open year-round; &), picnic area, rest rooms (&), restaurant (&), visitor centers (&), museum/exhibit, self-guided tour/trail. Entrance fee required. **Activities:** Camping, hiking, horseback riding, boating, fishing, bird-watching, wildlife viewing, float trips (outfitters just outside the park). **Special Features:** Mountains contrast with desert within the great bend of the Rio Grande, as the river waters rush through deep-cut canyons and the open desert for 118 miles. More than 450 species of birds have been seen in the park, with large migrations occurring in the spring. The fossil record at Big Bend spans a rich history of 35 million

See pages 16-17 for map of U.S. National Parks.

years within the Cretaceous Period. More than 90 dinosaur species, nearly 100 plant species, and more than two dozen fish, frogs, salamanders, turtles, crocodiles, lizards, and even early mammals have been discovered here, providing one of the most complete pictures of a prehistoric ecosystem known anywhere on earth.

★27★ BIG CYPRESS NATIONAL PRESERVE
33100 Tamiami Trail E
Ochopee, FL 34141
Web: www.nps.gov/bicy/
Phone: 239-695-2000; **Fax:** 239-695-3901
Size: 648,200 acres of federal land included within 720,056-acre park boundary. **History:** Authorized on October 11, 1974. **Location:** In South Florida approximately halfway between Miami and Naples. Extends from Everglades National Park northward to 7 miles north of I-75. Major highways crossing the preserve are I-75 and US 41, with Hwy 29 running north-south along its western boundary. **Facilities:** Campgrounds, picnic area, rest rooms (&), groceries, off-road vehicle trail, visitor center (&), museum/exhibit. **Activities:** Camping, hiking, fishing, hunting, canoeing, bicycling, bird-watching, wildlife viewing, off-road vehicle use (in designated areas). **Special Features:** Adjoining the northwest section of Everglades National Park (see separate entry for description), this large area protects the freshwaters of the Big Cypress Swamp, essential to the health of the neighboring Everglades and supporting the rich marine estuaries along Florida's southwest coast. Subtropical plant and animal life abounds in this ancestral home of the Seminole and Miccosukee Indians. The preserve includes 31 miles of the Florida National Scenic Trail (see separate entry in National Trails section).

★28★ BIG HOLE NATIONAL BATTLEFIELD
PO Box 237
Wisdom, MT 59761
Web: www.nps.gov/biho/
Phone: 406-689-3155; **Fax:** 406-689-3151
Size: 1,011 acres. **History:** Established as Big Hole Battlefield National Monument on June 23, 1910; changed to Big Hole National Battlefield on May 17, 1963. In 1992, legislation incorporated Big Hole National Battlefield with Nez Perce National Historical Park, making it part of a unique park consisting of 38 different sites located in five states: Oregon, Washington, Idaho, Montana, and Wyoming. **Location:** 10 miles west of Wisdom, Montana, on state highway 43. **Facilities:** Picnic area, visitor center, museum/exhibit, self-guided tour/trail. Entrance fee required. **Activities:** Guided tours and campfire programs (summer), hiking, fishing. **Special Features:** Park memorializes the Nez Perce Indians, the soldiers of the 7th U.S. Infantry, and the Bitterroot Volunteers who clashed at the Battle of the Big Hole in August of 1877 — a dramatic episode in the long struggle to confine the Nez Perce and other Indians to reservations.

★29★ BIG SOUTH FORK NATIONAL RIVER & RECREATION AREA
4564 Leatherwood Rd
Oneida, TN 37841
Web: www.nps.gov/biso/
Phone: 423-569-9778; **Fax:** 423-569-5505

Size: 125,310 acres. **History:** Authorized on May 7, 1974. **Location:** In southeastern Kentucky and northeastern Tennessee. Southbound on I-75 take KY 461 south to KY 80, take 80 west to US 27, take 27 south to Oneida and follow TN 297 west into the park. From I-75 northbound, take TN 63 west to US 27, take 27 north to Oneida and follow TN 297 west into the park. From I-40 westbound, exit at US 27, travel north to Oneida and follow TN 297 west into the park. From I-40 eastbound, exit at US 127 and travel north to TN 154, take 154 north to TN 297, and take 297 east into the park. **Facilities:** Campgrounds (&), primitive lodge (accessible only by foot or horseback), picnic area, rest rooms (&), boat ramp, visitor centers (&), museum/exhibit, horse trails (200+ miles). **Activities:** Camping, hiking, horseback riding, swimming, whitewater rafting, canoeing, kayaking, fishing, hunting, mountain biking. **Special Features:** The free-flowing Big South Fork of the Cumberland River and its tributaries pass through 90 miles of scenic gorges and valleys containing a wide range of natural and historical features. The U.S. Army Corps of Engineers, with its experience in managing river basins, was charged with land acquisition, planning and development of facilities, which have now been completed.

★30★ BIG THICKET NATIONAL PRESERVE
6044 FM420
Kountze, TX 77625
Web: www.nps.gov/bith/
Phone: 409-951-6700; **Fax:** 409-951-6868
Size: 97,246 acres. **History:** Authorized on October 11, 1974. Designated a Biosphere Reserve in 1981. Designated a Globally Important Bird Area by the American Bird Conservancy in 2001. **Location:** Preserve comprises 9 land units and 6 water corridors in eastern Texas. To reach information center, enter Beaumont via I-10 and then take US 69-287 north 7 miles past Kountze to FM 420, and then east for 2.5 miles. **Facilities:** Picnic area, rest rooms (&), boat ramp, information center (&), backcountry campground, self-guiding tour/trail. **Activities:** Hiking, camping, boating, canoeing, swimming, fishing, hunting, bird-watching, wildlife viewing, interpretive programs. **Special Features:** Big Thicket was the first Preserve established in the National Park System. A convergence of ecosystems occurred here during the last Ice Age, bringing together, in one geographical location, the eastern hardwood forests, the Gulf coastal plains, and the midwest prairies. A great number of plant and animal species coexist in this "biological crossroads of North America."

★31★ BIGHORN CANYON NATIONAL RECREATION AREA
PO Box 7458
Fort Smith, MT 59035
Web: www.nps.gov/bica/
Phone: 406-666-2412; **Fax:** 406-666-2415
Size: 120,296 acres. **History:** October 15, 1966. **Location:** In south-central Montana and north-central Wyoming. There are two visitor centers and other developed facilities in Fort Smith, Montana and near Lovell, Wyoming. To get to the north end of park, take I-90 to Hardin, MT, and Hwy 313 40 miles south to Fort Smith. To get to the south end of park, take US 310

See pages 16-17 for map of U.S. National Parks.

from Billings, MT or US 14A from Sheridan, WY to Lovell, and continue 2 miles east on Highway 14A to Highway 37, then north 9 miles. **Facilities:** Campgrounds (open all year; &); picnic area, rest rooms (&), groceries, boat rental, boat ramp, visitor centers (&), museum/exhibit, self-guided tour/trail. Entrance fee required. **Activities:** Camping, hiking, biking, swimming, boating, fishing, wildlife viewing, hunting, snowshoeing. **Special Features:** Bighorn Lake, formed by Yellowtail Dam on the Bighorn River, extends 71 miles through Wyoming and Montana, including 55 miles through spectacular Bighorn Canyon. The Crow Indian Reservation borders a large part of the area.

★32★ BISCAYNE NATIONAL PARK

9700 SW 328th St
Homestead, FL 33033
Web: www.nps.gov/bisc/
Phone: 305-230-1144; **Fax:** 305-230-1190
Size: 172,971 acres. **History:** Authorized as Biscayne National Monument on October 18, 1968; redesigned and enlarged on June 28, 1980. **Location:** Convoy Point (park headquarters and visitor center) is located 9 miles east of Homestead, Florida, on SW 328 Street. **Facilities:** Campgrounds (only accessible by boat), picnic area, rest rooms (&), visitor center (&), boat tours and rentals. **Activities:** Camping, hiking, swimming, boating, canoeing, snorkeling, scuba diving, fishing, glass bottom boat tours (&), snorkeling and dive trips, interpretive programs. **Special Features:** Subtropical islands form a north-south chain, with Biscayne Bay on the west and the Atlantic Ocean on the east. The park protects interrelated marine systems including the longest stretch of mangrove forest left on Florida's east coast, bay communities, more than 40 of the Florida Keys, and a portion of the world's third-longest living coral reef.

★33★ BLACK CANYON OF THE GUNNISON NATIONAL PARK

102 Elk Creek
Gunnison, CO 81230
Web: www.nps.gov/blca/
Phone: 970-641-2337; **Fax:** 970-641-3127
Size: 30,750 acres. **History:** Proclaimed a national monument on March 2, 1933. Wilderness designated on October 20, 1976. Redesignated as a national park on October 21, 1999. **Location:** 15 miles east of Montrose and 50 miles west of Gunnison in west-central Colorado. To reach South Rim from Montrose, take US 50 and CO 347; to reach North Rim, take CO 92 south from Crawford and then North Rim Road (closed in winter). **Facilities:** Campgrounds (&), picnic area, rest rooms (&), visitor center (&), museum/exhibit, self-guided tour/trail. Entrance fee required. **Activities:** Camping, hiking, mountaineering, horseback riding, fishing, rafting/kayaking, cross-country skiing, wildlife viewing, interpretive programs (summer months). The North Rim of the park is closed during the winter. **Special Features:** Park protects the most spectacular 14 miles of the 53-mile-long Black Canyon, which has been carved by the Gunnison River. The unique and spectacular landscape of this sheer-walled canyon was formed slowly by the action of water and rock scouring down through hard Proterozoic crystalline rock. No other canyon in North America combines the narrow opening, sheer walls, and startling depths offered by the Black Canyon of the Gunnison.

★34★ BLUE RIDGE PARKWAY

199 Hemphill Knob Rd
Asheville, NC 28803
Web: www.nps.gov/blri/
Phone: 828-271-4779; **Fax:** 828-271-4313
Size: 93,735 acres. **History:** Initial construction funds allocated under authority of the National Industrial Recovery Act of June 16, 1933; National Park Service administration authorized on June 30, 1936. **Location:** Parkway extends 469 miles along the crests of the southern Appalachians in Virginia and North Carolina, linking two eastern national parks — Shenandoah and Great Smoky Mountains (see separate listings for descriptions of each). The motor road is marked every mile by concrete mileposts beginning at MP 0 near Shenandoah NP and ending at MP 469 at Great Smoky Mountain NP. **Facilities:** Campgrounds (&), picnic area, rest rooms (&), cabin rental, lodging, groceries, restaurant/snacks, boat rental, visitor centers (&), museum/exhibit, self-guided tour/trail. **Activities:** Camping, hiking, bicycling, horseback riding, boating, fishing, bird-watching, wildlife viewing, auto touring, snowmobiling, cross-country skiing, ranger programs, historical and cultural demonstrations. **Special Features:** Following the crest of the Blue Ridge Mountains, this scenic parkway ranges in elevation from 649 to 6,047 feet above sea level and embraces several large recreational and natural history areas and Appalachian cultural sites in North Carolina and Virginia.

★35★ BLUESTONE NATIONAL SCENIC RIVER

104 Main St
PO Box 246
Glen Jean, WV 25846
Web: www.nps.gov/blue/
Phone: 304-465-0508; **Fax:** 304-465-0591
Size: 4,310 acres. The Bluestone River is 77 miles in length, of which 10.5 miles are designated national scenic river. **History:** Authorized on October 26, 1988. **Location:** Near Route 20 between Hinton and Athens, West Virginia. Accessible through its two neighboring state parks, Bluestone State Park to the north and Pipestem Resort State Park to the south (see separate entries in West Virginia state parks chapter), which are connected by trail. A tram takes visitors to the Bluestone River from Pipestem State Park. **Facilities:** Visitor center at nearby New River Gorge National River (see separate entry for description). **Activities:** Fishing, boating, hiking, mountain biking, horseback riding. The upper Bluestone River is a popular whitewater run during higher springtime flows. This upper is rated Class III-IV and is for experienced boaters; the lower section is suitable for beginning paddlers. **Special Features:** The Bluestone River, named for the deep blue limestone streamed of its upper reaches in Virginia, has created a gorge 1,000 feet deep. The section designated as a national scenic river preserves relatively unspoiled land in southwest West Virginia and contains natural and historic features of the Appalachian Plateau.

★36★ BOOKER T. WASHINGTON NATIONAL MONUMENT

12130 Booker T Washington Hwy
Hardy, VA 24101
Web: www.nps.gov/bowa/
Phone: 540-721-2094; **Fax:** 540-721-8311

See pages 16-17 for map of U.S. National Parks.

Size: 239 acres. **History:** Authorized on April 5, 1956. **Location:** On VA 122 (Booker T. Washington Hwy), 22 miles southeast of Roanoke, Virginia. From I-81, take I-581, then US 220 south from Roanoke to VA 122; from the Blue Ridge Parkway, take VA 43 south to VA 122; and from Lynchburg, take US 460 west to VA 122. **Facilities:** Picnic area, visitor center (&), museum/exhibit, self-guided tour/trail. **Activities:** Hiking, guided tour, educational programs. **Special Features:** On April 5, 1856, Booker T. Washington was born a slave on the 207-acre farm of James and Elizabeth Burroughs. This site was the birthplace and early childhood home of the famous black leader and educator.

★37★ BOSTON AFRICAN-AMERICAN NATIONAL HISTORIC SITE

14 Beacon St, Suite 401
Boston, MA 02108
Web: www.nps.gov/boaf/
Phone: 617-742-5415; **Fax:** 617-720-0848
Size: 0.6 acres. **History:** Authorized on October 10, 1980. **Location:** In the heart of Boston's Beacon Hill neighborhood. **Activities:** Self-guided tour and guided tour. **Special Features:** This site contains 15 pre-Civil War structures relating to the history of Boston's 19th century African-American community, including the African Meeting House, the oldest standing African-American church in the United States. The sites are linked by the 1.6-mile Black Heritage Trail.

★38★ BOSTON HARBOR ISLANDS NATIONAL RECREATION AREA

408 Atlantic Ave, Suite 228
Boston, MA 02110
Web: www.nps.gov/boha/
Phone: 617-223-8666; **Fax:** 617-223-8671
Size: 1,482 acres. **History:** Established on November 12, 1996. **Location:** An urban archipelago of 34 islands scattered across 50 square miles of the Boston Harbor; all the islands are located within four to ten miles of Boston. Passenger ferries link the islands to the mainland at several locations, including downtown Boston, South Boston, Quincy, and Hull. George's Island serves as the Park's central point of arrival and departure; from there, water shuttles take visitors to other islands. Private boats may anchor off-shore. **Facilities:** Discovery center, campgrounds, ferry service. **Activities:** Camping, hiking, fishing, beachcombing, kayaking, wildlife viewing, boat cruises, guided and self-guided walks. **Special Features:** The park is rich in natural and cultural resources, and includes the only drumlin field in the United States that intersects a coast, formed by the glaciers some 15,000 years ago. The 34 islands are managed by a unique, 13-member partnership that includes the National Park Service and other public and private organizations. George's Island is home to Fort Warren, a historic Civil War site and National Historic Landmark, and Little Brewster Island includes Boston Light, the oldest light station in the country.

★39★ BOSTON NATIONAL HISTORICAL PARK

Charlestown Navy Yard
Boston, MA 02129
Web: www.nps.gov/bost/
Phone: 617-242-5601; **Fax:** 617-242-6006

Size: 43 acres. **History:** Authorized on October 1, 1974. **Location:** In downtown Boston. Seven of the eight privately, municipally and federally owned and managed historic sites that comprise the historical park are connected by the Freedom Trail, a 2.5-mile walking tour of 16 sites and structures of historic importance in downtown Boston and Charlestown. **Facilities:** Picnic area, rest rooms (&), restaurant/snacks, visitor centers (&), museum/exhibit, self-guided tour/trail. Entrance fees required at some sites. **Activities:** Walking tours, historical talks. **Special Features:** The events and ideas associated with the American Revolution and the founding and growth of the United States provide the common thread linking the sites that comprise this park: Bunker Hill, Dorchester Heights, Old North Church, Paul Revere House, Faneuil Hall, Old State House, Old South Meeting House, and a portion of the Charlestown Navy Yard, including the *USS Cassin Young*, the *USS Constitution*, and the USS Constitution Museum.

★40★ BRICE'S CROSSROADS NATIONAL BATTLEFIELD SITE

2680 Natchez Trace Pkwy
Tupelo, MS 38804
Web: www.nps.gov/brcr/
Phone: 662-680-4025; **Fax:** 662-680-4033; **Toll Free:** 800-305-7417
Size: 1 acre. **History:** Established on February 21, 1929; transferred from War Department on August 10, 1933. **Location:** 6 miles west of Baldwyn on US 45 and MS 370. **Facilities:** Exhibit. **Activities:** Self-guided walks. Park interpreters are located at the Tupelo visitor center of the Natchez Trace Parkway (see separate entry for description). **Special Features:** The Confederate cavalry under the leadership of Major General Nathan Bedford Forrest defeated a much larger Union column under Brigadier General Samuel Sturgis at Brices Cross Roads on June 10, 1864.

★41★ BROWN VS BOARD OF EDUCATION NATIONAL HISTORIC SITE

1515 SE Monroe St
Topeka, KS 66612
Web: www.nps.gov/brvb/
Phone: 785-354-4273; **Fax:** 785-354-7213
Size: 1.85 acres. **History:** Established on October 26, 1992. **Location:** Historic site is located at Monroe Elementary School at the corner of 15th and Monroe streets in Topeka, Kansas. **Facilities:** Visitor center. **Activities:** Self-guided tour, ranger-led tours of Monroe School (reservations required). **Special Features:** Site commemorates the landmark 1954 U.S. Supreme Court decision that ended racial segregation in America's public schools. On May 17, 1954, the Supreme Court unanimously declared that "separate educational facilities are inherently unequal" and, as such, violate the 14th Amendment to the United States Constitution, which guarantees all citizens "equal protection of the laws."

★42★ BRYCE CANYON NATIONAL PARK

PO Box 640201
Bryce Canyon, UT 84764
Web: www.nps.gov/brca/
Phone: 435-834-5322; **Fax:** 435-834-4102

See pages 16-17 for map of U.S. National Parks.

Size: 35,835 acres. **History:** Proclaimed as Bryce Canyon National Monument on June 8, 1923; changed to Bryce Canyon National Park on February 25, 1928. **Location:** In southern Utah. From the north or south on US Hwy 89, turn east on UT 12 (7 miles south of Panguitch, Utah) and travel to the junction of UT 12 and 63. Then turn south onto UT 63 and travel 3 miles to park entrance. From the east, travel west on UT 12 to the intersection with UT 63. Then turn south to park entrance. **Facilities:** Lodge, campgrounds (&), picnic area, rest rooms (&), cabin rental, groceries, restaurant, visitor center (&), museum/exhibit, hiking trails (50+ miles). Entrance fee required. **Activities:** Camping, hiking, biking, horseback riding, cross-country skiing, guided hikes and interpretive programs, auto touring. **Special Features:** In horseshoe-shaped amphitheaters along the edge of the Paunsaugunt Plateau in southern Utah, erosion has shaped colorful Claron limestones, sandstones, and mudstones into thousands of spires, fins, pinnacles, and mazes, collectively called ''hoodoos.'' The 18-mile main park road affords outstanding views of the park and southern Utah scenery; from many overlooks you can see more than 100 miles on a clear day.

★43★ BUCK ISLAND REEF NATIONAL MONUMENT
2100 Church St #100
Christiansted
Saint Croix, VI 00820
Web: www.nps.gov/buis/
Phone: 340-773-1460; **Fax:** 340-773-5995
Size: 19,015 acres. **History:** Proclaimed on December 28, 1961. **Location:** 1.5 miles northeast of the Island of Saint Croix in the U.S. Virgin Islands. **Facilities:** Beaches, picnic area, bathhouse, self-guided trails. A visitor center is located in Fort Christiansvaern in dowtown Christiansted. **Activities:** Hiking, swimming, snorkeling, scuba diving, boating, boat tours, fishing, wildlife viewing. **Special Features:** The park features the finest marine garden in the Caribbean, as well as having coral grottoes, sea fans, gorgonias, and tropical fishes. The island, which has a nature trail and beaches, is a rookery for frigate birds and brown pelicans and is a nesting area for sea turtles.

★44★ BUFFALO NATIONAL RIVER
402 N Walnut St, Suite 136
Harrison, AR 72601
Web: www.nps.gov/buff/
Phone: 870-741-5443; **Fax:** 870-741-7286
Size: 94,293 acres. **History:** Authorized on March 1, 1972 as the country's first national river. Wilderness designated on November 10, 1978. **Location:** In northern Arkansas. Headquarters is located in Harrison, providing administrative services to the national river. The main visitor center for the park (Tyler Bend) is located 11 miles north of Marshall. The park has two other visitor contact stations: the Pruitt Ranger Station, located 5 miles north of Jasper on Hwy. 7, and Buffalo Point Ranger Station, located 17 miles south of Yellville on Hwy. 14. **Facilities:** Campgrounds (&), picnic area, rest rooms (&), cabin rental (Buffalo Point), restaurant/snacks, boat rental, canoe and johnboat put-in areas, trails, visitor center (&), museum/exhibit, trails (100+ miles). **Activities:** Camping, hiking, horseback riding, swimming, boating, canoeing, fishing, hunting, guided hikes, float trips, junior ranger programs. **Special Features:** Offering

both swift-running and placid stretches, the Buffalo is one of the few remaining unpolluted, free-flowing rivers in the lower 48 states. Following what is likely an ancient riverbed, it cuts its way through massive limestone bluffs traveling eastward through the Ozarks and into the White River. The National Park Service protects 135 miles of the 150-mile-long river.

★45★ CABRILLO NATIONAL MONUMENT
1800 Cabrillo Memorial Dr
San Diego, CA 92106
Web: www.nps.gov/cabr/
Phone: 619-557-5450; **Fax:** 619-226-6311
Size: 160 acres. **History:** Proclaimed on October 14, 1913; transferred from War Department on August 10, 1933. **Location:** Within the city of San Diego at the end of Point Loma. To get there, follow CA 209 south, from I-5 or I-8. **Facilities:** Picnic area, rest rooms (&), visitor center (&), museum/exhibit, self-guided tour/trail. Entrance fee required. **Activities:** Hiking, fishing, whale watching, interpretive programs. **Special Features:** Juan Rodriguez Cabrillo, Portuguese explorer who claimed the West Coast of the United States for Spain in 1542, is memorialized here. At the highest point of the park stands the Old Point Loma Lighthouse, which has been a San Diego icon since 1854 and has been restored to its most active period — the 1880s. Gray whales migrate offshore during the winter. Tidepools found on the west side of the park are excellent for studying southern California coastal ecology.

★46★ CANAVERAL NATIONAL SEASHORE
308 Julia St
Titusville, FL 32796
Web: www.nps.gov/cana/
Phone: 321-267-1110; **Fax:** 321-264-2906
Size: 57,662 acres. **History:** Established on January 3, 1975. **Location:** Near Titusville and New Smyrna Beach on Florida's east coast. Accessible via US 1, I-95, and Route 528 (Bee Line Expwy.). The northern access, New Smyrna Beach, is on Route A1A. The southern access, Titusville, is on Route 406/402. Playalinda Beach is reached via Route 402. **Facilities:** Primitive campgrounds, picnic area, rest rooms (&), boat ramp, visitor center (&), museum/exhibit, self-guided tour/trail. **Activities:** Camping, hiking, swimming, boating, fishing, bird-watching, horseback riding, wildlife viewing (including turtle watches in June and July), auto touring, guided tour. **Special Features:** Twenty-five miles of undeveloped barrier island preserve the natural beach, dune, marsh, and lagoon habitats for a variety of wildlife, including many species of birds. The Kennedy Space Center occupies the southern end of the island and temporary closures are possible due to launch-related activities. The area includes a portion of 140,393-acre Merritt Island National Wildlife Refuge (see separate entry in national wildlife refuges section), administered by the US Fish and Wildlife Service.

**★47★ CANE RIVER CREOLE NATIONAL
    HISTORICAL PARK**
400 Rapids Dr
Natchitoches, LA 71457
Web: www.nps.gov/cari/
Phone: 318-352-0383; **Fax:** 318-352-4549

See pages 16-17 for map of U.S. National Parks.

Size: 207 acres (park); 40,000 acres (heritage area). **History:** Authorized on November 2, 1994. **Location:** The Cane River National Heritage Area extends approximately a mile on either side of the Cane River from the southern boundary of the City of Natchitoches to Monette's Ferry, Louisiana. The headquarters for the national historical park is at Oakland Plantation in Natchitoches Parish. Take I-49 to Exit 127 (Flora/Cypress Exit), then east 1.5 miles on Hwy. 120. Cross over LA 1 onto LA 494, then 4 miles on Hwy. 494 to Oakland Plantation. The park will be to the west. **Facilities:** None at the present time. **Activities:** Ranger-guided tours of the Oakland Plantation and of the grounds of the Magnolia Plantation. **Special Features:** Park preserves significant landscapes, sites, and structures associated with the development of Creole culture in both urban and rural settings. Oakland Plantation, the outbuildings of Magnolia Plantation, Cane River corridor, the historic district of the town of Natchitoches, and the Fort Jessup and Las Adaes sites are important components.

★48★ CANYON DE CHELLY NATIONAL MONUMENT

PO Box 588
Chinle, AZ 86503
Web: www.nps.gov/cach/
Phone: 928-674-5500; **Fax:** 928-674-5507
Size: 83,840 acres. **History:** Authorized on February 14, 1931. **Location:** In northeastern Arizona. Visitor center is 3 miles from Route 191 in Chinle. **Facilities:** Lodge, campground, picnic area, groceries, restaurant/snacks, visitor center, museum/exhibit, horse rental, jeep tours. **Activities:** Camping, hiking, horseback riding, auto touring, interpretive programs, guided tours. **Special Features:** At the base of sheer red cliffs and in canyon wall caves are ruins of Indian villages built between AD 350 and 1300. Modern Navajo Indians live and farm here. Park offers a 34-mile (round trip) North Rim Drive, with views of some of the most beautiful Navajo cliff dwellings in the area, and a 37-mile (round trip) South Rim Drive, with panoramic views of the canyons, the Defiance Plateau, and the Chuska Mountains.

★49★ CANYONLANDS NATIONAL PARK

2282 S West Resource Blvd
Moab, UT 84532
Web: www.nps.gov/cany/
Phone: 435-719-2313; **Fax:** 435-719-2300
Size: 337,598 acres. **History:** Established on September 12, 1964. **Location:** In southeastern Utah. There are two paved entrances into the park: Hwy. 313 leads to the Island in the Sky District and is 10 miles north of Moab; and Hwy. 211 leads to the Needles District and is 40 miles south of Moab. **Facilities:** Campgrounds (&), picnic area, rest rooms (&), off-road vehicle trail, visitor centers (&), ranger station, self-guided tour/trail. Entrance fee required. **Activities:** Camping, hiking, biking, horseback riding, boating, kayaking, canoeing, interpretive programs, guided tours. **Special Features:** In this geological wonderland, rocks, spires, and mesas dominate the heart of the Colorado Plateau cut by canyons of the Green and Colorado rivers. Petroglyphs left by Indians hundreds of years ago are also present. The Colorado and Green rivers divide the park into four districts: the Island in the Sky, the Needles, the Maze, and the rivers themselves. While the districts share a primitive desert atmosphere, each retains its own character and offers different opportunities for exploration and the study of natural and cultural history.

★50★ CAPE COD NATIONAL SEASHORE

99 Marconi Site Rd
Wellfleet, MA 02667
Web: www.nps.gov/caco/
Phone: 508-349-3785; **Fax:** 508-349-9052
Size: 43,609 acres. **History:** Authorized on August 7, 1961; established on June 1, 1966. **Location:** Within the 40-mile-long section between Chatham and Provincetown, Cape Cod. From Boston area, take Route 3 south to the Sagamore Bridge in Bourne. Follow US 6 eastward to Eastham and Provincetown. From Providence, RI, take I-95 north to I-195. Follow US 6 eastward. **Facilities:** Six swimming beaches, picnic area, backcountry use permits, rest rooms (&), lodging, restaurant/snacks, off-road vehicle trail, bicycle trail, bathhouse, visitor centers (&), museum/exhibit, 11 self-guided nature trails. Entrance fee required. **Activities:** Hiking, bicycling, horseback riding, swimming, fishing, hunting, ranger-guided tours. **Special Features:** Ocean beaches, dunes, woodlands, freshwater ponds, and marshes make up this park on outer Cape Cod. A variety of historic structures are located within its boundaries, including lighthouses, a lifesaving station, numerous Cape Cod style houses, and Marconi's Wireless Station site.

★51★ CAPE HATTERAS NATIONAL SEASHORE

1401 National Park Dr
Manteo, NC 27954
Web: www.nps.gov/caha/
Phone: 252-473-2111; **Fax:** 252-473-2595
Size: 30,351 acres. **History:** Authorized on August 17, 1937. Its lands include 5,915-acre Pea Island National Wildlife Refuge (see separate entry in national wildlife refuges chapter), administered by the US Fish and Wildlife Service. **Location:** Cape Hatteras stretches north to south across three islands: Bodie, Hatteras, and Ocracoke. The islands are linked by NC 12, which is the only major route through the park. From the north, NC 158 accesses the Outer Banks at Kitty Hawk, and then intersects NC 12 at the park's northern entrance below Nags Head. US 64 comes in from the west at Roanoke Island, and also intersects NC 12 at the park's northern entrance. State-operated toll ferries access the park's southern entrance at Ocracoke Island from Cedar Island or Swan Quarter, NC. **Facilities:** Campgrounds, picnic area, rest rooms (&), groceries, off-road vehicle trail, boat ramp, bathhouse, visitor center (&), museum/exhibit, self-guided tour/trail. **Activities:** Camping, hiking, swimming, boating, fishing, crabbing, surfing, hunting, bicycling, bird-watching, interpretive programs. **Special Features:** Stretched over 70 miles of barrier islands, Cape Hatteras National Seashore includes a number of natural and cultural resources. Once dubbed the "Graveyard of the Atlantic" for its treacherous currents, shoals, and storms, Cape Hatteras has a wealth of history relating to shipwrecks, lighthouses, and the U.S. Lifesaving Service. The Ocracoke Lighthouse (built in 1823) is the oldest operating

See pages 16-17 for map of U.S. National Parks.

lighthouse in North Carolina and the 208-foot Cape Hatteras Lighthouse (built in 1870) is the tallest in the United States.

★52★ CAPE KRUSENSTERN NATIONAL MONUMENT

PO Box 1029
Kotzebue, AK 99752
Web: www.nps.gov/cakr/
Phone: 907-442-3890; Fax: 907-442-8316
Size: 649,085 acres. History: Proclaimed on December 1, 1978. Location: Bordering the Arctic Ocean and Chukchi Sea in northwestern Alaska. Commercial airlines provide service from Anchorage or Fairbanks to Nome or Kotzebue. There are scheduled flights to villages and chartered flights to specific park areas. Summer access may include motorized/non-motorized watercraft, aircraft, or by foot. Winter access may include snowmobiles, aircraft, or by foot. Facilities: Ranger station (seasonal). There are no roads, trails, or campgrounds within the monument. Activities: Primitive camping, hiking, boating, kayaking, fishing, snowmobiling, wildlife viewing. Special Features: The monument includes a representative example of the Arctic coastline along the Chukchi Sea, and archeological sites located along a succession of lateral beach ridges provide evidence of an estimated 5,000 years of human activity. Inupiat people continue to use the resources today. Large numbers of migratory birds come from all over the world to Cape Krusenstern to nest.

★53★ CAPE LOOKOUT NATIONAL SEASHORE

131 Charles St
Harkers Island, NC 28531
Web: www.nps.gov/calo/
Phone: 252-728-2250; Fax: 252-728-2160
Size: 28,243 acres. History: Authorized on March 10, 1966. Designated a Biosphere Reserve in 1986. Cape Lookout Lighthouse transferred from US Coast Guard to National Park Service as part of Cape Lookout National Seashore on June 14, 2003. Location: Visitor center is on the eastern end of Harkers Island, 20 miles east of Beaufort, NC and 30 miles south of the Cedar Island terminus of the North Carolina State Ferry route from Ocracoke Island to Cedar Island. From Beaufort, take US 70 east to Harkers Island Road (SR 1332/SR 1335). From Cedar Island, take SR 12 south past the Atlantic turnoff to US 70 west. Continue on US 70 to Harkers Island Road (SR 1332/SR 1335). Cape Lookout National Seashore is accessible only through private ferries leaving from Harkers Island, Davis, Atlantic, Beaufort, Morehead City and Ocracoke or by personal watercraft. Facilities: Picnic area, cabin rental, off-road vehicle trail, visitor center, museum/exhibit. Activities: Camping, hiking, swimming, boating, fishing, hunting, wildlife viewing, guided tour. Special Features: This series of undeveloped barrier islands extends 56 miles along the lower Outer Banks, embracing beaches, dunes, historic Portsmouth Village, and Cape Lookout Lighthouse. Seashore is home to many endangered and threatened species of plants and animals including the Seabeach Amaranth, Piping Plover, and Loggerhead sea turtle.

★54★ CAPITOL REEF NATIONAL PARK

HC 70 Box 15
Torrey, UT 84775
Web: www.nps.gov/care/
Phone: 435-425-3791; Fax: 435-425-3026
Size: 241,904 acres. History: Proclaimed as a national monument on August 2, 1937; established as a national park on December 18, 1971. Location: In south-central Utah on UT 24. Facilities: Campgrounds, picnic area, rest rooms (&), visitor center (&), museum/exhibit, self-guided tour/trail. Entrance fee required. Activities: Camping, hiking, bicycling, horseback riding, fishing, rock climbing, auto touring, ranger-guided walks and evening programs. Special Features: Park preserves the 100-mile-long Waterpocket Fold, an uplift of sandstone cliffs with highly colored sedimentary formations created 65 million years ago. Preserved also is rock art of the Fremont Culture and a historic Mormon settlement.

★55★ CAPULIN VOLCANO NATIONAL MONUMENT

PO Box 40
Capulin, NM 88414
Web: www.nps.gov/cavo/
Phone: 505-278-2201; Fax: 505-278-2211
Size: 793 acres. History: Proclaimed on August 9, 1916, as Capulin Mountain National Monument; name changed on December 31, 1987. Location: In the northeastern corner of New Mexico. Park entrance is via NM 325, 3 miles north of the town of Capulin. Capulin is 58 miles west of Clayton on US 64 and 87, and 30 miles east of Raton and I-25. Facilities: Picnic area, rest rooms (&), visitor center (&), museum/exhibit, self-guided tour/trail. Entrance fee required. Activities: Hiking, auto touring, ranger-led programs. Special Features: Approximately 60,000 years ago, the rain of cooling cinders formed Capulin Volcano, a nearly perfectly-symmetrical cinder cone, rising more than 1000 feet above the surrounding landscape. A two-mile paved road to the top of the volcano and paved trails into the crater and around its rim provide visitors an unusual opportunity to see the inside of a volcano.

★56★ CARL SANDBURG HOME NATIONAL HISTORIC SITE

81 Carl Sadburg Ln
Flat Rock, NC 28731
Web: www.nps.gov/carl/
Phone: 828-693-4178; Fax: 828-693-4179
Size: 264 acres. History: Authorized on October 17, 1968; established on October 27, 1972. Location: In Flat Rock, NC, 3 miles south of Hendersonville, off US 25. Facilities: Information station, rest rooms (&), hiking trails, museum/exhibit. Entrance fee required. Activities: Hiking, house tours and other ranger-led programs. Special Features: "Connemara" was the farm home of the noted poet-author for the last 22 years of his life (1945-1967). During his residence here, he published more than one-third of his works. The historic site consists of a 22-room house, barns, sheds, rolling pastures, mountainside woods, walking/hiking trails, two small lakes, ponds, flower and vegetable gardens, and an orchard.

See pages 16-17 for map of U.S. National Parks.

★57★ CARLSBAD CAVERNS NATIONAL PARK

3225 National Parks Hwy
Carlsbad, NM 88220
Web: www.nps.gov/cave/
Phone: 505-785-2232; **Fax:** 505-785-2133
Size: 46,766 acres. **History:** Proclaimed Carlsbad Cave National Monument on October 25, 1923; established as Carlsbad Caverns National Park on May 14, 1930; designated a World Heritage Site on December 9, 1995. **Location:** In southeastern New Mexico. Accessible by way of US 62/180 from either Carlsbad, New Mexico (23 miles to the northeast) or El Paso, Texas (150 miles to the west). A scenic seven-mile entrance road leads from the park gate at Whites City to the visitor center and cavern entrance. **Facilities:** Picnic area, rest rooms (&), restaurant/snacks, visitor center (&), museum/exhibit, backcountry trails (50+ miles). **Activities:** Camping, hiking, self-guided and guided cave tours, auto touring. **Special Features:** Established to preserve Carlsbad Cavern and numerous other caves within a Permian-age fossil reef, the park contains 113 known caves, including Lechuguilla Cave—the nation's deepest limestone cave at 1,567 feet and third longest. From early spring through October, nearly 400,000 Mexican free-tail bats call Carlsbad Caverns home and visitors can watch the evening bat flight from the outdoor amphitheater at the cave's natural entrance.

★58★ CASA GRANDE RUINS NATIONAL MONUMENT

1100 Ruins Dr
Coolidge, AZ 85228
Web: www.nps.gov/cagr/
Phone: 520-723-3172; **Fax:** 520-723-7209
Size: 473 acres. **History:** Authorized as Casa Grande Ruin Reservation on March 2, 1889; redesignated by proclamation on August 3, 1918. **Location:** In Coolidge, Arizona, about an hour southeast of Phoenix. From I-10, take Coolidge exits and follow signs to park entrance off AZ 87/287. **Facilities:** Picnic area, rest rooms (&), visitor center (&), museum/exhibit, self-guided tour/trail. Entrance fee required. **Activities:** Guided and self-guided tours. **Special Features:** The nation's first archeological preserve protects the Casa Grande (Big House), one of the largest and most mysterious prehistoric structures ever built in North America. This multi-storied, earthen-walled structure surrounded by the remains of smaller buildings and a compound wall was constructed by the Hohokam, who farmed the Gila Valley in the early 1200s. Casa Grande was abandoned by the mid-1400s.

★59★ CASTILLO DE SAN MARCOS NATIONAL MONUMENT

1 S Castillo Dr
Saint Augustine, FL 32084
Web: www.nps.gov/casa/
Phone: 904-829-6506; **Fax:** 904-823-9388
Size: 17.6 acres. **History:** Proclaimed as Fort Marion National Monument on October 15, 1924; changed to present name on June 5, 1942. **Location:** On A1A in downtown Saint Augustine, Florida. **Facilities:** Rest rooms (&), museum/exhibit, self-guided tour/trail. Entrance fee required. **Activities:** Guided and self-guided tours. **Special Features:** Castillo de San Marcos is the oldest masonry fort and best-preserved example of a Spanish colonial fortification in the continental United States. It was originally built (1672-1695) by the Spanish to protect Saint Augustine, the first permanent settlement by Europeans in the continental United States (established in 1565), and was for many years the northernmost outpost of Spain's vast New World Empire. The floor plan is the result of "modernization" work done in the 18th century.

★60★ CASTLE CLINTON NATIONAL MONUMENT

Battery Park
New York, NY 10004
Web: www.nps.gov/cacl/
Phone: 212-344-7220; **Fax:** 212-825-6874
Size: 1 acre. **History:** Authorized on August 12, 1946. **Location:** In Battery park at the southern tip of Manhattan, New York. **Facilities:** Rest rooms (&), visitor center (&), museum/exhibit, self-guided tour/trail. **Activities:** Self-guided tours, and ranger-led programs and tours. **Special Features:** Built from 1808-1811, this structure served successively as a defense for New York harbor, a promenade and entertainment center, and an immigration depot through which more than 8 million people entered the United States from 1855 to 1890. From 1896 until 1941, it served as the New York City Aquarium and was one of the city's most popular attractions.

★61★ CATOCTIN MOUNTAIN PARK

6602 Foxville Rd
Thurmont, MD 21788
Web: www.nps.gov/cato/
Phone: 301-663-9330; **Fax:** 301-271-2764
Size: 5,810 acres. **History:** Catoctin Recreation Demonstration Area transferred from Resettlement Administration on November 14, 1936; changed to Catoctin Mountain Park on July 12, 1954. **Location:** 20 miles east of Hagerstown, Maryland. From MD 15 North, exit onto Route 77 West, go 3 miles, and turn right onto Park Central Road. From Hagerstown, take Route 77 East and turn left onto Park Central Road. **Facilities:** Campgrounds (&), cabin rental, picnic area, rest rooms (&), visitor center (&), museum/exhibit, self-guided tour/trail. **Activities:** Camping, hiking, horseback riding, mountain climbing, swimming, fishing, cross-country skiing, auto touring, ranger-led programs. **Special Features:** Part of the forested ridge that forms the eastern rampart of the Appalachian Mountains in Maryland, this mountain park has sparkling streams and panoramic vistas of the Monocacy Valley. Camp David, the Presidential retreat, is located within the park. It is not visible from the roads and is closed to the public.

★62★ CEDAR BREAKS NATIONAL MONUMENT

2390 W Hwy 56, Suite 11
Cedar City, UT 84720
Web: www.nps.gov/cebr/
Phone: 435-586-9451; **Fax:** 435-586-3813
Size: 6,155 acres. **History:** Proclaimed on August 22, 1933. **Location:** In southwestern Utah. From I-15 southbound, take UT 143 east; from I-15 northbound, take UT 14 east for 18 miles, then UT 148 north for 4 miles. **Facilities:** Campground,

See pages 16-17 for map of U.S. National Parks.

picnic area, rest rooms (&), visitor center (&), self-guided tour/trail. Entrance fee required. **Activities:** Camping, hiking, snowmobiling, cross-country skiing, auto touring. **Special Features:** A huge natural amphitheater has eroded into the variegated Pink Cliffs (Wasatch Formation), 2,000 feet thick at this point. Millions of years of sedimentation, uplift and erosion have created a deep canyon of rock walls, fins, spires and columns, that spans some three miles.

★63★ CEDAR CREEK & BELLE GROVE NATIONAL HISTORICAL PARK

PO Box 700
Middletown, VA 22645
Web: www.nps.gov/cebe/
Phone: 540-868-9176; **Fax:** 540-869-4527
Size: 3,593 acres. **History:** Designated a national historical landmark in 1969; established as a national historical park on December 19, 2002. Includes the key partner sites of Belle Grove Plantation, Cedar Creek Battlefield Foundation lands and visitor center, Shenandoah Valley Battlefield Foundation lands, and a developing Shenandoah County Park. **Location:** At the intersection of I-81 and Route 66 in the northern Shenandoah Valley near Middletown and Strasburg, VA. The historic Valley Turnpike (Route 11) runs through the park, which is embedded within the Shenandoah Valley Battlefields National Historic District, a National Heritage Area (see separate listing in National Heritage Areas section). **Facilities:** Two major sites, Cedar Creek Battlefield Visitor Center and Belle Grove Plantation House, are open to the public. In addition, a private campground is located within the park. The National Park Service has no developed facilities at this time. **Activities:** The partner sites will continue to be owned and operated independently, allowing such activities as the annual Battle of Cedar Creek Reenactment (mid October) to continue within the park. Activities include camping, driving tours, and special events. **Special Features:** Park commemorates a nationally significant Civil War landscape and antebellum plantation by sharing the story of Shenandoah Valley history from early settlement through the Civil War and beyond. Throughout the area there are historic, natural, cultural, military, and scenic resources.

★64★ CHACO CULTURE NATIONAL HISTORICAL PARK

PO Box 280
Nageezi, NM 87037
Web: www.nps.gov/chcu/
Phone: 505-786-7014; **Fax:** 505-786-7061
Size: 33,960 acres. **History:** Proclaimed Chaco Canyon National Monument on March 11, 1907; redesignated and renamed on December 19, 1980. Designated a World Heritage Site on December 8, 1987. **Location:** In northwestern New Mexico. The recommended access route to the park is from the north via Hwy. 44/550. Turn off Hwy. 44/550 at CR 7900 (3 miles southeast of Nageezi) and go 21 miles to the park boundary (5 miles of paved road on CR 7900 and 16 miles of dirt road on CR 7950/7985). **Facilities:** Campgrounds (&), picnic area, rest rooms (&), bicycle trail, visitor center (&), museum/exhibit, self-guided tour/trail. Entrance fee required. **Activities:** Camping,

hiking, bicycling, ranger-led walks. **Special Features:** The canyon contains 13 major prehistoric sites and hundreds of smaller ones, built by the Ancestral Puebloan People during the 9th through 12th centuries. The Chaco Museum collection contains approximately one million artifacts from more than 120 sites in Chaco Canyon and the surrounding region.

★65★ CHAMIZAL NATIONAL MEMORIAL

800 S San Marcial St
El Paso, TX 79905
Web: www.nps.gov/cham/
Phone: 915-532-7273; **Fax:** 915-532-7240
Size: 55 acres. **History:** Authorized on June 30, 1966; established on February 4, 1974. **Location:** In south-central El Paso, Texas, just north of the Rio Grande and adjacent to the international boundary. Access is via San Marcial Street or Delta Drive. **Facilities:** Picnic area, rest rooms (&), visitor center (&), museum/exhibit, self-guided tour/trail. **Activities:** Guided tour. **Special Features:** The peaceful settlement of a 99-year boundary dispute between the United States and Mexico is memorialized here. The Chamizal Treaty, ending the dispute, was signed in 1963. An amphitheater and 500-seat auditorium are used by the theatrical groups from both sides.

★66★ CHANNEL ISLANDS NATIONAL PARK

1901 Spinnaker Dr
Ventura, CA 93001
Web: www.nps.gov/chis/
Phone: 805-658-5730; **Fax:** 805-658-5799
Size: 249,561 acres. **History:** Proclaimed a national monument on April 26, 1938; redesignated a national park on March 5, 1980. Designated a Biosphere Reserve in 1976. **Location:** Park consists of five islands off Southern California: Anacapa, San Miguel, Santa Barbara, Santa Cruz, and Santa Rosa. Access to islands is by private boat or concessionaire boat; air service is available to Santa Rosa. Mainland visitor centers are located in Ventura (70 miles north of Los Angeles) and Santa Barbara (100 miles north of Los Angeles). **Facilities:** Campgrounds, picnic area, rest rooms (&), visitor center (&), museum/exhibit, self-guided tour/trail. **Activities:** Camping, hiking, swimming, boating, kayaking, scuba diving, snorkeling, fishing, surfing, whale watching, bird-watching, boat tours, interpretive programs. **Special Features:** The Channel Islands are home to more than 2,000 terrestrial plants and animals, of which 145 are found nowhere else in the world. Anacapa, Santa Barbara, and Santa Rosa islands are owned and administered by the National Park Service; San Miguel is owned by the U.S. Navy and administered by the National Park Service (permit needed for visitation); Santa Cruz is owned primarily by the Nature Conservancy and managed in cooperation with the National Park Service. The ocean, 6 miles out around each island, has been designated as the Channel Islands National Marine Sanctuary (see separate entry in National Marine Sanctuaries section for further information).

See pages 16-17 for map of U.S. National Parks.

1. US National Parks

★67★ CHARLES PINCKNEY NATIONAL HISTORIC SITE

1214 Middle St
Sullivans Island, SC 29482
Web: www.nps.gov/chpi/
Phone: 843-881-5516; **Fax:** 843-881-7070
Size: 28.5 acres. **History:** Authorized on September 8, 1988. **Location:** 6 miles north of Charleston off US 17. **Facilities:** Visitor center, exhibits. **Activities:** Self-guided tours, educational programs. **Special Features:** Charles Pinckney (1757-1824) fought in the Revolutionary War and became one of the principal framers of the Constitution. He served as Governor of South Carolina, a member of both the U.S. Senate and House of Representatives, and was President Thomas Jefferson's minister to Spain. His estate, known as Snee Farm, is one of the only 8 actual primary dwellings left that can be directly associated with a signer of the Constitution. Park preserves 28 acres of the 715-acre estate.

★68★ CHATTAHOOCHEE RIVER NATIONAL RECREATION AREA

1978 Island Ford Pkwy
Atlanta, GA 30350
Web: www.nps.gov/chat/
Phone: 678-538-1200; **Fax:** 770-399-8087
Size: 9,359 acres. **History:** Established on August 15, 1978. **Location:** The national recreation area comprises a series of parklands along a 48-mile stretch of the Chattahoochee River, north of Atlanta. Shuttle bus service is available among the sites. **Facilities:** Picnic area, rest rooms (&), visitor contact station, canoe and raft rental, boat ramp, hiking trails (50 miles), fitness trail with exercise stations, restaurant/snacks. **Activities:** Hiking, canoeing, kayaking, rafting, fishing, horseback riding. **Special Features:** The 540-mile Chattahoochee River flows southwesterly from the north Georgia mountains to its Flint River confluence at Lake Seminole. The portion of the river that comprises the national recreation area lies within four counties. In addition to providing recreational opportunities, it contains a wide variety of natural habitats, flora and fauna, 19th-century historic sites, and Native American archeological sites.

★69★ CHESAPEAKE & OHIO CANAL NATIONAL HISTORICAL PARK

1850 Dual Hwy, Suite 100
Hagerstown, MD 21740
Web: www.nps.gov/choh/
Phone: 301-739-4200; **Fax:** 301-739-5275
Size: 19,682 acres. **History:** Placed under the National Park Service on September 23, 1938; proclaimed Chesapeake and Ohio Canal National Monument on January 18, 1961; changed to national historical park on January 8, 1971. **Location:** Park runs along the Potomac River from the mouth of Rock Creek in Georgetown, DC, to Cumberland, MD, encompassing portions of Maryland, West Virginia, and the District of Columbia. Various sections of the canal can be reached via Routes I-495, I-70, and I-68. **Facilities:** Campgrounds, picnic area, rest rooms (&), restaurant/snacks, bicycle trail, boat rental, boat ramp, 6 visitor centers (&), museum/exhibit, self-guided tour/trail. **Activities:** Camping, hiking, bicycling, horseback riding, boating,

fishing, ranger-led programs, mule-drawn canal boat ride. **Special Features:** The park follows the route of the 184.5-mile canal along the Potomac River between Washington, DC, and Cumberland, MD. Built between 1828-1850, the canal operated as a transportation route, primarily hauling coal from western Maryland to the port of Georgetown in Washington, DC, until 1924. Hundreds of original structures, including locks, lockhouses, and aqueducts serve as reminders of the canal's role as a transportation system during the Canal Era. In addition, park includes a continuous trail through the spectacular scenery of the Potomac River Valley.

★70★ CHICKAMAUGA & CHATTANOOGA NATIONAL MILITARY PARK

3370 Lafayette Rd
Fort Oglethorpe, GA 30742
Web: www.nps.gov/chch/
Phone: 706-866-9241; **Fax:** 423-752-5215
Size: 9,036 acres. **History:** Established on August 19, 1890; transferred from War Department on August 10, 1933. **Location:** Park encompasses portions of Georgia and Tennessee. The Chickamauga Visitor Center is located off of US 27 in Fort Oglethorpe, GA. Lookout Mountain Battlefield Visitor Center is located on East Brow Road atop Lookout Mountain, TN. **Facilities:** Picnic area, rest rooms (&), 2 visitor centers (&), museum/exhibit, self-guided tour/trail. Entrance fee required. **Activities:** Hiking, horseback riding, living history demonstrations, auto touring. **Special Features:** In 1863, Union and Confederate forces fought for control of Chattanooga, the gateway to the deep south. A major Confederate victory on Chickamauga Creek in Georgia, September 19-20, was countered by Union victories at Orchard Knob, Lookout Mountain, and Missionary Ridge in Chattanooga, Tennessee, November 23-25. This was the first and the largest national military park established by Congress at the end of the 19th century.

★71★ CHICKASAW NATIONAL RECREATION AREA

1008 W 2nd St
Sulphur, OK 73086
Web: www.nps.gov/chic/
Phone: 580-622-3165; **Fax:** 580-622-6931
Size: 9,860 acres. **History:** Authorized as Sulphur Springs Reservation on July 1, 1902; combined with Arbuckle National Recreation Area and redesignated March 17, 1976. **Location:** On OK 177, just south of the town of Sulphur, Oklahoma; 90 miles south of Oklahoma City and 120 miles north of Dallas. **Facilities:** Campgrounds (&), picnic area, rest rooms (&), boat ramp, information and nature center (&), museum/exhibit, self-guided tour/trail. **Activities:** Camping, hiking, bicycling, swimming, boating, water-skiing, fishing, hunting, wildlife viewing, interpretive programs. **Special Features:** Chickasaw is one of the most heavily visited parks for its size in the National Park System, with 3.4 million visitors a year. The park is named to honor the Chickasaw Indian Nation, the original occupants of this land. The Travertine Nature Center offers nature study for both organized school groups and the casual visitor. Many visitors still come to drink the water from several mineral springs.

See pages 16-17 for map of U.S. National Parks.

★72★ CHIRICAHUA NATIONAL MONUMENT

13063 East Bonita Canyon Rd
Wilcox, AZ 85643
Web: www.nps.gov/chir/
Phone: 520-824-3560; **Fax:** 520-824-3421
Size: 11,985 acres. **History:** Proclaimed on April 18, 1924; transferred from Forest Service on August 10, 1933. Wilderness designated on October 20, 1976. **Location:** 120 miles east of Tucson. Exit I-10 at Willcox, and follow State Route 186 for 36 miles to the monument. **Facilities:** Campground, picnic area, rest rooms (&), visitor center (&), museum/exhibit, trails (20+ miles). Entrance fee required. **Activities:** Camping, hiking, bird-watching, wildlife viewing, auto touring, interpretive programs. **Special Features:** This forest of rock spires was eroded from layers of ash deposited by the Turkey Creek Volcano eruption 27 million years ago. Faraway Ranch, an early dude ranch, has been restored, and daily tours of the house offer a chance to learn about Swedish immigrants Neil and Emma Erickson and their children, one of the first families to settle in the area. The park area and surrounding mountains were also the homeland of the Chiricahua Apaches.

★73★ CHRISTIANSTED NATIONAL HISTORIC SITE

2100 Church St #100
Christiansted
Saint Croix, VI 00820
Web: www.nps.gov/chri/
Phone: 340-773-1460; **Fax:** 340-773-4995
Size: 27 acres. **History:** Designated as Virgin Islands National Historic Site on March 4, 1952; changed to present name on January 16, 1961. **Location:** In Christiansted, on the northern end of the Island of Saint Croix, US Virgin Islands. **Facilities:** Picnic area, rest rooms (&), visitor center, museum. Entrance fee required. **Activities:** Self-guided tour. **Special Features:** Colonial development of the Virgin Islands is commemorated by 18th- and 19th-century structures in the heart of the capital of the former Danish West Indies on Saint Croix Island. Since its discovery by Christopher Columbus in 1493, seven flags have flown over Saint Croix.

★74★ CITY OF ROCKS NATIONAL RESERVE

PO Box 169
Almo, ID 83312
Web: www.nps.gov/ciro/
Phone: 208-824-5519; **Fax:** 208-824-5563
Size: 14,107 acres. **History:** Authorized on November 18, 1988. Managed cooperatively by the National Park Service and the Idaho Department of Parks and Recreation. **Location:** 45 miles south of Burley, Idaho. From Boise and the west, take I-84 to the Declo Exit 216 and south to ID 77 to Albion, Elba, and Almo. From Pocatello and Idaho Falls, take I-86 & I-84 to the Declo Exit and then south to Almo. **Facilities:** Primitive campsites, rest rooms. Headquarters is located outside the reserve in Almo. **Activities:** Camping, hiking, rock climbing, mountain biking, horseback riding, cross-country skiing, snowmobiling, interpretive and educational programs. **Special Features:** This unique geologic area became a landmark in 1843 for California-bound emigrants. They left wagon ruts across the landscape and their signatures in axle grease on Register Rock,

Camp Rock and many others. Among the scenic granite spires and sculptured rock formations that dominate this landscape, a few pinnacles and monoliths are in excess of sixty stories tall and 2.5 billion years old. The smooth granite faces offer exceptional rock climbing and more than 500 climbing routes have been identified. Remnants of the California National Historic Trail are still visible in the area (see separate entry in national trails section).

★75★ CLARA BARTON NATIONAL HISTORIC SITE

5801 Oxford Rd
Glen Echo, MD 20812
Web: www.nps.gov/clba/
Phone: 301-320-1410
Size: 8.5 acres. **History:** Authorized on October 26, 1974. **Location:** Off MacArthur Blvd., adjacent to Glen Echo Park in Glen Echo, Maryland, several miles northwest of Washington, D.C. Accessible from the Capital Beltway (I-495). **Facilities:** Bicycle trail, visitor center, museum/exhibit. **Activities:** Guided tours. **Special Features:** This 38-room home of the founder of the American Red Cross served as the organization's headquarters for 7 years (1897-1904) and as her place of residence for the last 15 years of her life (1897-1912).

★76★ COLONIAL NATIONAL HISTORICAL PARK

Rt 238 & Colonial Pkwy
Yorktown, VA 23690
Web: www.nps.gov/colo/
Phone: 757-898-3400; **Fax:** 757-898-6346
Size: 8,677 acres. **History:** Authorized as Colonial National Monument on July 3, 1930; established on December 30, 1930; redesignated on June 5, 1936. **Location:** On the Virginia peninsula between the James and York rivers, a short distance from I-64. The 23-mile Colonial Parkway connects Jamestown and Yorktown, passing near restored Colonial Williamsburg along the way. **Facilities:** Picnic area, rest rooms (&), bicycle trail, visitor centers(&), museum/exhibit, self-guided tour/trail. Entrance fee required. **Activities:** Bicycling, auto touring, ranger-guided tours. **Special Features:** This park encompasses most of Jamestown Island, site of the first permanent English settlement; Yorktown, scene of the culminating battle of the American Revolution in 1781; a 23-mile parkway connecting these and other colonial sites with Williamsburg; and Cape Henry Memorial, which marks the approximate site of the first landing of Jamestown's colonists in 1607. Yorktown National Cemetery adjoins the park.

★77★ COLORADO NATIONAL MONUMENT

Fruita, CO 81521
Web: www.nps.gov/colm/
Phone: 970-858-3617; **Fax:** 970-858-0372
Size: 20,534 acres. **History:** Established on May 24, 1911. **Location:** In western Colorado, 12 miles from Grand Junction. From the east, take I-70 to Grand Junction, exit at Horizon Drive, and take Exit 31 to the east entrance; from the west, take I-70 to Fruita, and Exit 19 to the west entrance. **Facilities:** Campground, picnic area, rest rooms (&), bicycle trail, visitor

See pages 16-17 for map of U.S. National Parks.

center (&), museum/exhibit, trails. Entrance fee required. **Activities:** Camping, hiking, bicycling, horseback riding, mountain climbing, cross-country skiing, interpretive programs. **Special Features:** Park is part of the greater Colorado Plateau, which also includes such geological wonders as the Grand Canyon, Bryce Canyon, and Arches national parks (see separate entries for descriptions of each). Sheer-walled canyons, towering monoliths, unusual formations, dinosaur fossils, and remains of prehistoric Indian cultures reflect the environment and history of this colorful sandstone country.

★78★ CONGAREE NATIONAL PARK

100 National Park Rd
Hopkins, SC 29061
Web: www.nps.gov/cosw/
Phone: 803-776-4396; **Fax:** 803-783-4241
Size: 21,890 acres. **History:** Authorized on October 18, 1976; wilderness designated on October 24, 1988. Designated a Biosphere Reserve in 1983. Status changed from Congaree Swamp National Monument to Congaree National Park in November of 2003. **Location:** 20 miles southeast of Columbia, South Carolina. Take Exit 5 off I-77 and follow signs (15 miles). **Facilities:** Campsites (&), rest rooms (&), visitor center, boardwalk (&), trails. **Activities:** Camping, hiking, canoeing, kayaking, fishing, guided walks, canoe trips. **Special Features:** Congaree Swamp preserves, in a wilderness state, the largest intact tract of old-growth bottomland hardwood forest in the United States as well as many other plant and animal species associated with an alluvial floodplain. It features some of the tallest trees in the East with one of the highest canopies in the world. Though not a true swamp, it is recognized as an International Biosphere Reserve and National Natural Landmark.

★79★ CONSTITUTION GARDENS

900 Ohio Drive SW
Washington, DC 20024
Web: www.nps.gov/coga/
Phone: 202-426-6841; **Fax:** 202-724-0764
Size: 52 acres. **History:** Dedicated in May of 1976 and designated a separate park unit in 1982. **Location:** At Constitution Ave. and 17th St. in Washington, D.C. **Facilities:** Picnic area, rest rooms (&). **Special Features:** Once located under the Potomac River, site housed naval office buildings from 1917-1970 and was later dedicated by President Nixon in honor of the Bicentennial of the American Revolution. In July of 1982, the 56 Signers of the Declaration of Independence Memorial was dedicated on the small island in the lake. Park hosts an annual naturalization ceremony for new citizens.

★80★ CORONADO NATIONAL MEMORIAL

4101 E Montezuma Canyon Rd
Hereford, AZ 85615
Web: www.nps.gov/coro/
Phone: 520-366-5515; **Fax:** 520-366-5705
Size: 4,750 acres. **History:** Authorized as International Memorial on August 18, 1941; redesignated on July 9, 1952; established on November 5, 1952. **Location:** In southeastern Arizona along the border of the United States and Mexico, at the southern end of the Huachuca Mountains. From Phoenix or Tucson, take I-10 east and exit south on Hwy. 90 to Sierra Vista, then south on Hwy. 92 to Coronado Memorial Hwy. **Facilities:** Picnic area, rest rooms (&), visitor center (&), museum, self-guided tour/trail. **Activities:** Hiking, horseback riding, bird-watching, spelunking, interpretive programs. **Special Features:** Our Hispanic heritage and the first European exploration of the Southwest by Francisco Vasquez de Coronado (1540-1542) are commemorated here, near the point where Coronado's expedition entered what is now the United States. The memorial also preserves a wide array of plant and animal life native to the Southwest.

★81★ COWPENS NATIONAL BATTLEFIELD

4001 Chesnee Hwy
Gaffney, SC 29341
Web: www.nps.gov/cowp/
Phone: 864-461-2828; **Fax:** 864-461-7795
Size: 842 acres. **History:** Established as national battlefield site on March 4, 1929; redesignated on April 11, 1972. **Location:** 11 miles northwest of I-85 and Gaffney, SC, and 2 miles southeast of US 221 and Chesnee, SC. **Facilities:** Picnic area, rest rooms (&), bicycle trail, visitor center (&), museum/exhibit, self-guided tour/trail. **Activities:** Hiking, bicycling, auto touring, self-guided walks, interpretive programs. **Special Features:** Brigadier General Daniel Morgan won a decisive Revolutionary War victory here over British Lieutenant Colonel Banastre Tarleton on January 17, 1781.

★82★ CRATER LAKE NATIONAL PARK

PO Box 7
Crater Lake, OR 97604
Web: www.nps.gov/crla/
Phone: 541-594-3000; **Fax:** 541-594-3010
Size: 183,224 acres. **History:** Established on May 22, 1902. **Location:** In southwestern Oregon, on the crest of the Cascade Mountain range, 100 miles east of the Pacific Ocean. From Roseburg, take Route 138 east to the park's north entrance; from Bend, take Route 97 south to Route 138 west to the park's north entrance; from Medford, take Route 62 north and east to the park's west entrance; from Klamath Falls, take Route 97 north to route 62 north and west to the park's south entrance. **Facilities:** Campgrounds (&), picnic area, rest rooms (&), lodge, motor inn, groceries, restaurant/snacks, visitor centers (&), museum/exhibit, self-guided tour/trail. Entrance fee required. **Activities:** Camping, hiking, fishing, boat tours, snowmobiling, cross-country skiing, auto touring, interpretive walks, evening programs. **Special Features:** Crater Lake is well known for its deep blue color. It lies within the caldera of Mount Mazama, a volcano of the Cascade Range that erupted about 7,700 years ago. The mountain collapsed, forming a caldera. With a maximum depth of 1,932 feet, it is the deepest lake in the United States. The 33-mile Rim Drive (open from late June to mid-October) circles the caldera rim, providing scenic lake vistas.

★83★ CRATERS OF THE MOON NATIONAL MONUMENT & PRESERVE

PO Box 29
Arco, ID 83213
Web: www.nps.gov/crmo/
Phone: 208-527-3257; **Fax:** 208-527-3073

See pages 16-17 for map of U.S. National Parks.

Size: 410,000 acres (park) and 304,727 acres (preserve). **History:** Proclaimed on May 2, 1924. Wilderness designated on October 23, 1970. **Location:** In south-central Idaho, 18 miles west of Arco and 24 miles east of Carey on Hwy. 20/26/93; 84 miles from Idaho Falls and 90 miles from Twin Falls. **Facilities:** Campground, picnic area, rest rooms (&), visitor center (&), museum/exhibit, self-guided tour/trail. Entrance fee required. **Activities:** Camping, hiking, auto touring, cross-country skiing, snowshoeing, interpretive programs. **Special Features:** The Craters of the Moon Lava Field covers 618 square miles and is the largest young basaltic lava field in the coterminous United States. The monument preserves 83 square miles of it, and features more than 20 volcanic cones including outstanding examples of spatter cones. The more than 60 different lava flows on the surface range in age from 15,000 to just 2,000 years old. Surprisingly, this seemingly desolate landscape is home to more than 350 species of plants, 160 species of birds, and 43 mammals.

★84★ CUMBERLAND GAP NATIONAL HISTORICAL PARK

US Hwy 25E S
PO Box 1848
Middlesboro, KY 40965
Web: www.nps.gov/cuga/
Phone: 606-248-2817; **Fax:** 606-248-7276
Size: 20,512 acres. **History:** Authorized on June 11, 1940. **Location:** Includes sections in southeastern Kentucky, northeastern Tennessee, and southwestern Virginia. Accessible via US 25E from Kentucky and Tennessee or US 58 from Virginia. **Facilities:** Campground (&), picnic area, rest rooms (&), visitor center (&), museum/exhibit, trails (70 miles). **Activities:** Camping, hiking, wildlife viewing, interpretive programs. **Special Features:** This mountain pass on the Wilderness Road, explored by Daniel Boone, developed into a main artery of the great trans-Allegheny migration for settlement of ''the Old West'' and an important military objective in the Civil War.

★85★ CUMBERLAND ISLAND NATIONAL SEASHORE

113 W Saint Mary's St
PO Box 1203
Saint Marys, GA 31558
Web: www.nps.gov/cuis/
Phone: 912-882-4335; **Fax:** 912-673-7747
Size: 36,347 acres. **History:** Established on October 23, 1972; wilderness designated on September 8, 1982. Designated a Biosphere Reserve in 1986. **Location:** 7 miles east of St. Marys, Georgia, accessible by a concession-operated passenger ferry. **Facilities:** Campgrounds, picnic area, rest rooms (&), bathhouse, visitor center (&), museum/exhibit, self-guided tour/trail. **Activities:** Camping, hiking, swimming, fishing, ranger-led tours. **Special Features:** Magnificent and unspoiled beaches and dunes, marshes, and freshwater lakes, along with historic sites, make up the largest of Georgia's Golden Isles.

★86★ CURECANTI NATIONAL RECREATION AREA

102 Elk Creek
Gunnison, CO 81230
Web: www.nps.gov/cure/
Phone: 970-641-2337; **Fax:** 970-641-3127

Size: 41,972 acres. **History:** Administered under cooperative agreement with Bureau of Reclamation since February 11, 1965. **Location:** In west-central Colorado, accessible via US 50 which runs the length of the recreation area between Montrose and Gunnison (200 miles southwest of Denver). **Facilities:** Campgrounds (&), picnic area, rest rooms (&), groceries, restaurant/snacks, boat rental, boat ramp, visitor centers (&), museum/exhibit, self-guided tour/trail. **Activities:** Camping, hiking, swimming, boating, fishing, hunting, horseback riding, snowmobiling, cross-country skiing, bird-watching, interpretive programs, boat tours. **Special Features:** Three lakes — Blue Mesa, Morrow Point, and Crystal — extend for 40 miles along the Gunnison River. When full, Blue Mesa Lake, with a surface area of 14 square miles, is the largest lake in Colorado. Morrow Point Lake is the beginning of the Black Canyon of the Gunnison and below, Crystal Lake is the site of the Gunnison Diversion Tunnel, a National Historic Civil Engineering Landmark.

★87★ CUYAHOGA VALLEY NATIONAL PARK

15610 Vaughn Rd
Brecksville, OH 44141
Web: www.nps.gov/cuva/
Phone: 216-524-1497; **Fax:** 440-546-5989; **Toll Free:** 800-445-9667
Size: 32,861 acres. **History:** Authorized as a national recreation area on December 27, 1974; established on June 26, 1975; redesignated as a national park on October 11, 2000. **Location:** 22 miles along the Cuyahoga River between Cleveland and Akron, Ohio. **Facilities:** Picnic area, rest rooms (&), lodging, bicycle trail, visitor centers (&), museum/exhibit, 4 golf courses, winter sports center, self-guided tour/trail. **Activities:** Hiking, bicycling, horseback riding, swimming, canoeing, fishing, golf, birdwatching, winter sports, scenic train rides, interpretive programs, concerts, artist-in-residence programs, lecture series. **Special Features:** Preserving the rural character of the Cuyahoga River Valley, park includes more than 125 miles of multipurpose trails, as well as a number of historically significant sites. The 20-mile Ohio & Erie Canal Towpath Trail follows the historic route of the canal. The Cuyahoga Valley Scenic Railroad offers various excursions through the park on a year-round basis.

★88★ DAYTON AVIATION HERITAGE NATIONAL HISTORICAL PARK

16 S Williams St
Dayton, OH 45402
Web: www.nps.gov/daav/
Phone: 937-225-7705; **Fax:** 937-222-4512
Size: 86 acres. **History:** Authorized on October 16, 1992. **Location:** The four park sites are located throughout Dayton, Ohio. **Facilities:** Restored museum and exhibits operated by the National Park Service are located at Wright-Dunbar Interpretive Center and Aviation Trail Visitor Center and Museum and the Wright Cycle Company building. Exhibits and visitor services are also available at the Paul Laurence Dunbar State Memorial and Carillon Historical Park. **Activities:** Ranger-guided and self-guided tours. **Special Features:** Park preserves the area's aviation heritage associated with Orville and Wilbur Wright, their invention and development of aviation, and the life and works

of poet Paul Laurence Dunbar, a friend and classmate of the Wright brothers. Sites includes: the Wright Cycle Company Complex, including the Wright Cycle Company building and the Wright-Dunbar Interpretive Center (restored Hoover Block) and the Aviation Trail Visitor Center and Museum; the Huffman Prairie Flying Field Interpretive Center; the Wright Memorial; the Wright Brothers Aviation Center, featuring the 1905 Wright Flyer III; and the Paul Laurence Dunbar House State Memorial.

★89★ DE SOTO NATIONAL MEMORIAL
3000 75th St NW
Bradenton, FL 34209
Web: www.nps.gov/deso/
Phone: 941-792-0458; **Fax:** 941-792-5094
Size: 27 acres. **History:** Authorized on March 11, 1948. **Location:** At the northern terminus of 75th St. NW in Bradenton, Florida. Visitors can reach the park from I-75 or I-275. **Facilities:** Visitor center (&), museum/exhibit, self-guided tour/trail. **Activities:** Nature walk, interpretive programs. **Special Features:** The landing of Spanish explorer Hernando de Soto in Florida in 1539 and the first extensive organized exploration of what is now the southern United States by Europeans are commemorated here. With an army of 600 soldiers, Soto had come to the new world with a license from the King of Spain to explore, colonize, and pacify the Indians of the area known as ''La Florida''.

★90★ DEATH VALLEY NATIONAL PARK
PO Box 579
Death Valley, CA 92328
Web: www.nps.gov/deva/
Phone: 760-786-3200; **Fax:** 760-786-3283
Size: 3,372,402 acres. **History:** Proclaimed on February 11, 1933. Designated a Biosphere Reserve in 1984. Name changed from Death Valley National Monument on October 31, 1994. **Location:** In eastern California and southern Nevada. US 395 passes west of Death Valley and connects with CA 178 and CA 190 to the park. US 95 passes east and connects with NV 267, 374, and 373 to the park. I-15 passes southeast and connects with CA 127. **Facilities:** Campgrounds (&), picnic area, rest rooms (&), lodges, groceries, restaurant/snacks, bicycle trail, bathhouse, visitor centers (&), museums/exhibits, self-guided tour/trail. Entrance fee required. **Activities:** Camping, hiking, bicycling, horseback riding, auto touring, swimming, interpretive programs. **Special Features:** Death Valley is the largest national park unit outside of Alaska and includes more than 3 million acres of wilderness area. This large desert, nearly surrounded by high mountains, contains the lowest point in the Western Hemisphere. The area includes Scotty's Castle, the grandiose home of a famous prospector, and other remnants of gold and borax mining.

★91★ DELAWARE NATIONAL SCENIC RIVER
Delaware Water Gap National Recreation Area
1 River Rd
Bushkill, PA 18324
Web: www.nps.gov/dela/
Phone: 570-588-2435; **Fax:** 570-588-2780

Size: 1,973 acres. **History:** Established on November 10, 1978. **Location:** Along the Pennsylvania/New Jersey border, approximately 90 miles from Philadelphia, PA, and 64 miles from Newark, NJ. **Facilities:** Campground. **Activities:** Camping, swimming, canoeing, tubing, fishing, hunting. **Special Features:** The National Scenic River designation covers the 41 miles of the Delaware River that lie within the boundaries of Delaware Water Gap National Recreation Area (see separate entry for description).

★92★ DELAWARE WATER GAP NATIONAL RECREATION AREA
1 River Rd
Bushkill, PA 18324
Web: www.nps.gov/dewa/
Phone: 570-588-2435; **Fax:** 570-588-2780
Size: 66,740 acres. **History:** Authorized on September 1, 1965. **Location:** On the Pennsylvania/New Jersey border, 90 miles from Philadelphia and 64 miles from Newark. **Facilities:** Campgrounds, picnic area, rest rooms (&), boat rental, boat ramp, visitor centers (&), museum/exhibit, self-guided tour/trail. **Activities:** Camping, hiking, bicycling, mountain climbing, swimming, canoeing, kayaking, tubing, fishing, hunting, auto touring, snowmobiling, cross-country skiing, wildlife viewing, guided tour. **Special Features:** This scenic area preserves relatively unspoiled land on both the New Jersey and Pennsylvania sides of the Middle Delaware River. The 40-mile river segment flows through the famous gap in the Appalachian Mountains. The park sponsors a craft village and several environmental education centers.

★93★ DENALI NATIONAL PARK & PRESERVE
PO Box 9
Denali Park, AK 99755
Web: www.nps.gov/dena/
Phone: 907-683-2294; **Fax:** 907-683-9617
Size: 4,740,912 acres (national park) and 1,334,118 acres (national preserve). **History:** Established as Mount McKinley National Park on February 26, 1917. Separate Denali National Monument proclaimed on December 1, 1978. Both incorporated into and established as Denali National Park and Preserve on December 2, 1980. Wilderness designated on December 2, 1980. Designated a Biosphere Reserve in 1976. **Location:** Park headquarters is located along AK 3 (George Parks Highway), 240 miles north of Anchorage, 125 miles south of Fairbanks, and 12 miles south of Healy, Alaska. The Alaska Railroad provides daily summer passenger service to the park from Anchorage and Fairbanks. **Facilities:** Campgrounds (&), rest rooms (&), visitor centers (&), ranger station, self-guided tour/trail. Entrance fee required. **Activities:** Camping, hiking, mountain climbing, fishing, wildlife viewing, interpretive programs, cross-country skiing, dog mushing, bus tour. **Special Features:** The park contains North America's highest mountain, 20,320-foot Mount McKinley. Large glaciers of the Alaska Range, caribou, Dall sheep, moose, grizzly bears, and timber wolves are other highlights of this complete sub-arctic ecosystem.

See pages 16-17 for map of U.S. National Parks.

★94★ DEVILS POSTPILE NATIONAL MONUMENT

PO Box 3999
Mammoth Lakes, CA 93545
Web: www.nps.gov/depo/
Phone: 760-934-2289; **Fax:** 760-934-2289
Size: 798 acres. **History:** Proclaimed on July 6, 1911; transferred from Forest Service on August 10, 1933. **Location:** In east-central California, between Yosemite and Kings Canyon/Sequoia national parks. Drive 10 miles west from US 395 on SR 203 to Minaret Summit and then 7 miles on mountain road. **Facilities:** Campgrounds, picnic area, ranger station (占). **Activities:** Camping, hiking, horseback riding, fishing, interpretive programs. **Special Features:** The formation of Devils Postpile was the result of hot lava cooling and cracking to form basalt columns 40 to 60 feet high, resembling a giant pipe organ. The monument also includes the 101-foot Rainbow Falls of the San Joaquin River, and sections of the 211-mile John Muir Trail (linking Yosemite and Kings Canyon national parks) and the 2,638-mile Pacific Crest Trail (spanning the Cascade and Sierra Nevada mountain ranges, from Canada to Mexico).

★95★ DEVILS TOWER NATIONAL MONUMENT

Hwy 110 Bldg 170
Devils Tower, WY 82714
Web: www.nps.gov/deto/
Phone: 307-467-5283; **Fax:** 307-467-5350
Size: 1,347 acres. **History:** Proclaimed on September 24, 1906. **Location:** Entrance is 33 miles northeast of Moorcroft, Wyoming; 27 miles northwest of Sundance, Wyoming, via US 14; and 52 miles southwest of Belle Fourche, South Dakota, via SD 34/WY 24. **Facilities:** Campground (占), picnic area, rest rooms (占), visitor center, museum/exhibit, self-guided tour/trail. Entrance fee required. **Activities:** Camping, hiking, rock climbing. **Special Features:** Devils Tower, the nation's first national monument, is a nearly vertical monolith of igneous rock that rises 1,267 feet above the meandering Belle Fourche River. Known by several northern plains tribes as ''Bear Lodge,'' it is a sacred site of worship for many American Indians. It was also used as a filming site in the 1977 movie *Close Encounters of the Third Kind.*

★96★ DINOSAUR NATIONAL MONUMENT

4545 E Hwy 40
Dinosaur, CO 81610
Web: www.nps.gov/dino/
Phone: 970-374-3000; **Fax:** 970-374-3003
Size: 210,278 acres. **History:** Proclaimed on October 4, 1915. **Location:** In northwestern Colorado and northeastern Utah. Visitor center is 2 miles east of Dinosaur, CO, off US 40. **Facilities:** Campgrounds, picnic area, rest rooms (占), visitor centers (占), museum/exhibit, self-guided tour/trail. Entrance fee required. **Activities:** Camping, hiking, kayaking, whitewater rafting, fishing, auto touring. **Special Features:** Spectacular canyons were cut in this area by the Green and Yampa rivers through upfolded mountains. The quarry here is the single most important Jurassic dinosaur paleontological site anywhere. The monument also has a nearly complete stratigraphic geological record.

★97★ DRY TORTUGAS NATIONAL PARK

PO Box 6208
Key West, FL 33041
Web: www.nps.gov/drto/
Phone: 305-242-7700; **Fax:** 305-242-7711
Size: 64,701 acres. **History:** Proclaimed on January 4, 1935. Name changed from Fort Jefferson National Monument on October 26, 1992. **Location:** 70 miles west of Key West, Florida. Accessible only by boat or seaplane. **Facilities:** Campground (占), picnic area, rest rooms (占), visitor center, museum/exhibit, self-guided tour/trail. **Activities:** Camping, swimming, boating, fishing, snorkeling, scuba diving, bird-watching, interpretive programs. **Special Features:** Park is a cluster of seven small keys, with less than 40 acres of dry land. Fort Jefferson on Garden Key is the largest all-masonry fortification in the Western world, built in 1846-1866 to help control the Florida Straits. It served as a federal military prison during and after the Civil War. Bush Key is also home to some 100,000 sooty terns between March and September for their nesting season.

★98★ EBEY'S LANDING NATIONAL HISTORICAL RESERVE

PO Box 774
162 Cemetery Rd
Coupeville, WA 98239
Web: www.nps.gov/ebla/
Phone: 360-678-6084; **Fax:** 360-678-2246
Size: 19,324 acres. **History:** Authorized on November 10, 1978. **Location:** On central Whidbey Island off the coast of western Washington. The island is easily accesible from the mainland by automobile via SR 20 from Anacortes. The Washington State Ferry System provides year-round service to the island from Port Townsend and Mukilteo. **Facilities:** Gas, food, and loding are available within the reserve in the town of Coupeville. Campsites are available at two state parks within the reserve (Fort Casey State Park and Fort Ebey State Park). **Activities:** Camping, hiking, scuba diving, self-guided walking, biking, auto touring. **Special Features:** This area of central Whidbey Island, encompassing the community of Coupeville, protects important natural and historic features. Reserve commemorates: the first thorough exploration of the Puget Sound area by Captain George Vancouver in 1792; settlement by Colonel Isaac Neff Ebey, who led the first permanent white settlers to Whidbey Island; the early active years to the Donation Land Law of 1850-55; and the growth since 1883 of the historic town of Coupeville.

★99★ EDGAR ALLAN POE NATIONAL HISTORIC SITE

532 N 7th St
Philadelphia, PA 19123
Web: www.nps.gov/edal/
Phone: 215-597-8780; **Fax:** 215-597-1901
Size: 0.5 acres. **History:** Authorized on November 10, 1978; established on August 14, 1980. **Location:** On North 7th Street in Philadelphia, Pennsylvania. **Facilities:** Museum/exhibit, self-guided tour/trail. **Activities:** Self-guided and ranger-guided tours, educational programs. **Special Features:** The life and work of this gifted American author are portrayed in this three-building complex where Poe lived from 1843 to 1844. Of his several Philadelphia homes, only this one survives.

See pages 16-17 for map of U.S. National Parks.

★100★ EDISON NATIONAL HISTORIC SITE

Main St & Lakeside Ave
West Orange, NJ 07052
Web: www.nps.gov/edis/
Phone: 973-324-9973; **Fax:** 973-736-8496
Size: 21 acres. **History:** Edison Home National Historic Site designated on December 6, 1955; Edison Laboratory National Monument proclaimed on July 14, 1956; areas combined as Edison National Historic Site on September 5, 1962. **Location:** In West Orange, New Jersey, 2 miles west of the Garden State Parkway (Exit 145) and 1/2 mile north of I-280. **Facilities:** Rest rooms (&), visitor center (&), museum/exhibit. Entrance fee required. **Activities:** Guided tours. **Special Features:** Thomas Edison's laboratory and his residence, Glenmont, were home to the inventor from 1887 until 1931. At his "Invention Factory" he developed the phonograph, invented the movie camera and the nickel-iron alkaline storage battery, and was awarded 500 patents. The complex includes his chemistry lab, machine shop, and library.

★101★ EFFIGY MOUNDS NATIONAL MONUMENT

151 Hwy 76
Harpers Ferry, IA 52146
Web: www.nps.gov/efmo/
Phone: 563-873-3491; **Fax:** 563-873-3743
Size: 2,526 acres. **History:** Proclaimed on October 25, 1949. **Location:** 3 miles north of Marquette, Iowa, off IA 76. **Facilities:** Rest rooms (&), visitor center (&), museum/exhibit, self-guided tour/trail. Entrance fee required. **Activities:** Hiking, cross-country skiing, guided trail walks. **Special Features:** The monument preserves more than 200 prehistoric American Indian mound sites built along the Mississippi River between 450 BC and AD 1300, including 31 effigy mounds in the shapes of birds and bears. The mounds are outstanding examples of a significant phase of mound-building culture.

★102★ EISENHOWER NATIONAL HISTORIC SITE

250 Eisenhower Farm Ln
Gettysburg, PA 17325
Web: www.nps.gov/eise/
Phone: 717-338-9114; **Fax:** 717-338-0821
Size: 690 acres. **History:** Designated on November 27, 1967; authorized by act of Congress on December 2, 1969. **Location:** Adjoins Gettysburg National Military Park (see separate entry for description) in southeastern Pennsylvania, 35 miles southwest of York. **Facilities:** Rest rooms (&), visitor center (&), museum/exhibit, self-guided tour/trail. Entrance fee required. **Activities:** Guided tours, interpretive programs. **Special Features:** This was the only home ever owned by General Dwight D. Eisenhower and his wife, Mamie. It served as a refuge when he was President and as a retirement home after he left office. It includes four farms, three of which were used by Eisenhower for his show herd of black Angus cattle.

★103★ EL MALPAIS NATIONAL MONUMENT

123 E Roosevelt Ave
Grants, NM 87020
Web: www.nps.gov/elma/
Phone: 505-285-4641; **Fax:** 505-285-5661
Size: 114,277 acres. **History:** Established on December 31, 1987. **Location:** In the high desert lands south of Grants, New Mexico. Two major state highways border the monument and conservation area, and both are accessed via I-40. **Facilities:** Visitor center, self-guided tour/trail. **Activities:** Camping, hiking, auto touring, interpretive programs. **Special Features:** El Malpais ("the badlands" in Spanish) is a spectacular volcanic area, featuring cinder cones, a 17 mile-long lava tube system, and ice caves. The area is also rich in ancient Pueblo and Navajo Indian history, and features diverse ecosystems.

★104★ EL MORRO NATIONAL MONUMENT

HC 61 Box 43
Ramah, NM 87321
Web: www.nps.gov/elmo/
Phone: 505-783-4226; **Fax:** 505-783-4689
Size: 1,279 acres. **History:** Proclaimed on December 8, 1906. **Location:** 125 miles west of Albuquerque, New Mexico. From I-40 at Gallup (56 miles), go south on NM 602, then east on NM 53 through Ramah. From I-40 at Grants (42 miles), go southwest on NM 53. **Facilities:** Campground (&), picnic area, rest rooms (&), visitor center (&), museum/exhibit, self-guided tour/trail. Entrance fee required. **Activities:** Camping, hiking. **Special Features:** Ancestral Puebloans settled on the mesa top over 700 years ago. Spanish and American travelers rested, drank from the pool and carved their signatures, dates and messages for hundreds of years. Today, the national monument protects more than 2,000 inscriptions and petroglyphs, as well as Ancestral Puebloan ruins.

★105★ ELEANOR ROOSEVELT NATIONAL HISTORIC SITE

4097 Albany Post Rd
Hyde Park, NY 12538
Web: www.nps.gov/elro/
Phone: 845-229-9115; **Fax:** 845-229-0739
Size: 181 acres. **History:** Authorized on May 27, 1977. **Location:** In Hyde Park, New York, on Route 9G about 6 miles north of Poughkeepsie. **Facilities:** Restrooms (&), museum/exhibit. **Activities:** Guided tour. **Special Features:** Val-Kill Cottage, the focal point of the historic site, was originally built as a factory building for Val-Kill Industries, and was converted to a home by Eleanor Roosevelt in 1937. Mrs. Roosevelt used Val-Kill as a personal retreat from her busy life. Stone Cottage was built for her by Franklin Delano Roosevelt in 1925. The grounds include flower gardens, fields, trails, wooded areas, and a pond.

★106★ EUGENE O'NEILL NATIONAL HISTORIC SITE

PO Box 280
Danville, CA 94526
Web: www.nps.gov/euon/
Phone: 925-838-0249; **Fax:** 925-838-9471
Size: 13 acres. **History:** Authorized on October 12, 1976. **Location:** Near Danville, California. From San Francisco/Oakland area take I-80 to CA 24, then south on I-680 to Danville; from San Jose take I-680 north to Danville. **Facilities:** Visitor center.

See pages 16-17 for map of U.S. National Parks.

Activities: Guided and self-guided tours. Plays are presented in the old barn twice a year by the Eugene O'Neill Foundation in the spring and fall. **Special Features:** Tao House was built for Eugene O'Neill, who lived here from 1937 to 1944. Several of his best known plays, including The Iceman Cometh, Long Day's Journey Into Night, and A Moon for the Misbegotten were written here. The site is preserved as a memorial to the playwright.

★107★ EVERGLADES NATIONAL PARK

40001 SR-9336
Homestead, FL 33034
Web: www.nps.gov/ever/
Phone: 305-242-7700; **Fax:** 305-242-7728
Size: 1,508,537 acres. **History:** Authorized on May 30, 1934; established on December 6, 1947. Wilderness designated on November 10, 1978. Designated a Biosphere Reserve in 1976, a World Heritage Site in 1979, and a Wetland of International Importance in 1987. **Location:** Spans the southern tip of the Florida peninsula and most of Florida Bay. Park headquarters is located near Florida City. The northern and western visitor centers are accessible via US 41 (Tamiami Trail). The boundaries of Everglades National Park protect only the southern one-fifth of the historic Everglades ecosystem. **Facilities:** Campgrounds (&), picnic area, rest rooms (&), cabin rental, lodging, groceries, restaurant/snacks, bicycle trail, boat rental, boat ramp, visitor centers (&), museum/exhibit, self-guided tour/trail. Entrance fee required. **Activities:** Camping, hiking, bicycling, boating, fishing, bird-watching, wildlife viewing, ranger-led walks, boat tours, tram tours, educational programs. **Special Features:** This largest remaining subtropical wilderness in the coterminous United States has extensive freshwater and saltwater areas, open Everglades prairies, and mangrove forests. Park wildlife includes rare and endangered species, such as the American crocodile, Florida panther, and West Indian manatee. Each year, between November and May, between 50,000 and 100,000 wading birds congregate in the expansive freshwater and estuarine wetlands of the park, attracted by the excellent feeding conditions created by the drying marshes.

★108★ FEDERAL HALL NATIONAL MEMORIAL

26 Wall St
New York, NY 10005
Web: www.nps.gov/feha/
Phone: 212-825-6888; **Fax:** 212-825-6874
Size: 0.5 acres. **History:** Designated as Federal Hall Memorial National Historic Site on May 26, 1939; changed to Federal Hall National Memorial on August 11, 1955. **Location:** At the corner of Wall and Nassau streets, just off Broadway, in downtown Manhattan, NY. **Facilities:** Restrooms (&), visitor center (&). **Activities:** Guided tour. **Special Features:** This building is on the site of the original Federal Hall where the trial of John Peter Zenger, involving freedom of the press, was held in 1735; the Stamp Act Congress convened in 1765; the Second Continental Congress met in 1785; and Washington took the oath as first U.S. President and the Bill of Rights was adopted in 1789. The present building was completed in 1842 as a federal customs house. The statue of Washington on the steps of the building is by John Quincy Adams Ward.

★109★ FIRE ISLAND NATIONAL SEASHORE

120 Laurel St
Patchogue, NY 11772
Web: www.nps.gov/fiis/
Phone: 631-289-4810; **Fax:** 631-289-4898
Size: 19,579 acres. **History:** Authorized on September 11, 1964. Wilderness designated on December 23, 1980. **Location:** Fire Island stretches 32 miles along Long Island's south shore, from Moriches Inlet on the east to Democrat Point on the west. It forms a barrier between Great South Bay and the Atlantic Ocean. **Facilities:** Campground (&), picnic area, rest rooms (&), groceries, restaurant/snacks, bathhouse, marina, visitor centers (&), museum/exhibit, self-guided tour/trail. **Activities:** Camping, hiking, swimming, boating, canoeing, fishing, snorkeling, wildlife viewing, interpretive programs. **Special Features:** This barrier island offers the opportunity for beach-oriented recreation and ecological observations. The Fire Island Lighthouse and the William Floyd Estate provide introductions to the cultural history of Long Island. Much of the land in the seashore has natural features unusual for its proximity to New York City, including the Otis Pike Fire Island Wilderness, the only federal wilderness in New York, and the Sunken Forest, a 300-year-old holly forest.

★110★ FIRST LADIES NATIONAL HISTORIC SITE

205 Market Ave S
Canton, OH 44702
Web: www.nps.gov/fila/
Phone: 330-452-0876; **Fax:** 330-456-3414
Size: 0.33 acres. **History:** Authorized on October 11, 2000. The site is managed by the National Park Service and operated by the National First Ladies' Library. **Location:** Located at the Saxton McKinley House in downtown Canton, Ohio. **Facilities:** Gift shop and research library (available by scheduled arrangement only). **Activities:** Costumed docents conduct tours of the historic Ida Saxton McKinley home and exhibits highlight the McKinley's story, display images and belongings of United States First Ladies, and reveal their supporting role in the lives of US Presidents. **Special Features:** Park was established to preserve and interpret the role and history of First Ladies and other notable women in American history. Two properties, the home of First Lady Ida Saxton McKinley and the seven-story 1895 City National Bank Building, are preserved at the site.

★111★ FLIGHT 93 NATIONAL MEMORIAL

National Park Service
109 W Main St, Suite 104
Somerset, PA 15501
Web: www.flight93memorialproject.org
Phone: 814-443-4557; **Fax:** 814-443-2180
Size: 2,262 acres. **History:** Authorized as a national memorial on September 24, 2002; General Management Plan written and reviewed during the summer of 2006. **Location:** Memorial to be built in Shanksville, Pennsylvania, 80 miles southeast of Pittsburgh. **Special Features:** Memorial will honor the 40 passengers and crew members of Flight 93 who lost their lives in a struggle with hijackers who had overtaken the plane on the morning of September 11th, 1991.

See pages 16-17 for map of U.S. National Parks.

★112★ FLORISSANT FOSSIL BEDS NATIONAL MONUMENT
PO Box 185
Florissant, CO 80816
Web: www.nps.gov/flfo/
Phone: 719-748-3253; **Fax:** 719-748-3164
Size: 5,998 acres. **History:** Authorized on August 20, 1969.
Location: 35 miles west of Colorado Springs, Colorado. From north/south on I-25, take US 24 west 35 miles to town of Florissant, then follow signs 2 miles south to the visitor center. **Facilities:** Picnic area, rest rooms (&), visitor center (&), museum/exhibit, self-guided tour/trail. Entrance fee required. **Activities:** Hiking, horseback riding, cross-country skiing, guided tours, interpretive programs. **Special Features:** A wealth of fossil insects, seeds, and leaves of the Oligocene Period are preserved here in remarkable detail. Here, too, is an unusual display of petrified redwood stumps up to 14 feet wide.

★113★ FORD'S THEATRE NATIONAL HISTORIC SITE
900 Ohio Drive SW
Washington, DC 20024
Web: www.nps.gov/foth/
Phone: 202-426-6924; **Fax:** 202-426-1845
Size: 0.29 acres. **History:** Act of April 7, 1866, provided for purchase of Ford's Theatre by Federal Government; designation changed to Lincoln Museum on February 12, 1932; redesignated Ford's Theatre (Lincoln Museum) on April 14, 1965. House Where Lincoln Died authorized on June 11, 1896. Both areas combined as Ford's Theatre National Historic Site on June 23, 1970. **Location:** Near the intersection of 10th and E streets in the northwest section of Washington, DC, a block north of the FBI building on Pennsylvania Ave. **Facilities:** Visitor center, museum/exhibit. **Activities:** Guided tour. **Special Features:** On April 14, 1865, President Lincoln was shot while attending a show here at 511 Tenth Street, NW. He was carried across the street to the Petersen house, where he died the next morning. The museum beneath the theater contains portions of the Olroyd Collection of Lincolniana.

★114★ FORT BOWIE NATIONAL HISTORIC SITE
3203 S Old Ft Bowie Rd
Bowie, AZ 85605
Web: www.nps.gov/fobo/
Phone: 520-847-2500; **Fax:** 520-847-2221
Size: 999 acres. **History:** Authorized on August 30, 1964; established on July 29, 1972. **Location:** In southeastern Arizona, 116 miles east of Tucson. From Wilcox (on I-10), go 22 miles south on AZ 186 and then onto dirt road leading east into Apache Pass; from Bowie (on I-10), drive south 12 miles to Apache Pass. **Facilities:** Rest rooms (&), museum/exhibit, self-guided tour/trail. **Activities:** Hiking, birdwatching, wildlife viewing. **Special Features:** Established in 1862, this fort was the focal point of military operations against Geronimo and his band of Apaches, eventually culminating in the surrender of Geronimo in 1886 and the banishment of the Chiricahuas to Florida and Alabama. The site also preserves part of the Butterfield Overland Mail Route. The ruins can be reached only by trail.

★115★ FORT CAROLINE NATIONAL MEMORIAL
12713 Fort Caroline Rd
Jacksonville, FL 32225
Web: www.nps.gov/foca/
Phone: 904-641-7155; **Fax:** 904-641-3798
Size: 138 acres. **History:** Authorized on September 21, 1950.
Location: Along the Saint Johns River, 13 miles east of downtown Jacksonville, Florida. Memorial is a unit of Timucuan Ecological and Historic Preserve (see separate entry). **Facilities:** Picnic area, rest rooms (&), visitor center (&), museum/exhibit, self-guided tour/trail. **Activities:** Hiking, guided tour. **Special Features:** Two centuries of French and Spanish colonial rivalry in North America began here with the establishment of a French Huguenot settlement in 1564-1565.

★116★ FORT DAVIS NATIONAL HISTORIC SITE
PO Box 1379
Fort Davis, TX 79734
Web: www.nps.gov/foda/
Phone: 432-426-3224; **Fax:** 432-426-3122
Size: 474 acres. **History:** Authorized on September 8, 1961; established on July 4, 1963. **Location:** On the northern edge of the town of Fort Davis, Texas. From I-10 on the north or US 90 on the south, the site can be reached via TX 17 and 118. **Facilities:** Picnic area, rest rooms (&), visitor center (&), museum/exhibit, self-guided tour/trail. Entrance fee required. Park trails connect with Davis Mountains State Park. **Activities:** Hiking, interpretive programs. **Special Features:** A key post in west Texas from 1854-1891, Fort Davis was strategically located to guard emigrants, mail coaches, and freight wagons on the Trans-Pecos portion of the San Antonio-El Paso Road and on the Chihuahua Trail. Today the fort is regarded as the best preserved Indian Wars' frontier military post in the Southwest.

★117★ FORT DONELSON NATIONAL BATTLEFIELD
PO Box 434
Dover, TN 37058
Web: www.nps.gov/fodo/
Phone: 931-232-5706; **Fax:** 931-232-4085
Size: 552 acres (park) and 15 acres (cemetery). **History:** Established as National Military Park on March 26, 1928; redesignated on August 9, 1985. **Location:** One mile west of Dover, Tennessee, and 3 miles east of Land Between the Lakes on US 79. **Facilities:** Rest rooms (&), visitor center (&), museum/exhibit, self-guided tour/trail. **Activities:** Hiking, auto touring. **Special Features:** The first major victory for the Union Army in the Civil War occurred here in February of 1862 under the leadership of Ulysses S. Grant. Fort Donelson (Dover) National Cemetery (1,842 interments; 504 unidentified) adjoins the park.

★118★ FORT FREDERICA NATIONAL MONUMENT
6515 Frederica Rd
Saint Simons Island, GA 31522
Web: www.nps.gov/fofr/
Phone: 912-638-3639; **Fax:** 912-634-5357

See pages 16-17 for map of U.S. National Parks.

Size: 241 acres. **History:** Authorized on May 26, 1936. **Location:** On Saint Simons Island, 12 miles from Brunswick, Georgia, accessible via US 17 and the Brunswick-Saint Simons (F.J. Torras) Causeway. Bloody Marsh Battle Site, a detached unit of the park, is 6 miles south of Frederica. **Facilities:** Rest rooms (&), visitor center (&), museum/exhibit, self-guided tour/trail. Entrance fee required. **Activities:** Guided tour. **Special Features:** General James E. Oglethorpe built this British town and fort in 1736-1748 during the Anglo-Spanish struggle for control of what is now the southeastern United States. Fort Frederica's troops defeated the Spanish, ensuring Georgia's future as a British colony.

★119★ FORT LARAMIE NATIONAL HISTORIC SITE
965 Grey Rocks Rd
Fort Laramie, WY 82212
Web: www.nps.gov/fola/
Phone: 307-837-2221; **Fax:** 307-837-2120
Size: 833 acres. **History:** Proclaimed as a national monument on July 16, 1938; changed to national historic site on April 29, 1960. **Location:** 3 miles southwest of the town of Fort Laramie, Wyoming, off US 26. **Facilities:** Rest rooms (&), visitor center (&), museum/exhibit, self-guided tour/trail. **Activities:** Guided tour, interpretive programs, birdwatching, fishing, hiking. **Special Features:** Fort Laramie, on the eastern Wyoming prairie, was a fur-trade post from 1834 to 1849 and a major military post from 1849 to 1890. It figured prominently in the covered wagon migrations to Oregon and California.

★120★ FORT LARNED NATIONAL HISTORIC SITE
Rt 3 Box 69
Larned, KS 67550
Web: www.nps.gov/fols/
Phone: 620-285-6911; **Fax:** 620-285-3571
Size: 718 acres. **History:** Authorized on August 31, 1964; established on October 14, 1966. **Location:** 6 miles west of the city of Larned, Kansas, on KS 156. **Facilities:** Picnic area, rest rooms (&), visitor center (&), museum/exhibit, self-guided tour/trail. Entrance fee required. **Activities:** Fishing, guided tours, interpretive programs. **Special Features:** This military outpost was established midway along the Santa Fe Trail in 1859 to protect the mail and travelers. The fort served as a bureau for the Indian Agency during much of the 1860s and was a key military base of operations during the Indian War of 1868-1869. The fort was deactivated in 1878 and sold at public auction in 1884. The stone buildings are among the best preserved vestiges of the Indian Wars era.

★121★ FORT MATANZAS NATIONAL MONUMENT
8635 A1A S
Saint Augustine, FL 32080
Web: www.nps.gov/foma/
Phone: 904-471-0116; **Fax:** 904-471-7605
Size: 300 acres. **History:** Proclaimed on October 15, 1924; transferred from War Department on August 10, 1933. **Location:** 14 miles south of Saint Augustine, Florida, accessible via FL A1A on Anastasia Island. **Facilities:** Visitor center (&), museum/exhibit, self-guided tour/trail. **Activities:** Swimming, fishing, boating, guided boat tours. **Special Features:** Matanzas Inlet was the scene of crucial events in Spanish colonial history. The massacre of French soldiers here in 1565 was Spain's opening move in establishing a colony in Florida. The construction of Fort Matanzas in 1740-1742 was Spain's last effort to ward off British encroachments on Saint Augustine.

★122★ FORT MCHENRY NATIONAL MONUMENT & HISTORIC SHRINE
2400 E Fort Ave
Baltimore, MD 21230
Web: www.nps.gov/fomc/
Phone: 410-962-4290; **Fax:** 410-962-2500
Size: 43 acres. **History:** Authorized as Fort McHenry National Park on March 3, 1925; redesignated on August 11, 1939. **Location:** 3 miles southeast of the Baltimore Inner Harbor and just off I-95. **Facilities:** Picnic area, rest rooms (&), visitor center (&), museum/exhibit, self-guided tour/trail. Entrance fee required. **Activities:** Self-guided tours, interpretive programs. **Special Features:** Successful defense of this fort in the War of 1812, September 13-14, 1814, inspired Francis Scott Key to write "The Star Spangled Banner."

★123★ FORT MOULTRIE NATIONAL MONUMENT
1214 Middle St
Sullivans Island, SC 29482
Web: www.nps.gov/fomo/
Phone: 843-883-3123; **Fax:** 843-883-3910
Size: Fort is 2.4 acres. **Location:** Fort Moultrie is administered as part of Fort Sumter National Monument (see separate entry for description). It is located on Sullivans Island, South Carolina. From Charleston, take US 17 (business) to Mount Pleasant and turn right on SC 703. **Facilities:** Rest rooms, visitor center, exhibits. Entrance fee required. **Activities:** Self-guided tours, ranger-led programs. **Special Features:** Fort Moultrie's history covers 171 years of seacoast defense, including the first decisive victory in the American Revolution and the firing onto Fort Sumter during the first battle of the Civil War. The third Fort Moultrie, built in 1809, stands today.

★124★ FORT NECESSITY NATIONAL BATTLEFIELD
1 Washington Pkwy
Farmington, PA 15437
Web: www.nps.gov/fone/
Phone: 724-329-5512; **Fax:** 724-329-8682
Size: 903 acres. **History:** Established as national battlefield site on March 4, 1931; redesignated on August 10, 1961. **Location:** 11 miles east of Uniontown, Pennsylvania, on US 40. **Facilities:** Group campsites, picnic area (&), rest rooms (&), visitor center (&), museum/exhibit, self-guided tour/trail. Entrance fee required. **Activities:** Hiking, cross-country skiing, interpretive programs. **Special Features:** Colonial troops commanded by Colonel George Washington, then 22 years old, were defeated here in the opening battle of the French and Indian War on July 3, 1754. The park includes the nearby monument to Major General Edward Braddock and the early 19th-century Mount Washington Tavern and Jumonville Glen, site of the first skirmishing of the French and Indian War, May 28, 1754.

See pages 16-17 for map of U.S. National Parks.

★125★ FORT POINT NATIONAL HISTORIC SITE

Fort Mason, Bldg 201
San Francisco, CA 94123
Web: www.nps.gov/fopo/
Phone: 415-556-1693; **Fax:** 415-561-4390
Size: 29 acres. **History:** Established as national historic site on October 16, 1970. Beginning in the Fall of 2001, the Golden Gate Bridge District will be doing bridge retrofitting. Until this work is completed, for the safety of the visitors underneath the bridge, Fort Point will only remain open three days a week. **Location:** Beneath the southern end of the Golden Gate Bridge in San Francisco, California. **Facilities:** Picnic area, rest rooms (&), visitor center (&), museum/exhibit. **Activities:** Fishing, guided tour. **Special Features:** This classic brick and granite mid-19th-century coastal fort is the only one of its style on the west coast of the United States. It was occupied throughout the Civil War, but the advent of faster, more powerful rifled cannon made brick forts such as Fort Point obsolete. Between 1933 and 1937 the fort was used as a base of operations for the construction of the Golden Gate Bridge.

★126★ FORT PULASKI NATIONAL MONUMENT

US Hwy 80 E
Savannah, GA 31410
Web: www.nps.gov/fopu/
Phone: 912-786-5787; **Fax:** 912-786-6023
Size: 5,623 acres. **History:** Proclaimed on October 15, 1924; transferred from War Department on August 10, 1933. **Location:** 15 miles east of Savannah, Georgia. Follow US 80 east toward Tybee Island. **Facilities:** Picnic area, rest rooms (&), visitor center (&), museum/exhibit, self-guided tour/trail. Entrance fee required. **Activities:** Hiking, bicycling, boating, fishing, self-guided tours, interpretive programs. **Special Features:** Bombardment of this early 19th-century fort by rifled cannon in April of 1862 first demonstrated the ineffectiveness of old-style masonry fortifications.

★127★ FORT RALEIGH NATIONAL HISTORIC SITE

1401 National Park Dr
Manteo, NC 27954
Web: www.nps.gov/fora/
Phone: 252-473-5772; **Fax:** 252-473-2595
Size: 513 acres. **History:** Designated on April 5, 1941. **Location:** On US 64/264, 3 miles north of Manteo, North Carolina. **Facilities:** Rest rooms (&), visitor center (&), museum/exhibit, self-guided tour/trail. **Activities:** Guided tour, hiking, interpretive programs. **Special Features:** The first English settlement in North America was attempted here (1585-1587). The fate of Sir Walter Raleigh's "Lost Colony" remains a mystery. Site also preserves the cultural heritage of the Native Americans, European Americans and African Americans who have lived on Roanoke Island.

★128★ FORT SCOTT NATIONAL HISTORIC SITE

PO Box 918
Fort Scott, KS 66701
Web: www.nps.gov/fosc/
Phone: 620-223-0310; **Fax:** 620-223-0188
Size: 16.7 acres. **History:** Authorized on October 19, 1978. **Location:** In downtown Fort Scott, Kansas, at the intersection of US 69 and 54. It is 90 miles south of Kansas City and 4 miles from the Kansas-Missouri border. **Facilities:** Picnic area, rest rooms (&), visitor center (&), museum/exhibit, self-guided tour/trail. Entrance fee required. **Activities:** Guided and self-guided tours. **Special Features:** Established in 1842 as a base for the U.S. Army's peacekeeping efforts along the "permanent Indian frontier," the fort was manned by U.S. Dragoons and infantry soldiers who served in the Mexican War, provided armed escorts for parties on the Santa Fe and Oregon trails, surveyed unmapped country, and maintained contact with Plains Indians. The post was abandoned in 1853 and reactivated during the Civil War as a supply and training center. The restored and reconstructed buildings preserve the U.S. frontier of the 1840s and 1850s. Today the site consists of 20 historic structures, a parade ground and five acres of restored tallgrass prairie.

★129★ FORT SMITH NATIONAL HISTORIC SITE

301 Parker Ave
Fort Smith, AR 72901
Web: www.nps.gov/fosm/
Phone: 479-783-3961; **Fax:** 479-783-5307
Size: 75 acres. **History:** Authorized on September 13, 1961. **Location:** In downtown Fort Smith, 6 miles south of I-40 off Hwy. 64. **Facilities:** Picnic area, visitor center, museum/exhibit, self-guided tour/trail. Entrance fee required. **Activities:** Hiking, guided and self-guided tours. **Special Features:** This was one of the first U.S. military posts in the Louisiana Territory and served as a base of operations for enforcing federal Indian policy from 1817 to 1896. The park contains the remains of two frontier military forts and the Federal Court for the Western District of Arkansas. Judge Isaac C. Parker served here for 21 years protecting the rights of Native Americans and helping to bring civilized society to lawless country. "Hanging Judge" Parker's courtroom has been restored with reproductions of 1880s furnishings.

★130★ FORT STANWIX NATIONAL MONUMENT

112 E Park St
Rome, NY 13440
Web: www.nps.gov/fost/
Phone: 315-338-7730; **Fax:** 315-334-5051
Size: 15.5 acres. **History:** Authorized on August 21, 1935; acquisition completed in 1973. **Location:** In downtown Rome, New York, at the corner of North James St. and Erie Blvd. To get to Rome from the New York Thruway, take Exit 32 at Westmoreland to Rt. 233 north to Rt. 365 west, following the signs to downtown Rome. **Facilities:** Rest rooms (&), visitor center (&), museum/exhibit. Entrance fee required. **Activities:** Interpretive and living history programs. **Special Features:** The American stand here in 1777 was a major factor in repulsing the British invasion from Canada. The fort was also the site of the treaty of Fort Stanwix with the Iroquois on November 5, 1768. The current fort is a complete reconstruction of the original, built in 1758.

See pages 16-17 for map of U.S. National Parks.

★131★ FORT SUMTER NATIONAL MONUMENT

1214 Middle St
Sullivans Island, SC 29482
Web: www.nps.gov/fosu/
Phone: 843-883-3123; **Fax:** 843-883-3910
Size: 200 acres. **History:** Authorized on April 28, 1948; accepted by the U.S. Department of the Interior from the Department of the Army on July 12, 1948. **Location:** In Charleston Harbor, South Carolina, accessible only by boat. The concession tour boats leave from Patriots Point in Mount Pleasant, or the City Marina on Lockwood Blvd., just south of US 17 in Charleston. **Facilities:** Rest rooms (&), visitor center (&), museum/exhibit, self-guided tour/trail. **Activities:** Concession boat tour, self-guided tour. **Special Features:** The first engagement of the Civil War took place here on April 12, 1861, when Confederate artillery opened fire on this Federal fort in Charleston Harbor. Fort Sumter surrendered 34 hours later. The park also embraces Fort Moultrie, scene of the patriot victory of June 28, 1776 — one of the early defeats of the British in the Revolutionary War. Together the forts reflect 171 years of seacoast defense.

★132★ FORT UNION NATIONAL MONUMENT

PO Box 127
Watrous, NM 87753
Web: www.nps.gov/foun/
Phone: 505-425-8025; **Fax:** 505-454-1155
Size: 721 acres. **History:** Established on June 28, 1954. **Location:** In Watrous, New Mexico, 8 miles north of I-25 at the end of NM 161. **Facilities:** Picnic area, rest rooms (&), visitor center (&), museum/exhibit, self-guided tour/trail. Entrance fee required. **Activities:** Self-guided tour, living history talks and demonstrations. **Special Features:** Fort Union was established in 1851 as the guardian of the Santa Fe Trail. During it's forty-year history, three different forts were constructed close together. The third Fort Union was the largest in the American Southwest, and functioned as a military garrison, territorial arsenal, and military supply depot for the southwest. A large network of Santa Fe Trail ruts is still visible on the prairie.

★133★ FORT UNION TRADING POST NATIONAL
HISTORIC SITE

15550 Hwy 1804
Williston, ND 58801
Web: www.nps.gov/fous/
Phone: 701-572-9083; **Fax:** 701-572-7321
Size: 444 acres. **History:** Authorized on June 20, 1966. **Location:** 25 miles southwest of Williston, North Dakota, and 24 miles north of Sidney, Montana. **Facilities:** Rest rooms (&), visitor center (&), museum/exhibit, self-guided tour/trail. **Activities:** Hiking, fishing, cross-country skiing, self-guided tour, interpretive programs. **Special Features:** The principal fur-trading post of the American Fur Company in the Upper Missouri River region from 1828 to 1867, Fort Union served the Assiniboine, Crow, Cree, Ojibway, and Blackfeet tribes. Park encompasses portions of North Dakota and Montana.

★134★ FORT VANCOUVER NATIONAL HISTORIC
SITE

612 E Reserve St
Vancouver, WA 98661
Web: www.nps.gov/fova/
Phone: 360-816-6230; **Toll Free:** 800-832-3599
Size: 209 acres. **History:** Authorized as a national monument on June 19, 1948; changed to a national historic site on June 30, 1961. **Location:** In the city of Vancouver, Washington, just east of I-5 on East Evergreen Blvd. **Facilities:** Picnic area, rest rooms (&), visitor center (&), museum/exhibit. Entrance fee required. **Activities:** Guided tours, living history demonstrations. **Special Features:** From 1825 to 1849, Fort Vancouver was the western headquarters of the Hudson's Bay Company's fur trading operations. Under the leadership of Dr. John McLoughlin, often called the ''Father of Oregon,'' the fort became the center of political, cultural, commercial, and manufacturing activities in the Pacific Northwest. When American pioneers arrived in the Oregon Country during the 1830s and 1840s, they came to Fort Vancouver for supplies to begin their farms. The McLoughlin House, where Dr. McLoughlin lived from 1847 to 1857, in Oregon City has been fully restored and is maintained as a unit of the Fort Vancouver National Historic Site.

★135★ FORT WASHINGTON PARK

13551 Fort Washington Rd
Fort Washington, MD 20744
Web: www.nps.gov/fowa/
Phone: 301-763-4600; **Fax:** 301-763-1389
Size: 341 acres. **History:** Transfer from the War Department authorized on May 29, 1930; effective on August 12, 1940. **Location:** On the Maryland shore of the Potomac River, south of Washington, DC. From I-95, the Capital Beltway, follow the signs for MD 210 Indian Head Hwy. Take Exit 3, go south on Indian Head Hwy., and turn right onto Fort Washington Rd. **Facilities:** Picnic area, bicycle trail, rest rooms, visitor center, museum/exhibit, self-guided tour/trail. Entrance fee required. **Activities:** Hiking, bicycling, fishing, guided tours, living history programs. **Special Features:** This fort across the Potomac from Mount Vernon was built to protect Washington, D.C. Construction was begun in 1814 to replace an 1809 fort destroyed during the War of 1812.

★136★ FOSSIL BUTTE NATIONAL MONUMENT

PO Box 592
Kemmerer, WY 83101
Web: www.nps.gov/fobu/
Phone: 307-877-4455; **Fax:** 307-877-4457
Size: 8,198 acres. **History:** Established on October 23, 1972. **Location:** In southwestern Wyoming, near the intersection of US 189 and US 30. **Facilities:** Picnic area, visitor center, museum/exhibit, self-guided tour/trail. **Activities:** Hiking, horseback riding, guided tour. **Special Features:** This 50-million-year-old lake bed is one of the richest fossil localities in the world. The most noteworthy record of freshwater fossil fish ever found in the United States is preserved here. Fossil insects, snails, turtles, birds, bats, and plant remains are also found in the 50-million-year-old rock layers. Today, Fossil Butte is a

See pages 16-17 for map of U.S. National Parks.

semi-arid landscape of flat-topped buttes and ridges dominated by sagebrush, other desert shrubs, and grasses.

★137★ FRANKLIN DELANO ROOSEVELT MEMORIAL

c/o National Capital Parks Central
900 Ohio Dr SW
Washington, DC 20024
Web: www.nps.gov/frde/
Phone: 202-426-6841
Size: 7.5 acres. **History:** Authorized as a park on September 5, 1959; dedicated on May 2, 1997. **Location:** In West Potomac Park, between the Tidal Basin and the Potomac River, near the National Mall in Washington, DC. **Facilities:** Information area, bookstore. **Special Features:** Twelve years of American history are traced through a sequence of four outdoor rooms, each devoted to one of FDR's four terms in office. Sculpture inspired by photographs depict the 32nd President: A 10-foot statue shows him in a wheeled chair; a bas-relief depicts him riding in a car during his first inaugural.

★138★ FREDERICK DOUGLASS NATIONAL HISTORIC SITE

1900 Anacostia Dr SE
Washington, DC 20020
Web: www.nps.gov/frdo/
Phone: 202-426-5961; **Fax:** 202-426-0880
Size: 8.5 acres. **History:** Authorized on September 5, 1962, as Frederick Douglass Home; redesignated on February 12, 1988. **Location:** On 'W' Street in Washington, DC. **Facilities:** Picnic area, rest rooms (&), bicycle trail, visitor center (&), museum/exhibit, self-guided tour/trail. **Activities:** Guided tour. **Special Features:** From 1877 to 1895, this was the home of the Nation's leading 19th-century black spokesman. Among his achievements included his efforts to abolish slavery and his struggle for rights for all oppressed people. He also served as US Marshal for the District of Columbia and held diplomatic positions in Haiti and the Dominican Republic.

★139★ FREDERICK LAW OLMSTED NATIONAL HISTORIC SITE

99 Warren St
Brookline, MA 02445
Web: www.nps.gov/frla/
Phone: 617-566-1689; **Fax:** 617-232-4073
Size: 7 acres. **History:** Authorized on October 12, 1979. **Location:** In Brookline, Massachusetts, 5 miles east of I-95 and just south of Boylston Street. **Facilities:** Museum/exhibit, self-guided tour/trail. Park is currently closed to visitors as it undergoes a major preservation project involving the buildings, grounds and collections. Normal operating hours and programs are anticipated to resume in the fall of 2008. **Activities:** Guided tours. **Special Features:** The great conservationist, landscape architect, and founder of city planning moved his home to suburban Boston in 1883 and established ''Fairstead,'' the world's first full-scale professional office for the practice of landscape design. Over the course of the next century, his sons and successors expanded and perpetuated Olmsted's design ideals, philosophy, and influence. The site includes the Olmsted Archives and the Olmsted Center for Landscape Preservation.

★140★ FREDERICKSBURG & SPOTSYLVANIA NATIONAL MILITARY PARK

120 Chatham Ln
Fredericksburg, VA 22405
Web: www.nps.gov/frsp/
Phone: 540-371-0802; **Fax:** 540-371-1907
Size: 8,374 acres. **History:** Established on February 14, 1927; park and cemetery transferred from War Department on August 10, 1933. **Location:** 50 miles south of Washington, DC, and 50 miles north of Richmond, Virginia. Park includes numerous areas on both sides of I-95 in the Fredericksburg area. **Facilities:** Picnic area, rest rooms (&), visitor centers (&), museum/exhibit, bookstore, self-guided tour/trail. **Activities:** Hiking, bicycling, guided and self-guided tours. **Special Features:** Portions of four major Civil War battlefields (Fredericksburg, Chancellorsville, the Wilderness, and Spotsylvania Court House), Chatham Manor (a former hospital for Union soldiers), and several smaller historic sites comprise the park. The four battles, fought in the vicinity of Fredericksburg, occurred between 1862 and 1864 and resulted in 110,000 casualties, making it the bloodiest ground on the North American continent. Fredericksburg National Cemetery (15,333 interments; 12,746 unidentified) is located in the park.

★141★ FRIENDSHIP HILL NATIONAL HISTORIC SITE

223 New Geneva Rd
Point Marion, PA 15474
Web: www.nps.gov/frhi/
Phone: 724-725-9190; **Fax:** 724-725-1999
Size: 675 acres. **History:** Authorized on November 10, 1978. **Location:** In southwestern Pennsylvania, 12 miles from Uniontown and 10 miles from Morgantown, West Virginia. **Facilities:** Picnic area, rest rooms (&), visitor center (&), museum/exhibit, self-guided tour/trail. **Activities:** Hiking, fishing, cross-country skiing, guided and self-guided tours. **Special Features:** This stone and brick home on the Monongahela River near Point Marion, Pennsylvania, belonged to Albert Gallatin, Secretary of the Treasury, 1801-1813, under Presidents Jefferson and Madison. Gallatin's accomplishments and contributions include reducing the national debt, purchasing the Louisiana Territory and funding the Lewis & Clark exploration.

★142★ GATES OF THE ARCTIC NATIONAL PARK & PRESERVE

4175 Geist Rd
Fairbanks, AK 99709
Web: www.nps.gov/gaar/
Phone: 907-457-5752; **Fax:** 907-455-0601; **Toll Free:** 866-869-6887
Size: 7,523,898 acres (park) and 948,608 acres (preserve). **History:** Proclaimed Gates of the Arctic National Monument on December 1, 1978; established as a national park and preserve

See pages 16-17 for map of U.S. National Parks.

on December 2, 1980. Wilderness designated on December 2, 1980. Portion of park and preserve designated a Biosphere Reserve in 1984. **Location:** In the central Brooks Mountain Range in north-central Alaska. There are no roads in the park, although the Dalton Hwy. comes within about 5 miles of the park's eastern boundary. Access into the park is by charter plane from Bettles or other locations. Commercial air service is available to Anaktuvuk Pass, just outside the park. **Facilities:** Ranger stations, exhibits. **Activities:** Camping, hiking, mountain climbing, dog mushing, boating, fishing, bird-watching, hunting, cross-country skiing, snowshoeing. **Special Features:** Lying entirely north of the Arctic Circle, the park-preserve includes a portion of the Central Brooks Range, the northernmost extension of the Rocky Mountains. Often referred to as the greatest remaining wilderness in North America, this second largest unit of the National Park System is characterized by jagged peaks, gentle arctic valleys, wild rivers, and numerous lakes. The forested southern slopes contrast to the barren northern reaches of the site at the edge of Alaska's ''north slope.'' The park-preserve contains the Alatna, John, Kobuk, part of the Noatak, the North Fork of the Koyukuk, and the Tinayguk wild rivers. Together with adjacent Kobuk Valley National Park and Noatak National Preserve, it comprises one of the largest park areas in the world.

★143★ GATEWAY NATIONAL RECREATION AREA

210 New York Ave
Staten Island, NY 10305
Web: www.nps.gov/gate/
Phone: 718-354-4606; **Fax:** 718-354-4605
Size: 26,607 acres. **History:** Established on October 27, 1972. **Location:** Park extends through three New York City boroughs (Breezy Point Unit, Jamaica Bay Unit, and Staten Island Unit) and into northern New Jersey (Sandy Hook Unit). **Facilities:** Campgrounds, picnic area, rest rooms (♿), restaurant/snacks, bicycle trail, boat ramp, bathhouse, visitor centers (♿), museum/exhibit, self-guided tour/trail. **Activities:** Camping, hiking, bicycling, horseback riding, swimming, boating, fishing, auto touring, ranger-led programs. **Special Features:** With beaches, marshes, islands, and adjacent waters in the New York harbor area, this park offers urban residents a wide range of recreational opportunities. The Sandy Hook Unit, in New Jersey, features beaches, plant and animal life, and historic structures, including Sandy Hook Lighthouse (1764), the oldest operational light in the United States.

★144★ GAULEY RIVER NATIONAL RECREATION AREA

104 Main St
PO Box 246
Glen Jean, WV 25846
Web: www.nps.gov/gari/
Phone: 304-465-0508; **Fax:** 304-465-0591
Size: 11,506 acres. **History:** Authorized on October 26, 1988. **Location:** Off US 19 between Summersville and Fayetteville, West Virginia. **Facilities:** None. **Activities:** Camping, hiking, whitewater rafting, boating, kayaking, fishing, hunting. **Special Features:** The 25 miles of free-flowing Gauley River and the 6 miles of the Meadow River pass through scenic gorges and valleys containing a wide variety of natural and cultural features.

The Gauley River contains several Class V+ rapids, making it one of the most adventurous whitewater boating rivers in the eastern United States.

★145★ GENERAL GRANT NATIONAL MEMORIAL

Riverside Dr & W 122nd St
New York, NY 10027
Web: www.nps.gov/gegr/
Phone: 212-666-1640; **Fax:** 212-932-9631
Size: 0.75 acres. **History:** Dedicated on April 27, 1897. National Park Service administration authorized on August 14, 1958. **Location:** Overlooks the Hudson River from the Mornside Heights section of Manhattan. Near the intersection of Riverside Dr. and West 122nd St. **Facilities:** Visitor center/museum. **Activities:** Ranger-guided programs and tours. **Special Features:** This memorial to Ulysses S. Grant, the Union commander who brought the Civil War to an end, includes the tombs of General and Mrs. Grant. As the President of the United States (1869-1877), Grant signed the act establishing the first national park, Yellowstone, on March 1, 1872.

★146★ GEORGE ROGERS CLARK NATIONAL HISTORICAL PARK

401 S 2nd St
Vincennes, IN 47591
Web: www.nps.gov/gero/
Phone: 812-882-1776; **Fax:** 812-882-7270
Size: 26 acres. **History:** Authorized on July 23, 1966. **Location:** Between South 2nd St. and the Wabash River in Vincennes, Indiana. **Facilities:** Rest rooms (♿), visitor center (♿), museum/exhibit. Entrance fee required. **Activities:** Living history programs. **Special Features:** This classic memorial building, located near the site of old Fort Sackville, commemorates the capture of the fort from the British by Lieutenant Colonel George Rogers Clark, February 25, 1779, and the subsequent settlement of the region north of the Ohio River. The statue was sculpted by Hermon MacNeil.

★147★ GEORGE WASHINGTON BIRTHPLACE NATIONAL MONUMENT

1732 Popes Creek Rd
Washington's Birthplace, VA 22443
Web: www.nps.gov/gewa/
Phone: 804-224-1732; **Fax:** 804-224-2142
Size: 662 acres. **History:** Established on January 23, 1930. **Location:** On the Potomac River, 38 miles east of Fredericksburg, Virginia; accessible via VA 3 and VA 204. **Facilities:** Picnic area, rest rooms (♿), visitor center (♿), museum/exhibit, self-guided tour/trail. Entrance fee required. **Activities:** Hiking, fishing, ranger-guided tours, interpretive programs. **Special Features:** Birthplace of the first U.S. President in 1732, this park includes a memorial mansion and gardens, and the tombs of his father, grandfather, and great-grandfather.

★148★ GEORGE WASHINGTON CARVER NATIONAL MONUMENT

5646 Carver Rd
Diamond, MO 64840
Web: www.nps.gov/gwca/
Phone: 417-325-4151; **Fax:** 417-325-4231

See pages 16-17 for map of U.S. National Parks.

Size: 210 acres. **History:** Authorized on July 14, 1943. **Location:** 2 miles west of Diamond, Missouri, on Highway V, then south 0.5 miles on Carver Road. **Facilities:** Picnic area, rest rooms (&), visitor center (&), museum/exhibit, self-guided tour/trail. **Activities:** Hiking, guided tours and programs. **Special Features:** The birthplace and childhood home of George Washington Carver, African-American agronomist, educator, and humanitarian, include a museum, Discovery Center, a trail passing the birthplace site, Boy Carver statue, restored 1881 Moses Carver House, and the Carver family cemetery.

★149★ GEORGE WASHINGTON MEMORIAL PARKWAY

Turkey Run Park
McLean, VA 22101
Web: www.nps.gov/gwmp/
Phone: 703-289-2500; **Fax:** 703-289-2598
Size: 7,241 acres. **History:** Act providing for acquisition of land, establishment, and development of the parkway authorized on May 29, 1930. The road in Maryland was renamed the Clara Barton Parkway on November 28, 1989. **Location:** Parkway includes two main sections: the 25-mile Virginia section that runs from Mount Vernon northward along the Potomac River to I-495; and the the Clara Barton Parkway in Maryland that follows the Potomac River for 7 miles from Chain Bridge in Washington, DC, to north of I-495. **Facilities:** Picnic area, rest rooms (&), restaurant/snacks, bicycle trail, boat ramp, visitor center, museum/exhibit, self-guided tour/trail. **Activities:** Hiking, bicycling, boating, fishing, auto touring. **Special Features:** This landscaped riverfront parkway links many landmarks in the life of George Washington, while preserving the natural scenery along the Potomac River. It connects historic sites from Mount Vernon, where George Washington lived, past the National Capital, which he founded, to the Great Falls of the Potomac, where he demonstrated his skill as an engineer.

★150★ GETTYSBURG NATIONAL MILITARY PARK

97 Taneytown Rd
Gettysburg, PA 17325
Web: www.nps.gov/gett/
Phone: 717-334-1124; **Fax:** 717-334-1891
Size: 5,990 acres. **History:** Park established on February 11, 1895; transferred from War Department, along with cemetery, on August 10, 1933. **Location:** In Adams County, Pennsylvania, 50 miles northwest of Baltimore. From north and south, follow US 15 to Gettysburg; from east and west, follow US 30. **Facilities:** Youth group campsites, picnic area, rest rooms (&), bicycle trail, visitor center and cycloroma center (&), museum, self-guided tour/trail. **Activities:** Camping, bicycling, auto tour, guided tours, interpretive programs. **Special Features:** The great Civil War battle fought here July 1-3, 1863, repulsed the second Confederate invasion of the North and resulted in more than 51,000 soldiers being killed, wounded or captured, making it the bloodiest battle of the Civil War. Gettysburg National Cemetery (more than 7,000 interments; 1,668 unidentified) adjoins the park. President Lincoln delivered his Gettysburg Address here in dedicating the cemetery on November 19, 1863.

★151★ GILA CLIFF DWELLINGS NATIONAL MONUMENT

HC 68 Box 100
Silver City, NM 88061
Web: www.nps.gov/gicl/
Phone: 505-536-9461; **Fax:** 505-536-9344
Size: 533 acres. **History:** Proclaimed on November 16, 1907; transferred from Forest Service on August 10, 1933; Forest Service resumed administration of National Park Service area on April 28, 1975. **Location:** 44 miles north of Silver City on NM 15. **Facilities:** Rest rooms (&), visitor center (&), museum/exhibit, self-guided tour/trail. Entrance fee required. **Activities:** Hiking, guided tours. **Special Features:** These well-preserved cliff dwellings in natural cavities on the face of an overhanging cliff offers a glimpse of the homes and lives of the people of the Mogollon culture who lived in the Gila Wilderness from the 1280s through the early 1300s. There are several popular hot springs in the area.

★152★ GLACIER BAY NATIONAL PARK & PRESERVE

1 Park Rd
PO Box 140
Gustavus, AK 99826
Web: www.nps.gov/glba/
Phone: 907-697-2230; **Fax:** 907-697-2654
Size: 3,224,840 acres (park) and 58,406 acres (preserve). **History:** Proclaimed Glacier Bay National Monument on February 25, 1925; established as a national park and preserve on December 2, 1980. Wilderness designated on December 2, 1980. Designated a Biosphere Reserve in 1986. **Location:** West of Juneau in southeastern Alaska. Park headquarters is at Bartlett Cove, 65 miles from Juneau. Park can be reached only by boat or plane; there are no roads to Glacier Bay and no Alaska state ferry service. Travel options include scheduled and charter air services, tour boats, cruise ships, and charter boats. **Facilities:** Campground, lodging, restaurant/snacks, exhibits. **Activities:** Camping, hiking, mountain climbing, kayaking, boating, fishing, wildlife viewing, hunting, interpretive programs, boat and kayak tours. **Special Features:** Park features great tidewater glaciers, a dramatic range of plant communities from rocky terrain recently covered by ice to lush temperate rain forest, and a large variety of animals, including brown and black bear, mountain goats, whales, seals, and eagles. Also included are Mount Fairweather, the highest peak in southeast Alaska, and the U.S. portion of the Alsek River.

★153★ GLACIER NATIONAL PARK

PO Box 128
West Glacier, MT 59936
Web: www.nps.gov/glac/
Phone: 406-888-7800; **Fax:** 406-888-7808
Size: 1,013,572 acres. **History:** Established on May 11, 1910. Designated a Biosphere Reserve in 1976. Authorized as part of Waterton-Glacier International Peace Park on May 2, 1932. Designated as part of Waterton-Glacier International Peace Park World Heritage Site in 1995. **Location:** In northwestern Montana on the U.S./Canadian border. Accessible from the east and west along US 2. Park headquarters is located in West Glacier.

See pages 16-17 for map of U.S. National Parks.

Facilities: Campgrounds (♿), picnic area, rest rooms (♿), cabin rental, lodging (most hotels/lodges are open only from late May through September), groceries, restaurant/snacks, boat rental, boat ramp, visitor center (♿), museum/exhibit, trails (700+ miles). Entrance fee required. **Activities:** Camping, hiking, bicycling, mountain climbing, horseback riding, swimming, boating, fishing, cross-country skiing, snowshoeing, naturalist programs. **Special Features:** With precipitous peaks ranging above 10,000 feet, this ruggedly beautiful land includes 27 glaciers, many lakes and streams, a wide variety of wildflowers, and wildlife. The 52-mile Going to the Sun Road (opened in 1932) connects 10-mile-long Lake McDonald in the west, across the 6,646-foot high Logan Pass over the Continental Divide, to Saint Mary Lake on the eastern border.

★154★ GLEN CANYON NATIONAL RECREATION AREA
PO Box 1507
691 Scenic View Dr
Page, AZ 86040
Web: www.nps.gov/glca/
Phone: 928-608-6200; **Fax:** 928-608-6259
Size: 1,254,429 acres. **History:** Administered under cooperative agreements between Bureau of Reclamation and U.S. Department of the Interior, April 18, 1958, and September 17, 1965. Established as a national recreation area on October 27, 1972. **Location:** In southeastern Utah and northern Arizona, encompassing the area surrounding Lake Powell, which stretches for 186 miles along the old Colorado River channel behind Glen Canyon Dam. Lees Ferry and the Navajo Bridge Interpretive Center are located on AZ 89A. Carl Hayden Visitor Center in Page, AZ is on AZ 89. The Bullfrog Visitor Center is located on UT 276. Halls Crossing is also reached by UT 276. Hite is located just off UT 95. **Facilities:** Campgrounds, picnic area, rest rooms (♿), lodging, groceries, restaurant/snacks, boat rental, boat ramp, visitor centers (♿), museum/exhibit, self-guided tour/trail. **Activities:** Camping, hiking, mountain biking, swimming, kayaking, boating, fishing, scuba diving, water-skiing, hunting, auto touring, ranger programs, guided tours. **Special Features:** This park lies in the midst of the most rugged canyon country on the Colorado Plateau. Lake Powell's 1,960 miles of shoreline provide a variety of water-based recreational opportunities.

★155★ GOLDEN GATE NATIONAL RECREATION AREA
Fort Mason, Bldg 201
San Francisco, CA 94123
Web: www.nps.gov/goga/
Phone: 415-561-4700; **Fax:** 415-561-4750
Size: 74,826 acres. **History:** Established on October 27, 1972. Designated a Biosphere Reserve in 1988. **Location:** Encompasses shoreline area of San Francisco, Marin, and San Mateo counties in California. Accessible by Highways 1, 101, 880, and 280. **Facilities:** Campgrounds (♿), picnic area, rest rooms (♿), restaurant/snacks, bicycle trail, bathhouse, visitor centers (♿), museum/exhibit, self-guided tour/trail. **Activities:** Camping, hiking, bicycling, horseback riding, swimming, fishing, auto touring, interpretive programs. **Special Features:** Featuring 28 miles of coastline, the largest urban national park in the world includes ocean beaches, redwood forest, lagoons, marshes, military properties, a cultural center at Fort Mason, and Alcatraz Island.

★156★ GOLDEN SPIKE NATIONAL HISTORIC SITE
PO Box 897
Brigham City, UT 84302
Web: www.nps.gov/gosp/
Phone: 435-471-2209; **Fax:** 435-471-2341
Size: 2,735 acres. **History:** Designated as a national historic site in nonfederal ownership on April 2, 1957; authorized for federal ownership and administration by act of Congress on July 30, 1965. **Location:** 32 miles west of Brigham City, Utah, via UT 13 and 83. **Facilities:** Picnic area, visitor center (♿), museum/exhibit, self-guided tour/trail. Entrance fee required. **Activities:** Interpretive and living history programs, auto touring. **Special Features:** Completion of the first transcontinental railroad in the United States was celebrated here where the Central Pacific and the Union Pacific railroads met on May 10, 1869, joining 1,776 miles of rail.

★157★ GOVERNORS ISLAND NATIONAL MONUMENT
10 South St, Slip #7
New York, NY 10004
Web: www.governorsislandnationalmonument.org
Phone: 212-825-3045; **Fax:** 212-825-3055
Size: 23 acres of the 172-acre island. **History:** Established on January 19, 2001; transferred to the National Park Service on January 31, 2003. The General Management Plan (GMP), when completed, will provide a long-term strategy to address resource preservation and use, public programs, and activities. The planning process for the island is being led by the National Park Service (NPS) and the Governors Island Preservation and Education Corporation (GIPEC). NPS is responsible for the monument and GIPEC is responsible for development of the rest of the island. **Location:** Governors Island is located in Upper New York Harbor at the mouth of the East River, 0.5 mile from the southern tip of Manhattan and the Brooklyn waterfront. The island is about a five-minute boat ride from lower Manhattan or Brooklyn. **Facilities:** In planning stages. **Activities:** Tours (June-September). **Special Features:** Located on Governors Island, NY, between the confluence of the Hudson and East Rivers, the monument is part of a larger 1985 National Historic Landmark District designation and contains two important historical objects: Castle William and Fort Jay. Between 1806 and 1811, these fortifications were constructed as part of the First and Second American Systems of Coastal Fortification to protect New York City from sea attack. Both Castle William and Fort Jay represent two of the finest types of defensive structure in use from the Renaissance to the American Civil War. The monument also played important roles in the War of 1812, the American Civil War, and World Wars I and II. During the past 200 years, Governors Island was managed by the U.S. Army and the U.S. Coast Guard but is no longer needed for military purposes.

See pages 16-17 for map of U.S. National Parks.

★158★ GRAND CANYON NATIONAL PARK

PO Box 129
Grand Canyon, AZ 86023
Web: www.nps.gov/grca/
Phone: 928-638-7888; **Fax:** 928-638-7797
Size: 1,217,403 acres. **History:** Grand Canyon Forest Reserve proclaimed on February 20, 1893; Grand Canyon Game Preserve proclaimed on November 28, 1906; Grand Canyon National Monument proclaimed on January 11, 1908; national park established on February 26, 1919. A separate Grand Canyon National Monument proclaimed on December 22, 1932. Marble Canyon National Monument proclaimed on January 20, 1969. All three units and portions of Glen Canyon and Lake Mead national recreation areas combined with additional lands as national park on January 3, 1975. Designated a World Heritage Site on October 24, 1979. **Location:** In northern Arizona. Grand Canyon Village (South Rim) is 60 miles north of I-40 at Williams via AZ 64, and 80 miles northwest of Flagstaff via US 180. Only ten miles from rim to rim as the crow flies, the North Rim is 215 miles (about 4 1/2 hours) from the South Rim by car. The North Rim is 44 miles south of Jacob Lake, Arizona, via AZ 67. The road from Jacob Lake to the North Rim (Highway 67) is subject to closure due to snow from mid-October to mid-May. **Facilities:** Campgrounds (&), picnic area, rest rooms (&), cabin rental, lodging, groceries, restaurant/snacks, visitor centers and observation station (&), museum/exhibit, self-guided tour/trail, shuttle bus services. Entrance fee required. Services and facilities at the South Rim are open year round. Services and facilities at the North Rim are open from mid-May through mid-October. Weather permitting, the North Rim is open for day use only from mid-October through mid-May. **Activities:** Camping, hiking, bicycling, horseback riding, fishing, whitewater rafting, auto touring, cross-country skiing, interpretive programs, guided tours. **Special Features:** The park, focusing on the world-famous Grand Canyon of the Colorado River, encompasses 277 miles of the river with adjacent uplands, from the southern terminus of Glen Canyon National Recreation Area to the eastern boundary of Lake Mead National Recreation Area (see separate entries for descriptions of each). The forces of erosion have exposed an immense variety of formations which illustrate vast periods of geological history.

★159★ GRAND PORTAGE NATIONAL MONUMENT

PO Box 668
Grand Marais, MN 55604
Web: www.nps.gov/grpo/
Phone: 218-387-2788; **Fax:** 218-387-2790
Size: 710 acres. **History:** Designated as a national historic site on September 15, 1951; changed to national monument by act of Congress on September 2, 1958. **Location:** On the northwestern shore of Lake Superior, 7 miles south of the United States-Canada border and 36 miles north of Grand Marias, Minnesota. Park entrance is one mile from MN 61. **Facilities:** Picnic area, rest rooms (&), boat dock, museum/exhibit, self-guided tour/trail. Entrance fee required. **Activities:** Hiking, fishing, cross-country skiing, guided tour. **Special Features:** This 9-mile portage was a vital link on one of the principal routes for Indians, explorers, missionaries, and fur traders heading for the Northwest. The Grand Portage post of the North West Company has

been reconstructed at the eastern terminus of the Grand Portage on Lake Superior.

★160★ GRAND TETON NATIONAL PARK

Teton Park Rd
PO Drawer 170
Moose, WY 83012
Web: www.nps.gov/grte/
Phone: 307-739-3300; **Fax:** 307-739-3438
Size: 309,995 acres. **History:** Established on February 26, 1929. **Location:** In northwestern Wyoming, just north of Jackson and south of Yellowstone National Park. Accesible via US 26/287 from the east, US 26/89 or 191 from the south, and US 89 or 191/287 from the north. **Facilities:** Campgrounds (&), picnic area, rest rooms (&), cabin rental, lodging, groceries, restaurant/snacks, boat rental, boat ramp, visitor centers (&), museum/exhibit, self-guided tour/trail. Entrance fee required. **Activities:** Camping, hiking, horseback riding, mountain climbing, swimming, boating, fishing, wildlife viewing, auto touring, snowmobiling, cross-country skiing, snowshoeing, guided tours, educational programs. **Special Features:** The most impressive part of the Teton Range, this series of blue-gray peaks rising more than a mile above the sagebrush flats and pristine lakes was once a noted landmark for Indians and ''mountain men.'' The park includes part of Jackson Hole, winter feeding ground of the largest American elk herd.

★161★ GRANT-KOHRS RANCH NATIONAL HISTORIC SITE

266 Warren Ln
Deer Lodge, MT 59722
Web: www.nps.gov/grko/
Phone: 406-846-2070; **Fax:** 406-846-3962
Size: 1,618 acres. **History:** Authorized on August 25, 1972. **Location:** At the north end of the town of Deer Lodge, Montana, off I-90. Deer Lodge is 40 miles north of Butte and 80 miles southeast of Missoula. **Facilities:** Rest rooms (&), visitor center (&), museum/exhibit, self-guided tour/trail. Entrance fee required. **Activities:** Guided tour. **Special Features:** Once the headquarters of a 10-million-acre, 19th-century cattle empire, the site preserves more than 80 structures and many historic artifacts associated with its operation, representing more than 125 years of ranching heritage. It is still a working cattle ranch.

★162★ GREAT BASIN NATIONAL PARK

100 Great Basin National Park
Baker, NV 89311
Web: www.nps.gov/grba/
Phone: 775-234-7331; **Fax:** 775-234-7269
Size: 77,180 acres. **History:** Lehman Caves National Monument proclaimed on January 24, 1922; transferred from Forest Service on August 10, 1933; made part of Great Basin National Park when established on October 27, 1986. **Location:** The main park entrance is 5 miles west of Baker, Nevada, near the Nevada-Utah border. **Facilities:** Campgrounds (&), picnic area, rest rooms (&), restaurant/snacks, visitor center (&), museum/exhibit, self-guided tour/trail. **Activities:** Camping, hiking, horseback riding, mountain climbing, fishing, auto touring, cross-country skiing, guided cave tours, stargazing. **Special Features:**

See pages 16-17 for map of U.S. National Parks.

A remnant icefield on 13,063-foot Wheeler Peak, 5,000-year-old bristlecone pine trees, 75-foot limestone Lexington Arch, and the tunnels and decorated galleries of Lehman Caves are the park's major features.

★163★ GREAT EGG HARBOR NATIONAL SCENIC & RECREATIONAL RIVER

c/o National Park Service
200 Chestnut St
Philadelphia, PA 19106
Web: www.nps.gov/greg/
Phone: 215-597-5823
Size: 43,311 acres. **History:** Authorized on October 27, 1992. The National Park Service manages the designated river in partnership with the State of New Jersey, four counties, and twelve municipalities. **Location:** 129 miles of the Great Egg Harbor River and its tributaries run through or along the Pine Barrens of southern New Jersey, near the urban centers of Philadelphia, Trenton, Camden, and Wilmington. **Activities:** Canoeing, kayaking, sailboating, fishing, hiking, birdwatching, and camping. **Special Features:** The Great Egg Harbor River has been recognized as the longest canoeable river in the Pinelands National Reserve. The freshwater and tidal wetlands serve as resting, feeding, and breeding areas for waterfowl throughout the year amid undisturbed forests and swamp areas. The river corridor is home to several threatened and endangered species of flora and fauna and is rated one of the top birding spots in North America.

★164★ GREAT SAND DUNES NATIONAL PARK & PRESERVE

11500 Hwy 150
Mosca, CO 81146
Web: www.nps.gov/grsa/
Phone: 719-378-6300; **Fax:** 719-378-6310
Size: 107,452 acres (park) and 41,686 acres (preserve). Park acreage includes ''The Baca'' section purchased on September 10, 2004. **History:** Proclaimed on March 17, 1932. Wilderness designated on October 20, 1976. Redesignated Great Sand Dunes National Monument and Preserve on November 22, 2000. Redesignated a national park on September 24, 2004. **Location:** 35 miles northeast of Alamosa, Colorado, reached by US 160 and CO 150 from the south; or from CO 17 and County Six Mile Lane from the west. **Facilities:** Campground (&), picnic area, rest rooms (&), visitor center (&), museum/exhibit, self-guided tour/trail. Entrance fee required. **Activities:** Camping, hiking, fishing, horseback riding, auto touring, stargazing, ranger-guided programs. **Special Features:** In this high mountain valley are the tallest dunes in North America, flanked by some of the highest peaks in the Rocky Mountains. The park and preserve protects much of the Great Sand Dunes' natural system, including alpine tundra and lakes, forests, streams, dunes, grasslands, and wetlands. The dunes were deposited over thousands of years by southwesterly winds blowing through the passes of the Sangre de Cristo Mountains. Depending on the time of day, the dunes turn different shades of rust, brown, pink, cream, gray, and gold.

★165★ GREAT SMOKY MOUNTAINS NATIONAL PARK

107 Park Headquarters Rd
Gatlinburg, TN 37738
Web: www.nps.gov/grsm/
Phone: 865-436-1200; **Fax:** 865-436-1220
Size: 521,495 acres. **History:** Authorized on May 22, 1926; established for full development on June 15, 1930. Designated a Biosphere Reserve in 1976 and a World Heritage Site in 1983. **Location:** In eastern Tennessee and western North Carolina. Several major highways lead to the park's three main entrances. In Tennessee, from I-40 take Exit 407 (Sevierville) to TN 66 South, and continue to US 441 South. In Tennessee, from I-40 in Knoxville take Exit 386B US 129 south to Alcoa/Maryville, then proceed on US 321 north through Townsend, and then straight on TN 73. In North Carolina, from I-40 take US 19 west through Maggie Valley and proceed to US 441 north at Cherokee. From Atlanta and points south, follow US 441 and 23 North. **Facilities:** Campgrounds (&), picnic area, rest rooms (&), lodging, groceries, bicycle trail, visitor centers (&), museum/exhibit, trails (800+ miles). **Activities:** Camping, hiking, bicycling, horseback riding, fishing, wildlife viewing, auto touring, ranger-led programs and other educational activities. **Special Features:** The loftiest range east of the Black Hills and one of the oldest uplands on Earth, the Smokies have a biological diversity that includes 1,400+ species of flowering plants and 4,000+ species of non-flowering plants, 100 species of native trees, 200+ species of birds, and 66 species of mammals. Besides the exquisite flora and fauna, the park also preserves structures representing southern Appalachian mountain culture. It is one of the largest protected areas in the eastern United States.

★166★ GREENBELT PARK

6565 Greenbelt Rd
Greenbelt, MD 20770
Web: www.nps.gov/gree/
Phone: 301-344-3948; **Fax:** 301-344-1012
Size: 1,175 acres. **History:** Transferred from Public Housing Authority on August 3, 1950. **Location:** In Greenbelt, Maryland, 12 miles from downtown Washington, DC, and 23 miles from Baltimore. The Baltimore-Washington Parkway passes through the park. **Facilities:** Campground (&), picnic area, rest rooms (&), self-guided nature trails. **Activities:** Camping (year-round), hiking, bicycling, horseback riding, guided programs. **Special Features:** This woodland park offers urban dwellers access to many forms of outdoor recreation.

★167★ GUADALUPE MOUNTAINS NATIONAL PARK

400 Pine Canyon Rd
Salt Flat, TX 79847
Web: www.nps.gov/gumo/
Phone: 915-828-3251; **Fax:** 915-828-3269
Size: 86,416 acres. **History:** Authorized on October 15, 1966; established on September 30, 1972. Wilderness designated on November 10, 1978. **Location:** In west Texas on US 62/180, 110 miles east of El Paso and 55 miles southwest of Carlsbad, New Mexico. **Facilities:** Campground (&), picnic area, rest rooms (&), off-road vehicle trail, visitor center, museum, trails

See pages 16-17 for map of U.S. National Parks.

1. US National Parks

(80+ miles). **Activities:** Camping, hiking, horseback riding, bird-watching, wildlife viewing, stargazing. **Special Features:** Rising from the Chihuahuan Desert, this mountain mass contains portions of the world's most extensive and significant Permian limestone fossil reef. Also featured are a tremendous earth fault, lofty peaks, unusual flora and fauna, and a colorful record of the past.

★168★ GUILFORD COURTHOUSE NATIONAL MILITARY PARK

2332 New Garden Rd
Greensboro, NC 27410
Web: www.nps.gov/guco/
Phone: 336-288-1776; **Fax:** 336-282-2296
Size: 229 acres. **History:** Established on March 2, 1917; transferred from War Department on August 10, 1933. **Location:** In northwest Greensboro, off Battleground Ave. (US 220). **Facilities:** Rest rooms (&), bicycle trail, visitor center (&), museum/exhibit, self-guided tour/trail. **Activities:** Hiking, self-guided auto/bicycle tour, living history programs. **Special Features:** The battle fought here on March 15, 1781, was the largest, most hotly-contested action of the Revolutionary War's climactic Southern Campaign and opened the campaign that led to Yorktown and the end of the Revolution. Twenty-eight monuments honoring Revolutionary heroes and heroines dot the battlefield.

★169★ GULF ISLANDS NATIONAL SEASHORE (FLORIDA)

1801 Gulf Breeze Pkwy
Gulf Breeze, FL 32563
Web: www.nps.gov/guis/
Phone: 850-934-2600; **Fax:** 850-932-9654
Size: 65,817 acres (Florida District). **History:** Authorized on January 8, 1971. **Location:** Gulf Islands National Seashore is a 12-unit park located in Mississippi and Florida. The two districts are about a two-hour drive apart. The Florida District of the national seashore is located just south of Pensacola, Florida. Historic mainland forts and the National Museum of Naval Aviation are accessible via FL 295, south of Barrancas Ave., through the main entrance of the Pensacola Naval Air Station. The Naval Live Oaks, Fort Pickens, and Santa Rosa areas can be reached via US 98 east from Pensacola. (See separate entry for information on the Mississippi District of Gulf Islands National Seashore.) **Facilities:** Campgrounds, picnic area, rest rooms (&), groceries, restaurant/snacks, bicycle trail, bathhouse, visitor centers (&), museum/exhibit, self-guided tour/trail. Entrance fee required. **Activities:** Camping, hiking, bicycling, swimming, boating, fishing, snorkeling, bird-watching, guided tour. **Special Features:** Offshore islands have sparkling white sand beaches, historic forts, and nature trails. Mainland features of this unit, which is located near Pensacola, include the Naval Live Oaks Reservation, beaches, and military forts. All areas are accessible by car.

★170★ GULF ISLANDS NATIONAL SEASHORE (MISSISSIPPI)

3500 Park Rd
Ocean Springs, MS 39564
Web: www.nps.gov/guis/
Phone: 228-875-0823; **Fax:** 228-872-2358

Size: 73,959 acres (Mississippi District). **History:** Authorized on January 8, 1971. Wilderness designated on November 10, 1978. **Location:** Gulf Islands National Seashore is a 12-unit park located in Mississippi and Florida. The two districts are about a two-hour drive apart. The park headquarters of the Mississippi District of the national seashore is located in Ocean Springs, Mississippi, and is accessible via I-10 and US 90. The islands in the Mississippi district are 10 miles offshore and can be reached only by boat. During the spring, summer, and fall, excursion boat trips from Gulfport to West Ship Island are offered by a concessionaire. (See separate entry for information on the Mississippi District of Gulf Islands National Seashore.) **Facilities:** Campground, picnic area, rest rooms (&), boat ramp, bathhouse, visitor center (&), museum/exhibit, self-guided tour/trail. Entrance fee required. **Activities:** Camping, hiking, swimming, boating, fishing, bird-watching, guided boat tours. **Special Features:** Sparkling beaches, historic ruins, and wildlife sanctuaries, accessible only by boat, can be found on the offshore islands of this unit, located near Pascagoula and Biloxi. On the mainland there is an urban park with a nature trail and a campground at Ocean Springs.

★171★ HAGERMAN FOSSIL BEDS NATIONAL MONUMENT

221 N State St
Hagerman, ID 83332
Web: www.nps.gov/hafo/
Phone: 208-837-4793; **Fax:** 208-837-4857
Size: 4,351 acres. **History:** Authorized on November 18, 1988. **Location:** In south-central Idaho near the town of Hagerman, off US 30. **Facilities:** Information center, boardwalk, overlook. **Activities:** Hiking, fishing, bicycling, hunting, ranger-guided tours, interpretive programs. **Special Features:** Site protects the world's richest known fossil deposits from the late Pliocene epoch, 3-4 million years ago. These 220+ species of plants and animals represent the last glimpse of time that existed before the Ice Age, and the earliest appearances of modern flora and fauna. The fossils, which are embedded in the banks of the Snake River, have been exposed by the carving action of the river.

★172★ HALEAKALA NATIONAL PARK

PO Box 369
Makawao, HI 96768
Web: www.nps.gov/hale/
Phone: 808-572-4400; **Fax:** 808-572-1304
Size: 29,111 acres. **History:** Authorized as part of Hawaii National Park on August 1, 1916; redesignated on September 13, 1960. Wilderness designated on October 20, 1976. Designated a Biosphere Reserve in 1980. **Location:** Park extends from the 10,023 foot summit of Haleakala down the southeast flank of the mountain to the Kipahulu coast near Hana on the Island of Maui, Hawaii. These two sections of the Park are not directly connected by road, but both can be reached from Kahului. The Summit area of Haleakala is a three-hour round trip drive from Kahului via roads 37, 377, and 378. The Kipahulu area of the park is at the east end of Maui between Hana and Kaupo. **Facilities:** Campgrounds, picnic area, rest rooms (&), cabin rental, visitor centers (&), museum/exhibit, self-guided tour/

See pages 16-17 for map of U.S. National Parks.

trail. Entrance fee required. **Activities:** Camping, hiking, horseback riding, swimming, stargazing, wildlife viewing, auto touring, ranger-led programs. **Special Features:** The park preserves the outstanding features of the upper slopes of the Haleakala Crater on the island of Maui and protects the unique and fragile ecosystems of Kipahulu Valley, the scenic pools along Oheo Gulch, and many rare and endangered species.

★173★ HAMILTON GRANGE NATIONAL MEMORIAL

287 Convent Ave
New York, NY 10031
Web: www.nps.gov/hagr/
Phone: 212-283-5154
Size: 1 acre. **History:** Authorized on April 27, 1962. **Location:** At Covenant Ave. and West 141st St. in Manhattan, New York. **Facilities:** Memorial is closed to the public as part of its restoration and will move to its new location, around the corner in Saint Nickolas Park. It is expected to reopen to the public in late 2008 or early 2009. **Special Features:** ''The Grange,'' named after his grandfather's estate in Scotland, was the home of Alexander Hamilton, American statesman and first Secretary of the Treasury.

★174★ HAMPTON NATIONAL HISTORIC SITE

535 Hampton Ln
Towson, MD 21286
Web: www.nps.gov/hamp/
Phone: 410-823-1309; **Fax:** 410-823-8394
Size: 62 acres. **History:** Designated on June 22, 1948. **Location:** North of Baltimore, Maryland. From I-695 take Exit 27B north (Dulaney Valley Road) and then a right on Hampton Lane. From downtown Baltimore take I-83 (Jones Fall Expwy.) to I-695 east toward Towson to Exit 27B. **Facilities:** Restaurant/snacks, visitor center (&), museum/exhibit, self-guided tour/trail. **Activities:** Guided and self-guided tours. **Special Features:** This is a fine example of the lavish Georgian mansions built in America during the latter part of the 18th century. When it was completed in 1790, Hampton was the largest house in the United States. Site includes mansion, gardens and grounds, and original stone slave quarters.

★175★ HARPERS FERRY NATIONAL HISTORIC PARK

PO Box 65
Harpers Ferry, WV 25425
Web: www.nps.gov/hafe/
Phone: 304-535-6029; **Fax:** 304-535-6244
Size: 3,646 acres. **History:** Authorized as a national monument on June 30, 1944; changed to national historical park on May 29, 1963. **Location:** Along US 340, 65 miles west of Washington, DC, and Baltimore, Maryland. The site encompasses portions of Maryland, Virginia, and West Virginia. **Facilities:** Rest rooms (&), visitor center (&), museums, self-guided tour/trail. Entrance fee required. **Activities:** Hiking, fishing, rock climbing, guided tours. **Special Features:** Because of its strategic location at the confluence of the Shenandoah and Potomac rivers,

this town changed hands eight times during the Civil War. John Brown's raid took place here in 1859.

★176★ HARRY S TRUMAN NATIONAL HISTORIC SITE

223 N Main St
Independence, MO 64050
Web: www.nps.gov/hstr/
Phone: 816-254-9929; **Fax:** 816-254-4491
Size: 6.7 acres. **History:** Established on May 23, 1983. **Location:** Site includes the Truman Home in Independence, Missouri, and the Truman Farm Home in Grandview, Missouri. Both units are within the Kansas City metropolitan area. The visitor center in Independence is located at the intersection of Truman Rd. and Main St., in historic Fire Station No.1. The Truman Farm Home in Grandview is located in the retail and commercial district along Blue Ridge Blvd. **Facilities:** Rest rooms (&), visitor center (&), museum/exhibit. Entrance fee required. **Activities:** Guided tours and self-guided walking tour. **Special Features:** The site preserves the residences of Harry S Truman, the 33rd President. The Truman Home was his residence from 1919 until his death in 1972, and was called the ''Summer White House'' during his administration (1945-1953). The site includes three other homes that were part of the family compound. The Truman Farm Home in Grandview was his residence from 1906 to 1917. It was the hub of a 600-acre family farming operation.

★177★ HAWAII VOLCANOES NATIONAL PARK

PO Box 52
Hawaii National Park, HI 96718
Web: www.nps.gov/havo/
Phone: 808-985-6000; **Fax:** 808-985-6004
Size: 323,431 acres. **History:** Established as part of Hawaii National Park on August 1, 1916; redesignated Hawaii Volcanoes National Park on September 22, 1961. Wilderness designated on November 10, 1978. Designated a Biosphere Reserve in 1980 and a World Heritage Site in 1987. **Location:** 96 miles from Kailua-Kona driving southeast on Hwy. 11, or 125 miles through Waimea and Hilo via Hwys. 19 and 11. The park is 30 miles from Hilo. **Facilities:** Campgrounds (&), picnic area, rest rooms (&), lodging, restaurant/snacks, visitor center (&), museum/exhibit, self-guided tour/trail. Entrance fee required. **Activities:** Camping, hiking, mountain climbing, auto touring, stargazing, ranger-led programs. **Special Features:** Active volcanism continues here, on the island of Hawaii, where at lower elevations luxuriant and often rare vegetation provides food and shelter for a variety of animals. An 11-mile drive circles Kilauea's summit caldera and craters, passes through rainforest and desert, and provides access to scenic stops.

★178★ HERBERT HOOVER NATIONAL HISTORIC SITE

110 Parkside Dr
West Branch, IA 52358
Web: www.nps.gov/heho/
Phone: 319-643-2541; **Fax:** 319-643-5367

See pages 16-17 for map of U.S. National Parks.

Size: 187 acres. **History:** Authorized on August 12, 1965. **Location:** In West Branch, Iowa. Visitor center is on Parkside Dr. and Main St., 0.5 miles north from Exit 254 off I-80. **Facilities:** Picnic area, rest rooms (&), visitor center (&), museum/exhibit, self-guided tour/trail. Entrance fee required. **Activities:** Hiking, cross-country skiing, guided tour. **Special Features:** The birthplace, Friends Meetinghouse, and boyhood neighborhood of the 31st President (1929-1933), the gravesite of President and Mrs. Hoover, and the Hoover Presidential Library and Museum are located within the park. The library and museum are administered by the National Archives and Records Administration.

★179★ HOHOKAM PIMA NATIONAL MONUMENT

c/o Casa Grande Ruins National Monument
PO Box 518
Coolidge, AZ 85228
Web: www.nps.gov/pima/
Phone: 520-723-3172; **Fax:** 520-723-7209
Size: 1,690 acres. **History:** Authorized on October 21, 1972. **Location:** In Sacaton, in south-central Arizona, north of Casa Grande. **Facilities:** Not open to the public. **Special Features:** Preserved here are the archeological remains of the Hohokam culture, including artwork, homes, irrigation canals, and tools dating from about 300 BC to AD 1200. Hohokam is a Pima Indian word meaning "those who have gone."

★180★ HOME OF FRANKLIN D. ROOSEVELT NATIONAL HISTORIC SITE

4097 Albany Post Rd
Hyde Park, NY 12538
Web: www.nps.gov/hofr/
Phone: 845-229-9115; **Fax:** 845-229-0739
Size: 800 acres. **History:** Designated on January 15, 1944. **Location:** On US 9 in Hyde Park, 8 miles north of the city of Poughkeepsie, New York. **Facilities:** Picnic area, rest rooms (&), visitor center (&), museum/exhibit, self-guided tour/trail. Entrance fee required. **Activities:** Hiking, cross-country skiing, guided tour. **Special Features:** "Springwood" was the birthplace, lifetime residence, and "Summer White House" of the 32nd President. He entertained many distinguished visitors here. The gravesites of President and Mrs. Roosevelt are in the Rose Garden.

★181★ HOMESTEAD NATIONAL MONUMENT OF AMERICA

8523 W State Hwy 4
Beatrice, NE 68310
Web: www.nps.gov/home/
Phone: 402-223-3514; **Fax:** 402-228-4231
Size: 211 acres. **History:** Authorized on March 19, 1936. **Location:** In southeastern Nebraska, 40 miles south of Lincoln and 4 miles west of Beatrice on NE 4. **Facilities:** Picnic area, rest rooms (&), visitor center (&), museum/exhibit, self-guided tour/trail. **Activities:** Hiking, cross-country skiing, wildlife viewing. **Special Features:** This park, which includes the 160-acre claim filed by Daniel Freeman under The Homestead Act of 1862, is a memorial to the pioneers who settled the Great West. Among

the features are a typical homestead cabin, a restored frontier school, and more than 100 acres of tallgrass prairie.

★182★ HOPEWELL CULTURE NATIONAL HISTORICAL PARK

16062 SR-104
Chillicothe, OH 45601
Web: www.nps.gov/hocu/
Phone: 740-774-1125; **Fax:** 740-774-1140
Size: 1,170 acres. **History:** Proclaimed on March 2, 1923. Name changed from Mound City Group National Monument on May 27, 1992. **Location:** In south-central Ohio. The park visitor center, located at Mound City Group, is on OH 104, 2 miles north of US 35 and 3 miles north of Chillicothe. **Facilities:** Picnic area, rest rooms (&), visitor center (&), museum/exhibit, self-guided tour/trail. Entrance fee required. **Activities:** Hiking, guided tour, interpretive programs. **Special Features:** Park contains nationally significant archeological resources including large earthwork and mound complexes that provide an insight into the social, ceremonial, political, and economic life of the Hopewell people. Finely crafted artifacts of the Hopewell Culture (200 BC - AD 500) show that highly skilled artisans used an extensive trade network east of the Rocky Mountains.

★183★ HOPEWELL FURNACE NATIONAL HISTORIC SITE

2 Mark Bird Ln
Elverson, PA 19520
Web: www.nps.gov/hofu/
Phone: 610-582-8773; **Fax:** 610-582-2768
Size: 848 acres. **History:** Designated Hopewell Village National Historic Site on August 3, 1938; renamed on September 19, 1985. **Location:** 5 miles south of Birdsboro, Pennsylvania, on PA 345; 10 miles from Morgantown interchange of the PA Turnpike, via PA 23 East and PA 345 North. **Facilities:** Rest rooms (&), visitor center (&), museum/exhibit, self-guided tour/trail. Entrance fee required. **Activities:** Hiking, self-guided tours, living history programs. **Special Features:** Founded by Mark Bird, the first ironmaster, Hopewell Furnace (1771-1883) was one of the finest examples of a rural American 19th-century iron plantation. Hopewell and other "iron plantations" laid the foundations for America's iron and steel industry. The buildings include a blast furnace, the ironmaster's mansion, and auxiliary structures.

★184★ HORSESHOE BEND NATIONAL MILITARY PARK

11288 Horseshoe Bend Rd
Daviston, AL 36256
Web: www.nps.gov/hobe/
Phone: 256-234-7111; **Fax:** 256-329-9905
Size: 2,040 acres. **History:** Authorized on July 25, 1956. **Location:** In east central Alabama, on AL 49, 12 miles north of the town of Dadeville. **Facilities:** Picnic area, rest rooms (&), boat ramp, visitor center (&), museum/exhibit, self-guided tour/trail. **Activities:** Hiking, canoeing, fishing, auto touring, living history programs. **Special Features:** On March 27, 1814, at the "horseshoe bend" in the Tallapoosa River, General Andrew Jackson's

See pages 16-17 for map of U.S. National Parks.

forces and an army of 3,300 men attacked 1,000 Upper Creek warriors and opened large parts of Alabama and Georgia for settlement. More than 800 Upper Creeks died defending their homeland.

★185★ HOT SPRINGS NATIONAL PARK

101 Reserve St
Hot Springs, AR 71901
Web: www.nps.gov/hosp/
Phone: 501-620-6715
Size: 5,550 acres. **History:** Hot Springs Reservation set aside on April 20, 1832; dedicated to public use as a park on June 16, 1880; redesignated as a national park on March 4, 1921. **Location:** In Hot Springs, Arkansas, 55 miles southwest of Little Rock, in the Zig Zag Mountains on the eastern edge of the Ouachita Range. **Facilities:** Campground (&), picnic area, rest rooms (&), bathhouse, visitor center (&), museum/exhibit, self-guided tour/trail. **Activities:** Camping, hiking, horseback riding, thermal bathing, auto touring, family programs, guided and self-guided tours. **Special Features:** The oldest park currently in the National Park System (40 years older than Yellowstone National Park) protects 47 hot springs and their watershed, numerous hiking trails, as well as eight historic bathhouses that compose ''Bathhouse Row,'' a National Historic Landmark District.

★186★ HOVENWEEP NATIONAL MONUMENT

McElmo Rt
Cortez, CO 81321
Web: www.nps.gov/hove/
Phone: 970-562-4282; **Fax:** 970-562-4283
Size: 785 acres. **History:** Proclaimed on March 2, 1923. **Location:** In southeastern Utah and southwestern Colorado. The only paved entrance road is UT 262, which runs east from US 191, 15 miles south of Blanding. Also accessible from Cortez, Colorado. **Facilities:** Campground (31 sites), picnic area, rest rooms (&), ranger station, museum/exhibit, self-guided tour/trail. **Activities:** Camping, hiking, interpretive programs. **Special Features:** Monument protects six prehistoric, Puebloan-era villages spread over a twenty-mile expanse of mesa tops and canyons along the Utah-Colorado border. The first reports of these structures were made by W.D. Huntington, the leader of a Mormon expedition into southeastern Utah in 1854.

★187★ HUBBELL TRADING POST NATIONAL HISTORIC SITE

PO Box 150
1/2 Mile W. Hwy 191 on Hwy 264
Ganado, AZ 86505
Web: www.nps.gov/hutr/
Phone: 928-755-3475; **Fax:** 928-755-3405
Size: 160 acres. **History:** Authorized on August 28, 1965. **Location:** One mile west of Ganado, Arizona, and 55 miles northwest of Gallup, New Mexico. Accessible via AZ 264 from the east and west and by US 191 from the north and south. **Facilities:** Picnic area, rest rooms (&), groceries, visitor center (&), museum/exhibit, self-guided tour/trail. **Activities:** Guided tour. **Special Features:** Established in 1878, Hubbell Trading Post is the oldest continuously operating trading post in the Navajo Nation. It was first established by John Lorenzo Hubbell who, alone or together with his two sons, owned 30 trading posts, wholesale houses, several ranches and farms, business properties, and stage and freight lines. The trading post here has served as a bridge between cultures for generations.

★188★ INDEPENDENCE NATIONAL HISTORICAL PARK

143 S 3rd St
Philadelphia, PA 19106
Web: www.nps.gov/inde/
Phone: 215-597-8787; **Fax:** 215-597-1548
Size: 45 acres. **History:** Authorized on June 28, 1948; established on July 4, 1956. Independence Hall designated a World Heritage Site on October 24, 1979. **Location:** Visitor center is located at Third and Chestnut streets in downtown Philadelphia, Pennsylvania. Park is accessible via I-76 and I-676, I-95, and US 30 (Benjamin Franklin Bridge). **Facilities:** Rest rooms (&), restaurant/snacks, visitor center (&), museum/exhibit, self-guided tour/trail. **Activities:** Guided tours, special programs. **Special Features:** Spanning more than 20 city blocks within the historic district of the City of Philadelphia, park includes structures and sites associated with the American Revolution and the founding and growth of the United States: Independence Hall (where both the Declaration of Independence and the U.S. Constitution were created), Congress Hall, Old City Hall, the Liberty Bell, the First and Second Banks of the United States, Franklin Court, Deshler-Morris House (in Germantown), and others. Park has about 20 buildings open to the public.

★189★ INDIANA DUNES NATIONAL LAKESHORE

1100 N Mineral Springs Rd
Porter, IN 46304
Web: www.nps.gov/indu/
Phone: 219-926-7561; **Fax:** 219-926-7561
Size: 15,067 acres. **History:** Authorized on November 5, 1966. **Location:** Stretches along southern Lake Michigan in northwestern Indiana. Accessible via I-94, the Indiana Toll Road, I-80/90, US 20, IN 12 and various state roads. The South Shore Railroad from Chicago or South Bend includes several stops within the park area. **Facilities:** Campground, picnic area, rest rooms (&), restaurant/snacks, bicycle trail, bathhouse, visitor centers (&), environmental learning center, museum/exhibit, self-guided tour/trail. **Activities:** Camping, hiking, bicycling, horseback riding, swimming, boating, fishing, cross-country skiing, snowshoeing, public programs. **Special Features:** Dunes rise 180 feet above Lake Michigan's southern shore with beaches, bogs, marshes, swamps, and prairie remnants as other natural features. Historic sites include an 1822 homestead and 1900s family farm. The Paul H. Douglas Center for Environmental Education and the Indiana Dunes Environmental Learning Center provide day-use and residential programs.

★190★ ISLE ROYALE NATIONAL PARK

800 East Lakeshore Dr
Houghton, MI 49931
Web: www.nps.gov/isro/
Phone: 906-482-0984; **Fax:** 906-422-8753

See pages 16-17 for map of U.S. National Parks.

Size: 571,790 acres. History: Authorized on March 3, 1931. Wilderness designated on October 20, 1976. Designated a Biosphere Reserve in 1980. Location: In the northwest corner of Lake Superior, accessible only by boat or seaplane. Passenger ferries are available from Houghton or Copper Harbor, Michigan, or from Grand Portage, Minnesota. Seaplane service is available from Houghton, Michigan to Rock Harbor or Windigo on Isle Royale. Facilities: Campgrounds, picnic area, rest rooms (&), cabin rental, lodging, groceries, restaurant/snacks, boat rental, visitor centers (&), self-guided tour/trail. Park is open to the public from mid-April through October. Activities: Camping, hiking, swimming, scuba diving, boating, canoeing, kayaking, fishing, wildlife viewing, sightseeing cruises. Special Features: This forested island, the largest in Lake Superior, is 45 miles long and 9 miles wide at its widest point, and includes submerged lands which extend 4.5 miles out into the lake. The roadless island is distinguished by its wilderness character, wildlife that includes timberwolves and moose, pre-Columbian copper mines, and historic lighthouses and shipwrecks.

★191★ JAMES A. GARFIELD NATIONAL HISTORIC SITE
8095 Mentor Ave
Mentor, OH 44060
Web: www.nps.gov/jaga/
Phone: 440-255-8722; Fax: 440-974-2045
Size: 7.8 acres. History: Authorized on December 28, 1980; established on July 15, 1996. Site is managed cooperatively by the Western Historical Society and the National Park Service. Location: In Mentor, Ohio, just northeast of Cleveland. From I-90 (east of Cleveland) take the SR 306 Mentor/Kirtland Exit. Travel north on SR 306, 2 miles to Mentor Ave. (US 20), then east 2 miles. Facilities: Visitor center, museum/exhibit. Activities: Guided tour. Special Features: This site preserves the family home and artifacts of the 20th US President. Named Lawnfield by reporters, it was the site of the first successful front porch campaign which saw Garfield elected President. Following his assassination, the Memorial Library wing was added by Mrs. Garfield and her family, setting the precedent for presidential libraries.

★192★ JEAN LAFITTE NATIONAL HISTORICAL PARK & PRESERVE
419 Rue Decatur
New Orleans, LA 70130
Web: www.nps.gov/jela/
Phone: 504-589-3882; Fax: 504-589-3851
Size: 20,005 acres. History: Chalmette Unit established as Chalmette Monument and Grounds on March 4, 1907; established as Chalmette National Historical Park on August 10, 1939. Redesignated and incorporated with other units on November 10, 1978. New park authorized on November 10, 1978. Location: Park consists of six physically separate sites in southwestern Louisiana and a headquarters in New Orleans. Facilities: Picnic area, rest rooms (&), bicycle trail, visitor centers (&), museum/exhibit, self-guided tour/trail. Activities: Hiking, bicycling, boating, fishing, hunting, cultural programs and living history demonstrations, walking tours. Special Features: Park preserves and interprets the cultural diversity of Louisiana's

Mississippi Delta Region. The sites in Lafayette, Thibodaux, and Eunice interpret the Acadian cultures of the area; the Barataria Preserve in Marrero interprets the natural and cultural history of the uplands, swamps, and marshlands of the region; the Chalmette Battlefield and National Cemetery is the site of the 1815 Battle of New Orleans and the final resting place for soldiers from the Civil War, Spanish-American War, World Wars I and II, and Vietnam War; and the historic French Quarter interprets the history of New Orleans and the diverse cultures of Louisiana's Mississippi Delta Region.

★193★ JEFFERSON NATIONAL EXPANSION MEMORIAL
11 N 4th St
Saint Louis, MO 63102
Web: www.nps.gov/jeff/
Phone: 314-655-1700; Fax: 314-655-1641
Size: 91 acres. History: Designated on December 21, 1935; authorized on May 17, 1954. Location: In the heart of downtown Saint Louis on the Mississippi River. Interstate routes 44, 55, 64, and 70 converge near the park. Facilities: Rest rooms (&), visitor center (&), museum/exhibit. Entrance fee required. Activities: Guided tour. Special Features: This park on Saint Louis' Mississippi riverfront memorializes Thomas Jefferson and others who directed territorial expansion of the United States. Eero Saarinen's prize-winning, stainless steel gateway arch commemorates westward pioneers. Visitors may ascend the 630-foot-high arch. In the nearby Old Courthouse, Dred Scott sued for freedom in the historic slavery case.

★194★ JEWEL CAVE NATIONAL MONUMENT
11149 US Hwy 16, Bldg B-12
Custer, SD 57730
Web: www.nps.gov/jeca/
Phone: 605-673-2288; Fax: 605-673-3294
Size: 1,274 acres. History: Proclaimed on February 7, 1908; transferred from Forest Service on August 10, 1933. Location: 13 miles west of Custer, South Dakota, on US 16 or 24 miles east of Newcastle, Wyoming, on US 16. Facilities: Picnic area, rest rooms (&), visitor center (&), museum/exhibit. Activities: Hiking, wildlife viewing, guided cave tours. Special Features: With more than 136 miles surveyed, Jewel Cave is recognized as the second longest cave in the world. Its limestone caverns consist of a series of chambers connected by narrow passages, with many side galleries and fine calcite crystal encrustations. More and more of the cave is discovered by explorers each year.

★195★ JIMMY CARTER NATIONAL HISTORIC SITE
300 N Bond St
Plains, GA 31780
Web: www.nps.gov/jica/
Phone: 229-824-4104; Fax: 229-824-3441
Size: 72 acres. History: Authorized on December 23, 1987. Location: 10 miles west of Americus, Georgia, on US 280. Facilities: Rest rooms (&), visitor center (&), museum/exhibit. Activities: Self-guided tour. Special Features: The site includes President Carter's residence and boyhood home. The Plains High School, where both Jimmy and Rosalynn Carter attended

See pages 16-17 for map of U.S. National Parks.

grammar and high school, serves as the park's visitor center. The railroad depot, which served as campaign headquarters during the 1976 election, houses additional exhibits. The Jimmy Carter National Preservation District, separate from the park, includes part of the town of Plains and its environs.

★196★ JOHN D. ROCKEFELLER JR. MEMORIAL PARKWAY

PO Box 170
Moose, WY 83012
Web: www.nps.gov/jodr/
Phone: 307-739-3300; **Fax:** 307-739-3438
Size: 23,777 acres. **History:** Authorized on August 25, 1972. **Location:** In northwestern Wyoming, linking West Thumb in Yellowstone National Park with the south entrance of Grand Teton National Park. **Facilities:** Campground (&), backcountry use permits, rest rooms (&), cabin rental, lodging, groceries, restaurant/snacks, self-guided tour/trail. **Activities:** Camping, hiking, horseback riding, boating, fishing, hunting, snowmobiling, cross-country skiing. **Special Features:** This scenic 82-mile corridor commemorates Rockefeller's role in aiding establishment of many parks, including Grand Teton (see separate entry for description).

★197★ JOHN DAY FOSSIL BEDS NATIONAL MONUMENT

32651 Hwy 19
Kimberly, OR 97848
Web: www.nps.gov/joda/
Phone: 541-987-2333; **Fax:** 541-987-2336
Size: 13,944 acres. **History:** Authorized on October 26, 1974. **Location:** Park is divided into three widely separated units in north-central Oregon: the Clarno Unit, located 20 miles west of Fossil, OR; the Sheep Rock Unit, located 6 miles west of Dayville, OR; and the Painted Hills Unit, located 9 miles northwest of Mitchell, OR. The park headquarters is at the visitor center in the Sheep Rock Unit. **Facilities:** Picnic area, rest rooms (&), visitor center (&), museum/exhibit, self-guided tour/trail. **Activities:** Hiking, fishing, river rafting, auto touring, ranger-led programs. **Special Features:** The heavily eroded volcanic deposits of the John Day River basin preserve a remarkably complete record of animal and plant life, spanning more than 40 of the 65 million years of the Cenozoic Era (the ''Age of Mammals and Flowering Plants'').

★198★ JOHN F KENNEDY NATIONAL HISTORIC SITE

83 Beals St
Brookline, MA 02446
Web: www.nps.gov/jofi/
Phone: 617-566-7937; **Fax:** 617-730-9884
Size: 0.1 acres. **History:** Authorized on May 26, 1967; established as a national historic site in 1969. **Location:** On Beals Street in the Boston, Massachusetts, suburb of Brookline. **Facilities:** Visitor center, museum/exhibit. Entrance fee required. **Activities:** Guided tours of the birthplace, as well as the nearby neighborhood including homes, schools, and church associated with the Kennedy family. **Special Features:** This house was the birthplace (in 1917) and early boyhood home of the 35th President, as well as the first home shared by the president's father and mother, Joseph P. and Rose Fitzgerald Kennedy.

★199★ JOHN MUIR NATIONAL HISTORIC SITE

4202 Alhambra Ave
Martinez, CA 94553
Web: www.nps.gov/jomu/
Phone: 925-228-8860; **Fax:** 925-228-8192
Size: 345 acres. **History:** Authorized on August 31, 1964. **Location:** In Martinez, California, northeast of Oakland. Accessible via I-80 east to CA 4, exiting at Alhambra Ave.; and via I-680 north to CA 4, then west to Alhambra Ave. Exit. **Facilities:** Picnic area, rest rooms (&), visitor center (&), museum/exhibit, self-guided tour/trail. Entrance fee required. **Activities:** Guided and self-guided tours, birdwatching. **Special Features:** Park preserves the 14-room residence where naturalist John Muir lived from 1890 until his death in 1914. Site also includes the historic Martinez Adobe and a 325-acre tract of oak woodland and grassland (including Mount Wanda) historically owned by the Muir family. The site today is just a small piece of the original 2,600-acre ranch.

★200★ JOHNSTOWN FLOOD NATIONAL MEMORIAL

733 Lake Rd
South Fork, PA 15956
Web: www.nps.gov/jofl/
Phone: 814-495-4643; **Fax:** 814-495-7463
Size: 178 acres. **History:** Authorized on August 31, 1964. **Location:** Along US 219 and PA 869 at the South Fork Dam site, 10 miles northeast of Johnstown near St. Michael, Pennsylvania. **Facilities:** Picnic area, visitor center, museum/exhibit, self-guided tour/trail. **Activities:** Hiking, guided tour, interpretive programs. **Special Features:** A total of 2,209 people died in the Johnstown Flood of 1889, caused by a break in the South Fork Dam. Clara Barton successfully led the Red Cross in its first disaster relief effort.

★201★ JOSHUA TREE NATIONAL PARK

74485 National Park Dr
Twentynine Palms, CA 92277
Web: www.nps.gov/jotr/
Phone: 760-367-5500; **Fax:** 760-367-6392
Size: 789,866 acres. **History:** Proclaimed on August 10, 1936. Wilderness designated on October 20, 1976. Designated a Biosphere Reserve in 1984. Name changed from Joshua Tree National Monument on October 31, 1994. **Location:** 140 miles east of downtown Los Angeles via I-10. The west and north entrances to the park are off CA 62 (Twentynine Palms Hwy.), at the towns of Joshua Tree and Twentynine Palms. The south entrance is at Cottonwood Spring, about 25 miles east of Indio off I-10. **Facilities:** Campgrounds (&), picnic area, rest rooms (&), visitor centers (&), museum/exhibit, self-guided tour/trail. Entrance fee required. **Activities:** Camping, hiking, rock climbing, horseback riding, bicyling, auto touring, ranger-led programs, wildflower viewing, stargazing. **Special Features:** Two

See pages 16-17 for map of U.S. National Parks.

1. US National Parks

deserts, two large ecosystems whose characteristics are determined primarily by elevation, come together in the park. Below 3,000 feet, the Colorado Desert encompasses the eastern part of the park and features natural gardens of creosote bush, ocotillo, and cholla cactus. The higher, moister, and slightly cooler Mojave Desert is the special habitat of the Joshua tree and includes some of the most interesting geological displays found in California's deserts. Five fan palm oases also dot the park, indicating those few areas where water occurs naturally and wildlife abounds.

★202★ KALAUPAPA NATIONAL HISTORICAL
   PARK
PO Box 2222
Kalaupapa, HI 96742
Web: www.nps.gov/kala/
Phone: 808-567-6802; Fax: 808-567-6729
Size: 10,779 acres. History: Authorized on December 22, 1980. Administered in cooperation with several Hawaii state agencies. Location: On the central northern coast of the Island of Molokai, Hawaii. Facilities: Museum/exhibit. Activities: The National Park Service does not offer any regularly scheduled interpretive programs or activities because of the restricted nature of visitation to the park. Tours of the park are offered through a commercial service, owned and operated by a Kalaupapa resident. Special Features: Park contains the site of the Molokai Island Hansen's disease (leprosy) settlement (1866-1969), areas relating to early Hawaiian settlement, scenic and geological resources, and habitats for rare and endangered species. The churches of Siloama, established in 1866 and St. Philomena, begun in 1872 and associated with the work of Father Damien (Joseph DeVeuster) are located at Kalawao. Father Damien's life and death among his people focussed the attention of the world on the problem of this disease and the plight of its victims.

★203★ KALOKO-HONOKOHAU NATIONAL
   HISTORICAL PARK
73-4786 Kanalani St, Suite 14
Kailua-Kona, HI 96740
Web: www.nps.gov/kaho/
Phone: 808-329-6881
Size: 1,161 acres. History: Established on November 10, 1978. Location: At the base of Hualälai Volcano, along the Kona coast of the island of Hawaii; it is 3 miles north of Kailua-Kona and 3 miles south of Keahole-Kona International Airport, along Highway 19 (the Queen Ka'ahumanu Highway). Facilities: Limited. Activities: Hiking, fishing, swimming, snorkeling, scuba diving, kayaking. Special Features: Park was established for the preservation, protection, and interpretation of traditional native Hawaiian activities and culture. It was the site of important Hawaiian settlements before the arrival of European explorers. It includes coastal areas, 3 large fishponds, a house site, and other archeological remnants.

★204★ KATMAI NATIONAL PARK & PRESERVE
#1 King Salmon Mall
PO Box 7
King Salmon, AK 99613
Web: www.nps.gov/katm/
Phone: 907-246-3305; Fax: 907-246-2116

Size: 3,674,530 acres (park) and 418,669 acres (preserve). History: Proclaimed as Katmai National Monument on September 24, 1918; established as a national park and preserve on December 2, 1980. Wilderness designated on December 2, 1980. Location: On the Alaska Peninsula, across from Kodiak Island. Park Headquarters is in King Salmon, about 290 air miles southwest of Anchorage. Several commercial airlines provide daily flights into King Salmon as there is no road access. Brooks Camp, along the Brooks River approximately 30 air miles from King Salmon, is a common destination for visitors to the park. Brooks Camp can only be reached via small float plane or boat. Facilities: Campground, picnic area, lodging, groceries, restaurant/snacks, boat rental, boat ramp, visitor centers (&), self-guided tour/trail. Activities: Camping, hiking, mountain climbing, boating, kayaking, whitewater rafting, boat tours, fishing, hunting, wildlife viewing, cross-country skiing, interpretive programs, ranger-led walks. Special Features: Variety marks this vast land with lakes, forests, mountains, and marshlands that all abound in wildlife. The Alaska brown bear, the world's largest carnivore, thrives here, feeding upon red salmon that spawn in the many lakes and streams. Wild rivers and renowned sport fishing add to the attractions of this subarctic environment. Here, in 1912, Novarupta Volcano erupted violently, forming the ash-filled "Valley of Ten Thousand Smokes" where steam rose from countless fumaroles. The park-preserve contains part of the Alagnak Wild River (see separate entry).

★205★ KENAI FJORDS NATIONAL PARK
PO Box 1727
Seward, AK 99664
Web: www.nps.gov/kefj/
Phone: 907-224-7500; Fax: 907-224-7505
Size: 669,983 acres. History: Proclaimed Kenai Fjords National Monument on December 1, 1978; established as a national park on December 2, 1980. Location: South and west of Seward and 130 miles south of Anchorage via the Seward Highway. The Alaska Marine Highway (ferry) System connects Seward with Homer and Seldovia via Kodiak, providing service to Valdez and Cordova. Bus services are available between Anchorage and Seward. The Alaska Railroad serves Seward from Anchorage during the summer months. Facilities: Camping sites, visitor center (&), ranger station, backcountry public use cabins. Activities: Camping, hiking, boating, kayaking, fishing, snowmobiling, cross-country skiing, boat tours, wildlife viewing, interpretive programs. Special Features: The park includes one of the four major ice caps in the United States, the 300-square-mile Harding Icefield, and coastal fjords. Here a rich, varied rain forest is home to tens of thousands of breeding birds and adjoining marine waters support a multitude of sea lions, sea otters, and seals.

★206★ KENNESAW MOUNTAIN NATIONAL
   BATTLEFIELD PARK
900 Kennesaw Mountain Dr
Kennesaw, GA 30152
Web: www.nps.gov/kemo/
Phone: 770-427-4686; Fax: 770-528-8398

See pages 16-17 for map of U.S. National Parks.

Size: 2,884 acres. History: Authorized as a national battlefield site on February 8, 1917; changed to a national battlefield park on June 26, 1935. Location: In Kennesaw, Georgia, just west of Marietta. Accessible via I-75 and the Barrett Pkwy. Facilities: Picnic area, rest rooms (&), visitor center (&), museum/exhibit, self-guided tour/trail. Activities: Hiking, horseback riding, interpretive programs, auto touring. Special Features: Eleven miles of Union and Confederate earthworks are preserved within the park, marking the site of the battles of Kolb's Farm (June 22, 1864) and Kennesaw Mountain (June 27, 1864) during the Atlanta Campaign. General William T. Sherman's southward advance was temporarily halted here by General Joseph T. Johnston and the stalwart defense of his Confederates. Park interprets the historic events in which more than 5,350 soldiers were killed in the battles fought here from June 19, 1864 through July 2, 1864.

★207★ KEWEENAW NATIONAL HISTORICAL PARK

25970 Red Jacket Rd
PO Box 471
Calumet, MI 49913
Web: www.nps.gov/kewe/
Phone: 906-337-3168; Fax: 906-337-3169
Size: 1,869 acres. Much of that area is, and will remain, in private ownership. Rather than purchasing all the land within the boundary, this park will own only limited areas where it will preserve key structures and sites and conduct its interpretive activities. History: Established on October 27, 1992. Location: The Quincy Unit of the park is located just north of Hancock, Michigan, along US 41. The Calumet Unit is located in and around the Village of Calumet, Michigan, 8 miles north of the Quincy Unit on US 41. Facilities: The National Park Service operates a seasonal visitor information desk at the Quincy Mine & Hoist Gift Shop located north of Hancock, Michigan along U.S. Highway 41. Most visitor services, such as guided tours or museums, are provided by the park's partners known as Keweenaw Heritage Sites. Activities: During the summer, park staff provide guided interpretive programs in both the Calumet and Quincy Units. A number of governmentally and privately-operated attractions, which are cooperating with the National Park Service, can also be visited. Sites stretch for more than 100 miles along the length of the Keweenaw Peninsula, from Copper Harbor to Ontonagon. These Heritage Sites include Quincy Mine Hoist and Underground Tours, Fort Wilkins State Park (see separate entry in Michigan state parks section), Keweenaw County Historical Museum, Keweenaw Heritage Center, Houghton County Historical Museum, Copper Range Historical Museum, Coppertown Mining Museum, Seaman Mineral Museum, Delaware Copper Mine, and Hanka Homestead. Special Features: Park was established to commemorate the rich history of copper mining on the Keweenaw Peninsula of Michigan — the only place in the world where commercially abundant quantities of elemental copper occurred. It has the oldest metal mining heritage in the western hemisphere, dating back 7,000 years, and was the site of America's first large-scale, hard-rock industrial mining operations.

KINGS CANYON NATIONAL PARK
(See Sequoia & Kings Canyon National Parks.)

★208★ KINGS MOUNTAIN NATIONAL MILITARY PARK

2625 Park Rd
Blacksburg, SC 29702
Web: www.nps.gov/kimo/
Phone: 864-936-7921; Fax: 864-936-9897
Size: 3,945 acres. History: Established on March 3, 1931; transferred from War Department on August 10, 1933. Location: On SC 216 in Blacksburg, South Carolina, just south of the North and South Carolina border. The park is 60 miles north of Greenville, SC and 39 miles south of Charlotte, NC. From I-85, take NC Exit 2 south onto SC 216. Facilities: Backcountry campsite, rest rooms (&), visitor center, museum/exhibit, self-guided tour/trail. Activities: Camping, hiking, horseback riding, evening programs (on summer weekends). Special Features: American frontiersmen defeated the British here on October 7, 1780, at a critical point during the Revolution. The battle was the first major patriot victory to occur after the British invasion of Charleston, SC in May 1780.

★209★ KLONDIKE GOLD RUSH NATIONAL HISTORICAL PARK

2nd St & Broadway
PO Box 517
Skagway, AK 99840
Web: www.nps.gov/klgo/
Phone: 907-983-2921; Fax: 907-983-9249
Size: 13,191 acres. History: Established on June 30, 1976. Location: Skagway is reached by the South Klondike Hwy. and is 96 air miles north of Juneau and 110 miles south of Whitehorse, Yukon Territory. It is served by the Alaska Marine Highway (ferry) System from Juneau and by public bus from Whitehorse. Facilities: Campground, picnic area, restaurant/snacks, visitor center (&), museum/exhibit, self-guided tour/trail. Activities: Camping, hiking, fishing, hunting, horseback riding, cross-country skiing, snowshoeing, ranger-guided tours. Special Features: Historic buildings in Skagway and portions of Chilkoot and White Pass Trails, all prominent in the 1898 gold rush, are included in the park. Hiking the 33-mile Chilkoot Trail from near the Dyea townsite provides an opportunity to experience some of the challenges goldseekers faced.

★210★ KLONDIKE GOLD RUSH NATIONAL HISTORICAL PARK - SEATTLE UNIT

319 2nd Ave S
Seattle, WA 98104
Web: www.nps.gov/klse/
Phone: 206-220-4240
History: Authorized on June 30, 1976. Location: Visitor center is located in the Pioneer Square Historic District in Seattle, Washington. Facilities: Rest rooms (&), visitor center (&), museum/exhibit. Activities: Interpretive programs including gold panning demonstrations and walking tours. Special Features: In 1897 news of a gold strike in the Canadian Yukon reached Seattle, triggering a stampede north to the Klondike gold fields.

See pages 16-17 for map of U.S. National Parks.

From 1897 to 1898, tens of thousands of people from across the United States and around the world descended upon Seattle's commercial district. While in Seattle, they purchased millions of dollars of food, clothing, equipment, pack animals, and steamship tickets, before leaving for the gold fields.

★211★ KNIFE RIVER INDIAN VILLAGES NATIONAL HISTORIC SITE

564 County Rd 37
PO Box 9
Stanton, ND 58571
Web: www.nps.gov/knri/
Phone: 701-745-3300; **Fax:** 701-745-3708
Size: 1,758 acres. **History:** Authorized on October 26, 1974. **Location:** One-half mile north of Stanton, North Dakota, and 60 miles north of Bismarck; accessible via US 83 and ND 200A. **Facilities:** Picnic area, rest rooms (&), visitor center (&), museum/exhibit, self-guided tour/trail. **Activities:** Hiking, fishing, cross-country skiing, self-guided tours, educational programs, cultural workshops. **Special Features:** Park preserves historic and archeological remnants of the culture and agricultural lifestyle of the Northern Plains Indians. More than 50 archeological sites suggest a possible 8,000 year span of inhabitation, ending with five centuries of Hidatsa earthlodge village occupation.

★212★ KOBUK VALLEY NATIONAL PARK

PO Box 1029
Kotzebue, AK 99752
Web: www.nps.gov/kova/
Phone: 907-442-3890; **Fax:** 907-442-8316; **Toll Free:** 800-478-7252
Size: 1,750,717 acres. **History:** Proclaimed Kobuk Valley National Monument on December 1, 1978; established as a national park on December 2, 1980. Wilderness designated on December 2, 1980. **Location:** Park occupies a broad valley along the central Kobuk River in northwest Alaska about 30 miles north of the Arctic Circle. There are no roads that provide access to the park. Commercial airlines provide service from Anchorage to Kotzebue or Fairbanks to Bettles. From either location, there are scheduled flights to villages and chartered flights to specific park areas. Summer access may include motorized/non-motorized watercraft, aircraft, or by foot. Winter access may include snowmobiles, aircraft, or by foot. **Facilities:** Information center (in Kotzebue). **Activities:** Camping, hiking, boating, canoeing and kayaking, fishing, wildlife viewing, cross-country skiing, dog mushing, interpretive programs. **Special Features:** Embracing the central valley of the Kobuk River, the park, located entirely north of the Arctic Circle, includes a blend of biological, geological, and cultural resources. Here, in the northernmost extent of the boreal forest, a rich array of arctic wildlife can be found, including caribou, grizzly and black bear, wolf, and fox. The 25-square-mile Great Kobuk Sand Dunes lie just south of the Kobuk River against the base of the Waring Mountains. Archeological sites revealing more than 12,500 years of human occupation are among the most significant sites known in the Arctic, and the Kobuk Valley remains an important area for native cultures and traditional subsistence.

★213★ KOREAN WAR VETERANS MEMORIAL

c/o National Capital Parks - Central
900 Ohio Dr SW
Washington, DC 20004
Web: www.nps.gov/kowa/
Phone: 202-426-6841
Size: 2.2 acres. **History:** Authorized on October 28, 1986; dedicated on July 27, 1995. **Location:** Southeast of the Lincoln Memorial on Independence Ave., Washington, DC. **Facilities:** Bookstore (near the Lincoln Memorial). **Activities:** Ranger talks. **Special Features:** Memorial honors the American men and women who served in the Korean War (1950-1953). A grouping of 19 statues of infantry soldiers, created by World War II veteran Frank Gaylord, stands before a polished granite wall bearing the images of support personnel. A granite curb on the north side of the statues lists the 22 countries of the United Nations that sent troops or gave medical support in defense of South Korea.

★214★ LAKE CHELAN NATIONAL RECREATION AREA

c/o North Cascades National Park
PO Box 7
Stehekin, WA 98852
Web: www.nps.gov/lach/
Phone: 509-682-2549; **Fax:** 360-856-1934
Size: 61,947 acres. **History:** Established on October 2, 1968. **Location:** 50 miles uplake from Chelan, Washington. Accessible year-round by passenger ferry or float-plane; there are no road connections between Lake Chelan National Recreation Area and the outside. There are a number of trails available for hiking to the area in the summer. **Facilities:** Campgrounds, picnic area, cabin rental, lodging, groceries, restaurant/snacks, boat rental, visitor center, self-guided tour/trail. **Activities:** Camping, hiking, horseback riding, mountain climbing, boating, fishing, hunting, cross-country skiing, boat tours. **Special Features:** Here the beautiful Stehekin Valley, with a portion of fjordlike Lake Chelan, adjoins the southern unit of North Cascades National Park (see separate entry for description). Lake Chelan rests in a trough carved by glaciers, and with a depth of nearly 1,500 feet, is one of the nation's deepest lakes.

★215★ LAKE CLARK NATIONAL PARK & PRESERVE

240 West 5th Ave, Suite 236
Anchorage, AK 99501
Web: www.nps.gov/lacl/
Phone: 907-644-3626; **Fax:** 907-644-3810
Size: 2,619,733 acres (park) and 1,410,292 acres (preserve). **History:** Proclaimed Lake Clark National Monument on December 1, 1978; established as a national park and preserve on December 2, 1980. Wilderness designated on December 2, 1980. **Location:** Occupies the north end of the Alaska Peninsula in south-central Alaska, where the Alaska and Aleutian mountain ranges meet. Access to the Lake Clark region is by small aircraft; there is no highway access. A one to two-hour flight from Anchorage, Kenai, or Homer will provide access to most points within the park and preserve. **Facilities:** Cabin rental, lodging (in Port Alsworth), visitor center, restaurant/snacks. **Activities:**

See pages 16-17 for map of U.S. National Parks.

Camping, hiking, mountain climbing, boating, rafting, kayaking, canoeing, fishing, wildlife viewing, hunting, snowmobiling, cross-country skiing. **Special Features:** Located in the heart of the Chigmit Mountains along the western shore of Cook Inlet, the park-preserve contains great geological diversity, including jagged peaks, granite spires, and two symmetrical active volcanoes. More than 20 glacial carved lakes rim the mountain mass. Lake Clark, more than 40 miles long, is not only the largest lake here, but also the headwaters for red salmon spawning. Merrill and Lake Clark passes cut through the mountains and are lined by dozens of glaciers and hundreds of waterfalls that cascade over rocky ledges. The park-preserve contains the Chilikadrotna, Mulchatna, and Tlikakila wild rivers.

★216★ LAKE MEAD NATIONAL RECREATION AREA

601 Nevada Hwy
Boulder City, NV 89005
Web: www.nps.gov/lame/
Phone: 702-293-8990; **Fax:** 702-293-8936
Size: 1,495,664 acres. **History:** Administered under cooperative agreements with Bureau of Reclamation on October 13, 1936, and July 18, 1947. Name changed from Boulder Dam National Recreation Area on August 11, 1947. Established on October 8, 1964. **Location:** In southeastern Nevada and northwestern Arizona. Headquarters is in Boulder City, NV, 27 miles southeast of Las Vegas. There are 9 paved access roads into the national recreation area. **Facilities:** Campgrounds (&), picnic area, rest rooms (&), lodging, groceries, restaurant/snacks, boat rental, boat ramp, marinas, ferry service, bathhouse, visitor center (&), museum/exhibit, self-guided tour/trail. **Activities:** Camping, hiking, bicycling, swimming, scuba diving, snorkeling, boating, water-skiing, fishing, kayaking, auto touring. **Special Features:** Lake Mead, formed by Hoover Dam, and Lake Mohave, by Davis Dam, on the Colorado River and more than one million acres of surrounding desert and mountains comprise this first national recreation area established by an act of Congress. Nine developed areas on both lakes offer a wide range of accommodations and services year-round.

★217★ LAKE MEREDITH NATIONAL RECREATION AREA

419 E Broadway
Fritch, TX 79036
Web: www.nps.gov/lamr/
Phone: 806-857-3151; **Fax:** 806-857-2319
Size: 44,978 acres. **History:** Administered under cooperative agreement with Bureau of Reclamation on March 15, 1965. Name changed from Sanford National Recreation Area on October 16, 1972. **Location:** On the Texas Panhandle near Fritch, adjoining the Alibates Flint Quarries National Monument (see separate entry for description). Includes multiple access points; visitors from Amarillo may take either TX 136 north or TX 287 north. **Facilities:** Campgrounds, picnic area, groceries, off-road vehicle trail, boat ramp, marina, boat rental, museum/exhibit. **Activities:** Camping, hiking, horseback riding, swimming, scuba diving, boating, windsurfing, fishing, water-skiing, hunting, off-road vehicle use. **Special Features:** A popular water recreation area in the Southwest, 10,000-acre Lake Meredith was created by Sanford Dam on the Canadian River and now fills many breaks whose walls are crowned with white limestone caprock, scenic buttes, pinnacles, and red-brown, wind-eroded coves.

★218★ LAKE ROOSEVELT NATIONAL RECREATION AREA

1008 Crest Dr
Coulee Dam, WA 99116
Web: www.nps.gov/laro/
Phone: 509-633-9441; **Fax:** 509-633-9332
Size: 100,390 acres. **History:** Coulee Dam Recreation Area administered under cooperative agreement with Bureau of Reclamation and Bureau of Indian Affairs (U.S. Department of the Interior), since December 18, 1946. Renamed on January 1, 1997. **Location:** In northeast Washington, stretching 130 miles along the length of Lake Roosevelt. **Facilities:** Campgrounds (&), picnic area, rest rooms (&), boat ramp, marina, bathhouse, visitor center (&), museum/exhibit, self-guided tour/trail. **Activities:** Camping, swimming, boating, kayaking, fishing, waterskiing, wildlife viewing, auto touring, hunting, interpretive programs. **Special Features:** Formed by Grand Coulee Dam (part of the Columbia River Basin Project), 130-mile-long Franklin D. Roosevelt Lake is the principal recreation feature here. Fort Spokane, situated at the confluence of the Columbia and Spokane rivers, was one of the last frontier forts built in the West (1880) and vividly illustrates changes in government policy towards Indian tribes at the turn of the century.

★219★ LASSEN VOLCANIC NATIONAL PARK

38050 Hwy 36 E
Mineral, CA 96063
Web: www.nps.gov/lavo/
Phone: 530-595-4444; **Fax:** 530-595-3262
Size: 106,372 acres. **History:** Proclaimed as Lassen Peak and Cinder Cone National Monuments on May 6, 1907; made part of Lassen Volcanic National Park when established on August 9, 1916. Wilderness designated on October 19, 1972. **Location:** In northern California, 50 miles northeast of Red Bluff on CA 36, and 50 miles east of Redding on CA 44. **Facilities:** Campgrounds (&), picnic area, rest rooms (&), cabin rental, groceries, restaurant/snacks, boat ramp, visitor center (&), self-guided tour/trail. Entrance fee required. **Activities:** Camping, hiking, bicycling, horseback riding, mountain climbing, swimming, boating, fishing, cross-country skiing, auto touring, ranger-led programs. **Special Features:** Lassen Peak erupted intermittently from 1914 to 1921 and, before the 1980 eruption of Mount Saint Helens in Washington, was the most recent volcanic outburst in the contiguous 48 states. Active volcanism at the park includes hot springs, steaming fumaroles, mud pots, and sulfurous vents.

★220★ LAVA BEDS NATIONAL MONUMENT

1 Indian Well Headquarters
Tulelake, CA 96134
Web: www.nps.gov/labe/
Phone: 530-667-8100
Size: 46,560 acres. **History:** Proclaimed on November 21, 1925; transferred from Forest Service on August 10, 1933. Wilderness

See pages 16-17 for map of U.S. National Parks.

designated on October 13, 1972. **Location:** In northern California, near the California-Oregon border. Visitors travelling south on Highway 139 (from Oregon) will see signs 4 miles south of Tulelake directing them into Lava Beds. Visitors travelling north on Highway 139 (from Alturas) will see signs 27 miles north of Canby directing them into Lava Beds. **Facilities:** Campground (&), picnic area, rest rooms (&), visitor center (&), museum/exhibit, self-guided tour/trail. Entrance fee required. **Activities:** Camping, hiking, cave tours, horseback riding, cross-country skiing, wildlife viewing, ranger-guided programs. **Special Features:** Volcanic activity spewed forth molten rock and lava here, creating an incredibly rugged landscape — a natural fortress used by the Indians in the Modoc Indian War, 1872-1873. The lava tube caves, of which there are more than 500 in the park, are a favorite underground destination for visitors to explore. Park also features a large concentration of raptor birds, including the bald eagle, that winters here in numbers greater than any place outside Alaska.

★221★ LEWIS & CLARK NATIONAL HISTORICAL PARK

92343 Fort Clatsop Rd
Astoria, OR 97103
Web: www.nps.gov/lewi/
Phone: 503-861-2471; **Fax:** 503-861-2585
Size: 1,415 acres. **History:** Authorized on October 30th, 2004, incorporating state parks in Washington and Oregon along with the current Fort Clatsop National Memorial, which was established on May 29, 1958. **Location:** Park comprises 12 sites located on a 40-mile stretch of the Pacific coast from Long Beach, WA to Cannon Beach, OR. Most of the sites are located near US 101. **Facilities:** Picnic area, rest rooms (&), visitor center (&), museum/exhibit, self-guided tour/trail, boat launch. **Activities:** Hiking, canoeing, kayaking, fishing, wildlife viewing, beachcombing, interpretive programs. **Special Features:** Preserves sites associated with the arrival and winter encampment of the Lewis and Clark Expedition in the lower Columbia River area in the winter of 1805-1806, following its successful crossing of the North American Continent. Fort Clatsop, which was the expedition's winter encampment from December 1805 to March 1806, was already a unit of the National Park Service and has been incorporated into the newly designated national historical park.

★222★ LINCOLN BOYHOOD NATIONAL MEMORIAL

2916 E. South St
PO Box 1816
Lincoln City, IN 47552
Web: www.nps.gov/libo/
Phone: 812-937-4541; **Fax:** 812-937-9929
Size: 200 acres. **History:** Authorized on February 19, 1962. **Location:** On IN 162, 2 miles east of Gentryville, Indiana, and 4 miles south of Dale, Indiana. **Facilities:** Rest rooms (&), visitor center (&), museum/exhibit, self-guided tour/trail. Entrance fee required. **Activities:** Hiking, guided tour. **Special Features:** On this southern Indiana farm, Abraham Lincoln spent 14 formative years of his life, from the ages of 7 to 21 (1816-1829). His mother, Nancy Hanks Lincoln, is buried here.

★223★ LINCOLN HOME NATIONAL HISTORIC SITE

413 S 8th St
Springfield, IL 62701
Web: www.nps.gov/liho/
Phone: 217-492-4241; **Fax:** 217-492-4673
Size: 12 acres. **History:** Authorized on August 18, 1971. **Location:** In Springfield, Illinois. Visitor center is located at 426 South Seventh St. **Facilities:** Picnic area, rest rooms (&), visitor center (&), museum/exhibit, self-guided tour/trail. **Activities:** Guided tours. **Special Features:** Abraham and Mary Lincoln resided in this house for 17 years (1844-1861) before he became President. The house was originally constructed in 1839 as a one-story cottage, but was later expanded by the Lincoln's into a full two-story house. The surrounding four-block historic neighborhood is being restored to capture the atmosphere the Lincolns knew.

★224★ LINCOLN MEMORIAL

c/o National Capitol Parks - Central
900 Ohio Dr SW
Washington, DC 20024
Web: www.nps.gov/linc/
Phone: 202-426-6841; **Fax:** 202-724-0764
Size: 107 acres. **History:** Authorized on February 9, 1911. Dedicated on May 30, 1922. Transferred from Office of Public Buildings and Public Parks of the National Capital on August 10, 1933. **Location:** On 23rd St., between Independence and Constitution avenues in Washington, DC. **Facilities:** Rest rooms (&), self-guided tour/trail. **Activities:** Interpretive programs, guided walks. **Special Features:** This classical structure contains a 19-foot-high marble seated statue of Abraham Lincoln by sculptor Daniel Chester French. Murals, painted by Jules Guerin depicting principles evident in Lincoln's life, are on the north and south walls of the memorial above inscriptions of Lincoln's Gettysburg Address and his Second Inaugural Address. The building is constructed primarily of Colorado Yule marble and Indiana limestone. Architect of the building was Henry Bacon.

★225★ LITTLE BIGHORN BATTLEFIELD NATIONAL MONUMENT

PO Box 39
Crow Agency, MT 59022
Web: www.nps.gov/libi/
Phone: 406-638-3204; **Fax:** 406-638-2623
Size: 765 acres. **History:** Ordered established as a national cemetery on January 29, 1879; proclaimed National Cemetery of Custer's Battlefield Reservation on December 7, 1886; changed to Custer Battlefield National Monument by act of Congress on March 22, 1946; changed to Little Bighorn Battlefield National Monument on December 10, 1991. **Location:** Within the Crow Indian Reservation in southeastern Montana, 1 mile west of I-90/US 87. Crow Agency, MT, is 2 miles north; Billings, MT, is 65 miles northwest; and Sheridan, WY, is 70 miles to the south. **Facilities:** Rest rooms (&), visitor center (&), museum/exhibit, self-guided tour/trail. Entrance fee required. **Activities:** Self-guided walking tours, bus tours, auto touring, interpretive talks. **Special Features:** The area memorializes one

See pages 16-17 for map of U.S. National Parks.

of the last armed efforts of the Northern Plains Indians to preserve their ancestral way of life. Here, the famous Battle of the Little Big Horn was fought between the 7th U.S. Cavalry and the Lakota and Cheyenne Indians on June 25-26, 1876. Lieutenant Colonel George A. Custer and more than 260 soldiers and attached personnel were killed.

★226★ LITTLE RIVER CANYON NATIONAL PRESERVE

2141 Gault Ave N
Fort Payne, AL 35967
Web: www.nps.gov/liri/
Phone: 256-845-9605; **Fax:** 256-997-9129
Size: 13,633 acres. **History:** Authorized October 24, 1992. **Location:** In northeast Alabama, 40 miles west of Rome, accessible via AL 35 east of Fort Payne. **Facilities:** Restrooms, picnic area. DeSoto State Park (see separate entry in Alabama State Parks section) adjoins the preserve and offers lodging, campsites, a restaurant, and other ammenities. **Activities:** Hiking, primitive camping, whitewater paddling, canoeing, swimming, fishing, mountain biking, horseback riding, hunting, wildlife viewing, auto touring. **Special Features:** Preserve protects Little River, the nation's longest mountaintop river, which flows for almost its entire length down the middle of Lookout Mountain. The river and canyon systems offer spectacular landscapes including upland forest, waterfalls, canyon rims and bluffs, stream riffles and pools, boulders, and sandstone cliffs.

★227★ LITTLE ROCK CENTRAL HIGH SCHOOL NATIONAL HISTORIC SITE

2125 Daisy L. Gatson Bates Dr
Little Rock, AR 72202
Web: www.nps.gov/chsc/
Phone: 501-374-1957; **Fax:** 501-376-4728
Size: 27 acres. **History:** Established on November 6, 1998. **Location:** At the intersection of 14th and Park streets in Little Rock, Arkansas. **Facilities:** Museum and visitor center. Site is administered in partnership with Little Rock Public Schools, the City of Little Rock, and others. The school will continue to function as an educational institution. **Activities:** Guided tours (by reservation only) and self-guided tours, special programs. **Special Features:** The admission in 1957 of nine black students to Central High School was a critical test of the implementation of the Supreme Court's *Brown v. Board of Education* decision three years earlier, and drew national and international attention. In 1999 the Little Rock Nine each received the Congressional Gold Medal — our nation's highest civilian honor — for their efforts to desegregate Little Rock Central High School.

★228★ LONGFELLOW NATIONAL HISTORIC SITE

105 Brattle St
Cambridge, MA 02138
Web: www.nps.gov/long/
Phone: 617-876-4491; **Fax:** 617-497-8718
Size: 2 acres. **History:** Authorized on October 9, 1972. **Location:** On Brattle St. in Cambridge, Massachusetts. **Facilities:** Visitor center, museum/exhibit. Entrance fee required. **Activities:** Guided and self-guided tours. **Special Features:** Poet

Henry Wadsworth Longfellow lived here from 1837 to 1882 while teaching at Harvard. Years earlier, George Washington, Commander-in-Chief of the newly-formed Continental Army, headquartered and planned the Siege of Boston here (July, 1775 and April, 1776).

★229★ LOWELL NATIONAL HISTORICAL PARK

67 Kirk St
Lowell, MA 01852
Web: www.nps.gov/lowe/
Phone: 978-970-5000; **Fax:** 978-275-1762
Size: 141 acres. **History:** Authorized on June 5, 1978. **Location:** In Lowell, Massachusetts. By car take the Lowell Connector from either Rt. 495 (Exit 35C) or Rt. 3 (Exit 30A southbound, 30B northbound) to Thorndike St. (Exit 5B) and follow signs. **Facilities:** Picnic area, rest rooms (&), visitor center (&), museum/exhibit, self-guided tour/trail. **Activities:** Ranger-led walks, guided tours (including canal boat tours and river tours). **Special Features:** The history of America's Industrial Revolution is commemorated in the heart of dowtown Lowell. The Boott Cotton Mills Museum with its operating weave room of 88 power looms, "mill girl" boardinghouses, the Suffolk Mill Turbine Exhibit, and guided tours tell the story of the transition from farm to factory, chronicle immigrant and labor history, and trace industrial technology. The park includes textile mills, worker housing, 5.6 miles of canals, and 19th-century commercial buildings. Park also host the Lowell Folk Festival, the largest free folk festival in the United States, at the end of July.

★230★ LYNDON B. JOHNSON NATIONAL HISTORICAL PARK

100 Lady Bird Ln
Johnson City, TX 78636
Web: www.nps.gov/lyjo/
Phone: 830-868-7128; **Fax:** 830-868-7863
Size: 1,570 acres. **History:** Authorized on December 2, 1969, as a national historic site; redesignated on December 28, 1980. **Location:** Park includes two distinct visitor areas. Park headquarters and visitor center are in Johnson City, Texas. The LBJ Ranch is 14 miles west of Johnson City and 3 miles east of Stonewall, on US290. **Facilities:** Rest rooms (&), visitor center (&), museum/exhibit, self-guided tour/trail. **Activities:** Self-guided and guided tours. **Special Features:** The park consists of the birthplace, boyhood home, and ranch of the 36th President (1963-1969), and his grandparents' cattle ranch.

★231★ LYNDON BAINES JOHNSON MEMORIAL GROVE ON THE POTOMAC

Turkey Run Park
George Washington Memorial Pkwy
McLean, VA 22101
Web: www.nps.gov/lyba/
Phone: 703-289-2500; **Fax:** 703-289-2598
Size: 17 acres. **History:** Authorized on December 28, 1973; dedicated on September 27, 1974. Formerly known as Columbia Island, this park was renamed in honor of Lady Bird Johnson and her campaign to beautify Washington D.C. **Location:** In Lady Bird Johnson Park, a Potomac River island in Washington,

See pages 16-17 for map of U.S. National Parks.

1. US National Parks

DC. **Facilities:** Picnic area, rest rooms (&), groceries, restaurant/snacks, marina. **Activities:** Boating, fishing, bicycling. **Special Features:** A living memorial to the 36th President, the park overlooks the Potomac River vista of the Capital. The design features 500 white pines and inscriptions on Texas granite. Easy access to the 18-mile Mount Vernon Trail makes the grove a popular staging area for bicyclists and in-line skaters.

★232★ MAGGIE L. WALKER NATIONAL HISTORIC SITE
3215 East Broad St
Richmond, VA 23223
Web: www.nps.gov/malw/
Phone: 804-771-2017; **Fax:** 804-771-2226
Size: 1.3 acres. **History:** Authorized on November 10, 1978. **Location:** In the Jackson Ward community of Richmond, Virginia; accessible via I-95 and I-64 at Exit 76A or 76B. **Facilities:** Visitor center, museum/exhibit. **Activities:** Guided tour. **Special Features:** This rowhouse at 110 1/2 E. Leigh Street, Richmond, was the home of the daughter of an ex-house slave who became the first woman to found and become president of a bank, and who was also a leading figure in the African-American community.

★233★ MAMMOTH CAVE NATIONAL PARK
1 Mammoth Cave Pkwy
PO Box 7
Mammoth Cave, KY 42259
Web: www.nps.gov/maca/
Phone: 270-758-2180; **Fax:** 270-758-2349
Size: 52,830 acres. **History:** Authorized on May 25, 1926; fully established on July 1, 1941. Designated a World Heritage Site on October 27, 1981, and an International Biosphere Reserve on September 26, 1990. **Location:** 9 miles north of I-65 and 85 miles from both Louisville, Kentucky, and Nashville, Tennessee. **Facilities:** Campgrounds (&), picnic area, rest rooms (&), cabin rental, lodging, groceries, restaurant/snacks, visitor center (&), museum/exhibit, self-guided tour/trail. **Activities:** Camping, hiking, bicycling, horseback riding, boating, canoeing, kayaking, fishing, boat tours, guided cave tours (advance reservations accepted). **Special Features:** The park was established to preserve the cave system, including Mammoth Cave, the scenic river valleys of the Green and Nolin rivers, and a section of the hilly country north of the Green River. This is the longest recorded cave system in the world with more than 365 miles explored and mapped. The park contains several species of endangered plants and animals, including Eggert's Sunflower, the Eyeless Cave Shrimp, and several species of river mussels, among others.

★234★ MANASSAS NATIONAL BATTLEFIELD PARK
12521 Lee Hwy
Manassas, VA 20109
Web: www.nps.gov/mana/
Phone: 703-361-1339; **Fax:** 703-361-7106

Size: 5,073 acres. **History:** Designated on May 10, 1940. **Location:** Just north of Manassas and I-66, 25 miles west of Washington, DC. **Facilities:** Picnic area, rest rooms (&), visitor center (&), museum/exhibit, self-guided tour/trail. Entrance fee required. **Activities:** Hiking, horseback riding, interpretive programs, self-guided walking tour (First Battle of Manassas site), self-guided driving tour (Second Battle of Manassas site). **Special Features:** The Battles of First and Second Manassas were fought here on July 21, 1861, and August 28-30, 1862. The 1861 battle was the first test of Northern and Southern military prowess. Here, Confederate Brigadier General Thomas J. Jackson acquired his nickname "Stonewall."

★235★ MANZANAR NATIONAL HISTORIC SITE
5001 Hwy 395
Independence, CA 93526
Web: www.nps.gov/manz/
Phone: 760-878-2932; **Fax:** 760-878-2949
Size: 814 acres. **History:** Established on March 3, 1992. **Location:** Just off US 395, 12 miles north of Lone Pine, California, and 5 miles south of Independence, California. **Facilities:** Interpretive center (&), including exhibits, a bookstore, and theaters. Campsites, lodging, and food are available nearby. **Activities:** Self-guided and guided walking tours and auto tour. **Special Features:** Site of the Manzanar War Relocation Center, one of ten camps at which more than 110,000 Japanese-American citizens and Japanese aliens were interned during World War II. Among the visible remains of the camp is the camp auditorium. In addition, the stonework shells of the pagoda-like police post and sentry house, and portions of other buildings in the administrative complex remain, as do concrete foundations, and portions of water and sewer systems throughout the camp.

★236★ MARSH-BILLINGS-ROCKEFELLER NATIONAL HISTORICAL PARK
54 Elm St
Woodstock, VT 05091
Web: www.nps.gov/mabi/
Phone: 802-457-3368; **Fax:** 802-457-3405
Size: 643 acres. **History:** Established as Marsh-Billings National Historical Park on August 26, 1992; renamed on October 21, 1998. **Location:** In Woodstock, Vermont, 10 miles west of the I-89/US 4 junction. **Facilities:** Rest rooms, visitor center (&), farm and museum, gift shop, self-guided tour/trail. **Activities:** Hiking, guided tours, cross-country skiing, snowshoeing. **Special Features:** Home to pioneer conservationist George Perkins Marsh, the park includes a model farm and forest developed by Frederick Billings and continued by granddaughter Mary French Rockefeller and her husband, Laurence S. Rockefeller. In partnership with the Billings Farm and Museum, the park focuses on conservation themes and the stewardship of working landscapes and agricultural countryside. The park is headquarters for the Conservation Study Institute, designed to enhance leadership in the field of conservation.

See pages 16-17 for map of U.S. National Parks.

★237★ MARTIN LUTHER KING JR. NATIONAL HISTORIC SITE

450 Auburn Ave NE
Atlanta, GA 30312
Web: www.nps.gov/malu/
Phone: 404-331-5190; **Fax:** 404-730-3112
Size: 39 acres. **History:** Established on October 10, 1980. **Location:** On Auburn Ave. in Atlanta, Georgia. Accessible via I-75/85 at Exit 248C (Freedom Parkway/Carter Center). **Facilities:** Visitor center (♿), museum/exhibit, self-guided tour/trail. **Activities:** Guided and self-guided tours. **Special Features:** The birthplace, church, and grave of Dr. Martin Luther King, Jr., civil rights leader, are parts of this park. The neighborhood also includes the Martin Luther King, Jr., Center for Nonviolent Social Change, Inc. The surrounding 68-acre preservation district includes Sweet Auburn, the economic and cultural center of Atlanta's African-American community during most of the 20th century.

★238★ MARTIN VAN BUREN NATIONAL HISTORIC SITE

1013 Old Post Rd
Kinderhook, NY 12106
Web: www.nps.gov/mava/
Phone: 518-758-9689; **Fax:** 518-758-6986
Size: 39.5 acres. **History:** Authorized on October 26, 1974. **Location:** Just south of the Village of Kinderhook, New York, on NY 9H. **Facilities:** Visitor center (♿), museum/exhibit. **Activities:** Guided tour. **Special Features:** Lindenwald was the retirement home of Martin Van Buren, 8th President of the United States, and one of the principal architects of the Democratic Party. The 36-room mansion, containing original wallpaper and furnishings, has been restored to the Van Buren period. Named for the linden trees on the estate, Lindenwald was Van Buren's home from 1841 until his death in 1862.

★239★ MARY MCLEOD BETHUNE COUNCIL HOUSE NATIONAL HISTORIC SITE

1318 Vermont Ave NW
Washington, DC 20005
Web: www.nps.gov/mamc/
Phone: 202-673-2402; **Fax:** 202-673-2414
Size: 0.07 acres. **History:** Designated on October 15, 1982. Established as a National Historic Site on December 11, 1991. **Location:** On Vermont Ave. in the Logan Circle Historic District, Washington, DC. **Activities:** Guided tours. **Special Features:** From 1943 to 1966, this 19th century townhouse served as headquarters for the National Council of Negro Women, founded by educator and activist Mary McLeod Bethune. Site also commemorates McLeod Bethune's leadership in black women's rights movements from 1943 to 1949. She was also the founder of Bethune-Cookman College in Florida.

★240★ MESA VERDE NATIONAL PARK

PO Box 8
Mesa Verde, CO 81330
Web: www.nps.gov/meve/
Phone: 970-529-4465; **Fax:** 970-529-4637
Size: 52,122 acres. **History:** Established on June 29, 1906 as the first national park set aside to "preserve the works of man". Wilderness designated on October 20, 1976. Designated a World Heritage Site on September 6, 1978. **Location:** In southwestern Colorado, midway between Cortez and Mancos, off US 160. It is a 21-mile drive from the entrance to the park headquarters and the Chapin Mesa archeological sites. **Facilities:** Campground (♿), picnic area, rest rooms (♿), lodging, groceries, restaurants, snack bar, visitor center (♿), museum, 5 hiking trails. Entrance fee required. **Activities:** Camping, hiking, guided and self-guided walks to ruins, stargazing, cross-country skiing and snoeshoeing. **Special Features:** Mesa Verde, Spanish for "green table," offers a spectacular look into the lives of the Ancestral Puebloan People who made it their home for over 700 years, from AD 600 to 1300. The park's world-famous cliff dwellings and other works among the most notable and best preserved in the United States. Most of the park's 600 cliff dwellings were built from the late 1190s to the late 1270s. They range in size from one-room houses to villages of more than 200 rooms (the Cliff Palace).

★241★ MINIDOKA INTERNMENT NATIONAL MONUMENT

PO Box 570
Hagerman, ID 83332
Web: www.nps.gov/miin/
Phone: 208-837-4793; **Fax:** 208-837-4857
Size: 73 acres. **History:** Authorized on January 17, 2001. **Location:** In south-central Idaho, 17 miles northeast of Twin Falls and 21 miles East of Jerome. **Facilities:** No visitor information at the monument. There is a display located at Hagerman Fossil Beds National Monument Visitor Center that includes historic and modern pictures, information, and brochures. **Activities:** Self-guided walk. **Special Features:** Park commemorates the hardships and sacrifices of Japanese Americans interned there during World War II. Also known as the 'Hunt Camp', the Minidoka Relocation Center was a 33,000-acre site with more than 600 buildings and a total population of about 13,000 internees held from Washington, Oregon, and Alaska. It was in operation from August 1942 until October 1945 and constituted the seventh largest city in Idaho while it was operational. Most of the site's buildings and structures of the original camp have been removed. The site includes the remains of the entry guard station, waiting room, ornamental rock garden and commemorative plaques.

★242★ MINUTE MAN NATIONAL HISTORICAL PARK

174 Liberty St
Concord, MA 01742
Web: www.nps.gov/mima/
Phone: 978-369-6993; **Fax:** 978-318-7800
Size: 961 acres. **History:** Designated a national historic site on April 14, 1959; redesignated on September 21, 1959. **Location:** Between Lexington and Concord, Massachusetts, off I-95 (Exit 30B). Park visitor center is located on Route 2A west, 1 mile west of I-95. **Facilities:** Rest rooms (♿), visitor center, museum/exhibit, self-guided tour/trail. Entrance fee required. **Activities:** Guided and self-guided tours, interpretive programs. **Special**

See pages 16-17 for map of U.S. National Parks.

Features: Scene of the fighting on April 19, 1775, that opened the American Revolution, the park includes North Bridge, the Minute Man statue by Daniel Chester French, a number of Colonial houses, and 4 miles of Battle Road between Lexington and Concord. The park also includes ''The Wayside,'' home of authors Louisa May Alcott, Nathaniel Hawthorne, and Margaret Sidney.

★243★ **MINUTEMAN MISSILE NATIONAL HISTORIC SITE**

21280 SD Hwy 240
Philip, SD 57567
Web: www.nps.gov/mimi/
Phone: 605-433-5552; **Fax:** 605-433-5558
Size: 15 acres. **History:** Established on December 2, 1999. Delta 9 missile site transferred from the Air Force to the National Park System on September 27, 2002. The National Historic Site will be administered with Badlands National Park (see separate entry). **Location:** Park headquarters is located on the south side of Exit 131 off I-90, 75 miles east of Rapid City. Launch Control Facility Delta-01 is 4 mile west of headquarters. Launch Facility Delta-09 (missile silo) is located south of I-90 just off exit 116, 15 miles west of park headquarters. **Facilities:** Visitor center. **Activities:** Ranger-guided tours and talks. **Special Features:** Park interprets how the Minuteman missile played a strategic role in the country's defense during the Cold War. It features Launch Control Facility Delta 01 and Launch Facility Delta 09, the sole remaining examples of the original Minuteman system, dating back to the Cuban Missile Crisis.

★244★ **MISSISSIPPI NATIONAL RIVER & RECREATION AREA**

111 E Kellogg Blvd, Suite 105
Saint Paul, MN 55101
Web: www.nps.gov/miss/
Phone: 651-290-4160; **Fax:** 651-290-3214
Size: 53,775 acres. **History:** Established on November 18, 1988. **Location:** A narrow corridor of land on either side of the Mississippi River extending from Dayton, Minnesota, on the north boundary through the Minneapolis/Saint Paul area and downstream to Hastings, Minnesota. **Facilities:** Partnering organizations and agencies of the National Park Service operate a number of facilities along the river corridor, including state, regional, and community parks, historical sites, and a national wildlife refuge. Facilities at these locations include marinas, boat ramps, hiking trails, historical exhibits, bike trails, picnic areas, and visitor centers. **Activities:** Camping, hiking, bicycling, boating, canoeing, kayaking, fishing, water-skiing, hunting, cross-country skiing, snowshoeing, environmental programs. **Special Features:** In this 72-mile stretch, the Mississippi River flows through a variety of landscapes that include nationally significant natural, cultural, historic, scenic, economic, and scientific resources. The entire length of the river spans 2,350 miles, from its origin at Lake Itasca, Minnesota, to the Gulf of Mexico.

★245★ **MISSOURI NATIONAL RECREATIONAL RIVER**

PO Box 591
O'Neill, NE 68763
Web: www.nps.gov/mnrr/
Phone: 402-336-3970; **Fax:** 402-667-2552
Size: 34,159 acres. **History:** Authorized on November 10, 1978; expanded on May 24, 1991. **Location:** Two stretches of the Missouri River, comprising 98 river miles, are protected in northeast Nebraska and southeast South Dakota. The area includes a 59-mile section from Gavins Point Dam near Yankton, South Dakota, to Ponca, Nebraska, and a 39-mile section from Fort Randall Dam near Pickstown, South Dakota, to Lewis and Clark Lake. **Facilities:** The National Park Service operates no campgrounds in the park. Nearby campgrounds are operated by the US Army Corps of Engineers in Nebraska (Cottonwood and Tailwaters), the South Dakota Division of Parks and Recreation, the Nebraska Game and Parks Commission, Niobrara State Park, and Ponca State Park. **Activities:** Canoeing, kayaking, boating, fishing. **Special Features:** The two reaches of the Missouri River protected here are segments of the nation's Wild and Scenic River System. The reach set aside in 1978 from Gavins Point Dam to the vicinity of Ponca State Park still exhibits the river's dynamic character in its islands, bars, and chutes. The reach set aside in 1991 from Fort Randall Dam to Lewis and Clark Lake represents the natural landscape of the Missouri of pre-settlement days. Included in the upper reach are the lower 20 miles of the Niobrara River and the lower 8 miles of Verdigre Creek.

★246★ **MOJAVE NATIONAL PRESERVE**

2701 Barstow Rd
Barstow, CA 92311
Web: www.nps.gov/moja/
Phone: 760-252-6100; **Fax:** 760-252-6174
Size: 1,529,927 acres. **History:** Established on October 31, 1994, by the California Desert Protection Act. **Location:** Easily reached via I-15 or I-40 east of Barstow, California, and west of Needles, California, and Las Vegas, Nevada. Six freeway exits provide visitor access. **Facilities:** Campgrounds, visitor center, trails. **Activities:** Camping, hiking, bicycling, horseback riding, auto touring, hunting, wildflower viewing, off-road driving, interpretive programs. **Special Features:** The preserve protects the fragile habitat of the desert tortoise, vast open spaces, and historic mining scenes, such as the Kelso Railroad Depot (built in 1924). It is also home to the world's largest Joshua tree forest and the 600-foot-high Kelso Dunes, the third tallest dunes in North America.

★247★ **MONOCACY NATIONAL BATTLEFIELD**

4801 Urbana Pike
Frederick, MD 21704
Web: www.nps.gov/mono/
Phone: 301-662-3515; **Fax:** 301-662-3420
Size: 1,647 acres. **History:** Authorized as Monocacy National Military Park on June 21, 1934. Law required land purchase by private funds. Federal purchase authorized and redesignated on October 21, 1976. **Location:** In Frederick, Maryland; accessible from the north, east, and west via I-70, Exit 54 (Market Street),

See pages 16-17 for map of U.S. National Parks.

and from the south, via I-270, Exit 26 (Urbana). **Facilities:** Visitor center (&), museum/exhibit. **Activities:** Auto touring, hiking, bicycling, cross-country skiing, interpretive programs. **Special Features:** In a battle here on July 9, 1864, Confederate General Jubal A. Early defeated Union forces commanded by Major General Lew Wallace. Wallace's troops delayed Early's advance on Washington, DC, however, enabling Union forces to marshal a successful defense of the capital.

★248★ MONTEZUMA CASTLE NATIONAL MONUMENT

527 South Main St
Camp Verde, AZ 86322
Web: www.nps.gov/moca/
Phone: 928-567-5276; **Fax:** 928-567-3597
Size: 858 acres. **History:** Proclaimed on December 8, 1906. **Location:** 50 miles south of Flagstaff, Arizona, off I-17. **Facilities:** Picnic area, rest rooms (&), visitor center (&), museum/exhibit, self-guided tour/trail. Entrance fee required. **Activities:** Hiking, diorama/audio program, ranger-led programs. **Special Features:** Built in the 12th and 13th centuries by Sinagua farmers, this five-story, 20-room cliff dwelling is one of the best preserved in North America and is a classic example of the last phase of southern Sinagua occupation of the Verde Valley. Early settlers to the area assumed that the imposing structure was associated with the Aztec emperor Montezuma, but the structure was abandoned almost a century before Montezuma was born.

★249★ MOORES CREEK NATIONAL BATTLEFIELD

40 Patriots Hall Dr
Currie, NC 28435
Web: www.nps.gov/mocr/
Phone: 910-283-5591; **Fax:** 910-283-5351
Size: 88 acres. **History:** Established on June 2, 1926, as a national military park; transferred from War Department on August 10, 1933; redesignated on September 8, 1980. **Location:** 20 miles northwest of Wilmington, North Carolina. From the city, take I-40 or US 421 north to the junction with NC 210, and then proceed west on US 210. **Facilities:** Picnic area, rest rooms (&), visitor center (&), museum/exhibit, self-guided tour/trail. **Activities:** Bicycling, fishing, bird-watching, battlefield tours, living history programs. **Special Features:** The battle on February 27, 1776, between North Carolina Patriots and Loyalists is commemorated here. The Patriot victory notably advanced the revolutionary cause in the South.

★250★ MORRISTOWN NATIONAL HISTORICAL PARK

30 Washington Pl
Morristown, NJ 07960
Web: www.nps.gov/morr/
Phone: 973-543-4030
Size: 1,711 acres. **History:** Authorized on March 2, 1933. **Location:** In Morristown, New Jersey, along I-287. **Facilities:** Rest rooms (&), visitor center (&), museum/exhibit, self-guided tour/trail. Entrance fee required. **Activities:** Hiking, cross-country skiing, guided tour. **Special Features:** Morristown was quarters for the Continental Army during two critical winters — January

of 1777 and 1779-1780. The park includes the Ford Mansion, Jockey Hollow, and Fort Nonsense.

★251★ MOUNT RAINIER NATIONAL PARK

55210 238th Ave E
Ashford, WA 98304
Web: www.nps.gov/mora/
Phone: 360-569-2211; **Fax:** 360-569-2170
Size: 235,625 acres. **History:** Established on March 2, 1899. Wilderness designated on November 16, 1988. **Location:** In west-central Washington. Year-round access is via SR 706 to the Nisqually entrance in the SW corner of the park. Limited winter access is available via Hwy. 123 in the SE corner of the park. The Carbon River/Mowich Lake area (NW corner) is accessed via SR 165 through Wilkeson. Summer access is available via Hwy. 410 on the north and east sides of the park. **Facilities:** Campgrounds, picnic area, rest rooms (&), lodging, groceries, restaurant/snacks, visitor centers (&), museum/exhibit, self-guided tour/trail. Entrance fee required. **Activities:** Camping, hiking, bicycling, horseback riding, mountain climbing, fishing, cross-country skiing, auto touring, wildlife viewing, ranger-led programs. **Special Features:** This greatest single-peak glacial system in the United States radiates from the summit and slopes of Mount Rainier, an ancient volcano. The 14,410' mountain is surrounded by lush old growth forests, subalpine meadows, and a National Historic Landmark District that showcases the log and boulder buildings typical of the ''NPS Rustic'' style architecture of the 1920s and 1930s.

★252★ MOUNT RUSHMORE NATIONAL MEMORIAL

13000 Hwy 244, Bldg 31 Suite 1
Keystone, SD 57751
Web: www.nps.gov/moru/
Phone: 605-574-2523; **Fax:** 605-574-2307
Size: 1,278 acres. **History:** Authorized on March 3, 1925. **Location:** Surrounded by the Black Hills National Forest, memorial is 25 miles southwest of Rapid City, South Dakota, via US 16; and 3 miles from Keystone, South Dakota, via US 16A and SD 244. **Facilities:** Rest rooms (&), restaurant/snacks, visitor center (&), museum/exhibit. **Activities:** Ranger-led programs, cultural events. **Special Features:** Colossal heads of Presidents George Washington, Thomas Jefferson, Abraham Lincoln, and Theodore Roosevelt were sculpted by Gutzon Borglum on the face of a granite mountain. A lighting ceremony is presented in the amphitheater during summer evenings.

★253★ MUIR WOODS NATIONAL MONUMENT

Mill Valley, CA 94941
Web: www.nps.gov/muwo/
Phone: 415-388-2596; **Fax:** 415-389-6957
Size: 554 acres. **History:** Proclaimed on January 9, 1908. **Location:** 12 miles north of California's Golden Gate Bridge, accessible via US 101 and CA 1. **Facilities:** Rest rooms (&), restaurant/snacks, visitor center (&), museum/exhibit, self-guided tour/trail. Entrance fee required. **Activities:** Hiking, wildlife viewing. **Special Features:** The virgin stand of coastal redwoods was purchased by Congressman William Kent and his wife, Elizabeth

See pages 16-17 for map of U.S. National Parks.

Thacher Kent in 1905. The land was subsequently donated to the federal government and declared a national monument by President Theodore Roosevelt in 1908, in honor of John Muir, writer and conservationist.

★254★ NATCHEZ NATIONAL HISTORICAL PARK

1 Melrose Montebello Pkwy
Natchez, MS 39120
Web: www.nps.gov/natc/
Phone: 601-446-5790; **Fax:** 601-442-9516
Size: 105 acres. **History:** Authorized on October 7, 1988. **Location:** In Natchez, Mississippi, near the intersection of US 61 and US 65/84. **Facilities:** Restrooms, museum/exhibit. **Activities:** Guided tours of mansion and self-guided tours of grounds. **Special Features:** European settlement of Natchez began with a French trading post in 1714. Control passed to Spain in 1779 and to the United States in 1798. In the decades before the Civil War, Natchez became a commercial, cultural, and social center of the South's "cotton belt." The city today represents one of the best preserved concentrations of significant antebellum properties in the United States. Within the park are Melrose, an excellent example of a planter's home, and the home of William Johnson, a free African-American businessman, whose diary tells the story of everyday life in antebellum Natchez.

NATCHEZ TRACE NATIONAL SCENIC TRAIL

(See separate listing in National Trails section.)

★255★ NATCHEZ TRACE PARKWAY

2680 Natchez Trace Pkwy
Tupelo, MS 38804
Web: www.nps.gov/natr/
Phone: 662-680-4025; **Fax:** 662-680-4036; **Toll Free:** 800-305-7417
Size: 51,824 acres. **History:** Emergency Appropriation Act of June 19, 1934, allocated initial construction funds; established as parkway under National Park Service by act of May 18, 1938. Ackia Battleground (now called Chickasaw Village) and Meriwether Lewis Park were added to the Natchez Trace Parkway by Act of August 10, 1961. **Location:** A 444-mile route between Nashville, Tennessee, and Natchez, Mississippi. The southern terminus of the Parkway is accessed off of Liberty Road in Natchez, which is the historical "beginning" of the Old Trace at milepost zero. **Facilities:** Campgrounds (&), picnic area, rest rooms (&), groceries, boat ramp, visitor center (&), museum/exhibit, self-guided tour/trail. **Activities:** Camping, hiking, bicycling, horseback riding, swimming, boating, fishing, auto touring, ranger-guided talks. **Special Features:** This historic route generally follows the old Indian trace or trail between Nashville, Tennessee, and Natchez, Mississippi that connected southern portions of the Mississippi River, through Alabama, to salt licks in today's central Tennessee.

★256★ NATIONAL MALL

c/o National Capitol Parks - Central
900 Ohio Dr SW
Washington, DC 20024
Web: www.nps.gov/nama/
Phone: 202-426-6841; **Fax:** 202-724-0764

Size: 146 acres. **History:** Approved on July 16, 1790, except for 42 acres transferred later from other agencies. Transferred from Office of Public Buildings and Public Parks of the National Capital on August 10, 1933. **Location:** In the area encompassed by Constitution and Pennsylvania avenues, NW on the north, First Street on the east, Independence and Maryland avenues on the south, and 14th Street on the west. **Activities:** Shuttle tour. **Special Features:** This landscaped park extending from the Capitol to the Washington Monument was envisioned as a formal park in L'Enfant's Plan for the city of Washington in 1791.

★257★ NATIONAL PARK OF AMERICAN SAMOA

Pago Pago, AS 96799
Web: www.nps.gov/npsa/
Phone: 684-633-7082; **Fax:** 684-633-7085
Size: 9,000 acres. **History:** Authorized on October 31, 1988. The national park is entirely on lands leased from the ten Samoan villages, which are the true landowners; a 50-year lease was signed on September 9, 1993. **Location:** In American Samoa, 2,600 miles southwest of Hawaii. Park lands are on three separate islands: Tutuila, Ofu and Tau. There are scheduled flights from Honolulu, Hawaii, to Pago Pago on Tutuila. Regularly scheduled flights serve park areas on Ofu and Tau. **Facilities:** Visitor center (in Pago Pago), lodging. Because the national park lies entirely on lands still owned by several rural Samoan villages, traditional cultures have an impact on all aspects of this park's operations and visitor opportunities. **Activities:** Hiking, swimming, kayaking, fishing, snorkeling, scuba diving, auto touring, wildlife viewing, guided tours. Overnight stays in Samoan villages are encouraged. **Special Features:** Two rain forest preserves and a coral reef are home to unique tropical animals including the flying fox, Pacific Boa, tortoises, and an array of birds and fish.

★258★ NATIONAL WORLD WAR II MEMORIAL

17th St & Independence Ave NW
Washington, DC 20001
Web: www.wwiimemorial.com
Phone: 202-426-6841
Size: 7.5 acres. **History:** Authorized on May 25, 1993; dedicated on May 29, 2004. **Location:** On 17th Street, between Constitution and Independence avenues, flanked by the Washington Monument to the east and the Lincoln Memorial to the west. **Activities:** The memorial is operated by the National Park Service and is open to visitors 24 hours a day, seven days a week. **Special Features:** The World War II Memorial honors the 16 million Americans who served during World War II, along with the millions who supported them on the home front. A wall contains 4,000 gold stars symbolizing the more than 400,000 Americans who died during the war.

★259★ NATURAL BRIDGES NATIONAL MONUMENT

HC 60 Box 1
Lake Powell, UT 84533
Web: www.nps.gov/nabr/
Phone: 435-692-1234; **Fax:** 435-692-1111

See pages 16-17 for map of U.S. National Parks.

Size: 7,636 acres. **History:** Proclaimed on April 16, 1908. **Location:** Park entrance is at the end of UT 275, 35 miles west of Blanding on UT 95. **Facilities:** Campground, picnic area, rest rooms (&), visitor center (&), museum/exhibit, self-guided tour/trail. Entrance fee required. **Activities:** Camping, hiking, bicycling, auto touring, interpretive talks. **Special Features:** Three natural bridges carved out of sandstone, including the second and third largest in the world, are protected here. Also present are Ancestral Puebloan rock art and ruins.

★260★ NAVAJO NATIONAL MONUMENT
HC 71 Box 3
Tonalea, AZ 86044
Web: www.nps.gov/nava/
Phone: 928-672-2700; **Fax:** 928-672-2703
Size: 360 acres. **History:** Proclaimed on March 20, 1909. Headquarters is on 245 acres of tribal land adjacent to the Betatakin section; used by agreement of May, 1962. A right-of-way of 4.6 acres was granted to the National Park Service in 1977. **Location:** 50 miles northeast of Tuba City or 20 miles southwest of Kayenta, Arizona. Accessible via US 160, and then 9 miles on AR 564. **Facilities:** Campground (&), picnic area, rest rooms (&), visitor center (&), museum/exhibit, self-guided tour/trail. **Activities:** Camping, hiking, guided and self-guided tours. **Special Features:** Monument preserves Betatakin, Keet Seel, and Inscription House, three cliff dwellings of the Ancestral Puebloan People. The monument is surrounded by Navajo Nation land.

**★261★ NEW BEDFORD WHALING NATIONAL
        HISTORICAL PARK**
33 William St
New Bedford, MA 02740
Web: www.nps.gov/nebe/
Phone: 508-996-4095; **Fax:** 508-984-1250
Size: 34 acres. **History:** Authorized on November 12, 1996. **Location:** In New Bedford, Massachusetts, 50 miles southeast of Boston and 30 miles east of Providence, Rhode Island. Accessible via I-195 (Exit 15). **Facilities:** Visitor center, museum/exhibit (&). **Activities:** Self-guided walks, guided tours. **Special Features:** Park commemorates the heritage of the world's preeminent whaling port during the 19th century. A variety of cultural landscapes, historic buildings, museum collections, and archives preserve this history and collectively recount the stories of a remarkable era. Sites spread over 13 city blocks include the New Bedford Whaling Museum, the Seamen's Bethel, the schooner *Ernestina,* the U.S. Customs House, and the Rotch-Jones-Duff House and Garden Museum.

**★262★ NEW ORLEANS JAZZ NATIONAL
        HISTORICAL PARK**
419 Rue Decatur
New Orleans, LA 70130
Web: www.nps.gov/jazz/
Phone: 504-589-4806; **Fax:** 504-589-3865; **Toll Free:** 877-520-0677
Size: 5.1 acres. **History:** Authorized on October 31, 1994. **Location:** A temporary visitor center is located in the French Quarter at 916 N. Peters, New Orleans, Louisiana. **Facilities:** Work is underway to develop permanent facilities at historic Armstrong Park bordering North Rampart St., Orleans Ave., North Villere, and St. Phillip. The complex, located at the northern edge of the French Quarter, will be renovated into a visitor center with exhibits, park headquarters, performance venue, education classrooms, and a resource center. **Activities:** Interpretive activities include musical performances, ranger-led demonstrations and talks, lectures, films, and exhibits on a wide variety of jazz-related topics. A walking tour of significant historical jazz sites in the French Quarter is held a few times per month (by reservation). **Special Features:** Park interprets jazz as it has evolved in New Orleans and assists a range of organizations involved with jazz and its history.

★263★ NEW RIVER GORGE NATIONAL RIVER
104 Main St
PO Box 246
Glen Jean, WV 25846
Web: www.nps.gov/neri/
Phone: 304-465-0508; **Fax:** 304-465-0591
Size: 72,189 acres. **History:** Authorized on November 10, 1978. **Location:** 53 miles of the New River between the towns of Hinton and Fayetteville in southern West Virginia. **Facilities:** Campgrounds, picnic area, rest rooms (&), boardwalks, cabin rental, visitor centers (&), museum/exhibit. **Activities:** Camping, hiking, horseback riding, mountain biking, swimming, boating, kayaking, whitewater rafting, fishing, hunting, climbing. **Special Features:** A rugged, whitewater river, flowing northward through deep canyons, the New is among the oldest rivers on the continent. The free-flowing river falls 750 feet in 50 miles from Bluestone Dam to Gauley Bridge, creating one of the finest whitewater rivers in the eastern United States. It is abundant in natural, scenic, historic, and recreational features.

★264★ NEZ PERCE NATIONAL HISTORICAL PARK
39063 US Hwy 95
Spalding, ID 83540
Web: www.nps.gov/nepe/
Phone: 208-843-2261; **Fax:** 208-843-2817
Size: 2,495 acres. **History:** Authorized on May 15, 1965. **Location:** Park includes 38 sites located in north-central Washington, northeast Oregon, north-central Idaho, and western Montana. Headquarters is located in Spalding, Idaho, 11 miles east of Lewiston. **Facilities:** Picnic area, rest rooms (&), visitor centers (&), museum/exhibit, self-guided tour/trail. **Activities:** Hiking, auto touring, fishing, swimming, cross-country skiing, ranger-led programs. **Special Features:** The history and culture of the Nez Perce Indian country are preserved, commemorated, and interpreted here. Of the park's original 24 sites, and the 14 additional sites added in 1992, the National Park Service owns 9 of the properties, including Big Hole National Battlefield (see separate entry for description) and Bear Paw Battlefield. Other properties are managed through cooperative agreements. Park includes a number of sites that Captains Meriwether Lewis and William Clark passed through or camped at on their journey across western Montana and central Idaho.

See pages 16-17 for map of U.S. National Parks.

1. US National Parks

★265★ NICODEMUS NATIONAL HISTORIC SITE

304 Washington Ave
Nicodemus, KS 67625
Web: www.nps.gov/nico/
Phone: 785-839-4233; **Fax:** 785-839-4325
Size: 161 acres. **History:** Established on November 12, 1996. **Location:** 45 miles northwest of Hays, Kansas, on US 24 between Hill City and Stockton. **Facilities:** Visitor center includes exhibits on the history of Nicodemus and Blacks in the West. **Activities:** Tours (during summer season). **Special Features:** Nicodemus, Kansas is the only remaining western town established by African Americans during the Reconstruction Period following the Civil War, and represents the western expansion and settlement of the Great Plains. It is the site of the oldest reported post office supervised by African Americans in the United States. The site includes five buildings: The First Baptist Church, St. Francis Hotel, Nicodemus School District Number One, African Methodist Episcopal Church, and Township Hall (all privately owned).

★266★ NINETY SIX NATIONAL HISTORIC SITE

1103 Hwy 248
Ninety Six, SC 29666
Web: www.nps.gov/nisi/
Phone: 864-543-4068; **Fax:** 864-543-2058
Size: 1,022 acres. **History:** Authorized on August 19, 1976. **Location:** 2 miles south of the town of Ninety Six, South Carolina, on SC 248. Accessible via I-26 and SC 34, I-20 and US 25, or I-85 and SC 178. **Facilities:** Picnic area, rest rooms (&), visitor center (&), museum/exhibit, self-guided tour/trail. **Activities:** Hiking, bicycling, fishing, wildlife viewing, interpretive programs. **Special Features:** This important colonial backcountry trading village and government seat (after 1769) was held briefly by the British during the Revolutionary War and is the scene of Nathanael Greene's siege in 1781. The site contains earthwork embankments of a 1781 fortification, the remains of two historic villages, a colonial plantation complex, and numerous prehistoric sites.

★267★ NIOBRARA NATIONAL SCENIC RIVER

PO Box 591
O'Neill, NE 68763
Web: www.nps.gov/niob/
Phone: 402-336-3970
Size: 23,074 acres. **History:** Authorized on May 24, 1991. **Location:** 76-mile stretch of the Niobrara River in north-central Nebraska, from the Borman Bridge southeast of Valentine, east to the NE 137 Bridge north of Newport. 5,993 acres. **Facilities:** No National Park Service facilities are available. The U.S. Fish and Wildlife Service operates a visitor center at the Fort Niobrara National Wildlife Refuge that explains Fort Niobrara history, local wildlife, and refuge management. The Nebraska Game and Parks Commission operates a visitor center at Smith Falls State Park. **Activities:** Canoeing, kayaking, tubing, rafting, fishing, swimming, hiking, horseback riding, wildlife viewing. **Special Features:** The river flows through an ecological crossroads where six distinct ecosystems mix. The upper reach of the designated river is recognized as one of the nation's premier canoeing rivers. The Niobrara Valley is also a remarkable cultural landscape dotted with historic resources and small ranches and farms that have been locally owned for generations.

★268★ NOATAK NATIONAL PRESERVE

PO Box 1029
Kotzebue, AK 99752
Web: www.nps.gov/noat/
Phone: 907-442-3890; **Fax:** 907-442-8316
Size: 6,569,904 acres. **History:** Proclaimed as Noatak National Monument on December 1, 1978; established as a national preserve on December 2, 1980. Wilderness designated on December 2, 1980. Designated a Biosphere Reserve in 1976. **Location:** In northwestern Alaska, in the western Brooks Range, encompassing more than 250 miles of the Noatak River. Daily jet service is available from Anchorage and Fairbanks to Kotzebue. From there, scheduled air service is available to the parklands and nearby villages. Summer access may include motorized/non-motorized watercraft, aircraft, or by foot. Winter access may include snowmobiles, aircraft, or by foot. **Facilities:** Ranger stations (seasonal). **Activities:** Camping, hiking, mountain climbing, boating, kayaking, canoeing, rafting, fishing, hunting, cross-country skiing, dog mushing, wildlife viewing. **Special Features:** The Noatak River basin is the largest mountain-ringed river basin in the nation still virtually unaffected by man. The preserve includes landforms of great scientific interest, including the 65-mile-long Grand Canyon of the Noatak, a transition zone and migration route for plants and animals between subarctic and arctic environments, and an array of flora among the most diverse anywhere in the earth's northern latitudes. The preserve contains part of the 400-mile Noatak Wild and Scenic River.

★269★ NORTH CASCADES NATIONAL PARK

810 SR 20
Sedro Woolley, WA 98284
Web: www.nps.gov/noca/
Phone: 360-856-5700; **Fax:** 360-856-1934
Size: 504,781 acres. **History:** Established on October 2, 1968. Wilderness designated on November 16, 1988. The Stephen Mather Wilderness Area extends into Lake Chelan and Ross Lake national recreation areas (see separate entries) and the three park units in this mountainous region are managed as one. **Location:** In northwestern Washington. Access to the Park is from I-5 at Burlington, west of the mountains, and Twisp, on the east, following WA 20 (North Cascades Scenic Highway). WA 20, the major access to Ross Lake NRA, is partially closed from approximately mid-November to mid-April due to the weather. **Facilities:** Campgrounds, picnic area, rest rooms (&), cabins, lodging, boat rentals, restaurant/snacks, visitor centers (&), museum/exhibit, self-guided tour/trail. **Activities:** Camping, hiking, horseback riding, mountain climbing, fishing, boating, kayaking, whitewater rafting, wildlife viewing, auto touring, cross-country skiing, snowshoeing. **Special Features:** In this wilderness park, high jagged peaks intercept moisture-laden winds, producing glaciers, waterfalls, rivers, lakes, lush forests and meadows, and a great diversity of flora and fauna. The park and adjacent recreation areas encompass more than 300 glaciers, more than any other national park in the contiguous United

See pages 16-17 for map of U.S. National Parks.

States. Almost 400 miles of trails and vast undeveloped wilderness allow visitors to experience nature with minimal human intrusion.

★270★ OBED WILD & SCENIC RIVER

208 N Maiden St
Wartburg, TN 37887
Web: www.nps.gov/obed/
Phone: 423-346-6294; **Fax:** 423-346-3362
Size: 5,073 acres. **History:** Authorized on October 12, 1976. **Location:** In east-central Tennessee. From Nashville and west, take I-40 to US 127 north. From Knoxville and east, take I-40 to US 27 north. Both US 27 and US 127 run north and south and connect with TN 62 that skirts the northern edge of the area. **Facilities:** Undeveloped campground, picnic area, rest rooms (&), visitor center (&), museum/exhibit. **Activities:** Camping, hiking, swimming, boating, kayaking, whitewater paddling, fishing, hunting, climbing, interpretive programs. **Special Features:** The Obed River and its two main tributaries, Clear Creek and Daddy's Creek, cut into the Cumberland Plateau of East Tennessee, providing some of the most rugged scenery in the Southeast. Forty-five miles of streams are protected within the park, offering Class II through IV whitewater.

★271★ OCMULGEE NATIONAL MONUMENT

1207 Emery Hwy
Macon, GA 31217
Web: www.nps.gov/ocmu/
Phone: 478-752-8257; **Fax:** 478-752-8259
Size: 702 acres. **History:** Authorized on June 14, 1934. **Location:** On the east side of Macon, Georgia, on US 80 east (Emery Highway). Main access is from I-75 to I-16 east, at the north end of Macon, and then the second exit from I-16 (Coliseum Exit). **Facilities:** Picnic area, rest rooms (&), visitor center (&), museum/exhibit, self-guided tour/trail. Entrance fee required. **Activities:** Hiking, fishing, ranger-led programs. **Special Features:** Traces of 12,000 years of Southeastern culture from Ice Age Indians to the historic Creek Confederacy are preserved here, including the massive temple mounds of a Mississippian Indian ceremonial complex that thrived between AD 900 and 1100 and many artifacts.

★272★ OLYMPIC NATIONAL PARK

600 E Park Ave
Port Angeles, WA 98362
Web: www.nps.gov/olym/
Phone: 360-565-3130; **Fax:** 360-565-3015
Size: 922,651 acres. **History:** Proclaimed as Mount Olympus National Monument on March 2, 1909; established as Olympic National Park on June 29, 1938. Wilderness designated on November 16, 1988. Designated a Biosphere Reserve in 1976 and a World Heritage Site in 1981. **Location:** On the Olympic Peninsula in western Washington, encircled by US 101. From the Seattle/Tacoma area, travelers may reach U.S. 101 by several different routes, either by crossing Puget Sound on one of the Washington state ferries or by driving south around Puget Sound. The main park visitor center and park headquarters are located in Port Angeles at the north end of the peninsula. **Facilities:**

Campgrounds (&), picnic area, rest rooms (&), cabin rental, lodging, groceries, restaurant, boat rental, boat ramp, bathhouse, visitor centers (&), museum/exhibit, self-guided tour/trail. Entrance fee required. **Activities:** Camping, hiking, bicycling, horseback riding, mountain climbing, swimming, boating, fishing, cross-country skiing, snowshoeing, wildlife viewing, auto touring, ranger-led programs. **Special Features:** Park encompasses three distinctly different ecosystems: rugged glacier capped mountains, more than 70 miles of wild Pacific coast (the largest section of wilderness coast in the lower 48 states), and majestic stands of old-growth and temperate rain forest. These diverse ecosystems are still largely pristine in character (about 95% of the park is designated wilderness). More than 600 miles of trails provide access to these wild areas. Archeological and historical records show that human habitation of the area goes back at least 12,000 years.

★273★ OREGON CAVES NATIONAL MONUMENT

19000 Caves Hwy
Cave Junction, OR 97523
Web: www.nps.gov/orca/
Phone: 541-592-2100; **Fax:** 541-592-3981
Size: 488 acres. **History:** Proclaimed on July 12, 1909; transferred from Forest Service on August 10, 1933. **Location:** 20 miles southeast of Cave Junction, Oregon, on OR 46. Park is 50 miles south of Grants Pass, Oregon, and 76 miles northeast of Crescent City, California, via US 199. **Facilities:** Picnic area, rest rooms (&), lodging, restaurant/snacks, self-guided tour/trail. **Activities:** Hiking, snowshoeing, ranger-led programs, guided cave tours (late March through November). **Special Features:** Groundwater dissolving marble bedrock formed these cave passages and intricate flowstone formations. Above ground, the monument encompasses a remnant old-growth coniferous forest. It harbors a remarkable array of plants and a Douglas-fir tree with the widest known girth in Oregon.

★274★ ORGAN PIPE CACTUS NATIONAL MONUMENT

10 Organ Pipe Dr
Ajo, AZ 85321
Web: www.nps.gov/orpi/
Phone: 520-387-6849
Size: 330,689 acres. **History:** Proclaimed on April 13, 1937. Wilderness designated on November 10, 1978. Designated a Biosphere Reserve in 1976. **Location:** In southern Arizona, along the Mexican border. From the north (I-8), follow AZ 85 through Ajo and Why. The Monument is 35 miles south of Ajo and 22 miles south of Why. **Facilities:** Campgrounds (&), picnic area, rest rooms (&), visitor center (&), museum/exhibit, self-guided tour/trail. Entrance fee required. **Activities:** Camping, hiking, bicycling, horseback riding, auto touring, interpretive programs. **Special Features:** Sonoran Desert plants and animals found nowhere else in the United States are protected here, as are traces of the Camino del Diablo Historic Trail. Included among the flora and fauna are the organ pipe cactus, saguaro, elephant tree, and creatures such as the kangaroo rat and javelina that have been able to adapt themselves to extreme temperatures, intense sunlight, and little rainfall.

See pages 16-17 for map of U.S. National Parks.

★275★ OZARK NATIONAL SCENIC RIVERWAYS

404 Watercress Dr
PO Box 490
Van Buren, MO 63965
Web: www.nps.gov/ozar/
Phone: 573-323-4236; **Fax:** 573-323-4140
Size: 80,785 acres. **History:** Authorized on August 27, 1964; established on June 10, 1972. **Location:** 134 miles of the Jacks Fork and Current rivers in south-central Missouri. Accessible via I-44 or US 60. **Facilities:** Campgrounds (&), picnic area, rest rooms (&), cabin rental, groceries, restaurant/snacks, boat rental, boat ramp, museum/exhibit. **Activities:** Camping, hiking, horseback riding, swimming, boating, canoeing, tubing, fishing, hunting, nature hikes. **Special Features:** The nation's first national scenic riverway protects 134 miles of the Current and Jacks Fork rivers in the Ozark Highlands. Much of the area is underlain by soluble limestone and dolomite, giving rise to sinkholes, caves, and springs of a classical karst topography. There are more than 300 recorded caves within the boundaries and nearly 100 springs that pour thousands of gallons of clear, cold water into the streams. Big Spring, one of the largest springs in the United States, has an average flow of 276 million gallons of water per day. Ozark culture is also preserved throughout the area.

★276★ PADRE ISLAND NATIONAL SEASHORE

PO Box 181300
Corpus Christi, TX 78480
Web: www.nps.gov/pais/
Phone: 361-949-8173; **Fax:** 361-949-8023
Size: 130,434 acres. **History:** Authorized on September 28, 1962; established on April 6, 1968. **Location:** Southeast of the city of Corpus Christi, Texas. From Corpus Christi, go east through the city on South Padre Island Dr. (Highway 358), past the JFK Causeway and the bridge onto Padre Island, and continue 10 miles south on Park Road 22. **Facilities:** Campgrounds (&), rest rooms (&), picnic areas, observation decks, boat ramp, bathhouse, visitor center (&), museum/exhibit, self-guided tour/trail. Entrance fee required. **Activities:** Camping, hiking, horseback riding, auto touring, swimming, boating, fishing, windsurfing, water-skiing, scuba diving, snorkeling, bird-watching, educational and interpretive programs. **Special Features:** The longest remaining undeveloped barrier island in the world (80.5 miles) is noted for its wide sand beaches, excellent fishing, and abundant bird and marine life. Because of its location on a major migratory route known as the Central Flyway, approximately 380 species of birds have been documented within the National Seashore, representing almost 45% of all bird species documented in North America.

★277★ PALO ALTO BATTLEFIELD NATIONAL HISTORIC SITE

1623 Central Blvd, Suite 213
Brownsville, TX 78520
Web: www.nps.gov/paal/
Phone: 956-541-2785; **Fax:** 956-541-6356
Size: 3,407 acres. **History:** Authorized on November 10, 1978. **Location:** At the northeast corner of the intersection of FM 1847 (Paredes Line Road) and FM 511, 5 miles north of downtown Brownsville, Texas. **Facilities:** Visitor center, exhibits, self-guided trail with interpretive battlefield markers. **Activities:** Guided tours and interpretive programs (on an irregular basis). **Special Features:** Park preserves the large battlefield on which the first battle of the 1846-1848 Mexican War took place. It portrays the battle and the war, as well as its causes and consequences, from the perspective of both the United States and Mexico.

★278★ PEA RIDGE NATIONAL MILITARY PARK

15930 Hwy 62 E
Garfield, AR 72732
Web: www.nps.gov/peri/
Phone: 479-451-8122; **Fax:** 479-451-0219
Size: 4,300 acres. **History:** Authorized on July 20, 1956. **Location:** 80 miles southwest of Springfield, Missouri, off US 62. **Facilities:** Picnic area, visitor center (&), museum/exhibit, self-guided tour/trail. Entrance fee required. **Activities:** Hiking, auto touring. **Special Features:** The park represents what might be the most well preserved Civil War battlefield in the United States. The Union victory here on March 7-8, 1862, in one of the major engagements of the Civil War west of the Mississippi, led to the Union's total control of Missouri. The park also includes a 2.5-mile segment of the Trail of Tears National Historic Site (see separate entry in National Trails section).

★279★ PECOS NATIONAL HISTORICAL PARK

PO Box 418
Pecos, NM 87552
Web: www.nps.gov/peco/
Phone: 505-757-6414; **Fax:** 505-757-8460
Size: 6,670 acres. **History:** Authorized as a national monument on June 28, 1965; redesignated on June 27, 1990. **Location:** 25 miles southeast of Santa Fe, New Mexico, off I-25. **Facilities:** Picnic area, rest rooms (&), visitor center (&), museum/exhibit, self-guided tour/trail (&). Entrance fee required. **Activities:** Self-guided and guided tours, cultural demonstrations. **Special Features:** Park preserves 12,000 years of human history, including the ruins of the Pecos Pueblo and many other American Indian structures, Spanish colonial missions, homesteads of the Mexican era, a section of the Santa Fe Trail, sites related to the Civil War Battle of Glorieta Pass, and 20th century ranch history of Forked Lightning Ranch.

★280★ PENNSYLVANIA AVENUE NATIONAL HISTORIC SITE

c/o National Capitol Parks - Central
900 Ohio Dr SW
Washington, DC 20024
Web: www.nps.gov/paav/
Phone: 202-606-9686
History: Designated a national historic site on September 30, 1965. Added to the National Register of Historic Places on October 15, 1966. **Location:** This site includes a portion of Pennsylvania Avenue and the area adjacent to it between the Capitol and the White House. **Special Features:** Referred to as "America's Main Street," Pennsylvania Avenue encompasses

See pages 16-17 for map of U.S. National Parks.

1. US National Parks

Ford's Theatre National Historic Site (see separate entry), several blocks of the Washington commercial district, the Old Post Office Tower, and a number of federal structures.

★281★ PERRY'S VICTORY & INTERNATIONAL PEACE MEMORIAL

93 Delaware Ave
PO Box 549
Put-in-Bay, OH 43456
Web: www.nps.gov/pevi/
Phone: 419-285-2184; **Fax:** 419-285-2516
Size: 25.4 acres. **History:** Monument construction began in October 1912; opened to the public on June 13 1915; established on June 2, 1936, as a national monument; redesignated on October 26, 1972. **Location:** On South Bass Island in Lake Erie, 3 miles from the Ohio mainland. Ferries operate daily from April-November from Catawba Point (3 miles) and Port Clinton (10 miles), making frequent roundtrips in the summer. There is year-round air service from Port Clinton and Sandusky airports. **Facilities:** Rest rooms (&), museum/exhibit, observation deck. Entrance fee required. **Activities:** Fishing, interpretive talks, living history demonstrations. **Special Features:** Commodore Oliver H. Perry won the greatest naval battle of the War of 1812 on Lake Erie. The memorial — the world's most massive Doric column — was constructed ''to inculcate the lessons of international peace by arbitration and disarmament.'' It was designed by Joseph Freedlander. The 317-foot-high observation gallery offers a panoramic view of western Lake Erie.

★282★ PETERSBURG NATIONAL BATTLEFIELD

1539 Hickory Hill Rd
Petersburg, VA 23803
Web: www.nps.gov/pete/
Phone: 804-732-3531; **Fax:** 804-732-0835
Size: 2,659 acres (battlefield) and 8.7 acres (cemetery). **History:** Established as a national military park on July 3, 1926; redesignated a national battlefield on August 24, 1962. **Location:** Visitor center of park's main unit is east of the City of Petersburg, Virginia, just off VA 36. The Five Forks Battlefield is 25 miles southwest of the visitor center at the intersection of VA 613 and 627. The City Point Unit is located in the City of Hopewell, accessible from the visitor center via VA 36 and 156 to VA 10. **Facilities:** Picnic area, bicycle trail, visitor center (&), museum/exhibit, self-guided tour/trail. Entrance fee required. **Activities:** Hiking, bicycling, horseback riding, auto tours, living history programs. **Special Features:** The Union Army waged a ten-month campaign here in 1864-1865 to seize Petersburg, center of the railroads supplying Richmond and General Robert E. Lee's army. Park includes City Point in Hopewell, Virginia, where Ulysses S. Grant made his headquarters at Appomattox Manor for the final ten months of the war; and the Five Forks Battlefield, where the Confederate collapse led to the fall of the city and ultimately of Richmond. Poplar Grove (Petersburg) National Cemetery — 6,315 interments; 4,110 unidentified — is near the park.

★283★ PETRIFIED FOREST NATIONAL PARK

PO Box 2217
Petrified Forest, AZ 86028
Web: www.nps.gov/pefo/
Phone: 928-524-6228; **Fax:** 928-524-3567
Size: 221,540 acres. **History:** Proclaimed as a national monument on December 8, 1906; established as a national park on December 9, 1962. Wilderness designated on October 23, 1970. **Location:** Stretches between I-40 and US 180 in eastern Arizona. North entrance to the park is 26 miles east of Holbrook off I-40, and south entrance to the park is 19 miles east of Holbrook off US 180. **Facilities:** Picnic area, rest rooms (&), restaurant/snacks, visitor center (&), museum/exhibit, self-guided tour/trail. Entrance fee required. **Activities:** Hiking, bicycling, horseback riding, auto touring, ranger-guided tours. **Special Features:** Park features one of the world's largest and most colorful concentrations of petrified wood. Also included are the multi-hued badlands of the Chinle Formation known as the Painted Desert, historic structures, archeological sites, and displays of 225 million-year-old fossils that feature some of the earliest known dinosaurs of North America.

★284★ PETROGLYPH NATIONAL MONUMENT

6001 Unser Blvd NW
Albuquerque, NM 87120
Web: www.nps.gov/petr/
Phone: 505-899-0205; **Fax:** 505-899-0207
Size: 7,232 acres. **History:** Established on June 27, 1990. Owned and managed jointly by the National Park Service, the City of Albuquerque, and the State of New Mexico. **Location:** In Albuquerque, New Mexico. Accessible from I-40 off Unser Blvd. **Facilities:** Visitor center, picnic area, self-guided trails, interpretive exhibits, rest rooms (&). **Activities:** Hiking. **Special Features:** More than 20,000 prehistoric and historic Native American and Hispanic petroglyphs (images carved in rock) stretch 17 miles along Albuquerque's West Mesa escarpment.

★285★ PICTURED ROCKS NATIONAL LAKESHORE

PO Box 40
N8391 Sandpoint Rd
Munising, MI 49862
Web: www.nps.gov/piro/
Phone: 906-387-2607; **Fax:** 906-387-4025
Size: 73,236 acres. **History:** Authorized on October 15, 1966; established on October 5, 1972. **Location:** Along Lake Superior on Michigan's Upper Peninsula, between Munising and Grand Marais. The Pictured Rocks National Lakeshore/Hiawatha National Forest visitor information center is at the junction of MI 28 and County Road H-58 in Munising. **Facilities:** Campgrounds (&), picnic area, rest rooms (&), boat ramp, visitor centers (&), museum/exhibit, self-guided tour/trail. **Activities:** Camping, hiking, swimming, boating, kayaking, canoeing, fishing, hunting, snowmobiling, cross-country skiing, snowshoeing, ice fishing. **Special Features:** Situated on Lake Superior, Pictured Rocks was established as the country's first national lakeshore. It features multicolored sandstone cliffs, broad beaches, sand dunes, waterfalls, inland lakes, wetlands, hardwood and coniferous forests, and a variety of wildlife. At its widest point

See pages 16-17 for map of U.S. National Parks.

the lakeshore is only 6 miles and hugs the Superior shoreline for more than 40 miles.

★286★ PINNACLES NATIONAL MONUMENT

5000 Hwy 146
Paicines, CA 95043
Web: www.nps.gov/pinn/
Phone: 831-389-4485
Size: 24,514 acres. **History:** Proclaimed on January 16, 1908. Wilderness designated on October 20, 1976. **Location:** In the Gabilan Mountains, east of central California's Salinas Valley. Monument consists of two districts. The West District is accessible from US 101 near the town of Soledad, then east along CA 146 to the Chaparral area. The East District entrance is reached via US 25, south of the city of Hollister, then west on CA 146. The two districts are connected by trails, not by a vehicle road. **Facilities:** Campground (private), picnic area, rest rooms (&), visitor center (&), museum/exhibit, self-guided tour/trail. Entrance fee required. **Activities:** Camping, hiking, rock climbing, wildlife viewing, interpretive programs. **Special Features:** Spire-like rock formations 500 to 1,200 feet high, with caves and a variety of volcanic features, rise above the smooth contours of the surrounding countryside. The monument is renowned for the beauty and variety of its spring wildflowers and is also a release site for the endangered California condor, which can sometimes be seen from its hiking trails.

★287★ PIPE SPRING NATIONAL MONUMENT

HC 65 Box 5
406 North Pipe Spring Rd
Fredonia, AZ 86022
Web: www.nps.gov/pisp/
Phone: 928-643-7105; **Fax:** 928-643-7583
Size: 40 acres. **History:** Proclaimed on May 31, 1923. **Location:** 14 miles southwest of Fredonia, Arizona, accessible from US 89A via AZ 389. **Facilities:** Rest rooms (&), visitor center (&), museum/exhibit, self-guided tour/trail. Entrance fee required. **Activities:** Self-guided tours, hiking, ranger-guided tours, living history demonstrations. **Special Features:** The springs at this location have sustained hundreds of years of cultural occupation in this dry, desert region. The Ancestral Puebloan culture thrived here, followed by the Kaibab Paiute and Mormon pioneers. Historic structures associated with the 1870s pioneer ranching operation remain.

★288★ PIPESTONE NATIONAL MONUMENT

36 Reservation Ave
Pipestone, MN 56164
Web: www.nps.gov/pipe/
Phone: 507-825-5464; **Fax:** 507-825-5466
Size: 282 acres. **History:** Established on August 25, 1937. **Location:** In southwestern Minnesota, just north of the city of Pipestone. Follow signs from US 75, MN 23, or MN 30. **Facilities:** Picnic area, rest rooms (&), visitor center (&), museum/cultural center, self-guided tour/trail. Entrance fee required. **Activities:** Hiking, ranger-led programs, cultural demonstrations. **Special Features:** For centuries American Indians have been obtaining materials for pipe making from these quarries, a practice that continues today. Although painter George Catlin was not the first white person to visit the quarries, he was the first person to describe them in print. Pipestone is known as Catlinite in his honor. The park includes the Upper Midwest Indian Cultural Center, which provides space for craftsmen to display their work and for demonstrations of traditional crafts to take place.

★289★ PISCATAWAY PARK

13551 Fort Washington Rd
Fort Washington, MD 20744
Web: www.nps.gov/pisc/
Phone: 301-763-4600; **Fax:** 301-763-1389
Size: 4,695 acres. **History:** Authorized on October 4, 1961. **Location:** Stretches for 6 miles from Piscataway Creek to Marshall Hall on the Potomac River, on the opposite shore from Mount Vernon. **Facilities:** Picnic area, fishing pier, boardwalks, nature trails. **Activities:** Hiking, fishing, wildlife viewing, educational programs. **Special Features:** The tranquil view from Mount Vernon of the Maryland shore of the Potomac is preserved as a pilot project in the use of easements to protect parklands from obtrusive urban expansion. The project began in 1952 to preserve the river view as in was during George Washington's day.

★290★ POINT REYES NATIONAL SEASHORE

1 Bear Valley Rd
Point Reyes Station, CA 94956
Web: www.nps.gov/pore/
Phone: 415-663-8522; **Fax:** 415-663-8132
Size: 71,068 acres. **History:** Authorized on September 13, 1962; established on October 20, 1972. Wilderness designated on October 18, 1976. Designated a Biosphere Reserve in 1988. **Location:** 22 miles north of San Francisco on CA 1 along the west coast of California. Travelers may approach the park from the winding, scenic CA 1, either northbound or southbound, or via Sir Francis Drake Blvd. or Point Reyes/Petaluma Rd. **Facilities:** Campgrounds, picnic area, rest rooms (&), restaurant/snacks, bicycle trail, visitor centers (&), museum/exhibit, self-guided tour/trail. **Activities:** Camping, hiking, bicycling, horseback riding, swimming, fishing, kayaking, auto touring, bird-watching, wildlife viewing, ranger-guided programs. **Special Features:** This peninsula near San Francisco is noted for its long beaches backed by tall cliffs, lagoons and esteros, forested ridges, and offshore bird and sea lion colonies. Nearly 20% of the state's flowering plant species are represented on the peninsula and more than 45% of the bird species in North America have been sighted here. Located inside the park, the Point Reyes Lighthouse is one of the best places along the California Coast from which to observe California Gray Whales on their annual migration from Alaska to Mexico.

POTOMAC HERITAGE NATIONAL SCENIC TRAIL

(See separate listing in National Trails section.)

★291★ POVERTY POINT NATIONAL MONUMENT

c/o Poverty Point State Historic Site
PO Box 276
Epps, LA 71237
Web: www.nps.gov/popo/
Phone: 318-926-5492; **Fax:** 318-926-5366; **Toll Free:** 888-926-5492

See pages 16-17 for map of U.S. National Parks.

Size: 911 acres. **History:** Authorized on October 31, 1988. **Location:** In northeastern Louisiana. From I-20, take the Delhi exit and travel north of LA 17, east on LA 134, and north on LA 577. **Facilities:** No federal facilities; managed by the State of Louisiana. State park facilities are open to the public. **Special Features:** Park commemorates a culture that thrived during the first and second millennia, BC. Today erosion and more than a century of agriculture have reduced what may have been the largest and most intricate geometrical earthwork in North America.

★292★ **PRESIDENT'S PARK (WHITE HOUSE)**
c/o White House Visitor Center
1450 Pennsylvania Ave NW
Washington, DC 20230
Web: www.nps.gov/whho/
Phone: 202-208-1631; **Fax:** 202-208-1643
Size: 18.1 acres. **History:** Transferred on August 10, 1933, to the National Park Service, the direct legal successor of three Federal Commissioners appointed by the President under act of July 16, 1790, who directed initial construction. **Location:** At 1600 Pennsylvania Ave., NW, in Washington, DC. **Facilities:** Rest rooms (&), museum/exhibit. **Activities:** Tours of the White House have been expanded to include parties of ten or more people, regardless of age or type of group. Tour requests must be submitted through one's Member of Congress and are accepted up to six months in advance. These self-guided group tours are scheduled approximately one month before the requested date. **Special Features:** The White House was originally constructed (1792-1800) on the site selected by George Washington and included in L'Enfant's Plan. It has been the residence and office of every US President since John Adams first took occupancy in November of 1800. Despite some additions and minor changes, the exterior of the main structure remains much as it was in 1800. The interior has been completely renovated using the historic floor plan.

★293★ **PRINCE WILLIAM FOREST PARK**
18100 Park Headquarters Rd
Triangle, VA 22172
Web: www.nps.gov/prwi/
Phone: 703-221-7181; **Fax:** 703-221-3258
Size: 16,003 acres. **History:** Chopawamsic Recreation Demonstration Area transferred from Resettlement Administration on November 14, 1936; changed to Prince William Forest Park on June 22, 1948. **Location:** In northeast Virginia, 32 miles south of Washington, DC, and 22 miles north of Fredericksburg. From I-95, take Exit 150. **Facilities:** Campgrounds, picnic area, rest rooms (&), cabin rental, bicycle trail, visitor center (&), museum/exhibit, hiking trail, playing fields. Entrance fee required. **Activities:** Camping, hiking, bicycling, fishing, wildlife viewing, cross-country skiing, snowshoeing, interpretive programs. **Special Features:** Prince William is the greatest expanse of a Piedmont forest in the National Park System and the largest natural park in the metropolitan Washington area. It includes a major portion of the Quantico Creek watershed.

★294★ **PU'UHONUA O HONAUNAU NATIONAL HISTORICAL PARK**
PO Box 129
Honaunau, HI 96726
Web: www.nps.gov/puho/
Phone: 808-328-2326; **Fax:** 808-328-9485
Size: 420 acres. **History:** Authorized as City of Refuge National Historical Park on July 26, 1955; renamed on November 10, 1978. **Location:** On the Kona Coast of the island of Hawaii. Take HI 11 to HI 160 and continue downhill 4 miles to park entrance. **Facilities:** Picnic area, rest rooms (&), bathhouse, visitor center (&), museum/exhibit, self-guided tour/trail. Entrance fee required. **Activities:** Hiking, swimming, fishing, scuba diving, snorkeling, wildlife viewing. **Special Features:** Until 1819, the year of the death of Kamehameha I, vanquished Hawaiian warriors, noncombatants, and kapu breakers could escape death by reaching this sacred ground. Park includes ancient house sites, royal fishponds, coconut groves, and spectacular shore scenery.

★295★ **PUUKOHOLA HEIAU NATIONAL HISTORIC SITE**
62-3601 Kawaihae Rd
Kawaihae, HI 96743
Web: www.nps.gov/puhe/
Phone: 808-882-7218; **Fax:** 808-882-1215
Size: 86 acres. **History:** Authorized on August 17, 1972. **Location:** On the northwestern coast of the island of Hawaii, 1 mile south of Kawaihae off HI 270. **Facilities:** Rest rooms (&), visitor center (&), self-guided tour/trail. **Activities:** Hiking, birdwatching, wildlife viewing, guided tour, cultural demonstrations. **Special Features:** Ruins of Puukohola Heiau ("Temple on the Hill of the Whale"), built by King Kamehameha the Great in 1790-1791 during his rise to power, are preserved.

★296★ **RAINBOW BRIDGE NATIONAL MONUMENT**
c/o Glen Canyon National Recreation Area
PO Box 1507
Page, AZ 86040
Web: www.nps.gov/rabr/
Phone: 928-608-6200; **Fax:** 928-608-6259
Size: 160 acres. **History:** Proclaimed on May 30, 1910. While Rainbow Bridge is a separate unit of the National Park Service, it is proximate to and administered by Glen Canyon National Recreation Area (see separate entry for description). **Location:** In southern Utah. Accessible only by boat or by a 13-mile hike (with permit from the Navajo Nation). By boat across Lake Powell, it is 50 miles (4.5 hours round-trip) from Wahweap, Bullfrog, or Halls Crossing to Rainbow Bridge. The two trails leading to the park originate near Navajo Mountain. **Facilities:** Boat dock, rest rooms. **Activities:** Hiking. **Special Features:** Largest of the world's known natural bridges, this symmetrical, salmon-pink sandstone span rises 290 feet above the floor of Bridge Canyon.

★297★ **REDWOOD NATIONAL AND STATE PARKS**
1111 2nd St
Crescent City, CA 95531
Web: www.nps.gov/redw/
Phone: 707-465-7306; **Fax:** 707-464-1812

See pages 16-17 for map of U.S. National Parks.

Size: Park area includes 131,983 acres (federal: 71,715; state: 60,268). Old-growth forest is 38,982 acres (federal: 19,640; state: 19,342). **History:** Prairie Creek Redwoods State Park was established on August 13, 1923. Del Norte Coast Redwoods State Park: October 26, 1925. Jedediah Smith Redwoods State Park: June 3, 1929. Redwood National Park: October 2, 1968. In 1994, the California Department of Parks and Recreation and the National Park Service agreed to manage the four-park area jointly for maximum resource protection. The four-park cluster was designated a World Heritage Site in 1980 and an International Biosphere Reserve in 1983. In December 2005, federal legislation was approved to expand Redwood National and State Parks by including the Mill Creek watershed within its boundary. **Location:** Along the northern California coast, just south of the Oregon border. Accessible via US 101 and 199. **Facilities:** Campgrounds, picnic area, rest rooms (占), visitor centers (占), museum/exhibit, self-guided tour/trail. **Activities:** Camping, hiking, bicycling, horseback riding, swimming, scuba diving, snorkeling, fishing, boating, kayaking, whitewater rafting, auto touring, wildlife viewing, interpretive programs. **Special Features:** Coastal redwood forests with virgin groves of ancient trees, including the world's tallest, thrive in the foggy and temperate climate. The park includes 40 miles of scenic Pacific coastline. The three California state parks (listed above) together with Redwood National Park comprise 45 percent of all the old-growth redwood forest remaining in California.

★298★ RICHMOND NATIONAL BATTLEFIELD PARK

3215 E Broad St
Richmond, VA 23223
Web: www.nps.gov/rich/
Phone: 804-226-1981; **Fax:** 804-771-8522
Size: 7,127 acres. **History:** Authorized on March 2, 1936. **Location:** In Richmond, Virginia, accessible via I-95 (Exit 75) or I-64. The park encompasses a large area with battlefield sites and visitor centers located in the City of Richmond, and Henrico, Hanover and Chesterfield counties. It consists of 13 separate sites, including the Civil War Visitor Center and the Chimborazo Medical Museum, with four visitor centers. A complete tour of the park involves an 80-mile drive. **Facilities:** Picnic area, visitor centers, museum/exhibit, self-guided tour/trail. **Activities:** Walking tours, auto touring, living history programs. **Special Features:** The park commemorates 11 different sites associated with Union campaigns from 1861-1865 to capture Richmond, the Confederate capital. These battlefield sites include Cold Harbor, Gaines Mill, and Malvern Hill.

★299★ RIO GRANDE WILD & SCENIC RIVER

PO Box 129
Big Bend National Park, TX 79834
Web: www.nps.gov/rigr/
Phone: 432-477-2251; **Fax:** 432-477-1175
Size: 9,600 acres. **History:** Authorized on November 10, 1978. **Location:** A 196-mile portion of the Rio Grande from the Chihuahua/Coahuila state line in Mexico to the Terrell/Val Verde county line in Texas is protected as part of the National Wild and Scenic Rivers System. The upper 69-mile section lies within Big Bend National Park. Several highways lead to the river area through Big Bend National Park, including TX 118 from Alpine to Study Butte, or FM 170 from Presidio through Study Butte, or US 90 or US 385 through Marathon. **Facilities:** No federal facilities outside Big Bend National Park. **Activities:** Fishing, whitewater rafting, wildlife viewing. **Special Features:** The Rio Grande Wild and Scenic River is part of a valuable ecological system that represents the major riparian and aquatic habitat associated with the Chihuahuan Desert.

★300★ ROCK CREEK PARK

3545 Williamsburg Ln NW
Washington, DC 20008
Web: www.nps.gov/rocr
Phone: 202-895-6000; **Fax:** 202-895-6015
Size: 1,755 acres. **History:** Authorized on September 27, 1890; transferred to National Park Service on June 10, 1933. **Location:** In Washington, DC, within 5 miles of the White House. **Facilities:** Picnic area, rest rooms (占), bicycle trail, visitor centers (占), nature center, playgrounds, tennis courts, golf course, exercise trails, museum/exhibit. **Activities:** Hiking, bicycling, horseback riding, fishing, tennis, golf, running, ranger-led programs. **Special Features:** One of the largest urban parks in the United States, this wooded preserve contains a wide range of natural, historical, and recreational features in the midst of Washington, D.C. Points of interest include: the Nature Center and Planetarium, the focal point for activities related to the park's natural history; the Old Stone House, the oldest house in Washington; Peirce Mill, a gristmill where corn and wheat were ground into flour using water power from Rock Creek; and the remains of Civil War earthen fortifications, including Fort Stevens, the site of the only battle within the District of Columbia during the Civil War.

★301★ ROCKY MOUNTAIN NATIONAL PARK

1000 Hwy 36
Estes Park, CO 80517
Web: www.nps.gov/romo/
Phone: 970-586-1206; **Fax:** 970-586-1256
Size: 265,828 acres. **History:** Established on January 26, 1915. Wilderness designated on December 22, 1980. Designated a Biosphere Reserve in 1976. **Location:** In north-central Colorado, two hours by car from Denver. Accessible via US 34, US 36, and CO 7 from the east, and US 34 from the west. **Facilities:** Campgrounds (占), picnic area, rest rooms (占), restaurant/snacks, visitor centers (占), museum/exhibit, self-guided tour/trail (占). Entrance fee required. **Activities:** Camping, hiking, horseback riding, mountain climbing, fishing, snowshoeing, cross-country skiing, auto touring, wildlife viewing, ranger-led programs. **Special Features:** The park's rich scenery, typifying the massive grandeur of the Rocky Mountains, is accessible by Trail Ridge Road, the highest road in any US National Park (12,183'), which crosses the Continental Divide. Peaks towering more than 14,000 feet shadow wildlife and wildflowers in these 415 square miles of the Rockies. Park features 360 miles of trails, offering endless opportunities to hikers, backpackers and horseback riders.Trail Ridge,

See pages 16-17 for map of U.S. National Parks.

★302★ ROGER WILLIAMS NATIONAL MEMORIAL
282 N Main St
Providence, RI 02903
Web: www.nps.gov/rowi/
Phone: 401-521-7266; **Fax:** 401-521-7239
Size: 4.5 acres. **History:** Authorized on October 22, 1965. **Location:** In the College Hill Historic District of Providence, Rhode Island. **Facilities:** Rest rooms (&), visitor center (&), museum/exhibit. **Activities:** Walking tours and ranger-guided programs. **Special Features:** This memorial is a landscaped urban park on the site of the founding of Providence by Roger Williams in 1636. Williams guaranteed religious freedom to all faiths and this colony served as a refuge where all could come to worship as their conscience dictated without interference from the state.

**★303★ ROSIE THE RIVETER/WORLD WAR II
HOME FRONT NATIONAL HISTORICAL PARK**
1401 Marina Way S, Suite C
Richmond, CA 94804
Web: www.nps.gov/rori/
Phone: 510-232-5050
Size: 145 acres. **History:** Authorized on October 25, 2000. **Location:** In Richmond, California. **Facilities:** In early development stages. Includes unstaffed visitor center in Richmond's City Hall. **Activities:** Interpretive tours (by appointment) and auto touring of City of Richmond's historic World War II sites. **Special Features:** This Richmond, California park was created to commemorate the mobilization of the workforce on the home front during World War II, while specifically recognizing the contributions of women and minorities to this effort. The four Richmond shipyards, with their combined 27 shipways, produced 747 ships, more than any other shipyard complex in the country. Park will consist of five sites in the city of Richmond where the original buildings still stand that housed employees and provided services to those working at the shipyards. It will include various areas along the waterfront of Richmond where a World War II Home Front Education Center will be established.

**★304★ ROSS LAKE NATIONAL RECREATION
AREA**
c/o North Cascades National Park
810 SR 20
Sedro Woolley, WA 98284
Web: www.nps.gov/rola/
Phone: 360-856-5700; **Fax:** 360-856-1934
Size: 117,575 acres. **History:** Established on October 2, 1968. **Location:** In northwestern Washington, adjacent to North Cascades National Park (see separate entry). Access to the park is from I-5 at Burlington, west of the mountains, and Twisp, on the east, following WA 20 (North Cascades Scenic Highway). WA 20, the major access to Ross Lake NRA, is partially closed from approximately mid-November to mid-April due to the weather. **Facilities:** Campgrounds (&), picnic area, rest rooms (&), cabin rental, groceries, restaurant/snacks, boat rental, boat ramp, self-guided tour/trail. **Activities:** Camping, hiking, horseback riding, mountain climbing, boating, fishing, hunting, cross-country skiing, snowshoeing, guided tour. **Special Features:** Ringed by mountains, this national recreation area offers many outdoor recreation opportunities along the upper reaches of the Skagit River, between the north and south units of North Cascades National Park. It includes three reservoirs: 12,000-acre Ross Lake, 910-acre Diablo Lake, and 210-acre Gorge Lake — water gateways to more remote areas.

★305★ RUSSELL CAVE NATIONAL MONUMENT
3729 County Rd 98
Bridgeport, AL 35740
Web: www.nps.gov/ruca/
Phone: 256-495-2672; **Fax:** 256-495-9220
Size: 310 acres. **History:** Proclaimed on May 11, 1961. **Location:** 8 miles west of Bridgeport, Alabama. From US 72, take CR 75 north 1 mile to CR 98, then CR 98 north 4 miles. **Facilities:** Picnic area, rest rooms (&), visitor center (&), museum/exhibit, self-guided tour/trail. **Activities:** Guided cave tours, hiking, craft demonstrations. **Special Features:** An almost continuous archeological record of human habitation from at least 6500 BC to about AD 1650 (Transitional Paleo to Mississippian cultural periods) is revealed in this cave.

**★306★ SAGAMORE HILL NATIONAL HISTORIC
SITE**
20 Sagamore Hill Rd
Oyster Bay, NY 11771
Web: www.nps.gov/sahi/
Phone: 516-922-4788; **Fax:** 516-922-4792
Size: 83 acres. **History:** Authorized on July 25, 1962. **Location:** At the end of Cove Neck Rd. in Oyster Bay, Long Island, New York. **Facilities:** Rest rooms (&), visitor center (&), museum/exhibit, self-guided tour/trail. Entrance fee required. **Activities:** Guided tours. **Special Features:** This estate was the home of Theodore Roosevelt from 1886 until his death in 1919 and was used as the "Summer White House" from 1902 until 1908. Twenty-three rooms of the house, most containing original furnishings, are open to the public. The Georgian-styled Old Orchard Museum is located on the grounds.

★307★ SAGUARO NATIONAL PARK
3693 S Old Spanish Trail
Tucson, AZ 85730
Web: www.nps.gov/sagu/
Phone: 520-733-5100; **Fax:** 520-733-5183
Size: 91,440 acres. **History:** Proclaimed a national monument on March 1, 1933; transferred from Forest Service on August 10, 1933. Wilderness designated on October 20, 1976. Redesignated a national park on October 14, 1994. **Location:** Park consists of two districts: the Tucson Mountain District or Saguaro West, and the much larger Rincon Mountain District or Saguaro East. The two areas, separated by the city of Tucson, Arizona, are 30 miles apart. **Facilities:** Picnic area, rest rooms (&), visitor centers (&), museum/exhibit, self-guided tour/trail. Entrance fee required. **Activities:** Backcountry camping, hiking, bicycling, auto touring, guided walks, environmental education programs. **Special Features:** Giant saguaro cacti, unique to the Sonoran Desert, cover the valley floor and rise into the neighboring Rincon and West Tucson mountains. Five biotic life zones are represented here, from desert to ponderosa pine forest.

See pages 16-17 for map of U.S. National Parks.

★308★ SAINT CROIX ISLAND INTERNATIONAL HISTORIC SITE

c/o Acadia National Park
PO Box 177
Bar Harbor, ME 04609
Web: www.nps.gov/sacr/
Phone: 207-288-3338; **Fax:** 207-288-8813
Size: 45 acres. **History:** Authorized as a national monument on June 8, 1949; redesignated on September 25, 1984. **Location:** On US 1, 6 miles south of Calais, Maine. Mainland access is by either by Route 9 from Bangor or US 1, the coastal route from Portland and points south. Access to the Saint Croix Island section of the park is by private boat only. **Facilities:** Picnic area, rest rooms (&), boat ramp. No federal facilities. **Activities:** Hiking, interpretive programs (seasonal). **Special Features:** The only designated international historic site in the National Park Service is a monument to the beginning of the United States and Canada. The attempted French settlement of 1604, which led to the founding of New France, is commemorated on Saint Croix Island in the Saint Croix River on the Canadian border.

★309★ SAINT CROIX NATIONAL SCENIC RIVERWAY

401 Hamilton St
PO Box 708
Saint Croix Falls, WI 54024
Web: www.nps.gov/sacn/
Phone: 715-483-3284; **Fax:** 715-483-3288
Size: 67,469 acres. **History:** Authorized on October 2, 1968; placed under National Park Service on September 4, 1969. Lower Saint Croix segment authorized as a national scenic riverway on October 25, 1972. **Location:** 252 miles of the Namekagon and Saint Croix rivers in northwestern Wisconsin and eastern Minnesota. MN 95 and WI 35 parallel the lower stretches, and WI 63 parallels the upper stretches. **Facilities:** Campgrounds (&), canoe access campsites (developed and primitive), picnic area, rest rooms (&), boat rental, boat ramp, visitor centers (&), museum/exhibit, self-guided tour/trail. **Activities:** Camping, hiking, boating, canoeing, kayaking, fishing, hunting, wildlife viewing, cross-country skiing, snowshoeing. **Special Features:** Established as one of the original eight rivers under the National Wild and Scenic Rivers Act, the Saint Croix National Scenic Riverway, which includes the Namekagon, flows through some of the most scenic and least developed country in the Upper Midwest.

★310★ SAINT-GAUDENS NATIONAL HISTORIC SITE

139 St Gaudens Rd
Cornish, NH 03745
Web: www.sgnhs.org
Phone: 603-675-2175; **Fax:** 603-675-2701
Size: 148 acres. **History:** Authorized on August 31, 1964; established on May 30, 1977. **Location:** Just off NH 12A in Cornish, New Hampshire, and 1.5 miles north of the Covered Bridge at Windsor, Vermont. **Facilities:** Picnic area, rest rooms (&), museum/exhibit, self-guided tour/trail. Entrance fee required. **Activities:** Hiking, cross-country skiing, self-guided audio tours, guided tours. **Special Features:** The park includes the home, studios, and gardens of Augustus Saint-Gaudens, America's foremost sculptor of the late 19th and early 20th centuries. This was Saint-Gaudens' summer residence from 1885-1897 and his permanent home from 1900 until his death in 1907. Original sculpture is on exhibit.

★311★ SAINT PAUL'S CHURCH NATIONAL HISTORIC SITE

897 S Columbus Ave
Mount Vernon, NY 10550
Web: www.nps.gov/sapa/
Phone: 914-667-4116; **Fax:** 914-667-3024
Size: 6.1 acres. **History:** Designated on July 5, 1943. National Park Service administration authorized on November 10, 1978. **Location:** In Mount Vernon, New York. Accessible via I-95 (Exit 13). **Facilities:** Rest rooms (&), visitor center (&), museum/exhibit. **Activities:** Self-guided tours, ranger-guided tours, interpretive programs. **Special Features:** This 18th-century church is one of New York's oldest parishes (1665-1980). It was used as a hospital following the Revolutionary War battle at Pell's Point in 1776. The church stood at the edge of Eastchester village green, the site of the "Great Election" (1733), which raised the issues of freedom of religion and the press. The adjoining cemetery contains burials dating from 1704.

★312★ SALEM MARITIME NATIONAL HISTORIC SITE

174 Derby St
Salem, MA 01970
Web: www.nps.gov/sama/
Phone: 978-740-1660; **Fax:** 978-740-1685
Size: 9 acres. **History:** Designated on March 17, 1938. **Location:** On Derby St. in Salem, Massachusetts, 20 miles northeast of Boston. **Facilities:** Rest rooms (&), visitor center (&), waterfront orientation center (&), museum/exhibit, self-guided tour/trail. **Activities:** Hiking, bicycling, boating, fishing, ranger-led tours. **Special Features:** Recalling the time when Salem traded in the East Indies and throughout the world, the site includes 18th- and 19th-century wharves, the Custom House, the bonded warehouse, the West India Goods Store, the 17th-century Narbonne-Hale House, and the home of 18th-century merchant E. H. Derby. Salem Maritime was the first national historic site established in the National Park System.

★313★ SALINAS PUEBLO MISSIONS NATIONAL MONUMENT

PO Box 517
Mountainair, NM 87036
Web: www.nps.gov/sapu/
Phone: 505-847-2585; **Fax:** 505-847-2441
Size: 1,071 acres. **History:** Proclaimed Gran Quivira National Monument on November 1, 1909; name changed to Salinas National Monument and area enlarged on December 19, 1980; two state monuments absorbed on November 2, 1981; name changed on October 28, 1988. **Location:** Visitor center can be reached by taking I-25 south from Albuquerque to Belen, then NM 47 diagonally to US 60, then east 21 miles to Mountainair. Park's three primary archeological sites are all located within

See pages 16-17 for map of U.S. National Parks.

25 miles of the visitor center. **Facilities:** Picnic area, rest rooms (&), visitor center (&), museum/exhibit, self-guided tour/trail. **Activities:** Hiking. **Special Features:** This park preserves and interprets the best remaining examples of 17th-century Spanish Franciscan mission churches and conventos remaining in the United States and three large Pueblo Indian villages. The Salinas sites have been abandoned since the 1670s.

★314★ SALT RIVER BAY NATIONAL HISTORICAL PARK & ECOLOGICAL PRESERVE

c/o Christiansted National Historic Site
2100 Church St #100
Saint Croix, VI 00820
Web: www.nps.gov/sari/
Phone: 340-773-1460; **Fax:** 340-773-5995
Size: 978 acres. **History:** Authorized on February 24, 1992. Preservation efforts will be carried out in partnership by the U.S. Virgin Islands Government and the U.S. National Park Service. **Location:** On northern Saint Croix in the U.S. Virgin Islands. **Facilities:** None. **Activities:** Swimming, kayaking, snorkeling, hiking. **Special Features:** Park contains the only known site where members of the Columbus expedition set foot on what is now U.S. territory. It also preserves upland watersheds, mangrove forests, and estuarine and marine environments. The site is marked by Fort Sale, a remaining earthworks fortification from the Dutch period of occupation.

★315★ SAN ANTONIO MISSIONS NATIONAL HISTORICAL PARK

2202 Roosevelt Ave
San Antonio, TX 78210
Web: www.nps.gov/saan/
Phone: 210-534-8833; **Fax:** 210-534-1106
Size: 826 acres. **History:** Authorized on November 10, 1978; established on April 1, 1983. **Location:** Visitor center is near the intersection of Roosevelt Ave. and New Napier Ave. in San Antonio, Texas. **Facilities:** Rest rooms, bicycle trail, museum/exhibit, self-guided tour/trail. **Activities:** Hiking, bicycling, guided tour. **Special Features:** Four Spanish frontier missions (Concepción, San Jose, San Juan, and Espada), part of a colonization system that stretched across the Spanish Southwest in the 17th, 18th, and 19th centuries, are preserved here. The four mission churches within the park are active catholic parishes and hold regular services.

★316★ SAN FRANCISCO MARITIME NATIONAL HISTORICAL PARK

Lower Fort Mason, Bldg E Rm 265
San Francisco, CA 94123
Web: www.nps.gov/safr/
Phone: 415-561-7000; **Fax:** 415-556-1624
Size: 50 acres. **History:** Established on June 27, 1988. **Location:** At the west end of Fisherman's Wharf in San Francisco, California. **Facilities:** Museum/exhibits. **Activities:** Guided tours, craft and other interpretive programs. **Special Features:** The square-rigged sailing ship *Balclutha*, steam schooner *Wapama*, three-masted schooner *C.A. Thayer*, walking-beam ferry *Eureka*, scow schooner *Alma*, steam tug *Hercules*, paddle wheel tug *Eppleton*

Hall, and numerous smaller craft are preserved. Many of the ships are at the Hyde Street Pier at Aquatic Park in San Francisco. Not far from the pier is the National Maritime Museum with displays of ship models and historic artifacts. The J. Porter Shaw Library and extensive collections of ship plans and photographs are at the nearby Fort Mason Center, as is the World War II Liberty Ship *SS Jeremiah O'Brien.*

★317★ SAN JUAN ISLAND NATIONAL HISTORICAL PARK

PO Box 429
Friday Harbor, WA 98250
Web: www.nps.gov/sajh/
Phone: 360-378-2240; **Fax:** 360-378-2615
Size: 1,752 acres. **History:** Authorized on September 9, 1966. **Location:** On San Juan Island in northwest Washington. Island is accessible via Washington State ferries from Anacortes, Washington, 83 miles north of Seattle; or from Sidney, British Columbia, 15 miles north of Victoria. Also accessible by private boat or by commercial flights from Bellingham and Seattle, Washington, to Friday Harbor. Park's two units include an English Camp, 9 miles northwest of Friday Harbor, and an American Camp, 6 miles southeast of Friday Harbor. Shuttle buses stop at both camps daily during the summer season with an abbreviated schedule during spring and fall. **Facilities:** Picnic area, rest rooms (&), visitor center (&), museum/exhibit, self-guided tour/trail (&). **Activities:** Hiking, living history programs, guided nature walks, bird-watching. **Special Features:** Park marks the historic events on the island from 1853 to 1872 in connection with final settlement of the Oregon Territory's northern boundary, including the so-called Pig War of 1859. As the largest tract of public land on San Juan Island, the park includes more than six miles of public shoreline and is also a primary destination of hikers with a network of trails exploring woodlands, prairie and uplands. As a stop along the Pacific flyway, the park also provides temporary homes for more than 200 species of migratory birds.

★318★ SAN JUAN NATIONAL HISTORIC SITE

501 Norzagaray St
San Juan, PR 00901
Web: www.nps.gov/saju/
Phone: 787-729-6960; **Fax:** 787-289-7972
Size: 75 acres. **History:** Designated a National Historic Site on February 14, 1949. Designated a World Heritage Site on December 9, 1983. **Location:** In the city of Old San Juan, Puerto Rico. **Facilities:** Museum/exhibit. **Activities:** Guided tour. **Special Features:** Park includes the forts of El Morro, San Cristóbal, and and San Juan de la Cruz (also called El Cañuelo), plus bastions, powder houses, and three fourths of the city walls. Surrounding the old, colonial portion of San Juan, these massive masonry fortifications, oldest in the territorial limits of the United States, were begun by the Spaniards beginning in 1539 to protect a strategic harbor guarding the sea lanes to the New World. Most of the walls we see today were added later in a period of tremendous construction from the 1760's to the 1780's.

See pages 16-17 for map of U.S. National Parks.

★319★ SAND CREEK MASSACRE NATIONAL HISTORIC SITE

PO Box 249
Eads, CO 81036
Web: www.nps.gov/sand/
Phone: 719-438-5916; **Fax:** 719-438-5410
Size: The National Park Service has acquired 920 acres within the authorized boundary, while the remainder of the 12,583 acres of land is under private and state ownership. **History:** Authorized on November 7, 2000, but will not be established until the NPS acquires enough land to provide for the preservation, commemoration, and interpretation of the Sand Creek Massacre. The NPS is working in partnership with The Conservation Fund, the Cheyenne and Arapaho tribes, Kiowa County, and the State of Colorado towards establishment of the site. **Location:** Along the banks of Big Sandy Creek in Kiowa County in southeastern Colorado. The southern boundary of the site is 20 miles northeast of Eads and 10 miles north of Chivington. **Facilities:** Not open to the public. **Special Features:** On November 29, 1864, Colonel John M. Chivington led approximately 700 U.S. volunteer soldiers to a village of about 500 Cheyenne and Arapaho people camped along the banks of Big Sandy Creek in southeastern Colorado. Although the Cheyenne and Arapaho people believed they were under the protection of the U.S. Army, Chivington's troops attacked and killed about 150 people, mainly women, children, and the elderly. Ultimately, the massacre was condemned following three federal investigations.

★320★ SANTA MONICA MOUNTAINS NATIONAL RECREATION AREA

401 W Hillcrest Dr
Thousand Oaks, CA 91360
Web: www.nps.gov/samo/
Phone: 805-370-2300; **Fax:** 805-370-1850
Size: 154,109 acres. **History:** Established on November 10, 1978. The national recreation area is a cooperative effort that joins federal, state, and local park agencies with private preserves and landowners to protect the natural and cultural resources of this transverse mountain range and seashore. **Location:** West of Griffith Park in Los Angeles County and to the east of the Oxnard Plain in Ventura County. US 101 (Ventura Freeway) borders the mountains on the north, and CA 1 (Pacific Coast Highway) and the Pacific Ocean form the southern boundary. **Facilities:** Campground (&), picnic area, rest rooms (&), bicycle trail, visitor center (&), Native American Indian culture center (&), museum/exhibit, self-guided tour/trail. Limited federal facilities. **Activities:** Camping, hiking, bicycling, horseback riding, swimming, surfing, boating, fishing, wildlife viewing, guided tour. **Special Features:** This recreation area near Los Angeles offers rugged mountains, a coastline with sandy beaches and rocky shores, canyons covered with chaparral, and abundant wildlife. It includes more than 580 miles of public trails and encompasses four California state parks.

★321★ SARATOGA NATIONAL HISTORICAL PARK

648 Route 32
Stillwater, NY 12170
Web: www.nps.gov/sara/
Phone: 518-664-9821; **Fax:** 518-664-3349
Size: 3,394 acres. **History:** Authorized on June 1, 1938. **Location:** 40 miles north of Albany and 15 miles southeast of Saratoga Springs, New York, on US 4 and NY 32. Park comprises three separate units: the 4-square-mile battlefield in Stillwater, the Saratoga Monument in the nearby village of Victory, and the General Philip Schuyler House, 8 miles north in Schuylerville. **Facilities:** Picnic area, rest rooms (&), bicycle trail, visitor center (&), museum/exhibit, self-guided tour/trail. Entrance fee required. **Activities:** Hiking, bicycling, cross-country skiing, auto touring, interpretive programs. **Special Features:** The decisive American victory here over the British in 1777, an event which led France to recognize the independence of the United States and enter the war as a decisive military ally, was the turning point of the Revolution. Major General Philip Schuyler's country home and the 155-foot Saratoga monument are nearby.

★322★ SAUGUS IRON WORKS NATIONAL HISTORIC SITE

244 Central St
Saugus, MA 01906
Web: www.nps.gov/sair/
Phone: 781-233-0050; **Fax:** 781-231-7345
Size: 8.5 acres. **History:** Authorized on April 5, 1968. **Location:** In Saugus, Massachusetts, 8.5 miles north of Boston. Accessible via I-95 (Walnut St. Exit), US 1 north (Main St. Exit), or US 1 south ((Walnut St. Exit). **Facilities:** Picnic area, rest rooms (&), visitor center (&), museum/exhibit, self-guided tour/trail. **Activities:** Educational programs and tours. **Special Features:** This is the site of the first integrated ironworks in North America (1646-1668). It includes the reconstructed blast furnace, the forge, the rolling and slitting mill, and a restored 17th-century house.

★323★ SCOTTS BLUFF NATIONAL MONUMENT

PO Box 27
Gering, NE 69341
Web: www.nps.gov/scbl/
Phone: 308-436-4340; **Fax:** 308-436-7611
Size: 3,005 acres. **History:** Proclaimed on December 12, 1919. **Location:** On the North Platte River, 3 miles west of Gering, Nebraska, and 5 miles southwest of the town of Scottsbluff. The visitor center is just off NE 92. **Facilities:** Rest rooms (&), bicycle trail, visitor center (&), museum/exhibit, self-guided tour/trail. Entrance fee required. **Activities:** Hiking, bicycling, auto touring, ranger-guided walks, interpretive programs. **Special Features:** Rising 800 feet above the valley floor, this massive promontory was a landmark for many peoples, and it served as the path marker for those on the Oregon, California, Mormon, and Pony Express trails. The monument museum contains exhibits about the human and natural history of the area and also houses the world's largest collection of paintings by the frontier photographer and artist William Henry Jackson.

★324★ SEQUOIA & KINGS CANYON NATIONAL PARKS

47050 Generals Hwy
Three Rivers, CA 93271
Web: www.nps.gov/seki/
Phone: 559-565-3341; **Fax:** 559-565-3730

See pages 16-17 for map of U.S. National Parks.

Size: 461,901 acres (Kings Canyon NP) and 404,051 acres (Sequoia NP). More than 723,000 of the parks' acres are officially designated as Wilderness. **History:** Although they were created by separate acts of Congress, Sequoia and Kings Canyon share miles of boundary and are managed as one park. Sequoia was the second national park designated in the United States. Sequoia NP: established on September 25, 1890; wilderness designated on September 28, 1984; designated a Biosphere Reserve in 1976. Kings Canyon NP: established as General Grant National Park on October 1, 1890; name changed and combined with additional land on March 4, 1940; wilderness designated on September 28, 1984; designated a Biosphere Reserve in 1976. **Location:** In east-central California. CA 180 leads to Kings Canyon National Park from Fresno; CA 198 leads to Sequoia National Park from the town of Visalia. The Generals Hwy. connects the two, making loop trips possible. There are no roads into Sequoia and Kings Canyon National Parks from the east side. **Facilities:** Campgrounds (&), picnic area, rest rooms (&), cabin rental, lodging, groceries, restaurant/snacks, visitor centers (&), museum/exhibit, self-guided tour/trail (&). Entrance fee required. **Activities:** Camping, hiking, horseback riding, mountain climbing, fishing, cross-country skiing, snowshoeing, wildlife viewing, ranger-led walks, guided cave tours, auto touring. **Special Features:** Ranging from 1500' to 14,494' in elevation, these adjoining parks protect immense mountains, deep canyons, huge trees, and diverse habitats. Great groves of giant sequoias, (including the General Sherman Tree, the world's largest living thing), Mineral King Valley, and Mount Whitney, the highest mountain in the U.S. outside of Alaska, are spectacular attractions in Sequoia National Park. Two enormous canyons of the Kings River and the summit peaks of the High Sierra dominate the mountain wilderness of Kings Canyon National Park. General Grant Grove, which includes the Nation's Christmas Tree, is a detached section of the park.

★325★ **SHENANDOAH NATIONAL PARK**
3655 US Hwy 211E
Luray, VA 22835
Web: www.nps.gov/shen/
Phone: 540-999-3500; **Fax:** 540-999-3601
Size: 199,074 acres. **History:** Authorized on May 22, 1926; fully established on December 26, 1935. Wilderness designated on October 20, 1976 and September 1, 1978. **Location:** Headquarters is 3 miles west of Thornton Gap and 4 miles east of Luray on US 211 in Virginia. Four entrances to the park are at I-66 and US 340 to the north entrance at Front Royal, US 211 to the central entrance at Thornton Gap, US 33 to Swift Run Gap, and I-64 to the Rockfish Gap entrance at the southern end of the park and the northern end of the Blue Ridge Parkway. **Facilities:** Campground (&), picnic area, rest rooms (&), cabin rental, lodging, groceries, restaurant/snacks, visitor centers (&), museum/exhibit, self-guided tour/trail. Entrance fee required. **Activities:** Camping, hiking, horseback riding, fishing, wildlife viewing, bicycling, auto touring, ranger-led walks, interpretive programs. **Special Features:** Skyline Drive, a 105-mile road, winds through hardwood forests along the crest of this outstanding portion of the Blue Ridge Mountains, with spectacular vistas of the Shenandoah Valley and the Piedmont. Park features more than 500 miles of trails, including 101 miles of the Appalachian Trail (see separate entry in national trails section).

★326★ **SHILOH NATIONAL MILITARY PARK**
1055 Pittsburg Landing Rd
Shiloh, TN 38376
Web: www.nps.gov/shil/
Phone: 731-689-5696; **Fax:** 731-689-5450
Size: 5,065 acres. **History:** Established on December 27, 1894; transferred from War Department on August 10, 1933. **Location:** 110 miles east of Memphis, Tennessee. Accessible from I-40 via TN 22 south and from Memphis along TN 57 east and TN 22 north. **Facilities:** Picnic area, rest rooms (&), bicycle trail, visitor center (&), museum/exhibit, self-guided tour/trail. Entrance fee required. **Activities:** Auto touring, hiking, bicycling, ranger programs, living history demonstrations. **Special Features:** The bitter battle fought here April 6-7, 1862, prepared the way for Major General U.S. Grant's successful siege of Vicksburg. Besides preserving the site of the battle in Tennessee, park commemorates the subsequent siege, battle, and occupation of the key railroad junction at nearby Corinth, Mississippi. Well-preserved prehistoric Indian mounds overlook the river. Shiloh (Pittsburg Landing) National Cemetery adjoins the park.

★327★ **SITKA NATIONAL HISTORICAL PARK**
103 Monastery St
Sitka, AK 99835
Web: www.nps.gov/sitk/
Phone: 907-747-6281; **Fax:** 907-747-5938
Size: 112 acres. **History:** Proclaimed a national monument on March 23, 1910; redesignated a national historical park on October 18, 1972. **Location:** In the town of Sitka on Baranof Island in Alaska's southeastern panhandle. Sitka is accessible only by air or sea. Commercial airlines fly directly from Seattle, Juneau, and Anchorage. Air taxi companies fly a network of routes that link Sitka to Juneau, Haines, Skagway, and other southeast Alaska towns. Sitka is also a port of call for cruise ships and ferries on the Alaska Marine Highway System. **Facilities:** Picnic area, visitor center (&), museum/exhibit, self-guided tour/trail. **Activities:** Hiking, fishing, ranger-led walks, interpretive programs. **Special Features:** Alaska's oldest federally-designated park is the site of the 1804 fort and battle that marked the last major Tlingit Indian resistance to Russian colonization. Tlingit totem poles and crafts are exhibited. The Russian Bishop's House, built in 1842, is the oldest intact piece of Russian-American architecture.

★328★ **SLEEPING BEAR DUNES NATIONAL LAKESHORE**
9922 Front St
Empire, MI 49630
Web: www.nps.gov/slbe/
Phone: 231-326-5134; **Fax:** 231-326-5382
Size: 71,291 acres. **History:** Authorized on October 21, 1970; established on October 21, 1977. **Location:** In Michigan, on the northwestern shore of Lake Michigan's lower peninsula. Many north-south highways approach the park, including US 31 along Lake Michigan, US 131 through Grand Rapids, and I-75, which runs the length of the state into the Upper Peninsula. **Facilities:** Campgrounds (&), picnic area, rest rooms, restaurant/snacks, boat rental, boat ramp, bathhouse, visitor center (&), museum/exhibit, self-guided tour/trail. **Activities:** Camping,

See pages 16-17 for map of U.S. National Parks.

hiking, swimming, boating, kayaking, fishing, scuba diving, snorkeling, hunting, cross-country skiing, snowshoeing, auto touring, ranger-led walks, campfire programs. **Special Features:** This diverse landscape features 35 miles of Lake Michigan's eastern coastline, massive sand dunes, birch-lined streams, white sand beaches, beech-maple forests, clear lakes, and rugged bluffs towering as high as 460 feet above Lake Michigan. Two offshore wilderness islands — North and South Manitou — offer tranquility and seclusion.

★329★ SPRINGFIELD ARMORY NATIONAL HISTORIC SITE

1 Armory Sq, Suite 2 Bldg 13
Springfield, MA 01105
Web: www.nps.gov/spar/
Phone: 413-734-8551; **Fax:** 413-747-8062
Size: 55 acres. **History:** Authorized on October 26, 1974; established on March 21, 1978. **Location:** Overlooks the Connecticut River in the city of Springfield, Massachusetts, accessible via I-91. **Facilities:** Rest rooms (&), museum/exhibit. **Activities:** Self-guided walking tour and seasonal historical programs. **Special Features:** From 1794 to 1968 Springfield Armory was a center for the manufacture of U.S. military small arms and the scene of many important technological advances. The Armory Museum protects one of ther world's most extensive firearm collections.

★330★ STATUE OF LIBERTY NATIONAL MONUMENT & ELLIS ISLAND

Liberty Island
New York, NY 10004
Web: www.nps.gov/stli/
Phone: 212-363-3200
Size: 61 acres. **History:** Proclaimed on October 15, 1924; transferred from War Department on August 10, 1933. Ellis Island proclaimed on May 11, 1965. Designated a World Heritage Site on October 31, 1984. **Location:** The Statue of Liberty on Liberty Island and the Ellis Island Immigration Museum on Ellis Island are located in Lower New York Harbor, slightly over one mile from Lower Manhattan. Liberty and Ellis islands are accessible by ferry service only. Ferries are operated by Circle Line-Statue of Liberty Ferry, Inc. from Battery Park in New York City and Liberty State Park in Jersey City, New Jersey. **Facilities:** Rest rooms (&), restaurant/snacks, visitor center (&), museum/exhibit, self-guided tour/trail. **Activities:** Guided tours. **Special Features:** The famous 152-foot copper statue bearing the torch of freedom was a gift of the French people in 1886 to commemorate the alliance of the two nations in the American Revolution. Designed by Frederick Bartholdi, the statue came to symbolize freedom for immigrants. Nearby Ellis Island, through which nearly 12 million immigrants passed (1892-1954), was reopened to the public in 1990 as the country's only museum devoted entirely to immigration.

★331★ STEAMTOWN NATIONAL HISTORIC SITE

150 S Washington Ave
Scranton, PA 18503
Web: www.nps.gov/stea/
Phone: 570-340-5200; **Fax:** 570-340-5328; **Toll Free:** 888-693-9391

Size: 62.5 acres. **History:** Authorized on October 30, 1986. **Location:** In downtown Scranton, Pennsylvania, at the intersection of Lackawanna and Cliff avenues. Accessible from the north and south via I-81, from the east via I-84 and I-380, and from the west via I-80. **Facilities:** Visitor center (&), museum/exhibit (&). **Activities:** Ranger-led tours, living history programs, passenger railroad excursions (seasonal). **Special Features:** The former Delaware, Lackawanna & Western Railroad yard — including the remains of the historic roundhouse, switchyard, and associated buildings — and a collection of steam locomotives and railroad cars preserve and interpret the story of early 20th-century steam railroading in America.

★332★ STONES RIVER NATIONAL BATTLEFIELD

3501 Old Nashville Hwy
Murfreesboro, TN 37129
Web: www.nps.gov/stri/
Phone: 615-893-9501; **Fax:** 615-893-9508
Size: 709 acres. **History:** Established as a national military park on March 3, 1927; transferred from the War Department on August 10, 1933. Redesignated as a national battlefield on April 22, 1960. **Location:** In Murfreesboro, Tennessee, 35 miles southeast of Nashville. Accessible via I-24 (Exit 78B). **Facilities:** Picnic area, rest rooms (&), visitor center (&), bicycle trail, museum/exhibit, self-guided tour/trail. **Activities:** Hiking, bicycling, ranger-led talks, living history programs, auto touring. **Special Features:** The fierce midwinter battle, which began the federal offensive to trisect the Confederacy, took place here December 31, 1862 through January 2, 1863. Stones River National Cemetery adjoins the park.

★333★ SUNSET CRATER VOLCANO NATIONAL MONUMENT

c/o Flagstaff Area National Monuments
6400 N Hwy 89
Flagstaff, AZ 86004
Web: www.nps.gov/sucr/
Phone: 928-526-0502; **Fax:** 928-714-0565
Size: 3,040 acres. **History:** Proclaimed on May 26, 1930; transferred from Forest Service on August 10, 1933. **Location:** From Flagstaff, Arizona, take US 89 north 12 miles, then right on Sunset Crater - Wupatki Loop Rd. for 2 miles to park visitor center. **Facilities:** Campground (&), picnic area, rest rooms (&), visitor center (&), museum/exhibit, self-guided tour/trail. Entrance fee required. **Activities:** Camping, hiking, interpretive programs. **Special Features:** This volcanic cinder cone with summit crater was formed by a series of eruptions sometime between AD 1040 and 1100. Its upper part is colored as if by a sunset.

★334★ TALLGRASS PRAIRIE NATIONAL PRESERVE

PO Box 585
226 Broadway
Cottonwood Falls, KS 66845
Web: www.nps.gov/tapr/
Phone: 620-273-6034; **Fax:** 620-273-6099
Size: 10,894 acres. **History:** Established on November 12, 1996.

See pages 16-17 for map of U.S. National Parks.

The federal government will own up to 180 acres, with the National Park Trust — the purchaser of the property in 1994 — retaining ownership of the rest of the preserve. The Nation Park Service will manage and operate the entire preserve under a public-private agreement. **Location:** Preserve headquarters is 2 miles north of Strong City, Kansas, on US 177, 18 miles west of Emporia and 85 miles northeast of Wichita. **Facilities:** Historic ranch headquarters area with buildings dating from the late 19th century; a late 19th century one-room school house; nature trail. **Activities:** Hiking, self-guided and ranger-guided tours, living history demonstrations. **Special Features:** Tallgrass prairie once covered 400,000 square miles of North America. Less than 4 % remains, mostly in the Flint Hills of Kansas. This nationally-significant example of the once vast tallgrass prairie ecosystem also includes historic buildings and cultural resources of the Spring Hill Ranch.

★335★ **THADDEUS KOSCIUSZKO NATIONAL MEMORIAL**
c/o Independence National Historical Park
143 S 3rd St
Philadelphia, PA 19106
Web: www.nps.gov/thko/
Phone: 215-597-9618; **Fax:** 215-597-0042
Size: .02 acres. **History:** Authorized on October 21, 1972. Administered through Independence National Historical Park (see separate entry). **Location:** At the corner of Third and Pine streets in downtown Philadelphia, Pennsylvania. Park is accessible via I-76 and I-676, I-95, and US 30 (Benjamin Franklin Bridge). **Facilities:** Museum/exhibit. **Activities:** Guided and self-guided tours. **Special Features:** One of the first foreign volunteers to come to the aid of the American revolutionary army, Kosciuszko made many significant contributions to the American Revolution including the fortifications at Saratoga and West Point. The life and work of this Polish-born patriot and hero of the American Revolution are commemorated here at the house where he resided during the winter of 1797-1798.

★336★ **THEODORE ROOSEVELT BIRTHPLACE NATIONAL HISTORIC SITE**
28 E 20th St
New York, NY 10003
Web: www.nps.gov/thrb/
Phone: 212-283-5154; **Fax:** 212-677-3587
Size: 0.11 acres. **History:** Authorized on July 25, 1962. **Location:** On East 20th St. in Manhattan, New York. **Facilities:** Museum/exhibit. Entrance fee required. **Activities:** Guided tour. **Special Features:** The 26th President was born in a brownstone house here on October 27, 1858. Demolished in 1916, it was reconstructed and rededicated in 1923 and furnished by the President's widow and sisters. Approximately forty percent of the furnishings come from the original house.

★337★ **THEODORE ROOSEVELT INAUGURAL NATIONAL HISTORIC SITE**
641 Delaware Ave
Buffalo, NY 14202
Web: www.nps.gov/thri/
Phone: 716-884-0095; **Fax:** 716-884-0330

Size: 1 acre. **History:** Authorized on November 2, 1966. **Location:** On Delaware Ave. in Buffalo, New York; accessible via I-90. **Facilities:** Visitor center (&), museum/exhibit. **Activities:** Guided tour. **Special Features:** Theodore Roosevelt took the oath of office as President of the United States on September 14, 1901, here in the Ansley Wilcox House after the assassination of President William McKinley.

★338★ **THEODORE ROOSEVELT ISLAND PARK**
c/o Turkey Run Park
George Washington Memorial Pkwy
McLean, VA 22101
Web: www.nps.gov/this/
Phone: 703-289-2500; **Fax:** 703-289-2598
Size: 88.5 acres. **History:** Authorized on May 21, 1932; transferred from Office of Public Buildings and Public Parks of the National Capital on August 10, 1933. Memorial dedicated on October 27, 1967. **Location:** In the Potomac River, accessible from the northbound lane of the George Washington Memorial Parkway. **Facilities:** Rest rooms (&), self-guided tour/trail. **Activities:** Hiking, fishing, guided tour. **Special Features:** On this wooded island sanctuary, trails lead to an imposing statue of Roosevelt, the conservation-minded 26th President. His tenets on nature, manhood, youth, and the state are inscribed on tablets.

★339★ **THEODORE ROOSEVELT NATIONAL PARK**
315 2nd Ave
Box 7
Medora, ND 58645
Web: www.nps.gov/thro/
Phone: 701-623-4466; **Fax:** 701-623-4840
Size: 70,447 acres. **History:** Established as Theodore Roosevelt National Memorial Park on April 25, 1947; redesignated on November 10, 1978. Wilderness designated on November 10, 1978. **Location:** Park's North and South units are in both in western North Dakota. The South Unit entrance and visitor center are in Medora, just off I-94 (Exits 23 & 27), 135 miles west of Bismarck. The Painted Canyon Visitor Center is 7 miles east of Medora, just off I-94 (Exit 32). The North Unit entrance is 16 miles south of Watford City along US 85. The distance between Medora at the South Unit and the North Unit is 70 miles, via I-94 and US 85. **Facilities:** Campgrounds, picnic area, rest rooms (&), visitor centers (&), museum/exhibit, self-guided tour/trail. Entrance fee required. **Activities:** Camping, hiking, horseback riding, boating, kayaking, fishing, cross-country skiing, snowshoeing, wildlife viewing, auto touring, interpretive programs. **Special Features:** The park includes scenic badlands along the Little Missouri River and part of Theodore Roosevelt's Elkhorn Ranch. It also includes one of the largest petrified forests in the United States and extensive paleontological deposits from the Paleocene era. The 120-mile Maah Daah Hey Trail connects the two units of the park.

★340★ **THOMAS JEFFERSON MEMORIAL**
c/o National Capital Parks - Central
900 Ohio Dr SW
Washington, DC 20024
Web: www.nps.gov/thje/
Phone: 202-426-6841; **Fax:** 202-426-1835

See pages 16-17 for map of U.S. National Parks.

1. US National Parks

Size: 18.4 acres. **History:** Authorized on June 26, 1934. Dedicated on April 13, 1943. **Location:** In East Potomac Park next to the Tidal Basin, Washington, DC. **Facilities:** Rest rooms (&), visitor center, museum/exhibit, self-guided tour/trail. **Activities:** Guided tour. **Special Features:** This circular, colonnaded structure in the classic style introduced in this country by Jefferson, memorializes the author of the Declaration of Independence and President from 1801 to 1809. The interior walls present inscriptions from his writings. The heroic statue was sculpted by Rudolph Evans.

★341★ THOMAS STONE NATIONAL HISTORIC SITE

6655 Rose Hill Rd
Port Tobacco, MD 20677
Web: www.nps.gov/thst/
Phone: 301-392-1776; **Fax:** 301-934-8793
Size: 328 acres. **History:** Authorized on November 10, 1978. **Location:** Near Port Tobacco, Maryland, between MD 6 and 225. **Facilities:** Picnic area, rest rooms (&), visitor center (&), museum/exhibits. **Activities:** Guided tour. **Special Features:** ''Haberdeventure,'' a Georgian mansion built in 1771 near Port Tobacco, Maryland, was the home of Thomas Stone from 1771 to 1787. A signer of the Declaration of Independence, Stone was a delegate to the Continental Congress, 1775-1778 and 1783-1784. Park contains the restored home of Thomas Stone, outbuildings and family cemetery.

★342★ TIMPANOGOS CAVE NATIONAL MONUMENT

RR 3 Box 200
American Fork, UT 84003
Web: www.nps.gov/tica/
Phone: 801-756-5239; **Fax:** 801-756-5661
Size: 250 acres. **History:** Proclaimed on October 14, 1922; transferred from Forest Service on August 10, 1933. **Location:** In north-central Utah, within 10 miles of Lehi, American Fork, and Pleasant Grove. UT 92 runs east-west through the monument. **Facilities:** Picnic area, restaurant/snacks (&), visitor center (&), museum/exhibit, self-guided tour/trail. **Activities:** Hiking, fishing, ranger-guided programs (including cave tours). **Special Features:** Three moderate-sized limestone caves sit high on the rocky slopes of American Fork Canyon in the shadow of Mount Timpanogos. They are decorated with a dazzling display of helictites, stalactites, stalagmites, and other unusual formations. Caves are generally open from mid-May through September.

★343★ TIMUCUAN ECOLOGICAL & HISTORIC PRESERVE

c/o Fort Caroline National Memorial
12713 Fort Caroline Rd
Jacksonville, FL 32225
Web: www.nps.gov/timu/
Phone: 904-641-7155; **Fax:** 904-641-3798
Size: 46,287 acres. **History:** Authorized on February 16, 1988. **Location:** 13 miles east of downtown Jacksonville, Florida. The Fort Caroline National Memorial (see separate entry) serves as the principal interpretive center for the preserve. **Facilities:** Picnic area, rest rooms. **Activities:** Hiking, kayaking and canoeing. **Special Features:** Named for the American Indians who lived here for more than 3,000 years, the preserve encompasses Atlantic coastal marshes, islands, mudflats, tidal creeks, and the estuaries of the Saint Johns and Nassau rivers. It is one of the last unspoiled coastal wetlands on the Atlantic Coast. Besides traces of Indian life, remains of Spanish, French, and English colonial ventures can be found as well as southern plantation life and 19th-century military activities.

★344★ TONTO NATIONAL MONUMENT

HC02 Box 4602
Roosevelt, AZ 85545
Web: www.nps.gov/tont/
Phone: 928-467-2241; **Fax:** 928-467-2225
Size: 1,120 acres. **History:** Proclaimed on December 19, 1907; transferred from Forest Service on August 10, 1933. **Location:** 110 miles east of Phoenix, Arizona, and 4 miles east of Roosevelt Dam. Accessible via AZ 88/188 west from Globe, AZ 188 east from AZ 87 (Beeline Hwy.), or AZ 88 (Apache Trail) beginning at Apache Junction. **Facilities:** Picnic area, rest rooms (&), visitor center (&), museum/exhibit, self-guided tour/trail. Entrance fee required. **Activities:** Hiking, ranger-led tours. **Special Features:** These well-preserved cliff dwellings were occupied during the 13th, 14th, and early 15th centuries by the Salado Culture who farmed the Salt River Basin.

★345★ TUMACACORI NATIONAL HISTORICAL PARK

1891 E Frontage Rd
PO Box 67
Tumacacori, AZ 85640
Web: www.nps.gov/tuma/
Phone: 520-398-2341
Size: 360 acres. **History:** Proclaimed on September 15, 1908. **Location:** Main unit of the park is 45 miles south of Tucson and 19 miles north of Nogales, Arizona, at Exit 29 off I-19. **Facilities:** Picnic area, rest rooms (&), visitor center (&), museum/exhibit, self-guided tour/trail. Entrance fee required. **Activities:** Hiking, guided tours. **Special Features:** This historic Spanish Catholic mission building stands near the site first visited by Jesuit Father Kino in 1691. The park includes two other separate mission ruins sites — Calabazas and Guevavi — that are not yet open to the public. The primary site at Tumacácori includes a partially restored Franciscan church that is still used to celebrate special events. These missions are among more than 20 established in the Pimería Alta by Father Kino and other Jesuits, and later expanded upon by Franciscan missionaries.

★346★ TUPELO NATIONAL BATTLEFIELD

c/o Natchez Trace Pkwy
2680 Natchez Trace Pkwy
Tupelo, MS 38804
Web: www.nps.gov/tupe/
Phone: 662-680-4025; **Fax:** 662-680-4033; **Toll Free:** 800-305-7417
Size: 1 acre. **History:** Established as a national battlefield site

See pages 16-17 for map of U.S. National Parks.

on February 21, 1929; transferred from the War Department on August 10, 1933; changed to national battlefield on August 10, 1961. Administered by the Natchez Trace Parkway. **Location:** Within the city limits of Tupelo, Mississippi, between US 45 and the Natchez Trace Parkway. **Facilities:** Museum/exhibit. **Special Features:** Here, on July 13-14, 1864, Lieutenant General Nathan Bedford Forrest tried to cut the railroad supplying the Union's March on Atlanta.

★347★ TUSKEGEE AIRMEN NATIONAL HISTORIC SITE

1616 Chappie James Ave
Tuskegee, AL 36083
Web: www.nps.gov/tuai/
Phone: 334-724-0922; **Fax:** 334-724-0952
Size: 90 acres. **History:** Established on November 6, 1998. **Location:** At Moton Field Municipal Airport in Tuskegee, Alabama. **Facilities:** Visitor center, exhibits. **Activities:** Guided walks. **Special Features:** The site preserves the airfield, historic hangar, and other buildings at Moton Field, where African-American pilots known as the Tuskegee Airmen received their initial flight training during World War II. The first Civilian Pilot Training Program students completed their instruction in May, 1940. The Tuskegee program was then expanded and became the center for African-American aviation during World War II.

★348★ TUSKEGEE INSTITUTE NATIONAL HISTORIC SITE

1212 W Montgomery Rd
Tuskegee Institute, AL 36088
Web: www.nps.gov/tuin/
Phone: 334-727-3200; **Fax:** 334-727-1448
Size: 58 acres. **History:** Authorized on October 26, 1974. **Location:** Along Old Montgomery Rd., 1.5 miles northwest of downtown Tuskegee, Alabama; 35 miles east of Montgomery and 20 miles west of Auburn. **Facilities:** Rest rooms (&), visitor center (&), museum/exhibit. **Activities:** Ranger-guided tours and interpretive programs. **Special Features:** Booker T. Washington founded this college for black Americans in 1881. Preserved here are the brick buildings the students constructed themselves, Washington's home, and the George Washington Carver Museum, which serves as park headquarters and visitor center. The college is still an active institution that owns most of the property within the national historic site.

★349★ TUZIGOOT NATIONAL MONUMENT

527 S Main St
Camp Verde, AZ 86322
Web: www.nps.gov/tuzi/
Phone: 928-634-5564; **Fax:** 928-567-3597
Size: 812 acres. **History:** Proclaimed on July 25, 1939. **Location:** 52 miles south of Flagstaff, Arizona, via US Alt. 89A, or 90 miles north of Phoenix. **Facilities:** Rest rooms (&), visitor center (&), museum/exhibit, self-guided tour/trail (&). Entrance fee required. **Activities:** Guided tours. **Special Features:** Tuzigoot includes a large pueblo built by the Sinagua culture that flourished in the Verde Valley between AD 1100 and 1450.

The Sinagua were agriculturalists with trade connections that spanned hundreds of miles.

★350★ ULYSSES S GRANT NATIONAL HISTORIC SITE

7400 Grant Rd
Saint Louis, MO 63123
Web: www.nps.gov/ulsg/
Phone: 314-842-3298; **Fax:** 314-842-1659
Size: 9.6 acres. **History:** Established on October 3, 1989. **Location:** On Grant Rd., off Route 30 (Gravois Rd.), in south Saint Louis County, Missouri. **Facilities:** Rest rooms (&), visitor center (&), museum/exhibit. **Activities:** Self-guided tours, ranger-led interpretive programs. **Special Features:** Site includes a portion of the 1,100-acre plantation where Ulysses S. Grant lived during the 1850s. Although Grant never returned as a permanent resident during the Civil War and his Presidency, he bought the property in 1863 from his father-in-law, Frederick Dent, and held it until a few months before his death in 1885. Five historic structures of Grant's home, known as "White Haven," remain, including a two-story residence, a barn, and a stone building believed to have housed Grant's father-in-law's slaves. Property was originally purchased by the Dent family in 1821.

★351★ UPPER DELAWARE SCENIC & RECREATIONAL RIVER

274 River Rd
Beach Lake, PA 18405
Web: www.nps.gov/upde
Phone: 570-685-4871; **Fax:** 570-729-8565
Size: 75,000 acres. Only 28 acres are federally owned; the remainder of the river corridor is nonfederal, with most land under private ownership. **History:** Authorized on November 10, 1978. **Location:** 73.4 miles of the Delaware River between Hancock and Sparrow Bush, New York, along the Pennsylvania-New York border. Access routes for the southern portion of the river include NY 17, I-84, and US 6. For the northern portion, access routes include NY 17 and NY 191. NY 97 follows the entire New York shore of the river area. **Facilities:** Campgrounds (privately owned), rest rooms (&), cabin rental, lodging, groceries, restaurant/snacks, boat rental, boat ramp, visitor center (&), museum/exhibit. **Activities:** Camping, hiking, horseback riding, swimming, boating, canoeing, kayaking, tubing, fishing, hunting, auto touring, guided tour. **Special Features:** The longest free-flowing river in the Northeast includes riffles and Class I and II rapids between placid pools and eddies. This unit of the National Park Service is also home to John Roebling's Delaware Aqueduct, the oldest surviving wire suspension bridge in the United States; and the Zane Grey Museum, located at the one-time home of the American west novelist in Lackawaxen, PA.

★352★ USS ARIZONA MEMORIAL

1 Arizona Memorial Pl
Honolulu, HI 96818
Web: www.nps.gov/usar/
Phone: 808-422-0561; **Fax:** 808-483-8608

See pages 16-17 for map of U.S. National Parks.

Size: 10.5 acres. **History:** Established on September 9, 1980. **Location:** On the shoreline overlooking Pearl Harbor directly off HI 99 (Kamehameha Highway) on the island of Oahu, Hawaii. **Facilities:** Rest rooms (&), restaurant/snacks, visitor center (&), museum/exhibit. **Activities:** Guided tour. **Special Features:** This 184-foot-long floating memorial marks the spot where the USS Arizona was sunk in Pearl Harbor on December 7, 1941, during the Japanese attack. The memorial structure, spanning the mid-portion of the sunken battleship, consists of three main sections: the entry and assembly rooms; a central area designed for ceremonies and general observation; and the shrine room, where the names of those 1,177 crewmen killed on the *USS Arizona* are engraved on the marble wall.

★353★ VALLEY FORGE NATIONAL HISTORICAL PARK

1400 N Outer Line Dr
King of Prussia, PA 19406
Web: www.nps.gov/vafo/
Phone: 610-783-1077; **Fax:** 610-783-1060
Size: 3,466 acres. **History:** Authorized on July 4, 1976. **Location:** 18 miles west of Philadelphia, Pennsylvania, near the Schuylkill Expressway (76 East) and the Pennsylvania Turnpike (Routes 276 East and 76 West). **Facilities:** Picnic area, rest rooms (&), restaurant/snacks, bicycle trail, boat ramp, visitor center (&), museum/exhibit, self-guided tour/trail. Entrance fee required. **Activities:** Hiking, bicycling, horseback riding, boating, fishing, auto touring, self-guided tours, interpretive programs. **Special Features:** Site of the Continental Army's winter encampment, 1777-1778, the park contains General Washington's headquarters, original earthworks, a variety of monuments and markers, reconstructed log buildings, and a replica cannon.

★354★ VANDERBILT MANSION NATIONAL HISTORIC SITE

4097 Albany Post Rd
Hyde Park, NY 12538
Web: www.nps.gov/vama/
Phone: 845-229-9115; **Fax:** 845-229-0739
Size: 212 acres. **History:** Designated on December 18, 1940. **Location:** In the Hudson River Valley in Hyde Park, New York, 90 miles north of New York City and 70 miles south of Albany. Accessible via US 9. **Facilities:** Rest rooms, picnic area, visitor center (&), museum/exhibit. Entrance fee required. **Activities:** Guided tour, hiking. **Special Features:** This 54-room palatial mansion is a fine example of homes built by 19th-century millionaires. This particular home was constructed by Frederick W. Vanderbilt, a grandson of Cornelius Vanderbilt.

★355★ VICKSBURG NATIONAL MILITARY PARK

3201 Clay St
Vicksburg, MS 39183
Web: www.nps.gov/vick/
Phone: 601-636-0583; **Fax:** 601-636-9497
Size: 1,795 acres. **History:** Established on February 21, 1899; transferred from War Department on August 10, 1933. **Location:** In the northeastern portion of Vicksburg, Mississippi, with three detached units south of the city along Washington St. near the Mississippi River bridges and one unit in Madison Parish, Louisiana. Park entrance is on US 80 (Clay St.), just off I-20. **Facilities:** Picnic area, rest rooms (&), visitor center (including small museum with full-size dioramas), sellf-guided tour/trail. Entrance fee required. **Activities:** Hiking, bicycling, auto touring. **Special Features:** Reconstructed forts and trenches evoke memories of the 47-day siege that ended in the surrender of the city on July 4, 1863. Victory gave the North control of the Mississippi River and cut the Confederacy in two. Today, the battlefield at Vicksburg is in an excellent state of preservation. It includes 1,330 historic monuments and markers, 20 miles of reconstructed trenches and earthworks, a 16-mile tour road, antebellum home, 144 emplaced cannons, restored Union gunboat 1USS Cairo, and the Vicksburg National Cemetery.

★356★ VIETNAM VETERANS MEMORIAL

c/o National Capitol Park - Central
900 Ohio Drive SW
Washington, DC 20024
Web: www.thewall-usa.com
Phone: 202-426-6841; **Fax:** 202-426-1844
Size: 2 acres. **History:** Authorized on July 1, 1980; dedicated on November 13, 1982. Vietnam Women's Memorial dedicated on November 11, 1993. **Location:** Near the Lincoln Memorial at the west end of Constitution Gardens in Washington, DC. **Facilities:** Rest rooms (&). **Activities:** Walking tours, interpretive programs. **Special Features:** The polished black granite wall is inscribed with the names of more than 58,000 persons who gave their lives or remain missing in the Vietnam War (1964-1973). The memorial was designed by Maya Ying Lin. The entrance plaza includes a flagstaff and bronze statue of three Vietnam servicemen sculpted by Frederick Hart. The Vietnam Women's Memorial features a multifigure bronze statue designed by Glenna Goodacre.

★357★ VIRGIN ISLANDS CORAL REEF NATIONAL MONUMENT

c/o Virgin Islands National Park
1300 Cruz Bay Creek
Saint John, VI 00830
Web: www.nps.gov/vicr/
Phone: 340-776-6201
Size: 13,893 acres. **History:** January 31, 2001. **Location:** In the submerged lands within the three-mile belt off the island of St. John in the U.S. Virgin Islands. The Monument extends eastward from Estate Hermitage to Haulover Bay along the southern shoreline of the Island. Once on St. John, the only part of the monument accessible by land is in Hurricane Hole; the other sections must be accessed by boat. **Facilities:** No separate facilities for this site. Administered by the management of Virgin Islands National Park (see separate entry for description). **Special Features:** The island of St. John rises from a platform that extends several miles from shore before plunging to abyssal depths in the deepest part of the Atlantic Ocean. The platform contains a multitude of species that exist in a delicate balance, interlinked through complex relationships that have developed over tens of thousands of years. The monument contains all the elements of a Caribbean tropical marine ecosystem and several threatened and endangered species. Humpback whales, pilot

See pages 16-17 for map of U.S. National Parks.

whales, four species of dolphins, brown pelicans, roseate terns, least terns, and the hawksbill, Leatherback, and green sea turtles all use portions of the monument.

★358★ VIRGIN ISLANDS NATIONAL PARK

1300 Cruz Bay Creek
Saint John, VI 00830
Web: www.nps.gov/viis/
Phone: 340-776-6201; **Fax:** 340-775-9592
Size: 14,686 acres. **History:** Authorized on August 2, 1956. Designated a Biosphere Reserve in 1976. The need to protect reefs from further degradation led to a Presidential Proclamation establishing the Virgin Islands Coral Reef National Monument (see separate entry) in January 1999. **Location:** Park encompasses about three-fifths of the island of Saint John and nearly all of Hassel Island in Charlotte Amalie harbor on St. Thomas in the US Virgin Islands. Visitor center is located in Cruz Bay at the western edge of Saint John. Ferry service to Saint John is available from both Red Hook and Charlotte Amalie, Saint Thomas. **Facilities:** Campground, picnic area, rest rooms (&), cabin rental, groceries, restaurant/snacks, boat and snorkeling equipment rental, bathhouse, visitor center (&), museum/exhibit, self-guided tour/trail. **Activities:** Camping, hiking, swimming, snorkeling, scuba diving, boating, fishing, guided tours. **Special Features:** Park includes coral reefs, quiet coves, blue-green waters, and white sandy beaches fringed by green hills. Here, too, are early Indian sites and the remains of Danish colonial sugar plantations.

★359★ VOYAGEURS NATIONAL PARK

3131 Hwy 53 S
International Falls, MN 56649
Web: www.nps.gov/voya/
Phone: 218-283-9821; **Fax:** 218-285-7407
Size: 218,200 acres. **History:** Authorized on January 8, 1971; established on April 8, 1975. **Location:** In northern Minnesota, near the US/Canadian border, 15 miles east of International Falls and 300 miles north of Minneapolis-Saint Paul. Voyageurs is a water-based park (nearly one-third of the park is water). Access to the Kabetogama peninsula, the islands, and nearly all of the park's shoreline is by watercraft. **Facilities:** Campgrounds, picnic area, rest rooms (&), lodging, groceries, restaurant/snacks, boat rental, boat ramp, visitor centers (&), museum/exhibit, self-guided tour/trail. **Activities:** Camping, hiking, swimming, boating, kayaking, fishing, snowmobiling, cross-country skiing, snowshoeing, wildlife viewing, interpretive programs. **Special Features:** This waterway of four large lakes connected by narrows was once the route of the French-Canadian voyageurs who paddled birch bark canoes full of animal pelts and trade goods on their way to Lake Athabaska in Canada. Park lies in the southern part of the Canadian Shield, representing some of the oldest exposed rock formations in the world.

★360★ WALNUT CANYON NATIONAL MONUMENT

c/o Flagstaff Area National Monuments
6400 N Hwy 89
Flagstaff, AZ 86004
Web: www.nps.gov/waca/
Phone: 928-526-3367; **Fax:** 928-527-0246

Size: 3,579 acres. **History:** Proclaimed on November 30, 1915; transferred from Forest Service on August 10, 1933. **Location:** 10 miles east of downtown Flagstaff, Arizona. From I-40, take Exit 204 to entrance road. **Facilities:** Picnic area, rest rooms (&), visitor center, museum/exhibit, self-guided tour/trail. Entrance fee required. **Activities:** Hiking, guided walks. **Special Features:** These cliff dwellings were built in shallow caves under ledges of limestone by the Sinagua People more than 700 years ago. Though the Sinagua were the canyon's only permanent residents, artifacts found here indicate that they were preceded by Archaic peoples who traveled throughout the Southwest thousands of years ago.

★361★ WAR IN THE PACIFIC NATIONAL HISTORICAL PARK

135 Murray Blvd, Suite 100
Hagåtña, GU 96910
Web: www.nps.gov/wapa/
Phone: 671-477-7278; **Fax:** 671-472-7281
Size: 2,037 acres. **History:** Authorized on August 18, 1978. **Location:** On the island of Guam in the North Pacific. Park includes several units on the west-central part of the island near the villages of Asan, Piti, and Agat. **Facilities:** Picnic area, rest rooms (&), groceries, restaurant/snacks, visitor center (&), museum/exhibit, self-guided tour/trail. **Activities:** Hiking, bicycling, horseback riding, swimming, snorkeling, scuba diving, boating, kayaking, fishing, guided tour. **Special Features:** The 1944 recapture of Guam by American forces during World War II is interpreted at seven units on this island, from the summit of Mount Tenjo (1,033 ft.) to the submerged war relics on the offshore coral reefs (132 ft. deep). Visitors can learn about the events that lead to the outbreak of the Pacific War, the Battle of Guam and the role the Mariana Islands played in helping to end World War II (1941-1945).

★362★ WASHINGTON MONUMENT

c/o National Capitol Park - Central
900 Ohio Dr SW
Washington, DC 20024
Web: www.nps.gov/wamo/
Phone: 202-426-6841
Size: 106 acres. **History:** Authorized on January 31, 1848; completed on December 6, 1884; transferred from Office of Public Buildings and Public Parks of the National Capital on August 10, 1933. **Location:** At Constitution Ave. and 15th St. in Washington, DC. **Facilities:** Rest rooms (&), museum/exhibit. **Activities:** Guided tour. **Special Features:** A dominating feature of the Nation's Capital, this 555-foot obelisk honors the country's first President, George Washington. The architect-designer was Robert Mills.

★363★ WASHITA BATTLEFIELD NATIONAL HISTORIC SITE

426 E Broadway
Cheyenne, OK 73628
Web: www.nps.gov/waba/
Phone: 580-497-2742; **Fax:** 580-497-2712
Size: 315 acres. **History:** Authorized on November 12, 1996.

See pages 16-17 for map of U.S. National Parks.

Location: Site is 2 miles west of Cheyenne, Oklahoma, on OK 47A. Park headquarters and Black Kettle Museum are near the intersection of US 283 and OK 47. **Facilities:** Picnic area, rest rooms (&), museum/exhibit. **Activities:** Hiking, ranger-led programs. **Special Features:** Site protects and interprets the site of the Southern Cheyenne village of Peace Chief Black Kettle that was attacked by the 7th US Cavalry under Lieutenant Colonel George A. Custer just before dawn on November 27, 1868 during the era of the Plains and Indian Wars. The controversial strike has been described as both a battle and a massacre.

★364★ WEIR FARM NATIONAL HISTORIC SITE

735 Nod Hill Rd
Wilton, CT 06897
Web: www.nps.gov/wefa/
Phone: 203-834-1896; **Fax:** 203-834-2421
Size: 74.3 acres. **History:** Authorized on October 31, 1990. **Location:** In southwestern Connecticut, between the towns of Ridgefield and Wilton; accessible via US 7 and CT 102. **Facilities:** Visitor center. **Activities:** Guided and self-guided tours, workshops, artists-in-residence programs, adult and children's art classes. **Special Features:** Site is named in honor of J. Alden Weir (1852-1919), a leading American Impressionist painter and a founder of The Ten. After his death, the cultural heritage at Weir Farm was carried on by a second generation of artists, including his daughter Dorothy Weir Young, an artist; her husband Mahonri Mackintosh Young, a sculptor; C. Sperry Andrews, a contemporary landscape painter; and his wife Doris Andrews, also an artist. A study collection of important primary materials on the artists who lived and worked at Weir Farm is being gathered, including personal letters, sketchbooks, drawings, and major works of art.

★365★ WHISKEYTOWN-SHASTA-TRINITY NATIONAL RECREATION AREA

PO Box 188
Whiskeytown, CA 96095
Web: www.nps.gov/whis/
Phone: 530-242-3400; **Fax:** 530-246-5154
Size: 42,503 acres. **History:** Authorized on November 8, 1965; established on October 21, 1972. Of the three parts of the Whiskeytown-Shasta-Trinity National Recreation Area, the Whiskeytown Unit is the only unit administered by the National Park Service. The Shasta and Trinity units are administered by the Forest Service. **Location:** The Whiskeytown Unit of the national recreation area is on CA 299 off I-5 near Redding, California. **Facilities:** Campgrounds (&), picnic area, rest rooms (&), groceries, restaurant/snacks, boat rental, boat ramp, bathhouse, visitor center (&), self-guided tour/trail. **Activities:** Camping, hiking, horseback riding, bicycling, swimming, boating, canoeing, water-skiing, scuba diving, snorkeling, fishing, hunting, gold panning (recreational), interpretive programs. **Special Features:** Whiskeytown Unit, with its mountainous backcountry and large reservoir, provides a multitude of outdoor recreation opportunities as well as remains of buildings built during the Gold Rush. Whiskeytown Lake provides 36 miles of shoreline and 3,200 surface acres for recreation.

★366★ WHITE SANDS NATIONAL MONUMENT

PO Box 1086
Holloman AFB, NM 88330
Web: www.nps.gov/whsa/
Phone: 505-679-2599
Size: 143,733 acres. **History:** Proclaimed on January 18, 1933. **Location:** On US 70, 15 miles southwest of Alamogordo and 52 miles east of Las Cruces, New Mexico. **Facilities:** Backcountry campsites, picnic area (&), rest rooms (&), visitor center (&), self-guided tour/trail. Entrance fee required. **Activities:** Camping, hiking, bicycling, auto touring, ranger-led walks and programs. **Special Features:** The park contains a significant portion of the world's largest gypsum dunefield. The glistening white dunes rise 60 feet high and cover 275 square miles. Small animals have adapted to this harsh environment by developing light, protective coloration. Plants also have adapted, extending root systems to remain atop the ever-shifting dunes.

★367★ WHITMAN MISSION NATIONAL HISTORIC SITE

328 Whitman Mission Rd
Walla Walla, WA 99362
Web: www.nps.gov/whmi/
Phone: 509-522-6360; **Fax:** 509-522-6355
Size: 139 acres. **History:** Authorized as Whitman National Monument on June 29, 1936; changed to current designation on January 1, 1963. **Location:** In southeastern Washington, 7 miles west of Walla Walla on US 12. **Facilities:** Picnic area, rest rooms (&), visitor center (&), museum/exhibit, self-guided tour/trail. Entrance fee required. **Activities:** Ranger-led programs, cultural demonstrations. **Special Features:** The mission of Marcus and Narcissa Whitman at Waiilatpu was an important way station in the early days of the Oregon Trail. The Whitmans labored to bring Christianity to the Cayuse, but deep cultural differences and a measles epidemic led to violence in which the Cayuse killed the Whitmans and 11 others.

★368★ WILLIAM HOWARD TAFT NATIONAL HISTORIC SITE

2038 Auburn Ave
Cincinnati, OH 45219
Web: www.nps.gov/wiho/
Phone: 513-684-3262; **Fax:** 513-684-3627
Size: 3.1 acres. **History:** Authorized on December 2, 1969. **Location:** In the Mount Auburn section of Cincinnati, Ohio, off I-71. **Facilities:** Rest rooms (&), visitor center (&), museum/exhibit, self-guided tour/trail. **Activities:** Guided tour. **Special Features:** William Howard Taft, the only person to serve as both President (1909-1913) and Chief Justice of the United States (1921-1930), was born and raised in this house, which has been restored.

★369★ WILSON'S CREEK NATIONAL BATTLEFIELD

6424 W Farm Rd 182
Republic, MO 65738
Web: www.nps.gov/wicr/
Phone: 417-732-2662; **Fax:** 417-732-1167

See pages 16-17 for map of U.S. National Parks.

Size: 2,365 acres. **History:** Authorized on April 22, 1960, as a national battlefield park; redesignated on December 16, 1970. **Location:** 3 miles east of Republic and 10 miles southwest of Springfield, Missouri. Accessible via US 60 and MO ZZ. **Facilities:** Picnic area, rest rooms (&), bicycle trail, visitor center (&), museum/exhibit, self-guided tour/trail. Entrance fee required. **Activities:** Hiking, bicycling, horseback riding, auto touring, living history programs. **Special Features:** The battle here on August 10, 1861, was the first major Civil War engagement west of the Mississippi and the scene of the death of Nathaniel Lyon, the first Union general killed in combat. The Confederate failure here resulted in keeping Missouri in the Union. Major features include a 5-mile automobile tour loop, the restored 1852 Ray House, and "Bloody Hill," the scene of the major battle. Wilson's Creek Civil War Museum (formerly the Sweeny Museum) contains an outstanding collection of artifacts relating to the war west of the Mississippi.

★370★ WIND CAVE NATIONAL PARK

26611 US Hwy 385
Hot Springs, SD 57747
Web: www.nps.gov/wica/
Phone: 605-745-4600; **Fax:** 605-745-4207
Size: 28,295 acres. **History:** Established on January 9, 1903. Wind Cave National Game Preserve established on August 10, 1912, and added to the park on June 15, 1935. **Location:** In southwestern South Dakota. From Rapid City, take US 79 south for 50 miles to US 18, then right onto US 385 North, which passes through Hot Springs and into the park. Also accessible via US 16 west out of Rapid City onto US 385 south. **Facilities:** Campground (&), picnic area, rest rooms (&), restaurant/snacks, visitor center (&), museum/exhibit, self-guided tour/trail. **Activities:** Camping, hiking, auto touring, guided cave tours and prairie hikes. **Special Features:** Here in the scenic Black Hills, one of the world's longest and most complex caves is well known for its outstanding display of boxwork, an unusual cave formation composed of thin calcite fins resembling honeycombs. The park's mixed grass prairie is one of the few remaining and is home to native wildlife such as bison, elk, pronghorn, mule deer, coyotes, and prairie dogs.

★371★ WOLF TRAP NATIONAL PARK FOR THE PERFORMING ARTS

1551 Trap Rd
Vienna, VA 22182
Web: www.nps.gov/wotr/
Phone: 703-255-1800; **Fax:** 703-255-1971
Size: 130 acres. **History:** Authorized on October 15, 1966. **Location:** Near Vienna, Virginia, outside I-495 (Capital Beltway), between VA 7 and VA 267 (Dulles Toll Rd.) **Facilities:** Picnic area, rest rooms (&), restaurant/snacks. **Activities:** Performances, educational programs, guided tour. **Special Features:** At this first national park for the performing arts, Filene Center can accommodate an audience of 7,000, including 3,000 on the sloping lawn in a setting of rolling hills and woods.

★372★ WOMEN'S RIGHTS NATIONAL HISTORICAL PARK

136 Fall St
Seneca Falls, NY 13148
Web: www.nps.gov/wori/
Phone: 315-568-2991; **Fax:** 315-568-2141
Size: 7.4 acres. **History:** Authorized on December 8, 1980. **Location:** In Seneca Falls, New York, accessible via the New York Thruway (I-90) off Exit 41. **Facilities:** Rest rooms (&), visitor center (&), museum/exhibit, self-guided tour/trail. **Activities:** Guided tours. **Special Features:** This park commemorates the beginning of the women's struggle for equal rights and includes the Wesleyan Methodist Chapel, the site of the first Women's Rights Convention in 1848, the home and office of Elizabeth Cady Stanton, the M'Clintock House where the Declaration of Sentiments was written, and other sites related to notable early women's rights activists, including the home of Richard and Jane Hunt in Waterloo.

★373★ WRANGELL-SAINT ELIAS NATIONAL PARK & PRESERVE

Mile 106.8 Richardson Hwy
Copper Center, AK 99573
Web: www.nps.gov/wrst/
Phone: 907-822-5234; **Fax:** 907-822-7216
Size: 8,323,148 acres (park) and 4,852,753 acres (preserve). **History:** Proclaimed as Wrangell-Saint Elias National Monument on December 1, 1978; established as a national park and preserve on December 2, 1980. Wilderness designated on December 2, 1980. Designated a World Heritage Site on October 24, 1979. **Location:** In southeastern Alaska. Park can be reached from Anchorage via Glenn Hwy. (AK 1). At Glennallen, Glenn Hwy. meets the Richardson Hwy., skirting the park's western boundary en route to the coastal city of Valdez. The Tok Cutoff coming south from the Alaska Hwy. borders the park's northwestern corner. From these highways, two unpaved roads penetrate the park. The Chitina-McCarthy Rd. extends 61 miles from Chitina to the Kennicott River, just west of McCarthy. The northern park area is reached via the Nabesna Rd., which extends 45 miles from Slana to Nabesna. A short flight on an air taxi from Glennallen, Chitina, Nabesna, or McCarthy can transport you into the heart of the park. **Facilities:** Campground, lodging, boat rental, visitor center, ranger stations. Limited federal facilities. **Activities:** Camping, hiking, horseback riding, mountain climbing, boating, kayaking, rafting, fishing, hunting, wildlife viewing, cross-country skiing. **Special Features:** The Chugach, Wrangell, and Saint Elias mountain ranges converge here in what is often referred to as the "mountain kingdom of North America." The largest unit of the National Park System and a day's drive east of Anchorage, the park-preserve includes the continent's largest assemblage of glaciers and the greatest collection of peaks above 16,000 feet, including Mount Saint Elias. At 18,008 feet, it is the second highest peak in the United States. Adjacent to Canada's Kluane National Park, the site is characterized by its remote mountains, valleys, and wild rivers, all rich in their concentrations of wildlife.

See pages 16-17 for map of U.S. National Parks.

★374★ WRIGHT BROTHERS NATIONAL MEMORIAL

1401 National Park Dr
Manteo, NC 27954
Web: www.nps.gov/wrbr/
Phone: 252-473-2111; **Fax:** 252-473-2595
Size: 428 acres. **History:** Authorized as Kill Devil Hill Monument National Memorial on March 2, 1927; transferred from War Department on August 10, 1933; redesignated on December 1, 1953. **Location:** On the Outer Banks of North Carolina in the town of Kill Devil Hills, midway between Kitty Hawk and Nags Head at milepost 7.5 on US158. **Facilities:** Rest rooms (占), visitor center (占), museum/exhibit, self-guided tour/trail. Entrance fee required. **Activities:** Guided tour. **Special Features:** The first sustained flight in a heavier-than-air machine was made here by Wilbur and Orville Wright on December 17, 1903. Site includes museum exhibits, reconstructed camp buildings, the first flight area, and a 60-foot granite monument perched atop 90-foot-tall Kill Devil Hill commemorating the achievement of these two visionaries from Dayton, Ohio.

★375★ WUPATKI NATIONAL MONUMENT

Flagstaff Area National Monuments
6400 N Hwy 89
Flagstaff, AZ 86004
Web: www.nps.gov/wupa/
Phone: 928-679-2365; **Fax:** 928-679-2349
Size: 35,422 acres. **History:** Proclaimed on December 9, 1924. **Location:** From Flagstaff, Arizona, take US 89 north for 12 miles and turn right at sign for Sunset Crater Volcano - Wupatki National Monuments. Visitor center is 21 miles from this junction. **Facilities:** Picnic area, visitor center (占), museum/exhibit, self-guided tour/trail. Entrance fee required. **Activities:** Hiking, auto touring, self-guided tour, interpretive programs. **Special Features:** Ruins of red sandstone pueblos built by farming Ancestral Puebloan People between 1120 and 1250 are preserved here.

★376★ YELLOWSTONE NATIONAL PARK

PO Box 168
Yellowstone National Park, WY 82190
Web: www.nps.gov/yell/
Phone: 307-344-7381; **Fax:** 307-344-2323
Size: 2,219,791 acres. **History:** Established on March 1, 1872. Designated a Biosphere Reserve in 1976 and a World Heritage Site in 1978. **Location:** In northwestern Wyoming, with sections in eastern Idaho and southern Montana. Park includes five main entrances: the north entrance is on US 89, near the gateway community of Gardiner, MT; the northeast entrance is on US 212, 69 miles from Red Lodge, WY; the west entrance is on US 20, near the town of West Yellowstone, MT; the east entrance is on US 20 and US 14/16, 53 miles from Cody, WY; and the south entrance is on US 89, 191 and 287, 64 miles from Jackson, WY. **Facilities:** Campgrounds (占), picnic area, rest rooms (占), cabin rental, lodging, groceries, restaurant/snacks, boat rental, boat ramp, horse rental, visitor centers (占), museum/exhibit, self-guided tour/trail. Entrance fee required. **Activities:** Camping, hiking, horseback riding, bicycling, boating, fishing, snowmobiling, cross-country skiing, wildlife viewing, auto touring, ranger-led programs, educational programs and courses. **Special Features:** Old Faithful and some 10,000 other thermal features make this the Earth's greatest geyser area. Here, too, are lakes, waterfalls, high mountain meadows, wildlife, and the Grand Canyon of the Yellowstone, all set apart in 1872 as the world's first national park.

★377★ YOSEMITE NATIONAL PARK

9039 Village Dr
PO Box 577
Yosemite, CA 95389
Web: www.nps.gov/yose/
Phone: 209-372-0200; **Fax:** 209-379-1800
Size: 761,266 acres. **History:** Yosemite Valley and Mariposa Big Tree Grove granted to State of California on June 30, 1864; park established on October 1, 1890; Federal Government accepted lands returned by state on June 11, 1906. Wilderness designated on September 28, 1984. Designated a World Heritage Site on October 31, 1984. **Location:** There are five entrances to the park: South entrance is on CA 41, 64 miles north of Fresno; Arch Rock entrance is on CA 140, 75 miles northeast of Merced; Big Oak Flat entrance is on CA 120, 88 miles from Manteca; Tioga Pass entrance is on Highway 120, 10 miles west of Lee Vining; and Hetch Hetchy entrance is accessible via CA 120 and Evergreen Rd. **Facilities:** Campgrounds (占), picnic area, rest rooms (占), cabin rental, lodging, groceries, restaurant/snacks, bicycle trail, boat rental, boat ramp, bathhouse, visitor centers (占), museum/exhibit, shuttle buses, self-guided tour/trail. Entrance fee required. **Activities:** Camping, hiking, bicycling, horseback riding, mountain climbing, swimming, boating, fishing, wildlife viewing, cross-country skiing, ranger-guided walks. **Special Features:** Park embraces a spectacular tract of scenic wildlands in the Sierra Nevada that stretches along California's eastern flank. Ranging from 2,000 feet above sea level to more than 13,000 feet, park encompasses alpine wilderness, mountains, lakes, waterfalls, and forests that include groves of giant sequoias. Park highlights include: Yosemite Valley with its high cliffs and waterfalls; Tuolumne Meadows, a high subalpine meadow surrounded by mountain peaks; Glacier Point, which offers a spectacular view of Yosemite Valley and the high country; and the Mariposa Grove, which contains hundreds of ancient giant sequoias.

★378★ YUCCA HOUSE NATIONAL MONUMENT

c/o Mesa Verde National Park
PO Box 8
Mesa Verde, CO 81330
Web: www.nps.gov/yuho/
Phone: 970-529-4465; **Fax:** 970-529-4637
Size: 34 acres. **History:** Proclaimed on December 19, 1919. **Location:** 15 miles south of Cortez, Colorado, off US 666. **Facilities:** None. **Special Features:** Yucca House is one of the largest archeological sites in southwest Colorado, and acted as an important community center for the Ancestral Puebloan people from A.D. 1150-1300. Ruins of these large prehistoric Indian pueblos are as yet unexcavated. Due to the size and extent of mounds, it is believed that, when excavated, they will prove of great archeological significance and educational interest. The name ''Yucca House'' was selected for the monument because

See pages 16-17 for map of U.S. National Parks.

the Indians of the Montezuma valley called Sleeping Ute Mountain by a name meaning yucca, due to the abundance of yucca plants growing on the mountainsides.

★379★ YUKON-CHARLEY RIVERS NATIONAL PRESERVE

4175 Geist Rd
Fairbanks, AK 99709
Web: www.nps.gov/yuch/
Phone: 907-457-5752; **Fax:** 907-455-0601
Size: 2,526,512 acres. **History:** Proclaimed Yukon-Charley National Monument on December 1, 1978; established as a national preserve on December 2, 1980. **Location:** 115 miles of the 1,800-mile Yukon River and the entire Charley River basin along the Canadian border in east-central Alaska. There is no road access, but two highways serve towns near the Preserve boundaries. The 161-mile Taylor Hwy. begins at Tetlin Junction on the Alaska Highway and ends at Eagle, 12 miles from the preserve. The 162-mile Steese Hwy. begins in Fairbanks and end in Circle, 14 miles from the preserve. Scheduled air taxis from Fairbanks serve Eagle and Circle, located upriver and downriver of the preserve, respectively. **Facilities:** Visitor center, public use cabins. **Activities:** Camping, hiking, boating, rafting, kayaking, canoeing, fishing, hunting, bird-watching, interpretive programs. **Special Features:** Most visitors to the preserve float the Yukon or Charley rivers. The Charley, an 88-mile wild river, is considered by many to be the most spectacular river in Alaska. Numerous rustic cabins and historic sites on the preserve are reminders of the importance of the Yukon River during the 1898 Gold Rush. Paleontological and archeological sites here add much to our knowledge of man and his environment thousands of years ago.

★380★ ZION NATIONAL PARK

SR 9
Springdale, UT 84767
Web: www.nps.gov/zion/
Phone: 435-772-3256; **Fax:** 435-772-3426
Size: 146,598 acres. **History:** Mukuntuweap National Monument proclaimed on July 31, 1909; incorporated in Zion National Monument by proclamation on March 18, 1918. Established as national park on November 19, 1919. **Location:** In southwestern Utah. The Visitor Center at the Kolob Canyons entrance is accessible from I-15, Exit 40. The eastern entrance to the park is from US-89 to UT 9. The Zion Canyon Visitor Center is a short distance from the Park's South Entrance adjacent to Springdale. **Facilities:** Campgrounds (&), picnic area, rest rooms (&), cabin rental, lodging, restaurant/snacks, visitor center (&), museum/exhibit, self-guided tour/trail. Entrance fee required. **Activities:** Camping, hiking, bicycling, horseback riding, mountain climbing, wildlife viewing, snowmobiling, cross-country skiing, tram tours, auto touring, ranger-led programs. **Special Features:** Colorful canyon and mesa scenery includes erosion and rock-fault patterns that create phenomenal shapes and landscapes. This includes the world's largest arch - Kolob Arch spanning 310 feet - and other natural wonders such as waterfalls and clear backcountry pools. The elevation differences at Zion provide habitat for extremely diverse plant

communities. Evidence of Ancestral Puebloans, known as the Anasazi, date from 2,000 years ago.

AFFILIATED AREAS

In an Act of August 18, 1970, the National Park System was defined in law as ''any area of land and water now or hereafter administered by the Secretary of the Interior through the National Park Service for park, monument, historic, parkway, recreational, or other purposes.'' The same law specifically excludes ''miscellaneous areas administered in connection therewith,'' that is, those properties that are neither federally owned nor directly administered by the National Park Service but which utilize NPS assistance.

The Affiliated Areas comprise a variety of locations in the United States and Canada that preserve significant properties outside the National Park System. Some of these have been recognized by Acts of Congress, others have been designated national historic sites by the Secretary of the Interior under authority of the Historic Sites Act of 1935. All draw technical or financial aid from the National Park Service.

★381★ ALEUTIAN WORLD WAR II NATIONAL HISTORIC AREA

c/o Ounalashka Corp
PO Box 149
Unalaska, AK 99685
Web: www.nps.gov/aleu/
Phone: 907-581-1276
Size: 81 acres. **History:** Authorized on November 12, 1996. **Location:** On Amaknak Island in the Aleutian Island Chain, 800 miles west of Anchorage, Alaska. **Activities:** Visitors to the area may explore the remaining structures and ruins, and sense the scope of the war effort mounted in the Aleutians to protect the United States from the Japanese invasion. **Special Features:** Interprets the history of the Aleut people and the role of the Aleut people and the Aleutian Islands in the defense of the United States during World War II. Property includes the U.S. Army base Fort Schwatka, one of four coastal defense posts built to protect Dutch Harbor (the back door to the United States) during World War II.

★382★ AMERICAN MEMORIAL PARK

PO Box 5198-CHRB
Saipan, MP 96950
Web: www.nps.gov/amme/
Phone: 670-234-7207; **Fax:** 670-234-6698
Size: 133 acres. **History:** Authorized on August 18, 1978. **Location:** On Tanapag Harbor, Saipan, in the Northern Mariana Islands. **Facilities:** Beaches, sports fields, picnic sites, boat marinas, playgrounds, walkways, and a 30-acre wetland and mangrove forest. **Activities:** Baseball, bicycling, running, tennis, swimming. **Special Features:** Park honors the American and Marianas people who gave their lives during the Marianas Campaign of World War II. More than 5,000 names are inscribed on a memorial which was dedicated June 15, 1994, during the 50th anniversary of the Invasion of Saipan.

See pages 16-17 for map of U.S. National Parks.

★383★ BENJAMIN FRANKLIN NATIONAL MEMORIAL

The Franklin Institute
222 N 20th St
Philadelphia, PA 19103
Web: sln.fi.edu/tfi/exhibits/memorial.html
Phone: 215-448-1200
Size: 0.01 acres. **History:** Designated on October 25, 1972. Owned and administered by the Franklin Institute. **Location:** In the rotunda of The Franklin Institute Science Museum in Philadelphia, Pennsylvania. **Activities:** Tours. **Special Features:** Memorial Hall features a 20-foot-high marble statue of of Franklin, by James Earle Fraser, honors the inventor-statesman. The statue weighs 30 tons and sits on a 92-ton pedestal of white Seravezza marble. Memorial Hall also houses many of Franklin's original possessions, including his composing table and several of his original publications.

★384★ CHICAGO PORTAGE NATIONAL HISTORIC SITE

c/o Cook County Forest Preserve
Cummings Sq
River Forest, IL 60305
Web: www.civiccenterauthority.org/pages/portsite.htm
Phone: 773-261-8400
Size: 91 acres. **History:** Designated on January 3, 1952. Administered by Cook County. **Location:** Near the intersection of Harlem Ave. and I-55 (Adlai Stevenson Expwy.) in Chicago, Illinois. **Special Features:** A portion of the portage between the Great Lakes and the Mississippi River, discovered by French explorers Jacques Marquette and Louis Jolliet, is preserved here. The portage was a major factor in the development of the United States interior. With the opening of the Illinois and Michigan Canal in 1848, the portage became the transportation link that spurred development of the city of Chicago.

★385★ CHIMNEY ROCK NATIONAL HISTORIC SITE

PO Box F
Bayard, NE 69334
Web: www.nps.gov/chro/
Phone: 308-586-2581
Size: 83 acres. **History:** Designated on August 2, 1956. Owned by state of Nebraska; administered by the city of Bayard, the Nebraska State Historical Society, and the National Park Service under a cooperative agreement of June 21, 1956. **Location:** 1.5 miles south of NE 92 on Chimney Rock Road in Bayard, Nebraska. **Facilities:** Visitor center with interpretive displays, video presentation, and group tours. Entrance fee required. **Special Features:** As they travelled west, pioneers camped near this famous landmark, which stands 500 feet above the Platte River along the Oregon and California trails.

★386★ FATHER MARQUETTE NATIONAL MEMORIAL

720 Church St
Saint Ignace, MI 49781
Web: www.nps.gov/fama/
Phone: 906-643-8620

Size: 52 acres. **History:** Authorized on December 20, 1975. **Location:** In Straits State Park near Saint Ignace, Michigan, just west of I-75 off US 2. **Facilities:** Current attractions include the memorial, an outdoor 15-station interpretive trail, and a panoramic view of the Mackinac Bridge. **Activities:** Modern camping (in Straits State Park). **Special Features:** The memorial pays tribute to the life and work of Father Jacques Marquette, French priest and explorer. He established Michigan's earliest European settlements at Sault Ste. Marie and St. Ignace in 1668 and 1671, and lived among the Great Lakes Indians from 1666 until his death in 1675.

★387★ GLORIA DEI (OLD SWEDES') CHURCH NATIONAL HISTORIC SITE

Columbus Blvd & Christian St
Philadelphia, PA 19147
Web: www.nps.gov/glde/
Phone: 215-389-1513; **Fax:** 215-597-1416
Size: 3.7 acres. **History:** Designated on November 17, 1942. **Location:** Along the Delaware River between the Benjamin Franklin and Walt Whitman bridges, 0.5 miles south of Penn's Landing in Philadelphia, Pennsylvania. **Facilities:** Gloria Dei is an active religious congregation, and is home to the parish minister. **Special Features:** Founded in 1677, Gloria Dei is the second oldest Swedish church in the United States and oldest church in Pennsylvania. The present structure, a splendid example of 17th-century Swedish church architecture, was built between 1698 and 1700. The Church is maintained by its congregation and contains important historic relics and artifacts.

★388★ GREEN SPRINGS NATIONAL HISTORIC LANDMARK DISTRICT

3655 US Hwy 211 E
Luray, VA 22835
Web: www.nps.gov/grsp/
Phone: 434-999-3402
Size: 14,004 acres. **History:** Declared a national historic landmark in 1974. Preservation easements accepted for nearly half the area in the district on December 12, 1977. **Location:** The district is located 1.5 miles north of I-64, on US 15 from exit 136, Zion Crossroads. It is 6.5 miles long and 4.5 miles wide, roughly bounded by US 15, VA 22, and VA 613 in the western end of Louisa County, Virginia. **Facilities:** There are no National Park Service facilities or other public facilities in the district. **Activities:** The rural cultural landscape of farms and houses can be viewed from the many public roads throughout the district. **Special Features:** This portion of Louisa County in Virginia's Piedmont is noted for its concentration of fine rural manor houses and related buildings in an unmarred landscape, representing many generations of agricultural, architectural, and social history.

★389★ HISTORIC CAMDEN REVOLUTIONARY WAR SITE

222 Broad St
PO Box 710
Camden, SC 29020
Web: www.historic-camden.net
Phone: 803-432-9841; **Fax:** 803-432-3815

See pages 16-17 for map of U.S. National Parks.

Size: 107 acres. **History:** Authorized on May 24, 1982. **Location:** Just south of Camden, South Carolina, off US 521. **Activities:** Guided and self-guided tours of the outdoor museum complex, which includes the town site of 18th century Camden, the restored and furnished 1785 John Craven House, Cunningham House circa 1830, two early 19th century logs cabins with exhibits, partially restored 1795 McCaa House, reconstructions of some of the military fortifications, the reconstructed and furnished Joseph Kershaw mansion, headquarters for Lord Cornwallis, a blacksmith exhibit and a .6-mile Nature Trail. Visitors can also enjoy walking the Old Camden Trace, a 3.5 mile route through Historic Camden, the Nature Trail, the 1758 Quaker Cemetery and numerous other landmarks of early Camden. **Special Features:** This early colonial village was established in the mid-1730s and was known as Fredericksburg Township. In 1768 the village was named Camden in honor of Charles Pratt, Lord Camden, a British Parliamentary champion of Colonial rights. The site was occupied by the British under Lord Cornwallis from May 1, 1780, until May 9, 1781. Camden was one of the few frontier settlements where two Revolutionary War battles were fought: August 16, 1780, and April 25, 1781. Restorations and reconstructions include fort sites, log cabins, and 18th- and 19th-century homes, including the Joseph Kershaw house where Lord Cornwallis made his headquarters.

★390★ ICE AGE NATIONAL SCIENTIFIC RESERVE

Wisconsin Dept of Natural Resources
Box 7921
Madison, WI 53707
Web: www2.nature.nps.gov/geology/parks/icag/index.cfm
Phone: 608-266-7616; **Fax:** 608-267-7474
Size: 32,500 acres. **History:** Authorized in October of 1964 and established in 1971. Unit is administered by the Wisconsin Department of Natural Resources. **Location:** Reserve comprises nine units throughout the state of Wisconsin. **Facilities:** State parks in the area are open to the public. **Special Features:** This first national scientific reserve contains nationally significant features of continental glaciation.

★391★ INTERNATIONAL PEACE GARDEN

Rt 1
Box 116
Dunseith, ND 58329
Web: www.peacegarden.com
Phone: 701-263-4390; **Fax:** 701-263-3169; **Toll Free:** 888-432-6733
Size: 2,339 acres. **History:** Originated by North Dakota in 1931. Federal aid authorized in acts of 1949, 1954, 1958, and 1974. North Dakota holds the 888-acre U.S. portion for International Peace Garden, Inc., which administers the area for North Dakota and Manitoba. **Location:** Park straddles the US/Canadian border between Dunseith, North Dakota, and Boissevain, Manitoba. **Facilities:** Interpretive center, gift shop, game warden museum, hiking trails, bike paths, cross-country ski trails, campgrounds. **Activities:** Interpretive programs, including garden tours, nature hikes, crafts programs, gardening classes, greenhouse tours, horticulturist talks, campfire programs, and environmental education activities. **Special Features:** Park commemorates the friendship between this continent's two largest nations — the

United States and Canada — along the longest unfortified border in the world. It encompasses magnificent floral displays, Lake Metigoshe, Lake Metigoshe State Park, Devil's Lake, and Sully's Hill National Game Preserve.

★392★ INUPIAT HERITAGE CENTER

PO Box 749
Barrow, AK 99723
Web: www.nps.gov/inup/
Phone: 907-852-5494
History: Designated on February 3, 1999. Center is owned and managed by the North Slope Borough on behalf of the whaling villages of the North Slope. **Location:** In Barrow, a community of approximately 4000, which is located on the shore of the Arctic Ocean in northern Alaska. **Facilities:** Exhibits, artifact collections, library, gift shop. **Special Features:** Center is affiliated with New Bedford Whaling National Historical Park (see separate entry) in New Bedford, Massachusetts, to commemorate more than 2,000 whaling voyages from New Bedford to the western Arctic during the late 19th and early 20th century. Many Alaska Natives, particularly Inupiat Eskimo people, participated in commercial whaling. Center collects, preserves, and exhibits historical material, art objects, and scientific displays, and houses a traditional room where people can demonstrate and teach traditional crafts in elders-in-residence and artists-in residence programs.

★393★ JAMESTOWN NATIONAL HISTORIC SITE

c/o Association for the Preservation of Virginia Antiquities
204 W Franklin St
Richmond, VA 23220
Web: www.apva.org/jr.html
Phone: 757-229-1733; **Fax:** 757-229-4273
Size: 22.5 acres. **History:** Designated on December 18, 1940. Owned and administered by the Association for the Preservation of Virginia Antiquities. The remainder of the Jamestown site and island are part of Colonial National Historical Park (see separate entry). **Location:** On the western end of Jamestown Island, Virginia, 7 miles from Colonial Williamsburg, off the Colonial Parkway. **Activities:** Visitor tours of the Old Towne; exploration of the New Towne; and driving and exploration of the island on the three- or five-mile wilderness loop drive. Interpretive signs and paintings along the way discuss some of the early industries attempted by the English. **Special Features:** Part of this site of the first permanent English settlement in North America (1607) is on the upper end of Jamestown Island, scene of the first representative legislative government on this continent, July 30, 1619.

★394★ KATE MULLANY NATIONAL HISTORIC SITE

c/o American Labor Studies Center
100 S Swan St
Albany, NY 12210
Phone: 518-331-4474
History: Designated a National Historic Landmark in 199; authorized as a national historic site on December 3, 2004. The house was privately owned until 2003, when it was purchased

See pages 16-17 for map of U.S. National Parks.

by the New York AFL-CIO on behalf of the American Labor Studies Center (ALSC). Under the authorized bill, the property is designated an affiliated area of the National Park System, which will provide the center with technical and financial assistance for planning, development, interpretation, and preservation of the site. The site will continue to be owned and operated by ALCS. **Location:** The Kate Mullany House is located at 350 Eighth Street in Troy, New York. **Facilities:** Not open to the public. **Special Features:** Catherine A. (Kate) Mullany was an Irish immigrant laundry worker who organized and led Troy's Collar Laundry Union during the 1860's, one of the first all-female labor unions in the United States. She lived in this house from 1869 to 1875, inherited the house when her mother died in 1876, moved away, returned in 1903, and died here in 1906.

★395★ LOWER EAST SIDE TENEMENT MUSEUM NATIONAL HISTORIC SITE

108 Orchard St
New York, NY 10002
Web: www.tenement.org
Phone: 212-431-0233
History: The Lower East Side Tenement Museum was chartered in 1988. On November 12, 1998, it was designated a National Historic Area affiliated with the National Park Service. **Location:** Located on Orchard St. in Manhattan's Lower East Side, New York City. **Activities:** Museum and tenement tours. **Special Features:** The heart of the Tenement Museum is its tenement building at 97 Orchard Street, home to an estimated 7,000 people from 20 nations between 1863 and 1935. The museum promotes tolerance and historical perspective through the presentation and interpretation of the variety of immigrant and migrant experiences at this "gateway to America."

★396★ NEW JERSEY COASTAL HERITAGE TRAIL ROUTE

389 Fortescue Rd
PO Box 568
Newport, NJ 08345
Web: www.nps.gov/neje/
Phone: 856-447-0103; **Fax:** 856-447-0108
History: Authorized on October 20, 1988, as a partnership project by the National Park Service in cooperation with the State of New Jersey and many other public and private organizations. **Location:** Extends for nearly 300 miles along coastal New Jersey, from Perth Amboy to Cape May on the Atlantic coast, and west along the Delaware Bay from Cape May to the Delaware Memorial Bridge at Deepwater, New Jersey. **Facilities:** Trail welcome centers are located at Fort Mott State Park (off State Route 49 between Salem and Pennsville in Salem County near the Delaware Memorial Bridge) and at the Ocean View Tourist Information Center (Milepost 18.3 on the Garden State Parkway in Cape May County north of Cape May). **Activities:** Intended primarily for vehicular tourism, with exhibits and special programs available. **Special Features:** Trail explores the diverse heritage of the Jersey Shore and Raritan and Delaware bays. Five themes define different aspects of coastal life: Maritime History, Coastal Habitats, Wildlife Migration, Historic Settlements, and Relaxation and Inspiration. Lighthouses, boardwalks, historic communities, and migratory flyways are all part of the trail.

★397★ OKLAHOMA CITY NATIONAL MEMORIAL

620 N Harvey Ave
Oklahoma City, OK 73102
Web: www.oklahomacitynationalmemorial.org
Phone: 405-235-3313; **Fax:** 405-235-3315; **Toll Free:** 888-542-4673
Size: 6.2 acres. **History:** Established on October 9, 1997; redesignated as an affiliated area of the National Park Service on January 23, 2004. The national memorial and museum are owned and operated by the Oklahoma City National Memorial Foundation. **Location:** In Oklahoma City, Oklahoma, between Robinson and Harvey streets on the east and west, and between Sixth and Fourth streets on the north and south. **Facilities:** Rest rooms (♿). **Activities:** Group tours (reservations available). **Special Features:** Memorial honors the victims, survivors, and rescuers of the Oklahoma City bombing of April 19, 1995. Site includes three separate components: the Outdoor Symbolic Memorial, the Memorial Center, and the National Memorial Institute for the Prevention of Terrorism (www.mipt.org).

★398★ PINELANDS NATIONAL RESERVE

c/o New Jersey Pinelands Commission
15 Springfield Rd, PO Box 7
New Lisbon, NJ 08064
Web: www.nps.gov/pine/
Phone: 609-894-7300; **Fax:** 609-894-7330
Size: 1,164,025 acres (7.8% federal). **History:** Authorized on November 10, 1978, as the nation's first national reserve. Designated a Biosphere Reserve in 1983. Protected by state and federal legislation through management by local, state, and federal governments and the private sector. **Location:** In southern New Jersey. It represents 22% of the state's total land area and includes portions of seven counties (Atlantic, Burlington, Camden, Cape May, Cumberland, Gloucester, and Ocean), and all or parts of 56 municipalities. **Facilities:** Public recreation facilities are provided within state parks and forests. **Activities:** Camping, hiking, fishing, boating, horseback riding, sightseeing. **Special Features:** This area, which is the largest essentially undeveloped tract on the Eastern seaboard, is a unique ecosystem of historic villages and berry farms amid vast oak-pine forests, extensive wetlands, and diverse species of plants and animals.

★399★ PORT CHICAGO NAVAL MAGAZINE NATIONAL MEMORIAL

PO Box 280
Danville, CA 94526
Web: www.nps.gov/poch/
Phone: 925-838-0249; **Fax:** 925-838-9471
History: Authorized on October 28, 1992 **Location:** At the Concord Naval Weapons Station near Concord, California (a one-hour drive from the Oakland/San Francisco area). **Activities:** Guided tour (advanced reservations required). **Special Features:** Memorial recognizes the critical role Port Chicago played in World War II by serving as the main facility for the War in the Pacific. It also commemorates the explosion that occurred at the Port Chicago Naval Magazine on July 17, 1944, which resulted in the largest domestic loss of life during World War II.

See pages 16-17 for map of U.S. National Parks.

1. US National Parks

★400★ RED HILL PATRICK HENRY NATIONAL MEMORIAL
1250 Red Hill Rd
Brookneal, VA 24528
Web: www.redhill.org
Phone: 434-376-2044; **Fax:** 434-376-2647; **Toll Free:** 800-514-7463
Size: 117 acres. **History:** Authorized on May 13, 1986. Owned and operated by the Patrick Henry Memorial Foundation. **Location:** Near Brookneal, Virginia, 35 miles southeast of Lynchburg, accessible via US 501 or VA 40. **Activities:** Guided tour. **Special Features:** The law office and grave of the fiery Virginia patriot, statesman, and orator are preserved at this small plantation along with a reconstruction of Patrick Henry's last home, several dependencies, and a museum.

★401★ ROOSEVELT CAMPOBELLO INTERNATIONAL PARK
PO Box 129
Lubec, ME 04652
Web: www.fdr.net/
Phone: 506-752-2922; **Fax:** 506-752-6000
Size: 2,722 acres. **History:** Established on January 22, 1964. Owned and administered by a United States-Canadian commission. **Location:** On the southern end of Campobello Island in New Brunswick, Canada. It is connected by the FDR International Bridge to Lubec on the easternmost tip of the state of Maine. Lubec is reached by ME 189 from US 1. During the summer, access to Campobello is also available by car ferry from Deer Island, New Brunswick. **Facilities:** Visitor center, theater, rest rooms. **Activities:** Guided and self-guided tours, birdwatching, hiking, sea kayaking, interpretive programs. **Special Features:** Park is a joint memorial by Canada and the United States and a symbol of the close relationship between the two countries. Here are the summer home and the grounds where President Franklin D. Roosevelt vacationed, the waters where he sailed, and the woods, bogs, and beaches where he tramped and relaxed. He was stricken by poliomyelitis here in his summer home at the age of 39.

★402★ SEWALL-BELMONT HOUSE NATIONAL HISTORIC SITE
144 Constitution Ave NE
Washington, DC 20002
Web: www.nps.gov/sebe/
Phone: 202-546-1210; **Fax:** 202-546-3997
Size: 0.35 acres. **History:** Authorized on October 26, 1974. **Location:** On Capitol Hill at the corner of Second St. and Constitution Ave., next to the Hart Senate Office Bldg., in Washington, DC. **Activities:** Group tours (open on a limited basis). **Special Features:** Originally built by Robert Sewall in 1799-1800, and rebuilt after fire damage from the War of 1812, this red brick house is one of the oldest on Capitol Hill. It has been the National Woman's Party headquarters since 1929 and commemorates the party's founder and women's suffrage leader, Alice Paul, and associates.

★403★ THOMAS COLE NATIONAL HISTORIC SITE
218 Spring St
Catskill, NY 12414
Web: www.thomascole.org
Phone: 518-943-7465; **Fax:** 518-943-0652
Size: 3.4 acres. **History:** Established on December 9, 1999. Owned, managed, and operated by the Greene County Historical Society of Greene County, New York. **Location:** At 218 Spring St. in the village of Catskill, New York. **Activities:** Guided tours. **Special Features:** Site includes the Hudson River home and studio of the eminent British-American landscape painter Thomas Cole (1801-1848), who is recognized as the founder of "Hudson River School," America's first indigenous school of landscape painting. Also known as Thomas Cole's Cedar Grove, the site is listed on the *National Register of Historic Places* and has been designated as a National Historic Landmark. Within a 15-mile radius of the Thomas Cole House, an area that forms a key part of the rich cultural and natural heritage of the Hudson River Valley region, significant landscapes and scenes painted by Thomas Cole and other Hudson River artists, such as Frederic Church, survive intact.

★404★ TOURO SYNAGOGUE NATIONAL HISTORIC SITE
85 Touro St
Newport, RI 02840
Web: www.tourosynagogue.org
Phone: 401-847-4794; **Fax:** 401-847-8121
Size: 0.23 acres. **History:** Designated on March 5, 1946. Owned by Congregation Shearith Israel, New York City. The National Park Service lends technical assistance for preservation of the building under a cooperative agreement with two congregations (Shearith Israel and Jeshuat Israel). **Location:** In Newport, Rhode Island. **Activities:** Guided tour. **Special Features:** Dedicated in 1762, it is the oldest synagogue in the United States and the only one that survives from the colonial era. Designed by noted colonial architect Peter Harrison, the synagogue is the present-day place of worship of Congregation Jeshuat Israel.

See pages 16-17 for map of U.S. National Parks.

2. CANADIAN NATIONAL PARKS

★405★ PARKS CANADA
25 Eddy St
Gatineau, Québec
Canada K1A 0M5
819-997-0055 - Phone
888-773-8888 - Toll-free for North America
Web: www.pc.gc.ca

Manages a system of national parks, national marine conservation areas, national historic sites and other heritage places, ensuring their long-term integrity, while encouraging public understanding and appreciation of Canada's heritage and history. There are 42 national parks, representing 28 of Canada's 39 distinct natural regions, and there are two operating sites in the national marine conservation areas system representing two of Canada's 29 marine regions. A primary objective of Parks Canada is to complete the national parks system by including at least one national park in each of Canada's natural regions. Work is underway to create these new parks, in cooperation with provinces, territories, aboriginal peoples, other federal departments, interest groups, and the public. Currently, the national parks and park reserves cover nearly 265,000 sq. km or about 2.9% of Canada's total land mass. When the system is complete it will cover just over 3% of Canada.

This section provides information on the individual park units that comprise the Canadian National Park System. Contact information, including mailing address, phone, fax, and web addresses are included for each listing, as well as a brief description of the park area.

Parks Canada National Volunteer Program
25 Eddy Street, 4th Floor
Hull, Quebec
Canada K1A 0M5

★406★ AULAVIK NATIONAL PARK
PO Box 29
Sachs Harbour, NT X0E0Z0
Web: www.pc.gc.ca/pn-np/nt/aulavik
Phone: 867-690-3904; **Fax:** 867-690-4808
Size: 12,200 sq. km. **Established:** 1992. **Location:** On northern Banks Island, the most western island of the Canadian Arctic Archipelago. Access is by air charter from Inuvik, which has daily air service from southern Canada. Sachs Harbour, the only community on Banks Island, is located 250 km southwest of the park. **Facilities:** None. **Activities:** Backcountry camping, hiking, rafting, canoeing, wildlife viewing, bird-watching. **Special Features:** Park features pristine Arctic wilderness, including broad river valleys, sheer cliffs, and rugged desert-like badlands. The Thomsen River, Canada's most northerly navigable river, provides more than 150 km for wilderness rafting and canoeing. Park includes a variety of wildlife, including a thriving population of more than 68,000 muskoxen and a stable population of the endangered Peary caribou that pass through each year as they migrate between their wintering grounds and summer calving grounds. The Banks Island Migratory Bird Sanctuary protects Brant and lesser snow geese sedge meadow molting habitat, and more than 40 other species of birds have been observed. Within the park boundaries there are more than 230 archeological sites that suggest the presence of human life in this part of the Arctic dates back more than 4,000 years.

★407★ AUYUITTUQ NATIONAL PARK
PO Box 353
Pangnirtung, NU X0A0R0
Web: www.pc.gc.ca/pn-np/ab/auyuittuq
Phone: 867-473-8828; **Fax:** 867-473-8612
Size: 19,089 sq. km. **Established:** 1972. Status was elevated from national park reserve to full-fledged national park in 1999. **Location:** Situated almost entirely above the Arctic Circle, on the north shore of Baffin Island's Cumberland Peninsula. Most visitors enter Auyuittuq through the park's southern entrance at Overlord, a 28-km trip from the community of Pangnirtung. Travel to the park from either Pangnirtung or Qikitarjuaq can be arranged with local outfitters; travel is either by boat or snowmobile, depending on the season. **Facilities:** Visitor center, boat charter, hiking trails. **Activities:** Camping, hiking, mountain climbing, fishing, cross-country skiing, snowmobiling, wildlife viewing (including whale watching). The majority of park visitors come in July and August and spend most of their time in the southern part of the park. **Special Features:** Auyuittuq (''the land that never melts'') is a rugged mountain tundra park featuring active glaciers, deep valleys, spectacular fjords, and many species of arctic mammals and birds. Park is dominated by the Penny Ice Cap, which covers one-third of the park area and is a vestige of the last Ice Age. With ice as thick as 300 meters in places, the ice cap provides an excellent record of past climates and has been the base for several major scientific studies into climate change and global warming. Auyuittuq has a rich legacy of prehistoric and historic cultural resources that tell the story of occupation by the modern Inuit and their ancestors for thousands of years.

★408★ BANFF NATIONAL PARK
Box 900
Banff, AB T1L1K2
Web: www.pc.gc.ca/pn-np/ab/banff
Phone: 403-762-1550; **Fax:** 403-762-3380; **Toll Free:** 877-737-3783

See pages 18-19 for map of Canadian National Parks.

Size: 6,641 sq. km. **Established:** 1885. **Location:** In the Canadian Rocky Mountains on the Alberta side of the Continental Divide, 128 km west of Calgary and 401 km southwest of Edmonton. The Trans-Canada Highway runs west from Calgary into the park and through Banff and Lake Louise, then continues west towards Vancouver. Buses to Banff and Lake Louise run year round. The 230-km Icefields Parkway connects Lake Louise with Jasper National Park (see separate entry for description). **Facilities:** Visitor centers, Banff Springs Hotel, park museum (established in 1895), 13 campgrounds, hot springs, rustic shelters, commercial backcountry lodges, Alpine Club of Canada huts, trails (1600+ km), commercial horse outfitters, and numerous guide services. The resort towns of Banff and Lake Louise are located in the park and each offers visitors a full range of services and facilities, including information centers. The Cave and Basin National Historic Site in Banff commemorates the establishment, growth, and development of Canada's national parks through interactive displays and exhibits. **Activities:** Camping, hiking, horseback riding, mountain biking, fishing (permit required), canoeing, kayaking, rafting, wildlife viewing, scenic touring, mountaineering, rock climbing, interpretive programs, guided tours, cross-country skiing, skating, snowshoeing. **Special Features:** Founded in 1885 following the discovery of the Cave and Basin Hot Springs, Banff is Canada's oldest and most famous national park, and is part of the UNESCO Rocky Mountain Parks World Heritage Site. It includes a variety of outstanding geological and ecological features, including rugged mountains, glaciers, icefields, alpine meadows, lakes, mineral hot springs, deep canyons and hoodoos. Its diverse wildlife features 53 species of mammals, including elk, bighorn sheep, black and grizzly bear, wolf, coyote, caribou, and mountain lion. The Castleguard Caves in the remote northwest corner of the park form Canada's longest cave system.

★409★ BRUCE PENINSULA NATIONAL PARK

20 Centennial Dr Hwy 6
PO Box 189
Tobermory, ON N0H2R0
Web: www.pc.gc.ca/pn-np/on/bruce
Phone: 519-596-2233; **Fax:** 519-596-2298
Size: 154 sq. km. **Established:** 1987. **Location:** On the northern tip of the Bruce Peninsula, between Georgian Bay and Lake Huron, in eastern Ontario. Accessible from the south along Highway 6 or from the north via Ontario Northland Ferry M.S. Chi-Cheemaun, which operates during the spring, summer and fall. Area is also accessible by private boat or by plane. **Facilities:** Campgrounds and backcountry campsites, hiking trails, interpretive centers. The village of Tobermory, 11 km northwest of Cyprus Lake, provides medical services, stores, private campgrounds, lodgings, and groceries. A full range of visitor services is also available along Highway 6. **Activities:** Hiking, camping (year-round), swimming, fishing, canoeing, kayaking, cross-country skiing, snowshoeing, wildlife and wildflower viewing, interpretive and educational programs. **Special Features:** Park protects a rugged limestone landscape and one of the largest remaining tracts of forest in southern Ontario. Its shoreline cliffs are part of Ontario's ''Great Wall'', the Niagara Escarpment, a World Biosphere Reserve that runs from Niagara Falls to Tobermory. The park features a 20-km segment of the Bruce Trail, which follows the Niagara Escarpment for 782 kms. Plant life in the park includes 43 species of orchids and more than 20 varieties of ferns, including the rare northern holly fern.

★410★ CAPE BRETON HIGHLANDS NATIONAL PARK

Ingonish Beach, NS B0C1L0
Web: www.pc.gc.ca/pn-np/ns/cbreton
Phone: 902-224-2306; **Fax:** 902-285-2866
Size: 948 sq. km. **Established:** 1936. **Location:** Park stretches across the northern tip of Cape Breton Island between the Gulf of St. Lawrence and the Atlantic Ocean. Entrances are located on the Cabot Trail north of Cheticamp (west side of the Island) and at Ingonish Beach (east). **Facilities:** Visitor center, 25 hiking trails, 6 campgrounds (including full hookups and showers), exhibits, 18-hole golf course. **Activities:** Hiking, camping (year-round), ocean and freshwater swimming, fishing, nature and interpretive programs, wildlife viewing, cross-country skiing (40 km of trails), tobogganing, bicycling, golfing, tennis. **Special Features:** Park is known for its spectacular highlands and ocean scenery. The first national park established in the Atlantic provinces features some of the last remaining protected wilderness in Nova Scotia. The 113-km Cabot Trail traverses the park from Chéticamp to Ingonish, offering numerous lookoffs, roadside exhibits, walking trails, and scenic side routes.

★411★ ELK ISLAND NATIONAL PARK

Site 4 RR 1
Fort Saskatchewan, AB T8L2N7
Web: www.pc.gc.ca/pn-np/ab/elkisland
Phone: 780-992-2950; **Fax:** 780-992-2951
Size: 194 sq. km. **Established:** 1906. **Location:** 35 km east of Edmonton, Alberta, on Yellowhead Hwy 16 east. **Facilities:** Visitor center, 2 campgrounds, 11 trails (90 km;&), picnic areas, restrooms, boat launch, 9-hole golf course. Services and facilities are concentrated in Astotin Lake area. **Activities:** Camping, hiking, wildlife viewing, boating, cross-country skiing, snowshoeing, golfing, environmental education programs. **Special Features:** Elk Island is one of four national parks that represent the Southern Boreal Plains and Plateau natural region. It protects a portion of the transitional grassland ecosystem, a landscape that once stretched across the central portion of the continent. In addition to wildlife that includes plains and wood bison, elk, moose, deer, coyote, and beaver, park is home to 250+ bird species.

★412★ FATHOM FIVE NATIONAL MARINE PARK

Box 189
Tobermory, ON N0H2R0
Web: www.pc.gc.ca/amnc-nmca/on/fathomfive
Phone: 519-596-2233; **Fax:** 519-596-2298
Size: 112 sq. km. **Established:** 1987. **Location:** At the tip of the Bruce Peninsula, accessible from the south along Highway 6 (four hours from Toronto) or from the north via Ontario Northland Ferry M.S. Chi-Cheemaun, which operates during the spring, summer, and fall. **Facilities:** Visitor center, diver registration center, and public facilities (on Flowerpot Island only) including docks, picnic shelter, hiking trails, and 6 campsites. **Activities:** Scuba diving, snorkeling, kayaking, swimming,

See pages 18-19 for map of Canadian National Parks.

hiking, bird watching, glass-bottom boat tours to Flowerpot Island (spring-fall), dive charters, interpretive programs (June-September). **Special Features:** Canada's first national marine park protects 22 islands at the mouth of Georgian Bay and a main ecosystem that extends from the surface water down 200 meters. The remains of 22 known sail and steam vessels from the mid-19th to the early 20th century lie within the park boundaries and may be viewed by diving or from one of the glass-bottom tours boats operating out of Tobermory. Flowerpot Island and the picturesque rock formations from which it derived its name are among Canada's most recognized and most popular natural attractions. Bruce Peninsula National Park is located nearby (see separate entry for description).

★413★ FORILLON NATIONAL PARK

122 Gaspe Blvd
Gaspe, QC G4X1A9
Web: www.pc.gc.ca/pn-np/qc/forillon
Phone: 418-368-5505; **Fax:** 418-368-6837; **Toll Free:** 888-773-8888
Size: 217 sq. km. **Established:** 1970. **Location:** At the eastern tip of the Gaspé Peninsula, accessible via Highway 132. **Facilities:** Visitor center, interpretation center, 367 semi-serviced campsites, group campground, 2 backcountry campgrounds, trails, exhibits, observation tower, amphitheater, playground area. **Activities:** Camping, hiking, bicycling, horseback riding, fishing, swimming, sea kayaking, scuba diving, snorkeling, wildlife viewing (including whale watching cruise), cross-country skiing, snowshoeing, dogsledding, snowmobiling (limited), interpretive programs. **Special Features:** Forillon takes in a narrow, mountainous peninsula that extends into the Gulf of St. Lawrence and marks the eastern end of the Appalachian mountain chain. Even though forest covers 95% of the park's land area, Forillon is noted for the diversity of its plant life, which can be partially attributed to the presence of 10 separate ecosystems. The park's 696 plant species include botanical communities such as the arctic-alpine flora of the cliffs, the plants of the salt marsh, and the vegetation of the dunes. More than 225 nesting and visiting species of land birds have been observed in the park, as well as grey seals and harbor seals, porpoises and dolphins, 7 species of whales, and several species of land mammals. The peninsula's prominent feature is the lighthouse at Pointe-au-Pere National Historic Site, which rises 30 meters above the St. Lawrence, guiding navigators past the formidable headland.

★414★ FUNDY NATIONAL PARK

PO Box 1001
Alma, NB E4H1B4
Web: www.pc.gc.ca/pn-np/nb/fundy
Phone: 506-887-6000; **Fax:** 506-887-6008; **Toll Free:** 877-737-3783
Size: 206 sq. km. **Established:** 1948. **Location:** Near the village of Alma in southeastern New Brunswick on the Bay of Fundy. From Fredericton, take Trans-Canada Hwy 2 east towards Moncton, then take Hwy 114 at exit 432; from Saint John, take Hwy 1 east, then Trans-Canada Hwy 2 east towards Moncton, and Hwy 114 at exit 432; and from Moncton, travel southwest on Hwy 114. **Facilities:** Visitor center (&), 4 frontcountry campgrounds (600+ sites), 13 backcountry and 4 group campgrounds (&), 53 housekeeping chalets, 20 motel units, 20-bed hostel, restaurant (&), hiking trails and walking trails (104 km.), 9-hole golf course, tennis courts, heated saltwater pool (&), lawn bowling greens, adventure playground, flower gardens. **Activities:** Camping, hiking, boating, swimming, mountain biking, golfing, cross-country skiing, interpretive programs (June-September), birdwatching, wildlife viewing. **Special Features:** Situated where the Caledonia Highlands meet the Bay of Fundy, park encompasses some of the last remaining wilderness in southern New Brunswick. The tidal fluctuation of the Bay of Fundy can be as much as 12 meters, the highest in the world. Because of its location along the Atlantic migration flyway, park is often the site of spectacular bird migrations in the spring and fall, and 255 species have been sighted in the park.

★415★ GEORGIAN BAY ISLANDS NATIONAL PARK

911 Wye Valley Rd
Box 9
Midland, ON L4R4K6
Web: www.pc.gc.ca/pn-np/on/georg
Phone: 705-526-9804; **Fax:** 705-526-5939
Size: 25.6 sq. km. **Established:** 1929. **Location:** 2 hours north of Toronto. Take Hwy. 400 north from Toronto to Muskoka Road 5 (Exit 156), then turn left on Muskoka Road 5 to Honey Harbour. Access is by boat only. Privately owned water taxis operate out of Honey Harbour. **Facilities:** Visitor center and 11 campgrounds (on Beausoleil Island), marina and other visitor services (in nearby town of Honey Harbour), boat dockage, trails, sand beaches, picnic areas. **Activities:** Boating, sailing, fishing, swimming, snorkeling, canoeing/kayaking, hiking, camping, bicycling, wildlife viewing, snowshoeing, cross-country skiing, interpretive programs. **Special Features:** Located in the transition zone between the northern Canadian Shield and the hardwood forests of the southern Great Lakes, the park's islands are home to both northern and southern species of plants and animals, and include the greatest diversity of reptiles and amphibians found in any Canadian national park.

★416★ GLACIER NATIONAL PARK

PO Box 350
Revelstoke, BC V0E2S0
Web: www.pc.gc.ca/pn-np/bc/glacier/index_E.asp
Phone: 250-837-7500; **Fax:** 250-837-7536
Size: 1,349 sq. km. **Established:** 1886. **Location:** On the Trans-Canada Hwy in south-central British Columbia. The nearest communities are Golden, 80 km to the east, and Revelstoke, 72 km to the west. Both Vancouver and Calgary have regular bus service to Rogers Pass, located in the heart of the park. **Facilities:** Visitor center, 50-room hotel (at Rogers Pass; open year-round), 2 frontcountry campgrounds (80 sites), 3 backcountry campsites, 3 backcountry cabins, 18 hiking trails (200 km), boardwalk. Heather Mountain Lodge, located 23 km east of Rogers Pass summit on the park boundary, includes 20 rooms and a restaurant. **Activities:** Camping, hiking, fishing (permit required), bicycling, mountain climbing, skiing, wildlife viewing, scenic touring, interpretive and educational programs. **Special Features:** Featuring more than 400 glaciers, park protects an

See pages 18-19 for map of Canadian National Parks.

area of the Selkirk and Purcell mountain ranges, including critical habitats for threatened and endangered wildlife species such as the grizzly bear and the mountain caribou. More than half of the park lies in the alpine tundra zone - above the limit of tree growth - with the rest of the park encompassing subalpine forests and meadows. Glacier's steep terrain and heavy snowfall have given the park a reputation as one of North America's premier road-accessible ski touring destinations from December to April. Rogers Pass in Glacier National Park has been designated a National Historic Site in commemoration of its role as an essential, yet perilous, link in the building of the transcontinental railway.

★417★ GRASSLANDS NATIONAL PARK

PO Box 150
Val Marie, SK S0N2T0
Web: www.pc.gc.ca/pn-np/sk/grasslands
Phone: 306-298-2257; **Fax:** 306-298-2042
Size: Planned for 906 sq. km. when fully established (land acquisition is about 50% complete). **Established:** 1981. **Location:** In southwestern Saskatchewan near the Saskatchewan-Montana border. The park's West Block centers on the Frenchman River Valley and can be accessed near the village of Val Marie (1.5-hour drive south of Swift Current) on Hwy. 4. The park's East Block centers on the Killdeer Badlands and can be accessed near the town of Wood Mountain on Hwy 18. **Facilities:** Visitor center, 8 hiking trails, no designated campgrounds in park. Village of Val Marie provides limited essential service such as groceries, restaurant, fuel and accommodations near the West Block of the park. Similar services are available in the villages of Glentworth and Wood Mountain, the nearest towns to the East Block. **Activities:** Primitive camping, hiking, horseback riding, bird watching, wildlife viewing, cross-country skiing, nature photography, self-guided auto tour, interpretive programs (limited). **Special Features:** One of the largest pieces of virtually undisturbed mixed-grass prairie in North America, park supports a wide range of fauna, including species rarely found elsewhere in the country. Park is located on the site where Sir George Mercier Dawson made the first recorded discovery of dinosaur remains in 1874 and where Sitting Bull and his Sioux followers took refuge from the U.S. Army after the battle of the Little Big Horn in 1876.

★418★ GROS MORNE NATIONAL PARK

PO Box 130
Rocky Harbour, NL A0K4N0
Web: www.pc.gc.ca/pn-np/nl/grosmorne
Phone: 709-458-2417; **Fax:** 709-458-2059; **Toll Free:** 877-737-3783
Size: 1,805 sq. km. **Established:** 1973. **Location:** On the west coast of the island of Newfoundland. If driving from the Canadian mainland, the shortest and fastest way to the park is via the ferry service between North Sydney and Port aux Basques. It is 300 km from Port aux Basques to the park entrance at Wiltondale, which is about a four-hour drive. **Facilities:** Visitor center (Rocky Harbour), Discovery Center (Woody Point), 5 frontcountry campgrounds and 7 wilderness campgrounds, trails (100+ km), swimming pool. **Activities:** Camping, hiking, boating, kayaking, fishing, swimming, wildlife and bird watching,

cross-country skiing, boat tours, interpretive programs, live theater. **Special Features:** Park protects Newfoundland's western highlands and Gulf of Saint Lawrence lowlands, and features rugged coastline, mountains, glacier-carved fjords, and ocean inlets and lakes. The park is considered a textbook illustration of plate tectonics, and due to its unique geological features, it was designated a UNESCO World Heritage Site in 1987. Its array of flora and fauna includes more than 25 species of land mammals, 239 species of birds, and more than 700 species of flowering plants.

★419★ GULF ISLANDS NATIONAL PARK RESERVE

2220 Harbour Rd
Sidney, BC V8L2P6
Web: www.pc.gc.ca/pn-np/bc/gulf
Phone: 250-654-4000; **Fax:** 250-654-4014
Size: 35 sq. km. **Established:** 2003. **Location:** Situated in the southern Strait of Georgia to the southeast of Vancouver Island (British Columbia), park is spread out over 15 islands and includes numerous islets and reefs. British Columbia Ferries provides vehicle and passenger service to Mayne Island, Saturna Island and North and South Pender Islands through their Southern Gulf Islands routes from the Swartz Bay (Vancouver Island) and Tsawwassen (Vancouver) ferry terminals. All other areas of the park are accessible only via powerboat, sailboat or kayak. **Facilities:** Services and facilities for visitors are limited. Parks Canada is working to develop a national park management plan that will take several years to complete. Privately-operated tourist services outside of the park are available on Saturna, Mayne, and North and South Pender islands. Arrangements for overnight accommodation on these islands should be made in advance. Fees are charged for campsites and overnight dockspace and mooring buoys. **Activities:** Camping, hiking, boating, and kayaking. **Special Features:** Located between BC's largest urban centers, Vancouver and Victoria, the islands and surrounding waters are key attractions for local residents and visitors. They provide habitat for great blue heron, numerous shorebirds and waterfowl, and haul-outs for harbour seals and sea lions.

★420★ GWAII HAANAS NATIONAL PARK RESERVE/HAIDA HERITAGE SITE

PO Box 37
Queen Charlotte, BC V0T1S0
Web: www.pc.gc.ca/pn-np/bc/gwaiihaanas
Phone: 250-559-8818; **Fax:** 250-559-8366
Size: 1,474 sq. km. of land on 138 islands. **Established:** 1988. **Location:** In the southern part of Haida Gwaii (Queen Charlotte Islands), a remote archipelago off the British Columbia coast, 640 km north of Vancouver. It is accessible only by boat or float plane. **Facilities:** Limited (no trails or designated campsites). Haida Gwaii Watchmen basecamps have been established at major sites of cultural and natural significance. Watchmen provide site security and protection of the cultural features, and also provide visitors with the opportunity to hear firsthand of the living Haida culture. **Activities:** Sea kayaking, boating, fishing (license required), hiking, camping, wildlife viewing. More than 50 commercial operators offer services in the Archipelago from May-September. Independent travellers to Gwaii Haanas must make an advance reservation or obtain a stand-by space. **Special**

See pages 18-19 for map of Canadian National Parks.

Features: The rugged San Christoval Mountains, rocky coastline, and the remnants of native village sites offer a unique experience combining wilderness, solitude, spirituality and Haida culture. One of the finest old-growth temperate rainforests left on the Pacific coast remains relatively intact. Diversity of wildlife includes gray whales (migrating north during the spring), killer whales, humpback, sei, finback and minke whales, dolphins, porpoises, and harbor seals. Gwaii Haanas also includes an estimated 750,000 nesting seabirds and a large breeding colony of Steller's sea lions, located near Cape St. James.

★421★ IVVAVIK NATIONAL PARK
Western Arctic Field Unit
PO Box 1840
Inuvik, NT X0E0T0
Web: www.pc.gc.ca/pn-np/yt/ivvavik
Phone: 867-777-8800; **Fax:** 867-777-8820
Size: 9,750 sq. km. **Established:** 1984. **Location:** On the north slope of the Yukon Territory. Access to the park is by air charter service from Inuvik, NT, which is 200 km east of the park. Inuvik, the largest community in the region, has daily flights from southern Canada and may also be reached via the Dempster Highway. **Facilities:** None. **Activities:** The most popular recreational activity in Ivvavik is whitewater rafting on the Firth River, which includes 130 navigable km from Margaret Lake to the Beaufort Sea. The rapids range from Class I to Class IV. Other activities include backcountry camping, hiking, wildlife viewing, fishing, and kayaking. **Special Features:** Ivvavik is the first national park in Canada to be established as a result of an Aboriginal land claim settlement. It encompasses a variety of arctic and subarctic ecosystems, which range from the height of land in the south, through mountains, foothills, and river valleys to the coastal plain and the Beaufort Sea. Park is the summer home of the 125,000+ Porcupine caribou herd, which migrates annually from the forested valleys of north-central Yukon to calving grounds on the Beaufort coast. Spring migration peaks at the end of May and early June. Archeologists have discovered the remains of eight distinct cultures that have traveled through the northern Yukon and there is evidence that human habitation could extend back 30,000 years.

★422★ JASPER NATIONAL PARK
PO Box 10
Jasper, AB T0E1E0
Web: www.pc.gc.ca/pn-np/ab/jasper
Phone: 780-852-6176; **Fax:** 780-852-5601; **Toll Free:** 877-737-3783
Size: 10,878 sq. km. **Established:** 1907. **Location:** On the eastern slopes of the Rocky Mountains of west-central Alberta, 370 km west of Edmonton along the Yellowhead Hwy 16, and 404 km northwest of Calgary via Trans-Canada Hwy 1 and the Icefields Parkway (Hwy 93). The town of Jasper is located in the middle of the park. **Facilities:** The townsite of Jasper includes a variety of hotels, restaurants, shops, gas stations, grocery and convenience stores, park information center, and a tramway. Park facilities also include 10 campgrounds (1770+ campsites; &), hot springs, and trails (1000 km). **Activities:** Camping, hiking, swimming, fishing, boating, bicycling, scenic driving,

wildlife viewing, horseback riding, climbing and mountaineering, cross-country skiing, downhill skiing, ice skating, snowboarding, snowshoeing, interpretive programs. **Special Features:** Jasper is the largest and most northerly of the four Canadian Rocky Mountain national parks that comprise the UNESCO World Heritage Site. It is located at the northern end of the spectacular Icefields Parkway, a 230-km scenic route that passes close to the Columbia Icefield and connects Jasper with Lake Louise in Banff National Park (see separate entry). Along the way, visitors can take a snocoach tour on the Athabasca Glacier, one of six large glaciers that cover more than 325 sq. km of mountain park. Park's rugged topography includes a number of mountains that rise to elevations above 3,000 meters, including Mt. Columbia, Alberta's highest peak at 3,782 meters. Among the five national historic sites located within the park's boundaries are the Jasper House (1813) and the Henry House (1811).

★423★ KEJIMKUJIK NATIONAL PARK
PO Box 236
Maitland Bridge, NS B0T1B0
Web: www.pc.gc.ca/pn-np/ns/kejimkujik
Phone: 902-682-2772; **Fax:** 902-682-3367; **Toll Free:** 877-737-3783
Size: 404 sq. km. **Established:** 1967. **Location:** Off Route 8 (Kejimkujik Scenic Drive), which traverses southwestern Nova Scotia between Liverpool and Annapolis Royal. The Seaside Adjunct is located off Hwy 103, 25 km southwest of Liverpool. **Facilities:** Visitor center, 360 regular campsites (Jeremys Bay), primitive campsites, canoe and bicycle rental, boat launch, viewing tower. **Activities:** Camping, hiking, canoeing (including guided trips), swimming, fishing, bicycling, guided walks, wildlife viewing, cross-country skiing, interpretive programs. **Special Features:** Park's numerous lakes and rivers afford some of the finest canoeing in eastern Canada. The Seaside Adjunct, a 22 sq km area on Nova Scotia's south shore, is noted for its abundant wildlife and spectacular scenery. More than 200 species of birds can be found within Kejimkujik and the park is also the most important national park for reptiles in Atlantic Canada, featuring five species of snakes and three species of turtles.

★424★ KLUANE NATIONAL PARK AND RESERVE
PO Box 5495
Haines Junction, YT Y0B1L0
Web: www.pc.gc.ca/pn-np/yt/kluane
Phone: 867-634-7250; **Fax:** 867-634-7208
Size: 22,061 sq. km. **Established:** 1972. **Location:** In the southwestern corner of the Yukon, near Haines Junction. The Alaska and Haines highways skirt the eastern boundary of the park along the frontal Kluane National Park & Reserve ranges. Visitors can reach Haines Junction by driving 160 km west of Whitehorse on the Alaska Highway, or by driving 249 km north of Haines, Alaska on the Haines Road. Whitehorse is serviced by daily commercial flights originating in Vancouver. There are also regular flights from Anchorage, Fairbanks and Juneau. **Facilities:** Visitor centers at Haines Junction (open mid-May to mid-September; &) and near Sheep Mountain (open year-round; &), campgrounds (most open from mid-May to mid-September),

See pages 18-19 for map of Canadian National Parks.

day-use area (at Kathleen Lake), hiking trails (ᔤ). **Activities:** Camping, hiking, guided walks and interpretive programs, mountain biking, horseback riding, fishing (license required), boating and canoeing, rafting (on the Alsek River), flying over the Icefield ranges, mountain climbing, wildlife viewing, cross-country skiing, snowshoeing, dog sledding, and snowmobiling. **Special Features:** Park is a land of high mountains, large icefields, and lush lower valleys that protect the greatest diversity of plant and wildlife in northern Canada. Mount Logan (5,959m; 19,545'), the highest mountain in Canada and the second highest peak in North America, is located within the park. The contiguous protected regions of Kluane National Park & Reserve, Wrangell-St. Elias and Glacier Bay national parks in Alaska (see separate entries), and the Tatshenshini-Alsek Provincial Park in British Columbia form the largest international protected area in the world and are recognized as a UNESCO World Heritage Site.

★425★ KOOTENAY NATIONAL PARK

PO Box 220
Radium Hot Springs, BC V0A1M0
Web: www.pc.gc.ca/pn-np/bc/kootenay
Phone: 250-347-9505; **Fax:** 250-347-9980; **Toll Free:** 877-737-3783
Size: 1,406 sq. km. **Established:** 1920. **Location:** Park lies in the southeastern corner of British Columbia, 888 km east of Vancouver and 170 km west of Calgary. It can be reached from the north at two access points on the Trans-Canada Highway: Castle Junction in Banff National Park (via Highway 93 South - the Kootenay Parkway) or Golden (via Highway 95); or from the south via Highway 93/95. The closest full service towns are Radium Hot Springs, just outside the park's West Gate, and Banff, 33 km east of the park's north entrance. **Facilities:** Kootenay Lodge (10 cabins and restaurant; open mid-May to late September), visitor centers at Radium Hot Springs and Vermilion Crossing, 4 campgrounds, 200+ km of trails, Radium Hot Springs Pools complex. **Activities:** Camping, hiking, mountaineering and climbing, wildlife viewing, boating, canoeing, rafting, fishing, mountain biking, horseback riding, interpretive programs, cross-country skiing, and snowshoeing. **Special Features:** Park is noted for its remarkable diversity of climate and landscape, from glacier-clad peaks along the Continental Divide in the north, to the dry, grassy slopes of the Columbia Valley in the south, where even cactus grows. Kootenay, Yoho, Banff and Jasper national parks, and Mt. Robson, Mt. Assiniboine and Hamber provincial parks, form UNESCO's Rocky Mountain Parks World Heritage Site, one of the world's largest protected wilderness areas. Open year-round, the Radium Hot Springs facility is home to Canada's largest hot springs pool.

★426★ KOUCHIBOUGUAC NATIONAL PARK

186 Rt 117
Kouchibouguac, NB E4X2P1
Web: www.pc.gc.ca/pn-np/nb/kouchibouguac
Phone: 506-876-2443; **Fax:** 506-876-4802; **Toll Free:** 877-737-3783
Size: 239 sq. km. **Established:** 1969. **Location:** On New Brunswick's central eastern shore in an area known as the Acadian Coastal Drive. It is located in Kent County, a one-hour drive north of Moncton or a four-hour drive from the Quebec border. Take Highway 15 to Shediac and then either Highway 11 heading north, or the more scenic Route 134. **Facilities:** Visitor center, frontcountry and backcountry campgrounds, group tenting area, nature trails, cycling paths (60 km), beaches and beach boardwalks, bicycle and boat rentals. **Activities:** Camping, hiking, bicycling, canoeing, kayaking, paddle boating, bird watching, wildlife viewing, cross-country skiing, snowshoeing, tobogganing, interpretive programs. **Special Features:** Park protect a unique ecosystem of sandy barrier islands on the Northumberland Strait, characterized by lagoons, bogs, salt marshes, beaches, dunes, and tall forests, and set on Canada's warmest ocean waters. Park features the second largest tern colony in North America. The Voyageur Canoe Program offers visitors the opportunity to explore isolated barrier islands where they'll see harbor and grey seals.

★427★ LA MAURICIE NATIONAL PARK

702 5th St
PO Box 160
Shawinigan, QC G9N6T9
Web: www.pc.gc.ca/pn-np/qc/mauricie
Phone: 819-538-3232; **Fax:** 819-536-3661; **Toll Free:** 877-737-3783
Size: 536 sq. km. **Established:** 1970. **Location:** 50 km north of the Saint Lawrence River, approximately 200 km from Montréal, 190 km from Québec City, and 60 km from Trois Rivieres. A good portion of the park is situated in the heart of the Laurentian Mountains. **Facilities:** 2 lodges (Andrew and Wabenaki), visitor center, 580+ campsites, trails (80 km, ᔤ), canoe and boat rental, boat ramps. **Activities:** Hiking, camping (year-round), swimming, canoeing, fishing, mountain biking, cross-country skiing, wildlife viewing, interpretive programs. **Special Features:** Park typifies the region of the Lauretians, a range of low mountains bordering the Saint Lawrence River along its entire course from the Great Lakes to Labrador. It includes a section of the Laurentian Trail and more than 150 lakes, including the 16-km-long Wapizagonke Lake. The diverse wildlife includes 50 species of mammals, 180 species of birds, 29 species of fish, and 19 species of reptiles and amphibians.

★428★ MINGAN ARCHIPELAGO NATIONAL PARK RESERVE

1340 de la Digue St
Havre-Saint-Pierre, QC G0G1P0
Web: www.pc.gc.ca/pn-np/qc/mingan
Phone: 418-538-3331; **Fax:** 418-538-3595; **Toll Free:** 888-773-8888
Size: 151 sq. km, comprising a coastal chain of some 1000 islands and islets. **Established:** 1984. **Location:** At Havre-Saint-Pierre, 870 km east of Québec City, along the north shore of the Gulf of Saint Lawrence. Lies between the mouths of the Saint-Jean River to the west and the Aguanish River to the east. Take Hwy 138 from Québec City. **Facilities:** Visitor/interpretive center (Havre-Saint-Pierre), Minganie Research and Interpretation Centre (Longue-Pointe-de-Mingan), campgrounds, hiking trails. **Activities:** Camping, hiking, sea kayaking, scuba diving, boat tours (May-October), bird watching, whale watching, guided hikes, interpretive programs. **Special Features:** Park's

See pages 18-19 for map of Canadian National Parks.

dramatic topography features Canada's largest concentration of shoreline arches and grottoes as well as distinctive 500-million-year-old limestone monoliths. More than 200 species of birds can be seen on the islands, including the Atlantic puffin and the common eider. Park also features three types of seals and nine species of cetaceans, including the minke, blue, and humpback whale.

★429★ MOUNT REVELSTOKE NATIONAL PARK

PO Box 350
Revelstoke, BC V0E2S0
Web: www.pc.gc.ca/pn-np/bc/revelstoke
Phone: 250-837-7500; **Fax:** 250-837-7536
Size: 262 sq. km. **Established:** 1914. **Location:** Park is adjacent to the City of Revelstoke, 148 km west of Golden. It is bounded on two sides by highways: The Trans-Canada Highway, which runs just inside the park's boundary for 13 km along the southeast perimeter of the park; and Provincial Highway #23 North, which skirts the park's west edge. **Facilities:** Two backcountry campgrounds, two backcountry cabins, 10 hiking trails; accommodations and services are available in the City of Revelstoke, located 1 km. from the park along the Trans-Canada Highway. **Activities:** Camping, hiking, bicycling, fishing, wildlife viewing, scenic touring, cross-country skiing, snowshoeing, interpretive programs. **Special Features:** The 26-km Meadows-in-the-Sky Parkway winds through forests of cedar and hemlock, spruce and fir to the subalpine wildflower meadows and the summit of Mount Revelstoke. This paved mountain road offers the only opportunity in the Canadian national park system for private vehicles to access a mountaintop environment. Winter is the dominant season and lingers on the summit until July or even August. During the brief summer, the mountaintop explodes into color when its wildflower meadows bloom in mid-August.

★430★ NAHANNI NATIONAL PARK RESERVE

PO Box 348
Fort Simpson, NT X0E0N0
Web: www.pc.gc.ca/pn-np/nt/nahanni
Phone: 867-695-3151; **Fax:** 867-695-2446
Size: 4,766 sq. km. **Established:** 1976. **Location:** In the heart of the Mackenzie Mountains, centered on the river valleys of the South Nahanni and Flat rivers, in the southwest part of the Northwest Territories. Accessible by air charter services from Fort Simpson, Fort Liard, Fort Nelson, Yellowknife, Watson Lake, and Muncho Lake. Virginia Falls and Rabbitkettle Lake are the only designated aircraft landing sites within the park reserve. **Facilities:** Visitor center, primitive campsites (Rabbitkettle Lake, Virginia Falls, and Kraus Hot Springs). **Activities:** Regarded as a premier wilderness river national park, Nahanni affords multi-day whitewater canoeing, kayaking, and rafting trips by licensed outfitters, ranging from ten days to three weeks. Other activities include camping, hiking (including guided hikes), flight-seeing day trips, and wildlife viewing. **Special Features:** In 1978, the park was designated the first ever UNESCO World Heritage Site, because of its spectacular scenery and unique geological features. It protects 200 miles of the 250-mile-long South Nahanni River, which originates as a small stream in the remote Mackenzie Mountains and grows dramatically in size and power as it winds its way through broad river valleys and steep-walled canyons. The river's spectacular scenery includes: Rabbitkettle Hotsprings, source of the largest known tufa mounds in Canada; Virginia Falls, with a vertical drop twice that of Niagara Falls; a series of canyons up to 1200 meters deep; and caves such as Grotte Valerie with its ancient skeletons of nearly a hundred Dall's sheep.

★431★ PACIFIC RIM NATIONAL PARK RESERVE

2185 Ocean Terrace Rd
Box 280
Ucluelet, BC V0R3A0
Web: www.pc.gc.ca/pn-np/bc/pacificrim
Phone: 250-726-7721; **Fax:** 250-726-4720; **Toll Free:** 877-737-3783
Size: 510 sq. km. **Established:** 1970. **Location:** Park is composed of three sections: Long Beach, the West Coast Trail and the Broken Group Islands. The Long Beach Unit is located on the west coast of Vancouver Island between the villages of Ucluelet and Tofino. The West Coast Trail includes the section of coast southeast of Barkley Sound between the villages of Bamfield and Port Renfrew. The Broken Group Islands consist of approximately 100 islands and rocks located in Barkley Sound. **Facilities:** Visitor center, campgrounds, 75-km. West Coast Trail (optional reservation system; mandatory trail use permit). **Activities:** Camping, hiking, canoeing and kayaking, scuba diving, fishing, wildlife viewing, interpretive programs. **Special Features:** Park's marine and forest environment features sand beaches, an island archipelago, old-growth coastal temperate rainforest, and significant archeological sites. The area is home to a variety of marine mammals, including seals, sea lions, and whales. The villages of Ucluelet and Tofino host their annual Whale Festival from mid-March to mid-April to mark the gray whale spring migration north through park waters. Approximately 250 species of birds, mostly spring and fall migrants, have also been identified within the park and bordering areas. The West Coast Trail, one of the best-known and most challenging hikes in North America, follows a rugged shoreline where approximately 66 ships have met their demise along this stretch of the ''Graveyard of the Pacific''.

★432★ POINT PELEE NATIONAL PARK

407 Monarch Ln, RR 1
Leamington, ON N8H3V4
Web: www.pc.gc.ca/pn-np/on/pelee
Phone: 519-322-2365; **Fax:** 519-322-1277; **Toll Free:** 888-773-8888
Size: 15.2 sq. km.(including Middle Island). **Established:** 1918. **Location:** 56 km southeast of Windsor on the most southern point on Canada's mainland — a large sandspit on the north shore of Lake Erie. **Facilities:** Visitor center (&), transit train, observation tower, boardwalk, trails (12 km; &.), theater program and exhibits, interpretive programs, food concession, boat and bicycle rentals. **Activities:** Hiking, swimming, fishing, canoeing, bicycling, skating, bird watching, butterfly watching cross-country skiing. **Special Features:** Point Pelee is one of Canada's smallest national parks, but still attracts nearly 400,000 visitors each year. Each spring, birders from around the world converge on Point Pelee to take part in the ''Festival of Birds.'' The month-long festival celebrates the arrival of some of the

See pages 18-19 for map of Canadian National Parks.

highest concentrations of migrating songbirds found in North America. Park is also a temporary home to thousands of migrating Monarch butterflies in the fall.

★433★ PRINCE ALBERT NATIONAL PARK

PO Box 100
Waskesiu Lake, SK S0J2Y0
Web: www.pc.gc.ca/pn-np/sk/princealbert
Phone: 306-663-4522; **Toll Free:** 877-737-3783
Size: 3,875 sq. km. **Established:** 1927. **Location:** In central Saskatchewan, 80 km north of Prince Albert. Park is accessible by highways 2/264 and 263 (scenic route). **Facilities:** Nature center, regular and backcountry campsites, as well as services and recreational facilities within the townsite of Waskesiu Lake, including lodging, food, and an 18-hole golf course. **Activities:** Camping, hiking, wildlife viewing, canoeing, kayaking, swimming, fishing, bicycling, cross-country skiing, snowshoeing, lake skating, golfing, interpretive programs. **Special Features:** Representative of the transition from aspen parkland to northern boreal forest, park is home to the second largest white pelican breeding colony in Canada and the only one afforded full protection by a national park. One third of Canada's remaining original fescue grasslands, part of a once vast prairie ecosystem, is located in pockets in the southwest corner of the park, where bison roam freely. Park also preserves the cabin of Grey Owl, woodsman, author, and orator who died in 1938.

★434★ PRINCE EDWARD ISLAND NATIONAL PARK

2 Palmers Lane
Charlottetown, PE C1A5V6
Web: www.pc.gc.ca/pn-np/pe/pei-ipe
Phone: 902-672-6350; **Fax:** 902-672-6370; **Toll Free:** 877-737-3783
Size: 27 sq. km. **Established:** 1937. **Location:** The park extends 40 km from Dalvay to Cavendish, along the north shore of Prince Edward Island (30 minutes north of Charlottetown). The Greenwich Dune System can be accessed by following Route 2 east through the village of St. Peters and then taking Route 313 to the site. **Facilities:** Visitor centers, 3 campgrounds, group tenting area, trails, 18-hole golf course (in Cavendish). **Activities:** Camping, hiking, bicycling, swimming, fishing, canoeing, kayaking, windsurfing, cross-country skiing, skating, interpretive programs. **Special Features:** Park protects a spectacular system of sand dunes, red sandstone cliffs, saltwater marshes, and 40 km of some of the finest salt-water beaches in Canada. It also features two cultural landmarks: Green Gables House, known internationally through L.M. Montgomery's classic novel, *Anne of Green Gables*; and Dalvay-by-the-Sea Hotel, a historic landmark built in 1895. In 1998, 6 km of the Greenwich Peninsula were added to the Park to protect unique dune formations, rare plants and animals, as well as archaeological findings dating back 10,000 years.

★435★ PUKASKWA NATIONAL PARK

Hwy 627
PO Box 212
Heron Bay, ON P0T1R0
Web: www.pc.gc.ca/pn-np/on/pukaskwa
Phone: 807-229-0801; **Fax:** 807-229-2097

Size: 1,878 sq. km. **Established:** 1978. **Location:** On the north shore of Lake Superior, 25 km east of the town of Marathon in northern Ontario. The only road access to Pukaskwa is at the north end near Hattie Cove. **Facilities:** Visitor center (&), Hattie Cove campground (67 sites, &), backcountry campsites (along Coastal Hiking Trail), interpretive trails, boardwalk. **Activities:** Camping, hiking, canoeing, kayaking, whitewater rafting, fishing, bicycling, interpretive programs, guided hikes (summer). **Special Features:** Pukaskwa is Ontario's only wilderness national park, and its rugged landscape includes volcanic rock, boreal forest, and Lake Superior coastline. The Coastal Hiking Trail meanders for 60 km and offers opportunities to traverse the Canadian Shield.

★436★ QUTTINIRPAAQ NATIONAL PARK

PO Box 278
Iqaluit, NU X0A0H0
Web: www.pc.gc.ca/pn-np/nu/quttinirpaaq
Phone: 867-975-4673; **Fax:** 867-975-4674
Size: 37,775 sq. km. **Established:** 1988. Name was officially changed from Ellesmere Island to Quttinirpaaq and status was elevated from national park reserve to full-fledged national park in 1999. **Location:** Park is situated on the north end of Ellesmere Island, the most northerly island of the Canadian Arctic archipelago. It covers half of the island that is north of Greely Fiord, and a third of the island's northern coastline, which is only 720 km from the North Pole. Park is accessible by plane through Resolute Bay (NWT), the second most northerly community in Canada. First Air offers jet services to Resolute Bay from Iqaluit or Ottawa. From Resolute Bay, charter services are offered to and from the park (a four-hour flight) by Kenn Borek Air. Make reservations well in advance for travel during the summer months. **Facilities:** Limited. **Activities:** Camping, hiking, fishing, dog sledding. Ward Hunt Island, along the park's northern coast, is the launching point for North Pole expeditions (usually in March or April). **Special Features:** Canada's northernmost and second-largest national park protects some of the most remote, fragile, and rugged land in North America with natural features that include high mountains, deeply cut plateaus, polar desert, and arctic tundra. Icefields up to 900 meters (3,000 ft.) thick cloak the mountains in the northern portion of the park. This ice is a remnant of the last continental glaciation that covered most of North America 10,000 years ago. Several ''nunataks'' (peaks protruding through the icecap) stand more than 2,500 meters (8,250 ft.) above sea level. The peak of the nunatak, Mount Barbeau, at 2,616 meters (8,633 ft.) is the highest mountain in eastern North America. Quttinirpaaq National Park is also one of the driest areas of the northern hemisphere, with an annual precipitation of only 6 centimeters (2.5 in.).

★437★ RIDING MOUNTAIN NATIONAL PARK

General Delivery
Wasagaming, MB R0J2H0
Web: www.pc.gc.ca/pn-np/mb/riding
Phone: 204-848-7275; **Fax:** 204-848-2596; **Toll Free:** 800-707-8480
Size: 2,968 sq. km. **Established:** 1933. **Location:** Highway 10 connects Brandon, 95 km to the south, with Wasagaming (the park's visitor services center) and continues to Dauphin, 13 km

See pages 18-19 for map of Canadian National Parks.

beyond the park's northern border. From the east, Highway 19 enters the park through the scenic escarpment region. **Facilities:** Visitor center, 5 family campgrounds, backcountry campsites, 400 km of hiking, biking, and horse trails; Wasagaming, the park's townsite, offers a full range of visitor services including accommodations, restaurants and shopping. **Activities:** Camping, hiking, horseback riding, boating, canoeing, swimming, fishing, wildlife viewing, guided hikes and interpretive programs, junior naturalist program, cross-country skiing, snowmobiling. **Special Features:** Forming part of the Manitoba Escarpment, park is situated at the crossroads where habitats characteristic of eastern, western, and northern Canada meet and mingle in a diverse pattern of forest and grasslands, hills and valleys. It offers the greatest mix of wildlife and plants in southwestern Manitoba, including 60 species of mammals and 260 species of birds. It also features a captive bison herd and some of the highest concentrations of moose and elk in the area.

★438★ SAGUENAY-SAINT LAWRENCE MARINE PARK

182 rue de l'Eglise
PO Box 220
Tadoussac, QC G0T2A0
Web: www.pc.gc.ca/amnc-nmca/qc/saguenay
Phone: 418-235-4703; **Fax:** 418-235-4686
Size: 1,138 sq. km. **Established:** 1990. The first marine conservation park in the Province of Québec is operated jointly by the governments of Québec and Canada. **Location:** At the juncture of the Saguenay River and the Saint Lawrence Estuary, approximately 205 km from Québec City. **Facilities:** Information center, observation sites, trails (96 km), marina, boat launch. **Activities:** Camping, hiking, fishing, boating, sea kayaking, scuba diving, whale watching, interpretive and educational programs. **Special Features:** Park protects the ecosystems of a representative portion of the Saguenay Fjord and the Saint Lawrence Estuary marine environment, an area rich and diverse in marine life. In all, more the 15 marine mammals inhabit the area on a regular basis or use it as a summer feeding ground including the harbor seal, harbor porpoise, beluga whale, minke whale, fin whale, and blue whale. Park also serves as the reproduction, feeding, and staging area for a number species of aquatic birds.

★439★ SAINT LAWRENCE ISLANDS NATIONAL PARK

2 County Rd 5
RR 3
Mallorytown, ON K0E1R0
Web: www.pc.gc.ca/pn-np/on/lawren
Phone: 613-923-5261; **Fax:** 613-923-1021
Size: 23.5 sq. km., including 24 islands, 90 inlets and shoals, and a mailand base. **Established:** 1904. **Location:** In the heart of the Thousand Islands area, an 80-km wide extension of granite hilltops joining the Canadian Shield of northern Ontario with the Adirondack Mountains in New York State. The mainland headquarters (Mallorytown Landing) is located on the Saint Lawrence River between Brockville and Gananoque, Ontario. Travelers on Hwy 401 take exit 675 south; U.S. visitors travel north on I-81 to 1000 Islands Pkwy, then turn east. Access to park islands is by private boat or commercial water taxi (by appointment only). **Facilities:** Saint Lawrence Islands is a water-oriented park with facilities at more than 20 island locations. Many park islands include docks, nature trails, primitive campsites (on 11 islands; available on a first-come-first-served basis), group campsites (on Grenadier Island and Mallorytown; reservations only), privies, and shelters. The day-use area at Mallorytown Landing (♿) includes a small beach, boat launch, picnic area, and restrooms. Exhibits on natural and cultural history are open to the public during the operating season and by appointment during the rest of the year. **Activities:** Camping, hiking, swimming, kayaking, canoeing, boating, boat tours, scuba diving, bicycling, interpretive programs, nature camps for children. Both power and sailboaters use the park islands as stopping off points for a day or overnight enroute down or up the St. Lawrence River. Cedar Island, off Kingston, is a stopover for boaters sailing into Lake Ontario or as a starting off point for cruising up the Rideau Canal. **Special Features:** The first Canadian national park east of the Rocky Mountains is the site of the preserved hull of a British gunboat from the War of 1812, raised from the St. Lawrence River near Mallorytown Landing. The presence of the Great Lakes to the west has the effect of a 'heat sink' which moderates the climate in the area immediately surrounding the Thousand Islands. As a result, many plants and animals reach the limits of their range in the Thousand Islands.

★440★ SIRMILIK NATIONAL PARK

PO Box 300
Pond Inlet, NU XOAOSO
Web: www.pc.gc.ca/pn-np/nu/sirmilik
Phone: 867-899-8092; **Fax:** 867-899-8104
Size: 22,200 sq. km. **Established:** 1999. **Location:** On northern Baffin Island, 700 km north of the Arctic Circle and 600 km west of Greenland in the High Arctic. Travel to and from Sirmilik from either Pond Inlet or Arctic Bay can be arranged with local outfitters, with service by either boat or snowmobile, depending on the season. Travel to Pond Inlet is generally through Iqaluit, the capital of Nunavut, which has direct connections with Montréal, Ottawa, and Yellowknife (First Air Ltd., Canadian North). First Air offers scheduled flights from Iqaluit to both Pond Inlet and Arctic Bay (via Nanisivik). Kenn Borek Air offers scheduled flights to Pond Inlet. **Facilities:** None at the present time. Services are available in Pond Inlet and Arctic Bay, located at the northern end of Baffin Island. **Activities:** Camping, hiking, dogsledding, snowmobiling, boating, canoeing, sea kayaking, fishing, cross-country skiing, wildlife viewing, mountain climbing, visiting archeological sites. **Special Features:** Sirmilik ("The Place of Glaciers") features high sea cliffs, glaciers dropping into the sea, rugged mountains, and deep fjords. It is also one of the richest areas for marine mammals and birds in all of Nunavut. Its marine life includes bowhead and beluga whales, narwhals, walruses, and several types of seals. The park encompasses the Bylot Island Bird Sanctuary, which protect the nesting grounds and large concentrations of snow geese, kittiwakes, and murres. The numerous archeological sites in the park are evidence of the prehistoric lives of Inuit and earlier inhabitants.

See pages 18-19 for map of Canadian National Parks.

★441★ TERRA NOVA NATIONAL PARK

General Delivery
Glovertown, NL A0G2L0
Web: www.pc.gc.ca/pn-np/nl/terranova
Phone: 709-533-2801; **Fax:** 709-533-2706; **Toll Free:** 877-737-3783
Size: 400 sq. km. **Established:** 1957. **Location:** 80 km east of Gander and 240 km west of St. John's. The Trans-Canada Highway runs through the park. **Facilities:** Marine interpretation center (open May-October, &), frontcountry and backcountry campsites, hiking trails (60 km), boat and bicycle rental. **Activities:** Camping, hiking, swimming, sea kayaking, canoeing, boat tours, golfing, bicycling, wildlife viewing, interpretive programs. **Special Features:** Park is representative of the easternmost section of the continent-wide belt of boreal forest zone, with diverse ground vegetation that includes more than 500 species of vascular plants, 200 species of moss, and hundreds of species of lichens. Terra Nova's Marine Interpretation Center includes a touch tank, aquariums, exhibits, interpretive programs, science camps, and videos.

★442★ TORNGAT MOUNTAINS NATIONAL PARK RESERVE

c/o Parks Canada
25 Eddy St
Gatineau, QC K1A0M5
Phone: 888-773-8888
Size: 9,700 sq. km. **Established:** 2005. It is expected that the national park reserve will move to full national park status in the near future, when a Park Impacts and Benefits Agreement is completed with the Nunavik Inuit of northern Quebec, who also have a land claim to the area of the national park reserve that has been accepted for negotiation by Canada. **Location:** In northern Labrador extending from Saglek Fjord in the south, to the very northern tip of Labrador; and from the provincial boundary with Quebec in the west, to the waters of the Labrador Sea in the east. **Facilities:** To be determined. **Activities:** Hiking, climbing, kayaking. **Special Features:** Canada's first national park in Labrador protects an area of spectacular Arctic wilderness, with mountains, fjords, river valleys and rugged coastal landscapes. Nachvak Fjord, which lies near the center of the park reserve, was formed by a glacier cutting through the Torngat Mountains as it flowed to the sea during the last ice age. Today, the Torngat Mountains include the highest peaks in continental eastern North America, and are dotted by many small glaciers. The park area has been home to the Inuit and their ancestors for thousands of years and is also home to abundant wildlife.

★443★ TUKTUT NOGAIT NATIONAL PARK

PO Box 91
Paulatuk, NT X0E1N0
Web: www.pc.gc.ca/pn-np/nt/tuktutnogait
Phone: 867-580-3233; **Fax:** 867-580-3234
Size: 18,181 sq. km. **Established:** Established by Parliament in 1998 as a result of an agreement signed in 1996 by the Federal and Northwest Territories governments, and the Inuvialuit. **Location:** Part of the Tundra Hills Natural Region in the Melville Hills, northeast of Inuvik. Access is by boat shuttle or on foot from Paulatuk, located 45 km to the west, or by air charter from the town of Inuvik, located 425 km to the southwest. Inuvik is the largest community in the region and is serviced daily by scheduled aircraft from southern Canada. Commercial flights are available from Inuvik to Paulatuk three times a week during the summer months. **Facilities:** This is a true wilderness park and visitors are required to be completely self-sufficient. There are no visitor facilities, campgrounds, or established hiking trails. **Activities:** Camping, hiking, canoeing, fishing, wildlife viewing. **Special Features:** Park protects the calving grounds of the Bluenose caribou herd and its cliffs and canyons provide a nesting habitat for one of the highest densities of birds of prey in North America, including peregrine falcons and golden eagles. The park's arctic tundra and barren lands are also home to populations of musk oxen, wolves, grizzly bears, red foxes, and wolverines. It includes more than 360 archaeological sites.

★444★ UKKUSIKSALIK NATIONAL PARK

c/o Nunavut Field Unit Office of Parks Canada
PO Box 278
Iqaluit, NU X0A0H0
Phone: 867-975-4673; **Fax:** 867-975-4674
Size: 20,558 sq. km. **Established:** 2003. **Location:** Park is located just south of the community of Repulse Bay and the Arctic Circle and surrounds Wager Bay, a 100-km-long saltwater inlet on the northwest coast of Hudson Bay in Nunavut. The park is accessible by scheduled flights from either Winnipeg or Yellowknife via Rankin Inlet, Baker Lake, and on to Repulse Bay. **Facilities:** None. **Activities:** Camping, hiking, wildlife viewing. It is highly recommended that visitors hire a local outfitter to take them into the park due to the high polar bear population. **Special Features:** Named after the soapstone found within its boundaries, the park protects important habitat for caribou, muskox, polar bear, grizzly bear, golden eagles and many other arctic wildlife species. The landscape of Ukkusiksalik features eskers, mudflats, cliffs, rolling tundra banks and unique coastal regions and it is the first national park to encompass almost an entire watershed. Wager Bay is important to local Inuit communities as a hunting ground, and also because of its cultural significance. More than 500 archeological sites are located within the park.

★445★ VUNTUT NATIONAL PARK

General Delivery
Old Crow, YT Y0B1N0
Web: www.pc.gc.ca/pn-np/yt/vuntut
Phone: 867-667-3910; **Fax:** 867-966-3432
Size: 4,345 sq. km. **Established:** 1995. **Location:** In the northwestern corner of the Yukon Territory, 50 km by air or 190 km by river north of the community of Old Crow. Old Crow is the most northerly and most isolated community in the Yukon (175 km from the Dempster Hwy.). Park is bounded by Ivvavik National Park (see separate entry) to the north and the U.S. border and Arctic National Wildlife Refuge (see separate entry in US National Parks section) to the west. **Facilities:** None. **Activities:** Hiking, canoeing, wildlife viewing, cross-country skiing. **Special Features:** Dedicated to wilderness preservation and the maintenance of aboriginal lifestyles, park will be developed according to conservation and preservation principles as well as the Vuntut Gwitchin's desire to share their natural and

See pages 18-19 for map of Canadian National Parks.

cultural heritage with others. Vuntut National Park, along with Ivvavik National Park and the Arctic National Wildlife Refuge represent international efforts to protect a major northern ecosystem defined in part by the Porcupine caribou herd. This herd is one of the largest in North America numbering approximately 160,000 animals.

★446★ WAPUSK NATIONAL PARK

PO Box 127
Churchill, MB R0B0E0
Web: www.pc.gc.ca/pn-np/mb/wapusk
Phone: 204-675-8863; **Fax:** 204-675-2026; **Toll Free:** 888-748-2928
Size: 11,475 sq. km. **Established:** 1996. **Location:** Located in the northeast corner of Manitoba on the shores of Hudson Bay. Park stretches south and inland along Hudson Bay towards the Nelson River. Boundary lies 45 km southeast of the town of Churchill. **Facilities:** Limited. **Activities:** Limited at present to polar bear viewing and flightseeing. Additional activities will be determined when a management plan is finalized for the park. Activities in the Churchill area include birdwatching, polar bear viewing, beluga whale viewing (in the Churchill River), and canoeing. **Special Features:** Park includes one of the largest known polar bear maternity denning sites in the world and vital habitat for hundreds of thousands of waterfowl and shorebirds that nest along the coast of Hudson Bay or gather and feed there during annual migrations. Traditional land use by aboriginal and other local users includes gathering of berries, deadwood, flowers and other natural products for domestic purposes, as well as trapping and hunting caribou for domestic consumption.

★447★ WATERTON LAKES NATIONAL PARK

Box 200
Waterton Park, AB T0K2M0
Web: www.watertonpark.com
Phone: 403-859-2224; **Fax:** 403-859-5152
Size: 505 sq. km. **Established:** 1895. **Location:** In the southwest corner of Alberta, 270 km south of Calgary and 130 km southeast of Lethbridge. From Calgary take Highway 2 south to Fort Macleod, then west on Highway 3 to Pincher Creek, then south again on Highway 6 (a 3-hour drive). From Lethbridge, drive south to Cardston on Highway 2, then west to the park via Highway 5 (a 1.25-hour drive). **Facilities:** Information center (May-October), heritage center (summer), 3 frontcountry campgrounds (390+ campsites), 9 wilderness campsites, trails (200 km), 18-hole golf course. Waterton Park Village, located inside the park, offers complete services including hotels, dining, and shopping. Interpretive guides, bicycle rentals, boat tours on Upper Waterton Lake, and canoe or rowboat rentals at Cameron Lake are also available. **Activities:** Camping, hiking, horseback riding, swimming, boating, boat tours, sailboarding, scuba diving, birdwatching, wildlife viewing, bicycling, mountain climbing, golfing (May-October), winter sports, interpretive and educational programs. **Special Features:** Park features some of the oldest rock in Canada's Rocky Mountains and Upper Waterton Lake, the deepest lake in the Canadian Rockies. In 1932, the Waterton Lakes National Park was joined with Montana's Glacier National Park to form the Waterton-Glacier International Peace Park. The International Peace Park, the first of its kind, symbolizes the peace and goodwill between the United States and Canada as exemplified by the world's longest undefended border. Although the two halves are administered separately, the parks cooperate on environmental initiatives and in protecting the alpine backcountry.

★448★ WOOD BUFFALO NATIONAL PARK

PO Box 750
Fort Smith, NT X0E0P0
Web: www.pc.gc.ca/pn-np/nt/woodbuffalo
Phone: 867-872-7900; **Fax:** 867-872-3910
Size: 44,792 sq. km. **Established:** 1922. **Location:** Park straddles the Alberta-Northwest Territories border. It may be reached from two communities: Fort Smith (NWT) and Fort Chipewyan (Alberta). The park headquarters in Fort Smith has year-round road access via the MacKenzie Highway and NT Highway 5. There is no all-weather road access to Fort Chipewyan; access is by air only. **Facilities:** Visitor centers (Fort Chipewyan and Fort Smith), hiking trails, frontcountry campground and group camp (Pine Lake, &), backcountry campsites (Rainbow Lakes and Sweetgrass), interpretive exhibits (&), educational programs. **Activities:** Camping, hiking, swimming, boating, canoeing, fishing, wildlife viewing, birdwatching, cross-country skiing, snowshoeing. **Special Features:** Canada's largest national park was originally established to protect the last remaining herds of wood bison in northern Canada. Today it is a designated UNESCO World Heritage Site that protects one of the largest free-roaming, self-regulating bison herds in the world and provides the last remaining natural nesting area for the endangered whooping crane. The Peace-Athabasca Delta is one of the largest inland freshwater deltas in the world and a major nesting and staging area for migratory waterfowl in North America. Migratory waterfowl from all four North American flyways pass through the delta in the spring and fall. Archeological evidence shows that aboriginal people have inhabited the Wood Buffalo region for more than 8,000 years.

★449★ YOHO NATIONAL PARK

PO Box 99
Field, BC V0A1G0
Web: www.pc.gc.ca/pn-np/bc/yoho
Phone: 250-343-6783; **Fax:** 250-343-6012
Size: 1,313 sq. km. **Established:** 1896. **Location:** On the western slopes of the Rocky Mountains near Field, British Columbia; 832 km. east of Vancouver, and 210 km west of Calgary on the Trans-Canada Hwy 1. Borders Banff National Park to the east and Kootenay National Park to the south (see separate entries). **Facilities:** The town of Field, located in the park, includes lodge, guest houses, restaurants, and other basic services. Park facilities also include Emerald Lake Lodge (24 cabin-style buildings), 4 frontcountry campgrounds, backcountry campgrounds, and hiking trails (400 km). **Activities:** Camping, hiking, canoeing and kayaking, rafting, fishing, horseback riding, bicycling, mountaineering, wildlife viewing, cross-country skiing, interpretive programs. **Special Features:** Park includes 28 mountain peaks over 3,000 meters and one of the world's most important fossil finds, the Burgess Shale Formation, that contains the fossilized remains of more than 120 marine animal species dating back 515 million years. The Burgess Shale World Heritage

See pages 18-19 for map of Canadian National Parks.

Site is now incorporated into the larger Canadian Rocky Mountain Parks World Heritage Site with Yoho, Kootenay, Banff and Jasper national parks, and Mt. Assiniboine, Mt. Robson and Hamber provincial parks. Other notable features at Yoho include the Spiral Tunnels, which were cut through the park's mountains to make way for the railroad; Takakkaw Falls, with a free fall of 254 meters, the third highest in Canada; and the Natural Bridge, where the Kicking Horse River has carved its way through solid rock.

See pages 18-19 for map of Canadian National Parks.

3. NATIONAL FORESTS AND GRASSLANDS

★450★ **FOREST SERVICE**
U.S. Department of Agriculture
1400 Independence Ave SW
Washington, DC 20250
202-205-8333 - Phone
202-205-1765 - Fax
Web: www.fs.fed.us

The Forest Service manages the nation's forests and grasslands, conducts forestry research, and provides technical and financial assistance to state and private forestry agencies. Forest Service lands comprise 193 million acres, or 8.5 percent of the total land area in the United States. When the national forest system was established in 1905, its mission was to restore and preserve forests for their renewable resources such as timber and water. Over time, the Forest Service's focus has expanded to include providing outdoor recreation areas and facilities for the public.

Publications: Numerous general and technical reports, bulletins, leaflets, brochures, pamphlets, books, fact sheets, and maps. For a publications list, write to: Forest Service Publications, 201 14th Street NW, Washington, DC 20250, or see the Forest Service's publications website: www.fs.fed.us/publications.

For local information about the national forest system contact the Forest Service at one their regional office locations listed below. For more specific information, contact the individual national forests and grasslands listed throughout this section.

Regional Offices:

Region 1 - Northern Region
PO Box 7669
Missoula, MT 59807
406-329-3511 - Phone
406-329-3347 - Fax
Web: www.fs.fed.us/r1
(northern Idaho, Montana, North Dakota, northwestern South Dakota, northeast Washington)

Region 2 - Rocky Mountain Region
740 Simms St
Golden, CO 80401
303-275-5350 - Phone
303-275-5754 - Fax
Web: www.fs.fed.us/r2
(Colorado, Kansas, Nebraska, South Dakota, eastern Wyoming)

Region 3 - Southwestern Region
333 Broadway Blvd SE
Albuquerque, NM 87102
505-842-3292 - Phone
505-842-3800 - Fax
Web: www.fs.fed.us/r3
(Arizona, New Mexico)

Region 4 - Intermountain Region
324 25th St
Ogden, UT 84401
801-625-5306 - Phone
801-625-5359 - Fax
Web: www.fs.fed.us/r4
(southern Idaho, Nevada, Utah, western Wyoming)

Region 5 - Pacific Southwest Region
1323 Club Dr
Vallejo, CA 94592
707-562-8737 - Phone
707-562-9091 - Fax
Web: fs.fed.us/r5
(California, Hawaii, Guam, Trust Territories of the Pacific Islands)

Region 6 - Pacific Northwest Region
333 SW 1st St
PO Box 3623
Portland, OR 97208
503-808-2468 - Phone
503-808-2210 - Fax
Web: www.fs.fed.us/r6
(Oregon, Washington)

(no Region 7)

Region 8 - Southern Region
1720 Peachtree Rd NW, Suite 760S
Atlanta, GA 30309
404-347-7226 - Phone
404-347-4821 - Fax
Web: www.southernregion.fs.fed.us
(Alabama, Arkansas, Florida, Georgia, Kentucky, Louisiana, Mississippi, North Carolina, Oklahoma, Puerto Rico, South Carolina, Tennessee, Texas, Virgin Islands, Virginia)

See pages 20-21 for map of U.S. National Forests and Grasslands.

Region 9 - Eastern Region
626 E Wisconsin Ave
Milwaukee, WI 53202
414-297-3600 - Phone
414-297-3608 - Fax
Web: www.fs.fed.us/r9
(Connecticut, Delaware, Illinois, Indiana, Iowa, Maine
Maryland, Massachusetts, Michigan, Minnesota, Missouri,
New Hampshire, New Jersey, New York, Ohio, Pennsylvania,
Rhode Island, Vermont, West Virginia, Wisconsin)

Region 10 -Alaska Region
PO Box 21628
Juneau, AK 99802
907-586-8806 - Phone
907-586-7892 - Fax
Web: www.fs.fed.us/r10

Forest Service research stations conduct basic and applied research to help sustain the health, productivity, and diversity of the nation's forests, rangelands, and related resources. Regional sites include:

North Central Research Station
1992 Folwell Ave
Saint Paul, MN 55108
651-649-5000 - Phone
651-649-5285 - Fax
Web: www.ncrs.fs.fed.us

Northeastern Research Station
11 Campus Blvd, Suite 200
Newtown Square, PA 19073
610-557-4017 - Phone
610-557-4095 - Fax
Web: www.fs.fed.us/ne

Pacific Northwest Research Station
333 SW 1st Ave
Portland, OR 97204
503-808-2592 - Phone
503-808-2130 - Fax
Web: www.fs.fed.us/pnw

Pacific Southwest Research Station
800 Buchanan St
Albany, CA 94710
510-559-6300 - Phone
510-559-6440 - Fax
Web: www.fs.fed.us/psw

Rocky Mountain Research Station
2150 Centre Ave, Bldg A
Fort Collins, CO 80526
970-295-5926 - Phone
970-295-5927 - Fax
Web: www.fs.fed.us/rm

Southern Research Station
200 WT Weaver Blvd
Asheville, NC 28802
828-257-4298 - Phone
828-257-4840 - Fax
Web: www.srs.fs.usda.gov

Forest Products Laboratory
1 Gifford Pinchot Dr
Madison, WI 53726
608-231-9200 - Phone
608-231-9592 - Fax
Web: www.fpl.fs.fed.us

International Institute of Tropical Forestry
Jardín Botánico Sur
1201 Calle Ceiba
San Juan, PR 00926
787-766-5335 - Phone
787-766-6302 - Fax
Web: www.fs.fed.us/global/iitf

★451★ ALLEGHENY NATIONAL FOREST
222 Liberty St
PO Box 847
Warren, PA 16365
Web: www.fs.fed.us/r9/allegheny
Phone: 814-723-5150; **Fax:** 814-726-1465
Size: 513,325 acres. **Location:** Northwestern Pennsylvania. Accessible by US 6, 62, and 219. Nearby cities/towns include Bradford, Kane, Ridgway, Sheffield, Tionesta, and Warren. **Facilities:** 20 campgrounds, 11 picnic sites, 4 beaches, 6 boat launches, trails. **Activities:** Camping, hunting, fishing, boating, canoeing, swimming, hiking, mountain biking, ORV riding, cross-country skiing, snowmobiling. **Special Features:** 700+ miles of streams and rivers including the Allegheny River, a designated Wild and Scenic river; Allegheny Islands Wilderness, 7 small river islands; Allegheny National Recreation Area; a 95-mile section of the North Country National Scenic Trail.

★452★ ANGELES NATIONAL FOREST
701 N Santa Anita Ave
Arcadia, CA 91006
Web: www.fs.fed.us/r5/angeles
Phone: 626-574-5200; **Fax:** 626-574-5233
Size: 654,000 acres. **Location:** Los Angeles County, north of

See pages 20-21 for map of U.S. National Forests and Grasslands.

the city of Los Angeles. Accessible by CA 2 and 39. **Facilities:** Three visitor centers, 54 campgrounds, picnic sites, shooting range, hiking and bridle trails (557 miles), ORV trails (364 miles), open ORV areas (364 acres). **Activities:** Camping, fishing, boating, swimming, canoeing, water-skiing, jet skiing, hiking, backpacking, hunting, target shooting, horseback riding, ORV riding, cross-country and downhill skiing. **Special Features:** Steep, rugged mountains adjoining the Los Angeles metropolitan area. Points of interest include Mount Baldy, San Gabriel Wilderness, Big Santa Anita Canyon, Pyramid Lake, and Castaic Lake.

★453★ ANGELINA NATIONAL FOREST

111 Walnut Ridge Rd
Zarvalla, TX 75980
Web: www.fs.fed.us/r8/texas
Phone: 936-897-1068; **Fax:** 936-897-3406
Size: 153,179 acres. **Location:** East-central Texas. Accessible by US 69, TX 63, and TX 147. Nearby cities/towns include Jasper, Lufkin, and San Augustine. **Facilities:** Campgrounds, picnic sites, boat launch, trails, archeological sites. **Activities:** Camping, hunting, fishing, boating, canoeing, swimming, water-skiing, hiking, horseback riding, ORV riding. **Special Features:** 114,500-acre Sam Rayburn Reservoir and Boykin Springs Recreation Area.

★454★ APACHE & SITGREAVES NATIONAL FORESTS

309 S Mountain Ave
PO Box 640
Springerville, AZ 85938
Web: www.fs.fed.us/r3/asnf
Phone: 928-333-4301; **Fax:** 928-333-5966
Size: 2,003,525 acres. **Location:** Central Arizona. Accessible by US 60, 180, and 666; AZ 77 and 260. Nearby cities/towns include Alpine, Clifton, Eagar, Greer, Heber, Holbrook, Pinetop-Lakeside, Show Low, Springerville, and Winslow. **Facilities:** 40 campgrounds, 2 group camps, picnic sites, trails (nearly 1,000 miles), scenic drives. **Activities:** Camping, hunting, fishing, hiking, mountain biking, horseback riding, cross-country skiing, snowshoeing, snowmobiling, ice fishing, tubing, wildlife viewing. **Special Features:** 34 lakes and reservoirs; 680 miles of streams; Mogollon Rim; White Mountains; prehistoric Blue River cliff dwellings.

★455★ APALACHICOLA NATIONAL FOREST

PO Box 579
Bristol, FL 32321
Web: www.fs.fed.us/r8/florida
Phone: 850-643-2282
Size: 564,000 acres. **Location:** Florida Panhandle. Accessible by US 98 and 319; FL 65. Nearby cities/towns include Apalachicola, Bristol, and Tallahassee. **Facilities:** 5 campgrounds, dispersed camping, picnic sites, trails (85 miles), boat ramps, swimming beaches, rifle range. **Activities:** Camping, hunting, fishing, boating, canoeing, swimming, hiking, mountain biking, horseback riding, ORV riding. **Special Features:** 64-mile segment of the Florida National Scenic Trail; Bradwell Bay Wilderness; Leon Sinks Geological Area; Fort Gadsden Historical Site.

★456★ ARAPAHO & ROOSEVELT NATIONAL FORESTS

2150 Centre Ave, Bldg E
Fort Collins, CO 80526
Web: www.fs.fed.us/r2/arnf
Phone: 970-295-6600
Size: 1,500,000 acres. **Location:** North-central Colorado. Accessible by US 34, 40, and 287; and CO 14 and 72. Nearby cities/towns include Boulder, Dillon, Fort Collins, Grandby, and Winter Park. **Facilities:** 53 campgrounds, 20 picnic areas, trails, 10 wilderness areas, scenic drives. **Activities:** Camping, big-game hunting, fishing, boating, hiking, bicycling, horseback riding, rock climbing, ORV riding, cross-country and downhill skiing, snowmobiling. **Special Features:** Forests surround Rocky Mountain National Park (see entry in national parks section). Points of interest include Mount Evans, Mount Goliath Natural Area, Peak-to-Peak Scenic Byway, Berthoud Pass, Continental Divide National Scenic Trail (see entry in national trails section), Moffat Tunnel, and Arapaho National Recreation Area.

★457★ ASHLEY NATIONAL FOREST

355 N Vernal Ave
Vernal, UT 84078
Web: www.fs.fed.us/r4/ashley
Phone: 435-789-1181; **Fax:** 435-781-5142
Size: 1,384,132 acres. **Location:** Northeastern Utah and southwestern Wyoming. Accessible by I-80; US 191; UT 530, 40, 44. Nearby cities/towns include Duchesne, Manila, and Vernal, UT; Green River, WY. **Facilities:** Lodges, cabins, 67 campgrounds, trails (1,000+ miles), boat ramps, marinas, scenic drives. **Activities:** Camping, hunting, fishing, boating, hiking, horseback riding, ORV riding, cross-country skiing, snowmobiling. **Special Features:** 13,528-foot Kings Peak, highest peak in Utah; Flaming Gorge National Recreation Area with its 91-mile-long reservoir; Flaming Gorge-Uintas National Scenic Byway; and Green River Corridor, a world-class fishery.

★458★ BEAVERHEAD-DEERLODGE NATIONAL FOREST

420 Barrett St
Dillon, MT 59725
Web: www.fs.fed.us/r1/b-d
Phone: 406-683-3900
Size: 3,320,000 acres. **Location:** Southwestern Montana. Accessible by US 10A; MT 38, MT 43 and MT 278. Nearby cities/towns include Anaconda, Butte, Deer Lodge, Dillon, Philipsburg, Jackson, Sheridan, and Wisdom. **Facilities:** 27 cabins, 50 campgrounds, dispersed camping, picnic sites, trails (2,750 miles), boat launch, scenic drives. **Activities:** Camping, hunting, fishing, boating, swimming, hiking, horseback riding, downhill and cross-country skiing. **Special Features:** Anaconda Pintlar Wilderness Area; segments of Continental Divide National Scenic Trail and Nez Perce Historic Trail; ghost towns including Elkhorn and Coolidge; Sheepshead Mountain Recreation Area,

See pages 20-21 for map of U.S. National Forests and Grasslands.

one of the nation's premier handicapped-accessible outdoor recreation sites.

★459★ BIENVILLE NATIONAL FOREST

3473 Hwy 35 S
Forest, MS 39074
Web: www.fs.fed.us/r8/mississippi/bienville/
Phone: 601-469-3811; **Fax:** 601-469-2513
Size: 178,400 acres. **Location:** East-central Mississippi. Accessible by I-20; US 80; MS 18 and 35. Nearby cities/towns include Forest, Raleigh, Jackson, and Meridian. **Facilities:** 2 campgrounds, picnic sites, boat launch, trails. **Activities:** Camping, hunting, fishing, swimming, hiking, mountain biking, horseback riding. **Special Features:** Harrell Prairie Hill Botanical Area, a remnant of Jackson Prairie natural grassland surrounded by forest; 3 designated wildlife management areas: Bienville, Caney Creek, and Tallahala. Bienville NF also contains a 189-acre tract that is the largest known block of old-growth timber in Mississippi.

★460★ BIGHORN NATIONAL FOREST

2013 Eastside 2nd St
Sheridan, WY 82801
Web: www.fs.fed.us/r2/bighorn
Phone: 307-674-2600; **Fax:** 307-674-2668
Size: 1,115,073 acres. **Location:** North-central Wyoming. Accessible by US 14, 16, and 87. Nearby cities/towns include Buffalo, Cody, and Sheridan. **Facilities:** 7 lodges, 32 campgrounds, 14 picnic areas, 2 ski areas, visitors centers, trails (1,500+ miles), lookout towers, boat ramps. **Activities:** Camping, hunting, fishing, boating, hiking, horseback riding, off-road driving, mountain climbing, cross-country and downhill skiing, snowmobiling. **Special Features:** Medicine Wheel National Historic Landmark; Fort Phil Kearney State Historic Site (see entry in Wyoming state parks section); Bighorn Mountains; three rivers, four natural lakes, ten reservoirs, and nine streams.

★461★ BITTERROOT NATIONAL FOREST

1801 N 1st St
Hamilton, MT 59840
Web: www.fs.fed.us/r1/bitterroot
Phone: 406-363-7100; **Fax:** 406-363-7159
Size: 1,600,000 acres. **Location:** Southwestern Montana and Idaho. Accessible by US 93; MT 43 and MT 12. Nearby cities/towns include Missoula, Florence, Stevensville, Victor, Corvallis, Hamilton, Darby, and Sula. **Facilities:** 5 cabins, 18 campgrounds, lookouts, picnic sites, trails (1,600 miles), environmental education center. **Activities:** Camping, hunting, fishing, swimming, whitewater rafting, hiking, biking, horseback riding, skiing, snowboarding, snowmobiling. **Special Features:** Two mountain ranges, Bitterroot in the west and Sapphire in the east, separated by Bitterroot River valley; miles of rivers including the Selway, Clearwater, and Bitterroot, with world-class whitewater rapids; wilderness areas including portions of Selway-Bitterroot, Anaconda Pintler, and Frank Church River of No Return.

★462★ BLACK HILLS NATIONAL FOREST

1019 N 5th St
Custer, SD 57730
Web: www.fs.fed.us/r2/blackhills
Phone: 605-673-9200; **Fax:** 605-673-9350
Size: 1,200,000 acres. **Location:** Southwestern South Dakota. Accessible by US 14, 16, 18, 85, and 385. Nearby cities/towns include Custer, Hill City, Hot Springs, Rapid City, Spearfish, and Sturgis, SD; New Castle, WY. **Facilities:** Visitor center, 30 campgrounds, 32 picnic areas, beaches, boat ramps, trails (450 miles), 2 scenic drives. **Activities:** Camping, hunting, fishing, boating, swimming, rock hounding, gold panning, interpretive programs. **Special Features:** Historic gold rush region. Points of interest include Harney Peak, at 7,242 feet South Dakota's highest point; Mount Rushmore National Memorial (see entry in national parks section); Jewel Cave National Monument (see entry in national parks section); Norbeck Wildlife Preserve; and Black Elk Wilderness.

★463★ BOISE NATIONAL FOREST

1249 S Vinnell Way, Suite 200
Boise, ID 83709
Web: www.fs.fed.us/r4/boise
Phone: 208-364-4100; **Fax:** 208-373-4111
Size: 2,612,000 acres. **Location:** North and east of Boise. Accessible by US 20; ID 21 and 22. Nearby cities/towns include Boise, Cascade, and Idaho City. **Facilities:** 14 cabins, 40 campgrounds, dispersed camping, picnic areas, trails (1,300+ miles), winter sports area. **Activities:** Camping, hunting, fishing, rafting, kayaking, sailing, water-skiing, hiking, horseback riding, mountain biking, ORV riding, cross-country and downhill skiing, snowmobiling. **Special Features:** Most of the land lies within the Idaho Batholith, a large and highly erosive geological formation that has created a rugged mountain region, with elevations ranging from 2,600 to 9,800 feet, and numerous lakes and streams. Points of interest include Lucky Peak Nursery, Bogus Basin Ski Area, and a portion of Frank Church River of No Return Wilderness area.

★464★ BRIDGER-TETON NATIONAL FOREST

340 N Cache Dr
PO Box 1888
Jackson, WY 83001
Web: www.fs.fed.us/btnf
Phone: 307-739-5500; **Fax:** 307-739-5010
Size: 3,500,000 acres. **Location:** Western Wyoming. Accessible by US 26, 89, 189, and 287. Nearby cities/towns include Pinedale and Jackson. **Facilities:** 3 ski resorts, 37 campgrounds, dispersed camping, cabins, picnic areas, 11 boating areas, trails (34 trailheads; 2,200 miles). **Activities:** Camping, hunting, fishing, boating, canoeing, rafting, swimming, hiking, mountain biking, horseback riding, ORV riding, rock climbing, cross-country and downhill skiing, snowmobiling, snowboarding, snowshoeing, ice climbing, dog sledding. **Special Features:** Comprises a large part of the Greater Yellowstone Ecosystem - the largest intact ecosystem in the lower 48 states. Points of interest include Teton and Wind River mountain ranges; a 200-mile segment of Continental Divide National Scenic Trail (see entry in national

See pages 20-21 for map of U.S. National Forests and Grasslands.

trails section); Gros Ventre Slide geological area; three nationally designated wilderness areas: Bridger, Gros Ventre, and Teton; Periodic Spring, largest of world's three known coldwater geysers. Forest adjoins Yellowstone and Grand Teton national parks (see entries in national parks section).

★465★ CARIBBEAN NATIONAL FOREST (EL YUNQUE)
HC 01 Box 13490
Rio Grande, PR 00745
Web: www.fs.fed.us/r8/caribbean
Phone: 787-888-1810; **Fax:** 787-888-5685
Size: 28,000 acres. **Location:** 25 miles northeast of the San Juan metropolitan area, in the Sierra de Luquillo Mountains. Accessible by PR 3, 191, and 186. **Facilities:** Visitor center with theater and gift shop, picnic sites, trails (24 miles), observation towers. **Activities:** Primitive camping, fishing, hiking, bird watching. **Special Features:** Only tropical forest in the U.S. National Forest System. Contains 23 tree species found nowhere else. Provides habitat for rare wildlife including the Puerto Rican parrot, found only on this part of the island. Three of the forest's rivers have been designated as Wild & Scenic: Río La Mina, Río Mameyes, and Río Icacos.

★466★ CARIBOU-TARGHEE NATIONAL FOREST
1405 Hollipark Dr
Idaho Falls, ID 83401
Web: www.fs.fed.us/r4/caribou-targhee
Phone: 208-524-7500
Size: 3,000,000 acres. **Location:** Southeastern Idaho, with small portions in Utah and Wyoming. Accessible by US 91 and 191. Nearby cities/towns include Ashton, Idaho Falls, Malad City, Montpelier, Pocatello, and Soda Springs. **Facilities:** Cabins, campgrounds, group camps, dispersed camping, trails (1,200 miles), 3 ski areas, interpretive displays. **Activities:** Camping, hunting, fishing, hiking, bicycling, horseback riding, boating, canoeing, rafting, cross-country and downhill skiing, snowmobiling. **Special Features:** Encompasses all or portions of several distinct mountain ranges including Lemhi, Beaverhead, Bitterroot, Centennial, Henry's Lake, Teton, Big Hole, Caribou, and Snake River ranges. Includes Minnetonka Cave, one of just two public caves managed by the US Fish & Wildlife Service; 115,000-acre Jedediah Smith Wilderness; 250 miles of streams and 8,100 total surface acres of lakes and reservoirs. Forest adjoins Yellowstone and Grand Teton national parks (see entries in national parks section).

★467★ CARSON NATIONAL FOREST
208 Cruz Alta Rd
Taos, NM 87571
Web: www.fs.fed.us/r3/carson
Phone: 505-758-6200; **Fax:** 505-758-6213
Size: 1,500,000 acres. **Location:** Northwestern and north-central New Mexico. Accessible by US 64, 285, and 84; NM 3, 75, and 38. Nearby cities/towns include Canjilon, Chama, Cimarron, El Rito, Tres Pidras, Penasco, Farmington, Taos, Questa, and Tierra Amarilla. **Facilities:** 30 campgrounds, dispersed camping, 8 picnic grounds, trails (330 miles), 3 ski areas. **Activities:** Camping, hunting, fishing, hiking, mountain biking, horseback riding, skiing, snowshoeing, snowmobiling. **Special Features:** 400 miles of streams and numerous lakes; Sangre de Cristo Mountains; Wheeler Peak (13,161 feet), highest in New Mexico; Ghost Ranch Living Museum; four wilderness areas.

★468★ CHATTAHOOCHEE-OCONEE NATIONAL FORESTS
1755 Cleveland Hwy
Gainesville, GA 30501
Web: www.fs.fed.us/conf
Phone: 770-297-3000; **Fax:** 770-297-3025
Size: 865,855acres. **Location:** Northern and central Georgia. Accessible by US 19, 23, 41, 76, 123, 129, 278, and 441; GA 5, 7, and 65. Nearby cities/towns include Atlanta, Dahlonega, Greensboro, Madison, and Dalton. **Facilities:** 21 campgrounds, dispersed camping, picnic areas, trails (530 miles), canoe trail, 6 swimming beaches, 4 shooting ranges, 2 scenic byways, 10 wilderness areas. **Activities:** Camping, hunting, fishing, boating, canoeing, whitewater rafting, hiking, horseback riding, ORV riding, swimming, rock hounding, gold panning. **Special Features:** Anna Ruby Falls, twin waterfalls that merge to form Smith Creek; Brasstown Bald, highest mountain in Georgia (4,784 feet) with a 360-degree view of four states; southern end of the Appalachian Mountains (including a segment of the Appalachian National Scenic Trail, see entry in national trails section); Chattooga Wild and Scenic River; Track Rock Archeological Area; a 37-mile segment of Bartram Trail, a National Recreation Trail; Scull Shoals historical area, featuring remnants of buildings, bridges, and factories of the once-prosperous town of Scull Shoals.

★469★ CHEQUAMEGON-NICOLET NATIONAL FOREST
1170 4th Ave S
Park Falls, WI 54552
Web: www.fs.fed.us/r9/cnnf
Phone: 715-762-2461; **Fax:** 715-762-5179
Size: 1,500,000 acres. **Location:** Northeastern and north-central Wisconsin. Accessible by US 2, 8, 45, and 63; WI 13, 32, 52, 55, 139, 64, and 70. Nearby cities/towns include Ashland, Eagle River, Hayward, Medford, Rhinelander, and Park Falls. **Facilities:** 41 campgrounds, 7 group camps, 19 cabins, picnic areas, trails (300+ miles), swimming beaches, boat ramps, scenic drives. **Activities:** Camping, hunting, fishing, boating, swimming, hiking, mountain biking, horseback riding, ORV riding, cross-country skiing, snowmobiling, ice fishing, snowshoeing. **Special Features:** Numerous large and small lakes, a wildlife area, and the North Country and Ice Age national scenic trails. Known as the Cradle of Rivers: headwaters of the Wolf, Pine, Popple, Oconto, Peshtigo, Deerskin, and Wisconsin rivers originate from within forest boundaries.

★470★ CHEROKEE NATIONAL FOREST
2800 N Ocoee St
Cleveland, TN 37312
Web: www.fs.fed.us/r8/cherokee
Phone: 423-476-9700; **Fax:** 423-476-9721

See pages 20-21 for map of U.S. National Forests and Grasslands.

Size: 640,000 acres. **Location:** Eastern Tennessee. Accessible by US 11, 64, 165, 321/11E, 411, and 421; TN 68, 70, and 81; I-40, I-75, and I-181. Nearby cities/towns include Chattanooga, Cleveland, Ducktown, Benton, Etowah, Knoxville, Newport, Greeneville, Johnson City, and Elizabethton. **Facilities:** 30 campgrounds, dispersed camping, 30 picnic sites, trails (700 miles), boat ramps. **Activities:** Camping, hunting, fishing, boating, swimming, rafting, hiking, mountain biking, horseback riding. **Special Features:** Ocoee Whitewater Center, site of the 1996 Olympic Games canoe and kayak competitions; 7 whitewater rivers; John Muir and Warrior's Passage national recreation trails; 170 miles of the Appalachian National Scenic Trail (see entry in national trails section). Forest is split into two sections by the Great Smoky Mountains National Park (see entry in national parks section).

★471★ CHIPPEWA NATIONAL FOREST

200 Ash Ave NW
Cass Lake, MN 56633
Web: www.fs.fed.us/r9/chippewa
Phone: 218-335-8600; **Fax:** 218-335-8637
Size: 666,542acres. **Location:** North-central Minnesota. Accessible by US 2 and 371; MN 6, 34, and 46. Nearby cities/towns include Blackduck, Cass Lake, Grand Rapids, Marcell, Remer, and Walker. **Facilities:** Visitor center, 21 campgrounds, dispersed camping, picnic sites, trails (160 miles), snowmobile trails (382 miles), 9 canoe routes, 9 beaches, 3 scenic byways, 57 boat ramps, fishing piers. **Activities:** Camping, fishing, boating, mountain biking, berry picking, swimming, water-skiing, hiking, cross-country skiing, snowshoeing, snowmobiling, ice fishing, OHV riding, bird watching, dog sledding, horseback riding. **Special Features:** Gilfillan Area, an undeveloped tract with an abundance of wild orchids; Lost Forty, a tract of virgin pines left untouched by loggers because early maps incorrectly showed the area was a lake; historic Rabideau CCC Camp, 13 buildings of a former Civilian Conservation Corps camp, on the *National Register of Historic Places*; Webster Lake Bog, an area with carnivorous plants along a self-guiding boardwalk trail; 150 pairs of breeding bald eagles.

★472★ CHUGACH NATIONAL FOREST

3301 C St, Suite 300
Anchorage, AK 99503
Web: www.fs.fed.us/r10/chugach
Phone: 907-743-9500; **Fax:** 907-743-9476
Size: 5,600,000 acres. **Location:** Extends south and east of Anchorage along the south-central Alaskan Coast. Accessible by highway to Anchorage, Seward, and Kenai. Nearby cities/towns include Anchorage, Cordova, Seward, Valdez, and Whittier. **Facilities:** 42 cabins, 15 campgrounds, dispersed camping, picnic sites, trails (200 miles). **Activities:** Camping, hunting, fishing, boating, hiking, heli-skiing, snowmobiling, dogsledding, salmon viewing. **Special Features:** Second largest national forest in the United States. Encompasses Kenai Peninsula, Prince William Sound, and Copper River Delta. At 700,000 acres, the delta is the largest contiguous wetland area remaining on the western coast of the U.S. Begich Boggs Visitor Center, located at the head of Portage Valley, features exhibits focusing on glaciers and Alaska wildlife.

★473★ CIBOLA NATIONAL FOREST

2113 Osuna Rd NE, Suite A
Albuquerque, NM 87113
Web: www.fs.fed.us/r3/cibola
Phone: 505-346-3900; **Fax:** 505-346-3901
Size: 1,949,637 acres. **Location:** 13 separate parcels in west and central New Mexico. Accessible by US 85, 66, and 60. Nearby cities/towns include Albuquerque, Datil, Gallup, Grants, Magdalena, Mountainair, and Socorro. **Facilities:** Visitor center, 22 campgrounds, dispersed camping, picnic sites, ski area, trails, boat launches. **Activities:** Camping, deer and antelope hunting, OHV riding, limited fishing, hiking, mountain biking, hang gliding, downhill skiing (at Sandia Peak). **Special Features:** Forest includes the Datil, Gallinas, Magdalena, Bear, Manzano, Sandia, San Mateo, Mount Taylor, and Zuni mountains. Minutes east of downtown Albuquerque, an aerial tram travels from the desert floor to the top of the forest's 10,378-foot Sandia Peak. The 2.7-mile Sandia Peak Tram, said to be the world's longest aerial tram, offers riders an 11,000-square-mile panoramic view of New Mexico.

★474★ CLEARWATER NATIONAL FOREST

12730 Hwy 12
Orofino, ID 83544
Web: www.fs.fed.us/r1/clearwater
Phone: 208-476-4541; **Fax:** 208-476-8329
Size: 1,800,000 acres. **Location:** North-central Idaho. Accessible by US 12 and 95. Nearby cities/towns include Kooskia, Lewiston, Orofino, and Moscow. **Facilities:** 2 visitor centers, 8 cabins, campgrounds, picnic sites, trails (1,700 miles), scenic drives. **Activities:** Camping, hunting, fishing, boating, kayaking, rafting, hiking, ORV riding, mountain biking, cross-country skiing, snowmobiling, snowshoeing. **Special Features:** Forest is composed mainly of deep forested canyons interspersed with high, rugged ridges. Attractions include the Lewis and Clark Highway (US 12), a scenic drive through some of Northern Idaho's most beautiful scenery, with interpretive stops along the way; Lewis and Clark and Nez Perce national historic trails (see separate entries in national trails section); Selway-Bitterroot Wilderness; Mallard-Larkins Pioneer Area.

★475★ CLEVELAND NATIONAL FOREST

10845 Rancho Bernardo Rd, Suite 200
San Diego, CA 92127
Web: www.fs.fed.us/r5/cleveland
Phone: 858-673-6180; **Fax:** 858-673-6192
Size: 460,000 acres. **Location:** Southwestern California, extending 35 miles from Orange County to within 5 miles of Mexico. Accessible by US 15 and 8. Nearby cities/towns include Corona, Escondido, Ramona, Alpine, and San Diego. **Facilities:** 15 campgrounds, 7 picnic sites, trails (356 miles), ORV areas (2,160 acres), shooting ranges. **Activities:** Camping, hunting, fishing, hiking, mountain biking, ORV riding, shooting, horseback riding, bird watching. **Special Features:** Includes Laguna and Palomar mountains and the famed Palomar Observatory with its 200-inch Hale telescope. The Pacific Crest National Scenic Trail passes through the forest (see entry in national trails section).

See pages 20-21 for map of U.S. National Forests and Grasslands.

3. National Forests and Grasslands

★476★ COCONINO NATIONAL FOREST

1824 S Thompson St
Flagstaff, AZ 86001
Web: www.fs.fed.us/r3/coconino
Phone: 928-527-3600; **Fax:** 928-527-3620
Size: 1,821,495 acres. **Location:** Northern Arizona. Accessible by US 89 and 89A. Nearby cities/towns include Camp Verde, Clarkdale, Flagstaff, and Sedona. **Facilities:** 3 cabins, 22 campgrounds, 5 group camps, dispersed camping, boat ramps, trails (300+ miles), 4 ski areas, scenic drives, ORV area (13,500 acres at Cinder Hill). **Activities:** Camping, hunting, fishing, boating, canoeing, rafting, hiking, horseback riding, ORV riding, cross-country and downhill skiing, snowshoeing, snowmobiling. **Special Features:** Includes Arizona's highest point at 12,633 feet atop Mount Humphreys; Oak Creek Canyon, with red and pink sandstone cliffs; Mogollan Rim, a rugged escarpment that forms the southern limit of the Colorado Plateau.

COEUR D'ALENE NATIONAL FOREST

(see Idaho Panhandle National Forests)

★477★ COLUMBIA RIVER GORGE NATIONAL SCENIC AREA

902 Wasco St, Suite 200
Hood River, OR 97031
Web: www.fs.fed.us/r6/columbia
Phone: 541-308-1700; **Fax:** 541-386-1916
Size: 292,000 acres. **Location:** Cuts through the Cascade Mountain Range in northern Oregon. Accessible by I-84 and OR 35. Nearby cities/towns include Hood River, OR, and White Salmon, WA. **Facilities:** 4 campgrounds, day-use areas, trails (200+ miles), scenic drives. **Activities:** Camping, fishing, hiking, mountain biking, boating, canoeing, kayaking, whitewater rafting, windsurfing, rock climbing, bird & wildlife watching. **Special Features:** The Columbia River Gorge is a spectacular river canyon cutting through the volcanic rock in the Cascade Mountain Range and is the only sea-level passage through the Cascades. The Gorge contains cities, farms, and industries, and has a population of 40,000. Points of interest include the Historic Columbia River Highway; Crown Point, with a 30-mile vista of the Gorge; Maryhill Museum of Art and a replica of England's Stonehenge, both built on the Gorge Cliffs; a wildflower refuge; Beacon Rock, an 800-foot volcanic remnant. Historic route of the Oregon Trail and the Lewis and Clark expedition.

★478★ COLVILLE NATIONAL FOREST

765 S Main St
Colville, WA 99114
Web: www.fs.fed.us/r6/colville
Phone: 509-684-7000; **Fax:** 509-684-7080
Size: 1,100,000 acres. **Location:** Northeast corner of Washington, bordering Canada. Accessible by US 395; CA 20 and 21. Nearby cities/towns include Colville, Newport, Metaline Falls, and Republic. **Facilities:** 28 campgrounds, 3 group camps, dispersed camping, 6 interpretive sites, picnic sites, trails (485+ miles), scenic drives, ski area, ORV area. **Activities:** Camping, hunting, fishing, boating, canoeing, rafting, hiking, ORV riding, mountain biking, swimming, water-skiing, cross-country and downhill skiing, snowmobiling. **Special Features:** Forest encompasses three mountain ranges, Okanogan, Kettle River, and Selkirk, considered foothills of the Rocky Mountains. Features include Salmo-Priest Wilderness, located in the wet, western slopes of the Selkirks and containing old-growth forests of red cedar, Douglas fir, and western hemlock; 49 Degrees North Ski, a full-service ski resort; Sherman Pass, the highest pass in Washington. The only herd of woodland caribou in Washington resides in the northeastern corner of the forest near Metaline Falls.

★479★ CONECUH NATIONAL FOREST

16375 US Hwy 29
Andalusia, AL 36420
Web: www.fs.fed.us/r8/alabama
Phone: 334-222-2555
Size: 83,883 acres. **Location:** Southern Alabama on the Florida border. Accessible by US 29 and AL 137. Nearby towns are Andalusia, Brewton, and Opp, AL; Crestview, FL. **Facilities:** Campground, picnic sites, trails, shooting range. **Activities:** Camping, hunting, fishing, bird watching, boating, swimming, hiking, mountain biking, horseback riding, shooting. **Special Features:** Open Pond Recreation Area, with CCC-built shelter; Conecuh Trail, a 20-mile trek through Alabama's coastal plains; Blue Spring, a large natural spring with icy, clear waters.

★480★ CORONADO NATIONAL FOREST

300 W Congress St
Tucson, AZ 85701
Web: www.fs.fed.us/r3/coronado
Phone: 520-388-8300; **Fax:** 520-388-8305
Size: 1,780,196 acres. **Location:** Southeastern Arizona. Accessible by US 80, 89, and 191; AZ 82. Nearby cities/towns include Benson, Bisbee, Douglas, Nogales, Patagonia, Safford, Tombstone, Tucson, and Wilcox. **Facilities:** Visitor centers, 32 campgrounds, dispersed camping, 31 picnic sites, trails, scenic drives, OHV area, 8 wilderness areas. **Activities:** Camping, hunting, fishing, boating, hiking, mountain biking, ORV riding, skiing, spelunking, rock climbing. **Special Features:** Forest protects 12 mountain ranges (Arizona's "sky islands"), which offer an unusual range of climates and vegetation, affording swimming and skiing opportunities just 40 miles apart. Mount Lemmon, just 25 miles northeast of downtown Tucson, is the southernmost ski area in the continental United States.

★481★ CROATAN NATIONAL FOREST

141 E Fisher Ave
New Bern, NC 28560
Web: www.cs.unca.edu/nfsnc
Phone: 252-638-5628
Size: 161,000 acres. **Location:** Eastern North Carolina, on the coast between Morehead City and New Bern. Accessible by US 17 and 70; NC 24 and 58. Nearby cities/towns include Morehead City, New Bern, and Swansboro. **Facilities:** 3 campgrounds, dispersed camping, picnic sites, boat ramps, fishing piers, nature trails, 4 wilderness areas. **Activities:** Camping, fresh and saltwater fishing, boating, canoeing, swimming, hiking. **Special Features:** Diverse ecosystems ranging from freshwater pocosins to

See pages 20-21 for map of U.S. National Forests and Grasslands.

longleaf pine savannas to salt marsh; Cedar Point Tideland Trail, a short National Recreation Trail that showcases the ecology of an estuary; Neusiok Trail, a 26-mile trek from the Newport River to the Neuse River; White Oak River, with some of the finest blackwater bass fishing in North Carolina.

★482★ CUSTER NATIONAL FOREST

1310 Main St
Billings, MT 59105
Web: www.fs.fed.us/r1/custer
Phone: 406-657-6200; **Fax:** 406-657-6222
Size: 1,278,279 acres. **Location:** In Montana, North Dakota, and South Dakota. Accessible by US 85 and 212. Nearby cities/towns include Absarokee, Ashland, Billings, Columbus, and Red Lodge. **Facilities:** 48 campgrounds, picnic areas, trails (100s of miles), scenic drives. **Activities:** Camping, hunting, fishing, boating, swimming, hiking, mountain biking, mountain climbing, cross-country skiing. **Special Features:** Diverse landscape of rugged mountains, rock outcrops, snowfields, ridges, grasslands, and mountain meadows. Areas of interest include Granite Peak, the highest point in Montana at 12,799 feet; Grasshopper Glacier, which contains millions of frozen grasshoppers believed to be 200 years old; Absaroka-Beartooth Wilderness Area, encompassing two distinctly different mountain ranges.

★483★ DANIEL BOONE NATIONAL FOREST

1700 Bypass Rd
Winchester, KY 40391
Web: www.fs.fed.us/r8/boone
Phone: 859-745-3100; **Fax:** 859-744-1568
Size: 706,000 acres. **Location:** Eastern Kentucky. Accessible by I-75 and I-64. Nearby cities/towns include Lexington, London, Morehead, and Stanton. **Facilities:** 20 campgrounds, 3 group camps, picnic sites, swimming beaches, marinas, boat ramps, trails. **Activities:** Camping, hunting, fishing, boating, swimming, water-skiing, hiking, horseback riding, rock climbing, spelunking. **Special Features:** Rugged land characterized by steep slopes, narrow valleys, and cliffs. Attractions include Lake Cumberland, Cave Run Lake, Laurel River Lake, and Red River Gorge Geological Area, containing more than 100 major natural arches and unusual vegetation. Cumberland Falls and Natural Bridge state resort parks (see separate entries in Kentucky State Parks section) are within the proclamation boundary of the forest.

★484★ DAVY CROCKETT NATIONAL FOREST

Rt 1
Box 55 FS
Kennard, TX 75847
Web: www.southernregion.fs.fed.us/texas
Phone: 936-655-2299; **Fax:** 936-655-2817
Size: 161,000 acres. **Location:** East-central Texas. Accessible by US 287; TX 7, 94, and 103. Nearby cities/towns include Crockett, Groveton, and Lufkin. **Facilities:** Campground, dispersed camping, picnic sites, trails, beach and bathhouse, amphitheater. **Activities:** Camping, hunting, fishing, boating, swimming, hiking, horseback riding. **Special Features:** Ratcliff Lake

Recreation Area, a camp built in 1936 by the Civilian Conservation Corps surrounding a 45-acre lake; 3,040-acre Big Slough Wilderness Area; 20-mile-long Four C National Recreation Trail.

★485★ DELTA NATIONAL FOREST

20380 Hwy 61
Rolling Fork, MS 39159
Web: www.fs.fed.us/r8/mississippi/delta
Phone: 662-873-6256; **Fax:** 662-873-2770
Size: 60,000 acres. **Location:** West-central Mississippi. Accessible by US 61. Nearby cities/towns include Rolling Rock and Vicksburg. **Facilities:** Dispersed camping, picnic sites, boat launches, trails, ATV trails (50+ miles). **Activities:** Camping, hunting, fishing, boating, bird watching, hiking, mountain biking, swimming. **Special Features:** A large, contiguous block of bottomland hardwood forest, seasonally flooded timber, and small sloughs draining into the Big and Little Sunflower rivers in the Yazoo Basin of the Mississippi River. It is the only bottomland hardwood ecosystem in the national forest system.

★486★ DESCHUTES & OCHOCO NATIONAL FORESTS

1645 Hwy 20 E
Bend, OR 97701
Web: www.fs.fed.us/r6/centraloregon
Phone: 541-383-5300; **Fax:** 541-383-5531
Size: Just over 2,500,000 acres. **Location:** Central Oregon. Accessible by US 97, 26, and 20; OR 126. Nearby cities/towns include Redmond and Sisters. **Facilities:** 125 campgrounds, dispersed camping, cabin rentals, day-use sites, trails, 8 wilderness areas, ski area. **Activities:** Camping, fishing, hiking, mountain biking, OHV riding, boating, rock hounding, wildlife viewing, snowmobiling, cross-country skiing, interpretive tours. **Special Features:** Alpine forests, volcanic remnants, dense evergreen forests, mountain lakes, caves, desert areas, and alpine meadows. Attractions include Lava Butte, Lava River Cave, the Upper Deschutes River Scenic Waterway, and Odell and Crescent Lakes, which straddle the Oregon Cascades. Forest also includes Steins Pillar, a 200-foot rock outcrop.

★487★ DESOTO NATIONAL FOREST

654 W Frontage Rd
Wiggins, MS 39577
Web: www.fs.fed.us/r8/mississippi/desoto
Phone: 601-928-4422; **Fax:** 601-928-5143
Size: 378,538 acres. **Location:** Southeastern Mississippi. Accessible by US 49 and 98; MS 67, 15, 57, 26, 29, 13, 63, and 42. Nearby cities/towns include Biloxi, Gulfport, Hattiesburg, and Laurel. **Facilities:** 25 campgrounds, cabins, dispersed camping, picnic sites, trails (230 miles), scenic drive, fishing pier, group camp. **Activities:** Camping, hunting, fishing, boating, canoeing, hiking, mountain biking, horseback riding, ORV riding. **Special Features:** Mississippi's only nationally designated scenic river, Black Creek, famous for its wide sandbars and relaxed floating pace; two wilderness areas, Black Creek and Leaf; Ashe Forest Tree Nursery, southern region's only tree nursery, built in 1936 by the Civilian Conservation Corps.

See pages 20-21 for map of U.S. National Forests and Grasslands.

3. National Forests and Grasslands

★488★ **DIXIE NATIONAL FOREST**
1789 Wedgewood Ln
Cedar City, UT 84720
Web: www.fs.fed.us/r4/dixie
Phone: 435-865-3700; **Fax:** 435-865-3791
Size: Nearly 2,000,000 acres. **Location:** Southern Utah. Accessible by US 89; UT 12, 14, 18, and 24. Nearby cities/towns include Cedar City, Enterprise, Escalante, Panguitch, and Saint George. **Facilities:** 4 visitor centers, 26 campgrounds, group camp, 5 picnic sites, trails. **Activities:** Camping, hunting, fishing, canoeing, sailing, swimming, water-skiing, hiking, biking, horseback riding, cross-country and downhill skiing, sledding, snowmobiling, spelunking, OHV riding. **Special Features:** Elevations ranging from 2,800 feet to 11,322 feet at Blue Bell Knoll on Boulder Mountain; Red Canyon, with red sandstone formations rivaling those of Bryce Canyon National Park (see entry in national parks section); Panguitch and Navajo lakes; and Powell Point, offering views of three states.

★489★ **ELDORADO NATIONAL FOREST**
100 Forni Rd
Placerville, CA 95667
Web: www.fs.fed.us/r5/eldorado
Phone: 530-622-5061; **Fax:** 530-621-5297
Size: 786,994 acres. **Location:** Eastern California, between Sacramento and Lake Tahoe. Accessible by US 50 and CA 88. Nearby cities/towns include Placerville and Sacramento. **Facilities:** Information centers, 70+ developed campgrounds, 4 cabins, dispersed camping, picnic sites, hiking trails, bridle trails, OHV trails, boat ramps, ski areas, scenic drives (&&). **Activities:** Camping, hunting, fishing, boating, swimming, whitewater rafting, water-skiing, hiking, mountain biking, horseback riding, OHV riding, cross-country and downhill skiing, snowmobiling. **Special Features:** Historic points of interest include Coloma, the actual site of the gold discovery in California on January 24, 1848; Bedford Park, the only municipally-owned gold mine in the U.S. that is open to the public; two wilderness areas totaling 169,000 acres.

★490★ **FINGER LAKES NATIONAL FOREST**
5218 SR 414
Hector, NY 14841
Web: www.fs.fed.us/r9/gmfl/fingerlakes
Phone: 607-546-4470; **Fax:** 607-546-4474
Size: 16,118 acres. **Location:** Lies on a ridge between Seneca and Cayuga Lakes in the Finger Lakes Region of New York State. Accessible by I-90 and I-81; VT 17. **Facilities:** Visitor center, 3 campgrounds, dispersed camping, picnic sites, trails (30+ miles). **Activities:** Camping, hunting, fishing, hiking, horseback riding, cross-country skiing, snowmobiling, blueberry picking. **Special Features:** Includes 12-mile Interloken National Recreation Trail. Five acres of forest are managed for blueberry production; apples, raspberries, and other fruits are also abundant. During the summer, cattle is allowed to graze on forest property to help create habitat for the tiny Henslow sparrow, a bird found in very few places in the world.

★491★ **FISHLAKE NATIONAL FOREST**
115 E 900 North
Richfield, UT 84701
Web: www.fs.fed.us/r4/fishlake
Phone: 435-896-9233; **Fax:** 435-896-9347
Size: 1,424,524 acres. **Location:** Central Utah. Accessible by US 50, 89, and 91; UT 24, 72, and 53; I-70 and I-15. Nearby cities/towns include Beaver, Fillmore, Kanosh, Loa, Monroe, Richfield, and Salina. **Facilities:** 15 campgrounds, 9 group camps, dispersed camping, picnic sites, boating area, trails (1,040 miles), scenic drives. **Activities:** Camping, hunting, fishing, boating, hiking, OHV riding. **Special Features:** Fish Lake Basin, a 13,700-acre area with 2,500 acres of lakes and 670 acres of reservoir; Tushar Mountains, with peaks exceeding 12,000 feet. Three concession-operated resorts are located on forest property: Bowery Haven Resort, Fishlake Lodge, and Lakeside Resort; Canyon of Gold driving tour, with stops of historical interest along the way.

★492★ **FLATHEAD NATIONAL FOREST**
1935 3rd Ave E
Kalispell, MT 59901
Web: www.fs.fed.us/r1/flathead
Phone: 406-758-5200; **Fax:** 406-758-5363
Size: 2,300,000 acres. **Location:** Northwestern Montana. Accessible by US 2 and 93; MT 35. Nearby cities/towns include Columbia Falls, Kalispell, and Whitefish. **Facilities:** 11 cabins, 34 campgrounds, dispersed camping, picnic sites, trails (2,600 miles), ski areas. **Activities:** Camping, hunting, fishing, boating, canoeing, rafting, swimming, hiking, mountain biking, horseback riding, cross-country and downhill skiing, huckleberry picking. **Special Features:** Second largest national forest outside of Alaska, Flathead lands include large parcels designated as wilderness areas: Bob Marshall (1,009,356 acres), Great Bear (285,771 acres), and Mission Mountain (74,000 acres). Attractions include Big Mountain ski and summer resort, Blacktail Ski area, and the Swan and Flathead mountain ranges. Wildlife seen at the time of Lewis and Clark's exploration are all still present today on forest lands.

★493★ **FRANCIS MARION & SUMTER NATIONAL FORESTS**
4931 Broad River Rd
Columbia, SC 29212
Web: www.fs.fed.us/r8/fms
Phone: 803-561-4000; **Fax:** 803-561-4004
Size: 629,258 total acres: 370,442 - Sumter NF; 258,816 - Francis Marion NF. **Location:** Francis Marion NF is in southeastern South Carolina; Sumter NF is in west-central and northwestern South Carolina. Accessible by US 17, 25, and 176; SC 41, 45, 72, and 107. Nearby cities/towns include Charleston, Edgefield, Moncks Corner, Newberry, Union, and Walhalla. **Facilities:** Visitor center (at Francis Marion), 26 campgrounds, dispersed camping, picnic sites, boat ramps, trails (500+ miles), 10 shooting ranges, 10 lookout towers, scenic drives, 5 wilderness areas, archeological sites. **Activities:** Camping, hunting, fishing, boating, canoeing, rafting, swimming, hiking, bird watching, mountain biking, horseback riding, ORV riding. **Special Features:** Piedmont and Blue Ridge Mountains; Chattooga

See pages 20-21 for map of U.S. National Forests and Grasslands.

River, a nationally designated Wild and Scenic River; 15 waterfalls including King Creek Falls, the forest's tallest at 70 feet; Sewee Visitor and Environmental Education Center, which features a red wolf exhibit; numerous archeological sites; seed orchard.

★494★ FREMONT-WINEMA NATIONAL FORESTS

1301 S 'G' St
Lakeview, OR 97630
Web: www.fs.fed.us/r6/frewin/
Phone: 541-947-2151; **Fax:** 541-947-6399
Size: 2,300,000 acres. **Location:** South-central Oregon. Accessible by US 395; OR 66 and 31. Nearby cities/towns include Klamath Falls, Lakeview, and Silver Lake. **Facilities:** 24 forest camps, 22 developed campgrounds, picnic sites, day-use areas, trails, 2 hang gliding launch sites, 3 ski areas, scenic drives, 3 wilderness areas, boat launch. **Activities:** Camping, hunting, fishing, hiking, boating, biking, horseback riding, birdwatching, hang gliding, cross-country and downhill skiing, snowmobiling. **Special Features:** Gearhart Mountain Wilderness, a 22,823-acre area surrounding Gearhart Mountain (7,500 feet above sea level); North Warner Viewpoint (6,300 feet above sea level); Slide Mountain Geologic Area, site of a giant prehistoric landslide. Several indigenous Native American groups inhabit the area.

★495★ GALLATIN NATIONAL FOREST

10 E Babcock Ave
PO Box 310
Bozeman, MT 59771
Web: www.fs.fed.us/r1/gallatin
Phone: 406-587-6701; **Fax:** 406-587-6758
Size: 1,800,000 acres. **Location:** Southwestern Montana. Accessible by US 20, 89, and 191. Nearby cities/towns include Bozeman, Livingston, and West Yellowstone. **Facilities:** Visitors centers, 44 campgrounds, 24 cabins, 25 picnic sites, trails (2,600+ miles), boat launches, 3 ski areas. **Activities:** Camping, hunting, fishing, boating, swimming, hiking, horseback riding, mountain biking, mountain climbing, cross-country and downhill skiing, snowmobiling. **Special Features:** Forest spans six mountain ranges, protects significant parcels of two wilderness areas (Absaroka-Beartooth and Lee Metcalf), and includes long stretches of the Yellowstone, Gallatin, and Madison rivers—which offer anglers ''blue ribbon'' trout fishing. Other features include the Avalanche Center, providing public avalanche advisories daily during mid-winter (406-587-6981) and OTO Dude Ranch, where volunteers learn skills to help restore and renovate a historic ranch built in 1912. Forest surrounds the northwest corner of Yellowstone National Park (see entry in national parks section).

★496★ GEORGE WASHINGTON & JEFFERSON NATIONAL FORESTS

5162 Valleypointe Pkwy
Roanoke, VA 24019
Web: www.fs.fed.us/r8/gwj
Phone: 540-265-5100; **Fax:** 540-265-5145; **Toll Free:** 888-265-0019

Size: 1,770,673 total acres: 1,061,080 - George Washington NF; 709,593 - Jefferson NF. **Location:** Jefferson NF is in western Virginia, crossing WV and KY state lines in places. Accessible by US 11, 220, 21, 52, and 58. Nearby cities/towns include Bristol, Bluefield, Lexington, Lynchburg, Radford, Roanoke, and Wytheville. George Washington NF lies on both sides of the Virginia-West Virginia line, extending from around Covington, VA, in the south up to near Winchester, VA, in the north. Accessible by I-64 and I-81; US 11, 33, and 220; VA 42 and 259. Nearby cities/towns include Front Royal, Luray, Harrisonburg, Lexington, and Waynesboro. **Facilities:** Visitor center (Sherando Lake), 30+ campgrounds, 3 group camps, dispersed camping, 40+ picnic areas, trails (2,000 miles) including 9 national recreation trails and 4 OHV trails, marina, fishing piers, swimming beaches, 7 shooting ranges, scenic drives (3,000 miles) (&&). **Activities:** Camping, hunting, fishing, boating, canoeing, rafting, swimming, hiking, mountain biking, ORV riding, wildlife viewing, bird watching, horseback riding, 14 historical/cultural sites. **Special Features:** Forests are located within eight major river basins (Potomac, James, Roanoke, New, Big Sandy, Holston, Cumberland, and Clinch) and comprise three mountain ranges (Shenandoah, Allegheny, and Blue Ridge). Points of interest include historic and scenic Shenandoah Valley; Elizabeth Furnace Recreation Area, with 150-year-old remnants of the pig iron industry that once flourish here; Reddish Knob (4,397 feet), offering a panoramic view of the Potomac Highlands; Elliot Knob, the highest spot in George Washington NF at 4,463 feet; scenic Blue Ridge Parkway; and a 300-mile segment of the Appalachian National Scenic Trail (see entry in national trails section).

★497★ GIFFORD PINCHOT NATIONAL FOREST

10600 NE 51st Cir
Vancouver, WA 98682
Web: www.fs.fed.us/gpnf
Phone: 360-891-5000; **Fax:** 360-891-5045
Size: 1,312,000 acres. **Location:** On the slopes of the Cascade Mountains in southwest Washington. Accessible by US 12 and I-5, WA 14 and SR 504. Nearby cities/towns include Vancouver, Stevenson, Longview, Centralia, and White Salmon. **Facilities:** Visitor centers and information stations, 40+ campgrounds, equestrian camps, dispersed camping, 2 cabins, day-use sites, trails (1,200 miles), observatory, scenic drives. **Activities:** Camping, fishing, hiking, horseback riding, mountain biking, canoeing, kayaking, berry picking, mountain climbing, cross-country skiing, snowmobiling. **Special Features:** Mount St. Helens National Volcanic Monument, 110,000 acres; Mount Adams, Washington's second highest peak and a designated wilderness area; Indian Heaven Wilderness, a wilderness area on a high plateau with more than 150 lakes; Big Lava Bed, a 14,000-acre lava flow field; Bear Meadow, on the edge of the Mount St. Helens blast zone; lava tubes and caves, including Ape Cave, the longest known lava tube in the continental U.S. at 12,810 feet.

★498★ GILA NATIONAL FOREST

3005 E Camino del Bosque
Silver City, NM 88061
Web: www.fs.fed.us/r3/gila
Phone: 505-388-8201; **Fax:** 505-388-8204

See pages 20-21 for map of U.S. National Forests and Grasslands.

Size: 3,321,101 acres. **Location:** West-central New Mexico. Accessible by US 180; NM 15, 32, 35, 78, 90, 152, and 159. Nearby cities/towns include Deming, Glenwood, Las Cruces, Lordsburg, Reserve, Silver City, and Truth or Consequences. **Facilities:** 30 campgrounds, group camp, picnic sites, trails (100s of miles). **Activities:** Camping, hunting, fishing, rafting, hiking, horseback riding, mountain biking, ORV riding, bird watching, cross-country skiing, snowshoeing. **Special Features:** Forest is semi-desert to alpine country, most of it remote and undeveloped, with elevations of 4,500 to 10,700 feet. Three wilderness areas: Gila Wilderness, the first designated wilderness in the nation, Aldo Leopold Wilderness, and Blue Range Wilderness. Major rivers include Gila River, Mimbres River, and San Francisco River. Points of interest include Catwalk National Recreation Trail, a unique trail of suspended walkways; Gila Cliff Dwellings National Monument (see entry in national parks section), well-preserved cliff dwellings dating back to 1200; natural hot springs.

★499★ GRAND MESA, UNCOMPAHGRE & GUNNISON NATIONAL FORESTS

2250 US Hwy 50
Delta, CO 81416
Web: www.fs.fed.us/r2/gmug
Phone: 970-874-6600; **Fax:** 970-874-6698
Size: 3,161,912 acres. **Location:** West-central Colorado. Accessible by US 6, 50, and 550. Nearby cities/towns include Delta and Grand Junction. **Facilities:** Visitor centers, 59 campgrounds, dispersed camping, picnic sites, trails (100s of miles), observatory, interpretive exhibits, scenic drives, boat ramps. **Activities:** Camping, fishing, boating, hiking, hunting, horseback riding, mountain biking, downhill and cross country skiing, snowmobiling, rafting. **Special Features:** Forest encompasses Grand Mesa, world's largest flat top mountain. Lands End Observatory, built in 1935 by Project Works Administration, overlooking the Grand and Gunnison River valleys with views of LaSal Mountains in Utah and the San Juan Mountains of Colorado; Slugmullion Earth Slide, a continually-moving natural earth flow which began over 700 years ago and created a dam across the Lake Fork of the Gunnison River to form Lake San Cristobal; Dry Mesa Dinosaur Quarry, located on the rim of a deep canyon.

★500★ GREEN MOUNTAIN NATIONAL FOREST

231 N Main St
Rutland, VT 05701
Web: www.fs.fed.us/r9/gmfl
Phone: 802-747-6700; **Fax:** 802-747-6766
Size: 375,000 acres. **Location:** Central and southern Vermont. Accessible by US 4 and 7. Nearby cities/towns include Brandon, Brattleboro, Bennington, Burlington, Manchester, Rochester, and Rutland. **Facilities:** Campgrounds, picnic sites, trail (512 miles), scenic drives, 3 ski areas. **Activities:** Camping, hunting, fishing, swimming, gold panning, hiking, mountain biking, horseback riding, cross-country and downhill skiing, snowmobiling, snowshoeing, snowboarding. **Special Features:** Landscapes range from rugged mountains to secluded hollows. Forest's Green Mountain Range is traversed by Vermont's ''Long Trail,'' the oldest formal hiking trail in the U.S. The trail's southern portion overlays the Appalachian National Scenic Trail

(see entry in national trails section). Forest and nearby Champlain Valley have numerous points of historic interest, including battlegrounds of Revolutionary and French and Indian Wars; 2000+ historic/archeological sites.

★501★ HELENA NATIONAL FOREST

2880 Skyway Dr
Helena, MT 59602
Web: www.fs.fed.us/r1/helena
Phone: 406-449-5201; **Fax:** 406-449-5436
Size: 976,000 acres. **Location:** West-central Montana. Accessible by US 12. Nearby cities/towns include Helena, Lincoln, Townsend, and Boulder. **Facilities:** 7 cabins, 13 campgrounds, picnic sites, trails (1000+ miles), scenic drives. **Activities:** Camping, hunting, fishing, boating, swimming, hiking, mountain biking, horseback riding, cross-country skiing, snowmobiling, OHV riding. **Special Features:** Blackfoot and Missouri rivers; Continental Divide National Scenic Trail (see entry in national trails section); wilderness areas Gates of the Mountains (28,562 acres, including a 38-mile stretch of river) and Scapegoat (239,936 acres); 300,000-acre Elkhorn Wildlife Management Unit.

★502★ HELLS CANYON NATIONAL RECREATION AREA

88401 Hwy 82
Enterprise, OR 97828
Web: www.fs.fed.us/hellscanyon
Phone: 541-426-5546; **Fax:** 541-426-5522
Size: 652,488 acres. **Location:** Northeast corner of Oregon and western Idaho. Accessible by OR 39, 86; ID 29, 71. Nearby towns include Joseph and Enterprise, OR, and Riggins and Grangeville, ID. **Facilities:** 36 campground/picnicking areas, trails (819 miles), boat launch sites, scenic overlooks and drives, lookout tower. **Activities:** Camping, hunting, fishing, canoeing, whitewater rafting, hiking, mountain biking, horseback riding, rock climbing, guided river tours (concession operated). **Special Features:** North America's deepest river gorge encompasses a vast and remote region with dramatic changes in elevation, terrain, climate, and vegetation. Carved by the Snake River, Hells Canyon plunges more than a mile below Oregon's west rim and 8,000 feet below He Devil Peak of Idaho's Seven Devils Mountains. No roads cross Hells Canyon's 10-mile wide expanse, and only three roads lead to the Snake River between the Hells Canyon Dam and the Oregon-Washington state line. Includes the Snake, Imnaha, and Rapid wild and scenic rivers. Hells Canyon NRA is part of Wallowa-Whitman, Nez Perce, and Payette national forests (see separate entries in this section).

★503★ HIAWATHA NATIONAL FOREST

2727 N Lincoln Rd
Escanaba, MI 49829
Web: www.fs.fed.us/r9/forests/hiawatha
Phone: 906-786-4062; **Fax:** 906-789-3311
Size: 879,000 acres. **Location:** Central and Eastern upper peninsula of Michigan. Accessible by US 2, 75, and 41; MI 28, 94, and 123. Nearby cities/towns include Escanaba, Manistique, Munising, Rapid River, Saint Ignace, and Sault Saint Marie.

See pages 20-21 for map of U.S. National Forests and Grasslands.

Facilities: Visitor center (Point Iroquois), 2 cabins, 24 campgrounds, group camp, 17 dispersed campsites, picnic sites, beaches, boat launches, fishing piers, trails (nearly 700 miles), scenic drives. **Activities:** Camping, hunting, fishing, boating, swimming, hiking, mountain biking, ORV riding, horseback riding, cross-country skiing, snowmobiling, ice fishing. **Special Features:** Access to 77 miles of shoreline of Lakes Superior, Michigan, and Huron; 775 miles of rivers and streams; 413 lakes; 150 waterfalls; numerous historic lighthouses.

★504★ HOLLY SPRINGS NATIONAL FOREST

1000 Front St
Oxford, MS 38655
Web: www.fs.fed.us/r8/mississippi/hollysprings
Phone: 662-236-6550; **Fax:** 662-234-8318
Size: 147,000 acres. **Location:** North-central Mississippi, southeast of Memphis. Accessible by US 72 and 78; MS 7, 4, 5, 6, 30, 349, 355, and 370. Nearby cities/towns include Holly Springs, New Albany, and Oxford. **Facilities:** Campgrounds, picnic sites, boat ramps, fishing pier (&), trails, playground. **Activities:** Camping, hunting, fishing, boating, swimming, hiking. **Special Features:** Historic Indian mounds, more than 40 lakes (originally built for flood and erosion control) including 260-acre Chewalla Lake. Nearby are state-owned Upper Sardis Wildlife Management Area and Wall Doxey State Park (see entry in Mississippi state parks section).

★505★ HOMOCHITTO NATIONAL FOREST

1200 Hwy 184 E
Meadville, MS 39653
Web: www.southernregion.fs.fed.us/mississippi/homochitto
Phone: 601-384-5876; **Fax:** 601-384-2172
Size: 189,000 acres. **Location:** Southwestern Mississippi. Accessible by US 98 and 84; MS 28, 33, 550, 551, and 563. Nearby cities/towns include Brookhaven, Gloster, Meadville, and Natchez. **Facilities:** Campground, dispersed camping, picnic sites, trails, scenic drive, playground. **Activities:** Camping, hunting, fishing, boating, swimming, hiking, mountain biking, horseback riding. **Special Features:** Popular hunting area, rich with turkey and deer; 12-acre Clear Spring Lake; sandy beach and a manicured grass area.

★506★ HOOSIER NATIONAL FOREST

811 Constitution Ave
Bedford, IN 47421
Web: www.fs.fed.us/r9/hoosier
Phone: 812-275-5987; **Fax:** 812-279-3423
Size: 200,000 acres. **Location:** South-central Indiana. Accessible by US 50 and 150; IN 37, 46, 62, and 64. Nearby cities/towns include Bedford, Bloomington, Tell City, and Evansville. **Facilities:** 5 campgrounds, equestrian camps, group camp, picnic sites, trails (239 miles), lookout tower, scenic drives. **Activities:** Camping, hunting, fishing, boating, swimming, hiking, mountain biking, horseback riding, rock collecting, berry picking, mushroom picking. **Special Features:** Pioneer Mothers Memorial Forest, 88 acres of virgin old-growth walnut and oak trees; Lick Creek Settlement, site of a town established in 1820 by freed slaves and probable waystation on the Underground

Railroad; Lake Monroe, Indiana's largest lake (a reservoir covering 10,750 acres) which abuts the forest's northwest corner.

★507★ HUMBOLDT-TOIYABE NATIONAL FOREST

1200 Franklin Way
Sparks, NV 89431
Web: www.fs.fed.us/r4/htnf
Phone: 775-331-6444; **Fax:** 775-355-5399
Size: 6,300,000 acres. **Location:** Scattered parcels across Nevada and into eastern California. Accessible by US 93, 395, 6, 50, and 95. Nearby cities/towns include Ely, Elko, Las Vegas, Reno, Tonopah, and Winnemucca. **Facilities:** 70+ campgrounds, dispersed camping, picnic areas, trails (2,000 miles). **Activities:** Camping, hunting, fishing, hiking, ORV riding, mountain biking, horseback riding, cross-country skiing, snowmobiling. **Special Features:** Largest national forest outside Alaska. Areas of interest include Jarbridge Wilderness, Ruby Mountains, crystal clear lakes high in the Sierra, aspen stands on Table Mountain, sagebrush lowlands, alpine meadows, streams, massive canyons, and Mount Charleston. The Pacific Crest National Scenic Trail (see entry in national trails section) passes through the forest south of Lake Tahoe.

★508★ HURON-MANISTEE NATIONAL FORESTS

1755 S Mitchell St
Cadillac, MI 49601
Web: www.fs.fed.us/r9/hmnf
Phone: 231-775-2421; **Fax:** 231-775-5551; **Toll Free:** 800-821-6263
Size: 964,000 acres. **Location:** Huron NF is in east-central Michigan; Manistee NF is in west-central Michigan. Accessible by US 10, 23, 27, 31, and 131; MI 20, 33, 37, 46, 55, 65, 72, and 82. Nearby cities/towns include Big Rapids, Cadillac, Manistee, Grayling, Harrisville, and Muskegon. **Facilities:** Visitor center, 20 campgrounds, 5 group camps, dispersed camping, picnic sites, boat launches, trails (330+ miles), scenic drives. **Activities:** Camping, fishing, boating, swimming, hiking, horseback riding, OHV riding, cross-country skiing, snowmobiling. **Special Features:** The historic Lumberman's Monument, erected in 1932; access to Lake Huron and Lake Michigan and their excellent beaches.

★509★ IDAHO PANHANDLE NATIONAL FORESTS

3815 Schreiber Way
Coeur d'Alene, ID 83815
Web: www.fs.fed.us/ipnf
Phone: 208-765-7223; **Fax:** 208-765-7307
Size: About 2,500,000 acres. **Location:** In Idaho, Montana, and Washington. Accessible by I-90; ID 3, 57, and 200; US 2, 10, 95, and 95A. Nearby cities/towns include Avery, Coeur d'Alene, Kellog, and Wallace. Consists of the Coeur d'Alene and portions of the Kaniksu and Saint Joe national forests. **Facilities:** 11 cabins, 42 campgrounds, dispersed camping, picnic sites, trails (1,984 miles), scenic drives, ski areas. **Activities:** Camping, hunting, fishing, boating, rafting, hiking, mountain biking, OHV riding, horseback riding, swimming, snowmobiling, snowshoeing, cross-country and downhill skiing, rock hounding, prospecting, fossil hunting, berry picking, mushroom collecting, wildlife

See pages 20-21 for map of U.S. National Forests and Grasslands.

viewing. **Special Features:** Situated in the east-central part of the Columbia Plateau, forests include portions of Idaho's most scenic mountain ranges: the Selkirk, Cabinet, Coeur d'Alene, and Bitterroot mountains. Points of interest include Emerald Creek Garnet Area, where visitors can dig for Idaho's state gem, and Lookout Pass Ski and Recreation Area.

★510★ **INYO NATIONAL FOREST**

351 Pacu Ln, Suite 200
Bishop, CA 93514
Web: www.fs.fed.us/r5/inyo
Phone: 760-873-2400; **Fax:** 760-873-2458
Size: 2,000,000 acres. **Location:** Extends 165 miles along the California and Nevada border between Ridgecrest and Reno. Accessible by US 6 and 395; CA 168. Nearby cities/towns include Bishop and Mammoth Lakes. **Facilities:** 4 visitors' centers, 16 resorts with cabins (concession operated), 71 campgrounds, 16 group camps, equestrian camps, hike-in camps, dispersed camping, picnic sites, trails, 2 alpine ski areas, 33 interpretive sites of historical or natural interest, 400 lakes. **Activities:** Camping, fishing, boating, swimming, water-skiing, hiking, mountain biking, horseback riding, cross-country and downhill skiing, snowmobiling, sledding, ice skating. **Special Features:** Mono Lake, a 60-square-mile lake 2.5 times as salty as seawater, estimated to be more than 700,000 years old; Mono Basin National Scenic Area, an area of unusual geological formations known as tufa; Ancient Bristlecone Pine Forest, world's oldest known living trees, some of which are more than 40 centuries old; Alabama Hills, a favorite location for Hollywood westerns, featuring unusual rock formations with Mount Whitney, California's highest peak (14,496 feet), in the background. Portions of John Muir Trail and Pacific Crest National Scenic Trail (see entry in national trails section) pass through the forest. Nearby are Sequoia National Park, Kings Canyon National Park, and Devil's Postpile National Monument (see separate entries in national parks section).

★511★ **KAIBAB NATIONAL FOREST**

800 S 6th St
Williams, AZ 86046
Web: www.fs.fed.us/r3/kai
Phone: 928-635-8200; **Fax:** 928-635-8208
Size: 1,600,000 acres. **Location:** Central and north-central Arizona. Accessible by US 89, 64, and 67. Nearby cities/towns include Ash Fork, Cottonwood, Flagstaff, Fredonia, Grand Canyon, and Williams. **Facilities:** 2 visitors centers, 8 campgrounds, picnic sites, trails, ski area, scenic drives. **Activities:** Camping, hunting, fishing, hiking, horseback riding, mountain biking, skiing, wildlife viewing. **Special Features:** The Grand Canyon divides the forest into North and South districts. Forest provides the only known habitat for Kaibab squirrels. Highway 67, also known as the Kaibab Plateau Scenic Byway, is described as "the most beautiful 44 miles in Arizona."

KANIKSU NATIONAL FOREST
(see Idaho Panhandle National Forests)

★512★ **KISATCHIE NATIONAL FOREST**

2500 Shreveport Hwy
Pineville, LA 71360
Web: www.fs.fed.us/r8/kisatchie
Phone: 318-473-7160
Size: 604,000 acres. **Location:** West-central Louisiana. Accessible by US 71, 165, 167, and 84. Nearby cities/towns include Alexandria, Minden, and Winnfield. **Facilities:** Campgrounds, picnic sites, trails (100+ miles), boat launches, scenic drives. **Activities:** Camping, hunting, fishing, boating, swimming, water-skiing, hiking, bicycling, horseback riding, OHV riding. **Special Features:** Sugar Cane National Recreation Trail and Wild Azalea National Recreation Trail; historic Fullerton Sawmill, one of the South's largest sawmills, which operated during the early 1900s; Longleaf Trail National Scenic Byway; 8,700-acre Kisatchie Hills Wilderness Area.

★513★ **KLAMATH NATIONAL FOREST**

1312 Fairlane Rd
Yreka, CA 96097
Web: www.fs.fed.us/r5/klamath
Phone: 530-842-6131; **Fax:** 530-398-4599
Size: 1,700,000 acres. **Location:** Straddles the California-Oregon border. Accessible by I-5. Nearby cities/towns include Etna, Happy Camp, and Orleans. **Facilities:** 36 campgrounds, dispersed camping, resorts (concession operated), picnic sites, trails (1,000+ miles), lookout towers, 5 wilderness areas. **Activities:** Camping, hunting, fishing, swimming, whitewater rafting, hiking, mountain biking, horseback riding, mountain climbing, spelunking, cross-country and downhill skiing, snowmobiling. **Special Features:** Marble Mountains and Trinity wilderness areas; 200 miles of river system for rafting and 152 miles of wild and scenic rivers; a 116-mile segment of Pacific Crest National Scenic Trail (see entry in national trails section); more than 100 glacial lakes. Forest houses the Living Memorial Sculpture Garden, ten stylized metal sculptures that honor veterans of all wars and people affected by war, both in the battle zone and at home.

★514★ **KOOTENAI NATIONAL FOREST**

506 Hwy 2 W
Libby, MT 59923
Web: www.fs.fed.us/r1/kootenai
Phone: 406-293-6211; **Fax:** 406-283-7709
Size: 2,200,000 acres. **Location:** Northwestern Montana. Accessible by US 2 and 93; MT 37, 56, 200, and 508. Nearby cities/towns include Eureka and Libby. **Facilities:** 6 rental cabins and lookout towers, 39 developed campgrounds, picnic sites, trails (1,343 miles), scenic drives. **Activities:** Camping, hunting, fishing, boating, swimming, water skiing, hiking, horseback riding, cross-country and downhill skiing, snowmobiling, rock climbing, bicycling, gold panning. **Special Features:** Portions of five mountain ranges: Whitefish Range, Purcell Mountains, Bitterroot Range, Salish Mountains, Cabinet Mountains; Kootenai and Clark Fork rivers; Lake Koocanusa, Cabinet Gorge, and

See pages 20-21 for map of U.S. National Forests and Grasslands.

3. National Forests and Grasslands

Noxon reservoirs; 100 lakes ranging from small alpine lakes to 1,240-acre McGregor Lake.

★515★ LAKE TAHOE BASIN MANAGEMENT UNIT

35 College Dr
South Lake Tahoe, CA 96150
Web: www.fs.fed.us/r5/ltbmu
Phone: 530-543-2600; **Fax:** 530-543-2693
Size: 151,300 acres. **Location:** In the Sierra Nevada Mountains. Accessible by US 50 and 89 (12 miles south of I-80). Nearby cities/towns include South Lake Tahoe and Truckee, CA, and Carson City and Reno, NV. **Facilities:** Visitor center, 9 Forest Service campgrounds and 10 other campgrounds, dispersed camping, picnic sites, trails (210 miles), beaches, boat ramps, historic sites. **Activities:** Camping, hunting, fishing, boating, swimming, water-skiing, hiking, mountain biking, horseback riding, OHV riding, cross-country and downhill skiing, snowmobiling. **Special Features:** Manages federal lands surrounding Lake Tahoe, including portions of Eldorado, Tahoe, and Toiyabe national forests (see separate entries). Lake Tahoe, which sits on the "bend" along the California-Nevada border, is 22 miles long and 12 miles wide, includes 71 miles of shoreline, and is the third deepest lake in North America. California and Nevada state parks are also located around the lake.

★516★ LAND BETWEEN THE LAKES NATIONAL
RECREATION AREA

100 Van Morgan Dr
Golden Pond, KY 42211
Web: www.lbl.org
Phone: 270-924-2000
Size: 170,000 acres. **Location:** Southwest Kentucky and northwest Tennessee. Accessible by I-24; US 62-641, 68, 79. Nearby cities/towns include Paduca, Princeton, Iuka, and Golden Pond, KY, and Paris, Buchanon, and Bumpus Mills, TN. **Facilities:** 3 visitors centers, 4 campgrounds, rental cabins, dispersed camping, 6 beaches, trails (200+ miles), boat ramps, docks, fishing piers, canoe rentals, stables, ORV area, planetarium, gift shop. **Activities:** Camping, hunting, fishing, boating, canoeing, hiking, mountain biking, horseback riding, ORV riding, guided tours, interpretive programs. **Special Features:** Inland peninsula between Kentucky Lake and Lake Barkley with 300 miles of undeveloped shoreline. Points of interest include Elk & Bison Prairie, 750 acres of restored prairie and home to the largest publicly owned bison herd east of the Mississippi; the Homeplace, a rural Tennessee farm circa 1850; Nature Station, an outdoor activity and environmental education center.

★517★ LASSEN NATIONAL FOREST

2550 Riverside Dr
Susanville, CA 96130
Web: www.fs.fed.us/r5/lassen
Phone: 530-257-2151; **Fax:** 530-252-6428
Size: 1,200,000 acres. **Location:** Northeastern California. Accessible by US 395; CA 36, 44, and 89. Nearby cities/towns include Chico, Mill Creek, Red Bluff, Redding, and Susanville. **Facilities:** Resort with cabins, campgrounds, dispersed camping, picnic sites, hiking trails, OHV trails, marina, boat ramps, 6

winter sports areas. **Activities:** Camping, fishing, boating, sailing, swimming, OHV riding, water-skiing, hiking, horseback riding, cross-country and downhill skiing, snowmobiling. **Special Features:** Forest surrounds Lassen Volcanic National Park (see entry in national parks section), and encompasses an area of California known as "the crossroads," where the Sierra Nevada, the Cascades, and the Great Basin converge. Points of interest include Eagle Lake, California's second largest natural lake; ancient pictographs and hieroglyphics; volcanic lava flow tubes; and 120 miles of the Pacific Crest National Scenic Trail (see entry in national trails section).

★518★ LEWIS & CLARK NATIONAL FOREST

1101 15th St N
Great Falls, MT 59401
Web: www.fs.fed.us/r1/lewisclark
Phone: 406-791-7700; **Fax:** 406-761-1972
Size: 1,800,000 acres. **Location:** West-central Montana. Accessible by US 12, 87, and 89. Nearby cities/towns include Choteau, Augusta, Stanford, Harlowton, White Sulphur Springs, and Great Falls. **Facilities:** Visitor center, 5 cabins, 29 campgrounds, picnic sites, trails, 2 ski areas, scenic drives, 14 boat camps. **Activities:** Camping, hunting, fishing, boating, canoeing, rafting, swimming, hiking, mountain biking, horseback riding, ORV riding, snowmobiling, downhill and cross-country skiing. **Special Features:** Lewis and Clark National Historic Trail Interpretive Center celebrates the accomplishments of the historic expedition, focusing on the challenges faced in trying to portage the Great Falls of the Missouri River and on Thomas Jefferson's vision for expanding the American West. Forest's Rocky Mountain Division includes rugged mountain peaks that often have snow for 10 months of the year; the Jefferson Division comprises six distinct mountain ranges. A segment of the 3,100-mile Continental Divide National Scenic Trail passes through the forest (see separate entry in national trails section).

★519★ LINCOLN NATIONAL FOREST

1101 New York Ave
Alamogordo, NM 88310
Web: www.fs.fed.us/r3/lincoln
Phone: 505-434-7200; **Fax:** 505-434-7218
Size: 1,103,441 acres. **Location:** South central New Mexico. Accessible by US 60, 70, and 380; NM 83, 24, 37, and 48. Nearby cities/towns include Ruidoso, Alamogordo, Artesia, Capitan, Carlsbad, Cloudcroft, and Roswell. **Facilities:** 14 campgrounds, 8 group camps, dispersed camping, picnic sites, trails (400 miles), 2 ski areas, scenic viewpoints, scenic drives. **Activities:** Camping, hunting, fishing, hiking, mountain biking, ORV riding, birdwatching, tubing, horseback riding, spelunking, cross-country and downhill skiing, snowmobiling. **Special Features:** Birthplace of "Smokey Bear," the symbol of wildfire prevention. In 1950, a black bear cub was found clinging to a tree during a wildfire in the northern part of the forest. The cub was nicknamed "Hot Foot Teddy" by firefighters, and, after being nursed back to health, he was flown to Washington, D.C., to reside in the National Zoo as "Smokey Bear." Unique attractions include Sitting Bull Falls, a 180-foot waterfall located in a bowl canyon; Sunspot Solar Observatory at Sacramento

See pages 20-21 for map of U.S. National Forests and Grasslands.

3. National Forests and Grasslands

Peak; and the Apache Point Lunar Observatory. Nearby is Carlsbad Caverns National Park (see entry in national parks section).

★520★ LOLO NATIONAL FOREST

Fort Missoula Bldg 24
Missoula, MT 59804
Web: www.fs.fed.us/r1/lolo
Phone: 406-329-3750; **Fax:** 406-329-3795
Size: 2,100,000 acres. **Location:** Western Montana surrounding Missoula. Accessible by I-90; US 83, 200, and 12. Nearby cities/towns include Missoula, Plains, Seeley Lake, and Superior. **Facilities:** 9 rental cabins and lookouts, 31 campgrounds, picnic sites, trails (2,500+ miles). **Activities:** Camping, hunting, fishing, boating, canoeing, rafting, swimming, water skiing, hiking, mountain biking, horseback riding, cross-country skiing, snowmobiling, wildlife viewing. **Special Features:** Remote, high alpine lakes, whitewater streams, heavily forested ridges, and smooth rolling meadows. Areas of interest include the Bitterroot Mountains and the Rattlesnake National Recreation Area; and the Lolo National Historic Trail, a section of the Nez Perce Tribe's traditional trail across the Bitterroot Range, which Lewis and Clark followed in 1805 and 1806.

★521★ LOS PADRES NATIONAL FOREST

6755 Hollister Ave, Suite 150
Goleta, CA 93117
Web: www.fs.fed.us/r5/lospadres
Phone: 805-968-6640; **Fax:** 805-961-5729
Size: 1,750,000 acres. **Location:** Western California between Ventura and Monterey. Accessible by US 101. Nearby cities/towns include Atascadero, Carmel, Frazier Park, King City, Monterey, Paso Robles, San Luis Obispo, Santa Barbara, Santa Maria, and Ventura. **Facilities:** 69 campgrounds (most have fewer than 10 campsites), picnic sites, trails (1,257 miles), OHV roads (459 miles), winter sports area. **Activities:** Camping, fishing, boating, canoeing, swimming, hiking, mountain biking, horseback riding, OHV riding, rock climbing, hang gliding, cross-country skiing, hunting, target shooting. **Special Features:** Home to the endangered California condor. Points of interest include La Panza Range, Santa Ynez River Recreation Area, Figueroa Mountain Recreation Area, Sierra Madre Mountains, and ten wilderness areas. Forest property comprises 400 miles of year-round and seasonal streams, 37 lakes and reservoirs (in or near the forest), and many miles of coastal shoreline, including the spectacular Big Sur Coast. Forest also contains rock art created by the Chumash Indians.

★522★ MALHEUR NATIONAL FOREST

431 Patterson Bridge Rd
John Day, OR 97845
Web: www.fs.fed.us/r6/malheur
Phone: 541-575-3000; **Fax:** 541-575-3001
Size: 1,700,000 acres. **Location:** In the Blue Mountains of eastern Oregon. Accessible by US 26 and 395. Nearby cities/towns include Burns and John Day. **Facilities:** 22 campgrounds, group camps, equestrian camps, hiking trails, snowmobile trails (502 trails), picnic sites, boat launches. **Activities:** Camping, hunting, fishing, boating, hiking, horseback riding, rock hounding, mountain biking, cross-country skiing, snowmobiling. **Special Features:** 68,700-acre Strawberry Mountain Wilderness Area, Cedar Grove Botanical Area, Vinegar Hill-Indian Rock Scenic Area, 50-acre Lake Magone, and stretches of federally designated Wild and Scenic River on the Malheur and North Fork.

★523★ MANTI-LA SAL NATIONAL FOREST

599 W Price River Dr
Price, UT 84501
Web: www.fs.fed.us/r4/mantilasal
Phone: 435-637-2817; **Fax:** 435-637-4940
Size: 1,413,111 acres. **Location:** Southeastern Utah. Accessible by US 89; UT 10, 29, 31, 46, and 95. Nearby cities/towns include Blanding, Ferron, Huntington, Manti, Moab, and Monticello. **Facilities:** Visitors centers, 25 campgrounds, dispersed camping, picnic sites, trails (100s of miles), winter sports area, scenic drives. **Activities:** Camping, hunting, fishing, boating, hiking, OHV riding, mountain biking, horseback riding, cross-country skiing, snowmobiling. **Special Features:** Huntington Creek, noted as one of the premiere fly-fishing streams in Utah; Joe's Valley, a 1200-acre reservoir; Wasatch Plateau; La Sal Mountains; Abajo (or Blue) Mountains; Dark Canyon Wilderness Area.

★524★ MARK TWAIN NATIONAL FOREST

401 Fairgrounds Rd
Rolla, MO 65401
Web: www.fs.fed.us/r9/forests/marktwain
Phone: 573-364-4621; **Fax:** 573-364-6844
Size: 1,472,667 acres. **Location:** South-central Missouri. Accessible by US 60 and 67; MO 21, 32, 49, and 72. Nearby cities/towns include Branson, Springfield, Van Buren, West Plains, and Willow Springs. **Facilities:** 23 campgrounds, 3 group camps, picnic sites, swimming beaches, trails (742 miles), boat ramps, fishing docks (&&). **Activities:** Camping, boating, canoeing, hunting, fishing, swimming, hiking, mountain biking, horseback riding, ORV riding, bird watching, wildlife viewing. **Special Features:** Forest encompasses 14 clear, fast-flowing streams, 16 lakes, and 7 wilderness areas comprising more than 63,000 acres. With an average flow of about 220 million gallons per day, Greer Spring is the second largest spring in Missouri.

★525★ MEDICINE BOW-ROUTT NATIONAL FORESTS

2468 Jackson St
Laramie, WY 82070
Web: www.fs.fed.us/r2/mbr
Phone: 307-745-2300; **Fax:** 307-745-2398
Size: Nearly 3,000,000 acres. **Location:** Extend from north central Colorado to central Wyoming. Nearby cities/towns include Casper, Cheyenne, Laramie, and Steamboat Springs. Accessible by US 30, US 40, WY 130 and 230, and CO 125. **Facilities:** Visitor center, 14 rental cabins and stations, 58 campgrounds, dispersed camping, picnic areas, boat ramps, lookout towers, scenic drives, ski areas. **Activities:** Camping, fishing, boating, hunting, hiking, mountain biking, ORV riding, rock

See pages 20-21 for map of U.S. National Forests and Grasslands.

climbing, rafting, water skiing, cross-country and downhill skiing, snowmobiling. **Special Features:** Encompasses portions of Medicine Bow Mountains, the Sierra Madre, and Laramie Range. Points of interest include sites with unusual geological formations (Devil's Playground, Turtle Rock, and Vedauwoo Glen), Black Mountain lookout station, and LaBonte Canyon. Rabbit Ears Pass, an historic landmark used by pioneers

★526★ MENDOCINO NATIONAL FOREST

825 N Humbolt Ave
Willows, CA 95988
Web: www.fs.fed.us/r5/mendocino
Phone: 530-934-3316; **Fax:** 530-934-7384
Size: 913,306 acres. **Location:** Northwestern California. Accessible by I-5, US 101, CA 20, and CA 162. Nearby cities/towns include Corning, Laytonville, Sacramento, Ukiah, and Willits. **Facilities:** 30 campgrounds, 4 group camps, dispersed camping, resorts (concession operated), picnic sites, hiking trails, OHV trails (350+ miles). **Activities:** Camping, hunting, fishing, boating, swimming, water-skiing, whitewater rafting, hiking, mountain biking, horseback riding, OHV riding, rock hounding, hang gliding, cross-country skiing, snowmobiling. **Special Features:** Only California national forest not crossed by paved roads. Features 300 miles of streams and 2,000 acres of lakes and ponds, mineral hot springs, Yolla Bolly-Middle Eel and Snow Mountain wilderness areas.

★527★ MODOC NATIONAL FOREST

800 W 12th St
Alturas, CA 96101
Web: www.fs.fed.us/r5/modoc
Phone: 530-233-5811; **Fax:** 530-233-8719
Size: 1,979,407 acres. **Location:** Northeastern corner of California. Accessible by US 299 and 395; CA 139. Nearby cities/towns include Adin, Alturas, Canby, Cedarville, and Tulelake. **Facilities:** Campgrounds, dispersed camping, boat launches, picnic sites, trails (175 miles), scenic drives. **Activities:** Camping, hunting, fishing, boating, hiking, mountain biking, wild horse viewing, horseback riding, hang gliding, rock hounding, cross-country and downhill skiing, sledding, snowmobiling, snowshoeing. **Special Features:** Mountains, pine forests and meadows, lakes, streams, rugged canyons, wetlands, lava beds, and high desert plateaus. Points of interest include Happy Camp and Sugar Hill Lookouts with panoramic views and exhibits of Forest Service history; stone circles, rock piles, and petroglyphs revealing 10,000 years of Native American occupation; tree carvings (arborglyphs) made by Basque shepherds during the late 19th and early 20th centuries; abandoned homesteads of early settlers.

★528★ MONONGAHELA NATIONAL FOREST

200 Sycamore St
Elkins, WV 26241
Web: www.fs.fed.us/r9/mnf
Phone: 304-636-1800; **Fax:** 304-636-1875
Size: 919,000+ acres. **Location:** Eastern West Virginia. Accessible by SR 55, US 33, 219, and 250. Nearby towns include Elkins, Petersburg, Parson, Marlinton, Richwood, Bartow, and White Sulphur Springs. **Facilities:** 2 visitor centers, 23 campgrounds, dispersed camping, 17 picnic sites, trails (500+ miles), scenic drives, historic sites, lookout towers. **Activities:** Camping, hunting, trapping, fishing, swimming, boating, canoeing, whitewater rafting, hiking, rock climbing, mountain biking, horseback riding, cross-country skiing. **Special Features:** Landscape of spectacular views, blueberry thickets, highland bogs, and open areas with exposed rocks. Features include Spruce Knob, West Virginia's highest peak (4,863 feet); Falls of Hills Creek Scenic Area, a 114-acre area with three waterfalls; Seneca Rocks Discovery Center; Smoke Hole Canyon, where the South Branch of the Potomac River has carved a 20-mile-long, half-mile deep canyon with nearly vertical walls.

★529★ MOUNT BAKER-SNOQUALMIE NATIONAL FOREST

21905 64th Ave W
Mountain Terrace, WA 98043
Web: www.fs.fed.us/r6/mbs
Phone: 425-775-9702; **Toll Free:** 800-627-0062
Size: 1,724,229 acres. **Location:** Northwest and west-central Washington state. Accessible by I-90 and US 2; WA 20, 542, 530, and 410. Nearby cities/towns include Bellingham, Everett, Seattle, and Tacoma. **Facilities:** 31 campgrounds, 14 group camps, 27 picnic areas, trails (1,500+ miles), 4 ski areas, lookout towers, scenic drives. **Activities:** Camping, hunting, fishing, boating, canoeing, whitewater rafting, hiking, mountain biking, horseback riding, mountain climbing, cross-country and downhill skiing, snowmobiling, snowshoeing. **Special Features:** Forest extends for more than 140 miles along the western slopes of the Cascade Mountains. Includes 8 wilderness areas, 2 volcanic peaks, Mount Baker and Glacier Peak, which tower thousands of feet above the adjacent ridges, and more glaciers and snow fields than any other national forest in the lower 48 states. Contains the Skagit Wild and Scenic River System, composed of 158 combined miles on the Skagit, Cascade, Sauk, and Suiattle rivers.

★530★ MOUNT HOOD NATIONAL FOREST

16400 Champion Way
Sandy, OR 97055
Web: www.fs.fed.us/r6/mthood
Phone: 503-668-1700; **Fax:** 503-668-1794
Size: 1,067,043 acres. **Location:** In the Cascade Mountain Range of northwestern Oregon. Accessible by US 26 and 35. Nearby cities/towns include Gresham, Hood River, and Portland. **Facilities:** 83 campgrounds, 1 cabin, 20 day-use sites, trails (1,000 miles), winter sports area, lookout tower, scenic drives, hot springs. **Activities:** Camping, fishing, boating, hiking, mountain biking, horseback riding, rafting, OHV riding, mountain climbing, snowboarding, snowmobiling, cross-country and downhill skiing, berry picking, mushroom collecting. **Special Features:** 189,200 acres of designated wilderness, featuring Mount Hood Wilderness, which includes the mountain's peak and upper slopes, and Olallie Scenic Area, a remote lake basin. Other points of interest include Timberline Lodge (built in 1937 high on Mount Hood), Lost Lake, Trillium Lake, Timothy Lake, Rock Creek Reservoir, and portions of the Old Oregon Trail including Barlow Road.

See pages 20-21 for map of U.S. National Forests and Grasslands.

3. National Forests and Grasslands

★531★ NANTAHALA NATIONAL FOREST

160A Zillicoa St
Asheville, NC 28802
Web: www.cs.unca.edu/nfsnc
Phone: 828-257-4200
Size: 531,286 acres. **Location:** Southwestern North Carolina. Accessible by US 19, 64, and 129; NC 28 and 107. Nearby cities/towns include Bryson City, Hayesville, Murphy, and Robbinsville. **Facilities:** Campgrounds, group camp, lodge, picnic sites, trails (1,734 miles), swimming beaches, boat ramps, lookout tower, scenic drives, ORV areas. **Activities:** Camping, hunting, fishing, boating, canoeing, whitewater rafting, swimming, hiking, mountain biking, horseback riding, ORV riding, rock climbing. **Special Features:** Because the sun penetrates the bottom of the gorge only at noon, the Cherokee named the area Nantahala, ''Land of the Noon-Day Sun.'' Attractions include Nantahala River Gorge, an 8.5-mile stretch of Nantahala River known as a world-class whitewater river; a portion of the Appalachian National Scenic Trail (see entry in national trails section); Joyce Kilmer Memorial Forest, a remnant old-growth forest that contains specimens of more than 100 tree species, many more than 400 years old. 411-foot Whitewater Falls, the highest falls east of the Rocky Mountains. Great Smoky Mountains National Park (see entry in national parks section) adjoins the forest at its northern boundary.

★532★ NEBRASKA & SAMUEL R. MCKELVIE NATIONAL FORESTS

125 N Main St
Chadron, NE 69337
Web: www.fs.fed.us/r2/nebraska
Phone: 308-432-0300; **Fax:** 308-432-0309
Size: 257,628 total acres: 141,549 acres - Nebraska NF, 116,079 acres - Samuel R McKelvie NF. **Location:** Tracts in northwest and central Nebraska. Accessible by US 20, 83, and 385; NE 2. Nearby towns are Chadron, Dunning, and Thedford. **Facilities:** Visitor centers, 9 campgrounds, picnic areas, trails (100+ miles), swimming pool, lookout tower, softball diamond. **Activities:** Camping, hunting, fishing, swimming, hiking, horseback riding, rock hounding, bird watching, OHV riding, wildlife watching. **Special Features:** Warbonnet and Yellow Hair monuments, memorializing a 1876 conflict between the U.S. Army's 5th calvary and a band of Cheyenne; Soldier Creek Wilderness, with a 15-mile loop trail; Merritt Reservoir, ranked among the best fishing lakes in Nebraska; and Merritt Reservoir State Recreation Area (see entry in Nebraska state parks section).

★533★ NEZ PERCE NATIONAL FOREST

1005 Hwy 13
Grangeville, ID 83530
Web: www.fs.fed.us/r1/nezperce
Phone: 208-983-1950; **Fax:** 208-983-4099
Size: 2,200,000 acres. **Location:** North-central Idaho. Accessible by US 12 and 95; ID 13 and 14. Nearby cities/towns include Grangeville and Kooskia. **Facilities:** 3 rental cabins, 70 campgrounds, hiking and bridle trails, snowmobile trails, boat launch, lookout tower, scenic drives. **Activities:** Camping, hunting, fishing, boating, canoeing, whitewater rafting, hiking, horseback riding, cross-country skiing, snowmobiling, ATV riding, mountain biking. **Special Features:** Five rivers designated as Wild and Scenic: Rapid, Salmon, Selway, Snake, and Middle Fork of the Clearwater; 4 wilderness areas, comprising nearly half of the forest's total acreage; Hells Canyon National Recreation Area (see separate entry in this section).

★534★ OCALA NATIONAL FOREST

17147 E Hwy 40
Silver Springs, FL 34488
Web: www.fs.fed.us/r8/florida
Phone: 352-625-2520
Size: 389,000 acres. **Location:** Central Florida. Accessible by US 17 and 301; FL 19, 40, 42, and 314. Nearby cities/towns include DeLand, Eustis, Ocala, and Palatka. **Facilities:** 2 cabins, 14 campgrounds, 3 group camps, dispersed camping, picnic sites, trails, canoe rentals, boat ramps, fishing piers, rifle range, visitor centers. **Activities:** Camping, hunting, fishing, boating, sailing, canoeing, water-skiing, swimming, snorkeling, hiking, mountain biking, horseback riding, OHV riding. **Special Features:** Nation's southernmost forest and oldest national forest east of the Mississippi. Points of interest include Big Scrub, largest stand of sand pine trees in the world; Juniper Springs, a semi-tropical environment unique in the national forest system; Alexander Springs Creek Wilderness, a hardwood swamp and sand scrub pine ecosystem that provides habitat for a wide variety of wildlife; a 67-mile segment of the Florida National Scenic Trail (see entry in national trails section).

★535★ OKANOGAN NATIONAL FOREST

1240 S 2nd Ave
Okanogan, WA 98841
Web: www.fs.fed.us/r6/oka
Phone: 509-826-3275; **Fax:** 509-826-3789
Size: 1,501,782 acres. **Location:** Northern Washington. Accessible by US 97 and WA 20. Nearby cities/towns include Conconully, Mazama, Okanogan, Twisp, and Winthrup. **Facilities:** 38 campgrounds, trails (1,285 miles), scenic overlooks, scenic drives, 55 lakes, picnic sites. **Activities:** Camping, fishing, boating, hiking, horseback riding, mountain biking, hunting, OHV riding, rock climbing, cross-country and downhill skiing, snowmobiling, heli-skiing. **Special Features:** 100-foot Cedar Creek Falls; Goat Wall, a huge granite outcropping above the western end of Methow Valley; North Cascades Scenic Highway; Pasayten and Lake Chelan-Sawtooth wilderness areas; Big Tree Botanical Area, featuring two 600-year-old western larch trees; a segment of the Pacific Crest Trail (see separate entry in national trails section).

★536★ OLYMPIC NATIONAL FOREST

1835 Black Lake Blvd SW
Olympia, WA 98512
Web: www.fs.fed.us/r6/olympic
Phone: 360-956-2402; **Fax:** 360-956-2330
Size: 633,677 acres. **Location:** Northwestern Washington. Accessible by US 101. Nearby cities/towns include Aberdeen, Olympia, Port Angeles, Quilcene, and Shelton. **Facilities:** 20 campgrounds, lodge, 3 cabins, trails (270 miles), picnic sites,

See pages 20-21 for map of U.S. National Forests and Grasslands.

scenic drives. **Activities:** Camping, boating, sailing, swimming, scuba diving, fishing, seasonal oyster and clam harvesting, hiking, mountain climbing, horseback riding, bicycling, beachcombing, bird watching. **Special Features:** Surrounded on three sides by saltwater; Quinault Rain Forest, a primeval zone of giant moss-covered trees and lush foliage; nation's largest population of Roosevelt elk; 5 wilderness areas; spectacular views of mountains, valleys, rivers, lakes, waterfalls, and beaches.

★537★ OSCEOLA NATIONAL FOREST
PO Box 70
Olustee, FL 32072
Web: www.fs.fed.us/r8/florida
Phone: 386-752-2577
Size: Nearly 200,000 acres. **Location:** Northeastern Florida. Accessible by I-10; US 41, 90, 441; FL 100. Nearby cities/towns include Jacksonville and Lake City. **Facilities:** Campgrounds, dispersed camping, 9 hunt camps, rifle range, picnic sites, trails. **Activities:** Camping, hunting, picnicking, fishing, hiking, OHV riding, wildlife viewing, horseback riding, boating, swimming. **Special Features:** Olustee Battlefield Historic Site, where one of the nation's largest reenactments of a Civil War battle is staged annually during Presidents' Day weekend in February; Big Gum Swamp Wilderness, a cypress-gum swamp with a perimeter of pine flatwoods; Ocean Pond, a 1,760-acre natural lake; a 23-mile section of the Florida National Scenic Trail (see entry in national trails section).

★538★ OTTAWA NATIONAL FOREST
E 6248 US 2
Ironwood, MI 49938
Web: www.fs.fed.us/r9/ottawa
Phone: 906-932-1330; **Fax:** 906-932-0122
Size: 1,000,000 acres. **Location:** Northwestern corner of Michigan's upper peninsula, near Wisconsin state line. Accessible by US 2 and 45; MI 28 and 64. Nearby cities/towns include Bessemer, Iron River, Ironwood, Kenton, Ontonagon, Trout Creek, Wakefield, and Watersmeet. **Facilities:** Visitor center, 22 campgrounds, group camps, dispersed camping, picnic sites, trails (200 miles), boat launches, scenic drives, ski areas. **Activities:** Camping, hunting, fishing, boating, canoeing, kayaking, swimming, hiking, mountain biking, cross-country and downhill skiing, snowmobiling, ice fishing, snowshoeing. **Special Features:** 500 named lakes, 2,000 miles of streams, and numerous waterfalls; 108 miles of the North Country National Scenic Trail (see entry in national trails section); Black River Harbor, the Forest Service's only Great Lakes harbor. Portions of the forest receive more than 200 inches of snow annually.

★539★ OUACHITA NATIONAL FOREST
100 Reserve St
PO Box 1270
Hot Springs, AR 71902
Web: www.fs.fed.us/r8/ouachita
Phone: 501-321-5202
Size: 1,800,000 acres. **Location:** West-central Arkansas and southeastern Oklahoma. Accessible by US 59, 70, 71, 270, and

271; AR 7 and 10. Nearby cities/towns include Booneville, Hot Springs, and Mena, AR; Heavener and Poteau, OK. **Facilities:** 21 campgrounds, group camps, picnic sites, trails (700 miles), 11 shooting ranges, scenic drives, 5 float camps, 2 historical sites. **Activities:** Camping, hunting, fishing, boating, swimming, hiking, mountain biking, ORV riding, horseback riding, rock hounding, rock climbing. **Special Features:** 4,000 miles of streams and 1,600 acres of lake and ponds; 192 miles (85%) of Ouachita National Recreation Trail; Robert S. Kerr Arboretum and Nature Center, with interpretive exhibits and self-guided trails; Winding Stair Mountain National Recreation Area.

★540★ OZARK-SAINT FRANCIS NATIONAL FORESTS
605 W Main
Russellville, AR 72801
Web: www.fs.fed.us/oonf/ozark
Phone: 479-964-7200
Size: 1,222,600 total acres. **Location:** Ozark NF is in northwestern and north-central Arkansas. Accessible by US 71; AR 7, 21, 22, and 23. Nearby cities/towns include Clarksville, Fort Smith, Harrison, Ozark, and Russellville. Saint Francis NF is in east-central Arkansas. Accessible by US 49; AR 44 and 242. Nearby cities/towns include Marianna and La Grange. **Facilities:** Visitor centers, 23 campgrounds, 9 cabins, 2 lodges, picnic sites, boat launches, hiking trails (395 miles), multi-use trails (130 miles), scenic drives. **Activities:** Camping, hunting, fishing, boating, canoeing, whitewater rafting, swimming, hiking, mountain biking, horseback riding, interpretive programs, spelunking. **Special Features:** Forest houses Blanchard Springs Caverns, which were described as ''the cave find of the century'' when the large, upper level was discovered in 1963. Guided tours of the developed caverns are regularly scheduled; tours of wild caves are available by reservation.

★541★ PAYETTE NATIONAL FOREST
800 W Lakeside Ave
PO Box 1026
McCall, ID 83638
Web: www.fs.fed.us/r4/payette
Phone: 208-634-0700; **Fax:** 208-634-0744
Size: 2,300,000 acres. **Location:** West-central Idaho. Accessible by US 95. Nearby cities/towns include Council, McCall, New Meadows, and Weiser. **Facilities:** 22 campgrounds, picnic sites, trails (2,125 miles), scenic drives, 4 airstrips. **Activities:** Camping, hunting, fishing, hiking, horseback riding, mountain biking, OHV riding, cross-country and downhill skiing, snowmobiling. **Special Features:** Portions of Hells Canyon National Recreation Area and Frank Church River of No Return wilderness; Salmon River, a designated Wild and Scenic River; remains of historic gold rush mining camps.

★542★ PIKE & SAN ISABEL NATIONAL FORESTS
2840 Kachina Dr
Pueblo, CO 81008
Web: www.fs.fed.us/r2/psicc
Phone: 719-553-1400; **Fax:** 719-553-1440
Size: 2,000,000+ acres. **Location:** Central Colorado. Accessible

See pages 20-21 for map of U.S. National Forests and Grasslands.

by US 24 and 285. Nearby cities/towns include Colorado Springs, Cripple Creek, and Denver. **Facilities:** Visitor center, 53 campgrounds, 4 group camps, 3 cabins, dispersed camping, picnic sites, trails, scenic drives. **Activities:** Camping, hunting, fishing, hiking, mountain biking, kayaking, rafting, OHV riding, mountain climbing, rock climbing, skiing, snowmobiling. **Special Features:** Pikes Peak, with highway to 14,000-foot summit; Sangre de Cristo Range, with 12 peaks above 14,000 feet, including Mount Elbert (14,433 feet), the highest point in Colorado; Mount Champion Mine and Mill, developed in the late 1890s and the major producer of ore in the Twin Lakes-Red Mountain area.

★543★ PISGAH NATIONAL FOREST

1001 Pisgah Hwy
Pisgah Forest, NC 28768
Web: www.cs.unca.edu/nfsnc
Phone: 828-877-3265; **Fax:** 828-884-7527
Size: 510,119 acres. **Location:** Western North Carolina. Accessible by US 19, 23, 64, 276, and the Blue Ridge Parkway. Nearby cities/towns include Brevard, Canton, and Waynesville. **Facilities:** Visitor center, campgrounds, picnic sites, boat ramp, trails, ORV area, scenic drives. **Activities:** Camping, fishing, boating, swimming, hiking, ORV riding, mountain biking, horseback riding, interpretive programs, rock climbing, berry picking. **Special Features:** The Cradle of Forestry in America, an outdoor museum on former grounds of George Washington Vanderbilt's estate, which depicts the history of forest conservation and honors leaders in its development; Looking Glass Falls, an unbroken rush of whitewater 30 feet wide and 60 feet high; Appalachian National Scenic Trail (see entry in national trails section); Roan Mountain Gardens, with spring displays of purple rhododendron; Shining Rock Wilderness, named for a rock outcrop filled with quartz deposits.

★544★ PLUMAS NATIONAL FOREST

159 Lawrence St
Quincy, CA 95971
Web: www.fs.fed.us/r5/plumas
Phone: 530-283-2050; **Fax:** 530-283-7746
Size: 1,146,000 acres. **Location:** Northeastern California. Accessible by US 395; CA 70, 89. Nearby cities/towns include Greenville, Portola, Quincy, and Sierraville. **Facilities:** 49 campgrounds, group camps, dispersed camping, picnic sites, trails (nearly 300 miles), lookouts, boat launch, scenic drives. **Activities:** Camping, fishing, boating, rafting, whitewater rafting, swimming, water-skiing, hiking, mountain biking, blackberry picking, hunting, horseback riding, OHV riding, cross-country skiing, snowmobiling. **Special Features:** Feather Falls, one of the highest (640 feet) and most picturesque waterfalls in the U.S.; Middle Fork of the Feather River, a designated Wild and Scenic River; a 75-mile segment of the Pacific Crest National Scenic Trail (see entry in national trails section); Butterfly Valley Botanical Area, a 500-acre preserve for carnivorous plants; Bucks Lake Wilderness, with elevations ranging from 2,000 feet in Feather River Canyon to 7,017 feet at Spanish Peak.

★545★ PRESCOTT NATIONAL FOREST

344 S Cortez St
Prescott, AZ 86303
Web: www.fs.fed.us/r3/prescott
Phone: 928-443-8000
Size: 1,237,061 acres. **Location:** Central Arizona. Accessible by US 89, 69, and I-17. Nearby cities/towns include Camp Verde, Chino Valley, Clarkdale, Cottonwood, Dewey, Jerome, Prescott Valley, and Prescott. **Facilities:** 10 campgrounds, 4 group camps, dispersed camping, cabin, picnic sites, trails (450 miles), 8 wildernesses, archeological sites, scenic drives. **Activities:** Camping, hunting, trout fishing, canoeing, whitewater rafting, hiking, mountain biking, horseback riding, rock climbing, hang gliding, gold panning. **Special Features:** Forest lies in a mountainous area between forested plateaus to the north and arid desert to the south. Features include Granite Mountain Wilderness and the Verde River, Arizona's only wild and scenic river.

★546★ RIO GRANDE NATIONAL FOREST

1803 W Hwy 160
Monte Vista, CO 81144
Web: www.fs.fed.us/r2/riogrande
Phone: 719-852-5941; **Fax:** 719-852-6250
Size: 1,860,000 acres. **Location:** Southwestern Colorado. Accessible by US 160 and 285. Nearby cities/towns include Alamosa, Monte Vista, and Saguache. **Facilities:** 24 campgrounds, dispersed camping, picnic grounds, waterfalls, scenic views, trails, winter sports area. **Activities:** Camping, fishing, boating, rafting, hiking, mountain biking, horseback riding, ORV driving, hunting, cross-country and downhill skiing, snowmobiling. **Special Features:** Contains portions of four wilderness areas: La Garita, Weminuche, San Juan, and Sangre de Cristo. Headwaters of the Rio Grande de Norte, third longest river in the United States, are within the forest. The Continental Divide runs for 236 miles along most of the western border of the forest.

★547★ ROGUE RIVER-SISKIYOU NATIONAL FOREST

333 W 8th St
PO Box 520
Medford, OR 97501
Web: www.fs.fed.us/r6/rogue-siskiyou
Phone: 541-858-2200; **Fax:** 541-858-2205
Size: Almost 1,800,000 acres. **Location:** Surrounds the Rogue Valley in southwestern Oregon. Accessible by I-5, OR 62, 140, and 66. Nearby cities/towns include Ashland, Grants Pass, Klamath Falls, and Medford. **Facilities:** 73 campgrounds, 10 cabin/lookout rentals, trails (more than 200), boat ramps, scenic drives, interpretive trails, 200 miles of wild and scenic rivers, picnic areas. **Activities:** Camping, fishing, canoeing, whitewater rafting, swimming, hiking, horseback riding, mountain biking, ORV riding, cross-country skiing, snowmobiling. **Special Features:** Upper reaches of the Rogue River in the Cascade Range; Sea stacks, isolated outcrops of rock standing in the ocean. They are remnants of rocky headlands that were eroded by wave action. Gin Lin Trail, which interprets the history of a Chinese emigrant's gold mining operation. Pacific Crest National Scenic

See pages 20-21 for map of U.S. National Forests and Grasslands.

Trail (see entry in national trails section) runs the entire length of the forest.

★548★ SABINE NATIONAL FOREST

201 S Palm
Hemphill, TX 75948
Web: www.fs.fed.us/r8/texas
Phone: 409-787-3870; **Fax:** 409-787-3878; **Toll Free:** 866-235-1750
Size: 160,656 acres. **Location:** Eastern Texas, near Louisiana state line. Accessible by US 96; TX 21 and 87. Nearby cities/towns include Hemphill and San Augustine. **Facilities:** Campgrounds, dispersed camping, picnic sites, boat launches, marina, trails. **Activities:** Camping, hunting, fishing, boating, swimming, hiking, horseback riding, mountain biking. **Special Features:** Toledo Bend Reservoir, nation's fifth-largest manmade reservoir; Indian Mounds Wilderness Area, 12,369 acres with a large stand of American beech and Southern magnolia forest; Red Hills Lake, 19-acre lake constructed by the Civilian Conservation Corps.

SAINT JOE NATIONAL FOREST

(see Idaho Panhandle National Forests)

★549★ SALMON-CHALLIS NATIONAL FOREST

50 Hwy 93 S
Salmon, ID 83467
Web: www.fs.fed.us/r4/sc
Phone: 208-756-5100; **Fax:** 208-756-5151
Size: 4,300,000 acres. **Location:** East-central Idaho, bordered by the Bitterroot Range of the Continental Divide on the east. Accessible by US 93 and ID 28. Nearby cities/towns include Challis, Leadore, Mackay, Salmon, and Stanley. **Facilities:** Cabins, campgrounds (mostly primitive), equestrian camp, picnic sites, trails (more than 800 miles). **Activities:** Camping, hunting, fishing, boating, canoeing, whitewater rafting, hiking, horseback riding, technical mountain climbing, OHV riding, cross-country and downhill skiing, snowmobiling. **Special Features:** Includes 1.3 million acres of the Frank Church River of No Return Wilderness, the largest wilderness area in the continental U.S.; parts of the Salmon River, a nationally designated Wild and Scenic River; Borah Peak (12,662 feet), Idaho's tallest mountain; segments of Continental Divide National Scenic Trail, Lewis and Clark National Historic Trail, and Nez Perce National Historic Trail (see separate entries in national trails section).

★550★ SAM HOUSTON NATIONAL FOREST

394 FM 1375 W
New Waverly, TX 77358
Web: www.fs.fed.us/r8/texas
Phone: 936-344-6205; **Fax:** 936-344-2123
Size: 163,037 acres. **Location:** East-central Texas. Accessible by US 59, 75, and 190; TX 105 and 150. Nearby cities/towns include Cleveland, Conroe, and Huntsville. **Facilities:** 3 campgrounds, group camp, dispersed camping, picnic sites, trails, boat ramps. **Activities:** Camping, hunting, fishing, boating, sailing, swimming, hiking, horseback riding, mountain biking, ORV riding. **Special Features:** Lake Conroe (22,000 acres) and Lake Livingston (82,600 acres); 128-mile-long Lone Star Hiking Trail; and 3,855-acre Little Lake Creek Wilderness Area, which supports a dense population of the endangered red-cockaded woodpecker.

★551★ SAN BERNARDINO NATIONAL FOREST

602 S Tippecanoe Ave
San Bernardino, CA 92408
Web: www.fs.fed.us/r5/sanbernardino
Phone: 909-382-2600; **Fax:** 909-383-5586
Size: 818,999 acres. **Location:** Southwestern California, east of Los Angeles. Accessible by US 60; CA 18 and 74. Nearby cities/towns include Palm Springs, Riverside, and San Bernardino. **Facilities:** 3 visitor centers, cabins, 23 campgrounds, 21 group camps, dispersed camping, 13 picnic areas, 5 equestrian campgrounds, 2 fishing piers, trails (598 miles), unpaved roads (1,178 miles), OHV areas, scenic drives, 3 shooting ranges, 5 downhill ski areas, snow play area. **Activities:** Camping, hunting, fishing, boating, swimming, water-skiing, hiking, mountain biking, horseback riding, OHV riding, cross-country and downhill skiing, snowmobiling, snowboarding. **Special Features:** 6 wilderness areas; top fishing lakes Big Bear and Lake Hemet; Rim of the World Scenic Byway; a 193-mile portion of the Pacific Crest National Scenic Trail (see entry in national trails section); natural hot springs. Geological evidence of the San Andreas Fault can be seen around Lost Lake, the forest's only natural lake, which formed in a ''sag'' in the earth's surface.

★552★ SAN JUAN NATIONAL FOREST

15 Burnett Ct
Durango, CO 81301
Web: www.fs.fed.us/r2/sanjuan
Phone: 970-247-4874; **Fax:** 970-385-1243
Size: 2,500,000 acres. **Location:** Southwestern Colorado. Accessible by US 160 and 550. Nearby cities/towns include Cortez, Durango, and Pagosa Springs. **Facilities:** 39 campgrounds, 8 group camps, dispersed camping, picnic grounds, boat ramps, trails, lookout towers, scenic drives. **Activities:** Camping, hunting, fishing, boating, canoeing, water-skiing, hiking, mountain biking, OHV riding, horseback riding, mountain climbing, rock climbing, snowmobiling, interpretive programs. **Special Features:** Chimney Rock Archeological Area, landmarked by a prominent spire atop a high mesa and featuring thousand-year-old dwellings of the Ancestral Puebloan people; Treasure Falls, a 105-foot drop of Fall Creek; three large reservoirs: McPhee, Lemon, and Vallecita; six wilderness areas; Durango Mountain Resort. Nearby are Canyon of the Ancients National Monument (on Bureau of Land Management lands) and Mesa Verde National Park (see entry in national parks section).

★553★ SANTA FE NATIONAL FOREST

1474 Rodeo Rd
Santa Fe, NM 87505
Web: www.fs.fed.us/r3/sfe
Phone: 505-438-7840; **Fax:** 505-438-7834
Size: 1,600,000 acres. **Location:** North-central New Mexico. Accessible by I-25, US 285, 85, 64, and 84; NM 4, 126, 96,

See pages 20-21 for map of U.S. National Forests and Grasslands.

3. National Forests and Grasslands

and 63. Nearby cities/towns include Albuquerque, Bernalillo, Cuba, Espanola, Las Vegas, Pecos, and Santa Fe. **Facilities:** 23 campgrounds, 13 picnic sites, trails (1,002 miles), scenic outlook. **Activities:** Camping, hunting, fishing, hiking, mountain biking, horseback riding, ORV riding, skiing, snowmobiling. **Special Features:** Southern Sangre de Cristo Range including 13,103-foot Truchas Peak; Jemez and San Pedro ranges, with 10,000 - 12,000 foot peaks; scenic Valles Caldera National Preserve (89,000 acres); 620 miles of mountain streams and lakes; East Fork of the Jemez River, a designated Wild and Scenic River.

★554★ SAWTOOTH NATIONAL FOREST

2647 Kimberly Rd E
Twin Falls, ID 83301
Web: www.fs.fed.us/r4/sawtooth
Phone: 208-737-3200; **Fax:** 208-737-3236
Size: 2,100,000 acres. **Location:** South-central Idaho and northern Utah. Accessible by US 84, 75, and 21. Nearby cities/towns include Burley and Twin Falls. **Facilities:** Visitor center, 50+ campgrounds, 12 group camps, picnic sites, boat ramps, trails, ski resort (concession operated), 4 winter sports areas, scenic drives, wildlife viewing sites with scopes. **Activities:** Camping, hunting, fishing, boating, canoeing, swimming, hiking, mountain biking, horseback riding, cross-country and downhill skiing, snowmobiling. **Special Features:** Four mountain ranges; headwaters of five major rivers; 967 miles of streams; more than 1,000 lakes; 756,000-acre Sawtooth National Recreation Area. The forest's 217,000-acre Sawtooth Wilderness contains more than 50 major peaks over 10,000 feet and more than 300 lakes.

★555★ SEQUOIA NATIONAL FOREST

1839 S Newcomb St
Porterville, CA 93257
Web: www.fs.fed.us/r5/sequoia
Phone: 559-784-1500; **Fax:** 559-781-4744
Size: 1,136,950 acres. **Location:** Southern end of the Sierra Nevada Mountain Range in central California. Accessible by US 395; CA 155, 178, 180, and 190. Nearby cities/towns include Porterville and Bakersfield. **Facilities:** 7 rental cabins, 50 campgrounds, 12 group camps, dispersed camping, resort (concession operated), picnic sites, trails (1,000+ miles), marina, scenic drives, lookout tower, 9-hole golf course. **Activities:** Camping, hunting, fishing, boating, canoeing, whitewater rafting, swimming, hiking, mountain biking, horseback riding, cross-country and downhill skiing. **Special Features:** 38 groves of giant sequoias, including Boole Tree, the largest tree on National Forest Service land and recognized as one of the largest trees in the world at 269 feet, with a diameter of 35 feet; Trail of a Hundred Giants; Wild and Scenic Rivers, including the North and South Forks of the Kern River and the King River; a 78-mile segment of Pacific Crest National Scenic Trail (see entry in national trails section).

★556★ SHASTA-TRINITY NATIONAL FOREST

3644 Avtech Pkwy
Redding, CA 96002
Web: www.fs.fed.us/r5/shastatrinity
Phone: 530-226-2500; **Fax:** 530-226-2470

Size: 2,100,000 acres. **Location:** Northern California. Accessible by I-5; US 97; and CA 3, 36, 89, and 299. Nearby cities/towns include Callahan, Dunsmuir, Hayfork, McCloud, Mount Shasta, Redding, and Weaverville. **Facilities:** 50+ campgrounds, group camps, boat-in camps, dispersed camps, cabin, lookout towers, picnic sites, trails (1,400 miles), marinas, boat ramps, winter sports areas, scenic drives. **Activities:** Camping, hunting, swimming, fishing, boating, water-skiing, whitewater rafting, hiking, horseback riding, mountain biking, cross-country and downhill skiing, snowboarding, snowmobiling, mountain climbing, interpretive programs. **Special Features:** Mount Shasta, a 14,162-foot volcano; 32 alpine lakes; Whiskeytown-Shasta-Trinity National Recreation Area (see entry in national parks section); 154 miles of the Pacific Crest National Scenic Trail (see entry in national trails section); and four wild and scenic rivers.

★557★ SHAWNEE NATIONAL FOREST

50 Hwy 145 S
Harrisburg, IL 62946
Web: www.fs.fed.us/r9/shawnee
Phone: 618-253-7114; **Fax:** 618-253-1060; **Toll Free:** 800-699-6637
Size: 270,000 acres. **Location:** Southern tip of Illinois. Accessible by US 45 and 51; IL 1, 3, 127, 145, 146, and 151. Nearby cities/towns include Cairo, Carbondale, Harrisburg, Marion, and Murphysboro. **Facilities:** 15 campgrounds, 2 group camps, dispersed camping, picnic sites, marina, boat launches, trails (300 miles), scenic drive. **Activities:** Camping, hunting, fishing, boating, swimming, hiking, horseback riding, rock climbing. **Special Features:** Little Grand Canyon, featuring cave-like overhangs, wildflowers, and unusual ferns; Millstone Bluff Archeological Area, with petroglyphs, a stone fort, cemetery, and village site from the Mississippian period; Inspiration Point Bluff, rising 350 feet above Mississippi River bottomland at the LaRue Pine Hills/Otter Pond Research Natural Area.

★558★ SHOSHONE NATIONAL FOREST

808 Meadow Ln
Cody, WY 82414
Web: www.fs.fed.us/r2/shoshone
Phone: 307-527-6241; **Fax:** 307-578-1212
Size: 2,466,555 acres. **Location:** Northwestern Wyoming. Accessible by US 14, 20, and 287; CO 120. Nearby cities/towns include Cody, Dubois, Lander, Meeteetse, and Powell. **Facilities:** 2 visitor centers, 30 campgrounds, dispersed camping, picnic areas, trails (700+ miles), winter sports areas, scenic drives. **Activities:** Camping, hunting, fishing, hiking, mountain biking, horseback riding, rafting, kayaking, OHV riding, mountain climbing, cross-country skiing, snowmobiling, ice climbing. **Special Features:** Includes portions of the Absaroka, Wind River, and Beartooth mountain ranges; 13,804-foot Gannett Peak, the highest point in Wyoming; 16 named glaciers and 140 unnamed ones; Continental Divide National Scenic Trail (see entry in national trails section).

See pages 20-21 for map of U.S. National Forests and Grasslands.

★559★ SIERRA NATIONAL FOREST

1600 Tollhouse Rd
Clovis, CA 93611
Web: www.fs.fed.us/r5/sierra
Phone: 559-297-0706; **Fax:** 559-294-4809
Size: 1,300,000 acres. **Location:** East-central California. Accessible by CA 41, 168, and 180. Nearby cities/towns include Fresno and North Fork. **Facilities:** 71 campgrounds, 11 group camps, dispersed camping, picnic areas, trails, winter sports areas, ski resort, scenic drives. **Activities:** Camping, fishing, boating, canoeing, sailing, whitewater rafting, swimming, water-skiing, windsurfing, hiking, mountain biking, horseback riding, hunting, OHV riding, cross-country and downhill skiing, snowmobiling, sledding, dog sledding, snow playing. **Special Features:** Sierra Vista Scenic Byway, a 100-mile open loop through the Sierra Nevada Mountain Range; five designated wilderness areas: Ansel Adams, Dinkey Lake, John Muir, Kaiser, and Monarch; geological features including Arch Rock, the Balls, and Globe Rock. Forest property abuts the southern boundary of Yosemite National Park (see entry in national parks section).

★560★ SIUSLAW NATIONAL FOREST

4077 SW Research Way
PO Box 1148
Corvallis, OR 97339
Web: www.fs.fed.us/r6/siuslaw
Phone: 541-750-7000; **Fax:** 541-750-7234
Size: More than 630,000 acres. **Location:** In the coastal mountain range of west-central Oregon. Accessible by US 20 and 101; OR 18, 34, 36, 38, and 126. Nearby cities/towns include Corvallis, Eugene, Florence, Reedsport, and Waldport. **Facilities:** Visitor center; almost 40 campgrounds, trails (230 miles), boat ramps, 2 ORV areas. **Activities:** Camping, salt and freshwater fishing, boating, canoeing, swimming, hiking, horseback riding, biking, ORV riding, beachcombing, whale watching. **Special Features:** One of only two national forests in the continental U.S. with oceanfront property; four major rivers that flow through the forest into the Pacific Ocean (the Nestucca, Alsea, Siuslaw, and Umpqua); Mary's Peak, highest point in the Coastal Range (4,097 feet). Points of interest include Cape Perpetua Scenic Area, Oregon Dunes National Recreation Area, Cascade Head Scenic Area, and the historic Heceta Head Lighthouse.

★561★ SIX RIVERS NATIONAL FOREST

1330 Bayshore Way
Eureka, CA 95501
Web: www.fs.fed.us/r5/sixrivers
Phone: 707-442-1721; **Fax:** 707-442-9242
Size: 957,590 acres. **Location:** Northwestern California. Accessible by US 101; CA 36, 96, and 299. Nearby cities/towns include Crescent City, Eureka, Fortuna, Klamath, Orick, and Orleans. **Facilities:** Campgrounds, group camp, rental cabin, dispersed camping, picnic sites, trails (400 miles), OHV areas, scenic drives. **Activities:** Camping, hunting, fishing, boating, kayaking, whitewater rafting, hiking, mountain biking, horseback riding, cross-country skiing. **Special Features:** Portions of four wilderness areas: Siskiyou, Trinity Alps, Yolla-Bolly, and North Fork; the undamed Smith River, one of the largest Wild and Scenic river systems (315 miles) in the U.S.; Smith River National Recreation Area.

★562★ STANISLAUS NATIONAL FOREST

19777 Greenley Rd
Sonora, CA 95370
Web: www.fs.fed.us/r5/stanislaus
Phone: 209-532-3671; **Fax:** 209-533-1890
Size: 1,090,039 acres. **Location:** East-central California. Accessible by US 395; CA 4, 108, and 120. Nearby cities/towns include Angels Camp, Groveland, Jamestown, and Sonora. **Facilities:** 55 campgrounds, dispersed camping, picnic sites, trails (1,000+ miles), ORV area, winter recreation area, 2 ski resorts. **Activities:** Camping, hunting, fishing, boating, canoeing, whitewater rafting, swimming, water-skiing, hiking, mountain biking, horseback riding, ORV riding, cross-country and downhill skiing, snowmobiling, interpretive programs. **Special Features:** Almost 5000 archeological and historical sites, 6 of which are on the *National Register of Historic Places*; Bower Cave, a limestone cavern sacred to Native Americans; and 29 miles of the Tuolumne and 11 miles of the Merced, both wild and scenic rivers.

★563★ SUPERIOR NATIONAL FOREST

8901 Grand Avene Pl
Duluth, MN 55808
Web: www.fs.fed.us/r9/forests/superior
Phone: 218-626-4300; **Fax:** 218-626-4398
Size: 3,000,000 acres. **Location:** Northeastern Minnesota. Accessible by I-35, MN 169, and US 53 and 61. Nearby cities/towns include Duluth, Ely, Grand Marais, and Virginia. **Facilities:** 39 campgrounds, group camps, dispersed camping, picnic sites, boat launches, trails (400+ miles), scenic drives. **Activities:** Camping, hunting, fishing, boating, canoeing, sailing, swimming, hiking, mountain biking, horseback riding, rock hounding, blueberry picking, cross-country and downhill skiing, snowmobiling, ice fishing, snowshoeing, dog sledding. **Special Features:** Boundary Waters Canoe Area Wilderness, a one-million-acre area with 1,500 miles of canoe trails, believed to be the most heavily used wilderness area in America; Superior Hiking Trail, a 205-mile trail that runs along the high ridgeline beside Lake Superior, rated as one of the best in trails in Midwestern America. Northern Minnesota is the last stronghold of the gray wolf in the lower 48 states; approximately 300-400 gray wolves live in the forest.

★564★ TAHOE NATIONAL FOREST

631 Coyote St
Nevada City, CA 95959
Web: www.fs.fed.us/r5/tahoe
Phone: 530-265-4531; **Fax:** 530-478-6109
Size: 845,094 acres. **Location:** In the North Central Sierra Nevada Range, between Lake Tahoe and the Sacramento Valley. Accessible by US 80 and CA 89. Nearby cities/towns include Downieville, Nevada City, and Sierra City. **Facilities:** Visitor center, 77 campgrounds, 12 group camps, dispersed camping, 20 picnic sites, 4 resorts, boat ramps, trail, ORV areas, 5 downhill

See pages 20-21 for map of U.S. National Forests and Grasslands.

3. National Forests and Grasslands

ski areas, snowshoeing, shooting range, scenic drives. **Activities:** Camping, hunting, fishing, boating, whitewater rafting, canoeing, swimming, water-skiing, hiking, mountain biking, horseback riding, rock climbing, cross-country and downhill skiing, snowmobiling, gold panning. **Special Features:** Northern end of California's Gold Country; elevations range from 1,500 feet, around the golden foothills on the western slope, to the 9,400-foot high peaks of the Sierra crest. Pacific Crest National Scenic Trail; North Fork of the American River, a Wild and Scenic river; three forks of the Yuba River; excellent fishing at Jackson Meadows and Stampede reservoirs; historic sites from the Donner Party, the Gold Rush era, and prehistoric Native Americans.

★565★ TALLADEGA NATIONAL FOREST

1001 North St
Talladega, AL 35160
Web: www.southernregion.fs.fed.us/alabama/talladega
Phone: 256-362-2909
Size: 391,531 acres. **Location:** Central Alabama. Accessible by US 78; AL 5. Nearby cities/towns include Anniston, Centreville, Heflin, Marion, Selma, Sylacauga, Talladega, and Tuscaloosa. **Facilities:** Campgrounds, dispersed camping, picnic sites, trails, shooting range, scenic drive. **Activities:** Camping, hunting, fishing, boating, swimming, hiking, mountain biking, horseback riding, ORV riding, geocaching. **Special Features:** Lake Chinnabee and Coleman Lake recreation areas; Chinnabee Silent Trail, a rigorous trek constructed by a Boy Scout troop from the Alabama Institute for the Deaf and Blind; 7,245-acre Cheaha Wilderness; Pinhoti Trail, a 100-mile-long National Recreation Trail. Cheaha State Park (see entry in Alabama state parks section) lies within forest boundaries.

★566★ TOMBIGBEE NATIONAL FOREST

PO Box 912
Hwy 15 S
Ackerman, MS 39735
Web: www.fs.fed.us/r8/mississippi/tombigbee
Phone: 601-285-3264; **Fax:** 601-285-3608
Size: 66,662 acres. **Location:** Northeastern Mississippi. Accessible by US 82; MS 12, 15, 25, 32, and 41. Nearby cities/towns include Ackerman, Houston, Starkville, and Tupelo. **Facilities:** 2 campgrounds, picnic sites, trails, boat ramps, scenic drives. **Activities:** Camping, hunting, fishing, boating, swimming, hiking, mountain biking, horseback riding, ORV riding. **Special Features:** Upper Coastal Plain pine and hardwood forests; prehistoric Mississippian-period mounds at Owl Creek; 26-mile Noxubee Crest Bike Trail; Davis and Choctaw lakes.

★567★ TONGASS NATIONAL FOREST

648 Mission St
Ketchikan, AK 99901
Web: www.fs.fed.us/r10/tongass
Phone: 907-225-3101; **Fax:** 907-228-6215
Size: 17,000,000 acres. **Location:** Southeast Alaska, comprising 80 percent of all land between the southern tip (near Ketchikan) to north of Yakutut. No road access; accessible by ferry, boat, or plane only. Nearby cities/towns include Juneau, Ketchikan, Sitka, Skagway, and Yakutut. **Facilities:** 3 visitor centers, 15 campgrounds, 150 cabins, picnic sites, trails, warming huts. **Activities:** Camping, hunting, fishing, boating, canoeing, kayaking, hiking, berry picking, mushroom collecting, flightseeing tours (concession operated), whale watching, ice skating, snowmobiling, cross-country and downhill skiing, snowshoeing, interpretive programs. **Special Features:** Largest national forest in the U.S., three times larger than the next largest national forest. (At 17,000,000 acres, forest is larger than the states of Delaware or Rhode Island.) Features glaciers, mountains, waterways, and islands separated by straits and channels. Points of interest include Mendenhall Glacier Visitor Center, Pack Creek Bear Viewing Area, and native arts displays at Southeast Alaska Discovery Center.

★568★ TONTO NATIONAL FOREST

2324 E McDowell Rd
Phoenix, AZ 85006
Web: www.fs.fed.us/r3/tonto
Phone: 602-225-5200; **Fax:** 602-225-5295
Size: Almost 3,000,000 acres. **Location:** Central Arizona. Accessible by I-17, AZ 87, 188, 288, and 260; US 60, 77, 80, and 89. Nearby cities/towns include Cave Creek, Globe, Mesa, Miami, Payson, Phoenix, Pine, Superior, Roosevelt, and Young. **Facilities:** Visitors center, 92 campgrounds, picnic areas, trails (nearly 900 miles), scenic drives. **Activities:** Camping, hunting, fishing, boating, sailing, canoeing, rafting, swimming, water-skiing, target shooting, hiking, mountain biking, horseback riding, OHV riding, rock hounding, interpretive programs. **Special Features:** Ranks among the most-visited national forests. Comprised of desert, canyons, chaparral, woodlands, and conifer forests. Points of interest include Roosevelt Lake Visitor Center; prehistoric sites Sears-Kay ruins and Shoofly Village; 8 wilderness areas totaling 589,300 acres; Salt and Verde rivers, portions of which are designated Wild and Scenic; lakes (Roosevelt, Apache, Canyon, and Saguaro) and reservoirs (Bartlett and Horseshoe).

★569★ TUSKEGEE NATIONAL FOREST

125 National Forest Rd 949
Tuskegee, AL 36083
Web: www.fs.fed.us/r8/alabama
Phone: 334-727-2652
Size: 11,252 acres. **Location:** East-central Alabama. Accessible by US 29 and 80; AL 81. Nearby cities/towns include Auburn and Tuskegee. **Facilities:** Hunter camps, dispersed camping, picnic sites, trails, shooting range. **Activities:** Camping, hunting, fishing, hiking, horseback riding, bicycling. **Special Features:** Taska Recreation Area, with log cabin replica of Booker T. Washington's birthplace; Tsinia Wildlife Viewing Area, with trails, viewing blind, and observation tower; an 8.5-mile section of Bartram Trail, a National Recreation Trail.

★570★ UINTA NATIONAL FOREST

88 W 100 North
PO Box 1428
Provo, UT 84601
Web: www.fs.fed.us/r4/uinta
Phone: 801-342-5100

See pages 20-21 for map of U.S. National Forests and Grasslands.

Size: Almost 1,000,000 acres. **Location:** Central Utah. Accessible by US 40, 50, 89, and 189; UT 35. Nearby cities/towns include American Fork, Heber, Pleasant Grove, Nephi, Provo, and Spanish Fork. **Facilities:** 28 campgrounds, group camps, 7 picnic sites, trails, boat ramps, fishing piers (&). **Activities:** Camping, hunting, fishing, hiking, horseback riding, rafting, berry picking, mountain biking, kayaking, cross-country and downhill skiing, snowmobiling, snow shoeing. **Special Features:** Ranges from high desert to the mountain summits of Mount Nebo (11,877 feet) and Mount Timpanogos (11,750 feet). Points of interest include Cascade Springs, large springs which cascade down in a series of limestone terraces and pools; Devil's Kitchen Geological Area, featuring eroded sandstone formations; Strawberry Reservoir, one of Utah's premier fishing reservoirs with 17,164 surface acres. Forest surrounds Timpanogos Cave National Monument (see entry in national parks section).

★571★ UMATILLA NATIONAL FOREST

2517 SW Hailey Ave
Pendleton, OR 97801
Web: www.fs.fed.us/r6/uma
Phone: 541-278-3716; **Fax:** 541-278-3730
Size: 1,406,178 acres. **Location:** In the Blue Mountains of northeastern Oregon and southeastern Washington. Accessible by US 395 and 12; OR 11. Nearby cities/towns include La Grande and Pendleton, OR; Clarkston, Pomeroy, and Walla Walla, WA. **Facilities:** 20+ campgrounds, dispersed camping, 11 rental cabins, trails (715 miles), winter sports areas, scenic drives. **Activities:** Camping, hunting, fishing, boating, whitewater rafting, kayaking, hiking, mountain biking, horseback riding, OHV riding, bird watching, huckleberry picking, mushroom gathering, cross-country and downhill skiing, snowmobiling, ice fishing, tobaggoning, dog sledding. **Special Features:** Blue Mountain Scenic Byway, a scenic alternative to I-84; Vinegar Hill-Indian Rock scenic area, with 360-degree vistas from several high elevation viewpoints; Fremont Powerhouse, Gibson Cave, and Target Meadows historic sites; North Fork of John Day River, a designated Wild and Scenic River; Table Rock Lookout (6,250 feet), with spectacular views of the surrounding area.

★572★ UMPQUA NATIONAL FOREST

2900 NW Stewart Pkwy
Roseburg, OR 97470
Web: www.fs.fed.us/r6/umpqua
Phone: 541-672-6601; **Fax:** 541-957-3495
Size: 984,602 acres. **Location:** Southwestern Oregon, from the summit of the Cascade Mountain range to the western lowlands. Accessible by OR 138. Nearby cities/towns include Canyonville, Cottage Grove, and Roseburg. **Facilities:** 54 campgrounds, 5 rental cabins, 4 resorts (concession operated), trails (757 miles), boat launches, scenic drives. **Activities:** Camping, hunting, fishing, boating, canoeing, whitewater rafting, hiking, rock climbing, mountain biking, horseback riding, cross-country and downhill skiing, snowmobiling. **Special Features:** 25-mile "Wild and Scenic" section of North Umpqua River; three wilderness areas; Emile Big Tree Botanical Area, a grove of giant, old-growth Douglas fir trees; historic Bohemia Mining District; Pacific Crest National Scenic Trail (see entry in national trails

section); Rogue-Umpqua Scenic Byway (Highway 138), nicknamed the "Highway of Waterfalls." Nearby is Crater Lake National Park (see entry in national parks section).

★573★ UWHARRIE NATIONAL FOREST

789 NC Hwy 24/27 E
Troy, NC 27371
Web: www.cs.unca.edu/nfsnc
Phone: 910-576-6391
Size: 50,189 acres. **Location:** In the Piedmont northeast of Charlotte. Accessible by US 220; NC 24, 27, 49, and 109. Nearby cities/towns include Albemarle, Asheboro, and Troy. **Facilities:** 9 campgrounds, group camp, hunter camps, dispersed camping, rental cabin, picnic sites, boat ramp, fishing pier, trails. **Activities:** Camping, hunting, fishing, boating, canoeing, sailing, swimming, hiking, ORV riding, mountain biking, horseback riding, gold panning, rock hounding. **Special Features:** 20-mile-long Uwharrie National Recreation Trail, featuring old homesites, cemeteries, and gold mines along or near the trail; Badin Lake, a 5,350-acre impoundment of the Yadkin River; Uwharrie River, one of the Piedmont's last unspoiled rivers.

★574★ WALLOWA-WHITMAN NATIONAL FOREST

1550 Dewey Ave
PO Box 907
Baker City, OR 97814
Web: www.fs.fed.us/r6/w-w
Phone: 541-523-6391
Size: 2,392,508 acres. **Location:** Northeastern Oregon and western Idaho. Accessible by I-84; US 26 and 95; OR 3, 7, 245, 82, and 86. Nearby cities/towns include Baker City, Halfway, Unity, Enterprise, La Grande, Union, and Riggins, ID. **Facilities:** 71 campgrounds, group camps, picnic areas, 6 cabins, trails (2,775 miles), 4 winter recreation areas, scenic drives, boat launches. **Activities:** Camping, hunting, fishing, boating, whitewater rafting, hiking, mountain biking, horseback riding, OHV riding, wildlife viewing, snowmobiling, cross-country and downhill skiing. **Special Features:** Comprising 294 miles of wild and scenic rivers, glacial lakes, 4 wilderness areas (Eagle Cap, North Fork John Day, Hell's Canyon, and Monument Rock), remnants of historic gold mining operations, and prehistoric sites. Points of interest include Hells Canyon National Recreation Area (see separate entry in this section) and the Wallowa Lake Tramway, which transports visitors 3,700 vertical feet to the summit of Mt. Howard.

★575★ WASATCH-CACHE NATIONAL FOREST

125 S State St
Salt Lake City, UT 84138
Web: www.fs.fed.us/r4/wcnf
Phone: 801-236-3400; **Fax:** 801-524-3172
Size: 1,908,437 acres. **Location:** In northeast and north-central Utah and southwestern Wyoming. Accessible by US 80, 91, and 189; UT 150. Nearby cities/towns include Brigham City, Kamas, Logan, Ogden, and Salt Lake City. **Facilities:** 4 visitor centers, 73 campgrounds, dispersed camping, 33 picnic areas, 2 marinas, boat ramps, trails (1,524 miles), 5 ski areas (concession operated), scenic drives. **Activities:** Camping, hunting, fishing,

See pages 20-21 for map of U.S. National Forests and Grasslands.

boating, swimming, hiking, mountain biking, horseback riding, OHV riding, rock climbing, wildlife viewing, cross-country and downhill skiing, snowshoeingm snowmobiling. **Special Features:** Seven designated wilderness areas including Lone Peak, Twin Peak, Mount Olympus, Deseret Peak, High Uinta, Wellsville, and Mount Naomi; Logan Canyon Scenic Byway, featuring 500 million years of geologic history; Bear Lake, a large scenic lake often called the ''Carribean of the Rockies'' for its turquoise blue water; and a segment of the Great Western Trail, a corridor running from Canada to Mexico.

★576★ WAYNE NATIONAL FOREST

13700 US Hwy 33
Nelsonville, OH 45764
Web: www.fs.fed.us/r9/wayne
Phone: 740-753-0101; **Fax:** 740-753-0118
Size: 236,858 acres. **Location:** Three separate parcels in southeastern Ohio. Accessible by US 33; OH 7 and 93. Nearby cities/towns include Athens and Marietta. **Facilities:** Visitor center, 7 campgrounds, dispersed camping, picnic sites, trails (300 miles), scenic drives. **Activities:** Camping, hunting, boating, canoeing, swimming, fishing, hiking, ORV riding, mountain biking, horseback riding, wildlife viewing. **Special Features:** Vesuvius Furnace, partially restored iron furnace built in 1833; Irish Run Natural Bridge, one of seven natural rock bridges in Ohio; three 100-year-old covered bridges; Shawnee Lookout Tower, constructed by the CCC in 1939; mounds and prehistoric earthworks from the Adena and Hopewell cultures; Leith Run Recreation Area, offering access to Ohio River. Wayne NF is Ohio's only national forest.

★577★ WENATCHEE NATIONAL FOREST

215 Melody Ln
Wenatchee, WA 98801
Web: www.fs.fed.us/r6/wenatchee
Phone: 509-664-9200; **Fax:** 509-664-9280
Size: 2,200,000 acres. **Location:** Central Washington. Accessible by I-90; US 2, 97, and 12. Nearby cities/towns include Chelan, Tonasket, Entiat, Naches, Ellensburg, Leavenworth, and Wenatchee. **Facilities:** 100+ campgrounds, group camps, dispersed camping, cabins, picnic areas, trails (2,500 miles), boat ramps, scenic overlooks, scenic drives, 7 wilderness areas. **Activities:** Camping, fishing, boating, canoeing, rafting, hiking, mushroom gathering, berry picking, horseback riding, mountain biking, skiing, snowmobiling, rock hounding, rock climbing, mountain climbing. **Special Features:** Some of the Northwest's best rock-climbing sites at Liberty Bell Mountain, Icicle Canyon, and Tumwater Canyon; Lake Chelan and Lake Wenatchee; Boulder Cave, a natural stone tunnel formed by erosion; Slate Peak, affording a 360-degree view of Mt. Baker and the surrounding Cascades.

★578★ WHITE MOUNTAIN NATIONAL FOREST

719 N Main St
Laconia, NH 03246
Web: www.fs.fed.us/r9/forests/white_mountain
Phone: 603-528-8721; **Fax:** 603-528-8783

Size: Nearly 800,000 acres. **Location:** Northern New Hampshire and southwestern Maine. Accessible by US 2, 3, and 302. Nearby cities/towns include Berlin, Conway, Gorham, Lancaster, and Littleton. **Facilities:** 3 cabins, 23 campgrounds, 3 group camps, 10 picnic sites, trails (1,200+ miles), 10 ski areas (concession operated), scenic drives, lighthouses, 5 wilderness areas. **Activities:** Camping, hunting, fishing, boating, canoeing, swimming, jet skiing, hiking, mountain biking, mountain climbing, horseback riding, cross-country and downhill skiing, snowshoeing, snowmobiling. **Special Features:** Cascading streams, more than 20 waterfalls, and landscape ranging from rugged treeless summits to wooded hollows. Among the forest's ranges and ridges are the Northeast's highest mountains — the Presidential Range — which culminate in the bare granite summit of 6,288-foot Mount Washington. A segment of the Appalachian National Scenic Trail passes through the forest (see entry in national trails section).

★579★ WHITE RIVER NATIONAL FOREST

900 Grand Ave
PO Box 948
Glenwood Springs, CO 81602
Web: www.fs.fed.us/r2/whiteriver
Phone: 970-945-2521
Size: 2,300,000 acres. **Location:** West-central Colorado. Accessible by US 70, 6, 24, 40, and 285; CO 82. Nearby cities/towns include Aspen, Dillon, Eagle, Glenwood Springs, Meeker, and Rifle. **Facilities:** Resorts, 37 campgrounds, 6 picnic areas, boat ramps, trails (1,895 miles), ski areas (concession operated), scenic drives. **Activities:** Camping, hunting, fishing, boating, rafting, mountain biking, inline skating, horseback riding, ORV riding, mountain climbing, cross-country and downhill skiing, snowmobiling, snowshoeing. **Special Features:** Among the most heavily used national forests in the country, White River includes: Vail, the largest ski resort in the country; ten mountain peaks above 14,000 feet in elevation; Glenwood Canyon, an 18-mile stretch of the Colorado River with 1,000-foot cliffs above the river; and 8 wilderness areas totaling more than 750,000 acres.

★580★ WILLAMETTE NATIONAL FOREST

211 E 7th Ave
Eugene, OR 97401
Web: www.fs.fed.us/r6/willamette
Phone: 541-225-6300
Size: 1,675,407 acres. **Location:** In the western Cascade mountains of western Oregon. Accessible by US 20; OR 58, 126, and 22. Nearby cities/towns include Salem, Albany, and Eugene. **Facilities:** 87 campgrounds, dispersed camping, picnic areas, trails, scenic drives, boat launch, 15 winter sports areas. **Activities:** Camping, fishing, boating, swimming, rafting, hiking, mountain biking, cross-country and downhill skiing, snowmobiling, tubing, snowshoeing, dog sledding. **Special Features:** Clear Lake, with its submerged forest; McKenzie River, a scenic whitewater river originating in the high Cascade Mountains; McKenzie River Trail, which follows the river for 27 miles; 286-foot Salt Creek Falls; Pacific Crest National Scenic Trail; and Waldo Lake, one of the purest lakes in the world. Seven major volcanic peaks exist within the forest's boundary.

See pages 20-21 for map of U.S. National Forests and Grasslands.

★581★ WILLIAM B. BANKHEAD NATIONAL FOREST

PO Box 278
Double Springs, AL 35553
Web: www.fs.fed.us/r8/alabama/forests
Phone: 205-489-5111
Size: 180,581 acres. **Location:** Northwest Alabama. Accessible by US 278; AL 5, 74, and 195. Nearby cities/towns include Decatur, Haleyville, Jasper, and Russellville. **Facilities:** Campgrounds, dispersed camping, trails, picnic sites, ballfields, shooting range, boat ramps. **Activities:** Camping, hunting, fishing, boating, swimming, hiking, bicycling, horseback riding, ORV riding. **Special Features:** 25,000-acre Sipsey Wilderness, the largest wilderness area east of the Mississippi River; Sipsey Fork, Alabama's only designated Wild and Scenic River; Lewis Smith Lake, excellent for bass and bluegill fishing.

NATIONAL GRASSLANDS

Totaling almost four million acres, our nation"s 20 publicly-owned National Grasslands are administered by the USDA Forest Service and managed for sustainable multiple uses as part of the National Forest System. Revegetated to provide for soil and water conservation, the grasslands also protect important wildlife habitat. They are rich in mineral, oil and gas resources and offer diverse recreational uses, such as mountain bicycling, hiking, hunting, fishing, photogratphing, bird-watching, and sightseeing. Fossils, prehistoric and historic resources, as well as many cultural sites have been discovered on the grasslands and they are being managed to protect these important legacy resources as well. For further information, visit the official National Grasslands web site at: http://www.fs.fed.us/grasslands/

★582★ BLACK KETTLE & MCCLELLAN CREEK NATIONAL GRASSLANDS

Rt 1 Box 55B
Cheyenne, OK 73628
Web: www.fs.fed.us/r3/cibola
Phone: 580-497-2143; **Fax:** 580-497-2379
Size: 32,749 total acres: 31,300 - Black Kettle NG; 1,449 - McClellan Creek NG. **Location:** Western Oklahoma and Texas Panhandle. Accessible by US 283; OK 30, 33, and 47; TX FM 2477. Nearby cities/towns include Cheyenne, Durham, Reydon, and Strong City, OK, and Canadian and Pampa, TX. **Facilities:** 5 campgrounds, dispersed camping, picnic areas, trails, boat ramps, dock. **Activities:** Camping, hunting, fishing, boating, hiking, horseback riding, bird watching. **Special Features:** Black Kettle NG sits on elevated tableland consisting of rolling sandhills with prairie grasses, sagebrush, and stands of cottonwood trees. Features include Lake Marvin Recreation Area and Washita Battlefield National Historic Site (see entry in national parks section). McClellan Creek NG is characterized by open grasslands, marshes, and woodlands. The grassland's 325-acre Lake McClellan is its primary attraction.

★583★ BUFFALO GAP, FORT PIERRE AND OGLALA NATIONAL GRASSLANDS

125 N Main St
Chadron, NE 69337
Web: www.fs.fed.us/r2/nebraska
Phone: 308-432-0300
Size: More than 800,000 total acres: 591,727 - Buffalo Gap NG; 94,400 - Oglala NG; 116,178 - Fort Pierre NG. **Location:** Buffalo Gap: southwestern South Dakota, abutting the north and west sides of Pine Ridge Indian Reservation. Accessible by SD 44, I-90, US 79/385, 18, and 14. Nearby cities/towns include Hot Springs, Kadoka, Scenic, and Wall. Fort Pierre: Central South Dakota. Accessible by US 83 and SD 1806. Oglala: in the Nebraska panhandle. Accessible from US 20, 385. **Facilities:** Visitor center, dispersed camping, picnic sites, trails, OHV recreation area, stocked ponds. **Activities:** Camping, hunting, fishing, hiking, mountain biking, OHV riding, bird watching, rock hounding. **Special Features:** Prairie Bike Trail, a 15-mile loop trail; reintroduction site for America's rarest mammal, the black-footed ferret. Richland Wildlife Area includes Richland Reservoir and over 500 acres of mixed grass prairie that is not grazed by livestock. Toadstool Park, where evidence of paleorivers, or ancient rivers, can be seen. Nearby are Badlands National Park and Wind Cave National Park (see entries in national parks section) and Black Hills National Forest (see separate entry in this section).

★584★ BUTTE VALLEY NATIONAL GRASSLAND

37805 Hwy 97
Macdoel, CA 96058
Phone: 530-398-4391
Size: 18,425 acres. **Location:** North-central California, near the Oregon border. Accessible by US 97. Nearby cities/towns include Dorris, Macdoel, and Yreka. **Facilities:** Scenic drive. **Activities:** Wildlife viewing, bird watching. **Special Features:** 2,000 acres of restored wetlands; resident wildlife includes pronghorn antelope, bald and golden eagles, red tailed hawks, sandhill cranes, Swanson's hawks, and pelicans.

★585★ CADDO & LYNDON B. JOHNSON NATIONAL GRASSLANDS

1400 N US Hwy 81/287
PO Box 507
Decatur, TX 76234
Web: www.fs.fed.us/r8/texas
Phone: 940-627-5475; **Fax:** 940-627-6558
Size: 38,035 total acres: 17,785 - Caddo NG; 20,250 - LBJ NG. **Location:** Northeastern Texas. Accessible by US 81/287, 380, and FM 100. Nearby cities/towns include Alvord, Decatur, Parris, and Bonham. **Facilities:** Campground, group camp, fishing piers (♿), picnic sites, trails (75+ miles), boat ramps, archery range. **Activities:** Camping, hunting, fishing, boating, swimming, hiking, mountain biking, horseback riding. **Special Features:** Caddo NG includes three fishing lakes, the largest of which is Lake Coffee Mill (651 acres). Lyndon B. Johnson NG features a 50-mile, multi-use trail that links several of the grassland's small lakes. Resident wildlife includes white-tailed deer, coyotes, bobcats, red fox, waterfowl, bobwhite quail, turkey, and songbirds.

See pages 20-21 for map of U.S. National Forests and Grasslands.

CEDAR RIVER NATIONAL GRASSLAND
(see Dakota Prairie National Grasslands)

★586★ CIMARRON NATIONAL GRASSLAND
242 Hwy 56 E
Elkhart, KS 67950
Web: www.fs.fed.us/r2/psicc/cim
Phone: 620-697-4621; **Fax:** 620-697-4340
Size: 108,175 acres. **Location:** Southwestern corner of Kansas. Accessible by US 56; KS 95, 27 and 51. Nearby cities/towns include Elkhart, Rolla, and Wilburton. **Facilities:** Campground, dispersed camping, picnic area, trails, fishing pier, livestock corral, scenic drive. **Activities:** Camping, fishing, hunting, hiking, horseback riding, mountain biking, OHV riding, bird watching. **Special Features:** A portion of the Santa Fe National Historic Trail (see entry in national trails section); Eightmile Historical Monument, where Kansas, Colorado, and Oklahoma share borders; Point of Rocks (3,540 feet), the third highest point in the state of Kansas.

★587★ COMANCHE NATIONAL GRASSLAND
27204 Hwy 287
PO Box 127
Springfield, CO 81073
Web: www.fs.fed.us/r2/psicc/coma
Phone: 719-523-6591; **Fax:** 719-523-4861
Size: 443,030 acres. **Location:** Southeastern Colorado. Accessible by US 160, 287/385, and 350; CO 109, and 50. Nearby cities/towns include Kim, Walsh, Lamar, Campo, Pritchett, and Vilas. **Facilities:** Dispersed camping, trails, 3 picnic areas, scenic drive. **Activities:** Camping, hunting, hiking, horseback riding, mountain biking, bird watching, wildlife viewing. **Special Features:** Vogel Canyon and Picture Canyon, which contain prehistoric Native American village sites and well-preserved examples of rock art; Picketwire Canyonlands, largest dinosaur track in North America with 1,300 footprints; a segment of Santa Fe National Historical Trail (see entry in national trails section), with historic water springs sites, scenic lookouts, and visible wagon ruts.

★588★ CROOKED RIVER NATIONAL GRASSLAND
813 SW Hwy 97
Madras, OR 97741
Web: www.fs.fed.us/r6/centraloregon
Phone: 541-475-9272
Size: 112,000 acres. **Location:** Central Oregon. Accessible by US 26 and 97; OR 26. Nearby cities/towns include Pineville, Warm Springs, Madras, Metolius, and Culver. **Facilities:** 2 campgrounds, trails. **Activities:** Camping, fishing, hunting, canoeing, kayaking, swimming, hiking, mountain biking, OHV riding, horseback riding, bird watching, rock hounding, cross-country skiing. **Special Features:** Rimrock Springs, an oasis in Oregon's arid high desert, featuring a 1.5-mile loop trail that leads to scenic overlooks with expansive views of the grassland; the Deschutes and Crooked wild and scenic rivers; Henderson Flat ORV Area.

★589★ CURLEW NATIONAL GRASSLAND
PO Box 146
Malad, ID 83252
Web: www.fs.fed.us/r4/caribou-targhee/about/curlew
Phone: 208-766-4743
Size: 47,000 acres. **Location:** South-central Idaho. Accessible by ID 37 and 38. Nearby cities/towns include Malad, Holbrook, Roy, and Stone. **Facilities:** Campgrounds, boat launches, scenic drive. **Activities:** Camping, hunting, fishing, hiking, swimming, boating, water-skiing, bird watching. **Special Features:** Remains of old homesteads, abandoned during Dust Bowl days; 250-acre Stone Reservoir; Hudspeth Cutoff Trail, a route used by California-bound emigrants as a shortcut to the Oregon Trail. The western edge of the grassland is a site where, in early March, male sharp-tail grouse perform their mating "dance."

★590★ DAKOTA PRAIRIE NATIONAL GRASSLANDS
240 W Century Ave
Bismarck, ND 58503
Web: www.fs.fed.us/r1/dakotaprairie
Phone: 701-250-4443; **Fax:** 701-250-4454
Size: 2,609,900 total acres, encompassing four national grasslands: Little Missouri NG (1,028,000 acres); Sheyenne NG (70,200 acres); Cedar River NG (6,700 acres); Grand River NG (155,000 acres). **Location:** Little Missouri NG: Western North Dakota; accessible by I-94, US 85; nearby towns include Grassy Butte and Medora. Sheyenne NG: Southeastern North Dakota; accessible by ND 27; nearby towns include Anselm, Lisbon, and McLeod. Cedar River NG: Southern North Dakota; accessible by ND 49; nearby towns include Lemmon, SD, and North Lemmon, ND. Grand River NG: Northwest South Dakota; accessible by SD 73 and SD 75; nearby towns include Bison, Lodgepole, and Shadehill. **Facilities:** 9 campgrounds (Little Missouri NG), dispersed camping, picnic and day-use areas, trails, scenic drives. **Activities:** Camping, hunting, canoeing, fishing, hiking, horseback riding, mountain biking, bird watching. **Special Features:** Four disparate grasslands each with their own characteristics. Little Missouri NG is the nation's largest grassland. It surrounds Teddy Roosevelt National Park (see entry in national parks section) and offers the most developed amenities. 100-mile-long Maah Daah Hey Trail traverses the area's scenic and rugged North Dakota badlands. The Little Missouri River, along the grassland's western edge, is popular for canoeing. Sheyenne NG contains a 25-mile segment of North Country National Scenic Trail (see entry in national trails section). Its long-grass prairie supports a large population of greater prairie chickens. Grand River NG's mixed-grass prairie is home to Shadehill Recreation Area (see entry in South Dakota state parks section) and the historic land of Sitting Bull. Cedar River NG is a mixed-grass prairie on plains and rolling hills, intersected by streams and dry draws. All but 400 acres of Cedar River NG lie within Standing Rock Sioux Reservation.

GRAND RIVER NATIONAL GRASSLAND
(see Dakota Prairie National Grasslands)

★591★ KIOWA & RITA BLANCA NATIONAL GRASSLANDS
714 Main St
Clayton, NM 88415
Web: www.fs.fed.us/r3/cibola
Phone: 505-374-9652; **Fax:** 505-374-9664

See pages 20-21 for map of U.S. National Forests and Grasslands.

3. National Forests and Grasslands

Size: Approximately 230,000 total acres: 136,505 acres - Kiowa NG; 93,323 acres - Rita Blanca NG. **Location:** Northeast New Mexico, northwest Texas Panhandle, and into Oklahoma. Accessible by US 87, 56/412; NM 39 and 402. Nearby towns include Clayton, Mills, and Seneca, NM, Kerrick and Texline, TX. **Facilities:** Campground, dispersed camping, picnic areas, trails. **Activities:** Camping, hunting, canoeing, rafting, fishing, hiking, horseback riding, mountain biking, bird watching, wildlife viewing. **Special Features:** 14-mile segment of the Canadian River; 2-mile section of the Santa Fe National Historic Trail; several paleontological, historic, and prehistoric cultural sites. Canadian River Canyon in the westernmost section of Kiowa NG is a wildlife ''island.'' Barbary sheep, native to Africa, and Rocky Mountain mule deer introduced in 1940s and 1950s have flourished here.

LITTLE MISSOURI NATIONAL GRASSLAND
(see Dakota Prairie National Grasslands)

★592★ MIDEWIN NATIONAL TALLGRASS PRAIRIE
30239 S SR 53
Wilmington, IL 60481
Web: www.fs.fed.us/mntp
Phone: 815-423-6370
Size: 19,165 acres. **Location:** Northeastern Illinois, 40 miles south of Chicago. Accessible by I-55 and IL 53. Nearby cities/towns include Elwood, Joliet, Manhattan, and Symerton. **Facilities:** Trails, picnic areas, hunting blinds (&). **Activities:** Hunting, hiking, bicycling, horseback riding, bird watching, guided tours, interpretive programs. **Special Features:** Nation's first federally designated tallgrass prairie. Former Army ammunition production site (Joliet Arsenal) where TNT was manufactured between 1940 and 1976. Midewin is the Potawatomi word for healing, an appropriate name for the site, which requires extensive environmental cleanup and restoration. The area is not open to unescorted public, but educational and recreational facilities are being developed.

★593★ PAWNEE NATIONAL GRASSLAND
660 'O' St
Greeley, CO 80631
Web: www.fs.fed.us/arnf
Phone: 970-346-5000
Size: 193,063 acres. **Location:** North-central Colorado, northeast of Greeley. Accessible by US 85 and CO 14. Nearby cities/towns include Ault, Eaton, Fort Collins, Grover, Greeley, and Sterling. **Facilities:** Campground, group camps, picnic areas, trails, ballfields, scenic drive and overlook. **Activities:** Camping, hiking, hunting, mountain biking, horseback riding, bird watching, stargazing. **Special Features:** Pawnee Buttes, a geological feature rising some 300 feet above the prairie; Crow Valley Recreation Area; old cemeteries and homesteads; nearby Grover Grassland Museum and Briggsdale Heritage House.

SHEYENNE NATIONAL GRASSLAND
(see Dakota Prairie National Grasslands)

★594★ THUNDER BASIN NATIONAL GRASSLAND
2250 E Richards St
Douglas, WY 82633
Web: www.fs.fed.us/r2/mbr
Phone: 307-358-4690; **Fax:** 307-358-3072
Size: 572,000 acres. **Location:** Northeastern Wyoming. Accessible by WY 59, 450, 116, 451, and US 16. Nearby cities/towns include Wright, Moorecroft, Gillete, Douglas, Newcastle, and Upton. **Facilities:** Dispersed camping, picnic areas, trails, reservoir, fishing pier, OHV roads (1,000+ miles). **Activities:** Camping, fishing, hunting, hiking, mountain biking, OHV riding, bird watching, wildlife viewing. **Special Features:** Where the Black Hills meet the prairie, site of one of the largest intact grassland habitats left in the Northern Great Plains. Numerous prehistoric and historic sites have been found here, ranging from Native American encampments, to historic trails and wagon roads, to more recent homesteads and pastoral camps. Current uses of the property include surface coal mining, oil and gas development, cattle grazing, and recreation.

See pages 20-21 for map of U.S. National Forests and Grasslands.

4. NATIONAL WILDLIFE REFUGES

★595★ **U.S. FISH & WILDLIFE SERVICE (USFWS)**
1849 'C' St NW, 3256 MIB
Washington, DC 20240
202-208-4717 - Phone
202-208-6965 - Fax
800-344-9453 - Toll free
Web: www.fws.gov

The U.S. Fish and Wildlife Service manages a system of more than 540 national wildlife refuges encompassing nearly 100 million acres of lands and waters nationwide. The Service's mission is to conserve, protect, and enhance fish, wildlife, and their habitats for the continuing benefit of the American people. While the needs of wildlife come first, most refuges offer a variety of wildlife-oriented recreation and education opportunities.

Publications: Numerous general and technical reports, bulletins, leaflets, posters, and brochures, both in print and online. These publications, including *National Wildlife Refuge System - A Visitor's Guide*, are available from the Publications Unit of the Fish and Wildlife Service in Shepherdstown, West Virginia. Call (800) 344-9453.

For further information on the national wildlife refuge system in the United States contact the Division of Refuges or its regional offices at the locations listed below.

Regional Offices:

Alaska Region
1011 E Tudor Rd
Anchorage, AK 99503
907-786-3309 - Phone
907-786-3495 - Fax
Web: alaska.fws.gov

Great Lakes-Big Rivers Region
1 Federal Dr
Fort Snelling, MN 55111
612-713-5360 - Phone
612-713-5284 - Fax
Web: fws.gov/midwest
(Illinois, Indiana, Iowa, Michigan, Missouri, Minnesota, Ohio, Wisconsin)

Mountain-Prairie Region
134 Union Blvd
Denver, CO 80228
303-236-7905 - Phone
303-236-8295 - Fax
Web: mountain-prairie.fws.gov
(Colorado, Kansas, Montana, Nebraska, North Dakota, South Dakota, Utah, Wyoming)

Northeast Region
300 Westgate Center Dr
Hadley, MA 01035
413-253-8200 - Phone
413-253-8308 - Fax
Web: fws.gov/northeast
(Connecticut, Delaware, Maine, Maryland, Massachusetts, New Hampshire, New Jersey, New York, Pennsylvania, Rhode Island, Vermont, Virginia, West Virginia)

Pacific Region
Eastside Federal Complex
911 NE 11th Ave
Portland, OR 97232
503-231-6118 - Phone
503-872-2716 - Fax
Web: fws.gov/pacific
(California, Hawaii, Idaho, Nevada, Oregon, Washington, Pacific Islands)

Southeast Region
1875 Century Blvd
Atlanta, GA 30345
404-679-4000 - Phone
404-679-4006 - Fax
Web: fws.gov/southeast
(Alabama, Arkansas, Florida, Georgia, Kentucky, Louisiana, Mississippi, North Carolina, South Carolina, Tennessee; Puerto Rico, Virgin Islands)

Southwest Region
500 Gold Ave SW
Albuquerque, NM 87102
505-248-6911 - Phone
505-248-6915 - Fax
Web: fws.gov/southwest
(Arizona, New Mexico, Oklahoma, Texas)

This section provides information on the individual refuges that comprise the National Wildlife Refuge System. Refuge conditions, regulations, and activities are subject to change, so users

See pages 22-23 for map of National Wildlife Refuges.

of this book are encouraged to contact the refuges for up-to-the-minute information. The phone number and address listed are those of the office that administers the refuge and do not necessarily reflect the location of the refuge.

★596★ ACE BASIN NATIONAL WILDLIFE REFUGE

8675 Willtown Rd
PO Box 848
Hollywood, SC 29449
Web: www.fws.gov/acebasin
Phone: 843-889-3084; **Fax:** 843-889-3282
Location: 25 miles south of Charleston, South Carolina. **Established:** 1990. **Habitat:** 11,815 acres of wetlands, early successional fields, and wooded uplands. Plans call for eventually increasing total acreage to about 18,000 acres. **Facilities:** Visitor center, hiking trails, observation towers, historic site. **Activities:** Canoeing, kayaking, hiking, hunting, fishing. **Access:** Year round during daylight hours. **Primary Wildlife:** American alligator, peregrine falcon, bald eagle, wood stork and other wading birds, waterfowl, deer. **Special Features:** Refuge is part of 350,000-acre ACE Basin, one of the largest undeveloped wetland ecosystems remaining on the Atlantic coast. Its name comes for the three rivers that flow into the basin, the Ashepoo, Combahee, and Edisto rivers. Two separate units comprise refuge lands: one along the Edisto River and the other along the Combahee River. A historic antebellum plantation home in the Edisto River unit serves as refuge headquarters.

★597★ AGASSIZ NATIONAL WILDLIFE REFUGE

22996 290th St NE
Middle River, MN 56737
Web: www.fws.gov/midwest/agassiz
Phone: 218-449-4115; **Fax:** 218-449-3241
Location: 12 miles north of Thief River Falls on Highway 32. **Established:** 1937. **Habitat:** 61,500 acres of wetland, shrubland, forestland, grassland, and cropland. **Facilities:** Visitor center, auto tour route, trails, observation tower. **Activities:** Hiking, hunting, educational programs, wildlife observation. **Access:** Open during daylight hours. **Primary Wildlife:** Moose, gray wolves, ducks, Canada geese, Franklin's gulls, herons, egrets, cormorants, grebes, and white-tailed deer. **Special Features:** The refuge is one of only two refuges in the lower 48 states with resident packs of eastern gray wolves.

★598★ ALAMOSA NATIONAL WILDLIFE REFUGE

9383 El Rancho Ln
Alamosa, CO 81144
Web: www.fws.gov/alamosa
Phone: 719-589-4021; **Fax:** 719-587-4705
Location: Four miles east of Alamosa in the San Luis Valley. **Established:** 1962. **Habitat:** 11,169 acres of dry uplands, wet meadows, river oxbows, and riparian corridors along the Rio Grande floodplain. **Facilities:** Visitor center, auto tour route, trail (2-mile loop). **Activities:** Hiking, hunting. **Access:** Year round during daylight hours. Visitor center open weekdays

March to November. **Primary Wildlife:** Songbirds, water birds, sandhill cranes, raptors, elk, deer, beaver, and coyotes. **Special Features:** A wide variety of avian species use the refuge. In late winter, bald eagles concentrate in the southern end of the refuge feeding in the open water of the Rio Grande. In the summer, black-necked stilts and avocets may be seen feeding on exposed mudflats.

★599★ ALASKA MARITIME NATIONAL WILDLIFE REFUGE

95 Sterling Hwy, Suite 1 MS 505
Homer, AK 99603
Web: alaskamaritime.fws.gov
Phone: 907-235-6546; **Fax:** 907-235-7783
Location: Chain of more than 2,500 islands, headlands, rocks, islets, spires, and reefs off the Alaskan coast. Stretches from Cape Lisburne on the Chukchi Sea to the tip of the Aleutians and eastward to Forrester Island on the border of British Columbia. **Established:** 1909. **Habitat:** 4.9 million acres, including tundra, rain forest, cliffs, volcanoes, beaches, lakes, and streams. More than half the refuge (2.64 million acres) is wilderness. **Facilities:** Visitor center. **Activities:** Camping, hiking, hunting, fishing, educational programs, wildlife viewing. **Access:** Refuge lands are open to the public at all times. Visitor center open mid-May through mid-September, Wednesday-Sunday. **Primary Wildlife:** Sea birds, sea lions, seals, walrus, sea otters, polar bears. **Special Features:** Includes the most diverse wildlife of all the refuges in Alaska. About 80 percent of Alaska's marine birds (15 to 30 million birds among 55 species) use the refuge.

★600★ ALASKA PENINSULA NATIONAL WILDLIFE REFUGE

PO Box 277 MS 545
King Salmon, AK 99613
Web: alaskapeninsula.fws.gov
Phone: 907-246-3339; **Fax:** 907-246-6696
Location: On the upper half of the Alaskan peninsula. **Established:** 1980. **Habitat:** 3.7 million acres of tundra, mountains, active volcanoes, glacial lakes, fjords, and rugged coastlines. **Facilities:** Visitor center. **Activities:** Camping, boating, canoeing, fishing, hiking, hunting, flightseeing. **Access:** Access to refuge lands is by small aircraft, boat or rugged cross-country hiking; there are no roads. Refuge is open year round. **Primary Wildlife:** Sea lion, seabirds, migratory waterfowl, bald eagle, hawk, falcon, owl, caribou, moose, brown bear, wolf, and salmon, migratory whales. **Special Features:** Refuge is dominated by the Aleutian Range and contains 8,400-foot Mount Veniaminof, a massive volcano with a base almost 30 miles across and larger than any active volcano on earth. The summit crater, about 5.2 miles in diameter, contains a 25-square-mile cupped ice field—the most extensive crater glacier in North America.

★601★ ALLIGATOR RIVER NATIONAL WILDLIFE REFUGE

PO Box 1969
Manteo, NC 27954
Web: alligatorriver.fws.gov
Phone: 252-473-1131; **Fax:** 252-473-1668

See pages 22-23 for map of National Wildlife Refuges.

Location: Northeastern North Carolina. **Established:** 1984. **Habitat:** 152,000 acres of marshland and pine and hardwood pine forests. **Facilities:** Trails, canoe trail, auto tour route. **Activities:** Boating, canoeing, fishing, hunting, educational programs. **Access:** Open during daylight hours. **Primary Wildlife:** Concentrations of ducks, geese, and swans. Also wading birds, shorebirds, American woodcock, raptors, black bears, American alligators, white-tailed deer, raccoons, rabbits, quail, river otters, red wolves, red-cockaded woodpeckers, and neotropical migratory birds. **Special Features:** Established to preserve and protect a unique wetland habitat (pocosin) and its associated wildlife species. Pocosin is a Native American word meaning 'swamp-on-a-hill' and is characterized by poorly drained soils high in organic material. One of the last remaining strongholds for black bear on the eastern seaboard, the refuge also provides habitat for the endangered red-cockaded woodpecker.

★602★ AMAGANSETT NATIONAL WILDLIFE REFUGE

c/o Long Island NWR Complex
PO Box 21
Shirley, NY 11967
Phone: 631-286-0485
Location: On Long Island's south fork, south of Amagansett. **Established:** 1968. **Habitat:** 36 acres of dunes, beach, and swale. **Activities:** Surf fishing, wildlife viewing, photography. **Access:** Open from dawn to dusk. Only beach area is open to the public. **Primary Wildlife:** Shorebirds and songbirds, hawks, owls, and the Eastern hognose snake. **Special Features:** Refuge preserves a portion of Long Island beach and dune habitat in a natural state.

★603★ ANAHO ISLAND NATIONAL WILDLIFE REFUGE

c/o Stillwater NWR
1000 Auction Rd
Fallon, NV 89406
Web: stillwater.fws.gov/anaho.html
Phone: 775-423-5128
Location: 30 miles northeast of Reno, Nevada, near the eastern shoreline of Pyramid Lake. **Established:** 1913. **Habitat:** 247-acre rocky island. **Access:** Closed to the public. Boating is not permitted within 500 feet of the island. **Primary Wildlife:** White pelicans, cormorants, great blue herons, and gulls. **Special Features:** Provides habitat for one of the largest white pelican nesting colonies in North America.

★604★ ANAHUAC NATIONAL WILDLIFE REFUGE

PO Box 278
Anahuac, TX 77514
Web: www.fws.gov/southwest/refuges/texas/anahuac
Phone: 409-267-3337; **Fax:** 409-267-4314
Location: An hour and a half east of Houston, along east Galveston Bay. **Established:** 1963. **Habitat:** More than 34,000 acres of coastal marsh and coastal prairie. **Facilities:** Visitor information station, trails, boardwalk, auto tour route, 2 boat ramps, rest rooms. **Activities:** Boating, canoeing, fishing, hunting, educational programs. **Access:** Open 24 hours. **Primary Wildlife:** 27 species of ducks, snow geese, wading birds, songbirds, American alligators, muskrat, nutria, bobcat, coyote. Marine species include white and brown shrimp, blue crab, flounder, and spotted sea trout. **Special Features:** The Willows, a seemingly insignificant stand of willow trees, provides crucial habitat for many of the neotropical migrants after their 600 mile journey across the Gulf of Mexico. Spring migration has been known to produce 17 species of migrants in a single tree.

★605★ ANKENY NATIONAL WILDLIFE REFUGE

2301 Wintel Rd
Jefferson, OR 97352
Web: www.fws.gov/willamettevalley/ankeny
Phone: 503-588-2701; **Fax:** 503-589-0954
Location: 10 miles south of Salem, Oregon. **Established:** 1965. **Habitat:** 2,796 acres of Willamette Valley agricultural bottomland. **Facilities:** Hiking trails, observation blinds, overlooks, auto tour route. **Activities:** Hiking, bicycling (only on roads open to vehicles), wildlife watching, educational programs. **Access:** Roads and trails are open sunrise to sunset; some trails close seasonally (October-March) to prevent disturbance to wintering waterfowl. **Primary Wildlife:** Dusky Canada geese and many other species of waterfowl; also hawks, vultures, quail, shorebirds, bald eagle, red fox, beaver, red-legged frog, and black-tailed deer. **Special Features:** Situated near the confluence of the Willamette and Santiam rivers, the refuge's fertile farmed fields, hedgerows, forests, and wetlands provide a variety of wildlife habitats.

★606★ ANTIOCH DUNES NATIONAL WILDLIFE REFUGE

c/o Don Edwards San Francisco Bay NWR
PO Box 524
Newark, CA 94560
Phone: 707-769-4200
Location: 30 miles west of Stockton, California. **Established:** 1980. **Habitat:** Two tracts of land totaling 55 acres of sand dunes along the San Joaquin River. **Activities:** Docent-led tours on the second Saturday of the month. **Access:** Closed to the public. **Primary Wildlife:** Critical habitat for Lange's metalmark butterfly (endangered) and two endangered flowers: Contra Costa wallflower and Antioch Dunes evening primrose. **Special Features:** Nation's first national wildlife refuge established to protect endangered plants and insects. The site preserves two sand dune areas left after the Mohave Desert receded in prehistoric times. Isolation of this sand dune habitat resulted in the development of subspecies of plants and insects found nowhere else in the world.

★607★ ARANSAS NATIONAL WILDLIFE REFUGE

PO Box 100
Austwell, TX 77950
Web: www.fws.gov/southwest/refuges/texas/aransas.html
Phone: 361-286-3559; **Fax:** 361-286-3722
Location: Northeast of Corpus Christi. **Established:** 1937. **Habitat:** More than 115,000 acres of low-lying coastal land and barrier island, covered with grasslands, wetlands, and woodlands. **Facilities:** Visitor center, observation tower, hiking trails,

See pages 22-23 for map of National Wildlife Refuges.

auto tour route (16 miles), picnic area with bathroom, boardwalk, photography blind. **Activities:** Fishing, hiking, hunting, biking, canoeing, kayaking, educational programs. **Access:** Open sunrise to sunset. **Primary Wildlife:** Whooping cranes and other migratory birds, butterflies, American alligator, armadillo, shrews, bats, wild boar, white-tailed deer. **Special Features:** More than 392 species of birds have been seen in Aransas NWR, which is home to the largest wild flock of whooping cranes each winter.

★608★ ARAPAHO NATIONAL WILDLIFE REFUGE
973 JC Rd #32
Walden, CO 80480
Web: arapaho.fws.gov
Phone: 970-723-8202
Location: 8 miles south of Walden, Colorado, off Highway 125. **Established:** 1967. **Habitat:** 24,804 acres of irrigated meadow, sagebrush grasslands, and streams in an intermountain glacial basin. **Facilities:** Viewing sites, hiking trails, auto tour route (6 miles). **Activities:** Fishing, hiking, hunting. **Access:** Open during daylight hours. **Primary Wildlife:** Mallard, pintail, gadwall, American wigeon, and other ducks. Also provides habitat for sage grouse, coyote, and pronghorn antelope. **Special Features:** The refuge produces about 9,000 ducklings and 150 to 200 goslings each year. When refuge lands are fully acquired and developed, waterfowl production is expected to increase significantly.

★609★ ARCHIE CARR NATIONAL WILDLIFE REFUGE
1339 20th St
Vero Beach, FL 32960
Web: www.fws.gov/archiecarr
Phone: 561-562-3909; **Fax:** 561-564-7393
Location: Between Melbourne and Wabasso along Florida's east coast. **Established:** 1991. **Habitat:** 900 acres (when acquisiton is complete) sandy beach coastline. **Activities:** Educational programs. **Access:** Limited by turtle activity; nest surveys are conducted April to September. **Primary Wildlife:** Loggerhead sea turtles, green sea turtles. **Special Features:** A linear refuge stretching for 20.5 miles, the site is the most important nesting area for loggerhead sea turtles in the Western Hemisphere and second most important nesting beach in the world. Twenty-five percent of all loggerhead sea turtle nests are laid along this strip of beach.

★610★ ARCTIC NATIONAL WILDLIFE REFUGE
101 12th Ave, Rm 236
Fairbanks, AK 99701
Web: arctic.fws.gov
Phone: 907-456-0250; **Fax:** 907-456-0428; **Toll Free:** 800-362-4546
Location: Inside the Arctic Circle, along the northernmost Alaska-Canada border. **Established:** 1960 as the Arctic National Wildlife Range. **Habitat:** 19.2 million acres of coastal lagoons, barrier islands, arctic tundra, foothills, mountains, and boreal forests cut by braided rivers and streams with clusters of shallow freshwater lakes and marshes. **Facilities:** Visitor contact station.

Activities: Boating, canoeing, fishing, hunting, camping, educational programs. **Access:** Unrestricted, except by weather. No roads inside the refuge, the nearest is Dalton Highway (a gravel road) which passes the western tip. Accessible primarily by aircraft. **Primary Wildlife:** Caribou, all 3 species of North American bears (black, grizzly, and polar), wolf, moose, wolverine, muskoxen, peregrine falcon, lynx, and snow geese. **Special Features:** One of the largest refuges within America's national wildlife refuge system, Arctic NWR is among the most complete, pristine, and undisturbed ecosystems on earth. It is home to more than 160 bird species, 36 kinds of land mammals, 9 marine mammal species, and 36 types of fish.

★611★ AROOSTOOK NATIONAL WILDLIFE REFUGE
c/o Moosehorn NWR
PO Box 554
Limestone, ME 04750
Web: northeast.fws.gov/me/aro.htm
Phone: 207-454-7161
Location: Located on part of the former Loring Air Force Base in Limestone, Maine. **Established:** 1998. **Habitat:** 4,295 acres of restored and forested wetlands. **Facilities:** Visitor contact station, trails. **Activities:** Hiking, fishing, canoeing, wildlife observation, cross-country skiing, snowshowing. **Access:** Year round during daylight hours. **Primary Wildlife:** Moose, beaver, bear, deer. **Special Features:** Once a part of Loring Air Force Base, the Aroostook property served as a storage site for weapons during the Cold War.

★612★ ARROWWOOD NATIONAL WILDLIFE REFUGE
7745 11th St SE
Pingree, ND 58476
Web: www.fws.gov/arrowwood/Arrowwood%5FNWR
Phone: 701-285-3341; **Fax:** 701-285-3350
Location: Along the James River in east central North Dakota. **Established:** 1935. **Habitat:** 15,934 acres of marshes, prairie grasslands, cultivated fields, and wooded ravines. **Facilities:** Viewing sites, picnic area, trails, auto tour route (5.5 miles), rest rooms. **Activities:** Boating (25 hp limit), canoeing, fishing, ice fishing, hunting, bow hunting, bird watching, horseback riding, bicycling, cross-country skiing, educational programs **Access:** Recreational areas are open April through September during daylight hours. **Primary Wildlife:** Geese, teal, wood ducks, gadwalls, mallards, canvasbacks, shorebirds, white-tailed deer, badger, mink. **Special Features:** Refuge is named for Native Americans who traveled here to obtain wood for arrow shafts.

★613★ ARTHUR R. MARSHALL LOXAHATCHEE NATIONAL WILDLIFE REFUGE
10216 Lee Rd
Boynton Beach, FL 33437
Web: www.fws.gov/loxahatchee
Phone: 561-734-8303; **Fax:** 561-369-7190
Location: 6 miles west of Boynton Beach in southeastern Florida. **Established:** 1951. **Habitat:** 147,392 acres of Everglades

See pages 22-23 for map of National Wildlife Refuges.

vegetation including cypress swamp, wet prairies, sloughs, sawgrass marshes, and tree islands. **Facilities:** Visitor center, boat ramp, boardwalk trails, observation tower, butterfly garden. **Activities:** Boating, canoeing, fishing, hiking, biking, hunting. **Access:** Open daily from sunrise to sunset. **Primary Wildlife:** Concentrations of migratory waterfowl, migratory passerines, and wading birds. Refuge includes rookeries for several species of herons and egrets, as well as anhinga and white ibis. **Special Features:** Occupying the last of the northern Everglades, the refuge provides habitat and protection for many endangered and threatened species, including the American alligator, snail kite, and wood stork.

★614★ ASH MEADOWS NATIONAL WILDLIFE REFUGE

HCR 70 Box 610-Z
Amargosa Valley, NV 89020
Web: www.fws.gov/desertcomplex/ashmeadows
Phone: 775-372-5435; **Fax:** 775-372-5436
Location: 90 miles northwest of Las Vegas. **Established:** 1984.
Habitat: Desert oasis, featuring 23,000 acres of alkaline Mohave desert interspersed with several free-flowing natural springs, outflow channels, and associated wetland habitat. **Facilities:** Visitor contact station, viewing sites, boardwalk, picnic areas. **Activities:** Swimming, wildlife watching, hunting, educational programs. **Access:** Open during daylight hours. **Primary Wildlife:** Endangered Ash Meadows Amargosa pupfish, Warm Springs pupfish, Devil's Hole pupfish, and Ash Meadows speckled dace; blacktail jackrabbit, chuckwalla lizards. **Special Features:** Set aside primarily for the protection and recovery of endangered fishes and plants, the refuge provides habitat for 24 species of plants and animals found nowhere else on earth.

★615★ ASSABET RIVER NATIONAL WILDLIFE REFUGE

73 Weir Hill Rd
Sudbury, MA 01776
Web: www.fws.gov/northeast/assabetriver
Phone: 978-443-4661
Location: 25 miles West of Boston. **Established:** 2000. **Habitat:** 2,230 acres of pine/hardwood forest, old field, and wetland. **Facilities:** Trails, visitor center. **Activities:** Hiking, hunting, fishing, wildlife observation, educational programs. **Access:** Refuge office and visitor center open daily 8 am to 4 pm. **Primary Wildlife:** Waterfowl, wading birds, raptors, shorebirds, passerines, white-tailed deer, wild turkey, and rabbit. **Special Features:** The refuge lands were formerly part of Fort Deavers, also known as the Sudbury Training Annex. The U.S. Army transferred 2,230 acres to the Fish & Wildlife Service in the fall of 2000.

★616★ ATCHAFALAYA NATIONAL WILDLIFE REFUGE

61389 Hwy 434
Lacombe, LA 70445
Web: www.fws.gov/atchafalaya
Phone: 985-882-2000; **Fax:** 985-882-9133
Location: 20 minutes west of Baton Rouge. **Established:** 1984.

Habitat: 15,222 acres of bottomland hardwood swamp, lakes, and bayous. **Facilities:** Visitor contact station, hiking trails. **Activities:** Fishing, hiking, wildlife viewing, hunting, photography, educational programs. **Access:** Open year round during daylight hours. **Primary Wildlife:** American bald eagle, Louisiana black bear, white-tailed deer, fox, and coyote, swallow-tailed kite, eastern wild turkey. **Special Features:** The 595,000-acre Atchafalaya River Basin is the nation's largest complex of forested wetlands and supports the nation's largest concentration of American woodcock. Refuge is located adjacent to the Louisiana's Sherburne Wildlife Management Area, which offers camping areas and boat launch facilities.

★617★ ATTWATER PRAIRIE CHICKEN NATIONAL WILDLIFE REFUGE

PO Box 519
Eagle Lake, TX 77434
Web: www.fws.gov/southwest/refuges/texas/attwater
Phone: 979-234-3021; **Fax:** 979-234-3278
Location: About 60 miles west of Houston, Texas. **Established:** 1972. **Habitat:** 10,528 acres of native prairie grasses bordered on the east by the San Bernard River. **Facilities:** Visitor center, auto tour route (5 miles), trails, picnic area. **Activities:** Hiking, educational programs. **Access:** Open sunrise to sunset. **Primary Wildlife:** Endangered Attwater's prairie chicken and nearly 250 other species of birds; also bison, raccoons, bobcat, coyote, armadillo, alligator, and snakes. **Special Features:** Refuge offers the last hope for survival for the endangered Attwater's prairie chicken, which once numbered over a million on the Texas and Louisiana gulf coastal prairies. Today, less than one percent of coastal prairies remain and in 1996, scientists estimated only about four dozen birds remained in the wild. Today a captive breeding program involving Texas A&M University, the Houston Zoo, the San Antonio Zoo, Sea World of Texas, Caldwell Zoo, and the Abilene Zoo is aimed at species repopulation on the prairie.

★618★ AUDUBON NATIONAL WILDLIFE REFUGE

3275 11th St NW
Coleharbor, ND 58531
Web: audubon.fws.gov
Phone: 701-442-5474
Location: In west-central North Dakota, on the south side of Lake Audubon. **Established:** 1955, as Snake Creek National Wildlife Refuge. **Habitat:** 14,735 total acres includes 10,421-acre Lake Audubon, 100 small islands in the lake, wetlands, and mixed-grass prairie. **Facilities:** Visitor center, viewing sites, hiking trails, auto tour route (7.5 miles), observation blind. **Activities:** Fishing, ice fishing, hunting, educational programs. **Access:** Open year round during daylight hours. **Primary Wildlife:** Sharp-tailed grouse, giant Canada goose, white pelican, mallard, teal, pintail, ring-necked pheasant, partridge, white-tailed deer, and painted turtle. **Special Features:** The refuge serves as an important feeding and resting area for waterfowl migrating in the Central Flyway. Nearby Lake Sakakawea and two state parks provide recreational opportunities including camping, picnicking, boating, and fishing.

See pages 22-23 for map of National Wildlife Refuges.

★619★ BACK BAY NATIONAL WILDLIFE REFUGE
4005 Sandpiper Rd
Virginia Beach, VA 23456
Web: www.fws.gov/backbay
Phone: 757-721-2412
Location: 20 miles south of Virginia Beach Virginia. **Established:** 1938. **Habitat:** More than 9,000 acres of coastline barrier island habitat including beach, dunes, woodland, farm fields, and marsh. **Facilities:** Visitor contact station, viewing sites, trails, tram tour. **Activities:** Canoeing, fishing, hiking, hunting, bicycling, educational programs. **Access:** Dawn to dusk year round. **Primary Wildlife:** Snow geese and ducks, as well as loggerhead sea turtles, piping plovers, peregrine falcons, and bald eagles. **Special Features:** Approximately 10,000 snow geese and a large variety of ducks visit Back Bay NWR during the peak of fall migration, usually in December.

★620★ BAKER HOWLAND & JARVIS ISLAND NATIONAL WILDLIFE REFUGES
c/o Pacific/Remote Islands NWR Complex
300 Ala Moana Blvd, Rm 5-231, PO Box 50167
Honolulu, HI 96850
Web: www.fws.gov/pacificislands/wnwr/pbakernwr.html
Phone: 808-792-9550; **Fax:** 808-792-9586
Location: Baker and Howland are just north of the equator in the central Pacific Ocean, about 1,600 miles southwest of Honolulu; Jarvis is 1,000 miles east of Baker and Howland. **Established:** 1974. **Habitat:** Baker is a 405-acre flat coral island surrounded by 30,504 acres of submerged land; Howland consists of a 455-acre island surrounded by 32,074 acres of submerged land; Jarvis is a 1,086 island surrounded by 35,297 acres of submerged land. **Access:** Access is restricted to protect nesting colonies; authorized visitation only by permit issued by refuge manager. **Primary Wildlife:** Nesting seabirds. **Special Features:** Feral cats once preyed heavily on the island's nesting seabirds; they were successfully eradicated from Baker Island in 1964.

★621★ BALCONES CANYONLANDS NATIONAL WILDLIFE REFUGE
24518 FM 1431
Marble Falls, TX 78654
Web: www.fws.gov/southwest/refuges/texas/balcones
Phone: 512-339-9432; **Fax:** 512-267-6530
Location: Northwest of Austin, Texas, in the Hill Country of central Texas. **Established:** 1992. **Habitat:** 21,836 acres of limestone hills, canyons, and springs. **Facilities:** Observation deck, restrooms, trails. **Activities:** Hiking, hunting, educational programs, birdwatching. **Access:** Open every day, sunrise to sunset, with some exceptions in specific areas. **Primary Wildlife:** Golden-cheeked warbler and black-capped vireo, jackrabbits, squirrels, butterflies. **Special Features:** Refuge protects nesting habitat for two endangered songbirds that nest almost exclusively in central Texas: the golden-cheeked warbler and the black-capped vireo.

★622★ BALD KNOB NATIONAL WILDLIFE REFUGE
1439 Coal Chute Rd
Bald Knob, AR 72010
Web: www.fws.gov/southeast/baldknob
Phone: 870-347-2614; **Fax:** 870-347-2908
Location: 50 miles southwest of Jonesboro, Arkansas. **Established:** 1993. **Habitat:** 14,800 acres of cropland, bottomland hardwood, sloughs, and oxbow lakes. **Activities:** Hiking, wildlife watching, fishing, hunting, educational programs. **Access:** Daylight hours year round. **Primary Wildlife:** Migratory waterfowl and other birds, river otters, bobcat, bald eagle, peregrine falcon. **Special Features:** On the site of a former rice farm, the refuge provides an important wintering area for puddle ducks, pintails, and geese and is key breeding habitat for wood ducks, hooded mergansers, herons, and neotropical birds. A pair of bald eagles have historically nested on the refuge.

★623★ BANDON MARSH NATIONAL WILDLIFE REFUGE
c/o Oregon Coast NWR Complex
2127 SE Marine Science Dr
Newport, OR 97365
Web: www.fws.gov/oregoncoast/bandonmarsh
Phone: 541-867-4550; **Fax:** 541-867-4551
Location: North of Bandon, Oregon, on the Pacific Coast. **Established:** 1983. **Habitat:** 889 acres of Coquille River estuary including salt marsh, mudflat, and beachgrass communities. **Facilities:** Trail (&). **Activities:** Boating, canoeing, fishing, bird watching, clamming, hunting. **Access:** Observation area and marsh are open daily, sunrise to sunset. **Primary Wildlife:** Shorebirds, wading birds, raptors, waterfowl, and seabirds, including common murres, tufted puffins, three species of cormorants, harbor seal, sea lions. **Special Features:** Bandon Marsh NWR is located along the picturesque southern Oregon coast near the mouth of the Coquille River.

★624★ BANKS LAKE NATIONAL WILDLIFE REFUGE
c/o Okefenokee NWR
Rt 2, Box 3330
Folkston, GA 31537
Web: www.fws.gov/southeast/bankslake
Phone: 912-496-7366; **Fax:** 912-496-3332
Location: 2 miles west of Lakeland in southern Georgia. **Established:** 1985. **Habitat:** 4,049 acres of cypress swamp, marsh, and lake. **Facilities:** Viewing sites, hiking trails, canoe trail, boat launch, boat rental concession. **Activities:** Boating, canoeing, fishing, hiking, wildlife watching. **Access:** Open during daylight hours. **Primary Wildlife:** Ducks, wading birds, and shorebirds. **Special Features:** Banks Lake is a natural pocosin, or mill pond, most likely created by the tidal action of the ocean and shaped by a more temperate climate thousands of years ago. The site's 1,000 acres of open water are popular for sport fishing.

★625★ BASKETT SLOUGH NATIONAL WILDLIFE REFUGE
10995 Hwy 22
Dallas, OR 97338
Web: www.fws.gov/WillametteValley/baskett
Phone: 503-623-2749; **Fax:** 503-623-7812

See pages 22-23 for map of National Wildlife Refuges.

Location: 10 miles west of Salem, Oregon. **Established:** 1965. **Habitat:** 2,492 acres of irrigated hillsides, oak-covered knolls, grass fields, and wetlands. **Facilities:** Interpretive and viewing kiosk, spotting scope, hiking trails, auto tour route, rest rooms. **Activities:** Hunting, educational programs, wildlife watching, hiking. **Access:** Some portions of the refuge are closed to the public while geese are present, from October through April. **Primary Wildlife:** Dusky Canada geese. Also several species of waterfowl, shorebirds, woodpeckers, and a variety of songbirds, Pacific tree frogs, black-tailed deer, raptors. **Special Features:** Baskett Slough NWR was created to provide vital wintering habitat for dusky Canada geese. Unlike other Canada geese, duskies have limited summer and winter ranges. They nest on Alaska's Copper River Delta and winter almost exclusively in the Willamette Valley. Refuge also provides habitat for 30 species of mammals, including red fox and black-tailed deer, eight species of amphibians, and ten species of reptiles.

★626★ BAYOU COCODRIE NATIONAL WILDLIFE REFUGE

PO Box 1772
Ferriday, LA 71334
Web: bayoucocodrie.fws.gov
Phone: 318-336-7119; **Fax:** 318-336-5610
Location: In Concordia Parish in east-central Louisiana, 3 miles south of Ferriday. **Established:** 1992. **Habitat:** 11,255 acres of bottomland hardwoods in the Mississippi River delta. **Activities:** Hunting, fishing, hiking, educational programs, bird watching. **Access:** Open during daylight hours. **Primary Wildlife:** Migratory waterfowl, swallows, herons, egrets, white-tailed deer, turkey, vultures, owls. **Special Features:** The bald eagle, peregrine falcon, and the Louisiana black bear can occasionally be found in the refuge.

★627★ BAYOU SAUVAGE NATIONAL WILDLIFE REFUGE

c/o Southeast Louisiana Refuges
61389 Hwy 434
Lacombe, LA 70445
Web: www.fws.gov/bayousauvage
Phone: 985-882-2000; **Fax:** 985-882-9133
Location: On the Louisiana gulf coast, just northeast of New Orleans. **Established:** 1990. **Habitat:** 23,000 acres of fresh and brackish marshes. **Facilities:** Hiking trails, cultural sites, boardwalk, pavilion, restrooms. **Activities:** Boating, canoeing, fishing, hiking, bicycling, crawfishing, crabbing, educational programs. **Access:** Open during daylight hours. **Primary Wildlife:** Brown pelican, peregrine falcon, bald eagle, as well as waterfowl, wading birds, shorebirds, swamp rabbits, and alligators. **Special Features:** As many as 50,000 waterfowl use the wetland areas of the refuge during the fall, winter, and early spring months. It is the largest urban wildlife refuge in the country.

★628★ BAYOU TECHE NATIONAL WILDLIFE REFUGE

10816A Hwy 182 E
Franklin, LA 70538
Web: www.fws.gov/bayouteche
Phone: 337-828-0092; **Fax:** 337-828-0061

Location: 55 miles from Lafayette, Louisiana. **Established:** 2001. **Habitat:** 9,028 acres of bottomland hardwoods and cypress-gum forests. **Activities:** Fishing, hunting, boating, wildlife observation, educational programs. **Access:** Sunrise to sunset. **Primary Wildlife:** Louisiana black bear, alligators, wading birds, bald eagles, ducks, white-tailed deer. **Special Features:** Bayou Teche is the only NWR with the specific mission of managing bears. The Louisiana black bear, a sub-species of the American black bear, is relatively abundant throughout the refuge.

★629★ BEAR LAKE NATIONAL WILDLIFE REFUGE

PO Box 9
Montpelier, ID 83254
Web: www.fws.gov/pacific/refuges/field/ID_Bearlk.htm
Phone: 208-847-1757
Location: 7 miles southwest of Montpelier, in the southeast corner of Idaho. **Habitat:** 19,000 acres of marsh, open water, and grasslands at an elevation of 5,900 feet. **Facilities:** Boat launch, hiking trails. **Activities:** Fishing, hunting, biking, horseback riding, boating. **Access:** Open during daylight hours. **Primary Wildlife:** Important as a nesting area for white-faced ibis, Canada geese, canvasback and redhead ducks. Feeding and nesting grounds for greater sandhill cranes, many species of ducks, and a variety of water and shorebirds. **Special Features:** Surrounded by mountains, the refuge lies in the Bear Lake Valley at elevations ranging from 5,925 feet on the marsh to 6,800 feet on the rocky slopes of Merkley Mountain.

★630★ BEAR RIVER MIGRATORY BIRD REFUGE

2155 W Forest St
Brigham City, UT 84302
Web: www.fws.gov/bearriver
Phone: 435-723-5887; **Fax:** 435-723-8873
Location: Northern tip of the Great Salt Lake, 15 miles west of Brigham City. **Established:** 1928. **Habitat:** 74,000 acres of marsh, open water, uplands, wet meadows, ponds, and mudflats. **Facilities:** Visitor contact station, viewing sites, auto tour route (12 miles), photography blinds, wildlife education center. **Activities:** Fishing, hunting, educational programs. **Access:** Auto tour route open sunrise to sunset year round. **Primary Wildlife:** Waterfowl and shore birds. **Special Features:** The new 28,000 square-foot wildlife education center features a 200-seat auditorium, and 3,500-square-foot exhibit hall, as well as classrooms and a research lab.

★631★ BEAR VALLEY NATIONAL WILDLIFE REFUGE

c/o Klamath Basin NWR Complex
4009 Hill Rd
Tulelake, CA 96134
Web: www.klamathnwr.org/bearvalley.html
Phone: 530-667-2231
Location: 12 miles southwest of Klamath Falls, Oregon. **Established:** 1978. **Access:** Closed to all public entry, except by foot during deer hunting season. From outside the refuge between December and mid-March, early morning visitors can observe

See pages 22-23 for map of National Wildlife Refuges.

large numbers of bald eagles and other raptors. **Primary Wildlife:** Wintering bald eagles. **Special Features:** Located on a northeast slope sheltered from winter winds, the refuge protects a night roosting site for wintering bald eagles. In recent years, as many as 300 bald eagles have used the roost in a single night. Several bald eagle pairs also nest at the site.

★632★ BECHAROF NATIONAL WILDLIFE REFUGE

PO Box 277
King Salmon, AK 99613
Web: becharof.fws.gov
Phone: 907-246-3339; **Fax:** 907-246-6696
Location: At the base of the Alaska Peninsula, 295 miles southwest of Anchorage, between Katmai National Park (see entry in national parks chapter) and Alaska Peninsula NWR (see separate entry). **Established:** 1980. **Habitat:** 1,157,000 acres with Becharof Lake covering one-fourth of the total area; the remainder of the refuge includes low rolling hills, tundra wetlands, volcanic peaks, and wilderness. **Facilities:** Visitor center (located in King Salmon near the airport). **Activities:** Camping, boating, canoeing, salmon fishing, hiking, bear hunting, educational programs. **Access:** Access to refuge lands is by small aircraft, boat or rugged cross country hiking; there are no roads. Refuge lands are open to the public at all times. **Primary Wildlife:** Heavy concentrations of brown bear, as well as moose, migrating caribou, eagles, falcons, and salmon. **Special Features:** The refuge is dominated by Becharof Lake, the second largest lake in Alaska. The lake and its tributaries contribute over ten million adult salmon annually to the Bristol Bay fishery. All five species of Pacific salmon inhabit the refuge, as do Arctic char and Arctic grayling.

★633★ BENTON LAKE NATIONAL WILDLIFE REFUGE

922 Bootlegger Trail
Great Falls, MT 59404
Web: bentonlake.fws.gov
Phone: 406-727-7400; **Fax:** 406-727-7432
Location: 12 miles north of Great Falls, on the western edge of the northern Great Plains. **Established:** 1929. **Habitat:** 12,383 acres of native shortgrass prairie surrounded by mountain ranges on three sides. Benton Lake is a 5,000-acre shallow marsh. **Facilities:** Visitor contact station, viewing sites, boardwalk, hiking trails, auto tour route. **Activities:** Fishing, hiking, hunting, cross-country skiing, ice skating, wildlife observation. **Access:** Open year round during daylight hours. **Primary Wildlife:** Water birds including snow geese, tundra swans, shorebirds, avocets, phalaropes, willets, and grebes. Also provides habitat for native prairie birds, bald eagles, peregrine falcons, and mammals such as raccoon, weasel, and coyote. **Special Features:** During spring and fall migrations, up to 150,000 ducks, 40,000 snow geese, 2,500 Canada geese, 5,000 tundra swans, and perhaps as many as 50,000 shorebirds use the marsh. During an average breeding season, the refuge produces 20,000 ducks, and 10,000 Franklin's gulls nests.

★634★ BIG BOGGY NATIONAL WILDLIFE REFUGE

6801 County Rd 306
Brazoria, TX 77422
Web: www.fws.gov/southwest/refuges/texas/texasmidcoast/bigboggy.htm
Phone: 979-964-3639; **Fax:** 979-964-3210
Location: Beside Matagorda Bay, about 20 miles southeast of Bay City. **Established:** 1983. **Habitat:** 5,000 acres of salt marsh. **Activities:** Waterfowl hunting. **Access:** Open to the public for waterfowl hunting season and for special activities. **Primary Wildlife:** Migratory waterfowl and other bird species, especially roseate spoonbill, white Ibis, snowy egret, and brown pelican. **Special Features:** Site includes Dressing Point Island, one of the major rookeries for colonial nesting birds on the Texas Gulf Coast.

★635★ BIG BRANCH MARSH NATIONAL WILDLIFE REFUGE

61389 Hwy 434
Lacombe, LA 70445
Web: www.fws.gov/bigbranchmarsh
Phone: 985-882-2000; **Fax:** 985-882-9133
Location: 15 miles north of New Orleans, on the north shore of Lake Pontchartrain. **Established:** 1994. **Habitat:** 17,094 acres of pine flatwoods, oak rides, and coastal marsh on the shoreline of Lake Pontchatrain. **Facilities:** Visitor center, viewing sites, trails, boat ramp. **Activities:** Boating, canoeing, fishing, hiking, bicycling, hunting, wildlife watching, educational programs, interpretive tours. **Access:** Daylight hours year round. **Primary Wildlife:** Turkey, deer, squirrels, red-cockaded woodpecker, bald eagle and osprey. **Special Features:** The marshes provide spawning and nursery habitat for a number of fresh and saltwater species, including shrimp, crabs, redfish, trout, bass and catfish.

★636★ BIG LAKE NATIONAL WILDLIFE REFUGE

PO Box 67
Manila, AR 72442
Web: www.fws.gov/biglake
Phone: 870-564-2429; **Fax:** 870-564-2573
Location: 2 miles east of Manila in northeastern Arkansas. **Established:** 1915. **Habitat:** 11,038 acres of water interspersed with timbered swampland. **Facilities:** Fishing pier, viewing sites, boat ramps, auto tour route, trail. **Activities:** Boating, canoeing, fishing, frogging, hunting, educational programs. **Access:** Lake is open to the public March through October during daylight hours. Auto tour route is open year round. **Primary Wildlife:** Wintering and migrating ducks, nesting bald eagles and osprey. **Special Features:** The refuge basin is thought to have formed as a result of the New Madrid earthquakes in the winter of 1811-12.

★637★ BIG MUDDY NATIONAL FISH & WILDLIFE REFUGE

4200 New Haven Rd
Columbia, MO 65201
Web: www.fws.gov/midwest/bigmuddy
Phone: 573-876-1826; **Fax:** 573-879-1839; **Toll Free:** 800-611-1826

See pages 22-23 for map of National Wildlife Refuges.

Location: On the Missouri River, near Columbia, Missouri. **Established:** 1994. **Habitat:** 10,400 acres (with plans to expand to 60,000 acres) of bottomland forests, lakes, sloughs, cropland, and marsh. **Facilities:** Undeveloped. **Activities:** Boating, canoeing, fishing, hunting. **Access:** Unrestricted. **Primary Wildlife:** Waterfowl, wading birds, shorebirds, and neotropical migratory birds. Also provides habitat for endangered and threatened species, including pallid sturgeon, decurrent false aster, bald eagle, piping plover, least tern, peregrine falcon, gray bat, and Indiana bat. **Special Features:** Refuge is located on six parcels in various counties along the Missouri River. Land along the river was covered with several feet of sand by 1993 flooding, and the property now is being purchased piecemeal. Refuge managers plan to let the river return to a natural course and create a variety of habitats in the process.

★638★ BIG OAKS NATIONAL WILDLIFE REFUGE

1661 W JPG Niblo Rd
Madison, IN 47250
Web: www.fws.gov/midwest/bigoaks
Phone: 812-273-0783; **Fax:** 812-273-0786
Location: 5 miles north of Madison on US Highway 421. **Established:** 2000. **Habitat:** 50,000 acres of grasslands, shrub, forests, and wetlands; 165-acre lake. **Facilities:** Interpretive exhibits, wildlife viewing sites, boat ramp. **Activities:** Boating, fishing, hunting, wild food products (mushrooms, nuts, berries, asparagus) for personal use, educational programs (by prior arrangement). **Access:** Open 10 days per month from mid-April until the end of November; contact refuge office for specific days and times. **Primary Wildlife:** River otter. Also a broad range of birds (200 species sighted), mammals (39 species), bats, reptiles and amphibians, fish, and butterflies. **Special Features:** Refuge contains at least 32 caves, all of which are closed to the public. During a recent survey of the caves and wells on the refuge, researchers discovered 6 previously unknown species of invertebrates.

★639★ BIG STONE NATIONAL WILDLIFE REFUGE

44843 County Rd 19
Odessa, MN 56276
Web: www.fws.gov/midwest/bigstone
Phone: 320-273-2191; **Fax:** 320-273-2231
Location: Near the Minnesota-South Dakota border, 0.5 miles west of Odessa, Minnesota. **Established:** 1975. **Habitat:** 11,521 acres of wetlands, woodlands, native prairie, and granite rock outcroppings. **Facilities:** Visitor contact station, viewing sites, hiking trails, auto tour route. **Activities:** Fishing, hunting, wildlife watching, educational programs. **Access:** Open during daylight hours. **Primary Wildlife:** Mallard, Canada geese, American bittern, partridge, beaver, otter, white-tailed deer. **Special Features:** Part of the Big Stone-Whetstone River Project of Minnesota and South Dakota, the refuge serves as a wintering area for as many as 1,200 whitetail deer and has a year-round population of river otters. Site also protects an area of ball cactus, which grows nowhere else in Minnesota.

★640★ BILL WILLIAMS RIVER NATIONAL WILDLIFE REFUGE

60911 Hwy 95
Parker, AZ 85344
Web: www.fws.gov/southwest/refuges/arizona/billwill.html
Phone: 928-667-4144
Location: In western Arizona, between Lake Havasu City and Parker, along the Lower Colorado River Valley. **Established:** 1941. **Habitat:** 6,105 acres of cattail marshes, open lake, riparian habitat, and desert upland. **Facilities:** Visitor contact station, viewing sites, auto tour route. **Activities:** Fishing, hiking, hunting, bicycling, horseback riding, boating. **Access:** Open during daylight hours. **Primary Wildlife:** More than 275 species of birds, including nesting neotropical birds such as summer tanagers, vermilion flycatchers, and yellow-billed cuckoos. Also rattlesnakes, razorback suckers, bonytail chubs, bighorn sheep and cottontail rabbit. **Special Features:** Refuge is one of only a few places in the world where one can see Saguaro cactus, a cattail stand, and a cottonwood tree together. This unique blend of upland desert, marsh, and desert riparian habitats provides for a diverse array of birds, mammals, and reptiles.

★641★ BITTER CREEK NATIONAL WILDLIFE REFUGE

c/o Hopper Mountain NWR
PO Box 5839
Ventura, CA 93005
Web: www.fws.gov/hoppermountain/Bitterck
Phone: 805-644-5185; **Fax:** 805-644-1732
Location: 40 miles southwest of Bakersfield, California, near Maricopa. **Established:** 1985. **Habitat:** 14,094 acres consisting primarily of bushlands and grasslands with a small area of juniper and scrub oak. **Facilities:** Auto tour route. **Access:** The refuge is closed to visitors except from a county road that bisects the refuge. **Primary Wildlife:** Traditional feeding and roosting habitat for the California condor. Also provides habitat for the San Joaquin kit fox, golden eagle, and the endangered blunt-nosed leopard lizard **Special Features:** Refuge is one of the centers for research aimed at assisting the recovery of the California condor.

★642★ BITTER LAKE NATIONAL WILDLIFE REFUGE

4067 Bittler Lake Rd
Roswell, NM 88201
Web: www.fws.gov/southwest/refuges/newmex/bitterlake
Phone: 505-622-6755; **Fax:** 505-622-4004
Location: Northeast of Roswell, New Mexico, in the middle of the Pecos River Valley. **Established:** 1937. **Habitat:** 24,536 acres where the Chihuahuan Desert, short grass prairie, Pecos River and the Rosewell artesian come together. **Facilities:** Viewing sites, picnic area, trails, auto tour route, endangered species tours (by appointment). **Activities:** Hiking, horseback riding, hunting, bicycling, educational programs. **Access:** Open daily from dawn to dusk. **Primary Wildlife:** Sandhill cranes and migratory waterfowl, dragonflies, damselflies, frogs, horned lizard, deer. **Special Features:** Site of the endangered interior least terns' only nesting area in New Mexico. The refuge supports one

See pages 22-23 for map of National Wildlife Refuges.

of the most diverse populations of dragonflies and damselflies in North America.

★643★ BLACK BAYOU LAKE NATIONAL WILDLIFE REFUGE

11372 Hwy 143
Farmerville, LA 71241
Web: www.fws.gov/northlouisiana/blackbayoulake
Phone: 318-726-4400; Fax: 318-726-4667
Location: In northern Louisiana, 4 miles north of Monroe. Established: 1997. Habitat: 4,200 acres of wetlands consisting of a shallow lake, riparian areas, and farm fields. Facilities: Visitor center, viewing sites, boardwalk trail (&), nature trails, boat launches, canoe trail, environmental education center. Activities: Boating, canoeing, fishing, hunting (with restrictions), wildlife watching, educational programs. Access: Open year round during daylight hours. Primary Wildlife: Endangered red-cockaded woodpeckers, as well as wading birds, squirrel, rabbit, deer, alligator, snakes, turtles. Special Features: Refuge property is operated by the Fish and Wildlife Service under a free 99-year lease with the City of Monroe.

★644★ BLACK COULEE NATIONAL WILDLIFE REFUGE

c/o Bowdoin NWR
HC 65, Box 5700
Malta, MT 59538
Phone: 406-654-2863
Location: North of Dodson in northeastern Blaine County, Montana. Established: 1938. Habitat: 1,494-acre native range with a large retention reservoir. Facilities: None. Activities: Hunting. Access: Refuge is fenced and gates are normally locked, but visitors may enter on foot. Roads in this remote region may be too dangerous to travel during winter. Primary Wildlife: Migratory birds; resident wildlife includes pronghorn antelope and raptors. Special Features: Waterfowl and upland game bird hunting is allowed on a portion of the refuge, east of the road, but hunters must walk in. In high-water years, a small boat may be carried to the reservoir during hunting season.

★645★ BLACKBEARD ISLAND NATIONAL WILDLIFE REFUGE

c/o Savannah Coastal Refuges Complex
1000 Business Center Dr, Suite 10
Savannah, GA 31405
Web: www.fws.gov/blackbeardisland/
Phone: 912-652-4415; Fax: 912-652-4385
Location: Off the Atlantic coast of Georgia, 50 miles south of Savannah. Established: Originally established as a wildlife preserve in 1924; redesignated as a wildlife refuge in 1940. Habitat: 5,618 acres of maritime forest, salt marsh, freshwater marsh, and beach. Facilities: Viewing sites, trails. Activities: Canoeing, sea kayaking, fishing, shrimping, crabbing, hiking, deer hunting, bicycling, wildlife watching, environmental programs. Access: Open year round during daylight hours; accessible by boat only. Primary Wildlife: Waterfowl, songbirds, raptors, alligators, loggerhead turtle, and deer. Special Features: Blackbeard Island was named for Edward Teach, popularly known as Blackbeard the Pirate. Legend tells of his murderous and plundering activities along the coast and his periodic retreats to the island for "banking" purposes. Rumors of Blackbeard's buried treasure still circulate, but no evidence of his fortune has ever been discovered.

★646★ BLACKWATER NATIONAL WILDLIFE REFUGE

2145 Key Wallace Dr
Cambridge, MD 21613
Web: blackwater.fws.gov
Phone: 410-228-2677
Location: On the eastern shore of Maryland, 12 miles south of Cambridge. Established: 1933. Habitat: 27,000 acres of tidal marsh, open water, woodlands, agricultural areas, and freshwater impoundments. Facilities: Visitor center, trails, auto tour route. Activities: Boating, canoeing, fishing, crabbing, hiking, biking, wildlife watching, hunting, educational programs. Access: Open from dawn to dusk. Primary Wildlife: Canada geese, snow geese, mallard, pintail, American wigeon, and teal. The bald eagle and Delmarva fox squirrel are seen regularly, as is the peregrine falcon during the migratory season. Also nutria, white tail deer, bats, muskrats, skunks, skinks, turtles. Special Features: Before its designation as a refuge, the marshland along Blackwater River was used for trapping muskrats. Remains of old drainage ditches and furrows in some areas indicate past agricultural use.

★647★ BLOCK ISLAND NATIONAL WILDLIFE REFUGE

c/o Rhode Island NWR Complex
3679 D Old Post Rd, PO Box 307
Charlestown, RI 02813
Web: www.fws.gov/blockisland
Phone: 401-364-9124
Location: On the northern tip of Block Island, 12 miles offshore south of Point Judith, Rhode Island. Established: 1973. Habitat: 127 acres of sandy beaches and rolling dunes. Facilities: Viewing sites, hiking trails. Activities: Fishing, hiking. Access: Open from dawn to dusk. Primary Wildlife: Migratory songbirds. Special Features: Refuge supports large concentrations of migratory songbirds (70+ species) which visit the area each fall. Many young, inexperienced songbirds "overfly" the mainland and stop over on Block Island before continuing their migration. The refuge also provides habitat for the endangered American burying beetle, the only known population east of the Mississippi River.

★648★ BLUE RIDGE NATIONAL WILDLIFE REFUGE

c/o Hopper Mountain NWR
PO Box 5839
Ventura, CA 93005
Web: www.fws.gov/hoppermountain/Blueridge
Phone: 805-644-5185; Fax: 805-644-1732
Location: In Los Padres National Forest, 45 miles northwest of

See pages 22-23 for map of National Wildlife Refuges.

4. National Wildlife Refuges

the Los Angeles metropolitan area. **Established:** 1982. **Habitat:** 897 acres of mountains, rock outcroppings, chaparral, and coniferous trees. **Access:** Refuge is closed to the public due to the sensitivity of California condors and the refuge's isolation. **Primary Wildlife:** Traditional summer roosting site for the endangered California condor; also quail, owls, bobcat, mountain lion, chipmunk. **Special Features:** Two observation points are maintained in the Los Padres National Forest (see entry in national forests section).

★649★ BOGUE CHITTO NATIONAL WILDLIFE REFUGE
61389 Hwy 434
Lacombe, LA 70445
Web: www.fws.gov/boguechitto
Phone: 985-882-2000; **Fax:** 985-882-9133
Location: Southeastern Louisiana along the Louisiana-Mississippi line, 9 miles north of Slidell. **Established:** 1980. **Habitat:** 36,600 acres of bottomland hardwood, bayous, and sloughs. **Facilities:** Primitive campsites, hiking trails, canoe trail. **Activities:** Camping, boating, canoeing, fishing, hunting, hiking, educational programs. **Access:** Open during daylight hours. Much of refuge is accessible by boat only. **Primary Wildlife:** Endangered and threatened species include bald eagle, ringed-sawback turtle, gopher tortoise, inflated heelsplitter mussel, and Gulf sturgeon. Other wildlife present are deer, turkey, neotropicals, rabbit, raccoon, several varieties of snake, mink, skunk, wading birds, and waterfowl. **Special Features:** Located in the Pearl River basin, the refuge protects one of the least disturbed southern swamplands in the nation, with sections in both Louisiana and Mississippi. Bogue Chitto means ''large stream'' as defined by the Choctaw Indians.

★650★ BOMBAY HOOK NATIONAL WILDLIFE REFUGE
2591 Whitehall Neck Rd
Smyrna, DE 19977
Web: www.fws.gov/northeast/bombayhook
Phone: 302-653-9345; **Fax:** 302-653-0684
Location: On the western shore of Delaware Bay about 10 miles northeast of Dover, Delaware. **Established:** 1937. **Habitat:** 15,978 acres primarily of tidal salt marsh, with creeks, rivers, croplands, freshwater impounds, wooded upland, swamp, and brush. **Facilities:** Visitor center, auto tour route, trails, observation towers, historic Allee House. **Activities:** Hiking, hunting, educational programs, bird and wildlife watching. **Access:** Open during daylight hours. Portions closed seasonally. **Primary Wildlife:** Migrating waterfowl, a variety of ducks, shorebirds, wading birds, frogs, turtles, whitetail deer, horseshoe crabs. **Special Features:** During May and June, when horseshoe crabs lay eggs along the bay shore and mud flats, thousands of shorebirds stop to feed before continuing their northward migration.

★651★ BON SECOUR NATIONAL WILDLIFE REFUGE
12295 State Hwy 180
Gulf Shores, AL 36542
Web: www.fws.gov/bonsecour
Phone: 251-540-7720; **Fax:** 251-540-7301

Location: 50 miles west of Pensacola, Florida, and 50 miles southeast of Mobile, Alabama, in the town of Gulf Shores. **Established:** 1980. **Habitat:** 7,000 acres of coastal lands, including beaches with sand dunes, scrub forest, fresh and saltwater marshes, freshwater swamps, and uplands. **Facilities:** Trails. **Activities:** Canoeing, fishing, hiking. **Access:** Open year round during daylight hours. **Primary Wildlife:** Endangered Alabama beach mouse, green and loggerhead turtles, ospreys, herons, pelicans, shorebirds, raccoon, coyote, flying squirrels, six-lined racerunner. **Special Features:** Loggerhead and green sea turtles nest on the refuge's beaches between mid-May and mid-August.

★652★ BOND SWAMP NATIONAL WILDLIFE REFUGE
c/o Piedmont NWR
718 Juliette Rd
Round Oak, GA 31038
Web: www.fws.gov/bondswamp
Phone: 478-986-5441; **Fax:** 478-986-9646
Location: 6 miles south of Macon, Georgia. **Established:** 1989. **Habitat:** 6,500 acres of bottomland hardwoods and swamp forests. **Facilities:** Trails, visitor center. **Activities:** Canoeing, hiking, fishing, hunting. **Access:** Daylight hours year round; shore fishing March 15-October 15. **Primary Wildlife:** Bald eagles, wood ducks, migratory waterfowl, wading birds, songbirds, white-tailed deer, turkeys, black bears, and alligators. **Special Features:** Refuge is located adjacent to the Ocmulgee River and is part of the Ocmulgee Heritage Greenway.

★653★ BOSQUE DEL APACHE NATIONAL WILDLIFE REFUGE
PO Box 1246
Socorro, NM 87801
Web: www.fws.gov/southwest/refuges/newmex/bosque
Phone: 505-835-1828; **Fax:** 505-835-0314
Location: 20 miles south of Socorro, New Mexico. **Established:** 1939. **Habitat:** 57,191 acres of moist bottomlands, wetlands, riparian forests, and farm fields. The Rio Grande flows through the center of the floodplain. **Facilities:** Visitor center, viewing sites, auto tour route, trails. **Activities:** Fishing, hiking, hunting, educational programs, special events. **Access:** Open one hour before sunrise until one hour after sunset. **Primary Wildlife:** Snow geese and other waterfowl, sandhill cranes, American kestral, ravens, roadrunner, oryx, mule deer, rabbits, and porcupine. **Special Features:** One of the most spectacular wildlife refuges in North America, tens of thousands of birds gather here each autumn and stay through the winter. Refuge encompasses three wilderness areas totaling 30,850 acres and five research natural areas totaling 18,500 acres.

★654★ BOWDOIN NATIONAL WILDLIFE REFUGE
194 Bowdoin Auto Tour Rd
Malta, MT 59538
Web: www.fws.gov/bowdoin
Phone: 406-654-2863; **Fax:** 406-654-2866
Location: 7 miles northeast of Malta in northeastern Montana. **Established:** 1936. **Habitat:** 15,551 acres of marsh and grassland. **Facilities:** Visitor contact station, wildlife viewing sites

See pages 22-23 for map of National Wildlife Refuges.

(&), photo blind, auto tour route (15 miles). **Activities:** Boating, canoeing, hunting, educational programs. **Access:** Open during daylight hours. **Primary Wildlife:** Canada geese, white pelicans, California gulls, ring-billed gulls, cormorants, great blue herons, turtles, snakes, gophers, coyotes, pronghorn antelope, and deer. **Special Features:** Although geologic history indicates that Lake Bowdoin was once an oxbow of the pre-glacial Missouri River channel, today the river lies nearly 70 miles south of the refuge.

★655★ BOYER CHUTE NATIONAL WILDLIFE REFUGE

3720 Rivers Way
Fort Calhoun, NE 68023
Web: www.fws.gov/boyerchute
Phone: 402-468-4313; **Fax:** 402-468-4316
Location: Beside the Missouri River, 8 miles north of Omaha, Nebraska. **Established:** 1997. **Habitat:** 3,350-acre river channel with a sand and sediment bed. **Facilities:** Hiking trails, picnic areas, fishing pier, 2 education pavilions. **Activities:** Fishing, hunting, wildlife watching, educational programs. **Access:** Open year round from 30 minutes before sunrise to 30 minutes after sunset. **Primary Wildlife:** Raptors, wild turkey, beaver, raccoon, snapping turtles, snakes, toads and frogs. **Special Features:** Site is undergoing restoration to recreate wildlife habitat that became scarce when the Missouri River was improved for navigation half a century ago. To recreate riverine habitat conditions, areas along the channel have been planted with trees and shrubs native to the area. Other areas have been seeded with a mix of native prairie grasses and forbs.

★656★ BRAZORIA NATIONAL WILDLIFE REFUGE

4430 Trammel
Freeport, TX 77541
Web: www.fws.gov/southwest/refuges/texas/texasmidcoast/ brazoria.htm
Phone: 979-239-3915; **Fax:** 979-239-1404
Location: On the Texas gulf coast at the west end of the Galveston Bay. **Established:** 1966. **Habitat:** 43,388 acres of fresh and salt marshes, sloughs, ponds, coastal prairies, and bottomland forests. **Facilities:** Visitor contact station, viewing sites, auto tour route (7 miles), trails, fishing pier. **Activities:** Boating, fishing, biking, crabbing, wildlife watching, hunting, educational programs. **Access:** Year round during daylight hours. **Primary Wildlife:** Wading and shorebirds such as herons and ibises; also roseate spoonbills, alligators, frogs, toads, salamanders, coyotes, bobcats, butterflies, dragonflies. **Special Features:** Birders often identify more than 200 species on and around the refuge during the Audubon Society's annual Christmas Bird Count in mid-December. This count usually ranks number one or two in the nation in the number of species sighted.

★657★ BRETON NATIONAL WILDLIFE REFUGE

61389 Hwy 434
Lacomb, LA 70445
Web: www.fws.gov/breton
Phone: 985-882-2000; **Fax:** 985-882-9133
Location: In the Gulf of Mexico, 20 miles south of Gulfport,

Mississippi, and 50 miles east of New Orleans, Louisiana. **Established:** 1904. **Habitat:** 13,000 acres include the Chandeleur Islands (south to Breton Island), barrier islands with low sandy beach whose size and shape are constantly altered by tropical storms, wind, and tidal action. The area above mean high tide is approximately 6,923 acres. **Facilities:** Primitive campsites, lighthouse. **Activities:** Camping (limited), boating, fishing, birdwatching. **Access:** Accessible only by boat. Nesting colonies are closed to visitors; other areas have unlimited access. **Primary Wildlife:** Brown pelicans, piping plover, terns, nutria, rabbits and loggerhead turtles. **Special Features:** Refuge is the second oldest in the nation, set aside by President Theodore Roosevelt, and is the only one he ever visited.

★658★ BROWNS PARK NATIONAL WILDLIFE REFUGE

1318 Hwy 318
Maybell, CO 81640
Web: www.fws.gov/brownspark
Phone: 970-365-3613; **Fax:** 970-365-3614
Location: On the Green River in the extreme northwestern corner of Colorado. **Established:** 1963. **Habitat:** 12,150acres that include riparian, wetlands, grasslands, uplands. **Facilities:** Visitor contact station, campgrounds, viewing sites, trails, auto tour route (11 miles), fishing pier, historic features. **Activities:** Camping, boating, canoeing, fishing, hunting, bicycling, horseback riding, wildlife watching, hiking. **Access:** Unrestricted. **Primary Wildlife:** Migratory Canada geese and ducks including mallards, redheads, teal, and canvasbacks. Bald eagles in winter and peregrine falcons and golden eagles in spring and summer. Also provides habitat for mule deer, antelope, chukar partridge, elk, and sage grouse. **Special Features:** Rich in cultural history, Brown's Park has been the site of human habitation since prehistoric times. The Fremont Indian culture lived in the valley around A.D. 600-1300. Fur trappers and traders established a thriving winter rendezvous site with the Shoshone in the 1830s. Evidence of the early settlers and Native Americans can still be seen throughout the Refuge. Three historical sites, including Lodore Hall (which still serves as a community center) and several old abandoned cabins and homesteads, attest to the rich history of the area.

★659★ BUCK ISLAND NATIONAL WILDLIFE REFUGE

3013 Estate Golden Rock, Suite 167
Christiansted, VI 08820
Web: www.fws.gov/southeast/buckisland
Phone: 340-773-4554
Location: 2 miles offshore of Saint Thomas in the U.S. Virgin Islands. **Established:** 1969. **Habitat:** 45-acre island comprised mostly of cactus, brush, grasslands, and a rocky shoreline. **Activities:** Boating, diving, snorkeling, hiking. **Access:** Open during daylight hours; accessible by boat only. **Primary Wildlife:** Refuge was transferred to Fish and Wildlife Service due to its value for migratory birds; however, birds rarely use the refuge because of an overwhelming abundance of black rats. Visitors may observe red-billed tropic birds, frigate birds, terns, and other species in the vicinity of the island. **Special Features:** Surrounding

See pages 22-23 for map of National Wildlife Refuges.

waters and bays contain reefs and a shipwreck that attracts boaters and divers.

★660★ **BUENOS AIRES NATIONAL WILDLIFE REFUGE**
PO Box 109
Sasabe, AZ 85633
Web: www.fws.gov/southwest/refuges/arizona/buenosaires
Phone: 520-823-4251
Location: 50 miles southwest of Tucson. **Established:** 1985. **Habitat:** 118,000 acres of grasslands, wetlands, riparian streams, and desert mountains. **Facilities:** Visitor contact station, viewing sites, boardwalk, auto tour route, trails, picnic sites, historic features, primitive campsites. **Activities:** Hiking, backpacking, camping, mountain biking, horseback riding, hunting, educational programs. **Access:** Open to public use 24 hours a day. **Primary Wildlife:** Masked bobwhite quail (endangered), pronghorn antelope, javelina, mountain lion, badger, and occasional jaguar. Provides habitat for many southeast Arizona specialty birds, including gray hawk, zone-tailed hawk, black hawk, and owls. **Special Features:** In addition to the masked bobwhite quail, Buenos Aires NWR protects habitat for six other endangered species: cactus ferruginous pygmy owl, Pima pineapple cactus, Kearney's bluestar, peregrine falcon, Southwest willow flycatcher, and razorback sucker.

★661★ **BUFFALO LAKE NATIONAL WILDLIFE REFUGE**
PO Box 179
Umbarger, TX 79091
Web: southwest.fws.gov/refuges/texas/buffalo.html
Phone: 806-499-3382; **Fax:** 806-499-3254
Location: 30 miles southeast of Amarillo, Texas. **Established:** 1958. **Habitat:** 7,664 acres of shortgrass prairie, brush, woodland, and dry lake bed. **Facilities:** Visitor contact station, viewing sites, auto tour route, trails, campsites, picnic areas. **Activities:** Wildlife watching, hiking, educational programs. **Access:** Year round. **Primary Wildlife:** Upland game birds, deer, neotropical migrant birds, bald eagle, peregrine falcon, wild turkey, bobcats, prairie dogs. **Special Features:** Buffalo Lake NWR contains some of the best remaining shortgrass prairie in the United States, including 175 acres designated a National Natural Landmark.

★662★ **CABEZA PRIETA NATIONAL WILDLIFE REFUGE**
1611 N 2nd Ave
Ajo, AZ 85321
Web: www.fws.gov/southwest/refuges/arizona/cabeza.html
Phone: 520-387-6483; **Fax:** 520-387-5359
Location: South of Gila Bend, Arizona. **Established:** 1939. **Habitat:** 860,010 acres of Sonoran Desert, consisting of low mountain ranges separated by broad alluvial valleys. **Facilities:** Visitor center, trails, primitive campsites. **Activities:** Hiking, hunting, camping, educational programs. **Access:** Year round with some restrictions; contact refuge office. **Primary Wildlife:** Bighorn sheep, Sonoran pronghorn, and lesser long-nosed bat,

desert tortoise, desert horned lizards, desert pocket mouse, red-tailed hawks, Gambrel's quail. **Special Features:** Cabeza Prieta, the third largest national wildlife refuge in the lower 48 states, shares a 56-mile border with Sonora, Mexico. Although the land is desert, it is not as barren as it appears; the refuge is home to 391 kinds of plants and more than 300 species of wildlife.

★663★ **CABO ROJO NATIONAL WILDLIFE REFUGE**
c/o Caribbean Islands NWR Complex
PO Box 510
Boqueron, PR 00622
Web: www.fws.gov/southeast/caborojo
Phone: 787-851-7258; **Fax:** 787-851-7440
Location: Coastal plain of southwestern Puerto Rico. **Established:** 1974. **Habitat:** 1,836 acres of grassland, forests, and scrub. **Facilities:** Visitor center, interpretive trail, hiking trails (12 miles). **Activities:** Hiking, wildlife watching, photography. **Access:** Monday through Friday, year round. **Primary Wildlife:** Endangered yellow-shouldered blackbird, Adelaide's warbler, Caribbean elaenia, troupial, Puerto Rican tody. **Special Features:** Other native birds using the refuge include the Puerto Rican tody, Adelaide's warbler, Caribbean elaenia, and troupial.

★664★ **CACHE RIVER NATIONAL WILDLIFE REFUGE**
26320 Hwy 33 S
Augusta, AR 72006
Web: cacheriver.fws.gov
Phone: 870-347-2614; **Fax:** 870-347-2908
Location: Along the Cache River and Bayou DeView in Jackson, Woodruff, Prairie, and Monroe counties. **Established:** 1986. **Habitat:** 62,000 acres of bottomland hardwood forest in the middle and lower Cache River Basin. **Facilities:** None. **Activities:** Boating, canoeing, fishing, hunting. **Access:** Unlimited. **Primary Wildlife:** Waterfowl, turkey, squirrel, rabbit, deer. **Special Features:** This area of the Cache River is nationally known for it excellent waterfowl hunting. It is the single most important wintering area for mallards in North America, and contains the only population of native black bears in Arkansas.

★665★ **CALOOSAHATCHEE NATIONAL WILDLIFE REFUGE**
c/o J. N. "Ding" Darling NWR
1 Wildlife Dr
Sanibel, FL 33957
Web: southeast.fws.gov/Caloosahatchee
Phone: 941-472-1100; **Fax:** 941-472-4061
Location: 7 miles east of Fort Myers, Florida. **Established:** 1920. **Habitat:** 40 acres consisting of three mangrove islands covered with fresh and brackish water vegetation. **Activities:** Canoeing, kayaking, fishing, wildlife watching. **Access:** By boat only. **Primary Wildlife:** West Indian manatee, wood stork, eastern indigo snake, American crocodile, and bald eagle. Site also provides roosting habitat for a wide diversity of shore birds, wading birds, waterfowl, raptors, and neotropical migratory bird species. **Special Features:** Refuge is located adjacent to Florida Power and Light Company's Orange River power plant. Warm

See pages 22-23 for map of National Wildlife Refuges.

155

water discharge from the power plant attracts manatees during the cool winter months.

★666★ CAMAS NATIONAL WILDLIFE REFUGE

2150 East 2350 North
Hamer, ID 83425
Web: www.fws.gov/pacific/refuges/field/ID_Camas.htm
Phone: 208-662-5423
Location: Southeastern Idaho, 36 miles north of Idaho Falls. **Established:** 1936. **Habitat:** 10,578 acres of marshes, meadows, and uplands. **Facilities:** Hiking roads. **Activities:** Hiking, cross-country skiing, wildlife watching. **Access:** Year round, daylight hours. **Primary Wildlife:** Mallards, pintails, gadwalls, wigeon, Canada geese, and trumpeter swan. Also moose, mule deer, and white-tailed deer, beaver, coyote, cottontail. **Special Features:** Refuge provides habitat for the endangered bald eagle in the winter and occasionally the peregrine falcon in the summer. The rare trumpeter swan also nests here.

★667★ CAMERON PRAIRIE NATIONAL WILDLIFE REFUGE

1428 Hwy 27
Bell City, LA 70630
Web: www.fws.gov/cameronprairie
Phone: 337-598-2216; **Fax:** 337-598-2492
Location: Southwestern Louisiana, 25 miles southeast of Lake Charles. **Established:** 1988. **Habitat:** 9,621 acres of cropland and marsh. **Facilities:** Visitor center, viewing sites, boardwalk, auto tour route, boat launch. **Activities:** Boating, canoeing, fishing, hiking, hunting, educational programs, wildlife watching. **Access:** Year round, sunrise to sunset. **Primary Wildlife:** Waterfowl, roseate spoonbills, herons, egrets, alligators, and furbearers. **Special Features:** The site's old rice fields have been converted to freshwater marshland, providing habitat for 45,000 ducks and 10,000 geese during the peak winter months.

★668★ CANAAN VALLEY NATIONAL WILDLIFE REFUGE

HC 70 Box 200
Davis, WV 26260
Web: www.fws.gov/canaanvalley
Phone: 304-637-7312
Location: Tucker County, West Virginia. **Established:** 1994. **Habitat:** 15,245 acres including wet soils, forests, shrub lands, open lands. Eventually, the refuge will include 24,000 acres. **Facilities:** Visitor center, trails. **Activities:** Hiking, hunting, fishing, bicycling, horseback riding, cross-country skiing, snowshoeing, educational programs. **Access:** Every day from 1 hour before sunrise to 1 hour after sunset. **Primary Wildlife:** American woodcock and many other migratory bird species. Also Cheat Mountain salamander (threatened) and northern Virginia flying squirrel (endangered), turtles, snakes, bats. **Special Features:** Drained by the Blackwater River and its tributaries, Canaan Valley comprises one of the largest freshwater wetlands in the Appalachians. The area contains 40 distinct plant communities with more than 580 plant species. These habitats support equally diverse wildlife populations—290 species of vertebrates have been observed.

★669★ CAPE MAY NATIONAL WILDLIFE REFUGE

24 Kimbles Beach Rd
Cape May Courthouse, NJ 08210
Web: capemay.fws.gov
Phone: 609-463-0994; **Fax:** 609-463-1667
Location: On the Cape May peninsula. **Established:** 1989. **Habitat:** More than 11,000 acres contains a wide range of habitats including upland and lowland forests, fields, barrier beach, salt marsh, and salt meadows cut through by meandering tidal creeks. Proposed acquisition would take the refuge to 21,200 acres. **Facilities:** Visitor contact station, viewing sites, hiking trails. **Activities:** Hiking, hunting, fishing, wildlife watching. **Access:** Daylight hours year round. **Primary Wildlife:** Red knots, ruddy turnstones, woodcock, and raptors, shellfish, snakes. **Special Features:** Two Mile Beach, transferred to the refuge from the Coast Guard in 1999, is a 507-acre site managed to protect one of the last remaining tracts of undeveloped maritime forest and beach in New Jersey. Thousands of Red Knots and Ruddy Turnstones rely on habitat along the Cape May Peninsula to rest and feed during migration.

★670★ CAPE MEARES NATIONAL WILDLIFE REFUGE

c/o Oregon Coast NWR Complex
2127 SE Marine Science Dr
Newport, OR 97365
Web: www.fws.gov/oregoncoast/capemeares
Phone: 541-867-4550; **Fax:** 541-867-4551
Location: South of Tillamook Bay, 8 miles west of Tillamook, Oregon. **Established:** 1938. **Habitat:** 138 acres of rocky Pacific Ocean headlands and an old growth forest of Sitka spruce and western hemlock. **Facilities:** Viewing sites, hiking trail, interpretive exhibits. **Activities:** Hiking, wildlife watching. **Access:** Public entry is permitted along the section of the Oregon Coast Trail that passes through the forest to Cape Meares State Park (see entry in Oregon state parks chapter). **Primary Wildlife:** Common murres, tufted puffins, pelagic cormorants, band-tailed pigeons, black-tailed deer, bald eagle, and peregrine falcon. **Special Features:** One of the best places on Oregon's north coast to observe migrating whales (November to December and March to May).

★671★ CAPE ROMAIN NATIONAL WILDLIFE REFUGE

5801 Hwy 17 N
Awendaw, SC 29429
Web: caperomain.fws.gov
Phone: 843-928-3264; **Fax:** 843-928-3803
Location: Along the coast of South Carolina in Charleston County. **Established:** 1932. **Habitat:** 64,229 acres of salt and freshwater marshes, live oak forest, beach and sand dunes, fresh and brackish impoundments. **Facilities:** Visitor center, viewing sites, hiking trails. **Activities:** Boating, canoeing, fishing, hiking, hunting, educational programs, shelling, beachcombing. **Access:** Open year round during daylight hours; accessible by boat. **Primary Wildlife:** Alligators, white-tailed deer, loggerhead sea turtles, brown pelicans, terns, gulls, waterfowl, wading birds, red wolves. **Special Features:** Refuge protects the largest nesting rookery for brown pelicans, terns, and gulls on South Carolina

See pages 22-23 for map of National Wildlife Refuges.

4. National Wildlife Refuges

coast and the largest nesting area for loggerhead sea turtles outside of Florida. Cape Romain also plays an integral role in the recovery of the endangered red wolf.

★672★ CAROLINA SANDHILLS NATIONAL WILDLIFE REFUGE

23734 US Hwy 1
McBee, SC 29101
Web: www.fws.gov/carolinasandhills
Phone: 843-335-8401; **Fax:** 843-375-8406
Location: Northeastern South Carolina. **Established:** 1939. **Habitat:** 45,348 acres of longleaf pine/wiregrass interspersed with scrub oak, creek bottom hardwoods, croplands, lakes, and ponds. **Facilities:** Visitor contact station, picnic area, auto tour route, trails, observation towers, photography blind. **Activities:** Bicycling, fishing, hiking, hunting, educational programs. **Access:** Open during daylight hours. **Primary Wildlife:** Red-cockaded woodpecker (endangered), mallards, black ducks, pintails, wood ducks, Canada geese, eastern wild turkey, raccoon, opossum, and beaver. **Special Features:** Refuge is one of the Southeast's premier sites for viewing the rapidly diminishing longleaf pine and wiregrass ecosystem. Site also offers habitat protection for the Pine Barrens tree frog, southern bald eagle, eastern cougar, and red-cockaded woodpecker.

★673★ CASTLE ROCK NATIONAL WILDLIFE REFUGE

c/o Humboldt Bay NWR
1020 Ranch Rd
Loleta, CA 95551
Web: www.fws.gov/refuges/profiles/index.cfm?id=11647
Phone: 707-733-5406; **Fax:** 707-733-1946
Location: 0.5 miles offshore of Crescent City, along California's northern coast. **Established:** 1981. **Habitat:** A 14-acre rock island with steep cliffs and sparse vegetation. **Access:** Closed to the public; wildlife can be observed from the mainland shore. **Primary Wildlife:** Endangered Aleutian Canada geese. **Special Features:** Refuge preserves the state's second largest seabird breeding colony and is a haul-out spot for a variety of marine mammals including California sea lion, Stellar sea lion, and northern elephant seal.

★674★ CAT ISLAND NATIONAL WILDLIFE REFUGE

401 Island Rd
Marksville, LA 71351
Web: www.fws.gov/catisland
Phone: 318-253-4238; **Fax:** 318-253-7139
Location: Near the town of Saint Francisville, about 25 miles north of Baton Rouge. **Established:** 2000. **Habitat:** 9,623 acres of forested wetlands in the Mississippi floodplain. The federally approved acquisition boundary encompasses 36,500 acres; additional acreage will be added as funding becomes available. **Facilities:** Trails (4 miles). **Activities:** Hunting, boating, fishing, hiking. **Access:** Open year round during daylight hours. However, the refuge is completely inundated by the Mississippi River annually (generally between January and June) and is inaccessible by vehicle once floodwaters cross the road. **Primary Wildlife:** Louisiana black bear (endangered) and neotropical migratory birds. Other wildlife found in the area are white-tailed deer, bobcat, mink, river otter, wild turkey, and several species of amphibians. **Special Features:** Refuge lands contain old-growth bald cypress trees estimated to be 500 to 1,000 years old, including the National Champion bald cypress. Bald cypress is the largest tree species east of the Sierra Nevada mountain range.

★675★ CATAHOULA NATIONAL WILDLIFE REFUGE

PO Drawer Z
Rhinehart, LA 71363
Web: www.fws.gov/catisland
Phone: 318-992-5261; **Fax:** 318-992-6023
Location: 20 miles northeast of Alexandria, Louisiana. **Established:** 1958. **Habitat:** 25,043 acres of lowland hardwood forest and abandoned farm fields. **Facilities:** Visitor contact station, observation towers, boardwalk trail (&), hiking trails, auto tour route, fishing pier (&). **Activities:** Fishing, hunting, hiking, educational programs. **Access:** Year round during daylight hours. **Primary Wildlife:** Migratory waterfowl (primarily mallards), wood ducks, songbirds, raptors, white-tailed deer, alligators, cricket frogs, and squirrel. **Special Features:** Refuge lies adjacent to Catahoula Lake, a state-owned wetland. The lake's water level is managed by the U.S. Fish and Wildlife Service in cooperation with the Louisiana Department of Wildlife and Fisheries and the U.S. Army Corps of Engineers.

★676★ CEDAR ISLAND NATIONAL WILDLIFE REFUGE

c/o Mattamuskeet NWR
38 Mattamuskeet Rd
Swanquarter, NC 27885
Web: www.fws.gov/cedarisland/
Phone: 252-926-4021; **Fax:** 252-926-1743
Location: 40 miles northeast of Beaufort, North Carolina, along the Atlantic coast. **Established:** 1964. **Habitat:** 14,480 acres of brackish coastal marsh, pocosin and woodlands. **Facilities:** 2 boat ramps. **Activities:** Boating, canoeing, fishing, hunting. **Access:** Year round. **Primary Wildlife:** Diving ducks (including lesser scaups, canvasbacks, redheads, and buffleheads), sea ducks, American black ducks, black rails, wading birds, and shore birds. **Special Features:** Refuge also provides habitat and protection for American alligators and brown pelicans.

★677★ CEDAR KEYS NATIONAL WILDLIFE REFUGE

c/o Lower Suwanee NWR
16450 NW 31st Pl
Chiefland, FL 32626
Web: www.fws.gov/cedarkeys
Phone: 352-493-0238; **Fax:** 352-493-1935
Location: Off Florida's Gulf coast in Levy County. **Established:** 1929. **Habitat:** 800 acres on 13 islands, ranging in size from 1 acre to 120 acres, four of which are designated wilderness areas. **Facilities:** Visitor contact center, viewing sites, hiking

See pages 22-23 for map of National Wildlife Refuges.

trails, dock. **Activities:** Boating, fishing, educational programs. **Access:** Beaches of all islands, except Seahorse Key, are open to the public year round during daylight hours. Interior of islands is closed to the public. Access is by boat only. **Primary Wildlife:** White ibis, snowy egret, tri-colored heron, brown pelican, great blue heron, and osprey, bald eagle, crabs, shellfish, bottlenose dolphin, manatees. **Special Features:** The refuge's Seahorse Key contains one of the largest colonial bird nesting sites in north Florida. An historic lighthouse, operated by the University of Florida as a Marine Science Lab, sits atop Seahorse Key.

★678★ **CEDAR POINT NATIONAL WILDLIFE REFUGE**
c/o Ottawa NWR
14000 W State Rt 2
Oak Harbor, OH 43449
Web: www.fws.gov/midwest/cedarpoint
Phone: 419-898-0014; **Fax:** 419-898-7895
Location: Northwestern Ohio where Maumee Bay meets Lake Erie. **Established:** 1965. **Habitat:** 2,445 acres, primarily marsh divided into 3 pools. **Activities:** Fishing. **Access:** Most of the refuge is closed to the public; however, a fishing area near Yondota Road gate is open from June to August. **Primary Wildlife:** Migrating waterfowl, herons, egrets, bald eagles. **Special Features:** Refuge property was donated to the U.S. Fish and Wildlife Service by owners of the Cedar Point Shooting Club. A bald eagle nest is located where the shooting club's lodge once stood.

★679★ **CHARLES M. RUSSELL NATIONAL WILDLIFE REFUGE**
PO Box 110
Lewistown, MT 59457
Web: cmr.fws.gov
Phone: 406-538-8706; **Fax:** 406-538-7521
Location: Along the Missouri River in north-central Montana. **Established:** 1936. **Habitat:** 1,100,000 acres of native prairies, forested coulees, river bottoms, and badlands. **Facilities:** Visitor contact station, viewing sites, campgrounds, picnic areas, boat launch, trails, auto tour route, historic features, wilderness area (20,000 acres). **Activities:** Camping, boating, fishing, bicycling, hiking, horseback riding, hunting, educational programs. **Access:** Unlimited. **Primary Wildlife:** Rocky Mountain bighorn sheep, mule deer, white-tailed deer, elk, pronghorn, and prairie dogs. Also raptors, double-crested cormorants, and blue herons. **Special Features:** Refuge's terrain is reminiscent of paintings by Charlie Russell, the western artist for whom the refuge is named. Site includes 250,000-acre Fort Peck Reservoir.

★680★ **CHASE LAKE NATIONAL WILDLIFE REFUGE**
5924 19th St SE
Woodworth, ND 58496
Web: www.fws.gov/arrowwood/chaselake_nwr
Phone: 701-752-4218
Location: In south-central North Dakota, 15 miles northwest of Medina. **Established:** 1908. **Habitat:** 4,385 acres of native

prairie grassland and wetlands. **Facilities:** Visitor contact station, viewing sites. **Activities:** Fishing, hunting, educational programs. **Access:** A special use permit is required to enter the refuge. **Primary Wildlife:** American white pelican, piping plover, Canada goose, tundra swan, fox, coyote, badger, long-tailed weasel. **Special Features:** Chase Lake NWR is the second oldest refuge in North Dakota, originally established to protect the native white pelican.

★681★ **CHASSAHOWITZKA NATIONAL WILDLIFE REFUGE**
1502 SE Kings Bay Dr
Crystal River, FL 34429
Web: www.fws.gov/chassahowitzka
Phone: 352-563-2088; **Fax:** 352-795-7961
Location: On Florida's Gulf coast, 65 miles north of Saint Petersburg. **Established:** 1941. **Habitat:** 31,000 acres of saltwater bays and estuaries, brackish marshes, and hardwood swamps. **Facilities:** Visitor contact station. **Activities:** Boating, canoeing, fishing, hunting, educational programs. **Access:** Unlimited; most of the refuge is accessible only by boat. **Primary Wildlife:** Endangered and threatened species include southern bald eagle, arctic peregrine falcon, brown pelican, wood stork, West Indian manatee, Florida black bear, American alligator, eastern indigo snake, gopher tortoise, green sea turtle, Kemp's Ridley sea turtle, and loggerhead sea turtle. Also raccoons, deer, bobcats, coyotes, cormorants, herons, egrets, osprey, and many species of ducks. **Special Features:** The refuge supports a healthy population of reptiles, including the Florida cottonmouth, Eastern diamondback rattlesnake, diamondback terrapin, and Florida box turtles. Atlantic bottlenose dolphins are often seen in the Chassahowitzka River.

★682★ **CHAUTAUQUA NATIONAL WILDLIFE REFUGE**
19031 E County Rd 2110N
Havana, IL 62644
Web: www.fws.gov/Midwest/Chautauqua
Phone: 309-535-2290; **Fax:** 309-535-3023
Location: Central Illinois, 25 miles southwest of Peoria. **Established:** 1936. **Habitat:** 6,200 acres, which include 3,400-acre Lake Chautauqua, and timbered bottomlands and bluffs. **Facilities:** Visitor contact station, viewing sites, hiking trails, auto tour route, picnic area, boat ramp. **Activities:** Boating, canoeing, fishing, hiking, hunting, mushroom and berry picking, educational programs. **Access:** Open sunrise to sunset. **Primary Wildlife:** Geese, mallards, wood ducks, eagles, herons, egrets, bald eagle, white pelican, white-tailed deer, and fox. **Special Features:** Along Lake Chautauqua's east shoreline are large seepage springs which keep strips of the shoreline from icing over even in the coldest weather.

★683★ **CHICKASAW NATIONAL WILDLIFE REFUGE**
1505 Sand Bluff Rd
Ripley, TN 38063
Web: www.fws.gov/chickasaw
Phone: 731-635-7621; **Fax:** 731-635-0178

See pages 22-23 for map of National Wildlife Refuges.

Location: 9 miles north of Ripley. **Established:** 1985. **Habitat:** 24,096 acres of bottomland hardwood forest, agricultural lands, grassland/shrub, and open water. **Facilities:** Visitor contact station, viewing sites, trails, auto tour route, boat ramps. **Activities:** Boating, canoeing, fishing, hiking, hunting. **Access:** Open year round during daylight hours. Waterfowl sanctuary closed November 15 - March 15. **Primary Wildlife:** Mallard, black duck, gadwall, pintail, wild turkey, and deer. **Special Features:** Refuge protects some of the last remaining bottomland hardwood forest in the Lower Mississippi Valley and provides a stopover for waterfowl migrating and wintering along the Mississippi River.

★684★ CHINCOTEAGUE NATIONAL WILDLIFE REFUGE

PO Box 62
Chincoteague, VA 23336
Web: chinco.fws.gov
Phone: 757-336-6122; **Fax:** 757-336-5273
Location: On Assateague Island. **Established:** 1943. **Habitat:** More than 14,000 acres of beach, dune marsh and maritime forest. **Facilities:** Visitor center (&), viewing sites, trails (15 miles). **Activities:** Surf fishing, clamming, crabbing, swimming (Memorial Day through Labor Day), boating, hiking, biking, hunting, interpretive programs. **Access:** Daylight hours year round. **Primary Wildlife:** Waterfowl, piping plover, Delmarva Peninsula fox squirrel, loggerhead sea turtle, and peregrine falcon. Also provides habitat for sika deer, white-tailed deer, muskrat, river otter, spotted and atlantic bottle nosed porpoises, common dolphin, quahogs, blue crabs, snakes, turtles, and the Chincoteague pony. **Special Features:** Descendants of colonial horses brought to Assateague Island in the 17th century, Chincoteague ponies have become adapted to their environment. The Chincoteague Volunteer Fire Company owns the entire herd (about 150 horses) and auctions off some foals and yearlings every July to benefit the town's ambulance and fire services.

★685★ CHOCTAW NATIONAL WILDLIFE REFUGE

PO Box 808
Jackson, AL 36545
Web: choctaw.fws.gov
Phone: 251-246-3583; **Fax:** 251-246-5414
Location: 80 miles north of Mobile. **Established:** 1964. **Habitat:** 4,218 acres plus 236 acres in perpetual conservation easements. One half of the refuge is made up of creeks, sloughs, lakes, and backwaters of the Tombigbee River; the other half is bottomland hardwoods. **Facilities:** Visitor contact station, hiking trails, auto tour route, scenic overlook, boat ramp. **Activities:** Boating, fishing, hiking, hunting. **Access:** Open year round during daylight hours. Between December 1 and March 1 some areas are closed to the public to provide sanctuary to wintering waterfowl. **Primary Wildlife:** Heron, raptor, otter, beaver, deer, turkey, raccoon, squirrel, American alligator, bald eagle, wood stork. **Special Features:** Two creeks (Okaktuppa Creek and Turkey Creek) divide the refuge into three sections. Thirty-five acres of black gum and bald cypress have been set aside as Tupelo Gum Natural Area.

★686★ CIBOLA NATIONAL WILDLIFE REFUGE

66600 Cibola Lake Rd
Rt 2, Box 1
Cibola, AZ 85328
Web: www.fws.gov/southwest/refuges/CibolaNWR
Phone: 928-857-3253; **Fax:** 928-857-3420
Location: Along the Colorado River, 20 miles south of Blythe, California. **Established:** 1964. **Habitat:** 16,600 acres of lower Colorado River floodplain, surrounded by desert ridges and washes. **Facilities:** Visitor center, viewing sites, auto tour route, nature trail. **Activities:** Boating, water skiing, canoeing, fishing, hunting. **Access:** Open during daylight hours. **Primary Wildlife:** More than 288 species of birds, including bald eagle, southwestern willow flycatcher, Yuma clapper rail, Gambel's quail, mourning and white-winged doves, greater sandhill cranes, Canada geese, desert mule deer, bobcat, and coyotes. **Special Features:** The refuge encompasses the historic Colorado River channel, which provides life-sustaining water to wildlife that survives in an environment that reaches 120 degrees in the summer and receives an average of only 2 inches of rain a year.

★687★ CLARENCE CANNON NATIONAL WILDLIFE REFUGE

c/o Great River NWR
PO Box 88
Annada, MO 63330
Web: midwest.fws.gov/greatriver/info/clacan.htm
Phone: 573-847-2333; **Fax:** 573-847-2269
Location: 50 miles northwest of Saint Louis, Missouri, beside the Mississippi River. **Established:** 1964. **Habitat:** 3,750 acres of wetlands, impoundments, forests, grasslands, and crop fields. **Facilities:** Visitor contact station, viewing sites, auto tour route. **Activities:** Educational programs, fishing, hunting, bicycling, berry and mushroom picking for personal consumption. **Access:** Open during daylight hours. Portions of the refuge are closed seasonally to the public based on waterfowl migrations. **Primary Wildlife:** Bald eagle, king rail, shorebirds, bats, rabbits, deer, snakes, turtles, frogs. **Special Features:** Site provides seasonal wetlands and permanent marshes by actively manipulating water levels and vegetative growth, which re-creates the changing habitats important to many types of migratory birds.

★688★ CLARKS RIVER NATIONAL WILDLIFE REFUGE

91 US Hwy 641 N
PO Box 89
Benton, KY 42025
Web: www.fws.gov/southeast/clarksriver
Phone: 270-527-5770; **Fax:** 270-527-5052
Location: In western Kentucky between Benton and Paducah on the East Fork of the Clarks River. **Established:** 1997. **Habitat:** 8,500 acres of wetland habitat formed by the river, creeks, beaver ponds, and natural ponding. The proposed boundary of the refuge is 18,000 acres. **Facilities:** Under development; in acquisition stages. **Activities:** Bicycling, horseback riding, fishing, hunting, hiking. **Access:** Open year-round; some areas closed seasonally. **Primary Wildlife:** Migrating waterfowl, wading birds, raptors and many species of migratory neotropical birds. Also home to migrating monarch butterflies, wild turkey,

See pages 22-23 for map of National Wildlife Refuges.

white-tailed deer, groundhogs, coyote, beaver, mink, salamanders, turtles, frogs, and snakes. **Special Features:** Clarks River is the only National Wildlife Refuge located solely within the state of Kentucky.

★689★ CLEAR LAKE NATIONAL WILDLIFE REFUGE

c/o Klamath Basin NWR Complex
4009 Hill Rd
Tulelake, CA 96134
Web: www.fws.gov/klamathbasinrefuges/clearlake/
clearlake.html
Phone: 530-667-2231; **Fax:** 530-667-3299
Location: In northern California near the Oregon border, 15 miles south of Tulelake. **Established:** 1911. **Habitat:** 46,460 acres consisting of a 20,000 acre lake surrounded by upland habitat of bunchgrass, low sagebrush, and juniper. **Activities:** Hunting, fishing. **Access:** Except for limited hunting, the refuge is closed to the public. **Primary Wildlife:** White pelicans, cormorants, sage grouse, pronghorn antelope, and mule deer. **Special Features:** Small, rocky islands in the lake provide nesting habitat for one of the few remaining American white pelican breeding colonies in the West. On average, about 1,400 pelicans are fledged each year.

★690★ COACHELLA VALLEY NATIONAL WILDLIFE REFUGE

c/o Sonny Bono Salton Sea NWR Complex
906 W Sinclair Rd
Calipatria, CA 92233
Web: www.fws.gov/pacific/coach
Phone: 760-348-5278; **Fax:** 760-348-7245
Location: West of Indio, California. **Established:** 1985. **Habitat:** 13,000 acres of palm oasis woodlands, perennial desert pools, and blow-sand habitat. **Facilities:** Trails. **Activities:** Hiking, horseback riding. **Access:** Closed to the public except for a trail on the north part of the refuge. **Primary Wildlife:** Coachella Valley fringe-toed lizard (threatened) and flat-tailed horned lizard. **Special Features:** The refuge contains the majority of critical habitat within the Coachella Valley Preserve for the Coachella Valley fringe-toed lizard. The area has the state's second largest grove of native fan palms and some Coachella Valley milk vetch, a plant with pinkish-purple flowers.

★691★ COKEVILLE MEADOWS NATIONAL WILDLIFE REFUGE

c/o Seedskadee NWR
PO Box 700
Green River, WY 82935
Phone: 307-875-2187; **Fax:** 307-875-4425
Location: About 10 miles south of Cokeville, Wyoming, on State Highway 30. **Established:** 1993. **Habitat:** A 20-mile stretch of the Bear River and its associated wetlands and uplands. The approved acquisition boundary totals 26,657 acres; to date 8,106 acres have been purchased or are protected through conservation easements. **Facilities:** None; still in acquisition stages. **Access:** Not yet open to public use. **Primary Wildlife:** Nesting waterfowl and colony-nesting bird species including white-faced

ibis and black terns; also antelope, elk, and mule deer. **Special Features:** The refuge supports one of the highest densities of nesting waterfowl in Wyoming.

★692★ COLD SPRINGS NATIONAL WILDLIFE REFUGE

c/o Mid-Columbia River National Wildlife Refuge Complex
3250 Port of Benton Blvd, PO Box 1447
Richland, WA 99352
Web: www.fws.gov/midcolumbiariver/Coldspringspage.htm
Phone: 509-371-9212
Location: Near the Washington border, 7 miles east of Hermiston, Oregon. **Established:** 1954. **Habitat:** 3,117 acres of open water, marsh, sagebrush, grasslands, and trees. **Facilities:** Trails. **Activities:** Boating (electric motors only), fishing, hiking, biking, horseback riding, hunting (fall and winter). **Access:** Year round during daylight hours. **Primary Wildlife:** Canada geese, ducks, pheasants, quail, mule deer. **Special Features:** Refuge wetlands support large numbers of wintering waterfowl while adjacent riparian habitat supports a rich abundance of songbirds and healthy populations of western mule deer and desert elk.

★693★ COLUMBIA NATIONAL WILDLIFE REFUGE

735 E Main St
PO Drawer F
Othello, WA 99344
Web: www.fws.gov/pacific/refuges/field/wa_columbia.htm
Phone: 509-488-2668
Location: 8 miles northwest of Othello, Washington. **Established:** 1944. **Habitat:** 23,000 acres in the Columbia River Basin scablands, with numerous small lakes surrounded by sagebrush and grassy uplands, canyons, and buttes. **Facilities:** Visitor contact station, hiking trails, overlook, auto tour route, boat ramps. **Activities:** Boating, canoeing, camping, fishing, hiking, hunting, educational programs. **Access:** Open during daylight hours. **Primary Wildlife:** Mallards, Canada geese, gadwalls, cinnamon teal, redheads, and coyote. **Special Features:** Refuge lies in the rain shadow of the Cascade Mountains where annual precipitation averages less than 8 inches, creating an arid desert environment.

★694★ COLUSA NATIONAL WILDLIFE REFUGE

c/o Sacramento NWR
752 County Rd 99W
Willows, CA 95988
Web: www.fws.gov/sacramentovalleyrefuges/colusa.htm
Phone: 530-934-2801
Location: 70 miles north of Sacramento, California. **Established:** 1945. **Habitat:** 4,626 acres of seasonal marsh, permanent ponds, watergrass, and uplands. **Facilities:** Viewing sites, hiking trails, auto tour route (3 miles). **Activities:** Hiking, hunting, educational programs. **Access:** Year round, sunrise to sunset. **Primary Wildlife:** Migratory waterfowl. **Special Features:** Thousands of waterfowl are present from September through March. Peak populations occur in December and January.

See pages 22-23 for map of National Wildlife Refuges.

★695★ CONBOY LAKE NATIONAL WILDLIFE REFUGE

100 Wildlife Refuge Rd
Box 5
Glenwood, WA 98619
Web: www.fws.gov/ridgefieldrefuges/CLNWRHome.htm
Phone: 509-364-3410
Location: 5 miles south of Glenwood, Washington. **Established:** 1964. **Habitat:** 6,500 acres of wetlands, lakebed, forests and grasslands. **Facilities:** Visitor contact station, hiking trails. **Activities:** Hunting, fishing, hiking. **Access:** Public access is limited to the Willard Springs Trail; public hunting area is open only during the hunting season. **Primary Wildlife:** Canada geese and ducks, tundra swans, sandhill cranes, bald eagles, elk, beaver, Oregon spotted frogs. **Special Features:** Refuge protects one of three known nesting areas for sandhill cranes in Washington.

★696★ CONSCIENCE POINT NATIONAL WILDLIFE REFUGE

c/o Long Island NWR Complex
PO Box 21
Shirley, NY 11967
Phone: 631-286-0485; **Fax:** 631-286-4003
Location: On Long Island's south fork, 1 mile north of North Sea. **Established:** 1971. **Habitat:** 60 acres of forests, grasslands, fresh and saltwater marshes. **Access:** Closed to the public to protect nesting waterfowl. **Primary Wildlife:** Red tailed hawk, American Kestral, osprey, great horned owl, gray squirrel, eastern cottontail, and red fox. **Special Features:** Refuge includes a prime example of maritime grassland, a native grassland composed of little bluestem grass, switch grass, poverty grass, and hairgrass. Prickly pear cactus is also a conspicuous component of the maritime grassland.

★697★ COPALIS NATIONAL WILDLIFE REFUGE

c/o Washington Maritime NWR Complex
33 S Barr Rd
Port Angeles, WA 98362
Web: www.fws.gov/pacific/refuges/field/wa_copalis.htm
Phone: 360-457-8451; **Fax:** 360-457-9778
Location: Along Washington's Pacific coast, offshore from Copalis Beach. **Established:** 1907. **Habitat:** A portion of 870 islands, rocks, and reefs. Many are rocky outcroppings exposed only during low tide; others are rock islands with salal, salmonberry, and a few stunted conifers. **Facilities:** Wildlife viewing sites. **Activities:** Bird watching. **Access:** Public access on the islands is not permitted. Observation from the mainland or by boat, which should stay at least 200 yards away to avoid disturbing nesting birds. **Primary Wildlife:** Pelagic birds including Leach's storm petrel, fork-tailed storm petrel, rhinoceros auklet, tufted puffin, common murre, glaucous-winged gull, western gull, Brandt's cormorant, pelagic cormorant, Cassin's auklet, black oystercatcher, pigeon guillemot, and double-crested cormorant. Also sea lions, harbor seals, sea otters and whales. **Special Features:** Interpretive panels at Lake Ozette, Rialto Beach, Second Beach, Ruby Beach, and Kalalock provide information about nearby islands.

★698★ CRAB ORCHARD NATIONAL WILDLIFE REFUGE

8588 Rt 148
Marion, IL 62959
Web: www.fws.gov/midwest/craborchard
Phone: 618-997-3344; **Fax:** 618-997-8961
Location: Between Carbondale and Marion in southern Illinois. **Established:** 1947. **Habitat:** 43,878 acres of fields, wetlands and rolling hills. **Facilities:** Visitor contact station, campgrounds, picnic areas, marina, auto tour route, trails, observation tower. **Activities:** Camping, boating, fishing, swimming, hiking, bicycling, hunting, educational programs. **Access:** Unlimited. **Primary Wildlife:** Canada geese, hawks, shorebirds, owls, white-tailed deer, raccoons, wild turkey, rabbit, turtles and frogs. **Special Features:** Refuge includes three manmade lakes (totaling 8,700 acres), 21,000 acres of forest, and a 4,050-acre wilderness area.

★699★ CRANE MEADOWS NATIONAL WILDLIFE REFUGE

19502 Iris Rd
Little Falls, MN 56345
Web: midwest.fws.gov/cranemeadows
Phone: 320-632-1575; **Fax:** 320-632-5471
Location: Central Minnesota, 30 miles north of St. Cloud and 6 miles southeast of Little Falls. **Established:** 1992. **Habitat:** 1,825 acres of native tallgrass prairie, oak savanna, and wetlands with dense stands of wild rice. **Facilities:** Wildlife viewing sites, trails. **Activities:** Hiking, wildlife watching, photography, cross-country skiing, snowshoeing. **Access:** Year round during daylight hours. **Primary Wildlife:** Sandhill cranes and other migrating birds, waterfowl, bald eagle, muskrat, beaver, river otter, northern cricket frog, snapping turtle, coyote, red fox, skunk, and snakes. **Special Features:** Located in a transition zone between tallgrass prairie and deciduous forest, refuge hosts one of the largest nesting populations of greater sandhill cranes in Minnesota.

★700★ CRESCENT LAKE NATIONAL WILDLIFE REFUGE

10630 Rd 181
Ellsworth, NE 69340
Web: crescentlake.fws.gov/crescentlake
Phone: 308-762-4893
Location: 28 miles from Oshkosh in the Nebraska panhandle. **Established:** 1931. **Habitat:** 45,818 acres of rolling sandhills, grasslands, and lakes. **Facilities:** Trails, auto tour route, photo blind. **Activities:** Fishing, ice fishing, hiking, hunting, educational programs. **Access:** Open year round during daylight hours. **Primary Wildlife:** Waterfowl, shorebirds, bald eagles, raccoon, striped skunk, pronghorn, eastern cottontail, mule and white-tailed deer. **Special Features:** Nebraska's sandhills are the largest continuous dune area in America and offer evidence that the land was once the shore of an ancient sea.

See pages 22-23 for map of National Wildlife Refuges.

★701★ CROCODILE LAKE NATIONAL WILDLIFE REFUGE

PO Box 370
Key Largo, FL 33037
Web: www.fws.gov/southeast/crocodilelake
Phone: 305-451-4223; **Fax:** 305-451-1508
Location: On north Key Largo, Florida, off Card Sound Road. **Established:** 1980. **Habitat:** 6,606 acres of tropical hardwood hammock, mangrove forests, manmade channels, and open water. **Activities:** Educational programs. **Access:** Closed to general public use, although limited special-use permits may be obtained. **Primary Wildlife:** Endangered species include American crocodile, Schaus' swallowtail butterfly, Key Largo woodrat, and Key Largo cotton mouse. **Special Features:** Refuge contains some of the Keys' last remaining stands of high tropical hardwood hammock.

★702★ CROSS CREEKS NATIONAL WILDLIFE REFUGE

643 Wildlife Rd
Dover, TN 37058
Web: crosscreeks.fws.gov
Phone: 931-232-7477; **Fax:** 931-232-5958
Location: 25 miles west of Clarksville, Tennessee. **Established:** 1963. **Habitat:** 8,862 acres of wetlands, woodlands, croplands, grasslands, and open water. **Facilities:** Visitor center, trails, auto tour route, boat launch. **Activities:** Boating, fishing, hiking, biking, hunting. **Access:** Closed to public entry from mid-November to mid-March 15 to minimize disturbances to wintering waterfowl and nesting bald eagles. During the remainder of the year, the refuge is open during daylight hours. **Primary Wildlife:** Geese, ducks, raptors, shorbirds, wading birds, neo-tropical migratory birds, white-tailed deer, squirrel, and turkey. **Special Features:** Refuge encompasses 12 miles of the Cumberland River (Lake Barkley) and is home to 650 species of plants and 490 species of birds, mammals, fish, reptiles, and amphibians.

★703★ CROSS ISLAND NATIONAL WILDLIFE REFUGE

c/o Maine Coastal Islands NWR
14 Water St, PO Box 279
Milbridge, ME 04658
Phone: 207-546-2124
Location: In Machias Bay, 52 miles east of Ellsworth, Maine. **Established:** 1980. **Habitat:** 6 offshore islands, comprising 1,703 acres of dense forests of red and white spruce with mixed hardwoods. **Activities:** Shellfishing, fishing. **Access:** Accessible by personal boat only. Cross and Scotch islands are open year round from sunrise to sunset. Mink, Inner and Outer Double Head Shots, and Old Man islands are open during daylight hours from September through March and closed during the nesting season, April through August. **Primary Wildlife:** White-tailed deer, bald eagles, waterfowl, shorebirds, songbirds, common eiders, razorbacks, and storm petrels. **Special Features:** Like many of the islands along the coast of Maine, those within the Cross Island NWR have a long history of human habitation. Known by the Native Americans as Sebohegonet, Cross Island was used for generations as a base for fishing activities.

★704★ CRYSTAL RIVER NATIONAL WILDLIFE REFUGE

c/o Chassahowitzka NWR
1502 SE Kings Bay Dr
Crystal River, FL 34429
Web: www.fws.gov/crystalriver
Phone: 352-563-2088; **Fax:** 352-795-7961
Location: Along Florida's gulf coast, 75 miles north of Saint Petersburg. **Established:** 1983. **Habitat:** 80 acres which include 20 small islands and several parcels of land surrounded by Kings Bay. **Activities:** Boating, canoeing, diving, snorkeling, fishing, educational programs. **Access:** Daylight hours; accessible by boat only. **Primary Wildlife:** Endangered West Indian manatee, wading birds, raptors, alligators and fish. **Special Features:** Refuge includes 30 springs from which 600 million gallons of fresh water flow daily, creating Florida's most significant naturally occurring warm water refugium for manatee. The site provides critical habitat for about one fourth of the nation's manatee population.

★705★ CULEBRA NATIONAL WILDLIFE REFUGE

PO Box 190
Culebra, PR 00622
Web: www.fws.gov/southeast/culebra
Phone: 787-742-0115; **Fax:** 787-742-0115
Location: 10 miles southeast of Machias, Puerto Rico, in Machias Bay. **Established:** 1909. **Habitat:** 1,568 acres comprising lands on Culebra and 22 smaller islands in the vicinity. The islands' diverse habitats include subtropical dry forest, mangroves, brush, and grasslands. **Facilities:** Visitor contact station, hiking trail. **Activities:** Boating, hiking. **Access:** Portions of refuge open daily sunrise to sunset; special-use permits are required for visitation to other areas. **Primary Wildlife:** Sooty terns, seabirds, hawksbill and leatherback sea turtles. **Special Features:** Refuge includes a large nesting colony for 60,000 sooty terns. Leatherback and hawksbill sea turtles use refuge beaches for nesting.

★706★ CURRITUCK NATIONAL WILDLIFE REFUGE

c/o MacKay Island NWR
316 Marsh Causeway
Knotts Island, NC 27950
Web: www.fws.gov/mackayisland/currituck
Phone: 252-429-3100
Location: On North Carolina's outer banks. **Established:** 1984. **Habitat:** 4,103 acres in six separate units made up of sandy beaches, grassy dunes, maritime forests, shrub thickets, and brackish and freshwater marshes. **Facilities:** None. **Activities:** Boating, canoeing, fishing, hunting, educational programs. **Access:** Open during daylight hours. **Primary Wildlife:** Wading birds, shore birds, piping plover, waterfowl, raptors, feral horses, feral hogs, crab and loggerhead sea turtle. **Special Features:** Monkey Island, now the site of a bird rookery, was once home to the Pamunkey Indians.

See pages 22-23 for map of National Wildlife Refuges.

★707★ **CYPRESS CREEK NATIONAL WILDLIFE REFUGE**

0137 Rustic Campus Dr
Ullin, IL 62992
Web: www.fws.gov/Midwest/CypressCreek
Phone: 618-634-2231
Location: Between the Mississippi River and Ohio River, 20 miles north of Cairo, Illinois. **Established:** 1990. **Habitat:** 15,000 acres of wetlands, bottomland forests, swamps, and oak barrens. Planning to expand to 36,000 acres. **Facilities:** Visitor contact station, viewing sites, trails (20+ miles). **Activities:** Boating, canoeing, fishing, hiking, hunting, educational programs. **Access:** Daylight hours. **Primary Wildlife:** Migratory waterfowl and other birds, green tree frogs, water snakes, deer, turkey, squirrels, and rabbits. **Special Features:** The area has been designated as a ''Wetlands of International Importance'' by the RAMSAR Convention. The reserve contains cypress tupelo trees believed to be more than 1,000 years old.

★708★ **DAHOMEY NATIONAL WILDLIFE REFUGE**

831 Hwy 446
Boyle, MS 38730
Web: dahomey.fws.gov
Phone: 662-742-9331; **Fax:** 662-742-3378
Location: In Bolivar County, 8 miles west of Boyle, Mississippi. **Established:** 1990. **Habitat:** 9,691 acres of bottomland that include wetlands and hardwood forests. **Facilities:** Auto tour route. **Activities:** Fishing, hunting. **Access:** Year round. **Primary Wildlife:** Migrating waterfowl and neotropical birds, squirrels, rabbits, white-tailed deer, and eastern wild turkey. **Special Features:** The refuge is the largest remaining tract of bottomland hardwood-forested wetlands in the northwest portion of Mississippi. Its network of gravel roads offers springtime visitors excellent opportunities to view migrating songbirds.

★709★ **D'ARBONNE NATIONAL WILDLIFE REFUGE**

11372 Hwy 143
Farmerville, LA 71363
Web: darbonne.fws.gov
Phone: 318-726-4400; **Fax:** 318-726-4667
Location: Northeastern Louisiana, 6 miles north of West Monroe. **Established:** 1975. **Habitat:** 17,419 acres of bottomland hardwood and pine and upland hardwood forests, moist soil and permanent water. **Facilities:** Visitor contact station, viewing sites, hiking trails, boat ramps, observation tower. **Activities:** Boating, canoeing, fishing, hunting, educational programs. **Access:** Year round, although about 75 percent of the refuge is subject to annual flooding from December through May. **Primary Wildlife:** Waterfowl, wading birds, shorebirds, red-cockaded woodpecker, neotropical songbirds, alligator, and white-tailed deer. **Special Features:** The central physical feature is Bayou D'Arbonne, 13 miles of which lies within the refuge. The bayou meanders through a 2- to 4-mile wide floodplain characterized by alluvial soils.

★710★ **DEEP FORK NATIONAL WILDLIFE REFUGE**

PO Box 816
Okmulgee, OK 74447
Web: www.fws.gov/southwest/refuges/oklahoma/
Deep%20Fork
Phone: 918-756-0815; **Fax:** 918-756-0275
Location: 35 miles south of Tulsa. **Established:** 1993. **Habitat:** 9,000 acres of hardwood forests, wetlands, and lakes. **Facilities:** Trails, boardwalk. **Activities:** Boating, canoeing, fishing, hiking, hunting. **Access:** Daylight hours. **Primary Wildlife:** Mallard, blue-winged teal, frogs, turtles, snakes, rabbits, deer, butterflies and dragonflies. **Special Features:** Refuge protects important wetlands along the Deep Fork River. The land is subject to flooding at least once a year, creating excellent conditions for waterfowl.

★711★ **DEER FLAT NATIONAL WILDLIFE REFUGE**

13751 Upper Embankment Rd
Nampa, ID 83686
Web: deerflat.fws.gov
Phone: 208-467-9278; **Fax:** 208-467-1019
Location: 4 miles southwest of Nampa, Idaho. **Established:** 1909. **Habitat:** 10,588 acres divided into two units: the 9,000-acre Lake Lowell sector made up of open water and wetlands, and the Snake River Island sector which includes 101 islands covered with sagebrush uplands, grasslands and riparian forests. **Facilities:** Visitor center, hiking trails, auto tour route (29.5 miles), picnic areas, boat launch. **Activities:** Fishing, swimming, mountain biking, hiking, horseback riding, hunting, educational programs. **Access:** Open from dawn to dusk. **Primary Wildlife:** Waterfowl, especially mallards and Canada geese. Also provides habitat for bald eagles, hawks, mule deer, yellow-bellied marmot, pocket gopher, gopher snake, bullfrog, and painted turtle. **Special Features:** The refuge's Lake Lowell is approximately 9,000 acres at full pool and is fed by water out of the Boise River through the New York Canal. Water in the lake is manipulated to create a variety of aquatic and upland habitats for wildlife.

★712★ **DELEVAN NATIONAL WILDLIFE REFUGE**

c/o Sacramento NWR
752 County Rd 99W
Willows, CA 95988
Web: www.fws.gov/sacramentovalleyrefuges/delevan.htm
Phone: 530-934-2801
Location: 80 miles north of Sacramento, California. **Established:** 1962. **Habitat:** 5,797 acres of seasonal marsh, permanent ponds, and uplands. **Facilities:** Viewing sites. **Activities:** Hunting, wildlife watching. **Access:** Daylight hours year round. **Primary Wildlife:** Migratory waterfowl, wintering peregrine falcon and bald eagle, tricolored blackbird and a large colony of the endangered palmate-bracted bird's beak. Also provides habitat for giant garter snake, beaver, muskrat, and black-tailed deer. **Special Features:** Hundreds of thousands of ducks and geese use the refuge from November through January.

★713★ **DELTA NATIONAL WILDLIFE REFUGE**

61389 Hwy 434
Lacombe, LA 70445
Web: southeastlouisiana.fws.gov/delta.html
Phone: 985-882-2000; **Fax:** 985-882-9133

See pages 22-23 for map of National Wildlife Refuges.

Location: At the southeastern tip of the Mississippi River Delta, 60 miles southeast of New Orleans. **Established:** 1935. **Habitat:** 49,000 acres of freshwater and brackish marsh, shallow ponds, channels, and bayous. **Facilities:** Visitor contact station. **Activities:** Boating, canoeing, camping, fishing, hunting. **Access:** Open year round during daylight hours. Access is by boat only. **Primary Wildlife:** Greater and lesser yellowlegs, long-billed dowitchers, dunlins, western sandpipers, northern harriers, red-tailed hawks, alligators, deer, and swamp rabbits. **Special Features:** Delta NWR is an extremely important nursery area for both fresh and saltwater species of fish and shellfish. Tens of thousands of wintering waterfowl take advantage of the rich food resources found in the delta.

★714★ **DES LACS NATIONAL WILDLIFE REFUGE**
PO Box 578
Kenmare, ND 58746
Web: deslacs.fws.gov/dsl.htm
Phone: 701-385-4046
Location: 1 mile west of Kenmare, North Dakota. **Established:** 1935. **Habitat:** 19,544 acres of marshes, lakes, grasslands, and woodlands. **Facilities:** Visitor contact station, viewing sites, observation blind, picnic areas, auto tour route, trails. **Activities:** Canoeing, fishing, hiking, hunting, cross-country skiing, snowshoeing. **Access:** Open during daylight hours. **Primary Wildlife:** Western grebes, American white pelican, Canada geese, short eared owl, deer, and occasional moose. **Special Features:** The refuge is a 28-mile-long river valley with three natural lakes. Early trappers originally called this area ''Riviere des Lacs,'' literally, ''River of the Lakes,'' which aptly describes its prominent features. The refuge is well known for spectacular snow goose populations of 200,000 to 300,000 in the fall.

★715★ **DESECHEO NATIONAL WILDLIFE REFUGE**
c/o Caribbean Islands NWR Complex
PO Box 510
Boqueron, PR 00622
Web: southeast.fws.gov/Desecheo
Phone: 787-851-7258; **Fax:** 787-851-7440
Location: 14 miles west of the northwest corner of Puerto Rico. **Established:** 1976. **Habitat:** 360 acres encompassing all of Desecheo Island. The island is extremely rugged and rocky, its highest peak at 676 feet. **Access:** Closed to the public due to the presence of unexploded military munitions. **Primary Wildlife:** Feral goats and cats, monkeys. **Special Features:** Three endemic species and subspecies of lizards are found on the island. Island once housed the largest red-footed booby and brown booby nesting colony in the eastern Caribbean.

★716★ **DESERT NATIONAL WILDLIFE RANGE**
HCR 38 Box 700
Las Vegas, NV 89124
Web: www.fws.gov/desertcomplex/desertrange
Phone: 702-879-6110; **Fax:** 702-879-6115
Location: 23 miles north of Las Vegas in southern Nevada. **Established:** 1936. **Habitat:** 1.5 million acres of desert shrub, desert woodlands, and coniferous forest in the Mohave Desert. **Facilities:** Primitive campsites, picnic areas, viewing sites,

trails, auto tour route, historic features. **Activities:** Camping, hiking, horseback riding, hunting, educational programs. **Access:** Unlimited; a four-wheel drive vehicle with high clearance is recommended. **Primary Wildlife:** Desert bighorn sheep. Also provides habitat for the endangered pahrump poolfish, mule deer, coyotes, and birds. **Special Features:** The largest national wildlife refuge in the 48 contiguous states includes six mountain ranges with elevations ranging from 2,500 feet to nearly 10,000 feet.

★717★ **DESOTO NATIONAL WILDLIFE REFUGE**
1434 316th Ln
Missouri Valley, IA 51555
Web: midwest.fws.gov/desoto
Phone: 712-642-4121
Location: 25 miles north of Omaha. **Established:** 1958. **Habitat:** 8,362 acres of forest, grassland, cropland and wetlands. **Facilities:** Visitor center, picnic areas, viewing sites, photo blind, boat ramp, auto tour route (12 miles), trails, historic features. **Activities:** Boating, canoeing, fishing, ice fishing, hunting, mushroom picking, educational programs. **Access:** Daily from 1/2 hour before sunrise to 1/2 hour after sunset. **Primary Wildlife:** Snow geese, wood ducks, mallards, pheasants, eagles, songbirds, and white-tailed deer. **Special Features:** Refuge lies in the fertile plain of the Missouri River Valley and includes 875-acre DeSoto Lake. Between 300,000 and 800,000 snow geese stop here during their annual fall migration.

★718★ **DETROIT RIVER INTERNATIONAL WILDLIFE REFUGE**
9311 Groh Rd
Grosse Ile, MI 48138
Web: midwest.fws.gov/DetroitRiver
Phone: 734-692-7608; **Fax:** 734-695-7603
Location: Lower Detroit River in Michigan and Canada. **Established:** 2001. **Habitat:** 4,211 acres of islands, coastal wetlands, marshes, shoals, and riverfront lands along 18 miles of the Lower Detroit River. **Facilities:** Undeveloped; refuge is in planning and remediation stages. **Activities:** Boating, bird watching, hunting, fishing, interpretation. **Access:** Not yet open to the public. **Primary Wildlife:** 29 species of migratory waterfowl and 300 other types of migratory birds. Also 65 species of fish. **Special Features:** North America's first international wildlife refuge seeks to restore lands that were once one of the most significant migratory staging areas for diving ducks. In the past 100 years, discharges from the steel and chemical industry and municipal sewage effluent, along with the effects of large, deep-draft vessels, have degraded the lower Detroit River ecosystem. Only a remnant of the once vast numbers of migratory waterfowl can be seen today.

★719★ **DON EDWARDS SAN FRANCISCO BAY NATIONAL WILDLIFE REFUGE**
9500 Thornton Ave
Newark, CA 94560
Web: www.fws.gov/desfbay
Phone: 510-792-0222
Location: Near the Dumbarton Bridge toll plaza in Fremont,

See pages 22-23 for map of National Wildlife Refuges.

California. **Established:** 1974. **Habitat:** 30,000 acres of mudflats, open water, salt marshes, salt ponds, and uplands. **Facilities:** Visitor center, viewing sites, hiking trails, fishing pier, boat ramps, historic features, (♿♿), environmental education center. **Activities:** Boating, canoeing, fishing, hunting, hiking, educational programs. **Access:** Year round during daylight hours. **Primary Wildlife:** Western snowy plover, California clapper rail, salt marsh harvest mouse, and brine shrimp. **Special Features:** Refuge protects habitat for the endangered California clapper rail and the salt marsh harvest mouse, as well as the California brown pelican, California least tern, and peregrine falcon.

★720★ DRIFTLESS AREA NATIONAL WILDLIFE REFUGE

401 Business Hwy 18 N
McGregor, IA 52157
Web: www.fws.gov/midwest/driftless
Phone: 563-873-3423
Location: Along Highway 18 between the towns of Marquette and McGregor, Iowa. **Established:** 1989. **Habitat:** 775 acres containing algific (cold air) talus (loose rocks) slopes on 7 separate tracts. **Activities:** Educational programs (by prior arrangement). **Access:** Limited areas open for fishing, hunting, and wildlife observation, granted by special arrangement with refuge staff prior to visit. **Primary Wildlife:** Endangered Iowa Pleistocene snail and eight other snails, fish, turtles, frogs, herons, wood ducks and water birds. **Special Features:** Refuge protects an unusual habitat called algific (cold air) talus (loose rock) slopes. On these slopes, constant cold air or cold groundwater exiting from a cliff or talus slope creates an cool microclimate, one that may be considerably different from areas only a few feet away. Refuge is home to nine endangered and threatened snail species and two threatened plant species, which generally are found only on algific talus slopes.

★721★ DUNGENESS NATIONAL WILDLIFE REFUGE

c/o Washington Maritime NWR Complex
33 S Barr Rd
Port Angeles, WA 98365
Web: pacific.fws.gov/refuges/field/wa_dungeness.htm
Phone: 360-457-8451
Location: Between Port Townsend and Port Angeles, Washington, at the eastern end of the Strait of Juan de Fuca. **Established:** 1915. **Habitat:** 631 acres of sand spit, tidelands, and forested uplands. **Facilities:** Viewing sites, boat launch, trails, historic features, interpretive exhibits. **Activities:** Boating, canoeing, fishing, crabbing, clamming, beachcombing, horseback riding, educational programs. **Access:** During daylight hours; access is by foot or horseback only. **Primary Wildlife:** Waterfowl, seabirds, shellfish, and seals. **Special Features:** Refuge includes the world's longest natural sand spit.

★722★ EASTERN NECK NATIONAL WILDLIFE REFUGE

1730 Eastern Neck Rd
Rock Hall, MD 21661
Web: easternneck.fws.gov
Phone: 410-639-7056; **Fax:** 410-639-2516

Location: 15 miles northeast of Annapolis, Maryland. **Established:** 1962. **Habitat:** 2,286 acres of woodland, grassland, open water, marsh and cropland. **Facilities:** Visitor contact station, observation tower, trails (♿), boardwalk (♿), picnic area, boat ramps, historic features. **Activities:** Boating, canoeing, fishing, crabbing, hiking, hunting, educational programs. **Access:** Open from dawn to dusk. **Primary Wildlife:** Waterfowl, songbirds, butterflies, Delmarva fox squirrel, and birds of prey, including the bald eagle. **Special Features:** Refuge is one of seven sites where remnant populations of the endangered Delmarva fox squirrel exist.

★723★ EASTERN SHORE OF VIRGINIA NATIONAL WILDLIFE REFUGE

5003 Hallett Cir
Cape Charles, VA 23310
Web: www.fws.gov/northeast/easternshore
Phone: 757-331-2760
Location: Southern tip of the Delmarva Peninsula, along Virginia's seaboard. **Established:** 1984. **Habitat:** 1,153 acres of maritime forests, thickets, grasslands, croplands, with fresh and brackish ponds. **Facilities:** Visitor center, viewing sites, hiking trails, photo blind. **Activities:** Hunting, hiking. **Access:** Year round during daylight hours. **Primary Wildlife:** Waterfowl, raptors, shorebirds, songbirds, star-nosed mole, little brown bat, snakes, turtles, frogs, white-tailed deer, and fox. **Special Features:** Each fall, migrating birds gather on refuge lands until favorable wind and weather conditions permit an easy crossing of Chesapeake Bay. This ''funneling effect'' offers excellent viewing opportunities for visitors between late August and early November.

★724★ EDWIN B. FORSYTHE NATIONAL WILDLIFE REFUGE

Greek Creek Rd
Oceanville, NJ 08231
Web: www.fws.gov/northeast/forsythe
Phone: 609-652-1665; **Fax:** 609-652-1474
Location: 9 miles north of Atlantic City, along southern New Jersey's Atlantic coast. **Established:** In 1984, two refuges were combined to create Edwin B. Forsythe NWR. **Habitat:** 43,000 acres of coastal habitats—primarily tidal salt meadow and marsh interspersed with shallow coves and bays. **Facilities:** Visitor contact station, viewing sites, hiking trails, boat ramp, auto tour route (8 miles). **Activities:** Fishing, crabbing, hunting, hiking, wildlife watching, boating, educational programs. **Access:** Daily, sunrise to sunset. **Primary Wildlife:** Migrating ducks and geese, wading birds, and shore birds. Also piping plover, peregrine falcons, ospreys, and bald eagles. **Special Features:** Refuge is located along one of the Atlantic Flyway's most active flight paths and has been designated a Wetland of International Importance under the RAMSAR Convention. A portion of the New Jersey Coastal Heritage Trail passes through the refuge.

See pages 22-23 for map of National Wildlife Refuges.

★725★ EGMONT KEY NATIONAL WILDLIFE REFUGE

c/o Chassahowitzka NWR
1502 SE Kings Bay Dr
Crystal River, FL 34429
Web: www.fws.gov/egmontkey
Phone: 352-563-2088; **Fax:** 352-795-7961
Location: Offshore from Saint Petersburg, Florida, at the mouth of Tampa Bay. **Established:** 1974. **Habitat:** 328-acre island. **Facilities:** Trails, beach, historic features. **Activities:** Boating, fishing, diving/snorkeling, hiking, educational programs. **Access:** Daylight hours; accessible by boat only. **Primary Wildlife:** Brown pelicans, terns, gopher tortoises, and other colonial nesting water birds. **Special Features:** Refuge includes the remains of Fort Dade, built to protect Tampa after the outbreak of the Spanish-American War. Egmont Key is also the site of a Florida state park (see Egmont Key entry in Florida state parks section).

★726★ ELIZABETH A. MORTON NATIONAL WILDLIFE REFUGE

c/o Long Island NWR Complex
784 Noyack Rd
Shirley, NY 11963
Phone: 631-286-0485
Location: On Long Island's south fork, 6 miles west of Sag Harbor. **Established:** 1954. **Habitat:** 187 acres of bay beach, brackish and freshwater ponds, kettle holes, tidal flats, salt and fresh water marshes, shrub, grassland, maritime oak forest and red cedar. **Facilities:** Viewing sites, trails. **Activities:** Fishing, hiking. **Access:** Every day from 1/2 hour before sunrise to 1/2 hour after sunset. The beach peninsula is closed from early April through mid-August to protect nesting piping plovers. **Primary Wildlife:** Waterfowl, wading birds, shorebirds, piping plover, and songbirds, white-tailed deer, red fox, eastern cottontail, chipmunks, and gray squirrels. **Special Features:** Beach habitat provides nesting areas for threatened piping plovers and least terns. The waters surrounding the refuge are considered critical for juvenile Kemp's Ridley sea turtles and are occasionally used by loggerhead sea turtles.

★727★ ELLICOTT SLOUGH NATIONAL WILDLIFE REFUGE

c/o Don Edwards San Francisco Bay NWR
PO Box 524
Newark, CA 94560
Web: www.fws.gov/pacific/refuges/field/
   CA_Ellicott_slough.htm
Phone: 510-792-0222
Location: 4 miles west of Watsonville, California, alongside Monterey Bay. **Established:** 1975. **Habitat:** 139 acres of coastal uplands. **Access:** Closed to the public. **Primary Wildlife:** Santa Cruz long-toed salamander and California tiger salamander. **Special Features:** The threatened California red-legged frog has been documented on the refuge in the past and is presumed to still exist.

★728★ EMIQUON NATIONAL WILDLIFE REFUGE

c/o Illinois River NWFR
19031 E County Rd 2110N
Havana, IL 62644
Web: www.fws.gov/midwest/emiquon
Phone: 309-535-2290; **Fax:** 309-535-3023
Location: At the confluence of the Spoon River and Illinois River, southwest of Peoria. **Established:** 1993. **Habitat:** 1,305 acres, a mix of backwater lakes, bottomland forests, and floodplain wetlands with a small amount of upland forest. When land acquisitions are complete, refuge will comprise more than 11,122 acres. **Facilities:** Viewing sites (&), hiking trail, boat launch. **Activities:** Boating, canoeing, fishing, hunting, hiking, environmental educational programs. **Access:** Daylight hours. **Primary Wildlife:** Migratory waterfowl. **Special Features:** When restored, Emiquon will provide habitat for migratory birds, fish and resident wildlife. An additional 1,100 acres will be retained for agricultural crops for wildlife.

★729★ ERIE NATIONAL WILDLIFE REFUGE

11296 Wood Duck Ln
Guys Mills, PA 16327
Web: www.fws.gov/northeast/erie
Phone: 814-789-3585; **Fax:** 814-789-2909
Location: 35 miles south of Erie in northwestern Pennsylvania. **Established:** 1959. **Habitat:** 8,777 acres consisting of beaver ponds, pools, marshland, and forested slopes interspersed with croplands, grasslands, and wet meadows. **Facilities:** Visitor center (&), viewing sites, trails, auto tour route, historic features, fishing dock (&), indoor bird viewing room with microphones to hear the birds. **Activities:** Fishing, hiking, hunting, cross-country skiing, snowshoeing, educational programs. **Access:** Open from dawn to dusk. **Primary Wildlife:** Black ducks, wood ducks, hooded mergansers, blue-winged teal, mallards, beaver, woodchuck, and white-tailed deer. **Special Features:** Erie NWR is the only refuge in the nation protecting endangered Northern riffleshell and clubshell mussels. It has also been designated an Important Bird Area by the National Audubon Society.

★730★ EUFAULA NATIONAL WILDLIFE REFUGE

367 Hwy 165
Eufaula, AL 36027
Web: www.fws.gov/eufaula
Phone: 334-687-4065; **Fax:** 334-687-5906
Location: 5 miles north of Eufala. **Established:** 1964. **Habitat:** 11,184 acres of open water, wetlands, woodlands, croplands and grasslands. **Facilities:** Visitor contact station, observation towers, trails, auto tour route. **Activities:** Boating, canoeing, fishing, hiking, hunting, educational programs. **Access:** Open year round during daylight hours. **Primary Wildlife:** Canada geese, raptors, sandhill cranes, American alligator, bald eagle, wood stork, squirrel, rabbit, and fox. **Special Features:** Refuge has several rookeries, with bald eagle and osprey nests.

★731★ FALLON NATIONAL WILDLIFE REFUGE

c/o Stillwater NWR
1000 Auction Rd
Fallon, NV 89406
Web: www.fws.gov/stillwater/fallon.html
Phone: 775-423-5128; **Fax:** 775-423-0416

See pages 22-23 for map of National Wildlife Refuges.

Location: 70 miles east of Reno. **Established:** 1931. **Habitat:** 15,000 acres of gently rolling to flat deser shrublands made up of greasewood and saltbush. **Facilities:** Undeveloped. **Activities:** Limited hunting. **Access:** Open to public but travel is limited to dirt roads. Four-wheel-drive vehicles are recommended. **Primary Wildlife:** Migratory shorebirds and waterfowl. **Special Features:** A system of both active and stable dunes accentuates the topography in this area.

★732★ **FARALLON NATIONAL WILDLIFE REFUGE**
c/o Don Edwards San Francisco Bay NWR
PO Box 524
Newark, CA 94560
Web: www.fws.gov/sfbayrefuges/farallon/farallon.htm
Phone: 510-792-0222
Location: Islands 28 miles west of the Golden Gate Bridge. **Established:** 1909. **Habitat:** 211 acres of rocky islands. **Access:** Closed to the public. Local conservation groups sponsor trips to the islands; contact refuge office. **Primary Wildlife:** Western gull, tufted puffin, American black oystercatchers, elephant seals, California sea lion, California brown pelican, and white sharks. **Special Features:** Refuge protects the largest seabird breeding colony on the Pacific coast south of Alaska, hosting more than 300,000 birds each summer.

★733★ **FEATHERSTONE NATIONAL WILDLIFE REFUGE**
c/o Mason Neck NWR
14344 Jefferson Davis Hwy
Woodbridge, VA 22191
Web: www.fws.gov/northeast/va/frs.htm
Phone: 703-490-4979; **Fax:** 709-490-5631
Location: South of Washington, D.C., where Neabsco Creek joins the Potomac River. **Established:** 1970. **Habitat:** 325 acres of wetlands and woodlands. **Access:** Closed to the public. **Primary Wildlife:** Neotropical migrants, waterfowl, ospreys, and bald eagles. Also provides habitat for white-tailed deer, red fox, raccoon, gray squirrel, and beaver. **Special Features:** Biological surveys monitor waterfowl and bald eagle feeding and nesting activity. Refuge lands have been identified as providing a possible route for the Potomac Heritage National Scenic Trail (see entry in national trails section).

★734★ **FELSENTHAL NATIONAL WILDLIFE REFUGE**
PO Box 1157
Crossett, AR 71635
Web: felsenthal.fws.gov
Phone: 870-364-3167; **Fax:** 870-364-3757
Location: 5 miles west of Crossett, Arkansas. **Established:** 1970. **Habitat:** 65,000 acres of sloughs, buttonbush swamps, lakes, bottomland hardwood forest and upland forest. **Facilities:** Visitor center, 11 primitive campsites, trails. **Activities:** Fishing, hunting, camping, educational programs. **Access:** Year round, 24-hour access. **Primary Wildlife:** Waterfowl, wild turkeys, songbirds, and deer. **Special Features:** Felsenthal is the world's largest green-tree reservoir. The 15,000-acre Felsenthal Pool more than doubles in size to 36,000 acres during winter flooding.

★735★ **FERN CAVE NATIONAL WILDLIFE REFUGE**
c/o Wheeler NWR
2700 Refuge Headquarters Rd
Decatur, AL 35603
Web: www.fws.gov/ferncave
Phone: 256-353-7243; **Fax:** 256-340-9728
Location: 20 miles west of Scottsboro, Alabama. **Established:** 1981. **Habitat:** 199 acres of upland hardwoods and limestone outcroppings. **Facilities:** Viewing sites, hiking trails. **Activities:** Wildlife observation, photography. **Access:** Fern Cave itself is not open to the public; other portions of the refuge are open, but limited, due to the terrain. **Primary Wildlife:** Gray bat, Indiana bat, deer, squirrels, turkey, and American Hart's-tongue fern. **Special Features:** Fern Cave contains the largest wintering colony of gray bats in the United States with more than one million bats hibernating there in the winter. Spectacular features, important paleological and archeological finds, and a diversity of cave fauna have contributed to Fern Cave being described as one of the most spectacular caves in the United States.

★736★ **FISH SPRINGS NATIONAL WILDLIFE REFUGE**
PO Box 568
Dugway, UT 84022
Web: www.fws.gov/fishsprings
Phone: 435-831-5353; **Fax:** 435-831-5354
Location: South edge of the Great Salt Lake Desert, 104 miles southwest of Tooele and 78 miles northwest of Delta. **Established:** 1959. **Habitat:** 17,992 acres of saline marsh. **Facilities:** Visitor contact station, picnic area, viewing sites, auto tour route (11 miles), historic features. **Activities:** Canoeing, hiking, hunting. **Access:** Open sunrise to sunset. However, refuge is extremely isolated and can be reached only by gravel roads across uninhabited desert. **Primary Wildlife:** Waterfowl, including swans, Canada geese, mallards, and teal. Also provides habitat for a variety of shore and wading birds, including great blue herons, avocets, and eared grebes. **Special Features:** Pony Express riders came to and left from the Fish Springs Pony Express Station twice a day. Retracing their route leads hundreds of enthusiasts through the refuge each year.

★737★ **FISHERMAN ISLAND NATIONAL WILDLIFE REFUGE**
c/o Eastern Shore of Virginia NWR
5003 Hallett Cir
Cape Charles, VA 23310
Web: www.fws.gov/refuges/profiles/index.cfm?id=51651
Phone: 757-331-2760; **Fax:** 757-331-3424
Location: Off the tip of the Delmarva Peninsula, 14 miles south of Cape Charles. **Established:** 1969. **Habitat:** 1,850-acre barrier island consisting of brackish marsh, beach, and upland. **Access:** Guided tours available by reservation on weekends between October and March. No other public access. **Primary Wildlife:** Waterfowl, shorebirds, songbirds, and raptors, including peregrine falcons and bald eagles. Other species include the sea turtle and tiger beetle. **Special Features:** Because there are no mammalian predators, the island provides protection for such species as the brown pelican and royal tern.

See pages 22-23 for map of National Wildlife Refuges.

★738★ FLATTERY ROCKS NATIONAL WILDLIFE REFUGE

c/o Washington Maritime NWR Complex
33 S Barr Rd
Port Angeles, WA 98362
Web: pacific.fws.gov/refuges/field/wa_Flatteryrocks.htm
Phone: 360-457-8451
Location: Off Washington's Pacific coast, south of Cape Flattery. **Established:** 1907. **Habitat:** A portion of 870 islands, rocks, and reefs. Many are rocky outcroppings exposed only during low tide; others are rock islands with salal, salmonberry; and a few stunted conifers. **Facilities:** Viewing sites. **Activities:** Bird watching. **Access:** Public access on the islands is not permitted. Observation from the mainland or by boat, which should stay at least 200 yards away to avoid disturbing nesting birds. **Primary Wildlife:** Pelagic birds including tufted puffins, black oystercatcher, pigeon guillemot, common murre, storm petrels, auklets, cormorants, and gulls. Waters around the islands are home to harbor and fur seals, California sea lions, river otters and whales, including right, grays and humpbacks. **Special Features:** Interpretive panels at Lake Ozette, Rialto Beach, Second Beach, Ruby Beach, and Kalalock provide information about refuge's offshore islands.

★739★ FLINT HILLS NATIONAL WILDLIFE REFUGE

PO Box 128
Hartford, KS 66854
Web: flinthills.fws.gov
Phone: 620-392-5553
Location: North of Emporia, Kansas, in the Neosho River Valley. **Established:** 1966. **Habitat:** 18,500 acres of native grassland and hardwood timber interspersed with shallow marshes, flooded sloughs, and croplands. **Facilities:** Visitor center, boat ramps, picnic areas, trails, auto tour route. **Activities:** Boating, canoeing, fishing, hiking, hunting, educational programs. **Access:** Open daylight hours. Waterfowl and bald eagle management requires that portions of the refuge be closed and that public access be restricted during periods of intensive waterfowl use. **Primary Wildlife:** Waterfowl, including blue-winged teal, wood ducks, green herons, and snowy egrets. Also provides habitat for beaver, muskrat, coyote, bobcat, and white-tailed deer. **Special Features:** Refuge lies upstream of John Redmond Reservoir on land owned by the U.S. Army Corps of Engineers.

★740★ FLORIDA PANTHER NATIONAL WILDLIFE REFUGE

3860 Tollgate Blvd, Suite 300
Naples, FL 34114
Web: www.fws.gov/floridapanther
Phone: 239-353-8442; **Fax:** 239-353-8640
Location: 20 miles east of Naples, Florida. **Established:** 1989. **Habitat:** 26,400 acres of cypress and mixed swamp forests, pine forests, hardwood hammock forests, and prairies, marshes, and sloughs. Permanent and seasonal wetlands comprise approximately 70% of the refuge acreage. **Access:** Restricted to designated trails in one portion of the refuge. **Primary Wildlife:** Florida panther, Florida black bear, Big Cypress fox squirrel, American alligator, eastern indigo snake. Also provides habitat

for Atlantic loggerhead sea turtle, striped mud turtle, Kemp's ridley sea turtle, wild turkey and white-tailed deer. **Special Features:** Refuge is situated in the upper segment of the Fakahatchee Strand of the Big Cypress Swamp. In any given month, 5-11 pathers use the refuge area to den, hunt, and travel through.

★741★ FORT NIOBRARA NATIONAL WILDLIFE REFUGE

Hidden Timber Rt
HC 14, Box 67
Valentine, NE 69201
Web: fortniobrara.fws.gov
Phone: 402-376-3789
Location: 4 miles east of Valentine, in north-central Nebraska. **Established:** 1912. **Habitat:** 19,131 acres of deep canyons, limestone rocks, sand dunes and mixed grass prairie. **Facilities:** Visitor center, viewing sites (&), hiking trails, auto tour route, historic features, hand launch boat ramp. **Activities:** Canoeing, river floating, hiking. **Access:** Open to the public during daylight hours. **Primary Wildlife:** Bison, elk, songbirds, wood ducks, grasshopper sparrow, and greater prairie chickens. **Special Features:** The site was originally Fort Niobrara Military Reservation, which was established in 1879 to keep peace between the Sioux Indians and settlers. Soldiers stationed here fought no battles, and the fort was abandoned in 1906. All that remains is one building (the red barn), old foundations and earth works.

★742★ FOX RIVER NATIONAL WILDLIFE REFUGE

c/o Horicon NWR
W4279 Headquarters Rd
Mayville, WI 53050
Web: www.fws.gov/midwest/foxriver
Phone: 920-387-2658; **Fax:** 920-387-2973
Location: In Marquette County, Wisconsin. **Established:** 1979. **Habitat:** 1,004 acres, consisting mostly of sedge meadow, wet prairie, and shallow marsh wetlands dominated by many species of sedges, grasses, and cattail. Other wetland types such as fens, lowland forest, shrub-carr thickets, deep marsh, and open water occur on the refuge as well. **Facilities:** Undeveloped. **Activities:** Deer hunting (with restrictions). **Access:** Closed to the public except for seasonal hunting. **Primary Wildlife:** Greater sandhill crane, herons, rails, songbirds, deer, turkey, and bobwhite quail. **Special Features:** Approximately 50 greater sandhill cranes use the refuge during the summer, but more than 300 cranes use it as a staging area during the fall migration.

★743★ FRANKLIN ISLAND NATIONAL WILDLIFE REFUGE

c/o Maine Coastal Islands NWR
PO Box 495
Rockport, ME 04856
Phone: 207-546-2124
Location: In Muscongus Bay, 25 miles east of Bath, Maine. **Established:** 1973. **Habitat:** Two islands comprising 12 total acres of open grasslands and stands of red spruce with a dense raspberry understory. **Access:** Open September through March, dawn to dusk; closed April through August during the seabird nesting season. Accessible by boat only. **Primary Wildlife:**

See pages 22-23 for map of National Wildlife Refuges.

4. National Wildlife Refuges

Colonial seabirds, including common eider, black-crowned night heron, black guillemot, Leach's storm petrel, and osprey. **Special Features:** The U.S. government built a lighthouse on the island in 1808; it was staffed by the Coast Guard until it was automated in 1967.

★744★ FRANZ LAKE NATIONAL WILDLIFE REFUGE

PO Box 1136
Washougal, WA 98671
Web: www.fws.gov/ridgefieldrefuges/flnwrhome.htm
Phone: 360-835-8767; **Fax:** 360-835-9780
Location: 35 miles east of Portland, Oregon. **Established:** 1990. **Habitat:** 590 acres that include wetlands, woodlands from lower elevation willows and cottonwoods to mid-elevation old growth fir and cedar. **Facilities:** Scenic overlook. **Access:** Group tours are available by arrangement. **Primary Wildlife:** Canada geese, tundra swans, and ducks, as well as western painted turtles, Pacific tree frogs, western toads, garter snakes, and California ground squirrels. **Special Features:** Several springs and seeps on the refuge have been identified as critical brood areas for Coho salmon and other salmon species.

★745★ GRAND BAY NATIONAL WILDLIFE REFUGE

PO Box 1062
Grand Bay, AL 36541
Web: www.fws.gov/grandbay
Phone: 228-497-6322; **Fax:** 228-497-5407
Location: 7 miles east of Pascagoula, Mississippi, and 20 miles west of Mobile, Alabama. **Established:** 1992. **Habitat:** 14,000 acres of tidal marsh and pine savanna. Proposed acquisition will encompass 32,000 acres. **Facilities:** Viewing sites. **Activities:** Boating, canoeing, fishing, hunting, educational programs. **Access:** Year round during daylight hours. **Primary Wildlife:** Gopher tortoise (threatened), bald eagle (threatened), red-cockaded woodpecker (endangered), brown pelican (endangered). **Special Features:** The refuge's coastal marshes contribute essential food and cover for many varieties of marine animals, including spotted seatrout, red drum, flounder, blue crab, and shrimp.

★746★ GRAND COTE NATIONAL WILDLIFE REFUGE

c/o Lake Ophelia NWR
401 Island Rd
Marksville, LA 71351
Web: www.fws.gov/grandcote
Phone: 318-253-4238; **Fax:** 318-253-7139
Location: Central Louisiana, 15 miles southwest of Alexandria. **Established:** 1989. **Habitat:** 6,077-acre basin, with forest, cropland, wetlands, moist soil, and open water. **Facilities:** Visitor contact station, viewing sites, hiking trails. **Activities:** Canoeing, fishing, crawfishing, hiking, hunting, educational programs. **Access:** Open daylight hours year round. **Primary Wildlife:** Migratory waterfowl, shorebirds such as spotted sandpiper, great blue herons, egrets, as well as white-tailed deer, raccoon, river otter, beavers, nutria and rabbits. Peregrine falcon and bald eagles

have also been known to use the refuge. **Special Features:** Refuge was once part of the large, contiguous Mississippi River bottomland hardwood forest. Today, much of the land is in the process of being reforested.

★747★ GRAYS HARBOR NATIONAL WILDLIFE REFUGE

c/o Nisqually NWR
100 Brown Farm Rd
Olympia, WA 98516
Web: www.fws.gov/graysharbor
Phone: 360-753-9467; **Fax:** 360-534-9302
Location: At the western city limits of Hoquiam, Washington, beside Grays Harbor bay. **Established:** 1988. **Habitat:** 1,500 acres of tidal flats, salt marsh, freshwater ponds, and deciduous woodlands. **Facilities:** Boardwalk trail, viewing sites. **Access:** Open during daylight hours. **Primary Wildlife:** Shorebirds, particularly western sandpipers, but also dunlins, black-footed albatross, and semipalmated plovers. **Special Features:** Grays Harbor is one of four major staging areas for shorebirds in North America. Each spring, up to one million shorebirds gather, or stage, here to store up fat reserves and rest for the nonstop flight to their northern breeding grounds. Peregrine falcons and merlins are also seen at that time.

★748★ GRAYS LAKE NATIONAL WILDLIFE REFUGE

74 Grays Lake Rd
Wayan, ID 83285
Web: pacific.fws.gov/refuges/field/ID_grayslk.htm
Phone: 208-574-2755
Location: 27 miles north of Soda Springs, in southeast Idaho. **Established:** 1965. **Habitat:** Grays Lake is 18,330 acres of what is actually a large, shallow marsh. It has little open water and is covered with dense vegetation, primarily bulrush and cattail. Wet meadows and grasslands surround the marsh. **Facilities:** Visitor center, viewing sites. **Activities:** Hiking, hunting, cross-country skiing. **Access:** Foot traffic (including cross-country skiing and snowshoeing) is allowed on the northern half of the refuge from October through March. **Primary Wildlife:** Greater sandhill cranes, Canada geese, ducks, Franklin's gulls, white-faced ibis, tumpeter swans, moose, elk, mule deer and badger. **Special Features:** Refuge is the largest hardstem bulrush marsh in North America, and protects the largest nesting population of greater sandhill cranes in the world.

★749★ GREAT BAY NATIONAL WILDLIFE REFUGE

100 Merimac Dr
Newington, NH 03801
Web: www.fws.gov/refuges/profiles/index.cfm?id=53570
Phone: 603-431-7511
Location: 3 miles west of Portsmouth, along the eastern shore of Great Bay in southeastern New Hampshire. **Established:** 1992. **Habitat:** 1,054 acres of forested uplands, open grasslands, shrub, fresh water, forested wetlands, and salt marsh. **Facilities:** Visitor contact station, hiking trails. **Activities:** Hiking, hunting. **Access:** Year round during daylight hours. **Primary Wildlife:** Bald eagle, peregrine falcon, common loon, pied-billed grebe,

See pages 22-23 for map of National Wildlife Refuges.

4. National Wildlife Refuges

osprey, common tern, northern harrier, as well as black ducks. **Special Features:** Refuge also administers the Karner Blue Butterfly Easement in Concord, providing habitat for the endangered species.

★750★ GREAT DISMAL SWAMP NATIONAL WILDLIFE REFUGE
3100 Desert Rd
Suffolk, VA 23434
Web: www.fws.gov/northeast/greatdismalswamp/
Phone: 757-986-3705; **Fax:** 757-986-2353
Location: In southeastern Virginia and northeastern North Carolina. **Established:** 1974. **Habitat:** 111,000 acres of forested wetland, with the 3,100-acre Lake Drummond located in the heart of the swamp. **Facilities:** Trails (100+ miles), boardwalk, viewing sites, boat ramp, auto tour route. **Activities:** Boating, canoeing, fishing, hiking, biking, hunting, educational programs. **Access:** Open from dawn to dusk. **Primary Wildlife:** Warblers, wood ducks, barred owls, pileated woodpeckers, robins, blackbirds, black bear, bobcat, foxes, and white-tailed deer. **Special Features:** Refuge is home to one of the most concentrated black bear populations on the east coast and the nation's largest remaining stand of Atlantic white cedar.

★751★ GREAT MEADOWS NATIONAL WILDLIFE REFUGE
73 Weir Hill Rd
Sudbury, MA 01776
Web: www.fws.gov/northeast/greatmeadows
Phone: 978-443-4661; **Fax:** 978-443-2898
Location: 20 miles west of Boston. **Established:** 1947. **Habitat:** 3,600 acres of freshwater wetlands along 12 miles of the Concord and Sudbury rivers. **Facilities:** Visitor center, trails, viewing sites. **Activities:** Fishing, hiking, hunting, canoeing, educational programs. **Access:** Open from dawn to dusk. **Primary Wildlife:** Wood ducks, black ducks, mallards, muskrats, red fox, raccoons, and weasels. **Special Features:** Minute Man National Historical Park and Thoreau's Walden Pond are both located nearby.

★752★ GREAT RIVER NATIONAL WILDLIFE REFUGE
County Rd 206
Annada, MO 63330
Web: www.fws.gov/midwest/greatriver
Phone: 573-847-2333
Location: East of Annada, Missouri, about 40 miles north of Saint Louis. **Established:** 1958, as the Annada District of the Mark Twain NWR; converted into a separate refuge in 2000. **Habitat:** 15,000 wetland and riparian acres spread over 100 miles of the Mississippi River. **Facilities:** Wildlife viewing sites, trails. **Activities:** Fishing, hunting, hiking, bicycling, berry and mushroom picking for personal consumption, wildlife watching. **Access:** Dawn to dusk year round. **Primary Wildlife:** Migratory birds, including shorebirds, songbirds and waterfowl as well as bald eagle, canvasback, geese, fish, mussels, Indiana bat, badger, shrew, frogs, toads, salamanders, snakes, lizards, and turtles.

Special Features: In 1998, the Great River Refuge was designated as a globally important bird area. The refuge's proximity to Saint Louis provides excellent educational opportunities to a large population.

★753★ GREAT SWAMP NATIONAL WILDLIFE REFUGE
241 Pleasant Plains Rd
Basking Ridge, NJ 07920
Web: www.fws.gov/northeast/greatswamp
Phone: 973-425-1222; **Fax:** 973-425-7309
Location: 26 miles west of New York City. **Established:** 1960. **Habitat:** 7,600 acres of swamp woodland, hardwood ridges, cattail marsh, grassland, ponds and streams. **Facilities:** Visitor contact station, viewing sites, trails, auto tour route, 2 environmental education centers. **Activities:** Hiking, hunting, educational programs. **Access:** Open from dawn to dusk. **Primary Wildlife:** Wood ducks, mallards, Canada goose, black duck, loons, eastern bluebird, turkey vultures, wild turkeys, eastern chipmunk, shrews, voles, and white-tailed deer. **Special Features:** Refuge supports more than 244 species of birds (including one of the largest breeding populations of eastern bluebirds in the state), 39 species of reptiles and amphibians, 29 species of fish, 33 species of mammals, and approximately 600 species of plants. Additionally, 26 of these species are state-listed as being threatened or endangered including the bog turtle, wood turtle, and blue-spotted salamander.

★754★ GREAT WHITE HERON NATIONAL WILDLIFE REFUGE
c/o Key Deer NWR
179 Key Deer Blvd
Big Pine Key, FL 33043
Web: southeast.fws.gov/greatwhiteheron
Phone: 305-872-2239; **Fax:** 305-872-2154
Location: Islands on the north side of the lower Florida Keys between Marathon and Key West. **Established:** 1938. **Habitat:** 6,207 acres of mangrove islands and wetlands, with some sandy beaches and dunes. An additional 123,900 acres of marine waters are managed but not owned by the Fish and Wildlife Service. **Facilities:** Visitor contact station (on Big Pine Key). **Activities:** Boating, canoeing, fishing. **Access:** By boat only; access to islands is restricted. **Primary Wildlife:** Great white heron and other wading birds, sea turtles. **Special Features:** Refuge consists of a 300-square-mile area of water and unpopulated islands. No raccoons live on the islands, thus providing a safe nesting, roosting, wading, and resting habitat critical for more than 250 bird species.

★755★ GREEN CAY NATIONAL WILDLIFE REFUGE
c/o Sandy Point NWR
3013 Estate Golden Rock, Suite 167
Christiansted, VI 00820
Web: www.fws.gov/southeast/greencay
Phone: 340-773-4554
Location: Off the north coast of Saint Croix, U.S. Virgin Islands. **Established:** 1977. **Habitat:** 14-acre island of volcanic rock. **Access:** Island refuge is closed due to fragile habitat. **Primary**

See pages 22-23 for map of National Wildlife Refuges.

4. National Wildlife Refuges

Wildlife: St. Croix ground lizard and colonial nesting birds
Special Features: Buried under the island's volcanic rock are 33,000 conch shells, revealing a history of human occcupancy dating back 1,000 years.

★756★ GRULLA NATIONAL WILDLIFE REFUGE

c/o Muleshoe NWR
PO Box 549
Muleshoe, TX 79347
Web: www.fws.gov/southwest/refuges/newmex/grulla.html
Phone: 806-946-3341; **Fax:** 806-946-3317
Location: 25 miles southeast of Portales, New Mexico. **Established:** 1969. **Habitat:** 3,236 acres of saline lake bed and grasslands. **Facilities:** Viewing sites, trail. **Activities:** Hiking. **Access:** Year round during daylight hours. **Primary Wildlife:** Lesser sandhill cranes, waterfowl, and shore birds. **Special Features:** In years that the lake holds water, lesser sandhill cranes may be seen throughout the fall and winter months.

★757★ GUADALUPE-NIPOMO DUNES NATIONAL WILDLIFE REFUGE

PO Box 9
Guadalupe, CA 93434
Web: www.fws.gov/hoppermountain/guadalupe
Phone: 805-343-9151; **Fax:** 805-343-9141
Location: Pacific coast in San Luis Obispo County, California. **Established:** 2000. **Habitat:** 2,550 acres of coastal dunes. **Facilities:** Visitor center, wildlife viewing stations, trails, auto tour route. **Activities:** Hiking, surf fishing, wildlife viewing, guided walks, educational programs. **Access:** Open year round. **Primary Wildlife:** Endangered and threatened species are California least tern, California red-legged frog, and Western snowy plover. Other wildlife include deer, black bear, bobcat, mountain lion (rarely), and migratory birds including the endangered California brown pelican. **Special Features:** Refuge protects part of California's Guadalupe-Nipomo Dunes complex, the largest, most bio-diverse, coastal dune-lagoon ecosystem on earth. The dunes system includes 1,400 known species of birds, plants, and animals, and the highest sand dunes on the Pacific coast.

★758★ GUAM NATIONAL WILDLIFE REFUGE

PO Box 8134 MOU-3
Dededo, GU 96912
Web: www.fws.gov/pacificislands/wnwr/guamnwrindex.html
Phone: 671-355-5096; **Fax:** 671-355-5098
Location: Northernmost point of Guam. **Established:** 1993. **Habitat:** 22,500 acres of volcanic Pacific island. **Facilities:** Visitor center. **Activities:** Education programs, fishing. **Access:** Refuge's 772-acre Ritidian Unit is open to public. **Primary Wildlife:** Endangered Mariana fruit bat, Mariana crow, island swiftlet, and Mariana common moorhen. **Special Features:** Most of the refuge is an "overlay" on lands administered by the U.S. Air Force and U.S. Navy. Although the military mission is given precedence on these lands, the U.S. Fish and Wildlife Service assists in protecting native species and habitats.

★759★ HAGERMAN NATIONAL WILDLIFE REFUGE

6465 Refuge Rd
Sherman, TX 75092
Web: southwest.fws.gov/refuges/texas/hagerman
Phone: 903-786-2826
Location: Along Lake Texoma, northwest of Sherman, Texas, near the Texas-Oklahoma border. **Established:** 1946. **Habitat:** 11,320 acres of lakeshore, ponds, and upland prairies. **Facilities:** Visitor center, viewing sites, picnic area, auto tour route (4 miles), trails, historical features. **Activities:** Boating, canoeing, fishing, hiking, hunting. **Access:** Open during daylight hours. **Primary Wildlife:** Canada geese, snow geese, white-fronted geese, ducks, squirrel, rabbit, deer. **Special Features:** In the early 1900s, the refuge was the location of Hagerman Townsite, population 250. It was abandoned in 1943 to make way for Lake Texoma.

★760★ HAKALAU FOREST NATIONAL WILDLIFE REFUGE

c/o Big Island Refuges
32 Kinoole St, Suite 101
Hilo, HI 96720
Web: www.fws.gov/pacificislands/wnwr/bhakalaunwr.html
Phone: 808-933-6915; **Fax:** 808-933-6917
Location: 12 miles northwest of Hilo, on the island of Hawaii. **Established:** 1985. **Habitat:** 32,733 acres on the windward (eastern) slope of Moana Loa. Habitats include grassland and open woodland at the highest elevations; a closed-canopy rain forest with an understory of native trees, shrubs, and ferns around 5,000 feet; and bogs, fern patches, and scrub dissected by deep gulches below 4,000 feet. **Facilities:** Visitor contact station. **Activities:** Birdwatching, hiking. **Access:** Open to the public on weekends and holidays. **Primary Wildlife:** Endangered forest birds, including the akiapola'au, the Hawaii akepa, Hawaii creeper, i'iwi, apapane, elepaio, and Hawaiian hoary bat. **Special Features:** Refuge's two units are located at elevations between 2,000 and 6,600 feet on the east and west sides of the island of Hawaii. The sloping terrain is forested with some of the finest remaining stands of native montane rainforest in the state.

★761★ HAMDEN SLOUGH NATIONAL WILDLIFE REFUGE

21212 210th St
Audubon, MN 56511
Web: www.fws.gov/midwest/hamdenslough
Phone: 218-439-6319
Location: One mile northeast of Audubon, Minnesota. **Established:** 1989. **Habitat:** 3,170 acres of rolling hills, grasslands, and small wetlands. A total of 5,944 acres are planned for acquision, and an additional 2,600 acres will be leased from private landowners. **Facilities:** Visitor contact station, viewing sites, hiking trails. **Activities:** Hiking, wildlife observation, educational programs. **Access:** Open year round during daylight hours. **Primary Wildlife:** More than 219 species of birds, including the Le Conte's sparrow, American avocet, sedge wren, American bittern, bald eagle, harriers, hawks, and merlins. **Special Features:** The goal of Hamden Slough NWR is to reestablish almost 6,000 acres of prairie wetland ecosystem. Early

See pages 22-23 for map of National Wildlife Refuges.

restoration efforts have already had a dramatic effect, with tremendous increases in bird diversity and abundance.

★762★ HANALEI NATIONAL WILDLIFE REFUGE

c/o Kilauea Point NWR
PO Box 1128
Kilauea, HI 96754
Web: pacificislands.fws.gov/wnwr/khanaleinwr.html
Phone: 808-828-1413; Fax: 808-828-1414
Location: In the Hanalei Valley on the northern coast of Kauai.
Established: 1972. Habitat: 917 acres of river bottom land, taro farms, and wooded slopes. Access: Closed to public use, but refuge wildlife is visible from an overlook on Highway 56. Primary Wildlife: Hawaiian birds, including the endangered Koloa (Hawaiian duck), Hawaiian moorhen, Hawaiian coot, Hawaiian stilt, and the Hawaiian hoary bat. Special Features: Refuge is located on the on the north side of picturesque Hanalei Valley, encircled by waterfall-draped mountains. Taro is grown on the refuge by local farmers, continuing a practice that stretches back more than 1,200 years in the valley.

★763★ HANDY BRAKE NATIONAL WILDLIFE REFUGE

c/o D'Arbonne NWR
11372 Hwy 143
Farmerville, LA 71241
Web: www.fws.gov/handybrake
Phone: 318-726-4222; Fax: 318-726-4667
Location: In northeastern Louisiana, 6 miles north of Bastrop. Established: 1990. Habitat: 20,000 acres of reforested and restored wetlands. Facilities: Observation tower, trails. Activities: Hiking, rabbit hunting (in February). Access: Year round during daylight hours. Primary Wildlife: Waterfowl, shore birds, raptors, wading birds, and other wetland species. Special Features: Once bottomland hardwood tracts that were cleared for agriculture, refuge lands have been reforested and wetlands have been restored.

★764★ HANFORD REACH NATIONAL MONUMENT

3520 Port of Benton Blvd
Richland, WA 99354
Web: www.fws.gov/hanfordreach/index-expanded.html
Phone: 509-371-1801; Fax: 509-375-0196
Location: Off I-182 in central Washington, north of Richland. Established: 2000. Habitat: 195,000 acres, primarily shrub-steppe with riparian, aquatic, and riverine habitats, including the Saddle Mountain NWR. Facilities: Boat launch, scenic overlook. Activities: Boating, canoeing, hunting, fishing, wildlife observation. Access: Most of the Columbia River corridor is open for public use, though some shoreline and islands are closed to visitation. A few day-use areas are open during daylight hours, but most areas are closed except for pre-approved ecological research and environmental education activities. Primary Wildlife: Chinook salmon. Species of concern include ferruginous hawk, burrowing owl, loggerhead shrike, sage sparrow, Brewer's sparrow, sage thrasher, greater sage grouse, long-billed curlew, sagebrush vole, Merriam's shrew, pygmy rabbit, Washington ground squirrel, black-tailed jack rabbit, sagebrush lizard,

and striped whipsnake. Special Features: The U.S. Fish and Wildlife Service's only national monument, Hanford Reach is a place of sweeping vistas and stark beauty with a chilling reminder of its dark history. The U.S. Department of Energy's "Hanford Site" was established during World War II as part of the Manhattan Project; plutonium from Hanford's reactors fueled "Fat Man," the atomic bomb dropped on Nagasaki, Japan, on August 9, 1945, killing as many as 150,000 people. The reactors are being dismantled, and the lands and waters are undergoing remediation.

★765★ HARBOR ISLAND NATIONAL WILDLIFE REFUGE

c/o Seney NWR
HCR 2 Box 1
Seney, MI 49883
Web: www.fws.gov/midwest/harborisland
Phone: 906-586-9851; Fax: 906-586-3800
Location: Northwest of Drummond Island in Potagannissing Bay on Lake Huron. Established: 1983. Habitat: 700-acre island with a marshy harbor, sandy beaches, and forest. Facilities: Trails. Activities: Fishing, swimming, hunting. Access: By boat only; open during daylight hours when weather permits. Primary Wildlife: A variety of birds and mammals, including fox, grouse, snowshoe hare, white-throated sparrow, gray jay, and eagles. Timber wolves may hunt in the refuge during the winter. Special Features: Harbor Island features mature stands of balsam fir, white cedar, paper birch, sugar maple and red oak.

★766★ HARRIS NECK NATIONAL WILDLIFE REFUGE

c/o Savannah Coastal Refuges Complex
1000 Business Center Dr, Suite 10
Savannah, GA 31405
Web: www.fws.gov/harrisneck
Phone: 912-832-4608; Fax: 912-832-4002
Location: 50 miles south of Savannah on the east coast of Georgia. Established: 1962. Habitat: 2,824 acres of saltwater marsh, grassland, mixed deciduous woods, and cropland. Facilities: Visitor contact station, trails, auto tour route (4 miles), fishing piers. Activities: Fishing, hiking, bicycling, hunting, educational programs. Access: Open during daylight hours. Some portions of the refuge may be closed seasonally to protect wildlife from human disturbance. Primary Wildlife: Egrets, herons, mallards, gadwalls, teals, wood storks, feral hogs, deer, alligators. Special Features: Boating access to refuge tidal waters and Blackbeard Island is available via public boat ramp located on the Barbour River (at the end of Harris Neck Road).

★767★ HART MOUNTAIN NATIONAL ANTELOPE REFUGE

PO Box 111
18 S G St
Lakeview, OR 97630
Web: www.fws.gov/sheldonhartmtn/Hart
Phone: 541-947-3315; Fax: 541-947-4414
Location: South-central Oregon, 68 miles northeast of Lakeview. Established: 1936. Habitat: 278,000 acres of high desert

See pages 22-23 for map of National Wildlife Refuges.

atop a ridge that rises an abrupt 3,000 feet on its west side and then slopes gently eastward. Terrain includes canyons, cliffs, steep slopes, and sharp crests, as well as low ridges, hills, and wide plains. **Facilities:** Visitor contact station, viewing sites, hiking trails, auto tour route, primitive campsites, historical features. **Activities:** Camping, bicycling, horseback riding, fishing, hiking, rockhounding, hunting. **Access:** Unlimited. **Primary Wildlife:** Pronghorn antelope, California bighorn sheep, mule deer, sage grouse, rattlesnakes, and sagebrush lizard. **Special Features:** Hart Mountain National Antelope Refuge is located on a massive fault block ridge that ascends abruptly nearly three-quarters of a mile above the Warner Valley floor in a series of rugged cliffs, steep slopes and knife-like ridges.

★768★ HATCHIE NATIONAL WILDLIFE REFUGE
6772 Hwy 76 S
Stanton, TN 38069
Web: www.fws.gov/hatchie
Phone: 731-772-0501; **Fax:** 731-772-7839
Location: Along the Hatchie Scenic River, 1 mile south of Brownsville, Tennessee. **Established:** 1964. **Habitat:** 11,556 acres of bottomland hardwood timber, agricultural land, timber uplands, shrub and wooded swamp, and open water. **Facilities:** Viewing sites, auto tour route. **Activities:** Canoeing, fishing, hiking, hunting, educational programs. **Access:** Daylight hours, year-round. Some parts of the refuge are closed to the public from November 15 to March 15 to provide sanctuary to waterfowl. **Primary Wildlife:** Migratory waterfowl, wading birds, shorebirds, deer, turkey, beaver, squirrels, and rabbits. **Special Features:** About 90 percent of the refuge lies within the floodplain of the Hatchie River. The Hatchie is the last unchannelized river of its type in the Lower Mississippi River Valley and still functions under near-normal wetland cycles.

★769★ HAVASU NATIONAL WILDLIFE REFUGE
PO Box 3009
Needles, CA 92363
Web: www.fws.gov/southwest/refuges/arizona/havasu
Phone: 760-326-3853; **Fax:** 760-326-5745
Location: On the Arizona side of the Colorado River, north of I-40. **Established:** 1941. **Habitat:** 37,515 acres of Topock marsh, Colorado River, backwater bays, desert mountains, and cliffs. **Facilities:** Visitor contact station, viewing sites, historic features, 3 boat launches, campground (concession). **Activities:** Boating, canoeing, water-skiing, jetskiing (with restriction), camping, fishing, hiking, hunting. **Access:** A small portion of Topock Marsh is closed to all entry from October through January to decrease disturbance to wildlife. **Primary Wildlife:** Endangered Yuma clapper rail, desert bighorn sheep, peregrine falcon, bald eagle, roadrunners and tanagers. **Special Features:** The refuge protects 30 river miles—300 miles of shoreline—from Needles, California, to Lake Havasu City, Arizona. Arizona's Desert Wilderness Act of 1990 and the California Desert Protection Act in 1994 together designated 17,606 acres, or 32 percent of the refuge, as wilderness.

★770★ HAWAIIAN ISLANDS NATIONAL WILDLIFE REFUGE
c/o Pacific Remote Islands NWR Complex
300 Ala Moana Blvd Rm 5-231, PO Box 50167
Honolulu, HI 96850
Web: www.fws.gov/pacificislands/wnwr/pnorthwestnwr.html
Phone: 808-792-9550; **Fax:** 808-792-9586
Location: A chain of nine islands, reefs, and atolls extending about 1,200 miles northwest from main Hawaiian Islands. **Established:** 1909. **Habitat:** 1,766 acres of emergent rocky islands, sandy islets, and rugged volcanic-remnant islands, and more than 600,000 of submerged lands. **Access:** Closed to public use. Special-use permits can be obtained for scientific research. **Primary Wildlife:** Endangered Laysan duck, Laysan finch, Nihoa finch and Nihoa millerbird, albatross, green and hawksbill sea turtles, O'ahu tree snail. **Special Features:** The refuge supports almost the entire population of the endangered Hawaiian monk seal and provides nesting beaches for virtually the entire Hawaiian population of threatened green sea turtles. Additionally, several thousand species of inshore tropical fish, algae, coral, and other marine organisms inhabit the marine habitat of the refuge.

★771★ HEWITT LAKE NATIONAL WILDLIFE REFUGE
c/o Bowdoin NWR
HC 65, Box 5700
Malta, MT 59538
Phone: 406-654-2863
Location: Northeastern Montana just west of Nelson Reservoir in Phillips County. **Established:** 1938. **Habitat:** 1,680 acres, comprising a shallow lake basin with little vegetation. **Activities:** Hunting. **Access:** Limited by private ownership of surrounding areas; call refuge office for specific details. **Primary Wildlife:** Migratory birds; also pronghorns and black-tailed prairie dogs. **Special Features:** A large shallow lake basin covers much of the refuge, with water absent some years. The alkaline nature of the lake precludes much vegetation growth.

★772★ HILLSIDE NATIONAL WILDLIFE REFUGE
1562 Providence Rd
Cruger, MS 38924
Web: www.fws.gov/hillside
Phone: 662-235-4989
Location: 13 miles north of Yazoo City, Mississippi. **Established:** 1975. **Habitat:** 15,572 acres of bottomland hardwoods, cypress sloughs, early successional reforested areas, croplands, ponds, and streams. **Facilities:** Viewing sites, hiking trails (&). **Activities:** Fishing, hunting, educational programs. **Access:** Year round during daylight hours. **Primary Wildlife:** Waterfowl and other migratory birds, including hooded mergansers, killdeer, snipe, sandpipers, yellowlegs, white-tailed deer, squirrel, rabbit, and American alligator. **Special Features:** As one of the largest forested tracts in the Mississippi Delta, the refuge provides important stop-over and nesting habitat for neotropical migratory birds.

See pages 22-23 for map of National Wildlife Refuges.

★773★ **HOBE SOUND NATIONAL WILDLIFE REFUGE**
PO Box 645
Hobe Sound, FL 33475
Web: hobesound.fws.gov
Phone: 772-546-6141; **Fax:** 772-546-7572
Location: In Martin County, off the east coast of Florida. **Established:** 1969. **Habitat:** 967 acres of beach, sand dunes, and mangroves on Jupiter Island and a sand pine scrub forest on the mainland. **Facilities:** Visitor center, viewing sites, trail, boat launch, nature center, museum. **Activities:** Fishing, hiking, educational programs. **Access:** Daylight hours year round. **Primary Wildlife:** Sea turtles, brown pelicans, ospreys, and a variety of shorebirds and songbirds. **Special Features:** One of the most productive sea turtle nesting areas in the United States, the refuge provides habitat to the endangered leatherback, green, and threatened loggerhead sea turtles.

★774★ **HOLLA BEND NATIONAL WILDLIFE REFUGE**
10448 Holla Bend Rd
Dardanelle, AR 72834
Web: www.fws.gov/southeast/hollabend
Phone: 479-229-4300; **Fax:** 479-229-4302
Location: 6 miles south of Dardanelle, Arkansas. **Established:** 1957. **Habitat:** 7,057 acres of farm fields, shallow water impoundments, and river channel. **Facilities:** Visitor contact station, boat ramps, auto tour route, trail, observation tower. **Activities:** Boating, canoeing, fishing, hunting, hiking. **Access:** Open year round during daylight hours. **Primary Wildlife:** Mallard, pintail, teal, wigeon, gadwall, and Canada and snow geese. Also provides habitat for white-tailed deer, turkey, bobcat, and coyote. **Special Features:** Refuge lies along the Arkansas River and is bounded by an old oxbow lake that was created when the U.S. Army Corps of Engineers cut a channel through the bend in the river to promote navigation and flood control.

★775★ **HOPPER MOUNTAIN NATIONAL WILDLIFE REFUGE**
PO Box 5839
Ventura, CA 93005
Web: www.fws.gov/hoppermountain/Hopper
Phone: 805-644-5185; **Fax:** 805-644-1732
Location: Northeast of Fillmore, California. **Established:** 1974. **Habitat:** 2,471 acres of rugged mountains, rock outcroppings, chaparral, hardwood groves, and open grasslands. **Access:** Closed to visitation. **Primary Wildlife:** California condor and other birds. **Special Features:** Area is a traditional feeding site for the endangered California condor. From October through May, the birds can occasionally be seen from observation points in the Los Padres National Forest (see entry in national forest section).

★776★ **HORICON NATIONAL WILDLIFE REFUGE**
W4279 Headquarters Rd
Mayville, WI 53050
Web: www.fws.gov/midwest/horicon
Phone: 920-387-2658
Location: 6 miles east of Waupun, Wisconsin. **Established:** 1941. **Habitat:** 21,417 acres of hemi-marsh surrounded by grasslands. **Facilities:** Visitor center, picnic area, viewing sites, hiking trails, auto tour route. **Activities:** Fishing, hiking, bicycling, cross-country skiing, hunting, educational programs. **Access:** Open from dawn to dusk. **Primary Wildlife:** Canada geese, herons, egrets, ducks, snapping turtles, river otters, and white-tailed deer. **Special Features:** Horicon Marsh, covering 32,000 acres, is the largest freshwater cattail marsh in the United States.

★777★ **HULEIA NATIONAL WILDLIFE REFUGE**
c/o Kilauea Point NWR
PO Box 1128
Kilauea, HI 96754
Web: www.fws.gov/pacificislands/wnwr/khuleianwr.html
Phone: 808-828-1413; **Fax:** 808-828-1414
Location: Kauai's north shore. **Established:** 1973. **Habitat:** 241 acres located in a relatively flat valley bordered by steep wooded hillside. **Access:** Not open to the public. **Primary Wildlife:** Endangered Koloa (Hawaiian ducks), Hawaiian moorhen, Hawaiian coot, and the Hawaiian stilt. **Special Features:** Refuge protects the largest population of Koloa (Hawaiian ducks) found on Kauai, which may be viewed from the Menehune Fish Pond overlook along Hulemalu Road out of Nawiliwili.

★778★ **HUMBOLDT BAY NATIONAL WILDLIFE REFUGE**
1020 Ranch Rd
Loleta, CA 95551
Web: www.fws.gov/humboldtbay
Phone: 707-733-5406
Location: On the northern California coast, near the cities of Arcata and Eureka. **Established:** 1971. **Habitat:** 3,700 acres of diked marshes, seasonal wetlands, salt marshes, mudflats, and open water. **Facilities:** Visitor contact station, viewing sites, interpretive trails. **Activities:** Boating, canoeing, fishing, hunting, hiking. **Access:** Open during daylight hours. **Primary Wildlife:** Waterfowl (including black brant and shorebirds), peregrine falcon, bald eagle, brown pelican, western snowy plover, Humboldt Bay wallflower and beach layia. **Special Features:** One of the largest remaining eelgrass beds south of Washington, Humboldt Bay is an important spawning, nursery, and feeding area for fish and other marine life. In winter, it is not unusual for more than 100,000 birds to use the Bay as a feeding and resting spot.

★779★ **HURON NATIONAL WILDLIFE REFUGE**
c/o Seney NWR
1674 Refuge Entrance Rd
Seney, MI 49883
Web: www.fws.gov/refuges/profiles/index.cfm?id=31511
Phone: 906-586-9851; **Fax:** 906-586-3800
Location: In Lake Superior, southeast of Michigan's Keweenaw Peninsula. **Established:** 1905. **Habitat:** 147 acres on 8 islands with habitats of ground-level vegetation, sparse red pines and white birch, and barren granite with scattered lichen growth. **Facilities:** Trails, historic features. **Activities:** Boating, fishing.

See pages 22-23 for map of National Wildlife Refuges.

Access: Only West Huron Island (Lighthouse Island) is open for public visitation. **Primary Wildlife:** Herring gulls, merlins, bald eagles, and gulls. **Special Features:** West Huron Island includes a lighthouse that was built in 1868 and is listed in the *National Register of Historic Places.*

★780★ HUTTON LAKE NATIONAL WILDLIFE REFUGE

c/o Arapaho NWR
953 Jackson County Rd 32
Walden, CO 80480
Web: www.fws.gov/refuges/profiles/index.cfm?id=65522
Phone: 970-723-8202; **Fax:** 970-723-8202
Location: 12 miles southwest of Laramie in southeastern Wyoming. **Established:** 1932. **Habitat:** 1,968 acres of greasewood/grassland uplands and 560 acres of open water and marsh. **Facilities:** Auto tour route, boat launch. **Access:** Daylight hours when weather permits. **Primary Wildlife:** Migratory waterfowl, shorebirds, raptors, pronghorn, and endangered Wyoming toad. **Special Features:** Site includes a semicircle of five small lakes: Hutton, Creighton, George, Rush, and Hoge.

★781★ IMPERIAL NATIONAL WILDLIFE REFUGE

PO Box 72217
Yuma, AZ 85365
Web: www.fws.gov/southwest/refuges/arizona/imperial.html
Phone: 928-783-3371; **Fax:** 928-783-0652
Location: North of Yuma, Arizona. **Established:** 1941. **Habitat:** 25,768 acres of desert uplands and riparian wetlands along 30 miles of the lower Colorado River in Arizona and California, including the last unchannelized section before the river enters Mexico. **Facilities:** Visitor center, observation tower, hiking trails, auto tour route, historic features. **Activities:** Boating, canoeing, fishing, hiking, hunting. **Access:** Most areas are open 24 hours a day year round. **Primary Wildlife:** Waterfowl, marsh and waterbirds, shorebirds, songbirds, mule deer, and desert bighorn sheep. **Special Features:** Wetland wildlife is most abundant in winter when /snowbirds' such as cinnamon teal and northern pintail use the refuge. During the summer months, visitors are likely to see permanent residents such as great egrets and muskrat. At dawn and dusk, desert bighorn sheep and mule deer can be seen near the river.

★782★ INNOKO NATIONAL WILDLIFE REFUGE

PO Box 69
McGrath, AK 99627
Web: innoko.fws.gov
Phone: 907-524-3251; **Fax:** 907-524-3141; **Toll Free:** 888-601-7970
Location: 300 miles northwest of Anchorage in the central Yukon River Valley. **Established:** 1980. **Habitat:** Two separate sections totaling 3.85 million acres. Half the refuge is made up of black spruce muskeg, wet meadows, and sedge or horsetail marshes with lakes and ponds. The other half is marked by hills of less than 1,000 feet. **Facilities:** Visitor contact station, primitive campsites. **Activities:** Camping, kayaking, river floating, fishing, hiking, hunting. **Access:** Primary means of access is by privately-owned aircraft, commercial guiding and outfitting

services, and commercial air taxi operators. Not accessible by car; and, due to the refuge's remote and isolated location, access by watercraft is usually not practical. **Primary Wildlife:** Canada geese, pintail, wigeon, shoveler, scaup, scoters, and red-necked grebes. Also provides habitat for salmon, Canada lynx, bear, moose, and wolf. **Special Features:** A float trip on the Innoko River offers excellent opportunities to view wildlife. Sport hunting for moose and black bear is popular, and fishing for northern pike is excellent.

★783★ IROQUOIS NATIONAL WILDLIFE REFUGE

1101 Casey Rd
Alabama, NY 14013
Web: www.fws.gov/northeast/iroquois
Phone: 585-948-5445
Location: Midway between Buffalo and Rochester, New York. **Established:** 1958. **Habitat:** 10,818 acres of marsh, wooded swamp, wet meadows, pasture, cropland, and upland forest. **Facilities:** Visitor contact station, viewing sites, trails. **Activities:** Canoeing, fishing, frogging, hunting, educational programs. **Access:** Open from dawn to dusk. Portions are closed from March to mid-July during waterfowl nesting season. **Primary Wildlife:** Waterfowl, wading birds, shorebirds, deer, fox, turkey, and frogs. **Special Features:** The refuge is located within the historic Oak Orchard Swamp, known locally as the "Alabama Swamp."

★784★ ISLAND BAY NATIONAL WILDLIFE REFUGE

c/o J. N. "Ding" Darling NWR Complex
1 Wildlife Dr
Sanibel, FL 33957
Web: www.fws.gov/southeast/islandbay
Phone: 239-472-1100; **Fax:** 239-472-4061
Location: On the north side of Charlotte Harbor in Turtle Bay, southwest of Punta Gorda, Florida. **Established:** 1908. **Habitat:** Six undeveloped tracts of land located in a complex mangrove islands surrounded by brackish waters. The land totals 20 acres. **Activities:** Boating, saltwater fishing. **Access:** Year round; accessible by boat only. **Primary Wildlife:** Shorebirds, gulls, and terns. Also, raccoons, marsh rabbits, manatees, sea turtles, American crocodile, bald eagle, wood stork and east indigo snake. **Special Features:** Administered as a satellite of the J.N. "Ding" Darling NWR (see separate entry). Occasionally, boaters visit some of the islands with uplands such as Bull Key, but mosquitoes are usually so numerous that visiting any of the islands is extremely uncomfortable.

★785★ IZEMBEK NATIONAL WILDLIFE REFUGE

PO Box 127
Cold Bay, AK 99571
Web: izembek.fws.gov
Phone: 907-532-2445; **Fax:** 907-532-2549
Location: Tip of the Alaska Peninsula. **Established:** 1960 as Izembek National Wildlife Range; became Izembek NWR in 1980. **Habitat:** 417,533 acres of lakes, rivers, valleys, glaciers, snowfields, thermal springs, active volcanoes, and an estuary.

See pages 22-23 for map of National Wildlife Refuges.

Facilities: Visitor contact station. **Activities:** Camping (no designated campsites), boating, kayaking, fishing, hiking, hunting. **Access:** Refuge headquarters is located in Cold Bay, a small remote community accessible only by aircraft or the state marine ferry system, which serves Cold Bay once a month from May to October. Limited vehicle access to the refuge is via 40 miles of gravel roads and trails; aircraft or boats are required for access elsewhere within the refuge. **Primary Wildlife:** Black brant, Canada geese, emperor geese, Steller's eiders, tundra swan, harbor seals, sea otters, sea lions, whales, brown bears, caribou and salmon. **Special Features:** Refuge protects the watershed of Izembek Lagoon, an estuary containing one of the largest eelgrass beds in the world, which serves as an international crossroad to migrating waterfowl and shorebirds. The world's population of Pacific brant, thousands of Canada geese, and other waterfowl congregate on the lagoon from late August through early November. Each spring and fall the entire population of emperor geese migrate through Izembek, with several thousand wintering here.

★786★ J. CLARK SALYER NATIONAL WILDLIFE REFUGE

PO Box 66
Upham, ND 58789
Web: www.fws.gov/jclarksalyer
Phone: 701-768-2548
Location: Along the lower reaches of the Souris River in north-central North Dakota. **Established:** 1935. **Habitat:** 58,700 acres of freshwater marshland. **Facilities:** Visitor contact station, viewing sites, trails, auto tour route, canoe trail. **Activities:** Canoeing, fishing, hunting, educational programs. **Access:** Open daily, 5am - 10pm. **Primary Wildlife:** Waterfowl, including Canada geese, gadwall, blue-winged teal, and mallard. Also provides habitat for butterflies, beaver, mink, raccoon, deer, and porcupine. **Special Features:** An important feeding and resting area on the Central Flyway, the refuge has developed into one of the most important duck production areas in the United States.

★787★ J. N. "DING" DARLING NATIONAL WILDLIFE REFUGE

1 Wildlife Dr
Sanibel, FL 33957
Web: dingdarling.fws.gov
Phone: 239-472-1100; **Fax:** 239-472-4061
Location: On Florida's west coast; 15 miles southwest of Ft. Myers, Florida, on Sanibel Island. **Established:** 1945. **Habitat:** 6,354 acres of mangrove forest, submerged seagrass beds, cordgrass marshes and West Indian hardwood hammocks. **Facilities:** Visitor center, canoe and kayak rentals, boat launches, auto tour route (5 miles), trails, observation tower, pavilion, historic features. **Activities:** Boating, canoeing, fishing, hiking, bicycling, educational programs, tram tours. **Access:** Open daily during daylight hours. **Primary Wildlife:** American crocodile, West Indian manatee, eastern indigo snake, and sea turtles. Also provides habitat for a wide diversity of shore birds, wading birds, waterfowl, wood stork, peregrine falcon, American alligator, and bald eagle. **Special Features:** Named after political cartoonist who was one of the pioneers of the conservation movement.

Darling is credited as one of the key people in the establishment of the National Wildlife Refuge System.

★788★ JAMES CAMPBELL NATIONAL WILDLIFE REFUGE

c/o Oahu NWR Complex
66-590 Kam Hwy, Room 2C
Haleiwa, HI 96712
Web: pacificislands.fws.gov/wnwr/ojamesnwr.html
Phone: 808-637-6330; **Fax:** 808-637-3578
Location: On Oahu's north shore in Haleiwa. **Established:** 1976. **Habitat:** 164 acres made up of a mix of naturally occurring spring-fed marsh and man-made ponds and impoundments. **Facilities:** Visitor contact station. **Activities:** Educational tours (by prior arrangement). **Access:** Open to the public from the third Saturday in October through the third Saturday in February. Guided tours are available. **Primary Wildlife:** Endangered Hawaiian moorhen, Hawaiian coot, and Hawaiian stilt. Also provides habitat for the Koloa (Hawaiian duck) and black-crowned night herons. **Special Features:** The refuge encompasses Punanmano Pond, a naturally occurring, spring-fed marsh, and man-made ponds formerly used as sugar cane waste settling basins.

★789★ JAMES RIVER NATIONAL WILDLIFE REFUGE

c/o Eastern Virginia Rivers NWR Complex
PO Box 1030, 336 Wilna Rd
Warsaw, VA 22572
Web: www.fws.gov/refuges/profiles/index.cfm?id=51621
Phone: 804-333-1470; **Fax:** 804-333-3396
Location: Beside the James River, southeast of Richmond, Virginia. **Established:** 1991. **Habitat:** 4,200 acres of river and riparian areas with upland hardwood forests of elm, gum, and oak, and softwood loblolly pine. **Facilities:** None. **Activities:** Hunting, hiking. **Access:** By reservation only. **Primary Wildlife:** Bald eagles, songbirds, raptors, shad, striped bass, beaver, red fox, and opossum. **Special Features:** Refuge is the largest summer roosting area for juvenile bald eagles east of the Mississippi River. As many as 2,000 eagles visit the refuge over the course of the summer. The refuge also provides a year-round roosting area for both mature and immature bald eagles and includes several bald eagle nests.

★790★ JOHN H. CHAFEE NATIONAL WILDLIFE REFUGE AT PETTAQUAMSCUTT COVE

c/o Rhode Island NWR Complex
PO Box 307
Charlestown, RI 02813
Web: www.fws.gov/refuges/profiles/index.cfm?id=53547
Phone: 401-364-9124
Location: In the towns of Narragansett and South Kingstown, Rhode Island. **Established:** 1988 as Pettaquamscutt Cove NWR; renamed in 1999. **Habitat:** 317 acres of salt marshes, tidal sandflats, grasslands, and shrub land. **Activities:** Saltwater fishing, environmental education. **Access:** Year round during daylight hours; not readily accessible by road, boat or kayak is the best way to get there. **Primary Wildlife:** Important migration and wintering habitat for a variety of waterfowl and other birds,

See pages 22-23 for map of National Wildlife Refuges.

including wading birds, shorebirds such as plovers and sandpipers, and osprey. **Special Features:** The refuge has been identified as the most important black duck migration and wintering habitat in Rhode Island.

★791★ JOHN HAY NATIONAL WILDLIFE REFUGE

c/o Great Bay NWR
336 Nimble Hill Rd
Newington, NH 03255
Web: www.thefells.org
Phone: 603-763-4789
Location: In New Hampshire, 30 miles west of Concord. **Established:** 1987. **Habitat:** 164 acres of forested hardwood uplands scattered with stands of white and red pine, hemlock, and spruce. **Facilities:** Trail, historic features. **Activities:** Educational programs, hiking, wildlife watching. **Access:** Trail is available for public use. **Primary Wildlife:** Migratory birds, white-tailed deer, black bear, ruffed grouse, and pileated woodpeckers. **Special Features:** Occupies the estate of John Hay, personal secretary to President Abraham Lincoln and Secretary of State under presidents William McKinley and Theodore Roosevelt. The historic buildings, grounds, and gardens, known as ''The Fells,'' are managed through an agreement with the Friends of John Hay NWR.

★792★ JOHN HEINZ NATIONAL WILDLIFE REFUGE AT TINICUM

8601 Lindbergh Blvd
Philadelphia, PA 19153
Web: www.fws.gov/northeast/heinz
Phone: 215-365-3118
Location: In Philadelphia and Delaware counties, one mile from the Philadelphia International Airport. **Established:** 1972 (as Tinicum National Environmental Center); renamed in 1991. **Habitat:** 1,200 acres (when acquisitions are complete) of freshwater tidal marsh, impoundments, upland fields, meadows, and woods. **Facilities:** Visitor contact station, observation platform (♿), trails, exhibits. **Activities:** Canoeing, fishing, hiking, bicycling, educational programs. **Access:** Open from dawn to dusk. **Primary Wildlife:** Waterfowl, sandpipers, herons, egrets, fox, deer, muskrat, turtles, fish, and frogs. **Special Features:** Refuge is a resting and feeding area for more than 280 species of birds, 80 of which nest here. Site also provides habitat for Pennsylvania's endangered red-bellied turtle and the coastal plain leopard frog.

★793★ JOHNSTON ISLAND NATIONAL WILDLIFE REFUGE

300 Ala Moana Blvd, Rm 5-231 Box 50167
Honolulu, HI 96850
Web: www.fws.gov/pacificislands/wnwr/pjohnsnwr.html
Phone: 808-792-9550; **Fax:** 808-792-9586
Location: 717 nautical miles west-southwest of Honolulu. **Established:** 1926. **Habitat:** Approximately 696 acres of land on four coral islands and a 9-mile-long emergent reef. **Access:** Closed to public access. **Primary Wildlife:** 14 species of seabirds including shearwaters, petrels, tropicbirds, frigatebirds, boobies, tern, and noddies; also three species of marine animals:

green sea turtle, Hawaiian monk seal, and humpback whale. **Special Features:** In an area with hundreds of thousands of square miles of open ocean, Johnston Atoll is the only shallow water and dry land, offering an oasis for reef and bird life. There are 33 known species of coral here.

★794★ JULIA BUTLER HANSEN REFUGE FOR THE COLUMBIAN WHITE-TAILED DEER

46 Steamboat Slough Rd
PO Box 566
Cathlamet, WA 98612
Web: www.fws.gov/willapa/JuliaButlerHansen
Phone: 360-795-3915
Location: In western Washington and Oregon. **Established:** 1972. **Habitat:** 6,000 acres of pastures, forested tidal swamps, brushy woodlots, marshes, and sloughs. **Facilities:** Viewing sites, boat launch. **Activities:** Boating, fishing, hiking, migratory bird hunting. **Access:** Open daily from dawn to dusk. **Primary Wildlife:** White-tailed deer, elk, swans, Canada geese, painted turtle, red-legged frogs, bald eagles and ospreys. **Special Features:** By the turn of the twentieth century, the Columbian white-tailed deer had disappeared from nearly all of its range, and in the 1930s it was thought to be extinct. Remnant populations were subsequently discovered, and the refuge was established with 230 of the remaining deer. The current population along the lower Columbia River is thought to be fewer than 800 animals, of which about half live on the refuge.

★795★ KAKAHAIA NATIONAL WILDLIFE REFUGE

c/o Maui NWR Complex
PO Box 1042
Kihei, HI 96753
Web: www.fws.gov/pacificislands/wnwr/mkakahaianwr.html
Phone: 808-875-1582; **Fax:** 808-875-2945
Location: 5 miles east of Kaunakakai along the south coast of Molokai. **Established:** 1977. **Habitat:** 44 acres of freshwater pond and marsh. **Activities:** Group educational tours (by prior arrangement). **Access:** Not open to the public except by special use permit. **Primary Wildlife:** Endangered Hawaiian coot and Hawaiian stilt. **Special Features:** Scenic coastline is a popular picnicking and shoreline fishing spot for local residents.

★796★ KANUTI NATIONAL WILDLIFE REFUGE

101 12th Ave, Rm 262
Fairbanks, AK 99701
Web: kanuti.fws.gov
Phone: 907-456-0329; **Fax:** 907-456-0428
Location: Inside the Arctic Circle, about 150 air miles northwest of Fairbanks. **Established:** 1980. **Habitat:** 1.6 million acres of streams, wetlands, muskeg, lakes, birch and poplar meadows, and boreal forests. **Facilities:** Visitor center. **Activities:** Camping (no designated campsites), boating, canoeing, river floating, hiking, fishing, hunting, flightseeing. **Access:** No road access. Refuge's headquarters and visitor center, shared with the National Park Service, is located in the small community of Bettles, which usually can be reached by commercial airline from Fairbanks. Visitors can also access the refuge during the summer and early fall via float trips from Dalton Highway, which runs

See pages 22-23 for map of National Wildlife Refuges.

4. National Wildlife Refuges

just east of the refuge. **Primary Wildlife:** 130 species of birds and 37 species of mammals including bears, wolves, moose, wolverine, beavers, muskrats, marten, and mink. Also migratory fish: sheefish and chinook, chum, and coho salmon. **Special Features:** The region's typically short, hot summers give rise to numerous thunderstorms and lightning strikes. This results in a continuous cycle of burn and recovery that creates diverse habitats with different plant species and levels of maturity within each species. The resulting mosaic of habitat types supports a unusually wide variety of wildlife.

★797★ KEALIA POND NATIONAL WILDLIFE REFUGE

c/o Maui NWR Complex
PO Box 1042
Kehei, HI 96753
Web: www.fws.gov/pacificislands/wnwr/mkealianwr.html
Phone: 808-875-1582
Location: Adjacent to Maalaea Bay, along the south-central coast of Maui. **Established:** 1992. **Habitat:** 700 acres of wetlands. **Facilities:** Visitor contact station, viewing sites, boardwalk trail. **Activities:** Educational programs, hiking, wildlife observation. **Access:** Year round during daylight hours. **Primary Wildlife:** Endangered Hawaiian stilt and Hawaiian coot, wintering migratory waterfowl, shorebirds; also provides nesting ground for the endangered hawksbill turtle. **Special Features:** In summer, the pond often shrinks to less than half its winter size, leaving a crust of pure crystalline salt at its margins. Kealia means "the salt-encrusted place," and Hawaiians gathered salt here for centuries.

★798★ KELLYS SLOUGH NATIONAL WILDLIFE REFUGE

c/o Devils Lake WMD
221 2nd St
Devils Lake, ND 58301
Web: www.fws.gov/refuges/profiles/index.cfm?id=62583
Phone: 701-662-8611
Location: 8 miles west of Grand Forks, North Dakota. **Established:** 1936. **Habitat:** 1,867 acres of wetlands and grasslands. **Facilities:** Viewing sites, hiking trails, auto tour route. **Activities:** Hiking, hunting, trapping, wildlife observation. **Access:** Daylight hours. **Primary Wildlife:** Migrating waterfowl, shorebirds, Canada geese, mallards, gadwalls, scaup, red fox, raccoon, and white-tailed deer. **Special Features:** Refuge provides important breeding grounds for migratory waterfowl and other wildlife.

★799★ KENAI NATIONAL WILDLIFE REFUGE

PO Box 2139
Soldotna, AK 99669
Web: kenai.fws.gov
Phone: 907-262-7021; **Fax:** 907-262-3599
Location: South-central Alaska on the Kenai Peninsula, 110 miles south of Anchorage. **Established:** 1941 (as Kenai National Moose Range); designated a NWR in 1980. **Habitat:** 2 million acres of ice fields and glaciers, forest, tundra, lakes, wetlands, rivers. **Facilities:** Visitor center, campsites, cabins, picnic areas,

viewing sites, trails, auto tour route, canoe trail. **Activities:** Camping, boating, fishing, hiking, horseback riding, hunting, cross-country skiing, snowmobiling, educational programs. **Access:** Open 24 hours a day; accessible from Sterling Highway. Developed facilities are available year round for day and overnight camping. **Primary Wildlife:** Moose, Dall sheep, mountain goat, caribou, coyote, wolf, bear, trumpeter swan, lynx, wolverine, and beaver. **Special Features:** The refuge is referred to as a "miniature Alaska" as it contains every major Alaskan habitat. The cultural history of the Peninsula spans 10,000 years and includes five distinct cultural traditions, with both Indian and Eskimo occupations.

★800★ KERN NATIONAL WILDLIFE REFUGE

PO Box 670
Delano, CA 93216
Web: natureali.org/KNWR.htm
Phone: 661-725-2767
Location: 18 miles west of Delano, in south-central California. **Established:** 1960. **Habitat:** 11,249 acres which include natural valley grasslands and developed marsh. **Facilities:** Visitor contact station, auto tour route. **Activities:** Hunting, wildlife observation. **Access:** Open daily, from dawn to dusk. **Primary Wildlife:** Migratory wildfowl and shorebirds, as well as endangered Buena Vista Lake shrew, San Joaquin kit fox, and the blunt-nosed leopard lizard. **Special Features:** Refuge provides suitable habitat for several endangered species and preserves a remnant example of the historic valley uplands in the San Joaquin Desert.

★801★ KEY CAVE NATIONAL WILDLIFE REFUGE

c/o Wheeler NWR
2700 Refuge Headquarters Rd
Decatur, AL 35603
Web: www.fws.gov/keycave
Phone: 256-353-7243; **Fax:** 256-340-9728
Location: 5 miles southwest of Florence in Lauderdale County, Alabama. **Established:** 1997. **Habitat:** 1,060 acres of hardwood forests, croplands, and a 38-acre sinkhole lake. **Facilities:** Undeveloped. **Activities:** Hiking, hunting, wildlife observation. **Access:** Open to public; entry into cave for research by permit only. **Primary Wildlife:** Alabama cavefish and gray bat. **Special Features:** Refuge protects habitat for only known population of the Alabama cavefish.

★802★ KEY WEST NATIONAL WILDLIFE REFUGE

c/o National Key Deer Refuge
179 Key Deer Blvd
Big Pine Key, FL 33043
Web: southeast.fws.gov/KeyWest
Phone: 305-872-2239; **Fax:** 305-872-2154
Location: West of Key West, Florida. **Established:** 1908. **Habitat:** Unpopulated mangrove islands totaling 189,497 acres with some sandy beaches, dunes, saltmarsh, and coastal berm hammocks, along with seagrass and coral reef communities. **Facilities:** Visitor contact station (on Big Pine Key). **Activities:** Boating, fishing, snorkeling, diving. **Access:** By boat only; portions of some islands are closed. **Primary Wildlife:** Wading birds,

See pages 22-23 for map of National Wildlife Refuges.

sea turtles. **Special Features:** All of the islands in the refuge are designated as part of the Wilderness Preservation System, and are managed to minimize human impact and influence.

★803★ KILAUEA POINT NATIONAL WILDLIFE REFUGE

PO Box 1128
Kilauea, HI 96754
Web: pacificislands.fws.gov/wnwr/kkilaueanwr.html
Phone: 808-828-1413; **Fax:** 808-828-1414
Location: On the north coast of Kauai, 1 mile north of Kilauea. **Established:** 1985. **Habitat:** 203 acres of cliffs and headlands jutting up to 200 feet above the surf. **Facilities:** Visitor center, viewing sites, trails, historic features. **Activities:** Educational programs, hiking, wildlife observation. **Access:** Open daily, 10am - 4pm. **Primary Wildlife:** Wedge-tailed shearwaters, red-footed boobies, Hawaiian monk seals, and the endangered nene or Hawaiian Goose, which is the state bird of Hawaii. **Special Features:** Refuge houses the historic Kilauea Lighthouse. Visitors may spot great frigatebirds, brown boobies, red-tailed and white-tailed tropicbirds, and Laysan albatrosses. Humpback whales and dolphins can often be sighted in the water off the Point.

★804★ KIRTLANDS WARBLER NATIONAL WILDLIFE REFUGE

c/o Seney NWR
1674 Refuge Entrance Rd
Seney, MI 49883
Web: www.fws.gov/refuges/profiles/index.cfm?id=31513
Phone: 906-586-9851; **Fax:** 906-586-3800
Location: Scattered across eight counties at 119 sites in the northern lower peninsula of Michigan. **Established:** Early 1980s. **Habitat:** 6,684 acres of jack pine growing on Grayling sands. **Facilities:** Viewing sites. **Activities:** Hunting, wildlife observation, birding tours. **Access:** Open during daylight hours. **Primary Wildlife:** Kirtland's warbler (endangered), spruce grouse, Nashville warbler, yellow-rumped warbler, eastern towhee, eastern bluebird, black-backed woodpecker, and brown thrasher. **Special Features:** Site is the only known nesting area of one of the world's rarest birds, the Kirtland's warbler, a small, blue-gray and yellow songbird.

★805★ KIRWIN NATIONAL WILDLIFE REFUGE

702 E Xavier Rd
Kirwin, KS 67644
Web: www.fws.gov/kirwin
Phone: 785-543-6673
Location: North-central Kansas. **Established:** 1954. **Habitat:** 10,778 acres of tallgrass prairie, shortgrass plains, riparian forest, wetlands, cropland and open water. **Facilities:** Visitor center, viewing sites, hiking trail, auto tour route. **Activities:** Fishing, hiking, hunting, educational programs. **Access:** Unlimited. **Primary Wildlife:** Waterfowl, waterbirds, shorebirds, rabbits, fox squirrels, black-tailed prairie dogs, and white-tailed deer. **Special Features:** In perfect conditions, the refuge can support approximately one million ducks and geese. Hundreds of great blue herons and double-crested cormorants nest in the flooded

timber under high water conditions, while interior least terns nest in times of low water.

★806★ KLAMATH MARSH NATIONAL WILDLIFE REFUGE

HC 63 Box 303
Chiloquin, OR 97624
Web: www.fws.gov/klamathbasinrefuges/klamathmarsh/
klamathmarsh.html
Phone: 541-783-3380
Location: 45 miles north of Klamath Falls, Oregon. **Established:** 1958 as Klamath Forest NWR. **Habitat:** 40,646 acres of marshes and grasslands with surrounding forests. **Facilities:** Visitor contact station, viewing sites, hiking trails, canoe trail, auto route. **Activities:** Canoeing, fishing, hunting, hiking, wildlife observation. **Access:** Open during daylight hours. **Primary Wildlife:** Sandhill cranes, white pelican, bald eagle, peregrine falcon, Great gray owl, Rocky Mountain elk, and spotted frog. **Special Features:** Refuge is named for the historic Klamath Marsh, which lies entirely within refuge boundaries. Its pine forests support diverse wildlife, including great gray owl and Rocky Mountain elk. The refuge appears to be one of the last remaining strongholds of the spotted frog, a candidate for the endangered species list.

★807★ KODIAK NATIONAL WILDLIFE REFUGE

1390 Buskin River Rd
Kodiak, AK 99615
Web: kodiak.fws.gov
Phone: 907-487-2600; **Fax:** 907-487-2144; **Toll Free:** 888-408-3514
Location: On the island of Kodiak, off the coast of southwestern Alaska. **Established:** 1941. **Habitat:** 1.932 million acres of lakes, marshes, bogs, and meadows. **Facilities:** Visitor center, cabins. **Activities:** Camping, boating, canoeing, rafting, fishing, hiking, hunting, educational programs. **Access:** Unlimited except by weather. Kodiak Island is served by commercial flights and Alaska State Ferry. **Primary Wildlife:** Brown bear, red fox, river otter, short-tailed weasel, little brown bat, tundra vole, eagle, mountain goat, Roosevelt elk, and salmon. **Special Features:** Refuge encompasses about two-thirds of Kodiak Island. In addition, the refuge includes a 50,000-acre portion of Afognak Island to the north of Kodiak Island.

★808★ KOFA NATIONAL WILDLIFE REFUGE

356 W 1st St
Yuma, AZ 85364
Web: southwest.fws.gov/refuges/arizona/kofa.html
Phone: 928-783-7861; **Fax:** 928-783-8611
Location: Northeast of Yuma, Arizona, in the Sonoran Desert. **Established:** 1939. **Habitat:** 665,400 acres of desert, with two small but steep and rugged mountain ranges. **Facilities:** Visitor contact station, hiking trails, primitive campgrounds. **Activities:** Camping, hiking, hunting, rockhounding (in limited area). **Access:** Open 24 hours. **Primary Wildlife:** Desert bighorn sheep, white-winged dove, desert tortoise, and desert kit fox. **Special Features:** Two mountain ranges dominate the landscape—the Kofa Mountains and the Castle Dome Mountains. Although

See pages 22-23 for map of National Wildlife Refuges.

not especially high, both ranges are extremely rugged and rise sharply from the surrounding desert plains, providing ideal big-horn sheep country.

★809★ KOOTENAI NATIONAL WILDLIFE REFUGE

HCR 60 Box 283
Bonners Ferry, ID 83805
Web: kootenai.fws.gov
Phone: 208-267-3888; **Fax:** 208-267-5570
Location: In Idaho's panhandle, 20 miles from the Canadian border. **Established:** 1964. **Habitat:** 2,774 acres of wetlands, meadows, riparian forests and agricultural fields. **Facilities:** Visitor contact station (&), viewing sites (&), photo blinds, trails (&), auto tour route (4.5 miles). **Activities:** Fishing, hunting, hiking, cross-country skiing, ice skating, educational programs. **Access:** Open daily during daylight hours. **Primary Wildlife:** Migratory waterfowl, including mallards, northern pintails, American wigeons, tundra swans, and Canada geese. Also provides habitat for mule and white-tailed deer, elk, moose, yellow pine chipmunk, western jumping mouse, and black bear. **Special Features:** Several marked trails provide views of wildlife habitats and access to observation points and photo blinds. 220 species of birds and 45 species of mammals have been observed in the refuge.

★810★ KOYUKUK NATIONAL WILDLIFE REFUGE

101 Front St
Galena, AK 99741
Web: koyukuk.fws.gov
Phone: 907-656-1231; **Fax:** 907-656-1706; **Toll Free:** 800-656-1231
Location: 270 miles west of Fairbanks, in the central Yukon Valley. **Established:** 1980. **Habitat:** Nearly 4 million acres of wetlands, boreal forest, and tundra. **Facilities:** Visitor contact station, historical features. **Activities:** Camping, boating, fishing, hiking, hunting, educational programs. **Access:** Unlimited except by weather; access is by boat, aircraft, or snowmobile. **Primary Wildlife:** Raptors including the bald eagle. Also provides habitat for owl, trumpeter swan, white-fronted goose, American wigeon, mallard, northern pintail, northern shoveler, lynx, black and grizzly bears, wolves, moose, and caribou. **Special Features:** Caribou from the migratory western arctic herd, which numbers more than 450,000, often move into the northern-most reaches of the refuge in winter. The refuge also supports a resident, non-migratory caribou population, the Galena Mountain herd, which numbers about 300.

★811★ LACASSINE NATIONAL WILDLIFE REFUGE

209 Nature Rd
Lake Arthur, LA 70549
Web: www.fws.gov/refuges/profiles/index.cfm?id=43610
Phone: 337-774-5923
Location: In Cameron Parish in southern Louisiana. **Established:** 1937. **Habitat:** Nearly 35,000 acres of water tolerant grasses, sedge, shrubs; vegetation in the undeveloped marshes is covered with maidencane and bull tongue. Refuge is dominated by Lacassine Pool, a 16,000-acre impounded freshwater marsh. **Facilities:** Visitor contact station, viewing sites, hiking trails. **Activities:** Boating, canoeing, hiking, fishing, hunting, educational programs. **Access:** Open year round from one hour before sunrise until one hour after sunset. **Primary Wildlife:** Bald eagle, peregrine falcon, ibis, alligator, nutria, Louisiana black bear, black-bellied whisting ducks, pintails, and wood ducks. **Special Features:** Several hundred thousand ducks and geese use the refuge as a wintering habitat. Wood ducks, fulvous and black-bellied whisting ducks, and mottled ducks nest here during the breeding season.

★812★ LACREEK NATIONAL WILDLIFE REFUGE

29746 Bird Rd
Martin, SD 57551
Web: www.fws.gov/lacreek
Phone: 605-685-6508
Location: 120 miles southeast of Rapid City in southwestern South Dakota. **Established:** 1935 as Lacreek Migratory Waterfowl Refuge. **Habitat:** 16,410 acres of native sandhills, sub-irrigated meadows, impounded freshwater marshes, and mixed grass prairie uplands. **Facilities:** Visitor contact station, viewing sites, hiking trails, campground, auto tour route. **Activities:** Boating, canoeing, swimming, water skiing, picnicking, camping, fishing, hunting. **Access:** Open during daylight hours. **Primary Wildlife:** Trumpeter swans, ducks, burrowing owls, prairie dogs, mule and white-tailed deer, pheasant, and occasional whooping cranes. **Special Features:** Average annual refuge production includes 80-100 trumpeter swans. Spring concentrations of 29,000 ducks and 37,000 geese are not uncommon.

★813★ LAGUNA ATASCOSA NATIONAL WILDLIFE REFUGE

PO Box 450
Rio Hondo, TX 78583
Web: southwest.fws.gov/refuges/texas/laguna.html
Phone: 956-748-3607; **Fax:** 956-748-3609
Location: East of Rio Hondo, Texas, in the lower Rio Grande Valley. **Established:** 1976. **Habitat:** 45,187 acres of temperate, subtropical, coastal and desert habitats. **Facilities:** Visitor center, viewing sites, campgrounds, hiking trails, boat launch, fishing pier, auto tour routes (16 miles). **Activities:** Hiking, fishing, boating, camping, wildlife observation, hunting, bicycling. **Access:** Open year round during daylight hours. **Primary Wildlife:** Ducks, grebe, javelina, green jays, roseate spoonbill, roadrunner, verdin, alligator, ocelot and Texas tortoise. **Special Features:** Laguna Atascosa NWR is the largest protected area of natural habitat left in the Lower Rio Grande Valley. The refuge marks the northern range for several species of birds.

★814★ LAGUNA CARTAGENA NATIONAL WILDLIFE REFUGE

c/o Caribbean Islands NWR Complex
PO Box 510
Boqueron, PR 00622
Web: www.fws.gov/southeast/lagunacartagena
Phone: 787-851-7258; **Fax:** 787-851-7440
Location: In the Lajas Valley of southwestern Puerto Rico. **Established:** 1989. **Habitat:** 1,059 acres of freshwater marsh, wetlands, sugar cane fields, and pastures. **Facilities:** Viewing

See pages 22-23 for map of National Wildlife Refuges.

4. National Wildlife Refuges

sites, hiking trails. **Activities:** Hiking, wildlife observation. **Access:** Year round during daylight hours. **Primary Wildlife:** Smooth-billed anis, Magnificent frigatebird, herons, and the endangered Yellow-shouldered blackbird. **Special Features:** The present lagoon is a remnant of what was once a large open expanse of water and one of the most important freshwater habitats for birds in Puerto Rico. Due to past agricultural practices, 90 percent of the lagoon is choked with aquatic plants which restrict nesting and feeding.

★815★ LAKE ALICE NATIONAL WILDLIFE REFUGE

c/o Devils Lake WMD
PO Box 908
Devils Lake, ND 58301
Web: www.fws.gov/lakealice
Phone: 701-662-8611
Location: 20 miles northwest of Devils Lake, North Dakota. **Established:** 1935. **Habitat:** 11,500 acres of wetlands and marshes. A mixture of grasses and legumes have been planted throughout the refuge to provide cover and food for various resident wildlife. **Facilities:** Viewing sites, trails, observation tower, auto tour route. **Activities:** Hiking, hunting, primitive camping, educational programs. **Access:** Open during daylight hours. **Primary Wildlife:** Franklin gulls, black-crowned night herons, mallards, pintails, gadwall, partridge, pheasant, grouse, woodpeckers, white-tailed deer, red fox, coyotes, and an occasional moose. **Special Features:** Lake Alice is an area of major waterfowl concentrations during spring and fall migrations, supporting hundreds of thousands of nesting waterfowl annually.

★816★ LAKE ANDES NATIONAL WILDLIFE REFUGE

38672 291st St
Lake Andes, SD 57356
Web: lakeandes.fws.gov
Phone: 605-487-7603; **Fax:** 605-487-7604
Location: Southern South Dakota. **Established:** 1936. **Habitat:** 5,638 acres of natural, shallow prairie lake and grasslands. **Facilities:** Visitor contact station, viewing sites, hiking trails. **Activities:** Fishing, hiking, hunting, educational group tours (by prior arrangement). **Access:** Open year round during daylight hours. **Primary Wildlife:** Colonial-nesting eared grebes, black terns, Franklin gulls, bald eagles, blue-winged teal, bobolinks, white-tailed deer, beaver, and muskrats. **Special Features:** The refuge occupies the southern portion of the Prairie Pothole regions, known as the "Duck Factory" as many ducks rely on this habitat to raise their young.

★817★ LAKE ILO NATIONAL WILDLIFE REFUGE

3275 11th St NW
Coleharbor, ND 58531
Web: lakeilo.fws.gov
Phone: 701-442-5474; **Fax:** 701-442-5546
Location: West-central North Dakota, 25 miles north of Dickinson. **Established:** 1939. **Habitat:** 4,034 acres of native prairie, planted grasslands, and wetlands. The uplands are characterized by gently sloping hills and terraces with creeks and an occasional slough. **Facilities:** Visitor contact station, picnic areas, hiking trails, fishing pier (&), boat ramp, historic features. **Activities:** Boating, canoeing, fishing, ice fishing, hiking. **Access:** Year round during daylight hours. **Primary Wildlife:** Canada geese, mallards, pintails, blue-winged teal, shovelers, plovers, and gadwall. Also present are deer, antelope, pheasants, and sharp-tail grouse. **Special Features:** Archeologicial findings show Lake Ilo has been continously inhabited for more than 11,000 years. On-site displays showcase artifacts with interpretive exhibits.

★818★ LAKE ISOM NATIONAL WILDLIFE REFUGE

c/o Reelfoot NWR
4343 Hwy 157
Union City, TN 38261
Web: www.fws.gov/refuges/profiles/recEdMore.cfm?ID=
42576
Phone: 731-286-0650
Location: Northwest Tennessee, 3 miles south of Reelfoot Lake. **Established:** 1938. **Habitat:** 1,850 acres of open water, forested wetlands, and croplands. **Facilities:** Trail, boat launch. **Activities:** Boating, fishing, hunting. **Access:** The refuge waters are open to the public from March 15 through November 15 for fishing and wildlife observation. The land portion of the refuge is open March 15 through November 15. **Primary Wildlife:** Geese, ducks, bald eagles, songbirds, white-tailed deer, raccoons, and squirrels. **Special Features:** Refuge maintains dozens of nest boxes for wood ducks.

★819★ LAKE NETTIE NATIONAL WILDLIFE REFUGE

c/o Audubon NWR
3275 11th St NW
Coleharbor, ND 58531
Phone: 701-442-5474; **Fax:** 701-442-5546
Location: West-central North Dakota, about 10 miles northwest of the community of Turtle Lake. **Established:** 1939. **Habitat:** 1,285 acres of wetland and 400-acre Lake Nettie. **Facilities:** Undeveloped. **Activities:** Deer hunting, wildlife observation, education programs. **Access:** Open year round to walk-ins. **Primary Wildlife:** Nesting and migratory waterfowl. **Special Features:** In the mid-1980s, eighteen islands were constructed in Mud Lake by Ducks Unlimited to provide protected nesting sites for water birds.

★820★ LAKE OPHELIA NATIONAL WILDLIFE REFUGE

401 Island Rd
Marksville, LA 71351
Web: www.fws.gov/lakeophelia
Phone: 318-253-4238
Location: In the Red River floodplain in east-central Louisiana, 18 miles north of Marksville. **Established:** 1988. **Habitat:** 18,000 acres of hardwood forest, cropland, wetlands, lakes and bayous. **Facilities:** Visitor contact station, viewing sites, boat launch, trails. **Activities:** Boating, fishing, hunting, hiking, educational programs. **Access:** Open during daylight hours; the lake is open for fishing from March to mid-October. **Primary Wildlife:** Wading birds, ducks, bobcats, alligators, and foxes.

See pages 22-23 for map of National Wildlife Refuges.

Special Features: Lake Ophelia is a 350-acre, cypress-lined lake that was once a channel of the Red River. The lake is a renowned warmwater fishery.

★821★ LAKE UMBAGOG NATIONAL WILDLIFE REFUGE

2756 Dam Rd
Errol, NH 03579
Web: www.fws.gov/northeast/lakeumbagog
Phone: 603-482-3415
Location: Along the northern New Hampshire-Maine border. **Established:** 1992. **Habitat:** Includes 8,500-acre Lake Umbagog and 16,300 acres of forests, wetlands, and rivers. **Facilities:** Visitor contact station, viewing sites, intrepretive trail (&). **Activities:** Boating, canoeing, fishing, hunting. **Access:** Trail open year round, dawn to dusk. **Primary Wildlife:** Bald eagle, peregrine falcon, black duck, scaups, scoters, northern harrier, woodcock, woodchuck, coyote, bear and moose. **Special Features:** In 1979 the Secretary of the Interior designated part of the wetlands at Harper's Meadow a National Natural Landmark, recognizing the floating bog and wetlands as a significant natural area.

★822★ LAKE WOODRUFF NATIONAL WILDLIFE REFUGE

2045 Mud Lake Rd
DeLeon Springs, FL 32130
Web: www.fws.gov/lakewoodruff/
Phone: 386-985-4673; **Fax:** 386-985-7926
Location: 30 miles north of Orlando in central Florida. **Established:** 1964. **Habitat:** 21,574 acres of freshwater marsh and hardwood swamp interspersed with canals, streams, and lakes. **Facilities:** Visitor contact station, observation tower, hiking trails. **Activities:** Boating, canoeing, fishing, bicycling, hiking, hunting, educational programs. **Access:** Open year round during daylight hours. **Primary Wildlife:** West Indian manatee, indigo snake, American alligator, snail kite, osprey, limpkin, gopher tortoise, and white-tailed deer. **Special Features:** Refuge protects ecologically sensitive lands along the Saint John River. It contains more than 5,000 acres of freshwater and more than 50 miles of waterways which are used by endangered Florida manatees as foraging, breeding and calving areas.

★823★ LAKE ZAHL NATIONAL WILDLIFE REFUGE

c/o Crosby WMD
PO Box 148
Crosby, ND 58730
Web: www.fws.gov/refuges/profiles/recEdMore.cfm?ID=62561
Phone: 701-965-6488; **Fax:** 701-965-6487
Location: 30 miles north of Williston, North Dakota; refuge is divided by State Highway 50. **Established:** 1939. **Habitat:** 3,739 acres of mostly native prairie around two large semi-permanent marshes. **Facilities:** Visitor contact station. **Activities:** Hunting, hiking, bird watching. **Access:** Open during hunting season; a special permit is required for other times. **Primary Wildlife:** Giant Canada geese, migratory and nesting waterfowl, pheasant, grouse, partridge, and deer. **Special Features:** The

Lake Zahl area was homesteaded in the late 1800s and early 1900s, primarily for farming purposes. The lake itself was established in 1939 following a decade of extreme drought.

★824★ LAS VEGAS NATIONAL WILDLIFE REFUGE

Rt 1 Box 399
Las Vegas, NM 87701
Web: southwest.fws.gov/refuges/newmex/lasvegas
Phone: 505-425-3581; **Fax:** 505-545-8510
Location: 7 miles southeast of Las Vegas, New Mexico. **Established:** 1965. **Habitat:** 8,672 acres of native grassland, cropland, marshes, ponds, forested canyons, and streams. **Facilities:** Visitor contact station, viewing sites, trail, auto tour routes (8 miles), historic sites. **Activities:** Hiking, fishing, hunting. **Access:** Dawn to dusk, 7 days a week. **Primary Wildlife:** Hawks, sandpipers, white-throated swifts, mule deer, pronghorn, wild turkeys, and rabbits. **Special Features:** Refuge's trail is a self-guided, half-mile nature walk that descends into a box canyon. To protect wildlife on the refuge and historic sites in the area, trail is open for day use only and requires a free, special-use permit.

★825★ LEE METCALF NATIONAL WILDLIFE REFUGE

PO Box 247
Stevensville, MT 59870
Web: leemetcalf.fws.gov
Phone: 406-777-5552; **Fax:** 406-777-4344
Location: Along the Bitterroot River, 25 miles south of Missoula, Montana. **Established:** 1963 as Ravalli NWR. **Habitat:** 2,800 acres of meadows, wetlands, and river bottom woodlands surrounded by mountains. **Facilities:** Visitor contact station, trails(&), auto tour route, historical features. **Activities:** Fishing, hiking, hunting. **Access:** Open year round during daylight hours. **Primary Wildlife:** Osprey, great blue herons, Canada geese, double-crested cormorants, bald eagles, belted kingfishers, deer, muskrat, striped skunk, gopher, beaver, and painted turtle. **Special Features:** Cradled between the Bitterroot and Sapphire Mountain ranges, and bounded on the west by the Bitterroot River, the refuge offers spectacular scenery.

★826★ LESLIE CANYON NATIONAL WILDLIFE REFUGE

c/o San Bernardino NWR
PO Box 3509
Douglas, AZ 85608
Web: www.fws.gov/Refuges/profiles/index.cfm?id=22524
Phone: 520-364-2104
Location: Southeast corner of Arizona. **Established:** 1988. **Habitat:** 2,770 acres of rough mountainous terrain. **Facilities:** Auto tour route. **Access:** A portion of the refuge is open daily during daylight hours; call refuge office for details. **Primary Wildlife:** Endangered Yaqui chub and Yaqui topminnow. Also provides habitat for mule deer, mountain lion, Madrean alligator lizard, checkered and mexican garter snakes, gila monster and 270 species of birds. **Special Features:** Refuge includes Leslie Creek and its valuable riparian habitat, which supports a rare velvet ash-cottonwood-black willow gallery forest.

See pages 22-23 for map of National Wildlife Refuges.

★827★ **LEWIS & CLARK NATIONAL WILDLIFE REFUGE**
46 Steamboat Slough Rd
Cathlamet, WA 98612
Web: www.fws.gov/pacific/refuges/field/wa_L&C.htm
Phone: 360-795-3915
Location: Islands in the lower Columbia River in western Oregon. **Established:** 1972. **Habitat:** 35,000 acres of tidelands and open water with 8,313 acres of islands and sand bars. **Facilities:** Boat launch. **Activities:** Boating, canoeing, fishing, hunting. **Access:** Open during daylight hours; accessible only by boat. **Primary Wildlife:** Tundra swans, ducks, harbor seals, sea lions, river otter, weasels, beaver and fish. **Special Features:** Estuarine waters provide vital food resources for juvenile salmon as they pause to become acclimated to salt water before entering the Pacific Ocean. Bald eagles are present year round and have established 30-35 active nest sites.

★828★ **LIDO BEACH NATIONAL WILDLIFE REFUGE**
Long Island NWR Complex
PO Box 21
Shirley, NY 11967
Web: www.fws.gov/northeast/longislandrefuges/lidobeach.html
Phone: 631-286-0485; **Fax:** 631-286-4003
Location: Off Meadowbrook State Parkway in Long Island, New York. **Established:** 1969. **Access:** Open to the public by special use permit. **Primary Wildlife:** Sandpipers, redwing blackbirds, clapper rails, osprey, black ducks. **Special Features:** The area is almost entirely tidal wetland, where shorebird and wading bird diversity is high. Wintering waterfowl such a black ducks and Atlantic brant make good use of the wetland.

★829★ **LITTLE PEND OREILLE NATIONAL WILDLIFE REFUGE**
1310 Bear Creek Rd
Colville, WA 99114
Web: www.fws.gov/littlependoreille
Phone: 509-684-8384; **Fax:** 509-684-8381
Location: In the northeast corner of Washington, along the Little Pend Oreille River. **Established:** 1939. **Habitat:** 40,198 acres of mountainous forests interspersed with grasslands, at elevations ranging from 1,800 to 5,600 feet. **Facilities:** Visitor contact station, viewing sites, hiking trails, campgrounds, auto tour route. **Activities:** Boating, canoeing, fishing, hunting, hiking, camping, horseback riding, mountain biking, cross-country skiing, snowshoeing, educational programs. **Access:** Open 24 hours a day. **Primary Wildlife:** Threatened Canada lynx, white-tailed deer. Also provides habitat for moose, black bear, great horned owl, woodpeckers, bluebirds, chipmunks, beavers, and wild turkey. **Special Features:** Refuge lakes and marshes provide a spring and fall stopover point for migratory waterfowl. In combination with adjacent lands, the refuge provides for species that require large tracts of forest.

★830★ **LITTLE RIVER NATIONAL WILDLIFE REFUGE**
PO Box 340
Broken Bow, OK 74728
Web: www.fws.gov/southwest/refuges/oklahoma/littleriver
Phone: 580-584-6211
Location: Southeastern Oklahoma in Broken Bow. **Established:** 1987. **Habitat:** 15,000 acres of low, wet bottomland with old oxbows and sloughs with cypress. **Facilities:** Boat ramps. **Activities:** Boating, canoeing, fishing, hunting, hiking. **Access:** Year round. **Primary Wildlife:** Migratory waterfowl, primarily mallards and wood ducks. Also Swainson's warbler, flycatchers, swallows, vireos, snakes, swamp rabbits, raccoons, alligator, and beaver. **Special Features:** Refuge is the only known nesting location in Oklahoma for Swainson's warbler, a secretive songbird that winters in the Caribbean.

★831★ **LOGAN CAVE NATIONAL WILDLIFE REFUGE**
c/o Holla Bend NWR
10448 Holla Bend Rd
Dardanelle, AR 72834
Web: southeast.fws.gov/logancave
Phone: 479-229-4300; **Fax:** 479-229-4302
Location: Between Siloan Springs and Springdale, Arkansas. **Established:** 1989. **Habitat:** 123-acre cave ecosystem. **Access:** Closed to public. **Primary Wildlife:** Gray bat (endangered), Ozark cave crayfish (endangered), Ozark cavefish (threatened). **Special Features:** Gray bats use the cave in the spring and summer as a maternity site.

★832★ **LONG LAKE NATIONAL WILDLIFE REFUGE**
12000 353rd St SE
Moffit, ND 58560
Web: www.fws.gov/longlake
Phone: 701-387-4397
Location: In south-central North Dakota. **Established:** 1932. **Habitat:** 22,300 acres of lake bottom, rolling prairie, and cultivated uplands. **Facilities:** Visitor center, viewing sites, trail, picnic area. **Activities:** Boating, canoeing, fishing, ice fishing, hunting, educational programs. **Access:** Open during daylight hours. **Primary Wildlife:** Canada geese, pintail, mallard, ring-necked pheasants, snowy owl, sandhill cranes, white-tailed deer, coyote, fox, rabbits, mink, and badger. **Special Features:** Refuge was designated a Globally Important Bird Area and a Western Hemisphere Shorebird Reserve Network site, because of its importance as both a breeding and migratory stopover for more than 20,000 shorebirds.

★833★ **LOST TRAIL NATIONAL WILDLIFE REFUGE**
6295A Pleasant Valley Rd
Marion, MT 59925
Web: bisonrange.fws.gov/losttrail
Phone: 406-858-2216
Location: About 25 air-miles west of Kalispell, Montana. **Established:** 1999. **Habitat:** 7,885 acres of mountain drainage

See pages 22-23 for map of National Wildlife Refuges.

consisting of wet meadows, prairie grasslands, and wooded slopes. **Facilities:** In planning and development stages. **Activities:** Wildlife observation, environmental study. **Access:** Limited; call refuge office. **Primary Wildlife:** Grebes, herons, gulls, killdeer, sandhill cranes, harriers, hawks, owls, lynx, wolverine, bobcat, grizzly bear, gray wolf, elk and moose. **Special Features:** Prior to acquisition, refuge lands were privately owned and operated as a cattle and horse ranch, dating back to the late 1800s. Indian pictographs are located on rock faces near the interior of the refuge.

★834★ LOSTWOOD NATIONAL WILDLIFE REFUGE

8315 Hwy 8
Kenmare, ND 58746
Web: lostwood.fws.gov
Phone: 701-848-2722
Location: Northwestern North Dakota. **Established:** 1935. **Habitat:** 26,747 acres of rolling hills, with short-grass and mixed grass prairie interspersed with numerous wetlands. **Facilities:** Viewing sites, trails, auto tour route. **Activities:** Canoeing, hunting, hiking, cross-country skiing, snowshoeing. **Access:** Year round during daylight hours. **Primary Wildlife:** Migratory waterfowl including blue-winged teal, mallard, gadwall, wigeon, lesser scaup, redheads, and canvasbacks. Other birds include Virginia rail, marbled godwit, Wilson's phalarope, American avocet, sparrows, upland sandpiper, sharp-tailed grouse, northern harriers, and giant Canada geese. Also home to white-tailed deer, badger, weasel, and white-tailed jackrabbit. **Special Features:** About 70% of Lostwood is virgin prairie. Most wetlands were not drained and remain as they were prior to settlement. In 1975, more than 5,500 acres were set aside as the Lostwood Wilderness Area.

★835★ LOWER HATCHIE NATIONAL WILDLIFE REFUGE

234 Fort Prudhomme Dr
Henning, TN 38041
Web: www.fws.gov/lowerhatchie
Phone: 731-738-2296; **Fax:** 731-738-2297
Location: Along the Hatchie Scenic River in western Tennessee. **Established:** 1980. **Habitat:** 9,451 acres of bottomland hardwood forest, cropland, water, and grasslands. **Facilities:** Viewing sites, hiking trails, auto tour route, boat ramps, historical features. **Activities:** Boating, canoeing, fishing, hiking, hunting, educational programs. **Access:** Open year round during daylight hours. Waterfowl sanctuary closed November 15 - March 15. **Primary Wildlife:** Bald eagles, Mississippi kites, wild turkey, neotropical songbirds, waterfowl, shorebirds, as well as mammals, reptiles, amphibians and fish. **Special Features:** The Hatchie River remains the longest continuous stretch of naturally meandering river in the lower Mississippi River Valley. As a result, wildlife and fisheries thrive in its almost pristine watershed ecosystems. The refuge helps protect and enhance the ever-diminishing bottomland hardwood forests.

★836★ LOWER KLAMATH NATIONAL WILDLIFE REFUGE

c/o Klamath Basin NWR Complex
4009 Hill Rd
Tulelake, CA 96134
Web: www.fws.gov/klamathbasinrefuges/lowerklamath/lowerklamath.html
Phone: 530-667-2231; **Fax:** 530-667-3299
Location: On the California-Oregon border, 5 miles west of Tulelake, California. **Established:** 1908. **Habitat:** 53,600 acres of shallow marshes, open water, grassy uplands, and croplands. **Facilities:** Visitor center, viewing sites, photography blinds, auto tour route (10 miles). **Activities:** Hunting, wildlife observation, educational programs. **Access:** Open during daylight hours. **Primary Wildlife:** Waterfowl, including gadwall, mallard, white pelicans, bald eagles, peregrine falcons, white-faced ibis, and herons. **Special Features:** The refuge is a fall staging area for 20-30 percent of the central valley population of sandhill crane. From 20,000 to 100,000 shorebirds use refuge wetlands during the spring migration. Winter wildlife populations include 500 bald eagle and 30,000 tundra swan.

★837★ LOWER RIO GRANDE VALLEY NATIONAL WILDLIFE REFUGE

c/o Santa Ana NWR
Rt 2, Box 202A
Alamo, TX 78516
Web: southwest.fws.gov/refuges/texas/lrgv.html
Phone: 956-784-7500; **Fax:** 956-787-8338
Location: 7 miles south of Alamo, Texas. **Established:** 1979. **Habitat:** 90,000 acres of coastal barrier islands, resacas (oxbow lakes), desert-like brushlands, riverside woodlands, and caliche hillsides. Still in an acquisition phase, the refuge will eventually encompass 132,500 acres. **Facilities:** Visitor center (at Santa Ana NWR). **Activities:** Canoeing, hiking hunting, fishing, bird-watching. **Access:** Portions of the refuge are open year round, from sunrise to sunset, to foot traffic only. **Primary Wildlife:** Two endangered cats: the ocelot and jaguarundi. Also provides habitat for speckled racer, plain chachalaca, green jay, great kiskadee, southern yellow bat, Kemp's Ridley turtle, white-tailed deer, and collared peccary. **Special Features:** Not only do the Central and Mississippi flyways converge here at the southern tip of Texas, but the area is also the northernmost range for many bird species. Considered one of the most biologically diverse NWRs in the continental United States, the site represents 11 distinct biotic communities that are host or home to 1,100 types of plants, 700 vertebrate species (including 484 bird species), and more than 300 species of butterflies.

★838★ LOWER SUWANNEE NATIONAL WILDLIFE REFUGE

16450 NW 31st Pl
Chiefland, FL 32626
Web: lowersuwannee.fws.gov
Phone: 352-493-0238; **Fax:** 352-493-1935
Location: Along the southern edge of the Big Bend Region of Florida's west coast. **Established:** 1979. **Habitat:** 53,000 acres of bottomland hardwood swamps, pine forests, cypress domes, tidal creeks, and salt marshes. **Facilities:** Visitor contact station,

See pages 22-23 for map of National Wildlife Refuges.

viewing sites, observation tower, trails, auto tour route, historic features, boat ramps, fishing pier. **Activities:** Boating, canoeing, fishing, hiking, biking, hunting, educational programs. **Access:** Unlimited. **Primary Wildlife:** White-tailed deer, wild turkeys, bobcats, alligators and river otters are year-round inhabitants. Gulf sturgeon, salt marsh voles, eastern indigo snakes, gopher tortoise, West Indian manatee and wood stork are some of the threatened or endangered species that live here. Birds such as swallow-tailed kite, bald eagle, osprey, and prothonotary warblers use the refuge seasonally. **Special Features:** The constant flow of nutrients from the Suwannee River and tidal creeks creates excellent wildlife habitat. Salt marshes and tidal flats act as a nursery for fish, shrimp, and shellfish, which attracts thousands of shore birds and diving ducks.

★839★ MACKAY ISLAND NATIONAL WILDLIFE REFUGE

316 Marsh Causeway
Knotts Island, NC 27950
Web: www.fws.gov/mackayisland
Phone: 252-429-3100
Location: Northeast corner of North Carolina on Knotts Island. **Established:** 1960. **Habitat:** 8,219 acres of freshwater and brackish marsh to upland and lowland eastern pine hardwood forest. **Facilities:** Visitor contact station, trails, fishing pier (&). **Activities:** Boating, canoeing, fishing, hiking, biking, deer hunting. **Access:** Open from sunrise to sunset; access to most of the refuge is closed from mid-October to mid-March. **Primary Wildlife:** Ducks, Canada geese, snow geese, herons, egrets, bald eagle, peregrine falcon, muskrat, nutria, river otter, gray and red fox, turtles and snakes, including the cottonmouth. **Special Features:** The refuge is strategically located along the Atlantic Flyway, making it an important wintering area for ducks, geese, and tundra swans. At times, flocks of over 12,000 snow geese may be observed on the refuge after their arrival in November.

★840★ MAINE COASTAL ISLANDS NATIONAL WILDLIFE REFUGE

PO Box 279
Milbridge, ME 04658
Web: www.fws.gov/northeast/mainecoastal
Phone: 207-546-2124
Location: 35 miles east of Ellsworth, Maine. **Established:** 1978. **Habitat:** More than 7,400 acres made up of 47 offshore islands and 3 coastal parcels, spanning more than 150 miles of Maine coastline. **Facilities:** Visitor contact station, trails. **Activities:** Hiking, hunting, berry picking, wildlife observation, education programs. **Access:** Mainland portions of the refuge are open from dawn to dusk; islands are closed to public entry during the nesting season. **Primary Wildlife:** Colonial seabirds including terns, puffins, razorbills, storm-petrels, laughing gulls, black guillemots, and common eiders; also bald eagles, white-tailed deer, and porcupine. **Special Features:** Eight lighthouse islands have been transferred to the refuge. Several species of seabirds nest on these islands.

★841★ MALHEUR NATIONAL WILDLIFE REFUGE

36391 Sodhouse Ln
Princeton, OR 97721
Web: www.fws.gov/malheur
Phone: 541-493-2612
Location: Southeastern Oregon. **Established:** 1908 as the Lake Malheur Reservation; renamed in 1935 as Malheur Migratory Bird Refuge and in 1940 as Malheur NWR. **Habitat:** More than 187,000 acres of uplands, wetlands, riparian areas, and meadows. **Facilities:** Visitor contact station, viewing sites, trails, auto tour routes, historic features. **Activities:** Canoeing, boating, horseback riding, fishing, hiking, bicycling, hunting. **Access:** Open daily from dawn to dusk. **Primary Wildlife:** Bald eagles, ravens, great horned owls, black-billed magpies, snow geese, trumpeter swans, and sandhill cranes. **Special Features:** Refuge provides important habitat to more than 320 species of birds and 58 species of mammals.

★842★ MANDALAY NATIONAL WILDLIFE REFUGE

3599 Bayou Black Dr
Houma, LA 73060
Web: www.fws.gov/southeast/mandalay
Phone: 985-853-1078; **Fax:** 985-853-1079
Location: About 5 miles southwest of Houma, Louisiana. **Established:** 1996. **Habitat:** 4,212 acres of freshwater marsh with ponds, levees, and manmade canals. **Activities:** Hunting (with restrictions), fishing, boating, canoeing. **Access:** By boat only; open year round. **Primary Wildlife:** Migrating waterfowl. Also alligators, wading birds, and bald eagles. **Special Features:** The refuge is composed primarily of freshwater marsh, which provides important habitat for wintering waterfowl of the Mississippi Flyway.

★843★ MARAIS DES CYGNES NATIONAL WILDLIFE REFUGE

24141 KS Hwy 52
Pleasanton, KS 66075
Web: maraisdescygnes.fws.gov
Phone: 913-352-8956
Location: On KS Highway 52, just north of Pleasanton, Kansas. **Established:** 1992. **Habitat:** 7,500 acres composed of the river and its adjacent streams and wetlands, bottomland hardwood forests, grasses, upland shrub and trees, cropland, and savanna. **Facilities:** Wildlife viewing sites. **Activities:** Hunting, fishing, boating (with restrictions), hiking. **Access:** Daylight hours year round. **Primary Wildlife:** Kentucky warbler, northern parula warbler, red shouldered hawk, turkey vulture, scissor-tailed flycatcher, and painted bunting. **Special Features:** The refuge is named after the Marais des Cygnes River, which runs through the middle of the refuge and is the dominant natural feature of the region. French for "Marsh of the Swans," the refuge was presumably named for trumpeter swans that were once a common sight here during their spring and fall migrations.

★844★ MARTIN NATIONAL WILDLIFE REFUGE

c/o Blackwater NWR
2145 Key Wallace Dr
Cambridge, MD 21613
Web: northeast.fws.gov/md/mrn.htm
Phone: 410-228-2692; **Fax:** 410-228-3261

See pages 22-23 for map of National Wildlife Refuges.

Location: Includes the northern half of Smith Island, which lies 11 miles west of Crisfield, Maryland, and Watts Island, which is located between the eastern shore of Virginia and Tangier Island. Both islands are situated in the lower Chesapeake Bay. **Established:** 1954. **Habitat:** 4,548 acres of tidal marsh, coves and creeks, and vegetated ridges. **Facilities:** Visitor contact station. **Access:** Varies; contact refuge office for specific dates and times. **Primary Wildlife:** Waterfowl, including black ducks, pintails, mallards, and Canada geese; also red fox, muskrat, mink, otter, voles, northern diamondback terrapin, crabs and oysters. **Special Features:** The tidal marsh, coves and creeks, and vegetated ridges of the refuge form an important stopover and wintering area for thousands of migratory waterfowl and nesting habitat for various wildlife species. Martin NWR is the largest unit of the Chesapeake Islands Refuges.

★845★ MASHPEE NATIONAL WILDLIFE REFUGE
73 Weir Hill Rd
Sudbury, MA 01773
Web: www.fws.gov/northeast/mashpee
Phone: 978-443-4661; **Fax:** 978-443-2898
Location: Located in the towns of Mashpee and Falmouth on Cape Cod, Massachusetts. **Established:** 1995. **Habitat:** 5,871 acres when complete; 335 acres are now in FWS ownership, comprised of saltwater marshes, cranberry bogs, swamps, freshwater marshes and a vernal pool. **Access:** Closed to the public. **Primary Wildlife:** Shorebirds, osprey, songbirds, white-tailed deer, red fox, and other small mammals. **Special Features:** Though closed to the public, environmental education and interpretive programs are occasionally offered by the Refuge Friends group.

★846★ MASON NECK NATIONAL WILDLIFE REFUGE
7603 High Point Rd
Lorton, VA 22079
Web: www.fws.gov/refuges/profiles/index.cfm?id=51610
Phone: 703-490-4979
Location: On the bank of the Potomac River 18 miles south of Washington, D.C. **Established:** 1969. **Habitat:** 2,277 acres of forest and marshlands with 4.4 miles of shoreline. **Facilities:** Viewing sites, hiking trails. **Activities:** Hunting, hiking, fishing, educational programs. **Access:** Public access is limited to trails and an environmental education site. **Primary Wildlife:** Bald eagles. Also provides habitat for great blue herons, wood thrush, ovenbirds, scarlet tanagers, northern parula warblers, and prothonotary warblers. **Special Features:** Seven bald eagle nests are located in or adjacent to the refuge and there is a wintering population of 50 to 60 birds. The refuge was listed as one of the top ten sites in the country for viewing bald eagles.

★847★ MASSASOIT NATIONAL WILDLIFE REFUGE
c/o Great Meadows NWR
73 Weir Hill Rd
Sudbury, MA 01776
Web: www.fws.gov/northeast/massasoit
Phone: 978-443-4661; **Fax:** 978-443-2898

Location: 40 miles southeast of Boston, Massachusetts. **Established:** 1983. **Habitat:** 184 acres of upland, lakeshore, and pond. **Access:** Closed to the public. **Primary Wildlife:** Plymouth red-bellied turtle. **Special Features:** A head-start program has been implemented on the refuge and surrounding ponds to expand the range of the Plymouth redbelly turtle into additional ponds, and increase the number of turtles in ponds with existing populations. From 1980 to 2002, more than 2,000 head-started turtles have been released in 22 sites.

★848★ MATHEWS BRAKE NATIONAL WILDLIFE REFUGE
c/o Hillside NWR
1562 Providence Rd
Cruger, MS 38924
Web: www.fws.gov/mathewsbrake
Phone: 662-235-4989; **Fax:** 662-235-5303
Location: Central Mississippi, 60 miles north of Jackson. **Established:** 1980. **Habitat:** 2,418 acres of bottomland hardwoods and young hardwood plantations, moist-soil plants around the Mathews Brake. **Facilities:** Boat ramp (&). **Activities:** Fishing, hunting, wildlife observation. **Access:** Open year round during daylight hours. **Primary Wildlife:** White-tailed deer, squirrel, rabbit, raccoon, largemouth bass, crappie, catfish, prothonotary warbler, cattle egret, ducks, bald eagles, and American alligator. **Special Features:** Each winter the brake provides habitat for more than 30,000 ducks. Neotropical migratory birds use the refuge during migration seasons throughout the year.

★849★ MATLACHA PASS NATIONAL WILDLIFE REFUGE
c/o J. N. ''Ding'' Darling NWR
1 Wildlife Dr
Sanibel, FL 33957
Web: www.fws.gov/southeast/matlachapass
Phone: 239-472-1100; **Fax:** 239-472-4061
Location: 10 miles northwest of Fort Myers, Florida, in the Matlacha Pass estuary. **Established:** 1908. **Habitat:** 512 acres consisting primarily of tidal wetlands with low sand and shell ridges and 23 islands. **Activities:** Boating, saltwater fishing. **Access:** All islands are closed to public access. **Primary Wildlife:** Endangered and threatened species including West Indian manatee, wood stork, eastern indigo snake, American crocodile, and bald eagle. Also provides habitat for sea turtles, osprey, shore birds, wading birds, raptors and neotropical migratory birds. **Special Features:** Refuge uplands and wetlands are maintained in their natural condition in order to provide undisturbed habitat for birds, fish, invertebrates, and other animals. The refuge is used as a nesting and roosting area by an assortment of colonial birds.

★850★ MATTAMUSKEET NATIONAL WILDLIFE REFUGE
38 Mattamuskeet Rd
Swanquarter, NC 27885
Web: mattamuskeet.fws.gov
Phone: 252-926-4021; **Fax:** 252-926-1743

See pages 22-23 for map of National Wildlife Refuges.

Location: 9 miles east of Swan Quarter, North Carolina. **Established:** 1934. **Habitat:** 50,180 acres total: Lake Mattamuskeet encompasses approximately 40,000 acres, and the remainder is marsh, timber, and croplands. **Facilities:** Visitor contact station, viewing sites, observation towers, hiking trails (under development), auto tour route, boat ramps. **Activities:** Boating, canoeing, fishing, crabbing, hunting, hiking, educational programs. **Access:** Year round during daylight hours. **Primary Wildlife:** Osprey, bald eagles, peregrine falcons, deer, bobcats, otters, gray foxes, occasionally black bear and red wolf. **Special Features:** Mattamuskeet lies in the middle of the Atlantic Flyway and provides a valuable wintering area for thousands of geese and 22 species of ducks.

★851★ MAXWELL NATIONAL WILDLIFE REFUGE

PO Box 276
Maxwell, NM 87728
Web: www.fws.gov/southwest/refuges/newmex/maxwell
Phone: 505-375-2331; **Fax:** 505-375-2332
Location: 100 miles northeast of Santa Fe, New Mexico. **Established:** 1936. **Habitat:** 3,700 acres of short-grass prairie, playa lakes, woodlots, wetlands and agricultural lands. **Facilities:** Visitor contact station, viewing sites. **Activities:** Boating, canoeing, fishing, educational programs. **Access:** Open 24 hours. **Primary Wildlife:** Ducks, geese, swans, sandhill cranes, bald and golden eagles, falcons, hawks, great horned owls, shorebirds, songbirds, prairie dogs, mule deer, and occasional mountain lion and black bear. **Special Features:** Maxwell NWR supports a wide variety of habitats and is home to more than 219 species of birds, 70 of which nest on the refuge.

★852★ MCFADDIN NATIONAL WILDLIFE REFUGE

PO Box 358
Sabine Pass, TX 77655
Web: www.fws.gov/southwest/refuges/texas/mcfaddin
Phone: 409-971-2909; **Fax:** 409-971-2104
Location: Along the Texas gulf coast, near the Louisiana border. **Established:** 1980. **Habitat:** 55,000 acres of freshwater and brackish marsh. **Facilities:** Visitor contact station, viewing sites, trails, boat ramps. **Activities:** Boating, canoeing, fishing, crabbing, hiking, hunting. **Access:** Open during daylight hours. **Primary Wildlife:** Warblers, vireos, grosbeaks, tanagers, orioles, American alligator, muskrat, river otter, raccoon, striped skunk, bobcat, gray fox, and coyote. **Special Features:** McFaddin NWR supports one of the largest populations of alligators in Texas.

★853★ MCKAY CREEK NATIONAL WILDLIFE REFUGE

c/o Mid-Columbia River Refuges
PO Box 1447
Richland, WA 99351
Web: www.fws.gov/midcolumbiariver/McKaypage.htm
Phone: 509-545-8588
Location: 8 miles south of Pendleton, Oregon. **Established:** 1954. **Habitat:** 1,837 acres of open water, marsh, and grasslands. **Facilities:** Boat ramp, trails, auto tour route. **Activities:** Boating, canoeing, fishing (March through September only), hiking, hunting. **Access:** Daylight hours; fishing is prohibited October through February. **Primary Wildlife:** Ducks, Canada geese, osprey, bald eagle, pheasant, and quail. **Special Features:** Refuge provides a resting and feeding area for thousands of Canada geese and ducks during the fall. Pheasants are common year round.

★854★ MCNARY NATIONAL WILDLIFE REFUGE

64 Maple St
Burbank, WA 99323
Web: midcolumbiariver.fws.gov/mcnarypage.htm
Phone: 509-547-4942
Location: Southern Washington, near the confluence of the Snake and Columbia rivers. **Established:** 1954. **Habitat:** More than 15,000 acres of backwater sloughs, seasonal wetlands, shrub-steppe uplands, irrigated farmlands, river islands, delta mudflats, and riparian areas. **Facilities:** Visitor center (&), viewing sites (&), hiking trails. **Activities:** Fishing, hunting, hiking, educational programs. **Access:** Open daily during daylight hours. **Primary Wildlife:** Migrating waterfowl, including Canada geese, mallards, American wigeon, pintails, long-billed curlews, and white pelicans. **Special Features:** Refuge visitors may see red-tailed, sharp-shinned, and Cooper's hawks, and northern harriers. Peregrine falcons are occasionally seen, particularly around the basalt cliffs in the Stateline and Juniper Canyon units.

★855★ MEDICINE LAKE NATIONAL WILDLIFE REFUGE

223 North Shore Rd
Medicine Lake, MT 59247
Web: medicinelake.fws.gov
Phone: 406-789-2305
Location: Northeastern Montana. **Established:** 1935. **Habitat:** 31,457 acres of prairie, sandhills, and wetlands. **Facilities:** Visitor contact station, viewing sites, observation tower, picnic areas, auto tour route, historic features. **Activities:** Canoeing, fishing, ice fishing, hunting, educational programs. **Access:** Open from sunrise to sunset. **Primary Wildlife:** Canada geese, white pelicans, sandhill cranes, and white-tailed deer, coyote, badger, and less often, moose, elk and pronghorn. **Special Features:** Large populations of rare grassland birds such as Baird's sparrows, Sprague's pipits, and chestnut collared longspurs nest on refuge prairies, attracting birdwatchers from across the country.

★856★ MERCED NATIONAL WILDLIFE REFUGE

c/o San Luis NWR
PO Box 2176
Los Banos, CA 93635
Web: pacific.fws.gov/refuges/field/CA_merced.htm
Phone: 209-826-3508
Location: 8 miles southwest of Merced. **Established:** 1951. **Habitat:** 7,035 acres of grasslands, agricultural fields, and wetlands. **Facilities:** Viewing sites, trails, auto tour route. **Activities:** Hunting, hiking, wildlife observation. **Access:** Open daily from 1/2 hour before sunrise to 1/2 hour after sunset. **Primary Wildlife:** Wintering waterfowl including pintails, shovelers,

See pages 22-23 for map of National Wildlife Refuges.

green-winged teal, lesser sandhill cranes, and Canada geese. **Special Features:** The refuge hosts up to 15,000 lesser sandhill cranes, the largest population in the Central Valley. Up to 100,000 geese (Ross', snow, white-fronted, and cackling Canada) use refuge marsh and croplands from November to March.

★857★ MEREDOSIA NATIONAL WILDLIFE REFUGE

c/o Illinois River NWFR
19031 E County Rd 2110N
Havana, IL 62644
Web: midwest.fws.gov/Meredosia
Phone: 309-535-2290; **Fax:** 309-535-3023
Location: Along the Illinois River, about 60 miles west of Springfield, Illinois. **Established:** 1973. **Habitat:** When complete, the refuge will total 5,255 acres of backwater lakes, bottomland forest, upland forest, prairie, seasonal wetland, and permanent marsh habitat. Its present size is 3,852 acres. **Facilities:** Viewing sites, hiking trails, interpretive display. **Activities:** Boating, canoeing, fishing, hiking, bicycling, educational programs. **Access:** Open daylight hours year round. **Primary Wildlife:** Grasshopper sparrows, dickcissels, meadowlarks, prothonotary warblers, woodpeckers, deer, turkeys, and squirrels. **Special Features:** Close up views of eagles from Beach Road.

★858★ MERRITT ISLAND NATIONAL WILDLIFE REFUGE

PO Box 6504
Titusville, FL 32782
Web: merrittisland.fws.gov
Phone: 321-861-0667; **Fax:** 321-861-1276
Location: East-central Florida next to NASA's space center. **Established:** 1963. **Habitat:** 140,000 acres of brackish marsh, with coastal dunes, scrub oaks, pine forests, and palm and oak hammocks. The refuge overlays John F. Kennedy Space Center and provides a buffer zone for NASA. **Facilities:** Visitor center, auto tour route, hiking trails, observation tower. **Activities:** Boating, canoeing, fishing, hiking, hunting, educational programs. **Access:** Open during daylight hours. Portions may be closed at times of NASA launch activity. **Primary Wildlife:** Great blue herons, great egrets, wood storks, cormorants, brown pelicans, bald eagles, manatees, Florida scrub jay, and alligators. **Special Features:** Coastal refuge consists of seven distinct habitat types and is positioned between the subtropic and temperate climatic zones. Over 500 species of wildlife inhabit the refuge, with 15 federally listed as threatened or endangered. The refuge is home to several wading bird rookeries, 10 active bald eagle nests, numerous osprey nests, up to 400 manatees during spring months, and an estimated 2,500 Florida scrub jays.

★859★ MIDDLE MISSISSIPPI RIVER NATIONAL WILDLIFE REFUGE

1293 Rocky Hollow Rd
Rockwood, IL 62280
Web: www.fws.gov/midwest/MiddleMississippiRiver
Phone: 618-763-4420; **Fax:** 618-763-4424
Location: Along the middle Mississippi River between St. Louis and Cairo, Illinois. **Established:** 2000. **Habitat:** 4,300 acres

floodplain forests, riverine wetlands of varous types and riverine aquatic habitat. **Facilities:** Trails, observation deck. **Activities:** Hunting, fishing, hiking, bicycling, mushroom and berry picking. **Access:** Year round during daylight hours. **Primary Wildlife:** Endangered pallid sturgeon, Indiana bat, northern crawfish frog, blue spotted salamander, and least tern, as well as hawks, eagles, herons, egrets, deer, lemmings, gophers, and mussels. **Special Features:** Refuge lands were purchased in response to the great flood of 1993 and are unique in the refuge complex. The former agricultural lands are being managed to restore the natural cycle of the Mississippi River floodplain and its riverine habitats. They will provide access to the floodplain for native fish during high water stages and create a corridor of floodplain forest habitat for migratory birds and resident wildlife.

★860★ MIDWAY ATOLL NATIONAL WILDLIFE REFUGE

PO Box 50167
Honolulu, HI 96850
Web: www.fws.gov/midway
Phone: 808-674-8237
Location: North-central Pacific Ocean, about 1,150 miles northwest of Honolulu. **Established:** In 1988 Midway became a NWR, subject to the U.S. Navy. In 1996, after the navy closed the facility, custody and accountability were transferred to the Department of the Interior. **Habitat:** 296,819 acres of ocean and three flat coral islands totaling about 1,549 acres. **Facilities:** Visitor contact station, viewing sites, hiking trail, historic features. **Activities:** Boating, fishing, hiking, educational programs. **Access:** Because of Midway Atoll's remote location in the middle of the north Pacific Ocean, it can only be accessed by air or sea under a special-use permit system. Permits may be obtained by contacting the Midway Phoenix Corp. **Primary Wildlife:** Laysan albatross, red-tailed noddies, white terns, also Hawaiian monk seals (endangered), green sea turtles (threatened), and Hawaiian spinner dolphins. **Special Features:** One of the most remote coral atolls in the world, Midway also has a fascinating history. It was the last link in a global telegraph system, inaugurated by a message from President Teddy Roosevelt on the fourth of July 1903; served as a landing site for Pan Am Clippers enroute across the Pacific Ocean in the late 1930s; and was the focus of a 1942 battle that changed the tide of the War in the Pacific.

★861★ MINGO NATIONAL WILDLIFE REFUGE

24729 State Hwy 51
Puxico, MO 63960
Web: midwest.fws.gov/Mingo
Phone: 573-222-3589
Location: 25 miles northeast of Poplar Bluff, Missouri. **Established:** 1945. **Habitat:** 21,676 acres of mostly hardwood bottomland swamp. **Facilities:** Visitor center, picnic areas, boat launch, auto tour route, trails, boardwalk, observation tower. **Activities:** Boating, fishing, hiking, hunting, horseback riding, educational programs, and collection of berries, nuts, pokeweed and mushrooms. **Access:** Daylight hours year round. **Primary Wildlife:** Ducks, geese, eagles, hawks, turkey, opossums, shrews, bats, deer, salamanders, frogs and turtles. **Special Features:** Refuge preserves the only remaining tract of native bottomland forest in the boothill of Missouri, which once covered

See pages 22-23 for map of National Wildlife Refuges.

4. National Wildlife Refuges

2.5 million acres. The tract was spared because draining Mingo Swamp proved too difficult for early 20th century technology.

★862★ MINIDOKA NATIONAL WILDLIFE REFUGE
961 E Minidoka Dam
Rupert, ID 83350
Web: pacific.fws.gov/refuges/field/ID_minidoka.htm
Phone: 208-436-3589
Location: 5 miles northeast of Rupert, Idaho. **Established:** 1909. **Habitat:** 20,721 acres (including 11,000 surface acres of Lake Walcott), with small bays and inlets and surrounding uplands of sagebrush and grassland. **Facilities:** Visitor contact station, hiking trails, boat ramp, campground. **Activities:** Boating, canoeing, fishing, ice fishing, hiking, hunting, camping. **Access:** Open during daylight hours. **Primary Wildlife:** Tundra swans, Canada geese, several duck species (including mallards, pintails, redheads, gadwall, wigeon), Idaho dunes tiger beetle, Utah valvata, river otters, mink and mule deer. **Special Features:** An important stopover in the Pacific Flyway, the refuge hosts concentrations of up to 100,000 ducks and geese during spring and fall migrations. Close to 500 tundra swans can be seen in the spring and bald eagles are regularly observed in fall and spring.

★863★ MINNESOTA VALLEY NATIONAL WILDLIFE REFUGE
3815 E 80th St
Bloomington, MN 55425
Web: www.fws.gov/midwest/minnesotavalley
Phone: 952-854-5900; **Fax:** 612-725-3279
Location: A corridor along the Minnesota River, from Fort Snelling State Park (near downtown Minneapolis) southwest to Jordan, Minnesota. **Established:** 1976. **Habitat:** 14,000 acres of riverine wetlands, fens, seeps, floodplain forests, oak savannas, forest, native grasslands. **Facilities:** Visitor center, auditorium, observation platform, trails, historic features. **Activities:** Fishing, hiking, biking, horseback riding, hunting, cross-country skiing, snowshoeing, snowmobiling, educational programs. **Access:** Open during daylight hours. **Primary Wildlife:** Owls, mallards, heron, egret, geese, American coots, doves, coyotes, badgers, and white-tailed deer. **Special Features:** Urban-area refuge is home to about 50 mammals, 30 species of reptiles and amphibians, and more than 200 species of birds.

★864★ MISSISQUOI NATIONAL WILDLIFE REFUGE
29 Tabor Rd
Swanton, VT 05488
Web: www.fws.gov/refuges/profiles/index.cfm?id=53520
Phone: 802-868-4781
Location: On the eastern shore of Lake Champlain near the Canadian border, 40 miles north of Burlington, Vermont. **Established:** 1943. **Habitat:** 6,642 acres of Missisquoi River delta. **Facilities:** Visitor contact station, viewing sites, nature trails, boat launch. **Activities:** Boating, canoeing, fishing, hiking, hunting, educational programs. **Access:** Open from dawn to dusk. **Primary Wildlife:** American woodcock, great blue heron, bobolink, black tern, osprey, and white tailed deer. **Special Features:**

Refuge lands also protect the Shad Island great blue heron rookery, one of the largest such colonies in Vermont.

★865★ MISSISSIPPI SANDHILL CRANE NATIONAL WILDLIFE REFUGE
7200 Crane Ln
Gautier, MS 39553
Web: www.fws.gov/mississippisandhillcrane
Phone: 228-497-6322
Location: Southern Mississippi, near the Gulf coast. **Established:** 1975. **Habitat:** Four separate parcels comprising more than 19,000 acres of wet pine savannas, pine scrub, forested swamps, and tidal marshes. **Facilities:** Visitor center, viewing sites, hiking trails. **Activities:** Educational programs. **Access:** Most of the refuge is closed to the public; the visitor center is open Monday through Friday from 8am to 3pm. **Primary Wildlife:** Endangered Mississippi sandhill crane. Also provides habitat for songbirds, harriers, and red-tailed hawks. **Special Features:** Mississippi sandhill cranes are a critically-endangered subspecies found nowhere else in the wild except on and adjacent to the Mississippi Sandhill Crane NWR. Only about 120 individuals remain, including about 20 breeding pairs.

★866★ MOAPA VALLEY NATIONAL WILDLIFE REFUGE
c/o Desert NWR
HCR 38, Box 700
Las Vegas, NV 89124
Web: desertcomplex.fws.gov/moapavalley
Phone: 702-879-6110; **Fax:** 702-879-6115
Location: 60 miles north of Las Vegas, Nevada. **Established:** 1979. **Habitat:** 106 acres of Mohave desert, palm trees, spring heads, and associated outflow channels and aquatic habitat. **Access:** Closed to the general public. **Primary Wildlife:** Endangered Moapa dace. **Special Features:** Refuge was established to secure habitat for the endangered Moapa dace, a small fish found in headwaters of the Muddy River. In the last decade, dace populations have declined due to habitat destruction.

★867★ MODOC NATIONAL WILDLIFE REFUGE
PO Box 1610
Alturas, CA 96101
Web: www.fws.gov/modoc
Phone: 530-233-3572; **Fax:** 530-233-4143
Location: Northeast corner of California, just south of Alturas. **Established:** 1961. **Habitat:** 7,000 acres of freshwater lakes and ponds, farmland and irrigated meadows, sagebrush upland and riparian corridors. **Facilities:** Visitor contact station, viewing sites, hiking trails, auto tour route. **Activities:** Boating, canoeing, fishing, hunting, educational programs. **Access:** Open daily during daylight hours. **Primary Wildlife:** Waterfowl, including Canada geese, mallards, cinnamon teal, wigeons, and pintails. Also provides habitat for white pelicans, rabbits, kangaroo rats, beaver, mule deer, pronghorn antelope, lizards, toads, frogs and snakes. **Special Features:** Fed by snowmelt from the Warner Mountains, the Pit River creates an oasis for wildlife in this high desert area of northeastern California.

See pages 22-23 for map of National Wildlife Refuges.

4. National Wildlife Refuges

★868★ MONOMOY NATIONAL WILDLIFE REFUGE

Wikis Way
Morris Island
Chatham, MA 02633
Web: www.fws.gov/northeast/monomoy
Phone: 508-945-0594; **Fax:** 508-945-9559
Location: In Nantucket Sound, south from the elbow of Cape Cod, Massachusetts. **Established:** 1944. **Habitat:** 7,604 acres on three barrier beach islands, consisting of sand dunes, freshwater ponds, and salt and freshwater marshes. **Facilities:** Visitor contact station, viewing sites, hiking trails. **Activities:** Fishing, shellfishing, hiking. **Access:** Open year round during daylight hours. A portion of Morris Island accessible by causeway; North and South Monomoy islands are accessible by boat only. **Primary Wildlife:** Migratory birds, including the threatened piping plover and endangered roseate tern, red knot and horseshoe crab. **Special Features:** Harbor and gray seals haul out on refuge beaches in winter. Ninety-four percent of the refuge is designated wilderness area.

★869★ MONTE VISTA NATIONAL WILDLIFE REFUGE

c/o Alamosa NWR
9383 El Rancho Ln
Alamosa, CO 81101
Web: alamosa.fws.gov/Monte%20Vista.html
Phone: 719-589-4021
Location: In south-central Colorado, about 4 miles east of Alamosa. **Established:** 1953. **Habitat:** 14,804 acres of artificially-created wetlands. **Facilities:** Viewing sites, trails, auto tour route (4 miles). **Activities:** Hunting, hiking, wildlife observation. **Access:** Open year round during daylight hours. **Primary Wildlife:** White-faced ibis, avocets, bald eagles, harriers, greater sandhill cranes, whooping cranes, deer, coyotes, beaver, porcupines, and elk. **Special Features:** Refuge is a major stopover for migrating greater sandhill cranes moving between their wintering grounds in the south and their breeding grounds in the north. Up to 20,000 cranes pass through the refuge every spring and fall.

★870★ MONTEZUMA NATIONAL WILDLIFE REFUGE

3395 Rts 5/20 E
Seneca Falls, NY 13148
Web: www.fws.gov/r5mnwr
Phone: 315-568-5987
Location: Upstate New York, 35 miles west of Syracuse. **Established:** 1938, as Montezuma Migratory Bird Refuge. **Habitat:** 7,068 acres of restored marsh, hardwood forest, and grassland. **Facilities:** Visitor center, nature trails, observation towers, auto tour route. **Activities:** Hiking, hunting, cross-country skiing, snowshoeing, educational programs. **Access:** Open from dawn to dusk. **Primary Wildlife:** Migratory waterfowl (Canada geese, snow geese, black ducks, mallards, and wood ducks), shore birds (killdeer, yellowlegs, herons, and egrets), butterflies, red fox, white-tailed deer, and muskrats. **Special Features:** With 7,000 acres of the former marshes restored, the area is once again attracting large flocks of waterfowl and many species of waterbirds each spring and fall.

★871★ MOOSEHORN NATIONAL WILDLIFE REFUGE

RR 1 Box 202, Suite 1
Baring, ME 04694
Web: www.fws.gov/refuges/profiles/index.cfm?id=53530
Phone: 207-454-7161; **Fax:** 207-454-2550
Location: Eastern Maine, 90 miles northeast of Bangor. **Established:** 1937. **Habitat:** 28,751 acres of rolling hills, large ledge outcrops, streams, lakes, bogs, marshes, hardwood forest, and rocky shoreline. **Facilities:** Visitor contact station, viewing sites, hiking trails. **Activities:** Fishing, hiking, mountain biking, hunting, cross-country skiing, snowshoeing, educational programs. **Access:** Open from dawn to dusk. **Primary Wildlife:** American woodcock. Also provides habitat for wood ducks, bald eagles, osprey, grouse, bear and moose. **Special Features:** The woodlands of the refuge are home to many songbirds, including neotropical migrants. In mid-May, a flush of migrating warblers fills the forest with song; 26 species of these little birds nest on the refuge. Northern forest species such as boreal chickadees and spruce grouse are also present.

★872★ MORGAN BRAKE NATIONAL WILDLIFE REFUGE

c/o Hillside NWR
1562 Providence Rd
Cruger, MS 38924
Web: morganbrake.fws.gov
Phone: 662-235-4989; **Fax:** 662-235-5303
Location: Central Mississippi, about 60 miles north of Jackson. **Established:** 1977. **Habitat:** 7,381 acres of bottomland and upland hardwoods, cypress/tupelo brakes, croplands, and ponds. **Activities:** Hunting, fishing, hiking, wildlife observation, educational programs. **Access:** Year round during daylight hours. **Primary Wildlife:** Ducks, cattle egret, black-crowned night heron, bald eagles, golden eagles, blue jay, butterflies, deer, squirrel, rabbit, American alligator, and raccoon. **Special Features:** Refuge is located on the former site of a commercial catfish farm that included 55 ponds. It is noted for large numbers of wintering waterfowl which have exceeded 100,000 in recent years. Approximately 250 species of birds use the refuge, which is an important migration stopover.

★873★ MOUNTAIN LONGLEAF NATIONAL WILDLIFE REFUGE

291 Jimmy Parks Blvd
Fort McClellan, AL 36205
Web: www.fws.gov/southeast/mountainlongleaf
Phone: 256-848-6833; **Fax:** 256-848-5517
Location: In the southern Appalachian Mountains between Atlanta, Georgia, and Birmingham, Alabama. **Established:** 2003. **Habitat:** 9,016 acres old-growth mountain longleaf pine forest. **Access:** 3,000 acres open during daylight hours. The other 6,000 acres will be open once environmental cleanup is complete. **Primary Wildlife:** Endangered gray bat and red-cockaded woodpecker, scarlet tanagers and ovenbirds. **Special Features:** Only mountain refuge in southeastern U.S. was formerly part of Fort McClellan military training base. Refuge is being surveyed to determine where unexploded ordnance exist and what must be done to make refuge lands safe for visitors.

See pages 22-23 for map of National Wildlife Refuges.

★874★ MULESHOE NATIONAL WILDLIFE REFUGE

PO Box 549
Muleshoe, TX 79347
Web: www.fws.gov/southwest/refuges/texas/muleshoe
Phone: 806-946-3341; **Fax:** 806-946-3317
Location: 20 miles south of Muleshoe, Texas. **Established:** 1935. **Habitat:** 5,809 acres of short grass rangeland with scattered mesquite and three lakes. **Facilities:** Visitor contact station, viewing sites, hiking trail, campgrounds, picnic area. **Activities:** Camping, hiking, wildlife observation. **Access:** Open during daylight hours. **Primary Wildlife:** Lesser sandhill cranes, pintails, green-winged teal, wigeon, mallard, northern shoveler, American kestrel, turkey vulture, prairie dogs, prairie rattlesnakes, coyote, bobcat, badger, cottontail and jackrabbits, and porcupine. **Special Features:** Muleshoe's three sink-type lakes depend entirely on runoff for water and are periodically dry. When the lakes are full, 600 acres of water are available for wildlife.

★875★ MUSCATATUCK NATIONAL WILDLIFE REFUGE

12985 E US Hwy 50
Seymour, IN 47274
Web: www.fws.gov/midwest/muscatatuck
Phone: 812-522-4352; **Fax:** 812-522-7802
Location: In southern Indiana, about 50 miles south of Indianapolis. **Established:** 1966. **Habitat:** 7,802 acres of farm lands, lakes, ponds, moist soil, grassland, forest. **Facilities:** Visitor center, viewing sites, hiking trails (&), auto tour route (9 miles), historic features. **Activities:** Boating, fishing, ice fishing, hiking, hunting, educational programs. **Access:** Open year round during daylight hours. **Primary Wildlife:** Canada geese, wood ducks, great blue herons, the rare copperbelly water snake, white-tailed deer, muskrat, beaver, and turkey. **Special Features:** On most of the refuge's lakes, fishing is permitted year round. Good catches of largemouth bass, bluegill, crappie, and channel catfish are not uncommon. Ice fishing is permitted when conditions are safe.

★876★ NANSEMOND NATIONAL WILDLIFE REFUGE

c/o Great Dismal Swamp NWR
PO Box 349
Suffolk, VA 23439
Web: www.fws.gov/refuges/profiles/index.cfm?id=51581
Phone: 757-986-3705
Location: On the Nansemond River in Suffolk, 10 miles west of Portsmouth. **Established:** 1973. **Habitat:** 207 acres of mostly salt marshland and an additional 204 acres of upland grassland and forested stream corridors (transferred from the US Navy in 1999). **Access:** Closed to the public since access is limited to a roadway passing through closed military areas. **Primary Wildlife:** Black ducks, mallards, canvasbacks, and wading, marsh, and shorebirds. **Special Features:** A satellite refuge managed by Great Dismal Swamp National Wildlife Refuge.

★877★ NANTUCKET NATIONAL WILDLIFE REFUGE

c/o Great Meadows NWR
73 Weir Hill Rd
Sudbury, MA 01776
Web: northeast.fws.gov/ma/nat.htm
Phone: 978-443-4661
Location: North tip of Nantucket Island, 4 miles east of Nantucket. **Established:** 1975. **Habitat:** 40 acres of sand dunes with low shrub vegetation and shifting sand. **Activities:** Fishing, wildlife observation. **Access:** Open from dawn to dusk; closed to vehicular access during nesting season. **Primary Wildlife:** Piping plovers, least tern, gray and harbor seals. **Special Features:** Refuge features the Great Point Lighthouse, originally constructed in 1784 and rebuilt several times, most recently in 1986.

★878★ NATIONAL BISON RANGE

132 Bison Range Rd
Moiese, MT 59824
Web: www.fws.gov/bisonrange
Phone: 406-644-2211; **Fax:** 406-644-2661
Location: Northwest of Missoula in western Montana. **Established:** 1908. **Habitat:** 18,500 acres of Palouse prairie, forests, wetlands, and streams. **Facilities:** Visitor center, picnic areas, hiking trails, auto tour routes, interpretive exhibits. **Activities:** Fishing, hiking, educational programs. **Access:** Open during daylight hours. **Primary Wildlife:** Bison, deer, elk, bighorn sheep, black bear, and pronghorn. **Special Features:** Protects one of the most important remaining herds of bison. The animals were reestablished here after the number of known wild bison was reduced to 20 from about 50 million in the early 1800s. The refuge maintains a herd of 350-500 animals.

★879★ NATIONAL ELK REFUGE

PO Box 510
Jackson, WY 83001
Web: www.fws.gov/nationalelkrefuge
Phone: 307-733-9212; **Fax:** 307-733-9729
Location: Northwestern Wyoming, north of Jackson. **Established:** 1912. **Habitat:** Nearly 25,000 acres of grass meadows, sagebrush flats, timbered foothills, and marshes. **Facilities:** Visitor center, viewing sites, hiking trails, auto tour route, picnic areas. **Activities:** Hunting, fishing, horse-drawn sleigh ride tours, educational programs. **Access:** Open during daylight hours. **Primary Wildlife:** Elk, bison, moose, bighorn sheep, mule deer, antelope, bald eagles, sandhill cranes, songbirds and waterfowl. **Special Features:** In late October and early November, about 7,500 elk begin migrating from their high summer range in Grand Teton National Park, southern Yellowstone National Park, and neighboring national forests to winter here at the refuge.

★880★ NATIONAL KEY DEER REFUGE

179 Key Deer Blvd
Big Pine Key, FL 33043
Web: nationalkeydeer.fws.gov
Phone: 305-872-2239; **Fax:** 305-872-2154

See pages 22-23 for map of National Wildlife Refuges.

Location: Florida Keys, about 30 miles northeast of Key West. **Established:** 1957. **Habitat:** 84,351 acres of upland forest, shrub wetland and wetland marsh. **Facilities:** Visitor contact station, viewing sites, hiking trails (&). **Activities:** Boating, canoeing, fishing, hiking, educational programs. **Access:** Open during daylight hours. **Primary Wildlife:** Key deer, a subspecies of the Virginia white-tailed deer. **Special Features:** The Key deer is the smallest of all white-tailed deer and is a species not found anywhere else in the world. In 1957, only 27 known deer existed. With the establishment of the refuge and intensive law enforcement efforts, the population has increased to about 800 deer.

★881★ NEAL SMITH NATIONAL WILDLIFE REFUGE

PO Box 399
Prairie City, IA 50228
Web: www.fws.gov/midwest/nealsmith
Phone: 641-994-3400
Location: 20 miles east of Des Moines, Iowa. **Established:** 1990 as Walnut Creek NWR. **Habitat:** 8,000 acres being restored to tallgrass prairie and oak savanna. **Facilities:** Visitor center, viewing sites, hiking trails, auto tour route. **Activities:** Hunting, hiking, biking, mushroom collecting, educational programs. **Access:** Year round during daylight hours. **Primary Wildlife:** Elk, bison, beaver, badger, weasel, plains pocket gopher, Henslow's sparrow, northern harrier, short-eared owl, bobolink and meadowlark. **Special Features:** Refuge is the largest re-creation of the tallgrass prairie ecosystem anywhere in the United States. Native grasses and prairie flowers are being nurtured, and more than 200 types of prairie seeds have been replanted.

★882★ NECEDAH NATIONAL WILDLIFE REFUGE

W7996 20th St W
Necedah, WI 54646
Web: www.fws.gov/midwest/necedah
Phone: 608-565-2551; **Fax:** 608-565-3160
Location: In central Wisconsin, 4 miles west of Necedah. **Established:** 1939. **Habitat:** 43,696 acres of forest, wetlands, and large tracts of rare oak barrens. **Facilities:** Visitor contact station, viewing sites, observation tower, auto tour route, trails. **Activities:** Fishing, hiking, hunting, berry picking, cross-country skiing, snowshoeing, educational programs. **Access:** Open during daylight hours. **Primary Wildlife:** Bald eagles, whooping cranes, tringed bog hunter dragonflies, turkey, white-tailed deer, ruffed grouse, beaver, and coyote. **Special Features:** Refuge also provides habitat for threatened, endangered, and rare species such as the Karner blue butterfly, Massasauga rattlesnake, Blanding's turtle, and gray wolf.

★883★ NESTUCCA BAY NATIONAL WILDLIFE REFUGE

c/o Oregon Coast NWR Complex
2127 SE Marine Science Dr
Newport, OR 97365
Web: www.fws.gov/oregoncoast/nestuccabay
Phone: 541-867-4550

Location: South of Pacific City, Oregon, just off Highway 101. **Established:** 1991. **Habitat:** 850 acres of tidal saltmarsh, mudflats, freshwater bogs, pasturelands, grasslands, and forested lagg. **Facilities:** Wildife viewing sites. **Access:** Closed to the public. **Primary Wildlife:** Dusky Canada goose and Aleutian cackling goose. It is also an important rest stop for migrating shorebirds and other waterfowl and is used by peregrine falcons and bald eagles. **Special Features:** The southernmost coastal sphagnum bog habitat on the Pacific Coast is contained in the refuge's Neskowin Marsh unit. This rare ecosystem is home to unusual plant species such as the carnivorous sundew.

★884★ NINEPIPE NATIONAL WILDLIFE REFUGE

c/o National Bison Range
132 Bison Range Rd
Moiese, MT 58924
Web: www.fws.gov/bisonrange/ninepipe
Phone: 406-644-2211; **Fax:** 406-644-2661
Location: Northwest Montana, 50 miles north of Missoula. **Established:** 1921. **Habitat:** 2,062 acres of upland habitat and rolling grassland interspersed with pothole wetlands. **Facilities:** Viewing sites, auto tour route, self-guided nature trail (&). **Activities:** Fishing, educational programs. **Access:** Daylight hours, although some areas of the refuge are closed seasonally. **Primary Wildlife:** Canada geese, red-necked grebes, song sparrows, yellow-headed and red-winged blackbirds, ring-necked pheasants, American bitterns, sora rails, osprey, double-crested cormorants, and great blue herons. Also provides habitat for muskrat, striped skunk, mink, badger, meadow voles, porcupine, and forage for grizzly bears. **Special Features:** Refuge is on tribal lands located in Flathead Valley, operated under agreement with the Salish and Kootenai tribes. No hunting is permitted.

★885★ NINIGRET NATIONAL WILDLIFE REFUGE

c/o Rhode Island NWR Complex
50 Bend Rd
Charlestown, RI 02813
Phone: 401-364-9124; **Fax:** 401-364-0170
Location: On Rhode Island's south shore, about halfway between Westerly and Naragannsett. **Established:** 1970. **Habitat:** 900 acres of saltmarshes, kettle ponds, freshwater wetlands, maritime shrublands and forests dominated by oak or maple. **Facilities:** Visitor center with interpretive exhibits and gift store, trails, observation platforms. **Activities:** Surf fishing, hiking, hunting, educational programs. **Access:** Open from dawn to dusk year round. **Primary Wildlife:** Piping plover, osprey, bluebirds, woodcock, common merganser, and red-breasted merganser. **Special Features:** Located on the site of a former naval air station, the refuge provides visitors with more than 3 miles of trails. Of the more than 250 bird species that visit the refuge, 70 nest here.

★886★ NISQUALLY NATIONAL WILDLIFE REFUGE

100 Brown Farm Rd
Olympia, WA 98516
Web: www.fws.gov/nisqually
Phone: 360-753-9467; **Fax:** 360-534-9302

See pages 22-23 for map of National Wildlife Refuges.

Location: 8 miles northeast of Olympia, Washington. **Established:** 1974. **Habitat:** 3,000 acres of salt and freshwater marshes, grasslands, riparian, and mixed forest habitats. **Facilities:** Visitor contact station, hiking trails (&), observation tower, viewing sites, historic features. **Activities:** Boating, fishing, hiking, hunting, educational programs. **Access:** Open daily during daylight hours. **Primary Wildlife:** Migratory birds, including wigeon, mallard, and blue-winged teal; also shrews, moles, otters, bats, whales, porpoises, snakes and newts. **Special Features:** Refuge is located in the Nisqually River Delta, a biologically rich and diverse area at the southern end of Puget Sound.

★887★ NORTH PLATTE NATIONAL WILDLIFE REFUGE

c/o Crescent Lake NWR
115 Railway St
Scottsbluff, NE 69363
Web: crescentlake.fws.gov/northplatte
Phone: 308-635-7851
Location: Panhandle of Western Nebraska. **Established:** 1916. **Habitat:** 2,722 acres of grassland and lakes. **Facilities:** Boat launch, hiking trails. **Activities:** Canoeing, fishing, ice fishing, hiking, educational programs. **Access:** Closed to public entry during October, November, and December. **Primary Wildlife:** Waterfowl and shorebirds; also bald eagles, bullsnake, western plains garter snake, northern leopard frog, black-tailed prairie dog, eastern cottontail, mule and white-tailed deer. **Special Features:** As many as 20 bald eagles and more than 200,000 waterfowl may concentrate on the refuge during fall migration. Well over 200 bird species have been observed on the refuge since 1975. Lake Alice has one of the oldest and most successful bald eagle nests in Nebraska.

★888★ NOWITNA NATIONAL WILDLIFE REFUGE

PO Box 287
Galena, AK 99741
Web: nowitna.fws.gov
Phone: 907-656-1231; **Fax:** 907-656-1708; **Toll Free:** 800-656-1231
Location: 150 miles west of Fairbanks, Alaska, in the central Yukon River Valley. **Established:** 1980. **Habitat:** More than 2,100,000 acres of river valley, wetlands, forest and tundra. **Facilities:** Visitor contact station (in Galena). **Activities:** Boating, canoeing, fishing, hunting, primitive camping. **Access:** Access to the refuge is possible by airplane, boat, snowmobile, dog sled, or on foot. **Primary Wildlife:** Moose, bear, caribou, martens, wolverine, ducks, geese, trumpeter swans, bald eagle, northern harrier, red-tailed hawk, salmon, sheefish and northern pike. **Special Features:** A 223-mile segment of the Nowitna River, a nationally designated Wild River, bisects the refuge and forms a broad meandering floodplain.

★889★ NOXUBEE NATIONAL WILDLIFE REFUGE

2970 Bluff Lake Rd
Brooksville, MS 39739
Web: www.fws.gov/noxubee
Phone: 662-323-5548; **Fax:** 662-323-6390

Location: East-central Mississippi. **Established:** 1940. **Habitat:** 47,000 acres of lakes, pine woodlands, and forested bottomlands. **Facilities:** Visitor contact station, viewing sites, observation tower, picnic areas, boat ramp, trails (&). **Activities:** Boating, fishing, hiking, hunting, educational programs. **Access:** Open year round during daylight hours. **Primary Wildlife:** Canada geese and waterfowl (primarily mallards), red-tailed hawk, bobwhite, American wigeons, teal, alligators, white-tailed deer, catfish, cottonmouth, copperhead, timber and pygmy rattlesnake. **Special Features:** Noxubee maintains an intensive red-cockaded woodpecker management program. Its 1/4-mile Woodpecker Trail offers the visitor an excellent opportunity to view this endangered bird.

★890★ OAHU FOREST NATIONAL WILDLIFE REFUGE

c/o Oahu NWR Complex
66-590 Kam Hwy
Haleiwa, HI 96712
Web: www.fws.gov/pacificislands/wnwr/oahuforestnwr.html
Phone: 808-637-6330; **Fax:** 808-637-3578
Location: South of the Schofield Barracks Military Reserve, in the northern Koolau Mountains on the eastern side of Oahu, Hawaii. **Established:** 2000. **Habitat:** 4,525 acres of forested land on the leeward slopes of Oahu's Kooalu Mountains. Habitat communities include mesic forest, rain forest, high-elevation cloud forest, and freshwater streams. **Access:** Closed to the public. **Primary Wildlife:** Oahu elepaio (endangered), Hawaiian owl, native honeycreepers, and other native Hawaiian forest birds. **Special Features:** Refuge protects some of the last remaining intact native forests on Oahu, and supports at least 17 species of endangered plants and four species of endangered tree snails.

★891★ OCCOQUAN BAY NATIONAL WILDLIFE REFUGE

c/o Mason Neck NWR
13950 Dawson Beach Rd
Woodbridge, VA 22191
Web: www.fws.gov/northeast/va/mro.htm
Phone: 703-490-4979; **Fax:** 703-490-5631
Location: In Woodbridge, Virginia, 20 miles south of Washington, D.C. **Established:** 1998. **Habitat:** 644-acre mix of wetlands, forest, and native grasslands. **Facilities:** Visitor contact station. **Activities:** Fishing, hunting (with restrictions), educational programs. **Access:** Year round during daylight hours. **Primary Wildlife:** White-tailed deer, woodcock, snipe, northern harrier, savanna sparrow, and great horned owl. **Special Features:** More than 220 species of birds and 600 species of plants, as well as 65 species of butterflies have been documented on the refuge.

★892★ OHIO RIVER ISLANDS NATIONAL WILDLIFE REFUGE

3004 7th St
PO Box 1811
Parkersburg, WV 26102
Web: northeast.fws.gov/wv/ori.htm
Phone: 304-422-0752; **Fax:** 304-422-0754

See pages 22-23 for map of National Wildlife Refuges.

Location: Extends nearly 400 river miles along the Ohio River. **Established:** 1990. **Habitat:** 3,300 acres of farm fields and old-growth timber on 22 Ohio River islands and three mainland tracts. **Facilities:** Visitor contact station, hiking trails, auto tour route. **Activities:** Boating, canoeing, fishing, hiking, hunting, educational programs. **Access:** Open for day use. One islands has bridge access; all others are accessible only by boat. **Primary Wildlife:** Prothonotary and cerulean warblers, great blue herons, osprey, ring-necked ducks, bald eagles, deer, rabbit, squirrel, and the endangered fanshell and pink mucket mussel. **Special Features:** Refuge protects land and water habitats used by 40 species of freshwater mussels, two of which are endangered. Most of the refuge is located in West Virginia; Pennsylvania and Kentucky each include two islands.

★893★ OKEFENOKEE NATIONAL WILDLIFE
  REFUGE
Rt 2 Box 3330
Folkston, GA 31537
Web: www.fws.gov/okefenokee
Phone: 912-496-7836
Location: Southern Georgia. **Established:** 1936. **Habitat:** 402,000 acres of freshwater swamp with numerous islands, lakes, forests, and prairies. **Facilities:** Visitor center, picnic area, boat launch, canoe trails, hiking trails, observation tower, auto tour route, historic features. **Activities:** Boating (10 hp limit), camping, canoeing, fishing, hiking, biking, hunting, educational programs. **Access:** Open year round. **Primary Wildlife:** Wading birds (herons, egrets, ibises, wood stork, sandhill cranes, and bitterns), American alligator, red-cockaded woodpeckers, Florida black bear, green anole. **Special Features:** Okefenokee Swamp remains one of the oldest and best-preserved freshwater areas in America, covering an area 38 miles long and 25 miles wide. The slow-moving waters form the Suwannee River, which flows southwesterly through Florida into the Gulf of Mexico. The swamp also drains into the Atlantic Ocean via the Saint Mary's River, which forms the boundary between Georgia and Florida.

★894★ OPTIMA NATIONAL WILDLIFE REFUGE
c/o Washita NWR
Rt 1 Box 68
Butler, OK 73625
Web: www.fws.gov/southwest/refuges/oklahoma/optima
Phone: 580-664-2205; Fax: 580-664-2206
Location: Oklahoma's panhandle. **Established:** 1978. **Habitat:** 4,333 acres of grasslands and wooded bottomland. **Activities:** Hunting, wildlife observation. **Access:** Open year round during daylight hours. **Primary Wildlife:** White-tailed deer, coyotes, Rio Grande turkeys, quail, turkey vulture, American Kestrel, hawks, bald and golden eagles. **Special Features:** Optima Dam was completed in 1978 but the impoundment never reached expected levels. To date, the lake has never risen enough to flood any of the refuge lands.

★895★ OREGON ISLANDS NATIONAL WILDLIFE
  REFUGE
c/o Oregon Coast NWR Complex
2127 SE Marine Science Dr
Newport, OR 97365
Web: www.fws.gov/oregoncoast/oregonislands
Phone: 541-867-4550
Location: Along Oregon's 320 miles of coastline. **Established:** 1935. **Habitat:** More than 1,853 coastal islands, rocks, and reefs. **Facilities:** At Coquille Point: visitor contact station, interpretive displays, trails, viewing sites. **Access:** Offshore sites are closed to public entry but can be viewed from scenic lookout points along the coast. **Primary Wildlife:** Tufted puffins, Leach's and fork-tailed storm-petrels, rhinoceros auklets, cormorants, harbor seals, California sea lions, Steller sea lions and northern elephant seals. **Special Features:** Refuge provides essential breeding and haulout areas for harbor seals, sea lions, and elephant seals.

★896★ OTTAWA NATIONAL WILDLIFE REFUGE
14000 W State Rt 2
Oak Harbor, OH 43449
Web: www.fws.gov/midwest/Ottawa
Phone: 419-898-0014; Fax: 419-898-7895
Location: 15 miles east of Toledo in northern Ohio. **Established:** 1961. **Habitat:** 6,350 acres of wetland, native prairie, wooded areas, and open estuary. **Facilities:** Visitor contact station, viewing sites, trails. **Activities:** Hunting, trapping, fishing, hiking, educational programs. **Access:** Open from dawn to dusk. **Primary Wildlife:** Canada geese, mallards, teal, wood ducks, American wigeon, canvasbacks, bald eagles, coyotes, and white-tailed deer. **Special Features:** Up to 70 percent of the Mississippi Flyway population of black ducks can be found in the Lake Erie marshes during fall migration. Large numbers of migrating songbirds stop in the area to rest during their spring migration.

★897★ OURAY NATIONAL WILDLIFE REFUGE
266 W 100 North, Suite 2
Vernal, UT 84078
Web: ouray.fws.gov
Phone: 435-789-0351
Location: Northeastern Utah. **Established:** 1960. **Habitat:** 11,987 acres along a 12-mile stretch of the Green River. Habitats include river, riparian woodlands, wetlands, artificial impoundments, croplands, semidesert shrublands, grasslands, and clay bluffs. **Facilities:** Visitor contact station, viewing sites, trails, auto tour route. **Activities:** Hiking, fishing, mountain biking, horseback riding, canoeing, rafting, hunting, educational programs. **Access:** Open during daylight hours. **Primary Wildlife:** Three endangered fish — Colorado pikeminnow, bonytail, and humpback chub — as well as beaver, muskrat, river otter, waterfowl, cottontail rabbits, raccoons, mule deer, elk, bobcats, bald and golden eagles, great horned owls and hawks. **Special Features:** The desert of northeastern Utah is a harsh environment, where less than 8 inches of rain falls per year, but the Green River transports water from the mountains of Wyoming to the area and as a result thousands of waterfowl, songbirds and other wildlife flock to the refuge.

See pages 22-23 for map of National Wildlife Refuges.

4. National Wildlife Refuges

★898★ OVERFLOW NATIONAL WILDLIFE REFUGE

c/o Felsenthal NWR
3858 Hwy 8E
Parkdale, AR 71661
Web: www.fws.gov/southeast/overflow
Phone: 870-473-2869; **Fax:** 870-473-5191
Location: South-central Arkansas. **Established:** 1980. **Habitat:** 12,247 acres of bottomland hardwoods, agriculture fields, and upland pine and hardwood forests. **Activities:** Hunting, hiking, wildlife observation, educational programs. **Access:** Year round during daylight hours. **Primary Wildlife:** Migratory waterfowl and other birds, deer, rabbit, squirrel. **Special Features:** The refuge's western boundary follows a 110-foot contour along the Mississippi Alluvial Valley excarpment, an abrupt rise in elevation separating the Mississippi River delta from the gulf coastal plain.

★899★ OXBOW NATIONAL WILDLIFE REFUGE

c/o Great Meadows NWR
73 Weir Hill Rd
Sudbury, MA 01776
Web: oxbow.fws.gov
Phone: 978-443-4661; **Fax:** 978-443-2898
Location: 35 miles northwest of Boston. **Established:** 1988. **Habitat:** 1,667 acres of freshwater marsh, oxbow wetland and upland habitat. **Facilities:** Hiking trails. **Activities:** Hiking, hunting, fishing, educational programs. **Access:** Open from dawn to dusk. **Primary Wildlife:** Migratory birds, American woodcock, turkey, white-tailed deer, and the Blanding's turtle. **Special Features:** The refuge hosts the highest density of nesting Blanding's turtle east of the Mississippi River.

★900★ OXFORD SLOUGH NATIONAL WILDLIFE REFUGE

4425 Burley Dr, Suite A
Chubbuck, ID 83202
Web: www.fws.gov/pacific/refuges/field/ID_oxford.htm
Phone: 208-237-6615
Location: 10 miles northwest of Preston, Idaho. **Habitat:** 1,878 acres of marshes, meadows, and uplands. **Activities:** Canoeing, kayaing, wildlife observation. **Access:** No developed facilities for public use. **Primary Wildlife:** Waterbirds. **Special Features:** Refuge includes nesting ducks and a variety of waterbirds including a colony of white-faced ibises.

★901★ OYSTER BAY NATIONAL WILDLIFE REFUGE

c/o Long Island NWR Complex
PO Box 21
Shirley, NY 11967
Phone: 631-286-0485; **Fax:** 631-286-4003
Location: On northwestern Long Island, New York. **Established:** 1968. **Habitat:** More than 3,000 acres of shallow bays and salt marshes. **Facilities:** None. **Activities:** Boating, canoeing, fishing, educational programs. **Access:** Open from dawn to dusk; accessible by boat only. **Primary Wildlife:** Migratory waterfowl, ducks and waterbirds; also marine invertebrates, shellfish, fish, harbor seals, and diamond terrapin. **Special Features:** Refuge is a marine sanctuary encompassing more water than land. New York's last remaining commercial oyster farm operates on the refuge, harvesting 90 percent of the state's oysters.

★902★ OZARK PLATEAU NATIONAL WILDLIFE REFUGE

Rt 1 Box 18A
Vian, OK 74962
Web: www.fws.gov/southwest/refuges/oklahoma/Ozark
Phone: 918-773-5251; **Fax:** 918-773-5598
Location: Northeastern Oklahoma. **Established:** 1985; originally known as Oklahoma Bat Caves NWR. **Habitat:** 16 tracts totaling 3,067 acres of forested areas with numerous caves. **Access:** Closed to recreational uses. **Primary Wildlife:** Ozark big-eared bats. Also, gray bats, blind cavefish, salamanders and crayfish. **Special Features:** Refuge protects critical maternity caves for bats as well as other cave-dwelling wildlife including blind cavefish, salamanders, and crayfish. Some of these creatures are only native to Oklahoma and some are even unique to a specific cave.

★903★ PABLO NATIONAL WILDLIFE REFUGE

c/o National Bison Range
132 Bison Range Rd
Moiese, MT 59824
Web: www.fws.gov/bisonrange/pablo
Phone: 406-644-2211; **Fax:** 406-664-2661
Location: Northwest Montana, 40 miles north of Missoula. **Established:** 1921. **Habitat:** 2,542 acres of rolling grassland interspersed with pothole wetlands, uplands and a small stand of cottonwoods. **Facilities:** Auto tour route. **Activities:** Fishing, ice fishing, wildlife observation. **Access:** Year round during daylight hours. **Primary Wildlife:** Migratory waterfowl, including Canada geese, mallards, and redheads. Pintail, American widgeon, shoveler, blue and green-winged teal, ruddy duck, gadwall, bald eagle, loons, muskrat, striped skunk, and meadow voles are also present. **Special Features:** The upland area is used by Confederated Salish and Kootenai Tribal members for farming and grazing.

★904★ PAHRANAGAT NATIONAL WILDLIFE REFUGE

PO Box 510
Alamo, NV 89001
Web: www.fws.gov/desertcomplex/pahranagat
Phone: 775-725-3417; **Fax:** 775-725-3389
Location: 90 miles north of Las Vegas, Nevada. **Established:** 1963. **Habitat:** 5,380 acres of marshes, meadows, lakes, and upland desert. **Facilities:** Primitive campsites, viewing sites, picnic areas, trails. **Activities:** Camping, fishing, hiking, hunting, educational programs. **Access:** Open year round, 24 hours a day. **Primary Wildlife:** Waterfowl and shorebirds, including pintails, mallards, redheads, and greater sandhill cranes. Also provides habitat for warblers, orioles, finches, sparrows, Gambel's quail, roadrunners, kit foxes, coyotes, mule deer and mountain lions. **Special Features:** Pahranagat's water originates from

See pages 22-23 for map of National Wildlife Refuges.

large springs north of the refuge. The site includes four main water impoundments—North Marsh, Upper and Lower Pahranagat Lakes, and the Middle Marsh.

★905★ PANTHER SWAMP NATIONAL WILDLIFE REFUGE

13695 River Rd
Yazoo City, MS 39194
Web: www.fws.gov/pantherswamp
Phone: 662-746-5060; **Fax:** 662-746-5055
Location: West-central Mississippi, 10 miles southwest of Yazoo City. **Established:** 1978. **Habitat:** 38,697 acres of bottomland hardwood forests interspersed with numerous wooded sloughs, cypress-tupelo brakes, and bayous. **Facilities:** Auto tour route. **Activities:** Canoeing, fishing hunting. **Access:** Year round during daylight hours. **Primary Wildlife:** Waterfowl and other migratory birds, American alligator, white-tailed deer, swamp rabbit, wild turkey, squirrel, and various small fur-bearers. **Special Features:** In addition to providing resting and feeding areas for more than 100,000 wintering waterfowl annually, the refuge also provides habitat for 200 species of neotropical migratory songbirds.

★906★ PARKER RIVER NATIONAL WILDLIFE REFUGE

6 Plum Island Tpke
Newburyport, MA 01950
Web: www.fws.gov/northeast/parkerriver
Phone: 978-465-5753
Location: 35 miles north of Boston, Massachusetts. **Established:** 1942. **Habitat:** 4,662 acres of sandy beach and dune, shrub/thicket, bog, swamp, freshwater marsh, salt marsh and associated creek, river, mud flat, and salt panne. **Facilities:** Visitor contact station, viewing sites, trails (&), beach, boat ramp, auto tour route. **Activities:** Fishing, shelling, hunting, bicycling, hiking, canoeing, kayaking, educational programs. **Access:** Open from dawn to dusk. Portions of beach are closed April through July. **Primary Wildlife:** American woodcock, piper plover, red-winged blackbird, osprey, purple martin, mourning cloak butterflies, pearl crescent butterflies, spring azure butterflies, white-tailed deer, coyote, hooded arctic seals, and harbor seals. **Special Features:** The refuge supports varied and abundant populations of resident and migratory wildlife including more than 300 species of birds as well as mammals, reptiles, amphibians, insects, and plants.

★907★ PASSAGE KEY NATIONAL WILDLIFE REFUGE

1502 SE Kings Bay Dr
Crystal River, FL 34429
Web: www.fws.gov/southeast/passagekey
Phone: 352-563-2088; **Fax:** 352-795-7961
Location: Offshore from Saint Petersburg, Florida, and accessible only by boat. **Established:** 1905. **Habitat:** 63 acres, including a 30-acre meandering barrier island. **Access:** Closed to the public. **Primary Wildlife:** Royal terns, sandwich terns, brown pelicans. **Special Features:** When first established, the refuge was a mangrove island with a freshwater lake. A 1920 hurricane

destroyed it and it is now a barrier island which houses the largest royal and sandwich tern nesting colonies in Florida.

★908★ PATHFINDER NATIONAL WILDLIFE REFUGE

c/o Arapaho NWR
953 Jackson County Rd 32
Walden, CO 80480
Web: www.fws.gov/refuges/profiles/index.cfm?id=65523
Phone: 970-723-8202; **Fax:** 970-723-8528
Location: 50 miles southwest of Casper, Wyoming. **Established:** 1928. **Habitat:** 16,807 acres in 4 units consisting of sagebrush/grassland and wetlands. **Facilities:** Viewing sites with interpretive signs. **Activities:** Boating, canoeing, fishing, hunting. **Access:** Open year round during daylight hours. **Primary Wildlife:** Willets, American Avocets, Wilson's phalaropes, American coots, great blue herons, pronghorn, mule deer, and rabbits. **Special Features:** Refuge overlays portions of the Bureau of Reclamation's Pathfinder Reservoir. It is an important waterfowl unit in the western edge of the Central Flyway.

★909★ PATOKA RIVER NATIONAL WILDLIFE REFUGE

510 1/2 W Morton St
PO Box 217
Oakland City, IN 47660
Web: www.fws.gov/midwest/patokariver
Phone: 812-749-3199; **Fax:** 812-749-3059
Location: In Pike and Gibson counties in southwest Indiana. **Established:** 1994. **Habitat:** 5,131 acres of river corridor with wetlands and bottomland hardwood forests. **Facilities:** Trails, wildlife viewing sites. **Activities:** Fishing, canoeing, hunting, hiking, wildlife observation, educational programs. **Access:** Daylight hours year round. **Primary Wildlife:** 380 species of wildlife including bald eagle, Indiana bat, and interior least tern. **Special Features:** Refuge provides some of the best wood duck production habitat in the state, and is home to the largest nesting colony of interior lest tern east of the Mississippi River.

★910★ PATUXENT RESEARCH REFUGE

12100 Beech Forest Rd
Laurel, MD 20708
Web: www.fws.gov/northeast/patuxent/
Phone: 301-497-5580; **Fax:** 301-497-5515
Location: In the Baltimore/Washington metropolitan corridor near Laurel. **Established:** 1936. **Habitat:** 12,750 acres of forest, meadow, and wetland. **Facilities:** Visitor center with interpretive exhibits, auditorium, gift shop, viewing sites, hiking trails, tram tours, auto tour route. **Activities:** Fishing, hunting, hiking, bicycling, horseback riding, educational programs. **Access:** Year round during daylight hours; some portions of the refuge are closed to public entry. **Primary Wildlife:** Migrant neotropical birds, waterfowl, raptors, bald eagles, fish including bluegill, largemouth bass, catfish, and white-tailed deer. **Special Features:** The refuge houses the National Wildlife Visitor Center, the largest science and environmental education center operated by the Department of the Interior. Interactive exhibits focus on global environmental issues, migratory bird studies, habitats,

See pages 22-23 for map of National Wildlife Refuges.

4. National Wildlife Refuges

endangered species, creature life cycles, and research techniques used by scientists.

★911★ PEA ISLAND NATIONAL WILDLIFE REFUGE

c/o Alligator River NWR
PO Box 1969
Manteo, NC 27954
Web: www.fws.gov/peaisland
Phone: 252-473-1131; **Fax:** 252-473-1668
Location: On Hatteras Island on the Outer Banks of North Carolina. **Established:** 1937. **Habitat:** 5,834 acres of ocean beach, barrier dunes, salt flats, salt marshes, and fresh and brackish water ponds. Site also include 25,700 acres of Proclamation Boundary waters. **Facilities:** Visitor center, viewing sites, hiking trails (&). **Activities:** Boating, canoeing, hiking, beachcombing, fishing, educational programs. **Access:** Open year round during daylight hours. **Primary Wildlife:** Ducks, geese, tundra swans, herons, egrets, terns, piping plovers, ospreys, peregrine falcons, loggerhead sea turtles, and muskrats. **Special Features:** Refuge is home to more than 365 species of birds, 25 species of mammals, 24 species of reptiles, and 5 species of amphibians.

★912★ PEARL HARBOR NATIONAL WILDLIFE REFUGE

c/o Oahu NWR Complex
66-590 Kam Hwy
Haleiwa, HI 96712
Web: www.fws.gov/pacificislands/wnwr/opearlnwr.html
Phone: 808-637-6330; **Fax:** 808-637-3578
Location: Within the Pearl Harbor Naval Base, 10 miles west of Honolulu. **Established:** 1972. **Habitat:** Two parcels totaling 62 acres of freshwater wetlands. **Access:** Limited access; contact refuge office. **Primary Wildlife:** Endangered Hawaiian moorhen, Hawaiian coot, Hawaiian duck, and the Hawaiian stilt. **Special Features:** Refuge is composed of two units: the Honouliuli Unit, which is extensively managed for a variety of waterbirds including Hawaii's endangered waterbirds and migrant waterfowl; and the Waiawa Unit, which is composed of two ponds, one of which is primarily managed for the endangered Hawaiian stilt.

★913★ PEE DEE NATIONAL WILDLIFE REFUGE

5770 US Hwy 52 N
Wadesboro, NC 28170
Web: www.fws.gov/peedee
Phone: 704-694-4424; **Fax:** 704-694-6570
Location: South-central North Carolina, 50 miles east of Charlotte. **Established:** 1963. **Habitat:** 8,443 acres of upland forest, bottomland hardwoods, and agricultural fields. **Facilities:** Visitor contact station, viewing sites, hiking trails, auto tour route. **Activities:** Boating, canoeing, fishing, hiking, hunting, educational programs. **Access:** Open during daylight hours. **Primary Wildlife:** Turkey, mourning dove, quail, wood ducks, squirrel, raccoon, opossum, and deer. **Special Features:** The diversity of habitats supports a broad range of wildlife, including more than 180 species of birds, 49 species of amphibians and reptiles, 28 species of mammals, and 20 species of fish.

★914★ PELICAN ISLAND NATIONAL WILDLIFE REFUGE

1330 20th St
Vero Beach, FL 32960
Web: www.fws.gov/pelicanisland
Phone: 772-562-3909; **Fax:** 772-299-3101
Location: In the Intracoastal Waterway near Sebastian Inlet, along Florida's east coast. **Established:** 1903. **Habitat:** 5,413 acres of seagrass beds, oyster bars, mangrove islands, salt marsh and maritime hammocks. **Facilities:** Observation tower, viewing sites, boardwalk trails. **Activities:** Boating, canoeing, fishing, boat tours, hiking. **Access:** Daily during daylight hours. **Primary Wildlife:** Wood storks, brown pelicans, egrets, herons, ibis, double-crested cormorants, Florida manatee, Green sea turtle, Hawksbill sea turtle, Kemp's ridley sea turtle, Loggerhead sea turtle, Eastern indigo snake, bald eagle, and piping plover. **Special Features:** Pelican Island is America's first officially designated national wildlife refuge. The island is surrounded by Indian River Lagoon, the most biologically diverse estuary in the United States.

★915★ PIEDMONT NATIONAL WILDLIFE REFUGE

718 Juliette Rd
Hillsboro, GA 31038
Web: www.fws.gov/piedmont
Phone: 478-986-5441; **Fax:** 478-986-9646
Location: In central Georgia, 25 miles north of Macon. **Established:** 1939. **Habitat:** 35,000 acres of hardwoods, streams, and ponds. **Facilities:** Visitor center, viewing sites, auto tour route, trails. **Activities:** Fishing, hiking, hunting, educational programs. **Access:** Open during daylight hours. **Primary Wildlife:** Woodpeckers (including the red-cockaded woodpecker), warblers, flycatchers, brown-headed nuthatches, chickadees, wood ducks, herons, belted kingfishers, and hawks; also provides habitat for white-tailed deer, squirrels, bats, foxes, coyotes, raccoons, and bobcats. **Special Features:** More than 30 cemeteries are located on the refuge, a historical link to the settlers that once inhabited the area. Headstones date as far back as the 1700's.

★916★ PIERCE NATIONAL WILDLIFE REFUGE

c/o Ridgefield NWR
PO Box 457
Ridgefield, WA 98642
Web: www.fws.gov/ridgefieldrefuges/PNWRHome.htm
Phone: 360-887-4106; **Fax:** 360-887-4109
Location: Adjacent to the Columbia River, 20 miles east of Washougal. **Established:** 1965. **Habitat:** 329 acres of river bottomland with riparian areas, wetlands, open pasture, and woodlands. **Access:** Limited to arranged group tours. **Primary Wildlife:** Waterfowl including Canada geese, chum salmon. **Special Features:** The refuge's Hardy Creek supports one of the last remaining chum salmon runs in the lower Columbia River drainage.

See pages 22-23 for map of National Wildlife Refuges.

★917★ PINCKNEY ISLAND NATIONAL WILDLIFE REFUGE

c/o Savannah Coastal Refuges Complex
1000 Business Center Dr, Suite 10
Savannah, GA 31405
Web: www.fws.gov/pinckneyisland
Phone: 912-652-4415
Location: Near Hilton Head, South Carolina. **Established:** 1975. **Habitat:** 4,053 acres of salt marsh, tidal creeks, forestland, brushland, fallow field, and freshwater ponds. **Facilities:** Viewing sites, trails. **Activities:** Fishing, hiking, bicycling, hunting (limited), educational programs. **Access:** Open sunrise to sunset. **Primary Wildlife:** Herons, egrets, alligators, deer, bald eagle, wood stork, and flatwoods salamander. **Special Features:** Pinckney Island NWR includes Corn Island, Big and Little Harry Islands, Buzzard Island, and numerous small hammocks. Picnkney Island is the largest and the only one open to public use.

★918★ PINE ISLAND NATIONAL WILDLIFE REFUGE

c/o J. N. "Ding" Darling NWR
1 Wildlife Dr
Sanibel, FL 33957
Web: www.fws.gov/southeast/PineIsland
Phone: 239-472-1100; **Fax:** 239-472-4061
Location: Southwest coast of Florida, north of Sanibel Island in Pine Island Sound. **Established:** 1908. **Habitat:** 548 acres on 17 islands of densely forested red and black mangrove. **Activities:** Boating, saltwater fishing, wildlife observation. **Access:** By boat only. The islands receive little public use because the most of the islands have no uplands and access is difficult in the mangrove areas. **Primary Wildlife:** Colonial birds, especially the brown pelican. Also several endangered or threatened species including wood stork, eastern indigo snake, American crocodile, West Indian manatee, and bald eagle, as well as raccoons, dolphins, and gopher tortoises. **Special Features:** Two of the original three islands first set aside by Teddy Roosevelt can be found southwest of the Intracoastal Waterway at day beacons 64 and 65.

★919★ PINELLAS NATIONAL WILDLIFE REFUGE

c/o Chassahowitzka NWR
1502 SE Kings Bay Dr
Crystal River, FL 34429
Web: www.fws.gov/southeast/pinellas
Phone: 352-563-2088; **Fax:** 352-795-7961
Location: In Pinellas County, Florida, offshore from Saint Petersburg. **Established:** 1951. **Habitat:** Several islands and their coastal sea grass beds, comprising 403 total acres. **Activities:** Non-motorized boating, saltwater fishing. **Access:** Accessible by boat only; islands closed to public use. **Primary Wildlife:** Colonial birds species including brown pelicans, herons, egrets, and cormorants. **Special Features:** Refuge hosts the largest brown pelican rookery in Florida.

★920★ PIXLEY NATIONAL WILDLIFE REFUGE

c/o Kern NWR
PO Box 670
Delano, CA 93216
Web: www.fws.gov/pacific/refuges/field/CA_Pixley.htm
Phone: 661-725-2767
Location: 35 miles south of Tulare, California, in the San Joaquin Valley. **Established:** 1956. **Habitat:** 6,192 acres of native valley grasslands and developed marshlands. **Access:** By special arrangement only; contact refuge office. **Primary Wildlife:** Blunt-nosed leopard lizard (endangered), Tipton kangaroo rat, and San Joaquin kit fox. **Special Features:** Wetlands provide habitat for wintering waterfowl.

★921★ PLUM TREE ISLAND NATIONAL WILDLIFE REFUGE

c/o Back Bay NWR
4005 Sandpiper Rd
Virginia Beach, VA 23456
Web: www.fws.gov/northeast/va/pti.htm
Phone: 757-721-2412; **Fax:** 757-721-6141
Location: Southwest corner of the Chesapeake Bay, just north of Hampton, Virginia. **Established:** 1974. **Habitat:** 3,450 acres of salt marsh, shrub scrub and wooded habitats. **Access:** Island is saturated with unexploded bombs and other munitions and is closed to public entry. **Primary Wildlife:** Waterfowl, marshbirds, and shorebirds. **Special Features:** Area was used as a gunnery and bombing practice range until the late 1950s. It remains an emergency jettison zone for the Air Force.

★922★ POCOSIN LAKES NATIONAL WILDLIFE REFUGE

205 S Ludington Dr
Columbia, NC 27925
Web: www.fws.gov/pocosinlakes
Phone: 252-796-3004
Location: Northeastern North Carolina. **Established:** 1990. **Habitat:** 113,674 acres of open water, riverine swamp, pocosin wetlands, croplands, grass fields, and pine hardwood forests. **Facilities:** Viewing sites, hiking trails, auto tour route. **Activities:** Fishing, hunting, hiking, wildlife observation. **Access:** Year round during daylight hours. **Primary Wildlife:** Ducks, geese, tundra swans, raptors, red-cockaded woodpecker, red wolf, and black bear. **Special Features:** Attempts to reintroduce the red wolf to the area have proven successful.

★923★ POND CREEK NATIONAL WILDLIFE REFUGE

c/o Felsenthal NWR
1958 Central Rd
Lockesburg, AR 71846
Web: www.fws.gov/southeast/pondcreek
Phone: 870-289-2126; **Fax:** 870-289-2127
Location: 30 miles north of Texarkana, Arkansas. **Established:** 1994. **Habitat:** 27,300 acres of bottomland hardwoods with oxbow lakes, rivers, and sloughs. **Facilities:** 4 primitive campsites, trails. **Activities:** Camping, hiking, fishing, hunting, wildlife observation. **Access:** Open year round. **Primary Wildlife:**

See pages 22-23 for map of National Wildlife Refuges.

Migratory and resident waterfowl, neotropical migratory birds, wading birds, deer, squirrel, rabbit, beaver, nutria, and coyote. **Special Features:** Refuge has abundant water resources in the form of rivers, lakes, sloughs and mature bottomland hardwoods with excellent species compositions.

★924★ POND ISLAND NATIONAL WILDLIFE REFUGE

PO Box 495
Rockport, ME 04656
Web: www.fws.gov/refuges/profiles/index.cfm?id=53537
Phone: 207-236-6970
Location: Coastal Maine, 16 miles northeast of Portland. **Established:** 1973. **Habitat:** 10-acre treeless island with grass, forb and shrub. **Activities:** Hunting, wildlife observation. **Access:** Boat access only. Visitation should be attempted only by experienced boaters—the mouth of the Kennebec River is known for strong currents, heavy seas, fog, and large tidal changes. Island is closed from April through August to prevent disturbance to nesting birds. **Primary Wildlife:** Common terns, Leach's storm petrels, eider ducks, and gulls. **Special Features:** A tern restoration program was initiated in 1996 in which tern decoys and recorded sounds were used to lure the birds to Pond Island. In 1999, ten pairs of common terns successfully nested, producing the first tern chick in more than 60 years. Today the island supports about 135 pairs of nesting terns.

★925★ PORT LOUISA NATIONAL WILDLIFE REFUGE

10728 County Rd X61
Wapello, IA 52653
Web: www.fws.gov/midwest/PortLouisa
Phone: 319-523-6982; **Fax:** 319-523-6960
Location: 5 miles east of Wapello on Country Road X61. **Established:** 1958, as the Wapello District of Mark Twain NWR Complex. Renamed in 2000. **Habitat:** 8,375 acres of bottomland timber, backwater sloughs, marshes, wet meadows and grasslands. **Activities:** Hunting, fishing, boating, canoeing, hiking, bicycling, berry and mushroom picking for personal use, environmental education, wildlife observation. **Access:** Daylight hours. Refuge's Big Timbers unit is open year round; other areas are closed part of the winter. **Primary Wildlife:** Migratory birds, Indiana and gray bats, bobcat, fox, white-tailed deer, rabbits, lemmings, moles, freckled madtom, catfish, slender glass lizard, copperhead, alligator snapping turtle, stinkpot turtle, frogs, and sirens. **Special Features:** Refuge comprises four divisions, each with unique characteristics, but all located within the Mississippi Flyway, one of the nation's most important bird migration routes. The primary refuge management objective is to provide waterfowl and migratory birds with food, water, and protection during the spring and fall migration.

★926★ PRESQUILE NATIONAL WILDLIFE REFUGE

c/o Eastern Virginia Rivers NWR Complex
PO Box 1030
Warsaw, VA 22572
Web: www.fws.gov/northeast/presquile
Phone: 804-333-1470; **Fax:** 804-333-3396

Location: About 20 miles south of Richmond, Virginia. **Established:** 1953. **Habitat:** 1,329-acre island in the James River, composed mostly of hardwood swamp with a fringe of marsh and about 300 acres of upland fields. **Facilities:** Visitor center, trails. **Activities:** Hunting, fishing (from boat only), educational programs. **Access:** By advance reservation. **Primary Wildlife:** Canada geese, wood ducks, black ducks, and mallards. **Special Features:** A 28-foot pontoon boat ferries visitors to the refuge during scheduled events.

★927★ PRIME HOOK NATIONAL WILDLIFE REFUGE

11978 Turkle Pond Rd
Milton, DE 19968
Web: www.fws.gov/northeast/primehook
Phone: 302-684-8419; **Fax:** 302-684-8504
Location: On the west shore of Delaware Bay, 32 miles southeast of Dover. **Established:** 1963. **Habitat:** 10,000 acres of freshwater and salt marshes, woodlands, grasslands, scrub-brush habitats, ponds, bottomland forest, agricultural lands, and a 7-mile creek. **Facilities:** Visitor center, viewing sites, hiking trails, boat launch, boardwalk. **Activities:** Canoeing, fishing, hiking, hunting, educational programs. **Access:** Open from dawn to dusk. **Primary Wildlife:** Geese, wood ducks, black ducks, mallards, gadwalls, salamanders, lizards, turtles, frogs, toads, horseshoe crabs, white-tailed deer, and wild turkey. **Special Features:** Forested lands are managed to provide habitat for the Delmarva fox squirrel and bald eagle.

★928★ PROTECTION ISLAND NATIONAL WILDLIFE REFUGE

c/o Washington Maritime NWR Complex
33 S Barr Rd
Port Angeles, WA 98362
Web: www.fws.gov/pacific/refuges/field/wa_protectionis.htm
Phone: 360-457-8451
Location: At the mouth of Discovery Bay in the Strait of Juan de Fuca. **Established:** 1982. **Habitat:** 364-acre island of high grassy slopes, low brush, and a small timbered area. **Access:** Island is closed to protect nesting seabirds and harbor seals. Commercial boat tours are available from nearby marinas. **Primary Wildlife:** Rhinoceros auklets, pigeon guillemots, pelagic cormorants, tufted puffins, black oystercatchers, and glaucous-winged gulls. **Special Features:** Approximately 70 percent of the nesting seabird population of Puget Sound nest on the island, which includes one of the largest nesting colonies of rhinoceros auklets in the world. The island also contains one of Washington's last nesting populations of tufted puffins. Harbor seals use the island as a pupping and haulout area.

★929★ QUIVIRA NATIONAL WILDLIFE REFUGE

Rt 3 Box 48 A
Stafford, KS 67578
Web: quivira.fws.gov
Phone: 620-486-2393
Location: South-central Kansas. **Established:** 1955. **Habitat:** 22,135 acres of mudflats and wetlands, marsh edges, croplands

See pages 22-23 for map of National Wildlife Refuges.

and prairie grasslands. **Facilities:** Visitor contact station, viewing sites, hiking trails, auto tour route. **Activities:** Fishing, hiking, hunting, educational programs. **Access:** Open during daylight hours. **Primary Wildlife:** Mallards, wood ducks, pintails, white egrets, white pelicans, bobcats, prairie dogs, and coyotes. **Special Features:** Twenty-one miles of canals and numerous water control structures divert water to over 34 wetlands ranging in size from 10 acres to 1,500 acres.

★930★ RACHEL CARSON NATIONAL WILDLIFE REFUGE

321 Port Rd
Wells, ME 04090
Web: www.fws.gov/northeast/rachelcarson
Phone: 207-646-9226; **Fax:** 207-646-6554
Location: Southern coast of Maine. **Established:** 1966. **Habitat:** 9,125 acres (when acquisition is complete) of freshwater wetlands, uplands and tidal habitats. **Facilities:** Visitor contact station, viewing sites, trail (&). **Activities:** Hunting, hiking, boating, educational programs. **Access:** Open from dawn to dusk. **Primary Wildlife:** Piping plover, least terns, peregrine falcons, bald eagles, raccoon, mink, gray fox, short-tailed weasel, woodchucks, and snowshoe hares. **Special Features:** Refuge comprises ten separate units stretching along 50 miles of coastline between Portsmouth, New Hampshire, and Portland, Maine. Refuge habitat lies within the transition zone of the northern boreal forest and eastern deciduous forest; many plant and animal species found here are at their northern or southern range limit.

★931★ RAPPAHANNOCK RIVER VALLEY NATIONAL WILDLIFE REFUGE

c/o Eastern Virginia Rivers NWR Complex
336 Wilna Rd
Warasaw, VA 22572
Web: www.fws.gov/refuges/profiles/index.cfm?id=51622
Phone: 804-333-1470
Location: 40 miles northeast of Richmond, Virginia. **Established:** 1996. **Habitat:** 7,393 (of 20,000 proposed) acres of cropland, upland, wetland, and marsh. **Facilities:** Outdoor classroom, trails (&), fishing pier (&). **Activities:** Hiking, canoeing, kayaking, hunting, fishing, educational programs. **Access:** Wilna unit is open daily, sunrise to sunset; access to all other units is limited. **Primary Wildlife:** American bald eagle, peregrine falcon, shortnose sturgeon, and sensitive joint vetch. Also provides habitat for wood thrush, Acadian flycatcher, grasshopper sparrow and northern bobwhite. **Special Features:** Archeological and historic sites are abundant on both sides of the Rappahannock River. Old pilings can still be seen from the days when steamboats made regular stops to pick up produce and passengers for transport to the Port of Baltimore.

★932★ RED ROCK LAKES NATIONAL WILDLIFE REFUGE

27820 Southside Centennial Rd
Lima, MT 59739
Web: redrocks.fws.gov
Phone: 406-276-3536; **Fax:** 406-276-3538

Location: Southeast corner of Montana, at the eastern end of the Centennial Valley. **Established:** 1935. **Habitat:** 43,500 acres of high-elevation mountain wetlands and riparian lands. **Facilities:** Visitor contact station, picnic areas, trails, campgrounds, boat launch. **Activities:** Canoeing, fishing, hiking, hunting, primitive camping, snowmobiling, educational programs. **Access:** Weekdays during daylight hours. **Primary Wildlife:** Trumpeter swans, sandhill cranes, badgers, wolverines, bears, wolves, Arctic grayling, westslope cutthroat trout, moose and pronghorn antelope. **Special Features:** Refuge is designated a National Natural Landmark, as well as one of the few marshland wilderness areas in the country. As such, it is managed for primitive wilderness values and no formal trails are designated or maintained.

★933★ REELFOOT NATIONAL WILDLIFE REFUGE

4343 Hwy 157
Union City, TN 38261
Web: www.fws.gov/reelfoot
Phone: 731-538-2481; **Fax:** 731-538-9760
Location: Northwest corner of Tennessee. **Established:** 1941. **Habitat:** 10,428 acres of farmland, moist soil, and forest. **Facilities:** Visitor center, observation towers, trails, boat launch, auto tour route. **Activities:** Boating, canoeing, fishing, hunting, hiking, educational programs. **Access:** Open year round during daylight hours, though some units are closed at various times throughout the year. **Primary Wildlife:** Eagles, mallards, gadwalls, American wigeons, Canada geese, white-tailed deer, and wild turkey. **Special Features:** Reelfoot Lake was formed during the winter of 1811-1812 as a result of the most violent series of earthquakes ever recorded in North America.

★934★ RICE LAKE NATIONAL WILDLIFE REFUGE

36289 SH 65
McGregor, MN 55760
Web: www.fws.gov/midwest/ricelake
Phone: 218-768-2402
Location: East-central Minnesota, 5 miles south of McGregor. **Established:** 1935. **Habitat:** 18,300 acres of bog lands, shallow lakes, glacial ridges, and 4,500-acre Rice Lake. **Facilities:** Visitor contact station, viewing sites, auto tour route, trails, picnic areas. **Activities:** Boating, canoeing, fishing, hiking, cross-country skiing, snowshoeing, hunting. **Access:** Daily during daylight hours. **Primary Wildlife:** Mallard, wigeon, wood duck, Canada geese, snow geese, sandhill crane, sharp-tailed grouse, red and gray fox, river otter, northern pike, buffalo fish, yellow perch, walleye and crappie. **Special Features:** Local Chippewa use traditional methods to harvest a portion of the wild rice crop from Rice Lake each year.

★935★ RIDGEFIELD NATIONAL WILDLIFE REFUGE

301 N 3rd Ave
Ridgefield, WA 98642
Web: www.fws.gov/ridgefieldrefuges/RNWRHome.htm
Phone: 360-887-4106
Location: Along the Columbia River, between Vancouver and Longview in southwestern Washington. **Established:** 1965.

See pages 22-23 for map of National Wildlife Refuges.

Habitat: 5,150 acres of marshes, grasslands, and woodlands. **Facilities:** Visitor contact station, viewing sites, trails, auto tour route. **Activities:** Fishing, hiking, hunting, wildlife observation, educational programs. **Access:** Open during daylight hours. **Primary Wildlife:** Canada geese, sandhill crane, mallard, great blue herons, red-tailed hawks, black-tailed deer, coyote, raccoon, skunk, beaver, river otter, and occasional brush rabbits. **Special Features:** Refuge contains the historic Cathlapotle townsite, which was visited by Lewis and Clark in 1806, and is one of the best-preserved Native American sites in the northwestern United States.

★936★ ROANOKE RIVER NATIONAL WILDLIFE REFUGE

114 W Water St
Windsor, NC 27983
Web: www.fws.gov/roanokeriver
Phone: 252-794-3808
Location: Northeastern North Carolina. **Established:** 1989. **Habitat:** 17,500 acres of bottomland hardwood forest and cypress-tupelo sloughs, and black and brown water streams. **Facilities:** Visitor contact station, hiking trails. **Activities:** Boating, canoeing, fishing, hunting, hiking, educational programs. **Access:** Open during daylight hours year round. **Primary Wildlife:** Raptors, osprey, and neo-tropical migrants, herons, bald eagle, shortnose sturgeon, wild turkey, and black bear. **Special Features:** Refuge consists of five different tracts of land along 70 miles of the Roanoke River and two distant satellite tracts in other river basins.

★937★ ROCKY MOUNTAIN ARSENAL NATIONAL WILDLIFE REFUGE

US Fish & Wildlife Service, Bldg 121
Commerce City, CO 80022
Web: www.fws.gov/rockymountainarsenal
Phone: 303-289-0232; **Fax:** 303-289-0579
Location: 11 miles northeast of Denver, Colorado. **Established:** 2000. **Habitat:** 17,000 acres of native prairie, woodlots and wetlands.. **Facilities:** Visitor center, trails, viewing sites. **Activities:** Hiking, catch-and-release fishing (during summer months), educational programs. **Access:** Weekends 8:00 a.m. to 4:30 p.m. **Primary Wildlife:** Bald eagles and other raptors, bats, burrowing owls, pocket gopher, meadow vole, prairie dogs, deer, waterfowl, and songbirds. **Special Features:** In 1986, a communal roost of bald eagles was discovered on an environmental cleanup site managed by the U.S. Army and Shell Oil. The discovery of the then-endangered species led to the creation of Rocky Mountain Arsenal NWR.

★938★ ROSE ATOLL NATIONAL WILDLIFE REFUGE

c/o Pacific Remote Islands NWR Complex
300 Ala Moana Blvd, PO Box 50167
Honolulu, HI 96850
Web: www.fws.gov/pacificislands/wnwr/prosenwr.html
Phone: 808-792-9550; **Fax:** 808-792-9586
Location: 2,700 miles south of Hawaii. **Established:** 1973. **Habitat:** Two small islets, about 15 acres in total size, and 39,236 acres of submerged land. **Access:** Restricted; contact refuge office. **Primary Wildlife:** 12 species of migratory seabirds, including red-footed boobies, great and lesser frigatebirds, black noddies, white terns, and sooty terns. Also provides habitat for the threatened green sea turtle and the endangered hawksbill turtle. **Special Features:** Refuge is part of the territory of American Samoa and is managed cooperatively by the U.S. Fish and Wildlife Service and the government of American Samoa. Rose Atoll NWR is the southernmost refuge in the National Wildlife Refuge system, and consists of two uninhabited islands on a doughnut-shaped reef. Diverse marine life in the atoll's lagoon includes numerous fish species and a population of rare giant clams.

★939★ RUBY LAKE NATIONAL WILDLIFE REFUGE

HC 60 Box 860
Ruby Valley, NV 89833
Web: www.fws.gov/pacific/refuges/field/NV_rubylk.htm
Phone: 775-779-2237
Location: 65 miles southeast of Elko in northeastern Nevada. **Established:** 1938. **Habitat:** 37,632 acres of marshes, open ponds, wet meadows, and sagebrush uplands. **Facilities:** Visitor center, auto tour route, boat launch. **Activities:** Boating, canoeing, fishing, hunting, educational programs. **Access:** Year round during daylight hours. **Primary Wildlife:** Sandhill cranes, canvasback and redhead ducks, trumpeter swans, mountain lions, and bobcats. **Special Features:** The marsh is a remnant of an ancient lake and is supplied with water from more than 160 springs emerging from the base of the Ruby Mountains.

★940★ RYDELL NATIONAL WILDLIFE REFUGE

17788 349 St SE
Erskine, MN 56635
Web: www.fws.gov/midwest/rydell
Phone: 218-687-2229; **Fax:** 218-687-2225
Location: Northwestern Minnesota, about 60 miles east of East Grand Forks. **Established:** 1992. **Habitat:** 2,120 acres of maple/basswood/oak forest, wetlands, tallgrass prairie and bogs; at least 19 old farmsteads make up the refuge lands, and five partial log buildings remain. **Facilities:** Visitor center, viewing sites, trails. **Activities:** Hunting, hiking, snowshoeing, cross-country skiing, educational programs. **Primary Wildlife:** Several ducks species, neotropical migratory birds, cormorants, ruffed grouse, red-eyed vireo, cedar waxwing, white-tailed deer, black bear, barred owl, otters, beavers, and foxes. **Special Features:** More than 170 wood duck boxes and 150 bluebird boxes have been erected and are actively maintained in order to provide habitat for cavity nesting birds.

★941★ SABINE NATIONAL WILDLIFE REFUGE

3000 Holly Beach Hwy
Hackberry, LA 70645
Web: www.fws.gov/sabine
Phone: 337-762-3816; **Fax:** 337-762-3780
Location: 22 miles south of Sulphur, Louisiana. **Established:** 1937. **Habitat:** 124,511 acres of open water, marshes, and grasslands. **Facilities:** Visitor center, boat ramps, observation tower,

See pages 22-23 for map of National Wildlife Refuges.

hiking trails (&). **Activities:** Boating, canoeing, fishing, crabbing, shrimping, hiking, hunting, trapping, educational programs. **Access:** Open year round, from sunrise to sunset. **Primary Wildlife:** Ducks, geese, alligators, muskrats, nutria, raptors, wading birds, shorebirds, blue crabs, and shrimp. **Special Features:** Refuge has been designated as an "Internationally Important Bird Area" due to the numerous wading, water, and marsh birds that utilize it throughout the year. The exhibits in the refuge visitor center and the Wetland Walkway are considered two of the principal tourist attractions in southwest Louisiana. More than 280,000 people visit the refuge annually and it is considered an integral part of the Creole Nature Trail All American Road.

★942★ SACHUEST POINT NATIONAL WILDLIFE REFUGE

c/o Rhode Island NWR Complex
3679 D Old Post Rd, PO Box 307
Charlestown, RI 02813
Web: www.fws.gov/refuges/profiles/index.cfm?id=53543
Phone: 401-364-9124
Location: In Middletown, 4 miles east of Newport, Rhode Island. **Established:** 1970. **Habitat:** 242 acres of saltmarsh, beach strand, and upland shrub. **Facilities:** Visitor center (&), trails, observation platforms. **Activities:** Surf fishing, hiking, educational programs. **Access:** Open from dawn to dusk. **Primary Wildlife:** More than 200 species of birds, including peregrine falcon, northern harrier, and the snowy owl. **Special Features:** Refuge includes a large concentration of wintering harlequin ducks.

★943★ SACRAMENTO NATIONAL WILDLIFE REFUGE

752 County Rd 99W
Willows, CA 95988
Web: www.fws.gov/sacramentovalleyrefuges/sac.htm
Phone: 530-934-2801
Location: Along I-5, about 85 miles north of Sacramento, California. **Established:** 1937. **Habitat:** 10,783 acres of seasonal marsh, permanent ponds, watergrass, and uplands. **Facilities:** Visitor center (with exhibits, gift shop, and learning center), viewing platforms, hiking trails, auto tour routes. **Activities:** Hiking, hunting, educational programs. **Access:** Open from sunrise to sunset year round. **Primary Wildlife:** Fairy shrimp, vernal pool tadpole shrimp, giant garter snake, peregrine falcon, bald eagle, tricolored blackbird, grebe, heron, golden eagle, beaver, muskrat, and black-tailed deer. **Special Features:** For thousands of years the Sacramento Valley has provided a winter haven for ducks, geese, and swans. Waterfowl migrate here by the millions from as far away as the Arctic regions of Alaska, Canada and Siberia.

★944★ SACRAMENTO RIVER NATIONAL WILDLIFE REFUGE

c/o Sacramento NWR
752 County Rd 99W
Willows, CA 95988
Web: www.fws.gov/sacramentovalleyrefuges/sacriver.htm
Phone: 530-934-2801

Location: North of Sacramento, California. **Established:** 1989. **Habitat:** About 10,000 acres of riparian habitat, wetlands, and uplands, with croplands and walnut, almond, and prune orchards. **Facilities:** Viewing sites, interpretive panels, hiking trail. **Activities:** Hiking, hunting, fishing, wildlife observation. **Access:** Currently limited to a portion of the Llano Seco unit: open year round from sunrise to sunset. **Primary Wildlife:** Migratory songbirds and waterfowl, river otter, turtles, beaver, American pelicans, ospreys, and bank swallows. **Special Features:** Refuge is composed of 26 properties along a 77-mile stretch of the Sacramento River between the cities of Red Bluff and Princeton.

★945★ SADDLE MOUNTAIN NATIONAL WILDLIFE REFUGE

3520 Port of Benton Rd
Richland, WA 99352
Phone: 509-371-1801
Location: East-central Washington. **Established:** 1953. **Habitat:** 195,000 acres of shrub upland, a 730-acre lake, and riparian lands along the Columbia River. **Access:** Closed to general public access. Use is limited to approved ecological research and environmental education activities. **Primary Wildlife:** Loggerhead shrike, burrowing owl, Canada geese, ducks, eagles, and northern grasshopper mouse. **Special Features:** Saddle Mountain NWR is a unit of Hanford Reach National Monument. The Monument/Refuge is the first of its kind under U. S. Fish and Wildlife Service management within the lower 48 states and managed as a unit of the National Wildlife Refuge System.

★946★ SAINT CATHERINE CREEK NATIONAL WILDLIFE REFUGE

PO Box 117
Sibley, MS 39165
Web: www.fws.gov/saintcatherinecreek
Phone: 601-442-6696; **Fax:** 604-442-8990
Location: In southwestern Mississippi, 7 miles south of Natchez. **Established:** 1990. **Habitat:** 24,445 acres of bottomland and upland hardwoods, cleared land, cypress swamps, and fallow fields. **Facilities:** Visitor contact station, viewing sites, hiking trails, auto tour route. **Activities:** Fishing, boating, hiking, hunting. **Access:** Open sunrise to sunset. **Primary Wildlife:** Migratory waterfowl, peregrine falcon, bald eagle, white-tailed deer, turkey, squirrels, chipmunks, and alligator. **Special Features:** Bounded to the west by the Mississippi River, refuge provides habitat for migratory waterfowl in the Mississippi Flyway.

★947★ SAINT MARKS NATIONAL WILDLIFE REFUGE

PO Box 68
Saint Marks, FL 32355
Web: www.fws.gov/saintmarks
Phone: 850-925-6121
Location: South of Tallahassee along the Big Bend coast of northwestern Florida. **Established:** 1931. **Habitat:** 68,000 acres of coastal marshes, islands, tidal creeks, and estuaries. **Facilities:** Visitor center, picnic areas, auto tour route, interpretive trails, historic features. **Activities:** Fishing, hiking, biking, hunting,

See pages 22-23 for map of National Wildlife Refuges.

4. National Wildlife Refuges

horseback riding, educational programs. **Access:** Open year round during daylight hours. **Primary Wildlife:** Waterfowl, ibis, white pelican, bald eagle, Atlantic green turtle, Atlantic loggerhead turtle, leatherback turtle, West Indian manatee, and alligator. **Special Features:** Refuge is home to Saint Marks Lighthouse, which was built in 1832 and is still in use today.

★948★ SAINT VINCENT NATIONAL WILDLIFE REFUGE

PO Box 447
Apalachicola, FL 32329
Web: southeast.fws.gov/stvincent
Phone: 850-653-8808; **Fax:** 850-653-9893
Location: 22 miles southwest of Apalachicola, Florida. **Established:** 1968. **Habitat:** 12,350-acre island of open water, wetlands, forest shrub, and sand dunes. **Facilities:** Visitor center, hiking trails. **Activities:** Boating, canoeing, fishing, hiking, hunting, educational programs. **Access:** Open during daylight hours; accessible only by boat. **Primary Wildlife:** Red wolf, bald eagle, peregrine falcon, piping plover, wood stork, American alligator, Eastern ndigo snake, loggerhead sea turtle, gopher tortoise and white-tailed deer. **Special Features:** Endangered red wolves, native to the southeast, are raised on Saint Vincent NWR as part of a recovery program. Wolves are allowed to roam the island to gain ''wild experience.'' They are then transferred to mainland wild release sites and captive sites, as needed.

★949★ SALINAS RIVER NATIONAL WILDLIFE REFUGE

c/o Don Edwards San Francisco Bay NWR
PO Box 524
Newark, CA 94560
Web: www.fws.gov/pacific/refuges/field/CA_salinas.htm
Phone: 510-792-0222
Location: 10 miles north of Monterey, California. **Established:** 1973. **Habitat:** 367 acres of ocean, beach, dunes, grassland, river, lagoon, and salt marsh. **Facilities:** Trails. **Activities:** Fishing, hiking, wildlife observation. **Access:** Open during daylight hours. **Primary Wildlife:** Endangered California brown pelican, Smith's blue butterfly, and the peregrine falcon. Also provides habitat for the rare snowy plover. **Special Features:** Refuge serves as a resting and feeding area for waterfowl, shorebirds, and other water birds.

★950★ SALT PLAINS NATIONAL WILDLIFE REFUGE

Rt 1 Box 76
Jet, OK 73749
Web: www.fws.gov/saltplains
Phone: 580-626-4794; **Fax:** 580-626-4793
Location: Northern Oklahoma, about 30 miles northwest of Enid. **Established:** 1930. **Habitat:** 32,000 acres of salt flats, open reservoir, woodlands, grasslands, and agricultural fields. **Facilities:** Visitor center, viewing sites, hiking trails, auto tour route. **Activities:** Boating, fishing, hunting, hiking, crystal digging, educational programs. **Access:** Open daylight hours. **Primary Wildlife:** Migratory ducks, geese, Whooping and Sandhill cranes, mountain lion, bobcat, coyote, white-tailed deer, toads

and frogs, turtles and snakes. **Special Features:** The salt plains are a unique geological area. Almost perfectly flat, the land is barren, with a wafer-thin salt crust. The salt was formed by repeated flooding by sea water millions of years ago. The sea water was cut off from the sea and evaporated, depositing thick layers of salt.

★951★ SAN ANDRES NATIONAL WILDLIFE REFUGE

PO Box 756
Las Cruces, NM 88004
Web: www.fws.gov/southwest/refuges/newmex/sanandres
Phone: 505-382-5047; **Fax:** 505-382-5454
Location: 30 miles northeast of Las Cruces. **Established:** 1941. **Habitat:** 57,215 acres of desert shrub, desert riparian, grass shrub, mountain shrub and pinon juniper. **Access:** Because the refuge lies within the boundaries of the White Sands Missile Range, it is closed to public entry and all recreational uses. **Primary Wildlife:** Bighorn sheep. Also Gambel's quail, mule deer, coyote, mountain lion, and golden eagle. **Special Features:** The refuge extends over 21 miles along the southern portion of the San Andres Mountains. This area is the northernmost extension of the Chihuahuan Desert and one of the largest contiguous, relatively-undisturbed Chihuahuan Desert land masses in the U.S.

★952★ SAN BERNARD NATIONAL WILDLIFE REFUGE

6801 CR 306
Brazoria, TX 77422
Web: www.fws.gov/southwest/refuges/texas/texasmidcoast/sanbernard.htm
Phone: 979-964-3639; **Fax:** 979-964-3210
Location: On the Texas gulf coast, about 50 miles southwest of Galveston. **Established:** 1968. **Habitat:** 27,414 acres of marshes, ponds, and bottomland forest. **Facilities:** Visitor contact station, viewing sites, hiking trails, auto tour route, boat ramp. **Activities:** Boating, canoeing, fishing, crabbing, hiking, waterfowl hunting, educational programs. **Access:** Open during daylight hours. **Primary Wildlife:** Snow geese, egrets terns, bald eagles, oysters, crabs, bobcats, and alligators. **Special Features:** Refuge bottomland forests and willow trees attract high numbers of warblers migrating north. When warm, moist air heading north from the Gulf collides with cold dry air heading south, conditions are good for a ''warbler fallout.'' Heavy winds and rain cause the tiny birds to drop from the sky to the shelter of trees, with hundred often falling into single locations.

★953★ SAN BERNARDINO NATIONAL WILDLIFE REFUGE

PO Box 3509
Douglas, AZ 85607
Web: www.fws.gov/southwest/refuges/arizona/sanbernardino.html
Phone: 520-364-2104; **Fax:** 520-364-2130
Location: In the southeast corner of Arizona, on the U.S.-Mexico border. **Established:** 1982. **Habitat:** 2,309 acres of Chihuahuan desert scrub, desert grassland, mesquite bosque,

See pages 22-23 for map of National Wildlife Refuges.

fallow fields, artesian wells and seeps, woodland, riparian scrub, marshlands and water. **Facilities:** Trails. **Activities:** Hunting, hiking. **Access:** Visits require a special-use permit, available at refuge office. **Primary Wildlife:** Endangered native fishes including Yaqui chub, Yaqui topminnow, Yaqui beautiful shiner, and Yaqui catfish. Also provides habitat for Virginia rail, ringneck duck, Mexican duck, sandhill cranes, great blue heron, green-backed heron, hummingbirds, javelina, mountain lion, coatimundi, rattlesnakes, gila monster, and Mandrean alligator lizard, and a number of raptors, including gray hawk, zone-tailed hawk, golden eagle, Swainson's hawk, kestrel, sharp-shinned hawk, and peregrine falcon. **Special Features:** The refuge features more than 270 species of birds and an abundance of butterflies, dragonflies, damselflies, and other invertebrates.

★954★ SAN DIEGO NATIONAL WILDLIFE REFUGE

13910 Lyons Valley Rd, Suite R
Jamul, CA 91935
Web: www.fws.gov/sandiegorefuges/Otay.htm
Phone: 619-669-7295
Location: Southwest California, about 15 miles southeast of San Diego. **Established:** 1997. **Habitat:** 4,224 acres of mainly coastal sage scrub, chapparal, freshwater marsh, and oak woodland. **Activities:** Hiking, wildlife observation, educational programs. **Access:** Limited; contact refuge office. **Primary Wildlife:** Least Bell's vireo, coastal California gnatcatcher, quino checkerspot (butterfly), and San Diego horned lizard. **Special Features:** A number of threatened and endangered plant species exist on refuge lands including San Diego mesa mint, San Diego button celery, California Orcutt grass, Otay Mesa mint, Del Mar manzanita, and Orcutt's spineflower.

★955★ SAN JOAQUIN RIVER NATIONAL WILDLIFE REFUGE

c/o San Luis NWR
PO Box 2176
Los Banos, CA 93635
Web: www.fws.gov/sanluis/sanjoaquin_info.htm
Phone: 209-826-3508; **Fax:** 209-826-1445
Location: 8 miles west of Modesto, California. **Established:** 1987. **Habitat:** 6,642 acres of riparian forests, pastures, agricultural fields, and wetlands. **Access:** Closed to the public. **Primary Wildlife:** Aleutian Canada geese, sandhill cranes, herons, egrets and neotropical migratory land birds. **Special Features:** Refuge played a key role in the recovery and 2001 delisting of the Aleutian Canada Goose by providing critical habitat for the species.

★956★ SAN JUAN ISLANDS NATIONAL WILDLIFE REFUGE

c/o Washington Maritime NWR Complex
33 S Barr Rd
Port Angeles, WA 98362
Web: www.fws.gov/pacific/refuges/field/wa_sanjuanis.htm
Phone: 360-457-8451
Location: Northern Puget Sound. **Established:** 1976. **Habitat:** 83 islands (reefs, rocks, grassy islands, and forested islands)

totaling 454 acres. **Facilities:** Primitive campsites, trail, picnic areas, and boat moorage (on Turn and Matia islands only). **Activities:** Camping, boating, fishing. **Access:** Best access is by boat from Anacortes or Friday Harbor. All islands except Turn Island and five acres on Matia Islands are closed to the public, but observation from boats is permitted on all the other islands. **Primary Wildlife:** Nesting seabirds including pigeon guillemots, double-crested cormorants, pelagic cormorants, and glaucous-winged gulls. **Special Features:** Several of the islands can be viewed from Washington State ferries that traverse the area.

★957★ SAN LUIS NATIONAL WILDLIFE REFUGE

PO Box 2176
Los Banos, CA 93635
Web: sanluis.fws.gov
Phone: 209-826-3508; **Fax:** 209-826-1445
Location: 10 miles north of Los Banos. **Established:** 1966. **Habitat:** 26,340 acres of managed seasonal and permanent wetlands, riparian habitat, native grasslands, alkali sinks, and vernal pools. **Facilities:** Hiking trails, auto tour route, observation tower. **Activities:** Fishing, hunting. **Access:** Open daily from 1/2 hour before sunrise to 1/2 hour after sunset. **Primary Wildlife:** Mallards, pintails, green-winged teal, hawks, owls, crayfish, frogs, and San Joaquin kit fox. **Special Features:** San Luis contains the most extensive network of pristine native grasslands, shrubs, and vernal pools that remain in the Central Valley.

★958★ SAN PABLO BAY NATIONAL WILDLIFE REFUGE

7715 Lakeville Hwy
Petaluma, CA 94954
Web: www.fws.gov/refuges/profiles/index.cfm?id=11644
Phone: 707-469-4200
Location: Along the northern shore of San Pablo Bay in northern California. **Established:** 1974. **Habitat:** More than 13,000 acres of open water, mudflats, salt marshes, and seasonal wetlands. **Facilities:** Trails. **Activities:** Boating, canoeing, fishing, hunting, educational programs. **Access:** Open during daylight hours. **Primary Wildlife:** California clapper rail, salt marsh harvest mouse, California black rail, San Pablo song sparrow, and Suisun shrew. Also migratory shorebirds and waterfowl, particularly diving ducks. **Special Features:** Refuge includes numerous threatened, endangered, and sensitive species requiring tidal marsh habitat for their survival, including 11 fish species that swim through San Pablo Bay to reach their freshwater spawning grounds.

★959★ SAND LAKE NATIONAL WILDLIFE REFUGE

39650 Sand Lake Dr
Columbia, SD 57433
Web: sandlake.fws.gov
Phone: 605-885-6320; **Fax:** 605-885-6333
Location: Northeast corner of South Dakota. **Established:** 1935. **Habitat:** 22,000 acres of marsh, open water, woodlands, grasslands, and croplands. **Facilities:** Visitor center, viewing sites, observation tower, hiking trails, auto tour route. **Activities:** Fishing, hiking, hunting, educational programs. **Access:** Open

4. National Wildlife Refuges

See pages 22-23 for map of National Wildlife Refuges.

from sunrise to sunset between early April and mid-October. **Primary Wildlife:** Giant Canada geese, ring-necked pheasants, red foxes, and white-tailed deer. **Special Features:** Refuge claims the largest nesting colony of Franklin's gulls in the world.

★960★ SANDY POINT NATIONAL WILDLIFE REFUGE

3013 Estate Golden Rock, Suite 167
Christiansted, VI 00820
Web: www.fws.gov/southeast/SandyPoint
Phone: 340-773-4554; **Fax:** 340-773-4554
Location: Southwestern end of St. Croix, south of the town of Frederiksted, Virgin Islands. **Established:** 1984. **Habitat:** 327 acres of beach, mangroves, and littoral woodland vegetation. **Activities:** Hiking, wildlife observation. **Access:** Open on weekends. **Primary Wildlife:** Endangered leatherback sea turtle, least tern, brown pelican, black-necked stilt, and black-whiskered vireo. **Special Features:** Sandy Point has the largest beach in the Virgin Islands and hosts the largest known nesting population of leatherback sea turtles under U.S. jurisdiction.

★961★ SANTA ANA NATIONAL WILDLIFE REFUGE

Rt 2 Box 202A
Alamo, TX 78516
Web: www.fws.gov/southwest/refuges/texas/santana.html
Phone: 956-784-7500; **Fax:** 956-787-8338
Location: Southern Texas, 7 miles south of Alamo. **Established:** 1943. **Habitat:** 2,088 acres of thorn forest. **Facilities:** Visitor center, viewing sites, trails (12 miles, &), auto tour route (7 miles), butterfly garden. **Activities:** Hiking, bicycling, tram tours (seasonal). **Access:** Open sunrise to sunset. **Primary Wildlife:** Black-bellied and fulvous whistling duck, blue-winged, green-winged, and cinnimon teal, anhinga, white ibis, northern harrier, peregrine falcon, hook-billed kite, buff-bellied hummingbird, roseate spoonbill, Mexican ground squirrel, and the endangered ocelot and jaguarundi. **Special Features:** Santa Ana is located where subtropical climate, gulf coast, great plains, and Chihuahuan desert converge. Thousands of birds from the Central and Mississippi flyways funnel through the area on their way to and from Central and South America. Area is also habitat for about half of all butterfly species found in North America.

★962★ SANTEE NATIONAL WILDLIFE REFUGE

2125 Fort Watson Rd
Summerton, SC 29148
Web: southeast.fws.gov/santee
Phone: 803-478-2217; **Fax:** 803-478-2314
Location: North side of Lake Marion. **Established:** 1942. **Habitat:** 15,095 acres of mixed hardwoods and pine hardwoods, pine plantations, marsh, croplands, old fields, ponds, impoundments, and open water. **Facilities:** Visitor center, trails, auto tour route, boat ramp. **Activities:** Boating, canoeing, fishing, hiking, hunting, educational programs. **Access:** Open during daylight hours. **Primary Wildlife:** Red-cockaded woodpecker, bald eagle, American alligator, ducks, geese, swans, shrews, moles bats, river otter, bobcat, long-tailed weasel, and white-tailed deer. **Special Features:** Refuge is a major wintering area for ducks,

geese and swans, as well as a nesting and stopover area for neotropical migratory birds, raptors, shore and wading birds.

★963★ SAUTA CAVE NATIONAL WILDLIFE REFUGE

c/o Wheeler NWR
2700 Refuge Headquarters Rd
Decatur, AL 35603
Web: www.fws.gov/sautacave
Phone: 256-353-7243; **Fax:** 256-340-9728
Location: 7 miles west of Scottsboro, Alabama, near Guntersville Reservoir. **Established:** 1978. **Habitat:** Hillside cave surrounded by 264 acres of hardwoods. **Facilities:** Viewing sites, trails. **Activities:** Hiking. **Access:** The cave is not open to the public; other portions of the refuge are open during daylight hours. **Primary Wildlife:** Endangered gray bats and Indiana bats. **Special Features:** The refuge's double-entrance cave has been a major maternity cave for gray and Indiana bats. In 1997, a summer count documented 300,000 to 400,000 gray bats emerging from the cave.

★964★ SAVANNAH NATIONAL WILDLIFE REFUGE

c/o Savannah Coastal Refuges Complex
1000 Business Center Dr, Suite 10
Savannah, GA 31405
Web: www.fws.gov/savannah
Phone: 912-652-4415
Location: Along the Atlantic coast, near the South Carolina-Georgia border. **Established:** 1927. **Habitat:** More than 29,000 acres of freshwater marshes, tidal rivers, creeks, and bottomland hardwoods. **Facilities:** Trails, auto tour route. **Activities:** Bicycling, fishing, hunting, educational programs **Access:** Open during daylight hours; about half of the refuge is accessible only by boat. **Primary Wildlife:** Mallards, pintails, teal, wood ducks, bald eagle, wood stork, flatwoods salamander, and American alligator. **Special Features:** Located on the Atlantic Flyway, refuge hosts thousands of mallards, pintails, teal and as many as ten other species of ducks during the winter months, joining resident wood ducks.

★965★ SEAL BEACH NATIONAL WILDLIFE REFUGE

PO Box 815
Seal Beach, CA 90740
Web: www.fws.gov/sandiegorefuges/Seal.htm
Phone: 562-598-1024
Location: On the California coast, about 30 miles south of downtown Los Angeles. **Established:** 1972. **Habitat:** 911 acres of salt marsh, tidal wetlands, and a small area of coastal uplands. **Access:** Limited; contact the visitor center for activities. **Primary Wildlife:** Endangered light-footed clapper rail, California least tern, brown pelican, peregrine falcon, and Belding's Savannah sparrow. **Special Features:** Seal Beach provides important habitat for a variety of migratory shorebirds, waterfowl, and seabirds. As part of the predator management program, monthly night surveys of mammals are conducted.

See pages 22-23 for map of National Wildlife Refuges.

★966★ SEAL ISLAND NATIONAL WILDLIFE REFUGE

c/o Maine Coastal Islands NWR
PO Box 495
Milbridge, ME 04656
Phone: 207-236-6970
Location: 58 miles east of Brunswick. **Established:** 1972. **Habitat:** 65-acre tree-less island with rocky shores and grassy areas. **Access:** Closed to the public. **Primary Wildlife:** Puffins, common terns, arctic terns, common eiders, black guillemots, and harbor and gray seals. **Special Features:** Through it Project Puffin, the National Audubon Society successfully reintroduced Atlantic puffins to the island after a 150-year absence.

★967★ SEATUCK NATIONAL WILDLIFE REFUGE

c/o Long Island NWR Complex
500 St Marks Ln
Islip, NY 11751
Phone: 631-286-0485
Location: On Long Island's south shore in Islip. **Established:** 1968. **Habitat:** 196 acres of tidal marsh, old fields, brush, woodland, grasslands and pine barren. **Access:** Closed to the public. **Primary Wildlife:** Migratory birds, particularly waterbirds, raptors, songbirds, white-tailed deer, and red fox. **Special Features:** Approximately one half of the refuge consists of tidal marsh, which serves a vast number of waterfowl in the winter months.

★968★ SEEDSKADEE NATIONAL WILDLIFE REFUGE

PO Box 700
Green River, WY 82935
Phone: 307-875-2187
Location: Southwest Wyoming, 40 miles north of Green River. **Established:** 1965. **Habitat:** 26,400-acre riparian, wetland, and upland shrub along the Green River. **Facilities:** Visitor center, viewing sites, trail, auto tour route, historic features. **Activities:** Fishing, hiking, hunting, educational programs. **Access:** Open year round, 1/2 hour before sunrise to 1/2 hour after sunset. **Primary Wildlife:** Rufous hummingbird, Wilson's warbler, yellow warbler, bullock's oriole, bald eagle, trumpeter swans, ruddy ducks, white-faced ibis, redheads, cinnamon teal, moose, mule deer, porcupine, pygmy rabbit, pronghorn, and muskrats. **Special Features:** The Oregon and Mormon national historic trails cross the refuge (see entries in national trails section). Segments of these trails, as well as the Pony Express Trail, can still be seen on and adjacent to the refuge.

★969★ SELAWIK NATIONAL WILDLIFE REFUGE

PO Box 270
Kotzebue, AK 99752
Web: www.fws.gov/refuges/profiles/index.cfm?id=75625
Phone: 907-442-3799
Location: Straddles the Arctic Circle in northwestern Alaska. **Established:** 1980. **Habitat:** 2.15 million acres of forests, lakes, wetlands, and tundra hills. **Activities:** Camping, rafting, fishing, hiking, hunting, cross-country skiing. **Access:** Open 24 hours a day. Refuge is roadless and is accessible only by boat, aircraft, or on foot. **Primary Wildlife:** Pacific golden plovers, semipalmated and western sandpipers, red-necked phalaropes, geese, cranes, swans, moose, caribou, brown bear, wolverine, and fox. **Special Features:** Two Inupiaq villages are within the refuge boundary and four other Inupiaq villages are located within 25 miles of the refuge. People of these villages, and from more distant Inupiaq villages, have traditionally used refuge resources for subsistence living.

★970★ SENEY NATIONAL WILDLIFE REFUGE

1674 Refuge Entrance Rd
Seney, MI 49883
Web: www.fws.gov/midwest/seney
Phone: 906-586-9851; **Fax:** 906-586-3800
Location: 5 miles south of Seney, Michigan. **Established:** 1935. **Habitat:** 95,212 acres of bogs, wetland, and forest. **Facilities:** Visitor center, viewing sites, auto tour route, trails. **Activities:** Fishing, hiking, biking, hunting, cross-country skiing, snowshoeing, educational programs. **Access:** Open during daylight hours. **Primary Wildlife:** Trumpeter swans, sandhill cranes, Canada geese, eagles, osprey, common loons, river otters, beavers, black bears, moose, and gray wolves. **Special Features:** More than 200 species of birds, 26 species of fish, 45 species of mammals, and 420 species of plants have been recorded on the refuge.

★971★ SEQUOYAH NATIONAL WILDLIFE REFUGE

Rt 1 Box 18-A
Vian, OK 74962
Web: www.fws.gov/southwest/refuges/oklahoma/sequoyah
Phone: 918-773-5251
Location: Southeast of Muskogee in east-central Oklahoma. **Established:** 1970. **Habitat:** 20,800 acres of open water, riverine, oxbow lakes, wooded sloughs, wetlands, agricultural lands, bottomland hardwoods, and shrub-scrub grasslands. **Facilities:** Visitor contact station, viewing sites, hiking trails, auto tour route (6 miles), historic features. **Activities:** Boating, canoeing, fishing, hunting, hiking, bicycling, educational programs. **Access:** Open sunrise to sunset. **Primary Wildlife:** Mallards, gadwall, pintail, teal, snow geese, bald eagles, bats, armadillo, rabbits, woodchuck, white-tailed deer, black bear, western cottonmouth, timber rattlesnake, skinks, newt, salamander and frogs. **Special Features:** The refuge name honors Sequoyah, a Native American, who invented a Cherokee alphabet consisting of syllables that allowed his tribe to preserve their traditions and history in writing.

★972★ SEVILLETA NATIONAL WILDLIFE REFUGE

PO Box 1248
Socorro, NM 87801
Web: www.fws.gov/southwest/refuges/newmex/sevilleta
Phone: 505-864-4021; **Fax:** 505-864-7761
Location: 20 miles north of Socorro, New Mexico. **Established:** 1973. **Habitat:** 229,700 acres covering a wide range of ecosystem types: Chihuahuan desert, Great Plains grassland, Great Basin shrub-steppe, piñon-juniper woodland, riparian forests, wetlands, and montane coniferous forest. **Access:** Refuge is

See pages 22-23 for map of National Wildlife Refuges.

managed primarily as a research area and closed to most recreational uses. However, limited waterfowl and dove hunting is available, and special tours may be arranged by contacting the refuge. **Primary Wildlife:** Desert bighorn sheep, pronghorn, mule deer, mountain lion, horned lizard, bald eagle, peregrine falcon, and several species of ducks, herons, cranes, and raptors. **Special Features:** Management has been devoted to restoring the refuge to the natural conditions that might have been seen around the turn of the 20th century. As a result, native animals like deer, elk, coyotes, mountain lions, and a wide variety of birds and reptiles have become more abundant and visible. The Mexican wolf captive management facility on the refuge has been used to re-acclimate these endangered species to their historical habitat.

★973★ SHAWANGUNK GRASSLANDS NATIONAL WILDLIFE REFUGE
c/o Wallkill River NWR
1547 Rt 565
Sussex, NJ 07461
Web: www.fws.gov/northeast/shawangunk
Phone: 973-702-7266; **Fax:** 973-702-7286
Location: About 12 miles northwest of the I-84/I-87 junction near the town of Wallkill, New Jersey. **Established:** 1999. **Habitat:** 565 acres, primarily grassland with some wooded areas. **Facilities:** Trails, wildlife viewing sites, visitor contact station. **Activities:** Wildlife observation, hiking, snowshoeing, cross-country skiing, educational programs. **Access:** Open during daylight hours, but access is restricted to existing roadway and runways. **Primary Wildlife:** Grassland-dependant birds including northern harrier, short-eared owl, upland sandpiper, horned lark, eastern meadowlark, bobolink, and several species of sparrow. **Special Features:** The grassland present today was created in the 1940s when the U.S. military filled a wetland to build an airstrip. Though manmade, the grassland is important to the survival of grassland birds and is one of only two large grasslands in the Hudson Valley.

★974★ SHELDON NATIONAL WILDLIFE REFUGE
c/o Hart Mountain National Antelope Refuge
PO Box 111
Lakeview, OR 97630
Web: www.fws.gov/sheldonhartmtn/Sheldon
Phone: 541-947-3315; **Fax:** 541-947-4414
Location: Northwestern corner of Nevada. **Established:** 1931. **Habitat:** More than 500,000 acres of rugged landscape, including narrow gorges, springs, waterfalls, and tablelands of sagebrush and mountain mahogany. Elevations range from 4,500 to 7,600 feet. **Facilities:** Visitor contact station, viewing sites, campsites, trails, auto tour route, historic features. **Activities:** Canoeing, fishing, ice fishing, horseback riding, hunting, camping, rock hounding. **Access:** Open 24 hours. **Primary Wildlife:** Pronghorn antelope, bighorn sheep, horses, burros, sage grouse, and mule deer. **Special Features:** The lure of fire opals draws miners and rock collectors to the Virgin Valley mining district.

★975★ SHELL KEYS NATIONAL WILDLIFE REFUGE
c/o Southeast Louisiana Refuges
61389 Hwy 434
Lacombe, LA 70445
Web: www.fws.gov/refuges/profiles/index.cfm?id=43613
Phone: 985-882-2000
Location: Off the south-central Louisiana coast in the Gulf of Mexico, 40 miles south of Lafayette. **Established:** 1907. **Habitat:** Small sand spit and shell barrier islands. **Activities:** Boating, fishing. **Access:** Restricted, due to its remote location. **Primary Wildlife:** Black skimmers, laughing gulls, white and brown pelicans, royal and sandwich terns. **Special Features:** Nearly submerged and regularly covered in storm overwash, Shell Keys are eroding away, exposing the state's vulnerable marsh coastline to the damaging effects of the ocean and storms.

★976★ SHERBURNE NATIONAL WILDLIFE REFUGE
17076 293rd Ave
Zimmerman, MN 55398
Web: www.fws.gov/midwest/sherburne
Phone: 763-389-3323; **Fax:** 763-389-3493
Location: East-central Minnesota, approximately 50 miles northwest of Minneapolis-Saint Paul. **Established:** 1965. **Habitat:** 30,700 acres of oak savanna, big woods, and wetlands. **Facilities:** Trails (&), viewing sites, auto tour route. **Activities:** Canoeing, fishing, hunting, hiking, cross-country skiing, snowshoeing, educational programs. **Access:** Open from dawn to dusk; designated wildlife sanctuary areas are closed to public access from March through August. **Primary Wildlife:** Canada geese, duck, owls, woodpeckers, snakes, lizards, turtles, frogs, coyote, wolf, vole, white-tailed deer, gray and red fox. **Special Features:** American Indian village sites discoverd on the refuge date back to 1300 A.D.

★977★ SHIAWASSEE NATIONAL WILDLIFE REFUGE
6975 Mower Rd
Saginaw, MI 48601
Web: midwest.fws.gov/Shiawassee
Phone: 989-777-5930; **Fax:** 989-777-9200
Location: Lower central Michigan, 25 miles south of Saginaw Bay. **Established:** 1953. **Habitat:** 9,427 acres consisting of bottomland-hardwood forests, rivers, marshes, managed pools, fields, and croplands. Authorized future land acquisitions would expand refuge's present boundaries by 7,500 acres. **Facilities:** Hiking trails (12 miles), wildlife viewing sites, learning center. **Activities:** Boating, fishing, hunting, hiking, educational programs. **Access:** Year round during daylight hours. **Primary Wildlife:** Trumpeter swan, tundra swan, wood duck, blue-winged teal, northern shoveler, bats, damselflies, dragonflies, butterflies, river otter, white-tailed deer, coyote, weasels, grasshoppers, and turtles. **Special Features:** More than 10,000 years ago much of the area, including present-day Shiawassee NWR, was covered by a large glacial lake. Evidence of the ancient lakebed can still be seen.

See pages 22-23 for map of National Wildlife Refuges.

★978★ SILETZ BAY NATIONAL WILDLIFE REFUGE

c/o Oregon Coast NWR Complex
2127 SE Marine Science Dr
Newport, OR 97365
Web: oregoncoast.fws.gov/siletzbay
Phone: 541-867-4550
Location: Just south of Lincoln City, Oregon. **Established:** 1991. **Habitat:** More than 500 acres of coastal habitats including salt marsh, brackish marsh, tidal sloughs, mudflats, and coniferous and deciduous forestland. **Facilities:** None. **Access:** Closed to the public, but wildlife can be viewed from the highway. **Primary Wildlife:** Coho and chinook salmon, steelhead and cutthroat trout. Also provides habitat for bald eagles, red-tailed hawk, osprey, great blue herons, and great egrets. **Special Features:** The primary ecological goal of the refuge is to allow the salt marsh to return to its natural tidally-influenced state.

★979★ SILVIO O. CONTE NATIONAL FISH & WILDLIFE REFUGE

52 Ave A
Turner Falls, MA 01376
Web: www.fws.gov/r5soc
Phone: 413-863-0209; **Fax:** 413-863-3070
Location: The entire length of the Connecticut River, from the northern tip of New Hampshire to the Atlantic Ocean. **Established:** 1997. **Habitat:** 7 parcels totalling 30,130 acres of tidal marshes, riparian areas, floodplain forests, and other wetlands. **Facilities:** Visitor centers, trails, viewing sites. **Activities:** Fishing, hunting, wildlife observation, snowmobiling, environmental education. **Access:** Year round during daylight hours. **Primary Wildlife:** Shrews, bats, rabbits and hare, chipmunks, coyotes, foxes, bobcats, lynx, black bear, white-tailed deer, moose, ducks, geese, swans, rails, grebes, and herons. **Special Features:** The refuge overlays the entire 7.2 million-acre Connecticut River Watershed and will eventually comprise state-owned lands in Massachusetts, Connecticut, New Hampshire, and Vermont, as well as property owned by federal agencies, private landowners, utility companies, corporations, and environmental organizations.

★980★ SLADE NATIONAL WILDLIFE REFUGE

c/o Long Lake NWR
12000 353rd St SE
Moffit, ND 58560
Web: www.fws.gov/longlake/slade.htm
Phone: 701-387-4397; **Fax:** 701-387-4767
Location: Kidder County, in south-central North Dakota. **Established:** 1940. **Habitat:** 3,000 acres of gently rolling prairie dotted by numerous lakes and marshes with 975 acres of wetland. **Activities:** Hunting. **Access:** Open year round. **Primary Wildlife:** Canada geese, snow geese, ring-necked pheasant, sharp-tailed grouse, gray partridge, coyotes, and red fox. **Special Features:** Refuge contains five semi-permanent lakes and marshes, plus 15 pothole areas, totalling over 900 acres.

★981★ SONNY BONO SALTON SEA NATIONAL WILDLIFE REFUGE

906 W Sinclair Rd
Calipatria, CA 92233
Web: www.fws.gov/pacific/refuges/field/CA_sbono.htm
Phone: 760-348-5278
Location: South-central California, about 90 miles east of San Diego. **Established:** 1930. **Habitat:** 35,484 acres of salt marsh and open water and 2,000 acres of pasture and freshwater marsh. **Facilities:** Visitor center, viewing sites, hiking trail, picnic area. **Activities:** Hiking, hunting, educational programs. **Access:** Open sunrise to sunset. **Primary Wildlife:** Canada geese, snow geese, fulvous whistling duck, wood stork, long-billed curley, mountain plover, western snowy plover, burrowing owl, white-faced ibis. Also provides habitat for the endangered Yuma clapper rail. **Special Features:** At 228 feet below sea level, Salton Sea is one of the lowest spots in the United States. It is a wintering area for waterfowl and other waterbirds, with peak populations in December and January.

★982★ SQUAW CREEK NATIONAL WILDLIFE REFUGE

PO Box 158
Mound City, MO 64470
Web: www.fws.gov/midwest/SquawCreek
Phone: 660-442-3187; **Fax:** 660-442-5248
Location: Northwestern Missouri in the Missouri River floodplain. **Established:** 1935. **Habitat:** 7,350 acres of wetland, grassland, and forest. **Facilities:** Visitor contact station, picnic area, trails, auto tour route. **Activities:** Fishing, hiking, hunting, mushroom picking, educational programs. **Access:** Open daily from sunrise to sunset. **Primary Wildlife:** Snow geese, eagles, ducks, coyotes, and white-tailed deer. **Special Features:** The refuge is home to a variety of animal species: wildlife recordings show more than 30 species of mammals, nearly 40 species of reptiles and amphibians, and more than 300 species of birds use the refuge.

★983★ STEIGERWALD LAKE NATIONAL WILDLIFE REFUGE

c/o Ridgefield NWR
PO Box 457
Ridgefield, WA 98642
Web: pacific.fws.gov/ridgefield/Steiger.htm
Phone: 360-887-4106
Location: On the Columbia River, 10 miles east of Vancouver, Washington. **Established:** 1984. **Habitat:** 1,059 acres of riverine floodplain, semi-permanent wetlands, cottonwood-dominated riparian corridors, pastures, and remnant stands of Oregon white oak. **Access:** Closed to the public, but can be viewed from State Highway 14. **Primary Wildlife:** Canada geese, songbirds, and waterfowl. **Special Features:** Refuge supports anadromous fish, breeding neotropical birds, and migrating and wintering ducks, geese, and other birds.

See pages 22-23 for map of National Wildlife Refuges.

★984★ STEWART B. MCKINNEY NATIONAL WILDLIFE REFUGE

733 Old Clinton Rd
Westbrook, CT 06498
Web: www.fws.gov/refuges/profiles/index.cfm?id=53546
Phone: 860-399-2513; **Fax:** 860-399-2515
Location: Eight units along 60 miles of the Connecticut coastal shore, consisting of five islands and three coastline locations. **Established:** 1972 as Salt Meadow NWR. Redesignated as Connecticut Coastal NWR in 1984. Renamed in 1987 to honor U.S. Congressman Stewart B. McKinney, who was instrumental in establishing the refuge. **Habitat:** More than 800 acres of varied habitat including grassy upland, tidal salt marsh, forest, and barrier beach. **Facilities:** Visitor contact station, viewing sites, trails, beach. **Activities:** Fishing, hiking, educational programs. **Access:** Portions of the refuge are closed periodically to protect nesting birds; contact refuge office for specific dates. **Primary Wildlife:** Wading birds, shorebirds, songbirds and terns (including the roseate tern), brant, scotes, American black duck, and piping plover. **Special Features:** Located in the Atlantic Flyway, the refuge provides important resting, feeding, and nesting habitat for many species of wading birds, shorebirds, songbirds and terns, including the endangered roseate tern. Adjacent waters serve as wintering habitat for brant, scoters, American black duck, and other waterfowl. Salt Meadow Unit, in Westbrook, CT, and Falkner Island Unit, three miles off the coast of Guilford, CT, have both been designation as an ''Important Bird Area'' by the National Audubon Society.

★985★ STEWART LAKE NATIONAL WILDLIFE REFUGE

c/o Audubon NWR
489 102nd Ave SW
Dunn Center, ND 58626
Phone: 701-548-8110
Location: Southwestern North Dakota, 8 miles southwest of Amidon. **Established:** 1941. **Habitat:** 1,590 acres of flowage wetlands (640 acres owned by FWS). **Activities:** Fishing, wildlife observation. **Access:** Year round during daylight hours. **Primary Wildlife:** Nesting waterfowl, shorebirds, and neo-tropical birds. **Special Features:** Refuge features a wide variety of native grasses and forbs.

★986★ STILLWATER NATIONAL WILDLIFE REFUGE

1000 Auction Rd
Fallon, NV 89406
Web: www.fws.gov/stillwater/stillwater.html
Phone: 775-423-5128; **Fax:** 775-423-0416
Location: West-central Nevada, 60 miles east of Reno. **Established:** 1948. **Habitat:** 88,000 acres of desert, marsh, and shrub. **Facilities:** Trails, auto tour route. **Activities:** Hunting, hiking, wildlife observation. **Access:** Open from 1/2 hour before sunrise until sunset, daily. **Primary Wildlife:** Long-billed dowitchers, black-necked stilts, American avocets, American white pelicans, double-crested cormorants, white-faced ibis, egrets, herons, gulls and terns. Also provides habitat for kit fox, lizards and kangaroo rats, White-tailed antelope squirrel, and rabbits. **Special Features:** Listed as a ''Globally Important Bird Area'' by

the American Bird Conservancy, the refuge's rich and diverse wetlands attract more than 250,000 waterfowl annually. More than 280 species of birds have been sighted on refuge lands.

★987★ STONE LAKES NATIONAL WILDLIFE REFUGE

1624 Hood-Franklin Rd
Elk Grove, CA 95758
Web: www.fws.gov/pacific/refuges/field/CA_stonelk.htm
Phone: 916-775-4420; **Fax:** 916-775-4407
Location: 10 miles south of Sacramento, California, off I-5, Hood-Franklin exit. **Established:** 1994. **Habitat:** More than 4,000 acres of seasonal and permanent wetlands, riparian forest, grasslands, and fresh water lakes. **Facilities:** Visitor contact station, nature trail and viewing platform (&). **Activities:** Hiking, education programs. **Access:** Open one or two weekends per month and for special events. Contact refuge office for schedule. **Primary Wildlife:** Migratory waterbirds and nesting colony birds including double-crested cormorants, great-blue herons, and great egrets. Also several endangered, threatened and special-status species, including valley elderberry longhorn beetle, giant garter snake, vernal pool tadpole, fairy shrimps, Sacramento splittail, western pond turtle, and American peregrine falcon. **Special Features:** Refuge is situated near a large, urban area at the north end of the Sacramento-San Joaquin delta. The delta attracts thousands of migrating waterfowl, shorebirds, and other water birds.

★988★ SULLYS HILL NATIONAL GAME PRESERVE

c/o Devils Lake WMD
PO Box 908
Devils Lake, ND 58301
Web: sullyshill.fws.gov
Phone: 701-662-8611; **Fax:** 701-662-8612
Location: Central North Dakota, on the south shore of Devils Lake. **Established:** 1931. **Habitat:** 1,674 acres of wooded hills and wetland marshes. **Facilities:** Visitor center, viewing sites, picnic area, trails, auto tour route (4 miles), historic features, amphitheater. **Activities:** Hiking, cross-country skiing, educational programs. **Access:** The auto tour route and nature trail are open from May through October, dawn to dusk. **Primary Wildlife:** Bison, elk, deer, prairie dog, turkey, and waterfowl. **Special Features:** Sullys Hill is one of four refuges for American bison and elk managed by the U.S. Fish and Wildlife Service. Its herd of bison was established in 1918 with just six animals brought in from Portland, Oregon.

★989★ SUNKHAZE MEADOWS NATIONAL WILDLIFE REFUGE

1168 Main St
Old Town, ME 04468
Web: www.fws.gov/refuges/profiles/index.cfm?id=53560
Phone: 207-827-6138; **Fax:** 207-827-6099
Location: 15 miles northeast of Bangor, Maine. **Established:** 1988. **Habitat:** 11,200 acres of wet meadows, shrub thickets, cedar swamps, red and silver maple floodplain forests and open freshwater streams. **Facilities:** Visitor contact station, hiking

See pages 22-23 for map of National Wildlife Refuges.

trails. **Activities:** Boating, canoeing, fishing, hunting, educational programs. **Access:** Open from dawn to dusk. **Primary Wildlife:** Frogs, toads, salamanders, neotropical land birds, grassland-nesting birds, marsh birds and American woodcock. **Special Features:** Refuge protects habitat used by many species of birds, as well as rare species such as the Tomah Mayfly and the Showy Lady's Slipper.

★990★ **SUPAWNA MEADOWS NATIONAL WILDLIFE REFUGE**
197 Lighthouse Rd
Pennsville, NJ 08070
Web: www.fws.gov/Refuges/profiles/index.cfm?id=52571
Phone: 609-463-0994
Location: 35 miles south of Philadelphia. **Established:** 1971. **Habitat:** 2,800 acres of brackish and tidal wetlands and uplands. **Facilities:** Trails, historic features. **Activities:** Fishing, crabbing, hunting (with restrictions), environmental education. **Access:** Daily during daylight hours. **Primary Wildlife:** Black ducks, mallards, herons, egrets, osprey, red fox, white-tailed deer, woodchuck, and muskrat. **Special Features:** Refuge includes a historic lighthouse, Finns Point Rear Range Light.

★991★ **SUTTER NATIONAL WILDLIFE REFUGE**
c/o Sacramento NWR
752 County Rd 99W
Willows, CA 95988
Web: www.fws.gov/refuges/profiles/index.cfm?id=11623
Phone: 530-934-2801
Location: North-central California, about 50 miles north of Sacramento. **Established:** 1945. **Habitat:** 2,591 acres of seasonal marsh, permanent ponds, and uplands. **Activities:** Waterfowl and pheasant hunting, wildlife observation. **Access:** Daylight hours year round. **Primary Wildlife:** Migratory waterfowl, ducks, geese, giant garter snake, Chinook salmon, yellow-billed cuckoo, and Sainson's hawk. **Special Features:** Refuge supports wintering populations of more than 175,000 ducks and 50,000 geese.

★992★ **SWAN LAKE NATIONAL WILDLIFE REFUGE**
16194 Swan Lake Ave
Sumner, MO 64681
Web: www.fws.gov/midwest/SwanLake
Phone: 660-856-3323; **Fax:** 660-856-3687
Location: North-central Missouri, near the town of Sumner. **Established:** 1937. **Habitat:** 10,795 acres of wetland, farmland, and old growth bottomland hardwood. **Facilities:** Visitor center, fishing piers, trails, observation tower, auto tour route. **Activities:** Boating, canoeing, fishing, hunting, hiking, educational programs. **Access:** Open during daylight hours; access to portions of the interior are limited. **Primary Wildlife:** Canada geese, waterfowl, eagles, coyotes, raccoons, muskrat, and white-tailed deer. **Special Features:** More than 100 bald eagles winter on refuge lands.

★993★ **SWAN RIVER NATIONAL WILDLIFE REFUGE**
c/o Lost Trail NWR
6900A Pleasant Valley Rd
Marion, MT 59925
Web: www.fws.gov/bisonrange/swan
Phone: 406-858-2216; **Fax:** 406-858-2218
Location: 38 miles southeast of Creston, Montana. **Established:** 1973. **Habitat:** 1,568 acres of grassland, forest, oxbow sloughs, and forest. **Facilities:** Viewing sites (&), trails. **Activities:** Boating, fishing, hunting, educational programs. **Access:** Open during daylight hours; portions may be closed to protect nesting birds. **Primary Wildlife:** Migratory birds; also elk, deer, moose, grizzly and black bears, beavers, river otters, and muskrats. **Special Features:** Swan River, which once meandered through the floodplain, has been forced toward the west by deposits of silt, leaving a series of oxbow sloughs within the refuge floodplain.

★994★ **SWANQUARTER NATIONAL WILDLIFE REFUGE**
c/o Mattamuskeet NWR
38 Mattamuskeet Rd
Swanquarter, NC 27885
Web: www.fws.gov/mattamuskeet/swanquarter
Phone: 252-926-4021
Location: Coastal North Carolina, on the north shore of Pamlico Sound. **Established:** 1932. **Habitat:** 16,411 acres of brackish marsh and forested wetlands. **Facilities:** Boat launch, fishing pier. **Activities:** Boating, fishing, crabbing, hunting, hiking, biking. **Access:** Open during daylight hours. **Primary Wildlife:** Wading birds, shorebirds, ducks, osprey, bald eagle, and American alligators. **Special Features:** Swanquarter NWR supports one of the northernmost populations of the American alligator.

★995★ **TALLAHATCHIE NATIONAL WILDLIFE REFUGE**
c/o Mississippi WMD
PO Box 1070
Grenada, MS 38901
Web: southeast.fws.gov/tallahatchie
Phone: 662-226-8286; **Fax:** 662-226-8488
Location: 9 miles west of Holcomb, Mississippi, along Tippo Bayou. **Established:** 1990. **Habitat:** 4,083 acres of former agricultural lands; about 1/3 of the property has been reforested with native bottomland trees. **Facilities:** Boat ramp. **Activities:** Boating, canoeing, hiking, fishing, hunting. **Access:** Year round during daylight hours. **Primary Wildlife:** Eastern screech owls, barred owls, loggerhead shrikes, red-tailed hawks, painted buntings, white-tailed deer, rabbits, squirrels, and raccoons. **Special Features:** Most of the agricultural land in the area is devoted to raising soybeans and rice for the benefit of waterfowl. The refuge is complemented on the south by the 9,483-acre Malmaison Wildlife Management Area, managed by the State of Mississippi.

See pages 22-23 for map of National Wildlife Refuges.

4. National Wildlife Refuges

★996★ TAMARAC NATIONAL WILDLIFE REFUGE

35704 County Hwy 26
Rochert, MN 56578
Web: www.fws.gov/midwest/tamarac
Phone: 218-847-2641
Location: Approximately 55 miles east of Fargo, North Dakota. **Established:** 1938. **Habitat:** Nearly 43,000 acres of forest, lakes, marshes, bogs, swamps and temporary ponds. **Facilities:** Visitor center, picnic areas, boat launch, fishing pier, auto tour route, trails, viewing sites. **Activities:** Boating, canoeing, fishing, hiking, bicycyling, horseback riding, mushroom and berry picking, hunting, cross-country skiing, educational programs. **Access:** Open year round, 5am to 10pm. **Primary Wildlife:** Ducks, geese, bald eagles, trumpeter swans, wild turkey, white-tailed deer, beaver, timber wolf, and porcupine. **Special Features:** The forests and waters of the refuge are home to an expanding bald eagle population; sightings are common during the breeding season.

★997★ TARGET ROCK NATIONAL WILDLIFE REFUGE

c/o Long Island NWR Complex
PO Box 21
Shirley, NY 11967
Web: www.fws.gov/refuges/profiles/index.cfm?id=52568
Phone: 631-286-0485
Location: On the north shore of Long Island, 25 miles east of New York City. **Established:** 1967. **Habitat:** 80 acres of upland forest, beach, a brackish pond and several vernal ponds. **Facilities:** Trails. **Activities:** Fishing, hiking. **Access:** Open 1/2 hour before sunrise to 1/2 hour after sunset. During the spring, a segment of the beach is closed to public use to allow bank swallows to nest undisturbed. **Primary Wildlife:** Owls, osprey, American Kestrel, puddle ducks, black ducks, double-crested cormorants, herons, egrets, sandpipers, plovers, red fox, gray squirrel, eastern chipmunk, eastern cottontail, white-tailed deer, and harbor seals. **Special Features:** State and federally protected piping plover, least tern, and common tern depend on the refuge's rocky shore for foraging and rearing young.

★998★ TEN THOUSAND ISLANDS NATIONAL WILDLIFE REFUGE

3860 Tollgate Blvd, Suite 300
Naples, FL 34114
Web: www.fws.gov/southeast/tenthousandisland
Phone: 239-353-8442; **Fax:** 239-353-8640
Location: 20 miles southeast of Naples, Florida, on the south side of State Road 41. **Established:** 1996. **Habitat:** 35,000 acres of mangrove forest, marine waters, and freshwater marshland. **Facilities:** Trail. **Activities:** Camping, hunting, boating, canoeing, fishing. **Access:** Year round. **Primary Wildlife:** Wood storks, wading birds, shore birds, manatees, sea turtles. **Special Features:** Refuge encompasses part of one of the largest expanses of mangrove estuary in North America, and its beaches provide a substantial nesting area for loggerhead sea turtles.

★999★ TENNESSEE NATIONAL WILDLIFE REFUGE

3006 Dinkins Ln
Paris, TN 38242
Web: www.fws.gov/tennesseerefuge
Phone: 731-642-2091; **Fax:** 731-644-3351
Location: West-central Tennessee. **Established:** 1945. **Habitat:** 50,997 acres of water (ponds, rivers, and streams), forests, farmland, and grasslands. **Facilities:** Visitor contact station, viewing sites, boat launch, auto tour routes, trails, historic site. **Activities:** Boating, canoeing, fishing, hunting, educational programs. **Access:** Open daily during daylight hours. **Primary Wildlife:** Canada geese, mallards, wigeon, black ducks, wood ducks, heron, frogs, toads, turtles, bats, rabbits, nine-banded armadillo, woodchuck, and white-tailed deer. **Special Features:** Several endangered or threatened species may be found on the refuge, including the bald eagle, least tern, woodstork and several species of mussels.

★1000★ TENSAS RIVER NATIONAL WILDLIFE REFUGE

2312 Quebec Rd
Tallulah, LA 71282
Web: www.fws.gov/tensasriver
Phone: 318-574-2664; **Fax:** 318-574-1624
Location: Northeastern Louisiana. **Established:** 1980. **Habitat:** 64,012 acres of open water, woodlands, croplands, reforested fields, and wetlands. **Facilities:** Visitor center, interpretive displays, trails, viewing sites, 2 observation towers. **Activities:** Boating, canoeing, fishing, hunting, educational programs. **Access:** Open 24 hours a day. **Primary Wildlife:** Black bears, ducks, geese, raptors, wading birds, and shorebirds. **Special Features:** Refuge is home to an estimated 100-120 Louisiana black bears, a threatened species.

★1001★ TETLIN NATIONAL WILDLIFE REFUGE

PO Box 779
Tok, AK 99780
Web: tetlin.fws.gov
Phone: 907-883-5312
Location: 94 miles northwest of the U.S./Canada border, and 205 miles southeast of Fairbanks, Alaska. **Established:** 1980. **Habitat:** 730,000 acres of mountains, rivers, forest, tundra, and wetlands. **Facilities:** Visitor center, viewing sites, hiking trails, auto tour route, campsites. **Activities:** Camping, boating, canoeing, fishing, hunting, educational programs. **Access:** Unlimited, except by weather. **Primary Wildlife:** Sandhill cranes, green-winged teal, ring-necked ducks, ruddy ducks, owls, hawks, black-billed magpie, and Pacific loons. Also red fox, snowshoe hare, spruce grouse, wolves, black and brown bear, lynx, moose, Dall sheep, and caribou. **Special Features:** Thousands of birds migrate through the refuge each spring on their way to other nesting areas throughout Alaska. At least 115 species remain on the refuge to nest and raise their young.

★1002★ TEWAUKON NATIONAL WILDLIFE REFUGE

9754 143 1/2 Ave SE
Cayuga, ND 58013
Web: www.fws.gov/tewaukon
Phone: 701-724-3598

See pages 22-23 for map of National Wildlife Refuges.

4. National Wildlife Refuges

Location: Southeast corner of North Dakota. **Established:** 1945. **Habitat:** 8,363 acres of prairie, grasslands, wooded and grassy stream corridors, wetlands, and croplands. **Facilities:** Visitor contact station, picnic area, trails, viewing sites, boat ramp (&), auto tour route, historic features. **Activities:** Boating, canoeing, fishing, ice fishing, hiking, hunting, educational programs. **Access:** Open daily from dawn until 10pm. **Primary Wildlife:** Waterfowl, white-tailed deer, red fox, skunk, muskrat, and mink. **Special Features:** Refuge is located astride the Wild Rice River, which flows from west to east and then north out of Lake Tewaukon. In the 1960s four dams were built to control the river, resulting in hundreds of acres of lakes and marshes, and creating nesting and migration habitat for waterfowl.

★1003★ **TEXAS POINT NATIONAL WILDLIFE REFUGE**

c/o McFaddin NWR
PO Box 358
Sabine Pass, TX 77655
Web: www.fws.gov/southwest/refuges/texas/mcfaddin
Phone: 409-971-2909; **Fax:** 409-971-2104
Location: On the Texas gulf coast, near the Louisiana border. **Established:** 1979. **Habitat:** 8,900 acres of fresh to salt marsh with some wooded uplands and prairie ridges. **Facilities:** Hiking trails, 5 boat ramps. **Activities:** Boating, canoeing, fishing, crabbing, hunting. **Access:** Open 24 hours a day. **Primary Wildlife:** Warblers, vireos, grosbeaks, tanagers, orioles, buntings, bobcat, gray fox, and American alligator. **Special Features:** Large concentrations of migrating songbirds fly through the upper Texas coast, with peak periods of migration occurring in April. Nearly 280 species of birds are found on the refuge.

★1004★ **THATCHER ISLAND NATIONAL WILDLIFE REFUGE**

c/o Parker River NWR
261 Northern Blvd, Plum Island
Newburyport, MA 01950
Web: www.fws.gov/northeast/ma/tis.htm
Phone: 978-465-5753; **Fax:** 978-465-2807
Location: About 25 miles northeast of Boston: 1 mile off the coast of Massachusetts on the north side of Thacher Island. **Established:** 1972. **Habitat:** 22 acres of rock edge, grass, and shrub. **Access:** Accessible by boat only. Open daily from sunrise to sunset but is subject to temporary closures. **Primary Wildlife:** Herring and great black-backed gulls, cormorants, common eider, and other waterfowl species. **Special Features:** Thacher Island is home to the Cape Ann Light Station, designated a National Historic Landmark. A unique feature of this site is its twin light towers; the North Tower is located on refuge property.

★1005★ **THEODORE ROOSEVELT NATIONAL WILDLIFE REFUGE**

728 Yazoo Refuge Rd
Hollandale, MS 38748
Web: www.fws.gov/trnwr
Phone: 662-839-2638; **Fax:** 662-839-2619
Location: In the Mississippi Flyway, near Onward, Mississippi.

Established: 2004. **Habitat:** 6,600 acres of bottomland hardwood forest and old agricultural land. **Access:** Not open to the public; future plans include public access. **Primary Wildlife:** Louisiana black bear, songbirds, wading birds, raptors. **Special Features:** Plans are underway to reforest additional acreage with native bottomland hardwood trees to help provide essential habitat for the endangered Louisiana black bear, a common visitor in the region.

★1006★ **THREE ARCH ROCKS NATIONAL WILDLIFE REFUGE**

c/o Oregon Coast NWR Complex
2127 SE Marine Science Dr
Newport, OR 97365
Web: www.fws.gov/oregoncoast/3archrocks
Phone: 541-867-4550
Location: Off Oregon's coastline, due west of Portland. **Established:** 1907. **Habitat:** 15 acres of rock islands (three large rocks and six smaller rocks). **Access:** Closed to public entry, but can be seen from the mainland at Cape Meares and in the town of Oceanside. Waters within 500 feet of the rocks are closed to all watercraft from May through mid-September. **Primary Wildlife:** Tufted puffins, common murres, cormorants, Steller sea lions. **Special Features:** The first national wildlife refuge established west of the Mississippi River, the site protects Oregon's largest seabird nesting colony, which has more than 230,000 birds.

★1007★ **TIJUANA SLOUGH NATIONAL WILDLIFE REFUGE**

301 Caspian Way
Imperial Beach, CA 91932
Web: sandiegorefuges.fws.gov/Tijuana.htm
Phone: 619-575-2704
Location: Southwestern corner of California. **Established:** 1994. **Habitat:** 1,051 acres of estuarine habitats: open water, tidal salt marsh, beach dune, riparian, vernal pool, and upland. **Facilities:** Visitor center, trails, viewing sites. **Activities:** Fishing, hiking, educational programs. **Access:** Open daily during daylight hours. **Primary Wildlife:** Endangered species include light-footed clapper rail, California least tern, Least Bell's vireo, and California brown pelican. **Special Features:** Refuge is part of the 2,700-acre Tijuana River National Estuarine Research Reserve. It is one of southern California's largest remaining salt marshes without a road or railroad trestle running through it.

★1008★ **TISHOMINGO NATIONAL WILDLIFE REFUGE**

12000 S Refuge Rd
Tishomingo, OK 73460
Web: www.fws.gov/southwest/refuges/oklahoma/tishomingo
Phone: 580-371-2402; **Fax:** 580-371-9312
Location: South-central Oklahoma. **Established:** 1946. **Habitat:** 16,464 acres of hardwood forests, wild plum thickets, grasslands, cropland, seasonally flooded flats and shallows, and the 4,500-acre Cumberland Pool. **Facilities:** Trails, viewing sites,

See pages 22-23 for map of National Wildlife Refuges.

(Left margin: 4. National Wildlife Refuges)

picnic areas, historic features. **Activities:** Boating, fishing, hiking, hunting. **Access:** Daylight hours, except for nighttime fishing. **Primary Wildlife:** White-tailed deer, wild turkeys, armadillos, opossums, fox squirrels, cottontails, hawks, warblers, vireos, red-headed woodpeckers, ducks, and bald eagles. **Special Features:** Farming has been a tradition at the refuge since 1848 when Methodist missionaries worked with the Chickasaw Nation to open a school to teach boys to write, as well as grow crops. Today, the refuge plants 700 to 900 acres of crops for wildlife to feed on.

★1009★ TOGIAK NATIONAL WILDLIFE REFUGE

PO Box 270
Dillingham, AK 99627
Web: togiak.fws.gov
Phone: 907-842-1063; **Fax:** 907-842-5402
Location: Between Kuskokwim and Bristol bays in southwestern Alaska. **Established:** 1980. **Habitat:** 4.7 million acres of mountains, tundra, forests, wetlands, lakes, rivers, streams, and coastal cliffs and beaches. **Facilities:** Visitor center, viewing sites. **Activities:** Camping, canoeing, kayaking, rafting, fishing, hiking, hunting, flightseeing, educational programs. **Access:** Open 24 hours; access is mainly by air. **Primary Wildlife:** Ptarmigan, moose, caribou, wolverines, brown bear, Pacific walrus, Steller's sea lions, harbor and spotted seals, chinook, sockeye, northern pintail, northern hawk owl, Steller's sea eagle, loons, grebes, geese, swans, teals, and eiders. **Special Features:** The northern 2.3 million acres of the refuge are designated as the Togiak Wilderness Area, constituting the second larges contiguous wilderness area withing the National Wildlife Refuge System.

★1010★ TOPPENISH NATIONAL WILDLIFE REFUGE

21 Pumphouse Rd
Toppenish, WA 98948
Web: www.fws.gov/midcolumbiariver/toppenish
Phone: 509-865-2405
Location: South-central Washington, 6 miles south of Toppenish. **Established:** 1964. **Habitat:** 1,978 acres of brushy creek bottoms, wet meadows, sagebrush uplands, and croplands. **Facilities:** Observation lookouts, trails. **Activities:** Hiking, hunting. **Access:** Open during daylight hours. **Primary Wildlife:** Waterfowl, raptors, and marsh birds, including eagles, hawks, herons, gulls, egrets, and terns. **Special Features:** Refuge provides resting and feeding area for up to 30,000 migrating waterfowl.

★1011★ TREMPEALEAU NATIONAL WILDLIFE REFUGE

W28488 Refuge Rd
Trempealeau, WI 54661
Web: www.fws.gov/midwest/trempealeau
Phone: 608-539-2311
Location: West-central Wisconsin. **Established:** 1936. **Habitat:** 6,226 acres of forested blufflands, riverine wetlands, and upland sand prairies. **Facilities:** Visitor contact station, viewing sites, trails, auto tour route. **Activities:** Canoeing, fishing, hunting, hiking, biking, cross-country skiing, snowshoeing, educational programs. **Access:** Open year round during daylight hours. **Primary Wildlife:** White pelicans, great blue herons, great egrets, black terns, grasshopper, lark and vesper sparrows, eastern meadowlarks, bald eagle, osprey, deer, coyote, muskrat, gray squirrels, pileated and red-headed woodpeckers, wild turkey, Blanding's turtle, and painted and snapping turtles. **Special Features:** The refuge is situated in a unique geological formation known as the driftless area. Thousands of years ago, glaciers surrounded but did not pass over the land. Blown into mounds, sand and silt from melting glaciers formed the rolling sand prairies of the refuge.

★1012★ TRINITY RIVER NATIONAL WILDLIFE REFUGE

1351 N Main
Liberty, TX 77575
Web: southwest.fws.gov/refuges/texas/trinityriver
Phone: 936-336-9786; **Fax:** 936-336-9847
Location: 48 miles east of Houston and 44 miles west of Beaumont, Texas, on Highway 90. **Established:** 1994. **Habitat:** 21,000 acres of floodplain/wetland including bottomland hardwood forests, forested swamps, cultivated pastures, open water, and wet pastures. **Facilities:** Boat ramp, fishing pier (&), butterfly/hummingbird garden, primitive trails. **Activities:** Fishing, hunting, wildlife observation, boating, canoeing, kayaking, hiking. **Access:** Public entry by walk-in is permitted year-round from sunrise to sunset. Some tracts may be closed during hunting season. **Primary Wildlife:** White-tailed deer, squirrels, freshwater turtles, alligators, snakes, river otters, bald eagle, butterflies, pelicans, cormorants, herons, yellow-bellied sapsucker, and woodpeckers. **Special Features:** Some 275 species of birds can be found in the bottomland forests and associated wetlands in eastern Texas and 100 bird species are known to breed there. It has been documented that Trinity River NWR is home to at least 620 plant species and more than 400 vertebrate species.

★1013★ TRUSTOM POND NATIONAL WILDLIFE REFUGE

c/o Rhode Island NWR Complex
PO Box 307
Charlestown, RI 02813
Web: www.fws.gov/northeast/trustompond
Phone: 401-364-9124
Location: South of Providence, in South Kingston. **Established:** 1987. **Habitat:** 800 acres of salt pond, upland forests, barrier beach, and grassland. **Facilities:** Trails (&), observation platforms. **Activities:** Surf fishing, hiking, hunting, wildlife observation, educational programs. **Access:** Open from dawn to dusk. Beach is closed to the public from April through mid-September to protect nesting birds. **Primary Wildlife:** Least tern, piping plover (threatened), osprey, common tern, bobolink, eastern meadowlark, yellow warbler, black duck, and Canada geese. **Special Features:** The refuge's beach provides nesting habitat for the piping plover and least tern. Ten species of fish, 40 species of mammals, and more than 20 species of amphibians and reptiles have also been seen on the refuge.

See pages 22-23 for map of National Wildlife Refuges.

★1014★ TUALATIN RIVER NATIONAL WILDLIFE REFUGE

16507 SW Roy Rogers Rd
Sherwood, OR 97140
Web: www.fws.gov/tualatinriver
Phone: 503-590-5811; **Fax:** 503-590-6702
Location: Northwestern Oregon, 15 miles southwest of downtown Portland. **Established:** 1992. **Habitat:** When acquisition is complete, the refuge will total over 3,000 acres of rivers and streams, seasonal and permanent wetlands, forested wetlands, riparian areas, grasslands, shrublands, and forested uplands. **Activities:** Guided canoe tours, guided bird walks, hiking. **Access:** Site is currently under development and access is limited; contact refuge office for details. **Primary Wildlife:** Migrating waterfowl, beaver, deer, heron, native fish, raptors, and songbirds. **Special Features:** Refuge is home to nearly 200 species of birds, more than 50 species of mammals, 25 species of reptiles and amphibians, and a wide variety of insects, fish, and plants.

★1015★ TULE LAKE NATIONAL WILDLIFE REFUGE

c/o Klamath Basin NWR Complex
4009 Hill Rd
Tulelake, CA 96134
Web: www.fws.gov/klamathbasinrefuges/tulelake/
tulelake.html
Phone: 530-667-2231; **Fax:** 530-667-8337
Location: Near the California-Oregon border. **Established:** 1928. **Habitat:** 39,116 acres of mostly open water and croplands. **Facilities:** Visitor center, viewing sites, photography blinds, hiking trails, auto tour route (10 miles), canoe trail. **Activities:** Canoeing, hunting, hiking, wildlife observation. **Access:** Open during daylight hours. **Primary Wildlife:** American bald eagle, golden eagle, American white pelican, white-faced ibis, peregrine falcon, pintail, mallard, gadwall, canvasback, grebes, black terns, tri-colored blackbird, and Snow, Ross' and Canada geese. **Special Features:** The Tule Lake canoe trail is open from July through September; canoes may be rented from nearby concessionaires.

★1016★ TURNBULL NATIONAL WILDLIFE REFUGE

26010 S Smith Rd
Cheney, WA 99004
Web: www.fws.gov/turnbull
Phone: 360-235-4723
Location: Eastern Washington, about 20 miles southwest of Spokane. **Established:** 1937. **Habitat:** Nearly 16,000 acres of channeled scabland with basalt outcrops, canyons, and ponderosa pine forests interspersed with marshes, wetlands, and lakes. **Facilities:** Visitor contact station, trails, auto tour route, observation points (&). **Activities:** Hiking, wildlife observation, biking, educational programs. **Access:** Open daily during daylight hours. **Primary Wildlife:** Duck, geese, white-tailed deer, elk, coyotes, beaver, badger, and moose. **Special Features:** Refuge is in an ecological transition zone between the dry, sagebrush-dotted grasslands of the Columbia Basin and the timbered Selkirk and Bitterroot mountain ranges to the east.

★1017★ TWO PONDS NATIONAL WILDLIFE REFUGE

c/o Rocky Mountain Arsenal NWR, Bldg 121
Commerce City, CO 80022
Web: www.fws.gov/twoponds
Phone: 303-289-0930
Location: 15 miles northwest of Denver, Colorado, in the suburban community of Arvada. **Established:** 1990. **Habitat:** 72 acres of grassy wetlands and uplands with three small ponds. **Facilities:** Trails, viewing sites. **Activities:** Hiking, wildlife observation, guided tours. **Access:** Open year round during daylight hours. **Primary Wildlife:** Deer, red fox, turtles, raccoon, sparrows, hawks, woodpeckers, magpies, warblers, and herons. **Special Features:** 113 species of birds have been observed on refuge land, mostly during the spring, summer, and fall; 22 nest here.

★1018★ TWO RIVERS NATIONAL WILDLIFE REFUGE

HCR 82 Box 107
Brussels, IL 62013
Web: www.fws.gov/midwest/TwoRivers
Phone: 618-883-2524; **Fax:** 618-883-2201
Location: 17 miles west of Alton, Illinois. **Established:** Originally established as the Brussels district of the Mark Twain NWR in 1958. In 2000 the Mark Twain NWR was split into 5 separate refuges, including Two Rivers. **Habitat:** 8,500 acres of bottomland forests, grasslands, lakes, sloughs, and cropland. **Facilities:** Visitor center (Calhoun unit), trails. **Activities:** Fishing, boating, bicycling, berry and mushroom picking (for personal consumption), hunting (Apple Creek unit only), educational programs (by appointment). **Access:** Open daylight hours except between October 15 and December 31 when refuge is closed to provide sanctuary for migrating birds. **Primary Wildlife:** Grebes, White pelicans, Canada geese, wood duck, bald eagle, red-tailed hawk, slender glass lizard, speckled kingsnake, gray and Indiana bat, spotted skunk, least shrew, freckled madtom, burbot, and chub. **Special Features:** Provides an important link in the chain of resting, feeding, and wintering areas for migratory birds using the Mississippi Flyway. More than 5 million ducks and 50,000 geese normally funnel through this river junction on their migration.

★1019★ TYBEE NATIONAL WILDLIFE REFUGE

c/o Savannah Coastal Refuges Complex
1000 Business Center Dr, Suite 10
Savannah, GA 31405
Web: www.fws.gov/tybee
Phone: 912-652-4415
Location: In the mouth of the Savannah River, adjacent to the Georgia state line. **Established:** 1938. **Habitat:** 100 acres covered with scrub vegetation and sand deposits and partly bordered by saltwater marsh. **Access:** Closed to the public. **Primary Wildlife:** Migratory birds. **Special Features:** Endangered species, including piping plovers and wood storks have been observed on refuge land, and shortnose sturgeon and manatees have been in observed in waters bordering the refuge.

See pages 22-23 for map of National Wildlife Refuges.

★1020★ **UL BEND NATIONAL WILDLIFE REFUGE**
c/o Charles M. Russell NWR
PO Box 110
Lewistown, MT 59457
Web: www.fws.gov/refuges/profiles/index.cfm?id=61529
Phone: 406-538-8706; **Fax:** 406-538-7521
Location: Within Charles M. Russell NWR in north-central Montana. **Established:** 1976. **Habitat:** 20,000 acres of designated wilderness: native prairie, forested coulees, river bottoms, and "breaks" badlands. **Activities:** Hiking, horseback riding, boating, fishing. **Access:** Limited; contact refuge office. **Primary Wildlife:** Black-footed ferret, prairie dogs, white-tailed deer, mule deer, elk, bighorn sheep, pronghorn, coyotes, waterfowl, game birds. **Special Features:** This "refuge-within-a-refuge" is the site of an effort to rescue the black-footed ferret, one of North America's most endangered animals. Since black-footed ferrets depend heavily on black-tailed prairie dogs, refuge staff has begun related efforts to increase the abundance and distribution of prairie dog towns.

★1021★ **UMATILLA NATIONAL WILDLIFE REFUGE**
c/o Mid-Columbia River Refuges
PO Box 1447
Pasco, WA 99352
Web: www.fws.gov/midcolumbiariver/Umatillapage.htm
Phone: 509-371-9212; **Fax:** 509-375-0196
Location: Several sites along the Columbia River around Irrigon, Oregon, and Paterson, Washington. **Established:** 1969. **Habitat:** 29,370 acres of marshes, sloughs, open water, cropland, and sagebrush uplands. **Facilities:** Visitor contact station, viewing sites, hiking trails, auto tour route, boat ramps. **Activities:** Boating, fishing, hunting, educational programs. **Access:** Open year round, dawn to dusk. **Primary Wildlife:** Great Basin Canada geese, ducks, long-billed curlews, and other marsh and water birds; also mule deer and coyote. **Special Features:** Refuge provides habitat for all species of ducks found in the West, except sea ducks. The largest number of ducks on the refuge at one time, estimated at 458,000 birds, occurred November 13, 1983.

★1022★ **UNION SLOUGH NATIONAL WILDLIFE REFUGE**
1710 360th St
Titonka, IA 50480
Web: www.fws.gov/midwest/unionslough
Phone: 515-928-2523; **Fax:** 515-928-2230
Location: Just south of the Minnesota border, about 50 miles west of Mason City, Iowa. **Established:** 1937. **Habitat:** 3,334 acres of open water, marsh, uplands, riverine bottomlands and woody vegetation. **Facilities:** Viewing sites, trails, auto tour route. **Activities:** Fishing, hiking, hunting, educational programs. **Access:** Open during daylight hours. Some portions close seasonally; contact refuge office. **Primary Wildlife:** American white pelicans, great blue herons, mallards, bald eagles, white-tailed deer, ring-necked pheasants, raccoons, and muskrats. **Special Features:** Refuge name is derived from the connection or "union" of two watersheds: the Blue Earth River of Minnesota and the East Fork of the Des Moines River. The terrain is nearly flat, allowing the flow of the water to be determined by the direction of the wind at times. Refuge is a major producer of wood ducks, with approximately 2,500 hatched annually.

★1023★ **UPPER KLAMATH NATIONAL WILDLIFE REFUGE**
c/o Klamath Basin NWR Complex
4009 Hill Rd
Tulelake, CA 96134
Web: www.klamathnwr.org/upperklamath.html
Phone: 530-667-2231; **Fax:** 530-667-8337
Location: 25 miles northwest of Klamath Falls, Oregon, along Highway 140. **Established:** 1928. **Habitat:** 15,000 acres of mostly freshwater marsh and open water. **Facilities:** Canoe trail, viewing sites. **Activities:** Canoeing, fishing, hunting. **Access:** Open during daylight hours. **Primary Wildlife:** Canada goose, ducks, white pelicans, grebes, herons, egrets, bald eagle, osprey, beavers, muskrats, river otters, and two endangered species, lost river sucker and short nosed sucker. **Special Features:** Bald eagle and osprey nest nearby and can sometimes be seen fishing in refuge waters. A boat is essential to visit this refuge.

★1024★ **UPPER MISSISSIPPI RIVER NATIONAL WILDLIFE & FISH REFUGE**
51 E 4th St
Winona, MN 55987
Web: www.fws.gov/midwest/UpperMississippiRiver
Phone: 507-452-4232; **Fax:** 507-452-0851
Location: Along 261 miles of the Mississippi River from Wabasha, Minnesota, to Rock Island, Illinois. **Established:** 1924. **Habitat:** 240,000 acres of broad pools, islands, braided channels, extensive bottomland forest, floodplain marshes and occasional sand prairie. **Facilities:** Visitor center, viewing sites, picnic areas, boat ramps, trails, historic features. **Activities:** Boating, canoeing, fishing, ice fishing, hunting, trapping, hiking, camping, educational programs. **Access:** Open 24 hours a day. **Primary Wildlife:** Tundra swans, canvasbacks, lesser scaup, mallards, wigeon, bald eagles, vireos, and deer. **Special Features:** More than 160 bald eagle nests and a yearly average of 15 active heron colonies with a total of 5,000 nests exist on the refuge. The refuge and river also support 119 fish species.

★1025★ **UPPER OUACHITA NATIONAL WILDLIFE REFUGE**
c/o D'Arbonne NWR
11372 Hwy 143
Farmerville, LA 71363
Web: www.fws.gov/upperouachita
Phone: 318-726-4400; **Fax:** 318-726-4667
Location: 6 miles north of West Monroe, Louisiana. **Established:** 1978. **Habitat:** More than 40,000 acres of bottomland hardwood forest, upland forest, shrub and wooded swamp, reforested farmland, and open water. **Facilities:** Visitor contact station, trails, boat ramps. **Activities:** Boating, canoeing, fishing, hunting, hiking, educational programs. **Access:** Year round, although 80% of the refuge is subject to annual flooding from December through May. **Primary Wildlife:** Concentrations of

ducks, geese, wading birds, raptors, and a small wintering population of bald eagles. **Special Features:** The site's central physical feature is the Ouachita River, which bisects the refuge and features a wide floodplain characterized by alluvial soils. The refuge provides excellent wintering habitat for tens of thousands of ducks and geese.

★1026★ UPPER SOURIS NATIONAL WILDLIFE REFUGE

17705 212th Ave NW
Berthold, ND 58718
Web: uppersouris.fws.gov
Phone: 701-468-5467
Location: In Souris River Valley in northwestern North Dakota. **Established:** 1935. **Habitat:** 32,092 acres including river bottom woodlands, flood plains, rolling hills with native mixed grasses, and steep, brush-covered coulees. **Facilities:** Visitor contact station, viewing sites, picnic areas, fishing piers, trails, auto tour route, (&). **Activities:** Boating, canoeing, fishing, hunting, hiking, berry picking, cross-country skiing, educational programs. **Access:** Daily between 5 a.m. to 10 p.m., year round. **Primary Wildlife:** Geese, tundra swans, pintails, canvasbacks, redheads, buffleheads, muskrats, and white-tailed deer. **Special Features:** Focal point of the refuge is 10,000-acre Lake Darling, constructed in 1936 to provide water to downstream marshes on J. Clark Salyer and Upper Souris NWRs.

★1027★ VALENTINE NATIONAL WILDLIFE REFUGE

HC 14 Box 67
Valentine, NE 69201
Web: www.fws.gov/valentine
Phone: 402-376-3789
Location: In the Sandhills area of north-central Nebraska. **Established:** 1935. **Habitat:** 71,516 acres of sand dunes, mid- and tall-grass prairies, marshes, and lakes. **Facilities:** Viewing sites, trails, boat ramps (&). **Activities:** Canoeing, fishing, hiking, hunting. **Access:** Open year round during daylight hours. **Primary Wildlife:** Waterfowl, including blue-winged teal, mallards, pintails, gadwalls, redheads, ruddy ducks, shovelers, prairie chicken, sharp-tailed grouse, and pelican. Mammals include deer, muskrat, and beaver. **Special Features:** In early spring, prairie chickens and sharp-tailed grouse gather on dancing grounds for their elaborate courtship display. During their spring and fall migrations, sandhill cranes pass over in great numbers, filling the sky with trailing Vs and musical rattling calls. Cold weather brings bald and golden eagles to hunt on the snow-covered prairie.

★1028★ VIEQUES NATIONAL WILDLIFE REFUGE

PO Box 1527
Vieques, PR 00765
Web: www.fws.gov/southeast/vieques
Phone: 787-741-2138; **Fax:** 787-741-2158
Location: On the island of Vieques, Puerto Rico. **Established:** 2001. **Habitat:** 17,673 acres of beaches, coastal lagoons, mangrove wetlands and upland forested areas. The marine environment around the refuge contains coral reefs and seagrass beds.

Facilities: Visitor center. **Activities:** Hiking, bicycling, fishing, beach activities, crabbing. **Access:** Certain areas of the refuge are open 7 days a week from sunrise to sunset. **Primary Wildlife:** Green, loggerhead, hawksbill and leatherback sea turtles, Antillean manatee, brown pelican, crabs, and migratory birds. **Special Features:** In addition to its ecological value, the refuge contains important resources of archeological and historic significance, including legacies of the Taino culture and sugar cane era.

★1029★ WACCAMAW NATIONAL WILDLIFE REFUGE

PO Box 1439
1601 N Fraser St
Georgetown, SC 29440
Web: www.fws.gov/waccamaw
Phone: 843-527-8069
Location: Portions of Horry, Georgetown, and Marion counties, South Carolina. **Established:** 1997. **Habitat:** 9,506 acres of black water forested wetlands to forested and emergent wetlands. **Activities:** Boating, canoeing, kayaking, fishing, hunting, educational programs. **Access:** Few refuge tracts are accessible by car. **Primary Wildlife:** Waterfowl, wading birds, deer, squirrel, hogs. **Special Features:** Refuge includes portions of Great Pee Dee, Little Pee Dee and Waccamaw rivers. It is the northernmost nesting area for swallow-tailed kites.

★1030★ WALLKILL RIVER NATIONAL WILDLIFE REFUGE

1547 County Rt 565
Sussex, NJ 07461
Web: www.fws.gov/northeast/wallkillriver
Phone: 973-702-7266; **Fax:** 973-702-7286
Location: Along the Wallkill River in northwestern New Jersey. **Established:** 1990. **Habitat:** 4,800 acres of swamps, fens, wet meadows, old fields and forests. Land acquistion is ongoing. **Facilities:** Visitor contact station, trails, hand-launch boat ramps, historic sites. **Activities:** Canoeing, kayaking, fishing, hunting, hiking, cross-country skiing, snowshoeing, educational programs. **Access:** Open dawn to dusk year round. **Primary Wildlife:** Songbirds, wading birds, migratory waterfowl, shorebirds, and raptors, butterflies, dragonflies, bog turtles, bobcat, opossum, foxes, river otter, eastern cottontail, bats, salamanders, snakes, and frogs. **Special Features:** Migratory birds on the Atlantic Flyway are naturally "funneled" through the valley, where the refuge's high-quality wetlands provide a resting and feeding area.

★1031★ WALLOPS ISLAND NATIONAL WILDLIFE REFUGE

c/o Chincoteague NWR
PO Box 62
Chincoteague, VA 23336
Phone: 757-336-6122; **Fax:** 757-336-5273
Location: 5 miles from Norfolk, Virginia. **Established:** 1975. **Habitat:** 373 acres of mostly salt marsh and woodlands. Additionally, the Fish & Wildlife Service uses 3,000 acres of NASA-owned land on Wallops Island for research and management of

See pages 22-23 for map of National Wildlife Refuges.

(margin) 4. National Wildlife Refuges

declining wildlife. **Activities:** Hiking, deer hunting (limited). **Access:** Closed to the public. **Primary Wildlife:** Snow geese, black ducks, dunlin, dowitchers, bald eagle, piping plover, Wilson's plover, American oystercatcher, white-tailed deer. **Special Features:** Refuge protects the Simoneston Bay sea-level fen. Sea-level fens are nutrient-poor maritime seepage wetlands, confined to a few sites with an unusual combintion of environmental conditions for the mid-Atlantic. Only four occurrences are known in Virginia.

★1032★ WAPACK NATIONAL WILDLIFE REFUGE

c/o Great Bay NWR
100 Merrimac Dr
Newington, NH 03801
Phone: 603-431-7511; **Fax:** 603-431-6014
Location: On North Pack Monadnock Mountain in New Hampshire, 20 miles west of Nashua. **Established:** 1972. **Habitat:** 1,672 acres of timbered mountain slopes, bare rock ledges and cliffs, bogs, and swamps. **Facilities:** Trails. **Activities:** Hiking, wildlife observation. **Access:** Open from dawn to dusk year round. **Primary Wildlife:** Tree sparrows, hawks, pine grosbeaks, white throated sparrow, deer, bear, coyote, fisher, fox, mink and weasel. **Special Features:** The 30-mile Wapack Trail, which crosses parts of Massachusetts and New Hampshire, passes through the center of refuge.

★1033★ WAPANOCCA NATIONAL WILDLIFE REFUGE

26320 Hwy 33S
Augusta, AR 72006
Web: www.fws.gov/refuges/profiles/index.cfm?id=43650
Phone: 870-347-2614
Location: 20 miles northwest of Memphis, Tennessee. **Established:** 1961. **Habitat:** 5,484 acres of lake, swamp, bottomland hardwoods, and agricultural land. **Facilities:** Visitor center, observation platform, boat ramp, canoe trail, auto tour route. **Activities:** Boating, fishing, hunting, educational programs. **Access:** Open during daylight hours. **Primary Wildlife:** Migrating ducks, geese, and raptors. Also provides habitat for fox squirrels, rabbits, and deer. **Special Features:** Bald eagles are present during the winter, and there is one active eagle nest on site.

★1034★ WASHITA NATIONAL WILDLIFE REFUGE

Rt 1 Box 68
Butler, OK 73625
Web: www.fws.gov/southwest/refuges/oklahoma/washita
Phone: 580-664-2205; **Fax:** 580-664-2206
Location: West-central Oklahoma, approximately 5 miles west of Butler, Oklahoma. **Established:** 1961. **Habitat:** 8,200 acres of hills, ravines, bottomlands, and water. **Facilities:** Visitor contact station, viewing sites. **Activities:** Boating, fishing, hunting (limited), educational programs. **Access:** Open during daylight hours. **Primary Wildlife:** Snow geese, Canada geese, mallards, common mergansers, bald eagles, Swainson's hawks, and sandhill cranes. Also provides habitat for black-tailed prairie dogs, coyotes, badgers, and bobcats. **Special Features:** Within the refuge, the slow-moving Washita River winds through prairie and farmlands to merge with Foss Reservoir, providing a home and resting area for geese and other waterfowl.

★1035★ WASSAW NATIONAL WILDLIFE REFUGE

c/o Savannah Coastal Refuges Complex
1000 Business Center Dr, Suite 10
Savannah, GA 31405
Web: www.fws.gov/wassaw
Phone: 912-652-4415; **Fax:** 912-652-4385
Location: On Georgia's northern coast, 14 miles southeast of Savannah. **Established:** 1969. **Habitat:** 10,053 acres of salt marshes and beaches with rolling dunes, live oak, and slash pine woodlands. **Facilities:** Trails (20 miles). **Activities:** Boating, kayaking, biking, beachcombing, fishing, hunting, hiking, educational programs. **Access:** Open during daylight hours; accessible only by boat. **Primary Wildlife:** Threatened or endangered species such as bald eagle, wood stork, piping plover, peregrine falcons, and loggerhead turtles. **Special Features:** Threatened loggerhead sea turtles nest here in the summer.

★1036★ WATERCRESS DARTER NATIONAL WILDLIFE REFUGE

c/o Wheeler NWR
2700 Refuge Headquarters Rd
Decauter, AL 35603
Web: southeast.fws.gov/watercressdarter
Phone: 256-353-7243; **Fax:** 256-340-9728
Location: Within city limits of Bessemer in Jefferson County, Alabama. **Established:** 1980. **Habitat:** 23 acres of bushy vegetation with a .25-acre pond. **Activities:** Hiking, wildlife observation. **Access:** Open during daylight hours. **Primary Wildlife:** Watercress darter **Special Features:** The watercress darter is a small, colorful fish found in the watercress zone of springs and spring runs. Just seven locations are known to support the 2-inch-long darter — all in the upper Black Warrior River drainage near Birmingham.

★1037★ WAUBAY NATIONAL WILDLIFE REFUGE

44401 134A St
Waubay, SD 57273
Web: waubay.fws.gov
Phone: 605-947-4521; **Fax:** 605-947-4524
Location: Northeastern South Dakota. **Established:** 1935. **Habitat:** 4,650 acres of lakes, grasslands, marshlands, and woodlands. **Facilities:** Visitor center, interpretive exhibits, trails, observation tower, picnic area. **Activities:** Hiking, deer hunting, cross-country skiing, ice fishing, educational programs. **Access:** Open during daylight hours. Visitor center hours are 8 a.m. to 4:30 p.m., Monday through Friday. **Primary Wildlife:** Canada geese, snow geese, gadwalls, redheads, shovelers, Baltimore orioles, orchard orioles, bats, deer, fox squirrels, cottontail rabbits, and gophers. **Special Features:** ''Waubay'' is the Sioux word meaning ''a nesting place for birds.'' More than 245 species of birds call the refuge home.

See pages 22-23 for map of National Wildlife Refuges.

4. National Wildlife Refuges

★1038★ WERTHEIM NATIONAL WILDLIFE REFUGE

c/o Long Island NWR Complex
PO Box 21
Shirley, NY 11967
Phone: 631-286-0485; **Fax:** 631-286-4003
Location: On Long Island's south shore. **Established:** 1947. **Habitat:** 2,550 acres of marine seagrass beds, intertidal saltmarsh, high saltmarsh, freshwater marsh, swamps, and upland pine and oak forests. **Facilities:** Visitor contact station, viewing sites, hiking trails. **Activities:** Boating, fishing, hiking, wildlife observation. **Access:** Open from dawn to dusk. **Primary Wildlife:** Waterfowl, primarily black duck. Also provides habitat for owls, hawks, butterflies, mice, voles, deer, weasel, and fox. **Special Features:** The refuge contains one of the last undeveloped estuary systems remaining on Long Island and includes Carmans River, a state-designated Wild and Scenic River.

★1039★ WHEELER NATIONAL WILDLIFE REFUGE

2700 Refuge Headquarters Rd
Decatur, AL 35603
Web: www.fws.gov/wheeler
Phone: 256-353-7243; **Fax:** 256-340-9728
Location: North-central Alabama, along the Tennessee River and its tributaries. **Established:** 1938. **Habitat:** 34,500 acres of unfarmed uplands, shoreline woodlands, open water, hardwood bottomlands, and pine plantations. **Facilities:** Visitor center, trails, boardwalk, viewing sites, auto tour route, historic features, boat ramp. **Activities:** Boating, canoeing, fishing, hiking, biking, horseback riding (on open graveled roads), hunting, educational programs. **Access:** Open during daylight hours. **Primary Wildlife:** Ducks, geese, hummingbirds, butterflies, American alligator, raccoon, and deer. **Special Features:** Refuge supports the southernmost and Alabama's only significant concentration of wintering Canada geese. In the fall, geese and ducks migrate to the refuge, where they rest and feed throughout the winter.

★1040★ WHITE RIVER NATIONAL WILDLIFE REFUGE

57 S CC Camp Rd
PO Box 205
Saint Charles, AR 72140
Web: www.fws.gov/whiteriver
Phone: 870-282-8200; **Fax:** 870-282-8234
Location: Eastern Arkansas, in the floodplain of the lower White River. **Established:** 1935. **Habitat:** 160,000 acres of bottomland hardwood forest, lakes, streams, and impoundments. **Facilities:** Visitor contact station, observation tower, campgrounds. **Activities:** Boating, fishing, frogging, hunting, camping. **Access:** Open 24 hours a day from March through October. From November to March, portions of the refuge may be closed to protect nesting wildlife or due to flooding; check with office. **Primary Wildlife:** Canada geese, mallard, turkey, bald eagle, black bear, and deer. **Special Features:** Ranging from 3-10 miles wide and almost 90 miles long, the refuge is one of the largest remaining bottomland hardwood forests in the Mississippi River Valley.

★1041★ WHITTLESEY CREEK NATIONAL WILDLIFE REFUGE

c/o Northern Great Lakes Visitor Center
29270 County Hwy G
Ashland, WI 54806
Web: www.fws.gov/midwest/WhittleseyCreek
Phone: 715-685-2678; **Fax:** 715-685-2680
Location: On State Highway 13, north of junction with U.S. Highway 2, in northern Wisconsin. **Established:** 1999. **Habitat:** Some 540 acres, to include spring-fed streams, coastal wetlands, sedge meadows, lowland hardwood swamps, black spruce swamps, and abandoned agricultural fields. **Activities:** Fishing, waterfowl hunting, wildlife observation. **Access:** Daylight hours year round. **Primary Wildlife:** Trout, salmon, waterfowl. **Special Features:** Currently in acquisition stages, the refuge is part of a large wetland complex on Lake Superior.

★1042★ WICHITA MOUNTAINS WILDLIFE REFUGE

32 Refuge Headquarters
Indiahoma, OK 73552
Web: www.fws.gov/southwest/refuges/wichitamountains
Phone: 580-429-3222
Location: 20 miles northwest of Lawton, Oklahoma, in Comanche County. **Established:** 1901. **Habitat:** 59,020 acres of prairie grasslands, rocky outcrops, and oak forest. **Facilities:** Campground, primitive campsites, youth camp, visitor center, trails, picnic areas. **Activities:** Camping, fishing, hiking, rock climbing. **Access:** Year round. **Primary Wildlife:** American bison, Rocky Mountain elk, white-tailed deer, and Texas longhorn cattle. **Special Features:** More than 50 mammal species, 240 bird species, 64 reptile and amphibian species, 36 fish species, and 806 plant species thrive at this refuge.

★1043★ WILLAPA NATIONAL WILDLIFE REFUGE

3888 SR 101
Ilwaco, WA 98624
Web: www.fws.gov/willapa/WillapaNWR
Phone: 360-484-3482
Location: On the shores of Willapa Bay near the Pacific Ocean in southwestern Washington. **Established:** 1937. **Habitat:** More than 15,000 acres of salt marshes, tideflats, old-growth forest, coastal dunes and beaches. **Facilities:** 5 primitive boat campsites (on Long Island), trails, viewing sites. **Activities:** Camping, boating, canoeing, fishing, hiking, hunting. **Access:** Daily from dawn to dusk. **Primary Wildlife:** Wintering waterfowl, including black brant, trumpeter swans, Canada geese, and canvasback. Also provides habitat for black bear, deer, elk, and shorebirds. **Special Features:** Refuge features FWS's first interpretive art trail, celebrating habitat restoration of a stream that is now home to sea-run cutthroat trout, chum salmon, and many other species. The trail is a meandering boardwalk with a 22-foot bronze sculpture of a salmon skeleton, the first of several planned art pieces depicting nature's life cycle. The bay is one of the most pristine estuaries in the United States.

See pages 22-23 for map of National Wildlife Refuges.

★1044★ WILLIAM L. FINLEY NATIONAL WILDLIFE REFUGE

26208 Finley Refuge Rd
Corvallis, OR 97333
Web: www.fws.gov/willamettevalley/finley
Phone: 541-757-7236; **Fax:** 541-757-4450
Location: 10 miles south of Corvallis, Oregon. **Established:** 1964. **Habitat:** 5,666 acres of riparian and upland forest, upland and wet prairie, wetlands, and farm fields. **Facilities:** Visitor contact station, interpretive trails, viewing sites, auto tour route, historic features. **Activities:** Fishing, hunting, hiking, biking, educational programs. **Access:** Open daily from sunrise to sunset. **Primary Wildlife:** Canada geese, great blue heron, mallards, pintails, red-tailed hawk, harriers, Roosevelt elk, red-legged frog, beaver, Pacific tree frog, grey tailed vole, and raccoons. **Special Features:** Refuge is named after the naturalist who helped persuade President Theodore Roosevelt to establish the National Wildlife Refuge System.

★1045★ WOLF ISLAND NATIONAL WILDLIFE REFUGE

c/o Savannah Coastal Refuges Complex
1000 Business Center Dr, Suite 10
Savannah, GA 31405
Web: www.fws.gov/wolfisland
Phone: 912-652-4415
Location: Central Georgia coast. **Established:** 1930. **Habitat:** 5,126 acre barrier island consisting of a narrow strip of oceanfront beach backed by a broad band of salt marsh. **Activities:** Fishing, shell fishing. **Access:** Refuge's saltwater areas are open to public use, but all beach, marsh, and upland areas are closed to the public. **Primary Wildlife:** Brown pelicans, loggerhead sea turtles, diamondback terrapins. **Special Features:** The strategic location of Wolf Island made it an important identification point on navigational charts of the 1800s. A Coast Guard lighthouse, which stood on the northern tip of Wolf Island, has long since disappeared into the ocean.

★1046★ YAZOO NATIONAL WILDLIFE REFUGE

728 Yazoo Refuge Rd
Hollandale, MS 38748
Web: www.fws.gov/yazoo
Phone: 662-839-2638; **Fax:** 662-839-2619
Location: West-central Mississippi, about 28 miles south of Greenville. **Established:** 1936. **Habitat:** 12,941 acres of marshes, swamps, sandy ridges, cropland, and bottomland hardwood forests. **Facilities:** Trails, viewing sites, observation tower. **Activities:** Hiking, wildlife observation, hunting, educational programs. **Access:** Open year round during daylight hours. **Primary Wildlife:** Mourning doves, wood ducks, Canada geese, wild turkey, Louisiana black bear, white-tailed deer, squirrel, rabbit, raccoon, and American alligator. **Special Features:** Refuge includes and surrounds Swan Lake, a 4,000+-acre oxbow lake which has silted in and contains mature cypress and ash woodlands.

★1047★ YUKON DELTA NATIONAL WILDLIFE REFUGE

PO Box 346
Bethel, AK 99559
Web: yukondelta.fws.gov
Phone: 907-543-3151
Location: 400 miles west of Anchorage. **Established:** 1980 with the consolidation of Clarence Rhode, Nunivak, and Hazen Bay refuges. **Habitat:** 19 million acres of rivers, sloughs, lakes, and ponds. **Facilities:** Visitor center. **Activities:** Camping, backpacking, boating, fishing, hiking, hunting, educational programs. **Access:** Accessible only by boat or aircraft; contact refuge staff before visiting. **Primary Wildlife:** Geese, swans, greater scaup, eider, gulls, cranes, loons, black and brown bear, caribou, musk ox, wolves, seals, walrus, North American Pacific salmon, and whale. **Special Features:** Yukon Delta is the nation's largest wildlife refuge, where the waters of the Yukon and Kuskokwim rivers flow through a vast "treeless plain," or tundra. In terms of both density and species diversity, the refuge is the most important shorebird nesting area in the United States. The Yukon and Kuskokwim rivers, and their many tributaries that weave their way through the refuge, provide hundreds of miles of spawning and rearing habitat for fish. A total of 44 species use the refuge's fresh and marine waters.

★1048★ YUKON FLATS NATIONAL WILDLIFE REFUGE

101 12th Ave
Box 264
Fairbanks, AK 99701
Web: www.fws.gov/refuges/profiles/index.cfm?id=75635
Phone: 907-456-0440
Location: 100 miles north of Fairbanks. **Established:** 1978. **Habitat:** 9 million acres of wetlands, uplands, and subalpine terrain. **Facilities:** Visitor contact station. **Activities:** Camping, boating, canoeing, kayaking, rafting, fishing, hunting, educational programs. **Access:** Open 24 hours a day; access is primarily by aircraft or boat. **Primary Wildlife:** Scaup, pintails, scoters, wigeons, moose, caribou, Dall sheep, black and brown bears, wolves, marten, and lynx. **Special Features:** In the spring, millions of migrating birds converge on the refuge which, with its 40,000 lakes and other wetlands, has one of the highest waterfowl nesting densities in North America. An estimated 1.6 million ducks, 10,000 geese, 11,000 sandhill cranes, 15,000 loons, at least 100,000 grebes, and hundreds of thousands of songbirds nest annually on the refuge.

See pages 22-23 for map of National Wildlife Refuges.

5. NATIONAL TRAILS

★1049★ National Park Service
Conservation and Outdoor Recreation
1849 C St NW (Org. code 2220)
Washington, DC 20240
202-354-6900 - Phone
202-371-5179 - Fax
Web: www.nps.gov/nts

★1050★ Bureau of Land Management
National Scenic and Historic Trails
1849 C St, Rm 406-LS
Washington, DC 20240
202-452-5125 - Phone
202-452-5124 - Fax
Web: www.blm.gov/nlcs/nsht/

★1051★ USDA Forest Service
Recreation, Heritage & Wilderness Resources
Mail Stop 1125
1400 Independence Ave. SW
Washington, D.C. 20090-1125
202-205-1706
Web: www.fs.fed.us/recreation/programs/trails/

In 1968, Congress passed the National Trails System Act in order to establish a national system of trails in both urban and rural settings for persons of all ages, interests, skills, and physical abilities. Originally the act specified three categories of national trails: scenic trails, recreation trails, and connecting or side trails. In 1978, historic trails were added as another category. These various trails are defined as follows:

National scenic trails are federally-administered long-distance trails that are located to maximize outdoor recreation potential while providing for the conservation and enjoyment of nationally significant scenic, historical, natural, or cultural qualities of areas through which the trails pass.

National historic trails are federally-administered trails that follow original trails or routes of travel of national historical significance, including exploration, migration, and military action. They are established to identify and protect a historic route, plus its historic remnants and artifacts, for public use and enjoyment. The historic trails generally consist of remnant sites and trail segments, and thus are not necessarily continuous.

National recreation trails are federally-recognized trails managed by public and private agencies at the local, state, and national levels and include nature trails, river routes, and historic tours. Today almost 1,000 of these trails have been designated throughout the country. A listing of National recreation trails may be found at: www.americantrails.org

Connecting or side trails encourage connections between trails, from trails to towns and cities, and link parks, forests, and historic sites.

National scenic and historic trails can only be authorized by Congress, through amendment of the National Trails System Act. Of the 24 national scenic and national historic trails so far established, 17 are administered by the National Park Service, four by the Forest Service, one by the Bureau of Land Management, and two jointly by the National Park Service and the Bureau of Land Management.

Recreation and connecting or side trails may be designated and established by the secretary of the interior or the secretary of agriculture, as appropriate. Each national scenic (NST) and historic trail (NHT) is a partnership between an administering federal agency and one or more non-profit trail organizations. In addition, state agencies, local communities, outing organizations, historical societies, individual landowners, and other groups often play critical roles in establishing and maintaining these trails. Roles vary along each trail. For example, the federal government carries out land protection along the Appalachian NST, but the State of Wisconsin and the Ice Age Park and Trail Foundation buy lands to protect the Ice Age NST. Trail information is usually available from both the non-profit organizations and the administering federal office(s).

The following pages provide descriptive information on the national scenic and historic trails that currently comprise the National Trails System.

★1052★ALA KAHAKAI NATIONAL HISTORIC
TRAIL
E Mau Na Ala Hele
PO Box 6384
Kamuela, HI 96743
Web: www.alakahakai.com

Trail Administrator
c/o Kaloko-Honokahau National Historical Park
73-4786 Kanalani St, Suite 14
Kailua-Kona, HI 96740
808-326-6012 - Phone
Web: www.nps.gov/alka/

Length: 175 miles. **Established:** November 14, 2000. **Description:** Ultimately, the ''Ala Kahakai'' (Trail by the Sea) will be a continuous walking path, extending along the coastline of Hawaii. It is proposed to extend from 'Upolu Point in North Kohala District to Waha'ula Heiau at the eastern boundary of Hawaii Volcanoes National Park. The exact location of the trail will be determined after consultation with native Hawaiians,

See pages 24-25 for map of National Trails.

5. National Trails

landowners, the Na Ala Hele State-wide Trail and Access System, the National Park Service, and other key stakeholders in every affected region or ahupua'a. The trail will traverse hundreds of ancient Hawaiian settlement sites and more than 200 ahupua'a, or traditional sea to mountain land divisions. It will tell the story of how Hawaiians flourished as a civilization, Captain Cook's historic landing, the rise of Kamehameha I, and subsequent changes leading to Hawaii's unique blend of cultures.

★1053★ APPALACHIAN NATIONAL SCENIC TRAIL
Appalachian Trail Conservancy
PO Box 807
Harpers Ferry, WV 25425
304-535-6331 - Phone
304-535-2667 - Fax
Web: www.appalachiantrail.org

Trail Manager - NPS Appalachian Park Trail Office
c/o Harpers Ferry Center
Harpers Ferry, WV 25425
304-535-6278 - Phone
304-535-6270 - Fax
Web: www.nps.gov/appa

Length: 2,171 miles. **Established:** October 2, 1968. **Description:** Trail hugs the crests of the Appalachian Mountains from Mount Katahdin, Maine south through New Hampshire, Vermont, Massachusetts, Connecticut, New York, New Jersey, Pennsylvania, Maryland, West Virginia, Virginia, Tennessee, and North Carolina, to Springer Mountain, Georgia. It is open only to hikers, and facilities along the way include campgrounds, picnic areas, cabin rentals, groceries, visitor centers (&), and exhibits. Shelters are spaced for convenient overnight stays. The Appalachian Trail Conservancy (ATC), established in 1925, developed the trail and maintains it today through 32 affiliated volunteer trail clubs. Only a few miles still need protection through public ownership. Almost 400 people each year hike the entire trail. Contact the Appalachian Trail Conservancy for guidebooks and maps.

★1054★ CALIFORNIA NATIONAL HISTORIC TRAIL
Oregon-California Trails Assn
PO Box 1019
Independence, MO 64051
816-252-2276 - Phone
816-836-0989 - Fax
Web: www.octa-trails.org

Trail Administrator
NPS National Trails System Office, Salt Lake City
324 S. State St, Suite 200
Salt Lake City, UT 84145
801-741-1012 - Phone
801-741-1102 - Fax
Web: www.nps.gov/cali

Length: 5,665 miles. **Established:** August 3, 1992. **Description:** Trail was the route of the greatest mass migration in

American history, and today remnants of the trail are reminders of the sacrifices, struggles, and triumphs of early American travelers and settlers. Trail includes portions that were pioneered and developed before the 1849 California Gold Rush. An estimated 320 historic sites along the entire trail include forts, trading posts, natural landmarks, river crossing sites, campsites, trail junctions, and gravesites.

★1055★ CONTINENTAL DIVIDE NATIONAL SCENIC TRAIL
Continental Divide Trail Alliance
PO Box 628
Pine, CO 80470
303-838-3760 - Phone
303-838-3960 - Fax
Web: www.cdtrail.org

Continental Divide Trail Society
3704 N Charles St, Suite 601
Baltimore, MD 21218
410-235-9610 - Phone
Web: www.cdtsociety.org

Trail Administrator - USDA Forest Service, Rocky Mountain Region
740 Simms St
Golden, CO 80401
303-275-5054 - Phone
303-275-5366 - Fax
Web: www.fs.fed.us/r2/trails/cdnst/

Length: 3,100 miles. **Established:** November 10, 1978. **Description:** In close proximity to the Continental Divide, the trail starts 14 miles north of the US-Canadian border in Waterton, Alberta, and extends southward into Glacier National Park, Montana (see separate entry in National Parks section), through Idaho, Wyoming, Colorado, and New Mexico to the Mexican border. Current plans call for completing the trail in 2008. It is open to hikers, pack and saddle animals, and in some places, off-road motorized vehicles. Trail provides spectacular backcountry travel and is the most rugged of the national scenic trails.

★1056★ EL CAMINO REAL DE LOS TEJAS NATIONAL HISTORIC TRAIL
El Camino Real de los Tejas Association
Web: www.elcaminorealtx.com

National Park Service
PO Box 728
Santa Fe, NM 87504
505-988-6888 - Phone
Web: www.elcaminorealtx.com

Length: 2,600 miles. **Established:** October 18, 2004. **Description:** This network of routes in Texas and Louisiana in the 18th and 19th centuries connected Mexico City and various provincial

See pages 24-25 for map of National Trails.

capitals and mission outposts. Along it, Spanish and Mexican influences moved northeastward. As the Old San Antonio Road, after Mexican independence in 1821, this route brought American immigrants south and west into what became the Texas Republic, the anexation of which precipitated the Mexican-American War of the late 1840's. The comprehensive management plan for developing this trail is just getting underway.

★1057★ EL CAMINO REAL DE TIERRA ADENTRO NATIONAL HISTORIC TRAIL
Bureau of Land Management
PO Box 27115
Santa Fe, NM 87502
505-438-7454 - Phone
505-438-7426 - Fax

Camino Real Trail Association
PO Box 20500
El Paso, TX 79998
Web: www.elcaminoreal.org

NPS National Trails System Office
PO Box 728
Santa Fe, NM 87504
505-988-6888 - Phone
Web: www.elcaminoreal.org

Length: 404 miles. **Established:** October 13, 2000. **Description:** The longest and oldest European road in North America, El Camino Real de Tierra Adentro (The Royal Road of the Interior Lands) was used for more than 300 years as the primary route between northern Mexico and what is now the southwestern United States. It was used by the Spanish for colonization, missionary supply, commerce, cultural exchange, and military campaigns. American Indian groups dating back into prehistoric times, especially the Pueblo Indians of the Rio Grande River Valley, also used the area and trail along the Rio Grande long before Europeans arrived. After Mexico gained independence from Spain in 1821, El Camino Real expanded its importance as a trade route and linked with the Santa Fe Trail. In 1846, it played an important part in the Mexican-American War and was also utilized during the U.S. Civil War, when three battles were fought in New Mexico. The historical period of the trail ended in 1882, when railroad connections replaced wagon trails across the West. The total mileage of El Camino Real from Mexico City to San Juan Pueblo is 1,500 miles. The trail is managed jointly by the Bureau of Land Management and the National Park Service.

★1058★ FLORIDA NATIONAL SCENIC TRAIL
Florida Trail Association
5415 SW 13th St
Gainesville, FL 32608
352-378-8823 - Phone
352-378-4550 - Fax
Web: www.floridatrail.org

Trail Administrator - USDA Forest Service
National Forests in Florida
325 John Knox Rd, Suite F-100
Tallahassee, FL 32303
850-523-8538 - Phone
850-523-8578 - Fax

Length: 1,300 miles. **Established:** March 28, 1983. **Description:** Trail was conceived and initiated by James A. Kern, who formed the Florida Trail Association in 1964. The trail extends from Big Cypress National Preserve (see separate entry in National Parks section) in South Florida through Florida's three national forests to Gulf Islands National Seashore (see separate entry in National Parks section) in the western panhandle. Trail is especially enjoyable for winter hiking and camping, passing through America's only subtropical landscape. Side loop trails connect to historic sites and other points of interest. More than 1,000 miles are completed and some 300 miles are officially open to public use.

★1059★ ICE AGE NATIONAL SCENIC TRAIL
Ice Age Park & Trail Foundation Inc
306 E. Wilson St, Lower Level
Madison, WI 53703
608-663-8278 - Phone
608-663-1283 - Fax
Web: www.iceagetrail.org

Trail Administrator - National Park Service
700 Rayovac Dr, Suite 100
Madison, WI 53711
608-441-5610 - Phone
608-441-5606 - Fax
Web: www.nps.gov/iatr

Length: 1,000 miles. **Established:** October 3, 1980. **Description:** Winding along a chain of moraine hills in Wisconsin, the trail links together six of the nine units of the Ice Age National Scientific Reserve. Trail was conceived by Ray Zillmer in the 1950s and publicized by Rep. Henry Reuss in his book On the Trail of the Ice Age. Today more than half the trail is open to public use. Certain sections are popular for marathons, ski races, and ultra-running.

★1060★ IDITAROD NATIONAL HISTORIC TRAIL
Trail Administrator - Bureau of Land Management, Anchorage District
6881 Abbott Loop Rd
Anchorage, AK 99507
907-267-1207 - Phone
907-267-1267 - Fax
Web: www.ak.blm.gov/iditarod/index.html

Iditarod National Historic Trail Inc
PO Box 2323
Seward, AK 99664
Web: www.iditarodnationalhistorictrail.org

Length: 2,450 miles; main route is 900 miles. **Established:**

See pages 24-25 for map of National Trails.

November 10, 1978. **Description:** The Iditarod is a system of historic trails made famous by Alaska gold prospectors and their dog teams during the late 19th and early 20th century Gold Rush. Most of the trail is only usable during Alaska's six-month winter when rivers and tundra are frozen. Each year the renowned 1,150-mile Iditarod Sled Dog Race is run along the trail from Anchorage to Nome. Other events include the 210-mile Iditasport race for skiers, mountain bikers, and snowshoers, and the Alaska Gold Rush Classic Snowmachine Race. A network of shelters is being installed for public use.

★1061★ JUAN BAUTISTA DE ANZA NATIONAL HISTORIC TRAIL

Amigos de Anza
c/o Heritage Trails Fund
1350 Castle Rock Rd
Walnut Canyon, CA 94598
925-937-7661 - Phone
Web: www.therapure.com/anza-trail/

Anza Trail Coalition of Arizona
PO Box 42612
Tucson, AZ 85733
520-792-0554 - Phone

Trail Administrator - National Park Service
1111 Jackson St, Suite 700
Oakland, CA 94607
510-817-1438 - Phone
510-817-1505 - Fax
Web: www.nps.gov/juba

Length: 1,200 miles. **Established:** August 15, 1990. **Description:** Trail follows the route over which a party of Spanish colonists, led by Captain Juan Bautista de Anza, set out from Mexico to establish an overland route to California in 1775. This party of 30 families, a dozen soldiers, and 1,000 cattle, horses,and mules spent three months traversing the deserts of the Southwestbefore reaching the missions of the California coast. Another threemonths were spent traveling up the Pacific coast to the Golden Gate,where the city of San Francisco now stands. They sought to build a presidio and mission overlooking the Golden Gate and secure it from threats by the Russians and British. In 1975 and 1976, an expedition reenactment took place from Horcasitas, Mexico, to San Francisco, CA.

★1062★ LEWIS & CLARK NATIONAL HISTORIC TRAIL

Lewis & Clark Trail Heritage Foundation Inc
PO Box 3434
Great Falls, MT 59403
406-454-1234 - Phone
406-454-0448 - Fax
Web: www.lewisandclark.org

Trail Administrator - National Park Service
Lewis & Clark National Historic Trail
601 Riverfront Dr
Omaha, NE 68102
402-661-1804 - Phone
402-661-1805 - Fax
Web: www.nps.gov/lecl

Length: 3,700 miles. **Established:** November 10, 1978. **Description:** Trail commemorates the route of the 1804-1806 Lewis and Clark Expedition from the Mississippi River to the Pacific Ocean at the mouth of the Columbia River, and return. Approximately 4,500 miles of water routes, planned trails, and marked highways follow the outbound and return routes. Almost 500 public and private recreation and historic sites along the trail provide for public use and interpretation of the expedition. From 2003 to 2006, the Bicentennial of the Lewis and Clark Expedition involved thousands of trail partners, with 15 signature events along the way.

★1063★ MORMON PIONEER NATIONAL HISTORIC TRAIL

Mormon Trails Association
4681 Villa View Dr, Unit C
West Valley City, UT 84120
801-526-4552 - Phone
Web: www.mormontrails.org

Trail Administrator - NPS National Trails System Office, Salt Lake City
Long Distance Trails Office - Salt Lake City
324 S State St, Suite 200
Salt Lake City, UT 84111
801-741-1012 - Phone
801-741-1102 - Fax
Web: www.nps.gov/mopi

Length: 1,300 miles. **Established:** November 10, 1978. **Description:** Trail follows the route over which Brigham Young led the Mormons to escape religious persecution from Nauvoo, Illinois (1846), to the site of Salt Lake City, Utah, in 1847. The 1,624-mile auto tour route in five states (Illinois, Iowa, Nebraska, Utah, and Wyoming) is generally marked with the trail logo and closely follows the trail's historic route.

★1064★ NATCHEZ TRACE NATIONAL SCENIC TRAIL

2680 Natchez Trace Pkwy
Tupelo, MS 38804
662-680-4014 - Phone
662-680-4034 - Fax
Web: www.nps.gov/natt

Length: 485 miles. **Established:** March 28, 1983. **Description:** Trail lies within the boundaries of the Natchez Trace Parkway (see separate entry in National Parks section), which extends from Natchez, Mississippi, to Nashville, Tennessee. The Parkway commemorates the historic Natchez Trace, an ancient path

See pages 24-25 for map of National Trails.

5. National Trails

that began as a series of animal tracks and Native American trails. It was later used by early explorers, ''Kaintuck'' boatmen, post riders, and military men, including General Andrew Jackson after his victory at the Battle of New Orleans. The Natchez Trace National Scenic Trail highlights existing segments of the original Natchez Trace wherever possible. In the trail's 1987 comprehensive plan, four segments near Nashville, Jackson, and Natchez totaling 110 miles were selected for development as hiking and horseback trails.

★1065★ NEZ PERCE (NEE-ME-POO) NATIONAL HISTORIC TRAIL
Nez Perce National Historical Park
Route 1, Box 100
Hwy 95 S
Spalding, ID 83540
208-843-2261 - Phone
208-843-2124 - Fax
Web: www.nps.gov/nepe

Nez Perce Trail Foundation
PO Box 2544
Orofino, ID 83544
208-756-4870 - Phone
Web: nezpercetrail.net

Trail Administrator - USDA Forest Service
12730 Hwy 12
Orofino, ID 83544
208-476-8334 - Phone
208-476-8329 - Fax
Web: www.fs.fed.us/npnht/news

Length: 1,170 miles. **Established:** October 6, 1986. **Description:** Trail route honors the heroic attempt by the ''non- treaty'' Nez Perce Indians to escape capture by the U.S. Army. In 1877, the Nez Perce were forced to leave their ancestral homelands and move to a reservation east of Lewiston, Idaho. During this journey, hostilities broke out between white settlers and some groups of the Nez Perce, and the U.S. Army was called in. The resisting bands headed east, crossed the Rocky Mountains, and hoped to find refuge in Canada. Led by several commanders, including Chief Joseph, they eluded capture for months, traveling through the newly established Yellowstone National Park (see separate entry in National Parks section) and out onto the Great Plains. Just short of reaching the Canadian border in Montana, most of the party were overtaken near the Bearpaw Mountains.

★1066★ NORTH COUNTRY NATIONAL SCENIC TRAIL
North Country Trail Association
229 E Main St
Lowell, MI 49331
616-897-5987 - Phone
616-897-6605 - Fax
Web: www.northcountrytrail.org

Trail Administrator - National Park Service
North Country National Scenic Trail
700 Rayovac Dr, Suite 100
Madison, WI 53711
608-441-5610 - Phone
608-441-5615 - Fax
Web: www.nps.gov/noco

Length: 3,200 miles. **Established:** March 5, 1980. **Description:** Conceived in the mid-1960s, this trail links upstate New York with the Missouri River in North Dakota. Trail journeys through a varietyof environments: the grandeur of the Adirondacks, Pennsylvania's hardwoodforests, the farmland and canals of Ohio, the Great Lakes shorelines ofMichigan, the glacier-carved forests, lakes, and streams of northern Wisconsinand Minnesota, and the vast plains of North Dakota. Today more than half thetrail is open for public use. Some of the longer segments cross nine nationalforests and two national park areas along the route.

★1067★ OLD SPANISH NATIONAL HISTORIC TRAIL
NPS National Trails System Office
PO Box 728
Santa Fe, NM 87504
505-988-6736 - Phone
Web: www.nps.gov/olsp

Old Spanish Trail Association
PO Box 7
Marysville, WA 98270
702-874-1410 - Phone
Web: www.oldspanishtrail.org

Bureau of Land Management
NM 930
PO Box 27115
Santa Fe, NM 87502
505-438-7454 - Phone
505-438-7426 - Fax

Length: 2,500 miles. **Established:** December 4, 2002. **Description:** Following three interbraided trail routes across the deserts of the Southwest, Mexican trade caravans conducted commerce between Santa Fe and Los Angeles from 1829 to 1848. This commerce in mules, horses, woolens (and even Indian slaves) was generated by the city of Santa Fe that then served as a hub of international trade, linked east by the Santa Fe Trail and south by El Camino Real de Tierra Adentro (both also now recognized as national historic trails; see separate entries for descriptions of each). Such trade created significant impact on the Mexican, Indian, and American populations of the Southwest. Part of the trail was also used by explorers, trappers, prospectors, and immigrants. The western sections of the trail became a Mormon road in 1847.

See pages 24-25 for map of National Trails.

★1068★ OREGON NATIONAL HISTORIC TRAIL
Oregon-California Trails Association
PO Box 1019
Independence, MO 64051
816-252-2276 - Phone
816-836-0989 - Fax
Web: www.octa-trails.org

Trail Administrator - National Park Service
NPS National Trails System Office, Salt Lake City
324 S State St, PO Box 45155
Salt Lake City, UT 84145
801-741-1012 - Phone
801-741-1102 - Fax
Web: www.nps.gov/oreg

Length: 2,170 miles. **Established:** November 10, 1978. **Description:** Trail was the pathway to the Pacific for fur traders, gold seekers, missionaries, and emigrants. Between 1841 and the mid 1860s, an estimated 300,000 pioneers followed this route from the Midwest to Oregon on a trip that took five months to complete. Today the trail corridor contains some 300 miles of discernible wagon ruts and 125 historic sites. The approximate route can be followed by automobile, and opportunities are available to travel by foot, horse, or bike in many places.

★1069★ OVERMOUNTAIN VICTORY NATIONAL HISTORIC TRAIL
Overmountain Victory Trail Association
PO Box 242421
Charlotte, NC 28224
770-382-2863 - Phone
Web: www.ovta.org

Trail Administrator - National Park Service
c/o Kings Mountain National Military Park
2435 Park Rd
Blacksburg, SC 29702
864-936-3477 - Phone
864-936-3477 - Fax
Web: www.nps.gov/ovvi

Length: 300 miles. **Established:** September 8, 1980. **Description:** In the fall of 1780, upcountry patriots from Virginia, Tennessee, and North Carolina formed a militia to respond to British threats. This trail marks their 14-day trek across the Appalachians to the Piedmont region of the Carolinas. There they defeated loyalist militia at the Battle of Kings Mountain, setting in motion events that led to the British surrender at Yorktown and the end of the Revolutionary War. Each year history buffs retrace this patriotic event. Much of the trail has become road and highway; only a 20-mile portion remains as a foot trail across the mountains. In most places roadside signs indicate proximity to the trail.

★1070★ PACIFIC CREST NATIONAL SCENIC TRAIL
Pacific Crest Trail Association
5325 Elkhorn Blvd
PMB 256
Sacramento, CA 95842
916-349-2109 - Phone
916-349-1268 - Fax
Web: www.pcta.org

Trail Administrator - USDA Forest Service, Pacific Southwest Region
1323 Club Dr
Vallejo, CA 94592
707-562-8837 - Phone
707-562-9055 - Fax
Web: www.fs.fed.us/pct

Length: 2,638 miles. **Established:** October 2, 1968. **Description:** Lying along the spectacular shoulders of the Cascade and Sierra Nevada mountain ranges from Canada to Mexico, the Pacific Crest is the West Coast counterpart of the Appalachian Trail. Inspired in the 1930s by the idea of a long-distance mountain trail, citizen activists worked with the Forest Service to establish the trail. It passes through 25 national forests and 7 national parks.

★1071★ PONY EXPRESS NATIONAL HISTORIC TRAIL
National Pony Express Association
601 S. Western Ave
Blue Rapids, KS 66411
Web: www.xphomestation.com

Trail Administrator - National Park Service
NPS National Trails System Office, Salt Lake City
324 S State St, PO Box 45155
Salt Lake City, UT 84145
801-741-1012 - Phone
801-741-1102 - Fax
Web: www.nps.gov/poex

Length: 1,966 miles. **Established:** August 3, 1992. **Description:** Trail recognizes the route of the Pony Express from April 1860 through October 1861 as a significant episode in the development of the American West. Organized by private entrepreneurs, the horse-and-rider relay system became the nation's most direct and practical means of east-west communications before the telegraph. During its 18 months of operation, the Pony Express carried mail between Saint Joseph, Missouri, and Sacramento, California, in the unprecedented time of only 10 days. Many segments of this trail may be followed today by horse or car. An annual Pony Express Re-Run is held in early June.

★1072★ POTOMAC HERITAGE NATIONAL SCENIC TRAIL
Allegheny Trail Alliance
419 College Ave
Greensburg, PA 15601
888-282-2453 - Phone
Web: www.atatrail.org

See pages 24-25 for map of National Trails.

C&O Canal Association
PO Box 366
Glen Echo, MD 20812
301-983-0825 - Phone
Web: www.candocanal.org

Potomac Heritage Trail Association
118 Park St., SE
Vienna, VA 22108
571-436-7801 - Phone
Web: www.potomactrail.org

Trail Administrator - National Park Service
Potomac Heritage National Scenic Trail Office
PO Box B
Harpers Ferry, WV 25425
304-535-4014 - Phone
304-535-4020 - Fax
Web: www.nps.gov/pohe

Length: 704 miles. **Established:** March 28, 1983. **Description:** Trail recognizes and commemorates the unique mix of history and recreation along the Potomac River. Much is already in place: the 184-mile towpath of the Chesapeake and Ohio Canal in the District of Columbia and Maryland, the 18-mile Mount Vernon Trail in Virginia, the 75-mile Laurel Highlands Trail in Pennsylvania, and the 150-mile Great Allegheny Passage from Cumberland, Maryland, to Pittsburgh, Pennsylvania. The trail begins at the mouth of the Potomac River and follows both banks to the District of Columbia. For 184 miles it coincides with the Chesapeake and Ohio Canal Towpath, then turns north, ending at Conemaugh Gorge. Trail encompasses portions of Maryland, Virginia, Pennsylvania, and the District of Columbia and is a catalyst for local recreation and conservation projects.

★1073★ SANTA FE NATIONAL HISTORIC TRAIL
Santa Fe Trail Association
Santa Fe Trail Center
RR 3
Larned, KS 67550
620-285-2054 - Phone
Web: www.santafetrail.org

Trail Administrator - National Park Service
NPS National Trails System Office, Santa Fe
PO Box 728
Santa Fe, NM 87504
505-988-6888 - Phone
505-986-5214 - Fax
Web: www.nps.gov/safe

Length: 1,203 miles. **Established:** May 8, 1987. **Description:** After Mexican independence in 1821, U.S. and Mexican traders developed the Santa Fe Trail, using American Indian travel and trade routes. It quickly became a commercial and cultural link between the two countries and also became a road of conquest during the Mexican and Civil wars. With the building of the railroad to Santa Fe in the 1880's, the trail was largely abandoned. Of the 1,203 miles of trail route between Old Franklin, Missouri, and Santa Fe, New Mexico, more than 200 miles of ruts and trace remain visible; some 30 miles of these are protected on federal lands.

★1074★ SELMA TO MONTGOMERY NATIONAL HISTORIC TRAIL
Trail Administrator - NPS Selma to Montgomery National Historic Trail Office
7001 US Hwy 80 W
Hayneville, AL 36040
334-877-1983 - Phone
334-727-0856 - Fax
Web: www.nps.gov/semo/

Established: November 12, 1996. **Description:** This historic trail includes city streets and US Highway 80 from Brown Memorial Chapel A.M.E. Church in Selma to the State Capitol Building in Montgomery, traveled by voting rights advocates during March of 1965 to dramatize the need for voting rights legislation. On ''Bloody Sunday,'' March 7, 1965, some 600 civil rights marchers headed east out of Selma on U.S. Route 80, but were driven back at the Edmund Pettus Bridge by state and local lawmen using billy clubs and tear gas. Two days later, on March 9, Martin Luther King, Jr., led a ''symbolic'' march to the bridge. After seeking and receiving court protection for a third, full-scale march, about 3,200 marchers set out for Montgomery on March 21, walking 12 miles a day and sleeping in fields. By the time they reached the capitol on March 25, they were 25,000 strong. Less than five months later, President Lyndon Johnson signed the Voting Rights Act of 1965. The route was also designated an ''All-American Road,'' the highest tribute a road can receive under the Federal Highway Administration's National Scenic Byways Program.

★1075★ TRAIL OF TEARS NATIONAL HISTORIC TRAIL
Trail of Tears Association
c/o American Indian Center of Arkansas
1100 N University, Suite 143
Little Rock, AR 72207
501-666-9032 - Phone
501-666-5875 - Fax
Web: www.nationaltota.org

Trail Administrator - National Park Service
NPS National Trails System Office, Santa Fe
PO Box 728
Santa Fe, NM 87504
505-988-6888 - Phone
505-986-5214 - Fax
Web: www.nps.gov/trte

Length: 2,200 miles. **Established:** 1987. **Description:** Two trail routes were used for the forced removal of more than 15,000 Cherokee Indians by the U.S. Army from their ancestral lands in the southeastern states to lands west of the Mississippi River

See pages 24-25 for map of National Trails.

in the late 1830s. Various detachments followed different routes west to the Oklahoma Territory. The journey lasted from June of 1838 to March of 1839 and thousands died along the way. Today, the designated trail follows: a water trail (1,226 miles) along the Tennessee, Ohio, Mississippi, and Arkansas rivers; and an overland route (826 miles) from Chattanooga, Tennessee, to Tahlequah, Oklahoma.

See pages 24-25 for map of National Trails.

6. NATIONAL MARINE SANCTUARIES

★1076★ NATIONAL MARINE SANCTUARY PROGRAM

1305 East-West Hwy, 11th Fl
Silver Springs, MD 20910
301-713-3125 - Phone
301-713-0404 - Fax
Web: www.sanctuaries.nos.noaa.gov/

The National Marine Sanctuaries Program was established by Congress in 1972 under the Marine Protection, Research, and Sanctuaries Act. The act authorized the designation of National Marine Sanctuaries to protect the ecological, historical, and recreational resources in specially designated coastal areas. The National Oceanic and Atmospheric Administrations (NOAA), an office of the Sanctuaries and Reserve Division within the Department of Commerce, is responsible for managing the nation's marine sanctuaries and protecting the complex marine ecosystems.

The National Marine Sanctuary System consists of 14 marine protected areas that encompass more than 150,000 square miles of marine and Great Lakes waters from Washington State to the Florida Keys, and from Lake Huron to American Samoa. The system includes 13 national marine sanctuaries and the Northwestern Hawaiian Islands Marine National Monument.

Sanctuary habitats include rocky reefs, kelp forests, whale migrations corridors, deep-sea canyons, and underwater archaeological sites. The sanctuaries can provide a safe habitat for species close to extinction or protect historically significant shipwrecks. Ranging in size from less than one square mile to 137,792 square miles, each sanctuary site is a unique place needing special protections.

The following section provides information on each the individual units that comprise the National Marine Sanctuary System.

★1077★ CHANNEL ISLANDS NATIONAL MARINE SANCTUARY

113 Harbor Way, Suite 150
Santa Barbara, CA 93109
Web: www.channelislands.noaa.gov
Phone: 805-966-7107; **Fax:** 805-568-1582
Year Designated: 1980. **Location:** 25 miles off the coast of Santa Barbara, California. **Description:** The Sanctuary protects 1,658 square miles of waters surrounding Anacapa, Santa Cruz, Santa Rosa, San Miguel, and Santa Barbara islands. Sanctuary boundaries extend from mean high tide to six nautical miles (seven miles) seaward. **Facilities:** A visitor center is located on the top floor of the Santa Barbara Maritime Museum. Visitors can learn more about the habitats and natural resources of the Channel Islands through interpretive exhibits, computer stations with internet access, and telescopes set up for island viewing. **Common Species:** California sea lion, elephant and harbor seal, rockfish, abalone, bocaccio rockfish, and the blue shark. **Environmental Issues:** Commercial and recreational fishing, oil and gas development, commercial shipping lanes in close waters, and non-point source pollution. **Habitats:** Seagrass meadows, kelp forests, rock shelves, tide pools, rubble piles, sandy beaches, and rocky shores. **Access:** The Islands are accessible via personal boats and scheduled cruises. **Activities:** Boating, diving, kayaking, spearfishing, bird-watching, camping, and wildlife cruises. **Special Features:** Since the end of the fur trade, researchers have documented the dramatic recovery of the pinniped population. Four types of pinnipeds currently breed in sanctuary waters: the California sea lion, the northern fur seal, the northern elephant seal, and the harbor seal. Twenty-seven species of whales and dolphins, 6 species of seals and sea lions, and more than 60 species of marine birds have been observed in sanctuary waters. The brown pelican, an endangered species, maintains its only Pacific breeding colony on Anacapa Island.

★1078★ CORDELL BANK NATIONAL MARINE SANCTUARY

One Bear Valley Rd
Point Reyes Station, CA 94956
Web: cordellbank.noaa.gov
Phone: 415-663-0314; **Fax:** 415-663-0315
Year Designated: 1989. **Location:** Rises from the sea floor about 52 miles northwest of the Golden Gate Bridge and at the edge of the continental shelf, just outside of San Francisco, California. **Description:** The Sanctuary encompasses 526 square miles of Pacific Ocean waters surrounding and including Cordell Bank. The Bank consists of a series of steep-sided ridges and narrow pinnacles resting on a plateau and lies in the middle of the California Current upwelling system, one of five major upwelling areas in the world. The waters depth around most of Cordell Bank is 200 feet, and along a few of its ridges and pinnacles this submerged island rises to within 120 feet of the ocean's surface. Cordell Bank is approximately 9.5 miles long and 4.5 miles wide. Waters are 6,000 feet deep to the west of the bank and about 300-400 feet deep to the east. **Common Species:** Dall's porpoise, shearwater, and the following engangered species: humpback whale, stellar sea lion, brown pelican, blue whale, and the short-tailed albatross. **Environmental Issues:** Protecting the upwelling region from commercial and recreational fishing. **Habitats:** Open ocean, rocky subtidal areas, and soft sediment continental shelf and slope. **Access:** This Sanctuary is one of the least accessible due to the depth of waters, strong currents, and its distance from the mainland.

See page 26 for map of National Marine Sanctuaries.

Access is only available by way of boat. **Activities:** Whale watching cruises, bird watching, fishing, and nature excursions. **Special Features:** Forty-seven species of seabirds have been identified and 26 species of marine mammals have been observed in sanctuary waters. It is one of the most important feeding grounds in the world for the endangered blue and humpback whales, which travel from their breeding areas in Mexico and Central America to feed on the abundant krill and schooling fish that aggregate near the bank. The sanctuary is known as the ''albatross capital of the northern hemisphere,'' as five of the fourteen albatross species have been documented here.

★1079★ **FAGATELE BAY NATIONAL MARINE SANCTUARY**
PO Box 4318
Pago Pago, AS 96799
Web: fagatelebay.noaa.gov
Phone: 684-633-7354; **Fax:** 684-633-7355
Year Designated: 1986. **Location:** Fagatele Bay is located within an eroded volcanic crater off the southwest coast of Tutuila Island, American Samoa. **Description:** The Sanctuary encompasses 163 acres (.25 square miles) of bay area off the southwest coast of Tutuila Island. It is the smallest and most remote of the national marine sanctuaries. Sanctuary borders extend from Steps Point, the southernmost point of the island, to Fagatele Point on the island's southwestern shore. Fagatele Bay embodies a fringing coral reef ecosystem with a terraced structure, which is typical of volcanic islands. The fringing coral reef contains nearly 200 species of coral, which provide shelter and habitat for a variety of marine life. It is the only true tropical reef in the sanctuary program. **Facilities:** The Sanctuary office is located in the village of Pago Pago. Although the staff does not sponsor or conduct diving or snorkeling tours, they will provide tour contact information for those interested in exploring the bay. **Common Species:** Many species of brightly-colored tropical fish, such as parrot fish and butterfly fish, octopus, giant clams, lobsters, crabs, and sharks. **Environmental Issues:** Illegal fish poaching with the use of dynamite, sewage outflow up-current of Fagatele Bay, rapid algal growth, and climate change. **Habitats:** Fringing coral reef. **Access:** Charter boats are available from Pago Pago Harbor for recreational diving and snorkeling trips. It is also possible to access the bay by foot. A trail runs north-south along the 200-foot-high Matautuloa Ridge. The trail opens up to a small sand beach. **Activities:** Diving and snorkeling. **Special Features:** The land side of Fagatele bay is bordered by 200-foot vertical cliffs. Along these steep slopes are some of America's rare paleotropical rainforests. Endangered hawksbill turtles, green sea turtles, humpback whales, and sperm whales find refuge in the bay's protected waters. From June to September, visitors can hear numerous underwater whale-songs which the males use to attract mates and the females use to communicate with their young.

★1080★ **FLORIDA KEYS NATIONAL MARINE SANCTUARY**
33 East Quay Rd
Key West, FL 33040
Web: floridakeys.noaa.gov
Phone: 305-809-4700; **Fax:** 305-293-5011

Year Designated: 1990. **Location:** Surrounds the entire archipelago of the Florida Keys, portions of Florida Bay, the Gulf of Mexico, and the Atlantic Ocean. **Description:** The Sanctuary encompasses 3,600 square miles of submerged lands and waters surrounding most of the 1,700 islands that make up the Florida Keys, a 220-mile-long string of islands extending south and west of the Florida mainland. The shoreward boundary of the sanctuary is the mean high-water mark. **Common Species:** Manatees, sea turtles, whales, American crocodiles, and wood storks. **Environmental Issues:** Deteriorating water quality, physical damage to coral reefs and sea grass communities, declining health of living coral reefs, and loss of essential marine resources. **Habitats:** Coral reefs, fringing mangroves and mangrove islands, seagrass meadows, hardbottom regions, patch reefs, and bank reefs. **Access:** More than 257 private and public recreational sites are available in the Florida Keys. Access points range from boat ramps along US Highway 1, the main road that spans the entire length of the Keys, to large public facilities such as John Pennekamp Coral Reef State Park (see separate entry in Florida State Parks section). **Activities:** Diving, snorkeling, fishing, boating, and swimming. **Special Features:** Approximately six miles seaward of the Florida Keys and within sanctuary boundaries is North America's only living coral barrier reef and the third longest barrier reef in the world. Cultural resources are also contained within the sanctuary. The proximity of coral reefs to centuries old shipping routes has resulted in a high concentration of shipwrecks and an abundance of artifacts.

★1081★ **FLOWER GARDEN BANKS NATIONAL MARINE SANCTUARY**
4700 Ave U, Bldg 216
Galveston, TX 77551
Web: flowergarden.noaa.gov
Phone: 409-621-5151; **Fax:** 409-621-1316
Year Designated: 1992. **Location:** The Sanctuary is comprised of the East Flower Garden Bank, the West Flower Garden Bank, and Stetson Bank. The Flower Garden Banks are located 105 miles south of the Texas/Louisiana border and Stetson Bank is 70 miles south of Galveston, Texas. **Description:** The northernmost coral reef in the continental United States, the Flower Garden Banks sit atop two salt domes rising above the ocean floor. The coral reefs ascend to within 66 feet of the ocean's surface. Including all three banks, the sanctuary encompasses approximately 49 square miles. Twenty-one species of coral are found in the sanctuary and more than 80 species of algae provide food for the marine animals, including more than 200 species of fish. Within the East Flower Garden Bank is the only known oceanic brine seep location in continental shelf waters. Unlike the coral development of the East and West Flower Garden Banks, the corals found in Stetson Bank do not build reefs. Stetson Bank supports a coral and sponge habitat. **Facilities:** Exhibit at the Audubon Aquarium of the Americas in New Orleans. **Common Species:** Manta ray, barracuda, whale shark, scalloped hammerhead shark, loggerhead, hawksbill, and leatherback turtles, and the golden smooth trunkfish. **Environmental Issues:** Vessel anchoring, oil and gas development, and the impact of increased recreational diving. **Habitats:** Brine seep, coral reef, and sponge habitats. **Access:** The Sanctuary is only accessible by boat. With favorable weather conditions it takes seven to eight hours to

See page 26 for map of National Marine Sanctuaries.

6. National Marine Sanctuaries

reach the Flower Garden Banks. **Activities:** Diving and recreational fishing. **Special Features:** Each August, the eighth day after the full moon, the waters of the Flower Garden Banks are engulfed in white as the coral reefs begin spawning. Coral spawning was rarely seen before 1990, when it occurred in the Flower Garden Banks. Due in part to this phenomenal occurrence, *Scuba Diving* magazine has ranked it among the top ten overall dive destinations in North America.

★1082★ GERRY E STUDDS STELLWAGEN BANK NATIONAL MARINE SANCTUARY

175 Edward Foster Rd
Scituate, MA 02066
Web: stellwagen.noaa.gov
Phone: 781-545-8026; **Fax:** 781-545-8036
Year Designated: 1992. **Location:** Sits at the mouth of Massachusetts Bay, 25 miles east of Boston, Massachusetts. **Description:** The Sanctuary protects an 842-square-mile area that begins three miles offshore at both its northern and southern borders. Boundaries include the submerged lands of Stellwagen Bank, a sand and gravel plateau formed by the slow retreat of Ice Age glaciers, Tillies Bank, and southern sections of Jeffrey's Ledge. Stellwagen Bank is the most prominent feature in the sanctuary. The bank covers the distance between northern Cape Cod and Cape Ann, Massachusetts, which is approximately 20 miles in length. The bank comes within 65 feet of the ocean's surface at its most shallow point and within 100 feet at the upper plateaus. The seaward side of the bank drops off to more than 600 feet. **Facilities:** Interpretive displays that highlight the living resources within sanctuary waters are located at various coastal points. **Common Species:** Atlantic white-sided dolphin, harbor porpoise, harbor seal, humpback whale, finback whale, minke whale, pilot whale, and the endangered northern right whale. **Environmental Issues:** Pollution from coastal towns, vessel traffic, sewage dumping, offshore mineral and gravel mining, and the impact of fishing and trawling on the ocean floor. **Habitats:** Sand and gravel banks, rocky ledges, muddy basins, and boulder fields. **Access:** Available via fishing or whale watching cruises. **Activities:** Fishing, boating, whale watching, and scuba diving. **Special Features:** Northern right whales can be seen passing through sanctuary waters during their annual migration, which occurs from January-April and October-November.

★1083★ GRAY'S REEF NATIONAL MARINE SANCTUARY

10 Ocean Science Circle
Savannah, GA 31411
Web: graysreef.noaa.gov
Phone: 912-598-2345; **Fax:** 912-598-2367
Year Designated: 1981. **Location:** 23 miles off Sapelo Island, Georgia. **Description:** Gray's Reef is one of the largest nearshore live-bottom reefs in the southeastern United States and is unique because it exists in waters where both temperate and subtropical elements are combined. The sanctuary is composed of a submerged hard bottom (limestone) area with sandstone outcroppings and ledges six to ten feet high. The rocky areas are separated by a series of sandy, flat-bottomed troughs. Seventy feet below the ocean's surface, the rocky platform is covered with attached organisms which gives the reef its live-bottom

designation. Seventeen square miles of open ocean are protected by sanctuary boundaries. **Facilities:** The sanctuary office and an interpretive center are located in the Georgia Marine Science Center on Skidway Island, just outside of Savannah, Georgia. **Common Species:** Black sea bass, snapper, grouper, barracuda, nurse shark, loggerhead sea turtle, and northern right whale. **Environmental Issues:** Protecting the North Atlantic right whale. **Habitats:** Flat bottom troughs, flat top ridge, ledges and crevices, slopes and sandy areas, waters above the reef, and scarps. **Access:** The reef is easily accessible by boat. Marinas and boat landing facilities are located along the coast between Savannah and Brunswick, Georgia. **Activities:** Recreational fishing, sport fishing, boating, underwater photography, and scuba diving. **Special Features:** Gray's Reef National Marine Sanctuary is part of the only known winter calving ground for the endangered North Atlantic right whale.

★1084★ GULF OF THE FARALLONES NATIONAL MARINE SANCTUARY

Fort Mason, Bldg 201
San Francisco, CA 94123
Web: farallones.noaa.gov
Phone: 415-561-6622; **Fax:** 415-561-6616
Year Designated: 1981. **Location:** North and west of San Francisco Bay in California, including offshore marine regions of the Gulf of the Farallones and the nearshore waters of Bodega Bay, Tomales Bay, Estero de San Antonio, Estero Americano, and Bolinas Lagoon. Part of the United Nations' Golden Gate Biosphere Reserve. **Description:** The Sanctuary encompasses 1,255 square miles and is comprised of open ocean, near shore tidal flats, rocky intertidal areas, wetlands, subtidal reefs, and coastal beaches. Boundaries include the coastline up to mean high tide. Thirty miles west of the Golden Gate Bridge are the Farallon Islands, a national wildlife refuge that offers protection and breeding sites for seabirds and marine mammals. The Sanctuary sea floor slopes gently for almost 35 miles, which makes it the widest continental shelf along the California coast, and then drops-off just beyond the Farallon Islands. **Facilities:** A citizens' group, The Farallones Marine Sanctuary Association, maintains visitors' centers in San Francisco and Pacifica. They also sponsor sanctuary displays in Point Reyes and Sausalito. **Common Species:** California gray whale, humpback whale, blue whale, Stellar sea lion, white shark, ashy storm-petrel, rockfish, and abalone. **Environmental Issues:** Sewage, pesticides, increased recreational use, fishing, the release of toxic materials, and the possibility of oil spills. **Habitats:** Deep ocean, estuaries, rocky intertidal zones, and sandy beaches. **Access:** Many local parks, as well as Tomales Bay State Park, Golden Gate National Recreation Area, and Point Reyes National Seashore, provide easy access to sanctuary waters. **Activities:** Kayaking, boating, surfing, bird-watching, sportfishing, and whale watching. **Special Features:** Thirty-three species of marine mammals have been observed in the Sanctuary and one fifth of California's harbor seals breed there. Home to 27 endangered or threatened species. Annually, on the Farallon Islands alone, there are nearly 400,000 breeding seabirds and 10,000 seals and sea lions.

6. National Marine Sanctuaries

See page 26 for map of National Marine Sanctuaries.

★1085★ HAWAIIAN ISLANDS HUMPBACK WHALE NATIONAL MARINE SANCTUARY

726 South Kihei Rd
Kihei, HI 96753
Web: hawaiihumpbackwhale.noaa.gov
Phone: 808-879-2818; **Fax:** 808-874-3815
Year Designated: 1992. **Location:** Coastal and open ocean waters surrounding all of the main islands of the Hawaiian Archipelago. **Description:** The Sanctuary encompasses 1,400 square miles of ocean surrounding the Hawaiian Islands. The boundary extends seaward from the shoreline to the 100-fathom isobath and includes the following areas: the four-island area of Maui County, the north and south coast of Oahu, the north shore of Kauai, and the northwest section of Hawaii. **Facilities:** The main office in Kihei (Maui) maintains a Sanctuary Education Center that offers informative displays about local culture and animals found in sanctuary waters. There is also a deck for whale watching. **Common Species:** North Pacific humpback whale, sea turtle, shark, monk seal, false killer whale, right whale, and the following dolphin species: rough-toothed, spinner, striped, and bottlenose. **Environmental Issues:** Protecting the endangered North Pacific humpback whales. **Habitats:** Coastal waters and open ocean. **Access:** Local beaches provide easy access to sanctuary waters. **Activities:** Whale watching cruises, boating, fishing, scuba diving, snorkeling, canoeing, and kayaking. **Special Features:** Sanctuary waters provide the only breeding ground for the endangered North Pacific humpback whale in the United States. Scientific research indicates that two-thirds of the North Pacific humpback whale population (approximately 4,000-5,000 whales) migrate from Alaska to the shallow, warm waters surrounding the main Hawaiian Islands to breed, calve, and nurse their young. Whales can be observed from November to May.

★1086★ MONITOR NATIONAL MARINE SANCTUARY

c/o The Mariners' Museum
100 Museum Dr
Newport News, VA 23606
Web: monitor.noaa.gov
Phone: 757-599-3122; **Fax:** 757-591-7353
Year Designated: The Monitor was placed on the *National Register of Historic Places* in October of 1974 as a resource of national significance. In January, 1975, it became the first National Marine Sanctuary. **Location:** 16 miles south southeast of Cape Hatteras, North Carolina. Sanctuary boundaries protect the wreck site of the USS Monitor and the waters above it, which total an area approximately one mile in diameter. **Description:** The USS Monitor was a prototype vessel built for the Union Navy that now rests 240 feet under water in a bow-down position on a flat, sandy seafloor. On March 9, 1862, the Monitor engaged in a four-hour battle with the confederate ship, the USS Virginia. The Monitor survived the battle, but sunk later that year in a storm off the coast of North Carolina. The vessel remained unveiled for more than 100 years before scientists discovered it in 1973. The USS Monitor is historically significant because it marked the end of an era of wooden-hulled sailing warships. After the 1862 battle, wars at sea would be won or lost with ironclad, turreted, and steam-powered vessels. **Facilities:** The Mariners' Museum in Newport News, Virginia, maintains a permanent USS Monitor exhibit. The museum also retains possession of artifacts, ship components, historical research materials, and scientific data obtained during expeditions and research activities. **Environmental Issues:** Protecting the wreck site and preventing further damage and deterioration from both natural processes and human activities, such as boat anchoring and fishing. **Access:** The USS Monitor wreck is accessible to divers when accompanied by a sanctuary observer. **Activities:** Diving. **Special Features:** The USS Monitor wreck site is listed on the National Register of Historic Places.

★1087★ MONTEREY BAY NATIONAL MARINE SANCTUARY

299 Foam St
Monterey, CA 93940
Web: montereybay.noaa.gov
Phone: 831-647-4201; **Fax:** 831-647-4250
Year Designated: 1992. **Location:** The waters of Monterey Bay and the Pacific Ocean, just off the coast of central California. **Description:** The Sanctuary stretches from Marin to Cambria, encompassing a shoreline length of 276 miles and 5,322 square miles of ocean. The shoreline boundary is mean high tide and the seaward boundary is 35 miles offshore. **Common Species:** Sea otter, seal, sea lion, gray whale, humpback whale, blue whale, king salmon, brown pelican, market squid, and rockfish. **Environmental Issues:** Effects of the disposal of dredge material, pollution, fishing and vessel traffic on water quality and living resources. **Habitats:** Kelp forests, coastal lagoons, open ocean, wetlands, sandy beaches, and rocky shores. **Access:** A 350-mile stretch of Highway 1 travels along the landward edge of the sanctuary and provides visitors with numerous access points. There are 25 public beaches and parks, 16 campgrounds, 17 wildlife areas, and more than 12 museums, aquariums, and research stations which make the sanctuary easily accessible. **Activities:** Kayaking, sailing, fishing, surfing, diving, whale watching, and wildlife observation excursions. **Special Features:** Monterey Bay National Marine Sanctuary is a migration corridor for 4 species of sea turtles, 26 species of marine mammals, 94 species of seabirds, 345 species of fish, and 450+ species of algae. The underwater canyon in sanctuary waters is 10,663 feet deep (more than 2 miles), deeper than the Grand Canyon.

★1088★ NORTHWESTERN HAWAIIAN ISLANDS MARINE NATIONAL MONUMENT

6600 Kalaniana'ole Hwy, Suite 300
Honolulu, HI 96825
Web: hawaiireef.noaa.gov
Phone: 808-397-2660; **Fax:** 808-397-2662
Year Designated: Established as a marine reserve in 2000; designated a marine national monument in 2006. **Location:** A chain of small islands, atolls, submerged banks, and reefs beginning approximately 138 miles west of the main Hawaiian islands, and stretching northwest for more than 1,242 nautical miles. **Description:** The diverse and expansive coral reef ecosystem of the Northwestern Hawaiian Islands encompasses an array of scientific and historic objects found nowhere else on Earth.

See page 26 for map of National Marine Sanctuaries.

6. National Marine Sanctuaries

Reserve includes 4,770 square nautical miles of coral reefs, which represents approximately 70% of all coral reefs in U.S. waters. It features a much greater diversity of reef habitats than the main Hawaiian Islands, including a unique assemblage of fish, invertebrates, birds, sea turtles, marine mammals and other species. Numerous archeological artifacts found on several of the islands establish a close relationship with the Hawaiian culture, with evidence of both prehistoric seasonal and permanent settlements, as well as use of the area for religious purposes. **Habitats:** The Northwestern Hawaiian Islands provide vital habitat for a variety of migratory species, including several species of marine mammals (e.g., spotted dolphins, humpback whales), sea turtles, the only remaining population of the endangered Hawaiian monk seal, and more than 14 million seabirds. **Facilities:** Mokupäpapa: Discovery Center for Hawaii's Remote Coral Reefs, an interactive educational facility, provides educational programs and teacher training on marine life, as well as the natural and cultural resources contained within the nation's largest conservation area. Located in Hilo, Mokupäpapa is a joint project of NOAA's National Marine Sanctuary Program and the University of Hawaii. **Activities:** Recreational fishing, boating, scuba diving. **Special Features:** The Marine National Monument is the second largest marine protected area in the world, and is the largest protected area in U.S. history. It encompasses 137,792 square miles of Pacific Ocean, an area larger than all the country's national parks combined.

★1089★ OLYMPIC COAST NATIONAL MARINE SANCTUARY
115 Railroad Ave East, Suite 301
Port Angeles, WA 98362
Web: olympiccoast.noaa.gov
Phone: 360-457-6622; **Fax:** 360-457-8496
Year Designated: 1994. **Location:** Sanctuary covers 135 miles along the Washington Coast from about Cape Flattery to the mouth of the Copalis River, sharing 65 miles of coastline with Olympic National Park (see separate entry in national parks section) and extending out 35 miles from the shoreline. Three national wildlife refuges are located within the Sanctuary: Flattery Rocks NWR, Quillayute Needles NWR and Copalis Rock NWR (see separate entries in national wildlife refuge section). **Description:** Olympic Coast National Marine Sanctuary encircles 3,310 square miles of Pacific Ocean. The sanctuary encompasses the entire continental shelf, extending out to the 100 fathom isobath, as well as deeper waters at the heads of Juan de Fuca, Quinault, and Nitnat submarine canyons. **Common Species:** Harbor seal, harbor porpoise, Pacific white-sided dolphin, Risso's dolphin, humpback whale, California gray whale, sea otter, tufted puffin. **Environmental Issues:** Vessel traffic, the impact of fishing on the environment, water quality, and the possibility of oil spills. **Habitats:** Sand and cobble beaches, rocks, subtidal reefs, offshore islands, sea stacks and arches, tidepools, submarine canyons, and plankton-rich upwelling zones. **Access:** Visitors can access the sanctuary waters through Neah Bay on the Makah Indian Reservation, La Push on the Quileute Reservation, Olympic National Park, and Pacific Beach State Park. Each area provides various routes to the sanctuary including marinas, boat launches, and walking trails. **Activities:** Whale watching, scuba diving, fishing, sea kayaking, surfing. **Special Features:** The sanctuary is home to one of the largest

bald eagle populations in the lower 48 states. During annual migrations, the number of seabirds, shorebirds, and waterfowl can easily exceed one million.

★1090★ THUNDER BAY NATIONAL MARINE SANCTUARY & UNDERWATER PRESERVE
500 W Fletcher St
Alpena, MI 49707
Web: thunderbay.noaa.gov
Phone: 989-356-8805; **Fax:** 989-354-0144
Year Designated: 2000. **Location:** Northwestern section of Lake Huron, near Alpena, Michigan. **Description:** Sanctuary encompasses 448 square miles of northwest Lake Huron, off the northeast coast of Michigan's Lower Peninsula. The landward boundary of the sanctuary/preserve is marked by the northern and southern limits of Alpena County, and the sanctuary/preserve extends east from the lakeshore to longitude 83 degrees west. An estimated 200 shipwrecks that span two centuries of Great Lakes maritime history are located in and around the sanctuary. **Facilities:** Great Lakes Maritime Heritage Center in Alpena, MI. **Activities:** Scuba diving, boating, kayaking, fishing. Visitors can also learn about seafaring on the Great Lakes aboard replicas of historic sailing vessels. **Special Features:** Thunder Bay National Marine Sanctuary and Underwater Preserve is the first sanctuary located in the Great Lakes region, the first one in fresh water, and only the second one designated to protect underwater cultural resources.

6. National Marine Sanctuaries

See page 26 for map of National Marine Sanctuaries.

7. NATIONAL HERITAGE AREAS

★1091★ NATIONAL HERITAGE AREAS PROGRAM
1201 Eye St NW, 8th Fl
Washington, DC 20005
202-354-2222 - Phone
202-371-6468 - Fax
Web: www.cr.nps.gov/heritageareas/

National Heritage Areas are regions in which entire communities live and work, and in which residents, businesses, and local governments have come together to conserve special landscapes and their own heritage. Through a number of independent authorities, Congress has established 37 National Heritage Areas in 27 states, in which conservation, interpretation and other activities are managed by partnerships among federal, state, and local governments and the private sector. These areas consist mainly of private property, though some include public parks and preserves. Protection and upkeep of these lands and properties, as well as the activities such as tours and festivals, are primarily accomplished through voluntary actions. Designation as a National Heritage Area brings no federal regulation of private property. The National Park Service provides technical assistance as well as financial assistance for a limited number of years following designation.

Each National Heritage Area is a settled landscape that tells the story of its residents. Over time the land and the local environment have shaped traditions and cultural values in the people who live there. All of these National Heritage areas are young and constitute an ambitious experiment – a new way of conserving and enjoying the nation's natural and cultural heritage. As such, the kinds of visitor experiences available vary widely. These areas are at different stages of implementing their plans for scenic byways, walking and cycling trails, scenic and recreational rivers, interpretive and educational activities, and rehabilitation of historic buildings and districts.

The National Heritage Areas Act of 2006 added ten new national heritage areas. These include:
  Arabia Mountain National Heritage Area (GA)
  Atchafalaya National Heritage Area (LA)
  Champlain Valley National Heritage Partnership (NY and VT)
  Crossroads of the American Revolution National Heritage Area (NJ)
  Freedom's Frontier National Heritage Area (KS and MO)
  Great Basin National Heritage Route (UT and NV)
  Gullah/Geechee Heritage Corridor (NC, SC, GA, and FL)
  Mormon Pioneer National Heritage Area (UT)
  Northern Rio Grande National Heritage Area (NM)
  Upper Housatonic Valley National Heritage Area (MA and CT)

Over the next several years, the local management entities of these National Heritage Areas will work closely with their national park partners, other federal agencies, and state and local partners to develop a management plan to conserve and interpret their regions' nationally significant stories and resources.

This section provides information on the 27 National Heritage Areas that have been established to date. Contact information, including mailing address, phone, fax, and web addresses are included for each listing, as well as a brief description of the designated area.

★1092★ AUGUSTA CANAL NATIONAL HERITAGE AREA
Augusta Canal Authority
PO Box 2367
Augusta, GA 30903
Web: www.augustacanal.com
Phone: 706-823-0440; **Fax:** 706-823-1045
Established: Authorized on November 12, 1996. **Location:** In Augusta, Georgia. **Special Features:** This nine-mile corridor follows the full length of the best preserved canal of its kind remaining in the southern United States. The canal transformed Augusta into an important regional industrial area on the eve of the Civil War, and was instrumental in the post-Civil War relocation of much of the nation's textile industry to the South.

★1093★ AUTOMOBILE NATIONAL HERITAGE AREA
300 River Pl, Suite 1600
Detroit, MI 48207
Web: www.experienceeverythingautomotive.org
Phone: 313-259-3425; **Fax:** 313-259-5254
Established: Authorized on November 6, 1998. **Location:** Encompasses almost 10,000 square miles, portions of 13 counties, and nearly 260 municipalities and townships in central and southeastern Michigan. **Special Features:** At the beginning of the 20th century, a small group of pioneer auto manufacturers assembled a few hundred ''horseless carriages'' in Michigan. By the time twenty years had passed, Michigan had more than 700 automotive-related companies on record, including 367 in Detroit alone. Southeast Michigan, which includes the ''Motor Cities'' of Detroit, Lansing and Flint, is the region that put the world on wheels. The heritage area consists of six significant corridors. This collection of auto-related museums, attractions, activities and events exists to preserve and interpret the story of the automobile.

★1094★ BLACKSTONE RIVER VALLEY NATIONAL HERITAGE CORRIDOR

1 Depot Sq
Woonsocket, RI 02895
Web: www.nps.gov/blac/
Phone: 401-762-0250; **Fax:** 401-762-0530
Established: Established on November 10, 1986. **Location:** A corridor of 24 cities and towns between Worcester County in central Massachusetts and Providence County in northern Rhode Island. Route 146 is the main highway running north and south between Providence and Worcester, with major intersections at I-95 and I-295 in Rhode Island. Exit 11 on I-90 (Massachusetts Turnpike) gives access to Route 122 and visitor information centers in Worcester and Uxbridge. **Special Features:** The American Industrial Revolution had its roots here along some 46 miles of river and canals running from Worcester, Massachusetts, to Providence, Rhode Island. The mills (including Slater Mill), villages, and associated transportation networks in the Blackstone Valley together tell the story of industrialization.

★1095★ BLUE RIDGE NATIONAL HERITAGE AREA

3 General Aviation Dr
Fletcher, NC 28732
Web: www.blueridgeheritage.com
Phone: 828-687-7234; **Fax:** 828-687-7552
Established: Authorized on November 10, 2003 **Location:** Includes 24 counties in the Blue Ridge Mountains of western North Carolina. **Special Features:** The rich natural and cultural heritage in this region has contributed significantly to the history and development of the United States. The Blue Ridge National Heritage Area works to preserve and interpret traditional instrumental and vocal folk music, folklife traditions, traditional arts, the heritage and influences of the Cherokee Indians, and various historic sites and collections of artifacts. The area is managed by a partnership of state, local, non-profit, and Cherokee Indian representatives.

★1096★ CACHE LA POUDRE RIVER CORRIDOR

1100 10th St, Suite 401
Greeley, CO 80631
Web: www.nature.nps.gov/cachelapoudre/index.htm
Phone: 970-350-9755; **Fax:** 970-350-9763
Established: Authorized on October 19, 1996. **Location:** In north-central Colorado, beginning at the eastern edge of the Arapaho-Roosevelt National Forest (see separate entry) and extending east through Fort Collins and Larimer County to Greeley and Weld County up to $\frac{1}{4}$ miles west of its confluence with the South Platte River. The boundary of the 40-mile Corridor is the river's 100-year floodplain. **Special Features:** Commemorates the role of water development and management in the American West. The legislation provides for the interpretation of the unique and significant contributions to national heritage of cultural and historical lands, waterways and structures within the Corridor.

★1097★ CANE RIVER NATIONAL HERITAGE AREA

PO Box 1201
Natchitoches, LA 71458
Web: www.caneriverheritage.org
Phone: 318-356-5555; **Fax:** 318-356-8222

Established: Authorized on November 2, 1994. **Location:** In northwestern Louisiana. The central corridor of the heritage area begins just south of Natchitoches, the oldest permanent settlement in the Louisiana Purchase, and extends along both sides of Cane River Lake for approximately 35 miles. **Special Features:** A largely rural, agricultural landscape known for its historic plantations, its distinctive Creole architecture, and its multi-cultural legacy. Historically this region was situated at the intersection of French and Spanish realms in the New World. Today it is home to a unique blend of cultures, including French, Spanish, African, American Indian, and Creole. The heritage area includes Cane River Creole National Historical Park (see separate entry), seven national historic landmarks, three state historic sites, and many other historic plantations, homes, and churches.

★1098★ DELAWARE & LEHIGH NATIONAL HERITAGE CORRIDOR

Delaware & Lehigh Canal National Heritage Corridor Commission
1 S Third St
Easton, PA 18042
Web: www.nps.gov/dele/
Phone: 610-923-3548; **Fax:** 610-923-0537
Established: Designated on November 18, 1988. Administered by a federal commission appointed by the Secretary of the Interior and the Governor of Pennsylvania working with a consortium of state, county, local, and private landowners. **Location:** Stretching 150 miles, the corridor follows the historic routes of the Delaware Canal and the Lehigh Navigation System, from Bristol to Wilkes-Barre, in eastern Pennsylvania. **Special Features:** These two 19th-century canals and their associated early railroads opened up the rich anthracite coal fields of eastern Pennsylvania and fueled the Industrial Revolution. The corridor includes museums dealing with the region's cultural and industrial history, as well as state parks and historic landmarks.

★1099★ ERIE CANALWAY NATIONAL HERITAGE CORRIDOR

c/o Peebles Island Resource Center
PO Box 219
Waterford, NY 12188
Web: www.nps.gov/erie/index.htm
Phone: 518-237-8643; **Fax:** 518-235-4248
Established: Authorized on December 21, 2000. **Location:** In upstate New York. **Special Features:** Few historic resources in the United States are equal to the Erie Canal in their impact on the creation of the American nation. The Erie Canalway National Heritage Corridor will work in partnership with the 230 communities in the heritage corridor to protect this treasured cultural and historic resource and promote the 524-mile New York State Canal System as a recreation destination for today's boaters and visitors.

★1100★ ESSEX NATIONAL HERITAGE AREA

221 Essex St, Suite 41
Salem, MA 01970
Web: www.essexheritage.org
Phone: 978-740-0444; **Fax:** 978-744-6473

7. National Heritage Areas

Established: Authorized on November 12, 1996. **Location:** A 550-square mile area between the Atlantic Coast and the Merrimack Valley in southeastern New Hampshire and northeastern Massachusetts. **Special Features:** Includes the thousands of historic sites and districts that illuminate colonial settlement, the growth and decline of the maritime industries, and the development of the shoe and textile industries. The area also features historic seaports and New England town commons; industrial mills and pristine beaches; renowned museums and wildlife refuges; working farms and natural trails.

★1101★ HUDSON RIVER VALLEY NATIONAL HERITAGE AREA

Hudson River Valley Greenway
Capitol Bldg, Room 254
Albany, NY 12224
Web: www.hudsonrivervalley.com
Phone: 518-473-3835; **Fax:** 518-473-4518
Established: Authorized on November 12, 1996. **Location:** From Troy to New York City. **Special Features:** The Hudson River Valley contains a rich assemblage of natural features and nationally significant cultural and historical sites. The valley has maintained the scenic, rural character that inspired the Hudson Valley School of landscape painting and the Knickerbocker writers. Recreational opportunities are found in local parks, protected open spaces, and greenways.

★1102★ ILLINOIS & MICHIGAN CANAL NATIONAL HERITAGE CORRIDOR

Canal Corridor Association
200 W 8th St
Lockport, IL 60441
Web: www.canalcor.org
Phone: 815-588-1100; **Fax:** 815-588-1101
Established: Designated on August 24, 1984, as the nation's first national heritage corridor. **Location:** A 100-mile-long cultural park between Chicago and Peru in northeastern Illinois. **Special Features:** The Illinois and Michigan Canal, completed in 1848, connected the Great Lakes to the Mississippi River watershed along a longstanding Indian portage route. The 97-mile canal extended from the Chicago River near Lake Michigan to the Illinois River at Peru, Illinois. It rapidly transformed Chicago from a small settlement to a critical transportation hub between the East and the developing Midwest. The towpath trail along the canal is a state park that runs through a rural and wooded landscape, linking a number of towns laid out by the original canal commission.

★1103★ LACKAWANNA VALLEY NATIONAL HERITAGE AREA

Lackawanna Heritage Valley
1300 Old Plank Rd
Mayfield, PA 18433
Web: www.lhva.org
Phone: 570-963-6730; **Fax:** 570-963-6732
Established: Authorized on November 6, 2000. **Location:** Along the Lackawanna River in northeastern Pennsylvania. **Special Features:** The 40-mile-long Lackawanna Heritage Valley

is at the center of what was once the world's most productive anthracite field. The heritage area features history and culture closely tied to the anthracite coal mining industry, a cornerstone of the American industrial legacy. A combination of trails, museums, and other visitor attractions help tell the nationally important story of anthracite.

★1104★ MISSISSIPPI GULF NATIONAL HERITAGE AREA

Mississippi Department of Marine Resources
1141 Bayview Ave
Biloxi, MS 39530
Web: www.dmr.state.ms.us
Phone: 228-523-4122
Established: Authorized on December 8, 2004. Management of the area will be coordinated by the Mississippi Department of Marine Resources in consultation with the Mississippi Department of Archives and History. **Location:** A six-county area within the Mississippi Coastal Plain that borders the Gulf of Mexico. **Special Features:** The area has been shaped by the natural coastal and riverine environment and a number of cultural influences, including those of early Native Americans and Spanish, French, and English settlers. Yhe area contains cultural and historical sites related to these cultures, including the first capital of the Louisiana Territory, in addition to natural, scenic, and recreational resources along the coast and wetlands.

★1105★ NATIONAL AVIATION HERITAGE AREA

Aviation Heritage Foundation, Inc.
PO Box 414
Dayton, OH 45409
Web: birthplaceofaviation.com
Phone: 937-222-6039
Established: Authorized on December 8, 2004. The area will be managed by the non-profit organization Aviation Heritage Foundation, Inc. **Location:** An eight-county region in Southwest Ohio. **Special Features:** Consisting of 9 historical sites and one member organization, NAHA builds upon the Wright Brothers' legacy and the aviation history that followed them in the Dayton, Ohio region. Partnership projects among federal, state and local governments and the private sector have been occurring since the passage of the Dayton Aviation Heritage Preservation Act in 1992. Heritage development, interpretation and preservation projects based on historic aviation resources and sites will be strengthened and enhanced by the new designation. Resources within the heritage area's boundaries include Wright-Patterson Air Force Base and Dayton Aviation Heritage National Historical Park.

★1106★ NATIONAL COAL HERITAGE AREA

Coal Heritage Highway Authority
PO Box 5176
Beckley, WV 25801
Web: www.coalheritage.org
Phone: 304-256-6941; **Fax:** 304-256-6994
Established: Authorized on November 12, 1996. **Location:** 11 counties in southern West Virginia. **Special Features:** The cultural geography here has been profoundly influenced over

7. National Heritage Areas

the last 125 years by the pervasive role of the coal mines. The communities in these 11 counties reflect their origins as ''company towns'' formed by local traditions, waves of immigrant workers, and the dominance of the mining companies. Ethnic neighborhoods and the physical infrastructure of the mines are still clearly seen throughout the region.

★1107★ OHIO & ERIE CANAL NATIONAL HERITAGE CORRIDOR

Ohio & Erie Canal Corridor Coalition
520 S Main St, Suite 2541-F
Akron, OH 44311
Web: www.ohioeriecanal.org
Phone: 330-434-5657; **Fax:** 330-434-5688
Established: Authorized on November 12, 1996. **Location:** 110-mile stretch in northeastern Ohio from Cleveland through New Philadelphia (including Akron and Canton). **Special Features:** This area of northeast Ohio celebrates the canal that enabled shipping between Lake Erie and the Ohio River and vaulted Ohio into commercial prominence in the early 1830s. The canal and towpath trail pass through agricultural lands and rural villages into industrial communities such as Akron, Canton, and Cleveland that trace their prosperity to the coming of the canal. Visitors can explore this 110-mile heritage greenway through three primary routes: The Ohio & Erie Canal Towpath Trail, the CanalWay Ohio National Scenic Byway, and the Cuyahoga Valley Scenic Railroad.

★1108★ OIL REGION NATIONAL HERITAGE AREA

Oil Region Alliance of Business, Industry & Tourism
PO Box 128
Oil City, PA 16301
Web: www.oilregion.org
Phone: 800-483-6264; **Fax:** 814-677-5206
Established: The Oil Region was designated a Pennsylvania Heritage Park in 1994 and authorized as a National Heritage Area on December 8, 2004. The national heritage area will be managed by the Oil Region Alliance of Business, Industry & Tourism. **Location:** Comprised of Venango County, Oil Creek Township in eastern Crawford County, and the City of Titusville, Pennsylvania. **Special Features:** The area contains remnants of the oil industry, in addition to historic valley and riverbed settlements, plateau developments, farmlands, and industrial landscapes. The area's cultural traditions have been shaped by Native Americans, frontier settlements, the French and Indian War, African Americans and the Underground Railroad, and Swedish and Polish immigration. The NHA designation will enhance the current efforts of the Commonwealth of Pennsylvania, volunteer organizations, and private businesses to interpret, preserve, enhance, and promote the cultural, national, and recreational resources of the region to residents and visitors.

★1110★ QUINEBAUG & SHETUCKET RIVERS VALLEY NATIONAL HERITAGE CORRIDOR

Quinebaug-Shetucket Heritage Corridor, Inc.
107 Providence St
Putnam, CT 06260
Web: www.thelastgreenvalley.org
Phone: 860-963-7226; **Fax:** 860-928-2189

Established: Authorized on November 2, 1994. **Location:** Encompasses 1,086 square miles and 35 towns in the Quinebaug and Shetucket Rivers Valley in northeastern Connecticut and south-central Massachusetts. **Special Features:** The Quinebaug and Shetucket Rivers Valley is one of the last unspoiled and undeveloped areas in the northeastern United States and has been called ''The Last Green Valley'' in the sprawling metropolitan Boston-to-Washington corridor. The region has retained its fundamental rural character, with lush woodlands and clean waterways, authentic sites representing distinct periods of American history (including architecturally significant mill structures and mill villages), and large tracts of parks and other permanent open spaces.

★1111★ RIVERS OF STEEL NATIONAL HERITAGE AREA

623 E 8th Ave
Bost Bldg
Homestead, PA 15120
Web: www.riversofsteel.com
Phone: 412-464-4020; **Fax:** 412-464-4417
Established: Authorized on November 12, 1996. **Location:** In southwestern Pennsylvania, encompassing 3,000 square miles in seven counties along the Allegheny, Monongahela, and Ohio rivers. **Special Features:** From 1875 to 1980, southwestern Pennsylvania was the Steel Making Capital of the World. The industry made possible railroads, skyscrapers, and shipbuilding, while altering corporate practice and labor organization. The heritage area preserves, interprets, and manages the historic, cultural, and natural resources related to Big Steel and its related industries. There are remains of numerous mills as well as communities founded by mill workers, many of which are linked by hiking trails and riverboat tours.

★1112★ SCHUYLKILL RIVER VALLEY NATIONAL HERITAGE AREA

140 College Dr
Pottstown, PA 19464
Web: www.schuylkillriver.org
Phone: 484-945-0200; **Fax:** 484-945-0240
Established: Authorized on November 6, 2000. **Location:** Encompasses the river valley associated with the 128-mile Schuylkill River in southeastern Pennsylvania. **Special Features:** The heritage area includes three national park areas, the historic city of Philadelphia, and many early communities and canal towns throughout the corridor. The Schuylkill River is central to the story of colonization and industrialization in America. The area provides pre-Revolutionary mills, late 19th-century factories, and numerous historic districts and cultural attractions throughout a five-county area.

★1113★ SHENANDOAH VALLEY BATTLEFIELDS NATIONAL HISTORIC DISTRICT

Shenandoah Valley Battlefields Foundation
PO Box 897
New Market, VA 22844
Web: www.shenandoahatwar.org
Phone: 540-740-4545; **Fax:** 540-740-4509

Established: Authorized on November 12, 1996. **Location:** In northern Virginia. **Special Features:** From 1861 to 1865 the Shenandoah Valley of Virginia was caught in the crossfire between the North and the South. Because of its strategic location, this fertile agricultural valley became a significant theater of war. Today 15 battlefields and more than 320 sites, towns, villages, and farms in this eight-county National Historic District attest to the struggle and perserverance of the soldiers and civilians who shaped this turning point in American history.

★1114★ **SILOS & SMOKESTACKS NATIONAL HERITAGE AREA**
Russell Lamson Bldg, 209 W 5th St, Suite E
PO Box 2845
Waterloo, IA 50704
Web: www.silosandsmokestacks.org
Phone: 319-234-4567; **Fax:** 319-234-8228
Established: Authorized on November 12, 1996. **Location:** 37-county region in northeastern Iowa. **Special Features:** Heritage area illustrates the transformation that took place as mechanization paved the way for a distinctly American system of industrialized agriculture. Tractor design and manufacture, mechanized farming, corn-hog production, dairying, beef cattle feeding, and meat packing continue to characterize the region. The unique cultural histories of family farming and agribusiness are equally well represented.

★1115★ **SOUTH CAROLINA NATIONAL HERITAGE CORRIDOR**
Heritage Tourism Development Office
1205 Pendleton St
Columbia, SC 29201
Web: www.sc-heritagecorridor.org
Phone: 803-734-1743; **Fax:** 803-734-0670
Established: Authorized on November 12, 1996. **Location:** Extends 240 miles across 14 counties in western South Carolina, stretching from the mountains of Oconee County, along the Savannah River, to the port city of Charleston. **Special Features:** This corridor, bounded at one end by the ancient port city of Charleston and at the other by the mountains of the Blue Ridge, contains historic, cultural, and natural resources that tell the story of South Carolina's — and the South's — centuries-long evolution and culture. Two routes begin in the mill villages, waterfalls, and mountains of the Up Country; run through historic courthouse towns and military sites and along the Savannah River; and follow the Edisto River and the South Carolina Railroad to the Low Country's wealth of African-American and antebellum history, centered in and around historic Charleston.

★1109★ **SOUTHWESTERN PENNSYLVANIA INDUSTRIAL HERITAGE ROUTE**
105 Zee Plaza
PO Box 565
Hollidaysburg, PA 16648
Web: www.sphpc.org
Phone: 814-696-9380; **Fax:** 814-696-9569
Established: Authorized on November 19, 1988. **Location:** 500-mile route across the Alleghenies through nine counties in southwestern Pennsylvania. **Special Features:** Features hundreds of sites relating to the nation's industrial story. Included are the Altoona Railyards, the Johnstown Flood National Memorial and Museum (see separate entry), the steel mills of Johnstown, and Horseshoe Curve, a 19th century engineering marvel built by the Pennsylvania Railroad.

★1116★ **TENNESSEE CIVIL WAR NATIONAL HERITAGE AREA**
Center for Historic Preservation, Middle Tennessee State University
Box 80
Murfreesboro, TN 37132
Web: histpres.mtsu.edu/tncivwar/
Phone: 615-898-2947; **Fax:** 615-898-5614
Established: Authorized on November 12, 1996. **Location:** Includes the entire state of Tennessee and features eight heritage corridors along river and railroad systems. **Special Features:** A number of areas throughout Tennessee preserve and interpret the legacy of the Civil War there. Heritage resources are focused on important events, geographic factors, decisive battles, engagements, and the strategic maneuvers of the war, as well as the impact of the Civil War and Reconstruction on Tennessee's residents.

★1117★ **WHEELING NATIONAL HERITAGE AREA**
1400 Main St
Wheeling, WV 26003
Web: www.wheelingheritage.org
Phone: 304-232-3087; **Fax:** 304-232-1812
Established: Authorized on October 11, 2000. **Location:** In Wheeling, West Virginia. **Special Features:** Once the capital of West Virginia, Wheeling marked the northernmost navigable port on the Ohio River. It became a thriving commercial, industrial, and cultural center, and by 1818 was the terminus of the National Road, the nation's first highway. A waterfront park plus a variety of venues throughout the city interpret the history and culture of the area.

★1118★ **YUMA CROSSING NATIONAL HERITAGE AREA**
180 W 1st St, Suite E
Yuma, AZ 85364
Web: www.yumaheritage.com
Phone: 928-373-5190; **Fax:** 928-373-5191
Established: Authorized on October 19, 2000. **Location:** In Yuma, Arizona. **Special Features:** Dedicated to conserving and interpreting the natural and cultural history of the Colorado River and the Yuma Crossing.

8. NATIONAL SCENIC BYWAYS

★1119★ National Scenic Byways Program
U.S. Department of Transportation
Federal Highway Administration
HEPN-50, Room 3232
400 Seventh St, SW
Washington DC 20590
202-366-1929 – Phone
800-429-9297 – Toll-free
Web: www.bywaysonline.org

The National Scenic Byways Program is part of the U.S. Department of Transportation, Federal Highway Administration. It was established to help recognize, preserve, and enhance selected roads throughout the United States. Since 1992, the National Scenic Byways Program has provided funding for more than 2,100 state and nationally designated byway projects in 50 states, Puerto Rico, and the District of Columbia.

The U.S. Secretary of Transportation recognizes certain roads as National Scenic Byways or All-American Roads. To be designated as a National Scenic Byway, a road must possess at least one of these six intrinsic qualities: historic, cultural, natural, scenic, recreational, or archaeological. In addition, the features contributing to the distinctive characteristics of the corridor's intrinsic qualities must possess regional significance.

To receive an All-American Road designation, a road must possess multiple intrinsic qualities that are nationally significant and contain one-of-a-kind features that do not exist elsewhere. The road must also be considered a "destination unto itself." That is, the Byway must be the primary destination for a trip, and must provide an exceptional travel experience. There are currently 99 National Scenic Byways and 27 All-American Roads, including 18 multi-state Byways.

This section provides information on the individual byways and All-American roads that comprise America's Byway System. In addition to descriptive information on each byway, contact information is provided for the organization or governing body that is deemed to be best suited to provide the traveler with detailed information on the byway itself and on nearby points of interest. This may include a convention & visitors bureau, an adjoining national park or forest, or some other relevant organization or agency. The web site listed for each byway provides the most detailed information available and doesn't necessarily correspond to the agency/organization listed.

Listings here are arranged by state and then alphabetically by byway name. Information included under the heading "Time to Allow" is the approximate drive time if traveling straight through from one end of the byway to the other. The actual travel time will, of course, depend on a number of factors, including the number and length of stops at points of interest along the way, weather and road conditions, and so on.

ALABAMA

★1120★ NATCHEZ TRACE PARKWAY - ALABAMA
Natchez Trace Parkway Visitor Center
2680 Natchez Trace Parkway
Tupelo, MS 38804
Web: www.nps.gov/natr/
Phone: 800-305-7417
Length: 32 miles (Alabama section); 444 miles (entire parkway). **Designation/Year:** All-American Road (1996). **Description:** The Alabama segment of the Natchez Trace Parkway is the middle leg of a byway that covers the entire length of the 444-mile Natchez Trace, which encompasses portions of Tennessee, Alabama, and Mississippi. Native Americans, Kaintuck boatmen, indians, post riders, soldiers and fortune seekers all travelled across this trail, charting new territory and creating a vital link between the Mississippi Territory and the United States. The Alabama section of the byway offers a wealth of early pioneer and Native American history, including nearby access to the Trail of Tears National Historic Trail, which tells the story of how more than 16,000 Cherokee Indians were forced to leave their homeland. **Start/Endpoint:** Parkway runs from Nashville, TN to Natchez, MS. The Alabama section cuts through the northwest corner of the state and is accessible from Highways 20 and 14, and also from Highway 72 going west.

★1121★ SELMA TO MONTGOMERY MARCH BYWAY
7001 US Hwy 80
Hayneville, AL 36040
Web: www.nps.gov/semo/
Phone: 334-877-1983
Length: 54 miles. **Designation/Year:** All-American Road (1996). **Description:** Historic trail marks the Selma to Montgomery March in 1965, led by Dr. Martin Luther King, Jr. The first of the three marches from Selma along Highway 80 ended in what became known as "Bloody Sunday"; the second march went to the foot of the Edmund Pettus Bridge where the marchers prayed and turned around; and the third ended successfully at the State Capitol in Montgomery. Also designated as a National Historic Trail. **Start/Endpoint:** From Selma to Montgomery, Alabama. **Time to Allow:** 1 hour.

★1122★ TALLADEGA SCENIC DRIVE
c/o USDA Forest Service
2946 Chestnut St
Montgomery, AL 36107
Web: www.byways.org/browse/byways/2057/
Phone: 334-832-4470
Length: 26 miles. **Designation/Year:** National Scenic Byway
(1998). **Description:** Traverses the backbone of Horseblock and
Cheaha Mountains, the southernmost extension of the Appalachian mountain range, to Alabama's highest peak at 2,407 feet
elevation. The entire route is located within the boundaries of
Talladega National Forest and Cheaha State Park is located at
the top of Cheaha Mountain near the midway point. **Start/
Endpoint:** Byway runs in a northeast/southwest direction from
near the intersection of I-20 and Highway 281 to Turnipseed
Hunt Camp near the southern end of Cheaha State Park. **Time
to Allow:** 1 hour.

ALASKA

★1123★ ALASKA'S MARINE HIGHWAY
6858 Glacier Highway
PO Box 112505
Juneau, AK 99801
Web: www.dot.state.ak.us/amhs/
Phone: 800-642-0066
Length: 8,834 miles. **Designation/Year:** All-American Road
(2005). **Description:** Scenic coastal ferry route in southern
Alaska that includes Alaska's Inside Passage, Prince William
Sound, Kodiak, and the Aleutian Islands. Scenery includes pristine islands, spectacular fjords, the Gulf of Alaska and Lower
Cook Inlet, snow-capped mountains, historical towns and villages, and abundant wildlife. **Start/Endpoint:** The ''Inside Passage'' extends from Queen Charlotte Islands of British Columbia
north to Skagway. The Gulf Coast Route extends from Juneau
to the Marine Highway's westernmost port, Unalaska, in the
Aleutians. **Time to Allow:** Running times for selected routes:
37 hours from Bellingham, WA to Ketchikan, AK; 5.5 hours
from Valdez to Cordova; 18.5 hours from Kodiak to Chignik

★1124★ GLENN HIGHWAY
c/o Alaska Public Lands Information Center
605 West 4th Ave, Suite 105
Anchorage, AK 99501
Web: www.dot.state.ak.us/stwdplng/scenic/
Phone: 907-271-2737
Length: 139 miles. **Designation/Year:** Scenic Byway (2002).
Description: Paralleling the Chugach Mountains along its entire
route, byway follows a path carved by ancient glaciers. It pro-
vides access to the 495,000-acre Chugach State Park at Eagle
River and follows the Matanuska River for over half its length.
Near the byway's end at Eureka Summit, visitors can observe
four of Alaska's major mountain ranges: the Alaska Range, the
Chugach Mountains, the Talkeetna Mountains and the Wrangell-
St. Elias Mountains. **Start/Endpoint:** From Anchorage to the
Little Nelchina River. **Time to Allow:** 2.5 hours to drive.

★1125★ SEWARD HIGHWAY
c/o Alaska Public Lands Information Center
605 West 4th Ave, Suite 105
Anchorage, AK 99501
Web: www.dot.state.ak.us/stwdplng/scenic/byways-
seward.shtml
Phone: 907-271-2737
Length: 127 miles. **Designation/Year:** All-American Road
(2000). **Description:** From Anchorage to Girdwood, the highway borders Turnagain Arm and Chugach State Park. From
Girdwood to Seward, it passes through Chugach National Forest
offering dramatic views of wild Alaska. The diversity of landscape and wildlife found along the route is the hallmark of the
highway corridor. **Start/Endpoint:** From Anchorage to Seward,
Alaska. **Time to Allow:** 5 hours.

ARIZONA

★1126★ CORONADO TRAIL SCENIC BYWAY
c/o Apache and Sitgreaves National Forests
PO Box 640
Springerville, AZ 85938
Web: www.fs.fed.us/r3/asnf/
Phone: 928-333-4301
Length: 123 miles. **Designation/Year:** National Scenic Byway
(2005). **Description:** Byway runs close to the 1540 route of
Spanish explorer Francisco Vasquez, who was seeking the riches
of the legendary Seven Cities of Cibola. Scenic points along
this eastern Arizona route feature the Sonoran Desert, the White
Mountains (including 7,951' Mitchell Peak and 8,786' Rose
Peak), and the Apache-Sitgreaves National Forest. **Start/End-
point:** From Springerville to Morenci in east-central Arizona.
Time to Allow: 4-5 hours (including more than 400 switch-
backs).

★1127★ HISTORIC ROUTE 66 - ARIZONA
c/o The Powerhouse Tourist Information & Visitor Center
120 W Route 66
Kingman, AZ 86401
Web: www.kingmantourism.org
Phone: 866-427-7866
Length: 370 miles (Arizona section); 1,410 miles (entire byway). **Designation/Year:** National Scenic Byway (2005). **Description:** Route 66 was designated in 1926 as a federal highway
linking Chicago, IL to Los Angeles, CA. The 2,448-mile route
passed through Illinois, Missouri, Kansas, Oklahoma, Texas,
New Mexico, Arizona, and California. The road was decommissioned in 1985 in favor of the new interstate highway system
and today only 1,410 miles of the original route in three states
(Illinois, New Mexico and Arizona) have been designated as
National Scenic Byway. Arizona's Historic Route 66 includes
the longest unbroken stretch of the original route and some of
the most picturesque scenery in the Southwest. Areas along the
way include the city of Flagstaff, Petrified Forest National Park,
Meteor Crater, Sunset Crater Volcanic National Monument,
Walnut Canyon National Monument, Grand Canyon Caverns,
as well as Homolovi Indian ruins and cliff dwellings of the
Sinagua Indians. **Start/Endpoint:** Runs east/west from Lupton

on the New Mexico/Arizona border to Topock on the Arizona-California border. **Time to Allow:** 7 hours (Arizona section); 5-6 days (entire byway).

★1128★ KAIBAB PLATEAU - NORTH RIM PARKWAY

c/o Kaibab National Forest
800 South Sixth St
Williams, AZ 86046
Web: www.fs.fed.us/r3/kai/
Phone: 928-635-8200
Length: 42 miles. **Designation/Year:** National Scenic Byway (1998). **Description:** Byway is the only route to the North Rim of the Grand Canyon and passes through the Kaibab National Forest, which offers opportunities for hiking, horseback riding, backpacking, wildlife viewing, and primitive camping. The byway is closed to traditional vehicles during the winter, but is accessible by snowmobile or cross-country skiing. **Start/Endpoint:** From Jacob Lake to the North Rim of the Grand Canyon in Arizona. **Time to Allow:** 1 hour.

★1129★ RED ROCK SCENIC BYWAY

c/o Sedona Chamber of Commerce
331 Forest Rd
Sedona, AZ 86336
Web: www.arizonascenicroads.com
Phone: 800-288-7336
Length: 7.5 miles. **Designation/Year:** All-American Road (2005). **Description:** The route through Cococino National Forest curves through the high desert country, a colorful mosaic of red soil and green junipers. Giant Rock formations include Castle Rock, Bell Rock, and Courthouse Butte, a popular spot for off-road mountain biking. **Start/Endpoint:** A stretch of SR 179 from Milepost 302.5 to 310, approximately 100 miles north of Phoenix. **Time to Allow:** 20 minutes.

★1130★ SKY ISLAND SCENIC BYWAY

c/o Coronado National Forest
300 W Congress St
Tucson, AZ 85701
Web: www.fs.fed.us/r3/coronado/
Phone: 520-388-8300
Length: 27 miles. **Designation/Year:** National Scenic Byway (2005). **Description:** The only paved road that leads to the upper reaches of 9,157-foot Mount Lemmon, the parkway rises dramatically, passing through five life zones, from Sonoran Desert lowlands all the way up to a mixed-conifer forest, the geographic equivalent of traveling from Mexico to Canada. It provides a range of recreational opportunities, including backcountry hiking, mountain biking, and horseback riding. Mount Lemmon offers alpine skiing in the during the winter months. **Start/Endpoint:** From the Sonoran Desert floor in Tucson to the village of Summerhaven near the top of Mount Lemmon in the Santa Catalina Mountains north of Tucson. **Time to Allow:** 3-6 hours (including backtracking).

ARKANSAS

★1131★ CROWLEY'S RIDGE PARKWAY - ARKANSAS

c/o Arkansas Delta Byways
PO Box 2050
State University, AR 72467
Web: www.deltabyways.com
Phone: 870-972-2803
Length: 212 miles, including a 198-mile section in Arkansas and a 14-mile section in Missouri. **Designation/Year:** National Scenic Byway (1998). **Description:** Route follows Crowley's Ridge, a series of rolling hills stretching north to south in the midst of the Arkansas delta. Area is abundant in wildlife and natural areas as the byway traverses the Chalk Bluff Natural Area, five state parks, and the Saint Francis National Forest. Area also includes remnants of Native American culture and Civil War history. **Start/Endpoint:** The Arkansas section of the byway runs from Saint Francis (near the Arkansas-Missouri border) to Helena (near the Arkansas-Tennessee border). **Time to Allow:** 5 hours (Arkansas section) and 30 minutes (Missouri section)

★1132★ GREAT RIVER ROAD - ARKANSAS

c/o Arkansas Delta Byways
PO Box 2050
State University, AR 72467
Web: www.deltabyways.com
Phone: 870-972-2803
Length: 362 miles (Arkansas section); 2,069 miles (entire byway). **Designation/Year:** National Scenic Byway (2002). **Description:** The 2,069-mile Great River Road borders the Mississippi River through the states of Mississippi, Arkansas, Iowa, Illinois, Wisconsin, and Minnesota. The 362-mile Arkansas segment features museums and monuments highlighting Civil War history and archeology of the ancient Mississippi mound-building cultures. It also offers opportunities for outdoor recreation including fishing and wildlife viewing. **Start/Endpoint:** The north-south route runs from the historic concrete arch that spans US 61 at the Missouri state line to US 65 at the Louisiana state line. Near the southern terminus of the Arkansas section of the byway, a spur route runs east on US 82 to the Mississippi River Bridge and the Mississippi state line.

★1133★ TALIMENA SCENIC DRIVE - ARKANSAS

c/o Ouachita National Forest
PO Box 1270
Hot Springs, AR 71902
Web: www.talimenascenicdrive.com
Phone: 501-321-5202
Length: 54 miles including 16-mile section in Arkansas and 38-mile section in Oklahoma. **Designation/Year:** National Scenic Byway (2005). **Description:** Byway stretches across the top of the Ouachita Mountains in eastern Oklahoma and western Arkansas, the highest mountain range between the Appalachians and the Rockies. The Arkansas section of the byway provides access to recreation destinations such as the Ouachita National Forest, as well as Queen Wilhelmina State Park and the Black

Fork Mountain Wilderness Trail. The Ouchita National Forest features more than 700 trails for hiking, backpacking, horseback riding, and off-road vehicles, including the Ouachita National Recreation Trail, a 194-mile trail that traverses the forest. **Start/Endpoint:** The Arkansas section of the byway runs from Mena, AR to the Arkansas-Oklahoma state line. **Time to Allow:** 30 minutes (Arkansas section) and 1 hour (Oklahoma section).

CALIFORNIA

★1134★ ARROYO SECO HISTORIC PARKWAY - ROUTE 110

c/o Mountains Recreation and Conservation Authority
570 West Ave 26, Suite 100
Los Angeles, CA 90065
Web: www.byways.org/browse/byways/10246/
Phone: 323-221-9944
Length: 9.5 miles. **Designation/Year:** National Scenic Byway (2002). **Description:** The route through the historic arts and crafts landscape of the Arroyo Seco passes through Chinatown and Elysian Park, the Cypress Park neighborhood, early 20th century landmarks (including Lummis House, Heritage Square, and the Southwest Museum), the Highland Park neighborhood, South Pasadena, and ends on Colorado Boulevard in the heart of historic Old Town Pasadena. **Start/Endpoint:** From Los Angeles to Pasadena along Arroyo Seco Parkway (110 Pasadena Freeway). **Time to Allow:** 20 minutes.

★1135★ BIG SUR COAST HIGHWAY - ROUTE 1

c/o Big Sur Chamber of Commerce
PO Box 87
Big Sur, CA 93920
Web: www.byways.org/browse/byways/2301/
Phone: 831-667-2100
Length: 72 miles. **Designation/Year:** All-American Road (1996). **Description:** Following the California coastline, route offers views of steep fog-shrouded sea cliffs and rugged canyons, redwood forests, and pristine coastline. Areas of interest include Los Padres National Forest, the Southern Redwood Botanical Area, Limekiln and Julia Pfeiffer Burns state parks, and the Big Sur area. **Start/Endpoint:** From north to south, follows Route 1 from Carmel to Ragged Point at the Monterey County line. The County line also marks the northern endpoint of the San Luis Obispo North Coast Scenic Byway (see separate listing), another ''All-American'' Road. **Time to Allow:** 1.5 hours.

★1136★ DEATH VALLEY SCENIC BYWAY

c/o Death Valley National Park
PO Box 579
Death Valley, CA 92328
Web: www.nps.gov/deva/
Phone: 760-786-3200
Length: 81.5 miles. **Designation/Year:** National Scenic Byway (2002). **Description:** Byway provides a great opportunity to explore Death Valley National Park, including landscapes of parched salt flats, colored volcanic rock, and sand dunes. Visitors can get out of their vehicles at several vista points/scenic overlooks and hiking trails. Dante's View, just off the main road, offers a viewpoint of Badwater, the lowest elevation in the United States at 282 feet below sea level, all the way up to Telescope Peak, the highest point in the park at 11,049 feet. **Start/Endpoint:** From the eastern entrance of Death Valley National Park, roughly 13 miles west of Death Valley Junction on Highway 190, to the western boundary of the park. **Time to Allow:** 2 hours.

★1137★ EBBETTS PASS SCENIC BYWAY

692 Marshall, Suite A
San Andreas, CA 95249
Web: www.scenic4.org
Phone: 209-754-2094
Length: 61 miles. **Designation/Year:** National Scenic Byway (2005). **Description:** Byway winds through untouched wilderness in the High Sierra past alpine meadows, lakes, pine forests and scenic vistas, ranging in elevation from 3000 to 8500 feet. The land surrounding the byway features two state parks, Stanislaus National Forest, and various designated wilderness areas. Six-thousand-acre Calaveras Big Trees State Park is home to two groves of Giant Sequoia, the most northern stands in the United States. **Start/Endpoint:** On SR 4 and SR 89 between Arnold and Markleeville in east-central California. **Time to Allow:** 2 hours.

★1138★ SAN LUIS OBISPO NORTH COAST BYWAY - ROUTE 1

c/o City of San Luis Obispo
990 Palm St
San Luis Obispo, CA 93401
Web: www.ci.san-luis-obispo.ca.us/
Phone: 805-781-7100
Length: 57 miles. **Designation/Year:** All-American Road (2002). **Description:** Route includes coastal scenic views and spectacular ocean vistas, as well as various cultural and historical sites. Points of interest include: San Luis Obispo, one of California's oldest communities (founded in 1772), Montaña de Oro State Park, Morro Bay, Estero Bay, Harmony Valley, San Simeon State Park, the Hearst Castle, and the Piedras Blancas Lighthouse. **Start/Endpoint:** From south to north, follows Route 1 from San Luis Obispo to Ragged Point at the Monterey county line. The County line also marks the southern endpoint of the Big Sur Coastal Highway (see separate listing), another ''All-American'' Road. **Time to Allow:** One hour.

★1139★ TIOGA ROAD/BIG OAK FLAT ROAD

c/o Yosemite National Park
PO Box 577
Yosemite National Park, CA 95389
Web: www.nps.gov/yose/
Phone: 209-372-0200
Length: 64 miles. **Designation/Year:** National Scenic Byway (1996). **Description:** Crossing the valleys and ridges of Yosemite National Park, the byway offers spectacular views of towering granite peaks, pristine lakes, wildflower-covered meadows, and lush evergreen forests with Giant Sequoia groves. The highest

automobile pass in California includes elevation changes of more than one mile from west to east. Highlights of the drive include the 9,945-foot Tioga Pass, Tuolumne Meadows, Crane and Big Oak Flat, the Merced and Tuolumne Sequoia Groves, Hetch Hetchy Reservoir, Yosemite Valley, Mariposa Grove, and Historic Wawona. **Start/Endpoint:** Traverses Yosemite National Park in an east/west direction from SR 120 at Tioga Pass to the western entrance of the park at Big Oak Flat. **Time to Allow:** 1.5 - 2 hours

★1140★ **VOLCANIC LEGACY SCENIC BYWAY - CALIFORNIA**
300 Pine St
Mount Shasta, CA 96067
Web: www.volcaniclegacybyway.org
Phone: 866-722-9929
Length: 360 miles (California section); 500 miles (total length).
Designation/Year: All-American Road (2002). **Description:** The byway's volcanic landscape includes a wide diversity of scenery, passing through or near dense forests, wetlands and habitat areas, grasslands, farms and ranches, and timber resource lands. Forests and mountains along the byway are home to hiking trails, including the Pacific Crest National Scenic Trail, ski slopes, and fishing and kayaking in clear mountain streams and lakes. Areas of interest include Lassen Volcanic National Park, Hat Creek, McArthur-Burney Falls State Park, the McCloud Waterfalls, and 14,162-foot Mount Shasta, the tallest volcano in California. **Start/Endpoint:** Byway includes sections in northern California and southern Oregon. In California, byway runs from Mount Lassen in Northern California to the California-Oregon border. **Time to Allow:** One day.

COLORADO

★1141★ **COLORADO RIVER HEADWATERS BYWAY**
c/o Granby Chamber of Commerce
PO Box 35
Granby, CO 80446
Web: www.coloradobyways.org
Phone: 970-887-2311
Length: 69 miles. **Designation/Year:** National Scenic Byway (2005). **Description:** Route follows the path of the Colorado River from its headwaters in Rocky Mountain National Park, passing through a diverse topography of high mountain passes, rugged mountains and canyons. Rocky Mountain National Park, the Arapaho and Roosevelt National Forests, Lake Granby, and Grand Lake offer a variety of recreational opportunities including camping, hiking, fishing, canoeing, and rafting. **Start/Endpoint:** Route follows a northeast/southwest direction from West Lake to State Bridge near Bond, Colorado. It includes sections of US 34, US 40, and CR 1. **Time to Allow:** 1.5 hours.

★1142★ **DINOSAUR DIAMOND PREHISTORIC HIGHWAY - COLORADO**
c/o Dinosaur Journey Museum
550 Jurassic Ct
Fruita, CO 81521
Web: www.dinosaurdiamond.org
Phone: 970-858-7282

Length: 152 miles (Colorado section); 328 miles (Utah section).
Designation/Year: National Scenic Byway (2002). **Description:** This route on the northern edge of the Colorado Plateau features some of the world's most significant dinosaur fossil quarries and museums. The Colorado section of the byway includes excavation sites such as Dinosaur Hill in Fruita, the Museum of Western Colorado, Dinosaur National Monument, and Colorado National Monument. Recreational opportunities along the route include biking, hiking, and camping. **Start/Endpoint:** The Colorado section of this two-state, 512-mile loop begins at Dinosaur, just over the Utah border, runs south on SR 64 to Rangely, south on SR 139 to Loma, then east to Fruita on US 6 and Grand Junction. The byway then loops back to the Utah section, west on I-70 to the Colorado-Utah border. **Time to Allow:** 3 hours (Colorado section); 10 hours (entire byway).

★1143★ **FRONTIER PATHWAYS SCENIC AND HISTORIC BYWAY**
c/o El Pueblo History Museum
301 North Union Ave
Pueblo, CO 81003
Web: www.frontierpathways.org
Phone: 719-583-8631
Length: 103 miles. **Designation/Year:** National Scenic Byway (1998). **Description:** Known for its topographic diversity, byway features historic homesteads, abandoned trading posts and stage stops, the pristine Wet Mountain Valley, and wildlife viewing pullouts. It passes through the San Isabel National Forest, which offers great opportunities for camping, hiking, biking, and wildlife viewing. It also offers views of the Sangre de Cristo Mountains, with 22 peaks reaching at least 13,000 feet. **Start/Endpoint:** Northern section of the byway runs from Pueblo along SR 96 through Wetmore, Silver Cliff, and Westcliffe. The southern section of the byway runs from Colorado City northwest on SR 165 for 52 miles to its junction with SR 96 at McKenzie Junction, then west along SR 96 to Westcliffe. **Time to Allow:** 2 hours.

★1144★ **GOLD BELT TOUR SCENIC AND HISTORIC BYWAY**
c/o BLM-Royal Gorge Resource Area
3170 East Main St
Canon City, CO 81212
Web: www.goldbeltbyway.com
Phone: 719-275-0631
Length: 135 miles. **Designation/Year:** National Scenic Byway (2000). **Description:** Byway follows historic railroad and stagecoach routes leading visitors to North America's greatest gold camp, three world class fossil sites, and numerous historic sites. Areas of interest include: Victor's National Historic District and Cripple Creek, the historical hub of the mining district; the Royal Gorge Railroad and the 1,053-foot suspension bridge spanning the Royal Gorge; and Florissant Fossil Beds National Monument and the Garden Park Fossil Area. Recreational opportunities include fishing, camping, hiking, mountain biking, and horseback riding. **Start/Endpoint:** Runs north/south from Florissant to Florence, Colorado, including three separate routes.

The 34-mile Phantom Canyon Road runs from Florence to Victor, the 26-mile Shelf Road runs from Cañon City to Cripple Creek, and the High Park Road segment connects Florence and Cañon City with Teller Road 1 and Teller Road 11. **Time to Allow:** 6 hours (including loops or backtracking)

★1145★ GRAND MESA SCENIC AND HISTORIC BYWAY

c/o Grand Mesa, Uncompahgre and Gunnison National Forests
USDA Forest Service - 2250 Highway 50
Delta, CO 81416
Web: www.grandmesabyway.org
Phone: 970-874-6600
Length: 63 miles. **Designation/Year:** National Scenic Byway (1996). **Description:** This 'playground in the sky' climbs through the dusty canyon of Plateau Creek to the evergreen forests of the mesa top, 11,000 feet above sea level. The impressive Grand Mesa, called Thunder Mountain by the Utes, was formed by lava flows, glaciers, and forces of erosion. It offers magnificent views of alpine forests and mountains of the surrounding region, and includes more than 300 lakes and reservoirs. It also offers views of the La Sal and the San Juan Mountains, both more than 60 miles away. **Start/Endpoint:** Follows CO 65 for its entirety from the northern end at the Mesa exit on I-70 to the southern terminus at Cedaredge. Also includes a spur route off CO 65 along Land's End Road to Land's End. **Time to Allow:** 2 hours.

★1146★ SAN JUAN SKYWAY

c/o San Juan National Forest
15 Burnett Ct
Durango, CO 81301
Web: www.fs.fed.us/r2/sanjuan/
Phone: 970-247-4874
Length: 233-mile loop. **Designation/Year:** All-American Road (1996). **Description:** Byway snakes through Old West towns like Durango, Silverton and Telluride, and twists through some of the most rugged mountains in the country on the famous Million Dollar Highway. It also passes along Mesa Verde National Park, all in the shadows of impressive 14,000-foot peaks. Skiing is one of the premier activities along the byway, and the five million acres of the San Juan and Uncompahgre National Forests offer opportunities for a variety of recreational activities. **Start/Endpoint:** From Durango, route runs north on US 550 past Hermosa, Silverton, and Ouray. It then follows CO 62 from near Ridgway to Placerville, then CO 145 to the southeast to the junction with US 160 near Cortez, then US 160 back to Durango to complete the entire loop. **Time to Allow:** 5 hours.

★1147★ SANTA FE TRAIL - COLORADO

PO Box 377
312 East Main St
Trinidad, CO 81082
Web: www.santafetrailscenicandhistoricbyway.org
Phone: 719-846-7217
Length: 184 miles (Colorado section); 565 miles (entire byway).

Designation/Year: National Scenic Byway (1998). **Description:** One of America's first great trade routes, the Santa Fe Trail (1821-1880) was also critical to the westward expansion of the United States. The section of the trail located in present-day Colorado traverses one of the last strongholds of the nomadic Plains Indians and one of the first toeholds of Anglo-American pioneers who began homesteading along the Arkansas River in the 1860s. **Start/Endpoint:** West on US 50 from the Kansas-Colorado state border to La Junta, then southwest on US 350 to the New Mexico-Colorado state border. **Time to Allow:** 4 hours (Colorado section); 12 hours (entire byway).

★1148★ TOP OF THE ROCKIES SCENIC AND HISTORIC BYWAY

c/o Leadville/Lake County Chamber of Commerce
809 Harrison Ave, PO Box 861
Leadville, CO 80461
Web: www.topoftherockiesbyway.org
Phone: 719-486-3900
Length: 75 miles. **Designation/Year:** National Scenic Byway (1998). **Description:** Byway climbs from 8,000 feet to over 11,300 feet above sea level where snowfall can exceed 360 inches per year. Travelers cross the 10,424-foot Tennessee Pass en route to the booming mining town of Leadville, the highest incorporated community in the US at 10,200 feet above sea level. Visitor activities include four-wheeling, mountain biking, horseback riding, and hiking on Colorado's highest mountains, Mount Elbert and Mount Massive, both reachng over 14,400 feet. The national forests surrounding Leadville offer opportunities for other outdoor activities such as snowmobiling, snowshoeing, fishing, wildlife viewing, and golf. **Start/Endpoint:** The Byway run east from Twin Lakes on SR 82 (Independence Pass Road), then north on US 24 to Leadville, where the byway forks into two routes. The northwest fork continues on US 24 north to Minturn. The northeast fork follows SR 91 to Copper Mountain. **Time to Allow:** 2.5 hours.

★1149★ TRAIL OF THE ANCIENTS - COLORADO

c/o Anasazi Heritage Center
27501 Highway 184
Dolores, CO 81323
Web: www.coloradobyways.org
Phone: 970-882-4811
Length: 112 miles (Colorado section); 480 miles (entire byway). **Designation/Year:** National Scenic Byway (2005). **Description:** The Trail provides access to numerous examples of Ancestral Puebloan culture and other aspects of the Four Corners history and culture. Areas of interest along the Colorado section of the byway include Mesa Verde National Park, Anasazi Heritage Center, Canyons of the Ancients National Monument (including Lowry Pueblo), and Hovenweep National Monument. **Start/Endpoint:** The Trail of the Ancients is a loop route in Colorado and Utah that may be started at any point along its length. From Mesa Verde National Park it runs west on US 160 toward Cortez and the junction with SR 145. In a counterclockwise direction, it then includes portions of SR 145, SR 184, US 491, county roads and spur routes, and MC Road 10 to Hovenweep National Monument at the Colorado-Utah state line. Completing the Colorado portion of the byway, from Cortez, the

route runs south on US 491, then west on US 160 to Four Corners Monument. **Time to Allow:** 3 hours (Colorado section); 9 hours including backtracking (entire byway).

★1150★ TRAIL RIDGE ROAD/BEAVER MEADOW ROAD
c/o Rocky Mountain National Park
1000 Highway 36
Estes Park, CO 80517
Web: www.nps.gov/romo/
Phone: 970-586-1206
Length: 48 miles. **Designation/Year:** All-American Road (1996). **Description:** Winding through the forests and mountains of Rocky Mountain National Park, Trail Ridge Road/Beaver Meadow Road is one of the most spectacular drives in the United States. Various overlooks offer views of wooded valleys, mountain peaks, a stunning array of wildflowers, and arctic climatic conditions. At 10,758-foot Milner Pass, the byway meets the Continental Divide National Scenic Trail, which ranges 3,100 miles from the Canada-Montana border to the Mexico-New Mexico border. The national park includes more than 350 miles of trails for hikers and backpackers of all skill levels. **Start/Endpoint:** Byway generally follows US 34 from Estes Park to Grand Lake, Colorado. **Time to Allow:** 2 hours.

CONNECTICUT

★1151★ CONNECTICUT STATE ROUTE 169
c/o Quinebaug-Shetucket Heritage Corridor Inc.
107 Providence St
Putnam, CT 06260
Web: www.thelastgreenvalley.org
Phone: 860-963-7226
Length: 32 miles. **Designation/Year:** National Scenic Byway (1996). **Description:** This 25-town historic route traverses one of the last unspoiled areas in the northeastern United States, with rustic farmlands, forests, farmsteads, open spaces, and historic structures and features. **Start/Endpoint:** Route runs north/south from the Connecticut-Massachusetts state line to Lisbon, Connecticut. **Time to Allow:** 1 hour.

★1152★ MERRITT PARKWAY
c/o Merritt Parkway Conservancy
PO Box 183
Westport, CT 06881
Web: www.merrittparkway.org
Phone: 203-661-3255
Length: 37 miles. **Designation/Year:** National Scenic Byway (1996). **Description:** Parkway was developed and designed with styles representative of American tastes of the 1930's with the idea of integrating the traveled way, roadside, and adjoining landscape together into a natural setting. It is one of the only roads listed on the National Register of Historic Places and includes a number of places along the way related to nature reservation, including the Audubon Center in Greenwich, with 15 miles of hiking trails and more than 500 acres of woodlands and meadows, and the 63-acre Bartlett Arboretum in North

Stamford. **Start/Endpoint:** Includes the portion of SR 15 from the New York state line north to the Sikorsky Bridge, which crosses the Housatonic River, at the Stratford-Milford town line. **Time to Allow:** 1 hour.

DELAWARE

★1153★ BRANDYWINE VALLEY SCENIC BYWAY
c/o Greater Wilmington Convention & Visitors Bureau
100 W 10th St
Wilmington, DE 19801
Web: www.visitwilmingtonde.com
Phone: 302-652-4088
Length: 12.25 miles. **Designation/Year:** National Scenic Byway (2005). **Description:** The Brandywine Valley shows the legacy of the prominent families in the industrial development of the nation for over two centuries, featuring a concentration of historic sites, estates, gardens and museums. Points of interest include the Hotel du Pont and the du Pont Theatre, the Nemours and Winterthur estates, Longwood Gardens, Hagley Museum and Library, Delaware Museum of Natural History, and Brandywine River Museum. **Start/Endpoint:** Begins at the Pennsylvania state line at DE 52 (Kennett Pike) and continues to Wilmington city limits. Also branches off DE 52 (Pennsylvania Avenue) to DE 100 (Montchanin Road) and continues to the Pennsylvania state line. **Time to Allow:** 1 hour.

FLORIDA

★1154★ A1A SCENIC & HISTORIC COASTAL BYWAY
c/o Saint Augustine, Ponte Vedra, & The Beaches Visitor and Convention Bureau
88 Riberia St, Suite 400
Saint Augustine, FL 32084
Web: www.scenica1a.org
Phone: 800-653-2489
Length: 72 miles. **Designation/Year:** National Scenic Byway (2002). **Description:** Paralleling a coastal barrier island and the Atlantic coast, byway offers breathtaking views of the Atlantic Ocean and includes important sites in Florida history such as the Colonial Spanish Quarter, Fort Matanzas, Castillo de San Marcos, and Fort Mose. The byway passes through Saint Augustine, the nation's oldest continually occupied European settlement. Recreational visitors traveling the byway can enjoy swimming, fishing, and wildlife viewing, including the Florida Birding Trail. **Start/Endpoint:** Begins at the Duval/Saint Johns County boundary line near Ponte Vedra Beach and continues south along State Road A1A until its terminus at the Flagler/Volusia County Line south of Flagler Beach. **Time to Allow:** 2 hours.

★1155★ INDIAN RIVER LAGOON SCENIC HIGHWAY
c/o Indian River County Chamber of Commerce
1216 21st St
Vero Beach, FL 32960
Web: www.byways.org/browse/byways/16199/
Phone: 772-567-3491

Length: 150 miles. **Designation/Year:** National Scenic Byway (2002). **Description:** Byway meanders through three national wildlife refuges, several state and local parks and sanctuaries, and the Kennedy Space Center. Recreational opportunities along the byway include swimming, surfing, sailing, boating, fishing, bird-watching, hiking, and biking. The Indian River Lagoon is the most biologically diverse estuary in North America, home to more than 4,000 species of plants and animals. **Start/Endpoint:** Runs along Florida's Atlantic Coast from the Canaveral National Seashore near Titusville south to Wabasso. It includes portions of A1A, US 1, SR 3, and SR 405. **Time to Allow:** 4 hours.

★1156★ TAMIAMI TRAIL SCENIC HIGHWAY

c/o Everglades Area Chamber of Commerce
PO Box 130
Everglades City, FL 34139
Web: www.byways.org/browse/byways/12130/
Phone: 239-695-3172
Length: 49.5 miles. **Designation/Year:** National Scenic Byway (2000). **Description:** Byway features scenic Florida landscapes with excellent opportunities for wildlife viewing, from alligators to birds. Tracts of public land along the route include Big Cypress National Preserve, Everglades National Park, Ten Thousand Islands National Wildlife Refuge, and the Fakahatchee and Collier-Seminole state parks. **Start/Endpoint:** Runs east/west along US 41 from Naples to Miami, Florida. **Time to Allow:** 4 hours.

GEORGIA

★1157★ RUSSELL-BRASSTOWN SCENIC BYWAY

c/o Chattahoochee-Oconee National Forests
1755 Cleveland Hwy
Gainesville, GA 30501
Web: www.fs.fed.us/conf/
Phone: 770-297-3000
Length: 41 miles. **Designation/Year:** National Scenic Byway (2000). **Description:** Encircled by the scenic beauty of the Chattahoochee National Forest, byway runs through the fertile valleys and mountain gaps of the southern Appalachians. Scenic areas along the route include Unicoi and Vogel state parks, Anna Ruby Falls Scenic Area, High Shoals Creek Falls Scenic Area, Raven Cliff Falls & Wilderness Area, Dukes Creek Falls, Smithgall-Woods Dukes Creek Conservation Area, and Tray Mountain Wilderness. **Start/Endpoint:** Byway runs from Robertstown north along SR 17/75, then southwest along SR 180, southeast along SR 348, completing the loop at SR 75 Alternate. **Time to Allow:** 3 hours.

IDAHO

★1158★ INTERNATIONAL SELKIRK LOOP - IDAHO

PO Box 920
Bonners Ferry, ID 83805
Web: www.selkirkloop.org
Phone: 888-823-2626

Length: 89 miles (Idaho section); 166 miles (US section); 280 miles (entire byway in the US and Canada). **Designation/Year:** All-American Road (2005). **Description:** Following rivers and lakeshores most of the way, the byway encircles the Selkirk Mountains in northeast Washington, north Idaho, and southeast British Columbia. This section of the byway passes through the Idaho panhandle's scenic recreation area, including several sections of the Panhandle National Forest and between Lake Pend Oreille and Priest Lake. The Panhandle National Forest provides a variety of year-round recreational opportunities, including downhill skiing and snowmobiling, snowboarding, bicycling, hiking, fishing, boating, horseback riding, and hunting. The public lands bordering the loop are home to the largest diversity of wildlife in the lower 48 states with more than 50 mammal and 265+ bird species. **Start/Endpoint:** A loop route through northern Idaho, northeastern Washington, and southeastern British Columbia. Idaho section of the byway runs from the Washington state border near Oldtown, east on US 2, then north on US 95 and SR 1 to the US-Canadian border near Porthill, Idaho. **Time to Allow:** 2 hours (Idaho section); 8-10 hours (entire byway including ferry ride and US-Canadian border crossings).

★1159★ NORTHWEST PASSAGE SCENIC BYWAY

c/o North Central Idaho Travel Association
PO Box 2018
Lewiston, ID 83501
Web: northcentralidaho.info
Phone: 877-364-3246
Length: 202 miles. **Designation/Year:** All-American Road (2005). **Description:** Byway traces the historic route of Meriwether Lewis and William Clark as they searched for a passage between the Missouri and Columbia rivers. The 1.8-million-acre Clearwater River offers opportunities for kayaking and whitewater rafting. Along the route visitors can explore Lewis and Clark Expedition campsites, numerous Nez Perce historical and cultural sites, and the Nez Perce National Historical Park Museum at Spalding. **Start/Endpoint:** Follows US 12 from Spalding along the Clearwater River to Kooskia, Idaho. From there it follows Idaho SR 13 to Grangeville. **Time to Allow:** 5.5 hours.

★1160★ PAYETTE RIVER SCENIC BYWAY

c/o Donnelly Chamber of Commerce
PO Box 83
Donnelly, ID 83615
Web: www.byways.org/browse/byways/2037/
Phone: 208-325-3545
Length: 112 miles. **Designation/Year:** National Scenic Byway (2002). **Description:** Passing through Boise and Payette National forests, this scenic route offers travelers views of mountain forests, Payette Lake, Cascade Reservoir, and Payette River, where visitors can enjoy whitewater rafting and other recreational activities. Points of interest include the resort towns of Cascade, McCall, and New Meadows, the Thunder Mountain Historic Train Ride and Horseshoe Bend, and Rainbow Bridge, which is listed on the National Register of Historic Places. **Start/Endpoint:** Route begins at the junction of US 95 and New

Meadows and parallels the Payette River along SR 55 south to a junction with SR 44 in Eagle. **Time to Allow:** 2.5 hours.

★1161★ PEND OREILLE SCENIC BYWAY

c/o Hope-Clark Fork Chamber of Commerce
PO Box 159
Clark Fork, ID 83811
Web: www.poby.org/
Phone: 208-266-1101
Length: 33 miles. **Designation/Year:** National Scenic Byway (2002). **Description:** Byway provides access to the region's rugged mountain scenery and abundant water recreation opportunities. It flanks the eastern edge of Lake Pend Oreille, the fifth deepest lake in the United States, and skirts the western side of Kaniksu National Forest, which offers opportunities for camping, hiking, and mountain biking. In the winter, the Schweitzer Mountain Resort offers skiing, snowboarding, and snowmobiling. **Start/Endpoint:** From west to east, byway runs from the junction of US 95 north of Sandpoint along ID 200 to the Montana state line. It passes through the small towns of Hope, East Hope, and Clark Fork. **Time to Allow:** 40 minutes.

★1162★ PIONEER HISTORIC BYWAY

c/o Pioneer Country Travel Council of Southeastern Idaho
PO Box 669
Lava Hot Springs, ID 83246
Web: www.seidaho.org
Phone: 888-201-1063
Length: 127 miles. **Designation/Year:** National Scenic Byway (2005). **Description:** Many of the historical and cultural milestones along the route can be traced to the mid 1800s, when Mormon pioneers began settling the area. Areas of interest include: Franklin, Idaho's oldest city; the Bear River Massacre National Historic Site, where 250 Native Americans were killed by an American army unit; Sheep Rock, the first split of the Oregon-California Trail; Hooper Springs Park in Soda Springs; Grays Lake National Wildlife Refuge and Caribou Mountain; Tincup Canyon in Caribou National Forest; and 500,000-year-old Niter Ice Cave. **Start/Endpoint:** Follows ID 34 from the Wyoming state line south to Soda Springs, where it crosses the Oregon Trail-Bear Lake Scenic Byway (US 30). From there it continues south on ID 34, then follows US 91 to the Utah state line. **Time to Allow:** 2.5 hours.

★1163★ WESTERN HERITAGE HISTORIC BYWAY

c/o Kuna Chamber of Commerce
PO Box 123
Kuna, ID 83634
Web: www.byways.org/browse/byways/2593/
Phone: 208-922-9254
Length: 40 miles. **Designation/Year:** National Scenic Byway (2005). **Description:** Byway traverses dramatic landscapes, historic sites, and 21 miles of the 600,000-acre Snake River Birds of Prey National Conservation Area, home to the densest population of breeding raptors in North America. The conservation area is used by 24 species of birds of prey including hawks, eagles, falcons, osprey, harriers, and owls. Areas of interest along the byway include historic Kuna, the Silver Trail, Swan

Falls Dam, and Celebration Park, Idaho's first archeological park. **Start/Endpoint:** From Meridian, byway runs along ID 69 to East Avalon Avenue in Kuna, then south on Swan Falls Road to Swan Falls Dam. **Time to Allow:** 1 hour.

ILLINOIS

★1164★ GREAT RIVER ROAD - ILLINOIS

c/o Western Illinois Tourism Development Office
581 South Deere Rd
Macomb, IL 61455
Web: www.greatriverroad-illinois.org
Phone: 877-477-7007
Length: 557 miles (Illinois section); 2,069 miles (entire byway). **Designation/Year:** National Scenic Byway (2000). **Description:** The 2,069-mile Great River Road borders the Mississippi River through the states of Mississippi, Arkansas, Iowa, Illinois, Wisconsin, and Minnesota. The Illinois section of the byway along the Mississippi River flood plain includes 29 state recreation and/or conservation areas. Areas of interest include: Cahokia Mounds, a designated World Heritage Site that features 68 man-made mounds; the historic town of Nauvoo; the John Deere Pavilion in Moline; 8000-acre Pere Marquette State Park; and Spring Lake/Upper Mississippi River National Wildlife Refuge. **Start/Endpoint:** Byway spans the entire western edge of Illinois from Galena south to Cairo.

★1165★ HISTORIC NATIONAL ROAD - ILLINOIS

c/o National Road Association of Illinois
800 East Industrial Dr
Toledo, IL 62468
Web: www.nationalroad.org
Phone: 217-849-3188
Length: 165 miles (Illinois); 824 miles (entire route). **Designation/Year:** All-American Road (2002). **Description:** America's first interstate highway, the National Road was built to to link the people and cities along the Eastern seaboard to those on the frontiers west of the Allegheny Mountains. Authorized by Congress in 1806, construction of the road began in Cumberland, Maryland in 1811. The road reached Vandalia, then the Illinois state capitol, in 1839 and later was completed to the Illinois border at East Saint Louis, opening a link to the water route of the Mississippi. Point of interest along the Illinois section of the route include Cahokia Mounds State Historic Site, Franciscan Monastery Museum, and Lincoln Log Cabin State Historic Site. The Eads Bridge, located on the western terminus of the National Road on the Mississippi River was built by the self-taught engineer, James Buchanan Eads. Completed in 1874, it was the the first bridge to span the Mississippi River and is still in use today. **Start/Endpoint:** The east/west route runs from Baltimore, Maryland, to the Mississippi River at the Eads Bridge in East Saint Louis, Illinois. It crosses six states: Maryland, West Virginia, Pennsylvania, Ohio, Indiana, and Illinois. The Illinois section of the byway runs along US 40, following the original route surveyed in 1828, beginning at the Indiana state line near Terre Haute.

★1166★ HISTORIC ROUTE 66 - ILLINOIS

c/o Illinois Route 66 Heritage Project, Inc.
CITDO - 700 E. Adams
Springfield, IL 62704
Web: www.illinoisroute66.org
Phone: 217-525-7980
Length: 436 miles (Illinois section); 1,410 miles (entire byway).
Designation/Year: National Scenic Byway (2005). **Description:** Route 66 was designated in 1926 as a federal highway linking Chicago, IL to Los Angeles, CA. The 2,448-mile route passed through Illinois, Missouri, Kansas, Oklahoma, Texas, New Mexico, Arizona, and California. The road was decommissioned in 1985 in favor of the new interstate highway system and today only 1,410 miles of the original route in three states (Illinois, New Mexico and Arizona) have been designated as National Scenic Byway.Traversing more than 70 Illinois communities, the ''Mother Road'' joins the urban cityscape of Chicago with the countryside of Illinois' heartland, presenting memories of an era in the development of the American highway through restored and preserved attractions. **Start/Endpoint:** The Illinois section of the byway runs from Chicago southwest to the Martin Luther King Memorial Bridge at the Missouri state line. **Time to Allow:** 8 hours (Illinois section); 5-6 days (entire byway).

★1167★ ILLINOIS RIVER ROAD: ROUTE OF THE
        VOYAGEURS

Peioria Area Convention & Visitors Bureau
456 Fulton St, Suite 300
Peoria, IL 61602
Web: www.fermatainc.com/voyageurs/
Phone: 800-747-0302
Length: 291 miles. **Designation/Year:** National Scenic Byway (2005). **Description:** Byway preserves the natural river country along the banks of the Illinois River, following the routes of some of the early French explorers (les Voyageurs). It parallels the Illinois River Country Nature Trail, a chain of 100+ nature-based destinations in the Illinois River Valley. Natural areas such as the Wildlife Prairie State Park and the Emiquon National Wildlife Refuge provide habitat for several of the species that have come to characterize the American frontier experience, such as buffalo, wild geese, and the American bald eagle. **Start/ Endpoint:** Byway is a series of roadways paralleling the Illinois River on both sides of the river from Ottawa, near the I&M Canal Corridor, southwest to Havana at the intersection of US 136 in central Illinois. **Time to Allow:** 7 hours.

★1168★ LINCOLN HIGHWAY

Illinois Lincoln Highway Coalition
200 South State St
Belvidere, IL 61008
Web: www.lincolnhwyil.com
Phone: 866-455-4249
Length: 179 miles. **Designation/Year:** National Scenic Byway (2000). **Description:** The historic byway follows the original alignment of the Lincoln Highway, the first paved, transcontinental highway in the United States. It was the site of the first ''seedling mile'' of paved roadway, conceived and promoted by Carl Fisher to demonstrate the superiority of pavement over dirt roads. Byway passes through several cities and historic sites, and preserves some of the original navigation markers, allowing visitors to get a sense of the original journey. **Start/Endpoint:** Byway crosses the width of northern Illinois from Lynwood, just south of Chicago on the Illinois-Indiana border, to Fulton on the Mississippi River. Most of the Illinois section of the byway follows US 30 and IL 38. **Time to Allow:** 3 hours.

★1169★ MEETING OF THE GREAT RIVERS SCENIC
        ROUTE

c/o Alton Regional Convention and Visitors Bureau
200 Piasa St
Alton, IL 62002
Web: www.byways.org/browse/byways/10393/
Phone: 800-258-6645
Length: 33 miles. **Designation/Year:** National Scenic Byway (1998). **Description:** Route allows visitors to discover the natural and historical heritage of southern Illinois, offering a view of the floodplain where the Mississippi, Missouri, and Illinois rivers join together. Areas of interest include: the Camp River Dubois State Historic Site, which commemorates the beginning of Lewis and Clark's expedition to the Pacific; the historic city of Alton, where Abraham Lincoln and Stephen Douglas held their final debate in the race for U.S. Senate; the 25-mile Sam Vadalabene Bike Trail, which parallels the Mississippi River and is one of the most scenic bike routes in the region; and the town of Elsah, one of the only towns to be put on the National Historic Register in its entirety. **Start/Endpoint:** The Byway runs from Pere Marquette State Park along IL 100, IL 143, and IL 3 to south of the city of Hartford.

★1170★ OHIO RIVER SCENIC BYWAY - ILLINOIS

c/o Southernmost Illinois Tourism Bureau
PO Box 378
Anna, IL 62906
Web: www.southernmostillinois.com
Phone: 800-248-4373
Length: 188 miles (Illinois section); 943 miles (entire byway)
Designation/Year: National Scenic Byway (1998). **Description:** Byway winds across Ohio, Indiana, and Illinois, telling the story of the Ohio River, which has shaped the landscape, people, and economics of the region since its beginning 10,000 years ago. The Illinois section of the byway includes: Fort Massac State Park, featuring a reconstruction of the timber fortification (built in 1794), a museum, interpretive programs, and opportunities for camping, hiking, boating, and hunting; Fort Defiance State Park, which commemorates the Civil War Fort Defiance, commanded by General U.S. Grant; the Trail of Tears, where the Cherokee passed through southern Illinois on their tragic journey; and Shawnee National Forest, which includes Garden of the Gods, named for its impressive rock formations. **Start/Endpoint:** Byway winds from Saline and Gallatin counties on SR 146, following the Ohio River south through Hardin and Pope counties. It then runs west through Massac and Pulaski counties, ending at the confluence of the Ohio and Mississippi rivers at Cairo. **Time to Allow:** 4 hours (Illinois section).

INDIANA

★1171★ HISTORIC NATIONAL ROAD - INDIANA

c/o Indiana National Road Association
PO Box 284
Cambridge City, IN 47327
Web: www.indiananationalroad.org
Phone: 765-478-3172
Length: 156 miles (Indiana); 824 miles (entire route). **Designation/Year:** All-American Road (2002). **Description:** America's first interstate highway, the National Road was built to to link the people and cities along the Eastern seaboard to those on the frontiers west of the Allegheny Mountains. Authorized by Congress in 1806, construction of the road began in Cumberland, Maryland in 1811. The road reached Vandalia, then the Illinois state capitol, in 1839 and later was completed to the Illinois border at East Saint Louis, opening a link to the water route of the Mississippi.Spanning the breadth of the state, the Indiana section of the National Road follows Highway 40 right through the heart of Indiana and its capital, Indianapolis. Points of interest include: Antique Alley, featuring more than 900 antique dealers in a 33-mile stretch; Children's Museum of Indianapolis, Indianapolis Motor Speedway, and the Richmond Railroad Depot Historic District. **Start/Endpoint:** The east/west route runs from Baltimore, Maryland, to the Mississippi River at the Eads Bridge in East Saint Louis, Illinois. It crosses six states: Maryland, West Virginia, Pennsylvania, Ohio, Indiana, and Illinois. The Indiana section of the road follows US 40 from Richmond, near the Ohio border, to West Terre Haute, near the Illinois border.

★1172★ OHIO RIVER SCENIC BYWAY - INDIANA

c/o Ohio River Scenic Route Inc.
315 Southern Indiana Ave
Jeffersonville, IN 47130
Web: www.ohioriverscenicroute.org
Phone: 812-282-6654
Length: 303 miles (Indiana section); 943 miles (entire byway). **Designation/Year:** National Scenic Byway (1996). **Description:** Byway winds across Ohio, Indiana, and Illinois, telling the story of the Ohio River, which has shaped the landscape, people, and economics of the region since its beginning 10,000 years ago. The Indiana section parallels the Ohio River, passing through the hills and farmlands of the southern part of the state. Areas of interest include: Howard Steamboat Museum, Carnegie Center for Art and History, Lincoln's Boyhood National Monument, and the Hoosier National Forest, which offers opportunities for hiking, sailing, boating, fishing, mountain biking, and horseback riding. **Start/Endpoint:** Extends from Lawrenceberg on US 50 over US 56, 62, 66 and I-164 to the Illinois state border. **Time to Allow:** 6 hours (Indiana section).

IOWA

★1173★ GREAT RIVER ROAD - IOWA

c/o Iowa Department of Tourism
200 East Grand Ave
Des Moines, IA 50309
Web: www.byways.org/browse/byways/2190/
Phone: 888-472-6035
Length: 326 miles (Iowa section); 2,069 miles (entire byway). **Designation/Year:** National Scenic Byway (2000). **Description:** The 2,069-mile Great River Road borders the Mississippi River through the states of Mississippi, Arkansas, Iowa, Illinois, Wisconsin, and Minnesota. The 326-mile stretch in Iowa preserves historic resources associated with the Mississippi River and the story of transportation. Visitors can explore the towns and cities along the route, experience the Mississippi River on steamboats, commercial barges, and recreational crafts, visit sacred sites and landscape effigies of Native Americans (including Effigy Mounds National Monument), and view bald eagles and the migration of 100,000 geese and ducks along the Mississippi Flyway. **Start/Endpoint:** Follows the Mississippi River along Iowa's eastern border from the Minnesota state line near New Albin south to the Missouri state line near Keokuk. **Time to Allow:** 6 hours (Iowa section); 6 days (entire byway).

★1174★ LOESS HILLS SCENIC BYWAY

c/o Harrison County Historical Village & Iowa Welcome Center
2931 Monroe Ave
Missouri Valley, IA 51555
Web: www.harrisoncountyparks.org
Phone: 712-642-2114
Length: 220 miles. **Designation/Year:** National Scenic Byway (2000). **Description:** Byway weaves through a landform of windblown silt deposits that formed a yellow soil called loess along the eastern edge of the Missouri River Valley. Strong windstorms deposited layers of loess several hundred feet thick on both sides of the Missouri River Valley, molding the soft soil into sheer ridges and rippled hills. The Loess Hills region includes many culturally and historically important sites, public parks, and recreation areas. **Start/Endpoint:** Byway follows the Missouri River along western Iowa from Akron near the South Dakota state line to the Missouri state line south of Hamburg. **Time to Allow:** 5 hours.

KANSAS

★1175★ FLINT HILLS SCENIC BYWAY

c/o Flint Hills Scenic Byway Committee
PO Box 387
Cottonwood Falls, KS 66845
Web: www.ksbyways.org/flint/index.html
Phone: 620-273-8686
Length: 48 miles. **Designation/Year:** National Scenic Byway (2005). **Description:** Byway offers panoramic vistas of the tallgrass prairie and an opportunity to learn what early pioneers experienced as they travelled the Santa Fe Trail. Areas of interest along the route feature: Tallgrass Prairie National Preserve; historic sites in Council Grove including the Kaw Mission State Historic Site and Museum, Council Oak, Santa Fe Trail, Old Cowboy Jail, Post Office Oak and Museum; and Cottonwood Falls, site of the Chase County Courthouse (in operation since 1873) and the Roniger Native American Museum. **Start/Endpoint:** Crosses the Flint Hills of Kansas on SH 177 between Council Grove and Cassoday. **Time to Allow:** 1 hour.

★1176★ WETLANDS AND WILDLIFE SCENIC BYWAY

c/o Great Bend Convention & Visitors Bureau
PO Box 274
Great Bend, KS 67530
Web: www.ksbyways.org/wetlands/index.html
Phone: 620-792-2750
Length: 77 miles. **Designation/Year:** National Scenic Byway (2005). **Description:** Byway winds around Cheyenne Bottoms and Quivira National Wildlife Refuge, two of the largest wetland ecosystems in the world. The Cheyenne Bottoms Wildlife Area covers 20,000 acres and is considered the largest marsh in the interior of the United States and the most important migration point for shorebirds in North America. Less than 20 miles away, the 22,135-acre Quivira National Wildlife Refuge is a staging area for more than 500,000 birds during their spring migration. Opportunities abound for bird and wildlife watching, hiking, and many other nature activities at both locations. **Start/Endpoint:** Byway begins 5 miles west of Hoisington, at the west junction of US 281 and SH 4; and end at the junction of Route 636 with with US 281. **Time to Allow:** 1.5 hours.

KENTUCKY

★1177★ COUNTRY MUSIC HIGHWAY

c/o Southern & Eastern Kentucky Tourism Development
 Association
2292 South Hwy 27
Somerset, KY 42501
Web: www.countrymusichighway.com
Phone: 606-677-6095
Length: 144 miles. **Designation/Year:** National Scenic Byway (2002). **Description:** Running almost the entire length of eastern Kentucky, byway was home to a large number of well-known country musicians who were born along an eight-county stretch of Highway US 23. These include Loretta Lynn, Wynonna Judd, Naomi Judd, Billy Ray Cyrus, Tom T. Hall, Ricky Skaggs, Keith Whitley, Dwight Yoakam, and Patty Loveless. Byway also passes through areas which are rich in the history of Native Americans, pioneers, the Civil War, and the mining industry. **Start/Endpoint:** Follows US 23 south from Ashland to Whitesburg, Kentucky. **Time to Allow:** 2.5 hours.

★1178★ RED RIVER GORGE SCENIC BYWAY

c/o Southern & Eastern Kentucky Tourism Development
 Association
2292 South Highway 27
Somerset, KY 42501
Web: www.byways.org/browse/byways/2482/
Phone: 606-677-6095
Length: 46 miles. **Designation/Year:** National Scenic Byway (2002). **Description:** Byway features more than a hundred natural stone arches, formed by the action of wind and water over 70 million years. It winds through the 700,000-acre Daniel Boone National Forest, a rugged area characterized by steep forested ridges, narrow valleys, and more than 3,400 miles of cliffline. Area provides opportunities for outdoor adventure such as canoeing, rock climbing, and kayaking. **Start/Endpoint:** Follows KY 11, KY 715, and KY 15 from Stanton to Zachariah, Kentucky. **Time to Allow:** 1 hour.

★1179★ WILDERNESS ROAD HERITAGE HIGHWAY

c/o Southern & Eastern Kentucky Tourism Development
 Association
2292 South Highway 27
Somerset, KY 42501
Web: www.byways.org/browse/byways/2566/
Phone: 606-677-6095
Length: 94 miles. **Designation/Year:** National Scenic Byway (2002). **Description:** Byway traces and interprets the migration of early pioneers and explorers through the Cumberland Gap and the subsequent development of Kentucky's nationally renowned folk art and country music heritage. Areas of interest include Cumberland Gap National Historic Park, which offers panoramic views of the Appalachians, as well as Berea, the ''Folk Arts & Crafts Capital of Kentucky.'' **Start/Endpoint:** Byway follows US 25E for 30 miles through Middlesboro and Pineville to the junction with KY 229 just north of Barbourville, then north on KY 229 for 21 miles to the junction with US 25 in London, and then north on US 25 through Laurel and Rockcastle counties to Berea in Madison County. **Time to Allow:** 2 hours.

LOUISIANA

★1180★ CREOLE NATURE TRAIL

c/o Southwest Louisiana Convention & Visitors Bureau
1205 N. Lakeshore Dr
Lake Charles, LA 70601
Web: www.creolenaturetrail.org
Phone: 800-456-7952
Length: 180 miles. **Designation/Year:** All-American Road (2002). **Description:** Byway passes through thousands of acres of untouched wetlands, including four national wildlife refuges, salt and freshwater resources. It also features Civil War and archeological digsites, and miles of natural beaches, marshlands, and prairie lands. Visitors can enjoy wildlife viewing, bicycling, hunting, boating, swimming and other recreational activities. Following Hurricane Rita, which hit southwest Louisiana on September 23, 2005, the Creole Nature Trail All-American Road has been in a state of recovery. **Start/Endpoint:** Beginning on SR 27 near Sulphur and Lake Charles, byway cuts through the marshlands of southern Calcasieu and Cameron parishes and hugs the coast of the Gulf of Mexico. Other entrances are located on LA 82 at the Texas state line and the Vermilion Parish line; exit 36 from I-10; and just north of the Lake Charles Regional Airport on LA 385. **Time to Allow:** 4.5 hours.

MAINE

★1181★ ACADIA BYWAY

Acadia National Park
P.O. Box 177 - Eagle Lake Road
Bar Harbor, ME 04609
Web: www.byways.org/browse/byways/13791/
Phone: 207-288-3338

8. National Scenic Byways

Length: 40 miles. **Designation/Year:** All-American Road (2000). **Description:** Scenic Loop road through Acadia National Park offers views of the rugged Maine coastline as well as access to Bar Harbor, Sand Beach, Thunder Hole, Otter Cliffs, Jordan Pond, Cadillac Mountain, and the ferry to the Cranberry Islands. The Park Loop Road was designed around biking and walking recreational activities. **Start/Endpoint:** Route begins in Trenton, Maine at the Thompson Island Bridge. The Park Loop Road is closed from late November to mid-April. **Time to Allow:** 3 hours.

★1182★ OLD CANADA ROAD SCENIC BYWAY
c/o Maine Office of Tourism
#59 State House Station
Augusta, ME 04333
Web: www.byways.org/browse/byways/11510/
Phone: 888-624-6345
Length: 78 miles. **Designation/Year:** National Scenic Byway (2000). **Description:** Byway winds alongside the Kennebec River, Wyman Lake, The Dead River, and vast forests, passing through villages and outposts that are much as they were at the turn of the century. It crosses the Appalachian National Scenic Trail at Caratunk and passes near Moxie Falls, the tallest waterfall in the state. **Start/Endpoint:** From Twelve Corners, where US 201 intersects with SR 43, north along US 201 to the Canadian border. **Time to Allow:** 2.5 hours.

★1183★ RANGELEY LAKES SCENIC BYWAY
c/o Rangeley Lakes Chamber of Commerce
P. O. Box 317
Rangely, ME 04970
Web: www.rangeleymaine.com
Phone: 800-685-2537
Length: 36 miles. **Designation/Year:** National Scenic Byway (2000). **Description:** Byway winds through the mountains of Maine, passing over 33,000 acres of conserved public access lands. It crosses the Appalachian Trail twice and runs along the shores of Rangeley Lake, the centerpiece of 112 interconnected lakes and ponds scattered throughout the region. Recreational activities include fishing, hiking, skiing, snowmobiling, wildlife viewing, and leaf watching. **Start/Endpoint:** From Small Falls, follows SR4 and SR17 to just south of Height of Land. **Time to Allow:** 2.5 hours.

★1184★ SCHOODIC SCENIC BYWAY
c/o Schoodic Area Chamber of Commerce
PO Box 381
Winter Harbor, ME 04693
Web: www.schoodicbyway.org
Phone: 207-963-7658
Length: 29 miles. **Designation/Year:** National Scenic Byway (2000). **Description:** Traversing an unspoiled region of northeastern Maine, byway passes along villages and waterfronts, several lighthouses, the only mainland portion of Acadia National Park, and close to Petit Manan National Wildlife Refuge. It offers views of Cadillac Mountain and Frenchman Bay, fields of blueberry, and wildflowers. **Start/Endpoint:** Begins on US 1 where the Hancock-Sullivan Bridge crosses Taunton Bay.

Continues through Sullivan to SR 186 in Gouldsboro, then follows SR 186 through Winter Harbor to the Schoodic Loop Road. After traversing the loop through Acadia National Park, the byway rejoins SR 186 in Birch Harbor and runs east, ending in Prospect Harbor. **Time to Allow:** 1.5 hours.

MARYLAND

★1185★ CATOCTIN MOUNTAIN SCENIC BYWAY
c/o Tourism Council of Frederick County
19 East Church St
Frederick, MD 21701
Web: www.fredericktourism.org
Phone: 800-999-3613
Length: 38 miles. **Designation/Year:** National Scenic Byway (2005). **Description:** Byway provides access to two national parks, the state's highest waterfall, abundant hiking and biking trails, as well as historic downtown areas and Civil War sites. Home to Camp David, the nearby Catoctin Mountain National Park (see separate entry in National Parks section) contains thousands of acres of federally protected land, including an extensive trail system and camping areas. **Start/Endpoint:** From the Pennsyvania state line, south on US 15 and US 340 to the Potomac River at the Virginia state line. **Time to Allow:** 1 hour.

★1186★ CHESAPEAKE COUNTRY SCENIC BYWAY
c/o Kent County Tourism Development Office
400 High St
Chestertown, MD 21620
Web: www.byways.org/browse/byways/2261/
Phone: 410-778-0416
Length: 85 miles. **Designation/Year:** National Scenic Byway (2002). **Description:** The network of routes that comprise this byway allows visitors to experience Colonial history, Revolutionary War battlefields, crossroad communities, rural farmland, water-based recreation, scenic vistas, and more. Situated along the Atlantic Flyway, it includes wildlife refuges and management areas that are major feeding and resting places for migratory and wintering waterfowl. Nowhere along this Byway is the visitor far from the tributaries that feed the Chesapeake Bay or from the Bay itself. **Start/Endpoint:** The Upper Eastern Shore section of the byway runs from the Chesapeake Bay Bridge to the Chesapeake and Delaware Canal. There are many main and secondary roads that lead to the byway, but starting at the northern or southern entrance will provide the most complete experience. **Time to Allow:** 2.5 hours.

★1187★ HISTORIC NATIONAL ROAD - MARYLAND
c/o Maryland Scenic Byways
State Highway Administration - 707 North Calvert Street
Baltimore, MD 21202
Web: www.sha.state.md.us/exploremd/oed/scenicByways/
  BywaysProgram.asp
Phone: 410-545-8637
Length: 170 miles (Maryland); 824 miles (entire route). **Designation/Year:** All-American Road (2002). **Description:** America's first interstate highway, the National Road was built to to

link the people and cities along the Eastern seaboard to those on the frontiers west of the Allegheny Mountains. Authorized by Congress in 1806, construction of the road began in Cumberland, Maryland in 1811. The road reached Vandalia, then the Illinois state capitol, in 1839 and later was completed to the Illinois border at East Saint Louis, opening a link to the water route of the Mississippi.The Maryland section of the byway offers access to the Blue Ridge Mountains, the B&O Railroad Museum in Baltimore, the C&O Canal, the 40,000-acre Green Ridge State Forest, and a number of cities including Baltimore, Frederick, Ellicott City, Hagerstown, and Cumberland. **Start/Endpoint:** The east/west route runs from Baltimore, Maryland, to the Mississippi River at the Eads Bridge in East Saint Louis, Illinois. It crosses six states: Maryland, West Virginia, Pennsylvania, Ohio, Indiana, and Illinois. The Maryland section of the road runs from the Inner Harbor in Baltimore west to the Pennsylvania state line near Keysers Ridge, including sections of Alt US 40 and MD 144.

MICHIGAN

★1188★ COPPER COUNTRY TRAIL

c/o Keweenaw Convention & Visitors Bureau
Calumet, MI 49913
Web: www.keweenaw.info
Phone: 906-337-4579
Length: 47 miles. **Designation/Year:** National Scenic Byway (2005). **Description:** Byway tells the story of copper on the Keweenaw Peninsula, featuring museums, former mining communities, and a national historic park along the way. Points of interest include: Keweenaw National Historical Park (two separate units); Fort Wilkins State Park, once an active US Army base built to keep peace in Michigan's Copper Country; Brockway Mountain, featuring a nine-mile scenic drive that offers spectacular views of Lake Superior; and the Eagle Harbor Lighthouse and Museums. **Start/Endpoint:** Byway begins at the Portage Lake Lift Bridge, the only road access to the Keweenaw Peninsula, then follows US 41 north to Copper Harbor. **Time to Allow:** 1 hour.

★1189★ RIVER ROAD SCENIC BYWAY

c/o Huron-Manistee National Forests
River Road, Oscoda - Hale
Oscoda, MI 48750
Web: www.byways.org/browse/byways/10781/
Phone: 989-739-0728
Length: 22 miles. **Designation/Year:** National Scenic Byway (2005). **Description:** Byway parallels the historic and scenic Au Sable River, providing overlooks of the diverse landscape of the Au Sable River Valley and the Huron National Forest. Visitors can enjoy a variety of recreational opportunities along this route, including fishing, camping, wildlife viewing, and snowmobiling. The Lumberman's Monument Visitor Center includes exhibits and hands-on displays that tell the stories of the lumberjacks who worked the woods and rode the rivers. **Start/ Endpoint:** Byway begins 7 miles northeast of Hale at the intersection of SR 65 and Rollways Road, continues 4 miles east on SR 65 to River Road, then 18 miles east on River Road to the intersection with US 23 in Oscoda, Michigan. **Time to Allow:** 1 hour.

★1190★ WOODWARD AVENUE (M-1)

c/o Detroit Metro Convention & Visitors Bureau
211 W. Fort St, Suite 1000
Detroit, MI 48226
Web: www.woodwardavenue.us
Phone: 313-202-1800
Length: 27 miles. **Designation/Year:** National Scenic Byway (2002). **Description:** Lined with historical landmarks and cultural institutions, Woodward Avenue follows the pathway of growth of the City of Detroit and is one of the few byways offering an urban experience. It passes through downtown Detroit, the Boston Edison neighborhood, past Highland Park, the Detroit Zoo, the City of Birmingham, the Cranbrook Educational Community in Bloomfield Hills, and ends in to the City of Pontiac. The foot of Woodward, the narrowest point of the Detroit River, served as the end of the road and a crossing to freedom into Canada for many runaway slaves using the underground railroad. **Start/Endpoint:** Also known as M-1, Woodward Avenue is a state route beginning at the Detroit River in the Detroit central business district and running linearly northwest to Pontiac.

MINNESOTA

★1191★ EDGE OF THE WILDERNESS SCENIC BYWAY

c/o Visit Grand Rapids
501 S Pokegama Ave, Suite 3
Grand Rapids, MN 55744
Web: www.byways.org/browse/byways/2455/
Phone: 800-355-9740
Length: 47 miles. **Designation/Year:** National Scenic Byway (1996). **Description:** Leaving the urban center of Grand Rapids, byway offers vistas of lowland meadows and lakes, then winds through mixed hardwoods and stands of conifers and aspens in the Chippewa National Forest. Within the byways corridor, visitors can enjoy popular recreational activities such as hiking, camping, fishing, cross-country skiing, and snowmobiling. **Start/Endpoint:** Byway begins at the intersection of US 2 and SR 38 in Grand Rapids and proceeds north on SR 38 through the Chippewa National Forest and the towns of Marcell and Bigfork, terminating in Effie, Minnesota. **Time to Allow:** 3 hours.

★1192★ GRAND ROUNDS SCENIC BYWAY

c/o Explore Minnesota Tourism
121 7th Place E - Metro Square Suite 100
Saint Paul, MN 55101
Web: www.byways.org/browse/byways/2243/
Phone: 888-868-7476
Length: 52 miles. **Designation/Year:** National Scenic Byway (1998). **Description:** Byway encompasses more than 50 miles of parks, parkways, bike paths and pedestrian paths, and greenways that encircle the city of Minneapolis and trace the

8. National Scenic Byways

Mississippi River, Minnehaha Creek, and a chain of several lakes. Points of interest include Butler Wildflower Garden at Theodore Wirth Park; a large rose garden at Lake Harriet; Minnehaha Park and Falls; Our Lady of Lourdes Church, the oldest continually used church in Minneapolis; Mill Ruins Park, with its stone arches, canals, and traces of 19th century flourmills; and Saint Anthony Falls Heritage Trail system, which connects several historic areas in the heart of the city. Byway passes near several museums and cultural centers including Orchestra Hall, Weisman Art Museum, Minneapolis Institute of Arts, Walker Art Center and Minneapolis Sculpture Garden, Guthrie Theater, and Mill City Museum. **Start/Endpoint:** Byway begins in downtown Minneapolis at the intersection of 8th Avenue and the James I Rice Memorial Parkway. It follows a series of connecting routes that include sections of the West River Parkway and East River Parkway, Godfrey Parkway, East Minnehaha Parkway and West Minnehaha Parkway, East Lake Harriet Parkway and West Lake Harriet Parkway, William Barry Parkway, East and West Lake Calhoun Parkways, West Lake of the Isles Parkway, Cedar Lake Parkway, Theodore Wirth Parkway, Victory Memorial Parkway, Webber Parkway, St. Anthony Parkway, Columbia Parkway, Stinson Parkway, and Ridgeway Parkway, with the byway designation ending at the edge of the Francis A. Gross Golf Course. **Time to Allow:** 3-4 hours.

★1193★ **GREAT RIVER ROAD - MINNESOTA**
c/o Minnesota Mississippi River Parkway Commission
PO Box 59159
Minneapolis, MN 55459
Web: www.mnmississippiriver.com
Phone: 763-212-2560
Length: 575 miles (Minnesota section); 2,069 miles (entire byway). **Designation/Year:** National Scenic Byway (2000). **Description:** The 2,069-mile Great River Road borders the Mississippi River through the states of Mississippi, Arkansas, Iowa, Illinois, Wisconsin, and Minnesota. The Minnesota section passes along a number of towns and urban areas along the banks of the Mississippi River, as well as the pristine lakes and forests of northern Minnesota. Route includes Lake Itasca State Park, the headwaters of the Mississippi River and Minnesota's first state park, established in 1891 to conserve its giant pines from logging. **Start/Endpoint:** Beginning at the ''Old Man River'' source at Lake Itasca, the Minnesota section of the byway runs east and then south, picking up segments of numerous state and county roads, and ending at the Minnesota-Iowa state line.

★1194★ **HISTORIC BLUFF COUNTRY SCENIC BYWAY**
c/o Historic Bluff Country
PO Box 609
Harmony, MN 55939
Web: www.bluffcountry.com
Phone: 800-428-2030
Length: 88 miles. **Designation/Year:** National Scenic Byway (2002). **Description:** Following the panoramic Root River Valley to the Mississippi River, byway offers scenic views of Minnesota's rich and rolling farmland and tree-covered bluffs. Most of the byway passes through the Richard J. Dryer Memorial Hardwood Forest, a two-million-acre natural area that offers

visitors opportunities for camping, hiking, backpacking, wildlife viewing, snowmobiling and cross-country skiing. Byway also offers access to underground attractions such as Niagara Cave in Harmony and Mystery Cave, which offers spelunking tours. Above Mystery Cave, the Forestville Historic Village portrays several restored period structures from the nineteenth century. **Start/Endpoint:** Byway follows SR16 from La Crescent on the Mississippi River west to I-90 near Dexter. **Time to Allow:** 3 hours.

★1195★ **MINNESOTA RIVER VALLEY SCENIC BYWAY**
c/o Saint Peter Tourism & Visitors Bureau
101 South Front St
Saint Peter, MN 56082
Web: www.mnrivervalley.com
Phone: 800-473-3404
Length: 287 miles. **Designation/Year:** National Scenic Byway (2002). **Description:** Byway follows the Minnesota River through the fertile region of western Minnesota and towns steeped in local history. Areas of interest along the route include: several state parks, including Lac qui Parle; the Lower Sioux Agency History Center, which provides a detailed history of the events of the US-Sioux Conflict of 1862; the Pioneer Village in Montevideo where 23 buildings tell the story of pioneer life in the late 1800's; Minnesota's Machinery Museum at Hanley Falls; Redwood Falls, home to the 200-acre wooded Alexander Ramsey Park; and Big Stone National Wildlife Refuge, which provides habitat for waterfowl, migratory birds and resident wildlife. **Start/Endpoint:** From east to west, byway begins at the junction of SR 25 near Belle Plaine and runs to the South Dakota state border at West Browns Valley.

★1196★ **NORTH SHORE SCENIC DRIVE**
c/o Duluth Convention & Visitors Bureau
21 West Superior St
Duluth, MN 55802
Web: www.superiorbyways.com/north-shore-scenic-drive/
Phone: 800-438-5884
Length: 154 miles. **Designation/Year:** All-American Road (2002). **Description:** Byway offers spectacular vistas of Lake Superior as it skirts the foothills of the Sawtooth Range to the northwest. It offers access to eight state parks, Superior National Forest, and the 200-mile Superior Hiking Trail, rated one of the most scenic trails in the country. Along the byway, visitors can enjoy water-based recreation including fishing, sailing, kayaking, and excursion boating. On the northern end of the byway, the Grand Portage National Monument features a reconstructed North-West Company fur-trading post. **Start/Endpoint:** Follows the shoreline of Lake Superior along SR 61 in northeastern Minnesota from Duluth to Grand Portage near the US-Canadian border. **Time to Allow:** 3 hours.

★1197★ **PAUL BUNYAN SCENIC BYWAY**
c/o Brainerd Lakes Area Chamber of Commerce
124 N 6th St
Brainerd, MN 56501
Web: explorebrainerdlakes.com
Phone: 800-450-2838

Length: 54 miles. **Designation/Year:** National Scenic Byway (2005). **Description:** Byway captures the spirit of the legendary giant lumberjack as it passes through tall forests, large lakes, and communities in northern Minnesota. Areas of interest include: the Uppgaard Wildlife Management Area, which includes 14 different habitats that draw in non-game wildlife for visitors to enjoy; the Paul Bunyan State Trail, connecting several of the local townships along the path of the old railway for bikers, hikers, and cross-country skiers; the Historic Fire Tower, offering visitors sweeping views of the surrounding forests; and the Crosslake Historical Society Museum and Historic Log Village, showcasing the life of the early settlers. **Start/Endpoint:** The byway is a double loop drive located about 150 miles north of the Minneapolis-Saint Paul area. Bounded on the west by US 371, it includes portions of Highways 1, 3, 11, 15, and 16. **Time to Allow:** 1.5 hours.

MISSISSIPPI

★1198★ GREAT RIVER ROAD - LOWER MISSISSIPPI

c/o Vicksburg Convention & Visitors Bureau
PO Box 110
Vicksburg, MS 39181
Web: www.byways.org/browse/byways/62295/
Phone: 800-221-3536
Length: 101 miles (Mississippi section); 2,069 miles (entire byway). **Designation/Year:** National Scenic Byway (2005). **Description:** The 2,069-mile Great River Road borders the Mississippi River through the states of Mississippi, Arkansas, Iowa, Illinois, Wisconsin, and Minnesota. The Mississippi section of the byway skirts the Mississippi River in the extreme southwest corner of the state, covering historically important terrain, including more than a thousand years of history from Native American civilizations to remnants of the Antebellum South to Civil War battlefields and ruins. Areas of interest include: Vicksburg National Military Park, Rosemont Plantation (childhood home of Jefferson Davis), the Grand Village of the Natchez Indians, Historic Jefferson College, Natchez National Historical Park, Clark Creek Natural Area, and the Coca-Cola Museum. **Start/Endpoint:** Byway runs along US 61 from the Issaquena County line south through Woodville to the Louisiana state line. **Time to Allow:** 2 hours (Mississippi section); 6 days (entire byway)

★1199★ NATCHEZ TRACE PARKWAY - MISSISSIPPI

Natchez Trace Parkway Visitor Center
2680 Natchez Trace Parkway
Tupelo, MS 38804
Web: www.nps.gov/natr/
Phone: 800-305-7417
Length: 312 miles (Mississippi section); 444 miles (entire parkway). **Designation/Year:** All-American Road (1996). **Description:** The Mississippi segment of the Natchez Trace Parkway covers roughly three-fourths of the 444-mile Natchez Trace, which encompasses portions of Tennessee, Alabama, and Mississippi. Native Americans, Kaintuck boatmen, indians, post

riders, soldiers and fortune seekers all travelled across this trail, charting new territory and creating a vital link between the Mississippi Territory and the United States. The Mississippi section of the byway includes a number of sites associated with mound-building cultures, the Chickasaw, and the Civil War. Points of interest include Brices Cross Roads National Battlefield Site, Chickasaw Council House and Chickasaw Village, Emerald Mound, and Grand Village of the Natchez State Historic Site. Homochitto and Tombigbee national forests offer opportunities for outdoor recreation. **Start/Endpoint:** The Mississippi section of the byway runs north from Natchez to just past Bear Creek Mound at the Alabama state line. From there, it continues north through Alabama and Tennessee, ending just south of Nashville.

MISSOURI

★1200★ CROWLEY'S RIDGE PARKWAY - MISSOURI

c/o Missouri Division of Tourism
PO Box 1055
Jefferson City, MO 65102
Web: www.byways.org/browse/byways/13752/
Phone: 573-751-4133
Length: 212 miles, including a 14-mile section in Missouri and a 198-mile section in Arkansas. **Designation/Year:** National Scenic Byway (2000). **Description:** The Missouri stretch of the byway runs alongside Jim Morris State Park, the grave of Billy DeMint, Gunnels Hill Civil War Cemetery, and the Four Mile House, an excellent example of early pioneer construction. **Start/Endpoint:** The Missouri section of the byway runs from Malden to the Arkansas state line along US 62. **Time to Allow:** 30 minutes (Missouri section) and 5 hours (Arkansas section).

★1201★ LITTLE DIXIE HIGHWAY OF THE GREAT RIVER ROAD

c/o Missouri Division of Tourism
PO Box 1055
Jefferson City, MO 65102
Web: www.visitmo.com
Phone: 573-751-4133
Length: 30 miles. **Designation/Year:** National Scenic Byway (2002). **Description:** Byway provides a opportunity to visit some of Missouri's historical districts and to get a feel for the Old South through the area's Victorian-era streetscapes and plantation-era mansions. Areas of interest include: the Clarksville Historic District, Georgia Street Historic District in the city of Louisiana; and the 6,705-acre Ted Shanks Conservation Area. Lock and Dam #24, near Clarksville, offers a vantage point from which to view the American bald eagle and other birds that pass through the corridor. **Start/Endpoint:** Byway parallels the Mississippi River along SR 79 from Clarksville to Pike County's northern boundary. **Time to Allow:** 1 hour.

MONTANA

★1202★ BEARTOOTH SCENIC BYWAY - MONTANA

c/o Friends of the Beartooth All-American Road
1108 14th St, #403
Cody, WY 82414
Web: www.beartoothhighway.com
Phone: 307-587-3669
Length: 30 miles (Montana section); 69 miles (entire byway).
Designation/Year: All-American Road (2002). Description: Regarded as one of the most spectacular national forest routes in North America, the Beartooth runs from the historic mining town of Red Lodge to the northeast entrance of Yellowstone National Park. Surrounded by the Custer, Gallatin, and Shoshone national forests, it offers travelers the opportunity to observe the transition from a lush forest ecosystem to alpine tundra in the space of a few miles. The Beartooths are one of the highest elevation and most rugged areas in the lower 48 states, with 20 peaks over 12,000 feet in elevation. The road itself is the highest elevation highway in Wyoming (10,947 feet) and Montana (10,350 feet), and is the highest elevation highway in the Northern Rockies. Start/Endpoint: Montana's section of the byway (US 212) is comprised of two segments: the western section runs through Gallatin National Forest, starting between Red Lodge and Gardiner, just north of Yellowstone National Park, and ending at the state line; the eastern section resumes about 40 miles later at the state line and runs through Custer National Forest, ending at Red Lodge, Montana. Time to Allow: 1.5 hours (Montana); 3 hours (entire byway).

NEVADA

★1203★ LAKE TAHOE EASTSHORE DRIVE

c/o Tahoe-Douglas Chamber of Commerce & Visitor Center
195 US Hwy 50, Round Hill Mall, PO Box 7139
Lake Tahoe, NV 89449
Web: www.tahoechamber.org
Phone: 775-588-4591
Length: 28 miles. Designation/Year: National Scenic Byway (1996). Description: The Eastshore Drive skirts the edges of Lake Tahoe, providing visitors with outstanding views of the Lake Tahoe Basin. The visitor center offers accounts of the pioneer and Indian history of the area. Outdoor enthusiasts can enjoy camping, hiking, biking, and skiing, as well as water-based recreation in Lake Tahoe, the largest alpine lake in North America. Areas of interest include Lake Tahoe Nevada State Park, Sand Harbor State Park, the Pony Express National Historic Trail, Cave Rock, and Incline Village, which is home to many events and festivals, including the Lake Tahoe Jazz Festival. Start/Endpoint: Byway follows US 50 north from Stateline, Nevada, and intersects NV 28. It then continues north to the northeast point of Lake Tahoe just beyond Incline Village. Time to Allow: 1 hour.

★1204★ LAS VEGAS STRIP

c/o Las Vegas Convention & Visitors Authority
3150 Paradise Rd
Las Vegas, NV 89109
Web: www.lvcva.com
Phone: 877-847-4858
Length: 4.5 miles. Designation/Year: All-American Road (2000). Description: Often referred to as "The Jewel of the Desert," Las Vegas has long been recognized as the entertainment vacation capital of the country. World-renowned for its neon glitter, the Strip features a diversity of hotels, casinos, and restaurants, providing opportunities to experience Las Vegas to its fullest. Start/Endpoint: Byway begins at the "Welcome to Fabulous Las Vegas" sign on Las Vegas Boulevard and Russell Road and ends on Las Vegas Boulevard and Sahara Avenue.

★1205★ PYRAMID LAKE SCENIC BYWAY

c/o Pyramid Lake Paiute Tribe Museum
709 State Street, PO Box 256
Nixon, NV 89424
Web: www.byways.org/browse/byways/2457/
Phone: 775-574-1088
Length: 96 miles. Designation/Year: National Scenic Byway (1996). Description: As the only Byway in the nation entirely within a tribal reservation, this route takes visitors to one of the largest desert lakes in the world and provides a unique opportunity to interact with the Paiute tribe. Famous for its unique natural tufa rock formations and crystal-clear water, Pyramid Lake provides habitat for deer, antelope, bighorn sheep, and migrating waterfowl, and with its large population of Lahontan cutthroat trout, offers excellent opportunities for fishing. Start/Endpoint: Byway begins at the Pyramid Lake Indian Reservation border. At its junction with NV 446, it forks and continues northwest to Sutcliffe or southeast, on NV 446, to Nixon. At Nixon the Byway forks again, north onto NV 447 to its nearby terminus or south onto NV 447 to Wadsworth. Time to Allow: 2 hours including backtracking.

NEW HAMPSHIRE

★1206★ CONNECTICUT RIVER SCENIC BYWAY - NEW HAMPSHIRE

c/o Connecticut River Scenic Byway Council
PO Box 1182
Charlestown, NH 03603
Web: www.ctrivertravel.net
Phone: 603-826-4800
Length: 265.5 miles (New Hampshire section); 499 miles (entire byway) Designation/Year: National Scenic Byway (2005). Description: Running along both sides of the Upper Connecticut River, byway includes numerous traditional New England historic and cultural sites in rural farming villages and urban centers, set in a landscape of sheltered valleys and mountains. Points of interest along the New Hampshire section of the byway include: Fort No. 4, a "Living History Museum" that offers 18th century craft demonstrations and reenactments of Revolutionary War battles; Charlestown's Historic Main Street, which features more than 60 historic structures; the Saint-Gaudens National Historic Site, comprised of the home, gardens, and studios of Augustus Saint-Gaudens (1848-1907), one of America's greatest sculptors; the Cornish-Windsor Covered Bridge, the longest wooden covered bridge in the United States; and Dartmouth College and Hood Museum of Art, New Hampshire's oldest

college and its museum. **Start/Endpoint:** Byway includes sections in New Hampshire and Vermont. From the New Hampshire-Massachusetts border, byway runs north along NH 63, NH 12, NH 12A, NH 10, NH 135, US 3, and NH 145 to the Canadian border. The Vermont section of the byway runs parallel on the west side of the Connecticut River. **Time to Allow:** 7 hours (New Hampshire section); 14 hours (entire byway).

★1207★ KANCAMAGUS SCENIC BYWAY

c/o White Mountains Attractions Visitors Bureau
200 Kancamagus Highway
North Woodstock, NH 03262
Web: www.byways.org/browse/byways/2458/
Phone: 603-745-8720
Length: 34.5 miles. **Designation/Year:** National Scenic Byway (1996). **Description:** Recognized as one the most spectacular fall-foliage trips, "The Kanc," as locals call it, passes through the heart of the White Mountains in New Hampshire, climbing to nearly 3,000 feet as it traverses the flank of Mount Kancamagus. Areas of interest include: Clark Trading Post, Loon Mountain Ski Resort, Passaconaway Historic Site, and Falls Pond and Rocky Gorge Scenic Area. **Start/Endpoint:** Byway follows SR 112 from its junction with I-93 in Lincoln (near the Pemigewasset River) east to the city of Conway at the junction of SR 112 and SR 16. While traveling the "Kanc," visitors can complete their loop by taking the White Mountains Trail National Scenic Byway (see separate entry for description). **Time to Allow:** 1 hour.

★1208★ WHITE MOUNTAIN TRAIL

c/o White Mountain Attractions
PO Box 1055
North Woodstock, NH 03262
Web: www.byways.org/browse/byways/2256/
Phone: 800-346-3687
Length: 100 miles. **Designation/Year:** National Scenic Byway (1998). **Description:** Byway is located almost entirely inside White Mountain National Forest in a region that was first home to the Abenaki Indians, and later the inspiration of artists and authors, including Nathaniel Hawthorne. Areas of interest include: Clark's Trading Post, Conway Scenic Railroad, Franconia Notch State Park, and Cannon Mountain Ski Area. Byway also offers access to nearby Mount Washington, the highest peak in the Northeast, and the Appalachain National Scenic Trail, which runs from Maine through Georgia. **Start/Endpoint:** Byway runs from Conway, north along NH 16 and US 302, then northwest on US 302 to Twin Mountain, west on US 3, and then south on I-93 and US 3 to North Woodstock. There is a spur that runs south from Bartlett, and follows Bear Notch Road for 8.5 miles. **Time to Allow:** 2.5 hours.

NEW MEXICO

★1209★ BILLY THE KID SCENIC BYWAY

c/o Lincoln National Forest
1101 New York Ave
Alamogordo, NM 88310
Web: www.fs.fed.us/r3/lincoln/
Phone: 505-434-7200

Length: 84 miles. **Designation/Year:** National Scenic Byway (1998). **Description:** The Billy the Kid Trail pays tribute to the infamous "Wild West" outlaw and several other western icons, including Smokey Bear, as it winds through the rugged beauty of the million-acre Lincoln National Forest. Points of interest include the Hubbard Museum of the American West, Fort Stanton, Lincoln State Monument, and Smokey Bear Museum and Park. **Start/Endpoint:** From Ruidoso, this loop route follows US 70 east to Hondo, then US 380 northwest to Capitan, then NM 48 south to Ruidoso. A separate section of the byway follows NM 220 from near Alto and NM 48 to just north of Fort Stanton at US 380. **Time to Allow:** 2 hours.

★1210★ EL CAMINO REAL NATIONAL SCENIC BYWAY

c/o El Camino Real International Heritage Center
PO Box 175
Socorro, NM 87801
Web: www.byways.org/browse/byways/2065/
Phone: 505-854-3600
Length: 299 miles. **Designation/Year:** National Scenic Byway (2005). **Description:** Beginning in the 16th century and spanning more than 300 years of active use, *El Camino Real* ("The Royal Highway") served as a major artery for travel and commerce from Mexico City through the provinces of New Spain to the Rio Grande Valley in the Santa Fe area, some 1500 miles to the north. Portions of the road follow the Rio Grande Pueblo Indian Trail, which was in use before the first Spanish settlers. Byway passes alongside a number of national historical sites, indian pueblos, historical towns, state parks, and wildlife refuges. Ranging from the low-lying flatlands of the south to the 10,000-foot peaks of the northern mountains, the byway also provides a gateway for a variety of recreational opportunities. **Start/Endpoint:** Follows the Rio Grande River from the US-Mexico border to San Juan Pueblo, just north of Santa Fe, New Mexico. **Time to Allow:** 9 hours.

★1211★ GERONIMO TRAIL SCENIC BYWAY

211 Main St
Truth or Consequences, NM 87901
Web: www.geronimotrail.com
Phone: 505-894-1968
Length: 154 miles **Designation/Year:** National Scenic Byway (2005). **Description:** From desert mountains to forested mountains and vast stretches of mesa lands in between, byway covers a variety of natural terrain of the Southwest and is home to many ethnic groups that have shaped the history of the region. In the town of Truth or Consequences, the Geronimo Trail Visitors Center and Geronimo Springs Museum offers information and exhibits on Geronimo and local history. Other areas of interest along the byway include Elephant Butte Lake State Park, Emory Pass Vista, Gila National Forest, and the historic communities of San Lorenzo, Kingston, Hillsboro, Cuchillo, and Winston. **Start/Endpoint:** The horseshoe-shaped byway runs from Beaverhead to San Lorenzo, New Mexico. From its midpoint at Truth or Consequences, the southern section follows NM 187 south to NM 152, then through Emory Pass in the Black Range Mountains, winding down to the village of San

Lorenzo. The northern route from Truth or Consequences includes small sections of NM 51, NM 179, and NM 181, then follows NM 52 to NM 59, then 31 miles along NM 59 to the Beaverhead Ranger Station. **Time to Allow:** 13 hours, including backtracking.

★1212★ HISTORIC ROUTE 66 - NEW MEXICO

c/o New Mexico Route 66 Association
1415 Central Ave NE
Albuquerque, NM 87106
Web: www.rt66nm.org
Phone: 505-852-2995
Length: 604 miles (New Mexico section); 1,410 miles (entire byway). **Designation/Year:** National Scenic Byway (2000). **Description:** Route 66 was designated in 1926 as a federal highway linking Chicago, IL to Los Angeles, CA. The 2,448-mile route passed through Illinois, Missouri, Kansas, Oklahoma, Texas, New Mexico, Arizona, and California. The road was decommissioned in 1985 in favor of the new interstate highway system and today only 1,410 miles of the original route in three states (Illinois, New Mexico and Arizona) have been designated as National Scenic Byway.The New Mexico section of the route offers a cultural mix of Native American heritage, old Spanish Pueblos, 19th Century ranches, and remnants of authentic Route 66-era tourist attractions. **Start/Endpoint:** The New Mexico section of the byway runs east/west across the state from the Texas state line to the Arizona state line. It includes a double loop near Albuquerque, which offers branch routes northeast to Santa Fe and southwest to Los Lunas. **Time to Allow:** 16 hours (New Mexico section); 5-6 days (entire byway).

★1213★ JEMEZ MOUNTAIN TRAIL

c/o Sandoval County Visitor Center
243 Camino del Pueblo, PO Box 40
Bernalillo, NM 87004
Web: www.jemezmountaintrail.org
Phone: 800-252-0191
Length: 163 miles. **Designation/Year:** National Scenic Byway (1998). **Description:** Byway offers opportunities to view ancient Indian ruins, an Indian Pueblo, as well as spectacular geological formations. Areas of interest include Bandelier National Monument, Jemez State Monument, Valles Caldera National Preserve, Soda Dam, Pueblo of Jemez, Cabezon, Battleship Rock and the Spence Hot Springs. Approximately 65 miles of the byway winds through the Santa Fe National Forest, including 40 miles through the Jemez National Recreation Area, offering visitors opportunities for recreational activities. **Start/Endpoint:** From Los Alamos, byway follows NM 4 west to La Cueva and then south to San Ysidro. From there it follows US 550 (the old NM 44) north to Cuba, then NM 126 to La Cueva, completing the loop, and then NM 4 back to Los Alamos. **Time to Allow:** 3 hours.

★1214★ SANTA FE TRAIL - NEW MEXICO

c/o Santa Fe Trail Association
RR 3
Larned, KS 67550
Web: santafetrailnm.org
Phone: 620-285-2054

Length: 381 miles (New Mexico section); 565 miles (entire byway). **Designation/Year:** National Scenic Byway (1998). **Description:** One of America's first great trade routes, the Santa Fe Trail (1821-1880) was also critical to the westward expansion of the United States. Featuring spectacular and rugged scenery, the section of the trail located in present-day New Mexico offers access to a number of state parks, Carson and Santa Fe national forests, Las Vegas National Wildlife Refuge, Capulin Volcano National Monument, Fort Union, Kit Carson Museum, and the Santa Fe Interpretive Center and Museum. The area around the Santa Fe Trail includes more than 20 Historic Districts and more than 30 individual sites on the National Register of Historic Places, most of which are directly related to the trail. **Start/Endpoint:** Byway runs from Santa Fe to Springer, following US 85, I-25, and several state highways, then forks into two routes. The northern route runs along NM 21 and US 64 to the Colorado state line near Raton; and the eastern route runs along US 56, NM 453, and NM 406 to Clayton, and then along NM 410 northeast to the Oklahoma State line. **Time to Allow:** 8 hours (New Mexico section); 12 hours (entire byway)

★1215★ TRAIL OF THE MOUNTAIN SPIRITS SCENIC BYWAY

PO Box 865
Silver City, NM 88062
Web: www.tmsbyway.com
Phone: 505-536-9459
Length: 110 miles. **Designation/Year:** National Scenic Byway (2005). **Description:** Byway passes through areas rich in scenic, historical and natural interest, including the Gila Cliff Dwellings National Monument, Gila National Forest and Gila Wilderness Area, the Continental Divide and Continental Divide National Scenic Trail, Wild Horse Mesa, Lake Roberts, Fort Bayard, and the historic community of Silver City. **Start/Endpoint:** From Silver City, byway runs north on NM 15, past the junction with NM 35, to the Gila Cliff Dwellings National Monument. At that turnaround point, it follows NM 15 back to the junction with NM 35, then east/southeast on NM 35 to NM 152, then west back to Silver City. **Time to Allow:** 3 hours.

★1216★ TURQUOISE TRAIL

c/o Turquoise Trail Association
PO Box 303
Sandia Park, NM 87047
Web: www.turquoisetrail.org
Phone: 888-263-0003
Length: 62 miles. **Designation/Year:** National Scenic Byway (2000). **Description:** Linking Albuquerque and Sante Fe, byway offers glimpses into the diverse culture, history, and scenic beauty of central New Mexico through its towns, museums, and natural landscapes. It features the Cerrillos Turquoise Mining Museum and the Museum of Archaeology and Material Culture; the ''ghost'' mining towns of Golden, Madrid, and Cerrillos; Sandia Cave, and Sandia Crest and Sandia Peak Tramway. With the Cibola National Forest, Cibola Mountain Wilderness Area, and other canyons, forests, and natural areas, visitors can enjoy year-round adventure, from hiking to cross-country skiing. **Start/Endpoint:** Byway runs from Tijeras north along NM 14 through Golden, Madrid, and Cerrillos to near the junction of

NM 14 and I-25, just south of Santa Fe. A side route runs from Sandia Park west on NM 536 past the junction with NM 165 to Sandia Crest. **Time to Allow:** 2 hours including backtracking.

NEW YORK

★1217★ LAKES TO LOCKS PASSAGE

c/o Lakes to Locks Passage Inc
814 Bridge Rd
Crown Point, NY 12928
Web: www.lakestolocks.com
Phone: 518-597-9660
Length: 234 miles. **Designation/Year:** All-American Road (2002). **Description:** Paralleling Lake Champlain and the Champlain Canal, byway offers scenic vistas and access to numerous historic sites that tell the story of North America's oldest commercial waterway and the Lake Champlain Region. Historic sites include Saratoga National Historical Park, Old Fort House Museum, Mount Defiance, Fort Ticonderoga, and Crown Point State Historic Site. State parks and preserves offer hiking trails, lakeside beaches, and opportunities for wildlife viewing. The Champlain Trail Bikeways are known as some of the best cycling trails in the country. **Start/Endpoint:** Byway runs in a north/south direction from Waterford to Rouses Point, NY, on the Canadian border.

★1218★ MOHAWK TOWPATH SCENIC BYWAY

c/o Mohawk Towpath Scenic Byway Coalition Inc
PO Box 90
Clifton Park, NY 12065
Web: www.mohawktowpath.homestead.com
Phone: 518-383-8565
Length: 28 miles. **Designation/Year:** National Scenic Byway (2005). **Description:** Byway follows both the Erie Canal and the Mohawk River through the Schenectady region, offering many scenic, recreational and historic resources. Architecture from the 18th and 19th centuries endures today, highlighting the canal culture era that changed this region. Today, bikers and hikers can travel the byway's canal-side paths where mules and horses once towed barges. **Start/Endpoint:** Paralleling the Mohawk River, byway begins at the intersection of NY 4 and NY 32 in Waterford, passes through Cohoes and Crescent, and ends at the intersection of State Street and NY 5 in Schenectady. An alternate loop route from NY 9 in Crescent returns to Waterford, joining the main designation at the intersection of NY 32. **Time to Allow:** 40 minutes.

★1219★ SEAWAY TRAIL SCENIC BYWAY - NEW YORK

c/o Seaway Trail, Inc.
PO Box 660
Sackets Harbor, NY 13685
Web: www.seawaytrail.com
Phone: 315-646-1000
Length: 454 (New York section); 518 miles (entire byway). **Designation/Year:** National Scenic Byway (1996). **Description:** Trail through New York and Pennsylvania runs along the scenic shoreline of Lake Erie, the Niagara River, Lake Ontario, and the Saint Lawrence River. New York section of the byway includes a mixture of historic sites, lighthouses, scenic landscapes, large cities, and quaint villages. The shores of Lake Ontario and Lake Erie also offer lots of opportunities for water-based recreation. Among the areas of interest include the 20-mile Chautauqua-Lake Erie Wine Trail, the Dunkirk Historical Lighthouse, Fort Niagara State Historic Park, Fort Ontario State Historic Site, Harriet Tubman's Home, Niagara Falls, the Strong Museum & National Toy Hall of Fame, Theodore Roosevelt Inaugural Historic Site, Thousand Islands, and the cities of Buffalo and Rochester. **Start/Endpoint:** New York section of byway runs from the Pennsylvania state line near Ripley along the shores of Lake Erie, then north along the Niagara River to the shores of Lake Ontario. From there it follows the entire southern and eastern shore of Lake Ontario to Cape Vincent and then runs along the Saint Lawrence River to its northern terminus at Rooseveltown, near the Canadian border.

NORTH CAROLINA

★1220★ BLUE RIDGE PARKWAY - NORTH CAROLINA

199 Hemphill Knob Road
Asheville, NC 28803
Web: www.nps.gov/blri/
Phone: 828-271-4779
Length: 252 miles (North Carolina section); 469 miles (entire parkway). **Designation/Year:** All-American Road (1996). **Description:** Built during the Depression, the Blue Ridge Parkway is the nation's longest rural parkway, extending along the crests of the Southern Appalachians and connecting Shenandoah National Park in Virginia with the Great Smoky Mountains National Park in North Carolina. The North Carolina section of the parkway runs through Pisgah National Forest, passing close to 6,684-foot Mount Mitchell, the highest point east of the Mississippi River. Other areas of interest include: the Cradle of Forestry in America, an information and discovery center dedicated to the beginning of forestry in the United States; Linville Caverns, which offers opportunities for caving on Humpback Mountain; Doughton Park, one of the best places along the parkway for viewing wildlife; and the Biltmore Estate in Asheville. **Start/Endpoint:** The North Carolina section of the parkway begins at the Virginia state line at milepost 216.9, and extends south to Cherokee, North Carolina, where it ends at milepost 469 and the Great Smoky Mountains National Park begins. It intersects with the city of Asheville just after milepost 380 at I-40. **Time to Allow:** 8 hours (North Carolina section); 14 hours (entire parkway).

★1221★ CHEROHALA SKYWAY - NORTH CAROLINA

c/o National Forests in North Carolina
160A Zillicoa St
Asheville, NC 28801
Web: www.byways.org/browse/byways/10500/
Phone: 828-257-4200
Length: 20.5 miles (North Carolina section); 43 miles (entire

8. National Scenic Byways

byway). **Designation/Year:** National Scenic Byway (1998). **Description:** Route displays natural and panoramic scenes of western North Carolina and offers opportunities for camping, hiking, horseback riding, and other recreation in Nantahala National Forest. The Junaluska Museum and Memorial Site, located in Robbinsville, is dedicated to preserving Cherokee history and culture with artifacts, artwork, and tools of the people who once lived here. **Start/Endpoint:** Byway spans portions of North Carolina and Tennessee. The route in North Carolina follows NC 143 west from Robbinsville, NC, through the Nantahala National Forest to the Tennessee border. The Tennessee section begins at the North Carolina border and runs along TN 165 through Cherokee National Forest to the information station just east of Tellico Plains. **Time to Allow:** 45 minutes (North Carolina section); 2 hours (entire byway).

NORTH DAKOTA

★1222★ NATIVE AMERICAN SCENIC BYWAY - NORTH DAKOTA

c/o Standing Rock Tourism Office
Bldg 1 - North Standing Rock Ave
Fort Yates, ND 58538
Web: www.standingrocktourism.com
Phone: 701-854-8500
Length: 51 miles (North Dakota section); 357 miles (entire byway). **Designation/Year:** National Scenic Byway (2005). **Description:** Byway crosses four Sioux Indian Reservations, linking cultural and recreational sites throughout North and South Dakota. Areas of interest along the North Dakota section of the byway include: Four Mile Creek, where Lewis & Clark camped on October 14, 1804; Standing Rock Buffalo Pasture, a thousand-acre preservation site that houses herds of buffalo, an animal that historically provided the Lakota with food, clothing, and shelter; the Fort Yates Stockade, the only building that remains intact from the military post established in 1874; and Standing Rock Monument from which the Standing Rock Reservation derived its name. **Start/Endpoint:** The North Dakota section of the byway is located in Sioux County in the south-central part of the state. The corridor lies entirely within the boundaries of the Standing Rock Indian Reservation and follows the Missouri River south to the South Dakota state line. The byway follows ND 1806 and ND 24. **Time to Allow:** 1.5 hours (North Dakota section); 5.5 hours (entire byway)

★1223★ SHEYENNE RIVER VALLEY SCENIC BYWAY

Scenic Byways Coordinator - North Dakota Parks and
   Recreation Department
1600 E. Century Ave, Suite 3
Bismarck, ND 58503
Web: byway.hellovalley.com
Phone: 701-328-5369
Length: 63 miles. **Designation/Year:** National Scenic Byway (2002). **Description:** Stretching along the Sheyenne River Valley, byway follows ancient Native American footpaths and pioneer wagon trails, including more than 30 recognized historic sites as well as gold rush and military installations, trails and

bridges. Fort Ransom State Park offers opportunities for outdoor recreation, including horseback riding, hiking, canoeing, and cross-country skiing. **Start/Endpoint:** Byway runs from County Road 17 near Baldhill Dam south to Lisbon, North Dakota.

OHIO

★1224★ AMISH COUNTRY BYWAY

c/o Holmes County Chamber of Commerce and Tourism
   Bureau
35 North Monroe St
Millersburg, OH 44654
Web: www.visitamishcountry.com
Phone: 330-674-3975
Length: 76 miles. **Designation/Year:** National Scenic Byway (2002). **Description:** Byway offers opportunities to learn about and experience the culture and history of the Amish and northern Appalachian people. Points of interest include: the Amish and Mennonite Heritage Center, which includes a cyclorama of Amish and Mennonite and Hutterite history; Historical Winesburg, founded in 1827; the Farmer's Produce Auction; Killbuck Museum and Victorian House Museum; and Amish Country antique stores and markets. The Killbuck Marsh Wildlife Area spans both Wayne and Holmes counties and is the state's largest remaining marshland outside of the Lake Erie Region. **Start/Endpoint:** Byway is located in Holmes County, Ohio and has four major access portals: from the northwest along SR 39 at Loudonville; from the northeast on US 62 near Wilmot; from the southwest on US 62 at Brinkhaven; and from the southeast along SR 39 near Sugarcreek/Shanesville. **Time to Allow:** 1.5 hours.

★1225★ HISTORIC NATIONAL ROAD - OHIO

c/o Ohio National Road Association
76 E High St
Springfield, OH 45502
Web: www.ohionationalroad.org
Phone: 937-324-7752
Length: 228 miles (Ohio); 824 miles (entire route). **Designation/Year:** All-American Road (2002). **Description:** America's first interstate highway, the National Road was built to to link the people and cities along the Eastern seaboard to those on the frontiers west of the Allegheny Mountains. Authorized by Congress in 1806, construction of the road began in Cumberland, Maryland in 1811. The road reached Vandalia, then the Illinois state capitol, in 1839 and later was completed to the Illinois border at East Saint Louis, opening a link to the water route of the Mississippi. The Ohio section of the byway was constructed during the 1820s and 1830s and today the route is defined by US 40. Points of interest include: the Blaine Hill Bridge, the state's oldest bridge built in 1828 and named the state Bicentennial Bridge; Dayton Aviation Heritage National Historical Park, which includes a collection of sites on the Wright brothers and Paul Laurence Dunbar; the National Road/Zane Grey Museum; and a number of stone S-bridges, a unique feature of the National Road, at Blaine Hill, Salt Fork, and Fox Creek. **Start/Endpoint:** The east/west route runs from Baltimore, Maryland, to the Mississippi River at the Eads Bridge in East Saint Louis, Illinois.

It crosses six states: Maryland, West Virginia, Pennsylvania, Ohio, Indiana, and Illinois. The Ohio section of the road runs from Bridgeport across the entire length of the state to the Indiana border.

★1226★ LAKE ERIE COASTAL OHIO TRAIL
c/o Lake Erie Coastal Ohio
PO Box 1639
Sandusky, OH 44870
Web: www.coastalohio.com
Phone: 419-609-0399
Length: 293 miles. **Designation/Year:** National Scenic Byway (2005). **Description:** The Byway links 300 museums and natural areas along Lake Erie's southern shore. It features: Perry's Victory and International Peace Memorial, which commemorates the War of 1812's Battle of Lake Erie and the 150 years of peace between the United States and Canada; the Magee Marsh Wildlife Area/Ottawa National Wildlife Refuge, consistently ranked a top 10 birding spot in North America; the Hubbard House, a stopover for refugee slaves fleeing to Canada; and Kelleys Island, which shows the effect of glaciation on the earth's surface. Byway also offers excellent opportunities for fishing, boating, and swimming. **Start/Endpoint:** Byway runs along the southern shore of Lake Erie from the Pennsylvania state line to just south of Toledo. **Time to Allow:** 8 hours.

★1227★ OHIO & ERIE CANALWAY
c/o Ohio & Erie Canalway Association
PO Box 609420
Cleveland, OH 44109
Web: www.ohioanderiecanalway.com
Phone: 216-520-1825
Length: 110 miles. **Designation/Year:** National Scenic Byway (2000). **Description:** Byway passes through a diverse cultural and natural landscape that is a direct legacy of the Canal Era. In 1832, when the Ohio & Erie Canal opened from Cleveland to Portsmouth, Ohio, it became part of a continuous link from the Atlantic Seaboard to the Gulf of Mexico, via the Great Lakes and the Ohio and Mississippi rivers. By offering a reliable transportation system for goods and passengers, the Canal helped to bring prosperity to new and existing communities along its route, to fuel westward expansion, and to change the national economic markets. Today, the Ohio & Erie Canalway is both a national byway and a national heritage area. The corridor includes a number of local, county, and federal recreation areas that offer opportunities for activities such as hiking and bicycling. **Start/Endpoint:** Byway runs in a north/south direction from Cleveland through the Cuyahoga Valley National Park, Akron, and Massillon, ending near Dover. In Cleveland the byway includes three forks, each about 10 miles in length. **Time to Allow:** 4.5 hours.

★1228★ OHIO RIVER SCENIC BYWAY - OHIO
c/o Ohio River Trails Inc.
1613 Washington Blvd
Belpre, OH 45714
Web: www.ohioriverway.org
Phone: 740-423-7233

Length: 452 miles (Ohio section); 943 miles (entire byway). **Designation/Year:** National Scenic Byway (1998). **Description:** Byway winds across Ohio, Indiana, and Illinois, telling the story of the Ohio River, which has shaped the landscape, people, and economics of the region since its beginning 10,000 years ago. Offering almost continuous views to the river, the Ohio section of the byway offers access to prehistoric American Indian burial mounds and other earthworks; the Campus Martius Museum in Marietta, where visitors can learn about the European settlement of Ohio, spanning the period from 1780 to 1970; Old Fort Steuben, a post Revolutionary War fort built for the protection of surveyors; the Ohio River Museum in Marietta; and the Harriet Beecher Stowe House, where she wrote Uncle Tom's Cabin. **Start/Endpoint:** The Ohio section of the byway runs from the Pennsylvania border on US 52 along the Ohio River to the Indiana state border. It comprises the entire southern border and part of the eastern border of Ohio. **Time to Allow:** 10 hours (Ohio section).

OKLAHOMA

★1229★ TALIMENA SCENIC DRIVE - OKLAHOMA
c/o Talimena Scenic Drive Association
Web: www.talimenascenicdrive.com
Phone: 918-567-3434
Length: 54 miles including 38-mile section in Oklahoma and 16-mile section in Arkansas. **Designation/Year:** National Scenic Byway (2005). **Description:** Stretches across the top of the Ouachita Mountains in eastern Oklahoma and western Arkansas, the highest mountain range between the Appalachians and the Rockies. Provides access to recreation destinations such as the Ouachita National Forest, the Winding Stair National Recreation Area, as well as Cedar Lake Recreation Area. The Ouachita National Forest features more than 700 trails for hiking, backpacking, horseback riding, and off-road vehicles, including the Ouachita National Recreation Trail, a 194-mile trail that traverses the forest. **Start/Endpoint:** The Oklahoma section runs from 8 miles east of Talihina, OK (at the western border of the Ouchita National Forest) to the Oklahoma-Arkansas state line. **Time to Allow:** 1 hour (Oklahoma section) and 30 minutes (Arkansas section).

OREGON

★1230★ CASCADE LAKES SCENIC BYWAY
c/o Central Oregon Visitors Association
661 SW Powerhouse Dr, Suite 1301
Bend, OR 97702
Web: www.byways.org/browse/byways/2144/
Phone: 541-389-8799
Length: 66 miles. **Designation/Year:** National Scenic Byway (1998). **Description:** The towering Cascade Mountains and Deschutes National Forest provide the backdrop for this scenic drive and offer outstanding opportunities for hiking and rock climbing. The byway's main feature is the numerous lakes including Devil's Lake, Sparks Lake, the Lava Lakes, the Cultus Lakes, Crane Prairie Reservoir, Wickiup Reservoir, and Davis

Lake. Byway provides outstanding viewpoints of Mount Bachelor and Three Sisters in the Cascade Range and crosses paths with early explorers and trappers like Kit Carson, John C. Fremont, and Nathaniel J. Wyeth. **Start/Endpoint:** From Bend, byway follows Forest Road 46 west, passing through Deschutes National Forest, turning south near Devil's Lake, and continuing south to the junction of FR 46 and SR 58 (near Crescent and Odell lakes.) **Time to Allow:** 3-5 hours.

★1231★ HELLS CANYON SCENIC BYWAY

c/o Hells Canyon Chamber of Commerce
P O Box 841
Halfway, OR 97834
Web: www.byways.org/browse/byways/2145/
Phone: 541-742-4222
Length: 218 miles. **Designation/Year:** All-American Road (2000). **Description:** Byway is an open loop through the Wallowa Mountains to the rim of Hells Canyon, North America's deepest river-carved canyon. From the river's edge up to the mountaintop and back down to the valley floor, the route offers the dramatic scenery of Wallowa-Whitman National Forest and Hells Canyon National Recreation Area. Recreational opportunities abound, including camping, fishing, rafting, hiking, bicycling, bird-watching, and cross-country skiing and snowmobiling. **Start/Endpoint:** Byway is a loop that encircles the Wallowa Mountains, intersecting with I-84 at La Grande and Baker City. It includes portions of SR 86, FS 39, and SR 82. **Time to Allow:** 6 hours.

★1232★ HISTORIC COLUMBIA RIVER HIGHWAY

c/o Columbia River Gorge Visitors Association
PO Box 271
North Bonneville, WA 98639
Web: www.byways.org/browse/byways/2141/
Phone: 800-984-6743
Length: 70 miles. **Designation/Year:** All-American Road (1998). **Description:** With scenery that includes the Columbia River, cascading waterfalls and deep gorges, this was the first scenic highway in the United States to be recognized as a National Historic Landmark. Points of interest include Multnomah Falls, the second highest year-round waterfall in the US and the most visited natural site in Oregon, as well as Bridal Veil Falls, Chanticleer Point, Wahkeena Falls, Horsetail Falls, and Ainsworth State Park. The Vista House at Crown Point serves as a memorial to Oregon's pioneers. During the spring, the Oneonta Gorge area erupts into magnificent wildflower displays, including many plants that only exist in this area. **Start/Endpoint:** Paralleling the Columbia River, byway includes two separate sections: from Troutdale to Dodson and from Mosier to The Dalles. **Time to Allow:** 2 hours.

★1233★ MCKENZIE PASS-SANTIAM PASS SCENIC BYWAY

c/o Deschutes National Forest
1001 SW Emkay Dr
Bend, OR 97702
Web: www.byways.org/browse/byways/2148/
Phone: 541-383-5300

Length: 82 miles. **Designation/Year:** National Scenic Byway (1998). **Description:** Byway features the highest concentration of snowcapped volcanoes and associated glaciers in the lower 48 states. Areas of interest include: Broken Top Mountain and The Three Sisters, along with their waterfalls, that tower above the route; Deschutes National Forest, which includes five wilderness areas, 157 lakes and reservoirs, and 1,400 miles of trails; the Dee Wright Observatory, which offers panoramic views of the Cascade Mountain Range as far north as Mount Hood; and the 2,638-mile Pacific Crest National Scenic Trail, which cuts across the byway in two places. **Start/Endpoint:** From Sisters, this loop byway runs northwest along US 20, then west on SR 126 near Suttle Lake, then south on SR 126 to the junction with SR 242, then east onto SR 242. The byway along SR 242 then passes through the Willamette and Deschutes National Forests and the Three Sisters Wilderness Area, then completes the full loop at Sisters. **Time to Allow:** 2 hours.

★1234★ MOUNT HOOD SCENIC BYWAY

c/o Clackamas County Tourism Development Council
2051 Kaen Rd, Suite 427
Oregon City, OR 97045
Web: www.mthoodterritory.com/byway.htm
Phone: 503-655-8490
Length: 105 miles. **Designation/Year:** National Scenic Byway (2005). **Description:** Byway is a panoramic route around 11,245-foot Mount Hood, offering exceptional views of geological diversity, ranging from pastoral valleys to temperate rain forest to semi-arid uplands. The route was traveled by the wagon trains carrying settlers to the Oregon Territory and on to the Willamette Valley. At either endpoint, byway connects to the Historic Columbia River Highway (an ''All-America Road''), making a natural loop around the mountain, and offering access to three of Oregon's unique natural wonders: Multnomah Falls, the Columbia River Gorge and Mount Hood. It also offers exceptional recreational opportunities, including year-round skiing on Mount Hood at Timberline and world-class wind surfing in the Hood River. **Start/Endpoint:** Byway runs along SR 35 from Troutdale to Hood River. **Time to Allow:** 3 hours.

★1235★ OUTBACK SCENIC BYWAY

c/o Lake County Chamber of Commerce
126 North E St
Lakeview, OR 97630
Web: www.byways.org/browse/byways/2142/
Phone: 541-947-6040
Length: 170 miles. **Designation/Year:** National Scenic Byway (1998). **Description:** Byway passes through Oregon's remote and rugged Great Basin Country, where visitors can explore volcanic remnants like Fort Rock, find fossils at Fossil Lake, see Old Perpetual Geyser, or visit Albert Rim, the largest geological fault in North America, which towers 2,500 feet above the valley floor. The Summer Lake Wildlife Area offers an abundance of lakes, hiking trails, scenic viewpoints, and archeological finds. **Start/Endpoint:** Byway runs from La Pine south along SR 31 past Silver Lake, Summer Lake and Paisely until route turns into US 395. From there it continues along US 395 until its endpoint just past Lakeview at the Oregon-California border. **Time to Allow:** 4 hours.

★1236★ PACIFIC COAST SCENIC BYWAY - OREGON

c/o Oregon Coast Visitors Association
137 NE First St, PO Box 74
Newport, OR 97365
Web: www.visittheoregoncoast.com
Phone: 888-628-2101
Length: 363 miles. **Designation/Year:** All-American Road (2002). **Description:** Byway runs along the full length of Oregon's coastline, offering access to beaches, temperate rain forest, sand dunes, rugged cliffs, and historic towns. More than 40 miles of coastline from Florence to Coos Bay make up the Oregon Dunes National Recreation Area. Numerous parks along the way offer opportunities for recreation and wildlife viewing, including Cape Blanco State Park, the Rogue River-Siskiyou National Forests, and six national wildlife refuges. Historic sites include the Fort Clatsop National Memorial, where the Lewis and Clark Expedition spent the winter of 1805-06. A number of lighthouses in the area include Cape Blanco, the oldest lighthouse on the Oregon coast as well as Yaquina Head and Heceta Head lighthouses. Other points of interest include the Oregon Coast Aquarium in Newport, Sea Lion Caves, and Cannon Beach, site of the annual Sandcastle Building Contest in early June. **Start/Endpoint:** Byway follows the Oregon coast along Highway 101 from Astoria south to the California border.

★1237★ ROGUE-UMPQUA SCENIC BYWAY

c/o Umpqua National Forest
2900 Stewart Pkwy
Roseburg, OR 97470
Web: www.fs.fed.us/r6/umpqua/
Phone: 541-672-6601
Length: 172 miles. **Designation/Year:** National Scenic Byway (2002). **Description:** Commonly known as the ''highway of waterfalls,'' byway features diverse river and mountain terrain, including rolling oak-covered hills, coniferous forests, inter-canyon lava flows, and whitewater rapids. About 18 miles east of Roseburg, the North Umpqua River crashes into the Little River at Colliding Rivers, one of the few places in the world where two rivers meet head-on. Park visitors can enjoy whitewater thrills and outstanding steelhead runs on the North Umpqua River as it tumbles through the Umpqua National Forest. Other areas of interest include Diamond Lake, near the base of 9,182-foot Mount Thielsen, which is located near the north entrance to Crater Lake National Park; and the Pacific Crest National Scenic Trail, which passes near the byway in Diamond Lake Recreation Area. **Start/Endpoint:** Byway runs from Roseburg, east on SR 138, then south/southwest on SR 230 and SR 62 to SR 234 just before Gold Hill, where the Byway ends.

★1238★ VOLCANIC LEGACY SCENIC BYWAY - OREGON

300 Pine St
Mount Shasta, CA 96067
Web: www.volcaniclegacybyway.org
Phone: 866-722-9929
Length: 140 miles (Oregon section); 500 miles (total length). **Designation/Year:** All-American Road (1998). **Description:** The Oregon section of the byway offers access to Crater Lake National Park, which features the deepest lake in the United States. Other areas of interes include: 90,000-acre Upper Klamath Lake, the largest body of fresh water west of the Rockies; Klamath Basin National Wildlife Refuges, where visitors can see more than a million birds during peak migrations in the fall; Favell Museum, offering displays of more than 100,000 artifacts from tribes around the world; Fort Klamath, established in 1863 to protect immigrant trains from Native American attack and to maintain peace in the region during the Civil War; and the Winema and Umpqua national forests, which offer many recreational opportunities. **Start/Endpoint:** Byway includes sections in northern California and southern Oregon. In Oregon, byway runs from the Diamond Lake Junction on US 97 about halfway between Bend and Klamath Falls south to the Oregon-California border on US 97. **Time to Allow:** 1 day.

★1239★ WEST CASCADES SCENIC BYWAY

c/o Mount Hood National Forest
16400 Champion Way
Sandy, OR 97055
Web: www.fs.fed.us/r6/mthood/
Phone: 503-668-1700
Length: 220 miles. **Designation/Year:** National Scenic Byway (2000). **Description:** Scenic byway between Portland and Eugene skirts the west side of the Cascade Mountain Range as it runs through both the Mount Hood and Willamette national forests. It offers scenic views of waterfalls, old growth forests, rushing whitewater, lakes, and the snowcapped mountain peaks of Mount Jefferson, Mount Washington, Three Fingered Jack, and the Three Sisters. **Start/Endpoint:** Byway begins in Estacada and runs south on SR 224, FR 46, SR 22, SR 126, and FR 19, ending in the town of Oakridge, Oregon.

PENNSYLVANIA

★1240★ HISTORIC NATIONAL ROAD - PENNSYLVANIA

c/o National Road Heritage Corridor
65 West Main St, 2nd Floor
Uniontown, PA 15401
Web: www.nationalroadpa.org
Phone: 724-437-9877
Length: 90 miles (Pennsylvania); 824 miles (entire route). **Designation/Year:** All-American Road (2002). **Description:** America's first interstate highway, the National Road was built to to link the people and cities along the Eastern seaboard to those on the frontiers west of the Allegheny Mountains. Authorized by Congress in 1806, construction of the road began in Cumberland, Maryland in 1811. The road reached Vandalia, then the Illinois state capitol, in 1839 and later was completed to the Illinois border at East Saint Louis, opening a link to the water route of the Mississippi.Points of interest along the Pennsylvania section of the route include Fort Necessity National Battlefield and Washington Tavern, Friendship Hill National Historic Site (the country estate of Albert Gallatin), Coal & Coke Heritage Center, Pennsylvania Trolley Museum, and historic Old Petersburg/Addison Tollhouse, one of only two tollhouses still remaining on the Historic National Road. **Start/**

8. National Scenic Byways

Endpoint: The east/west route runs from Baltimore, Maryland, to the Mississippi River at the Eads Bridge in East Saint Louis, Illinois. It crosses six states: Maryland, West Virginia, Pennsylvania, Ohio, Indiana, and Illinois. The Pennsylvania section of the route runs along US 40 from the Maryland state line near Addison to the West Virginia state line near West Alexander.

★1241★ SEAWAY TRAIL SCENIC BYWAY - PENNSYLVANIA

c/o Erie Area Convention & Visitors Bureau
208 East Bayfront Parkway, Suite 103
Erie, PA 16507
Web: www.visiteriepa.com
Phone: 800-524-3743
Length: 64 miles (Pennsylvania section); 518 miles (entire byway). **Designation/Year:** National Scenic Byway (2005). **Description:** Trail through New York and Pennsylvania runs along the scenic shoreline of Lake Erie, the Niagara River, Lake Ontario, and the Saint Lawrence River. Hugging the shore of Lake Erie, the Pennsylvania section of the byway features three state parks, including Presque Isle State Park, which is located on a peninsula in Lake Erie. Here visitors can enjoy fishing, swimming, windsurfing, and kayaking, as well as a visit to the War of 1812 historic site. The park is the rest stop for more than 320 species of migratory birds. Byway also includes several lighthouses and vineyards, some of which are available for tours. **Start/Endpoint:** The Pennsylvania section of the trail begins at the Ohio state line on US 20 and runs east along the shores of Lake Erie, primarily along PA 5, to the New York state line. The byway includes a spur route around the perimeter of Presque Isle in a 14 mile loop.

SOUTH CAROLINA

★1242★ ASHLEY RIVER ROAD

c/o Charleston Area Convention and Visitor Bureau
423 King St
Charleston, SC 29403
Web: www.byways.org/browse/byways/13794/
Phone: 843-853-8000
Length: 11 miles. **Designation/Year:** National Scenic Byway (2000). **Description:** Featuring Southern plantations and old churches, byway capture the history of the American South and the culture of South Carolina's low-country, including a rich African-American culture. Points of interest include: Drayton Hall, the only pre-Revolutionary plantation house remaining on the historic Ashley River Road; Fort Bull, Confederate earthworks constructed in 1863; and the Old St. Andrew's Church and Middleton Place, both National Historic Landmarks. **Start/Endpoint:** Following the Ashley River along SC 61, byway begins at milepost 5.84 (Charleston County) in Church Creek, follows SC 61, and ends at milepost 15.75 (Dorchester County) near SC 165. **Time to Allow:** 25 minutes.

★1243★ CHEROKEE FOOTHILLS SCENIC BYWAY

c/o Discover Upcountry Carolina Association
PO Box 3116
Greenville, SC 29602
Web: theupcountry.com
Phone: 800-849-4766

Length: 112 miles. **Designation/Year:** National Scenic Byway (1998). **Description:** Once known as ''Keowee Path'' or ''Cherokee Path,'' this route was once used by the Cherokees and the English and French fur traders. Adjoining the byway are the Nantahala and Sumter national forests, as well as a number of state parks that together offer a full range of recreational opportunities. Areas of interest include: Caesar's Head State Park, which includes Raven Cliff Falls, one of the highest waterfalls in the eastern United States; the 1,000-foot-high sheer rock face of Glassy Mountain; and Campbell's Covered Bridge, which is South Carolina's only remaining covered bridge. Two national park units can be found near the northern end of the byway: Cowpens National Battlefield and King's Mountain National Military Park. **Start/Endpoint:** Follows SR 11 from Gaffney at the northern end to just over the Georgia-South Carolina border at Exit 1. **Time to Allow:** 3 hours.

★1244★ SAVANNAH RIVER SCENIC BYWAY

c/o South Carolina Department of Parks, Recreation & Tourism
1205 Pendleton St
Columbia, SC 29201
Web: www.byways.org/browse/byways/2162/
Phone: 866-224-9339
Length: 110 miles. **Designation/Year:** National Scenic Byway (1998). **Description:** Winding along three major lakes and traversing four counties in western South Carolina, byway affords scenic views of the densely-wooded Hickory Knob State Park and Sumter National Forest, quaint towns such as McCormick and Willington, and rolling farmland dotted with historic churches. Located a short distance from the byway, the J. Strom Thurmond Reservoir and the Savannah River offer camping, fishing, and other recreational opportunities. In Abbeville, the Burt-Stark Mansion is a Civil War-era historic site that served as a meeting place for Jefferson Davis and his War Council. **Start/Endpoint:** From south to north, byway begins about 9 miles north of Augusta, Georgia, at the South Carolina-Georgia border. From there, it parallels the Savannah River along SC 28, SC 81, SC 187, and SC 24 to Oakway, South Carolina. **Time to Allow:** 3 hours.

SOUTH DAKOTA

★1245★ NATIVE AMERICAN SCENIC BYWAY - SOUTH DAKOTA

c/o Cheyenne River Sioux Tribe
Department of Game, Fish and Parks, PO Box 590, E. Hwy 212
Eagle Butte, SD 57625
Web: www.crstgfp.com
Phone: 605-964-7812
Length: 306 miles (South Dakota section); 357 miles (entire byway). **Designation/Year:** National Scenic Byway (2005). **Description:** Byway crosses four Sioux Indian Reservations, linking cultural and recreational sites throughout North and South Dakota. Areas of interest along the South Dakota section of the byway include: the Akta Lakota Museum and Cultural Center in Chamberlain, devoted to preserving and promoting Sioux

culture; the Lower Brule Indian Reservation and Crow Creek Indian Reservation, where visitors can learn about the history and modern customs of the Sioux; Lake Sharpe, which offers opportunities for water sports, hunting, and fishing; and Fort Pierre, where European traders and Native tribes once traded goods. **Start/Endpoint:** The South Dakota section of the byway runs from I-90 near Chamberlain and continue across the Missouri River to Oacoma. From there it picks up sections of SD 50, BIA 4, SD 47, BIA 5, BIA 10, SD 1806, US 83, US 14, SD 63, Highway 212, BIA 7, BIA 4, and SD 20, ending at the North Dakota border. **Time to Allow:** 3.5 hours (South Dakota section); 5.5 hours (entire byway)

★1246★ PETER NORBECK SCENIC BYWAY

c/o Black Hills National Forest
1019 N 5th St
Custer, SD 57730
Web: www.fs.fed.us/r2/blackhills/
Phone: 605-673-9200
Length: 68 miles. **Designation/Year:** National Scenic Byway (1996). **Description:** Named for South Dakota conservationist, Governor, and U.S. Senator, byway features historic Mount Rushmore and the rugged beauty of the Black Hills. Areas of interest include the Centennial Trail, climbing through 100+ miles of wilderness; Custer State Park, a 73,000-acre wildlife preserve; the Needles Highway, passing among straight stone spires; the Crazy Horse Monument, a mountain-size monument celebrating the life of one of the greatest Native American leaders; Harney Peak, the highest peak east of the Rocky Mountains; and Jewel Cave National Monument, featuring the second largest cave in the United States. **Start/Endpoint:** This double loop byway is accessible from Rapid City by following SD 16 southwest toward Keystone or following US 385 north from Hotsprings. The byway includes sections of SD 244, US 16A, SD 87, and SD 89. **Time to Allow:** 2-4 hours.

TENNESSEE

★1247★ CHEROHALA SKYWAY - TENNESSEE

c/o Monroe County Department. of Tourism
520 Cook St, Suite A
Madisonville, TN 37354
Web: www.cherohala.com
Phone: 800-245-5428
Length: 22.5 miles (Tennesse section); 43 miles (entire byway). **Designation/Year:** National Scenic Byway (1996). **Description:** Route in the southern Appalachian Mountains passes along cultural heritage and historic sites of the Cherokee tribe and early settlers. Situated entirely within Cherokee National Forest, it also offers opportunities for recreation such as camping, hiking, horseback riding, swimming, and kayaking. Nearby areas of interest include Tellico Lake, Craighead Caverns and the Lost Sea, Bald River Falls, Fort Loudoun State Park, and the Sequoyah Museum. **Start/Endpoint:** Byway spans portions of Tennessee and North Carolina. The Tennessee section of the byway begins at the information station just east of Tellico Plains and follows TN 165 east through Cherokee National Forest to the North Carolina state line. Skyway's route in North

Carolina follows NC 143 east from the Tennessee border through Nantahala National Forest to Robbinsville. **Time to Allow:** 1 hour (Tennessee section); 2 hours (entire byway).

★1248★ NATCHEZ TRACE PARKWAY - TENNESSEE

Natchez Trace Parkway Visitor Center
2680 Natchez Trace Parkway
Tupelo, MS 38804
Web: www.nps.gov/natr/
Phone: 800-305-7417
Length: 101 miles (Tennessee section); 444 miles (entire parkway). **Designation/Year:** All-American Road (1996). **Description:** The Tennessee segment of the Natchez Trace Parkway is the northern leg of the byway, covering the entire length of the 444-mile Natchez Trace, which encompasses portions of Tennessee, Alabama, and Mississippi. Native Americans, Kaintuck boatmen, indians, post riders, soldiers and fortune seekers all travelled across this trail, charting new territory and creating a vital link between the Mississippi Territory and the United States. Areas of interest near the Tennessee section of the byway include two national park units — Shiloh National Military Park and Stones River National Battlefield — Jackson Falls, and the Gordon House and Ferry Site. **Start/Endpoint:** The Tennessee section of the parkway begins just south of Nashville at its junction with TN 100 and runs south to the Alabama state line. The parkway continues south through sections of Alabama and Mississippi, ending in Natchez, MS.

UTAH

★1249★ DINOSAUR DIAMOND PREHISTORIC HIGHWAY - UTAH

c/o Dinosaurland Travel Board
55 East Main
Vernal, UT 84078
Web: www.dinoland.com
Phone: 800-477-5558
Length: 328 miles (Utah section); 152 miles (Colorado section). **Designation/Year:** National Scenic Byway (2002). **Description:** This route on the northern edge of the Colorado Plateau features some of the world's most significant dinosaur fossil quarries and museums. The Utah section of the byway passes near Arches and Canyonlands national parks, the Mill Canyon Dinosaur Trail and Copper Ridge Dinosaur Trackway, Cleveland-Lloyd Dinosaur Quarry, Utah Field House of Natural History, Flaming Gorge, and Dinosaur National Monument. The Green and Colorado rivers run through the area of southeastern Utah and western Colorado, providing excellent opportunities for water-based recreation including rafting and fishing. There are also excellent opportunities along this route for hiking, mountain biking, and horseback riding. **Start/Endpoint:** The Utah section of this two-state, 512-mile loop begins at the Colorado border on I-70 and runs in a clockwise direction west through Moab, Green River and Price, then turns northeast through Duchesne, Roosevelt and Vernal, before crossing back into Colorado again on US 40. **Time to Allow:** 6.5 hours (Utah section); 10 hours (entire byway).

8. National Scenic Byways

★1250★ **FLAMING GORGE-UINTAS SCENIC BYWAY**

c/o Ashley National Forest
355 North Vernal Ave
Vernal, UT 84078
Web: www.byways.org/browse/byways/2008/
Phone: 435-789-1181
Length: 82 miles. **Designation/Year:** National Scenic Byway (1998). **Description:** Designated as the state's first National Forest Scenic Byway in 1988, this route, known as ''The Drive Through the Ages,'' runs through the Ashley National Forest east of the Uinta Mountains, one of the few east-west ranges in the country. The Flaming Gorge National Recreation Area, created as a recreational destination, includes nearly half of the byway and offers opportunities for hiking, river rafting, swimming, canoeing, and camping. Byway is also located near Dinosaur National Monument and Quarry, one of the world's greatest sources for dinosaur skeletons. **Start/Endpoint:** From Vernal, byway runs north on US 191 to UT 44, where it forks: the left fork follows UT 44 to Manila, where the byway ends; the right fork continues on US 191 past the community of Dutch John to the Wyoming state line. **Time to Allow:** Two hours (including backtracking on Highway 44).

★1251★ **HIGHWAY 12 - A JOURNEY THROUGH TIME SCENIC BYWAY**

Scenic Byway 12
PO Box 132
Tropic, UT 84776
Web: www.scenicbyway12.com
Length: 124 miles. **Designation/Year:** All-American Road (2002). **Description:** The ''journey through time'' route connects national parks, monuments, and forests to preserve some of the most spectacular rock formations and stunning scenery in the United States. This includes the red rock formations of Red Canyon in Dixie National Forest, Grand Staircase-Escalante National Monument, the Escalante River, Calf Creek Canyon, and the Hogsback and 9,760-foot Boulder Mountain. At Boulder visitors can get a firsthand look at life in a prehistoric Native American village at the Anasazi Indian Village Park. Continuing north from Boulder, the route crosses the eastern flank of Boulder Mountain with spectacular views of Capitol Reef National Park, the Henry Mountains, Circle Cliffs, and Navajo Mountain on the far side of Lake Powell. On a clear day travelers can see more than 100 miles into Colorado and Arizona. **Start/Endpoint:** Byway connects Bryce Canyon National Park to Capitol Reef National Park. From west to east, it begins at the junction of US 89 and SR 12, 7 miles south of Panguitch and 8 miles north of Hatch in Garfield County. Byway ends at the junction of SR 12 and SR 24, just east of Torrey, in Wayne County. **Time to Allow:** 3 hours.

★1252★ **LOGAN CANYON SCENIC BYWAY**

c/o Cache Valley Visitors Bureau
199 North Main St
Logan, UT 84321
Web: www.tourcachevalley.com
Phone: 800-882-4433
Length: 41 miles. **Designation/Year:** National Scenic Byway (2002). **Description:** From historic Cache Valley on the west to picturesque Bear Lake on the east, byway winds northeast through the Wasatch-Cache National Forest. Along the way, 500 million years of geologic history unfold in rugged rock formations. Byway offers recreational opportunities for all seasons, including fishing on the Logan River, swimming, sailing and boating on Bear Lake, skiing, snowboarding and snowmobiling on Bear Mountain, and camping and hiking in Wasatch-Cache National Forest. **Start/Endpoint:** Byway runs from Logan to Garden City, Utah along US 89. The Logan River parallels US 89 much of the way. **Time to Allow:** 1 hour.

★1253★ **NEBO LOOP SCENIC BYWAY**

c/o Uinta National Forest
88 West 100 North, PO Box 1428
Provo, UT 84601
Web: www.fs.fed.us/r4/uinta/
Phone: 801-342-5100
Length: 37 miles. **Designation/Year:** National Scenic Byway (1998). **Description:** Route passes almost entirely through the Uinta National Forest, offering outstanding views of the Wasatch Mountains and 11,923-foot Mount Nebo, the tallest mountain in the range. Areas of interest include: Devil's Kitchen (a tiny replica of Bryce Canyon), the Mount Nebo Wilderness Area; and Payson Lake. **Start/Endpoint:** Byway connects Payson to Nephi along CR 015. **Time to Allow:** 1 hour.

★1254★ **THE ENERGY LOOP: HUNTINGTON & ECCLES CANYONS SCENIC BYWAY**

c/o Castle Country Travel Council
90 North 100 East #2
Price, UT 84501
Web: www.byways.org/browse/byways/13831/
Phone: 800-842-0789
Length: 86 miles. **Designation/Year:** National Scenic Byway (2000). **Description:** Deriving its name from the rich coal mining history of the area, the Energy Loop begins and ends at the eastern and western valleys below the Wasatch Plateau, traversing a variety of landscapes along the way. Areas of interest include: the Skyline Mine in Eccles Canyon, which extracts five million tons of coal per year; Helper's Western Mining and Railroad Museum; and the Cleveland-Lloyd Dinosaur Quarry, site of the densest concentration of Jurassic dinosaur bones ever found. **Start/Endpoint:** Byway runs from Fairview, east on UT 31 to its junction with UT 264 at the top of Fairview Canyon. Here, the Byway forks: the north route follows UT 264 east to Scofield, then north on UT 96 to UT 6 in Colton; the south route continues on UT 31 south to the end of the byway at Huntington. **Time to Allow:** 1.5 hours.

★1255★ **TRAIL OF THE ANCIENTS - UTAH**

c/o Utah's Canyon Country Travel Council
117 South Main St, PO Box 490
Monticello, UT 84535
Web: www.utahscanyoncountry.com
Phone: 800-574-4386
Length: 366 miles (Utah section); 480 miles (entire byway).

Designation/Year: National Scenic Byway (2005). **Description:** The Trail of the Ancients is an auto trail that offers access to numerous examples of Ancestral Puebloan culture, other aspects of the Four Corners history and culture, and scenic vistas. Areas of interest along the Utah section of the byway include: Edge of the Cedars State Park and Museum, Four Corners Monument (where Utah, Colorado, Arizona, and New Mexico meet at a common point), Grand Gulch Primitive Area, Hovenweep and Natural Bridges national monuments, Monument Valley Navajo Tribal Park, and Three Kiva Pueblo. **Start/Endpoint:** The Trail of the Ancients is a loop route in Colorado and Utah that may be started at any point along its length. The Utah section of the byway is accessible from Monticello south along US 191; from County Road 414 or UT 162 at the Colorado state line; and from Highway 163 north from the Arizona state line. The loop section in Utah includes sections of US 191, and UT 95, 261, and 163. **Time to Allow:** 6 hours (Utah section); 9 hours including backtracking (entire byway).

VERMONT

★1256★ CONNECTICUT RIVER SCENIC BYWAY - VERMONT

c/o Connecticut River Scenic Byway Council
PO Box 1182
Charlestown, NH 03603
Web: www.ctrivertravel.net
Phone: 603-826-4800
Length: 233 miles (Vermont section); 499 (entire byway). **Designation/Year:** National Scenic Byway (2005). **Description:** Running along both sides of the Upper Connecticut River, byway includes numerous traditional New England historic and cultural sites in rural farming villages and urban centers, set in a landscape of sheltered valleys and mountains. Points of interest along the Vermont section of the byway include: the Rockingham Meeting House, the earliest public building in Vermont, built in 1787; the American Precision Museum, housing the largest collection of historically significant machine tools in the country; the Marsh-Billings-Rockefeller National Historical Park and the Billings Farm & Museum; the Quechee Gorge, one of Vermont's most spectacular natural wonders; White River Junction, home to a historic railroad station and Old 494, a restored train engine; and the New England Transportation Museum, which details the region's railroading history. **Start/Endpoint:** Byway includes sections in New Hampshire and Vermont. From the New Hampshire-Massachusetts border, byway runs north along NH 63, NH 12, NH 12A, NH 10, NH 135, US 3, and NH 145 to the Canadian border. The New Hampshire section of the byway runs parallel on the east side of the Connecticut River. **Time to Allow:** 7 hours (Vermont section); 14 hours (entire byway).

VIRGINIA

★1257★ BLUE RIDGE PARKWAY - VIRGINIA

199 Hemphill Knob Road
Asheville, NC 28803
Web: www.nps.gov/blri/
Phone: 828-271-4779

Length: 217 miles (Virginia section); 469 miles (entire parkway). **Designation/Year:** All-American Road (2005). **Description:** Built during the Depression, the Blue Ridge Parkway is the nation's longest rural parkway, extending along the crests of the Southern Appalachians and connecting Shenandoah National Park in Virginia with the Great Smoky Mountains National Park in North Carolina. The Virginia section of the parkway passes through George Washington National Forest and offers access to the Appalachian National Scenic Trail. Areas of interest include: Cave Mountain Lake and Sherando Lake recreation areas, which offer opportunities for swimming, boating, camping, and other recreational activities; and Crabtree Falls, which is the largest vertical drop waterfall east of the Mississippi River. **Start/Endpoint:** Milepost 0 at Rockfish Gap near Waynesboro, Virginia, is the northern end of the Blue Ridge Parkway and the beginning of the scenic roadway that ends in North Carolina. To the north, the Parkway connects directly to Skyline Drive, which winds 105 miles through Shenandoah National Park. The byway crosses the North Carolina-Virginia state line at milepost 216.9, and extends south to Cherokee, North Carolina, where it ends and the Great Smoky Mountains National Park begins. **Time to Allow:** 6 hours (Virginia section); 14 hours (entire parkway).

★1258★ COLONIAL PARKWAY

c/o Colonial National Historical Park
PO Box 210
Yorktown, VA 23690
Web: www.byways.org/browse/byways/60441/
Phone: 757-898-2410
Length: 23 miles. **Designation/Year:** All-American Road (2005). **Description:** The Colonial Parkway takes in the 174-year period of British colonial history in North America. Beginning at Jamestown, site of the first permanent English settlement in North America, the Parkway leads first to Williamsburg, where America's democratic ideals matured in Virginia's 18th-century capital. The Parkway culminates at Yorktown, where English colonial America came to an end with the defeat of the British army in 1781, securing independence for the United States of America. Along the entire route it offers spectacular views of the James and York rivers, and turnouts offer glimpses of the area's rich natural and cultural history. **Start/Endpoint:** The Colonial Parkway runs from the Jamestown Settlement Visitor Center near the James River to the Visitor Center in Colonial National Historical Park on the York River. **Time to Allow:** 1 hour.

★1259★ GEORGE WASHINGTON MEMORIAL PARKWAY

Turkey Run Park
McLean, VA 22101
Web: www.nps.gov/gwmp/
Phone: 703-289-2500
Length: 25 miles. **Designation/Year:** All-American Road (2005). **Description:** Designed and managed as a memorial to the first President of the United States, the parkway passes monuments and memorials, wildlife preserves and historic homes, waterfalls and scenic overlooks. Points of interest include Mount Vernon Estate and Gardens, Fort Hunt, Dyke Marsh

Wildlife Preserve, Arlington House, Arlington National Cemetery, Claude Moore Colonial Farm, Fort Marcy, and Great Falls Park. In addition to its status as an All-American Road, the parkway is also a unit of the National Park System. **Start/Endpoint:** Starting at the Mount Vernon Estate, byway runs north, passing through the city of Alexandria, to its endpoint just past the Claude Moore Colonial Farm. **Time to Allow:** 1 hour.

★1260★ SKYLINE DRIVE

Shenandoah National Park
3655 US Highway 211 East
Luray, VA 22835
Web: www.nps.gov/shen/
Phone: 540-999-3500
Length: 105 miles. **Designation/Year:** National Scenic Byway (2005). **Description:** Skyline Drive is an integral element of Shenandoah National Park and is the only public road through the park. Together they were created to to provide outstanding views of the scenic and historic Shenandoah Valley and Piedmont Region of Virginia and to protect the natural and cultural resources of the northern Blue Ridge. Although best known for its vibrant fall foliage, the park is no less spectacular (and a lot less crowded) in the spring when the wildflowers and trees are in full bloom. Portions of Skyline Drive are periodically closed during inclement weather and at night during deer hunting season. Visitors can still enter the park on foot to hike even when the Drive is closed. **Start/Endpoint:** Beginning near the town of Waynesboro, Skyline Drive runs north through Shenandoah National Park and ends in the town of Front Royal. It is located 91 miles from Richmond, VA and 80 miles from Washington, DC.

WASHINGTON

★1261★ CHINOOK SCENIC BYWAY

c/o Mount Baker-Snoqualmie National Forest
21905 64th Avenue W
Mountlake Terrace, WA 98043
Web: www.fs.fed.us/r6/mbs/
Phone: 425-775-9702
Length: 85 miles. **Designation/Year:** All-American Road (1998). **Description:** Byway encompasses the unique beauty of both Mount Rainier National Park and the Mather Parkway. Working its way through scenic Mount Baker-Snoqualmie National Forest, it is the most accessible road for viewing 14,410-foot Mount Rainier. Areas of interest include Boulder Cave, Norse Peak Wilderness Area, Edgar Rock Historic CCC Camp, Chinook Pass Overlook, Boulder Cave Recreation Trail, Skookum Flats (one of the best bicycle trails in the country) and Federation Forest State Park. **Start/Endpoint:** Starting from Enumclaw, byway follows WA 410 through Greenwater and Cliffdell to Naches. **Time to Allow:** 3 hours.

★1262★ COULEE CORRIDOR SCENIC BYWAY

c/o Ephrata Chamber of Commerce
PO Box 275
Ephrata, WA 98823
Web: www.byways.org/browse/byways/54772/
Phone: 509-754-4656

Length: 150 miles. **Designation/Year:** National Scenic Byway (2005). **Description:** The entire corridor consists of a series of coulees, or dry canyons, which were shaped by the rushing torrents released when a 2000-foot natural ice dam melted in Montana. This Ice Age flood also left behind boulders, gravel bars and sand dunes, and carved out 900-foot basalt cliffs. Areas of interest include: Lake Roosevelt National Recreation Area, the Grand Coulee Dam, the Colville Tribal Museum, Dry Falls (the remains of a waterfall once ten times the size of Niagara Falls), Soap Lake, Moses Lake Museum & Art Center, and Columbia National Wildlife Refuge. **Start/Endpoint:** Located in north-central Washington, byway runs north/south from Omak along parts of three highway routes (SR 155, US 2 and SR 17) to Othello. **Time to Allow:** 3.5 hours.

★1263★ INTERNATIONAL SELKIRK LOOP - WASHINGTON

PO Box 920
Bonners Ferry, ID 83805
Web: www.selkirkloop.org
Phone: 888-823-2626
Length: 77 miles (Washington section); 166 miles (US section); 280 miles (entire byway in the US and Canada). **Designation/Year:** All-American Road (2005). **Description:** Following rivers and lakeshores most of the way, the byway encircles the Selkirk Mountains in northeast Washington, north Idaho, and southeast British Columbia. Historically, the waterways were used for transportation, but today they are a source of year-round recreation that includes boating, water skiing, windsurfing, swimming, fishing, canoeing, kayaking, and rafting. The Washington section of the route runs through river valleys along in the edge of Colville National Forest and enters the ''Forgotten Corner'' of Washington. **Start/Endpoint:** A loop route through northern Idaho, northeastern Washington, and southeastern British Columbia. Washington section of the byway runs from the Idaho state border near Newport, north on SR 20 and SR 31 to the US-Canadian border near Metaline. **Time to Allow:** 2 hours (Washington section); 8-10 hours (entire byway including ferry ride and US-Canadian border crossings).

★1264★ MOUNTAINS TO SOUND GREENWAY

c/o Mountains to Sound Greenway Trust
911 Western Ave, Suite 523
Seattle, WA 98104
Web: www.mtsgreenway.org
Phone: 206-382-5565
Length: 100 miles. **Designation/Year:** National Scenic Byway (1998). **Description:** Greenway features dramatically different landscapes, including the dry plateaus of eastern Washington, the rugged Cascade mountains, forestlands and rural farms, and the city of Seattle on Puget Sound. Along the way, travellers can visit historic logging and mining towns and enjoy numerous scenic spots for outdoor recreation. The I-90 right-of-way can be traveled by bicycle for the entire length of the greenway, including separated and landscaped trails along urban portions of the highway. Many recreational trails exist along the corridor in lands managed by the US Forest Service, the State Department of Natural Resources, State Parks, and private lands. **Start/Endpoint:** Byway runs along I-90 from Thorp west to Seattle,

passing through the towns of Easton, North Bend, and Issaquah. **Time to Allow:** 2 hours.

★1265★ STEVENS PASS GREENWAY

c/o Leavenworth Chamber of Commerce & Visitors Office
PO Box 327
Leavenworth, WA 98826
Web: www.byways.org/browse/byways/2231/
Phone: 509-548-5807
Length: 89 miles. **Designation/Year:** National Scenic Byway (2005). **Description:** This picturesque drive through a high mountain pass runs from a saltwater port to the rugged Cascades and through a historic railroad district. Byway is one of Washington's two year-round accessible mountain passes. It follows the wild and scenic Skykomish and Wenatchee rivers along most of its length. Originally developed for the Old Great Northern Railway, the route is rich in rail history and is now considered a major corridor for rail freight mobility. Year-round recreational opportunites along the corridor include whitewater rafting, skiing, hiking, fishing, camping, and auto touring. **Start/Endpoint:** Byway runs from Everett east along US 2 to Leavenworth, then southeast on US 2/97 to the town of Wenatchee. **Time to Allow:** 2.5 hours.

★1266★ STRAIGHT OF JUAN DE FUCA HIGHWAY

c/o North Olympic Peninsula Visitor and Convention Bureau
PO Box 670
Port Angeles, WA 98362
Web: www.olympicpeninsula.org
Phone: 800-942-4042
Length: 61 miles. **Designation/Year:** National Scenic Byway (2000). **Description:** Byway follows the shoreline of a glacial fjord that connects Puget Sound to the Pacific Ocean. It skirts Olympic National Park and Olympic National Forest, a unique area that includes temperate rain forest, mountain terrain, and saltwater beaches. Other areas of interest along the byway include: the Salt Creek Recreation Area, featuring the remnants of Fort Hayden; Sail and Seal Rocks, an offshore feeding area for gray whales; and the Makah Indian Reservation, which includes the Makah Cultural Museum and a hiking trail leading to the coast and to Cape Flattery, the most northwestern point of the contiguous United States. **Start/Endpoint:** Byway begins just west of Port Angeles at the Elwha River Overlook and follows SR 112 west to the Makah Indian Reservation. **Time to Allow:** 2 hours.

WEST VIRGINIA

★1267★ COAL HERITAGE TRAIL

c/o Coal Heritage Highway Authority/National Coal Heritage
  Area
PO Box 5176
Beckley, WV 25801
Web: www.coalheritage.org
Phone: 304-256-6941
Length: 98 miles. **Designation/Year:** National Scenic Byway (1998). **Description:** Route traverses four southern West Virginia counties in a region that commemorates the history and culture of the coal industry. Areas of interest include the Beckley Exhibition Coal Mine and the historic town of Bramwell. Byway also offers recreational opportunities, such as fishing on Bluestone Lake, hiking along the Appalachian National Scenic Trail, or camping at Camp Creek State Forest. It crosses the Bluestone National Scenic River near Bramwell and provides access to the New River Gorge east from the town of Beckley. **Start/Endpoint:** Byway runs from West Virginia-Virginia border north along US 52, which turns into SR 16, then continues north to the town of Beckley at the junction of SR 16 and I-77. **Time to Allow:** 3 hours.

★1268★ HIGHLAND SCENIC HIGHWAY

c/o Monongahela National Forest
200 Sycamore St
Elkins, WV 26241
Web: www.byways.org/browse/byways/2460/
Phone: 304-636-1800
Length: 43 miles. **Designation/Year:** National Scenic Byway (1996). **Description:** This route in the Monongahela National Forest passes through river valleys and onto mountain ridges, offering scenic views of the Allegheny Highlands as well as opportunities for walks through mountain bogs and cranberry glades. Areas of interest include the 35,846-acre Cranberry Wilderness and the 750-acre Cranberry Glades Botanical Area, the largest area of bogs in West Virginia. The Monongahela National Forest offers opportunities for camping, hiking, and fishing. **Start/Endpoint:** Byway runs from Richwood along SR 55 and then east on SR 150 until the route ends at the edge of the Monogahela National Forest, at the junction of SR 150 and US 219. **Time to Allow:** 2 hours.

**★1269★ HISTORIC NATIONAL ROAD - WEST
   VIRGINIA**

c/o National Road Alliance of West Virginia, Inc.
PO Box 6338
Wheeling, WV 26003
Web: www.historicwvnationalroad.org
Phone: 800-828-3097
Length: 15.7 miles (West Virginia); 824 miles (entire route). **Designation/Year:** All-American Road (2002). **Description:** America's first interstate highway, the National Road was built to to link the people and cities along the Eastern seaboard to those on the frontiers west of the Allegheny Mountains. Authorized by Congress in 1806, construction of the road began in Cumberland, Maryland in 1811. The road reached Vandalia, then the Illinois state capitol, in 1839 and later was completed to the Illinois border at East St. Louis, opening a link to the water route of the Mississippi.The West Virginia section of the byway passes through Wheeling, where visitors can see West Virginia Independence Hall; Wheeling's "Old Town," a neighborhood of Victorian homes overlooking the Ohio River; Capitol Music Hall, established in 1933 and home to Jamboree USA and the Wheeling Symphony; the Kruger Street Toy and Train Museum, where the annual Marx Toy Convention is held; Wheeling Park and the Wheeling Heritage Trails; and the Wheeling Suspension Bridge, the first to cross the Ohio River; and

the Elm Grove Stone Arch Bridge, the oldest extant bridge in the state. **Start/Endpoint:** The east/west route runs from Baltimore, Maryland, to the Mississippi River at the Eads Bridge in East Saint Louis, Illinois. It crosses six states: Maryland, West Virginia, Pennsylvania, Ohio, Indiana, and Illinois. The West Virginia section of the byway begins at the Pennsylvania-West Virginia state line on US 40 and continues into the city of Wheeling where it crosses the Wheeling Suspension Bridge. The byway continues onto Wheeling Island and ends across a bridge that leads to Bridgeport, Ohio.

★1270★ **MIDLAND TRAIL**

c/o Midland Trail Scenic Highway Association
237 Capitol St
Charleston, WV 25301
Web: www.midlandtrail.com
Phone: 304-343-6001
Length: 117 miles. **Designation/Year:** National Scenic Byway (2000). **Description:** Byway is a gateway to world-class whitewater rafting, with access to the New and Gauley rivers. Several outfitters in the area offer Class V-VI rafting. The area is also a mecca for outdoor activities such as rock climbing on the face of the New River Gorge. The trail itself was a warpath for both Union and Confederate armies during the Civil War and includes a number of historical sites. Other points of interest include the Greenbrier Hotel, a National Historic Landmark and West Virginia's only five-star resort, and the nearby Oakhurst Links, the oldest golf course in the country, built in 1884. **Start/Endpoint:** Route runs from the town of White Sulphur Springs northwest on US 60 to just past Charleston. **Time to Allow:** 2 hours.

★1271★ **STAUNTON-PARKERSBURG TURNPIKE**

c/o Staunton-Parkersburg Turnpike Alliance
PO Box 227
Beverly, WV 26253
Web: www.spturnpike.org
Phone: 304-637-7424
Length: 180 miles. **Designation/Year:** National Scenic Byway (2005). **Description:** Connecting the upper Shenandoah Valley with the Ohio River, the route was essential to early development and settlement of the area. It was also of prime importance in the political dissension that led to the separation and eventual statehood of the section of Virginia that became West Virginia. The historic byway and associated backways include such Civil War sites as the Rich Mountain Battlefield, Beverly Historic District, Cheat Summit Fort, Camp Bartow, and Camp Allegheny. Accompanying points of interest are the many historic sites, houses, and towns revealing the hardships of early life experienced by the settlers. **Start/Endpoint:** Byway follows US 250 west from the West Virginia-Virginia state line to Huttonsville, then US 219 north to Beverly, US 33 to near Troy, and SR 47 to Parkersburg.

★1272★ **WASHINGTON HERITAGE TRAIL**

c/o Jefferson County Convention and Visitors Bureau
37 Washington Ct
Harpers Ferry, WV 25425
Web: www.washingtonheritagetrail.org
Phone: 866-435-5698
Length: 137 miles. **Designation/Year:** National Scenic Byway (2000). **Description:** Byway traverses a landscape rich in historic, natural and scenic resources, from forest covered mountains and valley farmland to historic towns and remains of bygone industries. Near the byway visitors will find Harper's Ferry National Historical Park, 21 National Register Historic Districts, and 126 National Register Historic Sites, many of which are associated with George Washington's family. A number of live history programs, including artillery demonstrations and battle reenactments, are carried out throughout the year. **Start/Endpoint:** From the community of Pawpaw, byway runs north to Berkeley Springs along SR 9, where it become a loop route. The north loop follows SR 9, then several county roads and SR 480 southeast to Shepherdstown, then south on CR 230 and US 340 to Charlestown. The south loop runs southwest from Berkeley Springs on County Road 9/10 until it joins with US 522, then follows several county roads to Charlestown and US 340.

WISCONSIN

★1273★ **GREAT RIVER ROAD - WISCONSIN**

c/o Wisconsin Department of Tourism
PO Box 8690
Madison, WI 53708
Web: www.wigreatriverroad.org
Phone: 800-432-8747
Length: 249 miles (Wisconsin section); 2,069 miles (entire byway). **Designation/Year:** National Scenic Byway (2000). **Description:** The 2,069-mile Great River Road borders the Mississippi River through the states of Mississippi, Arkansas, Iowa, Illinois, Wisconsin, and Minnesota. The Wisconsin segment of the byway flanks the Mississippi River along the state's western border, displaying the culture and heritage of 33 river towns. Travelers can stop at the 30 or more state historical markers and archaeological sites, and also at the many local museums, which tell the stories of early Indian occupants, the French fur traders and explorers, the lead mining boom, the steamboat era, and the lumber barons. Recreational opportunities include 50 local parks and beaches, and 12 state and 3 national recreational resources. **Start/Endpoint:** The northern gateway of the Wisconsin Great River Road at Prescott is 30 miles southeast of Saint Paul, Minnesota, via US 10 and US 61. The southern gateway is near the east end of the US 20 Mississippi River bridge in Dubuque, Iowa at the Illinois state line. **Time to Allow:** 10 hours (Wisconsin section); 6 days (entire byway)

WYOMING

★1274★ **BEARTOOTH SCENIC BYWAY - WYOMING**

c/o Friends of the Beartooth All-American Road
1108 14th St, #403
Cody, WY 82414
Web: www.beartoothhighway.com
Phone: 307-587-3669
Length: 39 miles (Wyoming section); 69 miles (entire byway). **Designation/Year:** All-American Road (2000). **Description:**

Regarded as one of the most spectacular national forest routes in North America, the Beartooth runs from the historic mining town of Red Lodge to the northeast entrance of Yellowstone National Park. Surrounded by the Custer, Gallatin, and Shoshone national forests, it offers travelers the opportunity to observe the transition from a lush forest ecosystem to alpine tundra in the space of a few miles. The Beartooths are one of the highest elevation and most rugged areas in the lower 48 states, with 20 peaks over 12,000 feet in elevation. The road itself is the highest elevation highway in Wyoming (10,947 feet) and Montana (10,350 feet), and is the highest elevation highway in the Northern Rockies. **Start/Endpoint:** From the south, access to the Beartooth All-American Road is via WY 120 from Cody, Wyoming, and then WY 296 (the Chief Joseph Scenic Byway) to its intersection with the Beartooth Highway. **Time to Allow:** 1.5 hours (Wyoming); 3 hours (entire byway).

9. STATE PARKS

Alabama State Parks

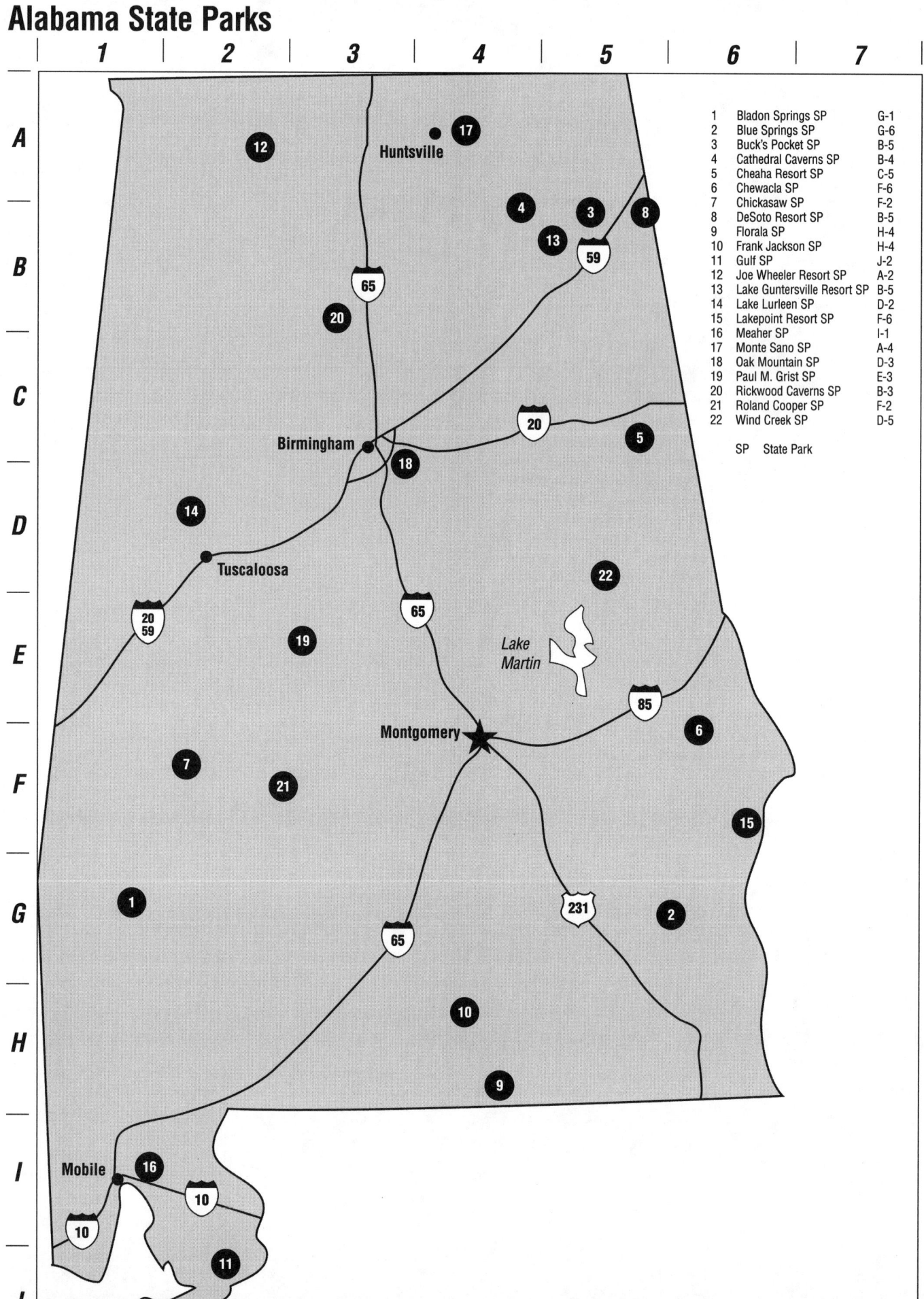

1	Bladon Springs SP	G-1
2	Blue Springs SP	G-6
3	Buck's Pocket SP	B-5
4	Cathedral Caverns SP	B-4
5	Cheaha Resort SP	C-5
6	Chewacla SP	F-6
7	Chickasaw SP	F-2
8	DeSoto Resort SP	B-5
9	Florala SP	H-4
10	Frank Jackson SP	H-4
11	Gulf SP	J-2
12	Joe Wheeler Resort SP	A-2
13	Lake Guntersville Resort SP	B-5
14	Lake Lurleen SP	D-2
15	Lakepoint Resort SP	F-6
16	Meaher SP	I-1
17	Monte Sano SP	A-4
18	Oak Mountain SP	D-3
19	Paul M. Grist SP	E-3
20	Rickwood Caverns SP	B-3
21	Roland Cooper SP	F-2
22	Wind Creek SP	D-5

SP   State Park

ALABAMA

★1275★ **Alabama Division of State Parks**
64 N Union St
Montgomery, AL 36130
(334) 242-3333 - Phone
(334) 242-2137 - Fax
(800) 252-7275 - Toll-free
Web: www.alapark.com
Mission of the Division is to acquire and preserve natural areas; to develop, furnish, operate and maintain recreational facilities; and to extend the public's knowledge of the state's natural environment. System covers nearly 48,000 acres and consists of 24 parks, including seven designated as resort parks. Parks include more than 200 miles of trails.

★1276★ **Alabama Division of Wildlife & Freshwater Fisheries**
64 N Union St
Montgomery, AL 36130
(334) 242-3469 - Phone
(334) 242-3032 - Fax
Web: www.conservation.alabama.gov/agfd
Responsible for management, protection, conservation, and enhancement of the wildlife and aquatic resources of Alabama. Administers hunting and fishing licensing; supports hunter education programs; enforces state wildlife laws. Maintains 34 wildlife management areas, 2 wildlife refuges, and 2 sanctuaries, covering nearly 789,000 acres. Monitors and stocks 23 public fishing lakes totaling 1,912 surface acres.

★1277★ **Alabama Historical Commission**
468 S Perry St
Montgomery, AL 36130-0900 (334) 242-3184 - Phone
(334) 240-3477 - Fax
Web: www.preserveala.org
Protects and preserves Alabama's historical properties; operates 12 historic sites open to the public.

Key to campsite classification:

- **Modern campsites** — Sites include water, electricity, and sewage hookups, picnic tables, and grills. At most parks, restrooms with showers, laundries, and dump stations are located nearby.
- **Primitive campsites** — No hookups. Water and restroom facilities are located nearby.

★1278★ **BLADON SPRINGS STATE PARK**
3921 Bladon Rd
Bladon Springs, AL 36919
Web: www.alapark.com/parks
Phone: 334-754-9207; **Fax:** 334-754-9207

Size: 357 acres. **Location:** 1 mile north of Bladon Springs in southwest Alabama. **Facilities:** 10 modern campsites, picnic areas, group pavilion (&), restrooms, playground. **Activities:** Camping, picnicking. **Special Features:** Park centers on four mineral springs, popular in the 19th century for their purported health benefits.

★1279★ **BLUE SPRINGS STATE PARK**
2595 Hwy 10
Clio, AL 36017
Web: www.alapark.com/parks
Phone: 334-397-4875; **Fax:** 334-397-4875
Size: 103 acres. **Location:** 6 miles east of Clio in southeast Alabama. **Facilities:** 50 modern campsites, primitive campsites, comfort station (&), picnic area (&), group pavilion, playground, snack bar. **Activities:** Camping, boating (nonmotorized), fishing, swimming. **Special Features:** Park's swimming pool is fed by a crystal clear underground spring.

★1280★ **BUCK'S POCKET STATE PARK**
393 County Rd 174
Grove Oak, AL 35975
Web: www.alapark.com/parks
Phone: 256-659-2000; **Fax:** 256-659-2000
Size: 2,000 acres. **Location:** 2 miles north of Grove Oak in northeast Alabama. **Facilities:** 36 modern campsites, primitive campsites, picnic area, group pavilion, comfort stations, camp store, snack bar, trails (hiking and bicycle trails and a 6-mile horseback trail), playground; boat launch nearby. **Activities:** Camping, boating, fishing, hiking, horseback riding. **Special Features:** Park lies in a secluded natural pocket of the Appalachian Mountain chain and its picnic area offers a canyon rim view into the pocket below.

★1281★ **CATHEDRAL CAVERNS STATE PARK**
637 Cave Rd
Woodville, AL 35776
Web: www.alapark.com/parks
Phone: 256-728-8193; **Fax:** 256-728-8193
Size: 461 acres. **Location:** 3 miles south of Hwy 72 off of Cathedral Caverns Highway between Woodville and Grant. **Facilities:** Primitive campsites, comfort station (&), group pavilion (&), picnic area, playground, welcome center with restrooms, gifts, and refreshments. **Activities:** Guided tours. **Special Features:** Cavern features include Big Rock Canyon, Mystery River, and Goliath, a huge stalagmite column that reaches the cave ceiling 45 feet above.

★1282★ **CHEAHA RESORT STATE PARK**
19644 Hwy 281
Delta, AL 36258
Web: www.alapark.com/parks
Phone: 256-488-5111; **Fax:** 256-488-5885; **Toll Free:** 800-610-5801

275

Size: 2,799 acres. Location: 12 miles south of I-20, off State Hwy 281 in northeast Alabama. Facilities: 73 modern campsites, primitive campsites, comfort stations, 15 family cottages (some pet-friendly), 30-room lodge, convention facilities, group lodge (32-person capacity), playground, trails, picnic area, group pavilions, restaurant, snack bar, camp store, gift shop (&&). Activities: Camping, boating (nonmotorized), fishing, swimming, hiking, mountain biking, nature programs. Special Features: The park is located atop Cheaha Mountain, the state's highest point at 2,407 feet, and is surrounded by Talladega National Forest. An observation tower at the summit affords a 360-degree panoramic view.

★1283★ CHEWACLA STATE PARK

124 Shell Toomer Pkwy
Auburn, AL 36830
Web: www.alapark.com/parks
Phone: 334-887-5621; Fax: 334-821-2439
Size: 696 acres. Location: 4 miles south of Auburn off I-85. Facilities: 36 modern campsites, primitive campsites, comfort stations, 6 family cottages, picnic area, group pavilions, 8 trails (including a mountain bike trail and a tree identification trail), boat rentals, snack bar, tennis courts, playground. Activities: Camping, boating (nonmotorized), fishing, swimming, hiking, mountain biking, tennis. Special Features: Recreational activities center on the park's 26-acre lake.

★1284★ CHICKASAW STATE PARK

26955 US Hwy 43
Gallion, AL 36742
Web: www.alapark.com/parks
Phone: 334-295-8230; Fax: 334-295-8230
Size: 520 acres. Location: On US 43, 4 miles north of Linden in west central Alabama. Facilities: 8 modern campsites, primitive campsites, comfort station, picnic areas, group pavilions, hiking trails, playground, wading pool. Activities: Camping, hiking. Special Features: Park is adjacent to a wheelchair-accessible state-operated hunting facility.

★1285★ DESOTO RESORT STATE PARK

13883 County Rd 89
Fort Payne, AL 35967
Web: www.alapark.com/parks
Phone: 256-845-0051; Fax: 256-845-8286
Size: 3,502 acres. Location: 8 miles northeast of Fort Payne in northeast Alabama. Facilities: 78 modern campsites, primitive campsites, comfort stations, 22 family cottages, 25-room lodge, meeting rooms, picnic area, group pavilions, hiking trails (12 miles), a boardwalk trail, nature center, restaurant, gift shop, snack bar, camp store, tennis courts, playground (&&). Activities: Camping, fishing, swimming, hiking, tennis, nature programs. Special Features: Situated atop Lookout Mountain, the park features spectacular views of waterfalls, including the 104-foot DeSoto Falls.

★1286★ FLORALA STATE PARK

22738 Azalea Dr
Florala, AL 36442
Web: www.alapark.com/parks
Phone: 334-858-6425; Fax: 334-858-6425
Size: 40 acres. Location: Located in the city of Florala in south central Alabama, on the Alabama/Florida state line. Facilities: 23 modern campsites, comfort stations, meeting room, picnic area, group pavilions, snack bar, boat launch, fishing pier, paddle boat rentals, playground. Activities: Camping, boating, fishing, water skiing, swimming. Special Features: Park is located along the shores of 500-acre Lake Jackson, which is considered one of the clearest and cleanest bodies of water in the state.

★1287★ FRANK JACKSON STATE PARK

100 Jerry Adams Dr
Opp, AL 36467
Web: www.alapark.com/parks
Phone: 334-493-6988; Fax: 334-493-2478
Size: 2,050 acres. Location: In the town of Opp, in south central Alabama. Facilities: 26 modern campsites (&), primitive campsites, comfort stations (&), picnic areas, group pavilion, walking trail, bathhouse, boat launch ramp, fishing platform (&), playground. Activities: Camping, boating, fishing, swimming, hiking. Special Features: A premier fishing destination, the park features a 1000-acre, stream-fed lake (Lake Frank Jackson). There's also a natural island, with a boardwalk and walking path.

★1288★ GULF STATE PARK

20115 State Hwy 135
Gulf Shores, AL 36542
Web: www.alapark.com/parks
Phone: 251-948-7275; Fax: 251-948-7726
Size: 6,150 acres. Location: In the city of Gulf Shores on the coast of Alabama. Facilities: 486 modern campsites, comfort stations (&), camp store (&), 21 family cottages (&), picnic areas, group pavilions, trails (temporarily closed due to Hurricane Katrina), marina, snack bar, 18-hole golf course, tennis courts, playground. Activities: Camping, boating, fishing (saltwater and freshwater), swimming, water skiing, hiking, bicycling, tennis, golf, nature programs. Special Features: The park is located along the Gulf of Mexico, with 2.5 miles of sugar white sand beach, and plans are currently being developed for a new hotel, restaurant, and conference center on the beach. The park's 825-foot fishing pier on the Gulf was destroyed by Hurricane Ivan, but plans also are underway to construct a new pier. The park also includes Lake Shelby, a 900-acre lake that offers good freshwater fishing as well as boating and swimming. The resort's 18-hole championship golf course is near the lake.

★1289★ JOE WHEELER RESORT STATE PARK

201 McLean Dr
Rogersville, AL 35652
Web: www.alapark.com/parks
Phone: 256-247-5466; Fax: 256-247-1449
Size: 2,550 acres. Location: 2 miles west of Rogersville, off US 72. Facilities: 116 modern campsites, primitive campsites, camp store (&), comfort stations, 25 family cottages, group

9. State Parks

lodge, 75-room resort lodge (&), restaurant (&), convention facilities (&), marina, boat ramps, boat rentals, 18-hole golf course, picnic area, group pavilion, trails (5 miles), snack bar, playground, tennis courts, gift shop. **Activities:** Camping, boating, fishing, swimming, hiking, bicycling, tennis. **Special Features:** The park is divided by the Tennessee River, with its main facilities on the shores of Wheeler Lake on the Tennessee River. The park's group lodge is located within a cove off of Elk River, about 10 miles from the main park area. The cabins are located on the south side of the Tennessee River, near Wheeler Dam, with access to both Wheeler Lake and Wilson Lake.

★1290★ LAKE GUNTERSVILLE RESORT STATE PARK
7966 Alabama Hwy 227
Guntersville, AL 35976
Web: www.dcnr.state.al.us/parks/lake_guntersville_1a.html
Phone: 256-571-5444
Size: 5,909 acres. **Location:** 6 miles northeast of Guntersville, off Highway 227, in northeast Alabama. **Facilities:** 364 modern campsites, primitive campsites, camp store, 35 family cottages (&), 100-room resort lodge with swimming pool, restaurant, convention facilities, gift shop, picnic area, group pavilions, trails, snack bar, 18-hole golf course, tennis courts, playground, nature center. **Activities:** Camping, boating, fishing, swimming, hiking, tennis, eagle watching. **Special Features:** Park is located in the Tennessee Valley overlooking the 69,000-acre Guntersville Reservoir. The resort inn, restaurant, and convention complex (closed for renovation 2004-2006) is situated at the pinnacle of Taylor Mountain, with a view of Lake Guntersville below.

★1291★ LAKE LURLEEN STATE PARK
13226 Lake Lurleen Rd
Coker, AL 35452
Web: www.alapark.com/parks
Phone: 205-339-1558; **Fax:** 205-339-8885
Size: 1,625 acres. **Location:** 12 miles northwest of Tuscaloosa in west central Alabama. **Facilities:** 91 modern campsites, comfort stations, picnic area, group pavilions, an activity building, beach with bathhouse, fishing piers, boat rentals and boat-launch areas, trails (10 miles, including 7 miles of a new multi-use single-track trail open only for foot and mountain bike traffic), playground, camp store, snack bar, playground. **Activities:** Camping, boating, fishing, swimming, hiking. **Special Features:** The park and its 250-acre lake were named for Alabama's only female governor, Lurleen B. Wallace.

★1292★ LAKEPOINT RESORT STATE PARK
104 Lakepoint Dr
Eufaula, AL 36027
Web: www.alapark.com/parks
Phone: 334-687-8011; **Fax:** 334-687-3273; **Toll Free:** 800-544-5253
Size: 1,220 acres. **Location:** 7 miles north of Eufaula, off Highway 431, in southeast Alabama on the Alabama-Georgia line. **Facilities:** 245 modern campsites, camp store, comfort stations,

bathhouses, 29 family cottages (&), 101-room resort lodge with swimming pool and game room, convention facilities, restaurant, gift shop, picnic area (&), group pavilions (&), hiking trails, marina, nature center, 18-hole golf course, snack bar, tennis courts, playground. **Activities:** Camping, boating, fishing, swimming, hiking, tennis, wildlife viewing. **Special Features:** Park is located on the banks of the 45,200-acre Lake Eufaula, "Bass Capital of the World," and adjoins Eufaula National Wildlife Refuge (see entry in national wildlife refuges section).

★1293★ MEAHER STATE PARK
5200 Battleship Pkwy E
Spanish Fort, AL 36577
Web: www.alapark.com/parks
Phone: 251-626-5529; **Fax:** 251-626-5529
Size: 1,327 acres. **Location:** 2 miles west of Spanish Fort on Highway 90 in southwest Alabama. **Facilities:** 11 modern campsites, picnic areas, group pavilion, nature trails, boat ramp, fishing pier, playground. **Activities:** Boating, fishing, hiking, wildlife viewing. **Special Features:** Located in the wetlands of Mobile Bay, the park's two nature trails include a boardwalk with a view of the Mobile Delta.

★1294★ MONTE SANO STATE PARK
5105 Nolen Ave
Huntsville, AL 35801
Web: www.alapark.com/parks
Phone: 256-534-3757; **Fax:** 256-539-7069
Size: 2,140 acres. **Location:** Within the city limits of Huntsville in northeast Alabama. **Facilities:** 89 modern campsites (&), primitive campsites, comfort stations, 14 family cottages, lodge with meeting facilities, picnic area, group pavilions, hiking trails (20 miles), mountain bike trail (8 miles), camp store, playground, amphitheater. **Activities:** Camping, hiking, mountain biking, wildlife viewing. **Special Features:** Monte Sano's mountaintop retreat combines the history of the 1930s Civilian Conservation Corps building projects with the technology of the modern Space and Rocket Center city of Huntsville. The lodge originally built by the CCC and destroyed by fire in 1947 has been reconstructed, restoring the facility's beauty while also modernizing it and keeping its original intent available to the public. Other developments of the CCC that are still in use include 11 stone cabins, the picnic area and pavilions, and an amphitheatre.

★1295★ OAK MOUNTAIN STATE PARK
200 Terrace Dr
PO Box 278
Pelham, AL 35124
Web: www.alapark.com/parks
Phone: 205-620-2520; **Fax:** 205-620-2531
Size: 9,940 acres. **Location:** Just off I-65, 15 miles south of Birmingham in central Alabama. **Facilities:** 150 modern campsites, primitive campsites, comfort stations, camp store, 10 family cottages (&), meeting rooms, picnic areas, group pavilions, playground, 50 miles of hiking, biking, and equestrian trails (&), horse stables, 18-hole golf course, pro shop and snack bar, demonstration farm. **Activities:** Camping, boating (no gas motors), fishing, swimming, hiking, horseback riding, mountain

9. State Parks

biking, golf, nature programs. **Special Features:** Oak Mountain is Alabama's largest park, with pine-studded ridges and lush green hardwood bottoms. The state's largest wildlife rehabilitation center is located in the park, and more than 2,000 injured and orphaned wild creatures are cared for there each year. Visitors may view the rehabilitation process through one way glass. In addition, the park's Treetop Nature Trail offers close-up views of unreleasable hawks and owls in natural habitat enclosures (&). The oldest continuously operating BMX track in the nation is also located at the park.

★1296★ PAUL M. GRIST STATE PARK

1546 Grist Rd
Selma, AL 36701
Web: www.alapark.com/parks
Phone: 334-872-5846; **Fax:** 334-872-5846
Size: 1,080 acres. **Location:** 15 miles north of Selma in the central section of Alabama. **Facilities:** 6 modern campsites (&), primitive campsites, comfort stations (&), picnic area (&), group pavilions (&), hiking trail, boat launch, snack bar. **Activities:** Camping, boating (no gas motors), fishing, swimming, hiking. **Special Features:** The park's centerpiece is a 100-acre lake stocked with bass, bluegill, redear sunfish, and catfish.

★1297★ RICKWOOD CAVERNS STATE PARK

370 Rickwood Park Rd
Warrior, AL 35180
Web: www.alapark.com/parks
Phone: 205-647-9692; **Fax:** 205-647-9692
Size: 380 acres. **Location:** 4 miles off I-65 at Exit 284 near Warrior in north central Alabama. **Facilities:** 13 modern campsites, comfort stations, picnic areas, group pavilions, hiking trails, Olympic-size swimming pool, gift shop, snack bar, playground (&)(&). **Activities:** Camping, swimming, hiking, miniature-train ride, spelunking, guided tours. **Special Features:** The park's caverns extend for a mile underground, with features that include colorful 260 million-year-old limestone formations, blind cave fish, and an underground pool. The park is open year round. Cavern tours are available week-ends March-May and September-October, with daily tours available from Memorial Day through Labor Day. The caverns are closed November-February.

★1298★ ROLAND COOPER STATE PARK

285 Deer Run Dr
Camden, AL 36726
Web: www.alapark.com/parks
Phone: 334-682-4838; **Fax:** 334-682-4050
Size: 236 acres. **Location:** 6 miles northeast of Camden in south central Alabama. **Facilities:** 47 modern campsites with bathhouse, laundry, and camp store, primitive campsites, 5 family cottages, picnic area, group pavilion, comfort station, trails, boat launch, 9-hole golf course, snack bar, playground. **Activities:** Camping, boating, fishing, hiking, golf. **Special Features:** The park is set in a pine forest along the 22,000-acre Millers Ferry Reservoir on the Alabama River and offers excellent fishing, especially for bass and crappie.

★1299★ WIND CREEK STATE PARK

4325 Alabama Hwy 128
Alexander City, AL 35010
Web: www.alapark.com/parks
Phone: 256-329-0845; **Fax:** 256-234-4870
Size: 1,445 acres. **Location:** 7 miles southeast of Alexander City in east central Alabama. **Facilities:** 626 modern campsites (&), comfort stations, picnic areas (&), group pavilions (&), hiking trails (about 8 miles total), marina, fishing pier, camp store, snack bar, playground; 10 camping cabins are under construction, with 3 now open. **Activities:** Camping, boating, fishing, swimming, hiking. **Special Features:** Park is situated along the shores of 41,000-acre Lake Martin and offers the nation's largest state-run campgrounds. Many of the campsites are waterfront, allowing campers to fish, swim, and launch boats from their own sites.

Alaska State Parks

1	Afognak Island SP	G-8
2	Alaska Chilkat Bald Eagle Preserve	F-12
3	Anchor River SRA	F-8
4	Baranof Castle SHS	F-13
5	Beecher Pass SMP	G-13
6	Bettles Bay SMP	F-9
7	Big Bear/Baby Bear SMP	G-13
8	Big Delta SHP	D-9
9	Big Lake North SRS	F-9
10	Big Lake South SRS	F-9
11	Birch Lake SRA	D-9
12	Black Sands Beach SMP	G-14
13	Blair Lake SRA	E-8
14	Blueberry Lake SRS	F-10
15	Boswell Bay SMP	F-10
16	Buskin River SRS	G-8
17	Caines Head SRA	F-9
18	Canoe Passage SMP	F-10
19	Captain Cook SRA	F-9
20	Chena River SRA	F-8
21	Chena River SRS	D-9
22	Chilkat Islands SMP	F-12
23	Chilkat SP	F-12
24	Chilkoot Lake SRS	E-12
25	Chugach SP	F-9
26	Clam Gulch SRA	F-9
27	Clearwater SRS	D-9
28	Crooked Creek SRS	F-9
29	Dall Bay SMP	G-14
30	Decision Point SMP	F-9
31	Deep Creek SRA	F-8
32	Delta SRS	D-9
33	Denali SP	E-8
34	Donnelly Creek SRS	D-9
35	Driftwood Bay SMP	F-9
36	Dry Creek SRS	E-9
37	Eagle Beach SRA	F-12
38	Eagle Trail SRS	E-10
39	Entry Cove SMP	F-9
40	Ernest Gruening SHP	F-13
41	Fielding Lake SRS	D-9
42	Finger Lake SRA	F-9
43	Fort Abercrombie SHP	G-8
44	Funter Bay SMP	F-13
45	Granite Bay SMP	F-9
46	Grindall Island SMP	G-14
47	Halibut Point SRS	F-13
48	Harding Lake SRA	D-9
49	Hatcher Pass East Management Area	E-9
50	Horseshoe Bay SMP	F-9
51	Independence Mine SHP	E-9
52	Jack Bay SMP	F-9
53	Joe Mace Island SMP	G-13

54	Johnson Creek SRS	F-13
55	Johnson Lake SRA	F-8
56	Juneau Trail System	F-13
57	Kachemak Bay SP	G-8
58	Kasilof River SRS	F-8
59	Kayak Island SMP	F-10
60	Kenai River Special Management Area	F-8
61	Kepler-Bradley Lakes SRA	E-9
62	King Mountain SRS	E-9
63	Lake Aleknagik SRS	F-5
64	Lake Louise SRA	E-9
65	Liberty Falls SRS	E-10
66	Lowell Point SRS	F-9
67	Lower Chatanika River SRA	C-9
68	Magoun Islands SMP	G-13
69	Matanuska Glacier SRS	E-9
70	Montana Creek SRS	E-8
71	Moon Lake SRS	D-10
72	Mosquito Lake SRS	E-12
73	Nancy Lake SRA	E-9
74	Nancy Lake SRS	E-9
75	Ninilchik SRA	F-8
76	Old Sitka SHP	F-13

Alaska State Parks

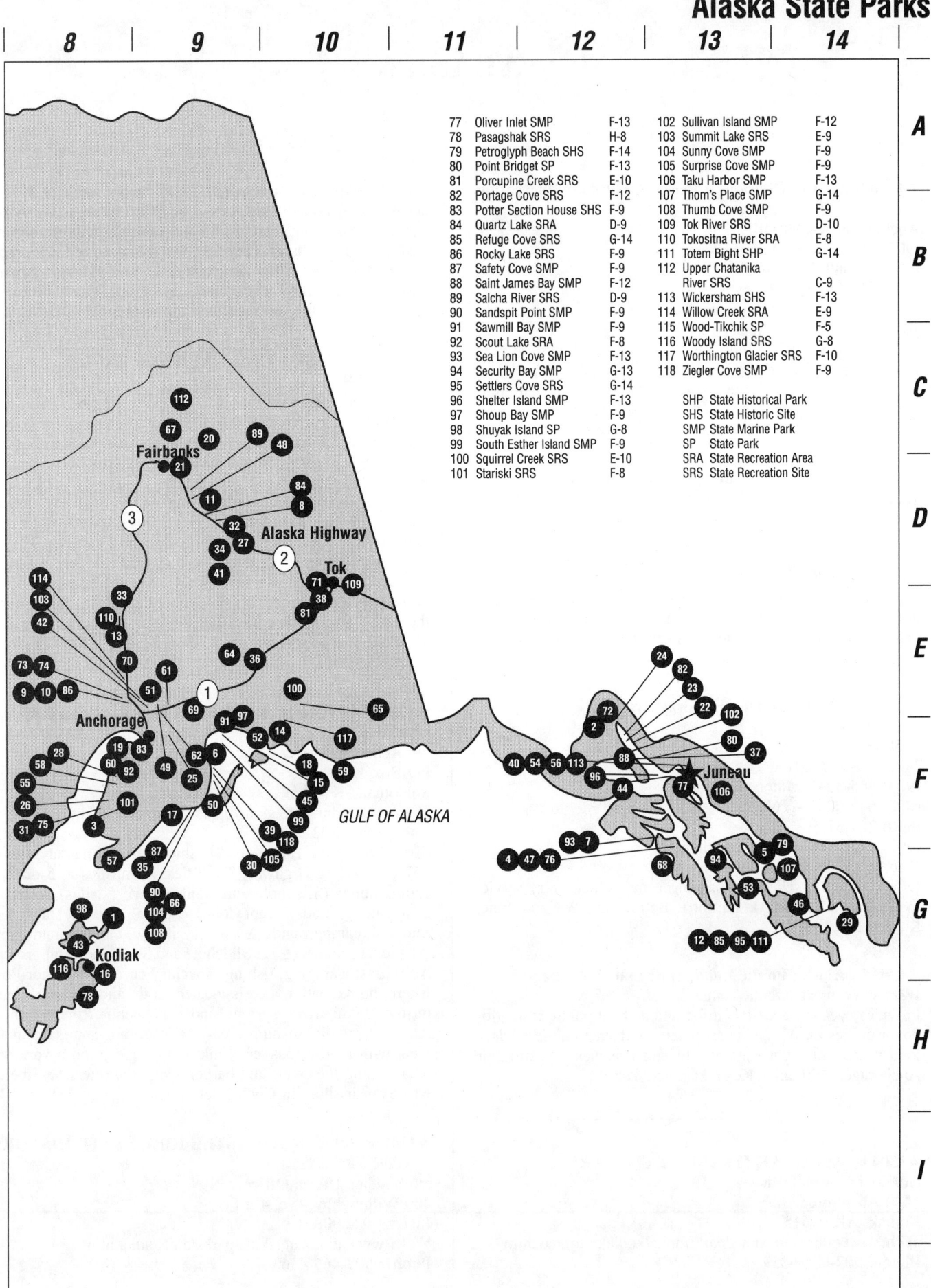

77	Oliver Inlet SMP	F-13
78	Pasagshak SRS	H-8
79	Petroglyph Beach SHS	F-14
80	Point Bridget SP	F-13
81	Porcupine Creek SRS	E-10
82	Portage Cove SRS	F-12
83	Potter Section House SHS	F-9
84	Quartz Lake SRA	D-9
85	Refuge Cove SRS	G-14
86	Rocky Lake SRS	F-9
87	Safety Cove SMP	F-9
88	Saint James Bay SMP	F-12
89	Salcha River SRS	D-9
90	Sandspit Point SMP	F-9
91	Sawmill Bay SMP	F-9
92	Scout Lake SRA	F-8
93	Sea Lion Cove SMP	F-13
94	Security Bay SMP	G-13
95	Settlers Cove SRS	G-14
96	Shelter Island SMP	F-13
97	Shoup Bay SMP	F-9
98	Shuyak Island SP	G-8
99	South Esther Island SMP	F-9
100	Squirrel Creek SRS	E-10
101	Stariski SRS	F-8

102	Sullivan Island SMP	F-12
103	Summit Lake SRS	E-9
104	Sunny Cove SMP	F-9
105	Surprise Cove SMP	F-9
106	Taku Harbor SMP	F-13
107	Thom's Place SMP	G-14
108	Thumb Cove SMP	F-9
109	Tok River SRS	D-10
110	Tokositna River SRA	E-8
111	Totem Bight SHP	G-14
112	Upper Chatanika River SRS	C-9
113	Wickersham SHS	F-13
114	Willow Creek SRA	E-9
115	Wood-Tikchik SP	F-5
116	Woody Island SRS	G-8
117	Worthington Glacier SRS	F-10
118	Ziegler Cove SMP	F-9

SHP State Historical Park
SHS State Historic Site
SMP State Marine Park
SP State Park
SRA State Recreation Area
SRS State Recreation Site

ALASKA

★1300★ Alaska Division of Parks & Outdoor Recreation
550 W 7th Ave, Suite 1380
Anchorage, AK 99501
(907) 269-8700 - Phone
(907) 269-8907 - Fax
(907) 269-8670 - Employment
(907) 269-8708 - Volunteering
Web: www.dnr.state.ak.us/parks
With more than 3.2 million acres, Alaska's park system is by far the largest, comprising nearly one-third of all state park land in the United States. Protected lands include recreation areas, marine parks, historical sites, and wildlife preserves and range in size from one-half acre to 1.6 million acres.

★1301★ Alaska Department of Fish & Game
1255 W 8th St
PO Box 115526
Juneau, AK 99811
(907) 465-4100
Web: www.adfg.state.ak.us/
Conserves and manages fish and wildlife resources. Regulates hunting and fishing licensing and enforces state wildlife laws. Oversees refuges, sanctuaries, and habitat areas essential to the propagation of native species.

★1302★ Alaska Marine Highway System
P.O. Box 112505
6858 Glacier Highway
Juneau, AK 99801
(907) 465-3941 - Phone (Juneau)
(800) 642-0066 - Toll-free
(800) 764-3779 - TTY
(907) 272-7116 - Phone (Anchorage)
Web: www.dot.state.ak.us/amhs
Offers regularly scheduled passenger and vehicle ferry service to 32 communities in Alaska, and to Bellingham, WA and Prince Rupert, BC.

★1303★ Alaska Public Lands Information Centers
Web: www.nps.gov/aplic/center
Provides one-stop access to information about public recreation opportunities on Alaska's vast federal and state public lands; a joint project of eight state and federal agencies. Locations in Anchorage, Fairbanks, Ketchikan, and Tok.

★1304★ AFOGNAK ISLAND STATE PARK
c/o Kodiak Area Office
1400 Abercrombie Dr
Kodiak, AK 99615
Web: www.dnr.state.ak.us/parks/units/kodiak/afognak.htm
Phone: 907-486-6339

Size: 75,049 acres. **Location:** 25 air miles north of Kodiak; accessible by boat or floatplane. **Facilities:** 2 cabins. **Activities:** Canoeing/kayaking, fishing, hiking, hunting, wildlife observation. **Special Features:** Park is known for its rugged topography, dense old-growth Sitka spruce forests, and salmon spawning habitat. Kodiak brown bear, Sitka black-tailed deer, Roosevelt elk, and the endangered marbled murrelet inhabit the park.

★1305★ ALASKA CHILKAT BALD EAGLE PRESERVE
c/o Southeast Area Office
400 Willoughby Ave, 4th Fl
Juneau, AK 99801
Web: www.dnr.state.ak.us/parks/units/eagleprv.htm
Phone: 907-465-4563
Size: 49,320 acres. **Location:** Along Haines Highway, between mileposts 8 and 30. **Facilities:** Picnic sites, toilets, water, boat launch. **Activities:** Eagle watching. **Special Features:** The preserve provides critical habitat for the world's largest concentration of bald eagles. The area is a year-round home for 200 to 400 eagles and seasonal home to more than 3,000 eagles during the Fall Congregation (October through February). The main viewing area is between miles 18 and 24 of Haines Highway, where the Chilkat River fans out and rarely freezes.

★1306★ ANCHOR RIVER STATE RECREATION AREA
c/o Kenai/PWS Area Office
PO Box 1247
Soldotna, AK 99669
Web: www.dnr.state.ak.us/parks/units/anchoriv.htm
Phone: 907-262-5581
Size: 228 acres. **Location:** Northwest of Homer at milepost 157 on Sterling Highway. **Facilities:** Campsites at 5 different campgrounds (Slidehole and Halibut have ♿ sites), toilets (♿ at all campgrounds except Coho), drinking water at Halibut and Slidehole campgrounds (♿), picnic sites at 3 campgrounds (some ♿), picnic shelters (♿) at Slidehole and Steelhead campgrounds. **Activities:** Camping, fishing. **Special Features:** Anchor Point, where the recreation area is located, is the most westerly point on the US highway system, and the Anchor River is one of Alaska's premier fishing areas. Wildlife are abundant in this area, with moose, beaver, mink, bald eagles, and a variety of ducks along the river, and harbor seals, sea otters, and beluga whales near shore in Cook Inlet.

★1307★ BARANOF CASTLE HILL STATE HISTORIC SITE
c/o Southeast Area Office
400 Willoughby Ave, 4th Fl
Juneau, AK 99801
Web: www.dnr.state.ak.us/parks/units/sitka.htm
Phone: 907-465-4563

Size: 1 acre. **Location:** In downtown Sitka on Lincoln Street. **Facilities:** Walkway (&) to site, interpretive panels. **Special Features:** Castle Hill is the site of the transfer of the Alaska territory from Russia to the United States in 1867. Tlingit natives originally inhabited this area and built a strategic fortification at this site. A walk to the top of the hill provides spectacular views of downtown Sitka and the waterfront.

★1308★ BEECHER PASS STATE MARINE PARK
c/o Southeast Area Office
400 Willoughby Ave, 4th Fl
Juneau, AK 99801
Phone: 907-465-4563
Size: 660 acres. **Location:** West of Wrangell; no road access. **Facilities:** Undeveloped. **Activities:** Fishing, hunting. **Special Features:** Park consists of a series of small islands and coves used extensively by the local population for fishing and hunting. Fishing here is excellent.

★1309★ BETTLES BAY STATE MARINE PARK
c/o Kenai/PWS Area Office
PO Box 1247
Soldotna, AK 99669
Web: www.dnr.state.ak.us/parks/units/pwssmp/smpwhit2.htm
Phone: 907-262-5581
Size: 680 acres. **Location:** One of several state marine parks that can be reached from Whittier; accessible only by boat. **Facilities:** Undeveloped. **Activities:** Boating, fishing, wildlife viewing. There are campsites here, but camping is generally poor due to the wetlands. **Special Features:** Park is well protected from winds and has a good soft holding bottom, making it an excellent anchorage. The park affords excellent views of the scenic Bettles Glacier, and attractions include an old stamp press and gold mine located just southeast of the park.

★1310★ BIG BEAR/BABY BEAR STATE MARINE PARK
c/o Southeast Area Office
400 Willoughby Ave, 4th Fl
Juneau, AK 99801
Web: www.dnr.state.ak.us/parks/units/sitka.htm
Phone: 907-465-4563
Size: 1,032 acres. **Location:** Near Peril Straits, about 35 miles north of Sitka; no road access. **Facilities:** Undeveloped. **Activities:** Camping, fishing, hunting. **Special Features:** Access to this park is primarily by boat and it has no visitor facilities. However, the protected anchorage here provides opportunities for camping, hunting, and fishing.

★1311★ BIG DELTA STATE HISTORICAL PARK
c/o Northern Area Office
3700 Airport Way
Fairbanks, AK 99709
Web: www.dnr.state.ak.us/parks/units/deltajct/bigdelta.htm
Phone: 907-451-2695
Size: 11 acres. **Location:** 8 miles north of Delta Junction at milepost 274.5 on Richardson Highway. **Facilities:** 23 RV campsites, picnic area, toilets (&), drinking water, trails, museum, gift shop, restaurant. **Activities:** Camping, picnicking, hiking, tours. **Special Features:** This site was an important crossroad for travelers, traders, and the military during the early days of the 20th century. Rika's Roadhouse, the centerpiece of the park, served travelers of the historic Valdez-to-Fairbanks Trail from 1909 to 1947.

★1312★ BIG LAKE NORTH STATE RECREATION SITE
c/o Mat-Su/CB Area Office
HC 32 Box 6706
Wasilla, AK 99654
Phone: 907-745-3975
Size: 19 acres. **Location:** Southwest of Wasilla, at milepost 5 on North Big Lake Rd. **Facilities:** Campsites (limit 7 nights), picnic areas and shelters (&), toilet facilities (&), drinking water (&), boat launch. **Activities:** Camping, boating, fishing, and other water recreation. **Special Features:** Big Lake is the largest lake in the Matanuska-Susitna Valley, and Big Lake North and South both offer numerous camping and water recreation opportunities.

★1313★ BIG LAKE SOUTH STATE RECREATION SITE
c/o Mat-Su/CB Area Office
HC 32 Box 6706
Wasilla, AK 99654
Phone: 907-745-3975
Size: 22 acres. **Location:** Southwest of Wasilla, at milepost 5.2 on South Big Lake Road. **Facilities:** Campsites (limit 7 nights), picnic areas (&), toilet facilities (&), drinking water, boat launch. **Activities:** Camping, boating, fishing, and other water recreation. **Special Features:** Big Lake is the largest lake in the Matanuska-Susitna Valley, and Big Lake North and South both offer numerous camping and water recreation opportunities.

★1314★ BIRCH LAKE STATE RECREATION AREA
c/o Northern Area Office
3700 Airport Way
Fairbanks, AK 99709
Web: www.dnr.state.ak.us/parks/units/birch.htm
Phone: 907-451-2695
Size: 48 acres. **Location:** Off Richardson Highway, via the military recreation area road at Milepost 305.2. **Facilities:** 20 trailer/RV campsites, 5 tent camping sites, public-use cabin, picnic area, toilets, drinking water, courtesy dock (&) and boat launch, ice fishing hut rentals. **Activities:** Camping, fishing, ice fishing, boating, jet skiing, water-skiing, snowmobiling. **Special Features:** Park is situated between a lilypad-covered lake and forested wetlands. Lake offers excellent fishing for stocked species year round..

★1315★ BLACK SANDS BEACH STATE MARINE PARK
c/o Southeast Area Office
400 WIlloughby Ave, 4th Fl
Juneau, AK 99801
Phone: 907-465-4563

Size: 640 acres. Location: On Gravina Island, south of Ketchikan; accessible by boat only. Facilities: Undeveloped. Activities: Fishing. Special Features: Park is a popular stop for sea kayakers from Ketchikan.

★1316★ BLAIR LAKE STATE RECREATION SITE
c/o Mat-Su/CB Area Office
HC 32 Box 6706
Wasilla, AK 99654
Phone: 907-745-3975
Size: 400 acres. Location: Adjacent to south side of Denali State Park; no road access. Facilities: Undeveloped. Activities: Fishing. Special Features: Blair Lake has good fishing for rainbow trout.

★1317★ BLUEBERRY LAKE STATE RECREATION
   SITE
c/o Kenai/PWS Area Office
PO Box 1247
Soldotna, AK 99669
Phone: 907-262-5581
Size: 192 acres. Location: East of Valdez, at milepost 23 on Richardson Highway. Facilities: Campsites, trails, toilets (&), drinking water. Activities: Camping, fishing, hiking, wildlife viewing. Special Features: Site offers a panoramic view of a large portion of the Chugach Range, several glaciers, and the Keystone Canyon area. Trans-Alaska Oil Pipeline passes near the site.

★1318★ BOSWELL BAY STATE MARINE PARK
c/o Kenai/PWS Area Office
PO Box 1247
Soldotna, AK 99669
Web: www.dnr.state.ak.us/parks/units/pwssmp/smpcord.htm
Phone: 907-262-5581
Size: 799 acres. Location: On the eastern tip of Hinchinbrook Island. Facilities: Undeveloped. Activities: Beachcombing, wildlife observation, fishing, hunting. Special Features: The southern edge of the park is a high-energy beach exposed to the Gulf of Alaska. As a result of the 1964 earthquake, the former shoreline is now inland by more than a mile. Areas of the park are adjacent to the Copper River Delta State Critical Habitat.

★1319★ BUSKIN RIVER STATE RECREATION SITE
c/o Kodiak Area Office
1400 Abercrombie Dr
Kodiak, AK 99615
Web: www.dnr.state.ak.us/parks/units/kodiak/buskin.htm
Phone: 907-486-6339
Size: 168 acres. Location: 4 miles west of Kodiak on Rezanof Drive; near the state airport. Facilities: 15 campsites, picnic sites, 2 picnic shelters (&), trails, toilets (&), drinking water (&), historical features, beach, fishing platform (&). Activities: Camping, fishing, hiking, mountain biking. Special Features: Buskin River supports the most productive and popular sport fishery along the Kodiak Island road system. The north end of

the park is the site of Miller Army Air Field (1941-1944) and contains military remnants of the World War II era.

★1320★ CAINES HEAD STATE RECREATION AREA
c/o Kenai/PWS Area Office
PO Box 1247
Soldotna, AK 99669
Web: www.dnr.state.ak.us/parks/units/caineshd.htm
Phone: 907-262-5581
Size: 5,961 acres. Location: South of Seward; accessible by boat or on foot via the Coastal Trail. (Flooding in Seward during the month of October 2006 caused extensive trail damage at this SRA.) Facilities: Camping area, cabins, toilets, trails, picnic sites, picnic shelters, historical features. Activities: Camping, fishing, hiking. Special Features: Terrain features a massive headland rising 650 feet above Resurrection Bay, against a backdrop of rolling alpine meadows and sharp peaks. Park is the site of Fort McGilvray, an abandoned World War II fort, and other historical military structures. (Early in World War II, the territory of Alaska was attacked and occupied by Imperial Japanese ground forces, so Caines Head and other Resurrection Bay vantages became strategic spots for defending the Port of Seward.)

★1321★ CANOE PASSAGE STATE MARINE PARK
c/o Kenai/PWS Area Office
PO Box 1247
Soldotna, AK 99669
Web: www.dnr.state.ak.us/parks/units/pwssmp/smpcord.htm
Phone: 907-262-5581
Size: 2,735 acres. Location: On Hawkins Island, 8 miles west of Cordova. Facilities: Undeveloped. Activities: Fishing. Special Features: Park encompasses the natural low pass on the Hawkins Island. Forested uplands and considerable wetlands line Canoe Passage, and the seas to the south are shallow. Most of the island is private land.

★1322★ CAPTAIN COOK STATE RECREATION
   AREA
c/o Kenai/PWS Area Office
PO Box 1247
Soldotna, AK 99669
Web: www.dnr.state.ak.us/parks/units/captcook.htm
Phone: 907-262-5581
Size: 3,466 acres. Location: 25 miles north of Kenai, at milepost 36 on the North Kenai Road. Facilities: Drive-in campsites, tent camping area, boat-in campsites, picnic sites (mostly in day-use areas), picnic shelter (&), trails, boat launch, canoe landing, beach, toilets, drinking water. Activities: Camping, swimming, boating, canoeing, fishing, ice fishing, hiking, cross-country skiing, bow hunting (in season), ATV riding (restricted areas), beachcombing, bird-watching, wildlife observation. Special Features: Park's diverse terrain features saltwater beaches on Cooks Inlet, forests, lakes, and streams. The beaches are popular with agate hunters.

★1323★ CHENA RIVER STATE RECREATION AREA

c/o Northern Area Office
3700 Airport Way
Fairbanks, AK 99709
Web: www.dnr.state.ak.us/parks/units/chena
Phone: 907-451-2695
Size: 254,080 acres. **Location:** 26 miles east of Fairbanks on Chena Hot Springs Road. **Facilities:** 73 campsites, 7 cabins, 4 backcountry shelters, picnic sites, picnic shelters, toilets (&), drinking water, trails, shooting range. **Activities:** Camping, fishing, swimming, canoeing, kayaking, hiking, horseback riding, cross-country skiing, dog sledding, ATV riding, mountain biking, shoeshowing, snowmobiling, rock climbing, hunting, trapping, wildlife observation. **Special Features:** Park encompasses 397 square miles of forests, rivers, and alpine tundra, and offers a wide range of recreational activities year round. The park follows the class II Chena River, with numerous entry and exit points for canoeing, kayaking, and fishing. Four small ponds have also been stocked, and fish caught in those can be kept (river fishing is catch and release only). Wildlife here are abundant; black and grizzly bears inhabit the area but are seldom seen.

★1324★ CHENA RIVER STATE RECREATION SITE

c/o Northern Area Office
3700 Airport Way
Fairbanks, AK 99709
Web: www.dnr.state.ak.us/parks/units/chenasrs.htm
Phone: 907-451-2695
Size: 27 acres. **Location:** At 221 University Avenue in downtown Fairbanks. **Facilities:** 67 campsites (11 with electric and water hookups; some &), 5 walk-in tent campsites, 10 picnic sites along the river, picnic shelter (&) and playfield, 4 restrooms with flush toilets (&), nature trail, boat launch. Camping is limited to 5 consecutive nights from June 10 through August 10. **Activities:** Camping, boating. **Special Features:** Park is located on the banks of the Chena River on the west side of Fairbanks. It is operated by a private company.

★1325★ CHILKAT ISLANDS STATE MARINE PARK

c/o Southeast Area Office
400 Willoughby Ave, 4th Fl
Juneau, AK 99801
Web: www.dnr.state.ak.us/parks/units/haines.htm
Phone: 907-465-4563
Size: 6,560 acres. **Location:** 13 air miles south of Haines and just south of Chilkat State Park (see separate entry). **Facilities:** Undeveloped. **Special Features:** Access to this park is difficult because of high and unpredictable winds. Kayaks work best, because they can be brought on shore and have a shallow draft.

★1326★ CHILKAT STATE PARK

c/o Southeast Area Office
400 Willoughby Ave, 4th Fl
Juneau, AK 99801
Web: www.dnr.state.ak.us/parks/units/haines.htm
Phone: 907-465-4563
Size: 9,837 acres. **Location:** 7 miles south of Haines on Mud Bay Road. **Facilities:** 32 campsites, picnic sites, picnic shelter,
trails, boat launch, toilets (&), drinking water, visitor center. **Activities:** Camping, fishing, hiking, wildlife observation. **Special Features:** The log-cabin visitor center affords spectacular views of Chilkat Inlet and Rainbow and Davidson glaciers. The center offers viewing scopes for spotting marine wildlife in the inlet such as seals, porpoises, and whales. Visitors may also glimpse bears and mountain goats on the other side of the inlet.

★1327★ CHILKOOT LAKE STATE RECREATION SITE

c/o Southeast Area Office
400 Willoughby Ave, 4th Fl
Juneau, AK 99801
Web: www.dnr.state.ak.us/parks/units/haines.htm
Phone: 907-465-4563
Size: 80 acres. **Location:** 10 miles northeast of Haines via Lukat and Chilkoot River roads, or 5 miles past the ferry terminal, at the south end of Chilkoot Lake. **Facilities:** 32 campsites (7 nights limit), picnic shelter, trails, toilets (&), drinking water, boat launch, historical features (&). **Activities:** Camping, fishing. **Special Features:** The park and surrounding area offers some of the best salmon fishing in Southeast Alaska, with four salmon runs, starting in mid-June and ending in mid-October.

★1328★ CHUGACH STATE PARK

c/o Chugach Area Office
HC 52 Box 8999
Indian, AK 99540
Web: www.dnr.state.ak.us/parks/units/chugach
Phone: 907-345-5014; **Fax:** 907-345-6982
Size: 495,204 acres. **Location:** East of Anchorage, along Glenn and Seward Highways. **Facilities:** 135 campsites (all 3 campgrounds have overflow areas), group use area, 2 cabins, yurt, picnic areas and shelters, trails, nature center, gift shop, restrooms, snack bar. **Activities:** Camping, fishing, boating, wind surfing, hiking, ATV riding, bicycling, horseback riding, whitewater rafting, whale watching, mountain climbing, glacier travel, interpretive programs, guided nature walks, guided backcountry wilderness hikes, wildlife viewing, cross-country and downhill skiing, snowshoeing, dogsledding, snowmobiling, ice climbing. **Special Features:** One of the largest state parks in the United States, Chugach ranges in elevation from sea level to 8,000 feet and includes vegetation zones that vary from dense forest to alpine tundra. Although the predominant feature of the park is the breathtaking alpine scenery, the park offers other remarkable phenomena such as the bore tide in Turnagain Arm — twice a day, a wall of water up to six feet high races up the channel as the tide comes in. The park supports an abundance of wildlife, maintains an extensive trail system, and offers a variety of recreational opportunities year round.

★1329★ CLAM GULCH STATE RECREATION AREA

c/o Kenai/PWS Area Office
PO Box 1247
Soldotna, AK 99669
Web: www.dnr.state.ak.us/parks/units/clamglch.htm
Phone: 907-262-5581
Size: 495 acres. **Location:** 21 miles southwest of Soldotna, at

9. State Parks

milepost 117 on Sterling Highway. **Facilities:** Tent campsites, picnic area, picnic shelter (&), latrines (&), drinking water. **Activities:** Camping, fishing, clamming, ATV riding (restricted areas). **Special Features:** Situated on the bluffs overlooking scenic Cook Inlet, Clam Gulch offers visitors a panoramic view of the Aleutian Mountain Range and its three tallest peaks—Mount Iliamna, Mount Redoubt, and Mount Spurr. The region is famous for the hundreds of thousands of razor clams harvested annually from the sandy beaches adjacent to the state recreation area.

★1330★ CLEARWATER STATE RECREATION SITE

c/o Northern Area Office
3700 Airport Way
Fairbanks, AK 99709
Web: www.dnr.state.ak.us/parks/units/deltajct/clearwtr.htm
Phone: 907-451-2695
Size: 27 acres. **Location:** 8.5 miles from Milepost 1415 of the Alaska Highway on Clearwater Road; or 11 miles from Milepost 268 of the Richardson Highway on Jack Warren Road. **Facilities:** 17 campsites, picnic area, trails, toilets, drinking water, boat launch. **Activities:** Camping, fishing, hiking, river floating. **Special Features:** The Delta Clearwater River provides good fishing and river float opportunities, as well as access to the Tanana and Goodpaster rivers. A boardwalk at the site allows for up-close viewing of plants and wildlife. In spring and fall, the site is an excellent place to see sandhill cranes, swans, geese, and other migratory birds.

★1331★ CROOKED CREEK STATE RECREATION SITE

c/o Kenai/PWS Area Office
PO Box 1247
Soldotna, AK 99669
Web: www.dnr.state.ak.us/parks/units/kasilof.htm
Phone: 907-262-5581
Size: 105 acres. **Location:** Near Kasilof, on Coho Loop Road; the town of Kasilof is 15 miles south of Soldotna. **Facilities:** 80 campsites (7-nights limit), picnic sites, trails (&), toilets (&), drinking water (&). **Activities:** Camping, fishing, hiking. **Special Features:** Located near the confluence of Crooked Creek and the Kasilof River, the site offers outstanding king salmon fishing from the bank of the Kasilof River in May and June.

★1332★ DALL BAY STATE MARINE PARK

c/o Southeast Area Office
400 Willoughby Ave, 4th Fl
Juneau, AK 99801
Phone: 907-465-4563
Size: 585 acres. **Location:** Off Gravina Island. **Facilities:** Undeveloped; no road access. **Activities:** Fishing. **Special Features:** Park is located in a sheltered cove on Cook Inlet, south of Ketchikan.

★1333★ DECISION POINT STATE MARINE PARK

c/o Kenai/PWS Area Office
PO Box 1247
Soldotna, AK 99669
Web: www.dnr.state.ak.us/parks/units/pwssmp/smpwhit1.htm
Phone: 907-262-5581
Size: 460 acres. **Location:** At the eastern end of Passage Canal, 8 miles from Whittier; no road access. **Facilities:** 2 camping beaches, latrine. **Activities:** Primitive tent camping, kayaking, fishing. **Special Features:** Park is generally used by kayakers and small boat users as there is no adequate anchorage. Bountiful intertidal life on the rocks at Decision Point may be viewed during minus tides.

★1334★ DEEP CREEK STATE RECREATION AREA

c/o Kenai/PWS Area Office
PO Box 1247
Soldotna, AK 99669
Web: www.dnr.state.ak.us/parks/units/deepck.htm
Phone: 907-262-5581
Size: 172 acres. **Location:** 36 miles north of Homer, at milepost 138 on Sterling Highway. **Facilities:** 2 campgrounds, toilets (&), drinking water (&), picnic sites (&) in day-use area, beach, scenic overlooks, tractor-assisted boat launching services (from private company). **Activities:** Camping, boating, fishing, clamming, beachcombing, ATV riding (on saltwater beaches only), wildlife observation, bird watching. **Special Features:** Deep Creek offers legendary halibut and king salmon fishing, as well as razor clams, and has salt water access. Whales, seals and otters can be seen offshore. Bald eagles are visible here year round, and sandhill cranes and other shore birds inhabit the saltwater marsh in May.

★1335★ DELTA STATE RECREATION SITE

c/o Northern Area Office
3700 Airport Way
Fairbanks, AK 99709
Web: www.dnr.state.ak.us/parks/units/deltajct/deltasrs.htm
Phone: 907-451-2695
Size: 23 acres. **Location:** At milepost 267 on Richardson Highway, in Delta Junction. **Facilities:** 25 developed campsites, picnic area, covered picnic shelter (&), toilets (&), drinking water (&), adjacent airstrip, stores nearby. **Activities:** Camping, picnicking. **Special Features:** A popular campground for those traveling between Tok and Fairbanks, this site features spectacular views of the Alaska Range, including Mount Hayes (elevation 13,832 feet).

★1336★ DENALI STATE PARK

c/o Mat-Su/CB Area Office
HC 32 Box 6706
Wasilla, AK 99654
Web: www.dnr.state.ak.us/parks/units/denali1.htm
Phone: 907-745-3975
Size: 324,240 acres. **Location:** About 100 air miles north of Anchorage on Parks Highway. **Facilities:** 123 campsites, 2 public-use cabins, picnic sites, picnic shelter (&), toilets (some &), drinking water (some &), hiking trails (some &), 2 boat launches,

9. State Parks

canoe/kayak rentals (at Byers Lake Campground only), informational bulletin boards. **Activities:** Camping, fishing, boating, hiking, rock climbing, wildlife viewing. **Special Features:** Situated between the Talkeetna Mountains to the east and the Alaska Range to the west, the park's spectacular landscape varies from meandering lowland streams to alpine tundra. Dominating this diverse terrain are Curry and Kesugi ridges, which together form a north-south alpine ridge 35 miles long. Roadside vantage points offer excellent views of Mount McKinley and the heart of the Alaska Range. The park borders on Denali National Park and Preserve (see separate entry in national parks section) to the west, and, except for roadside facilities, is essentially a wilderness.

★1337★ DONNELLY CREEK STATE RECREATION SITE
c/o Northern Area Office
3700 Airport Way
Fairbanks, AK 99709
Web: www.dnr.state.ak.us/parks/units/deltajct/donnelly.htm
Phone: 907-451-2695
Size: 46 acres. **Location:** 32 miles south of Delta Junction, at milepost 238 on Richardson Highway. **Facilities:** 12 campsites, trails, toilets, drinking water. **Activities:** Camping, hiking, wildlife observation. **Special Features:** Park features a secluded wilderness campground (one of the state's most scenic), with views of some of the tallest peaks in the Alaska Range. On occasion, caribou are sighted browsing in the area, and the Delta bison herd can often be seen across the Delta River on their summer calving grounds.

★1338★ DRIFTWOOD BAY STATE MARINE PARK
c/o Kenai/PWS Area Office
PO Box 1247
Soldotna, AK 99669
Web: www.dnr.state.ak.us/parks/units/pwssmp/smpsewd.htm
Phone: 907-262-5581
Size: 1,480 acres. **Location:** Along the southwest coast of Day Harbor to the east of Resurrection Bay, a 23-mile boat ride from Seward. **Facilities:** Undeveloped. Fresh water availability is limited to runoff during wet weather. **Activities:** Fishing, wildlife viewing. **Special Features:** Driftwood Bay, the largest of the area's marine parks, offers excellent mountain views. This is a popular fair-weather anchorage for recreational boaters and also offers good protection from Day Harbor's often rough seas.

★1339★ DRY CREEK STATE RECREATION SITE
c/o Mat-Su/CB Area Office
HC 32 Box 6706
Wasilla, AK 99654
Phone: 907-745-3975
Size: 360 acres. **Location:** Just north of Glennallen, at milepost 117.5 on Richardson Highway. **Facilities:** 58 campsites, picnic sites, picnic shelters, trails, toilets (&), drinking water (&). **Activities:** Camping, fishing, hiking. **Special Features:** Park is in a forested setting in the Copper Valley.

★1340★ EAGLE BEACH STATE RECREATION AREA
c/o Southeast Area Office
400 Willoughby Ave, 4th Fl
Juneau, AK 99801
Phone: 907-465-4563
Size: 590 acres. **Location:** North of Juneau, at milepost 29 on Glacier Highway. **Facilities:** Campsites, picnic sites, trails, boat launch, toilets, drinking water (&&). **Activities:** Camping, hiking, fishing, wildlife viewing. **Special Features:** Park offers views of Lynn Canal, Chilkat Mountains, and Juneau Mountains. Whales, sea lions, and seals can often be sighted offshore.

★1341★ EAGLE TRAIL STATE RECREATION SITE
c/o Northern Area Office
3700 Airport Way
Fairbanks, AK 99709
Web: www.dnr.state.ak.us/parks/units/tok.htm
Phone: 907-451-2695
Size: 280 acres. **Location:** 16 miles south of Tok, at milepost 109.5 of the Tok Cut-off Highway. **Facilities:** 35 campsites, picnic sites, picnic shelter, latrines (&), drinking water, hiking and nature trails, historical features. **Activities:** Camping, hiking, wildlife viewing. **Special Features:** Eagle Trail campground offers most highway travelers their first opportunity to explore the Alaska Range. An eight-hour hike up the bordering creek brings backpackers within close viewing distance of Dall sheep in the Tok Trophy Sheep Management Area.

★1342★ ENTRY COVE STATE MARINE PARK
c/o Kenai/PWS Area Office
PO Box 1247
Soldotna, AK 99669
Web: www.dnr.state.ak.us/parks/units/pwssmp/smpwhit1.htm
Phone: 907-262-5581
Size: 370 acres. **Location:** 2 miles east of Decision Point on the northeast corner where Passage Canal and Port Wells meet. No road access. **Facilities:** Undeveloped. **Activities:** Primitive tent camping, kayaking. **Special Features:** Park features a natural arch located on the east shore of the cove and offers a beautiful view of Tebenkof Glacier. The lagoon is a good site for clamming, but the entrance is shallow and can only be accessed by small boats on full high tide.

★1343★ ERNEST GRUENING STATE HISTORICAL PARK
c/o Southeast Area Office
400 Willoughby Ave, 4th Fl
Juneau, AK 99801
Phone: 907-465-4563
Size: 12 acres. **Location:** North of Juneau, at milepost 24 on Glacier Highway. **Facilities:** Trail, boat ramp, historical features. **Activities:** Fishing, hiking. **Special Features:** Trail passes through meadows and along the seashore—a popular spot with anglers, picnickers, and boaters. Park is named for Ernest Gruening, governor of the Territory of Alaska from 1939-1953.

9. State Parks

★1344★ FIELDING LAKE STATE RECREATION SITE

c/o Northern Area Office
3700 Airport Way
Fairbanks, AK 99709
Web: www.dnr.state.ak.us/parks/units/deltajct/fielding.htm
Phone: 907-451-2695
Size: 605 acres. **Location:** South of Delta Junction, 2 miles west of milepost 200.5 on Richardson Highway. **Facilities:** 7 campsites, cabin, toilets (&), drinking water, boat launch, trails. **Activities:** Camping, fishing, hiking. **Special Features:** Campground is located at an elevation of 2,973 feet in the Alaska Range, above the treeline. Fishing here is excellent — the fish population is natural and not stocked — though ice often remains on the lake until July due to the site's high elevation.

★1345★ FINGER LAKE STATE RECREATION AREA

c/o Mat-Su/CB Area Office
HC 32 Box 6706
Wasilla, AK 99654
Phone: 907-745-3975
Size: 69 acres. **Location:** Just west of Palmer on Bogard Road. **Facilities:** Camping sites (7-day limit), picnic sites, toilets (&), drinking water, trails, boat launch. **Activities:** Camping, fishing. **Special Features:** Finger Lake is a put-in point for Seven Mile Canoe Trail, which traverses Finger, Cottonwood, Mud, and Wasilla lakes.

★1346★ FORT ABERCROMBIE STATE HISTORICAL PARK

c/o Kodiak Area Office
1400 Abercrombie Dr
Kodiak, AK 99615
Web: www.dnr.state.ak.us/parks/units/kodiak/ftaber.htm
Phone: 907-486-6339
Size: 186 acres. **Location:** 3.7 miles east of Kodiak, on Rezanof Drive. **Facilities:** 13 campsites (7-day limit), toilets (&), drinking water (&), picnic sites, picnic shelter (&), trails, historical features (&), beach, visitor center. **Activities:** Camping, canoeing, kayaking, swimming, fishing, hiking. **Special Features:** This seaside park features remnants of a World War II military installation, foot trails leading to a rugged coastline, and a lake stocked with rainbow trout and grayling. The park overlooks Mill Bay and Monashka Bay, offering spectacular views from steep rock cliffs.

★1347★ FUNTER BAY STATE MARINE PARK

c/o Southeast Area Office
400 Willoughby Ave, 4th Fl
Juneau, AK 99801
Phone: 907-465-4563
Size: 162 acres. **Location:** Toward the north end of Admiralty Island; no road access. **Facilities:** Undeveloped. **Activities:** Fishing, hunting. **Special Features:** Located in the northern part of Admiralty Island, which has the world's highest concentration of brown bears. Funter Bay's weather is relatively mild, with warm summers and cool and wet winters.

★1348★ GRANITE BAY STATE MARINE PARK

c/o Kenai/PWS Area Office
PO Box 1247
Soldotna, AK 99669
Web: www.dnr.state.ak.us/parks/units/pwssmp/smpwhit2.htm
Phone: 907-262-5581
Size: 2,105 acres. **Location:** On the northwest corner of Esther Island, 25 mile from Whittier. Park is one of several state marine parks that can be reached from Whittier and is accessible only by boat. **Facilities:** Undeveloped. **Activities:** Primitive tent camping in selected areas, boating, fishing, hiking, climbing, wildlife observation. **Special Features:** Park includes two bays, protective islands, muskeg and old growth forest uplands. Anchorage is excellent in both bays and can accommodate many boats at once. Most of the shoreline is steep granite cliffs, boulders, and slabs. The surrounding hills afford panoramic views and provide excellent hiking and climbing opportunities. Tange Lake is stocked with rainbow trout.

★1349★ GRINDALL ISLAND STATE MARINE PARK

c/o Southeast Area Office
400 Willoughby Ave, 4th Fl
Juneau, AK 99801
Phone: 907-465-4563
Size: 240 acres. **Location:** In southeast Alaska, west of Ketchikan. Accessible only by plane or boat. **Facilities:** Public-use cabin, trails, toilets. **Activities:** Boating, fishing, hiking, scuba diving, beachcombing. **Special Features:** Grindall Island is a protected holdover spot for small boats venturing across Clarence Strait from Ketchikan during stormy weather. The southern tip of the island is an established sea lion haul-out site.

★1350★ HALIBUT POINT STATE RECREATION SITE

c/o Southeast Area Office
400 Willoughby Ave, 4th Fl
Juneau, AK 99801
Web: www.dnr.state.ak.us/parks/units/sitka.htm
Phone: 907-465-4563
Size: 40 acres. **Location:** 4 miles north of downtown Sitka, on Halibut Road. **Facilities:** Picnic sites, 3 covered shelters, hiking trail, toilets (&), drinking water, historical feature. **Activities:** Fishing, hiking, beachcombing. **Special Features:** This day-use recreation site is situated along the ocean, with a half-mile trail through coastal spruce and hemlock forest.

★1351★ HARDING LAKE STATE RECREATION AREA

c/o Northern Area Office
3700 Airport Way
Fairbanks, AK 99709
Web: www.dnr.state.ak.us/parks/units/harding.htm
Phone: 907-451-2695
Size: 335 acres. **Location:** 45 miles south of Fairbanks at milepost 321.4 on Richardson Highway. **Facilities:** More than 90 campsites, including 5 walk-in group campsites, picnic sites, 2 picnic shelters (&), trails, toilets (&), drinking water (&), boat

9. State Parks

launch, game field with areas for baseball, volleyball, and horse-shoes. **Activities:** Camping, fishing, boating, jet skiing, canoeing, hiking. **Special Features:** Established in 1967, Harding Lake is one of the longest-standing park facilities in the Alaska State Parks system.

★1352★ HATCHER PASS EAST MANAGEMENT AREA
c/o Mat-Su/CB Area Office
HC 32 Box 6706
Wasilla, AK 99654
Phone: 907-745-3975
Size: 75,000 acres. **Location:** North of Palmer on Hatcher Pass Road. **Facilities:** Camping sites (at Gold Mint Trailhead), picnic sites (at Gold Mint Trailhead and Government Peak), trails, toilets (at Fishhook and Gold Mint trailheads). **Activities:** Camping, picnicking, hiking. **Special Features:** Area is used for summer and winter recreation.

★1353★ HORSESHOE BAY STATE MARINE PARK
c/o Kenai/PWS Area Office
PO Box 1247
Soldotna, AK 99669
Web: www.dnr.state.ak.us/parks/units/pwssmp/smpwhit2.htm
Phone: 907-262-5581
Size: 970 acres. **Location:** In southwestern Prince William Sound on Latouche Island, 3 miles northeast of the town of Chenega Bay; accessible only by boat. **Facilities:** Undeveloped. **Activities:** Primitive camping, boating. **Special Features:** This bay is one of the only anchorages left with public uplands in this area of the sound. Active and historic mine plots can be found around the park. All lands surrounding the park are private.

★1354★ INDEPENDENCE MINE STATE HISTORICAL PARK
c/o Mat-Su/CB Area Office
HC 32 Box 6706
Wasilla, AK 99654
Web: www.dnr.state.ak.us/parks/units/indmine.htm
Phone: 907-745-3975
Size: 761 acres. **Location:** North of Palmer at mile post 17.3 on Hatcher Pass Road. **Facilities:** Visitor center (closed in winter), toilets (&), drinking water, picnic sites, trails (&). **Activities:** Tours, hiking, sledding, snowboarding, cross-country skiing. **Special Features:** Park features the abandoned buildings and machinery of a 300-man camp and hardrock goldmine operation dating from the 1930s and 1940s. In 1974, Independence Mine was entered into the *National Register of Historic Places.*

★1355★ JACK BAY STATE MARINE PARK
c/o Kenai/PWS Area Office
PO Box 1247
Soldotna, AK 99669
Web: www.dnr.state.ak.us/parks/units/pwssmp/smpvald.htm
Phone: 907-262-5581
Size: 811 acres. **Location:** 15 miles from Valdez, southeast of

Valdez Narrows. **Facilities:** Tent platforms and other campsites, fire ring, latrine. No drinking water near campsites. **Activities:** Camping, boating, fishing. **Special Features:** Located within an hour's boat ride of Valdez, park offers visitors a wilderness experience including island camping.

★1356★ JOE MACE ISLAND STATE MARINE PARK
c/o Southeast Area Office
400 Willoughby Ave, 4th Fl
Juneau, AK 99801
Phone: 907-465-4563
Size: 62 acres. **Location:** In Sumner Strait, near Point Baker; no road access. **Facilities:** Undeveloped. **Activities:** Fishing. **Special Features:** Park is a small island near the community of Point Baker, used primarily as an anchorage and recreation site. Fishing here is excellent.

★1357★ JOHNSON CREEK STATE RECREATION SITE
c/o Southeast Area Office
400 Willoughby Ave, 4th Fl
Juneau, AK 99801
Phone: 907-465-4563
Size: 65 acres. **Location:** In Juneau, at milepost 15.5 on North Douglas Highway. **Facilities:** Undeveloped. **Special Features:** Historic gold lode site.

★1358★ JOHNSON LAKE STATE RECREATION AREA
c/o Kenai/PWS Area Office
PO Box 1247
Soldotna, AK 99669
Web: www.dnr.state.ak.us/parks/units/kasilof.htm
Phone: 907-262-5581
Size: 332 acres. **Location:** 2 miles south of Kasilof, at milepost 110 on Sterling Highway. **Facilities:** 48 campsites, group use picnic area with shelter (&), toilets (&), drinking water (&), boat launch. **Activities:** Camping, trout fishing, canoeing. **Special Features:** Site is located in a wooded area surrounding Johnson Lake, where fishing for rainbow trout is popular.

★1359★ JUNEAU TRAIL SYSTEM
c/o Southeast Area Office
400 Willoughby Ave, 4th Fl
Juneau, AK 99801
Phone: 907-465-4563
Size: 15 miles. **Location:** In the Juneau area. **Facilities:** Trails, historical features. **Activities:** Hiking. **Special Features:** System consists of several separate trails. Popular segments include Mount Juneau Trail (3 miles), Mount Roberts Trail (4 miles), Perseverance Trail (3 miles), Granite Creek Trail (3.5 miles), and Sheep Creek Trail (3.5 miles).

9. State Parks

★1360★ KACHEMAK BAY STATE PARK & STATE WILDERNESS PARK

c/o Kenai/PWS Area Office
PO Box 1247
Soldotna, AK 99669
Web: www.dnr.state.ak.us/parks/units/kbay/kbay.htm
Phone: 907-262-5581
Size: 370,399 acres. Location: Across the bay from the town of Homer. Access is by plane or boat; there are no roads to the park. Facilities: Camping permitted in most areas of the park, with some developed sites, 3 public-use cabins, toilets (no drinking water), trails (80 miles), boat dock, mooring buoys. Activities: Camping, fishing, boating, kayaking, hiking, mountaineering, skiing, hunting, bird watching. Special Features: Alaska's first state park, and only wilderness park, contains nearly 400,000 acres of mountains, glaciers, forests, and ocean. Kachemak Bay is a critical habitat area, supporting many species of marine life, including sea otters, seals, porpoise, and whales. Land mammals include moose, black bear, mountain goats, coyotes, and wolves, and the many species of birds that inhabit the bay include eagles, gyrfalcons, and puffins. Above the timberline, visitors will find glaciers and snowfields stretching for miles.

★1361★ KASILOF RIVER STATE RECREATION SITE

c/o Kenai/PWS Area Office
PO Box 1247
Soldotna, AK 99669
Web: www.dnr.state.ak.us/parks/units/kasilof.htm
Phone: 907-262-5581
Size: 30 acres. Location: Southwest of Soldotna, along the Kasilof River at milepost 109.5 on Sterling Highway, adjacent to the Sterling Highway bridge. Facilities: 1Camping area, toilets (&), drinking water, boat launch. Activities: Camping, fishing. Special Features: Site is a popular put-in and take-out spot for drift fishing on the Kasilof River. Bank fishing for most species is available both up and down stream from the camping area.

★1362★ KAYAK ISLAND STATE MARINE PARK

c/o Kenai/PWS Area Office
PO Box 1247
Soldotna, AK 99669
Web: www.dnr.state.ak.us/parks/units/pwssmp/smpcord.htm
Phone: 907-262-5581
Size: 1,437 acres. Location: In the Gulf of Alaska, 50 miles southeast of Cordova. Facilities: Undeveloped. Activities: Fishing. Special Features: Park sits on a large dagger of land thrust out into the cold, unpredictable waters of the Gulf of Alaska at the approximate site of the landing of the Bering Expedition in 1741, when Europeans first set foot in Alaska. Few people visit this park due to the exposed shores and bad weather.

★1363★ KENAI RIVER SPECIAL MANAGEMENT AREA

c/o Kenai/PWS Area Office
PO Box 1247
Soldotna, AK 99669
Web: www.dnr.state.ak.us/parks/units/kenairiv.htm
Phone: 907-262-5581
Size: 848 acres. Location: Day use area on Kalifornsky Beach Road; boat launch at 4.2 Kenai Spur Highway. Facilities: Restrooms, boat launch. Activities: Camping (in developed campsites at adjacent parks along the river), fishing, boating, wildlife observation. Special Features: Area consists of more than 105 linear miles of rivers and lakes, including Kenai Lake, Skilak Lake, and the Kenai River from river mile 82 downstream to four miles above the river's mouth on Cook Inlet. The Kenai River is one of the most popular freshwater fisheries in Alaska, featuring major runs of four Pacific salmon species (king, red, silver, and pink) as well as trophy-sized rainbow trout and Dolly Varden. The area also supports large concentrations of bald eagles and many species of migratory waterfowl.

★1364★ KEPLER-BRADLEY LAKES STATE RECREATION AREA

c/o Mat-Su/CB Area Office
HC 32 Box 6706
Wasilla, AK 99654
Phone: 907-745-3975
Size: 349 acres. Location: Southwest of Palmer, at milepost 38 on Glenn Highway. Facilities: Camping and picnicking sites (at Long Lake only), trails (except at Matanuska Lake); most of the lakes have toilets (&) and/or water (&). Activities: Camping, fishing. Special Features: Area encompasses four lakes that have excellent fishing: Canoe, Irene, Long, and Matanuska.

★1365★ KING MOUNTAIN STATE RECREATION SITE

c/o Mat-Su/CB Area Office
HC 32 Box 6706
Wasilla, AK 99654
Phone: 907-745-3975
Size: 20 acres. Location: North of Palmer, at milepost 76 on Glenn Highway. Facilities: Camping sites, picnic sites, picnic shelter, toilets, drinking water. Activities: Camping, picnicking. Special Features: Site offers an excellent view of King Mountain and the glacier-fed Matanuska River.

★1366★ LAKE ALEKNAGIK STATE RECREATION SITE

550 W 7th Ave, Suite 1380
Anchorage, AK 99510
Phone: 907-269-8698; Fax: 907-269-8698
Size: 7 acres. Location: At milepost 22 on Lake Road, north of Dillingham and south of Wood-Tikchik. Facilities: Picnic site with shelter, toilet, boat launch. Activities: Fishing. Special Features: Lake Aleknagik offers excellent fishing.

9. State Parks

★1367★ **LAKE LOUISE STATE RECREATION AREA**
c/o Mat-Su/CB Area Office
HC 32 Box 6706
Wasilla, AK 99654
Phone: 907-745-3975
Size: 511 acres. **Location:** Northwest of Glennallen, at milepost 160 on Glenn Highway. **Facilities:** 60 campsites (15-day limit), picnic shelters (占), toilets (占), drinking water, boat launch. **Activities:** Camping, fishing, boating, wildlife viewing. **Special Features:** Park provides access to Lake Louise and its adjoining lakes, which together are over 20 miles long. Fishing for lake trout and grayling is excellent.

★1368★ **LIBERTY FALLS STATE RECREATION SITE**
c/o Mat-Su/CB Area Office
HC 32 Box 6706
Wasilla, AK 99654
Phone: 907-745-3975
Size: 10 acres. **Location:** Southeast of Glenallen, near Chitina, at milepost 23.5 on Edgerton Highway. **Facilities:** 10 campsites (4-night limit), picnic shelter, toilets (占), trails. **Activities:** Camping, hiking. **Special Features:** A short loop road affords a good view of the thundering waterfalls.

★1369★ **LOWELL POINT STATE RECREATION SITE**
c/o Kenai/PWS Area Office
PO Box 1247
Soldotna, AK 99669
Phone: 907-262-5581
Size: 19 acres. **Location:** 2 Lowell Point Road, south of Seward. **Facilities:** Trails, toilet (占). **Activities:** Fishing, kayaking, wildlife watching. **Special Features:** Located on Resurrection Bay, the area's plentiful marine life includes sea otters and sea lions, as well as bald eagles and a variety of sea birds. Occasionally, orcas or humpback whales are sighted.

★1370★ **LOWER CHATANIKA RIVER STATE RECREATION AREA**
c/o Northern Area Office
3700 Airport Way
Fairbanks, AK 99709
Web: www.dnr.state.ak.us/parks/units/chatanik.htm
Phone: 907-451-2695
Size: 400 acres. **Location:** North of Fairbanks, at milepost 11 on Elliott Highway. **Facilities:** Campsites (占), picnic sites (占), picnic shelter (占), latrines (占), drinking water (占), boat ramp. **Activities:** Camping, canoeing, river floating, fishing. **Special Features:** Park is situated on the Chatanika River and has a boat ramp for people floating the river.

★1371★ **MAGOUN ISLANDS STATE MARINE PARK**
c/o Southeast Area Office
400 Willoughby Ave, 4th Fl
Juneau, AK 99801
Web: www.dnr.state.ak.us/parks/units/sitka.htm
Phone: 907-465-4563
Size: 1,135 acres. **Location:** In Krestof Sound, approximately 12 miles northwest of Sitka; no road access. **Facilities:** Undeveloped. **Activities:** Camping, hunting, fishing, beachcombing. **Special Features:** Access to this park is primarily by boat. There are no developed visitor facilities, but island-sheltered bays provide opportunities for exploring and other recreation. Fishing here is excellent.

★1372★ **MATANUSKA GLACIER STATE RECREATION SITE**
c/o Mat-Su/Copper Basin Area Office
HC 32 Box 6706
Wasilla, AK 99654
Phone: 907-745-3975
Size: 229 acres. **Location:** 54 miles east of Palmer, at milepost 101 on Glenn Highway. **Facilities:** Camping sites, picnic sites, toilets (占), drinking water (占), trails. **Activities:** Camping, hiking. **Special Features:** Park affords panoramic views of Matanuska Glacier and the surrounding Chugach Mountains.

★1373★ **MONTANA CREEK STATE RECREATION SITE**
c/o Mat-Su/CB Area Office
HC 32 Box 6706
Wasilla, AK 99654
Phone: 907-745-3975
Location: North of Wasilla, at milepost 96.6 on Parks Highway. **Facilities:** Camping and picnic sites, toilets, water, trails. **Activities:** Camping, fishing. **Special Features:** Site is one of several rivers and creeks in this area of Alaska that offer great fishing.

★1374★ **MOON LAKE STATE RECREATION SITE**
c/o Northern Area Office
3700 Airport Way
Fairbanks, AK 99709
Web: www.dnr.state.ak.us/parks/units/tok.htm
Phone: 907-451-2695
Size: 22 acres. **Location:** 15 miles northwest of Tok, at milepost 1332 of the Alaska Highway. **Facilities:** 15 campsites, latrines (占), drinking water, picnic area, boat launch (small boats), sandy beach. **Activities:** Camping, boating, water-skiing, swimming. **Special Features:** Park is a popular get-away destination for local residents. Local float planes, flown by Alaskan bush pilots, land on Moon Lake.

★1375★ **MOSQUITO LAKE STATE RECREATION SITE**
c/o Southeast Area Office
400 Willoughby Ave, 4th Fl
Juneau, AK 99801
Web: www.dnr.state.ak.us/parks/units/haines.htm
Phone: 907-465-4563
Size: 10 acres. **Location:** 27 miles northwest of Haines, off Haines Highway at milepost 27.2. **Facilities:** 13 campsites, picnic shelter, toilets, drinking water, dock, boat launch. **Activities:** Camping, fishing, boating. **Special Features:** Park is set alongside the lake, in a Sitka spruce and Western hemlock forest.

Visitors are warned that the park is appropriately named, so they should bring plenty of insect repellant.

★1376★ **NANCY LAKE STATE RECREATION AREA**
c/o Mat-Su/CB Area Office
HC 32 Box 6706
Wasilla, AK 99654
Web: www.dnr.state.ak.us/parks/units/nancylk/nancylk.htm
Phone: 907-745-3975
Size: 22,685 acres. **Location:** North of Wasilla (and a 90-minute drive north of Anchorage), on Nancy Lake Parkway, off Parks Highway at milepost 67.2. **Facilities:** 98 campsites, several rustic cabins, picnic sites and shelter at campground area, toilets, drinking water (campground area), boat launch (small boats), ranger station, canoe trails. **Activities:** Camping, fishing, ice fishing, canoeing, cross-country skiing, snowmobiling, dog sledding. **Special Features:** Area is one of the few flat, lake-studded landscapes in Alaska preserved for recreation purposes. The clear waters are ringed with unspoiled forests, and the area features a well-developed canoe trail system.

★1377★ **NANCY LAKE STATE RECREATION SITE**
c/o Mat-Su/CB Area Office
HC 32 Box 6706
Wasilla, AK 99654
Phone: 907-745-3975
Size: 36 acres. **Location:** Milepost 66.5 on Parks Highway, at the north edge of Nancy Lake State Recreation Area. **Facilities:** More than 30 campsites, picnic sites and shelter, toilets, drinking water, boat launch. **Activities:** Camping, fishing. **Special Features:** Site adjoins Nancy Lake State Recreation Area and has its own campground.

★1378★ **NINILCHIK STATE RECREATION AREA**
c/o Kenai/PWS Area Office
PO Box 1247
Soldotna, AK 99669
Web: www.dnr.state.ak.us/parks/units/nilchik.htm
Phone: 907-262-5581
Size: 93 acres. **Location:** On the west side of the Kenai Peninsula, about 40 miles south of Soldotna on Sterling Highway. **Facilities:** 4 camping areas (some sites &), picnic sites at Ninilchik Campground (&) and Ninilchik Overlook, picnic shelter (&) at Ninilchik Campground, toilets (&), drinking water, boat launch at Ninilchik Beach site, scenic overlook. **Activities:** Camping, fishing (except at Ninilchik View Campground), clamming, ATV riding (on saltwater beaches only). **Special Features:** Ninilchik is the site of world class salmon and halibut fishing. Park vistas include Mount Iliamna and Mount Redoubt, both active volcanoes. Nearby is historical Ninilchik Village, originally settled by Russian colonists, and a Russian Orthodox Church built in 1900. The name Ninilchik means ''peaceful settlement by a river.''

★1379★ **OLD SITKA STATE HISTORIC SITE**
c/o Southeast Area Office
400 Willoughby Ave, 4th Fl
Juneau, AK 99801
Web: www.dnr.state.ak.us/parks/units/sitka.htm
Phone: 907-465-4563
Size: 212 acres. **Location:** 7 miles north of downtown Sitka, on Halibut Road. **Facilities:** Historical features (&), interpretive exhibits, toilets (&), trails (&), boat launch and dock. **Activities:** Fishing, boating, hiking. **Special Features:** The Russians built a settlement at this site along Starrigavan Bay in the early 1800s.

★1380★ **OLIVER INLET STATE MARINE PARK**
c/o Southeast Area Office
400 Willoughby Ave, 4th Fl
Juneau, AK 99801
Phone: 907-465-4563
Size: 560 acres. **Location:** 12 miles south of Juneau, between Seymour Canal and Stephens Passage, on Admiralty Island. **Facilities:** Public use cabin, toilets, trails. **Activities:** Fishing, wildlife viewing. **Special Features:** Located within the Admiralty Island National Monument and Federal Wilderness Area, Oliver Inlet provides access to not only Seymour Canal, but other portions of the national monument as well. Humpback and killer whales, seals, sea lions, porpoises, Sitka deer, and brown bear are found within the area.

★1381★ **PASAGSHAK RIVER STATE RECREATION SITE**
c/o Kodiak Area Office
1400 Abercrombie Dr
Kodiak, AK 99615
Web: www.dnr.state.ak.us/parks/units/kodiak/pasagshak.htm
Phone: 907-486-6339
Size: 20 acres. **Location:** 40 miles west of Kodiak via Rezanof Drive to Pasagshak Road. **Facilities:** 10 campsites, picnic sites, toilets (&), drinking water (&). **Activities:** Camping, fishing. **Special Features:** This small riverside park on the mouth of the Pasagshak River is a popular fishing area.

★1382★ **PETROGLYPH BEACH STATE HISTORIC SITE**
c/o Southeast Area Office
400 Willoughby Ave, 4th Fl
Juneau, AK 99801
Phone: 907-465-4563
Size: 7 acres. **Location:** In Wrangell. **Facilities:** Boardwalk trail, historic features. **Activities:** Fishing. **Special Features:** Site has the highest concentration of petroglyphs in southeastern Alaska; visitors can find as many as 40 designs. A deck overlooking Petroglyph Beach features cast replicas of the site's petroglyphs for visitors to make rubbings on.

★1383★ **POINT BRIDGET STATE PARK**
c/o Southeast Area Office
400 Willoughby Ave, 4th Fl
Juneau, AK 99801
Web: www.dnr.state.ak.us/parks/units/ptbridg1.htm
Phone: 907-465-4563
Size: 2,850 acres. **Location:** 40 miles north of Juneau, at milepost 38.5 on Glacier Highway. **Facilities:** 2 cabins, trails, toilets. **Activities:** Fishing, hiking, beachcombing, wildlife observation,

cross-country skiing, snowshoeing. **Special Features:** Park features meadows of wildflowers, forested mountains, cliffs, salmon spawning streams, rocky beaches, and the sea.

★1384★ PORCUPINE CREEK STATE RECREATION
   SITE
c/o Mat-Su/Copper Basin Area Office
HC 32 Box 6706
Wasilla, AK 99654
Phone: 907-745-3975
Size: 240 acres. **Location:** Southwest of Tok, at milepost 64 on the Tok Cut-off. **Facilities:** 12 campsites, trails, toilets, drinking water (&). **Activities:** Camping, fishing, hiking. **Special Features:** Park is located in the foothills of the south slope of the Alaska Range. Copper River Valley and the Wrangell Mountains lie to the south.

★1385★ PORTAGE COVE STATE RECREATION
   SITE
c/o Southeast Area Office
400 Willoughby Ave, 4th Fl
Juneau, AK 99801
Web: www.dnr.state.ak.us/parks/units/haines.htm
Phone: 907-465-4563
Size: 7 acres. **Location:** At 1 Beach Road in downtown Haines. **Facilities:** Tent camping sites for bicycle or walk-in camping, picnic sites, toilets, drinking water. **Activities:** Camping, fishing. **Special Features:** Park offers a great view of Chilkoot Inlet and surrounding mountains.

★1386★ POTTER SECTION HOUSE STATE
   HISTORIC SITE
c/o Chugach Area Office
HC 52 Box 8999
Indian, AK 99540
Phone: 907-345-5014
Size: 0.5 acres. **Location:** In Anchorage, at milepost 115 on Seward Highway. **Facilities:** Historical features (&), picnic sites, toilets (&). **Special Features:** Built in 1929 to serve a section of the Alaska Railroad, the house is the only one of its kind still standing along the route. Displays include a rotary snow plow and rail work car.

★1387★ QUARTZ LAKE STATE RECREATION
   AREA
c/o Northern Area Office
3700 Airport Way
Fairbanks, AK 99709
Web: www.dnr.state.ak.us/parks/units/deltajct/quartz.htm
Phone: 907-451-2695
Size: 556 acres. **Location:** 10 miles north of Delta Junction; access via a 3-mile road at milepost 277.8 on Richardson Highway. **Facilities:** 115 campsites, 2 cabins, 4 ice fishing huts, picnic areas, picnic shelters, toilets (&), drinking water, 2 boat launches, fishing docks (&), boat rentals, swimming area, beach

volleyball court, trails. **Activities:** Camping, swimming, waterskiing, fishing, ice fishing, hiking, wildlife viewing, snowmobiling, dog mushing, skijoring. **Special Features:** Fishing is the main attraction of the Quartz Lake Recreation Area. Quartz Lake, which has some of the best road accessible fishing in Interior Alaska, is stocked annually with more than 300,000 fingerling rainbow trout, as well as coho salmon. Lost Lake, which is also part of the recreation area, is also well-stocked and has some good fishing, especially canoe or dock fishing.

★1388★ REFUGE COVE STATE RECREATION SITE
c/o Southeast Area Office
400 Willoughby Ave, 4th Fl
Juneau, AK 99801
Phone: 907-465-4563
Size: 13 acres. **Location:** 6 miles northwest of Ketchikan, at milepost 8.7 on Tongass Road. **Facilities:** Picnic sites, toilet facilities. **Activities:** Fishing. **Special Features:** Site features one of the few road-accessible sandy beaches near Ketchikan.

★1389★ ROCKY LAKE STATE RECREATION SITE
c/o Mat-Su/CB Area Office
HC 32 Box 6706
Wasilla, AK 99654
Phone: 907-745-3975
Size: 49 acres. **Location:** Southwest of Wasilla, at milepost 3.5 on Big Lake Road. **Facilities:** Campsites (7 nights limit), toilets, drinking water, boat launch. **Activities:** Camping, fishing. **Special Features:** Lake offers good rainbow trout fishing.

★1390★ SAFETY COVE STATE MARINE PARK
c/o Kenai/PWS Area Office
PO Box 1247
Soldotna, AK 99669
Web: www.dnr.state.ak.us/parks/units/pwssmp/smpsewd.htm
Phone: 907-262-5581
Size: 960 acres. **Location:** Along the west side of Day Harbor, east of Resurrection Bay, a 28-mile boat ride from Seward. **Facilities:** Undeveloped. **Activities:** Primitive beach camping, boating, fishing. **Special Features:** Park features the marine environment of the cove, an upland forest of spruce, hemlock, and alder, and a three-acre freshwater lake. It also offers excellent views of Ellsworth Glacier, an arm of the Sargent Icefield, near the cove's entrance.

★1391★ SAINT JAMES BAY STATE MARINE PARK
c/o Southeast Area Office
400 Willoughby Ave, 4th Fl
Juneau, AK 99801
Phone: 907-465-4563
Size: 1,002 acres. **Location:** On the west side of Lynn Canal; no road access. **Facilities:** Undeveloped. **Activities:** Fishing, hunting. **Special Features:** The largest state marine park in Alaska, Saint James Bay is both a destination recreational area as well as an overnight stop for boaters en route between Haines and Juneau. The bay has been identified by the Alaska Department of Fish and Game as the best waterfowl habitat and hunting

9. State Parks

area on Lynn Canal. Resident wildlife includes populations of black and brown bear and mountain goats.

★1392★ SALCHA RIVER STATE RECREATION SITE
c/o Northern Area Office
3700 Airport Way
Fairbanks, AK 99709
Web: www.dnr.state.ak.us/parks/units/salcha.htm
Phone: 907-451-2695
Size: 62 acres. Location: At milepost 323.3 on Richardson Highway, southeast of Fairbanks. Facilities: Campsites, public-use cabin, picnic sites, toilets, drinking water, boat launch. Activities: Camping, fishing. Special Features: Park was designed primarily to provide boat access to the Salcha and Tanana rivers. King salmon, arctic grayling, and northern pike are the most common species of fish caught in the Salcha River.

★1393★ SANDSPIT POINT STATE MARINE PARK
c/o Kenai/PWS Area Office
PO Box 1247
Soldotna, AK 99669
Web: www.dnr.state.ak.us/parks/units/pwssmp/smpsewd.htm
Phone: 907-262-5581
Size: 560 acres. Location: 12 miles southeast of Seward, in Resurrection Bay at the northeast tip of Fox Island (Renard Island). Facilities: Undeveloped. Fresh water is not available. Activities: Primitive beach camping, kayaking, fishing. Special Features: Park includes steep, inaccessible uplands to the west and a half-mile long spit to the east, with spectacular panoramic views of Resurrection Bay and Eldorado Narrows. The north beach of the spit is fine sand, and the variety of marine life found in tide pools there, the ease of launching and landing, and suitability for beach camping make this a popular destination for kayakers. The southern beach on the spit is not recommended for landings due to its rocky nature and the often heavy surf.

★1394★ SAWMILL BAY STATE MARINE PARK
c/o Kenai/PWS Area Office
PO Box 1247
Soldotna, AK 99669
Web: www.dnr.state.ak.us/parks/units/pwssmp/smpvald.htm
Phone: 907-262-5581
Size: 2,320 acres. Location: 15 miles southwest of Valdez, on the northern shoreline of Port Valdez, and 3 miles west of Valdez Narrows. Facilities: Campsites, toilet facilities. Activities: Camping, fishing, boating, wildlife viewing. Special Features: This picturesque bay is surrounded by 4,000-foot peaks, providing protected anchorage in the southwest arm of the bay. Viewable wildlife include land and sea otters, seals, bears, and a variety of birds.

★1395★ SCOUT LAKE STATE RECREATION AREA
c/o Kenai/PWS Area Office
PO Box 1247
Soldotna, AK 99669
Phone: 907-262-5581

Size: 164 acres. Location: Just west of the community of Sterling, at milepost 85 on Sterling Highway. Facilities: Picnic sites, picnic shelter, toilet facilities, drinking water, trails. Activities: Picnicking, hiking, fishing. Special Features: Site is used primarily for fishing and other day-use activities.

★1396★ SEA LION COVE STATE MARINE PARK
c/o Southeast Area Office
400 Willoughby Ave, 4th Fl
Juneau, AK 99801
Web: www.dnr.state.ak.us/parks/units/sitka.htm
Phone: 907-465-4563
Size: 630 acres. Location: On the north end of Kruzof Island, 25 miles northwest of Sitka; no road access. Facilities: Trails. Activities: Camping, fishing, hiking, beachcombing, birdwatching. Special Features: Park has no developed facilities, but offers more adventurous visitors the opportunity to explore a remote sandy beach on the Gulf of Alaska. Access to the park is by boat to Kallinin Bay, where a trail begins along a river estuary that leads 2.5 miles through forest and muskegs to Sea-lion Cove.

★1397★ SECURITY BAY STATE MARINE PARK
c/o Southeast Area Office
400 Willoughby Ave, 4th Fl
Juneau, AK 99801
Web: www.dnr.state.ak.us/parks/units/sitka.htm
Phone: 907-465-4563
Size: 500 acres. Location: On the north end of Kuiu Island facing Frederick Sound and Catham Strait; no road access. Facilities: Undeveloped. Activities: Fishing, beachcombing. Special Features: Provides safe haven anchorage for vessels in an area of large open water.

★1398★ SETTLERS COVE STATE RECREATION SITE
c/o Southeast Area Office
400 Willoughby Ave, 4th Fl
Juneau, AK 99801
Phone: 907-465-4563
Size: 76 acres. Location: North of Ketchikan, at milepost 18 on North Tongass Road. Facilities: Campsites (limit 7 nights), public-use cabins, picnic sites, picnic shelter (&), toilets (&), drinking water (&), trails, boat launch access. Activities: Camping, fishing, hiking, beachcombing. Special Features: Site includes a sandy beach and salmon stream.

★1399★ SHELTER ISLAND STATE MARINE PARK
c/o Southeast Area Office
400 Willoughby Ave, 4th Fl
Juneau, AK 99801
Phone: 907-465-4563
Size: 3,560 acres. Location: 20 miles northwest of downtown Juneau; no road access. Facilities: Picnic sites, toilet facilities, trails. Activities: Fishing, kayaking, boating, hiking, diving, beachcombing, hunting. Special Features: Park features two sandy coves.

9. State Parks

★1400★ SHOUP BAY STATE MARINE PARK

c/o Kenai/PWS Area Office
PO Box 1247
Soldotna, AK 99669
Web: www.dnr.state.ak.us/parks/units/pwssmp/smpvald.htm
Phone: 907-262-5581
Size: 4,560 acres. **Location:** 5 miles southwest of the Port of Valdez; no road access. **Facilities:** Campsites (including good sites for large groups), 3 cabins, toilets, trails. **Activities:** Camping, fishing, hiking, wildlife observation. **Special Features:** Park highlights include Shoup Glacier, and the black-legged kittiwake rookery in the lagoon. Anchorage here is fair to poor in the bay but good for small boats in the lagoon; the lagoon can only be reached during high tide with small boats. Visitors are cautioned to be on the lookout for icebergs and allow plenty of room to get around these potentially dangerous navigation hazards. A foot trail runs from Valdez to this park (the only state marine park with foot access in Prince William Sound).

★1401★ SHUYAK ISLAND STATE PARK

c/o Kodiak Area Office
1400 Abercrombie Dr
Kodiak, AK 99615
Web: www.dnr.state.ak.us/parks/units/kodiak/shuyak.htm
Phone: 907-486-6339
Size: 47,000 acres. **Location:** 54 miles north of Kodiak; accessible only by air or water. **Facilities:** 4 cabins, trails. **Activities:** Fishing, boating, kayaking, hiking, hunting, wildlife viewing. **Special Features:** This wilderness park encompasses part of a coastal forest system that is unique to the Kodiak Archipelago, containing only one tree species, the Sitka spruce. The island is only 12 miles long and 11 miles wide, but it has more sheltered waterways than anywhere else in the Archipelago. The lands and waters of the area host seabirds, whales, harbor seals, sea lions, and porpoises. Shuyak also has a limited number of Kodiak brown bear, which are potentially fierce.

★1402★ SOUTH ESTHER ISLAND STATE MARINE PARK

c/o Kenai/PWS Area Office
PO Box 1247
Soldotna, AK 99669
Web: www.dnr.state.ak.us/parks/units/pwssmp/smpwhit2.htm
Phone: 907-262-5581
Size: 3,360 acres. **Location:** On the southern end of Esther Island, 20 miles east of Whittier. **Facilities:** Undeveloped. **Activities:** Boating, fishing, hiking. **Special Features:** Park includes two bays, Lake and Quillian. Quillian Bay remains relatively undisturbed, while Lake Bay houses one of the world's largest fish hatcheries. The hatchery is owned and operated by a non-profit corporation, and tours of the facility are offered to visitors at no charge. Fishing here is good, but sport fishermen should avoid getting in the way of the daily operations of the hatchery. During commercial openings the fishing fleet crowds the area and visitors are advised to stay clear of the nets and boat traffic. During the height of the fish run, black bears can be seen near the hatchery.

★1403★ SQUIRREL CREEK STATE RECREATION SITE

c/o Mat-Su/CB Area Office
HC 32 Box 6706
Wasilla, AK 99654
Phone: 907-745-3975
Size: 160 acres. **Location:** South of Glenallen, at milepost 79.5 on Richardson Highway. **Facilities:** 23 campsites, toilets, drinking water. **Activities:** Camping, fishing. **Special Features:** An accesible pathway leads to the beach.

★1404★ STARISKI STATE RECREATION SITE

c/o Kenai/PWS Area Office
PO Box 1247
Soldotna, AK 99669
Phone: 907-262-5581
Size: 60 acres. **Location:** 20 miles north of Homer at milepost 151 on Sterling Highway. **Facilities:** 9 campsites, picnic shelter, toilets (&), drinking water. **Activities:** Camping. **Special Features:** Site is five miles north of Anchor Point, on a high bluff overlooking Cook Inlet, with spectacular views of three volcanoes that border the inlet.

★1405★ SULLIVAN ISLAND STATE MARINE PARK

c/o Southeast Area Office
400 Willoughby Ave, 4th Fl
Juneau, AK 99801
Web: www.dnr.state.ak.us/parks/units/haines.htm
Phone: 907-465-4563
Size: 2,163 acres. **Location:** At the south end of Sullivan Island, south of Chilkat State Marine Park and 20 air miles south of Haines; no road access. **Facilities:** Undeveloped. **Activities:** Fishing. **Special Features:** Two bays on the east side of the island provide access to the park but no anchorages. Weather and winds in Lynn Canal are unpredictable, making anchoring very difficult, so kayaks are the best bet because they can be brought on shore and have a shallow draft.

★1406★ SUMMIT LAKE STATE RECREATION SITE

c/o Mat-Su/CB Area Office
HC 32 Box 6706
Wasilla, AK 99654
Web: www.dnr.state.ak.us/parks/units/summit.htm
Phone: 907-745-3975
Size: 360 acres. **Location:** Northwest of Palmer, at milepost 19.2 on Hatcher Pass Road. **Facilities:** Trails. **Activities:** Hiking, hang gliding, backcountry skiing, snow boarding, snowshoeing, snowmobiling. **Special Features:** Summit Lake is a tarn (small steep-banked mountain lake or pool) with a depth of 20 feet. West of the lake, a trail leads up a to to a bluff overlook, with views of Willow Creek drainage, the Susitna Valley, and the western arc of the Alaska Range. The overlook is a popular launch site for paragliders in the summer. The area above and east of the lake, April Bowl, is popular in winter for backcountry skiing, snow boarding, and snowshoeing. Park is also open to snowmobiling in winter.

9. State Parks

★1407★ SUNNY COVE STATE MARINE PARK
c/o Kenai/PWS Area Office
PO Box 1247
Soldotna, AK 99669
Web: www.dnr.state.ak.us/parks/units/pwssmp/smpsewd.htm
Phone: 907-262-5581
Size: 960 acres. **Location:** 14 miles south of Seward at the south end of Fox Island (Renard Island) in Resurrection Bay. **Facilities:** Undeveloped. Fresh water supply is available seasonally . **Activities:** Beach camping, fishing, wildlife viewing. **Special Features:** With the exception of the south beach of Sunny Cove, vertical rock cliffs characterize the park's coastline. The south shore of the cove has a good camping beach and is popular as an anchorage for sailboats and power boats. The cove also offers a good view of Callisto Head, Bear Glacier, and Kenai Fjords National Park, and wildlife viewing along the vertical cliffs is excellent.

★1408★ SURPRISE COVE STATE MARINE PARK
c/o Kenai/PWS Area Office
PO Box 1247
Soldotna, AK 99669
Web: www.dnr.state.ak.us/parks/units/pwssmp/smpwhit1.htm
Phone: 907-262-5581
Size: 2,280 acres. **Location:** On the western side of the mouth of Cochrane Bay, 15 miles east of Whittier; accessible by boat. **Facilities:** 7 camping areas, latrine, trail. **Activities:** Camping, fishing, boating, sailing, kayaking, hiking. **Special Features:** Park is one of the most popular anchorages in western Prince William Sound. Weekends draw the most use, with eight or more boats in the cove.

★1409★ TAKU HARBOR STATE MARINE PARK
c/o Southeast Area Office
400 Willoughby Ave, 4th Fl
Juneau, AK 99801
Phone: 907-465-4563
Size: 700 acres. **Location:** In Stephens Passage, southeast of Juneau; no road access. **Facilities:** Undeveloped. **Activities:** Fishing. **Special Features:** Park features a protected harbor with a floating dock.

★1410★ THOM'S PLACE STATE MARINE PARK
c/o Southeast Area Office
400 Willoughby Ave, 4th Fl
Juneau, AK 99801
Phone: 907-465-4563
Size: 1,198 acres. **Location:** On Wrangell Island. **Facilities:** Undeveloped. **Activities:** Fishing. **Special Features:** Park features a sheltered cove, an excellent fishing stream, and tidal flats.

★1411★ THUMB COVE STATE MARINE PARK
c/o Kenai/PWS Area Office
PO Box 1247
Soldotna, AK 99669
Web: www.dnr.state.ak.us/parks/units/pwssmp/smpsewd.htm
Phone: 907-262-5581
Size: 720 acres. **Location:** 9 miles south of Seward on the east side of Resurrection Bay. **Facilities:** Beach campsites, 2 public-use cabins (1 &), toilets, trails, 2 mooring buoys. Fresh water is available from a stream that flows from a glacier. **Activities:** Camping, fishing, boating. **Special Features:** The most striking geological feature in the area is Porcupine Glacier, which towers above the park and provides a dramatic backdrop. Thumb Cove offers good protection from the often unstable weather of Resurrection Bay.

★1412★ TOK RIVER STATE RECREATION SITE
c/o Northern Area Office
3700 Airport Way
Fairbanks, AK 99709
Web: www.dnr.state.ak.us/parks/units/tok.htm
Phone: 907-451-2695
Size: 9 acres. **Location:** 4.5 miles east of Tok, at milepost 1309 of the Alaska Highway. **Facilities:** 43 campsites, picnic sites, picnic shelter (&), drinking water, latrines (&), walking trail. **Activities:** Camping, hiking, canoeing, floating. **Special Features:** Situated on the east bank of the Tok River, this park provides river boating and float trip opportunities to visitors. Across the river from the campground is the burned area of the 1990 Tok River Fire.

★1413★ TOKOSITNA RIVER STATE RECREATION SITE
c/o Mat-Su/CB Area Office
HC 32 Box 6706
Wasilla, AK 99654
Phone: 907-745-3975
Size: 600 acres. **Location:** At milepost 70.8 on Parks Highway. **Facilities:** Undeveloped. **Activities:** Camping, fishing. **Special Features:** Park is under development.

★1414★ TOTEM BIGHT STATE HISTORICAL PARK
c/o Southeast Area Office
400 Willoughby Ave, 4th Fl
Juneau, AK 99801
Web: www.dnr.state.ak.us/parks/units/totembgh.htm
Phone: 907-465-4563
Size: 33 acres. **Location:** North of Ketchikan, at milepost 10 on North Tongass Road. **Facilities:** Historical features, trails, toilets, drinking water (&&). **Special Features:** In the 1930s the US Forest Service hired skilled carvers among Native Americans to salvage and reconstruct the native totem poles that had been left to rot when Natives moved to non-Native settlements to find work. The fragments of old poles were laid beside freshly-cut cedar logs, and every attempt was made to copy them traditionally. By the end of World War II, 14 totem poles and a clanhouse, or community house, were in place and are now preserved at the Totem Bight site.

★1415★ UPPER CHATANIKA RIVER STATE RECREATION SITE
c/o Northern Area Office
3700 Airport Way
Fairbanks, AK 99709
Web: www.dnr.state.ak.us/parks/units/chatanik.htm
Phone: 907-451-2695

9. State Parks

Size: 73 acres. **Location:** North of Fairbanks at mile 39 on Steese Highway. **Facilities:** 25 campsites, 4 picnic sites, toilets, drinking water, latrines, boat ramp. **Activities:** Camping, fishing, canoeing, river rafting. **Special Features:** Canoeists and rafters launch their boats here for an all-day float to the Lower Chatanika River State Recreation Area (see separate entry).

★1416★ **WICKERSHAM STATE HISTORIC SITE**
c/o Southeast Area Office
400 Willoughby Ave, 4th Fl
Juneau, AK 99801
Web: www.dnr.state.ak.us/parks/units/wickrshm.htm
Phone: 907-465-4563
Size: 0.5 acres. **Location:** At 213 7th Street in Juneau. **Facilities:** Historical features, toilet facilites (&). **Special Features:** The first large Victorian home built on "Chicken Ridge" in Juneau, the House of Wickersham was the home of Alaska's pioneer Judge James Wickersham. The history of Wickersham and the Gold Rush era is told through old photos, Alaskan artifacts, memorabilia, and the period furnishings on display at the house.

★1417★ **WILLOW CREEK STATE RECREATION AREA**
c/o Mat-Su/CB Area Office
HC 32 Box 6706
Wasilla, AK 99654
Phone: 907-745-3975
Size: 3,583 acres. **Location:** North of Wasilla, at milepost 70.8 on Parks Highway. **Facilities:** 2 campgrounds (some sites &), picnic shelters, toilets (&), drinking water (&), trails. **Activities:** Camping, fishing, cross-country skiing, snowmobiling. **Special Features:** The Willow area encompasses lands north of Nancy Lake to the Talkeetna River Drainage. Willow is well-known for its fishing, and during winter it becomes a training ground for area dog mushers to prepare for races such as the Iditarod.

★1418★ **WOOD-TIKCHIK STATE PARK**
550 W 7th Ave, Suite 1390
Anchorage, AK 99510
Web: www.dnr.state.ak.us/parks/units/woodtik.htm
Phone: 907-269-8698
Size: 1.5 million acres. **Location:** 33 miles north of Dillingham; accessible by boat or plane only. **Facilities:** Trails, toilets. **Activities:** Primitive camping, fishing, hunting, boating, canoeing, kayaking. **Special Features:** Park is the largest state park in the US. It has just a few rustic facilities — emphasis here is on low impact camping and "pack it in, pack it out" practices. The park is named for its two separate systems of lakes and is characterized by its water-based ecosystems. All five species of Pacific salmon spawn here, and freshwater sportfish are generally prolific throughout the area. Wildlife is also abundant, from moose, caribou, and brown bear to small animals such as beaver, muskrat, otter, fox, wolverine, and mink. The entire park is open to camping, though some areas require a permit, and all but one of the lakes are open to motorized boating.

★1419★ **WOODY ISLAND STATE RECREATION SITE**
c/o Kodiak Area Office
1400 Abercrombie Dr
Kodiak, AK 99615
Phone: 907-486-6339
Size: 112 acres. **Location:** 2 miles east of Kodiak; accessible by water only. **Facilities:** Undeveloped. **Activities:** Canoeing, kayaking, fishing, hunting. **Special Features:** Woody Island is a rugged and pristine state recreation area.

★1420★ **WORTHINGTON GLACIER STATE RECREATION SITE**
c/o Kenai/PWS Area Office
PO Box 1247
Soldotna, AK 99669
Phone: 907-262-5581
Size: 113 acres. **Location:** East of Valdez, at milepost 28.7 on Richardson Highway. **Facilities:** Picnic sites, picnic shelter, trail to glacier (&), toilets (&). **Activities:** Picnicking, scenic views. **Special Features:** This scenic recreation site is one of the few parks in the U.S. where visitors can actually touch a glacier. Its 2,700-foot elevation provides a view of smaller glaciers which dot the surrounding mountains.

★1421★ **ZIEGLER COVE STATE MARINE PARK**
c/o Kenai/PWS Area Office
PO Box 1247
Soldotna, AK 99669
Web: www.dnr.state.ak.us/parks/units/pwssmp/smpwhit1.htm
Phone: 907-262-5581
Size: 720 acres. **Location:** On the northern side at the mouth of Pigot Bay, 18 miles from Whittier; accessible by boat. **Facilities:** Undeveloped. **Activities:** Camping, fishing, wildlife observation. **Special Features:** Park has protected anchorage in the cove, where a maximum of four boats can safely anchor at one time. A picnic site with a fire ring is located on the east corner of the cove, and a campsite can be found on the north corner of the cove at the edge of the forest. There is drinking water further up in Pigot Bay.

9. State Parks

Arizona State Parks

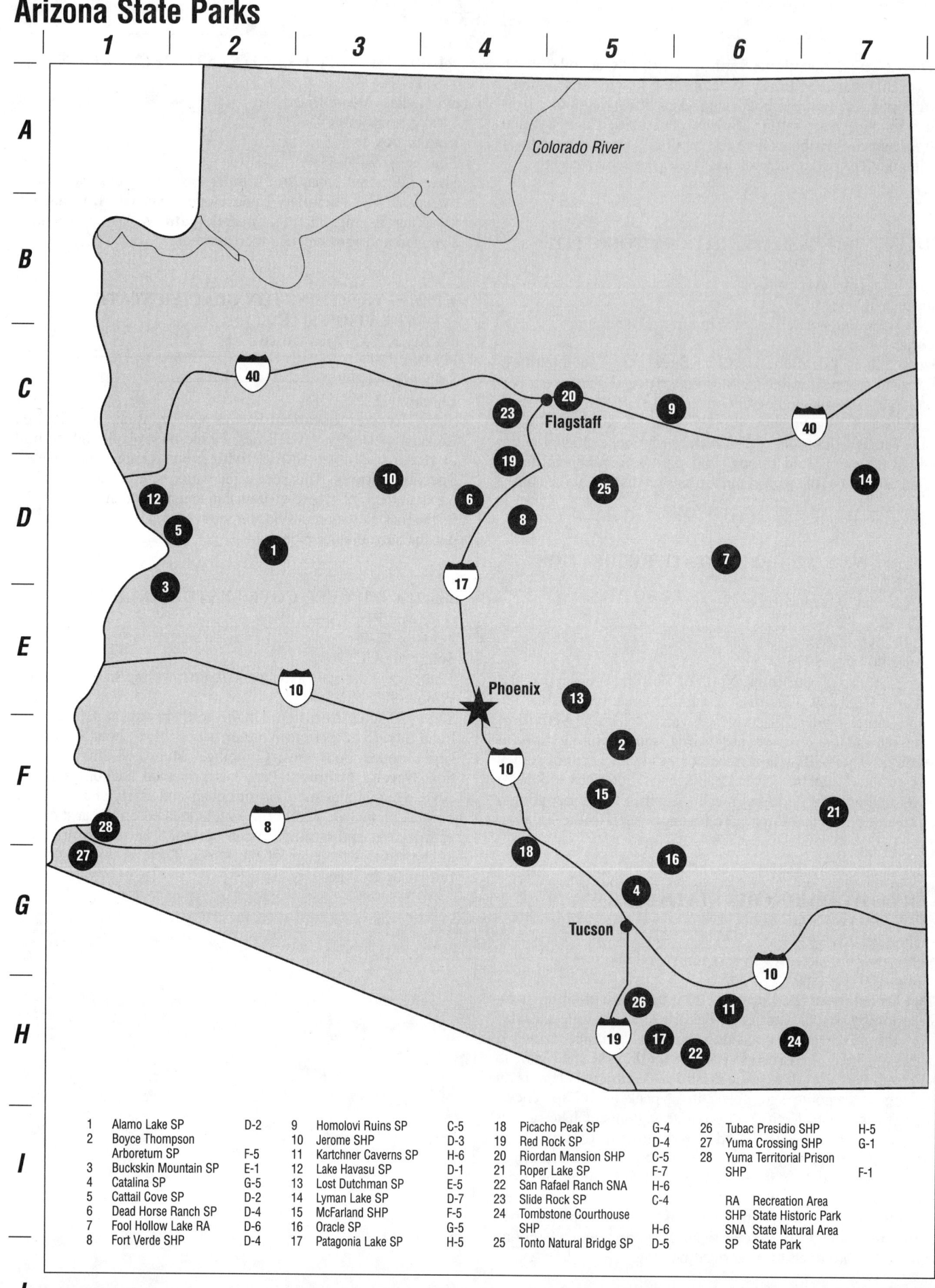

1	Alamo Lake SP	D-2	9	Homolovi Ruins SP	C-5	18	Picacho Peak SP	G-4	26	Tubac Presidio SHP	H-5
2	Boyce Thompson		10	Jerome SHP	D-3	19	Red Rock SP	D-4	27	Yuma Crossing SHP	G-1
	Arboretum SP	F-5	11	Kartchner Caverns SP	H-6	20	Riordan Mansion SHP	C-5	28	Yuma Territorial Prison	
3	Buckskin Mountain SP	E-1	12	Lake Havasu SP	D-1	21	Roper Lake SP	F-7		SHP	F-1
4	Catalina SP	G-5	13	Lost Dutchman SP	E-5	22	San Rafael Ranch SNA	H-6			
5	Cattail Cove SP	D-2	14	Lyman Lake SP	D-7	23	Slide Rock SP	C-4	RA	Recreation Area	
6	Dead Horse Ranch SP	D-4	15	McFarland SHP	F-5	24	Tombstone Courthouse		SHP	State Historic Park	
7	Fool Hollow Lake RA	D-6	16	Oracle SP	G-5		SHP	H-6	SNA	State Natural Area	
8	Fort Verde SHP	D-4	17	Patagonia Lake SP	H-5	25	Tonto Natural Bridge SP	D-5	SP	State Park	

ARIZONA

★1422★ Arizona State Parks
1300 W Washington St
Phoenix, AZ 85007
(602) 542-4174 - Phone
(602) 542-4180 - Fax
(602) 542-6900 - Employment
(602) 542-7152 - Volunteering
Web: www.pr.state.az.us
Manages 28 state properties, including outdoor recreation parks, historic sites, and natural areas. Offers financial assistance and technical advise to public agencies and private groups for the development of a statewide trail system. Jointly administers the state's off-highway vehicle program with the Arizona Fish and Game Department.

★1423★ Arizona Fish & Game Department
2221 W Greenway Rd
Phoenix, AZ 85023
(602) 942-3000
Web: www.azgfd.com
Directs wildlife programs for game and non-game species. Conducts fishing programs, operates fish hatcheries, stocks lake and ponds. Administers boat registration as well as hunting and fishing licensing.

★1424★ ALAMO LAKE STATE PARK
PO Box 38
Wenden, AZ 85357
Web: www.pr.state.az.us/Parks/parkhtml/alamo.html
Phone: 928-669-2088
Size: 8,400 acres. **Elevation:** 1,300 feet. **Location:** 38 miles north of Wenden and US 60. **Facilities:** 250 campsites (developed and undeveloped), electrical and water hookups, showers, restrooms, picnic area, picnic shelters, group-use area, biking trails, marina, boat ramps, boat rental, visitor center, playground (&&). **Activities:** Camping, boating, canoeing, fishing, swimming, bicycling, rock hounding, wildlife viewing. **Special Features:** Alamo Lake is located on the Bill Williams River where the Big Sandy River and Santa Maria River come together and is considered one of the state's best for largemouth bass fishing. The park is home to a wide variety of wildlife, including waterfowl, mule deer, foxes, coyotes, bald and golden eagles, and wild burros.

★1425★ BOYCE THOMPSON ARBORETUM STATE PARK
37615 US Hwy 60
Superior, AZ 85273
Web: www.pr.state.az.us/Parks/parkhtml/boyce.html
Phone: 520-689-2811; **Fax:** 520-689-5858
Size: 323 acres. **Elevation:** 2,400 feet. **Location:** 3 miles west of Superior on US 60, 50 miles east of Phoenix. **Facilities:** Picnic areas, picnic shelters, nature trails, visitor center, interpretive center, demonstration garden, restrooms, gift shop (&&). **Special Features:** Established in the early 1920s by botanical enthusiast William Boyce Thompson, the Arboretum is Arizona's oldest and largest botanical garden. Paths through the garden grounds showcase arid-region plants and trees from around the world.

★1426★ BUCKSKIN MOUNTAIN STATE PARK
5476 Hwy 95
Parker, AZ 85344
Web: www.pr.state.az.us/Parks/parkhtml/buckskin.html
Phone: 928-667-3231
Size: 1,677 acres. **Elevation:** 420 feet. **Location:** On the Colorado River, 12 miles north of Parker, on AZ 95; the Park's River Island unit is 1 mile north of the park. **Facilities:** 68 campsites and 21 cabana sites, electric hookups, showers, restrooms, picnic areas, picnic shelters, restaurant, clothing boutique, campstore, hiking trails, boat ramp, boat rental, gas dock, visitor center, playground, basketball and volleyball courts, arcade (&&); River Island has 37 camp sites, restroom and showers, group use area, beach, boat launch. **Activities:** Camping, boating, fishing, swimming, jet skiing, hiking, wildlife viewing. **Special Features:** Scenically located between the Buckskin Mountains and the Colorado River, the park attracts both nature lovers and water enthusiasts. Challenging trails ascend steep bluffs to panoramic overlooks.

★1427★ CATALINA STATE PARK
PO Box 36986
Tucson, AZ 85740
Web: www.pr.state.az.us/Parks/parkhtml/catalina.html
Phone: 520-628-5798; **Fax:** 520-628-5797
Size: 5,493 acres. **Elevation:** 2,650 feet. **Location:** 9 miles north of Tucson on AZ 77 (Oracle Road) at mile marker 81. **Facilities:** 120 campsites (95 with electric and water hookups), showers, restrooms, group-use area, picnic areas, picnic shelters, multi-use trails, equestrian center, visitor center (&&). **Activities:** Camping, hiking, backpacking, bicycling, horseback riding, plant and wildlife viewing. **Special Features:** Park's high desert terrain includes foothills, canyons, and streams which support a vast array of desert plants and wildlife, including more than 150 species of birds. Park is located within Coronado National Forest (see entry in national forests section).

★1428★ CATTAIL COVE STATE PARK
PO Box 1990
Lake Havasu City, AZ 86405
Web: www.pr.state.az.us/Parks/parkhtml/cattail.html
Phone: 928-855-1223; **Fax:** 928-855-1730

Size: 2,000 acres. Elevation: 480 feet. Location: 15 miles south of Lake Havasu City, off AZ 95. Facilities: 61 campsites, 28 boat-in campsites, electric hookups, showers, restrooms, picnic areas, picnic shelters, hiking trails, boat ramps, boat rental, swimming beach (&&). Activities: Camping, boating, fishing, swimming, water skiing, jet skiing, hiking, rock hounding. Special Features: Park is located on Lake Havasu, a 45-mile-long lake created by a dam on the Colorado River near Parker.

★1429★ DEAD HORSE RANCH STATE PARK

675 Dead Horse Ranch Rd
Cottonwood, AZ 86326
Web: www.pr.state.az.us/Parks/parkhtml/deadhorse.html
Phone: 928-634-5283
Size: 328 acres. Elevation: 3,300 feet. Location: Across the Verde River from Cottonwood. The Verde River Greenway, a 6-mile stretch between the Tuzigoot and Bridgeport bridges, is also managed as a unit of the park. Facilities: A 22-site campground (most can accommodate 2 camping units), including both electric and non-electric hookup sites, showers, restrooms, dump station, picnic areas, picnic shelters, group day-use areas, boat ramp, multi-use trails, concession/gift shop, visitor center (&&) . Activities: Camping, canoeing, fishing, hiking, horseback riding, mountain biking, wildlife viewing. Special Features: The park's 3,300-foot elevation means mild temperatures for outdoor activities, and the Verde River Greenway within the park features a Cottonwood/Willow riparian gallery forest and abundant wildlife.

★1430★ FOOL HOLLOW LAKE RECREATION AREA

1500 N Fool Hollow Lake Rd
Show Low, AZ 85901
Web: www.pr.state.az.us/Parks/parkhtml/foolhollow.html
Phone: 928-537-3680
Size: 800 acres. Elevation: 6,300 feet. Location: 2 miles north of US 60 off Highway 260 in Show Low. Facilities: 123 campsites (electric hookups or tents), restrooms, private showers, dump station fish cleaning station, boat ramp, picnic area, picnic shelters, playground, visitors center (&&). Activities: Camping, boating (8 HP limit), fishing, picnicking, wildlife viewing. More than 103 miles of hiking trails are available in the White Mountain Trail System, located within 15 miles of the recreation area in the adjacent Apache-Sitgreaves National Forest. Special Features: Show Low Creek flows into 150-acre Fool Hollow Lake, which is a natural feeding ground for a variety of wildlife and a diverse fishery. The lake supports populations of rainbow trout, brown trout, large and small mouth bass, black crappie, green sunfish, channel catfish, and walleye.

★1431★ FORT VERDE STATE HISTORIC PARK

PO Box 397
Camp Verde, AZ 86322
Web: www.pr.state.az.us/Parks/parkhtml/fortverde.html
Phone: 928-567-3275; Fax: 928-567-4036
Size: 11 acres. Elevation: 3,100 feet. Location: 3 miles east of I-17, at 125 E Holloman St in Camp Verde. Facilities: 3 historic house museums, visitor center, picnic areas, restrooms

(&&). Activities: Living history programs, self-guided tours. Special Features: Park is considered the best preserved example of an Indian Wars period fort in Arizona. Fort Verde was the primary base for General George Crook's US Army scouts and soldiers, and visitors today can experience 3 historic house museum — Commanding Officer's Quarters, Bachelors' Quarters, and Doctor's Quarters on Officer's row — all furnished in the 1880s period. Interpretive exhibits with period artifacts on military life, Indian Scouts, and Indian Wars history are located in the former Administration uilding.

★1432★ HOMOLOVI RUINS STATE PARK

HCR 63, Box 5
Winslow, AZ 86047
Web: www.pr.state.az.us/Parks/parkhtml/homolovi.html
Phone: 928-289-4106; Fax: 928-289-2021
Size: 4,000 acres. Elevation: 4,900 feet. Location: Just off I-40 outside Winslow. Facilities: Pueblo ruins, visitor center, bookstore, exhibits; 53 campsites with electric hook-ups, dump station, restrooms, and showers; picnic areas, picnic shelters, trails (&&). Activities: Camping, hiking, picnicking, wildlife viewing, interpretive programs. Special Features: Park serves as a center of archeological research for the late migration period of the Hopi from the 1200s to the late 1300s and is a sacred place to the Hopi. At the same time, the park provides an opportunity for visitors to visit the sites, which consist of three main pueblo ruins, and to use other park facilities.

★1433★ JEROME STATE HISTORIC PARK

PO Box D
Jerome, AZ 86331
Web: www.pr.state.az.us/Parks/parkhtml/jerome.html
Phone: 928-634-5381
Size: 3 acres. Elevation: 5,000 feet. Location: In the town of Jerome just off SR 89A, on Douglas Road. Facilities: Historic mansion, antique mining equipment, history exhibits, visitor center, restrooms, picnic area, picnic shelters (&&). Special Features: Park features the mansion of James S. ''Rawhide'' Douglas, built in 1916, which sits atop a hill overlooking the scenic Verde Valley. Exhibits recount the story of this once flourishing copper mining community, including the people, places, and technology that played a major role in Arizona's mining history.

★1434★ KARTCHNER CAVERNS STATE PARK

PO Box 1849
Benson, AZ 85602
Web: www.pr.state.az.us/Parks/parkhtml/kartchner.html
Phone: 520-586-4100
Size: 550 acres. Elevation: 4,600 feet. Location: 9 miles south of I-10, off AZ 90, exit 302. Facilities: 60 campsites, electric hookups, showers, restrooms, picnic areas, picnic shelters, hiking trails, visitors center, exhibits, amphitheater, gift shop (&&). Activities: Camping, hiking, cave tours, educational programs. Special Features: The cave was discovered in 1974, but its existence did not become public knowledge until its purchase was approved as an Arizona State Park in 1988. A trained guide leads all tours of the cave, and facilities at the park's Discovery

9. State Parks

Center include information on the tours as well as interactive displays and a theater with a video program. During the summer months, the cave's Big Room serves as a nursery for about 1,000 female cave myotis bats.

★1435★ LAKE HAVASU STATE PARK

699 London Bridge Rd
Lake Havasu City, AZ 86403
Web: www.pr.state.az.us/Parks/parkhtml/havasu.html
Phone: 928-855-2784; **Fax:** 928-453-9358
Size: 6,200 acres. **Elevation:** 480 feet. **Location:** Off AZ 95 and Industrial Blvd. **Facilities:** 42 campsites, showers, restrooms, group-use area, picnic areas, picnic shelters, nature trails, 3 boat ramps (&&). **Activities:** Camping, boating, fishing, swimming, hiking, water skiing, jet skiing. **Special Features:** Park features Arroyo-Camino Interpretive Garden, showcasing the diverse plants life that exists in the surrounding desert. London Bridge, which once spanned the Thames River in London, is located about a mile from the park's Windsor Beach unit; it now crosses a manmade channel in the Colorado River.

★1436★ LOST DUTCHMAN STATE PARK

6109 N Apache Tr
Apache Junction, AZ 85219
Web: www.pr.state.az.us/Parks/parkhtml/dutchman.html
Phone: 480-982-4485
Size: 292 acres. **Elevation:** 2,000 feet. **Location:** 5 miles northeast of Apache Junction, off AZ 88. **Facilities:** 70 campsites (no hookups), showers, restrooms, group-use areas, picnic areas, picnic shelters, multi-use trails, visitor center (&&). **Activities:** Camping, hiking, horseback riding, mountain biking, wildlife viewing, interpretive exhibits. **Special Features:** Park is located in the Sonoran Desert, at the base of the Superstition Mountains, and is named after a fabled lost gold mine. The area is dotted with ancient cliff dwellings and caves.

★1437★ LYMAN LAKE STATE PARK

PO Box 1428
Saint Johns, AZ 85936
Web: www.pr.state.az.us/Parks/parkhtml/lyman.html
Phone: 928-337-4441
Size: 1,200 acres. **Elevation:** 6,000 feet. **Location:** 11 miles south of Saint Johns on US 191. **Facilities:** 61 campsites (38 hookup, 23 non-hookup), showers, restrooms, 6 cabins, 4 yurts, group-use area, picnic areas, picnic shelters, snack bar, nature trails, boat ramps, boat rentals, camp store, horshoe pits, volleyball court (&&). **Activities:** Camping, boating, canoeing, fishing, swimming, water-skiing, hiking, rock hounding, interpretive programs. **Special Features:** Lyman Lake is a 1,500-acre reservoir on the Little Colorado River. Because of its size, the lake is one of the few bodies of water in northeastern Arizona with no size restrictions on boats. During the summer months, interpretive programs include ranger-guided tours of a petroglyph trail.

★1438★ MCFARLAND STATE HISTORIC PARK

PO Box 109
Florence, AZ 85232
Web: www.pr.state.az.us/Parks/parkhtml/mcfarland.html
Phone: 520-868-5216
Size: 2.5 acres. **Elevation:** 1,200 feet. **Location:** Downtown Florence, at Main and Ruggles. **Facilities:** Historic buildings, exhibits, picnic area, restrooms (&). **Activities:** Interpretive programs; guided walking tours of Florence's downtown historic district. **Special Features:** The park's building represents a transition between Sonoran and Anglo-American architecture with its wood-shingled pitched roof and traditional adobe brick walls. During the 1800s the building was a courthouse and later a county hospital. Former governor Ernest W. McFarland purchased the building from the Pinal County Historical Society in 1974 and donated it to the Arizona State Parks Board for a historic park. In 1982 an archives building was completed and now houses his papers.

★1439★ ORACLE STATE PARK

3820 Wildlife Dr
Oracle, AZ 85623
Web: www.pr.state.az.us/Parks/parkhtml/oracle.html
Phone: 520-896-2425
Size: 4,000 acres. **Elevation:** 4,500 feet. **Location:** In the northern foothills of the Santa Catalina Mountains near the community of Oracle in southern Pinal County (about 45 minutes from Tucson). **Facilities:** Visitor and education center, a 7-mile section of the Arizona Trail, historic ranch house, picnic area, restrooms (&&) **Activities:** Picnicking, birding, hiking, biking, horseback riding, nature study, educational programs, guided tours. **Special Features:** Purpose of the park is to act as a wildlife refuge and environmental learning center. It contains a variety of native plant communities, interesting geographic formations, wildlife resources, and the historic Kannally Ranch House. The park's environmental programs are available to schools and organized groups; these educational programs must be scheduled in advance.

★1440★ PATAGONIA LAKE STATE PARK

400 Patagonia Lake Rd
Patagonia, AZ 85624
Web: www.pr.state.az.us/Parks/parkhtml/patagonia.html
Phone: 520-287-6965
Elevation: 3,750 feet. **Location:** 12 miles northeast of Nogales on AZ 82, in the Sonoita Valley. **Facilities:** 107 campsites, 12 boat-in campsites, 34 electric hookups, showers, restrooms, group-use area, picnic areas, picnic shelter, nature trails, marina, beach, boat ramps, boat rental, fishing pier, visitor center, playground, camp store (&&). **Activities:** Camping, boating, fishing, swimming, hiking, bird watching. **Special Features:** Patagonia Lake, a 250-acre manmade lake in southeastern Arizona, is popular for a variety of recreational activities. Located within the park is the 5,000-acre Sonoita Creek State Natural Area, which is unique in that seven distinct vegetative communities, ranging from semi-desert grasslands to riparian deciduous forests, are present within a relatively small area. It also supports numerous rare and endangered wildlife species.

★1441★ PICACHO PEAK STATE PARK

PO Box 275
Picacho, AZ 85241
Web: www.pr.state.az.us/Parks/parkhtml/picacho.html
Phone: 520-466-3183
Size: 3,502 acres. **Elevation:** 2,000 feet. **Location:** Off I-10, exit 219; 60 miles south of Phoenix and 40 miles north of Tucson. **Facilities:** 100 campsites, electric and non-electric hookups, showers, restrooms, group-use area (by reservation), picnic area, trails, historical markers, playground (&&). **Activities:** Camping, hiking, wildlife viewing. **Special Features:** Used as a landmark by travelers for centuries, Picacho Peak stands 1,500 feet above the desert floor. The most significant Civil War battle in Arizona took place near Picacho Peak in April of 1862, when an advance detachment of Union forces from California attacked a Confederate scouting party. The battle is reenacted here each year.

★1442★ RED ROCK STATE PARK

4050 Red Rock Loop Rd
Sedona, AZ 86336
Web: www.pr.state.az.us/Parks/parkhtml/redrock.html
Phone: 928-282-6907; **Fax:** 928-282-5972
Size: 286 acres. **Elevation:** 3,900 feet. **Location:** 5 miles southwest of Sedona on Lower Red Rock Loop Road. **Facilities:** Group-use area, restrooms, picnic areas, picnic shelters, multi-use trails, visitor center, exhibits, auditorium, gift shop (&&). **Activities:** Hiking, birding, exhibits, Ranger-led and self-guided interpretive walks, video and slide programs. **Special Features:** Park is a center for environmental education on the northern Arizona landscape. Plants and wildlife are abundant at Red Rock due to the land-based ecosystem provided by Oak Creek, which meanders throughout the park.

★1443★ RIORDAN MANSION STATE HISTORIC
  PARK

409 Riordan Rd
Flagstaff, AZ 86001
Web: www.pr.state.az.us/Parks/parkhtml/riordan.html
Phone: 928-779-4395; **Fax:** 928-556-0253
Size: 6 acres. **Elevation:** 6,900 feet. **Location:** Next to Northern Arizona University on Riordan Road in Flagstaff. **Facilities:** Historic mansion, visitor center, restrooms, picnic areas, picnic shelters (&&). **Activities:** Guided tours of the mansion; visitor center has an exhibit area, slide program, and a children's "touch table." **Special Features:** The mansion is actually two separate homes connected by a common area. It was built in 1904 for the Riordan brothers, Timothy and Michael, who operated a successful logging business and played a significant role in the development of the social and economic structure of Flagstaff and northern Arizona. The building is an example of Arts and Crafts style architecture, featuring a rustic exterior of log-slab siding, volcanic stone arches, and hand-split wooden shingles. The home has 40 rooms, more than 13,000 square feet of living area, and servants' quarters.

★1444★ ROPER LAKE STATE PARK

101 E Roper Lake Rd
Safford, AZ 85546
Web: www.pr.state.az.us/Parks/parkhtml/roper.html
Phone: 928-428-6760; **Fax:** 928-428-7879
Size: 400 acres. **Elevation:** 3,130 feet. **Location:** 6 miles south of Safford off US Route 191. **Facilities:** 71 campsites, electric hookups, cabins, showers, restrooms, group-use area, picnic areas, picnic shelters, hiking trails, boat ramp, natural mineral water hot springs hot tub, day-use island, beach, visitor center, playground (&&). **Activities:** Camping, boating (no gas motors), fishing, swimming. **Special Features:** Park consists of two units: the main Roper Lake Unit and the Dankworth Pond Unit, 3 miles south. Roper Lake features a 30-acre stocked lake and a natural stone hot tub with water from the park's mineral hot springs. Dankworth Pond (15 acres) was once a fish hatchery for rearing catfish; it features a replica Indian Village.

★1445★ SAN RAFAEL RANCH STATE PARK

HC 2, Box 200
Patagonia, AZ 85624
Web: www.pr.state.az.us/Parks/parkhtml/sanrafael.html
Phone: 520-394-2447
Size: 3,500 acres state-owned. **Elevation:** 4,750 feet. **Location:** 23 miles southeast of Patagonia in southern Santa Cruz County. **Facilities:** Historic pre-territorial ranch house with barns and windmills. **Activities:** Park is not currently open to the public. Scenic driving and picture taking of the Valley are the only activities available. **Special Features:** A joint effort of the Nature Conservancy and AZ State Parks, this site protects a pristine 35-square mile area of rolling short-grass prairie along the Santa Cruz River, free of electric wires and paved highways. The ranch house is not currently open to visitors, but nature walks, an historic house tour, and other activities are to be offered to the public in the future on the southern portion of the property owned by AZ State Parks.

★1446★ SLIDE ROCK STATE PARK

PO Box 10358
Sedona, AZ 86336
Web: www.pr.state.az.us/Parks/parkhtml/sliderock.html
Phone: 928-282-3034
Size: 43 acres. **Elevation:** 4,930 feet. **Location:** 7 miles north of Sedona, at 6871 N Hwy 89A. **Facilities:** Natural rock water slides, picnic areas, picnic shelters, nature trail, volleyball court, restrooms (&). In addition, the park is close to several Coconino National Forest campgrounds and hiking trails. **Activities:** Swimming, wading, bird watching, fishing. **Special Features:** Park is a historic apple farm nestled in Oak Creek Canyon and features an 80-foot natural water slide. In season, apples grown here can be purchased at an on-site fruit market.

★1447★ TOMBSTONE COURTHOUSE STATE
  HISTORIC PARK

PO Box 216
Tombstone, AZ 85638
Web: www.pr.state.az.us/Parks/parkhtml/tombstone.html
Phone: 520-457-3311

Size: 1 acre. **Elevation:** 4,539 feet **Location:** In Tombstone, at the corner of Toughnut and 3rd Streets, 2 blocks off US 80. **Facilities:** Picnic area, visitor center, museum (the courthouse) exhibits, restrooms (&). **Special Features:** Tombstone was the West's wildest silver mining town and was the site of the famous gunfight at the OK Corral. The Victorian-style courthouse was built in 1882 at a cost of nearly $50,000, and some of the state's most notorious criminal cases were tried here. Today the Courthouse is a museum, with antiques, artifacts, and exhibits, including tax licenses for operating a brothel and an invitation to a hanging.

★1448★ TONTO NATURAL BRIDGE STATE PARK
PO Box 1245
Payson, AZ 85547
Web: www.pr.state.az.us/Parks/parkhtml/tonto.html
Phone: 928-476-4202; **Fax:** 928-476-2264
Size: 160 acres. **Elevation:** 4,500 feet. **Location:** 10 miles north of Payson, off Highway 87. **Facilities:** Group-use area, picnic area, picnic shelters, hiking trails, scenic viewpoints, historic structures, gift shop, portable restrooms (&&). **Activities:** Hiking, picnicking, guided tours of the historic lodge. The lodge has a dining room and restrooms and can be rented overnight (maximum 12-20 people). All hiking trails descend into Pine Canyon and are steep and strenuous. **Special Features:** Tonto Natural Bridge is believed to be the world's largest natural travertine bridge. It stands 183 feet high over a 400-foot long tunnel that measures 150 feet at its widest point.

★1449★ TUBAC PRESIDIO STATE HISTORIC PARK
PO Box 1296
Tubac, AZ 85646
Web: www.pr.state.az.us/Parks/parkhtml/tubac.html
Phone: 520-398-2252
Size: 10 acres. **Elevation:** 3,500 feet. **Location:** 45 miles south of Tucson, on I-19. **Facilities:** Visitor center, museum, 1885 schoolhouse, underground archeology exhibit, picnic areas, picnic shelters, restrooms (&), multi-use trail, gift shop. **Activities:** Hiking, birding, interpretive programs. **Special Features:** Park preserves remnants of Arizona's first European settlement, a military fort founded by the Spanish in 1752. An underground display features portions of the original foundation, walls, and plaza floor of the Presidio de San Ignacio de Tubac. Museum exhibits highlight the contributions Native Americans, Spanish, Mexican, and Anglo cultures have made to Arizona's development. A segment of the Juan Bautista de Anza National Historic Trail (see entry in national trails section) passes through the park.

★1450★ YUMA CROSSING STATE HISTORIC PARK
201 N 4th Ave
Yuma, AZ 85364
Web: www.pr.state.az.us/Parks/parkhtml/yumacross.html
Phone: 928-329-0471
Size: 9 acres. **Elevation:** 120 feet. **Location:** On 4th Ave, 1/2 mile south of the 4th Ave exit off I-8. **Facilities:** Transportation museum, visitor center, gift shop, picnic area, restrooms (&). **Activities:** Interpretive programs. **Special Features:** Park is located on the grounds of the old Yuma Quartermaster Depot, built during the 1860s to store and distribute supplies to all of the military forts in Arizona, Nevada, Utah, New Mexico, and Texas. Historic features at park include the Depot's Commanding Officer's Quarters and a 1907 Southern Pacific Steam Locomotive and Coach Car.

★1451★ YUMA TERRITORIAL PRISON STATE HISTORIC PARK
PO Box 10792
Yuma, AZ 85366
Web: www.pr.state.az.us/Parks/parkhtml/yuma.html
Phone: 928-783-4771
Size: 7 acres. **Elevation:** 120 feet. **Location:** On Prison Hill Road in Yuma, off I-8. **Facilities:** Territorial Prison built in 1876, museum, gift shop, video room, restrooms (&). **Activities:** Historic exhibits. **Special Features:** Arizona Territorial Prison was home to 3,069 prisoners, including 29 women, from 1876 through 1909. The park's museum details the prison's development and tells stories of prisoners who served time there. Artifacts preserved include strap-iron cell doors, crude bunk beds, and numerous ball and chain devices.

9. State Parks

Arkansas State Parks

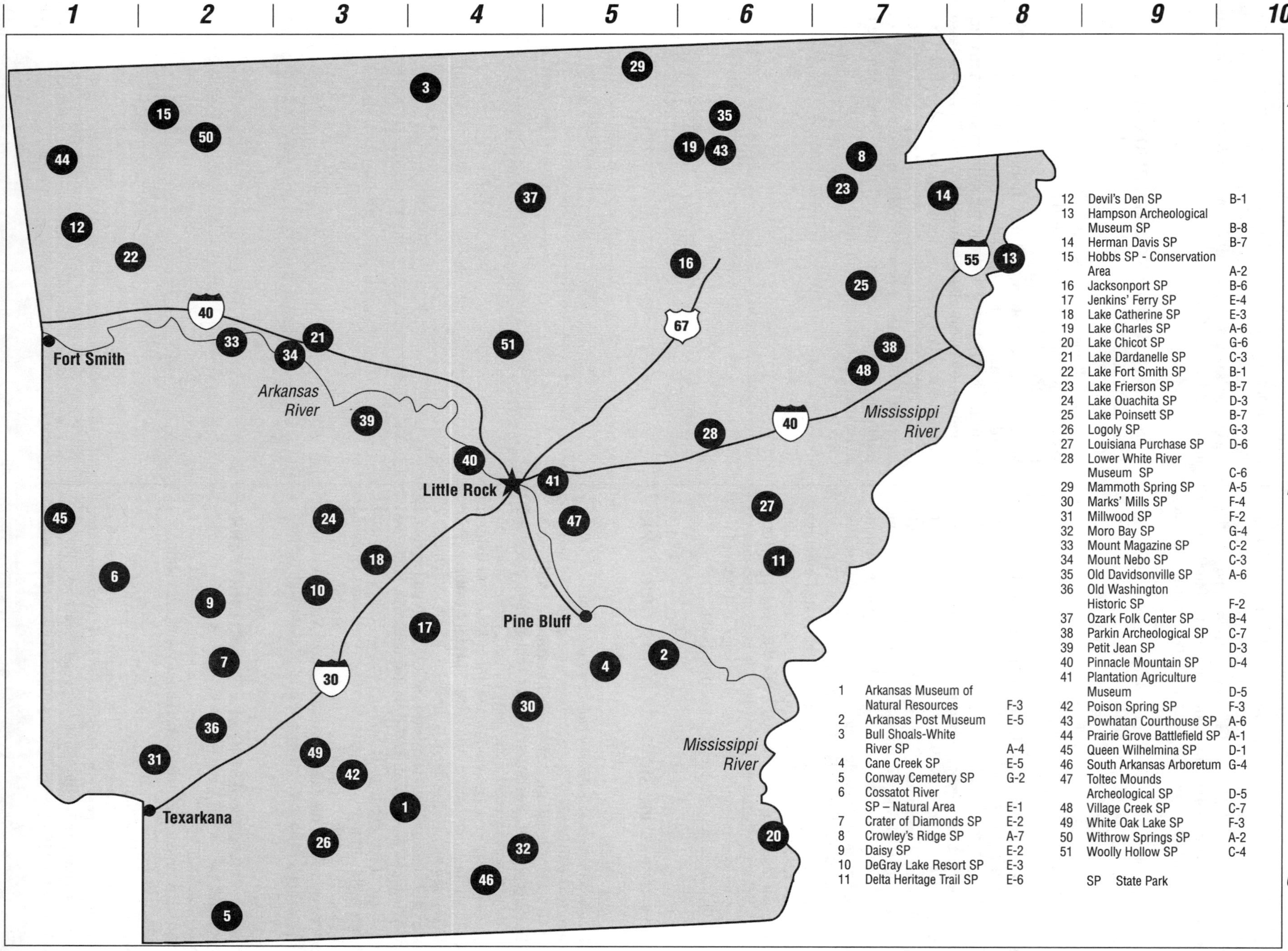

12	Devil's Den SP	B-1
13	Hampson Archeological	
	Museum SP	B-8
14	Herman Davis SP	B-7
15	Hobbs SP – Conservation	
	Area	A-2
16	Jacksonport SP	B-6
17	Jenkins' Ferry SP	E-4
18	Lake Catherine SP	E-3
19	Lake Charles SP	A-6
20	Lake Chicot SP	G-6
21	Lake Dardanelle SP	C-3
22	Lake Fort Smith SP	B-1
23	Lake Frierson SP	B-7
24	Lake Ouachita SP	D-3
25	Lake Poinsett SP	B-7
26	Logoly SP	G-3
27	Louisiana Purchase SP	D-6
28	Lower White River	
	Museum SP	C-6
29	Mammoth Spring SP	A-5
30	Marks' Mills SP	F-4
31	Millwood SP	F-2
32	Moro Bay SP	G-4
33	Mount Magazine SP	C-2
34	Mount Nebo SP	C-3
35	Old Davidsonville SP	A-6
36	Old Washington	
	Historic SP	F-2
37	Ozark Folk Center SP	B-4
38	Parkin Archeological SP	C-7
39	Petit Jean SP	D-3
40	Pinnacle Mountain SP	D-4
41	Plantation Agriculture	
	Museum	D-5
42	Poison Spring SP	F-3
43	Powhatan Courthouse SP	A-6
44	Prairie Grove Battlefield SP	A-1
45	Queen Wilhelmina SP	D-1
46	South Arkansas Arboretum	G-4
47	Toltec Mounds	
	Archeological SP	D-5
48	Village Creek SP	C-7
49	White Oak Lake SP	F-3
50	Withrow Springs SP	A-2
51	Woolly Hollow SP	C-4

SP State Park

1	Arkansas Museum of	
	Natural Resources	F-3
2	Arkansas Post Museum	E-5
3	Bull Shoals-White	
	River SP	A-4
4	Cane Creek SP	E-5
5	Conway Cemetery SP	G-2
6	Cossatot River	
	SP – Natural Area	E-1
7	Crater of Diamonds SP	E-2
8	Crowley's Ridge SP	A-7
9	Daisy SP	E-2
10	DeGray Lake Resort SP	E-3
11	Delta Heritage Trail SP	E-6

304

ARKANSAS

★1452★ Arkansas Division of State Parks
1 Capitol Mall
Little Rock, AR 72201
(501) 682-1191 - Phone
(501) 682-1364 - Fax
(888) 287-2757 - Toll-free
(501) 682-7742 - Employment
Web: arkansasstateparks.com
Oversees 51 state parks totaling more than 50,000 acres. Also maintains more than 300 miles of trails including a segment of the 223-mile Ouachita National Recreation Trail.

★1453★ Arkansas Game & Fish Commission
2 Natural Resources Dr
Little Rock, AR 72205
(501) 223-6300 - Phone
(501) 223-6444 - Fax
(800) 364-4263 - Toll-free
Web: www.agfc.com
Manages 52 lakes and nearly 100 wildlife management areas with public access for hunting and other outdoor related sports. Conducts boater education courses and other informational programs, operates fish hatcheries, and administers hunting and fishing licensing.

Key to campsite classification:

- **Class A campsites** — Include picnic tables, grills, water and electricity hookups. Sites designated as ''premium'' include sewer hookups; ''preferred'' sites offer a scenic view. Restrooms with flush toilets and hot showers are nearby. Most campgrounds also have a trailer dump station.
- **Class B campsites** — Sites include picnic tables and grills. No utility hookups, but drinking water is nearby. Restrooms have flush toilets and may include hot showers.
- **Primitive campsites** — Limited facilities; may include pit or chemical toilets and a drinking water supply.
- **Overflow** — These are not designated campsites, but space in parking lots or open fields that may be assigned when all developed campsites are occupied.

★1454★ ARKANSAS MUSEUM OF NATURAL RESOURCES
PO Box 7
Smackover, AR 71762
Web: www.arkansasstateparks.com/parks/park.asp?id=42
Phone: 870-725-2877; **Fax:** 870-725-2161

Size: 19 acres. **Location:** On AR 7, 2 miles south of Smackover. **Facilities:** Museum with state-of-the-art exhibits and an adjacent Oil Field Park with working equipment. **Special Features:** Museum features a 25,000-square-foot main exhibition/research building that includes a 10,500-square-feet exhibit hall, orientation theater, exhibit work area, research center, and museum store/gift shop. Displays and exhibits at the Oil Field Park emphasize petroleum and brine recovered for bromine extraction.

★1455★ ARKANSAS POST MUSEUM
5530 Hwy 165 S
Gillett, AR 72055
Web: www.arkansasstateparks.com/parks/park.asp?id=45
Phone: 870-548-2634
Location: 6 miles south of Gillett on US 165 at the junction of AR 169. **Facilities:** Museum. **Special Features:** Museum is made up of five exhibit buildings where visitors can explore life as it was on Arkansas's southern Grand Prairie from the end of the Civil War to the present day.

★1456★ BULL SHOALS-WHITE RIVER STATE PARK
129 Bull Shoals Park
Bull Shoals, AR 72642
Web: www.arkansasstateparks.com/parks/park.asp?id=8
Phone: 870-431-5521
Size: 663 acres. **Location:** From Mountain Home, 6 miles north on AR 5, then 8 miles west on AR 178. **Facilities:** 107 campsites (most with hookups but 20 are tent sites with no hookups), 2 rent-a-camp sites, 2 rent-an-RV sites, picnic areas, pavilions, hiking trails (2.5 miles), boat dock with motor, kayak, and canoe rentals as well as supplies, equipment, and gifts; new visitor center has an exhibit hall, theater, and gift shop (♿♿). **Activities:** Camping, fishing, boating, water sports, hiking, interpretive programs. **Special Features:** Park is located in the scenic Ozark Mountains along the shores of White River and Bull Shoals Lake. The White River is one of mid-America's premier rainbow streams. A dam on the river forms the 45,440-acre Bull Shoals Lake, which is also popular for fishing as well as other watersports.

★1457★ CANE CREEK STATE PARK
50 State Park Rd
Star City, AR 71667
Web: www.arkansasstateparks.com/parks/park.asp?id=34
Phone: 870-628-4714; **Fax:** 870-628-3611
Size: 2,053 acres. **Location:** From Star City, 5 miles east on AR 293; lake access is by county road off AR 11, east of Star City. **Facilities:** 30 Class A campsites and 1 Rent-an-RV site, showers, restrooms, picnic areas, pavilions (including 1 screened and 1 enclosed/climate-controlled), trails, bathhouse, boat ramp,

fishing piers, visitor center with exhibits and gift shop, playground (占占). **Activities:** Camping, fishing, hiking, bicycling, kayaking, interpretive programs, bird watching. **Special Features:** Park is located where the West Gulf Coastal Plain and the Mississippi Delta meet, providing opportunities to explore two distinct natural settings — the park's rolling woodlands in the Gulf Coastal Plain or a timbered Delta lake on the 1,675-acre Cane Creek Lake.

★1458★ CONWAY CEMETERY STATE PARK
c/o Arkansas State Parks
1 Capitol Mall
Little Rock, AR 72201
Web: www.arkansasstateparks.com/parks/park.asp?id=54
Phone: 888-287-2757
Size: 11 acres. **Location:** From Bradley, 2 miles west on AR 160 to Walnut Hill, then south on the county road for 0.5 miles. (Park is located in extreme southwestern Arkansas.) **Facilities:** None. **Special Features:** Historic park preserves the gravesite of James Sevier Conway (1796-1855), Arkansas' first governor. The cemetery is the family plot of the former Conway homesite and cotton plantation, Walnut Hill. Forty gravesites lie within the graveyard.

★1459★ COSSATOT RIVER STATE PARK-NATURAL AREA
1980 Hwy 278 W
Wickes, AR 71973
Web: www.arkansasstateparks.com/parks/park.asp?id=39
Phone: 870-385-2201; **Fax:** 870-385-7858
Size: 5,484 acres. **Location:** South of Mena in west central Arkansas. Northern route is via AK 246 between Vandervoort and Athens; southern route is via US 278 between Wickes and Umpire. **Facilities:** Tent campsites with no hookups (Cossatot Falls and Sandbar areas); picnic sites, restrooms, river access points (Brushy Creek Recreation Area at the Hwy 246 bridge); hiking trails; visitor center with exhibits, gift shop, meeting rooms. **Activities:** Whitewater canoeing and kayaking, hiking, interpretive programs. **Special Features:** Parkland extends for 12 miles along the Cossatot River, reputed to have the best whitewater float stream in mid-America. The river forms Cossatot Falls, a rugged and rocky canyon with Class IV rapids. (Flow levels are dependent on rainfall, so floatable river levels usually are limited to late fall, winter, and spring.)

★1460★ CRATER OF DIAMONDS STATE PARK
209 State Park Rd
Murfreesboro, AR 71958
Web: www.craterofdiamondsstatepark.com
Phone: 870-285-3113; **Fax:** 870-285-4169
Size: 887 acres. **Location:** 2 miles southeast of Murfreesboro on AR 301. **Facilities:** 59 campsites with water and electric hookups, showers, restrooms, picnic areas, screened pavilion, aquatic playground, trails, restaurant, laundry, gift shop, visitor center, exhibits. **Activities:** Camping, hiking, prospecting for diamonds and other gems, interpretive programs. **Special Features:** First discovered here in 1906, the diamonds come from the eroded surface of an ancient volcanic pipe. Visitors can

search a 37-acre plowed field to prospect for and keep any gems they find, which may include diamonds, amethyst, garnet, jasper, agate, or quartz. Since Crater of Diamonds became a state park in 1972, more than 25,000 diamonds have been carried home by visitors. Notable diamonds found here include the largest diamond ever unearthed in the US (40.23 carats) and the Strawn-Wagner Diamond, a flawless diamond with the highest grade a diamond can achieve.

★1461★ CROWLEY'S RIDGE STATE PARK
2092 Hwy 168 N
Paragould, AR 72450
Web: www.arkansasstateparks.com/parks/park.asp?id=7
Phone: 870-573-6751
Size: 271 acres. **Location:** 15 miles north of Jonesboro on AR 141; or 9 miles west of Paragould on US 412, then 2 miles south on AR 168. **Facilities:** 18 campsites with electric and water, 8 tent sites, showers, restrooms, 4 duplex cabins, group lodge, picnic areas, pavilions, snack bar, trails, 31-acre fishing lake. **Activities:** Camping, fishing, boating (no gas motors), swimming, interpretive programs. **Special Features:** Park occupies the former homestead of Benjamin Crowley, whose family first settled the area, and features native log and stone structures constructed by the Civilian Conservation Corps.

★1462★ DAISY STATE PARK
103 E Park
Kirby, AR 71950
Web: www.arkansasstateparks.com/parks/park.asp?id=12
Phone: 870-398-4487
Size: 272 acres. **Location:** On the northern end of Lake Greeson, just off off US 70, 1/4 mile south of Daisy. **Facilities:** 82 campsites with electric and water hookups, 21 tent sites, showers, restrooms, picnic area, screened pavilion, launch ramp, trails (including a motorcycle/mountain bike/ATV trail), playground. **Activities:** Camping, fishing, swimming, water sports, hiking, mountain biking, motorcycling. **Special Features:** Park is located in the Ouachita Mountain foothills. The 7,000-acre Lake Greeson is popular with watersports enthusiasts as well as anglers, and the Little Missouri River and four other float streams offer spring and early summer trout fishing.

★1463★ DEGRAY LAKE RESORT STATE PARK
2027 State Park Entrance Rd
Bismarck, AR 71929
Web: www.degray.com
Phone: 501-865-2801
Size: 938 acres (land). **Location:** Exit 78 off I-30 at Caddo Valley/Arkadelphia, then 7 miles north on Scenic 7 Byway; or, from Hot Springs, 21 miles south on Scenic 7 Byway. **Facilities:** 113 campsites with electric and water hookups, 3 Rent-a-Yurts; 96-room lodge and convention center with swimming pool, hot tub, fitness room, restaurant, business center, meeting rooms; 18-hole championship golf course with driving range, practice range, and pro shop; full-service marina with tackle, dock space, fuel, and boat rentals; swim beaches, boat launches, pavilions, trails, bicycle rentals, store, tennis court, basketball court, laundry (占占). **Activities:** Camping, fishing, swimming, snorkeling,

9. State Parks

scuba diving, other water sports, hiking, bicycling, horseback riding (guided trail rides), tennis, golf, interpretive programs. **Special Features:** Park is situated in the Ouachita Mountain foothills on the north shore of 13,800-acre DeGray Lake. It combines the amenities of a resort with outdoor activities of a park.

★1464★ DELTA HERITAGE TRAIL STATE PARK
PO Box 193
Watson, AR 71674
Web: www.arkansasstateparks.com/parks/park.asp?id=55
Phone: 870-644-3474
Size: 73.5-mile linear park (when complete). **Location:** Between Lexa (6 miles west of Helena) and Cypress Bend (5 miles northeast of McGehee) in southeastern Arkansas. **Facilities:** Trail (the first 4 miles of the 73-mile trail have been completed, from Helena junction to Barton, with trailheads at both Helena junction and Walnut Corner). **Activities:** Hiking, bicycling, wildlife viewing. **Special Features:** A rails-to-trails conversion of a former Union Pacific railroad route, the Delta Heritage Trail is being developed in phases and will traverse some of the most remote and scenic areas in the Mississippi Delta region of Arkansas.

★1465★ DEVIL'S DEN STATE PARK
11333 W Arkansas Hwy 74
West Fork, AR 72774
Web: www.arkansasstateparks.com/parks/park.asp?id=4
Phone: 479-761-3325; **Fax:** 479-761-3676
Size: 2,047 acres. **Location:** 8 miles south of Fayetteville; from I-540 take exit 53 (West Fork), then 17 miles southwest on AR 170. **Facilities:** 144 campsites (most with hookups), several tent-only campsites (including 8 hike-in), 16 cabins, group camp, pavilion, meeting room, playground, store, cafe (seasonal), swimming pool (seasonal), water sports rentals, hiking and mountain bike trails (&&); a horse camp at the park has 43 campsites with water/electric hookups and access to about 20 miles of riding trails. **Activities:** Camping, fishing, canoeing, kayaking, pedal boating, swimming, hiking, backpacking, mountain biking, horseback riding, interpretive programs. **Special Features:** Located in Lee Creek Valley in the Ozark Mountains, the park features rustic-style wood and stone structures crafted by the Civilian Conservation Corps. These structures include a native stone dam spanning Lee Creek in the heart of the park. The park's 8-acre Devil's Lake is formed by the dam.

★1466★ HAMPSON ARCHEOLOGICAL MUSEUM STATE PARK
PO Box 156
Wilson, AR 72395
Web: www.arkansasstateparks.com/parks/park.asp?id=31
Phone: 870-655-8622; **Fax:** 870-655-8061
Size: 5 acres. **Location:** At the junction of US 61 and Lake Drive in Wilson. **Facilities:** Museum, restrooms, picnic sites, playground. **Special Features:** Museum exhibits artifacts from the Nodena culture, a civilization of art, religion, political structure, and trading networks developed in this area from 1400-1650.

★1467★ HERMAN DAVIS STATE PARK
c/o Arkansas State Parks
1 Capitol Mall
Little Rock, AR 72201
Web: www.arkansasstateparks.com/parks/park.asp?id=56
Phone: 888-287-2757
Size: 1 acre. **Location:** On AR 18 in the community of Manila. **Special Features:** Park surrounds a monument to Private Herman Davis, an Arkansas farm boy and war hero. Davis ranked fourth on General John J. Pershing's list of World War I's 100 greatest heroes and received the Distinguished Service Cross. He also received the Croix de Guere and Medaulle Militaire from the French government for his heroic acts.

★1468★ HOBBS STATE PARK-CONSERVATION AREA
21392 E Hwy 12
Rogers, AR 72756
Web: www.arkansasstateparks.com/parks/park.asp?id=38
Phone: 479-789-2380
Size: 11,750 acres. **Location:** 10 miles east of Rogers on AR 12. **Facilities:** 4 hiking trails, including a 1/4 mile, barrier-free historical trail and a 16-mile multi-use trail; public firing range; regulated seasonal hunting; undeveloped access to Beaver Lake. **Activities:** Hiking, shooting, hunting, interpretive programs. **Special Features:** Park is located along the southern shore of 28,370-acre Beaver Lake and is Arkansas's largest state park in land area. It is presently in its initial development phase; future development is to include a visitor/educational center, cabins, pavilions, and picnic areas. Managed jointly by Arkansas State Parks, Arkansas Natural Heritage Commission, and Arkansas Game and Fish Commission.

★1469★ JACKSONPORT STATE PARK
205 Avenue St
Newport, AR 72112
Web: www.arkansasstateparks.com/parks/park.asp?id=17
Phone: 870-523-2143; **Fax:** 870-523-4620
Size: 160 acres. **Location:** On AR 69 in Jacksonport, 3 miles north of Newport. **Facilities:** 20 Class A campsites, swim beach on the White River, pavilion, picnic sites, playground, riverwalk trail, museums. **Activities:** Camping, fishing, boating, swimming, hiking. **Special Features:** A thriving river port in the 1800s, Jacksonport was occupied by both Confederate and Union armies during the Civil War due to its strategic location. Park includes a restored 1872 courthouse with exhibits of Jackson County's history and the *Mary Woods No 2*, a sternwheel paddleboat.

★1470★ JENKINS' FERRY STATE PARK
c/o Arkansas State Parks
1 Capitol Mall
Little Rock, AR 72201
Web: www.arkansasstateparks.com/parks/park.asp?id=28
Phone: 888-287-2757
Size: 40 acres. **Location:** 13 miles south of Sheridan on AR 46. Contact Information **Facilities:** Exhibits, picnic areas, pavilion (no electricity), swimming area, boat launch. **Activities:**

Interpretive programs, picnicking, swimming, boating. **Special Features:** Jenkins' Ferry is one of three Civil War battlegrounds in south central Arkansas that were part of the Union Army's Red River Campaign, the purpose of which was to take Texas away from the Confederate troops. The other two battlegrounds are Marks' Mills State Park and Poison Spring State Park (see separate listings).

★1471★ LAKE CATHERINE STATE PARK

1200 Catherine Park Rd
Hot Springs, AR 71913
Web: www.arkansasstateparks.com/parks/park.asp?id=2
Phone: 501-844-4176
Size: 2,180 acres. **Location:** Exit 97 off I-30 near Malvern, then 12 miles north on AR 171. **Facilities:** 73 campsites with hookups (including preferred sites), 2 rent-a-camp sites, 18 cabins, picnic sites, pavilion, playgrounds, marina (seasonal), boat rentals, boat launch ramp, laundry, trails, nature center (seasonal), visitor center with groceries, ice, snacks, and gifts (&&). **Activities:** Camping, fishing, swimming, water sports, hiking, horseback riding, scenic boat tours, interpretive programs. **Special Features:** Park is situated in the Ouachita Mountains on the shore of 1,940-acre Lake Catherine, one of the Hot Springs area's Diamond Lakes. The park features rustic-style facilities of native stone and wood constructed by the Civilian Conservation Corps in the 1930s.

★1472★ LAKE CHARLES STATE PARK

3705 Hwy 25
Powhatan, AR 72458
Web: www.arkansasstateparks.com/parks/park.asp?id=14
Phone: 870-878-6595
Size: 140 acres. **Location:** From Hoxie, 8 miles northwest on US 63, then 6 miles south on AR 25. **Facilities:** 60 campsites (electric and water hookups), 1 Rent-An-RV, showers, restrooms, picnic area, screened pavilion with ceiling fans, hiking trails, swimming beach, boat ramp, playground, visitor center with gift shop, camping supplies, and snacks (&&). **Activities:** Camping, fishing, swimming, hiking. **Special Features:** Park is located in the foothills of the Ozark Mountains on Lake Charles, a 645-acre, spring-fed lake. Anglers will find good fishing for crappie, bass, bream, and catfish year round.

★1473★ LAKE CHICOT STATE PARK

2542 Hwy 257
Lake Village, AR 71653
Web: www.arkansasstateparks.com/parks/park.asp?id=10
Phone: 870-265-5480
Size: 132 acres. **Location:** 8 miles northeast of Lake Village on AR 144. **Facilities:** 122 campsites with hookups, 14 cabins (many with a fishing dock), picnic areas, screened pavilions, swimming pool (seasonal), meeting hall with kitchen, laundry, store/marina, bicycle rentals, playground, visitor center with exhibits (&&). **Activities:** Camping, fishing, swimming, boating, bird watching, interpretive programs (including lake tours, levee tours, and other opportunities for bird and wildlife viewing). **Special Features:** Park is located in the Mississippi Delta region adjacent to Arkansas' largest natural lake. Lake Chicot

is a 20-mile-long oxbow lake, cut off centuries ago when the Mississippi River changed course. The park is located in the Mississippi Flyway and offers some of the state's best year-round birding opportunities.

★1474★ LAKE DARDANELLE STATE PARK

100 State Park Dr
Russellville, AR 72802
Web: www.arkansasstateparks.com/parks/park.asp?id=6
Phone: 479-967-5516
Size: 294 acres **Location:** Two separate areas on opposite sides of Lake Dardanelle: the Russellville area is located off I-40, exit 81, south and then immediately west for 5 miles on AR 326; the Dardanelle Area is 4 miles west of Dardanelle on AR 22. **Facilities:** 84 campsites with hookups (65 at Russellville and 19 at Dardanelle), picnic areas, pavilions, bathhouses, marina, boat ramps. In addition, the Russellville area has a fishing pier (&), trail, kayak and bicycle rentals, and visitor center with exhibits. **Activities:** Camping, fishing, swimming, water sports, hiking, interpretive programs. **Special Features:** Lake Dardanelle is a 34,000-acre reservoir on the Arkansas River. The park is a National Park Service Certified Trail of Tears site, and guided kayak and party barge tours led by park interpreters allow visitors to learn about the history of the area, including land routes where the Trail of Tears crossed here.

★1475★ LAKE FORT SMITH STATE PARK

PO Box 4
Mountainburg, AR 72946
Web: www.arkansasstateparks.com/parks/park.asp?id=18
Phone: 479-369-2469
Size: 125 acres. **Facilities:** Park closed in 2002 due to relocation but is expected to reopen in 2007. Facilities will include campsites, camping cabins, group lodging, cabins, picnic sites, trails, a visitor center, pavilion, swimming pool, and marina. **Special Features:** Park is being relocated due to the enlarging of Lake Fort Smith and Lake Shepherd Springs into a single reservoir to provide additional water storage for the Fort Smith municipal water supply. The new park will be located on the western side of the enlarged reservoir. For updated information, contact the park.

★1476★ LAKE FRIERSON STATE PARK

7904 Hwy 141
Jonesboro, AR 72401
Web: www.arkansasstateparks.com/parks/park.asp?id=33
Phone: 870-932-2615
Size: 114 acres. **Location:** 10 miles north of Jonesboro on AR 141. **Facilities:** 4 campsites with water and electric hookups, 3 campsites with no hookups, restrooms, picnic area, pavilion, playground, trail, boat ramp, boat rentals (fishing boat, kayak, pedal boats), fishing pier (&), visitor center with exhibits. **Activities:** Camping, fishing, boating, hiking. **Special Features:** Situated on Crowley's Ridge in northeast Arkansas, on the shore of 335-acre Lake Frierson, this park is known for its year-round fishing and springtime displays of wild dogwood blossoms.

9. State Parks

★1477★ **LAKE OUACHITA STATE PARK**
5451 Mountain Pine Rd
Mountain Pine, AR 71956
Web: www.arkansasstateparks.com/parks/park.asp?id=9
Phone: 501-767-9366
Size: 370 acres. **Location:** From Hot Springs, 3 miles west on US 270, then 12 miles north on AR 227. **Facilities:** 65 campsites with electric and water hookups, 24 campsites with no hookups, 12 hike-in tent sites, 8 cabins, swimming area, picnic areas, trails, full-service marina with boat rentals, bait, and supplies, visitor center with exhibits and a store (દદ). **Activities:** Camping, fishing, swimming, water-skiing, scuba diving, boating. **Special Features:** Surrounded by the Ouachita National Forest (see listing in section on National Forests), Lake Ouachita is Arkansas's largest lake (40,000 acres) within the state's borders and is considered a mecca for watersports. At the lake's eastern tip is historic Three Sisters' Springs, once thought to have curative powers.

★1478★ **LAKE POINSETT STATE PARK**
5752 State Park Ln
Harrisburg, AR 72432
Web: www.arkansasstateparks.com/parks/park.asp?id=13
Phone: 870-578-2064
Size: 112 acres. **Location:** From Harrisburg, 1 mile east on AR 14, then 3 miles south on AR 163. **Facilities:** 29 campsites with hookups, picnic areas, screened pavilion, trail, boat ramp, boat and kayak rentals, playground (દદ). **Activities:** Camping, fishing, boating. **Special Features:** The park and its 640-acre Lake Poinsett are situated atop Crowley's Ridge in northeast Arkansas.

★1479★ **LOGOLY STATE PARK**
PO Box 245
McNeil, AR 71752
Web: www.arkansasstateparks.com/parks/park.asp?id=27
Phone: 870-695-3561
Size: 368 acres. **Location:** 6 miles north of Magnolia on Logoly Road (County Road 47), just off US 79 near the McNeil Highway junction. **Facilities:** 6 group tent sites, a bathhouse with showers, picnic areas, pavilion, playground, trails, visitor center with exhibits and an indoor classroom. **Activities:** Camping, hiking, workshops/interpretive programs. **Special Features:** Arkansas' first environmental education state park, most of Logoly comprises a State Natural Area with unique plant species and mineral springs.

★1480★ **LOUISIANA PURCHASE STATE PARK**
c/o Arkansas State Parks
1 Capitol Mall
Little Rock, AR 72201
Web: www.arkansasstateparks.com/parks/park.asp?id=37
Phone: 888-287-2757
Size: 36 acres. **Location:** From I-40 at Brinkley, 21 miles south on US 49 to AR 362, then 2 miles east. Located at the junction of Lee, Monroe, and Phillips counties. **Facilities:** Boardwalk trail (દ), exhibits. **Activities:** Interpretive programs. **Special Features:** A National Historic Landmark, the park preserves the point from which all surveys of property acquired through the Louisiana Purchase of 1803 initiated. The granite monument marking the survey's initial point lies within a headwater swamp. To reach the monument, visitors must walk along an elevated boardwalk that features wayside exhibits telling about the Louisiana Purchase and the swamp's flora and fauna.

★1481★ **LOWER WHITE RIVER MUSEUM STATE PARK**
2009 Main St
Des Arc, AR 72040
Web: www.arkansasstateparks.com/parks/park.asp?id=43
Phone: 870-256-3711; **Fax:** 870-256-9202
Size: 0.5 acres. **Location:** In Des Arc at the western end of Main Street. **Facilities:** Museum exhibits, restrooms, visitor center (દદ). **Special Features:** Museum interprets the role of Arkansas's White River, with emphasis on the Lower White, as one of the vital transportation routes for the earliest settlers arriving in the Arkansas frontier. Exhibits and artifacts tell of the river's influence on the settlements along its banks and their subsequent commerce.

★1482★ **MAMMOTH SPRING STATE PARK**
PO Box 36
Mammoth Spring, AR 72554
Web: www.arkansasstateparks.com/parks/park.asp?id=25
Phone: 870-625-7364; **Fax:** 870-625-3255
Size: 62 acres. **Location:** On US 63 in Mammoth Spring; 2 miles south the Missouri border. **Facilities:** Historic exhibits, picnic area, pavilion, trail, ball field, playground (દદ). **Activities:** Fishing, hiking, bird watching, interpretive programs. **Special Features:** Mammoth Spring, Arkansas's largest spring and a National Natural Landmark, flows nine million gallons of water hourly. The waters form a 10-acre lake and then flow southward as Spring River, a popular Ozark trout and float stream. Historic attractions located near the spring include the 1886 Frisco depot, which houses a collection of railroad memorabilia, and a Frisco caboose. Remnants of a mill and hydroelectric plant are also located at the park, and the information center has additional exhibits on the area's history and natural resources.

★1483★ **MARKS' MILLS STATE PARK**
c/o Arkansas State Parks
1 Capitol Mall
Little Rock, AR 72201
Web: www.arkansasstateparks.com/parks/park.asp?id=29
Phone: 888-287-2757
Size: 6.2 acres. **Location:** Southeast of Fordyce at the junction of AR 97 and AR 8. **Facilities:** Interpretive exhibits, picnic sites. **Special Features:** Marks' Mills is one of three Civil War battlegrounds in south central Arkansas that were part of the Union Army's Red River Campaign, the purpose of which was to take Texas away from the Confederate troops. The other two battlegrounds are Jenkins' Ferry State Park and Poison Spring State Park (see separate listings).

9. State Parks

★1484★ MILLWOOD STATE PARK

1564 Hwy 32 E
Ashdown, AR 71822
Web: www.arkansasstateparks.com/parks/park.asp?id=26
Phone: 870-898-2800; Fax: 870-898-2632
Size: 823 acres. Location: From junction of I-30 and US 71 at Texarkana, 16 miles north on US 71 to Ashdown, then 9 miles east on AR 32. Facilities: 116 campsites (including 112 with hookups, 3 primitive sites, and 1 Rent-An-RV), showers, restrooms, picnic areas, pavilion, playground, hiking and bicycle trails, a marina that has groceries, gifts, and boat rentals in addition to bait and gas, visitor center (&&). Activities: Camping, fishing, boating, hiking, mountain biking, bird watching, interpretive programs. Special Features: Park is situated alongside Millwood Lake, a 29,260-acre fishing hotspot known nationwide. The lake regularly hosts bass tournaments; many trophy fish of over 10 pounds have been recorded and 4- and 5-pound catches are common.

★1485★ MORO BAY STATE PARK

6071 Hwy 600
Jersey, AR 71651
Web: www.arkansasstateparks.com/parks/park.asp?id=20
Phone: 870-463-8555
Size: 117 acres. Location: 29 miles southwest of Warren on US 63; or 23 miles northeast of El Dorado on US 63. Facilities: 20 campsites with electric and water hookups, bathhouse, picnic areas, screened pavilion, playground, hiking trails, marina, boat rentals, store (&&). Activities: Camping, fishing, water sports, hiking. Special Features: Located in south central Arkansas where Moro Bay and Raymond Lake join the Ouachita River, Park is especially popular for fishing and water sports.

★1486★ MOUNT MAGAZINE STATE PARK

16878 Hwy 309 S
Paris, AR 72855
Web: www.arkansasstateparks.com/parks/park.asp?id=41
Phone: 479-963-8502; Fax: 479-963-1031
Size: 2,200 acres. Location: On Scenic Highway 309 approximately 17 miles south of Paris; or, from Danville, 9 miles west on AR 10 to Havana, then 10 miles north on Scenic Highway 309. Facilities: 60-room mountain lodge with restaurant, conference center, enclosed swimming pool, fitness center and 13 fully equipped cabins (all-new lodge and cabins opened Spring 2006); 18 campsites, scenic overlook, hiking trails, pavilion, picnic area, restrooms, visitor center with exhibit gallery and gift shop (&&). Activities: Camping, hiking, mountain biking, horseback riding, rock climbing, rappelling, hang gliding, ORV adventure, backpacking, interpretive programs. Special Features: Park is located in the Ozark National Forest atop Magazine Mountain, the state's highest mountain, offering panoramic vistas of river valleys, canyons, and distant mountains. The park is a destination for outdoor sports and extreme adventure enthusiasts and is the state parks system's most dramatic location for technical rock climbing.

★1487★ MOUNT NEBO STATE PARK

16728 W State Hwy 155
Dardanelle, AR 72834
Web: www.arkansasstateparks.com/parks/park.asp?id=5
Phone: 479-229-3655
Size: 2,893 acres. Location: 7 miles west of Dardanelle on AR 155. (Highway 155 zigzags up the mountain and includes hairpin curves; not recommended for trailers longer than 15 feet.) Facilities: 24 Class B campsites, 10 hike-in campsites (no dump station), 14 cabins, picnic areas, pavilion, hiking trails (14 miles), swimming pool, tennis courts, ball field, playgrounds, visitor center with exhibits, store, and bicycle rentals (&&). Activities: Camping, swimming, hiking, bicycling, tennis, interpretive programs. Special Features: Rising 1,350 feet, Mount Nebo offers sweeping views of the Arkansas River Valley. Native logs and stones from the mountain were used by the Civilian Conservation Corps to construct many of the park's cabins, pavilions, bridges, and trails.

★1488★ OLD DAVIDSONVILLE STATE PARK

7953 Hwy 166 S
Pocahontas, AR 72455
Web: www.arkansasstateparks.com/parks/park.asp?id=23
Phone: 870-892-4708
Size: 173 acres. Location: From Pocahontas, 2 miles west on US 62, then 9 miles south on AR 166; or, from Black Rock, US 63 to AR 361, then 6 miles north. Facilities: 24 campsites with electric and water hookups, 25 tent sites, showers, restrooms, picnic areas, 2 screened pavilions, playgrounds, trails (including a self-guided trail through the old town site), boat launch ramp (Black River only), boat rentals, fishing pier (&), visitor center, exhibits, gift shop. Activities: Camping, fishing, boating, hiking, interpretive programs. Special Features: Park preserves the locale of historic Davidsonville (established in 1815), the site of the Arkansas Territory's first post office, courthouse, and land office. In addition to its historic significance, the park borders the Black River and a 12-acre fishing lake, and fishing is a major activity here.

★1489★ OLD WASHINGTON HISTORIC STATE PARK

PO Box 98
Washington, AR 71862
Web: www.oldwashingtonstatepark.com
Phone: 870-983-2684
Size: 90 acres. Location: Exit 30 off I-30 at Hope, 9 miles northwest on US 278. Facilities: Historic buildings, restaurant, group rental facilities (&&). Special Features: Established in 1824, Washington was an important stop on the Southwest Trail for pioneers traveling to Texas. Later it became a major service center for area planters, merchants, and professionals, and from 1863-1865 it was the Confederate capital of Arkansas. The park interprets everyday life in Washington from 1824 to 1889, with the 1874 Courthouse serving as the visitor center. Other restored structures include an 1836 Courthouse, blacksmith shop, weapons museum, several residences, and an 1832 tavern/restaurant where Southern country fare is served daily for lunch. The park also houses the Southwest Arkansas Regional Archives, a

9. State Parks

resource center for historical and genealogical research. Operated in conjunction with Pioneer Washington Restoration Foundation.

★1490★ OZARK FOLK CENTER STATE PARK

PO Box 500
Mountain View, AR 72560
Web: www.ozarkfolkcenter.com
Phone: 870-269-3851; **Fax:** 870-269-2909
Size: 637 acres. **Location:** One mile north of Mountain View on Spur 382 (Jimmy Driftwood Parkway) off Highways 5, 9, and 14. Street address is 1032 Park Avenue. **Facilities:** 60-room lodge, restaurant, snack bar, conference and meeting facilities, music theater, crafts village, outdoor stage, snack bar, exhibits, gift shop, picnic areas. **Activities:** Craft exhibitions and demonstrations, music programs, contests, workshops, festivals. **Special Features:** Park is America's only facility that preserves the Ozark heritage and presents its living history. Facilities and programs at the Center focus on the cultural and social history of the Ozark region, particularly in the areas of pioneer crafts and mountain music.

★1491★ PARKIN ARCHEOLOGICAL STATE PARK

PO Box 1110
Parkin, AR 72373
Web: www.arkansasstateparks.com/parks/park.asp?id=40
Phone: 870-755-2500; **Fax:** 870-755-2676
Size: 61 acres. **Location:** In the community of Parkin, at the junction of US 64 and AR 184 north. **Facilities:** Interpretive trails; visitor center with exhibit area, archeological laboratory, and gift shop; picnic area, playground, enclosed pavilion. **Activities:** Interpretive programs. **Special Features:** A National Historic Landmark, Park interprets the Mississippi Period Native American village located here from AD 1000 to 1550 and visited by the Hernando de Soto expedition in 1541. The mound site is jointly managed by Arkansas State Parks and the Arkansas Archeological Survey as a research station, museum, and interpretive center.

★1492★ PETIT JEAN STATE PARK

1285 Petit Jean Mountain Rd
Morrilton, AR 72110
Web: www.petitjeanstatepark.com
Phone: 501-727-5441
Size: 2,656 acres. **Location:** Exit 108 off I-40 at Morrilton, 9 miles south on AR 9, then 12 miles west on AR 154. **Facilities:** 125 Class A campsites, 5 tent-only fly-in campsites (&), group camp area, rent-a-camp sites, tepee rentals, 33 cabins, 24-room lodge with restaurant, picnic areas, pavilions, recreation hall, hiking trails (20+ miles), boathouse with snack bar, boat rentals, and supplies, a boat launch ramp, fishing pier (&), swimming pool, tennis courts, playgrounds, antique/classic cars museum, airport (daytime use only). **Activities:** Camping, fishing, swimming, boating, hiking, interpretive programs. **Special Features:** Petit Jean Mountain rises 1,100 feet above the Arkansas River Valley, between the Ouachitas and Ozarks, offering panoramic views. Mather Lodge, the park's focal point, is situated on a bluff overlooking Cedar Creek Canyon, which features a 95-foot waterfall and a rock dam that forms the 100-acre Lake Bailey. The rustic-style log and stone facilities at the park were constructed by the Civilian Conservation Corps.

★1493★ PINNACLE MOUNTAIN STATE PARK

11901 Pinnacle Valley Rd
Little Rock, AR 72223
Web: www.arkansasstateparks.com/parks/park.asp?id=3
Phone: 501-868-5806; **Fax:** 501-868-5018
Size: 1,801 acres. **Location:** Exit 9 off I-430 at Little Rock, 7 miles west on AR 10, then 2 miles north on AR 300. **Facilities:** Picnic area, pavilion, launch ramps, hiking trails, visitor center with exhibits, meeting room, and gift shop (&&). **Activities:** Fishing, hiking, interpretive programs. **Special Features:** Pinnacle Mountain is a day-use park dedicated to environmental education, recreation, and preservation. The area offers a great diversity of habitats, from high upland peaks to bottomlands along the Big and Little Maumelle rivers. Park includes the Arkansas Arboretum, a 71-acre site with exhibits on native flora from each of Arkansas' six natural divisions.

★1494★ PLANTATION AGRICULTURE MUSEUM

PO Box 87
Scott, AR 72142
Web: www.arkansasstateparks.com/parks/park.asp?id=44
Phone: 501-961-1409
Size: 4.5 acres. **Location:** In the community of Scott at the junction of US 165 and AR 161. **Facilities:** Museum. **Special Features:** Museum focuses on the history of cotton agriculture in Arkansas from statehood in 1836 through World War II, when agricultural practices became mechanized. The museum interprets rural life during the plantation era and also includes the Dortch Gin Exhibit Building, where visitors can learn how cotton was grown and ginned.

★1495★ POISON SPRING STATE PARK

c/o Arkansas State Parks
1 Capitol Mall
Little Rock, AR 72201
Web: www.arkansasstateparks.com/parks/park.asp?id=47
Phone: 888-287-2757
Size: 85 acres. **Location:** 10 miles west of Camden on AR 76. Contact Information **Facilities:** Outdoor interpretive exhibits, picnic areas **Special Features:** Poison Spring is one of three Civil War battlegrounds in south central Arkansas that were part of the Union Army's Red River Campaign, the purpose of which was to take Texas away from the Confederate troops. The other two battlegrounds are Jenkins' Ferry State Park and Marks' Mills State Park (see separate listings).

★1496★ POWHATAN HISTORIC STATE PARK

PO Box 93
Powhatan, AR 72458
Web: www.arkansasstateparks.com/parks/park.asp?id=46
Phone: 870-878-6765
Size: 3.5 acres. **Location:** On AR 25 in Powhatan. **Facilities:**

9. State Parks

Restored 1888 courthouse, other historic buildings, related exhibits. **Special Features:** During the 1800s Powhatan was a busy river port on the Black River. Its Victorian courthouse was built in 1888 from bricks made on site and today serves as a regional archive containing some of the oldest records in Arkansas. Other historic buildings at the site include a jail, a log house, and a two-room schoolhouse called the Powhatan Male and Female Academy. Exhibits interpret the rich history of technology, politics, and lifestyles that shaped northern Arkansas.

★1497★ PRAIRIE GROVE BATTLEFIELD STATE PARK

506 E Douglas St
Prairie Grove, AR 72753
Web: www.arkansasstateparks.com/parks/park.asp?id=30
Phone: 479-846-2990
Size: 194 acres. **Location:** On US 62 in the community of Prairie Grove. **Facilities:** Exhibits, small pavilion. **Activities:** Guided tours or self-guided tours, including a one-mile Battlefield Trail or a five-mile driving tour. **Special Features:** Park protects one of America's most intact Civil War battlefields where, on December 7, 1862, the Confederate army clashed with Union troops. In one day of fierce fighting, casualties on both sides numbered about 2,700. Exhibits, tours, and other programs describe the battle and its local effects. A battle reenactment takes place biennially on even-numbered years the first week-end in December.

★1498★ QUEEN WILHELMINA STATE PARK

3877 Hwy 88 W
Mena, AR 71953
Web: www.arkansasstateparks.com/parks/park.asp?id=11
Phone: 479-394-2863
Size: 460 acres. **Location:** On the Talimena Scenic Drive, 13 miles west of Mena on AR 88. **Facilities:** 35 campsites with electric and water hookups, 6 tent sites, showers, restrooms, 38-room lodge, restaurant, meeting rooms, picnic areas, playground, hiking trails, exhibits (&&). A miniature train, miniature golf course, and a native plant/wildlife center are open seasonally. **Activities:** Camping, hiking, interpretive programs. **Special Features:** The first inn to open here in 1898 was built by the Kansas City, Pittsburg, and Gulf Railroad as a resort retreat for its passengers. Since Dutch interests largely financed the railroad, the inn was named in honor of The Netherlands' reigning monarch at the time, Queen Wilhelmina. (Two inns have since replaced the original one.)

★1499★ SOUTH ARKANSAS ARBORETUM

c/o South Arkansas Community College
PO Box 7010
El Dorado, AR 71731
Web: www.arkansasstateparks.com/parks/park.asp?id=52
Phone: 870-862-8131
Size: 13 acres. **Location:** From AR Hwy 82B in El Dorado, north 1 mile to 501 Timberlane, adjacent to the El Dorado High School. **Facilities:** Walking trails, pavilion, restrooms. **Activities:** Guided tours (by appointment). **Special Features:**

Operated by South Arkansas Community College, the arboretum exhibits plants indigenous to Arkansas's West Gulf Coastal Plain region, as well as exotic species such as flowering azaleas and camellias.

★1500★ TOLTEC MOUNDS ARCHEOLOGICAL STATE PARK

490 Toltec Mounds Rd
Scott, AR 72142
Web: www.arkansasstateparks.com/parks/park.asp?id=24
Phone: 501-961-9442; **Fax:** 501-961-9221
Size: 182 acres. **Location:** From Little Rock, take Exit 7 off I-440 and go 10 miles southeast on US 165, then 1/4 mile south on AR 386. **Facilities:** Interpretive trails; visitor center with exhibits, an AV theater, archeological research laboratory, and meeting room; restrooms and picnic areas (&&). **Activities:** Hiking, guided archeological tours, interpretive programs. **Special Features:** This archeological park preserves and interprets Arkansas' tallest Indian mounds, the remains of a large ceremonial and governmental complex that was inhabited from AD 600 to 1050. The site (a National Historic Landmark) is managed by Arkansas State Parks and the Arkansas Archeological Survey.

★1501★ VILLAGE CREEK STATE PARK

201 County Rd 754
Wynne, AR 72396
Web: www.arkansasstateparks.com/parks/park.asp?id=21
Phone: 870-238-9406; **Fax:** 870-238-9415
Size: 6,909 acres. **Location:** Exit 242 off I-40 at Forrest City, 13 miles north on AR 284. **Facilities:** 96 campsites with electric and water hookups (for RVs, tents, and horse campers), showers, restrooms, 10 cabins, picnic areas, 4 pavilions (2 enclosed), playgrounds, baseball/multi-use fields, driving range, tennis courts, swimming beach, hiking trails, horse trails, boat docks, boat rentals, visitor center with store, gift shop, and bicycle rentals, interpretive center with meeting facility and exhibits (&&). **Activities:** Camping, fishing, swimming, hiking, interpretive programs. **Special Features:** Located in the unique geological region of Crowley's Ridge, the park features lush forests of oak, sugar maple, beech, butternut, and tulip poplar. Its two lakes offer fishing for bass, bream, catfish, and crappie.

★1502★ WHITE OAK LAKE STATE PARK

563 Hwy 387
Bluff City, AR 71722
Web: www.arkansasstateparks.com/parks/park.asp?id=16
Phone: 870-685-2748
Size: 666 acres. **Location:** From I-30 at Prescott, 20 miles east on AR 24, then 2 miles southeast on AR 387. **Facilities:** 41 campsites with electric and water hookups, 4 tent sites, bathhouse, restrooms, picnic areas, pavilion, hiking trails, marina with boat rentals, boat ramp, fishing pier, playground, store, visitor center with exhibits and bicycle rentals (&&). **Activities:** Camping, fishing, boating, hiking, bird watching, interpretive programs. **Special Features:** Park is adjacent to Poison Spring State Forest on the shore of 2,765-acre White Oak Lake. The park has an abundance of wildlife, with regular sightings of

great blue heron, green heron, egret, and osprey, and, in winter, bald eagles.

★1503★ WITHROW SPRINGS STATE PARK
33424 Spur 23
Huntsville, AR 72740
Web: www.arkansasstateparks.com/parks/park.asp?id=15
Phone: 479-559-2593
Size: 774 acres. **Location:** 5 miles north of Huntsville on AR 23; or 20 miles south of Eureka Springs on AR 23. **Facilities:** 47 campsites with electric and water hookups, group camps, showers, restrooms, picnic areas, pavilions, hiking trails, canoe rental, tennis courts, ball fields, crossbow range, swimming pool, snack bar, gift shop, playground. **Activities:** Camping, fishing, swimming, tennis, hiking, baseball and softball, archery. **Special Features:** Park is located in the heart of the Ozark Mountains along War Eagle River and is a peaceful setting for camping and quiet river floats. Canoes/shuttle service are available.

★1504★ WOOLLY HOLLOW STATE PARK
82 Woolly Hollow Rd
Greenbrier, AR 72058
Web: www.arkansasstateparks.com/parks/park.asp?id=35
Phone: 501-679-2098
Size: 399 acres. **Location:** Exit 125 off I-40 at Conway, 12 miles north on US 65, then 6 miles east on AR 285. **Facilities:** 30 campsites (20 with hookups, 10 without), bathhouse with showers, boat rentals, boat launch ramp, snack bar, swim beach, picnic area, pavilion, trail, gift shop (&&). **Activities:** Camping, boating, fishing, swimming, hiking. **Special Features:** Park is a peaceful retreat nestled in the Ozark foothills and includes 40-acre Lake Bennett, a popular spot for fishing, swimming, and floating. Park property includes the 1882 Woolly Cabin, the one-room log home of the area's first settlers.

California State Parks

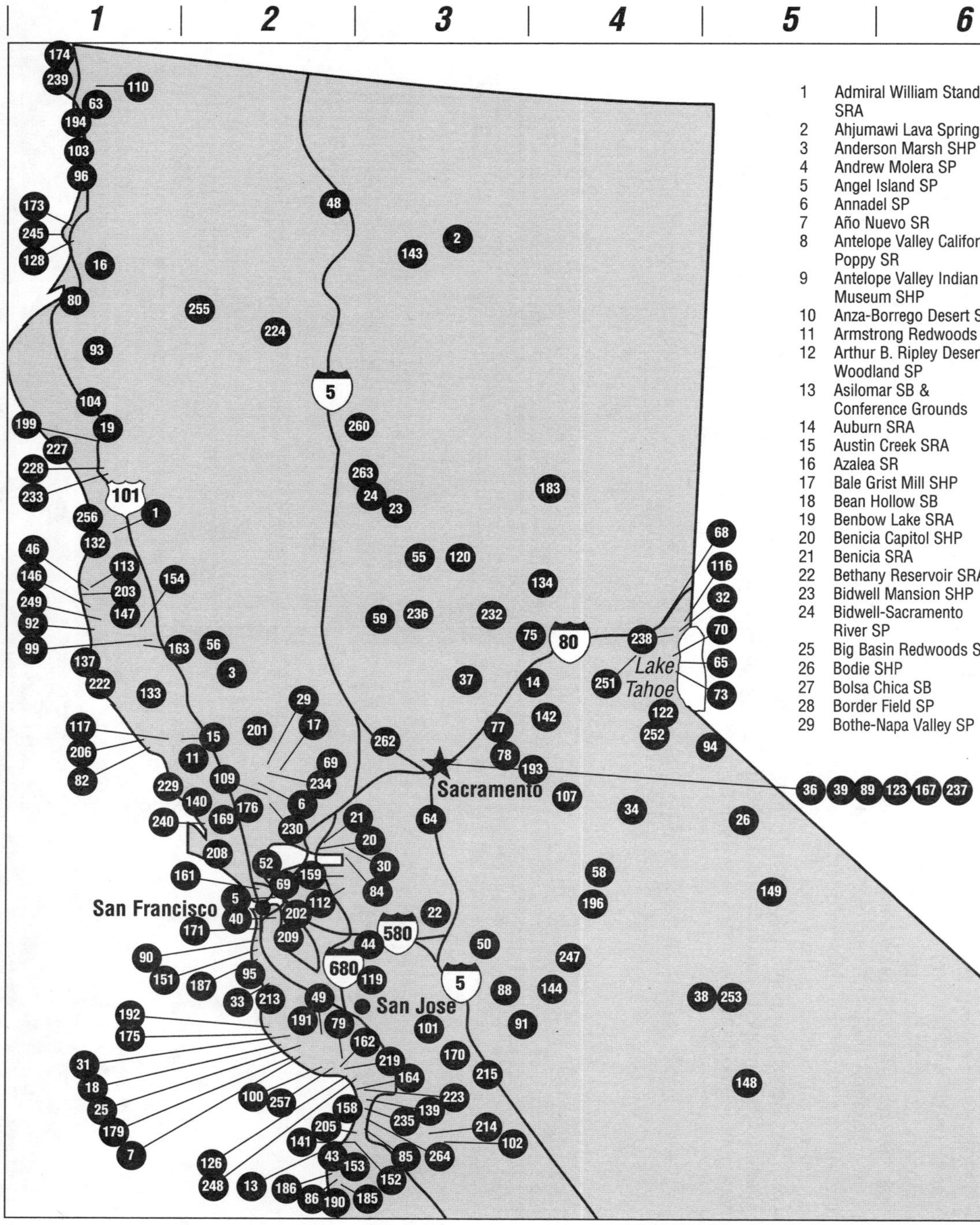

#	Park	Grid
1	Admiral William Standley SRA	C-1
2	Ahjumawi Lava Springs SP	B-3
3	Anderson Marsh SHP	D-2
4	Andrew Molera SP	H-2
5	Angel Island SP	F-2
6	Annadel SP	E-2
7	Año Nuevo SR	G-2
8	Antelope Valley California Poppy SR	I-6
9	Antelope Valley Indian Museum SHP	I-6
10	Anza-Borrego Desert SP	K-8
11	Armstrong Redwoods SR	E-2
12	Arthur B. Ripley Desert Woodland SP	J-6
13	Asilomar SB & Conference Grounds	G-2
14	Auburn SRA	D-4
15	Austin Creek SRA	E-2
16	Azalea SR	B-1
17	Bale Grist Mill SHP	E-2
18	Bean Hollow SB	F-2
19	Benbow Lake SRA	C-1
20	Benicia Capitol SHP	E-2
21	Benicia SRA	E-2
22	Bethany Reservoir SRA	F-3
23	Bidwell Mansion SHP	C-3
24	Bidwell-Sacramento River SP	C-3
25	Big Basin Redwoods SP	F-2
26	Bodie SHP	E-5
27	Bolsa Chica SB	K-6
28	Border Field SP	L-7
29	Bothe-Napa Valley SP	E-2
30	Brannan Island SRA	E-2
31	Burleigh H. Murray Ranch	F-2
32	Burton Creek SP	D-4
33	Butano SP	F-2
34	Calaveras Big Trees SP	E-4
35	California Citrus SHP	K-7
36	California State Capitol Museum	E-3
37	California State Indian Museum	D-3
38	California State Mining & Mineral Museum	F-5
39	California State Railroad Museum	E-3
40	Candlestick Point SRA	F-2
41	Cardiff SB	L-7
42	Carlsbad SB	K-7
43	Carmel River SB	G-2
44	Carnegie SVRA	F-3
45	Carpinteria SB	J-5
46	Caspar Headlands SB & SR	D-1
47	Castaic Lake SRA	J-5
48	Castle Crags SP	A-2
49	Castle Rock SP	F-2
50	Caswell Memorial SP	F-3
51	Cayucos SB	H-3
52	China Camp SP	E-2
53	Chino Hills SP	J-7
54	Chumash Painted Cave SHP	J-4
55	Clay Pit SVRA	D-3
56	Clear Lake SP	D-2
57	Colonel Allensworth SHP	H-5
58	Columbia SHP	E-4
59	Colusa-Sacramento River SRA	D-3
60	Corona del Mar SB	K-6
61	Crystal Cove SP	K-6
62	Cuyamaca Rancho SP	L-8
63	Del Norte Coast Redwoods SP	A-1
64	Delta Meadows	E-3
65	DL Bliss SP	D-4
66	Dockweiler SB	K-6
67	Doheny SB	K-7
68	Donner Memorial SP	D-4
69	Eastshore SP	F-2
70	Edward Z'Berg Sugar Pine Point SP	D-4
71	El Capitan SB	J-4
72	El Presidio de Santa Barbara SHP	J-4
73	Emerald Bay SB	D-4
74	Emma Wood SB	J-5
75	Empire Mine SHP	D-4
76	Estero Bay SB	H-3
77	Folsom Lake SRA	E-3
78	Folsom Powerhouse SHP	E-3
79	Forest of Nisene Marks SP	G-2
80	Fort Humboldt SHP	B-1
81	Fort Ord Dunes SP	G-2
82	Fort Ross SHP	E-1
83	Fort Tejon SHP	I-5
84	Franks Tract SRA	E-2
85	Fremont Peak SP	G-3
86	Garrapata SP	G-2
87	Gaviota SP	J-4
88	George J. Hatfield SRA	F-3
89	Governor's Mansion SHP	E-3
90	Gray Whale Cove SB	F-2
91	Great Valley Grasslands SP	F-3
92	Greenwood SB	D-1
93	Grizzly Creek Redwoods SP	B-1
94	Grover Hot Springs SP	E-5
95	Half Moon Bay SB	F-2
96	Harry A. Merlo SRA	A-1
97	Hearst San Simeon SHM	H-3
98	Heber Dunes SVRA	L-8
99	Hendy Woods SP	D-1
100	Henry Cowell Redwoods SP	G-2
101	Henry W. Coe SP	F-3
102	Hollister Hills SVRA	G-3
103	Humboldt Lagoons SP	A-1
104	Humboldt Redwoods SP	C-1
105	Hungry Valley SVRA	I-5
106	Huntington SB	K-6
107	Indian Grinding Rock SHP	E-4
108	Indio Hills Palms	K-8
109	Jack London SHP	E-2
110	Jedediah Smith Redwoods SP	A-1
111	John Little SR	H-3
112	John Marsh Home	F-2
113	Jug Handle SR	D-1
114	Julia Pfeiffer Burns SP	H-3
115	Kenneth Hahn SRA	J-6
116	Kings Beach SRA	D-4
117	Kruse Rhododendron SR	E-1
118	La Purisima Mission SHP	I-4
119	Lake del Valle SRA	F-3
120	Lake Oroville SRA	D-3
121	Lake Perris SRA	K-7
122	Lake Valley SRA	D-4
123	Leland Stanford Mansion SHP	E-3

Map labels: Lake Tahoe · Sacramento · San Jose · San Francisco

California State Parks

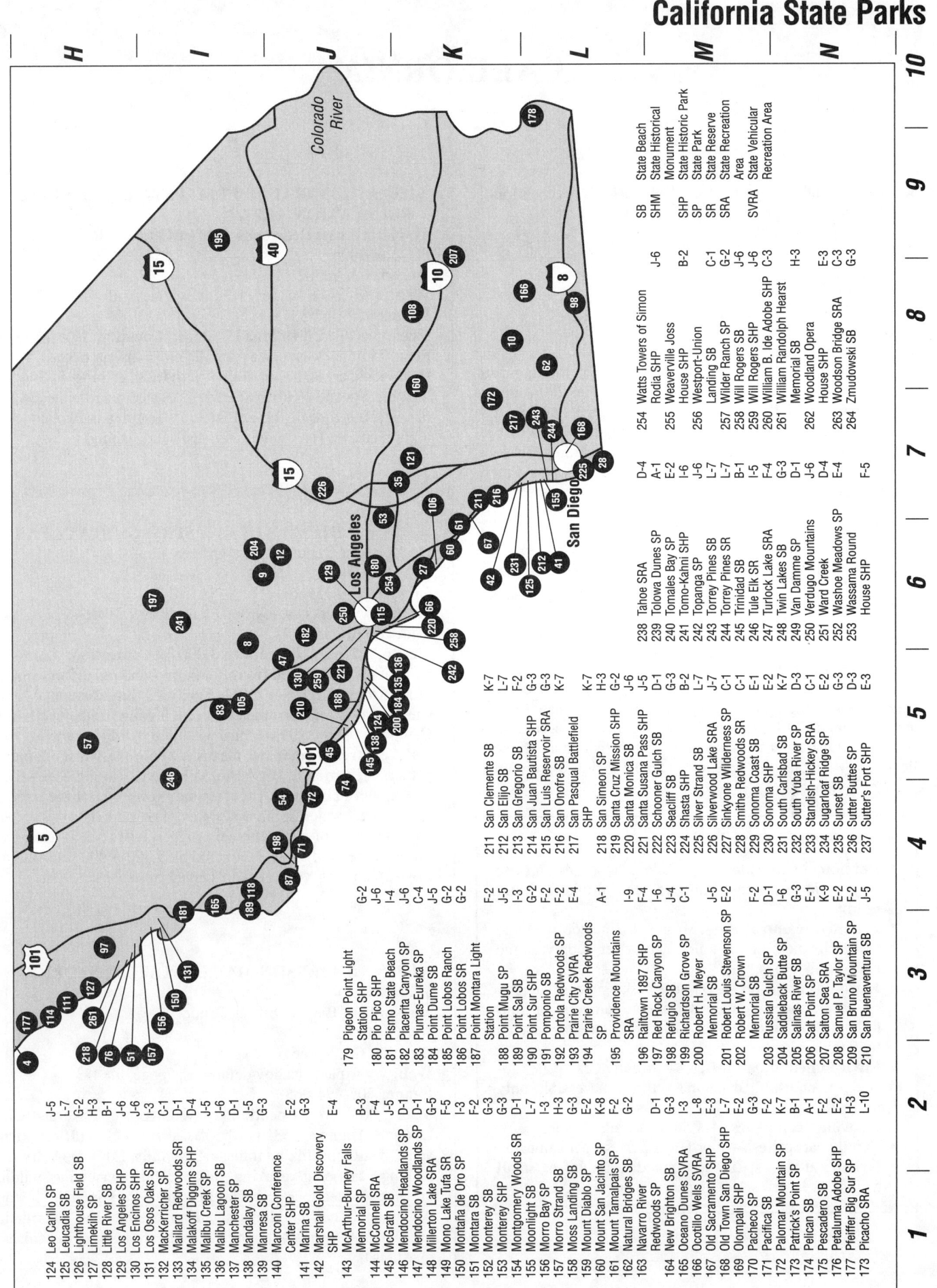

124	Leo Carrillo SP	J-5	
125	Leucadia SB	L-7	
126	Lighthouse Field SB	G-2	
127	Limekiln SP	H-3	
128	Little River SB	B-1	
129	Los Angeles SHP	J-6	
130	Los Encinos SHP	J-6	
131	Los Osos Oaks SR	I-3	
132	MacKerricher SP	C-1	
133	Maillard Redwoods SR	D-1	
134	Malakoff Diggins SHP	D-4	
135	Malibu Creek SP	J-5	
136	Malibu Lagoon SB	J-6	
137	Manchester SP	D-1	
138	Mandalay SB	J-5	
139	Manresa SB	G-3	
140	Marconi Conference Center SHP	E-2	
141	Marina SB	G-3	
142	Marshall Gold Discovery SHP	E-4	
143	McArthur-Burney Falls Memorial SP	B-3	
144	McConnell SRA	F-4	
145	McGrath SB	J-5	
146	Mendocino Headlands SP	D-1	
147	Mendocino Woodlands SP	D-1	
148	Millerton Lake SRA	G-5	
149	Mono Lake Tufa SR	F-5	
150	Montaña de Oro SP	I-3	
151	Montara SB	F-2	
152	Monterey SB	G-3	
153	Monterey SHP	G-3	
154	Montgomery Woods SR	D-1	
155	Moonlight SB	L-7	
156	Morro Bay SP	I-3	
157	Morro Strand SB	H-3	
158	Moss Landing SB	G-3	
159	Mount Diablo SP	E-2	
160	Mount San Jacinto SP	K-8	
161	Mount Tamalpais SP	F-2	
162	Natural Bridges SB	G-2	
163	Navarro River Redwoods SP	D-1	
164	New Brighton SB	G-3	
165	Oceano Dunes SVRA	I-3	
166	Ocotillo Wells SVRA	L-8	
167	Old Sacramento SHP	E-3	
168	Old Town San Diego SHP	L-7	
169	Olompali SHP	E-2	
170	Pacheco SP	G-3	
171	Pacifica SB	F-2	
172	Palomar Mountain SP	K-7	
173	Patrick's Point SP	B-1	
174	Pelican SB	A-1	
175	Pescadero SB	F-2	
176	Petaluma Adobe SHP	E-2	
177	Pfeiffer Big Sur SP	H-3	
173	Picacho SRA	L-10	

179	Pigeon Point Light Station SHP	F-2	
180	Pio Pico SHP	J-5	
181	Pismo State Beach	I-3	
182	Placerita Canyon SP	J-6	
183	Plumas-Eureka SP	C-4	
184	Point Dume SB	J-5	
185	Point Lobos Ranch	G-2	
186	Point Lobos SR	G-2	
187	Point Montara Light Station	F-2	
188	Point Mugu SP	J-5	
189	Point Sal SB	I-3	
190	Point Sur SHP	G-2	
191	Pomponio SB	F-2	
192	Portola Redwoods SP	F-2	
193	Prairie City SVRA	E-4	
194	Prairie Creek Redwoods SP	A-1	
195	Providence Mountains SRA	I-9	
196	Railtown 1897 SHP	F-4	
197	Red Rock Canyon SP	I-6	
198	Refugio SB	J-4	
199	Richardson Grove SP	C-1	
200	Robert H. Meyer Memorial SB	J-5	
201	Robert Louis Stevenson SP	E-2	
202	Robert W. Crown Memorial SB	F-2	
203	Russian Gulch SP	D-1	
204	Saddleback Butte SP	I-6	
205	Salinas River SB	G-3	
206	Salt Point SP	E-1	
207	Salton Sea SRA	K-9	
208	Samuel P. Taylor SP	E-2	
209	San Bruno Mountain SP	F-2	
210	San Buenaventura SB	J-5	

211	San Clemente SB	K-7	
212	San Elijo SB	L-7	
213	San Gregorio SB	F-2	
214	San Juan Bautista SHP	G-3	
215	San Luis Reservoir SRA	G-3	
216	San Onofre SB	K-7	
217	San Pasqual Battlefield SHP		
218	San Simeon SP	K-7	
219	Santa Cruz Mission SHP	H-3	
220	Santa Monica SB	G-2	
221	Santa Susana Pass SHP	J-6	
222	Schooner Gulch SB	D-1	
223	Seacliff SB	G-3	
224	Shasta SHP	B-2	
225	Silver Strand SB	L-7	
226	Silverwood Lake SRA	J-7	
227	Sinkyone Wilderness SP	C-1	
228	Smithe Redwoods SR	C-1	
229	Sonoma Coast SB	E-1	
230	Sonoma SHP	E-2	
231	South Carlsbad SB	K-7	
232	South Yuba River SP	D-3	
233	Standish-Hickey SRA	C-1	
234	Sugarloaf Ridge SP	E-2	
235	Sunset SB	G-3	
236	Sutter Buttes SP	D-3	
237	Sutter's Fort SHP	E-3	

238	Tahoe SRA	D-4	
239	Tolowa Dunes SP	A-1	
240	Tomales Bay SP	E-2	
241	Tomo-Kahni SHP	I-6	
242	Topanga SP	J-6	
243	Torrey Pines SB	L-7	
244	Torrey Pines SR	L-7	
245	Trinidad SB	B-1	
246	Tule Elk SRA	I-5	
247	Turlock Lake SRA	F-4	
248	Twin Lakes SB	G-3	
249	Van Damme SB	D-1	
250	Verdugo Mountains	J-6	
251	Ward Creek	D-4	
252	Washoe Meadows SP	E-4	
253	Wassama Round House SHP	F-5	
254	Watts Towers of Simon Rodia SHP	J-6	
255	Weaverville Joss House SHP	B-2	
256	Westport-Union Landing SB	C-1	
257	Wilder Ranch SP	G-2	
258	Will Rogers SB	J-6	
259	Will Rogers SHP	J-6	
260	William B. Ide Adobe SHP	C-3	
261	William Randolph Hearst Memorial SB	H-3	
262	Woodland Opera House SHP	E-3	
263	Woodson Bridge SRA	C-3	
264	Zmudowski SB	G-3	

SB	State Beach	
SHM	State Historical Monument	
SHP	State Historic Park	
SP	State Park	
SR	State Reserve	
SRA	State Recreation Area	
SVRA	State Vehicular Recreation Area	

CALIFORNIA

★1505★ California Department of Parks & Recreation
PO Box 942896
Sacramento, CA 942896
(916) 653-6995 - Information Line
(916) 654-6374 – Fax
(800) 777-0369 - Reservations
(916) 653-6995 - Employment
(916) 653-9069 - Volunteering
Web: www.parks.ca.gov
System consists of more than 270 state park properties comprising 1.4 million acres, which includes more than 280 miles of coastline and 625 miles of lake and river frontage. Parks include areas for active recreation, ecologically sensitive lands that require protection, and numerous historic sites including missions, battlefields, ethnic settlements, ghost towns, and Native American sites and artifacts.

★1506★ California Department of Fish & Game
1416 9th St
Sacramento, CA 95814
(916) 445-0411 - Phone
(916) 653-1856 - Fax
Web: www.dfg.ca.gov
Manages 108 state wildlife areas totaling more than 683,000 acres and 124 ecological reserves totaling more than 173,000 acres. Maintains 180 public fishing and boating access sites, operates 20 fish hatcheries, and administers fishing and hunting licensing. Promotes the state's Watchable Wildlife program.

Key to campsite classification:

- **Developed campsites** — Include picnic table and fire ring with restrooms, showers, and drinking water nearby.
- **Primitive campsites** — Most sites include a picnic table, chemical or pit toilet, and water supply; some have no facilities.
- **En route campsites** — Day-use parking areas that may be used by self-contained trailers, campers, or motorhomes on an overnight basis. Site must be vacated by 9:00 a.m.
- **Environmental campsites** — Primitive campsites located in undisturbed natural settings, accessible only by foot.
- **Hike/bike campsites** — Primitive trailside sites.
- **Family campsites** — 8 or fewer persons per campsite.
- **Group camps** — Can accommodate groups as small as 9 or as large as 100, depending on location.

★1507★ ADMIRAL WILLIAM STANDLEY STATE RECREATION AREA
c/o North Coast Redwoods District Office
PO Box 2006
Eureka, CA 95502
Web: www.parks.ca.gov/default.asp?page_id=424
Phone: 707-247-3318
Size: 45 acres. **Elevation:** 1,700 feet. **Location:** North of Santa Rosa, 14 miles west of Laytonville on Branscomb Road. **Facilities:** Picnic areas, hiking trails. **Activities:** Fishing, hiking, picnicking. **Special Features:** Park is located near the headwaters of the south fork of the Eel River. It features redwoods and is a popular spot for salmon and steelhead fishing.

★1508★ AHJUMAWI LAVA SPRINGS STATE PARK
c/o Northern Buttes District Office
400 Glen Dr
Oroville, CA 95966
Web: www.parks.ca.gov/default.asp?page_id=464
Phone: 530-335-2777
Size: 6,415 acres. **Elevation:** 3,000 feet. **Location:** Accessible by boat only, launched from Rat Farm Landing, 3.5 miles north of McArthur (Highway 299E). **Facilities:** Environmental campsites, boat-in camps, picnic areas, hiking trails. **Activities:** Camping, fishing, hiking, bird watching, wildlife viewing. **Special Features:** Ahjumawi means ''where the waters come together,'' referring to Big Lake, Tule River, Ja-She Creek, Lava Creek, and Fall River. Together they form one of the nation's largest freshwater springs systems. The park is a wilderness area and most of it is extremely rugged lava rock — over two-thirds of the park's area is covered by 3,000-5,000 year-old lava flows, including vast areas of jagged black basalt.

★1509★ ANDERSON MARSH STATE HISTORIC PARK
c/o Northern Buttes District Office
400 Glen Dr
Oroville, CA 95966
Web: www.parks.ca.gov/default.asp?page_id=483
Phone: 707-994-0688
Size: 1,065 acres. **Location:** Between Lower Lake and Clear Lake on Highway 53, north of Calistoga. **Facilities:** Picnic areas, restrooms, hiking trails, nature trails, exhibits. **Activities:** Fishing, canoeing/kayaking, hiking, bird watching, wildlife viewing, guided tours. **Special Features:** Park includes historic Anderson Ranch buildings and Native American sites dating back 10,000 years. A popular blackberry festival is held here in August.

★1510★ ANDREW MOLERA STATE PARK
c/o Monterey District Office
2211 Garden Rd
Monterey, CA 93940
Web: www.parks.ca.gov/default.asp?page_id=582
Phone: 831-667-2315
Size: 4,766 acres. Location: 20 miles south of Carmel on Highway 1. Facilities: Primitive walk-in trail camp with 24 sites (limit 4 people per site), hiking trails, biking trails, horseback trails, picnic areas, visitor center, exhibits, restrooms. Activities: Camping, fishing, hiking, swimming, surfing, horseback riding, beachcombing. Special Features: Located in the Big Sur area, this park is still relatively undeveloped and offers visitors great hiking, fishing, and beachcombing. The beach is located a mile from the highway at its closest point and is rarely crowded.

★1511★ ANGEL ISLAND STATE PARK
c/o North Bay District Office
PO Box 123
Duncan Mills, CA 95430
Web: www.angelisland.com
Phone: 415-435-1915
Size: 756 acres. Location: Park is located in San Francisco Bay and is accessible only by private boat or public ferry from San Francisco, Tiburon, or Vallejo. Facilities: 9 environmental campsites (campers should be prepared to carry equipment up to two miles), picnic areas, hiking trails, bike trails, boat mooring, visitor center, restrooms, exhibits, food service (&&). Activities: Camping, fishing, hiking, boating, bicycling, interpretive programs, guided tram tours, guided kayak trips around the island. Special Features: The island is rich in history and, among other things, has been a Miwok Indian hunting ground, a Civil War encampment, a World War II POW camp, an Immigration Station, and a Nike Missile Base (1952-1962). Situated in the middle of San Francisco Bay, the park offers spectacular views of the San Francisco skyline, the Marin Headlands, and Mount Tamalpais.

★1512★ ANNADEL STATE PARK
c/o Diablo Vista District Office
845 Casa Grande Rd
Petaluma, CA 94954
Web: www.parks.ca.gov/default.asp?page_id=480
Phone: 707-938-1519
Size: 5,093 acres. Location: East of Santa Rosa and south of Highway 12, at 6201 Channel Drive, via Mission Boulevard and Montgomery Drive. Facilities: Picnic areas, multi-use trails, restrooms. Activities: Fishing, hiking, horseback riding, mountain biking, bird watching, guided tours. Special Features: This park preserves significant native and early California quarry industry sites (cobblestone quarries in this area once supplied paving material for San Francisco) as well as the most outstanding example of northern oak woodland in existence.

★1513★ AÑO NUEVO STATE RESERVE
c/o Santa Cruz District Office
303 Big Trees Park Rd
Felton, CA 95018
Web: www.parks.ca.gov/default.asp?page_id=523
Phone: 650-879-2025
Size: 1,319 acres (reserve); 2,896 acres (undeveloped Año Nuevo State Park). Location: 27 miles south of Half Moon Bay on Highway 1. Facilities: Visitor center, restrooms, exhibits, picnic area, hiking trails, nature trails (&&). Activities: Fishing, hiking, guided tours. Special Features: Reserve is the site of the world's largest mainland breeding colony of northern elephant seals. During the breeding season (mid-December to March), daily access to the reserve is available only via guided walks; reservations are recommended.

★1514★ ANTELOPE VALLEY CALIFORNIA POPPY
  RESERVE
c/o Inland Empire District Office
17801 Lake Perris Dr
Perris, CA 92571
Web: www.parks.ca.gov/default.asp?page_id=627
Phone: 661-724-1180
Size: 1,781 acres. Location: 15 miles west of Lancaster on Avenue I. Facilities: Picnic areas, hiking and nature trails (8 miles), restrooms, visitor center, exhibits (&&). Activities: Hiking, wildflower photography, guided tours, interpretive program (seasonal). Special Features: After winter and spring rains, this high-desert reserve is transformed into fields of golden poppies and other wildflowers. The wildflower season generally lasts from mid-March through mid-May, but the park is open year-round from sunrise to sunset. Visitors should be prepared for very high winds and should be aware of the high numbers of Mojave Green rattlesnakes in this area.

★1515★ ANTELOPE VALLEY INDIAN MUSEUM
  STATE HISTORIC PARK
c/o Inland Empire District Office
17801 Lake Perris Dr
Perris, CA 92571
Web: www.avim.parks.ca.gov
Phone: 661-946-3055
Size: 147 acres. Location: 19 miles east of the Antelope Valley Freeway (State Highway 14), at 15701 East Avenue M in Lancaster. Facilities: Museum, picnic areas, restrooms, visitor center, hiking trail. Special Features: Museum, which houses objects created by the American Indian cultures of the western Great Basin, California, and the Southwest, is closed indefinitely for stabilization. Comprehensive interpretive and research information and a complete catalogue of artifacts are available at www.avim.parks.ca.gov.

★1516★ ANZA-BORREGO DESERT STATE PARK
c/o Colorado Desert District Office
200 Palm Canyon Dr
Borrego Springs, CA 92004
Web: www.anzaborrego.statepark.org
Phone: 760-767-4205; Fax: 760-767-3427
Size: 584,065 acres. Elevation: 15 to 6,193 feet. Location: North of San Diego via I-8 from the south or Highways 78 & 79 from the east and west. Facilities: 3 campgrounds that include developed and full-hookup sites, tent sites, primitive sites, and & sites; group campsites; picnic areas; hiking trails, horseback trails, nature trails; restrooms, visitor center, exhibits (&&).

Activities: Camping, hiking, horseback riding, wildlife viewing, guided tours. **Special Features:** Anza-Borrego Desert State Park is the largest state park in California, with 500 miles of dirt roads, 12 wilderness areas, and miles of hiking trails affording visitors the opportunity to experience the wonders of the Colorado Desert. The park features washes, wildflowers, palm groves, cacti, and sweeping vistas, as well as a wide range of animal life, from roadrunners to mule deer and bighorn sheep to the red diamond rattlesnake.

★1517★ ARMSTRONG REDWOODS STATE RESERVE

c/o North Bay District Office
PO Box 123
Duncan Mills, CA 95430
Web: www.parks.ca.gov/default.asp?page_id=450
Phone: 707-869-2015; **Fax:** 707-869-5629
Size: 752 acres. **Location:** 2 miles north of Guerneville, at 170000 Armstrong Woods Road. **Facilities:** Picnic areas (&), hiking/nature trails (&), horseback trails, restrooms (&), visitor center (&), outdoor amphitheater. **Activities:** Picnicking, hiking, horseback riding, interpretive programs. **Special Features:** Reserve is a redwood grove set aside as a natural park and botanical garden by lumberman Colonel James Armstrong. The ancient coast redwood is the tallest living thing on Earth, and the Reserve's tallest tree measures more than 310 feet high. The oldest tree in the grove is estimated to be more than 1,400 years old.

★1518★ ARTHUR B. RIPLEY DESERT WOODLAND STATE PARK

c/o Inland Empire District Office
17801 Lake Perris Dr
Perris, CA 92571
Web: www.parks.ca.gov/default.asp?page_id=634
Phone: 661-942-0662
Size: 567 acres. **Location:** On Lancaster Road, 5 miles west of the Antelope Valley California Poppy Reserve and 1 mile south of State Highway 138 via 210th Street West. **Facilities:** Undeveloped; picnic table and self-guided nature trail. **Activities:** Hiking, picnicking. **Special Features:** Reserve protects and preserves an impressive stand of native Joshua trees and junipers which once grew in great abundance throughout the valley. Today, only remnant parcels of this woodland community remain in the valley; most of it was cleared for farming and housing.

★1519★ ASILOMAR STATE BEACH & CONFERENCE GROUNDS

c/o Monterey District Office
2211 Garden Rd
Monterey, CA 93940
Web: www.parks.ca.gov/default.asp?page_id=566
Phone: 831-646-6440
Size: 107 acres. **Location:** Adjacent to Sunset Drive in Pacific Grove. **Facilities:** Beach, conference center (including meeting halls, 314 guest rooms, and dining facilities), hiking trails, nature trails (&&). **Activities:** Fishing, hiking, wildlife viewing. **Special Features:** Asilomar Beach is a narrow one-mile strip of

sandy beach and rocky coves with no restrooms or picnic areas. A boardwalk across the dunes gives access to the conference grounds, which are located in a beautiful setting of dunes and pines in Monterey Bay. The original buildings, established in 1913, were designed by noted San Francisco architect Julia Morgan.

★1520★ AUBURN STATE RECREATION AREA

c/o Gold Fields District Office
7806 Folsom-Auburn Rd
Folsom, CA 95630
Web: www.parks.ca.gov/default.asp?page_id=502
Phone: 530-885-4527
Size: 42,000 acres. **Location:** South of I-80, between Auburn and Colfax. Main access is south of Auburn, via Highway 49 or Auburn-Foresthill Road. **Facilities:** Boat-in and primitive campsites, picnic areas, multi-use trails, boat mooring, boat ramps; no drinking water available. **Activities:** Camping, fishing, hiking, swimming, boating, whitewater rafting, horseback riding, mountain biking, off-highway vehicle (OHV) riding, gold panning. **Special Features:** Area includes more than 40 miles of the North and Middle Forks of the American river. Whitewater rafting is popular on both forks of the river, with Class II, III, and IV runs. More than 30 private outfitters are licensed to offer whitewater trips in Auburn SRA.

★1521★ AUSTIN CREEK STATE RECREATION AREA

c/o North Bay District Office
PO Box 123
Duncan Mills, CA 95430
Web: www.parks.ca.gov/default.asp?page_id=452
Phone: 707-865-2391
Size: 5,927 acres. **Elevation:** 150 to 1,500 feet. **Location:** 2 miles north of Guerneville on Armstrong Woods Road. Access is via a steep and narrow winding mountain road; vehicles more than 20 feet long and all towed vehicles are prohibited. **Facilities:** 24 family campsites with flush toilets and potable water (no showers), primitive back country campsites, picnic areas, multi-use trails (22 miles). **Activities:** Camping, hiking, horseback riding. **Special Features:** The Austin Creek SRA is adjacent to Armstrong Redwoods State Reserve and is accessed through the same entrance, but the recreation area's topography is a strong contrast to the primeval redwood forest. Here the deep ravines, grassy hillsides, and rocky mountaintops provide an excellent resource for hikers and equestrians, with miles of trails and panoramic wilderness views.

★1522★ AZALEA STATE RESERVE

c/o North Coast Redwoods District Office
PO Box 2006
Eureka, CA 95502
Web: www.parks.ca.gov/default.asp?page_id=420
Phone: 707-677-3132
Size: 30 acres. **Location:** 5 miles north of Arcata via US 101 and North Bank Road (Highway 200). **Facilities:** Picnic area, hiking/nature trail (1 mile). **Activities:** Picnicking, hiking. **Special Features:** Reserve protects an area where western azaleas

9. State Parks

grow. At peak blooming season in April and May, the flowers provide a stunning display.

★1523★ BALE GRIST MILL STATE HISTORIC PARK

c/o Diablo Vista District Office
845 Casa Grande Rd
Petaluma, CA 94954
Web: www.parks.ca.gov/default.asp?page_id=482
Phone: 707-942-4575
Size: 0.75 acre. **Location:** 3 miles north of Saint Helena on Highway 29. **Facilities:** Visitor center, exhibits, picnic area, trails. **Special Features:** Site of a partially-restored water-powered grist mill with a 36-foot water wheel. Built in 1846, the mill remained in use until the early 1900s, and was a center of social activity for Napa Valley settlers. A 2-mile trail connects this park to Bothe-Napa Valley State Park (see separate entry).

★1524★ BEAN HOLLOW STATE BEACH

c/o Santa Cruz District Office
303 Big Trees Park Rd
Felton, CA 95018
Web: www.parks.ca.gov/default.asp?page_id=527
Phone: 650-879-2170
Size: 44 acres. **Location:** On the San Mateo coast, 17.5 miles south of Half Moon Bay and 3 miles south of Pescadero on Highway 1. **Facilities:** Picnic areas, hiking trail, self-guiding nature trail, restrooms. **Activities:** Fishing, picnicking, beachcombing. **Special Features:** The beach includes numerous tide pools with anemones, crab, sea urchins, and other marine life. Swimming is dangerous because of cold water, rip currents, and heavy surf.

★1525★ BENBOW LAKE STATE RECREATION AREA

c/o North Coast Redwoods District Office
PO Box 2006
Eureka, CA 95502
Web: www.parks.ca.gov/default.asp?page_id=426
Phone: 707-923-3238
Size: 1,142 acres. **Elevation:** 400 feet. **Location:** 2 miles south of Garberville at 1600 US 101. **Facilities:** Developed family campsites (&), en route campsites, hike/bike campsites, restrooms, showers, RV hookups, picnic areas (&), hiking trails, boat launch, boat rentals. **Activities:** Camping, fishing, hiking, swimming, canoeing, cultural programs, guided tours. **Special Features:** Benbow Lake was created by construction of a dam across the south fork of the Eel River in 1928 and is located near the historic Benbow Inn.

★1526★ BENICIA CAPITOL STATE HISTORIC PARK

c/o Diablo Vista District Office
845 Casa Grande Rd
Petaluma, CA 94954
Web: www.parks.ca.gov/default.asp?page_id=475
Phone: 707-745-3385
Size: 0.86 acre. **Location:** In Benicia at 115 West G Street. **Facilities:** Visitor center, exhibits. **Activities:** Guided tours. **Special Features:** Benicia Capitol was the third seat of California's state government (1853-1854) and is the only pre-Sacramento capitol that survives. The original building has been restored with reconstructed period furnishings and exhibits.

★1527★ BENICIA STATE RECREATION AREA

c/o Diablo Vista District Office
845 Casa Grande Rd
Petaluma, CA 94954
Web: www.parks.ca.gov/default.asp?page_id=476
Phone: 707-648-1911
Size: 447 acres. **Location:** 1.5 miles west of Benicia on I-780. **Facilities:** En route campsites (motorhomes or trailers only; no tents), picnic areas, multi-use trails (2.5 miles). **Activities:** Fishing, hiking, bicycling, picnicking, wildlife viewing. **Special Features:** The area consists of marshland, grassy hillsides, and rocky beaches along the narrowest section of Carquinez Strait.

★1528★ BETHANY RESERVOIR STATE RECREATION AREA

c/o Central Valley District Office
22708 Broadway St
Columbia, CA 95310
Web: www.parks.ca.gov/default.asp?page_id=562
Phone: 209-874-2056
Size: 609 acres. **Location:** Northeast of Livermore, 7 miles off I-580 at the Grant Line Road exit. **Facilities:** Picnic areas (&), boat mooring, boat ramps, fishing platforms (&), bike trail, restrooms (&). **Activities:** Fishing, boating, windsurfing, bicycling. **Special Features:** Recreation area is located at the northern end of the San Joaquin Valley at the terminus of the California Aqueduct and includes the northernmost trailhead for the California Aqueduct Bikeway. It also features many windmills.

★1529★ BIDWELL MANSION STATE HISTORIC PARK

c/o Northern Buttes District Office
400 Glen Dr
Oroville, CA 95966
Web: www.parks.ca.gov/default.asp?page_id=460
Phone: 530-895-6144
Size: 5 acres. **Location:** At 525 The Esplanade in Chico, next to the campus of California State University. **Facilities:** Visitor center, restrooms, exhibits (&), picnic area. **Activities:** Guided tours. **Special Features:** John Bidwell was an agriculturalist, social activist, and politician. He built his 3-story brick home in the 1860s in the overall style of an Italian villa. The mansion contains 26 rooms and measures 10,000 square feet.

★1530★ BIDWELL-SACRAMENTO RIVER STATE PARK

c/o Northern Buttes District Office
400 Glen Dr
Oroville, CA 95966
Web: www.parks.ca.gov/default.asp?page_id=463
Phone: 530-342-5185

Size: 329 acres. **Location:** 5 miles west of Chico on River Road (off W. Sacramento Avenue). **Facilities:** Family campsites, day use areas (&), picnic areas, restrooms, hiking/nature trails. **Activities:** Fishing, river rafting, canoeing, kayaking, tubing, swimming, hiking. **Special Features:** Park includes 4 miles of riverfront and preserves a fine example of the riverine habitat, featuring a riparian community once common along the river—tall oaks and cottonwoods with a thick undergrowth of elderberry, wild grape, blackberry, and wild rose. The most popular activity at the park is bank or boat fishing for salmon, steelhead, and shad, but it is also popular for "cruising down the river" on inner tubes, canoes, or kayaks.

★1531★ BIG BASIN REDWOODS STATE PARK

21600 Big Basin Way
Boulder Creek, CA 95006
Web: www.parks.ca.gov/default.asp?page_id=540
Phone: 831-338-8860
Size: 18,033 acres. **Elevation:** Sea level to 2,000 feet. **Location:** 25 miles northwest of Santa Cruz via Highway 9 and Highway 236. **Facilities:** 147 developed family campsites, 5 trail camps, 35 tent cabins, restrooms, showers, picnic areas, trails (80+ miles), visitor center, exhibits, food service, lodging, supplies (&&). **Activities:** Camping, hiking, horseback riding, mountain biking, swimming, wildlife viewing, guided tours. **Special Features:** California's oldest state park, Big Basin Redwoods was established in 1902 and in 1928 became the first unit of the newly formed California State Park System. (Actually, Yosemite, through 1864 federal legislation became California's and the nation's first state park, but it was later transferred to federal jurisdiction.) Park is home to the largest contiguous stand of ancient coast redwoods south of San Francisco and features more than 80 miles of trails, including some that link Big Basin to Castle Rock State Park (see separate entry) and the eastern reaches of the Santa Cruz Mountains.

★1532★ BODIE STATE HISTORIC PARK

PO Box 515
Bridgeport, CA 93517
Web: www.parks.ca.gov/default.asp?page_id=509
Phone: 760-647-6445
Size: 1,064 acres. **Elevation:** 8,375 feet. **Location:** Northeast of Yosemite, 13 miles east of Highway 395 on Bodie Road. **Facilities:** Visitor center, exhibits, picnic areas, restrooms. **Activities:** Self-guided tours. **Special Features:** Park preserves a genuine California gold-mining ghost town. When the Standard Company struck pay dirt in 1877, a gold rush transformed Bodie from a tiny hamlet into a boomtown of 10,000 people. A small part of the town survives, preserved in a state of "arrested decay." Bodie is open all year; however, because of the high elevation, it is accessible only by over-snow equipment during the winter months. The park's visitor center/museum is open only during the summer months, from Memorial Day to Labor Day.

★1533★ BOLSA CHICA STATE BEACH

c/o Orange Coast District Office
3030 Avenida del Presidente
San Clemente, CA 92672
Web: www.parks.ca.gov/default.asp?page_id=642
Phone: 714-846-3460
Size: 169 acres. **Location:** On Pacific Coast Highway, in Huntington Beach between Golden West Street and Warner Avenue. **Facilities:** Campsites with hookups (self-contained vehicles only), beach, picnic areas, multi-use trails, restrooms, food service (&&). **Activities:** Camping, fishing, swimming, surfing, bicycling, skating, wildlife viewing, birdwatching. **Special Features:** The beach extends for 3 miles from Seal Beach to the Huntington Beach city pier. Popular for surf fishing for perch, corbina, croaker, cabezon, and sand shark, the beach is also popular in the summer for bare-handed fishing for California grunion, a species of fish that spawns only on sandy southern California beaches. Bolsa Chica State Beach is connected to Huntington State Beach (see separate entry) by a 7-mile bike trail.

★1534★ BORDER FIELD STATE PARK

c/o San Diego Coast District Office
4477 Pacific Hwy
San Diego, CA 92110
Web: www.parks.ca.gov/default.asp?page_id=664
Phone: 619-575-3613
Size: 1,310 acres. **Location:** 15 miles south of San Diego via I-5, Dairy Mart Road, and Monument Road. **Facilities:** Picnic areas, trails (&), restrooms (&), visitor center (3 miles north in Imperial Beach), exhibits (&). **Activities:** Surf fishing, swimming, hiking, horseback riding, wildlife viewing, birding. **Special Features:** Located in the extreme southwest corner of the continental United States, park includes an obelisk set into the border fence that marks the international boundary established with Mexico by the Treaty of Guadalupe Hidalgo in 1848. The park contains much of the Tijuana River National Estuarine Reserve, an important wildlife habitat. The salt and freshwater marshes provide refuge for several species of migrating waterfowl and resident wading birds, including the black-necked stilt, avocet, teal, American widgeon, and pelican.

★1535★ BOTHE-NAPA VALLEY STATE PARK

c/o Diablo Vista District Office
845 Casa Grande Rd
Petalulma, CA 94954
Web: www.parks.ca.gov/default.asp?page_id=477
Phone: 707-942-4575
Size: 1,991 acres. **Elevation:** 300 to 2,000 feet. **Location:** 5 miles north of Saint Helena and 4 miles south of Calistoga on Highway 29/128. **Facilities:** Developed family campsites, developed group camp, hike/bike campsites, picnic areas, trails, swimming pool (open summer only), horseback riding concession (summer and fall), visitor center, exhibits (&&). **Activities:** Camping, hiking, bicycling, swimming, horseback riding, picnicking, wildlife viewing, interpretive programs. **Special Features:** Park is located in the heart of Napa Valley wine country, with trails that go through stands of coastal redwoods as well as forests of Douglas-fir, tanoak, and madrone. The area was

home to the Wappo Indians until the 1840s, and a Native American Garden near the visitor center displays some of the plants that were important to the people of this area. A Pioneer Cemetery is located near the day use/picnic area.

★1536★ BRANNAN ISLAND STATE RECREATION AREA

c/o Gold Fields District Office
7806 Folsom-Auburn Rd
Folsom, CA 95630
Web: www.parks.ca.gov/default.asp?page_id=487
Phone: 916-777-7701
Size: 329 acres. Location: 3 miles south of Rio Vista on Highway 160. Facilities: 140+ campsites (including family campsites, group campsites, hike/bike campsites), boat-in camps, lodging, restrooms, showers, picnic areas, beach, boat mooring (32 slips), boat launch, visitor center (open weekends). Activities: Camping, hiking, fishing, swimming, boating, windsurfing, wildlife viewing, guided tours. Special Features: Park is located northeast of San Francisco Bay in the the Sacramento-San Joaquin Delta, a web of waterways, islands, and marshes that offer prime wildlife habitat and outstanding fishing.

★1537★ BURLEIGH H. MURRAY RANCH

c/o Santa Cruz District Office
303 Big Trees Park Rd
Felton, CA 95018
Web: www.parks.ca.gov/default.asp?page_id=535
Phone: 650-726-8819
Size: 1,325 acres. Location: On the San Mateo coast, near Half Moon Bay; 1 mile south of the intersection of Highways 1 and 92. Facilities: Picnic areas, hiking trails, biking trails, horseback trails. There is no drinking water available in the park. Activities: Hiking, bicycling, horseback riding, picnicking. Special Features: Historic ranch is located in a pristine valley south of Half Moon Bay. Mills Barn, built in the late 1800s, is a good representation of an English Lake County Bank Barn and is the only building of this type in California. The foundation of the barn and other buildings, including an unreinforced arched stone bridge, was constructed using masonry techniques dating back to Roman times.

★1538★ BURTON CREEK STATE PARK

c/o Sierra District Office
PO Box 266
Tahoma, CA 96142
Web: www.parks.ca.gov/default.asp?page_id=512
Phone: 530-583-5475
Size: 1,890 acres. Location: On the northeast side of Tahoe City. Facilities: Trails. Activities: Hiking, mountain biking, cross-country skiing. Special Features: Park consists of nearly 2,000 acres of undeveloped forest, meadows, and streams between Lake Tahoe and Tahoe National Forest, with 6 miles of unpaved roadway for hiking and cross-country skiing.

★1539★ BUTANO STATE PARK

c/o Santa Cruz District Office
303 Big Trees Park Rd
Felton, CA 95018
Web: www.parks.ca.gov/default.asp?page_id=536
Phone: 650-879-2040
Size: 4,628 acres. Elevation: 500 feet. Location: On the San Mateo coast, off Highway 1, 3 miles northeast of the Gazos Creek Coastal Access Point by way of Gazos Creek Road, and about 4.5 miles southeast of Pescadero by way of the Pescadero and Cloverdale Roads. Facilities: 39 family campsites (21 developed, 18 walk-in sites), environmental campsites, hike/bike campsites, picnic areas, hiking trails, restrooms, visitor center (&), exhibits. Activities: Camping, picnicking, hiking, bicycling, interpretive programs (seasonal). Special Features: Park is located in a redwood-filled canyon in the Santa Cruz Mountains, just three miles from the ocean. Trails meander through coastal scrub and redwood forests, and the higher mountains afford coastal views.

★1540★ CALAVERAS BIG TREES STATE PARK

c/o Central Valley District Office
22708 Broadway St
Columbia, CA 95310
Web: www.parks.ca.gov/default.asp?page_id=551
Phone: 209-795-2334
Size: 6,498 acres. Elevation: 4,700 feet. Location: Northeast of Stockton, 4 miles northeast of Arnold on Highway 4. Facilities: 129 developed family campsites, group camp, showers, restrooms, picnic areas, hiking trails, nature trails, visitor center, exhibits (&&). Activities: Camping, fishing, swimming, hiking, mountain biking, cross-country skiing, interpretive programs. Special Features: Located on the western slope of the Sierra Nevada, the park features two large groves of some of the oldest living redwoods in California. The North Grove includes the "Discovery Tree," the first Sierra redwood noted by Augustus T. Dowd in 1852.

★1541★ CALIFORNIA CITRUS STATE HISTORIC PARK

c/o Inland Empire District Office
17801 Lake Perris Dr
Perris, CA 92571
Web: www.parks.ca.gov/default.asp?page_id=649
Phone: 951-780-6222
Size: 248 acres. Location: In Riverside, 1 mile east of Highway 91, at 9400 Dufferin Avenue. Facilities: Picnic areas (&), visitor center (&), amphitheater, demonstration groves, hiking trails, restrooms (&). Activities: Guided tours. Special Features: This unique historic park recaptures the time when citrus was "King" in California and interprets the importance of the citrus industry in southern California. The land contained within the park still continues to produce high-quality fruits.

9. State Parks

★1542★ CALIFORNIA STATE CAPITOL MUSEUM

c/o Capital District Office
101 J St
Sacramento, CA 95814
Web: www.parks.ca.gov/parkindex/results.asp?ckAlpha3= on&searchtype=14
Phone: 916-324-0333
Location: Downtown Sacramento at 10th and L streets. **Facilities:** Historic building, visitor center, exhibits, restrooms, nature trail, gardens, food service (&&). **Activities:** Guided tours. **Special Features:** Home of the California legislature since 1869, the capitol building underwent a major renovation that restored much of its original appearance. The surrounding Capitol Park includes 40 acres of gardens, featuring trees from around the world and memorials to significant events involving California.

★1543★ CALIFORNIA STATE INDIAN MUSEUM

c/o Capital District Office
101 J St
Sacramento, CA 95814
Web: www.parks.ca.gov/default.asp?page_id=486
Phone: 916-324-0971; **Fax:** 916-322-5231
Location: At 2618 K St in downtown Sacramento, adjacent to Sutter's Fort State Historic Park. **Facilities:** Museum, visitor center, exhibits, restrooms (&&). **Activities:** Self-guided tours; guided tours for groups by reservation. **Special Features:** Museum reflects the rich heritage and ongoing traditions of California's many Native American groups, which numbered in the hundreds before the arrival of European settlers. The museum contains a fine collection of native artifacts, including basketry, beadwork, and clothing. Several Native American structures have been built in an outdoor demonstration area, and visitors can try using Native American tools in a hands-on area of the museum.

★1544★ CALIFORNIA STATE MINING & MINERAL MUSEUM

c/o Central Valley District Office
22708 Broadway St
Columbia, CA 95310
Web: www.parks.ca.gov/default.asp?page_id=588
Phone: 209-742-7625
Location: Mariposa fairgrounds, 1.8 miles south of Mariposa on historic Highway 49. **Facilities:** Museum, exhibits, gift shop, restrooms (&&). **Special Features:** Museum houses California's official mineral collection, established in 1880 to educate the public about the significance of the state's mineral resources. The collection includes nearly 20,000 specimens, including many rarities discovered during the mid- to late 1800s. Displays include the Fricot Nugget, the largest crystalline gold specimen discovered during the Gold Rush era.

★1545★ CALIFORNIA STATE RAILROAD MUSEUM

c/o Capital District Office
101 J St
Sacramento, CA 95814
Web: www.csrmf.org
Phone: 916-445-7387; **Fax:** 916-327-5655

Location: In Old Sacramento at 125 'I' Street. **Facilities:** Museum, exhibits, restrooms, food service. **Activities:** Guided tours, excursion train rides (seasonal). **Special Features:** Museum interprets the role of the "iron horse" in connecting California to the rest of the nation. Housed in one large building are more than 21 fully-restored historic locomotives and cars. A full-scale diorama depicts the building of a section of the transcontinental railroad in the 1860s. A block from the museum is a reconstructed passenger station and freight depot circa 1867. During the summer, a steam train takes visitors from the depot to Miller Park and back along the Sacramento River.

★1546★ CANDLESTICK POINT STATE RECREATION AREA

c/o Diablo Vista District Office
845 Casa Grande Rd
Petaluma, CA 94954
Web: www.parks.ca.gov/default.asp?page_id=519
Phone: 415-671-0145
Size: 205 acres. **Location:** In San Francisco, off the 3Com Park exit from US 101. **Facilities:** Picnic areas (&), restrooms, hiking trail (&), bike trail, fitness course (for seniors), 2 fishing piers, community gardens area. **Activities:** Fishing, bicycling, hiking, skating, windsurfing, cultural programs, special events. **Special Features:** Candlestick Point received its name from the days when early settlers burned wooden ships off the point here. As the flaming masted vessels sank, the last part going down into the water resembled a candlestick. Park includes "Windharp Hill," where unique wind and metal musical instruments fill the air with music on breezy days.

★1547★ CARDIFF STATE BEACH

c/o San Diego Coast District Office
4477 Pacific Hwy
San Diego, CA 92110
Web: www.parks.ca.gov/default.asp?page_id=656
Phone: 760-753-5091
Size: 507 acres. **Location:** 1 mile south of Cardiff on Old Highway 101, across from San Elijo Lagoon. **Facilities:** Lifeguard stations, restrooms (&). **Activities:** Fishing, swimming, surfing, beachcombing. **Special Features:** This gently sloping beach with warm water has some of the most popular surfing locations in the state.

★1548★ CARLSBAD STATE BEACH

c/o San Diego Coast District Office
4477 Pacific Hwy
San Diego, CA 92110
Web: www.parks.ca.gov/default.asp?page_id=653
Phone: 760-438-3143
Size: 28 acres. **Location:** On Carlsbad Boulevard, Highway S21 at Tamarack in Carlsbad **Facilities:** Picnic areas (&) **Activities:** Fishing, swimming, surfing, scuba diving, beachcombing. **Special Features:** Beach is located at the foot of coastal bluffs.

★1549★ CARMEL RIVER STATE BEACH
c/o Monterey District Office
2211 Garden Rd
Monterey, CA 93940
Web: www.parks.ca.gov/default.asp?page_id=567
Phone: 831-624-4909
Size: 297 acres. Location: From Highway 1 in Carmel via Ocean Avenue and Scenic Road. Facilities: Trails. Activities: Fishing, hiking, birdwatching. Special Features: Near the mouth of the Carmel River, a lagoon provides sanctuary for a wide variety of waterfowl and song birds. Ocean swimming and even wading are considered extremely dangerous here.

★1550★ CARNEGIE STATE VEHICULAR RECREATION AREA
c/o Twin Cities District Office
13300 White Rock Rd
Rancho Cordova, CA 95742
Web: www.parks.ca.gov/default.asp?page_id=410
Phone: 925-447-9027
Size: 5,075 acres. Location: On Tesla-Corral Hollow Road between Tracy and Livermore. Facilities: Campground, picnic area, restrooms, visitor center. Activities: Primitive camping, OHV riding. Special Features: Characterized by dry rocky washes, rolling hills, and steep rugged canyons, the park provides a setting for off-highway vehicle (OHV) users of all skill levels. Carnegie offers two motocross tracks, an ATV/MC track, a 90cc track for younger riders, and a 4X4 obstacle course.

★1551★ CARPINTERIA STATE BEACH
c/o Channel Coast District Office
911 San Pedro St
Ventura, CA 93001
Web: www.parks.ca.gov/default.asp?page_id=599
Phone: 805-684-2811
Size: 62 acres. Location: 12 miles south of Santa Barbara off US 101. Facilities: Family campsites (tent camping; RV camping with hookups), hike/bike campsites, en route campsites, group camp, restrooms, showers, picnic areas, visitor center, exhibits (&&). Activities: Camping, fishing, swimming, wildlife viewing, interpretive programs. Special Features: Seals and sea lions, as well as an occasional gray whale, can be seen in this area December through May, and tidepools contain starfish, sea anemones, crabs, snails, octopi, and sea urchins. The Spanish named the area "Carpinteria" because the Chumash tribe had a large, oceangoing canoe-building enterprise or "carpentry shop" located here. The Chumash chose the spot because of the naturally-occurring surface tar they used to seal their boats.

★1552★ CASPAR HEADLANDS STATE BEACH & STATE RESERVE
c/o Mendocino District Office
PO Box 440
Mendocino, CA 95460
Web: www.parks.ca.gov/parkindex
Phone: 707-937-5804
Size: 75 acres (beach); 2.7 acres (reserve). Location: Reserve is 4 miles north of Mendocino on the Pacific Coast; Beach is 2 miles north of Russian Gulch on the coast access road (Point Cabrillo Drive). Facilities: Beach. Activities: Fishing, whale watching. Special Features: Beach consists of miles of undeveloped beach adjacent to the headlands, which offer a panoramic ocean view. It's a good place to watch for migrating gray whales. The reserve contains a small strip of rugged coastline featuring sculpted rocks, wildflowers, and surf. A permit is needed to enter the reserve.

★1553★ CASTAIC LAKE STATE RECREATION AREA
c/o Angeles District Office
1925 Las Virgenes
Calabasas, CA 91302
Web: www.parks.ca.gov/default.asp?page_id=628
Phone: 213-798-2961
Size: 4,224 acres. Location: 41 miles northeast of downtown Los Angeles; from I-5, exit at Hughes Lake Road. Facilities: Campsites (including group camping), picnic areas, trails, 3 boat ramps, boat rentals, bait and tackle shop, fishing pier (&), playgrounds, restrooms. Activities: Camping, boating, jet skiing, water skiing, kayaking, fishing, swimming, hiking, mountain biking. Special Features: Castaic Lake is a reservoir of the State Water Project. It includes 29 miles of shoreline and two bodies of water. The lower lake is used for non-powered boating and swimming. The larger upper lake is suitable for fishing, power boating, sailing, and water- and jet skiing.

★1554★ CASTLE CRAGS STATE PARK
c/o Northern Buttes District Office
400 Glen Dr
Oroville, CA 95966
Web: www.parks.ca.gov/default.asp?page_id=454
Phone: 530-235-2684
Size: 3,905 acres. Location: 6 miles south of Dunsmuir on I-5. Facilities: 76 developed campsites, 6 environmental campsites, restrooms, showers, picnic areas, hiking trails (28 miles), visitor center, exhibits. Activities: Camping, fishing, hiking, swimming, horseback riding. Special Features: Park is named for the 6,000 feet tall granite spires (glacier-polished crags) that tower above the Sacramento River. Park also offers a view of Mount Shasta to the northeast. A section of the 2,650-mile Pacific Crest National Scenic Trail passes through the park (see separate entry in the national trails section), and a 2.7 mile access trail leads to Castle Crags Wilderness, which is part of the Shasta-Trinity National Forest.

★1555★ CASTLE ROCK STATE PARK
c/o Santa Cruz District Office
303 Big Trees Park Rd
Felton, CA 95018
Web: www.parks.ca.gov/default.asp?page_id=538
Phone: 408-867-2952
Size: 5,242 acres. Elevation: 3,215 feet. Location: 2.5 miles south of junction of Highways 9 & 35 on Skyline Road. Facilities: 23 primitive backpacking campsites, picnic areas, trails (32 miles). Activities: Camping, hiking, horseback riding, rock climbing. Special Features: Situated along the crest of the Santa

9. State Parks

Cruz Mountains, the park retains a wild and natural atmosphere of steep canyons with interesting rock formations and a dense, mossy forest of coast redwood, Douglas fir, and madrone. The park's trails are part of a more extensive system that links the Santa Clara and San Lorenzo valleys with Castle Rock State Park, Big Basin Redwoods State Park (see separate entry), and the Pacific Coast.

★1556★ CASWELL MEMORIAL STATE PARK
c/o Central Valley District Office
22708 Broadway St
Columbia, CA 95310
Web: www.parks.ca.gov/default.asp?page_id=557
Phone: 209-599-3810
Size: 258 acres. Location: Along the Stanislaus River, near the town of Ripon, south on Austin Road off Highway 99. Facilities: Family and group campsites, picnic areas (&), hiking and nature trails, beaches and swimming areas, restrooms (&), exhibits. Activities: Camping, fishing, hiking, swimming, wildlife viewing, bird watching, interpretive programs (seasonal). Special Features: Park protects a fine example of the oak riparian woodlands that once flourished throughout the Central California Valley. It is home to several endangered animal species, including the riparian brush rabbit, which is not known to occur anywhere else, and bird watching is a popular activity there.

★1557★ CAYUCOS STATE BEACH
c/o San Luis Obispo Coast District Office
750 Hearst Castle Rd
San Simeon, CA 93452
Web: www.parks.ca.gov/default.asp?page_id=596
Phone: 805-549-3312
Size: 16 acres. Location: At the foot of Cayucos Drive in the town of Cayucos, 5 miles north of Morro Bay. Facilities: Beach, restrooms, picnic area, playground, fishing pier. Activities: Swimming, fishing, surfing. Special Features: Beach features a half mile of sandy beach along the Pacific and a lighted pier for night fishing. The town of Cayucos has a number of historical buildings left over from the old town that now house shops, restaurants, and antique stores.

★1558★ CHINA CAMP STATE PARK
c/o North Bay District Office
PO Box 123
Duncan Mills, CA 95430
Web: www.parks.ca.gov/default.asp?page_id=466
Phone: 415-456-0766
Size: 1,514 acres. Location: 4 miles east of San Rafael, off US 101 on North San Pedro Road. Facilities: 30 walk-in tent campsites, showers, restrooms, 25 developed picnic sites and a group picnic area, hiking trails (15 miles), horseback trails, bike trails, visitor center, exhibits, food service (&&). Activities: Camping, fishing, hiking, boating (small boats only), water-skiing, windsurfing, bicycling, horseback riding, wildlife viewing, guided tours. Special Features: Park includes the historic remains of Chinese immigrants' shrimp fishing village from the 1880s. The property is a natural watershed along the shores of San Francisco Bay with an extensive inter-tidal ecosystem, as

well as salt marsh, meadow, and oak wood habitats which support a wide variety of wildlife. The area has some of the best weather in the San Francisco Bay area, with an average of more than 200 fog-free days per year.

★1559★ CHINO HILLS STATE PARK
c/o Inland Empire District Office
17801 Lake Perris Dr
Perris, CA 92571
Web: www.parks.ca.gov/default.asp?page_id=648
Phone: 951-780-6222
Size: 14,173 acres. Elevation: 1,000 feet. Location: 10 miles northwest of the Corona; from the 91 Freeway take Highway 71 north to Soquel Canyon west, then south on Elinvar. Facilities: Picnic area, equestrian staging area, pipe corrals, a historic barn, water spigots, restrooms, multi-use trails (55 miles). Activities: Primitive camping, hiking, horseback riding, mountain biking. Special Features: A natural open-space area in the hills of Santa Ana Canyon near Riverside, Park is a critical link in the Puente-Chino Hills biological corridor. It encompasses stands of oaks, sycamores, and rolling, grassy hills that stretch nearly 31 miles, from the Santa Ana Mountains to the Whittier Hills.

★1560★ CHUMASH PAINTED CAVE STATE
   HISTORIC PARK
c/o Channel Coast District Office
911 San Pedro St
Ventura, CA 93001
Web: www.parks.ca.gov/default.asp?page_id=602
Phone: 805-968-1033
Size: 7.5 acres. Elevation: 1,750 feet. Location: 3 miles south of San Marcos Pass on Painted Cave Road, off Highway 154. Special Features: Park features a sandstone cave with fine examples of Native American art on the walls. The scenes include religious drawings by Chumash Indians, as well as depictions of coastal fishermen that date back to the 1600s.

★1561★ CLAY PIT STATE VEHICULAR
   RECREATION AREA
c/o Northern Buttes District Office
400 Glen Dr
Oroville, CA 95966
Web: www.parks.ca.gov/default.asp?page_id=409
Phone: 530-538-2200
Size: 220 acres. Location: 3 miles west of Oroville; west of Highway 70 on Oroville Dam Boulevard (Highway 162), then 2 miles south on Larkin Road to entrance. Facilities: Trails and dirt roads, rifle range. Activities: ORV riding, target practice. Special Features: Clay used to build the Lake Oroville impoundment was taken from this site in the Feather River Valley. The resulting depression—a large shallow pit ringed with low hills—provides good beginner terrain for off-road motorcycle, all-terrain vehicle, and dune buggy enthusiasts.

★1562★ CLEAR LAKE STATE PARK
c/o Northern Buttes District Office
400 Glen Dr
Oroville, CA 95966
Web: www.parks.ca.gov/default.asp?page_id=473
Phone: 707-279-4293

Size: 590 acres. **Location:** 3.5 miles northeast of Kelseyville on Soda Bay Road, north of Calistoga in the wine country. **Facilities:** 147 developed family campsites (including 2 hike/bike campsites; some sites &), group camp, showers, restrooms (&), picnic areas (&), hiking and nature trails, swimming area, boat ramps, boat moorage, visitor center (&). **Activities:** Camping, fishing, hiking, swimming, boating, water-skiing, wildlife viewing, guided tours, interpretive programs (seasonal). **Special Features:** Clear Lake is the largest natural lake entirely within the state. Most of the water in the lake comes from runoff, though some comes from springs in Soda Bay. Bass fishing is so good here that some fishing organizations have designated Clear Lake as the best bass lake in the nation, based on numbers of fish caught. The lake also contains catfish, blackfish, Sacramento perch, hitch, crappie, and bluegill.

★1563★ COLONEL ALLENSWORTH STATE HISTORIC PARK

c/o Central Valley District Office
22708 Broadway St
Columbia, CA 95310
Web: www.parks.ca.gov/default.asp?page_id=583
Phone: 661-849-3433
Size: 947 acres. **Location:** North of Bakersfield, 7 miles west of Earlimart and Highway 99 on County Road J22, or 20 miles north of Wasco on Highway 43. **Facilities:** 15 developed family campsites, picnic areas, showers, restrooms, visitor center, exhibits, historic structures. **Activities:** Camping, group tours (by reservation). **Special Features:** Established in 1908, the small farming community of Allensworth was the only California town to be founded, financed, and governed by African Americans. Its founding father, Colonel Allen Allensworth, was a former slave, Union soldier, army chaplain, and the highest ranking black officer of his time. Uncontrollable circumstances, including a drop in the area's water table, resulted in the town's demise, but, with continuing restoration and special events, the town is coming back to life as a state historic park.

★1564★ COLUMBIA STATE HISTORIC PARK

c/o Central Valley District Office
22708 Broadway St
Columbia, CA 95310
Web: www.parks.ca.gov/default.asp?page_id=552
Phone: 209-588-9128
Size: 273 acres. **Location:** 3 miles north of Sonora, off Highway 49. **Facilities:** Historic structures, visitor center, exhibits, restaurants, lodging, picnic areas, restrooms (&). **Activities:** Gold panning, stagecoach rides, mine tours, interpretive programs. **Special Features:** Park preserves an example of one of the most colorful eras in American history, a typical 1850s gold rush town. For a time Columbia was California's second largest city, but unlike many other settlements that disappeared due to fire, vandalism, and time, Columbia was never completely deserted. In 1945, the state legislature proclaimed the town a state historic park. The town's old Gold Rush-era business district has been preserved with shops, restaurants, and two hotels for today's visitors.

★1565★ COLUSA-SACRAMENTO RIVER STATE RECREATION AREA

c/o Northern Buttes District Office
400 Glen Dr
Oroville, CA 95966
Web: www.parks.ca.gov/default.asp?page_id=461
Phone: 530-458-4927
Size: 66 acres. **Location:** Near downtown Colusa, 9 miles east of I-5 on Highway 20, north of Sacramento. **Facilities:** 14 developed campsites (2 &), showers, restrooms, picnic area, hiking trails, boat ramp. **Activities:** Camping, fishing, hiking. **Special Features:** Park features some of the finest fishing in California, including king salmon, steelhead, rainbow trout, and striped bass. The river is also a major migratory route along the Pacific flyway and the area is home to a large number of bird species.

★1566★ CORONA DEL MAR STATE BEACH

c/o Orange Coast District Office
3030 Avenida del Presidente
San Clemente, CA 92672
Web: www.parks.ca.gov/default.asp?page_id=652
Phone: 949-492-0802
Size: 30 acres. **Location:** In Corona del Mar, near the intersection of Iris Street and Ocean Boulevard. **Facilities:** Beach. **Activities:** Swimming, surfing, diving. **Special Features:** This half-mile-long sandy beach is framed by cliffs and a rock jetty that forms the east entrance to Newport Harbor.

★1567★ CRYSTAL COVE STATE PARK

c/o Orange Coast District Office
3030 Avenida del Presidente
San Clemente, CA 92672
Web: www.parks.ca.gov/default.asp?page_id=644
Phone: 949-494-3539
Size: 3,936 acres. **Location:** Off the Pacific Coast Highway between Corona del Mar and Laguna Beach. **Facilities:** 21 environmental campsites (hike-in), picnic areas, trails, beach, lodging, restaurant, visitor center, exhibits, restrooms (&&). **Activities:** Hiking, mountain biking, horseback riding, fishing, swimming, surfing, scuba diving, snorkeling, interpretive programs. **Special Features:** Park includes 3.5 miles of shoreline and 2,000 acres of undeveloped woodland. Beyond the shore, the park's boundary extends underwater to where the ocean is 120 feet deep; the offshore waters have been designated as an underwater park. The first phase of the 12.3-acre historic cottage district opened in June 2006, with rental cottages and a restaurant.

★1568★ CUYAMACA RANCHO STATE PARK

c/o Colorado Desert District Office
200 Palm Canyon Dr
Borrego Springs, CA 92004
Web: www.parks.ca.gov/default.asp?page_id=667
Phone: 760-765-0755; **Toll Free:** 800-444-7275
Size: 24,693 acres. **Elevation:** 6,000 feet. **Location:** East of San Diego, 5 miles north of I-8 on Highway 79. **Facilities:** 167

developed family campsites (no hookups) with restrooms and pay showers, group camps, including an equestrian family camp, picnic areas (&), trails (100+ miles), visitor center (&&). Campgrounds are seasonal (closed December-March). **Activities:** Camping, fishing, hiking, backpacking, horseback riding, mountain biking, wildlife viewing, interpretive programs. **Special Features:** Park offers acres of meadows, mountains, and oak woodlands, with more than 100 miles of multi-use trails. Though the park sustained serious damage in an October 2003 wildfire, the meadows are still abundant with summer wildflowers and native grasses,oaks are thriving, and pine seedlings are flourishing.

★1569★ **DEL NORTE COAST REDWOODS STATE PARK**

c/o North Coast Redwoods District Office
PO Box 2006
Eureka, CA 95502
Web: www.parks.ca.gov/default.asp?page_id=414
Phone: 707-464-6101
Size: 31,168 acres. **Location:** 7 miles south of Crescent City on US 101. **Facilities:** Campground with family, hike/bike, and 8 & campsites, restrooms (&), picnic areas, trails, exhibits. **Activities:** Camping, hiking, mountain biking. **Special Features:** Established in 1929, Park combines spectacular Pacific coastline with dense stands of old-growth redwoods. A half-mile of sandy beach provides excellent tidepool viewing at low tide but is not safe for swimming. The bulk of the rocky sea coast is generally inaccessible except by Damnation and Footsteps Rock trails. Together, Del Norte Coast Redwoods State Park, Jedediah Smith Redwoods State Park, Prairie Creek Redwoods State Park, and Redwood National Park (see separate entries) make up 45 percent of all the old-growth redwood forest remaining in California.

★1570★ **DELTA MEADOWS**

c/o Gold Fields District Office
7806 Folsom-Auburn Rd
Folsom, CA 95630
Web: www.parks.ca.gov/default.asp?page_id=492
Phone: 916-777-7701
Size: 472 acres. **Location:** 1 mile east of Locke. Access is mainly by boat; limited vehicle access is off River Road by way of a small gravel road just east of the cross channel. **Facilities:** Undeveloped; boat mooring, trails. **Activities:** Fishing, boating, hiking, guided tours (by appointment). **Special Features:** Delta Meadows preserves a remnant of the Sacramento River Delta as it was before dams and leeves controlled the annual flooding. The property's waterways contain permanent and seasonal water areas, as well as adjacent uplands that support a variety of riparian plant and animal life, including the river otter, the delta smelt and the Sacramento chub. The property contains Native American occupancy sites, as well as remnants of such early farming and ranching activities as slough dredging and levee building.

★1571★ **DL BLISS STATE PARK**

c/o Sierra District Office
PO Box 266
Tahoma, CA 96142
Web: www.parks.ca.gov/default.asp?page_id=505
Phone: 530-525-3345
Size: 2,149 acres. **Location:** 17 miles south of Tahoe City on Highway 89. **Facilities:** Campsites for family, group, and hike/bike camping (seasonal), picnic areas (&), hiking and nature trails, restrooms. **Activities:** Camping, fishing, hiking, swimming. **Special Features:** Park includes one of Lake Tahoe's finest and most popular beaches. A self-guided trail leads to Balancing Rock, a large granite rock that has long been a natural attraction on Lake Tahoe's western shore. The granite of this large rock has weathered more rapidly at the joint plane, leaving a 130-ton overlying rock balanced on the rock below. From promontories such as Rubicon Point, visitors can see over one hundred feet into the depths of Lake Tahoe.

★1572★ **DOCKWEILER STATE BEACH**

c/o Los Angeles County Dept of Beaches & Harbors
13837 Fiji Way
Marina del Rey, CA 90292
Web: www.parks.ca.gov/default.asp?page_id=617
Phone: 310-305-9503
Size: 91 acres. **Location:** At the western terminus of Imperial Highway in Playa del Rey. **Facilities:** Beach, picnic area, concession stand, showers, restrooms, fire rings; RV park and hang gliding facility nearby. **Activities:** Swimming, surfing, volleyball. **Special Features:** This wide beach, located beneath the takeoff path for the Los Angeles International Airport, features a 3-mile long shoreline. The park is operated by Los Angeles County.

★1573★ **DOHENY STATE BEACH**

25300 Dana Point Harbor Dr
Dana Point, CA 92629
Web: www.parks.ca.gov/default.asp?page_id=645
Phone: 949-496-6172
Size: 254 acres. **Location:** On Del Obispo/Dana Harbor Drive, approximately 1 mile north of I-5 and about 3 miles from San Juan Capistrano Mission. . **Facilities:** 120 developed campsites for family or hike/bike camping, showers, restrooms, picnic areas, volleyball courts, trails, food service, supplies, visitor center, exhibits (&&). **Activities:** Camping, fishing, swimming, surfing, tide pool exploring, hiking, bicycling. **Special Features:** Doheny State Beach is divided into two sections: a campground in the southern area (with some campsites only steps away from the beach); and a day-use area in the northern area, with a 5-acre lawn for volleyball and picnicking.

★1574★ **DONNER MEMORIAL STATE PARK**

c/o Sierra District Office
PO Box 266
Tahoma, CA 96142
Web: www.parks.ca.gov/default.asp?page_id=503
Phone: 530-582-7892
Size: 2,953 acres. **Location:** 100 miles east of Sacramento via

I-80, just west of downtown Truckee, on the south side of the freeway. **Facilities:** 154 developed family campsites, picnic areas, hiking and ski trails, nature trails, boat ramp access, visitor center, museum, exhibits (&&). **Activities:** Camping, fishing, boating, sailing, hiking, swimming, windsurfing, water-skiing, cross-country skiing, snowshoeing. **Special Features:** The ill-fated Donner Party, halted by heavy snows, camped here during the winter of 1846. Park's Emigrant Trail Museum features exhibits on the Donner Party and area history. Near the museum is the Pioneer Monument and the Donner Party's Murphy family cabin site.

★**1575**★ **EASTSHORE STATE PARK**
c/o Diablo Vista District Office
845 Casa Grande Rd
Petaluma, CA 94954
Web: www.parks.ca.gov/default.asp?page_id=520
Phone: 707-989-9548
Size: 442 acres. **Location:** Park extends from the City of Richmond in the north to Emeryville and Oakland in the south, ending near the east anchorage of the San Francisco Bay Bridge. **Facilities:** Under development. **Activities:** Hiking, bicycling, bird watching. **Special Features:** Park includes tidelands and upland property along 8.5 miles of shoreline of the San Francisco Bay. The park is not yet fully developed, though some areas are open to the public.

★**1576**★ **EDWARD Z'BERG SUGAR PINE POINT STATE PARK**
c/o Sierra District Office
PO Box 266
Tahoma, CA 96142
Web: www.parks.ca.gov/default.asp?page_id=510
Phone: 530-525-7232
Size: 2,324 acres. **Elevation:** 6,250 feet. **Location:** On the west shore of Lake Tahoe, 10 miles south of Tahoe City on Highway 89. **Facilities:** Developed family campsites and group camps, restrooms (&), picnic areas, swimming beach, trails (&), nature center, exhibits. **Activities:** Camping, fishing, hiking, mountain biking, swimming, cross-country skiing, snowshoeing, winter camping, guided tours, interpretive programs. **Special Features:** Park contains one of the finest remaining natural areas on Lake Tahoe. With nearly two miles of lake frontage, the park has dense forests of pine, fir, aspen, and juniper. The park also features Hellman-Ehrman Mansion, built in 1903 as a summer home for financier Isaias W. Hellman, which provides an interesting view into the lifestyles of the wealthy on Lake Tahoe.

★**1577**★ **EL CAPITAN STATE BEACH**
c/o Channel Coast District Office
911 San Pedro St
Ventura, CA 93001
Web: www.parks.ca.gov/default.asp?page_id=601
Phone: 805-968-1033
Size: 2,634 acres. **Location:** 17 miles west of Santa Barbara off US 101. **Facilities:** Campsites for family, group, en route, or hike/bike camping (some & sites), restrooms (&), picnic areas, hiking trails, nature trails, bike trails, food service, supplies. **Activities:** Camping, hiking, bicycling, fishing, swimming, surfing, guided tours. **Special Features:** Terrain includes a sandy beach, rocky tidepools, and stands of sycamore and oaks along El Capitán Creek. A stairway provides access from the bluffs to the beach area, and a bike trail connects the park with Refugio State Beach (see separate entry) 2.5 miles away.

★**1578**★ **EL PRESIDIO DE SANTA BARBARA STATE HISTORIC PARK**
c/o Channel Coast District Office
911 San Pedro St
Ventura, CA 93001
Web: www.parks.ca.gov/default.asp?page_id=608
Phone: 805-965-0093
Size: 5.4 acres. **Location:** 123 East Canon Perdido, between Anacapa and Santa Barbara streets in downtown Santa Barbara. **Facilities:** Visitor center, exhibits. **Activities:** Guided tours. **Special Features:** Built in 1782, the Presidio served as the military and government headquarters for the lands between Los Angeles and San Luis Obispo until 1846. El Cuartel, the oldest existing building in Santa Barbara, is all that remains of the last of four Royal Presidios (Spanish military outposts) built in Alta California. Two original buildings have been restored and five others reconstructed.

★**1579**★ **EMERALD BAY STATE PARK**
c/o Sierra District Office
PO Box 266
Tahoma, CA 96142
Web: www.parks.ca.gov/default.asp?page_id=506
Phone: 530-525-7277
Size: 1,533 acres. **Location:** 22 miles south of Tahoe City. **Facilities:** Developed family campsites, boat-in campsites, picnic areas, hiking trails, boat mooring, visitor center, exhibits. **Activities:** Camping, fishing, hiking, swimming, scuba diving, boating, wildlife viewing, guided tours. **Special Features:** Emerald Bay was designated a National Natural Landmark in 1969 for its brilliant panorama of mountain-building processes and glacier carved granite. The park includes Vikingsholm, an eclectic combination of Scandinavian building types considered one of the finest examples of Scandinavian architecture in the western hemisphere. Emerald Bay is the resting place for many boats, launches, and barges used in the lake before the turn of the century (including those used in the construction of Vikingsholm) and was designated an underwater state park in 1994.

★**1580**★ **EMMA WOOD STATE BEACH**
c/o Channel Coast District Office
911 San Pedro St
Ventura, CA 93001
Web: www.parks.ca.gov/default.asp?page_id=604
Phone: 805-968-1033
Size: 112 acres. **Location:** West of Ventura; family campsites are 2 miles west on US 101 and the group camp is at the west end of Main Street in Ventura. **Facilities:** 90 primitive family campsites for self-contained vehicles (no tents permitted), 4 developed group campsites (tent camping and primitive RV camping), picnic areas, hiking trails, bike trails. Group camp

facilities include restrooms and water (no hook-ups); primitive campsites have no restrooms or water. **Activities:** Camping, fishing, swimming, surfing, hiking, bicycling. **Special Features:** The Ventura River Estuary at the southeast end of the beach attracts a variety of wildlife, including raccoons, songbirds, and great blue heron, and dolphins are occasionally seen just offshore. Site also includes the crumbling ruins of a World War II coastal artillery site.

★1581★ EMPIRE MINE STATE HISTORIC PARK

c/o Sierra District Office
PO Box 266
Tahoma, CA 96142
Web: www.parks.ca.gov/default.asp?page_id=499
Phone: 530-273-8522
Size: 853 acres. **Location:** At 10791 East Empire Street in Grass Valley, 24 miles north of Auburn on Highway 49. **Facilities:** Historic structures, visitor center/museum (&), exhibits (&), restrooms, picnic tables, multi-use trails (8 miles). **Activities:** Hiking, mountain biking, horseback riding, guided tours. **Special Features:** For more than 100 years, Empire Mine was one of the largest, deepest, longest-operating, and richest gold mines in North America, producing nearly 5.6 million ounces of gold before it closed in 1956. The park includes many of the mine's original buildings, the owner's home and restored gardens, as well as the entrance to 367 miles of abandoned and flooded mine shafts.

★1582★ ESTERO BAY STATE BEACH

c/o San Luis Obispo Coast District Office
750 Hearst Castle Rd
San Simeon, CA 93452
Web: www.parks.ca.gov/default.asp?page_id=22263
Phone: 805-772-7434
Size: 1,152 acres. **Location:** West of Cayucos, along Estero Bay. **Facilities:** Nature trails. **Special Features:** Purpose of this property is to preserve a diverse and particularly scenic area of the Pacific Ocean coast, with sea stacks and intertidal areas, a substantial area of wetlands, low bluffs, and coastal terraces punctuated by a number of perennial and intermittent streams, and containing a pocket cove and beach at Villa Creek. The property also includes Native American occupancy sites.

★1583★ FOLSOM LAKE STATE RECREATION AREA

c/o Gold Fields District Office
7806 Folsom-Auburn Rd
Folsom, CA 95630
Web: www.parks.ca.gov/default.asp?page_id=500
Phone: 916-988-0205
Size: 19,562 acres. **Elevation:** 456 feet. **Location:** In the Sierra-Nevada foothills about 25 miles east of Sacramento; can be reached via Highway 50 or I-80. **Facilities:** Tent and RV campsites (family, group, and environmental camping), showers, restrooms (&), picnic areas (&), multi-use trails (60 miles), paved bike/hike path (&), food service, boat ramps, marina (seasonal), fishing pier (&), visitor center (&). **Activities:** Camping, fishing,

hiking, swimming, boating, canoeing, kayaking, sailing, water-skiing, jet skiing, bicycling, mountain biking, horseback riding, wildlife viewing, interpretive programs (by appointment). **Special Features:** The park's 12,000-acre reservoir is the busiest recreational lake in the state park system, and smaller Lake Natoma, downstream from Folsom Lake, is popular for crew races, sailing, kayaking, and other aquatic sports. For cyclists, the American River Bicycle Path is a 32-mile-long route that connects Folsom Lake with many Sacramento County parks and ends in Old Sacramento.

★1584★ FOLSOM POWERHOUSE STATE HISTORIC PARK

c/o Folsom Lake State Recreation Area
7806 Folsom-Auburn Rd
Folsom, CA 95630
Web: www.parks.ca.gov/default.asp?page_id=501
Phone: 916-985-4843
Size: 35 acres. **Location:** The recreation area, located near the town of Folsom, can be reached via either Highway 50 or I-80. **Facilities:** Historic structures, picnic areas, trails, restrooms (&). **Activities:** Guided tours (by appointment), hiking, fishing. **Special Features:** Built by H.P. Livermore in 1895, Folsom Powerhouse is one of the oldest hydroelectric facilities in the United States and represents a major advance in the commercial application of electricity. Vintage generators are still in place at the powerhouse, as is the control switchboard, faced with Tennessee marble. Visitors touring the powerhouse can see the massive General Electric transformers, each capable of conducting from 800 to 11,000 volts of electricity, in addition to the forebays and canal system that brought the water from the dam.

★1585★ FOREST OF NISENE MARKS STATE PARK

c/o Santa Cruz District Office
303 Big Trees Park Rd
Felton, CA 95018
Web: www.parks.ca.gov/default.asp?page_id=666
Phone: 831-763-7062
Size: 10,222 acres. **Elevation:** Sea level to 2,600 feet. **Location:** 4 miles north of Aptos on Aptos Creek Road. **Facilities:** Environmental campsites, picnic areas, trails. **Activities:** Camping, hiking, biking, horseback riding. **Special Features:** Park offers rugged semi-wilderness, rising from sea level to steep coastal mountains. Standing on land that was once clear-cut during a 40-year logging frenzy (1883-1923), today the park is a monument to forest regeneration.

★1586★ FORT HUMBOLDT STATE HISTORIC PARK

c/o North Coast Redwoods District Office
PO Box 2006
Eureka, CA 95502
Web: www.parks.ca.gov/default.asp?page_id=665
Phone: 707-445-6567
Size: 18 acres. **Location:** On the south side of Eureka on Highland Avenue, just off US 101. **Facilities:** Visitor center/museum, exhibits, historic structures, picnic areas, restrooms (&&). **Activities:** Self-guided tours, group tours by appointment. **Special Features:** Fort was established in 1853 to assist in conflict

resolution between Native Americans and gold-hungry settlers. The partially reconstructed outpost features a historical museum with military and native displays depicting then-common events of the region. The park also has a logging museum and exhibit and two operational steam engines.

★1587★ **FORT ORD DUNES STATE PARK**
c/o Monterey District Office
2211 Garden Rd
Monterey, CA 93940
Web: www.parks.ca.gov/default.asp?page_id=580
Phone: 831-649-2836
Location: On Monterey Bay. **Facilities:** Under development. **Special Features:** Park is still in the planning stages and is not yet open to the public.

★1588★ **FORT ROSS STATE HISTORIC PARK**
c/o North Bay District Office
PO Box 123
Duncan Mills, CA 95430
Web: www.parks.ca.gov/default.asp?page_id=449
Phone: 707-847-3286
Size: 3,393 acres. **Location:** 12 miles north of Jenner on Highway 1. **Facilities:** Primitive campsites, picnic area, hiking trails, visitor center, exhibits (&), restrooms (&). **Activities:** Camping, fishing, hiking, scuba diving, guided tours. **Special Features:** Fort Ross was in operation from 1812 to 1841 as a trading outpost for the Russian-American Company. It was the southernmost settlement in the Russian colonization of the North American continent, established as an agricultural base to supply Alaska. Fort Ross was the site of California's first windmills and shipbuilding, and Russian scientists were among the first to record California's cultural and natural history. Today, one original building and five reconstructed structures exist within the stockade walls.

★1589★ **FORT TEJON STATE HISTORIC PARK**
c/o Central Valley District Office
22708 Broadway St
Columbia, CA 95310
Web: www.parks.ca.gov/default.asp?page_id=585
Phone: 661-248-6692; **Fax:** 661-248-8373
Size: 647 acres. **Location:** 70 miles north of Los Angeles on I-5, near the top of Grapevine Canyon. **Facilities:** Visitor center/museum (&), exhibits (&), picnic areas (&), group campsites. **Activities:** Guided and self-guided tours, living history demonstrations (monthly). **Special Features:** Fort Tejon (1854-1864) was established by the U.S. Army to protect and control Native Americans living on the Sebastian Indian Reservation, and to protect both native and white settlers from raids by the Paiutes, Chemeheui, Mojave, and other Indian groups of the desert regions to the southeast. This post is one of the significant remaining links to the historic period of early European occupation of California. Park includes restored adobes from the original fort and museum exhibits on army life and local history.

★1590★ **FRANKS TRACT STATE RECREATION AREA**
c/o Gold Fields District Office
7806 Folsom-Auburn Rd
Folsom, CA 95630
Web: www.parks.ca.gov/default.asp?page_id=490
Phone: 916-777-7701
Size: 3,523 acres. **Location:** 5 miles southeast of Brannan Island between False River and Bethel Island; accessible by boat only. **Facilities:** Undeveloped. **Activities:** Fishing, waterfowl hunting (with restrictions), swimming, boat-in camping. **Special Features:** Franks Tract flooded twice during the 1930s and today most of the area remains underwater. The tract is located in the Sacramento-San Joaquin Delta along the Pacific flyway. During the fall and winter months, a large variety of migrating waterfowl can be found here. Year-round residents include gulls, great blue herons, terns, swallows, crows, blackbirds, cormorants, and kingfishers.

★1591★ **FREMONT PEAK STATE PARK**
c/o Monterey District Office
2211 Garden Rd
Monterey, CA 93940
Web: www.parks.ca.gov/default.asp?page_id=564
Phone: 831-623-4255
Size: 162 acres. **Elevation:** 2,750 feet. **Location:** Off Highway 156, 11 miles south of San Juan Bautista on San Juan Canyon Road. Trailers are not recommended. **Facilities:** Camping and picnic facilities, hiking and nature trails, observatory with 30-inch telescope. **Activities:** Camping, hiking, educational exhibits. **Special Features:** At 3,169 feet in elevation, peak offers vistas of San Benito Valley, Monterey Bay, and the Santa Lucia Mountains east of Big Sur. The Fremont Peak Observatory is open for public programs on selected evenings.

★1592★ **GARRAPATA STATE PARK**
c/o Monterey District Office
2211 Garden Rd
Monterey, CA 93940
Web: www.parks.ca.gov/default.asp?page_id=579
Phone: 831-624-4909
Size: 2,940 acres. **Location:** On Highway 1, 6.5 miles south of Rio Road in Carmel (18 miles north of Big Sur). **Facilities:** Hiking trails. **Activities:** Fishing, hiking, wildlife viewing. **Special Features:** Park includes two miles of beachfront and features diverse coastal vegetation, with trails running from ocean beaches into dense redwood groves. Sea lions, harbor seals, and sea otters frequent the coastal waters, and California gray whales pass close by during their yearly migration.

★1593★ **GAVIOTA STATE PARK**
c/o Channel Coast District Office
911 San Pedro St
Ventura, CA 93001
Web: www.parks.ca.gov/default.asp?page_id=606
Phone: 805-968-1033
Size: 2,744 acres. **Location:** 33 miles west of Santa Barbara on US 101. **Facilities:** Family campsites, picnic area, restrooms/

9. State Parks

showers (占), hiking trails, horseback trails, food service, supplies; no drinking water. **Activities:** Camping, fishing, hiking, swimming, diving, surfing, horseback riding. **Special Features:** This section of the coast was first called *gaviota* (seagull) by soldiers of the Portola Expedition in 1769. A railroad trestle crosses the park's creek above the day-use parking lot; a trailhead there allows entry to the upland portions of the park, where Gaviota Peak (2,458 feet) affords panoramic views of the coast and the Channel Islands.

★1594★ GEORGE J. HATFIELD STATE RECREATION AREA

c/o Central Valley District Office
22708 Broadway St
Columbia, CA 95310
Web: www.parks.ca.gov/default.asp?page_id=556
Phone: 209-632-1852
Size: 46.5 acres. **Location:** At 4394 North Kelly Road in Hilmar; from I-5, take the Newman exit and continue east on County Road J-18 for 5 miles. Park entrance is just past the San Joaquin River Bridge. **Facilities:** Family and group campsites, picnic areas. **Activities:** Camping, fishing, swimming. **Special Features:** Recreation area is situated in the San Joaquin Valley, near the confluence of the San Joaquin and Merced rivers.

★1595★ GOVERNOR'S MANSION STATE HISTORIC PARK

c/o Capital District Office
101 J St
Sacramento, CA 95814
Web: www.parks.ca.gov/default.asp?page_id=498
Phone: 916-323-3047
Size: 0.78 acre. **Location:** At 1526 H Street in Sacramento (corner of 16th and H streets). **Facilities:** Historic building, visitor center, exhibits, restrooms (占占). **Activities:** Guided tours. **Special Features:** Built by hardware store owner Albert Gallatin in 1878, mansion became the official residence for California's governors in 1903 and was used by all subsequent governors (13 in all) until 1967 when Ronald Reagan became the last governor to reside there. The mansion is an example of Second Empire-Italianate architecture and has more than 30 rooms.

★1596★ GRAY WHALE COVE STATE BEACH

c/o Santa Cruz District Office
303 Big Trees Park Rd
Felton, CA 95018
Web: www.parks.ca.gov/default.asp?page_id=528
Phone: 650-726-8819
Size: 3.1 acres. **Location:** On the San Mateo Coast, north of Montara on Highway 1. **Facilities:** Beach, trail, restrooms. **Activities:** Fishing, sunbathing, hiking, wildlife viewing. **Special Features:** Small, isolated beach where clothing is optional. During their annual migration, gray whales can be seen close to shore.

★1597★ GREAT VALLEY GRASSLANDS STATE PARK

c/o Central Valley District Office
22708 Broadway St
Columbia, CA 95310
Web: www.parks.ca.gov/default.asp?page_id=559
Phone: 209-826-1197
Size: 2,826 acres. **Location:** 20 miles west of Merced, 1 mile south of Highway 140 on Highway 165. **Facilities:** Undeveloped. **Activities:** Fishing, wildlife watching. **Special Features:** Park preserves one of the few intact examples of native grasslands on the floor of the Central Valley. The park is part of the larger Grasslands Ecological Area (GEA), a 180,000-acre complex of federal, state, and private lands managed for wildlife habitat protection. The GEA is the largest remaining contiguous block of wetlands in California. Several rare and endangered plant and animal species inhabit the park.

★1598★ GREENWOOD STATE BEACH

c/o Mendocino District Office
PO Box 440
Mendocino, CA 95460
Web: www.parks.ca.gov/default.asp?page_id=447
Phone: 707-937-5804
Size: 47 acres. **Location:** 15 miles north of Point Arena on Highway 1, along the Mendocino County coast. **Facilities:** Visitor center, exhibits, restrooms, picnic area, beach access, hiking trails. **Activities:** Fishing, hiking. **Special Features:** Once the site of a redwood lumber mill, a 75-year-old mill office building serves as visitor center and museum, interpreting the history of Greenwood as a lumber town in the late 1800s through the early 1900s.

★1599★ GRIZZLY CREEK REDWOODS STATE PARK

c/o North Coast Redwoods District Office
PO Box 2006
Eureka, CA 95502
Web: www.parks.ca.gov/default.asp?page_id=421
Phone: 707-777-3683
Size: 429 acres. **Location:** Off US 101 southeast of Eureka at 16949 Highway 36 in Carlotta. **Facilities:** 30 developed family campsites (some 占), restrooms/showers (占), group camp, environmental camp, picnic areas (占), horseshoe pit, hiking trails (4.5 miles), visitor center with exhibits and bookstore (占). **Activities:** Camping, canoeing, kayaking, fishing, hiking, swimming, guided tours. **Special Features:** This quiet, secluded park includes the Cheatham Grove, an exceptional stand of coast redwoods.

★1600★ GROVER HOT SPRINGS STATE PARK

c/o Sierra District Office
PO Box 266
Tahoma, CA 96142
Web: www.parks.ca.gov/default.asp?page_id=508
Phone: 530-694-2248
Size: 553 acres. **Elevation:** 5,840 feet. **Location:** 4 miles west of Markleeville at the end of Hot Springs Road. **Facilities:**

Campground, picnic areas, hiking trails. **Activities:** Camping, fishing, hiking, swimming, cross-country skiing, snowshoeing. **Special Features:** Located on the east side of the Sierra at the edge of the Great Basin Province, Park is famous for its hot springs mineral pool and is open year round. The weather here is highly variable, and visitors should be prepared for a full range of potential conditions. It is extremely windy at any time.

★1601★ HALF MOON BAY STATE BEACH

c/o San Mateo Coast Sector Office
95 Kelly Ave
Half Moon Bay, CA 94019
Web: www.parks.ca.gov/default.asp?page_id=531
Phone: 650-726-8819; **Fax:** 650-726-8816
Size: 181 acres. **Location:** 0.5 miles west of Highway 1 on Kelly Avenue in Half Moon Bay. **Facilities:** 52 campsites (tent and RV sites, no hookups), group campground, showers (coin-operated), restrooms, picnic areas, trails, visitor center (&&). **Activities:** Camping, fishing, surfing, hiking, horseback riding, bicycling. **Special Features:** Beach offers four miles of broad, sandy coastline along crescent-shaped Half Moon Bay. Water temperatures here are extremely cold and not suitable for swimming.

★1602★ HARRY A. MERLO STATE RECREATION AREA

c/o North Coast Redwoods District Office
PO Box 2006
Eureka, CA 95502
Web: www.parks.ca.gov/default.asp?page_id=431
Phone: 707-677-3132
Size: 955 acres. **Location:** 32 miles north of Eureka on US 101. **Activities:** Fishing (small boats allowed), windsurfing. **Special Features:** Harry A. Merlo SRA and the adjacent Humboldt Lagoons State Park (see separate entry) include three lagoons that can overflow into the ocean during heavy storms, carving a deep channel that can drop their water levels by as much as 6 feet an hour. Later, the surf and tide reform the beach.

★1603★ HEARST SAN SIMEON STATE HISTORICAL MONUMENT

750 Hearst Castle Rd
San Simeon, CA 93452
Web: www.parks.ca.gov/default.asp?page_id=591
Phone: 805-927-2020; **Toll Free:** 800-444-4445
Size: 209 acres. **Location:** On Highway 1, halfway between Los Angeles and San Francisco. **Facilities:** Historic structures/museums, visitor center, exhibits, gift shops, food service, picnic area, restrooms (&&). **Activities:** Guided tours. **Special Features:** The famous "Castle" was designed by noted architect Julia Morgan and built by William Rudolph Hearst between 1919 and 1947. It includes a 115-room main house, guest houses, theater, tennis courts, pools, and 127 acres of gardens, terraces, and walkways. It remains as Hearst left it, furnished with fabulous antiquities and artwork. More than a million visitors a year tour Hearst Castle®.

★1604★ HEBER DUNES STATE VEHICULAR RECREATION AREA

c/o Ocotillo Wells District Office
PO Box 356
Borrego Springs, CA 92004
Web: www.parks.ca.gov/default.asp?page_id=408
Phone: 760-768-9379
Size: 342 acres. **Location:** 8 miles east of Heber on Heber Road; access park via I-8 to State Highway 111 or 86. **Facilities:** Camping ramadas, restrooms, showers, picnic areas, baseball field. **Activities:** Camping, baseball, ORV riding. **Special Features:** Park includes the riverbed of the old Alamo River, where tamarisk trees have taken root in deposits of sand. The international border crossing into Mexico is located three miles south of the park.

★1605★ HENDY WOODS STATE PARK

c/o Mendocino District Office
PO Box 440
Mendocino, CA 95460
Web: www.parks.ca.gov/default.asp?page_id=438
Phone: 707-895-3141
Size: 816 acres. **Location:** 8 miles northwest of Boonville, 0.5 mile south of Highway 128 on Philo-Greenwood Road. **Facilities:** 92 developed campsites (4 & sites), hike/bike campground, cabins (1 &), hermit huts, restrooms and showers (&), 25 picnic sites, multi-use trail (&), nature trails (2 miles), visitor center, exhibits. **Activities:** Camping, canoeing, kayaking, swimming, hiking, biking, horseback riding. Fishing is not allowed in the park but is permitted in the Navarro River watershed down river from the bridge at the park entrance. **Special Features:** Park features two virgin coast redwood groves: 80-acre Big Hendy, with a self-guided, wheelchair-accessible discovery trail; and 20-acre Little Hendy. Park is well-known for a fallen redwood stump that was home for a man known locally as the Hendy Woods Hermit. Located in the middle of the Anderson Valley wine district, this park is warmer and less foggy than redwood parks along the coast.

★1606★ HENRY COWELL REDWOODS STATE PARK

c/o Santa Cruz District Office
303 Big Trees Park Rd
Felton, CA 95018
Web: www.parks.ca.gov/default.asp?page_id=546
Phone: 831-335-4598
Size: 4,316 acres. **Location:** Near Felton on Highway 9 in the Santa Cruz Mountains. **Facilities:** Family and hike/bike campsites, restrooms and showers, picnic area, trails (20 miles), self-guided nature path, nature center with exhibits, gift shop, food service (&&). **Activities:** Camping, hiking, biking, horseback riding, guided tours. Fishing is permitted in the San Lorenzo River during the steelhead and salmon season, approximately November through February. **Special Features:** Park features 15 miles of trails through a forest of coast redwoods, Douglas fir, madrone, oak, and a stand of Ponderosa pine. The main park area contains old-growth redwoods. The tallest tree in the park is about 285 feet tall; the oldest trees are 1400-1800 years old.

★1607★ **HENRY W. COE STATE PARK**
c/o Monterey District Office
2211 Garden Rd
Monterey, CA 93940
Web: www.parks.ca.gov/default.asp?page_id=561
Phone: 408-779-2728
Size: 89,264 acres. **Elevation:** 2,600 feet. **Location:** 13 miles east of Morgan Hill on East Dunne Avenue. **Facilities:** Camping areas, including 20 drive-in campsites, 10 hike-in group campsites, backpacking campsites, and 8 designated horse camps with pipe corrals, hiking trails (250 miles), mountain bike trails (100 miles), horseback trails, nature trails, picnic areas (&), visitor center, exhibits. **Activities:** Camping, fishing, hiking, backpacking, horseback riding, mountain biking, interpretive programs (seasonal). **Special Features:** Park's terrain is rugged, varied, and beautiful, with lofty ridges and steep canyons. It is the largest state park in northern California, encompassing the headwaters of Coyote Creek, long stretches of the Pacheco and Orestimba creeks, and a wilderness area. The park's Pine Ridge Museum interprets ranch life in the late 1880s.

★1608★ **HOLLISTER HILLS STATE VEHICULAR
RECREATION AREA**
c/o Hollister Hills District Office
7800 Cienega Rd
Hollister, CA 95023
Web: www.parks.ca.gov/default.asp?page_id=404
Phone: 831-637-3874
Size: 6,621 acres. **Elevation:** 660-2,425 feet. **Location:** 6 miles south of Hollister. **Facilities:** Family and group campsites (some &), showers (&), restrooms (&), picnic areas (&), hiking and biking trails, nature trails, visitor center, food service, supplies. **Activities:** Camping, hiking, mountain biking, ORV riding. **Special Features:** This vehicle recreation area includes 64 miles of trails as well as motocross, vintage, TT, and mini-bike tracks for motorcycles and ATVs, and 24 miles of trails and a custom-designed obstacle course for four-wheel-drive vehicles. The area also offers self-guided natural history walks through Azalea Canyon and along the San Andreas Fault.

★1609★ **HUMBOLDT LAGOONS STATE PARK**
c/o North Coast Redwoods District Office
PO Box 2006
Eureka, CA 95502
Web: www.parks.ca.gov/default.asp?page_id=416
Phone: 707-677-3132
Size: 2,217 acres. **Location:** On US Highway 101, 40 miles north of Eureka and 55 miles south of Crescent City. **Facilities:** Boat-in and environmental campsites, picnic areas, hiking trails, boat ramps, visitor center, bookstore. **Activities:** Camping, fishing, boating, hiking, beachcombing, wildlife viewing. **Special Features:** Humboldt Lagoons State Park and the adjacent Harry A. Merlo SRA (see separate entry) include three lagoons. Dry Lagoon was drained for farmland in the early 1900s, and Stone Lagoon was the site of dairy farms. Today the marshland habitat has returned and supports a rich variety of marsh plants, birds, and other animals. The beach here provides access to six miles of beachcombing, bird watching, whale watching, and agate

hunting, or visitors can bring their own boats and explore the lagoon.

★1610★ **HUMBOLDT REDWOODS STATE PARK**
c/o North Coast Redwoods District Office
PO Box 2006
Eureka, CA 95502
Web: www.parks.ca.gov/default.asp?page_id=425
Phone: 707-946-2409
Size: 51,590 acres. **Location:** 45 miles south of Eureka and 20 miles north of Garberville off of Highway 101. The visitor center is located on the Avenue of the Giants, State Route 254, between the towns of Weott and Myers Flat. **Facilities:** More than 250 developed family campsites as well as environmental camps, group camps, trail camps, and a horse camp, picnic areas, trails (100+ miles), boat ramps, restrooms, visitor center, exhibits (&&). **Activities:** Camping, fishing, swimming, boating, hiking, horseback riding, mountain biking, interpretive programs (seasonal). **Special Features:** Park is California's largest redwood state park and includes the Rockefeller Forest, the largest remaining contiguous old-growth coast redwood forest in the world. The Avenue of the Giants parallels 33 miles of US 101 through the park, and is California's showplace for the magnificent coast redwoods.

★1611★ **HUNGRY VALLEY STATE VEHICULAR
RECREATION AREA**
c/o Hungry Valley District Office
PO Box 1360 46001 Orwin Way
Gorman, CA 93534
Web: www.parks.ca.gov/default.asp?page_id=405
Phone: 661-248-7007
Size: 18,401 acres. **Elevation:** 2,600-8,000 feet. **Location:** On Peace Valley Road in Gorman, 60 miles north of Los Angeles and 55 miles south of Bakersfield. **Facilities:** Camping areas, picnic areas, restrooms (vault toilets), visitor center; drinking water is not available. **Activities:** Camping, ORV riding, hiking. **Special Features:** Recreation area features more than 130 miles of scenic trails for motorcycles, ATVs, dune buggies, and four-wheel drive vehicles, including a practice mini-track for beginning riders. A 60-acre preserve protects valley oaks and native bunchgrasses.

★1612★ **HUNTINGTON STATE BEACH**
c/o Orange Coast District Office
3030 Avenida del Presidente
San Clemente, CA 92672
Web: www.parks.ca.gov/default.asp?page_id=643
Phone: 714-846-3460
Size: 121 acres. **Location:** In Huntington Beach, opposite Magnolia Avenue on Pacific Coast Highway. **Facilities:** Picnic areas, beach, multi-use trails, food service, beach access ramp, restrooms (&&). **Activities:** Camping, surf fishing, swimming, surfing, windsurfing, hiking, skating, bicycling. **Special Features:** Beach is the site of a nesting sanctuary for the California least tern, a rare and endangered species, and the threatened snowy plover. A bike trail connects Huntington State Beach to

Bolsa Chica State Beach (see separate entry), forming five miles of sandy beach.

★1613★ INDIAN GRINDING ROCK STATE HISTORIC PARK
c/o Central Valley District Office
22708 Broadway St
Columbia, CA 95310
Web: www.parks.ca.gov/default.asp?page_id=553
Phone: 209-296-7488
Size: 135 acres. **Location:** Northeast of Stockton, 8 miles east of Jackson at 14881 Pine Grove-Volcano Road in Pine Grove. **Facilities:** 23 developed family campsites with showers and restrooms, 7 bark houses for primitive/environmental camping, picnic areas, hiking and nature trails, museums, historical features (&&). **Activities:** Camping, interpretive programs, living history demonstrations, special events. **Special Features:** Park preserves a great outcropping of marbleized limestone with 1,185 mortar holes—the largest collection of bedrock mortars in North America—used many centuries ago by a Native American group now referred to as the Northern Sierra Miwok. The park includes the Chaw'se Regional Indian Museum, featuring an outstanding collection of Sierra Nevada Indian artifacts. Present-day descendents of the Miwok designed and helped reconstruct a typical Miwok village in the park, which includes bark houses, a ceremonial round house, acorn granaries, and shade ramadas.

★1614★ INDIO HILLS PALMS
c/o Colorado Desert District Office
200 Palm Canyon Dr
Borrego Springs, CA 92004
Web: www.parks.ca.gov/default.asp?page_id=640
Phone: 619-393-3059
Size: 5,644 acres. **Location:** East of Palm Springs on Thousand Palms Road, 2 miles north of Ramon Road. There are currently no marked access roads to the property. **Activities:** Covered wagon tours of oases. **Special Features:** Along a line where the San Andreas Fault captures groundwater, native California fan palms thrive in great numbers. Indio Palms is a wild parkland that is part of the adjacent Coachella Valley Preserve. The nearest palm groves are relatively easy to reach from a trailhead and parking area 4-miles north of Indio.

★1615★ JACK LONDON STATE HISTORIC PARK
c/o Diablo Vista District Office
845 Casa Grande Rd
Petaluma, CA 94954
Web: www.parks.ca.gov/default.asp?page_id=478
Phone: 707-938-5216
Size: 1,611 acres. **Location:** 2400 London Ranch Road in Glen Ellen (about 20 minutes north of Sonoma). **Facilities:** Historic home, museum, exhibits, picnic areas, horse rentals (seasonal), multi-use trails, self-guiding history trail (&&). **Activities:** Hiking, horseback riding, bicycling, group tours. **Special Features:** Author Jack London made the Valley of the Moon his home in 1905. From his cottage, he wrote numerous short stories, novels, and articles while overseeing ambitious agricultural enterprises.

Park includes the cottage, ranch, and gravesite of Jack London, and the ruins of London's dream house, Wolf House.

★1616★ JEDEDIAH SMITH REDWOODS STATE PARK
c/o North Coast Redwoods District Office
PO Box 2006
Eureka, CA 95502
Web: www.parks.ca.gov/default.asp?page_id=413
Phone: 707-464-6101
Size: 10,447 acres. **Location:** 9 miles east of Crescent City on Highway 199. **Facilities:** 106 developed campsites (some &), hike/bike campsites, showers, restrooms (&), picnic areas, hiking and nature trails (20 miles), river access, visitor center, exhibits. **Activities:** Camping, fishing, hiking, swimming, horseback riding, mountain biking, interpretive programs. **Special Features:** This predominately old growth coast redwoods park is bisected by the last major free flowing river in California, the Smith River, which is known for its runs of king salmon and steelhead trout in the fall and winter. Park is named for Jedediah Smith, the first white man to explore the interior of northern California, who pioneered a trail southwest from the Great Salt Lake across the Mojave Desert through the San Bernadino Mountains into California.

★1617★ JOHN LITTLE STATE RESERVE
c/o Monterey District Office
2211 Garden Rd
Monterey, CA 93940
Web: www.parks.ca.gov/default.asp?page_id=568
Phone: 831-667-2315
Size: 21 acres. **Location:** Monterey County, between State Highway 1 and the Pacific Ocean. **Facilities:** Undeveloped. **Special Features:** Situated on a scenic point of land, the site preserves and protects a section of steep, rugged cliffs on the Big Sur coast where Lime Creek enters the Pacific Ocean. The reserve contains the original 1917 cabin of early conservationist Elizabeth K. Livermore.

★1618★ JOHN MARSH HOME
c/o Diablo Vista District Office
845 Casa Grande Rd
Petaluma, CA 94954
Web: www.parks.ca.gov/default.asp?page_id=525
Phone: 707-989-9548
Size: 3,663 acres. **Location:** Eastern Contra Costa County. **Facilities:** Under development. **Special Features:** The John Marsh/Cowell Ranch property encompasses nearly 4,000 acres of natural habitat, wildlife, and unique cultural features, including the historic John Marsh Home.

★1619★ JUG HANDLE STATE RESERVE
c/o Mendocino District Office
PO Box 440
Mendocino, CA 95460
Web: www.parks.ca.gov/default.asp?page_id=441
Phone: 707-937-5804

Size: 776 acres. **Location:** 1 mile north of Caspar on Highway 1. **Facilities:** Picnic areas, hiking and nature trails. **Activities:** Hiking, picnicking, scuba diving. **Special Features:** Reserve's "ecological staircase" offers a firsthand look at 500,000 years of California's geological history. A 2.5-mile self-guiding nature trail leads through five wave-cut terraces formed by glacier, sea, and tectonic activity that built the coast range. Each of the terraces was uplifted from sea level about 100,000 years before the one below it. The lowest terrace still battles ocean waves, the third terrace has a unique pygmy forest, and terraces above display more advanced vegetation.

★1620★ JULIA PFEIFFER BURNS STATE PARK

c/o Monterey District Office
2211 Garden Rd
Monterey, CA 93940
Web: www.parks.ca.gov/default.asp?page_id=578
Phone: 831-667-2315
Size: 3,762 acres. **Location:** 37 miles south of Carmel on Highway 1. **Facilities:** Environmental campsites, picnic areas, restrooms, hiking trails. **Activities:** Camping, hiking, scuba diving (with permit), wildlife viewing. **Special Features:** Park stretches from the Big Sur coastline into nearby 3,000-foot ridges and features redwood, tan oak, madrone, chaparral, and an 80-foot waterfall that drops from granite cliffs into the ocean from the Overlook Trail. A spot at the end of Overlook Trail is a great place to see gray whales in December and January. A panoramic view of the ocean and miles of rugged coastline is available from the higher elevations along the trails east of Highway 1. A portion of the park is an Underwater Area for scuba diving.

★1621★ KENNETH HAHN STATE RECREATION AREA

c/o Angeles District Office
1925 Las Virgenes
Calabasas, CA 91302
Web: www.parks.ca.gov/default.asp?page_id=612
Phone: 323-298-3660
Size: 401 acres. **Location:** At 4100 South La Cienega Boulevard in Baldwin Hills. **Facilities:** Picnic areas, footpaths and trails (5 miles), playgrounds, sports fields, fishing lake, Japanese garden, community center, restrooms. **Activities:** Fishing, swimming, volleyball, hiking, bicycling/mountain biking. **Special Features:** Recreation area features Olympic Forest, which was planted with one tree for each of the 140 nations that participated in the 1984 games in Los Angeles. The area was also the site of the 1932 Olympic Village for athletes in the 10th Olympiad. Operated by Los Angeles County.

★1622★ KINGS BEACH STATE RECREATION AREA

c/o Sierra District Office
PO Box 266
Tahoma, CA 96142
Web: www.parks.ca.gov/default.asp?page_id=511
Phone: 530-546-4212
Size: 7.7 acres. **Elevation:** 6,225 feet. **Location:** In downtown Kings Beach, on the northeast side of Tahoe City. **Facilities:** Beach, picnic area (♿), restrooms (♿) **Activities:** Swimming and other water sports, volleyball. **Special Features:** This day-use only recreation area features ponderosa pine and small brush along 700 feet of frontage on Lake Tahoe.

★1623★ KRUSE RHODODENDRON STATE RESERVE

c/o North Bay District Office
PO Box 123
Duncan Mills, CA 95430
Web: www.parks.ca.gov/default.asp?page_id=448
Phone: 707-847-2391
Size: 317 acres. **Location:** 20 miles north of Jenner, near milepost 43 on Highway 1. **Facilities:** Hiking, nature, and horseback trails (5 miles). **Activities:** Hiking, horseback riding. **Special Features:** Reserve features acres of wild rhododendrons, which bloom from April through June, as well as second-growth redwood, Douglas fir, and tan oak. In addition to the rhododendrons, other understory plants include ferns, salals, pacific wax myrtle, and California huckleberry. The rhododendrons grew here after a forest was destroyed by a severe forest fire.

★1624★ LA PURISIMA MISSION STATE HISTORIC PARK

c/o Channel Coast District Office
911 San Pedro St
Ventura, CA 93001
Web: www.parks.ca.gov/default.asp?page_id=598
Phone: 805-733-3713
Size: 1,934 acres. **Location:** 2 miles northeast of Lompoc at 2295 Purisima Road. **Facilities:** Picnic areas, trails, restrooms, visitor center, museum, historic buildings. **Activities:** Hiking, bicycling, horseback riding, guided tours. **Special Features:** Founded by Father Presidente Fermin de Lasuén in 1787, La Purisima Mission was the eleventh of 21 Franciscan missions in what is now California. It is considered the most completely restored mission in California, with ten of the original buildings fully restored and furnished, including the church, shops, quarters, and blacksmith shop.

★1625★ LAKE DEL VALLE STATE RECREATION AREA

c/o Diablo Vista District Office
845 Casa Grande Rd
Petaluma, CA 94954
Web: www.parks.ca.gov/default.asp?page_id=537
Phone: 510-635-0135
Size: 3,732 acres. **Location:** On Del Valle Road, a few miles south of I-580 in Livermore. **Facilities:** 150 developed family campsites (21 with water and sewage hookups; no electrical), showers and restrooms, youth group camps, 2 swimming beaches, stocked lake, picnic areas, trails, boat ramp, boat rentals, visitor center, exhibits. **Activities:** Camping, swimming, fishing, boating, sailing, canoeing, hiking, horseback riding, guided lake tours. **Special Features:** Park is operated by the East Bay Regional Park District and its centerpiece is a lake five miles long. Del Valle also is the eastern gateway to the

Ohlone Wilderness Trail, which comprises 28 miles of scenic backcountry trail.

★1626★ LAKE OROVILLE STATE RECREATION AREA

c/o Northern Buttes District Office
400 Glen Dr
Oroville, CA 95966
Web: www.parks.ca.gov/default.asp?page_id=462
Phone: 530-538-2200
Size: 29,447 acres. **Location:** 7 miles east of Oroville via Highway 162. **Facilities:** More than 200 family campsites (with and without hookups), overnight sites for self-contained vehicles, 6 group sites, a horsecamp with 15 campsites, 10 floating campsites for people with their own boats, 6 areas designated for boat-in camping, restrooms and showers, 2 marinas, boat launch ramps, snack bars, boat rentals, boat mooring, picnic areas (including designated sites for boaters), swimming beaches, hiking and horseback trails, nature trails, fish hatchery with underwater viewing windows, visitor center complex with displays and a 47-foot viewing tower (&&). **Activities:** Camping, fishing, sailing and power boating, swimming, water-skiing, windsurfing, hiking, horseback riding, mountain biking, hunting (with restrictions). **Special Features:** Lake Oroville is the largest state water facility in northern California. It is primarily a boater's park, with 167 miles of shoreline and more than 15,500 surface acres. The lake was created by construction of the Oroville Dam, at 770 feet the nation's tallest earthen dam. One arm of the lake reaches to within 0.25 miles of 640-foot Feather Falls, one of the highest waterfalls in North America.

★1627★ LAKE PERRIS STATE RECREATION AREA

c/o Inland Empire District Office
17801 Lake Perris Dr
Perris, CA 92571
Web: www.parks.ca.gov/default.asp?page_id=651
Phone: 951-657-0676
Size: 6,675 acres. **Location:** 11 miles southeast of Riverside, in the Moreno Valley, via Highway 60 or I-215. **Facilities:** 431 developed family campsites (167 tent sites with no hookups and 264 RV sites with water and electric hookups), primitive horse camp (7 camping units), 6 group camps, picnic areas (including group picnic sites), 2 designated swimming areas with showers and changing rooms, restrooms, boat ramps, boat mooring, marina, snack bar, museum (@d&). **Activities:** Camping, fishing, hiking, swimming, boating, sailing, windsurfing, water-skiing, jet skiing, horseback riding, mountain biking, rock climbing, wildlife viewing. **Special Features:** Set amid unusual rock formations, Lake is the last of the reservoirs built in conjunction with the California Aqueduct. In addition to the many recreational activities available here, the park hosts a regional Indian Museum.

★1628★ LAKE VALLEY STATE RECREATION AREA

c/o Sierra District Office
PO Box 266
Tahoma, CA 96142
Web: www.parks.ca.gov/default.asp?page_id=515
Phone: 530-577-0802

Size: 155 acres. **Elevation:** 6,000+ feet. **Location:** 3.5 miles southwest of city of South Lake Tahoe, off Highway 50. **Facilities:** 18-hole championship golf course, snowmobile rentals, food service, restrooms. **Activities:** Golf, snowmobiling, cross-country skiing. **Special Features:** Park features golf during the summer months and snowmobiling and cross-country skiing in winter. The golf course lies at an elevation of 6,000 plus feet, and shots carry farther in the thin mountain air.

★1629★ LELAND STANFORD MANSION STATE HISTORIC PARK

c/o Capital District Office
101 J St
Sacramento, CA 95814
Web: www.stanfordmansion.org
Phone: 916-324-0575; **Fax:** 916-324-5885
Size: 0.88 acre. **Location:** At 800 'N' Street in downtown Sacramento, just a few blocks from the State Capitol. **Facilities:** Historic mansion and gardens, visitor center, exhibits. **Activities:** Guided tours. **Special Features:** The office of three California governors (including Leland Stanford) during the 1860s, the mansion now serves as a museum and as California's official reception center, where the Governor and legislative leaders meet with dignitaries and business leaders from other states and countries. The 19,000-square-foot mansion has recently undergone a $22 million restoration.

★1630★ LEO CARILLO STATE PARK

c/o Angeles District Office
1925 Las Virgenes
Calabasas, CA 91302
Web: www.parks.ca.gov/default.asp?page_id=616
Phone: 818-880-0350
Size: 2,516 acres. **Location:** 28 miles northwest of Santa Monica on Highway 1 (Pacific Coast Highway). **Facilities:** 135 developed family campsites (some & sites), group campground, showers, restrooms, picnic areas (&), hiking trails, supplies, visitor center, displays. **Activities:** Camping, fishing, swimming, surfing, windsurfing, scuba diving, beachcombing, hiking, interpretive programs. **Special Features:** Park includes 1.5 miles of beach, with tide pools, coastal caves, and offshore reefs. It is named after Leo Carrillo (1880-1961), actor, preservationist, and conservationist best known for his portrayal of Pancho, the Cisco Kid's sidekick, in an early 1950s TV series.

★1631★ LEUCADIA STATE BEACH

c/o San Diego Coast District Office
4477 Pacific Hwy
San Diego, CA 92110
Web: www.parks.ca.gov/default.asp?page_id=661
Phone: 760-633-2740
Size: 10.6 acres. **Location:** In Encinitas, west of I-5 at 948 Neptune Avenue. Beach access is via an improved trail at the foot of Leucadia Boulevard. **Facilities:** None. **Activities:** Swimming, fishing, surfing, picnicking. **Special Features:** This small rocky beach, locally known as Beacon's Beach, is operated by the city of Encinitas.

★1632★ **LIGHTHOUSE FIELD STATE BEACH**
c/o Santa Cruz District Office
303 Big Trees Park Rd
Felton, CA 95018
Web: www.parks.ca.gov/default.asp?page_id=550
Phone: 831-420-5270
Size: 37.6 acres. **Location:** On West Cliff Drive in downtown Santa Cruz; operated by the city of Santa Cruz. **Facilities:** Picnic tables, restrooms, beach access, trails, museum. **Activities:** Surfing, windsurfing, birding, hiking, bicycling. **Special Features:** Also known as Point Santa Cruz, this area forms the northern boundary of Monterey Bay and is one of the last open headlands in any California urban area. This is one of the places along the California coast where Monarch butterflies spend the winter. The rare Black Swift is also drawn to the area, and sea lions populate the offshore rocks. The lighthouse is home to California's first surfing museum, tracing more than 100 years of surfing history in Santa Cruz.

★1633★ **LIMEKILN STATE PARK**
c/o San Luis Obispo Coast District Office
750 Hearst Castle Rd
San Simeon, CA 93452
Web: www.parks.ca.gov/default.asp?page_id=577
Phone: 831-667-2403
Size: 711 acres. **Location:** 56 miles south of Carmel and 2 miles south of Lucia off Highway 1. **Facilities:** 33 family campsites, restrooms, showers, hiking trails. **Activities:** Camping, hiking, fishing. **Special Features:** This rugged area includes redwoods, crashing surf, and the unique history of limekilns, with breathtaking views of the Big Sur coast.

★1634★ **LITTLE RIVER STATE BEACH**
c/o North Coast Redwoods District Office
PO Box 2006
Eureka, CA 95502
Web: www.parks.ca.gov/default.asp?page_id=419
Phone: 707-677-3132
Size: 112 acres. **Location:** 13 miles north of Eureka and 5 miles south of Trinidad, just off US 101. **Facilities:** Beach; borders Clam Beach County Park, which has camping and day use facilities. **Special Features:** Beach features dunes and a broad open beach.

★1635★ **LOS ANGELES STATE HISTORIC PARK**
c/o Angeles District Office
1925 Las Virgenes
Calabasas, CA 91302
Web: www.parks.ca.gov/default.asp?page_id=22272
Phone: 213-620-6152
Size: 32 acres. **Location:** In Los Angeles, between North Broadway and North Spring Street, near the Los Angeles river and El Pueblo de Los Angeles Historical Monument. **Facilities:** Under development; an 18-acre interim park area includes a one-mile trail. **Activities:** Hiking, bicycling. **Special Features:** Park is the result of the efforts of a diverse coalition of local citizens, activists, and environmental justice advocates who worked together in a community effort to protect the land from industrial development and save it as a public park. The site ((formerly known as the "Cornfield Property") has significance and associations at many levels in the history of Los Angeles.

★1636★ **LOS ENCINOS STATE HISTORIC PARK**
c/o Angeles District Office
1925 Las Virgenes
Calabasas, CA 91302
Web: www.parks.ca.gov/default.asp?page_id=619
Phone: 818-784-4849
Size: 4.7 acres. **Location:** In Encino at the corner of Balboa and Ventura Boulevard. **Facilities:** Picnic areas, historic structures, exhibits (&&). **Activities:** Guided tours. **Special Features:** Park is an early California rancho that includes the original nine-room de la Osa Adobe, several other period historic structures, and a lake shaped like a Spanish guitar. The park contains exhibits on early California ranch life. This historically valuable location passed through many hands, going from Indian to Mission to Californio to French Basque control through the 19th Century.

★1637★ **LOS OSOS OAKS STATE RESERVE**
c/o San Luis Obispo Coast District
750 Hearst Castle Rd
San Simeon, CA 93452
Web: www.parks.ca.gov/default.asp?page_id=597
Phone: 805-772-7434
Size: 85 acres. **Location:** On Los Osos Valley Road in the Los Osos Valley, just outside the town of Los Osos, about halfway between Los Angeles and San Francisco. **Facilities:** Hiking and nature trails. **Activities:** Hiking, nature study. **Special Features:** Reserve features ancient sand dunes covered with centuries-old coast live oak trees. Five major plant communities thrive within the reserve: coastal sage scrub, central coastal scrub, dune oak scrub, coast live oak forest, and riparian (streamside).

★1638★ **MACKERRICHER STATE PARK**
c/o Mendocino District Office
PO Box 440
Mendocino, CA 95460
Web: www.parks.ca.gov/default.asp?page_id=436
Phone: 707-964-9112
Size: 2,519 acres. **Location:** 3 miles north of Fort Bragg on Highway 1, near the town of Cleone. **Facilities:** 139 developed family campsites (tent or RV; 8 sites &), 10 walk-in campsites, showers and restrooms, picnic area, hiking and bike trails, horse trails, nature trail (&), visitor center (&). **Activities:** Camping, fishing, hiking, horseback riding, bicycling, wildife viewing. **Special Features:** Park encompasses 8 miles of beach and bluff, headland, dune, forest, and wetlands habitats. At one time the park was part of the Mendocino Indian Reservation as well as a part of the Union Lumber Company. During winter and spring, the park's headland offers a great vantage point to view migrating whales.

9. State Parks

★1639★ MAILLARD REDWOODS STATE RESERVE

c/o Mendocino District Office
PO Box 440
Mendocino, CA 95460
Web: www.parks.ca.gov/default.asp?page_id=439
Phone: 707-937-5804
Size: 242 acres. **Location:** In Mendocino County, 20 miles northwest of Cloverdale on Fish Rock Road, 3.5 miles from Highway 128. **Special Features:** Purpose of this small reserve is to preserve and protect, in essentially natural condition, the coast redwood forest and associated wildlife habitat along the Garcia River and adjacent watersheds.

★1640★ MALAKOFF DIGGINS STATE HISTORIC PARK

c/o Sierra District Office
PO Box 266
Tahoma, CA 96142
Web: www.parks.ca.gov/default.asp?page_id=494
Phone: 530-265-2740
Size: 3,143 acres. **Location:** 26 miles northeast of Nevada City on North Bloomfield Road (steep gravel road). **Facilities:** Family and group campsites, environmental campsites, rustic cabins, picnic areas, hiking and bike trails, horseback trails, fishing pier, visitor center, exhibits (&&). **Activities:** Camping, fishing, hiking, swimming, horseback riding, mountain biking, interpretive programs (seasonal). **Special Features:** The devastating force of ''hydraulic'' mining, employed in the 1800s, is still evident in the hills of this park. The gold-mining technique which used powerful streams of water to wash away entire mountains was ended after years of legal battles between mine owners and downstream farmers and communities. The park also contains a 7,847-foot bedrock tunnel that served as a drain.

★1641★ MALIBU CREEK STATE PARK

c/o Angeles District Office
1925 Las Virgenes
Calabasas, CA 91302
Web: www.parks.ca.gov/default.asp?page_id=614
Phone: 818-880-0367
Size: 8,017 acres. **Location:** Entrance is at 1925 Las Virgenes Road, 4 miles south of Highway 101 in Calabasas. **Facilities:** 60 developed family campsites (some sites &), group camp, restrooms (&), picnic areas (&), hiking, equestrian, and mountain bike trails (15 miles), interpretive trail (&), visitor center (&), exhibits. **Activities:** Fishing, swimming, hiking, horseback riding, mountain biking, wildlife viewing, guided tours. **Special Features:** Set in the rugged Santa Monica Mountains, this area was for centuries the center of Chumash Native American life. Part of the park's land was once owned by Twentieth Century Fox, and evidence of productions such as *M*A*S*H* and *Planet of the Apes* can still be seen.

★1642★ MALIBU LAGOON STATE BEACH

c/o Angeles District Office
1925 Las Virgenes
Calabasas, CA 91302
Web: www.parks.ca.gov/default.asp?page_id=835
Phone: 818-880-0350
Size: 110 acres. **Location:** 23200 Pacific Coast Highway in Malibu. **Facilities:** Picnic areas, restrooms, trails, historic home, exhibits (&&). **Activities:** Fishing, swimming, hiking, wildlife viewing, guided tours. **Special Features:** Beach is located where Malibu Creek runs into the Pacific Ocean forming a saltwater marsh. Guided tours of the wetlands and other natural elements such as grunion, the monarch butterfly, tidepools, and gray whale are scheduled seasonally. Site also includes the historic Adamson House, built in 1929, a beachfront home that combines design motifs from several cultures, including Spanish, Moorish, and Persian.

★1643★ MANCHESTER STATE PARK

c/o Mendocino District Office
PO Box 440
Mendocino, CA 95460
Web: www.parks.ca.gov/default.asp?page_id=437
Phone: 707-937-5804
Size: 5,272 acres. **Location:** Park surrounds the town of Manchester, which is located in Mendocino County on Coast Highway 1 about 7 miles north of Point Arena; park entrance is 0.5 miles north of town. **Facilities:** Environmental campsites (family and group sites), picnic areas, hiking trails (&). **Activities:** Camping, fishing, hiking, wildlife viewing. **Special Features:** Park has 5 miles of sandy beach, sand dunes, and flat grasslands, with nearly 18,000 feet of ocean frontage. Excellent steelhead and salmon fishing are available in the park's two streams, Brush Creek and Alder Creek. The park features a variety of coastal wildflowers, including sea pinks, poppies, lupines, baby blue eyes, and blue irises. The San Andreas Fault runs into the sea at the park.

★1644★ MANDALAY STATE BEACH

c/o Channel Coast District Office
911 San Pedro St
Ventura, CA 93001
Web: www.parks.ca.gov/default.asp?page_id=609
Phone: 805-968-1033
Size: 92 acres. **Location:** In Oxnard, off US Highway 101 at the western end of Fifth Street. **Facilities:** Undeveloped. **Activities:** Swimming, fishing, beachcombing. **Special Features:** This day-use facility generally makes available to the public all beach-related recreational activities that can be accommodated without impairing the scenic or natural integrity of the site.

★1645★ MANRESA STATE BEACH

c/o Santa Cruz District Office
303 Big Trees Park Rd
Felton, CA 95018
Web: www.parks.ca.gov/default.asp?page_id=545
Phone: 831-761-1795
Size: 138 acres. **Location:** 13 miles south of Santa Cruz; from south of Aptos, take San Andreas Road southwest to Manresa. **Facilities:** 64 walk-in tent campsites, picnic tables. **Activities:** Camping, surfing, surf fishing. **Special Features:** Manresa

Beach supports coastal scrub and coastal strand plant communities and associated wildlife. Dangerous rip currents, cold temperatures, and deep offshore holes make swimming and surfing here hazardous activities for any but the most experienced surfers.

★1646★ MARCONI CONFERENCE CENTER STATE HISTORIC PARK

PO Box 789
Marshall, CA 94940
Web: www.parks.ca.gov/default.asp?page_id=467
Phone: 415-663-9020
Size: 62.4 acres. Location: Off Highway 1, 2 miles south of Marshall. Facilities: Lodging, meeting rooms, food service, jogging trail with a paracourse, volleyball and badminton courts, horseshoe pits. Activities: Bicycling, hiking, birdwatching, fishing. Special Features: Center is situated on wooded hills overlooking scenic Tomales Bay in Marin County, north of San Francisco. The site is operated as a non-profit conference facility so that the grounds are preserved and protected while historical buildings at the site are being reconstructed. This was once the site of Gugliemo Marconi's historic 1913-1920 Trans-Pacific Wireless Station, and the station's main building, which once housed station workers and Marconi's guests, is undergoing a complete restoration. When completed, the building is predicted to become a grand landmark.

★1647★ MARINA STATE BEACH

c/o Monterey District
2211 Garden Rd
Monterey, CA 93940
Web: www.parks.ca.gov/default.asp?page_id=581
Phone: 831-384-7695
Size: 171 acres. Location: At the foot of Reservation Road in Marina, 10 miles north of Monterey. Facilities: Boardwalk (&), picnic area, restrooms, concession building. Activities: Hang gliding, kite flying, radio-controlled model airplane flying. Special Features: The beach is wheelchair accessible via a boardwalk trail that winds through the Marina Dunes Natural Preserve. Water recreation here is extremely hazardous due to strong rip currents.

★1648★ MARSHALL GOLD DISCOVERY STATE HISTORIC PARK

c/o Gold Fields District Office
7806 Folsom-Auburn Rd
Folsom, CA 95630
Web: www.parks.ca.gov/default.asp?page_id=484
Phone: 530-622-3470
Size: 513 acres. Location: On Highway 49 in Coloma, between Placerville and Auburn. Facilities: Historic buildings, museum, exhibits, restrooms, picnic areas, hiking trails, nature trails (&&). Activities: Interpretive programs, living history demonstrations, guided tours, fishing, hiking, gold panning. Special Features: Park encompasses most of the historic town of Coloma, where James Marshall's discovery of gold in 1848 was the start of the famous California Gold Rush. Historic buildings on exhibit include a full-sized replica of Sutter's sawmill.

★1649★ MCARTHUR-BURNEY FALLS MEMORIAL STATE PARK

c/o Northern Buttes District Office
400 Glen Dr
Oroville, CA 95966
Web: www.parks.ca.gov/default.asp?page_id=455
Phone: 530-335-2777
Size: 910 acres. Elevation: 3,000 feet. Location: Northeast of Redding on Highway 89 near Burney, 6 miles north of Highway 299. Facilities: 128 family campsites (no hookups), 7 primitive campsites, showers, restrooms, picnic areas, hiking trails (5 miles), boat ramps, boat rentals, fishing pier, visitor center, food service, supplies (&&). Activities: Camping, fishing, hiking, swimming, boating, water-skiing, horseback riding, wildlife viewing. Special Features: Park is located on the eastern edge of the Cascade Mountains, on the Modoc plateau halfway between Mount Shasta and Lassen Peak. The park's centerpiece is a 129-foot-high waterfall, flowing at 100 million gallons of water a day. Additional water emerges from springs across the face of the falls, which joins to create a mist-filled basin of lush, green vegetation. A section of the 2,650-mile Pacific Crest Trail passes through the park (see entry in national trails section).

★1650★ MCCONNELL STATE RECREATION AREA

c/o Central Valley District Office
22708 Broadway St
Columbia, CA 95310
Web: www.parks.ca.gov/default.asp?page_id=554
Phone: 209-394-7755
Size: 74 acres. Location: 5 miles southeast of Delhi on Highway 99, south of Turlock. Facilities: Family and group campsites, modern restrooms and showers, picnic areas, children's play areas (&&). Activities: Camping, fishing, swimming. Special Features: Park is located on the banks of the Merced River where fishing is good for catfish, black bass, and perch.

★1651★ MCGRATH STATE BEACH

c/o Channel Coast District Office
911 San Pedro St
Ventura, CA 93001
Web: www.parks.ca.gov/default.asp?page_id=607
Phone: 805-654-4744
Size: 314 acres. Location: 5 miles south of Ventura off Highway 101 via Harbor Boulevard. Facilities: Family campsites and group campsites (some sites &), restrooms (&), showers, hiking and nature trails (&), beach (&), visitor center. Activities: Camping, fishing, hiking, swimming, surfing, wildlife viewing. Special Features: Beach is considered one of the best bird-watching areas in California, encompassing the riverbanks of Santa Clara River and sand dunes along the shore. A nature trail leads to the Santa Clara Estuary Natural Preserve.

★1652★ MENDOCINO HEADLANDS STATE PARK

c/o Mendocino District Office
PO Box 440
Mendocino, CA 95460
Web: www.parks.ca.gov/default.asp?page_id=442
Phone: 707-937-5804

Size: 7,709 acres. **Location:** Just off Highway 1, surrounding the town of Mendocino. **Facilities:** Visitor center, exhibits, restrooms, hiking trails (3 miles), scenic vista. **Activities:** Fishing, hiking, surfing, scuba diving, wildlife viewing. **Special Features:** Park's trails wind along the cliffs, affording spectacular views of the rugged coastline with sea arches and hidden grottos.

★1653★   MENDOCINO WOODLANDS STATE PARK

c/o Mendocino District Office
PO Box 440
Mendocino, CA 94560
Web: www.parks.ca.gov/default.asp?page_id=443
Phone: 707-937-5755
Size: 720 acres. **Location:** 9 miles east of Mendocino and 7 miles inland from the coast. **Facilities:** Three group camps, each with kitchens, dining and recreation halls, 2- and 4-bedroom cabins, and communal restrooms with hot showers; trails. **Activities:** Hiking, swimming. **Special Features:** Park is situated in the heart of a redwood forest and features 200 wood and stone buildings built by the WPA and the Civilian Conservation Corps (CCC) in the 1930s. Buildings throughout the Park feature walls of old growth redwood, hand-hewn beams, and hand-crafted stone fireplaces.

★1654★   MILLERTON LAKE STATE RECREATION
   AREA

c/o San Joaquin District
PO Box 205
Friant, CA 93626
Web: www.parks.ca.gov/default.asp?page_id=587
Phone: 559-822-2225
Size: 6,857 acres. **Location:** 20 miles northeast of Fresno via Highway 41 and Highway 145. **Facilities:** 148 developed family campsites (27 with electrical hookups; 11 ♿ sites), 2 group campgrounds, 25 boat-in campsites, showers, restrooms (♿), picnic areas (♿), hiking and mountain biking trails, 3 boat launch ramps, marina, boat rentals, exhibit center. **Activities:** Camping, fishing, hiking, swimming, boating, windsurfing, wildlife viewing. **Special Features:** Park has more than 40 miles of shore land for water sports, and the hills surrounding the lake provide good hiking opportunities. During winter, special boat tours are offered for viewing bald and golden eagles. Park also contains the original Millerton County courthouse, built in 1867.

★1655★   MONO LAKE TUFA STATE RESERVE

PO Box 99
Lee Vining, CA 93541
Web: www.parks.ca.gov/default.asp?page_id=514
Phone: 760-647-6331
Size: 55,300 acres. **Location:** On Highway 395, 13 miles east of Yosemite National Park, near the town of Lee Vining. **Facilities:** Trails, picnic areas. **Activities:** Hiking, swimming, boating, cross-country skiing, wildlife viewing, guided tours. **Special Features:** Surrounded by the Sierra Crest, volcanoes, and the Great Basin desert, the Reserve offers spectacular scenery, including unusual tufa formations that have developed under the lake's surface. These "tufa towers" are calcium-carbonate spires and knobs formed by interaction of freshwater springs

and alkaline lake water. The ancient Mono Lake, more than a million years old, is one of the oldest in North America and is about 2.5 times as salty and 80 times as alkaline as the ocean.

★1656★   MONTAÑA DE ORO STATE PARK

c/o San Luis Obispo Coast District Office
750 Hearst Castle Rd
San Simeon, CA 93452
Web: www.parks.ca.gov/default.asp?page_id=592
Phone: 805-528-0513
Size: 8,357 acres. **Location:** 6 miles southwest of Morro Bay and 7 miles south of Los Osos on Pecho Road. **Facilities:** Primitive, environmental, and equestrian campsites, restrooms, picnic areas, trails, visitor center. **Activities:** Camping, fishing, hiking, mountain biking, horseback riding, wildlife viewing. **Special Features:** Park features rugged cliffs, secluded sandy beaches, coastal plains, streams, canyons, and hills, including 1,347-foot Valencia Peak. The park's name, "Mountain of Gold," comes from the golden wildflowers that bloom in spring.

★1657★   MONTARA STATE BEACH

c/o Santa Cruz District Office
303 Big Trees Park Rd
Felton, CA 94018
Web: www.parks.ca.gov/default.asp?page_id=532
Phone: 650-726-8819
Size: 780 acres. **Location:** 8 miles north of Half Moon Bay on Highway 1. **Facilities:** Trails, beach. **Activities:** Surf fishing, hiking, mountain biking, horseback riding, tide pool exploring. **Special Features:** Beach is bounded by low hills both to the north and south. Point Montara (see separate entry) has a lighthouse with overnight accommodations. Montara Mountain, which is part of the State Beach, is a northern spur of the Santa Cruz Mountains and features the only undisturbed coastal mountain habitat found over 100 miles of coastline.

★1658★   MONTEREY STATE BEACH

c/o Monterey District Office
2211 Garden Rd
Monterey, CA 93940
Web: www.parks.ca.gov/default.asp?page_id=576
Phone: 831-384-7695
Size: 100 acres. **Location:** At the Seaside exit off Highway 218, west of Highway 1. **Facilities:** Picnic areas, hiking trails, beach, restrooms. **Activities:** Fishing, kayaking, hiking, tide pool exploring, surfing, scuba diving, kite flying, volleyball, beachcombing. **Special Features:** The park includes 3 separate beaches, approximately a mile apart.

★1659★   MONTEREY STATE HISTORIC PARK

c/o Monterey District Office
2211 Garden Rd
Monterey, CA 93940
Web: www.parks.ca.gov/default.asp?page_id=575
Phone: 831-649-7118
Size: 9.7 acres. **Location:** 20 Custom House Plaza in Monterey.

9. State Parks

Facilities: Historic buildings, museum, exhibits, restrooms, icnic areas, food services, trails (&&). **Activities:** Guided tours, picnicking, fishing, hiking. **Special Features:** Monterey is a showplace of early California history, having served as capitol under Spanish, Mexican, and US rule. Ten buildings, including the Custom House built in 1827 and California's First Theatre (1846-47), as well as several residences built in the 1830s, preserve the area's rich history.

★1660★ MONTGOMERY WOODS STATE RESERVE

c/o Mendocino District Office
PO Box 440
Mendocino, CA 95460
Web: www.parks.ca.gov/default.asp?page_id=434
Phone: 707-937-5804
Size: 2,581 acres. **Location:** 15 miles east of the town of Comptche; or 13 miles west from Ukiah, past Orr's Mineral Hot Springs resort. **Facilities:** Picnic areas, hiking and nature trails. **Activities:** Hiking, picnicking. **Special Features:** One of the more remote of California's redwood parks, Montgomery Woods' groves include the two main species of redwoods of the western United States, the Sierra Redwood and the Coast Redwood. The reserve is also a fern forest.

★1661★ MOONLIGHT STATE BEACH

c/o San Diego Coast District Office
4477 Pacific Hwy
San Diego, CA 92110
Web: www.parks.ca.gov/default.asp?page_id=659
Phone: 858-642-4200
Size: 12.7 acres. **Location:** West of I-5 on Encinitas Boulevard in Encinitas. **Facilities:** Beach, tennis and volleyball courts, snack bar, recreational equipment rentals. **Activities:** Swimming, surfing, fishing, tennis, volleyball. **Special Features:** This wide, sandy beach has been known as Moonlight Beach since the early 1900s when local residents came to the area for midnight picnics.

★1662★ MORRO BAY STATE PARK

c/o San Luis Obispo Coast District Office
750 Hearst Castle Rd
San Simeon, CA 93452
Web: www.parks.ca.gov/default.asp?page_id=594
Phone: 805-772-7434
Size: 2,785 acres. **Location:** From Highway 1, exit at the Los Osos - Baywood Park offramp and go left about 1 mile. **Facilities:** 135 campsites (30 with water and electrical hookups), 2 group camps, pay showers, restrooms, picnic facilities, hiking/mountain biking trails, nature trails, marina, mooring space, canoe and kayak rentals, food service, 18-hole golf course, museum (&&). **Activities:** Camping, fishing, golf, hiking, mountain biking, swimming, boating, sailing, birding, interpretive programs. **Special Features:** Park includes a lagoon and natural bay habitat, and a saltwater marsh that supports a thriving bird population. The bay's most prominent feature is Morro Rock. The Museum of Natural History is located at the park, with exhibits covering natural and cultural history, Native American life, geology, and oceanography.

★1663★ MORRO STRAND STATE BEACH

c/o San Luis Obispo Coast District Office
750 Hearst Castle Rd
San Simeon, CA 93452
Web: www.parks.ca.gov/default.asp?page_id=593
Phone: 805-772-7434
Size: 183 acres. **Location:** 2 miles south of Cayucos on Highway 1. **Facilities:** Family campsites, picnic areas. **Activities:** Camping, fishing, swimming, surfing, windsurfing, kite flying. **Special Features:** This coastal park includes a 3-mile stretch of beach. Kite flying is popular here due to the reliable wind gusts.

★1664★ MOSS LANDING STATE BEACH

c/o Monterey District Office
2211 Garden Rd
Monterey, CA 93940
Web: www.parks.ca.gov/default.asp?page_id=574
Phone: 831-384-7695
Size: 60 acres. **Location:** On Jetty Road in Moss Landing, 16 miles north of Monterey via Highway 1. **Facilities:** Trails. **Activities:** Fishing, surfing, windsurfing, picnicking, hiking, horseback riding, birding. **Special Features:** Surfing and surf fishing are popular here, but water recreation is dangerous because of strong rip currents. Picnicking on the beach is also popular, because the dunes protect it from afternoon winds. The area is also an important migratory stop along the Pacific Flyway.

★1665★ MOUNT DIABLO STATE PARK

c/o Diablo Vista District Office
845 Casa Grande Rd
Petaluma, CA 94954
Web: www.parks.ca.gov/default.asp?page_id=517
Phone: 925-837-2525
Size: 20,103 acres. **Elevation:** 3,849 feet. **Location:** 5 miles east of I-680 in Danville, on Mount Diablo Scenic Boulevard. **Facilities:** 56 campsites with hot showers and flush toilets, group camping sites (some with horse facilities), restrooms, showers, picnic areas (&), trails, museum/visitor center (&), interpretive center (&), exhibits and displays, gift shop. **Activities:** Camping, hiking, horseback riding, mountain biking, rock climbing, wildlife watching. **Special Features:** The summit of Mount Diablo affords a spectacular 360-degree panoramic view of more than 20,000 square miles of California, including Lassen Peak, the Farallon Islands, the Sierra Nevada, and San Francisco's Golden Gate Bridge. The park's extensive trails also feature good viewing locations.

★1666★ MOUNT SAN JACINTO STATE PARK

c/o Inland Empire District Office
17801 Lake Perris Dr
Perris, CA 92571
Web: www.parks.ca.gov/default.asp?page_id=636
Phone: 951-659-2607
Size: 13,718 acres. **Elevation:** 6,000-10,000 feet. **Location:** Off Highway 243 near Idyllwild. **Facilities:** 81 developed campsites (31 with hot showers and flush toilets, 50 with vault toilets), 48 primitive wilderness campsites (hike-in), group wilderness

sites (maximum of 15 people per group), picnic areas, trails, visitor center, food service, gift shop, aerial tram. Permit required for wilderness camping. **Activities:** Camping, hiking, backpacking, horseback riding, cross-country skiing, wildlife viewing. **Special Features:** Mount San Jacinto stands at 10,804 feet in an area of magnificent granite peaks, subalpine forests, and fern-bordered mountain meadows. Most of the park is a designated wilderness area used by hikers and backpackers; a segment of the 2,650-mile Pacific Crest Trail passes through the park (see entry in national trails section). An aerial tram from Palm Springs takes passengers from Valley Station (2,643 feet) to Mountain Station (8,516 feet) along the edge of the wilderness area.

★1667★ MOUNT TAMALPAIS STATE PARK

c/o North Bay District Office
PO Box 123
Duncan Mills, CA 95430
Web: www.parks.ca.gov/default.asp?page_id=471
Phone: 415-388-2070
Size: 6,243 acres. **Elevation:** 0-2,571 feet. **Location:** At 801 Panoramic Highway in Mill Valley, north of San Francisco's Golden Gate; from Highway 101 take Highway 1 to the Stinson Beach Exit and follow signs up the mountain. **Facilities:** 16 developed walk-in campsites, 10 rustic cabins, picnic areas, trails (50+ miles), visitor center, exhibits, food service, 3,750-seat stone amphitheater, restrooms (&&). **Activities:** Camping, fishing, hiking, horseback riding, mountain biking, wildlife viewing, interpretive programs. **Special Features:** Park includes 6,300 acres of redwood groves and oak woodlands, with a spectacular view from the 2,571-foot peak of Mount Tamalpais. On a clear day visitors can see the Farallon Islands 25 miles out to sea, the Marin County Hills, San Francisco and the bay, and Mount Diablo.

★1668★ NATURAL BRIDGES STATE BEACH

c/o Santa Cruz District Office
303 Big Trees Park Rd
Felton, CA 95018
Web: www.parks.ca.gov/default.asp?page_id=541
Phone: 831-423-4609
Size: 59 acres. **Location:** On West Cliff Drive in Santa Cruz. **Facilities:** Beach, picnic areas, trails, visitor center, bookstore, restrooms (&&). **Activities:** Fishing, swimming, windsurfing, hiking, wildlife viewing, interpretive programs. **Special Features:** Named for the picturesque water-worn rock formations just off its coastal bluffs, the beach property includes Monarch Butterfly Natural Preserve, winter home to some 100,000 Monarch butterflies every year.

★1669★ NAVARRO RIVER REDWOODS STATE PARK

c/o Mendocino District Office
PO Box 440
Mendocino, CA 95460
Web: www.parks.ca.gov/default.asp?page_id=435
Phone: 707-937-5804
Size: 727 acres. **Location:** On Highway 128, 5 miles west of Boonville. **Facilities:** 25 developed campsites, 10 primitive campsites, picnic areas. **Activities:** Camping, fishing, swimming, canoeing. **Special Features:** Park lies alongside the crystal-clear waters of the Navarro River, with walking paths through redwood groves. During summer, the weather here is considerably warmer than on the coast.

★1670★ NEW BRIGHTON STATE BEACH

c/o Santa Cruz District Office
303 Big Trees Park Rd
Felton, CA 95018
Web: www.parks.ca.gov/default.asp?page_id=542
Phone: 831-464-6330
Size: 157 acres. **Location:** In the town of Capitola, 4 miles south of Santa Cruz on Highway 1. **Facilities:** Tent and RV campsites (including 10 RV sites with hookups; some sites &), picnic areas, hiking trails, restrooms (&). **Activities:** Camping, fishing, swimming, hiking. **Special Features:** Near the beach is a forest of Monterey pine and coastal live oak. The camping area is on a bluff overlooking northern Monterey Bay.

★1671★ OCEANO DUNES STATE VEHICULAR RECREATION AREA

c/o Oceano Dunes District Office
575 Camino Mercado
Arroyo Grande, CA 93420
Web: www.parks.ca.gov/default.asp?page_id=406
Phone: 805-473-7230
Size: 2,685 acres. **Location:** In Oceano, 3 miles south of the city of Pismo Beach, off Highway 1. **Facilities:** Primitive camping on beach and open dune area, vault and chemical toilets, picnic areas, trails, beach wheelchair rentals. **Activities:** Camping, OHV riding, hiking, swimming, surf fishing, horseback riding, bird watching. **Special Features:** Area is among the most popular and unique of California state parks, attracting visitors from across the United States. Five and a half miles of beach are open for vehicle use, and 1,500 acres of sand dunes are available for off-highway motor vehicle riding. Oceano Dunes is the only California state park where vehicles may be driven on the beach. Four wheel drive vehicles are recommended for driving to the camping and off highway vehicle use areas in the park. OHV's must be transported to this point before unloading.

★1672★ OCOTILLO WELLS STATE VEHICULAR RECREATION AREA

c/o Ocotillo Wells District Office
PO Box 356
Borrego Springs, CA 92004
Web: www.parks.ca.gov/default.asp?page_id=407
Phone: 760-767-5391
Size: 54,198 acres. **Location:** 35 miles east of Julian via Highway 78, or about 20 miles west of Highway 86. **Facilities:** Picnic tables, pay showers; no drinking water. **Activities:** Tent camping, ORV riding. **Special Features:** Ocotillo Wells SVRA is a motorcycle, four-wheel drive, all-terrain vehicle, and dune buggy use area, with more than 70,000 acres of desert available for off-highway exploration and recreation. The wash-and-ridge

9. State Parks

terrain includes a butte with dunes and a sand bowl, a blow-sand dune, springs, and a camp on a former homestead site. Area is adjacent to Anza-Borrego Desert State Park (see separate entry).

★1673★ OLD SACRAMENTO STATE HISTORIC PARK

c/o Capital District Office
101 J St
Sacramento, CA 95814
Web: www.parks.ca.gov/default.asp?page_id=497
Phone: 916-442-7644
Size: 293 acres. **Location:** Downtown Sacramento; take I-5 to J Street exit and follow signs to historic district. **Facilities:** Historic buildings, museum, visitor center, exhibits, restrooms, food service, picnic areas, bike trails (&&). **Special Features:** Park is part of the Old Sacramento Historic District, all of which has been designated a National Historic Landmark. The park includes original and reconstructed Gold Rush-era buildings, displays, shops, and the California State Railroad Museum. Among the historic structures is the Big Four Building, where much of the transcontinental railroad was planned, and the BF Hastings Building, which was the western terminus of the Pony Express.

★1674★ OLD TOWN SAN DIEGO STATE HISTORIC PARK

c/o San Diego Coast District Office
4477 Pacific Hwy
San Diego, CA 92110
Web: www.parks.ca.gov/default.asp?page_id=663
Phone: 619-220-5422; **Fax:** 619-688-3229; **Toll Free:** 800-777-0369
Size: 29 acres. **Location:** On San Diego Avenue and Twiggs Street in San Diego. **Facilities:** Historic buildings, visitor center, exhibits, restaurants, shops, restrooms, picnic areas (&&). **Activities:** Guided tours. **Special Features:** San Diego became California's first Spanish settlement when a mission and fort were established there in 1769. The historic park recreates life in the Mexican and early American periods of 1821 to 1872. Historic buildings include homes with artifacts that reflect ordinary life of the period, a schoolhouse, a blacksmith shop, San Diego's first newspaper office, and a stable with a carriage collection. Five original adobes are part of the complex.

★1675★ OLOMPALI STATE HISTORIC PARK

PO Box 1016
Novato, CA 94948
Web: www.parks.ca.gov/default.asp?page_id=465
Phone: 415-892-3383
Size: 700 acres. **Location:** On US 101, 3 miles north of Novato. **Facilities:** Picnic area, hiking and horseback trails, visitor center, exhibits; no drinking water available. **Activities:** Hiking, horseback riding, guided tours. **Special Features:** Park is on land that once supported a large village of the Coast Miwok Indians. Discovery here of a 16th-century English coin suggests that villagers may have had contact with either Sir Francis Drake or with people who had traded with the early English explorer.

A project is underway to build several structures representative of a Coast Miwok village, which will be used as an interpretive and educational site.

★1676★ PACHECO STATE PARK

c/o Central Valley District Office
22708 Broadway St
Columbia, CA 95310
Web: www.parks.ca.gov/default.asp?page_id=560
Phone: 209-826-6283
Size: 6,894 acres. **Location:** 24 miles west of Los Banos or 20 miles east of Gilroy, at 38787 Dinosaur Point Road in Hollister, off Highway 152. **Facilities:** Trails (28 miles); no drinking water. **Activities:** Hiking, horseback riding, mountain biking. **Special Features:** Park is the last remaining section of a Mexican land grant under which Francisco Pacheco and his son built the first house in Merced County in 1843. Among the historic features of the park are an old line shack used by Henry Miller's cattle company in the late 1800s, part of the old Butterfield stage line route, and the remains of the original Pacheco adobe. Only about a third of the park's property (2,600 acres) is open for public use at present.

★1677★ PACIFICA STATE BEACH

c/o Santa Cruz District Office
303 Big Trees Park Rd
Felton, CA 95018
Web: www.parks.ca.gov/default.asp?page_id=524
Phone: 650-738-7381
Size: 20.7 acres. **Location:** Off Highway 1 in downtown Pacifica. **Facilities:** Beach. **Special Features:** This wide, crescent-shaped beach marks the northern gateway to the coastline that stretches south of San Francisco.

★1678★ PALOMAR MOUNTAIN STATE PARK

c/o Colorado Desert District Office
200 Palm Canyon Dr
Borrego Springs, CA 92004
Web: www.parks.ca.gov/default.asp?page_id=637
Phone: 760-742-3462
Size: 1,909 acres. **Elevation:** Average of 5,000 feet. **Location:** Off Highway 76, up Highway S6, then left on Highway S7 at the junction near the mountaintop. **Facilities:** 31 family campsites with hot showers and flush toilets, 3 group camps, stocked pond, picnic areas, hiking/nature trails. **Activities:** Camping, fishing, hiking, wildlife viewing, interpretive programs. **Special Features:** Park preserves some of the finest coniferous woodland in the Peninsular Range and offers spectacular views of the Pacific Ocean when coastal fog is not present. In 1928, the builders of what was then the world's largest telescope selected 6,100-foot Mount Palomar for their observatory. The observatory (located outside the park's boundaries) is open to the public.

★1679★ PATRICK'S POINT STATE PARK

4150 Patrick's Point Dr
Trinidad, CA 95570
Web: www.parks.ca.gov/default.asp?page_id=417
Phone: 707-677-3570

9. State Parks

Size: 652 acres **Location:** 25 miles north of Eureka on US 101. **Facilities:** Family and group campsites, showers, restrooms, picnic areas, hiking trails (6 miles), visitor center, exhibits (க்க்). **Activities:** Camping, fishing, hiking, wildlife viewing, agate hunting, guided tours, interpretive programs. **Special Features:** Located in the heart of California's coast redwood country, the park features a reconstructed Yurok Indian Village and a native plant garden, as well as Agate Beach, where visitors can hunt for semi-precious stones at low tide. A dramatic shoreline ranging from broad sandy beaches to sheer cliffs that rise high above the Pacific Ocean offers great opportunities to explore tide pools, search for agates and driftwood, or watch whales and sea lions.

★1680★   PELICAN STATE BEACH

c/o North Coast Redwoods District Office
PO Box 2006
Eureka, CA 95502
Web: www.parks.ca.gov/default.asp?page_id=412
Phone: 707-464-6101
Size: 5.2 acres. **Location:** 21 miles north of Crescent City on US 101. **Facilities:** Undeveloped. **Activities:** Fishing, picnicking, beachcombing. **Special Features:** Situated on the Oregon border, this small, secluded beach is California's northernmost state beach.

★1681★   PESCADERO STATE BEACH

c/o Santa Cruz District Office
303 Big Trees Park Rd
Felton, CA 95018
Web: www.parks.ca.gov/default.asp?page_id=522
Phone: 650-726-8819
Size: 700 acres. **Location:** 14.5 miles south of Half Moon Bay on Highway 1. **Facilities:** Picnic area, hiking trails. **Activities:** Fishing, hiking, birding, wildlife viewing. **Special Features:** Beach's mile-long shoreline includes sandy coves, rocky cliffs, and tide pools. Across the highway is Pescadero Marsh Natural Preserve, a refuge for blue heron, kites, deer, raccoons, foxes, and other wildlife. Dogs are prohibited on the beach or in the Preserve at all times.

★1682★   PETALUMA ADOBE STATE HISTORIC
   PARK

c/o Diablo Vista District Office
845 Casa Grande Rd
Petaluma, CA 94954
Web: www.parks.ca.gov/default.asp?page_id=474
Phone: 707-762-4871
Size: 41 acres. **Location:** At the east edge of Petaluma, off Highway 116 and Adobe Road. **Facilities:** Historic site, exhibits, picnic areas. **Activities:** Guided tours. **Special Features:** General Mariano Guadalupe Vallejo's adobe, the largest private rancho in California between 1834 and 1846, was the center of activity on one of the most prosperous private estates established during the Mexican period. The adobe contains authentic furniture and exhibits depicting early rancho life.

★1683★   PFEIFFER BIG SUR STATE PARK

c/o Monterey District Office
2211 Garden Rd
Monterey, CA 93940
Web: www.parks.ca.gov/default.asp?page_id=570
Phone: 831-667-2315
Size: 1,107 acres. **Location:** 26 miles south of Carmel on Highway 1. **Facilities:** Family and group campsites; lodge with 61 guest rooms, conference center, meeting rooms, cafe, and grocery store; picnic areas, hiking trails, self-guided nature trail (க்க்). **Activities:** Camping, hiking, swimming. **Special Features:** Park features redwoods, conifers, oaks, open meadows and great views of the Pacific and Big Sur gorge.

★1684★   PICACHO STATE RECREATION AREA

c/o Colorado Desert District Office
200 Palm Canyon Dr
Borrego Springs, CA 92004
Web: www.picacho.statepark.org
Phone: 760-393-3052
Size: 6,759 acres. **Location:** 24 miles off Interstate 8, north of Winterhaven, just east of Yuma, AZ. Park's remote location requires visitors to drive over 18 miles of dirt roads that are passable for cars and vehicles with trailers and motorhomes, but can be impassable in summer thunderstorms. Travelers on this road should carry extra water and other essential supplies. **Facilities:** 54 primitive family campsites (1 site க்), group camp, 2 boat-in group camps, solar showers, chemical toilets (க்), picnic areas (க்), hiking trails, boat ramps. **Activities:** Camping, fishing, hiking, boating, swimming, water-skiing, wildlife viewing, guided tours. **Special Features:** Area was the site of a gold mining town in the 1800s, and visitors can hike to the ruins of the mill sites. Eight miles of the lower Colorado River are the recreation area's eastern border, providing opportunities for fishing and water sports. Temperatures at Picacho range from a wintertime low of 20 degrees to a summertime high of 120; the ideal time to visit is from mid-October to the end of April.

★1685★   PIGEON POINT LIGHT STATION STATE
   HISTORIC PARK

210 Pigeon Point Rd
Pescadero, CA 94060
Web: www.parks.ca.gov/default.asp?page_id=533
Phone: 650-879-0633
Size: 75.5 acres. **Location:** On Highway 1, 20 miles south of Half Moon Bay and 27 miles north of Santa Cruz. **Facilities:** Historic structures, youth hostel, visitor center, hiking trails, picnic areas. **Activities:** Guided tours, fishing, hiking. **Special Features:** Set on a cliff on the central California coast, the 115-foot lighthouse is one of the tallest in the US. It is currently closed for restoration, but the grounds remain open. The restored lighthouse keeper's house is operated as a youth hostel.

★1686★   PIO PICO STATE HISTORIC PARK

c/o Angeles District Office
1925 Las Virgenes
Calabasas, CA 91302
Web: www.parks.ca.gov/default.asp?page_id=621
Phone: 562-695-1217

Size: 3.4 acres. **Location:** In Whittier, west of I-605 at Pioneer and Whittier boulevards. **Facilities:** Historic home, picnic areas (&&). **Activities:** Guided tours. **Special Features:** Park commemorates the life of California's last Mexican governor before the American takeover of 1846. Once the headquarters of Pico's 8,894-acre ranch, the park includes a 19th century adobe that has recently been structurally stabilized, and facilities and grounds that have been completely renovated.

★1687★ PISMO STATE BEACH

c/o Oceano Dunes District Office
575 Camino Mercado
Arroyo Grande, CA 93420
Web: www.parks.ca.gov/default.asp?page_id=595
Phone: 805-489-2684
Size: 1,343 acres. **Location:** Off Highway 1 in the town of Oceano. **Facilities:** Family campsites (including RV hookups), showers, restrooms, picnic areas, trails (including a paved nature trail), nature center, exhibits (&&). **Activities:** Camping, surf fishing, swimming, surfing, hiking, horseback riding, wildlife viewing, clamming, interpretive programs. **Special Features:** Park has six miles of sandy beach and tree-lined dunes, as well as a nature center. This park is one of the largest over-wintering monarch butterfly sites in the US.

★1688★ PLACERITA CANYON STATE PARK

c/o Angeles District Office
1925 Las Virgenes
Calabasas, CA 91302
Web: www.parks.ca.gov/default.asp?page_id=622
Phone: 213-620-6152
Size: 342 acres. **Location:** In Los Angeles County, at 19152 Placerita Canyon Road, Newhall, CA. **Facilities:** Nature center and natural area. **Activities:** Hiking, picnicking, interpretive and educational programs. **Special Features:** Park preserves and protects the site of the first discovery of gold in California, in 1842. Designated as a State Historic Landmark, the park is situated in the transition zone between the San Gabrial Mountains and the Mojave Desert and contains sandstone formations, streams, and woodlands. Park is operated by Los Angeles County and includes a nature center with gardens (including one of the largest displays of camellias in the world), a lake, and pools and waterfalls.

★1689★ PLUMAS-EUREKA STATE PARK

310 Johnsville Rd
Blairsden, CA 96103
Web: www.parks.ca.gov/default.asp?page_id=507
Phone: 530-836-2380
Size: 4,424 acres. **Location:** 5 miles west of Blairsden on County Road A-14. **Facilities:** Historic buildings, family and group campsites, picnic areas, hiking and nature trails, restrooms, visitor center, exhibits (&&). **Activities:** Camping, fishing, hiking, mountain biking, downhill skiing, cross-country skiing, guided tours (seasonal), demonstrations. **Special Features:** Mining began here in the 1850s and continued until World War II. The focal point of the park is museum building, which was originally constructed as the miners' bunkhouse and

now serves as the park's visitor center. Other historic buildings, which have been maintained in a "near restored" condition, include stamp mills, stable, mine office, and the blacksmith shop.

★1690★ POINT DUME STATE BEACH

c/o Angeles District Office
1925 Las Virgenes
Calabasas, CA 91302
Web: www.parks.ca.gov/default.asp?page_id=623
Phone: 310-457-8143
Size: 36 acres. **Location:** At the south end of Westward Beach Road in Malibu. **Facilities:** Undeveloped beach and nature preserve with trails. **Activities:** Fishing, swimming, surfing, scuba diving, hiking, whale watching (December to March). **Special Features:** Adjacent to the beach area is Point Dume State Preserve, an area of headlands, cliffs, rocky coves, and beach access. On a clear day, visitors can enjoy a scenic view of the entire Santa Monica Bay, north Malibu Coast, inland Santa Monica Mountains, and distant Catalina Island.

★1691★ POINT LOBOS RANCH

c/o Monterey District Office
2211 Garden Rd
Monterey, CA 93940
Web: www.parks.ca.gov/default.asp?page_id=569
Phone: 831-624-4909
Size: 1,329 acres. **Location:** South of Monterey, in Carmel-by-the-Sea. **Facilities:** Under development. **Special Features:** This property is new and not yet open to the public. Its purpose is to preserve an extremely scenic portion of the northern Big Sur Coast, an area offering spectacular views of Carmel Bay and the Pacific Ocean coastline. The property contains one of the world's largest native Monterey Pine forests, examples of the rare Gowen cypress, and areas of the rare maritime chaparral plant community. It also provides mountain lion habitat.

★1692★ POINT LOBOS STATE RESERVE

c/o Monterey District Office
2211 Garden Rd
Monterey, CA 93940
Web: www.parks.ca.gov/default.asp?page_id=571
Phone: 831-624-4909
Size: 1,325 acres. **Location:** In Monterey County, 3 miles south of Carmel on Highway 1. **Facilities:** Picnic areas, restrooms, trails (&&). **Activities:** Hiking, wildlife viewing, scuba diving, guided tours. **Special Features:** Once the home of a turn-of-the-century whaling and abalone industry, Reserve contains headlands, coves, and rolling meadows and is known for its exceptional beauty. Wildlife includes seals, sea lions, sea otters, and migrating gray whales (from December to May), and thousands of seabirds also make the reserve their home. The offshore area, popular with divers, forms one of the richest underwater habitats in the world.

★1693★ POINT MONTARA LIGHT STATION

c/o Santa Cruz District Office
303 Big Trees Park Rd
Felton, CA 95018
Web: www.parks.ca.gov/default.asp?page_id=534
Phone: 650-728-7177

9. State Parks

Size: 6 acres. **Location:** 25 miles south of San Francisco on Highway 1 between Montara and Moss Beach. **Facilities:** 45-bed youth hostel (&), picnic areas. **Special Features:** Point Montara Fog Signal and Light Station was established in 1875. The historic lighthouse and turn-of-the-century buildings have been restored and are operated by Hostelling International-American Youth Hostels and California State Parks, in cooperation with the US Coast Guard.

★1694★ POINT MUGU STATE PARK

c/o Angeles District Office
1925 Las Virgenes
Calabasas, CA 91302
Web: www.parks.ca.gov/default.asp?page_id=630
Phone: 805-488-5223
Size: 13,947 acres. **Location:** 15 miles south of Oxnard on Highway 1. **Facilities:** Family campsites (tent and RV; some @ sites), group campsites, picnic areas (&), trails (70+ miles). **Activities:** Camping, surf fishing, hiking, swimming, body surfing, horseback riding, bicycling, wildlife viewing. **Special Features:** Located in the Santa Monica Mountains, the park features five miles of ocean shoreline with sandy beaches, sand dunes, rocky bluffs, rugged hills and uplands, two river canyons, and wide grassy valleys. Park also encompasses the jagged pinnacles of the Boney Mountains State Wilderness Area.

★1695★ POINT SAL STATE BEACH

c/o Channel Coast District Office
911 San Pedro St
Ventura, CA 93001
Web: www.parks.ca.gov/default.asp?page_id=605
Phone: 805-733-3713
Size: 84 acres. **Location:** In the northwestern part of Santa Barbara County, near the city of Guadalupe. **Facilities:** None. In addition, portions of the main access road were destroyed by heavy rains in 1998, and the beach remains inaccessible. **Activities:** When accessible, activities have included fishing, beachcombing, hiking, nature study, and picnicking. Because of extremely dangerous rip currents, occasional shark sightings, and the absence of lifeguard service, swimming is not recommended. Persons found camping in the park are subject to citation, arrest, or eviction by Park Rangers. Because of security concerns at adjacent Vandenberg Air Force Base, Air Police also strictly enforce the no camping rule. **Special Features:** Park includes 2 miles of ocean frontage. Lands above the beach and rocky shoreline have extremely steep slopes, and numerous landslides are evident. Prime examples of coastal sage and chaparral communities occur on these slopes. Views of the coastline, beach, and rugged mountain slopes are exceptional.

★1696★ POINT SUR STATE HISTORIC PARK

c/o Monterey District Office
2211 Garden Rd
Monterey, CA 93940
Web: www.parks.ca.gov/default.asp?page_id=565
Phone: 831-625-4419
Size: 92 acres. **Location:** 19 miles south of Carmel off Highway 1. **Facilities:** Historic structures, restrooms. **Activities:** Guided tours. **Special Features:** Point Sur is the only complete turn-of-the century Lightstation open to the public in California and is on the *National Register of Historic Places*. First lit on August 1, 1889, the lighthouse has remained in continuous operation. The Lightstation buildings are currently being restored to their turn-of-the-century appearance. The Lightstation is open to the public only through docent-led tours (year round on week-ends and seasonally on Wednesdays).

★1697★ POMPONIO STATE BEACH

c/o Santa Cruz District Office
303 Big Trees Park Rd
Felton, CA 95018
Web: www.parks.ca.gov/default.asp?page_id=521
Phone: 831-335-6318
Size: 421 acres. **Location:** 12 miles south of Half Moon Bay along Highway 1. **Facilities:** Picnic area, trails, restrooms. **Activities:** Fishing, hiking, picnicking. **Special Features:** Day-use beach offers access to miles of gently sloping, sandy beaches at the base of high sandstone bluffs.

★1698★ PORTOLA REDWOODS STATE PARK

c/o Santa Cruz District Office
303 Big Trees Park Rd
Felton, CA 95018
Web: www.parks.ca.gov/default.asp?page_id=539
Phone: 650-948-9098
Size: 2,608 acres. **Location:** On Portola State Park Road, 3 miles west of Highway 35 via Alpine Road. **Facilities:** 53 developed family campsites, 3 group campgrounds (tents only), 6 hike-in campsites, showers, picnic areas, hiking trails (18 miles), nature trails, visitor center. **Activities:** Camping, hiking. **Special Features:** A rugged, natural basin forested by Douglas firs, oaks, and giant coast redwoods, park includes one of the tallest redwoods (300 feet high) in the Santa Cruz Mountains. Trails crisscross the canyon and its two streams, Peters Creek and Pescadero Creek.

★1699★ PRAIRIE CITY STATE VEHICULAR RECREATION AREA

c/o Twin Cities District Office
13300 White Rock Rd
Rancho Cordova, CA 95742
Web: www.parks.ca.gov/default.asp?page_id=411
Phone: 916-985-7378
Size: 2,785 acres. **Location:** At the base of the Sierra Nevada foothills, 20 miles east of downtown Sacramento and 3 miles south of Highway 50. **Facilities:** OHV trails, motocross track, race tracks, picnic areas, restrooms, supplies. **Activities:** OHV riding. **Special Features:** Site features motorcycle, ATV, and 4-wheel-drive open areas as well as a midget track, go-cart track, clay oval track, mud drags, and a four-wheel drive obstacle course.

★1700★ PRAIRIE CREEK REDWOODS STATE PARK

c/o North Coast Redwoods District Office
PO Box 2006
Eureka, CA 95502
Web: www.parks.ca.gov/default.asp?page_id=415
Phone: 707-464-6101

9. State Parks

Size: 14,187 acres. **Location:** 50 miles north of Eureka and 25 miles south of Crescent City on Newton B. Drury Scenic Parkway off of Highway 101. **Facilities:** 100 developed family campsites, environmental campsites, 3 hike/bike campgrounds, picnic areas, trails (75 miles), visitor center, exhibits, nature store (&&). **Activities:** Camping, fishing, hiking, bicycling, backpacking, wildlife viewing, birding, interpretive programs, guided walks. **Special Features:** One of California's most popular redwood parks, Prairie Creek features herds of Roosevelt elk and a network of trails, including accessible trails for individuals with physical or visual limitations. Near the north end of Gold Bluffs Beach is Fern Canyon, a narrow canyon whose high, vertical walls are completely covered with ferns. Together, Prairie Creek Redwoods State Park, Jedediah Smith Redwoods State Park, Del Norte Coast Redwoods State Park, and Redwood National Park (see separate entries) are managed cooperatively by the National Park Service and the California Department of Parks and Recreation. These parks make up 45 percent of all the old-growth redwood forest remaining in California.

★1701★ PROVIDENCE MOUNTAINS STATE RECREATION AREA

c/o Inland Empire District Office
17801 Lake Perris Dr
Perris, CA 92571
Web: www.parks.ca.gov/default.asp?page_id=615
Phone: 760-928-2586
Size: 5,890 acres. **Elevation:** 4,300 feet. **Location:** In the eastern Mojave Desert off of Interstate 40, 16 miles northwest of the Essex Road exit. **Facilities:** 6 primitive family campsites, hiking trails, self-guided nature trails, picnic areas, restrooms, visitor center, exhibits (&&). **Activities:** Camping, hiking, guided tours. **Special Features:** Park is located on the east side of the Providence Mountain range, with dramatic views of the surrounding Mojave Desert. Features include Mitchell Caverns, the only limestone caverns in California's state park system; and the Mary Beale Nature Trail, offering a self-guided walk through the desert.

★1702★ RAILTOWN 1897 STATE HISTORIC PARK

c/o Capital District Office
101 J St
Sacramento, CA 95814
Web: www.railtown1897.org
Phone: 209-984-3953
Size: 24.2 acres. **Location:** At 5th Avenue and Reservoir Road in Jamestown, 3 miles south of Sonora. **Facilities:** Historical buildings and exhibits, interpretive center, gift shop, picnic areas (&&) **Activities:** Steam train excursion rides (seasonal), guided tours. **Special Features:** Park is home to the Historic Jamestown Shops and Roundhouse—an intact and still-functioning steam locomotive repair and maintenance facility, portions of which date back to 1897. This one-of-a-kind attraction combines industrial heritage and railroad history with the lore of Hollywood's film industry — the park's historic locomotives and railroad cars have appeared in more than 200 films, TV productions, and commercials.

★1703★ RED ROCK CANYON STATE PARK

c/o Inland Empire District Office
17801 Lake Perris Dr
Perris, CA 92571
Web: www.parks.ca.gov/default.asp?page_id=631
Phone: 661-942-0662
Size: 25,325 acres. **Location:** 25 miles northeast of Mojave on Highway 14, near Cantil. **Facilities:** 50 primitive campsites (&) with potable water and pit toilets, picnic areas, hiking trails, nature trails, visitor center (&), restrooms (&). **Activities:** Camping, hiking, interpretive programs. **Special Features:** Park features scenic desert cliffs, buttes, and colorful rock formations that were a landmark and watering hole for 19th-century stagecoaches and freight wagons. Significant paleontologic sites, the remains of an 1890s mining operation, and many arid-adapted plants and animals are protected here. Park also has been the site for a number of movies.

★1704★ REFUGIO STATE BEACH

c/o Channel Coast District Office
911 San Pedro St
Ventura, CA 93001
Web: www.parks.ca.gov/default.asp?page_id=603
Phone: 805-968-1033
Size: 905 acres. **Location:** 20 miles west of Santa Barbara on US 101, at 10 Refugio Beach Road in Goleta. **Facilities:** Family and group campsites, restrooms, picnic areas, bike trail, food service, supplies (&&). **Activities:** Camping, fishing, bicycling, swimming. **Special Features:** A bike trail along the beach bluff connects with El Capitán State Beach (see separate entry), 2.5 miles away. Palm trees planted near Refugio Creek give a distinctive look to the beach and camping area.

★1705★ RICHARDSON GROVE STATE PARK

c/o North Coast Redwoods District Office
PO Box 2006
Eureka, CA 95502
Web: www.parks.ca.gov/default.asp?page_id=422
Phone: 707-247-3318
Size: 1,772 acres. **Location:** 7 miles south of Garberville on US 101. **Facilities:** 170 developed family campsites (1 site for hikers and cyclists), 1 developed group camp, showers, restrooms, picnic areas, hiking trails, nature trail, visitor center, exhibits (&&). **Activities:** Camping, fishing, hiking, swimming, interpretive programs (seasonal). **Special Features:** Named after Friend W. Richardson, the 25th governor of California, this park is where northbound travelers first encounter significant old growth redwood forest.

★1706★ ROBERT H. MEYER MEMORIAL STATE BEACH

c/o Angeles District Office
1925 Las Virgenes
Calabasas, CA 91302
Web: www.parks.ca.gov/default.asp?page_id=633
Phone: 310-457-8143
Size: 37 acres. **Location:** 10 miles west (upcoast) of Malibu on Highway 1. **Facilities:** Picnic areas, beach, visitor center,

restrooms. **Activities:** Swimming, surfing. **Special Features:** Beach is made up of three cove or cliff-foot strands known as ''pocket beaches'' along the west end of the city of Malibu: El Pescador, La Piedra, and El Matador. Parking is on a bluff, and the beaches are accessed by long descending staircases and trails.

★1707★ ROBERT LOUIS STEVENSON STATE PARK

c/o Diablo Vista District Office
845 Casa Grande Rd
Petaluma, CA 94954
Web: www.parks.ca.gov/default.asp?page_id=472
Phone: 707-942-4575
Size: 6,026 acres. **Location:** 7 miles north of Calistoga on Highway 29. **Facilities:** Picnic areas, hiking trails, vista point; no drinking water or restrooms. **Activities:** Hiking. **Special Features:** In 1880, author Robert Louis Stevenson spent his honeymoon on the slopes of 4,343-foot Mount Saint Helena. Although nothing remains of Stevenson's cabin, the site is identified on the trail to the summit. Today's hikers can climb the 5-mile trail to the mountain's summit for spectacular views of the Bay area and, on clear days, the top of Mount Shasta.

★1708★ ROBERT W. CROWN MEMORIAL STATE BEACH

c/o Diablo Vista District Office
845 Casa Grande Rd
Petaluma, CA 94954
Web: www.parks.ca.gov/default.asp?page_id=526
Phone: 510-562-7275
Size: 132 acres, including 2.5 miles of beach. **Location:** In the city of Alameda; visitor center is on McKay Avenue **Facilities:** Beach, bathhouse, picnic area, sailboard rentals, visitor center, exhibits (占占). **Activities:** Swimming, windsurfing, wildlife viewing, interpretive programs. **Special Features:** The Elsie Roemer Bird Sanctuary, a refuge for aquatic birds and other salt marsh creatures, is located at the east edge of the beach. At the north end of the beach is a marine reserve. Crab Cove Visitor Center includes exhibits of the area's colorful past, when it was an amusement center known as the ''Coney Island of the West.'' The visitor center also has displays and aquaria highlighting flora and fauna of San Francisco Bay and other marine areas.

★1709★ RUSSIAN GULCH STATE PARK

c/o Mendocino District Office
PO Box 440
Mendocino, CA 95460
Web: www.parks.ca.gov/default.asp?page_id=432
Phone: 707-937-4296
Size: 1,305 acres. **Location:** 2 miles north of Mendocino on Highway 1. **Facilities:** 30 developed family campsites with showers and restrooms (占), group camp with recreation hall (占), horsemen's camp (primitive), picnic areas, hiking trails, paved bicycle trail, horseback trail. **Activities:** Camping, fishing, swimming, scuba diving, hiking, mountain biking, horseback riding, interpretive programs. **Special Features:** Park is known for the heavily forested Russian Gulch Creek Canyon,

a headland that features the Devil's Punch Bowl, a large, collapsed sea cave with churning water that gives the appearance of a boiling cauldron. Inland, the park has a 36-foot-high waterfall.

★1710★ SADDLEBACK BUTTE STATE PARK

c/o Inland Empire District Office
17801 Lake Perris Dr
Perris, CA 92571
Web: www.parks.ca.gov/default.asp?page_id=618
Phone: 661-942-0662
Size: 2,954 acres. **Location:** 17 miles east of Lancaster on East Avenue J and 170th Street East. **Facilities:** 50 family campsites, group camp, restrooms, picnic areas, nature trails, hiking trails, equestrian trail (4.5 miles), visitor center, exhibits. **Activities:** Camping, hiking, horseback riding. **Special Features:** Saddleback Butte is a 3,651-foot-high granite mountaintop that stands 1,000 feet above Antelope Valley on the western edge of the Mojave Desert. The state park, which surrounds the butte, was created to protect the butte as well as examples of native Joshua Tree woodlands and other plants and animals that were once common throughout this high desert area.

★1711★ SALINAS RIVER STATE BEACH

c/o Monterey District Office
2211 Garden Rd
Monterey, CA 93940
Web: www.parks.ca.gov/default.asp?page_id=573
Phone: 831-384-7695
Size: 282 acres. **Location:** 1 mile south of Moss Landing (take Potrero from Highway 1). **Facilities:** Picnic areas, restrooms, trails. **Activities:** Fishing, hiking, horseback riding, birding. **Special Features:** A popular fishing spot, this state beach protects one of Monterey Bay's most interesting sand dune areas and includes protected habitats of snowy plover and other native dune animals and plants.

★1712★ SALT POINT STATE PARK

c/o North Bay District Office
PO Box 123
Duncan Mills, CA 95430
Web: www.parks.ca.gov/default.asp?page_id=453
Phone: 707-847-3221
Size: 5,685 acres. **Location:** On Highway 1, 90 miles north of San Francisco. **Facilities:** 109 family campsites, 20 walk-in campsites,10 hike/bike campsites, group camp, restrooms, picnic areas, hiking and equestrian trails (20 miles), paved mountain bike trails, underwater park, visitor center. **Activities:** Camping, fishing, scuba diving, skin diving, hiking, horseback riding, mountain biking, wildlife viewing. **Special Features:** Park has 6 miles of rugged coastline with rocky promontories, pounding surf, and panoramic views, as well as grasslands, prairies, and pygmy forests. The park includes Gerstle Cove Marine Reserve, one of the first underwater parks in California, where marine life is completely protected.

9. State Parks

★1713★ SALTON SEA STATE RECREATION AREA
c/o Colorado Desert District Office
200 Palm Canyon Dr
Borrego Springs, CA 92004
Web: www.saltonsea.statepark.org
Phone: 760-393-3052
Size: 16,901 acres. Location: 30 miles south of Indio on High-way 111, on the northeastern side of the Salton Sea. Facilities: 150 developed family campsites (some ♿), RV hookups, 3 prim-itive campgrounds, picnic areas (♿), hiking and nature trails, boat ramps, boat mooring, restrooms, visitor center. Activities: Camping, fishing, swimming, boating, water-skiing, windsurf-ing, kayaking, birding, guided boat tours. Special Features: One of the world's largest inland seas, Salton Sea resulted from an accidental break in a hastily constructed dike supplying Colorado River water to the Imperial Valley. The 360-square-mile basin is one of southern California's most popular boating areas — because of the sea's low altitude (228 feet below sea level), atmospheric pressure improves speed and ski boat engine performance.

★1714★ SAMUEL P. TAYLOR STATE PARK
PO Box 251
Lagunitas, CA 94938
Web: www.parks.ca.gov/default.asp?page_id=469
Phone: 415-488-9897
Size: 2,707 acres. Location: 15 miles west of San Rafael on Sir Francis Drake Boulevard. Facilities: Family campsites (6 sites ♿), 2 group camps (75-person capacity), horsemen's camp, picnic areas (♿), hiking trails, paved bike trail (♿), restrooms (♿), visitor center. Activities: Camping, swimming, hiking, mountain biking, horseback riding. Special Features: Park fea-tures wooded countryside with a unique mix of coast redwoods groves and open grassland in the rolling hills of Marin County north of San Francisco. In the 1870s and 1880s, the resort area known as Camp Taylor was one of the first places in the nation to offer outdoor camping as a form of recreation. Today the site of Camp Taylor lies within the boundaries of the state park.

★1715★ SAN BRUNO MOUNTAIN STATE PARK
c/o Diablo Vista District Office
845 Casa Grande Rd
Petaluma, CA 94954
Web: www.parks.ca.gov/default.asp?page_id=518
Phone: 707-989-9548
Size: 298 acres. Location: On Guadalupe Canyon Parkway, off the Bayshore Boulevard/Brisbane exit from Highway 101 or the Mission Street exit off Highway 280. Facilities: Hiking trails, picnic areas, restrooms (♿). Activities: Hiking, wildlife viewing. Special Features: Park is located at the northern reaches of the Santa Cruz range and is home to a wide variety of birds and animals, as well as several endangered plant and butterfly species.

★1716★ SAN BUENAVENTURA STATE BEACH
c/o Channel Coast District Office
911 San Pedro St
Ventura, CA 93001
Web: www.parks.ca.gov/default.asp?page_id=600
Phone: 805-648-3918

Size: 110 acres. Location: In the city of Ventura, on San Pedro Street off Highway 101. Facilities: Beach (♿), picnic areas, bicycle trails, beach equipment rentals, food service. Activities: Fishing, swimming, surfing, bicycling. Special Features: Beach includes a 1,700-foot-long pier with a snack bar, restaurant, and bait shop. Bike trails connect to other nearby beaches.

★1717★ SAN CLEMENTE STATE BEACH
c/o Orange Coast District Office
3030 Avenida del Presidente
San Clemente, CA 92672
Web: www.parks.ca.gov/default.asp?page_id=646
Phone: 949-492-3156
Size: 117 acres. Location: Near the south end of San Clemente on I-5 (Basilone Road) via the Avenida Calafia exit. Facilities: 160 campsites (including 72 RV sites with full hookups), group camping area, showers, restrooms, picnic areas, nature trail, butterfly trail (♿♿). Activities: Camping, surf fishing, swim-ming, surfing, snorkeling, skin diving, hiking, interpretive pro-grams (seasonal). Special Features: The north end of this mile-long beach is popular with surfers.

★1718★ SAN ELIJO STATE BEACH
c/o San Diego Coast District Office
4477 Pacific Hwy
San Diego, CA 92110
Web: www.parks.ca.gov/default.asp?page_id=662
Phone: 760-753-5091
Size: 588 acres. Location: Along Coast Highway 101, 0.75 miles north from San Elijo Lagoon's entrance channel, near the community of Cardiff-by-the-Sea. Facilities: Campsites, show-ers, restrooms, supplies (♿♿). Activities: Camping, fishing, swimming, surfing. Special Features: Beach is a narrow, bluff-backed stretch of sand on the San Diego Coast. A nearby reef is popular with snorkelers and divers.

★1719★ SAN GREGORIO STATE BEACH
c/o Santa Cruz District Office
303 Big Trees Park Rd
Felton, CA 95018
Web: www.parks.ca.gov/default.asp?page_id=529
Phone: 650-726-8819
Size: 172 acres. Location: 10.5 miles south of Half Moon Bay on Highway 1. Facilities: Picnic areas, restrooms, historical marker. Activities: Fishing, birding. Special Features: San Gre-gorio Creek empties into the sea here, leaving a protected estuary at the back of a wide, sandy beach. The estuary is home to many birds and small animals.

★1720★ SAN JUAN BAUTISTA STATE HISTORIC
      PARK
c/o Monterey District Office
2211 Garden Rd
Monterey, CA 93940
Web: www.parks.ca.gov/default.asp?page_id=563
Phone: 831-623-4881
Size: 6.1 acres. Location: On Highway 156, 7 miles west of

9. State Parks

Hollister, in the city of San Juan Bautista. **Facilities:** Picnic area, restrooms, visitor center, exhibits (&&). **Special Features:** Adjacent to one of California's 21 Franciscan missions, this location was once the largest town in central California and the hub of travel between northern and central California. The mission is owned and operated by the Catholic Church and has been in continuous use since July 1, 1812. The park includes several structures built in the 1800s, including the Plaza Hotel, stable, blacksmith shop, granary, jail, and several houses. Museum exhibits depict California life of the Mission, Mexican, and early American periods.

★1721★ SAN LUIS RESERVOIR STATE RECREATION AREA

c/o Central Valley District Office
22708 Broadway St
Columbia, CA 95310
Web: www.parks.ca.gov/default.asp?page_id=558
Phone: 209-826-1196
Size: 26,036 acres. **Location:** 7 miles west of I-5, or 33 miles east of Highway 101 from Gilroy. **Facilities:** 132 developed family campsites (53 with electric and water hookups; some sites &), more than 500 undeveloped campsites, group camp, primitive horse campground, showers, restrooms (&), picnic areas (&), visitor center (&), exhibits, trails, boat ramps. **Activities:** Camping, fishing, swimming, boating, jet skiing, water-skiing, windsurfing, sailboarding, hiking, bicycling, horseback riding, hunting (seasonal). **Special Features:** San Luis Reservoir is part of the California Aqueduct System and comprises three artificial lakes: San Luis Reservoir, O'Neill Forebay, and Los Banos Creek Reservoir. Fishing is excellent with large populations of striped bass, largemouth bass, rainbow trout, and channel catfish.

★1722★ SAN ONOFRE STATE BEACH

c/o Orange Coast District Office
3030 Avenida del Presidente
San Clemente, CA 92672
Web: www.parks.ca.gov/default.asp?page_id=647
Phone: 714-492-4872
Size: 2,107 acres. **Location:** 3 miles south of San Clemente on I-5 (Basilone Road). **Facilities:** 328 campsites (173 developed sites with no hookups; 65 sites with electric and water hookups; 90 tent sites; some sites &), hiking trails (some parts &). **Activities:** Camping, swimming, surfing, hiking. **Special Features:** Site features 3.5 miles of sandy beaches with six access trails cut into the bluff above; a marshy area where San Mateo Creek meets the shoreline; and Trestles Beach, a well-known California surfing site. Whales, dolphins, and sea lions can be seen offshore from time to time.

★1723★ SAN PASQUAL BATTLEFIELD STATE HISTORIC PARK

15808 San Pasqual Valley Rd
Escondido, CA 92027
Web: www.parks.ca.gov/default.asp?page_id=655
Phone: 760-737-2201
Size: 60.4 acres. **Location:** 8 miles south of Escondido on Highway 78, next to the San Diego Wild Animal Park. **Facilities:** Visitor center, exhibits, restrooms (&&), hiking and nature trails. **Special Features:** Park honors soldiers who fought in the battle between US and Californio forces on December 6, 1846 during the Mexican-American War. The battle proved to be one of the bloodiest and most controversial in California history, as General Stephen Kearny and General Andres Pico both claimed victory. The park has been set aside, not as a monument to war, but as a reminder of the passions that can lead nations to war.

★1724★ SAN SIMEON STATE PARK

c/o San Luis Obispo Coast District Office
750 Hearst Castle Rd
San Simeon, CA 93452
Web: www.parks.ca.gov/default.asp?page_id=590
Phone: 805-927-2020
Size: 2,281 acres. **Location:** 35 miles north of San Luis Obispo on Highway 1 and 5 miles south of the Hearst San Simeon State Historical Monument. **Facilities:** 134 developed campsites (tent or RV; some sites &), 68 primitive campsites (some sites &), showers, restrooms (&), picnic areas, boat ramps, hiking trails (portion &). **Activities:** Camping, boating, kayaking, fishing, hiking. **Special Features:** The coastal bluffs and promontories of this scenic park offer unobstructed views of the ocean and rocky shore. The park includes three natural preserves and is a convenient place to camp for Hearst Castle visitors. (See separate entry for description of Hearst San Simeon State Historical Monument.)

★1725★ SANTA CRUZ MISSION STATE HISTORIC PARK

c/o Santa Cruz District Office
303 Big Trees Park Rd
Felton, CA 95018
Web: www.parks.ca.gov/default.asp?page_id=548
Phone: 831-335-6318
Size: 1.9 acres. **Location:** One block off the Mission Plaza on School Street in downtown Santa Cruz. **Facilities:** Visitor center, exhibits. **Activities:** Group tours (by reservation). **Special Features:** Misión la Exaltacion de la Santa Cruz, the twelfth mission built in California, was completed during the 1790s. After suffering damage from several earthquakes, it collapsed in 1857. This park is the site of a complex of buildings that were erected around the original Santa Cruz Mission. Part of the cluster, the Neary-Rodriguez Adobe was built in 1791 and is the last of the mission's many buildings to survive. The lovely, single-story adobe has been restored to its original appearance.

★1726★ SANTA MONICA STATE BEACH

c/o Angeles District Office
1925 Las Virgenes
Calabasas, CA 91302
Web: www.parks.ca.gov/default.asp?page_id=624
Phone: 310-458-8974
Size: 48.5 acres. **Location:** Along the Pacific Coast Highway in Santa Monica. **Facilities:** Beach, picnic area, shops, pier. **Activities:** Swimming, surfing, volleyball, basketball. **Special**

9. State Parks

Features: This 2-mile-long beach is operated by the City of Santa Monica.

★1727★ SANTA SUSANA PASS STATE HISTORIC PARK
c/o Angeles District Office
1925 Las Virgenes
Calabasas, CA 91302
Web: www.parks.ca.gov/default.asp?page_id=611
Phone: 213-620-6152
Size: 671 acres. **Elevation:** 1,000-1,850 feet. **Location:** About 1 mile south of Highway 118; follow Topanga Canyon Boulevard south and turn right on Devonshire to entrance to Chatsworth Park South. The hills surrounding the community park are the parklands for Santa Susana Pass State Park. **Facilities:** Trails. **Activities:** Hiking, horseback riding, interpretive programs, guided hikes. **Special Features:** Here in the western part of the Transverse Ranges, the land is dominated by high, narrow ridges and deep canyons covered with an abundant variety of plant life. The park offers panoramic views of the rugged natural landscape as a striking contrast to the developed communities nearby.

★1728★ SCHOONER GULCH STATE BEACH
c/o Mendocino District Office
PO Box 440
Mendocino, CA 95460
Web: www.parks.ca.gov/default.asp?page_id=446
Phone: 707-937-5804
Size: 53.6 acres. **Location:** 3 miles south of Point Arena off Highway 1. **Facilities:** Picnic areas, hiking trails. **Activities:** Fishing, hiking, windsurfing, scuba diving, beachcombing. **Special Features:** The beach and headlands preserve a scenic spot along the Mendocino Coast. The area was frequented by Russians and native Alaskan hunters as early as 1812, and by Mexican land owners in the 1840s.

★1729★ SEACLIFF STATE BEACH
c/o Santa Cruz District Office
303 Big Trees Park Rd
Felton, CA 95018
Web: www.parks.ca.gov/default.asp?page_id=543
Phone: 831-685-6500
Size: 87 acres. **Location:** 5.5 miles south of Santa Cruz, off Highway 1 at the State Park Drive exit in the neighborhood of Aptos. **Facilities:** 26 campsites (RVs only; all sites have full hookups), picnic areas, showers, restrooms, hiking trails, visitor center, exhibits, fishing pier, food service (&&). **Activities:** Camping, fishing, swimming, interpretive programs. **Special Features:** Seacliff State Beach is known for its fishing pier and concrete freighter, the *Palo Alto*, docked at the end of the pier. Unfortunately, the ship is unsafe and closed to the public.

★1730★ SHASTA STATE HISTORIC PARK
c/o Northern Buttes District Office
400 Glen Dr
Oroville, CA 95966
Web: www.parks.ca.gov/default.asp?page_id=456
Phone: 530-243-8194

Size: 23 acres. **Location:** 6 miles west of downtown Redding on Highway 299. **Facilities:** Historical features, visitor center, exhibits (&), restrooms (&), picnic areas. **Special Features:** The park preserves the ruins of Shasta City, the "Queen City" of California's northern mining district which was once the center of the 1850s gold rush. The Shasta County Courthouse has been restored to its 1861 appearance and serves as a museum, with historical exhibits and a collection of historic California artwork featuring more than 100 paintings by early California artists.

★1731★ SILVER STRAND STATE BEACH
c/o San Diego Coast District Office
4477 Pacific Hwy
San Diego, CA 92110
Web: www.parks.ca.gov/default.asp?page_id=654
Phone: 619-435-5184
Size: 3,749 acres. **Location:** 4.5 miles south of the city of Coronado on Highway 75. **Facilities:** 136 en route campsites (self-contained vehicles only; no hookups), picnic areas with ramadas (&), restrooms (&). **Activities:** Fishing, swimming, surfing, sailing, kiteboarding, water-skiing. **Special Features:** Silver Strand's beaches serve as a peninsula separating San Diego Bay from the Pacific Ocean. Three pedestrian tunnels under the highway lead to the bay side of the park. Water in the bay is usually warmer and calmer than on the Pacific side, safer for family swimming and sailing. An Aquatics Center at the park specializes in instructional classes for select water sports.

★1732★ SILVERWOOD LAKE STATE RECREATION AREA
c/o Inland Empire District Office
17801 Lake Perris Dr
Perris, CA 92571
Web: www.parks.ca.gov/default.asp?page_id=650
Phone: 760-389-2281
Size: 2,201 acres. **Elevation:** 3,350 feet. **Location:** 20 miles north of San Bernardino via Highways 18 and 138. **Facilities:** 136 developed campsites with showers and restrooms, group camps, picnic areas (including 3 that are reached by boat), hiking and biking trails, nature trails, swimming beaches, marina with launching ramp, boat and equipment rentals, boat mooring, marina store, visitor center, exhibits, food service (&&). **Activities:** Camping, fishing, hiking, swimming, boating, water-skiing, windsurfing, bicycling, wildlife viewing, interpretive programs. **Special Features:** Silverwood Lake was formed by Cedar Springs Dam and is located in an area between desert and pine-covered mountains. At an elevation of 3,350 feet, Silverwood Lake is the highest reservoir in the state water system. A segment of the 2,650-mile Pacific Crest Trail passes through the park (see entry in national trails section).

★1733★ SINKYONE WILDERNESS STATE PARK
PO Box 245
Whitethorn, CA 95489
Web: www.parks.ca.gov/default.asp?page_id=429
Phone: 707-986-7711

9. State Parks

Size: 7,937 acres. **Location:** North end of wilderness: 36 miles southwest of Garberville/Redway on Briceland Road. South end of wilderness (Usal Beach): 15 miles west of Leggett on PCH from Highway 101. Last few miles of both routes are unpaved, steep, and narrow, and may be impassable in wet weather. **Facilities:** Primitive campsites, walk-in tent campsites, picnic areas, hiking and backpacking trails (20 miles), horseback trails, visitor center; no drinking water. **Activities:** Camping, backpacking, fishing, hiking, horseback riding, wildlife viewing. **Special Features:** The park's rugged Lost Coast Trail winds 21 miles through a coastal plateau, with access to ocean vistas, waterfalls, cliffs, black sand beaches, tide pools, and trail campsites.

★1734★ SMITHE REDWOODS STATE RESERVE
c/o North Coast Redwoods District Office
PO Box 2006
Eureka, CA 95502
Web: www.parks.ca.gov/default.asp?page_id=427
Phone: 707-247-3318
Size: 689 acres. **Location:** 4 miles north of Leggett on US 101. **Facilities:** Picnic areas. **Activities:** Fishing, swimming. **Special Features:** Formerly a private resort, the reserve features a 60-foot waterfall on the south fork of the Eel River and the Frank and Bess Smithe Grove of redwoods.

★1735★ SONOMA COAST STATE BEACH
c/o North Bay District Office
PO Box 123
Duncan Mills, CA 95430
Web: www.parks.ca.gov/default.asp?page_id=451
Phone: 707-875-3483
Size: 9,711 acres. **Location:** Between Jenner and Bodega Bay on Highway 1. **Facilities:** 125 developed campsites, 31 primitive/environmental campsites, showers and restrooms, picnic areas, hiking trails, horseback trails, boat launch (&&). **Activities:** Camping, fishing, hiking, horseback riding, beachcombing, wildlife viewing. **Special Features:** Sonoma Coast State Beach, which is actually a series of beaches separated by rock bluffs and headlands, extends 17 miles from Bodega Head to Vista Trail (4 miles north of Jenner). Visitors can access the beach at more than a dozen points along Highway 1. The high cliffs of Bodega Head are an excellent vantage point for watching migrating gray whales.

★1736★ SONOMA STATE HISTORIC PARK
c/o Diablo Vista District Office
845 Casa Grande Rd
Petalulma, CA 94954
Web: www.parks.ca.gov/default.asp?page_id=479
Phone: 707-938-9560
Size: 63.6 acres. **Location:** Park's main office is at 363 3rd Street West in Sonoma. **Facilities:** Historic sites, visitor center, exhibits (&), restrooms (&), picnic areas. **Activities:** Guided tours. **Special Features:** Park is made up of six historic sites in separate locations within the picturesque town of Sonoma: the Mission San Francisco Solano de Sonoma, the Blue Wing Inn, the Sonoma Barracks, the Toscano Hotel, and La Casa Grande and Lachryma Montis, the homes of General Mariano Guadalupe Vallejo, Military Commander and Director of Colonization of the Northern Frontier. The 1823 Mission was the northernmost Franciscan Mission in California and the last to be established.

★1737★ SOUTH CARLSBAD STATE BEACH
c/o San Diego Coast District
9609 Waples St, Suite 200
San Diego, CA 92121
Web: www.parks.ca.gov/default.asp?page_id=660
Phone: 760-438-3143
Size: 118 acres. **Location:** 3 miles south of Carlsbad on Carlsbad Boulevard. **Facilities:** Family campsites, concessions building, picnic areas, restrooms (&&). **Activities:** Camping, fishing, swimming, snorkeling, skin diving, surfing. **Special Features:** Park's large blufftop campground is very popular, especially during the summer. A staircase leads down to the beach.

★1738★ SOUTH YUBA RIVER STATE PARK
17660 Pleasant Valley Rd
Penn Valley, CA 95946
Web: www.parks.ca.gov/default.asp?page_id=496
Phone: 530-432-2546
Size: 8,720 acres. **Location:** North of Nevada City, off Highway 49. **Facilities:** Picnic areas, hiking and nature trails, restrooms (&&). **Activities:** Fishing, hiking, swimming, gold panning, guided tours. **Special Features:** This 20-mile portion of the south fork of the Yuba River canyon stretches from Malakoff Diggins State Historic Park (see separate entry) to Bridgeport. The area includes Bridgeport Covered Bridge, the longest single-span covered bridge in the world, and Independence Trail, a wheelchair-accessible trail that follows the Old Excelsior Ditch. Visitors can pan for gold or hike trails leading to historic mining sites.

★1739★ STANDISH-HICKEY STATE RECREATION AREA
c/o North Coast Redwoods District Office
PO Box 206
Eureka, CA 95502
Web: www.parks.ca.gov/default.asp?page_id=423
Phone: 707-925-6482
Size: 1,021 acres. **Location:** 1.5 miles north of Leggett on US 101. **Facilities:** Developed family campsites (includes & site), hike/bike campsite, picnic areas, hiking trails. **Activities:** Camping, fishing, hiking, swimming, interpretive programs (seasonal). **Special Features:** Standish-Hickey stands at the gateway to ''tall trees country'' and features nearly two miles of the South Fork of the Eel River. One of the few virgin coast redwood stands remaining in this area can be seen on the Grove Trail.

★1740★ SUGARLOAF RIDGE STATE PARK
c/o Diablo Vista District Office
845 Casa Grande Rd
Petaluma, CA 94954
Web: www.parks.ca.gov/default.asp?page_id=481
Phone: 707-833-5712

Size: 3,783 acres. **Location:** 7 miles east of Santa Rosa. **Facilities:** Family and group campsites, picnic areas (&), trails (25 miles), horseback riding concession (seasonal), observatory (&), visitor center (&), exhibits (&). **Activities:** Camping, hiking, horseback riding. **Special Features:** Park is located in an area where the headwaters of the Sonoma Creek run through gorge and canyon, then across the meadow floor beneath scenic rock outcroppings surrounded by redwoods and saddleback ferns. On clear days, from the 2,729-foot summit of Bald Mountain visitors can see the Sierra Nevada and the Golden Gate. An observatory located within the park offers year-round astronomy education and interpretive programs.

★1741★ SUNSET STATE BEACH

c/o Santa Cruz District Office
303 Big Trees Park Rd
Felton, CA 95018
Web: www.parks.ca.gov/default.asp?page_id=544
Phone: 831-763-7062
Size: 302 acres. **Location:** 16 miles south of Santa Cruz via Highway 1 and San Andreas Road. **Facilities:** 90 developed family campsites (no hookups), restrooms, picnic areas (&), hiking trails, glider port for remote control gliders. **Activities:** Camping, fishing, hiking, interpretive programs (seasonal). **Special Features:** Sunset State Beach features pine trees, large sand dunes, and oceanside picnic spots. Strong currents make swimming hazardous here.

★1742★ SUTTER BUTTES STATE PARK

c/o Northern Buttes District Office
400 Glen Dr
Oroville, CA 95966
Web: www.parks.ca.gov/lat_long_map/default.asp?lvl_id=352
Phone: 530-538-2200
Size: 1,784 acres. **Location:** North of Highway 20 between Colusa and Yuba City. **Special Features:** Park is not yet open to the public, and it has not been officially named yet.

★1743★ SUTTER'S FORT STATE HISTORIC PARK

c/o Capital District, Historic Sites Sector
101 J St
Sacramento, CA 95814
Web: www.parks.ca.gov/default.asp?page_id=485
Phone: 916-445-4422; **Fax:** 916-447-9318
Size: 5.8 acres. **Location:** In midtown Sacramento between K and L Streets and 26th and 28th Streets. **Facilities:** Restored fort, visitor center, exhibits, restrooms (&&). **Activities:** Guided and self-guided tours. **Special Features:** Sutter's Fort was Sacramento's earliest settlement. John Sutter, a Swiss immigrant, received a 48,000-acre Mexican land grant in the Sacramento Valley in 1839 and used the land to create a flourishing agricultural empire. However, less than a decade after they were established, Sutter's properties were overrun by gold seekers and the fort is all that remains. The fort has been restored to its 1846 appearance.

★1744★ TAHOE STATE RECREATION AREA

c/o Sierra District Office
PO Box 266
Tahoma, CA 96142
Web: www.parks.ca.gov/default.asp?page_id=504
Phone: 530-583-3074
Size: 61.7 acres. **Location:** 0.25 miles east of Tahoe City on Highway 28. **Facilities:** 27 lakeside family campsites, restrooms, showers, picnic areas. **Activities:** Camping, fishing, swimming. **Special Features:** Park offers excellent views of Lake Tahoe and direct access to the lake shoreline.

★1745★ TOLOWA DUNES STATE PARK

1375 Elk Valley Rd
Crescent City, CA 95531
Web: www.parks.ca.gov/default.asp?page_id=430
Phone: 707-465-2145
Size: 4,399 acres. **Location:** 2 miles north of Crescent City via Northcrest Drive, north off US Highway 101. **Facilities:** 2 primitive campgrounds, including a ride-in horse camp and 6 walk-in sites, picnic areas, trails, boat launch. **Activities:** Camping, fishing, hiking, horseback riding, mountain biking, birding, wildlife viewing, interpretive programs. **Special Features:** Park encompasses some of the finest wetlands habitat on California's northern coast. Tolowa Dunes is an ancient sand dune complex that has evolved into several distinct ecological communities: ocean beach, river, open and vegetated sand dunes, wooded ridges, and wetlands. A diverse assortment of birds, animals, and plant life thrive here, and the area serves as an important stopover on the Pacific flyway for thousands of migrating ducks, geese, and swans.

★1746★ TOMALES BAY STATE PARK

c/o North Bay District Office
PO Box 123
Duncan Mills, CA 95430
Web: www.parks.ca.gov/default.asp?page_id=470
Phone: 415-669-1140
Size: 2,443 acres. **Location:** 40 miles north of San Francisco, adjacent to Point Reyes National Seashore; 8 miles from Highway One on the west side of the bay and 4 miles north of Inverness on Pierce Point Road. **Facilities:** Picnic areas (&), trails, restrooms (&). **Activities:** Swimming, boating, kayaking, clamming, hiking. **Special Features:** This day-use park features four gently sloping, surf-free beaches, protected from winds by Inverness Ridge, the backbone of the Point Reyes Peninsula. The park also includes forests, hills, meadows, and marshes as well as one of the finest remaining virgin groves of Bishop pine in California.

★1747★ TOMO-KAHNI STATE HISTORIC PARK

c/o Inland Empire District Office
17801 Lake Perris Dr
Perris, CA 92571
Web: www.parks.ca.gov/default.asp?page_id=610
Phone: 661-942-0662
Size: 400 acres. **Location:** 12 miles outside Tehachapi; Tomo-Kahni Resource Center at 112 F Street, Suite A, Tehachapi.

9. State Parks

Facilities: Remains of Native American village. **Activities:** Guided tours only, on weekends during the spring and fall (by appointment). **Special Features:** Overlooking Sand Canyon to the east and the Tehachapi valley to the west, Tomo-Kahni, or "Winter Village," was the site of a Kawaiisu (Nuooah) village. The Kawaiisu migrated from the Great Basin and made the Tehachapi their home for two to three thousand years. They are noted for their finely woven baskets of intricate and colorful design.

★1748★ TOPANGA STATE PARK
c/o Angeles District Office
1925 Las Virgenes
Calabasas, CA 91302
Web: www.parks.ca.gov/default.asp?page_id=629
Phone: 310-455-2465
Size: 12,666 acres. **Elevation:** 1,500 feet. **Location:** On Entrada Road, off Topanga Canyon Boulevard. **Facilities:** Hike/bike campsites, picnic areas (&), restrooms (&), trails, nature center (&). **Activities:** Camping, hiking, horseback riding, mountain biking (on fire roads). **Special Features:** Located in the cliffs and canyons of the Santa Monica Mountains, park includes 36 miles of trails through open grassland, live oaks, and scenic views of the Pacific Ocean. The park is located entirely within the Los Angeles city limits and is considered the world's largest wildland within the boundaries of a major city.

★1749★ TORREY PINES STATE BEACH
c/o San Diego Coast District
9609 Waples St, Suite 200
San Diego, CA 92121
Web: www.parks.ca.gov/default.asp?page_id=658
Phone: 858-755-2063
Size: 61.4 acres. **Location:** 1 mile south of Del Mar on North Torrey Pines Road. **Facilities:** Beach, picnic areas, restrooms (&&). **Activities:** Fishing, swimming, surfing, beachcombing, hiking. **Special Features:** This wide, sandy beach stretches 4.5 miles from Del Mar past Los Peñasquitos Lagoon to the base of sandstone cliffs at Torrey Pines Mesa. The beach can also be reached by trail from Torrey Pines State Reserve (see separate entry).

★1750★ TORREY PINES STATE RESERVE
c/o San Diego Coast District
12600 N Torrey Pines Rd
San Diego, CA 92121
Web: www.parks.ca.gov/default.asp?page_id=657
Phone: 858-755-2063
Size: 1,461 acres. **Location:** North of San Diego, between La Jolla and Del Mar. **Facilities:** Hiking trails, interpretive trail (&), visitor center (&), exhibits (&), restrooms (&). **Activities:** Nature study, wildlife viewing. **Special Features:** Reserve is home of North America's rarest pine tree, *Pinus torreyana*, which grows only here and on Santa Rosa Island off the coast near Santa Barbara. The reserve also protects the last salt marshes and waterfowl refuges in Southern California.

★1751★ TRINIDAD STATE BEACH
c/o North Coast Redwoods District Office
PO Box 2006
Eureka, CA 95502
Web: www.parks.ca.gov/default.asp?page_id=418
Phone: 707-677-3132
Size: 159 acres. **Location:** 19 miles north of Eureka, just off US 101. **Facilities:** Picnic areas, restrooms, trails. **Activities:** Fishing, hiking, horseback riding. **Special Features:** Trinidad State Beach is located in a secluded cove, with a natural arch at the north end of the beach. It's a short hike through the woods and across open bluffs to the beach. Low tide is the best time to visit.

★1752★ TULE ELK STATE RESERVE
c/o Central Valley District Office
22708 Broadway St
Columbia, CA 95310
Web: www.parks.ca.gov/default.asp?page_id=584
Phone: 661-764-6881
Size: 984 acres. **Location:** North of Gorman, south of Buttonwillow, and west of I-5 via Stockdale Highway. **Facilities:** Picnic areas, visitor center, exhibits, viewing platform (&&). **Activities:** Wildlife viewing. **Special Features:** Reserve protects a herd of tule elk, once in danger of extinction. The elk are most active from late summer through early autumn. Visitors are encouraged to bring binoculars for better viewing.

★1753★ TURLOCK LAKE STATE RECREATION AREA
c/o Central Valley District Office
22708 Broadway St
Columbia, CA 95310
Web: www.parks.ca.gov/default.asp?page_id=555
Phone: 209-874-2056
Size: 3,559 acres. **Location:** 25 miles east of Modesto on the south side of the Tuolumne River. **Facilities:** 66 developed family campsites (no hookups), hot showers, restrooms, picnic areas (&), swimming beach (&), boat dock, boat launch ramp. **Activities:** Camping, fishing, swimming, boating, water-skiing. **Special Features:** Bounded on the north by the Tuolumne River and on the south by Turlock Lake, the recreation area provides an ideal setting for water-oriented outdoor activities. It features a 3,500-surface-acre lake with 26 miles of shoreline, and 228 acres of foothill country.

★1754★ TWIN LAKES STATE BEACH
c/o Santa Cruz District Office
303 Big Trees Park Rd
Felton, CA 95018
Web: www.parks.ca.gov/default.asp?page_id=547
Phone: 831-427-4868
Size: 95.4 acres. **Location:** In Santa Cruz near the small craft harbor. **Facilities:** Trails, food service. **Activities:** Fishing, swimming, picnicking, hiking, birding. **Special Features:** Beach offers a mile of sandy shoreline. The adjacent Schwan Lake is a good location for bird watching.

9. State Parks

★1755★ VAN DAMME STATE PARK
c/o Mendocino District Office
PO Box 440
Mendocino, CA 95460
Web: www.parks.ca.gov/default.asp?page_id=433
Phone: 707-937-5804
Size: 2,337 acres. Location: 3 miles south of the town of Mendocino on Highway 1. Facilities: Family campground, environmental campground, hike/bike campground, group campground, picnic areas, trails (10 miles), visitor center, restrooms (&&). Activities: Camping, fishing, hiking, bicycling, scuba diving, guided kayak tours. Special Features: Park features a protected cove for divers, a fern canyon for hikers, and a unique forest of Mendocino pygmy cypress. The park's sheltered and easily reached beach is a gathering place for abalone divers.

★1756★ VERDUGO MOUNTAINS
c/o Angeles District Office
1925 Las Virgenes
Calabasas, CA 91302
Web: www.parks.ca.gov/default.asp?page_id=635
Phone: 213-620-6152
Size: 251 acres. Location: In Los Angeles County, near Sun Valley. Facilities: Undeveloped. Special Features: Purpose of this property is to preserve and protect as urban open space a remnant of natural lands located near the city of Glendale in the north portion of the heavily urbanized Los Angeles basin. The property is a geologically detached piece of the San Gabriel Mountains and offers vistas towards the main range.

★1757★ WARD CREEK
c/o Sierra District Office
PO Box 366
Tahoma, CA 96142
Web: www.parks.ca.gov/default.asp?page_id=513
Phone: 530-525-7232
Size: 173 acres. Location: South of Tahoe City. Special Features: Purpose of the property is to preserve and protect an area of undeveloped upland forest and meadowland on the west side of the Lake Tahoe Basin.

★1758★ WASHOE MEADOWS STATE PARK
c/o Sierra District Office
PO Box 266
Tahoma, CA 96142
Web: www.parks.ca.gov/default.asp?page_id=516
Phone: 530-525-3345
Size: 628 acres. Location: 3.5 miles southeast of South Lake Tahoe on US 50. Facilities: Undeveloped. Special Features: Park consists of meadows and woodlands in a valley at the base of the escarpment leading to Echo Summit. It was named for the Native Americans who inhabited the area for thousands of years.

★1759★ WASSAMA ROUND HOUSE STATE HISTORIC PARK
c/o Central Valley District Office
22708 Broadway St
Columbia, CA 95310
Web: www.parks.ca.gov/default.asp?page_id=586
Phone: 559-822-2332
Size: 27 acres. Location: 5 miles northwest of Oakhurst off Highway 49. Facilities: Picnic area, exhibits and programs. Special Features: Park is used primarily by local Native Americans as a ceremonial meeting place. Gathering Day, held the third Saturday of October, includes demonstrations of dancing, crafts, and basket weaving.

★1760★ WATTS TOWERS OF SIMON RODIA STATE HISTORIC PARK
c/o Angeles District Office
1925 Las Virgenes
Calabasas, CA 91302
Web: www.parks.ca.gov/default.asp?page_id=613
Phone: 213-847-4646
Size: 0.11 acre. Location: 1765 East 107th Street, Los Angeles. Managed by the city of Los Angeles Cultural Affairs Department. Activities: Cultural programs, including tours, lectures, exhibits, and studio workshops for teachers and school children. Special Features: Watts Towers, which consists of a complex set of 17 separate sculptural pieces built on a residential lot in the community of Watts, is the work of Italian immigrant Simon Rodia. Using steel pipes and rods, wrapped with wire mesh, coated with mortar, and decorated with pieces of porcelain, tile, and glass, Rodia spent more than 30 years, beginning in 1921, building this tribute to his adopted country. Watts Towers is one of only nine works of folk art listed on the National Register of Historic Places.

★1761★ WEAVERVILLE JOSS HOUSE STATE HISTORIC PARK
c/o Northern Buttes District Office
400 Glen Dr
Oroville, CA 95966
Web: www.parks.ca.gov/default.asp?page_id=457
Phone: 530-623-5282
Size: 2.8 acres. Location: 50 miles west of Redding, at the southwest corner of Highway 299 and Oregon Street in the community of Weaverville. Facilities: Historical and cultural exhibits, visitor center. Activities: Guided tours. Special Features: Still used as a place of worship, this Taoist temple is the oldest continuously used Chinese temple in California. Exhibits displayed at the temple interpret the role played by Chinese immigrants in early California history and include art objects, pictures, mining tools, and weapons used in the 1854 Tong War.

★1762★ WESTPORT-UNION LANDING STATE BEACH
c/o Mendocino District Office
PO Box 440
Mendocino, CA 95460
Web: www.parks.ca.gov/default.asp?page_id=440
Phone: 707-937-5804

Size: 57.8 acres. Location: 2 miles north of Westport, 19 miles north of Fort Bragg, on Highway 1. Facilities: 46 primitive campsites, picnic area, restrooms, hiking trails. Activities: Camping, fishing. Special Features: Beach features more than 3 miles of rugged and scenic coastline, with campsites on the bluff overlooking the Pacific Ocean. It is a haven for tide pool explorers, surf fishermen, abalone divers, and spear fishing enthusiasts.

★1763★ WILDER RANCH STATE PARK

c/o Santa Cruz District Office
303 Big Trees Park Rd
Felton, CA 95018
Web: www.parks.ca.gov/default.asp?page_id=549
Phone: 831-426-0505
Size: 8,341 acres. Location: Just north of Santa Cruz city limits, immediately west of Highway 1. Facilities: Picnic areas, restrooms, trails, visitor center, historic structures and exhibits (&). Activities: Hiking, horseback riding, bicycling, guided tours, living history demonstrations. Special Features: Park has 34 miles of hiking, biking, and equestrian rails winding through coastal terraces and valleys. The site was originally the main rancho supplying the Santa Cruz Mission and later became a successful and innovative dairy ranch. Surrounding grounds include Victorian homes, gardens, and historic adobe.

★1764★ WILL ROGERS STATE BEACH

c/o Angeles District Office
1925 Las Virgenes
Calabasas, CA 91302
Web: www.parks.ca.gov/default.asp?page_id=625
Phone: 310-305-9503
Size: 82 acres. Location: Off the Pacific Coast Highway, near the intersection with Temescal Canyon Road. Facilities: Beach, bike path, restrooms (&), food service, volleyball courts, playground. Activities: Swimming, surfing, skin diving, fishing, bicycling, volleyball. Special Features: Beach, which encompasses 1.75 miles of sandy shoreline, is operated by the Los Angeles County Department of Beaches and Harbors. Several movies and TV shows have been filmed here.

★1765★ WILL ROGERS STATE HISTORIC PARK

c/o Angeles District Office
1925 Las Virgenes
Calabasas, CA 91302
Web: www.parks.ca.gov/default.asp?page_id=626
Phone: 310-454-8212
Size: 189 acres. Location: In Pacific Palisades off Sunset Boulevard at 1501 Will Rogers State Park Road, just east of the Pacific Ocean. Facilities: Picnic areas (&), trails, horse training ring, restrooms (&), visitor center (&), exhibits. Activities: Hiking, horseback riding, guided tours. Special Features: The 31-room home of the famous humorist and actor includes exhibits of Rogers' memorabilia and art collection. Other structures at the site include a stable, corrals, riding ring, roping arena, and polo field.

★1766★ WILLIAM B. IDE ADOBE STATE HISTORIC PARK

c/o Northern Buttes District Office
400 Glen Dr
Oroville, CA 95966
Web: www.parks.ca.gov/default.asp?page_id=458
Phone: 530-529-8599
Size: 3.9 acres. Location: South of Redding, 2 miles northeast of Red Bluff on Adobe Road. Facilities: Picnic area, hiking trails, restrooms, visitor center, exhibits (&&). Activities: Fishing, hiking. Special Features: Park overlooks the Sacramento River and features the old adobe home, carriage shed, and blacksmith shop of California pioneer William B. Ide, who was president of the short-lived (22 days) California Bear Republic.

★1767★ WILLIAM RANDOLPH HEARST MEMORIAL STATE BEACH

c/o San Luis Obispo Coast District Office
750 Hearst Castle Rd
San Simeon, CA 93452
Web: www.parks.ca.gov/default.asp?page_id=589
Phone: 805-927-2020
Size: 8.1 acres. Location: In the town of San Simeon, directly across Highway 1 from the Hearst Castle. Facilities: Picnic area (&), fishing pier, boat ramps, kayak rentals, restrooms (&), food service, charter boat service. Activities: Fishing, swimming, boating, ocean kayaking, beachcombing, hiking.. Special Features: A popular beach spot, this protected cove offers visitors pier fishing and deep-sea fishing from chartered boats.

★1768★ WOODLAND OPERA HOUSE STATE HISTORIC PARK

c/o Capital District Office
101 J Street
Sacramento, CA 95814
Web: www.parks.ca.gov/default.asp?page_id=488
Phone: 530-666-9617
Size: 0.26 acre. Location: At the corner of Main and Second streets in historic downtown Woodland. Facilities: Opera house (&). Activities: Tours, classes. Special Features: The Woodland Opera House is the last of the once-numerous opera houses of California's early small towns. Before it closed in 1913, it was a stopping place for more than 300 touring companies. The opera house became a state historic park in 1976, and since then its interior has been restored to the grandeur it enjoyed at the turn of the century. Live entertainment is offered there on a year-round basis.

★1769★ WOODSON BRIDGE STATE RECREATION AREA

c/o Northern Buttes District Office
400 Glen Dr
Oroville, CA 95966
Web: www.parks.ca.gov/default.asp?page_id=459
Phone: 530-839-2112
Size: 323 acres. Location: On South Avenue 3 miles west of Highway 99 at Vina, or 6 miles east of I-5 at Corning. Facilities: Family and environmental campsites, picnic areas, hiking and

9. State Parks

nature trails, nature preserve, boat ramp nearby. **Activities:** Camping, fishing, hiking. **Special Features:** This oak woodland park is nestled along the Sacramento River between Chico and Red Bluff. The park includes a preserve that features some of the last remaining riparian habitat in California and provides a winter home for bald eagles and a summer nest site for the yellow billed cuckoo.

★1770★ **ZMUDOWSKI STATE BEACH**
c/o Monterey District Office
2211 Garden Rd
Monterey, CA 93940
Web: www.parks.ca.gov/default.asp?page_id=572
Phone: 831-384-7695
Size: 194 acres. **Location:** 20 miles northwest of Monterey off Highway 1; take Stuve Road and turn onto Giberson Road. **Facilities:** Trails. **Activities:** Fishing, hiking, horseback riding, birdwatching. **Special Features:** Beach is popular with anglers, equestrians, and bird watchers and includes the Pájaro River estuary, where a natural preserve has been set aside. Swimming and water sports are hazardous at this beach because of strong rip-currents.

9. State Parks

Map grid: A B C D E F G (columns) / 1 2 3 4 5 6 7 8 9 10 (rows)

Labels on map: Denver, Colorado Springs, Pueblo, Aspen, Grand Junction, Colorado River, Arkansas River

No.	Park	Grid
1	Arkansas Headwaters RA	D-4
2	Barr Lake SP	B-6
3	Bonny Lake SP	B-8
4	Boyd Lake SP	A-5
5	Castlewood Canyon SP	C-5
6	Chatfield SP	C-5
7	Cherry Creek SP	D-5
8	Cheyenne Mountain SP	D-2
9	Crawford SP	B-4
10	Eldorado Canyon SP	
11	Eleven Mile SP	C-4
12	Golden Gate Canyon SP	B-4
13	Harvey Gap SP	B-2
14	Highline SP	C-1
15	Jackson Lake SP	A-6
16	James M. Robb – Colorado River SP	C-1
17	John Martin Reservoir SP	E-7
18	Lake Pueblo SP	E-5
19	Lathrop SP	E-5
20	Lory SP	C-4
21	Mancos SP	B-4
22	Mueller SP	B-2
23	Navajo SP	C-1
24	North Sterling SP	A-7
25	Paonia SP	C-3
26	Pearl Lake SP	A-3
27	Ridgway SP	D-2
28	Rifle Falls SP	C-2
29	Rifle Gap SP	B-2
30	Roxborough SP	C-5
31	Saint Vrain SP	A-5
32	San Luis SP & Wildlife Area	E-4
33	Spinney Mountain SP	C-4
34	Stagecoach SP	A-3
35	State Forest SP	A-4
36	Steamboat Lake SP	A-3
37	Sweitzer Lake SP	D-2
38	Sylvan Lake SP	C-3
39	Trinidad SP	F-6
40	Vega SP	C-2
41	Yampa River SP	A-2

RA Recreation Area
SP State Park

COLORADO

★1771★ Colorado Division of Parks & Outdoor Recreation

1313 Sherman St, Suite 618
Denver, CO 80203
(303) 866-3437 - Phone
(303) 866-3206 - Fax
(800) 678-2267 - Reservations
Web: parks.state.co.us

Manages more than 270,000 acres of land at 41 state parks. Trail program maintains more than 500 miles of trails for hiking, biking, wildlife watching, horseback riding, cross-country skiing, snowshoeiing, snowmobiling, and off-roading. Snowmobile program provides 2,700 miles of groomed and marked winter trails for winter enthusiasts.

★1772★ Colorado Division of Wildlife

6060 Broadway
Denver, CO 80216
(303) 297-1192
Web: wildlife.state.co.us

Oversees the state's 960 wildlife species. Develops programs to protect and recover threatened and endangered species, regulates hunting and fishing licensing, and manages more than 230 wildlife areas.

Key to campsite classification:

Campsites — 14 x 14 tent pads, table, fire ring. Some campgrounds include electrical hook-ups, showers, laundry, and dump station facilities.

Camper Cabins — offer a variety of accommodations, featuring wood-burning, propane or electric heaters and are available year-round at select sites.

★1773★ ARKANSAS HEADWATERS RECREATION AREA

307 W Sackett Ave
Salida, CO 81201
Web: parks.state.co.us
Phone: 719-539-7289
Size: 18,000 acres. **Elevation:** 4,000-9,400 feet. **Location:** Extends south from the mining town of Leadville to the Pueblo Reservoir. Main roads of access include Highways 285/24 and 50/291. **Facilities:** 102 campsites (no drinking water available), group campground (with restrictions), 108 picnic sites, 14 bathhouses, trails (27 miles total), boat launches, visitor/nature center (&&). **Activities:** Camping (year-round), fishing, ice fishing, boating, river rafting and kayaking, swimming, hiking, mountain biking, horseback riding, hunting (with restrictions), rock climbing, sightseeing, interpretive programs. **Special Features:** Park

stretches nearly 150 miles along the Arkansas River, with spectacular views and abundant opportunities for outdoor recreation, including white-water boating.

★1774★ BARR LAKE STATE PARK

13401 Picadilly Rd
Brighton, CO 80603
Web: parks.state.co.us
Phone: 303-659-6005
Size: 815 acres land; 1,918 acres water. **Elevation:** 5,100 feet. **Location:** I-76 northeast from Denver to Bromley Lane, east 1 mile to Picadilly Road, and south 2 miles to park entrance. **Facilities:** 32 picnic sites, multi-use trails, boat ramp, visitor/nature center (&), restrooms (&). **Activities:** Boating (10-hp limit), sailboarding, fishing, hiking, mountain biking, horseback riding, hunting (with restrictions), cross-country skiing, snowshoeing, ice fishing, wildlife viewing, bird watching, guided tram tours (seasonal), interpretive programs. **Special Features:** Barr Lake is home to the Rocky Mountain Bird Observatory and is an important wildlife refuge, with more than 300 species of birds sighted on park lands. The southwest side of the lake and the marshes along its edge provide habitat for great blue herons, bald eagles, and pelicans. A family of eagles nests in the park each spring.

★1775★ BONNY LAKE STATE PARK

30010 County Rd 3
Idalia, CO 80735
Web: parks.state.co.us
Phone: 970-354-7306
Size: 5,000 acres land, 1,900 acres water. **Elevation:** 3,700 feet. **Location:** 23 miles north of Burlington on Highway 385, then east on County Road 2 or 3 for about 1.5 miles. **Facilities:** 190 campsites (100 with electrical hookups), group campground, showers, laundry, restrooms, 98 picnic sites, group picnic area, nature trail, snack bar, camp store, 6 boat ramps, fish cleaning station, marina, mooring/docking, boat rental, jet ski rental, visitor/nature center, (&&). **Activities:** Camping, boating, fishing, swimming, water-skiing, windsurfing, jet skiing, hunting (with restrictions), cross-country skiing, ice skating, ice fishing, winter camping, hiking, bird watching, interpretive programs. **Special Features:** An oasis on the plains, the lake offers a welcomed change from the rolling prairie and grasslands that surround the park. Bonny Lake is Colorado's easternmost state park.

★1776★ BOYD LAKE STATE PARK

3720 N County Rd 11-C
Loveland, CO 80539
Web: parks.state.co.us
Phone: 970-669-1739

Size: 400 acres land; 1,750 acres water. **Elevation:** 5,000 feet. **Location:** 23 miles north of Burlington on Highway 385, then east on County Road 2 or 3 for about 1.5 miles. **Facilities:** 148 campsites with electrical hookups, laundry, showers, restrooms, 90 picnic sites, group picnic area, snack bar, hiking trails, bike trails, bathhouse, 2 boat ramps, marina, mooring/docking, boat rental, sailboard and jet ski rental, visitor/nature center (රර). **Activities:** Camping, boating, fishing, swimming, water-skiing, jet skiing, sailboarding, hiking, bicycling, hunting (with restrictions), cross-country skiing, ice skating, ice fishing, winter camping, interpretive programs. **Special Features:** A family-oriented park in northern Colorado, Boyd Lake offers not only a modern water sports facility, but also features an introduced grassland community of species tolerant of sandy soils and drought, including a thriving prairie dog community. More than 200 species of migratory and resident birds also inhabit the park.

★1777★ CASTLEWOOD CANYON STATE PARK
2989 S Hwy 83
Franktown, CO 80116
Web: parks.state.co.us
Phone: 303-688-5242
Size: 2,136 acres. **Elevation:** 6,300 feet. **Location:** From I-25 at Castle Rock, east on Hwy 86 6miles to Franktown, then south on Hwy 83 (S Parker Rd) 5 miles to the park entrance. **Facilities:** 32 picnic sites, group picnic area, hiking trails (12 miles), bike trails (2.25 miles), horseback trail (1 mile), visitor/nature center, restrooms (රර). **Activities:** Hiking, mountain biking, rock climbing, bird watching, cross-country skiing, interpretive programs. **Special Features:** Located in the Black Forest in central Colorado, the park's attractions include dramatic canyon walls and ruins of a century-old dam.

★1778★ CHATFIELD STATE PARK
11500 N Roxborough Park Rd
Littleton, CO 80125
Web: parks.state.co.us
Phone: 303-791-7275
Size: 3,768 acres land; 1,550 acres water. **Elevation:** 5,430 feet. **Location:** From Denver, south on Wadsworth Ave (CO 121), south past C-470, then east into park at Deer Creek entrance; or south on Santa Fe to Titan Pkwy, then west to Roxborough Park Rd and turn north to Plum Creek entrance. **Facilities:** 153 campsites with electrical hookups, showers, laundry, restrooms, group campgrounds, 139 picnic sites, group picnic area, snack bar, multi-use trails (18 miles), bridle trails (24 miles), stables/horse rental, 3 boat ramps, marina, mooring/docking, boat rental, jet ski rental, model airplane field (රර). **Activities:** Camping, boating, fishing, swimming, water-skiing, sailboarding, jet skiing, hiking, bicycling, horseback riding, cross-country skiing, ice skating, ice fishing, winter camping, interpretive programs. **Special Features:** Located just outside the Denver metro area, Chatfield features rolling foothills, an expansive reservoir, and abundant wildlife. In addition to the wide range of other activities available here, the park is one of the most popular hot-air balloon launch areas on the Front Range.

★1779★ CHERRY CREEK STATE PARK
4201 S Parker Rd
Aurora, CO 80014
Web: parks.state.co.us
Phone: 303-699-3860; **Fax:** 303-699-3864
Size: 4,200 acres land; 880 acres water. **Elevation:** 5,550 feet. **Location:** 1 mile south of I-225 on Parker Road, adjacent to south Denver. **Facilities:** 102 campsites (80 with electrical hookups), showers, restrooms, laundry, 3 group campgrounds, 106 picnic sites, 5 group picnic areas, 2 snack bars, multi-use trails (12 miles), stables/horse rental, bathhouse, 2 boat ramps, marina, mooring/docking, boat rental, jet ski and sailboard rentals, model airplane field, shooting range (රර). **Activities:** Camping, boating, fishing, swimming, water-skiing, jet skiing, sailboarding, hiking, bicycling, horseback riding, cross-country skiing, ice skating, ice fishing, interpretive programs (seasonal). **Special Features:** Park features a natural prairie environment and an 880-acre lake that together provide complete range of outdoor recreation opportunities in the midst of a densely populated urban area. Crowded on summer weekends.

★1780★ CHEYENNE MOUNTAIN STATE PARK
4255 Sinton Rd
Colorado Springs, CO 80907
Web: parks.state.co.us
Phone: 719-227-5256
Location: In Colorado Springs, west of Highway 115. **Facilities:** Master plan is in development stages. **Special Features:** Colorado's newest state park, Cheyenne Mountain opened to the public in the fall of 2006. At that time it opened for day-use only, with a Visitor Center, trails, and picnic sites available. The campgrounds are expected to open late in the summer of 2007, and additional facilities will open as the construction progresses.

★1781★ CRAWFORD STATE PARK
PO Box 147
Crawford, CO 81415
Web: parks.state.co.us
Phone: 970-921-5721
Size: 337 acres land; 397 acres water. **Elevation:** 6,600 feet. **Location:** From Delta, CO 92 east to Hotchkiss and then 10 miles to Crawford; park is 1 mile south of town. **Facilities:** 66 campsites, electrical hookups, restrooms, 40 picnic sites, group picnic area, 2 boat ramps, multi-use trails, visitor/nature center (රර). **Activities:** Camping, boating, fishing, swimming, water-skiing, jet skiing, sailboarding, hiking, bicycling, hunting (with restrictions), snowmobiling, cross-country skiing, ice fishing, snowtubing, winter camping, interpretive programs. **Special Features:** Park lies adjacent to the Smith Fork River on Colorado's western slope, near Black Canyon of the Gunnison and Blue Mesa Reservoir.

★1782★ ELDORADO CANYON STATE PARK
9 Kneale Rd
Box B
Eldorado Springs, CO 80025
Web: parks.state.co.us
Phone: 303-494-3943; **Fax:** 303-499-2729

9. State Parks

Size: 1,441 acres. **Elevation:** 6,000 feet. **Location:** South from Boulder on CO 93 to CO 170, then on to park entrance west of the town of Eldorado Springs, about 8 miles southwest of Boulder. **Facilities:** 35 picnic sites, group picnic area, stables/horse rental, hiking and bridle trails (12 miles), bike trails (9 miles), visitor/nature center, restrooms. **Activities:** Fishing, hiking, mountain biking, horseback riding, rock climbing, hunting (with restrictions), cross-country skiing, interpretive programs. **Special Features:** Eldorado Canyon features sheer rock formations rising 1,500 feet above the canyon floor, affording some of the best technical rock climbing in the country. Park includes more than 500 different climbing routes.

★1783★ ELEVEN MILE STATE PARK

4229 County Rd 92
Lake George, CO 80827
Web: parks.state.co.us
Phone: 719-748-3401
Size: 4,075 acres land; 3,405 acres water. **Elevation:** 8,597 feet. **Location:** From Colorado Springs, US 24 west for 38 miles to1 mile west of the town of Lake George, then south 6 miles on County Road 90 to County Road 92, then south 5 miles to park. **Facilities:** 349 campsites (51 with electrical hookups), primitive backcountry campsites, showers, restrooms, laundry, 20 picnic sites, hiking and mountain bike trails (5 miles), 3 boat ramps, boat rentals, marina, mooring/docking, visitor/nature center (&&). **Activities:** Camping, boating, fishing, sailboarding, jet skiing, hiking, mountain biking, hunting (with restrictions), cross-country skiing, ice skating, ice fishing, snowtubing, winter camping, interpretive programs (seasonal). **Special Features:** One of Colorado's largest reservoirs, Eleven Mile offers uncrowded boating, ideal wind conditions, and some of the state's best trout and northern pike fishing.

★1784★ GOLDEN GATE CANYON STATE PARK

92 Crawford Gulch Rd
Golden, CO 80403
Web: parks.state.co.us
Phone: 303-582-3707; **Fax:** 303-582-3712
Size: 12,350 acres land; 20 acres water. **Elevation:** 9,100 feet. **Location:** Hwy 93 north from Golden, left on Golden Gate Canyon Road 13 miles. **Facilities:** 156 campsites (59 with electrical hookups), group campground, showers, restrooms, 7 cabins/yurts, 125 picnic sites, group picnic area, hiking trails (35 miles), mountain biking/horseback riding trails (22 miles) 20 backcountry campsites, 4 backcountry shelters, visitor/nature center (&&). **Activities:** Camping, fishing, hiking, mountain biking, horseback riding, rock climbing, hunting (with restrictions), cross-country skiing/snowshoeing, ice skating, ice fishing, winter camping, interpretive programs. **Special Features:** Wildflower meadows, autumn colors, and a panoramic view of more than 100 miles of the Continental Divide make this park ideal for sightseers and photographers. Park is located just 30 miles from Denver..

★1785★ HARVEY GAP STATE PARK

c/o Rifle Gap State Park
5775 Hwy 325
Rifle, CO 81650
Web: parks.state.co.us
Phone: 970-625-1607
Size: 160 acres land; 160 acres water. **Elevation:** 6,400 feet. **Location:** From I-70, exit to Silt, then 0.1 miles east on Main and then north 1.2 miles on 7th, which will become CR 214 (peach valley); turn west on CR 233 (Silt Mesa) for 1.1 miles, then north on CR 237 (Harvey Gap Rd) 3.3 miles to park entrance. **Facilities:** 30 picnic sites, boat ramp, restrooms. **Activities:** Boating (20-hp limit), sailboardng, fishing, swimming, ice fishing, ice skating, cross-country skiing, snowmobiling, snowtubing, hunting (with restrictions). **Special Features:** The lake at Harvey Gap sits in an area of cedar and sagebrush habitat, but the lakeshore has many shady cottonwood trees. The Grand Hogback, the ridge that marks the edge of the Rocky Mountains, runs along the south end of the 190-acre reservoir. The park, which is for day use only, offers easy access for all kinds of water recreation, and the reservoir is a favorite with anglers.

★1786★ HIGHLINE LAKE STATE PARK

1800 11.8 Rd
Loma, CO 81524
Web: parks.state.co.us
Phone: 970-858-7208
Size: 580 acres land; 174 acres water. **Elevation:** 4,700 feet. **Location:** From Grand Junction, west on I-70 to Loma exit, then north on CO 139 for 6 miles, west on Q Road 1.2 miles, north onto 11.8 Road for 1 mile to park entrance. **Facilities:** 28 campsites, showers, restrooms, laundry, 78 picnic sites, group picnic area, multi-use trails (5 miles), bathhouse, 2 boat ramps, boat rental, jet ski rental, observation deck, snack bar (&&). **Activities:** Camping, boating, fishing, swimming, water-skiing, sailboarding, jet skiing, hunting (with restrictions), hiking, mountain biking, horseback riding, ice skating, ice fishing, winter camping, bird watching. **Special Features:** Park features two lakes: Highline Lake is designated for water-skiers and boaters, and Mack Mesa Lake is designated for wakeless boating only. Both offer great fishing. The park is the center for water sports in the Grand Valley of western Colorado and makes an ideal base camp for exploring the Grand Junction area.

★1787★ JACKSON LAKE STATE PARK

26363 County Rd 3
Orchard, CO 80649
Web: parks.state.co.us
Phone: 970-645-2551
Size: 440 acres land; 2,700 acres water. **Elevation:** 4,440 feet. **Location:** From US 34 & I-76 interchange, take CO 39 north 7.25 miles through Goodrich, then west on Y5 for 2.5 miles. **Facilities:** 260 campsites (163 with electrical hookups), showers, restrooms, group campground, 60 picnic sites, group picnic area, snack bar, nature trail, swimming beach, boat ramp, marina, mooring/docking, boat rental, jet ski rental, sailboard rental, visitor/nature center (&&). **Activities:** Camping, boating, fishing, swimming, water-skiing, jet skiing, sailboarding, hunting (with restrictions), cross-country skiing, ice skating, ice fishing,

winter camping, bird watching, interpretive programs (seasonal). **Special Features:** Once known primarily for the hunting around its banks, Jackson Lake has become a site for outdoor recreation and water sports. The park is also known for its warm water, with sandy bottom and shore, and for its abundance of diverse bird species.

★1788★ JAMES M. ROBB - COLORADO RIVER
STATE PARK
PO Box 700
Clifton, CO 81520
Web: parks.state.co.us
Phone: 970-434-3388
Size: 335 total acres land; 103 total acres water. **Elevation:** 4,498-4,700 feet **Location:** Island Acres: I-70 to Exit 47, five miles east of Palisade; Fruita: I-70 to Exit 19 at Fruita, then south 1/4 mile on Hwy 340; Connected Lakes: from southwest portion of Grand Junction, go northwest on Dike Road from Broadway; Corn Lake: Exit 37 off I-70 to 32 Rd, then south 2 miles on Hwy 141; Wildlife Area: On D Road at 30 1/4 Road **Facilities:** Island Acres: 80 campsites, electric/sewer hookups, showers, laundry, 50 picnic sites, group picnic area, trails. Fruita: 63 campsites, electric/sewer hookups, group campground, showers, laundry, 11 picnic areas, group picnic area, bathhouse, boat ramp, trails, visitor/nature center. Connected Lakes: 24 picnic sites, hiking & mountain biking trails, boat ramp. Corn Lake: 20 picnic sites, multi-use trails, boat ramp. Wildlife Area: Multi-use trails. All locations have restrooms and ♿. **Activities:** Island Acres and Fruita: Camping, boating, fishing, sailboarding, swimming, ice fishing, ice skating, winter camping, interpretive programs. Connected Lakes: Picnicking, hiking, mountain biking, boating, fishing, sailboarding, ice fishing, ice skating, interpretive programs. Corn Lake: Picnicking, hiking, mountain biking, horseback riding, fishing, ice fishing, ice skating, interpretive programs. Wildlife Area: Hiking, mountain biking, horseback riding, fishing, interpretive programs. No gas motors permitted for boating/fishing. **Special Features:** Colorado River State Park is actually five separate parcels along the Colorado River where it flows through the Grand Junction area. Starting from the east going down river, the sections are Island Acres, Corn Lake, Wildlife Area, Connected Lakes, and Fruita. Each of the five sections has its own specialty, providing five unique outdoor opportunities.

★1789★ JOHN MARTIN RESERVOIR STATE PARK
30703 County Rd 24
Hasty, CO 81044
Web: parks.state.co.us
Phone: 719-829-1801; **Fax:** 719-829-1807
Size: 1,727 acres land; 11,450 acres water. **Elevation:** 3,851 feet. **Location:** From the East: US 50 west 20 miles to Hasty, then south on School Street for 2 miles. From the West: US 50 east 20 miles from La Junta to Las Animas, continue through Las Animas 16 miles to Hasty, then south on School Street for 2 miles. **Facilities:** 213 campsites, 163 electrical/sewer hookups, showers, laundry, group campground, 17 picnic areas, 3 group picnic areas, trails, 2 boat ramps, restrooms, visitor/nature center (♿). **Activities:** Camping, hiking, mountain biking, boating,

fishing, jet skiing, sailboarding, swimming, water-skiing, cross-country skiing/snowshoeing, ice fishing, ice skating, winter camping, interpretive programs. **Special Features:** Located in the Lower Arkansas River Valley in southeastern Colorado, John Martin is a large reservoir that accommodates all forms of water recreation. The park also supports a diverse community of wildlife and is a nesting place for the threatened piping plover and endangered interior least tern from mid-April to late August each year. Bald eagles can be seen here in the winter months.

★1790★ LAKE PUEBLO STATE PARK
640 Pueblo Reservoir Rd
Pueblo, CO 81005
Web: parks.state.co.us
Phone: 719-561-9320
Size: 9,045 acres land; 4,646 acres water. **Elevation:** 4,880 feet.
Location: I-25 to Pueblo, then US 50 west for 4 miles. Turn south on Pueblo Blvd and go 4 miles to Thatcher Ave, and west 6 miles to park. **Facilities:** 401 campsites, electrical hookups, 3 group campgrounds, showers, restrooms, 348 picnic sites, 4 group picnic areas, snack bar, hiking/mountain biking trails (18 miles), horseback trails (10 miles), swimming beach with waterslide, bathhouse, fishing piers, fish cleaning station, 2 boat ramps, 2 full-service marinas, mooring/docking, boat rental, jet ski rental, visitor/nature center (♿). **Activities:** Camping, boating, fishing, swimming, water-skiing, sailboarding, jet skiing, hiking, mountain biking, horseback riding, hunting (with restrictions), cross-country skiing, ice fishing, winter camping, interpretive programs. **Special Features:** With the Greenhorn and Sangre de Cristo mountain ranges as a background to the south and west and Pikes Peak to the north, Lake Pueblo is an area of contrasts. Miles of trails make it easy to discover the beauty of the area, but the park's 11-mile-long reservoir also makes it a prime destination for water sports enthusiasts.

★1791★ LATHROP STATE PARK
70 County Rd 502
Walsenburg, CO 81089
Web: parks.state.co.us
Phone: 719-738-2376
Size: 1,594 acres land, 320 acres water. **Elevation:** 6,400 feet.
Location: 3 miles west of Walsenburg on US 160. **Facilities:** 100 campsites, electrical hookups, group campgrounds, showers, restrooms, 40 picnic sites, group picnic area, hiking trails (5 miles), multi-use paved trail, 9-hole golf course, bathhouse, 3 boat ramps, visitor/nature center (♿). **Activities:** Camping, boating, fishing , swimming, water-skiing, sailboarding, jet skiing, hiking, bicycling, hunting (with restrictions), cross-country skiing, winter camping, interpretive programs. **Special Features:** Colorado's first state park, Lathrop has a 2-mile interpretive trail that winds through sandstone formations, then climbs up Hogback Ridge along the park's northern boundary, affording panoramic views of the Spanish Peaks, Sangre de Cristo, and Wet Mountain ranges. The park has two lakes, Martin Lake and Horshoe Lake, and the Visitors Center features artists' murals that showcase the area's history and heritage.

9. State Parks

★1792★ LORY STATE PARK

708 Lodgepole Dr
Bellvue, CO 80512
Web: parks.state.co.us
Phone: 970-493-1623
Size: 2,479 acres. **Elevation:** 7,015 feet. **Location:** From Ft Collins, take US 287 north through LaPorte, then left at the Bellvue exit onto County Road 23N, left 1.4 miles to County Road 25G, right 1.6 miles to park entrance. **Facilities:** 6 backcountry campsites, restrooms (&), 20 picnic sites (&), group picnic area, hiking trails (25 miles), bike trails (15 miles), bridle trails (15 miles), stables/horse rentals, visitor/nature center. **Activities:** Camping, hiking, mountain biking, horseback riding, rock climbing, hunting (with restrictions), cross-country skiing, snowtubing, winter camping, interpretive programs. Park borders Horsetooth Reservoir, where boating, fishing, water-skiing, and sailboarding are permitted. **Special Features:** Park is located along the edge of Horsetooth Reservoir in Larimer County, near Fort Collins. It features extensive trails, and its diverse terrain is home to a variety of wildlife, such as mule deer, wild turkey, black bear, mountain lion, coyote, blue grouse, and many reptile species.

★1793★ MANCOS STATE PARK

42545 County Rd N
Mancos, CO 81328
Web: parks.state.co.us
Phone: 970-533-7065
Size: 334 acres land; 216 acres water. **Elevation:** 7,800 feet. **Location:** From Durango take US 160 west 27 miles to the town of Mancos, north on Highway 184 about 0.25 miles, east onto County Road 42 about 4 miles, then west on County Road ''N'' 0.5 miles to the park entrance. **Facilities:** 32 campsites, 2 yurts, 12 picnic sites, group picnic area, volleyball court, horseshoe pits, restrooms, trails (5 miles), boat ramp (&&). **Activities:** Camping, boating, fishing, hiking, mountain biking, horseback riding, cross-country skiing, ice fishing, snowmobiling, winter camping, interpretive programs. **Special Features:** Mancos is located in southwest Colorado, surrounded by the San Juan mountains, 10 miles from Mesa Verde National Park (see entry in national parks section). The area is rich in western history, especially that of the Ancestral Puebloans whose ruins are preserved and displayed at the nearby Anasazi Heritage Center, 20 miles northwest in town of Dolores.

★1794★ MUELLER STATE PARK

PO Box 39
Divide, CO 80814
Web: parks.state.co.us
Phone: 719-687-2366
Size: 5,121 acres land; 10 acres water. **Elevation:** 9,500 feet. **Location:** 25 miles west of Colorado Springs on US 24 to Divide, then south 3.5 miles on CO 67 to the park entrance. **Facilities:** 132 campsites (110 with electrical hookups), showers, restrooms, 3 cabins, 41 picnic sites, stables/horse rental, hiking trails (55 miles), mountain biking trails (19 miles), horseback trails (27 miles), visitor/nature center (&&). **Activities:** Camping, fishing, hiking, mountain biking, horseback riding, hunting (with restrictions), cross-country skiing, ice fishing, snowtubing, winter camping, wildlife viewing, interpretive programs. **Special Features:** Park encompasses some of the most beautiful land in the state and is a favorite with photographers and sightseers. It's a popular wildlife watching area, including elk, black bear, eagles, and hawks, and features almost 55 miles of scenic trails.

★1795★ NAVAJO STATE PARK

1526 County Road 982
Box 1697
Arboles, CO 81121
Web: parks.state.co.us
Phone: 970-883-2208
Size: 2,672 acres land; 15,600 acres water. **Elevation:** 6,100 feet. **Location:** US 160 west from Pagosa Springs for 17 miles, southwest onto CO 151 for 18 miles to the town of Arboles, then 2 miles south on County Road 982. **Facilities:** 138 campsites, electrical and sewer hookups, showers, 3 cabins, camp store, 25 picnic sites, 2 group picnic areas, snack bar, hiking trail, boat ramp, marina, boat rentals, jet ski rentals, visitor/nature center (&&). **Activities:** Camping, boating, fishing, swimming, water-skiing, sailboarding, jet skiing, hiking, mountain biking, hunting (with restrictions), winter camping, interpretive programs. **Special Features:** Navajo Lake extends for 35 miles south into New Mexico and yields record-size fish in open waters without crowds. While the lake is the focal point of many of the activities at the park, visitors can also view wildlife and see interesting artifacts of the Anasazi Indians, who were the original inhabitants of this area.

★1796★ NORTH STERLING STATE PARK

24005 County Rd 330
Sterling, CO 80751
Web: parks.state.co.us
Phone: 970-522-3657
Size: 2,351 acres land; 2,880 acres water. **Elevation:** 4,065 feet. **Location:** From W Main Street in Sterling (Hwy 240), turn north 12 miles on N 7th Ave (CR 39) to the reservoir. **Facilities:** 141 campsites (97 with electrical hookups), showers, restrooms, 38 picnic sites, group picnic area, multi-use trails, snack bar, swimming beach, 3 boat ramps, marina, boat rentals, jet ski rentals, visitor/nature center (&&). **Activities:** Camping, boating, swimming, fishing, water-skiing, sailboarding, jet skiing, hunting (with restrictions), ice fishing, winter camping, interpretive programs. **Special Features:** Located in the eastern grasslands of Colorado, the park features scenic bluffs and expansive views of the surrounding high plains. North Sterling Reservoir is a popular boating area, with an array of coves and fingers to explore.

★1797★ PAONIA STATE PARK

PO Box 147
Crawford, CO 81415
Web: parks.state.co.us
Phone: 970-921-5721
Size: 1,507 acres land; 350 acres water. **Elevation:** 6,500 feet. **Location:** From Glenwood Springs take CO 82 south to Carbondale, then south and southwest on CO 133 for 46 miles. From

9. State Parks

Delta, take Highway 92 east to Hotchkiss, then north on Highway 133, 16 miles past Paonia. **Facilities:** 15 campsites (&), 10 picnic sites (&), restrooms (&), boat ramp. No drinking water available. **Activities:** Camping, picnicking, boating, fishing, water-skiing, sailboarding, jet skiing, cross-country skiing, snowtubing. **Special Features:** Park is surrounded by Gunnison National Forest (see entry in national forests section) and features views of the Ragged Mountains. An abundance of wildflowers makes the park a popular destination for photographers.

★1798★ PEARL LAKE STATE PARK
PO Box 750
Clark, CO 80428
Web: parks.state.co.us
Phone: 970-879-3922
Size: 169 acres land; 167 acres water. **Elevation:** 8,065 feet. **Location:** From Steamboat Springs go west 2 miles on US 40 to CR 129, north 23 miles to Pearl Lake Road, and east 2 miles to park entrance. **Facilities:** 38 campsites (&), 2 yurts, restrooms (&), 7 picnic sites, boat ramp, trails. **Activities:** Camping (late May to mid-October), boating, fishing, hunting (with restrictions), snowmobiling, cross-country skiing/snowshoeing, ice fishing. **Special Features:** Park is located in the mountains north of Steamboat Springs and features excellent fly and lure fishing for native cutthroat trout. Fishing at Pearl Lake is restricted to flies and artificial lures; bait fishing is prohibited. The best fishing of the year tends to be mid- to late May during ice off.

★1799★ RIDGWAY STATE PARK
28555 Hwy 550
Ridgway, CO 81432
Web: parks.state.co.us
Phone: 970-626-5822
Size: 2,200 acres land; 1,000 acres water. **Elevation:** 6,870 feet. **Location:** From Montrose, 22 miles south on US 550. **Facilities:** 280 campsites, electrical hookups, showers, laundry, restrooms, 3 yurts, 87 picnic sites, group picnic area, snack bar, stables/horse rental, multi-use trails (14 miles), swimming beach, bathhouse, boat ramp, marina, mooring/docking, boat rental, 2 fish cleaning stations, visitor/nature center (&&). **Activities:** Camping, boating, fishing, swimming, water-skiing, sailboarding, jet skiing, hiking, mountain biking, horseback riding, hunting, rock climbing, cross-country skiing/snowshoeing, ice skating, ice fishing, snowtubing, winter camping, interpretive programs. **Special Features:** Visitors to Ridgway enjoy exceptional scenery, including Mount Sneffels (14,149 feet above sea level), the San Juan Mountains to the south, and the Cimarron Range to the east. The park is known as one of the nation's most accessible recreation areas for people with disabilities.

★1800★ RIFLE FALLS STATE PARK
5775 Hwy 325
Rifle, CO 81650
Web: parks.state.co.us
Phone: 970-625-1607
Size: 93 acres. **Elevation:** 6,800 feet. **Location:** I-70 to Rifle exit, Highway 13 north through Rifle for 3 miles, then right

onto CO 325 for 10 miles. **Facilities:** 20 campsites (13 with electrical hookups), 9 picnic sites, trails (2 miles), restrooms (&&). **Activities:** Camping, fishing, hiking, mountain biking, spelunking, cross-country skiing, winter camping. **Special Features:** Park is in a lush valley with limestone caves and an 80-foot triple waterfall.

★1801★ RIFLE GAP STATE PARK
5775 Hwy 325
Rifle, CO 81650
Web: parks.state.co.us
Phone: 970-625-1607
Size: 1,700 acres land; 359 acres water. **Elevation:** 6,000 feet. **Location:** I-70 to Rifle exit, Highway 13 north through Rifle for 3 miles, then right onto CO 325 for 6 miles. **Facilities:** 49 campsites, restrooms (&), 24 picnic sites, group picnic area, trails, boat ramp, visitor/nature center (&). **Activities:** Camping, boating, fishing, swimming, scuba diving, water-skiing, sailboarding, jet skiing, cross-country skiing, ice skating, ice fishing, snowmobiling, snow tubing, winter camping, interpretive programs. **Special Features:** The clean, clear waters of the park's 350-acre reservoir offer some of the best water-sport opportunities in the state, including scuba diving. In addition, Rifle Gap is close to many ski areas, only 40 miles from Glenwood's famous hot springs, and is home to a variety of wildlife, including deer and elk.

★1802★ ROXBOROUGH STATE PARK
4751 N Roxborough Dr
Littleton, CO 80125
Web: parks.state.co.us
Phone: 303-973-3959
Size: 3,329 acres. **Elevation:** 6,500 feet. **Location:** Take C-470 to the Wadsworth exit, then go about 5 miles south and turn left onto Waterton Road for 1.6 miles until it ends at N Rampart Range Road. Go south on N Rampart Range Road for 2.3 miles to Roxborough Park Road and take the next right (about 50 yards away) to enter the park. **Facilities:** Hiking trails (12 miles), visitor/nature center, restrooms (&&). **Activities:** Hiking, cross-country skiing, interpretive programs. **Special Features:** Park preserves and protects an unusual geological feature—tilted, red sandstone towers—which have earned the park recognition as a National Natural Landmark. These red rock formations represent more than 1.2 billion years of geologic time.

★1803★ SAINT VRAIN STATE PARK
3525 State Hwy 119
Longmont, CO 80504
Web: parks.state.co.us
Phone: 303-678-9402
Size: 50 acres land; 80 acres water. **Elevation:** 4,900 feet. **Location:** 7 miles east of Longmont; from I-25, west on CO 119, then north on CR 7. **Facilities:** 60 campsites, hiking trail, 15 picnic sites, 3 fishing piers, restrooms (&&). **Activities:** Camping, boating (electric motors only), fishing, ice skating, ice fishing, cross-country skiing, winter camping, interpretive programs (by appointment). **Special Features:** Located in the

shadow of Long's Peak, the park offers great fishing and outstanding opportunities for bird watching, especially in the winter when bald eagles visit.

★1804★ SAN LUIS STATE PARK & WILDLIFE AREA

County Ln 6 N
PO Box 175
Mosca, CO 81146
Web: parks.state.co.us
Phone: 719-378-2020
Size: 2,054 acres land; 890 acres water. **Elevation:** 7,525 feet.
Location: Take Highway 160 west from Walsenburg for 60 miles, then north on Highway 150 for 13.5 miles, left on Six Mile Lane for 8 miles, and north a short distance to park entrance. **Facilities:** 51 campsites, electrical hookups, laundry, showers, restrooms, 27 picnic sites, multi-use trails, boat ramp (&&). **Activities:** Camping, boating, fishing, water-skiing, sailboarding, jet skiing, hiking, mountain biking, hunting (with restrictions), cross-country skiing/snowshoeing, ice skating, ice fishing, bird watching, interpretive programs. **Special Features:** Park is a unique desert area near Great Sand Dunes National Monument (see entry in national parks section), with a natural playa lake located amid rolling sand hills and flats. The park is also a wildlife area, with waterfowl, shorebirds, songbirds, and raptors as well as big game such as deer and elk. There's also a bison ranch nearby.

★1805★ SPINNEY MOUNTAIN STATE PARK

c/o Eleven Mile State Park
4229 County Rd 92
Lake George, CO 80827
Web: parks.state.co.us
Phone: 719-748-3401
Size: 3,400 acres land; 2,520 acres water. **Elevation:** 8,686 feet.
Location: From Colorado Springs take US 24 west for 55 miles over Wilkerson Pass. Turn left on Park County Road 23 and go 2.8 miles, then right on County Road 59 and continue on to park entrance. **Facilities:** 20 picnic sites (&), trails, 2 boat ramps, boat rental, restrooms (&). **Activities:** Boating, fishing, sailboarding, jet skiing, picnicking, bicycling, hunting (with restrictions), interpretive programs. **Special Features:** The park's reservoir is a Gold Medal Fishery, known for cutthroat, rainbow, brown trout, and northern pike. Adjacent to Eleven Mile State Park (see separate entry). This is a day-use park (no camping) that is open from approximately May to mid-November.

★1806★ STAGECOACH STATE PARK

PO Box 98
Oak Creek, CO 80467
Web: parks.state.co.us
Phone: 970-736-2436
Size: 866 acres land; 780 acres water. **Elevation:** 7,250 feet.
Location: From Steamboat Springs, 4 miles east on US 40, then south on CO 131 for 5 miles to Routt County Road 14 and then 7 miles south to park entrance. **Facilities:** 92 campsites (65 with electrical hookups), group campground, laundry, showers, restrooms, 50 picnic sites, group picnic area, snack bar, multi-use trails, swimming beach, bathhouse, 2 boat ramps,

marina, boat rentals (&&). **Activities:** Camping, boating, fishing, swimming, water-skiing, jet skiing, sailboarding, hiking, mountain biking, horseback riding, hunting (with restrictions), snowmobiling, cross-country skiing/snowshoeing, ice fishing, snowmobiling (with restrictions) snowtubing, winter camping, bird watching, interpretive programs. **Special Features:** Located in Yampa Valley, south of Steamboat Springs, the park is centered around a 780-acre reservoir with a full-service marina. This is also an area known for its mining and logging history.

★1807★ STATE FOREST STATE PARK

56750 Hwy 14
Walden, CO 80480
Web: parks.state.co.us
Phone: 970-723-8366; **Fax:** 970-723-8325
Size: 70,708 acres land; 130 acres water. **Elevation:** 9,100 feet.
Location: 75 miles west of Fort Collins on CO 14, over Cameron Pass. **Facilities:** 152 campsites, 32 electrical hookups, restrooms, 14 cabins and yurts, 9 picnic sites, hiking trails (94 miles), bike and bridle trails (130 miles), stables/horse rental, 2 boat ramps, mooring/docking, visitor/nature center (&&). **Activities:** Camping, boating, sailboarding, fishing, hiking, mountain biking, horseback riding, ATV riding, hunting (with restrictions), rock climbing, snowmobiling, cross-country skiing, ice skating, ice fishing, winter camping, interpretive programs. **Special Features:** Park presents the natural landscape of classic Colorado with soaring peaks, alpine lakes, and vast stretches of forest.

★1808★ STEAMBOAT LAKE STATE PARK

PO Box 750
Clark, CO 80428
Web: parks.state.co.us
Phone: 970-879-3922
Size: 1,505 acres land; 1,053 acres water. **Elevation:** 8,100 feet.
Location: From Steamboat Springs go west 2 miles on US 40 to County Road 129, turn north, and go 26 miles. **Facilities:** 198 campsites (83 with electrical hookups), 5 camper cabins, showers, restrooms, 25 picnic sites, snack bar, hiking trails (4.5 miles), bicycling trails (3.4 miles), bridle trails (6 miles), 3 boat ramps, marina, mooring/docking, boat rentals, visitor/nature center, wildlife viewing deck (&&). **Activities:** Camping, boating, fishing, swimming, water-skiing, jet skiing, sailboarding, hiking, bicycling, horseback riding, hunting (with restrictions), snowmobiling, cross-country skiing, ice fishing, winter camping, wildlife viewing, interpretive programs (seasonal). **Special Features:** Located at the base of Hahn's Peak, Park features spectacular scenery as well as excellent recreational opportunities, including access to 60 miles of premier snowmobiling trails in the adjacent Routt National Forest (see separate entry in national forests section).

★1809★ SWEITZER LAKE STATE PARK

1735 E Rd
PO Box 173
Delta, CO 81416
Web: parks.state.co.us
Phone: 970-874-4258

Size: 73 acres land; 137 acres water. **Elevation:** 5,000 feet. **Location:** 1 mile south of Delta on US 50; or 20 miles north of Montrose on US 50. **Facilities:** 32 picnic sites, group picnic areas, multi-use trail (1.5 miles), showers, boat ramp, restrooms, visitor/nature center (&&). **Activities:** Picnicking, boating, fishing (fish are not edible), swimming, water-skiing, jet skiing, hiking, sailboarding, hunting, bird watching, cross-country skiing, interpretive programs. **Special Features:** Sweitzer Lake, "the oasis on the edge of the desert," was developed solely for recreation,

★1810★ SYLVAN LAKE STATE PARK

10200 Brush Creek Rd
PO Box 1475
Eagle, CO 81631
Web: parks.state.co.us
Phone: 970-328-2021
Size: 1,427 acres land; 40 acres water. **Elevation:** 8,500 feet. **Location:** I-70 west to the Eagle exit, south through the town of Eagle to Brush Creek Road, then turn right and go 15 miles to the park. **Facilities:** 46 campsites, group campground, 9 cabins, 3 yurts, showers, restrooms, 30 picnic sites, multi-use trail (1 mile), boat ramp, boat rental, visitor/nature center (&&). **Activities:** Camping, boating (non-motorized or electric trolling motors only), fishing, sailboarding, hiking, mountain biking, hunting, snowmobiling, cross-country skiing, ice skating, ice fishing, snowtubing, winter camping, interpretive programs. **Special Features:** Park features a small mountain lake and is surrounded by the White River National Forest (see entry in national forests section).

★1811★ TRINIDAD LAKE STATE PARK

32610 State Hwy 12
Trinidad, CO 81082
Web: parks.state.co.us
Phone: 719-846-6951
Size: 1,600 acres land; 900 acres water. **Elevation:** 6,300 feet. **Location:** 3 miles west of Trinidad on CO 12. **Facilities:** 62 campsites, electrical hookups, group campground, laundry, showers, restrooms, 46 picnic sites, group picnic area, hiking/bicycle trails (10 miles), bridle trails (4 miles), boat ramp, mooring/docking, visitor/nature center (&&). **Activities:** Camping, boating, fishing, water-skiing, windsurfing, jet skiing, hiking, bicycling, horseback riding, hunting (with restrictions), cross-country skiing, ice skating, ice fishing, winter camping, interpretive programs (seasonal). **Special Features:** Park is located in the foothills of southern Colorado, bordered by the historic Santa Fe Trail and the scenic Highway of Legends. The nearby city of Trinidad was home and resting place to such famous names of the Old West as Wyatt Earp, Bat Masterson, Kit Carson, and Billy the Kid.

★1812★ VEGA STATE PARK

PO Box 186
Collbran, CO 81624
Web: parks.state.co.us
Phone: 970-487-3407
Size: 898 acres land; 900 acres water. **Elevation:** 8,000 feet.

Location: About 55 miles east of Grand Junction, turn south off I-70 onto CO 65, then east on CO 330 through Collbran and continue 12 miles to park entrance. **Facilities:** 108 campsites, electrical hookups, showers, restrooms, 5 camper cabins, group campground, 50 picnic sites, group picnic area, multi-use trails (2 miles), 3 boat ramps, visitor/nature center (&&). **Activities:** Camping, boating, fishing, water-skiing, jet skiing, sailboarding, hiking, mountain biking, ATV riding, hunting (with restrictions), snowmobiling, snowshoeing, ice fishing, snowtubing, winter camping, interpretive programs (seasonal). **Special Features:** Vega Lake sits in an alpine meadow on the west edge of Grand Mesa National Forest (see entry in national forests section).

★1813★ YAMPA RIVER STATE PARK

PO Box 759
Hayden, CO 81639
Web: parks.state.co.us
Phone: 970-276-2061
Size: 70 acres. **Elevation:** 6,300 feet. **Location:** All sites and the reservoir can be accessed from CO 40. The headquarters is located 2 miles west of Hayden. **Facilities:** 25 developed campsites and limited dispersed camping at Elkhead; 50 sites at a new campground near the Colorado State Parks Headquarters site; boat ramps; 47 picnic areas (20 at Elkhead); restrooms; multi-use trails; group picnic area, visitor center (&), educational facility, and observation decks at Headquarters site. **Activities:** Camping, whitewater rafting, canoeing, boating, water-skiing, jet skiing, sailboarding, fishing, hiking, mountain biking, horseback riding, cross-country skiing, snowmobiling, snow tubing, ice skating, ice fishing, winter camping, wildlife viewing. **Special Features:** Parks protects a 172-mile stretch of the Yampa River from Stagecoach Reservoir to Dinosaur National Monument, encompassing the entire Yampa Valley. The Yampa River is recognized as one of the most biologically intact river systems remaining in the West. Park includes the river, 8 public access sites, and Elkhead Reservoir, a 600-acre manmade lake just north of the river.

9. State Parks

Connecticut State Parks

CONNECTICUT

★1814★ **Connecticut State Parks Division**
79 Elm St
Hartford, CT 06106
(860) 424-3200 - Phone
(860) 424-4070 - Fax
(866) 287-2757 - Toll-free (Connecticut only)
(877) 668-2267 - Toll-free Reservations (860) 424-3006 - Employment
(860) 424-3200 - Volunteering
Web: www.dep.state.ct.us/stateparks
Oversees a system of more than 60 state parks and forests. Operates 100+ boat access sites at lakes, streams, and Long Island Sound. Also, maintains the state trail system, manages and operates historic and cultural sites, and interprets historic and natural resources.

★1815★ **Connecticut Wildlife Division**
79 Elm St
Hartford, CT 06106
(860) 424-3011 - Phone
(860) 424-4070 - Fax
Web: http://www.dep.state.ct.us/burnatr/wildlife/wdhome.htm
Manages the wildlife management areas. Also, promotes appreciation of wildlife, monitors wildlife habitat on state lands, and regulates hunting practices.

Key to campsite classification:

- **Campsites** — Showers, toilets, and drinking water are provided in most areas. Sewer connections and electrical hookups are not available.
- **Backpack campsites** — Primitive sites with few or no facilities along established trails. Small, Adirondack-type shelters available at some locations; stays are limited to one night.
- **Canoe campsites** — Primitive, with few or no facilities, on the Connecticut River. Stays limited to one night.
- **Horse camp** — Primitive campgrounds for equestrians, which include horse corral or tie-up areas.
- **Youth group camp** — Facilities vary; available free to recognized non-profit youth organizations.

★1816★ **AMERICAN LEGION & PEOPLES STATE FORESTS**
PO Box 161
Pleasant Valley, CT 06063
Web: www.dep.state.ct.us/stateparks/forests/amerlegion.htm
Phone: 860-379-2469
Size: 782 acres. **Location:** 1 mile north of Pleasant Valley on West River Road. **Facilities:** 30 campsites (open mid-April through Columbus Day), youth group camp, flush toilets (campground only) (&), hiking trails, picnic tables (&), picnic shelter (&), nature museum (seasonal). **Activities:** Camping, canoeing and kayaking, freshwater fishing, hiking, bicycling (roads only), hunting, cross-country skiing/snowshoeing, snowmobiling, field sports, interpretive programs (seasonal). **Special Features:** Forests are located in the Pleasant Valley section of Barkhamsted. The west branch of the Farmington River, a designated Wild and Scenic River, is the center of riverbased recreational activities. American Legion Forest features rugged terrain with steep, rocky hillsides and views of unusual rock formations and the river valley. Attractions at Peoples State Forest include the Barkhamsted Lighthouse and other cultural and historic sites. Campsites are at American Legion only.

★1817★ **BECKLEY FURNACE INDUSTRIAL MONUMENT**
c/o Burr Pond State Park
385 Burr Mountain Rd
Torrington, CT 06790
Web: dep.state.ct.us/stateparks/parks/beckley.htm
Phone: 860-482-1817
Size: 6 acres. **Location:** Lower Road off Route 44 in the East Canaan section of the Town of North Canaan. **Activities:** Picnicking, fishing, historical tours, interpretive programs. **Special Features:** Built in 1847, the Beckley blast furnace produced iron primarily for the manufacture of railroad car wheels that were known for their excellence and durability. The furnace closed in 1919 and stands today as the best preserved example of a technology that has long since vanished.

★1818★ **BIGELOW HOLLOW STATE PARK & NIPMUCK STATE FOREST**
c/o Shenipsit State Forest
166 Chestnut Hill Rd
Stafford Springs, CT 06076
Web: www.dep.state.ct.us/stateparks/parks/bigelow.htm
Phone: 860-684-3430
Size: 9,000 acres (Park and adjoining Forest). **Location:** Park is 2 miles east of Union on Route 197. **Facilities:** Picnic tables (&), hiking trails, boat launch ramp, pit toilets. **Activities:** Pond fishing, hiking, boating, scuba diving, mountain biking, cross-country skiing, snowmobiling, hunting (Forest only). **Special Features:** Scenic, natural setting includes access to two popular trout ponds, Bigelow Pond and Lake Mashapaug. The Bigelow Hollow and Nipmuck Forest lie within one of the largest unbroken forest areas in Eastern Connecticut. Forest includes a mountain laurel sanctuary.

★1819★ BLACK ROCK STATE PARK

c/o Topsmead State Forest
PO Box 1081
Litchfield, CT 06759
Web: www.dep.state.ct.us/stateparks/parks/blackrock.htm
Phone: 860-567-5694
Size: 443 acres. **Location:** 2 miles west of Thomaston on Route 6. **Facilities:** 96 campsites, restrooms (&), picnic tables (&), hiking trails, food concession. **Activities:** Camping (week-ends only mid-April through Memorial Day, then daily to October 1), pond and stream fishing, swimming, hiking, field sports. **Special Features:** The name Black Rock is derived from the local graphite deposits that resident Native Americans allowed the early settlers of Naugatuck Valley to mine. Early use of the area by Native Americans has been confirmed by the discovery of numerous arrowheads and stone implements once used by Mohegan, Paugussett, and Tunxis tribes.

★1820★ BLUFF POINT STATE PARK

c/o Fort Trumbull State Park
90 Walbach St
New London, CT 06320
Web: www.dep.state.ct.us/stateparks/parks/bluffpoint.htm
Phone: 860-444-7591
Size: 806 acres. **Location:** Exit I-95 at Route 117, then right onto US 1, left on Depot Road, and continue under railroad overpass to parking area. **Facilities:** Picnic tables, restrooms, boat launch. **Activities:** Saltwater fishing, shellfishing, hiking, picnicking, mountain biking, boating. **Special Features:** Park is a designated Coastal Reserve, which means it has been established ''for the purpose of preserving its native ecological associations, unique faunal and floral characteristics, geological features, and scenic qualities in a condition of undisturbed integrity.''

★1821★ BURR POND STATE PARK

384 Burr Mountain Rd
Torrington, CT 06790
Web: www.dep.state.ct.us/stateparks/parks/burrpond.htm
Phone: 860-482-1817
Size: 436 acres. **Location:** 5 miles north of Torrington on old Route 8. **Facilities:** Boat launch, picnic shelter, picnic tables (&), restrooms (&), food concessions. **Activities:** Fishing, boating, swimming, hiking, mountain biking. **Special Features:** Burr Pond is the site of Borden's first condensed milk factory in the United States, built in 1857. A scenic path encircles the 88-acre pond contained in the park.

★1822★ CAMPBELL FALLS STATE PARK RESERVE

c/o Burr Pond State Park
385 Burr Mountain Rd
Torrington, CT 06790
Web: dep.state.ct.us/stateparks/reserves/campbell.htm
Phone: 860-482-1817
Size: 102 acres. **Location:** Route 272 north from Norfolk center, then left onto Tobey Hill Road. **Activities:** Stream fishing, hiking. **Special Features:** Park is a natural reserve area with no developed facilities. It was donated to the State of Connecticut

and the Commonwealth of Massachusetts by the White Memorial Foundation of Litchfield, CT, and the two states cooperate in its care and maintenance.

★1823★ CHATFIELD HOLLOW STATE PARK

381 Rt 80
Killingworth, CT 06419
Web: www.dep.state.ct.us/stateparks/parks/chatfield.htm
Phone: 860-663-2030
Size: 356 acres. **Location:** 1.5 miles west of Killingworth on Route 80. **Facilities:** Picnic table (&), picnic shelters, trails, restrooms (&). **Activities:** Picnicking, pond and stream fishing, swimming, hiking, cross-country skiing. **Special Features:** Park is situated in a heavily wooded hollow with natural caves and rocky ledges. The park's trail system extends into adjoining Cockaponset State Forest (see separate entry).

★1824★ COCKAPONSET STATE FOREST

c/o Chatfield Hollow State Park
381 Rt 80
Killingworth, CT 06419
Web: www.dep.state.ct.us/stateparks/forests/cockaponset.htm
Phone: 860-663-2030
Size: 15,652 acres. **Location:** 3 miles west of Chester on Route 148, in Haddam. **Facilities:** Youth group camping area, pit toilets. **Activities:** Youth group camping, pond fishing, swimming, hiking, mountain biking, horseback riding, cross-country skiing, snowmobiling, hunting. **Special Features:** Named after an Algonquin chief who's buried in the Ponset section of Haddam, Cockaponset is the second largest state forest in Connecticut.

★1825★ COLLIS P. HUNTINGTON STATE PARK

c/o Putnam Memorial State Park
492 Black Road Tpke
Redding, CT 06896
Web: www.dep.state.ct.us/stateparks/parks/huntington.htm
Phone: 203-938-2285
Size: 878 acres. **Location:** Take Route 58 to Sunset Hill Road; park entrance is on the east side. **Facilities:** Trails, pit toilets. **Activities:** Canoeing, fishing (5 ponds), hiking, horseback riding, mountain biking, cross-country skiing. **Special Features:** Park was a gift from Archer and Anna Hyatt Huntington in memory of Archer Huntington's stepfather, Collis P. Huntington, a railroad tycoon. Anna Huntington was a world-famous sculptor, and her sculptures of bears and wolves welcome visitors at the park entrance.

★1826★ CONNECTICUT VALLEY RAILROAD STATE PARK

1 Railroad Ave
PO Box 452
Essex, CT 06426
Web: www.essexsteamtrain.com
Phone: 860-767-0103; **Fax:** 860-767-0104
Size: 300 acres. **Location:** Exit 3 off of Route 9 onto Railroad Avenue. **Special Features:** The park's land is owned by the

State of Connecticut and leased to the Connecticut Valley Railroad. From May through October, a vintage steam train takes visitors on an hour-long round trip to Chester. The train connects with an optional riverboat cruise at Deep River landing.

★1827★ DAY POND STATE PARK

c/o Eastern District HQ
209 Hebron Rd
Marlborough, CT 06447
Web: www.dep.state.ct.us/stateparks/parks/daypond.htm
Phone: 860-295-9523
Size: 180 acres. **Location:** 5.5 miles west of Colchester off Route 149. **Facilities:** Picnic shelter (&), trail, bathrooms (&). **Activities:** Picnicking, pond fishing, swimming, hiking, field sports. **Special Features:** Central feature of the park is a trout-stocked pond originally constructed by a pioneer family named Day.

★1828★ DENNIS HILL STATE PARK

c/o Burr Pond State Park
385 Burr Mountain Rd
Torrington, CT 06790
Web: www.dep.state.ct.us/stateparks/parks/dennishill.htm
Phone: 860-482-1817
Size: 240 acres. **Location:** 2 miles south of Norfolk on Route 272. **Facilities:** Picnic shelter (&), hiking trails, pit toilets. **Activities:** Picnicking, hiking. **Special Features:** Park is an estate that was owned by New York surgeon Frederick Shepherd Dennis and given to the state in 1935. The 1,627-foot summit pavilion (formerly a summer residence) offers views of Haystack Mountain, Mount Greylock in Massachusetts, the Green Mountains, and a portion of the state of New Hampshire. The park is especially beautiful during the fall foliage season.

★1829★ DEVIL'S HOPYARD STATE PARK

366 Hopyard Rd
East Haddam, CT 06423
Web: www.dep.state.ct.us/stateparks/parks/devilshopyard.htm
Phone: 860-873-8566
Size: 860 acres. **Location:** 3 miles north of the intersection of Route 82 and Route 156. **Facilities:** 21 wooded campsites, fishing platform (&), picnic shelters, picnic tables (&), trails, pit toilets (&). Camping is available from mid-April through Memorial Day weekend. **Activities:** Camping (including youth group camping), stream fishing, hiking, bicycling, birding. **Special Features:** Park's focal point is Chapman Falls, where water drops 60 feet into a pool, then continues on as Eight Mile River.

★1830★ DINOSAUR STATE PARK

400 West St
Rocky Hill, CT 06067
Web: www.dep.state.ct.us/stateparks/parks/dinosaur.htm
Phone: 860-529-8423; **Fax:** 860-257-1405
Size: 60 acres. **Location:** 1 mile east of Exit 23 off I-91. **Facilities:** Exhibit center (&), gift shop, picnic tables (&), arboretum, nature trails, bathrooms (&). **Activities:** Interpretive programs. **Special Features:** The park's geodesic dome exhibit center encloses a rock exposure that bears about 500 tracks made by dinosaurs of the Jurassic period (200 million years ago), an 80-foot-long diarama depicting the setting in which the tracks were made, and related interactive exhibits. From May 1 through October 31, visitors can make a cast of dinosaur tracks but must bring their own materials for this, including 10 pounds of plaster of paris.

★1831★ FORT GRISWOLD BATTLEFIELD STATE PARK

c/o Fort Trumbull State Park
90 Walbach St
New London, CT 06320
Web: www.dep.state.ct.us/stateparks/parks/fort_griswold.htm
Phone: 860-444-7591
Size: 16 acres. **Location:** 2 miles from Clarence B Sharp Highway exit off I-95 at 57 Fort Street in Groton. **Facilities:** Revolutionary War museum, picnic tables, portable toilets (&&). **Special Features:** Historic site where, on September 6, 1781, the British forces commanded by Benedict Arnold captured the Fort and massacred 88 of the 165 defenders stationed there. The home that sheltered the wounded after the battle, the Ebenezer Avery House, has been restored on park grounds.

★1832★ FORT TRUMBULL STATE PARK

90 Walbach St
New London, CT 06320
Web: www.dep.state.ct.us/stateparks/parks/fort_trumbull.htm
Phone: 860-444-7591
Size: 16 acres. **Location:** In New London, south of I-95 on the west side of Thames River. (Northbound I-95, Exit 83; southbound I-95, Exit 84). **Facilities:** Walking trail, fishing pier, conference center, visitor center, restrooms (&&). **Activities:** Fishing, tours of historic fort, including the ramparts, interactive exhibits. **Special Features:** Built from 1839 to 1852, Fort Trumbull is one of a group of 42 forts built to defend of the east coast of the United States. The visitor center's state-of-the-art exhibits and displays interpret more than 225 years of military history and technological advances, from the Revolutionary War to the Cold War. (The visitor center is closed between Columbus Day and Memorial Day Weekend.) Park also boasts one of the finest fishing piers on the east coast.

★1833★ GAY CITY STATE PARK

c/o Eastern District HQ
209 Hebron Rd
Marlborough, CT 06447
Web: www.dep.state.ct.us/stateparks/parks/gaycity.htm
Phone: 203-295-9523
Size: 1,569 acres. **Location:** 3 miles south of Bolton on Route 85. **Facilities:** Picnic tables (&), trails, bathrooms. **Activities:** Pond fishing, swimming, youth group camping, picnicking, hiking, mountain biking, field sports, cross-country skiing. **Special Features:** Park centers on the remains of an 18th-century, abandoned mill village. Stone foundations of mills, water ditches, and houses can be seen along wooded roads. The park adjoins Meshomasic State Forest.

9. State Parks

★1834★ GILLETTE CASTLE STATE PARK

67 River Rd
East Haddam, CT 06423
Web: www.dep.state.ct.us/stateparks/parks/gillettecastle.htm
Phone: 860-526-2336
Size: 184 acres. Location: 4 miles south of East Haddam off Route 82. Facilities: Primitive riverside camp sites, hiking trails, picnic shelter, picnic tables, restrooms, food concessions, scenic vista, historic building, visitor center (&&). Activities: Castle tours. Special Features: The park and its 24-room castle have recently undergone an $11 million renovation and restoration. The rugged stone castle, which was designed by actor William Gillette, sits atop a cliff high above the Connecticut River. Travelers to and from the west may want to take the Chester-Hadlyme ferry across the river.

★1835★ HADDAM MEADOWS STATE PARK

c/o Chatfield Hollow State Park
381 Rt 80
Killingworth, CT 06419
Web: www.dep.state.ct.us/stateparks/parks/
  haddammeadows.htm
Phone: 203-663-2030
Size: 175 acres. Location: 3 miles south of Higganum off Route 9A. Situated in the Connecticut River flood plain. Facilities: Picnic tables (&), boat launch, pit toilets. Activities: Boating, fishing, picnicking, field sports. Special Features: In colonial times the broad floodplain that is now Haddam Meadows State Park played an important role in the agricultural economy of the area. Fertilized each year by spring flooding along the banks of the Connecticut River, it yielded abundant crops of hay and grain. After the harvest, the meadow was used as common pasture for all who owned livestock in Haddam. Today the meadow is a popular spot for all types of field sports, and the Connecticut River offers water-based recreation.

★1836★ HALEY FARM STATE PARK

c/o Fort Trumbull State Park
90 Walbach St
New London, CT 06320
Web: dep.state.ct.us/stateparks/parks/haleyfarm.htm
Phone: 860-444-7591
Size: 198 acres. Location: Route 215 south to Brook Street, in Groton. Facilities: Bike trail (&), pit toilets. Activities: Hiking, bicycling, jogging, cross-country skiing. Special Features: A segment of the 7-mile Haley Farm Bike Trail from Mystic to Groton passes through the park.

★1837★ HAMMONASSET BEACH STATE PARK

1288 Boston Post Rd
PO Box 271
Madison, CT 06443
Web: www.dep.state.ct.us/stateparks/parks/hammonasset.htm
Phone: 203-245-2785; Fax: 203-245-9201
Size: 919 acres. Location: 1 mile south of Exit 62 from I-95. Facilities: 558 open campsites, showers, restrooms, picnic shelter, picnic tables, beach, walking trails, boardwalk, car top boat launch, food concession, nature center (&&). A limited number of specialized beach wheelchairs are available for disabled visitors. Activities: Camping (seasonal; mid-April-Columbus Day), carry-in boating, saltwater fishing, swimming, scuba diving, hiking, bicycling, interpretive programs. Special Features: Connecticut's largest public beach facility offers visitors two miles of white sandy beach.

★1838★ HARKNESS MEMORIAL STATE PARK

275 Great Neck Rd
Waterford, CT 06385
Web: www.dep.state.ct.us/stateparks/parks/harkness.htm
Phone: 203-443-5725
Size: 116 acres. Location: 4 miles south of New London on Route 213. Facilities: Mansion and formal gardens, picnic tables, bathrooms (&&). Activities: Mansion tours. Special Features: Eolia, the elegant 42-room Italian mansion that was once the summer home of the Edward S Harkness family, offers panoramic views of Long Island Sound. The mansion is available to rent for private events.

★1839★ HAYSTACK MOUNTAIN STATE PARK

c/o Burr Pond State Park
385 Burr Mountain Rd
Torrington, CT 06790
Web: www.dep.state.ct.us/stateparks/parks/haystack.htm
Phone: 860-482-1817
Size: 224 acres. Location: 1 mile north of Norfolk on Route 272. Facilities: Observation tower, scenic overlook, picnic tables (&), pit toilets. Activities: Hiking. Special Features: The 34-foot-high stone tower at the summit of Haystack Mountain (1,716 feet above sea level) allows visitors to see Long Island Sound, the Berkshires, and peaks in Massachusetts and New York.

★1840★ HOPEVILLE POND STATE PARK

193 Roode Rd
Jewett City, CT 06351
Web: www.dep.state.ct.us/stateparks/parks/hopeville.htm
Phone: 860-376-2920
Size: 554 acres. Location: 3 miles east of Jewett City on Route 201, off Exit 86 of Route 52. Facilities: 80 wooded campsites, 16 open sites, bathrooms (&), showers, concessions, picnic tables (&), boat launch ramp. Activities: Camping (seasonal, from mid-April to October 1), boating, pond fishing, swimming, hiking, bicycling, field sports. Special Features: Park was developed in the 1930s by the Civilian Conservation Corps around a former woolen mill pond. Pachaug State Forest (see separate entry) is nearby.

★1841★ HOUSATONIC MEADOWS STATE PARK

c/o Macedonia Brook State Park
159 Macedonia Brook Rd
Kent, CT 06757
Web: www.dep.state.ct.us/stateparks/parks/housatonic.htm
Phone: 860-927-3238
Size: 451 acres. Location: 1 mile north of Cornwall Bridge on Route 7. Facilities: 95 campsites with bathrooms and showers,

concession, picnic tables (&&). **Activities:** Camping (seasonal, from mid-April to December 31), youth camping, canoeing, fly fishing, hiking. **Special Features:** Park is located in the rock-strewn valley of the Housatonic River amid the rugged hills of the northwestern uplands. A two-mile stretch of river (including the park shore) is limited to fly fishing. A segment of the Appalachian National Scenic Trail passes through the park (see entry in national trails section).

★1842★ HURD STATE PARK

c/o Gillette Castle State Park
67 River Rd
East Haddam, CT 06423
Web: dep.state.ct.us/stateparks/parks/hurd.htm
Phone: 860-526-2336
Size: 884 acres. **Location:** 3 miles south of the center of Colbalt on Route 151. **Facilities:** Picnic shelters, picnic tables, pit toilets; primitive riverside campsites are available for people traveling on the river. **Activities:** Youth group camping, boat camping, hiking, mountain biking, picnicking, birding, freshwater fishing, cross-country skiing, rock climbing, field sports. **Special Features:** Situated on the high east bank of the Connecticut River, park affords scenic views of the river in spring and summer and of colorful foliage in autumn.

★1843★ INDIAN WELL STATE PARK

c/o Osbornedale State Park
PO Box 113
Derby, CT 06418
Web: www.dep.state.ct.us/stateparks/parks/indianwell.htm
Phone: 203-735-4311
Size: 153 acres. **Location:** 2 miles north of Shelton on Route 110. **Facilities:** Picnic shelter (&), bathrooms (&), boat launch. **Activities:** Boating, river fishing, swimming, picnicking, hiking, field sports. **Special Features:** Park is named Indian Well because of the Romeo and Juliet-like Native American legend surrounding the Park's scenic waterfalls and the splash pool at the bottom of the falls. Local Native Americans never actually used the area as a well. The park's primary attraction, however, is its location on the western bank of the Housatonic River.

★1844★ JAMES L. GOODWIN STATE FOREST

Goodwin Forest Conservation Education Center
23 Potter Rd
Hampton, CT 06226
Web: dep.state.ct.us/educ/goodwin/goodwinforest.htm
Phone: 860-455-9534; **Fax:** 860-455-9857
Size: 2,171 acres. **Location:** 3 miles east of South Chaplin on Route 6. **Facilities:** Pavilion, trails. **Activities:** Pond fishing, boating (non-motorized only), youth group camping, hiking, horseback riding, snowshoeing, cross-country skiing. **Special Features:** Forest features a butterfly garden, seasonal museum, and pond. The Goodwin Forest Conservation Education Center offers programs for the public, schools, and educators.

★1845★ JOHN A. MINETTO STATE PARK

c/o Burr Pond State Park
385 Burr Mountain Rd
Torrington, CT 06790
Web: www.dep.state.ct.us/stateparks/parks/minetto.htm
Phone: 860-482-1817
Size: 678 acres. **Location:** 6 miles north of Torrington on Route 272. **Facilities:** Picnic tables, bathrooms. **Activities:** Picnicking, pond and stream fishing, cross-country skiing. **Special Features:** The rolling, open land formerly known as Hall Meadow was renamed John A Minetto State Park in honor of the former state senator from Torrington.

★1846★ KENT FALLS STATE PARK

c/o Macedonia Brook State Park
159 Macedonia Brook Rd
Kent, CT 06757
Web: www.dep.state.ct.us/stateparks/parks/kentfalls.htm
Phone: 860-927-3238
Size: 295 acres. **Location:** 3 miles north of Kent on Route 7. **Facilities:** Picnic tables, trail, bathrooms (&&). **Activities:** Hiking, fishing, picnicking, photography. **Special Features:** One of Connecticut's most scenic parks, with a cascading waterfall that draws thousands of visitors each year, especially during the spring and fall. A stairway provides views of all levels of the casade.

★1847★ KETTLETOWN STATE PARK

1400 Georges Hill Rd
Southbury, CT 06488
Web: www.dep.state.ct.us/stateparks/parks/kettletown.htm
Phone: 203-264-5678
Size: 605 acres. **Location:** 5 miles south of Southbury, Exit 15 off I-84. **Facilities:** 68 partly wooded and open campsites (open mid-May to October 1), picnic tables (&), bathrooms (&). **Activities:** Camping, youth group camping (must apply in writing), freshwater fishing, swimming, hiking. **Special Features:** Park borders Lake Zoar, an impoundment of the Housatonic River. When settlers first arrived in this area, they purchased a large tract of land from the Native Americans for one brass kettle, so the name Kettletown was given to it. All of the state park lies within the boundaries of the original purchase.

★1848★ LAKE WARAMAUG STATE PARK

30 Lake Waramaug Rd
New Preston, CT 06777
Web: www.dep.state.ct.us/stateparks/parks/lakewaramaug.htm
Phone: 860-868-2592
Size: 95 acres. **Location:** 5 miles north of New Preston on Lake Waramaug Road (Route 478). **Facilities:** 78 wooded and open campsites (available mid-May through September), showers, bathrooms (&), food concession, picnic tables (&), canoe and kayak rentals. **Activities:** Camping (seasonal), lake fishing, swimming, scuba diving, boating. **Special Features:** Park features one of Connecticut's most scenic lakes. In autumn, vivid fall foliage is mirrored in the lake surface.

9. State Parks

★1849★ MACEDONIA BROOK STATE PARK
159 Macedonia Brook Rd
Kent, CT 06757
Web: www.dep.state.ct.us/stateparks/parks/macedonia.htm
Phone: 860-927-3238
Size: 2,300 acres. **Location:** 4 miles northwest of Kent off Route 341. **Facilities:** 51 campsites (open mid-April through September) with bathrooms (&), picnic shelter (&), picnic tables (&), trails, pit toilets. **Activities:** Camping, stream fishing, hiking, cross-country skiing. **Special Features:** Two peaks within the park are near 1,400 feet in elevation and offer outstanding views of the Catskills and Taconics. A segment of the Appalachian National Scenic Trail passes through the park (see entry in national trails section).

★1850★ MANSFIELD HOLLOW STATE PARK
c/o Mashamoquet Brook State Park
RFD 1 147 Wolf Den Rd
Pomfret Center, CT 06259
Web: dep.state.ct.us/stateparks/parks/mansfield.htm
Phone: 860-928-6121
Size: 2,328 acres. **Location:** 1 mile east of Mansfield Center off Route 89. **Facilities:** Boat launch ramp, nature trail, picnic tables, pit toilets. **Activities:** Boating, fishing, picnicking, hiking, mountain biking, field sports (&), cross-country skiing. **Special Features:** Damming of the Natchaug River by the Army Corps of Engineers has created a 500-acre lake for boating and fishing. No swimming is allowed since part of the lake is used for public water supply.

★1851★ MASHAMOQUET BROOK STATE PARK
147 Wolf Den Dr
Pomfret Center, CT 06259
Web: www.dep.state.ct.us/stateparks/parks/mashamoquet.htm
Phone: 860-928-6121
Size: 860 acres. **Location:** 5 miles southwest of Putnam on Route 44. **Facilities:** 20 wooded campsites and 35 open campsites (campgrounds open mid-April through September; available for youth camping), showers, bathrooms, picnic shelters, picnic tables, nature trail. **Activities:** Camping, fishing, swimming, hiking. **Special Features:** Park was formed by combining three smaller parks: Mashamoquet Brook, Wolf Den, and Saptree Run. The region was once the domain of the Mohegan chief Uncas.

★1852★ MILLERS POND STATE PARK RESERVE
c/o Chatfield Hollow State Park
381 Rt 80
Killingworth, CT 06419
Phone: 860-663-2030
Size: 15,642 acres. **Location:** Off of Foothills Road in Durham. **Facilities:** Park is a designated walk-in facility, with gravel parking at the main gate and pit toilets. **Activities:** Hiking, fishing. **Special Features:** Park is located in Cockaponsett State Forest. Millers Pond is unique in that its principal source of water comes from large springs which create a body of unpolluted water. The original dam at the pond was erected some time before 1704.

★1853★ MOHAWK STATE FOREST
20 Mohawk Mountain Rd
Goshen, CT 06756
Web: www.dep.state.ct.us/stateparks/forests/mohawk.htm
Phone: 860-491-3620
Size: 3,351 acres. **Location:** 4 miles west of Goshen on Route 4. **Facilities:** Lookout tower and overlook; pit toilets. **Activities:** Youth group camping, pond and stream fishing, hiking, snowmobiling. **Special Features:** A wildlife sanctuary with panoramic views, Forest contains a black spruce bog that gives visitors the opportunity to view a rare plant community. A segment of the Appalachian National Scenic Trail passes through the forest (see entry in national trails section).

★1854★ MOUNT TOM STATE PARK
c/o Lake Waramaug State Park
30 Lake Waramaug Rd
New Preston, CT 06777
Web: www.dep.state.ct.us/stateparks/parks/mounttom.htm
Phone: 860-868-2592
Size: 232 acres. **Location:** 3.5 miles west of Bantam off Route 202. **Facilities:** Picnic tables (&), food concession (&), hiking trail, bathhouse, observation tower, bathrooms (&). **Activities:** Boating (non-motorozed), fishing, swimming, scuba diving, hiking. **Special Features:** Park is one of the oldest in Connecticut's state park systems. The summit of Mount Tom is 1,325 feet, and a hiking trail ascends 500 feet along a one-mile route to a stone tower on top of the mountain.

★1855★ NATCHAUG STATE FOREST
c/o Mashamoquet Brook State Park
RFD #1 Wolf Den Rd
Pomfret Center, CT 06259
Web: www.dep.state.ct.us/stateparks/forests/natchaug.htm
Phone: 860-928-6121
Size: 12,935 acres. **Location:** 4 miles south of Phoenixville on Route 198 in Eastford. The entrance road bridge off Route198 in Eastford was closed to both vehicles and pedestrians in 2005 and will remain closed indefinitely until structural repairs have been made. General access to the Forest is available through the entrance located off of Pilfershire Road in Eastford. Parking for picnicking and fishing access along the Natchaug River is still off Route 198. **Facilities:** Primitive camping area for serious backpackers, horse camp sites (basic facilities only), picnic tables (&), trails, pit toilets. **Activities:** Horse and backpack camping, fishing (the Natchaug River is a designated Trout Park fishing area), hiking, mountain biking, horseback riding, cross-country skiing, snowmobiling, hunting. **Special Features:** Natchaug means "land between the rivers" and refers to the land at the junction of the Bigelow and Still Rivers, which join to form the Natchaug River. Of historic interest is a large stone fireplace and chimney, which are the remains of the birthplace of General Nathaniel Lyon, the first Union general killed in the Civil War.

★1856★ **NEHANTIC STATE FOREST**
c/o Gillette Castle State Park
67 River Rd
East Haddam, CT 06423
Web: dep.state.ct.us/stateparks/forests/nehantic.htm
Phone: 860-526-2336
Size: 5,062 acres. **Location:** Off Route 156 in Lyme. **Facilities:** Boat launch, picnic tables (&), pit toilets. **Activities:** Boating, hiking, picnicking, swimming. **Special Features:** The first state forest in New London County, Nehantic has all been purchased since 1925 and is mostly covered with a second growth of hardwoods. There are a number of good trout streams in the forest.

★1857★ **OSBORNEDALE STATE PARK**
555 Roosevelt Dr
Derby, CT 06418
Web: www.dep.state.ct.us/stateparks/parks/osbornedale.htm
Phone: 203-735-4311
Size: 350 acres. **Location:** 1 mile northwest of Derby off Route 34. **Facilities:** Picnic shelters, picnic tables (&), bathrooms (&), environmental center (&), historic home. **Activities:** Pond fishing, ice skating, field sports, hiking, museum tours, educational programs. **Special Features:** Park is located in the Naugatuck Valley hills just east of the Housatonic River, on land once owned by Mrs. Frances Osborne Kellogg. The recently renovated house and grounds that comprised her estate, the Osborne Homestead Museum, are located adjacent to the park, and guided tours are available to the public. The Kellog Environmental Center at Osbornedale State Park offers a number of programs and activities for the general public as well.

★1858★ **PACHAUG STATE FOREST**
Route 49
PO Box 5
Voluntown, CT 06384
Web: www.dep.state.ct.us/stateparks/forests/pachaug.htm
Phone: 860-376-4075
Size: 22,938 acres. **Location:** 1 mile north of the center of Voluntown on Route 49. **Facilities:** Forest has two principal areas, Chapman and Green Falls. Both areas have campsites (22 at Chapman, 18 at Green Falls), trails, boat launches, and picnic tables. The Chapman Area also has pit toilets and a horse camp with 18 campsites. The campgrounds at Green Falls are open from late April through September only. **Activities:** Camping, boating, freshwater fishing (& at Chapman Area), hiking, hunting, mountain biking (both areas); in addition, the Chapman Area offers backpack, horse, and youth camping, horseback riding, motorcycling, cross-country skiing, and snowmobiling. **Special Features:** The largest state forest in Connecticut, Pachaug contains southern white cedar swamps and a rhododendron sanctuary. The Chapman Area includes Mt Misery Overlook, the highest point in the vicinity (elevation 441 feet).

★1859★ **PENWOOD STATE PARK**
57 Gunn Mill Rd
Bloomfield, CT 06002
Web: www.dep.state.ct.us/stateparks/parks/penwood.htm
Phone: 860-242-1158

Size: 787 acres. **Location:** 4 miles west of Bloomfield on Route 185. **Facilities:** Picnic shelter, picnic tables, bathrooms (&&), trails. **Activities:** Hiking, mountain biking, cross-country skiing, picnicking. **Special Features:** Park has an extensive trail system, with most of the trails starting and ending in the main picnic area. A nature trail built by the Youth Conservation Corps encircles Lake Louise and passes by the pinnacle overlook. At the donor's request, ground fires, horses, and camping are specifically excluded from activities at this park.

★1860★ **PUTNAM MEMORIAL STATE PARK**
429 Black Rock Tpke
Redding, CT 06896
Web: www.dep.state.ct.us/stateparks/parks/putnam.htm
Phone: 203-938-2285
Size: 183 acres. **Location:** 3 miles south of Bethel on Route 58. **Facilities:** Youth group camping areas, museum, interpretive trail, pit toilets. **Activities:** Pond fishing, ice skating, hiking, field sports, picnicking. **Special Features:** Park is the site of the Continental Army's 1779 winter encampment under the command of General Israel Putnam. The site includes remains of the encampment, reconstructed log buildings, and a museum.

★1861★ **QUADDICK STATE PARK**
c/o Mashamoquet Brook State Park
147 Wolf Den Dr
Pomfret Center, CT 06259
Web: dep.state.ct.us/stateparks/parks/quaddick.htm
Phone: 860-928-6121
Size: 116 acres. **Location:** 7 miles northeast of Putnam via East Putnam Road off Route 44, at 818 Town Farm Road in Thompson. **Facilities:** Picnic shelters, picnic tables (&), bathrooms, bathhouses, boat launch. **Activities:** Boating, fishing, swimming, hiking, field sports (&), ice skating. **Special Features:** Park is located along Quaddick Reservoir in the northeast corner of the state.

★1862★ **ROCKY NECK STATE PARK**
PO Box 676
Niantic, CT 06357
Web: www.dep.state.ct.us/stateparks/parks/rockyneck.htm
Phone: 860-739-5471
Size: 708 acres. **Location:** 3 miles west of Niantic (Exit 72 from the Connecticut Turnpike), at 244 W Main Street (Rte 156) in East Lyme. **Facilities:** 160 wooded and open campsites (open May-September), showers, bathrooms (&), picnic tables (&), pavilion, food concession, hiking trails. **Activities:** Camping, hiking, saltwater fishing, swimming, scuba diving, field sports, interpretive programs. **Special Features:** Park's stone-free, mile-long beach on Long Island Sound is one of Connecticut's finest saltwater swimming beaches.

★1863★ **SALMON RIVER STATE FOREST**
c/o Eastern District HQ
209 Hebron Rd
Marlborough, CT 06447
Web: www.dep.state.ct.us/stateparks/forests/salmon.htm
Phone: 860-295-9523

9. State Parks

Size: 6,115 acres. **Location:** In Colchester, 2 miles west of Route 149 on River Road, adjacent to Day Pond State Park. **Facilities:** Picnic tables (&), fishing platform (&), pit toilets. **Activities:** River fishing, fly fishing, white water kayaking and canoeing (early spring), hiking, mountain biking, horseback riding, cross-country skiing, hunting (big and small game), sports field. **Special Features:** Forest includes a long stretch of the Salmon River, which is known for its excellent trout fishing and features an area designated for fly fishing. Kayak and canoe enthusiasts come in early spring for whitewater rapids.

★1864★ SELDEN NECK STATE PARK

c/o Gillette Castle State Park
67 River Rd
East Haddam, CT 06423
Web: dep.state.ct.us/stateparks/camping/rvrcmp.htm
Phone: 860-526-2336
Size: 528 acres. **Location:** An island in the Connecticut River, accessible by water only, in Lyme, CT. **Facilities:** Primitive campsites (May-September), fireplaces, pit toilets. **Activities:** River camping, hiking. **Special Features:** The only inhabitants of this island park are deer, wild turkey, and other wildlife.

**★1865★ SETH LOW PIERREPONT STATE PARK
        RESERVE**

c/o Putnam Memorial State Park
492 Black Rock Tpke
Redding, CT 06896
Web: dep.state.ct.us/stateparks/reserves/sethlow.htm
Phone: 203-938-2285
Size: 305 acres. **Location:** Off of Route 116, on Barlow Mountain Road in Ridgefield. **Facilities:** Boat launch, pit toilets. **Activities:** Hiking, fishing boating (small boats). **Special Features:** Reserve was a gift to the Connecticut State Park and Forest Commission from Seth Low Pierrepont, a millionaire and ex-diplomat, upon his death in 1956. It is a designated walk-in facility.

★1866★ SHENIPSIT STATE FOREST

166 Chestnut Hill Rd
Stafford Springs, CT 06076
Web: www.dep.state.ct.us/stateparks/forests/ctforests.htm
Phone: 860-684-3430
Size: 6,126 acres. **Location:** Off Route 190 in Stafford. **Facilities:** Civilian Conservation Corps museum, observation tower, outhouses. **Activities:** Hiking, fishing, picnicking, hunting (with restrictions), cross-country skiing, snowmobiling. **Special Features:** One of Connecticut's premiere places for viewing fall foliage.

★1867★ SHERWOOD ISLAND STATE PARK

PO Box 188
Greens Farms, CT 06436
Web: www.dep.state.ct.us/stateparks/parks/sherwood.htm
Phone: 203-226-6983
Size: 234 acres. **Location:** 2 miles south of Westport (Exit 18 off Connecticut Turnpike). **Facilities:** Picnic tables, picnic shelter, food concession, bathrooms, showers, pavilion, surf chairs (&&). **Activities:** Saltwater fishing, shellfishing, swimming, field sports, scuba diving, interpretive programs. **Special Features:** Park features large open fields and 1.5 miles of beach frontage on Long Island Sound. Park is a Viewpoint Exhibit Host Site, with outdoor exhibits that reproduce 19th Century works of art and provide information about the artist and the location.

★1868★ SILVER SANDS STATE PARK

c/o Osbornedale State Park
PO Box 113
Derby, CT 06418
Web: www.dep.state.ct.us/stateparks/parks/silversands.htm
Phone: 203-735-4311
Size: 310 acres. **Location:** Exit 35 off I-95. **Facilities:** Boardwalk (&), portable toilets (&). **Activities:** Saltwater fishing, swimming, picnicking. **Special Features:** Captain Kidd is reputed to have buried his treasure somewhere near here in 1699. State Park acquisition, ultimately involving over 300 parcels, began after Hurricane Diane destroyed 75 homes in 1955. The park's plan seeks to return the site to its historic past of interior tidal wetlands separated from the sound by sand dunes.

★1869★ SLEEPING GIANT STATE PARK

200 Mount Carmel Ave
Hamden, CT 06518
Web: www.dep.state.ct.us/stateparks/parks/sleepinggiant.htm
Phone: 203-789-7498
Size: 1,439 acres. **Location:** 2 miles north of Hamden off Route 10. **Facilities:** Youth group camping areas (written application required), picnic shelter, picnic tables (&), hiking trails, nature trail, bathrooms, observation tower, scenic vista. **Activities:** Stream fishing, hiking. **Special Features:** The ''sleeping giant'' is a 2-mile stretch of mountain top resembling a large man lying in repose. A 1.5 mile scenic trail leads to the stone observation tower on the peak of Mount Carmel, affording excellent views of Long Island Sound and the New Haven area. Park is a designated Trout Park.

★1870★ SOUTHFORD FALLS STATE PARK

Quaker Farms Rd
Rt 188
Southbury, CT 06488
Web: www.dep.state.ct.us/stateparks/parks/southford.htm
Phone: 203-264-5169
Size: 120 acres. **Location:** 4 miles southwest of Southbury on Route 188. **Facilities:** Picnic tables (&), bathrooms. **Activities:** Pond and stream fishing, hiking, field sports, cross-country skiing, ice skating. **Special Features:** At the turn of the century, Park was the site of the Diamond Match Company. Scenic waterfalls are located at the southeast end of the park on Eight Mile River. The Larkin Bridle Trail is nearby. Park is a designated Trout Park.

9. State Parks

★1871★ SQUANTZ POND STATE PARK

178 Shortwoods Rd
New Fairfield, CT 06810
Web: www.dep.state.ct.us/stateparks/parks/squantz.htm
Phone: 203-797-4165
Size: 172 acres. **Location:** 4 miles north of New Fairfield on Route 39. **Facilities:** Bathrooms (&), boat launch, fishing platform (&), picnic tables (&), food concession. **Activities:** Boating, pond fishing, swimming, scuba diving, hiking, ice skating. **Special Features:** In autumn, the park's pond is a favorite subject for photographers, capturing colorful reflections of foliage in the mirrored surface of the water.

★1872★ STRATTON BROOK STATE PARK

57 Gun Mill Rd
Bloomfield, CT 06002
Web: www.dep.state.ct.us/stateparks/parks/stratton.htm
Phone: 860-658-1388
Size: 148 acres. **Location:** 2 miles west of Simsbury, at 194 Stratton Brook Road, on Route 305. **Facilities:** Picnic shelters, picnic tables, bathhouses, bathrooms, bike trail, seasonal interpretive displays (&&). **Activities:** Fishing, swimming, hiking, bicycling, field sports, cross-country skiing, ice skating. **Special Features:** Connecticut's first totally wheelchair-accessible state park is one of the better-known small parks in the state because of its proximity to the Hartford metropolitan area. It is a designated Trout Park.

★1873★ TALCOTT MOUNTAIN STATE PARK

c/o Penwood State Park
57 Gunn Mill Rd
Bloomfield, CT 06002
Web: www.dep.state.ct.us/stateparks/parks/talcott.htm
Phone: 860-242-1158
Size: 557 acres. **Location:** 3 miles south of Simsbury on Route 185. **Facilities:** Picnic shelter, trails, observation tower, bathrooms. **Activities:** Hiking, picnicking. **Special Features:** A 1.5-mile hike brings the visitor to what is considered one of the most scenic vistas in the state. On the peak of the mountain is Heublein Tower, 1,000 feet above the Farmington River Valley. On clear days, visibility can be as great as 50 miles. The tower is open on a seasonal basis.

★1874★ TOPSMEAD STATE FOREST

PO Box 1081
Litchfield, CT 06759
Web: www.dep.state.ct.us/stateparks/forests/topsmead.htm
Phone: 860-567-5694
Size: 514 acres. **Location:** Off Route 118, 2 miles west of Route 8, less than 1 mile east of Litchfield Center. **Facilities:** Historic cottage, hiking trails, ecology trail with interpretive signs, pit toilets. **Activities:** Cottage tours (2x/month, June through October), hiking, hunting (permitted north of Route 118 only), cross-country skiing, birding. **Special Features:** Topsmead State Forest is the former summer estate of Miss Edith Morton Chase, who died in 1972. The estate includes an English Tudor style house surrounded by plantings of holly, lilac, and juniper as well as formal gardens.

★1875★ WADSWORTH FALLS STATE PARK

c/o Chatfield Hollow State Park
381 Rt 80
Killingworth, CT 06419
Web: www.dep.state.ct.us/stateparks/parks/wadsworth.htm
Phone: 860-663-2030
Size: 285 acres. **Location:** 2 miles southwest of Middletown on Route 157, at 721 Wadsworth St, Middlefield. **Facilities:** Picnic tables (&), hiking trails, bathrooms (&). **Activities:** Stream fishing, swimming, hiking, mountain biking. **Special Features:** Park features a scenic waterfall with an overlook and wooded trails through mountain laurel.

★1876★ WEST ROCK RIDGE STATE PARK

c/o Sleeping Giant State Park
200 Mount Carmel Ave
Hamden, CT 06518
Web: www.dep.state.ct.us/stateparks/parks/westrock.htm
Phone: 203-789-7498
Size: 1,533 acres. **Location:** On Wintergreen Avenue in Hamden. From Route 10 (Dixwell Avenue) turn west onto Benham, south onto Main Street, and then west onto Wintergreen. **Activities:** Hiking, canoeing, fishing, mountain biking, fall foliage viewing. **Special Features:** Rising up to 627 feet above sea level, West Rock Ridge is one of the most prominent physiographic features of the New Haven region. West Rock affords the visitor a spectacular view; it is estimated that one can see approximately 200 square miles from various locations on the ridge, with excellent views of New Haven Harbor and Long Island Sound. There are no bathroom facilities at this park.

★1877★ WHARTON BROOK STATE PARK

c/o Sleeping Giant State Park
200 Mount Carmel Ave
Hamden, CT 06518
Web: dep.state.ct.us/stateparks/parks/wharton.htm
Phone: 203-789-7498
Size: 96 acres. **Location:** 2 miles south of Wallingford on Route 5. **Facilities:** Picnic shelter (&), bathhouse, food concession, bathrooms. **Activities:** Fishing, swimming. **Special Features:** In 1918-1920, this site was known as a traveler's wayside, a forerunner of today's highway rest areas. Located on wooded, sandy knolls, Wharton Brook is still a good spot for a peaceful picnic. It is also a designated Trout Park.

Delaware State Parks

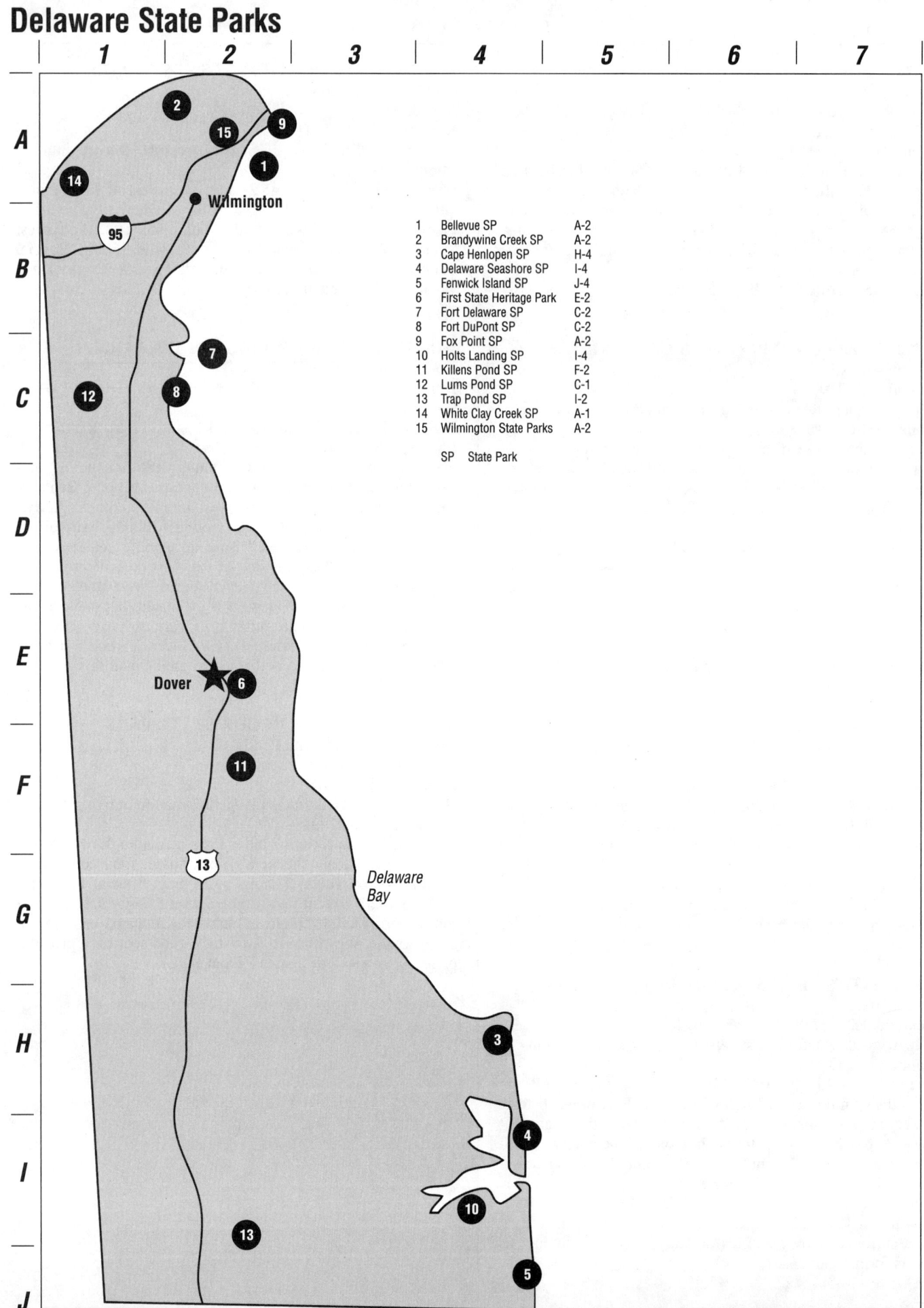

1	Bellevue SP	A-2
2	Brandywine Creek SP	A-2
3	Cape Henlopen SP	H-4
4	Delaware Seashore SP	I-4
5	Fenwick Island SP	J-4
6	First State Heritage Park	E-2
7	Fort Delaware SP	C-2
8	Fort DuPont SP	C-2
9	Fox Point SP	A-2
10	Holts Landing SP	I-4
11	Killens Pond SP	F-2
12	Lums Pond SP	C-1
13	Trap Pond SP	I-2
14	White Clay Creek SP	A-1
15	Wilmington State Parks	A-2

SP   State Park

Wilmington

Dover

Delaware Bay

DELAWARE

★1878★ Delaware Division of Parks & Recreation
89 Kings Hwy
Dover, DE 19901
(302) 739-9200 - Phone
(302) 739-3817 - Fax
(877) 987-2757 - Reservations
(302) 739-9200 - Volunteers
Web: www.destateparks.com
Operates and maintains 14 state parks (including related preserves and greenways) totaling more than 20,000 acres. Develops educational and interpretive programs and oversees the protection of natural areas.

★1879★ Delaware Division of Fish & Wildlife
89 Kings Hwy
Dover, DE 19901
(302) 739-9910
Web: www.fw.delaware.gov
Protects fish and wildlife resources and enforces laws and regulations designed to protect and conserve these resources. Offers hunter and boater safety education programs and provides environmental education programs and public outreach

---

★1880★ BELLEVUE STATE PARK
800 Carr Rd
Wilmington, DE 19809
Web: www.destateparks.com/bvsp/bvsp.htm
Phone: 302-761-6963; **Fax:** 302-761-6951
Size: 328 acres. **Location:** 2 miles north of Wilmington, off I-95, near the Marsh Road Exit. **Facilities:** Picnic areas, pavilions, playground, nature trails, fitness track, tennis courts, equestrian facilities (indoor and outdoor arenas), fishing pond, gardens, refreshments, restrooms (&&). **Activities:** Fishing (catch and release), hiking, bicycling, horseback riding, disc golf, guided tours, recreational and cultural programs (year round). **Special Features:** Once the family home of the William DuPont, Jr, Bellevue Hall is an elegant country estate situated on acres of parkland and surrounded by formal gardens. Available for rent for receptions, meetings, and other group functions, the mansion offers guests the charm of a historic setting with the amenities of a modern facility.

★1881★ BRANDYWINE CREEK STATE PARK
PO Box 3782
Greenville, DE 19807
Web: www.destateparks.com/bcsp/bcsp.asp
Phone: 302-577-3534
Size: 933 acres. **Location:** 3 miles north of Wilmington at the intersection of DE routes 100 and 92 in Greenville. **Facilities:**

Picnic area, pavilions, trails (14 miles), disc golf course, nature center, restrooms, gift shop (&&). **Activities:** Youth camping, canoeing/kayaking, tubing, fishing (&), hiking, bicycling, sledding, cross-country skiing, bird watching, kite flying, interpretive nature programs. **Special Features:** Delaware's first two nature preserves are located within the park — Tulip Tree Woods, a majestic stand of 190-year-old tulip poplar, and Freshwater Marsh.

★1882★ CAPE HENLOPEN STATE PARK
42 Cape Henlopen Dr
Lewes, DE 19958
Web: www.destateparks.com/chsp/chsp.htm
Phone: 302-645-8983
Size: 5,193 acres. **Location:** In Lewes, 1 mile east of the Cape May-Lewes Ferry. **Facilities:** 139 family campsites with water hookups, 17 family campsites with no hookups, youth group campsites (primitive; tents only), restrooms, showers, laundry, swimming beach/pool, fishing pier, fishing center, boat rentals, picnic area, pavilions, dune crossing, bike trail, nature trails, horse trails, nature center, disc golf course, game courts, ball fields, auditorium, gift shop, food concessions (&&). **Activities:** Family camping, youth camping, surf and pier fishing (&), swimming, hiking, bicycling, tennis, basketball, softball, picnicking, birdwatching, nature programs. **Special Features:** Located at the mouth of Delaware Bay, Cape Henlopen includes four miles of bay and ocean beaches as well as a pond wildlife area with a unique saltwater inpoundment and a broad salt marsh. Along the coast, the Great Dune rises 80 feet above sea level, and ''walking dunes'' slowly move across pine forests. The variety of habitats within the park make it a good home for many species of wildlife.

★1883★ DELAWARE SEASHORE STATE PARK
130 Coastal Hwy
Rehoboth Beach, DE 19971
Web: www.destateparks.com/dssp/dssp.asp
Phone: 302-227-2800
Size: 2,825 acres. **Location:** Between the Atlantic Ocean and Rehoboth Bay, on DE 1, between Dewey Beach and Bethany Beach. **Facilities:** 145 campsites with water, electric, and sewer hookups (some camping areas in the park are closed due to bridge construction that is expected to extend through 2009; these 145 sites are still open, but campers should be aware that there will be noise and dust from the construction work during this period), beach cottages, picnic areas, pavilions, restrooms, showers, swimming beaches, bathhouse, marina, fuel dock, boat ramp, charter and dive boat rentals, dune crossing, horse trails, nature trails, food concession (&&). **Activities:** Camping, boating, sailing, sailboarding, windsurfing, fishing (&), swimming, surfing, nature programs (seasonal). **Special Features:** Park is bounded on the west by Rehoboth Bay and Indian River Bay,

and on the east by nearly 7 miles of Atlantic Ocean beach. Thompson Island Preserve, northwest of the inlet, is a salt marsh habitat where osprey have established nesting areas.

★1884★ FENWICK ISLAND STATE PARK

c/o Delaware Seashore State Park
Inlet 850
Rehoboth Beach, DE 19971
Web: www.destateparks.com/fenwick/fisp.asp
Phone: 302-227-2800
Size: 344 acres. **Location:** Along the Atlantic Ocean on DE 1, between South Bethany Beach and the town of Fenwick Island. **Facilities:** Picnic area, swimming beach, bathhouse, shower facilities, restrooms, boat rentals, food concession, gift shop (&&). **Activities:** Swimming, fishing, crabbing, clamming, boating, sailing, surfing, windsurfing. **Special Features:** Park is a 3-mile stretch of barrier island along the Atlantic coast, and activities there are water-oriented.

★1885★ FIRST STATE HERITAGE PARK

c/o Delaware Division of Parks & Recreation
152 S State St
Dover, DE 19901
Web: www.destateparks.com/heritagepark
Phone: 302-739-9194
Facilities: Historical and cultural sites in Dover; visitor center, exhibits. **Activities:** Self-guided and guided tours. **Special Features:** Established by Governor Ruth Ann Minner in 2004, Park represents a partnership between the Delaware Dept of State, the Delaware Dept of Natural Resources & Environmental Control, and the Delaware Economic Development Office. The state's first "park without boundaries" links historical and cultural sites within the capital city of Dover. Included among the sites are Legislative Hall, the Delaware Public Archives, State House Museum, Museum Square, Biggs Museum of American Art, Woodburn/Hall House (governor's residence), and the Delaware State Visitor Center.

★1886★ FORT DELAWARE STATE PARK

PO Box 170
Delaware City, DE 19706
Web: www.destateparks.com/fdsp
Phone: 302-834-7941; **Fax:** 302-836-2539
Size: 288 acres. **Location:** On Pea Patch Island in the Delaware River between DE and NJ, 20 miles south of Wilmington. Access is by ferry located on Clinton Street in Delaware City; Delaware City is on the north side of the Chesapeake and Delaware Canal off Rte 9. **Facilities:** Civil War sites and exhibits, picnic area (&), nature trails, concession stand, restrooms (&), bird observation platform. **Activities:** Interpretive programs, picnicking, birdwatching. **Special Features:** Originally built in 1859 to protect the ports of Wilmington and Philadelphia, Fort Delaware served as a makeshift prison for 32,300 Confederate soldiers and Union deserters during the Civil War. Disease, malnutrition, and exposure killed more than 2,400 prisoners; many were buried across the river at what is now Finn's Point National Cemetery. (Fort Delaware closed in 2006 for historic preservation but is expected to reopen in the Spring of 2007.)

★1887★ FORT DUPONT STATE PARK

c/o Fort Delaware State Park
PO Box 170
Delaware City, DE 19706
Web: www.destateparks.com/fdsp/fdpp.htm
Phone: 302-834-7941
Size: 322 acres. **Location:** Along the Delaware River just south of Delaware City, off Route 9. **Facilities:** Picnic areas, trails, boat ramp, tennis courts, basketball courts, ball field, meeting facility, restrooms. **Activities:** Hiking, fishing, tennis, basketball, birdwatching, self-guided tours. **Special Features:** Named for Rear Admiral Samuel Francis duPont, the Fort was actively used as a military base from the Civil War through World War II. In this area also is the Port Penn Interpretive Center, which offers displays and programs that explain the folk life of the historic wetland communities along the shores of the Delaware. The Center also offers walking tours featuring the historic homes of Port Penn as well as the marshlands that surround the town of Delaware City.

★1888★ FOX POINT STATE PARK

c/o Bellevue State Park
800 Carr Rd
Wilmington, DE 19809
Web: www.destateparks.com/foxpt/foxpt.htm
Phone: 302-761-6963
Size: 171 acres. **Location:** East of I-495 at the Edgemoor Road north of Wilmington. **Facilities:** Picnic area, pavilions, playground, volleyball courts, horseshoe pits, restrooms (&). **Activities:** Picnicking, walking, biking, river viewing. **Special Features:** Formerly a toxic waste dump site, the property has been remediated and now offers a "window on the Delaware River," where visitors can watch commercial ships traveling to and from the port of Philadelphia. On clear days it's possible to see all the way north to Philadelphia and south past the Delaware Memorial Bridge.

★1889★ HOLTS LANDING STATE PARK

PO Box 76
Millville, DE 19970
Web: www.destateparks.com/holts/hlsp.htm
Phone: 302-539-9060
Size: 203 acres. **Location:** On Indian River Bay, off DE 26, just north of the towns of Millville and Ocean View. **Facilities:** Picnic area, pavilions, youth group campsites (tent only), restrooms, nature trail, boat ramp, playground, crabbing pier (&&). **Activities:** Boating, windsurfing, fishing, clamming, crabbing, hiking, bicycling, nature programs (seasonal). **Special Features:** Located on the south shore of Indian River Bay, the park has the only pier on Delaware's Inland Bay that was built specifically for crabbing. In addition, the park's Seahawk Nature Trail passes through four distinct habitats: broad-leaf forest, meadow, cordgrass marsh, and beach bay front.

★1890★ KILLENS POND STATE PARK

5025 Killens Pond Rd
Felton, DE 19943
Web: www.destateparks.com/kpsp/kpsp.htm
Phone: 302-284-4526

Size: 1,444 acres. **Location:** One mile east of US 13, south of Felton, DE. **Facilities:** 59 campsites (with water and electric hookups), 17 primitive campsites, 10 camping cabins, 1 cottage, restrooms, shower facilities, picnic area, pavilions, nature trails, boat ramp, boat rentals, fishing piers, swimming beach, waterslide park with swimming and wading pools, concession stand, game courts, ball fields, disc golf course, playground (&&). **Activities:** Camping, boating, fishing, swimming, hiking, bicycling, softball, volleyball, shuffleboard, nature programs. **Special Features:** Park's centerpiece is the 66-acre Killen pond, which features boating and fishing, but it also has a waterslide park with two 27-foot-high spiraling slides, 3 lap lanes for serious swimmers, toddler areas, and interactive water features.

★1891★ LUMS POND STATE PARK
1068 Howell School Rd
Bear, DE 19701
Web: www.destateparks.com/lpsp/lpsp.asp
Phone: 302-368-6989
Size: 1,790 acres. **Location:** On DE 71 south of Newark, just off DE 896. **Facilities:** 6 campsites with electric hookups, 66 campsites without hookups (4 are horse sites), 2 yurts, showers, restrooms, picnic area, pavilions, nature trails, multi-use trails, marina, boat rentals, boat ramp, fishing pier, nature center, game courts, ball fields, disc golf course, playground, food concession (&&). **Activities:** Family camping, youth group camping, boating, fishing, hiking, bicycling, horseback riding, baseball, softball, basketball, football, soccer, tennis, volleyball, nature programs (seasonal). **Special Features:** Park is built around the largest freshwater pond in Delaware, and includes the Whale Wallow Nature Center and a unique 0.1-mile Sensory Trail.

★1892★ TRAP POND STATE PARK
33587 Baldcypress Ln
Laurel, DE 19956
Web: www.destateparks.com/tpsp/tpsp.htm
Phone: 302-875-5153
Size: 3,106 acres. **Location:** 5 miles east of Laurel, off DE 24. **Facilities:** 130 campsites (with electric and water hookups), 12 walk-in tent sites, 2 yurts, 8 camping cabins, shower facilities, restrooms, laundry, picnic area, pavilions, food concession, boat ramp, boat rentals, nature trails, game courts, ball fields, playground (&&). **Activities:** Family camping, youth group camping, boating, fishing, hiking, horseback riding, nature programs. **Special Features:** Park features the northernmost natural stand of baldcypress trees in the US. The pond was originally created to power a sawmill during the harvest of large baldcypress from the area. During the 1930s the government purchased the pond and surrounding farmland, and the Civilian Conservation Corps began developing the area for recreation.

★1893★ WHITE CLAY CREEK STATE PARK
425 Wedgewood Rd
Newark, DE 19711
Web: www.destateparks.com/wccsp
Phone: 302-368-6900
Size: 3,384 acres. **Location:** 2 miles north of Newark on DE 896. **Facilities:** Picnic area, pavilions, hiking and shared-use trails, historical sites, nature programs, food concession, restrooms (&&). **Activities:** Hiking, mountain biking, horseback riding, picnicking, fishing, hunting, cross-country skiing, sledding, nature programs, birdwatching. **Special Features:** Park includes four linked sections: the Carpenter Recreation Area, White Clay Creek Preserve (see entry in Pennsylvania state parks section), Possum Hill, and the Judge Morris Estate. It is known especially for its excellent birdwatching.

★1894★ WILMINGTON STATE PARKS
1021 W 18th St
Wilmington, DE 19802
Web: www.destateparks.com/wilmsp/wilmsp.htm
Phone: 302-577-7020; **Fax:** 302-577-7084
Location: In downtown Wilmington, along the Brandywine River. **Facilities:** Picnic areas, pavilions, trails, game courts, sports fields, food concessions, restrooms, playgrounds (&&). (These facilities are mainly at Brandywine and Rockford parks; Fletcher Brown and Alapocas are mainly areas to relax and enjoy the scenery.) **Activities:** Hiking, bicycling, inline skating, tennis, basketball, hockey, baseball, softball, football, soccer. **Special Features:** Wilmington State Parks is made up of both city- and state-owned land and is managed by the Delaware Division of Parks and Recreation. The park is actually a cluster of four urban parks connected by trails: Brandywine Park (including the Brandywine Zoo and Baynard Stadium), Rockford Park, H. Fletcher Brown Park, and Alapocas Woods Natural Area.

9. State Parks

Florida State Parks

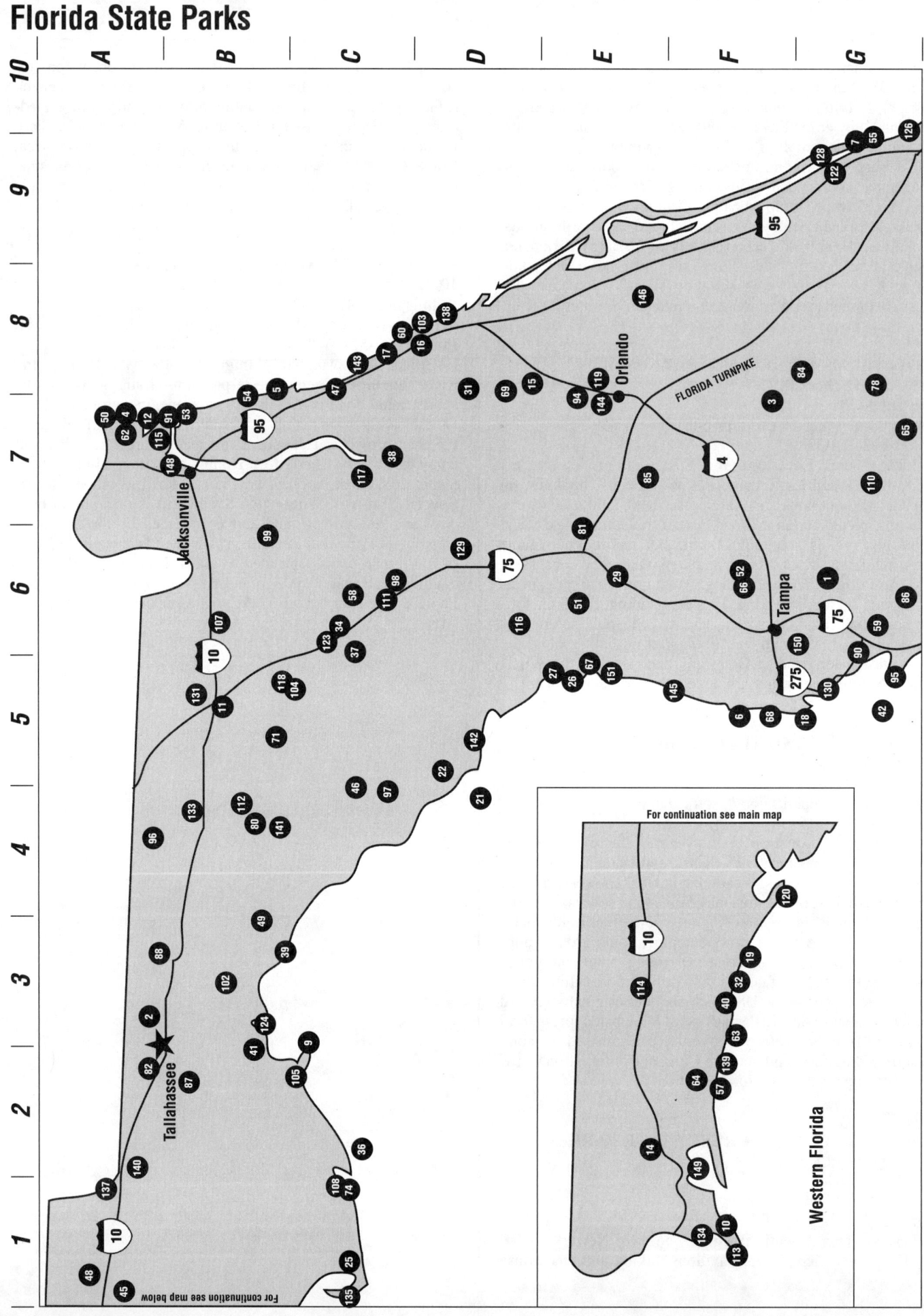

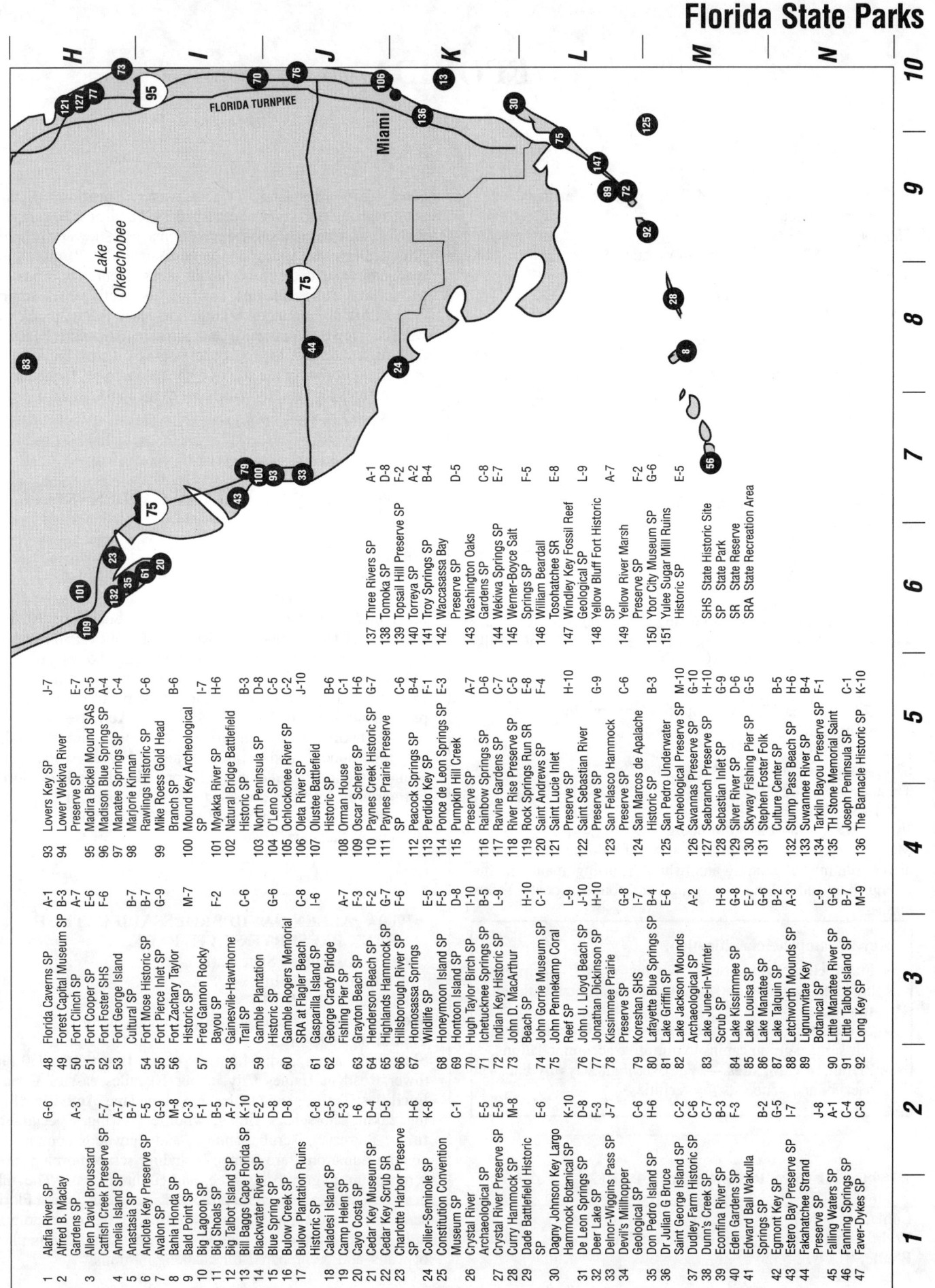

Florida Turnpike
Lake Okeechobee
Miami

#	Park	Grid
1	Alafia River SP	G-6
2	Alfred B. Maclay Gardens SP	A-3
3	Allen David Broussard Catfish Creek Preserve SP	F-7
4	Amelia Island SP	A-7
5	Anastasia SP	B-7
6	Anclote Key Preserve SP	F-5
7	Avalon SP	G-9
8	Bahia Honda SP	M-8
9	Bald Point SP	C-3
10	Big Lagoon SP	F-1
11	Big Shoals SP	B-5
12	Big Talbot Island SP	A-7
13	Bill Baggs Cape Florida SP	K-10
14	Blackwater River SP	E-2
15	Blue Spring SP	D-8
16	Bulow Creek SP	D-8
17	Bulow Plantation Ruins Historic SP	C-8
18	Caladesi Island SP	G-5
19	Camp Helen SP	F-3
20	Cayo Costa SP	I-6
21	Cedar Key Museum SP	D-4
22	Cedar Key Scrub SR	D-5
23	Charlotte Harbor Preserve SP	H-6
24	Collier-Seminole SP	K-8
25	Constitution Convention Museum SP	C-1
26	Crystal River Archaeological SP	E-5
27	Crystal River Preserve SP	E-5
28	Curry Hammock SP	M-8
29	Dade Battlefield Historic SP	E-6
30	Dagny Johnson Key Largo Hammock Botanical SP	K-10
31	De Leon Springs SP	D-8
32	Deer Lake SP	F-3
33	Delnor-Wiggins Pass SP	J-7
34	Devil's Millhopper Geological SP	C-6
35	Don Pedro Island SP	H-6
36	Dr Julian G Bruce Saint George Island SP	C-2
37	Dudley Farm Historic SP	C-6
38	Dunn's Creek SP	C-7
39	Econfina River SP	B-3
40	Eden Gardens SP	F-3
41	Edward Ball Wakulla Springs SP	B-2
42	Egmont Key SP	G-5
43	Estero Bay Preserve SP	I-7
44	Fakahatchee Strand Preserve SP	J-8
45	Falling Waters SP	A-1
46	Fanning Springs SP	C-4
47	Faver-Dykes SP	C-8
48	Florida Caverns SP	A-1
49	Forest Capital Museum SP	B-3
50	Fort Clinch SP	A-7
51	Fort Cooper SP	E-6
52	Fort Foster SHS	F-6
53	Fort George Island Cultural SP	B-7
54	Fort Mose Historic SP	B-7
55	Fort Pierce Inlet SP	G-9
56	Fort Zachary Taylor Historic SP	M-7
57	Fred Gannon Rocky Bayou SP	F-2
58	Gainesvile-Hawthorne Trail SP	C-6
59	Gamble Plantation Historic SP	G-6
60	Gamble Rogers Memorial SRA at Flagler Beach	C-8
61	Gasparilla Island SP	I-6
62	George Crady Bridge Fishing Pier SP	A-7
63	Grayton Beach SP	F-3
64	Henderson Beach SP	F-2
65	Highlands Hammock SP	G-7
66	Hillsborough River SP	F-6
67	Homosassa Springs Wildlife SP	E-5
68	Honeymoon Island SP	F-5
69	Hontoon Island SP	D-8
70	Hugh Taylor Birch SP	I-10
71	Ichetucknee Springs SP	B-5
72	Indian Key Historic SP	L-9
73	John D. MacArthur Beach SP	H-10
74	John Gorrie Museum SP	C-1
75	John Pennekamp Coral Reef SP	K-10
76	John U. Lloyd Beach SP	J-10
77	Jonathan Dickinson SP	H-10
78	Kissimmee Prairie Preserve SP	G-8
79	Koreshan SHS	I-7
80	Lafayette Blue Springs SP	B-4
81	Lake Griffin SP	E-6
82	Lake Jackson Mounds Archaeological SP	A-2
83	Lake June-in-Winter Scrub SP	H-8
84	Lake Kissimmee SP	G-8
85	Lake Louisa SP	E-7
86	Lake Manatee SP	G-6
87	Lake Talquin SP	B-2
88	Letchworth Mounds SP	A-3
89	Lignumvitae Key Botanical SP	L-9
90	Little Manatee River SP	G-6
91	Little Talbot Island SP	B-7
92	Long Key SP	M-9
93	Lovers Key SP	J-7
94	Lower Wekiva River Preserve SP	E-7
95	Madira Bickel Mound SAS	G-5
96	Madison Blue Springs SP	A-4
97	Manatee Springs SP	C-4
98	Marjorie Kinnan Rawlings Historic SP	C-6
99	Mike Roess Gold Head Branch SP	B-6
100	Mound Key Archeological SP	I-7
101	Myakka River SP	H-6
102	Natural Bridge Battlefield Historic SP	B-3
103	North Peninsula SP	D-8
104	O'Leno SP	C-5
105	Ochlockonee River SP	C-2
106	Oleta River SP	J-10
107	Olustee Battlefield Historic SP	B-6
108	Orman House	C-1
109	Oscar Scherer SP	H-6
110	Paynes Creek Historic SP	G-7
111	Paynes Prairie Preserve SP	C-6
112	Peacock Springs SP	B-4
113	Perdido Key SP	F-1
114	Ponce de Leon Springs SP	E-3
115	Pumpkin Hill Creek Preserve SP	A-7
116	Rainbow Springs SP	D-6
117	Ravine Gardens SP	C-7
118	River Rise Preserve SP	C-5
119	Rock Springs Run SR	E-8
120	Saint Andrews SP	F-4
121	Saint Lucie Inlet Preserve SP	H-10
122	Saint Sebastian River Preserve SP	G-9
123	San Felasco Hammock Preserve SP	C-6
124	San Marcos de Apalache Historic SP	B-3
125	San Pedro Underwater Archeological Preserve SP	M-10
126	Savannas Preserve SP	H-10
127	Seabranch Preserve SP	H-10
128	Sebastian Inlet SP	G-9
129	Silver River SP	D-6
130	Skyway Fishing Pier SP	G-5
131	Stephen Foster Folk Culture Center SP	B-5
132	Stump Pass Beach SP	H-6
133	Suwannee River SP	B-4
134	Tarkiln Bayou Preserve SP	F-1
135	TH Stone Memorial Saint Joseph Peninsula SP	C-1
136	The Barnacle Historic SP	K-10
137	Three Rivers SP	A-1
138	Tomoka SP	D-8
139	Topsail Hill Preserve SP	F-2
140	Torreya SP	A-2
141	Troy Springs SP	B-4
142	Waccasassa Bay Preserve SP	D-5
143	Washington Oaks Gardens SP	C-8
144	Wekiwa Springs SP	E-7
145	Werner-Boyce Salt Springs SP	F-5
146	William Beardall Tosohatchee SR	E-8
147	Windley Key Fossil Reef Geological SP	L-9
148	Yellow Bluff Fort Historic SP	A-7
149	Yellow River Marsh Preserve SP	F-2
150	Ybor City Museum SP	G-6
151	Yulee Sugar Mill Ruins Historic SP	E-5

SHS State Historic Site
SP State Park
SR State Reserve
SRA State Recreation Area

FLORIDA

★1895★ **Florida Division of Recreation & Parks**
3900 Commonwealth Blvd
Tallahassee, FL 32399
(850) 245-2157 – State Parks Information Center
(850) 245-3038 - Fax
(800) 326-3521 - Reservations
(850) 245-3098 - Volunteering
Web: www.floridastateparks.org
Comprising more than 723,000 acres and 100 miles of beach, system includes 159 state properties including parks, museums, preserves, gardens, trails, and areas designated as historic, archeological, and cultural sites. Parks include beaches rated among the best in the world, as well as underwater preserves and archeological sites for divers.

★1896★ **Florida Division of Forestry**
3125 Conner Blvd
Tallahassee, FL 32399
(850) 488-4274 - Phone
(850) 488-0863 - Fax
Web: www.fl-dof.com
Manages 33 state forests comprising 1,045,000 acres. Operates and maintains developed facilities for camping, swimming, hiking, horseback riding, fishing, and hunting.

★1897★ **Florida Fish & Wildlife Conservation Commission**
Farris Bryant Bldg
620 S Meridian St
Tallahassee, FL 32399
(850) 488-4676
Web: www.floridaconservation.org
Manages more than five million acres of wildlife management areas. Administers hunting and fishing licensing, maintains numerous boat and fishing access sites, and conducts boater safety classes.

> **Key to campsite classification:**
> - **Full-facility campsites** — For tent or RV; electricity hookups, water spigots, and nearby restrooms with hot showers.
> - **Group and Youth group camps** — Facilities vary from full-service group cabins to primitive accommodations.
> - **Primitive campsites** — For overnight stays by backpackers and canoeists; no facilities.

★1898★ **ALAFIA RIVER STATE PARK**
14326 S County Rd 39
Lithia, FL 33547
Web: www.floridastateparks.org/alafiariver
Phone: 813-672-5320

Size: 6,258 acres land; 54 acres water. **Location:** 10 miles southeast of Tampa on County Road 39. **Facilities:** 30 campsites with water, electrical service, restrooms, and showers, primitive group campsites, hiking and equestrian trails (20 miles), off-road mountain bike trails, picnic areas, picnic pavilions (&), playground, volleyball area, horshoe pits.. **Activities:** Camping, fishing, hiking, mountain biking, horseback riding, picnicking, wildlife viewing, canoeing and kayaking. **Special Features:** Park offers some of the most challenging off-road bicycle trails in Florida. Formerly the site of a phosphate mine, the reclaimed land features topography with some of the most radical elevation changes in the state.

★1899★ **ALFRED B. MACLAY GARDENS STATE PARK**
14326 S County Rd 39
Lithia, FL 33547
Web: www.floridastateparks.org/alafiariver
Phone: 813-672-5320
Size: 6,258 acres land; 54 acres water. **Location:** 10 miles southeast of Tampa on County Road 39. **Facilities:** 30 campsites with water, electrical service, restrooms, and showers, primitive group campsites, hiking and equestrian trails (20 miles), off-road mountain bike trails, picnic areas, picnic pavilions (&), playground, volleyball area, horshoe pits.. **Activities:** Camping, fishing, hiking, mountain biking, horseback riding, wildlife viewing, canoeing and kayaking. **Special Features:** Park offers some of the most challenging off-road bicycle trails in Florida. Formerly the site of a phosphate mine, the reclaimed land features topography with some of the most radical elevation changes in the state.

★1900★ **ALLEN DAVID BROUSSARD CATFISH CREEK PRESERVE STATE PARK**
c/o Lake Kissimmee State Park
14248 Camp Mack Rd
Lake Wales, FL 33853
Web: www.floridastateparks.org/catfishcreek
Phone: 863-696-1112
Size: 8,022 acres land; 64.5 acres water. **Location:** 3950 Firetower Road in Haines City, about 10 miles east of Dundee. **Facilities:** Trails, picnic tables in parking area. **Activities:** Fishing, hiking, horseback riding, wildlife viewing. **Special Features:** Preserve's scrub, sandhill, and flatwoods communities contain numerous rare plants, including scrub morning glory, scrub plum, pygmy fringe tree, and cutthroat grass. They also provide a habitat for several protected species, including Florida scrub-jays, bald eagles, gopher tortoises, and Florida scrub lizards. Park conditions are rugged — visitors should bring plenty of water and be prepared for challenging trails.

★1901★ AMELIA ISLAND STATE PARK

12157 Heckscher Dr
Jacksonville, FL 32226
Web: www.floridastateparks.org/ameliaisland
Phone: 904-251-2320
Size: 230 acres. Location: 7 miles north of Little Talbot Island State Park (or 8 miles south of Fernandina Beach), on A1A. Facilities: Beach, horse rental. Activities: Saltwater fishing, canoeing/kayaking, horseback riding, wildlife viewing. Special Features: Pristine beaches, salt marshes, and coastal maritime forests provide a glimpse of the original Florida. This park is also one of the few locations on the East Coast that offers horseback riding on the beach, a 45-minute riding tour along the shoreline.

★1902★ ANASTASIA STATE PARK

1340-A A1A S
Saint Augustine, FL 32080
Web: www.floridastateparks.org/anastasia
Phone: 904-461-2033; Fax: 904-461-2033
Size: 1,425 acres land; 218 acres water. Location: Exit 311 from I-95, go east on SR 207, then right on SR 312, and left on A1A; or from US 1, left onto SR 312 and then north (left) on A1A. Facilities: 139 full-facility campsites (&), bathhouses, beach (&), picnic area, trails, canoe and sailboard rentals, food concessions, camp store, playground, interpretive exhibits, restrooms. Activities: Camping, boating, canoeing/kayaking, fishing, swimming, surfing, windsurfing, hiking, horseback riding, bicycling, wildlife viewing. Special Features: Located just south of Saint Augustine on Anastasia Island, the park has a broad beach, tidal salt marsh, and maritime and upland hammock. In addition to the many water sports available, the park is a great place to see birds, marsh life, or even whales or other sea creatures.

★1903★ ANCLOTE KEY PRESERVE STATE PARK

c/o Honeymoon Island State Park
1 Causeway Blvd
Dunedin, FL 34698
Web: www.floridastateparks.org/anclotekey
Phone: 727-469-5942
Size: 403 acres land; 11,774 acres water. Location: 3 miles off the coast of Tarpon Springs; accessible only by private boat. Facilities: Primitive campsites, picnic areas, pavilions, restrooms. Activities: Camping, swimming, boating, wildlife viewing. Special Features: Park is home to at least 43 species of birds, including the American oystercatcher, bald eagle, piping plover. A picturesque 1887 federal lighthouse is located at the southern end of the island.

★1904★ AVALON STATE PARK

c/o Fort Pierce Inlet State Park
Fort Pierce, FL 34949
Web: www.floridastateparks.org/avalon
Phone: 772-468-3985
Size: 645 acres land; 11 acres water. Location: Along A1A on North Hutchinson Island in Saint Lucie County, 4 miles north of Fort Pierce Inlet State Park. Facilities: Beach, restroom, showers, nature trails, picnic area with pavilions. Activities: Swimming, snorkeling, fishing, canoeing/kayaking, hiking. Special Features: Avalon is one of the state's newest seaside parks, with more than a mile of undeveloped beachfront. Swimmers and snorkelers at the park are advised to be cautious of underwater obstacles left behind by amphibious warfare exercises during World War II.

★1905★ BAHIA HONDA STATE PARK

36850 Overseas Hwy
Big Pine Key, FL 33043
Web: www.floridastateparks.org/bahiahonda
Phone: 305-872-2353
Size: 474 acres land, 17 acres water. Location: 12 miles south of Marathon on US 1. Facilities: 80 campsites (most full-facility), 3 duplex cabins (6 units), bathhouses, beach, showers, restrooms, picnic areas/pavilions, nature trails, food concession, boat ramp, canoe/kayak rental, interpretive exhibits. Activities: Camping, boating, canoeing/kayaking, fishing, swimming, snorkeling, scuba diving, hiking, bicycling, in-line skating, boat tours, birding, interpretive programs. Special Features: Park is known for its beautiful beaches, magnificent sunsets, and excellent snorkeling. It's also a good place to see wading birds and showbirds, as well as unique plants and animals.

★1906★ BALD POINT STATE PARK

146 Box Cut
Alligator Point, FL 32346
Web: www.floridastateparks.org/baldpoint
Phone: 850-349-9146
Size: 4,065 acres land; 794 acres water. Location: Off US 98, 1 mile south of Ochlockonee Bay, on SR 370. Facilities: Beaches, boat ramp, nature trails, picnic areas/pavilions, restrooms. Activities: Fishing, canoeing and kayaking, swimming, bicycling, birding. Special Features: Located on Alligator Point where Ochlockonee Bay meets the Apalachee Bay, the park features coastal marshes, pine flatwoods, and oak thickets that foster a diversity of biological communities. In the fall, bald eagles and other raptors, as well as monarch butterflies, are commonly sighted as they fly south for the winter.

★1907★ BIG LAGOON STATE PARK

12301 Gulf Beach Hwy
Pensacola, FL 32507
Web: www.floridastateparks.org/biglagoon
Phone: 850-492-1595
Size: 684 acres land; 48 acres water. Location: On County Road 292A, 10 miles southwest of Pensacola. Facilities: 75 campsites with electrical and water hookups, showers, picnic tables, beaches, boat ramp, nature trails, interpretive exhibits. Activities: Camping, boating, canoeing, fishing, crabbing, swimming, hiking, wildlife viewing, nature study. Special Features: Park sits on the northern shoreline of Big Lagoon, which separates the mainland from Perdido Key and the Gulf of Mexico. An observation tower at the east beach area gives visitors a panoramic view of Big Lagoon and Gulf Islands National Seashore (see entry in national parks section) across the Intracoastal Waterway.

9. State Parks

★1908★ BIG SHOALS STATE PARK
PO Drawer G
White Springs, FL 32096
Web: www.floridastateparks.org/bigshoals
Phone: 386-397-4331
Size: 1,652 acres. **Location:** On County Road 135, 1 mile northeast of US 41 in White Springs. **Facilities:** Picnic areas, pavilion, restrooms, nature trails (33 miles), bicycle trails, horseback trails. **Activities:** Kayaking and canoeing, fishing, hiking, horseback riding, bicycling, hunting (with restrictions), birding, wildlife viewing. **Special Features:** Park features largest whitewater rapids in Florida. When the water level is around 60 feet mean sea level, the Big Shoals rapids are rated Class III. For much of the year, the water is too low to create rapids, but the riverbed and banks reveal overhangs, small caves, sandbars, and an abundance of wildlife. Limestone bluffs that rise 80 feet above the banks of the Suwanee River provide scenic vistas not found anywhere else in Florida.

★1909★ BIG TALBOT ISLAND STATE PARK
12157 Heckscher Dr
Jacksonville, FL 32226
Web: www.floridastateparks.org/bigtalbotisland
Phone: 904-251-2320
Size: 1,694 acres land; 15 acres water.. **Location:** 20 miles east of downtown Jacksonville on A1A North, immediately north of Little Talbot Island State Park. **Facilities:** Beaches (nonbathing), boat ramp, nature trails, picnic area, pavilions. **Activities:** Boating, canoeing/kayaking, fishing, bicycling, hiking. **Special Features:** Located on one of the sea islands unique to Northeast Florida, the park is primarily a natural preserve. Centuries of wind and water have created a 20-foot bluff along the shore, and the park's famous boneyard beach is covered with the skeletons of live oak and cedar trees that one grew near the ocean.

★1910★ BILL BAGGS CAPE FLORIDA STATE PARK
1200 S Crandon Blvd
Key Biscayne, FL 33149
Web: www.floridastateparks.org/capeflorida
Phone: 305-361-5811; **Fax:** 305-365-0003
Size: 414 acres land; 17 acres water. **Location:** On the southern end of Key Biscayne, off the Rickenbacker Causeway, south of downtown Miami. **Facilities:** 18 picnic pavilions, playground, beach, showers, restrooms, concessions, restaurant, hiking/nature trails, bicycle rentals, youth camping area, overnight boat camping. **Activities:** Saltwater fishing, canoeing/kayaking, swimming, hiking, bicycling, guided tours, wildlife viewing, boat camping. **Special Features:** Bill Baggs was a Miami newspaper editor who championed this area for a state park. The historic lighthouse on Cape Florida, which was built in 1825 and reconstructed in 1846, is the oldest standing structure in Miami-Dade County. Guided tours of the lighthouse and of the lighthouse keeper's cottage are given twice daily, Thursday through Monday.

★1911★ BLACKWATER RIVER STATE PARK
7720 Deaton Bridge Rd
Holt, FL 32564
Web: www.floridastateparks.org/blackwaterriver
Phone: 850-983-5363; **Fax:** 850-983-5364
Size: 615 acres land; 21 acres water. **Location:** 15 miles northeast of Milton, off US 90. **Facilities:** 30 full-facility campsites (electric and water hookups), pavilions and other picnic areas and shelters, nature trails. **Activities:** Camping, canoeing/kayaking (Blackwater River is a designated canoe trail), tubing, swimming, freshwater fishing, hiking, wildlife viewing, interpretive programs (seasonal). **Special Features:** Blackwater River is considered to be one of the purest sandbottom rivers in the US. One of the Atlantic white cedars that line the shore of river was recognized in 1982 as a Florida Champion tree, one of the oldest and largest of its species.

★1912★ BLUE SPRING STATE PARK
2100 W French Ave
Orange City, FL 32763
Web: www.floridastateparks.org/bluespring
Phone: 386-775-3663
Size: 2,202 acres land; 442 acres water. **Location:** 2 miles west of Orange City on French Avenue. **Facilities:** 51 full-facility campsites, primitive campsite, (4-mile hike-in), 6 cabins, restrooms (&), picnic areas/pavilions, concessions, restaurant, fishing pier, canoe rentals, nature trails, interpretive exhibit. **Activities:** Camping, boating, canoeing/kayaking, freshwater fishing, swimming, snorkeling, scuba diving, hiking, guided boat tours, wildlife viewing. **Special Features:** The largest spring on the Saint Johns River, Blue Spring is a designated Manatee Refuge and winter home to a growing population of West Indian manatees. The spring's 73 degree water is crystal clear.

★1913★ BULOW CREEK STATE PARK
2099 N Beach St
Ormond Beach, FL 32174
Web: www.floridastateparks.org/bulowcreek
Phone: 386-676-4050
Size: 3,689 acres land; 1,432 acres water. **Location:** 5 miles north of Ormond Beach on Old Dixie Highway. **Facilities:** Picnic areas/pavilions, trails, restrooms. **Activities:** Canoeing, hiking, wildlife viewing. **Special Features:** Park preserves one of the largest remaining stands of southern live oak forest along the east coast of Florida and is home to the Fairchild oak, one of the largest live oak trees in the south.

★1914★ BULOW PLANTATION RUINS HISTORIC
        STATE PARK
PO Box 655
Bunnell, FL 32110
Web: www.floridastateparks.org/bulowplantation
Phone: 386-517-2084
Size: 150 acres land; 2 acres water. **Location:** 3 miles west of Flagler Beach off County Road 2001 (Old King's Road), between SR 100 and Old Dixie Highway. **Facilities:** Picnic area, screened pavilion, restrooms, nature trails, canoe rentals, boat

ramp (boats more than 16 feet not recommended on Bulow Creek), interpretive center. **Activities:** Canoeing/kayaking, fishing, picnicking, hiking. **Special Features:** Once the site of the Bulow family's plantation of sugar cane, cotton, rice, and indigo, the Bulow Plantation was destroyed in 1836 during the Second Seminole War. Ruins of the former plantation include a sugar mill, spring house, several wells, and the crumbling foundations of the plantation house and slave cabins. A scenic walking trail leads visitors to the ruins of the sugar mill, and an interpretive center tells the plantation's history.

★1915★ CALADESI ISLAND STATE PARK

1 Causeway Blvd
Dunedin, FL 34698
Web: www.floridastateparks.org/caladesiisland
Phone: 727-469-5918; **Fax:** 727-469-5703
Size: 661 acres land; 1,809 acres water. **Location:** 1 mile west of Dunedin off the Gulf coast. Accessible only by private boat or scheduled ferry service. **Facilities:** Beaches, marina, overnight boat docking with electric and water hookups, food concession, restrooms, hiking trails, picnic tables, playground, public showers. **Activities:** Boating, canoeing/kayaking, fishing, swimming, hiking, wildlife viewing. **Special Features:** One of the few completely natural islands on Florida's Gulf Coast, Caladesi's white sand beaches have been rated among the best in the US.

★1916★ CAMP HELEN STATE PARK

23937 Panama City Beach Pkwy
Panama City Beach, FL 32413
Web: www.floridastateparks.org/camphelen
Phone: 850-233-5059; **Fax:** 850-236-3204
Size: 182 acres. **Location:** In Panama City Beach just west of the Phillips Inlet bridge on the Bay and Walton county line. **Facilities:** Beaches, nature trails, interpretive exhibits, picnic tables, visitor center. **Activities:** Fishing (in designated areas), swimming, hiking. Boating opportunities exist at the park, but there is no public boat ramp, canoe launch facilities, or tie-ups, and caution is advised to any boater not familiar with these waters. It is recommended that boating be limited to smaller craft such as canoes, kayaks, John Boats, pontoon boats, or bass boats. **Special Features:** Park is bordered on three sides by the Gulf of Mexico and Lake Powell, one of the largest coastal dune lakes in Florida. (Coastal dune lakes are rare worldwide, and in the US are found only along the Gulf Coast.) Between 1945 and 1987, Camp Helen was a company resort for employees of an Alabama textile mill, and some of those buildings are now being restored.

★1917★ CAYO COSTA STATE PARK

PO Box 1150
Boca Grande, FL 33921
Web: www.floridastateparks.org/cayocosta
Phone: 941-964-0375; **Fax:** 941-964-1154
Size: 2,421 acres land; 34 acres water. **Location:** Directly south of Boca Grande and west of Pine Island and North Fort Myers; accessible only by private boat or passenger ferry. **Facilities:** Primitive campsites (tents, cabins, yurts), restrooms, showers,

bayside dockage, kayak rental, picnic tables, pavilions, beach, trails, amphitheater, gift shop. **Activities:** Camping, boating, canoeing/kayaking, fishing, swimming, snorkeling, scuba diving, hiking, bicycling, shelling, wildlife viewing, interpretive programs. **Special Features:** Park is a barrier island with more than 9 miles of beaches and acres of pine forests, oak-palm hammocks, and mangrove swamps, as well as a spectacular assortment of birds. Visitors might also see manatees or pods of dolphins in the waters around the park.

★1918★ CEDAR KEY MUSEUM STATE PARK

12231 SW 166 Ct
Cedar Key, FL 32625
Web: www.floridastateparks.org/cedarkeymuseum
Phone: 352-543-5350
Size: 13 acres land; 6 acres water. **Location:** Off SR 24 on Museum Drive in Cedar Key. **Facilities:** Museum, nature trail. **Special Features:** Museum exhibits depict Cedar Key's colorful history as a port city and railroad connection during the 19th Century. The museum also houses a shell collection assembled by Saint Clair Whitman, founder of the first museum in Cedar Key. His house is located at the park and has been restored to reflect 1920s life.

★1919★ CEDAR KEY SCRUB STATE RESERVE

PO Box 187
Cedar Key, FL 32625
Web: www.floridastateparks.org/cedarkeyscrub
Phone: 352-543-5567
Size: 4,156 acres land; 907 acres water. **Location:** 6 miles northeast of Cedar Key on SR 24, just north of Waccassa Bay State Preserve (see separate entry). **Facilities:** Picnic area, multiuse trails, canoe and kayak rental. **Activities:** Boating, canoeing/kayaking, fishing, picnicking, hiking, bicycling, horseback riding, wildlife viewing. **Special Features:** Reserve consists of diverse habitats of salt marsh, swamps, hardwood forests, pine flatwoods, and scrub, which support a variety of wildlife.

★1920★ CHARLOTTE HARBOR PRESERVE STATE PARK

12301 Burnt Store Rd
Punta Gorda, FL 33955
Web: www.floridastateparks.org/charlotteharbor
Phone: 941-575-5861
Size: 42,600 acres. **Location:** Approximately 3 miles south of US 41/Tamiami Trail, on Burnt Store Road (County Road 786) in Punta Gorda. **Facilities:** About 6 miles of marked trails, visitor center. **Activities:** Boating/canoeing/kayaking, fishing, hiking, interpretive programs. **Special Features:** Most of the park is made up of mangrove forests and salt marshes, but public access is available at strategic upland points in each area of the park. Information is available from the Charlotte Harbor Environmental Center, which is located within the park at 10941 Burnt Store Road.

9. State Parks

★1921★ COLLIER-SEMINOLE STATE PARK
20200 E Tamiami Trail
Naples, FL 34114
Web: www.floridastateparks.org/collier-seminole
Phone: 239-394-3397; Fax: 239-394-5113
Size: 6,767 acres land; 505 acres water. Location: On US 41, 17 miles south of Naples. Facilities: Full-facility campsites, primitive campsites (including youth group camping), showers, picnic area, pavilions, playground, restrooms, nature trails, off-road biking course, boat ramp, interpretive exhibits, concession, visitor/nature center. Activities: Camping, canoeing/kayaking, fishing, boat tours, bicycling, hiking, guided tours, wildlife viewing. Special Features: Park features vegetation and wildlife typical of the Everglades as well as a forest of tropical trees. Nature trails wind through pine flatwoods and cypress swamp, and one trail has a boardwalk system and observation platform overlooking the salt marsh. Common wildlife sightings along the trails include alligator, raccoons, osprey, white ibis, and other wading birds.

★1922★ CONSTITUTION CONVENTION MUSEUM
STATE PARK
200 Allen Memorial Way
Port Saint Joe, FL 32456
Web: www.floridastateparks.org/constitutionconvention
Phone: 850-229-8029
Size: 13 acres. Location: In Port Saint Joe, off US 98. Facilities: Museum. Activities: Guided tours, interpretive programs. Special Features: Museum commemorates the work of the 56 territorial delegates who drafted Florida's first state constitution in 1838. After four more constitution conventions, Florida was admitted to the Union in 1845 as the 27th state.

★1923★ CRYSTAL RIVER ARCHAEOLOGICAL
STATE PARK
3400 N Museum Pointe
Crystal River, FL 34428
Web: www.floridastateparks.org/crystalriver
Phone: 352-795-3817
Size: 61.5 acres. Location: On Museum Pointe in Crystal River. Special Features: The six-mound complex, built by pre-Columbian mound builders, is considered one of the longest continuously occupied sites in Florida. For 1,600 years (200 BC to AD 1400), this area included an imposing prehistoric ceremonial center. It is estimated that 7,500 Indians might have visited the complex annually. Site is a National Historic Landmark.

★1924★ CRYSTAL RIVER PRESERVE STATE PARK
3266 N Sailboat Ave
Crystal River, FL 34428
Web: www.floridastateparks.org/crystalriverpreserve
Phone: 352-563-0450; Fax: 352-563-0246
Size: 25,355 acres. Location: West of US 19, in Crystal River. Facilities: 9 miles of hiking/bicycling trails, 2.5 miles nature/interpretive trail, visitor center with displays and exhibits. Activities: Bicycling, canoeing, fishing, hiking, nature study, wildlife viewing, birdwatching. Special Features: Park borders 20 miles of the northern Gulf Coast between Yankeetown and Homosassa. Its undisturbed islands, inlets, backwaters, and forests provide a place of exceptional natural beauty, making it a favorite for nature lovers and photographers.

★1925★ CURRY HAMMOCK STATE PARK
56200 Overseas Hwy
Marathon, FL 33050
Web: www.floridastateparks.org/curryhammock
Phone: 305-289-2690
Size: 579 acres land; 391 acres water. Location: On both sides of US 1, starting at Little Crawl Key (Mile Marker 56.2), 11 miles west of Long Key. Facilities: 28 full-facility campsites (open November-May), campers-only bathhouse with hot showers (&), cold-water outdoor showers (for day-use visitors), picnic area, pavilions (&), playground, nature trail. Activities: Camping, swimming, snorkeling, canoeing, saltwater fishing, bicycling, hiking, inline skating, wildlife viewing. No launching of powerboats is permitted at this park. Special Features: Park is made up of a group of tropical islands in the Middle Keys with hardwood hammocks that support one of the largest populations of thatch palms in the US. Mangrove swamps, seagrass beds, and wetlands on the islands provide habitats for tropical wildlife.

★1926★ DADE BATTLEFIELD HISTORIC STATE
PARK
7200 County Rd 603
S Battlefield Dr
Bushnell, FL 33513
Web: www.floridastateparks.org/dadebattlefield
Phone: 352-793-4781
Size: 80.5 acres. Location: Off I-75 and SR 48, west of Highway 301. Facilities: Picnic area, nature trail, restrooms, playground, visitor center, historical exhibits, recreation hall. Activities: Picnicking, wildlife viewing. Special Features: Site of the 1835 battle that marked the beginning of the Second Seminole Indian War. Of the 108 soldiers led by Major Francis L Dade, only three survived.

★1927★ DAGNY JOHNSON KEY LARGO
HAMMOCK BOTANICAL STATE PARK
PO Box 487
Key Largo, FL 33037
Web: www.floridastateparks.org/keylargohammock
Phone: 305-451-1202
Size: 2,344 acres land; 77 acres water. Location: On County Road 905, 0.25 miles north of its intersection with Overseas Highway (US 1). Facilities: Nature trails, picnic tables. Activities: Hiking, bicycling, wildlife viewing, picnicking. Special Features: Comprising one of the largest contiguous tracts of tropical West Indian hardwood hammock found in the U.S., the site is home to 84 protected species of plants and animals including wild cotton, mahogany mistletoe, and the American crocodile.

★1928★ DE LEON SPRINGS STATE PARK

601 Ponce De Leon Blvd
PO Box 1338
De Leon Springs, FL 32130
Web: www.floridastateparks.org/deleonsprings
Phone: 386-985-4212
Size: 592 acres land, 14 acres water. Location: At the corner of Ponce De Leon and Burt Parks Road, 5 miles north of DeLand on US 17. Facilities: Picnic tables, 4 pavilions (2 with electrical service), restaurant, food concessions, nature trails, interpretive exhibits, boat ramp, canoe, kayak, and paddleboat rentals, Eco/History boat tours, playground, restrooms (占). Activities: Boating, canoeing/kayaking, freshwater fishing, swimming, snorkeling, hiking, wildlife viewing. Special Features: De Leon Springs, a second-magnitude spring, delivers 19 million gallons of water daily. In the 1880s the springs became a winter resort, where tourists were promised ''a fountain of youth impregnated with a deliciously healthy combination of soda and sulphur.''

★1929★ DEER LAKE STATE PARK

357 Main Park Rd
Santa Rosa Beach, FL 32459
Web: www.floridastateparks.org/deerlake
Phone: 850-231-0337; Fax: 850-231-1879
Size: 1,956.5 acres land; 38 acres water. Location: On County Road 30A in Santa Rosa Beach. Facilities: Beach, picnic areas, boardwalk, 10-mile walking/biking trail. Activities: Fishing, swimming, hiking, biking, wildlife viewing. Special Features: Park shares its name with the coastal dune lake within its boundaries. Coastal dune lakes occur rarely throughout the world and only on the Gulf Coast in the US. A boardwalk across the dunes offers easy access to the beach as well as a view of the dune ecosystem. The habitat at Deer Lake includes such rare plants as gulf coast lupine, spoonflower, pitcher plants, and one of the largest Florida populations of Curtiss' sand grass.

★1930★ DELNOR-WIGGINS PASS STATE PARK

11100 Gulf Shore Dr
Naples, FL 34108
Web: www.floridastateparks.org/delnor-wiggins
Phone: 239-597-6196; Fax: 239-597-8223
Size: 136 acres land; 30 acres water. Location: In North Naples, 5 miles west of I-75, Exit 111. Facilities: Beach (占), boat ramp (docks there are 占), picnic areas, pavilion, concessions, restaurant, restrooms (占), showers, interpretive exhibits. Activities: Boating, fishing, swimming, snorkeling, scuba diving, wildlife viewing, guided tours. Special Features: One of the most popular seashore destinations in Naples, the park's mile-long beach has been rated one of the best in the US. A tower at the north end of the island provides an excellent view of Wiggins Pass and the surrounding coastal habitat.

★1931★ DEVIL'S MILLHOPPER GEOLOGICAL STATE PARK

4732 Millhopper Rd
Gainesville, FL 32653
Web: www.floridastateparks.org/devilsmillhopper
Phone: 352-955-2008
Size: 67 acres. Location: 2 miles northwest of Gainesville, off SR 232. Facilities: Picnic area, visitor center, nature trails (including a boardwalk system that descends to the bottom of the Devil's Millhopper). Activities: Picnicking, wildlife viewing, guided tours. Special Features: Designated a National Natural Landmark, Devil's Millhopper is a significant geological formation that has been visited since the early 1880s. It is a bowl-shaped cavity 120 feet deep that leads down to a miniature rainforest. Researchers have learned a great deal about Florida's natural history by studying fossil shark teeth, marine shells, and the fossilized remains of extinct land animals found in this limestone sinkhole.

★1932★ DON PEDRO ISLAND STATE PARK

PO Box 1150
Boca Grande, FL 33921
Web: www.floridastateparks.org/donpedroisland
Phone: 941-964-0375; Fax: 941-964-1154
Size: 223 acres land; 8 acres water. Location: Off the coast of Cape Haze, about 9 miles south of Englewood; accessible only by private boat. Facilities: Beach, boat docks, restrooms, pavilions, nature trails. Activities: Boating, canoeing/kayaking, saltwater fishing, swimming, snorkeling, scuba diving, shelling, wildlife viewing, interpretive programs. Special Features: Located between Knight Island and Little Gasparilla Island, Don Pedro is part of an extensive chain of barrier islands along the Gulf Coast of Florida. Boat docks are located on the bay side of the island, which is lined with mangroves, and the island's mile of white sand beach is on the Gulf side.

★1933★ DR. JULIAN G. BRUCE SAINT GEORGE ISLAND STATE PARK

1900 E Gulf Beach Dr
Saint George Island, FL 32328
Web: www.floridastateparks.org/stgeorgeisland
Phone: 850-927-2111
Size: 2,023 acres. Location: On Saint George Island, 10 miles southeast of Eastpoint, off US 98. Facilities: Beach, picnic areas, playground, nature trails, showers, boat ramps. Activities: Canoeing/kayaking, saltwater fishing, swimming, hiking, wildlife viewing. Special Features: The park was seriously damaged in 2005 by Hurricane Dennis and is presently undergoing reconstruction. The park will remain open during construction, and some facilities were completed during the summer of 2006, but camping was closed until further notice. Call the park office for construction updates and other information.

★1934★ DUDLEY FARM HISTORIC STATE PARK

18730 W Newberry Rd
Newberry, FL 32669
Web: www.floridastateparks.org/dudleyfarm
Phone: 352-472-1142
Size: 327 acres. Location: 4 miles east of Newberry on SR 26. Facilities: Picnic area, nature trail, interpretive exhibits. Activities: Self-guided tours, group tours (by appointment), birdwatching. Special Features: Dudley Farm is a living-history, working farm once owned by the Dudley family. The farmstead is made up of 18 historic structures, most of which

were built during the late 1800s and early 1900s. Costumed interpreters demonstrate daily farm activities.

★1935★ DUNN'S CREEK
320 Cisco Rd
Pomona Park, FL 32181
Web: www.floridastateparks.org/dunnscreek
Phone: 386-329-3721; Fax: 386-329-3718
Size: 6,235 acres. Location: 13 miles south of Palatka on US 17 between Pomona Park and Satsuma. Facilities: Picnic tables, trails. Activities: Hiking, biking, horseback riding, wildlife viewing. Special Features: A new addition to Florida's state park system, Dunn's Creek is located south of a sharp bend in the Saint Johns River. The park's natural communities include sand dunes as well as sandhills covered with longleaf pines and wiregrass.

★1936★ ECONFINA RIVER STATE PARK
4384 Econfina Rd
Lamont, FL 32336
Web: www.floridastateparks.org/econfinariver
Phone: 850-922-6007
Size: 4,396 acres land; 132 acres water. Location: At the end of SR 14, south of US 98, in Taylor County. Facilities: Picnic areas, boat ramp, trails, food concession. Activities: Boating, canoeing, fishing, bicycling, hiking, horseback riding, wildlife viewing. Special Features: Located on the Gulf of Mexico, the park offers scenic vistas and a variety of landscapes: pine flatwoods, oak and palm forests, and salt marshes dotted with pine islands.

★1937★ EDEN GARDENS STATE PARK
PO Box 26
Point Washington, FL 32454
Web: www.floridastateparks.org/edengardens
Phone: 850-231-4214
Size: 162 acres. Location: In Point Washington, off US 98 on County Road 395. Facilities: Picnic areas, interpretive exhibits. Activities: Guided tours, fishing, boating. Special Features: Park is part of an estate owned in the 1800s by a wealthy Florida timber family. Its focal point is the beautifully renovated two-story house surrounded by moss-draped live oaks and ornamental gardens. The house has elegant white columns and wrap-around porch, and its collection of Louis XVI furniture is one of the largest in the US.

★1938★ EDWARD BALL WAKULLA SPRINGS STATE PARK
550 Wakulla Park Dr
Wakulla Springs, FL 32327
Web: www.floridastateparks.org/wakullasprings
Phone: 850-224-5950
Size: 5,969 acres land; 86 acres water. Location: On SR 267 14 miles south of Tallahassee, at the intersection of SR 267 with SR 61. Facilities: Lodge, meeting rooms, restaurant, interpretive exhibits, picnic areas, nature trails, food concession, gift shop.

Activities: Guided tours, boat tours, swimming, snorkeling, hiking, wildlife viewing. Special Features: Park has one of the largest and deepest freshwater springs in the world as well as an abundance of wildlife, including alligators, turtles, deer, and birds. The Wakulla Springs Lodge, with 27 individually unique guestrooms, was built by Edward Ball in 1937 and is listed on the *National Register of Historic Places*.

★1939★ EGMONT KEY STATE PARK
4905 34th St S #5000
Saint Petersburg, FL 33711
Web: www.floridastateparks.org/egmontkey
Phone: 727-893-2627; Fax: 727-893-2627
Size: 272 acres. Location: At the mouth of Tampa Bay, southwest of Fort DeSoto Beach; accessible only by private boat. Facilities: Beach, nature trails, picnic tables. Activities: Boating, fishing (in designated areas), swimming (in designated areas), hiking, wildlife viewing. Special Features: Though it is primarily a wildlife refuge, Egmont Key has a working lighthouse that has stood since 1858. During the 19th Century, the island was a camp for captured Seminoles at the end of the Third Seminole War, and later it was occupied by the Navy during the Civil War. In 1898 Fort Dade was built there and remained active until 1923.

★1940★ ESTERO BAY PRESERVE STATE PARK
PO Box 7
Estero, FL 33928
Web: www.floridastateparks.org/esteroBay
Phone: 239-463-3240
Size: 10,457 acres. Location: Near Estero, between Fort Myers and Naples. Go west off I-75 onto Corkscrew Road, then right onto US 41 and left on Broadway West. Public access point is on the north side of the road next to the Florida Power & Light substation. Facilities: Trails. Activities: Boating/canoeing/kayaking (must launch from Koreshan State Historic Site nearby), fishing, hiking, bicycling, wildlife viewing. Special Features: The first acquatic preserve established in Florida and one of the state's most productive estuaries, the preserve protects the water, inlets, and islands along 10 miles of Estero Bay.

★1941★ FAKAHATCHEE STRAND PRESERVE STATE PARK
PO Box 548
Copeland, FL 34137
Web: www.floridastateparks.org/fakahatcheestrand
Phone: 239-695-4593
Size: 75,693 acres. Location: On Janes Memorial Scenic Drive, just west of Copeland on SR 29. Facilities: A 2,000-foot-long boardwalk at Big Cypress Bend provides a trail through the old growth cypress. Activities: Wildlife viewing, guided canoe trips. Special Features: Fakahatchee Strand is a linear swamp forest that has been sculpted by the movement of water for thousands of years. Beneath a protective canopy of bald cypress trees is a slow-moving slough that shields the forest interior from extreme cold temperatures, and this fosters a high level of rare and endangered tropical plant species. The Strand is the only place in the world where bald cypress and royal palm trees share the

forest canopy, and it also contains 44 native orchids and 14 native bromeliad species. It's a haven for wildlife as well, and Florida panthers, Florida black bears, Eastern indigo snakes, Everglades minks, and diamondback terrapins can still be found here. The migratory bird life is quite spectacular as well.

★1942★ FALLING WATERS STATE PARK

1130 State Park Rd
Chipley, FL 32428
Web: www.floridastateparks.org/fallingwaters
Phone: 850-638-6130
Size: 173 acres. **Location:** 3 miles south of Chipley, off SR 77A. **Facilities:** 24 full-facility campsites, primitive camping, including youth group camping, pavilions, picnic tables, showers, restrooms, nature trails. **Activities:** Camping, swimming, fishing, hiking, wildlife viewing. **Special Features:** The boardwalk trail that leads visitors to Florida's highest waterfall is lined with fern-covered sinkholes. Falling Waters Sink is a 100-foot deep, 20-foot wide cylindrical pit into which flows a small stream that drops 73 feet to the bottom of the sink. The water's final destination is unknown. The park also has a butterfly garden where visitors can see native and migrating butterflies.

★1943★ FANNING SPRINGS STATE PARK

18020 NW Hwy 19
Fanning Springs, FL 32693
Web: www.floridastateparks.org/fanningsprings
Phone: 352-463-3420; **Fax:** 352-463-3420
Size: 193 acres land; 5 acres water. **Location:** On US Highway 19/98 in the town of Fanning Springs. **Facilities:** Cabins (each accommodates up to 6 people; one ৬), canoe and kayak rental, picnic tables and pavilions, nature trails. **Activities:** Fishing (designated areas), boating, canoeing, swimming, snorkeling, scuba diving, hiking, wildlife viewing. **Special Features:** Located on the historic Suwannee River, Fanning Spring is a first magnitude spring, producing approximately 65 million gallons of water daily. Red-shouldered hawks, pileated woodpeckers, barred owls, and white-tailed deer are among the animals seen at the park.

★1944★ FAVER-DYKES STATE PARK

1000 Faver Dykes Rd
Saint Augustine, FL 32086
Web: www.floridastateparks.org/faver-dykes
Phone: 904-794-0997; **Fax:** 386-446-6781
Size: 4,291 acres land; 38 acres water. **Location:** 15 miles south of Saint Augustine at the intersection of I-95 and US 1. **Facilities:** 30 full-facility campsites, primitive youth group camping area, picnic areas, pavilions, playground, nature trails, boat ramp, canoe rentals, restrooms (৬). **Activities:** Camping, boating, canoeing, freshwater and saltwater fishing, hiking, wildlife viewing. **Special Features:** Park lies along Pellicer Creek, a popular site for birding. The park is also home to deer, turkeys, hawks, bobcats, and river otters.

★1945★ FLORIDA CAVERNS STATE PARK

3345 Caverns Rd
Marianna, FL 32446
Web: www.floridastateparks.org/floridacaverns
Phone: 850-482-9598
Size: 1,280 acres. **Location:** 3 miles north of Marianna on SR 166. **Facilities:** 38 campsites with electric and water hookups, a primitive youth group camp, picnic areas, pavilions, playground, multi-use trails, equestrian facility/stables, boat ramp, canoe rentals, showers, restrooms, food concession, visitor center. **Activities:** Camping, boating, canoeing, freshwater fishing, swimming, hiking, bicycling, horseback riding, interpretive programs, guided tours. **Special Features:** Park is one of the few state parks with dry (air-filled) caves and is the only Florida state park to offer cave tours to the public. The cave has formations of limestone stalactites, stalagmites, soda straws, flowstones, and draperies. Tours last about 45 minutes and are considered to be moderately strenuous.

★1946★ FOREST CAPITAL MUSEUM STATE PARK

204 Forest Park Dr
Perry, FL 32348
Web: www.floridastateparks.org/forestcapital
Phone: 850-584-3227
Size: 14 acres. **Location:** South of Perry on US 19. **Facilities:** Museum, exhibits, pavilions, visitor center with gift shop. **Activities:** Guided tours. **Special Features:** Museum celebrates the heritage of Florida's forest industry, with the heart of the museum dedicated to longleaf pines and the products manufactured from them. Outside the museum, longleaf pines more than 50 years old provide a canopy over the grounds. An authentic 19th Century cracker homestead is adjacent to the museum.

★1947★ FORT CLINCH STATE PARK

2601 Atlantic Ave
Fernandina Beach, FL 32034
Web: www.floridastateparks.org/fortclinch
Phone: 904-277-7274; **Fax:** 904-277-7225
Size: 1,428 acres land; 9 acres water. **Location:** North of Fernandina Beach, off A1A. **Facilities:** 62 full-facility campsites with restrooms and hot showers, youth group campsites with restrooms, beaches, restrooms/changing rooms, showers, fishing pier, nature trails, picnic areas, visitor center. **Activities:** Camping, saltwater fishing, swimming, shelling, hiking, bicycling, wildlife viewing, guided tours. **Special Features:** Part of the state park system since 1935, Fort Clinch is one of the best-preserved 19th Century forts in the US. Although no battles were fought here, it was garrisoned during both the Civil War and the Spanish-American War. Tours of the fort are held daily, with period reenactments that depict garrison life.

★1948★ FORT COOPER STATE PARK

3100 S Old Floral City Rd
Inverness, FL 34450
Web: www.floridastateparks.org/fortcooper
Phone: 352-726-0315
Size: 682 acres land; 55 acres water. **Location:** Off US 41 on

South Old Floral City Road, 2 miles south of Inverness. **Facilities:** Primitive tent campsite, nature trails, picnic areas/pavilions (including one that accommodates up to 70 people), canoe and paddleboat rentals (private boats prohibited), playground, recreation hall. **Activities:** Camping, canoeing, freshwater fishing, swimming, hiking, wildlife viewing, birding. **Special Features:** In 1836 the First Georgia Battalion of Volunteers built a stockade here, enabling the soldiers to withstand several skirmishes with Seminole Indians led by Chief Osceola. Today many of the activities at the park center around Lake Holathlikaha, and a new 2,300-foot long multi-use paved trail makes the park a major trailhead for access to the Withlacoochee State Trail. The park is also part of the Great Florida Birding Trail.

★1949★ FORT FOSTER STATE HISTORIC SITE
Hillsborough River State Park
15402 US 301 N
Thonotosassa, FL 33592
Web: www.floridastateparks.org/fortfoster
Phone: 813-987-6771
Location: Fort is part of Hillsborough River State Park (see separate entry) but is located on the east side of US 301 from the park. **Facilities:** Interpretive center at Hillsborough River State Park has exhibits about the fort. **Activities:** Guided tours (weekends only); interpretive programs at the Ranger Station at Hillsborough River State Park. **Special Features:** Fort Foster is a replica wood picket style fort constructed on the site of the original fort, which was one of the Seminole War forts constructed during the early 1800s.

★1950★ FORT GEORGE ISLAND CULTURAL STATE PARK
12157 Heckscher Dr
Jacksonville, FL 32226
Web: www.floridastateparks.org/fortgeorgeisland
Phone: 904-251-2320
Size: 630 acres land; 29 acres water. **Location:** 16 miles east of downtown Jacksonville on SR A1A; or 3 miles south of Little Talbot Island State Park. **Facilities:** Boat ramp, nature trails, visitor center, meeting rooms, interpretive exhibits, gift store. **Activities:** Canoeing, shoreline fishing, hiking, bicycling, guided tours. **Special Features:** Huge shell mounds found on the island are evidence of Indian habitation dating back thousands of years. Fort George was built in 1736 by General James Oglethorpe, founder of the Georgia Colony. The fort no longer stands, and its actual location is not known. A key attraction of the park today is the recently restored Ribault Club. An exclusive resort in the 1920s, it now houses the park's visitor center, with meeting space available for special occasions.

★1951★ FORT MOSE HISTORIC STATE PARK
c/o Anastasia State Park
1340-A A1A S
Saint Augustine, FL 32080
Web: www.floridastateparks.org/fortmose
Phone: 904-461-2033
Size: 41 acres land; 0.25 acres water. **Location:** 2 miles north of Castillo de San Marcos near Saint Augustine city gates on US 1. **Facilities:** A new visitor center is under construction, and the park's pavilion and boardwalk are closed until the center is completed. Call 904-461-2033 for information. **Activities:** When park is open: Boating/canoeing (no boat landings at the park), picnicking, hiking, wildlife viewing. **Special Features:** Park has been closed to visitors during construction of a new visitor center. When it is open, the boardwalk in the park provides a view of the original Fort Mose site. Although nothing remains of the fort, the site is listed on the *National Register of Historic Places* because of its importance in American history. In 1738, the Spanish governor of Florida chartered Fort Mose as a settlement for freed Africans who had fled slavery in the British Carolinas. When Spain ceded Florida to Britain in 1763, the inhabitants of Fort Mose migrated to Cuba.

★1952★ FORT PIERCE INLET STATE PARK
905 Shorewinds Dr
Fort Pierce, FL 34949
Web: www.floridastateparks.org/fortpierceinlet
Phone: 772-468-3985
Size: 812 acres land; 329 acres water. Includes Jack Island. **Location:** 4 miles east of Fort Pierce, via North Causeway. **Facilities:** Camping area (primitive) for organized youth groups, covered pavilions, trails, beach, showers, restrooms, playground. **Activities:** Youth group camping, canoeing, saltwater fishing, swimming, surfing, snorkeling, scuba diving, shelling, hiking, bicycling, birding. **Special Features:** Located on the north shore of Fort Pierce Inlet, this park features Atlantic beach, dunes, and coastal hammock. Dynamite Point, which was a training site for Navy Frogmen during World War II, is a haven for birdwatchers. Jack Island Preserve, located 1.5 miles north of the park, has trails for hiking, biking, and nature study.

★1953★ FORT ZACHARY TAYLOR HISTORIC STATE PARK
PO Box 6560
Key West, FL 33041
Web: www.floridastateparks.org/forttaylor
Phone: 305-292-6713
Size: 36 acres land; 19 acres water. **Location:** At the end of Southard Street in Key West, on Truman Annex. **Facilities:** Picnic areas, beach, showers, restrooms, food concession, kayak and snorkeling gear rental, interpretive exhibits, hiking trails. **Activities:** Saltwater fishing, kayaking, swimming, snorkeling, scuba diving, hiking, bicycling, wildlife viewing, guided tours. **Special Features:** Construction of the fort began in 1845, shortly after Florida became a state, but took 21 years to complete due to yellow fever, shortages of material and men, remoteness, and hurricanes. Fort Taylor remained in Union hands throughout the Civil War, and was again used during the Spanish-American War. Beginning in the late 1960s, excavations for old armaments uncovered a buried arsenal from Civil War times. In recognition of the fort's large collection of Civil War cannons, it was placed on the *National Register of Historic Places* and designated a National Historic Landmark.

★1954★ FRED GANNON ROCKY BAYOU STATE PARK

4281 Hwy 20
Niceville, FL 32578
Web: www.floridastateparks.org/rockybayou
Phone: 850-833-9144
Size: 346 acres. Location: On SR 20, 5 miles east of Highway 85. Facilities: 42 full-facility campsites, showers, pavilions, playground, trails, boat ramp. Activities: Camping, boating, canoeing/kayaking, saltwater and freshwater fishing, hiking, bicycling, wildlife viewing. Special Features: Rocky Bayou, the main feature of the park, is the trailing arm of Choctawhatchee Bay. The property also preserves the old-growth (some over 300 years old) longleaf pines that once dominated this part of Florida. US Air Force Colonel Fred Gannon, for whom the park is named, was instrumental in transforming the site from a World War II bombing practice range to a picturesque state park.

★1955★ GAINESVILLE-HAWTHORNE STATE TRAIL

3400 SE 15th St
Gainesville, FL 32641
Web: www.floridastateparks.org/gainesville-hawthorne
Phone: 352-466-3397
Size: 16-mile trail. Location: Starts on SE 15th Street in Gainesville and extends to Hawthorne near US 301. Facilities: Paved trail. Activities: Hiking, bicycling, horseback riding. Special Features: Trail stretches from Boulware Springs Park in Gainesville through Paynes Prairie State Preserve and the Lochloosa Wildlife Management Area into downtown Hawthorne. It was built on a historic railroad line established in 1850 which was important in the founding and history of Gainesville. The 21,000-acre Paynes Prairie State Preserve (see separate entry) offers additional off-road bicycle trails.

★1956★ GAMBLE PLANTATION HISTORIC STATE PARK

3708 Patten Ave
Ellenton, FL 34222
Web: www.floridastateparks.org/gambleplantation
Phone: 941-723-4536
Size: 16 acres. Location: In Ellenton on US 301 East. Facilities: Historic home, picnic tables, restrooms (&), visitor center. Activities: Guided tours. Special Features: The only surviving plantation house in South Florida, the antebellum mansion was the home of Major Robert Gamble and headquarters to an extensive sugar plantation. It is believed that Confederate Secretary of State Judah P. Benjamin took refuge in the house after the fall of the Confederacy, until his safe passage to England could be secured.

★1957★ GAMBLE ROGERS MEMORIAL STATE RECREATION AREA AT FLAGLER BEACH

3100 S A1A
Flagler Beach, FL 32136
Web: www.floridastateparks.org/gamblerogers
Phone: 386-517-2086
Size: 111 acres land; 22 acres water. Location: In Flagler Beach, off A1A, bordered by the Atlantic Ocean and the Intracoastal Waterway. Facilities: 34 full-facility campsites, dune walkovers, picnic tables, nature trail, beach, showers, restrooms (&), boat ramp, boat basin, kayak rentals. Activities: Camping, saltwater fishing, boating, canoeing, swimming, bicycling, hiking, wildlife viewing. Special Features: Daily low tide is a good time to observe shore birds feeding in tidal ponds. At night during the summer months, sea turtles crawl onto the beach to lay their eggs. The park is named for Florida folk singer Gamble Rogers and railroad entrepreneur Henry Flagler.

★1958★ GASPARILLA ISLAND STATE PARK

PO Box 1150
Boca Grande, FL 33921
Web: www.floridastateparks.org/gasparillaisland
Phone: 941-964-0375; Fax: 941-964-1154
Size: 126.5 acres land; 0.5 acres water. Location: South end of Gasparilla Island via the Boca Grande Causeway (private toll) at County Road 775 and Placida. Facilities: Beach, showers, restrooms (&), nature trails, picnic areas, museum (lighthouse), visitor center. Activities: Saltwater fishing, canoeing/kayaking, swimming, snorkeling, shelling, hiking, bicycling, wildlife viewing, interpretive programs (seasonal). Special Features: A barrier island on Florida's southwest coast, Gasparilla Island is the site of the restored Boca Grande Lighthouse, built in 1890.

★1959★ GEORGE CRADY BRIDGE FISHING PIER STATE PARK

12157 Heckscher Dr
Jacksonville, FL 32226
Web: www.floridastateparks.org/nassausound
Phone: 904-251-2320
Size: 1.5 acres. Location: 7 miles north of Little Talbot Island State Park on SR A1A. Facilities: Fishing pier, bait and tackle shop. Activities: Fishing. Special Features: Located northeast of Jacksonville, pier is a mile-long, pedestrian-only fishing bridge spanning Nassau Sound. The bridge is open 24 hours a day year-round, and there is a tackle shop at the north end of the bridge. Nassau Sound is considered one of the best fishing areas in the state and is home of the state record flounder.

★1960★ GRAYTON BEACH STATE PARK

c/o Deer Lake State Park
357 Main Park Rd
Santa Rosa Beach, FL 32459
Web: www.floridastateparks.org/graytonbeach
Phone: 850-231-4210
Size: 1,988 acres land, 183 acres water. Location: Near the town of Grayton Beach on SR 30A, south of US 98. Facilities: Full-facility campsites, 30 duplex cabins (2 &), picnic pavilion, trails, boat ramp, beaches, showers, amphitheater. Activities: Camping, canoeing/kayaking, saltwater fishing, swimming, hiking, bicycling, wildlife viewing, interpretive programs (seasonal). Special Features: Located in one of the oldest townships on Florida's Gulf Coast, the park's beaches have consistently been ranked among the best in the nation.

9. State Parks

391

★1961★ HENDERSON BEACH STATE PARK

17000 Emerald Coast Pkwy
Destin, FL 32541
Web: www.floridastateparks.org/hendersonbeach
Phone: 850-837-7550
Size: 219 acres. **Location:** Just east of Destin on US 98. **Facilities:** 60 full-facility campsites, beach, bathhouses, showers, food concessions, 2 picnic pavilions, playground, nature trails. **Activities:** Camping, saltwater fishing, swimming, bicycling, in-line skating, hiking, wildlife viewing. **Special Features:** Park features sugar white sand beaches and more than 6,000 feet of shoreline along the Gulf of Mexico. Boardwalks allow visitors easy access to the beach while protecting the dunes and vegetation.

★1962★ HIGHLANDS HAMMOCK STATE PARK

5931 Hammock Rd
Sebring, FL 33872
Web: www.floridastateparks.org/highlandshammock
Phone: 863-386-6094; **Fax:** 863-386-6095
Size: 9,220 acres land; 31 acres water. **Location:** On County Road 634, 4 miles west of Sebring. **Facilities:** 138 full-facility campsites (&), youth group campground, primitive camping, restrooms (&), showers, picnic area (&), playgrounds, trails, interpretive exhibits, museum (&), restaurant. **Activities:** Camping, hiking, bicycling, horseback riding, in-line skating, birding, wildlife viewing, interpretive programs, tram tours (seasonal). **Special Features:** Highlands Hammock is one of Florida's oldest parks and is one of the earliest examples of grassroots support for environmental preservation. Concerned about plans to turn the hammock into farmland, local citizens acquired the property and pledged to protect it. When Florida's state park system was established in 1935, Highlands Hammock became one of the four original parks, and the Civilian Conservation Corps (CCC) built a camp there as a base for development.

★1963★ HILLSBOROUGH RIVER STATE PARK

15402 US 301 N
Thonotosassa, FL 33592
Web: www.floridastateparks.org/hillsboroughriver
Phone: 813-987-6771
Size: 3,728 acres land; 60.5 acres water. **Location:** 12 miles north of Tampa and 6 miles south of Zephyrhills on US 301. **Facilities:** 108 full-facility campsites, youth group camping area, primitive campsites, showers, 6 picnic pavilions, 2 playgrounds, swimming pool (&), trails, canoe rentals, restrooms (&), interpretive center, food concession. **Activities:** Camping, canoeing, freshwater fishing, swimming, hiking, bicycling, guided tours, wildlife viewing. **Special Features:** Park includes Fort Foster (see separate entry), the only standing replica of a Second Seminole War fort in the US. Nature trails border scenic Hillsborough River, leading through hammocks of live oaks, sabal palms, and hickories.

★1964★ HOMOSASSA SPRINGS WILDLIFE STATE PARK

4150 S Suncoast Blvd
Homosassa, FL 34446
Web: www.floridastateparks.org/homosassasprings
Phone: 352-628-5343; **Fax:** 352-628-4243

Size: 195 acres land; 5 acres water. **Location:** In Homosassa Springs, 75 miles north of Tampa, on US 19. **Facilities:** Picnic area, nature trails, visitor center, exhibits, restaurant, snack bar, gift shops. **Activities:** Hiking, wildlife viewing, birding, educational programs, boat tours. **Special Features:** Park showcases native Florida wildlife, including manatees, black bears, bobcats, white-tailed deer, American alligators, American crocodiles, and river otters. Visitors can view the manatees year-round from an underwater observatory in Homosassa's main spring. Snakes and other native animals are featured at Wildlife Encounter programs and at the park's Reptile House and Children's Education Center. The park also features wading birds, birds of prey, and songbirds.

★1965★ HONEYMOON ISLAND STATE PARK

1 Causeway Blvd
Dunedin, FL 34698
Web: www.floridastateparks.org/honeymoonisland
Phone: 727-469-5942
Size: 1,303 acres land; 1,507 acres water. **Location:** At the west end of State Route 586, north of Dunedin. **Facilities:** Beach, showers, restrooms (&), nature trail, interpretive exhibits, picnic areas, 2 covered pavilions, playground, food concession, kayak rental. **Activities:** Saltwater fishing, swimming, shelling, surfing, kayaking, hiking, wildlife viewing, guided tours. **Special Features:** Honeymoon Island is one in the chain of barrier islands that extends from Anclote Key south to Cape Romano. Originally called Hog Island, it became Honeymoon Isle in 1939 when a New York developer built 50 palm-thatched bungalows for honeymooners. Today visitors can enjoy the park's Gulf beaches, mangrove swamps, and tidal flats, as well as one of South Florida's few remaining virgin slash pine forests.

★1966★ HONTOON ISLAND STATE PARK

2309 River Ridge Rd
DeLand, FL 32720
Web: www.floridastateparks.org/hontoonisland
Phone: 386-736-5309
Size: 1,528 acres land; 120 acres water. **Location:** 6 miles west of Deland, off SR 44; accessible only by private boat or park ferry. **Facilities:** Youth group camp area, 12 primitive campsites (tent sites), 6 rustic cabins, bathhouses and showers (for campers only), restrooms (&), picnic area, pavilion, playground, overnight boat slips, canoe and kayak rental, nature trail, visitor center. **Activities:** Camping, boating, canoeing/kayaking, fishing, hiking, bicycling, wildlife viewing. **Special Features:** Snails gathered from the shallows of the Saint Johns River were a staple food of the Timucuan Indians who first inhabited this island. Through the years, the discarded shells of the snails accumulated to form large mounds on the island, one of which can be viewed from the park's nature trail.

★1967★ HUGH TAYLOR BIRCH STATE PARK

3109 E Sunrise Blvd
Fort Lauderdale, FL 33304
Web: www.floridastateparks.org/hughtaylorbirch
Phone: 954-564-4521; **Fax:** 954-762-3737

9. State Parks

Size: 174 acres land; 1.25 acres water. **Location:** On East Sunrise Boulevard in Fort Lauderdale, just west of A1A. **Facilities:** Youth camp with 6 air-conditioned cabins (each with restrooms and kitchens), primitive youth camping area, picnic areas, pavilions, playgrounds, restrooms, canoe rental, nature trails, visitor center. **Activities:** Group camping, canoeing, fishing, swimming, hiking, bicycling, inline skating, birding, guided tours (seasonal). **Special Features:** An island of trees and greenery in the middle of urban Fort Lauderdale, the park sits between the Atlantic Ocean and the Intracoastal Waterway, adjacent to Fort Lauderdale Beach. It contains several distinct native biological communities, including a maritime hammock and a freshwater lagoon. The Terramar Visitor Center, which was Hugh Taylor Birch's home, has displays of the area's history and of its unique ecosystem.

★1968★ **ICHETUCKNEE SPRINGS STATE PARK**
12087 SW US Hwy 27
Fort White, FL 32038
Web: www.floridastateparks.org/ichetuckneesprings
Phone: 386-497-2511
Size: 2,512 acres land; 22.5 acres water. **Location:** 4 miles northwest of Fort White, off State Roads 47 and 238. **Facilities:** Picnic areas, covered pavilions, hiking trails, food concession, in-park shuttle, visitor center. **Activities:** Canoeing, tubing, swimming, scuba diving (only at Blue Hole Spring, and divers must be cave certified), snorkeling, hiking, wildlife viewing, interpretive programs. **Special Features:** Ichetucknee's head spring was declared a National Natural Landmark by the US Dept of the Interior in 1972. It is one of a series of named springs along the Ichetucknee River that produce 233 million gallons of fresh water daily.

★1969★ **INDIAN KEY HISTORIC STATE PARK**
c/o Lignumvitae Key Botanical State Park
PO Box 1052
Islamorada, FL 33036
Web: www.floridastateparks.org/indiankey
Phone: 305-664-2540
Size: 13 acres land; 98 acres water. **Location:** On the ocean side of US 1 at Mile Marker 78.5. Park is usually accessible by private boat or charter boat, but the island's dock sustained considerable storm damage and, as of the summer of 2006, accessibility was by canoe or kayak only. **Facilities:** Nature trails. **Activities:** Boating, canoeing, fishing, snorkeling, scuba diving, boat tours, guided tours, hiking. **Special Features:** During the 1800s, Indian Key was the site of a lucrative business salvaging cargo from wrecked ships, and remains of this activity can still be seen there. The island was also Dade County's first county seat (1836).

★1970★ **JOHN D. MACARTHUR BEACH STATE PARK**
10900 SR 703 (A1A)
North Palm Beach, FL 33408
Web: www.floridastateparks.org/macarthurbeach
Phone: 561-624-6950
Size: 317 acres land; 120.5 acres water. **Location:** In northern Palm Beach County, 2.8 miles south of the intersection of US 1 and PGA Boulevard on A1A. **Facilities:** Beach, picnic areas, pavilions, playground restrooms, trails, nature center (visitor center). **Activities:** Saltwater fishing, canoeing, swimming, hiking, scuba diving, snorkeling, wildlife viewing, interpretive programs. **Special Features:** Park is a barrier island, featuring a unique mixture of coastal and tropical hammock and mangrove forest. MacArthur Beach is a prime nesting area for sea turtles, including loggerhead, green, and leatherback turtles.

★1971★ **JOHN GORRIE MUSEUM STATE PARK**
PO Box 267
Apalachicola, FL 32329
Web: www.floridastateparks.org/johngorriemuseum
Phone: 850-653-9347
Size: 1 acre. **Location:** On 6th Street in Apalachicola, off US 98. **Facilities:** Museum. **Activities:** Interpretive exhibits. **Special Features:** John Gorrie was a young physician who served as Apalachicola's postmaster, city treasurer, town councilman, and bank director in the early 1800s. Concern for his yellow fever patients led Gorrie to develop a method for cooling their rooms. By inventing a machine that made ice, he became a pioneer in the field of air conditioning and refrigeration and in 1851 received the first US patent for mechanical refrigeration. A replica of his ice-making machine is on display at the museum.

★1972★ **JOHN PENNEKAMP CORAL REEF STATE PARK**
PO Box 487
Key Largo, FL 33037
Web: www.floridastateparks.org/pennekamp
Phone: 305-451-1202
Size: 3,169 acres land, 60,667 acres water. **Location:** At Mile Marker 102.5 in Key Largo. **Facilities:** 47 full-facility campsites (for tents and RV campers), youth camping area (available for organized youth or adult groups), picnic areas, pavilions, playground, trails, beaches, showers, restrooms, food concession, deep-water boat ramp, boat rentals, dive shop, visitor center. **Activities:** Camping, boating, canoeing, saltwater fishing, swimming, snorkeling, scuba diving, hiking, boat tours, snorkeling excursions, scuba lessons and tours, wildlife viewing. **Special Features:** The first underwater state park in the United States, John Pennekamp Coral Reef State Park covers approximately 70 nautical square miles. Visitors can enjoy the coral reefs and their associated marine life by scuba diving or snorkeling, or they can view the reefs from a glass-bottom boat. In addition, the visitor center has a 30,000-gallon saltwater aquarium and a theater showing nature videos.

★1973★ **JOHN U. LLOYD BEACH STATE PARK**
6503 N Ocean Dr
Dania, FL 33004
Web: www.floridastateparks.org/lloydbeach
Phone: 954-923-2833
Size: 285.5 acres land; 25 acres water. **Location:** North of Hollywood, off A1A. **Facilities:** Beach, 2 boat ramps, canoe/

9. State Parks

kayak rental, restaurant, concessions, 7 picnic pavilions, playground, restrooms, nature trails, visitor center. **Activities:** Boating, canoeing, saltwater fishing, swimming, snorkeling, scuba diving, hiking, wildlife viewing. **Special Features:** Located adjacent to busy Port Everglades, this beachfront park preserves some of South Florida's vanishing natural resources including dunes, coastal hammock, and mangroves.

★1974★ JONATHAN DICKINSON STATE PARK

16450 SE Federal Hwy
Hobe Sound, FL 33455
Web: www.floridastateparks.org/jonathandickinson
Phone: 772-546-2771
Size: 10,692 acres land, 787 acres water. **Location:** 12 miles south of Stuart on US 1. **Facilities:** 135 full-facility campsites, primitive campsites, youth group camp, 12 cabins, swimming beach, picnic area, 4 pavilions, playground, trails, concession store, restrooms, boat ramp, canoe/kayak and motorboat rentals. **Activities:** Camping, boating, canoeing, freshwater fishing, swimming, hiking, backpacking, bicycling, horseback riding, guided tours, boat excursions, wildlife viewing, interpretive programs. **Special Features:** One of the largest parks in south Florida, Jonathan Dickinson consists of sand pine scrub, pine flatwoods, mangroves, river swamps, and the Loxahatchee River, Florida's first designated Wild and Scenic River.

★1975★ KISSIMMEE PRAIRIE PRESERVE STATE PARK

33104 NW 192 Ave
Okeechobee, FL 34972
Web: www.floridastateparks.org/kissimmeeprairie
Phone: 239-462-5360
Size: 51,913 acres land; 1,853 acres water. **Location:** 25 miles northwest of Okeechobee via US 441 and County Road 724. **Facilities:** Full-facility campsites (including a horseback campground) with restrooms (&) and showers, primitive campsites, 2 large Port-o-lets, restroom at park office (&), picnic tables, trails. **Activities:** Camping, fishing, hiking, bicycling, horseback riding, birding, wildlife viewing, guided swamp buggy tours. **Special Features:** Preserve is one of the largest remaining stretches of Florida dry prairie, reminiscent of the Great Plains of the Midwest. The preserve offers excellent seasonal birding opportunities and is home to the endangered Florida grasshopper sparrow, as well as the crested caracara and sandhill crane. This is also one of the few areas in the state that is far enough from urban and suburban locations to eliminate light pollution, which creates a setting for outstanding stargazing.

★1976★ KORESHAN STATE HISTORIC SITE

PO Box 7
Estero, FL 33928
Web: www.floridastateparks.org/koreshan
Phone: 239-992-0311; **Fax:** 239-992-1607
Size: 163 acres land; 0.5 acres water. **Location:** At the intersection of US 41 and Corkscrew Road at Estero. **Facilities:** 60 full-facility wooded campsites, picnic area, playground, trails, interpretive exhibits, boat ramp, restrooms (&). **Activities:**

Camping, canoeing/kayaking, freshwater fishing, hiking, wildlife viewing, guided tours. **Special Features:** In 1894, Cyrus Reed Teed brought his followers to Estero to build New Jerusalem for his faith, Koreshanity. The colony, known as Koreshan Unity, believed that the entire universe existed within a giant, hollow sphere. After Teed's death the colony began fading, and in 1961 the last four members deeded the land to the state.

★1977★ LAFAYETTE BLUE SPRINGS STATE PARK

799 NW Blue Spring Rd
Mayo, FL 32066
Web: www.floridastateparks.org/lafayettebluesprings
Phone: 386-294-3667
Size: 195 acres. **Location:** 7 miles northwest of Mayo on the west side of the Suwannee River. **Facilities:** Primitive walk-in tent campsites, portable restrooms, boat ramp, trails, picnic areas, pavilions, **Activities:** Camping, swimming, snorkeling, boating, canoeing/kayaking, fishing, hiking, wildlife viewing. For certified scuba divers, cave diving is available in the Green Sink cave system. Sometimes during rainy seasons dark river water backs up into the springs, making the water appear to be black in color. When this happens, swimming and diving is prohibited. **Special Features:** The first magnitude spring, which produces 168 million gallons of water daily, is the focal point of most recreational activities at the park. A short spring-run with a natural limestone land bridge connects one spring bank to the other. The park also contains a mile of Suwannee River shoreline, and a series of sinkholes are located throughout the park.

★1978★ LAKE GRIFFIN STATE PARK

3089 US 441-27
Fruitland Park, FL 34731
Web: www.floridastateparks.org/lakegriffin
Phone: 352-360-6760
Size: 521 acres land, 38 acres water. **Location:** 3 miles north of Leesburg and 30 miles south of Ocala. **Facilities:** 40 full-facility campsites, bathhouse(&), restrooms (&), picnic area, covered shelter, playground, nature trail, boat ramp, canoe rentals. **Activities:** Camping, boating, canoeing, freshwater fishing, wildlife viewing. **Special Features:** Located near the park's entrance is one of the state's largest live oak trees, measuring 150 feet in height and 10 feet around.

★1979★ LAKE JACKSON MOUNDS ARCHAEOLOGICAL STATE PARK

3600 Indian Mounds Rd
Tallahassee, FL 32303
Web: www.floridastateparks.org/lakejacksonmounds
Phone: 850-922-6007; **Fax:** 850-488-0366
Size: 164 acres land; 41 acres water. **Location:** Off US 27, 2 miles north of I-10 in Tallahassee. **Facilities:** Picnic tables, trails, interpretive exhibits. **Activities:** Guided tours, interpretive programs, hiking. **Special Features:** Park site is part of an area now known as the Southeastern Ceremonial Complex, which was occupied by the Lake Jackson Indians during the period 1200-1500 AD. The Complex encompasses six earthen temple mounds and one possible burial mound. The largest mound is

9. State Parks

approximately 36 feet high and measures 278 feet by 312 feet at the base. Artifacts of pre-Columbian societies that have been found here include burial objects such as copper breastplates, shell beaded necklaces, bracelets, anklets, and cloaks, along with the remains of important tribal members.

★1980★ LAKE JUNE-IN-WINTER SCRUB STATE PARK

c/o Highlands Hammock State Park
5931 Hammock Rd
Sebring, FL 33872
Web: www.floridastateparks.org/lakejuneinwinter
Phone: 863-386-6099
Size: 845 acres. **Location:** 12 miles south of Sebring off US 27. **Facilities:** Hiking trails, picnic tables. There is no drinking water at the park. **Activities:** Hiking, wildlife viewing, fishing. **Special Features:** Park protects one of the state's most endangered natural communities, sand scrub (sometimes called Florida's desert). Some of Florida's rarest plants and animals are found in the scrub, including the Florida scrub-jay, Florida scrub lizard, Florida mouse, deer, gopher tortoise, and bobcat. This park is relatively new and is still being developed; it's best suited to those seeking a remote wilderness experience and nature study.

★1981★ LAKE KISSIMMEE STATE PARK

14248 Camp Mack Rd
Lake Wales, FL 33853
Web: www.floridastateparks.org/lakekissimmee
Phone: 863-696-1112
Size: 5,643 acres land; 291 acres water.. **Location:** Off SR 60, 15 miles east of Lake Wales. **Facilities:** 60 full-facility campsites, youth group camp, 2 primitive campsites, picnic area, playground, observation tower, trails (13 miles), boat ramp, marina. **Activities:** Camping, boating, freshwater fishing, hiking, backpacking, horseback riding, interpretive and living history programs. **Special Features:** Park is located on the shores of lakes Kissimmee, Tiger, and Rosalie, and offers outstanding fishing. A "cow camp" is the focus of the park's living history program, where visitors can learn about the life of a cow hunter circa 1876 and see Florida Cracker cattle, descendants of the Spanish cattle brought to Florida by early explorers and settlers. Park also features some of Florida's darkest night skies and several star watching programs are offered throughout the year.

★1982★ LAKE LOUISA STATE PARK

7305 US Hwy 27
Clermont, FL 34714
Web: www.floridastateparks.org/lakelouisa
Phone: 352-394-3969
Size: 3,960 acres land; 448 acres water. **Location:** On US 27, 7 miles south of SR 50. **Facilities:** 60 full-facility campsites, including 2 bathhouses (&), 2 fishing piers, a pavilion, and an amphitheater; 3 primitive campsites, an equestrian primitive camp, and 3 primitive youth campsites; 20 cabins (&); 3 equestrian trails and a 0.5-mile nature trail; canoe/kayak launch.

(Available facilities vary at the three lakes that are most accessible at the park.) **Activities:** Camping, canoeing/kayaking, fishing, swimming, hiking, horseback riding. **Special Features:** Park is known for its six beautiful lakes, rolling hills, and scenic landscapes. Lake Louisa is the largest in a chain of 13 lakes connected by the Palatlakaha River, which is designated as an Outstanding Florida Waterway.

★1983★ LAKE MANATEE STATE PARK

20007 Hwy 64 E
Bradenton, FL 34202
Web: www.floridastateparks.org/lakemanatee
Phone: 941-741-3028
Size: 556 acres land; 22.5 acres water. **Location:** 15 miles east of Bradenton on SR 64. **Facilities:** 60 full-facility campsites, picnic area, pavilion, playground, swimming beach, showers, boat ramp, restrooms (&). **Activities:** Camping, boating (20 HP limit), freshwater fishing, swimming, wildlife viewing. **Special Features:** Park extends along 3 miles of the south shore of Lake Manatee, which serves as a water reservoir for Manatee and Sarasota counties. The rest of the park is mostly pine flatwoods and sand pine scrub, with some depression marshes and hardwood forests.

★1984★ LAKE TALQUIN STATE PARK

1022 DeSoto Park Dr
Tallahassee, FL 32301
Web: www.floridastateparks.org/laketalquin
Phone: 850-922-6007
Size: 481 acres land; 5.5 acres water. **Location:** 15 miles west of Tallahassee on SR 20, on Jack Vause Landing Road. **Facilities:** Large pavilion, trails. **Activities:** Fishing, boating, canoeing, picnicking, hiking, wildlife viewing. **Special Features:** Lake Talquin was formed in 1927 when Jackson Bluff Dam was constructed on the Ochlockonee River to produce hydroelectric power. The lake offers outstanding fishing for largemouth bass, bream, shellcracker, and speckled perch.

★1985★ LETCHWORTH MOUNDS STATE PARK

4500 Sunray Rd S
Monticello, FL 32344
Web: www.floridastateparks.org/letchworthmounds
Phone: 850-922-6007; **Fax:** 850-488-0366
Size: 188 acres. **Location:** 15 miles east of Tallahassee, off US 90 on Sunray Road South. **Facilities:** Boardwalk leading to the park's tallest mound (&), hiking trails, picnic tables. Visitor Center is planned. **Activities:** Hiking, wildlife viewing, picnicking; guided tours available with two weeks notice. **Special Features:** Part of an archeological complex that extends beyond the park's boundaries, the Letchworth Mounds include a small burial mound recorded in 1972 as well as a larger mound complex recorded five years later. Florida's tallest Native American ceremonial mound, which is 46 feet tall, is located here. It's believed that the people who built the mound were members of the Weedon Island Culture, a group of Native Americans who lived in North Florida between 200 and 800 AD.

★1986★ LIGNUMVITAE KEY BOTANICAL STATE PARK

PO Box 1052
Islamorada, FL 33036
Web: www.floridastateparks.org/lignumvitaekey
Phone: 305-664-2540
Size: 846 acres land; 9,971 acres water. **Location:** 1 mile west of US 1 at Mile Marker 78.5; accessible only by private or charter boat. **Facilities:** Visitor center (the Matheson house, built in 1919), restrooms. **Activities:** Boating, canoeing, fishing, snorkeling, wildlife viewing, guided boat tours, guided walking tours. **Special Features:** Island was acquired in 1919 by William J. Matheson, a wealthy chemist who lived in Miami. The virgin tropical hardwood hammock that thrives here is typical of the kind that once covered most of the Upper Keys. The site preserves the lignumvitae, a tree that produces an especially hard wood, and other native trees.

★1987★ LITTLE MANATEE RIVER STATE PARK

215 Lightfoot Rd
Wimauma, FL 33598
Web: www.floridastateparks.org/littlemanateeriver
Phone: 813-671-5005
Size: 2,416 acres. **Location:** 4 miles south of Sun City, off US 301 on Lightfoot Road. **Facilities:** 34 full-facility campsites, 4 of which are specifically designed for horse camping, youth/group camping area, primitive camping, picnic area, pavilions, playground, hiking trails (6.5 miles), equestrian trail (8 miles), canoe rental, restrooms (&). **Activities:** Camping, canoeing, freshwater fishing, hiking, horseback riding, wildlife viewing, interpretive programs. **Special Features:** Little Manatee River begins in a swampy area east of Fort Lonesome in southeastern Hillsborough County and flows about 40 miles before emptying into Tampa Bay. The river has been designated an Outstanding Florida Water and is part of the Cockroach Bay Aquatic Preserve.

★1988★ LITTLE TALBOT ISLAND STATE PARK

12157 Heckscher Dr
Jacksonville, FL 32226
Web: www.floridastateparks.org/littletalbotisland
Phone: 904-251-2320; **Fax:** 904-251-2325
Size: 1,872 acres land; 44 acres water. **Location:** 17 miles east of I-95 on Heckscher Drive (Milepost Exit 358A off I-95). **Facilities:** 40 full-facility campsites with 2 bathhouses, launch for small boats, nature trail, and playground at the campground; primitive youth/group camping area; beaches with boardwalks, bathhouses, and outdoor showers; picnic areas and pavilions; nature trails. **Activities:** Camping, canoeing (rental provider near park), saltwater fishing, swimming, surfing, shelling, hiking, bicycling, wildlife viewing, interpretive programs. **Special Features:** More than 5 miles of sandy beaches, undisturbed salt marshes, and vegetated dunes have been preserved on this Atlantic coast barrier island. Wildlife at the park includes river otters, marsh rabbits, bobcats, and a variety of shorebirds.

★1989★ LONG KEY STATE PARK

PO Box 776
Long Key, FL 33001
Web: www.floridastateparks.org/longkey
Phone: 305-664-4815
Size: 832 acres land, 148 acres water. **Location:** At Mile Marker 67.5, 67400 Overseas Highway, in the Florida Keys. **Facilities:** 60 full-facility campsites, picnic areas, playground, nature trails, showers, restrooms, canoe rentals. **Activities:** Camping, canoeing, saltwater fishing, swimming, snorkeling, hiking, wildlife viewing, interpretive programs. **Special Features:** Spanish explorers named the island ''Cayo Vivora'' (Rattlesnake Key) to describe its shape, which resembles a snake with its jaws open.

★1990★ LOVERS KEY STATE PARK

8700 Estero Blvd
Fort Myers Beach, FL 33931
Web: www.floridastateparks.org/loverskey
Phone: 239-463-4588
Size: 545 acres land; 918 acres water. **Location:** On County Road 865 between Fort Myers Beach and Bonita Beach in Lee County. **Facilities:** Beaches, bathhouses, showers, canoe/kayak rental, boat ramp, bicycle rental, food concession, picnic areas/shelters, pavilions, volleyball courts, playgrounds, restrooms (&), trails (8 miles total), **Activities:** Boating, canoeing, saltwater fishing, picnicking, shelling, swimming, hiking, bicycling, birding, wildlife viewing, Eco-tours. **Special Features:** Park is made up of 4 barrier islands: Black Island, Lovers Key, Inner Key, and Long Key. For years Lovers Kay was accessible only by boat, and it was said that only lovers traveled there to enjoy its remote and solitary beach. Today, the islands and their waters are not only a place for park visitors to enjoy, they're also a haven for wildlife, including West Indian manatees, bottlenose dolphins, roseate spoonbills, marsh rabbits, and bald eagles.

★1991★ LOWER WEKIVA RIVER PRESERVE STATE PARK

1800 Wekiwa Cir
Apopka, FL 32712
Web: www.floridastateparks.org/lowerwekivariver
Phone: 407-884-2008; **Fax:** 407-884-2039
Size: 16,991 acres land; 413.5 acres water. **Location:** 9 miles west of Sanford on SR 46. **Facilities:** Primitive horse camping area with bathhouse/showers (&) and restroom (&); multiuse trails. **Activities:** Horse camping, canoeing (must launch from outside locations), bicycling, hiking, horseback riding, wildlife viewing. **Special Features:** Central Florida nature in its purest form is found in this preserve, which borders more than 6 miles of the Saint Johns River and 4 miles of the Wekiva River and Blackwater Creek. The area's system of blackwater streams and wetlands provides a habitat for black bear, river otter, alligator, wood stork, and sandhill crane.

★1992★ MADIRA BICKEL MOUND STATE ARCHEOLOGICAL SITE

3708 Patten Ave
Ellenton, FL 34222
Web: www.floridastateparks.org/madirabickelmound
Phone: 941-723-4536

9. State Parks

Size: 5.5 acres land; 4 acres water. Location: Approximately 1.5 miles off US 19 , in Palmetto; entrance is about 1 mile south of I-275. Facilities: Under development. Picnic tables are available now; nature trails and kiosks with historical information are planned. Activities: Picnicking. Special Features: Site was the first in Florida to be designated a State Archeological Site, in 1948. The flat-topped ceremonial mound is composed of sand, shell, and village debris and is 20 feet high. Excavations have disclosed at least three periods of Native American cultures, with the earliest dating back 2,000 years.

★1993★ MADISON BLUE SPRINGS STATE PARK

8300 NE State Road 6
Lee, FL 32059
Web: www.floridastateparks.org/madison
Phone: 850-971-5003
Size: 44 acres. Location: 10 miles east of Madison on the Withlacoochee River, off SR 6. Facilities: Canoe launch, picnic areas and shelters, showers. Activities: Canoeing, swimming, scuba diving (certified divers), fishing, wildlife viewing. Special Features: The park's first magnitude spring is about 82 feet wide and 25 feet deep and bubbles up into a limestone basin along the west bank of the Withlacoochee River. This park is one of Florida's newest state parks.

★1994★ MANATEE SPRINGS STATE PARK

11650 NW 115th St
Chiefland, FL 32626
Web: www.floridastateparks.org/manateesprings
Phone: 352-493-6072
Size: 2,423 acres land; 20 acres water. Location: At the end of SR 320, off US 98, 6 miles west of Chiefland. Facilities: 92 full-facility campsites for tents or RVs, group/youth campsites (primitive), picnic areas, pavilions, playground, food concession, canoe/kayak rentals, nature trails (8.5 miles). Activities: Camping, boating (motor boats), canoeing, freshwater fishing, swimming, scuba diving and cave diving (for certified divers), snorkeling, hiking, bicycling, wildlife viewing, boat tours, guided walking tours. Special Features: Manatee Springs is one of Florida's first-magnitude springs, producing more than 100 million gallons of fresh water daily. In winter, manatees swim upriver to spend nights in the warm waters of the head-spring.

★1995★ MARJORIE KINNAN RAWLINGS HISTORIC STATE PARK

18700 S County Road 325
Cross Creek, FL 32640
Web: www.floridastateparks.org/marjoriekinnanrawlings
Phone: 352-466-3672
Size: 77 acres. Location: In Cross Creek, off County Road 325. Facilities: Historic home, farmyard, groves, hiking trails. Activities: Guided tours, interpretive programs, hiking. Special Features: Site preserves the cracker-style home and farm of Marjorie Kinnan Rawlings, author of the Pulitzer Prize-winning novel *The Yearling*.

★1996★ MIKE ROESS GOLD HEAD BRANCH STATE PARK

6239 SR 21
Keystone Heights, FL 32656
Web: www.floridastateparks.org/goldhead
Phone: 352-473-4701
Size: 2,250 acres land; 115 acres water. Location: 6 miles northeast of Keystone Heights on SR 21. Facilities: 74 full-facility campsites (all have water, but 10 of the sites do not have electrical hookups), 2 primitive campsites, and 3 group campsites (with restrooms, but no electrical hookups); cabins with amenities, including CCC cabins, block cabins, and new 2-bedroom cabins (&); beach, picnic area, 8 covered shelters, playground; canoe rentals; hiking and equestrian trails. Activities: Camping, canoeing, freshwater fishing, swimming, hiking, horseback riding, wildlife viewing. Special Features: Park is located on rolling sandhills in an area known as the central ridge of Florida. A deep ravine with springs issuing from its side bisects the area and forms Gold Head Branch. The park was developed by the Civilian Conservation Corps in the 1930s, and the CCC's craftsmanship can still be seen at the park today.

★1997★ MOUND KEY ARCHEOLOGICAL STATE PARK

PO Box 7
Estero, FL 33928
Web: www.floridastateparks.org/moundkey
Phone: 239-992-0311; Fax: 239-992-1607
Size: 172 acres. Location: In Estero Bay, several miles by boat from Koreshan State Historic Site or Lovers Key State Park. Accessible by boat only. Facilities: Under development. A trail that has interpretive displays spans the width of the island. Park has no restroom facilities. Activities: Boating, fishing, hiking, wildlife viewing. Special Features: Mound Key is believed to have been the ceremonial center of the Calusa Indians when the Spaniards first attempted to colonize Southwest Florida in the 1500s. Rising more than 30 feet above the waters of Estero Bay, the shell mounds and ridges on the island were probably created by prehistoric Native Americans from seashells, fish bones, and pottery.

★1998★ MYAKKA RIVER STATE PARK

13207 SR 72
Sarasota, FL 34241
Web: www.floridastateparks.org/myakkariver
Phone: 941-361-6511; Toll Free: 800-326-3521
Size: 36,079 acres land; 1,120 acres water. Location: 9 miles east of Sarasota on SR 72. Facilities: 76 full-facility campsites, 3 youth/group camps, 6 primitive campsites, and 5 historic log cabins (modernized); concession with canoe and bicycle rentals, food, supplies, and souvenirs; picnic areas, pavilions, playgrounds; boat ramp, fishing pier (&); horse trail, nature trail with observation tower; visitor center, restrooms (&). Activities: Camping, canoeing, freshwater fishing, hiking, backpacking, horseback riding, bicycling, wildlife viewing, birding, tram tours, canoe tours, airboat rides, interpretive programs. Special Features: The Myakka River, designated as a Florida Wild and Scenic River, flows through 58 square miles of wetlands,

9. State Parks

397

prairies, hammocks, and pinelands. The park features an elevated, canopied walkway that offers visitors a walk ''through the tree tops'' and panoramic views over a vast expanse of forest. In addition to the river, the park also has two lakes.

★1999★ NATURAL BRIDGE BATTLEFIELD HISTORIC STATE PARK

7502 Natural Bridge Rd
Tallahassee, FL 32305
Web: www.floridastateparks.org/naturalbridge
Phone: 850-922-6007; **Fax:** 850-488-0366
Size: 9 acres. **Location:** 6 miles east of Woodville, off SR 363 on Natural Bridge Road. **Facilities:** Picnic tables. **Activities:** A reenactment of the battle is held here every year in March. **Special Features:** It was here at the Battle of Natural Bridge that volunteers and Confederate forces repelled three attacks and several skirmishes against Union forces to keep Tallahassee as the only Confederate capital east of the Mississippi River not captured by the Union. Natural Bridge is also the area where the Saint Marks River drops into a sinkhole and flows underground for a quarter mile before re-emerging.

★2000★ NORTH PENINSULA STATE PARK

c/o Gamble Rogers Memorial State Recreation Area
3100 S A1A
Flagler Beach, FL 32136
Web: www.floridastateparks.org/northpeninsula
Phone: 386-517-2086
Size: 547 acres land; 2 acres water. **Location:** 40 Highbridge Road, Ormond by the Sea, 4 miles south of Flagler Beach on SR A1A. **Facilities:** Beach, picnic area, hiking trail, restrooms. **Activities:** Swimming, shelling, fishing, hiking, wildlife viewing. **Special Features:** Park features more than two miles of Atlantic beaches and provides a haven for such rare creatures as the Florida scrub-jay, Indigo snake, and gopher tortoise.

★2001★ OCHLOCKONEE RIVER STATE PARK

PO Box 5
Sopchoppy, FL 32358
Web: www.floridastateparks.org/ochlockoneeriver
Phone: 850-962-2771
Size: 528 acres land; 15 acres water. **Location:** 4 miles south of Sopchoppy on US 319, 10 miles from the Gulf Coast. **Facilities:** 30 full-facility campsites, youth group camp, picnic tables, boat ramp, nature trails. **Activities:** Camping, boating, canoeing, freshwater and saltwater fishing, swimming, hiking, bicycling, wildlife viewing. **Special Features:** From the park, boaters have access to the Ochlockonee River, Ochlockonee Bay, and the Gulf of Mexico. Ochlockonee, which means ''yellow waters,'' is a mix of brackish, tidal surge, and fresh water. The park's diverse biological communities feature small grass ponds, bayheads, and oak thickets which provide habitat for deer, fox squirrel, bobcat, gray fox, as well as numerous species of birds including the endangered red-cockaded woodpecker.

★2002★ O'LENO STATE PARK

410 SE Oleno Park Rd
High Springs, FL 32643
Web: www.floridastateparks.org/oleno
Phone: 386-454-1853
Size: 1,714 acres land; 27 acres water. **Location:** On US 441, 6 miles north of High Springs. **Facilities:** 61 full-facility campsites, primitive camping (3 youth camps, 1 hike-in camp, 1 horse camping area), group camp with 17 cabins, dining hall, kitchen, recreation hall, bathhouses; picnic area, shelters, playground areas; hiking, biking, and horse trails; canoe and bicycle rentals. **Activities:** Camping, canoeing, freshwater fishing, swimming, hiking, backpacking, horseback riding, bicycling, wildife viewing. **Special Features:** Park is located on the banks of the scenic Santa Fe River, a tributary of the Suwannee River. Inside park property, the Santa Fe River disappears and flows underground for three miles before resurfacing again. Other interesting natural features include sinkholes, hardwood hammock, river swamp, and sandhill communities. The park was first developed by the Civilian Conservation Corps in the 1930s and the suspension bridge they built still spans the river.

★2003★ OLETA RIVER STATE PARK

3400 NE 163rd St
North Miami Beach, FL 33160
Web: www.floridastateparks.org/oletariver
Phone: 305-919-1846
Size: 1,013 acres land; 20 acres water. **Location:** On Biscayne Bay, at 3400 NE 163rd Street, off I-95 in Miami. **Facilities:** 14 primitive cabins, bathhouse, youth group camping area, beach, fishing pier, 9 covered picnic pavilions, playground, mountain biking trails, hiking trails, concession offering bicycle and canoe/kayak rentals as well as snacks, public showers, restrooms. **Activities:** Camping, boating, canoeing, saltwater fishing, swimming, bicycling, hiking, wildlife viewing. **Special Features:** Florida's largest urban park, Oleta River is located on Biscayne Bay in the Miami metropolitan area. Although it offers a variety of recreation, it is best known for its miles of off-road bicycling trails, ranging from novice trails to more than 10 miles challenging trails for experienced mountain bikers.

★2004★ OLUSTEE BATTLEFIELD HISTORIC STATE PARK

PO Box 40
Olustee, FL 32072
Web: www.floridastateparks.org/olustee
Phone: 386-758-0400
Size: 691 acres. **Location:** 2 miles east of Olustee on US 90. **Facilities:** Picnic tables, nature trail, interpretive center, visitor center. **Activities:** Interpretive programs. **Special Features:** Site commemorates Florida's largest Civil War battle, in which more than 10,000 soldiers fought for five hours on February 20, 1864. Three US Colored Troops, including the now-famous *54th Massachusetts*, participated in the battle, which ended with the retreat of the Union soldiers to Jacksonville for the remainder of the war. Casualties that day totaled more than 2,800. The battle is reenacted each year, and scenes for Civil War movies (including Glory) have been filmed during the reenactments.

★2005★ ORMAN HOUSE
177 5th St
Apalachicola, FL 32325
Web: www.floridastateparks.org/ormanhouse
Phone: 850-653-1209
Size: 1.5 acres. **Location:** In the downtown historical section of Apalachicola, off US 98. **Facilities:** Historic house, interpretive exhibits. **Activities:** Guided tours. **Special Features:** This antebellum home overlooking the Apalachicola River was built by cotton merchant Thomas Orman in 1838 and was used for both business and social gatherings. The house features details of both federal and Greek revival styles, with wooden mantelpieces, molded plaster cornices, and wide heart-pine floorboards.

★2006★ OSCAR SCHERER STATE PARK
1843 S Tamiami Trail
Osprey, FL 34229
Web: www.floridastateparks.org/oscarscherer
Phone: 941-483-5956; **Fax:** 941-480-3007
Size: 1,377 acres land; 4.5 acres water. **Location:** On US 41, 2 miles south of Osprey. **Facilities:** Full-facility campsites, primitive camping area (tents only) for youth/adult groups, beach, boat ramp (canoes and kayaks only), canoe/kayak rentals, multi-use trails, nature trail with butterfly gardens (&), pavilions, picnic areas, 3 playgrounds (&), restrooms (&), showers, visitors/nature center. **Activities:** Camping, canoeing/kayaking, freshwater and saltwater fishing, swimming, snorkeling, hiking, bicycling, wildlife viewing, guided canoe tours, interpretive programs. **Special Features:** Park's extensive scrubby flatwoods provide habitat for the threatened Florida scrub-jay as well as other declining species, including the gopher tortoise, gopher frog, and indigo snake.

★2007★ PAYNES CREEK HISTORIC STATE PARK
888 Lake Branch Rd
Bowling Green, FL 33834
Web: www.floridastateparks.org/paynescreek
Phone: 863-375-4717; **Fax:** 863-375-4510
Size: 396 acres. **Location:** 0.5 mile southeast of Bowling Green on Lake Branch Road. **Facilities:** Youth camping area, picnic tables, pavilions, playground, trails, visitor center, restrooms (&). **Activities:** Fishing, canoeing, hiking, wildlife viewing, interpretive programs. **Special Features:** Fort Chokonikla was the first in a chain of forts constructed in the 1840s to control the Seminoles. The Seminoles didn't want war and never attacked the fort, but the Army was nearly defeated by disease-carrying mosquitoes. A museum at the park's visitor center depicts the lives of Florida's Seminole Indians and the pioneers in this area during the 19th Century.

★2008★ PAYNES PRAIRIE PRESERVE STATE PARK
100 Savannah Blvd
Micanopy, FL 32667
Web: www.floridastateparks.org/paynesprairie
Phone: 352-466-3397
Size: Nearly 21,000 acres land; 188 acres water. **Location:** On US 441, 10 miles south of Gainesville. **Facilities:** Full-facility campsites (tents, trailers, or motorized vehicles up to 40 feet long), picnic areas, covered pavilions, multi-use trails, boat ramp, visitor center. **Activities:** Camping, boating (no gasoline motors), canoeing/kayaking, fishing, hiking, backpacking, bicycling, horseback riding, wildlife viewing, interpretive programs (seasonal). **Special Features:** Park became Florida's first state preserve in 1971 and has since been designated as a National Natural Landmark. The preserve contains more than 20 distinct biological communities, which provide an array of habitats for various kinds of wildlife, including alligators, bison, wild horses, and some 270 species of birds.

★2009★ PEACOCK SPRINGS STATE PARK
Administration Office
18081 185th Rd
Live Oak, FL 32060
Web: www.floridastateparks.org/peacocksprings
Phone: 386-776-2194
Size: 277.5 acres. **Location:** 16 miles southwest of Live Oak on State Route 51; 2 miles east of Luraville on Peacock Springs Road. **Facilities:** Picnic areas. **Activities:** Swimming, snorkeling, scuba diving (proof of certification required). **Special Features:** Park includes one of the longest underwater cave systems in the continental United States. About 28,000 feet of its underwater passages have been explored and surveyed by cave divers. Park's natural features include two major springs, a major spring run, and six sinkholes.

★2010★ PERDIDO KEY STATE PARK
12301 Gulf Beach Hwy
Pensacola, FL 32507
Web: www.floridastateparks.org/perdidokey
Phone: 850-492-1595
Size: 273 acres land; 17 acres water. **Location:** 15 miles southwest of Pensacola, off SR 292. **Facilities:** Beach, showers, picnic tables. **Activities:** Fishing, swimming, wildlife viewing. **Special Features:** Perdido Key is a barrier island on the Gulf of Mexico, with white sand beaches and rolling dunes covered with sea oats.

★2011★ PONCE DE LEON SPRINGS STATE PARK
2860 Ponce de Leon Springs Rd
Ponce de Leon, FL 32455
Web: www.floridastateparks.org/poncedeleonsprings
Phone: 850-836-4281
Size: 420 acres. **Location:** 0.5 miles south of US 90 on County Road 181-A. **Facilities:** Picnic area with shelters, trails. **Activities:** Swimming, snorkeling, freshwater fishing, hiking, wildlife viewing, ranger-guided walks (seasonal). **Special Features:** The main natural spring is a convergence of two underground water flows and produces 14 million gallons of crystal-clear water daily. The temperature of the springs is 68 degrees year-round.

★2012★ PUMPKIN HILL CREEK PRESERVE STATE PARK
13802 Pumpkin Hill Rd
Jacksonville, FL 32226
Web: www.floridastateparks.org/pumpkinhill
Phone: 904-696-5980

9. State Parks

Size: 3,895.5 acres. **Location:** Exit Heckscher Drive north from I-95 or 9A, then north on New Berlin and east on Cedar Point Road for about 10 miles, then north again on Pumpkin Hill Road. **Facilities:** Hand launch area for canoes and kayaks, multi-use trails. **Activities:** Canoeing/kayaking, fishing, hiking, bicycling, horseback riding, wildlife viewing. **Special Features:** Located east of the city of Jacksonville and west of the beaches, Park preserves one of the largest contiguous areas of coastal uplands remaining in Duval County. The uplands protect the water quality of Nassau and Saint Johns rivers, providing an important refuge for birds. Both wildlife and wildflowers are abundant at the park.

★2013★ RAINBOW SPRINGS STATE PARK

19158 SW 81st Place Rd
Dunnellon, FL 34432
Web: www.floridastateparks.org/rainbowsprings
Phone: 352-465-8555
Size: 1,459 acres land; 13 acres water. **Location:** 3 miles north of Dunnellon on the east side of US 41. **Facilities:** Full-facility campground with camp store, recreation hall, showers, restrooms, pool, and playground (located about 6 miles by car from the park's day use area), picnic area, pavilions, canoe/kayak rental, gardens, trails. **Activities:** Camping, canoeing, swimming, tubing, snorkeling, birding, hiking. **Special Features:** Rainbow Springs was formerly the site of a privately owned attraction that lost most of its business when Disney World opened. In the early 1990s volunteers cleared the area and opened it as a park on week-ends, and the Florida Park Service officially opened it as a state park in 1995. The springs are referred to as the headsprings of the Rainbow River, which has been designated a National Natural Landmark and an Outstanding Florida Waterway.

★2014★ RAVINE GARDENS STATE PARK

1600 Twigg St
Palatka, FL 32177
Web: www.floridastateparks.org/ravinegardens
Phone: 386-329-3721; **Fax:** 386-329-3718
Size: 139 acres land; 7.5 acres water. **Location:** At 1600 Twigg Street in Palatka. **Facilities:** Gardens, picnic areas, playground, trails, interpretive exhibits, restrooms (&), civic center complex with covered pavilion, auditorium, and meeting rooms. **Activities:** Hiking, bicycling, picnicking, wildlife viewing. **Special Features:** Ravine Gardens was created in the 1930s by the federal Works Project Administration, which planted the ravines with more than 95,000 azaleas (64 varieties), 11,000 palm trees, and 250,000 ornamental plants. Much of the WPA's original landscaping still exists as the park's formal gardens and extensive trail system. The peak flowering period is azalea season, late January to April.

★2015★ RIVER RISE PRESERVE STATE PARK

410 SE O'Leno Park Rd
High Springs, FL 32643
Web: www.floridastateparks.org/riverrise
Phone: 386-454-1853
Size: 4,425 acres land; 56 acres water. **Location:** Off US 441, 6 miles north of High Springs, within O'Leno State Park. **Facilities:** Primitive campsites with a centrally located bathhouse and 20-stall horse barn, 20 miles of horseback riding trails, picnic pavilion. **Activities:** Camping, horseback riding, fishing. **Special Features:** From the 1500s to the 1700s a natural land bridge formed a crossroad between the Santa Fe River Sink and the River Rise that was traveled by Spanish explorers, Indians, and settlers. Today visitors can see where the Santa Fe River disappears within O'Leno State Park and then reemerges more than three miles away at River Rise. From there it continues its journey on to the Suwannee River.

★2016★ ROCK SPRINGS RUN STATE RESERVE

c/o Wekiwa Springs State Park
1800 Wekiwa Cir
Apopka, FL 32712
Web: www.floridastateparks.org/rockspringsrun
Phone: 407-884-2008; **Fax:** 407-884-2039
Size: 13,843 acres. **Location:** In Sorrento, off State Route 46. **Facilities:** 2 canoe campsites and an equestrian campsite (all primitive), multi-use trails, restroom and shower facility (&). **Activities:** Camping, hiking, canoeing, horseback riding, bicycling, wildlife viewing. Swimming is not permitted. **Special Features:** Reserve features extensive trails through pine scrub, pine flatwoods, bayheads, hammocks, and swamps, but its most striking natural feature is the spring/run river system that surrounds most of its perimeter. This system is formed from the discharge of several artesian springs together with the tannic runoff from the surrounding watershed and is accessible from the hiking trails, but it also creates one of the most scenic canoe trails in central Florida. (Canoes and kayaks cannot be launched from within the Reserve, but there are several launching places outside the Reserve.)

★2017★ SAINT ANDREWS STATE PARK

4607 State Park Ln
Panama City, FL 32408
Web: www.floridastateparks.org/standrews
Phone: 850-233-5140
Size: 1,104 acres land; 65.5 acres water. **Location:** 3 miles east of Panama City Beach, off SR 392 (Thomas Drive). **Facilities:** 176 full-facility campsites, youth/group primitive camping area, bathhouses, beach, showers, picnic areas and pavilions, playgrounds, food and other concessions, canoe/kayak rental, boat ramp, 2 fishing piers and jetties, hiking trails, visitor center, restroom. **Activities:** Camping, boating, canoeing/kayaking, saltwater fishing, swimming, snorkeling, scuba diving, surfing, hiking, bicycling, boat excursions, living history demonstrations, interpretive programs. **Special Features:** Park is located on a peninsula between the Gulf of Mexico and Grand Lagoon. During World War II it was part of a military reservation, and circular cannon platforms are still in place near the jetties on the beach. A parcel of the park that remains undeveloped is Shell Island, a barrier island just across the ship's channel from the mainland. Shuttle boats run to the island during the spring and summer.

★2018★ SAINT LUCIE INLET PRESERVE STATE PARK

4810 SE Cove Rd
Stuart, FL 34997
Web: www.floridastateparks.org/stlucieinlet
Phone: 772-219-1880
Size: 946 acres land; 3,888 acres water. **Location:** In Port Salerno, on the Intracoastal Waterway, 0.67 miles south of the inlet; accessible only by private boat. **Facilities:** Beach, showers, picnic shelter, boat dock, hiking/nature trail, restrooms. **Activities:** Boating, canoeing, saltwater fishing, swimming, snorkeling, scuba diving, hiking, wildlife viewing. **Special Features:** A 3,300-foot boardwalk on this barrier island leads visitors from the dock through mangrove forests and coastal hammocks of live oaks, cabbage palms, paradise trees, and wild limes to 2.7 miles of Atlantic beach. In summer months the preserve's beaches are an important nesting area for loggerhead, green, and leatherback turtles.

★2019★ SAINT SEBASTIAN RIVER PRESERVE STATE PARK

1000 Buffer Preserve Dr
Fellsmere, FL 32948
Web: www.floridastateparks.org/stsebastian
Phone: 321-953-5004; **Fax:** 321-953-5006
Size: 21,348 acres. **Location:** Off Babcock Street (County Road 507) just north of the C-54 Canal (north entrance/visitor center); or off Fellsmere Road (County Road 512) 1.8 miles east of I-95 (south entrance). **Facilities:** 5 primitive tent campsites for group camping, 6 hike-in primitive tent campsites, 3 primitive campsites for horse camping, 2 picnic pavilions, 1 remote picnic area, multi-use trails (60 miles), a Port-o-Let toilet facility (&), small unmanned visitor center (&). **Activities:** Camping, horseback riding, hiking, bicycling, fishing, canoeing/kayaking (no launch facilities in park), wildlife viewing, birding, guided tours (seasonal). **Special Features:** Park preserves open grassy forests of longleaf pine and other biological communities, including cypress domes, scrubby flatwoods, sandhills, and a strand swamp. These habitats are home to many native plants and animals, including more than 50 protected species. Several cultural, historical, and archeological resources also are found at the park.

★2020★ SAN FELASCO HAMMOCK PRESERVE STATE PARK

12720 NW 109 Ln
Alachua, FL 32615
Web: www.floridastateparks.org/sanfelascohammock
Phone: 386-462-7905
Size: 6,908.5 acres land; 18.5 acres water. **Location:** Hiking trailhead is 4 miles northwest of Gainesville on SR 232; equestrian/mountain bike trailhead is of US 441 just south of Alachua. **Facilities:** Hiking trails (southern two-thirds of the park); equestrian, mountain biking, and hiking trails (northern third of park). **Activities:** Hiking, horseback riding, mountain biking, wildlife viewing. **Special Features:** Preserve has one of the few remaining mature forests in Florida. The limestone outcrops and extreme changes in elevation provide conditions for many species of hardwood trees. Bobcats, white-tailed deer, gray foxes, turkeys, and many species of songbirds make their homes in the preserve, which also features sinkholes, steephead springs, ponds, and small lakes.

★2021★ SAN MARCOS DE APALACHE HISTORIC STATE PARK

148 Old Fort Rd
Saint Marks, FL 31355
Web: www.floridastateparks.org/sanmarcos
Phone: 850-925-6216
Size: 16 acres. **Location:** In Saint Marks, off SR 363, on Old Fort Road. **Facilities:** Museum, trails. **Special Features:** The history of this National Landmark began in 1528 when Spanish explorer Panfilo de Narvaez arrived in the area with 300 men, but the first fort was not built here until 1679. The museum at the park displays pottery and tools unearthed near the original fort and explains the site's history.

★2022★ SAN PEDRO UNDERWATER ARCHAEOLOGICAL PRESERVE STATE PARK

PO Box 1052
Islamorada, FL 33036
Web: www.floridastateparks.org/sanpedro
Phone: 305-664-2540
Size: 644 acres water. **Location:** In 18 feet of water approximately 1.25 nautical miles south from Indian Key at GPS coordinates 24 degrees 51.802'N, 80 degrees 40.795'W. **Facilities:** Underwater shipwreck site with mooring buoys. **Activities:** Boating, canoeing, snorkeling, scuba diving, swimming. **Special Features:** Part of a Spanish flotilla, the *San Pedro* was a 287-ton Dutch-built ship that sank in a hurricane in 1733. After major salvage efforts in the 1960s, all that remains of the *San Pedro* is a large pile of ballast stones covering an area 90 feet long and 30 feet wide. The underwater site has been enhanced with seven replica cannons, an anchor, and an information plaque. Its location in a white sand pocket surrounded by prolific marine life makes it one of the most picturesque of the 1733 wreck sites.

★2023★ SAVANNAS PRESERVE STATE PARK

9551 Gumbo Limbo Ln
Jensen Beach, FL 34957
Web: www.floridastateparks.org/savannas
Phone: 772-398-2779
Size: 7,062 acres land; 123 acres water. **Location:** 2 miles east of US 1 on Walton Road in Port Saint Lucie. **Facilities:** Picnic areas/pavilions, canoe/kayak rentals (seasonal), restrooms, multi-use trails, Education Center. **Activities:** Freshwater fishing, canoeing, hiking, bicycling, horseback riding, wildlife viewing, educational programs. **Special Features:** Freshwater marshes, or "savannas," once extended all along Florida's southeast coast. The Savannas Preserve, which stretches more than 10 miles from Fort Pierce to Jensen Beach, is the largest and most intact remnant of Florida's east coast savannas.

9. State Parks

★2024★ SEABRANCH PRESERVE STATE PARK
4810 SE Cove Rd
Stuart, FL 34997
Web: www.floridastateparks.org/seabranch
Phone: 772-219-1880
Size: 922 acres. **Location:** Near Hobe Sound in eastern Martin County, 10 miles south of Stuart. **Facilities:** 8 miles of hiking trails, bathroom facilities, picnic area (no drinking water). Other facilities are under development. **Activities:** Hiking, wildlife viewing. **Special Features:** Preserve provides an opportunity to experience several different natural communities in a relatively short distance. Within the space of one mile, visitors can see rare sand pine scrub, scrubby flatwoods, a baygall community, and a mangrove swamp. Protected species of plants found here include hand fern, Curtiss' milkweed, yellow bachelor button, and golden polypody.

★2025★ SEBASTIAN INLET STATE PARK
9700 S A1A
Melbourne Beach, FL 32951
Web: www.floridastateparks.org/sebastianinlet
Phone: 321-984-4852; **Fax:** 321-984-4854
Size: 774 acres land; 143 acres water. **Location:** On SR A1A 15 miles south of Melbourne Beach. **Facilities:** 51 full-facility campsites, 4 waterfront picnic pavilions, picnic areas on both sides of the inlet, playground, beaches, showers, restrooms (&), boat ramps, boat rentals, canoe/kayak rentals, snack bar, gift shop, hiking trails, mountain bike trails, 40-mile-long multi-use paved path, interpretive exhibits. **Activities:** Camping, boating, canoeing, saltwater fishing, swimming, surfing, snorkeling, scuba diving, shelling, birding, wildlife viewing, boat excursion tours, hiking, bicycling. **Special Features:** Park is situated on the tips of two barrier islands, with the Atlantic Ocean to the east, Indian River Lagoon to the west, and Sebastian Inlet between the two. It is a premier saltwater fishing location and offers some of the best surfing on Florida's east coast. The park also contains the Sebastian Fishing Museum, which tells the history of Sebastian's fishing industry, and the McLarty Treasure Museum, featuring the history of the 1715 Spanish treasure fleet.

★2026★ SILVER RIVER STATE PARK
1425 NE 58th Ave
Ocala, FL 34470
Web: www.floridastateparks.org/silverriver
Phone: 352-236-7148; **Fax:** 352-236-7150
Size: 4,164 acres land; 66 acres water. **Location:** East of Ocala, 1 mile south of SR 40 on SR 35. **Facilities:** 59 full-facility campsites, youth group camping area (primitive), 10 luxury cabins, biking and hiking trails, equine trails, interpretive exhibits, picnic area with pavilions, playground, restrooms, showers. **Activities:** Camping, canoeing/kayaking, off-road biking, hiking, horseback riding, wildlife viewing. **Special Features:** The park includes 14 distinct natural communities, dozens of springs, and miles of trails. It also houses an 1800s Florida Cracker replica pioneer village with a house, school, church, and other homestead structures, as well as the Silver River Museum and Environmental Center.

★2027★ SKYWAY FISHING PIER STATE PARK
4905 34th St S, Suite 5000
Saint Petersburg, FL 33711
Web: www.floridastateparks.org/skyway
Phone: 727-865-0668; **Fax:** 727-893-1292
Size: 20.5 acres. **Location:** North and south of the Skyway Bridge on I-275 (US 19). **Facilities:** Fishing pier, food concession. **Activities:** Fishing. **Special Features:** When the new Sunshine Skyway bridge was built over Tampa Bay, linking Saint Petersburg with Sarasota, the old bridge was turned into the world's longest fishing pier. The pier is open 24 hours a day year-round and is lighted at night.

★2028★ STEPHEN FOSTER FOLK CULTURE
  CENTER STATE PARK
PO Drawer G
White Springs, FL 32096
Web: www.floridastateparks.org/stephenfoster
Phone: 386-397-2733
Size: 846 acres. **Location:** In White Springs, off US 41 North, on the banks of the Suwannee River. **Facilities:** 45 full-facility campsites, 5 fully-equipped riverside cabins, youth group camping area, picnic tables, multi-use trails, museum. **Activities:** Camping, canoeing/kayaking, fishing, hiking, bicycling, horseback riding, wildlife viewing, guided tours. **Special Features:** Appropriately situated on the Suwannee River, the Stephen Foster Folk Culture Center honors the memory of Foster, whose song "Old Folks at Home" made famous a river Foster never actually saw. Dioramas that depict scenes from Foster's most famous songs are housed in the Stephen Foster Museum and Carillon Tower, and his music can be heard from the 97-bell carillon throughout the day. Rare pianos and priceless musical instruments also are on exhibit at the museum. The park hosts the Florida Folk Festival annually on Memorial Day week-end, and other special events are held here throughout the year.

★2029★ STUMP PASS BEACH STATE PARK
Barrier Islands State Parks
PO Box 1150
Boca Grande, FL 33921
Web: www.floridastateparks.org/stumppass
Phone: 941-964-0375; **Fax:** 941-964-1154
Size: 219.5 acres land; 36 acres water. **Location:** South end of Manasota Key, at Exit 191 off I-75. **Facilities:** Beach, showers, boat ramp, picnic tables, pavilions, nature trails, restrooms (&), visitor center, interpretive exhibits. **Activities:** Swimming, shelling, snorkeling, scuba diving, fishing, boating, canoeing/kayaking, hiking, wildlife viewing. **Special Features:** Park is located at the southern end of Manasota Key, in the southwest corner of Sarasota County. Its most outstanding feature is its mile-long, Gulf-front beach, which is the main focal point for recreational activity at the park.

★2030★ SUWANNEE RIVER STATE PARK
20185 County Rd 132
Live Oak, FL 32060
Web: www.floridastateparks.org/suwanneeriver
Phone: 386-362-2746

9. State Parks

Size: 1,870 acres land; 64 acres water. **Location:** 13 miles west of Live Oak, off US 90. **Facilities:** 30 full-facility campsites, 5 fully-equipped cabins, 2 youth group tent camping areas, 2 picnic pavilions (in addition to picnic tables at the campsites), nature trails, boat ramp. **Activities:** Camping, boating, canoeing, freshwater fishing, hiking, wildlife viewing, tram tours. **Special Features:** A high bluff in the park overlooks the spot where the Withlacoochee River flows into the Suwannee on its way to the Gulf of Mexico. Other features at the park that show the Suwanee's importance to Florida history include long mounds of earthworks built during the Civil War by Confederate troops to guard against incursions by Union Navy gunboats, a cemetery that's one of the state's oldest, and a paddlewheel shaft from a 19th Century steamboat.

★2031★ TARKILN BAYOU PRESERVE STATE PARK

c/o Big Lagoon State Park
Pensacola, FL 32507
Web: www.floridastateparks.org/tarkilnbayou
Phone: 850-492-1595
Size: 4,165 acres land; 32 acres water.. **Location:** In Escambia County, 1.5 miles south of the intersection of US 98 and SR 293. **Facilities:** Hiking trails, picnic tables. **Activities:** Hiking, wildlife viewing, picnicking. **Special Features:** Park is home to four species of endangered pitcher plants, including the rare, carnivorous, white-top pitcher plant that is unique to the Gulf Coast and found only between the Apalachicola and Mississippi rivers. The preserve is also home to other rare and endangered plant species, and almost 100 plant and animal species depend on its wet prairie habitat. This includes the alligator snapping turtle, sweet pitcher plant, and Chapman's butterwort.

★2032★ TH STONE MEMORIAL SAINT JOSEPH PENINSULA STATE PARK

8899 Cape San Blas Rd
Port Saint Joe, FL 32456
Web: www.floridastateparks.org/stjoseph
Phone: 850-227-1327; **Fax:** 850-227-1488
Size: 2,602.5 acres land; 113 acres water. **Location:** Near Port Saint Joe, off County Road 30-E, off US 98. **Facilities:** 119 full-facility campsites, a primitive site for youth/group camping, primitive camping areas in the park's Wilderness Preserve, 8 fully-equipped cabins, 10 miles of white sand beach, public showers, boat ramp, canoe and other watercraft rental, picnic tables, playground, hiking trails. **Activities:** Camping, boating, canoeing, saltwater fishing, swimming, snorkeling, hiking, bicycling, birding, wildlife viewing. **Special Features:** Park is bounded on three sides by the waters of Saint Joe Bay and the Gulf of Mexico and has one of the top-rated beaches in the US. The park is also an excellent bird watching area, with sightings of more than 209 species currently recorded. It is a premier location for observing hawks during their fall migration, including the endangered peregrine falcon. Monarch butterflies can also be seen making their fall migration from the northern United States to wintering sites in Mexico.

★2033★ THE BARNACLE HISTORIC STATE PARK

3485 Main Hwy
Coconut Grove, FL 33133
Web: www.floridastateparks.org/thebarnacle
Phone: 305-442-6866
Size: 5 acres land; 4 acres water. **Location:** In Coconut Grove (Miami) at 3485 Main Highway. **Facilities:** Interpretive exhibits, picnic tables, restrooms. **Activities:** Guided tours, wildlife viewing. **Special Features:** Built in 1891, The Barnacle was the home of Ralph Middleton Munroe, yacht designer, naturalist, photographer, and one of Coconut Grove's most influential pioneers. The house is surrounded by a tropical hardwood forest that is one of the last remnants of the once vast Miami Hammock.

★2034★ THREE RIVERS STATE PARK

7908 Three Rivers Park Rd
Sneads, FL 32460
Web: www.floridastateparks.org/threerivers
Phone: 850-482-9006
Size: 610.5 acres land; 57.5 acres water. **Location:** On SR 271 (River Road), 2 miles north of Sneads. **Facilities:** Campground with 30 full-facility campsites and a log cabin (for rent), youth/group camp, picnic area with 3 pavilions, playground, boat ramps canoe rentals, hiking trails. **Activities:** Camping, boating, canoeing, fishing, bicycling, hiking, wildlife viewing. **Special Features:** Where Florida meets the southwest corner of Georgia, the Chattahochee and Flint rivers converge to form Lake Seminole, which provides the setting for this park. The hilly terrain is covered by hardwood hammock and pine forests that make an excellent home for white-tailed deer, fox squirrels, gray foxes, and abundant bird life. Because the park is on the northern border of the state, rare plant species not found in other parts of the state grow here.

★2035★ TOMOKA STATE PARK

2099 N Beach St
Ormond Beach, FL 32174
Web: www.floridastateparks.org/tomoka
Phone: 386-676-4050
Size: 1,497 acres land; 123 acres water. **Location:** 3 miles north of Ormond Beach on North Beach Street. **Facilities:** 100 full-facility campsites, youth group camp, 5 separate picnic areas with pavilions, playground, restrooms (&), 3 bathhouses with hot showers, nature trails, interpretive exhibits, boat ramp, canoe rentals, museum. **Activities:** Camping, boating, canoeing, saltwater fishing, hiking, wildlife viewing, historical and interpretive programs. **Special Features:** Located near the confluence of the Tomoka and Halifax rivers, park sits where early Native Americans once lived off the fish-filled lagoons. A museum at the park houses artworks by Fred Dana Marsh, wildlife displays, Native American artifacts, and exhibits about Florida history.

★2036★ TOPSAIL HILL PRESERVE STATE PARK

7525 W Scenic Hwy 30A
Santa Rosa Beach, FL 32459
Web: www.floridastateparks.org/topsailhill
Phone: 850-267-0299
Size: 1,473 acres land; 170 acres water. **Location:** In Santa

Rosa Beach on Route 30A, 1 mile off US 98. **Facilities:** RV Resort area with 156 full-facility campsites, including electric, cable, and sewer hookups, swimming pool, laundry, bathhouses, shuffleboard and tennis courts; furnished bungalows (at the RV campgrounds); beaches, showers, pavilions, picnic areas, restrooms (&), nature trails; visitor center with concession; tram service to beach. **Activities:** Camping, saltwater and freshwater fishing, swimming, hiking, bicycling, wildlife viewing. **Special Features:** Park has 3.2 miles of secluded beaches with dunes over 25 feet tall. It's named for the tallest dune in the preserve which, when viewed from the Gulf, resembles a ship's topsail. The park also contains five coastal dune lakes, which are now found only in the Florida Panhandle and nowhere else in the US. The park's dune ecosystem makes it one of the few remaining homes of the Choctawhatchee Beach Mouse.

★2037★ TORREYA STATE PARK
2576 NW Torreya Park Rd
Bristol, FL 32321
Web: www.floridastateparks.org/torreya
Phone: 850-643-2674
Size: 13,204 acres. **Location:** Off SR 12, on County Road 1641, 13 miles north of Bristol. **Facilities:** 30 full-facility campsites, a yurt, primitive and youth/group camping areas, 3 picnic pavilions, restrooms, playground, nature trails, interpretive exhibits. **Activities:** Camping, boating (no boat access from park due to bluffs), hiking, wildlife viewing, guided tours of historic home. **Special Features:** Park is named for a rare species of Torreya tree that only grows on the bluffs along the Apalachicola River. Other rare plants found in the park include the Florida yew tree and the US champion winged elm, and forests of hardwood trees provide the best display of fall color found in Florida. Gregory House, a fully-furnished plantation home built in 1849, is also on park grounds.

★2038★ TROY SPRINGS STATE PARK
674 NE Troy Springs Rd
Branford, FL 32008
Web: www.floridastateparks.org/troyspring
Phone: 386-935-4835
Size: 72 acres land; 6 acres water. **Location:** Off County Road 425, 1.3 miles north of US 27. **Facilities:** Boat dock, picnic tables, restrooms, walkway (&). Hiking and equestrian trails are under construction. The horse trail will include a 14-stall barn, wash rack, public restroom, and a primitive camping area. **Activities:** Boating/canoeing/kayaking, fishing, swimming, snorkeling, scuba diving (proof of certification required). **Special Features:** Troy Springs is a recent addition to the Florida state park system. The depths of the 70-feet deep, first magnitude spring contain the remains of a Civil War-era steamboat that was scuttled in the spring run in 1863 to keep it from being captured.

★2039★ WACCASASSA BAY PRESERVE STATE PARK
PO Box 187
Cedar Key, FL 32625
Web: www.floridastateparks.org/waccasassabay
Phone: 352-543-5567
Size: 27,962 acres land; 6,136 acres water. **Location:** Accessible only by boat, from County Road 40 in Yankeetown, County Road 326 in Gulf Hammock, or Cedar Key. **Facilities:** Primitive canoe campsite on the river. **Activities:** Boating, canoeing, fishing, wildlife viewing (from canoes; no marked foot trails in park). **Special Features:** Preserve is popular with anglers because it has both saltwater and freshwater fishing. The park's extensive salt marshes and tidal creeks provide habitats for saltwater fish, crabs, and shellfish. Several endangered species, including West Indian manatees, bald eagles, American alligators, and Florida black bear live or feed within the preserve.

★2040★ WASHINGTON OAKS GARDENS STATE PARK
6400 N Oceanshore Blvd
Palm Coast, FL 32173
Web: www.floridastateparks.org/washingtonoaks
Phone: 386-446-6780; **Fax:** 386-446-6781
Size: 415 acres land; 10.5 acres water. **Location:** 2 miles south of Marineland, off A1A **Facilities:** Beach, picnic area, covered pavilion, playground, restrooms (&), nature trails, interpretive exhibits, visitor center. **Activities:** Saltwater fishing (surf fishing or from the seawall), bicycling, hiking, picnicking, wildlife viewing. **Special Features:** Situated between the Atlantic Ocean and the Matanzas River, this property was once owned by a distant relative of George Washington, but the gardens were established by Louise and Owen Young, who bought the land in 1936. The gardens make use of both native and exotic species, from azaleas and camellias to birds of paradise. Although the formal gardens are the centerpiece of the park, it is also known for the unique shoreline of coquina rock formations that line its Atlantic beach.

★2041★ WEKIWA SPRINGS STATE PARK
1800 Wekiwa Cir
Apopka, FL 32712
Web: www.floridastateparks.org/wekiwasprings
Phone: 407-884-2008; **Fax:** 407-884-2039
Size: 7,664 acres land, 73 acres water. **Location:** Exit 94 off I-4, then west on SR 434 to Wekiwa Springs Road. **Facilities:** 60 full-facility campsites (&), primitive campsites (including 2 canoe sites), primitive youth camp, and youth/group camp with 20 cabins, recreation hall, dining hall, swimming pool, amphitheater, pavilion, and baseball field; canoe rentals; picnic areas, playground, pavilions, restrooms (&); food concession (&), recreation and dining hall (if not in use by youth camping group); boardwalk nature trail (&), hiking trails (13.5 miles), equestrian trail (8 miles), bike trail (9 miles); nature center (&). **Activities:** Camping, canoeing, freshwater fishing, swimming, snorkeling, hiking, horseback riding, bicycling, wildlife viewing. **Special Features:** Park is located at the headwaters of the Wekiva River, an hour's drive from most Central Florida attractions. The springs' name, Wekiwa, is from the Creek Indian word for "bubbling water." Wekiva, the river's name, means "flowing water." The springs are one of the region's most familiar and popular geologic features.

★2042★ WERNER-BOYCE SALT SPRINGS STATE PARK

PO Box 490
Port Richey, FL 34673
Web: www.floridastateparks.org/werner-boyce
Phone: 727-816-1890; **Fax:** 727-816-1888
Size: 2,615 acres land; 1,384 acres water. **Location:** Off Scenic Drive in Port Richey. **Facilities:** Under development. Current facilities include picnic tables, a pavilion, a short hiking trail (0.5 miles), and a self-composting toilet facility (&). **Activities:** Fishing, boating (no launch or dockage in park), picnicking. **Special Features:** Park protects four miles of coastline along the Gulf of Mexico in western Pasco County. The salt spring appears to be small but is actually 320 feet deep. The park is a new addition to the Florida state park system, and only a portion of it has been opened to the public while additional recreational opportunities are being developed.

★2043★ WILLIAM BEARDALL TOSOHATCHEE STATE RESERVE

3365 Taylor Creek Rd
Christmas, FL 32709
Web: www.floridastateparks.org/tosohatchee
Phone: 407-568-5893; **Fax:** 407-568-1704
Size: 32,060 acres land; 1,970 acres water. **Location:** East of Orlando, south of State Road 50 on the west bank of the Saint Johns River. **Facilities:** Primitive campsites, including a horseback campsite and a youth/group camping area, multi-use trails. **Activities:** Camping, fishing, hiking, horseback riding, bicycling, wildlife viewing, hunting (with restrictions). **Special Features:** Reserve borders 19 miles of the Saint Johns River. Alternating cycles of fire and flooding have created a mosaic of marshes, swamps, pine flatwoods, and hammocks, a diverse habitat that supports a variety of wildlife.

★2044★ WINDLEY KEY FOSSIL REEF GEOLOGICAL STATE PARK

c/o Lignumvitae Key Botanical State Park
PO Box 1052
Islamorada, FL 33036
Web: www.floridastateparks.org/windleykey
Phone: 305-664-2540
Size: 32 acres. **Location:** At Mile Marker 85.5 on Windley Key near Islamorada. **Facilities:** Environmental Education Center with displays and meeting room, restroom facilities, nature trails, picnic tables. **Activities:** Hiking, wildlife viewing, guided tours. **Special Features:** Formed of Key Largo limestone (fossilized coral), this land was sold to the Florida East Coast Railroad, which used the stone to to build Henry Flagler's Overseas Railroad in the early 1900s. After the railroad's completion, the site was used to quarry a decorative stone called Keystone. Visitors today can walk along the quarry walls, where they can see cross sections of the ancient coral and learn about the quarry and its operation.

★2045★ YBOR CITY MUSEUM STATE PARK

1818 9th Ave
Tampa, FL 33605
Web: www.floridastateparks.org/Yborcity
Phone: 813-247-6323
Size: 1 acre. **Location:** At the corner of 9th Avenue and 19th Street in Tampa. **Facilities:** Museum, gardens, restrooms (&). **Activities:** Guided tours, interpretive programs. **Special Features:** In the late 1800s, Don Vicente Martinez Ybor came to the Tampa area and built a city that became the "Cigar Capital of the World." From the opening of the first cigar factory in 1886 until the 1930s, Ybor City was a flourishing community, but competition from machines, popularity of cigarettes, and the Depression combined to bring about the decline of the city's cigar industry. The park is dedicated to preserving Ybor City's unique cultural heritage, and the museum traces the history of the city and its cigar-making industry.

★2046★ YELLOW BLUFF FORT HISTORIC STATE PARK

12157 Heckscher Dr
Jacksonville, FL 32226
Web: www.floridastateparks.org/yellowbluff
Phone: 904-251-2320
Size: Nearly 2 acres. **Location:** On Yellow Bluff peninsula on the north side of the Saint Johns River (on New Berlin Road). **Facilities:** Historic site, picnic tables. **Special Features:** Located near the mouth of the Saint Johns River, this site was an important military position during the Civil War because it allowed access to the inland areas of Florida's east coast. Though there never was an actual fort on Yellow Bluff, an encampment constructed here in 1862 was fortified and equipped with large guns. The site was occupied by both Confederate and Union troops during the war and at its peak housed more than 250 soldiers.

★2047★ YELLOW RIVER MARSH PRESERVE STATE PARK

c/o Blackwater River State Park
7720 Deaton Bridge Rd
Holt, FL 32564
Web: www.floridastateparks.org/yellowriver
Phone: 850-983-5363
Size: 815 acres. **Location:** On County Road 191, 1 mile north of the intersection with County Road 281 and along both sides of the highway on Blackwater Bay. **Special Features:** Park protects one of Florida's last remaining tracts of wet prairie, including the largest community of carnivorous pitcher plants in the state. There are no recreational facilities at the preserve, but the pitcher plant prairies provide excellent opportunities for photography and nature appreciation.

★2048★ YULEE SUGAR MILL RUINS HISTORIC STATE PARK

c/o Crystal River Archaeological State Park
3400 N Museum Pointe
Crystal River, FL 34428
Web: www.floridastateparks.org/yuleesugarmill
Phone: 352-795-3817
Size: 9 acres. **Location:** On County Road 490 (Yulee Drive), about 2.5 miles west of Homosassa Springs. **Facilities:** Picnic area, pavilion, restsrooms. **Special Features:** Site was once part of a thriving sugar plantation owned by David Levy Yulee, and

9. State Parks

the park contains such remnants of the plantation as a 40-foot limestone masonry chimney, iron gears, and a cane press. The steam-driven sugar mill operated from 1851 to 1864 and supplied sugar products for southern troops during the Civil War. After Florida gained statehood, Yulee served in the US House of Representatives and the US Senate.

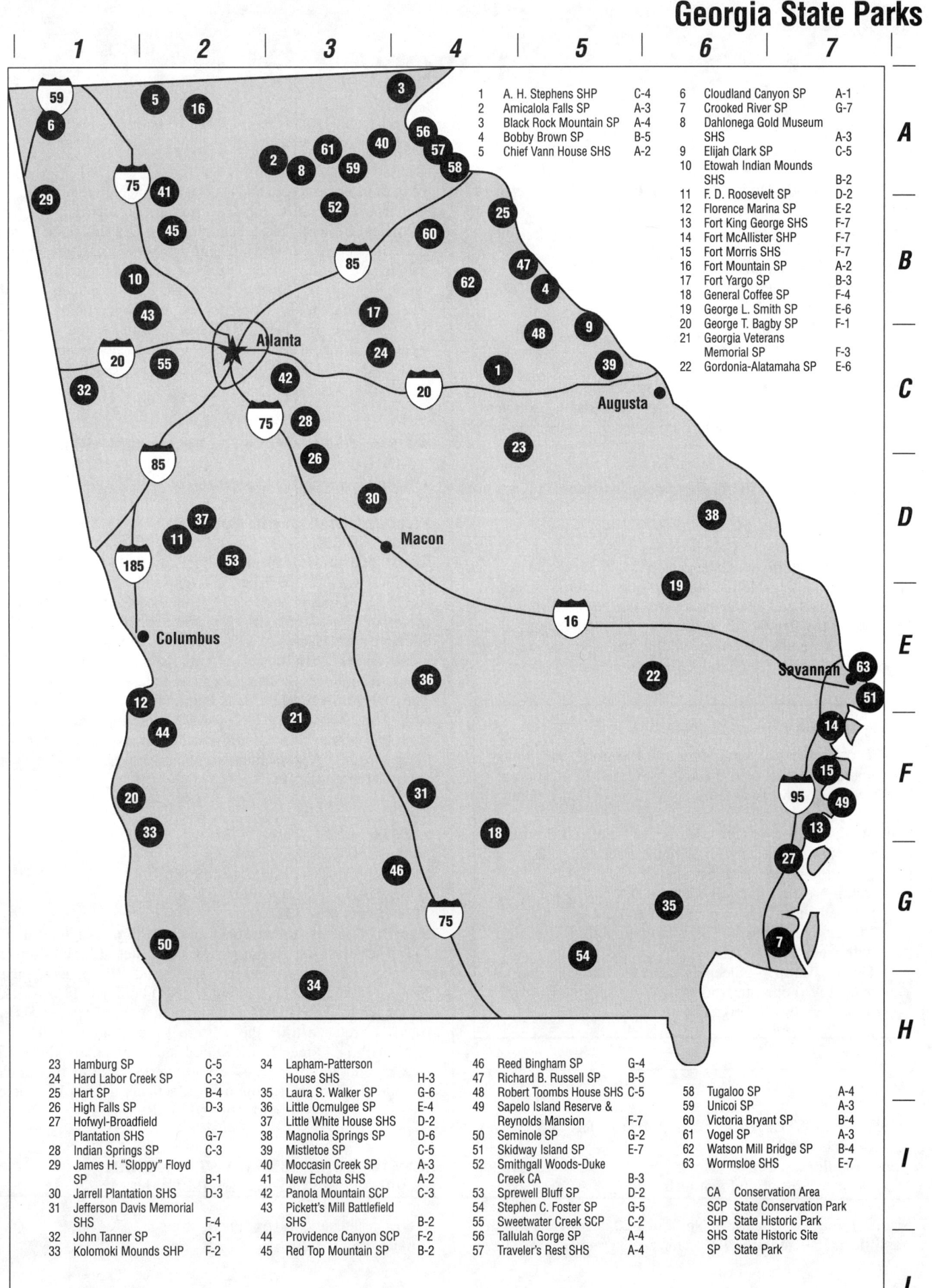

Georgia State Parks

1	A. H. Stephens SHP	C-4
2	Amicalola Falls SP	A-3
3	Black Rock Mountain SP	A-4
4	Bobby Brown SP	B-5
5	Chief Vann House SHS	A-2
6	Cloudland Canyon SP	A-1
7	Crooked River SP	G-7
8	Dahlonega Gold Museum SHS	A-3
9	Elijah Clark SP	C-5
10	Etowah Indian Mounds SHS	B-2
11	F. D. Roosevelt SP	D-2
12	Florence Marina SP	E-2
13	Fort King George SHS	F-7
14	Fort McAllister SHP	F-7
15	Fort Morris SHS	F-7
16	Fort Mountain SP	A-2
17	Fort Yargo SP	B-3
18	General Coffee SP	F-4
19	George L. Smith SP	E-6
20	George T. Bagby SP	F-1
21	Georgia Veterans Memorial SP	F-3
22	Gordonia-Alatamaha SP	E-6

23	Hamburg SP	C-5
24	Hard Labor Creek SP	C-3
25	Hart SP	B-4
26	High Falls SP	D-3
27	Hofwyl-Broadfield Plantation SHS	G-7
28	Indian Springs SP	C-3
29	James H. "Sloppy" Floyd SP	B-1
30	Jarrell Plantation SHS	D-3
31	Jefferson Davis Memorial SHS	F-4
32	John Tanner SP	C-1
33	Kolomoki Mounds SHP	F-2
34	Lapham-Patterson House SHS	H-3
35	Laura S. Walker SP	G-6
36	Little Ocmulgee SP	E-4
37	Little White House SHS	D-2
38	Magnolia Springs SP	D-6
39	Mistletoe SP	C-5
40	Moccasin Creek SP	A-3
41	New Echota SHS	A-2
42	Panola Mountain SCP	C-3
43	Pickett's Mill Battlefield SHS	B-2
44	Providence Canyon SCP	F-2
45	Red Top Mountain SP	B-2
46	Reed Bingham SP	G-4
47	Richard B. Russell SP	B-5
48	Robert Toombs House SHS	C-5
49	Sapelo Island Reserve & Reynolds Mansion	F-7
50	Seminole SP	G-2
51	Skidway Island SP	E-7
52	Smithgall Woods-Duke Creek CA	B-3
53	Sprewell Bluff SP	D-2
54	Stephen C. Foster SP	G-5
55	Sweetwater Creek SCP	C-2
56	Tallulah Gorge SP	A-4
57	Traveler's Rest SHS	A-4
58	Tugaloo SP	A-4
59	Unicoi SP	A-3
60	Victoria Bryant SP	B-4
61	Vogel SP	A-3
62	Watson Mill Bridge SP	B-4
63	Wormsloe SHS	E-7

CA	Conservation Area
SCP	State Conservation Park
SHP	State Historic Park
SHS	State Historic Site
SP	State Park

GEORGIA

★2049★ **Georgia Division of State Parks & Historic Sites**
2 ML King Jr Dr
Suite 1352 East
Atlanta, GA 30334
(404) 656-3530 - Phone
(404) 651-5871 - Fax
(800) 864-7275 - Toll-free Reservations
(404) 656-2695 - Employment
(404) 656-6539 - Volunteering
Web: www.gastateparks.org
Operates 63 state parks and historic sites. Maintains hundreds of miles of trails and greenways. Interprets the state's natural and cultural resources through publications, exhibits, and programs.

★2050★ **Georgia Wildlife Resources Division**
2070 US Hwy 278 SE
Social Circle, GA 30025
(770) 918-6400
Web: georgiawildlife.dnr.state.ga.us
Administers hunting and fishing licensing; supports hunter education programs and boater safety courses; enforces state wildlife laws. Manages 9 fish hatcheries, 9 public fishing areas, and 112 boat ramps. Oversees wildlife management areas and coordinates the state's natural heritage program.

Key to campsite classification:

- **Tent/trailer/RV campsites** — Electrical and water hookups, grills, or fire rings, picnic tables. Restrooms with hot showers within easy walking distance. Dump stations.
- **Walk-in sites** — Tent pad, picnic table, and fire ring; no water or electricity. Within easy walking distance to restrooms and parking area.
- **Primitive backpacking sites** — Designated but undeveloped sites. Gear is packed in and out by hiker.
- **Pioneer camping** — Tent campgrounds for groups, with water and pit toilets.
- **Group Camp** — Sleeping quarters, kitchens, dining/assembly rooms, restrooms, activity areas, and swimming facilities for organized groups.

★2051★ **AH STEPHENS STATE HISTORIC PARK**
456 Alexander St N
Crawfordville, GA 30631
Web: gastateparks.org/info/ahsteph
Phone: 706-456-2602
Size: 1,177 acres. **Location:** North of I-20 near Crawfordville.
Facilities: 25 tent/trailer/RV campsites, group camp (sleeps 120), pioneer campground, 4 cottages, 3 picnic shelters, 1 group shelter, walking trails (3 miles; 1 trail ♿), horseback riding trails (12 miles) 2 fishing lakes, boat rentals, swimming pool, historic home, museum. **Activities:** Camping, boating (no gas motors), fishing, swimming, hiking, horseback riding, guided tours, educational programs. **Special Features:** Park is named after the vice president of the Confederacy and governor of Georgia. Stephens's home, Liberty Hall, has been renovated to its 1875 style and is open for tours. The Confederate Museum at the park houses one of the finest collections of Civil War artifacts in Georgia.

★2052★ **AMICALOLA FALLS STATE PARK & LODGE**
418 Amicalola Falls State Park Rd
Dawsonville, GA 30534
Web: gastateparks.org/info/amicalola
Phone: 706-265-4703
Size: 829 acres. **Location:** 15 miles northwest of Dawsonville on GA Hwy 52. **Facilities:** 24 tent/trailer/RV campsites, 14 cottages, 57-room lodge and conference center, 20-room inn (accessible only on foot), 4 picnic shelters, 1 group shelter, hiking trails (12 miles), ropes course, restaurant, gift shops, visitor center. **Activities:** Camping, fishing, hiking, interpretive programs, outdoor skills classes (seasonal). **Special Features:** The 729-foot Amicalola Falls is the tallest cascading waterfall east of the Mississippi River. An 8-mile approach trail leads from the falls to Springer Mountain, the southern terminus of the 2,144-mile Appalachian National Scenic Trail, which runs from Georgia to Maine.

★2053★ **BLACK ROCK MOUNTAIN STATE PARK**
3085 Black Rock Mountain Pkwy
Mountain City, GA 30562
Web: gastateparks.org/info/blackrock
Phone: 706-746-2141
Size: 1,743 acres. **Location:** 3 miles north of Clayton, off US 441. **Facilities:** 48 tent/trailer/RV campsites, 12 walk-in sites, 4 backcountry sites, pioneer campground, 10 cottages, picnic areas, 2 picnic shelters, hiking trails (11 miles), 17-acre lake, visitor center. **Activities:** Camping, fishing, hiking. **Special Features:** Located astride the Eastern Continental Divide at an altitude of 3,640 feet, Black Rock Mountain is the highest state park in Georgia. Numerous scenic overlooks offer spectacular 80-mile views of the southern Appalachians. The park is named for its sheer cliffs of dark-colored biotite gneiss.

★2054★ **BOBBY BROWN STATE PARK**
2509 Bobby Brown State Park Rd
Elberton, GA 30635
Web: gastateparks.org/info/bobbybrown
Phone: 706-213-2046

Size: 665 acres. **Location:** 21 miles southeast of Elberton, off GA 72. **Facilities:** 61 tent/trailer/RV campsites, pioneer campground, 5 yurts, picnic areas, 2 picnic shelters, 1 group shelter, hiking trail (1.9 miles), swimming pool, boat ramp, boat dock, canoe and fishing boat rentals, concessions (seasonal). **Activities:** Camping, boating, fishing, swimming, hiking. **Special Features:** Park is located where the old town of Petersburg was situated in the 1790s, where the Broad and Savannah rivers flow into the Clarks Hill Reservoir. The 70,000-acre manmade lake is one of the largest east of the Mississippi.

★2055★ CHIEF VANN HOUSE STATE HISTORIC SITE

82 GA Hwy 225 N
Chatsworth, GA 30705
Web: gastateparks.org/info/chiefvann
Phone: 706-695-2598
Size: 99 acres. **Location:** On the outskirts of Chatsworth at the intersection of Georgia highways 225 and 52-A. **Facilities:** Picnic tables, nature trail, visitor center, gift shop. **Special Features:** Built by James Vann in 1804, this was the first brick home within the Cherokee Nation and is one of the best-preserved Cherokee plantation homes. The two-story mansion is decorated with hand carvings and features a remarkable ''floating'' staircase and many fine antiques.

★2056★ CLOUDLAND CANYON STATE PARK

122 Cloudland Canyon Park
Rising Fawn, GA 30738
Web: gastateparks.org/info/cloudland
Phone: 706-657-4050
Size: 3,485 acres. **Location:** On GA 136, 8 miles east of Trenton and I-59 and 18 miles west of Lafayette. **Facilities:** 73 tent/trailer/RV campsites, 30 walk-in sites, 11 backcountry sites, pioneer campground, 16 cottages, a group lodge that sleeps 40, 6 picnic shelters, 2 group shelters, hiking trails, tennis courts, gift shop. **Activities:** Camping, hiking, tennis, disc golf. **Special Features:** Located on the western edge of Lookout Mountain, the park straddles a deep gorge cut into the mountain by Sitton Gulch Creek. Spectacular views into the canyon can be seen from the picnic area and from the park's rim trail.

★2057★ CROOKED RIVER STATE PARK

6222 Charlie Smith Sr Hwy
Saint Mary's, GA 31558
Web: gastateparks.org/info/crookriv
Phone: 912-882-5256
Size: 500 acres. **Location:** 7 miles north of Saint Mary's, on GA Spur 40; or 8 miles east of I-95 exit 3. **Facilities:** 62 tent/trailer/RV campsites, pioneer campground, 11 cottages, 5 picnic shelters, winterized group shelter, hiking trails (4 miles), bathhouse, boat ramp and dock, bicycle rental, miniature golf course, nature center. **Activities:** Camping, boating, kayaking, saltwater fishing, hiking, bicycling, birding. **Special Features:** Park is located on the south bank of the Crooked River on Georgia's Colonial Coast. Nearby are the ruins of the McIntosh Sugar Works mill, built around 1825; also nearby is the ferry and visitor center for Cumberland Island National Seashore.

★2058★ DAHLONEGA GOLD MUSEUM STATE HISTORIC SITE

1 Public Sq
Dahlonega, GA 30533
Web: gastateparks.org/info/dahlonega
Phone: 706-864-2257
Size: 0.7 acres. **Location:** 5 miles west of GA Hwy 400, on the Public Square in Dahlonega. **Facilities:** Museum. **Activities:** Goldpanning, shopping, sightseeing. **Special Features:** In the 1830s, thousands of gold seekers flocked to the Cherokee Nation in north Georgia, beginning the nation's first major gold rush. Between 1838 and 1861, more than $6 million was coined by the U.S. Mint branch in Dahlonega from gold mined nearby. The Dahlonega Gold Museum, located in the old Lumpkin County Courthouse, offers visitors a look at the mining history of Georgia.

★2059★ ELIJAH CLARK STATE PARK

2959 McCormick Hwy
Lincolnton, GA 30817
Web: gastateparks.org/info/elijah
Phone: 706-359-3458
Size: 447 acres. **Location:** 7 miles northeast of Lincolnton, on US 378. **Facilities:** 165 tent/trailer/RV campsites, pioneer campground, 20 cottages, 5 picnic shelters, 2 group shelters, nature trails (3.75 miles), swimming beach, 4 boating/skiing ramps, fishing pier, miniature golf course, shuffleboard courts, playground, museum. **Activities:** Camping, boating, fishing, swimming, water-skiing, hiking, guided tours (seasonal). **Special Features:** Located on the western shore of 70,000-acre Clarks Hill Lake, the park is named for a Georgia frontiersman and Revolutionary War hero. A renovated and furnished log cabin museum displays furniture, utensils, and tools from the period around 1780.

★2060★ ETOWAH INDIAN MOUNDS STATE HISTORIC SITE

813 Indian Mounds Rd SW
Cartersville, GA 30120
Web: gastateparks.org/info/etowah
Phone: 770-387-3747
Size: 54 acres. **Location:** 5 miles southwest of I-75 exit 288. **Facilities:** Museum, gift shop, picnic tables, riverside benches. **Activities:** Interpretive programs. **Special Features:** Believed to be the most intact Mississippian Culture site in the southeastern United States, the site contains six earthen mounds, a plaza, village area, borrow pits, and a defensive ditch. The area was likely a major political and religious center and home to several thousand Native Americans between A.D. 1000 and 1550. To date only about ten percent of the site has been excavated. The park's museum interprets daily life in the community with exhibits of stone effigies, wooden figures, objects made of sea shell and stone, and other artifacts.

★2061★ FD ROOSEVELT STATE PARK

2970 GA Hwy 190
Pine Mountain, GA 31822
Web: gastateparks.org/info/fdr
Phone: 706-663-4858

9. State Parks

Size: 9,049 acres. **Location:** Off I-185 near Calloway Gardens, west of Warm Springs on GA 190; or south of Pine Mountain, off US 27. **Facilities:** 140 tent/trailer/RV campsites, backcountry campsites, pioneer campground, 2 group camps, 22 cottages, 2 picnic shelters, group shelter, hiking trails (37 miles), equestrian trails (20 miles), 2 lakes, boat rentals, horse rental, swimming pool, camp store. **Activities:** Camping, hiking, backpacking, horseback riding, fishing, boating, swimming, guided hikes. **Special Features:** Park is deeply rooted in the historical era of four-time US president Franklin D. Roosevelt. Seeking a place for treatment after he was stricken with polio in 1921, Roosevelt traveled to Warm Springs and built his Little White House, now a state historic site (see separate entry). Several park structures, including a stone swimming pool, were built by the Civilian Conservation Corps during the 1930s.

★2062★ **FLORENCE MARINA STATE PARK**
Rt 1, Box 36
Omaha, GA 31821
Web: gastateparks.org/info/flormarin
Phone: 229-838-4244
Size: 173 acres. **Location:** 16 miles west of Lumpkin at the end of GA 39C. **Facilities:** 43 tent/trailer/RV campsites, 6 cottages, 8 efficiency units, picnic shelter, group shelter, 2 playgrounds, nature trail, swimming pool, marina, boat ramps, docks, boat rentals, lighted fishing pier, interpretive center, 2 tennis courts, miniature golf course. **Activities:** Camping, boating, fishing, swimming, birding, interpretive programs. **Special Features:** Florence Marina lies at the north end of 45,000-acre Lake Walter F. George, adjacent to a natural deep-water marina. Park includes Kirbo Interpretive Center, with artifacts from the prehistoric Paleo-Indian period through the early 20th century.

★2063★ **FORT KING GEORGE STATE HISTORIC SITE**
1600 Wayne St
Darien, GA 31305
Web: gastateparks.org/info/ftkinggeorge
Phone: 912-437-4770
Size: 22 acres. **Location:** 3 miles east of I-95 exit 49, in Darien. **Facilities:** Historic buildings, museum. **Special Features:** From 1721 until 1736, Fort King George was the southernmost outpost of the British Empire in North America. His Majesty's Independent Company garrisoned the fort for seven years, but after enduring hardships from disease, threats of Spanish and Indian attacks, and the harsh, unfamiliar coastal environment, they eventually abandoned it. The 18th century frontier fortification has been reconstructed from old records and drawings, and structures available for public tour include a blockhouse, officers' quarters, barracks, a guardhouse, moat, and palisades.

★2064★ **FORT MCALLISTER STATE HISTORIC PARK**
3894 Fort McAllister Rd
Richmond Hill, GA 31324
Web: gastateparks.org/info/ftmcallister
Phone: 912-727-2339; **Fax:** 912-727-3614; **Toll Free:** 800-864-7275

Size: 1,725 acres. **Location:** 10 miles east of I-95 on GA Spur 144 (I-95 exit 90). **Facilities:** 65 tent/trailer/RV campsites, backcountry campsites, pioneer campground, 3 cottages, 2 picnic shelters, group shelter, playgrounds, hiking/biking trails (4.3 miles), boat ramps and dock, fishing pier, earthwork fort, Civil War museum, gift shop. **Activities:** Camping, saltwater fishing, hiking, bicycling, birding, fort tours. **Special Features:** Located on the south bank of the Great Ogeechee River, this park features the best-preserved earthwork fortification of the Confederacy. The sand and mud earthworks were attacked seven times by Union ironclads but did not fall until captured in 1864 by Gen. William T. Sherman during his "March to the Sea." The park's Civil War museum features an interior designed to resemble a bombproof and contains exhibits, artifacts, and a gift shop.

★2065★ **FORT MORRIS STATE HISTORIC SITE**
2559 Fort Morris Rd
Midway, GA 31320
Web: gastateparks.org/info/ftmorris
Phone: 912-884-5999
Size: 70 acres. **Location:** 7 miles east of I-75 exit 76, via Island Highway and Fort Morris Road. **Facilities:** Pioneer campground (groups only), 7 picnic sites, 1-mile nature trail, visitor center, gift shop. **Activities:** Birdwatching, educational programs. **Special Features:** When the Continental Congress convened in 1776, local delegates recognized the need to protect their growing seaport from the British. Soon afterwards, a low bluff on the Medway River at Sunbury was fortified and garrisoned by 200 patriots. When the British demanded the fort's surrender on November 25, 1778, a defiant Col. John McIntosh replied "Come and take it!" The British refused, and withdrew to Florida. However, 45 days later they returned with a superior force, and on January 9, 1779, Fort Morris fell after a short but heavy bombardment. Under the name Fort Defiance, the bulwark was once again used against the British during the War of 1812.

★2066★ **FORT MOUNTAIN STATE PARK**
181 Fort Mountain Park Rd
Chatsworth, GA 30705
Web: gastateparks.org/info/fortmt
Phone: 706-695-2621
Size: 3,712 acres. **Location:** 8 miles east of Chatsworth via GA 52 (take Exit 333 off I-75). **Facilities:** 70 tent/trailer/RV campsites, 4 walk-in campsites, 6 platform campsites, pioneer campground, backcountry campsites, 15 cottages, 117 picnic sites, 7 picnic shelters, group shelter, hiking trails (14 miles), mountain biking trails (30 miles), equestrian trails (18 miles), stables, horse rentals, fishing and pedal boat rental, lake with swimming beach, miniature golf course. . **Activities:** Camping, fishing, swimming, hiking, backpacking, horseback riding, mountain biking. **Special Features:** Fort Mountain derives its name from an ancient 855-foot-long rock wall of unknown origin that stands at the highest point of the mountain. The wall is thought to have been built by Indians as fortification against other more hostile Indians or for ancient ceremonies.

★2067★ FORT YARGO STATE PARK

210 S Broad St
Winder, GA 30680
Web: gastateparks.org/info/ftyargo
Phone: 770-867-3489
Size: 1,814 acres. **Location:** 1 mile south of Winder on GA 81. **Facilities:** 40 tent/trailer/RV campsites, 7 walk-in campsites, pioneer campground, group camp(special populations), 3 cottages, 5 picnic shelters, 2 group shelters, multi-use trails (15 miles), lake with beach, 2 boat ramps, boat rentals, 2 tennis courts, miniature golf course. **Activities:** Camping, boating, fishing, swimming, hiking, bicycling. **Special Features:** Park features a log fort built by settlers in 1792 for protection against Creek and Cherokee Indians. Within the park also is Will-A-Way Recreation Area, an accessible facility specifically designed for challenged populations

★2068★ GENERAL COFFEE STATE PARK

46 John Coffee Rd
Nicholls, GA 31554
Web: gastateparks.org/info/gencoffee
Phone: 912-384-7082
Size: 1,511 acres. **Location:** 6 miles east of Douglas on GA 32. **Facilities:** 50 tent/trailer/RV campsites, pioneer camping, 5 cottages, 32-bed group lodge (&), 7 picnic shelters, winterized group shelter, playgrounds, trails (4 miles), swimming pool and bathhouse, canoe rental, outdoor amphitheater, camp store. **Activities:** Camping, fishing, canoeing, swimming, hiking, interpretive programs. **Special Features:** Park includes Heritage Farm, where agricultural history is interpreted with log cabins, a corn crib, tobacco barn, cane mill, farm animals, and other exhibits. One of the overnight cottages available at the park is Burnham House, an elegantly decorated 19th-century cabin. The park is named for General John Coffee, a planter, US Congressman, and military leader.

★2069★ GEORGE L. SMITH STATE PARK

371 George L Smith State Park Rd
Twin City, GA 30471
Web: gastateparks.org/info/georgels
Phone: 478-763-2759
Size: 1,634 acres. **Location:** 4 miles southeast of Twin City off GA 23. **Facilities:** 25 tent/trailer/RV campsites, pioneer campground, 4 cottages, 4 picnic shelters, winterized group shelter, trails (7 miles), lake, boat ramp, canoe/pedal boat rentals. **Activities:** Camping, boating (10 HP limit), fishing, canoeing, hiking, biking, birding. **Special Features:** Named after one of Georgia's great legislators, the park is best known for the newly refurbished Parrish Mill, a combination grist mill, saw mill, covered bridge, and a dam built in 1880 (open for tours).

★2070★ GEORGE T. BAGBY STATE PARK & LODGE

330 Bagby Pkwy
Fort Gaines, GA 31751
Web: gastateparks.org/info/georgetb
Phone: 229-768-2571
Size: 700 acres. **Location:** 3.5 miles north of Fort Gaines off GA 39. **Facilities:** 60-room lodge and conference center, 5 cottages, group lodge, picnic shelter, group shelter, trails (3 miles), swimming beach, marina, gas dock, boat ramp, canoe/fishing boat rentals, bicycle rentals, restaurant, 18-hole golf course, pro shop. **Activities:** Boating, fishing, water-skiing, swimming, golf, hiking, bicycling, birding, volleyball. **Special Features:** This resort-style park is situated on the shore of 48,000-acre Lake Walter F George (also known as Lake Eufala) in southwest Georgia, along the Georgia-Alabama state line.

★2071★ GEORGIA VETERANS STATE PARK

2459 US 280 W
Cordele, GA 31015
Web: gastateparks.org/info/georgiavet
Phone: 229-276-2371
Size: 1,308 acres. **Location:** 9 miles west of I-75 (exit 101) near Cordele on US 280. **Facilities:** 77 tent/trailer/RV campsites, pioneer campground, 10 cottages, resort lodgings, restaurant, meeting rooms, 18-hole golf course, swimming pool, full-service marina, boat rental, 4 picnic shelters, group shelter, nature trail, R/C model airplane flying field, disc golf course. **Activities:** Camping, boating, fishing, swimming, water-skiing, model airplane flying, golf, disc golf, birding. **Special Features:** Established as a memorial to US veterans, the park features a museum with aircraft, armored vehicles, uniforms, weapons, medals, and other items from the Revolutionary War through the Gulf War. The Lake Blackshear Resort and and Golf Club is a privately operated conference center at the park, with 78 lodge rooms, 10 cottages, and a restaurant. The SAM Shortline Excursion Train runs through the park on its way from Cordele to Plains, allowing riders to see an antique telephone museum, Habitat for Humanity's Global Village, President Jimmy Carter's boyhood farm, and other attractions.

★2072★ GORDONIA-ALATAMAHA STATE PARK

322 Park Ln
US 280 W
Reidsville, GA 30453
Web: gastateparks.org/info/gordonalt
Phone: 912-557-7744
Size: 462 acres. **Location:** Near Reidsville just off US 280. **Facilities:** 27 tent/trailer/RV campsites, 4 picnic shelters, group shelter, swimming pool, lake, boat rentals, 9-hole golf course, pro shop, miniature golf course. **Activities:** Camping, fishing, swimming, golf, boating (no private boats). **Special Features:** Gordonia-Alatamaha's unusual name comes from the nearly extinct Gordonia tree, a member of the bay family, and the original spelling of nearby Altamaha River. Recreational activities at the park center around a 12-acre lake.

★2073★ HAMBURG STATE PARK

6071 Hamburg State Park Rd
Mitchell, GA 30820
Web: gastateparks.org/info/hamburg
Phone: 478-552-2393
Size: 741 acres. **Location:** 20 miles north of Sandersville via Hamburg State Park Road off GA102. **Facilities:** 30 tent/trailer/RV campsites, pioneer campground, 2 picnic shelters, group

shelter, trails (3.5 miles), 225-acre lake, boat rentals, historic grist mill and museum, country store. **Activities:** Camping, boating (no gas motors), canoeing, fishing, hiking. **Special Features:** Park offers a mix of outdoor recreation and history. A 1920s water-powered grist mill is still operating today, and a museum at the park displays old agricultural tools and appliances used in rural Georgia.

★2074★ HARD LABOR CREEK STATE PARK

Knox Chapel Rd
Rutledge, GA 30663
Web: gastateparks.org/info/hardlabor
Phone: 706-557-3001
Size: 5,804 acres. **Location:** I-20 exit 105 into Rutledge, then north 3 miles on Fairplay Road. **Facilities:** 63 tent/trailer/RV campsites, 12 equestrian campsites, pioneer campground, 20 cottages, 2 group camps, 5 picnic shelters, 2 group shelters, hiking trails (2.5 miles), equestrian trail (22 miles), horse stalls, riding ring, 2 lakes, beach and bathhouse (seasonal), boat rentals, 18-hole golf course. **Activities:** Camping, boating, fishing, swimming, hiking, horseback riding. **Special Features:** Hard Labor Creek cuts through the park's championship golf course, creating water hazards on five holes. The creek is thought to have been named by slaves who tilled summer fields or by Native Americans who found it difficult to ford.

★2075★ HART STATE PARK

330 Hart Park Rd
Hartwell, GA 30643
Web: gastateparks.org/info/hart
Phone: 706-376-8756
Size: 147 acres. **Location:** 3 miles north of Hartwell off US 29. **Facilities:** 78 tent/trailer/RV campsites, 16 walk-in sites, 5 cottages, 3 picnic shelters, trail (1.5 miles), swimming beaches, 2 boat ramps, docks, canoe rentals, jon boat and pontoon boat rentals, music theater. **Activities:** Camping, boating, fishing, swimming, water skiing, hiking, bicycling, music programs. **Special Features:** Recreational activities at the park center around the 55,590-acre Lake Hartwell.

★2076★ HIGH FALLS STATE PARK

76 High Falls Park Dr
Jackson, GA 30233
Web: gastateparks.org/info/highfall
Phone: 478-993-3053
Size: 1,050 acres. **Location:** 1.8 miles east of I-75 exit #198 at High Falls Road. **Facilities:** 112 tent/trailer/RV campsites, pioneer campground, 5 picnic shelters, screened group shelter, trails (4 miles), swimming pool, 650-acre lake, 2 boat ramps, docks, canoe and fishing boat rentals, miniature golf course. **Activities:** Camping, boating, canoeing, fishing, swimming (pool only), hiking. **Special Features:** In the early 1800s, this site was a prosperous industrial town with several stores, a grist mill, cotton gin, blacksmith shop, shoe factory, and hotel, but High Falls became a ghost town in the 1880s when a major railroad bypassed it. Today, park visitors can enjoy the scenic waterfall on the Towaliga River and hike to the remaining grist mill foundation.

★2077★ HOFWYL-BROADFIELD PLANTATION STATE HISTORIC SITE

5556 US Hwy 17 N
Brunswick, GA 31525
Web: gastateparks.org/info/hofwyl
Phone: 912-264-7333
Size: 1,270 acres. **Location:** Between Brunswick and Darien on US Highway 17, 1 mile east of I-95 exit 42. **Facilities:** Historic home, museum, gift shop, nature trail, picnic area. **Activities:** Guided house tours, interpretive programs. **Special Features:** The plantation and its inhabitants were part of the genteel low country society that developed during the antebellum period. Originally a rice plantation along the Altamaha River, the home is furnished with antiques, and its exhibits depict plantation life in the mid-1800s.

★2078★ INDIAN SPRINGS STATE PARK

678 Lake Clark Rd
Flovilla, GA 30216
Web: gastateparks.org/info/indspr
Phone: 770-504-2277
Size: 528 acres. **Location:** 4 miles southeast of Jackson on GA 42. **Facilities:** 88 tent/trailer/RV campsites, pioneer campground, 10 cottages, group camp, 7 picnic shelters, group shelter, nature trail, 105-acre lake and swimming beach, boat ramp, docks, pedal boat rentals, museum, miniature golf course. **Activities:** Camping, boating (10 HP limit), fishing, swimming, miniature golf. **Special Features:** Indian Springs is thought to be the oldest state park in the United States — it was acquired by the state in 1825 and became an official "State Forest Park" in 1927. A museum at the park highlights the Creek Indians, who used the springs for centuries to heal the sick, as well as the park's resort history in the 1800s and the structures built by the Civilian Conservation Corps during the Great Depression.

★2079★ JAMES H. "SLOPPY" FLOYD STATE PARK

2800 Sloppy Floyd Lake Rd
Summerville, GA 30747
Web: gastateparks.org/info/sloppy
Phone: 706-857-0826
Size: 561 acres. **Location:** 3 miles southeast of Summerville via US 27. **Facilities:** 25 tent/trailer/RV campsites, pioneer campground, 4 cottages, 4 picnic shelters, 2 playgrounds, 2 stocked lakes, boardwalk, boat ramps and docks, boat rentals, fishing pier (&). **Activities:** Camping, boating (no gas motors), fishing, hiking. **Special Features:** Park was named for James H "Sloppy" Floyd, who served in the Georgia House of Representatives from 1953 until 1974. It is surrounded by the Chattahoochee National Forest (see entry in national forests section), which has miles of hiking and bridle trails.

★2080★ JARRELL PLANTATION STATE HISTORIC SITE

711 Jarrell Plantation Rd
Juliette, GA 31046
Web: gastateparks.org/info/jarrell
Phone: 478-986-5172
Size: 233 acres. **Location:** Southeast of Juliette, 18 miles east

of I-75 Forsyth exit 185; or 18 miles north of Macon exit 171. **Facilities:** Museum, historic buildings, gift shop, picnic area. **Special Features:** This cotton plantation was owned by the Jarrell family for more than 140 years. In 1847 John Fitz Jarrell built the simple heart pine house typical of most plantations and made many of the furnishings visitors see today. John's son later diversified the farm, adding a sawmill, cotton gin, gristmill, shingle mill, planer, sugar cane press, syrup evaporator, workshop, barn, and outbuildings.

★2081★ JEFFERSON DAVIS MEMORIAL STATE HISTORIC SITE

338 Jeff Davis Park Rd
Fitzgerald, GA 31750
Web: gastateparks.org/info/jeffd
Phone: 229-831-2335
Size: 13 acres. **Location:** Off GA Highway 32 in Irwinville. **Facilities:** Civil War museum, monument, gift shop, picnic sites, group shelter, playground, nature trail. **Special Features:** A monument at this site marks the spot where Confederate President Jefferson Davis was captured and arrested by Union soldiers May 9, 1865.

★2082★ JOHN TANNER STATE PARK

354 Tanner's Beach Rd
Carrollton, GA 30117
Web: gastateparks.org/info/jtanner
Phone: 770-830-2222
Size: 138 acres. **Location:** 6 miles west of Carrollton on GA 16. **Facilities:** 32 tent/trailer/RV campsites, pioneer campground, 6-unit motor lodge, group lodge (sleeps 40), 4 picnic shelters, 2 group shelters, trails, swimming beach, 2 lakes, boat rentals, miniature golf course. **Activities:** Camping, boating (no gas motors), fishing, swimming, hiking. **Special Features:** Park features two lakes and the largest sand beach of any Georgia state park.

★2083★ KOLOMOKI MOUNDS STATE HISTORIC PARK

205 Indian Mounds Rd
Blakely, GA 39823
Web: gastateparks.org/info/kolomoki
Phone: 229-724-2150
Size: 1,293 acres. **Location:** 6 miles north of Blakely off US 27. **Facilities:** 43 tent/trailer/RV campsites (&), pioneer campgrounds, group camp, 7 picnic shelters, 2 group shelters, trails (5 miles), swimming pool, 2 lakes, boat ramp, dock, boat and canoe rentals, miniature golf course, museum, gift shop, amphitheater. **Activities:** Camping, boating (10 HP limit), fishing, swimming, hiking, astronomy programs (seasonal). **Special Features:** Park is an important archeological site as well as a scenic recreational area. Seven mounds within the park were built around 250-950 AD by the Swift Creek and Weeden Island Indians. The mounds include Georgia's oldest great temple mound, two burial mounds, and four ceremonial mounds. The park's museum is partially situated inside an excavated mound, providing an unusual setting for viewing artifacts.

★2084★ LAPHAM-PATTERSON HOUSE STATE HISTORIC SITE

626 N Dawson St
Thomasville, GA 31792
Web: gastateparks.org/info/lapham
Phone: 229-225-4004
Size: 1 acre. **Location:** On Dawson Street in Thomasville. **Facilities:** Historic house, picnic area, gift shop. **Activities:** Guided house tour. **Special Features:** The Lapham-Patterson House is an outstanding example of a Victorian era home. Built between 1884-85 as a winter cottage for prosperous shoe merchant C.W. Lapham of Chicago, the residence was equipped with its own gas lighting system, hot and cold running water, indoor plumbing, and modern closets. Architectural features include fish-scale shingles, oriental-style porch decorations, long-leaf pine inlaid floors, cantilevered balcony, and a double-flue chimney with a walk-through stairway. Lapham-Patterson House was named a National Historic Landmark in 1975.

★2085★ LAURA S. WALKER STATE PARK

5653 Laura Walker Rd
Waycross, GA 31503
Web: gastateparks.org/info/lwalker
Phone: 912-287-4900
Size: 626 acres. **Location:** 9 miles southeast of Waycross on GA 177. **Facilities:** 44 tent/trailer/RV campsites, 2 pioneer campgrounds, group camp, 9 picnic shelters, 5 group shelters, nature trails, 120-acre lake, swimming pool, boat ramp, docks, canoe rentals, wildlife observation platform, 18-hole golf course, clubhouse, and golf pro. **Activities:** Camping, boating, fishing, swimming, water-skiing, hiking, golf. **Special Features:** Located near the famous Okefenokee Swamp, the park is home to alligators, carnivorous pitcher plants, saw palmettos, yellow shafted flickers, great blue heron, and other flora and fauna native to Georgia's swampland. Park was named for Laura Walker, a Georgia writer, teacher, civic leader, and naturalist who was a great lover of trees and worked for their preservation.

★2086★ LITTLE OCMULGEE STATE PARK & LODGE

PO Drawer 149
McRae, GA 31055
Web: gastateparks.org/info/liocmulgee
Phone: 229-868-7474
Size: 1,360 acres. **Location:** 2 miles north of McRae via US 319 and US 441. **Facilities:** 55 tent/trailer/RV campsites, pioneer campground, 10 cottages, 60-room lodge and conference center, restaurant, swimming pool (overnight guests only), 18-hole golf course and pro shop, 7 picnic shelters, group shelter, trails (2.6 miles) and boardwalk, 265-acre lake with beach, boating/skiing ramp, canoe and pedal boat rentals, bicycle rental, volleyball courts, miniature golf course, tennis courts, meeting facilities, amphitheater. **Activities:** Camping, boating, fishing, swimming, water-skiing, hiking, bicycling, golfing. **Special Features:** Located in south Georgia, this park features a variety of amenities, including a newly renovated lodge with hotel-style guest rooms, meeting facilities, and restaurant with a golf course view.

★2087★ **LITTLE WHITE HOUSE STATE HISTORIC SITE**
401 Little White House Rd
Warm Springs, GA 31830
Web: gastateparks.org/info/littlewhite
Phone: 706-655-5870; **Fax:** 706-655-5872
Size: 160 acres. **Location:** .25 mile south of Warm Springs on GA 85 Alt and GA 27 Alt. **Facilities:** Historic home, therapeutic pools and springs complex, museum, picnic areas. **Activities:** House tours. **Special Features:** Franklin Delano Roosevelt built the Little White House in 1932 while still governor of New York. He had first come to Warm Springs in 1924 hoping that the spring waters would provide a cure for the infantile paralysis (polio) that had struck him in 1921. During FDR's presidency and the Great Depression, he developed many New Deal Programs (such as the Rural Electrification Administration) based upon his experiences in this small town. On April 12, 1945, FDR suffered a stroke while his portrait was being painted and died a short while later. Today, the Unfinished Portrait is a focal point of the Little White House tour. The house and furnishings have been preserved much as Roosevelt left them in 1945.

★2088★ **MAGNOLIA SPRINGS STATE PARK**
1053 Magnolia Springs Dr
Millen, GA 30442
Web: gastateparks.org/info/magspr
Phone: 478-982-1660
Size: 1,071 acres. **Location:** 5 miles north of Millen on US 25. **Facilities:** 26 tent/trailer/RV campsites, 3 walk-in sites, 2 pioneer campgrounds, a group camp, 6 cottages, 8 picnic shelters, 3 group shelters, 3 playgrounds, trails (10 miles), boat rentals, boat ramp, fishing dock (&), swimming pool, freshwater aquarium. **Activities:** Camping, boating, fishing, swimming (pool only), hiking, bicycling. **Special Features:** Park is known for its crystal-clear springs that flow 7 million gallons of water a day and the lovely boardwalk that spans the water. A freshwater aquarium at the park features native species.

★2089★ **MISTLETOE STATE PARK**
3723 Mistletoe Rd
Appling, GA 30802
Web: gastateparks.org/info/mistletoe
Phone: 706-541-0321
Size: 1,920 acres. **Location:** 8 miles north of I-20 exit 175, off GA 150. **Facilities:** 92 tent/trailer/RV campsites, 4 walk-in sites, a backcountry site, pioneer campground, 10 cottages, camper cabin, 5 picnic shelters, group shelter, nature trail (3.5 miles), backpacking trail (12 miles), lake, swimming beach, beach house (seats 75), 3 boat ramps, fishing dock (&), boat rentals, wildlife observation area. **Activities:** Camping, boating, fishing, swimming, water-skiing, hiking, bicycling, wildlife viewing. **Special Features:** Located on 76,000-acre Clarks Hill Lake near Augusta, this park is known as one of the finest bass fishing spots in the nation.

★2090★ **MOCCASIN CREEK STATE PARK**
3655 Hwy 197
Clarkesville, GA 30523
Web: gastateparks.org/info/moccasin
Phone: 706-947-3194

Size: 32 acres. **Location:** 20 miles north of Clarkesville on GA 197. **Facilities:** 55 tent/trailer/RV campsites, picnic shelter, interpretive trail (1 mile), hiking trail (2 miles), observation tower, lake, boat dock and ramp, fishing pier (&), canoe and jon boat rentals, playground. **Activities:** Camping, boating, lake fishing, stream fishing (restricted to children under 12 and seniors 65 and older), hiking, wildlife viewing. **Special Features:** Moccasin Creek is known as the park "where spring spends the summer." It sits nestled in the Blue Ridge Mountains beside the shores of Lake Burton, deep within Chattahoochee National Forest (see entry in national forests section).

★2091★ **NEW ECHOTA STATE HISTORIC SITE**
1211 Chatsworth Hwy NE
Calhoun, GA 30701
Web: gastateparks.org/info/echota
Phone: 706-624-1321
Size: 191 acres. **Location:** 1 miles east of I-75 exit 317, in Calhoun. **Facilities:** Visitor center, gift shop, nature trail, boat ramp. **Activities:** Self-guided tour, fishing. **Special Features:** In 1825, the Cherokee national legislature established a capital called New Echota at the headwaters of the Oostanaula River. During its short history, New Echota was the site of the first Indian-language newspaper office, a court case which carried to the US Supreme Court, one of the earliest experiments in national self-government by an Indian tribe, the signing of a treaty which relinquished Cherokee claims to lands east of the Mississippi River, and the assembly of tribal members for removal west on the infamous Trail of Tears. Today, visitors can see several original and reconstructed buildings including the Council House, court house, print shop, and an 1805 store.

★2092★ **PANOLA MOUNTAIN STATE PARK**
2600 Hwy 155 SW
Stockbridge, GA 30281
Web: gastateparks.org/info/panolamt
Phone: 770-389-7801
Size: 1,026 acres. **Location:** 18 miles southeast of Atlanta on GA 155 via I-20 (exit 68). **Facilities:** 4 picnic shelters, playground, hiking trails, nature trail, fitness trail, interpretive center, conference room. **Activities:** Hiking, guided hikes, educational programs. **Special Features:** Park was created to protect a 100-acre granite monadnock (mountain) that shelters rare plants of the Piedmont region. Panola Mountain is designated as a National Natural Landmark.

★2093★ **PICKETT'S MILL BATTLEFIELD STATE HISTORIC SITE**
4432 Mt Tabor Church Rd
Dallas, GA 30157
Web: gastateparks.org/info/picketts
Phone: 770-443-7850
Size: 765 acres. **Location:** 5 miles northeast of Dallas off GA Highway 381. **Facilities:** Visitor center with artifacts and exhibits, earthworks, hiking trails (4 miles), picnic tables, group shelter. **Special Features:** Pickett's Mill is one of the best preserved Civil War battlefields in the nation. During the spring of 1864, Federal forces, while advancing toward Atlanta, reached the

vicinity of Pickett's Mill, where they attacked Confederate troops. The Confederate victory delayed the Federal advance on Atlanta for one week, but it resulted in more than 2,000 combined casualties. Today, visitors can travel roads used by Union and Confederate troops and see earthworks constructed by the soldiers.

★2094★ PROVIDENCE CANYON STATE PARK

Rt 1, Box 158
Lumpkin, GA 31815
Web: gastateparks.org/info/providence
Phone: 229-838-6202
Size: 1,003 acres. **Location:** 7 miles west of Lumpkin on GA 39C. **Facilities:** 6 backcountry campsites, pioneer campground, 2 picnic shelters, group shelter, hiking trails (10 miles), visitor center. **Activities:** Hiking, backpacking, photography. **Special Features:** Multi-colored soils, along with the rare plumleaf azalea and other wildflowers, form the layers of Georgia's ''Little Grand Canyon.'' The park's visitor center explains how the massive gullies (the deepest being 150 feet) were caused by erosion due to poor farming practices in the 1800s.

★2095★ RED TOP MOUNTAIN STATE PARK & LODGE

50 Lodge Rd SE
Cartersville, GA 30121
Web: gastateparks.org/info/redtop
Phone: 770-975-0055
Size: 1,562 acres. **Location:** 1.5 miles east of I-75 exit 285, near Cartersville (about 45 minutes north of Atlanta). **Facilities:** 92 tent/trailer/RV campsites, pioneer campground, 18 cottages, a yurt, 33-room lodge and conference center, restaurant, swimming pool (lodge and cottage guests only), lake, swimming beach, tennis courts, 7 picnic shelters, 2 group shelters, wooded trails (15.5 miles), paved trail (&), marina, 2 boat ramps, 2 docks, meeting facilities, miniature golf course. **Activities:** Camping, boating, water skiiing, fishing, swimming, hiking, interpretive programs. **Special Features:** Once an important mining area for iron, the park is named for the rich red earth color of the soil caused by its high iron-ore content. The park is surrounded by Lake Allatoona, a 12,000-acre reservoir on the Etowah River, and includes a reconstructed 1860s log cabin (open and staffed on Saturdays).

★2096★ REED BINGHAM STATE PARK

542 Reed Bingham Rd
Adel, GA 31620
Web: gastateparks.org/info/reedbing
Phone: 229-896-3551
Size: 1,613 acres. **Location:** 6 miles west of Adel on GA 37, via I-75 exit 39. **Facilities:** 46 tent/trailer/RV campsites, pioneer campground, 6 picnic shelters, 4 group shelters, hiking trails (4 miles), lake, swimming beach, 3 boat ramps, fishing pier (&), canoe rental, dock and boat rental, bicycle rental, playground, miniature golf course. **Activities:** Camping, boating, canoeing, fishing (including competitions), swimming, water-skiing, hiking, bicycling, birding. **Special Features:** Park surrounds a 375-acre lake and is a major boating and water skiing attraction in

south Georgia. It is also the largest winter vulture roost in Georgia, with thousands of black vultures and turkey vultures arriving there each November and staying through early April.

★2097★ RICHARD B. RUSSELL STATE PARK

2650 Russell State Park Rd
Elberton, GA 30635
Web: gastateparks.org/info/richbruss
Phone: 706-213-2045
Size: 2,508 acres. **Location:** 8 miles northeast of Elberton, off GA 77 on Ruckersville Road. **Facilities:** 28 tent/trailer/RV campsites, 17 cottages, 3 picnic shelters, group shelter, trails (6 miles), lake, swimming beach, rowing area, boat ramp, canoe and pedal boat rentals, 18-hole golf course, disc golf course (&&). **Activities:** Camping, boating, rowing, fishing, swimming, water-skiing, beach volleyball, hiking, bicycling, golfing. **Special Features:** Located on a 26,500-acre lake, Park has excellent fishing and boating. It also features an 18-hole golf course, and its nature trail follows the shoreline to one of the oldest steel pin bridges in the area. The park's facilities are all designed to be totally wheelchair accessible, including the swimming beach.

★2098★ ROBERT TOOMBS HOUSE STATE HISTORIC SITE

216 E Robert Toombs Ave
Washington, GA 30673
Web: gastateparks.org/info/rtoombs
Phone: 706-678-2226
Size: 4.3 acres. **Location:** 216 East Robert Toombs Avenue in Washington, GA. **Facilities:** Museum, gift shop, picnic area. **Special Features:** Robert Toombs was a successful planter and lawyer who served as state legislator, US Congressman, and Senator. ''Defend yourselves; the enemy is at your door!'' thundered Toombs from the Senate floor on January 24, 1860. The following year, Georgia seceded from the Union and, for many, Toombs personified the South's fervent secessionist movement. In 1870, as the Reconstruction Era drew to a close, Toombs felt that Georgia should live under a constitution of its own making. His last service to Georgia citizens was to help create the Constitution of 1877, which was not amended until 1945.

★2099★ SAPELO ISLAND RESERVE & REYNOLDS MANSION

Sapelo Island Visitors Center
Rt 1 Box 1500
Darien, GA 31305
Web: gastateparks.org/info/sapelo
Phone: 912-437-3224
Size: 6,110-acre reserve on a 16,006-acre barrier island. **Location:** Sapelo ferry and visitor center are located in Meridian, 8 miles northeast of Darien, off GA 99. **Facilities:** Pioneer campground, 13 lodge rooms (Reynolds Mansion), visitor center (in Meridian). **Activities:** Guided tours (by reservation), marsh and beach walks. **Special Features:** Guided tours of Sapelo Island highlight the African-American community of Hog Hammock, University of Georgia Marine Institute, Reynolds Mansion, and a restored lighthouse built in 1820. Historic Reynolds

9. State Parks

Mansion is historical estate that can be used for conferences, retreats, and other functions (groups only, from 16-29 people). A campground on the island is also available only for groups (15-25 people).

★2100★ SEMINOLE STATE PARK

7870 State Park Dr
Donalsonville, GA 39845
Web: gastateparks.org/info/seminole
Phone: 229-861-3137
Size: 604 acres. **Location:** 16 miles south of Donalsonville via GA 39; or 23 miles west of Bainbridge on GA 253. **Facilities:** 50 tent/trailer/RV campsites, pioneer campground, 14 cottages (&), 5 picnic shelters, group shelter, hiking trail, lake, swimming beach, 4 boating/skiiing ramps, 4 fishing docks, canoe rentals, miniature golf course, gift shop. **Activities:** Camping, boating, fishing, swimming, water-skiing, hiking. **Special Features:** Park is located on Lake Seminole, a 37,500-acre reservoir in southwest Georgia, near the Alabama and Florida borders. The lake is shallow, but natural lime sink ponds have left areas of cool water with a variety of fish. The park is also near one of Georgia's largest wildlife management areas, providing excellent duck and deer hunting.

★2101★ SKIDAWAY ISLAND STATE PARK

52 Diamond Cswy
Savannah, GA 31411
Web: gastateparks.org/info/skidaway
Phone: 912-598-2300; **Fax:** 912-598-2365
Size: 588 acres. **Location:** 15 miles southeast of Savannah on Diamond Causeway. **Facilities:** 88 tent/trailer/RV campsites, 3 pioneer campgrounds, 5 picnic shelters, group shelter, trails, swimming pool, playground, nature trails, observation towers, visitor center. **Activities:** Camping, swimming, hiking, bicycling, birding, interpretive programs. **Special Features:** This barrier island park includes both salt and freshwater habitats due to estuaries and marshes that flow through the area. The park borders Skidaway Narrows, part of the Intracoastal Waterway. Two nature trails wind through marshes, live oaks, cabbage-palmettos, and longleaf pines, offering visitors the opportunity to look for deer, raccoon, shore birds, and rare migrating birds such as the painted bunting. The park's visitor/interpretive center has a birding station, nature exhibits, and a gift shop.

★2102★ SMITHGALL WOODS CONSERVATION AREA & LODGE

61 Tsalaki Trail
Helen, GA 30545
Web: gastateparks.org/info/smithgall
Phone: 706-878-3087
Size: 5,663 acres. **Location:** 3 miles west of Helen on GA 75-Alt., just south of the Richard B Russell Scenic Highway (GA 348). **Facilities:** Lodge, pioneer campground (youth groups only), 3 picnic shelters, trails (4 miles), wildlife viewing stands, visitor center. **Activities:** Group camping, trout fishing (reservation required), hiking, bicycling, hunting (with restrictions), wildlife viewing, nature photography, guided tours, educational programs. **Special Features:** Duke's Creek, north Georgia's premier catch-and-release trout fishing stream, runs through Smithgall Woods, and trout fishing and van tours are offered certain days of the week (call for schedule). The lodge at Smithgall Woods is actually five separate cottages, making this mountain retreat ideal for romantic getaways or corporate retreats.

★2103★ SPREWELL BLUFF STATE PARK

740 Sprewell Bluff Rd
Thomaston, GA 30286
Web: gastateparks.org/info/sprewell
Phone: 706-646-6026
Size: 1,372 acres. **Location:** 10 miles west of Thomaston, off GA 74. **Facilities:** Picnic area, playground, boat ramp, hiking trail (3 miles). **Activities:** Fishing, canoeing, rafting, hiking, picnicking, horshoe pitching, volleyball. **Special Features:** This day-use park offers a scenic trail along the banks of the Flint River and up rocky bluffs, offering excellent views from high above the river.

★2104★ STEPHEN C. FOSTER STATE PARK

17515 Hwy 177
Fargo, GA 31631
Web: gastateparks.org/info/scfoster
Phone: 912-637-5274
Size: 80 acres. **Location:** 18 miles northeast of Fargo via GA 177. **Facilities:** 66 tent/trailer/RV campsites, pioneer campground, 9 cottages, 3 picnic shelters, nature trail, 25 miles of day-use waterways, boat ramp, canoe and fishing boat rentals, visitor/interpretive center. **Activities:** Camping, boating, fishing, wildlife viewing, swamp boat tours, interpretive programs. **Special Features:** Named after well-known songwriter Stephen Foster, the park is located within Okefenokee National Wildlife Refuge (see entry in national wildlife refuge section) and is a primary entrance to the famed Okefenokee Swamp. Visitors can view lush vegetation or look for alligators, turtles, raccoon, black bear, deer, birds, and other creatures while on the park's elevated boardwalk trail or on a guided boat trip; or they can rent a boat or canoe to explore the swamp further.

★2105★ SWEETWATER CREEK STATE PARK

Lithia Springs, GA 30122
Web: gastateparks.org/info/sweetwater
Phone: 770-732-5871
Size: 2,549 acres. **Location:** 15 miles west of Atlanta, off I-20 exit 44. **Facilities:** 11 picnic shelters, group shelter, playgrounds, hiking trails (9 miles), lake, boat ramps, 2 fishing docks, canoe and fishing boat rentals, visitor center and museum. **Activities:** Camping, boating (no gas motors), lake and stream fishing, hiking, interpretive programs. **Special Features:** Only minutes from downtown Atlanta, Sweetwater Creek is a peaceful tract of wilderness with miles of trails, shady streams, and 215-acre George Sparks Reservoir. The site includes the ruins of the New Manchester Manufacturing Company, a textile mill burned down during the Civil War.

★2106★ TALLULAH GORGE STATE PARK

338 Jane Hurt Yarn Dr
Tallulah Falls, GA 30573
Web: gastateparks.org/info/tallulah
Phone: 706-754-7970
Size: 2,689 acres. **Location:** On US Highway 441, within Tallulah Falls city limits. **Facilities:** 50 tent/trailer/RV campsites, pioneer campground, backcountry Adirondack shelter, 2 picnic shelters, hiking trails (20+ miles), paved ''Rails to Trails'' path, 63-acre lake, swimming beach, tennis courts, interpretive center, gift shop. **Activities:** Camping, fishing, whitewater paddling (seasonal/limited), swimming, aesthetic water releases (spring and fall), hiking, bicycling (including mountain biking), rock climbing/rappelling (requires permit), interpretive programs. **Special Features:** One of the most spectacular canyons in the eastern US, the gorge is two miles long and nearly 1,000 feet deep. A suspension bridge crosses 80 feet above the gorge, affording breathtaking views of the river and waterfalls. Visitors must obtain a free permit (limit 100 per day) from the visitor center before hiking down to the gorge floor. The park's interpretive center features an award-winning film that takes viewers on a journey through the gorge.

★2107★ TRAVELER'S REST STATE HISTORIC SITE

11 Stage Coach Private Dr
Toccoa, GA 30577
Web: gastateparks.org/info/travelers
Phone: 706-886-2256
Size: 5.5 acres. **Location:** 6 miles east of Toccoa via US Highway 123. **Activities:** Guided tours. **Special Features:** Traveler's Rest was the plantation home of Devereaux Jarrett, one of the richest men in the Tugaloo Valley. Jarrett bought the site in 1833 as part of his plantation and created an inn to accommodate the growing number of travelers to northeast Georgia. The home, which was recognized as a National Historic Landmark in 1965, features a 90-foot-long porch and hand-numbered rafters, and most of its furnishings are original antiques.

★2108★ TUGALOO STATE PARK

1763 Tugaloo State Park Rd
Lavonia, GA 30553
Web: gastateparks.org/info/tugaloo
Phone: 706-356-4362
Size: 393 acres. **Location:** 6 miles north of Lavonia (I-85 exit 173), off GA 328. **Facilities:** 108 tent/trailer/RV campsites (&), 5 primitive campsites, pioneer campground, 20 cottages, 7 picnic shelters, group shelter, hiking trails (4 miles), lake, swimming beach and bathhouse, 2 boat ramps, canoe rentals (seasonal),tennis courts, miniature golf course. **Activities:** Camping, fishing, sailing, boating, canoeing, swimming, water-skiing, hiking, tennis, volleyball, horseshoe pitching, miniature golf. **Special Features:** The name ''Tugaloo'' comes from an Indian name for the river that flowed here prior to the construction of Hartwell Dam. The park is situated on a rugged peninsula that juts into 55,590-acre Hartwell Reservoir. Fishing is excellent year round, and largemouth bass are plentiful.

★2109★ UNICOI STATE PARK & LODGE

1788 Highway 356 Rd
Helen, GA 30545
Web: gastateparks.org/info/unicoi
Phone: 800-573-9659
Size: 1,050 acres. **Location:** 2 miles northeast of Helen via GA 356. **Facilities:** 82 tent/trailer/RV campsites, 33 walk-in campsites, camping shelters, 30 cottages, 100-room lodge, restaurant, 6 picnic shelters, hiking trails (12 miles), mountain biking trails (8 miles), 53-acre lake, beach, beach house (seats 75), fishing dock (&), canoe and pedal boat rentals, tennis courts, meeting facilities. **Activities:** Camping, canoeing, fishing, swimming, hiking, mountain biking, guided hikes, interpretive programs. **Special Features:** Park is located near the alpine village of Helen in the north Georgia mountains. Created by artist John Pollack and local businessmen, quaint Helen is one of the state's most popular tourist destinations. The gift shop at the lodge specializes in handmade quilts and local pottery.

★2110★ VICTORIA BRYANT STATE PARK

1105 Bryant Park Rd
Royston, GA 30662
Web: gastateparks.org/info/vicbryant
Phone: 706-245-6270
Size: 502. **Location:** 2 miles north of Franklin Springs on GA 327. **Facilities:** 27 tent/trailer/RV campsites, 8 platform tent sites, 2 pioneer campgrounds, 6 picnic shelters, 3 playgrounds, trails (8 miles), swimming pool, 1 fishing pond for campers, 1 fishing pond for disabled visitors only, 18-hole golf course and pro shop. **Activities:** Camping, fishing, swimming, hiking, mountain biking. **Special Features:** Nestled in the rolling hills of Georgia's upper piedmont, park features two stocked fishing ponds.

★2111★ VOGEL STATE PARK

7485 Vogel State Park Rd
Blairsville, GA 30512
Web: gastateparks.org/info/vogel
Phone: 706-745-2628
Size: 233 acres. **Location:** 11 miles south of Blairsville via US 19/129. **Facilities:** 103 tent/trailer/RV campsites, 18 walk-in campsites, primitive backpacking sites, pioneer campground, 35 cottages, 4 picnic shelters, group shelter, trails (17 miles), 20-acre lake, swimming beach, pedal boat rental, miniature golf course, CCC museum, general store. **Activities:** Camping, pedal boating, fishing, swimming, hiking, backpacking. **Special Features:** One of Georgia's oldest and most popular state parks, Vogel is located at the base of Blood Mountain in Chattahoochee National Forest (see entry in national forests section). Driving from the south, visitors pass through Neel Gap, a beautiful mountain pass near Brasstown Bald, the highest point in Georgia. Many visitors come during the fall when the Blue Ridge Mountains are blanketed with red, yellow, and gold leaves. A segment of the Appalachian National Scenic Trail passes through the park (see entry in national trails section).

9. State Parks

★2112★ WATSON MILL BRIDGE STATE PARK

650 Watson Mill Rd
Comer, GA 30629
Web: gastateparks.org/info/watson
Phone: 706-783-5349
Size: 1,018 acres. **Location:** 3 miles south of Comer off GA 22. **Facilities:** 32 tent/trailer/RV campsites (horse stalls with 11 of the sites), pioneer campground, log cabin bunkhouse, 3 picnic shelters, group shelter, hiking trails (7 miles), bicycling trails (5 miles), equestrian trails (12 miles), 5-acre mill pond, canoe and pedal boat rentals, historic structures. **Activities:** Camping, canoeing, fishing, hiking, bicycling, horseback riding. **Special Features:** Park contains the longest original-site covered bridge in Georgia, with four spans stretching 229 feet across the South Fork River. Built in 1885, the bridge is supported by a town lattice truss system held together with wooden pins.

★2113★ WORMSLOE STATE HISTORIC SITE

7601 Skidaway Rd
Savannah, GA 31406
Web: gastateparks.org/info/wormsloe
Phone: 912-353-3023
Size: 1,233 acres. **Location:** 10 miles southeast of Savannah's historic district on Skidaway Road. **Facilities:** Tabby ruins, museum, gift shop, nature trail, picnic area. **Activities:** Living history programs. **Special Features:** Site preserves the tabby ruins of a colonial estate constructed by Noble Jones, one of Georgia's first settlers. Jones was an English physician and carpenter who prospered in the colonial wilderness. He came to Savannah with James Oglethorpe in 1733 and commanded a company of Marines charged with Georgia's coastal defense. Jones served as constable, Indian agent, and surveyor (laying out New Ebenezer and Augusta). Museum exhibits include artifacts excavated at Wormsloe as well as a film about the founding of the 13th colony.

9. State Parks

Hawaii State Parks

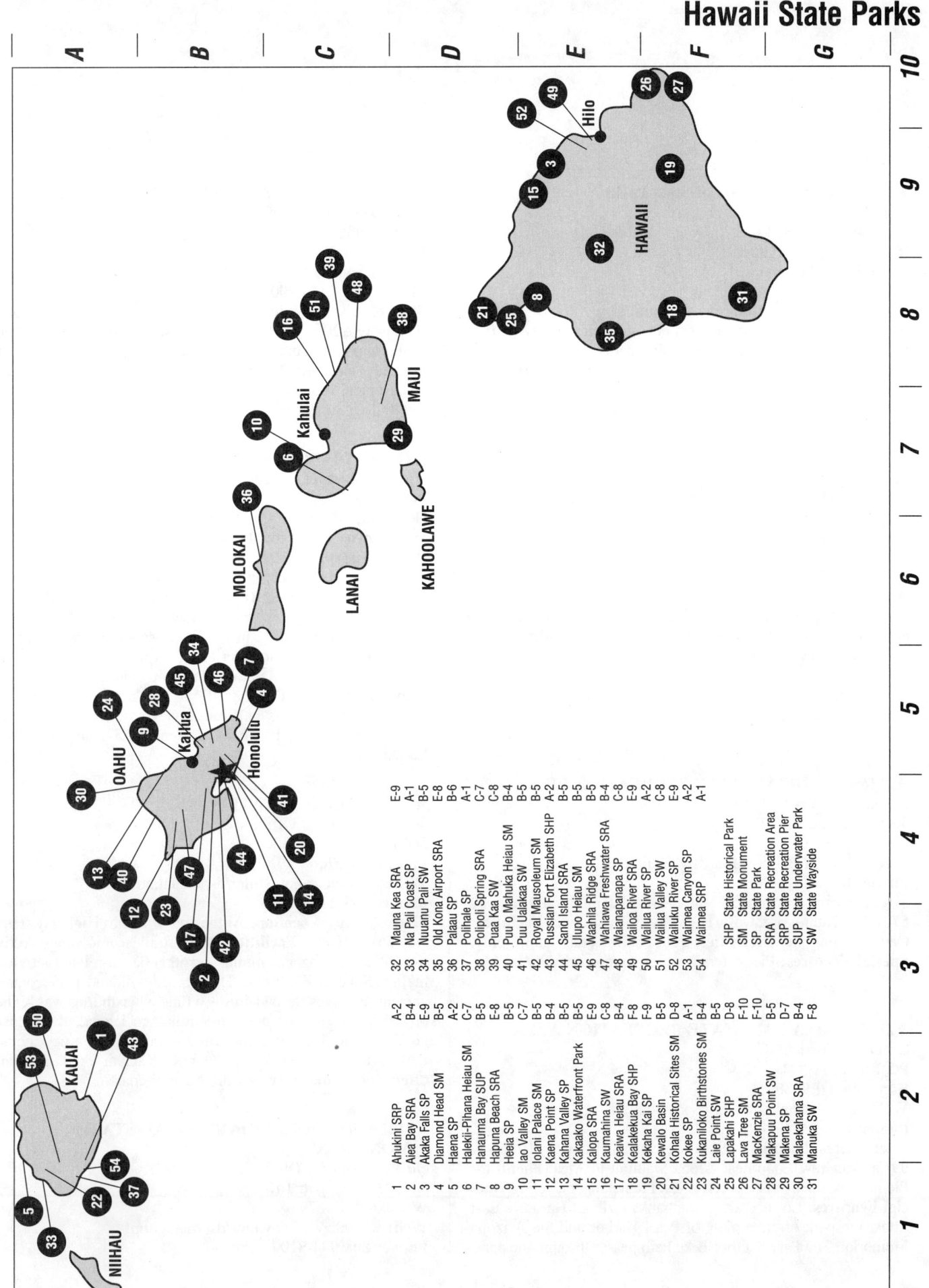

1	Ahukini SRP	A-2	32	Mauna Kea SRA	E-9
2	Aiea Bay SRA	B-4	33	Na Pali Coast SP	A-1
3	Akaka Falls SP	E-9	34	Nuuanu Pali SW	B-5
4	Diamond Head SM	B-5	35	Old Kona Airport SRA	E-8
5	Haena SP	A-2	36	Palaau SP	B-6
6	Halekii-Pihana Heiau SM	C-7	37	Polihale SP	A-1
7	Hanauma Bay SUP	B-5	38	Polipoli Spring SRA	C-7
8	Hapuna Beach SRA	E-8	39	Puaa Kaa SW	C-8
9	Heeia SP	B-5	40	Puu o Mahuka Heiau SM	B-4
10	Iao Valley SM	C-7	41	Puu Ualakaa SW	B-5
11	Iolani Palace SM	B-5	42	Royal Mausoleum SM	B-5
12	Kaena Point SP	B-4	43	Russian Fort Elizabeth SHP	A-2
13	Kahana Valley SP	B-5	44	Sand Island SRA	B-5
14	Kakaako Waterfront Park	B-5	45	Ulupo Heiau SM	B-5
15	Kalopa SRA	E-9	46	Waahila Ridge SRA	B-5
16	Kaumahina SW	C-8	47	Wahiawa Freshwater SRA	B-4
17	Keaiwa Heiau SRA	B-4	48	Waianapanapa SP	C-8
18	Kealakekua Bay SHP	F-9	49	Wailoa River SRA	E-9
19	Kekaha Kai SP	F-9	50	Wailua River SP	A-2
20	Kewalo Basin	B-5	51	Wailua Valley SW	C-8
21	Kohala Historical Sites SM	D-8	52	Wailuku River SP	E-9
22	Kokee SP	A-1	53	Waimea Canyon SP	A-2
23	Kukaniloko Birthstones SM	B-4	54	Waimea SRP	A-1
24	Laie Point SW	B-5			
25	Lapakahi SHP	D-8		SHP	State Historical Park
26	Lava Tree SM	F-10		SM	State Monument
27	MacKenzie SRA	F-10		SP	State Park
28	Makapuu Point SW	B-5		SRA	State Recreation Area
29	Makena SP	D-7		SRP	State Recreation Pier
30	Malaekahana SRA	B-4		SUP	State Underwater Park
31	Manuka SW	F-8		SW	State Wayside

HAWAII

★2114★ Hawaii Division of State Parks
1151 Punchbowl St
Honolulu, HI 96813
(808) 587-0300 - Phone
(808) 587-0311 - Fax
(808) 587-0180 - Employment
Web: www.state.hi.us/dlnr/dsp/dsp.html
System consists of 52 state parks encompassing nearly 25,000 acres on the 5 major islands. Hawaii's parks protect the state's cultural and archeological sites, and allow visitors to experience the islands' unique geological features and scenic wonders. Visitors wishing to camp or hike on state park land must contact park office to obtain a permit.

★2115★ Hawaii Division of Forestry & Wildlife
1151 Punchbowl St, Rm 325
Honolulu, HI 96813
(808) 587-0166 - Phone
(808) 587-0160 - Fax
Web: www.dofaw.net
Oversees state-owned forests, natural areas, public hunting areas, and plant and wildlife sanctuaries. Develops and maintains trails and issues hunting permits.

★2116★ AHUKINI STATE RECREATION PIER
c/o Kauai District Office
3060 Eiwa St, Rm 306
Lihue, HI 96766
Web: www.hawaii.gov/dlnr/dsp/kauai.html
Phone: 808-274-3444
Size: 0.9 acres. **Location:** At the end of Ahukini Road (Highway 570), off Kuhio Highway (Highway 56) in Lihue. **Facilities:** Ocean fishing pier. **Activities:** Pole fishing, crab netting only. **Special Features:** Pier offers a sweeping coastal view.

★2117★ AIEA BAY STATE RECREATION AREA
c/o Oahu District Office
PO Box 621
Honolulu, HI 96809
Web: www.hawaii.gov/dlnr/dsp/oahu.html
Phone: 808-587-0300
Size: 6 acres. **Location:** Off Kamehameha Highway (Highway 99) at McGrew Loop near Aloha Stadium in Aiea. **Facilities:** Picnic area, scenic vistas. **Activities:** Picnicking, bicycling. **Special Features:** Located along the banks of Pearl Harbor's East Lock, the park offers a view of Pearl Harbor and the Arizona Memorial. The Pearl Harbor Bike Path passes through the park.

★2118★ AKAKA FALLS STATE PARK
c/o Hawaii District Office
PO Box 936
Hilo, HI 96721
Web: www.hawaii.gov/dlnr/dsp/hawaii.html
Phone: 808-974-6200
Size: 65.4 acres. **Location:** At the end of Akaka Falls Road (Highway 220), 3.6 miles southwest of Honomu. **Facilities:** Walking path, scenic lookout. **Activities:** Hiking, nature study. **Special Features:** A self-guided walk takes visitors through lush tropical vegetation to views of cascading Kahuna Falls and free-falling Akaka Falls, which plunges 442 feet into a gorge.

★2119★ DIAMOND HEAD STATE MONUMENT
c/o Oahu District Office
PO Box 621
Honolulu, HI 96809
Web: www.hawaii.gov/dlnr/dsp/oahu.html
Phone: 808-587-0300
Size: 475 acres. **Location:** Off Diamond Head Road between Makapuu Avenue and 18th Avenue in Honolulu. **Facilities:** Picnic area, hiking trail, scenic views. **Activities:** Hiking. **Special Features:** Hawaii's most famous landmark is a large tuff cone formed by a short series of explosive eruptions some 100,000 years ago. Diamond Head's picnic area is in a landscaped meadow on the crater floor; a hike to the summit (0.7 miles one way) offers panoramic views of Honolulu and the Kahala plain. Park has been designated a National Natural Landmark.

★2120★ HAENA STATE PARK
c/o Kauai District Office
3060 Eiwa St, Rm 306
Lihue, HI 96766
Web: www.hawaii.gov/dlnr/dsp/kauai.html
Phone: 808-274-3444
Size: 66 acres. **Location:** At the end of Kuhio Highway (Highway 56) in Haena. **Facilities:** Beach, trail, scenic views. **Activities:** Shore fishing, swimming and other beach-related activities, hiking. **Special Features:** This scenic wildland park contains ancient sea caves formed during a time when the sea was higher, probably 4,000 years ago. (According to legend, the volcano goddess Pele dug the caves while searching for a new home.) Park is the trailhead for the 11-mile Kalalau Trail. Park also offers spectacular views of the Na Pali coast.

★2121★ HALEKII-PIHANA HEIAU STATE MONUMENT
c/o Maui District Office
54 S High St, Rm 101
Wailuku, HI 96793
Web: www.hawaii.gov/dlnr/dsp/maui.html
Phone: 808-984-8109

Size: 10.2 acres. **Location:** In Wailuku at the end of Hea Place, off Kuhio Place from Waiehu Beach Road (Highway 340). **Facilities:** Cultural site; no drinking water. **Special Features:** Monument preserves the remains of two important *heiau* (places of worship) that were rededicated as war temples by Kahekili, Maui's last ruling chief. Site offers a view of central Maui and the Wailuku Plain.

★2122★ HANAUMA BAY STATE UNDERWATER PARK

c/o Oahu District Office
PO Box 621
Honolulu, HI 96809
Web: www.hawaii.gov/dlnr/dsp/oahu.html
Phone: 808-587-0300
Size: 101 acres. **Location:** At Hanauma Bay Beach Park, 0.3 miles east of Hawaii Kai, off Kalanianaole Highway (Highway 72). **Activities:** Swimming, snorkeling, scuba diving. **Special Features:** Park offers novice divers the opportunity to observe reef fishes and corals. The adjoining area is a City and County beach park with interpretive kiosk.

★2123★ HAPUNA BEACH STATE RECREATION AREA

c/o Hawaii District Office
PO Box 936
Hilo, HI 96721
Web: www.hawaii.gov/dlnr/dsp/hawaii.html
Phone: 808-974-6200
Size: 62 acres. **Location:** On Queen Kaahumanu Highway (Highway 19), 2.3 miles south of Kawaihae. **Facilities:** A-frame shelters with pavilion and comfort stations (cold showers and restrooms), picnic areas, food concession, beach, trails. **Activities:** Swimming, bodysurfing, other beach activities. **Special Features:** Hapuna is a landscaped beach park offering a variety of beach activities, but visitors are cautioned to be aware of dangerous rip currents and pounding shore breaks during periods of high surf. The site also offers access to the historic coastal trail, Ala Kahakai.

★2124★ HEEIA STATE PARK

c/o Oahu District Office
PO Box 621
Honolulu, HI 96809
Web: www.hawaii.gov/dlnr/dsp/oahu.html
Phone: 808-587-0300
Size: 18.5 acres. **Location:** At 46-465 Kamehameha Highway (Highway 83) at Kealohi Point in Heeia. **Facilities:** Picnic area, scenic vistas. **Special Features:** Coastal park offers good views of Kaneohe Bay and Heeia Fishpond. A party hall at the park is available for weekend rental; contact the Friends of Heeia State Park at (808) 247-3156.

★2125★ IAO VALLEY STATE MONUMENT

c/o Maui District Office
54 S High St, Rm 101
Wailuku, HI 96793
Web: www.hawaii.gov/dlnr/dsp/maui.html
Phone: 808-984-8109

Size: 6.2 acres. **Location:** At the end of Iao Valley Road (Highway 32) in Iao Valley. **Facilities:** Paved walking path, scenic overlook, botanical garden; no drinking water. **Activities:** Nature study. **Special Features:** Park offers a scenic view of Iao Needle, an erosion feature that rises 1,200 feet from the valley floor. A botanical garden contains plants brought by the Hawiians who settled in Iao Valley, an area rich in cultural and spiritual values. It also is the site of the Battle of Kepaniwai, where Kamehameha I's forces conquered Maui's army in an effort to unite the islands in 1790.

★2126★ IOLANI PALACE STATE MONUMENT

c/o Oahu District Office
PO Box 621
Honolulu, HI 96809
Web: www.hawaii.gov/dlnr/dsp/oahu.html
Phone: 808-587-0300
Size: 11 acres. **Location:** Corner of South King Street and Richards Street, downtown Honolulu. **Facilities:** Cultural site. **Activities:** Guided tours (reservation required; contact Friends of Iolani Palace at 808-522-0832). **Special Features:** Officially dedicated in 1882, Iolani Palace was the royal palace of the Hawaiian monarchy and served as the setting for monarchs and their courts on formal occasions. The park is a National Historic Landmark. Palace grounds are popular for informal picnics and weekly band concerts.

★2127★ KAENA POINT STATE PARK

c/o Oahu District Office
PO Box 621
Honolulu, HI 96809
Web: www.hawaii.gov/dlnr/dsp/oahu.html
Phone: 808-587-0300
Size: 779 acres. **Location:** At the end of Farrington Highway (Highway 930) in Makua. **Facilities:** Beach with lifeguard services, trail (2.7 miles), scenic lookout; no drinking water. **Activities:** Shore fishing, board surfing and bodysurfing (for experts only), swimming (only during completely calm conditions in summer), hiking. **Special Features:** Park features a mile-long sandy beach along a remote and wild section of the coastline. It is hot and dry here, with little shade. The park's trail is along the volcanic coast, with tide pools and natural stone arches along the way, and offers scenic views of the Makua coastline. Porpoises are sighted during the early morning hours from a point near the mouth of Kaluakauila stream. A large sea cave, Kaneana, is the legendary home of Nanue, the shark man.

★2128★ KAHANA VALLEY STATE PARK

c/o Oahu District Office
PO Box 621
Honolulu, HI 96809
Web: www.hawaii.gov/dlnr/dsp/oahu.html
Phone: 808-587-0300
Size: 5,229 acres. **Location:** At 55-222 Kamehameha Highway (Highway 83) in Kahana. **Facilities:** Campgrounds, picnic areas, beach, hiking trails, cultural site, public hunting area. **Activities:** Camping, hiking, swimming, bodysurfing, other beach-related activities, pig hunting. **Special Features:** This scenic wildland

9. State Parks

valley offers visitors a glimpse of the islands before the arrival of Westerners. The park features a historic fishpond along the shoreline of the bay, and a short hike leads to a fishing shrine known as a *koa*. In addition to the beach-related activities available, visitors can pick fruit in a lushly vegetated forest or picnic in a coconut grove.

★2129★ KAKAAKO WATERFRONT PARK

c/o Oahu District Office
PO Box 621
Honolulu, HI 96809
Web: www.hawaii.gov/dlnr/dsp/oahu.html
Phone: 808-587-0300
Size: 28 acres. **Location:** At the end of Ahui or Ohe streets off Ala Moana Boulevard, in Honolulu. **Facilities:** Picnic areas, amphitheater, waterfront promenade, ocean access, observation areas. **Activities:** Shore fishing, bodysurfing. **Special Features:** This waterfront park is built over a former municipal landfill. Observation areas along the waterfront provide excellent views of Waikiki and Diamond Head.

★2130★ KALOPA STATE RECREATION AREA

c/o Hawaii District Office
PO Box 936
Hilo, HI 96721
Web: www.hawaii.gov/dlnr/dsp/hawaii.html
Phone: 808-974-6200
Size: 100 acres. **Elevation:** 2,000 feet. **Location:** 5 miles southeast of Honokaa, at the end of Kalopa Road 3 miles inland from Mamalahoa Highway (Highway 19). **Facilities:** Campground, lodging, picnic areas, nature trail (0.7-mile loop). **Activities:** Camping, hiking, horseback riding, nature study. **Special Features:** Park's nature trail has the beginnings of an arboretum of the Island's native plants. A forest reserve that adjoins the park has additional trails, including a 2-mile horse loop trail.

★2131★ KAUMAHINA STATE WAYSIDE

c/o Maui District Office
54 S High St, Rm 101
Wailuku, HI 96793
Web: www.hawaii.gov/dlnr/dsp/maui.html
Phone: 808-984-8109
Size: 8 acres. **Location:** On Hana Highway (Highway 360), approximately 28 miles east of Kahului Airport (2-hour drive). **Facilities:** Picnic area, scenic lookout; no drinking water. **Special Features:** This forested rest stop has showy exotic plants and a view of the northeast Maui coastline.

★2132★ KEAIWA HEIAU STATE RECREATION AREA

c/o Oahu District Office
PO Box 621
Honolulu, HI 96809
Web: www.hawaii.gov/dlnr/dsp/oahu.html
Phone: 808-587-0300
Size: 385 acres. **Location:** At the end of Aiea Heights Drive in Aiea Heights. **Facilities:** Campground, picnic areas, hiking trail (4.8-mile loop), cultural site. Rustic facilities. **Activities:** Camping, hiking, nature study. **Special Features:** Park offers forest recreation and includes the remains of a *heiau ho'ola*, a temple where healers trained and treated various illnesses.

★2133★ KEALAKEKUA BAY STATE HISTORICAL PARK

c/o Hawaii District Office
PO Box 936
Hilo, HI 96721
Web: www.hawaii.gov/dlnr/dsp/hawaii.html
Phone: 808-974-6200
Size: 4 acres. **Location:** At the end of Napopoo Beach Road, off Government Road from Puuhonua Road (Highway 160) or Lower Government Road from Mamalahoa Highway (Highway 11) at Captain Cook or Keei Junction. **Facilities:** Historic site, scenic lookout. **Special Features:** Site features Hikiau Heiau, a place of worship where priests offered reverence to Captain Cook in 1779, believing he was the god Lono returning to them as promised. Site also offers a panoramic view of Kealakekua Bay, with the Captain Cook Monument visible at a distance across the bay.

★2134★ KEKAHA KAI (KONA COAST) STATE PARK

c/o Hawaii District Office
PO Box 936
Hilo, HI 96721
Web: www.hawaii.gov/dlnr/dsp/hawaii.html
Phone: 808-974-6200
Size: 1,643 acres. **Location:** On Queen Kaahumanu Highway (Highway 19), 2.6 miles north of Keahole Airport. **Facilities:** Beach, picnic area, portable toilets, trails, scenic vista; no drinking water. **Activities:** Hiking, swimming, other beach-related activities. **Special Features:** This wilderness park includes the Mahaiula and Kua Bay sections, two beach areas linked by a 4.5 mile segment of the historic coastal trail, Ala Kahakai. Visitors can also hike to the summit of Puu Kuili, a 342-foot hgih cinder cone that offers an excellent view of the coastline.

★2135★ KEWALO BASIN

c/o Oahu District Office
PO Box 621
Honolulu, HI 96809
Web: www.hawaii.gov/dlnr/dsp/oahu.html
Phone: 808-587-0300
Size: 3 acres. **Location:** Off Ala Moana Boulevard at Ward Avenue in Honolulu; adjacent to Ala Moana Beach Park. **Facilities:** Picnic areas, promenade, outdoor showers. **Activities:** Picnicking. **Special Features:** This oceanside park near downtown Honolulu features a pedestrian promenade and trellised picnic areas.

★2136★ KOHALA HISTORICAL SITES STATE MONUMENT

c/o Hawaii District Office
PO Box 936
Hilo, HI 96721
Web: www.hawaii.gov/dlnr/dsp/hawaii.html
Phone: 808-974-6200

9. State Parks

Size: 6.7 acres. **Location:** On a coastal dirt road off Upolu Airport road from Akoni Pule Highway (Highway 270), 1.6 miles from Upolu Airport. **Facilities:** Historic sites. **Special Features:** Two sites are located here: the Mookini Heiau, a National Historic Landmark that is one of the most famous sacrificial temples on the island; and the Kamehameha I Birthsite, a memorial to Hawaii's greatest king, who united all the island chiefdoms into a kingdom.

★2137★ **KOKEE STATE PARK**
c/o Kauai District Office
3060 Eiwa St, Rm 306
Lihue, HI 96766
Web: www.hawaii.gov/dlnr/dsp/kauai.html
Phone: 808-274-3444
Size: 4,345 acres. **Location:** 15 miles north of Kekaha on Kokee Road (Highway 550). **Facilities:** Housekeeping cabins, campground, picnic areas, trails, scenic lookouts, public hunting area, food concession, museum. **Activities:** Tent and trailer camping, hiking, nature study, pig hunting, trout fishing (seasonal), plum picking (seasonal). **Special Features:** Park adjoins Waimea Canyon State Park (see separate entry) and offers spectacular views of lush Kalalau Valley from a lookout at 4,000 feet elevation. The park is an excellent area for learning about native plants and rain forest birds.

★2138★ **KUKANILOKO BIRTHSTONES STATE MONUMENT**
c/o Oahu District Office
PO Box 621
Honolulu, HI 96809
Web: www.hawaii.gov/dlnr/dsp/oahu.html
Phone: 808-587-0300
Size: 5 acres. **Location:** At the intersection of Kamehameha Highway (Highway 99) and Whitmore Avenue on the north side of Wahiawa. **Facilities:** Cultural site, exhibits. **Special Features:** This site is a place where royalty came for the birth of their children and is considered one of the most important cultural sites on Oahu. The birthsite consisted of two rows of 18 stones (representing Oahu's 36 chiefs) and a stone backrest where the chieftess would give birth. Today, the area is covered with 180 stones over an area of about a half acre.

★2139★ **LAIE POINT STATE WAYSIDE**
c/o Oahu District Office
PO Box 621
Honolulu, HI 96809
Web: www.hawaii.gov/dlnr/dsp/oahu.html
Phone: 808-587-0300
Size: 1.4 acres. **Location:** Off Kamehameha Highway (Highway 83) at Laie town via Anemoku Street to the end of Naupaka Street. **Facilities:** Scenic lookout. **Activities:** Shore fishing. **Special Features:** Coastal cliff wayside offers scenic views of an offshore sea arch and seabird sanctuary island.

★2140★ **LAPAKAHI STATE HISTORICAL PARK**
c/o Hawaii District Office
PO Box 936
Hilo, HI 96721
Web: www.hawaii.gov/dlnr/dsp/hawaii.html
Phone: 808-974-6200
Size: 262 acres. **Location:** On Akoni Pule Highway (Highway 270), 12.4 miles north of Kawaihae. **Facilities:** Cultural site; marine reserve. **Activities:** Self-guided tours, interpretive programs. **Special Features:** Park contains the partially-restored ruins of an ancient Hawaiian coastal settlement. Visitors here can learn about early Hawaiian lifestyle through re-enactments of daily activities, story telling, and a self-guided walk through the remains. A marine preserve is located in nearby ocean waters, with various activities regulated.

★2141★ **LAVA TREE STATE MONUMENT**
c/o Hawaii District Office
PO Box 936
Hilo, HI 96721
Web: www.hawaii.gov/dlnr/dsp/hawaii.html
Phone: 808-974-6200
Size: 17 acres. **Location:** Off Pahoa-Pohoiki Road (Highway 132), 2.7 miles southeast of Pahoa. **Facilities:** Picnic area, walking path; no drinking water. **Activities:** Nature study. **Special Features:** Park preserves a forest of lava trees, an unusual volcanic feature that resulted when a lava flow swept through this forested area and left behind lava molds of the tree trunks.

★2142★ **MACKENZIE STATE RECREATION AREA**
c/o Hawaii District Office
PO Box 936
Hilo, HI 96721
Web: www.hawaii.gov/dlnr/dsp/hawaii.html
Phone: 808-974-6200
Size: 13 acres. **Location:** On Kalapana-Kapoho Beach Road (Highway 137), 9 miles northeast of Kaimu. **Facilities:** Campsites, picnic area, trail; no drinking water. **Activities:** Tent camping, picnicking, hiking, shore fishing. **Special Features:** Park features low cliffs, a wild volcanic coastline, and an ironwood grove. An old Hawaiian coastal trail traverses the park.

★2143★ **MAKAPUU POINT STATE WAYSIDE**
c/o Oahu District Office
PO Box 621
Honolulu, HI 96809
Web: www.hawaii.gov/dlnr/dsp/oahu.html
Phone: 808-587-0300
Size: 38 acres. **Location:** Off Kalanianaole Highway (Highway 72) from either Waimanalo or Hawaii Kai. **Facilities:** Scenic lookout; no drinking water, no restrooms. **Activities:** Hiking. **Special Features:** A one-mile hike (one way) along a former roadway leads to a lighthouse. Various points along the way offer sweeping views of southeastern Oahu's coastline, where whales can sometimes be seen offshore. The hike is an uphill climb to a 500-foot elevation under hot, dry, and windy conditions.

9. State Parks

★2144★ MAKENA STATE PARK

c/o Maui District Office
54 S High St, Rm 101
Wailuka, HI 96793
Phone: 808-984-8109
Size: 164 acres. **Location:** South of Wailea at the end of Wailea Alanui Road. **Facilities:** Beach, pit toilets, scenic vistas; no drinking water. **Activities:** Swimsing, bodysurfing, board surfing, shore fishing. **Special Features:** Rugged and scenic beach park includes the Puu Olai cinder cone and a wide white sand beach.

★2145★ MALAEKAHANA STATE RECREATION AREA

c/o Oahu District Office
PO Box 621
Honolulu, HI 96809
Web: www.hawaii.gov/dlnr/dsp/oahu.html
Phone: 808-587-0300
Size: 110 acres. **Location:** Off Kamehameha Highway (Highway 83) at Malaekahana Beach. Kalanai Point section is 0.6 miles north of Laie town; Kahuka section is 1.3 miles north of Laie town. **Facilities:** Campgrounds, lodging (Kahuku Section), picnic areas, beach. **Activities:** Camping, swimming, bodysurfing, beach-related activities, shore fishing. **Special Features:** Area is a wooded beach park, with activities available at two locations.

★2146★ MANUKA STATE WAYSIDE

c/o Hawaii District Office
PO Box 936
Hilo, HI 96721
Web: www.hawaii.gov/dlnr/dsp/hawaii.html
Phone: 808-974-6200
Size: 13.4 acres. **Location:** On Mamalahoa Highway (Highway 11), 19 miles west of Naalehu. **Facilities:** Picnic facilities; no drinking water. **Activities:** Open shelter camping, picnicking. **Special Features:** Site provides a rest stop for the touring public among a collection of native and introduced trees in the Manuka Natural Area Reserve.

★2147★ MAUNA KEA STATE RECREATION AREA

c/o Hawaii District Office
PO Box 936
Hilo, HI 96721
Web: www.hawaii.gov/dlnr/dsp/hawaii.html
Phone: 808-974-6200
Size: 20.5 acres. **Elevation:** 6,500 feet. **Location:** 35 miles west of downtown Hilo in central Hawaii, on Saddle Road (Highway 200). **Facilities:** Housekeeping cabins, picnic areas, scenic views. **Activities:** Picnicking; pig, sheep, and bird hunting nearby. **Special Features:** At 6,500 feet, park's elevation provides good views of Mauna Loa and Mauna Kea. The area has clear, dry weather with cold nights. Period military training nearby may disrupt the peace and quiet of the area. (Note: Car rental companies may prohibit the use of their vehicles on the road that leads to the park, Saddle Road.)

★2148★ NA PALI COAST STATE PARK

c/o Kauai District Office
3060 Eiwa St, Rm 306
Lihue, HI 96766
Web: www.state.hi.us/dlnr/dsp/NaPali/na_pali.htm
Phone: 808-274-3444
Size: 6,175 acres. **Location:** Along the northwestern coast of Kauai, accessible only on foot or by boat. Land access is by the Kalalau Trail, which begins in Haena State Park at the northwest end of Kuhio Highway (Route 56). Kalalau Valley is also accessible by commercial boats from May15 through September 15. **Facilities:** Hiking trails, primitive campsites; no drinking water. **Activities:** Hiking, backpacking, primitive camping, shore fishing, seasonal goat hunting, commercial boat tours. **Special Features:** Park features exceptionally scenic sea cliffs and valleys that can be viewed by land along the coastal Kalalau Trail or by air and sea with commercial operators. It offers a primitive recreational experience with either a 2-mile (one way) day hike or a strenuous 11-mile backpacking trip to a primitive camp with an overnight stopover. Portions of the trail are strenuous and are recommended for experienced hikers only, and knowledge and skills of primitive outdoor living are required for backpacking and camping along this coast. Swimming and wading are not recommended as ocean conditions here can be dangerous.

★2149★ NUUANU PALI STATE WAYSIDE

c/o Oahu District Office
PO Box 621
Honolulu, HI 96809
Web: www.hawaii.gov/dlnr/dsp/oahu.html
Phone: 808-587-0300
Size: 3 acres. **Location:** Off Pali Highway (Highway 61) via marked access road. **Facilities:** Scenic lookout. **Special Features:** Site features an impressive view of windward Oahu from *pali* (cliffs) at 1,200-foot elevation along the Koolau Range. Winds here are so strong one can lean against a ''wall'' of wind.

★2150★ OLD KONA AIRPORT STATE RECREATION AREA

c/o Hawaii District Office
PO Box 936
Hilo, HI 96721
Web: www.hawaii.gov/dlnr/dsp/hawaii.html
Phone: 808-974-6200
Size: 104 acres. **Location:** At the end of Kuakini Highway (Highway 11) in Kailua-Kona. **Facilities:** Beach, picnic area, rental pavilion, jogging path. **Activities:** Surfing, snorkeling, tidepooling, shore and spear fishing, and other beach-related activities. **Special Features:** This day-use beach park offers a variety of water-related recreation opportunities, but lifeguard services are not provided. The park gate fronts on the runway of the old airport.

★2151★ PALAAU STATE PARK

c/o Oahu District Office
PO Box 621
Honolulu, HI 96809
Web: www.hawaii.gov/dlnr/dsp/molokai.html
Phone: 808-587-0300

Size: 234 acres. **Location:** At the end of Kalae Highway (Highway 47), Palaau, on the island of Molokai. **Facilities:** Campground, picnic area, cultural site, scenic lookout; no drinking water. **Activities:** Camping. **Special Features:** Park provides a scenic overlook of historic Kalaupapa, which was once a residential colony to which persons with leprosy were banished. A short trail leads to a phallic stone thought to enhance fertility.

★2152★ **POLIHALE STATE PARK**
c/o Kauai District Office
3060 Eiwa St, Rm 306
Lihue, HI 96766
Web: www.hawaii.gov/dlnr/dsp/kauai.html
Phone: 808-274-3444
Size: 138 acres. **Location:** At the end of a 5-mile-long dirt road from Mana Village, off Kaumualii Highway (Highway 50) past the Pacific Missile Range facility. **Facilities:** Campground, picnic shelters, beach, scenic vista. **Activities:** Tent camping, shore fishing, swimming (in summer, during calm conditions). **Special Features:** Park is situated on a wild coastline with a large sand beach backed by dunes and offers good views of the high sea cliffs of Na Pali Coast.

★2153★ **POLIPOLI SPRING STATE RECREATION AREA**
c/o Maui District Office
54 S High St, Rm 101
Wailuku, HI 96793
Web: www.hawaii.gov/dlnr/dsp/maui.html
Phone: 808-984-8109
Size: 10 acres. **Elevation:** 6,200 feet. **Location:** In Kula Forest Reserve, 10 miles upland from Kula on Waipoli Road off Kekaulike Avenue (Highway 377); four-wheel-drive vehicle recommended. **Facilities:** Campground (no showers), cabin (10-person capacity), picnic area, trails; no drinking water. **Activities:** Camping, hiking, pig and seasonal bird hunting. **Special Features:** Camping and lodging at Polipoli Spring are located within the fog belt of the Kula Forest Reserve at an elevation of 6,200 feet, and nights here are generally cold, often below freezing in winter. An extensive trail system in the Reserve includes an area of conifer forest reminiscent of the Pacific Northwest.

★2154★ **PUAA KAA STATE WAYSIDE**
c/o Maui District Office
54 S High St, Rm 101
Wailuku, HI 96793
Web: www.hawaii.gov/dlnr/dsp/maui.html
Phone: 808-984-8109
Size: 5 acres. **Location:** On Hana Highway (Highway 360), approximately 38 miles east of Kahului Airport (2.5-hour drive). **Facilities:** Picnic area, scenic overlook; no drinking water. **Special Features:** This rest stop is located in a rain forest and includes small scenic waterfalls and pools.

★2155★ **PUU O MAHUKA HEIAU STATE MONUMENT**
c/o Oahu District Office
PO Box 621
Honolulu, HI 96809
Web: www.hawaii.gov/dlnr/dsp/oahu.html
Phone: 808-587-0300
Size: 5.7 acres. **Location:** Off Pupukea Homestead Road (Highway 835) from Kamehameha Highway in Pupukea. **Facilities:** Cultural site. **Special Features:** Site contains Oahu's largest *heiau* (place of worship), a low-walled court platform-type temple with two adjoining smaller independent structures. It's likely that the site was used as a sacrificial temple, and it has been suggested that three of Captain George Vancouver's men may have been sacrificed here in 1792, when they came ashore to collect water.

★2156★ **PUU UALAKAA STATE WAYSIDE**
c/o Oahu District Office
PO Box 621
Honolulu, HI 96809
Web: www.hawaii.gov/dlnr/dsp/oahu.html
Phone: 808-587-0300
Size: 50 acres. **Location:** Off Round Top Drive off Makiki Street in Honolulu. **Facilities:** Picnic area, picnic shelters, scenic view. **Activities:** Picnicking, hiking (in adjacent forest reserve). **Special Features:** Scenic wayside lies in a forested area on a cinder cone close to downtown Honolulu, with sweeping views of southern Oahu from Diamond Head to Pearl Harbor, including Honolulu and Manoa Valley. It is the trailhead for Ualakaa Loop Trail (1-mile loop).

★2157★ **ROYAL MAUSOLEUM STATE MONUMENT**
c/o Oahu District Office
PO Box 621
Honolulu, HI 96809
Web: www.hawaii.gov/dlnr/dsp/oahu.html
Phone: 808-587-0300
Size: 10 acres. **Location:** At 2261 Nuuanu Avenue in Honolulu. **Facilities:** Cultural site, exhibits. **Activities:** Guided tours (by advance reservation), interpretive programs; picnicking not allowed. **Special Features:** Mausoleum is the burial place of Hawaiian royalty— members of the Kamehameha and Kalakaua dynasties with their retainers.

★2158★ **RUSSIAN FORT ELIZABETH STATE HISTORICAL PARK**
c/o Kauai District Office
3060 Eiwa St, Rm 306
Honolulu, HI 96766
Web: www.hawaii.gov/dlnr/dsp/kauai.html
Phone: 808-274-3444
Size: 17.3 acres. **Location:** Off Kaumualii Highway (Highway 50), on the east bank of Waimea rivermouth. **Facilities:** Historic fort, walking path. **Activities:** Self-guided tours. **Special Features:** This fort built of boulders stands as a reminder of Russia's short-lived adventure (1815-1817) in the Hawaiian Islands. The

massive stacked stone walls of the fort are a mix of Hawaiian construction and Russian fort design.

★2159★ SAND ISLAND STATE RECREATION AREA
c/o Oahu District Office
PO Box 621
Honolulu, HI 96809
Web: www.hawaii.gov/dlnr/dsp/oahu.html
Phone: 808-587-0300
Size: 140 acres. Location: At the end of Sand Island Access Road, off Nimitz Highway (Highway 92), Sand Island, Honolulu. Facilities: Campground, picnic area, beach, scenic vista; boat ramp nearby. Activities: Camping, shore fishing, board surfing. Special Features: Area lies on the west side of Honolulu Harbor and includes a small sand beach popular with local residents. It offers a good view of the harbor and sunsets.

★2160★ ULUPO HEIAU STATE MONUMENT
c/o Oahu District Office
PO Box 621
Honolulu, HI 96809
Web: www.hawaii.gov/dlnr/dsp/oahu.html
Phone: 808-587-0300
Size: 1.4 acres. Location: Off Kailua Road (Highway 61) via Uluoa, Manu-Aloha, and Manu-Oo Roads to the Windward YMCA parking lot; 0.4 miles northeast of Castle Hospital in Kailua. Facilities: Cultural site. Special Features: Site contains the ruins of a large, open-platform *heiau* (place of worship) overlooking Kawai Nui Marsh and Kailua Bay in the distance.

★2161★ WAAHILA RIDGE STATE RECREATION AREA
c/o Oahu District Office
PO Box 621
Honolulu, HI 96809
Web: www.hawaii.gov/dlnr/dsp/oahu.html
Phone: 808-587-0300
Size: 50 acres. Location: At the end of Ruth Place in the Saint Louis Heights area of Honolulu, off Waialae Avenue via Saint Louis Drive and Peter Street. Facilities: Picnic area, scenic lookout, trails. Activities: Hiking, picnicking. Special Features: Area is located on a ridge forested with Norfolk Island pines and offers views of Palolo and Manoa valleys.

★2162★ WAHIAWA FRESHWATER STATE RECREATION AREA
c/o Oahu District Office
PO Box 621
Honolulu, HI 96809
Web: www.hawaii.gov/dlnr/dsp/oahu.html
Phone: 808-587-0300
Size: 66 acres. Location: At 380 Walker Avenue, off Avocado Street or California Avenue from Kamehameha Highway (Highway 80), Wahiawa. Facilities: Picnic area, boat ramp. Activities: Freshwater fishing from shore or boat (no boating except for fishing purposes). Special Features: Recreation area is located along the wooded shore of Wahiawa Reservoir, with year-round

freshwater fishing. Neither swimming nor water skiing are permitted here.

★2163★ WAIANAPANAPA STATE PARK
c/o Maui District Office
54 S High St, Rm 101
Wailuku, HI 96793
Web: www.hawaii.gov/dlnr/dsp/maui.html
Phone: 808-984-8109
Size: 122 acres. Location: Off Hana Highway (Highway 360) at the end of Waianapanapa Road, 53 miles east of Kahului Airport (3-hour drive). Facilities: Campground, cabins, picnic areas, hiking trails, beach, cultural sites. Activities: Camping, shore fishing, hiking, nature study. Special Features: Located on a remote, wild, low-cliffed volcanic coastline, the park offers an excellent opportunity to study a seabird colony or hike along an ancient Hawaiian coastal trail. Park features also include native hala forest, a legendary cave, a *heiau* (place of worship), natural stone arch, sea stacks, blow holes, and a small black sand beach.

★2164★ WAILOA RIVER STATE RECREATION AREA
c/o Hawaii District Office
PO Box 936
Hilo, HI 96721
Web: www.hawaii.gov/dlnr/dsp/hawaii.html
Phone: 808-964-6200
Size: 132 acres. Location: In downtown Hilo; parking lot is at the end of Piilani Street and visitor center access road is off Pauahi Street. Facilities: Picnic area, boat ramp, visitor center. Activities: Picnicking, boat fishing (with restrictions). Special Features: The visitor center at this urban landscaped park on the Wailoa River contains cultural displays as well as visitor services.

★2165★ WAILUA RIVER STATE PARK
c/o Kauai District Office
3060 Eiwa St, Rm 306
Lihue, HI 96766
Web: www.hawaii.gov/dlnr/dsp/kauai.html
Phone: 808-274-3444
Size: 1,093 acres. Location: Along the Wailua River, off Kuhio Highway (Highway 56); historic sites and scenic overlooks on Kuamoo Road (Highway 580); and Wailua Falls at end of Maalo Road (Highway 583) from Kapaia. Facilities: Scenic vistas, cultural sites, marina with dining and gift shop. Activities: Boat excursions, river fishing, picnicking. Special Features: Park is set in a lush river valley, with scenic vistas of waterfalls and the Wailua River Valley as well as a riverboat cruise (fee charged) to Fern Grotto, a fern-covered cave situated in a tropical garden. This area was once an important seat of chiefly power in old Hawaii, and the park contains the remains of places of worship, places of refuge, and birthstones.

9. State Parks

★2166★ WAILUA VALLEY STATE WAYSIDE

c/o Maui District Office
54 S High St, Rm 101
Wailuku, HI 96793
Web: www.hawaii.gov/dlnr/dsp/maui.html
Phone: 808-984-8109
Size: 1.5 acres. **Location:** On Hana Highway (Highway 360), approximately 32 miles east of Kahului Airport (2.25-hour drive). **Facilities:** Scenic lookout; no drinking water. **Special Features:** Wayside offers views of Keanae Valley, Koolau Gap in Haleakala's rim, and Wailua Village and old taro fields.

★2167★ WAILUKU RIVER STATE PARK

c/o Hawaii District Office
PO Box 936
Hilo, HI 96721
Web: www.hawaii.gov/dlnr/dsp/hawaii.html
Phone: 808-974-6200
Size: 16.3 acres. **Location:** Off Waianuenue Avenue, Hilo. The Boiling Pots area is at the end of Peepee Falls Drive; Rainbow Falls is on Rainbow Drive. **Facilities:** Scenic overlooks, walking paths. **Special Features:** Park features viewpoints of geologic and scenic interest along Wailuku River. Boiling Pots is a succession of big pools connected by underground flow or cascades, with waters that roll and bubble as if boiling. Hexagonal columns that line the pools were formed by the slow cooling of basalt lava. The 80-foot Rainbow Falls is known for the rainbow often visible in its mist; legend says that a cave behind the waterfall was the home of Hina, mother of the demigod Maui.

★2168★ WAIMEA CANYON STATE PARK

c/o Kauai District Office
3060 Eiwa St, Rm 306
Lihue, HI 96766
Web: www.hawaii.gov/dlnr/dsp/kauai.html
Phone: 808-274-3444
Size: 1,866 acres. **Location:** 11 miles north of Kekaha on Kokee Road (Highway 550); adjoins Kokee State Park (see separate entry). **Facilities:** Picnic areas, nature trail, scenic lookout. **Activities:** Trout fishing (seasonal), wildland picnicking, hiking; pig and seasonal goat hunting nearby. **Special Features:** Rim overlooks one of the state's scenic treasures—the deep, colorful gorge of Waimea Canyon. The site also offers a good view of Niihau Island. Visitors can hike into and out of the canyon through an adjacent forest reserve. The hike is a long one, and strenuous.

★2169★ WAIMEA STATE RECREATION PIER

c/o Kauai District Office
3060 Eiwa St, Rm 306
Lihue, HI 96766
Phone: 808-274-3444
Size: 2 acres. **Location:** On Laau Road in the town of Waimea, off Pokole Road or Moana Road from Kaumualii Highway (Highway 50). **Facilities:** Fishing pier, picnic facilities. **Activities:** Pole fishing (with restrictions) and crabbing. **Special Features:** Site is an ocean fishing pier.

9. State Parks

Idaho State Parks

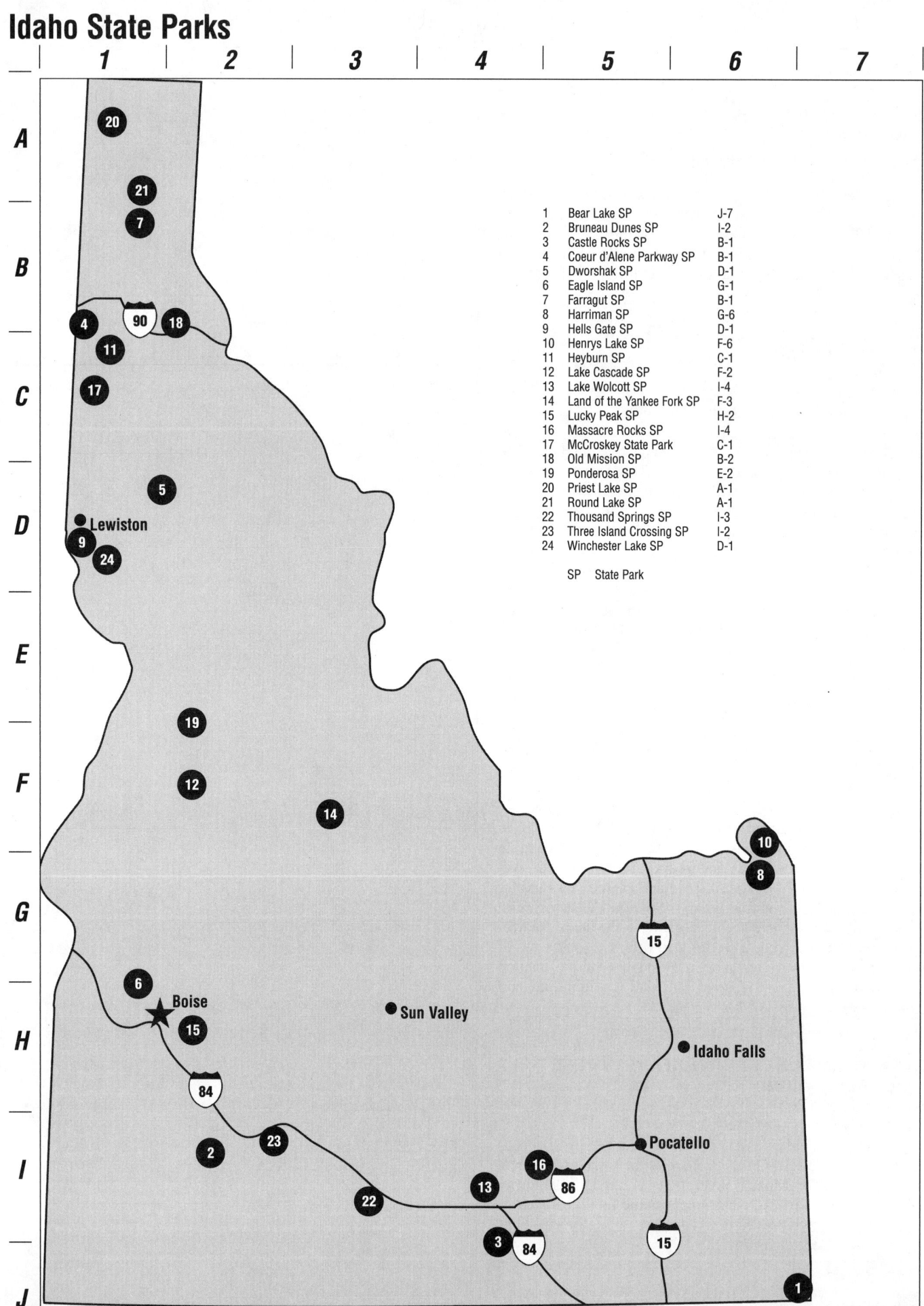

1	Bear Lake SP	J-7
2	Bruneau Dunes SP	I-2
3	Castle Rocks SP	B-1
4	Coeur d'Alene Parkway SP	B-1
5	Dworshak SP	D-1
6	Eagle Island SP	G-1
7	Farragut SP	B-1
8	Harriman SP	G-6
9	Hells Gate SP	D-1
10	Henrys Lake SP	F-6
11	Heyburn SP	C-1
12	Lake Cascade SP	F-2
13	Lake Wolcott SP	I-4
14	Land of the Yankee Fork SP	F-3
15	Lucky Peak SP	H-2
16	Massacre Rocks SP	I-4
17	McCroskey State Park	C-1
18	Old Mission SP	B-2
19	Ponderosa SP	E-2
20	Priest Lake SP	A-1
21	Round Lake SP	A-1
22	Thousand Springs SP	I-3
23	Three Island Crossing SP	I-2
24	Winchester Lake SP	D-1

SP   State Park

IDAHO

★2170★ **Idaho Department of Parks & Recreation**
5657 Warm Springs Ave
Boise, ID 83716
(208) 334-4199 - Phone
(208) 334-3741 - Fax
(208) 514-2490 - Employment
(208) 334-4180 - Volunteering
Web: www.idahoparks.org
Manages 26 state parks (including historic sites and natural areas) and three visitor centers where interstate highways cross into Idaho. Develops and maintains trails and provides facilities for trail users. Administers registration program for boats, snowmobiles, and other off-road vehicles. Promotes boating safety programs, and monitors water quality issues of the state's rivers, streams, and lakes.

★2171★ **Idaho Department of Fish & Game**
PO Box 25
Boise, ID 83707
(208) 334-3700 - Phone
(208) 334-2114 - Fax
Web: www.state.id.us/fishgame
Operates 35 wildlife management areas for hunting, fishing, and other public uses. Administers licenses for fishing and hunting, offers hunter education programs, and manages 19 fish hatcheries.

Key to campsite classification:

- **Primitive campsites** — No amenities at site; camping area not defined.
- **Standard campsites** — Any defined campsite, either tent pad or RV pad/area (may include: table, and/or grill).
- **Serviced campsites** — Any defined campsite, either tent pad or RV pad/area, with water, electricity and/or sewer at site (may include: table, and/or grill).

★2172★ **BEAR LAKE STATE PARK**
PO Box 297
Paris, ID 83261
Web: www.idahoparks.org/parks/bearlake.aspx
Phone: 208-847-1045; **Fax:** 208-847-1056; **Toll Free:** 866-634-3246
Size: 966 acres. **Elevation:** 5,900 feet. **Location:** In southeastern Idaho, 20 miles south of Montpelier. **Facilities:** 48 campsites, including standard campsites (some with electricity), 1 primitive group camp, and 2 group camps with water and electricity; group picnic shelter; boat ramp, beaches, volleyball area.

Activities: Camping, swimming, fishing, boating, water skiing, snowmobiling, interpretive programs. **Special Features:** Park is located in a high mountain valley in the southeast corner of Idaho. Bear Lake is 20 miles long and 8 miles wide, with half of the lake in Idaho and half in Utah. In summer the lake draws water sports enthusiasts, and in winter visitors to the park can snowmobile or fish for the Bonneville cisco, which is found nowhere else on earth. Bear Lake National Wildlife Refuge is located adjacent to the park (see entry in national wildlife refuges section).

★2173★ **BRUNEAU DUNES STATE PARK**
27608 Sand Dunes Rd
Mountain Home, ID 83647
Web: www.parksandrecreation.idaho.gov/parks/
    bruneaudunesstatepark.aspx
Phone: 208-366-7919; **Fax:** 208-366-2844
Size: 4,800 acres. **Elevation:** 2,470 feet. **Location:** 18 miles southwest of Mountain Home, in southwestern Idaho. **Facilities:** 98 campsites, including 82 with water and electricity, group campsite, 2 rental cabins, showers, flush toilets, hiking trails, equestrian trails, equestrian facility, boat ramps, group picnic shelter, observatory, educational center, nature store. **Activities:** Camping, swimming, fishing, boating (electric motors only), hiking, horseback riding, sledding, sky watching, guided nature walks, interpretive programs. **Special Features:** Park features a 470-foot-tall sand dune, the tallest single-structured sand dune in North America. Visitors are allowed to climb the dunes, but vehicles are not allowed on them. Visitors to the park can also view stars at the state's only public observatory, which is located here. In addition, the park is part of the world-famous Snake River Birds of Prey Area, and the visitor center has information on all birds of prey as well as insects, fossils, wildlife, and sand dunes.

★2174★ **CASTLE ROCKS STATE PARK**
Box 69
Almo, ID 83312
Web: www.idahoparks.org/parks/castlerocks.aspx
Phone: 208-824-5519
Size: 1,240 acres. **Elevation:** 5,620-6,540 feet. **Location:** In Almo, in south central Idaho, south of Burley. **Facilities:** Under development. Primitive camping available at nearby City of Rocks National Reserve. **Activities:** Hiking, mountain biking, horseback riding, picnicking, wildlife viewing, rock climbing. **Special Features:** Idaho's newest state park, located adjacent to City of Rocks National Reserve, is a former ranch that includes examples of early 20th Century ranching structures, irrigated pastures, and striking scenery. Some of its spires rival those at City of Rocks and offer exceptional rock climbing. The park also protects some of the most pristine archeological sites in southern Idaho. Wildlife found here include mule deer, mountain

lion, bighorn sheep, and the state's first recorded ringtail. Bird-watching is also excellent.

★2175★ COEUR D'ALENE PARKWAY STATE PARK
2750 Kathleen Ave, Suite 1
Coeur d'Alene, ID 83815
Web: www.idahoparks.org/parks/coeurdaleneparkway.aspx
Phone: 208-699-2224
Size: 34 acres. Elevation: 2,187 feet. Location: Adjacent to Coeur d'Alene Drive in the city of Coeur d'Alene, which is located in northern ID, east of Spokane, WA. Facilities: Roadside picnic tables, group picnic area, an exercise course, restrooms, trails, boat launch facility, docks. Activities: Boating, fishing, hiking, bicycling. Special Features: The Coeur d'Alene Parkway lies along the north shore of Lake Coeur d'Alene, following Centennial Trail east from Coeur d'Alene to Higgens Point. More than 1,000 feet of public shoreline parallels the path of this linear park.

★2176★ DWORSHAK STATE PARK
PO Box 2028
Orofino, ID 83544
Web: www.idahoparks.org/parks/dworshak.aspx
Phone: 208-476-5994; Fax: 208-476-7225; Toll Free: 866-634-3246
Size: 850 acres. Elevation: 1,600 feet. Location: In north central Idaho, 24 miles northwest of Orofino. Facilities: 105 campsites (many with water and electricity), 4 camping cabins, group camp (lodge with 8 bunk-style group cabins, another cabin that sleeps 4, and modern kitchen facilities), showers, flush toilets, group shelter, fish cleaning station, meeting facility, marina with 101 boat slips, boat ramps, playground, volleyball area, horseshoe pits, archery range, hiking trails. Activities: Camping, swimming, fishing, boating, water-skiing, hiking, interpretive programs. Special Features: Located among trees and open meadows on the western shore of the 54-mile-long Dworshak Reservoir.

★2177★ EAGLE ISLAND STATE PARK
4000 W Hatchery Rd
Eagle, ID 83616
Web: www.idahoparks.org/parks/eagleisland.aspx
Phone: 208-939-0696; Fax: 208-939-9708
Size: 545 acres. Elevation: 2,724 feet. Location: 8 miles west of Boise. Facilities: Swimming beach, waterslide, picnic area, group shelters, trails (including hard paths, nature trail, and 5-mile equestrian trail), horseshoe pit, volleyball area, snack bar, restrooms. Activities: Swimming, fishing, boating (non-motorized), picnicking, wildlife viewing, hiking, bicycling, horseback riding. Special Features: Day-use park with a waterslide open on week-ends during the summer.

★2178★ FARRAGUT STATE PARK
13550 E Hwy 54
Athol, ID 83801
Web: www.idahoparks.org/parks/farragut.aspx
Phone: 208-683-2425; Fax: 208-683-7416

Size: 4,000 acres. Elevation: 2,054 feet. Location: In northern Idaho, 30 miles north of Coeur d'Alene. Facilities: 184 individual campsites 6 equestrian sites, 10 camping cabins, and 4 group camps (camping sites include primitive, standard, and serviced sites with electricity and water), showers, flush toilets, group picnic shelters, playground, volleyball area, disc golf course, trails (including paved), boat ramps and docks, shooting range, model airplane flying field, education center, museum. Activities: Camping, swimming, fishing, boating, water-skiing, hiking, bicycling, horseback riding, snowmobiling, sledding, cross-country skiing, radio-controlled model airplane flying, guided walks, interpretive programs. Special Features: Park is located on the shores of Lake Pend Oreille, Idaho's largest lake, at the foot of the Coeur d'Alene Mountains in the Bitterroot Range. This was formerly the site of the world's second-largest Naval training center, the Farragut Naval Training Station, and the park includes a Naval Training Center Museum and a historic brig.

★2179★ HARRIMAN STATE PARK
3489 Green Canyon Rd
Island Park, ID 83429
Web: www.idahoparks.org/parks/harriman.aspx
Phone: 208-558-7368; Fax: 208-558-7045; Toll Free: 866-634-3246
Size: 11,000 acres. Elevation: 6,120 feet. Location: Eastern Idaho, 18 miles north of Ashton on US 20. Facilities: Yurts, rental cabins (4-bedroom log home and 3-bedroom cabin, both fully furnished), dormitory facility with meeting room and kitchen (for groups of 15-40), showers, restrooms, trails, picnic area, warming hut for skiers, historic buildings. Activities: Fishing, hiking, mountain biking, horseback riding, cross-country skiing, wildlife viewing, guided nature walks, historic building tours. Special Features: Park lies within an 11,000-acre wildlife refuge in the greater Yellowstone ecosystem. Moose, elk, and sandhill cranes are common here, as is North America's largest waterfowl, the trumpeter swan. Henrys Fork, which meanders through the park, is considered one of the best fly-fishing streams in the country. From 1902 to 1977 the park acreage was owned by Union Pacific Railroad investors and served as a cattle ranch and private retreat of the Harriman and Guggenheim families. Tours of the railroad ranch buildings are available during the summer months.

★2180★ HELLS GATE STATE PARK
5100 Hells Gate Rd
Lewiston, ID 83501
Web: www.idahoparks.org/parks/hellsgate.aspx
Phone: 208-799-5015; Fax: 208-799-5187; Toll Free: 866-634-3246
Size: 960 acres. Elevation: 733 feet. Location: North central Idaho, 4 miles south of Lewiston on Snake River Avenue. Facilities: 93 campsites (including both standard sites and serviced sites with electricity), group camping, cabins, camp store, picnic sites, group shelter, playground, trails (including paved), marina with more than 100 slips, public boat launch, convenience store, boat rentals, beach, volleyball area, interpretive center, gift shop. Activities: Camping, swimming, fishing, boating, jet boat rides, hiking, horseback riding, mountain biking, guided nature walks, interpretive programs. Special Features: Park is a gateway to

Hells Canyon, the deepest river gorge in North America, and jet boat excursions into the canyon leave on a regular basis from the park's docks. The park is also a gateway to Lewis and Clark country, and the Discovery Center at the park features indoor educational displays, a two-acre outdoor interpretive plaza along the banks of the Snake River, and a film on the journey of Lewis and Clark through Idaho. The park has a long season of warm weather, and it does not snow there in winter. (For additional information about Hells Canyon, see entry on the Hells Canyon National Recreation Area in the national forests section.)

★2181★ HENRYS LAKE STATE PARK

3917 E 5100 North
Island Park, ID 83429
Web: www.idahoparks.org/parks/henryslake.aspx
Phone: 208-558-7532; **Toll Free:** 866-634-3246
Size: 585 acres. **Elevation:** 6,470 feet. **Location:** In eastern Idaho, 15 miles from Yellowstone National Park **Facilities:** 45 campsites (some with electricity and water), camping cabins, showers, flush toilets, modern fish cleaning station, boat ramp, trails. **Activities:** Camping, fishing, hiking, mountain biking, guided nature walks. **Special Features:** Henrys Lake is a high mountain lake where the trout fishing is considered among the finest in the west. The park opens the Thursday before Memorial day and closes on October 31st, weather permitting.

★2182★ HEYBURN STATE PARK

1291 Chatcolet Rd
Plummer, ID 83851
Web: www.idahoparks.org/parks/heyburn.aspx
Phone: 208-686-1308; **Fax:** 208-686-3003; **Toll Free:** 866-634-3246
Size: 5,744 acres land; 2,332 acres water. **Elevation:** 2,128-3,366 feet. **Location:** Northern Idaho, south of Coeur d'Alene. **Facilities:** 132 campsites (some with electricity), 2 rental cottages, picnic shelters, trails, restrooms, showers, boat ramp, marina, store, cruise boat, volleyball area, playground, developed wildlife viewing site, interpretive center. **Activities:** Camping, swimming, fishing, boating, water-skiing, sailing, canoeing, hiking, mountain biking, horseback riding, cross-country skiing, waterfowl hunting, guided nature walks, wildlife observation, interpretive programs. **Special Features:** Created in 1908, Heyburn is the oldest state park in the Pacific Northwest and includes 3 lakes: Chatcolet, Benewah, and Hidden lakes. In addition, the Saint Joe River meanders along the eastern boundary of the park. Before it was a park, this area was a gathering place for the Coeur d'Alene Indian tribe.

★2183★ LAKE CASCADE STATE PARK

PO Box 709
Cascade, ID 83616
Web: www.idahoparks.org/parks/lakecascade.aspx
Phone: 208-382-6544; **Fax:** 208-382-4071; **Toll Free:** 866-634-3246
Size: 4,450 acres. **Elevation:** 4,825 feet. **Location:** In southwestern Idaho, 75 miles north of Boise on Hwy 55. **Facilities:** 300 standard campsites, including a group camp and a yurt group complex, 175 individual sites in 6 developed campgrounds, and primitive camping areas; restrooms; trails (including paved); group picnic shelter, playground, horseshoe pits; 6 boat launch ramps, boat docks. **Activities:** Camping, boating, sailing, windsurfing, fishing, hiking, mountain biking, cross-country skiing, ice fishing. **Special Features:** Park is nestled in the mountains of central Idaho and offers year-round recreational opportunities.

★2184★ LAKE WALCOTT STATE PARK

959 E Minidoka Dam
Rupert, ID 83350
Web: www.idahoparks.org/parks/lakewalcott.aspx
Phone: 208-436-1258; **Fax:** 208-436-1268
Size: 65 acres. **Elevation:** 4,700 feet. **Location:** In south central Idaho, 11 miles northeast of Rupert. **Facilities:** 23 campsites, including standard sites as well as an RV campground with water and electric hookups; showers and restrooms; paved trails; boat ramp; 3 picnic shelters, disc golf course, volleyball area, horseshoe pits, playground. **Activities:** Camping, boating, fishing, hiking, bicycling, wildlife viewing, disc golf. **Special Features:** Park is located at the northwest end of the Bureau of Reclamation's Lake Walcott Project and serves as a convenient base from which to explore the Minidoka National Wildlife Refuge (see entry in national wildlife refuges section), which has some of the best birding in southern Idaho.

★2185★ LAND OF THE YANKEE FORK STATE PARK

PO Box 1086
Challis, ID 83226
Web: www.idahoparks.org/parks/yankeefork.aspx
Phone: 208-879-5244; **Fax:** 208-879-5243
Size: 21 acres. **Elevation:** 5,001 feet. **Location:** Central Idaho, south of Challis. **Facilities:** Museum store, restroom facilities, walking path (&), hiking trail, interpretive center. Camping opportunities are available at Forest Service and Bureau of Land Management campgrounds nearby. Whitewater rafting is also available nearby. **Activities:** Museum exhibits, gold panning station, interpretive programs, special events. **Special Features:** Park is part of the larger Land of the Yankee Fork Historic Area managed jointly by the Idaho Department of Parks and Recreation, the Salmon-Challis National Forest, and the Bureau of Land Management. The Interpretive Center in Challis has museum exhibits and provides information on local mining history and area attractions.

★2186★ LUCKY PEAK STATE PARK

9725 E Hwy 21
Boise, ID 83716
Web: www.idahoparks.org/parks/luckypeak.aspx
Phone: 208-334-2432
Size: 240 acres. **Elevation:** 2,750 feet. **Location:** 10 miles southeast of Boise. **Facilities:** Camping and hiking (backcountry yurts); full-service marina, 2 boat ramps, watercraft rental, convenience store (Spring Shores); beach, restrooms, changing areas, showers, picnic tables (Sandy Point); picnic tables, 3 group shelters, restrooms (Discovery). **Activities:** Backcountry camping, hiking, boating, fishing, swimming, ice fishing. **Special Features:** Park consists of four distinct units, three of which

9. State Parks

are located near Lucky Peak Reservoir: 1) Discovery, a roadside park; 2) Sandy Point, a popular beach below the foot of Lucky Peak Dam; 3) Spring Shores, which has lakeside access for water enthusiasts; and 4) Idaho City Backcountry Yurts, with camping opportunities and a trail system.

★2187★ MASSACRE ROCKS STATE PARK
3592 N Park Ln
American Falls, ID 83211
Web: www.idahoparks.org/parks/massacrerocks.aspx
Phone: 208-548-2672; Fax: 208-548-2671; Toll Free: 866-634-3246
Size: 990 acres. Elevation: 4,400 feet. Location: Southeastern Idaho, 10 miles west of American Falls. Facilities: 43 campsites (including sites with water and electrical hookups), restrooms, showers, camp store, horse rest area, trails, nature trail, boat launch area, docks, visitor center. Activities: Camping, fishing, boating, hiking, bicycling, mountain biking, rock climbing, wildlife viewing, interpretive programs. Special Features: Situated on the Snake River, Park is a popular place for birdwatching, with more than 200 species of birds sighted here. The park also has cottontail, jackrabbit, coyote, muskrat, and beaver, as well as some 300 species of desert plants. Located two miles from the park is Register Rock, a huge boulder that has the signatures of Oregon Trail emigrants.

★2188★ MCCROSKEY STATE PARK
2750 Kathleen Ave
Coeur d'Alene, ID 83815
Web: www.idahoparks.org/parks/maryminervamccroskey.aspx
Phone: 208-666-6711
Size: 5,300 acres. Elevation: 3,039-4,324 feet. Location: Northern Idaho, 26 miles north of Moscow. Facilities: 9 campsites (primitive and standard), group picnic shelter, multi-use trails. Activities: Camping, hiking, mountain biking, horseback riding. Special Features: The highlight of this ridgeline park is an 18-mile skyline drive on unimproved roads that provides spectacular views of the Palouse prairie as well as access to 32 miles of trails. (The road is not recommended for RVs and may also be too rough for some cars.) The park is named for Mary Minerva McCroskey and is dedicated to the memory of frontier women and the hardships they endured.

★2189★ OLD MISSION STATE PARK
Box 30
Cataldo, ID 83810
Web: www.idahoparks.org/parks/oldmission.aspx
Phone: 208-682-3814; Fax: 208-682-4032
Size: 18 acres. Elevation: 2,200 feet. Location: Northern Idaho, 1 mile east of Cataldo. Facilities: Historic buildings, picnic areas, restrooms, trails, boat ramp, interpretive center. Activities: Fishing, boating, hiking, guided walks, interpretive programs. Special Features: Park features the oldest standing building in Idaho, the Mission of the Sacred Heart. The mission was built between 1850 and 1853 by the Coeur d'Alene Indians and Jesuit missionaries. The building has walls 18 inches thick and was built entirely without nails. The Coeur d'Alene Indians

still consider it their mission and return each year on August 15 to celebrate the Feast of the Assumption.

★2190★ PONDEROSA STATE PARK
Box 89
McCall, ID 83638
Web: www.idahoparks.org/parks/ponderosa.aspx
Phone: 208-634-2164; Fax: 208-634-5370
Size: 1,515 acres. Elevation: 5,050 feet. Location: Southwestern Idaho, 2 miles northeast of McCall city center. Facilities: 117 primitive and developed campsites (some with electricity), rental cabins and yurts, group picnic shelters, trails, restrooms, showers, boat ramps, volleyball area, horseshoe pits, interpretive center. Activities: Camping, swimming, fishing, boating, hiking, mountain biking, cross-country skiing, snowshoeing, guided walks, interpretive programs. Special Features: Park covers most of a peninsula that juts into Payette Lake near McCall, and a scenic overlook offers a spectacular view of the lake. The park's namesake Ponderosa pines—some 500 years old and 150 feet high—are the most noticeable species of tree here, but Douglas fir, grand fir, lodgepole pine, and western larch also grow in the park. The park has more than 14 miles of groomed Nordic ski trails and has been selected as the venue for the 2008 Masters World Cup, a prestigious Nordic skiing event.

★2191★ PRIEST LAKE STATE PARK
314 Indian Creek Park Rd
Coolin, ID 83821
Web: www.idahoparks.org/parks/priestlake.aspx
Phone: 208-443-2200; Fax: 208-443-3893; Toll Free: 866-634-3246
Size: 755 acres. Elevation: 2,440 feet. Location: Northern Idaho, 33 miles north of Priest River. Facilities: 151 primitive, basic, and developed campsites (some with electricity), 5 camping cabins, isolated group camp with its own beach, restrooms, showers, group picnic shelter, trails, swimming beach, boat ramps, docks, boat rentals, horseshoe pits, volleyball area. Activities: Camping, swimming, fishing, boating, water-skiing, hiking, cross-country skiing, ice fishing, snowmobiling, guided nature walks, interpretive programs. Special Features: Park lies just 30 miles from the Canadian border, below the crest of the Selkirk Mountains. It sits along the shores of Priest Lake, which is 19 miles long and more than 300 feet deep. Summer activities focus around the lake, but in winter the park offers more than 200 miles of marked, groomed snowmobile trails.

★2192★ ROUND LAKE STATE PARK
PO Box 170
Sagle, ID 83860
Web: www.idahoparks.org/parks/roundlake.aspx
Phone: 208-263-3489; Toll Free: 866-634-3246
Size: 142 acres. Elevation: 2,122 feet. Location: Northern Idaho, 10 miles south of Sandpoint. Facilities: 51 standard campsites with central water, showers, and restroom facilities, group picnic shelter, horseshoe pits, hiking trails, boat dock, boat launch, information center. Activities: Camping, swimming, fishing, boating (electric motors only), bicycling, hiking, wildlife viewing, cross-country skiing, ice fishing, ice skating,

guided nature walks, interpretive programs. **Special Features:** Surrounded by a forest of towering pine, hemlock, larch, and red cedar, 58-acre Round Lake is the product of glacial activity dating back to the Pleistocene Epoch. The lake is relatively shallow, only about 37 feet at its deepest, and offers good trout fishing. Hikers on the park's trails will find beaver lodges, dams, and ponds, and might glimpse a resident moose.

★2193★ THOUSAND SPRINGS STATE PARK

Box 149
Hagerman, ID 83332
Web: www.idahoparks.org/parks/thousandsprings.aspx
Phone: 208-837-4505
Size: 110 acres. **Elevation:** 2,800 feet. **Location:** 1074 E 2350 South in Hagerman. **Facilities:** Malad Gorge: trails, picnic areas; Billingsley Creek: indoor horse riding arena; Box Springs Canyon: hiking trail, viewing platform; Niagara Springs: restrooms, picnic tables, group picnic shelter. **Activities:** Primitive camping, hiking, wildlife viewing, fishing, picnicking. **Special Features:** Thousand Springs is located in an area known as Magic Valley and encompasses four individual units: 1) Malad Gorge, where the Malad River runs down stairstep falls into the Devils Washbowl, then cuts through a 250-foot gorge on its way to the Snake River, 2-1/2 miles downstream. Views of the gorge are best from a sturdy bridge that crosses the canyon. 2) Billingsley Creek, located in the Hagerman Valley, was formerly known as Emerald Valley Ranch and used primarily for agriculture. It was purchased for state park use in 2001. 3) Earl M Hardy Box Canyon Springs Nature Preserve, which features a 20-foot waterfall and springs that flow at a rate of 180,000 gallons per minute. 4) Niagara Springs, which tumble down the canyon side at 250 cubic feet per second, with water the icy blue of glaciers.

★2194★ THREE ISLAND CROSSING STATE PARK

Box 609
Glenns Ferry, ID 83623
Web: www.idahoparks.org/parks/threeislandcrossing.aspx
Phone: 208-366-2394; **Fax:** 208-366-7913; **Toll Free:** 866-634-3246
Size: 613 acres. **Elevation:** 2,484 feet. **Location:** Southwestern Idaho, south of Mountain Home, 4 miles off I-84. **Facilities:** 82 full-service campsites, cabins, showers, restrooms, group picnic shelter, hiking trail, interpretive center. **Activities:** Camping, fishing, hiking, interpretive programs. **Special Features:** Pioneer travelers on the Oregon Trail crossed the Snake River at this site, one of the most famous river crossings on the historic trail. The Glenns Ferry community sponsors a crossing reenactment the second Saturday of each August. Visitors to the park can learn about pioneer emigrants and Native American history at the park's Oregon Trail History and Education Center.

★2195★ WINCHESTER LAKE STATE PARK

PO Box 186
Winchester, ID 83555
Web: www.idahoparks.org/parks/winchesterlake.aspx
Phone: 208-924-7563; **Fax:** 208-924-5941; **Toll Free:** 866-634-3246
Size: 418 acres. **Elevation:** 3,900 feet. **Location:** North central

Idaho, 36 miles south of Lewiston. **Facilities:** 69 campsites (many with electricity), 4 rental yurts, restrooms, showers, group picnic shelter, playground, trails, boat ramp. **Activities:** Camping, fishing, boating (electric motors only), hiking, mountain biking, cross-country skiing, ice fishing, ice skating, guided nature walks, interpretive programs. **Special Features:** Winters at this park are long and cold with ample snowfall, while summers are short, with warm days and cool nights. The park offers year-round recreation activities, with a primitive camping area and yurts available all year. Wildlife at the park includes white-tailed deer, Canada geese, muskrats, Steller's jay, osprey, and Columbian ground squirrels. The Wolf Education and Research Center is located one mile from the entrance to the park.

Illinois State Parks

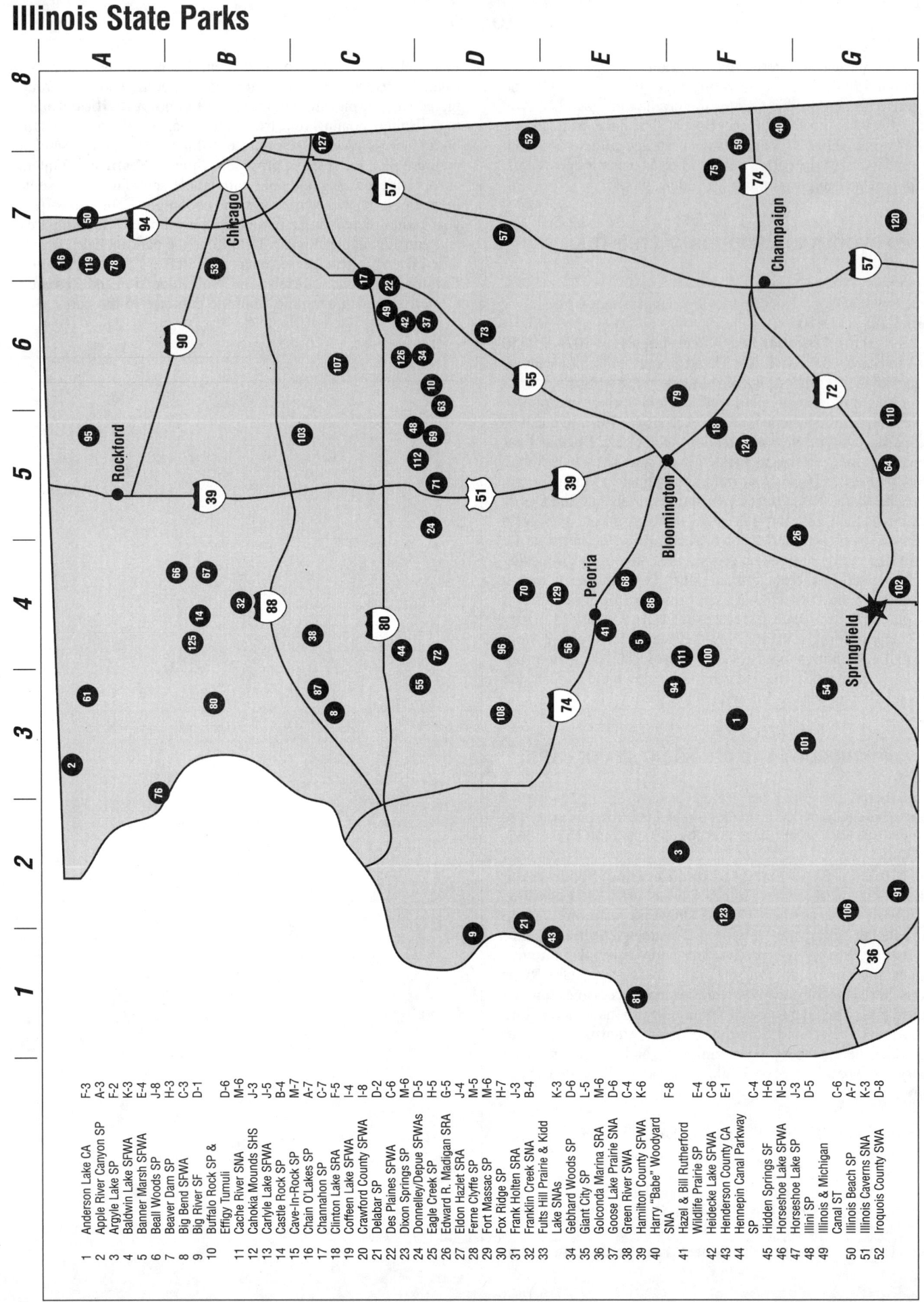

1	Anderson Lake CA	F-3
2	Apple River Canyon SP	A-3
3	Argyle Lake SP	F-2
4	Baldwin Lake SFWA	K-3
5	Banner Marsh SFWA	E-4
6	Beall Woods SP	J-8
7	Beaver Dam SP	H-3
8	Big Bend SFWA	C-3
9	Big River SF	D-1
10	Buffalo Rock SP &	
	Effigy Tumuli	D-6
11	Cache River SNA	M-6
12	Cahokia Mounds SHS	J-3
13	Carlyle Lake SFWA	J-5
14	Castle Rock SP	B-4
15	Cave-In-Rock SP	M-7
16	Chain O'Lakes SP	A-7
17	Channahon SP	C-7
18	Clinton Lake SRA	F-5
19	Coffeen Lake SFWA	I-4
20	Crawford County SFWA	I-8
21	Delabar SP	D-2
22	Des Plaines SFWA	C-6
23	Dixon Springs SP	M-6
24	Donnelley/Depue SFWAs	D-5
25	Eagle Creek SP	H-5
26	Edward R. Madigan SRA	G-5
27	Eldon Hazlet SRA	J-4
28	Ferne Clyffe SP	M-5
29	Fort Massac SP	M-6
30	Fox Ridge SP	H-7
31	Frank Holten SRA	J-3
32	Franklin Creek SNA	B-4
33	Fults Hill Prairie & Kidd	
	Lake SNAs	K-3
34	Gebhard Woods SP	D-6
35	Giant City SP	L-5
36	Golconda Marina SRA	M-6
37	Goose Lake Prairie SNA	D-6
38	Green River SWA	C-4
39	Hamilton County SFWA	K-6
40	Harry "Babe" Woodyard	
	SNA	F-8
41	Hazel & Bill Rutherford	
	Wildlife Prairie SP	E-4
42	Heidecke Lake SFWA	C-6
43	Henderson County CA	E-1
44	Hennepin Canal Parkway	
	SP	C-4
45	Hidden Springs SF	H-6
46	Horseshoe Lake SFWA	N-5
47	Horseshoe Lake SP	J-3
48	Illini SP	D-5
49	Illinois & Michigan	
	Canal ST	C-6
50	Illinois Beach SP	A-7
51	Illinois Caverns SNA	K-3
52	Iroquois County SWA	D-8

434

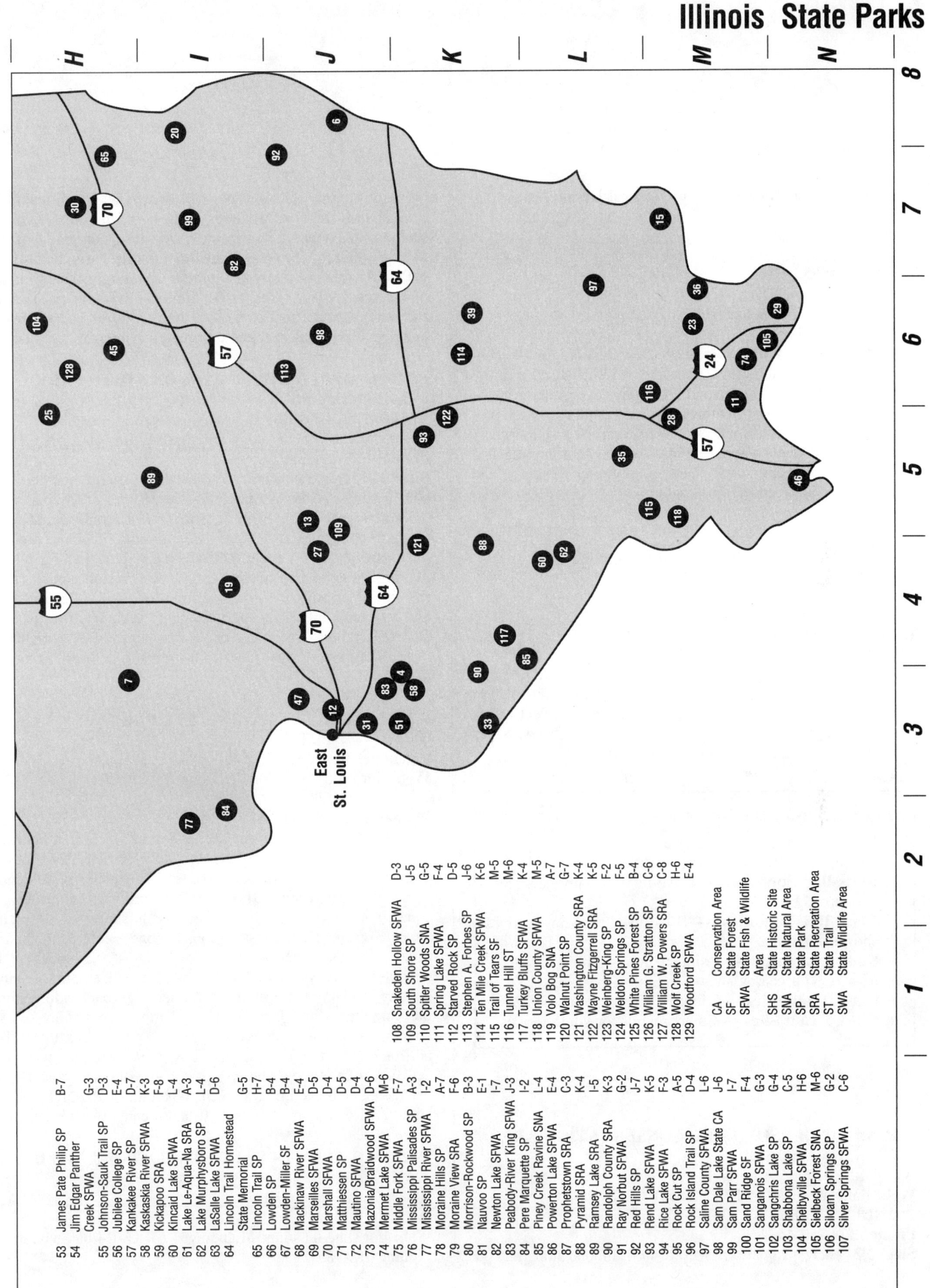

East
St. Louis

53	James Pate Philip SP	B-7
54	Jim Edgar Panther	
	Creek SFWA	G-3
55	Johnson-Sauk Trail SP	D-3
56	Jubilee College SP	E-4
57	Kankakee River SP	D-7
58	Kaskaskia River SFWA	K-3
59	Kickapoo SRA	F-8
60	Kincaid Lake SFWA	L-4
61	Lake Le-Aqua-Na SRA	A-3
62	Lake Murphysboro SP	L-4
63	LaSalle Lake SFWA	D-6
64	Lincoln Trail Homestead	
	State Memorial	G-5
65	Lincoln Trail SP	H-7
66	Lowden SP	B-4
67	Lowden-Miller SF	B-4
68	Mackinaw River SFWA	E-4
69	Marseilles SFWA	D-5
70	Marshall SFWA	D-4
71	Matthiessen SP	D-5
72	Mautino SFWA	D-4
73	Mazonia/Braidwood SFWA	D-6
74	Mermet Lake SFWA	M-6
75	Middle Fork SFWA	F-7
76	Mississippi Palisades SP	A-3
77	Mississippi River SFWA	I-2
78	Moraine Hills SP	A-7
79	Moraine View SRA	F-6
80	Morrison-Rockwood SP	B-3
81	Nauvoo SP	E-1
82	Newton Lake SFWA	I-7
83	Peabody-River King SFWA	J-3
84	Pere Marquette SP	I-2
85	Piney Creek Ravine SNA	L-4
86	Powerton Lake SFWA	E-4
87	Prophetstown SRA	C-3
88	Pyramid SRA	K-4
89	Ramsey Lake SRA	I-5
90	Randolph County SRA	K-3
91	Ray Norbut SFWA	G-2
92	Red Hills SP	J-7
93	Rend Lake SFWA	K-5
94	Rice Lake SFWA	F-3
95	Rock Cut SP	A-5
96	Rock Island Trail SP	D-4
97	Saline County SFWA	L-6
98	Sam Dale Lake State CA	J-6
99	Sam Parr SFWA	I-7
100	Sand Ridge SF	F-4
101	Sanganois SFWA	G-3
102	Sangchris Lake SP	G-4
103	Shabbona Lake SP	C-5
104	Shelbyville SFWA	H-6
105	Sielbeck Forest SNA	M-6
106	Siloam Springs SP	G-2
107	Silver Springs SFWA	C-6

108	Snakeden Hollow SFWA	D-3
109	South Shore SP	J-5
110	Spitler Woods SNA	G-5
111	Spring Lake SFWA	F-4
112	Starved Rock SP	D-5
113	Stephen A. Forbes SP	J-6
114	Ten Mile Creek SFWA	K-6
115	Trail of Tears SF	M-5
116	Tunnel Hill ST	M-6
117	Turkey Bluffs SFWA	K-4
118	Union County SFWA	M-5
119	Volo Bog SNA	A-7
120	Walnut Point SP	G-7
121	Washington County SRA	K-4
122	Wayne Fitzgerrell SRA	K-5
123	Weinberg-King SP	F-2
124	Weldon Springs SP	F-5
125	White Pines Forest SP	B-4
126	William G. Stratton SP	C-6
127	William W. Powers SRA	C-8
128	Wolf Creek SP	H-6
129	Woodford SFWA	E-4

CA	Conservation Area
SF	State Forest
SFWA	State Fish & Wildlife
	Area
SHS	State Historic Site
SNA	State Natural Area
SP	State Park
SRA	State Recreation Area
ST	State Trail
SWA	State Wildlife Area

ILLINOIS

★2196★ **Illinois Department of Natural Resources**
1 Natural Resources Way
Springfield, IL 62702
(217) 782-6302 - Phone
(217) 782-9552 - Fax
(217) 782-9175 - TDD
(618) 462-1181 - Volunteering
Web: dnr.state.il.us
Manages parks and other recreation sites, including trails, conservation areas, state forests, fish and wildlife areas, wildlife management areas, and state parks. Operates two state museums and four fish hatcheries. Conducts environmental education programs and promotes the state's nature preserves system to protect wildlife resources and habitats. Administers hunting and fishing licensing and offers hunting, trapping, boating, and snowmobile safety education programs.

★2197★ **Illinois Historic Preservation Agency**
313 S 6th St
Springfield, Illinois 62701
(217) 785-1511 - Phone
(217) 785-7937 - Fax
Web: www.state.il.us/HPA
Operates more than 60 historic site and memorials, offers educational services, and oversees federally-mandated preservation programs. Administers the Abraham Lincoln Presidential Library in Springfield, a museum and research facility devoted to the study of Abraham Lincoln and the Civil War.

Key to campsite classification:

- **Class A campsites** — Drive-in sites with electrical hookups and nearby shower facilities.
- **Class B/E campsites** — Drive-in sites with electrical hookups.
- **Class B/S campsites** — Drive-in sites with nearby shower facilities.
- **Class C campsites** — Primitive drive-in sites; or walk-in sites with nearby shower facilities.
- **Class D campsites** — Primitive hike-in or boat-in sites.
- **Class Y campsites** — Campgrounds for youth groups.

★2198★ **ANDERSON LAKE CONSERVATION AREA**
647 N IL Hwy 100
Astoria, IL 61501
Web: dnr.state.il.us/Lands/Landmgt/PARKS/R1/
ANDERSON.HTM
Phone: 309-759-4484
Size: 2,247 acres. **Location:** West central Illinois, along IL 100 in Fulton County, 11 miles north of Browning. **Facilities:** Class C campsites (tents or trailers), showers, picnic areas, 2 picnic shelters, boat docks, 2 boat ramps. **Activities:** Camping, boating, fishing, hunting. **Special Features:** In the early half of the 1900s, Anderson Lake was a private shooting grounds for one of the many duck clubs in the Illinois River valley. Today's recreational opportunities include dove, squirrel, and waterfowl hunting, as well as exceptional bluegill fishing.

★2199★ **APPLE RIVER CANYON STATE PARK**
8763 E Canyon Rd
Apple River, IL 61001
Web: dnr.state.il.us/Lands/Landmgt/PARKS/R1/APPLE.HTM
Phone: 815-745-3302
Size: 297 acres. **Location:** In Jo Daviess County, near the Wisconsin border in the extreme northwest corner of Illinois, about 2.5 hours west of Chicago. **Facilities:** 45 Class C campsites, 2 Class C campsites (&), youth campground, 4 picnic areas, 3 picnic shelters (2 &), trails. **Activities:** Camping, fishing, hiking, hunting. **Special Features:** Centuries of erosion helped create the park's landscape of massive limestone cliffs, deep ravines, and timbered hills. The park contains such wildlife as deer, squirrels, rabbits, raccoons, eagles, hawks, and 47 varieties of birds. More than 165 varieties of flowers can be seen throughout the park.

★2200★ **ARGYLE LAKE STATE PARK**
640 Argyle Park Rd
Colchester, IL 62326
Web: dnr.state.il.us/Lands/Landmgt/PARKS/R1/
ARGYLE.HTM
Phone: 309-776-3422
Size: 1,710 acres. **Location:** 7 miles east of Macomb. **Facilities:** 86 Class A campsites with showers and electricity, 24 Class B/E sites (electrical hookups), 18 Class C campsites with vehicle access and restrooms, 31 Class D (primitive) campsites, an equestrian campground, restrooms with showers, 10 picnic areas, 3 group shelters, playground, concession stand, hiking trails (5 miles), equestrian trails (7 miles), boat and canoe rentals, boat launch, docks, visitor center. **Activities:** Camping, fishing, boating (10 HP limit), canoeing, hiking, horseback riding, hunting, snowmobiling, sledding, ice skating, ice fishing, cross-country skiing, interpretive programs. **Special Features:** The portion of the park now occupied by its 93-acre lake was once called Argyle Hollow and was part of the old stagecoach route between Galena and Beardstown. When the state purchased the land in 1948, a dam was erected that created the lake.

★2201★ **BALDWIN LAKE STATE FISH & WILDLIFE AREA**
10981 Conservation Rd
Baldwin, IL 62217
Web: dnr.state.il.us/lands/Landmgt/PARKS/R4/baldwin.htm
Phone: 618-785-2555

Size: 2,018-acre lake. **Location:** Within the Kaskaskia River State Fish & Wildlife area, near Baldwin, Illinois, off Risdon School Road. **Facilities:** Primitive camping areas, picnic facilities, toilets and drinking water, boat ramps, boat docks. **Activities:** Camping, fishing, boating (50 HP limit), picnicking, waterfowl viewing. **Special Features:** Baldwin Lake is a cooling lake owned by the Illinois Power Company and leased to the state for public recreational use. The lake and adjoining lands are designated as a waterfowl and wildlife refuge, with peak populations of 10,000 geese and 20,000 ducks seen in the area during winter. Approximately 200 resident giant Canada geese nest on the lake levees, and, starting in April, broods of goslings begin to appear.

★2202★ BANNER MARSH STATE FISH & WILDLIFE AREA

19721 N US 24
Canton, IL 61520
Web: dnr.state.il.us/Lands/Landmgt/PARKS/R1/banner.htm
Phone: 309-647-9184
Size: 4,363 acres. **Location:** 25 miles southwest of Peoria on US 24. **Facilities:** Picnic areas, boat ramps, restrooms, area for training hunting dogs and conducting field trials. **Activities:** Boating, canoeing, fishing, hunting, youth group camping (walk-in or boat-in). **Special Features:** Banner Marsh is made up of more than 200 individual bodies of water that, together with its land resources, provide habitat for migrating and local waterfowl, numerous species of fish, and other wildlife.

★2203★ BEALL WOODS STATE PARK

9285 Beall Woods Ave
Mount Carmel, IL 62863
Web: dnr.state.il.us/Lands/Landmgt/PARKS/R5/BEALL.HTM
Phone: 618-298-2442
Size: 636 acres. **Location:** Southeastern Illinois, in Wabash County, 6 miles south of Mount Carmel on Route 1 near Keensburg. **Facilities:** 16 class C campsites with restrooms, picnic areas with shelters and playgrounds, hiking trails, visitor center. **Activities:** Camping, boating (electric motors only), fishing, hiking, hunting, interpretive programs. **Special Features:** Located on the banks of the Wabash River, Beall Woods has one of the few remaining tracts of virgin timber east of the Mississippi River, with trees over 120 feet tall and more than three feet in diameter.

★2204★ BEAVER DAM STATE PARK

14548 Beaver Dam Ln
Plainview, IL 62685
Web: dnr.state.il.us/Lands/Landmgt/PARKS/R4/beaver.htm
Phone: 217-854-8020
Size: 750 acres. **Location:** West central Illinois, in Macoupin County, 7 miles south of Carlinville. **Facilities:** Class A trailer camping area with electricity at each pad and a shower building with flush toilets, a separate tent camping area with nearby restrooms and water, group camping area, rental cabin, picnic area, playground, 4 pavilions, concession stand, boat rentals, boat ramp and docks, 59-acre stocked lake, hiking trails (8 miles), archery range. **Activities:** Camping, boating (electric motors only), fishing, hiking, archery (broadhead points prohibited), cross-country skiing, sledding, ice skating, ice fishing. **Special Features:** Although the beaver is virtually gone from this area, the park was named for beaver dams which formed the lake more than a century ago.

★2205★ BIG BEND STATE FISH & WILDLIFE AREA

PO Box 181
Prophetstown, IL 61277
Web: dnr.state.il.us/lands/Landmgt/PARKS/R1/BIGBEND.HTM
Phone: 815-537-2270
Size: 1,188 acres. **Location:** In northwest Illinois, in Whiteside County, 4 miles west of Prophetstown, along the Rock River on VanDamme Road and Banks Road. **Facilities:** None. **Activities:** Fishing (limited), hiking, hunting. **Special Features:** Area is located beside a bend in the Rock River.

★2206★ BIG RIVER STATE FOREST

RR 1, Box 118
Keithsburg, IL 61442
Web: dnr.state.il.us/Lands/Landmgt/PARKS/R1/BIGRIVER.HTM
Phone: 309-374-2496
Size: 2,900 acres. **Location:** Western Illinois, in Henderson County, 6 miles north of Oquawka on the Oquawka-Keithsburg blacktop. **Facilities:** Tent and trailer campsites (primitive), equestrian campground, horse rentals, picnic areas, shelters, 3 boat ramps, hiking trail, horseback riding trails, snowmobile trails, scenic roadways. **Activities:** Camping (including equestrian and group camping), boating, fishing, ice fishing, hiking, horseback riding, hunting, snowmobiling. **Special Features:** Forest is managed primarily to demonstrate sound forestry practices. A prominent landmark in the forest is its fire tower. In addition, to separate the forest into manageable components, 60 miles of firebreaks interlace Big River State Forest. When fires aren't a threat, hikers and horseback riders use the firebreaks as trails.

★2207★ BUFFALO ROCK STATE PARK & EFFIGY TUMULI

PO Box 2034
1300 N 27th Rd
Ottawa, IL 61350
Web: dnr.state.il.us/Lands/Landmgt/PARKS/I&M/EAST/BUFFALO/Home.htm
Phone: 815-433-2220
Size: 298 acres. **Location:** Northeastern Illinois, in LaSalle County, about 3 miles west of Ottawa on the bluffs of the Illinois River. **Facilities:** Primitive camping areas (no restrooms or drinking water), picnic areas, 2 shelters with restrooms and drinking water near each, playground, baseball diamond, nature trails, 2 observation decks. **Activities:** Camping, picnicking, hiking, wildlife viewing. **Special Features:** Park includes five contemporary earthen sculptures on the site of a former surface coal mine. Titled ''Effigy Tumuli'' in tribute to the Native American burial grounds that inspired it, this unique ''earth art''

9. State Parks

is one of the largest earthen sculptures ever built and the largest since Mount Rushmore. The five sculptures—a snake, a turtle, a catfish, a frog, and an insect called a water strider—represent animals native to the Illinois River region.

★2208★ CACHE RIVER STATE NATURAL AREA
930 Sunflower Ln
Belknap, IL 62908
Web: dnr.state.il.us/lands/landmgt/PARKS/R5/
    CACHERVR.HTM
Phone: 618-634-9678
Size: 14,314 acres. Location: In southernmost Illinois, just west of US 45 and south of IL 146, near Vienna. Facilities: Canoe trail (3-6 miles), bicycle trail (8 miles of the Tunnel Hill State Bicycle Trail), hiking trails (18 miles), wetlands center. Activities: Canoeing, fishing, hiking, bicycling, birding, wildlife viewing, hunting, interpretive programs. Special Features: Among the outstanding natural features in the area are massive cypress trees with bases that exceed 40 feet in circumference. Many are more than 1,000 years old, including one that has been designated as a state champion due to its huge trunk girth, towering height, and heavily branched canopy. Wetlands in the area are so important to migratory waterfowl and shorebirds that they've been designated a Wetland of International Importance.The area provides habitat for more than 100 plant and animal species that are listed by the state of Illinois as endangered or threatened.

★2209★ CAHOKIA MOUNDS STATE HISTORIC SITE
30 Ramey St
Collinsville, IL 62234
Web: www.cahokiamounds.com
Phone: 618-346-5160; Fax: 618-346-5162
Size: 2,200 acres. Location: Between Collinsville and East Saint Louis, off Highway 5570 (8 miles from downtown Saint Louis). Facilities: Interpretive center, gift shop. Activities: A variety of special events, craft classes, lecture series, tours, and interpretive programs year round. Special Features: Cahokia Mounds preserves the remains of the most sophisticated prehistoric native civilization north of Mexico. The site was inhabited from around AD 700-1400 and at its peak covered nearly six square miles and had a population of as many as 10-20,000 people. The largest of the earthen mounds preserved within the historic area is Monks Mound, which at 100 feet is the largest prehistoric earthen mound in the New World. Cahokia Mounds is recognized as a US Natural Historic Landmark and has also been designated a World Heritage Site by the United Nations Educational and Scientific Organization (UNESCO). The site is administered by the Illinois Historic Preservation Agency.

★2210★ CARLYLE LAKE STATE FISH & WILDLIFE AREA
RR 2
Vandalia, IL 62471
Web: dnr.state.il.us/lands/Landmgt/PARKS/R4/
    CARLYLE.HTM
Phone: 618-425-3533
Size: 9,500 acres. Location: West central Illinois, 60 miles east of Saint Louis, near Vandalia at the southwestern tip of Fayette County. Facilities: Boat ramps. Activities: Hunting, trapping (with restrictions), fishing, birdwatching. Special Features: As a major stopping point for migrating ducks and geese, area offers excellent waterfowl hunting opportunities. Fishing is available on more than 2,000 acres of the lake and on the Kaskaskia River.

★2211★ CASTLE ROCK STATE PARK
1365 W Castle Rd
Oregon, IL 61061
Web: dnr.state.il.us/Lands/Landmgt/PARKS/R1/
    CASTLE.HTM
Phone: 815-732-7329
Size: 1,995 acres. Location: Northwestern Illinois, 3 miles south of Oregon on Highway 2 in Ogle County. Facilities: Primitive canoe camping area; 3 picnic areas with shelters, playgrounds, toilets, and drinking water; hiking trails (6 miles); boat ramp. Additional campsites, picnic areas, and trails are planned. Activities: Boating, canoeing, fishing, hiking, hunting (limited), cross-country skiing, sledding. Special Features: Park lies along the west bank of the Rock River and is representative of the Rock River Hills area, with rock formations, ravines, and unique northern plant associations. Castle Rock is a large sandstone butte situated between Rock River and Highway 2. The rock is made up of Saint Peter sandstone and is one of the few places in Illinois where this type of sandstone comes to the surface, even though it underlies almost the whole state.

★2212★ CAVE-IN-ROCK STATE PARK
1 New State Park Rd
Box 338
Cave-In-Rock, IL 62919
Web: dnr.state.il.us/Lands/Landmgt/PARKS/R5/
    CAVEROCK.HTM
Phone: 618-289-4325
Size: 204 acres. Location: Southern Illinois, on the Ohio River in Hardin County, off IL 1. Facilities: 34 Class A campsites (with electricity), 25 Class B/S campsites, showers and restrooms in both camping areas, lodge with 4 duplex guest houses, restaurant, picnic areas, 4 picnic shelters, 3 developed playground areas, hiking trails, 2 boat ramps, full-service marina (nearby). Activities: Camping, boating, fishing, hiking. Special Features: Park is named for a 55-foot-wide cave atop the high bluffs overlooking the Ohio River. From 1797 to the mid-1830s, the cave served as a lair for outlaws, bandits, and river pirates who preyed on those traveling along the Ohio River.

★2213★ CHAIN O'LAKES STATE PARK
8916 Wilmot Rd
Spring Grove, IL 60081
Web: dnr.state.il.us/Lands/Landmgt/PARKS/R2/
    CHAINO.HTM
Phone: 847-587-5512
Size: 2,793 acres, with another 3,230 acres in the adjoining conservation area. Location: Northeastern Illinois, 60 miles northwest of Chicago and 4 miles south of the Illinois-Wisconsin border. Facilities: 151 campsites in Class A-Premium camping areas, 87 campsites in 3 Class B-premium areas, and 1 youth

group camping area, 3 cabins (no restroom facilities in cabins), 1 rent-a-tent site, 7 picnic areas (1 &), 4 picnic shelters, 3 playgrounds, hiking trail (2.25 miles), hiking/biking trail (6 miles), equestrian trail (8 miles), trail designed for disabled users (.25 miles), horse rentals (seasonal), concession stand, boat and canoe rentals, boat ramp, fishing piers. **Activities:** Camping, boating, canoeing, fishing, hiking, bicycling, horseback riding, hunting, ice skating, ice fishing, cross-country skiing, sledding. **Special Features:** Located in the heart of Illinois' largest concentration of natural lakes, the park borders three natural lakes (Grass, Marie, and Nippersink) and the Fox River, which connects another seven lakes that make up the chain. In addition, the park contains a 44-acre lake within its boundaries.

★2214★ CHANNAHON STATE PARK

PO Box 54
Channahon, IL 60410
Web: dnr.state.il.us/Lands/Landmgt/PARKS/I&M/EAST/
CHANNAHO/Park.htm
Phone: 815-467-4271
Size: 25 acres. **Location:** Northeastern Illinois, Rt 6 Channahon exit off I-55. **Facilities:** Primitive camping (no vehicle access) with pit toilets and drinking water in camping area, access to 61 miles of hiking trail, picnic areas, shelter, playground. **Activities:** Boating (electric motors only), canoeing, fishing, hiking, picnicking, interpretive programs. **Special Features:** Park is the official trailhead for the 96-mile Illinois & Michigan Canal State Trail (see separate entry). Channahon is an Indian word meaning "the meeting of the waters" and refers to the joining of the DuPage, Des Plaines, and Kankakee rivers.

★2215★ CLINTON LAKE STATE RECREATION AREA

RR 1, Box 4
DeWitt, IL 61735
Web: dnr.state.il.us/Lands/Landmgt/PARKS/R3/
CLINTON.HTM
Phone: 217-935-8722
Size: 9,307 acres. **Location:** 3 miles east of Clinton in central Illinois. **Facilities:** 17 Class AA campsites (electric, water, sewer hookups; showers), 286 Class A campsites (electric hookups, showers), 5 Class B/S sites (with showers; adaptable to tents, trailers, or motorhomes), a youth or adult group camp area (accommodates up to 75; no showers), picnic areas, shelters, playgrounds, restrooms, 3 hiking trails, multi-use trail, 6 boat ramps, canoe launch, fishing pier, beach, food concession (&&). **Activities:** Camping, boating, canoeing, sailing, fishing, swimming, water-skiing, hiking, horseback riding, hunting, ice skating, ice fishing, snowmobiling, cross-country skiing. **Special Features:** Park's 4,900-acre lake features excellent fishing for crappie, catfish, walleye, and striped bass. The property actually belongs to Illinois Power Company, which operates a nuclear power plant in the area, and has been operated as a state park since 1978 through a long-term lease with the utility company. Note: Effective 5/18/05 the Valley Mill Bank fishing area, Peninsula and Lane day use areas, and West Side shelter are closed indefinitely.

★2216★ COFFEEN LAKE STATE FISH & WILDLIFE AREA

15084 N 4th Ave
Coffeen, IL 62017
Web: dnr.state.il.us/Lands/Landmgt/PARKS/R4/Coffeen.htm
Phone: 217-537-3351
Size: 2,750 acres. **Location:** In Montgomery County in west central Illinois, 3 miles east northeast of Donnellson and I-127 or 2 miles west southwest of Coffeen and IL185. **Facilities:** Picnic facilities, toilets, drinking water, boat ramps (&), docks (&). **Activities:** Boating (25 HP limit), fishing, hunting, trapping. **Special Features:** Site operates under a longterm lease with Ameren Energy Generating company. Twenty-two species of fish are found in Coffeen Lake, including largemouth and striped bass, white crappie, and channel catfish. Power plant operation noticeably affects fishing activity and success, but fish growth appears to be faster than in many other lakes.

★2217★ CRAWFORD COUNTY STATE FISH & WILDLIFE AREA

12609 E 1700th Ave
Hutsonville, IL 62433
Web: dnr.state.il.us/Lands/Landmgt/PARKS/R5/Crawford.htm
Phone: 618-563-4405
Size: 1,129 acres. **Location:** In southern Illinois, 2 miles west and 1 mile south of Hutsonville. **Facilities:** Picnic area, shelter. **Activities:** Hunting, fishing (pole and line only), picnicking. **Special Features:** Area contains 9 small ponds, ranging in size from one-half to two acres, with largemouth bass, bluegill, redear, and channel catfish. Game species for hunting include squirrel, deer, dove, woodcock, quail, furbearers, rabbit, and common snipe.

★2218★ DELABAR STATE PARK

RR 2, Box 27
Oquawka, IL 61469
Web: dnr.state.il.us/Lands/Landmgt/PARKS/R1/
DELABAR.HTM
Phone: 309-374-2496
Size: 89 acres. **Location:** Along the Mississippi River in northwest Illinois, 1.5 miles of north of Oquawka, near IL 164. **Facilities:** Campsites for tent or trailer camping (some primitive, some with electric and water hookups), group camping area, showers, 3 picnic areas, picnic shelter, restrooms, playground, trails (2 miles), boat ramp, 2 docks. **Activities:** Camping, boating, fishing, hiking, ice fishing, ice skating. **Special Features:** Much of the park is forested, providing habitat for a variety of wildlife species including squirrel, rabbit, raccoon, deer, groundhog, and quail. More than 50 species of birds have been identified at Delabar.

★2219★ DES PLAINES STATE FISH & WILDLIFE AREA

24621 N River Rd
Wilmington, IL 60481
Web: dnr.state.il.us/Lands/Landmgt/PARKS/I&M/EAST/
DESPLAIN/PARK.HTM
Phone: 815-423-5326

9, State Parks

Size: 5,500 acres. **Location:** In Will County in northeast Illinois, 10 miles south of Joliet and 55 miles southwest of Chicago, off I-55. **Facilities:** Class C campsites with water and pit toilets, 2 picnic areas, picnic shelter, playground, 2 boat ramps, handtrap range, archery range, dog field-trial training area. **Activities:** Camping, boating (10 HP maximum on backwaters, unlimited on river, no boats on Milliken lake), fishing, hiking, hunting, ice fishing. **Special Features:** The largest pheasant hunting facility in the state of Illinois is located at this site, and Milliken Lake, along with several ponds and river backwaters, offer panfish, catfish, and bass fishing. In addition, the Kankakee River borders the site on the south, with 3 miles of shoreline providing access to boating enthusiasts as well as walleye and northern pike fishing. The area also includes an 80-acre nature preserve containing remnants of natural prairie.

★2220★ DIXON SPRINGS STATE PARK

RR 2, Box 178
Golconda, IL 62938
Web: dnr.state.il.us/Lands/Landmgt/PARKS/R5/
DIXON.HTM
Phone: 618-949-3394
Size: 801 acres. **Location:** Southern Illinois, 10 miles west of Golconda on IL 146 near its junction with IL 145. **Facilities:** Class B trailer camping area with electricity available, 10 primitive camping sites, 3 picnic areas, 2 picnic shelters, playgrounds, drinking water, swimming pool, bathhouse, 45-foot water slide, concession stand, 2 hiking trails, 2 basketball courts, 2 volleyball courts, 3 horshoe pits, archery range. **Activities:** Camping, swimming, hiking, hunting, basketball, volleyball, archery. **Special Features:** Park is located in the Illinois Shawnee Hills and sits on a giant block of rock that was dropped 200 feet along a fault line extending across Polk County. This part of the state was once an Indian Reservation, but all of the Indians were gone by the 1830s. During the 19th century, Dixon Springs became a health spa, with visitors attracted to its seven springs of mineral-enriched water.

★2221★ DONNELLEY/DEPUE STATE FISH & WILDLIFE AREAS

1001 W 4th St
PO Box 52
DePue, IL 61322
Web: dnr.state.il.us/Lands/Landmgt/PARKS/R1/Don.htm
Phone: 815-447-2353
Size: 3,015 acres. **Location:** Northwest Illinois. The Donnelly Area is 2 miles north of Hennepin on Putnam County Highway 1; the DePue Area is near the village of DePue, in Bureau County. **Facilities:** Hiking and equestrian trails. **Activities:** Boating, fishing, hiking, horseback riding, hunting, bird watching, nature study. **Special Features:** Complex is an important North American waterfowl migration corridor and is managed primarily for migratory waterfowl. Both areas border the Illinois River.

★2222★ EAGLE CREEK STATE RECREATION AREA

PO Box 16
Findlay, IL 62534
Web: dnr.state.il.us/Lands/Landmgt/PARKS/R3/
EAGLECRK.HTM
Phone: 217-756-8260
Size: 2,200 acres. **Location:** East central Illinois, 4 miles southeast of Findlay on the west side of Lake Shelbyville. **Facilities:** 35 Class A campsites (with electricity, showers and other facilities), Class B/S campsites (with showers and vehicle access), Class D campsites (primitive), organized group camp area, 138-room resort, conference center, restaurant, lounge, swimming pool, picnic areas, 3 nature trails, backpacking trail (12 miles), cross-country ski trail (3 miles), boat ramp, 2 marinas. **Activities:** Camping, boating, fishing, swimming, hiking, hunting, cross-country skiing. **Special Features:** The Flood Control Act of 1958 authorized the Shelbyville Reservoir Project, which involved construction of a dam and creation of a lake. This natural resource management area includes both Eagle Creek State Recreation Area and Wolf Creek State Park (see separate entry), which face each other across Lake Shelbyville.

★2223★ EDWARD R. MADIGAN STATE FISH & WILDLIFE AREA

1366 1010th Ave
Lincoln, IL 62656
Web: dnr.state.il.us/Lands/Landmgt/PARKS/R4/Edmad.htm
Phone: 217-735-2424
Size: 974 acres. **Location:** West central Illinois, along Salt Creek in Logan County, on the south edge of Lincoln. **Facilities:** Picnic area, shelters, playground areas, horseshoe pits, hiking/bicycle trail (7 miles), jogging trail. **Activities:** Canoeing, fishing, picnicking, hiking, mountain biking, hunting. **Special Features:** Formerly known as Railsplitter State Park, the park now honors Edward R. Madigan (1936-1994) for his lifelong dedication to state and national public service. The park is the home of the largest sycamore tree in the state and is located near several state historic sites in and around the city of Lincoln.

★2224★ ELDON HAZLET STATE RECREATION AREA

20100 Hazlet Park Rd
Carlyle, IL 62231
Web: dnr.state.il.us/Lands/Landmgt/PARKS/R4/
ELDON.HTM
Phone: 618-594-3015
Size: 3,000 acres. **Location:** West central Illinois, 5 miles north of Carlyle and 3 miles east of IL 127 in Clinton County. **Facilities:** 328 Class A campsites (electrical hookups; 7 &), 36 Class C sites (walk-in tent camping), and 2 rustic rent-a-cabins, with camp store, 3 shower buildings, numerous privy toilets, playgrounds, basketball court, sand volleyball court, horshoe pits, and an amphitheater in the main campground area; youth campground; 20 lakefront cottages; 40-acre sailboat harbor with showers, picnic tables, play equipment, day-use docks, picnic shelter, boat launching ramp, and 3 electric hoists; day-use areas with boat ramps, courtesy dock (&), picnic shelters, play equipment, privy toilets, fish cleaning station (&); swimming pool,

hiking trails (9 miles), fishing piers. **Activities:** Camping, fishing, boating, sailing, swimming, hiking, hunting, interpretive programs. **Special Features:** Park includes the largest campground (Illini campground) in the Illinois state park system on the largest manmade lake (Carlyle Lake) in the state. Strong wind conditions and the large expanse of water—18 miles long and 5 miles wide—make Carlyle Lake very popular for sailing.

★2225★ FERNE CLYFFE STATE PARK
PO Box 10
Goreville, IL 62939
Web: dnr.state.il.us/Lands/Landmgt/PARKS/R5/FERNE.HTM
Phone: 618-995-2411
Size: 2,430 acres. **Location:** On IL 37 in southern Illinois, 1 mile south of Goreville and 12 miles south of Marion. **Facilities:** Class A campground (electricity, showers, flush toilets), walk-in primitive campground with toilets and drinking water nearby, youth group campground (drinking water and toilets), backpack campsites with showers and toilets, equestrian campground (showers, drinking water, toilets), 7 picnic areas (some with shelters, drinking water, and playgrounds), 18 trails, nature preserve. **Activities:** Camping, bank fishing, hiking, horseback riding, hunting, rock climbing, nature study. **Special Features:** An abundance of ferns, unique geological features, and unusual plant communities make Ferne Clyffe an especially scenic area. Impressive rock formations can be seen from most of the trails, including a 150-foot- long shelter bluff (Hawks' Cave) and a 100-foot-tall intermittent waterfall. The park also has more than 700 specifies of plants.

★2226★ FORT MASSAC STATE PARK
1308 E 5th St
Metropolis, IL 62960
Web: dnr.state.il.us/Lands/Landmgt/PARKS/R5/frmindex.htm
Phone: 618-524-4712
Size: 1,450 acres. **Location:** In southern Illinois, off I-24 in Metropolis. **Facilities:** 50 Class A campsites (electrical hookups), tent camping, group campground, picnic areas, 4 covered picnic shelters, 3 playgrounds, trails, boat dock, launch ramp, visitor center. **Activities:** Camping, boating, fishing, hiking, hunting, interpretive programs. **Special Features:** Overlooking the Ohio River on the southern tip of Illinois, Fort Massac was dedicated as the first Illinois state park in 1908. The fort's military history pre-dates the Revolutionary War. The current historic site is a replica of the 1802 American fort that was located there and also has the archeological outline of the French fort that was there in 1757.

★2227★ FOX RIDGE STATE PARK
18175 State Park Rd
Charleston, IL 61920
Web: dnr.state.il.us/Lands/Landmgt/PARKS/R3/FOX/
FOX.HTM
Phone: 217-345-6416
Size: 2,064 acres. **Location:** 8 miles south of Charleston in east-central Illinois. **Facilities:** 43 Class A campsites, 3 cabins, picnic areas, 8 shelters, pavilion, restrooms, playgrounds, 2 baseball diamonds, sand volleyball courts, hiking trails (2 &), equestrian trail (4 miles), fitness trail, fishing pier (&), canoe launches. **Activities:** Camping, canoeing, fishing, hiking, horseback riding, hunting, baseball, volleyball. **Special Features:** Unlike the flat prairies found in most of this part of Illinois, Fox Ridge is known for its steep, thickly wooded ridges, broad valleys, and miles of scenic trails.

★2228★ FRANK HOLTEN STATE RECREATION AREA
4500 Pocket Rd
East Saint Louis, IL 62205
Web: dnr.state.il.us/Lands/Landmgt/PARKS/R4/frank.htm
Phone: 618-874-7920
Size: 1,180 acres. **Location:** Within sight of Saint Louis' Gateway Arch, park is almost entirely surrounded by East Saint Louis. **Facilities:** Picnic areas with shelters, 18-hole golf course, food concession (in the golf clubhouse), boat ramps, sports fields. **Activities:** Boating (10 HP limit), fishing, golf, picnicking, field sports. **Special Features:** Park was established in 1964 and originally named Grand Marais. In 1967 the name was changed to Frank Holten in honor of a distinguished legislator from East Saint Louis who served 48 years in the Illinois General Assembly. The park is one of the largest day-use facilities in the surrounding area and can accommodate up to 2,000 patrons per day.

★2229★ FRANKLIN CREEK STATE NATURAL AREA
1872 Twist Rd
Franklin Grove, IL 61031
Web: dnr.state.il.us/Lands/Landmgt/PARKS/R1/
FRANKLIN.HTM
Phone: 815-456-2878
Size: 664 acres. **Location:** Northwest Illinois, 1 mile northwest of the village of Franklin Grove and 8 miles east of Dixon, just north of IL 38. **Facilities:** Picnic areas, picnic shelters (some &), restrooms, drinking water, trails (including &); equestrian area with trails, picnic shelter, restrooms, drinking water, outdoor show areal; visitor center. **Activities:** Fishing, hiking, horseback riding, hunting (limited), cross-country skiing, snowmobiling, interpretive programs. **Special Features:** A 180-acre nature preserve where high, rocky bluffs shelter a perennial creek, creating an environment in which a variety of flora and fauna thrive, is the cornerstone from which the rest of this recreation area has been built. A reconstructed 1847 grist mill that became operational in 1999 serves as the visitor center for the natural area.

★2230★ FULTS HILL PRAIRIE & KIDD LAKE STATE NATURAL AREAS
c/o Randolph County State Recreation Area
4301 S Lake Dr
Chester, IL 62233
Web: dnr.state.il.us/Lands/Landmgt/PARKS/R4/fhp.htm
Phone: 618-826-2706
Size: 997 acres total. **Location:** Along the Mississippi River

bluff near the town of Fults, 25 miles south of Belleville. **Activities:** Birdwatching, nature study. **Special Features:** Fults Hills Prairie contains the largest complex of high-quality loess hill prairie in Illinois, and was recognized as a National Natural Landmark in 1986. Kidd Lake is an example of the type of wetlands once common in the Mississippi floodplain. It is an important rest stop for migrating waterfowl and provides critical habitiat to a diverse range of birds, amphibians, and reptiles.

★2231★ **GEBHARD WOODS STATE PARK**

401 Ottawa St
PO Box 272
Morris, IL 60450
Web: dnr.state.il.us/Lands/Landmgt/PARKS/I&M/EAST/
GEBHARD/Park.htm
Phone: 815-942-0796
Size: 30 acres. **Location:** Northeast Illinois, along the I & M Canal in the city of Morris. **Facilities:** Primitive walk-in camping area, 5 picnic areas, 2 picnic shelters with restrooms, playground, baseball diamond, horseshoe pits, 3 fishing ponds, trails, information center. **Activities:** Camping, boating (no gas motors), canoeing, fishing, hiking, bicycling, cross-country skiing, snowmobiling, interpretive programs. **Special Features:** Park is bordered on the south by the Illinois & Michigan Canal and to the north by Nettle Creek. A footbridge connects the park to the historic I & M Canal State Trail, a 61-mile trail on an old canal towpath. The trail includes interpretive exhibits that describe the canal and the era of canal travel. A stone aqueduct that was originally built to carry the canal over Nettle Creek adds to the history of the area.

★2232★ **GIANT CITY STATE PARK**

235 Giant City Rd
Makanda, IL 62958
Web: dnr.state.il.us/lands/Landmgt/PARKS/R5/GC.HTM
Phone: 618-457-4836
Size: 4,055 acres. **Location:** Southern Illinois, in the hills of the Shawnee National Forest (see entry in the national forests chapter) near Carbondale. **Facilities:** Class A campground with water, electricity, showers, and sanitary facilities for tent or trailer camping, Class A equestrian campground near the park's horse trail, 14 primitive walk-in sites; lodge with 34 cabins, restaurant, lounge, swimming pool, children's pool; picnic areas and shelters, playgrounds; hiking trails, equestrian trails, horse stables, fishing ponds; visitor center with gift shop, natural and cultural exhibits, and discovery corner for children. **Activities:** Camping, boating (10 HP limit), canoeing, fishing, hiking, horseback riding, hunting, rock climbing, interpretive programs. **Special Features:** The name "Giant City" is derived from an area in the park where unique impressions have been made by massive sandstone structures. Formed 12,000 years ago, the huge sandstone bluffs have created walls so precise they seem almost manmade, with sections that appear to form streets or alleys for a city of giants.

★2233★ **GOLCONDA MARINA STATE RECREATION AREA**

RR 2
Golconda, IL 62958
Web: dnr.state.il.us/lands/Landmgt/PARKS/R5/
GOLCONDA.HTM
Phone: 618-683-5875
Size: 274 acres. **Location:** In southeastern Pope County in southern Illinois, along the Ohio River at Golconda. **Facilities:** Camping area, picnic area, marina, boat ramps, trails. **Activities:** Camping, boating, water-skiing, fishing, hiking. **Special Features:** The full-service Golconda Marina serves as the gateway to the Smithland Pool, a 23,000-acre recreational area of fingered tributaries off the Ohio River. A large bluff above the marina features camping and picnic areas that overlook the river, as well as a hiking trail that goes up historic steps registered with the National Historical Society.

★2234★ **GOOSE LAKE PRAIRIE STATE NATURAL AREA**

5010 N Jugtown Rd
Morris, IL 60450
Web: dnr.state.il.us/Lands/Landmgt/PARKS/I&M/EAST/
GOOSE/HOME.HTM
Phone: 815-942-2899
Size: 2,537 acres. **Location:** Northeast Illinois, in Grundy County, 50 miles southwest of Chicago and 1 mile southwest of the confluence of the Kankakee and Des Plaines rivers. **Facilities:** Picnic areas, restrooms, hiking trails (7 miles), visitor center. A boat launch and boat rental concession is available at Heidecke Lake, a 2,000-acre cooling pond that lies adjacent to Goose Lake Prairie. **Activities:** Hiking, picnicking, interpretive programs; fishing and hunting at Heidecke Lake. **Special Features:** At one time more than half of the state of Illinois was covered with prairie, which is how it earned the nickname "the Prairie State." Today, the 2,500-acre Goose Lake Prairie is the largest remnant of prairie left in Illinois. Goose Lake itself was drained by settlers in 1890 in order to gain more farmland, leaving only the ponds and marshes that remain at the site today. Most of the prairie is now made up of tall prairie grasses, and the rest consists of broad-leaved flowering plants known collectively as forbs.

★2235★ **GREEN RIVER STATE WILDLIFE AREA**

375 Game Rd
Harmon, IL 61042
Web: dnr.state.il.us/Lands/Landmgt/PARKS/R1/green.htm
Phone: 815-379-2324
Size: 2,565 acres. **Location:** Northwest Illinois, about 6 miles northwest of Ohio, IL, off IL 26. **Facilities:** Primitive campsites with vehicle access (Class C), equestrian trail (10 miles), check station for hunters. **Activities:** Hunting, camping, horseback riding, bird watching. **Special Features:** Site is a wildlife restoration area, with topography that ranges from flat to gently rolling. About one-third of the acreage is dominated by swampy sloughs; remaining portions are prairie restorations, open fields, cultivated areas, or timberlands. Many of these areas have been specially planted and managed to provide food and cover for a variety of wildlife species.

★2236★ HAMILTON COUNTY STATE FISH & WILDLIFE AREA

RR 4, Box 242
McLeansboro, IL 62859
Web: dnr.state.il.us/Lands/Landmgt/PARKS/R5/ HAMILTON.HTM
Phone: 618-773-4340
Size: 1,683 acres. Location: 8 miles southeast of McLeansboro, off Route 14 in southern Illinois. Facilities: Tent and trailer campsites with electricity and showers, boat launch, boat rental, picnic areas, playground, trails, concession stand. Activities: Camping, fishing, (10 HP limit for boats), hiking, horseback riding, hunting, ice fishing. Special Features: The park's main attraction is 75-acre Dolan Lake, which has 3 miles of shoreline and a maximum depth of 18 feet. The lake contains largemouth bass, bluegill, sunfish, crappie, channel catfish, and bullheads.

★2237★ HARRY "BABE" WOODYARD STATE NATURAL AREA

19284 E 670 North
Georgetown, IL 61846
Web: dnr.state.il.us/Lands/Landmgt/PARKS/R3/hbw.htm
Phone: 217-442-4915
Size: 1,104 acres. Location: East central Illinois, about 12 miles south from exit 215 off I-74. Facilities: None. Activities: Hiking, fishing, hunting. Special Features: Area supports 12 state-designated endangered or threatened species and provides habitat for 23 forest interior species.

★2238★ HAZEL & BILL RUTHERFORD WILDLIFE PRAIRIE STATE PARK

3826 N Taylor Rd
Hanna City, IL 61536
Web: www.wildlifeprairiestatepark.org
Phone: 309-676-0998; Fax: 309-676-7783
Size: 2,000 acres. Location: 10 miles west of downtown Peoria on I-74 (exit 82 south). Facilities: On-site lodging (cabins, cottages, converted horse stables, rail cars, hotel room [&]), banquet facilities, meeting rooms, dining room, cafe, gift shops, picnic areas, walking trails, restrooms. Activities: Wildlife viewing, fishing, interpretive programs. Special Features: Zoological park showcases Illinois native wildlife: wolves, bison, black bear, elk, cougar, otters, waterfowl, and other wildlife. Other features include a butterfly garden, a restored prairie, Pioneer Farmstead with petting area and historic buildings, and train rides.

★2239★ HEIDECKE LAKE STATE FISH & WILDLIFE AREA

5010 N Jugtown Rd
Morris, IL 60450
Web: dnr.state.il.us/Lands/Landmgt/PARKS/R2/Heidecke.htm
Phone: 815-942-6352
Size: 1,300 acres. Location: Exit 240 off I-55 (Lorenzo Road/ Pine Bluff Road), then west to Jugtown Road; lake is 1 mile north on Jugtown Road. Facilities: Boat launch facility, concession with rental boats and motors. Other facilities available at Goose Lake Prairie State Natural Area, adjacent to Heidecke Lake. Activities: Hunting, fishing (bank or boat fishing; size and catch limits). Only boats for fishing or waterfowl hunting are permitted on the lake. Boats must have gasoline-powered motors, and no water skiing, swimming, wading, sailboating, or personal watercraft are allowed at the lake. Special Features: Lake is managed by the state specifically for hunting and fishing. The fish-stocking program there produces trophy-size bass. Both shotgun and archery hunting are offered at Heidecke Lake.

★2240★ HENDERSON COUNTY CONSERVATION AREA

RR 1, Box 118
Keithsburg, IL 61442
Web: dnr.state.il.us/lands/Landmgt/PARKS/R1/ HENDERSO.HTM
Phone: 309-374-2496
Size: 87 acres. Location: 20 miles southwest of Monmouth and 5 miles east of the Mississippi River. Facilities: Tent and trailer campsites, picnic area, boat launch. Activities: Camping (individuals and adult groups), boating (electric motors only), fishing, ice skating, ice fishing. Special Features: Area includes Gladstone Lake, a 27-acre lake with 1.5 miles of shoreline and a maximum depth of 25 feet.

★2241★ HENNEPIN CANAL PARKWAY STATE PARK

16006 875 E St
Sheffield, IL 61361
Web: dnr.state.il.us/Lands/Landmgt/PARKS/R1/ HENNPIN.HTM
Phone: 815-454-2328
Size: 104.5-mile linear park spanning 5 counties. Location: Parkway basically parallels I-80 in Bureau and Henry counties in west central Illinois. Visitor Center is near Sheffield, off I-80 exit 45. Facilities: Class C and youth group camping at 6 of the locks and 2 bridges (drinking water at some), equestrian camping on the south side of Lock 21, picnic areas, picnic shelters (main complex only), playground (main complex), outdoor toilet facilities, multi-use trails, boat ramp (main complex), visitor center. Activities: Camping, boating, canoeing, fishing, hiking, bicycling, horseback riding, hunting, snowmobiling, cross-country skiing, ice skating. Special Features: Historic waterway connects the Illinois and Mississippi rivers. The canal flows south from Rock Falls and then splits, flowing east to the Illinois River at Bureau and west to the Mississippi River at Milan. The recreational corridor that straddles the 80-foot canal averages a quarter-mile in width. Boats must be carried about 300 feet around each of the canal's 33 locks. Seventeen miles of the former towpath are paved with crushed stone and are wheelchair accessible. A museum and visitor center in Sheffield details the history of the canal.

★2242★ HIDDEN SPRINGS STATE FOREST

RR 1, Box 200
Strasburg, IL 62465
Web: dnr.state.il.us/Lands/Landmgt/PARKS/R3/ HSFOREST.HTM
Phone: 217-644-3091

Size: 1,299 acres. **Location:** East central Illinois, 10 miles southeast of Shelbyville, near Clarksburg. **Facilities:** Class C campsites, picnic areas, shelter, playground, fishing ponds, trails. **Activities:** Camping, fishing, hiking, hunting, bird watching. **Special Features:** Forest was named after the seven known springs on the property which were used for drinking water by the Indians and early settlers. Over the years these springs have been covered over by natural siltation and vegetation. The entire forest area was originally planned as a state lake but was designated instead as a state forest when construction of Shelbyville Reservoir began. It is managed under the concept of multiple use (timber/resource management and and compatible recreation).

★2243★ **HORSESHOE LAKE STATE FISH & WILDLIFE AREA (ALEXANDER COUNTY)**
PO Box 85
Miller City, IL 62962
Web: dnr.state.il.us/Lands/Landmgt/PARKS/R5/ HORSHU.HTM
Phone: 618-776-5689
Size: 10,200 acres. **Location:** Southern Illinois, in Alexander County, just east of IL 3, 7 miles north of Cairo. **Facilities:** 38 Class A campsites with electricity and showers, 40 Class B/E campsites with electricity only, 10 Class C campsites, 4 picnic areas, playground. **Activities:** Camping, fishing, boating (10 HP limit), hunting. **Special Features:** The natural features of the area are similar to those found in the Deep South, with bald cypress, tupelo gum, and swamp cottonwood trees surrounding the lake. Horseshoe Island, Horseshoe Lake, and all areas not designated for public hunting are used to maintain the Canada goose population, and up to 150,000 geese winter at the site each year.

★2244★ **HORSESHOE LAKE STATE PARK (MADISON COUNTY)**
3321 Hwy 111
Granite City, IL 62040
Web: dnr.state.il.us/Lands/Landmgt/PARKS/R4/ HORSESP.HTM
Phone: 618-931-0270
Size: 2,960 acres. **Location:** Southwestern Illinois, in Madison County, off IL 111. **Facilities:** 48 Class C tent or trailer campsites, picnic areas, 5 shelters, 3 playgrounds, 2 volleyball areas, hiking trails (4 miles), fishing pier (&), 3 boat ramps. **Activities:** Camping, boating (50 HP limit), fishing, hiking, hunting. **Special Features:** Horseshoe Lake is very old, as illustrated by its 3-foot depth. It has been inhabited by various American Indian groups throughout time. The earliest evidence of activity at this site dates to 8000 BC. During the Woodland period (1000 BC-1000 AD), 30-40,000 mound builders farmed the surrounding area and relied on Horseshoe Lake as a supplemental food source.

★2245★ **ILLINI STATE PARK**
2660 E 2350th Rd
Marseilles, IL 61341
Web: dnr.state.il.us/Lands/Landmgt/PARKS/I&M/EAST/ ILLINI/PARK.HTM
Phone: 815-795-2448

Size: 510 acres. **Location:** On the southern bank of the Illinois River, south from Marseilles and US 6, in northwestern Illinois. **Facilities:** Tent and trailer campsites, including sites with electricity and sanitation service, youth camping area, picnic areas and shelters, playgrounds, restrooms, drinking water, concession stand, trails, baseball diamond, horseshoe pits, boat ramp, warming shelter. **Activities:** Camping, boating, fishing, hiking, ice skating, sledding. **Special Features:** Park features rustic Civilian Conservation Corps buildings and riverside picnic areas, offering both beautiful views and a sense of history. The northern edge of the park is bordered by the Great Falls of the Illinois River. In two miles, the river drops three feet, creating roaring rapids. The east end of the park was once the site of a prestigious country club organized by WD Boyce, founder of the Boy Scouts of America. The historic Illinois & Michigan Canal is less than one mile north of the park.

★2246★ **ILLINOIS BEACH STATE PARK**
Lake Front
Zion, IL 60099
Web: dnr.state.il.us/Lands/Landmgt/PARKS/R2/ ILBEACH.HTM
Phone: 847-662-4811; **Fax:** 847-662-6433
Size: 4,160 acres. **Location:** In northeastern Illinois, on Lake Michigan, near the Wisconsin border. **Facilities:** 244 Class A Premium sites with electricity and access to showers and sanitation facilities, camp store, swimming beach, fishing pier (&), trails (5 miles), picnic areas, interpretive center, 96-room resort lodge with conference center, restaurant, lounge, swimming pool, and health club. **Activities:** Camping, boating, water-skiing, fishing, swimming, hiking, bicycling, cross-country skiing (but not in nature preserve), interpretive programs. **Special Features:** Park is part of a dune complex that once stretched from south of Chicago to the Wisconsin line. Today the park contains the only beach ridge shoreline remaining in the state and a dramatic variety of vegetation and wildlife.

★2247★ **ILLINOIS CAVERNS STATE NATURAL AREA**
10981 Conservation Rd
Baldwin, IL 62217
Web: dnr.state.il.us/Lands/Landmgt/PARKS/R4/ILC.HTM
Phone: 618-458-6699
Size: Cave entrance is on a tract of 9.25 acres. **Location:** Monroe County is southwestern Illinois, 35 miles south of Saint Louis, Missouri. **Activities:** Spelunking, hiking. **Special Features:** Cave contains an extensive array of cave formations, many of which are still actively growing with the continued deposition of calcium carbonate. Cave is also home to a the largest number of cave-adapted animals known in the state, including the cave salamander and at least two species of bats. Approximately 6 miles of the cave's passages have been mapped. Days and hours of operation vary seasonally, but, when open, no one is allowed to enter the cave after 2:30 p.m.

★2248★ ILLINOIS & MICHIGAN CANAL STATE
TRAIL

PO Box 272
Morris, IL 60450
Web: dnr.state.il.us/Lands/Landmgt/PARKS/I&M/Main.htm
Phone: 815-942-0796
Size: 61 miles long. **Location:** From Lockport in the east to
LaSalle, parallel to the Illinois River. The I & M Canal Visitor
Center is located in the historic Gaylord Building, 200 West 8th
Street, Lockport. **Activities:** Hiking, bicycling, snowmobiling.
Special Features: Trail follows the historic route of the I & M
Canal, which was built between 1836 and 1848 and became the
final link in an all-water route between the east coast and the
Gulf of Mexico. Completion of the canal helped transofrm Illi-
nois from a sparsely settled wilderness to a prosperous, popu-
lous state.

★2249★ IROQUOIS COUNTY STATE WILDLIFE
AREA

RR 1
2803 East 3300 North Rd
Beaverville, IL 60912
Web: dnr.state.il.us/Lands/Landmgt/PARKS/R3/
IROQUOIS.HTM
Phone: 815-435-2218
Size: 2,480 acres. **Location:** About 80 miles south of Chicago,
2 miles north and 3 miles east of Beaverville. **Facilities:** Picnic
areas, sanitary facilities, trails, dog training area, archery range,
shooting range, concession (during hunting season). **Activities:**
Hiking, hunting, archery, snowmobiling. **Special Features:** The
area exhibits some of the finest and most extensive prairie marsh,
sedge meadow, and sand dune vegetation remaining in Illinois.
The majority of the area, 2,000 acres, is managed as a public
hunting area (primarily permit pheasant hunting). The remainder
is a dedicated nature preserve.

★2250★ JAMES "PATE" PHILIP STATE PARK

2050 W Stearns Rd
Bartlett, IL 30103
Web: dnr.state.il.us/lands/Landmgt/PARKS/R2/
JPatePhillip.htm
Phone: 847-608-3100
Size: 501 acres. **Location:** In northeast Illinois, in Bartlett, on
Stearns Road, west of Powis Road. **Facilities:** Picnic area, shel-
ter, multi-purpose trails (5 miles), restrooms, drinking water,
visitor/education center (♿). **Activities:** Environmental educa-
tion programs, hiking, horseback riding, bicycling, cross-coun-
try skiing. **Special Features:** Purpose of the park is to blend
the forest, marshland, and grasslands of Pratt's Wayne Woods
Forest Preserve, which lies south of James "Pate" Philips State
Park, with the park's conservation lands in order to establish
native vegetation that will create new opportunities for wildlife
corridors and greenway connections to neighboring counties.
The park's visitor center serves as an environmental education
facility, with exhibits and programs that illustrate the park's
restoration story.

★2251★ JIM EDGAR PANTHER CREEK STATE
FISH & WILDLIFE AREA

10149 County Hwy 11
Chandlerville, IL 62627
Web: dnr.state.il.us/Lands/Landmgt/PARKS/R4/jepc.htm
Phone: 217-452-7741
Size: 16,550 acres. **Location:** Cass County in west central Illinois, 25 miles northwest of Springfield off IL 125. **Facilities:**
84 Class A and AA campsites (all but 19 have electricity), 9
cabins, equestrian campground (51 sites with electricity), primitive camping area, shower building, picnic areas, restrooms,
shelters, hiking/jogging trails (3 miles), equestrian trail (26
miles), mountain bike/hiking trail (24 miles). **Activities:** Camping, boating, sailing, canoeing, fishing, hiking, bicycling, horseback riding, hunting. **Special Features:** At 26 square miles, site
is Department of Natural Resource's largest block of property.
It is composed of rolling hills with mature forest, agricultural
fields, and grasslands, and dissected by Panther and Cox creeks
and their tributaries. The area is home to a rich assortment of
wildlife, including the Indiana bat, northern harrier, and red-
shouldered hawk—all endangered species—and game species
such as the white-tailed deer, wild turkey, ring-neck pheasant,
and mourning dove.

★2252★ JOHNSON-SAUK TRAIL STATE PARK

28616 Sauk Trail Rd
Kewanee, IL 61443
Web: dnr.state.il.us/Lands/Landmgt/PARKS/R1/
JOHNSON.HTM
Phone: 309-853-5589
Size: 1,365 acres. **Location:** Northwest Illinois, off IL 78, 6
miles south of I-80 and 5 miles north of Kewanee. **Facilities:**
71 Class A campsites with electrical hookups for trailers, 25
Class C tent sites, showers, youth campground, 10 picnic areas,
2 shelters, playground, fishing piers, marina, boat rentals, restaurant, multi-use trails, historic barn. **Activities:** Camping, boating
(electric motors only), canoeing, fishing, hiking, hunting, cross-
country skiing, snowmobiling, sledding, ice skating, ice fishing.
Special Features: Park is situated along a trail once used by
the Winnebago Indians; the area was also used for hunting by
the Sauk and Fox Indians. The park's centerpiece is a 58-acre
lake with 2.5 miles of shoreline. The park also features one of
the largest round barns in the country, measuring more than 80
feet high and 85 feet in diameter, with a full-size silo inside.
Tours of the barn may be arranged through the park office.

★2253★ JUBILEE COLLEGE STATE PARK

13921 W Rt 150
Brimfield, IL 61517
Web: dnr.state.il.us/Lands/Landmgt/PARKS/R1/
JUBILEE.HTM
Phone: 309-446-3758
Size: 3,184 acres. **Location:** 15 miles northwest of Peoria, be-
tween the towns of Kickapoo and Brimfield, just off US 150.
Facilities: Class A (electric) and Class C campsites for RVs or
tents (Apr 15-Nov 1), with showers, flush toilets, and privies,
winter campground (Class B) with electricity and primitive priv-
ies (no running water), equestrian campground with drinking
water, toilet facilities, shelter house, picnic areas with shelters

(with electric), playgrounds, and restrooms, multi-use trails. **Activities:** Camping, fishing, horseback riding, hunting, cross-country skiing, snowmobiling. **Special Features:** Founded in 1839, Jubilee College was one of the earliest educational enterprises in Illinois. The college closed in 1862, and in 1933 the property was turned over to the state of Illinois. The college building, placed on the *National Register of Historic Places* in 1972, has been restored to its original appearance and is managed by the Illinois Historic Preservation Agency.

★2254★ KANKAKEE RIVER STATE PARK

5314 W Rt 102
PO Box 37
Bourbonnais, IL 60914
Web: dnr.state.il.us/Lands/Landmgt/PARKS/R2/
KANKAKEE.HTM
Phone: 815-933-1383
Size: 3,932 acres. **Location:** Northeast Illinois, 6 miles northwest of Kankakee, just south of IL 102 and north of IL 113; accessible from I-55 and I-57. **Facilities:** 110 Class A campsites, 2 cabins, more than 150 Class B (with electric) and C campsites, equestrian campground (seasonal), youth group camping area, trails, picnic areas and shelters, concession stand, 2 boat ramps, visitor center. **Activities:** Camping, boating (10 HP limit), canoeing, fishing, hiking, bicycling, horseback riding, hunting, cross-country skiing, snowmobiling, interpretive programs. **Special Features:** Park straddles the Kankakee River for 11 miles, in an area used for recreation since the 1890s. Several prehistoric sites are documented within the park's boundaries.

★2255★ KASKASKIA RIVER STATE FISH & WILDLIFE AREA

10981 Conservation Rd
Baldwin, IL 62217
Web: dnr.state.il.us/Lands/Landmgt/PARKS/R4/kaskas.htm
Phone: 618-785-2555
Size: 20,000 acres. **Location:** 35 miles southeast of Saint Louis, Missouri. **Facilities:** Primitive camping and picnic areas on land adjacent to the river, multi-use trails (12 miles), boat ramps. **Activities:** Boating, canoeing, fishing, hiking, camping, hunting, interpretive programs. **Special Features:** Park is one of the largest state-owned and managed sites in Illinois, with 36 miles of river, 2,018-acre Baldwin Lake, and diversified wildlife populations.

★2256★ KICKAPOO STATE RECREATION AREA

10906 Kickapoo Park Rd
Oakwood, IL 61858
Web: dnr.state.il.us/Lands/Landmgt/PARKS/R3/
KICKAPOO.HTM
Phone: 217-442-4915
Size: 2,842 acres. **Location:** Vermilion County, near Danville; accessible via I-74. **Facilities:** 184 sites for tent and trailer camping (about half with electrical hookups), a limited number of primitive walk-in sites, 2 shower buildings, 12 boat ramps, boat and canoe rentals, concession, restaurant, hiking and biking trails, 6 main picnic areas with shelters, drinking water, and

playground equipment, horse rentals. **Activities:** Camping, boating (electric motors only), canoeing, fishing, hunting, scuba diving, hiking, mountain biking, horseback riding, cross-country skiing, sledding, ice fishing, ice skating. **Special Features:** Kickapoo State Recreation Area is apparently the first park in the nation built on strip-mine land. Through the rejuvenative powers of nature, a landscape once devastated by nearly a century of strip mining now features 22 clear, deep-water ponds and thickly forested land that provides habitat for a variety of birds, animals, and wildflowers.

★2257★ KINKAID LAKE STATE FISH & WILDLIFE AREA

52 Cinder Hill Dr
Murphysboro, IL 62966
Web: dnr.state.il.us/lands/landmgt/PARKS/R5/Kinkaid.htm
Phone: 618-684-2867
Size: Lake encompasses 2,750 acres. 4,000 acres of the surrounding land is managed by the Illinois Dept of Natural Resources; 5,000 acres by the US Forest Service; 300 acres by Kinkaid-Reed's Creek Conservancy District. **Location:** Southwestern Illinois, in Jackson County, 5 miles north of Murphysboro and 100 miles southeast of Saint Louis, Missouri. **Facilities:** Picnic tables, shelters, restrooms, playground area, 4 boat ramps, full-service marina. (No camping on DNR property.) **Activities:** Boating, picnicking, fishing, hunting. **Special Features:** Site consists of sandstone bluffs, rolling hills, and an oak-hickory forest beside 2,750-acre Kinkaid Lake.

★2258★ LAKE LE-AQUA-NA STATE RECREATION AREA

8542 N Lake Rd
Lena, IL 61048
Web: dnr.state.il.us/Lands/Landmgt/PARKS/R1/
LEAQUANA.HTM
Phone: 815-369-4282
Size: 715 acres. **Location:** Northwest Illinois, in Stephenson County, just west of IL 73, 6 miles south of the Illinois-Wisconsin state line and 3 miles north of Lena. **Facilities:** RV and tent campsites (many with electrical hookups), equestrian campground, youth group camping area, restrooms, picnic areas, 2 picnic shelters, concession, trails (8.5 miles), canoe and paddleboat rentals, boat ramp, small swimming beach, fishing pier (&). **Activities:** Camping, boating (electric motors only), canoeing, fishing, swimming, hiking, bicycling, horseback riding, hunting (limited), ice fishing, sledding, cross-country skiing. **Special Features:** Park is named for the nearby village of Lena and the Latin word for water. A good variety of woodland wildflowers, including Dutchman's breeches, blood root, and bluebells, cover the ground in the spring and early summer. Squirrels, chipmunks, rabbits, and other small animals are often seen in the wooded areas, and deer are also frequently sighted. Observant visitors might also catch a glimpse of a badger. At the center of the park is a stocked, manmade lake.

★2259★ LAKE MURPHYSBORO STATE PARK

52 Cinder Hill Dr
Murphysboro, IL 62966
Web: dnr.state.il.us/Lands/Landmgt/PARKS/R5/
MURPHYSB.HTM
Phone: 618-684-2867
Size: 1,022 acres. **Location:** Southern Illinois, in Jackson County, 1 mile west of Murphysboro off IL 149. **Facilities:** 54 trailer campsites with electricity (3 ♿), 20 tent sites (1 ♿), showers, picnic area, picnic shelters, restrooms (♿), playground, fishing pier (♿), concession area, hiking trail, boat rentals, archery range. **Activities:** Camping, boating (10 HP limit), canoeing, fishing, hiking. **Special Features:** The 145-acre Lake Murphysboro (a manmade, stocked lake) is a tributary of Indian Creek and has a watershed of about 4,500 acres. The lake has 7.5 miles of shoreline, with a maximum water depth of 36 feet. A 600-foot dam is located at the south end of the park.

★2260★ LASALLE LAKE STATE FISH & WILDLIFE AREA

2660 E 2350th Rd
Marseilles, IL 61341
Web: dnr.state.il.us/Lands/Landmgt/PARKS/R1/
LASALLE.HTM
Phone: 815-357-1608
Size: 2,058 acres. **Location:** Northwest Illinois, 8 miles southeast of Marseilles. **Facilities:** Fishing pier (♿), boat ramp. **Activities:** Boating, fishing (with catch limits). **Special Features:** This manmade lake serves as a cooling lake for a nearby power station. Formed by levees that rise above the surrounding land, LaSalle Lake's ''perched'' construction helps the lake catch the wind to cool the impounded water, but sudden high winds can result in extremely hazardous conditions for unwary boaters. Due to the riprapped shoreline, there also is no natural shoreline for beaching boats. All boaters are responsible for their own safety, and swimming, wading, and water-skiing are prohibited, as are sailboats, sailboards, and surfboards.

★2261★ LINCOLN TRAIL HOMESTEAD STATE MEMORIAL

c/o Spitler Woods State Natural Area
705 Spitler Park Dr
Mount Zion, IL 62549
Web: dnr.state.il.us/lands/Landmgt/PARKS/R3/
LINCTRL.HTM
Phone: 217-864-3121
Size: 162 acres. **Location:** 8 miles south of Decatur, bisected by the Sangamon River. **Facilities:** Memorial, picnic area, drinking water, restrooms (♿♿). **Activities:** Youth group camping, fishing, hiking. **Special Features:** The site of Abraham Lincoln's first home in Illinois, with a memorial commemorating the beginnings of Lincoln's life in Illinois.

★2262★ LINCOLN TRAIL STATE PARK

16985 E 1350th Rd
Marshall, IL 62441
Web: dnr.state.il.us/lands/Landmgt/PARKS/R3/
LINCOLN.HTM
Phone: 217-826-2222

Size: 1,023 acres. **Location:** West of IL 1, 2 miles south of Marshall in Clark County, IL. **Facilities:** 2 Class A campgrounds with electricity, showers, toilet facilities, water, and playground equipment; a Class C tent camping area; a camping area for organized adult or youth groups; picnic areas with water and toilet facilities, 2 shelters, playgrounds; boat docks, boat ramp, boat rentals; concession stand; hiking trails. **Activities:** Camping, boating (10 HP limit), fishing, hiking, ice fishing, ice skating, cross-country skiing. **Special Features:** The focal point of the park is Lincoln Trail Lake, with 146 acres of surface area and more than 7 miles of thickly wooded shoreline. Park also includes the American Beech Woods Nature Preserve, with ravines filled with beech-maple forest similar to those existing in pioneer days. The area is named after the trail Abraham Lincoln's family followed en route from Indiana to Illinois in 1831.

★2263★ LOWDEN-MILLER STATE FOREST

1365 W Castle Rock Rd
Oregon, IL 61061
Web: dnr.state.il.us/Lands/Landmgt/PARKS/R1/
LOWDENMI.HTM
Phone: 815-732-7329
Size: 2,225 acres. **Location:** Northwest Illinois, along the eastern shore of the Rock River, 4 miles south of IL 64 at Oregon. **Facilities:** None. **Activities:** Hunting, hiking, cross-country skiing. **Special Features:** Forest provides excellent deer and turkey habitat.

★2264★ LOWDEN STATE PARK

1411 N River Rd
Oregon, IL 61061
Web: dnr.state.il.us/Lands/Landmgt/PARKS/R1/
LOWDENSP.HTM
Phone: 815-732-6828
Size: 207 acres. **Location:** Along the Rock River, just north of Oregon, in Ogle County. **Facilities:** Individual and group campsites (limited electricity), showers, concession stand, picnic areas, outdoor toilets, drinking water, hiking trails (4 miles), boat ramp and docks (adjacent to the park). **Activities:** Camping, boating, water skiing, fishing, hiking. (Swimming in the river is not permitted.) **Special Features:** Park features a 50-foot-tall concrete-reinforced statue of a Native American that towers above the Rock River on the bluffs north of Oregon. Although the sculptor, Lorado Taft, dedicated the statue to Native Americans, it has become most commonly associated with Chief Black Hawk. According to legend, as he was leaving the area after the Black Hawk War, the Sauk warrior talked of the great beauty of the Rock River Valley and admonished his captors to care for the land as his people had.

★2265★ MACKINAW RIVER STATE FISH & WILDLIFE AREA

15470 Nelson Rd
Mackinaw, IL 61755
Web: dnr.state.il.us/Lands/Landmgt/PARKS/R1/
MACKINA.HTM
Phone: 309-963-4969

9. State Parks

Size: 1,448 acres. **Location:** 4.5 miles northeast of Mackinaw, off IL 9. **Facilities:** Nature preserve, canoe access. **Activities:** Hunting, canoeing, fishing, hiking. **Special Features:** Diverse terrain consists of timbered hills, open meadows, and river bottoms.

★2266★ MARSEILLES STATE FISH & WILDLIFE AREA

2660 E 2350th Rd
Marseilles, IL 61341
Phone: 815-795-2448
Size: 2,550 acres. **Location:** South of the Illinois River, near Grand Ridge. **Facilities:** None. **Activities:** Hunting. **Special Features:** Site is predominantly wooded, with rugged terrain. There is no interior vehicle access, so hunters should be prepared for strenuous walking if they use the interior. The area is jointly used by the Illinois National Guard as a training facility, and all hunting programs are dependent on national security considerations.

★2267★ MARSHALL STATE FISH & WILDLIFE AREA

236 State Rt 26
Lacon, IL 61540
Web: dnr.state.il.us/Lands/Landmgt/PARKS/R1/ MARSHALL.HTM
Phone: 309-246-8351
Size: 5,922 acres. **Location:** Along the Illinois River near East Peoria, off IL 26. **Facilities:** Tent and trailer campsites (some with electricity and water), canoe campsites, picnic area with shelters (no drinking water), multi-use trail (3.5 miles), boat ramp. **Activities:** Camping, boating, canoeing, fishing, wildlife viewing, birdwatching, hiking, hunting, backpacking, cross-country skiing, ice fishing. **Special Features:** Park lies along 10 miles of Illinois River backwaters, bottomlands, and bluffs in the heart of the mallard duck flyway. The backwater lakes attract large flights of waterfowl during migration, but only the wood duck remains during summer to nest and raise young. Great blue heron also are found on the backwaters, and during the winter it's possible to see bald eages there.

★2268★ MATTHIESSEN STATE PARK

PO Box 509
Utica, IL 61373
Web: dnr.state.il.us/Lands/Landmgt/PARKS/R1/mttindex.htm
Phone: 815-667-4868
Size: 1,938 acres. **Location:** Central LaSalle County, 4 miles south of Utica and 3 miles east of Oglesby. **Facilities:** Equestrian campground, picnic areas, playground, restrooms, marked hiking trails (5 miles), horseback riding trails (9 miles), cross-country ski trails (6 miles), horse rentals, ski rental (Dec-Mar), historic site, field archery range, radio-controlled model airplane field. **Activities:** Hiking (on marked trails only; unmarked areas are dangerous), horseback riding, camping (equestrian only), wildlife viewing, hunting, cross-country skiing. **Special Features:** Bluffs composed of 425-million-year-old sandstone, canyons formed by water erosion, and Cascade Falls are among the park's striking natural features. An added attraction is a

restored fort and stockade buildings representative of the type of forts built by the French in the midwest during the 1600s and early 1700s.

★2269★ MAUTINO STATE FISH & WILDLIFE AREA

16006-875 E St
Sheffield, IL 61361
Web: dnr.state.il.us/Lands/Landmgt/PARKS/R1/ MAUTINO.HTM
Phone: 815-454-2328
Size: 911 acres. **Location:** 6 miles south of I-80, off IL 40 near Buda. **Facilities:** 15 stocked lakes, boat ramp, canoe access, restrooms (&). **Activities:** Boating (electric motors only), canoeing, fishing, hunting, hiking. **Special Features:** Area is mostly non-reclaimed strip-mined land with 15 stocked lakes for fishing. Shore access is limited, and shorelines drop abruptly into deep water.

★2270★ MAZONIA-BRAIDWOOD STATE FISH & WILDLIFE AREAS

PO Box 126
Braceville, IL 60407
Web: dnr.state.il.us/lands/Landmgt/PARKS/R2/ MAZONIA.HTM
Phone: 815-237-0063
Size: Two parcels: 1,017 acres (Mazonia) and 2,640 acres (Braidwood Lake). **Location:** Mazonia: In Grundy County, 3 miles southwest of Braidwood on IL 53 and Huston Road. Braidwood Lake: In Will County, off IL 53 south of Braidwood. **Facilities:** Under development. Plans include a paved access road to the main lakes, boat launches, ramps, parking lots, and toilets. **Activities:** Fishing, hunting, fossil collecting (permit required). **Special Features:** Mazonia encompasses 200 water impoundments, ranging in size from 3/4 acre to 30 acres, which contain bass, crappie, channel cat, and other species. Lake Braidwood is much larger and is potentially dangerous when winds reach 25 mph or higher.

★2271★ MERMET LAKE STATE FISH & WILDLIFE AREA

1812 Grinnell Rd
Belknap, IL 62908
Web: dnr.state.il.us/Lands/Landmgt/PARKS/R5/ MERMET.HTM
Phone: 618-524-5577
Size: 2,630 acres. **Location:** Southern Illinois, just north of the Ohio River, 0.5 miles southwest of Mermet on US 45. **Facilities:** Picnic tables, shelter, pit toilets, trails, 4 boat launch ramps, rental boats, paddles, and life jackets. **Activities:** Hunting, boating (10 HP limit), fishing, hiking. **Special Features:** Area is an old cypress swamp that has been converted into a waterfowl hunting area, with 30 permanent waterfowl blinds and 2 flooded walk-in areas. The area was developed mainly for duck hunting, but several thousand Canada, blue, and snow geese frequent the area each winter, and the lake is productive for largemouth bass, channel catfish, and most panfish.

★2272★ MIDDLE FORK STATE FISH & WILDLIFE AREA

10906 Kickapoo Park Rd
Oakwood, IL 61858
Web: dnr.state.il.us/Lands/Landmgt/PARKS/R3/Middle.htm
Phone: 217-442-4915
Size: 2,700 acres. **Location:** 6 miles north of I-74, Oakwood exit. **Facilities:** Class C, D, and equestrian camping facilities, multi-use trails (35 miles), canoe access, picnic tables and rustic sanitary facilities, trap range, archery trail. **Activities:** Camping, canoeing, fishing, hunting, hiking, horseback riding, cross-country skiing, snowmobiling. **Special Features:** Area is bounded on the east by the Kennekuk Cove County Park and on the south by Illinois Power Company's Vermilion Station. The site is named for the Middle Fork branch of the Vermilion River. The Middle Fork River is considered by ecological experts to be one of the most pristine in the state and is a designated National Wild and Scenic River.

★2273★ MISSISSIPPI PALISADES STATE PARK

16327A IL Rt 84
Savanna, IL 61074
Web: dnr.state.il.us/Lands/Landmgt/PARKS/R1/
PALISADE.HTM
Phone: 815-273-2731
Size: 2,500 acres. **Location:** North of Savanna, near the confluence of the Mississippi and Apple rivers in northwest Illinois. **Facilities:** 241 Class A and B campsites (110 with electrical hookups), showers and flush toilets (seasonal), camp convenience store, 2 youth camping areas, picnic areas, shelters, playgrounds, restrooms, hiking trails (15 miles), boat ramps. **Activities:** Camping, boating, fishing, hiking, hunting, cross-country skiing, sledding, ice fishing. **Special Features:** Park preserves palisades, or high, steep cliffs, along the Mississippi River. Erosion has carved intriguing rock formations on the bluff tops, including Indian Head and Twin Sisters, a pair of humanoid figures.

★2274★ MISSISSIPPI RIVER STATE FISH & WILDLIFE AREA

17836 State Highway 100 N
Grafton, IL 62037
Web: dnr.state.il.us/Lands/Landmgt/PARKS/R4/MISS.HTM
Phone: 618-376-3303
Size: 24,386 acres. **Location:** Headquarters located on IL 100, 11 miles north of Grafton. **Facilities:** Picnic areas. **Activities:** Boating, canoeing, fishing, hunting, birdwatching. **Special Features:** Area includes 15 wildlife management areas and 13 public access sites, scattered along 75 miles of two major rivers, the Mississippi and the Illinois. Most of the area is actively managed for wetland habitat enhancement and public recreation. The primary species of concern is waterfowl.

★2275★ MORAINE HILLS STATE PARK

914 S River Rd
McHenry, IL 60051
Web: dnr.state.il.us/Lands/Landmgt/PARKS/R2/
MORHILLS.HTM
Phone: 815-385-1624

Size: 2,200 acres. **Location:** 3 miles south of McHenry in the northeast corner of the state. **Facilities:** Picnic areas with drinking water and rustic toilet facilities, picnic shelters, concession building with restrooms, multi-use trails (10 miles), fishing piers (&), boat rentals (private watercraft prohibited), interpretive center, playground, restrooms. **Activities:** Boating (electric motors only), canoeing, fishing, hunting, hiking, bicycling, cross-country skiing, wildlife viewing. **Special Features:** Park derives its name from a geological formation known as a moraine, which is an accumulation of boulders, stones, and other debris deposited by a glacier. As glacial ice melted here following the Wisconsin glaciation period, it left gravel-rich deposits called kames that make up the park's wooded hills and ridges. The 48-acre Lake Defiance near the center of the park was formed when a large portion of ice broke away from the main glacier and melted. This lake, which is gradually filling in with peat from its unstable shoreline, is one of the few glacial lakes in Illinois that has remained largely undeveloped, maintaining a near-natural condition.

★2276★ MORAINE VIEW STATE RECREATION AREA

27374 Moraine View Park Rd
LeRoy, IL 61752
Web: dnr.state.il.us/lands/Landmgt/PARKS/R3/
MORAINE.HTM
Phone: 309-724-8032
Size: 1,687 acres. **Location:** Near LeRoy, just east of Bloomington/Normal, off I-74. **Facilities:** 137 Class A trailer campsites with water and electricity, 32 primitive Class D campsites, 2 group camping areas, and 30 Class A horsemen's campsites with water, electricity, and hitching racks; 8 picnic areas, 5 picnic shelters, 4 playgrounds; swimming beach, fishing pier (&), boat ramp, dock, boat rentals; restaurant and concession stand; hiking trails, bridle trails (10 miles), ski trails (7 miles), snowmobile trails, horse rentals for trail rides. **Activities:** Camping, boating (10 HP limit), canoeing, fishing, swimming, hiking, horseback riding, hunting, cross-country skiing, snowmobiling, ice fishing, ice skating. **Special Features:** When the glaciers of the last Ice Age moved through central Illinois 15,000 years ago, they pushed massive amounts of rock and earth before them, leaving in their wake long and expansive ridges across the landscape called moraines. Moraine View is located in the middle of one of the largest moraines in the state of Illinois.

★2277★ MORRISON-ROCKWOOD STATE PARK

18750 Lake Rd
Morrison, IL 61270
Web: dnr.state.il.us/Lands/Landmgt/PARKS/R1/
MORRISON.HTM
Phone: 815-772-4708
Size: 1,164 acres. **Location:** Northern Illinois, in Whiteside County, north of Morrison off IL 78. **Facilities:** 92 Class A campsites (with electricity), shower building with flush toilets, equestrian camping area, picnic areas, shelters, 9 fishing piers, boat ramp, dock, boat rental, concession, restaurant, hiking trails (3.5 miles), equestrian trail (14 miles), ski trails (14 miles). **Activities:** Camping, boating (10 HP limit), canoeing, fishing,

9. State Parks

hiking, horseback riding, hunting, ice fishing, ice skating, cross-country skiing, sledding, wildlife viewing, birdwatching. **Special Features:** Park includes Lake Carlton, reputed to be one of the best fishing spots in Illinois, and abundant wildlife, including deer, fox, coyote, and muskrat, as well as more than 150 species of birds, including pheasant and quail.

★2278★ NAUVOO STATE PARK

PO Box 426
Nauvoo, IL 62354
Web: dnr.state.il.us/Lands/Landmgt/PARKS/R4/
NAUVOO.HTM
Phone: 217-453-2512
Size: 148 acres. **Location:** In western Illinois, in Hancock County, on the south edge of Nauvoo, along IL 96. **Facilities:** 150 Class A and B campsites, youth group camping area, 2 picnic and playground areas, 2 shelter houses (1 with modern toilet facilities), ball diamond, hiking trails (&), boat launch (primitive), nature preserve, museum. **Activities:** Camping, boating (electric motors only), canoeing, fishing, picnicking, hiking, sledding, cross-country skiing. **Special Features:** When Mormons (including LDS founder Joseph Smith) settled in the Hancock County community of Commerce City in 1839, they changed its name to ''Nauvoo,'' a Hebrew word for ''pleasant land.'' A house built by Mormons in the 1840s serves as the Nauvoo State Park Museum.

★2279★ NEWTON LAKE STATE FISH & WILDLIFE AREA

3490 E 500th Ave
Newton, IL 62448
Web: dnr.state.il.us/Lands/Landmgt/PARKS/R5/
NEWTON.HTM
Phone: 618-783-3478
Size: 2,315 acres (1,775 acres lake; 540 acres shoreline). **Location:** In Jasper County, in southern Illinois, via the Effingham exit off I-57 and I-70. **Facilities:** Multi-use trails (22 miles), mountain bike trail (5 miles), boat ramp, concession. **Activities:** Boating (25 HP limit), fishing (size and catch limits), hiking, cross-country skiing, mountain biking, horseback riding. **Special Features:** Park operates as a day-use conservation area under lease from Central Illinois Public Service Company, with recreational activities limited by agreement. Jasper County has the largest of three prairie chicken flocks still existing in Illinois, and CIPSC has designated a portion of the property as an additional prairie chicken sanctuary.

★2280★ PEABODY RIVER KING STATE FISH & WILDLIFE AREA

10981 Conservation Rd
Baldwin, IL 62217
Web: dnr.state.il.us/Lands/Landmgt/PARKS/R4/
PEABODY.HTM
Phone: 618-785-2555
Size: 2,220 acres. **Location:** 0.5 miles east of New Athens via Old Highway 13 and Darmstadt Road, adjacent to the Kaskaskia River State Fish & Wildlife Area. **Facilities:** Boat ramp, canoe access, restrooms. **Activities:** Boating (10 HP limit), canoeing, fishing, hunting. **Special Features:** A former coal mining site, the area is dominated by lakes and ponds, with more than 20 fishing lakes and a waterfowl refuge.

★2281★ PERE MARQUETTE STATE PARK

Rt 100 , PO Box 158
Grafton, IL 62037
Web: dnr.state.il.us/lands/Landmgt/PARKS/R4/Peremarq.htm
Phone: 618-786-3323
Size: 8,000 acres. **Location:** Northwest of Saint Louis, Missouri, near the Illinois community of Grafton, about 20 miles from Alton. **Facilities:** 80 Class A campsites (2 &) with electrical hookups, drinking water, and shower access, 2 rent-a-camp cabins, youth camping area, 3 fully-equipped organized group camps (2 have swimming pools); lodge with 50 guest rooms and 22 guest cabins, conference center/meeting rooms, gift shop, dining room, cocktail lounge, indoor swimming pool, whirlpool/saunas, game room, and tennis court; picnic areas, 3 picnic shelters, boat ramps and docks, hiking trails (12 miles), equestrian trails (20 miles), horse rentals, and bike trail (20 miles, paved); visitor center with 300-gallon aquarium, exhibits, and displays. **Activities:** Camping, boating, fishing, hiking, bicycling, horseback riding, bird watching, hunting, interpretive programs. **Special Features:** The park overlooks a wide expanse of the Mississippi River and is famous for the exceptional beauty of its fall colors and, during winter, for its bald eagles. The park was named for Father Jacques Marquette, a French Jesuit missionary who, in 1673, was among the first group of Europeans to reach the confluence of the Mississippi and Illinois rivers. A large stone cross stands just east of the park entrance commemorating the historic landing.

★2282★ PINEY CREEK RAVINE STATE NATURAL AREA

c/o Randolph SFWA
4301 S Lake Dr
Chester, IL 62233
Web: dnr.state.il.us/lands/Landmgt/PARKS/R4/pcr.htm
Phone: 618-826-2706
Size: 198 acres. **Location:** West of Du Quoin and south of Steeleville on the Randolph-Jackson county line. **Activities:** Hiking, sightseeing, bird watching. (Because Piney Creek Ravine is a dedicated nature preserve, no hunting or consumptive use is allowed, and camping is expressly prohibited.) **Special Features:** Piney Creek Ravine is a dedicated state nature preserve and is one of only two locations in the state where short-leaf pine grows naturally. The preserve also contains the largest collection of prehistoric rock art in Illinois, with almost 200 designs believed to date back to the late Woodland (AD 500-1000) and Mississippian (AD 1000-1550) periods. Designs include both petroglyphs (carved) and pictographs (painted) of human figures, deer, birds, snakes, and symbols.

★2283★ POWERTON LAKE STATE FISH & WILDLIFE AREA

7982 S Park Rd
Manito, IL 61546
Web: dnr.state.il.us/lands/Landmgt/PARKS/R1/
POWERTON.HTM
Phone: 309-968-7135

Size: 1,426 acres. **Location:** 2 miles southwest of Pekin along Manito Road. **Activities:** Fishing, hunting. **Special Features:** Lake was built on the floodplain of the Illinois River in 1971 by Commonwealth Edison Company as a cooling reservoir for a fossil-fuel power plant. Approximately 60% of the area is open to waterfowl hunting, and the rest is maintained as a waterfowl rest area.

★2284★ PROPHETSTOWN STATE RECREATION AREA

Riverside Dr
PO Box 181
Prophetstown, IL 61277
Web: dnr.state.il.us/Lands/Landmgt/PARKS/R1/
PROPHET.HTM
Phone: 815-537-2926
Size: 53 acres. **Location:** On the northeast edge of the city of Prophetstown, along the south bank of the Rock River, in Whiteside County. **Facilities:** Tent and trailer campsites with some electrical outlets and a shower building with flush toilets, picnic area (with privy toilets), shelter, playground, horseshoe courts, boat ramp, nature trail. **Activities:** Camping, boating, fishing, hiking, hunting. **Special Features:** Park derives its name from the prophet Wa-bo-kie-shiek (White Cloud), a Native American of mixed Winnebago and Sauk descent who served as an advisor to the great Sauk war chief Black Hawk.

★2285★ PYRAMID STATE RECREATION AREA

1562 Pyramid Park Rd
Pinckneyville, IL 62274
Web: dnr.state.il.us/Lands/Landmgt/PARKS/R5/
PYRAMID.HTM
Phone: 618-357-2574
Size: 19,701 acres. **Location:** 6 miles south of Pinckneyville off IL 127, then 2 miles west on Pyatts Blacktop in Perry County. **Facilities:** Tent and trailer campsites (no electrical hookups), including 3 Class C camping areas, Class D walk-in sites, small equestrian camp, and youth group camping area; small picnic areas, shelter, pit toilets; multi-use trails (16.5 miles), boat ramps (at larger lakes). **Activities:** Camping, boating (10 HP limit), canoeing, fishing, hiking, horseback riding, mountain biking, hunting. **Special Features:** Formerly the site of coal strip mines, the park is on reclaimed land that now consists of heavily forested hills with many lakes and ponds.

★2286★ RAMSEY LAKE STATE RECREATION AREA

Ramsey Lake Rd
PO Box 97
Ramsey, IL 62080
Web: dnr.state.il.us/Lands/Landmgt/PARKS/R5/
RAMSEY.HTM
Phone: 618-423-2215
Size: 1,980 acres. **Location:** Southern Illinois, 1 mile northwest of Ramsey in Fayette County. **Facilities:** 90 campsites with electricity, flush toilet, and showers, 24 sites (with electricity) for organized group camping, 45 primitive sites, youth group campground, small campground for horses, picnic areas, shelters, playgrounds, privies, hiking trail, horse trail (13 miles), boat ramp, boat dock, boat rentals, concession. **Activities:** Camping, boating (electric motors only), canoeing, fishing, hiking, horseback riding, hunting, ice fishing, cross-country skiing, sledding, ice skating, snowmobiling. **Special Features:** Once known as the "Old Fox Chase Grounds," park used to be a popular place for fox and raccoon hunters. It was also the site of one of the largest dog trial events.

★2287★ RANDOLPH COUNTY STATE RECREATION AREA

4301 S Lake Dr
Chester, IL 62233
Web: dnr.state.il.us/Lands/Landmgt/PARKS/R4/RAND.HTM
Phone: 618-826-2706
Size: 1,101 acres. **Location:** 5 miles northeast of Chester, in Randolph County. **Facilities:** 95 Class C campsites, group camp area with shelter and electricity, 6 picnic areas with shelters and drinking water, concession, hiking trails, equestrian trails (11.6 miles), boat rentals (seasonal). **Activities:** Camping, boating (10 HP limit), canoeing, fishing, hiking, horseback riding, hunting, cross-country skiing. **Special Features:** Park is situated in the rolling hill country of southern Illinois, in an area is known for its wooded areas and abundant wildlife and songbirds.

★2288★ RAY NORBUT STATE FISH & WILDLIFE AREA

RR 1, Box 55C
Griggsville, IL 62340
Web: dnr.state.il.us/lands/Landmgt/PARKS/R4/ray.htm
Phone: 217-833-2811
Size: 1,140 acres. **Location:** Along the Illinois River, 5 miles east of Griggsville and 2 miles south of Valley City in Pike County. **Facilities:** None. **Activities:** Bank fishing, hunting, hiking, bald eagle watching (in winter). **Special Features:** Site provides exceptional habitat for a wide range of plants and animals, including the endangered bald eagle and the jeweled shooting star, a rare pre-glacial wildflower species. Notable geographic features include Big Blue Island, a narrow, 100-acre strip of land in the river, and two east-west flowing streams, Blue Creek (a river tributary) and Napoleon Hollow Creek (spring-fed). Portions of the river bluff areas are closed to the public seasonally to provide a refuge for the wintering bald eagles, but viewing is allowed from specified locations.

★2289★ RED HILLS STATE PARK

1100 N and 400 E
RR 2 Box 252A
Sumner, IL 62466
Web: dnr.state.il.us/Lands/Landmgt/PARKS/R5/
REDHLS.HTM
Phone: 618-936-2469
Size: 967 acres. **Location:** Southeastern Illinois, midway between Olney and Lawrenceville on US 50. **Facilities:** More than 100 Class A campsites with electricity, water, and access to a shower building with flush toilets (&), primitive tent camping area, rent-a-cabin, equestrian campground, youth group tent

camping area, picnic areas, shelters, playgrounds, restrooms (&), trails (8 miles), boat ramp, boat rentals, concession, restaurant, gift shop. **Activities:** Camping, boating (electric motors only), canoeing, fishing, hiking, bicycling, horseback riding, hunting, ice fishing, sledding, ice skating. **Special Features:** Park is situated at the westernmost edge of the first land in Illinois ceded by Native Americans to the United States. Red Hills is the highest point of land between Saint Louis and Cincinnati, with a 120-foot tower and cross at the summit. At the base is an open-air tabernacle where interdenominational worship services are held Sunday evenings during the summer.

★2290★ REND LAKE STATE FISH & WILDLIFE AREA

10885 E Jefferson Rd
Bonnie, IL 62816
Web: dnr.state.il.us/Lands/Landmgt/PARKS/R5/
   RENDLAKE/REND.HTM
Phone: 618-279-3110
Size: 20,000 acres land; 18,900 acres water. **Location:** Between Mount Vernon and Benton, just off I-57. **Facilities:** Boat ramps. (Additional facilities are located at Wayne Fitzgerrell State Park, which is also situated on Rend Lake. See separate entry for details.) **Activities:** Boating, fishing, hunting, wildlife viewing. **Special Features:** Property is managed to provide valuable habitat for a variety of animals and waterfowl, including great blue herons and many species of shorebirds. The area's main attraction is Rend Lake, with 19 public access areas, eight of which provide launching ramps. It was built as a joint project of the Illinois Dept of Natural Resources, the Rend Lake Conservancy District, and the US Corps of Engineers to provide a dependable domestic water supply for the two-county area.

★2291★ RICE LAKE STATE FISH & WILDLIFE AREA

19721 N US Hwy 24
Canton, IL 61520
Web: dnr.state.il.us/Lands/Landmgt/PARKS/R1/Rice.htm
Phone: 309-647-9184
Size: 5,660 acres. **Location:** Near the Illinois River, 3 miles south of Banner along US 24 in Fulton County. **Facilities:** Tent and trailer camping areas, including 32 sites with electrical hookups (2 &), restrooms (&), picnic area, boat ramp. **Activities:** Camping, boating, fishing, wildlife observation, hunting. **Special Features:** Because of an extensive habitat management program, this backwater wetland area is used by thousands of ducks and geese as they move through central Illinois during the changing seasons.

★2292★ ROCK CUT STATE PARK

7318 Harlem Rd
Loves Park, IL 61111
Web: dnr.state.il.us/Lands/Landmgt/PARKS/R1/
   ROCKCUT.HTM
Phone: 815-885-3311
Size: 3,092 acres. **Location:** Northern Illinois, 1.5 miles north of the Riverside Blvd exit off I-90, north of Rockford in Winnebago County. **Facilities:** 208 Class A-Premium campsites, 60 Class B-Premium campsites, primitive cabin (has electricity but no water or plumbing facilities), equestrian campground, showers and flush toilets (&) in campground area, picnic areas with pit toilets, playgrounds, concession, restaurant, hiking trails (40 miles), mountain bike trails (23 miles), equestrian trails (14 miles), swimming beach, 2 boat ramps, boat docks, fishing piers (&). **Activities:** Camping, boating (10 HP limit), fishing, swimming, hiking, horseback riding, mountain biking, hunting, cross-country skiing, ice fishing. **Special Features:** Blasting operations through rock, conducted by railroad crews in 1859, gave Rock Cut State Park its name. Park includes both a fishing lake and a separate lake especially for swimming.

★2293★ ROCK ISLAND TRAIL STATE PARK

311 E Williams St
PO Box 64
Wyoming, IL 61491
Web: dnr.state.il.us/Lands/Landmgt/PARKS/R1/
   ROCKISLE.HTM
Phone: 309-695-2228
Size: 26-mile linear park; 392 acres. **Location:** Between Alta (Peoria County) to Toulon (Stark County). **Facilities:** Class D primitive campsites (in Kickpoo Creek Recreation Area) with picnic tables, shelter, and water; parking, water, and pit toilets at all access sites along the trail; visitor center/railroad museum. **Activities:** Camping, hiking, bicycling, cross-country skiing, interpretive programs. **Special Features:** Following the abandoned Rock Island Railroad line, the trail travels through five towns (Alta, Dunlap, Princeville, Wyoming, and Toulon) over several bridges, including a trestle bridge over the Spoon River. The trail is lined with trees for much of the way, passing farmland, prairie grass, and wildflower meadows, and is considered one of the finest in Illinois. A restored train depot in Wyoming, Illinois, serves as trail headquarters.

★2294★ SALINE COUNTY STATE FISH & WILDLIFE AREA

85 Glen O Jones Rd
Equality, IL 62934
Web: dnr.state.il.us/Lands/Landmgt/PARKS/R5/
   SALINE.HTM
Phone: 618-276-4405
Size: 1,270 acres. **Location:** 5 miles southeast of Equality in southeastern Illinois, bordering the Shawnee National Forest (see separate entry in national forests chapter). **Facilities:** Tent and trailer campsites (no electricity), horsemen's campground, picnic areas, concession, hiking trails (9 miles), equestrian trails, boat rentals, boat ramps, 2 docks. **Activities:** Camping, boating (10 HP limit), fishing, hiking, horseback riding, hunting. **Special Features:** Site of springs and wells that furnished brine for one of the two salt works in the area. Before the first settlers arrived, Native Americans also produced salt from the springs here. Extracting salt from the springs' water became too expensive once commercial producers began manufacturing salt, and the land that was once so highly prized was sold off.

★2295★ SAM DALE LAKE STATE CONSERVATION AREA

RR 1
Johnsonville, IL 62850
Web: dnr.state.il.us/Lands/Landmgt/PARKS/R5/
    SAMDALE.HTM
Phone: 618-835-2292
Size: 1,302 acres. **Location:** 1.5 miles west of Johnsonville and 0.5 miles north of Ext 161 in northwest Wayne County. **Facilities:** 2 Class B/E campgrounds (with electrical hookups), tent and group camping areas (1 &), picnic areas, shelter, playgrounds, swimming beach, concession stand, nature trail, boat rentals, 2 boat ramps, docks. **Activities:** Camping, boating (10 HP limit), canoeing, fishing, hiking, swimming, hunting, ice fishing. **Special Features:** Park features Sam Dale Lake, a 194-acre lake with 8.5 miles of shoreline. The lake is long and narrow with many curves and fingers, making it a prime fishing spot.

★2296★ SAM PARR STATE FISH & WILDLIFE AREA

13225 E State Hwy 33
Newton, IL 62448
Web: dnr.state.il.us/Lands/Landmgt/PARKS/R5/
    SAMPARR.HTM
Phone: 618-783-2661
Size: 1,180 acres. **Location:** Southern Illinois, 3 miles northeast of Newton. **Facilities:** Class B/E, C, and D campsites, youth camping area, 4 day-use picnic areas with shelters, hiking trails (2 miles), equestrian trails (13 miles), 2 boat ramps, docks. **Activities:** Camping, boating (10 HP limit), fishing, hiking, horseback riding, hunting. **Special Features:** Area features a 183-acre manmade lake with 9 miles of shoreline.

★2297★ SAND RIDGE STATE FOREST

PO Box 111
Forest City, IL 61532
Web: dnr.state.il.us/Lands/Landmgt/PARKS/R4/SAND.HTM
Phone: 309-597-2212
Size: 7,200 acres. **Location:** Southwest of Peoria and 1.5 miles northwest of Forest City in Mason County. **Facilities:** 27 Class C campsites, 12 backcountry primitive sites, organized group campground, equestrian camping area with hitching rails, water, pit toilets, and a shelter area, picnic area with shelter, hiking trails (44 miles), equestrian trails (55 miles), snowmobile trails (26 miles), historic site, archery range, hand trap shooting range. **Activities:** Camping, hiking, horseback riding, snowmobiling, shooting, hunting, birdwatching. **Special Features:** Largest of the state forests in Illinois, Sand Ridge is the result of a prehistoric dry period when more desert-like conditions existed. It is one of the few places in the state with a variety of plants and animals more commonly associated with the southwest than the midwest, including the badger, pocket gopher, silvery bladderpod, and prickly pear cactus. Sand Ridge Forest is also an important nesting area for such neo-tropical migratory birds as the ovenbird, indigo bunting, veery, and scarlet tanager.

★2298★ SANGANOIS STATE FISH & WILDLIFE AREA

3594 County Road 200 N
Chandlerville, IL 62627
Web: dnr.state.il.us/Lands/Landmgt/PARKS/R4/
    SANGILL.HTM
Phone: 309-546-2628
Size: 10,360 acres. **Location:** At the junction of the Sangamon and Illinois rivers, 8 miles northwest of Chandlerville off Rt 78, mostly in Cass and Mason counties. **Facilities:** Boat ramp. **Activities:** Hunting. **Special Features:** Managed primarily as a refuge for migratory waterfowl and as a public duck and goose hunting area, Sanganois is one of the few state-owned refuges and public hunting areas along the Illinois River. Prior to state acquisition the lands and waters within the area were owned and operated as private duck clubs, the largest being the Sanganois Gun Club. Public access is mainly by boat.

★2299★ SANGCHRIS LAKE STATE PARK

9898 Cascade Rd
Rochester, IL 62563
Web: dnr.state.il.us/Lands/Landmgt/PARKS/R4/
    SANGCH.HTM
Phone: 217-498-9208
Size: 5,280 acres. **Location:** East of Springfield in central Illinois. **Facilities:** 135 Class A campsites (with electricity and showers), 40 Class B/S sites (showers), 15 Class C campsites (tent camping, walk-in or backpack, with showers), 5 equestrian campsites, group camping area, 2 cabins, playground, restrooms, 8 picnic areas, shelters, nature trails (3 miles), equestrian trail (5 miles), snowmobile trail (11 miles), boat ramps, docks, dog training area. (&&) **Activities:** Camping, boating (25 HP limit), canoeing, fishing, hiking, horseback riding, hunting, snowmobiling, interpretive programs. **Special Features:** The park's 3,000-acre, three-fingered lake, with 120 miles of shoreline, extends into both Sangamon and Christian counties, earning it the name ''Sangchris.''

★2300★ SHABBONA LAKE STATE PARK

4201 Shabbona Grove Rd
Shabbona, IL 60550
Web: dnr.state.il.us/Lands/Landmgt/PARKS/R1/
    SHABBONA.HTM
Phone: 815-824-2106
Size: 1,546 acres. **Location:** West of Chicago via I-88. **Facilities:** 150 Class A campsites (electricity, shower building with flush toilets), 2 cabins (no water or toilet facilities), 3 picnic areas, restrooms, horseshoe pits, concessions, trails (8 miles), fishing pier, boat rentals, boat ramp, restaurant (&&). **Activities:** Camping, boating (10 HP limit), canoeing, fishing, hiking, hunting, cross-country skiing, snowmobiling, ice fishing, sledding, ice skating, tobogganing. **Special Features:** Park was named for the Potawatomi chief who briefly held a small parcel of land here 10 years after the 1832 Black Hawk War. Shabbona Lake is a pilot site for disabled visitor accessibility, and all facilities, including a specially designed fishing pier, are totally accessible.

9. State Parks

★2301★ SHELBYVILLE STATE FISH & WILDLIFE AREA

RR 1, Box 42A
Bethany, IL 61914
Web: dnr.state.il.us/Lands/Landmgt/PARKS/R3/
SHELBY.HTM
Phone: 217-665-3112
Size: 6,200 acres. **Location:** Along the Kaskaskia and West Okaw rivers near Sullivan, off IL 121. **Facilities:** 6 small boat launch facilities in the wildlife areas, nature trails. **Activities:** Fishing, hunting, hiking, nature study. **Special Features:** Area is composed of two separate units, both managed primarily to promote diverse wildlife habitats and to provide opportunities for hunting and fishing.

★2302★ SIELBECK FOREST STATE NATURAL AREA

c/o Mermet Lake State Fish & Wildlife Area
1812 Grinnell Rd
Belknap, IL 62908
Phone: 618-524-5577
Size: 385 acres. **Location:** In southern Illinois, 3 miles northwest of Metropolis and 2 miles east of IL 45 on Upper Salem Road in Massac County. **Facilities:** Sielbeck Forest is maintained in its natural state and has no day-use areas, trails, or major improvements of any kind. **Activities:** Hunting, fishing, hiking. **Special Features:** Within this land and water reserve are 100 acres of floodplain forest dominated by cherrybark oak, sweetgum, and pin oak, and within this soggy forest are 35 acres of forested swamp dominated by cypress and tupelo. Many of the trees in this old-growth remnant are more than 200 years old and nearly 4 feet in diameter. The swamp rabbit makes its home here, and pileated and red-headed woodpeckers, nuthatches, and tree swallows are abundant. Also found in the Forest are two species found only in southern Illinois, in high quality floodplain forests and swamps, the storax (a small tree also known as American snowbell) and the giant sedge

★2303★ SILOAM SPRINGS STATE PARK

938 E 3003rd Ln
Clayton, IL 62324
Web: dnr.state.il.us/Lands/Landmgt/PARKS/R4/
SILOAMSP.HTM
Phone: 217-894-6205
Size: 3,323 acres. **Location:** Just east of Quincy near Clayton. **Facilities:** 98 Class A campsites (with electricity, restrooms, and showers), 84 Class B campsites (with showers and restrooms), 4 primitive backpack campsites, group campground, equestrian camping area, picnic areas, shelters, playground, restrooms, horseshoe pits, hiking trails (12), equestrian trails (23 miles), concession stand, 6 fishing piers, boat and canoe rentals, boat ramp. **Activities:** Camping, boating (electric motors only), canoeing, fishing, hiking, horseback riding, hunting, cross-country skiing, ice skating, ice fishing, sledding. **Special Features:** Area was once the site of a resort popular for the alleged curative value of its springs.

★2304★ SILVER SPRINGS STATE FISH & WILDLIFE AREA

13608 Fox Rd
Yorkville, IL 60560
Web: dnr.state.il.us/Lands/Landmgt/PARKS/R2/
SILVERSP.HTM
Phone: 630-553-6297
Size: 1,314 acres. **Location:** Northeastern Illinois, 5 miles west of Yorkville, off IL 47, in Kendall County. **Facilities:** Youth group camping area (no vehicle access), picnic area, shelters, restrooms, refreshment stand, nature trails (4 miles), equestrian trail (7 miles), snowmobile trail (4 miles). **Activities:** Camping, boating (no gas motors), canoeing, fishing, hiking, horseback riding, wildlife viewing, hunting, cross-country skiing, sledding, ice skating, snowmobiling. **Special Features:** Area is named for the pool of clear bubbling water located here, which does not freeze even on the coldest winter days. The area also features a segment of the Fox River and several small manmade lakes. A 45-acre natural prairie restoration project gives visitors a sense of the area's original landscape, with native wildflowers, songbirds, waterfowl, and upland game.

★2305★ SNAKEDEN HOLLOW STATE FISH & WILDLIFE AREA

1936 State Hwy 167
Victoria, IL 61485
Web: dnr.state.il.us/Lands/Landmgt/PARKS/R1/
SNAKE.HTM
Phone: 309-879-2607
Size: 2,497 acres. **Location:** 1 mile east of Victoria on IL 167. **Facilities:** Boat ramp, restrooms. **Activities:** Boating (10 HP limit), fishing, hunting. **Special Features:** With the exception of 160-acre Snakeden Hollow Lake, the area's 125 lakes and ponds were formed as a result of surface mining operations. Restoration efforts, begun in 1987, have developed the once-stripped land into diverse fish and wildlife habitats offering exceptional fishing and hunting opportunities. Site is named for a small creek that "snakes" its way through the property.

★2306★ SOUTH SHORE STATE PARK

c/o Eldon Hazlet State Recreation Area
20100 Hazlet Park Rd
Carlyle, IL 62231
Web: dnr.state.il.us/Lands/Landmgt/PARKS/R4/sts.htm
Phone: 618-594-3015
Size: 3 miles long. **Location:** 3 miles east of Carlyle on Route 50, along the southeast side of Carlyle Lake (across the lake from Eldon Hazlet State Park; see separate entry). **Facilities:** 33 Class C tent or trailer campsites (now electrical hookups or showers), 5 day-use picnic areas, boat ramp, restrooms, nature trails (closed for use as 3-D archery ranges several times a year). **Activities:** Camping, boating, sailing, fishing, hiking, wildlife viewing (especially white-tailed deer). **Special Features:** Because of the size of Lake Carlyle (it is the largest manmade reservoir in Illinois), there is no horsepower limit on boat motors, making the 26,000-acre lake a popular weekend destination for boaters. Sailboats are welcome here as well.

★2307★ SPITLER WOODS STATE NATURAL AREA

705 Spitler Park Dr
Mount Zion, IL 62549
Web: dnr.state.il.us/Lands/Landmgt/PARKS/R3/
    SPITLER.HTM
Phone: 217-864-3121
Size: 202.5 acres. **Location:** 8 miles southeast of Decatur and 0.5 miles east of Mount Zion, off IL 121. **Facilities:** Youth group campsites, restrooms, picnic areas, nature preserve, trails. **Activities:** Youth group camping, hiking. **Special Features:** Two-thirds of the area is a dedicated nature preserve containing one of the few remaining stands of climax-growth timber in central Illinois.

★2308★ SPRING LAKE STATE FISH & WILDLIFE AREA

7982 S Park Rd
Manito, IL 61546
Web: dnr.state.il.us/Lands/Landmgt/PARKS/R1/SPL.HTM
Phone: 309-968-7135
Size: 2,032 acres. **Location:** 25 miles southwest of Peoria on the east side of the Illinois River, in Tazewell County. **Facilities:** 70 Class C tent or trailer campsites (no showers or electric hookups), primitive walk-in tent campground (group camping permitted here), 5 day-use picnic areas, shelters, hiking trails (7.5 miles), concession stand, boat rentals, boat ramps. **Activities:** Camping, boating (25 HP limit), fishing, hiking, hunting, ice fishing. **Special Features:** Overlooked by a large sandstone bluff, Spring Lake is a long, narrow lake created by a meander of the Illinois River. The lake covers an area of 1,285 acres, with 18 miles of shoreline and a maximum depth of 10 feet.

★2309★ STARVED ROCK STATE PARK

PO Box 509
Utica, IL 61373
Web: dnr.state.il.us/Lands/Landmgt/PARKS/I&M/EAST/
    STARVE/PARK.HTM
Phone: 815-667-4726
Size: 2,630 acres. **Location:** On the south side of the Illinois River, 1 mile south of Utica, and midway between the cities of LaSalle-Peru and Ottawa. **Facilities:** Lodge with 72 luxury hotel rooms and 22 cabin rooms, restaurant, conference area, meeting rooms, indoor swimming pool, children's pool, whirpool, saunas, and sunning patio; 133 Class A-Premium campsites with electricity, showers, and flush toilets, youth group camping area, children's playground, camp store; picnic areas, 8 shelters, restrooms; hiking trails through park's bluffs and canyons (13 miles), horse rentals (nearby), boat ramps; visitor center. **Activities:** Camping, boating, canoeing, fishing, hiking, horseback riding, hunting, eagle viewing, interpretive programs. **Special Features:** The backdrop for activities at Starved Rock is 18 canyons formed by glacial meltwater and stream erosion that slice through tree-covered sandstone bluffs. The end-of-winter thaw and spring rains combine to create waterfalls at the heads of all 18 canyons, and vertical walls of moss-covered stone create a setting of natural geographic beauty uncommon in Illinois.

★2310★ STEPHEN A. FORBES STATE PARK

6924 Omega Rd
Kinmundy, IL 62854
Web: dnr.state.il.us/Lands/Landmgt/PARKS/R5/
    STEPHEN.HTM
Phone: 618-547-3381
Size: 3,103 acres. **Location:** Southern Illinois, 15 miles northeast of Salem in Marion County. **Facilities:** 115 campsites with electricity, water, and showers, 10 primitive walk-in campsites, youth group camping area, group rent-a-camp site with cabin, 21-site equestrian campground with electricity, picnic areas, sports field, playground, hiking trails, equestrian trails (15 miles), restaurant, marina, store, boat ramps, boat rentals, docks, floating walkway (&), swimming beach, aquatic laboratory (open for public tours). **Activities:** Camping, boating, canoeing, fishing, swimming, water-skiing, hiking, horseback riding, hunting, interpretive programs. **Special Features:** Park is named for natural scientist Stephen A. Forbes, whose more than 400 scientific publications are still used extensively in the study of aquatic biology, ichthyology, ornithology, and ecology. Park has more than 1,100 acres of oak and hickory forest surrounding a large lake with 18 miles of shoreline.

★2311★ TEN MILE CREEK STATE FISH & WILDLIFE AREA

RR 1, Box 179
McLeansboro, IL 62859
Web: dnr.state.il.us/Lands/Landmgt/PARKS/R5/TEN.HTM
Phone: 618-643-2862
Size: 5,824 acres. **Location:** In southeastern Jefferson County and western sections of Hamilton County, with access via rural roads leading from IL 142 and IL 14. **Facilities:** Archery range, hand trap range (shotgun use only), rifle range. **Activities:** Fishing (fish size and catch limits; boats 10 HP motor limit), hunting, trapping, wildlife viewing, hiking, target shooting. **Special Features:** About one-third of the land that is now part of Ten Mile Creek was once strip-mined. Since 1988 when the land was purchased, the site been reclaimed to varying degrees, with some areas being returned to flat agriculture land and others to steeply sloped areas interspersed with ponds and lakes. The remainder of the site, which was not mined, is a mixture of fields and forest bisected by small streams.

★2312★ TRAIL OF TEARS STATE FOREST

3240 State Forest Rd
Jonesboro, IL 62952
Web: dnr.state.il.us/Lands/Landmgt/PARKS/R5/
    TRLTEARS.HTM
Phone: 618-833-4910
Size: 5,114 acres. **Location:** Southern Illinois, 5 miles northwest of Jonesboro and 20 miles south of Murphysboro. **Facilities:** Class C tent camping and Class D backpack campsites, group camping areas, picnic areas, shelters, privies, ball diamond, trails (40 miles). **Activities:** Camping, hiking, horseback riding, hunting. **Special Features:** In the winter of 1838-1839, the Cherokee, Creek, and Chickasaw nations were forced by the US Army to move from the Southeast to reservations in Oklahoma Territory. They had to stop for the winter in southern Illinois, just south of the present-day state forest, because of floating ice

9. State Parks

455

in the Mississippi River. Hundreds died of cold and starvation during this cruel trek, which came to be known as the Trail of Tears (see separate entry on Trail of Tears National Historic Trail in national trails section). Today, Trail of Tears Forest in Illinois is a multiple-use site managed for timber, wildlife, ecosystem preservation, watershed protection, and recreation.

★2313★ TUNNEL HILL STATE TRAIL

Highway 146 E
PO Box 671
Vienna, IL 62995
Web: dnr.state.il.us/Lands/Landmgt/PARKS/R5/tunnel.htm
Phone: 618-658-2168
Size: 45-mile linear park. Location: Southern Illinois, between the communities of Harrisburg in Saline County and Karnak in Pulaski County. Facilities: Day-use trail with drinking water, privy toilets, and parking at access areas. Activities: Hiking, bicycling. Special Features: Located in southern Illinois, the trail offers access and facilities in communities of Harrisburg, Carrier Mills, Stonefort, New Burnside, Tunnel Hill, Vienna, and Karnak. It passes over 21 trestles, through a 543-foot tunnel, and through the Shawnee National Forest (see entry in national forests section). Interpretive signs along the route point out abandoned coal mines, a sandstone quarry, and other sites of interest.

★2314★ TURKEY BLUFFS STATE FISH & WILDLIFE AREA

4301 S Lakeside Dr
Chester, IL 62233
Phone: 618-826-2706
Size: 2,264 acres. Location: 2 miles south of Chester. Facilities: Trails, toilet facilities. Activities: Fishing, hunting, hiking, horseback riding, wildlife viewing. Special Features: Area is located on the Mississippi River bluffs in southwestern Illinois.

★2315★ UNION COUNTY STATE FISH & WILDLIFE AREA

2755 Refuge Rd
Jonesboro, IL 62952
Web: dnr.state.il.us/Lands/Landmgt/PARKS/R5/
   UNIONCO.HTM
Phone: 618-833-5175
Size: 6,202 acres. Location: 7 miles west of Jonesboro off Route 146 in Union County. Activities: Fishing (on Grassy Lake, Mar 1-Oct 15; 10 HP limit for boats), hunting (only in designated Public Hunting Area at south end of site), sightseeing and wildlife photography in Refuge area. Special Features: Area is winter home for 50,000 to 100,000 Canada geese each year. White-tailed deer, bald and golden eagles, and other waterfowl are also commonly found in the area.

★2316★ VOLO BOG STATE NATURAL AREA

28478 W Brandenburg Rd
Ingleside, IL 60041
Web: dnr.state.il.us/Lands/Landmgt/PARKS/R2/
   VOLOBOG.HTM
Phone: 815-344-1294

Size: 1,200 acres. Location: In northeastern Illinois, 4 miles south of Fox Lake in Lake and McHenry counties, on West Brandenburg Road. Facilities: Visitor center with displays, restrooms, picnic area, nature trail. Activities: Hiking, cross-country skiing, hunting, interpretive programs. Special Features: Volo Bog was created by the melting of large blocks of ice pushed deep into the ground 12,000 years ago. Among the bog's interesting plant life are sphagnum moss, cattails, leatherleaf, and a tamarack forest.

★2317★ WALNUT POINT STATE PARK

2331 E County Rd 370 N
Oakland, IL 61943
Web: dnr.state.il.us/lands/Landmgt/PARKS/R3/
   WALNUTPT.HTM
Phone: 217-346-3336
Size: 671 acres. Location: 20 miles northeast of Charleston, in east central Illinois, near I-57, US 36, and IL 133. Facilities: Class A campsites with electrical hookups and shower building with flush toilets, Class C walk-in tent sites, group camping area (youth and adult), 8 picnic areas with privies, 5 shelters, 2 playgrounds, horseshoe pits, nature preserve, hiking trails (&), floating docks, fishing piers, boat rentals, 2 boat ramps, concession. Activities: Camping, boating (electric motors only), fishing, hiking, hunting, cross-country skiing, ice skating, ice fishing, birdwatching, wildlife viewing, interpretive programs. Special Features: The focal point of the park is a 59-acre lake with 6.3 miles of shoreline and an average depth of 12.5 feet. The many-fingered lake is formed by an earthen dam located on the south side of the recreation area.

★2318★ WASHINGTON COUNTY STATE RECREATION AREA

18500 Conservation Dr
Nashville, IL 62263
Web: dnr.state.il.us/Lands/Landmgt/PARKS/R4/
   WASHCO.HTM
Phone: 618-327-3137
Size: 1,440 acres. Location: In southern Illinois, 4 miles south of Nashville. Facilities: Tent and trailer campsites, showers, 7 picnic areas with playgrounds, trails (7 miles), 2 boat ramps, boat docks, boat rentals, concession stand. Activities: Camping, boating (10 HP limit), fishing, hiking, hunting. Special Features: The area's 248-acre lake is long and narrow with 13 miles of shoreline.

★2319★ WAYNE FITZGERRELL STATE RECREATION AREA

11094 Ranger Rd
Whittington, IL 62897
Web: dnr.state.il.us/Lands/Landmgt/PARKS/R5/
   WAYNE.HTM
Phone: 618-629-2320
Size: 3,300 acres. Location: 6 miles north of Benton, just off I-57. Facilities: 243 modern campsites with electrical hookups, 40 tent sites, 3 shower buildings, resort lodge with 105 rooms and cabins, conference center, restaurant, swimming pool, tennis court, convenience store, gift shop, pontoon boat and wave

9. State Parks

runner rentals, picnic areas (&), shelters, playgrounds, restrooms, hiking/biking trail (4 miles), equestrian trail (9 miles), boat ramps, courtesy dock. **Activities:** Camping, boating, fishing, swimming, hiking, horseback riding, bicycling, hunting, tennis. **Special Features:** Park overlooks the US Army Corps of Engineers' 19,000-acre Rend Lake, and about 75% of the park's boundary is shoreline, providing excellent bankfishing opportunities. The park is noted for its extensive sporting dog field trial programs, hosting more than 25 field-trial events annually in which some of the best-trained retrievers, beagles, and bird dogs compete for regional and national honors.

★2320★ WEINBERG-KING STATE PARK

PO Box 203
Augusta, IL 62311
Web: dnr.state.il.us/Lands/Landmgt/PARKS/R4/
WEINBERG.HTM
Phone: 217-392-2345
Size: 772 acres. **Location:** 3 miles east of Augusta, north of IL 101. **Facilities:** Camping is mainly in the equestrian area and includes 19 electrical hookups, 4 picnic areas with pit toilets, playground, equestrian trails (30 miles). **Activities:** Camping, fishing, horseback riding, hunting, snowmobiling. **Special Features:** William Creek meanders through the park, providing habitat for a variety of wildlife.

★2321★ WELDON SPRINGS STATE PARK

1159 500 N
RR 2 Box 87
Clinton, IL 61727
Web: dnr.state.il.us/Lands/Landmgt/PARKS/R3/
WELDONRA.HTM
Phone: 217-935-2644
Size: 550 acres. **Location:** 3 miles southeast of Clinton, in DeWitt County. **Facilities:** 75 Class A campsites (electrical hookups, shower building, pit toilets), 9 Class C sites, tent, backpack, large group, and youth camping areas, picnic areas, shelters, restrooms, playgrounds, horseshoe pits, fishing platforms, boat ramp, boat rentals, concession stand, 2 outdoor amphitheaters, restaurant, historic site, museum/interpretive center, visitor center. **Activities:** Camping, boating (electric motors only), fishing, hiking, backpacking, wildlife viewing, cross-country skiing, ice fishing, sledding, tobogganing, interpretive programs. **Special Features:** Between 1901 and 1921, the property was the site of an annual gathering known as the Chautauqua Assembly. For ten days each summer, area residents created a temporary tent city as they came to hear some of the best public speakers and entertainers of the day. Representing every field of interest, programs were presented for the entertainment, education, and ''moral elevation'' of the participants. Among the many speakers were former President William Taft, Vice President Adlai Stevenson, William Jennings Bryan, evangelist Sam Jones, Rev. Billy Sunday, Helen Keller, and Carrie Nation.

★2322★ WHITE PINES FOREST STATE PARK

6712 W Pines Rd
Mount Morris, IL 61054
Web: dnr.state.il.us/Lands/Landmgt/PARKS/R1/
WHITEPNS.HTM
Phone: 815-946-3717

Size: 385 acres. **Location:** 12 miles north of Dixon, in the heart of Rock River Valley. **Facilities:** 103 Class B/S campsites, 2 youth group campgrounds (6 & sites), lodge with 16 cabins (25 guest rooms total), restaurant, lounge, gift shop, picnic areas, shelters, trails (&). **Activities:** Camping, hiking, cross-country skiing. **Special Features:** Forming the southern boundary of the park is the old Chicago-Iowa Trail, for years the principal route east and west across the northern part of the state. The park is in Black Hawk country and is rich in American Indian history. Among the park's most interesting features are the concrete fords that span its creeks, allowing visitors to literally drive through the flowing streams.

★2323★ WILLIAM G. STRATTON STATE PARK

401 Ottawa St
Morris, IL 60450
Phone: 815-942-0796
Size: 6 acres. **Location:** In the town of Morris, in northeastern Illinois. **Facilities:** 4 public boat launching ramps, jet ski launching area, picnic tables and benches along the water, multi-use trail. **Activities:** Boating, water-skiing, jet skiing, hiking, bicycling, snowmobiling. **Special Features:** Park was developed in 1959 to provide boat access to the Illinois River. Along the park's northern border is the Illinois & Michigan Canal State Trail (see separate entry), a 61-mile trail for hikers, bicyclists, and snowmobilers.

★2324★ WILLIAM W. POWERS STATE RECREATION AREA

12949 Avenue O
Chicago, IL 60633
Web: dnr.state.il.us/Lands/Landmgt/PARKS/R2/Wmpow.htm
Phone: 773-646-3270
Size: 580 acres. **Location:** On Chicago's far southeast side, along the Indiana border. **Facilities:** Picnic area, 4 shelters, 3 boat ramps. **Activities:** Boating (10 HP limit), fishing, picnicking, waterfowl hunting, ice fishing. **Special Features:** Main attraction is Wolf Lake, segmented by dikes and featuring six miles of shoreline for bank fishing.

★2325★ WOLF CREEK STATE PARK

RR 1, Box 99
Windsor, IL 61957
Web: dnr.state.il.us/Lands/Landmgt/PARKS/R3/
WOLFCREK.HTM
Phone: 217-459-2831
Size: 1,967 acres. **Location:** 8 miles northwest of Windsor. **Facilities:** 304 Class A campsites with showers, restrooms, and electricity, 78 Class C campsites, 2 family camping areas, organized group camp, equestrian campground, picnic areas (&), shelters, hiking trails, equestrian trail (15 miles), snowmobile trail (16.5 miles), swimming beach, boat ramp. **Activities:** Camping, boating, swimming, water-skiing, fishing, hiking, horseback riding, snowmobiling, hunting. **Special Features:** The Flood Control Act of 1958 authorized the Shelbyville Reservoir Project, which involved construction of a dam and creation of a lake. This natural resource management area includes both

9. State Parks

Wolf Creek State Park and Eagle Creek State Park (see separate entry), which face each other across Lake Shelbyville.

★2326★ WOODFORD STATE FISH & WILDLIFE AREA
RR 1
Low Point, IL 61545
Web: dnr.state.il.us/lands/Landmgt/PARKS/R1/
    WOODFORD.HTM
Phone: 309-822-8861
Size: 2,901 acres. **Location:** East of the Illinois River, northeast of Peoria, on IL 26. **Facilities:** Tent and trailer campsites, picnic tables, shelter, trails (3 miles; closed during fall migration), boat ramp, docks. **Activities:** Camping, boating, fishing, hiking, hunting. **Special Features:** Located in a picturesque spot along the east side of the Illinois River, the area features many artesian wells.

9. State Parks

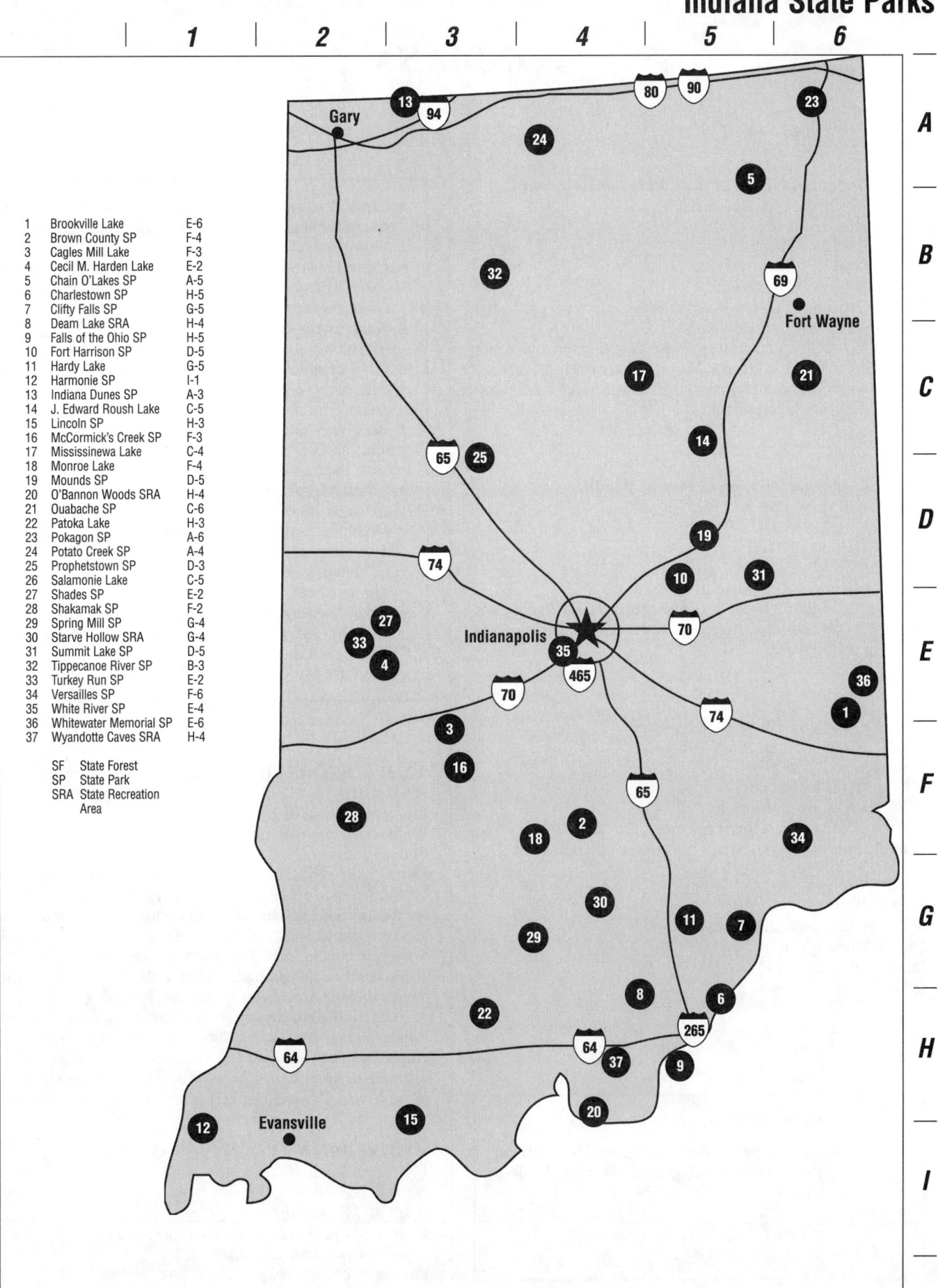

Indiana State Parks

1	Brookville Lake	E-6
2	Brown County SP	F-4
3	Cagles Mill Lake	F-3
4	Cecil M. Harden Lake	E-2
5	Chain O'Lakes SP	A-5
6	Charlestown SP	H-5
7	Clifty Falls SP	G-5
8	Deam Lake SRA	H-4
9	Falls of the Ohio SP	H-5
10	Fort Harrison SP	D-5
11	Hardy Lake	G-5
12	Harmonie SP	I-1
13	Indiana Dunes SP	A-3
14	J. Edward Roush Lake	C-5
15	Lincoln SP	H-3
16	McCormick's Creek SP	F-3
17	Mississinewa Lake	C-4
18	Monroe Lake	F-4
19	Mounds SP	D-5
20	O'Bannon Woods SRA	H-4
21	Ouabache SP	C-6
22	Patoka Lake	H-3
23	Pokagon SP	A-6
24	Potato Creek SP	A-4
25	Prophetstown SP	D-3
26	Salamonie Lake	C-5
27	Shades SP	E-2
28	Shakamak SP	F-2
29	Spring Mill SP	G-4
30	Starve Hollow SRA	G-4
31	Summit Lake SP	D-5
32	Tippecanoe River SP	B-3
33	Turkey Run SP	E-2
34	Versailles SP	F-6
35	White River SP	E-4
36	Whitewater Memorial SP	E-6
37	Wyandotte Caves SRA	H-4

SF	State Forest
SP	State Park
SRA	State Recreation Area

INDIANA

2327★ Indiana Division of State Parks & Reservoirs
402 W Washington St, Rm W298
Indianapolis, IN 46204
(317) 232-4124 - Phone
(317) 232-4132 - Fax
(800) 622-4931 - Toll-free
(866) 622-6746 - Toll-free Reservations
Web: www.in.gov/dnr/parklake
System includes nine reservoirs, 24 parks, and seven inns which cover more than 212,000 acres. Manages, interprets, and protects natural, wildlife, and cultural resources and provides for compatible recreational opportunities.

★2328★ Indiana Division of Fish & Wildlife
402 W Washington St, Rm W273
Indianapolis, IN 46204
(317) 232-4080 - Phone
(317) 232-8150 - Fax
Web: www.in.gov/dnr/fishwild
Manages 19 wildlife areas designed primarily for fishing and hunting. Many sites also offer wildlife viewing, picnicking, and camping opportunities.

★2329★ Indiana Division of Forestry
402 W Washington St, Rm W296
Indianapolis, IN 46204
(317) 232-4105 - Phone
Web: www.in.gov/dnr/forestry
Conserves and protects forest resources. Provides outdoor recreation facilities at 15 properties comprising 150,000 acres.

★2330★ Indiana State Museum
650 W Washington St
Indianapolis, IN 46204
(317) 232-1637 - Phone
(317) 233-8268 - Fax
Web: www.in.gov/ism
Manages and operates 14 historic sites.

Key to campsite classification:

- **Class AA campsites** — Sewage, water, and electrical hookup. Picnic table, parking spur, fire ring. Modern restrooms/showers.
- **Class A campsites** — Electrical hookup. Picnic table, fire ring, parking spur. Drinking water supply in area. Modern restrooms/showers.

- **Class B campsites** — Picnic table, fire ring, parking spur. Drinking water supply in area. Modern restrooms/showers.
- **Class C campsites** — Picnic table, fire ring, parking spur. Drinking water supply in area. Pit toilet (no showers or restrooms).
- **Horsemen's campground** — Class A or C campsites with tie-up for six horses at each site.
- **Rally campground** — Groups of five or more camping units (families). Drinking water supply near campground. Pit toilets. Advance reservation required.
- **Backpack and canoe campground** — Located in remote areas or near waterways. Water source in general area. Picnic tables, fire ring.
- **Youth tent areas** — Groups of ten or more with campers under 21 years old and their adult leaders. Available to public, semi-public, and not-for-profit groups only. Tent camping only. Fire rings, picnic tables. Pit toilets; no showers or restrooms. Drinking water supply near campground.
- **Housekeeping cabins** — Offer bedrooms, living areas, kitchens, and modern bathroom facilities. Other amenities, such as dishes and utensils, pillows, and linens, may or may not be provided.

★2331★ BROOKVILLE LAKE
PO Box 100
Brookville, IN 47012
Web: www.in.gov/dnr/parklake/properties/res_brookville.html
Phone: 765-647-2657
Size: 16,445 acres land; 5,260 acres water. **Location:** In southeastern Indiana, off Highways 1, 44, and 101. **Facilities:** Campground (located in Mounds SRA) with 388 sites with electric hookups and 62 sites with full hookups (electric, water, sewer), 5 shower houses, and 3 comfort stations; camp store, picnic areas, shelters, playground, hiking trails, 9 boat ramps, 4 marinas, swimming beach, shooting range, horseshoe pits, volleyball court. **Activities:** Camping, swimming, fishing, boating, waterskiing, hiking, ice fishing, shooting, hunting, interpretive programs. **Special Features:** Lake area encompasses Mounds State Recreation Area (not to be confused with Mounds State Park in Anderson, IN) and Quakertown State Recreation Area.

★2332★ BROWN COUNTY STATE PARK
1405 State Road 46 W
PO Box 608
Nashville, IN 47448
Web: www.in.gov/dnr/parklake/properties/
park_browncounty.html
Phone: 812-988-6406

Size: 15,696 acres. **Location:** In Brown County, off IN 46. **Facilities:** 429 campsites (401 with electric hookups), 204 equestrian campsites (118 with electric hookups), 60 rally campsites, youth tent areas, flush toilets and showers, camp store, family cabins, 84-room lodge (34 in Main Lodge, others in new addition) with restaurant and meeting/conference facilities, picnic areas with playgrounds/playfields, picnic shelters, hiking trails (18 miles), equestrian trails (70 miles), saddle barn, mountain bike trails (6 miles), tennis courts, swimming pool, nature center. **Activities:** Camping, swimming, fishing, ice fishing, hiking, horseback riding, mountain bike riding, tennis, interpretive programs. **Special Features:** Park is the largest state park in Indiana and is open year-round. In addition to the many recreational opportunities at the park, nearby Nashville features quaint specialty shops, art galleries, entertainment, and historic homes.

★2333★ CAGLES MILL LAKE

1317 W Lieber Rd, Suite 1
Cloverdale, IN 46120
Web: www.in.gov/dnr/parklake/properties/res_caglesmill.html
Phone: 765-795-4576
Size: 8,075 acres land; 1,400 acres water. **Location:** In south central Indiana, midway between Indianapolis and Terre Haute. **Facilities:** 120 electric and 96 non-electric campsites, campground grocery and concession (open summers), picnic areas (&), shelters, playgrounds, playfields, hiking and fitness trails, fishing pier, marina, 2 boat ramps, boat rentals, swimming pool and waterslide (at Lieber SRA), activity center, basketball court, horseshoe pits. **Activities:** Camping, swimming, fishing, boating, water-skiing, hiking, hunting, fishing trips (&), boat tours, interpretive and recreational programs. **Special Features:** The lake area includes Cataract Falls State Recreation Area and Lieber State Recreation Area. Cataract Falls, the largest waterfall in the state, are at the lake's headwaters.

★2334★ CECIL M. HARDEN LAKE

1588 S Raccoon Pkwy
Rockville, IN 47872
Web: www.in.gov/dnr/parklake/properties/res_cecil.html
Phone: 765-344-1412
Size: 4,065 acres land; 2,060 acres water. **Location:** Off I-36, east of Rockville. **Facilities:** 235 electric and 40 non-electric campsites, 35 primitive campsites, youth tent camping areas, camp store, picnic area, shelter, playground, horseshoe pits, basketball and volleyball courts, archery range, trails, 5 boat ramps, boat rental, fishing pier, swimming beach. **Activities:** Camping, swimming, fishing, boating, hiking, water-skiing, ice fishing, hunting, interpretive programs, tours and corn grinding demonstrations at 1880s roller mill. **Special Features:** Lake area includes Raccoon State Recreation Area and Historic Mansfield Roller Mill.

★2335★ CHAIN O'LAKES STATE PARK

2355 E 75 South
Albion, IN 46701
Web: www.in.gov/dnr/parklake/properties/
  park_chainolakes.html
Phone: 260-636-2654

Size: 2,718 acres. **Location:** Noble County, 5 miles south of Albion, off Highway 9. **Facilities:** 331 campsites with electric hookups, 49 nonelectric campsites, 33 primitive campsites, rally camp with 4 sites, youth tent areas, showers and flush toilets, camp store, family cabins, picnic areas with playgrounds, playfields, and toilet facilities, shelters, swimming beach, refreshment stand, hiking trails (10 miles), nature center, naturalist services, boat, canoe, and paddleboat rentals, boat ramp. **Activities:** Camping, fishing, swimming, boating (electric motors only), canoeing, hiking, cross-country skiing, ice fishing, interpretive programs. **Special Features:** Park is about a mile wide and four miles long, with more than seven miles of widely varying shoreline. The lakes in the chain are known as kettles and were once huge blocks of ice; the rivers of water formed by the melting ice carved the channels that connect 8 of the 11 lakes in the chain. The park's nature center is a restored schoolhouse that was originally built in 1915 and was actually in use until the early 1950s.

★2336★ CHARLESTOWN STATE PARK

PO Box 38
Charlestown, IN 47111
Web: www.in.gov/dnr/parklake/properties/
  park_charlestown.html
Phone: 812-256-5600
Size: 2,400 acres. **Location:** Along the Ohio River, near Charlestown, at 12500 State Road 62. **Facilities:** 132 campsites with electric hookups, flush toilets, showers, hiking trails (8 miles; moderate to rugged), picnic areas with shelters, playgrounds. **Activities:** Camping, hiking, fishing, bird watching, interpretive programs (seasonal). **Special Features:** Park features Fourteenmile Creek valley and elevation changes of more than 200 feet, with topography that includes Devonian fossil outcrops and areas of karst sinkholes.

★2337★ CLIFTY FALLS STATE PARK

1501 Green Rd
Madison, IN 47250
Web: www.in.gov/dnr/parklake/properties/
  park_cliftyfalls.html
Phone: 812-273-8885
Size: 1,416 acres. **Location:** Just west of Madison, with entrances off state roads 56 and 62. **Facilities:** 106 campsites with electricity available, 59 primitive campsites, youth tent areas; an inn with 64 rooms and 7 suites, a dining room (open to the public), indoor pool and hot tub (for inn guests), gift shop, banquet and conference rooms; picnic areas, playgrounds, playfields, toilet facilities, shelters; hiking trails (12 miles), swimming pool and water slide, tennis courts, nature center. **Activities:** Camping, swimming, hiking, tennis, interpretive programs. **Special Features:** Park features a narrow valley, sheer cliffs, and plunging waterfalls. Its shale and limestone rocks contain numerous marine fossils and are among the oldest bedrock exposures in the state.

★2338★ DEAM LAKE STATE RECREATION AREA

1217 Deam Lake Rd
Borden, IN 47106
Web: www.in.gov/dnr/forestry/stateforests/deamlake.htm
Phone: 812-246-5421

Size: 1,300 acres. **Location:** 5 miles southeast of New Providence (also known as Borden) on State Road 60. **Facilities:** 275 campsites with electrical hookup, restrooms, and showers (&), picnic areas, shelters, 2 playgrounds, hiking and mountain bike trails, nature center (&), boat ramp, rowboat rental, swimming beach (&), bathhouse, restrooms, food concessions. **Activities:** Camping, swimming, fishing, boating (electric motors only), hiking, mountain biking, hunting, interpretive programs. **Special Features:** Park was named in honor of Indiana's first state forester, Charles Deam, who is best known for his book *Trees of Indiana*. The area is forest property designed for recreational activities and is managed by the Indiana Division of Forestry. It is not part of Indiana's state parks system.

★2339★ FALLS OF THE OHIO STATE PARK

201 W Riverside Dr
Clarksville, IN 47129
Web: www.in.gov/dnr/parklake/properties/
park_fallsoftheohio.html
Phone: 812-280-9970; **Fax:** 812-280-7110
Size: 144 acres. **Location:** On the banks of the Ohio River in Clarksville. **Facilities:** Picnic areas, boat ramp, hiking trails, interpretive center. **Activities:** Fishing, hiking, fossil exploring (fossil collecting is prohibited), interpretive programs. **Special Features:** The 386-million-year-old fossil beds are among the largest exposed Devonian fossil beds in the world. Access to the fossil beds is best from August through October, when the river is at its lowest level.

★2340★ FORT HARRISON STATE PARK

5753 Glenn Rd
Indianapolis, IN 46216
Web: www.in.gov/dnr/parklake/properties/
park_fortharrison.html
Phone: 317-591-0904
Size: 1,700 acres. **Location:** Post Road and 59th Street in northeast Indianapolis. **Facilities:** 18-hole golf course, resort suites, conference/meeting rooms, dining hall, trails, nature center, picnic areas, playgrounds, play fields, shelters, saddle barn, nature shop/store, historic sites. **Activities:** Golfing, fishing, ice fishing, hiking, bicycling, interpretive programs, horse trail rides (guided rentals; seasonal), bird watching, sledding, cross-country skiing. **Special Features:** An active army fort until 1995, Fort Harrison is the former site of the Citizen's Military Training Camp and a World War II prisoner-of-war camp. These camps are preserved at the park's headquarters location.

★2341★ HARDY LAKE

4171 E Harrod Rd
Scottsburg, IN 47170
Web: www.in.gov/dnr/parklake/properties/res_hardy.html
Phone: 812-794-3800
Size: 2,178 acres land; 741 acres water. **Location:** In southeastern Indiana; accessible via State Roads 256 and 3. **Facilities:** 149 campsites with electricity, flush toilets, and showers, 19 primitive campsites, picnic shelter, hiking trails, marina, 4 boat ramps, 2 fishing piers, rowboat rentals, swimming beach, archery range, basketball and volleyball courts, open playfield.

Activities: Camping, swimming, fishing, ice fishing, boating, water-skiing, hiking, hunting, interpretive and recreational programs. **Special Features:** Hardy Lake is the smallest of Indiana's state-operated reservoirs but has the largest state-operated dam.

★2342★ HARMONIE STATE PARK

3451 Harmonie State Park Rd
New Harmony, IN 47631
Web: www.in.gov/dnr/parklake/properties/
park_harmonie.html
Phone: 812-682-4821
Size: 3,465 acres. **Location:** 25 miles northwest of Evansville and 4 miles south of New Harmony. **Facilities:** 200 campsites with electric hookups (6 &), youth tent camping areas, camp store, 11 family cabins (2 &), 6 picnic areas (&), 5 shelters, modern restrooms, playgrounds, playfields, bike trails (3 miles), hiking trails (8 miles), horse trails (3.5 miles; day use only), swimming pool, water slide, boat ramp, nature center. **Activities:** Camping, swimming, fishing, hiking, bicycling, horseback riding, interpretive programs. **Special Features:** Located along the banks of the Wabash River, the park offers scenic hiking and biking trails. The historic town of New Harmony, located nearby, honors two unique communities that settled here in the early 1800s. Fleeing religious persecution, the Rappites arrived in 1814 to await the impending millenium. Ten years later, the Owenites purchased the Rappite holdings and brought many great scientists and philosophers into the area.

★2343★ INDIANA DUNES STATE PARK

1600 North 25 East
Chesterton, IN 46304
Web: www.in.gov/dnr/parklake/properties/park_dunes.html
Phone: 219-926-1952
Size: 2,182 acres. **Location:** 7 miles north of Chesterton, along Lake Michigan, at the northern terminus of Highway 49. **Facilities:** 140 campsites (all with 50 amp electrical service), youth tent camping area, camp store, restrooms and showers, picnic areas with shelters, playgrounds, trails, nature center, swimming beach. **Activities:** Camping, swimming, fishing (smelt only), hiking, cross-country skiing (no ski rental), interpretive programs. **Special Features:** Park's unique environment includes sand dunes, a variety of desert plants, and 1,800 wooded acres, as well as 3 miles of shoreline along Lake Michigan.

★2344★ J. EDWARD ROUSH LAKE

517 N Warren Rd
Huntington, IN 46750
Web: www.in.gov/dnr/parklake/reservoirs/huntington.html
Phone: 260-468-2165
Size: 8,217 acres land; 870 acres water. **Location:** Off state roads 224 and 5, east and south of Huntington. **Facilities:** 130 primitive campsites, youth tent camping areas, shelterhouse, hiking trails, mountain bike trail, sled dog trail, swimming beach, 2 boat ramps, fishing piers (2 &), radio-controlled flying field, archery range, 3 basketball courts (beach and campground), shooting range, playground, interpretive services. **Activities:** Camping, swimming, fishing, boating, water-skiing, hiking,

mountain biking, ice fishing, hunting (pheasant). **Special Features:** Lake area includes Little Turtle State Recreation Area and Kil-So-Quah State Recreation Area.

★2345★ **LINCOLN STATE PARK**
Highway 162 Box 216
Lincoln City, IN 47552
Web: www.in.gov/dnr/parklake/properties/park_lincoln.html
Phone: 812-937-4710
Size: 1,747 acres. **Location:** Along State Road 162 south of Lincoln City. **Facilities:** 150 campsites with electrical hookups, 120 primitive campsites, youth tent camping areas, flush toilets, showers, group camp, 15 camping cottages, 10 family cabins, picnic areas with playgrounds, playfields, and toilet facilities, 5 shelters, hiking trails, swimming beach, beach bathhouse, general store, boat rentals (rowboats, paddleboats, canoes), boat launch ramp, historic home, amphitheater, nature preserve, nature center, naturalist services. **Activities:** Camping, swimming, fishing, boating (electric motors only), canoeing, hiking, interpretive programs. **Special Features:** During the summer season, the story of Abraham Lincoln is presented in the park's 1,500-seat outdoor amphitheater. The adjacent Lincoln Boyhood National Memorial (see entry in national parks section) features a working pioneer farm, the Lincoln cabin site, family cemetery, and the Historic Trail of Stones honoring major events in the Lincoln family history. The historic home of Colonel Jones, a merchant who employed Lincoln, is located at Lincoln State Park.

★2346★ **MCCORMICK'S CREEK STATE PARK**
250 McCormick's Creek Rd
Spencer, IN 47460
Web: www.in.gov/dnr/parklake/properties/
  park_mccormick.html
Phone: 812-829-2235
Size: 1,924 acres. **Location:** Along the White River, 14 miles northwest of Bloomington, IN. **Facilities:** 189 campsites with electrical hookups, modern restrooms, hot showers, 32 primitive sites, youth tent camping areas, group camp with sleeping barracks, camp store, family cabins; inn accommodations (Canyon Inn), including restaurant (open to the public), swimming pool (inn guests only), recreation center, and meeting and conference facilities; picnic areas with toilet facilities, playgrounds, and playfields, 7 shelters, 4 recreation buildings; hiking trails (10.7 miles), saddle barn, nature center, naturalist services. **Activities:** Camping, hiking, trail rides, tennis, interpretive programs. **Special Features:** Established in 1916, McCormick's Creek is Indiana's first state park, featuring unique limestone formations and scenic waterfalls.

★2347★ **MISSISSINEWA LAKE**
4673 S 625 East
Peru, IN 46970
Web: www.in.gov/dnr/parklake/properties/
  res_mississinewa.html
Phone: 765-473-6528
Size: 14,386 acres land; 3,210 acres water. **Location:** North central Indiana, on the Mississinewa River, 7 miles southeast

of Peru on State Road 13. **Facilities:** 335 campsites with electricity, 39 sites with full hookups (electric, water, and sewage), and 57 non-electric campsites, showers, flush toilets, picnic areas, shelters, playgrounds, hiking trails, 4 boat ramps, marina, fish cleaning station, 2 fishing piers, swimming beach, bathhouse, restrooms, concession, basketball and volleyball court (at campground), horseshoe pits (at campground), disc golf course, radio-control flying field. **Activities:** Camping, swimming, fishing, boating, water-skiing, hiking, ice fishing, hunting, interpretive programs (summer). **Special Features:** Lake area encompasses Frances Slocum, Miami, Pearson Mill, and Red Bridge state recreation areas.

★2348★ **MONROE LAKE**
4850 S State Rd 446
Bloomington, IN 47401
Web: www.in.gov/dnr/parklake/properties/res_monroe.html
Phone: 812-837-9546
Size: 23,952 acres land; 10,750 acres water. **Location:** South central Indiana, 10 miles south and east of Bloomington; accessible from State Roads 37, 46, 446, and 50 via local roads. **Facilities:** 226 electric and 94 non-electric campsites, modern restrooms and showers at campground, camp store, picnic areas, shelters, playgrounds, hiking trails, 9 boat ramps, fishing piers, marinas, gas dock, pontoon and fishing boat rentals, food concessions, 2 swimming beaches, bathhouses with showers, restrooms, nature center. **Activities:** Camping, swimming, fishing, boating, water-skiing, hiking, ice fishing, hunting, interpretive programs. **Special Features:** Lake area includes Allen's Creek, Cutright, Fairfax, Moore's Creek, Paynetown, and Salt Creek state recreation areas.

★2349★ **MOUNDS STATE PARK**
4306 Mounds Rd
Anderson, IN 46017
Web: www.in.gov/dnr/parklake/properties/park_mounds.html
Phone: 765-642-6627
Size: 290 acres. **Location:** Off I-69, east of Anderson. **Facilities:** 75 campsites with electric hookups, flush toilets, and showers, primitive youth tent camping area, camp store, hiking trails (6 miles), picnic areas with playgrounds and playfields, 2 shelters, recreation building (rental), swimming pool, bathhouse, concession, restrooms, visitor center with exhibits and wildlife viewing. **Activities:** Camping, swimming, fishing, hiking, interpretive programs. **Special Features:** Park features 10 unique earthworks built by a group of prehistoric Indians known as the Adena-Hopewell people. The largest earthwork, ''The Great Mound,'' is believed to have been constructed around 160 B.C. Archeological surveys indicate it was used as a gathering place for religious ceremonies.

★2350★ **O'BANNON WOODS STATE PARK**
7240 Old Forest Rd
Corydon, IN 47112
Web: www.in.gov/dnr/forestry/stateforests/harcraw.htm
Phone: 812-738-8232
Size: 2,000 acres. **Location:** In central and extreme southern

9. State Parks

Indiana, bordering the Ohio River, within the 24,000-acre Harrison-Crawford State Forest. **Facilities:** 281 campsites with electricity, modern restrooms, and showers, 47 equestrian campsites (primitive), group camping area (primitive) with 100-bed self-contained structures, picnic areas, 9 shelters, hiking trails (15.8 miles of short day-use trails and access to a 24-mile backpacking trail in Harrison-Crawford State Forest), horse trails, access sites for boaters, nature center, naturalist services. **Activities:** Camping, fishing, boating, hiking, horseback riding, interpretive programs. **Special Features:** Park, which is located within the Harrison-Crawford State Forest, features natural escarpments overlooking the Ohio River. Wyandotte Caves State Recreation Area (see separate entry) is also located in the Harrison-Crawford State Forest. The park was previously known as Wyandotte Woods State Recreation Area; the name was changed in 2004 to honor the late Governor Frank O'Bannon and his family.

★2351★ OUABACHE STATE PARK

4930 E State Rd 201
Bluffton, IN 46714
Web: www.in.gov/dnr/parklake/properties/
  park_ouabache.html
Phone: 260-824-0926
Size: 1,104 acres. **Location:** 5 miles southeast of Bluffton, off IN 201. **Facilities:** 77 campsites with electric hookups, showers, flush toilets, youth group camping area with 47 primitive tent sites, picnic areas, shelters, playgrounds, hiking trails, paved bike trail, swimming pool and waterslide, boat ramp, boat rental (rowboats, paddleboats, canoes), lodge recreation building (rental), 100-foot fire tower, nature center, naturalist services. **Activities:** Camping, swimming, fishing, boating (electric motors only), hiking, biking, interpretive programs. **Special Features:** Ouabache (pronounced ''wabash'') is the French spelling of the Indian word for Wabash, the river that forms the southwest boundary of the park.

★2352★ PATOKA LAKE

3084 N Dillard Rd
Birdseye, IN 47513
Web: www.in.gov/dnr/parklake/properties/res_patoka.html
Phone: 812-685-2464
Size: 25,800 acres land; 8,800 acres water. **Location:** On the Patoka River in southern Indiana; accessible via State Roads 164, 145, and 56. **Facilities:** 455 campsites with electricity, flush toilets, showers, asphalt pads, camp store, and fish cleaning station, 45 primitive campsites, picnic areas with shelters and toilet facilities (some sites &), swimming beach, bathhouse with showers and modern restrooms, food concessions, 2 marinas, 9 boat ramps, boat rentals, hiking, biking, and fitness trails, archery range, disc golf course. **Activities:** Camping, swimming, fishing, boating, water-skiing, hiking, bicycling, cross-country skiing, ice fishing, hunting, interpretive and recreational programs. **Special Features:** Lake area encompasses Jackson, Lick Fork, Little Patoka, Newton-Stewart, Painter Creek, South Lick Fork, and Walls Lake state recreation areas.

★2353★ POKAGON STATE PARK

450 Ln 100 Lake James
Angola, IN 46703
Web: www.in.gov/dnr/parklake/properties/park_pokagon.html
Phone: 260-833-2012
Size: 1,260 acres. **Location:** Near Angola, off I-69. **Facilities:** 200 campsites with electricity, 73 campsites with no electricity, campground showers and toilet facilities, group camp, youth tent areas; inn accommodations (Potawatomi Inn), including rooms and cabins, restaurant, cafe, swimming pool, meeting and conference rooms; picnic areas with shelters, playgrounds, play fields, toilet facilities; general store; hiking trails (11 miles), boat rentals (paddleboat, rowboat, and pontoon boats), swimming beach with bathhouse, recreation building rental, saddle barn, toboggan run, nature center, naturalist services. **Activities:** Camping, swimming, fishing, boating, hiking, horseback riding, cross-country skiing, tobogganing, interpretive programs. **Special Features:** Park has a quarter-mile toboggan run, a refrigerated twin track that offers speeds from 35-40 mph. The tobaggan run is open weekends from the Friday after Thanksgiving through February, depending on the weather (closed Christmas Eve and Christmas day).

★2354★ POTATO CREEK STATE PARK

25601 State Rd 4
PO Box 908
North Liberty, IN 46554
Web: www.in.gov/dnr/parklake/properties/
  park_potatocreek.html
Phone: 574-656-8186
Size: 3,840 acres. **Location:** North-central Indiana, 12 miles southwest of South Bend. **Facilities:** 287 campsites with electricity, showers, and flush toilets, 70 horsemen's campsites (also with electricity), youth tent areas, camp store, 17 family cabins, picnic areas, shelters, playgrounds, bicycle trail (3.2 miles), hiking trails, equestrian trails (9.6 miles), ski trails (8 miles), tubing hill, 2 boat ramps, boat rentals (rowboats, paddleboats, canoes), fishing pier, fish cleaning station, bicycle rental, recreation building rental, wildlife viewing area, nature center, naturalist services. **Activities:** Camping, swimming, fishing, boating (electric motors only), hiking, bicycling, horseback riding (no horse rental), cross-country skiing (no ski rental), ice fishing, sledding, tubing, wildlife viewing, interpretive programs. **Special Features:** Park is a blend of habitats, including 327-acre Worster Lake, prairies, forests, and an 80-acre wetland that offers excellent plant, bird, flower, and wildlife viewing opportunities.

★2355★ PROPHETSTOWN STATE PARK

PO Box 327
Battle Ground, IN 47920
Web: www.in.gov/dnr/parklake/properties/
  park_prophetstown.html
Phone: 765-567-4919
Size: 1,800 acres. **Location:** Exit 178 off I-65 onto State Road 43, left onto Burnett Road, then right on 9th Street to Swisher Road and Park gatehouse. **Facilities:** 110 campsites, all with electricity (half also have water and sewer hookups), picnic areas, shelters, playground, modern restrooms, asphalt biking

and hiking trail, nature trail, interpretive services (seasonal); historic Native American village and 1920s living history museum nearby. **Activities:** Camping, hiking, bicycling, interpretive programs. **Special Features:** Dedicated in 2004, the park is named for a Native American village located between the Tippecanoe and Wabash rivers. The village was established by Tecumseh and his brother, Tenskwatawa (The Prophet) in 1808 and was destroyed in an 1811 battle between tribes that had gathered there to repel further European settlement and troops sent by William Henry Harrison, then-governor of Indiana Territory. Visitors to the park can explore the re-created village at nearby Historic Prophetstown.

★2356★ **SALAMONIE LAKE**
9214 West-Lost Bridge W
Andrews, IN 46702
Web: www.in.gov/dnr/parklake/properties/res_salamonie.html
Phone: 260-468-2125
Size: 11,594 acres land, 2,855 acres water. **Location:** Northeastern Indiana on the Salamonie River in Huntington and Wabash counties; accessible via Rt 524, US 24, I-69, and State Road 124. **Facilities:** 246 campsites with electricity, 30 primitive campsites, horsemen's camp (38 primitive sites), youth tent camping areas, picnic areas with shelters and toilet facilities, trails, 5 boat ramps, marina, swimming beach with restrooms and food concessions, volleyball and basketball courts, playgrounds, horseshoe pits, wildlife viewing areas, amphitheater. **Activities:** Camping, swimming, fishing, boating, water-skiing, hiking, horseback riding, cross-country skiing, ice fishing, snowmobiling, hunting, nature center, interpretive programs. **Special Features:** Lake area encompasses Dora-New Holland, Lost Bridge East, Lost Bridge West, Mount Etna, and Mount Hope state recreation areas.

★2357★ **SHADES STATE PARK**
Rt 1 Box 72
Waveland, IN 47989
Web: www.in.gov/dnr/parklake/properties/park_shades.html
Phone: 765-435-2810
Size: 3,082 acres. **Location:** 17 miles southwest of Crawfordsville, off State Road 47. **Facilities:** 105 non-electric campsites with showers and flush toilets, youth tent camping areas, backpack and canoe campsites (seasonal), picnic areas, shelters, toilet facilities, playgrounds, playfields, hiking trails (15 miles), naturalist services (seasonal), canoe access. **Activities:** Camping, fishing, canoeing, hiking. **Special Features:** Park's sandstone cliffs overlook Sugar Creek and numerous shady ravines. Adjacent to the park is Pine Hills Nature Preserve.

★2358★ **SHAKAMAK STATE PARK**
6265 W State Rd 48
Jasonville, IN 47438
Web: www.in.gov/dnr/parklake/properties/park_shakamak.html
Phone: 812-665-2158
Size: 1,766 acres. **Location:** 25 miles south of Terre Haute on Highway 48. **Facilities:** Campground with 122 electric and 42 nonelectric campsites, showers, flush toilets (&), youth tent camping areas, group camp with dormitory rooms, 7 rent-a-camps with modern restrooms and showers, family cabins, camp store, picnic areas, shelters, playgrounds, playfields, tennis courts, hiking trails, saddle barn, swimming pool and waterslide, boat launch ramp at each of the 3 lakes, boat rental (rowboats and paddleboats), recreation building rental, nature center, naturalist services (seasonal). **Activities:** Camping, swimming, fishing, boating (electric motors only), hiking, horseback riding, tennis, ice fishing, interpretive programs. **Special Features:** Park includes a family aquatic center and three manmade lakes with 400 acres for fishing and boating.

★2359★ **SPRING MILL STATE PARK**
Box 376
Mitchell, IN 47446
Web: www.in.gov/dnr/parklake/properties/park_springmill.html
Phone: 812-849-4129
Size: 1,319 acres. **Location:** 3 miles east of Mitchell at 3333 State Road 60 East. **Facilities:** 187 campsites with electricity, restrooms, showers, 36 primitive campsites, youth tent camping areas, camp store, inn accommodations (Spring Mill Inn), restaurant (open to all park visitors), meeting and conference facilities, picnic areas with shelters, hiking trails, swimming pool, historic sites, nature center, naturalist services. **Activities:** Camping, swimming, volleyball and other games, fishing, ice fishing, boating (electric motors only), hiking, cave exploration, boat rides into Twin Caves, interpretive programs. **Special Features:** A memorial to Virgil I "Gus" Grissom is adjacent to the park gate, with a museum that houses the Gemini space capsule and space suit along with other items related to both Grissom's life and NASA. Other special features of the park include a restored Pioneer Village with a water-powered grist mill; and a cave ecosystem with northern blind cave fish, an endangered species.

★2360★ **STARVE HOLLOW STATE RECREATION AREA**
4345 S County Rd 275 W
Vallonia, IN 47281
Web: www.in.gov/dnr/forestry/stateforests/starvhlw.htm
Phone: 812-358-3464
Size: 500 acres. **Location:** 6 miles south of Brownstown, Indiana. **Facilities:** 55 electric and 125 nonelectric campsites, all with restrooms and showers, picnic areas, shelterhouses, playground, horseshoe pits, softball field, basketball and volleyball courts, mountain bike trails, nature center, 3 boat ramps, boat rental (rowboats and canoes), swimming beach, restrooms, food concessions. **Activities:** Camping, swimming, fishing, boating (electric motors only), mountain biking, hunting, interpretive programs. **Special Features:** Once the largest body of water in Indiana, Starve Hollow Lake offers some of the best fishing in the southern part of the state. The area is managed by the Indiana Division of Forestry and is not part of the state parks system.

★2361★ **SUMMIT LAKE STATE PARK**
5993 N Messick Rd
New Castle, IN 47362
Web: www.in.gov/dnr/parklake/properties/park_summitlake.html
Phone: 765-766-5873

9. State Parks

Size: 2,680 acres. **Location:** About 8 miles east of Mount Summit, off I-36. **Facilities:** 125 campsites with electricity, showers, and flush toilets, youth tent camping area, picnic areas, shelters, playgrounds, hiking trails, boat ramp, boat rentals (rowboats, paddleboats, canoes), swimming beach, bathhouse, concession, restrooms, nature preserve, naturalist services (seasonal). **Activities:** Camping, swimming, fishing, boating, hiking, ice fishing, cross-country skiing (no ski rental), wildlife viewing, birdwatching, interpretive programs. **Special Features:** Park has an excellent observation area for birdwatching and wildlife viewing.

★2362★ TIPPECANOE RIVER STATE PARK
4200 N US Hwy 35
Winamac, IN 46996
Web: www.in.gov/dnr/parklake/properties/
    park_tippecanoeriver.html
Phone: 574-946-3213
Size: 2,761 acres. **Location:** East of US 35, near Winamac. Winamac Fish & Wildlife Area (see separate entry) adjoins the park, on the west side of the highway. **Facilities:** 112 campsites with electricity, showers, and flush toilets, canoe camp with 10 primitive campsites (tent only), horsemen's camp with 56 primitive sites, youth tent camping area, group camp, picnic areas with shelters, playgrounds, playfields, recreation building rental, hiking trails (22.6 miles), equestrian trails (14 miles), boat ramp, 90-foot fire tower (open seasonally), naturalist services (seasonal). **Activities:** Camping, fishing, canoeing (no rentals), hiking, horseback riding, cross-country skiing (no ski rental). **Special Features:** The Tippecanoe River was once a major highway for the Potawatomie Indians and for Canadian fur traders. Today, the slow and winding river is ideal for canoeists.

★2363★ TURKEY RUN STATE PARK
8121 E Park Rd
Marshall, IN 47859
Web: www.in.gov/dnr/parklake/properties/
    park_turkeyrun.html
Phone: 765-597-2635
Size: 2,382 acres. **Location:** West central Indiana, along State Road 47 southwest of Crawfordsville, two miles east of State Road 41. **Facilities:** 213 campsites with electricity, showers, and flush toilets, youth tent camping areas, camp store, inn accommodations (Turkey Run Inn), including rooms and cabins, a restaurant, and meeting and conference facilities, picnic area, playground, tennis courts, playfields, shelters, trails, saddle barn, swimming pool, historic homes and buildings, nature center with planetarium, naturalist services. **Activities:** Camping, swimming, fishing, hiking, bicycling, horseback riding, tennis, guided tours, interpretive programs. **Special Features:** A number of historic structures are preserved at the park, including the Lusk Home, built in 1841, and Lieber Cabin, which was built in the 1840s of virgin timber and is the oldest of its kind in the state. The park is also the final resting place of Colonel Richard Lieber, who is considered the father of Indiana State Parks.

★2364★ VERSAILLES STATE PARK
Box 205 US Hwy 50
Versailles, IN 47042
Web: www.in.gov/dnr/parklake/properties/
    park_versailles.html
Phone: 812-689-6424
Size: 5,988 acres. **Location:** 0.5 miles east of Versailles on US 50. **Facilities:** 226 campsites with electricity, showers, and flush toilets, youth tent camping area, group camp that includes sleeping cabins, recreation hall, shower house, and dining hall , camp store, picnic areas, shelters, playground, playfields, recreation building rental, hiking trails, equestrian trails (day use only), saddle barn, swimming pool complex with waterslide, bathhouse, concession, boat ramp, boat rentals (rowboats, paddleboats, canoes), nature center, naturalist services (seasonal). **Activities:** Camping, swimming, fishing, boating (electric motors only), canoeing, hiking, trail rides, hayrides, interpretive programs. **Special Features:** Running directly through the park is Laughery Creek, named for Colonel Archibald Lochry, a Revolutionary War soldier. In 1781 Lochry and his men were killed in an Indian battle where Laughery Creek enters the Ohio River just south of Aurora, Indiana. Construction of 230-acre Versailles Lake began in 1954, and the lake was opened to the public for fishing and boating a few years later. A 25-meter swimming pool with a 100-foot waterslide was added to the park in 1987.

★2365★ WHITE RIVER STATE PARK
801 W Washington St
Indianapolis, IN 46204
Web: www.in.gov/whiteriver
Phone: 317-233-2434; **Fax:** 317-233-2367; **Toll Free:** 800-665-9056
Size: 250 acres. **Location:** 1 block west of the RCA Dome in downtown Indianapolis. **Special Features:** This large urban park includes a zoo, a botanical garden, a 15,000-seat natural grass ballpark (Victory Field), an IMAX Theater, the Eiteljorg Museum of American Indians and Western Art, and the NCAA Hall of Champions. The park is governed by the White River State Park Development Commission, which is composed of the mayor of Indianapolis, president of Indiana University, and the director of the Department of Natural Resources, as well as seven citizens appointed by the governor.

★2366★ WHITEWATER MEMORIAL STATE PARK
1418 S State Rd 101
Liberty, IN 47353
Web: www.in.gov/dnr/parklake/properties/
    park_whitewater.html
Phone: 765-458-5565
Size: 1,710 acres. **Location:** 1.5 miles south of Liberty, off IN 101. **Facilities:** 236 electric and 45 non-electric campsites with modern restrooms and showers, 37 primitive horsemen's campsites, youth tent camping areas (primitive), 20 family cabins, camp store, picnic areas, shelters, playgrounds, playfields, hiking trails (9 miles), equestrian trails (9 miles), saddle barn, 2 boat ramps, boat rentals (rowboats, paddleboats, canoes), swimming beach, bathhouse, naturalist services (seasonal). **Activities:**

Camping, swimming, fishing, ice fishing, boating (electric motors only on Whitewater Lake), hiking, horseback riding, guided trail rides, interpretive programs. **Special Features:** Park was established in 1949 as a living memorial to the men and women who served in World War II. The land for the park was originally purchased through a joint effort by Fayette, Franklin, Union, and Wayne counies.

★2367★ WYANDOTTE CAVES STATE RECREATION AREA
7315 S Wyandotte Cave Rd
Leavenworth, IN 47137
Web: www.in.gov/dnr/forestry/stateforests/wyandtcv.htm
Phone: 812-738-2782
Size: 26,000 acres. **Location:** 5 miles east of Leavenworth; located within the Harrison-Crawford State Forest, adjacent to the Wyandotte Woods State Recreation Area (see separate entries). **Facilities:** Campsites (at Wyandotte Woods). **Activities:** Spelunking. **Special Features:** Caves feature immense passageways and huge rooms as well as delicate formations and crystals.

Iowa State Parks

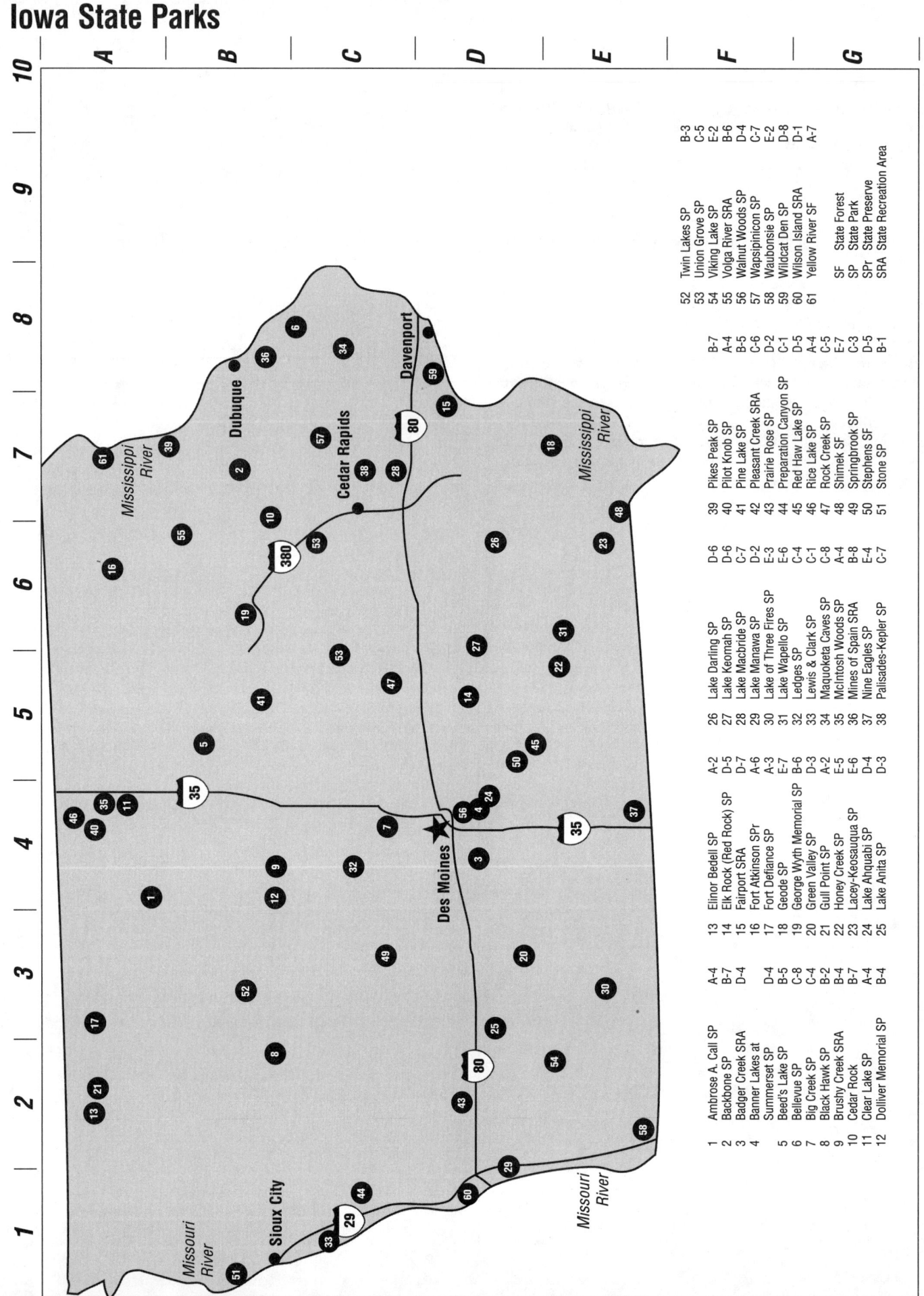

52	Twin Lakes SP	B-3
53	Union Grove SP	C-5
54	Viking Lake SP	E-2
55	Volga River SRA	B-6
56	Walnut Woods SP	D-4
57	Wapsipinicon SP	C-7
58	Waubonsie SP	E-2
59	Wildcat Den SP	D-8
60	Wilson Island SRA	D-1
61	Yellow River SF	A-7

SF	State Forest	
SP	State Park	
SPr	State Preserve	
SRA	State Recreation Area	

39	Pikes Peak SP	B-7
40	Pilot Knob SP	A-4
41	Pine Lake SP	B-5
42	Pleasant Creek SRA	C-6
43	Prairie Rose SP	D-2
44	Preparation Canyon SP	C-1
45	Red Haw Lake SP	D-5
46	Rice Lake SP	A-4
47	Rock Creek SP	C-5
48	Shimek SF	E-7
49	Springbrook SP	C-3
50	Stephens SF	D-5
51	Stone SP	B-1

26	Lake Darling SP	D-6
27	Lake Keomah SP	D-6
28	Lake Macbride SP	C-7
29	Lake Manawa SP	D-2
30	Lake of Three Fires SP	E-3
31	Lake Wapello SP	E-6
32	Ledges SP	C-4
33	Lewis & Clark SP	C-1
34	Maquoketa Caves SP	C-8
35	McIntosh Woods SP	A-4
36	Mines of Spain SRA	B-8
37	Nine Eagles SP	E-4
38	Palisades-Kepler SP	C-7

13	Elinor Bedell SP	A-2
14	Elk Rock (Red Rock) SP	B-7
15	Fairport SRA	D-4
16	Fort Atkinson SPr	A-6
17	Fort Defiance SP	A-3
18	Geode SP	E-7
19	George Wyth Memorial SP	B-6
20	Green Valley SP	D-3
21	Gull Point SP	A-2
22	Honey Creek SP	E-5
23	Lacey-Keosauqua SP	E-6
24	Lake Ahquabi SP	D-4
25	Lake Anita SP	D-3

1	Ambrose A. Call SP	A-4
2	Backbone SP	B-7
3	Badger Creek SRA	D-4
4	Banner Lakes at Summerset SP	D-4
5	Beed's Lake SP	B-5
6	Bellevue SP	C-8
7	Big Creek SP	C-4
8	Black Hawk SP	B-2
9	Brushy Creek SRA	B-4
10	Cedar Rock	B-7
11	Clear Lake SP	A-4
12	Dolliver Memorial SP	B-4

468

IOWA

★2368★ Iowa Department of Natural Resources
Conservation & Recreation Division
Wallace State Office Bldg
502 E 9th St
Des Moines, IA 50319
(515) 281-5918 - Phone
(515) 281-6794 - Fax
(515) 281-3087 - Employment
(515) 281-0878 - Volunteering
Web: www.iowadnr.com/parks
Operates and maintains 84 state parks and recreation areas. Administers more than 90 state preserve sites with archeological, geological, biological, and scenic significance. Manages state forests and nurseries totaling more than 40,000 acres. Oversees wildlife management areas encompassing nearly 300,000 acres.

★2369★ State Historical Society of Iowa
600 E Locust St
Des Moines, IA 50319
(515) 281-5111 - Phone
Web: www.iowahistory.org
Operates 8 historic sites, coordinates Iowa's National Register of Historic Places process, and educates the public on how to protect and restore historic property.

Key to campsite classification:

- **Modern campsites** — Include nearby showers and flush toilets. May or may not have electrical hookup.
- **Non-modern campsites** — No showers or modern restroom facilities; may or may not have electrical hookup.
- **Cabins** — Include electricity, water, furniture, refrigerator, kitchen range, and cooking utensils. Renters must provide bedding, dishes, and bathroom necessities. Accommodate four to eight persons.
- **Rustic cabins** — Include bunkbeds, furniture, outdoor grill, and picnic table. Showers and restroom facilities nearby.

★2370★ AMBROSE A. CALL STATE PARK
Rt 1, Box 264
Algona, IA 50511
Web: www.iowadnr.com/parks/state_park_list/ambrose.html
Phone: 515-295-3669
Size: 138 acres. **Location:** 1.5 miles southwest of Algona. **Facilities:** 16 campsites (13 with electric hookups; &), day-use lodge (&), trails, playground. **Activities:** Camping, hiking, cross-country skiing. **Special Features:** Park features an authentic log cabin typical of cabins built by the original settlers. It is constructed of elm logs, some exceeding 18 inches in diameter, which required four men to lift into place.

★2371★ BACKBONE STATE PARK
1347 129th St
Dundee, IA 52038
Web: www.iowadnr.com/parks/state_park_list/backbone.html
Phone: 563-924-2527; **Fax:** 563-924-2827
Size: 2,001 acres. **Location:** 4 miles southwest of Strawberry Point, off IA 410. **Facilities:** 125 campsites (49 with electrical hookups; &), year-round (&) and seasonal rental cabins, picnic areas, open picnic shelters, stone lodge, hiking and multi-use trails (21 miles), boat ramp, boat rentals, swimming beach, food concession, Civilian Conservation Corps museum, playground. **Activities:** Camping, swimming, lake and stream fishing, boating (electric motors only), hiking, mountain biking, rock climbing, cross-country skiing, snowmobiling, hunting (designated areas). **Special Features:** Iowa's first state park, Backbone was named for its narrow and steep ridge of bedrock carved by a loop of the Maquoketa River. The park is heavily wooded and provides a refuge for deer, raccoon, fox, turkeys, ruffed grouse, and songbirds.

★2372★ BADGER CREEK STATE RECREATION AREA
c/o Walnut Woods State Park
8951 SW 52nd Ave
North Des Moines, IA 50265
Phone: 515-285-4502
Size: 1,162 acres. **Location:** 6 miles southeast of Van Meter. **Facilities:** Boat ramp. **Activities:** Lake fishing, hunting. **Special Features:** Recreation area includes a 276-acre manmade lake.

★2373★ BANNER LAKES AT SUMMERSET STATE PARK
13084 Elkhorn St
Indianola, IA 50125
Web: www.iowadnr.com/parks/state_park_list/banner.html
Phone: 515-961-7101
Size: 222 acres. **Location:** 6 miles south of Indianola and 6 miles north of Des Moines, on Hwy 65/69. **Facilities:** Picnic areas, concession, boat ramps, restrooms, paved bicycle loop; a 5-mile mountain bike trail is planned. A shooting range and hunting area adjoin the park. **Activities:** Boating, fishing, picnicking, bicycling, shooting, hunting. **Special Features:** Iowa's newest state park, Banner Lakes was formerly the site of a coal mining operation and was known locally as Banner Pits.

★2374★ BEED'S LAKE STATE PARK
1422 165th St
Hampton, IA 50441
Web: www.iowadnr.com/parks/state_park_list/beeds.html
Phone: 641-456-2047
Size: 319 acres. Location: 3 miles northwest of Hampton. Facilities: 144 campsites (99 with electric hookups; &), restrooms, showers, picnic areas, picnic shelters (&), playground, multi-use trails (2 miles), fishing jetties and docks (&), boat rentals, boat ramp, swimming beach, food concession. Activities: Camping, swimming, lake fishing, boating, hiking, snowmobiling. Special Features: Park's 99-acre lake features an unusual 170-foot-long spillway with horizontal layers of limestone dropping abruptly 40 feet. Another unique feature is a causeway that crosses the lake near the lodge, providing more than a third of a mile of shoreline fishing as well as a convenient pathway for hikers and joggers.

★2375★ BELLEVUE STATE PARK
24668 Hwy 52
Bellevue, IA 52031
Web: www.iowadnr.com/parks/state_park_list/bellevue.html
Phone: 563-872-4019; Fax: 563-872-4773
Size: 770 acres. Location: 2.5 miles south of Bellevue on US 52. Facilities: 46 campsites (31 with electrical hookups; &) with modern restrooms and showers, day-use lodge, open picnic shelters (&), trails, nature center (&), butterfly garden, playground. Activities: Camping (all at Dyas Unit; camping not allowed at Nelson Unit), hiking, cross-country skiing. Special Features: Park features include high bluffs with scenic views of the Mississippi River, a unique butterfly sanctuary, and an enclosed nature center. The park lies in two separate tracts, the Nelson Unit and the Dyas Unit.

★2376★ BIG CREEK STATE PARK
12397 NW 89th Ct
Polk City, IA 50226
Web: www.iowadnr.com/parks/state_park_list/big_creek.html
Phone: 515-984-6473; Fax: 515-984-9320
Size: 3,550 acres. Location: 2 miles north of Polk City, off IA 415. Facilities: Picnic areas, open picnic shelters (&), paved multi-use trail (26 miles), snowmobile trails (13 miles), swimming beach, 5 boat ramps, boat rentals, jetty, fishing pier (&), dry dock storage, playground (&), multi-purpose sports field, food concession. Activities: Swimming, lake fishing, boating, sailing, hiking, bicycling, cross-country skiing, snowmobiling, hunting (with restrictions). Special Features: Park's 866-acre Big Creek Lake was created as part of the Saylorville project to protect Polk City from floods, but it also provides a wide variety of recreation. The fishing here is excellent year round.

★2377★ BLACK HAWK STATE PARK
228 S Blossom
Lake View, IA 51450
Web: www.iowadnr.com/parks/state_park_list/black_hawk.html
Phone: 712-657-8712; Fax: 712-657-0999
Size: 86 acres. Location: In Lake View, off IA 175 and 71.

Facilities: 176 campsites (68 with electric hookups; &) with showers and restrooms, picnic areas, 4 open picnic shelters, nature trail, fishing pier (&), 3 boat ramps, boat rentals, volleyball court, disc golf course, playground. Activities: Camping, swimming (designated areas only), lake fishing, boating, hiking. Special Features: 957-acre Black Hawk Lake is the southernmost glacier-formed lake in Iowa.

★2378★ BRUSHY CREEK STATE RECREATION AREA
3175 290th St
Lehigh, IA 50557
Web: www.iowadnr.com/parks/state_park_list/brushy_creek.html
Phone: 515-543-8298; Fax: 515-843-8395
Size: 6,500 acres. Location: 4 miles south of Duncombe, off County Road P-73. Facilities: 2 equestrian campgrounds (&) with a combined total of 230 campsites (120 electrical), showers and restrooms, playgrounds, horse wash areas, hitch rails at each site, and arena; equestrian day-use staging areas near each campground; non-equestrian campground with 47 campsites (37 with electric and 10 with full water and sewer hookups); multi-use trails (50 miles), picnic areas, 2 open shelters (&), boat ramp, fishing jetties, fishing pier, swimming beach, 2 shooting ranges. Activities: Camping, fishing, boating, swimming, horseback riding, hiking, mountain biking, cross-country skiing, snowmobiling, shooting, hunting. Special Features: Brushy Creek is one of Iowa's largest tracts of public outdoor recreation land. The park's equestrian camping facilities are among the most modern in the Midwest, and the creek and Des Moines River offer both scenic beauty and some great fishing. Expansion plans include construction of a 690-acre reservoir and associated facilities.

★2379★ CEDAR ROCK
PO Box 250
Quasqueton, IA 52326
Web: www.iowadnr.com/parks/state_park_list/cedar_rock.html
Phone: 319-934-3572
Size: 423 acres. Location: 3 miles northwest of Quasqueton. Facilities: Frank Lloyd Wright-designed home, visitor center. Activities: Free guided tours are given daily from May through October (Tues-Sun). Special Features: Designed by Frank Lloyd Wright in the late 1940s, Cedar Rock is an excellent example of Wright's "Usonian" style of architecture. Nearly everything at Cedar Rock bears the architect's imprint—he designed the furniture, selected the carpets, chose the draperies, and even picked out the accessories. Cedar Rock is one of seven Iowa residences designed by Wright. The home and grounds were given to the state in 1981 by its original owners, Mr and Mrs Lowell Walter.

★2380★ CLEAR LAKE STATE PARK
2730 S Lakeview Dr
Clear Lake, IA 50428
Web: www.iowadnr.com/parks/state_park_list/clear_lake.html
Phone: 641-357-4212; Fax: 641-357-4242

9. State Parks

Size: 55 acres. Location: 2 miles south of Clear Lake, off IA 106. Facilities: 176 campsites (most with electrical hookups; &) with restrooms and showers, more than 10 acres of picnic grounds, open picnic shelter, day-use lodge (&), playground, trails, swimming beach. Activities: Camping, swimming, lake fishing, boating, sailing, jet skiing, windsurfing, water-skiing, hiking. Special Features: Park is located on the southeast shore of 3,684-acre Clear Lake, one of the major outdoor recreation features of northern Iowa. The park is characterized by rolling land with mature groves of oak trees, with small draws and thickets that provide habitat for small wildlife. Scenic Woodford Island is managed primarily for wildlife habitat and is an excellent spot for fishing.

★2381★ DOLLIVER MEMORIAL STATE PARK

2757 Dolliver Park Ave
Lehigh, IA 50557
Web: www.iowadnr.com/parks/state_park_list/dolliver.html
Phone: 515-359-2539; Fax: 515-359-2542
Size: 600 acres. Location: 3 miles northwest of Lehigh, off IA 50. Facilities: 33 campsites with electrical hookups, restrooms, and showers; group camp with dining hall, showers, modern restrooms, and 10 sleeping cabins; family rental cabin that sleeps 4; picnic areas, 2 day-use lodges (&), open picnic shelter (&), hiking trail, boat ramp, playground. Activities: Camping, fishing, boating, hiking. Special Features: Natural and cultural features at the park include bluffs, canyons, the Des Moines River, Prairie Creek, and Indian mounds. A unique facet of the sandstone formations at Dolliver are the ''Copperas Beds.'' The 100-foot bluff on Prairie Creek is a cross-sectional view of an ancient river bed that's over 150 million years old.

★2382★ ELINOR BEDELL STATE PARK

c/o Gull Point State Park
1500 Harpen St
Milford, IA 51351
Web: www.iowadnr.com/parks/state_park_list/
  elinor_bedell.html
Phone: 712-337-3211
Size: 80 acres. Location: 2 miles east of Spirit Lake, on 250th Ave. Facilities: 8 RV campsites with full hookups and a modern restroom (&), youth group tent camping area, rental shelter with restrooms and kitchenette (&), fishing pier, bicycle and hiking trails, playground (&). Activities: Camping, boating, fishing, swimming, hiking, bicycling, wildlife viewing. Special Features: Located on the shores of East Lake Okoboji, park preserves one of the last open spaces in a region that is among Iowa's most popular tourist destinations - the Iowa Great Lakes. The land was given to the people of Iowa by Berkley and Elinor Bidell. Berkley Bidell represented northwest Iowa for 12 years in the US Congress.

★2383★ ELK ROCK STATE PARK

811 146th Ave
Knoxville, IA 50138
Web: www.iowadnr.com/parks/state_park_list/elk_rock.html
Phone: 641-842-6008
Size: 850 acres. Location: 7 miles north of Knoxville, off IA

14. Facilities: 21 campsites (12 with electrical hookups) with modern shower building, 60 equestrian campsites (24 with electrical hookups) with modern shower building, horse stalls, hitching rails, and riding arena, picnic area (1 mile north of the main park) with open picnic shelter, playground, multi-use trails (13 miles), 2 boat ramps. Activities: Camping, swimming, fishing, boating, hiking, horseback riding, mountain biking. Special Features: Park is located on 19,000-acre Lake Red Rock, one of Iowa's largest impoundments. The lake is a major ''rest stop'' for waterfowl and other migratory bird species (including white pelicans and bald eagles) during fall and spring migrations.

★2384★ FAIRPORT STATE RECREATION AREA

c/o Wildcat Den State Park
1884 Wildcat Den Rd
Muscatine, IA 52761
Web: www.iowadnr.com/parks/state_park_list/fairport.html
Phone: 563-263-4337; Fax: 563-264-8329
Size: 17 acres. Location: 5 miles east of Muscatine on IA 22. Facilities: 42 campsites (&) with electrical hookups, showers, and restrooms, boat ramps, docks, fish cleaning station, playground. Activities: Camping, fishing, boating. Special Features: Recreation area is located right on the Mississippi River, providing excellent river access and viewing.

★2385★ FORT ATKINSON STATE PRESERVE

c/o Volga River State Recreation Area
10225 Ivy Rd
Fayette, IA 52142
Web: www.iowadnr.com/parks/state_park_list/
  fort_atkinson.html
Phone: 563-425-4161
Size: 5 acres. Location: Adjoins the town of Fort Atkinson, off IA 24. Activities: An annual rendezvous recreates life on the 1840s Iowa frontier with authentic buckskinners, US Army dragoons, black powder shoots, crafts people, contests, and demonstrations. Special Features: The original Fort Atkinson (1840-1849) was built to keep the Winnebago on neutral ground after their removal from Wisconsin in 1840 and to provide protection for them from other native tribes. When the Winnebago were removed from Iowa there was no longer a reason for the fort and it ceased to exist. The fort was reconstructed and dedicated in 1968 as part of the State Preserve System because of its geological, archeological, and historical value.

★2386★ FORT DEFIANCE STATE PARK

c/o Gull Point State Park
1500 Harpen St
Milford, IA 51351
Web: www.iowadnr.com/parks/state_park_list/
  fort_defiance.html
Phone: 712-337-3211
Size: 191 acres. Location: 1 mile west of Estherville, off IA 9. Facilities: 16 non-modern campsites (no flush toilets or showers, but 8 sites have electric hookups), day-use rental lodge (&) constructed in the style of an old army outpost, open picnic shelter, trails. Activities: Camping, hiking, horseback riding, cross-country skiing, snowmobiling. Special Features: Park's

rugged woodland, with its trails and scenic overlooks, provides a good place to relax.

★2387★ GEODE STATE PARK

3249 Racine Ave
Danville, IA 52623
Web: www.iowadnr.com/parks/state_park_list/geode.html
Phone: 319-392-4601
Size: 1,641 acres. **Location:** 4 miles southwest of Danville. **Facilities:** 186 campsites (96 with electrical hookups; 2 camp pads &) with two modern shower buildings and restrooms (&) in campground, picnic areas (1 site &), open picnic shelters, hiking trails, nature trail, 186-acre lake, boat ramp, boat rentals, playground. **Activities:** Camping, swimming, fishing, boating, hiking, cross-country skiing. **Special Features:** Park is named for the geode stone, and a display of geodes, with mysterious crystal formations in their hollow cavities, can be seen at the campground.

★2388★ GEORGE WYTH MEMORIAL STATE PARK

3659 Wyth Rd
Waterloo, IA 50703
Web: www.iowadnr.com/parks/state_park_list/
george_wyth.html
Phone: 319-232-5505; **Fax:** 319-232-1508
Size: 1,200 acres. **Location:** On the Cedar River, within the Waterloo-Cedar Falls metropolitan area, off IA 218. **Facilities:** 58 campsites with modern showers and restrooms, day-use lodge (&), 3 open picnic shelters (&), multi-use paved trails (&), grass hiking trails (6 miles), swimming beach, fishing pier (&), fishing jetties (&), boat ramps, boat rentals, playground (&). **Activities:** Camping, swimming, lake and river fishing, boating, sailing, windsurfing, hiking, bicycling/mountain biking, inline skating, cross-country skiing, snowmobiling, mushroom hunting. **Special Features:** Park features several water areas: Brinker Lake (120 acres), open for power boating; George Wyth Lake, a 75-acre, no-wake lake with a wheelchair-accessible fishing pier and fishing jetties; Fisher Lake, a 40-acre natural lake; Alice Wyth Lake (60 acres), for boats with electric motors only; and the Cedar River. The park is also a National Urban Wildlife Sanctuary. More than 200 species of birds have been observed here, and white-tailed deer can be seen year round.

★2389★ GREEN VALLEY STATE PARK

1480 130th St
Creston, IA 50801
Web: www.iowadnr.com/parks/state_park_list/
green_valley.html
Phone: 641-782-5131; **Fax:** 641-782-8330
Size: 990 acres. **Location:** 2.5 miles northwest of Creston, off IA 186. **Facilities:** 145 campsites (85 with electrical hookups) with showers and modern restrooms (&), rustic camper cabins, open picnic shelters (&), self-guided nature trail, hiking trails, swimming beach, fishing jetties, 2 fishing piers (&), 2 fish cleaning stations, 4 boat ramps. **Activities:** Camping, swimming, lake fishing, boating, water-skiing, hiking. Inboard motors (including jet skis and jet boats) are not allowed on the lake.

Special Features: Recreational activities center around Green Valley's 390-acre lake.

★2390★ GULL POINT STATE PARK

1500 Harpen St
Milford, IA 51351
Web: www.iowadnr.com/parks/state_park_list/gull_point.html
Phone: 712-337-3211
Size: 195 acres. **Location:** 3.5 miles north of Milford, off IA 86. **Facilities:** Campground with 112 campsites (60 with electrical hookups; &), paved roads, modern restroom and shower facilities, and playground equipment, day-use lodge (&), open picnic shelters (&), interpretive trail, swimming beach, fishing pier. **Activities:** Camping, swimming, lake fishing, boating, sailing, water-skiing, hiking, cross-country skiing, wildlife viewing. **Special Features:** Located on West Lake Okoboji, this park serves as headquarters for the Gull Point Complex of state parks and recreation areas around northwestern Iowa's lakes region. The park features the Gulf Point Lodge, built in the 1930s by the Civilian Conservation Corps. It is the largest historic lodge in the state and includes full kitchen facilities and seating for 140 people. The lodge can be reserved for a variety of group activities.

★2391★ HONEY CREEK STATE PARK

12194 Honey Creek Pl
Moravia, IA 52571
Web: www.iowadnr.com/parks/state_park_list/
honey_creek.html
Phone: 641-724-3739; **Fax:** 641-724-9846
Size: 828 acres. **Location:** 12 miles southeast of Moravia. **Facilities:** 155 modern campsites (&) with showers and restrooms (80 sites have electrical hookups; 28 sites have full hookups with water, sewer, and electricity), open picnic shelters (&), interpretive trail, hiking trails, boat ramps. **Activities:** Camping, swimming, fishing, boating, hiking. **Special Features:** Honey Creek sits alongside Iowa's largest lake, Rathbun Lake, and is a part of the Rathbun Lake recreation complex consisting of 11,000 acres with eight parks, 155 miles of shoreline, two marinas, and 21,000 acres of public land. The Iowa Department of Natural Resources also manages the Rathbun Fish Hatchery and Fisheries Research Facility located below the dam.

★2392★ LACEY-KEOSAUQUA STATE PARK

PO Box 398
Keosauqua, IA 52565
Web: www.iowadnr.com/parks/state_park_list/lacey_keo.html
Phone: 319-293-3502; **Fax:** 319-293-3329
Size: 1,653 acres. **Location:** Adjoins Keosauqua, off IA 1. **Facilities:** 113 campsites (45 with electrical hookups) with modern restrooms and showers, 6 family cabins (rentals), day-use lodge (&), 3 open picnic shelters (&), playground, hiking trails, swimming beach and bathhouse, boat ramp, boat rentals, 30-acre lake. **Activities:** Camping, swimming, fishing, boating, hiking, cross-country skiing. **Special Features:** Lacey-Keosauqua is one of Iowa's largest and most picturesque state parks, whose natural features include hills, bluffs, and valleys along the Des Moines River. Overlooking the river in the northwest

section of the park are 19 burial mounds, built by an ancient group of Woodland Culture Indians.

★2393★ LAKE AHQUABI STATE PARK

1650 118th Ave
Indianola, IA 50125
Web: www.iowadnr.com/parks/state_park_list/
lake_ahquabi.html
Phone: 515-961-7101; **Fax:** 515-962-9424
Size: 770 acres. **Location:** 5.5 miles southwest of Indianola, off IA 349. **Facilities:** 141 campsites (85 with electrical hookups; &), modern restrooms, and showers, youth group camping area (&), day-use lodge, 3 open picnic shelters, multi-use trails, fishing jetties, fishing pier (&), boat ramps, boat rentals, concession, 115-acre manmade lake, swimming beach, playground. **Activities:** Camping, swimming, fishing, boating, hiking, mountain biking, cross-country skiing, snowmobiling. **Special Features:** "Ahquabi" is a Sauk and Fox word meaning "resting place."

★2394★ LAKE ANITA STATE PARK

55111 750th St
Anita, IA 50020
Web: www.iowadnr.com/parks/state_park_list/lake_anita.html
Phone: 712-762-3564; **Fax:** 712-762-4352
Size: 1,062 acres. **Location:** 5 miles south of I-80 from the Anita interchange. **Facilities:** 161 campsites (&; includes 52 sites with electrical hookups and 40 with full hookups, including water and sewer), 2 modern shower/restroom buildings in campground, picnic areas, 8 open picnic shelters (&), trails, swimming beach, playground, fishing jetty, 2 boat ramps, playground. **Activities:** Camping, swimming, fishing, boating, hiking, bicycling. **Special Features:** Park features a 171-acre manmade lake created by a dam on a branch of the Nishnabotna River. The lake offers excellent fishing for largemouth bass, crappies, and bluegills.

★2395★ LAKE DARLING STATE PARK

111 Lake Darling Rd
Brighton, IA 52540
Web: www.iowadnr.com/parks/state_park_list/
lake_darling.html
Phone: 319-694-2323
Size: 1,417 acres. **Location:** 3 miles west of Brighton, off IA 78 & 1. **Facilities:** 118 campsites (&; 81 with electrical hookups) with 2 modern restroom buildings, seasonal camping cabins (&), picnic areas and an open picnic shelter, trails, fishing jetty, boat ramp, boat rentals, 302-acre lake, swimming beach, food concession, playground. **Activities:** Camping, swimming, fishing, boating, hiking, mountain biking. **Special Features:** Park was named in honor of JN "Ding" Darling, an early 20th-century editorial cartoonist for the Des Moines Register and a champion of conservation.

★2396★ LAKE KEOMAH STATE PARK

2720 Keomah Ln
Oskaloosa, IA 52577
Web: www.iowadnr.com/parks/state_park_list/
lake_keomah.html
Phone: 641-673-6975; **Fax:** 641-673-0647

Size: 366 acres. **Location:** 6 miles east of Oskaloosa, off IA 371. **Facilities:** 65 campsites (41 with electrical hookups), modern showers and restrooms in campground, group camping area, day-use lodge, open picnic shelters (&), multi-use trails, swimming beach, fishing jetty (&), 2 boat ramps, 83-acre man-made lake. **Activities:** Camping, swimming, fishing, boating (electric motors only), hiking, snowmobiling, ice fishing. **Special Features:** Though it sounds like an Indian word, the name "Keomah" is actually derived from the first syllables of the two counties that originally helped finance the park, Keokuk and Mahaska. The park was dedicated in 1934, and many of the its facilities were built by the Civilian Conservation Corps.

★2397★ LAKE MACBRIDE STATE PARK

3525 Hwy 382 NE
Solon, IA 52333
Web: www.iowadnr.com/parks/state_park_list/
lake_macbride.html
Phone: 319-624-2200; **Fax:** 319-624-2188
Size: 2,180 acres. **Location:** 4 miles west of Solon, off IA 382. **Facilities:** 50 modern campsites (&) with shower and restroom (37 sites have electrical hookups), 60 non-modern campsites with non-flush restroom; open picnic shelters (&), day-use lodge (&), playground; multi-use trails, Volksport trail; fishing jetty, 7 boat ramps, boat rentals, swimming beach, food concession, 812-acre artificial lake. **Activities:** Camping, swimming, lake fishing, boating, hiking, bicycling, cross-country skiing, snowmobiling, bird watching. **Special Features:** Park is named for Dr Thomas Huston Macbride, an early Iowa conservationist credited with helping to establish Iowa's state park system.

★2398★ LAKE MANAWA STATE PARK

1100 South Shore Dr
Council Bluffs, IA 51501
Web: www.iowadnr.com/parks/state_park_list/
lake_manawa.html
Phone: 712-366-0220; **Fax:** 712-366-0474
Size: 1,529 acres. **Location:** 1 mile south of IA 92 in Council Bluffs. **Facilities:** 72 campsites (&; 37 with electrical hookups) with modern shower and restroom in campground, open picnic shelters (&), hiking and biking trails, nature trail (&), swimming beach, fishing pier (&), boat ramps, boat rentals, food concession, 660-acre natural lake, playground (&). **Activities:** Camping, swimming, lake fishing, boating, hiking, bicycling, mountain biking. **Special Features:** Lake Manawa was formed during a flood in 1881 when a portion of the river channel was cut off by the meandering of the Missouri River. Over the years, the resulting oxbow lake became a major outdoor recreation center. "Manawa" is a Native American term meaning "peace and comfort."

★2399★ LAKE OF THREE FIRES STATE PARK

2303 Lake Rd
Bedford, IA 50833
Web: www.iowadnr.com/parks/state_park_list/
lake_three_fires.html
Phone: 712-523-2700; **Fax:** 712-523-3104

Size: 1,155 acres. **Location:** 3 miles northeast of Bedford. **Facilities:** 140 campsites (&; 30 with electrical hookups)with restroom and showers in campground, equestrian campground with 22 campsites (8 with electrical hookups) and 15 holding pens, modern rental cabins (seasonal), day-use lodge (&), 2 open picnic shelters (&), multi-use trails (8 miles), swimming beach, playground, boat ramps, 85-acre artificial lake, 2 public hunting areas. **Activities:** Camping, hunting, swimming, lake fishing, boating, hiking, horseback riding, snowmobiling, hunting (in designated areas only). **Special Features:** Lake is nearly a mile long and half a mile wide and is surrounded by woodlands.

★2400★ LAKE WAPELLO STATE PARK

15248 Campground Rd
Drakesville, IA 52552
Web: www.iowadnr.com/parks/state_park_list/
lake_wapello.html
Phone: 641-722-3371; **Fax:** 641-722-3384
Size: 1,150 acres. **Location:** 6 miles west of Drakesville, off IA 273. **Facilities:** 89 campsites (&; 44 with electrical hookups), modern shower and restroom facilities, 14 family rental cabins, picnic areas, open picnic shelter (&), multi-use trails, nature trail, swimming beach, playground, fishing pier (&), boat ramp, boat rentals, restaurant (seasonal), concession. **Activities:** Camping, swimming, lake fishing, boating, hiking, snowmobiling, cross-country skiing. **Special Features:** Park has a newly remodeled stone and timber 1930s beach building that includes a seasonal restaurant, a lake observation deck, and restrooms, as well as a concession area. A portion of the building is available for rent. In addition, the facilities of a former Boy Scout camp are now owned by the Camp Wapello Preservation Group. These facilities include 10 separate tent camping areas, a dining hall with cooking facilities, and a shower building.

★2401★ LEDGES STATE PARK

1519 250th St
Madrid, IA 50156
Web: www.iowadnr.com/parks/state_park_list/ledges.html
Phone: 515-432-1852; **Fax:** 515-432-0757
Size: 1,200 acres. **Location:** 6 miles south of Boone, off IA 164; 15 miles from Ames. **Facilities:** 94 campsites (40 with electrical hookups, 42 non-electric, 12 hike-in) with modern restrooms, showers, and a playground in the campground (2 electrical sites &), 2 open picnic shelters (&), interpretive trail (&), hiking trails (13 miles). **Activities:** Camping and hiking; canoeing and fishing in the Des Moines River, which flows through the west edge of the park. **Special Features:** Park features sandstone cliffs (''ledges''), native plant communities, and a deep wooded river valley. Trails lead up and down steep slopes to scenic overlooks, and a winding road along Pea's Creek offers motorists breathtaking views of the ''canyon'' and the Des Moines River Valley.

★2402★ LEWIS & CLARK STATE PARK

21914 Park Loop
Onawa, IA 51040
Web: www.iowadnr.com/parks/state_park_list/
lewis_clark.html
Phone: 712-423-2829
Size: 176 acres. **Location:** 5 miles west of Onawa, off IA 175. **Facilities:** 82 modern campsites with electrical hookups (&), day-use lodge (&), more than 30 acres of picnic grounds, open picnic shelter (&), hiking trails, self-guided nature trail, swimming beach, playground, 2 boat ramps, 250-acre natural lake, historic exhibit. **Activities:** Camping, swimming, lake fishing, boating, hiking. **Special Features:** Park lies on the shores of Blue Lake, an oxbow lake formed by the meanderings of the Missouri River many years ago. It was the site of an 1804 Lewis and Clark encampment and includes a full-scale replica of the expedition's 55-foot keelboat <i>Discovery</i>.

★2403★ MAQUOKETA CAVES STATE PARK

10970 98th St
Maquoketa, IA 52060
Web: www.iowadnr.com/parks/state_park_list/
maquoketa_caves.html
Phone: 563-652-5833; **Fax:** 563-652-0061
Size: 323 acres. **Location:** 7 miles northwest of Maquoketa. **Facilities:** 29 campsites (&; 17 with electrical hookups), modern shower facility, picnic areas, open picnic shelters (&), playground, hiking trails (6 miles), interpretive center. **Activities:** Camping, hiking, interpretive programs. **Special Features:** Park contains more caves than any other state park in Iowa. An extensive trail system links the park's caves, overlooks, and other geological formations including ''Natural Bridge,'' which stands nearly 50 feet above Raccoon Creek, and 17-ton ''Balanced Rock.''

★2404★ MCINTOSH WOODS STATE PARK

1200 E Lake St
Ventura, IA 50482
Web: www.iowadnr.com/parks/state_park_list/
mcintosh_woods.html
Phone: 641-829-3847; **Fax:** 641-829-3841
Size: 62 acres. **Location:** 0.75 miles east of Ventura, off US 18. **Facilities:** 49 campsites (&; 45 with electrical hookups), modern restroom and shower building, playground, 2 yurts (&; seasonal rental), picnic areas, open picnic shelter, nature trail, swimming beach, fishing jetty, fish cleaning station, boat ramp. **Activities:** Camping, swimming, fishing, boating, hiking. **Special Features:** Park is located on the northwest shore of 3,684-acre Clear Lake and is one of its major boating access points.

★2405★ MINES OF SPAIN STATE RECREATION AREA

8991 Bellevue Heights
Dubuque, IA 52003
Web: www.iowadnr.com/parks/state_park_list/
mines_spain.html
Phone: 563-556-0620; **Fax:** 563-556-8474
Size: 1,380 acres. **Location:** Off US 52, on the south edge of Dubuque. **Facilities:** Historic sites, visitor/interpretive center, hiking trails (14 miles), ski trails (4 miles), 5 nature walks, bird and butterfly garden, observation blind, picnic facilities. **Activities:** Hiking, cross-country skiing, interpretive programs, hunting, wildlife viewing. **Special Features:** Rich in history,

9. State Parks

abundant wildlife, and unique plant communities, the park features the EB Lyons Interpretive Center and 600-acre Catfish Creek Preserve. It has been named a National Historic Landmark, a National Wildlife Federation Nature Area, and one of Iowa's Watchable Wildlife Areas.

★2406★ NINE EAGLES STATE PARK

RR 1
Davis City, IA 50065
Web: www.iowadnr.com/parks/state_park_list/
nine_eagles.html
Phone: 641-442-2855; **Fax:** 641-442-2856
Size: 1,119 acres. **Location:** 6 miles southeast of Davis City. **Facilities:** 68 campsites (&; 28 with electrical hookups), modern showers and restrooms, 7 primitive equestrian campsites, picnic areas, 2 open shelters (&), hiking trails (9 miles), equestrian trails (6 miles), swimming beach, playground, boat ramp, fish cleaning station. **Activities:** Camping, swimming, lake fishing, boating (electric motors only), hiking, horseback riding. **Special Features:** The park's 64-acre lake is one of the clearest impoundments in the state and is popular for bass, northern pike, tiger muskie, channel catfish, bluegill, and crappie fishing. White-tailed deer can be seen nearly every morning and evening along the park's roads.

★2407★ PALISADES-KEPLER STATE PARK

700 Kepler Dr
Mount Vernon, IA 52314
Web: www.iowadnr.com/parks/state_park_list/palisades.html
Phone: 319-895-6039; **Fax:** 319-895-9660
Size: 840 acres. **Location:** 3.5 miles west of Mount Vernon, off US 30. **Facilities:** 44 campsites (26 with electrical hookups) with modern shower and restroom facilities, 4 family cabins (seasonal rental), day-use lodge (&), picnic areas, open picnic shelter, hiking trails (6 miles), boat ramp. **Activities:** Camping, fishing, hiking. **Special Features:** Park lies along the scenic Cedar River and features river bluffs, deep ravines, hardwood forests, masses of wildflowers, and an abundance of wildlife. The area is also noted for its prehistoric significance; a molar tooth of a mammoth was once found here, and exposed rocks along the river contain fossils millions of years old.

★2408★ PIKES PEAK STATE PARK

15316 Great River Rd
McGregor, IA 52157
Web: www.iowadnr.com/parks/state_park_list/
pikes_peak.html
Phone: 563-873-2341; **Fax:** 563-873-3167
Size: 970 acres. **Location:** 3 miles southeast of McGregor, on County Road X-56. **Facilities:** 77 campsites (&; 60 with electrical hookups) with modern shower and restroom facilities, concession, picnic areas, open picnic shelters (&), playground, trails (&), scenic overlooks and viewing platforms. **Activities:** Camping, hiking, mountain biking. **Special Features:** From the top of a 500-foot bluff, the highest bluff on the Mississippi River, visitors can view the confluence of the Wisconsin and Mississippi rivers to the south and the twin suspension bridges connecting Iowa and Wisconsin to the north.

★2409★ PILOT KNOB STATE PARK

2148 340th St
Forest City, IA 50436
Web: www.iowadnr.com/parks/state_park_list/pilot_knob.html
Phone: 641-581-4835
Size: 528 acres. **Location:** 4 miles east of Forest City, off IA 9. **Facilities:** 60 campsites (&; 48 with electrical hookups) with modern shower and restroom facilities, playground, picnic areas, open picnic shelters (&), hiking and equestrian trails, open air amphitheater, warming house. **Activities:** Camping, lake fishing, hiking, horseback riding, cross-country skiing, ice fishing, ice skating, snowmobiling. Pilot Knob Recreation Area, just north of the park, is available for public hunting, hiking, snowmobiling, and other activities. **Special Features:** Pilot Knob is the second highest point in Iowa. In earlier times it served as a guide for pioneers traveling west, which is how it got its name. Today, an observation tower atop the knob affords visitors a panoramic view of the surrounding farmland. Hidden within the park is Dead Man's Lake, a four-acre floating sphagnum bog, the only one of its kind in Iowa.

★2410★ PINE LAKE STATE PARK

22620 County Hwy S56
Eldora, IA 50627
Web: www.iowadnr.com/parks/state_park_list/pine_lake.html
Phone: 641-858-5832; **Fax:** 641-858-5641
Size: 585 acres. **Location:** 0.5 miles northeast of Eldora, off County Road 556. **Facilities:** 128 modern campsites (76 with electrical hookups; &), 4 rental cabins (&), day-use lodge, open picnic shelters, interpretive trails, hiking trails (10 miles), swimming beach, fishing jetty, boat ramps, boat rentals, 9-hole golf course. **Activities:** Camping, swimming, fishing, boating (electric motors only), hiking, bicycling (&). **Special Features:** Park encompasses two lakes: 50-acre Lower Pine Lake and 69-acre Upper Pine Lake. A 50-mile bike trail, the Lake-to-Lake State Park Bike Route, connects Pine Lake to George Wyth Memorial State Park (see separate entry).

★2411★ PLEASANT CREEK STATE RECREATION AREA

4530 McClintock Rd
Palo, IA 52324
Web: www.iowadnr.com/parks/state_park_list/
pleasant_creek.html
Phone: 319-436-7716; **Fax:** 319-436-7715
Size: 1,927 acres. **Location:** 4 miles north and 0.5 miles west of Palo. **Facilities:** 69 campsites (&; 43 with electrical hookups), 2 modern shower and restroom facilities, 4 rustic camper cabins (&), picnic areas, open shelters, multi-use trails (10 miles), swimming beach, fishing jetties, 7 boat ramps, boat rentals, concession, playground. **Activities:** Camping, swimming, fishing, boating, hiking, bicycling, horseback riding, cross-country skiing, snowmobiling, hunting (with restrictions). **Special Features:** 410-acre Pleasant Creek Lake is one of the most popular boating spots in eastern Iowa and is one of the highest-quality fishing lakes in the region. Park is also a popular site for organized dog field trials.

9. State Parks

★2412★ PRAIRIE ROSE STATE PARK

680 Rd M47
Harlan, IA 51537
Web: www.iowadnr.com/parks/state_park_list/
prairie_rose.html
Phone: 712-773-2701; **Fax:** 712-773-2702
Size: 661 acres. **Location:** 6 miles southeast of Harlan. **Facilities:** 61 campsites with electrical hookups and modern shower and restroom facilities (&), 36 campsites with non-modern restroom facilities, picnic areas, 2 open picnic shelters (&), trails, swimming beach, playground, 6 fishing jetties, 2 fish cleaning docks, 2 boat ramps, 218-acre lake. **Activities:** Camping, swimming, fishing, canoeing, boating, sailing, ice boating, hiking, snowmobiling, cross-country skiing. **Special Features:** Located in a region of rolling hills, Prairie Rose is one of the most attractive outdoor recreation areas in western Iowa.

★2413★ PREPARATION CANYON STATE PARK

c/o Lewis and Clark State Park
21914 Park Loop
Onawa, IA 51040
Web: www.iowadnr.com/parks/state_park_list/
preparation_canyon.html
Phone: 712-423-2829
Size: 344 acres. **Location:** 5 miles southwest of Moorhead, off IA 183. **Facilities:** 9 hike-in campsites, picnic areas, open picnic shelter, hiking trails. **Activities:** Primitive camping, picnicking, hiking. **Special Features:** Park derives its name from the town of Preparation, so named because a group of Mormons who settled there in 1853 considered the area their ''School of Preparation for the Life Beyond.'' Their leader, Charles B Thompson, cheated them out of their valuable farmland and fled the area. The Iowa Supreme Court divided the remaining land equally among the remaining families, but the town faded and eventually disappeared. Descendents of the original Mormon families later sold the land where Preparation once stood to the state. Now a state park, the area is located in Loess Hills and surrounded on three sides by dramatic ridges.

★2414★ RED HAW STATE PARK

24550 US Hwy 34
Chariton, IA 50049
Web: www.iowadnr.com/parks/state_park_list/red_haw.html
Phone: 641-774-5632; **Fax:** 641-774-8821
Size: 649 acres. **Location:** 1 mile east of Chariton, off US 34. **Facilities:** Campground with 80 campsites (&; 60 with electrical hookups), paved roads, modern restrooms, showers, and playground; picnic areas, open picnic shelters (&), hiking and multi-use trails, 72-acre lake, swimming beach, 2 boat ramps, fishing jetty. **Activities:** Camping, boating (electric motors only), swimming, fishing, ice fishing, hiking, snowmobiling; an additional 229 acres south of the park are designated for public hunting. **Special Features:** Park's trees, including hawthorns, oaks, maples, and pines, make it a lovely place to visit in all seasons.

★2415★ RICE LAKE STATE PARK

c/o Ambrose A. Call State Park
Rt 1, Box 264
Algona, IA 50511
Phone: 641-581-4835

Size: 15 acres. **Location:** 2.5 miles southeast of Lake Mills. **Facilities:** Open picnic shelters, playground, boat ramp. **Activities:** Swimming, fishing, boating. **Special Features:** This day-use park has a 900-acre natural lake.

★2416★ ROCK CREEK STATE PARK

5627 Rock Creek E
Kellogg, IA 50135
Web: www.iowadnr.com/parks/state_park_list/
rock_creek.html
Phone: 641-236-3722; **Fax:** 641-236-5599
Size: 1,697 acres. **Location:** 6 miles northeast of Kellogg. **Facilities:** 200 campsites (&; 101 with electrical hookups) with modern restrooms, showers, and a playground, picnic areas, open picnic shelter, multi-use trails, fishing jetty, boat ramp. **Activities:** Camping, swimming, fishing, ice fishing, boating, hiking, horseback riding, cross-country skiing, snowmobiling, bird watching, hunting. **Special Features:** Park is a haven for many species of wildlife, including thousands of migrating ducks, and the large concentrations of teal, bluebills, and mallards provide excellent opportunities for birdwatching. At the lake's far north end, the Iowa Department of Natural Resources maintains a game management area open to public hunting in season.

★2417★ SHIMEK STATE FOREST

33653 Route J56
Farmington, IA 52626
Web: www.iowadnr.com/forestry/shimek.html
Phone: 319-878-3811
Size: 9,148 acres. **Location:** Southeast Iowa, 1 mile east of Farmington. **Facilities:** Forest comprises 5 units, 4 with recreation facilities: Farmington Unit has 8 campsites, boat ramp, picnic area (&), fishing dock, parking area, restrooms, and hiking trails (18.9 miles); Donnellson Unit has 11 campsites, 1 walk-in site, boat ramp, nature trail, picnic areas, and hiking trails (6.2 miles); Lick Creek Unit has 35 equestrian campsites, hitching rails, horse stalls, pit toilets, picnic tables, day-use area, and equestrian trails (25 miles); Keosauqua Unit has hiking trails (7.7 miles). Entire forest is open to hunting (except camping areas) and hiking. **Activities:** Camping, fishing, hiking, horseback riding, hunting. **Special Features:** Shimek has the largest continuous stand of forest cover in the state.

★2418★ SPRINGBROOK STATE PARK

2437 160th Rd
Guthrie Center, IA 50115
Web: www.iowadnr.com/parks/state_park_list/
springbrook.html
Phone: 641-747-3591; **Fax:** 641-747-8401
Size: 920 acres. **Location:** 8 miles northeast of Guthrie Center, off IA 25 and 384. **Facilities:** 118 campsites ((&); 81 with electrical hookups) with modern showers and restrooms, 6 family rental cabins, picnic areas with restroom facilities, open picnic shelters (&), hiking trails (12 miles), swimming beach, fishing jetties, boat ramps, boat rentals, playground, concession. **Activities:** Camping, hunting, swimming, fishing (lake and river), boating (electric motors only), hiking, bicycling, snowmobiling. **Special Features:** Park includes an abundance of

9. State Parks

476

wildlife, including deer, red and gray fox, coyote, raccoon, beaver, muskrat, and wild turkey.

★2419★ STEPHENS STATE FOREST

1111 N 8th St
Chariton, IA 50049
Web: www.iowadnr.com/forestry/stephens.html
Phone: 641-774-4559
Size: 7 units totaling 14,112 acres. **Location:** Forest headquarters office is located near the north edge of Chariton, 1 block west of Highway 14. **Facilities:** Some units have campgrounds, including equestrian campgrounds, stocked ponds for fishing, and developed trails. **Activities:** Camping, picnicking, fishing, horseback riding, cross-country skiing, snowmobiling, hiking, and backpacking in designated areas; most of the forest is open to hunting. **Special Features:** Forest was a base of operations for the Civilian Conservation Corps demonstration plantings of hardwoods and conifers in the 1930s. Over the years, ongoing practices have continued to improve forest production, as well as create wildlife habitat, control erosion, and protect the watershed.

★2420★ STONE STATE PARK

5001 Talbot Rd
Sioux City, IA 51103
Web: www.iowadnr.com/parks/state_park_list/stone.html
Phone: 712-255-4698
Size: 1,132 acres. **Location:** In the northwest of Sioux City, along IA 12. **Facilities:** 30 non-modern campsites (9 with electrical hookups), day-use lodge, 3 open picnic shelters (&), playground, hiking and cross-country skiing trails (8 miles), mountain bike and snowmobile trails (6 miles), equestrian trails (6 miles), nature center. **Activities:** Camping, lake and river fishing, hiking, horseback riding, mountain biking, cross-country skiing, snowmobiling, interpretive programs. **Special Features:** Stone is a nationally recognized urban wildlife sanctuary where wild turkeys, white-tailed deer, coyotes, and red foxes can be found, as well as a variety of bird life, including turkey vultures, barred owls, rufous-sided towhees, and ovenbirds. Rare butterflies, such as the Pawnee skipper and Olympia white, are found on the prairie ridges. The park's Dorothy Pecaut Nature Center features a ''walk-under'' prairie, a 400-gallon aquarium of native fish, a children's discovery center, natural history dioramas, and other interpretive displays.

★2421★ TWIN LAKES STATE PARK

c/o Black Hawk Lake State Park
PO Box 618
Lake View, IA 51450
Phone: 712-657-8712
Size: 15 acres. **Location:** 7.5 miles north of Rockwell City, off IA 4-124. **Facilities:** Boat ramp, open picnic shelter (&), playground. **Activities:** Fishing, swimming. **Special Features:** Day-use park has a 569-acre natural lake.

★2422★ UNION GROVE STATE PARK

1215 220th St
Gladbrook, IA 50635
Web: www.iowadnr.com/parks/state_park_list/union_grove.html
Phone: 641-473-2556; **Fax:** 641-473-3059
Size: 282 acres. **Location:** 4 miles southwest of Gladbrook. **Facilities:** 25 campsites (7 with electrical hookups) with non-modern restroom facilities, picnic areas, open picnic shelter, hiking trails, swimming beach, fishing jetty (&), 2 boat ramps. **Activities:** Camping, swimming, fishing, boating, hiking, snowmobiling. **Special Features:** Focal point of the park is its 110-acre lake. A restored prairie and a pine plantation are located in the northeast corner of the park, just off the main roadway.

★2423★ VIKING LAKE STATE PARK

2780 Viking Lake Rd
Stanton, IA 51573
Web: www.iowadnr.com/parks/state_park_list/viking_lake.html
Phone: 712-829-2235; **Fax:** 712-829-2842
Size: 1,000 acres. **Location:** 4 miles southeast of Stanton. **Facilities:** 120 campsites (&; 94 with electrical hookups, 22 full-service, 9 buddy sites, 26 non-electrical) with modern restrooms, showers, and a playground in the campground, open picnic shelter (&), nature trail (1 mile), hiking trails (6 miles), swimming beach, boat rentals, boat ramp, fishing jetty. **Activities:** Camping, swimming, fishing, boating, hiking, snowmobiling. **Special Features:** Viking Lake is one of the most popular state parks in southwest Iowa. A large portion of the park has been left in its natural state and has an abundance of wild flowers, plants, and wildlife.

★2424★ VOLGA RIVER STATE RECREATION AREA

10225 Ivy Rd
Fayette, IA 52142
Web: www.iowadnr.com/parks/state_park_list/volga_river.html
Phone: 563-425-4161; **Fax:** 563-425-3004
Size: 5,500 acres. **Location:** 4 miles north of Fayette, off IA 150. **Facilities:** 49 non-modern campsites (&), with an area for equestrian camping (campground has no flush toilets or showers, but a modern campground is planned), 2 main picnic areas, trails, boat ramp. Beach and swimming area planned. **Activities:** Camping, lake and river fishing, boating, canoeing, hiking, horseback riding, mountain biking, cross-country skiing, snowmobiling, hunting. **Special Features:** Park's scenic features include the Volga River and the old steel bridges that cross it, striking rock formations, prairie areas, and natural woodlands with unusual stands of aspen and Canadian yew. The area provides excellent habitat for a variety of fish and wildlife.

★2425★ WALNUT WOODS STATE PARK

3155 Walnut Woods Dr
West Des Moines, IA 50265
Web: www.iowadnr.com/parks/state_park_list/walnut_woods.html
Phone: 515-285-4502; **Fax:** 515-285-7476

9. State Parks

Size: 250 acres. **Location:** Within the metropolitan area of Des Moines, at the southern edge of West Des Moines, off IA 5. **Facilities:** 23 campsites (&; 8 with electrical hookups), modern restrooms (but no showers), day-use lodge (&), picnic areas, trails (2.5 miles), boat ramp. **Activities:** Camping, fishing, canoeing, hiking, horseback riding, cross-country skiing. **Special Features:** Park encompasses 250 acres of wooded bottomland along the Raccoon River. Within the park lies a large surviving natural stand of black walnut trees.

★2426★ **WAPSIPINICON STATE PARK**

21301 County Rd E34
Anamosa, IA 52205
Web: www.iowadnr.com/parks/state_park_list/
wapsipinicon.html
Phone: 319-462-2761; **Fax:** 319-462-4878
Size: 394 acres. **Location:** Just south of Anamosa on the Wapsipinicon River. **Facilities:** 30 campsites (&; 15 with electrical hookups), modern restrooms and showers in campground, 2 day-use lodges (&), open picnic shelters (&), nature trail, multi-use trails, boat ramp, 9-hole golf course. **Activities:** Camping, hunting, fishing, hiking, bicycling, cross-country skiing, snowmobiling, cave exploring. **Special Features:** One of Iowa's first state parks, Wapsipinicon affords hikers views of rocky staircases, crevices, and caves from its bluffs. Mushrooms, nuts, and berries may be harvested in the park.

★2427★ **WAUBONSIE STATE PARK**

2585 Waubonsie Park Rd
Hamburg, IA 51640
Web: www.iowadnr.com/parks/state_park_list/waubonsie.html
Phone: 712-382-2786; **Fax:** 712-382-9860
Size: 1,247 acres. **Location:** 7 miles southwest of Sidney, off IA 239-2. **Facilities:** 40 campsites (24 with electrical hookups) with modern shower and restroom facilities, 32-site equestrian campground with non-modern restroom facilities, open picnic shelter (&), interpretive trail, hiking trails (7 miles), equestrian trails (8 miles). **Activities:** Camping, hiking, horseback riding. **Special Features:** Park is located in the unique "Loess Hills," a landform found only along the Missouri River in Iowa and Missouri and in China. The Lewis and Clark National Historical Trail passes through the park.

★2428★ **WILDCAT DEN STATE PARK**

1884 Wildcat Den Rd
Muscatine, IA 52761
Web: www.iowadnr.com/parks/state_park_list/
wildcat_den.html
Phone: 563-263-4337; **Fax:** 563-264-8329
Size: 423 acres. **Location:** 10 miles east of Muscatine, off IA 22. **Facilities:** 28 campsites with non-modern restroom facilities, picnic areas, 2 open picnic shelters (&), trails. **Activities:** Camping, fishing, hiking. **Special Features:** Park's trail system winds through a variety of terrain and leads to scenic bluffs and outcroppings that provide hikers with spectacular views. Historical structures preserved at the park include Pine Creek Grist Mill, which is considered one of the finest examples of mid-19th

Century mills in the US and is on the *National Register of Historic Places.*

★2429★ **WILSON ISLAND STATE RECREATION AREA**

32801 Campground Ln
Missouri Valley, IA 51555
Web: www.iowadnr.com/parks/state_park_list/
wilson_island.html
Phone: 712-642-2069; **Fax:** 712-642-4390
Size: 544 acres. **Location:** 5 miles west of Loveland, off County Road G12. **Facilities:** 135 campsites, including a modern camping area with 63 electric sites, showers, flush toilets, and 2 youth group camps, a rustic rental cabin, playground, picnic area with shelters, multi-use trails (5 miles), boat ramp. **Activities:** Camping, fishing, hiking, mountain biking, cross-country skiing, snowmobiling, hunting. **Special Features:** Named after George Wilson, former governor of Iowa, Wilson Island came into existence as an island sandbar around 1900. Today the park encompasses dense cottonwood stands and has an abundance of wildlife, including deer, snow geese, and bald eagles. Immediately north of Wilson Island is the DeSoto National Wildlife Refuge (see entry in national wildlife refuges section).

★2430★ **YELLOW RIVER STATE FOREST**

729 State Forest Rd
Harpers Ferry, IA 52146
Web: www.iowadnr.com/forestry/yellowriver.html
Phone: 563-586-2254
Size: 8,503 acres. **Location:** 14 miles southeast of Waukon, off IA 76. **Facilities:** Most of the Forest's recreation activities are at its Paint Creek Unit, which has 168 equestrian campsites, Big Paint Creek, Little Paint Creek, 6 miles of stocked trout stream, hiking, snowmobile, and equestrian trails, cross-country ski trails, scenic overlooks, boat ramp. **Activities:** Camping, picnicking, fishing, hiking, horseback riding, cross-country skiing, and snowmobiling at Paint Creek Unit; entire forest is open to hunting (except for campgrounds), hiking, and cross-country skiing. **Special Features:** The park's 25-mile trail system passes through oak, hickory, and maple forests and features a view of Paint Creek Valley. The backpack trail at Yellow River was chosen as the best hike in the state.

Kansas State Parks

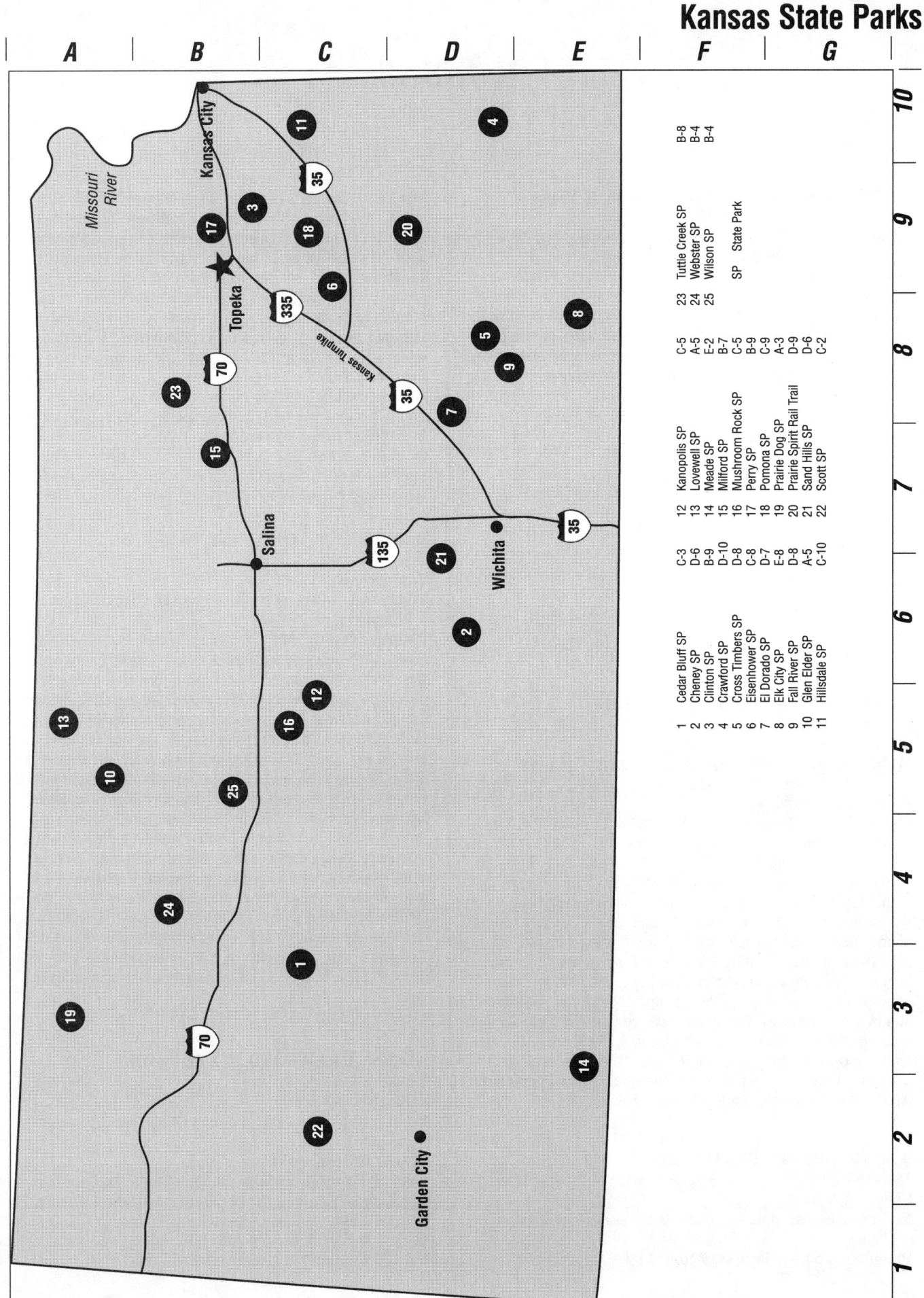

1	Cedar Bluff SP	C-3
2	Cheney SP	D-6
3	Clinton SP	B-9
4	Crawford SP	D-10
5	Cross Timbers SP	C-8
6	Eisenhower SP	D-7
7	El Dorado SP	E-8
8	Elk City SP	D-8
9	Fall River SP	A-5
10	Glen Elder SP	C-10
11	Hillsdale SP	

12	Kanopolis SP	C-5
13	Lovewell SP	A-5
14	Meade SP	E-2
15	Milford SP	B-7
16	Mushroom Rock SP	C-5
17	Perry SP	B-9
18	Pomona SP	C-9
19	Prairie Dog SP	A-3
20	Prairie Spirit Rail Trail	D-9
21	Sand Hills SP	D-6
22	Scott SP	C-2

23	Tuttle Creek SP	B-8
24	Webster SP	B-4
25	Wilson SP	B-4

SP State Park

KANSAS

★2431★ Kansas Department of Wildlife & Parks
1020 S Kansas Ave, Suite 200
Topeka, KS 66612
(785) 296-2281 - Phone
(785) 296-6953 - Fax
Web: www.kdwp.state.ks.us
Operates 24 state parks. Maintains an extensive system of trails which utilize park lands, wildlife areas, and other public property. Manages 4 fish hatcheries and more than 60 reservoirs, lakes, and other fishing areas. Administers fishing and hunting licensing and boat registration.

★2432★ Kansas State Historical Society
6425 SW 6th Ave
Topeka, KS 66615
(785) 272-8681 - Phone
(785) 272-8682 - Fax
Web: www.kshs.org
Preserves, manages, and operates 16 historical sites throughout the state.

★2433★ CEDAR BLUFF STATE PARK
Rt 2, Box 76A
Ellis, KS 67637
Web: www.kdwp.state.ks.us/news/state_parks/locations/
cedar_bluff
Phone: 785-726-3212
Size: 900 acres. **Location:** Trego County, 13 miles south of I-70, exit 135, on Highway 147. **Facilities:** 121 utility campsites (10 sites with full hookups, 91 with electric and water hookups, 20 with electric only), 300 non-utility sites, group campground with 12 utility sites, 2 primitive and 3 modern rental cabins, 5 showerhouses, 4 shelterhouses (2 reservable), 3 vault toilets, picnic areas, BMX track, basketball court, horseshoe pit, 2 fishing docks, 2 fish cleaning stations, 5 boat ramps, 5 courtesy docks, swimming beach. **Activities:** Camping, fishing, boating, windsurfing, water-skiing, jet skiing, swimming, basketball, hunting (♿). **Special Features:** Park consists of two distinct areas, Bluffton (350 acres) and Page Creek (500 acres). Located on the north side of the 6,000-acre Cedar Bluff Reservoir, Bluffton is the most developed of the two areas. The Page Creek Area is located on the south side of the reservoir.

★2434★ CHENEY STATE PARK
16000 NE 50th St
Cheney, KS 67570
Web: www.kdwp.state.ks.us/news/state_parks/locations/
cheney
Phone: 316-542-3664; **Fax:** 316-542-9979

Size: 1,913 acres. **Location:** 25 miles west of Wichita (54/400 to KS 251, then north 4 miles). **Facilities:** 223 utility camping sites, more than 400 primitive campsites, group camping area with 20 utility sites, 7 modern cabins, 7 modern pit toilets, 9 showerhouses, 1 shelter with restrooms, picnic/day use areas, group picnic shelters, 4 designated swimming areas, 6 boat ramps (22 launching lanes), 3 courtesy docks, 2 fish cleaning stations, marina, 2 nature trails. **Activities:** Camping, sailing, windsurfing, fishing (♿), boating, swimming, hiking. **Special Features:** Park occupies the shores of one of the top sailing lakes in the US, with the Ninnescah Sailing Center on the West Shore Area of the park as headquarters for sailing at Cheney. In addition to the recreational activities available at the lake, the 5,200-acre wildlife area adjacent to the park provides opportunities for wildlife watching, nature photography, and hunting.

★2435★ CLINTON STATE PARK
798 N 1415 Rd
Lawrence, KS 66049
Web: www.kdwp.state.ks.us/news/state_parks/locations/
clinton
Phone: 785-842-8562
Size: 1,425 acres. **Location:** 4 miles west of Lawrence. **Facilities:** 240 utility campsites, 220 primitive, non-utility campsites, restrooms and showers near campground, 6 picnic shelters, day-use picnic area, 4 playgrounds, sand volleyball area, archery range, 2 9-hole disc golf courses, 6 shower buildings, hiking and biking trails (25 miles), cross-country ski trail (5 miles), self-guided nature trail (1 mile), swimming beach with showerhouse, 16 boat ramp lanes, 8 courtesy docks, separate launch areas for windsurfers and personal watercraft, marina with floating restaurant, boat rentals. **Activities:** Camping, boating, fishing, swimming, water-skiing, hiking, mountain biking, cross-country skiing, wildlife viewing. **Special Features:** Park is situated on the north shore of the Clinton Reservoir in the scenic Osage Questas region of Kansas. The park is well-known for its extensive trails system, and the park staff work closely with Lawrence and University of Kansas individuals and organizations to present several concerts and other special events each year.

★2436★ CRAWFORD STATE PARK
1 Lake Rd
Farlington, KS 66734
Web: www.kdwp.state.ks.us/news/state_parks/locations/
crawford
Phone: 620-362-3671
Size: 500 acres. **Location:** On the edge of the Ozarks in southeast Kansas, 9 miles north of Girard in Crawford County. **Facilities:** 74 utility campsites (water and electricity), 425 primitive sites, 7 shelter houses, nature trail, hiking and mountain bike trails, horseshoe pits, sand volleyball, playgrounds, swimming

beach, 2 bathhouses, 2 boat ramps, 2 courtesy docks, full-service marina, restaurant. **Activities:** Camping, boating (limited times), fishing, swimming, scuba diving, hiking, mountain biking. **Special Features:** Two recorded archeological sites have been identified within the boundaries of the park, including remnants of a 19th century US military outpost. An interpretive trail connects the park with the Farlington Fish Hatchery, which was built in the 1930s shortly after the Civilian Conservation Corps completed construction of the park's 150-acre lake.

★2437★ CROSS TIMBERS STATE PARK

144 Hwy 105
Toronto, KS 66777
Web: www.kdwp.state.ks.us/news/state_parks/locations/
  cross_timbers
Phone: 620-637-2213
Size: 1,075 acres. **Location:** 12 miles west of Yates Center in Woodson County. **Facilities:** 62 utility campsites (15 full hookups, 37 with water and electric hookups, 10 with electric only), 180 primitive, non-utility sites, modern bathroom and shower facilities, backcountry camping on Chautauqua Hills Trail (by special permit), 2 rental cabins, trails, swimming beach, 6 boat ramp lanes, 2 courtesy docks. **Activities:** Camping, boating, fishing, swimming, hiking, backpacking, mountain biking, wildlife viewing. **Special Features:** Park is located in the Verdigris River Valley in southeast Kansas, in a region that was once a favored hunting and camping ground of the Native Americans of the Osage Nation. This area is in the northern reaches of the physiographic region known to early pioneers as Cross Timbers. The park provides numerous access points to the 2,800-acre Toronto Reservoir.

★2438★ EISENHOWER STATE PARK

29810 S Fairlawn Rd
Lyndon, KS 66523
Web: www.kdwp.state.ks.us/news/state_parks/locations/
  eisenhower
Phone: 785-528-4102
Size: 1,785 acres. **Location:** In southern Osage County, on the north shore of Melvern Lake. **Facilities:** 190 utility campsites, primitive campsites, group camping area, equestrian camping area, rental cabin (&), 4 shower houses, swimming beach, horseshoe pits, playgrounds, volleyball courts, picnic shelters, 18 boat ramp lanes, equestrian trail (20 miles) in undeveloped area of the park. **Activities:** Camping, boating, fishing, swimming, hiking, horseback riding, hunting. **Special Features:** Formerly known as Melvern State Park, the park was renamed in 1990 to honor Dwight David Eisenhower, the only US President from Kansas. The park is located on the eastern fringe of the Flint Hills and features 1,000 acres of tallgrass prairie, 400 acres of woodland, and a full range of recreational facilities.

★2439★ EL DORADO STATE PARK

618 NE Bluestem Rd
El Dorado, KS 67042
Web: www.kdwp.state.ks.us/news/state_parks/locations/
  el_dorado
Phone: 316-321-7180
Size: 4,000 acres. **Location:** 3 miles east and 1 mile north of the city of El Dorado on Highway 54. **Facilities:** More than 1,000 campsites, including 128 sites with full hookups, 352 with water and electric hookups, and 566 non-utility campsites, a 24-site group campground, a designated horse campground, 10 rental cabins, laundry facility, 13 showerhouses, picnic areas, 10 group shelters, trails, 2 swimming beaches, 17 boat ramp lanes, 5 courtesy docks, marina, sailing club, boat rentals, amphitheater with indoor-outdoor stage. **Activities:** Camping, boating, fishing, swimming, hiking, bicycling, horseback riding, hunting. **Special Features:** Kansas's largest state park, El Dorado is also one of its most handicapped-accessible. Among the park's many facilities is a large amphitheater with dual stages that accommodates a variety of concerts and festivals each year.

★2440★ ELK CITY STATE PARK

4825 Squaw Creek Rd
Independence, KS 67301
Web: www.kdwp.state.ks.us/news/state_parks/locations/
  elk_city
Phone: 620-331-6295
Size: 857 acres. **Location:** 5 miles northwest of Independence, KS. **Facilities:** 95 utility campsites (11 sites with full hookups, 84 with electric and water hookups), 55 primitive non-utility sites, restrooms and showers, 3 group shelters, nature trails, exercise trail, swimming beach, 3-lane boat ramps, 2 courtesy docks, fishing pier (&), disc golf course. **Activities:** Camping, fishing, swimming, boating, hiking, mountain biking, nature study. **Special Features:** Park has a nationally recognized trail system, including the 3-mile Table Mound Trail, which is named for the park's most prominent feature, a sheer limestone bluff. The park property is leased for public park and recreational purposes through an ageement between the state and the US Army Corps of Engineers.

★2441★ FALL RIVER STATE PARK

144 Hwy 105
Toronto, KS 66777
Web: www.kdwp.state.ks.us/news/state_parks/locations/
  fall_river
Phone: 620-637-2213
Size: 980 acres. **Location:** Southeastern Greenwood County, between the Cross Timbers region and the Flint Hills. **Facilities:** 45 utility campsites with water and electric hookups as well as modern restroom and shower facilities, more than 100 primitive campsites, 6 hiking trails, swimming beach, 4 boat ramp lanes, 4 courtesy docks, 14 picnic shelters. **Activities:** Camping, boating, canoeing, fishing, swimming, water-skiing, hiking, wildlife viewing, birdwatching, interpretive programs. **Special Features:** Park is a blend of forested flood plains, blackjack savannahs, and tallgrass prairie, and features a diversity of plant and animal life. More than 8,000 acres of public wildlife area adjoining the park are managed for a variety of game and nongame species.

★2442★ GLEN ELDER STATE PARK

2131 180 Rd
Glen Elder, KS 67446
Web: www.kdwp.state.ks.us/news/state_parks/locations/
glen_elder
Phone: 785-545-3345
Size: 1,391 acres. **Location:** 12 miles west of Beloit in Mitchell County, on the shores of Waconda Lake. **Facilities:** 121 campsites with electrical hookups (most with water), 240 non-utility sites, modern restroom and shower buildings, full-service marina (Apr-Oct), 6 boat ramp lanes, 2 courtesy docks (&), boat rental, fish cleaning station (&), group shelter, sports field, volleyball courts, swimming beach, nature trails (under development), historic site. **Activities:** Camping, boating, fishing, swimming, hiking, bicycling, baseball, softball, volleyball, interpretive programs. **Special Features:** Park's 12,500-acre Waconda Lake is one of the largest in the state and offers numerous recreational opportunities. In addition, Waconda Heritage Village, an area depicting pioneer heritage and Native American lore, is being developed on park property. Historic Hopewell Church has been reconstructed on the site, providing historical displays and a room that can be reserved for group events.

★2443★ HILLSDALE STATE PARK

26001 W 255th St
Paola, KS 66071
Web: www.kdwp.state.ks.us/news/state_parks/locations/
hillsdale
Phone: 913-783-4507
Size: 2,830 acres. **Location:** 3 miles west of Hillsdale, in Miami County. **Facilities:** 160 campsites with water and electric hookups, 40 non-utility sites, restrooms and showers, equestrian area with marked trails, swimming beach and bathhouse, picnic shelters, 10 boat ramp lanes, 5 courtesy docks, model airplane flying field for radio-controlled planes. **Activities:** Boating, fishing, swimming, hiking, horseback riding, bird watching, hunting (on adjacent lands), radio-controlled model airplane flying. **Special Features:** Located in the fastest-growing area of the state, the park is heavily used by residents of nearby Kansas City.

★2444★ KANOPOLIS STATE PARK

200 Horsethief Rd
Marquette, KS 67464
Web: www.kdwp.state.ks.us/news/state_parks/locations/
kanopolis
Phone: 785-546-2565
Size: 1,585 acres. **Location:** 33 miles southwest of Salina. **Facilities:** 119 utility campsites and more than 200 primitive sites in 14 campgrounds, full-service marina, 6 boat ramp lanes, 2 courtesy docks, beaches, picnic areas and shelters, nature trail (1.8 miles), multi-use trails (27.4 miles). **Activities:** Camping (including equestrian camping), boating, fishing, swimming, hiking, horseback riding, mountain biking. **Special Features:** Kansas' first state park, Kanopolis is situated in the rolling hills, bluffs, and woods of the scenic Smoky Hills region of Kansas.

★2445★ LOVEWELL STATE PARK

2446 250 Rd
Webber, KS 66970
Web: www.kdwp.state.ks.us/news/state_parks/locations/
lovewell
Phone: 785-753-4971
Size: 1,126 acres. **Location:** 14 miles northeast of Mankato, in northern Jewell County. **Facilities:** 23 campsites with full hookups, 13 sites with water and electric hookups, 82 campsites with electrical only, 306 primitive non-utility sites, 6 semimodern cabins, 4 shower/toilet buildings, 2 vault toilets, fish cleaning stations, picnic areas, playground, sand volleyball, softball diamond, horseshoe pits, group shelter, swimming beach, marina, 6 boat ramp lanes, 4 courtesy docks, archery range, trails, historic landmark, visitor center. **Activities:** Camping, boating, fishing, swimming, wildlife viewing. **Special Features:** Park hosts fishing tournaments and various other special events throughout the year, including a Kids Fishing Derby in early June, fireworks and a sand castle contest in July, and a Lovewell Fun Day in August. Church services are held at the historic limestone schoolhouse at the park during the summer months.

★2446★ MEADE STATE PARK

13051 V Rd
Meade, KS 67864
Web: www.kdwp.state.ks.us/news/state_parks/locations/
meade
Phone: 620-873-2572
Size: 443 acres. **Location:** 13 miles southwest of Meade, on Highway 23. **Facilities:** 42 campsites with with water and electrical hookups, 150 primitive campsites, nature trail, swimming beach and bathhouse, boat ramp, courtesy dock, day use areas, picnic shelters. **Activities:** Camping, boating (fishing boats only), fishing, swimming, hunting (on adjacent lands). **Special Features:** Located in the shortgrass prairie region of the state, Meade is the only state park in southwest Kansas. The park is situated around Meade State Fishing Lake, which offers excellent fishing for bluegill, crappie, channel cat, and largemouth bass. (Boats with motors must be used for fishing only, and no skiing or pleasure boating is permitted on the lake.)

★2447★ MILFORD STATE PARK

8811 State Park Rd
Milford, KS 66514
Web: www.kdwp.state.ks.us/news/state_parks/locations/
milford
Phone: 785-238-3014
Size: 1,084 acres. **Location:** 9 miles northwest of Exit 295 from I-70. **Facilities:** 141 utility campsites with water and electrical hookups (51 also have sewer hookups), 120 non-utility sites, 3 modern cabins, picnic areas and shelters, multi-purpose trails, swimming beach and bathhouse, 10 boat ramp lanes, 3 courtesy docks, full-service marina, viewing tower. **Activities:** Camping, boating, fishing, swimming, horseback riding, hiking, hunting (on adjacent lands). **Special Features:** Park is located near Junction City on the shores of 16,000-acre Milford Reservoir, the state's largest lake. The park houses a large yacht club, and nearby Milford Nature Center and Milford Fish Hatchery offer a variety of interpretive exhibits and displays.

★2448★ MUSHROOM ROCK STATE PARK

200 Horsethief Rd
Marquette, KS 67464
Web: www.kdwp.state.ks.us/news/state_parks/locations/
mushroom_rock
Phone: 785-546-2565
Size: 5 acres. **Location:** 12 miles east of Ellsworth, near Kanopolis State Park (see separate entry). **Facilities:** Day use area only, with historic landmark. **Special Features:** Kansas' smallest state park features unusual mushroom-shaped rocks that served as landmarks and meeting places for Native Americans and early pioneers. The rocks are a geological phenomenon of sandstone spheres balanced on softer pedestals of sandstone, with the largest rock measuring 27 feet in diameter.

★2449★ PERRY STATE PARK

5441 Westlake Rd
Ozawkie, KS 66070
Web: www.kdwp.state.ks.us/news/state_parks/locations/perry
Phone: 785-246-3449; **Fax:** 785-246-0224
Size: 1,597 acres. **Location:** In the southwest portion of Perry Reservoir, 4 miles north of Highway 24 on Highway 237. **Facilities:** 102 utility campsites (water and electric hookups), 200 non-utility sites (primitive), 5 shower buildings, trails, picnic shelters, swimming beach and bathhouse, 10 boat ramp lanes, 2 courtesy docks. **Activities:** Camping, boating, fishing, hiking, mountain biking, horseback riding, swimming, hunting (nearby). **Special Features:** Perry Reservoir is best known for its crappie and channel cat fishing. The marshes in the adjacent 11,000-acre wildlife area provide early hunting of migrating birds, and the deep water areas supply late-season mallard and diving duck hunting.

★2450★ POMONA STATE PARK

22900 S Hwy 368
Vassar, KS 66543
Web: www.kdwp.state.ks.us/news/state_parks/locations/
pomona
Phone: 785-828-4933
Size: 490 acres. **Location:** 30 miles south of Topeka, in Osage County. **Facilities:** 47 campsites with full hookups (water, electric, sewer), 97 campsites with water and electrical hookups, 200 non-utility sites, picnic shelters, group shelter facility, playgrounds, volleyball courts, horseshoe pits, 9-hole disc golf course, trails (2.5 miles), swimming beach and bathhouse, full-service marina, 5 boat ramp lanes, 2 courtesy docks. **Activities:** Camping, boating, fishing, swimming, water-skiing, hiking, hunting (nearby). **Special Features:** Park is well-known by northeast Kansas residents for its great family atmosphere. A popular destination for fisherman, the 4,000-acre Pomona Reservoir offers some of the best crappie and catfish angling in the state.

★2451★ PRAIRIE DOG STATE PARK

PO Box 431
Norton, KS 67654
Web: www.kdwp.state.ks.us/news/state_parks/locations/
prairie_dog
Phone: 785-877-2953

Size: 1,150 acres. **Location:** On the north shore of Keith Sebelius Reservoir in Norton County. **Facilities:** 58 utility campsites, more than 130 non-utility sites, rental cabin, group campground, 2 shower buildings, nature trail, picnic shelters, swimming beach and bathhouse, 2 boat ramp lanes, courtesy dock, museum. **Activities:** Camping, boating, fishing, swimming, hiking, wildlife viewing, interpretive programs. **Special Features:** Park is home to a thriving prairie dog colony and is the site of one of the last remaining adobe house in Kansas. In addition to the renovated adobe house (originally built in the 1890s), a one-room schoolhouse is also preserved at the park.

★2452★ PRAIRIE SPIRIT TRAIL STATE PARK

419 S Oak St
Garnett, KS 66032
Web: www.kdwp.state.ks.us/news/state_parks/locations/
prairie_spirit_trail
Phone: 785-448-6767
Size: 33-mile trail. **Location:** North-south trail runs from Ottawa to Welda. Main trailhead located in the Santa Fe depot near the town square in Garnett. **Facilities:** Day-use trail with rest areas along the route. **Activities:** Hiking, bicycling. **Special Features:** Trail is built on a railroad Right-of-Way that was the first north-south rail line in Kansas (the rail line was constructed in the 1860s). The trail is a hard packed limestone screening surface in rural areas, with portions asphalted through Garnett and Ottawa. Average width of the trail is a minimum of 8 feet, and the grades are moderate and follow original railroad grades. A per-person trail permit is required.

★2453★ SAND HILLS STATE PARK

4207 E 56th
Hutchinson, KS 67502
Web: www.kdwp.state.ks.us/news/state_parks/locations/
sand_hills
Phone: 316-542-3664
Size: 1,123 acres. **Location:** In Hutchinson, off KS 61. **Facilities:** 8 distinct trails, ranging from 1 mile to almost 4 miles and broken down as hiking, horseback riding, and interpretive trails; 2 vault toilets are the park's only modern facilities. **Activities:** Hiking, horseback riding, jogging, wildflower walks, birdwatching, hunting. **Special Features:** Park is a natural area that has been preserved for its sand dunes, grasslands, wetlands, and woodlands, and visitors are limited to walk-in access to help protect the park's natural features. (Per person permit required.)

★2454★ SCOTT STATE PARK

520 W Scott Lake Dr
Scott City, KS 67871
Web: www.kdwp.state.ks.us/news/state_parks/locations/scott
Phone: 620-872-2061
Size: 1,120 acres. **Location:** West of Highway 83, between Oakley and Scott City on KS 95. **Facilities:** 55 utility campsites, 100 non-utility sites, equestrian camping area, 3 modern shower buildings, vault toilets, multi-use trails, swimming beach and bathhouse, playground, shelters, concession facility, 100-acre fishing lake, 2 boat ramp lanes, 2 courtesy docks, canoe and paddle boat rentals, historical sites. **Activities:** Camping, boating

9. State Parks

(fishing boats only), fishing, swimming, hiking, horseback riding, interpretive programs, hunting (on adjacent lands). **Special Features:** Located in the western Kansas prairie, park is an oasis of natural springs, deep wooded canyons, and craggy bluffs. The park is also rich in history and includes the home of the original settlers in the area (Steele home), which has been preserved much as it was 100 years ago. Park is also the site of El Cuartelejo, the northernmost pueblo in the US.

★2455★ **TUTTLE CREEK STATE PARK**
5800-A River Pond Rd
Manhattan, KS 66502
Web: www.kdwp.state.ks.us/news/state_parks/locations/
tuttle_creek
Phone: 785-539-7941
Size: 1,196 acres. **Location:** 10 miles north of Manhattan, in northeast Kansas. **Facilities:** 198 utility campsites (154 with water and electric hookups; 44 electric-only sites), 500 primitive non-utility campsites, 4 rental cabins, picnic areas, 39 shelters, volleyball courts, horseshoe pits, 18-hole disc golf course, nature trails, mountain biking and equestrian trails, swimming beach and bathhhouse, 11 boat ramp lanes, 3 courtesy docks, marina, canoe rentals, restroom and shower facilities, shooting range. **Activities:** Camping, boating, canoeing, fishing, swimming, hiking, mountain biking, horseback riding, hunting (on adjacent lands). **Special Features:** Park is located on the banks of the state's second largest lake, Tuttle Creek Reservoir, with 12,500 acres of water and about 100 miles of rugged, wooded shoreline. Four individual units (River Pond, Spillway, Fancy Creek, and Randolph) make up the 1,200-acre park.

★2456★ **WEBSTER STATE PARK**
1210 Nine Rd
Stockton, KS 67669
Web: www.kdwp.state.ks.us/news/state_parks/locations/
webster
Phone: 785-425-6775
Size: 880 acres. **Location:** 8 miles west of Stockton on Highway 24. **Facilities:** 74 utility campsites, 100 non-utility sites (primitive), 2-bedroom rental cabin, picnic shelters, swimming beach, sand volleyball court, horseshoe pits, playgrounds, hiking trail, 5 boat ramp lanes, 3 courtesy docks, floating fishing docks, fishing pier (&), amphitheater. **Activities:** Camping, boating, fishing, swimming, water skiing, windsurfing, hiking, wildlife viewing, hunting (on adjacent lands). **Special Features:** Park is situated in the Solomon River Valley of north-central Kansas and comprises two separate tracts, one on the north shore of Webster Reservoir and the other on the south shore.

★2457★ **WILSON STATE PARK**
Rt 1, Box 181
Sylvan Grove, KS 67481
Web: www.kdwp.state.ks.us/news/state_parks/locations/
wilson
Phone: 785-658-2465
Size: 927 acres. **Location:** 9 miles west of Sylvan Grove. **Facilities:** 135 utility campsites (99 with electric and water hookups; 36 electric-only sites), 100 non-utility sites, picnic/day use areas, shelters, trails (including & trail), swimming beach and bathhouse, sand volleyball and basketball equipment and facilities, horseshoe pits, 5 boat ramp lanes, 2 courtesy docks (&), marina. **Activities:** Camping, boating, fishing, swimming, sand volleyball, hiking, bicycling, hunting (on adjacent lands). **Special Features:** Located in the heart of the Smoky Hills region, Wilson is considered by many to be Kansas' most beautiful park. The park and surrounding wildlife area offer opportunities to view and photograph deer, pheasant, waterfowl, and songbirds.

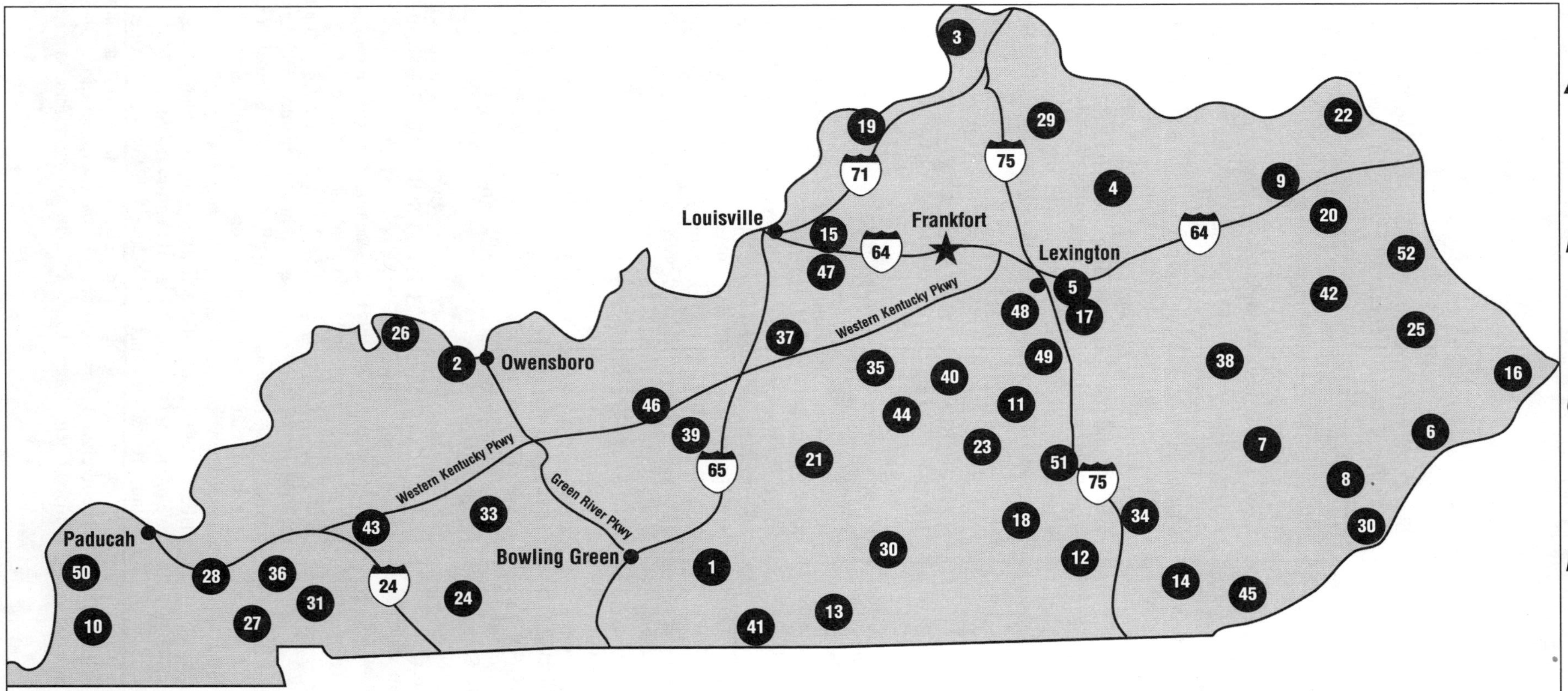

1 Barren River Lake SRP D-5
2 Ben Hawes SP C-3
3 Big Bone Lick SP A-6
4 Blue Licks Battlefield SRP B-7
5 Boone Station SHS C-9
6 Breaks Interstate Park C-8
7 Buckhorn Lake SRP D-9
8 Carr Creek SP D-9
9 Carter Caves SRP B-8
10 Columbus-Belmont SP D-1
11 Constitution Square SHS C-7
12 Cumberland Falls SRP D-7
13 Dale Hollow Lake SRP D-6
14 Dr. Thomas Walker SHS D-8
15 E. P. "Tom" Sawyer SP B-6
16 Fishtrap Lake SP C-10
17 Fort Boonesborough SP B-7

18 General Burnside Island SP D-7
19 General Butler SRP A-6
20 Grayson Lake SP B-9
21 Green River Lake SP C-5
22 Greenbo Lake SRP A-9
23 Isaac Shelby Cemetery SHS C-6
24 Jefferson Davis Monument SHS D-3
25 Jenny Wiley SRP C-9
26 John James Audubon SP C-3
27 Kenlake SRP D-2
28 Kentucky Dam Village SRP D-2
29 Kincaid Lake SP A-7
30 Kingdom Come SP D-9
31 Lake Barkley SRP D-2
32 Lake Cumberland SRP D-6

33 Lake Malone SP D-7
34 Levi Jackson SP C-7
35 Lincoln Homestead SP C-6
36 Mineral Mound SP D-2
37 My Old Kentucky Home SP C-5
38 Natural Bridge SRP C-8
39 Nolin Lake SP C-5
40 Old Fort Harrod SP C-6
41 Old Mulkey Meetinghouse SHS D-5
42 Paintsville Lake SP B-9
43 Pennyrile Forest SRP D-3
44 Perryville Battlefield SHS C-6
45 Pine Mountain SRP D-8
46 Rough River Dam SRP C-4
47 Taylorsville Lake SP B-6

48 Waveland Museum SHS B-7
49 White Hall SHS C-7
50 Wickliffe Mounds SHS D-1
51 William Whitley House SHS C-7
52 Yatesville Lake SP B-9

SHS State Historic Site
SP State Park
SRP State Resort Park

KENTUCKY

★2458★ **Kentucky Department of Parks**
500 Mero St
Frankfort, KY 40601
(502) 564-4270 - Phone
(502) 564-6100 - Fax
(800) 255-7275 - Toll-free
Web: www.kystateparks.com
Manages and maintains 52 state parks, including 17 resort parks, and 22 state historic sites. Cooperatively operates Breaks Interstate Park with Virginia. Sponsors numerous history and nature educational programs, dramas and musical entertainment, contests, tournaments, and festivals.

★2459★ **Kentucky Department of Fish & Wildlife Resources**
1 Game Farm Rd
Frankfort, KY 40601
(502) 564-3400 - Phone
(502) 564-6508 - Fax
(800) 858-1549 - Toll-free
Web: www.kdfwr.state.ky.us
Manages wildlife management areas for hunting, fishing, boating, and other nature-related recreation. Directs conservation education programs and develops wheelchair-accessible areas for hunting, fishing, and wildlife observation. Administers hunting and fishing licensing and boater certification.

Key to camping and lodging classifications:

- **Campsites** — Include electric and water hookups, camp store, playground, and central service buildings with restrooms and showers.
- **Primitive campsites** — Do not include electrical hookups. May have central service buildings with restrooms and showers, or sites may have nearby vault toilets.
- **Lodge rooms** — Two double beds, bath, phone, color TV, air conditioning, and daily maid service. A limited number of rooms have queen or king size beds. Some rooms have wet bars.
- **Cottages** — All cottages have a living room, bath, furnished kitchen, phone, color TV, air conditioning, and heat. Fresh linen is provided; no daily maid service. Some include a dining area.

★2460★ **BARREN RIVER LAKE STATE RESORT PARK**
1149 State Park Rd
Lucas, KY 42156
Web: www.parks.ky.gov/resortparks/br
Phone: 800-325-0057; **Fax:** 270-646-3645; **Toll Free:** 800-325-0057

Size: 1,099 acres land; 10,000 acres water. **Location:** 44 miles southeast of Bowling Green; I-65 to the Cumberland Parkway east, to US 31E south. **Facilities:** 51-room lodge, 22 cottages, 146-seat dining room, 99 campsites with showers and restrooms, 18-hole golf course, meeting rooms, swimming pool (for lodge and cottage guests only), public beach and bathhouse, picnic areas, 2 picnic shelters with restrooms, playgrounds, hiking trails (4 miles), horseback riding concession and stables, marina, boat ramp, boat rentals, lighted basketball court, 2 lighted tennis courts, shuffleboard, volleyball courts, gift shop. Inn and cottages open year-round; campground open Apr-Oct. **Activities:** Camping, swimming, water skiing, fishing, boating, hiking, bicycling, guided trail rides, golfing, shuffleboard, tennis, planned recreation activities.. **Special Features:** Park's lodge and cottages curve around the 10,000-acre lake, providing resort guests with spectacular views of sunsets.

★2461★ **BEN HAWES STATE PARK**
400 Boothfield Rd
Owensboro, KY 42301
Web: www.parks.ky.gov/stateparks/bh
Phone: 270-684-9808
Size: 547 acres. **Location:** Off US 60, 4 miles west of Owensboro. **Facilities:** Picnic shelter with restrooms, hiking trail (1.5 miles), 18-hole golf course, 9-hole golf course, softball fields, basketball courts, archery range, playground, meeting facilities. **Activities:** Golf, picnicking, hiking, archery, basketball, softball. **Special Features:** Park features two golf courses, an 18-hole par-71 course and a 9-hole par-3 course, with a fully-stocked pro shop.

★2462★ **BIG BONE LICK STATE PARK**
3380 Beaver Rd
Union, KY 41091
Web: www.parks.ky.gov/stateparks/bb
Phone: 859-384-3522
Size: 525 acres land; 7 acres water. **Location:** 22 miles southwest of Covington on KY 338, off US 71 and US 75. **Facilities:** 62-site campground with utility hookups, swimming pool (for campground guests only), and central service building with showers, restrooms, and laundry facilties; 7.5-acre fishing lake, nearly 40 acres of picnic grounds, 2 picnic shelters, playgrounds, softball fields, horseshoe pits, 18-hole miniature golf course, hiking trails (3.5 miles), tennis, volleyball, and basketball courts; gift shop, outdoor museum and discovery trail, buffalo herd. **Activities:** Camping, fishing, swimming, hiking, tennis, volleyball, basketball, softball, recreation programs (daily), interpretive programs (seasonal). **Special Features:** The scientific community recognizes this site as the ''Birthplace of American Vertebrate Paleontology.'' Great herds of prehistoric mammals once roamed this area, attracted by the warm salt springs. Many perished here, trapped in a swampy quagmire, and over time

9. State Parks

their skeletons fossilized. Park features Discovery Trail, a paved path that takes visitors through the area that was once a vast swampland past dramatic Ice Age dioramas featuring life-size models of prehistoric animals.

★2463★ BLUE LICKS BATTLEFIELD STATE RESORT PARK

Highway 68
Mount Olivet, KY 41064
Web: www.parks.ky.gov/resortparks/bl
Phone: 800-443-7008
Size: 580 acres. **Location:** 48 miles northeast of Lexington on US 68. **Facilities:** 32-room lodge with meeting facilities, 2 modern cottages, dining room that seats up to 255 people, 51 campsites with utility hookups, showers, and restrooms, picnic areas, picnic shelters (1 with restroom), hiking trails, nature preserve, swimming pool, 18-hole miniature golf course, playgrounds, museum, gift shop. **Activities:** Camping, swimming, fishing, hiking, boating, interpretive programs. **Special Features:** The salt springs at Blue Licks have attracted prehistoric animals, American Indians, pioneers (including Daniel Boone), and 19th-century southerners, who came for the rejuvenating effects of the therapeutic, bubbling waters. However, Blue Licks is more widely known as the site of the last Revolutionary War battle in Kentucky, where Kentuckians suffered great losses at the hands of British and Indian forces.

★2464★ BOONE STATION STATE HISTORIC SITE

240 Gentry Rd
Lexington, KY 40502
Web: parks.ky.gov/statehistoricsites/bs
Phone: 859-263-1073
Size: 46 acres. **Location:** Off I-75 at exit 104, south of Lexington. **Facilities:** Historic site, markers, picnic tables. **Special Features:** After leaving Fort Boonesborough, Daniel Boone established a pioneer station on this site in 1779. However, the Boone family suffered many hardships during the three years they lived here, including the deaths of their son Israel and nephew Thomas at the Battle of Blue Licks. Buried at the site are two of Boone's brothers, Samuel and Edward, and Samuel's wife, Sarah.

★2465★ BREAKS INTERSTATE PARK

PO Box 100
Breaks, VA 24607
Web: www.parks.ky.gov/stateparks/bi
Phone: 800-982-5122
Size: 4,500 acres. **Location:** Park sits astride the state line shared by both Kentucky and Virginia. It is located 8 miles north of Haysi, Virginia, and 7 miles east of Elkhorn, Kentucky, on KY-VA 80. **Facilities:** Lodge with 82 rooms and 1 suite (seasonal), cottages (year-round), restaurant (seasonal), convention center (seasonal), 122 campsites with utilities, showers, and restrooms (seasonal), picnic area, picnic shelters, hiking trails (12 miles), bike trails (2 miles), riding stables and trails, Olympic-sized swimming pool, concession stand, boat dock, pedal boat rental, visitor/interpretive center (seasonal), amphitheater,

gift shop (seasonal). **Activities:** Camping, boating (electric motors only), whitewater rafting, fishing, swimming, hiking, mountain biking, horseback riding, interpretive programs. **Special Features:** Often referred to as "The Grand Canyon of the South," Breaks Canyon, the deepest gorge east of the Mississippi River, is 5 miles long, 1,600 feet deep, and 250 million years old. The gorge was carved by the Russell Fork River, a tributary of the Big Sandy. The park is operated by a separate commission comprising members from both Virginia and Kentucky.

★2466★ BUCKHORN LAKE STATE RESORT PARK

4441 Kentucky Hwy 1833
Buckhorn, KY 41721
Web: www.parks.ky.gov/resortparks/bk
Phone: 800-325-0058
Size: 856 acres land; 1,200 acres water. **Location:** 20 miles northwest of Hazard, on KY 28. **Facilities:** 36-room lodge, 3 cottages, 210-seat dining room, meeting rooms, swimming pool (for lodge and cottage guests only), public beach and bathhouse, picnic areas, playground, hiking trails, self-guided nature trail (1.5 miles), marina (seasonal), 2 boat ramps, pontoon and fishing boat rentals, 18-hole miniature golf course, tennis court, shuffleboard court, sand volleyball court, horseshoe pits, gift shop. **Activities:** Fishing, boating, swimming, hiking, tennis, shuffleboard, recreational programs (seasonal), special events. **Special Features:** Park is located in the lush eastern Kentucky mountains along the edge of Daniel Boone National Forest (see entry in national forests section).

★2467★ CARR CREEK STATE PARK

Highway 15
Sassafras, KY 41759
Web: www.parks.ky.gov/stateparks/ck
Phone: 606-642-4050
Size: 29 acres land; 750 acres water. **Location:** 15 miles southeast of Hazard on KY 15. **Facilities:** 39 campsites with water and electric hookups, showers and restrooms, full-service marina, pontoon and fishing boat rentals, snack bar, beach, picnic facilities. **Activities:** Camping, boating, fishing, swimming. **Special Features:** Park has the longest lakefront sand beach in the Kentucky State Park system, with miles of shoreline and good fishing for bass, crappie, and walleye.

★2468★ CARTER CAVES STATE RESORT PARK

344 Caveland Dr
Olive Hill, KY 41164
Web: www.parks.ky.gov/resortparks/cc
Phone: 800-325-0059
Size: 1,850 acres land; 45 acres water. **Location:** 5 miles northwest of I-64 Exit 161 (Olive Hill). **Facilities:** 28-room fieldstone lodge, 10 cottages, 96-seat dining room, 2 group camping buildings, 89 campsites with utilities, restrooms, and showers, 9-hole regulation golf course, public swimming pool (free to lodge and cottage guests), picnic areas, 2 picnic shelters, playgrounds, hiking trails (26 miles), multi-use trail (10 miles), horse stable and rental concession, 18-hole miniature golf course, 2 tennis courts, meeting facilities, welcome center, gift shop. **Activities:**

Camping, swimming, fishing, boating (no motors), guided canoe trips, hiking, mountain biking, horseback riding, guided trail rides, golfing, tennis, guided cave tours. **Special Features:** Park features more than 20 caverns, including Cascade Cave, with an underground waterfall 30 feet high, and X Cave, which features luminous stone fans, pipes, and spirals. Bat Cave (the largest cave in the park) is the winter home to thousands of rare bats and is shown only during the summer.

★2469★ COLUMBUS-BELMONT STATE PARK

350 Park Rd
Columbus, KY 42032
Web: www.parks.ky.gov/stateparks/cb
Phone: 270-677-2327
Size: 156 acres. **Location:** 36 miles southwest of Paducah on KY 58 and KY 123/80. **Facilities:** 38 campsites with utility hookups, restrooms, showers, laundry facilities, 4 picnic shelters, playground, hiking trails (2.5 miles), activity center (with meeting rooms, dance floor, stage, banquet facilities, and kitchen), miniature golf course, historic sites, museum, snack bar, gift shop. **Activities:** Camping, hiking, interpretive displays. **Special Features:** Columbus-Belmont was the site of a major Civil War battle, and visitors to the park can see the massive chain and anchor the South used to block the passage of Union gunboats on the Mississippi River, as well as the earthen trenches dug to protect the Confederate troops. Ulysses S. Grant was the Union General who forced the evacuation of the Confederates in 1862.

★2470★ CONSTITUTION SQUARE STATE HISTORIC SITE

134 S 2nd St
Danville, KY 40422
Web: parks.ky.gov/statehistoricsites/cs
Phone: 859-239-7089
Size: 3 acres. **Location:** Off US 127 in Danville. **Facilities:** Historic buildings, picnic area. **Activities:** Guided and self-guided tours. **Special Features:** Constitution Square is the site of the 10 constitutional conventions that led to Kentucky's statehood in 1792. The square includes reproductions of the meetinghouse, courthouse, and jail, as well as the site's original post office, the first west of the Alleghenies, and other historic structures.

★2471★ CUMBERLAND FALLS STATE RESORT PARK

7351 Hwy 90
Corbin, KY 40701
Web: www.parks.ky.gov/resortparks/cf
Phone: 800-325-0063
Size: 1,776 acres. **Location:** 20 miles southwest of Corbin, off I-75. **Facilities:** 52-room lodge, cottages, 300-seat dining room, 50 campsites with electric and water hookups, showers and restrooms, and grocery, picnic areas, playgrounds, picnic shelter, hiking trails (17 miles), swimming pool, game courts, horse stables/concession, museum, meeting rooms, gift shop, snack shop, visitor center. **Activities:** Camping, swimming, guided whitewater rafting trips, fishing, hiking, tennis, shuffleboard,

guided horseback trail rides, guided tours, recreational and interpretive programs. **Special Features:** Known as the Niagara of the South, the waterfall forms a 125-foot-wide curtain that drops 60 feet into the gorge below. The mist of Cumberland Falls creates a unique "moonbow," visible only on clear nights during a full moon.

★2472★ DALE HOLLOW LAKE STATE RESORT PARK

6371 State Park Rd
Burkesville, KY 42717
Web: www.parks.ky.gov/resortparks/dh
Phone: 800-325-2282
Size: 3,398 acres land; 27,700 acres water. **Location:** South of Burkesville, on the Kentucky-Tennessee border. **Facilities:** 60-room lodge, 150-seat dining room, campground with 144 campsites, including 24 equestrian campsites, restrooms, and showers, multi-use trails (15 miles), picnic shelter, swimming pool (in campground), marina, boat ramp, fishing and pontoon boat rentals, conference center, gift shop. **Activities:** Camping, boating, swimming, scuba diving, water-skiing, fishing, spear fishing, hiking, mountain biking, horseback riding, recreational programs. **Special Features:** Park's lodge is perched clifftop 300 feet above Dale Hollow Lake at one of its widest points, providing spectacular views for guests. The lake was formed in 1943 by damming Tennessee's Obey River and has 620 miles of shoreline, with plenty of shoals, small tributaries, and clean, clear water to encourage healthy fish growth. The park's campground is insulated by thousands of acres of pristine forest.

★2473★ DR. THOMAS WALKER STATE HISTORIC SITE

4929 KY 459
Barbourville, KY 40906
Web: parks.ky.gov/statehistoricsites/dt
Phone: 606-546-4400
Size: 12 acres. **Location:** On KY 459, 5 miles southwest of Barbourville. **Facilities:** Historic site, gift shop, picnic shelters, playground, basketball court, 9-hole miniature golf course, concession stand (seasonal). **Activities:** Site tours, picnicking, miniature golf. **Special Features:** Park was named for Dr Thomas Walker, a physician and surveyor who led the first expedition through Cumberland Gap in 1750. He built the first cabin in Kentucky near the river (a replica of that cabin is at the site), which he gave the name Cumberland. Although Daniel Boone is remembered as Kentucky's most famous pioneer, Dr Walker actually arrived here more than 17 years earlier than Boone.

★2474★ EP "TOM" SAWYER STATE PARK

3000 Freys Hill Rd
Louisville, KY 40241
Web: www.parks.ky.gov/stateparks/ep
Phone: 502-426-8950; **Fax:** 502-429-7273
Size: 369 acres. **Location:** In Louisville (Westport Rd exit west off the Gene Snyder Freeway). **Facilities:** Picnic facilities, restrooms, activity center (with gymnasium, basketball courts, volleyball and badminton courts, weight room, locker and shower facilities, game area, and meeting room), fitness trail (1

mile), nature trail (1.25 miles; &), 10 soccer fields, 3 lighted softball fields, 12 lighted tennis courts, swimming pool, bathhouse, BMX (bicycle motocross) track, model airplane airfield, food concession, dog park. **Activities:** Swimming, hiking, jogging, tennis, BMX racing, exercise classes, gymnastics, tumbling, and physical education classes, league activities, sports clinics, arts and crafts programs. **Special Features:** Park is named in honor of Erbon Powers ''Tom'' Sawyer, a Louisville leader and father of television news woman Diane Sawyer.

★2475★ FISHTRAP LAKE STATE PARK

2204 Fishtrap Rd
Pikeville, KY 41501
Web: www.parks.ky.gov/stateparks/ft
Phone: 606-437-7496
Location: 7 miles south of Pikeville. **Facilities:** Group and individual picnic sites, shelters, basketball court. **Activities:** Fishing, picnicking. **Special Features:** The man-made Fishtrap Lake was created during the 1960s to help control flooding along the Ohio and Big Sandy Rivers. The park is situated among mountains and dense forests, and the natural protection of the area drew early settlers of all types here, including Kentucky pioneers as well as Native Americans. Throughout years of periodic excavation, more than 65,000 relics from early inhabitants have been found.

★2476★ FORT BOONESBOROUGH STATE PARK

4375 Boonesborough Rd
Richmond, KY 40475
Web: parks.ky.gov/stateparks/fb
Phone: 859-527-3131
Size: 153 acres. **Location:** Near Richmond, on KY 627. Take exit 95 off I-75 or exit at Winchester off I-64. **Facilities:** 167 campsites with water and electric hookups, primitive campsites, activities building, showers, restrooms, laundry, grocery store, 3 picnic shelters, playground, interpretive trail, swimming pool with water slide, wading pool, and rain tree, snack bar,18-hole miniature golf course, boat ramps, museum, meeting room, gift shop. **Activities:** Camping, fishing, boating, swimming, water skiing, hiking, recreational programs (seasonal), fort tours (seasonal). **Special Features:** In 1775 Daniel Boone and his company reached the Kentucky River, where they established Kentucky's second settlement. That settlement, Fort Boonesborough, has been reconstructed as a working fort with cabins, blockhouses, and furnishings, and resident artisans perform craft demonstrations and give modern-day visitors a true sense of what life was like for pioneers in Kentucky.

★2477★ GENERAL BURNSIDE ISLAND STATE PARK

8801 S Highway 27
Burnside, KY 42519
Web: parks.ky.gov/stateparks/ge
Phone: 606-561-4104
Size: 430 acres land; 50,250 acres water. **Location:** 8 miles south of Somerset on US 27. **Facilities:** 94 campsites with utility hookups, 2 central service buildings with showers and restrooms, 18-hole golf course, picnic areas, 2 picnic shelters (one with restrooms), playground, swimming pool, concession stand, boat ramp, marina with boat rentals (nearby). **Activities:** Camping, swimming, fishing, boating, golf. **Special Features:** Park is named for General Ambrose Burnside, who led patrols along the Cumberland River and circled this island while on the lookout for Confederate soldiers.

★2478★ GENERAL BUTLER STATE RESORT PARK

1608 Highway 227
Carrollton, KY 41008
Web: www.parks.ky.gov/resortparks/gb
Phone: 866-462-8853
Size: 791 acres land; 30 acres water. **Location:** 44 miles northeast of Louisville, off I-71. **Facilities:** 53-room lodge, 24 cottages, 176-seat dining room, swimming pool (for lodge and cottage guests only), conference center, 111 campsites with utility hookups, showers, restrooms, and laundry facilities, boat dock, boat rentals (pedal boats, canoes, rowboats, surfbikes), public beach, 9-hole regulation golf course with pro shop, miniature golf course, picnic area, shelter, playground, tennis and basketball courts, scenic overlook, trails, historic home, gift shop. **Activities:** Camping, fishing, boating, swimming, hiking, mountain biking, tennis, golf, recreational and interpretive programs, special events. **Special Features:** Park is situated at the confluence of the Ohio and Kentucky rivers. It is named for General William Orlando Butler, whose family's military fame spans from colonial times through the American Revolution, the War of 1812, the Mexican War, and the Civil War. Built in 1859, the Butler-Turpin house displays the family's 18th and 19th century heirlooms.

★2479★ GRAYSON LAKE STATE PARK

314 Grayson Lake Park Rd
Olive Hill, KY 41164
Web: parks.ky.gov/stateparks/gl
Phone: 606-474-9727
Size: 1,512 acres land; 1,500 acres water. **Location:** Exit 172 on I-64 onto KY 7 south. **Facilities:** 71 campsites with utility hookups, showers, and restrooms, picnic area, 2 picnic shelters, 3 playgrounds, hiking trail, beach, bathhouse, boat ramp. **Activities:** Camping, swimming, fishing, boating, hiking, nature study, golf. **Special Features:** Majestic sandstone bluffs form a walled canyon above Grayson Lake, where Shawnee and Cherokee Indians once camped under the cliffs as they hunted game in the area. The park's 18-hole, par-72 golf course, Hidden Cove, was named one of 2004's best new affordable golf courses by *Golf Digest*.

★2480★ GREEN RIVER LAKE STATE PARK

179 Park Office Rd
Campbellsville, KY 42718
Web: parks.ky.gov/stateparks/gr
Phone: 270-465-8255
Size: 1,331 acres land; 1,500 acres water. **Location:** On KY 55, 8 miles south of Campbellsville. **Facilities:** 157 campsites, utility hookups, showers, restrooms, laundry facility, camp store, picnic shelter, 2 playgrounds, multi-use trail (28 miles), beach, bathhouse, boat ramp, marina with boat and jet ski rentals

(nearby), 18-hole miniature golf course, basketball and volley-ball courts, gift shop. **Activities:** Camping, fishing, boating, jet skiing, water-skiing, hiking, mountain biking. **Special Features:** Park is situated along the shores of Green River Lake and offers a range of water sports opportunities.

★2481★ **GREENBO LAKE STATE RESORT PARK**

HC 60, Box 562
Greenup, KY 41144
Web: www.parks.ky.gov/resortparks/go
Phone: 800-325-0083
Size: 3,008 acres land; 225 acres water. **Location:** 18 miles north of I-64 from the Grayson exit. **Facilities:** 36-room lodge, 232-seat dining room, 63 utility and 35 primitive campsites, shower and restroom bulding, grocery store, 2 picnic shelters, playground, hiking trails (25 miles), 2 swimming pools (1 community pool, 1 pool for lodge guests only), beach (swimming not allowed in lake), marina (seasonal), boat ramp, boat rentals, fishing pier, 18-hole miniature golf course, tennis and basketball courts, horseshoe pits, gift shop, library and reading room. **Activities:** Camping, swimming, fishing, boating (no-wake speed limit), hiking, tennis, basketball, miniature golf, recreational programs. **Special Features:** The fieldstone lodge at this rustic resort is named in honor of Jesse Hilton Stuart (1906-1984), Kentucky's Poet Laureate and a native of Greenup County.

★2482★ **ISAAC SHELBY CEMETERY STATE HISTORIC SITE**

6725 Kentucky Hwy 300
Stanford, KY 40484
Web: parks.ky.gov/statehistoricsites/is
Phone: 859-239-7089
Size: 0.25 acres. **Location:** 5 miles south of Danville, off US 127. **Facilities:** Picnic tables and shelter. **Special Features:** Burial place of Isaac Shelby (1750-1826), Kentucky's first and fifth governor. Shelby was so highly esteemed for his military, political, and educational accomplishments that counties in nine states are named after him.

★2483★ **JEFFERSON DAVIS MONUMENT STATE HISTORIC SITE**

Highway 68 E
Fairview, KY 42221
Web: parks.ky.gov/statehistoricsites/jd
Phone: 270-886-1765
Size: 20 acres. **Location:** 9 miles east of Hopkinsville on US 68. **Facilities:** Visitor center with exhibits and gift shop, picnic area, 2 picnic shelters, playground. **Special Features:** Site is a memorial to Jefferson Davis, the President of the Confederacy, who was born here in June 3, 1808. The 351-foot monument constructed on this site marks Davis' birthplace and rests on a foundation of solid Kentucky limestone. An elevator takes visitors to an observation room at the top of the structure, affording visitors a panoramic view of the surrounding countryside.

★2484★ **JENNY WILEY STATE RESORT PARK**

75 Theatre Ct
Prestonsburg, KY 41653
Web: www.parks.ky.gov/resortparks/jw
Phone: 800-325-0142
Size: 1,498 acres land; 1,150 acres water. **Location:** In Prestonsburg, off US 23/460 on KY 3. **Facilities:** 49-room lodge, 224-seat dining room, cottages, 117-site campground with utility hookups, showers, restrooms, and grocery store, picnic shelters, playgrounds, hiking trails (10+ miles), 2 swimming pools (one for lodge and cottage guests only), boat dock, 3 boat launch ramps, pontoon boat rentals, 18-hole disc golf course, skylift, meeting rooms, 2 private dining facilities that seat up to 70, performing arts theater. **Activities:** Camping, swimming, fishing, boating, hiking, bicycling, theater programs, recreational programs. **Special Features:** Jenny Wiley was a pioneer woman who was taken captive by Indians in 1789 and endured the slaying of her brother and her children. She escaped captivity 11 months later. The mountain resort named for her is located alongside Dewey Lake and features summer musical theater presentations in Jenny Wiley Theatre.

★2485★ **JOHN JAMES AUDUBON STATE PARK**

3100 US Hwy 41 N
Henderson, KY 42419
Web: www.parks.ky.gov/stateparks/au
Phone: 270-826-2247
Size: 692 acres land; 40 acres water. **Location:** On US 41 in the northern outskirts of Henderson, 0.5 miles south of the US 41 bridge over the Ohio River. **Facilities:** 6 cottages (1 ♿), 69-site campground with utilities, showers, and restrooms, 4 picnic shelters (1 with restrooms), trails, pedal boat rentals, 9-hole golf course, tennis court (seasonal), playgrounds, museum and nature center with wildlife observatory and Discovery Center, meeting room, gift shop. **Activities:** Camping, fishing, boating (non-motorized only), hiking, golf, tennis, interpretive programs. **Special Features:** Naturalist John James Audubon lived in Henderson from 1810-1819, where he studied birds that became the subjects of his paintings. The park's museum interprets Audubon's life through his art and personal memorabilia, framed within a timeline of world events.

★2486★ **KENLAKE STATE RESORT PARK**

542 Kenlake Rd
Hardin, KY 42048
Web: www.parks.ky.gov/resortparks/kl
Phone: 800-325-1043
Size: 1,795 acres land; 128,807 acres water. **Location:** 40 miles southeast of Paducah via I-24. **Facilities:** 48-room hotel, cottages, 182-seat dining room, swimming pool (for lodge and cottage guests only), 90-site campground with utility hookups, showers, and restrooms, 2 picnic shelters, playgrounds, nature trails (2 miles), beach (no swimming in lake), marina, boat ramp, boat and jet ski rentals, 9-hole golf course, tennis center (indoor and outdoor courts), meeting rooms, gift shop, scenic gardens. **Activities:** Camping, swimming, fishing, boating, sailing, jet skiing, hiking, golfing, tennis, recreational and interpretive programs (year round). **Special Features:** Kenlake's seasonal tennis center features 4 indoor, temperature-controlled

courts, locker room facilities, and a fully-equipped pro shop. Four outdoor lighted courts are located adjacent to the tennis center, and another court is available near the lodge.

★2487★ KENTUCKY DAM VILLAGE STATE RESORT PARK

166 Upper Village Dr
Gilbertsville, KY 42044
Web: www.parks.ky.gov/resortparks/kd
Phone: 800-325-0146
Size: 1,351 acres land; 28,807 acres water. **Location:** 21 miles southeast of Paducah (exit 27 off I-24). **Facilities:** 72-room lodge, 346-seat dining room, 14-room inn (near the golf course; can be rented as an entire unit), 68 cottages, swimming pool (for lodge, inn, and cottage guests only); 221 paved campsites with water and electric hookups, 4 buildings with showers and restrooms, and grocery store; air camp that allows camping by visitor's aircraft; picnic shelters, playground, tennis courts, riding stables (seasonal), 18-hole golf course; marina, boat ramp, boat rentals (including pedal boats); paved, lighted airstrip, convention center, meeting rooms, gift shop. **Activities:** Camping, swimming, fishing, boating, water-skiing, horseback riding, golfing, tennis, recreational programs. **Special Features:** Park features the largest marina in the state park system on the largest lake in the state. Nearby is Land Between the Lakes National Recreation Area, a 170,000-acre wooded peninsula bounded by Kentucky Lake and Lake Barkley, which offers more than 200 miles of hiking trails (see entry in national forests section).

★2488★ KINCAID LAKE STATE PARK

565 Kincaid Park Rd
Falmouth, KY 41040
Web: parks.ky.gov/stateparks/kn
Phone: 859-654-3531
Size: 919 acres land; 183 acres water. **Location:** On KY 159, 48 miles southeast of Covington and 61 miles northeast of Lexington. **Facilities:** 84 campsites with electric and water hookups, campstore, and central service building with showers and restrooms, picnic shelter with restrooms, playground, hiking trails (2.25 miles), swimming pool, bathhouse, marina, boat ramp, boat rentals, 9-hole miniature golf course, basketball, tennis, handball, volleyball, and shuffleboard courts, multi-purpose building with meeting room. **Activities:** Camping, swimming, fishing, boating, hiking, tennis, shuffleboard, volleyball, basketball, recreational programs (seasonal). **Special Features:** Park has a new 9-hole golf course as well as an onsite marina with boat rentals and camping with all the modern conveniences.

★2489★ KINGDOM COME STATE PARK

502 Park Rd
Cumberland, KY 40823
Web: parks.ky.gov/stateparks/kc
Phone: 606-589-2479
Size: 1,283 acres land; 3 acres water. **Location:** 65 miles northeast of Middlesboro. From I-75, take US 25E to US 119 to Cumberland. **Facilities:** Picnic areas, 2 picnic shelters with vending machines and restrooms, pedal boat rentals, hiking trails

(14 miles), 9-hole miniature golf course, playgrounds, 2 basketball courts, rental equipment for horseshoes and volleyball, cave amphitheater, nature preserve, gift shop. Lodging is available at the Benham Schoolhouse Inn Bed and Breakfast in Benham, Ky, and a campground is available nearby in Lynch, KY. Primitive camping is permitted in designated areas of the park not on park trails. **Activities:** Primitive camping, fishing, hiking. **Special Features:** On the crest of Pine Mountain, at an elevation of 2,700 feet, Kingdom Come is Kentucky's highest state park. A unique feature of the park is its extraordinary rock formations, including Log Rock, a natural sandstone bridge, and Raven Rock, a gigantic slab of stone jutting some 290 feet into the air at a 45-degree angle. The park is named for John Fox, Jr's novel *The Little Shepherd of Kingdom Come*, a book about an orphaned youth and his journey through the hills and into the furor of the Civil War.

★2490★ LAKE BARKLEY STATE RESORT PARK

3500 State Park Rd
Cadiz, KY 42211
Web: www.parks.ky.gov/resortparks/lb
Phone: 800-325-1708
Size: 3,700 acres land; 57,920 acres water. **Location:** 29 miles west of Hopkinsville via US 68. **Facilities:** Main lodge with 120 rooms and 4 suites, small lodge with 10 rooms and 1 suite (may be rented as a whole unit), 9 cottages, 2 log cabins, 331-seat dining room, 18-hole golf course, 2 lighted tennis courts (overnight guests only), swimming pool (for lodge and cottage guests only); 78 campsites with utility hookups, restrooms, and showers; picnic shelter, playground, hiking trails (9 miles), swimming beach with bathhouse and volleyball court, lighted trap range, fitness center (with weight room, indoor pool, racquetball court, sauna, locker room); marina, boat ramp, boat rentals; paved, lighted airstrip, convention center/meeting rooms, gift shop. **Activities:** Camping, swimming, fishing, boating, water skiing, hiking, mountain biking, horseback riding, golfing, tennis, recreational programs and events. **Special Features:** Lake Barkley Lodge, designed by Edward Durrell Stone, features grand scale post-and-beam wood construction with more than 3.5 acres of glass that offer outstanding views of the lake. The world-class lodge has both indoor and outdoor swimming pools, a state-of-the-art fitness center, and an 18-hole, par-71 golf course.

★2491★ LAKE CUMBERLAND STATE RESORT PARK

5465 State Park Rd
Jamestown, KY 42629
Web: www.parks.ky.gov/resortparks/lc
Phone: 800-325-1709
Size: 3,117 acres land; 50,250 acres water. **Location:** 45 miles west of Somerset. Take the Cumberland Parkway to US 127. **Facilities:** 2 lodges (63 rooms in main lodge and 13 rooms in the other), 30 cottages, dining room (in main lodge), 147 campsites with utility hookups, showers, restrooms, and grocery store, indoor pool complex with spa and exercise room, outdoor public pool, 9-hole golf course, picnic shelters, playgrounds, hiking trails, marina, boat ramp, boat rentals, horse stables and concession, tennis and shuffleboard courts, 18-hole miniature golf

course, meeting rooms, gift shop. **Activities:** Camping, swimming, fishing, boating, water-skiing, hiking, horseback riding, golfing, tennis, shuffleboard, recreational and interpretive programs. **Special Features:** With more than 50,000 acres of water and 1,225 miles of shoreline, Lake Cumberland is considered one of the finest boating and fishing areas in the eastern United States.

★2492★ LAKE MALONE STATE PARK

331 State Rd 8001
Dunmor, KY 42339
Web: parks.ky.gov/stateparks/lm
Phone: 270-657-2111
Size: 349 acres land; 788 acres water. **Location:** 22 miles south of Central City, off the Western Kentucky Parkway. **Facilities:** 20 campsites with electric and water hookups, showers, restrooms, and laundry facilities, 100 primitive tent campsites, 2 picnic shelters with restrooms, playground, hiking trail (1.5 miles), beach, bathhouse, vending area, boat dock, boat ramp, boat rentals. **Activities:** Camping, fishing, swimming, boating, water skiing, hiking. **Special Features:** The lake is surrounded by 50-foot sandstone bluffs and a dense forest of hardwood trees. Mountain laurel, holly, dogwood, and wildflowers provide a rich tapestry of native flora.

★2493★ LEVI JACKSON STATE PARK

998 Levi Jackson Mill Rd
London, KY 40744
Web: parks.ky.gov/stateparks/lj
Phone: 606-878-8000
Size: 896 acres. **Location:** South of London on US 25 south (exit 38 off I-75). **Facilities:** 146 campsites with utility hookups, camp store, and 3 central service buildings with an activities room, showers, restrooms, and laundry facilities; group camping area with cabins, bathhouse, and clubhouse; picnic areas, 4 picnic shelters, playgrounds, hiking trails that include original portions of Wilderness Road and Boone's Trace (8.5 miles), horseshoe pits, volleyball and basketball courts, 18-hole miniature golf course, swimming pool with waterslides, museum, historic sites, 1,500-seat amphitheater. **Activities:** Camping, swimming, hiking, basketball, volleyball, recreational and interpretive programs (seasonal). **Special Features:** Two historic trails at the park, Wilderness Road and Boone's Trace, were the throughways used by more than 200,000 settlers who moved from the eastern colonies into the western frontier between 1774 and 1796. Kentucky's worst Indian massacre, McNitt's Defeat, took place here in 1786, and the Defeated Camp Pioneer Burial Ground is among the park's historic sites. Other sites include McHargue's Mill and the Mountain Life Museum, which brings visitors into a pioneer settlement.

★2494★ LINCOLN HOMESTEAD STATE PARK

5079 Lincoln Park Rd
Springfield, KY 40069
Web: parks.ky.gov/stateparks/lh
Phone: 859-336-7461
Size: 230 acres land; 41 acres water. **Location:** On KY 438, 5 miles north of Springfield. **Facilities:** 18-hole golf course with pro shop and snack bar, picnic shelter, playground, restrooms, historic buildings, gift shop. **Activities:** Golf. **Special Features:** Park's historic features include the original home of Nancy Hanks, Abraham Lincoln's mother, and replicas of the 1782 cabin and blacksmith shop where Lincoln's father, Thomas Lincoln, was raised and learned his trade.

★2495★ MINERAL MOUND STATE PARK

48 Finch Ln
Eddyville, KY 42038
Web: parks.ky.gov/stateparks/mm
Phone: 270-388-3673
Size: 541 acres land; 57,920 acres water. **Location:** 1 mile south of Eddyville via exit 40 on I-24. **Facilities:** 18-hole, par-72 golf course with pro shop, picnic area, boat ramp, hiking trails under development. **Activities:** Boating, fishing, water-skiing, jet skiing, hiking, picnicking, golf. **Special Features:** Situated on the shores of Lake Barkley, the property was once owned by the grandfather of F Scott Fitzgerald's wife, Zelda.

★2496★ MY OLD KENTUCKY HOME STATE PARK

501 E Stephen Foster Ave
Bardstown, KY 40004
Web: parks.ky.gov/stateparks/mk
Phone: 502-348-3502
Size: 290 acres. **Location:** In Bardstown on US 150. **Facilities:** 39 campsites with utility hookups, restrooms, showers, picnic area, restrooms, playground, 18-hole regulation golf course, visitor center, historic house and grounds, gift shop. **Activities:** Camping, golfing, tours of antebellum mansion and gardens by costumed guides, outdoor musical theatre production (in summer), Christmas candlelight tours. **Special Features:** The park's familiar name comes from the song by Stephen Foster (Kentucky's official state song), who was inspired to write it during a visit here at his cousins' plantation, Federal Hill. The park features the restored Rowan family estate, carriage house, smokehouse, and formal gardens.

★2497★ NATURAL BRIDGE STATE RESORT PARK

2135 Natural Bridge Rd
Slade, KY 40376
Web: www.parks.ky.gov/resortparks/nb
Phone: 800-325-1710
Size: 2,250 acres land; 60 acres water. **Location:** 52 miles southeast of Lexington off the Mountain Parkway on KY 11. **Facilities:** 35-room mountainside lodge, 11 cottages, 175-seat dining room, 82 campsites with utilities and 12 primitive campsites, central service buildings with showers and restrooms, 4 picnic shelters with restrooms, playground, hiking trails, swimming pool, bathhouse, watercraft rentals, 18-hole miniature golf course, nature center, nature preserve, meeting rooms, gift shop, open-air dance patio (Hoedown Island), sky lift, 2 snack bars. **Activities:** Camping, swimming, fishing, boating, hiking, naturalist programs. **Special Features:** Located adjacent to the Daniel Boone National Forest (see separate entry in national forests section) and the Red River Gorge Geological Area, Natural Bridge is a sandstone arch that spans 78 feet across and is 65 feet high.

★2498★ NOLIN LAKE STATE PARK
PO Box 340
Bee Spring, KY 42207
Web: parks.ky.gov/stateparks/nl
Phone: 270-286-4240
Size: 333 acres land; 5,795 acres water. Location: North of Bowling Green, off KY 1827. Facilities: 32 campsites with water and electricity, 20 primitive campsites, 3 sites ♿, restroom/shower building in campground, playground, picnic area, boat ramp, beach. Activities: Camping, fishing, boating. Special Features: Park lies along the northern border of Mammoth Cave National Park (see entry in national parks section).

★2499★ OLD FORT HARROD STATE PARK
100 S College St
Harrodsburg, KY 40330
Web: parks.ky.gov/stateparks/fh
Phone: 859-734-3314
Size: 32 acres. Location: 32 miles southwest of Lexington on US 68 in Harrodsburg. Facilities: Reconstructed historic fort, other historic sites, museum, picnic shelter with restrooms, playground, gift shop. Special Features: James Harrod built the first permanent settlement west of the Alleghenies at this site in 1774. The park's fort is an exact replica, with costumed craftspeople portraying pioneers and demonstrating crafts.

★2500★ OLD MULKEY MEETINGHOUSE STATE
HISTORIC SITE
1819 Old Mulkey Park Rd
Tompkinsville, KY 42167
Web: parks.ky.gov/statehistoricsites/om
Phone: 270-487-8481
Size: 60 acres. Location: On KY 1446 in Tompkinsville, about 25 miles south of the Edmonton exit on the Cumberland Parkway. Facilities: Historic building, pioneer cemetery, gift shop, picnic area, playground. Activities: Tours (free). Special Features: Site preserves the oldest log meetinghouse in Kentucky, built in 1804 during a period of religious revival. Many Revolutionary War soldiers and early pioneers, including Daniel Boone's sister, Hannah, are buried in the churchyard. The structure has 12 corners in the shape of a cross and three doors, symbolic of the Holy Trinity.

★2501★ PAINTSVILLE LAKE STATE PARK
PO Box 920
Staffordsville, KY 41256
Web: parks.ky.gov/stateparks/pl
Phone: 606-297-8486
Size: 242 acres land; 1,139 acres water. Location: 4 miles west of Paintsville. Take US 23 to US 460 to KY 40 to KY 2275. Facilities: 32-site RV campground with full hookups (2 sites ♿), 10 primitive campsites, restrooms, showers, playgrounds, horseshoe pits, sand volleyball court, and basketball court in campground, 2 picnic shelters, 2 sheltered pavilions, full-service marina, boat ramp, boat rentals. Activities: Camping, fishing, boating, water-skiing. Special Features: Located in the mountains of eastern Kentucky, Paintsville Lake features steep cliffs and wooded coves and offers excellent fishing.

★2502★ PENNYRILE FOREST STATE RESORT
PARK
20781 Pennyrile Lodge Rd
Dawson Springs, KY 42408
Web: www.parks.ky.gov/resortparks/pf
Phone: 800-325-1711
Size: 863 acres land; 56 acres water. Location: 20 miles northwest of Hopkinsville, on KY 109 N. Facilities: 24-room rustic wood and stone lodge, 12 cottages, dining room, 18-hole golf course with pro shop, swimming pool (for lodge and cottage guests only), 68 campsites with utility hookups, showers, restrooms, and laundry facility, picnic shelters, playgrounds, 7 nature trails, public beach, bathhouse, boat dock, boat rentals, 18-hole miniature golf course, tennis courts, meeting room, gift shop. Activities: Camping, swimming, fishing, boating, hiking, golfing, tennis, recreational programs. Special Features: Park is named for the tiny Pennyroyal plant found in the woodlands surrounding this resort.

★2503★ PERRYVILLE BATTLEFIELD STATE
HISTORIC SITE
1825 Battlefield Rd
Perryville, KY 40468
Web: parks.ky.gov/statehistoricsites/pb
Phone: 606-332-8631
Size: 630 acres. Location: 45 miles southwest of Lexington; take US 68 west to US 150 west. Facilities: Museum, monuments, gift shop, self-guided walking trails, picnic shelter with restrooms, playground. Activities: Living history demonstrations, including an annual Civil War re-enactment. Special Features: The most destructive Civil War battle in the state took place here October 8, 1862, with more than 6,000 killed, wounded, or missing. It was the South's last serious attempt to gain possession of Kentucky. The battlefield is one of the most unaltered Civil War sites in the nation, and a self-guided walking tour interprets battle events. The park's museum features battle relics and battleground maps.

★2504★ PINE MOUNTAIN STATE RESORT PARK
1050 State Park Rd
Pineville, KY 40977
Web: www.parks.ky.gov/resortparks/pm
Phone: 800-325-1712
Size: 1,519 acres. Location: 1 mile south of Pineville on US 25E or 10 miles north of Middlesboro, KY. Facilities: 30-room lodge, 20 cottages, 120-seat dining room, swimming pool (♿; for overnight guests only), 18-hole golf course, picnic shelters, playgrounds, restrooms, hiking trails (14 miles), bike trail, miniature golf course, a natural forest cove transformed into a 2,000-seat amphitheater (Laurel Cove), meeting rooms, gift shop. Activities: Camping, swimming, hiking, bicycling, golfing, interpretive programs. Special Features: Established in 1924, Kentucky's first state park is a mountaintop resort overlooking the Kentucky Ridge State Forest. The park's 18-hole championship golf course, Wasioto Winds, was ranked as one of the best new affordable public courses in the nation by *Golf Digest*. A collection of 180 prints by wildlife artist Ray Harm are on permanent display throughout the lodge, dining room, and convention center.

9. State Parks

493

★2505★ ROUGH RIVER DAM STATE RESORT
PARK

450 Lodge Rd
Falls of Rough, KY 40119
Web: www.parks.ky.gov/resortparks/rr
Phone: 800-325-1713
Size: 637 acres land; 4,860 acres water. Location: In Falls of
Rough, on KY 79, 15 miles north of the Western Kentucky
Parkway. Facilities: 40-room lodge, 17 cottages, 167-seat dining
room, 9-hole par-three golf course, swimming pool (for lodge
and cottage guests only), 66-site campground with utility hookups, showers, and restrooms, airplane camp with showers and
restrooms, paved airstrip (lighted), picnic areas, picnic shelter,
playgrounds, hiking trail (1 mile), interpretive trail (nearby),
tennis, volleyball, and shuffleboard courts, beach, bathhouse,
marina, boat ramp, boat rentals, 18-hole miniature golf course,
meeting rooms, gift shop. Activities: Camping, fishing, boating,
water-skiing, jet skiing, hiking, golfing, tennis, shuffleboard,
recreational and interpretive programs (year round). Special
Features: With a lake surface area of nearly 5,000 acres, Rough
River Dam offers ample recreational opportunity for watersports enthusiasts and some of the finest fishing in the state.

★2506★ TAYLORSVILLE LAKE STATE PARK
1320 Park Rd
Taylorsville, KY 40071
Web: parks.ky.gov/stateparks/tl
Phone: 502-477-8713
Size: 2,650 acres land; 3,050 acres water. Location: From Louisville, take the Gene Snyder Freeway south and KY 155 to
Taylorsville, then east on KY 44 3 miles to park. From Bluegrass
Parkway, take KY exit 55 to Taylorsville. Facilities: Campground with 45 RV sites and 10 equestrian campsites, utility
hookups, showers, restrooms, and laundry facilities in campground, multi-use trails (16 miles), marina, 4 boat ramps, pontoon boat rentals. Activities: Camping, fishing, boating, water
skiing, hiking, horseback riding, mountain biking. Special Features: Not far from Louisville, Kentucky's biggest city, this
park features a 3,050-acre lake for anglers and equestrian camping and riding trails for horse lovers.

★2507★ WAVELAND MUSEUM STATE HISTORIC
SITE

225 Waveland Museum Ln
Lexington, KY 40514
Web: parks.ky.gov/statehistoricsites/wv
Phone: 859-272-3611
Size: 10 acres. Location: 5 miles south of Lexington off Nicho-
lasville Road/US 27. Facilities: Historic home; picnic tables
and playground on the Waveland lawn. Activities: Guided tours.
Special Features: This beautiful Greek Revival mansion, built
in 1847 by Joseph Bryan, grandnephew of Daniel Boone, recreates the surroundings of the landed gentry in antebellum Kentucky. Guided tours of Waveland include the outbuildings,
where guests learn about slave life in Kentucky.

★2508★ WHITE HALL STATE HISTORIC SITE
500 White Hall Shrine Rd
Richmond, KY 40475
Web: parks.ky.gov/statehistoricsites/wh
Phone: 859-623-9178
Size: 13 acres. Location: In Richmond, off I-75 at exit 95.
Facilities: Historic mansion, gift shop, picnic tables and shelter.
Activities: Tours with costumed guides. Special Features:
White Hall was the home of Cassius Marcellus Clay, emancipa-
tionist, newspaper publisher, minister to Russia, and friend to
Abraham Lincoln. The restored 44-room Italianate mansion was
built in 1799 and remodeled in the 1860s. In addition to the
heirlom and period furnishings, it has many unique features for
its day, including indoor running water and central heating.
Clay's daughter, Laura, was politically active for women's suffrage and states rights, and in 1920 she became the first woman
to be nominated for US president by a major political party.

★2509★ WICKLIFFE MOUNDS STATE HISTORIC
SITE

94 Green St
Wickliffe, KY 42087
Web: www.parks.ky.gov/statehistoricsites/wm
Phone: 270-335-3681
Size: 26 acres. Location: In the community of Wickliffe, about
30 miles west of Paducah on highways 51-60-62 west, near
the confluence of the Mississippi and Ohio rivers. Facilities:
Museum, welcome center, gift shop, hiking trail, and picnic
area. Special Features: Wickliffe Mounds is the archaeological
site of a prehistoric Native American village of the Mississippian
mound builders. The village was occupied from about AD 1100
to 1350. The settlement here was complex, with permanent
houses and earthen mounds situated around a central plaza.
Visitors to the site can see the excavated features of the mounds;
displays of Mississippian pottery, stone tools, bone and shell
implements; the architecture of the mounds and houses; and the
burial practices of the Mississippians.

★2510★ WILLIAM WHITLEY HOUSE STATE
HISTORIC SITE

625 William Whitley Rd
Stanford, KY 40484
Web: parks.ky.gov/statehistoricsites/ww
Phone: 606-355-2881
Size: 40 acres. Location: About 10 miles south of Stanford off
US 150. Facilities: Historic home, gift shop, picnic area, 2
picnic shelters, playground. Activities: Guided tours. Special
Features: Completed in 1794, this was the first brick home and
circular racetrack built in Kentucky. The house was built in the
Flemish bond pattern for greater strength and has a secret chamber for hiding in the event of an Indian attack. The racetrack
was unique in the nation because it was the first circular design
and was built of clay instead of using turf. It is believed that
the American practice of racing counter-clockwise began at this
track, in response to anti-British feeling at the time — the British
raced in a clockwise direction.

★2511★ YATESVILLE LAKE STATE PARK
PO Box 767
Louisa, KY 41230
Web: parks.ky.gov/stateparks/yl
Phone: 606-673-1492
Size: 808 acres land; 2,300 acres water. **Location:** From Louisa, west on KY 3 for 3 miles. (Note: Marina and campgrounds/ golf course are about 15 miles apart.) **Facilities:** 27 campsites with full hookups, 20 primitive sites (4 hike-in and 16 boat-in), 18-hole, par-71 golf course, miniature golf course, picnic pavilion with 2 shelters, playground area, hiking trails, multi-use trail (20+ miles), marina, 2 boat ramps, swimming beach, restrooms and showers, snack bar. **Activities:** Camping, boating, fishing, swimming, hiking; backpacking, mountain biking, and horseback riding, as well as hiking, on park's multi-use trail.
Special Features: Yatesville Lake, an impoundment of the Big Sandy River, is the largest lake in eastern Kentucky and offers excellent bluegill crappie, and bass fishing.

Louisiana State Parks

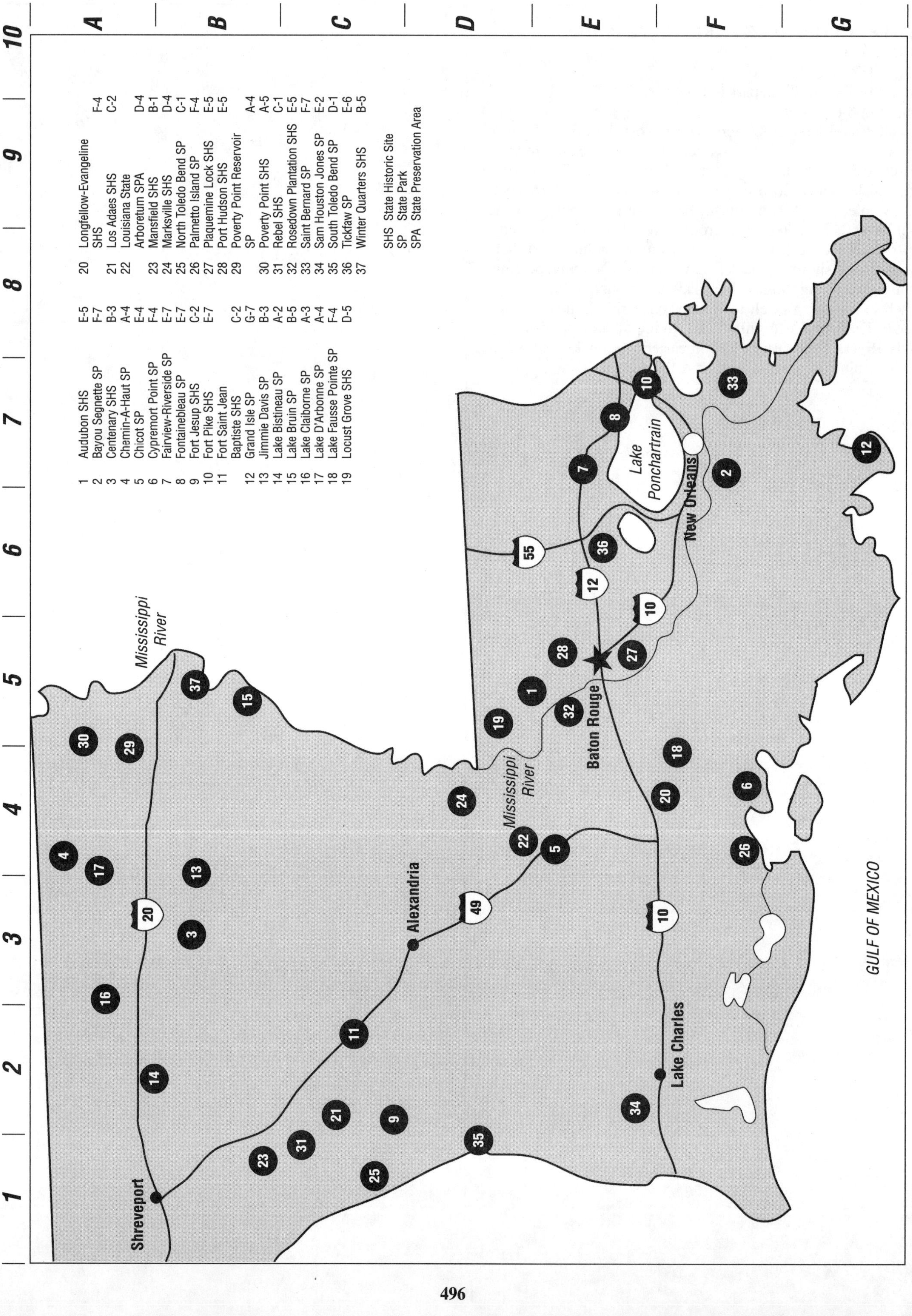

1 Audubon SHS E-5
2 Bayou Segnette SP F-7
3 Centenary SHS B-3
4 Chemin-A-Haut SP A-4
5 Chicot SP E-4
6 Cypremort Point SP F-4
7 Fairview-Riverside SP E-7
8 Fontainebleau SP E-7
9 Fort Jesup SHS C-2
10 Fort Pike SHS E-7
11 Fort Saint Jean Baptiste SHS C-2
12 Grand Isle SP G-7
13 Jimmie Davis SP B-3
14 Lake Bistineau SP A-2
15 Lake Bruin SP B-5
16 Lake Claiborne SP A-3
17 Lake D'Arbonne SP A-4
18 Lake Fausse Pointe SP F-4
19 Locust Grove SHS D-5
20 Longfellow-Evangeline SHS F-4
21 Los Adaes SHS C-2
22 Louisiana State Arboretum SPA D-4
23 Mansfield SHS B-1
24 Marksville SHS D-4
25 North Toledo Bend SP C-1
26 Palmetto Island SP F-4
27 Plaquemine Lock SHS E-5
28 Port Hudson SHS E-5
29 Poverty Point Reservoir SP A-4
30 Poverty Point SHS A-5
31 Rebel SHS C-1
32 Rosedown Plantation SHS E-5
33 Saint Bernard SP F-7
34 Sam Houston Jones SP E-2
35 South Toledo Bend SP D-1
36 Tickfaw SP E-6
37 Winter Quarters SHS B-5
SHS State Historic Site
SP State Park
SPA State Preservation Area
A
B
C
D
E
F
G
1
2
3
4
5
6
7
8
9
10
Shreveport
Alexandria
Lake Charles
Baton Rouge
New Orleans
Lake Ponchartrain
Mississippi River
Mississippi River
GULF OF MEXICO
20
49
10
10
12
55

LOUISIANA

★2512★ Louisiana Office of State Parks

PO Box 44426
Baton Rouge, LA 70804
(225) 342-8111 - Phone
(225) 342-8107 - Fax
(888) 677-1400 - Toll-free
(877) 226-7652 - Toll-free Reservations
Web: www.lastateparks.com

System consists of some three dozen properties. Sites include 19 state parks with a focus on outdoor recreation, 16 historic sites that preserve state's cultural and historic resources, and a preservation area that protects the state's natural heritage.

★2513★ Louisiana Department of Wildlife & Fisheries

2000 Quail Dr
Baton Rouge, LA 70808
(225) 765-2800 - Phone
(225) 765-2892 - Fax
Web: www.wlf.state.la.us

Operates and manages 61 wildlife management areas which offer hunting, fishing, camping, hiking, and wildlife study opportunities. Administers hunting and fishing licensing, supports hunter education programs, and enforces state wildlife laws.

Key to campsite classification:

- **Improved campsites** — Designated sites with water and electricity hookups, picnic table, grill or fire ring, and nearby comfort station.
- **Unimproved campsites** — No designated site, no utilities, but may have comfort station nearby.
- **Tent sites** — Tend pad, fire ring, lantern post with comfort station nearby.
- **Group camp** — Designated sites for large groups, has no utilities.
- **Cabins** — Fully furnished with heating and air conditioning; some may include fireplaces. Cookware, cooking utensils, dinnerware, silverware, and bed linens are provided. Visitors must provide their own towels, food, and personal supplies.
- **Lodges** — Equipped with kitchen, bath, and sleeping quarters. Can accommodate a large family or several family groups. Cookware, cooking utensils, dinnerware, silverware, and bed linens are provided. Visitors must bring their own towels, food, and personal items.

★2514★ AUDUBON STATE HISTORIC SITE

11788 Louisiana Hwy 965
Saint Francisville, LA 70775
Web: www.crt.state.la.us/parks/iaudubon.aspx
Phone: 225-635-3739; **Fax:** 225-784-0578; **Toll Free:** 888-677-2838

Size: 100 acres. **Location:** Off LA 965 near Saint Francisville, in West Feliciana Parish (25 minutes north of Baton Rouge). **Facilities:** Museum/historic home, formal gardens, exhibits, restrooms, picnic area, group pavilion, nature trails, visitor center. **Activities:** Guided tours, interpretive programs. **Special Features:** A 100-acre natural forest surrounds the nearly 200-year-old Oakley House where John James Audubon was hired in 1821 to teach drawing to Miss Eliza Pirrie, daughter of the plantation owners. Although the naturalist and painter spent only four months at Oakley, it was here that he began or completed 32 paintings featured in his *Birds of America* collection.

★2515★ BAYOU SEGNETTE STATE PARK

7777 Westbank Expy
Westwego, LA 70094
Web: www.crt.state.la.us/parks/ibyusegne.aspx
Phone: 504-736-7140; **Fax:** 504-436-4788; **Toll Free:** 888-677-2296

Size: 580 acres. **Location:** On US 90, just outside New Orleans, on the west bank of the Mississippi River. **Facilities:** Closed until further notice due to the impact of Hurricanes Katrina and Rita. **Special Features:** Park includes both swamp and marshlands, with abundant wildlife and interesting vegetation. Due to its unique location, it offers both saltwater and freshwater fishing.

★2516★ CENTENARY STATE HISTORIC SITE

3522 College St
Jackson, LA 70748
Web: www.crt.state.la.us/parks/icentenary.aspx
Phone: 225-634-7925; **Toll Free:** 888-677-2364

Size: 40 acres. **Location:** 4 blocks off LA 10, at East College and Pine streets in Jackson. **Facilities:** Historic buildings, exhibits, restrooms, trails, picnic area. **Activities:** Guided tours, interpretive programs. **Special Features:** Once the site of Centenary College, which originally opened in 1826 as the College of Louisiana, the school was closed during the Civil War. Its buildings were used by both Confederate and Union troops, and for a time the dormitories served as a hospital. Although the college reopened after the war, it never regained its former prosperity and later moved to Shreveport, where it remains today. The West Wing dormitory and a professor's cottage are the only buildings of the original college still standing, and these have been preserved to interpret the history of higher education in Louisiana.

★2517★ CHEMIN-A-HAUT STATE PARK

14656 State Park Rd
Bastrop, LA 71220
Web: www.crt.state.la.us/parks/icheminah.aspx
Phone: 318-283-0812; **Toll Free:** 888-677-2436

9. State Parks

Size: 503 acres. **Location:** Just east of LA 139, 10 miles north of Bastrop in Morehouse Parish. **Facilities:** 26 improved campsites, primitive camping area, comfort stations, 14 cabins (2 &), group camp, picnic area, 3 picnic shelters, 2 playgrounds, hard-surfaced trail, swimming pool, boat rentals, boat launch, meeting room, visitor center. **Activities:** Camping, boating, fishing, swimming, hiking. **Special Features:** Park is situated at the intersection of Bayous Chemin-A-Haut and Bartholomew, on a high bluff overlooking Bayou Bartholomew. Centuries ago, American Indians used this area for their seasonal migrations south.

★2518★ CHICOT STATE PARK
3469 Chicot Park Rd
Ville Platte, LA 70586
Web: www.crt.state.la.us/parks/ichicot.aspx
Phone: 337-363-2403; **Toll Free:** 888-677-2442
Size: 6,400 acres. **Location:** In Evangeline Parish, 7 miles north of Ville Platte on LA 3042. **Facilities:** 208 improved campsites, backpacking campsites, comfort stations, group camp, 15 cabins, 3 lodges, picnic areas, group shelters, playgrounds, trails, swimming pool, boathouse, 3 boat launches, boat rentals, fishing piers, restrooms, meeting room, concession area. **Activities:** Camping, boating, fishing, swimming, hiking, bicycling, backpacking. **Special Features:** Park features rolling hills surrounding a 2,000-acre manmade lake stocked with bream, bass, and crappie. Louisiana State Arboretum (see separate entry) is located 1.5 miles from the park entrance.

★2519★ CYPREMORT POINT STATE PARK
306 Beach Ln
Cypremort Point, LA 70538
Web: www.crt.state.la.us/parks/iCyprempt.aspx
Phone: 337-867-4510; **Toll Free:** 888-867-4510
Size: 185 acres. **Location:** 24 miles southwest of Jeanerette off LA 319 in Iberia and Saint Mary parishes. **Facilities:** 6 rental cabins (2 &), picnic area, group shelters, restrooms, swimming beach, sailboat launch, fishing pier. **Activities:** Boating, sailing, fishing, crabbing, swimming, water-skiing, windsurfing, wildlife viewing. **Special Features:** Park offers easy access to the Gulf of Mexico and includes a half-mile stretch of manmade beach. Sailing and swimming facilities here are excellent, as is the wildlife viewing.

★2520★ FAIRVIEW-RIVERSIDE STATE PARK
119 Fairview Dr
Madisonville, LA 70447
Web: www.crt.state.la.us/parks/iFairview.aspx
Phone: 985-845-3318; **Toll Free:** 888-677-3247
Size: 99 acres. **Location:** Off LA 22, 2 miles east of Madisonville in Saint Tammany Parish, on the north shore of Lake Pontchartrain. **Facilities:** 22 premium campsites (prime location sites, all with water and electric hookups), 59 improved campsites, 20 tent sites, comfort stations, picnic area, group shelters, playground, fishing pier, boat launch (nearby), museum. **Activities:** Camping, fishing, museum tours. **Special Features:** Park is located amid moss-draped oaks and woodlands on the bank of the Tchefuncte River. Near the entrance to the park is the

Otis House, which was originally built in the 1880s as the family home of a sawmill owner. In the 1930s it was purchased and renovated by Frank Otis and served as his summer home until his death in 1962, when the property was left to the State of Louisiana to be developed into a recreational site for visitors. The house was placed on the *National Register of Historic Places* in 1999.

★2521★ FONTAINEBLEAU STATE PARK
67825 US Hwy 190
Mandeville, LA 70448
Web: www.crt.state.la.us/parks/iFontaine.aspx
Phone: 985-624-4443; **Toll Free:** 888-677-3668
Size: 2,809 acres. **Location:** Southeast of Mandeville in Saint Tammany Parish on US 190, on the north shore of Lake Pontchartrain. **Facilities:** 23 premium campsites (19 pull-through sites and 4 campsites with sewerage hookups, all with water and electrical hookup), 103 improved campsites, 37 unimproved campsites, primitive group camping area, comfort stations, picnic area, group shelters, nature trail, swimming beach, sailboat ramp, playground. Availability of some facilities may be affected by status of hurricane cleanup and reconstruction efforts. **Activities:** Camping, sailing, fishing, swimming, hiking, bicycling, wildlife viewing, birding, interpretive programs. **Special Features:** Near the park entrance are crumbling ruins of an old sugar mill built in 1829. Bernard de Marigny de Mandeville developed the area as a sugar plantation, and the income from it helped support his lavish lifestyle. He named his large land holding Fontainebleau after the forest near Paris. A portion of the 31-mile Tammany Trace rails-to-trails route passes through the park.

★2522★ FORT JESUP STATE HISTORIC SITE
32 Geoghagan Rd
Many, LA 71449
Web: www.crt.state.la.us/parks/iFtjesup.aspx
Phone: 318-256-4117; **Toll Free:** 888-677-5378
Size: 22 acres. **Location:** In Sabine Parish, 6 miles east of Many on LA 6. **Facilities:** Historic buildings, picnic area, visitor's center with exhibits, restrooms, and gift shop. **Activities:** Guided tours, interpretive programs. **Special Features:** Colonel Zachary Taylor established and commanded the garrison at Fort Jesup, which was built as a border outpost in 1822. Taylor's troops established law and order in the area, and Fort Jesup remained an important military post for nearly 25 years. The original kitchen/mess hall is the only historic structure remaining from the large reservation that once spread across the frontier. The reconstructed officers' quarters building now houses the site's visitor center. In 1961, Fort Jesup was designated a National Historic Landmark

★2523★ FORT PIKE STATE HISTORIC SITE
27100 Chef Menteur Hwy
New Orleans, LA 70129
Web: www.crt.state.la.us/parks/iFortpike.aspx
Phone: 504-662-5703; **Toll Free:** 888-662-5703
Size: 94 acres. **Location:** Adjacent to the Old Spanish Trail (US 90) in eastern New Orleans. **Facilities:** Closed indefinitely

9. State Parks

due to extensive damage suffered during Hurricane Katrina. **Special Features:** Fort was constructed shortly after the War of 1812 to defend navigational channels leading into the city of New Orleans.

★2524★ FORT SAINT JEAN BAPTISTE STATE HISTORIC SITE

155 Rue Jefferson
Natchitoches, LA 71457
Web: www.crt.state.la.us/parks/iftstjean.aspx
Phone: 318-357-3101; **Toll Free:** 888-677-7853
Size: 7 acres. **Location:** On the banks of the Cane River between downtown Natchitoches and Northwestern State University. **Facilities:** Historic structures, exhibits, visitor center, restrooms, picnic area. **Activities:** Guided tours, interpretive programs. **Special Features:** Park features a full-scale replica of a French fort built in 1732 and the site of first the permanent European settlement in the territory later known as the Louisiana Purchase. The fort was a strategic outpost that evolved into a primary trading center for the French in the Lower Mississippi Valley.

★2525★ GRAND ISLE STATE PARK

Admiral Craig Dr
Grand Isle, LA 70358
Web: www.crt.state.la.us/parks/igrdisle.aspx
Phone: 985-787-2559; **Toll Free:** 888-787-2559
Size: 120 acres. **Location:** At the southern end of LA 1 in Jefferson Parish. **Facilities:** 49 premium campsites (all pull-through with water and electric hookups; 1 ♿), restrooms, picnic areas, beach and bathhouse, nature trail, observation tower, visitor center. The main fishing pier at Grand Isle was destroyed in Hurricane Katrina; construction of a new pier is expected to be completed by 2008. In addition, all beach camping has been curtailed to allow erosion damage from the storm to correct itself. The beach is still open for day use, however. **Activities:** Camping, boating, fishing, swimming, crabbing, birdwatching. **Special Features:** Park is located on a barrier island off the coast of Louisiana, in the Gulf of Mexico. More than 280 species of fish are known to make their home in the waters off Grand Isle, and it's a great launching point for deep-sea fishing.

★2526★ JIMMIE DAVIS STATE PARK

1209 State Park Rd
Chatham, LA 71226
Web: www.crt.state.la.us/parks/ijimmiedavis.aspx
Phone: 318-249-2595; **Toll Free:** 888-677-2263
Size: 294 acres. **Location:** 12 miles east of Jonesboro off LA 4. **Facilities:** 9 premium campsites (all prime waterfront locations with water and electric hookups), 64 improved campsites, 17 cabins, 17 lodges, group camp, comfort stations, picnic area, group shelters, playground, trails, swimming beach and bathhouse, 2 fishing piers, bait shop, 2 boat launches. **Activities:** Camping, boating, fishing, swimming, hiking, bicycling, birding. **Special Features:** Park sits on a peninsula that juts into 4,970-acre Caney Lake. It is named for Jimmie Davis, who was governor of Louisiana from 1944-48 and 1960-64 and was also famous as a country-western and gospel singer.

★2527★ LAKE BISTINEAU STATE PARK

103 State Park Rd
Doyline, LA 71023
Web: www.crt.state.la.us/parks/ibistino.aspx
Phone: 318-745-3503; **Toll Free:** 888-677-2478
Size: 750 acres. **Location:** 40 minutes south of Shreveport, off LA 163 in Webster Parish. **Facilities:** 17 premium campsites (5 pull-through campsites and 12 with prime locations, all with water and electric hookups), 44 improved campsites, comfort stations, 14 cabins, rental lodge, 2 group camps, picnic area, group shelters, playgrounds, restrooms, hiking trails, bike trails, canoe trail (11 miles), 2 swimming pools, beach, 2 boat launches, boat rentals, baseball field, visitor/nature center. **Activities:** Camping, fishing, boating, canoeing, swimming, hiking, bicycling. **Special Features:** Lake Bistineau got its start in 1800 when a gigantic log jam on the Red River flooded the area. A permanent dam was built in 1935, increasing the lake's surface area to 27 square miles.

★2528★ LAKE BRUIN STATE PARK

201 State Park Rd
Saint Joseph, LA 71366
Web: www.crt.state.la.us/parks/iLkbruin.aspx
Phone: 318-766-3530; **Toll Free:** 888-677-2784
Size: 53 acres. **Location:** East of US 65 near Saint Joseph in Tensas Parish, on the eastern border of Louisiana. **Facilities:** 12 premium campsites (5 pull-through campsites, 12 prime location campsites, all with water and electrical hookup), 13 improved campsites, 2 primitive campsites, group camping area, comfort stations, picnic area, covered pavilion, playgrounds, restrooms, swimming beach, bathhouse, boat launch, boat rentals, 3 fishing piers (♿♿). **Activities:** Camping, boating, fishing, swimming. **Special Features:** Park features a clear oxbow lake (once part of the Mississippi River) with ancient cypress trees along the shoreline. The site was originally established as a fish hatchery in 1928.

★2529★ LAKE CLAIBORNE STATE PARK

225 State Park Rd
Homer, LA 71040
Web: www.crt.state.la.us/parks/iClaiborn.aspx
Phone: 318-927-2976; **Toll Free:** 888-677-2524
Size: 620 acres. **Location:** 7 miles southeast of Homer off LA 146. **Facilities:** 20 premium campsites (12 pull-through campsites, 8 prime location campsites, all with water and electrical hookup), 67 improved campsites, 2 unimproved campsites (no hookups), primitive camping area, comfort stations, picnic area, group shelters, playground, hiking trails, bike trails, concession area, nature trails, swimming beach, boat launch, boat rentals, fishing piers. **Activities:** Camping, boating, canoeing, swimming, fishing, water-skiing, jet skiing, bicycling, hiking, interpretive programs. **Special Features:** Park's natural attractions includes piney woods, rolling hills, steep ravines, and the clear waters of 6,400-acre Lake Claiborne. The beach is situated on an inlet of the lake and is protected from boaters and water-skiiers.

9. State Parks

★2530★ LAKE D'ARBONNE STATE PARK
3628 Evergreen Rd
Farmerville, LA 71241
Web: www.crt.state.la.us/parks/iDarbonne.aspx
Phone: 318-368-2086; **Toll Free:** 888-677-5200
Size: 655 acres. **Location:** 5 miles west of Farmerville on LA 2. **Facilities:** 7 premium campsites (all prime location campsites, with water and electrical hookup), 51 improved campsites, 16 cabins (1 ♿), 2 lodges (1 ♿), group camp (52-person capacity), comfort stations, picnic areas, group pavilions, playgrounds, trails, swimming pool, boat rentals, boat launch, 5 fishing piers, meeting room, 4 lighted tennis courts, visitor center. **Activities:** Camping, boating, water-skiing, fishing, hiking, bicycling, interpretive programs. **Special Features:** Park features excellent fishing and water sports on a 15,250-acre manmade lake. Five fishing piers and record catches of bass, crappie, catfish and bream make the park especially popular with fishermen.

★2531★ LAKE FAUSSE POINTE STATE PARK
5400 Levee Rd
Saint Martinville, LA 70582
Web: www.crt.state.la.us/parks/ilakefaus.aspx
Phone: 318-229-4764; **Toll Free:** 888-677-7200
Size: 6,127 acres. **Location:** Off the West Atchafalaya Protection Levee Road, 18 miles southeast of Saint Martinville, in Iberia Parish. **Facilities:** 17 premium campsites (all prime location campsites, with water and electrical hookup), 33 improved campsites, 5 uimproved campsites, primitive camping area, comfort stations, 16 cabins (3 ♿), picnic areas, picnic pavilions, playground, nature trails, canoe trail, boat launch, boat dock, boat rentals, meeting room, visitor center, nature center. **Activities:** Camping, boating, canoeing, fishing, hiking, wildlife viewing, interpretive programs. **Special Features:** Park lies at the edge of one of the legendary features of Cajun Louisiana, the Atchafalaya Basin. Prior to the 20th century, the Basin was a vast swamp enclosed by the natural levees of Bayou Teche and the Mississippi River. The area surrounding the park was formerly the home site of the Chitimacha Indians, French and Acadian farmers and trappers, Spaniards, and Canary Islanders (called Isleños), each group contributing to the cultural diversity of this section of Louisiana.

★2532★ LOCUST GROVE STATE HISTORIC SITE
c/o Audubon State Historic Site
PO Box 546
Saint Francisville, LA 70775
Web: www.crt.state.la.us/parks/ilocust.aspx
Phone: 225-635-3739; **Toll Free:** 888-677-2838
Size: 1 acre. **Location:** North of Saint Francisville in West Feliciana Parish, on Bains-Ristroph Road, off LA 10. **Special Features:** Locust Grove is the site of a small cemetery with only 27 plots and is all that remains of what was once Locust Grove Plantation, owned by the sister of Jefferson Davis. In 1835 the future President of the Confederacy brought his young bride here for a visit. Both contracted malaria, and Mrs. Davis, who was also the daughter of Zachary Taylor, died. Her grave is here among other Davis family members.

★2533★ LONGFELLOW-EVANGELINE STATE HISTORIC SITE
1200 N Main St
Saint Martinville, LA 70582
Web: www.crt.state.la.us/parks/ilongfell.aspx
Phone: 337-394-3754; **Toll Free:** 888-677-2900
Size: 157 acres. **Location:** On LA 31 in Saint Martinville along the banks of Bayou Teche, 30 minutes southeast of Lafayette. **Facilities:** Historic structures, amphitheater, outdoor exhibits, visitor center, crafts shop, restrooms, picnic area, group pavilion. **Activities:** Guided tours, living history demonstrations, educational programs. **Special Features:** The first park of the Louisiana State Parks system, Longfellow-Evangeline interprets the history of the French-speaking people of the state. The park's centerpiece is Maison Olivier, a Creole plantation home built around 1815. The site also features an Acadian Farmstead depicting the lifestyle of Acadian settlers.

★2534★ LOS ADAES STATE HISTORIC SITE
6354 Hwy 485
Robeline, LA 71469
Web: www.crt.state.la.us/parks/iLosadaes.aspx
Phone: 318-472-9449; **Toll Free:** 888-677-5378
Size: 14 acres. **Location:** 1 mile northeast of Robeline on LA 485, just off LA 6. **Facilities:** Archeological site, visitor center, restrooms. **Activities:** Guided tours, interpretive programs. **Special Features:** Dating back to the early 1700s, Los Adaes was the symbol of New Spain in Louisiana, a former capital of Texas, and the scene of a unique cooperation among the French, the Spanish and the indigenous Native Americans. Today, archeological finds in the area and exhibits tell the story of this era in Louisiana history.

★2535★ LOUISIANA STATE ARBORETUM
4213 Chicot Park Rd
Ville Platte, LA 70586
Web: www.crt.state.la.us/parks/iarbor.aspx
Phone: 337-363-6289; **Toll Free:** 888-677-6100
Size: 300 acres. **Location:** On LA 3042, 8 miles north of Ville Platte and 1.5 miles from the entrance to Chicot State Park (see separate entry). **Facilities:** Herbarium, outdoor exhibits, trails (3 miles), restrooms. **Activities:** Nature study, guided tours, interpretive programs. **Special Features:** Established in 1961, the Louisiana State Arboretum was the first state-supported arboretum in the United States. The arboretum offers visitors a living botanical museum with natural growth and plantings grown for scientific or educational purposes. Trees, shrubs, and flowers are labeled for observation along an extensive network of trails. Due to its great variation in topography, almost every type of Louisiana vegetation, except coastal marsh and prairie, is represented on the site.

★2536★ MANSFIELD STATE HISTORIC SITE
15149 Hwy 175
Mansfield, LA 71052
Web: www.crt.state.la.us/parks/iMansfld.aspx
Phone: 318-872-1474; **Toll Free:** 888-677-6267
Size: 178 acres. **Location:** In DeSoto Parish, 4 miles south of

the town of Mansfield on LA 175. **Facilities:** Museum, outdoor exhibits, interpretive trails, visitor center, craft shop, restrooms, picnic area. **Activities:** Guided tours, living history demonstrations, interpretive programs. **Special Features:** Site commemorates the most important battle of the Civil War fought west of the Mississippi, and the museum's impressive collection includes Civil War weapons, arms, uniforms, letters, diaries, documents, and other related artifacts. The Confederate victory here prevented complete Union control of Louisiana and the progression of the war into Texas — and may have prolonged the war by several months. In 1973 the site was placed on the *National Register of Historic Places.*

★2537★ MARKSVILLE STATE HISTORIC SITE
837 ML King Dr
Marksville, LA 71351
Web: www.crt.state.la.us/parks/iMarksvle.aspx
Phone: 318-253-8954; **Toll Free:** 888-253-8954
Size: 42 acres. **Location:** In the town of Marksville, southeast of Alexandria, off LA 1. **Facilities:** Museum, archeological exhibits, picnic area, trails, restrooms. **Activities:** Guided tours, interpretive programs. **Special Features:** Site preserves the 1,600-year-old Marksville ceremonial center, a significant archeological resource and designated National Historic Landmark. The main portion of the site is surrounded by a semicircular earthwork which is 3,300 feet long and ranges from three to seven feet in height. The Marksville culture is a southeastern variant of the Hopewell culture, centered in Ohio and Illinois.

★2538★ NORTH TOLEDO BEND STATE PARK
2907 N Toledo Park Rd
Zwolle, LA 71486
Web: www.crt.state.la.us/parks/intoledo.aspx
Phone: 318-645-4715; **Toll Free:** 888-677-6400
Size: 900 acres. **Location:** 9 miles southwest of Zwolle, off LA 3229 (90 minutes south of Shreveport or 45 minutes west of Natchitoches). **Facilities:** 8 premium campsites (all prime location campsites, with water and electrical hookup), 55 improved campsites, comfort stations, 10 cabins, group camp with 5 dormitories, trails, picnic areas, group shelters, playground, swimming pool and bathhouse, boat launch, boat rentals, 2 fishing piers, visitor center, concession area, laundry, meeting room. **Activities:** Camping, boating, fishing, hiking, swimming. **Special Features:** Park is located on a peninsula along the eastern shore of one of the country's largest manmade reservoirs, 185,000-acre Toledo Reservoir. Organizations associated with the reservoir host numerous freshwater fishing competitions that attract fishermen from around the country.

★2539★ PALMETTO ISLAND STATE PARK
c/o Louisiana Office of State Parks
PO Box 44426
Baton Rouge, LA 70804
Web: www.crt.state.la.us/parks/iconstruction.aspx
Phone: 225-342-8111; **Toll Free:** 888-677-1400
Size: 1,299 acres. **Location:** Off LA 82 between Abbeville and Intracoastal City. **Facilities:** Under development; not open to public. **Special Features:** Park's amenities will include a visitor/nature center, 75 campsites, 15 two-bedroom cabins, group camp, meeting lodge, 4 picnic pavilions and numerous picnic sites, swimming pool, playground, 3 comfort stations, boat launch, canoe launch and trail, and hiking trail.

★2540★ PLAQUEMINE LOCK STATE HISTORIC SITE
57730 Main St
Plaquemine, LA 70764
Web: www.crt.state.la.us/parks/iPlaqlock.aspx
Phone: 225-687-7158; **Toll Free:** 877-987-7158
Size: 25 acres. **Location:** Off LA 1 in downtown Plaquemine in Iberville Parish, 13 miles south of Baton Rouge, on historic Main Street. **Facilities:** Visitor center, museum, historic structure, exhibits, observation tower, restroom. **Activities:** Guided tours, interpretive programs. **Special Features:** At the time of its completion in 1909, Plaquemine Lock on the Mississippi River had the highest water lift of any lock in the world. It was engineered by Colonel George W. Goethals, who also designed the Panama Canal. The site includes the original lockhouse and a working scale model of the lock.

★2541★ PORT HUDSON STATE HISTORIC SITE
236 Hwy 61
Jackson, LA 70748
Web: www.crt.state.la.us/parks/ipthudson.aspx
Phone: 225-654-3775; **Fax:** 225-654-4413; **Toll Free:** 888-677-3400
Size: 899 acres. **Location:** On US 61 in East Feliciana Parish, 14 miles north of Baton Rouge. **Facilities:** Museum, observation towers, outdoor displays, walking trails (6 miles), picnic area, visitor center, restrooms. **Activities:** Guided tours, living history demonstrations, interpretive programs. **Special Features:** Site includes original Civil War earthworks used by Confederate forces during the 1863 siege of Port Hudson by Union forces, a pivotal battle for control of the Mississippi River. The siege lasted 48 days and is believed to be the longest in American military history. The site is a National Historic Landmark.

★2542★ POVERTY POINT RESERVOIR STATE PARK
1500 Poverty Point Pkwy
Delhi, LA 71232
Web: www.crt.state.la.us/parks/ireservoir.aspx
Phone: 318-878-7536; **Toll Free:** 800-474-0392
Size: 2,700 acres water. **Location:** Off LA 17, just north of Delhi in Richland Parish. **Facilities:** 37 premium campsites (water, electrical and sewerage hookup), 17 improved campsites, 4 rental lodges (1 ♿), picnic area, trails, swimming beach, comfort stations, marina with covered boat slips, 2 boat launches, 2 fishing piers, fish-cleaning stations, concession area. **Activities:** Camping, boating, fishing, swimming, hiking. **Special Features:** Fish and wildlife species migrating through the reservoir are numerous, and the region falls within the Mississippi flyway for many species of birds. The eastern edge of the park along Bayou Macon contains attractive bear habitat, and visitors are cautioned that special attention should be given to any Louisiana black bear sightings on or near the reservoir.

★2543★ POVERTY POINT STATE HISTORIC SITE

6859 Hwy 577
Pioneer, LA 71266
Web: www.crt.state.la.us/parks/ipvertypt.aspx
Phone: 318-926-5492; Toll Free: 888-926-5492
Size: 400 acres. Location: East of Monroe on LA 577 in West Carroll Parish. Facilities: Museum, observation tower, outdoor exhibits, visitor center, restrooms, picnic area, trails. Activities: Guided tours, archeological workshop, interpretive programs, tram tours (seasonal). Special Features: Poverty Point preserves one of North America's most significant archeological sites, dating between 1650 and 700 BC. A highly civilized group, the Poverty Point inhabitants built a complex array earthen mounds and ridges overlooking the Mississippi River floodplain. The central construction consists of six rows of concentric ridges, which at one time were five feet high. The five aisles and six sections of ridges form a partial octagon, with the diameter of the outermost ridges measuring three-quarters of a mile. In 1962, Poverty Point was designated a National Historic Landmark.

★2544★ REBEL STATE HISTORIC SITE

1260 Hwy 1221
Marthaville, LA 71450
Web: www.crt.state.la.us/parks/irebel.aspx
Phone: 318-472-6255; Toll Free: 888-677-3600
Size: 46 acres. Location: 3 miles northwest of Marthaville on LA 1221. Facilities: Museum, exhibits, library, performance amphitheater, visitor center, restrooms, picnic areas, group pavilion, trails. Activities: Guided tours, interpretive programs, community outreach programs, musical performances. Special Features: Rebel is the home of the Louisiana Country Music Museum, with exhibits that interpret the development of the various folk music traditions in the region, from early gospel and string band music to today's country music sounds. The museum contains costumes, instruments, and pictures that have been donated by prominent country music and gospel performers, including Roy Acuff's fiddle and yo-yo as well as one of Hank Williams Jr's shirts. The building's architectural design depicts a stringed musical instrument.

★2545★ ROSEDOWN PLANTATION STATE HISTORIC SITE

12501 LA Hwy 10
Saint Francisville, LA 70775
Web: www.crt.state.la.us/parks/irosedown.aspx
Phone: 225-635-3322; Toll Free: 888-376-1867
Size: 371 acres. Location: In Saint Francisville on LA 10, off US 61. Facilities: Historic structures and gardens, picnic area, restrooms. Activities: Guided tours, interpretive programs. Special Features: Rosedown Plantation is located along one of the most historic corridors of South Louisiana. The site includes the restored antebellum home, 28 acres of formal gardens, and 13 other historic buildings. The home is furnished with many of the plantation's original contents.

★2546★ SAINT BERNARD STATE PARK

501 St Bernard Pkwy
Braithwaite, LA 70040
Web: www.crt.state.la.us/parks/iStbernrd.aspx
Phone: 504-682-2101; Toll Free: 888-677-7823
Size: 358 acres. Location: 18 miles southeast of New Orleans off LA 39 in Saint Bernard Parish. Facilities: Closed until further notice due to the impact of Hurricanes Katrina and Rita. Special Features: Located right along the Mississippi River, the park contains a network of man-made lagoons that provide a peaceful, natural setting for relaxation.

★2547★ SAM HOUSTON JONES STATE PARK

107 Sutherland Rd
Lake Charles, LA 70611
Web: www.crt.state.la.us/parks/iShjones.aspx
Phone: 337-855-2665; Toll Free: 888-677-7264
Size: 1,087 acres. Location: 12 miles north of Lake Charles off LA 378 in Calcasieu Parish. Facilities: 20 premium campsites (full hookups, including sewer), 42 improved campsites, 19 improved tent-only campsites, comfort stations, 12 cabins (2 &), picnic area, group shelter, playground, hiking trails, 2 boat launches, boat rentals. Activities: Camping, boating, canoeing, fishing, hiking, bird watching, interpretive programs. Special Features: Park's caretakers have worked to keep the land in its natural state, with tree-filled lagoons and a mixed pine and hardwood forest environment. The park was originally named for the Texas folk hero but was later changed to honor the state's 37th governor, who was instrumental in setting aside this tract of land for public use.

★2548★ SOUTH TOLEDO BEND STATE PARK

120 Bald Eaglel Rd
Anacoco, LA 71403
Web: www.crt.state.la.us/parks/istb.aspx
Phone: 337-286-9075; Toll Free: 888-398-4770
Size: 1,023 acres. Location: 16 miles west of Anacoco, on LA 191, in Sabine Parish, toward the southern end of Toledo Bend Reservoir. Facilities: 12 premium campsites (4 pull-through sites, 9 prime location sites, all with water and electrical hookup), 42 improved campsites, 5 tent campsites (no hookups), comfort stations, 19 cabins (2 &), picnic area, 3,000-foot surfaced nature trail, boat launch, visitor center with exhibits on local animal and plant life, observation deck. Activities: Camping, fishing, boating, hiking, bicycling, bird watching, interpretive programs. Special Features: Park is located on several small bluffs that extend over and into the South Toledo Reservoir, offering scenic, waterfront views to visitors. The area is a common nesting ground for bald eagles, which feed from the reservoir's plentiful supply of fish. The reservoir also is a nationally recognized destination for bass fishing tournaments.

★2549★ TICKFAW STATE PARK

27225 Patterson Rd
Springfield, LA 70462
Web: www.crt.state.la.us/parks/itickfaw.aspx
Phone: 225-294-5020; Toll Free: 888-981-2020
Size: 1,200 acres. Location: 32 miles southeast of Baton Rouge and 7 miles from the center of Springfield on LA 1037. Facilities: 30 improved campsites, 20 unimproved tent sites, comfort stations, 14 cabins (2 &), group camp, picnic areas, group shelters, playground, canoe rentals, water playground, trails (&),

exhibits, outdoor amphitheater, nature center, gift shop. **Activities:** Camping, canoeing, hiking, bicycling, skating, birding, wildife viewing, guided canoe tours, interpretive programs. **Special Features:** Park is a nature-based recreational site, designed for nature study and conservation education. Its mile-long boardwalk trail passes through four distinct ecosystems: cypress-tupelo swamp, bottomland hardwood forest, mixed pine and hardwood forest, and the riparian area of Tickfaw River.

★2550★ WINTER QUARTERS STATE HISTORIC SITE
4929 Hwy 608
Newellton, LA 71357
Web: www.crt.state.la.us/parks/iwinter.aspx
Phone: 318-467-9750; **Toll Free:** 888-677-9468
Size: 4 acres. **Location:** 8 miles southeast of Newellton on LA 608 in Tensas Parish. **Facilities:** Historic home, picnic area, restroom. **Activities:** Guided tours, interpretive programs. **Special Features:** Spared destruction in 1863 by Union forces following Sherman's orders to destroy everything not needed by Union troops, Winter Quarters was the only surviving plantation home out of 15 that lined the banks of Lake Saint Joseph. The restored house is furnished in the style of the period and includes a rare and perfectly preserved billiard table made by the Brunswick-Balke-Collender Company around 1845. Other items housed there include diaries and other personal records that provide a valuable link to the Antebellum period.

9. State Parks

Maine State Parks

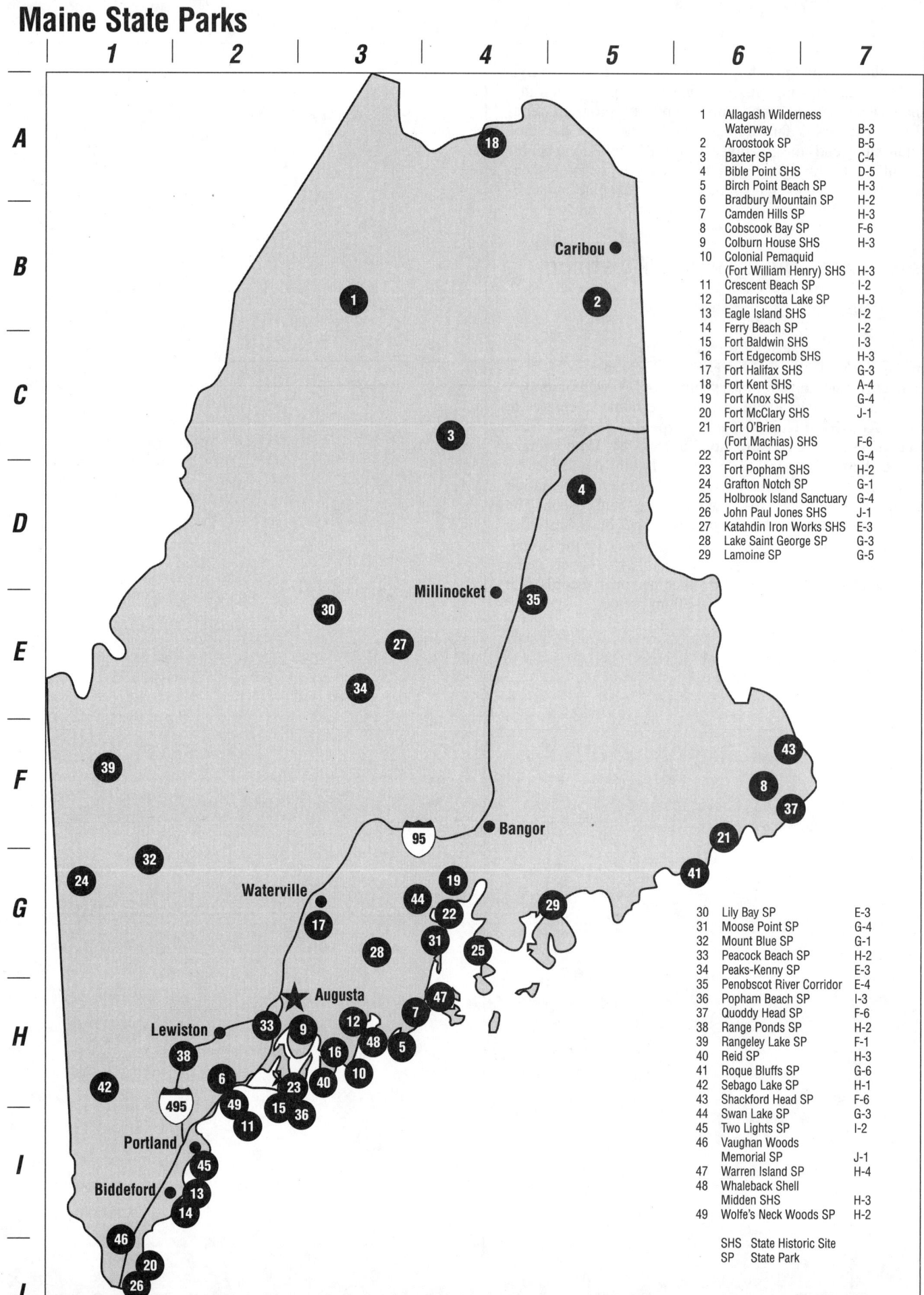

1	Allagash Wilderness Waterway	B-3
2	Aroostook SP	B-5
3	Baxter SP	C-4
4	Bible Point SHS	D-5
5	Birch Point Beach SP	H-3
6	Bradbury Mountain SP	H-2
7	Camden Hills SP	H-3
8	Cobscook Bay SP	F-6
9	Colburn House SHS	H-3
10	Colonial Pemaquid (Fort William Henry) SHS	H-3
11	Crescent Beach SP	I-2
12	Damariscotta Lake SP	H-3
13	Eagle Island SHS	I-2
14	Ferry Beach SP	I-2
15	Fort Baldwin SHS	I-3
16	Fort Edgecomb SHS	H-3
17	Fort Halifax SHS	G-3
18	Fort Kent SHS	A-4
19	Fort Knox SHS	G-4
20	Fort McClary SHS	J-1
21	Fort O'Brien (Fort Machias) SHS	F-6
22	Fort Point SP	G-4
23	Fort Popham SHS	H-2
24	Grafton Notch SP	G-1
25	Holbrook Island Sanctuary	G-4
26	John Paul Jones SHS	J-1
27	Katahdin Iron Works SHS	E-3
28	Lake Saint George SP	G-3
29	Lamoine SP	G-5

30	Lily Bay SP	E-3
31	Moose Point SP	G-4
32	Mount Blue SP	G-1
33	Peacock Beach SP	H-2
34	Peaks-Kenny SP	E-3
35	Penobscot River Corridor	E-4
36	Popham Beach SP	I-3
37	Quoddy Head SP	F-6
38	Range Ponds SP	H-2
39	Rangeley Lake SP	F-1
40	Reid SP	H-3
41	Roque Bluffs SP	G-6
42	Sebago Lake SP	H-1
43	Shackford Head SP	F-6
44	Swan Lake SP	G-3
45	Two Lights SP	I-2
46	Vaughan Woods Memorial SP	J-1
47	Warren Island SP	H-4
48	Whaleback Shell Midden SHS	H-3
49	Wolfe's Neck Woods SP	H-2

SHS State Historic Site
SP   State Park

MAINE

★2551★ Maine Bureau of Parks & Lands
22 State House Stn
Augusta, ME 04333
(207) 287-3821 - Phone
(207) 287-3823 - Fax
(800) 332-1501 – Toll-free Reservations (in Maine only)
Web: www.maine.gov/doc/parks
Oversees nearly 600,000 acres of land, including more than 30 state parks, state historic sites, and 29 units designated as Public Reserved Lands. Provides boat access to lakes, rivers, and the coast at almost 400 locations, and maintains many miles of off-road vehicle trails for use by ATVs, snowmobiles, and mountain bikes.

★2552★ Maine Department of Inland Fisheries & Wildlife
41 State House Stn
Augusta, ME 04333
(207) 287-8000 - Phone
Web: www.state.me.us/ifw
Manages the state's fish and wildlife conservation programs including hunting and fishing licensing, hunter education, and data collection. Enforces laws and rules governing the management and protection of fisheries and wildlife resources. Also administers registration of watercraft, snowmobiles, and ATVs.

Key to campsite classification:

• **Campsites —** No state park campground offers water or electrical hookups. Some sites have sanitary dump stations. Reservations for campsites at the state's twelve camping parks may be made by phone, mail, or through the Parks Bureau reservations web site. The camping season runs from mid-May to mid-October.

★2553★ ALLAGASH WILDERNESS WATERWAY
c/o Bureau of Parks & Lands Northern Region
106 Hogan Rd
Bangor, ME 04401
Web: www.maine.gov/doc/parks/programs/db_search
Phone: 207-941-4014
Size: 22,840 acres. **Location:** Northern Maine, from Telos Landing to Allagash (near the Canadian border). **Facilities:** 80 marked campsites, hiking trails. **Activities:** Low-impact, primitive camping, canoeing, hiking, hunting (in season), fishing, ice fishing, snowmobiling (no groomed trails). **Special Features:** Allagash Wilderness Waterway is a 92-mile-long ribbon of lakes, ponds, rivers, and streams winding through the heart of northern Maine's vast commercial forests. Hiking trails to fire

towers offer visitors spectacular views of the surrounding lakes and woodlands.

★2554★ AROOSTOOK STATE PARK
87 State Park Rd
Presque Isle, ME 04769
Web: www.maine.gov/doc/parks/programs/db_search
Phone: 207-768-8341
Size: 664 acres. **Location:** West off US 1 south of Presque Isle. **Facilities:** Campsites, showerhouse, kitchen shelter, picnic tables, trails, beach, bathhouse, canoe and paddleboat rentals (in summer), boat launch (点点). Open May 15-October 15. **Activities:** Camping, swimming, boating, canoeing, fishing, hiking, cross-country skiing, snowmobiling. **Special Features:** Popular activities at Maine's first state park include hiking on Quaggy Jo Mountain and trout fishing on Echo Lake. The park's natural areas are typical of northern Maine, consisting of spruce, fir, beech, and maple along with younger stands of poplar, birch, and other hardwoods. In low swampy areas, dense stands of cedar can be found.

★2555★ BAXTER STATE PARK
64 Balsam Dr
Millinocket, ME 04462
Web: www.baxterstateparkauthority.com
Phone: 207-723-5140
Size: 202,064 acres. **Location:** 50 miles north of Greenville. **Facilities:** Primitive campsites (lean-to/tent, wilderness cabins), trails. **Activities:** Low-impact camping and hiking, fishing, skiing (winter only), snowmobiling, mountain climbing. **Special Features:** Park is not part of Maine's state park system. It was given in trust to the people of Maine by former Governor Percival Baxter and is managed by an independent authority. The park consists of 200,000 acres of mountains, lakes, streams, and forest maintained in its natural wild state. It includes Mount Katahdin, the highest mountain in Maine, and the northern terminus of the 2,144-mile-long Appalachian National Scenic Trail (see separate entry in national trails section).

★2556★ BIBLE POINT STATE HISTORIC SITE
c/o Bureau of Parks & Lands
106 Hogan Rd
Bangor, ME 04401
Web: www.maine.gov/doc/parks/programs/db_search
Phone: 207-941-4014
Size: 27 acres. **Location:** From Island Falls, take the Merriman Road to its end, then follow the hiking trail along the western shore of the West Branch of the Mattawamkeag River, approximately 1 mile. The site is not staffed. **Special Features:** As a young man, Teddy Roosevelt camped, hunted, and fished in this area. It was reported that each day he would take his Bible

and hike to a point of land on the Mattawamkeag River and First Brook, where he would read the Bible. A plaque at the site commemorates Roosevelt's love for the area.

★2557★ BIRCH POINT STATE PARK
c/o Bureau of Parks & Lands
106 Hogan Rd
Bangor, ME 04401
Web: www.maine.gov/doc/parks/programs/db_search
Phone: 207-941-4014
Size: 62 acres. **Location:** In Owl's Head. **Facilities:** Picnic area, beach. Open Memorial Day-Labor Day. **Activities:** Swimming, fishing. **Special Features:** Park overlooks Penobscot Bay and has a crescent-shaped sand beach.

★2558★ BRADBURY MOUNTAIN STATE PARK
528 Hallowell Rd
Pownal, ME 04069
Web: www.maine.gov/doc/parks/programs/db_search
Phone: 207-688-4712
Size: 590 acres. **Location:** 5 miles from the Freeport-Durham exit off I-95. **Facilities:** 41 campsites, picnic area and shelter, trails, ballfields, playground. Open year-round. **Activities:** Camping, hiking, cross-country skiing, horseback riding, mountain biking, snowmobiling. **Special Features:** Park is one of Maine's five original state parks. Bradbury Mountain, which was sculpted by a glacier, is the park's most outstanding natural feature.

★2559★ CAMDEN HILLS STATE PARK
280 Belfast Rd
Camden, ME 04843
Web: www.maine.gov/doc/parks/programs/db_search
Phone: 207-236-3109
Size: 5,710 acres. **Location:** 2 miles north of Camden on US 1. **Facilities:** 107 campsites with showers and flush toilets (&), picnic area, hiking trails (30 miles). Open May 15-October 15. **Activities:** Camping, hiking, snowmobiling. **Special Features:** Park's signature location is the scenic vista atop Mount Battie, which offers sweeping views of Camden Harbor, Penobscot Bay, and surrounding islands. An easy foot trail leads up Mount Megunticook, highest of the Camden Hills. Harbor cruises and whale and puffin watches are available daily in nearby Camden, just a few minutes from the park.

★2560★ COBSCOOK BAY STATE PARK
RR 1, Box 127
Dennysville, ME 04628
Web: www.maine.gov/doc/parks/programs/db_search
Phone: 207-726-4412
Size: 888 acres. **Location:** 4 miles south of Dennysville on US 1. **Facilities:** 106 campsites, showers (&), restroom, picnic tables (&), trails, scenic road, boat launch. Open May 15-October 15. **Activities:** Camping, boating, fishing, clamming, hiking, cross-country skiing, snowmobiling. **Special Features:** ''Cobscook'' is a derivation of a Maliseet-Passamaquoddy word for waterfall,

referring to the falls that reverse with each change of the 24-foot tides, the highest in Maine. Park is located near Quoddy Head State Park (see separate entry), Moosehorn National Wildlife Refuge (see separate entry in national wildlife refuges section), and Franklin D. Roosevelt International Park on Campobello Island in New Brunswick.

★2561★ COLBURN HOUSE STATE HISTORIC SITE
Historic Site Specialist Bureau of Parks & Lands
22 State House Stn
Augusta, ME 04333
Web: www.maine.gov/doc/parks/programs/db_search
Phone: 207-287-3821
Location: Along the Kennebec River in Pittston, just south of Gardiner on Route 27. **Facilities:** Historic home. Open weekends in July and August. **Special Features:** Built in 1765, this colonial Federal-style house was home to several generations of the Colburn family. In 1775 Colonel Benedict Arnold led an expedition of more than 1,000 colonial soldiers up the Kennebec River to attack the British stronghold of Quebec City. Reuben Colburn helped plan and carry out this attack, and the Colburn house was Arnold's headquarters and launching point for the expedition against Quebec.

★2562★ COLONIAL PEMAQUID STATE HISTORIC SITE
PO Box 117
New Harbor, ME 04554
Web: www.maine.gov/doc/parks/programs/db_search
Phone: 207-677-2423
Size: 19 acres. **Location:** 4 miles on ME 129 from Damariscotta, then 9 miles on ME 130 and bear right 1 mile. **Facilities:** Museum, historic buildings, picnic area, snack bar, boat launch. Open Memorial Day through Labor Day. **Activities:** Guided tours (in summer); fishing. **Special Features:** Archeological excavations have unearthed 14 foundations of 17th- and 18th-century structures and the officers' quarters for Fort William Henry and Fort Frederick. A museum at the site displays hundreds of artifacts found there, dating from prehistoric times through the colonial period. Musket balls, old coins, pottery, and early hardware are among items of interest. The site includes a reconstruction of Fort William Henry, which also houses museum exhibits.

★2563★ CRESCENT BEACH STATE PARK
66 Two Lights Rd
Cape Elizabeth, ME 04107
Web: www.maine.gov/doc/parks/programs/db_search
Phone: 207-799-5871
Size: 244 acres. **Location:** 8 miles south of Portland on ME 77 in Cape Elizabeth. **Facilities:** Picnic areas, playground, trails, snack bar, beach, bathhouse (cold water showers), unpaved shallow boat launch, restrooms (&&). Open Memorial Day-Columbus Day (park is closed to vehicles in winter, but visitors can hike or ski the trails then). **Activities:** Swimming, fishing, hiking, wildlife viewing, bird watching, cross-country skiing. **Special Features:** Park's signature feature is a mile-long crescent-shaped beach. The beach and dunes provide nesting areas for

endangered piping plovers and resting and feeding areas for other shorebirds. The diverse habitats also support a host of wildlife.

★2564★ DAMARISCOTTA LAKE STATE PARK

8 State Park Rd
Jefferson, ME 04348
Web: www.maine.gov/doc/parks/programs/db_search
Phone: 207-549-7600
Size: 19 acres. Location: Off Route 32 in Jefferson. Facilities: Picnic area (&), group use shelter, playing field, playground, beach, changing rooms. Open Memorial Day-Labor Day. Activities: Swimming, fishing. Special Features: Park features a large freshwater lake and a lifeguard-protected swimming beach.

★2565★ EAGLE ISLAND STATE HISTORIC SITE

PO Box 161
South Harpswell, ME 04079
Web: www.maine.gov/doc/parks/programs/db_search
Phone: 207-624-6075
Size: 17 acres. Location: 3 miles off the coast of Harpswell. Facilities: Historic home and gardens, picnic area, pier, trails. Contact the Maine Bureau of Parks and Recreation for information concerning boats for hire providing transportation to the island. Open June 15-Labor Day. Activities: Tours. Special Features: Purchased in 1881 for $200, Eagle Island was the summer home of North Pole explorer, Admiral Robert Peary.

★2566★ FERRY BEACH STATE PARK

95 Bayview Rd
Saco, ME 04072
Web: www.maine.gov/doc/parks/programs/db_search
Phone: 207-283-0067
Size: 117 acres. Location: Off ME 9 on Bay View Road between Old Orchard Beach and Camp Ellis in Saco. Facilities: Beaches, changing room, picnic area (&), nature trails. Open Memorial Day-October 1. Activities: Swimming, hiking, nature programs. Special Features: Park includes a sheltered beach, dunes, and sweeping views of the white sand beaches between the Saco River and Pine Point. Trails highlight a variety of ecosystems, including Tupelo swampland, extremely rare at this latitude.

★2567★ FORT BALDWIN STATE HISTORIC SITE

c/o Popham Beach State Park
10 Perkins Farm Ln
Phippsburg, ME 04562
Web: www.maine.gov/doc/parks/programs/db_search
Phone: 207-389-1335
Size: 17 acres. Location: In the Popham Village section of Phippsburg. Special Features: Fort was built between 1905 and 1912 and named for Jeduthan Baldwin, an engineer for the Colonial army during the Revolutionary War. The fort was manned during World War I and World War II. It is open to the public year round.

★2568★ FORT EDGECOMB STATE HISTORIC SITE

66 Fort Rd
Edgecomb, ME 04556
Web: www.maine.gov/doc/parks/programs/db_search
Phone: 207-882-7777
Size: 3 acres. Location: Off US 1 at the Edgecomb end of the Wicasset bridge, on Eddy Road. Facilities: Historic structures, interpretive panels, picnic facilities. Open Memorial Day-Labor Day. Activities: Guided tours and special events in summer; fishing. Special Features: Located on Davis Island in the Sheepscott River, Fort was built prior to the War of 1812 to protect the Maine coast and its shipping interest. The centerpiece of the fort is the Blockhouse, which was built in 1809 and repre-sent's the nation's best-preserved blockhouse of this period.

★2569★ FORT HALIFAX STATE HISTORIC SITE

c/o Bureau of Parks & Lands
106 Hogan Rd
Bangor, ME 04401
Web: www.maine.gov/doc/parks/programs/db_search
Phone: 207-941-4014
Size: Less than 1 acre. Location: 1 mile south of Winslow-Waterville bridge on US 201. Activities: Picnicking. Special Features: The oldest blockhouse in the US is all that remains of Fort Halifax, which was built in 1754 to protect colonial settlements along the Kennebec River. In 1987 the blockhouse was dismantled by flood waters, but boat crews recovered the log timbers and the blockhouse was reassembled the following year. It is designated as a National Historic Landmark. Open Memorial Day-Labor Day.

★2570★ FORT KENT STATE HISTORIC SITE

c/o Bureau of Parks & Lands
106 Hogan Rd
Bangor, ME 04401
Web: www.maine.gov/doc/parks/programs/db_search
Phone: 207-941-4014
Size: 3 acres. Location: Off US 1 in the town of Fort Kent. Special Features: Fort served as Maine's northern post during the international border dispute during the Aroostook War and is a National Historic Landmark. It was Maine's first state-owned historic site and was named for Governor Edward Kent. Open Memorial Day-Labor Day.

★2571★ FORT KNOX STATE HISTORIC SITE

711 Fort Knox Rd
Prospect, ME 04981
Web: www.maine.gov/doc/parks/programs/db_search
Phone: 207-469-7719
Size: 124 acres. Location: On Route 174, just off US 1, west of the Waldo-Hancock Bridge. Facilities: Historic fort, interpretive center, picnic facilities. Open May 1-October 31. Activities: Guided tours in summer. Special Features: Fort Knox is New England's finest unmodified specimen of military architecture and features master granite craftsmanship. Maine's largest historic fort as well as the state's first granite fort, it was constructed between 1844 and 1864 but was never fully completed. The fort was strategically located on the narrows of the Penobscot

River to protect the river valley from naval attack and was manned during the Civil and Spanish-American Wars but never saw combat.

★2572★ FORT MCCLARY STATE HISTORIC SITE

28 Oldfields Rd
South Berwick, ME 03908
Web: www.maine.gov/doc/parks/programs/db_search
Phone: 207-384-5160
Size: 27 acres. **Location:** 2.5 miles from US 1 and the Maine Turnpike on Kittery Point Road (Route 103). **Facilities:** Historic structures, picnic tables, restrooms (&). Open Memorial Day-September 30. **Special Features:** Fort McClary was manned during five wars, from the American Revolution through World War I, though it saw little conflict. Its buildings represent several different periods of construction as the fort was upgraded to meet the area's defensive needs, preserving evidence of military history as well as changes in military architecture and technology.

★2573★ FORT O'BRIEN STATE HISTORIC SITE

c/o Bureau of Parks & Lands
106 Hogan Rd
Bangor, ME 04401
Web: www.maine.gov/doc/parks/programs/db_search
Phone: 207-941-4014
Size: 2 acres. **Location:** 5 miles from Machias on Route 92. **Facilities:** Historic structures; picnic tables. Open Memorial Day-Labor Day. **Special Features:** Fort was built in 1775 and destroyed by the British in the same year. It was refortified in 1777 and destroyed once again by the British in 1814. Well-preserved earthworks which overlook Machias Bay were erected for a battery of guns in 1863. The first naval engagement of the Revolution was fought offshore in 1775, five days before the battle at Bunker Hill. Fort is one of a few in Maine that were active during three wars.

★2574★ FORT POINT STATE PARK

c/o Bureau of Parks & Lands
106 Hogan Rd
Bangor, ME 04401
Web: www.maine.gov/doc/parks/programs/db_search
Phone: 207-941-4014
Size: 156 acres. **Location:** Off US 1 in Stockton Springs, on the tip of a peninsula jutting into Penobscot Bay. **Facilities:** Picnic area, remains of historic fort with interpretive panels. Open Memorial Day-Labor Day. **Activities:** Fishing, boating, hiking, bicycling, cross-country skiing (when roads are closed in winter). **Special Features:** Park features more than a mile of rocky shore, a tidal sandbar, and diverse habitat for a variety of plants and animals. It also includes Fort Point State Historic Site (the remains of Fort Pownall) and the Fort Point Light Station, which was built in 1836 as the first river light in Maine.

★2575★ FORT POPHAM STATE HISTORIC SITE

10 Perkins Farm Ln
Phippsburg, ME 04562
Web: www.maine.gov/doc/parks/programs/db_search
Phone: 207-389-1335

Size: 4 acres. **Location:** 15 miles from Bath on Route 209 (2 miles from Popham Beach State Park). **Activities:** Picnicking, surf fishing. **Special Features:** Fort Popham was built solely for the protection of Bath Iron Works and the state capital, Augusta. It was constructed of massive cut granite blocks and is crescent-shaped, with defenses on all sides. Construction began in 1862 for use during the Civil War, but the work stopped in 1869 and the fort was never completed. Modifications were made and it was used again in the Spanish American War and World War I. Historical records conclude that earlier fortifications, probably wooden, had existed here and protected the Kennebec settlements during the Revolutionary War and the War of 1812. It was nearby that the English made their first attempt to colonize New England in 1607. Open Memorial Day-September 30.

★2576★ GRAFTON NOTCH STATE PARK

1941 Bear River Rd
Newry, ME 04261
Web: www.maine.gov/doc/parks/programs/db_search
Phone: 207-824-2912
Size: 3,192 acres. **Location:** Bordering ME 26 between Upton and Newry. **Facilities:** Picnic areas, trails, scenic road. Open May 15-October 15. A main artery snowmobile trail, maintained by a local club, is open in winter. **Activities:** Fishing, hiking, snowmobiling. **Special Features:** Several hiking trails extend through this scenic area at the end of the Mahoosuc Range, including a segment of the Appalachian Trail (see separate entry in national trails section). Sights include Screw Auger Falls, Spruce Meadow, Mother Walker Falls, Old Speck Mountain, and Moose Cave.

★2577★ HOLBROOK ISLAND SANCTUARY

PO Box 35
Brooksville, ME 04617
Web: www.maine.gov/doc/parks/programs/db_search
Phone: 207-326-4012
Size: 1,345 acres. **Location:** Borders Penobscot Bay south of Bucksport in Brooksville. **Facilities:** Picnic tables, trails, area for launching canoes and kayaks. Open year-round. **Activities:** Canoeing/kayaking, hiking, fishing, swimming, cross-country skiing, wildlife watching. **Special Features:** Bordering Penobscot Bay, Holbrook Island Sanctuary is a scenic natural area of upland forests, rocky shores, and an offshore island.

★2578★ JOHN PAUL JONES STATE HISTORIC SITE

c/o Bureau of Parks & Lands
107 State House Stn
Augusta, ME 04333
Web: www.maine.gov/doc/parks/programs/db_search
Phone: 207-384-5160
Size: 2 acres. **Location:** On US 1 in the center of Kittery. **Special Features:** Site is the location of the granite and bronze sculpture established as a memorial to Maine's sailors and soldiers who served during World War I. The park was named for John Paul Jones, the Revolutionary War naval hero who commanded the sloop *Ranger*, which was built and launched from nearby Badger's Island. Open year-round.

9. State Parks

★2579★ KATAHDIN IRON WORKS STATE HISTORIC SITE

c/o Bureau of Parks & Lands
106 Hogan Rd
Bangor, ME 04401
Web: www.maine.gov/doc/parks/programs/db_search
Phone: 207-941-4014
Size: 23 acres. **Location:** 5 miles north of Brownville Junction on ME 11, then 6 miles on gravel road. **Special Features:** Site of a once-thriving iron works (built in 1843) that produced nearly 2,000 tons of raw iron annually for half a century. A blast furnace (originally there were 16) and charcoal kiln are all that remain of the iron works. Two National Natural Landmarks are located nearby: Gulf Hagas, a 3-mile-long gorge that is part of the Appalachain Trail, and The Hermitage, a 35-acre preserve with some of Maine's oldest white pines. Site is open Memorial Day-Labor Day.

★2580★ LAKE SAINT GEORGE STATE PARK

278 Belfast Augusta Rd
Liberty, ME 04949
Web: www.maine.gov/doc/parks/programs/db_search
Phone: 207-589-4255
Size: 358 acres. **Location:** Adjacent to Route 3 in Liberty, 16 miles west of Belfast and 25 miles east of Augusta. **Facilities:** 38 campsites with showers and flush toilets, beach, bathhouse (&), boat and canoe rentals, boat launch, trails, day-use area with picnic tables and playground. Open May 15-October 1. **Activities:** Camping, swimming, boating, fishing, hiking, snowmobiling. **Special Features:** Park is located on the shore of a crystal-clear, spring-fed lake often visited by loons. A groomed snowmobile trail from the park to Frye Mountain Game Management Area connects to several local club trails.

★2581★ LAMOINE STATE PARK

23 State Park Rd
Ellsworth, ME 04605
Web: www.maine.gov/doc/parks/programs/db_search
Phone: 207-667-4778
Size: 55 acres. **Location:** 8 miles southeast of Ellsworth on ME 184. **Facilities:** 61 campsites, hot showers, flush toilets, picnic area, boat launch, fishing pier, playground. **Activities:** Camping, boating, fishing, clamming. **Special Features:** Park is located on Frenchman's Bay, near Acadia National Park (see separate entry in national parks section). This location also provides easy access to Bar Harbor, rockbound islands, and area lighthouses.

★2582★ LILY BAY STATE PARK

13 Myrle's Way
Greenville, ME 04441
Web: www.maine.gov/doc/parks/programs/db_search
Phone: 207-695-2700
Size: 924 acres. **Location:** 8 miles north of Greenville. **Facilities:** 91 campsites, picnic area, playground, trails, 2 boat launch sites with boat slips, swim area. **Activities:** Camping (including group camping), swimming, boating, fishing, hiking, cross-country skiing, snowmobiling, ice fishing, bird watching, wildlife viewing. **Special Features:** Park is located on the shore of Moosehead Lake, the largest lake in New England. In the middle of the lake, Mount Kineo rises 800 feet above the water.

★2583★ MOOSE POINT STATE PARK

310 W Main St
Searsport, ME 04974
Web: www.maine.gov/doc/parks/programs/db_search
Phone: 207-548-2882
Size: 183 acres. **Location:** On US 1 between Belfast and Searsport. **Facilities:** Picnic area, trails. Open Memorial Day-September 30. **Activities:** Hiking, picnicking. **Special Features:** Park offers a panoramic view of Penobscot Bay.

★2584★ MOUNT BLUE STATE PARK

299 Center Hill Rd
Weld, ME 04285
Web: www.maine.gov/doc/parks/programs/db_search
Phone: 207-585-2347
Size: 7,489 acres. **Location:** 14 miles northwest of Wilton off ME 156 in Weld. **Facilities:** 136 tent or trailer campsites (&), walk-in group campsites, Adirondack shelters (for large group use), picnic area, playground, multi-use trails, beach, bathhouse, hot showers (&), restrooms (&), boat launch, canoe rentals, ice rink, amphitheater, nature center. **Activities:** Camping, swimming, boating, canoeing, fishing, hiking, mountain biking, horseback riding, ATV riding, cross-country skiing, snowmobiling, ice skating, wildlife viewing, interpretive programs. **Special Features:** Park offers spectacular views of Mount Blue and surrounding mountains that ring the area. The park is open year-round and offers four-season outdoor recreational opportunities.

★2585★ PEACOCK BEACH STATE PARK

RR 1, Box 2305
Richmond, ME 04357
Web: www.maine.gov/doc/parks/programs/db_search
Phone: 207-582-2813
Size: 93 acres. **Location:** Off Route 201 on Pleasant Pond in Richmond, about 10 miles from Augusta. **Facilities:** Beach. **Activities:** Swimming, picnicking. **Special Features:** A small beach and swimming area with a lifeguard make this a good spot for family outings.

★2586★ PEAKS-KENNY STATE PARK

401 State Park Rd
Dover-Foxcroft, ME 04426
Web: www.maine.gov/doc/parks/programs/db_search
Phone: 207-564-2003
Size: 839 acres. **Location:** 6 miles from Dover-Foxcroft on ME 153. **Facilities:** 56 campsites, flush toilets, hot showers, picnic area, beach, beach and bathhouse, hiking trails, amphitheater. Open May 15-October 1. **Activities:** Camping, swimming, fishing, hiking, nature programs. **Special Features:** Park is located in the mountains on the shore of Sebec Lake.

9. State Parks

★2587★ PENOBSCOT RIVER CORRIDOR
Bureau of Parks & Lands
106 Hogan Rd
Bangor, ME 04401
Web: www.maine.gov/doc/parks/programs/db_search
Phone: 207-941-4014
Special Features: Located in the heart of Maine's undeveloped forest land, the Penobscot River Corridor provides opportunities for remote canoe trips, fishing excursions, and whitewater rafting (provided by commercial operators). It is managed by the state's Bureau of Parks and Lands in cooperation with several landowners. Open year round.

★2588★ POPHAM BEACH STATE PARK
10 Perkins Farm Ln
Phippsburg, ME 04562
Web: www.maine.gov/doc/parks/programs/db_search
Phone: 207-389-1335
Size: 605 acres. **Location:** In Phippsburg, 14 miles south of Bath on ME 209. **Facilities:** Beach, bathhouses, showers, picnic area, trails (&&). Open April 15-October 30. **Activities:** Swimming, surfing, shell collecting, fishing, hiking, wildlife viewing. **Special Features:** Park features a long stretch of sand beach with views of Fox and Wood islands offshore. The Kennebec and Morse rivers border each end of the beach.

★2589★ QUODDY HEAD STATE PARK
973 S Lubec Rd
Lubec, ME 04652
Web: www.maine.gov/doc/parks/programs/db_search
Phone: 207-733-0911
Size: 541 acres. **Location:** 4 miles off ME 189 in Lubec. **Facilities:** Picnic area, trail; visitor center and museum at West Quoddy Head Light adjacent to the park. Park is open May 15-October 15. **Activities:** Hiking, whale watching, fishing. **Special Features:** The easternmost point of land and lighthouse in the United States are adjacent to the park. Originally built in 1808 and then rebuilt in 1858, West Quoddy Head Light and its fog cannon warned mariners of Quoddy's dangerous cliffs, ledges, and Sail Rock, greatly reducing shipwrecks in this foggy area.

★2590★ RANGE PONDS STATE PARK
PO Box 475
Poland Spring, ME 04274
Web: www.maine.gov/doc/parks/programs/db_search
Phone: 207-998-4104
Size: 750 acres. **Location:** Just off Empire Road in Poland. **Facilities:** Picnic area (&), group shelter, playground, ballfield, beach (&), swimming area, boat launch, trails. Open May 15-October 15. **Activities:** Swimming, boating (10 HP limit), canoeing/kayaking, windsurfing, fishing. **Special Features:** Most of the park's activity centers on the waterfront, which is easily accessible because of the smooth, surfaced promenade that parallels the pond for 1,000 feet immediately next to the beach.

★2591★ RANGELEY LAKE STATE PARK
HC 32, Box 5000
Rangeley, ME 04970
Web: www.maine.gov/doc/parks/programs/db_search
Phone: 207-864-3858
Size: 869 acres. **Location:** 30 miles north of Rumford via Route 17. **Facilities:** 50 campsites (&), picnic area, playground, restrooms (&) and hot showers (&), hiking trails, boat launch. Open May 15-October 1. **Activities:** Camping, swimming, boating, fishing, hiking, wildlife viewing, photography, snowmobiling. **Special Features:** Located in an area famous for trout and landlocked salmon fishing, this region of mountains and lakes offers some of the most beautiful scenery in the state.

★2592★ REID STATE PARK
375 Seguinland Rd
Georgetown, ME 04548
Web: www.maine.gov/doc/parks/programs/db_search
Phone: 207-371-2303
Size: 770 acres. **Location:** 13 miles south of Route 1 in Woolwich via Route 127. **Facilities:** Picnic areas, group shelter, 2 snack bars, bathhouses with showers and flush toilets (&), trails. Open year-round. **Activities:** Swimming, fishing. **Special Features:** Park is Maine's first saltwater beach, featuring long, wide sand beaches and large sand dunes, which are rare in Maine. Besides serving as a recreation resource, the beaches here are essential nesting areas for endangered least terns and piping plovers, as well as resting and feeding areas for other shorebirds.

★2593★ ROQUE BLUFFS STATE PARK
145 Schoppee Point Rd
Roque Bluffs, ME 04654
Web: www.maine.gov/doc/parks/programs/db_search
Phone: 207-255-3475
Size: 274 acres. **Location:** 6 miles off US 1 in Roque Bluffs. **Facilities:** Picnic area, pebble beach, freshwater pond, changing rooms, playground. Open May 15-October 1. **Activities:** Swimming, fishing. **Special Features:** Park is a unique day use area with both freshwater and saltwater swimming.

★2594★ SEBAGO LAKE STATE PARK
11 Park Access Rd
Casco, ME 04055
Web: www.maine.gov/doc/parks/programs/db_search
Phone: 207-693-6613
Size: 1,342 acres. **Location:** Off US 302 between Naples and South Casco, 30 miles northwest of Portland. **Facilities:** 250 campsites, picnic area, trails, beaches, bathhouses, hot showers, restrooms, boat ramp, snack bar, amphitheater. Open May 1-October 15. **Activities:** Camping, swimming, boating, sport fishing, hiking, bicycling, cross-country skiing. **Special Features:** Park is located on the north shore of Sebago Lake near the foothills of the White Mountains. In addition to its many recreational opportunities, the clear water of Sebago Lake supplies water for the greater Portland area.

9. State Parks

★2595★ SHACKFORD HEAD STATE PARK
c/o Bureau of Parks & Lands
106 Hogan Ave
Bangor, ME 04401
Web: www.maine.gov/doc/parks/programs/db_search
Phone: 207-941-4014
Size: 87 acres. Location: Off US 1 on ME 190 on Moose Island, in Eastport (the most eastern city in the US). Facilities: Hiking trail, scenic views. Activities: Hiking. Special Features: Park is an undeveloped peninsula with beaches, protected coves, and a bold headland. A trail through the woods to the rocky headland affords beautiful views of Cobscook Bay. Shackford Head Overlook offers a spectacular view of the Canadian islands of Campobello and Grand Manan, New Brunswick. Park is open year-round.

★2596★ SWAN LAKE STATE PARK
100 W Park Ln
Swanville, ME 04915
Web: www.maine.gov/doc/parks/programs/db_search
Phone: 207-525-4404
Size: 67 acres. Location: North of Swanville on ME 141. Facilities: Picnic area (&), group picnic shelter, playground, swimming area, walking trails, changing facilities, toilet facilities (&). Open Memorial Day-Labor Day. Activities: Swimming, fishing. Special Features: Located at the head of Swan Lake, the park is a favorite for family outings.

★2597★ TWO LIGHTS STATE PARK
7 tower Dr
Cape Elizabeth, ME 04107
Web: www.maine.gov/doc/parks/programs/db_search
Phone: 207-799-5871
Size: 41 acres. Location: Off ME 77 in Cape Elizabeth. Facilities: Picnic areas (60 sites), group shelters and sites with horseshoe courts. Open year-round. Activities: Picnicking. Special Features: Park features rocky headlands and sweeping views of Casco Bay and the open Atlantic Ocean. Its name originated from the twin lighthouses located nearby. Built in 1828, one of the lighthouses is now an active, automated light station, visible 17 miles at sea. The other is a private home.

★2598★ VAUGHAN WOODS STATE PARK
28 Oldfields Rd
South Berwick, ME 03908
Web: www.maine.gov/doc/parks/programs/db_search
Phone: 207-384-5160
Size: 250 acres. Location: Just south of South Berwick via Route 236. Facilities: Picnic facilities, hiking trails. Open Memorial Day-Labor Day. Activities: Hiking. Special Features: Park protects stands of old-growth pine and hemlock along scenic Salmon Falls River.

★2599★ WARREN ISLAND STATE PARK
PO Box 105
Lincolnville, ME 04849
Web: www.maine.gov/doc/parks/programs/db_search
Phone: 207-941-4014
Size: 70 acres. Location: In Penobscot Bay off Lincolnville. Accessible by private boat only. Facilities: 10 campsites, 2 Adirondack shelters, fresh drinking water, docking and mooring facilities. Activities: Camping, fishing, boating, hiking. Special Features: Park is a spruce-covered island designed for the boating public, with docking and mooring facilities on the lee side. There is no public ferry transportation to the island. There also are no telephones available on the island. Open Memorial Day-September 15.

★2600★ WHALEBACK SHELL MIDDEN STATE HISTORIC SITE
c/o Damariscotta River Assn
PO Box 333
Damariscotta, ME 04543
Web: www.maine.gov/doc/parks/programs/db_search
Phone: 207-563-1393
Size: 11 acres. Location: Just north of Damariscotta along Business Route 1, near the Round Top Center for the Arts. Facilities: Scenic walking trail (maintained by the Damariscotta River Association). Activities: Hiking, bird watching, nature and archeological study. Special Features: Site features an oyster shell mound created by Native Americans roughly between 2,200 and 1,000 years ago. Named ''Whaleback'' because of its size and shape, the mound (midden) consists mainly of discarded shells along with related cultural materials. Studies of the many bones found among the shells shows that the midden-builders were skilled hunters and fishermen with a well-rounded diet that included large game, different kinds of fish, and wild birds.

★2601★ WOLFE'S NECK WOODS STATE PARK
426 Wolfe's Neck Rd
Freeport, ME 04032
Web: www.maine.gov/doc/parks/programs/db_search
Phone: 207-865-4465
Size: 244 acres. Location: 4.5 miles from US 1 in downtown Freeport. Facilities: Picnic areas, restrooms, hiking trails (&&). Open April-October. Activities: Hiking, nature programs. Special Features: Dedicated to nature appreciation, the park offers interpretive trails through the woods, along the shore of Casco Bay, and beside the Harraseeket River. Its signature residents are the ospreys who nest on nearby Googins Island. Visitors who participate in a guided nature walk can view the baby birds in their nest through a high-powered lens and learn more about the osprey, who mate for life.

Maryland State Parks

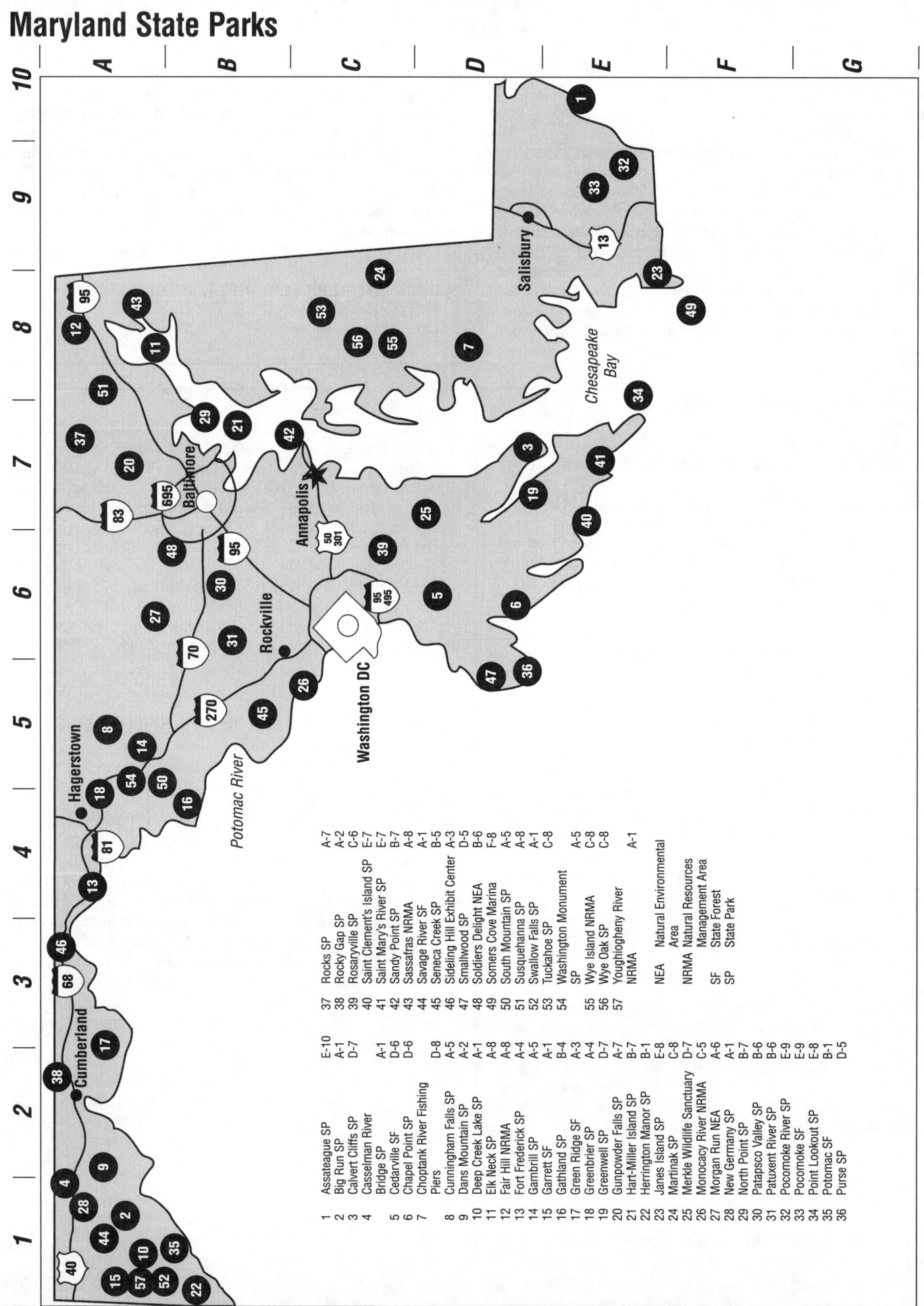

1	Assateague SP	E-10
2	Big Run SP	A-1
3	Calvert Cliffs SP	D-7
4	Casselman River Bridge SP	A-1
5	Cedarville SF	D-6
6	Chapel Point SP	D-6
7	Choptank River Fishing Piers	D-8
8	Cunningham Falls SP	A-5
9	Dans Mountain SP	A-2
10	Deep Creek Lake SP	A-1
11	Elk Neck SP	A-8
12	Fair Hill NRMA	A-8
13	Fort Frederick SP	A-4
14	Gambrill SP	A-5
15	Garrett SF	A-1
16	Gathland SP	B-4
17	Green Ridge SF	A-3
18	Greenbrier SP	A-4
19	Greenwell SP	D-7
20	Gunpowder Falls SP	A-7
21	Hart-Miller Island SP	B-7
22	Herrington Manor SP	B-1
23	Janes Island SP	E-8
24	Martinak SP	C-8
25	Merkle Wildlife Sanctuary	D-7
26	Monocacy River NRMA	C-5
27	Morgan Run NEA	A-6
28	New Germany SP	A-1
29	North Point SP	B-7
30	Patapsco Valley SP	B-6
31	Patuxent River SP	B-6
32	Pocomoke River SP	E-9
33	Pocomoke SF	E-9
34	Point Lookout SP	E-8
35	Potomac SF	B-1
36	Purse SP	D-5
37	Rocks SP	A-7
38	Rocky Gap SP	A-2
39	Rosaryville SP	C-6
40	Saint Clement's Island SP	E-7
41	Saint Mary's River SP	E-7
42	Sandy Point SP	B-7
43	Sassafras NRMA	A-8
44	Savage River SF	A-1
45	Seneca Creek SP	B-5
46	Sideling Hill Exhibit Center	A-3
47	Smallwood SP	D-5
48	Soldiers Delight NEA	B-6
49	Somers Cove Marina	F-8
50	South Mountain SP	A-5
51	Susquehanna SP	A-8
52	Swallow Falls SP	A-1
53	Tuckahoe SP	C-8
54	Washington Monument SP	A-5
55	Wye Island NRMA	C-8
56	Wye Oak SP	C-8
57	Youghiogheny River NRMA	A-1

NEA   Natural Environmental Area
NRMA Natural Resources Management Area
SF   State Forest
SP   State Park

MARYLAND

★2602★ **Maryland Department of Natural Resources**
Forest & Park Service
Tawes State Office Bldg
580 Taylor Ave
Annapolis, MD 21401
(410) 260-8367 - Phone
(800) 830-3974 - Toll-free Park Information
(888) 432-2267 - Toll-free Reservations
(301) 743-5928 - Volunteering
Web: www.dnr.state.md.us/publiclands
Manages state parks, forests, natural environmental and resources management areas, as well as exhibit centers, sanctuaries, state piers, and marinas. The system includes state parks, wildlife management areas, natural environment areas, and state. Offers organized tours and self-guided outdoor recreation programs for hiking, mountain biking, canoeing, kayaking, and other special activities.

★2603★ **Maryland Department of Natural Resources**
Wildlife & Heritage Service
Tawes State Office Bldg
580 Taylor Ave
Annapolis MD 21401
(410) 260-8540 - Phone
(410) 260-8596 - Fax
Web: www.dnr.state.md.us/wildlife
Oversees 41 wildlife management areas (WMAs) totaling 104,000 acres. Primarily managed for hunting, other recreational opportunities on WMA lands include fishing, hiking, bird watching, and nature photography.

Key to campsite classification:

- **Improved campsites** — Picnic table and grill at each site, with potable water located nearby. Centrally located wash houses with toilets, lavatories, and showers with hot water.
- **Unimproved campsites** — Tables and fireplaces at each site, with potable water and comfort station nearby.
- **Primitive campsites** — Portable or pit toilets nearby.
- **Camper cabins** — Basic one-room cabins with beds. Cooking is done outside on fireplace or grill. Wash house is centrally located.
- **Full service cabins** — Separate bedroom and kitchen with electricity, stove, refrigerator, and furniture. Most have bathrooms with showers.
- **Youth group camp** — Reserved for recognized organizations of youth 17 years of age and younger.

★2604★ **ASSATEAGUE STATE PARK**
7307 Stephen Decatur Hwy
Berlin, MD 21811
Web: www.dnr.state.md.us/publiclands/eastern/
assateague.html
Phone: 410-641-2120
Size: 859 acres. **Location:** In Worcester County, 6 miles south of Ocean City Inlet; accessible by Route 50 via MD 611. **Facilities:** 350 improved campsites (some with electric hookups), youth group camping areas, picnic area and shelter, bicycle trail, food concessions, camp store, boat launch, nature center (ᵔᵔ). **Activities:** Camping, boating, canoeing, saltwater fishing, ocean swimming, surfing, crabbing, bicycling, nature programs. **Special Features:** Maryland's only ocean park is a barrier island bordered on the east by two miles of Atlantic Ocean beach and on the west by Sinepuxent Bay. The park's marsh areas have a variety of wildlife, including deer and feral horses.

★2605★ **BIG RUN STATE PARK**
c/o New Germany State Park
349 Headquarters Ln
Grantsville, MD 21536
Web: www.dnr.state.md.us/publiclands/western/bigrun.html
Phone: 301-895-5453
Size: 300 acres. **Location:** In Garrett County, on the northern tip of the Savage River Reservoir, 16 miles from exit 24 off I-68. **Facilities:** 30 unimproved campsites (ᵔ), youth group camping area, picnic area and shelters, hiking trail, boat launch ramps nearby. **Activities:** Camping, flatwater canoeing, freshwater fishing, hiking. **Special Features:** Park is surrounded by Savage River State Forest with access to additional fishing, camping, hiking, and hunting opportunities. Big Run serves as trailhead for the 6-mile Monroe Run Trail.

★2606★ **CALVERT CLIFFS STATE PARK**
c/o Smallwood State Park
2750 Sweden Point Rd
Marbury, MD 20658
Web: www.dnr.state.md.us/publiclands/southern/
calvertcliffs.html
Phone: 301-743-7613
Size: 1,313 acres. **Location:** In Calvert County, 14 miles south of Prince Frederick on MD routes 2 and 4. **Facilities:** 6 youth group camping areas (open Apr 24-Oct 30), picnic tables, pavilion, playground (ᵔ), foot trails (13 miles). **Activities:** Youth group camping, fishing, hiking, bicycling (on service road only), hunting. **Special Features:** Calvert Cliffs, which dominate the shoreline of Chesapeake Bay for 30 miles in Calvert County, were formed over 15 million years ago, when all of southern Maryland was covered by a shallow sea. More than 600 species of fossils have been identified from these cliffs, with the teeth of various species of shark the most abundant. Visitors may

hunt for fossils on the open beach area and keep what they find, but access to the cliffs is not permitted due to their constant erosion.

★2607★ CASSELMAN RIVER BRIDGE STATE PARK
c/o New Germany State Park
349 Headquarters Ln
Grantsville, MD 21536
Web: www.dnr.state.md.us/publiclands/western/
    casselman.html
Phone: 301-895-5453
Size: 4 acres. **Location:** In Garrett County, east of Grantsville, on US 40. **Facilities:** Historic structure, picnic area. **Activities:** Freshwater fishing. **Special Features:** The 80-foot, single-span stone arch bridge once served the old National Road, which linked Cumberland, Maryland with the Ohio River. It was the largest bridge of its type at the time of its construction (1813-1814).

★2608★ CEDARVILLE STATE FOREST
10201 Bee Oak Rd
Brandywine, MD 20613
Web: www.dnr.state.md.us/publiclands/southern/
    cedarville.html
Phone: 301-888-1410
Size: 3,697 acres. **Location:** In Prince George and Charles counties, 25 miles south of Washington, DC. Reached via Cedarville Road off US 301. **Facilities:** Family camping sites (April 29-Sept 6), youth group camping area, picnic area, 2 pavilions, comfort stations (&), 4-acre stocked pond, multiuse trails (19.5 miles). **Activities:** Camping, freshwater fishing, hiking, bicycling, horseback riding, hunting, special programs. **Special Features:** A visitor center at the state's only warmwater fish hatchery is open during the summer. The headwaters of the Zekiah Swamp are located in Cedarville, and the swamp is a haven for wildlife.

★2609★ CHAPEL POINT STATE PARK
c/o Smallwood State Park
2750 Sweden Point Rd
Marbury, MD 20658
Web: www.dnr.state.md.us/publiclands/southern/
    chapelpoint.html
Phone: 301-743-7613
Size: 600 acres. **Location:** In southern Charles County, about 5 miles south of La Plata. **Facilities:** Paddle-in campsite (available by permit only). **Activities:** Fishing, hunting. **Special Features:** Located on the Port Tobacco River, a tributary of the Potomac, the park is an undeveloped multi-use site.

★2610★ CHOPTANK RIVER FISHING PIERS
29761 Bolingbroke Point Dr
Trappe, MD 21673
Web: www.dnr.state.md.us/publiclands/eastern/
    choptankpier.html
Phone: 410-820-1668
Size: 24 acres. **Location:** Adjacent to MD 50 at the Frederick

C Malkus Bridge near Cambridge. A 0.5-mile pier extends south from Talbot County and a 0.75-mile pier extends north from Dorchester County. **Facilities:** Lighted fishing piers (&). **Activities:** Saltwater fishing and crabbing; also picnicking, bicycling, walking, jogging, sunbathing. **Special Features:** The piers are the two ends of an old bridge over the Choptank River. The Talbot County side includes 25 acres of land extending upriver from the pier, with a walking path along the Choptank River and Bolingbroke Creek. The piers are open for fishing 24 hours a day year round.

★2611★ CUNNINGHAM FALLS STATE PARK
14039 Catoctin Hollow Rd
Thurmont, MD 21788
Web: www.dnr.state.md.us/publiclands/western/
    cunninghamfalls.html
Phone: 301-271-7574
Size: 4,946 acres. **Location:** In Frederick County, 15 miles north of Frederick. Park has 2 main developed areas: the Manor Area is located on the west side of US 15 at Thurmont; the William Houck Area is 3 miles west of Thurmont, off Route 77, on Catoctin Hollow Road. **Facilities:** 171 improved campsites (some with electric hookups), 9 camper cabins, bathhouses with showers and flush toilets, camp store, picnic areas, shelter, food concession, hiking trails, fishing pier (&), boat launch, canoe and rowboat rental, playground, historic site (&). **Activities:** Camping, boating, flatwater canoeing, freshwater fishing, swimming, hiking, hunting, cross-country skiing. **Special Features:** Cunningham Falls, for which the park is named, is a 78-foot cascading waterfall in a rocky gorge, located in the Houck Area of the park. Of historic interest is the Catoctin Iron Furnace, which operated from 1776 until 1903. A segment of the 2,144-mile Appalachian National Scenic Trail passes through the park (see entry in national trails section).

★2612★ DANS MOUNTAIN STATE PARK
c/o Rocky Gap State Park
12500 Pleasant Valley Rd
Flintstone, MD 21530
Web: www.dnr.state.md.us/publiclands/western/
    dansmountain.html
Phone: 301-722-1480
Size: 481 acres. **Location:** In Allegany County, 9 miles south of Frostburg, east of MD 36. **Facilities:** Stocked fishing pond, picnic areas, 4 picnic shelters, hiking trails, Olympic-size swimming pool, waterslide, bathhouse, playground, food concession, scenic overlook (&&). **Activities:** Freshwater fishing, swimming, hiking, nature programs. **Special Features:** Located on a 16-mile long mountain, Park is a seasonal day-use facility. Dan's Rock Overlook, located nearby, affords a panoramic view of the surrounding region from a height of 2,898 feet.

★2613★ DEEP CREEK LAKE STATE PARK &
     NATURAL RESOURCES MANAGEMENT AREA
898 State Park Rd
Swanton, MD 21561
Web: www.dnr.state.md.us/publiclands/western/
    deepcreeklake.html
Phone: 301-387-5563; **Fax:** 301-387-4462

Size: 1,818 acres. Location: In Garrett County, 10 miles northeast of Oakland on the east side of Deep Creek Lake and 2 miles east of Thayerville off US 219. Facilities: 112 improved campsites (26 with electric hookups; &), 2 mini-camper cabins, a Yurt, and an Adirondck-style shelter, hot showers, restrooms (&), picnic areas and shelters, playgrounds, hiking trails, snowmobile trails, fishing piers (&), boat launch, boat rentals, educational/interpretive center. Activities: Camping, boating, flatwater canoeing, freshwater fishing, swimming, hiking, mountain biking, cross-country skiing, snowmobiling, hunting, interpretive programs. Special Features: Park features 1 mile of shoreline on the state's largest manmade lake, which has a 6-square-mile surface. The park's Discovery Center showcases the natural resources of western Maryland and the cultural and historical heritage that changed a former logging and coal-mining region into a popular vacation destination.

★2614★ ELK NECK STATE PARK

4395 Turkey Point Rd
North East, MD 21901
Web: www.dnr.state.md.us/publiclands/central/elkneck.html
Phone: 410-287-5333

Size: 2,188 acres. Location: In Cecil County, 9 miles south of North East, on MD 272. Facilities: 270 improved campsites (some with full hookups), 8 cabins, 6 camper cabins, 6 youth group camps, camp store, picnic area and shelters, hiking trails, mountain bike trails, boat launch, boat rentals, food concession, historic site (lighthouse), visitor center (&&). Activities: Camping, boating, flatwater canoeing, fishing, swimming, hiking, mountain biking, hunting. Special Features: Park is located on the peninsula formed by the Northeast and Elk rivers and the Chesapeake Bay. The site presents a great variety of topography, from sandy beaches and marshlands to heavily wooded bluffs.

★2615★ FAIR HILL NATURAL RESOURCES MANAGEMENT AREA

300 Tawes Dr
Elkton, MD 21921
Web: www.dnr.state.md.us/publiclands/central/fairhill.html
Phone: 410-398-1246

Size: 5,613 acres. Location: In Cecil County, at the intersections of Routes 273 and 213. Bordered by Pennsylvania to the north and less than 0.5 miles west of Delaware. Facilities: Fairgrounds, race track, picnic areas and shelters, multi-use trails (75 miles), stables, nature center, activity hall, restrooms (&). Activities: Horse races, fishing, hiking, bicycling, horseback riding, cross-country skiing, hunting. Special Features: Fair Hill's attractions include a turf course, where steeplechase, timber course, and flat races are held with pari-mutuel wagering. The fairgrounds host the annual Cecil County Fair. The area's open expanses of land are composed of pristine fields and woodlands and offer a diverse range of outdoor recreational activities.

★2616★ FORT FREDERICK STATE PARK

11100 Fort Frederick Rd
Big Pool, MD 21711
Web: www.dnr.state.md.us/publiclands/western/
    fortfrederick.html
Phone: 301-842-2155

Size: 585 acres. Location: In Washington County, 18 miles west of Hagerstown off I-70 via MD 56. Facilities: 29 unimproved campsites (&), youth group camping area, camp store (&), picnic area and shelters (&), playground, hiking trail, boat launch, boat rental, concessions, visitor center (&), historic fort and related displays. Activities: Camping, boating, flatwater canoeing, freshwater fishing, hiking, cross-country skiing, living history programs. Special Features: Fort Frederick was erected in 1756, during the French and Indian War, and is considered the best preserved pre-Revolutionary stone fort in the country. The fort's stone wall and two barracks have been restored to their 1758 appearance. Military reenactments are held annually. The 23-mile Western Maryland Rail Trail begins one-half mile west of the park.

★2617★ GAMBRILL STATE PARK

c/o Cunningham Falls State Park
14039 Catoctin Hollow Rd
Thurmont, MD 21702
Web: www.dnr.state.md.us/publiclands/western/gambrill.html
Phone: 301-271-7574

Size: 1,137 acres. Location: In Frederick County, 6 miles northwest of Frederick, off I-70. Facilities: 28 improved campsites (&), 4 camper cabins, picnic area and shelters (&), playground, restrooms, hiking and nature trails (13 miles), nature center (&), scenic overlooks. Activities: Camping, freshwater fishing, hiking, mountain biking, interpretive programs. Special Features: Park is located on Catoctin Mountain. Three native stone overlooks located on the 1600-foot summit of High Knob, midway between the Mason-Dixon Line and the Potomac River, afford excellent views of the surrounding area.

★2618★ GARRETT STATE FOREST

1431 Potomac Camp Rd
Oakland, MD 21550
Web: www.dnr.state.md.us/publiclands/western/garrett.html
Phone: 301-334-2038

Size: 7,066 acres. Location: In Garrett County, 5 miles northwest of Oakland, off US 219. Facilities: 17 primitive campsites, primitive group and shelter sites, trails. Activities: Camping, freshwater fishing, hunting, hiking, horseback riding, bicycling, cross-country skiing, snowmobiling, ATV riding, birding. Special Features: In 1906, a portion of this forest was given to the state, which became the foundation of Maryland's present public lands system.

★2619★ GATHLAND STATE PARK

c/o Greenbrier State Park
21843 National Pike
Boonsboro, MD 21713
Web: www.dnr.state.md.us/publiclands/western/gathland.html
Phone: 301-791-4767

Size: 140 acres. Location: In Washington and Frederick counties, 1 mile west of Burkittsville, off MD 17. Facilities: Picnic area and shelter (&), hiking trails, visitor center, historic sites, museum (&). Activities: Hiking, interpretive programs. Special Features: Park was once the mountain home of George Alfred Townsend, a Civil War journalist and reporter. Site includes a unique collection of buildings and structures Townsend designed and constructed, some of which have been restored. Attractions include a large stone monument dedicated to war correspondents and a visitor center containing some of Townsend's writings and papers. The Appalachian National Scenic Trail passes through the park (see entry in national trails section). Park is also the site of the first major battle of the Civil War fought in Maryland.

★2620★ GREEN RIDGE STATE FOREST

28700 Headquarters Dr NE
Flintstone, MD 21530
Web: www.dnr.state.md.us/publiclands/western/
greenridge.html
Phone: 301-478-3124
Size: 44,000 acres. Location: In eastern Allegany County, 22 miles east of Cumberland, exit 64 off I-68. Facilities: 100 primitive campsites, 7 group camping sites, adirondack shelters, horse areas, picnic facilities, extensive trails, stocked fishing area, boat launches, shooting range (&), visitor center (&), scenic overlooks. Activities: Camping, boating, flatwater canoeing, freshwater fishing, hiking, mountain biking, horseback riding, hunting, snowmobiling, ATV riding, nature tourism programs. Special Features: Forest is located in the Ridge and Valley Province of the Allegheny Mountain chain and includes Town Hill, Green Ridge, and Polish Mountains. Several overlooks offer magnificent views. The forest features a challenging single-track 11.6-mile bike loop, suitable for intermediate to advanced riders. It winds up and down the ridges and valleys of the forest and includes technical obstacles such as stream crossings, fallen trees, steep turns, and sustained climbs. Four "easy-out" routes are incorporated into the trail, allowing riders to shorten their ride and return to the start/finish point.

★2621★ GREENBRIER STATE PARK

21843 National Pike
Boonsboro, MD 21713
Web: www.dnr.state.md.us/publiclands/western/
greenbrier.html
Phone: 301-791-4767
Size: 1,288 acres. Location: In Washington County, 10 miles east of Hagerstown, on US 40. Accessible from I-70 via the Myersville Interchange. Facilities: 165 improved campsites (some with electric hookups; &), bathhouses with hot showers, picnic areas (&), 4 reservable lakefront gazebos, hiking trails, mountain bike trails, 42-acre lake, boat launch, boat rentals, camp store, food concessions, playgrounds, visitor center (&). Activities: Camping, boating, flatwater canoeing, freshwater fishing, swimming, hiking, mountain biking, hunting, cross-country skiing. Special Features: Park is located in the Appalachian Mountains, one of the earth's oldest mountain ranges. Rock outcrops and "mountain stones" found at Greenbrier reveal much about earth's geologic history. The Appalachian National Scenic Trail (see entry in national trails section) enters the eastern edge of the park on Bartman's Hill.

★2622★ GREENWELL STATE PARK

25420 Rosedale Manor Ln
Hollywood, MD 20636
Web: www.dnr.state.md.us/publiclands/southern/
greenwell.html
Phone: 301-373-9775
Size: 596 acres. Location: In Saint Mary's County, on Steerhorn Neck Road, 3 miles off MD 235 in Hollywood, on MD 245. Facilities: Picnic area and pavilion, trails (6 miles), 191-foot fishing pier (&), rental lodge. Activities: Fishing, canoeing, swimming, hiking, horseback riding, bicycling, hunting. Special Features: Situated along the Patuxent River, the park features Rosedale Manor House, chapel, and gardens, which can be reserved for special events.

★2623★ GUNPOWDER FALLS STATE PARK

2813 Jerusalem Rd
PO Box 480
Kingsville, MD 21087
Web: www.dnr.state.md.us/publiclands/central/
gunpowder.html
Phone: 410-592-2897
Size: 18,500 acres. Location: Between Harford and Baltimore counties, in the Gunpowder River Valley. Facilities: Youth group camps, 2 camper cabins, rental cottage, picnic areas and shelters, playgrounds, trails (100 miles), swimming beach, marina, boat launch, boat rentals, food concessions, visitor center, museum (&&). Activities: Boating, flatwater and whitewater canoeing, tubing, windsurfing, freshwater and saltwater fishing, swimming, hiking, bicycling, horseback riding, hunting, cross-country skiing, interpretive programs. Special Features: Park areas include the Hereford Area, where there is a vacation rental cottage and world-class trout fishing; the 21-mile Northern Central Railroad Trail for hiking and bicycling; the Hammerman Area, which has swimming beaches and watercraft rentals; Dundee Creek Marina, which offers boat and slip rentals as well as boat launching in the Gunpowder River; and the Central Area, which includes the historic village of Jerusalem and has Jerusalem Mill as the park headquarters and visitor center. Gunpowder Falls is primarily a day-use park.

★2624★ HART-MILLER ISLAND STATE PARK

c/o Gunpowder Falls State Park
2813 Jerusalem Rd PO Box 480
Kingsville, MD 21087
Web: www.dnr.state.md.us/publiclands/central/hartmiller.html
Phone: 410-592-2897
Size: 244 acres. Location: In Baltimore County, in the Chesapeake Bay, near the mouth of Middle River. Accessible only by boat. Facilities: 22 primitive campsites, picnic area, hiking trails. Activities: Camping, saltwater fishing, swimming, hiking. Special Features: The western shore of the island offers safe mooring and access to a 3,000-foot sandy beach.

★2625★ HERRINGTON MANOR STATE PARK

222 Herrington Ln
Oakland, MD 21550
Web: www.dnr.state.md.us/publiclands/western/
herringtonmanor.html
Phone: 301-334-9180

Size: 365 acres. **Location:** In Garrett County, 5 miles northwest of Oakland. **Facilities:** 20 log cabins (2 ⑤), picnic areas (⑤) and shelters, trails, 53-acre lake, fishing pier (⑤), boat launch, boat rentals, ski, snowshoe, and sled rentals, food concession (⑤), tennis and volleyball courts, visitor center (⑤). **Activities:** Boating (rowboats, canoes, paddleboats), freshwater fishing, swimming, hiking, mountain biking, tennis, volleyball, cross-country skiing, interpretive programs. **Special Features:** Park is located within Garrett State Forest and offers miles of wilderness hiking and cross-country ski trails. Special events such as maple syrup demonstrations and apple butter making are held throughout the year.

★2626★ JANES ISLAND STATE PARK

26280 Alfred Lawson Dr
Crisfield, MD 21817
Web: www.dnr.state.md.us/publiclands/eastern/
  janesisland.html
Phone: 410-968-1565; **Fax:** 410-968-2515
Size: 3,147 acres. **Location:** In Somerset County, near Crisfield via MD 13 to MD 413 in Westover, then 11 miles to Plantation Road, turn right, then 1.5 miles to park entrance. **Facilities:** 104 improved campsites (tent or vehicle campers; 5 sites ⑤), 4 log cabins (1 ⑤), 5 camper cabins, picnic area, 2 pavilions, canoe trail, boat launch, canoe/kayak rentals, camp store, restrooms (⑤), nature/environmental education center (⑤), conference center. **Activities:** Camping, canoeing, saltwater fishing, crabbing, swimming, hiking, hunting, interpretive programs. **Special Features:** Almost completely surrounded by the waters of the Chesapeake Bay and its inlets, the park includes the developed mainland section (with cabins and camping areas) and an island accessible only by boat. Most of the waterways are protected from wind and current, providing ideal conditions for the novice as well as the experienced canoeist.

★2627★ MARTINAK STATE PARK

137 Deep Shore Rd
Denton, MD 21629
Web: www.dnr.state.md.us/publiclands/eastern/martinak.html
Phone: 410-820-1668
Size: 107 acres. **Location:** In Caroline County, 2 miles south of Denton, off MD 404. **Facilities:** 63 improved campsites (30 with electric hookups; some sites ⑤), bathhouse, 4 camper cabins, 1 full-service cabin, picnic area and shelters (⑤), playground, restrooms, hiking trails, boat launch, fishing pier, canoe rental, nature center (⑤). **Activities:** Camping, boating, flatwater canoeing, freshwater fishing, swimming, hiking, interpretive programs. **Special Features:** Bordered by the Choptank River and Watts Creek, the park is situated in hardwood and pine forests that support a wide variety of wildlife.

★2628★ MERKLE WILDLIFE SANCTUARY

11704 Fenno Rd
Upper Marlboro, MD 20772
Web: www.dnr.state.md.us/publiclands/southern/merkle.html
Phone: 301-888-1410
Size: 1,670 acres. **Location:** In Prince George's County; off US 301, follow signs east on Croom Road. **Facilities:** Visitor center (⑤) with exhibits and children's Discovery Room; trails. **Activities:** Bird watching, fishing, hiking, bicycling, horseback riding. **Special Features:** Sanctuary is the wintering ground for thousands of Canada geese, who arrive in mid-October and stay until late February or early March. About 100 geese stay there year round. The sanctuary also offers habitat to other birds and wildlife. In the summer, ospreys nest near the Visitor Center, and hummingbirds, finches, and purple martins are abundant.

★2629★ MONOCACY RIVER NATURAL RESOURCES MANAGEMENT AREA

c/o Seneca Creek State Park
11950 Clopper Rd
Gaithersburg, MD 20878
Web: www.dnr.state.md.us/publiclands/central/
  monocacy.html
Phone: 301-924-2127
Size: 1,800 acres. **Location:** Frederick County, near Dickerson. Access at Park Mills Road and Rt 28 where the roads cross the Monocacy River. **Facilities:** Boat ramp, unmarked trails. **Activities:** Hunting (in season), fishing, hiking, horseback riding. **Special Features:** Site consists of natural areas and farmlands.

★2630★ MORGAN RUN NATURAL ENVIRONMENT AREA

c/o Patapsco Valley State Park
8020 Baltimore National Pike
Ellicott City, MD 21043
Web: www.dnr.state.md.us/publiclands/central/
  morganrun.html
Phone: 410-461-5005
Size: 1,500 acres. **Location:** Carroll County, off MD 97, right on Bartholow Road, 0.1 miles to left on Jim Bowers Road, then left on Ben Rose Lane. **Facilities:** Trails, shooting range, fishing platform (⑤). **Activities:** Fishing, hiking, horseback riding, cross-country skiing, bow and muzzleloader hunting. **Special Features:** Morgan Run is a catch-and-release trout stream.

★2631★ NEW GERMANY STATE PARK

349 Headquarters Ln
Grantsville, MD 21536
Web: www.dnr.state.md.us/publiclands/western/
  newgermany.html
Phone: 301-895-5453
Size: 455 acres. **Location:** In Garrett County, 5 miles south of Grantsville, off I-68. **Facilities:** 37 improved campsites (⑤), 11 camper cabins, bathhouses with hot showers, camp store, restrooms (⑤), picnic area and shelters (⑤), hiking trails, boat launch, boat rentals (rowboats, kayaks, paddleboats, surf bikes), nature center. **Activities:** Camping, boating, flatwater canoeing, freshwater fishing, swimming, hiking, mountain biking (but not when trails have snow), cross-country skiing, interpretive programs. **Special Features:** Park lies within the boundaries of Savage River State Forest (see separate entry). It was built on the site of a former milling center on the Savage River and features a 13-acre lake.

★2632★ NORTH POINT STATE PARK

c/o Gunpowder Falls State Park
2813 Jerusalem Rd PO Box 480
Kingsville, MD 21087
Web: www.dnr.state.md.us/publiclands/central/
northpoint.html
Phone: 410-592-2897
Size: 1,310 acres. Location: In Baltimore County, off Old North Point Road in Edgemere. Facilities: Picnic area and shelter (&), trails, wading beach, fishing pier, historic interest, visitor center. Activities: Flatwater canoeing, saltwater fishing, hiking, bicycling. Special Features: Park is located on the shores of Chesapeake Bay and is the site of the historical Bay Shore Amusement Park, which operated here from 1906-1947. The original trolley shelter and fountain have been restored, and the trolley shelter can be reserved for special events. Another historic feature here is The Defenders' Trail, which was used during the War of 1812 and passes through the park.

★2633★ PATAPSCO VALLEY STATE PARK

8020 Baltimore National Pike
Ellicott City, MD 21043
Web: www.dnr.state.md.us/publiclands/central/
patapscovalley.html
Phone: 410-461-5005
Size: 14,500 acres. Location: In Baltimore, Howard, Carroll, and Anne Arundel counties, on the western outskirts of Baltimore City. Patapsco has five separate recreation areas: Avalon-Glenn Artney-Orange Grove Area, Hilton Area, Hollofield Area, Pickall Area, and McKeldin Area. Facilities: 73 improved campsites with electrical hookups, 14 family campsites (tent only, no electricity), 6 camper cabins, youth group camping, picnic areas and shelters, hiking, mountain biking, and equestrian trails, self-guiding nature trails, ball fields, playgrounds, disc golf course, historic sites, visitor center (&&). Activities: Camping, canoeing, freshwater fishing, hiking, horseback riding, mountain biking, nature walks, cross-country skiing, hunting, interpretive programs. Special Features: Park extends along 32 miles of the Patapsco River and is nationally known for its trail opportunities and scenery. Among its many features are the world's longest multiple-arched stone railroad bridge, a 300-foot suspension bridge over the river, and the Avalon Visitor Center with exhibits covering 300 years of local history.

★2634★ PATUXENT RIVER STATE PARK

c/o Seneca Creek State Park
11950 Clopper Rd
Gaithersburg, MD 20878
Web: www.dnr.state.md.us/publiclands/central/
patuxentriver.html
Phone: 301-924-2127
Size: 14,752 acres. Location: On Howard/Montgomery county line, along the Patuxent River Valley between MD routes 27 and 97; accessible from Baltimore via I-70 west. Facilities: Hiking and equestrian trails (unmarked). Activities: Flatwater canoeing, freshwater fishing, hiking, horseback riding, hunting, cross-country skiing. Special Features: Park is an undeveloped stream valley, a portion of which is designated as a State Wildlands Area. Trails lead to stream crossings along the length of the river.

★2635★ POCOMOKE RIVER STATE PARK

3461 Worcester Hwy
Snow Hill, MD 21863
Web: www.dnr.state.md.us/publiclands/eastern/
pocomokeriver.html
Phone: 410-632-2566
Size: 914 acres. Location: Along the banks of the Pocomoke River, in two separate sections: Shad Landing (544 acres), 3.5 miles south of Snow Hill near Rt 113; and Milburn Landing (370 acres), 7 miles northeast of Pocomoke City via Rt 364 or 12, within Pocomoke State Forest. Facilities: 223 improved campsites (some with electric hookups), hot showers, flush toilets, 12 mini-cabins, youth group camping sites, camp store, picnic areas and shelters, playgrounds, comfort stations, multiuse trails, swimming pool, fishing piers, marina, boat launch, boat rental (rowboats and canoes), food concession, visitor center (&&). Activities: Camping, boating, flatwater canoeing, freshwater fishing, swimming, hiking, bicycling, interpretive programs. Special Features: The park's combination of swamp and upland offers a great variety of plant and animal life, including white dogwood and pink laurel in the spring, river otters and bald eagles, and more than 50 species of fish. The Shad Landing area was a historically important link in a chain of refuges for runaway slaves seeking freedom in the north.

★2636★ POCOMOKE STATE FOREST

6572 Snow Hill Rd
Snow Hill, MD 21863
Web: www.dnr.state.md.us/publiclands/eastern/
pocomokeforest.html
Phone: 410-632-3732
Size: 14,753 acres. Location: In Worcester County, between Snow Hill and Pocomoke City. Facilities: Trails. Activities: Fishing, flatwater canoeing, hiking, mountain biking, horseback riding, off-road vehicle riding (motorcycles and ATVs). Special Features: Forest is famous for its stand of loblolly pine trees. Cypress swamps border the Pocomoke River and the nearby waters provide good fishing. Five areas in the forest, including the swamp, are designated State Wildlands Areas.

★2637★ POINT LOOKOUT STATE PARK

11175 Point Lookout Rd
Scotland, MD 20687
Web: www.dnr.state.md.us/publiclands/southern/
pointlookout.html
Phone: 301-872-5688; Fax: 301-872-5084
Size: 1,042 acres. Location: On the southern tip of Saint Mary's County, at the junction of the Potomac River and the Chesapeake Bay. Reached by MD 5. Facilities: 143 improved campsites (27 with electric hookups, 26 with full hookups; some sites &), 6 camper cabins, cottage, youth group camp, camp store, showers, restrooms, picnic areas (&), pavilion, playground, hiking trails, fishing pier (&), boat launch, boat rentals, museum, nature center, visitor center. Activities: Camping, boating, flatwater canoeing, windsurfing, saltwater fishing, swimming, hiking, bicycling, interpretive programs. Special Features: The park's peaceful surroundings belie its history as the site of a prison camp that held as many as 52,264 Confederate soldiers during the Civil War. Park facilities include a Civil War Museum

as well as the Marshland Nature Center. In 2006, the park sustained significant damage from Tropical Storm Ernesto. Though most facilities were reopened during the 2006 season, it is recommended that visitors contact the park to check on the status prior to making travel plans.

★2638★ POTOMAC STATE FOREST

1431 Potomac Camp Rd
Oakland, MD 21550
Web: www.dnr.state.md.us/publiclands/western/
    potomacforest.html
Phone: 301-334-2038
Size: 11,535 acres. **Location:** In southeastern Garrett County, off MD 135. **Facilities:** 22 primitive campsites, 1 primitive group camping site and 1 shelter site, picnic facilities, hiking trails, equestrian trails. **Activities:** Camping, freshwater fishing, hunting, hiking, bicycling, horseback riding, cross-country skiing, snowmobiling, ATV riding. **Special Features:** The headwaters of the Potomac River originate here in this rugged mountain forest. It also contains the highest point in any Maryland state forest, Backbone Mountain, with an elevation of 3,220 feet.

★2639★ PURSE STATE PARK

c/o Smallwood State Park
2750 Sweden Point Rd
Marbury, MD 20658
Web: www.dnr.state.md.us/publiclands/southern/purse.html
Phone: 301-743-7613
Size: 79 acres. **Location:** On Route 224; follow Rt 301 south to Rt 225 west. At the intersection of routes 225 and 224, go left about 15 miles to park. **Facilities:** Undeveloped. **Activities:** Hunting, fishing, bird watching, fossil hunting. **Special Features:** Park is located on the Potomac River, on Wade's Bay, and has no developed public facilities.

★2640★ ROCKS STATE PARK

3318 Rocks Chrome Hill Rd
Jarrettsville, MD 21084
Web: www.dnr.state.md.us/publiclands/central/rocks.html
Phone: 410-557-7994
Size: 855 acres. **Location:** In Harford County, 30 miles north of Baltimore and 8 miles northwest of Bel Air on MD 24. **Facilities:** Picnic areas (&) with shelters, playgrounds, and restroom facilities, hiking trails. **Activities:** Canoeing, tubing, freshwater fishing, rock climbing, rapelling, hiking, hunting. **Special Features:** Forests and boulders flank Deer Creek, and a natural 190-foot outcrop above the creek, called the King and Queen Seat, was once a ceremonial gathering place of the Susquehannock Nation.

★2641★ ROCKY GAP STATE PARK

12500 Pleasant Valley Rd
Flintstone, MD 21530
Web: www.dnr.state.md.us/publiclands/western/
    rockygap.html
Phone: 301-722-1480
Size: 3,400 acres. **Location:** In Allegany County, 6 miles east of Cumberland on I-68, exit 50. **Facilities:** 278 improved campsites (30 with electric hookups; some sites &), bathhouses, family group campsite with mini-cabin, 3 youth group camping areas, 10 mini-cabins, 3-bedroom chalet, picnic area and shelters (&), hiking trails, swimming beaches, fishing piers (&), boat ramp, boat rentals (canoes, kayaks, rowboats, paddle boats), amphitheater (&; available for rental), camp store, food concessions, game room, nature center, aviary; also located at the park is a 220-room lodge with meeting rooms, full-service restaurant and lounge, private dining room, fitness room, swimming pool, tennis and volleyball courts, gazebo dock, and18-hole golf course. **Activities:** Camping, boating (electric motors only), flatwater canoeing, freshwater fishing, swimming, hiking, hunting, interpretive programs. **Special Features:** Park is surrounded by rugged mountains and features 243-acre Lake Habeeb, where boating is permitted 24 hours a day. The lake is fed by Rocky Gap Run, which winds through a mile-long gorge with sheer cliffs, overlooks, and a hemlock forest dense with rhododendron. The Rocky Gap Lodge and Golf Resort is situated in the heart of the park.

★2642★ ROSARYVILLE STATE PARK

8714 Rosaryville Rd
Upper Marlboro, MD 20772
Web: www.dnr.state.md.us/publiclands/southern/
    rosaryville.html
Phone: 301-856-9656
Size: 982 acres. **Location:** In Prince George's County, 4 miles south of Upper Marlboro off US 301. **Facilities:** Historic mansion, 2 rental pavilions, restroom, day-use trails. **Activities:** Hiking, bicycling, horseback riding. **Special Features:** This day-use park is the site of Mount Airy Mansion Plantation, one of the oldest Calvert mansions in Maryland and rich in history. The oldest section of the mansion was built in the 1600s, and in 1774 George Washington attended his stepson's wedding there. The mansion can be rented for special events.

★2643★ SAINT CLEMENT'S ISLAND STATE PARK

c/o Point Lookout State Park
11175 Point Lookout Rd
Scotland, MD 20687
Web: www.dnr.state.md.us/publiclands/southern/
    stclements.html
Phone: 301-872-5688
Size: 40 acres. **Location:** On the Potomac River, near Saint Clement's and Breton bays. Accessible only by boat. **Facilities:** Picnic areas and shelters, hiking trails, portajohn. **Activities:** Saltwater fishing, hiking, hunting. Boat tours to the island are offered on week-ends by the Potomac River Museum. **Special Features:** On March 25, 1634, the first English settlers under the Baltimore proprietorship landed on Saint Clement's Island in the *Ark* and the *Dove*. The park contains a memorial cross dedicated to the memory of the first Marylanders.

9. State Parks

★2644★ SAINT MARY'S RIVER STATE PARK

c/o Point Lookout State Park
11175 Point Lookout Rd
Scotland, MD 20687
Web: www.dnr.state.md.us/publiclands/southern/
stmarysriver.html
Phone: 301-872-5688
Size: 2,450 acres. **Location:** 3 miles north of Great Mills, off MD 5 on Camp Cosoma Road (24 miles north of Point Lookout State Park). **Facilities:** Picnic tables, playground, boat launch ramps, trail (7.5 miles), comfort station. **Activities:** Boating (electric motors only), flatwater canoeing, freshwater fishing, hiking, mountain biking, horseback riding, hunting. **Special Features:** Park consists of 2 main areas: Site 1 holds the 250-acre Saint Mary's Lake (a trophy bass lake); Site 2 covers about 2,200 acres and is a wildlands area and a managed hunting area. Site 2 is primarily undeveloped, but Site 1 has some public facilities.

★2645★ SANDY POINT STATE PARK

1100 E College Pkwy
Annapolis, MD 21401
Web: www.dnr.state.md.us/publiclands/southern/
sandypoint.html
Phone: 410-974-2149; **Fax:** 410-974-2647
Size: 786 acres. **Location:** In Anne Arundel County, at the western terminus of the Bay Bridge, off US 50/301 at exit 32. **Facilities:** Picnic areas, 12 picnic shelters, hiking trails, swimming beaches, showers, restrooms, marina, 22 boat launches, boat rentals, fishing piers, food concession (&&). **Activities:** Boating, saltwater fishing, swimming, hiking, bird watching. **Special Features:** The park's beaches and picnic areas provide excellent views of the Chesapeake Bay Bridge and the ocean-going vessels and sailing regattas on their way in and out of Baltimore Harbor. The park's location on the eastern flyway also makes it a good location for viewing a large variety of woodland, marsh, and migratory waterfowl.

★2646★ SASSAFRAS NATURAL RESOURCES
MANAGEMENT AREA

c/o Tuckahoe State Park
13070 Crouse Mill Rd
Queen Anne, MD 21657
Web: www.dnr.state.md.us/publiclands/sassafrasplan.html
Phone: 410-820-1668
Size: 991 acres. **Location:** Northern Kent County along the Sassafras River. **Facilities:** No developed facilities. **Activities:** Hiking, bicycling, horseback riding, nature study, hunting, fishing, group camping (limited). **Special Features:** Area consists of rolling woodland, farmlands, wetlands, and nearly three miles of shoreline along the Sassafras River and Turner's Creek. It is managed to conserve, protect, and enhance existing wildlife habitat, fisheries, and other natural resources and offers only low-impact recreational opportunities.

★2647★ SAVAGE RIVER STATE FOREST

127 Headquarters Ln
Grantsville, MD 21536
Web: www.dnr.state.md.us/publiclands/western/
savageriver.html
Phone: 301-895-5759
Size: 54,000 acres. **Location:** In Garrett County, generally south of I-68. **Facilities:** 52 primitive roadside campsites, backpack camping throughout the forest, picnic facilities, bicycle and hiking trails, boat launch, shooting range. **Activities:** Camping, canoeing, freshwater fishing, hiking, mountain biking, hunting, cross-country skiing, snowmobiling, ATV riding. **Special Features:** Forest is the largest facility in the state forest system. The forest is classified as a mixed hardwood forest, and it preserves a strategic watershed. More than 12,000 acres of the forest have been designated as Wildlands.

★2648★ SENECA CREEK STATE PARK

11950 Clopper Rd
Gaithersburg, MD 20878
Web: www.dnr.state.md.us/publiclands/central/seneca.html
Phone: 301-924-2127
Size: 6,290 acres. **Location:** In Montgomery County, 1.5 miles west of Gaithersburg, off I-270. **Facilities:** Picnic areas and shelters (&), playgrounds, restrooms (&), trails, boat rentals, visitor center with auditorium, museum, disc golf course, shooting range. **Activities:** Boating, flatwater canoeing, freshwater fishing, hiking, horseback riding, mountain biking, hunting, cross-country skiing, interpretive programs. **Special Features:** Park includes 90-acre Clopper Lake. Sites of historical interest include a partially restored mill with outdoor exhibits and a one-room schoolhouse.

★2649★ SIDELING HILL EXHIBIT CENTER

c/o Fort Frederick State Park
11100 Fort Frederick Rd
Big Pool, MD 21711
Web: www.dnr.state.md.us/publiclands/western/
sidelinghill.html
Phone: 301-842-2155
Location: In Washington County, 6 miles west of Hancock, on I-68. **Facilities:** Visitor center, picnic area, food concession, scenic overlook; exhibit center (&) has exhibits, an orientation program, and tourism information. **Activities:** Interpretive programs. **Special Features:** The four-story exhibit center offers a unique opportunity to view one of the best rock exposures in the northeastern United States. Highway construction cut through the mountain, exposing almost 850 vertical feet of syncline, which formed 350 million years ago. The exhibit center is located within the state's 3,000-acre Sideling Hill Wildlife Management Area.

★2650★ SMALLWOOD STATE PARK

2750 Sweden Point Rd
Marbury, MD 20658
Web: www.dnr.state.md.us/publiclands/southern/
smallwood.html
Phone: 301-743-7613

Size: 629 acres. **Location:** In Charles County, 4 miles west of Pisgah, off MD 224. **Facilities:** 15 improved campsites (all with electric hookups), 4 camper cabins, 2 youth group camping sites, picnic areas and shelters, playground, hiking trails (2 miles), fishing piers, marina, boat launch ramps, boat rentals, food concession, historic home (&&). **Activities:** Camping, boating, flatwater canoeing, fishing, hiking, cross-country skiing, interpretive programs. **Special Features:** Smallwood was the home of General William Smallwood, a Revolutionary War officer and the fourth governor of Maryland. His house, called Smallwood Retreat, has been restored and is open to visitors.

★2651★ SOLDIERS DELIGHT NATURAL ENVIRONMENT AREA
c/o Patapsco Valley State Park
8020 Baltimore National Pike
Ellicott City, MD 21043
Web: www.dnr.state.md.us/publiclands/central/soldiers.html
Phone: 410-461-5005
Size: 1,900 acres. **Location:** In Baltimore County, on Deer Park Road north of MD 26. **Facilities:** Hiking trails (7 miles), visitor center. **Activities:** Hiking, interpretive programs. **Special Features:** Area the only undisturbed serpentine barren in Maryland, with more than 39 rare, threatened, or endangered plant species as well as rare insects, rocks, and minerals.

★2652★ SOMERS COVE MARINA
715 Broadway
PO Box 67
Crisfield, MD 21817
Web: www.dnr.state.md.us/publiclands/eastern/somerscove.html
Phone: 410-968-0925; Fax: 410-968-1408; Toll Free: 800-967-3474
Size: 485 slips. **Location:** In Somerset County, via US 13 to MD 413. By sea, call Channel 16 for directions. **Facilities:** Annual slips to 65 feet, 100 transient births to 150 feet, covered dry-storage sheds, pavilion, swimming pool, 7 modern comfort stations, 3 laundry rooms, picnic facilities, charter and head boats, 3 boat launch ramps, 2 pump-out stations, 3 oil and anti-freeze stations, fuel dock (gas and diesel), 2 stainless steel fish cleaning stations, meeting area and banquet room. **Activities:** Boating, sailing, fishing, swimming, charter fishing, cruises to Smith or Tangier Islands.. **Special Features:** Full-service public marina with access to many of Somerset County's finest attractions and located in historic Crisfield.

★2653★ SOUTH MOUNTAIN STATE PARK
c/o Greenbrier State Park
21843 National Pike
Boonsboro, MD 21713
Web: www.dnr.state.md.us/publiclands/western/southmountain.html
Phone: 301-791-4767
Size: 8,039 acres. **Location:** In Washington and Frederick counties. **Facilities:** 9 primitive campsites, hiking trails. **Activities:** Camping, hiking, cross-country skiing, hunting. **Special Features:** South Mountain, a ridge composed largely of resistant

quartzite, posed a formidable obstacle to the early settlers until 1755, when General Edward Braddock and a young surveyor named George Washington constructed a road over one of its passes. Park includes 40 miles of the 2,178-mile Appalachian National Scenic Trail (see entry in national trails section) and a historic Civil War battlefield.

★2654★ SUSQUEHANNA STATE PARK
c/o Rocks State Park
3318 Rocks Chrome Hill Rd
Jarrettsville, MD 21084
Web: www.dnr.state.md.us/publiclands/central/susquehanna.html
Phone: 410-557-7994
Size: 2,639 acres. **Location:** In Harford County, 3 miles north of Havre de Grace off Route 155. **Facilities:** 69 improved campsites (6 with electric hookups; some &), 6 camper cabins, picnic area, picnic shelters, restrooms, playground, archery range, multi-use trails (15 miles), boat ramps (&), historic sites. Campground open May-September. **Activities:** Camping, boating, flatwater canoeing, tubing, fishing, hiking, mountain biking, horseback riding, cross-country skiing, bow hunting (deer only), interpretive programs. **Special Features:** In addition to its many recreational opportunities, the Park features a number of historic sites, including: the restored Rock Run Historical Area with a working grist mill where visitors can watch cornmeal being ground by water power; the Jersey Toll House, which at one time was the collection point for travelers crossing the covered bridge spanning the Susquehanna River; and remnants of the Susquehanna Tidewater Canal.

★2655★ SWALLOW FALLS STATE PARK
c/o Herrington Manor State Park
222 Herrington Ln
Oakland, MD 21550
Web: www.dnr.state.md.us/publiclands/western/swallowfalls.html
Phone: 301-387-6938
Size: 257 acres. **Location:** In Garrett County, 9 miles northwest of Oakland on Swallow Falls Rd. **Facilities:** 65 improved campsites (3 with full hookups; &), 3 youth group sites, modern bathhouses (&), picnic area (&), pavilion, playground, hiking trails. **Activities:** Camping, freshwater fishing, hiking, cross-country skiing, interpretive programs (seasonal). **Special Features:** This mountain park contains some of Maryland's most spectacular scenery. The wild and scenic Youghiogheny River flows along the park's borders, passing through shaded rocky gorges and creating rippling rapids. Park scenery also includes Muddy Creek Falls, a 63-foot waterfall.

★2656★ TUCKAHOE STATE PARK
13070 Crouse Mill Rd
Queen Anne, MD 21657
Web: www.dnr.state.md.us/publiclands/eastern/tuckahoe.html
Phone: 410-820-1668
Size: 3,498 acres. **Location:** In Caroline and Queen Anne's counties, 6 miles north of Queen Anne, off Maryland 404 via MD 480. **Facilities:** Family camping area with 51 sites (33 with

electric hookups), youth group camping area with 4 sites, 4 camper cabins, bathhouses with showers and toilet facilities, 2 picnic areas, rental pavilions, playgrounds, multi-use trails, boat launch, mountain bike, kayak, paddleboat, and canoe rentals, arboretum, visitor center (&&). **Activities:** Camping, boating (electric motors only), canoeing/kayaking, fishing, hiking, mountain biking, horseback riding, hunting. **Special Features:** Park features the 500-acre Adkins Arboretum with almost 3 miles of surfaced walkways leading through native species trees and shrubs. Tuckahoe Creek runs through the length of the park, and a 60-acre lake offers boating and fishing.

★2657★ WASHINGTON MONUMENT STATE PARK

c/o Greenbrier State Park
21843 National Pike
Boonsboro, MD 21713
Web: www.dnr.state.md.us/publiclands/western/
washington.html
Phone: 301-791-4767
Size: 147 acres. **Location:** In Washington County, 3 miles southeast of Boonsboro, off Alternate Route 40. **Facilities:** Youth group campsites, picnic area (&) and shelters, playground, playing fields, hiking trails, historic structure, museum (&). **Activities:** Camping, hiking, cross-country skiing, bird watching, interpretive programs. **Special Features:** Park gets its name from the first monument dedicated to George Washington. It is a rugged stone tower, erected on a craggy mountainside by the citizens of Boonsboro in 1827. The Appalachian National Scenic Trail (see entry in national trails section) passes the base of the monument.

★2658★ WYE ISLAND NATURAL RESOURCES MANAGEMENT AREA

632 Wye Island Rd
Queenstown, MD 21658
Web: www.dnr.state.md.us/publiclands/eastern/
wyeisland.html
Phone: 410-827-7577
Size: 2,800 acres. **Location:** In Queen Anne's County, 5 miles south of US 50 via Carmichael Road in Queenstown. **Facilities:** 3 primitive group campsites for youth and adult group camping, rental conference lodge, multi-use trails. **Activities:** Hiking, wildlife viewing, horseback riding, bicycling, primitive group camping, boating (no launch facilities), fishing, hunting. **Special Features:** Located in the tidal recesses of the Chesapeake Bay between the Wye River and the Wye East River, the area provides habitat for wintering waterfowl populations and other native wildlife. A holly tree that can be seen along one of the trails is more than 275 years old.

★2659★ WYE OAK STATE PARK

c/o Tuckahoe State Park
13070 Crouse Mill Rd
Queen Anne, MD 21657
Web: www.dnr.state.md.us/publiclands/eastern/wyeoak.html
Phone: 410-820-1668
Size: 29 acres. **Location:** On State Route 662 in the community of Wye Mills in Talbot County. **Facilities:** Limited picnic facilities (&). **Special Features:** Park was established primarily to protect the Wye Oak Tree, estimated to be over 450 years old, which toppled in June 2002. A structure dating to colonial times that was used as a one-room school house exists near the tree site.

★2660★ YOUGHIOGHENY RIVER NATURAL RESOURCES MANAGEMENT AREA

c/o Deep Creek Lake State Park
898 State Park Rd
Swanton, MD 21561
Web: www.dnr.state.md.us/publiclands/western/
youghiogheny.html
Phone: 301-387-5563; **Fax:** 301-387-4462
Size: 21 miles long. **Location:** Far western Garrett County between Friendsville and Oakland. **Activities:** Whitewater canoeing, fishing, hunting, hiking. **Special Features:** This is the first Maryland river to be classified "wild and scenic." Visitors are cautioned that the river is extremely difficult and potentially dangerous and must be treated with respect. Public access points can be found at Swallow Falls State Park, in the Sang Run area off Sang Run Road, and in Friendsville. For information regarding other points of access, contact Deep Creek Lake State Park.

Massachusetts State Parks

Grid columns: 1 2 3 4 5 6 7

Pittsfield · Quabbin Reservoir · Massachusetts Turnpike · Worcester · Springfield

1	Ames Nowell SP	D-10	
2	Ashland SP	D-8	
3	Ashuwillticook Rail Trail	B-2	
4	Bash Bish Falls SP	D-1	
5	Beartown SF	D-1	
6	Blackstone River & Canal Heritage SP	E-7	
7	Blue Hills Reservation	C-10	
8	Borderland SP	E-9	
9	Bradley Palmer SP	B-10	
10	Brimfield SF	E-5	
11	CM Gardner SP	D-2	
12	Callahan SP	C-8	
13	Cape Cod Rail Trail	G-13	
14	Chester-Blandford SF	D-2	
15	Clarksburg SP	A-2	
16	Cochituate SP	D-8	
17	Connecticut River Greenway SP	C-3	
18	D.A.R. SF	C-3	
19	Demarest Lloyd SP	G-10	
20	Dighton Rock SP	F-10	
21	Douglas SF	E-7	
22	Dunn SP	B-6	
23	Ellisville Harbor SP	F-12	
24	Erving SF	B-4	
25	F. Gilbert Hills SF	E-9	
26	Fall River Heritage SP	F-9	
27	Federated Women's Club SF	C-5	
28	Fort Phoenix SR	G-10	
29	Freetown-Fall River SF	F-10	
30	Gardner Heritage SP	B-6	
31	Georgetown-Rowley SF	A-10	
32	Granville SF	E-2	
33	Great Brook Farm SP	B-8	
34	Halibut Point SP	B-11	
35	Hampton Ponds SP	D-3	
36	Harold Parker SF	B-10	
37	Holyoke Heritage SP	D-4	
38	Hopkinton SP	D-8	
39	Horseneck Beach SR	H-10	
40	JA Skinner SP	D-4	
41	Jug End SR & WMA	D-1	
42	Kenneth Dubuque Memorial SF	B-3	
43	Lake Dennison RA	B-6	
44	Lake Lorraine SP	D-4	
45	Lawrence Heritage SP	A-9	
46	Leominster SF	B-7	
47	Lowell Heritage SP	B-9	
48	Lowell-Dracut-Tyngsboro SF	B-8	
49	Manuel F. Correllus SF	H-11	
50	Massasoit SP	F-10	
51	Maudslay SP	A-10	
52	Mohawk Trail SF	B-2	
53	Monroe SF	B-2	
54	Moore SP	C-6	
55	Mount Everett SR	E-1	
56	Mount Grace SF	B-5	
57	Mount Greylock SR	B-2	
58	Mount Holyoke Range SP	D-4	
59	Mount Sugarloaf SR	C-4	
60	Mount Tom SR	D-4	
61	Mount Washington SF	E-1	
62	Myles Standish Monument SR	E-11	
63	Myles Standish SF	F-11	
64	Nashua River Rail Trail	B-8	
65	Nasketucket Bay SR	G-11	
66	Natural Bridge SP	A-2	
67	Nickerson SP	F-13	
68	Norwottuck Rail Trail	C-4	
69	October Mountain SF	C-2	
70	Otter River SF	B-6	
71	Pearl Hill SP	B-7	
72	Pilgrim Memorial (Plymouth Rock) SP	E-11	
73	Pittsfield SF	C-1	
74	Purgatory Chasm SR	D-7	
75	Quabbin Reservoir Watershed	C-5	
76	Quinsigamond SP	D-7	
77	Robinson SP	E-4	
78	Rutland SP	C-6	
79	Salisbury Beach SR	A-10	
80	Sandisfield SF	D-2	
81	Sandy Point SR	A-11	
82	Savoy Mountain SF	B-2	
83	Schooner Ernestina	G-10	
84	Scusset Beach SR	F-12	
85	Shawme-Crowell SF	F-12	
86	South Cape Beach SP	G-12	
87	Spencer SF	D-6	
88	Streeter Point RA	E-5	
89	Tolland SF	D-2	
90	Upton SF	D-8	
91	Wachusett Mountain SR	C-7	
92	Wahconah Falls SP	C-2	
93	Walden Pond SR	C-9	
94	Watson Pond SP	E-9	
95	Wells SP	D-6	
96	Wendell SF	B-5	
97	Western Gateway Heritage SP	B-2	
98	Whitehall SP	D-7	
99	Willard Brook SF	B-7	
100	Willowdale SF	B-10	
101	Windsor SF	B-2	
102	Wompatuck SP	D-11	
103	Wyola SP	B-4	

RA   Recreation Area
SF   State Forest
SP   State Park
SR   State Reservation
WMA Wildlife Management Area

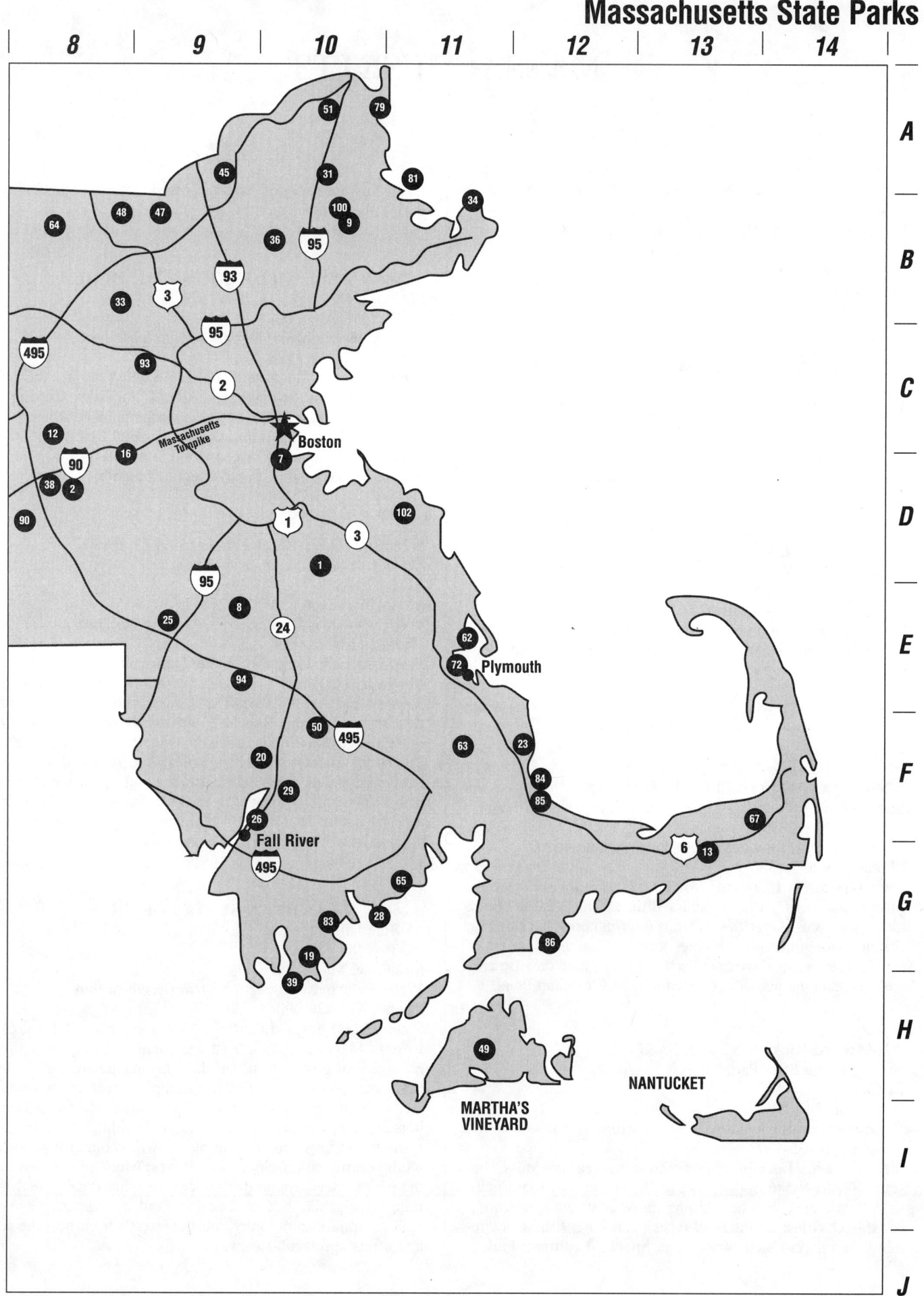

★2661★ **Massachusetts Department of Conservation & Recreation**
Division of State Parks & Recreation
251 Causeway St, Suite 600
Boston, MA 02114
(617) 626-1250 - Phone
(617) 626-1351 - Fax
(877) 422-6762 – Reservations
Web: www.state.ma.us/dem
System includes more than 135 state parks and state forests, along with several other sites designated as reservations, recreation areas, historic heritage sites, and trails. Although one of the smallest states in terms of size, Massachusetts has one of the largest state park systems, managing or overseeing 450,000 acres of state lands (about five percent of the state).

★2662★ **Massachusetts Department of Fish and Game**
251 Causeway St, Suite 400
Boston, MA 02114-2152
(617) 626-1500 - Phone
Web: www.state.ma.us/dfwele
Has five components made up of fisheries, wildlife, heritage and endangered species, realty and public information, and education. Maintains approximately 250 boat access sites.

★2663★ **AMES NOWELL STATE PARK**
Linwood St
Abington, MA 02351
Web: www.mass.gov/dcr/parks/southeast/ames.htm
Phone: 781-857-1336
Size: 607 acres. **Location:** South of Boston, in southeastern Massachusetts, off Rt 123 west. **Facilities:** Picnic area, ball field, trails, restrooms. **Activities:** Boating (non-motorized), canoeing, fishing, hiking, mountain biking, horseback riding, cross-country skiing. **Special Features:** Park is a year-round day-use area with recreational activity centered around Cleveland Pond.

★2664★ **ASHLAND STATE PARK**
c/o Hopkinton State Park
71 Cedar St
Hopkinton, MA 01748
Web: www.mass.gov/dcr/parks/northeast/ashl.htm
Phone: 508-435-4303
Size: 470 acres. **Location:** West of Boston, in eastern Massachusetts; take Rt 495 to Hopkinton exit, then east on Rt 135. **Facilities:** Picnic area, beaches, hiking trails, boat ramp, restrooms (&&). **Activities:** Boating (all types), canoeing, fishing, swimming, hiking, cross-country skiing. **Special Features:** Park is

located on the banks of Ashland Reservoir and is operated only during the summer months.

★2665★ **ASHUWILLTICOOK RAIL TRAIL**
PO Box 1433
Pittsfield, MA 01202
Web: www.mass.gov/dcr/parks/western/asrt.htm
Phone: 413-442-8928
Size: 11.2 miles. **Location:** Parallel to Route 8 through the towns of Cheshire, Lanesborough, and Adams. **Facilities:** Parking lots and restrooms at selected locations along trail. **Activities:** Walking/hiking, bicycling, inline skating. **Special Features:** Trail is a former railroad corridor converted into a 10-foot wide paved, universally accessible, passive recreation path.

★2666★ **BASH BISH FALLS STATE PARK**
c/o Mount Washington State Forest
RD 3 East St
Mount Washington, MA 01258
Web: www.mass.gov/dcr/parks/western/bash.htm
Phone: 413-528-0330
Size: 200 acres. **Location:** In the southern Berkshires of western Massachusetts, next to Mount Washington State Forest (see separate entry). **Facilities:** Trails, scenic viewing area. **Activities:** Fishing, hiking. **Special Features:** Bash Bish Falls is one of the state's most dramatic and the highest single-drop waterfall. The water tumbles through a series of gorges and a hemlock hardwood ravine forest, then drops about 60 feet into a pool below. The park is located in the extreme southwest corner of the state, next to Mount Washington State Forest, and also adjoins New York's Taconic State Park.

★2667★ **BEARTOWN STATE FOREST**
69 Blue Hill Rd
PO Box 97
Monterey, MA 01245
Web: www.mass.gov/dcr/parks/western/bear.htm
Phone: 413-528-0904
Size: 12,000 acres. **Location:** In the southern Berkshires in western Massachusetts, off Rt 23. **Facilities:** Campground (&; no cabins or group sites), beaches (&), picnic area, trails, boat ramp, restrooms (&). **Activities:** Camping, boating (non-motorized), canoeing, fishing, swimming, hiking, mountain biking, horseback riding, motorcycle and ATV riding, hunting (with restrictions), cross-country skiing, snowmobiling, snowshoeing, wildlife observation. **Special Features:** Much of the activity at the park centers around the 35-acre Benedict Pond. The 2,144-mile Appalachian National Scenic Trail (see separate entry in national trails section) intersects the forest's trails near the pond and offers spectacular views.

★2668★ BLACKSTONE RIVER & CANAL HERITAGE STATE PARK

287 Oak St
Uxbridge, MA 01569
Web: www.mass.gov/dcr/parks/central/blst.htm
Phone: 508-278-7604
Size: 1,005 acres. Location: In Uxbridge, off Rt 146 south via the Massachusetts Turnpike, Worcester/Providence exit (10A). Facilities: Picnic area, restrooms (&), trails, visitor center, historic site, scenic viewing area. Activities: Canoeing, hiking, mountain biking, hunting (with restrictions), cross-country skiing, wildlife observation, interpretive programs (seasonal). Special Features: The Blacksone Canal was built in the early 1800s to link Central Massachusetts to the Atlantic via Providence, RI. Most of the canal structures are now gone, but the remains of lock chambers, dams, bridges, workers' housing, and a company store are reminders of the area's industrial heritage. Visitors to the park can walk along restored sections of the canal and towpath from the River Bend Farm Visitor's Center.

★2669★ BLUE HILLS RESERVATION

695 Hillside St
Milton, MA 02186
Web: www.mass.gov/dcr/parks/metroboston/blue.htm
Phone: 617-698-1802
Size: 7,000 acres. Location: In Milton, .25 miles north of Houghton's Pond, off Rt 93 (exit 3). Facilities: Camping at the Appalachian Mountain Club; 36-hole golf course (in Canton); hiking trails (125 miles), skating rink, mountain bike rentals; picnic tables, softball fields, and swimming beach at Houghton's Pond; trailside museum, observatory and science center. Activities: Camping, boating (non-motorized only), fishing, golfing, hiking, horseback riding, ice skating, mountain biking, rock climbing, cross-country and downhill skiing, swimming, educational programs. Special Features: Reservation is located just minutes from downtown Boston, and visitors can view the entire metro area from the summit of Great Blue Hill, the highest of the 22 hills in the Blue Hills chain. The Metropolitan Parks Commission purchased the land for the reservation in 1893, making it one of the first areas in the state set aside for public recreation. It is rich in both archeological and historic resources, with 16 structures listed on the *National Register of Historic Places*, and it features scenic views, varied terrain, and more than 125 miles of trails.

★2670★ BORDERLAND STATE PARK

Massapoag Ave
North Easton, MA 02356
Web: www.mass.gov/dcr/parks/southeast/bord.htm
Phone: 508-238-6566
Size: 1,570 acres. Location: On the border of Sharon and Easton, in the Greater Boston area. Facilities: Historic home, group day-use area, hiking trails (&), equestrian trails, restrooms (&), visitor center. Activities: Boating (non-motorized), canoeing, fishing, hiking, horseback riding, disc golf, cross-country skiing, ice skating, sledding, scheduled tours. Special Features: Borderland is an English-style stone mansion built in 1910 by artist and suffragist Blanche Ames and her botanist husband Oakes.

Its 20 rooms are restored and furnished in their original style, and many of Blanche Ames's paintings grace the walls.

★2671★ BRADLEY PALMER STATE PARK

40 Asbury St
Topsfield, MA 01983
Web: www.mass.gov/dcr/parks/northeast/brad.htm
Phone: 978-887-5931
Size: 721 acres. Location: Route 1 to Topsfield, right on Ipswich Road, then right on Asbury Street. Facilities: Trails, picnic area, beaches (&), restrooms (&). Activities: Canoeing, fishing, hiking, mountain biking, horseback riding, cross-country skiing. Special Features: Formerly a private estate, this park features pine needle paths, rolling meadows, and hundreds of rhododendrons, which line old carriage roads and reach their peak blooming season in mid-June. The park is named for Bradley Palmer, the attorney who represented Sinclair Oil in the Teapot Dome Scandal and President Wilson at the Versailles Peace Conference after World War I.

★2672★ BRIMFIELD STATE FOREST

100 Dearth Hill Rd
Brimfield, MA 01010
Web: www.mass.gov/dcr/parks/central/brim.htm
Phone: 413-267-9687
Size: 3,250 acres. Location: South-central Massachusetts. Take Mass Pike (I-90) to Exit 8, Route 32 south to Route 20 east, right on Monson Road. Follow signs. Facilities: Group day-use area, trails, restrooms (&). Activities: Fishing, walking/hiking, mountain biking, horseback riding, hunting (with restrictions), swimming, cross-country skiing. Special Features: Rolling, densely forested property includes over 20 miles of roads and trails. Located in the western portion of the forest is Dean Pond Recreation Area, an isolated, peaceful spot for picnicking and swimming.

★2673★ CALLAHAN STATE PARK

93 Commonwealth Rd
Wayland, MA 01778
Web: www.mass.gov/dcr/parks/northeast/call.htm
Phone: 508-653-9641
Size: 819 acres. Location: West of Boston, on Millwood Street in Framingham; access via Rt 9 west to Rt 30 exit. Facilities: Trails, bicycle paths. Activities: Hiking, horseback riding, bicycling, cross-country skiing. Special Features: Property is a day-use park with seven miles of marked trails and nearly 100 acres of open fields.

★2674★ CAPE COD RAIL TRAIL

c/o Nickerson State Park
3488 Main St
Brewster, MA 02631
Web: www.mass.gov/dcr/parks/southeast/ccrt.htm
Phone: 508-896-3491
Size: 22 miles. Location: In the mid-Cape area, in southeastern Massachusetts. Facilities: Bicycle paths, hand-cycle rentals (&), scenic viewing area, restrooms available on trail. Activities:

9. State Parks

Bicycling, hiking, walking, running, horseback riding, cross-country skiing. **Special Features:** This paved trail follows a former railroad right-of-way from Dennis to Wellfleet. A wide unpaved shoulder accommodates horseback riding, walking, and running. Food and water, restrooms, and rental bikes are readily available along the trail.

★2675★ CHESTER-BLANDFORD STATE FOREST

PO Box 105
Chester, MA 01011
Web: www.mass.gov/dcr/parks/western/chbl.htm
Phone: 413-354-6347
Size: 2,308 acres. **Location:** In the eastern Berkshire Hills of western Massachusetts, off Rt 20; accessible via Mass Pike (I-90). **Facilities:** 12 campsites, trails, scenic viewing area, restrooms. **Activities:** Camping (May-Labor Day), fishing, picnicking, hiking, horseback riding, mountain biking, cross-country skiing. **Special Features:** Forest offers a rustic park experience and the opportunity to view the 60-foot cascade at Sanderson Brook Falls and other scenic vistas.

★2676★ CHICOPEE MEMORIAL STATE PARK

570 Burnett Rd
Chicopee Falls, MA 01020
Web: www.mass.gov/dcr/parks/central/chip.htm
Phone: 413-594-9416
Size: 575 acres. **Location:** In south-central Massachusetts, off Exit 6 from Mass Pike (I-90). **Facilities:** Group day-use area, picnic facilities, beaches (&), scenic viewing area, walking trails, restrooms (&). **Activities:** Fishing, swimming. **Special Features:** Park includes two 25-acre ponds. It was formerly the Cooley Brook Reservoir and Watershed.

★2677★ CLARKSBURG STATE PARK

1199 Middle Rd
Clarksburg, MA 01247
Web: www.mass.gov/dcr/parks/western/clsp.htm
Phone: 413-664-8345
Size: 368 acres. **Location:** In the northern Berkshires, in western Massachusetts. **Facilities:** 45 campsites, showers, restrooms (&), picnic area, pavilion, trails. **Activities:** Camping, boating (non-motorized), canoeing, fishing, swimming, hiking, hunting (nearby, with restrictions), cross-country skiing. **Special Features:** Park includes abundant, unspoiled forestland with spectacular views of Hoosac Range, Mount Greylock, and the Green Mountains. The park's Mausert Pond has a landscaped day-use area and is surrounded by 9.5 miles of trails. Three miles west of the park is Clarksburg State Forest, a 3,011-acre tract that is popular with hunters and hikers and offers wilderness camping at three designated sites.

★2678★ CM GARDNER STATE PARK

PO Box 105
Chester, MA 01011
Web: www.mass.gov/dcr/parks/western/gdsp.htm
Phone: 413-354-6347
Size: 29 acres. **Location:** In the eastern Berkshire foothills in western Massachusetts, off MA 112 north in Huntington. **Facilities:** Picnic area, walking trails, restrooms. **Activities:** Fishing, canoeing, hunting (with restrictions). **Special Features:** Park is situated in the rolling Berkshire foothills along a scenic section of the Westfield River East Branch.

★2679★ COCHITUATE STATE PARK

93 Commonwealth Rd
Wayland, MA 01778
Web: www.mass.gov/dcr/parks/northeast/coch.htm
Phone: 508-653-9641
Size: 1,126 acres. **Location:** In Natick, in the Greater Boston area, off Route 30 (Exit 13 off Mass Pike). **Facilities:** Beaches (&), picnic area, boat ramp, restrooms (&). **Activities:** Boating (all types), canoeing, fishing, swimming, mountain biking. **Special Features:** Park is a popular regional day-use facility with three lakes. Boat launching is limited to the middle lake; boaters gain access to the other lakes through channels under roadways.

★2680★ CONNECTICUT RIVER GREENWAY STATE PARK

136 Damon Rd
Northampton, MA 01060
Web: www.mass.gov/dcr/parks/central/crgw.htm
Phone: 413-586-8706
Size: 3,900 acres. **Location:** There are numerous access points along the river. **Facilities:** Picnic areas, restrooms (&). **Activities:** Boating (motorized and non-motorized), canoeing, fishing. **Special Features:** Greenway connects open spaces, parks, natural areas, scenic vistas, cultural features, and archeological and historic sites along the length of the Connecticut River.

★2681★ DAR STATE FOREST

c/o 555 East St
Williamsburg, MA 01096
Web: www.mass.gov/dcr/parks/western/darf.htm
Phone: 413-268-7098
Size: 1,770 acres. **Location:** On Route 112 in Goshen. **Facilities:** 51 campsites, 1 group camp, group day-use area, showers, restrooms, swimming beach, picnic area, pavilion, trails, boat ramp (&&). **Activities:** Camping, boating (non-motorized), fishing, swimming, hiking, mountain biking, horseback riding, cross-country skiing, snowshoeing, ice fishing, skating, snowmobiling, bird watching, interpretive programs (seasonal). **Special Features:** Park is located in the eastern foothills of the Berkshires, and the Goshen fire tower offers spectacular views of the Connecticut River Valley and into 5 states. More than 15 miles of marked mixed-use trails wind through the woods for year-round hiking and winter activities.

★2682★ DEMAREST LLOYD STATE PARK

Barney's Joy Rd
Dartmouth, MA 02748
Web: www.mass.gov/dcr/parks/southeast/deml.htm
Phone: 508-636-8816
Size: 222 acres. **Location:** Route 24 south to I-95, east to Exit 12, cross Route 6 and follow signs. **Facilities:** Beach, picnic

area, walking trails, restrooms, showers, scenic viewing area. **Activities:** Fishing, swimming, canoeing/kayaking. **Special Features:** Park features an 1,800-foot saltwater beach backed by rambling hills of beach grass and shaded picnic sites. A broad, scenic marsh borders the Slocum River on the park's eastern edge.

★2683★ **DIGHTON ROCK STATE PARK**
c/o Freetown State Forest
PO Box 171
Assonet, MA 02702
Web: www.mass.gov/dcr/parks/southeast/digr.htm
Phone: 508-822-7537
Size: 85 acres. **Location:** Near Fall River in southeastern Massachusetts, on Bay View Ave in Berkley. **Facilities:** Picnic area, trails, restrooms, museum (open by appointment). **Activities:** Boating (no motors), canoeing, fishing, hiking, mountain biking, cross-country skiing. **Special Features:** Dighton Rock is an 11-foot-tall boulder that once rested on the shore of the Taunton River adjacent to this park. Covered with carved designs of ancient and uncertain origin, the rock is now installed in a small museum on park grounds.

★2684★ **DOUGLAS STATE FOREST**
107 Wallum Lake Rd
Douglas, MA 01516
Web: www.mass.gov/dcr/parks/central/doug.htm
Phone: 508-476-7872
Size: 5,730 acres. **Location:** On the southern border of central Massachusetts, bordering both Connecticut and Rhode Island. Accessible via Mass Pike (I-90). **Facilities:** Picnic area, pavilion, group day-use area, trails, 2 boat ramps, swimming beach (&) and bathhouses, restrooms (&), interpretive center. **Activities:** Boating (all types), canoeing, fishing, swimming, hiking, mountain biking, horseback riding, hunting (with restrictions), cross-country skiing, snowmobiling, interpretive programs (seasonal). **Special Features:** Forest includes a rare example of Atlantic white cedar swampland. A 5-acre portion of the swamp is designated as a Massachusetts Wildland and is accessible to the public via a boardwalk trail. The Midstate Trail, a long-distance hiking trail that extends through the central part of the state to Mount Watatic in the north, runs through the forest.

★2685★ **DUNN STATE PARK**
Route 101
Gardner, MA 01440
Web: www.mass.gov/dcr/parks/central/dunn.htm
Phone: 978-632-7897
Size: 120 acres. **Location:** In the northern part of central Massachusetts, off Route 2 to Exit 24 (Rt 140 north). **Facilities:** Picnic facilities, play equipment, trails, boat ramp, visitor center (&&). **Activities:** Boating (non-motorized), canoeing, fishing, swimming, hiking, cross-country skiing, ice skating, interpretive programs (seasonal). **Special Features:** Park is situated on a 20-acre pond, and activities (all wheelchair accessible) are available year round.

★2686★ **ELLISVILLE HARBOR STATE PARK**
Rt 3A
Plymouth, MA 02360
Web: www.mass.gov/dcr/parks/southeast/ells.htm
Phone: 508-866-2580
Size: 101 acres. **Location:** In southeastern Massachusetts. From Boston, Route 3 south to Exit 2, right to Route 3A north; park is 2 miles on right. **Facilities:** Trails, scenic viewing area. **Activities:** Fishing, hiking, cross-country skiing. **Special Features:** One of the most scenic spots on the South Shore coastline, the park's natural attractions include a barrier beach, salt marsh, sphagnum bog, a red pine forest, and open meadows. In fall and winter, harbor seals can be seen just offshore.

★2687★ **ERVING STATE FOREST**
200 E Main St
Rt 2A
Erving, MA 01344
Web: www.mass.gov/dcr/parks/central/ervf.htm
Phone: 978-544-3939
Size: 4,479 acres. **Location:** In northern central Massachusetts, accessible via I-91 from north or south or Rt 2 from east or west. **Facilities:** 29 campsites, picnic area, group day-use area, beaches (&), restrooms (&), trails, boat ramp, scenic viewing area. **Activities:** Camping, boating (all types), canoeing, fishing, swimming, hiking, mountain biking, horseback riding, hunting (with restrictions), cross-country skiing, snowmobiling, interpretive programs (seasonal). **Special Features:** The woodlands contain 8 miles of forested roads, and numerous trails lead to points of scenic interest. Springtime brings beautiful displays of the flowering mountain laurel.

★2688★ **F. GILBERT HILLS STATE FOREST**
45 Mill St
Foxboro, MA 02035
Web: www.mass.gov/dcr/parks/southeast/fgil.htm
Phone: 508-543-5850
Size: 1,027 acres. **Location:** In southeastern Massachusetts. From the north, take I-95 south to Route 140 north; from Rt 495, take exit 14 (which is Rt 1) north. **Facilities:** Picnic area, trails, restrooms (&). **Activities:** Hiking, horseback riding, mountain biking, off-road vehicle riding, hunting (with restrictions), cross-country skiing. **Special Features:** A "passive use" pine and oak forest, F Gilbert Hills has 23 miles of trails, including a portion of Warner Trail, a long-distance hiking trail that travels through Norfolk County enroute to Rhode Island.

★2689★ **FALL RIVER HERITAGE STATE PARK**
200 Davol St
Fall River, MA 02720
Web: www.mass.gov/dcr/parks/southeast/frhp.htm
Phone: 508-675-5759
Size: 8.5 acres. **Location:** Off Route 24, on Route 79 in Fall River. **Facilities:** Visitor center, picnic area, restrooms (&), scenic viewing area. **Activities:** Public sailing programs, other programs and events. **Special Features:** Park is located on the shore of the Taunton River (Mount Hope Bay), overlooking Battleship Cove, home of the World War II battleship, *USS*

Massachusetts. The park includes a boardwalk, benches, groves of trees, an antique carousel, and a 3-acre meadow for concerts and other outdoor activities.

★2690★ **FEDERATED WOMEN'S CLUB STATE FOREST**
Rt 122
Baldwinville, MA 01436
Web: www.mass.gov/dcr/parks/central/fwsf.htm
Phone: 978-939-8962
Size: 984 acres. **Location:** In Petersham and New Salem. Take Route 202 to Route 122. Follow signs. **Facilities:** Limited service campsites, trails, scenic viewing areas. **Activities:** Camping (first come, first served), fishing, hiking, hunting (with restrictions), cross-country skiing, wildlife observation. **Special Features:** A 140-acre wildlife sanctuary has been set aside in the center of the forest, and a dammed pond on Fever Brook attracts migrating and native wildfowl. The road along Fever Brook offers outstanding scenery. The forest's chief geological feature, the Gorge, is located in the southwest section.

★2691★ **FORT PHOENIX STATE RESERVATION**
Green St
Fairhaven, MA 02719
Web: www.mass.gov/dcr/parks/southeast/ftph.htm
Phone: 508-992-4524
Size: 23 acres. **Location:** On the southeast coast of Massachusetts, off Route 6 west. **Facilities:** Picnic area, restrooms (&), showers, historic site, scenic viewing. **Activities:** Swimming, hiking. **Special Features:** Reservation is located minutes from downtown New Bedford and includes a half-mile of Buzzard Bay beachfront. The reservation is named for Fort Phoenix, a national landmark adjacent to the park that is managed by the Town of Fairhaven. From the fort's remnant ramparts, visitors can view the bay where the first naval battle of the Revolutionary War was fought.

★2692★ **FREETOWN-FALL RIVER STATE FOREST**
Slab Bridge Rd
Assonet, MA 02702
Web: www.mass.gov/dcr/parks/southeast/free.htm
Phone: 508-644-5522
Size: 5,441 acres. **Location:** In southeast Massachusetts, near Fall River and Taunton; access via Rt 24 south to Exit 10. **Facilities:** Picnic area, wading pool, fields, restrooms (&), trails, historic site, scenic views. **Activities:** Fishing, hiking, horseback riding, mountain biking, motorcycle riding (no ATVs), hunting (with restrictions), snowmobiling, dog sledding, cross-country skiing. **Special Features:** Forest is the site of a 227-acre Wampanoag Indian Reservation. Profile Rock, a 50-foot natural rock outcropping, shows a profile that the Wampanoags believe to be Chief Massasoit.

★2693★ **GARDNER HERITAGE STATE PARK**
265 Center St
Gardner, MA 01440
Web: www.mass.gov/dcr/parks/central/ghsp.htm
Phone: 978-632-7897

Location: On Lake Street in Gardner, in mid-central Massachusetts. From Route 2 take Exit 23 to Gardner. Follow signs. **Facilities:** Exhibits, restrooms. **Activities:** Self-guided exhibits. **Special Features:** Park is located in a restored 19th-century fire station, where exhibits trace the history of the silversmith and furniture making industry in Gardner (which is known as "Chair City").

★2694★ **GEORGETOWN-ROWLEY STATE FOREST**
40 Asbury St
Topsfield, MA 01983
Web: www.mass.gov/dcr/parks/northeast/grow.htm
Phone: 978-887-5931
Size: 1,112 acres. **Location:** In Georgetown, via I-95 north to Route 97 west (Exit 53B). **Facilities:** Trails. **Activities:** Hiking, mountain biking, horseback riding, off-road vehicle riding, hunting (with restrictions), cross-country skiing, snowmobiling. **Special Features:** The forest's extensive trail system is open year round.

★2695★ **GRANVILLE STATE FOREST**
323 W Hartland Rd
Granville, MA 01034
Web: www.mass.gov/dcr/parks/western/gran.htm
Phone: 413-357-6611
Size: 2,426 acres. **Location:** Off Route 57 in Granville, along the southern border of Massachusetts. **Facilities:** 22 campsites (no hookups), restrooms (&), showers, trails. **Activities:** Camping, fishing, hiking, mountain biking, horseback riding, hunting (with restrictions), cross-country skiing, bird watching, wildlife viewing. Camping is permitted only at designated sites; wilderness camping and swimming are prohibited. **Special Features:** Forest includes rustic campgrounds along the Hubbard River, named for the first English pioneer who settled here in 1749. The river cascades through natural rock formations, forming pools and waterfalls and dropping 450 feet in 2.5 miles.

★2696★ **GREAT BROOK FARM STATE PARK**
984 Lowell Rd
PO Box 0829
Carlisle, MA 01741
Web: www.mass.gov/dcr/parks/northeast/gbfm.htm
Phone: 978-369-6312
Size: 975 acres. **Location:** In northeastern Massachusetts, via Rt 128 or Rt 495. **Facilities:** Visitor center, restrooms (&), trails, canoe launch, ski rentals (seasonal), historic site, ice cream stand (seasonal). **Activities:** Canoeing, fishing, hiking, mountain biking, horseback riding, cross-country skiing, interpretive programs (&). **Special Features:** The farm and buildings at this park comprise a classic eastern Massachusetts agricultural landscape. An active dairy farm operates year-round, and guided barn tours are available from May to October. Park includes 20 miles of trails, from which notable Native American sites can be seen.

★2697★ HALIBUT POINT STATE PARK

16 Gaffield Ave
Rockport, MA 01966
Web: www.mass.gov/dcr/parks/northeast/halb.htm
Phone: 978-546-2997
Size: 56 acres. **Location:** In Cape Ann in northeastern Massachusetts; accessibale via I-95 north. **Facilities:** Picnic area, walking trails, restrooms (&), visitor center, historic site, scenic viewing area. **Activities:** Fishing, interpretive programs (seasonal), cross-country skiing. **Special Features:** The site of a former granite mining operation, this quarry area offers spectacular views of the rocky northern Massachusetts coastline and the Atlantic Ocean. Park interprets the history of granite and its many uses.

★2698★ HAMPTON PONDS STATE PARK

1048 North Rd
Westfield, MA 01085
Web: www.mass.gov/dcr/parks/central/hamp.htm
Phone: 413-532-3985
Size: 42 acres. **Location:** In the City of Westfield, in the southwestern part of central Massachusetts; Mass Pike (I-90) exit 3 to Route 202. **Facilities:** Picnic area, boat ramp, beaches (&), restrooms (&). **Activities:** Boating (all types), canoeing, fishing, swimming. **Special Features:** Park offers water-based recreation and picnicking.

★2699★ HAROLD PARKER STATE FOREST

1951 Turnpike St
North Andover, MA 01845
Web: www.mass.gov/dcr/parks/northeast/harp.htm
Phone: 978-686-3391
Size: 3,000 acres. **Location:** 20 miles north of Boston, in Andover, North Andover, North Reading, and Middleton. **Facilities:** 91 campsites (some & sites; no hookups), hot showers, restrooms (&), picnic area, beach (&), bathhouse, trails, nature center (seasonal). **Activities:** Camping, canoeing, fishing, swimming, hiking, mountain biking, horseback riding, hunting (with restrictions), cross-country skiing, interpretive programs (seasonal). **Special Features:** Situated in one of the state's oldest woodlands, the forest includes 11 ponds and more than 35 miles of trails and logging roads.

★2700★ HOLYOKE HERITAGE STATE PARK

221 Appleton St
Holyoke, MA 01040
Web: www.mass.gov/dcr/parks/central/hhsp.htm
Phone: 413-534-1723; **Fax:** 413-534-0909
Size: 8.5 acres. **Location:** Mass Pike (I-90) to Exit 4, Route 91 north to Route 202 north (Exit 16). Right at Appleton Street. **Facilities:** Picnic area, restrooms (&), visitor center, scenic viewing areas. **Activities:** Interpretive programs. **Special Features:** Park's visitor center features exhibits about paper manufacturing and Holyoke's industrial history, and special programs are offered year round. At the park also are an antique carousel, a children's museum, and the Volleyball Hall of Fame.

★2701★ HOPKINTON STATE PARK

71 Cedar St
Hopkinton, MA 01748
Web: www.mass.gov/dcr/parks/northeast/hpsp.htm
Phone: 508-435-4303
Size: 1,450 acres. **Location:** In the towns of Hopkinton and Ashland, in the Greater Boston area. **Facilities:** Picnic area, group day-use area (includes pavilion, restrooms, and playing field), trails, boat ramp, beaches, restrooms (&). **Activities:** Boating (non-motorized), canoeing, fishing, swimming, hiking, mountain biking, horseback riding, cross-country skiing, snowmobiling. **Special Features:** Park is located on Hopkinton Reservoir, which offers excellent trout fishing.

★2702★ HORSENECK BEACH STATE RESERVATION

PO Box 328
Westport, MA 02791
Web: www.mass.gov/dcr/parks/southeast/hbch.htm
Phone: 508-636-8816
Size: Nearly 600 acres. **Location:** In the southernmost part of eastern Massachusetts, at the western end of Buzzard's Bay. **Facilities:** 100 campsites (including some & sites), showers, restrooms (&), picnic areas (&), beaches (&), boat ramp, historic site. **Activities:** Camping, boating (all types), fishing, swimming, windsurfing, bird watching. **Special Features:** This 2-mile-long sandy beach is breezy year round and is one of the most popular ocean beaches on the Massachusetts South Shore. Its combination of ocean beach and estuary habitat makes it an excellent birding location as well.

★2703★ JA SKINNER STATE PARK

PO Box 91
Hadley, MA 01035
Web: www.mass.gov/dcr/parks/central/skin.htm
Phone: 413-586-0350
Size: 390 acres. **Location:** In the western part of central Massachusetts, on Rt 47 via Mass Pike (I-90). **Facilities:** Picnic area, trails, restrooms (&), historic site, scenic viewing areas, visitor center. **Activities:** Hiking, hawk watching, hang gliding, fall foliage viewing, interpretive programs (seasonal). **Special Features:** Park is located atop Mount Holyoke and offers outstanding views of the Connecticut River Valley. Summit House, a popular mountaintop hotel in the 1880s, is open for tours during the summer months, offering historic displays as well as special events. Park is named for Joseph Allen Skinner, a wealthy industrialist who donated the park's land and the hotel to the state in 1940.

★2704★ JUG END STATE RESERVATION & WILDLIFE MANAGEMENT AREA

c/o Mount Washington State Forest
RD 3 East St
Mount Washington, MA 01258
Web: www.mass.gov/dcr/parks/western/juge.htm
Phone: 413-528-0330
Size: 1,158 acres. **Location:** In the southern Berkshires of western Massachusetts, on Jug End Road in Egremont. **Facilities:**

Undeveloped. **Activities:** Hiking, hunting (with restrictions). **Special Features:** Located in one of the most scenic areas in Berkshire County, this recent acquisition—once a popular resort—is now managed for passive recreation and environmental research.

★2705★ KENNETH DUBUQUE MEMORIAL STATE FOREST
c/o Mohawk State Forest
PO Box 7
Charlemont, MA 01339
Web: www.mass.gov/dcr/parks/western/dubq.htm
Phone: 413-339-5504
Size: 7,882 acres. **Location:** Within Hawley, Plainfield, and Savoy, in the northern Berkshires in western Massachusetts; entrance is off Route 8A in Hawley. **Facilities:** Wilderness campsites, mixed-use trails (35 miles), hiking trails (6 miles), interpretive trail (1 mile, around Hallockville Pond), historic sites. **Activities:** Camping, canoeing, fishing, hiking, mountain biking, horseback riding, hunting (with restrictions), cross-country skiing, snowmobiling. **Special Features:** Park has many historic and archeological features, including remains of the long-abandoned village of South Hawley, a rare ''beehive'' charcoal kiln, and a natural mineral spring said to have healing attributes.

★2706★ LAKE DENNISON RECREATION AREA
Rt 202
Winchendon, MA 01475
Web: www.mass.gov/dcr/parks/central/lden.htm
Phone: 978-939-8962
Size: 4,221 acres. **Location:** In north-central Massachusetts, in Winchendon, off Route 202 via Route 2. **Facilities:** 150 campsites, showers, restrooms, beaches (&), picnic area, trails, boat ramp. **Activities:** Camping, boating (non-motorized), canoeing, fishing, swimming, hiking, horseback riding, cross-county skiing, hunting (with restrictions), interpretive program. **Special Features:** This rustic park, which offers waterfront camping beside an 85-acre freshwater lake, is a section of an Army Corps of Engineers flood control project.

★2707★ LAKE LORRAINE STATE PARK
44 Lake Dr
Springfield, MA 01118
Phone: 413-543-6628
Size: 2 acres. **Location:** In south-central Massachusetts, via Mass Pike (I-90) Exit 6. **Facilities:** Picnic areas, restrooms, scenic vista. **Activities:** Fishing, swimming. **Special Features:** Park is a freshwater swimming area and regional boat safety training center.

★2708★ LAKE WYOLA STATE PARK
94 Lake View Rd
Shutesbury, MA 01072
Web: www.mass.gov/dcr/parks/central/lwsp.htm
Phone: 413-367-0317
Size: 40 acres. **Location:** In the town of Shutesbury, just north of Amherst. **Facilities:** Picnic area, play fields, volleyball court, horseshoe pits, nature trails, beaches (&), boat ramp, restrooms (&). **Activities:** Fishing, swimming, boating (non-motorized), hiking. **Special Features:** Park is a day-use area on the shores of 128-acre Lake Wyola.

★2709★ LAWRENCE HERITAGE STATE PARK
1 Jackson St
Lawrence, MA 01840
Web: www.mass.gov/dcr/parks/northeast/lwhp.htm
Phone: 978-794-1655
Size: 74 acres. **Location:** From I-495 in Lawrence, take Exit 45 (Marston Street), left on Canal Street, then 3 blocks to Jackson Street. **Facilities:** Visitor center, picnic area, bicycle paths, hiking trails, restrooms (&), boat ramp, historic sites. **Activities:** Boating (&), canoeing, fishing, hiking, bicycling, interpretive programs. **Special Features:** This heritage park explains the role the city of Lawrence (one of America's first planned industrial cities) had in creating the labor unions of America. The mills of Lawrence were the site of the nation's first labor strikes. The visitor center is located in a restored 1840s boarding house and features two floors of exhibits. Nearby is 5-acre Pemberton Park, with walking trails, benches, and views of the city's mills and historic dam. Lawrence Riverfront State Park has tennis, basketball, and street hockey courts, a children's play area, walking trails, and a sledding hill.

★2710★ LEOMINSTER STATE FOREST
90 Fitchburg Rd
Rt 31
Westminster, MA 01473
Web: www.mass.gov/dcr/parks/central/lmsf.htm
Phone: 978-874-2303
Size: 4,300 acres. **Location:** Off Route 2, Exit 28. **Facilities:** Picnic areas, beach (at Crow Hill Pond only), trails, scenic viewing areas, restrooms. **Activities:** Boating (non-motorized), canoeing, fishing, swimming, hiking, mountain biking, horseback riding, rock climbing, hunting (with restrictions), cross-country skiing, snowshoeing, snowmobiling. **Special Features:** Forest is located in the five towns of Westminster, Princeton, Leominster, Fitchburg, and Sterling in north central Massachusetts. It contains five ponds, with more than 135 acres of total surface area, and offers a range of recreational opportunities, both summer and winter.

★2711★ LOWELL-DRACUT-TYNGSBORO STATE FOREST
PO Box 0829
Carlisle, MA 01741
Web: www.mass.gov/dcr/parks/northeast/ldtf.htm
Phone: 978-369-6312
Size: 1,140 acres. **Location:** In Lowell, in northeast Massachusetts; access via Route 495. **Facilities:** Trails (6 miles). **Activities:** Boating (non-motorized), fishing, hiking, bicycling, horseback riding, hunting (with restrictions), cross-country skiing, snowmobiling. **Special Features:** Prior to colonial settlement, this was probably the site of a Native American village. Later,

9. State Parks

the land was acquired to obtain granite for canals and factory foundations.

★2712★ LOWELL HERITAGE STATE PARK
PO Box 0829
Carlisle, MA 01741
Web: www.mass.gov/dcr/parks/northeast/llhp.htm
Phone: 978-369-6312
Size: 35 acres. Location: In Lowell, via I-495 or Route 3 to Lowell Connector. Follow signs to park. Facilities: Picnic area, trails, bike paths, boat ramp, restrooms (&), historic sites, visitor center. Activities: Boating, canoeing, fishing, swimming, hiking, bicycling, interpretive programs. Special Features: Lowell features a network of 19th century canals that were created to provide power for the textile mills that lined the water's edge. The buildings also still remain there. The park offers canal rides, exhibits about Lowell's role in America's industrial history, a Victorian Garden, more than two miles of landscaped esplanade where summer concerts are held, and swimming and boating in the Merrimack River.

★2713★ MANUEL F. CORRELLUS STATE FOREST
PO Box 1612
Vineyard Haven, MA 02568
Web: www.mass.gov/dcr/parks/southeast/corr.htm
Phone: 508-693-2540
Size: 5,146 acres. Location: On Martha's Vineyard in southeastern Massachusetts via Vineyard Haven/Edgartown Road. Facilities: Trails. Activities: Hiking, bicycling, mountain biking, horseback riding, hunting (with restrictions), cross-country skiing. Special Features: Forest is the focus of one of the largest environmental restoration projects in the U.S., through which the State Forest is working to bring back the site's native ecosystem. It is managed for passive recreation, mostly bicycling and hiking.

★2714★ MASSASOIT STATE PARK
1361 Middleboro Ave
East Taunton, MA 02718
Web: www.mass.gov/dcr/parks/southeast/mass.htm
Phone: 508-822-7405
Size: 1,500 acres. Location: In southeastern Massachusetts, off I-495. Facilities: 126 campsites (most with electrical or water hookups; some & sites), showers, restrooms (&), picnic area, trails, beaches (&), boat ramp, visitor center. Activities: Camping, boating (non-motorized), canoeing, fishing, swimming (camping patrons only), hiking, mountain biking, horseback riding, hunting (with restrictions), cross-country skiing. Special Features: Four lakes in this heavily wooded park afford many recreational opportunities as well as scenic beauty, especially in the fall, when the scarlet cranberry bogs contrast vividly with the evergreen pines.

★2715★ MAUDSLAY STATE PARK
Curzon Mill Rd
Newburyport, MA 01950
Web: www.mass.gov/dcr/parks/northeast/maud.htm
Phone: 978-465-7223

Size: 480 acres. Location: In northeast Massachusetts, on the North Shore. Access via Rt 95 or I-495. Facilities: Trails, bicycle paths, restrooms (&), historic site, scenic views. Activities: Fishing, picnicking, hiking, bicycling, mountain biking, horseback riding, cross-country skiing, group day use activities, interpretive programs (seasonal). Special Features: Formerly a private estate on the banks of the Merrimack River, the park features 19th-century gardens with masses of azaleas and rhododendrons (peak bloom is in May and June), as well as one of the largest naturally-occurring stands of mountain laurel in the state.

★2716★ MOHAWK TRAIL STATE FOREST
175 Mohawk Trail/ Rt 2
PO Box 7
Charlemont, MA 01339
Web: www.mass.gov/dcr/parks/western/mhwk.htm
Phone: 413-339-5504
Size: 6,457 acres. Location: In the northern Berkshires of western Massachusetts, off Route 2. Facilities: 56 campsites (some & sites), 6 log cabins (some &), group camping area, showers, restrooms (&), picnic area (&), trails. Activities: Camping, canoeing, fishing, swimming, hiking, hunting (with restrictions), cross-country skiing, interpretive programs (seasonal). Special Features: One of the most scenic woodlands in Massachusetts, the forest is located along and named for the Mohawk Trail, a historic Native American footpath that connected the Connecticut and Hudson River Valleys. Sections of this route are open today as the Mahican-Mohawk Trail.

★2717★ MONROE STATE FOREST
c/o Mohawk Trail State Forest
PO Box 7
Charlemont, MA 01339
Web: www.mass.gov/dcr/parks/western/mnro.htm
Phone: 413-339-5504
Size: 4,321 acres. Location: In the northern Berkshires of western Massachusetts, on Tilda Hill Road in Monroes, off MA 2. Facilities: Trails. Activities: Wilderness camping, fishing, hiking, horseback riding, hunting (with restrictions), cross-country skiing, snowmobiling. Special Features: This wild and rugged state forest features deep valleys, steep mountains, and tall trees. From the summit of Spruce Mountain or Raycroft Lookout hikers can view magnificent panoramas of the surrounding Hoosac and Green Mountains and Deerfield River. Dunbar Brook drops 700 feet in two miles, over huge moss-covered boulders that form waterfalls, rapids, and pools.

★2718★ MOORE STATE PARK
Mill St
Paxton, MA 01612
Web: www.mass.gov/dcr/parks/central/more.htm
Phone: 508-792-3969
Size: 432 acres. Location: In mid-central Massachusetts. From Worcester, take Rt 122 west, then Rt 31 south to park. Facilities: Historic site, walking trails. Activities: Canoeing, fishing, hunting (with restrictions), hiking, cross-country skiing, interpretive programs. Special Features: A peaceful retreat in the heart of central Massachusetts, Moore was the site of grist and saw mills

from 1747 through the early part of the 20th century, when it became a private estate. Today, visitors can see the stone mill foundations, a restored sawmill, and mountains of azaleas, rhododendron, and mountain laurel.

★2719★ MOUNT EVERETT STATE RESERVATION
c/o RD 3 East St
Mount Washington, MA 01258
Web: www.mass.gov/dcr/parks/western/meve.htm
Phone: 413-528-0330
Size: 1,356 acres. Elevation: 2,624 feet. Location: In the extreme southwest corner of Massachusetts, accessible via MA 41. Facilities: Day use area, including picnic area, near Guilder Pond, trails, restrooms, scenic viewing areas. Activities: Canoeing, hiking, cross-country skiing. Special Features: The top of Mount Everett offers a 360-degree panorama of Massachusetts, New York, and Connecticut. A segment of the Appalachian National Scenic Trail passes through the reservation (see separate entry in national trails section).

★2720★ MOUNT GRACE STATE FOREST
Winchester Rd
Warwick, MA 01378
Web: www.mass.gov/dcr/parks/central/mgrc.htm
Phone: 978-544-3939
Size: 1,458 acres. Elevation: 1,625 feet. Location: In northern central Massachusetts, on Winchester Road in Warwick, off Route 78. Facilities: Picnic area, restrooms, trails. Activities: Hiking, mountain biking, horseback riding, cross-country skiing, hunting (with restrictions), snowmobiling. Special Features: In 1676, during the era of Colonial skirmishes against the Wampanoag Indians known as King Phillip's War, Mary Rowland and her infant daughter Grace were captured by a band of King Phillip's warriors. On a march toward Canada the baby died, and it is said that she was buried by her mother's hands at the foot of the mountain that now bears her name.

★2721★ MOUNT GREYLOCK STATE
RESERVATION
Rockwell Rd
PO Box 138
Lanesborough, MA 01237
Web: www.mass.gov/dcr/parks/western/mgry.htm
Phone: 413-499-4262
Size: 12,500 acres. Elevation: 3,491 feet. Location: On Rockwell Road, off US 7, in Lanesborough. Facilities: 35 campsites, 5 group camps, backpack shelters, lodge accommodations, snack bar, restrooms (&), picnic sites, pavilion, trails, visitor center, scenic vista (&). Activities: Wilderness camping, hiking, backpacking, mountain biking, bird watching, hunting (with restrictions), cross-country skiing, snowmobiling, interpretive programs (seasonal). Special Features: Mount Greylock, the state's highest peak, offers spectacular views of up to 100 miles. Mountain summit includes the historic Bascom Lodge and the 92-foot-high War Veterans' Memorial Tower. The property was acquired by the Commonwealth in 1898 and became its first state park. A 14-mile segment of the Appalachian National Scenic Trail passes through the reservation.

★2722★ MOUNT HOLYOKE RANGE STATE PARK
Rt 116
Amherst, MA 01059
Web: www.mass.gov/dcr/parks/central/hksp.htm
Phone: 413-586-0350
Size: More than 3,000 acres. Location: In Amherst, off Route 116, in central Massachusetts. Facilities: Visitor center, picnic area, trails, restrooms (&), scenic viewing areas. Activities: Hiking, mountain biking, horseback riding, hunting (with restrictions), cross-country skiing, snowmobiling, displays and interpretive programs (seasonal). Special Features: Park straddles the 7-mile ridge that runs from Hadley to Belchertown. The ridge's steep slopes and east-west orientation create a number of forest types, including birch-beech-hemlock on the north side and oak-hickory on the south.

★2723★ MOUNT SUGARLOAF STATE
RESERVATION
Rt 116
South Deerfield, MA 01373
Web: www.mass.gov/dcr/parks/central/msug.htm
Phone: 413-545-5993
Size: 532 acres. Location: In the western part of central Massachusetts, on Route 116 in South Deerfield. Take Mass Pike (I-90) to Exit 4, I-91 north to Exit 24, then Route 116 east. Park is 1 mile on left. Facilities: Picnic area, restrooms (&), trails, scenic vista (&). Activities: Hiking. Special Features: Mount Sugarloaf consists of two peaks, North and South Sugarloaf, with an auto road that goes to the summit of South Sugarloaf. The mountain is composed of a prominent sandstone rock called Sugarloaf Arkose, and the view from its summit takes in the Connecticut River, the Pioneer Valley, and the Pelham and Berkshire Hills.

★2724★ MOUNT TOM STATE RESERVATION
125 Reservation Rd
Holyoke, MA 01027
Web: www.mass.gov/dcr/parks/central/mtom.htm
Phone: 413-534-1186
Size: 2,082 acres. Location: In Easthampton/Holyoke, in the western part of central Massachusetts. Facilities: Visitor center, picnic areas, playground, hiking and walking trails (20 miles), restrooms, scenic vistas (&&). Activities: Canoeing, fishing (&), hiking, cross-country skiing, ice skating, hawk watching. Special Features: Reservation is one of the premier hawk watching spots in New England. Each fall thousands of hawks and other birds fly past the mountain.

★2725★ MOUNT WASHINGTON STATE FOREST
RD 3
East St
Mount Washington, MA 01258
Web: www.mass.gov/dcr/parks/western/mwas.htm
Phone: 413-528-0330
Size: 4,169 acres. Location: In the extreme southwest corner of the state, in the southern Berkshires of western Massachusetts. Facilities: Wilderness campsites, restrooms, picnic area, trails (30 miles), scenic viewing area. Activities: Wilderness camping,

canoeing, fishing, hiking, mountain biking, horseback riding, hunting (with restrictions), cross-country skiing. **Special Features:** Situated on a mountain plateau, much of this forest was clear-cut between the late 1700s and mid-1800s to produce charcoal fuel for local iron forges. The red oak-northern hardwood forest has since regrown and offers 30 miles of trails over rugged terrain as well as wilderness camping.

★2726★ MYLES STANDISH MONUMENT STATE RESERVATION

Plymouth, MA 02360
Web: www.mass.gov/dcr/parks/southeast/mssm.htm
Phone: 508-866-2580
Size: 32 acres. **Location:** In southeastern Massachusetts, on Cresent Street in South Duxbury Center, off Route 3A north. **Facilities:** Historic site, picnic area. **Activities:** Mountain biking, interpretive programs (seasonal). **Special Features:** Built in the late 1800s, the monument is a 116-foot granite shaft crowned by a 14-foot statue of Captain Myles Standish, military leader of Plymouth Colony, and stands atop Captain's Hill, 200 feet above sea level. When the monument building is open (on weekends and during summer), visitors can climb 125 steps to a small viewing area at the top, but even from the base of the monument the view is spectacular.

★2727★ MYLES STANDISH STATE FOREST

PO Box 66
South Carver, MA 02366
Web: www.mass.gov/dcr/parks/southeast/mssf.htm
Phone: 508-866-2526
Size: 14,651 acres. **Location:** In southeastern Massachusetts, across the southern sections of Plymouth and Carver; access via Rt 3 or Rt 495. **Facilities:** 5 camping areas, including a section for horse camping, showers, restrooms (&), picnic area, boat ramp, hiking trails (13 miles), bicycle trails (15 miles), equestrian trails (35 miles). **Activities:** Camping, boating (non-motorized), canoeing, fishing, swimming, hiking, bicycling, horseback riding, hunting (with restrictions), cross-country skiing, snowmobiling, interpretive programs (seasonal). **Special Features:** Myles Standish is the largest publicly owned recreation area in southeastern Massachusetts, with 16 ponds and one of the largest contiguous pitch pine/scrub oak communities north of Long Island. Wildlife management areas within the forest are stocked with game birds in October and November. In the summer, interpretive programs such as pond shore walks, cranberry bog explorations, and fire tower tours acquaint visitors with the forest's unique natural, cultural, and historical aspects.

★2728★ NASHUA RIVER RAIL TRAIL

595 Main St
Townsend, MA 01474
Web: www.mass.gov/dcr/parks/northeast/nash.htm
Phone: 978-597-8802
Size: 11 miles. **Location:** Runs through Ayer, Groton, Pepperell, and Dunstable, with access at Ayer Center, Groton Center, Groton Sand Hill Road, and Dunstable at state line. **Facilities:** Scenic overlooks, rest stops; drinking water at Groton Town Hall; non-flush public toilets at trailhead in Ayer. **Activities:**

Walking/hiking, bicycling, inline skating, horseback riding, cross-country skiing. **Special Features:** Trail offers a 10-foot wide paved surface for the entire length, and a five-foot wide gravel equestrian path for seven miles of the trail from Groton Center to the New Hampshire boarder in Dunstable. The trail is universally accessible.

★2729★ NASKETUCKET BAY STATE RESERVATION

c/o Fort Phoenix State Reservation
Green St
Fairhaven, MA 02719
Web: www.mass.gov/dcr/parks/southeast/nbsr.htm
Phone: 508-992-4524
Size: 209 acres. **Location:** On the coastline of southeastern Massachusetts, in Mattapoisett, on Brandt Point Road. **Facilities:** Trails. **Activities:** Hiking. **Special Features:** Park offers wooded trails, open fields, and a rocky shoreline.

★2730★ NATURAL BRIDGE STATE PARK

PO Box 1757
North Adams, MA 01247
Web: www.mass.gov/dcr/parks/western/nbdg.htm
Phone: 413-663-6392
Size: 48 acres. **Location:** On McCauley Road, off Route 8 in North Adams, in the northern Berkshires of western Massachusetts. **Facilities:** Historic site, picnic area, walking trails, restrooms (&), scenic viewing areas. **Activities:** Fishing; interpretive programs (seasonal). **Special Features:** Park's 30-foot naturally-formed white marble bridge, created centuries ago by melting glaciers, is unique in North America. The bridge spans Hudson Brook as it tumbles through a steep 60-foot deep gorge.

★2731★ NICKERSON STATE PARK

3488 Main St
Brewster, MA 02631
Web: www.mass.gov/dcr/parks/southeast/nick.htm
Phone: 508-896-3491; **Toll Free:** 877-422-6762
Size: 1,955 acres. **Location:** In southeastern Massachusetts on the mid-Cape, on Route 6A west near Brewster. **Facilities:** 420 campsites (including & sites and yurt camping), showers, restrooms (&), picnic area (&), stocked ponds, beaches (&), trails, boat ramp, amphitheater. **Activities:** Camping, boating (non-motorized), canoeing, fishing, swimming, hiking, bicycling, mountain biking, horseback riding, cross-country skiing, birdwatching, interpretive and recreational programs (seasonal). **Special Features:** Park features eight crystal clear freshwater ponds known as "kettle ponds," which are among more than 300 such ponds that were formed as glaciers retreated from Cape Cod more than 10,000 years ago. These ponds are not fed by rivers or streams, but are completely dependent on groundwater and precipitation. An 8-mile bike path in the park connects to the 25-mile Cape Cod Rail Trail.

★2732★ NORWOTTUCK RAIL TRAIL

c/o Connecticut River Greenway State Park
136 Damon Rd
Northampton, MA 01060
Web: www.mass.gov/dcr/parks/central/nwrt.htm
Phone: 413-586-8706

Size: 8.5 miles. **Location:** West end access at Elwell Recreation Area in Northampton, at US 91 and Route 9. East end access at Warren Wright Road in Belchertown. **Facilities:** Trail (&), restrooms (&). **Activities:** Bicycling, skating, jogging, hiking, cross-country skiing. **Special Features:** Trail is part of Connecticut River Greenway State Park. It links Northampton, Hadley, and Amherst along the former Boston & Main Railroad right-of-way, with a level terrain that provides safe passage for pedestrians, wheelchairs, joggers, skaters, bicyclists, and cross-country skier of all ages and abilities. Motorized vehicles and horses are prohibited.

★2733★ OCTOBER MOUNTAIN STATE FOREST
317 Woodland Rd
Lee, MA 01238
Web: www.mass.gov/dcr/parks/western/octm.htm
Phone: 413-243-1778
Size: 16,500 acres. **Location:** In the central Berkshires in western Massachusetts, via US 20. **Facilities:** 46 campsites (including some & sites), showers, restrooms (&), trails, boat ramp and public landing. **Activities:** Camping, boating (non-motorized), canoeing, fishing, hiking, mountain biking, off-road vehicle riding (including ATVs), hunting (with restrictions), cross-country skiing, snowmobiling. **Special Features:** October Mountain is the largest state forest in Massachusetts, with trails for every level of experience. One of the most scenic trails leads to Schermerhorn Gorge, a natural feature that has intrigued generations of geologists. The forest also includes a segment of the Appalachian Trail.

★2734★ OTTER RIVER STATE FOREST
New Winchendon Rd
Baldwinville, MA 01436
Web: www.mass.gov/dcr/parks/central/ottr.htm
Phone: 978-939-8962
Size: 12,788 acres. **Location:** In north central Massachusetts. Take Rt 2 to Exit 20, turn onto Baldwinville Road and then turn right onto Rt 202 north. **Facilities:** 85 campsites (including yurt camping), showers, restrooms), showers, picnic areas, pavilion, swimming beach, ball field, trails. **Activities:** Camping, fishing, swimming, hiking, mountain biking, hunting (with restrictions), cross-country skiing, interpretive programs (seasonal). **Special Features:** Site is a popular camping and day-use facility centered around Beaman Pond. This property was the first land acquired by the State Forest Commission in 1915.

★2735★ PEARL HILL STATE PARK
595 Main St
Townsend, MA 01474
Web: www.mass.gov/dcr/parks/central/phil.htm
Phone: 508-597-8802
Size: 1,000 acres. **Location:** In the northeastern part of central Massachusetts, on New Fitchburg Road in West Townsend, off MA 119. **Facilities:** 51 campsites, bathhouse, restrooms, picnic area, group day-use area, trails. **Activities:** Camping, fishing, swimming, hiking, mountain biking, hunting (with restrictions),

cross-country skiing, snowmobiling, interpretive programs (seasonal). **Special Features:** Park is open seasonally, from Memorial Day through Labor Day, and has some of the largest and most private campsites in Massachusetts.

★2736★ PILGRIM MEMORIAL (PLYMOUTH ROCK) STATE PARK
Water St
Plymouth, MA 02360
Web: www.mass.gov/dcr/parks/southeast/plgm.htm
Phone: 508-866-2580
Size: 9 acres. **Location:** Route 3 south to Route 44 (Plymouth). Follow 44 east to waterfront. **Facilities:** Historic site, restrooms (&), scenic viewing area. **Activities:** Interpretive programs. **Special Features:** Park is the site of Plymouth Rock, where the Pilgrims landed on December 26, 1620. A waterfront park provides scenic views of Plymouth Harbor, where a replica of the *Mayflower* is anchored.

★2737★ PITTSFIELD STATE FOREST
1041 Cascade St
Pittsfield, MA 01201
Web: www.mass.gov/dcr/parks/western/pitt.htm
Phone: 413-442-8992
Size: 10,000 acres. **Location:** In the central Berkshires in western Massachusetts, off Route 20. **Facilities:** 31 campsites (13 rustic sites atop Berry Mountain, 12 sites with flush toilets at the mountain's base, and 6 open-field sites), restrooms (&), picnic area (&), group day-use area, trails (including nature and birding trails; some &), scenic vista (&). **Activities:** Camping, boating (non-motorized), fishing, swimming, hiking, mountain biking, horseback riding, off-road vehicle riding (including ATVs), hunting (with restrictions), cross-country skiing, snowmobiling. **Special Features:** Forest follows the crest of the Taconic Mountain Range separating Massachusetts and New York. It includes 65 acres of wild azalea fields that are a profusion of pink blossoms in June, and Berry Pond, which, at 2,150 feet, is one of the highest natural bodies of water in Massachusetts. The forest also includes Balance Rock, a 165-ton limestone rock with a diameter of only three feet at the point of balance.

★2738★ PURGATORY CHASM STATE RESERVATION
Purgatory Rd
Sutton, MA 01590
Web: www.mass.gov/dcr/parks/central/purg.htm
Phone: 508-234-3733
Size: 2,660 acres. **Location:** In the southeastern part of central Massachusetts, off Route 146 to Sutton. **Facilities:** Visitor center, picnic area, restrooms (&), trails, scenic viewing area. **Activities:** Hiking, cross-country skiing, rock climbing, hunting (with restrictions), interpretive programs. **Special Features:** Chasm is a unique natural landmark that runs for a quarter-mile between granite walls that rise to 70 feet. Trails lead to a wide variety of rock formations.

★2739★ QUABBIN RESERVOIR WATERSHED
Quabbin Visitor Center
495 Ware Rd
Belchertown, MA 01007
Web: www.mass.gov/dcr/parks/central/quabbin.htm
Phone: 413-323-7221
Size: 39 square miles water area. **Location:** Off Route 9 in Belchertown. **Facilities:** Visitor center, walking trails, scenic views. **Activities:** Shoreline fishing (with restrictions), hunting (with restrictions), hiking, bicycling (limited), bird watching, snowshoeing, picnicking (carry in, carry out), bird watching. **Special Features:** Created in the 1930s, Reservoir is one of the largest man-made public water supplies in the U.S. In order to flood the Swift River Valley, the entire population of four towns had to be relocated, including a railroad line and more than 6,000 graves. The primary purpose of the reservoir and surrounding lands is to supply drinking water, so public access is carefully regulated and controlled.

★2740★ QUINSIGAMOND STATE PARK
10 N Lake Ave
Worcester, MA 01605
Web: www.mass.gov/dcr/parks/central/quin.htm
Phone: 508-755-6880; **Fax:** 508-755-5347
Size: 51 acres. **Location:** Near Worcester, in central Massachusetts. **Facilities:** Picnic areas, swimming beach, tennis courts, restrooms (&), showers. **Activities:** Boating (nonmotorized), sailing, fishing (&), swimming. **Special Features:** Lake Quinsigamond's 2,000-meter rowing course is internationally recognized as one of the best courses in the world.

★2741★ ROBINSON STATE PARK
428 North St
Agawam, MA 01001
Web: www.mass.gov/dcr/parks/central/robn.htm
Phone: 413-786-2877
Size: 811 acres. **Location:** In the southwestern part of central Massachusetts. Take Mass Pike (I-90) to Exit 4, I-91 south, Route 57 west, Route 187 north to North Street. Follow signs. **Facilities:** Picnic areas, trails (&), restrooms (&), scenic viewing areas. **Activities:** Fishing, canoeing, swimming, hiking, bicycling, mountain biking, cross-country skiing. **Special Features:** Located just minutes from Springfield on the Westfield River, this urban park serves as a major day-use area. It features five miles of frontage on the river, and one of its most picturesque spots is a 17-acre island west of the falls at Mittineague.

★2742★ RUTLAND STATE PARK
Rt 122A
Rutland, MA 01543
Web: www.mass.gov/dcr/parks/central/rtld.htm
Phone: 508-886-6333
Size: 300 acres. **Location:** In mid-central Massachusetts, on Route 122A. **Facilities:** Picnic area, group day-use area, trails, restrooms. **Activities:** Boating (non-motorized), canoeing, fishing, swimming, hiking, mountain biking, hunting (with restrictions), cross-country skiing. **Special Features:** Park includes Whitehall Pond, which has a beach and freshwater swimming.

★2743★ SALISBURY BEACH STATE RESERVATION
PO Box 5303
Salisbury, MA 01952
Web: www.mass.gov/dcr/parks/northeast/salb.htm
Phone: 978-462-4481
Size: 521 acres. **Location:** On the coast of northeastern Massachusetts, on Route 1A in Salisbury. **Facilities:** 484 campsites (many with electrical hookups; some &), bathhouses, beach (&), comfort stations, boardwalk, restrooms (&), picnic area, pavilions, playground, 2 boat ramps. **Activities:** Camping, boating (all types), fishing, swimming, hunting (with restrictions), interpretive programs. **Special Features:** Park's beach extends 3.8 miles along the Atlantic Ocean, and in the fall and winter harbor seals sun themselves on the jetty. The town of Salisbury has many activities for children, including an amusement park and video arcade.

★2744★ SANDISFIELD STATE FOREST
PO Box 97
Monterey, MA 01245
Web: www.mass.gov/dcr/parks/western/sand.htm
Phone: 413-229-8212
Size: 7,785 acres. **Location:** In the southern Berkshires in western Massachusetts, off MA 57 in New Marlborough. **Facilities:** Picnic area, boat ramp, restrooms, trails. **Activities:** Boating (non-motorized), canoeing, fishing, swimming, hunting (with restrictions), hiking, cross-country skiing. **Special Features:** Within the hardwood forest are six lakes, ranging in size from 10 to 60 acres. York Lake is a popular day-use area with a 300-foot sandy beach.

★2745★ SANDY POINT STATE RESERVATION
PO Box 5303
Salisbury, MA 01952
Web: www.mass.gov/dcr/parks/northeast/sndp.htm
Phone: 978-462-4481
Size: 77 acres. **Location:** On the northeast coast of Massachusetts, 35 miles north of Boston, near the City of Newburyport in Parker River Wildlife Refuge (about 6 miles from the entrance of the refuge). **Facilities:** Walking trails. **Activities:** Fishing, birding, walking, beachcombing, hunting (with restrictions). **Special Features:** Reservation is at the southern tip of Plum Island, a classic Atlantic Ocean barrier island, with access through the adjacent Parker River National Wildlife Refuge (see entry in national wildlife refuges section). Sandy Point is an important nesting area for the endangered piping plover as well for the least tern, which is a species of special concern in Massachusetts. Recreation opportunities at the reservation are passive.

★2746★ SAVOY MOUNTAIN STATE FOREST
260 Central Shaft Rd
Florida, MA 01247
Web: www.mass.gov/dcr/parks/western/svym.htm
Phone: 413-663-8469
Size: 11,118 acres. **Location:** In the northern Berkshires of

western Massachusetts, off MA 2. **Facilities:** 45 campsites (including & sites), 1 group camp, 4 log cabins (available for year-round rental), showers, restrooms (&), picnic area (&), hiking trails (&), nature and birding trails, boat ramp, historic site. **Activities:** Camping, boating (non-motorized), canoeing, fishing, swimming, hiking, mountain biking, hunting (with restrictions), birdwatching, cross-country skiing, interpretive programs (seasonal). **Special Features:** Natural features include Bog Pond, with its floating bog islands, and Tannery Falls, where Ross Brook flows through a deep chasm and then cascades over 50 feet to a clear pool below.

★2747★ **SCHOONER ERNESTINA**
New Bedford State Pier
PO Box 2010
New Bedford, MA 02741
Web: www.mass.gov/dcr/parks/southeast/schern.htm
Phone: 508-992-4900
Location: Exit 15 off Rt 195 to Route 118 South, then left at second traffic light to State Pier. **Facilities:** Historic site. **Special Features:** A designated National Historic Landmark, the schooner was built in 1894 at the James and Tarr Yard in Essex, Massachusetts and is one of six remaining Essex-built schooners. She reached within 600 miles of the North Pole and is the last ship to bring immigrants to this country under sail from the Cape Verde Islands.

★2748★ **SCUSSET BEACH STATE RESERVATION**
140 Scusset Beach Rd
Sagamore Beach, MA 02562
Web: www.mass.gov/dcr/parks/southeast/scus.htm
Phone: 508-888-0859
Size: 380 acres. **Location:** In southeastern Massachusetts, on Cape Cod Bay at the east end of the Cape Cod Canal. **Facilities:** 98 campsites (mostly trailer sites; some &), showers, restrooms (&), picnic area, beaches, fishing pier, hiking trails (&), walking trails, historic site, interpretive center. **Activities:** Camping, fishing, swimming, bicycling, hiking, hunting (with restrictions), interpretive programs. **Special Features:** This popular swimming and camping area includes 1.5 miles of frontage along Cape Cod Canal, with views of the variety of boats and ships that pass through the canal.

★2749★ **SHAWME-CROWELL STATE FOREST**
PO Box 621
Sandwich, MA 02563
Web: www.mass.gov/dcr/parks/southeast/schr.htm
Phone: 508-888-0351
Size: 742 acres. **Location:** On Cape Cod in southeastern Massachusetts. **Facilities:** 285 campsites (some & sites), including yurt camping, showers, restrooms (&), picnic area, trails. **Activities:** Camping, swimming, hiking, horseback riding, hunting (with restrictions), cross-country skiing, interpretive programs. **Special Features:** More than 15 miles of roads and trails provide access to over 700 acres of pitch pine and scrub oak landscape.

★2750★ **SOUTH CAPE BEACH STATE PARK**
Great Neck Rd
Mashpee, MA 02649
Web: www.mass.gov/dcr/parks/southeast/socp.htm
Phone: 508-457-0495
Size: 401 acres. **Location:** In southeastern Massachusetts, on the southern part of Cape Cod, between between Waquoit Bay and Vineyard Sound. **Facilities:** Beaches (&), trails, restrooms (&). **Activities:** Boating (all types), canoeing, fishing, swimming, hiking, hunting (with restrictions), interpretive programs. **Special Features:** Park contains a wide variety of coastal environments, including barrier beach and dunes, salt marsh, scrub oak/pitch pine woodland and "kettle" ponds. Its white sand beach is over a mile long and features over-the-dune boardwalks.

★2751★ **SPENCER STATE FOREST**
Howe Pond Rd
Spencer, MA 01562
Web: www.mass.gov/dcr/parks/central/spen.htm
Phone: 508-886-6333
Size: 965 acres. **Location:** In mid-central Massachusetts; take Route 9 west to Route 31 south to Howe Pond Road and follow signs. **Facilities:** Picnic area, trails, restrooms. **Activities:** Canoeing, fishing, swimming, hiking, horseback riding, hunting (with restrictions), cross-country skiing, snowmobiling. **Special Features:** Forest features Howe Pond, the focal point for much of the forest's recreational activity.

★2752★ **STREETER POINT RECREATION AREA**
Rt 20
Sturbridge, MA 01566
Web: www.mass.gov/dcr/parks/central/stpt.htm
Phone: 508-347-9257
Size: 10 acres. **Location:** In south central Massachusetts. Take Mass Pike (I-90) to Exit 9, Route 20 west, and follow signs. **Facilities:** Picnic area, restrooms (&&). **Activities:** Fishing, swimming, hunting (with restrictions). Boating access available on US Army Corps of Engineers-mainted ramps on Route 20. **Special Features:** Activities and facilities center around the 400-acre East Brimfield Reservoir.

★2753★ **TOLLAND STATE FOREST**
410 Tolland Rd
PO Box 342
East Otis, MA 01029
Web: www.mass.gov/dcr/parks/western/toll.htm
Phone: 413-269-6002
Size: 4,893 acres. **Location:** In the southern Berkshires in western Massachusetts; accessible via Mass Pike (I-90) or from MA 8. **Facilities:** Campground, showers, restrooms (&), beach, picnic area, trails, boat ramp. **Activities:** Camping, fishing, swimming, hiking, mountain biking, ATV riding (on designated trails only), hunting (with restrictions), cross-country skiing, snowmobiling, interpretive programs (seasonal). **Special Features:** The centerpiece of this state forest is 1,065-acre Otis Reservoir, which provides a variety of recreation opportunities. The campground is situated on a scenic and wooded peninsula.

In season, hunting is open for all kinds of game, including turkey, deer, and bear.

★2754★ UPTON STATE FOREST

205 Westboro Rd
Upton, MA 01568
Web: www.mass.gov/dcr/parks/northeast/uptn.htm
Phone: 508-278-6486
Size: 2,600 acres. **Location:** In the southeastern part of central Massachusetts. Take Mass Pike (I-90) to I-495 south (Upton Exit 21B). **Facilities:** Trails. **Activities:** Hiking, mountain biking, horseback riding, hunting (with restrictions), cross-country skiing. **Special Features:** Forest features nearly 15 miles of multi-use trails, open year round.

★2755★ WACHUSETT MOUNTAIN STATE RESERVATION

Mountain Rd
PO Box 248
Princeton, MA 01541
Web: www.mass.gov/dcr/parks/central/wach.htm
Phone: 978-464-2987
Size: 2,849 acres. **Location:** In central Massachusetts; principal routes to the forest are via Rt 2 or Rt 190. **Facilities:** Visitor center, picnic area (&), restrooms (&), trails, historic sites, scenic vistas (&). **Activities:** Hiking, cross-country skiing, downhill skiing, hunting (with restrictions), hawk watching, nature study. **Special Features:** The reservation surrounds the summit of Mount Wachusett, from which there are views of Mount Monadnock in New Hampshire, the Berkshires to the west, and the Boston skyline to the east. Wachusett Mountain is part of an extensive greenway area and is also the location of the largest known area of old growth forest east of the Connecticut River in Massachusetts, with trees dating over 350 years old.

★2756★ WAHCONAH FALLS STATE PARK

c/o Pittsfield State Forest
1041 Cascade St
Pittsfield, MA 01201
Web: www.mass.gov/dcr/parks/western/wahf.htm
Phone: 413-442-8992
Size: 104 acres. **Location:** In the central Berkshires in western Massachusetts, off Route 9/8A in Dalton. **Facilities:** Trails. **Activities:** Fishing, hiking, picnicking. **Special Features:** Wahconah Falls Brook flows over several smaller tiered falls, then cascades about 40 feet into a deep pool. A hiking trail at the park goes through open woods and along upper portions of the falls.

★2757★ WALDEN POND STATE RESERVATION

915 Walden St
Concord, MA 01742
Web: www.mass.gov/dcr/parks/northeast/wldn.htm
Phone: 978-369-3254
Size: 400 acres. **Location:** Near Lincoln and Concord in the Greater Boston area. **Facilities:** Historic site, beaches (&), picnic area, boat ramp, trails. **Activities:** Boating (non-motorized), canoeing, fishing, swimming, hiking, cross-country skiing, guided tours and educational programs. **Special Features:** Henry David Thoreau lived at Walden Pond from July 1845 to September 1847, and his experience at Walden provided material for his book *Walden*, which inspired public awareness and respect for the natural environment. Because of Thoreau's legacy, Walden Pond has been designated a National Historic Landmark and is considered the birthplace of the conservation movement. A replica of Thoreau's house and the location of his modest home are available for viewing by the public. The number of visitors at Walden Pond is limited to no more than 1,000 people at a time, so visitors are advised to call the park in advance to check on availability.

★2758★ WATSON POND STATE PARK

Bay Rd
Taunton, MA 02783
Web: www.mass.gov/dcr/parks/southeast/wpsp.htm
Phone: 508-884-8280
Size: 10 acres. **Location:** I-495 to Taunton exit. Follow signs. **Facilities:** Beach, picnic area, small pavilion, bathhouse. **Activities:** Swimming. **Special Features:** Park is seasonal and is operated only during the summer months (late May to early September).

★2759★ WELLS STATE PARK

PO Box 602
Sturbridge, MA 01566
Web: www.mass.gov/dcr/parks/central/well.htm
Phone: 508-347-9257
Size: 1,471 acres. **Location:** In south central Massachusetts, off Route 49 north. **Facilities:** 60 campsites, showers, restrooms, swimming beach (for campers' use only), hiking trails, equestrian trails, boat ramp, scenic viewing areas. **Activities:** Camping, boating (all types), canoeing, fishing, swimming, hiking, mountain biking, horseback riding, hunting (with restrictions), cross-country skiing, interpretive programs (seasonal). **Special Features:** Wells State Park is a woodland park with more than 10 miles of hiking trails. Old Sturbridge Village, a nationally-renowned living history museum of New England village life in and around 1800, is a 5-mile drive from the park.

★2760★ WENDELL STATE FOREST

Montague Rd
Wendell, MA 01379
Web: www.mass.gov/dcr/parks/central/wndl.htm
Phone: 413-659-3797
Size: 7,566 acres. **Location:** In the northeast part of central Massachusetts, on Montague Road in Wendell. Take Rt 2 to Rt 63 south through Miller Falls. **Facilities:** Picnic sites, pavilion, ball field, trails, boat ramp, restrooms, scenic vistas (&&). **Activities:** Boating (non-motorized), canoeing, fishing, swimming, hiking, mountain biking, horseback riding, hunting (with restrictions), cross-country skiing. **Special Features:** The main day-use area in the Forest is Ruggles Pond, a 10-acre natural pond

9. State Parks

with crystal-clear water for swimming and fishing. The Metacomet-Monadnock Trail traverses the forest boundaries, and there is a small Adirondack shelter for trail users.

★2761★ WESTERN GATEWAY HERITAGE STATE PARK

9 Furnace St Bypass, Bldg 4
North Adams, MA 01247
Web: www.mass.gov/dcr/parks/western/wghp.htm
Phone: 413-663-6312
Size: 7 acres. **Location:** In North Adams, in the northern part of the Berkshires in western Massachusetts. Take Route 2 to North Adams, then Route 8 south and follow signs. **Facilities:** Historic site, picnic area, restrooms, visitor center (&&). **Activities:** Interpretive programs. **Special Features:** Park is at a former railroad yard, where exhibits and artifacts tell the history of the controversial and dangerous Hoosac Tunnel, one of the greatest engineering feats of the19th century. The tunnel, which is still in use today, was dug 4.75 miles through Hoosac Mountain, linking Massachusetts to Albany, NY, and 200 men lost their lives building it.

★2762★ WHITEHALL STATE PARK

71 Cedar St
Hopkinton, MA 01748
Web: www.mass.gov/dcr/parks/northeast/whit.htm
Phone: 508-435-4303
Size: 909 acres. **Location:** In east-central Massachusetts, on Route 135 west of Hopkinton Center. **Facilities:** Trails, boat ramp. **Activities:** Boating (all types), canoeing, fishing, hiking. **Special Features:** The 592-acre Whitehall Reservoir was once a source of drinking water for nearby communities, and the park consists almost entirely of water.

★2763★ WILLARD BROOK STATE FOREST

595 Main St
Townsend, MA 01474
Web: www.mass.gov/dcr/parks/central/wilb.htm
Phone: 978-597-8802
Size: 2,597 acres. **Location:** In north central Massachusetts, 50 miles from Boston, in Ashby and Townsend on Route 119. **Facilities:** 21 campsites, restrooms, picnic area, trails. **Activities:** Camping, fishing, swimming, hiking, mountain biking, horseback riding, hunting (with restrictions), cross-country skiing, snowmobiling. **Special Features:** Situated on the Massachusetts-New Hampshire border, the campground here lies beneath a pine canopy. A 4-mile trail connects Damon Pond of Willard Brook State Forest with nearby Pearl Hill State Park (see separate entry).

★2764★ WILLOWDALE STATE FOREST

40 Asbury St
Topsfield, MA 01983
Web: www.mass.gov/dcr/parks/northeast/wild.htm
Phone: 978-887-5931
Size: 2,400 acres. **Location:** In northeastern Massachusetts, on Topsfield Road in Ipswich. **Facilities:** No developed recreational facilities. **Activities:** Hiking, mountain biking, horseback riding, cross-country skiing, hunting (with restrictions). **Special Features:** Forest features 40 miles of trails.

★2765★ WINDSOR STATE FOREST

East St
Williamsburg, MA 01096
Web: www.mass.gov/dcr/parks/western/wnds.htm
Phone: 413-684-0948
Size: 1,743 acres. **Location:** In the northern part of the Berkshires in western Massachusetts, on River Road near West Cummington. **Facilities:** 24 limited-service campsites (no showers or flush toilets), picnic area, trails, scenic viewing area, restrooms (&). **Activities:** Camping, fishing, swimming, hiking, mountain biking, horseback riding, hunting (with restrictions), cross-country skiing, snowmobiling. **Special Features:** Forest features the cascading falls at Windsor Jambs, where a brook plunges through a 25-foot-wide gorge, with 80-foot granite walls rising straight up on both sides.

★2766★ WOMPATUCK STATE PARK

Union St
Hingham, MA 02536
Web: www.mass.gov/dcr/parks/southeast/womp.htm
Phone: 781-749-7160
Size: 3,500 acres. **Location:** Near Hingham on Boston's South Shore (35 minutes from downtown Boston). **Facilities:** 262 campsites (including 140 sites with electrical hookups and some & sites), showers, restrooms (&), boat ramp, bike paths (&), trails, visitor center. **Activities:** Camping, boating (non-motorized), fishing, hiking, bicycling, mountain biking, horseback riding, hunting (with restrictions), cross-country skiing, interpretive programs (seasonal). **Special Features:** One of the park's attractions is Mountain Blue Spring, a popular source of fresh drinking water, which visitors can help themselves to for free.

Michigan State Parks

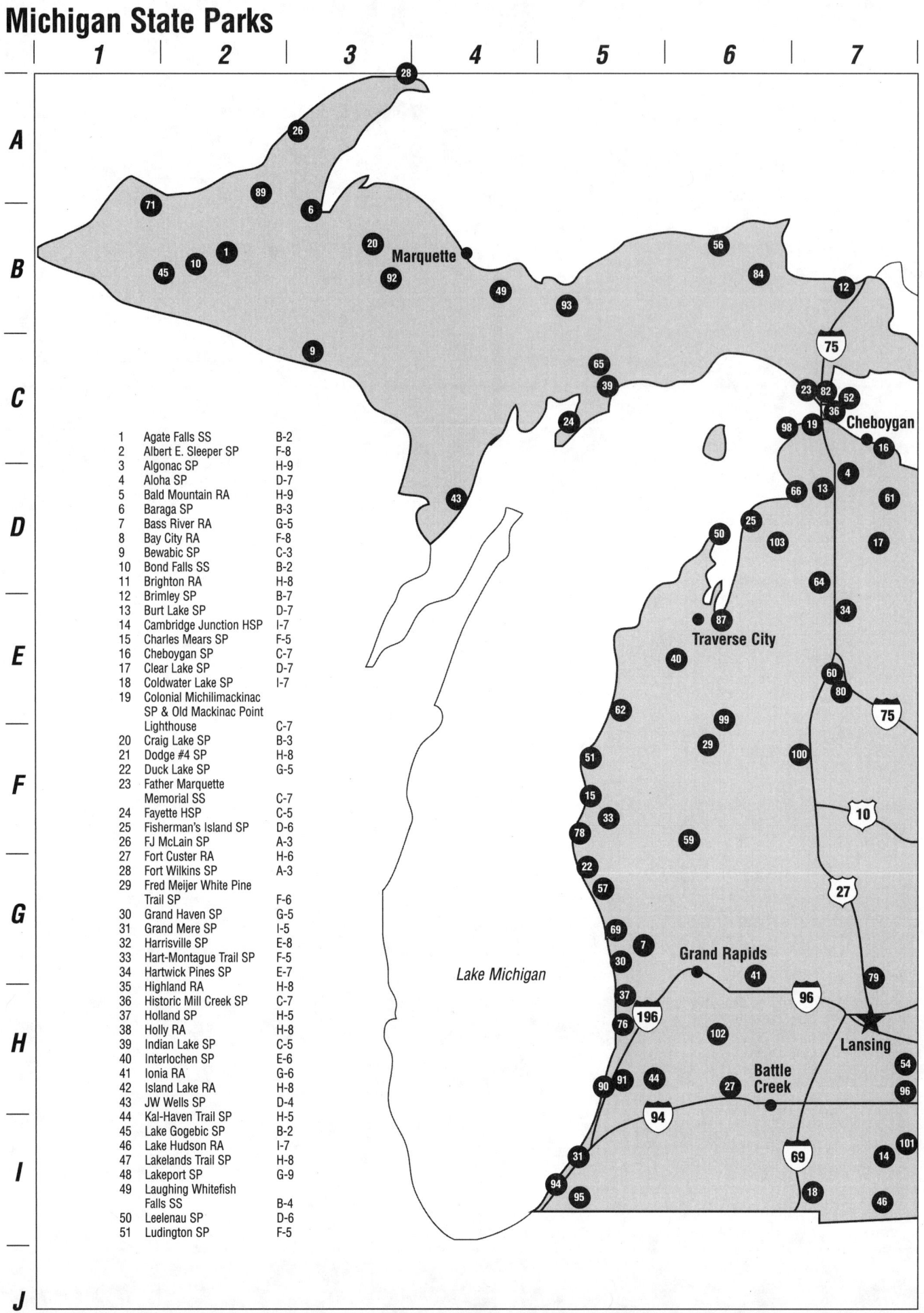

Marquette

Cheboygan

Traverse City

Grand Rapids

Lansing

Battle Creek

Lake Michigan

1	Agate Falls SS	B-2
2	Albert E. Sleeper SP	F-8
3	Algonac SP	H-9
4	Aloha SP	D-7
5	Bald Mountain RA	H-9
6	Baraga SP	B-3
7	Bass River RA	G-5
8	Bay City RA	F-8
9	Bewabic SP	C-3
10	Bond Falls SS	B-2
11	Brighton RA	H-8
12	Brimley SP	B-7
13	Burt Lake SP	D-7
14	Cambridge Junction HSP	I-7
15	Charles Mears SP	F-5
16	Cheboygan SP	C-7
17	Clear Lake SP	D-7
18	Coldwater Lake SP	I-7
19	Colonial Michilimackinac SP & Old Mackinac Point Lighthouse	C-7
20	Craig Lake SP	B-3
21	Dodge #4 SP	H-8
22	Duck Lake SP	G-5
23	Father Marquette Memorial SS	C-7
24	Fayette HSP	C-5
25	Fisherman's Island SP	D-6
26	FJ McLain SP	A-3
27	Fort Custer RA	H-6
28	Fort Wilkins SP	A-3
29	Fred Meijer White Pine Trail SP	F-6
30	Grand Haven SP	G-5
31	Grand Mere SP	I-5
32	Harrisville SP	E-8
33	Hart-Montague Trail SP	F-5
34	Hartwick Pines SP	E-7
35	Highland RA	H-8
36	Historic Mill Creek SP	C-7
37	Holland SP	H-5
38	Holly RA	H-8
39	Indian Lake SP	C-5
40	Interlochen SP	E-6
41	Ionia RA	G-6
42	Island Lake RA	H-8
43	JW Wells SP	D-4
44	Kal-Haven Trail SP	H-5
45	Lake Gogebic SP	B-2
46	Lake Hudson RA	I-7
47	Lakelands Trail SP	H-8
48	Lakeport SP	G-9
49	Laughing Whitefish Falls SS	B-4
50	Leelenau SP	D-6
51	Ludington SP	F-5

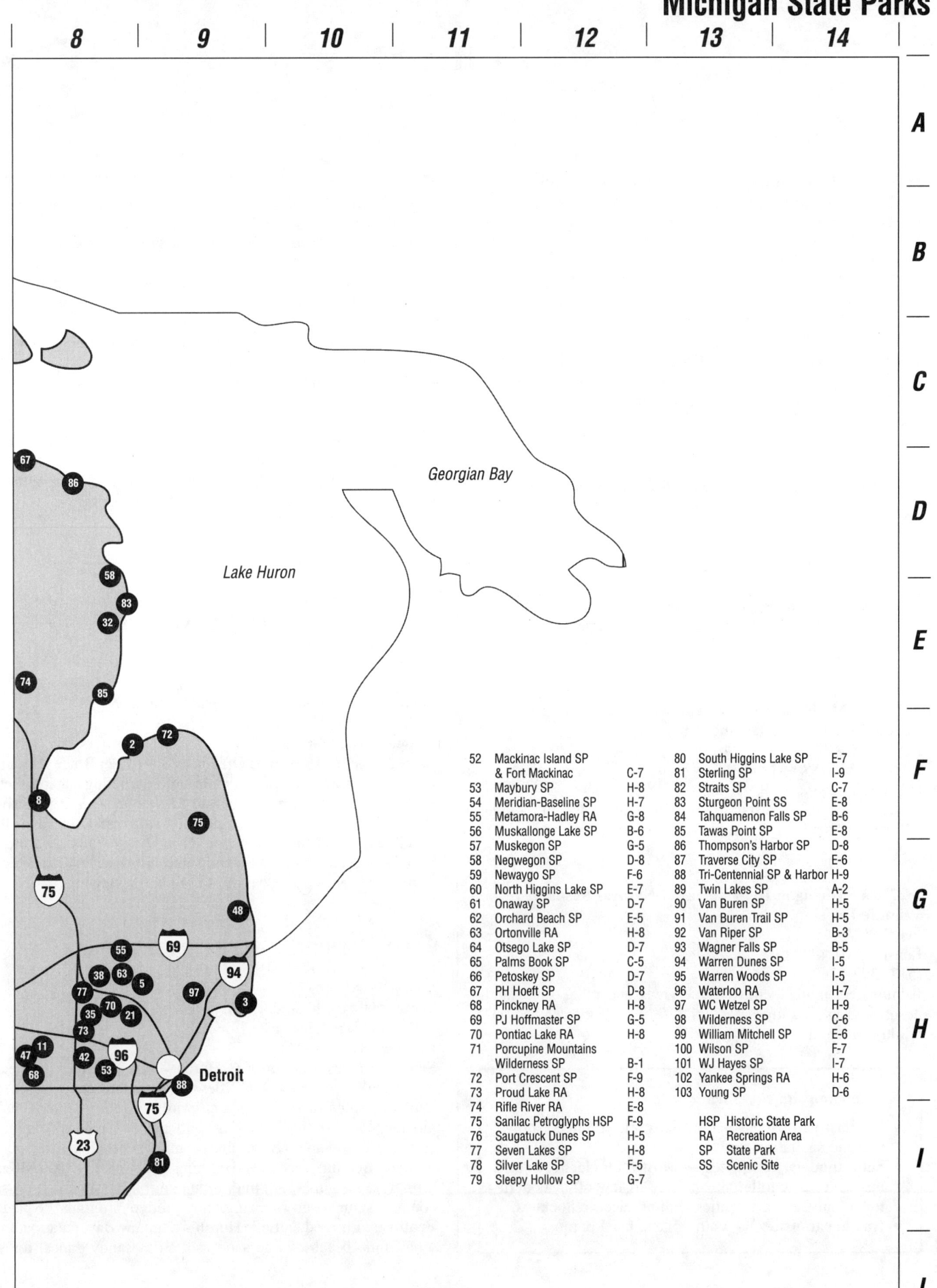

Georgian Bay

Lake Huron

Detroit

52	Mackinac Island SP		80	South Higgins Lake SP	E-7
	& Fort Mackinac	C-7	81	Sterling SP	I-9
53	Maybury SP	H-8	82	Straits SP	C-7
54	Meridian-Baseline SP	H-7	83	Sturgeon Point SS	E-8
55	Metamora-Hadley RA	G-8	84	Tahquamenon Falls SP	B-6
56	Muskallonge Lake SP	B-6	85	Tawas Point SP	E-8
57	Muskegon SP	G-5	86	Thompson's Harbor SP	D-8
58	Negwegon SP	D-8	87	Traverse City SP	E-6
59	Newaygo SP	F-6	88	Tri-Centennial SP & Harbor	H-9
60	North Higgins Lake SP	E-7	89	Twin Lakes SP	A-2
61	Onaway SP	D-7	90	Van Buren SP	H-5
62	Orchard Beach SP	E-5	91	Van Buren Trail SP	H-5
63	Ortonville RA	H-8	92	Van Riper SP	B-3
64	Otsego Lake SP	D-7	93	Wagner Falls SP	B-5
65	Palms Book SP	C-5	94	Warren Dunes SP	I-5
66	Petoskey SP	D-7	95	Warren Woods SP	I-5
67	PH Hoeft SP	D-8	96	Waterloo RA	H-7
68	Pinckney RA	H-8	97	WC Wetzel SP	H-9
69	PJ Hoffmaster SP	G-5	98	Wilderness SP	C-6
70	Pontiac Lake RA	H-8	99	William Mitchell SP	E-6
71	Porcupine Mountains		100	Wilson SP	F-7
	Wilderness SP	B-1	101	WJ Hayes SP	I-7
72	Port Crescent SP	F-9	102	Yankee Springs RA	H-6
73	Proud Lake RA	H-8	103	Young SP	D-6
74	Rifle River RA	E-8			
75	Sanilac Petroglyphs HSP	F-9	HSP	Historic State Park	
76	Saugatuck Dunes SP	H-5	RA	Recreation Area	
77	Seven Lakes SP	H-8	SP	State Park	
78	Silver Lake SP	F-5	SS	Scenic Site	
79	Sleepy Hollow SP	G-7			

MICHIGAN

★2767★ Michigan Department of Natural Resources
Parks & Recreation Bureau
PO Box 30031
Lansing, MI 48909
(517) 373-9900 - Phone
(517) 373-4625 - Fax
(800) 447-2757 - Reservations
(517) 373-3034 - Volunteering
Web: www.michigan.gov/dnr
Operates 97 parks, including linear trail parks, historic sites, and wilderness areas. Also manages the state's boating program, operates public access sites, mooring facilities, and marinas, and promotes the use of the Great Lakes by recreational boaters.

★2768★ Michigan Department of Natural Resources
Fisheries Division
PO Box 30446
Lansing, MI 48909
(517) 373-1280 - Phone
(800) 275-3474 - Fishing Hotline
Oversees 11,000 lakes, 36,000 miles of rivers and streams, and 6 fish hatcheries. Administers licenses, inventories fish communities, and monitors water resources.

★2769★ Michigan Department of Natural Resources
Forest Resource Management Division
PO Box 30452
Lansing, MI 48909-7952
(517) 373-1275
Manages six state forests on 3.9 million acres, which includes 145 campgrounds, trails, and canoe and trout streams.

★2770★ Michigan Department of Natural Resources
Wildlife Division
PO Box 30444
Lansing, MI 48909
(517) 373-1263
Administers more than 70 game areas and other state lands designated as wildlife areas, wildlife management areas, and wildlife research areas.

Key to campsite classification:

- **Modern campsites** — Electricity, flush toilets, showers, and sanitation station.
- **Semi-modern campsites** — Most offer electric hookups with rustic toilet, no showers. A few offer modern toilet and shower facilities with no electric hookups.
- **Rustic campsites** — Vault toilets, hand pump.

- **Equestrian campsites** — Rustic campsites with hitching posts for horses.
- **Rustic Cabins** — Equipped with single size beds or bunks with mattresses, table, chairs, and wood stoves for heat. There are outside hand pumps for water and vault toilets. Cabins vary in size to accommodate 4 to 24 people.
- **Mini-Cabins** — Sleep four, furnished with bunk beds, table, and electricity.
- **Organization campground** — Large area for youth groups only. Include vault toilets with running water or hand pumps.
- **Outdoor centers** — Specialized camping facilities for organized groups. Generally, each center has buildings for sleeping, a modern dining hall, kitchen, and a bathhouse serving groups of 30 to 120 campers.

★2771★ AGATE FALLS SCENIC SITE
c/o Baraga State Park
1300 US 41 S
Baraga, MI 49908
Web: www.michigandnr.com/parksandtrails/
ParksandTrailsInfo.aspx?id=413
Phone: 906-353-6558
Size: 213 acres. **Location:** Off Hwy 28 between Bruce Crossing and Trout Creek. **Facilities:** Picnic tables, drinking water, toilets, trail (&). Generally open from mid-May to late October. **Activities:** Hiking; scenic views. **Special Features:** Located in the middle branch of the Ontonagon River, Agate Falls are a broad band of interlacing cascades and small falls nearly 40 feet high. A foot trail provides access to the falls for viewing.

★2772★ ALBERT E. SLEEPER STATE PARK
6573 State Park Rd
Caseville, MI 48725
Web: www.michigandnr.com/parksandtrails/
ParksandTrailsInfo.aspx?id=494
Phone: 989-856-4411
Size: 723 acres. **Location:** In Huron County, 5 miles northeast of Caseville on M-25. **Facilities:** 226 modern campsites (&), outdoor center (a secluded area with 13 cabins, dining hall, kitchen, toilet/shower building, and picnic pavilion), day-use picnic area, shelter (&), trails (4 miles), beach house, playground. Boating access and fishing piers nearby. **Activities:** Camping, swimming, hiking, mountain biking, hunting, cross-country skiing, snowshoeing, interpretive programs. **Special Features:** Located on Lake Huron's Saginaw Bay, park features a half-mile beach of fine sand as well as sandy dunes, forest,

and wetlands. It is named for the Michigan governor (1917-1920) who signed into law the statute that created the state park system.

★2773★ ALGONAC STATE PARK
8732 River Rd
Marine City, MI 48039
Web: www.michigandnr.com/parksandtrails/
    ParksandTrailsInfo.aspx?id=433
Phone: 810-765-5605
Size: 1,450 acres. Location: In Saint Clair County, 22 miles northeast of I-94 Exit 243 (23 Mile Road). Facilities: 296 modern campsites, organization camp, semi-modern winter camping (includes electric service and vault toilets), picnic area and shelter (&), playground, trails, shooting/archery range, boating access sites nearby. Activities: Camping, fishing, hiking, biking, hunting, cross-country skiing. Special Features: Interpretive trails lead through the park's rare lake-plain prairie and oak savannah habitats, home to 19 plants on the state list of endangered, threatened, and special concern species.

★2774★ ALOHA STATE PARK
4347 3rd St
Cheboygan, MI 49721
Web: www.michigandnr.com/parksandtrails/
    ParksandTrailsInfo.aspx?id=434
Phone: 231-625-2522
Size: 106 acres. Location: 5 miles south of Cheboygan on M-33; 1 mile west via M-212. Facilities: 285 modern campsites, picnic area and shelter (&), 3 play areas with softball field, horseshoe pits, and volleball and basketball courts, swimming beaches, boat launch, multi-use trail. Activities: Camping, boating, fishing, swimming, ice fishing, hiking, bicycling, horseback riding, snowmobiling. Special Features: Park is located on Mullett Lake in the heart of the Inland Lakes Waterways, and campsites are near the Park's boat launch for those traveling this route. Mackinaw to Hawks Rails to Trails runs through the park.

★2775★ BALD MOUNTAIN RECREATION AREA
1330 E Greenshield Rd
Lake Orion, MI 48360
Web: www.michigandnr.com/parksandtrails/
    ParksandTrailsInfo.aspx?id=435
Phone: 248-693-6767
Size: 4,637 acres. Location: In Oakland County. Beach and day use areas are on M-24, about 2.5 miles from I-75; headquarters is 1.5 miles east of M-24 on Greenshield Road. Facilities: 2 rustic cabins, picnic area, 2 picnic shelters (&), playground, multi-use trails (15 miles), swimming beach, beach house, 2 fishing piers (&), 5 boat launching sites, shooting/archery range (&), snowmobile area. Activities: Boating, canoeing, fishing, swimming, hiking, hunting, mountain biking, cross-country skiing, snowmobiling. Special Features: This picturesque park area has some of the steepest hills and most rugged terrain in southeastern Michigan.

★2776★ BARAGA STATE PARK
1300 US 41 S
Baraga, MI 49908
Web: www.michigandnr.com/parksandtrails/
    ParksandTrailsInfo.aspx?id=408
Phone: 906-353-6558
Size: 56 acres. Location: 0.5 miles south of Baraga on US 41. Facilities: 116 modern campsites, 10 semi-modern campsites, picnic area, lighted pavilion, playground, nature trail. Activities: Camping, fishing, hiking, cross-country skiing, wildlife viewing, interpretive programs. Special Features: Park overlooks Lake Superior's scenic Keweenaw Bay. Area attractions include Bishop Baraga Shrine, the Sturgeon River Gorge, and Mount Arvon (Michigan's highest point).

★2777★ BASS RIVER RECREATION AREA
c/o P. J. Hoffmaster State Park
6585 Lake Harbor Rd
Muskegon, MI 49441
Web: www.michigandnr.com/ParksandTrails/
    ParksandTrailsInfo.aspx?id=436
Phone: 231-798-3711
Size: 1,665 acres. Location: Central Ottawa County, off M-45 to 104th Ave, then north 2.5 miles to west park entrance. Facilities: Boat launch, multi-use trails. Activities: Boating, hiking, mountain biking, horseback riding, cross-country skiing, hunting. Special Features: Park consists of open meadows, brush land, mature hardwoods, small ponds, and a 300-acre lake as well as about 3 miles of frontage on the Grand River.

★2778★ BAY CITY RECREATION AREA
3582 State Park Dr
Bay City, MI 48706
Web: www.michigandnr.com/parksandtrails/
    ParksandTrailsInfo.aspx?id=437
Phone: 989-684-3020
Size: 2,100 acres. Location: In Bay County, north of Bay City, 5 miles east of I-75 Exit 168 (Beaver Road). Facilities: 193 modern campsites, mini-cabins, organization campground, picnic areas (&), 5 shelters (&), 3-acre enclosed playground (&), beach house, fishing pier (&), bicycle trail (3 miles), hiking trails (7 miles), 3 observation towers, boardwalk, viewing platforms, shoreline spotting scopes, visitor center with exhibits, displays, and programs. Activities: Camping, hunting, fishing, ice fishing, swimming, hiking, biking, skating, cross-country skiing, wildlife observation, interpretive programs. Special Features: Situated on the shores of the Saginaw Bay, the park has one of the largest remaining freshwater coastal wetlands on the Great Lakes, the Tobico Marsh. With a mile of sandy shoreline as well as wetland woods, wet meadows, cattail marshes, and oak savannah prairies, the park is an ideal staging area for migratory birds and is known for its outstanding variety of wetland plants and wildlife.

★2779★ BEWABIC STATE PARK
720 Idlewild Rd
Crystal Falls, MI 49920
Web: www.michigandnr.com/parksandtrails/
    ParksandTrailsInfo.aspx?id=411
Phone: 906-875-3324

Size: 315 acres. **Location:** 4 miles west of Crystal Falls on US 2. **Facilities:** 133 modern campsites, 4 semi-modern campsites, picnic area and shelter, 2 playgrounds, tennis courts, trail, beach house, boat launch. **Activities:** Camping, fishing, swimming, hiking, cross-country skiing, tennis, horseshoes, volleyball. **Special Features:** Points of interest near the park include Pentoga Park, with its Indian burial ground, and Iron County Museum in Caspian.

★2780★ BOND FALLS SCENIC SITE

c/o Baraga State Park
1300 US 41 S
Baraga, MI 49908
Web: www.michigandnr.com/parksandtrails/
ParksandTrailsInfo.aspx?id=413
Phone: 906-353-6558
Size: 90 acres. **Location:** US 2 to US 45 north to Paulding, then 4 miles east on Bond Falls Road. **Facilities:** Picnic tables, boardwalk with 6 viewing locations (&). **Activities:** Hiking, scenic views. **Special Features:** The falls are created as the middle branch of the Ontonagon River tumbles over a thick belt of fractured rock, dividing it into numerous small cascades. Total drop of the falls is approximately 50 feet.

★2781★ BRIGHTON RECREATION AREA

6360 Chilson Rd
Howell, MI 48843
Web: www.michigandnr.com/parksandtrails/
ParksandTrailsInfo.aspx?id=438
Phone: 810-229-6566
Size: 4,947 acres. **Location:** In Livingston County, 6 miles southwest of Brighton off I-96. **Facilities:** 144 modern campsites, 50 rustic campsites, 19 equestrian campsites with stable and staging area, organization campground, 5 rustic cabins, hiking trails (7 miles), mountain bike trails (14 miles), equestrian trails (18 miles), picnic areas (&), 4 picnic shelters, playgrounds, beach house, fishing pier (&), boat launches, canoe rentals, horse rentals. **Activities:** Camping, fishing, swimming, hiking, mountain biking, horseback riding, hunting, cross-country skiing, bird watching, wildlife observation, interpretive programs. **Special Features:** Area has a combination of high, irregular ranges of hills interspersed with a number of lakes. Upland areas consist of oak forest, thick hedgerows, and open space, while lowland areas have grassy marshes, shrub marshes and dense swamp timber.

★2782★ BRIMLEY STATE PARK

9200 W 6-Mile Rd
Brimley, MI 49715
Web: www.michigandnr.com/parksandtrails/
ParksandTrailsInfo.aspx?id=414
Phone: 906-248-3422
Size: 160 acres. **Location:** I-75, Exit 386, west to M-28; turn right at intersection of M-28 and M-221 and go 2 miles to 6-Mile Road. **Facilities:** 237 modern campsites, picnic area and shelter, beach house, boat launch, playground. **Activities:** Camping, fishing, swimming, hiking, interpretive programs. **Special Features:** Located on Lake Superior's Whitefish Bay,

Park is a short drive from Tahquamenon Falls, the Hiawatha National Forest, the Tower of History, the Soo Locks, and a number of other area attractions.

★2783★ BURT LAKE STATE PARK

6635 State Park Dr
Indian River, MI 49749
Web: www.michigandnr.com/parksandtrails/
ParksandTrailsInfo.aspx?id=439
Phone: 231-238-9392
Size: 406 acres. **Location:** In Cheboygan County, on the southern end of Burt Lake, just south of the village of Indian River off I-75. **Facilities:** 306 modern campsites (&), mini-cabin (&), organization campground, trail (1 mile), picnic area and shelter &), boat launch (&), playground, concession/store. **Activities:** Camping, boating, fishing, swimming, hiking, cross-country skiing, interpretive programs. **Special Features:** Located on the southeast corner of Burt Lake with 2,000 feet of sandy shoreline, the park offers excellent fishing for perch, pike, and walleye. The park is open from early April to early November.

★2784★ CAMBRIDGE JUNCTION HISTORIC STATE PARK

13220 M-50
Brooklyn, MI 49230
Web: www.michigandnr.com/parksandtrails/
ParksandTrailsInfo.aspx?id=440
Phone: 517-467-4414
Size: 80 acres. **Location:** At the intersection of M-50 and US 12 in Lenawee County. **Facilities:** Historic tavern, visitor center, picnic tables. **Activities:** Exhibits, displays, nature programs. **Special Features:** Park is the site of Walker Tavern, a major stopping place for stagecoaches traveling between Detroit and Chicago in the early 19th century. The visitor center and restored tavern with period furniture tell the story of taverns and stagecoach travel for early Michigan residents. Site is operated in cooperation with the Department of History, Arts, and Libraries and is open May through October.

★2785★ CHARLES MEARS STATE PARK

W Lowell St
PO Box 370
Pentwater, MI 49449
Web: www.michigandnr.com/parksandtrails/
ParksandTrailsInfo.aspx?id=470
Phone: 231-869-2051
Size: 50 acres. **Location:** In Oceana County, east of the village of Pentwater, off US 31 (Monroe Rd exit). **Facilities:** 175 modern campsites, picnic area, shelter, playground, nature trail, beach house, beach volleyball court and horseshoe pits, concession/store, snowmobile area. **Activities:** Camping, fishing, swimming, hiking, snowmobiling, cross-country skiing, ice fishing, interpretive programs. **Special Features:** Park is located just outside the quaint resort village of Pentwater along the Lake Michigan shoreline.

★2786★ CHEBOYGAN STATE PARK
4490 Beach Rd
Cheboygan, MI 49721
Web: www.michigandnr.com/parksandtrails/
ParksandTrailsInfo.aspx?id=441
Phone: 231-627-2811
Size: 1,250 acres. **Location:** In Cheboygan County, 3 miles northeast of Cheboygan off US 23 on Duncan Bay (Lake Huron). **Facilities:** 76 modern campsites, organization campground, rustic cabins, tepees, trails, picnic area and shelter, playground, beach house, carry-in boat launch. **Activities:** Camping, boating, fishing, swimming, hiking, mountain biking, hunting, cross-country skiing, wildlife observation. **Special Features:** Park is located on the Lake Huron Straits of Mackinac and features scenic views. One of the main focal points of the park is the site of historic lighthouse ruins. The park is open year round.

★2787★ CLEAR LAKE STATE PARK
20500 M-33 North
Atlanta, MI 49709
Web: www.michigandnr.com/parksandtrails/
ParksandTrailsInfo.aspx?id=442
Phone: 989-785-4388
Size: 290 acres. **Location:** In Montmorency County, 10 miles north of Atlanta on M-33. **Facilities:** 200 modern campsites, organization campground, trails, picnic area, shelter, playground, horseshoe courts, beach, 2 boat launches. **Activities:** Camping, boating, fishing, swimming, hiking, mountain biking, wildlife viewing, hunting (on state forest land), cross-country skiing, interpretive programs. **Special Features:** Park is located within the boundaries of Mackinaw State Forest, which covers the northern eight counties of Michigan's Lower Peninsula. This is elk country, and elk can be seen and heard throughout the area in the early morning and evening, especially during the spring and fall. The park also has a sandy beach with a shallow swimming area that makes it ideal for children.

★2788★ COLDWATER LAKE STATE PARK
Copeland Rd
Coldwater, MI 49036
Web: www.michigandnr.com/parksandtrails/
ParksandTrailsInfo.aspx?id=443
Phone: 517-780-7866
Size: 400 acres. **Location:** About 2.5 miles east of Old 27, on Copeland Road. **Facilities:** Undeveloped. **Activities:** Hunting, bank fishing, hiking, cross-country skiing, snowmobiling. **Special Features:** Terrain is a mixture of swamp and farmland leading up to a natural lake.

★2789★ COLONIAL MICHILIMACKINAC STATE PARK & OLD MACKINAC POINT LIGHTHOUSE
c/o Mackinac State Historic Parks
PO Box 370
Mackinac Island, MI 49757
Web: www.mackinacparks.com
Phone: 231-436-4100
Location: Near southern end of Mackinac Bridge (Exit 339 off I-75) on the west side of Mackinaw City. **Facilities:** Historic fort.

Activities: Interpretive programs. **Special Features:** Colonial Michilimackinac is a reconstructed colonial fur-trading village and military outpost of the 1700s, with 15 buildings "inhabited" by a regiment of redcoats as well as traders and colonial ladies who demonstrate cooking, sewing, and other domestic arts of the time. The reconstruction is based on information gathered during the nation's longest archaeological excavation.

★2790★ CRAIG LAKE STATE PARK
851 County Rd AKE
PO Box 88
Champion, MI 49814
Web: www.michigandnr.com/parksandtrails/
ParksandTrailsInfo.aspx?id=415
Phone: 906-339-4461
Size: 6,983 acres. **Location:** 1 mile west of Michigamme to Craig Lake Road; follow signs 8 miles north. **Facilities:** Rustic (primitive) campsites, 2 rustic cabins, trails, snowmobile area, boat launch (on Keewaydin Lake only). **Activities:** Backpack camping, hunting, fishing, hiking, snowmobiling, cross-country skiing. **Special Features:** Michigan's most remote state park contains numerous small ponds and six lakes, including 374-acre Craig Lake, with six islands and high granite bluffs along its northern shoreline. The park normally has nine months of snow conditions and provides habitat for a variety of wildlife including deer, black bear, beaver, loons, and a portion of the Upper Peninsula moose herd.

★2791★ DODGE #4 STATE PARK
4250 Parkway Dr
Waterford, MI 48327
Web: www.michigandnr.com/parksandtrails/
ParksandTrailsInfo.aspx?id=445
Phone: 248-682-7323; **Fax:** 248-682-5587
Size: 139 acres. **Location:** In Oakland County, 6 miles southwest of Pontiac and 1 mile from Cass Elizabeth Road and Waterford Township. **Facilities:** Picnic area, shelter &), playground, swimming beach, fishing pier (&), boat launch site (&), concession/store. **Activities:** Boating, fishing, swimming, hiking, cross-country skiing. **Special Features:** Park features a white sandy beach and a one-mile shoreline on Cass Lake, and has an excellent reputation for bass, pike, bluegill, perch, and trout fishing.

★2792★ DUCK LAKE STATE PARK
3560 Memorial Dr
North Muskegon, MI 49445
Web: www.michigandnr.com/parksandtrails/
ParksandTrailsInfo.aspx?id=446
Phone: 231-744-3480
Size: 728 acres. **Location:** In Muskegon County, off US 31 (exit at Whitelake Drive and follow signs to park). **Facilities:** Picnic area and shelter, paved footpath, beach house, boat launch (access to Duck Lake only), snowmobile area. **Activities:** Fishing, swimming, hiking, hunting, cross-country skiing, snowmobiling. **Special Features:** This secluded day-use park stretches from the northern shore of Duck Lake to Lake Michigan and features a towering sand dune.

★2793★ FATHER MARQUETTE MEMORIAL SCENIC SITE
c/o Straits State Park
720 Church St
Saint Ignace, MI 49781
Web: www.michigandnr.com/parksandtrails/
ParksandTrailsInfo.aspx?id=416
Phone: 906-643-8620
Size: 58 acres. **Location:** In Straits State Park in Saint Ignace, just west of I-75 off US 2. **Facilities:** Picnic facilities. **Special Features:** Memorial honors the Jesuit priest who established Michigan's first permanent settlement. (See entry in National Parks section for additional details.) Site is open from Memorial Day through Labor Day.

★2794★ FAYETTE HISTORIC STATE PARK
13700 13.25 Ln
Garden, MI 49835
Web: www.michigandnr.com/parksandtrails/
ParksandTrailsInfo.aspx?id=417
Phone: 906-644-2603
Size: 711 acres. **Location:** Off US 2, turn south on M-183 at Garden Corners; 18 miles to park entrance on right. **Facilities:** 61 semi-modern campsites (with electric hookups), cottage, picnic area and shelter, playground, trails (5 miles), boat launch, visitor center, historic village. **Activities:** Camping, fishing, swimming, boating, scuba diving, hiking, hunting, cross-country skiing, guided and self-guided tours, interpretive programs. **Special Features:** Park features a restored iron-smelting company town (1867-1891). Located on Michigan's upper peninsula, the park includes three miles of shoreline on Big Bay De Noc with a beach on Sand Bay. The protected waters of Snail Shell Harbor offer limited boat camping and an interesting site for divers to explore.

★2795★ FISHERMAN'S ISLAND STATE PARK
PO Box 456
Bells Bay Rd
Charlevoix, MI 49720
Web: www.michigandnr.com/parksandtrails/
ParksandTrailsInfo.aspx?id=447
Phone: 231-547-6641
Size: 2,678 acres. **Location:** Just south of Charlevoix, off US-31 on Bell's Bay Road. **Facilities:** 81 rustic campsites, picnic area, trails (3 miles). **Activities:** Camping, swimming, hiking, cross-country skiing, hunting. **Special Features:** Park is not an island itself but is situated on five miles of undeveloped Lake Michigan shoreline and encompasses the tiny Fisherman's Island, which is a short distance offshore.

★2796★ FJ MCLAIN STATE PARK
18350 Hwy M-203
Hancock, MI 49930
Web: www.michigandnr.com/parksandtrails/
ParksandTrailsInfo.aspx?id=423
Phone: 906-482-0278
Size: 443 acres. **Location:** 9 miles north of US 41 in Hancock on Hwy M-203, between Calument and Hancock. **Facilities:**

98 modern campsites, rustic cabin, 2 picnic areas, 3 shelters (&), 2 playgrounds, swimming beach, trails. **Activities:** Camping, hunting, fishing, swimming, hiking, cross-country skiing, interpretive programs. **Special Features:** Park is situated on Lake Superior in the heart of the Keweenaw Peninsula and offers spectacular sunsets and a great view of the Keweenaw Waterway Lighthouse.

★2797★ FORT CUSTER RECREATION AREA
5163 Fort Custer Dr
Augusta, MI 49012
Web: www.michigandnr.com/parksandtrails/
ParksandTrailsInfo.aspx?id=448
Phone: 269-731-4200
Size: 3,033 acres. **Location:** In Kalamazoo County, between Battle Creek and Kalamazoo, off M-96 via I-94 Exit 92. **Facilities:** 219 modern campsites (&), organization campground, 3 rustic cabins, 2 mini-cabins (&), picnic area, shelter (&), multiuse trails (25 miles), beach house (&), boat launch sites (&), fishing pier (&), snowmobile area. **Activities:** Camping, fishing, boating, swimming, hiking, mountain biking, horseback riding, cross-country skiing, snowmobiling, dog sledding, hunting, interpretive programs. **Special Features:** Park's terrain is typical of southern Michigan farm country, with second growth forests and remnant areas of prairie. Praire restoration is in progress with excellent results. The area features three lakes, the Kalamazoo River, and an excellent trail system, and is considered one of the best mountain biking areas in the Midwest.

★2798★ FORT WILKINS STATE PARK
15223 US Hwy 41
Copper Harbor, MI 49918
Web: www.michigandnr.com/parksandtrails/
ParksandTrailsInfo.aspx?id=419
Phone: 906-289-4215
Size: 698 acres. **Location:** Northern terminus of US 41 in the tip of the Keweenaw Peninsula, northeast of Copper Harbor. **Facilities:** 159 modern campsites, 4 group use camping areas, mini-cabin, picnic area, shelters (&), playgrounds, trails, boat launch, concession/store (&). **Activities:** Camping, boating, fishing, swimming, hiking, bicycling, mountain biking, cross-country skiing, wildlife viewing, interpretive programs, living history demonstrations, boat tours of the Copper Harbor Lighthouse (Memorial Day - mid-June). **Special Features:** Located in the northern Keweenaw Peninsula, Park features a restored 1844 military outpost and a lighthouse built in 1866 that was one of the first on Lake Superior. (See also Keweenaw National Historical Park in national parks section.)

★2799★ FRED MEIJER WHITE PINE TRAIL STATE PARK
6093 M-115
Cadillac, MI 49601
Web: www.michigandnr.com/parksandtrails/
ParksandTrailsInfo.aspx?id=508
Phone: 231-775-7911
Size: 92-mile linear park. **Location:** Between Cadillac and Grand Rapids. Take US 131 north to Post Drive, turn right onto

Belmont Road and continue to Rogue River Road, where park entrance is on the left. **Facilities:** Trail is open from Cadillac to Comstock Park. The trail surface is natural ballast and hard packed gravel, with 13 miles of asphalt pavement from Reed City to Big Rapids and 7 miles of asphalt pavement from just north of Rockford to Belmont. **Activities:** Hiking, bicycling, cross-country skiing, snowmobiling. **Special Features:** The corridor of the trail was formerly Penn Central Railroad, also known as the Michigan Northern. There are 14 open-deck bridges along the route. The largest bridge is 319 feet long and crosses the Muskegon River one mile north of Big Rapids.

★2800★ GRAND HAVEN STATE PARK

1001 Harbor Ave
Grand Haven, MI 49417
Web: www.michigandnr.com/ParksandTrails/
    ParksandTrailsInfo.aspx?id=449
Phone: 616-847-1309
Size: 48 acres. **Location:** In Ottawa County, in Grand Haven, off US 31 (park signage directs path from US 31). **Facilities:** 174 modern campsites, picnic area, shelter, playground (swingsets only), beach house, fishing pier, concession/store (&&). **Activities:** Camping, fishing, swimming, hiking, cross-country skiing. **Special Features:** Park has the broad, sandy shore of Lake Michigan along its west side and the Grand River along the north side. The park consists entirely of beach sand and provides scenic views of Lake Michigan and the Grand Haven pier and lighthouse.

★2801★ GRAND MERE STATE PARK

c/o Warren Dunes State Park
12032 Red Arrow Hwy
Sawyer, MI 49125
Web: www.michigandnr.com/parksandtrails/
    ParksandTrailsInfo.aspx?id=450
Phone: 269-426-4013
Size: 985 acres. **Location:** Off I-94, in southwestern Michigan. **Facilities:** Picnic area (&), shelter (&), boat launch, nature trail (&). **Activities:** Hunting (no rifles or handguns), hiking, swimming, cross-country skiing. **Special Features:** Park features one mile of Lake Michigan shoreline characterized by large sand dunes with deep blowouts. Three inland lakes lie in the undeveloped natural area behind the dunes.

★2802★ HARRISVILLE STATE PARK

248 State Park Rd
PO Box 326
Harrisville, MI 48740
Web: www.michigandnr.com/parksandtrails/
    ParksandTrailsInfo.aspx?id=451
Phone: 989-724-5126
Size: 107 acres. **Location:** In Alcona County, 0.5 miles south of the M-72 intersection in Harrisville on US 23. **Facilities:** 195 modern campsites, mini-cabins, picnic area and shelter (&), playground, nature trail (2 miles), boat launch (nearby). **Activities:** Camping, swimming, hiking, cross-country skiing, interpretive program. **Special Features:** Park is situated in a stand of pine and cedar trees along the sandy shores of Lake Huron.

Park does not offer any fishing or boating facilities, but there is a Dept of Natural Resources boating access site in Harrisville.

★2803★ HART-MONTAGUE TRAIL STATE PARK

c/o Silver Lake State Park
9679 W State Park Dr
Mears, MI 49436
Web: www.michigandnr.com/parksandtrails/
    ParksandTrailsInfo.aspx?id=452
Phone: 231-873-3083
Size: 22-mile linear trail. **Location:** .25 miles east of the Hart Exit off US 31 (Polk Road). **Facilities:** Separate biking and hiking/cross-country skiing lanes, designated snow-mobile paths, scenic overlooks, picnic areas along route. **Activities:** Hiking, bicycling, cross-country skiing, snowmobiling, wildlife viewing. **Special Features:** The paved, 22-mile linear trail is on an abandoned C&O railroad corridor and passes through rural and forested lands with scenic overlooks and picnic areas located along the route.

★2804★ HARTWICK PINES STATE PARK

4216 Ranger Rd
Grayling, MI 49738
Web: www.michigandnr.com/parksandtrails/
    ParksandTrailsInfo.aspx?id=453
Phone: 989-348-7068
Size: 9,762 acres. **Location:** In Crawford County, 3 miles north of I-75 Exit 259 on M-93, northeast of Grayling. **Facilities:** 100 modern campsites, organization campground, rustic cabin, picnic area and shelter, modern restrooms, trails, fishing piers, visitor center/museum (&&). **Activities:** Camping, fishing, hiking, hunting, cross-country skiing, mountain biking, wildlife observation, interpretive programs. **Special Features:** Park's principal feature is a 49-acre forest of Old Growth Pines, one of the last remaining tracts of virgin pines in the Midwest. The Hartwick Pines Logging Museum (closed in winter) is located near the park's Michigan Forest Visitor Center, which offers exhibits and displays relating to Michigan's forests.

★2805★ HIGHLAND RECREATION AREA

5200 E Highland Rd
White Lake, MI 48383
Web: www.michigandnr.com/parksandtrails/
    ParksandTrailsInfo.aspx?id=455
Phone: 248-889-3750
Size: 5,903 acres. **Location:** 17 miles west of Pontiac on M-59, 12 miles east of US 23 or 14 miles west of I-75. **Facilities:** 30 rustic and equestrian campsites, organization campground, a modern lodge, picnic areas, picnic shelters (&), hiking trails (17 miles), mountain bike trails (16 miles), equestrian trails (12 miles), riding stable, swimming beach, beach house, 2 fishing piers, 3 dog field-trial areas, snowmobile area. **Activities:** Camping, boating, fishing, swimming, hiking, horseback riding, mountain biking, hunting, cross-country skiing, snowmobiling, wildlife observation. **Special Features:** Park includes three day-use areas and access sites on four lakes. It also includes 546-acre Haven Hill Natural Area, which has all of Michigan's forest

types as well as some unusual flora and fauna, providing an excellent educational facility.

★2806★ **HISTORIC MILL CREEK STATE PARK**
c/o Mackinac State Historic Parks
PO Box 370
Mackinac Island, MI 49757
Web: www.mackinacparks.com
Phone: 231-436-4100
Size: 625 acres. **Location:** In Cheboygan County, 3.5 miles southeast of Mackinaw City, on US 23. **Facilities:** Historic site, nature trails, interpretive center, museum store. **Activities:** Interpretive programs. **Special Features:** Mill Creek was the Straits of Mackinac's first industrial complex, providing lumber for the settlement of Mackinac Island in the 1790s. Demonstrations of hand-saw techniques and the power of a water-driven sawmill are provided at the site. Park also has scenic trails, and beaver dams may be seen along the western edge of the creek.

★2807★ **HOLLAND STATE PARK**
2215 Ottawa Beach Rd
Holland, MI 49424
Web: www.michigandnr.com/ParksandTrails/
ParksandTrailsInfo.aspx?id=458
Phone: 616-399-9390
Size: 142 acres. **Location:** In Ottawa County, 7 miles west of Holland. **Facilities:** 309 modern campsites (includng full hookup sites), picnic area and shelter, playground, beach house, boat launch (nearby), concession/store (点点). **Activities:** Camping, fishing, swimming, ice fishing, interpretive programs. **Special Features:** Park is divided into two units, one along Lake Michigan and the other along Lake Macatawa. The Holland area of Michigan is well known for tulips, and the annual Tulip Time Festival held each spring features the widest variety and greatest number of tulips grown anywhere in America.

★2808★ **HOLLY RECREATION AREA**
8100 Grange Hall Rd
Holly, MI 48442
Web: www.michigandnr.com/parksandtrails/
ParksandTrailsInfo.aspx?id=459
Phone: 248-634-8811
Size: 7,817 acres. **Location:** In the northern portion of Oakland County, between Pontiac and Flint, via I-75 or US 23. **Facilities:** 144 modern campsites, 15 semi-modern campsites, organization campground, rustic cabin, 2 mini-cabins, picnic area, 3 shelters (点), beach house (点), boat launches, boat and canoe/kayak rentals, fishing piers, snowmobile areas, trails. **Activities:** Camping, fishing, swimming, boating, canoeing, hiking, mountain biking (点), hunting, cross-country skiing, snowmobiling, interpretive programs. **Special Features:** Area's rolling hills provide scenic lake overlooks and excellent fall color viewing.

★2809★ **INDIAN LAKE STATE PARK**
8970W County Rd 442
Manistique, MI 49854
Web: www.michigandnr.com/parksandtrails/
ParksandTrailsInfo.aspx?id=420
Phone: 906-341-2355

Size: 847 acres. **Location:** Take US 2 to Thompson, then M-149 north 3 miles to County road 442 and east .5 miles to park. **Facilities:** 145 modern campsites (点), 72 semi-modern campsites (with electric hookups), picnic area (点), 2 picnic shelters (点), playground, beach house (点), boat launch, trails (点). **Activities:** Camping, boating, fishing, swimming, hiking, hunting, cross-country skiing, interpretive programs. **Special Features:** Park includes two separate units that are three miles apart and separated by Indian Lake. The lake is 6 miles long and 3 miles wide and has a surface area of 8,400 acres, but it is shallow, with a maximum depth of 18 feet, and is best suited for smaller boats.

★2810★ **INTERLOCHEN STATE PARK**
M-137
Interlochen, MI 49643
Web: www.michigandnr.com/parksandtrails/
ParksandTrailsInfo.aspx?id=460
Phone: 231-276-9511
Size: 187 acres. **Location:** In Grand Traverse County, 15 miles southwest of Traverse City on M-137. **Facilities:** 428 modern campsites (点), 52 rustic campsites, organization campground, mini-cabins (点), picnic area and shelter (点), playground (点), nature trail, 3 boat launches (点), boat rentals, concession/store/cafe (点) with video arcade. **Activities:** Camping, boating, fishing, swimming, hiking, cross-country skiing, ice fishing, interpretive programs. **Special Features:** Established in 1917, Michigan's first state park is situated between two well-known swimming and fishing lakes, Duck Lake and Green Lake. Adjacent to the park is Interlochen National Music Camp, which offers nightly performances by world-renowned artists.

★2811★ **IONIA RECREATION AREA**
2880 W David Hwy
Ionia, MI 48846
Web: www.michigandnr.com/ParksandTrails/
ParksandTrailsInfo.aspx?id=461
Phone: 616-527-3750
Size: 4,500 acres. **Location:** In Ionia County, 3 miles north of I-96 Exit 64 (Jordan Lake Road). **Facilities:** 100 modern campsites (点), 49 equestrian campsites, mini-cabins, organization campground, picnic areas and shelters, playground, hiking trails (3.5 miles), mountain bike trails (9 miles), equestrian trails (15 miles), beach house (点), rustic boat launch, hard-surface boat launch, dog field-trial area. **Activities:** Camping, fishing, swimming, canoeing, hiking, mountain biking, horseback riding, hunting, cross-country skiing, snowmobiling, bird watching, interpretive programs. **Special Features:** Area includes rolling hills, open meadows, forested ridges, a deep lake, and a four-mile stretch of the Grand River. Birding is excellent, with more than 400 species identified by the Audubon Society.

★2812★ **ISLAND LAKE RECREATION AREA**
12950 E Grand River Rd
Brighton, MI 48116
Web: www.michigandnr.com/parksandtrails/
ParksandTrailsInfo.aspx?id=462
Phone: 810-229-7067

Size: 4,000 acres. Location: In Livingston County, just south of the Kensington Road exit (151) off I-96. Facilities: Organization campground, 2 rustic cabins, picnic areas, 7 shelters, playground, volleyball courts, 2 beaches, beach house, fishing pier, canoe rentals (also rowboats and paddleboats, paved bicycle trails (4 miles), mountain bike trails (14 miles), hiking trails (18 miles), shooting/archery range, snowmobile area (&&). Activities: Camping, canoeing, fishing, hunting, swimming, hiking, biking, cross-country skiing, snowmobiling, wildlife observation, interpretive programs. Special Features: Huron River winds through the area and is popular with canoeists. Park also has the only balloon port in the state park system.

★2813★ JW WELLS STATE PARK

N7670 Hwy M-35
Cedar River, MI 49887
Web: www.michigandnr.com/parksandtrails/
    ParksandTrailsInfo.aspx?id=432
Phone: 906-863-9747
Size: 678 acres. Location: 30 miles south of Escanaba or 25 miles north of Menominee on M-35; 1 mile south of County Road G-12 and Cedar River. Facilities: 150 modern campsites, rustic cabins (&), lodge, picnic area (&), 2 picnic shelters (&), playground, 2 volleyball courts, horseshoe courts, beach house, trails (7 miles), rustic trailside shelters; boat ramp and charter fishing services in nearby Cedar River. Camping is seasonal, but the park is open year round. Activities: Camping, fishing, hunting, swimming, hiking, cross-country skiing, interpretive programs. Special Features: Park is located on Green Bay, with three miles of shoreline and a sandy beach.

★2814★ KAL-HAVEN TRAIL STATE PARK

c/o Van Buren State Park
23960 Ruggles Rd
South Haven, MI 49090
Web: www.michigandnr.com/parksandtrails/
    ParksandTrailsInfo.aspx?id=463
Phone: 269-637-2788
Size: 85 acres. Location: Trail connects Kalamazoo and South Haven. To reach the Kalamazoo trailhead, take US 31 west of Kalamazoo to M-43, then west .25 miles and north on 10th Street 2 miles. Activities: Hiking, bicycling, horseback riding, cross-country skiing, snowmobiling, wildlife viewing. Special Features: Trail is a is a 34-mile crushed limestone path made from old railroad corridors. It meanders through wooded areas, past farm lands, and over rivers and streams, and includes a camelback bridge and a covered bridge.

★2815★ LAKE GOGEBIC STATE PARK

N9995 State Hwy M-64
Marenisco, MI 49947
Web: www.michigandnr.com/parksandtrails/
    ParksandTrailsInfo.aspx?id=421
Phone: 906-842-3341
Size: 360 acres. Location: On M-64, between US 2 and M-28. Facilities: 105 modern and semi-modern (with electric hookups) campsites, 22 semi-modern rustic campsites (no hookups), picnic area and shelter, playground, beach house, boat launch, nature trail (2 miles). Activities: Camping, boating, fishing, swimming, hiking, cross-country skiing. Special Features: Park is located in an area with many spectacular waterfalls and includes nearly a mile of frontage on Lake Gogebic, the largest inland lake in the Upper Peninsula.

★2816★ LAKE HUDSON RECREATION AREA

5505 Morey Hwy
Clayton, MI 49235
Web: www.michigandnr.com/parksandtrails/
    ParksandTrailsInfo.aspx?id=464
Phone: 517-445-2265
Size: 2,796 acres. Location: In Lenawee County, 1.25 miles south of M-34 (Beecher Rd) on M-156. Facilities: 50 semi-modern campsites, picnic area and shelter, swimming beach, boat launch, volleyball nets. Activities: Camping, fishing, swimming, hunting. Special Features: Area includes 700-acre, man-made Lake Hudson and is designated a ''dark sky preserve'' for stargazing.

★2817★ LAKELANDS TRAIL STATE PARK

8555 Silver Hill Rd
8555 Silver Hill Rt 1
Pinckney, MI 48169
Web: www.michigandnr.com/parksandtrails/
    ParksandTrailsInfo.aspx?id=465
Phone: 734-426-4913
Size: 13-mile linear park. Location: Between Stockbridge and Pinckney. Trailheads are located .5 miles north of Pinckney on D-19 and .5 miles south of Stockbridge on M-106. Facilities: Trail. Activities: Hiking, bicycling, horseback riding, cross-country skiing. Special Features: Trail has a gravel surface and follows an abandoned rail corridor through wooded areas and rolling farmland. It is designed for hiking, bicycling, and wheelchair use on the north side and horseback riding on the south side.

★2818★ LAKEPORT STATE PARK

7605 Lakeshore Rd
Lakeport, MI 48059
Web: www.michigandnr.com/parksandtrails/
    ParksandTrailsInfo.aspx?id=466
Phone: 810-327-6224
Size: 565 acres. Location: In Saint Clair County, 10 miles north of Port Huron on M-25. Facilities: 250 modern campsites, mini-cabins, organization campground, picnic areas and shelter, playgrounds, concession/store. Activities: Camping, swimming, interpretive programs. Special Features: Park includes nearly a mile of Lake Huron beach. The park has two distinct units separated by the village of Lakeport.

★2819★ LAUGHING WHITEFISH FALLS SCENIC SITE

c/o Indian Lake State Park
8970W County Rd 442
Manistique, MI 49854
Web: www.michigandnr.com/parksandtrails/
    ParksandTrailsInfo.aspx?id=422
Phone: 906-341-2355

Size: 960 acres. **Location:** 2.8 miles north off M-94 at Sundell in Alger County (not far from Marquette). **Facilities:** Picnic area, trails, observation decks. **Activities:** Hiking, fishing, hunting, wildlife observation, scenic viewing areas. **Special Features:** Site features one of the Upper Peninsula's many impressive waterfalls. The North Country Trail, a national scenic trail, runs through the north end of this site, with a side trail to the falls.

★2820★ **LEELANAU STATE PARK**
15310 N Lighthouse Point Rd
Northport, MI 49670
Web: www.michigandnr.com/parksandtrails/
    ParksandTrailsInfo.aspx?id=467
Phone: 231-386-5422
Size: 1,350 acres. **Location:** In Leelanau County, north of Traverse City via M-22 to M-201, through Northport to County Road 629. **Facilities:** 52 rustic campsites, 2 mini-cabins, picnic area and shelter (&), playground, hiking trails (8.5 miles), museum. **Activities:** Camping, swimming, hiking, cross-country skiing, hunting. **Special Features:** ''Leelanau'' is a Native American word meaning ''A Land of Delight.'' Leelanau State Park is located on the tip of the little finger on Leelanau Peninsula and includes the Grand Traverse Lighthouse Museum, a restored lighthouse and fog signal building.

★2821★ **LUDINGTON STATE PARK**
PO Box 709
Ludington, MI 49431
Web: www.michigandnr.com/parksandtrails/
    ParksandTrailsInfo.aspx?id=468
Phone: 231-843-2423
Size: 5,300 acres. **Location:** In Mason County, 8.5 miles north of Ludington, on M-116 and Lakeshore Drive. **Facilities:** 3 modern campgrounds with a combined total of 352 campsites (&), 10 remote tent sites (hike-in), 3 mini-cabins (&), picnic areas, picnic shelter (&), playground, trails (&), swimming beaches, 2 beach houses, boat rentals (rowboat, kayak, canoe, or paddle boat), boat launch (&), 2 concessions, camp store, visitor center. **Activities:** Camping, boating, canoeing, fishing (&), hunting, swimming, hiking, bicycling, cross-country skiing, wildlife observation, lighthouse tours, interpretive programs. **Special Features:** Park is situated between Hamlin Lake and Lake Michigan, with several miles of shoreline and beaches on both bodies of water. The Great Lakes Visitor Center at the park features exhibits, displays, and programs about the wildlife, geology, and history unique to the Great Lakes.

★2822★ **MACKINAC ISLAND STATE PARK & FORT MACKINAC**
c/o Mackinac State Historic Parks
PO Box 370
Mackinac Island, MI 49757
Web: www.michigandnr.com/parksandtrails/
    ParksandTrailsInfo.aspx?id=418
Phone: 231-436-4100; **Fax:** 231-436-4210
Size: 1,800 acres. **Location:** In Mackinac County on an island in the Straits of Mackinac. Accessible by ferry from Mackinaw City and Saint Ignace; also accessible by plane to Mackinac

Island Airport. **Facilities:** Picnic area, playground, trails, concessions/store, historic fort, visitor center and museum. Open year round. **Activities:** Walking, hiking, horseback riding, bicycling, swimming, wildlife viewing, interpretive programs. **Special Features:** Park is Michigan's first state park and one of three state sites operated by Mackinac State Historic Parks. The park recreates life in the 1700s and early 1800s and features Fort Mackinac (built in 1780), Michigan's only revolutionary war-era fort. Other attractions on the island include a nature center, a scenic shoreline road, and inland trails with view of unusual geological formations. Cars are not permitted on the island.

★2823★ **MAYBURY STATE PARK**
20145 Beck Rd
Northville, MI 48167
Web: www.michigandnr.com/parksandtrails/
    ParksandTrailsInfo.aspx?id=469
Phone: 248-349-8390
Size: 944 acres. **Location:** In northwest Wayne County, at 8 Mile Road and Beck Road (5 miles west of I-275; 4 miles north of M-14; or 4 miles south of I-96). **Facilities:** Picnic area, 4 picnic shelters (&), playground, fishing pier, multi-use trails (some &), equestrian trail (11 miles), riding stable and horse staging area, ski trail (10 miles). **Activities:** Fishing, hiking (&), bicycling (&), mountain biking, horseback riding, cross-country skiing. **Special Features:** Maybury is a day-use park that provides a state park setting within a metropolitan area. Emphasis is on introducing the natural features of the environment to people who may not otherwise be able to experience it.

★2824★ **MERIDIAN-BASELINE STATE PARK**
c/o Waterloo Recreation Area
16345 McClure Rd
Chelsea, MI 48118
Web: www.michigandnr.com/parksandtrails/
    ParksandTrailsInfo.aspx?id=471
Phone: 734-475-8307
Size: 88 acres. **Location:** On Meridian Road, east from Leslie Exit off US 127, 20 miles south of Lansing. **Special Features:** This unique, landlocked park preserves the spot where measurements for all of Michigan's townships, ranges, and sections begin. The park is not accessible to the public, but is preserved for its historic value.

★2825★ **METAMORA-HADLEY RECREATION AREA**
3871 Hurd Rd
Metamora, MI 48455
Web: www.michigandnr.com/parksandtrails/
    ParksandTrailsInfo.aspx?id=472
Phone: 810-797-4439
Size: 723 acres. **Location:** In Lapeer County, 8 miles south of the city of Lapeer, off M-24. **Facilities:** 214 modern campsites, mini-cabins, picnic area and shelter, hiking trails (6 miles), beach house, boat launch, boat rentals (rowboats, paddleboats, canoes), 2 fishing piers (1 &), playground, concession/store, snowmobile area. **Activities:** Camping, hunting, boating, canoeing, fishing, swimming, hiking, cross-country skiing, snowmobiling, interpretive programs. **Special Features:** Park features rolling hills, vast wooded areas, and 80-acre Lake Minnewanna.

9. State Parks

★2826★ MUSKALLONGE LAKE STATE PARK

30042 County Rd 407
Newberry, MI 49868
Web: www.michigandnr.com/parksandtrails/
ParksandTrailsInfo.aspx?id=424
Phone: 906-658-3338
Size: 217 acres. Location: 28 miles northwest of Newberry in Luce County. Facilities: 159 modern campsites, picnic area, playground, boat launch, trails, snowmobile area. Activities: Camping, boating, fishing, swimming, hiking, rock hunting (especially agate), ice fishing, cross-country skiing, snowshoeing, snowmobiling, interpretive programs. Special Features: Park is situated between the shores of Muskallonge Lake and Lake Superior in an area known for its forests, lakes, and streams. There are about 70 lakes and 5 rivers within a 20-mile radius of the park.

★2827★ MUSKEGON STATE PARK

3560 Memorial Dr
North Muskegon, MI 49445
Web: www.michigandnr.com/parksandtrails/
ParksandTrailsInfo.aspx?id=475
Phone: 231-744-3480
Size: 1,165 acres. Location: In Muskegon County, 4 miles west of North Muskegon via the M-120 exit off US 31. Facilities: 244 modern campsites, 2 mini-cabins, organization campground (8 sites), picnic area and shelter (&), playground, hiking/ski trails (12 miles), luge run, beach house (&), lighted boat launch (&), fishing pier (&). Activities: Camping, boating, fishing, swimming, hiking, cross-country skiing, wildlife viewing, interpretive programs. Special Features: Park features more than 2 miles of sandy dune beach on Lake Michigan and more than 1 mile of frontage on Muskegon Lake, as well as a luge run and lighted ski trails. Attractions near the park include Michigan Adventure amusement park and the USS Silversides, a World War II submarine that is open for tours.

★2828★ NEGWEGON STATE PARK

c/o Harrisville State Park
PO Box 326
Harrisville, MI 48740
Web: www.michigandnr.com/parksandtrails/
ParksandTrailsInfo.aspx?id=476
Phone: 989-724-5126
Size: 2,469 acres. Location: In Alcona and Alpena Counties, off Black River Road, 15 miles northeast of Harrisville via US 23. Facilities: Undeveloped; there is a vault toilet and an Artesian well for drinking water. Activities: Hiking, hunting, wildlife observation. Special Features: A rustic, undeveloped area along the Lake Huron shore.

★2829★ NEWAYGO STATE PARK

2793 Beech St
Newaygo, MI 49337
Web: www.michigandnr.com/parksandtrails/
ParksandTrailsInfo.aspx?id=477
Phone: 231-856-4452
Size: 257 acres. Location: 5 miles west of US 131 Exit 125 to Beech Street, then north to park. Facilities: 99 rustic campsites, picnic areas, playgrounds, small beach, boat launch (&). Activities: Camping, boating, fishing, swimming, water-skiing. Special Features: Park's campground sits atop 20-foot embankments overlooking Hardy Dam Pond, with a 20-30 foot forested buffer between campsites.

★2830★ NORTH HIGGINS LAKE STATE PARK

11747 N Higgins Lake Dr
Roscommon, MI 48653
Web: www.michigandnr.com/parksandtrails/
ParksandTrailsInfo.aspx?id=478
Phone: 989-821-6125
Size: 429 acres. Location: In Crawford County; 5 miles west of I-75 Exit 244 or 1 mile east of the Military Road exit off US 27. Facilities: 174 modern campsites, picnic area, shelter (&), playground, multi-use trails (11 miles), boat launch (&). Activities: Camping, boating, fishing, swimming, hiking, biking, cross-country skiing. Special Features: Park is located on what was once the world's largest seedling nursery and offers a variety of tree, plant, bird, and animal species. The park also features a Civilian Conservation Corps Museum, and the Ralph A McMullen Conference Center is located nearby.

★2831★ ONAWAY STATE PARK

3622 N M-211
Onaway, MI 49765
Web: www.michigandnr.com/parksandtrails/
ParksandTrailsInfo.aspx?id=479
Phone: 989-733-8279
Size: 158 acres. Location: In Presque Isle County, 6 miles north of Onaway on M-211. Facilities: 96 modern campsites, picnic area, pavilion, swimming beach, boat launch, playground, nature trail. Activities: Camping, fishing, swimming, hiking, cross-country skiing. Special Features: Park is located on the southeast shore of Black Lake, in an area once frequented by Chippewa Indians, and features sand cobblestone beaches, large unique rock out-croppings, and a diverse variety of trees. The park is known for its variety of gamefish, including the elusive lake sturgeon. Ocqueoc Falls, the largest waterfall in Michigan's Lower Peninsula, is located just 10 miles east of the park.

★2832★ ORCHARD BEACH STATE PARK

2064 N Lakeshore Rd
Manistee, MI 49660
Web: www.michigandnr.com/parksandtrails/
ParksandTrailsInfo.aspx?id=480
Phone: 231-723-7422
Size: 201 acres. Location: In Manistee County, 2 miles north of Manistee on M-110. Facilities: 166 modern campsites, mini-cabin, trails, picnic area, pavilion with restroom, playground. Activities: Camping, swimming, hiking, cross-country skiing.. Special Features: Park is situated on a bluff overlooking Lake Michigan and has a self-guided nature trail.

★2833★ ORTONVILLE RECREATION AREA

5779 Hadley Rd
Ortonville, MI 48462
Web: www.michigandnr.com/parksandtrails/
ParksandTrailsInfo.aspx?id=481
Phone: 810-797-4439
Size: 5,400 acres. **Location:** In Oakland and Lapeer counties, just northeast of the village of Ortonville, off M-15. **Facilities:** 25 equestrian campsites (rustic, with vault toilets and a hand pump for water), a rustic cabin, picnic area, 2 shelters (&), playgrounds, horseshoe pits, hiking/biking trail (3.5 miles), equestrian trails (6.5 miles), beach house, boat launch sites (&), shooting/archery range (includes hand trap). **Activities:** Camping, boating, fishing, swimming, hiking, mountain biking, horseback riding, hunting, cross-country skiing, snowmobiling. **Special Features:** Park contains high wooded hills and offers a variety of recreational activities. Fishing and boating access sites are located on Algoe, Davidson, Round, and Today lakes.

★2834★ OTSEGO LAKE STATE PARK

7136 Old 27 S
Gaylord, MI 49735
Phone: 989-732-5485
Size: 62 acres. **Location:** In Otsego County. Take I-75 to the village of Waters, then go west to Old 27 and north about 5 miles to the park. **Facilities:** 155 modern campsites (most in the North Campground), picnic area and shelter (&), playground, volleyball and horseshoe courts, beach with boardwalk (&), beach house (&), boat launch (&), fishing pier, concession/store. **Activities:** Camping, boating, fishing, swimming. **Special Features:** The ''Alpine Village'' of Gaylord is easily accessible from this quiet, secluded family park, which is shaded by large oak, maple, and pine trees.

★2835★ PALMS BOOK STATE PARK

c/o Indian Lake State Park
8970W County Rd 442
Manistique, MI 49854
Web: www.michigandnr.com/parksandtrails/
ParksandTrailsInfo.aspx?id=425
Phone: 906-341-2355
Size: 388 acres. **Location:** At the northern terminus of M-149, north of US 2 at Thompson. **Facilities:** Picnic area (&), concession/store, observation raft and a trail leading to it (&). **Activities:** Nature study; hunting. **Special Features:** Park features the state's largest freshwater spring, Kitch-iti-ki-pi, the Big Spring, which measures 200 feet across and 40 feet deep. More than 10,000 gallons per minute gush from fissures in the spring's underlying limestone. A self-operated raft guides visitors to vantage points overlooking underwater features.

★2836★ PETOSKEY STATE PARK

2475 M-119 Hwy
Petoskey, MI 49712
Web: www.michigandnr.com/parksandtrails/
ParksandTrailsInfo.aspx?id=483
Phone: 231-347-2311
Size: 303 acres. **Location:** In Emmet County, 1.5 miles north of Petoskey off US 31 on the north end of Little Traverse Bay. **Facilities:** 168 modern campsites (&), mini-cabins (&), organization campground, picnic area with a 1-mile beach, playground, beach house, hiking trails, paved bicycle path nearby (&). **Activities:** Camping, swimming, hiking, cross-country skiing. **Special Features:** Park is located on Little Traverse Bay and features a beautiful sandy beach. Old Baldy Trail, one of two trails that run through the park, includes a stairway that leads up a stable dune (Old Baldy), which is one of the park's attractions. The view of the bay from the top of this dune is spectacular. Park is also a great spot to hunt for Petoskey stones.

★2837★ PH HOEFT STATE PARK

5001 US 23 N
Rogers City, MI 49779
Web: www.michigandnr.com/parksandtrails/
ParksandTrailsInfo.aspx?id=456
Phone: 989-734-2543
Size: 301 acres. **Location:** In Presque Isle County, 5 miles north of Rogers City on US 23. **Facilities:** 144 modern campsites, mini-cabin, organization campground, picnic area and shelter, 2 playgrounds, hiking trails (4.5 miles), paved bike trail. **Activities:** Camping, fishing, swimming, bicycling, hiking, hunting, cross-country skiing, interpretive programs. **Special Features:** Park is heavily wooded, with one mile of sandy Lake Huron shoreline. The moderating effect of the lake causes temperatures to be less extreme during both summer and winter and also causes up to two weeks delay in season changes compared to a few miles inland.

★2838★ PINCKNEY RECREATION AREA

8555 Silver Hill
Pinckney, MI 48169
Web: www.michigandnr.com/parksandtrails/
ParksandTrailsInfo.aspx?id=484
Phone: 734-426-4913
Size: 11,000 acres. **Location:** In Washtenaw County, off US 23 at Exit 49 (N Territorial Rd). **Facilities:** 186 modern campsites, 30 rustic campsites (25 at Crooked Lake and 5 at Blind Lake), picnic areas and shelters, playground, volleyball courts, horseshoe pits, beaches, beach houses, extensive system of hiking/mountain biking trails, equestrian trails, snowmobile area, boat launches and ramps (&), boat and canoe/kayak rentals (seasonal), fishing piers, concession/store. **Activities:** Camping, boating, canoeing/kayaking, fishing, swimming, hiking, mountain biking, horseback riding, hunting, cross-country skiing, snowmobiling, wildlife observation, interpretive programs. **Special Features:** Park features a chain of seven lakes and has three major use areas: Silver Lake Day Use Area, Bruin Lake Modern Campground, and the Halfmoon Day Use facility. The landscape of the park is a terminal moraine area formed during the last glaciation period.

★2839★ PJ HOFFMASTER STATE PARK

6585 Lake Harbor Rd
Muskegon, MI 49441
Web: www.michigandnr.com/parksandtrails/
ParksandTrailsInfo.aspx?id=457
Phone: 231-798-3711

Size: 1,043 acres. **Location:** In Muskegon and Ottawa counties, 3 miles west of US 31 via the Pontaluna Road exit. **Facilities:** 293 modern campsites, organization campground (2 sites), picnic area, shelter (&), trails, beach house, visitor center (&). **Activities:** Camping, swimming, hiking, cross-country skiing, wildlife observation, interpretive programs. **Special Features:** Park includes 2.5 miles of shoreline along Lake Michigan, towering sand dunes, and a stairway leading to the top of a high dune overlook. The Gillette Sand Dune Visitor Center offers programs, exhibits, and hands-on displays explaining the story of Michigan's sand dunes.

★2840★ PONTIAC LAKE RECREATION AREA

7800 Gale Rd
Waterford, MI 48327
Web: www.michigandnr.com/parksandtrails/
ParksandTrailsInfo.aspx?id=485
Phone: 248-666-1020
Size: 3,745 acres. **Location:** In Oakland County, 7 miles west of Pontiac on M-59, along the shore of Pontiac Lake. **Facilities:** 176 modern campsites, 24 equestrian campsites, picnic areas, picnic shelters (&), playground, ball field, concession/store, beach house, fishing piers (&), boat launch (&), hiking trail (2 miles), mountain bike trail (11 miles), equestrian trails (17 miles), horse rentals, pony rides, shooting/archery ranges (&). **Activities:** Camping, boating, water-skiing, tubing, fishing, swimming, hiking, mountain biking, horseback riding, hunting, snowmobiling, interpretive programs. **Special Features:** The area is a mixture of marshes, ponds, heavy forests, old farm fields, river bottom, and lakes. It supports a wide variety of animals, with excellent hunting as well as fishing for bass, pike, and panfish. The park's 11-mile mountain bike trail is ranked among the top 100 in the US.

★2841★ PORCUPINE MOUNTAINS WILDERNESS STATE PARK

33303 Headquarters Rd
Ontonagon, MI 49953
Web: www.michigandnr.com/parksandtrails/
ParksandTrailsInfo.aspx?id=426
Phone: 906-885-5275
Size: 59,020 acres. **Location:** 3 miles west of Silver City on M-107. **Facilities:** 100 modern campsites, 70 rustic campsites, a rental lodge, 19 rustic cabins, organization campground, picnic area and shelter, trails (100+ miles), beach house, canoe/kayak rentals (seasonal), 2 boat launches, concession/store, visitor center (open mid-May to mid-October), ski lodge, ski rentals. **Activities:** Camping, hunting, boating, fishing, swimming, hiking, mountain biking, cross-country skiing, downhill skiing, wildlife observation, interpretive programs. **Special Features:** Located 15 miles west of Ontonagon in the Upper Peninsula, Michigan's largest state park (and only state-designated wilderness) is one of the few remaining large wilderness areas in the Midwest. Set on the shores of Lake Superior, the park includes old-growth forest and varied scenic vistas. Areas of attraction within the "Porkies" include the Lake of the Clouds viewing area, Summit Peak observation tower, and the scenic Presque Isle River corridor, which has the state's second largest waterfall. The park also contains the Porcupine Mountains Ski Area, a major Michigan winter sports area.

★2842★ PORT CRESCENT STATE PARK

1775 Port Austin Rd
Port Austin, MI 48467
Web: www.michigandnr.com/parksandtrails/
ParksandTrailsInfo.aspx?id=486
Phone: 989-738-8663
Size: 565 acres. **Location:** In Huron County, 5 miles southwest of Port Austin on M-25. **Facilities:** 137 modern campsites, mini-cabin, trails (7 miles), picnic area and shelter, beach house, playground, fishing deck (&&). **Activities:** Camping, hunting, fishing, swimming, hiking, cross-country skiing, wildlife observation (&), interpretive programs. **Special Features:** Park is located at the tip of Michigan's "thumb" along three miles of sandy shoreline on Saginaw Bay.

★2843★ PROUD LAKE RECREATION AREA

3540 Wixom Rd
Commerce Township, MI 48382
Web: www.michigandnr.com/parksandtrails/
ParksandTrailsInfo.aspx?id=487
Phone: 248-685-2433
Size: 4,700 acres. **Location:** 6 miles north of I-96 at exit 159; 35 miles northwest of Detroit. **Facilities:** 130 modern campsites, organization campgrounds, picnic area and shelters, multi-use trails, boat launch sites, canoe/kayak rentals, concession/store. **Activities:** Camping, boating, canoeing, fishing, hiking, mountain biking, horseback riding, hunting, cross-country skiing, snowmobiling, interpretive programs. **Special Features:** Proud Lake is one of a chain of lakes linked by the Huron River, which runs for 4 miles through the park. The area has a distinct character of the North Country and features diverse plant life with striking autumn colorations.

★2844★ RIFLE RIVER RECREATION AREA

2550 E Rose City Rd
PO Box 98
Lupton, MI 48635
Web: www.michigandnr.com/parksandtrails/
ParksandTrailsInfo.aspx?id=489
Phone: 989-473-2258
Size: 4,449 acres. **Location:** In Ogemaw County, 4.5 miles east of Rose City off M-33. **Facilities:** 75 modern campsites, 99 rustic campsites, 5 rustic cabins (&), organization campground, picnic area, shelter (&), playground, multi-use trails, boat launch, snowmobile area. **Activities:** Camping, boating, canoeing, fishing, swimming, hiking, mountain biking, hunting, cross-country skiing, snowmobiling, snowshoeing, wildlife observation, interpretive programs. **Special Features:** Area is a wilderness located within the AuSable State Forest and provides a variety of recreational opportunities. It was formerly a private hunting and fishing retreat (Grousehaven) owned by the late HM Jewett, a pioneer auto manufacturer.

★2845★ SANILAC PETROGLYPHS HISTORIC STATE PARK

c/o Sleeper State Park
6573 State Park Rd
Caseville, MI 48725
Web: www.michigandnr.com/parksandtrails/
ParksandTrailsInfo.aspx?id=490
Phone: 989-856-4411
Size: 240 acres. Location: In Sanilac County, off Germania Road in Ubly, near Bad Axe. Facilities: Self-guided trail. Activities: Hiking, cross-country skiing. Special Features: Etched into a sandstone outcrop by Native American artists 300 to 1,000 years ago, the carvings depict panthers, deer, an archer, and more. They were discovered after forest fires swept the Lower Peninsula in 1881 and are the only known ancient petroglyphs in Michigan. They are very fragile and are available for viewing only via a use permit. The area containing the petroglyphic rock is fenced and is generally closed to the public, but the trail is open year round.

★2846★ SAUGATUCK DUNES STATE PARK

6575 138th Ave
Saugatuck, MI 49453
Web: www.michigandnr.com/parksandtrails/
ParksandTrailsInfo.aspx?id=491
Phone: 269-637-2788
Size: 880 acres. Location: In Allegan County, west of Highway 196 via Exit to 64th Street, then west on 138th Avenue to park. Facilities: Picnic area and shelter, trails (13 miles). Activities: Hiking, cross-country skiing, wildlife observation. Special Features: Saugatuck Dunes is a day use park along a secluded strip of Lake Michigan shoreline. The park's major attractions are the long sandy beaches and the 300-acre natural area, which contains a coastal dune system as well as three endangered plant species. Some of the dunes are more than 200 feet tall.

★2847★ SEVEN LAKES STATE PARK

14390 Fish Lake Rd
Holly, MI 48442
Web: www.michigandnr.com/parksandtrails/
ParksandTrailsInfo.aspx?id=492
Phone: 248-634-7271
Size: 1,434 acres. Location: In Oakland County, 5 miles west of I-75, Exit 101 or 5 miles east of US 23, Exit 79. Facilities: 70 modern campsites, picnic areas, shelters, playgrounds, beach house, boat launch sites on two lakes, boat rentals, concession/ store, snowmobile area, multi-use trails, fishing pier (&&). Activities: Camping, fishing, swimming, boating, canoeing, hiking, mountain biking, hunting, cross-country skiing, snowmobiling. Special Features: Park features a variety of ecosystems and topography, including rolling hills, forest, and sandy swimming beach.

★2848★ SILVER LAKE STATE PARK

9679 W State Park Rd
Mears, MI 49436
Web: www.michigandnr.com/parksandtrails/
ParksandTrailsInfo.aspx?id=493
Phone: 231-873-3083
Size: 2,936 acres. Location: In Oceana County. Follow signs west from US 31 at either the Hart or Shelby exit. Facilities: 200 modern campsites (&), picnic area, shelter (&), beach house, boat launch (&), off-road vehicle trails/routes. Activities: Camping, boating, fishing, swimming, hiking, hunting, ORV/ATV riding, interpretive programs. Special Features: Park features extensive frontage on Lake Michigan and includes acres of mature forest as well as dune country. The park's 450-acre vehicle "scramble" area is the only sand dunes site in Michigan that allows off-road vehicles.

★2849★ SLEEPY HOLLOW STATE PARK

7835 E Price Rd
Laingsburg, MI 48848
Web: www.michigandnr.com/parksandtrails/
ParksandTrailsInfo.aspx?id=495
Phone: 517-651-6217
Size: 2,678 acres. Location: In Clinton County, 15 miles northeast of Lansing off US 27. Facilities: 181 modern campsites, youth group campground, picnic areas, picnic shelters (&), playground, hiking/biking trails (16 miles), equestrian trails (6 miles), beach house (&), 2 fishing piers (&), boat launches (&), concession/store. Activities: Camping, boating, canoeing, fishing, swimming, hiking, mountain biking, horseback riding, hunting, cross-country skiing, snowshoeing, snowmobiling, bird watching, interpretive programs. Special Features: Park features Lake Ovid, a 410-acre manmade lake, and Little Maple River. More than 228 species of birds have been recorded in Sleepy Hollow, including the rarely recorded Bonaparte's Gull or Bald Eagle.

★2850★ SOUTH HIGGINS LAKE STATE PARK

106 State Park Dr
Roscommon, MI 48653
Web: www.michigandnr.com/parksandtrails/
ParksandTrailsInfo.aspx?id=496
Phone: 989-821-6374
Size: 962 acres. Location: On County Road 100 via Exit 239 off I-75 or US 127 to Higgins Lake Exit E. Facilities: 400 modern campsites (&), picnic area (&), 2 shelters (di), playground, self-guided nature trail (South Higgins, hiking trails (5 miles; Marl Lake), beach house (&), boat launch/ramp (&), boat rentals (seasonal), concession/store (&). Activities: Camping (Higgins Lake), boating, fishing (both lakes), ice fishing, swimming (Higgins Lake), hiking, hunting (Marl Lake), cross-country skiing, wildlife observation, interpretive programs. Special Features: Park is split by County Road 100, with Higgins Lake to the north and Marl Lake to the south. Most of the park's facilities are in the Higgins Lake area; the Marl Lake area is less developed.

★2851★ STERLING STATE PARK

2800 State Park Rd
Monroe, MI 48162
Web: www.michigandnr.com/parksandtrails/
ParksandTrailsInfo.aspx?id=497
Phone: 734-289-2715
Size: 1,300 acres. Location: In Monroe County, northeast of

I-75 Exit 15, **Facilities:** 256 modern campsites, picnic area, 2 picnic shelters, playground, 3 fishing piers, boat launch, multi-use trails (&&). **Activities:** Camping, boating, fishing, swimming, hiking, biking, cross-country skiing, wildlife viewing, interpretive programs. **Special Features:** Michigan's only state park on Lake Erie, Park is along the major flyway for migratory birds and a great place to see waterfowl, raptors, song birds, and wetland plants.

★2852★ STRAITS STATE PARK

720 Church St
Saint Ignace, MI 49781
Web: www.michigandnr.com/parksandtrails/
    ParksandTrailsInfo.aspx?id=427
Phone: 906-643-8620
Size: 181 acres. **Location:** In the city of Saint Ignace, on Church Street, south of US 2. **Facilities:** 255 modern campsites, 15 semi-modern campsites, mini-cabin, 2 organization campgrounds, picnic area, playground, national memorial, interpretive trail, observation deck. **Activities:** Camping, hiking, swimming. **Special Features:** Park is the site of the Father Marquette National Memorial and also offers panoramic views of Mackinac Bridge and the Straits of Mackinac.

★2853★ STURGEON POINT SCENIC SITE

c/o Harrisville State Park
PO Box 326
Harrisville, MI 48740
Web: www.michigandnr.com/parksandtrails/
    ParksandTrailsInfo.aspx?id=451
Phone: 989-724-5126
Size: 76 acres. **Location:** In Alcona County; take US 23 about 3 miles out of Harrisville to Lakeshore Drive, then 1 mile to Point Road and turn east to parking area. **Facilities:** Undeveloped. **Activities:** Swimming, hiking, wildlife watching. **Special Features:** Located on the site property is the Sturgeon Point Lighthouse and Maritime Museum. Lighthouse is owned by the US Coast Guard and maintained by the Alcona Historical Society.

★2854★ TAHQUAMENON FALLS STATE PARK

41382 W M-123
Paradise, MI 49768
Web: www.michigandnr.com/parksandtrails/
    ParksandTrailsInfo.aspx?id=428
Phone: 906-492-3415
Size: 46,179 acres. **Location:** In Chippewa County, on M-123, which can be reached via Mackinac Bridge (north from the bridge to Exit 352), Marquette (east on M-28), or Escanaba (US 2 east to M-117, then north to M-28 and east 3 miles to M-123). **Facilities:** 260 modern campsites (&), 36 semi-modern/rustic campsites, group camping area, picnic areas (&), shelter (&), playgrounds (&), boat launch (&), canoe/kayak rentals (seasonal), concession/store (&), hiking trails (&), snowmobile area. **Activities:** Camping, canoeing, fishing, hiking, hunting, cross-country skiing, snowmobiling, wildlife observation (&), interpretive programs. **Special Features:** Park stretches over 13 miles, most of which is undeveloped woodland with no roads, buildings, or power lines. The park's centerpiece, and the reason it exists, is the Tahquamenon River and its waterfalls. The Upper Falls, one of the largest waterfalls east of the Mississippi, has a drop of nearly 50 feet and is more than 200 feet across. Four miles downstream is the Lower Falls, a series of 5 smaller falls that cascade around an island.

★2855★ TAWAS POINT STATE PARK

686 Tawas Beach Rd
East Tawas, MI 48730
Web: www.michigandnr.com/parksandtrails/
    ParksandTrailsInfo.aspx?id=499
Phone: 989-362-5041
Size: 183 acres. **Location:** In Iosco County, 2.5 miles southeast of East Tawas off US 23. **Facilities:** 193 modern campsites, 2 mini-cabins, picnic area and shelter (&), playground, horseshoe pits, volleyball area, swimming beach, beach house (&), hiking trail, historic site. **Activities:** Camping, fishing, swimming, hiking, bird watching, interpretive programs. **Special Features:** Park is situated on the peninsula separating Tawas Bay from Lake Huron. It is a stopover point for hundreds of species of migratory birds, making it a favorite spot for bird watchers from all over the Midwest. The Tawas Point Lighthouse, built in 1876, is located at the park, with a museum store that's open May-October. The lighthouse is open for tours on week-ends Memorial Day through Labor Day, and the walk to the top of the tower offers a spectacular view of the bay.

★2856★ THOMPSON'S HARBOR STATE PARK

c/o Cheboygan Field Office
120 A St PO Box 117
Cheboygan, MI 49721
Web: www.michigandnr.com/parksandtrails/
    ParksandTrailsInfo.aspx?id=500
Phone: 231-627-9011
Size: 5,109 acres. **Location:** In Presque Isle County, 12 miles southeast of Rogers City via US 23. **Facilities:** Undeveloped. **Activities:** Hiking, hunting, fishing, wildlife observation, cross-country skiing. **Special Features:** Situated along 7.5 miles of Lake Huron shoreline, this park provides a rustic retreat for hikers exploring its 6 miles of trails.

★2857★ TRAVERSE CITY STATE PARK

1132 US-31 N
Traverse City, MI 49686
Web: www.michigandnr.com/parksandtrails/
    ParksandTrailsInfo.aspx?id=501
Phone: 231-922-5270
Size: 47 acres. **Location:** In Grand Traverse County, 3 miles east of downtown Traverse City on US 31. **Facilities:** 343 modern campsites, organization campground, picnic area, beach house (&), playground, food concession/store, boat rentals, multi-use trail. **Activities:** Camping, fishing, boating (power boating and sailing), canoeing, swimming, bicycling, hiking, cross-country skiing; fishing charters available in Grand Traverse Bay. **Special Features:** This urban park is just a few miles from Traverse City, one of the most popular resort towns in

Michigan, and features a quarter-mile of beach on Grand Traverse Bay. The original inhabitants of this area were the Ottawa branch of the Algonquin Indians.

★2858★ TRI-CENTENNIAL STATE PARK & HARBOR

1900 Atwater St
Detroit, MI 48207
Web: www.michigandnr.com/parksandtrails/
ParksandTrailsInfo.aspx?id=697
Phone: 313-396-0217
Size: 31 acres. Location: Along the Detroit River in the city of Detroit. Facilities: Picnic area, 2 sail-covered shelters, toilets, showers (for harbor guests only), 52-slip boat harbor (&&). Activities: Picnicking, shore fishing. Special Features: Located in the heart of downtown Detroit, Tricentennial is Michigan's first state park in an urban setting and its newest state park. Though not used for navigation, a 62-foot safety light tower (a replica of the lighthouse at Tawas Point State Park) provides a distinctive entry to the harbor.

★2859★ TWIN LAKES STATE PARK

6204 E Poyhonen Rd
Toivola, MI 49965
Web: www.michigandnr.com/parksandtrails/
ParksandTrailsInfo.aspx?id=429
Phone: 906-288-3321
Size: 175 acres. Location: 26 miles southwest of Houghton/Hancock on Highway M-26. Facilities: 62 modern campsites, picnic area and shelters, playground, horseshoe pit, volleyball net, nature trail, snowmobile area, beach house, boat launch. Activities: Camping, boating, fishing, swimming, hiking, cross-country skiing, snowmobiling. Special Features: The twin lakes, Lake Roland and Lake Gerald, offer anglers a chance at 16 different species found there. Lake Roland is shallow with a sandy beach and is one of the warmest inland lakes in the Upper Peninsula.

★2860★ VAN BUREN STATE PARK

23960 Ruggles Rd
South Haven, MI 49090
Web: www.michigandnr.com/parksandtrails/
ParksandTrailsInfo.aspx?id=502
Phone: 269-637-2788
Size: 400 acres. Location: In Van Buren County. Take Exit 13 off I-96 0.5 miles to Old Blue Star Highway, then north 4 miles and left onto County Road 380 and left again onto Ruggles Road. Facilities: 220 modern campsites, organization campground, picnic area and shelter (&), playground (&). Activities: Camping, swimming, hunting, interpretive programs. Special Features: Park features nearly a mile of sandy beach along Lake Michigan and high dune formations.

★2861★ VAN BUREN TRAIL STATE PARK

c/o Van Buren State Park
23960 Ruggles Rd
South Haven, MI 49090
Web: www.michigandnr.com/parksandtrails/
ParksandTrailsInfo.aspx?id=503
Phone: 269-637-2788
Size: 15-mile linear park. Location: Entrance to Trail is through Van Buren State Park (see separate entry). Facilities: Multi-use trail. Activities: Hiking, bicycling, cross-country skiing, snowmobiling. Special Features: Trail runs between Hartford and South Haven. Its surface is packed dirt or gravel.

★2862★ VAN RIPER STATE PARK

851 County Rd AKE
PO Box 88
Champion, MI 49814
Web: www.michigandnr.com/parksandtrails/
ParksandTrailsInfo.aspx?id=430
Phone: 906-339-4461
Size: 1,044 acres. Location: 35 miles west of Marquette on US 41. Facilities: 147 modern campsites (&), 40 rustic campsites (&), rustic cabin, mini-cabin, picnic area and shelter, playground, beach house (&), boat launch (&), concession/store, snowmobile area. Activities: Camping, boating, fishing, swimming, hiking, biking, snowmobiling, cross-country skiing, wildlife observation, interpretive programs. Special Features: Park contains a half-mile of frontage on the east end of Lake Michigamme, which has a fine sand beach and also is one of the top walleye lakes in the Upper Peninsula. Iron ore was first discovered in this area in 1845, a few miles east of the park, and evidence of early mining ventures can still be seen along the foot trails that wander through the hills on the north side of the highway.

★2863★ WAGNER FALLS SCENIC SITE

c/o Indian Lake State Park
8970W County Rd 442
Manistique, MI 49854
Web: www.michigandnr.com/parksandtrails/
ParksandTrailsInfo.aspx?id=431
Phone: 906-341-2355
Size: 22 acres. Location: In Alger County, M-28 (just east of Munising) to M-94, then west .25 miles. Facilities: Undeveloped. Activities: Hiking. Special Features: The scenic waterfall at this site is nestled among virgin pine and hemlock trees. An observation deck overlooks the falls.

★2864★ WARREN DUNES STATE PARK

12032 Red Arrow Hwy
Sawyer, MI 49125
Web: www.michigandnr.com/parksandtrails/
ParksandTrailsInfo.aspx?id=504
Phone: 269-426-4013
Size: 1,952 acres. Location: In Berrien County, 2.5 miles south of Bridgman on the west side of Red Arrow Highway. Facilities: 180 modern campsites, 36 rustic campsites, mini-cabins, organization campground, picnic area, shelter (&), beach house (&), hiking trails (6 miles), concession/store. Activities: Camping, swimming, hiking, hunting, cross-country skiing, wildlife observation. Special Features: Park is located along the shores of Lake Michigan and features a rugged dune formation rising 260 feet above the lake, offering great views and excellent hang gliding. Park is open year round.

9. State Parks

★2865★ **WARREN WOODS STATE PARK**
c/o Warren Dunes State Park
12032 Red Arrow Hwy
Sawyer, MI 49125
Web: www.michigandnr.com/parksandtrails/
ParksandTrailsInfo.aspx?id=505
Phone: 269-426-4013
Size: 311 acres. **Location:** In Berrien County in southwestern Michigan, southwest of Red Arrow Highway and Warren Dunes State Park). **Facilities:** Picnic area, hiking trail. **Activities:** Hiking. **Special Features:** Park is an undistrubed natural area, two-thirds of which is beech and maple climax forest. The hiking trail leads over a bridge that crosses the Galien River.

★2866★ **WATERLOO RECREATION AREA**
16345 McClure Rd
Chelsea, MI 48118
Web: www.michigandnr.com/parksandtrails/
ParksandTrailsInfo.aspx?id=506
Phone: 734-475-8307
Size: 20,500 acres. **Location:** Between Jackson and Chelsea, off I-94. **Facilities:** 290 modern campsites, 25 rustic campsites, 25 equestrian campsites, 3 rustic cabins, organization campground, picnic areas and shelters (&), playgrounds, hiking trails (&; 38 miles), mountain bike trails (5 miles), equestrian trails (12 miles), snowmobile area, beach house (&), fishing piers (&), boat launches, concession/store, visitor/discovery center (&). **Activities:** Camping, boating, fishing, swimming, hiking, mountain biking, horseback riding, hunting, cross-country skiing, snowmobiling, wildlife observation, interpretive programs. **Special Features:** The largest park in the Lower Peninsula, Waterloo Recreation Area includes 4 separate campgrounds, a day use area, beaches, 11 fishing lakes, and 8 boat launches, as well as miles of trails for a variety of uses. The park's Discovery Center offers exhibits, interactive displays, and nature programs. The park is large and spread out, with different routes leading to different types of facilities.

★2867★ **WC WETZEL STATE RECREATION AREA**
28681 Old North River Rd
Harrison Township, MI 48045
Web: www.michigandnr.com/parksandtrails/
ParksandTrailsInfo.aspx?id=507
Phone: 810-765-5605
Size: 900 acres. **Location:** In McComb County, west of I-94 at 26 Mile Road. **Facilities:** Undeveloped. **Activities:** Hiking, hunting, cross-country skiing, snowmobiling, radio-controlled model airplane flying. **Special Features:** Radio-controlled flying groups regularly fly their crafts and host events here.

★2868★ **WILDERNESS STATE PARK**
903 Wilderness Park Dr
Carp Lake, MI 49718
Web: www.michigandnr.com/parksandtrails/
ParksandTrailsInfo.aspx?id=509
Phone: 231-436-5381
Size: 10,369 acres. **Location:** In Emmet County, 11 miles west of Mackinaw City. **Facilities:** 250 modern campsites, 6 rustic cabins, 3 rustic bunkhouses (group use), picnic area, playground, multi-use trails (16 miles), boat launch, snowmobile area. **Activities:** Camping, fishing, swimming, bicycling (including mountain biking), hiking, hunting, cross-country skiing, snowmobiling, wildlife observation, birdwatching, interpretive programs. **Special Features:** Park features wilderness areas, 26 miles of Lake Michigan shoreline, and 16 miles of trails. Much of the terrain is dense forest, and anyone going into the forest is advised to take a map and compass as it's easy to get lost there. (Some sections of the interior show little evidence of ever having been occupied by man.)

★2869★ **WILLIAM MITCHELL STATE PARK**
6093 E M-115
Cadillac, MI 49601
Web: www.michigandnr.com/parksandtrails/
ParksandTrailsInfo.aspx?id=474
Phone: 231-775-7911
Size: 334 acres. **Location:** In Wexford County, 3 miles north of US 131, on M-115. **Facilities:** 221 modern campsites (&), mini-cabin (&), picnic area and shelter (&), playground, nature trail, beach house, boat launches, visitor center (&). **Activities:** Camping, boating, fishing, swimming, hiking, cross-country skiing, wildlife observation, interpretive programs. **Special Features:** Located between Cadillac and Mitchell lakes, the park houses the Carl T Johnson Hunting and Fishing Center, which showcases the history of hunting and fishing in Michigan.

★2870★ **WILSON STATE PARK**
910 N 1st St
PO Box 333
Harrison, MI 48625
Web: www.michigandnr.com/parksandtrails/
ParksandTrailsInfo.aspx?id=510
Phone: 989-539-3021
Size: 36 acres. **Location:** In Clare County, on the north end of Budd Lake, off US 1-27 at the Harrison exit. **Facilities:** 160 modern campsites, rental cottage, organization campground, picnic area and shelter (&), beach house, boat launch ramp. **Activities:** Camping, boating, water-skiing, fishing, swimming, cross-country skiing, snowmobiling, ice fishing. **Special Features:** Park is located on Budd Lake, a 175-acre lake known for its muskie fishing. This was originally the site of the Wilson Brothers Sawmill and Company Store, which thrived in the late 1800s.

★2871★ **WJ HAYES STATE PARK**
1220 Wampler's Lake Rd
Onsted, MI 49265
Web: www.michigandnr.com/parksandtrails/
ParksandTrailsInfo.aspx?id=454
Phone: 517-467-7401
Size: 654 acres. **Location:** On US 12, 9 miles west of Clinton and 4 miles east of M-50; M-124 cuts directly through the middle of the park. **Facilities:** 185 modern campsites, mini-cabins, picnic area, picnic shelter (&), playground, beach house, boat launch (&), concession/store. **Activities:** Camping, boating, fishing, ice fishing, swimming, interpretive programs. **Special Features:** Located in the heart of the Irish Hills, Park is bordered

9. State Parks

by a group of inland lakes, including Wampler's Lake. The Michigan International Speedway is just a short drive from the park.

★2872★ YANKEE SPRINGS RECREATION AREA

2104 S Briggs Rd
Middleville, MI 49333
Web: www.michigandnr.com/parksandtrails/
    ParksandTrailsInfo.aspx?id=511
Phone: 269-795-9081
Size: 5,200 acres. **Location:** In Barry County. From US-131 Exit 61, go 7 miles east on M-179, then south 1 mile on Briggs Road. **Facilities:** 200 modern campsites (on Gun Lake; &), 120 rustic campsites (at Deep Lake), equestrian campground with 25 sites, youth organization campground, picnic areas and shelters (&), playground, hiking trails (30 miles), mountain bike trails (12 miles), equestrian trails (9 miles), Nordic ski trails (10 miles), snowmobile area, fishing pier (&), boat launch sites (&), concession/store (&). **Activities:** Camping, boating, fishing, swimming, hiking, mountain biking, horseback riding, hunting, cross-country skiing, snowmobiling, wildlife observation, interpretive programs. **Special Features:** Park has nine lakes within its boundaries, two public beaches, and an extensive trail system. Special points of interest accessible from the trails include the Graves Hill scenic overlook and a glacially carved kettle formation called the Devil's Soupbowl.

★2873★ YOUNG STATE PARK

02280 Boyne City Rd
Boyne City, MI 49712
Web: www.michigandnr.com/parksandtrails/
    ParksandTrailsInfo.aspx?id=512
Phone: 231-582-7523
Size: 563 acres. **Location:** In Charlevoix County, on C56 northwest of Boyne City and M-75. **Facilities:** 240 modern campsites (&), mini-cabins, picnic area, playground (&), beach house (&), boat launch (for boats under 16 feet), concession/store (&), nature trails. **Activities:** Camping, boating, fishing, swimming, hiking, cross-country skiing, interpretive programs. **Special Features:** Park is located at the east end of Lake Charlevoix, a beautiful inland lake with access to Lake Michigan.

9. State Parks

Minnesota State Parks

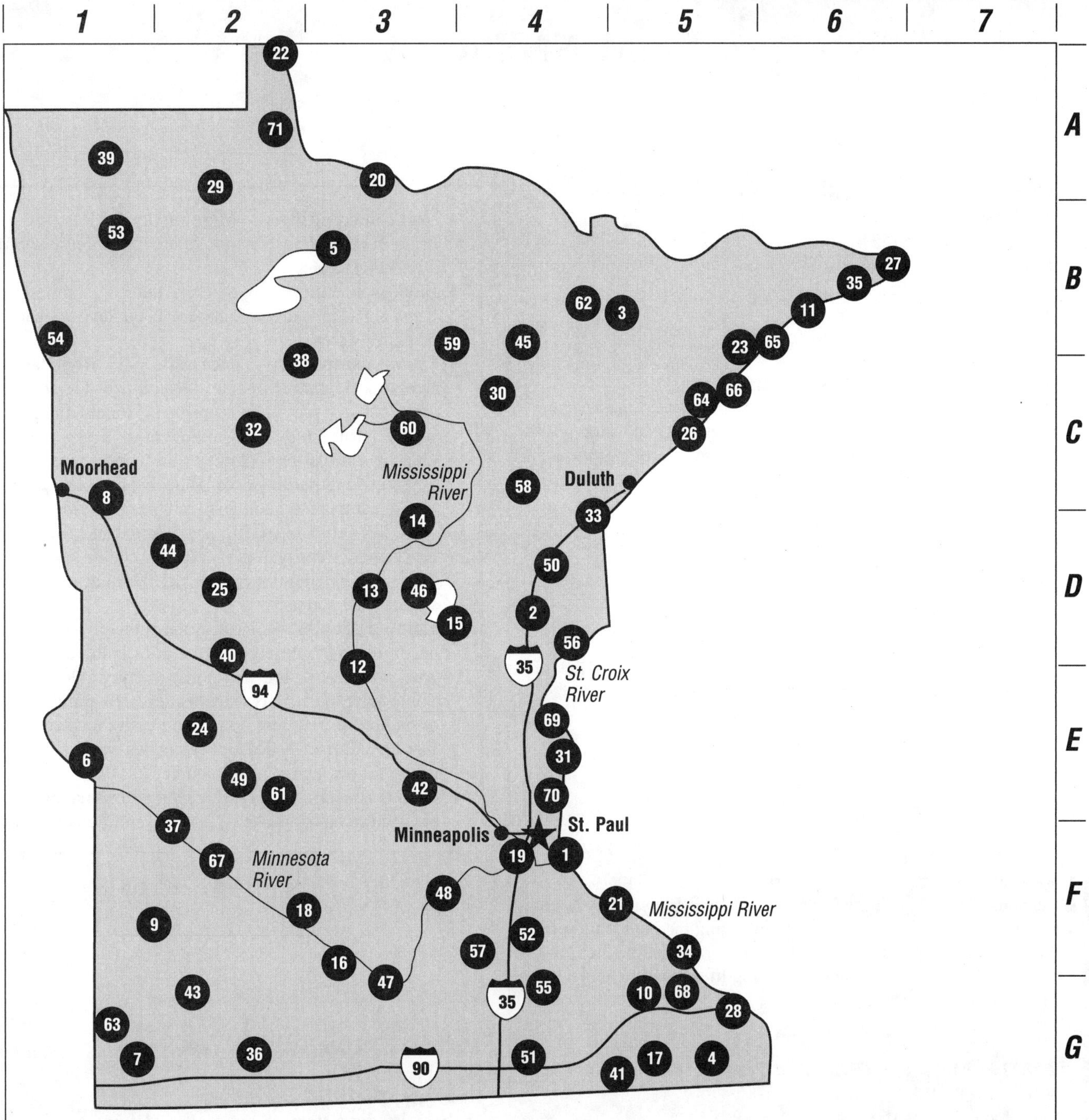

1	Afton SP	F-4	20	Franz Jevne SP	A-3	38	Lake Bemidji SP	C-2	57	Sakatah Lake SP	F-4
2	Banning SP	D-4	21	Frontenac SP	F-5	39	Lake Bronson SP	A-1	58	Savanna Portage SP	C-4

1 Afton SP — F-4
2 Banning SP — D-4
3 Bear Head Lake SP — B-5
4 Beaver Creek Valley SP — G-5
5 Big Bog SRA — B-3
6 Big Stone Lake SP — E-1
7 Blue Mounds SP — G-1
8 Buffalo River SP — C-1
9 Camden SP — F-1
10 Carley SP — G-5
11 Cascade River SP — B-6
12 Charles A. Lindbergh SP — E-3
13 Crow Wing SP — D-3
14 Cuyuna Country SRA — D-3
15 Father Hennepin SP — D-3
16 Flandrau SP — F-3
17 Forestville/Mystery Cave SP — G-5
18 Fort Ridgely SP — F-2
19 Fort Snelling SP — F-4

20 Franz Jevne SP — A-3
21 Frontenac SP — F-5
22 Garden Island SRA — A-2
23 George H. Crosby Manitou SP — B-5
24 Glacial Lakes SP — E-2
25 Glendalough SP — D-2
26 Gooseberry Falls SP — C-5
27 Grand Portage SP — B-6
28 Great River Bluffs SP — G-5
29 Hayes Lake SP — A-2
30 Hill Annex Mine SP — C-4
31 Interstate SP — E-4
32 Itasca SP — C-2
33 Jay Cooke SP — D-4
34 John A. Latsch SP — F-5
35 Judge CR Magney SP — B-6
36 Kilen Woods SP — G-2
37 Lac Qui Parle SP — F-2

38 Lake Bemidji SP — C-2
39 Lake Bronson SP — A-1
40 Lake Carlos SP — D-2
41 Lake Louise SP — G-5
42 Lake Maria SP — E-3
43 Lake Shetek SP — G-2
44 Maplewood SP — D-2
45 McCarthy Beach SP — B-4
46 Mille Lacs Kathio SP — D-3
47 Minneopa SP — G-3
48 Minnesota Valley SRA — F-3
49 Monson Lake SP — E-2
50 Moose Lake SP — D-4
51 Myre-Big Island SP — G-4
52 Nerstrand-Big Woods SP — F-4
53 Old Mill SP — B-1
54 Red River SRA — B-1
55 Rice Lake SP — G-4
56 Saint Croix SP — D-4

57 Sakatah Lake SP — F-4
58 Savanna Portage SP — C-4
59 Scenic SP — B-3
60 Schoolcraft SP — C-3
61 Sibley SP — E-2
62 Soudan Underground Mine SP — B-4
63 Split Rock Creek SP — G-1
64 Split Rock Lighthouse SP — C-5
65 Temperance River SP — B-6
66 Tettegouche SP — C-5
67 Upper Sioux Agency SP — F-2
68 Whitewater SP — G-5
69 Wild River SP — E-4
70 William O'Brien SP — E-4
71 Zippel Bay SP — A-2

SP   State Park
SRA   State Recreation Area

MINNESOTA

★2874★ **Minnesota Division of Parks & Recreation**
500 Lafayette Rd
Saint Paul, MN 55155
(651) 296-6157 - Phone
(651) 297-3618 - Fax
(888) 646-6367 - Toll-free
(866) 857-2757 - Toll-free Reservations
(651) 259-5249 - Volunteering
Web: www.dnr.state.mn.us/state_parks
Oversees more than 260,000 acres of the state's most scenic lands comprising 72 state parks, recreation areas and state waysides. Also manages Minnesota's state forests' campgrounds.

★2875★ **Minnesota Division of Fisheries**
500 Lafayette Rd
Saint Paul, MN 55155
(651) 259-5180 - Phone
(651) 297-7272 - Fax
Web: www.dnr.state.mn.us/fisheries
Manages the state's 5,400 game fish lakes and 15,000 miles of streams and rivers; administers fishing licensing.

★2876★ **Minnesota Division of Forestry**
500 Lafayette Rd
Saint Paul, MN 55155
(651) 259-5300 - Phone
(651) 296-5954 - Fax
Web: www.dnr.state.mn.us/forestry
Responsible for providing long-term, sustainable yield of forest resources from state forest lands; improving the health and productivity of other public and private forest lands (including community forest lands); and protecting life, property, and natural resources from wildfires.

★2877★ **Minnesota Division of Trails & Waterways**
500 Lafayette Rd
Saint Paul, MN 55155
(651) 297-1151 - Phone
(651) 297-5475 - Fax
Web: www.dnr.state.mn.us/trails_and_waterways
Develops and maintains 1,100 miles of state trails, 1,560 public water access sites, 280 fishing piers and shore fishing sites, and 26 designated canoe and boating routes (comprising more than 3,400 river miles).

Key to campsite classification:
- **Drive-in campsites** — Some parks have RV length limits. Many parks offer electrical hook-ups, dumping stations, and pull-through sites.

- **Walk-in campsites** — More rustic and less busy than drive-in campsites. Not more than 0.25 miles away from a parking area.
- **Backpack campsites** — More than 0.25 miles away from a parking area. Campers may have to carry in drinking water.
- **Canoe campsites** — Accessible only from lakes or rivers in the park. Most are located near the shore and are secluded, providing vault or pit toilets and a water source (which may need treatment).
- **Cart-in campsites** — Located in wooded areas 200 to 500 feet from parking area. Wheeled carts are provided free to campers to haul gear from parking area to campsites. No vehicular traffic is permitted in campground.
- **Horsemen's campsites** — Accommodate trailer units, and most are equipped with a hitching area, water source, and toilets.
- **Camper Cabins** — Rustic one-room log cabins that accommodate 5-6 people. Amenities include bunk beds with mattresses, screened porch, picnic table, fire ring. Some have electricity and heating. No running water or bathrooms, but restroom facilities are located nearby.
- **Group camps** — Rustic campsites with tables, fire rings, toilets, and a water source.
- **Group centers** — Facilities include cabins, hot showers, dining halls, kitchens, and private recreation areas.

★2878★ **AFTON STATE PARK**
6959 Peller Ave S
Hastings, MN 55033
Web: www.dnr.state.mn.us/state_parks/afton
Phone: 651-436-5391; **Fax:** 651-436-6912
Size: 1,695 acres. **Location:** From Saint Paul, go 9 miles east on I-94, then 7 miles south on Highway 95 and 3 miles east on County Road 20. **Facilities:** 24 backpack campsites, canoe campsite, flush toilets (&), 2 group campsites, picnic area and picnic shelters (&), hiking trails (20 miles), self-guided trail (0.75 mile), paved bike trail (4 miles), equestrian trails (5 miles), ski trails (18 miles), swimming beach, volleyball court, horseshoe pit, warming house, visitor center (&), interpretive exhibits, gift shop. **Activities:** Camping, swimming, river fishing, hiking, horseback riding, bicycling, cross-country skiing, snowshoeing, interpretive programs. **Special Features:** The park's rugged, rolling landscape includes remnant and restored prairies, deep ravines, and bluffs overlooking the Saint Croix River.

★2879★ BANNING STATE PARK

61101 Banning Park Rd
PO Box 643
Sandstone, MN 55072
Web: www.dnr.state.mn.us/state_parks/banning
Phone: 320-245-2668; Fax: 320-245-0251
Size: 6,201 acres. Location: Off I-35, Exit 195. Facilities: 33 drive-in campsites (11 with electrical hookups), showers (&), flush toilets (&), 1 backpack campsite, 4 canoe-in campsites, camper cabin (seasonal), picnic area (&), playground, hiking trails (17 miles), self-guided trails (2 miles), paved bike trail (1 mile), ski trails (12 miles), snowmobile trails (6 miles), boat access, interpretive exhibits, historic site, gift shop. Activities: Camping, river fishing, boating, canoeing, kayaking, hiking, bicycling, cross-country skiing, snowshoeing, snowmobiling. Special Features: Park features include dramatic sandstone rock formations and the Kettle River, where daring canoeists and kayakers shoot the turbulent rapids at Blueberry Slide, Mother's Delight, Dragon's Tooth, and Hell's Gate.

★2880★ BEAR HEAD LAKE STATE PARK

9301 Bear Head State Park Rd
Ely, MN 55731
Web: www.dnr.state.mn.us/state_parks/bear_head_lake
Phone: 218-365-7229; Fax: 218-365-7204
Size: 4,523 acres. Location: From the town of Tower, 9 miles east on US 169 to County Highway 128, then south 7 miles. Facilities: 73 drive-in campsites (26 with electric hookups), showers (&), flush toilets (&), 4 backpack campsites, canoe campsite, 2 canoe-in/boat-in campsites, group camp, camper cabin, guest house, hiking trails (17 miles), ski trail (9 miles), snowmobile trail (1 mile), picnic area, picnic shelter (&), swimming beach, boat ramp, fishing pier (&), boat and canoe/kayak rental, gift shop. Activities: Camping, swimming, lake and stream fishing, boating, canoeing, hiking, cross-country skiing, snowshoeing, snowmobiling, wildlife viewing. Special Features: Park is located in the secluded Northwoods, with pristine lakes and stands of white and red pines that tower over the birch, aspen, and fir trees. Wildlife at the park include black bears, nesting eagles, timber wolves, and moose. The park is just south of the Boundary Waters Canoe Area, and its trails link up with Taconite State Trail.

★2881★ BEAVER CREEK VALLEY STATE PARK

15954 County Rd 1
Caledonia, MN 55921
Web: www.dnr.state.mn.us/state_parks/beaver_creek_valley
Phone: 507-724-2107; Fax: 507-724-2107
Size: 1,187 acres. Location: From I-90, 24 miles south on MN 76, then west 4 miles on Houston County 1. Facilities: 42 drive-in campsites (16 with electrical hookups), showers, 6 walk-in campsites, group camp (3 sites), camper cabin (seasonal), picnic area (&), enclosed picnic shelter (&), interpretive exhibits, volleyball court, playground, warming house, hiking trails (8 miles), gift shop. Activities: Camping, stream fishing, hiking, bird watching. Special Features: Situated in the blufflands of southeastern Minnesota, the park is known for its clear streams fed by the "Big Spring." In spring, wildflowers that blanket the woodland hills and valleys attract migratory songbirds like the rare Acadian flycatcher, Cerulean warbler, and Louisiana waterthrush, which nest in the park.

★2882★ BIG BOG STATE RECREATION AREA

55716 Hwy 72 NE
Waskish, MN 56685
Web: www.dnr.state.mn.us/state_parks/big_bog
Phone: 218-647-8592; Fax: 218-647-8730
Size: 9,459 total acres. Location: On Hwy 72, just north of Waskish. Facilities: 31 campsites (26 with electric hookups), 5 winterized camper cabins (2 &), showers (&), flush toilets (&), picnic aea, picnic shelter (&), self-guided trail (1 mile), hiking trail (.5 miles), snowmobile trails (10 miles), swimming beach, fishing pier (&), boat ramp, horseshoe pit, interpretive exhibits, nature store. Activities: Camping, lake and river fishing, swimming, birdwatching, hiking, snowmobiling. Special Features: Park's 500-square-mile peat bog is the largest in the lower 48 states. The area includes such features as ovoid islands, water tracks, and rare species of orchids and birds unique to peat bogs.

★2883★ BIG STONE LAKE STATE PARK

35889 Meadowbrook State Park Rd
Ortonville, MN 56278
Web: www.dnr.state.mn.us/state_parks/big_stone_lake
Phone: 320-839-3663; Fax: 320-839-3676
Size: 986 acres. Location: 7 miles northwest of Ortonville on Highway 7. Facilities: 37 drive-in campsites (10 with electrical hookups), showers (&), flush toilets (&), group camp, picnic area, playground, horseshoe pit, swimming beach, hiking trail (3 miles), boat ramp, canoe rental, visitor center (&). Activities: Camping, swimming, lake fishing, boating, canoeing, hiking, showshoeing. Special Features: Located on the South Dakota-Minnesota border, 30-mile-long Big Stone Lake is the source of the Minnesota River. It attracts anglers who catch walleye, northerns, and bluegills.

★2884★ BLUE MOUNDS STATE PARK

1410 161st St
Luverne, MN 56156
Web: www.dnr.state.mn.us/state_parks/blue_mounds
Phone: 507-283-1307; Fax: 507-283-1306
Size: 1,826 acres. Location: 3 miles north of Luverne, just off US 75. Facilities: 73 drive-in campsites (40 with electrical hookups), showers (&), flush toilets (&), 14 walk-in campsites, group camp, picnic area (&), enclosed picnic shelter (&), playground, volleyball court, horseshoe pit, swimming beach, hiking trails (13 miles), self-guided trail (1 miles), paved bike trail (2.2 miles), snowmobile trail (3 miles), carry-in boat access, canoe rentals, historic site, gift shop. Activities: Camping, swimming, lake fishing, boating (no motors), canoeing, hiking, bicycling, snowshoeing, snowmobiling, rock climbing, bird watching. Special Features: Park is named for a large Sioux quartzite cliff that rises 100 feet above the plains. A small herd of bison graze on the prairie, and prickly pear cactus blooms here in June and July.

★2885★ **BUFFALO RIVER STATE PARK**
155 South St Hwy 10
PO Box 352
Glyndon, MN 56547
Web: www.dnr.state.mn.us/state_parks/buffalo_river
Phone: 218-498-2124; **Fax:** 218-498-2583
Size: 1,322 acres. **Location:** 14 miles east of Moorhead, just off US 10. **Facilities:** 44 drive-in campsites (35 with electrical hookups), showers (&), flush toilets (&), group camp, picnic area, enclosed picnic shelter (&), swimming beach, hiking trails (12 miles), self-guided trail (1 mile), ski trails (6 miles), warming house, gift shop. **Activities:** Camping, swimming, river fishing, hiking, cross-country skiing, snowshoeing. **Special Features:** Just 14 miles from the large metropolitan area of Fargo, North Dakota - Moorhead, Minnesota, Park is located amid one of Minnesota's finest and largest remnant prairies.

★2886★ **CAMDEN STATE PARK**
1897 County Rd
Lynd, MN 56157
Web: www.dnr.state.mn.us/state_parks/camden
Phone: 507-865-4530; **Fax:** 507-865-4608
Size: 2,245 acres. **Location:** 10 miles south of Marshall off MN 23. **Facilities:** 80 drive-in campsites (29 with electrical hookups), showers (&), flush toilets (&), 12 horsemen's campsites, group camp, picnic area (&), picnic shelters (&), playground, horseshoe pits, hiking trails (15 miles), self-guided trail (1.7 miles), mountain bike trails (4.25 miles), equestrian trails (10 miles), cross-country ski trails (5 miles), skate-ski trails (1.4 miles), snowmobile trails (7.6 miles), warming house, swimming beach, fishing pier &), boat ramp, canoe rentals, historic site, gift shop. **Activities:** Camping, swimming, lake and river fishing, boating (electric motors only), canoeing, hiking, mountain biking, horseback riding, cross-country skiing, snowshoeing, snowmobiling. **Special Features:** In the fall, Camden's woodlands and prairies blaze red, yellow, and gold as leaves of maple, basswood, ash, cottonwood, and hackberry trees begin to turn and the goldenrod, aster, and gentian bloom.

★2887★ **CARLEY STATE PARK**
c/o Whitewater State Park
19041 Hwy 74
Altura, MN 55910
Web: www.dnr.state.mn.us/state_parks/carley
Phone: 507-932-3007; **Fax:** 507-932-5938
Size: 209 acres. **Location:** 4 miles south of Plainview on Wabasha County Road 4 (about 15 miles northeast of Rochester). **Facilities:** 20 drive-in campsites, 3 group camps, hiking trails (5 miles), self-guided trail (1 mile), ski trail (5 miles), sliding hill, picnic area (&), shelter (&), playground. **Activities:** Camping, stream fishing, hiking, cross-country skiing. **Special Features:** Bluebells and other wildflowers carpet the valley with color each spring. The park's nature trail winds around the north branch of the Whitewater River.

★2888★ **CASCADE RIVER STATE PARK**
3481 W Hwy 61
Lutsen, MN 55612
Web: www.dnr.state.mn.us/state_parks/cascade_river
Phone: 218-387-3053; **Fax:** 218-387-3054
Size: 2,865 acres. **Location:** 10 miles southwest of Grand Marais, just off Highway 61 at mile post 101. **Facilities:** 40 drive-in campsites, showers, flush toilets, 5 backpack campsites, 2 group camps, picnic area, enclosed picnic shelter, hiking trails (18 miles), ski trails (17 miles), snowmobile trails (2 miles), warming house. **Activities:** Camping, fishing (lake, river, and stream), hiking, cross-country skiing, snowshoeing, snowmobiling. **Special Features:** The Cascade River drops 900 feet in its last three miles to Lake Superior. Visitors standing on a footbridge that spans the river, or at any of the viewing spots above the river, can feel the vibration of the rushing torrent of water as it cascades down the canyon.

★2889★ **CHARLES A. LINDBERGH STATE PARK**
1615 Lindbergh Dr S
PO Box 364
Little Falls, MN 56345
Web: www.dnr.state.mn.us/state_parks/charles_a_lindbergh
Phone: 320-616-2525; **Fax:** 320-616-2526
Size: 569 acres. **Location:** 1 mile southwest of Little Falls on Lindbergh Drive South. **Facilities:** 38 drive-in campsites (15 with electrical hookups), showers (&), flush toilets (&), 1 backpack campsite, 1 canoe-in campsite, group camp, picnic area (&), enclosed picnic shelter (&), playground, volleyball court, horseshoe pits, boat ramp, canoe rentals, snowshoe rentals, hiking trails (7 miles), ski trails (5 miles), warming house, historic site, visitor center (&), gift shop. **Activities:** Camping, river fishing, boating, canoeing, hiking, cross-country skiing, snowshoeing. **Special Features:** Park is located on the Mississippi River, and its picnic area features a historic shelter and stone water tower built by the Work Projects Administration. Adjacent to the park is the historic home of Charles A. Lindbergh, Sr., father of the famous aviator.

★2890★ **CROW WING STATE PARK**
3124 State Park Rd
Brainerd, MN 56401
Web: www.dnr.state.mn.us/state_parks/crow_wing
Phone: 218-825-3075; **Fax:** 218-825-3077
Size: 2,871 acres. **Location:** 9 miles south of Brainerd on US 371. **Facilities:** 59 drive-in campsites (12 with electrical hookups), showers (&), flush toilets (&), canoe campsite, group camp, camper cabin (seasonal), picnic area (&), enclosed picnic shelter (&), hiking trails (18 miles), self-guided trail (0.5 mile), paved bike trails (nearby), ski trails (6 miles), snowmobile trail (6 miles), boat ramp, boat and canoe rental, historic site, welcome center, interpretive exhibits, gift shop. **Activities:** Camping, river fishing, boating, canoeing, hiking, cross-country skiing, snowmobiling, snowshoeing, wildlife observation. **Special Features:** Park is located at the confluence of the Crow Wing and Mississippi rivers, and the historic and picturesque "Chippewa Lookout" overlooks the Mississippi. The park also contains a section of the famous Woods Trail, which served ox cart traffic carrying supplies between Saint Paul and the Red River settlements.

★2891★ CUYUNA COUNTRY STATE RECREATION AREA

307 3rd St
PO Box 404
Ironton, MN 56455
Web: www.dnr.state.mn.us/state_parks/cuyuna_country
Phone: 218-546-5926; **Fax:** 218-546-7369
Size: 1,824 acres. **Location:** 15 miles northeast of Brainerd on Hwy 210. **Facilities:** 16 drive-in campsites, surfaced bike trail (5 miles), bike rentals, ski and snowshoe rentals, picnic area, swimming beach, fishing pier, boating access (drive in or carry in), canoe/kayak rentals, historic site, interpretive exhibits. **Activities:** Camping, lake fishing, canoeing, swimming, bicycling, tours. **Special Features:** This area of former mining pits and rock deposit stockpiles has regenerated vegetation and clear lakes with 25 miles of undeveloped shoreline that can be explored by boat or canoe. Croft Mine Historical Park, in Ironton, offers tours and interpretive programs. Most of the facilities at the park are privately owned and operated.

★2892★ FATHER HENNEPIN STATE PARK

41294 Father Hennepin Park Rd
PO Box 397
Isle, MN 56342
Web: www.dnr.state.mn.us/state_parks/father_hennepin
Phone: 320-676-8763; **Fax:** 320-676-3748
Size: 320 acres. **Location:** Just west of Isle off State Highway 27. **Facilities:** 103 drive-in campsites (41 with electrical hookups), showers (&), flush toilets (&), group camp (6 sites), picnic area (&), picnic shelters (&), volleyball court, horseshoe pits, hiking trails (4 miles), wheelchair-accessible trail (0.25 mile), ski trails (2.5 miles), warming house, swimming beach, 2 fishing piers (&), boat launch, gift shop. **Activities:** Camping, swimming, lake fishing, boating, hiking, cross-country skiing, snowshoeing, snowmobiling, wildlife viewing (park has several albino deer). **Special Features:** Located on the southeast shore of Mille Lacs Lake, the park was named in honor of a French Jesuit priest who visited the area with a French expedition in 1680. Throughout his trip, he kept a journal describing the untamed wilderness he encountered.

★2893★ FLANDRAU STATE PARK

1300 Summit Ave
New Ulm, MN 56073
Web: www.dnr.state.mn.us/state_parks/flandrau
Phone: 507-233-9800; **Fax:** 507-359-1544
Size: 1,006 acres. **Location:** In New Ulm on Summit Avenue. **Facilities:** 89 drive-in campsites (34 with electrical hookups), showers(&), flush toilets (&), 3 walk-in campsites, modern group center, picnic area (&), enclosed picnic shelter (&), playground, volleyball court, horseshoe pits, hiking trails (8 miles), ski trails (8 miles), warming house, swimming beach, carry-in boat access, snowshoe and ski rentals, interpretive exhibits, gift shop. **Activities:** Camping, swimming, river fishing, boating, hiking, cross-country skiing, snowshoeing. **Special Features:** Big Cottonwood River meanders through this park, which features a sand-bottom swimming pond.

★2894★ FORESTVILLE/MYSTERY CAVE STATE PARK

21071 County 118
Preston, MN 55965
Web: www.dnr.state.mn.us/state_parks/forestville_mystery_cave
Phone: 507-352-5111; **Fax:** 507-352-5113
Size: 3,170 acres. **Location:** 6 miles south of Wykoff on Fillmore County 118. **Facilities:** 73 drive-in campsites (23 with electrical hookups), showers (&), flush toilets (&), horsemen's campground (including a specific day use area for day riders), group camp, picnic area (&), picnic shelters (&), hiking trail (17 miles), horse trails (15 miles), ski trails (11 miles), snowmobile trails (6 miles), warming house, historic site, interpretive exhibits, visitor center (&), gift shop. **Activities:** Camping, stream fishing, hiking, horseback riding, cave tours, cross-country skiing, snowmobiling, snowshoeing, interpretive programs (seasonal). **Special Features:** Park naturalists provide tours of Mystery Cave, where the temperature stays at a constant 48 degrees Fahrenheit, throughout the summer and on weekends in the spring and fall. Historic Forestville is a restored 1800s village operated by the Minnesota Historical Society.

★2895★ FORT RIDGELY STATE PARK

72158 County Rd 30
Fairfax, MN 55332
Web: www.dnr.state.mn.us/state_parks/fort_ridgely
Phone: 507-426-7840; **Fax:** 507-426-7112
Size: 1,040 acres. **Location:** 6 miles south of Fairfax off State Highway 4. **Facilities:** 31 drive-in campsites (15 with electrical hookups), showers (&), flush toilets (&), 3 walk-in campsites, 20 horsemen's campsites, group camp, picnic area, picnic shelters (&), playground, volleyball court, horseshoe pits, hiking trails (11 miles), paved bike trail (0.5 miles), horse trails (10 miles), ski trails (5 miles), snowmobile trails (8 miles), warming house, 9-hole golf course, historic site, interpretive exhibits, visitor center, gift shop. **Activities:** Camping, stream fishing, hiking, bicycling, horseback riding, snow sledding, cross-country skiing, snowmobiling, snowshoeing, golfing. **Special Features:** This historic fort and outpost, built in 1855 and manned until 1872, played a role in the US-Dakota Conflict of 1862, a major event in the state's history. An old farmhouse at the park has recently been renovated and is now available as a rental cabin.

★2896★ FORT SNELLING STATE PARK

101 Snelling Lake Rd
Saint Paul, MN 55111
Web: www.dnr.state.mn.us/state_parks/fort_snelling
Phone: 612-725-2389; **Fax:** 612-725-2391
Size: 2,931 acres. **Location:** Off State Highway 5 at the Post Road exit. **Facilities:** Picnic area (&), picnic shelters (&), flush toilets (&), hiking trails (18 miles), self-guided trail (1 mile), paved bike trail (5 miles), mountain bike trails (20 miles), ski trails (12 miles), skate-ski trails (6 miles), warming house, swimming beach (&), fishing pier (&), boat ramp, canoe rental, 9-hole golf course, volleyball court, playground, visitor center, interpretive exhibits, historic site, gift shop. **Activities:** Swimming, lake and river fishing, boating (electric motors only),

9. State Parks

canoeing, golfing, hiking, bicycling, mountain biking, cross-country skiing, snowshoeing, nature programs. **Special Features:** This day-use park is located in the heart of the Twin Cities and has extensive hiking, bike, and ski trails that link to Minnehaha Park and the Minnesota Valley National Wildlife Refuge (see separate entry in national refuges section). Visitors also can hike on Pike Island, where the Mississippi and Minnesota rivers converge, or follow the trails up to the historic Fort Snelling for a view of military life in the 1820s.

★2897★ FRANZ JEVNE STATE PARK
c/o Zippel State Park
3684 54th Ave NW
Williams, MN 56686
Web: www.dnr.state.mn.us/state_parks/franz_jevne
Phone: 218-783-6252; **Fax:** 218-783-6253
Size: 118 acres. **Location:** East of Birchdale on State Highway 11. **Facilities:** 18 drive-in campsites (2 with electric hookups), 3 walk-in campsites, pit toilets, picnic area (&), picnic shelter (&), hiking trails (2.5 miles), ski trails (3.5 miles), boat launch. **Activities:** Camping, river fishing, boating, cross-country skiing, snowshoeing. **Special Features:** Located between International Falls and Baudette, this small park offers picturesque views of Ontario and the Rainy River.

★2898★ FRONTENAC STATE PARK
29223 County 28 Blvd
Frontenac, MN 55026
Web: www.dnr.state.mn.us/state_parks/frontenac
Phone: 651-345-3401; **Fax:** 651-345-3694
Size: 2,237 acres. **Location:** 10 miles southeast of Red Wing on Highway 61. **Facilities:** 58 drive-in campsites (19 with electrical hookups), showers, flush toilets (&), 6 cart-in campsites, group camp, picnic area (&), picnic shelters (&), hiking trails (13 miles), self-guided trail (2.5 miles), paved bike trail (1 mile), ski trails (5 miles), snowmobile trail (5 miles), winter sliding hill, warming house, historic site, gift shop. **Activities:** Camping, lake and river fishing, hiking, cross-country skiing, snowmobiling, snow sledding, bird watching. Swimming and boating nearby. **Special Features:** Lake Pepin's diverse habitats—bluff land, prairie, floodplain forest, and upland hardwood forest—attract numerous warblers, hawks, waterfowl, and shorebirds, making this one of the best bird watching places in the US. Of the 260 different species of birds that have been counted here, some make the park their home, while others just stop by on their way up or down the Mississippi River flyway.

★2899★ GARDEN ISLAND STATE RECREATION AREA
c/o Zippel Bay State Park
3684 54th Ave NW
Williams, MN 56686
Web: www.dnr.state.mn.us/state_parks/garden_island
Phone: 218-783-6252; **Fax:** 218-783-6253
Size: 734 acres. **Location:** On Lake of the Woods, 19 nautical miles north of Zippel Bay. **Facilities:** Picnic area, enclosed picnic shelter, swimming beach, boat docks (summer and fall only), pit toilets. No running water. **Activities:** Swimming, lake fishing, boating. **Special Features:** Garden Island provides a day-use rest area and shore lunch stop for boaters on Lake of the Woods.

★2900★ GEORGE H. CROSBY MANITOU STATE PARK
c/o Tettegouche State Park
5702 Hwy 61
Silver Bay, MN 55614
Web: www.dnr.state.mn.us/state_parks/george_crosby_manitou
Phone: 218-226-6365; **Fax:** 218-226-6366
Size: 6,682 acres. **Location:** 7 miles north of the village of Finland on Lake County Road 7. **Facilities:** 21 backpack campsites, vault toilets, picnic area, hiking trails (24 miles), boat launch. **Activities:** Camping, lake and river fishing, boating (no motors), hiking, snowshoeing, wildlife viewing. **Special Features:** This park is located along Benson Lake and Manitou River in a north-country wilderness, where waterfalls cascade through a volcanic canyon surrounded by forest, and where bears, wolves, moose, and deer share the trails with hikers. The trails are challenging but offer spectacular views.

★2901★ GLACIAL LAKES STATE PARK
25022 County Rd 41
Starbuck, MN 56381
Web: www.dnr.state.mn.us/state_parks/glacial_lakes
Phone: 320-239-2860; **Fax:** 320-239-4605
Size: 2,423 acres. **Location:** From the town of Starbuck, 3 miles south on State Highway 29, then 2 miles south on County Road 41. **Facilities:** 38 drive-in campsites (14 with electrical hookups), showers (&), flush toilets (&), 4 backpack campsites, 2 walk-in campsites, 8 horsemen's campsites, 3 group camps, camper cabin (seasonal), picnic area, picnic shelter, playground, volleyball court, hiking trails (16 miles), self-guided trail (0.5 mile), horse trails (11 miles), ski trails (6 miles), snowmobile trail (11 miles), swimming beach, boat ramp, fishing pier, boat and canoe/kayak rentals, ski and snowshoe rentals, interpretive exhibits, gift shop. **Activities:** Camping, swimming, lake fishing, boating (electric motors only), canoeing, hiking, horseback riding, cross-country skiing, snowmobiling, snowshoeing. **Special Features:** Park features 56-acre Mountain Lake and a network of trails which lead to glacial formations, prairie potholes, marshes, woodlands, and creeks.

★2902★ GLENDALOUGH STATE PARK
25287 Whitetail Ln
Battle Lake, MN 56515
Web: www.dnr.state.mn.us/state_parks/glendalough
Phone: 218-644-0110; **Fax:** 218-864-0587
Size: 1,931 acres. **Location:** 23 miles east of Fergus Falls, near Battle Lake. **Facilities:** 22 cart-in tent campsites, 5 canoe-in campsites, flush toilets (&), showers (&), group camp (tents only), 4 camper cabins, picnic area, picnic shelters (&), playground, hiking trails (8 miles), self-guided trail (2 miles), paved bike trail (1.5 miles), mountain bike trails (5.5 miles), ski trails (6 miles), skate-ski trail (1.5 miles), warming house, swimming

beach, fishing pier (&), boat launch, boat and canoe/kayak rentals, ski and snowshoe rentals, historic site, interpretive exhibits. **Activities:** Camping, swimming, lake fishing, boating (with restrictions), canoeing, hiking, bicycling, mountain biking, cross-country skiing, snowshoeing. **Special Features:** Park features 9 miles of undeveloped shoreline and six lakes, and is one of the last large tracts of undeveloped lakeshore and land in west central Minnesota. The fishing here is excellent, with typical motorized boating and fishing opportunities offered on Molly Stark Lake. Annie Battle Lake is designated as a Heritage Fishery Lake and does not allow boat motors of any kind, including electric trolling motors. Other restrictions apply as well.

★2903★ GOOSEBERRY FALLS STATE PARK

3206 Hwy 61
Two Harbors, MN 55616
Web: www.dnr.state.mn.us/state_parks/gooseberry_falls
Phone: 218-834-3855; **Fax:** 218-834-3787
Size: 1,687 acres. **Location:** 13 miles northeast of Two Harbors on Highway 61. **Facilities:** 70 drive-in campsites, showers (&), flush toilets (&), group camp, kayak campsite, picnic area (&), enclosed picnic shelter (&), hiking trails (18 miles), mountain bike trails (12 miles), wheelchair-accessible trail (1.5 miles), ski trails (12 miles), snowmobile trails (1.5 miles), warming house, ski and snowshoe rentals, historic structures, visitor center (&), interpretive exhibits, gift shop. **Activities:** Camping, lake and river fishing, hiking, mountain biking, cross-country skiing, snowmobiling, snowshoeing, nature programs (year round). **Special Features:** Park is known for its spectacular waterfalls, river gorge, Lake Superior shoreline, Civilian Conservation Corps log and stone structures, and North Woods wildlife.

★2904★ GRAND PORTAGE STATE PARK

9393 E Hwy 61
Grand Portage, MN 55605
Web: www.dnr.state.mn.us/state_parks/grand_portage
Phone: 218-475-2360; **Fax:** 218-475-2365
Size: 278 acres. **Location:** On the US/Canada border, 36 miles north of the town of Grand Marais on Highway 61. **Facilities:** Hiking trails (4 miles), wheelchair-accessible trail (0.75 miles), snowshoe rentals, picnic area, historic site, visitor center (&), interpretive exhibits, gift shop. **Activities:** Hiking, snowshoeing, picnicking. **Special Features:** A boardwalk trail leads to an overlook of Minnesota's highest waterfall and the steep gorge into which the Pigeon River plunges. The falls presented a serious obstacle to river travel, so a "carrying place," or portage, was necessary, and American Indians created the ancient nine-mile trail from Lake Superior to bypass the falls. This trail became known as "The Grand Portage." The park lies within Grand Portage Indian Reservation and is bordered by Canada on the north and east. Lake Superior is about one mile east of the park.

★2905★ GREAT RIVER BLUFFS STATE PARK

43605 Kipp Dr
Winona, MN 55987
Web: www.dnr.state.mn.us/state_parks/great_river_bluffs
Phone: 507-643-6849; **Fax:** 507-643-6849

Size: 3,067 acres. **Location:** Off County Road 3, 20 miles southeast of Winona at the junction of US Highway 61 and I-90. **Facilities:** 31 drive-in campsites, showers (&), flush toilets (&), 5 bike-in campsites, group camp, picnic area (&), playground (&), hiking trails (6.5 miles), self-guided trails (2.5 miles), ski trails (9 miles), skate-ski trail (1 mile), sliding hill, snowshoe rentals, gift shop. **Activities:** Camping, hiking, cross-country skiing, skate-skiing, snow sledding, snowshoeing, birdwatching. **Special Features:** Park contains two Scientific and Natural Areas, King's and Queen's Bluff. The King's Bluff trail offers a breathtaking view of the Mississippi River Valley, which is a major flyway for waterfowl, eagles, and hawks.

★2906★ HAYES LAKE STATE PARK

48990 County Rd 4
Roseau, MN 56751
Web: www.dnr.state.mn.us/state_parks/hayes_lake
Phone: 218-425-7504; **Fax:** 218-425-7971
Size: 2,958 acres. **Location:** 15 miles south of the town of Roseau on State Highway 89, then 9 miles east on Roseau County Road 4. **Facilities:** 35 drive-in campsites (18 with electrical hookups), showers (&), flush toilets (&), 2 backpack campsites, 2 camper cabins (seasonal), group camp, hiking trails (13 miles), self-guided trail (2.5 miles), mountain bike trail (5 miles), horse trails (7 miles), ski trails (6 miles), snowmobile trails (6 miles), picnic area (&), enclosed picnic shelter (&), playground (&), swimming beach, fishing pier (&), boat launch, canoe and kayak rentals, historic site, interpretive exhibits, gift shop. **Activities:** Camping, swimming, lake and river fishing, boating (electric motors only), hiking, mountain biking, horseback riding, cross-country skiing, snowmobiling, snowshoeing, wildlife viewing. **Special Features:** Area wildlife includes loons, moose, beaver, fish, otter, lynx, black bear, and timberwolves.

★2907★ HILL ANNEX MINE STATE PARK

PO Box 376
Calumet, MN 55716
Web: www.dnr.state.mn.us/state_parks/hill_annex_mine
Phone: 218-247-7215; **Fax:** 218-247-7449
Size: 635 acres. **Location:** On the north edge of Calumet along State Highway 169, halfway between Grand Rapids and Hibbing. **Facilities:** Mine site, museum, exhibits, visitor center (&), gift shop, picnic area, picnic shelter, playground, flush toilets (&). **Activities:** Mine tours, interpretive programs (seasonal), fossil hunting. **Special Features:** Historic open-pit mine was one of the richest iron ore mines in the nation and is now a tribute to the mining industry. Tours into the pit offer visitors views of the mine pits, lakes, and rock walls in various shades of red, and tell about the mine operation, the people who worked here, and where they came from.

★2908★ INTERSTATE STATE PARK

307 Milltown Rd
PO Box 254
Taylors Falls, MN 55084
Web: www.dnr.state.mn.us/state_parks/interstate
Phone: 651-465-5711; **Fax:** 651-465-0517

Size: 298 acres. **Location:** 45 miles northeast of Minneapolis-St. Paul on US Highway 8 (1 mile south of Taylors Falls). **Facilities:** 37 drive-in campsites (22 with electrical hookups), showers (&), flush toilets (&), group camp, picnic area (&), enclosed picnic shelter (&), open shelter, volleyball court, hiking trails (4 miles), self-guided trail (3 miles), wheelchair-accessible trail (0.5 miles), boat launch, canoe rentals, canoe shuttle, visitor center (&), interpretive exhibits, historic site, gift shop. **Activities:** Camping, river fishing, boating (with restrictions), hiking, canoeing, excursion boat tours, rock climbing. **Special Features:** Geologically, the park is one of the most significant sites in Minnesota. Features include at least 10 different lava flows, two distinct glacial deposits, and traces of old streams, valleys, and faults.

★**2909**★ **ITASCA STATE PARK**
36750 Main Park Dr
Park Rapids, MN 56470
Web: www.dnr.state.mn.us/state_parks/itasca
Phone: 218-266-2100; **Fax:** 218-266-3942
Size: 32,690 acres. **Location:** 21 miles north of Park Rapids and 30 miles south of Bemidji on US 71. **Facilities:** 224 drive-in campsites (100 with electrical hookups), showers (&), flush toilets (&), 11 backpack campsites, 11 cart-in campsites, group camp, group center, cabins, lodge and restaurant, picnic areas and shelters (&), playground (&), volleyball court, hiking trails (49 miles), self-guided trail (3.5 miles), wheelchair-accessible trail (1.5 miles), paved bike trails (16 miles), ski trails (31 miles), snowmobile trails (31 miles), warming house, swimming beach, fishing pier (&), boat ramps, boat and motor rentals, pontoon and paddleboat rentals, canoe and kayak rentals, bike rentals, snowshoe rentals, visitor center (&), historic site, observation tower, snack bar, gift shops. **Activities:** Camping, swimming, lake fishing, boating (speed limit restrictions), canoeing, hiking, bicycling, cross-country skiing, snowmobiling, snowshoeing, excursion boat tours, nature programs. **Special Features:** Established in 1891, Itasca is the oldest state park in Minnesota. The Mississippi River begins its 2,552-mile journey to the Gulf of Mexico here. Points of interest include Preacher's Grove, Peace Pipe Vista, the Itasca Indian Mounds, Wegmann Cabin, and more than 100 lakes.

★**2910**★ **JAY COOKE STATE PARK**
780 Hwy 210
Carlton, MN 55718
Web: www.dnr.state.mn.us/state_parks/jay_cooke
Phone: 218-384-4610; **Fax:** 218-384-4851
Size: 8,781 acres. **Location:** 3 miles east of Carlton on State Highway 210. **Facilities:** 80 drive-in campsites (21 with electrical hookups), showers (&), flush toilets (&), 4 backpack campsites, 3 walk-in campsites, group camp, camper cabin (year round), picnic area and shelters (&), volleyball court, horseshoe pits, hiking trails (50 miles), paved bike trails (9 miles), mountain bike trails (13 miles), horse trail (6 miles), wheelchair accessible trail (0.5 miles), ski trails (32 miles), snowmobile trails (6 miles), warming house, snowshoe rentals, visitor center (&), interpretive exhibits, historic sites, gift shop. **Activities:** Camping, river and stream fishing, hiking, bicycling, mountain biking, horseback riding, cross-country skiing, snowmobiling,

snowshoeing, nature programs. **Special Features:** Park features an extensive network of trails, including one that leads over a swinging suspension bridge high above Saint Louis River.

★**2911**★ **JOHN A. LATSCH STATE PARK**
c/o Whitewater State Park
19041 Hwy 74
Altura, MN 55910
Web: www.dnr.state.mn.us/state_parks/john_latsch
Phone: 507-932-3007; **Fax:** 507-932-5938
Size: 1,871 acres. **Location:** 12 miles northwest of Winona on US Highway 61. **Facilities:** 7 walk-in campsites, vault toilet, picnic area (&), hiking trail (0.5 miles). **Activities:** Camping, hiking, snowshoeing. **Special Features:** John A Latsch, a Minnesota businessman, was the founder of the Izaak Walton League and often fished in the Mississippi below the bluffs of Faith, Hope, and Charity. A half-mile hike up a deep ravine affords a grand view of the Mississippi River Valley from these peaks.

★**2912**★ **JUDGE CR MAGNEY STATE PARK**
4051 E Hwy 61
Grand Marais, MN 55604
Web: www.dnr.state.mn.us/state_parks/judge_cr_magney
Phone: 218-387-3039; **Fax:** 218-387-3051
Size: 4,643 acres. **Location:** 14 miles northeast of Grand Marais on State Highway 61. **Facilities:** 27 drive-in campsites, showers (&), flush toilets (&), picnic area, hiking trails (9 miles), ski trails (5 miles), historic site. Park is open seasonally (April 1-October 31). **Activities:** Camping, fishing (lake, river, stream), hiking, cross-country skiing, snowshoeing. **Special Features:** Park features the Devil's Kettle waterfall, where the Brule River splits around a mass of volcanic rock. Half of the river plunges 50 feet into a pool, while the rest pours into a huge pothole.

★**2913**★ **KILEN WOODS STATE PARK**
50200 860th St
Rt 1 Box 122
Lakefield, MN 56150
Web: www.dnr.state.mn.us/state_parks/kilen_woods
Phone: 507-662-6258; **Fax:** 507-662-5501
Size: 548 acres. **Location:** On County Road 24, 8 miles northeast of Lakefield and 5 miles east of Highway 86. **Facilities:** 33 drive-in campsites (11 with electrical hookups), showers (&), 4 cart-in campsites, picnic area, enclosed picnic shelter (&), volleyball court, horseshoe pit, hiking trails (5 miles), ski trails (1.5 miles), snowmobile trails (3.5 miles), sliding hill, warming house. **Activities:** Camping, river fishing, hiking, cross-country skiing, snowmobiling, bird watching, snow sledding. **Special Features:** Trails meander along the tranquil Des Moines River and up to the Dinosaur Ridge Overlook, which affords a scenic view of the river valley.

★**2914**★ **LAC QUI PARLE STATE PARK**
14047 20th St NW
Watson, MN 56295
Web: www.dnr.state.mn.us/state_parks/lac_qui_parle
Phone: 320-752-4450; **Fax:** 320-734-4452

Size: 1,055 acres. **Location:** Approximately 0.5 miles north of Watson on US 59 and State Highway 7, then west on Chippewa County Road 13. **Facilities:** 85 drive-in campsites (58 with full hookups), showers (&), flush toilets (&), 3 cart-in campsites, group camp (6 sites), picnic area, picnic shelters (&), horseshoe pits, swimming beach, fishing pier (&), boat launch, hiking trails (6 miles), horse trails (5 miles), ski trails (5 miles), warming house, visitor center (&), historic site, gift shop. **Activities:** Camping, swimming, lake and river fishing, boating, canoeing, hiking, horseback riding, cross-country skiing, snowshoeing, bird watching, hunting. **Special Features:** In French, Lac Qui Parle means "lake which speaks," referring to the noise made by the thousands of migratory Canada geese and other waterfowl which descend on the lake in the spring and fall.

★2915★ LAKE BEMIDJI STATE PARK

3401 State Park Rd NE
Bemidji, MN 56601
Web: www.dnr.state.mn.us/state_parks/lake_bemidji
Phone: 218-755-3843; **Fax:** 218-755-4073
Size: 1,726 acres. **Location:** On the northeast shore of Lake Bemidji, on County Road 20 (north of Bemidji via US 71). **Facilities:** 95 drive-in campsites (43 with electrical hookups), showers (&), flush toilets (&), 2 group camps, group center, picnic area and enclosed shelter (&), hiking trails (15 miles), self-guided trail (1 mile), paved bike trails (6 miles), mountain bike trail (5 miles), wheelchair accessible trail (2 miles), ski trails (11 miles), snowshoe rentals, snowmobile trails (3 miles), warming house, fishing pier (&), boat launch, boat and canoe rentals, volleyball court, visitor center (&), interpretive exhibits, gift shop. **Activities:** Camping, swimming, lake fishing, boating, canoeing, hiking, bicycling, mountain biking, cross-country skiing, snowmobiling, eagle/osprey viewing, nature programs. **Special Features:** A boardwalk through a tamarack bog offers visitors in late spring a chance to see showy native plants, including lady's slippers, pitcher plants, dragon's mouth, grass pink, and insect-eating sundews.

★2916★ LAKE BRONSON STATE PARK

Box 9
Lake Bronson, MN 56734
Web: www.dnr.state.mn.us/state_parks/lake_bronson
Phone: 218-754-2200; **Fax:** 218-754-6141
Size: 3,598 acres. **Location:** 2 miles east of the town of Lake Bronson on County Highway 28. **Facilities:** 160 drive-in campsites (35 with electrical hookups), showers (&), flush toilets (&), 4 backpack campsites, 2 canoe-in campsites, group camp, picnic area and shelters (&), hiking trails (14 miles), self-guided trail (1.5 miles), paved bike trail (2 miles), mountain bike trails (5 miles), wheelchair accessible trail (2 miles), ski trails (7 miles), snowmobile trails (3 miles), warming house, swimming beach, fishing pier (&), boat launch, boat and canoe rentals, volleyball court, playground (&), observation tower, historic structures, visitor center (&), interpretive exhibits, gift shop. **Activities:** Camping, swimming, lake and river fishing, boating, canoeing, hiking, bicycling, mountain biking, cross-country skiing, snowmobiling, snowshoeing. **Special Features:** Located in a transition area between prairie and forest, this park supports a variety of wildlife. An observation tower in the park allows

visitors to view the prairie and aspen-oak forests or watch for deer, sharp-tailed grouse, moose, and sandhill cranes.

★2917★ LAKE CARLOS STATE PARK

2601 County Rd 38 NE
Carlos, MN 56319
Web: www.dnr.state.mn.us/state_parks/lake_carlos
Phone: 320-852-7200; **Fax:** 320-852-7349
Size: 1,236 acres. **Location:** 10 miles north of Alexandria off State Highway 29, then 2 miles west on County Road 38. **Facilities:** 124 drive-in campsites (81 with electrical hookups), showers (&), flush toilets (&), 2 walk-in campsites, 7 horsemen's campsites, 2 group camps, group center, picnic area, picnic shelter, hiking trails (14 miles), self-guided trails (3 miles), horse trails (9 miles), wheelchair accessible trail (0.5 miles), ski trails (6 miles), snowmobile trails (9 miles), snowshoe rentals, warming house, swimming beach, boat launch, interpretive exhibits, gift shop. **Activities:** Camping, swimming, lake fishing, boating, hiking, horseback riding, cross-country skiing, snowmobiling, snowshoeing, birdwatching. **Special Features:** In minutes, visitors can hike or ski from a tamarack bog to a maple-basswood stand or from open grassland to forested ridges.

★2918★ LAKE LOUISE STATE PARK

c/o Forestville/Mystery Cave State Park
21071 County Road 118
Preston, MN 55965
Web: www.dnr.state.mn.us/state_parks/lake_louise
Phone: 507-352-5111; **Fax:** 507-352-5113
Size: 1,147 acres. **Location:** 1.5 miles north of LeRoy on County Road 14. **Facilities:** 20 drive-in campsites (11 with electrical hookups), shower, 6 horsemen's campsites, group camp, picnic area (&), picnic shelter (&), hiking trails (11.5 miles), paved bike trail (10 miles), horse trails (10 miles), ski trails (3 miles), snowmobile trails (9.6 miles), swimming beach, hand launch boat ramp. **Activities:** Camping, swimming, lake and stream fishing, boating (electric motors only), canoeing, hiking, bicycling, horseback riding, cross-country skiing, snowmobiling, snowshoeing. **Special Features:** Park is situated at the confluence of the Little Iowa and Upper Iowa Rivers where they flow into Lake Louise. Park is open seasonally.

★2919★ LAKE MARIA STATE PARK

11411 Clementa Ave NW
Monticello, MN 55362
Web: www.dnr.state.mn.us/state_parks/lake_maria
Phone: 763-878-2325; **Fax:** 763-878-2620
Size: 1,614 acres. **Location:** Access via Highway 39 and Wright County Road 1 from the south; from the north, take Highway 8 to Highway 39 and Wright County Road. **Facilities:** 17 secluded backpack campsites, 2 group camps, 3 remote ski-in/walk-in camper cabins, flush toilets (&), picnic area (&), enclosed picnic shelter (&), hiking trails (14 miles), self-guided trail (1.5 miles), horse trails (6 miles), ski trails (14 miles), skate-ski trail (2 miles), snowshoe rentals, warming house, fishing pier, boat launch, boat and canoe rentals, visitor center (&), interpretive exhibits, gift shop. **Activities:** Camping, lake fishing, boating, canoeing, hiking, horseback riding, cross-country skiing, ice

skating, snowshoeing. **Special Features:** Park includes one of the few remaining stands of the "Big Woods," a maple, oak, and basswood forest that once covered part of southern Minnesota. The park is also home to the Blandings turtle, one of Minnesota's threatened species.

★2920★ **LAKE SHETEK STATE PARK**
163 State Park Rd
Currie, MN 56123
Web: www.dnr.state.mn.us/state_parks/lake_shetek
Phone: 507-763-3256; **Fax:** 507-763-3330
Size: 1,108 acres. **Location:** North of Currie via County Road 38. **Facilities:** 97 drive-in campsites (66 with electrical hookups), showers (占), flush toilets (占), 10 walk-in campsites, 2 group camps, group center, camper cabin, picnic area (占), picnic shelters (占), volleyball court, playground (占), horseshoe pits, hiking trails (14 miles), self-guided trail (1 mile), wheelchair-accessible trails (7.5 miles), paved bike trail (6 miles), ski trails (3 miles), snowmobile trails (5 miles), warming house, swimming beach, boat launch, boat and canoe rentals, historic site, interpretive exhibits, visitor center (占), gift shop. **Activities:** Camping, swimming, lake fishing, boating, canoeing, hiking, cross-country skiing, snowmobiling. **Special Features:** Park contains the largest lake in southwestern Minnesota, which forms the headwaters of the Des Moines River. "Shetek" is an Ojibwe word meaning "pelican," a bird that visits Lake Shetek during the summer and fall. Loon Island, a 45-acre bird sanctuary, is accessible on foot via a causeway and includes an interpretive trail.

★2921★ **MAPLEWOOD STATE PARK**
39721 Park Entrance Rd
Pelican Rapids, MN 56572
Web: www.dnr.state.mn.us/state_parks/maplewood
Phone: 218-863-8383; **Fax:** 218-863-8384
Size: 9,264 acres. **Location:** 7 miles east of Pelican Rapids on State Highway 108. **Facilities:** 71 drive-in campsites (32 with electrical hookups), showers (占), flush toilets (占), 3 backpack campsites, 50 horsemen's campsites, camper cabin (seasonal), group camp, picnic area (占), hiking trails (25 miles), self-guided trail (2.2 miles), horse trails (20 miles), ski trails (13 miles), snowmobile trails (20 miles), swimming beach, fishing pier, boat launch, boat and canoe rentals, interpretive exhibits, gift shop. **Activities:** Camping, swimming, lake fishing, boating, canoeing, hiking, horseback riding, cross-country skiing, snowmobiling. **Special Features:** Eight major lakes provide excellent opportunities for fishing and other water recreation. The maple forest turns brilliant shades of orange, gold, and red in the fall.

★2922★ **MCCARTHY BEACH STATE PARK**
7622 McCarthy Beach Rd
Side Lake, MN 55781
Web: www.dnr.state.mn.us/state_parks/mccarthy_beach
Phone: 218-254-7979; **Fax:** 218-254-7980
Size: 2,359 acres. **Location:** From the town of Hibbing, take US 169 north to County Road 5, then 16 miles to the park. **Facilities:** 86 drive-in campsites (18 with electrical hookups), showers (占), flush toilets (占), 3 walk-in campsites, group camp,

picnic area, enclosed picnic shelter, hiking trails (18 miles), horse trails (12 miles), mountain bike trails (17 miles), ski trails (9 miles), snowmobile trails (12 miles), swimming beach, horseshoe pits, fishing pier (占), boat launch, boat and canoe rentals, interpretive exhibits, gift shop. **Activities:** Camping, swimming, lake fishing, boating, canoeing, hiking, horseback riding, cross-country skiing, snowmobiling, snowshoeing. **Special Features:** The sandy beach on Sturgeon Lake has been rated one of the top 17 beaches in North America by *Highways Magazine*. Park also includes Side Lake and the four connected lakes of the Sturgeon chain.

★2923★ **MILLE LACS KATHIO STATE PARK**
15066 Kathio State Park Rd
Onamia, MN 56359
Web: www.dnr.state.mn.us/state_parks/mille_lacs_kathio
Phone: 320-532-3523; **Fax:** 320-532-3529
Size: 10,554 acres. **Location:** 8 miles north of Onamia off US 169. **Facilities:** 70 drive-in campsites (22 with electrical hookups), showers (占), flush toilets (占), 3 walk-in campsites, 10 horsemen's campsites, group camp, 5 camper cabins, hiking trails (35 miles), self-guided trail (1 mile), horse trails (27 miles), wheelchair accessible trail (1 mile), ski trails (20 miles), snowmobile trails (19 miles), snowshoe trails (7.5 miles), sliding hill, warming house, picnic area, enclosed picnic shelter, playground, swimming beach, boat launch, boat and canoe rentals, ski and snowshoe rentals, visitor center (占), historic sites, interpretive exhibits, gift shop, 100-foot fire/observation tower. **Activities:** Camping, swimming, lake and river fishing, boating, canoeing, hiking, horseback riding, cross-country skiing, snowmobiling, snowshoeing, snow sledding, nature programs. **Special Features:** The park, a registered National Historic Landmark due to its 9000 years of human history and archaeological significance, lies along the Rum River and encompasses Ogechie and Shakopee lakes. The river, lakes, and trails provide visitors the chance to see bald eagles, osprey, otters, beavers, loons, deer, bears, coyotes, and many other animals.

★2924★ **MINNEOPA STATE PARK**
54497 Gadwall Rd
Mankato, MN 56001
Web: www.dnr.state.mn.us/state_parks/minneopa
Phone: 507-389-5464; **Fax:** 507-389-5174
Size: 2,691 acres. **Location:** 5 miles west of Mankato on State Highway 68 and US Highway 169. **Facilities:** 61 drive-in campsites (6 with electrical hookups), showers (占), flush toilets (占), group camp, camper cabin, picnic area, picnic shelter (占), volleyball court, horseshoe pit, hiking trails (4 miles), ski trails (3.5 miles), hand launch boat ramp, visitor center, interpretive exhibits, historic site, gift shop. **Activities:** Camping, stream and river fishing, boating, canoeing, hiking, cross-country skiing. **Special Features:** The word Minneopa comes from the Dakota language and is interpreted to mean "water falling twice," referring to the beautiful waterfalls of the Minneopa Creek. Visitors can walk a trail that encircles the falls and leads down a limestone stairway to the valley below and then scend the opposite side for a panoramic view of the valley. Another park attraction is Seppmann Mill, a wind-driven grist mill fashioned in German style from native stone and lumber.

9. State Parks

★2925★ MINNESOTA VALLEY STATE RECREATION AREA

c/o Fort Snelling State Park
101 Snelling Lake Rd
Saint Paul, MN 55111
Web: www.dnr.state.mn.us/state_parks/minnesota_valley
Phone: 612-725-2389
Size: 5,501 acres. **Location:** 25 miles southwest of Minneapolis-Saint Paul off US Highway 169 in Jordan. **Facilities:** 25 drive-in campsites, 8 walk-in campsites, 8 horsemen's campsites, picnic area, picnic shelters (&), hiking trails (41 miles), self-guided trails (4.5 miles), paved bike trails (6 miles), mountain bike trails (29 miles), horse trails (29 miles), wheelchair accessible trail (1 mile), ski trails (5 miles), snowmobile trails (39 miles), boat launch, historic site. **Activities:** Camping, river fishing, boating, hiking, bicycling, mountain biking, horseback riding, cross-country skiing, snowmobiling, snowshoeing, wildlife observation. **Special Features:** The park's location on the Minnesota River includes diverse habitats: wetlands, floodplain forest, and blufftop oak savanna. Wildlife observation and bird-watching are popular activities year round.

★2926★ MONSON LAKE STATE PARK

1690 15th St NE
Sunburg, MN 56289
Web: www.dnr.state.mn.us/state_parks/monson_lake
Phone: 320-366-3797; **Fax:** 320-366-3882
Size: 187 acres. **Location:** Off State Highway 9, just west of Sunburg, via County Road 95. **Facilities:** 20 drive-in campsites, showers, flush toilets, picnic area, picnic shelter (&), hiking trail (1 mile), fishing pier, boat launch, canoe rental, historic site. **Activities:** Camping, lake fishing, boating, canoeing. **Special Features:** Park was established in 1923 as a memorial to two families who died in the US-Dakota Conflict of 1862.

★2927★ MOOSE LAKE STATE PARK

4252 County Rd 137
Moose Lake, MN 55767
Web: www.dnr.state.mn.us/state_parks/moose_lake
Phone: 218-485-5420; **Fax:** 218-485-5422
Size: 1,199 acres. **Location:** Off County Road 137, 0.25 miles east of I-35 at Moose Lake (Exit 214). **Facilities:** 33 drive-in campsites (20 with electrical hookups), showers (&), flush toilets (&), 2 walk-in campsites, group camp, hiking trails (5 miles), paved bike trail (2 miles) wheelchair-accessible trail (0.33 miles), ski trails (5 miles), snowmobile trail (2 miles), picnic area (&), volleyball court, horseshoe pit, swimming beach, fishing pier (&), boat launch, boat and canoe rentals, interpretive center (&), gift shop. **Activities:** Camping, swimming, lake fishing, boating, canoeing, hiking, bicycling, cross-country skiing, snowmobiling, snowshoeing. **Special Features:** The park's visitor center, which opened in 2003 and is officially named Moose Lake Agate and Geological Interpretive Center (MAGIC), showcases Minnesota's state gemstone, the Lake Superior agate. A small sandy beach is located beside Echo Lake, which is known for its bass, northern pike, and panfish.

★2928★ MYRE-BIG ISLAND STATE PARK

19499 780th Ave
Albert Lea, MN 56007
Web: www.dnr.state.mn.us/state_parks/myre_big_island
Phone: 507-379-3403; **Fax:** 507-379-3405
Size: 2,028 acres. **Location:** 3 miles southeast of Albert Lea on County Highway 38. **Facilities:** 93 drive-in campsites (32 with electrical hookups), showers (&), flush toilets (&), 4 backpack campsites, group camp, group center, camper cabin (seasonal), picnic area, open picnic shelter (&), enclosed picnic shelter, hiking trails (16 miles), self-guided trails (8.25 miles), wheelchair-accessible trail (0.5 miles), mountain bike trails (7 miles), ski trails (8 miles), snowmobile trails (7 miles), warming house, boat launch, canoe rental, gift shop. **Activities:** Camping, lake fishing, boating (with restrictions), canoeing, hiking, mountain biking, cross-country skiing, snowmobiling, snowshoeing, birdwatching. **Special Features:** Park is one of many good birding spots in southern Minnesota, especially during spring and fall migration. Regular avian visitors include birds of prey, shore birds, ducks, geese, and songbirds, including the indigo bunting, eastern bluebird, rose-breasted grosbeak, northern oriole, and eastern wood pewee. Unique features at the park include the 116-acre Big Island, which is covered with maple/basswood forest, and a glacial esker located in the northeast section of the park.

★2929★ NERSTRAND-BIG WOODS STATE PARK

9700 170th St E
Nerstrand, MN 55053
Web: www.dnr.state.mn.us/state_parks/nerstrand_big_woods
Phone: 507-333-4840; **Fax:** 507-333-4852
Size: 2,882 acres. **Location:** 10 miles south of Northfield on County Road 40. **Facilities:** 51 drive-in campsites (27 with electrical hookups), showers (&), flush toilets (&), 4 walk-in campsites, 3 group camps, picnic area (&), picnic shelters (&), playground, volleyball court, horseshoe pit, self-guided trails (13 miles), ski trails (7 miles), snowmobile trails (5 miles), warming house, snowshoe rental, visitor center (&), interpretive exhibits, gift shop. **Activities:** Camping, hiking, cross-country skiing, snowmobiling, snowshoeing. **Special Features:** Park is home to a large variety of spring wildflowers, including the rare sharp-lobed hepatica and the endangered dwarf trout lily, which is only found here.

★2930★ OLD MILL STATE PARK

33489 240th ave NW
Rt 1 Box 43
Argyle, MN 56713
Web: www.dnr.state.mn.us/state_parks/old_mill
Phone: 218-437-8174; **Fax:** 218-437-8104
Size: 407 acres. **Location:** 1 mile off County State Aid Hwy 4, between Newfolden and Argyle. **Facilities:** 26 drive-in campsites (10 with electrical hookups), showers (&), flush toilets (&), group camp, picnic area (&), enclosed picnic shelter (&), playground, volleyball court, horseshoe pit, hiking trails (7 miles), self-guided trail (1 mile), ski trails (7 miles), snowmobile trail (1.5 miles), sliding hill, ski and snowshoe rentals, warming house, swimming beach, hand launch boat ramp, historic sites, interpretive exhibits, gift shop. **Activities:** Camping, swimming,

9. State Parks

river fishing, hiking, cross-country skiing, snow sledding, snow-mobiling. **Special Features:** Park contains a historic log cabin and steam-powered flour mill, powered up annually to demonstrate how grain was ground into flour and bran.

★2931★ **RED RIVER STATE RECREATION AREA**
515 2nd St NW
East Grand Forks, MN 56721
Web: www.dnr.state.mn.us/state_parks/red_river
Phone: 218-773-4950; **Fax:** 218-773-4951
Size: 1,230 acres. **Location:** On the Red River in the city of East Grand Forks, 1 mile south of Highway 2. **Facilities:** 72 drive-in campsites (48 with full hookups), flush toilets (&), picnic area, picnic shelter (&), boat launch, paved multi-use trails, wheelchair accessible trail (2 miles), historic site, nature store, dining and shopping nearby. **Activities:** Camping, river fishing, boating, birding, hiking, bicycling, cross-country skiing, snowshoeing, snowmobiling. **Special Features:** Creation of this recreation area resulted from the 1997 flood that devastated the communities of East Grand Forks, MN and Grand Forks, ND. The land is now a 1,200-acre greenway set in an urban area.

★2932★ **RICE LAKE STATE PARK**
8485 Rose St
Owatonna, MN 55060
Web: www.dnr.state.mn.us/state_parks/rice_lake
Phone: 507-455-5871; **Fax:** 507-446-2326
Size: 1,071 acres. **Location:** 7 miles east of Owatonna on Rose Street. **Facilities:** 42 drive-in campsites (16 with electrical hookups), showers (&), flush toilets (&), 5 walk-in campsites, 4 cart-in campsites, 5 canoe-in campsites, 2 group camps, picnic area (&), picnic shelters (&), playground, hiking trails (5 miles), wheelchair-accessible trail (0.5 miles), ski trails (2.5 miles), snowmobile trails (3 miles), warming house, boat launch, canoe rental, interpretive exhibits, gift shop, observation deck. **Activities:** Camping, river fishing, boating, canoeing, hiking, cross-country skiing, snowmobiling, snowshoeing, nature observation, birdwatching. **Special Features:** American Indians once harvested wild rice from this lake, a major wetland that attracts many waterfall during migrations.

★2933★ **SAINT CROIX STATE PARK**
30065 St Croix Park Rd
Hinckley, MN 55037
Web: www.dnr.state.mn.us/state_parks/st_croix
Phone: 320-384-6591; **Fax:** 320-384-7070
Size: 33,895 acres. **Location:** 15 miles east of Hinckley on State Highway 48. **Facilities:** 211 drive-in campsites (42 with electrical hookups), showers (&), flush toilets (&), 4 walk-in campsites, 2 backpack campsites, 10 canoe-in campsites, 40 horsemen's campsites, group camp, 2 group centers, 5 cabins, 2 guest houses, picnic area, picnic shelter, playground, volleyball court, horseshoe pits, hiking trails (127 miles), self-guided trail (1.5 miles), wheelchair-accessible trail (1.5 miles), paved bike trails (5.5 miles), mountain bike trails (21 miles), horse trails (75 miles), ski trails (11 miles), snowmobile trails (80 miles), warming house, swimming beach, boat launch, canoe rentals, bike rentals, snowshoe rentals, historic structures, interpretive

exhibits, gift shop, fire tower. **Activities:** Camping, swimming, river and stream fishing, canoeing, hiking, bicycling, mountain biking, horseback riding, cross-country skiing, snowmobiling, snowshoeing, birding and wildlife observation. **Special Features:** Minnesota's largest state park is bounded by two great rivers: the Saint Croix River, a National Scenic Riverway, and the Kettle River, a State Wild and Scenic River.

★2934★ **SAKATAH LAKE STATE PARK**
50499 Sakatah Lake State Park Rd
Waterville, MN 56096
Web: www.dnr.state.mn.us/state_parks/sakatah_lake
Phone: 507-362-4438; **Fax:** 507-362-4558
Size: 842 acres. **Location:** Off State Highway 60, 1 mile east of the intersection of State Highway 13 and 60 at Waterville; or 14 miles west of Faribault. **Facilities:** 62 drive-in campsites (14 with electrical hookups), showers (&), flush toilets (&), 4 bike-in campsites, 2 group camps, camper cabin (seasonal), picnic area (&), horseshoe pit, hiking trails (5 miles), paved bike trails (3 miles), wheelchair accessible trail (0.36 miles), ski trails (5 miles), snowmobile trail (3 miles), fishing pier (&), boat launch, boat and canoe rentals, gift shop. **Activities:** Camping, lake fishing, boating, canoeing, hiking, bicycling (access to Sakatah State Trail), cross-country skiing, snowmobiling. **Special Features:** Sakatah-Singing Hills State Trail, stretching 39 miles from Mankato to Faribault, runs through the park.

★2935★ **SAVANNA PORTAGE STATE PARK**
55626 Lake Pl
McGregor, MN 55760
Web: www.dnr.state.mn.us/state_parks/savanna_portage
Phone: 218-426-3271; **Fax:** 218-426-4437
Size: 15,818 acres. **Location:** Off County Road 14 via Highway 65 north. **Facilities:** 61 drive-in campsites (18 with electrical hookups), showers (&), flush toilets (&), 6 backpack campsites, 2 canoe-in campsites, group camp, camper cabin, guest house, picnic area (&), picnic shelter (&), playground, horseshoe pits, volleyball court, hiking trails (17 miles), self-guided trails (5 miles), mountain bike trails (10 miles), ski trails (12 miles), snowmobile trails (34 miles), warming house, swimming beach, fishing pier, boat launch, boat and motor rentals, canoe rentals, historic site, visitor center (&), interpretive exhibits, gift shop. **Activities:** Camping, swimming, lake and river fishing, boating (electric motors only), canoeing, hiking, cross-country skiing, snowmobiling, snowshoeing. **Special Features:** Park contains the historic Savanna Portage Trail once traveled by fur traders, Dakota and Ojibwe Indians, and explorers. The trail required a six-mile portage across marsh, swamp, and forest, which took an average of five days to reach the West Savanna River. Today, visitors can hike the Savanna Portage Trail as well as the Continental Divide Trail.

★2936★ **SCENIC STATE PARK**
56956 Scenic Hwy 7
Bigfork, MN 56628
Web: www.dnr.state.mn.us/state_parks/scenic
Phone: 218-743-3362; **Fax:** 218-743-1362
Size: 3,360 acres. **Location:** 7 miles east of Bigfork on County

Road 7. **Facilities:** 95 drive-in campsites (20 with electrical hookups), showers (&), flush toilets (&), 2 backpack campsites, 5 canoe-in campsites, group camp, rental cabin (rustic), guest house, picnic area, enclosed picnic shelter (&), hiking trails (14 miles), self-guided trail (2 miles), paved bike trails (2 miles), ski trails (5 miles), snowmobile trail (10 miles), swimming beach, fishing pier (&), boat launch, boat and canoe rentals, historic structures, visitor center (&), interpretive exhibits, gift shop. **Activities:** Camping, swimming, lake fishing, canoeing, hiking, bicycling, cross-country skiing, snowmobiling, snowshoeing. **Special Features:** With seven pristine lakes, virgin pines, and more than 40 species of animals, Scenic State Park is well deserving of its name.

★2937★ SCHOOLCRAFT STATE PARK

c/o Hill Annex Mine State Park
PO Box 376
Calumet, MN 55716
Web: www.dnr.state.mn.us/state_parks/schoolcraft
Phone: 218-247-7215; **Fax:** 218-247-7449
Size: 295 acres. **Location:** State Highway 6 to County Road 28 west (turns into 65 W), then north on County Road 74. **Facilities:** 28 drive-in campsites, canoe-in campsite, group camp, picnic area, hiking trails (2 miles), boat access. **Activities:** Camping, river fishing, canoeing, hiking, showshoeing. **Special Features:** Located within Chippewa National Forest (see separate entry in national forests section), this quiet and peaceful park includes a virgin pine forest with trees more than 300 years old. The park was named for Henry Rowe Schoolcraft, who, with Anishinabe guide Ozawindib, charted the headwaters of the Mississippi River.

★2938★ SIBLEY STATE PARK

800 Sibley Park Rd NE
New London, MN 56273
Web: www.dnr.state.mn.us/state_parks/sibley
Phone: 320-354-2055; **Fax:** 320-354-2372
Size: 2,509 acres. **Location:** 15 miles north of Willmar on US 71. **Facilities:** 132 drive-in campsites (53 with electrical hookups), showers (&), flush toilets (&), 9 horsemen's campsites, group camp, modern group center, picnic area (&), picnic shelter, volleyball court, horseshoe pits, hiking trails (18 miles), self-guided trail (2 miles), wheelchair-accessible trail (2 miles), paved bike trails (5 miles), horse trails (9 miles), ski trail (10 miles), skate-ski trails (2 miles), snowmobile trails (6 miles), sliding hill, warming house, swimming beach, fishing pier (&), boat ramp, boat and canoe rental, interpretive center (&), historic site, interpretive exhibits, gift shop. **Activities:** Camping, swimming, lake and stream fishing, boating, canoeing, hiking, bicycling, horseback riding, cross-country skiing, snowmobiling, snowshoeing, snow sledding, nature programs. **Special Features:** Mount Tom, one of several high points in a 50-mile radius, affords a view of the surrounding patchwork of forest, farmland, prairie knolls, and lakes.

★2939★ SOUDAN UNDERGROUND MINE STATE PARK

PO Box 335
Soudan, MN 55782
Web: www.dnr.state.mn.us/state_parks/
soudan_underground_mine
Phone: 218-753-2245; **Fax:** 218-753-2246
Size: 1,250 acres. **Location:** Take US 169 to Soudan and follow the signs. **Facilities:** Picnic area (&), flush toilets (&), hiking trails (5 miles), self-guided trail (0.5 miles), boat access, visitor center (&), historic site, interpretive exhibits, gift shop. **Activities:** Lake fishing, boating, hiking, mine tours, nature programs, wildlife observation, birding. **Special Features:** For the hour-and-a-half tour, visitors don hard hats and descend by elevator a half-mile down into the mine, then board a rail car to see the deepest areas. Above ground, visitors can explore the dry house, drill shop, crusher house, and engine house and walk the boardwalk past one of the deepest open mine pits.

★2940★ SPLIT ROCK CREEK STATE PARK

336 50th Ave
Jasper, MN 56144
Web: www.dnr.state.mn.us/state_parks/split_rock_creek
Phone: 507-348-7908; **Fax:** 507-348-8940
Size: 1,303 acres. **Location:** 7 miles southwest of Pipestone off State Highway 23. **Facilities:** 28 drive-in campsites (19 with electrical hookups), showers (&), flush toilets (&), 6 walk-in campsites, group camp, picnic area (&), enclosed picnic shelter (&), playground, volleyball court, horseshoe pit, self-guided hiking trail (4.5 miles), wheelchair accessible trail (0.5 miles), sliding hill, warming house, swimming beach, fishing pier (&), boat ramp, boat, paddleboat, and canoe rentals, visitor center, interpretive exhibits, historic site, gift shop. **Activities:** Camping, swimming, lake fishing, boating (with restrictions), canoeing, hiking, snowshoeing, snow sledding. **Special Features:** Split Rock Lake, the largest body of water in Pipestone County, is the predominant feature of the park. The Pipestone National Monument (see separate entry in national parks section) is located 7 miles north of the park.

★2941★ SPLIT ROCK LIGHTHOUSE STATE PARK

3755 Split Rock Lighthouse Rd
Two Harbors, MN 55616
Web: www.dnr.state.mn.us/state_parks/split_rock_lighthouse
Phone: 218-226-6377; **Fax:** 218-226-6378
Size: 2,200 acres. **Location:** 20 miles northeast of Two Harbors on Highway 61. **Facilities:** 20 cart-in tent sites, 4 backpack campsites, showers (&), flush toilets (&), picnic area (&), picnic shelters (&), hiking trails (12 miles), self-guided trails (6 miles), wheelchair-accessible trail (0.25 miles), mountain bike trails (6 miles), paved bike trail (8 miles), ski trails (8 miles), warming house, visitor center (&), interpretive exhibits, historic site, gift shop. **Activities:** Camping, fishing (lake, river, and stream), hiking, bicycling, mountain biking, cross-country skiing, snowshoeing, lighthouse tours. **Special Features:** Park is located on the North shore of Lake Superior and is best known for its historic lighthouse. For 59 years, the keepers at Split Rock warned ships away from the rocks and treacherous North Shore with the lighthouse's 370,000-candlepower beacon.

★2942★ TEMPERANCE RIVER STATE PARK

7620 W Hwy 61
Box 33
Schroeder, MN 55613
Web: www.dnr.state.mn.us/state_parks/temperance_river
Phone: 218-663-7476; **Fax:** 218-663-7374
Size: 5,070 acres. **Location:** 1 mile north of Schroeder on Highway 61. **Facilities:** 54 drive-in campsites (18 with electrical hookups), 3 cart-in campsites, showers (&), flush toilets (&), picnic area, hiking trails (22 miles), self-guided trail (0.5 miles), ski trails (12 miles), snowmobile trails (8 miles), hand launch boat ramp, gift shop. **Activities:** Camping, lake and river fishing, boating, hiking, cross-country skiing, snowmobiling, snowshoeing, rock climbing. **Special Features:** Park includes the narrow Temperance River gorge with its many waterfalls. The trailhead for Superior Hiking Trail and North Shore Corridor Trail is located in the park.

★2943★ TETTEGOUCHE STATE PARK

5702 Hwy 61
Silver Bay, MN 55614
Web: www.dnr.state.mn.us/state_parks/tettegouche
Phone: 218-226-6365; **Fax:** 218-226-6366
Size: 9,349 acres. **Location:** 4.5 miles east of Silver Bay on Highway 61. **Facilities:** 28 drive-in campsites, showers (&), flush toilets (&), 5 backpack campsites, 6 walk-in campsites, 14 cart-in campsites, 5 kayak-in campsites, 4 cabins, guest house, picnic area (&), enclosed picnic shelter (&), hiking trails (23 miles), self-guided trail (2 miles), ski trails (15.5 miles), snowmobile trails (12 miles), fishing pier, hand launch boat ramp, canoe rentals, snowshoe rentals, visitor center (&), historic site, interpretive exhibits, gift shop. **Activities:** Camping, lake and river fishing, boating (no motors), canoeing, hiking, cross-country skiing, snowmobiling, snowshoeing, rock climbing, wildlife/peregrine falcon observation. **Special Features:** Park provides a great sense of the North Shore, with spectacular overlooks at Shovel Point; rocky, steep cliffs and inland bluffs; and the High Falls of the Baptism River. Park serves as one of the headquarters for information on the North Shore.

★2944★ UPPER SIOUX AGENCY STATE PARK

5908 Hwy 67
Granite Falls, MN 56241
Web: www.dnr.state.mn.us/state_parks/upper_sioux_agency
Phone: 320-564-4777; **Fax:** 320-564-4838
Size: 1,281 acres. **Location:** 8 miles southeast of Granite Falls on State Highway 67. **Facilities:** 34 drive-in campsites (14 with electrical hookups), 3 walk-in campsites, showers (&), flush toilets (&), 33 horsemen's campsites, 2 tipis, picnic area, picnic shelter, playground, volleyball court, horseshoe pits, hiking trails (18 miles), self-guided trail (2 miles), horse trails (16 miles), ski trails (2 miles), snowmobile trails (14 miles), sliding hill, warming house, snowshoe rentals, canoe rentals, boat launch, visitor center, interpretive exhibits, historic site, gift shop. **Activities:** Camping, river fishing, canoeing, hiking, horseback riding, snowmobiling, snow sledding, snowshoeing, birdwatching. **Special Features:** An 1851 treaty moved the Dakota Indians from Iowa and Minnesota to a reservation 20 miles wide along the Minnesota River Valley, and the Upper Sioux, or Yellow Medicine, Agency was established to administer the terms of the treaty. In the summer of 1862, the Agency was destroyed during the US-Dakota Conflict. The park exists today to preserve the old agency site, and to provide recreational opportunities in the scenic Minnesota River Valley.

★2945★ WHITEWATER STATE PARK

19041 Hwy 74
Altura, MN 55910
Web: www.dnr.state.mn.us/state_parks/whitewater
Phone: 507-932-3007; **Fax:** 507-932-5938
Size: 2,745 acres. **Location:** 3 miles south of Elba on State Highway 74. **Facilities:** 106 drive-in campsites (47 with electric hookups), showers (&), flush toilets (&), 4 walk-in campsites, camper cabin (seasonal), group camp, group center, picnic area (&), picnic shelter (&), volleyball court, horseshoe pits, hiking trails (10 miles), self-guided trails (3 miles), wheelchair-accessible trail (2 miles), ski trails (8 miles), snowshoe rentals, warming house, swimming beach, fishing pier (&), visitor center (&), interpretive exhibits, historic site, gift shop. **Activities:** Camping, swimming, stream fishing, hiking, cross-country skiing, snowshoeing, nature programs. **Special Features:** Picturesque limestone bluffs, deep ravines, spring-fed streams, and a noticeable lack of mosquitoes make this park in southeastern Minnesota very popular.

★2946★ WILD RIVER STATE PARK

39797 Park Trail
Center City, MN 55012
Web: www.dnr.state.mn.us/state_parks/wild_river
Phone: 651-583-2125; **Fax:** 651-583-3101
Size: 6,767 acres. **Location:** I-35 Exit 147 to State Highway 95, then east to County Road 12. **Facilities:** 96 drive-in campsites (17 with electrical hookups), showers (&), flush toilets (&), 7 backpack campsites, 5 canoe-in campsites, 20 horsemen's campsites, group camp, 2 camper cabins, modern guest house, picnic area (&), picnic shelters (&), hiking trails (35 miles), self-guided trail (2.7 miles), wheelchair-accessible trail (2.6 miles), paved bike trail (2.6 miles), horse trails (18 miles), ski trails (35 miles), warming house, boat ramp, canoe rentals, ski and snowshoe rentals, visitor center (&), interpretive exhibits, historic site, gift shop. **Activities:** Camping, river fishing, boating, hiking, horseback riding, mountain biking, cross-country skiing, snowshoeing, nature programs. **Special Features:** Park is located along 18 miles of the Saint Croix River, one of the eight original National Wild and Scenic Rivers. An all-season trail center provides a place to relax after hiking or cross-counry skiing the park's 35-mile trail system.

★2947★ WILLIAM O'BRIEN STATE PARK

16821 O'Brien Trail N
Marine-on-Saint Croix, MN 55047
Web: www.dnr.state.mn.us/state_parks/william_obrien
Phone: 651-433-0500; **Fax:** 651-433-0504
Size: 1,620 acres. **Location:** 12 miles north of Stillwater on

State Highway 95, near the town of Marine-on-St. Croix. **Facilities:** 124 drive-in campsites (60 with electrical hookups), showers (&), flush toilets (&), 2 walk-in campsites, camper cabin, 2 group camps, picnic area (&), picnic shelter (&), volleyball court, horseshoe pit, hiking trails (12 miles), self-guided trail (1.5 miles), wheelchair-accessible trail (2 miles), paved bike trail (1 mile), ski trails (12 miles), warming house, swimming beach, fishing pier (&), boat access, canoe rentals, visitor center (&), interpretive exhibits, gift shop. **Activities:** Camping, swimming, lake and river fishing, boating (with restrictions), canoeing, hiking, bicycling, cross-country skiing, snowshoeing, birdwatching, nature programs. **Special Features:** A great "getaway" park only one hour from the Twin Cities, the park offers a beautiful setting for recreation along the banks of the Saint Croix River.

★2948★ **ZIPPEL BAY STATE PARK**
3684 54th Ave NW
Williams, MN 56686
Web: www.dnr.state.mn.us/state_parks/zippel_bay
Phone: 218-783-6252; **Fax:** 218-783-6253
Size: 2,906 acres. **Location:** On County Road 8, about 18 miles northwest of Baudette. **Facilities:** 57 drive-in campsites, group camp, showers (&), picnic area (&), picnic shelter (&), volleyball court, hiking trails (9 miles), ski trails (9 miles), skate-ski trails (3 miles), snowmobile trails (5 miles), warming house, swimming beach, fishing pier (&), marina, boat access, visitor center, interpretive exhibits, gift shop. **Activities:** Camping, swimming, lake and river fishing, boating, hiking, cross-country skiing, snowmobiling, bird watching. **Special Features:** Park is located on the shores of Lake of the Woods, one of the world's largest lakes. Because of its size, the lake freezes much later than most lakes and remains ice covered much later in the spring. Park includes a two-mile sand beach on the lake shoreline.

Mississippi State Parks

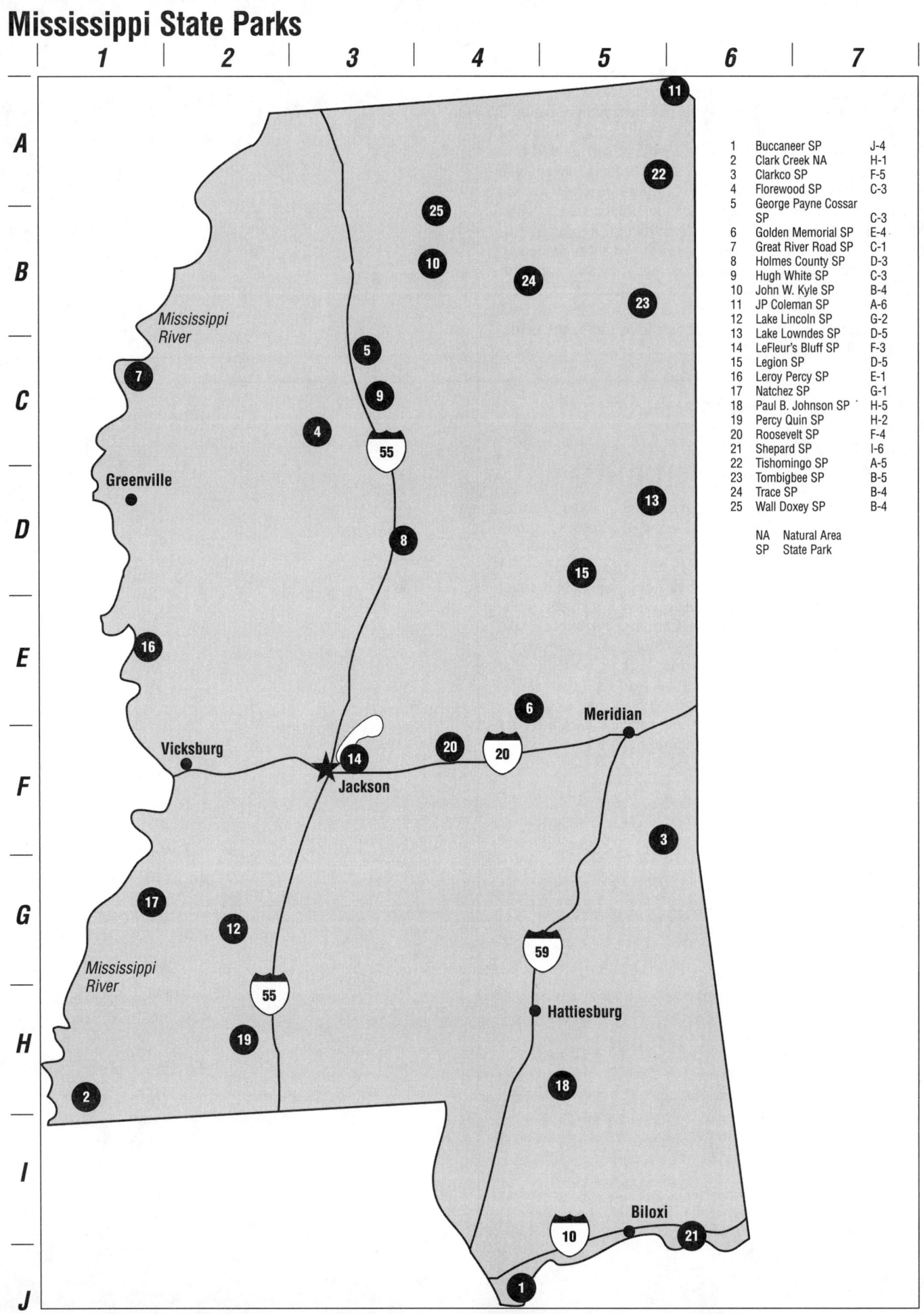

1	Buccaneer SP	J-4
2	Clark Creek NA	H-1
3	Clarkco SP	F-5
4	Florewood SP	C-3
5	George Payne Cossar SP	C-3
6	Golden Memorial SP	E-4
7	Great River Road SP	C-1
8	Holmes County SP	D-3
9	Hugh White SP	C-3
10	John W. Kyle SP	B-4
11	JP Coleman SP	A-6
12	Lake Lincoln SP	G-2
13	Lake Lowndes SP	D-5
14	LeFleur's Bluff SP	F-3
15	Legion SP	D-5
16	Leroy Percy SP	E-1
17	Natchez SP	G-1
18	Paul B. Johnson SP	H-5
19	Percy Quin SP	H-2
20	Roosevelt SP	F-4
21	Shepard SP	I-6
22	Tishomingo SP	A-5
23	Tombigbee SP	B-5
24	Trace SP	B-4
25	Wall Doxey SP	B-4

NA   Natural Area
SP   State Park

Mississippi River

Greenville

Vicksburg

Jackson

Meridian

Hattiesburg

Biloxi

Mississippi River

MISSISSIPPI

★2949★ Mississippi Department of Wildlife, Fisheries & Parks
Office of Parks
1505 Eastover Dr
Jackson, MS 39211
(601) 432-2400 - Phone
(800) 467-2757 - Toll-free
Web: www.mdwfp.com
Operates 29 parks, including three with golf courses. The department also manages 42 wildlife management areas and 24 state lakes.

Key to campsite classification:

- **Developed campsites** — May include water and electric hookups, or electricity only. Comfort stations with bathhouses and laundry facilities are located close by.
- **Tent campsites** — No utility connections; comfort stations nearby.
- **Group camps** — Accommodate 35 to 200 persons. Sleeping accommodations are in separate dormitory facilities or small group cabins. Campers furnish bed linens and bath articles. Meals are served cafeteria style in a dining hall.
- **Cabins** — All are heated and air-conditioned. Each cabin is furnished with bed and bath linens, soap, and basic kitchen equipment.

★2950★ BUCCANEER STATE PARK
1150 S Beach Blvd
Waveland, MS 39576
Web: www.mdwfp.com/parkView/parks.asp?ID=6841
Phone: 228-467-3822
Size: 398 acres. **Location:** 2 miles off US 90 on Beach Boulevard in Waveland on the Gulf Coast. **Special Features:** Park is closed due to Hurricane Katrina.

★2951★ CLARK CREEK NATURAL AREA
366 Fort Adams Pond Rd
Jackson, MS 39669
Web: www.mdwfp.com/parkView/parks.asp?ID=5852
Phone: 601-888-6040
Size: 700 acres. **Location:** 13 miles west of Woodville off Highway 24 at the Pond Community. **Facilities:** Trails. **Activities:** Hiking, birdwatching, photography. **Special Features:** Located in southwestern Mississippi, this Natural Area features some 50 waterfalls, ranging in size from 10 to more than 30 feet high, as well as a variety of uncommon plants and animals, including the threatened black bear. Hunting is not permitted here, and only foot traffic is allowed (no camping or motorized vehicles permitted). Clark Creek is in a remote area and offers no potable water or other amenities, so visitors should be medically fit and are cautioned to bring plenty of water on any outing here.

★2952★ CLARKCO STATE PARK
386 Clarkco Rd
Quitman, MS 39355
Web: www.mdwfp.com/parkView/parks.asp?ID=4842
Phone: 601-776-6651
Size: 816 acres. **Location:** 5 miles north of Quitman off US 45, on MS 145. **Facilities:** 43 developed campsites with full hookups, 3 bathhouses with hot showers, 15 tent campsites, 20 vacation cabins (each with private pier), camp store, picnic areas, 3 large pavilions, playground, nature trail (5 miles), playing field, 2 lighted tennis courts, boat launch, disc golf course, visitor center, meeting rooms. **Activities:** Camping, swimming, fishing, boating, water-skiing (115 HP limit; no jet skis), tennis. **Special Features:** Park is located near the Mississippi-Alabama state line, just south of Meridian. Its centerpiece is a 65-acre lake, which is stocked with bass, bluegill, bream, and catfish.

★2953★ FLOREWOOD STATE PARK
1999 County Rd 145
Greenwood, MS 38930
Web: www.mdwfp.com/parkView/parks.asp?ID=3822
Phone: 662-455-3821
Size: 104 acres. **Location:** 2 miles west of Greenwood off US 82. **Facilities:** Picnic tables (covered and uncovered). **Activities:** Picnicking. **Special Features:** Florewood is a day-use only park.

★2954★ GEORGE PAYNE COSSAR STATE PARK
165 County Rd 170
Oakland, MS 38948
Web: www.mdwfp.com/parkView/parks.asp?ID=2811
Phone: 662-623-7356
Size: 836 acres. **Location:** 8 miles east of Oakland off MS 32 (Exit 227 off I-55). **Facilities:** 84 developed campsites with water and electrical hookups, 2 bathhouses with hot showers, 13 vacation cabins, group camp, picnic area, 2 pavilions, full-service restaurant, nature trail (2.5 miles), swimming pool, boat launch ramps, playgrounds, 18-hole miniature golf course, 18-hole disc golf course, visitor center with meeting/banquet room, concession stand. **Activities:** Camping, swimming, fishing, boating, water-skiing, miniature and disc golf. **Special Features:** Park is situated on the shore's of Lake Enid, where the world record crappie, weighing in at over five pounds, was caught in 1954. Most of the land around the lake and in nearby Holly Springs National Forest is open for public hunting and is abundant in a variety of game.

★2955★ GOLDEN MEMORIAL STATE PARK
2104 Damascus Rd
Walnut Grove, MS 39189
Web: www.mdwfp.com/parkView/parks.asp?ID=4843
Phone: 601-253-2237
Size: 120 acres. **Location:** On MS 492, 5 miles east of Walnut Grove off MS 35. **Facilities:** Picnic area, 2 covered pavilions, playground, nature trail, fishing boat rentals. **Activities:** Picnicking, fishing. **Special Features:** Park memorializes the Old Golden School, a post-Civil War one-room schoolhouse that was once located here. A 15-acre spring-fed lake at the park is stocked with bass and bream.

★2956★ GREAT RIVER ROAD STATE PARK
PO Box 292
Rosedale, MS 38769
Web: www.mdwfp.com/parkView/parks.asp?ID=3823
Phone: 662-759-6762
Size: 756 acres. **Location:** Off MS 1 in Rosedale, 35 miles north of Greenville. **Facilities:** 61 developed campsites (RV or tent camping) with electric and water hookups, bathhouse with hot showers, picnic area and shelter, nature trails, boat launch, playing field, playground, 18-hole disc golf course, visitor center with concession stand, banquet room, and souvenir shop. **Activities:** Camping, fishing. **Special Features:** Park's 75-foot overlook tower provides panoramic views of the Mississippi River and the delta. Several of the park's trails lead to the sandbar, which at low water forms one of the largest beaches in the state. The sandbars are visited by a variety of birds and animals. The park is named for Great River Road, a scenic parkway the follows the Mississippi from its beginning as a small Canadian creek to its end at the Gulf of Mexico.

★2957★ HOLMES COUNTY STATE PARK
5369 State Park Rd
Durant, MS 39063
Web: www.mdwfp.com/parkView/parks.asp?ID=3824
Phone: 662-653-3351
Size: 537 acres. **Location:** 4 miles south of Durant off I-55, Exit 150. **Facilities:** 28 developed campsites with water and electric hookups, bathhouse with hot showers, 12 tent campsites with water, 12 vacation cabins (6 rustic, 6 duplex), group camp, 3 picnic areas, 3 pavilions, snack bar, nature trails (4 miles), swimming beach, boat launch (at English Lake only), playing fields, playgrounds, skating rink, disc golf course, outdoor amphitheater, worship services. **Activities:** Camping, fishing, hiking, skating. **Special Features:** Park is conveniently located, with easy access to I-55, and features two fishing lakes stocked with bass, bream, and catfish.

★2958★ HUGH WHITE STATE PARK
PO Box 725
Grenada, MS 38902
Web: www.mdwfp.com/parkView/parks.asp?ID=2812
Phone: 662-226-4934
Size: 1,321 acres. **Location:** 5 miles east of Grenada, off MS 8. **Facilities:** 173 developed campsites with water and electric hookups, bathhouses with hot showers, 3 primitive tent camping areas, group camp(includes meeting room, playground, and boat launch), 12 duplex vacation cabins (24 units), swimming pool (for cabin guests only), picnic area, pavilion, nature trail, boat launch, playgrounds, visitor center with meeting room. **Activities:** Camping, swimming, fishing, boating, water-skiing. **Special Features:** Park is located on 64,000-acre Grenada Lake and is known for its excellent crappie fishing. The lake is also stocked with bass, bream, and catfish. The park is midway between Memphis, Tennessee, and Jackson, Mississippi.

★2959★ JOHN W. KYLE STATE PARK
4235 State Park Rd
Sardis, MS 38666
Web: www.mdwfp.com/parkView/parks.asp?ID=2813
Phone: 662-487-1345
Size: 558 acres. **Location:** 8 miles east of Sardis, off MS 315; exit off I-55 at Sardis (Exit 252). **Facilities:** 200 developed campsites (RV or tent) with water and electric hookups, bathhouses, 22 vacation cabins (including 2 on golf course), group camp, picnic areas, 2 nature trails, swimming pool, boat launch ramps, playground, 2 lighted tennis courts,18-hole championship golf course, visitor center with ballroom, dining room, and indoor recreational facilities for group campers. **Activities:** Camping, swimming, fishing, boating, water-skiing, tennis, golf. **Special Features:** Park is situated on the shores of 58,500-acre Sardis Reservoir and includes Mallard Point, a championship golf course with a driving range and teaching course.

★2960★ JP COLEMAN STATE PARK
613 County Rd 321
Iuka, MS 38852
Web: www.mdwfp.com/parkView/parks.asp?ID=1814
Phone: 662-423-6515
Size: 637 acres. **Location:** Off MS 25 4 miles north of Iuka, turn onto CR 989, then go right on CR 321 and continue 1 mile to park entrance. **Facilities:** 69 developed campsites with full hookups and bathhouse with restrooms and hot showers, 17 tent campsites, 20 vacation cabins, motel with 16 rooms (2 ♿) and 3 townhouses, picnic area and shelter, boat launch, marina with slip rentals, miniature golf course (seasonal), visitor center with convention center and meeting rooms. **Activities:** Camping, swimming, fishing, boating, sailing, water-skiing, jet skiing, miniature golf. **Special Features:** Park is situated on a rocky bluff overlooking the Tennessee River and offers a wide range of water recreation activities.

★2961★ LAKE LINCOLN STATE PARK
2573 Sunset Dr
Wesson, MS 39191
Web: www.mdwfp.com/parkView/parks.asp?ID=5853
Phone: 601-643-9044
Size: 1,000 acres. **Location:** 4.5 miles east off Highway 51, near Wesson. **Facilities:** 71 developed campsites with electric hookups, 2 bathhouses with hot showers, 14 tent campsites, vacation cabin, picnic area, 2 open-air pavilions, comfort station, nature trails, swimming beach, beach volleyball court, playground, boat ramp with floating dock, 3 fishing piers, 18-hole disc golf course. **Activities:** Camping, hiking, boating, fishing,

swimming, water-skiing. **Special Features:** A serene environment nestled in the shade of towering hardwood trees, Park features a 550-acre lake with a 1.5-acre sand beach in an area separate from fishing and boating areas.

★2962★ LAKE LOWNDES STATE PARK
3319 Lake Lowndes Rd
Columbus, MS 39702
Web: www.mdwfp.com/parkView/parks.asp?ID=1815
Phone: 662-328-2110
Size: 709 acres. **Location:** 8 miles southeast of Columbus, off MS 69. **Facilities:** 50 developed campsites with water and electric hookups (23 sites also have sewer hookups), comfort station with hot showers, laundry facilities, and vending machines, primitive tent camping area, 4 vacation cabins with boat dock available, picnic area, pavilion, nature trail (3.5 miles), equestrian trail (7 miles), boat launch, 18-hole disc golf course, softball complex, tennis complex with 6 lighted courts, playground, visitor center with a multi-sports center, game room, meeting rooms, and amphitheater. **Activities:** Camping, swimming, fishing, boating, water-skiing (week-ends and holidays only), hiking, horseback riding, tennis. **Special Features:** Park is located on a 150-acre lake and its recreational complex includes indoor tennis, basketball, volleyball, and badminton courts, as well as outdoor softball fields and tennis courts.

★2963★ LEFLEUR'S BLUFF STATE PARK
2140 Riverside Dr
Jackson, MS 39202
Web: www.mdwfp.com/parkView/parks.asp?ID=5844
Phone: 601-987-3923; **Fax:** 601-354-6930
Size: 305 acres. **Location:** Off I-55 at Lakeland Drive in Jackson. **Facilities:** 30 developed campsites (tent or RV camping) with water and electrical hookups, bathhouse with hot showers, 2 executive-style 4-bedroom cabins, picnic area, 16,000-square-foot playground, 5 nature trails (1 paved), boat launch, 18-hole disc golf course, 9-hole public golf course, driving range, clubhouse. **Activities:** Camping, fishing, boating (electric motors only), golf. **Special Features:** Park provides a lush green spot in the heart of urban Jackson. Located within the park is the Mississippi Museum of Natural History, featuring aquariums, hands-on exhibits, 2.5 miles of nature trails, and an open-air amphitheater.

★2964★ LEGION STATE PARK
635 Legion State Park Rd
Louisville, MS 39339
Web: www.mdwfp.com/parkView/parks.asp?ID=1831
Phone: 662-773-8323
Size: 440 acres. **Location:** 2 miles north of Louisville on North Columbus Avenue. **Facilities:** 15 developed campsites with full hookups and a bathhouse with hot showers, tent campsites, 5 vacation cabins, picnic area and shelter, trails, playground, swimming beach, 2 lakes, fishing boat rental, visitor center. **Activities:** Camping, swimming, fishing, hiking. **Special Features:** Located in the red hill country of Mississippi, this park was the fourth of the original state parks developed by the Civilian Conservation Corps in the 1930s. The man-made structures in the park were designed to complement the natural beauty of the area. One such structure is the Legion Lodge, which serves as the park's visitor center.

★2965★ LEROY PERCY STATE PARK
PO Box 176
Hollandale, MS 38748
Web: www.mdwfp.com/parkView/parks.asp?ID=3825
Phone: 662-827-5436
Size: 1,792 acres. **Location:** 5 miles west of Hollandale, off MS 12. **Facilities:** 16 developed campsites with water and electrical hookups, bathhouse with hot showers, primitive tent camping area, 5 vacation cabins, group camp, picnic area, pavilion, 3 nature trails, 2 observation towers, boat launch, volleyball area, playground, disc golf course, restaurant, snack bar. **Activities:** Camping, fishing, hunting, wildlife viewing. **Special Features:** The oldest of Mississippi's state parks, Leroy Percy is characterized by artesian springs, cypress trees, and ancient oaks dripping with Spanish moss. This is the only state park in Mississippi with a wildlife preserve, and visitors can safely observe alligators from two observation towers.

★2966★ NATCHEZ STATE PARK
230-B Wickcliff Rd
Natchez, MS 39120
Web: www.mdwfp.com/parkView/parks.asp?ID=5845
Phone: 601-442-2658
Size: 3,641 acres. **Location:** 10 miles north of Natchez, off US 61 at Stanton. **Facilities:** 50 developed campsites with water and electrical hookups (6 also have sewage hookups), bathhouses with hot showers, 8 primitive tent campsites, 10 vacation cabins, picnic areas, pavilion, playground, nature trail, boat launch, visitor center, meeting room. **Activities:** Camping, fishing. **Special Features:** Park is located 10 miles north of historic Natchez, the oldest settlement on the Mississippi River. Before the Civil War, more than half the millionaires in the US lived in Natchez, and many of these elegant antebellum homes are now open for tours.

★2967★ PAUL B. JOHNSON STATE PARK
319 Geiger Lake Rd
Hattiesburg, MS 39401
Web: www.ohwy.com/ms/p/paulbjoh.htm
Phone: 601-582-7721; **Fax:** 601-545-5611; **Toll Free:** 800-467-2757
Size: 969 acres. **Location:** 15 miles south of Hattiesburg on Highway 49. **Facilities:** 108 developed campsites (85 with water and electric hookups), 25 tent campsites, bathhouses with restrooms and hot showers, 16 vacation cabins, group camp, picnic area, 6 pavilions, self-guided nature trail with 2 lookout towers, swimming beach, boat ramp, dock, disc golf course, playing fields, playground, visitor center with game room, meeting room, and exhibits. **Activities:** Camping, swimming, fishing, boating, water-skiing. **Special Features:** Park is located in the heart of the state's pine belt region, featuring longleaf and loblolly pines as well as dogwoods and ancient oaks. The University of Southern Mississippi is a short drive from the park.

9. State Parks

★2968★ PERCY QUIN STATE PARK

2036 Percy Quin Dr
McComb, MS 39648
Web: www.mdwfp.com/parkView/parks.asp?ID=5847
Phone: 601-684-3938
Size: 1,701 acres. Location: 6 miles south of McComb, off I-55 (Exit 13). Facilities: 100 developed campsites with water and electrical hookups, 4 bathhouses with hot showers, sand beach (for registered guests only), camp store (seasonal); 22 tent campsites with water and restrooms nearby; 25 vacation cabins and 2 executive golf villas; 9-unit lodge/motel; group camp; picnic area, 4 pavilions, comfort stations; nature trail (8 miles); swimming pool, 5 lighted tennis courts, playground, marina, boat launch, fish cleaning station; 18-hole golf course, 9-hole executive golf course, driving range, putting green; visitor center, convention center. Activities: Camping, hiking, swimming, fishing, boating, water-skiing, jet skiing, golf, tennis. Special Features: Park features loblolly pines, magnolia trees, rolling hills, spectacular seasonal flowers, and a mild climate year round. The 700-acre Lake Tangipahoa is stocked with bass, bream, catfish, and crappie, and both water-skiing and jet-skiing are permitted on the lake.

★2969★ ROOSEVELT STATE PARK

2149 Hwy 13 S
Morton, MS 39117
Web: www.mdwfp.com/parkView/parks.asp?ID=4848
Phone: 601-732-6316
Size: 691 acres. Location: Off I-20 at Exit 77 (Morton exit). Facilities: 109 developed campsites (81 with full hookups, 28 with electric and water hookups), bathhouse with hot showers, primitive tent camping area, group camp, 15 vacation cabins, 20-unit motel lodge (1 unit ♿), picnic areas, 5 pavilions, playground, lighted softball field, 2 lighted tennis courts, nature trails, boat launch, swimming pool, visitor center with video game room and souvenir shop. Activities: Camping, swimming, fishing, boating, water-skiing (Memorial Day-Labor Day), tennis. Special Features: Located between Meridian and Jackson, Park features a scenic overlook that provides a panoramic view of Bienville National Forest.

★2970★ SHEPARD STATE PARK

1034 Graveline Rd
Gautier, MS 39553
Web: www.mdwfp.com/parkView/parks.asp?ID=6849
Phone: 228-497-2244
Size: 307 acres. Location: 3 miles west of Pacagoula, south of US 90 at Gautier. Facilities: 28 developed campsites with water and electric hookups and a bathhouse, 10 primitive tent campsites, group camp (tents only), restrooms, picnic areas, pavilion, nature trails (5 miles), playground, soccer/recreation field, 18-hole disc golf course, visitor center, gift shop. Activities: Camping, hiking. Special Features: Park is located in a scenic coastal area, in Pascagoula River country, where legend has it that members of the Pascagoula Indian nation linked hands and walked into the river rather than being taken captive by hostile tribes. Their mournful death chant gave the river its nickname, the ''Singing River.''

★2971★ TISHOMINGO STATE PARK

PO Box 880
Tishomingo, MS 38873
Web: www.mdwfp.com/parkView/parks.asp?ID=1816
Phone: 662-438-6914
Size: 1,386 acres. Location: 2 miles south of Tishomingo off MS 25 at Milepost 304 on the Natchez Trace Parkway. Facilities: 62 developed campsites (with electrical hookups, restrooms, and showers), primitive tent camping area, 6 vacation cabins, group camp, picnic areas, 3 pavilions with electricity, nature trails (13 miles), swimming pool, boat launch, canoe rental, volleyball area, playgrounds, 18-hole disc golf course, compass course, worship services, museum/interpretive center. Activities: Camping, swimming, fishing, rock climbing, hiking, canoeing, float trips (daily from mid-April through mid-October). Special Features: Park takes its name from Chief Tishomingo, leader of the Chickasaw nation. Located in the foothills of the Appalachians, the park features a landscape of massive rock formations and fern-filled crevices found nowhere else in Mississippi. Massive moss-covered boulders dot the hillsides, and colorful wildflowers border trails once walked by Native Americans. The scenic Natchez Trace Parkway runs directly through the park.

★2972★ TOMBIGBEE STATE PARK

264 Cabin Dr
Tupelo, MS 38804
Web: www.mdwfp.com/parkView/parks.asp?ID=1817
Phone: 662-842-7669
Size: 522 acres. Location: 6 miles southeast of Tupelo, off MS 6. Facilities: 20 developed campsites with full hookups and bathhouse with hot showers, primitive tent camping, 7 vacation cabins, group camp, picnic area, 2 picnic pavilions, 3 nature trails, boat launch, paddleboat rentals, soft ball/soccer field, tennis court, 18-hole disc golf course, playground, visitor center with meeting and banquet room. Activities: Camping, swimming, fishing, boating, tennis, disc golf. Special Features: Park is just minutes from Tupelo, site of the biannual Tupelo Furniture Market, Elvis Presley's Birthplace, and the headquarters of the Natchez Trace Parkway.

★2973★ TRACE STATE PARK

2139 Faulkner Rd
Belden, MS 38826
Web: www.mdwfp.com/parkView/parks.asp?ID=1818
Phone: 662-489-2958
Size: 2,506 acres. Location: 10 miles east of Pontotoc and 9 miles west of Tupelo, off MS 6. Facilities: 52 developed campsites with electric and water hookups as well as 2 bathhouses with hot showers, 10 primitive tent campsites, 6 vacation cabins, picnic area with large pavilion, playground, multi-use trails (25 miles), stocked lake, boat ramps, fishing boat rentals, 18-hole disc golf course. Activities: Camping, swimming, fishing, water-skiing, hiking, mountain biking, horseback riding, ATV riding. Special Features: Park provides a quiet retreat together with the attractions of the fast-growing city of Tupelo nearby. Trace Lake offers 600 acres of freshwater for fishing and other water recreation.

9. State Parks

★2974★ WALL DOXEY STATE PARK
3946 Hwy 7 S
Holly Springs, MS 38635
Web: www.mdwfp.com/parkView/parks.asp?ID=2819
Phone: 662-252-4231
Size: 810 acres. **Location:** 7 miles south of Holly Springs, off MS 7. **Facilities:** 64 developed campsites with water and electric hookups, bathhouses with hot showers, 18 tent campsites, 9 vacation cabins, group camp, picnic area, 4 picnic pavilions, nature trail (2.5 miles), boat launch, playing fields, playground, disc golf course, visitor center with meeting and banquet rooms. **Activities:** Camping, swimming, fishing, boating. **Special Features:** Park is situated on a 60-acre spring-fed lake and offers fishing as well as other water sports. It's just a short drive from the park to the antebellum homes of Holly Springs.

9. State Parks

Missouri State Parks

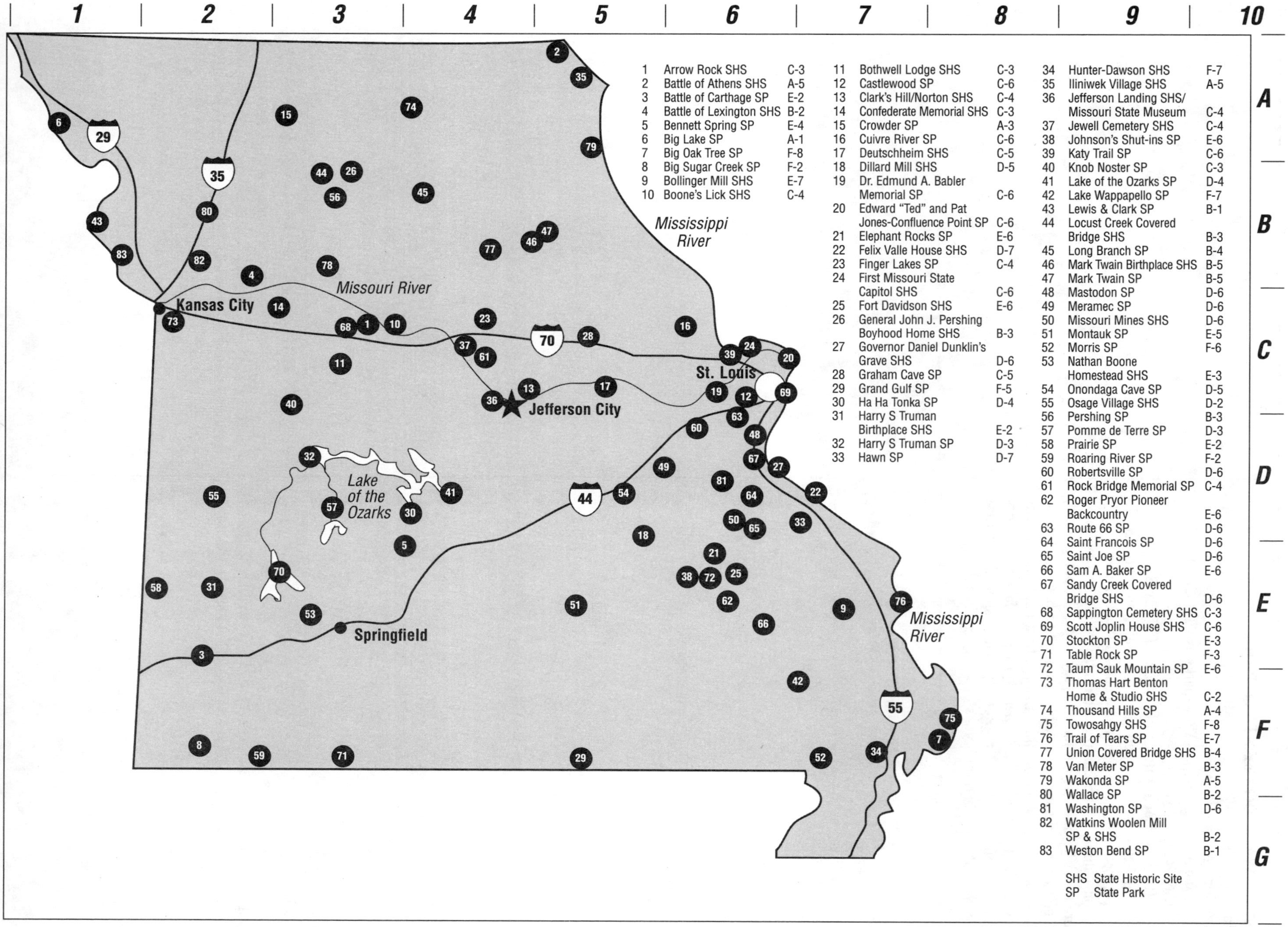

SHS State Historic Site
SP State Park

Mississippi River

Mississippi River

Missouri River

St. Louis

Jefferson City

Kansas City

Springfield

Lake of the Ozarks

MISSOURI

★2975★ **Missouri Department of Natural Resources Division of State Parks**
PO Box 176
Jefferson City, MO 65102
(573) 751-2479 - Phone
(877) 422-6766 - Toll-free Reservations
(800) 379-2419 – Toll-free
(800) 334-6946 - Volunteering
Web: www.mostateparks.com
Manages 83 parks, including 36 historical sites and a linear trail park. Preserves and interprets the state's natural landscapes and cultural landmarks while providing a variety of outdoor recreational opportunities.

Key to campsite classification:

- **Campsites** — Include a parking pad, table, grill, and lantern post. Some have electricity, water, and sewer hookups. In most campgrounds, water is turned off between November 1 and March 31; electricity stays on year round.
- **Group camps** — Include cabins, dining lodge and kitchen facilities, and rest rooms with showers. Can accommodate from 40 to 200 campers. Available from April 15 to October 15.

★2976★ **ARROW ROCK STATE HISTORIC SITE**
PO Box 1
Arrow Rock, MO 65320
Web: www.mostateparks.com/arrowrock.htm
Phone: 660-837-3330
Size: 167 acres. **Location:** 13 miles north of I-70 on Highway 41 in Saline County. **Facilities:** 12 basic campsites, 34 electric campsites, 1 campsite with full hookup, showers, special-use area, picnic sites, picnic shelter, restaurant, hiking trails, interpretive center, museum. **Activities:** Camping, lake fishing, hiking, interpretive programs, guided historical tours. **Special Features:** This historic village depicts the 19th-century character of Missouri's frontier years. Buildings include a one-room jail, the old courthouse, the home of artist George Caleb Bingham, and the Old Tavern where visitors can dine in an 1800s atmosphere. The Arrow Rock Lyceum is a noted summer theater that provides entertainment for visitors to the historic site. (See also Sappington Cemetery State Historic Site.)

★2977★ **BATTLE OF ATHENS STATE HISTORIC SITE**
Rt 1, Box 26
Revere, MO 63465
Web: www.mostateparks.com/athens.htm
Phone: 660-877-3871

Size: 408 acres. **Location:** 10 miles north of Kahoka on Highway 81, 4 miles east on Highway CC in Clark County. **Facilities:** 14 basic campsites, 15 electric campsites, picnic sites, picnic shelter, hiking trails, boat ramp, interpretive center. **Activities:** Camping, fishing, hiking, guided historical tours. **Special Features:** Site interprets the northernmost battle fought west of the Mississippi River during the Civil War. Union troops defeated the pro-South Missouri State Guard here in 1861.

★2978★ **BATTLE OF CARTHAGE STATE PARK**
c/o Harry S Truman Birthplace State Historic Site
1009 Truman
Lamar, MO 64759
Web: www.mostateparks.com/carthage.htm
Phone: 417-682-2279
Size: 7.4 acres. **Location:** Garrison exit off US 71 in Carthage, on the north side of East Chestnut Street, next to Carter Park. **Facilities:** Undeveloped except for interpretive shelter. **Special Features:** Site of the final confrontation in a 12-hour Civil War battle which began north of the town on the morning of July 5, 1861, preceding the Battle of Bull Run by 11 days. Missouri's Governor Claiborne Fox Jackson commanded the 6,000 Southern troops that forced General Franz Sigel and his 1,000 Union troops down the stagecoach road to Sarcoxie. The site remains as it was when the Southern troops camped there after the battle.

★2979★ **BATTLE OF LEXINGTON STATE HISTORIC SITE**
1300 N John Shea Dr
Lexington, MO 64067
Web: www.mostateparks.com/lexington
Phone: 660-259-4654
Size: 95 acres. **Location:** On John Shea Drive in Lexington, Lafayette County. **Facilities:** Historic home and battlegrounds, picnic sites, hiking trails, visitor center. **Activities:** Picnicking, interpretive programs, guided historical tours. **Special Features:** Oliver Anderson's mansion was the fiercely contested prize in a Civil War battle between the Missouri State Guard and the Union army. During three days of bloody battles, the house changed hands three times. Today the mansion is restored, as are the gardens and orchards that surround it, but visitors can still see damage from the shot and shell that hammered the house as well as remnants of the trenches and graves of unknown Union soldiers. Preserved also at the site are 100 acres of battlefield.

★2980★ **BENNETT SPRING STATE PARK**
26250 Hwy 64A
Lebanon, MO 65536
Web: www.mostateparks.com/bennett.htm
Phone: 417-532-4338

583

Size: 3,217 acres. **Location:** 12 miles west of Lebanon on Highway 64 in Dallas and Laclede counties. **Facilities:** 15 basic campsites, 128 electric campsites, 46 campsites with full hook-ups, showers, special use area, 3 cabins, 40 duplex/fourplex units, 22 motel rooms, picnic sites, 2 picnic shelters, dining lodge, hiking trails, swimming pool, canoe and raft rentals, nature center. **Activities:** Camping, canoeing, rafting, trout fishing, swimming, hiking, interpretive programs. **Special Features:** Nearly 100 million gallons of water gush daily from Bennett Spring, Missouri's third largest spring.

★2981★ BIG LAKE STATE PARK

204 Lake Shore Dr
Craig, MO 64437
Web: www.mostateparks.com/biglake.htm
Phone: 660-442-3770
Size: 407 acres. **Location:** 11 miles southwest of Mound City on Highway 111 in Holt County. **Facilities:** 18 basic campsites, 57 electric campsites, showers, 8 cabins, 12 motel rooms and 5 suites, picnic sites, picnic shelter, restaurant, swimming pool, boat ramp. **Activities:** Camping, lake fishing, swimming, bird watching, interpretive programs. **Special Features:** Park is located in northwest Missouri, midway between Kansas City and Omaha, on the state's largest oxbow lake, which was formed by the Missouri River before its course was controlled by channelization. The park also has a large marsh, and Squaw Creek National Wildlife Refuge (see separate entry in national wildlife refuges section) is nearby.

★2982★ BIG OAK TREE STATE PARK

13640 S Hwy 102
East Prairie, MO 63845
Web: www.mostateparks.com/bigoak.htm
Phone: 573-649-3149
Size: 1,029 acres. **Location:** East on Hwy 80 off I-55, 14 miles south of East Prairie on Highway 102 in Mississippi County. **Facilities:** Day-use park with picnic sites, picnic shelter, hiking and interpretive trails (&), boat ramp, nature center, interpretive exhibits. **Activities:** Lake fishing, hiking, picnicking. **Special Features:** Park derives its name from giant trees, some of which have been identified as the largest of their species within the state, and two that are national champions. The park's cypress swamp, with its bald cypress trees, is the only one of its kind in the state. A boardwalk through the park allows visitors a close-up view of this remnant of the vast swamp forest that once covered Missouri's "bootheel" region.

★2983★ BIG SUGAR CREEK STATE PARK

c/o Roaring River State Park
Rt 4 Box 4100
Cassville, MO 65625
Web: www.mostateparks.com/bigsugar.htm
Phone: 417-847-2539
Size: 2,082 acres. **Location:** Exit on Hwy W off Hwy 7 and follow 8th Street east out of Pineville 5 miles; in McDonald County. **Facilities:** Hiking trail. Park is still in the development stage; planned amenities include a day-use area, special-use area for organized youth groups, and a canoe launch. **Activities:**

Hiking. **Special Features:** Park preserves a portion of the Elk River Section of Missouri's Ozarks and features heavily forested hillsides, streams, and solitude. The area contains plants and animals that are less common or absent in other parts of the state, including armadillos, the chinquapin tree, and the Neosho orangethroat darter.

★2984★ BOLLINGER MILL STATE HISTORIC SITE

113 Bollinger Mill Rd
Burfordville, MO 63739
Web: www.mostateparks.com/bollinger.htm
Phone: 573-243-4591
Size: 43 acres. **Location:** On Highway HH in Cape Girardeau County. **Facilities:** Picnic sites. **Activities:** Guided historical tours, interpretive programs. **Special Features:** The location of grain milling for almost 200 years, the present four-story stone and brick gristmill and 140-foot covered bridge were completed around 1867. Visitors to the mill can still observe corn being ground into meal by water power. The Burfordville Covered Bridge, which crosses the river that powers the mill, is the oldest of only four covered bridges remaining in the state.

★2985★ BOONE'S LICK STATE HISTORIC SITE

c/o Arrow Rock State Historic Site
PO Box 1
Arrow Rock, MO 65320
Web: www.mostateparks.com/booneslick.htm
Phone: 660-837-3330
Size: 51 acres. **Location:** 12 miles northwest of Boonville on Highway 187, 2 miles west of Highway 87 in Howard County. **Facilities:** Picnic area, interpretive trail. **Special Features:** One of the earliest centers of industry in central Missouri, Boone's Lick is the site of the salt manufacturing business once owned and operated by Daniel Boone's sons, Daniel M. and Nathan Boone. A self-guided wooded trail leads down the hillside to the salt springs where the Boone brothers began their business. Wood remnants of the salt works and an iron kettle are still visible there.

★2986★ BOTHWELL LODGE STATE HISTORIC SITE

19349 Bothwell State Park Rd
Sedalia, MO 65301
Web: www.mostateparks.com/bothwell.htm
Phone: 660-827-0510
Size: 247 acres. **Location:** 7 miles north of Sedalia, east of US 65 in Pettis County. **Facilities:** Picnic sites, picnic shelter, playground, hiking and mountain biking trails. **Activities:** Hiking, mountain biking, guided tours. **Special Features:** Park features the 12,000-square-foot Bothwell Lodge, built between 1897 and 1928 as the country estate of former State Representative and prominent Sedalia lawyer John Homer Bothwell. The 31-room stone lodge was built in four sections on top of three natural caves, using native rock from the estate grounds. Near the lodge are a stone gazebo and a small three-sided shelter.

★2987★ CASTLEWOOD STATE PARK
1401 Kiefer Creek Rd
Ballwin, MO 63021
Web: www.mostateparks.com/castlewood.htm
Phone: 636-227-4433
Size: 1,803 acres. Location: At intersection of Kiefer Creek and Ries roads in Saint Louis County. Facilities: Picnic sites, 2 picnic shelters, hiking trails, mountain biking trails, equestrian trails. Activities: River fishing, hiking, mountain biking, horseback riding. Special Features: Park stretches for five miles along both sides of the Meramec River, with white limestone bluffs towering above the river. The park incorporates much of an old resort area that existed here between 1915 and 1940, including a grand staircase that once led up to hotels and clubs.

★2988★ CLARK'S HILL/NORTON STATE HISTORIC SITE
c/o Rock Bridge Memorial State Park
5901 S Hwy 63
Columbia, MO 65203
Web: www.mostateparks.com/clarkshill.htm
Phone: 573-449-7402
Size: 13 acres. Location: Northeast of Osage City, off Highway J in Cole County. Facilities: Trails. Activities: Hiking. Special Features: Site preserves a site recorded in the journal of William Clark in 1804. The Lewis and Clark Expedition had camped nearby, and Clark ascended the hill for a view of the confluence of the Missouri and Osage Rivers. Some Indian burial mounds observed by Clark lie along the wooded trail that takes visitors to the overlook of the rivers.

★2989★ CONFEDERATE MEMORIAL STATE HISTORIC SITE
211 W 1st St
Higginsville, MO 64037
Web: www.mostateparks.com/confedmem.htm
Phone: 660-584-2853
Size: 135 acres. Location: 1 mile north of Higginsville on Business Highway 13 in Lafayette County. Facilities: Historic site, picnic sites. Activities: Lake fishing, picnicking, interpretive programs. Special Features: Site preserves the grounds of the Confederate Home of Missouri, which once housed Civil War veterans and their families. Today, the site is a memorial to the 40,000 Missourians who fought under the Confederate flag and includes a historic chapel and cemetery.

★2990★ CROWDER STATE PARK
76 Hwy 128
Trenton, MO 64683
Web: www.mostateparks.com/crowder.htm
Phone: 660-359-6473
Size: 1,912 acres. Location: 4 miles west of Trenton on Highway 146 in Grundy County. Facilities: 10 basic campsites, 31 electric campsites, showers, organized group camp, special use area, picnic sites, 2 open picnic shelters, enclosed shelter, hiking , equestrian, and mountain biking trails, beach. Activities: Camping, boating, lake fishing, swimming, hiking, horseback riding, mountain biking. Special Features: The rolling hills of

northern Missouri serve as a scenic memorial to Major General Enoch H. Crowder, the Missourian who founded the Selective Service System in 1917. Much of the park is covered with forest where wild turkeys, deer, raccoons, and other wildlife live. The park also includes a 20-acre stocked lake with sand beach.

★2991★ CUIVRE RIVER STATE PARK
678 State Rt 147
Troy, MO 63379
Web: www.mostateparks.com/cuivre.htm
Phone: 636-528-7247
Size: 6,394 acres. Location: 3 miles east of Troy on Highway 47 in Lincoln County. Facilities: 52 basic campsites, 23 electric campsites, 31 campsites with full hookups, 5 walk-in sites, showers, organized group camp, special-use area, 5 basic and 8 electric equestrian campsites, picnic sites, 2 picnic shelters, hiking trails, backpacking trails, equestrian trails, beach, boat ramp, visitor center, exhibits. Activities: Camping, lake and stream fishing, swimming, hiking, horseback riding, backpacking, wildlife observation, interpretive programs. Special Features: Park includes two wild areas as well as three natural areas with high-quality ecosystems that feature native prairie, sinkhole ponds, woodlands, and a clear, rock-bottomed stream.

★2992★ DEUTSCHHEIM STATE HISTORIC SITE
109 W 2nd St
Hermann, MO 65041
Web: www.mostateparks.com/deutschheim.htm
Phone: 573-486-2200
Size: 0.69 acres. Location: In Hermann on 2nd Street, west of Market Street/Hwy 19 in Gasconade County. Activities: Guided tours. Special Features: Park includes four buildings in Hermann's historic district which reflect the culture and contributions of Missouri's early German immigrants. Strehly House was the site of the first print shop west of Saint Louis. Pommer-Genter House is restored and furnished as in 1840, and its barn displays early German tools and implements. Tour also includes a winery and two period gardens.

★2993★ DILLARD MILL STATE HISTORIC SITE
142 Dillard Mill Rd
Davisville, MO 65456
Web: www.mostateparks.com/dillardmill.htm
Phone: 573-244-3120
Size: 132 acres. Location: 1 mile south of Dillard, off Highway 49 in Crawford County. Facilities: Picnic sites, hiking trails. Activities: Fishing, hiking, guided tours. Special Features: Mill is one of Missouri's best preserved examples of a water-powered gristmill. The mill, which has been restored to operational order, was built around 1900 and continued to grind grain until the 1960s.

★2994★ DR. EDMUND A BABLER MEMORIAL STATE PARK
800 Guy Park Dr
Chesterfield, MO 63005
Web: www.mostateparks.com/babler.htm
Phone: 636-458-3813

Size: 2,441 acres. **Location:** 20 miles west of Saint Louis on Highway BA, between US 40 and Highway 100 in Saint Louis County. **Facilities:** 30 basic campsites, 43 electric campsites, showers, special use area, picnic sites, 3 picnic shelters, hiking trails (13 miles), bicycle trails, equestrian trails, swimming pool, visitor center. **Activities:** Camping, swimming, hiking, bicycling, horseback riding, interpretive programs. **Special Features:** Park sits in a wooded area of the Missouri River hills and features the Jacob L Babler Outdoor Education Center for the Disabled, a resident camp designed to accommodate campers with special needs.

★2995★ EDWARD "TED" AND PAT JONES-
    CONFLUENCE POINT STATE PARK
1000 Riverlands Way
West Alton, MO 63386
Web: www.mostateparks.com/confluence.htm
Phone: 636-899-1135
Size: 1,118 acres. **Location:** Off Highway 67 east, on Riverlands Way just before Clark's Bridge, in Saint Charles County. **Facilities:** Interpretive trail, exhibits. **Special Features:** Missouri's newest state park is situated at the point where the Mississippi and Missouri rivers meet. The history of the rivers and the role they played in the Lewis and Clark Expedition are interpreted at the park in outdoor exhibits, and a short trail takes visitors to the confluence point. Future plans for the park include restoration of a natural floodplain, which will emphasize native vegetation and natural wetlands suitable for the site's current soil, topography, and hydrology. This will include forests, prairies, and marshes.

★2996★ ELEPHANT ROCKS STATE PARK
c/o Fort Davidson State Historic Site
PO Box 509
Pilot Knob, MO 63663
Web: www.mostateparks.com/elephantrock.htm
Phone: 573-546-3454
Size: 132 acres. **Location:** On Highway 21, 2 miles north of the junction of Highway W and Highway 21 in Iron County. **Facilities:** Picnic sites, trails. **Activities:** Hiking, picnicking. **Special Features:** Giant red granite rocks one billion years old stand end-to-end like a train of circus elephants in this state park. One of the largest rocks weighs 680 tons. The first self-guiding Braille trail for the visually handicapped in Missouri state parks winds through the geological wonder.

★2997★ FELIX VALLE HOUSE STATE HISTORIC
    SITE
198 Merchant St
Sainte Genevieve, MO 63670
Web: www.mostateparks.com/felixvalle.htm
Phone: 573-883-7102
Size: 10 acres. **Location:** On the corner of Merchant and Second streets in Sainte Genevieve. **Facilities:** Historic site. **Activities:** Guided tours. **Special Features:** The Felix Valle House was built in 1818 as an American-Federal style residence and mercantile store. Restored and furnished to reflect the 1830s, the home today interprets the American influence on the French

community following the Louisiana Purchase. The house is located in the National Historic Landmark District of Sainte Genevieve, which preserves some of the finest examples of French colonial architecture in the nation.

★2998★ FINGER LAKES STATE PARK
1505 E Peabody Rd
Columbia, MO 65202
Web: www.mostateparks.com/fingerlakes.htm
Phone: 573-443-5315
Size: 1,131 acres. **Location:** 10 miles north of Columbia, off US 63 in Boone County. **Facilities:** 19 basic campsites, 16 electric campsites, showers, picnic sites, mountain bike and ORV trails (70 miles), beach, boat ramp. **Activities:** Camping, canoeing, lake fishing, swimming, scuba diving, bicycling, ATV and motorcycle riding (all ATVs must have orange flags). **Special Features:** Park was built on reclaimed strip-mine land. One of two state parks that allows off-road motorcycling, the park hosts races throughout the summer.

★2999★ FIRST MISSOURI STATE CAPITOL STATE
    HISTORIC SITE
200-216 S Main St
Saint Charles, MO 63301
Web: www.mostateparks.com/firstcapitol.htm
Phone: 800-334-6946; **Fax:** 636-940-3324; **Toll Free:** 800-334-6946
Size: 0.66 acres. **Location:** In the Saint Charles Historic District in Saint Charles County (5th Street exit north off I-70, then right on Booneslick and left on Main Street). **Facilities:** Historic site, interpretive center. **Activities:** Tours. **Special Features:** Missouri's first legislators met in this restored Federal-style row building to reorganize Missouri's territorial government into a state system. Sessions were held June 4, 1821, through October 1, 1826, when the new capitol in Jefferson City became ready for use. Governmental chambers, two residences, a general store, and a carpenter shop have been restored to their 1820s appearance.

★3000★ FORT DAVIDSON STATE HISTORIC SITE
PO Box 509
Pilot Knob, MO 63663
Web: www.mostateparks.com/ftdavidson.htm
Phone: 573-546-3454
Size: 86 acres. **Location:** In Pilot Knob, Highway 21 at Highway V in Iron County. **Facilities:** Picnic sites, 3 picnic shelters, playground, visitor center. **Activities:** Interpretive programs. **Special Features:** Site preserves Fort Davidson and the Pilot Knob battlefield, the scene in 1864 of one of the largest and most hard-fought Civil War battles in the state.

★3001★ GENERAL JOHN J. PERSHING BOYHOOD
    HOME STATE HISTORIC SITE
1100 Pershing Dr
Laclede, MO 64651
Web: www.mostateparks.com/pershingsite.htm
Phone: 660-963-2525

Size: 3 acres. **Location:** In Laclede, 1 mile north of US 36 on Highway 5 in Linn County. **Facilities:** Historic sites, picnic area. **Activities:** Guided tours. **Special Features:** General John "Black Jack" Pershing was the highest ranking military officer in United States history and was named General of the Armies of the US by a special act of Congress after World War I. Pershing grew up in Laclede, and his boyhood home, a Gothic 9-room house, features displays related to local history and to Pershing's life and career. The site also includes the one-room Prairie Mound School.

★3002★ **GOVERNOR DANIEL DUNKLIN'S GRAVE STATE HISTORIC SITE**

c/o Southern Missouri Historic District
2901 Hwy 61
Festus, MO 63028
Web: www.mostateparks.com/dunklinsgrave.htm
Phone: 636-937-3697
Size: 1.37 acres. **Location:** In Herculaneum, in Jefferson County. **Special Features:** Governor Daniel Dunklin was Missouri's fifth governor. The historic site interprets the role of Dunklin as the Father of Public Schools and provides a scenic overlook of the Mississippi River.

★3003★ **GRAHAM CAVE STATE PARK**

217 Hwy TT
Montgomery City, MO 63361
Web: www.mostateparks.com/grahamcave.htm
Phone: 573-564-3476
Size: 360 acres. **Location:** 2 miles west of Danville, off I-70, on Highway TT in Montgomery County. **Facilities:** 34 basic campsites, 18 electric campsites, showers, picnic sites, picnic shelter, playground areas, hiking trails, mountain bike trails, boat ramp, visitor center, exhibits. **Activities:** Camping, stream fishing, boating, hiking, mountain biking, interpretive programs.. **Special Features:** Park features an unusual sandstone cave where archaeologists uncovered artifacts revealing human use dating back to as early as 10,000 years ago. Clues to the lifestyle of the ancient Dalton and Archaic period Native Americans were uncovered, and exhibits at a visitor contact center describe the area's natural history and prehistoric occupation.

★3004★ **GRAND GULF STATE PARK**

Rt 3, Box 3554
Thayer, MO 65791
Web: www.mostateparks.com/grandgulf.htm
Phone: 417-264-7600
Size: 322 acres. **Location:** 6 miles west of Thayer, off Highway W in Oregon County. **Facilities:** Picnic sites, hiking trails, scenic overlooks. **Activities:** Hiking, picnicking. **Special Features:** Often referred to as Missouri's "Little Grand Canyon," Grand Gulf was created when the ceiling of a giant cave collapsed. A section of remaining roof forms one of the largest natural bridges in Missouri, spanning 200 feet with an opening 75 feet high and 50 feet wide. The gulf winds for a mile through vertical walls as high as 130 feet. Boardwalks allow visitors to descend partway into the chasm.

★3005★ **HA HA TONKA STATE PARK**

1491 State Rd D
Camdenton, MO 65020
Web: www.mostateparks.com/hahatonka.htm
Phone: 573-346-2986
Size: 3,680 acres. **Location:** 5 miles southwest of Camdenton, off US 54, on Highway D in Camden County. **Facilities:** Picnic sites, 2 picnic shelters, special use area, hiking and backpacking trails (15 miles), 2 courtesy boat docks (for visitors who arrive by boat). **Activities:** Lake fishing, hiking, backpacking, nature programs. **Special Features:** One of Missouri's geologic and scenic wonders, Ha Ha Tonka overlooks the Lake of the Ozarks from high limestone bluffs. The Osage River hills area is a classic example of a topography known as "karst," characterized by caves, sinks, underground streams, large springs, and natural bridges. The park also contains one of the state's best remaining examples of savanna and the remains of a huge stone castle.

★3006★ **HARRY S TRUMAN BIRTHPLACE STATE HISTORIC SITE**

1009 Truman St
Lamar, MO 64759
Web: www.mostateparks.com/trumansite.htm
Phone: 417-682-2279
Size: 2.5 acres. **Location:** In Lamar, 2 miles east of US 71, one block north off Highway 160 on Truman Street in Barton County. **Facilities:** Historic home. **Activities:** Guided tours. **Special Features:** Harry Truman, the only Missourian ever elected US president, was born here on May 8, 1884. Truman's family stayed in the six-room frame home, built between 1880 and 1882, until Harry was almost one year old. Furnishings represent those typically found in homes during the period when the Trumans lived here. In addition to the house, which had neither indoor plumbing nor electricity, visitors can view the smokehouse, well, and outhouse in the back.

★3007★ **HARRY S TRUMAN STATE PARK**

28761 State Park Rd
Warsaw, MO 65355
Web: www.mostateparks.com/trumanpark.htm
Phone: 660-438-7711
Size: 1,440 acres. **Location:** West of Warsaw 6 miles on Highway 7, then right on Highway UU 2 miles to the park, in Benton County. **Facilities:** 100 basic campsites, 98 electric campsites, showers, picnic sites, picnic shelter, hiking trails, beach with bathhouse and restrooms, marina, store, boat ramp, boat rentals, playgrounds. **Activities:** Camping, boating, lake fishing, swimming, water-skiing, hiking, interpretive programs. **Special Features:** Park encompasses the tip of a peninsula that juts into 55,600-acre Truman Lake.

★3008★ **HAWN STATE PARK**

12096 Park Dr
Sainte Genevieve, MO 63670
Web: www.mostateparks.com/hawn.htm
Phone: 573-883-3603
Size: 4,953 acres. **Location:** I-55 south from Saint Louis to

9. State Parks

Exit 150, then 11 miles west on Highway 32 in Sainte Genevieve County. **Facilities:** 19 basic campsites, 26 electric campsites, 5 walk-in campsites, showers, special use area, picnic sites, picnic shelter, hiking and backpacking trails. **Activities:** Camping, stream fishing, hiking, backpacking, birdwatching, nature study. **Special Features:** Park is one of Missouri's loveliest, with lush stands of native pines and hardwoods as well as a generous amount of flowering dogwood, redbud, and wild azalea. Other natural features include sandstone bluffs and canyons, clear sand-bottom streams, and a wide variety of rock types.

★3009★ **HUNTER-DAWSON STATE HISTORIC SITE**
PO Box 308
New Madrid, MO 63869
Web: www.mostateparks.com/hunterdawson.htm
Phone: 573-748-5340
Size: 20 acres. **Location:** On Dawson Road in New Madrid, New Madrid County. **Facilities:** Historic home. **Activities:** Guided tours. **Special Features:** This 15-room, antebellum home reflects the splendor of the fine mansions that once were common along the Great River Road. The house was built from 1859 to 1860 by the William and Amanda Hunter family and contains the original furniture, as well as many of the family's personal possessions.

★3010★ **ILINIWEK VILLAGE STATE HISTORIC SITE**
c/o Battle of Athens State Historic Site
Rt 1 Box 26
Revere, MO 63465
Web: www.mostateparks.com/iliniwek.htm
Phone: 660-877-3871
Size: 127 acres. **Location:** 2 miles north of Wayland on Highway B in Clark County (take gravel roads to site). **Facilities:** Picnic sites. **Activities:** Interpretive programs. **Special Features:** The site of a village once inhabited by the Indians of the Iliniwek Confederacy. The Iliniwek, or Illinois, were one of the three most significant native groups occupying Missouri at the time of first European contact. This site is the only known Ilinewek village in Missouri, and historians believe it was visited by explorers Marquette and Joliet on their 1673 expedition down the Mississippi River.

★3011★ **JEFFERSON LANDING STATE HISTORIC SITE & MISSOURI STATE MUSEUM**
Jefferson St & Capitol Ave
Jefferson City, MO 65101
Web: www.mostateparks.com/jeffersonland.htm
Phone: 573-751-2854
Size: 1 acre. **Location:** In Jefferson City, in Cole County. **Facilities:** Visitor center, exhibits. **Activities:** Guided tours. **Special Features:** Jefferson Landing, one of the few remaining 19th-century riverfront landings on the Missouri River, was a busy center of commerce in Jefferson City during the mid-1800s. Steamboats traveling from Saint Louis to Kansas City often docked in front of the Lohman Building, which today houses a visitor center, museum, and public meeting room. Nearby is the Missouri State Capitol, in which the Missouri State Museum

houses an impressive collection of exhibits portraying the state's history, legends, and cultural achievements.

★3012★ **JEWELL CEMETERY STATE HISTORIC SITE**
c/o Rock Bridge Memorial State Park
5901 S Hwy 163
Columbia, MO 65203
Web: www.mostateparks.com/jewellcem.htm
Phone: 573-449-7402
Size: 0.5 acres. **Location:** In southern Columbia, off Highway 163, in Boone County. **Special Features:** This is the burial place of Governor Charles Hardin, who served from 1875-1877, and descendants of George Jewell. The most well known member of the Jewell family buried in the cemetery is William Jewell, who died while establishing a college in Liberty, Missouri, that bears his name.

★3013★ **JOHNSON'S SHUT-INS STATE PARK**
HCR 1, Box 126
Middlebrook, MO 63656
Web: www.mostateparks.com/jshutins.htm
Phone: 573-546-2450
Size: 8,550 acres. **Location:** 8 miles north of Lesterville, off Hwy 21, 13 miles on Hwy N in Reynolds County. **Facilities:** In December 2005, the nearby Taum Sauk Reservoir breached, sending 1.3 billion gallons of water through the major day-use area of the park and destroying or damaging most of the facilities along the East Fork of the Black River. Cleanup began immediately, and longterm plans for major redevelopment of the park are in progress. Facilities available during the 2006 season included picnic tables, a playground, and a park store, as well as a boardwalk that takes visitors to an observation deck overlooking the shut-ins. **Activities:** Picnicking, interpretive programs. **Special Features:** Swift waters of the Black River flowing around some of the oldest exposed rocks in the nation have formed a series of canyonlike gorges or "shut-ins." Most of the park has been left as wilderness, and even under normal conditions, access to the park is limited and some restrictions apply.

★3014★ **KATY TRAIL STATE PARK**
c/o Boonville Area Office
320 1st St
Boonville, MO 65233
Web: www.mostateparks.com/katytrail
Phone: 660-882-8196; **Toll Free:** 800-334-6946
Size: 225-mile linear park. **Location:** From Saint Charles to Clinton. **Activities:** Walking/hiking, mountain biking, bicycling; horseback riding permitted from the State Fairgrounds in Sedalia to Calhoun. **Special Features:** Park is built on the former corridor of the Missouri-Kansas-Texas (MKT) Railroad, known as the "Katy." Much of the trail lies alongside the Missouri River, traveling through dense forests, wetlands, deep valleys, remnant prairies, open pastureland, and gently rolling farm fields. Trailheads are located about every 10 miles along the route.

★3015★ KNOB NOSTER STATE PARK

873 SE 10th
Knob Noster, MO 65336
Web: www.mostateparks.com/knobnoster.htm
Phone: 660-563-2463
Size: 3,567 acres. **Location:** At Knob Noster, off US 50, on Highway 23 in Johnson County. **Facilities:** 39 basic campsites, 37 electric campsites, 6 equestrian campsites (basic), organized group camp, special-use area, showers, picnic sites, 3 picnic shelters, hiking trails, mountain bike trails, equestrian trails, nature center. **Activities:** Camping, lake and stream fishing, hiking, mountain biking, horseback riding, nature programs. **Special Features:** Park includes Pin Oak Slough Natural Area, a four-acre forested oxbow slough that forms a wetland along Clearfork Creek.

★3016★ LAKE OF THE OZARKS STATE PARK

PO Box 170
Kaiser, MO 65047
Web: www.mostateparks.com/lakeozark.htm
Phone: 573-348-2694
Size: 17,442 acres. **Location:** 5 miles east on Highway 42 from US 54 to Highway 134 in Camden and Miller counties. **Facilities:** 101 basic campsites, 88 electric campsites, organized group camp, showers, 8 camper cabins, yurt, picnic sites, 2 picnic shelters, hiking trails, mountain bike trails, equestrian trails, backpacking trails, 2 swimming beaches, marinas, boat ramp, boat rentals, stables, park stores, visitor center. **Activities:** Camping, boating, sailing, lake fishing, swimming, hiking, mountain biking, horseback riding, backpacking, guided cave tours, nature programs. **Special Features:** Missouri's largest state park includes a visitor center and tours of Ozark Caverns, informing visitors about the cave's Angel's Showers—streams of water that continuously pour from the stalactites—and its other features.

★3017★ LAKE WAPPAPELLO STATE PARK

HC 2, Box 102
Williamsville, MO 63967
Web: www.mostateparks.com/lakewappapello.htm
Phone: 573-297-3232
Size: 1,854 acres. **Location:** 16 miles north of Poplar Bluff on US 67, and 8 miles east on Highway 172 in Wayne County. **Facilities:** 7 basic campsites, 71 electric campsites, showers, 8 cabins, 4 camper cabins, picnic sites, picnic shelters, playgrounds, hiking trails, mountain bike trails, equestrian trails, backpacking trails, swimming beach, boat ramps. **Activities:** Camping, boating, lake fishing, swimming, hiking, mountain biking, horseback riding, backpacking, interpretive programs. **Special Features:** Park is located in southeastern Missouri on Lake Wappapello, which features scenic lakeside coves and great fishing.

★3018★ LEWIS & CLARK STATE PARK

801 Lake Crest Blvd
Rushville, MO 64484
Web: www.mostateparks.com/lewisandclark.htm
Phone: 816-579-5564
Size: 189 acres. **Location:** 20 miles southwest of Saint Joseph, on Highway 138 in Buchanan County. **Facilities:** 7 basic campsites, 63 electric campsites, showers, picnic sites, picnic shelter, playground, swimming beach, boat ramp, 365-acre lake. **Activities:** Camping, boating, lake fishing, swimming. **Special Features:** Park is dedicated to explorers Meriwether Lewis and William Clark, who visited the area on their epic westward journey.

★3019★ LOCUST CREEK COVERED BRIDGE STATE HISTORIC SITE

c/o Gen. John J Pershing Boyhood Home State Historic Site
1100 Pershing Dr
Laclede, MO 64651
Web: www.mostateparks.com/locustbridge.htm
Phone: 660-963-2525
Size: 32 acres. **Location:** 3 miles west of Laclede on US 36, and 1 mile northeast on a gravel road (Danube Drive) in Linn County. **Facilities:** Picnic area. **Special Features:** Originally known as the Linn County Bridge, at 151 feet this bridge is the longest of the four remaining covered bridges in the state. The Howe-truss bridge was built in 1868 and housed America's first transcontinental road, Route 8. Bridge is reached by a quarter-mile walk down a historic road.

★3020★ LONG BRANCH STATE PARK

28615 Visitor Center Rd
Macon, MO 63552
Web: www.mostateparks.com/longbranch.htm
Phone: 660-773-5229
Size: 1,828 acres. **Location:** 2 miles west of the US 63 and US 36 junction in Macon County. **Facilities:** 9 basic campsites, 64 electric campsites, 9 walk-in campsites, showers, special use area, picnic sites, 2 picnic shelters, hiking trails, swimming beach, 3 boat ramps, fishing dock (&), boat rentals. **Activities:** Camping, boating, water-skiing, lake fishing, swimming, hiking. **Special Features:** Park is located along the banks of Long Branch Lake and includes wooded areas and restored prairie.

★3021★ MARK TWAIN BIRTHPLACE STATE HISTORIC SITE

37352 Shrine Rd
Florida, MO 65283
Web: www.mostateparks.com/twainsite.htm
Phone: 573-565-3449
Size: 13 acres. **Location:** In Mark Twain State Park, off Highway 107 in Monroe County, adjacent to the village of Florida. **Facilities:** Historic site, museum. **Activities:** Guided tours. **Special Features:** A modern museum surrounds the two-room 1830s cabin where author-humorist Samuel Langhorne Clemens (later known as Mark Twain) was born. The museum's exhibits, which include first editions of his books and a handwritten manuscript of *The Adventures of Tom Sawyer*, cover his childhood and his adult life as an author and businessman. In the village of Florida, a red granite monument marks the original location of the cabin. (Also see Mark Twain State Park.)

9. State Parks

★3022★ **MARK TWAIN STATE PARK**
20057 State Park Rd
Stoutsville, MO 65283
Web: www.mostateparks.com/twainpark.htm
Phone: 573-565-3440
Size: 2,775 acres. **Location:** On Highway 107 in Monroe County, near the village of Florida. **Facilities:** 22 basic campsites, 75 electric campsites, showers, organized group camp, special use area, 6 camper cabins, picnic sites, 2 picnic shelters (1 open, 1 enclosed), hiking trails, swimming beach, 2 boat ramps. **Activities:** Camping, lake fishing, boating, swimming, hiking, interpretive programs. **Special Features:** Park is located in the Salt River Hills of northeast Missouri, with rugged terrain reminiscent of southern parts of the state. Limestone bluffs and woodlands overlook the 18,000-acre Mark Twain Lake. The Mark Twain Birthplace State Historic Site (see separate entry) is located adjacent to the park.

★3023★ **MASTODON STATE HISTORIC SITE**
1050 Museum Dr
Imperial, MO 63052
Web: www.mostateparks.com/mastodon.htm
Phone: 636-464-2976; **Toll Free:** 800-334-6946
Size: 425 acres. **Location:** 20 miles south of Saint Louis, off I-55 Exit 186 in Jefferson County. **Facilities:** Museum, picnic sites, picnic shelter, special use campground, hiking trails. **Activities:** Hiking, picnicking, interpretive programs, tours. **Special Features:** Site contains the Kimmswick Bone Bed, an important archeological and paleontological site where the bones of mastodons and other now-extinct animals were first found in the 1800s. In 1979 scientists excavated a stone spear point made by hunters of the Clovis culture (14,000-10,000 years ago), providing the first solid evidence of the coexistence of people and mastodons. A museum at the site displays ancient artifacts, fossils, and a full-size replica of a mastodon skeleton.

★3024★ **MERAMEC STATE PARK**
115 Meramec Park Dr
Sullivan, MO 63080
Web: www.mostateparks.com/meramec.htm
Phone: 573-468-6072
Size: 6,896 acres. **Location:** 3 miles south of Sullivan on Highway 185, in Franklin, Washington, and Crawford counties. **Facilities:** 52 basic campsites, 125 electric campsites, 14 campsites with electric and water hookups, 18 campsites with full hookups, showers, group tenting area, 10 cabins, 10 duplex/fourplex units, 22 motel rooms, picnic sites, 4 picnic shelters, dining lodge, hiking and backpacking trails, boat ramp, canoe and raft rental, visitor center, exhibits, camp store, conference center. Some services and facilities are available on a seasonal basis. **Activities:** Camping, canoeing, rafting, river fishing, swimming, hiking, backpacking, cave tours. **Special Features:** Park includes several miles of shoreline along the Meramec River and features bluffs, forests, several springs, and more than 40 caves. Exhibits at the Visitor Center include large aquariums that display the variety of aquatic life found in the river.

★3025★ **MISSOURI MINES STATE HISTORIC SITE**
PO Box 492
Park Hills, MO 63601
Web: www.mostateparks.com/momines.htm
Phone: 573-431-6226
Size: 25 acres. **Location:** In Park Hills, on the south side of Highway 32 at Flat River Drive overpass, 1.5 miles west of Highway 67 in Saint Francois County. **Facilities:** Museum, shop. **Activities:** Tours. **Special Features:** For more than 100 years, the Old Lead Belt of Missouri provided nearly 80 percent of the nation's mined lead. When Saint Joe Minerals Corp. ceased operation, its largest mine-mill complex was donated to the state. The site features a museum with restored underground mining equipment, a display of mineral specimens, and exhibits on mining history.

★3026★ **MONTAUK STATE PARK**
RR 5, Box 279
Salem, MO 65560
Web: www.mostateparks.com/montauk.htm
Phone: 573-548-2201
Size: 1,396 acres. **Location:** 21 miles southwest of Salem on Highway 119 in Dent County. **Facilities:** 31 basic campsites, 123 electric campsites, showers, 3 cabins, 8 sleeping cabins, 16 fourplex units, 18 motel rooms, picnic sites, 2 picnic shelters, dining lodge (seasonal), store, hiking trails. **Activities:** Camping, river and stream fishing, hiking, nature programs. **Special Features:** The headwaters of the Current River are generated where Pigeon Creek merges with the 40 million gallons of water that pour daily from Montauk Springs. The park is developed around the springs and is a popular spot for rainbow trout fishing. An old gristmill built in 1896 is open for tours (seasonal). Visitors can also tour the park's trout hatchery.

★3027★ **MORRIS STATE PARK**
c/o Hunter-Dawson State Historic Site
PO Box 308
New Madrid, MO 63869
Web: www.mostateparks.com/morris.htm
Phone: 573-748-5340
Size: 161 acres. **Location:** 5 miles north of Campbell on Route WW in Dunklin County. **Facilities:** Hiking trail, scenic overlook, restroom, parking area, interpretive kiosks. **Activities:** Hiking. **Special Features:** Park's predominant feature is Crowley's Ridge, which extends well beyond the park's boundaries and consists of a strip of low hills that contain unusual soil types and rare plant species. The park is one of several sites with natural, cultural, or historical significance that can be visited along Crowley's Ridge Parkway, a 42-mile scenic byway.

★3028★ **NATHAN BOONE HOMESTEAD STATE HISTORIC SITE**
7850 N State Hwy V
Ash Grove, MO 65604
Web: www.mostateparks.com/boonehome.htm
Phone: 417-751-3266
Size: 400 acres. **Location:** West of Springfield, near Ash Grove in Greene County. **Activities:** Guided tours. **Special Features:**

This one-and-one-half story log house was the home of Daniel Boone's youngest child, Colonel Nathan Boone, a hunter, soldier, surveyor, and entrepreneur. Boone's three sons and two of his slaves built the house in 1837, which was the hub of a 720-acre farm. He, his wife, and other family members are buried near the house, while another cemetery near Boone's grave contains the remains of at least 16 men, women, and children who were kept as slaves on the farm.

★3029★ ONONDAGA CAVE STATE PARK

7556 Hwy H
Leasburg, MO 65535
Web: www.mostateparks.com/onondaga.htm
Phone: 573-245-6576
Size: 1,318 acres. **Location:** 7 miles south of the I-44 Leasburg exit (214), on Highway H in Crawford County. **Facilities:** 19 basic campsites, 47 campsites with electric and water hookups, showers, special use area, picnic sites, picnic shelter, hiking trails, boat ramp, visitor center, exhibits, store. **Activities:** Camping, canoeing, river fishing, swimming, hiking, guided cave tours. **Special Features:** Onondaga Cave is recognized as one of the most spectacular caves in the nation because of the quality of its formations. Guided tours of this National Natural Landmark as well as Cathedral Cave are available daily, March through October.

★3030★ OSAGE VILLAGE STATE HISTORIC SITE

c/o Harry S Truman Birthplace State Historic Site
1009 Truman
Lamar, MO 64759
Web: www.mostateparks.com/osagevillage.htm
Phone: 417-682-2279
Size: 100 acres. **Location:** 9 miles east of Nevada on Highway 54 (near Walker), 6 miles north on Highway C, then 3 miles on a gravel road in Vernon County. **Facilities:** Self-guiding walking trail, exhibits. **Special Features:** This site contains what was once a Big Osage Indian village occupied between 1700 and 1775. Included on the *National Register of Historic Places*, the site marks the location where the Osage were living when first encountered by Europeans. Pottery, weapons, and tools excavated from the site have provided information about the daily lives of the villagers, who hunted, planted crops, processed hides, and were very successful traders with the Europeans.

★3031★ PERSHING STATE PARK

29277 Hwy 130
Laclede, MO 64651
Web: www.mostateparks.com/pershingpark.htm
Phone: 660-963-2299
Size: 3,566 acres. **Location:** 7 miles west of Brookfield or 18 miles east of Chillicothe, off US 36 on Highway 130 in Linn County. **Facilities:** 12 basic campsites, 26 electric campsites, showers, special use area, picnic sites, picnic shelters (1 open, 1 enclosed), swimming beach, hiking and backpacking trails. **Activities:** Camping, river and stream fishing, swimming, hiking, backpacking, interpretive programs. **Special Features:** Park

was established in honor of John J. Pershing, commanding general of the American Expeditionary Forces during World War I. A hike down Riparian Trail provides a glimpse of pre-settlement Missouri, and four small lakes and Locust Creek offer anglers a variety of fish. Along the creek are forested bottomlands, shrub swamps, marshes, and a 1,000-acre wet prairie.

★3032★ POMME DE TERRE STATE PARK

HC 77, Box 890
Pittsburg, MO 65724
Web: www.mostateparks.com/pommedeterre.htm
Phone: 417-852-4291
Size: 734 acres. **Location:** In 2 areas, Pittsburg and Hermitage, that are 8 miles apart; both are south of US 54 in Hickory County. **Facilities:** 41 basic campsites, 193 electric campsites, 20 electric/water campsites, showers, special use area, picnic sites, picnic shelter, hiking trails, 2 public swimming beaches, fishing pier, marina, store, boat ramp, boat rentals. **Activities:** Camping, boating, fishing, swimming, hiking, nature programs (in summer). **Special Features:** Park lies along the banks of the 7,800-acre Pomme de Terre Reservoir and includes remnants of a pre-settlement savanna landscape dotted with stunted old-growth oak trees and native grasses.

★3033★ PRAIRIE STATE PARK

128 NW 150th Ln
Liberal, MO 64769
Web: www.mostateparks.com/prairie.htm
Phone: 417-843-6711
Size: 3,942 acres. **Location:** 16 miles west of Lamar in Barton County, off Highway 160, north on Highway NN to Central Road for 3 miles, then north on 150th Lane. **Facilities:** 2 basic campsites, picnic sites, hiking and backpacking trails, visitor center, exhibits. **Activities:** Camping, hiking, backpacking, wildlife observation, interpretive programs. **Special Features:** Park preserves Missouri's largest remaining tallgrass prairie, with grasses that grow as high as eight feet in the fall. The grass is strewn with ever-changing wildflowers and provides a home for bison and elk.

★3034★ ROARING RIVER STATE PARK

Rt 4, Box 4100
Cassville, MO 65625
Web: www.mostateparks.com/roaringriver.htm
Phone: 417-847-2539
Size: 3,973 acres. **Location:** 7 miles south of Cassville on Highway 112 in Barry County. **Facilities:** 48 basic campsites, 137 electric campsites, showers, organized group camp, 10 cabins, 16 duplex/fourplex units, 24 motel rooms and 2 suites, conference center, meeting rooms, restaurant, gift shop, picnic sites, 2 picnic shelters, hiking trails, swimming pool, park store, nature center. **Activities:** Camping, river fishing, swimming, hiking, interpretive programs. **Special Features:** Roaring River is known for its premier trout fishing. More than 20 million gallons of water gush daily from Roaring River Spring to form the headwaters of Roaring River, which is stocked daily during trout season.

★3035★ ROBERTSVILLE STATE PARK

PO Box 186
Robertsville, MO 63072
Web: www.mostateparks.com/robertsville.htm
Phone: 636-257-3788
Size: 1,225 acres. **Location:** 5 miles east of I-44, on Highway O near the junction of Highway N in Franklin County. **Facilities:** 12 basic campsites, 14 electric campsites, showers, picnic sites, 2 picnic shelters, playground, hiking trail, boat ramp. **Activities:** Canoeing, river fishing, hiking. **Special Features:** With the Meramec River and several oxbow sloughs of Calvey Creek along its border, the park features a wetland habitat that attracts many kinds of waterfowl.

★3036★ ROCK BRIDGE MEMORIAL STATE PARK

5901 S Hwy 163
Columbia, MO 65203
Web: www.mostateparks.com/rockbridge.htm
Phone: 573-449-7402
Size: 2,273 acres. **Location:** 5 miles south of downtown Columbia on Highway 163 in Boone County. **Facilities:** Picnic sites, 2 picnic shelters, playground, hiking trails, mountain bike trails, equestrian trails, special use area. **Activities:** Stream fishing, hiking, mountain biking, horseback riding, interpretive programs. **Special Features:** Natural geological formations are the principal features at this day-use park. A natural rock bridge, Devil's Icebox Cave, and numerous sinkholes are part of the large limestone cave system dating back thousands of years. A boardwalk and other trails lead visitors to the geological formations and through prairie and woods.

★3037★ ROGER PRYOR PIONEER BACKCOUNTRY

c/o Johnson's Shut-Ins State Park
HC Route 1 Box 126
Middlebrook, MO 63656
Web: www.mostateparks.com/rogerpryor.htm
Phone: 573-546-2450; **Toll Free:** 800-334-6946
Size: 61,000 acres. **Location:** In Shannon County; call park for location. **Facilities:** Hiking and backpacking trails (27 miles). **Activities:** Hiking, backpacking. **Special Features:** The state's largest undeveloped area is located within the state's largest privately owned forest (Pioneer Forest) in a remote area of the Ozarks. In addition to its 27 miles of trails, the area includes nearly 15 miles of frontage on the Current River, considered by many to be the finest float stream in the state. The area also includes two designated natural areas with impressive old-growth trees, some as old as 400 years.

★3038★ ROUTE 66 STATE PARK

97 N Outer Rd, Suite 1
Eureka, MO 63025
Web: www.mostateparks.com/route66.htm
Phone: 636-938-7198; **Fax:** 636-938-7804
Size: 419 acres. **Location:** 2 miles east of Eureka in St. Louis County. **Facilities:** Picnic area, 2 shelters, boat ramp, hiking trails, bicycle trails, equestrian trails, visitor center. **Activities:** Fishing, hiking, bicycling, horseback riding. **Special Features:** Park commemorates US Route 66, the historic highway that ran from Chicago to Los Angeles. A portion of the original Route 66, including a historic bridge across the Meramec River, lies within park boundaries. Bridgehead Inn, a restored 1935 roadhouse, serves as visitor center, with interpretive exhibits about the highway. The park sits on the site of the former resort community of Times Beach, abandoned and demolished after dioxin contamination made it uninhabitable.

★3039★ SAINT FRANCOIS STATE PARK

8920 US Hwy 67 N
Bonne Terre, MO 63628
Web: www.mostateparks.com/stfrancois.htm
Phone: 573-358-2173
Size: 2,735 acres. **Location:** On US 67, 4 miles north of Bonne Terre, in Saint Francois County. **Facilities:** 47 basic campsites, 63 electric campsites, showers, special use area, picnic sites, 2 picnic shelters, hiking, backpacking, and equestrian trails. **Activities:** Camping, stream fishing, canoeing, swimming, hiking, backpacking, horseback riding, interpretive programs. **Special Features:** Park, which comprises the Pike Run Hills surrounding Coonville Creek and along Big River, is a popular put-in point for float trips on Big River. The Coonville Creek Wild Area can be explored on horseback or on foot.

★3040★ SAINT JOE STATE PARK

2800 Pimville Rd
Park Hills, MO 63601
Web: www.mostateparks.com/stjoe.htm
Phone: 573-431-1069
Size: 8,243 acres. **Location:** From US Highway 67 to Highway 32 west, go 3 miles to Pimville Road in Saint Francois County. **Facilities:** 43 basic campsites, 53 electric campsites, showers, 25 equestrian campsites (12 basic, 13 electric), picnic sites, 6 picnic shelters, hiking/bicycling trails, equestrian trails, ATV trails, beach, boat ramp. **Activities:** Camping, lake fishing, swimming, hiking, bicycling, mountain biking, horseback riding, ATV riding. **Special Features:** Missouri's third largest state park, Saint Joe has the largest and one of the most popular off-road-vehicle areas in the Midwest, with about 2,000 acres for riding. The park is located in the old "Lead Belt" of southeast Missouri, where much of the nation's lead ore was extracted for more than a century. (See separate entry on Missouri Mines State Historic Site).

★3041★ SAM A. BAKER STATE PARK

Rt 1, Box 113
Patterson, MO 63956
Web: www.mostateparks.com/baker.htm
Phone: 573-856-4411
Size: 5,324 acres. **Location:** 4 miles north of Patterson on Highway 143 in Wayne County. **Facilities:** 66 basic campsites, 132 electric campsites, 21 equestrian campsites (10 with electricity), special use area, showers, 17 cabins, 1 sleeping cabin, picnic sites, 3 picnic shelters, playground, dining lodge, hiking trails, backpacking trails, equestrian trails, bicycle trails, canoe and raft rentals, boat ramp, visitor/nature center. **Activities:** Camping, canoeing, river and stream fishing, swimming, hiking, bicycling, horseback riding, nature programs. **Special Features:**

Set in the Saint Francois Mountain area, Park features an expansive, unspoiled wilderness that surrounds Mudlick Mountain.

★3042★ SANDY CREEK COVERED BRIDGE STATE HISTORIC SITE

c/o Mastodon State Historic Site
1050 Museum Dr
Imperial, MO 63052
Web: www.mostateparks.com/sandybridge.htm
Phone: 636-464-2976
Size: 206 acres. **Location:** Near Goldman, off Highway 21, in Jefferson County. **Facilities:** Historic bridge, picnic area. **Activities:** Picnicking. **Special Features:** Bridge was built in 1872 as part of a Jefferson County building program after the Civil War. It was destroyed by floodwaters in 1886 and rebuilt the following year. The bridge's appearance is that of an old red barn.

★3043★ SAPPINGTON CEMETERY STATE HISTORIC SITE

c/o Arrow Rock State Historic Site
PO Box 1
Arrow Rock, MO 65320
Web: www.mostateparks.com/sappingtoncem.htm
Phone: 660-837-3330
Size: 2 acres. **Location:** 5 miles southwest of Arrow Rock on Route AA in Saline County. **Special Features:** Sappington Cemetery is the resting place of several prominent Arrow Rock citizens, including Dr John Sappington, along with two Missouri governors who served in the 1800s. Dr Sappington was a pioneer in the use of quinine to treat malaria.

★3044★ SCOTT JOPLIN HOUSE STATE HISTORIC SITE

2658 Delmar Blvd
Saint Louis, MO 63103
Web: www.mostateparks.com/scottjoplin.htm
Phone: 314-340-5790; **Fax:** 314-340-5793
Size: 4 acres. **Location:** On Delmar Boulevard between Grand and Jefferson in Saint Louis. **Facilities:** Historic home. **Activities:** Guided tours. **Special Features:** In 1902 ragtime composer Scott Joplin and his wife lived in an apartment in this four-family structure, which today houses exhibits on Joplin's life and work. Eight of his compositions were published that year, including ''The Entertainer.'' The modest upstairs flat where Joplin lived has been restored to its turn-of-the-century appearance, and an antique player piano fills the home with his music.

★3045★ STOCKTON STATE PARK

19100 S Hwy 215
Dadeville, MO 63635
Web: www.mostateparks.com/stockton.htm
Phone: 417-276-4259
Size: 2,176 acres. **Location:** South of Stockton on Highway 215 in Cedar County. **Facilities:** 14 basic campsites, 60 electric campsites, showers, sleeping cabin, 5 camper cabins, 4 duplex units, 10 motel rooms, picnic sites, 2 picnic shelters, hiking trails, bicycle trail, dining lodge, swimming beach, marina, 2 boat ramps, boat rentals. **Activities:** Camping, boating, sailing, lake fishing, swimming, water-skiing, scuba diving, hiking, bicycling, bird watching. **Special Features:** Park is situated along Springfield plateau overlooking the 25,000-acre Stockton Reservoir. The steady breeze there makes it a favorite for those who enjoy sailing.

★3046★ TABLE ROCK STATE PARK

5272 State Hwy 165
Branson, MO 65616
Web: www.mostateparks.com/tablerock.htm
Phone: 417-334-4704
Size: 356 acres. **Location:** 7 miles southwest of Branson via US 65, then 5 miles west on Highway 165 in Taney County. **Facilities:** 43 basic campsites, 89 electric campsites, 20 sites with full hookups, showers, picnic sites, picnic shelter, hiking and biking trails, marina, personal watercraft rentals, boat rentals, boat ramp, store. **Activities:** Camping, boating, canoeing, sailing, lake fishing, scuba diving, swimming, jet skiing, parasailing, hiking, bicycling. **Special Features:** Park is located on the 43,000-acre Table Rock Lake and is near Branson, one of the most popular tourist destinations in the US.

★3047★ TAUM SAUK MOUNTAIN STATE PARK

c/o Johnson's Shut-Ins State Park
HC Route 1 Box 126
Middlebrook, MO 63656
Web: www.mostateparks.com/taumsauk.htm
Phone: 573-546-2450
Size: 7,501 acres. **Location:** 9 miles southwest of Ironton, off Highway 21, 5 miles on Highway CC in Iron and Reynolds counties. **Facilities:** 12 primitive walk-in campsites, special use area, picnic sites, hiking and backpacking trails. **Activities:** Camping, hiking, backpacking. **Special Features:** Park is located in the Saint Francois Mountains, one of the most rugged and scenic areas of the state. Rising to 1,772 feet, Taum Sauk Mountain is the highest in the state. A trail from the top of the mountain leads to Mina Sauk Falls, which drops 132 feet over a series of rocky ledges. Farther along on the trail is the Devil's Toll Gate, an 8-foot-wide passage through volcanic rhyolite standing 30 feet high.

★3048★ THOMAS HART BENTON HOME & STUDIO STATE HISTORIC SITE

3616 Belleview
Kansas City, MO 64111
Web: www.mostateparks.com/benton.htm
Phone: 816-931-5722
Size: 0.32 acres. **Location:** 2 blocks west of SW Trafficway, off of Valentine on Belleview, in Kansas City, Jackson County. **Facilities:** Historic home. **Activities:** Guided tours, interpretive programs. **Special Features:** Missouri's most noted 20th-century artist, Thomas Hart Benton lived in this 2 1/2 story, late Victorian-style house from 1939 until his death in 1975, and several of his paintings and sculptures can be viewed there. Benton converted half of the carriage house into his art studio, which is where he died. The studio remains as he left it, with

coffee cans full of paintbrushes, paints, and a stretched canvas waiting to be painted.

★3049★ THOUSAND HILLS STATE PARK

20431 State Hwy 157
Kirksville, MO 63501
Web: www.mostateparks.com/thousandhills.htm
Phone: 660-665-6995
Size: 3,080 acres. **Location:** West from Kirksville on Rt 6, then south 2 miles on Highway 157 in Adair County. **Facilities:** 15 basic campsites, 42 electric campsites, showers, special use area, outpost cabin, 4 duplex/fourplex units, picnic sites, 5 picnic shelters (4 open, 1 enclosed), hiking trails, mountain biking trails, backpacking trails, beach, full-service marina, boat ramp, boat rentals, dining lodge, interpretive shelter. **Activities:** Camping, boating, water-skiing, canoeing, lake fishing, swimming, hiking, mountain biking, interpretive programs. **Special Features:** Park centers around 573-acre Forest Lake, which also supplies water for the Kirksville community. An interpretive shelter at the park displays petroglyphs, rock carvings created by Native American inhabitants more than 1,500 years ago.

★3050★ TOWOSAHGY STATE HISTORIC SITE

c/o Hunter-Dawson State Historic Site
312 Dawson Rd
New Madrid, MO 63869
Web: www.mostateparks.com/towosahgy.htm
Phone: 573-748-5340
Size: 64 acres. **Location:** 13 miles southeast of East Prairie, off Highway 77 on County Road 502 in Mississippi County. **Facilities:** Interpretive exhibits. **Special Features:** This state historic site preserves the remains of a once-fortified Indian village, which also was an important ceremonial center. Indians of the Mississippian Culture inhabited the site between AD 1000 and 1400.

★3051★ TRAIL OF TEARS STATE PARK

429 Moccasin Springs
Jackson, MO 63755
Web: www.mostateparks.com/trailoftears.htm
Phone: 573-334-1711
Size: 3,415 acres. **Location:** 10 miles east of Fruitland, off Highway 61 N on Highway 177, in Cape Girardeau County. **Facilities:** 35 basic campsites, 10 electric campsites, 7 campsites with full hookups, showers, special use area, picnic sites, 2 picnic shelters, hiking and backpacking trails, equestrian trails, beach, boat ramp, visitor center. **Activities:** Camping, lake and river fishing, swimming, hiking, horseback riding, interpretive programs. **Special Features:** A portion of this wilderness once was part of the route known as the Trail of Tears, a trail taken by Cherokee Indians in their forced march to the West. (See Trail of Tears National Historic Trail entry in national trails section.)

★3052★ UNION COVERED BRIDGE STATE HISTORIC SITE

c/o Mark Twain Birthplace State Historic Site
37352 Shrine Rd
Florida, MO 65283
Web: www.mostateparks.com/unionbridge.htm
Phone: 573-565-3449
Size: 1 acre. **Location:** 5 miles west of Paris on US 24 and 3 miles south on Highway C, then west 0.25 miles on a county road in Monroe County. **Special Features:** This covered bridge is the only surviving example in Missouri of the Burr-arch truss system. Built in 1871 to span the Elk Fork of the Salt River, the bridge served travelers on the Paris-to-Fayette Road through Monroe County for 99 years.

★3053★ VAN METER STATE PARK

Rt 1, Box 47
Miami, MO 65344
Web: www.mostateparks.com/vanmeter.htm
Phone: 660-886-7537
Size: 983 acres. **Location:** 12 miles northwest of Marshall on Highway 122 in Saline County. **Facilities:** 9 basic campsites, 12 electric campsites, showers, picnic sites, 2 picnic shelters, hiking trails, visitor center. **Activities:** Camping, lake fishing, hiking, interpretive programs. **Special Features:** Park land was once the home of Missouri Indians, for whom the state and the river are named. The Missouri inhabited the area through the early 1700s. Predating the Missouri were prehistoric native tribes, whose burial mounds are located in the park. A feature of interest is the "old fort," a six-acre, Missouri Indian earthwork construction of unknown purpose.

★3054★ WAKONDA STATE PARK

32836 State Park Rd
LaGrange, MO 63448
Web: www.mostateparks.com/wakonda.htm
Phone: 573-655-2280
Size: 1,054 acres. **Location:** 3 miles south of LaGrange on US 61 in Lewis County. **Facilities:** 49 basic campsites, 29 electric campsites, showers, 10 recreational trailers, picnic sites, beach, boat ramps, nonmotorized jonboat and canoe rentals, hiking trails, mountain biking trails. **Activities:** Camping, boating (10 HP limit), canoeing, lake fishing, swimming, hiking, mountain biking. **Special Features:** Once composed of land that was mined for gravel used to surface the state's secondary highways, Park has been transformed into a recreation area that includes six lakes, trails, and a rare sand prairie.

★3055★ WALLACE STATE PARK

10621 NE Hwy 121
Cameron, MO 64429
Web: www.mostateparks.com/wallace.htm
Phone: 816-632-3745
Size: 502 acres. **Location:** 2 miles east of I-35 Exit 48, on Highway 21 in Clinton County. **Facilities:** 35 basic campsites, 42 electric campsites, showers, playground, special use area, travel camp, picnic sites, 2 picnic shelters (1 open, 1 enclosed),

hiking trails, beach. **Activities:** Camping, lake fishing, swimming, hiking. **Special Features:** Park's principal attraction is its peacefulness. The campground is favored by families and senior citizens and includes a travel camping area as well as a special use area popular with youth organizations. Twenty miles southwest of the park is Trice-Dedman Memorial Woods, a significant example of the northern Missouri hardwood forests that existed before European settlement. Trice-Dedman is owned by the Nature Conservancy and administered by the state's Department of Natural Resources.

★3056★ WASHINGTON STATE PARK
13041 State Hwy 104
DeSoto, MO 63020
Web: www.mostateparks.com/washington.htm
Phone: 636-586-2995
Size: 2,148 acres. **Location:** 9 miles south of DeSoto on Highway 21 in Washington County. **Facilities:** 26 basic campsites, 24 electric campsites, showers, special use area, 11 cabins, picnic sites, 2 picnic shelters, hiking and backpacking trails, swimming pool, canoe and raft rentals, boat ramp. **Activities:** Camping, canoeing, rafting, river fishing, swimming, hiking, backpacking, interpretive programs. **Special Features:** Park features include petroglyphs that are believed to have been made around AD 1000 and provide clues about the lives of prehistoric Indians that once inhabited this part of Missouri. Many of the buildings at the park were constructed by African-American Civilian Conservation Corps stonemasons during the 1930s, including stone steps that make up the 1,000 Steps Trail.

★3057★ WATKINS WOOLEN MILL STATE PARK & STATE HISTORIC SITE
26600 Park Rd N
Lawson, MO 64062
Web: www.mostateparks.com/wwmill
Phone: 816-580-3387
Size: 1,467 acres. **Location:** 7 miles east of I-35 on Highway 92, then north 1 mile on Highway RA in Clay County. **Facilities:** 23 basic campsites, 75 electric campsites, showers, special use area, picnic sites, picnic shelter, hiking trails, paved bicycle trail, equestrian trails, beach, bathhouse, boat ramp, visitor center. **Activities:** Camping, lake fishing, swimming, hiking, bicycling, horseback riding, interpretive programs, tours. **Special Features:** Site is dedicated to interpreting the 19th century landholdings of Waltus Locket Watkins and to providing a variety of outdoor recreation options. Watkins' house and outbuildings, the woolen factory and gristmill, and the nearby church and schoolhouse have been restored to create an 1870s farm, and a living history program is offered during the summer months. The mill is a National Historic Landmark and is the only 19th century American woolen mill with its original machinery still intact. The park is adjacent to the plantation buildings and features a 100-acre lake and other recreational facilities.

★3058★ WESTON BEND STATE PARK
16600 Hwy 45 N
Weston Bend b, MO 64098
Web: www.mostateparks.com/westonbend.htm
Phone: 816-640-5443
Size: 1,133 acres. **Location:** Exit 20 off I-29 to Highway 273, to Highway 45 in Platte County. **Facilities:** 4 basic campsites, 32 electric campsites, showers, picnic sites, picnic shelters (1 open, 1 enclosed), playground, hiking trail, paved bicycle trail, scenic overlook (&). **Activities:** Camping, fishing, hiking, bicycling. **Special Features:** Park lies adjacent to the Missouri River in an area once known for producing tobacco. Five tobacco barns remain in the park, and one has been converted to a reservable enclosed shelter. A scenic overlook at the park provides a view of the Missouri River, Fort Leavenworth, and beyond.

9. State Parks

Montana State Parks

1	Ackley Lake SP	C-5
2	Anaconda Smoke	
	Stack SP	D-3
3	Bannack SP	E-3
4	Beaverhead Rock SP	E-3
5	Beavertail Hill SP	C-3
6	Big Arm SP	B-2
7	Black Sandy SP	C-3
8	Brush Lake SP	A-10

9	Chief Plenty Coups SP	E-6
10	Clark's Lookout SP	E-3
11	Cooney Reservoir SP	E-6
12	Council Grove SP	C-2
13	Elkhorn SP	D-3
14	Finley Point SP	B-2
15	Fort Owen SP	C-2
16	Frenchtown Pond SP	C-2
17	Giant Springs SP	B-4

18	Granite Ghost Town SP	D-3
19	Greycliff Prairie Dog	
	Town SP	D-5
20	Hell Creek SP	B-8
21	Lake Elmo SP	D-6
22	Lake Mary Ronan SP	B-2
23	Lewis & Clark Caverns SP	D-4
24	Logan SP	B-1
25	Lone Pine SP	A-2

26	Lost Creek SP	D-3
27	Madison Buffalo	
	Jump SP	D-4
28	Makoshika SP	C-10
29	Medicine Rocks SP	D-9
30	Missouri Headwaters SP	D-4
31	Painted Rocks SP	D-2
32	Parker Homestead SP	D-4
33	Pictograph Cave SP	D-7
34	Pirogue Island SP	C-9
35	Placid Lake SP	C-3
36	Rosebud Battlefield SP	E-8
37	Salmon Lake SP	C-2
38	Sluice Boxes SP	C-5

39	Smith River SP	C-4
40	Spring Meadow Lake SP	C-3
41	Thompson Falls SP	B-1
42	Tongue River Reservoir SP	E-8
43	Tower Rock SP	C-4
44	Travelers Rest SP	C-2
45	Ulm Pishkun SP	B-4
46	Wayfarers SP	B-2
47	West Shore SP	B-2
48	Whitefish Lake SP	A-2
49	Wild Horse Island SP	B-2
50	Yellow Bay SP	B-2
	SP State Park	

MONTANA

★3059★ **Montana Fish, Wildlife & Parks Department**
Park Division
1420 E 6th Ave
PO Box 200701
Helena, MT 59620
(406) 444-2535 - Phone
(406) 444-4952 - Fax
(406) 444-5653 - Employment
(406) 444-3750 - Volunteering
Web: fwp.mt.gov/parks
Preserves, enhances, and interprets a diverse representation of natural, cultural/historic, and recreational resources in the state's 50 parks.

★3060★ **Montana Fish, Wildlife & Parks Department**
Wildlife Division
1420 E 6th Ave
PO Box 200701
Helena, MT 59620
(406) 444-2612 - Phone
Web: www.fwp.state.mt.us/habitat
Manages wildlife management areas, for the protection of the species and enjoyment of the public.

Key to campsite classification:

- **Campsites** — Include garbage collection and either flush or vault toilet. Some have drinking water nearby. Can accommodate only one group per site.
- **Group campsites** — Same facilities as regular campsites, but can accommodate multiple groups per site.
- **Cavern cabins** — At Lewis and Clark Caverns State Park. One room rental cabins consisting of one double bed, one bunk bed with two single mattresses, a dining table, electricity, and baseboard heat.
- **Yurts** — Sleep up to six people; waterproof canvas covering, reflective insulation and an outdoor wooden deck. Electrical outlets, lights, electric heat and a propane barbecue for outdoor cooking are also provided.
- **Tipis** — Sleep 6-8 people; no furnishings, picnic table and fire grill located outside.

★3061★ **ACKLEY LAKE STATE PARK**
4600 Giant Springs Rd
Great Falls, MT 59405
Web: fwp.mt.gov/lands/site_282450.aspx
Phone: 406-454-5840
Size: 160 acres. **Elevation:** 4,331 feet. **Location:** 17 miles west of Lewistown on Highway 87 to Hobson, then 5 miles south on MT 400 and 2 miles southwest on county road. **Facilities:** 23 campsites (3 tent, 20 trailer), group campsite, picnic area, vault toilets, boat ramp. **Activities:** Camping, boating, fishing, swimming, water-skiing. **Special Features:** Ackley Lake is a grassland park with excellent rainbow and brown trout fishing..

★3062★ **ANACONDA SMOKE STACK STATE PARK**
3201 Spurgin Rd
Missoula, MT 59804
Web: fwp.mt.gov/lands/site_280918.aspx
Phone: 406-542-5500
Size: 12 acres. **Elevation:** 5,758 feet. **Location:** On the eastern edge of Anaconda at the junction of Park Street (MT 1) and Monroe Street, adjacent to Goodman Park. **Facilities:** Interpretive signs at viewing site. **Special Features:** The old Anaconda Copper Company smelter stack, completed on May 5, 1919, is one of the tallest free-standing brick structures in the world, standing just over 585 feet. The inside diameter at the bottom is 75 feet and at the top 60 feet. The stack may be viewed and photographed only from a distance.

★3063★ **BANNACK STATE PARK**
4200 Bannack Rd
Dillon, MT 59725
Web: fwp.mt.gov/lands/site_281798.aspx
Phone: 406-834-3413
Size: 1,528 acres. **Elevation:** 5,837 feet. **Location:** 26 miles southwest of Dillon. **Facilities:** 28 campsites (14 tent, 14 trailer), group camping and picnicking facilities, rental tipi, picnic area, horseshoe pit, trails, wildlife viewing, visitor center, interpretive displays (♿♿). **Activities:** Camping, fishing, hiking, bicycling, horseback riding, wildlife viewing, tours (self-guided and guided), interpretive programs. **Special Features:** The ghost town of Bannack was the site of Montana's first major gold discovery in 1862. The main street is lined with more than 50 historic log and frame structures that recall Montana's formative years. Bannack is the best preserved of the Montana ghost towns being preserved rather than restored and is a registered National Historic Landmark.

★3064★ **BEAVERHEAD ROCK STATE PARK**
c/o Bannack State Park
4200 Bannack Rd
Dillon, MT 59725
Web: fwp.mt.gov/lands/site_281875.aspx
Phone: 406-834-3413
Size: 71 acres. **Elevation:** 5,098 feet. **Location:** 14 miles south of Twin Bridges on MT 41. **Facilities:** None. Undeveloped, unsigned, day use only. **Special Features:** Sacagawea recognized this huge landmark, resembling the head of a swimming beaver, while traveling with the Lewis and Clark Expedition in 1805. Site is listed in the *National Register of Historic Places.*

★3065★ BEAVERTAIL HILL STATE PARK

3201 Spurgin Rd
Missoula, MT 59804
Web: fwp.mt.gov/lands/site_280871.aspx
Phone: 406-542-5500
Size: 65 acres. **Elevation:** 3,615 feet. **Location:** 26 miles southeast of Missoula on I-90 to Beavertail Hill exit (130), then 0.25 miles south on county road. **Facilities:** 28 campsites (14 tent, 14 trailer, 1 ♿), 2 rental tipis, picnic area, hand launch boat access, interpretive trail (♿), amphitheater, flush toilets. **Activities:** Camping, fishing, hiking, bicycling, boating (non-motorized), wildlife viewing, interpretive programs. **Special Features:** Park is situated on the Clark Fork River, and its facilities include a one-mile self-guided trail that points out many of the natural features of the riparian zone in which the park is located. The park is open seasonally, from May 1 through September 30.

★3066★ BIG ARM STATE PARK

490 N Meridian Rd
Kalispell, MT 59901
Web: fwp.mt.gov/lands/site_280041.aspx
Phone: 406-752-5501
Size: 505 acres. **Elevation:** 2,953 feet. **Location:** 14 miles north of Polson on US 93. **Facilities:** 40 campsites (9 tent, 31 trailer), group camping area, 3 rental yurts, showers, flush toilets, picnic area (♿), picnic shelters (♿), hiking trail (2.5 miles), boat dock, boat ramp. **Activities:** Camping, hiking, boating, fishing, swimming, windsurfing, scuba diving, water-skiing, bird watching. **Special Features:** Park is located on Flathead Lake's Big Arm Bay and is a popular launching spot to access Wild Horse Island (see separate entry).

★3067★ BLACK SANDY STATE PARK

930 Custer Ave W
Helena, MT 59601
Web: fwp.mt.gov/lands/site_281944.aspx
Phone: 406-495-3270
Size: 44 acres. **Elevation:** 3,835 feet. **Location:** 7 miles north of Helena on I-15, then 4 miles east on Secondary 453, and north 3 miles. **Facilities:** 33 campsites (4 tent, 29 trailer, 2 ♿; no hookups), flush toilets (♿), picnic area, double-wide boat ramp (♿), boat dock, hiking trail (1 mile), interpretive displays. **Activities:** Camping, boating, fishing, swimming, water-skiing, hiking, bicycling. **Special Features:** Black Sandy is one of the few public parks located on the shores of Hauser Lake.

★3068★ BRUSH LAKE STATE PARK

c/o Region 6 Office
54078 US Hwy 2 W
Glasgow, MT 59230
Web: fwp.mt.gov/lands/site_7022011.aspx
Phone: 406-228-3700
Size: 450 acres. **Elevation:** 1,952 feet. **Location:** 31 miles southeast of Plentywood. **Facilities:** Under development. Facilities are to include interior road improvements, parking, boat ramp and dock, vault toilet, picnic tables, and a designated swimming area with a dock and floating platform **Special Features:** Park is northeastern Montana's first state park. Because of the lake's mineral content, there are no fish and very little aquatic vegetation, making it ideal for swimming, motorized boating, and water-skiing.

★3069★ CHIEF PLENTY COUPS STATE PARK

PO Box 100
Pryor, MT 59066
Web: fwp.mt.gov/lands/site_283264.aspx
Phone: 406-252-1289
Size: 491 acres. **Elevation:** 4,042 feet. **Location:** 35 miles south of Billings exit 447 off I-90 to Pryor, then 1 mile west. **Facilities:** Picnic area, horseshoe pit, trails, interpretive displays, visitor center. **Activities:** Fishing, swimming, hiking, bicycling, interpretive tours (reservations required). **Special Features:** Situated within the Crow Reservation in south-central Montana, this day-use park preserves the log home, sacred spring, and farmstead of Chief Plenty Coups, last chief of the Crow.

★3070★ CLARK'S LOOKOUT STATE PARK

c/o Bannack State Park
4200 Bannack Rd
Dillon, MT 59725
Web: fwp.mt.gov/lands/site_281963.aspx
Phone: 406-834-3413
Size: 8 acres. **Elevation:** 5,102 feet. **Location:** 1 mile north of Dillon, off Highway 91. **Facilities:** Undeveloped site. **Special Features:** In 1805, Captain William Clark climbed this rock outcropping overlooking the Beaverhead River to scout what lay ahead for the Lewis and Clark Expedition. Visitors can drive to the site and walk the trail to the top.

★3071★ COONEY STATE PARK

PO Box 254
Joliet, MT 59041
Web: fwp.mt.gov/lands/site_283293.aspx
Phone: 406-445-2326
Size: 318 acres. **Elevation:** 4,252 feet. **Location:** 22 miles southwest of Laurel on US 212, then 8 miles west of Boyd on county road. **Facilities:** 76 campsites (6 tent, 70 trailer, 2 ♿), flush toilets (♿), showers (seasonal), picnic area, boat ramp, boat dock, fish cleaning station, information kiosk. **Activities:** Camping, boating, fishing, swimming, water-skiing, wildlife viewing, birding, ice fishing, cross-country skiing, ice skating. **Special Features:** This irrigation reservoir, near Red Lodge and Beartooth Mountains, is the most popular recreation area in south-central Montana. Attractions include good walleye and rainbow trout fishing.

★3072★ COUNCIL GROVE STATE PARK

3201 Spurgin Rd
Missoula, MT 59804
Web: fwp.mt.gov/lands/site_280907.aspx
Phone: 406-542-5500
Size: 187 acres. **Elevation:** 3,064 feet. **Location:** 10 miles west of Missoula on Mullan Road. **Facilities:** Picnic area, vault toilets (♿), birdwatching, interpretive displays. **Activities:** Fishing, bird watching, hiking, bicycling, interpretive programs. **Special**

9. State Parks

Features: Park marks the site of the 1855 council between Isaac Stevens and the Salish, Kootenai, and Pend d'Oreille Indians. Here tribal leaders signed the Hellgate Treaty, which created the Flathead Indian Reservation.

★3073★ ELKHORN STATE PARK

930 Custer Ave W
Helena, MT 59601
Web: fwp.mt.gov/lands/site_281892.aspx
Phone: 406-495-3270
Size: 1 acre. **Elevation:** 6,437 feet. **Location:** I-15 at Boulder exit, 7 miles south on Montana 69, then 11 miles north on country road. **Facilities:** Interpretive displays. **Special Features:** Two structures from the 1880s silver-mining ghost town, Fraternity Hall and Gillian Hall, have been preserved as outstanding examples of frontier architecture.

★3074★ FINLEY POINT STATE PARK

490 N Meridian Rd
Kalispell, MT 59901
Web: fwp.mt.gov/lands/site_280032.aspx
Phone: 406-887-2715
Size: 28 acres. **Elevation:** 2,913 feet. **Location:** 11 miles north of Polson on MT 35, then 4 miles west on county road. **Facilities:** 20 campsites (4 tent, 16 trailer with electric and water hookups, 1 ♿), flush toilets, picnic area, boat dock (with hookups), boat ramp (♿). **Activities:** Camping, boating, fishing, swimming. **Special Features:** Park is located in a secluded, mature pine forest near the south end of Flathead Lake. The park is open seasonally, from May 1-September 30.

★3075★ FORT OWEN STATE PARK

3201 Spurgin Rd
Missoula, MT 59804
Web: fwp.mt.gov/lands/site_280846.aspx
Phone: 406-542-5500
Size: 2 acres. **Elevation:** 3,284 feet. **Location:** 25 miles south of Missoula on US 93 at Stevensville Junction, then 0.5 miles east on Secondary 269. **Facilities:** Interpretive displays, picnic table, vault toilets. **Activities:** Bicycling. **Special Features:** Built of adobe and logs, Fort Owen preserves the first permanent white settlement in Montana. Major John Owen established the fort as a regional trade center in 1850, and period furnishings and artifacts are displayed in the restored rooms of the east barracks. Fort is also the site of the first Catholic Church in Montana, founded in 1841 by Father DeSmet.

★3076★ FRENCHTOWN POND STATE PARK

3201 Spurgin Rd
Missoula, MT 59804
Web: fwp.mt.gov/lands/site_280880.aspx
Phone: 406-542-5500
Size: 41 acres. **Elevation:** 3,022 feet. **Location:** 15 miles west of Missoula on I-90 (exit 89), then 1 mile west on Frontage Road. **Facilities:** Picnic area, picnic shelter, playground, information kiosk, hiking trail (1 mile), flush toilets, drinking water. **Activities:** Boating (non-motorized), fishing, swimming, scuba diving, hiking, bicycling. **Special Features:** This day-use park is located on a spring-fed lake with a maximum depth of about 18 feet. The park is open seasonally, from May 1 through September 30.

★3077★ GIANT SPRINGS STATE PARK

4600 Giant Springs Rd
Great Falls, MT 59405
Web: fwp.mt.gov/lands/site_282690.aspx
Phone: 406-454-5840
Size: 851 acres. **Elevation:** 3,314 feet. **Location:** 2 miles east of US 87 on Giant Springs Road in Great Falls. **Facilities:** Picnic area, picnic shelters, playground, hiking trails (15 miles), bike trail, interpretive trail, information kiosk, visitor center (♿). **Activities:** Boating, fishing, hiking, bicycling, wildlife viewing. **Special Features:** Park is the site of one of the largest freshwater springs in the world, discovered by the Lewis and Clark Expedition in 1805. The springs flows at a measured rate of 338 million gallons of water per day. A state fish hatchery is located on park grounds, and the Rainbow Falls overlook is nearby.

★3078★ GRANITE GHOST TOWN STATE PARK

3201 Spurgin Rd
Missoula, MT 59804
Web: fwp.mt.gov/lands/site_280883.aspx
Phone: 406-542-5500
Size: .7 acres. **Elevation:** 6,549 feet. **Location:** 6 miles east of Philipsburg on forest road. **Facilities:** Interpretive displays. **Special Features:** Park preserves remnants of a once-thriving 1890s silver boomtown, comprising the Granite Mine superintendent's house and the ruins of the old miners' union hall, which reputedly had the "Northwest's Finest Dance Floor." The park is open seasonally, from May 1-September 30.

★3079★ GREYCLIFF PRAIRIE DOG TOWN STATE PARK

2300 Lake Elmo Dr
Billings, MT 59105
Web: fwp.mt.gov/lands/site_283312.aspx
Phone: 406-247-2940
Size: 98 acres. **Elevation:** 4,006 feet. **Location:** 9 miles east of Big Timber off I-90 at Greycliff exit. **Facilities:** Picnic area, interpretive displays. **Activities:** Wildlife viewing. **Special Features:** Park features a protected community of black-tailed prairie dogs.

★3080★ HELL CREEK STATE PARK

PO Box 1630
Miles City, MT 59301
Web: fwp.mt.gov/lands/site_283992.aspx
Phone: 406-234-0900
Size: 392 acres. **Elevation:** 2,231 feet. **Location:** 25 miles north of Jordan on county road. **Facilities:** 55 campsites (15 tent sites, 40 trailer sites, flush toilets (♿), showers, group campsite, motel rooms, rental cabins, picnic area, picnic shelters, playground, concessions, full-service marina and store, fish cleaning station,

boat ramp (&), boat rentals. **Activities:** Camping, boating, fishing, swimming, hiking, bicycling, wildlife viewing. **Special Features:** Located on the Hell Creek arm of Fort Peck Lake, Park has more than 1,600 miles of shoreline and is known for its walleye fishing. The park also serves as a launching point for boat camping in the wild and scenic Missouri Breaks area.

★3081★ **LAKE ELMO STATE PARK**
2300 Lake Elmo Dr
Billings, MT 59105
Web: fwp.mt.gov/lands/site_283333.aspx
Phone: 406-247-2955
Size: 184 acres. **Elevation:** 3,199 feet. **Location:** In Billings, Main Street (US 87) north to Pemberton Lane, then 0.5 miles west. **Facilities:** Picnic area, group pavilion, trails, showers, restrooms, boat ramp, fishing pier, volleyball court, interpretive center. **Activities:** Boating (non-motorized), fishing, swimming, windsurfing, sailboarding, hiking, bicycling, wildlife viewing, interpretive programs, cross-country skiing, ice fishing. **Special Features:** This urban day-use park is open year round.

★3082★ **LAKE MARY RONAN STATE PARK**
490 N Meridian Rd
Kalispell, MT 59901
Web: fwp.mt.gov/lands/site_280125.aspx
Phone: 406-849-5082
Size: 120 acres. **Elevation:** 3,770 feet. **Location:** US 93 at Dayton, then 7 miles northwest. **Facilities:** 36 campsites (12 tent, 24 trailer sites), group camp, flush toilets (&), showers, picnic area, boat ramp, boat docks. **Activities:** Camping, boating, fishing, swimming, bird watching. **Special Features:** Located seven miles west of Flathead Lake, Lake Mary Ronan is a shady park where visitors can pick huckleberries, hunt for mushrooms, or spot interesting birds. Park is open from May 31 through February 28.

★3083★ **LEWIS & CLARK CAVERNS STATE PARK**
PO Box 489
Whitehall, MT 59759
Web: fwp.mt.gov/lands/site_281895.aspx
Phone: 406-287-3541
Size: 2,920 acres. **Elevation:** 5,010 feet. **Location:** On MT 2, 22 miles west of Three Forks or 18 miles east of Whitehall. **Facilities:** 40 campsites (20 tent, 20 trailer, 1 &), group camp, 3 rustic cabins, rental tipi, picnic areas, group-use shelter, flush toilets, showers, hiking trail (9 miles), interpretive trails, visitor center, cafe, gift shop, amphitheater. **Activities:** Camping, fishing (limited river access, foot traffic only), hiking, bicycling, wildlife viewing, guided tours, interpretive programs. **Special Features:** Located in the rugged Jefferson River Canyon, Montana's first and best-known state park features some of the deepest and most spectacular caverns in the Northwest. Guided cave tours are available daily, May 1 through September 30.

★3084★ **LOGAN STATE PARK**
490 N Meridian Rd
Kalispell, MT 59901
Web: fwp.mt.gov/lands/site_280148.aspx
Phone: 406-293-7190

Size: 18 acres. **Elevation:** 3,333 feet. **Location:** 45 miles west of Kalispell on US 2. **Facilities:** 46 campsites (5 tent, 41 trailer, 2 & sites), group camp, restrooms (&), showers (&), picnic area, playground, horseshoe pit, hiking trail, boat launch, dock, boat rental. **Activities:** Camping, boating, fishing, swimming, waterskiing, hiking, birdwatching. **Special Features:** Park is located on the north shore of Middle Thompson Lake in an area heavily forested with western larch, Douglas fir, and ponderosa pine. It's surrounded by the Thompson Chain of Lakes, providing more than 15 fishable lakes within a short range from the park.

★3085★ **LONE PINE STATE PARK**
490 N Meridian
Kalispell, MT 59901
Web: fwp.mt.gov/lands/site_280065.aspx
Phone: 406-752-5501
Size: 243 acres. **Elevation:** 3,520 feet. **Location:** 4 miles southwest of Kalispell on Foy Lake Road, then 1 mile east on Lone Pine Road. **Facilities:** Picnic area, picnic shelters, hiking, bicycling, horseback riding, and interpretive trails, horseshoe pit, volleyball court, visitor center (&&). **Activities:** Hiking, horseback riding, bicycling, wildlife viewing, interpretive programs. **Special Features:** Three scenic overlooks at this day-use park provide views from Flathead Lake to Big Mountain Ski Area. Park is open from April 15 through November 1.

★3086★ **LOST CREEK STATE PARK**
3201 Spurgin Rd
Missoula, MT 59804
Web: fwp.mt.gov/lands/site_280851.aspx
Phone: 406-542-5500
Size: 974 acres. **Elevation:** 6,211 feet. **Location:** 1.5 miles east of Anaconda on Montana 1, then 2 miles north on Secondary 273, then 6 miles west. **Facilities:** 25 campsites, picnic area, interpretive trail, information kiosk. **Activities:** Camping, fishing, hiking, wildlife viewing. **Special Features:** Spectacular gray limestone cliffs and pink and white granite formations rise 1,200 feet above the canyon's narrow floor. A short trail leads to Lost Creek Falls, where water cascades over a 50-foot drop. Mountain goats and bighorn sheep are frequently seen on the cliffs above. Park is open May 1 through November 30.

★3087★ **MADISON BUFFALO JUMP STATE PARK**
1400 S 19th St
Bozeman, MT 59715
Web: fwp.mt.gov/lands/site_281935.aspx
Phone: 406-994-4042
Size: 638 acres. **Elevation:** 4,482 feet. **Location:** 23 miles west of Bozeman on I-90 at Logan exit, then 7 miles south on Buffalo Jump Road. **Facilities:** Picnic area, trails, interpretive displays. **Activities:** Hiking, bicycling. **Special Features:** Prior to the arrival of the horse and gun, native peoples stampeded herds of bison over this cliff to their death. They then used all parts of the buffalo for their food, clothing, and shelter. A hike to the top of the jump affords impressive views of the Madison River Valley.

9. State Parks

★3088★ MAKOSHIKA STATE PARK
PO Box 1242
Glendive, MT 59330
Web: fwp.mt.gov/lands/site_283890.aspx
Phone: 406-377-6256
Size: 27,166 acres. **Elevation:** 2,415 feet. **Location:** Follow signs through town on Snyder Avenue in Glendive. **Facilities:** 22 campsites (8 tent, 14 trailer, 1 ♿), group camp, picnic areas and shelters (♿), hiking and interpretive trails, archery range, rifle range, visitor center, amphitheater. **Activities:** Camping, hiking, bicycling, wildlife viewing, recreational shooting, archery, interpretive programs. **Special Features:** To the Sioux, Ma-ko-shi-ka meant ''bad earth'' or ''bad land,'' descriptive of the weird rock formations and stunted trees that characterize the area. These formations house the fossil remains of 10 species of dinosaurs, including tyrannosaurus and triceratops. The park's visitor center has exhibits explaining the site's geologic, fossil, and prehistoric features.

★3089★ MEDICINE ROCKS STATE PARK
PO Box 1630
Miles City, MT 59301
Web: fwp.mt.gov/lands/site_283951.aspx
Phone: 406-234-0900
Size: 333 acres. **Elevation:** 3,379 feet. **Location:** 25 miles south of Baker on MT 7, mile post 10, then 1 mile west on county road. **Facilities:** 12 campsites (6 tent, 6 trailer), group camp, picnic area, hiking trail. **Activities:** Camping, hiking, bicycling, wildlife viewing. **Special Features:** According to legend, Native American hunters congregated among the park's unique sandstone formations to conjure up magical spirits.

★3090★ MISSOURI HEADWATERS STATE PARK
c/o Region 3 Office
1400 S 19th St
Bozeman, MT 59715
Web: fwp.mt.gov/lands/site_281910.aspx
Phone: 406-994-4042
Size: 535 acres. **Elevation:** 4,045 feet. **Location:** 4 miles northeast of Three Forks, off Highway 205, then onto Highway 286. **Facilities:** 23 campsites (3 tent sites, 20 trailer site, 1 ♿ site), group facilities for camping and picnicking, 1 rental tipi, picnic area (♿), hiking trails (4 miles), interpretive trail, boat ramp (day-use only), restrooms, interpretive displays. **Activities:** Camping, boating (♿), fishing (♿), hiking, bicycling (♿). **Special Features:** Park encompasses the confluence of the Jefferson, Madison, and Gallatin rivers where they converge to form the Missouri River. In 1805, Captain Lewis stood on a limesone cliff and saw the three rivers, which he named after the US President and two cabinet members who financed the Lewis and Clark expedition.

★3091★ PAINTED ROCKS STATE PARK
3201 Spurgin Rd
Missoula, MT 59804
Web: fwp.mt.gov/lands/site_280864.aspx
Phone: 406-542-5500
Size: 323 acres. **Elevation:** 4,724 feet. **Location:** 17 miles south of Hamilton on US 93, then 23 miles southwest on Route 473. **Facilities:** 25 campsites (5 tent, 20 trailer sites), picnic area, picnic shelter, boat ramp (♿), dock. **Activities:** Camping, boating, fishing, swimming, wildlife viewing, snowshoeing, cross-country skiing. **Special Features:** Park is located in a remote pine-forest setting in the scenic Bitterroot Mountains, on Painted Rocks Reservoir.

★3092★ PARKER HOMESTEAD STATE PARK
c/o Lewis & Clark Caverns State Park
PO Box 489
Whitehall, MT 59759
Web: fwp.mt.gov/lands/site_281960.aspx
Phone: 406-287-3541
Size: 1.7 acres. **Elevation:** 4,147 feet. **Location:** 8 miles west of Three Forks on MT 2. **Facilities:** Interpretive displays, picnic table. **Activities:** Picnicking, bicycling. **Special Features:** Park preserves a sod-roofed log cabin built in the early 1900s that is representative of the frontier homes of pioneers who settled in Montana.

★3093★ PICTOGRAPH CAVE STATE PARK
c/o Region 5 Office
2300 Lake Elmo Dr
Billings, MT 59105
Web: fwp.mt.gov/lands/site_283286.aspx
Phone: 406-247-2955
Size: 93 acres. **Elevation:** 3,478 feet. **Location:** In Billings on I-90 at Lockwood exit, then 5miles south on county road. **Facilities:** Picnic area, trails, vault toilet, interpretive displays. **Activities:** Hiking, wildlife viewing. **Special Features:** The Pictograph, Middle, and Ghost cave complex was home to generations of prehistoric hunters, and more than 30,000 artifacts have been identified from the park. A short paved trail allows visitors to view the ancient rock paintings still visible in Pictograph Cave. Site is a National Historic Landmark. The park is open May 1 through September 30.

★3094★ PIROGUE ISLAND STATE PARK
PO Box 1630
Miles City, MT 59301
Web: fwp.mt.gov/lands/site_283962.aspx
Phone: 406-234-0900
Size: 210 acres. **Elevation:** 2,343 feet. **Location:** 1 mile north of Miles City on MT 59, 2 miles east on Kinsey Road, then 2 miles south on county road. **Facilities:** Picnic area, bike trail, hiking trail (2.4 miles), horseback riding trail. **Activities:** Fishing, hiking, bicycling, wildlife viewing, boating (non-motorized only), agate collecting. **Special Features:** This typical cottonwood-covered island on the Yellowstone River provides a natural haven for waterfowl, bald eagles, and white-tailed and mule deer, making it an excellent site for wildlife viewing. It's also a good place to hunt for moss agates. During low water, a small channel can be accessed by foot to get to the island by foot, and access is always available by floating the river. Captain Clark and his men, along with Sacagawea and baby Pomp, are believed to have camped on the island on their return trip east to Saint Louis in 1806.

★3095★ PLACID LAKE STATE PARK

3201 Spurgin Rd
Missoula, MT 59804
Web: fwp.mt.gov/lands/site_280895.aspx
Phone: 406-677-6804
Size: 32 acres. **Elevation:** 4,134 feet. **Location:** 3 miles south of Seeley Lake on MT 83, then 3 miles west on county road. **Facilities:** 41 campsites (20 tent stites, 20 trailer sites, 2 & sites), showers (&), flush toilets, picnic area, picnic shelters, horseshoe pit, volleyball court, boat ramp (single lane), dock, interpretive displays. **Activities:** Camping, boating, fishing, water-skiing, swimming, birdwatching. **Special Features:** Park is located in the Clearwater/Swan River Valley. Interpretive displays at the park explain early logging practices, attested to by giant western larch stumps in the area. Birdwatchers might spot red-necked grebes, osprey or common loons, as well as other waterfowl. The park is open May 1 through November 30.

★3096★ ROSEBUD BATTLEFIELD STATE PARK

PO Box 1630
Miles City, MT 59301
Web: fwp.mt.gov/lands/site_283981.aspx
Phone: 406-234-0900
Size: 3,055 acres. **Elevation:** 4,337 feet. **Location:** 25 miles east of Crow Agency on US 212, 20 miles south on Secondary 314, then 3 miles west on county road. **Facilities:** Picnic area, vault toilet, interpretive displays. **Activities:** Hiking, bicycling, wildlife viewing. **Special Features:** Battlefield is the site of the June 17, 1876 battle in which the Sioux and Cheyenne fought General George Crook's soldiers. This was one of the most intense battles ever waged between Native Americans and the US Army, setting the stage for the Battle of Little Bighorn that would occur eight days later.

★3097★ SALMON LAKE STATE PARK

3201 Spurgin Rd
Missoula, MT 59804
Web: fwp.mt.gov/lands/site_280904.aspx
Phone: 406-677-6804
Size: 42 acres. **Elevation:** 3,917 feet. **Location:** 5 miles south of Seeley Lake on MT 83. **Facilities:** 20 campsites (10 tent, 10 trailer, 1 & site), showers (&), flush toilets (&), picnic area, picnic shelters, horseshoe pit, hiking trail, boat ramp (&), amphitheater, interpretive displays. **Activities:** Camping (seasonal), boating, canoeing, fishing, water-skiing, swimming, hiking, birdwatching, interpretive programs. **Special Features:** The park is set in a woodland area directly adjacent to MT 83 and provides an access point to one of the lakes in the Clearwater River chain of lakes. The park is open May 1 through November 30.

★3098★ SLUICE BOXES STATE PARK

4600 Giant Springs Rd
Great Falls, MT 59406
Web: fwp.mt.gov/lands/site_282818.aspx
Phone: 406-454-5840
Size: 1,451 acres. **Elevation:** 4,216 feet. **Location:** 5 miles south of Belt on US 89, then 0.5 miles west on County Road 340. **Facilities:** Picnic area, backcountry campsite, hiking trail (3 miles). **Activities:** Backcountry camping (permit required), fishing, hiking, river floating, wildlife viewing. **Special Features:** Remains of mines, a railroad, and historic cabins line Belt Creek as it winds through a beautiful canyon carved in limestone. A primitive trail provides access to fishing, challenging floats, and wildlife viewing.

★3099★ SMITH RIVER STATE PARK

4600 Giant Springs Rd
Great Falls, MT 59405
Web: fwp.mt.gov/lands/site_-1.aspx
Phone: 406-454-5840
Location: 16 miles northwest of White Sulphur Springs on Secondary 360, then 7 miles north on county road. **Facilities:** Boat camping areas along the river canyon. **Activities:** Back country camping, fishing, boating, swimming, picnicking, wildlife viewing. **Special Features:** Smith River is a unique 59-mile river corridor with only one public put-in and one public take-out for the entire 59-mile segment of the river. The launch site is at Camp Baker and the take-out site at Eden Bridge, and a permit is required to float the stretch between these two points.

★3100★ SPRING MEADOW LAKE STATE PARK

930 Custer Ave W
Helena, MT 59620
Web: fwp.mt.gov/lands/site_281949.aspx
Phone: 406-495-3270
Size: 62 acres. **Elevation:** 3,911 feet. **Location:** From Helena, travel west on MT 12, then north on Joslyn to Country Club Avenue. **Facilities:** Picnic area, picnic shelters, restrooms, self-guided interpretive trail. **Activities:** Boating (non-motorized), fishing, swimming, scuba diving, hiking, wildlife viewing, interpretive programs. **Special Features:** This urban day-use park, just minutes from Helena, features a view of Mount Helena and a spring-fed lake.

★3101★ THOMPSON FALLS STATE PARK

490 N Meridian Rd
Kalispell, MT 59901
Web: fwp.mt.gov/lands/site_280084.aspx
Phone: 406-752-5501
Size: 36 acres. **Elevation:** 2,362 feet. **Location:** 1 mile northwest of Thompson Falls on MT 200. **Facilities:** 17 campsites (3 tent, 14 trailer sites), group camping area, vault toilets, picnic area, picnic shelters, boat ramp (&). **Activities:** Camping, boating, fishing, swimming, bird watching. **Special Features:** Park is located in a mature pine forest on the Clark Fork River, with excellent fishing and boating opportunities on the river or on Noxon Rapids Reservoir. The park is open May 1 through September 30.

★3102★ TONGUE RIVER RESERVOIR STATE PARK

PO Box 1630
Miles City, MT 59301
Web: fwp.mt.gov/lands/site_283967.aspx
Phone: 406-234-0900
Size: 642 acres. **Elevation:** 3,468 feet. **Location:** 6 miles north

9. State Parks

of Decker on Secondary 314, then 1 mile east on county road. **Facilities:** 106 campsites (16 tent sites, 90 trailer sites), vault toilets, picnic area, picnic shelters, food concession, fish cleaning station, marina, boat rentals (seasonally), boat ramp (占). **Activities:** Camping, boating, fishing, swimming, wildlife viewing. **Special Features:** Park's 12-mile-long reservoir is set amid scenic red shale, juniper canyons, and open prairies of southeastern Montana.

★3103★ TOWER ROCK STATE PARK

4600 Giant Springs
Great Falls, MT 59405
Web: fwp.mt.gov/lands/site_6844284.aspx
Phone: 406-454-5840
Size: 140 acres. **Elevation:** 3,796 feet. **Location:** Hardy Creek exit off I-15, about 40 miles south of Great Falls, between Craig and Pelican Point. **Facilities:** Undeveloped, with only an nterpretive trail and information kiosk. **Activities:** Hiking, wildlife viewing. **Special Features:** Tower Rock is a landmark noted by Captain Meriweather Lewis in his journal in 1805. The rock formation is 424 feet high and stands in the mouth of the canyon where the Missouri River flows from the mountains to the plains. Plans are to leave the park basically undeveloped except for a small parking area, hiking trails, and interpretive signs.

★3104★ TRAVELERS REST STATE PARK

PO Box 995
Lolo, MT 59847
Web: fwp.mt.gov/lands/site_2233810.aspx
Phone: 406-273-4253
Size: 73 acres. **Elevation:** 3,176 feet. **Location:** 8 miles south of Missoula to Lolo, then 0.5 miles west on US 12. **Facilities:** Picnic area, picnic shelter, interpretive trail, information kiosk, vault toilets. **Activities:** Fishing, hiking, wildlife viewing, interpretive programs. **Special Features:** Lewis and Clark's expedition twice camped at this site, in 1805 and 1806. Site is one of only two in the US with physical proof that Lewis and Clark were there. Travelers Rest Preservation & Heritage Association manages the site for Montana Fish, Wildlife and Parks Department.

★3105★ ULM PISHKUN STATE PARK

PO Box 109
Ulm, MT 59485
Web: fwp.mt.gov/lands/site_282807.aspx
Phone: 406-866-2217
Size: 1,599 acres. **Elevation:** 3,593 feet. **Location:** 10 miles south of Great Falls on I-15 at Ulm Exit, then 6 miles northwest on Ulm-Vaughn road. **Facilities:** Picnic area, trails, visitor center, meeting room. **Activities:** Hiking, wildlife viewing, interpretive programs. **Special Features:** This prehistoric bison kill site consists of a mile-long buffalo jump, or ''pishkun,'' thought to be the largest in the United States. The modern visitor center features displays and activities that explain the importance of the buffalo to the native people of the Plains. The top of the jump offers panoramic views of the Rocky Mountain Front, the

Missouri River, and the buttes and grasslands that characterize the area.

★3106★ WAYFARERS STATE PARK

490 N Meridian Rd
Kalispell, MT 59901
Web: fwp.mt.gov/lands/site_280159.aspx
Phone: 406-752-5501
Size: 68 acres. **Elevation:** 2,923 feet. **Location:** 0.5 miles south of Bigfork on MT 35. **Facilities:** 30 campsites (7 tent sites, 23 trailer sites, 1 占 site), showers, flush toilets, picnic area, group-use shelter, hiking trail, boat ramp, dock. **Activities:** Camping, boating, fishing, hiking, swimming, wildlife viewing. **Special Features:** Park is situated on the northeast shore of Flathead Lake, within walking distance of Bigfork. It offers nature walks along the rocky shoreline to the cliffs, with excellent views of the lake and summer wildflowers. Visitors are cautioned to be aware this is bear country, so items should not be stored in tents or soft-topped vehicles.

★3107★ WEST SHORE STATE PARK

490 N Meridian Rd
Kalispell, MT 59901
Web: fwp.mt.gov/lands/site_280091.aspx
Phone: 406-752-5501
Size: 129 acres. **Elevation:** 3,130 feet. **Location:** 20 miles south of Kalispell on US 93. **Facilities:** 26 campsites (6 tent sites, 20 trailer sites, 1 占 site), vault toilets, picnic area, boat ramp (占). **Activities:** Camping, boating, fishing, swimming. **Special Features:** Park is considered the most private on Flathead Lake. It is located in a mature pine, fir, and larch forest, and the park's glacially-carved rock outcrops offer spectacular views of Flathead Lake and the Swan and Mission mountain ranges. Visitors are cautioned to be aware this is bear country, so items should not be stored in tents or soft-topped vehicles.

★3108★ WHITEFISH LAKE STATE PARK

490 N Meridian Rd
Kalispell, MT 59901
Web: fwp.mt.gov/lands/site_280100.aspx
Phone: 406-862-3991
Size: 11 acres. **Elevation:** 3,012 feet. **Location:** 1 mile west of Whitefish on US 93, then 1 mile north. **Facilities:** 31 campsites (6 tent sites, 25 trailer sites, 1 占 site), showers, flush toilets, primitive hike-in/bike-in site, picnic area, picnic shelters, boat ramp (占), boat dock. **Activities:** Camping, boating, fishing, swimming, water-skiing, bicycling. **Special Features:** Park is located along the shore of Whitefish Lake in a mature forest just outside Whitefish. The lake is rarely windy, so it provides an excellent place for water-skiing.

★3109★ WILD HORSE ISLAND STATE PARK

490 N Meridian Rd
Kalispell, MT 59901
Web: fwp.mt.gov/lands/site_280179.aspx
Phone: 406-752-5501
Size: 2,164 acres. **Elevation:** 3,392 feet. **Location:** On Flathead

Lake, across from Big Arm State Park via boat to Little Skeeko Bay on the northwest side of the island. **Facilities:** Hiking trails (1 mile), vault toilet (composting). **Activities:** Fishing, swimming, hiking, wildlife viewing. **Special Features:** Island is the largest on Flathead Lake, and boat access is regulated to protect it. It preserves an endangered palouse prairie environment, historic resources, and wildlife, including bighorn sheep, mule deer, and wild horses. The Salish-Kootenai Indians were reported to have used the island to pasture horses to keep them from being stolen by other tribes.

★3110★ YELLOW BAY STATE PARK
490 N Meridian Rd
Kalispell, MT 59901
Web: fwp.mt.gov/lands/site_280115.aspx
Phone: 406-752-5501
Size: 15 acres. **Elevation:** 2,907 feet. **Location:** 15 miles north of Polson on MT 35. **Facilities:** 4 walk-in tent campsites, flush toilets, picnic area, picnic shelter, marina, dock, boat ramp (&). **Activities:** Camping, boating, fishing, swimming, scuba diving, bird watching. **Special Features:** Park is situated on Flathead Lake in the heart of Montana's sweet cherry orchards. Visitors can enjoy the cherry blossoms that color the hillsides in spring or sample the cherries in season at a nearby fruit stand.

Nebraska State Parks

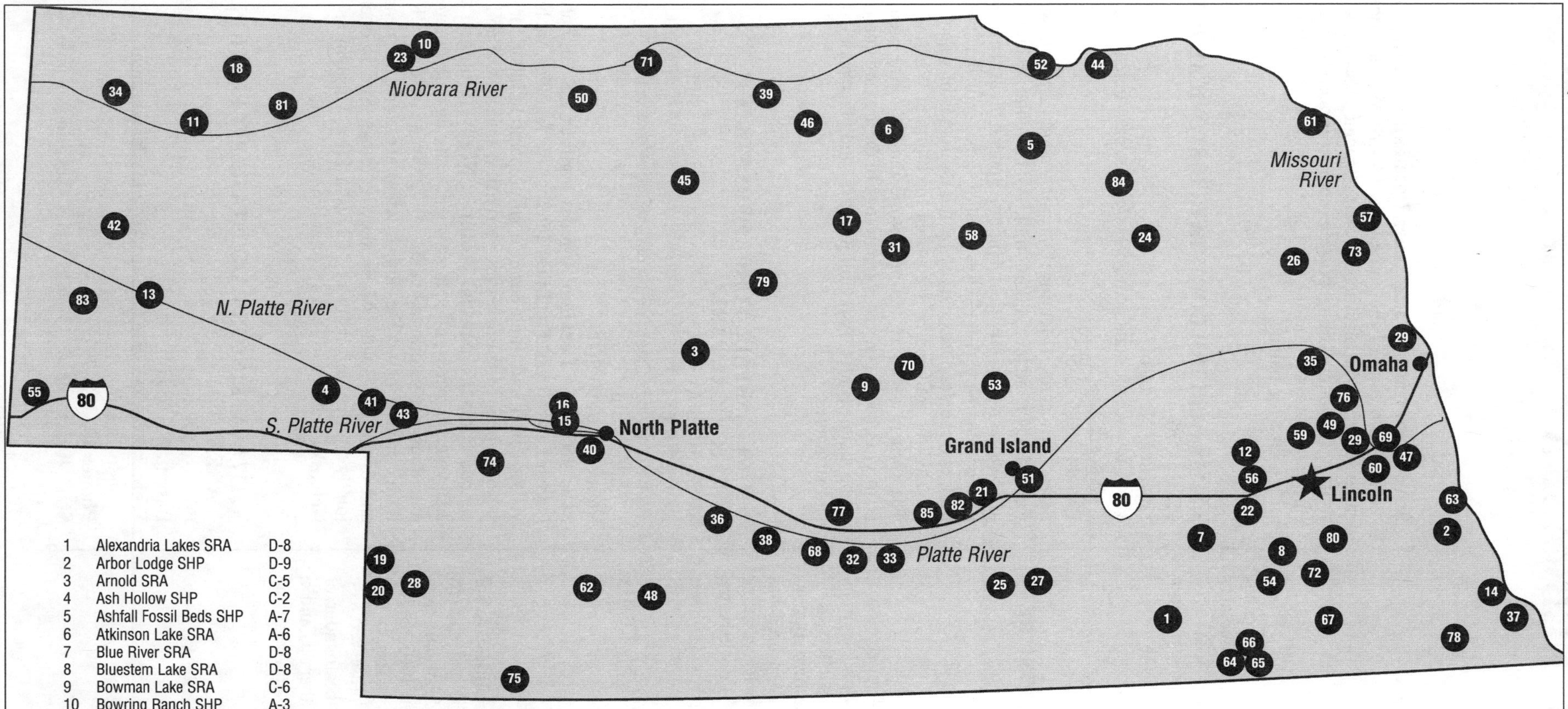

Map labels: Missouri River · Niobrara River · N. Platte River · S. Platte River · Platte River · Omaha · Lincoln · Grand Island · North Platte · I-80

#	Park	Grid
1	Alexandria Lakes SRA	D-8
2	Arbor Lodge SHP	D-9
3	Arnold SRA	C-5
4	Ash Hollow SHP	C-2
5	Ashfall Fossil Beds SHP	A-7
6	Atkinson Lake SRA	A-6
7	Blue River SRA	D-8
8	Bluestem Lake SRA	D-8
9	Bowman Lake SRA	C-6
10	Bowring Ranch SHP	A-3
11	Box Butte Reservoir SRA	A-2
12	Branched Oak SRA	C-8
13	Bridgeport SRA	B-1
14	Brownville SRA	D-10
15	Buffalo Bill Ranch SHP	C-4
16	Buffalo Bill Ranch SRA	C-4
17	Calamus Reservoir SRA	B-6
18	Chadron SP	A-2
19	Champion Lake SRA	D-3
20	Champion Mill SHP	D-3
21	Cheyenne SRA	D-6
22	Conestoga Lake SRA	D-8
23	Cottonwood Lake SRA	A-3
24	Cowboy State Recreation Trail	B-7
25	Crystal Lake SRA	D-7
26	Dead Timber SRA	B-8
27	DLD SRA	D-7
28	Enders Reservoir SRA	D-3
29	Eugene T. Mahoney SP	C-9
30	Fort Atkinson SHP	C-9
31	Fort Hartsuff SHP	B-6
32	Fort Kearny SRA	D-6
33	Fort Kearny SHP	D-6
34	Fort Robinson SP	A-1
35	Fremont Lakes SRA	C-8
36	Gallagher Canyon SRA	D-5
37	Indian Cave SP	D-10
38	Johnson Lake SRA	D-5
39	Keller Park SRA	A-5
40	Lake Maloney SRA	C-4
41	Lake McConaughy SRA	C-3
42	Lake Minatare SRA	B-1
43	Lake Ogallala SRA	C-3
44	Lewis & Clark SRA	A-7
45	Long Lake SRA	B-5
46	Long Pine SRA	A-5
47	Louisville SRA	C-9
48	Medicine Creek SRA	D-4
49	Memphis SRA	C-9
50	Merritt Reservoir SRA	A-4
51	Mormon Island SRA	C-7
52	Niobrara SP	A-7
53	North Loup SRA	C-7
54	Olive Creek Lake SRA	D-8
55	Oliver Reservoir SRA	C-1
56	Pawnee SRA	C-8
57	Pelican Point SRA	B-9
58	Pibel Lake SRA	B-6
59	Pioneer SRA	C-8
60	Platte River SP	C-9
61	Ponca SP	A-8
62	Red Willow Reservoir SRA	D-4
63	Riverview Marina SRA	D-9
64	Rock Creek Lake SRA	E-8
65	Rock Creek Station SHP	E-8
66	Rock Creek Station SRA	E-8
67	Rockford Lake SRA	D-9
68	Sandy Channel SRA	D-5
69	Schramm Park SRA	C-9
70	Sherman Reservoir SRA	C-6
71	Smith Falls SP	A-4
72	Stagecoach Lake SRA	D-8
73	Summit Lake SRA	B-9
74	Sutherland Reservoir SRA	C-3
75	Swanson Reservoir SRA	E-4
76	Two Rivers SRA	C-9
77	Union Pacific SRA	D-6
78	Verdon SRA	D-9
79	Victoria Springs SRA	B-5
80	Wagon Train SRA	D-9
81	Walgren Lake SRA	A-2
82	War Axe SRA	D-6
83	Wildcat Hills SRA	B-1
84	Willow Creek SRA	B-7
85	Windmill SRA	D-6

SHP   State Historical Park
SP   State Park
SRA   State Recreation Area

NEBRASKA

★3111★ Nebraska Game & Parks Commission
2200 N 33rd St
PO Box 30370
Lincoln, NE 68503
(402) 471-0641 - Phone
Web: www.ngpc.state.ne.us/parks
Manages 87 park properties, including state parks, historic sites, and numerous state recreation areas. Oversees wildlife management areas and operates fish hatcheries. Administers boat registrations and hunting and fishing licenses. Promotes outdoor safety education and facilitates state trail development.

★3112★ ALEXANDRIA STATE RECREATION AREA
57426 710th Rd
Fairbury, NE 68352
Web: www.ngpc.state.ne.us/parks/guides/parksearch/
findpark.asp
Phone: 402-729-5777
Size: 55 acres land; 46 acres water. **Location:** 4 miles east of Alexandria. **Facilities:** 46 non-pad campsites with electrical hookups, modern restrooms, picnic tables, picnic shelters, food concession. **Activities:** Camping, boating (non-motorized), fishing, mountain biking. **Special Features:** Recreation area has two lakes for fishing and is about 22 miles from Rock Creek Station State Historical Park, where Wild Bill Hickok began his career as a gunfighter.

★3113★ ARBOR LODGE STATE HISTORICAL PARK
PO Box 15
Nebraska City, NE 68410
Web: www.ngpc.state.ne.us/parks/guides/parksearch/
findpark.asp
Phone: 402-873-7222
Size: 72 acres. **Location:** In Nebraska City. **Facilities:** Arbor Lodge Museum, modern restrooms, picnic areas and shelter, trail, arboretum. **Special Features:** A stately, 52-room, neo-colonial mansion, Arbor Lodge was completed in 1903 by Joy Morton, founder of the Morton Salt Company. House and grounds were donated to the state in 1923 to be preserved as a monument to Joy's father, J. Sterling Morton, the founder of Arbor Day. Furnishings in the mansion are authentic, and a collection of antique carriages and wagons is displayed in the carriage house.

★3114★ ARNOLD STATE RECREATION AREA
HC 69, Box 117
Anselmo, NE 68813
Web: www.ngpc.state.ne.us/parks/guides/parksearch/
findpark.asp
Phone: 308-749-2235

Size: 10 acres land; 22 acres water. **Location:** In Custer County, on the south edge of the community of Arnold. **Facilities:** 80 campsites (20 with electrical hookups), picnic areas, dock. **Activities:** Camping, fishing, boating (nonpower or electric motor). **Special Features:** Arnold SRA is a primitive recreation area with a lake for fishing.

★3115★ ASH HOLLOW STATE HISTORICAL PARK
PO Box 70
Lewellen, NE 69147
Web: www.ngpc.state.ne.us/parks/guides/parksearch/
findpark.asp
Phone: 308-778-5651
Size: 1,001 acres. **Location:** 3.5 miles southeast of Lewellen. **Facilities:** Picnic area, hiking trail, visitor center, exhibits, historic structures. **Activities:** Hiking. **Special Features:** Sweet spring water made Ash Hollow a major stopover on the Overland trail, and the deep ruts carved by the thousands of wagons that traveled the trail can be seen from the bluffs at Windlass Hill. The springs also attracted prehistoric Indians to the area. The history, archaeology, and paleontology of the area are interpreted at the visitor center, Ash Hollow Cave, and other park exhibits and structures.

★3116★ ASHFALL FOSSIL BEDS STATE HISTORICAL PARK
86930 517th Ave
Royal, NE 68773
Web: www.ngpc.state.ne.us/parks/guides/parksearch/
findpark.asp
Phone: 402-893-2000
Size: 360 acres. **Location:** 6 miles north of US 20, between Orchard and Royal. **Facilities:** Interpretive facilities, including visitor center and rhino barn, fossil preparation laboratory, restrooms, picnic facilities, trail. **Activities:** Interpretive and educational programs. **Special Features:** Nearly 12 million years ago, volcanic ash engulfed this ancient watering hole, entombing numerous prehistoric animals. A 2,000-square-foot ''Rhino Barn'' protects part of the deposit, where skeletons are unearthed and displayed exactly where they're found. Site is operated jointly by the University of Nebraska State Museum and the Nebraska Game and Parks Commission.

★3117★ ATKINSON LAKE STATE RECREATION AREA
PO Box 508
Bassett, NE 68714
Web: www.ngpc.state.ne.us/parks/guides/parksearch/
findpark.asp
Phone: 402-684-2921
Size: 40 acres land; 14 acres water. **Location:** 1 mile west of

the town of Atkinson, just off US 20 and Holt county road. **Facilities:** 28 campsites (8 with electrical hookups), vault toilets, drinking water, hiking trail (1 miles), picnic areas, 2 picnic shelters, playground. **Activities:** Camping, boating (nonpower or electric motor), fishing, wildlife viewing. **Special Features:** Recreation area includes the Bluebird Trail, a half-mile trail with 12 bluebird houses and four benches on which visitors can rest and view these rare birds.

★3118★ BLUE RIVER STATE RECREATION AREA
3019 Apple St
Lincoln, NE 68503
Web: www.ngpc.state.ne.us/parks/guides/parksearch/
findpark.asp
Phone: 402-471-0641
Size: 14 acres. **Location:** 5 miles north of Dorchester, in Seward County. **Facilities:** Picnic areas, drinking water, river access. **Activities:** Fishing, picnicking. **Special Features:** This is a day use area located next to the Big Blue River. No camping is allowed.

★3119★ BLUESTEM STATE RECREATION AREA
3019 Apple St
Lincoln, NE 68503
Web: www.ngpc.state.ne.us/parks/guides/parksearch/
findpark.asp
Phone: 402-471-5545
Size: 417 acres land; 325 acres water. **Location:** 2.5 miles west of Sprague. **Facilities:** 219 campsites (19 with pads; none with electrical hookups), primitive restrooms, drinking water, picnic areas, 3 boat ramps, 4 docks, swimming beach, archery range. **Activities:** Camping, boating (all types, but 5 mph limit), fishing, swimming, hunting. **Special Features:** Lake's diverse fish population includes largemouth bass, bluegill, channel catfish, walleye, northern pike, and other species.

★3120★ BOWMAN LAKE STATE RECREATION AREA
RR 2, Box 117
Loup City, NE 68853
Web: www.ngpc.state.ne.us/parks/guides/parksearch/
findpark.asp
Phone: 308-745-0230
Size: 23 acres land; 20 acres water. **Location:** 0.5 miles west of Loup City. **Facilities:** 10 primitive campsites, drinking water, picnic tables and grills. **Activities:** Camping, boating (nonpower or electric motor), fishing. **Special Features:** Area is adjacent to the Loup River and features a man-made lake.

★3121★ BOWRING RANCH STATE HISTORICAL PARK
PO Box 38
Merriman, NE 69218
Web: www.ngpc.state.ne.us/parks/guides/parksearch/
findpark.asp
Phone: 308-684-3428
Size: 325 acres. **Location:** Just north and east of Merriman.

Facilities: Visitor center, picnic tables, modern restrooms. **Special Features:** Site is a Hereford demonstration ranch donated to the state by former US Senator Eve Bowring in memory of her husband. The ranch house displays include memorabilia from their public service careers, and the visitor center interprets ranching, homesteading, geology, wildlife, and other areas related to the Sandhills and the Bowrings.

★3122★ BOX BUTTE RESERVOIR STATE RECREATION AREA
PO Box 392
Crawford, NE 69339
Web: www.ngpc.state.ne.us/parks/guides/parksearch/
findpark.asp
Phone: 308-665-2903
Size: 612 acres land; 1,600 acres water. **Location:** 9.5 miles north of Hemmingford, in Dawes County. **Facilities:** 54 campsites (14 with pads and electrical hookups), vault toilets, drinking water, picnic areas, 4 picnic shelters, 2 boat ramps, 2 docks, fish cleaning station, swimming beach. **Activities:** Camping, boating (no restrictions), fishing, swimming, hiking. **Special Features:** Area is located on the west edge of the Sandhills in the Nebraska panhandle. Box Butte Reservoir is an impoundment on the Niobrara River.

★3123★ BRANCHED OAK STATE RECREATION AREA
12000 W Branched Oak Rd
Raymond, NE 68428
Web: www.ngpc.state.ne.us/parks/guides/parksearch/
findpark.asp
Phone: 402-783-3400
Size: 3,795 acres land; 1,800 acres water. **Location:** 2.5 miles north of Malcolm, off S-55M, 4 miles west of Raymond. **Facilities:** 599 campsites (320 have camping pads, 287 with electrical hookups; 12 sites have full hookups), modern restrooms, showers, equestrian camping area, picnic areas, 41 picnic shelters (1 with electricity), playgrounds, hiking trails (7 miles), mountain bike trails (6 miles), equestrian trails (3 miles), marina, camp store, restaurant, boat rentals, 9 boat ramps, 49 docks, 2 fish cleaning stations, 2 swimming beaches (unsupervised), dog trial area. **Activities:** Camping, boating (no restrictions), fishing, swimming, hiking, horseback riding, mountain biking. **Special Features:** Branched Oak is the largest of the Salt Valley lakes near Lincoln.

★3124★ BRIDGEPORT STATE RECREATION AREA
PO Box 65
Gering, NE 69341
Web: www.ngpc.state.ne.us/parks/guides/parksearch/
findpark.asp
Phone: 308-436-2383
Size: 119 acres land; 78 acres water. **Location:** On the north edge of the town of Bridgeport, on US 26-US 385. **Facilities:** 130 primitive campsites, vault toilets, drinking water, picnic areas, picnic shelter, playground, 2 boat ramps, 2 docks, swimming beach (unsupervised). **Activities:** Primitive camping, boating (all types), fishing, swimming. **Special Features:** Area was

once a sand and gravel pumping operation and now has 4 sandpit lakes. All boat types are permitted on Center Lake, but all must travel in a counter clockwise direction and speeds are limited to 5 mph in the bay area at the southwest edge of the lake. Boating in the other lakes is limited to electric or non-powered boats.

★3125★ BROWNVILLE STATE RECREATION AREA

c/o Indian Cave State Park
RR 1, Box 30
Shubert, NE 68437
Web: www.ngpc.state.ne.us/parks/guides/parksearch/
findpark.asp
Phone: 402-883-2575
Size: 22 acres. **Location:** Southeast of Brownville, off Highway 136. **Facilities:** 14 campsites, latrines, drinking water, picnic tables, picnic shelter, river access, boat ramp. **Activities:** Primitive camping, boating (all types), fishing. **Special Features:** Located on the Missouri River, the area is home of historic Meriwether Lewis Dredge Museum, operated by the Meriwether Lewis Foundation.

★3126★ BUFFALO BILL RANCH STATE HISTORICAL PARK

2921 Scouts Rest Ranch Rd
North Platte, NE 69101
Web: www.ngpc.state.ne.us/parks/guides/parksearch/
findpark.asp
Phone: 308-535-8035
Size: 25 acres. **Location:** 1 mile west of North Platte. **Facilities:** Museum. **Special Features:** Colonel William F. ''Buffalo Bill'' Cody (1846-1917) built his North Platte home during the heyday of his famous Wild West Show. Cody owned some 4,000 acres here, named Scout's Rest Ranch. The park includes the house and barn, which have been restored, as well as a wealth of Cody memorabilia.

★3127★ BUFFALO BILL RANCH STATE RECREATION AREA

2921 Scouts Rest Ranch Rd
North Platte, NE 69101
Web: www.ngpc.state.ne.us/parks/guides/parksearch/
findpark.asp
Phone: 308-535-8035
Size: 233 acres. **Location:** 1 mile west of North Platte, off I-80 at the North Platte interchange. **Facilities:** 43 campsites (23 are camping pads with electrical hookups), modern restrooms, picnic tables, picnic shelter, hiking trails (5 miles), river access. **Activities:** Camping, fishing, hiking. **Special Features:** Park is adjacent to Buffalo Bill Ranch State Historical Park, site of Buffalo Bill Cody's ranch home (see separate entry).

★3128★ CALAMUS STATE RECREATION AREA

HC 79, Box 20L
Burwell, NE 68823
Web: www.ngpc.state.ne.us/parks/guides/parksearch/
findpark.asp
Phone: 308-346-5666
Size: 4,958 acres land; 5,124 acres water. **Location:** 6 miles northwest of Burwell on Highway 96. **Facilities:** 177 campsites (122 camping pads with electrical hookups), modern restrooms, showers, vault toilets, picnic areas, swimming beach, food concession, 5 boat ramps, 5 docks, 2 fish cleaning stations, fish hatchery. **Activities:** Camping, boating (all types; 5 mph limit), fishing, swimming, hunting, self-guided tours of hatchery. **Special Features:** Located in the heart of the Sandhills, Calamus is Nebraska's newest major reservoir and the site of a state fish hatchery.

★3129★ CHADRON STATE PARK

15951 Hwy 385
Chadron, NE 69337
Web: www.ngpc.state.ne.us/parks/guides/parksearch/
findpark.asp
Phone: 308-432-6167
Size: 972 acres. **Location:** 9 miles south of Chadron on US 385. **Facilities:** 88 campsites (70 with electrical hookups), modern restrooms, showers, 22 cabins, picnic areas, 5 picnic shelters, playground, craft center, snack bar, swimming pool, hiking trails (6 miles), mountain bike trails (4 miles), mountain bike rentals, paddleboat rentals, concessions. **Activities:** Camping, fishing, swimming, hiking, mountain biking, horseback trail rides, interpretive programs. **Special Features:** At an elevation of nearly 5,000 feet, park lies in the heart of the Nebraska National Forest (see separate entry in national forests section) and is dominated by ponderosa pines.

★3130★ CHAMPION LAKE STATE RECREATION AREA

73122 338 Ave
Enders, NE 69027
Web: www.ngpc.state.ne.us/parks/guides/parksearch/
findpark.asp
Phone: 308-394-5118
Size: 2 acres land; 11 acres water. **Location:** 0.5 miles west of Champion, off US 6 or S-15A. **Facilities:** 8 campsites (all non-pad, 1 with electrical hookup), drinking water, picnic tables and grills, dock. **Activities:** Primitive camping, boating (nonpower or electric motor), fishing. **Special Features:** Area is located on an 11-acre lake near Champion Mill State Historical Park (see separate entry).

★3131★ CHAMPION MILL STATE HISTORICAL PARK

73122 338 Ave
Enders, NE 69027
Web: www.ngpc.state.ne.us/parks/guides/parksearch/
findpark.asp
Phone: 308-394-5118
Size: 4 acres. **Location:** In the town of Champion, west of Ogallala. **Facilities:** 3 picnic tables, trail, park office; camping available at the adjacent Champion Lake State Recreational Area (see separate entry). **Activities:** Tours of the mill building and grounds. **Special Features:** The last functional water-powered mill in Nebraska, Champion Mill stands as a symbol of the settlement and development of Nebraska and the West.

★3132★ CHEYENNE STATE RECREATION AREA
PO Box 944
Grand Island, NE 68832
Web: www.ngpc.state.ne.us/parks/guides/parksearch/
findpark.asp
Phone: 308-385-6210
Size: 18 acres land; 15 acres water. Location: At Wood River Interchange off I-80 (Exit 300). Facilities: 15 campsites, modern restrooms, picnic tables and grills, 3 picnic shelters. Activities: Primitive camping, boating (nonpower or electric motor), fishing. Special Features: Cheyenne SRA is a former wayside area.

★3133★ CONESTOGA STATE RECREATION AREA
RR 4, Box 41B
Lincoln, NE 68524
Web: www.ngpc.state.ne.us/parks/guides/parksearch/
findpark.asp
Phone: 402-796-2362
Size: 486 acres land; 230 acres water. Location: 2 miles north of Denton. Facilities: 57 campsites (33 with camping pads, of which 25 have electrical hookups), drinking water, hiking and mountain bike trails (2 miles), picnic areas, 2 picnic shelters, boat ramp, 8 docks, fish cleaning station. Activities: Camping, boating (all types), fishing, wildlife viewing. Special Features: Conestoga is a flood-control reservoir that offers power boating. It is located just 20 miles from Lincoln.

★3134★ COTTONWOOD LAKE STATE
RECREATION AREA
PO Box 38
Merriman, NE 69218
Web: www.ngpc.state.ne.us/parks/guides/parksearch/
findpark.asp
Phone: 308-684-3428
Size: 180 acres land; 60 acres water. Location: 0.5 miles east and 0.5 miles south of Merriman, off US 20. Facilities: 30 campsites, water, picnic areas and shelters, boat ramp, boat dock, playground. Activities: Camping, boating (all types), fishing. Special Features: Cottonwood has a typical sandhills lake and allows power boating. It is located near Bowring Ranch State Historical Park (see separate entry).

★3135★ COWBOY STATE RECREATION TRAIL
c/o District III Office
2201 N 13th St
Norfolk, NE 68701
Web: www.ngpc.state.ne.us/infoeduc/cowboy.html
Phone: 402-370-3374
Size: 321 linear miles when finished; 3,893 acres. Location: From Norfolk to Chadron, parallel to US 275 and US 20. Facilities: Finished trail segments include a 34-mile section between Norfolk and Nehigh, 8 miles between Inman and O'Neill, 4 miles through Valentine toward the east, and through the towns of Long Pine and Ainsworth. Activities: Hiking, bicycling, horseback riding, cross-country skiing. Special Features: On the historic route of Chicago and Northwestern Railroad, the Cowboy State Recreation Trail will lead through most of the

length of Nebraska, making it the longest rails-to-trails conversion in the U.S. Along its route, the trail will eventually pass over 221 bridges and through 29 communities.

★3136★ CRYSTAL LAKE STATE RECREATION
AREA
7425 S US Hwy 281
Doniphan, NE 68832
Web: www.ngpc.state.ne.us/parks/guides/parksearch/
findpark.asp
Phone: 308-385-6210
Size: 33 acres land; 30 acres water. Location: 1.5 miles north of Ayr, off US 281. Facilities: 70 campsites (20 with electrical hookups), water, picnic areas and shelters, dock, swimming beach, tennis court, playground, river access. Activities: Camping, boating (nonpower or electric motor), fishing, swimming, tennis. Special Features: In addition to its own 30-acre lake, recreation area is adjacent to Little Blue River and offers access to it.

★3137★ DEAD TIMBER STATE RECREATION AREA
227 County Rd & 12 Blvd
Scribner, NE 68057
Web: www.ngpc.state.ne.us/parks/guides/parksearch/
findpark.asp
Phone: 402-664-3597
Size: 150 acres land; 50 acres water. Location: 4 miles north of Scribner on US 275, then 1.5 miles east and 0.5 miles south. Facilities: 42 campsites (including 17 camping pads with electrical hookups), drinking water, latrines, picnic areas, 4 picnic shelters (1 with electricity), river access. Activities: Camping, boating (non-motorized), fishing. Special Features: Area is adjacent to the Elkhorn River.

★3138★ DLD STATE RECREATION AREA
7425 S US Hwy 281
Doniphan, NE 68832
Web: www.ngpc.state.ne.us/parks/guides/parksearch/
findpark.asp
Phone: 308-385-6211
Size: 7 acres. Location: 5 miles east of Hastings on US 6. Facilities: 4 campsites, 3 picnic tables with grills, picnic shelter. Activities: Primitive camping, picnicking. Special Features: Site was formerly designated a wayside area and offers US Highway 6 travelers a roadside rest.

★3139★ ENDERS RESERVOIR STATE RECREATION
AREA
73122 338th Ave
Enders, NE 69027
Web: www.ngpc.state.ne.us/parks/guides/parksearch/
findpark.asp
Phone: 308-394-5118
Size: 3,278 acres land (including waterfowl refuge); 1,707 acres water. Location: South of the village of Enders on US 6 - NE 61; 5 miles east and 4.5 miles south of Imperial. Facilities: 232 campsites (32 with electrical hookups; 8 of these have camping

pads), modern restrooms as well as vault toilets, coin-operated showers, picnic areas, 7 picnic shelters, boat ramp, dock, fish cleaning station. **Activities:** Camping, boating (all types), water-skiing, fishing, hunting, winter sports. **Special Features:** A portion of the land along the western side of the lake is designated a waterfowl refuge.

★3140★ EUGENE T. MAHONEY STATE PARK

28500 W Park Hwy
Ashland, NE 68003
Web: www.ngpc.state.ne.us/parks/guides/parksearch/
findpark.asp
Phone: 402-944-2523
Size: 690 acres land; 16 acres water. **Location:** 2 miles from Ashland, just off I-80 at Exit 426. **Facilities:** 149 campsites with electrical hookups, modern restrooms, showers, 51 cabins, 40-room lodge (with restaurant, gift shop, and meeting rooms), picnic areas, 10 picnic shelters, hiking trail (7 miles), swimming pool with 2 waterslides, marina, camp store, paddleboat rental, docks, observation tower, mini-theater, nature conservatory, driving range, miniature golf course, tennis and basketball courts, softball fields, activity center with indoor playground, ice skating rink, and concession stand, visitor center. **Activities:** Camping, fishing, hiking, swimming, tennis, softball, volleyball, miniature golf, cross-country skiing, horseback trail rides, ice skating, sledding, interpretive and entertainment programs. **Special Features:** The park is situated along the Platte River and is designed for year-round recreational activities and accommodations.

★3141★ FORT ATKINSON STATE HISTORICAL PARK

PO Box 240
Fort Calhoun, NE 68023
Web: www.ngpc.state.ne.us/parks/guides/parksearch/
findpark.asp
Phone: 402-468-5611; **Fax:** 402-468-5066
Size: 157 acres. **Location:** 1 mile east of Fort Calhoun and 9 miles northeast of Omaha. **Facilities:** Historic structures, visitor center, picnic tables, hiking trails, modern restrooms. **Activities:** Living history demonstrations, picnicking, hiking. **Special Features:** Established in 1820 on the recommendation of the Lewis and Clark Expedition, Fort Atkinson was the first US military post west of the Missouri River and was important to early fur trade, river traffic, and Indian relations. Much of the historic outpost has been reconstructed, and living history demonstrations are scheduled during the summer months.

★3142★ FORT HARTSUFF STATE HISTORICAL PARK

RR 1, Box 37
Burwell, NE 68823
Web: www.ngpc.state.ne.us/parks/guides/parksearch/
findpark.asp
Phone: 308-346-4715
Size: 18 acres. **Location:** Near Elyria, between Ord and Burwell on Highway 11. **Facilities:** Historic site, visitor center, gift shop, picnic tables, restrooms. **Special Features:** Built in the style

typical of Plains infantry outposts, Fort Hartsuff stood as a buffer between settlers and Indians in the North Loup River valley from 1874-1881. Park has been restored to its 1870s appearance, when soldiers patrolled the Loup and Cedar river valleys and pioneered a new trail to the Black Hills gold fields.

★3143★ FORT KEARNY STATE HISTORICAL PARK

1020 'V' Rd
Kearney, NE 68847
Web: www.ngpc.state.ne.us/parks/guides/parksearch/
findpark.asp
Phone: 308-865-5305
Size: 39 acres. **Location:** 6 miles southeast of Kearney. **Facilities:** Interpretive center; camping and other facilities available at nearby Fort Kearny State Recreation Area (see separate entry). **Special Features:** Built to protect Overland Trail travelers, Fort Kearney was a stagecoach station, a Pony Express home station, a military depot to outfit soldiers for Indian campaigns, and home of the Pawnee Scouts. The stockade, parade grounds, and blacksmith shop have been rebuilt, and exhibits in the interpretive center provide insights into conditions and events during the time the American West was settled.

★3144★ FORT KEARNY STATE RECREATION AREA

c/o Fort Kearny State Historical Park
1020 'V' Rd
Kearney, NE 68847
Web: www.ngpc.state.ne.us/parks/guides/parksearch/
findpark.asp
Phone: 308-865-5305
Size: 163 acres land; 23 acres water. **Location:** 1 mile east and 1 mile north of the Fort Kearney State Historical Park. **Facilities:** 110 campsites (75 with electrical hookups), modern restrooms, showers, picnic areas, 3 picnic shelters (1 with electricity), trails (5 miles), swimming beach, fishing pier (&), river access. **Activities:** Camping, boating (non-power), fishing, swimming, hiking, mountain biking. **Special Features:** In spring, the recreation area is a popular destination for bird watchers who come to see the world's largest concentration of sandhill cranes, as the cranes and other migratory waterfowl congregate in the central Platte River Valley. The camping area is shaded by stately cottonwood trees, some of which are more than 100 years old. Eight sandpit lakes are available for fishing, and the Fort Kearney State Historical Park is located nearby.

★3145★ FORT ROBINSON STATE PARK

PO Box 392
Crawford, NE 69339
Web: www.ngpc.state.ne.us/parks/guides/parksearch/
findpark.asp
Phone: 308-665-2900
Size: 22,605 acres land; 68 acres water. **Location:** 3 miles west of Crawford on US 20. **Facilities:** 125 campsites (100 with electrical hookups), modern restrooms, showers, group camping and equestrian facilities, 35 cabins, 22 lodge rooms, restaurant, camp store, activities center, meeting facilities, picnic areas and shelters, hiking trails (60 miles), mountain bike trails (20 miles),

equestrian trails (20 miles), food concession, indoor swimming pool, visitor center, nature center, museums and exhibit buildings. **Activities:** Camping, boating (nonpower or electric motor), fishing, swimming, hiking, horseback riding, mountain biking, jeep and stagecoach rides, interpretive programs. **Special Features:** Fort Robinson blends history and natural beauty with abundant recreational opportunities. The park also has its own buffalo and longhorn herds. The fort was an outpost that served from the days of the Indian Wars until after World War II and was the site of the 1879 Cheyenne Outbreak and the death of famed Sioux Chief Crazy Horse. Over the years, the fort served the Red Cloud Indian Agency as a cavalry remount station, K-9 dog training center, POW camp, and beef research station.

★3146★ FREMONT LAKES STATE RECREATION AREA

2351 County Rd 18
Ames, NE 68621
Web: www.ngpc.state.ne.us/parks/guides/parksearch/
findpark.asp
Phone: 402-727-3290 ·
Size: 40 acres land; 297 acres water. **Location:** 3 miles west of Fremont, off US 30. **Facilities:** 812 campsites (200 camping pads with electrical hookups; 12 non-pad sites with electrical hookups), modern restrooms as well as latrine buildings, showers, picnic areas, 5 picnic shelters, playground equipment, 6 boat ramps, 3 docks, fishing pier (&), 4 swimming beaches, country store, food concession. **Activities:** Camping, boating (all types), water-skiing, fishing, swimming. **Special Features:** Fremont's 20 sandpit lakes offer a variety of water recreation activities. One of the lakes has been specially redesigned for use by personal watercraft, and a ramp has been installed to allow the watercraft to back into the water.

★3147★ GALLAGHER CANYON STATE RECREATION AREA

1 East Park Dr 25A
Elwood, NE 68937
Web: www.ngpc.state.ne.us/parks/guides/parksearch/
findpark.asp
Phone: 308-785-2685
Size: 24 acres land; 400 acres water. **Location:** 10 miles south of Cozad on US 21, then 2 miles east, 1 mile north, and 1 mile west on county roads. **Facilities:** 72 primitive campsites, picnic tables and grills, playground, boat ramp, dock. **Activities:** Camping, boating (all types), fishing. **Special Features:** Although challenging to reach, Gallagher Canyon offers outstanding scenery and some of the state's best fishing for crappie, flathead, and channel catfish. The area provides access to more than 10 miles of canal that's open to all boats; the canal connects to Plum Creek Canyon Reservoir and Johnson Lake. The campground at Gallagher Canyon is heavily wooded and is rarely full.

★3148★ INDIAN CAVE STATE PARK

65296 720 Rd
Shubert, NE 68437
Web: www.ngpc.state.ne.us/parks/guides/parksearch/
findpark.asp
Phone: 402-883-2575

Size: 4,000 acres. **Location:** 10 miles south of Brownville, then 5 miles east on Spur 64E. **Facilities:** 274 campsites (134 pad sites and 10 non-pad sites with electrical hookups), modern restrooms, showers, equestrian camp, trailside adirondack shelters, picnic areas, 17 picnic shelters, hiking trails (22 miles), equestrian trails (16 miles), mountain bike trails (22 miles), boat ramp, river access. **Activities:** Camping (including equestrian and group camping), fishing, hiking, backpacking, horseback riding, mountain biking, trail rides (seasonal), historic sites, interpretive programs (seasonal). **Special Features:** Bordering the Missouri River, the park is a pristine wilderness area with a variety of hardwood trees, shrubs, and flora. Historic features include a restored schoolhouse and general store from the old river town of Saint Deroin where old-time crafts demonstrations are held during summer months.

★3149★ JOHNSON LAKE STATE RECREATION AREA

1 East Park Dr 25A
Elwood, NE 68937
Web: www.ngpc.state.ne.us/parks/guides/parksearch/
findpark.asp
Phone: 308-785-2685
Size: 68 acres land; 2,060 acres water. **Location:** 7 miles south of Lexington. **Facilities:** 207 campsites (113 are camping pads with electrical hookups), modern restrooms as well as vault toilets, showers, picnic areas, 5 picnic shelters, boat ramp, 8 docks, 2 fish cleaning stations, swimming beach, fishing piers (&). **Activities:** Camping, boating (all types), fishing, swimming. **Special Features:** Area is the heart of a complex of lakes on the Tri-County Canal system between Lexington and Cozad and provides three access points to Johnson Lake.

★3150★ KELLER PARK STATE RECREATION AREA

PO Box 508
Bassett, NE 68714
Web: www.ngpc.state.ne.us/parks/guides/parksearch/
findpark.asp
Phone: 402-684-2921
Size: 186 acres land; 10 acres water. **Location:** 3 miles west and 9 miles north of Long Pine, northwest of Ainsworth on Bone Creek. **Facilities:** 35 campsites (25 camping pads with electrical hookups; 10 tent sites), water, vault toilets, picnic areas, picnic shelter. **Activities:** Camping, boating (electric motor, non-powered), fishing, hiking, wildlife viewing. **Special Features:** Area includes five fishing ponds and is one of the few spots in Nebraska where anglers can catch rainbow trout along with warm water fish.

★3151★ LAKE MALONEY STATE RECREATION AREA

301 E State Farm Rd
North Platte, NE 69101
Web: www.ngpc.state.ne.us/parks/guides/parksearch/
findpark.asp
Phone: 308-535-8025
Size: 132 acres land; 1,000 acres water. **Location:** 6 miles south of North Platte, off Highway 83. **Facilities:** 256 campsites (56

with electrical hookups), vault toilets, showers, picnic areas, 4 boat ramps, 2 docks, 2 swimming beaches, 2 fish cleaning stations. **Activities:** Camping, boating (all types), fishing, swimming. **Special Features:** Area is near North Platte, which is the home of Buffalo Bill Ranch State Historical Park.

★3152★ **LAKE MCCONAUGHY STATE RECREATION AREA**
1450 Hwy 61N
Ogallala, NE 69153
Web: www.ngpc.state.ne.us/parks/guides/parksearch/
  findpark.asp
Phone: 308-284-8800
Size: 5,492 acres land; 35,700 acres water. **Location:** 11 miles north of Ogallala. **Facilities:** 268 campsites (camping pads) with electrical hookups, 58 camping pads without electricity, 2,647 primitive campsites, modern restrooms as well as vault toilets, coin-operated showers, picnic areas, 4 picnic shelters, concessions (including lodging), 15 boat ramps, 11 docks, 3 fish cleaning stations, boat rentals, swimming beach, visitor center. **Activities:** Camping, boating (all types), fishing, swimming. **Special Features:** Lake McConaughy (known locally as "Big Mac") is the state's largest reservoir and offers excellent opportunities for water sports, especially fishing. The Visitor/Water Interpretive Center at the lake features aquariums, a theater, and displays that interpret the benefits of the Platte River and the High Plains Aquifer.

★3153★ **LAKE MINATARE STATE RECREATION AREA**
PO Box 188
Minatare, NE 69356
Web: www.ngpc.state.ne.us/parks/guides/parksearch/
  findpark.asp
Phone: 308-783-2911
Size: 812 acres land; 2,158 acres water. **Location:** 12 miles northeast of Scottsbluff. **Facilities:** 52 campsites with electrical hookups, 110 primitive campsites, modern restrooms as well as vault toilets, showers, drinking water, picnic areas, 7 picnic shelters, 3 boat ramps, 4 docks, 2 fish cleaning stations, swimming beach (unsupervised). **Activities:** Camping, boating (all types), fishing, swimming. **Special Features:** Lake Minatare is the home of Nebraska's only lighthouse and a federal waterfowl refuge. The recreation area is also located near Scotts Bluff National Monument (see entry in national parks section) and Chimney Rock.

★3154★ **LAKE OGALLALA STATE RECREATION AREA**
1450 Hwy 61N
Ogallala, NE 69153
Web: www.ngpc.state.ne.us/parks/guides/parksearch/
  findpark.asp
Phone: 308-284-8800
Size: 239 acres land; 320 acres water. **Location:** 9 miles north of Ogallala, off NE 61, just below Kingsley Dam. **Facilities:** 262 campsites (62 with electrical hookups), modern restrooms, showers, picnic areas, 2 boat ramps, hiking trail (2 miles), 2

docks, boat rentals, fish cleaning station, fishing pier (&), concessions (including lodging). **Activities:** Camping, boating (all types; 5 mph limit), fishing, hiking. **Special Features:** Known locally as the "little lake," Lake Ogallala is just below the much larger Lake McConaughy, at the base of Kingsley Dam. Water enters Lake Ogallala from the bottom of Lake McConaughy and is extremely cold.

★3155★ **LEWIS & CLARK STATE RECREATION AREA**
54731 897 Rd
Crofton, NE 68730
Web: www.ngpc.state.ne.us/parks/guides/parksearch/
  findpark.asp
Phone: 402-388-4169
Size: 1,315 acres land; 7,982 acres water. **Location:** 9 miles north of Crofton on NE 121, along the northeast border with South Dakota. **Facilities:** 314 campsites (150 camping pads with electrical hookups; 24 non-pad sites with electrical hookups), modern restrooms, showers, 10 housekeeping cabins, playgrounds, picnic areas, picnic shelter with electricity, trails, swimming beach, fish cleaning station, 4 boat ramps, marina, boat slip rentals (seasonal). **Activities:** Camping, boating (all types; 5 mph limit in some areas), sailing, fishing, swimming, waterskiing, jet skiing, hunting, hiking, mountain biking, horseback riding, wildlife viewing, bird watching, ice fishing, ice skating, snowmobiling. **Special Features:** Straddling the border with South Dakota, Lewis and Clark is 35 miles long with 90 miles of shoreline. The site includes boating access points at five areas on the south side: Weigand-Burbach (the most developed section), Miller Creek, South Shore, Bloomfield, and Deep Water.

★3156★ **LONG LAKE STATE RECREATION AREA**
524 Panzer St
PO Box 508
Bassett, NE 68714
Web: www.ngpc.state.ne.us/parks/guides/parksearch/
  findpark.asp
Phone: 402-684-2921
Size: 30 acres land; 50 acres water. **Location:** 2 miles east of Johnstown, then 22 miles south on county road. **Facilities:** 10 campsites, vault toilets, picnic area. **Activities:** Primitive camping, boating (all types; 5 mph limit), fishing, hunting (primarily waterfowl). **Special Features:** Recreation area is located in Nebraska's Sandhills region, and Long Lake is a natural sandhill lake.

★3157★ **LONG PINE STATE RECREATION AREA**
524 Panzer St
PO Box 508
Bassett, NE 68714
Web: www.ngpc.state.ne.us/parks/guides/parksearch/
  findpark.asp
Phone: 402-684-2921
Size: 153 acres. **Location:** 1 mile west of Long Pine, just off US 20. **Facilities:** 28 campsites (8 with camping pads; no electricity), water, picnic tables and grills, 5 picnic shelters, hiking

trails (1 mile), archery range. **Activities:** Primitive camping, fishing, hiking, wildlife viewing. **Special Features:** Recreation area is located on a tract of Pine Ridge land that straddles Long Pine Creek.

★3158★ LOUISVILLE STATE RECREATION AREA

15810 Hwy 50
Louisville, NE 68037
Web: www.ngpc.state.ne.us/parks/guides/parksearch/
findpark.asp
Phone: 402-234-6855
Size: 142 acres land; 50 acres water. **Location:** 0.5 miles northwest of the community of Louisville, off NE 50. **Facilities:** 296 campsites (223 with electrical hookups; 236 sites have camping pads), modern restrooms, showers, trails, picnic areas, 5 picnic shelters, playground, swimming beach, bathhouse, camp store, river access. **Activities:** Camping, boating (electric motors or non-powered only), fishing, swimming, hiking, mountain biking, cross-country skiing. **Special Features:** Recreation area features 5 sandpit lakes and canoe access to the Platte River. It is located near Platte River State Park (see separate entries) and serves as an adjunct to it, with an excellent complex for RV camping.

★3159★ MEDICINE CREEK STATE RECREATION AREA

40611 Rd 728
Cambridge, NE 69022
Web: www.ngpc.state.ne.us/parks/guides/parksearch/
findpark.asp
Phone: 308-697-4667
Size: 1,200 acres land; 1,768 acres water. **Location:** 2 miles west of Cambridge on Highway 6 and 34, then 7 miles north on county road. **Facilities:** 316 campsites (70 with electrical hookups; 76 sites have camping pads), modern restrooms as well as latrines, showers, picnic areas, 11 picnic shelters, concession (restaurant, grocery, supplies, fuel, cabins), boat rentals, 3 boat ramps, 3 docks, 2 fish cleaning stations, swimming beach. **Activities:** Camping, boating (all types), fishing, swimming, hunting. **Special Features:** The recreation area and associated wildlife land encompass some 8,500 acres of public land and water. Located in the heart of southwest Nebraska's quail and pheasant range, this area is one of the finest public hunting areas in the state.

★3160★ MEMPHIS STATE RECREATION AREA

3019 Apple St
Lincoln, NE 68503
Web: www.ngpc.state.ne.us/parks/guides/parksearch/
findpark.asp
Phone: 402-471-5566
Size: 163 acres land; 48 acres water. **Location:** In the town of Memphis, off NE 63. **Facilities:** 150 campsites, water, picnic areas, 4 picnic shelters, hiking trails (1 mile), restaurant, playgrounds, boat ramp. **Activities:** Camping, boating (nonpower or electric motor), fishing, hiking. **Special Features:** The 48-acre lake is stocked with largemouth bass, bluegills, and channel catfish..

★3161★ MERRITT RESERVOIR STATE RECREATION AREA

420 E 1st St
Valentine, NE 69201
Web: www.ngpc.state.ne.us/parks/guides/parksearch/
findpark.asp
Phone: 402-376-3320
Size: 6,147 acres land; 2,906 acres water. **Location:** 26 miles southwest of Valentine on NE 97. **Facilities:** 218 campsites (28 with electrical hookups), modern restrooms as well as latrines, showers, picnic areas, 8 picnic shelters, concession (restaurant, rentals), boat rentals, 5 boat ramps, 2 fish cleaning stations. **Activities:** Camping, boating (all types), fishing, wildlife viewing. **Special Features:** Located in a narrow valley of the Snake River, the reservoir offers some of Nebraska's premiere fishing. Adjacent is McKelvie National Forest, with thousands of acres for hunting and hiking. Other nearby attractions include Valentine National Wildlife Refuge, Snake River Falls, the Valentine State Fish Hatchery, and Fort Niobrara Wildlife Refuge.

★3162★ MORMON ISLAND STATE RECREATION AREA

7425 S Hwy 281
Doniphan, NE 68832
Web: www.ngpc.state.ne.us/parks/guides/parksearch/
findpark.asp
Phone: 308-385-6211
Size: 92 acres land, 61 acres water. **Location:** At Grand Island Interchange, off I-80 (Exit 312). **Facilities:** 38 campsites (34 with electrical hookups), modern restrooms, showers, picnic shelters, trail rides, swimming beach, bathhouse, playground (♿♿). **Activities:** Camping, boating (non-motorized), fishing, swimming, bird watching. **Special Features:** Park was named for the winter stopover used by Mormon emigrants heading westward in 1884-1885. Mormon Island lies on the eastern edge of the great spring sandhill crane migration route in central Platte River Valley. The cranes begin arriving in early February and spend their days feeding and engaging in colorful courtship dances. After the first of April, the birds start flying to northern breeding grounds and are usually gone by mid-April.

★3163★ NIOBRARA STATE PARK

89261 522 Ave
Niobrara, NE 68760
Web: www.ngpc.state.ne.us/parks/guides/parksearch/
findpark.asp
Phone: 402-857-3373
Size: 1,640 acres. **Location:** 2 miles west of Niobrara, off NE 12. **Facilities:** 119 campsites (69 with electrical hookups), modern restrooms, showers, 19 cabins, picnic areas and shelters, hiking trails (14 miles), mountain bike trails (14 miles), swimming pool, 3 boat ramps, playground. **Activities:** Camping, boating (non-powered or electric), fishing, swimming, hiking, horseback trail rides, mountain biking, river raft trips (seasonal), wildlife viewing, bird watching, interpretive center. **Special Features:** Park is situated at the confluence of the Niobrara and Missouri rivers, on the northeastern border of Nebraska. The park has a large population of white-tailed deer as well as wild turkeys that roam freely throughout the camping area. Beaver,

9. State Parks

muskrat, and mink can be seen along the river banks. Adjacent to the park is Bazile Creek Wildlife Management Area, which offers additional opportunities for wildlife viewing, fishing, boating, and hunting in season. The park's interpretive center highlights the area's history, including the story of the Ponca Indians.

★3164★ NORTH LOUP STATE RECREATION AREA
7425 S US Hwy 281
Doniphan, NE 68832
Web: www.ngpc.state.ne.us/parks/guides/parksearch/
findpark.asp
Phone: 308-385-6211
Size: 13 acres land; 7 acres water. Location: 4 miles north of Saint Paul on US 281. Facilities: 10 campsites, water, picnic area, playground, river access. Activities: Primitive camping, fishing, boating (electric motor or non-powered). Special Features: Area is located along the North Loup River and is also near Marsh Wren and Leonard A. Koziol Wildlife Management Area.

★3165★ OLIVE CREEK STATE RECREATION AREA
3019 Apple St
Lincoln, NE 68503
Web: www.ngpc.state.ne.us/parks/guides/parksearch/
findpark.asp
Phone: 402-471-5566
Size: 437 acres land; 175 acres water. Location: 1.5 miles southeast of Kramer. Facilities: 50 campsites, water, picnic areas, 2 boat ramps, 8 docks. Activities: Primitive camping, boating (all types; 5 mph limit), fishing, hunting. Special Features: Although small, the lake supports a variety of fish: large-mouth bass, bluegill, and two kinds of catfish.

★3166★ OLIVER RESERVOIR STATE RECREATION AREA
210615 Hwy 71
Gering, NE 69341
Web: www.ngpc.state.ne.us/parks/guides/parksearch/
findpark.asp
Phone: 308-436-3777
Size: 917 acres land; 270 acres water. Location: 10 miles west of Kimball on US 30. Facilities: 175 campsites (75 are camping pads), drinking water, vault toilets, picnic areas, 2 picnic shelters with electricity, 2 boat ramps, 8 docks, swimming beach, bathhouses. Activities: Camping, boating (all types; some restrictions), fishing, swimming, water-skiing, hiking, hunting. Special Features: Oliver Reservoir is the only water-based recreational facility in the southwest Panhandle of Nebraska. The reservoir is a two-level lake that supports both cold water and warm water species, including walleye, yellow perch, largemouth bass, channel catfish, bluegill, and limited numbers of rainbow trout. The south side of the lake is maintained in a primitive state for hiking, hunting, and fishing.

★3167★ PAWNEE STATE RECREATION AREA
RR 4, Box 41B
Lincoln, NE 68524
Web: www.ngpc.state.ne.us/parks/guides/parksearch/
findpark.asp
Phone: 402-796-2362
Size: 1,804 acres land; 740 acres water. Location: 3 miles north and 2 miles west of Emerald. Facilities: 199 campsites (68 with electrical hookups; 102 camping pads), modern restrooms, showers, picnic areas, 2 picnic shelters, trails, food concession, 3 boat ramps, 4 docks, fish cleaning station, 2 swimming beaches. Activities: Camping, boating (all types), fishing, swimming, hiking, mountain biking, hunting, wildlife viewing. Special Features: Area has the second largest lake in the Salt Valley. Four docks provide easy access to the lake and good fishing for northern pike, walleye, largemouth bass, bluegill, and catfish.

★3168★ PELICAN POINT STATE RECREATION AREA
640 County Rd 19
Craig, NE 68019
Web: www.ngpc.state.ne.us/parks/guides/parksearch/
findpark.asp
Phone: 402-374-1727
Size: 36 acres. Location: 7 miles east and 5 miles north of Tekamah. Facilities: 17 campsites (camping pads), water, picnic area and shelter, boat ramp, dock, river access. Activities: Camping, boating (all types), fishing. Special Features: Area provides boating and fishing access to the Missouri River.

★3169★ PIBEL LAKE STATE RECREATION AREA
HC 79, Box 20L
Burwell, NE 68823
Web: www.ngpc.state.ne.us/parks/guides/parksearch/
findpark.asp
Phone: 308-346-5666
Size: 48 acres land; 24 acres water. Location: 9 miles south and 1 mile east of Bartlett, off US 281. Facilities: 30 campsites, water, picnic area, playground, boat ramp, dock. Activities: Primitive camping, boating (all types; 5 mph limit), fishing. Special Features: Pibel Lake is in a secluded area on the edge of the Sandhills. The lake has been renovated and stocked and has a dock for smaller boats.

★3170★ PIONEER STATE RECREATION AREA
3019 Apple St
Lincoln, NE 68503
Web: www.ngpc.state.ne.us/parks/guides/parksearch/
findpark.asp
Phone: 402-471-5566
Size: 8 acres. Location: 1.5 miles south of Swedeburg, in the southeastern part of the state. Facilities: Vault latrine, parking lot. Activities: Picnicking. Special Features: Pioneer SRA was formerly a wayside area. It is a day-use area only, and camping is not permitted here.

9. State Parks

★3171★ **PLATTE RIVER STATE PARK**
14421 346th St
Louisville, NE 68037
Web: www.ngpc.state.ne.us/parks/guides/parksearch/
 findpark.asp
Phone: 402-234-2217
Size: 519 acres. **Location:** Halfway between Lincoln and Omaha, about 2.5 miles south of Louisville. **Facilities:** 31 camper cabins, 21 housekeeping cabins, tepee rentals, modern restrooms, showers, group camp, restaurant, snack bar, picnic areas, hiking trails (10 miles), mountain bike trails (10 miles), fishing dock (&), swimming pool, paddleboat rentals, crafts center, amphitheater, archery range, observation deck; golf course nearby. **Activities:** Swimming, hiking, horseback trail rides, mountain biking, campfire programs. **Special Features:** Situated along the Platte River, park was formed by merging the sites of two private summer camps and a large wooded area. An 85-foot tower at the park includes a large observation deck that affords scenic views of the Platte Valley. Park management is aimed at providing excellent facilities for family recreation activities while keeping costs to a minimum.

★3172★ **PONCA STATE PARK**
PO Box 688
Ponca, NE 68770
Web: www.ngpc.state.ne.us/parks/guides/parksearch/
 findpark.asp
Phone: 402-755-2284
Size: 859 acres. **Location:** 2 miles north of Ponca. **Facilities:** 157 campsites (72 with electrical hookups), 14 housekeeping cabins, modern restrooms, showers, picnic areas, picnic shelters, hiking trails (20 miles), mountain bike trails (17 miles), swimming pool, boat ramp, docks, resource and education center with exhibit area, field laboratory, and conference rooms; golf course with clubhouse nearby. **Activities:** Camping, boating, fishing, swimming, hiking, mountain biking, guided horseback trail rides, hayrides and other planned group events, education programs. **Special Features:** Park is situated along the Missouri River bluffs in northeastern Nebraska and is the eastern gateway to a 59-mile section of the Missouri National Recreational River. Located at the park is the Missouri National Recreational River Resource and Education Center, and the park offers one of the state's most comprehensive outdoor/environmental education programs. The park is named for the Ponca Indians, whose chief (Standing Bear) fought and won the court battle to have the Indian declared a person under American Law.

★3173★ **RED WILLOW RESERVOIR STATE RECREATION AREA**
RR 1, Box 145
McCook, NE 69001
Web: www.ngpc.state.ne.us/parks/guides/parksearch/
 findpark.asp
Phone: 308-345-5899
Size: 1,358 acres land; 1,628 acres water. **Location:** 11 miles north of McCook. **Facilities:** 205 campsites (45 with electrical hookups; 95 camping pads), modern restrooms, showers, picnic areas, 20 picnic shelters, swimming beach, 4 boat ramps, mooring docks, concession with restaurant, grocery, supplies, gas, and boat rentals. **Activities:** Camping, boating (all types), swimming, fishing, hunting. **Special Features:** Area offers some of the best fishing and hunting in the state.

★3174★ **RIVERVIEW MARINA STATE RECREATION AREA**
PO Box 15
Nebraska City, NE 68410
Web: www.ngpc.state.ne.us/parks/guides/parksearch/
 findpark.asp
Phone: 402-873-7222
Size: 37 acres. **Location:** In Nebraska City, in the southeastern part of the state. **Facilities:** 46 campsites (16 are camping pads with electrical hookups), modern restrooms, showers, picnic areas, picnic shelter, 2 boat ramps, dock, river access. **Activities:** Camping, boating (all types), fishing. **Special Features:** Park provides boating and fishing access to the Missouri River. Arbor Lodge State Historical Park (see separate entry) is located nearby.

★3175★ **ROCK CREEK LAKE STATE RECREATION AREA**
73122 338 Ave
Enders, NE 69027
Web: www.ngpc.state.ne.us/parks/guides/parksearch/
 findpark.asp
Phone: 308-394-5118
Size: 54 acres land; 50 acres water. **Location:** 4 miles north and 1 mile west of Parks. **Facilities:** 43 campsites, water, picnic area, boat ramp, dock. **Activities:** Primitive camping, boating (nonpower or electric motor), fishing. **Special Features:** Rock Creek Fish Hatchery is located nearby.

★3176★ **ROCK CREEK STATION STATE HISTORICAL PARK**
57426 710th Rd
Fairbury, NE 68352
Web: www.ngpc.state.ne.us/parks/guides/parksearch/
 findpark.asp
Phone: 402-729-5777
Size: 353 acres. **Location:** 6 miles east of Fairbury. **Facilities:** Visitor/interpretive center, picnic areas, hiking and nature trails, restrooms; camping and other facilities available at the adjacent Rock Creek Station State Recreation Area (see separate entry). **Activities:** Picnicking, hiking. **Special Features:** Once a stage and Pony Express station, Rock Creek was also the place where "Wild Bill" Hickok shot David McCanles, beginning his bloody career as a gunfighter. Archeologists have investigated and excavated sites of two ranches dating back to 1858-1860, and the reconstruction of the buildings and corrals at both ranches is now complete. The park's visitor center interprets the ranches and other aspects of the history of the area.

★3177★ **ROCK CREEK STATION STATE RECREATION AREA**
57426 710th Rd
Fairbury, NE 68352
Web: www.ngpc.state.ne.us/parks/guides/parksearch/
 findpark.asp
Phone: 402-729-5777

9. State Parks

Size: 40 acres. **Location:** 6 miles east of Fairbury. **Facilities:** 35 campsites (25 sites are camping pads with electrical hookups), modern restrooms, showers, equestrian camping area with vault toilets, picnic areas, 3 picnic shelters, multi-use trails (4 miles). **Activities:** Camping, hiking, mountain biking, horseback riding. **Special Features:** Rock Creek SRA is a campground adjacent to Rock Creek Station State Historical Park (see separate entry).

★3178★ ROCKFORD STATE RECREATION AREA
3019 Apple St
Lincoln, NE 68503
Web: www.ngpc.state.ne.us/parks/guides/parksearch/
findpark.asp
Phone: 402-471-5566
Size: 286 acres land; 150 acres water. **Location:** 7 miles east and 2 miles south of Beatrice. **Facilities:** 107 campsites (30 with electrical hookups; 32 camping pads), water, picnic areas and 2 shelters, trail, swimming beach, boat ramp, dock. **Activities:** Camping, boating (all types), fishing, swimming, hiking.. **Special Features:** Homestead National Monument, where Daniel Freeman claimed one of the first homesteads under the Homestead Act of 1862, is located nearby.

★3179★ SANDY CHANNEL STATE RECREATION AREA
1020 'V' Rd
Kearney, NE 68847
Web: www.ngpc.state.ne.us/parks/guides/parksearch/
findpark.asp
Phone: 308-865-5305
Size: 87 acres land; 47 acres water. **Location:** 1.5 miles south of the Elm Creek interchange off I-80. **Facilities:** 30 campsites, water, river access. **Activities:** Camping, boating (non-motorized), fishing. **Special Features:** Area is adjacent to the Platte River and contains 47 acres of ponds.

★3180★ SCHRAMM PARK STATE RECREATION AREA
15810 Hwy 50
Louisville, NE 68037
Web: www.ngpc.state.ne.us/parks/schramm.html
Phone: 402-234-6855
Size: 332 acres land; 5 acres water. **Location:** On Highway 31, 6 miles south of I-80 Exit 432; 9 miles south of Gretna. **Facilities:** Picnic areas, 10 picnic shelters, nature trails (3 miles), visitor center, aquarium, museum, geological display. **Activities:** Fishing, hiking, mountain biking, picnicking. **Special Features:** This day use park is home to the Ak-Sar-Ben Aquarium, with 12 viewing tanks, a large terrarium, and a theater. Park is also the site of the state's first fish hatchery (1882), which is now a fish management museum, and an interesting geological display is located nearby.

★3181★ SHERMAN RESERVOIR STATE RECREATION AREA
RR 2, Box 117
Loup City, NE 68853
Web: www.ngpc.state.ne.us/parks/guides/parksearch/
findpark.asp
Phone: 308-745-0230

Size: 1,541 acres land; 2,845 acres water. **Location:** 4 miles east and 1 mile north of Loup City. **Facilities:** 360 campsites, primitive and modern restrooms, showers, picnic shelters, marina, 3 boat ramps, 3 docks, 2 fish cleaning stations. **Activities:** Primitive camping, boating (all types), fishing. **Special Features:** Sherman Dam creates a reservoir with 65 miles of shoreline, with rugged drainage ways branching off the main reservoir body that create interesting bays and coves for outstanding fishing. Powerboating and fishing are the mainstays of this recreation area.

★3182★ SMITH FALLS STATE PARK
HC 13, Box 25
Valentine, NE 69201
Web: www.ngpc.state.ne.us/parks/guides/parksearch/
findpark.asp
Phone: 402-376-1306
Size: 244 acres land; 8 acres water. **Location:** 15 miles east on Highway 12 from the town of Valentine, then 4 miles south on gravel road. **Facilities:** 23 primitive tent campsites, modern restrooms, pay showers, food concession, picnic sites, picnic shelter with electricity, 1-mile hiking trail. **Activities:** Camping, canoeing, fishing, hiking (on established trails only). **Special Features:** Nebraska's newest state park straddles the Niobrara National Scenic River (see entry in national parks section). It protects biological and scenic features of the location and allows visitors a view of the state's highest waterfall. Facilities are located on the north side of the Niobrara, with a footbridge across the river providing a link to the falls, which are located on the south side of the river.

★3183★ STAGECOACH STATE RECREATION AREA
3019 Apple St
Lincoln, NE 68503
Web: www.ngpc.state.ne.us/parks/guides/parksearch/
findpark.asp
Phone: 402-471-5566
Size: 607 acres land; 195 acres water. **Location:** 1.5 miles south and 0.5 miles west of Hickman. **Facilities:** 72 campsites (22 are camping pads with electrical hookups), drinking water, toilets, picnic facilities, boat ramp, dock, 2 fishing piers (1 pier ♿). **Activities:** Camping, boating (all types; 5 mph limit), fishing, hunting. **Special Features:** A portion of the recreation area's land is open to hunting for pheasant, quail, and dove in season.

★3184★ SUMMIT LAKE STATE RECREATION AREA
640 County Rd 19
Craig, NE 69019
Web: www.ngpc.state.ne.us/parks/guides/parksearch/
findpark.asp
Phone: 402-374-1727
Size: 345 acres land; 190 acres water. **Location:** 2 miles west of Tekamah. **Facilities:** 58 campsites (26 camping pads; no hookups), water, picnic areas, picnic shelters, hiking trail, 2 boat ramps, 3 docks, fish cleaning station, swimming beach. **Activities:** Camping, boating (all types; 5 mph limit), fishing, swimming, hiking, hunting. **Special Features:** Summit Lake is

stocked with largemouth bass, bluegill, channel catfish, walleye, and crappie.

★3185★ SUTHERLAND RESERVOIR STATE RECREATION AREA

301 E State Farm Rd
North Platte, NE 69101
Web: www.ngpc.state.ne.us/parks/guides/parksearch/
findpark.asp
Phone: 308-535-8025
Size: 37 acres land; 3,017 acres water. **Location:** 2 miles south of Sutherland. **Facilities:** 85 campsites (50 camping pads), water, picnic facilities, swimming beach, 3 boat ramps, 2 docks, fish cleaning station. **Activities:** Primitive camping, boating (all types), fishing, swimming, ice fishing. **Special Features:** In addition to the recreation opportunities offered at the recreation area, the Oregon Trail 9-hole golf course is located just a few minutes north of the lake.

★3186★ SWANSON RESERVOIR STATE RECREATION AREA

RR 2, Box 20
Stratton, NE 69043
Web: www.ngpc.state.ne.us/parks/guides/parksearch/
findpark.asp
Phone: 308-276-2671
Size: 3,957 acres land; 4,974 acres water. **Location:** 2 miles west of Trenton on US 34, on the Republican River. **Facilities:** 204 campsites (54 sites are camping pads with electrical hookups), modern restrooms as well as vault toilets, showers, picnic areas, 16 picnic shelters, concession (food, groceries, gas, supplies, water ski rentals), 7 boat ramps, mooring dock, 2 fish cleaning stations. **Activities:** Camping, boating (all types), fishing, hunting, water-skiing. **Special Features:** The largest of the four reservoirs in southwestern Nebraska, Swanson is known for its numerous walleye and growing population of black bass. Trophy-size northern pike can also be found here.

★3187★ TWO RIVERS STATE RECREATION AREA

27702 'F' St
Waterloo, NE 68069
Web: www.ngpc.state.ne.us/parks/guides/parksearch/
findpark.asp
Phone: 402-359-5165
Size: 302 acres land; 320 acres water. **Location:** 1 mile south and 1 mile west of Venice. **Facilities:** 223 campsites (61 with electrical hookups; camping pads at 213 sites), modern restrooms, showers, 10 cabins, picnic areas and shelters, hiking trail, swimming beach, food concession, bicycle and paddleboat rentals, fishing pier (&), 2 fish cleaning stations, river access. **Activities:** Camping, fishing (including put-and-take trout fishing), swimming, hiking. **Special Features:** The 10 cabins available at this recreation area are authentic Union Pacific cabooses that have been restored for park lodging. The cabooses are permanently sidetracked on actual rails. Each caboose sleeps six.

★3188★ UNION PACIFIC STATE RECREATION AREA

1020 'V' Rd
Kearney, NE 68847
Web: www.ngpc.state.ne.us/parks/guides/parksearch/
findpark.asp
Phone: 308-865-5305
Size: 26 acres land; 12 acres water. **Location:** Off the Odessa Interchange on I-80 (Exit 263). **Facilities:** 5 campsites, modern restrooms, picnic area, 3 shelters. **Activities:** Camping, boating (nonpower or electric motor), fishing. **Special Features:** Union Pacific is a former wayside area near Kearney, with easy access to restaurants, shopping, and the Museum of Nebraska Art.

★3189★ VERDON STATE RECREATION AREA

c/o Indian Cave State Park
RR 1, Box 30
Shubert, NE 68437
Web: www.ngpc.state.ne.us/parks/guides/parksearch/
findpark.asp
Phone: 402-883-2575
Size: 30 acres land; 45 acres water. **Location:** 0.5 miles west of Verdon, off US 73. **Facilities:** 20 campsites, water, picnic facilities. **Activities:** Camping, fishing. **Special Features:** Located in the southeast corner of Nebraska, Verdon features a small, clear, spring-fed lake.

★3190★ VICTORIA SPRINGS STATE RECREATION AREA

HC 69, Box 117
Anselmo, NE 68813
Web: www.ngpc.state.ne.us/parks/guides/parksearch/
findpark.asp
Phone: 308-749-2235
Size: 55 acres land; 5 acres water. **Location:** 6 miles east of Anselmo on Highway 21. **Facilities:** 81 campsites (21 are camping pads with electrical hookups), 2 housekeeping cabins, modern restrooms, showers, picnic areas, picnic shelter with electricity. **Activities:** Camping, boating (non-powered only), fishing. **Special Features:** Named for the mineral springs located there, Victoria Springs (established in 1925) is the third oldest area in Nebraska's state park system.

★3191★ WAGON TRAIN STATE RECREATION AREA

3019 Apple St
Lincoln, NE 68503
Web: www.ngpc.state.ne.us/parks/guides/parksearch/
findpark.asp
Phone: 402-471-5566
Size: 746 acres land; 315 acres water. **Location:** 2 miles east of Hickman. **Facilities:** 108 campsites (20 are camping pads with electrical hookups, water, picnic areas, 3 picnic shelters, swimming beach, boat ramp, dock, trails. **Activities:** Camping, boating (all types; 5 mph limit), fishing, swimming, hiking. **Special Features:** Wagon Trail is a Corps of Engineers watershed impoundment.

9. State Parks

★3192★ WALGREN LAKE STATE RECREATION AREA
15951 Hwy 385
Chadron, NE 69337
Web: www.ngpc.state.ne.us/parks/guides/parksearch/
findpark.asp
Phone: 308-432-6167
Size: 80 acres land; 50 acres water. **Location:** 2.5 miles east and 2.5 miles south of Hay Springs on gravel roads. **Facilities:** 40 campsites, water, picnic area, picnic shelter, 2 boat ramps, 2 docks, fishing pier (&). **Activities:** Primitive camping, boating (all types; 5 mph limit), fishing. **Special Features:** Walgren Lake contains black bullheads, bluegills, largemouth bass, walleyes, white crappies, and yellow perch, but heavy vegetation in late summer usually limits fishing.

★3193★ WAR AXE STATE RECREATION AREA
PO Box 427
Gibbon, NE 68840
Web: www.ngpc.state.ne.us/parks/guides/parksearch/
findpark.asp
Phone: 308-468-5700
Size: 9 acres land; 16 acres water. **Location:** On I-80 at the Shelton Interchange, Exit 291. **Facilities:** 8 campsites, modern restrooms, picnic area, 3 picnic shelters. **Activities:** Primitive camping, boating (nonpower or electric motor), fishing. **Special Features:** War Axe is a former wayside area along I-80.

★3194★ WILDCAT HILLS STATE RECREATION AREA
210615 Hwy 71
Gering, NE 69341
Web: www.ngpc.state.ne.us/parks/guides/parksearch/
findpark.asp
Phone: 308-436-3777
Size: 705 acres. **Location:** 10 miles south of Gering, off NE 71. **Facilities:** 5 campsites, modern restrooms, picnic areas, 3 picnic shelters, trails, playground, visitor/nature center. **Activities:** Primitive camping, hiking, mountain biking, wildlife viewing. **Special Features:** Located in the rugged rocky buttes and pine-covered canyons of western Nebraska, this recreation area features Wildcat Hills Nature Center, a museum and teaching center with exhibits of the area's unique flora and fauna. A 310-acre game reserve south of the recreation area holds a small herd of buffalo, elk, and longhorn cattle. Visitors are not permitted within the fenced reserve.

★3195★ WILLOW CREEK STATE RECREATION AREA
54876 852 Rd
Pierce, NE 68767
Web: www.ngpc.state.ne.us/parks/guides/parksearch/
findpark.asp
Phone: 402-329-4053
Size: 933 acres land; 700 acres water. **Location:** 1.5 miles southwest of Pierce. **Facilities:** 102 campsites (84 sites are camping pads with electrical hookups), modern restrooms, showers, picnic areas, 6 picnic shelters (2 with electricity), 2 playgrounds, multi-use trail (8 miles), swimming beach, 4 boat ramps, 3 docks, 7 rock fishing jetties. **Activities:** Camping, boating (all types), fishing, swimming, water-skiing, hiking, horseback riding, mountain biking, hunting (with restrictions), snowmobiling, birdwatching. **Special Features:** The reservoir lake is fairly shallow, measuring only about 35 feet at the deepest point, with good fishing for crappie, bluegill, bass, catfish, walleye, northern pike, tiger musky, and bullheads.

★3196★ WINDMILL STATE RECREATION AREA
PO Box 427
Gibbon, NE 68840
Web: www.ngpc.state.ne.us/parks/guides/parksearch/
findpark.asp
Phone: 308-468-5700
Size: 154 acres land; 14 acres water. **Location:** At the Gibbon Interchange off I-80 (Exit 285), between Kearney and Grand Island. **Facilities:** 89 campsites (69 are camping pads with electrical hookups), modern restrooms, showers, picnic areas, 4 picnic shelters (1 with electricity), swimming beach. **Activities:** Camping, boating (electric motor or non-powered only), fishing, swimming. **Special Features:** Site features an assortment of antique windmills that have been restored to working order. The largest is a railroad windmill that stands more than 60 feet tall.

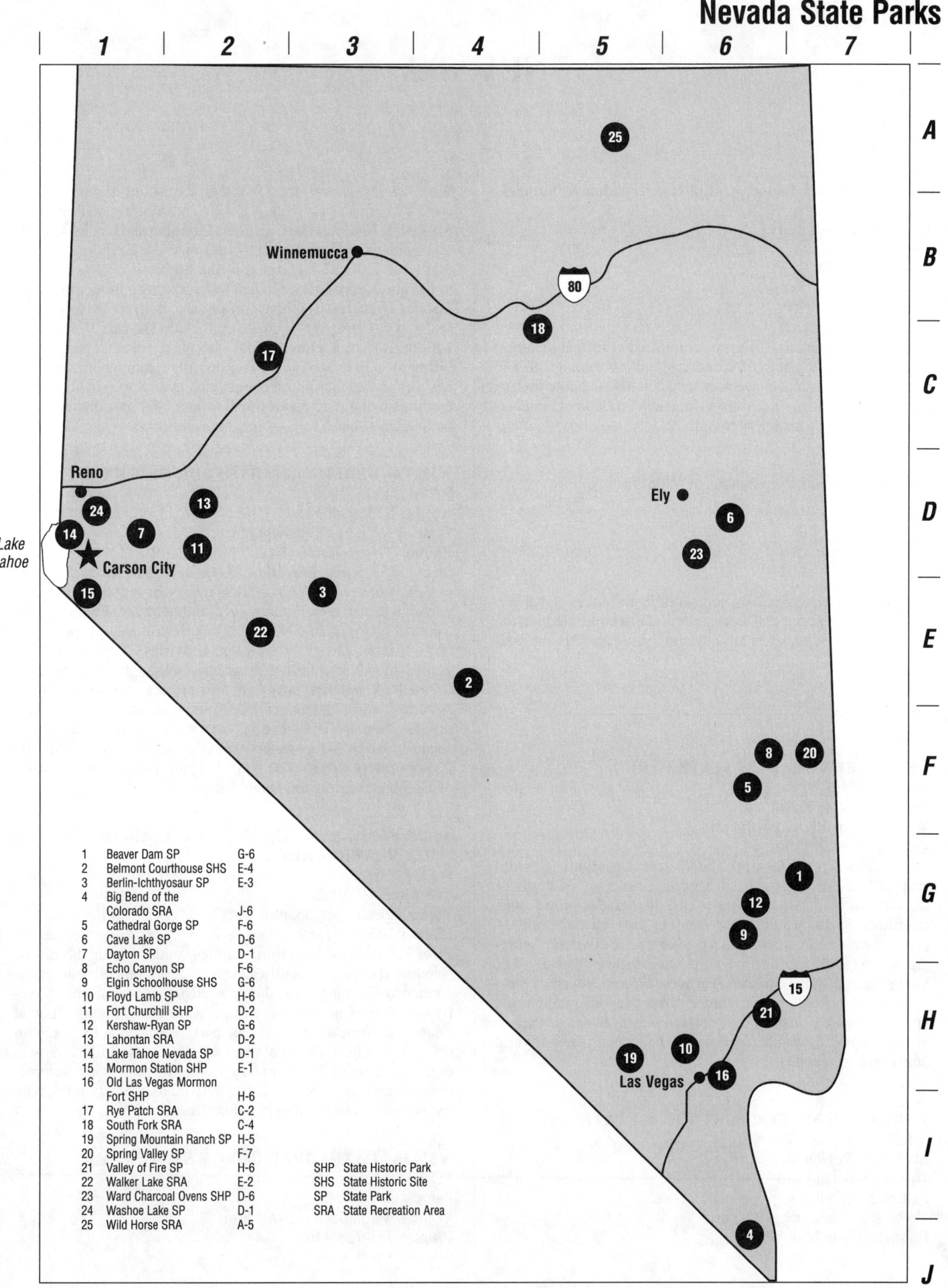

Nevada State Parks

1	Beaver Dam SP	G-6
2	Belmont Courthouse SHS	E-4
3	Berlin-Ichthyosaur SP	E-3
4	Big Bend of the Colorado SRA	J-6
5	Cathedral Gorge SP	F-6
6	Cave Lake SP	D-6
7	Dayton SP	D-1
8	Echo Canyon SP	F-6
9	Elgin Schoolhouse SHS	G-6
10	Floyd Lamb SP	H-6
11	Fort Churchill SHP	D-2
12	Kershaw-Ryan SP	G-6
13	Lahontan SRA	D-2
14	Lake Tahoe Nevada SP	D-1
15	Mormon Station SHP	E-1
16	Old Las Vegas Mormon Fort SHP	H-6
17	Rye Patch SRA	C-2
18	South Fork SRA	C-4
19	Spring Mountain Ranch SP	H-5
20	Spring Valley SP	F-7
21	Valley of Fire SP	H-6
22	Walker Lake SRA	E-2
23	Ward Charcoal Ovens SHP	D-6
24	Washoe Lake SP	D-1
25	Wild Horse SRA	A-5

SHP	State Historic Park
SHS	State Historic Site
SP	State Park
SRA	State Recreation Area

NEVADA

★3197★ Nevada Department of Conservation & Natural Resources
Division of State Parks
1300 S Curry St
Carson City, NV 89703
(775) 684-2770 - Phone
(775) 6842777 - Fax
Web: www.parks.nv.gov
Manages and maintains 24 parks, comprised of recreation areas, historic sites, and places of scenic, cultural, archeological, and scientific significance. Develops educational and interpretive programs, and oversees the design, acquisition, and implementation of the state's trail system.

★3198★ Nevada Department of Wildlife
1100 Valley Rd
Reno, NV 89512
(775) 688-1500 - Phone
(775) 688-1595 - Fax
Web: ndow.org
Restores and manages fish and wildlife resources. Oversees 11 wildlife management areas, offers conservation education programs, and administers hunting and fishing licenses and boat registrations.

★3199★ BEAVER DAM STATE PARK
PO Box 985
Caliente, NV 89008
Web: www.parks.nv.gov/bd.htm
Phone: 775-728-4460
Size: 2,393 acres. **Elevation:** 5,000 feet. **Location:** 34 miles east of Caliente, near the Utah border; go 6 miles north of Caliente on US 93, then 28 miles east on a graded gravel road. **Facilities:** 33 campsites, group camping area, chemical toilets, picnic areas (at campsites), interpretive trail. **Activities:** Camping, fishing (only with artificial lures with single barbless hooks), hiking, nature study. **Special Features:** Eastern Nevada's most remote and primitive park features deep canyons, pinyon and juniper forests, a stream, and numerous beaver dams. Park is open year round, weather permitting, but travel is not advised during winter months.

★3200★ BELMONT COURTHOUSE STATE HISTORIC SITE
c/o Fallon Region Headquarters
16799 Lahontan Dam
Fallon, NV 89406
Web: www.parks.nv.gov/bc.htm
Phone: 775-867-3001

Size: 2 acres. **Elevation:** 8,000 feet. **Location:** 45 miles northeast of Tonopah via US 6, NV 376, and Monitor Valley Road. **Facilities:** No developed facilities. Camping and picnic facilities are available on nearby public lands or at the US Forest Services's Pine Creek Campground in the Monitor Valley, 20 miles to the north. **Activities:** Guided tours (during summer months). **Special Features:** Belmont Courthouse, built in 1876, was the seat of Nye County government until 1905. The partially restored building offers a glimpse into Nevada's colorful past, when Belmont was a boomtown due to silver mining in the area. Visitors to the courthouse are advised that there no public park facilities or tourist services in Belmont, and gasoline may not be available there.

★3201★ BERLIN-ICHTHYOSAUR STATE PARK
HC 61, Box 61200
Austin, NV 89310
Web: www.parks.nv.gov/bi.htm
Phone: 775-964-2440; **Fax:** 775-964-2012
Size: 1,153 acres. **Elevation:** 7,000 feet. **Location:** 23 miles east of Gabbs, via NV 844. Park is open year round, but extreme winter weather conditions may prohibit travel. **Facilities:** 14 campsites (some suitable for RVs), restrooms, picnic areas, trails, historic sites, visitor center. **Activities:** Camping, hiking, guided tours, interpretive programs (seasonal). **Special Features:** Park was first established to protect and display North America's most abundant concentration and largest known Ichthyosaur fossils. Ichthyosaurs were giant marine reptiles that swam in warm ocean waters that covered this part of Nevada 225 million years ago. The park also preserves the mining town of Berlin as well as the Diana Mine.

★3202★ BIG BEND OF THE COLORADO STATE RECREATION AREA
PO Box 32850
Laughlin, NV 89028
Web: parks.nv.gov/bb.htm
Phone: 702-298-1859
Size: 2,336 acres. **Location:** 5 miles south of Laughlin on the Needles Highway. **Facilities:** Under development; some self-contained RV campsites, showers, picnic areas with shade. **Activities:** Camping, boating, fishing, swimming, hiking. **Special Features:** Nevada's newest state park is located at the southern tip of the state along the shore of the Colorado River, with dramatic views of the river and surrounding mountains. Summer temperatures here can reach 120°F; winters are very mild, with temperatures rarely dipping below freezing.

★3203★ CATHEDRAL GORGE STATE PARK
PO Box 176
Panaca, NV 89042
Web: www.parks.nv.gov/cg.htm
Phone: 775-728-4460

Size: 1,633 acres. **Elevation:** 4,800 feet. **Location:** 2 miles north of Panaca, just west of US 93. **Facilities:** 22 campsites, restrooms, showers, picnic area, group use facilities (camping, picnicking), trails (5 miles), visitor center. **Activities:** Camping, hiking, nature study, interpretive programs. **Special Features:** Park is located in a long, narrow valley where erosion has carved unique patterns in the soft bentonite clay of the canyon walls. Remote areas of cave-like formations and cathedral-like spires are accessible by trail, and a scenic overlook offers excellent views of the canyon. A Nevada Regional Visitor Center is located at the entrance to the park.

★3204★ CAVE LAKE STATE PARK
PO Box 151761
Ely, NV 89315
Web: www.parks.nv.gov/cl.htm
Phone: 775-728-4460
Size: 1,240 acres. **Elevation:** 7,300 feet. **Location:** 15 miles southeast of Ely via US 50/6/93 and Success Summit Road. **Facilities:** 2 campgrounds (each includes 1 group campsite), restrooms, showers, picnic areas, hiking trails, boat launch. **Activities:** Camping, boating, fishing, hiking, nature study, ice fishing, cross-country skiing, snowshoeing ice skating, sledding. **Special Features:** The park is located in the middle of the Schell Creek Range, adjacent to Humboldt National Forest, and features a 32-acre reservoir.

★3205★ DAYTON STATE PARK
PO Box 1478
Dayton, NV 89403
Web: parks.nv.gov/dsp.htm
Phone: 775-687-5678
Size: 152 acres. **Location:** On US 50, in the town of Dayton, 12 miles east of Carson City. **Facilities:** 10 campsites, restrooms, picnic facilities, group-use pavilion, interpretive trail, historic sites. **Activities:** Camping, fishing, hiking, bird watching, nature study, historical tours, interpretive programs. **Special Features:** Park is located in the town of Dayton, one of Nevada's first permanent settlements. Remnants of the Rock Point Mill, one of the largest of the stamp mills built along the Carson River to process silver ore, can be seen at the park.

★3206★ ECHO CANYON STATE PARK
HC 74, Box 295
Pioche, NV 89043
Web: www.parks.nv.gov/ec.htm
Phone: 775-962-5103
Size: 1,080 acres. **Elevation:** 5,200 feet. **Location:** 12 miles east of Pioche via State Routes 322 and 323. **Facilities:** 33 campsites, flush toilets and drinking water, picnic areas, group picnic area, hiking trail, boat ramp, historic features. **Activities:** Camping, fishing, hiking, interpretive programs. **Special Features:** Park features a 65-acre reservoir, abundant wildlife, a wide variety of native plants, and unique rock formations.

★3207★ ELGIN SCHOOLHOUSE STATE HISTORIC SITE
c/o Kershaw-Ryan State Park
PO Box 985
Caliente, NV 89008
Phone: 775-726-3564
Location: 20 miles south of Caliente in Rainbow Canyon on NV 317. **Special Features:** This one-room schoolhouse was built in 1922 for children in remote railroad siding and outlaying ranches south of Caliente. It was last used in 1967 and has since been restored to its original appearance. It was approved as a state historic site in 2005 and is managed as a unit of Kershaw-Ryan State Park.

★3208★ FLOYD LAMB STATE PARK
9200 Tule Springs Rd
Las Vegas, NV 89131
Web: www.parks.nv.gov/fl.htm
Phone: 702-486-5413; **Fax:** 702-486-5423
Size: 2,038 acres. **Location:** 10 miles north of Las Vegas via US 95 to Durango and then Tule Springs Road. **Facilities:** Picnic areas (including 2 for group use), restrooms, walking/bicycle path. **Activities:** Fishing, hiking, bicycling. **Special Features:** Originally known as Tule Springs, this park was an early watering stop for Native Americans. It later became a privately-owned working ranch, then a guest/dude ranch (circa 1950) where one could wait out the six week residency requirement to obtain a quick divorce. In addition to the Ranch Historic Area, the park offers tree-shaded groves alongside four small fishing lakes.

★3209★ FORT CHURCHILL STATE HISTORIC PARK
1000 Hwy 95A
Silver Springs, NV 89429
Web: www.parks.nv.gov/fc.htm
Phone: 775-577-2345
Size: 4,461 acres. **Location:** 8 miles south of Silver Springs on US 95A. **Facilities:** 20 campsites (no hookups), group area (camping or picnicking), picnic areas, trails, historic sites, visitor center, restrooms. **Activities:** Camping, fishing, swimming, hiking, canoeing, birdwatching, interpretive programs. **Special Features:** The US Army's Fort Churchill was built in 1860 to provide protection for early settlers but was abandoned nine years later. The ruins of the fort are preserved in a state of "arrested decay." Nearby is Buckland Station, which was a Pony Express stop. The Overland Telegraph also passed through this area at one time.

★3210★ KERSHAW-RYAN STATE PARK
PO Box 985
Caliente, NV 89008
Web: www.parks.nv.gov/kr.htm
Phone: 775-726-3564
Size: 264 acres. **Elevation:** 4,312 to 5,080 feet. **Location:** 2 miles south of Caliente via US 93 and State Route 317. **Facilities:** Picnic area, group use areas, restrooms, trails. **Activities:** Hiking, picnicking. **Special Features:** Park is situated in a colorful, scenic canyon at the northern end of Rainbow Canyon.

9. State Parks

Flash floods are not uncommon in Kershaw Canyon; flooding destroyed the park's facilities in 1984.

★3211★ LAHONTAN STATE RECREATION AREA
16799 Lahontan Dam
Fallon, NV 89406
Web: www.parks.nv.gov/lah.htm
Phone: 775-577-2235
Size: 30,522 acres. Location: On the Carson River, 18 miles west of Fallon and 45 miles east of Carson City via US 50. Facilities: 1 developed campground (primitive on-the-beach camping is permitted throughout most of the park), picnic areas, restrooms, boat launch facilities. Activities: Camping, hunting (with restrictions), boating, canoeing, fishing, swimming, water-skiing, hiking, horseback riding, wildlife observation. Special Features: Lahontan Reservoir is almost 17 miles long, with 69 miles of shoreline. When full, it covers 12,000 surface acres.

★3212★ LAKE TAHOE NEVADA STATE PARK
PO Box 8867
Incline Village, NV 89452
Web: www.parks.nv.gov/lt.htm
Phone: 775-831-0494; Fax: 775-831-2514
Size: 14,242 acres. Location: Located on the northeast side of Lake Tahoe, between parcels of Humboldt-Toiyabe National Forest (see entry in national forests chapter). Facilities: 2 primitive backcountry campsites (hike-in), picnic areas (&), group use areas, restrooms, nature trails (&), backcountry trails, ski trails, swimming beaches, boat launch facilities, concession services (seasonal bike and ski rentals, bike tours, snacks, cabin rentals), visitor center, scenic overlooks. Activities: Boating, fishing, hunting (with restrictions), swimming, scuba diving, hiking, mountain biking, horseback riding, cross-country skiing. Special Features: Park consists of several different units, including Sand Harbor, Spooner Lake, Cave Rock, Memorial Point, and Hidden Beach. The majority of the park is backcountry, spanning 13,000 acres within the Carson Range, stretching north from Spooner Lake to Incline Village. The extensive backcountry trail system offers exceptional opportunities for hiking, biking, and horseback riding.

★3213★ MORMON STATION STATE HISTORIC PARK
Genoa, NV 89411
Web: www.parks.nv.gov/ms.htm
Phone: 775-782-2590
Size: 3 acres. Location: In Genoa, 12 miles south of Carson City via US 395. Facilities: Historic site, visitor center, restrooms, picnic and group facilities. Activities: Historical programs, events. Special Features: Park is the site of Nevada's first permanent non-native settlement. A replica of a trading post built in 1851 now houses a small museum that displays relics of early pioneer days. (The museum is open April through October.)

★3214★ OLD LAS VEGAS MORMON FORT STATE HISTORIC PARK
500 E Washington Ave
Las Vegas, NV 89101
Web: www.parks.nv.gov/olvmf.htm
Phone: 702-486-3511; Fax: 702-486-3734
Size: 3 acres. Location: In downtown Las Vegas, at the corner of Washington Avenue and Las Vegas Boulevard. Facilities: Visitor center, historic site, exhibits. Activities: Interpretive programs. Special Features: The focus of this park is historic interpretation. The first permanent non-native settlers in the Las Vegas Valley were a group of Mormon missionaries who built an adobe fort along Las Vegas Creek in 1855. Today, the park includes a remnant of the original adobe fort with interpretive displays as well as a full-scale visitor center.

★3215★ RYE PATCH STATE RECREATION AREA
2505 Rye Patch Reservoir Rd
Lovelock, NV 89419
Web: www.parks.nv.gov/rp.htm
Phone: 775-538-7321
Size: 20,517 acres. Location: 22 miles east of Lovelock on I-80. Facilities: 25 improved campsites (no hookups), primitive campsites (boat-in or hike-in), 3 group camping areas, restrooms, showers, picnic areas, swimming beach, boat ramps, dock. Activities: Camping, boating, fishing, swimming, water-skiing, winter sports. Special Features: Area includes a 22-mile long reservoir on the Humboldt River, with 72 miles of shoreline and 11,000 acres of water surface when full.

★3216★ SOUTH FORK STATE RECREATION AREA
353 Lower South Fork Unit 8
Spring Creek, NV 89815
Web: www.parks.nv.gov/sf.htm
Phone: 775-744-4346
Size: 3,924 acres. Location: 16 miles south of Elko on State Route 228. Facilities: 25 campsites (open May-November 15), primitive shoreline camping, restroom, showers, trails, boat ramps. Activities: Camping, picnicking (no developed facilities), hunting (with restrictions), boating, fishing, swimming, wildlife observation, ice fishing, winter sports. Special Features: South Fork Reservoir covers 1,650 acres and is surrounded by wildlife-filled meadowlands and rolling hills. The park is known for its trophy-class trout and bass fishery.

★3217★ SPRING MOUNTAIN RANCH STATE PARK
PO Box 124
Blue Diamond, NV 89004
Web: www.parks.nv.gov/smr.htm
Phone: 702-875-4141
Size: 840 acres. Location: 15 miles west of Las Vegas on State Route 159 (the Blue Diamond Highway). Facilities: Historic sites, visitor center, picnic area, group use area, restrooms. Activities: Guided tours, living history demonstrations, cultural events, nature study. Special Features: Historic Spring Mountain Ranch is located within Red Rock Canyon National Conservation Area, beneath the cliffs of the Wilson Range. The mountain springs provided water for the Paiute and later brought

mountain men and early settlers to the area. The area was developed into a combination working ranch and luxury retreat by a string of owners, including Chester Lauck of the comedy team "Lum and Abner," actress Vera Krupp, and Howard Hughes.

★3218★ SPRING VALLEY STATE PARK

HC 74, Box 201
Pioche, NV 89043
Web: www.parks.nv.gov/sv.htm
Phone: 775-962-5102
Size: 1,563 acres. **Location:** 20 miles east of Pioche via NV 322. **Facilities:** 42 campsites, group use area, restrooms, showers, picnic areas, hiking trail, historic sites, fish cleaning station, boat ramp, dock with temporary slips. **Activities:** Camping, boating, fishing, swimming, hiking, winter sports, wildlife observation. **Special Features:** Park features 65-acre Eagle Valley Reservoir, which attracts a variety of waterfowl and shore birds to the park including mallards, teals, herons, avocets, and an occasional trumpeter swan. Eagles, hawks, songbirds, ravens, and road runners inhabit the canyons and valleys. A number of ranch buildings from the late 19th century still exist in the park, one of which is used as park headquarters.

★3219★ VALLEY OF FIRE STATE PARK

Valley Fire Rd
PO Box 515
Overton, NV 89040
Web: www.parks.nv.gov/vf.htm
Phone: 702-397-2088; **Fax:** 702-397-2621
Size: 35,300 acres. **Location:** 55 miles northeast of Las Vegas via I-15 off Exit 75; or via Lake Mead Northshore Road. **Facilities:** 51 campsites, 3 group use areas, restrooms, showers, picnic areas, hiking trails, historic sites, visitor center, interpretive displays. **Activities:** Camping, hiking, nature study, interpretive events. **Special Features:** Park is Nevada's oldest and largest state park, dedicated in 1935. The valley derives its name from red sandstone formations and the stark beauty of the Mojave Desert. Petrified wood and 3,000-year-old petroglyphs give witness to the trees and people that occupied the area long ago.

★3220★ WALKER LAKE STATE RECREATION AREA

c/o Fallon Region Headquarters
16799 Lahontan Dam
Fallon, NV 89406
Web: www.parks.nv.gov/walk.htm
Phone: 775-867-3001
Size: 280 acres. **Location:** 11 miles north of Hawthorne on US 95. **Facilities:** Picnic areas, restrooms, beach, boat ramps. **Activities:** Boating, fishing, swimming. **Special Features:** Walker Lake is one of the last remnants of an ancient inland sea that covered much of western Nevada nearly 10,000 years ago.

★3221★ WARD CHARCOAL OVENS STATE HISTORIC PARK

PO Box 151761
Ely, NV 89315
Web: www.parks.nv.gov/ww.htm
Phone: 775-728-4460
Size: 682 acres. **Elevation:** 7,000 feet. **Location:** 7 miles south of Ely via US 50/6/93, then 11 miles southwest on Cave Valley Road (a graded dirt road). **Facilities:** 14 campsites (2 large pull-through sites; 1 ♿ site), 2 vault-type restrooms, potable water (seasonal), rental yurt (in remote area), trails (interpretive, overlook, riparian trails; ATV-OHV multi-use trail), picnic sites, historic features. **Activities:** Camping, hiking, fishing. **Special Features:** Park is located in a setting of pinyon-juniper woodlands, lush riparian areas, and outstanding views of the Steptoe Valley and surrounding mountains. It is known for its six beehive-shaped ovens, used in the late 19th century to generate charcoal for use in the silver mines of nearby Ward.

★3222★ WASHOE LAKE STATE PARK

4855 East Lake Blvd
Carson City, NV 89704
Web: www.parks.nv.gov/wl.htm
Phone: 775-687-4319
Size: 8,053 acres. **Elevation:** 5,029 feet. **Location:** 10 miles north of Carson City and 15 miles south of Reno via US 395, then to East Lake Blvd. **Facilities:** 49 campsites (7-day limit; no hookups), group use area, restrooms, showers, picnic areas, trails, boat ramps, docks, observation tower. **Activities:** Camping, hunting (with restrictions), fishing, boating, catamaran sailing, swimming, windsurfing, water skiing, jet skiing, hiking, horseback riding, nature study, bird watching, interpretive programs. **Special Features:** Park is located in the heart of scenic Washoe Valley, with views of the majestic Sierra Nevadas and Carson Range. Features include a wetlands area with a viewing tower and interpretive displays.

★3223★ WILD HORSE STATE RECREATION AREA

HC 31, Box 265
Elko, NV 89801
Web: www.parks.nv.gov/wh.htm
Phone: 775-758-6493
Size: 120 acres. **Elevation:** 6,205 feet. **Location:** 67 miles north of Elko on State Route 225. **Facilities:** 33 campsites (no hookups), restrooms, showers, picnic area, boat ramp, beach. **Activities:** Camping, boating, fishing, swimming, hiking, hunting (nearby), interpretive programs, ice fishing, snowmobiling, skiing. **Special Features:** Area is situated on the northeast shore of Wild Horse Reservoir and commonly registers the state's lowest winter temperatures.

9. State Parks

New Hampshire State Parks

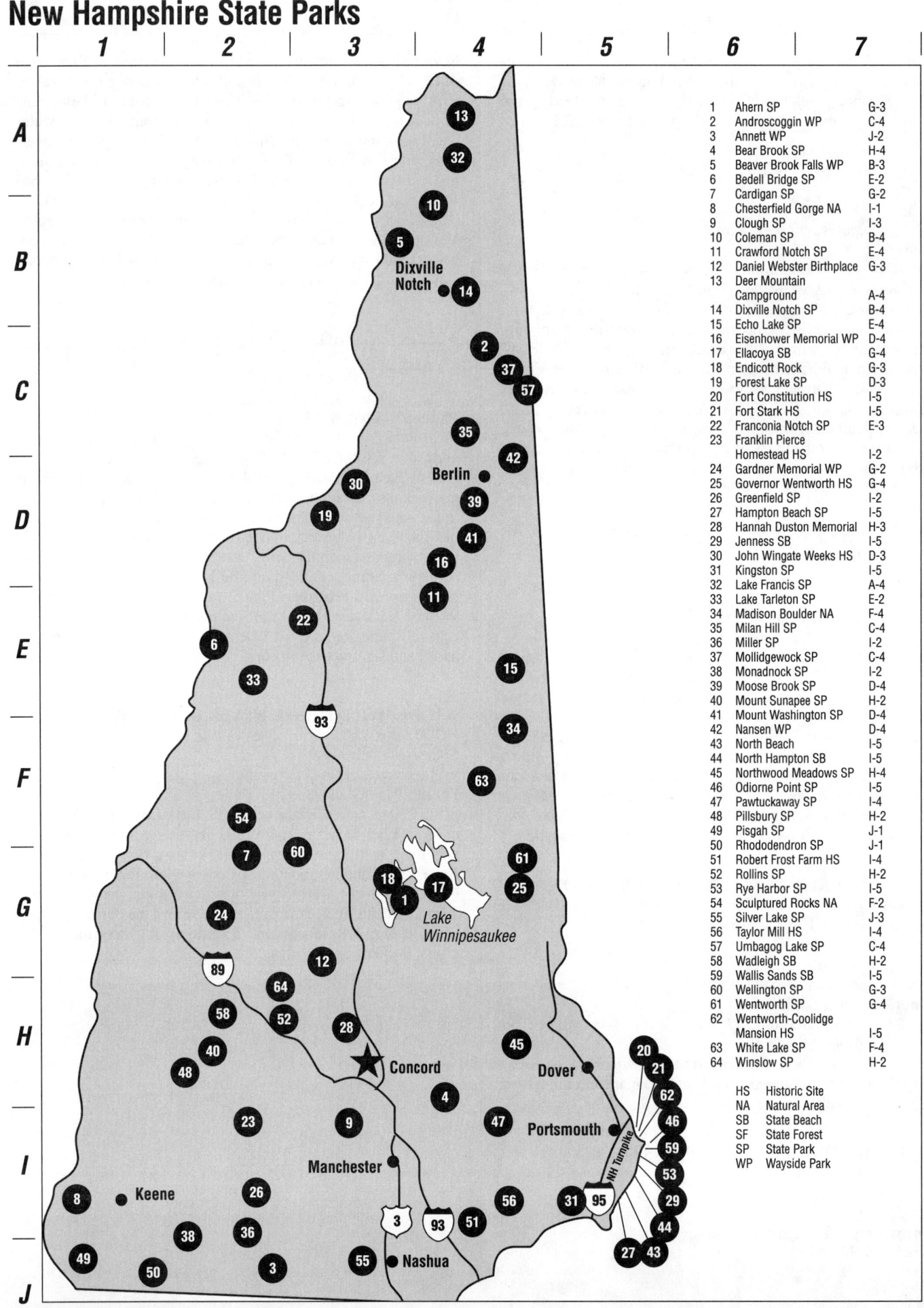

1	Ahern SP	G-3
2	Androscoggin WP	C-4
3	Annett WP	J-2
4	Bear Brook SP	H-4
5	Beaver Brook Falls WP	B-3
6	Bedell Bridge SP	E-2
7	Cardigan SP	G-2
8	Chesterfield Gorge NA	I-1
9	Clough SP	I-3
10	Coleman SP	B-4
11	Crawford Notch SP	E-4
12	Daniel Webster Birthplace	G-3
13	Deer Mountain Campground	A-4
14	Dixville Notch SP	B-4
15	Echo Lake SP	E-4
16	Eisenhower Memorial WP	D-4
17	Ellacoya SB	G-4
18	Endicott Rock	G-3
19	Forest Lake SP	D-3
20	Fort Constitution HS	I-5
21	Fort Stark HS	I-5
22	Franconia Notch SP	E-3
23	Franklin Pierce Homestead HS	I-2
24	Gardner Memorial WP	G-2
25	Governor Wentworth HS	G-4
26	Greenfield SP	I-2
27	Hampton Beach SP	I-5
28	Hannah Duston Memorial	H-3
29	Jenness SB	I-5
30	John Wingate Weeks HS	D-3
31	Kingston SP	I-5
32	Lake Francis SP	A-4
33	Lake Tarleton SP	E-2
34	Madison Boulder NA	F-4
35	Milan Hill SP	C-4
36	Miller SP	I-2
37	Mollidgewock SP	C-4
38	Monadnock SP	I-2
39	Moose Brook SP	D-4
40	Mount Sunapee SP	H-2
41	Mount Washington SP	D-4
42	Nansen WP	D-4
43	North Beach	I-5
44	North Hampton SB	I-5
45	Northwood Meadows SP	H-4
46	Odiorne Point SP	I-5
47	Pawtuckaway SP	I-4
48	Pillsbury SP	H-2
49	Pisgah SP	J-1
50	Rhododendron SP	J-1
51	Robert Frost Farm HS	I-4
52	Rollins SP	H-2
53	Rye Harbor SP	I-5
54	Sculptured Rocks NA	F-2
55	Silver Lake SP	J-3
56	Taylor Mill HS	I-4
57	Umbagog Lake SP	C-4
58	Wadleigh SB	H-2
59	Wallis Sands SB	I-5
60	Wellington SP	G-3
61	Wentworth SP	G-4
62	Wentworth-Coolidge Mansion HS	I-5
63	White Lake SP	F-4
64	Winslow SP	H-2

HS	Historic Site
NA	Natural Area
SB	State Beach
SF	State Forest
SP	State Park
WP	Wayside Park

NEW HAMPSHIRE

★3224★ New Hampshire Division of Parks & Recreation
PO Box 1856
Concord, NH 03302
(603) 271-3556 - Phone
(603) 271-2747 - Fax
(603) 271-3628 - Reservations
Web: www.nhparks.state.nh.us
Operates 72 state parks, historic sites, and numerous state beaches, natural areas, marinas and fishing piers, waysides, and miscellaneous areas. Protects and preserves unusual scenic, scientific, historic, recreational, and natural areas and makes them accessible to the public.

★3225★ New Hampshire Fish & Game Department
11 Hazen Dr
Concord, NH 03301
(603) 271-3511 - Phone
(603) 271-1438 - Fax
Web: wildlife.state.nh.us
Guards fish, wildlife, and marine resources by conserving and protecting their habitats. Provides the public education and access to fishing and hunting areas. Works to protect non-game species.

★3226★ New Hampshire Bureau of Trails
PO Box 1856
Concord, NH 03302
(603) 271-3254 - Phone
Web: www.nhtrails.org
Administers trails on state and federal lands, helps municipalities and organizations develop trails on public and private lands. Manages 250 miles of off-highway recreational vehicle trails, more than 300 miles of state-owned rail-trails, and 6,830 miles of snowmobile trails.

> **Key to campsite classification:**
> - **RV campsites** — Full-hookups sites (water, electric, sewer).
> - **Tent campsites** — No hookups.

★3227★ AHERN STATE PARK
Rt 106
Laconia, NH 03246
Web: www.nhstateparks.org/ParksPages/Ahern/Ahern.html
Phone: 603-823-7722
Size: 129 acres. **Location:** On Right Way Path Road, off Route 106 north. **Facilities:** Trails, pit toilets. **Activities:** Biking, hiking, fishing, picnicking. **Special Features:** Park is located on the shore of Lake Winnisquam, with 3,500 feet of shoreline in the park.

★3228★ ANDROSCOGGIN WAYSIDE PARK
Rt 16
Errol, NH 03579
Web: www.nhstateparks.org/ParksPages/Androscoggin/
Androscoggin.html
Phone: 603-538-6707
Location: Off NH Route 16 in Errol. **Activities:** Fishing, picnicking. **Special Features:** Park is located in 13 Mile Woods, on a bluff overlooking Androscoggin River rapids.

★3229★ ANNETT WAYSIDE PARK
Cathedral Rd
Rindge, NH 03461
Web: www.nhstateparks.org/ParksPages/Annett/Annett.html
Phone: 603-485-2034
Size: 1,336 acres. **Location:** Off NH Route 119 in Annett State Forest. **Facilities:** Picnic area, hiking trail. **Activities:** Hiking, picnicking. **Special Features:** Park is part of the 1,494-acre Arnett State Forest and is located near the Cathedral of the Pines National Shrine. Open mid-May to mid-November.

★3230★ BEAR BROOK STATE PARK
157 Deerfield Rd
Allenstown, NH 03275
Web: www.nhstateparks.org/ParksPages/BearBrook/
BearBrk.html
Phone: 603-485-9874
Size: 10,083 acres. **Location:** Off NH Route 28. **Facilities:** Campground is remotely located in the park (5 miles from day-use area, on Beaver Pond) and has: 95 campsites (no hookups), showers, camp store, and a small beach reserved for campers only. Park also offers: picnic area, group picnic shelter, trails (40 miles), 1.25-mile fitness course, canoe and rowboat rentals, playground, 2 archery ranges, ballfield, horseshoe area, 4-H camp, museum complex, nature center. **Activities:** Camping, boating (non-motorized only), fishing (including fly fishing), swimming, hiking, mountain biking, horseback riding, interpretive programs, snowmobiling, cross-country skiing. **Special Features:** Bear Brook is the largest developed state park in New Hampshire. It features a museum complex that includes three museums, a nature center, and a historic meeting house (open during the summer).

★3231★ BEAVER BROOK FALLS WAYSIDE PARK
Colebrook, NH 03576
Web: www.nhstateparks.org/ParksPages/BeaverBrook/
BeaverBrook.html
Phone: 603-538-6707

Size: 7 acres. **Location:** Off NH Route 145 near Colebrook. **Facilities:** Picnic area with shelters, group use area. **Activities:** Picnicking, hiking. **Special Features:** This scenic area is popular for hiking.

★3232★ BEDELL BRIDGE STATE PARK
Haverhill, NH 03765
Web: www.nhstateparks.org/ParksPages/BedellBridge/
   BedellBridge.html
Phone: 603-823-7722
Size: 74 acres. **Location:** Between NH Routes 10 and 25 in Haverhill. **Facilities:** Picnic area, boat launch. **Activities:** Boating, fishing. **Special Features:** Located along the Connecticut River, Park was the site of the second longest two-span covered bridge in the US. The Burrtuss bridge, which connected New Hampshire to Vermont, was destroyed by wind in 1979.

★3233★ CARDIGAN STATE PARK
Orange, NH 03741
Web: www.nhstateparks.org/ParksPages/Cardigan/
   Cardigan.html
Phone: 603-823-7722
Size: 5,798 acres. **Location:** Off NH Routes 4 and 118, via I-93, I-95, I-89, or I-91. **Facilities:** Picnic area, hiking trails. **Activities:** Hiking, winter use (with restrictions). **Special Features:** Park is an excellent area for hiking and includes a trail to Mount Cardigan's 3,121-foot treeless granite summit, which affords outstanding views.

★3234★ CHESTERFIELD GORGE NATURAL AREA
Rt 9
Chesterfield, NH 03443
Web: www.nhstateparks.org/ParksPages/ChesterfieldGorge/
   Chesterfield.html
Phone: 603-363-8373
Size: 13 acres. **Location:** On NH Route 9 in Chesterfield. **Facilities:** Visitor center, trails; picnic tables and flush toilets available in summer months. **Activities:** Hiking, picnicking. **Special Features:** Area has footpaths for hiking along the gorge and offers scenic views.

★3235★ CLOUGH STATE PARK
Weare, NH 03281
Web: www.nhstateparks.org/ParksPages/Clough/Clough.html
Phone: 603-529-7112
Location: Off NH Route 13, 5 miles east of Weare. **Facilities:** Picnic area, 900-foot beach, 2 bathhouses, flush toilets, changing areas, boat launch, playing fields. **Activities:** Boating (no motors), fishing, swimming, winter use. **Special Features:** Park is located on the shore of 150-acre Everett Lake, which was formed by a dam on the Piscataquog River.

★3236★ COLEMAN STATE PARK
Rt 26
Little Diamond Pond Rd
Stewartstown, NH 03597
Web: www.nhstateparks.org/ParksPages/Coleman/
   Coleman.html
Phone: 603-237-5382

Size: 1,573 acres. **Location:** Off NH Route 26, 12 miles east of Colebrook. **Facilities:** 24 primitive campsites (no hookups), flush toilets, playground, picnic area, group use area, boat launch (small boats only; speed restricted), boat rentals. **Activities:** Camping, boating, canoeing, fishing, hiking, hunting, cross-country skiing, snowmobiling. **Special Features:** Park is located on Little Diamond Pond in New Hampshire's remote north country and has excellent trout fishing. The park is at the northern terminus of the Androscoggin Trail, a hiking path that extends 55 miles south to Berlin.

★3237★ CRAWFORD NOTCH STATE PARK
Rt 302
Harts Location, NH 03812
Web: www.nhstateparks.org/ParksPages/CrawfordNotch/
   CrawfordNotch.html
Phone: 603-374-2272
Size: 5,950 acres. **Location:** Along US 302. **Facilities:** 36 tent campsites, flush toilets, showers, hiking trails, historic site, visitor center, snack bar, gift shop. **Activities:** Camping, fishing, hiking, picnicking, wildlife viewing. **Special Features:** Park encompasses six miles of rugged beauty in a scenic mountain pass, with numerous hiking trails, waterfalls, and mountain views. A plaque marks the site of the Willey House, which escaped damage from an 1826 landslide, but the Willey family perished as they sought shelter away from the house. The house later became an inn but burned down in 1898.

★3238★ DANIEL WEBSTER BIRTHPLACE
Franklin, NH 03235
Web: www.nhstateparks.org/ParksPages/DanWebster/
   DanielWebster.html
Phone: 603-934-5057
Size: 147 acres. **Location:** Off NH Route 127, 1 mile south of Franklin. **Facilities:** Grounds are open to the public, but buildings are currently closed and unstaffed, and there are no facilities available. **Special Features:** The two-room frame structure where Daniel Webster, one of the nation's most distinguished statemen and orators, was born, provides a view not only of Webster's early life, but also of life in the early years of the US. Restored in 1913, the home contains antique furnishings, utensils of the period (1782-1852), and Webster mementos.

★3239★ DEER MOUNTAIN CAMPGROUND
5309 N Main St
Pittsburg, NH 03592
Web: www.nhstateparks.org/ParksPages/DeerMountain/
   DeerMountainCmp.html
Phone: 603-538-6965
Size: 1,548 acres. **Location:** Off US Route 3, just south of the Canadian border, in Connecticut Lakes State Forest. Campground is adjacent to the Connecticut River, between Second and Third Connecticut lakes. **Facilities:** 25 primitive tent campsites, picnic tables. **Activities:** Camping, boating (no motors), hiking, fishing, wildlife viewing, winter use. **Special Features:** Park is adjacent to the stretch of Route 3 north of Pittsburg known as Moose Alley and is a prime location for moose viewing. It also

provides a good base for organized youth groups exploring the north country.

★3240★ DIXVILLE NOTCH STATE PARK

Rt 26
Dixville, NH 03576
Web: www.nhstateparks.org/ParksPages/DixvilleNotch/
Dixville.html
Phone: 603-538-6707
Size: 137 acres. **Location:** On NH Route 26 in Dixville; access via I-93, I-95, and I-91. **Facilities:** Picnic area, hiking trails, pit toilets. **Activities:** Hiking, picnicking. **Special Features:** Within the park is a scenic gorge and waterfalls on two mountain brooks. Hiking trails lead to Table Rock and nearby mountains. Park is open year round.

★3241★ ECHO LAKE STATE PARK

Conway, NH 03818
Web: www.nhstateparks.org/ParksPages/EchoLake/
EchoLake.html
Phone: 603-356-2672
Size: 118 acres. **Location:** Off NH 302, near North Conway. **Facilities:** Beach, bathhouse, picnic tables, hiking trails, scenic auto road. **Activities:** Swimming, fishing, boating (non-motorized only), hiking, rock climbing, ice climbing. **Special Features:** A scenic trail around the lake affords great views of sheer, 700-foot Cathedral Ledge, which towers over the lake. A mile-long auto road and hiking trails lead to the top of Cathedral Ledge, with views across the Saco River Valley to the White Mountains. Park is open weekends only starting Memorial Day, and then daily from June 24 to Labor Day.

★3242★ EISENHOWER MEMORIAL WAYSIDE PARK

Rt 302
Carroll, NH 03598
Web: www.nhstateparks.org/ParksPages/Eisenhower/
Eisenhower.html
Phone: 603-323-2087
Size: 0.7 acres. **Location:** On NH Route 302. **Facilities:** Picnic tables. **Special Features:** Park honors President Dwight D. Eisenhower. A short walk leads to views of the Presidential Range in the White Mountain National Forest.

★3243★ ELLACOYA STATE PARK

280 Scenic Dr
Gilford, NH 03246
Web: www.nhstateparks.org/ParksPages/Ellacoya/
Ellacoya.html
Phone: 603-293-7821
Size: 83 acres. **Location:** Off Route 11 in Gilford on the southwest shore of Lake Winnipesaukee. **Facilities:** 37 RV-only campsites with full hookups, laundromat, park store (refreshments and souvenirs), bathhouse with showers and changing rooms (&), beach, boat launch area (small boats only). **Activities:** Camping (no tents), boating, canoeing, fishing (with restrictions), swimming, picnicking. **Special Features:** Park is situated

on the shore of Lake Winnipesaukee, with a 600-foot sandy beach that offers views of the Ossipee and Sandwich mountains across the lake.

★3244★ ENDICOTT ROCK

Rt 3
Laconia, NH 03246
Web: www.nhstateparks.org/ParksPages/Endicott/
Endicott.html
Phone: 603-823-7722
Size: 0.1 acres. **Location:** Off US Route 3 in Laconia, at the south end of Weirs Beach. **Activities:** Picnicking. **Special Features:** This is the site of a large boulder that was inscribed in 1652 with the name John Endicott, Governor of Massachusetts Bay, and the initials of two Massachusetts Bay Colony commissioners and two surveyors. The rock marked the assumed headwaters of the Merrimack River — under the original Bay Charter of 1629, the northern boundary of the colony was fixed as a line three miles north of the Merrimack.

★3245★ FOREST LAKE STATE PARK

Dalton, NH 03598
Web: www.nhstateparks.org/ParksPages/ForestLake/
ForestLake.html
Phone: 603-837-9150
Size: 420 acres. **Location:** Off NH Route 116. **Facilities:** Picnic areas, playground, group use area, flush toilets, beach, bathhouse. **Activities:** Swimming, mountain biking, fishing, boating. **Special Features:** Created in 1935, Park is one of New Hampshire's ten original state parks. The park features a mountain lake with a 200-foot sandy beach in a woodland setting.

★3246★ FORT CONSTITUTION HISTORIC SITE

25 Wentworth Rd
New Castle, NH 03854
Web: www.nhstateparks.org/ParksPages/FortConstitution/
FortConstitution.html
Phone: 603-436-1552
Size: 2 acres. **Location:** Off NH Route 1B, at the US Coast Guard Station in New Castle. **Facilities:** Historic site, interpretive exhibits. **Activities:** Self-guided tours. **Special Features:** Fort is located on a peninsula on the northeast corner of New Castle Island overlooking the Pisquatua River and the Atlantic Ocean. It was originally a British stronghold known as Fort William and Mary. In December 1774, colonists raided the fort, an important event in the chain of events leading to the Revolution. Site is listed on the *National Register of Historic Places.*

★3247★ FORT STARK HISTORIC SITE

Wildrose Ln
New Castle, NH 03854
Web: www.nhstateparks.org/ParksPages/FortStark/
FortStark.html
Phone: 603-436-1552
Size: 10 acres. **Location:** Off NH Route 1B in the southeast corner of New Castle Island. **Facilities:** Historic site, unmarked

walking trail. **Special Features:** This historic military fortification overlooking the Piscataqua River, Atlantic Ocean, and Little Harbor was used as an active fort in every war from the Revolutionary War through World War II. The fort is named for John Stark, commander of New Hampshire forces in the Battle of Bennington (1777). The gates to the fort are locked for winter on November 1st.

★3248★ FRANCONIA NOTCH STATE PARK

Franconia, NH 03580
Web: www.franconianotchstatepark.com
Phone: 603-745-8391
Size: 6,693 acres. **Location:** On I-93 (Franconia Notch Parkway), in the heart of the White Mountain National Forest (see separate entry in national forests chapter). **Facilities:** 7 RV campsites with hookups (at Cannon RV Park), 97 wooded tent sites, showers, camp store, picnic areas, food service, trails, beach, bathhouse, boat launch, museum, historic site, visitor center, gift shop, aerial tramway, restrooms. **Activities:** Camping, boating, fishing, swimming, hiking, bicycling, mountain biking, rock climbing, winter sports, interpretive programs (seasonal). **Special Features:** Over time, fluvial and glacial erosive forces have formed spectacular scenery and natural geologic formations at this site. Park was home to New Hampshire's famous Old Man of the Mountain, a granite outcropping that looked like a profile of a man. Sadly, the formation collapsed May 3, 2003. Attractions at Franconia Notch include Flume Gorge, New England Ski Museum, and an aerial tramway to the summit of 4,180-foot Cannon Mountain. The Appalachian National Scenic Trail passes through the park (see separate entry in national trails section).

★3249★ FRANKLIN PIERCE HOMESTEAD HISTORIC SITE

c/o Hillsborough Historical Society
PO Box 896
Hillsboro, NH 03244
Web: www.nhstateparks.org/ParksPages/FranklinPierce/
FranklinPierce.html
Phone: 603-478-3165
Size: 13 acres. **Location:** Off Route 31 in Hillsborough. **Facilities:** Historic home, gift shop, restrooms. Open week-ends only. **Activities:** Guided tours (seasonal), picnicking. **Special Features:** The boyhood home of Franklin Pierce, 14th US President, is a spacious federal-style country home. Built by Pierce's father in 1804, the stately home reflects the gracious and affluent living of the 19th century.

★3250★ GARDNER MEMORIAL WAYSIDE PARK

Rt 4A
Wilmot, NH 03287
Web: www.nhstateparks.org/ParksPages/Gardner/
Gardner.html
Phone: 603-485-2034
Location: On NH Route 4A, 4 miles north of Wilmot. **Facilities:** Picnic area. **Activities:** Picnicking, hiking. **Special Features:** Park is part of the 6,675-acre Gile State Forest and includes a

memorial is to Walter C. Gardner II, whose father established Gile State Forest.

★3251★ GOVERNOR WENTWORTH HISTORIC SITE

Rt 109
Wolfeboro, NH 03894
Web: www.nhstateparks.org/ParksPages/GovWentworth/
GovWentworth.html
Phone: 603-823-7722
Size: 96 acres. **Location:** Off NH Route 109, near Wolfeboro. **Activities:** Picnicking. **Special Features:** Site holds the remains of the former summer estate of Royal Governor John Wentworth, last of New Hampshire's colonial governors. The mansion burned to the ground in 1820. An archeological dig there unearthed artifacts that reveal details about daily life and work methods of the privileged class of the period.

★3252★ GREENFIELD STATE PARK

Rt 136
Greenfield, NH 03047
Web: www.nhstateparks.org/ParksPages/Greenfield/
Grnfld.html
Phone: 603-547-3497
Size: 401 acres. **Location:** On NH Route 136, 1 mile west of Greenfield. **Facilities:** 257 campsites (mostly tents; 5 sites reserved for youth groups), showers, flush toilets, picnic area, park store, trails, beaches (separate beach for campers), boat launch (with restrictions), boat rentals. **Activities:** Camping, boating (with restrictions), fishing, swimming, hiking, biking, winter use. **Special Features:** Tucked away in the southwest corner of the state, the park features ponds, bogs, and a forest that extends to the shore of undeveloped Otter Lake.

★3253★ HAMPTON BEACH STATE PARK

Rt 1A
Hampton, NH 03842
Web: www.nhstateparks.org/ParksPages/Hampton/
Hampton.html
Phone: 603-926-3784
Size: 50 acres. **Location:** On Route 1A on the Atlantic coast. **Facilities:** 28 RV campsites, park store, picnic facilities, beach, amphitheater, public information services, comfort station, first aid station. **Activities:** Camping, fishing, swimming, whale watching. **Special Features:** This oceanfront park features miles of sandy beaches and entertainment during the summer season. The campground here is the only RV campground directly on the New Hampshire coast.

★3254★ HANNAH DUSTON MEMORIAL

Boscawen, NH 03303
Web: www.nhstateparks.org/ParksPages/HannahDuston/
HannahDuston.html
Phone: 603-485-2034
Size: 0.4 acres. **Location:** West of I-93 (Exit 17), near Boscawen. **Facilities:** Picnic area. **Special Features:** Erected in 1874, Memorial was the first publicly-funded statue in New Hampshire. It commemorates the courage of Hannah Duston, who

escaped after being taken prisoner in 1697 during the French and Indian War. The monument is located on a small island at the confluence of the Contoocook and Merrimack rivers.

★3255★ JENNESS STATE BEACH
Rt 1A
Rye, NH 03870
Web: www.nhstateparks.org/ParksPages/Jenness/Jenness.html
Phone: 603-436-1552
Size: 1.3 acres. Location: On NH Route 1A south of Rye. Facilities: Beach, bathhouse. Activities: Swimming. Special Features: This ocean beach offers bathroom facilities, metered parking, and lifeguard service.

★3256★ JOHN WINGATE WEEKS HISTORIC SITE
Lancaster, NH 03584
Web: www.nhstateparks.org/ParksPages/Weeks/Weeks.html
Phone: 603-788-4004
Size: 446 acres. Location: Off US 3, just south of Lancaster. Facilities: Historic home, picnic tables, scenic auto tour. Activities: Guided tours, picnicking, hiking, biking. Special Features: Site preserves the home of John Wingate Weeks, leading conservationist, US congressman, US senator, and Secretary of War under Presidents Harding and Coolidge. The house is set at the top of Mt. Prospect in Lancaster, and the house and grounds offer a panoramic view of the surrounding mountains. The site is open week-ends through October, and there is a fee to tour it.

★3257★ KINGSTON STATE PARK
124 Main St
Kingston, NH 03848
Web: www.nhstateparks.org/ParksPages/Kingston/Kingston.html
Phone: 603-642-5471
Size: 44 acres. Location: Off Route 125, south of Kingston. Facilities: Picnic areas, group use area, playground, softball field, horseshoe and volleyball areas, swimming area (300 feet), 2 bathhouses, flush toilets. Activities: Swimming, fishing, boating (with restrictions). Special Features: Just 14 miles from New Hampshire's seacoast, Park is close to many area attractions, including antique shops, mall, and restaurants.

★3258★ LAKE FRANCIS STATE PARK
439 River Rd
Pittsburg, NH 03592
Web: www.nhstateparks.org/ParksPages/LakeFrancis/LakeFrancis.html
Phone: 603-538-6965
Size: 38 acres. Location: Off Route 3, via I-93 or I-95. Facilities: 43 tent campsites (includes 5 walk-in sites with tent platforms), running water and flush toilets, group use area, picnic area, playground, boat launch, boat rentals. Activities: Camping (including youth group camping), boating, canoeing, fishing, hunting. Special Features: Park is located in the northern wilderness Connecticut Lakes region, on 2,000-acre Lake Francis. Fishing here is excellent, especially for rainbow trout, salmon, and pickerel.

★3259★ LAKE TARLETON STATE PARK
Route 25C
Piermont, NH 03779
Web: www.nhstateparks.org/ParksPages/LakeTarleton/LakeTarleton.html
Phone: 603-823-7722
Size: 48 acres. Location: Near Piedmont, on NH Route 25C. Facilities: Undeveloped. Activities: Swimming, picnicking, fishing, hunting (in season). Special Features: Park is surrounded by national forest and conservation lands, with outstanding views of the White Mountain National Forest across the lake.

★3260★ MADISON BOULDER NATURAL AREA
Madison, NH 03849
Web: www.nhstateparks.org/ParksPages/MadisonBoulder/MadisonBoulder.html
Phone: 603-823-7722
Size: 17 acres. Location: Off NH Route 113, near Madison. Activities: Picnicking. Special Features: This granite boulder, a National Natural Landmark, stands 83 feet long, 23 feet in height above the ground (part of the rock is buried), and 37 feet wide, and weighs more than 5,000 tons. It is one of the largest glacial erratics in the world.

★3261★ MILAN HILL STATE PARK
Rt 16
Milan, NH 03588
Web: www.nhstateparks.org/ParksPages/MilanHill/MilanHill.html
Phone: 603-466-3860
Size: 102 acres. Location: Off NH Route 16 to Milan via I-93 or I-95. Facilities: 10 primitive campsites with flush toilets, showers, and potable water source, fire tower. Note: Campground may be closed due to emergency repairs. Call for status. Activities: Camping, picnicking, hiking, fishing, canoeing, kayaking (in nearby Androscoggin River), wildlife viewing. Special Features: The fire tower at the summit of Milan Hill affords sweeping views of Canada, the White Mountains, and mountains of Maine.

★3262★ MILLER STATE PARK
Rt 101E
Peterborough, NH 03458
Web: www.nhstateparks.org/ParksPages/Miller/Miller.html
Phone: 603-924-3672
Size: 533 acres. Location: Off NH Route 101, 3 miles east of Peterborough. Facilities: Picnic sites, trails, scenic auto road, fire tower. Activities: Hiking, winter use. Special Features: Established in 1891, Park is the oldest state park in New Hampshire. It is named for General James Miller, hero of the Battle of Lundy's Lane in the War of 1812. A scenic auto road to the top of Pack Monadnock has great views, and a climb to the top of the fire tower offers a panoramic view of the surrounding countryside. Three trails provide hikers with access from the base to the 2,290-foot summit.

9. State Parks

★3263★ **MOLLIDGEWOCK STATE PARK**
Rt 16
Errol, NH 03579
Web: www.nhstateparks.org/ParksPages/Mollidgewock/
Mollidgewock.html
Phone: 603-482-3373
Size: 46 acres. **Location:** Off NH Route 16, 3 miles south of Errol and 28 miles north of Berlin. **Facilities:** 47 primitive tent campsites (5 are remote sites), group use area, camp store, picnic area, boat rentals (non-motorized). **Activities:** Camping, canoeing, kayaking, fishing, wildlife viewing. **Special Features:** Park is located within the 13-Mile Woods Scenic Area, along the shore of the Androscoggin River, an area popular for viewing moose and other wildlife.

★3264★ **MONADNOCK STATE PARK**
Rt 124
Jaffrey, NH 03452
Web: www.nhstateparks.org/ParksPages/Monadnock/
Monadnock.html
Phone: 603-532-8862
Size: 1,017 acres. **Location:** Off NH 124, 4 miles north of Jaffrey. **Facilities:** 21 tent sites (open year round, with limited services from November-March), youth group camping area, showers, flush toilets, picnic area, park store, trails, visitor center. **Activities:** Camping (including winter camping), hiking, cross-country skiing. **Special Features:** Mount Monadnock, a National Natural Landmark and a mecca for hikers, offers 40 miles of trails leading to its 3,165-foot summit. From the summit visitors have a 100-mile view to points in all six New England states. Mount Monadnock is one of the most climbed mountains in the world.

★3265★ **MOOSE BROOK STATE PARK**
RFD 1
30 Jimtown Rd
Gorham, NH 03581
Web: www.nhparks.state.nh.us/ParksPages/MooseBrook/
MooseBrook.html
Phone: 603-466-3860
Size: 744 acres. **Location:** Off US 2, 2 miles west of Gorham. **Facilities:** 59 campsites (wooded, open, remote, and pull-through sites; no hookups), showers, flush toilets, camp store, youth group area, trails. **Activities:** Camping, fishing, swimming, picnicking, hiking, biking, winter use. **Special Features:** Park serves as an excellent base for hiking the Crescent and Presidential ranges of the White Mountains, or for visiting the 6,288-foot Mount Washington.

★3266★ **MOUNT SUNAPEE STATE PARK**
Newbury, NH 03255
Web: www.nhstateparks.org/ParksPages/Sunapee/
Sunapee.html
Phone: 603-763-5561
Size: 2,893 acres. **Location:** Off Route 103 north of Newbury. **Facilities:** 5 lean-to campsites with pit toilets and water, beach, bathhouse, canoe and kayak rentals, store, playground, boat launch (some restrictions), restrooms with flush toilets and showers (at beach). **Activities:** Camping, picnicking, boating, fishing, swimming, hiking, alpine skiing (at Mount Sunapee Resort). **Special Features:** Park is a major recreation area in the Dartmouth-Lake Sunapee Region and includes an area for primitive family camping and the Mount Sunapee State Park Beach. Park is open in summer-fall months only, but winter skiing is available at Mount Sunapee Resort, which is owned by the state and managed by Okemo Mountain Resort.

★3267★ **MOUNT WASHINGTON STATE PARK**
Rt 302
Sargent's Purchase, NH 03581
Web: www.nhstateparks.org/ParksPages/MtWash/
MtWash.html
Phone: 603-466-3347
Size: 52 acres. **Location:** Near US 302, north of Crawford Notch and Route 16 at Pinkham Notch. Surrounded by White Mountain National Forest (see separate entry in national forests chapter). **Facilities:** Visitor center, cafeteria, restrooms, gift shop, observatory, museum, historic site, hiking trails, scenic auto road, cog railway. **Activities:** Hiking. **Special Features:** Mount Washington, the highest mountain in the northeast (6,288 feet), experiences some of the worst weather in the world and is the site of the highest land wind speed ever recorded (231 mph). Wind exceeds hurricane force (75 mph) more than 100 days a year. Park includes the restored Tip Top House and the Mount Washington Observatory Museum. A segment of the Appalachian National Scenic Trail passes through the park (see separate entry in national trails section). Park can be reached by auto road, cog railway, or hiking trails.

★3268★ **NANSEN WAYSIDE PARK**
Rt 16
Milan, NH 03588
Web: www.nhstateparks.org/ParksPages/Nansen/Nansen.html
Phone: 603-823-7722
Size: 6 acres. **Location:** On NH Route 16, 4 miles north of Berlin. **Facilities:** Picnic area, boat launch, pit toilets. **Activities:** Boating, fishing. **Special Features:** Park is located on the banks of the Androscoggin River and is the site of the historic 170-foot steel-framed Nansen Ski Jump (no longer in use), which towers over the area.

★3269★ **NORTH BEACH**
Rt 1A
Hampton, NH 03842
Web: www.nhparks.state.nh.us/ParksPages/NorthBeach/
NorthBeach.html
Phone: 603-436-1552
Location: Off NH Route 1A. **Facilities:** Bathhouse. **Activities:** Swimming. **Special Features:** Beach includes a bathhouse that's open year round and lifeguard service.

★3270★ **NORTH HAMPTON STATE BEACH**
Rt 1A
Hampton, NH 03862
Web: www.nhstateparks.org/ParksPages/NHampton/
NHampton.html
Phone: 603-436-1552

Size: 1.1 acres. Location: On NH Route 1A. Facilities: Bathhouse. Activities: Swimming. Special Features: Beach amenities include lifeguard service in the summer months.

★3271★ NORTHWOOD MEADOWS STATE PARK

Northwood, NH 03261
Web: www.nhstateparks.org/ParksPages/NorthwoodMeadows/
NorthwoodMdws.html
Phone: 603-485-2034
Size: 664 acres. Location: Off NH Route 4, in Northwood. Facilities: Trails (&). Activities: Fishing, boating (no motors), picnicking, biking, hiking, snowmobiling, cross-country skiing. Special Features: This wooded park in a wilderness setting has a large wetlands area and is an excellent place for nature walks. The park includes a pond created by a dammed brook.

★3272★ ODIORNE POINT STATE PARK

Rt 1A
Rye, NH 03870
Web: www.nhstateparks.org/ParksPages/Odiorne/
Odiorne.html
Phone: 603-436-7406
Size: 334 acres. Location: On NH Route 1A, 3 miles south of Portsmouth. Facilities: Picnic areas, group use area, large playground, trails, paved bike path, boat launch, restrooms, science center, interpretive displays. Activities: Boating, fishing, hiking, bicycling, cross-country skiing, educational programs. Special Features: Park offers sweeping views of the ocean and rocky shore and a network of trails through dense vegetation. The Seacoast Science Center, which is located in the park, has exhibits relating to the natural and human history of Odiorne and this seacoast area. The Center's programs include opportunities to learn about tide pool animals in an indoor touch tank or watch deep ocean fish swim the 1,000-gallon Gulf of Maine tank.

★3273★ PAWTUCKAWAY STATE PARK

128 Mountain Rd
Nottingham, NH 03290
Web: www.nhstateparks.org/ParksPages/Pawtuckaway/
Pawtuckaway.html
Phone: 603-895-3031
Size: 5,536 acres. Location: Off NH Route 156, near Nottingham. Facilities: 195 campsites (mainly for tents), youth group campsites, showers, flush toilets, camp store, picnic area, group use area with picnic shelter, ballfield, playground, beach, bathhouse, park store, boat launch, canoe rentals. Activities: Camping, boating, canoeing, fishing, swimming, hiking, biking, horseback riding (with restrictions), cross-country skiing, snowmobiling, wildlife viewing. Special Features: Park offers a variety of landscapes and points of interest, including an 803-acre lake, a mountaintop fire tower, a marsh where beavers, deer, and great blue herons can be seen, and a geologically unique field with large boulders called glacial erratics that were deposited there at the end of the last Ice Age.

★3274★ PILLSBURY STATE PARK

Washington, NH 03280
Web: www.nhstateparks.org/ParksPages/Pillsbury/
Pillsbury.html
Phone: 603-863-2860
Size: 5,561 acres. Location: 3.5 miles north of Washington off Route 31. Facilities: 41 primitive tent campsites (including 7 walk-in, 1 hike-to, and 2 boat-in sites and 1 youth group site) with pit toilets, playground, canoe rentals; hiking and mountain bike trails. Activities: Camping, canoeing, fishing, picnicking, hiking, mountain biking; winter use with some restrictions. Special Features: Park is heavily wooded, with several ponds and wetlands, and is one of New Hampshire's more primitive parks. Its network of hiking trails provides a major link in the Monadnock-Sunapee Greenway, a 51-mile hiking trail that connects the two mountains.

★3275★ PISGAH STATE PARK

PO Box 242
Winchester, NH 03470
Web: www.nhstateparks.org/ParksPages/Pisgah/Pisgah.htmll
Phone: 603-239-8153
Size: 13,361 acres. Location: Off Routes 10, 119, and 63 in Winchester, Chesterfield, and Hinsdale. Facilities: Visitor center (limited schedule), trails. Activities: Boating (with restrictions), fishing, hiking, mountain biking, horseback riding, snowmobiling, ATV riding. Special Features: Park is New Hampshire's largest state park, with 21 square miles of rough, forested terrain that encompasses an entire watershed as well as ponds, highland ridges, and numerous wetlands.

★3276★ RHODODENDRON STATE PARK

Rt 119W
Fitzwilliam, NH 03447
Web: www.nhstateparks.org/ParksPages/Rhododendron/
Rhododendron.html
Phone: 603-532-8862
Size: 766 acres. Location: Off NH Route 119W, north of Fitzwilliam. Facilities: Trails (including a & trail). Activities: Hiking, picnicking. Special Features: Park is named for the 16-acre grove of *Rhododendron Maximum*, a National Natural Landmark that is the park's focal point. A trail (&) encircles the grove, allowing visitors to observe the flowers close-up. Peak bloom is usually in mid-July. Wildflowers bloom throughout the park, and a wildflower trail winds through the forest adjacent to the rhododendron grove.

★3277★ ROBERT FROST FARM HISTORIC SITE

Route 28
Derry, NH 03038
Web: www.nhstateparks.org/ParksPages/FrostFarm/Frost.html
Phone: 603-432-3091
Size: 64 acres. Location: On Route 28, south of Derry. Facilities: Historic home, displays, trail, children's garden, visitor center. Activities: Guided tours, video presentations, poetry readings, picnicking. Special Features: Site was the home of poet Robert Frost and his family from 1900 to 1911. The structure is a simple, two-story white clapboard house, typical of

New England in the 1880s. The farmhouse and barn are open to the public week-ends from Memorial Day to Labor Day; grounds are open year round.

★3278★ ROLLINS STATE PARK
Warner, NH 03278
Web: www.nhstateparks.org/ParksPages/Rollins/Rollins.html
Phone: 603-456-3808
Size: Park of 4,965-acre Kearsarge Mountain State Forest. **Location:** Off Route 103 in the town of Warner. **Facilities:** Picnic area, hiking trails, scenic auto road. **Activities:** Hiking; winter use (with restrictions). **Special Features:** Park is situated on the south slope of Mount Kearsarge, with a 3.5 mile scenic auto road rising from the park's entrance to the parking and picnic area, which offers spectacular views. A half-mile hiking trail leads from the picnic area to the summit.

★3279★ RYE HARBOR STATE PARK
Rye, NH 03870
Web: www.nhstateparks.org/ParksPages/RyeHarbor/RyeHarbor.html
Phone: 603-436-1552
Size: 63 acres. **Location:** Off NH Route 1A. **Facilities:** Picnic tables, group use area, restrooms. **Activities:** Saltwater fishing, picnicking. **Special Features:** Park affords scenic views of the Atlantic Ocean, the Isles of Shoals, and Rye Harbor.

★3280★ SCULPTURED ROCKS NATURAL AREA
Groton, NH 03241
Web: www.nhstateparks.org/ParksPages/SculpturedRocks/SculpturedRocks.html
Phone: 603-823-7722
Size: 274 acres. **Location:** Between Routes 3A and 118 in Groton. **Special Features:** Park features interesting potholes eroded into curious shapes during the last Ice Age by water-borne stones and sediment.

★3281★ SILVER LAKE STATE PARK
Rt 122
Hollis, NH 03049
Web: www.nhstateparks.org/ParksPages/SilverLake/SilverLake.html
Phone: 603-465-2342
Size: 80 acres. **Location:** On Route 122, 1 mile north of Hollis. **Facilities:** Beach, bathhouse, picnic tables, kayak and paddleboat rentals, park store, restrooms. **Activities:** Swimming, boating (no motors), fishing, hiking. **Special Features:** Park's sandy 1,000-foot beach curves along a 34-acre lake. The park is open May-September.

★3282★ TAYLOR MILL HISTORIC SITE
Island Pond Rd
Derry, NH 03038
Phone: 603-431-6774
Size: 71 acres (Ballard State Forest). **Location:** In Ballard State Forest, near Derry on Island Pond Road. **Activities:** Picnicking,

boating (no motors), fishing, guided tours. **Special Features:** The renovated 1800s ''up and down'' sawmill is situated in Ballard State Forest in Derry. It is operated for demonstrations on certain week-ends during the summer.

★3283★ UMBAGOG LAKE STATE PARK
Rt 26
Cambridge, NH 03579
Web: www.nhstateparks.org/ParksPages/Umbagog/Umbagog.html
Phone: 603-482-7795
Size: 1,360 acres. **Location:** 7 miles east of Errol on Route 26. **Facilities:** 35 campsites with electrical and water hook-ups, 34 primitive remote campsites (mostly boat-in), 3 rental cabins, pit and flush toilets, camp store, boat launch, fuel sales, canoe and boat rentals, swimming beach. **Activities:** Camping, boating, fishing, swimming, picnicking, wildlife viewing, guided tours. **Special Features:** Park is one of the state's newer parks in the Great North Woods Region. Wildlife viewing here includes deer, moose, and a variety of birds.

★3284★ WADLEIGH STATE PARK
Rt 114
Sutton, NH 03260
Web: www.nhstateparks.org/ParksPages/Wadleigh/Wadleigh.html
Phone: 603-927-4724
Size: 43 acres. **Location:** On NH Route 114 in North Sutton. **Facilities:** Picnic areas, group use area, bathhouse, playing fields, flush toilets. **Activities:** Fishing, swimming, boating (some restrictions), biking; winter use (with restrictions). **Special Features:** Talls pines shade picnic sites adjacent to the beach on Kezar Lake.

★3285★ WALLIS SANDS STATE BEACH
Rt 1A
Rye, NH 03870
Web: www.nhstateparks.org/ParksPages/Wallis/Wallis.html
Phone: 603-436-9404
Size: 30 acres. **Location:** Off NH Route 1A south. **Facilities:** Store concession (food, drinks, other items), bathhouse with hot and cold showers, picnic tables (fires not allowed). **Activities:** Swimming. **Special Features:** This oceanfront beach offers views of the Isles of Shoals.

★3286★ WELLINGTON STATE PARK
Bristol, NH 03222
Web: www.nhstateparks.org/ParksPages/Wellington/Wellington.html
Phone: 603-744-2197
Size: 220 acres. **Location:** Off NH Route 3A, on West Shore Road in Bristol. **Facilities:** Picnic areas, 2 group picnic pavilions, swimming beach, bathhouse, volleyball and horseshoe courts, snack bar, boat launch (nearby), hiking trails, nature trail. **Activities:** Youth group camping, fishing, boating, swimming, hiking, winter use. **Special Features:** Located on the shore of

Newfound Lake, Park has the largest freshwater swimming beach in the New Hampshire State Park system.

★3287★ WENTWORTH-COOLIDGE MANSION HISTORIC SITE

375 Little Harbor Rd
Portsmouth, NH 03801
Web: www.nhparks.state.nh.us/ParksPages/
WentworthCoolidge/WentCoolHom.html
Phone: 603-436-6607
Size: 64 acres. **Location:** At the end of Little Harbor Road, 2 miles from downtown Portsmouth, off Route 1A. **Facilities:** Historic home, picnic area, restrooms, visitor center. **Activities:** Guided tours. **Special Features:** This 40-room mansion was the home of Benning Wentworth, New Hampshire's first royal governor, who served from 1741-1767. The house contains the council chamber where the state's first provincial government conducted its affairs in the pre-Revolutionary War period. The mansion is one of the most outstanding homes still remaining from the colonial era and is designated a National Historic Landmark.

★3288★ WENTWORTH STATE PARK

Wolfeboro, NH 03894
Web: www.nhstateparks.org/ParksPages/Wentworth/
Wentworth.html
Phone: 603-569-3699
Size: 51 acres. **Location:** On NH 109, 5 miles east of Wolfeboro. **Facilities:** Picnic tables, group use area, flush toilets, boat launch. **Activities:** Boating, fishing, swimming. **Special Features:** This small beach park is located on the shore of scenic Lake Wentworth. Open seasonally.

★3289★ WHITE LAKE STATE PARK

Rt 16
Tamworth, NH 03886
Web: www.nhstateparks.org/ParksPages/WhiteLake/
WhiteLake.html
Phone: 603-323-7350
Size: 903 acres. **Location:** On NH Route 16, 20 miles south of North Conway. **Facilities:** 200 tent sites, showers, flush toilets, camp store, canoe rentals, picnic area, group shelter, trails, beach, canoe rentals. **Activities:** Camping (including organized youth group camping), boating (with restrictions), fishing, swimming, hiking, canoeing, winter use. **Special Features:** Park's campground is well-located to serve as a base for a number of area activities — the Kancamagus National Scenic Byway, White Mountain National Forest hiking trails, and North Conway's tax-free shopping outlets are all within 20 minutes of the campground. In addition, a walking trail in the park leads to a 72-acre stand of pitch pines that has been designated a National Natural Landmark.

★3290★ WINSLOW STATE PARK

Kearsarge Mountain Rd
Wilmot, NH 03287
Web: www.nhstateparks.org/ParksPages/Winslow/
Winslow.html
Phone: 603-526-6168
Size: Park of 4,965-acre Kearsarge Mountain State Forest. **Location:** Off NH Route 11 in Wilmot. **Facilities:** Picnic area, hiking trails, scenic auto road. **Activities:** Hiking; fishing and winter use with some restrictions. **Special Features:** Park is located on the northwest slope of Mount Kearsarge. The picnic area is on a 1,820-foot plateau with views of the White Mountains to the north and the taller of the southern and central Vermont peaks. Trails lead to the summit.

9. State Parks

New Jersey State Parks

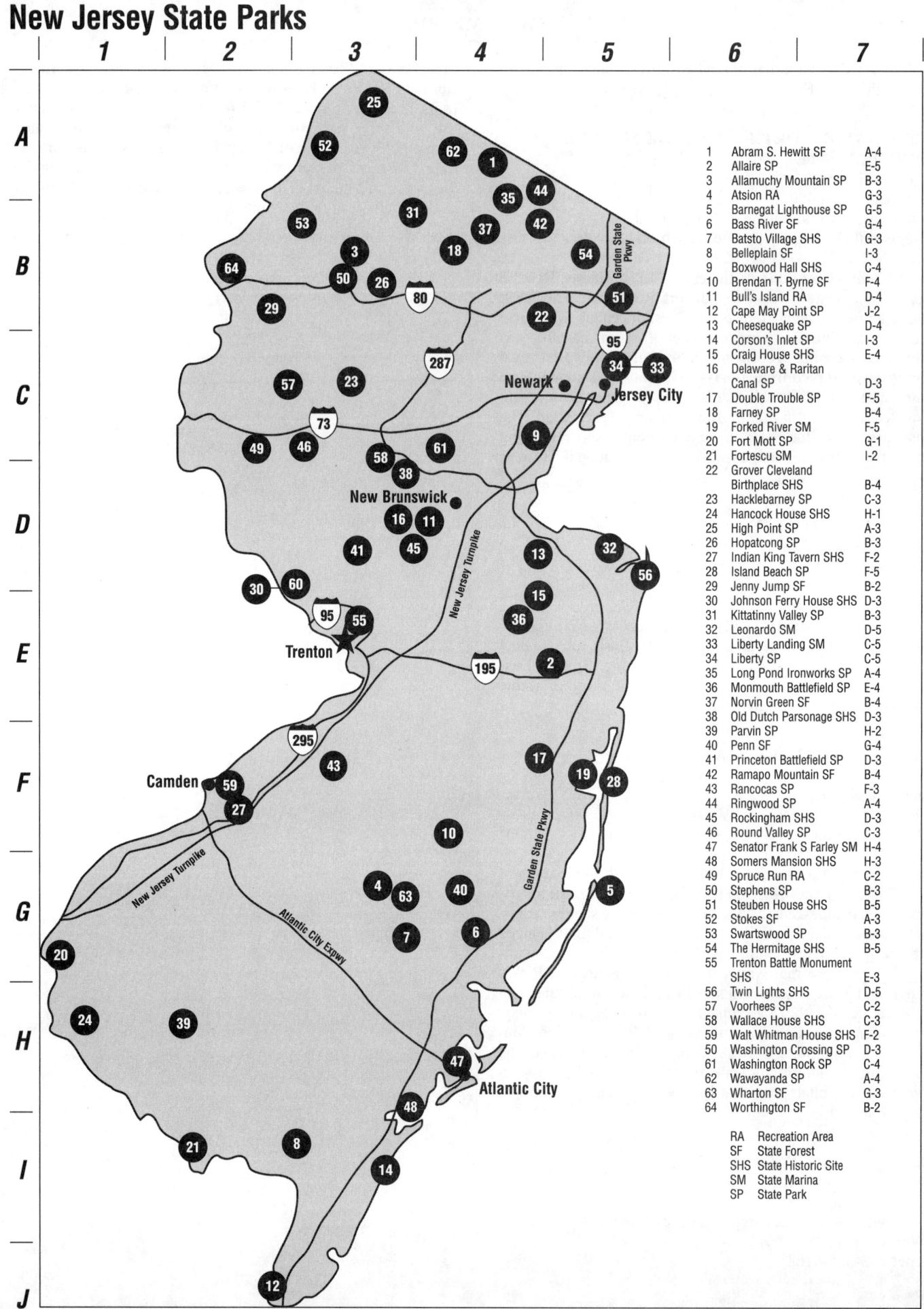

1	Abram S. Hewitt SF	A-4
2	Allaire SP	E-5
3	Allamuchy Mountain SP	B-3
4	Atsion RA	G-3
5	Barnegat Lighthouse SP	G-5
6	Bass River SF	G-4
7	Batsto Village SHS	G-3
8	Belleplain SF	I-3
9	Boxwood Hall SHS	C-4
10	Brendan T. Byrne SF	F-4
11	Bull's Island RA	D-4
12	Cape May Point SP	J-2
13	Cheesequake SP	D-4
14	Corson's Inlet SP	I-3
15	Craig House SHS	E-4
16	Delaware & Raritan Canal SP	D-3
17	Double Trouble SP	F-5
18	Farney SP	B-4
19	Forked River SM	F-5
20	Fort Mott SP	G-1
21	Fortescu SM	I-2
22	Grover Cleveland Birthplace SHS	B-4
23	Hacklebarney SP	C-3
24	Hancock House SHS	H-1
25	High Point SP	A-3
26	Hopatcong SP	B-3
27	Indian King Tavern SHS	F-2
28	Island Beach SP	F-5
29	Jenny Jump SF	B-2
30	Johnson Ferry House SHS	D-3
31	Kittatinny Valley SP	B-3
32	Leonardo SM	D-5
33	Liberty Landing SM	C-5
34	Liberty SP	C-5
35	Long Pond Ironworks SP	A-4
36	Monmouth Battlefield SP	E-4
37	Norvin Green SF	B-4
38	Old Dutch Parsonage SHS	D-3
39	Parvin SP	H-2
40	Penn SF	G-4
41	Princeton Battlefield SP	D-3
42	Ramapo Mountain SF	B-4
43	Rancocas SP	F-3
44	Ringwood SP	A-4
45	Rockingham SHS	D-3
46	Round Valley SP	C-3
47	Senator Frank S Farley SM	H-4
48	Somers Mansion SHS	H-3
49	Spruce Run RA	C-2
50	Stephens SP	B-3
51	Steuben House SHS	B-5
52	Stokes SF	A-3
53	Swartswood SP	B-3
54	The Hermitage SHS	B-5
55	Trenton Battle Monument SHS	E-3
56	Twin Lights SHS	D-5
57	Voorhees SP	C-2
58	Wallace House SHS	C-3
59	Walt Whitman House SHS	F-2
50	Washington Crossing SP	D-3
61	Washington Rock SP	C-4
62	Wawayanda SP	A-4
63	Wharton SF	G-3
64	Worthington SF	B-2

RA	Recreation Area
SF	State Forest
SHS	State Historic Site
SM	State Marina
SP	State Park

NEW JERSEY

★3291★ **New Jersey Department of Environmental Protection**
Division of Parks & Forestry
401 E State St, 7th Fl
Trenton, NJ 08625
(609) 984-0370 - Phone
(609) 292-7695 - Fax
(609) 984-6085 - Volunteering
Web: www.njparksandforests.org
Administers 42 parks, 11 forests, 3 recreation areas, and more than 50 historic sites. Manages the state trail system. Supports efforts to improve park access for people with disabilities.

Key to campsite classification:

- **Tent and trailer campsites** — Equipped with picnic table and fire ring. Sanitary facilities and water are nearby. No trailer hookups.
- **Cabins** — Accommodate four to six people (limited number can sleep eight persons). Contain living room area, sleeping quarters, kitchen, bathroom, running water, and electricity.
- **Camp shelters** — Small cabins with living room area, sleeping quarters, outside cooking equipment, and central toilet and shower facilities.
- **Lean-tos** — 4 sided, with wood-burning stove or propane heater.
- **Wilderness campsites** — Primitive campsites accessible only by hiking, canoe, or small boat. (Wharton offers wilderness campsites accessible by horseback.)
- **Group camps** — Minimum of seven persons per night.
- **Group cabins** — Furnished living room with fireplace, full kitchen, bunkrooms with double bunks, bathrooms with showers. Accommodates 12-30 people.

★3292★ **ABRAM S. HEWITT STATE FOREST**
c/o Wawayanda State Park
885 Warwick Tpke
Hewitt, NJ 07421
Web: www.njparksandforests.org/parks/abram.html
Phone: 973-853-4462
Size: 2,001 acres. **Location:** In Hewitt, off the Warwick Turnpike; access via Route 23 to Union Valley Road into West Milford. **Facilities:** Trails, lookout point. **Activities:** Hiking, hunting, cross-country skiing. **Special Features:** Isolated and untouched, the forest includes marshes and wetlands with several brooks and streams crisscrossing the lower areas. A section of the Appalachian National Scenic Trail (see separate entry in national trails section) passes through the forest, ascending Bearfort Ridge and offering scenic views eastward to Greenwood Lake.

★3293★ **ALLAIRE STATE PARK**
PO Box 220
Farmingdale, NJ 07727
Web: www.njparksandforests.org/parks/allaire.html
Phone: 732-938-2371
Size: 3,086 acres. **Location:** In Monmouth County, off the Garden State Parkway (Exit 98) or I-195 (Exit 31B). **Facilities:** 45 tent and trailer campsites with flush toilets and showers, 4 yurts (♿), 6 shelters (♿), 6 group sites with pit toilets, picnic tables and shelters, playground, food concession, equestrian trails, nature trails, historic sites, visitor center and museum, nature center. **Activities:** Camping, canoeing/kayaking, fishing, limited deer hunting, hiking, mountain biking, horseback riding, cross-country skiing, bird watching, historical programs, nature programs. **Special Features:** Park features historic Allaire Village, a restored 19th-century ironmaking village, and Pine Creek Railroad, with live-steam and diesel, narrow-gauge trains. The Manasquan River winds through the park and through Spring Meadow Golf Course, which is located adjacent to the park.

★3294★ **ALLAMUCHY MOUNTAIN STATE PARK**
c/o Stephens State Park
800 Willow Grove St
Hackettstown, NJ 07840
Web: www.njparksandforests.org/parks/allamuch.html
Phone: 908-852-3790
Size: 8,461 acres. **Location:** 3 miles north of Hackettstown between Willow Grove/Waterloo Road (Route 604) on the east, Route 517 on the west, and Cranberry Lake (Route 206) on the north. **Facilities:** Multi-use trails, cartop boat launch, lookout point, historic village. **Activities:** Camping, boating (electric motors only), canoeing, fishing, hunting, picnicking, hiking, horseback riding, mountain biking, winter sports (ice skating, ice fishing, ice boating, sledding, cross-country skiing), historical programs (seasonal), music programs (seasonal). **Special Features:** Park includes the Musconetcong River, with some of the best trout fishing in the state, and historic Waterloo Village, an early 19th-century restored village containing a working mill complex with gristmills and sawmills, a general store, blacksmith shop, and several historic houses.

★3295★ **ATSION RECREATION AREA**
c/o Wharton State Forest
4110 Nesco Rd
Hammonton, NJ 08037
Web: www.njparksandforests.org/parks/wharton.html
Phone: 609-268-0444
Location: On Route 206 in Shamong Township. **Facilities:** 50

9. State Parks

635

tent and trailer campsites with modern restrooms and showers, 9 cabins, group camp with pit toilets, picnic area, playground, swimming area, bathhouse, boat launch, hiking trails, food concession. **Activities:** Camping, fishing, boating (electric or non-powered only), swimming, hiking, mountain biking, horseback riding, interpretive programs (seasonal). **Special Features:** Atsion Recreation Area is located in Wharton State Forest (see separate entry).

★3296★ **BARNEGAT LIGHTHOUSE STATE PARK**
PO Box 167
Barnegat Light, NJ 08006
Web: www.njparksandforests.org/parks/barnlig.html
Phone: 609-494-2016
Size: 32 acres. **Location:** On the northern tip of Long Beach Island in Ocean County via the Garden State Parkway (Exit 63) or Route 72 east. **Facilities:** Picnic areas (&), picnic shelter, nature trail, lookout point, interpretive center. **Activities:** Fishing, bird watching, picnicking, hiking/walking, historical programs (seasonal). **Special Features:** The site of Barnegat Lighthouse on the northern tip of Long Beach in Ocean County was regarded as one of the most crucial "change of course" points for coastal vessels, which depended on the lighthouse to avoid offshore shoals. The story of Barnegat Lighthouse is showcased in the park's Interpretive Center.

★3297★ **BASS RIVER STATE FOREST**
762 Stage Rd
Tuckerton, NJ 08087
Web: www.njparksandforests.org/parks/bass.html
Phone: 609-296-1114
Size: 26,764 acres. **Location:** 25 miles north of Atlantic City and 6 miles west of Tuckerton via the Garden State Parkway. **Facilities:** 176 tent and trailer campsites (no hookups), 6 group campsites with pit toilets, 9 lean-tos (&), 6 lakeside shelters, 6 cabins, showers, flush toilets, laundry facilities, picnic area, picnic shelter, playground, trails (including a segment of the state's 50-mile Batona Trail), bathhouse, boat launch, rowboat concession (seasonal), food concession. **Activities:** Camping, boating (electric motors only), canoeing, fishing, swimming, hiking, horseback riding, hunting, snowmobiling, cross-country skiing. **Special Features:** Forest includes the Absegami Natural Area, a white cedar swamp with a half-mile nature trail, and West Pine Plains Natural Area, a rare stunted forest ecosystem, with pine and oak trees that may reach a canopy height of only four feet at maturity. Lake Absegami is the center of the forest's recreational activities.

★3298★ **BATSTO VILLAGE STATE HISTORIC SITE**
RD 9
Hammonton, NJ 08037
Web: www.njparksandforests.org/historic/index.html
Phone: 609-561-0024
Size: 40 acres. **Location:** On Route 542, 8 miles east of Hammonton, in Wharton State Forest (see separate entry). **Special Features:** Batsto Village is the site of a former bog iron and glassmaking industrial center (1766-1867) that now reflects the agricultural and commercial enterprises of Joseph Wharton during the years 1876-1909. The village consists of 33 historic buildings and structures, including Batsto Mansion, a gristmill, sawmill, general store, workers' homes, and a post office.

★3299★ **BELLEPLAIN STATE FOREST**
County Rt 50
PO Box 450
Woodbine, NJ 08270
Web: www.njparksandforests.org/parks/belle.html
Phone: 609-861-2404
Size: 21,034 acres. **Location:** Off the Garden State Parkway, Exit 17 southbound to Routes 9 and 550 or Exit 13 northbound; follow signs to forest. **Facilities:** 169 tent and trailer campsites, 2 group campsites with chemical toilets, 14 lean-tos (&), group cabin (&), 5 yurts (&), flush toilets, showers, group picnic area with shelter, ballfields, and playground, food concession, trails (including fitness trail), lookout point, bathhouse, boat launch, canoe rental, interpretive center. **Activities:** Camping, boating (electric motors only), canoeing, fishing, swimming, hiking, bicycling, mountain biking, horseback riding, hunting, trapping, ice fishing, snowmobiling, cross-country skiing . **Special Features:** Site includes Lake Nummy, a popular swimming, boating, and fishing area.

★3300★ **BOXWOOD HALL STATE HISTORIC SITE**
1073 E Jersey St
Elizabeth, NJ 07201
Web: www.njparksandforests.org/historic/index.html
Phone: 908-282-7167
Location: On East Jersey Street in Elizabeth. **Special Features:** Built in 1750, Boxwood Hall became the residence of Elias Boudinot, president of the Continental Congress that signed the Peace Treaty with Great Britain. George Washington visited Boudinot's home on his way to New York in 1789 for his first inauguration.

★3301★ **BRENDAN T. BYRNE STATE FOREST**
PO Box 215
New Lisbon, NJ 08064
Web: www.njparksandforests.org/parks/byrne.html
Phone: 609-726-1191
Size: 34,725 acres. **Location:** 30 miles east of Camden; accessible via the New Jersey Turnpike. **Facilities:** 82 tent and trailer campsites with flush toilets and showers, 3 group sites with water and flush toilets, 3 cabins, 3 yurts (&), picnic areas, picnic shelters, playground, multi-use trails (including a segment of the state's Batona Trail), historic village. **Activities:** Camping, fishing, hunting, hiking, bicycling, mountain biking, horseback riding, cross-country skiing, bird watching, environmental programs. **Special Features:** Forest (formerly known as Lebanon State Forest) is the site of historic Whitesbog Village, which is undergoing restoration. Founded in the 1870s, Whitesbog was once the largest cranberry farm in the state and is the birthplace of the cultivated blueberry. Forest also contains the 735-acre Cedar Swamp Natural Area, which supports the threatened swamp pink and other endangered plant species.

9. State Parks

★3302★ BULL'S ISLAND RECREATION AREA

2185 Daniel Bray Hwy
Stockton, NJ 08559
Web: www.njparksandforests.org/parks/bull.html
Phone: 609-397-2949
Size: 80 acres. **Location:** Take I-287 or Route 22 to the intersection with Route 202 in Somerville. Follow Route 202 south for 26 miles to the exit for Route 29 north. Go north for about 6 miles. Park entrance is on the left. **Facilities:** 69 tent and trailer campsites, flush toilet, showers, picnic area, playground, canoe launch, trails, lookout point. **Activities:** Camping, boating (electric motors only), canoeing, hiking, bicycling, mountain biking, cross-country skiing. **Special Features:** Area includes the Bull's Island Natural Area, which comprises a portion of a small forested island surrounded by the Delaware River and the Delaware & Raritan Canal.

★3303★ CAPE MAY POINT STATE PARK

PO Box 107
Cape May Point, NJ 08212
Web: www.njparksandforests.org/parks/capemay.html
Phone: 609-884-2159
Size: 235 acres. **Location:** In Cape May County, off the southern end of the Garden state Parkway. **Facilities:** Picnic tables and shelters, trails (including ⅃ trail), historic sites, interpretive/visitor center. **Activities:** Picnicking, surf fishing, hiking, bird watching, nature study, interpretive programs. **Special Features:** The 157-foot-high Cape May Point Lighthouse near the park entrance is still commissioned as an aid to navigation. The top of the lighthouse affords a panoramic view of the Cape May peninsula.

★3304★ CHEESEQUAKE STATE PARK

300 Gordon Rd
Matawan, NJ 07747
Web: www.njparksandforests.org/parks/cheesequake.html
Phone: 732-566-2161
Size: 1,361 acres. **Location:** Off the Garden State Parkway at Exit 120 or via Route 34; follow signs. **Facilities:** 53 tent and trailer campsites with flush toilets and showers, 6 group campsites with water and flush toilets, picnic areas, group picnic areas with shelter, playfields, and playground, hiking and multiuse trails, bathhouse, food concession, interpretive center. **Activities:** Camping, boating (electric motors only; cartop boat launch only), canoeing, lake fishing, swimming, hiking, bicycling, mountain biking, cross-country skiing, snow shoeing, sledding. **Special Features:** Park is located in the middle of the urban north and suburban south, in a transitional zone between two different ecosystems. Open fields, saltwater and freshwater marshes, a white cedar swamp, Pine Barrens, and a northeastern hardwood forest are its principal characteristics.

★3305★ CORSON'S INLET STATE PARK

c/o Belleplain State Forest
County Rt 550, PO Box 450
Woodbine, NJ 08270
Web: www.njparksandforests.org/parks/corsons.html
Phone: 609-861-2404

Size: 341 acres. **Location:** Park is bisected by Ocean Drive (Route 619), connecting Ocean City and Strathmere-Sea Isle City; accessible via the Garden State Parkway. **Facilities:** Hiking trails, boat ramp, point-of-interest site. **Activities:** Boating, sailing, jet skiing, saltwater fishing, crabbing, hiking, interpretive tours. **Special Features:** Park protects and preserves one of the last undeveloped tracts of land along the state's oceanfront.

★3306★ CRAIG HOUSE STATE HISTORIC SITE

347 Freehold-Englishtown Rd
Manalapan, NJ 07726
Web: www.njparksandforests.org/historic/index.html
Phone: 732-462-9616
Location: In Monmouth Battlefield State Park (see separate entry). **Special Features:** The Craig House, built in 1710 and restored to its 18th century appearance, exhibits the architecture, grounds, and setting of a landowner's home of the period. House was used as a field hospital and headquarters during the battle of Monmouth. Tours of the house and grounds are offered.

★3307★ DELAWARE & RARITAN CANAL STATE PARK

145 Mapleton Rd
Princeton, NJ 08540
Web: www.njparksandforests.org/parks/drcanal.html
Phone: 609-924-5705
Size: 4,476 acres. **Location:** Spans 5 counties in central New Jersey. Park office is located at Blackwells Mills. **Facilities:** Picnic tables, trails; boat launch at Bull's Island Recreation Area. **Activities:** Boating (no restrictions on the Delaware River, but only electric motors, cartop launches, and canoes permitted on the canal), fishing, hiking, bicycling, mountain biking, horseback riding, cross-country skiing, nature and history programs. **Special Features:** This 70-mile linear park is a popular recreational corridor as well as a valuable wildlife corridor connecting fields and forests. With its 19th-century bridges, bridgetender houses, locks, cobblestone spillways, and hand-built stone-arched culverts, the canal is also a great attraction to history lovers.

★3308★ DOUBLE TROUBLE STATE PARK

PO Box 175
Bayville, NJ 08721
Web: www.njparksandforests.org/parks/double.html
Phone: 732-341-6662
Size: 7,881 acres. **Location:** Off the Garden State Parkway (Exit 77) south on Double Trouble Road, across Pinewald Kessick Road. **Facilities:** Trails, historic village. **Activities:** Fishing, hunting, canoeing, kayaking, hiking, horseback riding, biking, picnicking (no tables or grills provided). **Special Features:** Park includes Double Trouble Village, originally a cranberry farm and packing plant. The one-time company town consists of 14 original historic structures dating from the late 19th century through the early 20th century, including a general store, a schoolhouse, and cottages, as well as a restored sawmill and cranberry sorting and packing house.

9. State Parks

★3309★ FARNY STATE PARK

c/o Ringwood State Park
1304 Sloatsburg Rd
Ringwood, NJ 07456
Web: www.njparksandforests.org/parks/farny.html
Phone: 973-962-7031
Size: 3,951 acres. **Location:** Next to Splitrock Reservoir, Rockaway Township, Morris County. Take Route 287 to Route 23 to Green Pond Road in Newfoundland. Turn left onto Upper Hibernia Road, then left onto Split Rock Road and follow it across Splitrock Reservoir Dam to parking area on left. **Facilities:** Undeveloped. **Activities:** Hiking, birdwatching, fishing (from boats only; no shoreline fishing permitted), ice fishing, hunting, cartop boat launching (no gas motors permitted), cross-country skiing. **Special Features:** Park is a forested wilderness of watershed lands crossed by an old logging road. Trail entry is through the Farny Natural Area. Split Rock Reservoir is adjacent to the park.

★3310★ FORKED RIVER STATE MARINA

311 S Main St
Forked River, NJ 08731
Web: www.njparksandforests.org/parks/
    marinas.html#forkedriver
Phone: 609-693-5045
Location: On Route 9, off the Garden State Parkway at Exit 74. **Facilities:** 125 berths; water, electricity, cable TV, and telephone hookups; laundry, shower/sanitary facilities, holding tank pumppout. **Special Features:** Facilities for bait and tackle, gas and diesel fuel, ice, ship store, restaurant, and repairs are located near the marina.

★3311★ FORT MOTT STATE PARK

454 Fort Mott Rd
Pennsville, NJ 08070
Web: www.njparksandforests.org/parks/fortmott.html
Phone: 856-935-3218
Size: 104 acres. **Location:** On Fort Mott Road, 3 miles off Route 49 East. **Facilities:** Historic site, picnic area, picnic shelter, group picnic area with playfields and playground, nature trail (&), welcome center with displays. **Activities:** Fishing, cross-country skiing, sledding, historical programs. **Special Features:** Fort was part of a coastal defense system built to defend the Delaware River. Fortifications seen there today were built in 1896 in anticipation of the Spanish-American War. Visitors can follow interpretive signs with detailed descriptions through the old batteries.

★3312★ FORTESCU STATE MARINA

Fortescu, NJ 08321
Web: www.njparksandforests.org/parks/
    marinas.html#fortescue
Phone: 609-447-5115
Location: On Delaware Bay 23 miles northwest of Cape May. **Facilities:** 125 berths, water, electricity, gas and diesel fuel, holding tank pumpout, launch ramp, charter and head boats. **Special Features:** Marina is operated through a lease agreement.

Ice, bait and tackle, restaurant, and repair facilities are located nearby.

★3313★ GROVER CLEVELAND BIRTHPLACE STATE HISTORIC SITE

207 Bloomfield Ave
Caldwell, NJ 07006
Web: www.njparksandforests.org/historic/grover_cleveland/
    gc_home.htm
Phone: 973-226-0001
Location: On Bloomfield Avenue in Caldwell. **Activities:** Guided tours. **Special Features:** The house in which US President Grover Cleveland was born was built in 1832 as The Manse, or Pastor's residence, for the First Presbyterian Church at Caldwell. The Cleveland family lived there during the time Grover Cleveland's father was minister to the church, from 1834-1841. Most of the first floor rooms portray the house as it was in 1837, the year President Cleveland was born.

★3314★ HACKLEBARNEY STATE PARK

c/o Voorhees State Park
119 Hacklebarney Rd
Long Valley, NJ 07853
Web: www.njparksandforests.org/parks/hackle.html
Phone: 908-638-6969
Size: 977 acres. **Location:** Route 206 to Chester, then 1 mile west via Route 24/513 to State Park Road and 2 miles on State Park Road to Hacklebarney Road. **Facilities:** Picnic tables, playground, hiking trails. **Activities:** Fishing, hunting, hiking, cross-country skiing. **Special Features:** The Black River and two of its tributaries cut through rocky Hacklebarney State Park, cascading around boulders in deep, hemlock-lined ravines.

★3315★ HANCOCK HOUSE STATE HISTORIC SITE

3 Front St
Hancock's Bridge, NJ 08038
Web: www.njparksandforests.org/historic/hancockhouse/
    hancockhouse-index.htm
Phone: 856-935-4373
Location: In the town of Hancock's Bridge. **Activities:** Guided tours (call for tour availability). **Special Features:** Built in 1734 by Judge William Hancock, the house is an excellent example of English Quaker patterned end wall brick houses associated with the lower Delaware Valley and southwestern New Jersey. It was also the scene of a British-led massacre during the Revolutionary War.

★3316★ HIGH POINT STATE PARK

1480 Rt 23
Sussex, NJ 07461
Web: www.njparksandforests.org/parks/highpoint.html
Phone: 973-875-4800
Size: 15,413 acres. **Location:** 7 miles north of the town of Sussex via Route 23; or 4 miles south of Port Jervis, NY. **Facilities:** 50 tent campsites (no trailers), flush toilets, 2 group camps with pit toilets, 2 cabins, 1 group cabin, picnic areas,

group picnic facilities with shelters, playgrounds, food concessions, cross-country ski center, ski rentals, multi-use trails, self-guided nature trail, bathhouse, boat launch, visitor center. **Activities:** Camping, boating (electric motors only), canoeing, fishing, swimming, hiking, horseback riding, mountain biking, cross-country skiing, ice skating, ice fishing, snowmobiling, special deer hunt (November), historical programs (seasonal), nature programs (year round). **Special Features:** High Point Monument, dedicated to the memory of all war veterans, is 220 feet high and is located 1,803 feet above sea level. The view from the top of the monument is a panorama of farmland and forest, hills and valleys, in three states. A segment of the Appalachian National Scenic Trail passes through the park (see separate entry in national trails section).

★3317★ HOPATCONG STATE PARK

PO Box 8519
Landing, NJ 07850
Web: www.njparksandforests.org/parks/hopatcong.html
Phone: 973-398-7010
Size: 107 acres. **Location:** At the southwest end of Lake Hopatcong. Take Exit 28 from Route 80 or follow Route 183 in Netcong. **Facilities:** Picnic areas, shelter, playgrounds, basketball courts, sand volleyball courts, playing field, refreshments, bathhouse, boat ramps, lookout point, playground. **Activities:** Boating, canoeing, sailing, sailboarding, jet skiing, fishing, swimming, ice skating, ice fishing, ice boating, ice sailing, sledding, snowmobiling. **Special Features:** Lake Hopatcong was originally created as part of Morris Canal, a 90-mile waterway that ran from Newark to Phillipsburg and was the chief means of transporting coal, iron, and zinc across New Jersey in the 1860s. The lake is 9 miles long with 2,500 surface acres.

★3318★ INDIAN KING TAVERN STATE HISTORIC SITE

233 Kings Hwy
Haddonfield, NJ 08033
Web: www.njparksandforests.org/historic/indianking/
index.html
Phone: 856-429-6792
Location: On Kings Highway in Haddonfield. **Activities:** Tours (call ahead for availability). **Special Features:** Indian King Tavern was the site of two important meetings of the New Jersey Assembly. At the first meeting, on March 10, 1777, the Assembly approved the adoption of the Great Seal of New Jersey. Six months later, the Assembly met again at the tavern and enacted a law substituting the word ''state'' for ''colony'' in all commissions, writs, and indictments.

★3319★ ISLAND BEACH STATE PARK

PO Box 37
Seaside Park, NJ 08752
Web: www.njparksandforests.org/parks/island.html
Phone: 732-793-0506
Size: 3,002 acres. **Location:** Between the Atlantic Ocean and Barnegat Bay. Take Route 37 east to Route 35 south to park entrance. **Facilities:** Self-guided trails, bike path (5 miles), bird observation blind, beach with designated swimming area, access ramp (&), bathhouses, concessions, interpretive center. **Activities:** Boating (car top launch only), canoeing, fishing, swimming, surfing, sailboarding, scuba diving, picnicking (no tables or grills provided), hiking, bicycling, horseback riding, waterfowl hunting. **Special Features:** Park occupies a narrow barrier island stretching for 10 miles between the Atlantic Ocean and Barnegat Bay, preserving one of New Jersey's last remaining undeveloped barrier beaches.

★3320★ JENNY JUMP STATE FOREST

PO Box 150
Hope, NJ 07844
Web: www.njparksandforests.org/parks/jennyjump.html
Phone: 908-459-4366
Size: 4,244 acres. **Location:** Near the town of Hope. To reach Hope, take Exit 12 off Route 80. **Facilities:** 22 tent and trailer campsites, showers and toilets, 8 shelters, 2 group camps with pit toilets, picnic area, boat launches, trails, observatory. **Activities:** Camping, boating (electric motors only), canoeing, fishing, hunting, hiking, mountain biking, cross-country skiing, ice fishing, interpretive programs (seasonal). **Special Features:** A climb to the top of Jenny Jump Mountain offers visitors panoramic vistas of the Highlands and the Kittatinny Mountains and Valley to the west, and scenic views of the Great Meadows to the east. In 1995, United Astronomy Clubs of New Jersey completed construction of Greenwood Observatory on leased park property. They offer public astronomy programs from April through October when weather permits.

★3321★ JOHNSON FERRY HOUSE STATE HISTORIC SITE

c/o Washington Crossing State Park
355 Washington Crossing-Pennington Rd
Titusville, NJ 08560
Web: www.njparksandforests.org/parks/washcros.html
Phone: 609-737-2515
Location: 8 miles north of Trenton in Washington Crossing State Park (see separate entry). **Special Features:** This 18th-century farmhouse was owned by Garret Johnson, who operated a 490-acre colonial plantation and a ferry service across the river in the 1700s. It is thought that the house was probably used by General George Washington and other officers the night they crossed the Delaware River.

★3322★ KITTATINNY VALLEY STATE PARK

PO Box 621
Andover, NJ 07821
Web: www.njparksandforests.org/parks/kittval.html
Phone: 973-786-6445
Size: 3,348 acres. **Location:** 8 miles north and 1 mile east of I-80, via Route 206. **Facilities:** Picnic areas, multi-use trails, self-guided nature trail. **Activities:** Boating (electric motors only), canoeing, fishing, hunting, hiking, horseback riding, mountain biking, cross-country skiing, dog sledding. **Special Features:** Park offers access to two popular trails: the Paulinskill Valley Trail, a 27-mile trail that traverses rural landscapes, deciduous forests, wetlands, and towns; and the Sussex Branch Trail, a 20-mile route that skirts swamps, lakes, fields, and

several small communities. Both are former railroads that have been converted to multi-use trails.

★3323★ LEONARDO STATE MARINA

102 Concord Ave
Leonardo, NJ 07737
Web: www.njparksandforests.org/parks/
marinas.html#leonardo
Phone: 732-291-1333
Location: 4 blocks off Route 36 in Leonardo. By water, it is due southwest of Sandy Hook and is the closest marina to the Sandy Hook Bay entrance. **Facilities:** 179 berths; water, electricity, and telephone hookups; launch ramp, winter wet storage, gas and diesel fuel, holding tank pumpout, ice, bait and tackle, luncheonette, shower/sanitary facilities, charter and head boats. **Special Features:** Marina's proximity to the east of the Earle Naval Pier makes it easily identifiable when entering Sandy Hook Bay from either New York Bay or the Atlantic Ocean.

★3324★ LIBERTY LANDING STATE MARINA

Liberty State Park
Audrey Zapp Dr
Jersey City, NJ 07305
Web: www.njparksandforests.org/parks/
marinas.html#libertylanding
Phone: 201-985-8000
Location: In Liberty State Park. Follow signs to park off New Jersey Turnpike Exit 14B. **Facilities:** 200 berths; travel lift, holding tank pumpout, sailing school. **Special Features:** Marina is operated through a lease agreement.

★3325★ LIBERTY STATE PARK

Morris Pesin Dr
Jersey City, NJ 07305
Web: www.njparksandforests.org/parks/liberty.html
Phone: 201-915-3440; **Fax:** 201-915-3408
Size: 1,211 acres. **Location:** Exit 14B off the New Jersey Turnpike; follow signs to park. **Facilities:** Picnic areas, playgrounds, nature and fitness trails, food concession, marina, boat launch, visitor center, interpretive center, science center, ferry service to Statue of Liberty and Ellis Island. **Activities:** Boating, canoeing, fishing, crabbing, bicycling, inline skating, hiking, jogging, cross-country skiing, sightseeing, environmental and historical education programs. **Special Features:** Park is located in a metropolitan area, with the Manhattan skyline as a backdrop. During the 19th and early 20th centuries, the park's site was a major industrial port with an extensive freight and passenger transportation network. Located in the north end of the park is the Central Railroad of New Jersey Terminal (CRRNJ). From 1892 to 1954, throngs of immigrants from northern, southern, and eastern Europe passed through Ellis Island and onto the CRRNJ to disperse into the United States. The park also includes Liberty Landing Marina (see separate entry).

★3326★ LONG POND IRONWORKS STATE PARK

c/o Ringwood State Park
1304 Sloatsburg Rd
Ringwood, NJ 07456
Web: www.njparksandforests.org/parks/longpond.html
Phone: 973-962-7031
Size: 2,591 acres. **Location:** On the border of Ringwood and West Milford, off Highway 511 (Greenwood Lake Turnpike). **Facilities:** Boat launch facilities, boat and canoe rentals, historic site. **Activities:** Fishing, boating (10 HP limit), canoeing, hiking, mountain biking, cross-country skiing, ice fishing, hunting, historical programs (seasonal). **Special Features:** Park is located at the site of a former ironworking community founded in 1766, and remnants of the industrial structures include furnaces, casting house ruins, charging areas, ice houses, waterwheels and other structures. The area is undergoing renovation, and the ''Old Country Store'' now houses the Long Pond Ironworks Museum.

★3327★ MONMOUTH BATTLEFIELD STATE PARK

347 Freehold-Englishtown Rd
Manalapan, NJ 07726
Web: www.njparksandforests.org/parks/monbat.html
Phone: 732-462-9616
Size: 1,810 acres. **Location:** On Route 23 in Monmouth County, 12 miles east of New Jersey Turnpike Exit 8. **Facilities:** Historic site, visitor center, picnic tables, playground, interpretive center, trails. **Activities:** Picnicking, hiking, horseback riding, cross-country skiing, sledding, special deer hunting. **Special Features:** One of the largest battles of the American Revolution took place in the fields and forests that now make up Monmouth Battlefield State Park. The park preserves a rural 18th-century landscape of hilly farmland and hedgerows that encompasses miles of hiking and horseback riding trails, picnic areas, and a restored Revolutionary War farmhouse.

★3328★ NORVIN GREEN STATE FOREST

c/o Ringwood State Park
1304 Sloatsburg Rd
Ringwood, NJ 07456
Web: www.njparksandforests.org/parks/norvin.html
Phone: 973-962-7031
Size: 4,365 acres. **Location:** Bordering Ringwood, West Milford, and Bloomingdale, off Highway 511. Parking at Weis Ecology Center on Snake Den Road, or along Burnt Meadow Road and Glen Wild Road. **Facilities:** Hiking trails, scenic vistas. **Activities:** Hiking, fishing, ice fishing, hunting, cross-country skiing, birdwatching. **Special Features:** Part of the Wyanokie Wilderness Area, the forest is near Wanaque Reservoir and features an extensive trail system developed from old logging roads. Several trails link up with public and private facilities, including the Weis Ecology Center and reservoir property.

★3329★ OLD DUTCH PARSONAGE STATE HISTORIC SITE

71 Somerset St
Somerville, NJ 08876
Phone: 908-725-1015

Location: On Somerset Street in Somerville. **Special Features:** Parsonage is a historic colonial structure that was built in 1751 with funds from three Dutch Reformed Church congregations of the Raritan Valley. The second parson who lived here, the Reverend Mr. Jacob Hardenbergh, was instrumental in the founding of Queen's College, which later became Rutgers, The State University of New Jersey.

★3330★ PARVIN STATE PARK

701 Almond Rd
Pittsgrove, NJ 08318
Web: www.njparksandforests.org/parks/parvin.html
Phone: 856-358-8616
Size: 1,309 acres. **Location:** Between Centerton and Vineland on Route 540 (Almond Road). **Facilities:** 56 tent and trailer campsites, showers, flush toilets, laundry facilities, playground, 4 group camping sites with flush toilets, 16 cabins, picnic area, group picnic shelter, food concession, multi-use trails (including ♿ trail), nature trails, bathhouse (♿), boat launch facilities, boat/canoe rentals, visitor center. **Activities:** Camping, boating (electric motors only), canoeing, fishing, swimming, hiking, biking, cross-country skiing, nature programs (seasonal). **Special Features:** Situated on the edge of the Pine Barrens, Park not only has pine forests typical to the area but also a swamp hardwood forest. Wildlife is varied here and includes the state-threatened barred owl and the endangered swamp pink.

★3331★ PENN STATE FOREST

c/o Bass River State Forest
762 Stage Rd
Tuckerton, NJ 08087
Web: www.njparksandforests.org/parks/penn.html
Phone: 609-296-1114
Size: 3,366 acres. **Location:** Take Route 563 to Lake Oswego Road in Jenkin's Neck, then follow for 3 miles. **Facilities:** Trails. **Activities:** Boating (electric motors only), canoeing, fishing, hiking, mountain biking, horseback riding, hunting. **Special Features:** This undeveloped wilderness area contains a rare forest community of stunted pine and oak, known locally as the ''Pygmy Forest.''

★3332★ PRINCETON BATTLEFIELD STATE PARK

500 Mercer Rd
Princeton, NJ 08540
Web: www.njparksandforests.org/parks/princeton.html
Phone: 609-921-0074
Size: 681 acres. **Location:** On Mercer Road (Princeton Pike) in Princeton, 1.5 miles south of Princeton University and 3.8 miles north of I-295/95. **Facilities:** Historic sites, trails. **Activities:** Historical programs, cross-country skiing, birdwatching. **Special Features:** Park commemorates the historic Battle of Princeton, fought on January 3, 1777, in which General George Washington won his first victory against the British Regulars on the field. In addition to the battlefield, the park includes the Clarke House Museum, a state historic site containing period furniture as well as Revolutionary War exhibits, and the Ionic Colonnade designed by Thomas U. Walter (architect of the US Capitol Building), a stone patio marking the grave of 21 British and 15 American soldiers killed in the battle.

★3333★ RAMAPO MOUNTAIN STATE FOREST

c/o Ringwood State Park
1304 Sloatsburg Rd
Ringwood, NJ 07456
Web: www.njparksandforests.org/parks/ramapo.html
Phone: 973-962-7031
Size: 4,200 acres. **Location:** From I-287 take exit 57 and follow Skyline Drive to park entrance. **Facilities:** Multi-use trails. **Activities:** Canoeing, fishing, hunting, birdwatching, hiking, mountain biking, horseback riding, cross-country skiing, ice fishing. **Special Features:** Forest includes Ramapo Lake Natural Area, with a 120-acre mountain lake and spectacular views from numerous rock outcroppings and ledges. Many of the forest's challenging trails offer a view of the New York City skyline as well.

★3334★ RANCOCAS STATE PARK

c/o Brendan T. Byrne State Forest
PO Box 215
New Lisbon, NJ 08064
Web: www.njparksandforests.org/parks/rancocas.html
Phone: 609-726-1191
Size: 1,252 acres. **Location:** Access via I-295 Exit 45A or via Route 38 into Mount Holly. **Facilities:** Hiking trails, nature center, replica Native American village. **Activities:** Hiking, nature programs (sponsored by the New Jersey Audubon Society). **Special Features:** A network of trails leads through hardwood forests along Rancocas Creek and an extensive freshwater tidal marsh. A portion of the park is leased to the Powhatan Indians, and a replica of the Indian village of the 1600s has been constructed on this site.

★3335★ RINGWOOD STATE PARK

1304 Sloatsburg Rd
Ringwood, NJ 07456
Web: www.njparksandforests.org/parks/ringwood.html
Phone: 973-962-7031
Size: 4,044 acres. **Location:** Off Route 287 Exit 57. Follow signs to park. **Facilities:** Picnic areas, playground, multi-use trails, nature trails, bathhouse, boat launch, boat rentals, food concession, skeet range, lookout point, historic homes, formal gardens, visitor center. **Activities:** Fishing, ice fishing, hunting, boating, canoeing, swimming, picnicking, hiking, mountain biking, horseback riding, cross-country skiing, snowmobiling, sledding, historical programs. **Special Features:** Park includes two historic homes, the New Jersey State Botanical Garden, and the Shepherd Lake Recreation Area. The two homes are Ringwood Manor, a mansion once owned by Abraham S. Hewitt, one of America's foremost iron masters, and Skylands Manor, a historically accurate reproduction of an English Jacobean mansion. Most of the recreational activities at the park are centered around Shepherd Lake.

★3336★ ROCKINGHAM STATE HISTORIC SITE

PO Box 496
Kingston, NJ 08528
Web: www.rockingham.net
Phone: 609-683-7132
Location: On County Route 603 (Laurel Avenue) in Franklin Township, Somerset County, NJ, between County Route 518 and NJ 27. Activities: Group tours. Special Features: In 1783, while the Continental Congress was meeting at Nassau Hall in nearby Princeton, Congress rented the house from the widow of Judge John Berrien for use by General George Washington from August 23 to November 10, 1783. Martha Washington joined him there during this period, and it was here that he got word that the Treaty of Paris had been signed and the Thirteen Colonies were independent of Great Britain.

★3337★ ROUND VALLEY RECREATION AREA

1220 Lebanon-Stanton Rd
Lebanon, NJ 08833
Web: www.njparksandforests.org/parks/round.html
Phone: 908-236-6355
Size: 3,669 acres. Location: East of Clinton off Route 22 via I-78. Facilities: 85 wilderness tent campsites (hike or bike-in; no vehicle access) and 8 group wilderness sites with drinking water and pit toilets nearby, picnic area, picnic shelters, playground, food concession, multi-use trails, bathhouse, boat launch facilities. Activities: Camping, boating (10 HP limit), canoeing, fishing, swimming, scuba diving, skin diving, hiking, mountain biking, horseback riding, cross-country skiing, hunting (waterfowl only), cross-country skiing, ice fishing, sledding. Special Features: Park includes New Jersey's deepest lake, the 2,000-acre Round Valley Reservoir, which is 180 feet deep, has exceptionally clear water, and is stocked with lake trout.

★3338★ SENATOR FRANK S. FARLEY STATE MARINA

600 Huron Ave
Atlantic City, NJ 08401
Web: www.njparksandforests.org/parks/marinas.html#senator
Phone: 609-441-8482
Location: On Clam Creek, a short distance from the Atlantic Ocean via Absecon Inlet or the Intracoastal Waterway. Facilities: 640 berths; water, electric, cable TV, and telephone hookups dockside; ice, laundry, shower/sanitary facilities, restaurant, lounge, luncheonette, bait and tackle, charter boats, ship store, gas and diesel fuel, holding tank pumpout. Special Features: Marina is operated through a lease agreement.

★3339★ SOMERS MANSION STATE HISTORIC SITE

1000 Shore Rd
Somers Point, NJ 08244
Web: www.njparksandforests.org/historic/index.html
Phone: 609-927-2212
Location: A block from Great Egg Harbor Bay on Somers Point Circle. Special Features: Mansion was built in 1725 by Richard Somers, who operated the first ferry across Great Egg Harbor Bay. It is the oldest existing house in Atlantic County.

★3340★ SPRUCE RUN RECREATION AREA

68 Van Syckel's Rd
Clinton, NJ 08809
Web: www.njparksandforests.org/parks/spruce.html
Phone: 908-638-8572
Size: 2,012 acres. Location: In Hunterdon County, off Route 31N, on Van Syckel's Road. Facilities: 67 tent and trailer campsites, flush toilets, showers, picnic areas, group picnic area with shelter, playgrounds, play fields, basketball courts, food concession, bathhouse, boat launch, boat rentals (seasonal), trails. Activities: Camping, boating (10 HP limit), canoeing/kayaking, fishing, swimming, sailing, windsurfing, bicycling, in-line skating, cross-country skiing, hunting (waterfowl), ice fishing, ice boating. Special Features: Surrounded by rolling hills, the park is situated on 1,290-acre Spruce Run Reservoir.

★3341★ STEPHENS STATE PARK

800 Willow Grove St
Hackettstown, NJ 07840
Web: www.njparksandforests.org/parks/stephens.html
Phone: 908-852-3790
Size: 805 acres. Location: 2 miles east of Hackettstown or 7.5 miles west of Route 206 on Waterloo Road. Facilities: 40 tent and small trailer campsites, flush toilets, picnic areas, playground, playfield, mutil-use trails. Activities: Camping, river fishing, hunting (with restrictions), hiking, horseback riding, bicycling, mountain biking, cross-country skiing, interpretive programs (seasonal). Special Features: A walking path along the Musconetcong River leads to shaded picnic spots.

★3342★ STEUBEN HOUSE STATE HISTORIC SITE

1209 Main St
River Edge, NJ 07661
Web: www.njparksandforests.org/historic/index.html
Phone: 201-487-1739
Location: On Main Street in River Edge. Special Features: This residence was presented to Baron Von Steuben in 1783 in gratitude for his assistance to the colonies during the Revolutionary War. The house contains a fine collection of colonial and early New Jersey furnishings owned by the Bergen County Historical Society.

★3343★ STOKES STATE FOREST

1 Coursen Rd
Branchville, NJ 07826
Web: www.njparksandforests.org/parks/stokes.html
Phone: 973-948-3820
Size: 15,996 acres. Location: Four miles north of Branchville via Route 206. Facilities: 50 tent and trailer campsites, 10 lean-tos, 9 group camping sites, 10 cabins, group cabin, picnic areas, picnic shelter, food concession, trails, scenic overlook, bathhouse. Activities: Camping, boating (electric motors only; car top boat launch), hunting, fishing, swimming, hiking, horseback riding, mountain biking, cross-country skiing, snowmobiling, ice skating, ice fishing. Special Features: Renowned for its beauty, Stokes features Tillman Ravine, with views of waterfalls and ferns clinging to rock crevices, and Sunrise Mountain, which offers breathtaking panoramic views.

9. State Parks

★3344★ SWARTSWOOD STATE PARK

PO Box 123
Swartswood, NJ 07877
Web: www.njparksandforests.org/parks/swartswood.html
Phone: 973-383-5230
Size: 2,272 acres. **Location:** 5 miles west of Newton and US Route 206 in Sussex County. **Facilities:** 65 tent and trailer campsites, flush toilets, showers, laundry facilities, 3 group camping sites, 6 yurts, picnic areas, picnic shelters, group picnic area, playground, food concession, hiking trails, multi-use trail (&), bathhouse, boat launch, boat and canoe rentals, bird observation facility. **Activities:** Camping, boating (electric motors only), canoeing, sailing, fishing, swimming, hiking, bicycling, horseback riding, mountain biking, inline skating, hunting, cross-country skiing, snowmobiling, ice skating, ice fishing, sledding, bird watching, nature programs (seasonal). **Special Features:** Established in 1914, Swartswood was New Jersey's first state park and is known for its tranquil surroundings and great fishing. Both Little Swartswood and Swartswood Lake have been the focus of water quality improvement efforts, including invasive aquatic weed control and watershed protection.

★3345★ THE HERMITAGE STATE HISTORIC SITE

335 N Franklin Tpke
Ho-Ho-Kus, NJ 07423
Web: www.thehermitage.org
Phone: 201-445-8311; **Fax:** 201-445-0437
Location: On North Franklin Turnpike in Ho-Ho-Kus. **Special Features:** The original section of The Hermitage House was built in the mid-18th century and visited by George Washington and his staff during the Revolutionary War. In 1845, the house was transformed by architect William Ranlett into one of the finest examples of Gothic Revival architecture in North America. Operated by the Friends of the Hermitage, Inc.

★3346★ TRENTON BATTLE MONUMENT STATE HISTORIC SITE

348 N Warren St
Trenton, NJ 08638
Web: www.njparksandforests.org/historic/
    Trentonbattlemonument/index.htm
Phone: 609-737-0623
Location: At 348 South Warren Street in Trenton. **Special Features:** Monument marks the site of the American artillery emplacements that contributed to the defeat of three Hessian regiments at the Battle of Trenton on December 26, 1776. The site is administered by Washington Crossing State Park (see separate entry).

★3347★ TWIN LIGHTS STATE HISTORIC SITE

Lighthouse Rd
Highlands, NJ 07732
Web: twin-lights.org
Phone: 732-872-1886
Location: On Lighthouse Road in Highlands. **Special Features:** Twin Lights has been used as an aid to navigation over the coastal waters of NJ since 1828. It was used as the primary lighthouse for New York Harbor and was known as the best

and the brightest light in North America. The current lighthouse was built in 1862 and replaced the earlier lights, which were beginning to deteriorate.

★3348★ VOORHEES STATE PARK

251 County Rd 513
Glen Gardner, NJ 08826
Web: www.njparksandforests.org/parks/voorhees.html
Phone: 908-638-6969
Size: 1,036 acres. **Location:** 2 miles north of High Bridge off County Road 513 in northern Hunterdon County. **Facilities:** 47 tent and trailer campsites, 2 group campsites, modern toilets, showers, picnic areas, picnic shelters, group picnic facilities, playground, multi-use trails, fitness trail (&), scenic overlook, observatory. **Activities:** Camping, fishing, hunting, hiking, bicycling, mountain biking, cross-country skiing, sledding, astronomy programs (seasonal). **Special Features:** From 1933-1941 Park was a camp for Civilian Conservation Corps (CCC) work crews, who planted trees, constructed shelters and picnic sites, and developed trails. Park's features include the New Jersey Astronomical Association's observatory, which has a 26-inch Newtonian reflector telescope that is one of the largest privately owned telescopes in New Jersey. For information about sky-watching programs, call (908) 638-8500.

★3349★ WALLACE HOUSE STATE HISTORIC SITE

71 Somerset St
Somerville, NJ 08876
Web: www.njparksandforests.org/historic/olddutch-wallace/
    odwh-wallacehouse.htm
Phone: 908-725-1015
Location: In Somerville. **Special Features:** General George Washington leased this house for use as his headquarters during the Middlebrook Winter Encampment from December of 1778 to June of 1779. It is one of the best examples of Georgian architecture in New Jersey.

★3350★ WALT WHITMAN HOUSE STATE HISTORIC SITE

330 Mickle Blvd
Camden, NJ 08103
Web: www.njparksandforests.org/historic/whitman/index.html
Phone: 609-964-5383
Location: On Mickle Blvd in Camden. **Special Features:** Poet Walt Whitman lived in this house from 1884 until his death in 1892. The house is furnished with a number of pieces owned and used by Whitman.

★3351★ WASHINGTON CROSSING STATE PARK

355 Washington Crossing-Pennington Rd
Titusville, NJ 08560
Web: www.njparksandforests.org/parks/washcros.html
Phone: 609-737-0623
Size: 2,009 acres. **Location:** Take Route 29 north from I-95 and follow the signs. **Facilities:** 4 group camps with portable toilets, picnic tables, picnic shelters, group picnic facilities, playground, trails (15 miles), visitor center, museum, nature center,

open-air theater (&), historic sites. **Activities:** Camping, hiking, mountain biking, horseback riding, fishing, cross-country skiing, snowshoeing, interpretive programs (seasonal). **Special Features:** The Continental Army, under the command of General George Washington, landed here after their historic crossing of the Delaware River on Christmas night, 1776. The exhibit galleries at the park's visitor center museum explore many facets of America's revolutionary conflict, and living history demonstrations are often held on week-ends at the Johnson Ferry House (see separate entry). Originally preserved for its historical significance, the park is also well known for its trails and wildlife habitat. A wide variety of migrating birds use the stream and ravine as a resting place and for nesting.

★3352★ WASHINGTON ROCK STATE PARK

c/o Liberty State Park
Morris Pesin Dr
Jersey City, NJ 07305
Web: www.njparksandforests.org/parks/washrock.html
Phone: 201-915-3401
Size: 52 acres. **Location:** Off Route 22 in Greenbrook Township on Washington Rock Road. **Facilities:** Picnic tables, scenic overlook. **Special Features:** The strategic location of Washington Rock made it a valuable lookout point during the American Revolution for General George Washington in June of 1777 when the British army, under General William Howe, was moving toward Westfield. From the vantage point of this natural rock outcropping, General Washington had a 30-mile panoramic view of the valley and was able to instruct his troops to circle behind Howe's troops and cut off their retreat.

★3353★ WAWAYANDA STATE PARK

885 Warwick Tpke
Hewitt, NJ 07421
Web: www.njparksandforests.org/parks/wawayanda.html
Phone: 973-853-4462
Size: 18,235 acres. **Location:** Along the Warwick Turnpike just east of Highland Lakes, near the New Jersey-New York state line. **Facilities:** 3 group camping sites with a clivus restroom, picnic tables, playground, food concession, trails (60 miles), boat launch, boat and canoe rentals, restroom adjacent to beach, viewing points. **Activities:** Group camping, boating (electric motors only), canoeing, hunting, fishing, swimming, hiking, bicycling, mountain biking, horseback riding, cross-country skiing, ice skating, ice fishing, snowmobiling. **Special Features:** Park is crisscrossed by a network of trails including a 19.6-mile segment of the Appalachian National Scenic Trail (see separate entry in national trails section).

★3354★ WHARTON STATE FOREST

4110 Nesco Rd
Hammonton, NJ 08037
Web: www.njparksandforests.org/parks/wharton.html
Phone: 609-561-0024
Size: 114,793 acres. **Location:** Batsto Village office: 8 miles east of Hammonton on Route 542. Atsion Recreation Area office: 8 miles north of Hammonton on Route 206. **Facilities:** 50 tent & trailer campsites with potable water, flush toilets, and showers (Atsion), 49 tent and trailer campsites with water and pit toilets (Godfrey Bridge), wilderness campsites (group, individual, and family sites), 9 cabins, picnic areas, picnic shelters, group picnic facilities, playgrounds, food concession, multi-use trails, nature trails, bathhouse, boat launch, visitor center, exhibit gallery, museum shop, interpretive center, historic village. **Activities:** Camping, boating (electric motors only), canoeing, fishing, swimming, hiking, mountain biking, horseback riding, cross-country skiing, hunting. **Special Features:** Forest is the largest single tract of land within the New Jersey state park system. Throughout Wharton are rivers and streams for canoeing, hiking trails (including a major section of New Jersey's Batona Trail), 500 miles of unpaved roads for mountain biking and horseback riding, and numerous lakes, ponds, and fields for wildlife observation. Forest also includes historic Batso Village, Atsion Recreation Area (see separate entries), Batsto Natural Area, and Oswego River Natural Area.

★3355★ WORTHINGTON STATE FOREST

HC 62, Box 2
Columbia, NJ 07832
Web: www.njparksandforests.org/parks/worthington.html
Phone: 908-841-9575
Size: 6,421 acres. **Location:** Three miles from the last exit in New Jersey off Route 80 west. **Facilities:** 69 tent and trailer campsites with modern toilets and showers, 3 group camps with modern toilets, picnic area, hiking trails, boat launch, visitor center. **Activities:** Camping, boating (electric motors only except in Delaware River), canoeing, fishing, hiking, hunting, cross-country skiing, snowmobiling, biking on Old Mine Road. **Special Features:** Situated in the Delaware Water Gap area, the forest contains some of the most rugged terrain found in the state. Heading north from Pennsylvania, the Appalachian National Scenic Trail (see entry in national trails section) enters New Jersey at Worthington State Forest.

New Mexico State Parks

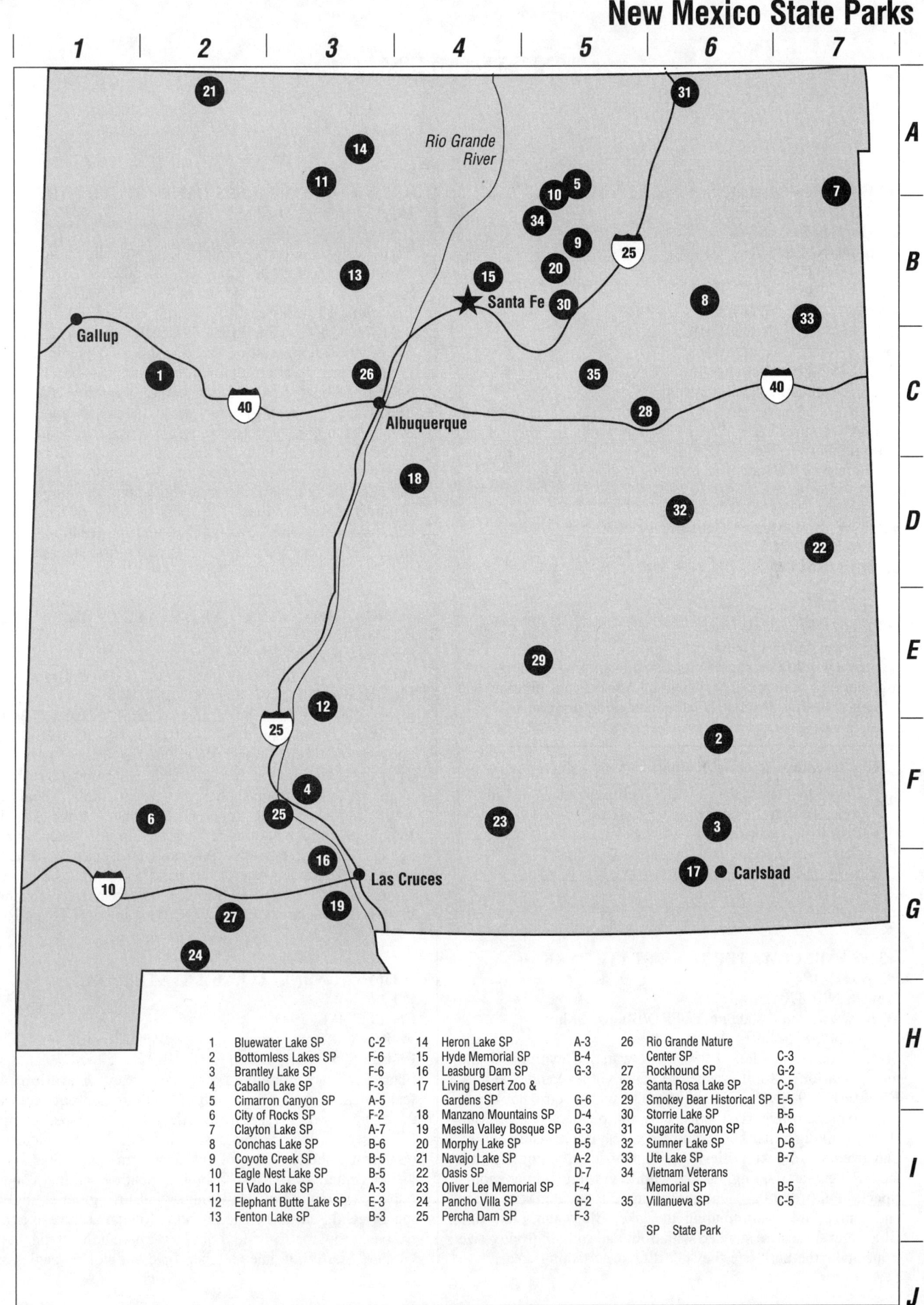

1	Bluewater Lake SP	C-2	14	Heron Lake SP	A-3	26	Rio Grande Nature	
2	Bottomless Lakes SP	F-6	15	Hyde Memorial SP	B-4		Center SP	C-3
3	Brantley Lake SP	F-6	16	Leasburg Dam SP	G-3	27	Rockhound SP	G-2
4	Caballo Lake SP	F-3	17	Living Desert Zoo &		28	Santa Rosa Lake SP	C-5
5	Cimarron Canyon SP	A-5		Gardens SP	G-6	29	Smokey Bear Historical SP	E-5
6	City of Rocks SP	F-2	18	Manzano Mountains SP	D-4	30	Storrie Lake SP	B-5
7	Clayton Lake SP	A-7	19	Mesilla Valley Bosque SP	G-3	31	Sugarite Canyon SP	A-6
8	Conchas Lake SP	B-6	20	Morphy Lake SP	B-5	32	Sumner Lake SP	D-6
9	Coyote Creek SP	B-5	21	Navajo Lake SP	A-2	33	Ute Lake SP	B-7
10	Eagle Nest Lake SP	B-5	22	Oasis SP	D-7	34	Vietnam Veterans	
11	El Vado Lake SP	A-3	23	Oliver Lee Memorial SP	F-4		Memorial SP	B-5
12	Elephant Butte Lake SP	E-3	24	Pancho Villa SP	G-2	35	Villanueva SP	C-5
13	Fenton Lake SP	B-3	25	Percha Dam SP	F-3			

SP   State Park

NEW MEXICO

9. State Parks

★3356★ **New Mexico State Parks Division**
1220 S Saint Francis Dr
PO Box 1147
Santa Fe, NM 87504
(505) 476-3355 - Phone
(505) 476-3361 - Fax
(888) 667-2757 - Toll-free
(877) 664-7787 - Reservations
(505) 476-7777 - Employment
(505) 476-3391 - Volunteering
Web: www.emnrd.state.nm.us/prd
The state's 34 parks protect significant historical, geological, and archeological sites. Parks Division works to preserve and interpret these resources. The division also develops, maintains, and improves the state's recreational trail system.

★3357★ **New Mexico Department of Fish & Game**
PO Box 25112
Santa Fe, NM 87504
(505) 827-7911 - Phone
(505) 827-7915 - Fax
(800) 862-9310 - Toll-free
Web: www.gmfsh.state.nm.us
Oversees wildlife management areas for camping, boating, fishing, hunting, and wildlife viewing. Administers hunting and fishing licensing. Promotes safety education programs.

Key to campsite classification:

- **Developed campsites** — Sites include picnic tables and concrete slabs.
- **Primitive campsites** — No special facilities, only a cleared area for pitching a tent.

★3358★ **BLUEWATER LAKE STATE PARK**
PO Box 3419
Prewitt, NM 87045
Web: www.emnrd.state.nm.us/PRD/Bluewater.htm
Phone: 505-876-2391
Size: 3,000 acres land; 1,200 acres water. **Elevation:** 7,400 feet. **Location:** 28 miles west of Grants via I-40 and NM 412. **Facilities:** 149 developed campsites (14 with electric hookups), primitive campsites, restrooms, showers, picnic areas, 2 group shelters, hiking trails, 3 boat ramps, courtesy dock, visitor center, playground (&&). **Activities:** Camping, boating, sailing, fishing, ice fishing, water-skiing, hiking, wildlife viewing, winter sports. **Special Features:** Park features rolling hills studded with piñon and juniper trees surrounding the lake. Bluewater Lake and Bluewater Creek are stocked with trout and catfish; trophy-size trout make the park one the state's favorite fishing areas.

★3359★ **BOTTOMLESS LAKES STATE PARK**
HC 12, Box 1200
Roswell, NM 88201
Web: www.emnrd.state.nm.us/PRD/bottomless.htm
Phone: 505-624-6058; **Fax:** 505-624-6029
Size: 1,400 acres land; 45 acres water. **Elevation:** 3,500 feet. **Location:** 12 miles east of Roswell on US 380, then south 3 miles on NM 409. **Facilities:** 37 developed campsites (32 with electric hookups), restrooms (&), showers, picnic areas (&), group shelter, playground, trails, swimming beach, courtesy dock, pedal boat rentals, visitor center/interpretive center. **Activities:** Camping, boating (under 3 hp), fishing, swimming, scuba diving, hiking, interpretive programs (seasonal). **Special Features:** Bordered by high red bluffs, the seven small lakes at this park were formed when circulating water dissolved gypsum and salt deposits in underlying rock formations, creating a network of underground cavities. The roofs of some of those caverns collapsed under their own weight, and the resulting sinkholes filled with water. Park is New Mexico's first state park.

★3360★ **BRANTLEY LAKE STATE PARK**
PO Box 2288
Carlsbad, NM 88221
Web: www.emnrd.state.nm.us/PRD/ParksPages/Brantley.htm
Phone: 505-457-2384; **Fax:** 505-457-2385
Size: 3,000 acres land; 4,000 acres water. **Elevation:** 3,300 feet. **Location:** 12 miles north of Carlsbad via US 285, then 4.5 miles northeast on Eddy County Road 30. **Facilities:** 51 developed campsites (all with electric hookups), restrooms (&), showers, picnic areas (&), group shelter, playground, trails, 2 boat ramps, courtesy dock, fishing dock, visitor center (&&). **Activities:** Camping, boating, sailing, fishing, swimming, water-skiing, jet skiing, hiking, interpretive programs (seasonal). **Special Features:** Park is a southern desert park, and Brantley Lake is the southernmost lake in New Mexico. The visitor center includes historical exhibits about the Wild West town of Seven Rivers.

★3361★ **CABALLO LAKE STATE PARK**
PO Box 32
Caballo, NM 87931
Web: www.emnrd.state.nm.us/PRD/caballo.htm
Phone: 505-743-3942
Size: 5,300 acres land; 11,500 acres water. **Elevation:** 4,100 feet. **Location:** 16 miles south of Truth or Consequences via I-25 exit 59 and NM 187. **Facilities:** 135 developed campsites (63 with electric hookups), restrooms (&), showers, picnic areas (&), group shelter, playground, 2 boat ramps, 3 docks (1 &), visitor center. **Activities:** Camping, boating, sailing, canoeing, fishing, swimming, water-skiing, windsurfing, jet skiing, birding. **Special Features:** The Caballo Mountains serve as a majestic backdrop for Caballo Lake, an impoundment on the Rio Grande. Starting in late October, bald and golden eagles arrive

to nest in and around the park. The park also features two cactus gardens where visitors can stroll among yuccas, century plants, ocotillos, cow tongues, and prickly pears, most of which bloom in late March and early April.

★3362★ CIMARRON CANYON STATE PARK
PO Box 185
Eagle Nest, NM 87718
Web: www.emnrd.state.nm.us/PRD/CimarronCanyon.htm
Phone: 505-377-6271
Size: 33,000 acres land. Elevation: 8,000 feet. Location: 3 miles east of Eagle Nest via US 64. Facilities: 88 developed campsites, restrooms (&), picnic area (&), trails. Activities: Camping, fishing, hiking, mountain biking, cross-country skiing, hunting (seasonal), wildlife viewing. Special Features: Park is part of a 33,116-acre wildlife area in New Mexico's high country and features spectacular palisade cliffs along the Cimarron River. Trout fishing here is excellent.

★3363★ CITY OF ROCKS STATE PARK
PO Box 50
Faywood, NM 88034
Web: www.emnrd.state.nm.us/PRD/cityrocks.htm
Phone: 505-536-2800
Size: 1,230 acres land. Elevation: 5,250 feet. Location: 24 miles northwest of Deming on US 180, then 4 miles northeast on NM 61. Facilities: 42 developed campsites (10 with electric hookups), restrooms (&), showers, picnic area (&), group shelter, trails, desert botanical garden, observatory, visitor center, interpretive exhibits. Activities: Camping, hiking, wildlife viewing. Special Features: Park was named for its incredible rock formations, which were formed of volcanic ash welded together 30 million years ago, then sculpted by wind and water into rows of monolithic blocks. A new addition to the park is a public night sky observatory where star parties are to be held.

★3364★ CLAYTON LAKE STATE PARK
141 Clayton Lake Rd
Clayton, NM 88415
Web: www.emnrd.state.nm.us/PRD/Clayton.htm
Phone: 505-374-8808
Size: 471 acres land; 170 acres water. Elevation: 5,040 feet. Location: 12 miles north of Clayton via NM 370. Facilities: 37 developed campsites (7 with electric hookups), 12 primitive campsites, restrooms, showers (&), playground, picnic shelters (&), including group shelter, trails, boat ramp, 3 docks, visitor center. Activities: Camping, boating (trolling speed only), canoeing, fishing, windsurfing, hiking, wildlife viewing. Special Features: Along the lake's spillway is an internationally significant dinosaur trackway where more than 500 dinosaur footprints dating back 100 million years have been identified and preserved. The park also offers outstanding fishing, and several duck species frequent the lake.

★3365★ CONCHAS LAKE STATE PARK
PO Box 976
Conchas Dam, NM 88416
Web: www.emnrd.state.nm.us/PRD/Conchas.htm
Phone: 505-868-2270
Size: 290 acres land; 9,600 acres water. Elevation: 4,200 feet. Location: 34 miles northwest of Tucumcari via NM 104. Facilities: 105 developed campsites (40 with electric hookups), restrooms (&), showers, picnic areas (&), playground, marina, 8 boat ramps, docks, slip rentals, full-service restaurant, lounge, store, overnight mobile home rentals, visitor center. Activities: Camping, boating, sailing, windsurfing, personal watercraft, fishing, swimming, water-skiing, snorkeling, scuba diving, wildlife viewing. Special Features: The park's 25-mile-long reservoir is one of the state's largest lakes and includes 60 miles of varied shoreline with secluded coves, canyons, and sandy beaches.

★3366★ COYOTE CREEK STATE PARK
PO Box 477
Guadalupita, NM 87722
Web: www.emnrd.state.nm.us/PRD/CoyoteCreek.htm
Phone: 505-387-2328
Size: 83 acres. Elevation: 7,700 feet. Location: 17 miles north of Mora via NM 434. Facilities: 47 developed campsites (17 with electric hookups), restrooms, showers, picnic areas (&), group shelter, playground, hiking trails, visitor center. Activities: Camping, fishing, hiking, wildlife viewing. Special Features: The park is nestled in the Sangre de Cristo Mountain foothills along a meandering stream. Coyote Creek has the most densely stocked waters in New Mexico, offering excellent opportunities for trout fishing.

★3367★ EAGLE NEST LAKE STATE PARK
PO Box 185
Eagle Nest, NM 87718
Web: www.emnrd.state.nm.us/PRD/EaglesNest.htm
Phone: 505-377-1594
Size: 2,485 acres land; 2,400 acres water. Elevation: 8,300 feet. Location: In northeastern New Mexico, 32 miles east of Taos off US 64. Facilities: Boat ramps, restrooms. Activities: Boating, fishing, ice fishing, picnicking, snowmobiling (on lake surface only), wildlife viewing. Special Features: Park is an excellent location for wildlife viewing, with an abundance of elk, bear, mule deer, eagles, turkeys and other birds.

★3368★ EL VADO LAKE STATE PARK
PO Box 367
Tierra Amarilla, NM 87575
Web: www.emnrd.state.nm.us/PRD/elvado.htm
Phone: 505-588-7247
Size: 1,730 acres land; 3,200 acres water. Elevation: 6,900 feet. Location: 17 miles southwest of Tierra Amarilla via NM 112. Facilities: 80 developed campsites (19 with electric hookups), restrooms (&), showers, picnic areas/shelters (&), group shelter, playground, hiking trails, 2 boat ramps, 2 courtesy docks, visitor center. Activities: Camping, boating, sailing, windsurfing, fishing, swimming, water-skiing, jet skiing, hiking, winter sports. Special Features: A 5.5-mile scenic trail along the Rio Chama connects El Vado with nearby Heron Lake. The lake and surrounding area serve as a major wintering ground for bald eagles and other birds such as red-tail hawks, water ouzels, and ospreys.

★3369★ **ELEPHANT BUTTE LAKE STATE PARK**

PO Box 13
Elephant Butte, NM 87935
Web: www.emnrd.state.nm.us/PRD/elephant.htm
Phone: 505-744-5923
Size: 24,500 acres land; 36,500 acres water. **Elevation:** 4,500 feet. **Location:** 5 miles north of Truth or Consequences via I-25, Exit 83. **Facilities:** 132 developed campsites (98 with electric hookups), restrooms (&), showers, picnic areas (&), group shelters, playground, hiking trails, marina, houseboat rentals, ski boat rentals, pontoon and kayak rentals, 4 boat ramps, 5 courtesy docks, visitor center, interpretive exhibits. **Activities:** Camping, boating, sailing, windsurfing, fishing, water-skiing, jet skiing, swimming, hiking, winter sports. **Special Features:** New Mexico's largest and most popular state park is situated beside 36,000-acre Elephant Butte Reservoir. The name ''Elephant Butte'' was derived from the eroded core of an ancient volcano, now an island in the reservoir, in the shape of an elephant. Though not related to the park's name, fossils of stegomastodon (a primitive relative of today's elephant) have been discovered near the reservoir, and the area was also a favorite hunting ground of the tyrannosaurus rex dinosaur.

★3370★ **FENTON LAKE STATE PARK**

455 Fenton Lake
Jemez Springs, NM 87025
Web: www.emnrd.state.nm.us/PRD/Fenton.htm
Phone: 505-829-3630
Size: 700 acres land; 37 acres water. **Elevation:** 7,900 feet. **Location:** 33 miles northwest of San Ysidro via NM 4 and 126. **Facilities:** 37 developed campsites (5 with electric hookups), restrooms (&), picnic tables and grills (&), 2 group shelters, playground, cross-country ski and biathlon trail, fishing platforms (&), boat ramp. **Activities:** Camping, boating (non- and electric-motored boats only), fishing, hiking, wildlife viewing, ice fishing, cross-country skiing. **Special Features:** Fenton Lake is a high mountain lake surrounded by ponderosa ines in the valley of the Rio Cebolla of the Jemez Mountains. The park was formerly a nesting area for migratory waterfowl and a wildlife refuge, and waterfowl, turkey, deer, muskrat, elk, and bobcat can still be observed.

★3371★ **HERON LAKE STATE PARK**

PO Box 159
Los Ojos, NM 87551
Web: www.emnrd.state.nm.us/PRD/heron.htm
Phone: 505-588-7470
Size: 4,100 acres land, 5,900 acres water. **Elevation:** 7,200 feet. **Location:** 11 miles west of Tierra Amarilla via US 64 and 84 and NM 95. **Facilities:** 250 developed campsites (54 with electric hookups), primitive campsites, restrooms (&), showers, picnic areas (&), 2 group shelters, trails, marina, mast-up sailboat storage facility, boat ramps, 4 courtesy docks, visitor center. **Activities:** Camping, boating (no-wake speeds only), sailing, fishing, ice fishing, swimming, windsurfing, paddlesports, hiking, wildlife viewing, cross-country skiing. **Special Features:** Lake Heron is a picturesque lake set among tall pines. A hiking and fishing trail along Rio Chama is accessed by a dramatic caprock stairway near Heron Dam. The 5.5-mile trail to El Vado Lake State Park (see separate entry) crosses the river by suspension bridge and offers scenic views along the route.

★3372★ **HYDE MEMORIAL STATE PARK**

740 Hyde Park Rd
Santa Fe, NM 87501
Web: www.emnrd.state.nm.us/PRD/Hyde.htm
Phone: 505-983-7175
Size: 350 acres. **Elevation:** 8,500 feet. **Location:** 8 miles northeast of Santa Fe Plaza via Hyde Park Road. **Facilities:** 50 developed campsites (7 with electric hookups), Adirondack shelters, restrooms (&), picnic areas (&), 3 group shelters, playground, hiking trails, rental lodge, visitor center. **Activities:** Camping, hiking, sledding, snowshoeing, cross-country skiing. **Special Features:** Located in the Sangre de Cristo Mountains, Park has dense stands of evergreens, as well as aspen and shrubs, and is a natural refuge for wildlife. The park also serves as a good base camp for excursions into the surrounding Santa Fe National Forest.

★3373★ **LEASBURG DAM STATE PARK**

PO Box 6
Radium Springs, NM 88054
Web: www.emnrd.state.nm.us/PRD/leasburg.htm
Phone: 505-524-4068; **Fax:** 505-526-5420
Size: 240 acres land. **Elevation:** 4,000 feet. **Location:** 15 miles north of Las Cruces off I-25, Exit 19. **Facilities:** 31 developed campsites (some with electric hookups), restrooms (&), showers, picnic areas, group shelter, playground, hiking trails, visitor center (&), interpretive exhibits. **Activities:** Camping, canoeing, kayaking, fishing, hiking, bird watching. **Special Features:** Park is a desert oasis, featuring the Cactus Patch botanical gardens as well as other cactus gardens. The Leasburg Diversion Dam, built in 1908, channels water from the Rio Grande to irrigate the vast farming area of the Upper Mesilla Valley. Nearby Fort Selden Monument has a museum and trails at the site of an 19th century army outpost.

★3374★ **LIVING DESERT ZOO & GARDENS STATE PARK**

PO Box 100
Carlsbad, NM 88221
Web: www.emnrd.state.nm.us/PRD/LivingDesert.htm
Phone: 505-887-5516; **Fax:** 505-885-4478
Size: 1,500 acres land. **Elevation:** 3,200 feet. **Location:** Off US 285, on the northwest edge of Carlsbad. **Facilities:** Visitor center with gift shop and book store, exhibits, restrooms (&), picnic area, trails. **Activities:** Wildlife viewing, education programs. **Special Features:** Dedicated to the interpretation of the Chihuahuan Desert, Park is an indoor/outdoor museum displaying more than 40 native animal species and hundreds of succulent plants from around the world. Display areas include a walk-through aviary, a greenhouse, and a 1.3 mile self-guided interpretive tour. One of the park's highlights is the endangered gray wolf. (Park is not affiliated or associated with the Living Desert in Palm Desert, CA.)

★3375★ MANZANO MOUNTAINS STATE PARK

HC 66, Box 202
Mountainair, NM 87036
Web: www.emnrd.state.nm.us/PRD/Manzano.htm
Phone: 505-847-2820
Size: 160 acres land. **Elevation:** 7,600 feet. **Location:** 16 miles northwest of Mountainair via NM 55 and 131. **Facilities:** 37 developed campsites (8 with electric hookups), restrooms (&), picnic area, group shelter, hiking trails, nature trail. **Activities:** Camping, hiking, birding, wildlife viewing, cross-country skiing. **Special Features:** Park is set in a forest of ponderosa pine, Gambel's oak, and alligator juniper, which provide a rich habitat for a variety of wildlife. In addition, the park is situated along an important raptor flyway and has a field checklist available for visitors who enjoy birding. Park is closed from November through early April.

★3376★ MESILLA VALLEY BOSQUE STATE PARK

PO Box 6
Radium Springs, NM 88054
Web: www.emnrd.state.nm.us/PRD/mesillavalley.htm
Phone: 505-524-4068
Size: 305 acres. **Elevation:** 3,900 feet. **Facilities:** Under development. **Special Features:** Park is a remnant of riverside woodland and restored wetland along the Rio Grande and is designed as a day-use park for walking, bicycling, and wildlife watching. Estimated completion date for the park's visitor center, offices, and associated facilities is fall of 2007.

★3377★ MORPHY LAKE STATE PARK

PO Box 477
Guadalupita, NM 87722
Web: www.emnrd.state.nm.us/PRD/MorphyLake.htm
Phone: 505-387-2328
Size: 30 acres land; 15 acres water. **Elevation:** 8,000 feet. **Location:** 7 miles south of Mora on NM 94, then 4 miles west on paved access road. **Facilities:** 20 developed campsites, picnic sites, trails, boat ramp, toilet facilities; no drinking water. **Activities:** Camping, hiking, boating (no gas motors), canoeing, fishing, ice fishing. **Special Features:** Located in the heart of the Sangre de Cristo Mountains, Park is set in a forest of pine trees at the end of a steep access road. The park's small, scenic lake is stocked with trout.

★3378★ NAVAJO LAKE STATE PARK

1448 NM 511 #1
Najavo Dam, NM 87419
Web: www.emnrd.state.nm.us/PRD/navajo.htm
Phone: 505-632-2278
Size: 21,000 acres land; 15,590 acres water. **Elevation:** 6,100 feet. **Location:** 25 miles east of Bloomfield via NM 64 and NM 511. **Facilities:** 246 developed campsites (98 with electric hookups; some with full hookups), restrooms (&), showers, picnic areas (&), group shelters, playgrounds, hiking trails, full-service marina, boat ramps, courtesy docks, visitor center with interpretive exhibits. **Activities:** Camping, boating, sailing, fishing (&), swimming, scuba diving, water-skiing, hiking, hunting, winter sports. **Special Features:** Navajo Lake is the state's second largest and offers the full gamut of water sports and services. The park comprises three separate areas: Pine River is the most developed and includes a visitor center with interpretive exhibits; Sims Mesa is on the east side of the lake, accessible by NM 527; and the San Juan River area below the dam is world renowned for excellent trout fishing and includes wheelchair-accessible fishing facilities on the river.

★3379★ OASIS STATE PARK

1891 Oasis Rd
Portales, NM 88130
Web: www.emnrd.state.nm.us/PRD/Oasis.htm
Phone: 505-356-5331; **Fax:** 505-356-5331
Size: 193 acres land; 3 acres water. **Elevation:** 4,000 feet. **Location:** 6.5 miles north of Portales via NM 467. **Facilities:** 23 developed campsites (13 with electric hookups), restrooms (&), showers, picnic areas (&), group shelter, playground, hiking trails. **Activities:** Camping, fishing, hiking, bird watching. **Special Features:** Located on the grassy plains of east-central New Mexico, Park provides a true oasis, with cottonwood trees and shifting sand dunes. The park also features a small fishing lake, prairie trails, and numerous birds.

★3380★ OLIVER LEE MEMORIAL STATE PARK

409 Dog Canyon Rd
Alamogordo, NM 88310
Web: www.emnrd.state.nm.us/PRD/oliverlee.htm
Phone: 505-437-8284; **Fax:** 505-439-1290
Size: 640 acres land. **Elevation:** 4,300 feet. **Location:** 12 miles south of Alamogordo via US 54, then east 4 miles on Alamogordo Road. **Facilities:** 48 developed campsites (18 with electric hookups), restrooms (&), showers, picnic area (&), group shelter, trails, historic structures, desert garden, visitor center, interpretive exhibits. **Activities:** Camping, hiking, wildlife viewing, education programs. **Special Features:** Park features historic exhibits and a fully restored 19th century ranch house, once the headquarters of Oliver Milton Lee (1865-1941), a colorful figure in New Mexico's history. Park is also the trailhead for the Dog Canyon National Recreational Trail in the adjacent Lincoln National Forest (see entry in section on national forests). This difficult, 6-mile trail has splendid views of the surrounding desert and White Sands National Monument.

★3381★ PANCHO VILLA STATE PARK

PO Box 450
Columbus, NM 88029
Web: www.emnrd.state.nm.us/PRD/PanchoVilla.htm
Phone: 505-531-2711
Size: 60 acres land. **Elevation:** 4,000 feet. **Location:** In the village of Columbus, 35 miles south of Deming via NM 11. **Facilities:** 62 developed campsites (all with electric hookups), restrooms (&), showers, picnic sites (&), group shelter, playground, trails, desert botanical gardens, historic buildings, visitor center, interpretive exhibits. **Activities:** Camping, hiking, wildlife viewing. **Special Features:** Park commemorates the 1916 raid of the small New Mexico border town and military camp at Columbus by guerrillas of the Mexican Revolution under General Francisco ''Pancho'' Villa. The park is located on the

grounds of the former Camp Furlong, and it was from here that General John ''Black Jack'' Pershing launched his punitive expedition into Mexico in retaliation against Villa. The park's historical exhibits depicting the raid and the US Army's subsequent punitive expedition are now housed in the park's $1.8 million, 7,000-square-foot Exhibit Hall. Several other buildings at the park date from the time of Villa's raid and are listed on the *National Register of Historic Places.*

★3382★ PERCHA DAM STATE PARK

PO Box 32
Caballo, NM 87931
Web: www.emnrd.state.nm.us/PRD/Percha.htm
Phone: 505-743-3942
Size: 80 acres land. **Elevation:** 4,100 feet. **Location:** 21 miles south of Truth or Consequences via I-25, Exit 59. **Facilities:** 50 developed campsites (30 with electric hookups), restrooms (&), showers, picnic areas (&), group shelter, playground, visitor center, interpretive exhibits. **Activities:** Camping, fishing, swimming, hiking, bird watching. **Special Features:** Park sits alongside the Rio Grande in the shade of tall cottonwood trees and offers excellent fishing and bird watching opportunities.

★3383★ RIO GRANDE NATURE CENTER STATE PARK

2901 Candelaria Rd NW
Albuquerque, NM 87107
Web: www.emnrd.state.nm.us/PRD/RGNC.htm
Phone: 505-344-7240; **Fax:** 505-344-4505
Size: 170 acres land. **Elevation:** 5,000 feet. **Location:** In Albuquerque, at the west end of Candelaria Road; take Exit 157A (Rio Grande Blvd) off I-40 or Exit 227 (Frontage Road) off I-25. **Facilities:** Nature trails, group shelter, visitor/nature center, classrooms, library, viewing areas, restrooms &). **Activities:** Naturalist-led hikes, wildlife viewing, nature study programs. **Special Features:** Park is a wildlife refuge and nature study center in the heart of Albuquerque, with a trail system along the river, classrooms, and a glass-walled library with viewing areas . It lies along the Rio Grande Flyway, an important migratory route for Canada geese, sandhill cranes, and various species of ducks and other waterfowl.

★3384★ ROCKHOUND STATE PARK

PO Box 1064
Deming, NM 88030
Web: www.emnrd.state.nm.us/PRD/Rockhound.htm
Phone: 505-546-6182
Size: 1,100 acres land. **Elevation:** 4,500 feet. **Location:** 5 miles south of Deming on NM 11, then east on NM 141 for 9 miles. **Facilities:** 29 developed campsites (18 with electric hookups), restrooms (&), showers, picnic areas (&), group shelter, playground, hiking trails, visitor center, interpretive exhibits. **Activities:** Camping, hiking, rock hounding, wildlife viewing. **Special Features:** Located on the western slope of the Little Florida Mountains, Park is popular with ''rock hounds'' because of the abundant agates and quartz crystals found here. Other minerals and specimens of volcanic origin are scattered around the park as well, including chalcedony and common opal.

★3385★ SANTA ROSA LAKE STATE PARK

PO Box 384
Santa Rosa, NM 88433
Web: www.emnrd.state.nm.us/PRD/santarosa.htm
Phone: 505-472-3110; **Fax:** 505-472-5956
Size: 500 acres land; 3,800 acres water. **Elevation:** 4,800 feet. **Location:** 7 miles north of Santa Rosa via NM 91. **Facilities:** 76 developed campsites (25 with electric hookups), restrooms (&), showers, picnic areas (&), group shelter, hiking trail, boat ramps, courtesy dock, visitor center. **Activities:** Camping, boating, sailing, canoeing, fishing, swimming, water-skiing, jet skiing, windsurfing, scuba diving, hiking, wildlife viewing. **Special Features:** Located on the plains of eastern New Mexico, Park's centerpiece is the Pecos River reservoir, which offers a variety of water recreation opportunities. In addition, the nearby town of Santa Rosa is known for its natural sinkhole lakes, where divers from around the country come to learn scuba skills.

★3386★ SMOKEY BEAR HISTORICAL STATE PARK

PO Box 591
Capitan, NM 88316
Web: www.SmokeyBearPark.com
Phone: 505-354-2748
Size: 3 acres. **Location:** In the village of Capitan on US 380 (also known as 118 Smokey Bear Blvd). **Facilities:** Visitor center, exhibits, amphitheater, picnic area, group picnic shelters, playground, train depot, Smokey Bear's gravesite and plaque. **Activities:** Educational programs. **Special Features:** Park commemorates the history of Smokey Bear as the national symbol of forest fire prevention. The original Smokey was found as a cub with burned paws near the site of a 17,000-acre forest fire near Capitan in 1950. He lived in the National Zoo for 26 years but was returned to Capitan for burial when he died. Park is administered by New Mexico Division of Forestry.

★3387★ STORRIE LAKE STATE PARK

HC 33, Box 109 #2
Las Vegas, NM 87701
Web: www.emnrd.state.nm.us/PRD/StorrieLake.htm
Phone: 505-425-7278
Size: 80 acres land; 1,100 acres water. **Elevation:** 6,600 feet. **Location:** 4 miles north of Las Vegas via NM 518. **Facilities:** 45 developed campsites (21 with electric hookups), restrooms (&), showers, picnic areas (&), 3 group shelters, playground, trails, boat ramps, courtesy dock, visitor center. **Activities:** Camping, boating, sailing, personal watercraft, fishing, swimming, water-skiing, windsurfing, wildlife viewing. **Special Features:** Storrie Lake's consistent winds provide excellent conditions for sailing and windsurfing. The park's visitor center features historical photos of the Santa Fe Trail and 19th century Las Vegas, which was a hangout for such notorious Old West characters as Doc Holliday, Billy the Kid, and Wyatt Earp.

★3388★ SUGARITE CANYON STATE PARK

HC 63, Box 386
Raton, NM 87740
Web: www.emnrd.state.nm.us/PRD/Sugarite.htm
Phone: 505-445-5607

Size: 3,600 acres land; 120 acres water. **Elevation:** 7,800 feet. **Location:** About 5.5 miles northeast of Raton via NM 72 east and 526 north. **Facilities:** 40 developed campsites (12 with electric hookups), restrooms (&), showers, picnic areas (&), group shelter, hiking trails, interpretive trail, boat ramp, courtesy dock, visitor center, exhibits. **Activities:** Camping, boating (no gas motors), canoeing and kayaking, fishing, hiking, rock climbing, cross-country skiing, wildlife viewing. **Special Features:** Located on the New Mexico-Colorado border, this heavily wooded, mountainous park was formerly the site of a coal-mining camp. An interpretive trail winds through the camp, and the visitor center provides information about the coal camp and the area's history. An extended cliff of basaltic rock columns, often referred to as "caprock," is the dominant geologic feature at the park, and rock climbing is permitted on the caprock.

★3389★ **SUMNER LAKE STATE PARK**

HC 64, Box 125

Fort Sumner, NM 88119

Web: www.emnrd.state.nm.us/PRD/SumnerLake.htm

Phone: 505-355-2541; **Fax:** 505-355-2542

Size: 6,700 acres land; 4,500 acres water. **Elevation:** 4,300 feet. **Location:** 10 miles northwest of Fort Sumner via US 84, then west for 6 miles on NM 203. **Facilities:** 50 developed campsites (18 with electric hookups), restrooms (&), showers, picnic areas (&), group shelter, trails, 3 boat ramps, boat docks, visitor center. **Activities:** Camping, swimming, boating, fishing, water-skiing, jet skiing, hiking, mountain biking, wildlife viewing. **Special Features:** In addition to the recreation activities available at the park, it also serves as a base for exploring 19th century history at nearby attractions. These include the Bosque Redondo Memorial and Fort Sumner State Monument, a Civil War era outpost that was the destination of the historical "Long Walk." Nearby also is the gravesite of the notorious outlaw Billy the Kid.

★3390★ **UTE LAKE STATE PARK**

PO Box 52

Logan, NM 88426

Web: www.emnrd.state.nm.us/PRD/UteLake.htm

Phone: 505-487-2284

Size: 1,500 acres land; 8,200 acres water. **Elevation:** 3,900 feet. **Location:** 3 miles west of Logan via NM 540. **Facilities:** 142 developed campsites (77 with electric hookups), restrooms (&), showers, picnic areas (&), group shelters, trails, marina, boat rentals, 5 boat ramps, courtesy docks, visitor center. **Activities:** Camping, boating, sailing, fishing, swimming, water-skiing, jet skiing, hiking, wildlife viewing, interpretive programs (seasonal). **Special Features:** Ute Lake, an impound on the Canadian River, is one of the longest lakes in the state at nearly 13 miles. It is also narrow, with its width never exceeding one mile. The lake offers some of the best walleye fishing in New Mexico, and visitors can fish 24 hours a day every day of the year.

★3391★ **VIETNAM VETERANS MEMORIAL STATE PARK**

Box 608

Angel Fire, NM 87710

Web: www.emnrd.state.nm.us/PRD/VietnamVets.htm

Phone: 505-377-6900; **Fax:** 505-377-3223

Size: 30 acres. **Elevation:** 8,500 feet. **Location:** In Angel Fire, 30 miles east from Taos on US 64. **Facilities:** Visitor center/museum, exhibits, chapel. **Activities:** Group tours by appointment. **Special Features:** Park is the only state park in the US dedicated solely as a Vietnam veterans memorial. It was originally established in 1968 by Victor and Jeanne Westphall to honor their son, Lt. David Westphall, who was killed in Vietnam in May 1968. The memorial was transferred to New Mexico State Parks in 2005 as the state's 33rd park. The memorial is open 7 days a week from 9 a.m. to 5 p.m. The chapel is open 24 hours a day, 7 days a week.

★3392★ **VILLANUEVA STATE PARK**

PO Box 40

Villanueva, NM 87583

Web: www.emnrd.state.nm.us/PRD/Villanueva.htm

Phone: 505-421-2957

Size: 1,600 acres land. **Elevation:** 5,600 feet. **Location:** 23 miles south of Las Vegas, NM, via I-25 to Exit 323, then south 15 miles on NM 3. **Facilities:** 33 developed campsites (12 with electric hookups), restrooms (&), showers, picnic shelters (&), playground, hiking trails, visitor center. **Activities:** Camping, fishing, canoeing and rafting (spring), hiking, wildlife viewing. **Special Features:** Near the picturesque Spanish-colonial village of Villanueva, this riverside park is situated in a canyon of red and yellow sandstone cliffs. Trails along the river lead to a prehistoric Indian ruin and a cliff-top vantage point.

9. State Parks

New York State Parks

1 Allan H. Treman SMP G-6
2 Allegany SP H-2
3 Battle Island SP E-7
4 Bayard Cutting Arboretum SP I-3
5 Bayswater Point SP J-2
6 Bear Mountain SP I-11
7 Beaver Island SP F-2
8 Belmont Lake SP I-2
9 Bennington Battlefield SHS E-12
10 Bethpage SP I-2
11 Betty & Wilbur Davis SP F-9
12 Big Six Mile Creek Marina SP F-2
13 Blauvelt SP I-1
14 Bonavista SP Golf Course E-7
15 Bowman Lake SP G-8
16 Buckhorn Island SP E-2
17 Burnham Point SP C-7
18 Buttermilk Falls SP G-6
19 Caleb Smith SPPr I-3
20 Camp Hero SP H-5
21 Canandaigua Lake SMP F-5
22 Canoe-Picnic Point SP B-7
23 Captree SP I-3
24 Caumsett SHP I-2
25 Cayuga Lake SP F-6
26 Cedar Island SP B-8
27 Cedar Point SP C-7
28 Chenango Valley SP G-8
29 Cherry Plain SP F-12
30 Chimney Bluffs SP D-6
31 Chittenango Falls SP E-8
32 Clarence Fahnestock SP I-12
33 Clark Reservation SP E-7
34 Clay Pit Ponds SPPr J-1
35 Clermont SHS H-11
36 Clinton House SHS I-11
37 Cold Spring Harbor SP I-2
38 Coles Creek SP A-9
39 Connetquot River SPPr I-3
40 Crailo SHS F-12
41 Crown Point SHS C-12
42 Cumberland Bay SP A-12
43 Darien Lakes SP F-3
44 Darwin Martin House SHS F-2
45 De Veaux Woods SP E-2
46 Delta Lake SP E-8
47 Devil's Hole SP E-2
48 DeWolf Point SP B-7
49 Earl W. Brydges Artpark SP E-2
50 Eel Weir SP A-8
51 Empire-Fulton Ferry SP J-1
52 Evangola SP F-2
53 Fair Haven Beach SP E-6
54 Fillmore Glen SP F-7
55 Fort Montgomery SHS I-11
56 Fort Niagara SP E-2
57 Fort Ontario SHS D-6
58 Four Mile Creek SP E-2
59 Franklin D. Roosevelt SP J-12
60 Ganondagan SHS E-5
61 Gantry Plaza SP I-2
62 Gilbert Lake SP F-9
63 Glimmerglass SP F-9
64 Golden Hill SP E-3
65 Goosepond Mountain SP I-11
66 Governor Alfred E. Smith/ Sunken Meadow SP I-3
67 Grafton Lakes SP F-12
68 Grant Cottage SHS E-11
69 Grass Point SP B-7
70 Green Lakes SP E-7
71 Hamlin Beach SP E-4
72 Harriet Hollister Spencer SRA F-5
73 Harriman SP J-11
74 Heckscher SP I-3
75 Hempstead Lake SP J-2
76 Herkimer Home SHS E-9
77 High Tor SP J-11
78 Highland Lakes SP I-10
79 Higley Flow SP B-9
80 Hither Hills SP H-5
81 Honeoye Lake SHS F-5
82 Hudson Highlands SP I-11
83 Hudson River Islands SP G-11
84 Hunts Pond SP F-8
85 Hyde Hall SHS F-9
86 Irondequoit Bay SMP E-5
87 Jacques Cartier SP B-8
88 James Baird SP I-12
89 John Boyd Thacher SP F-11
90 John Brown Farm SHS A-11
91 John Burroughs Memorial SHS G-10
92 John Jay Homestead SHS J-12
93 Johnson Hall SHS E-10
94 Jones Beach SP J-2
95 Joseph Davis SP E-2
96 Keewaydin SP B-8
97 Keuka Lake SP F-5
98 Knox Farm SP F-5
99 Knox's Headquarters SHS I-11
100 Kring Point SP B-8
101 Lake Erie SP G-1
102 Lake Superior SP I-9
103 Lake Taghkanic SP H-12
104 Lakeside Beach SP E-3
105 Letchworth SP F-4

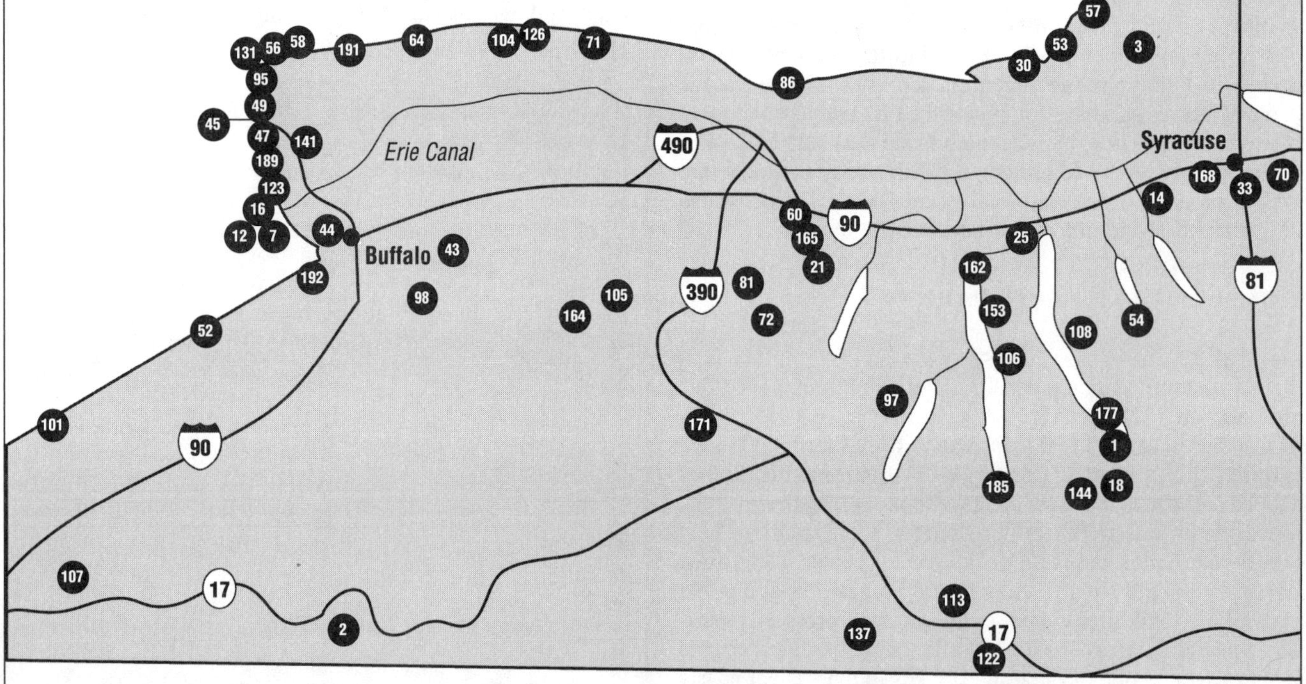

Syracuse
Erie Canal
Buffalo

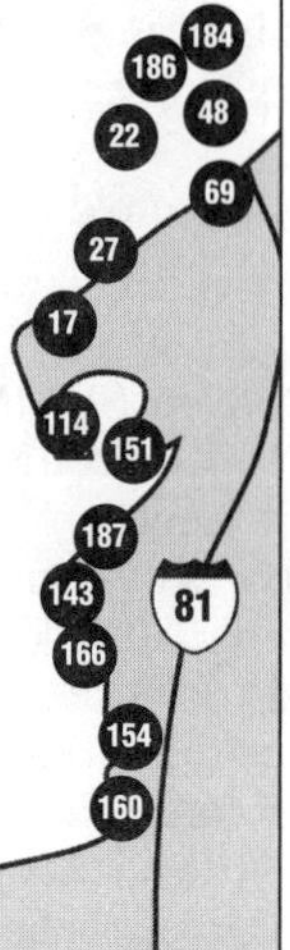

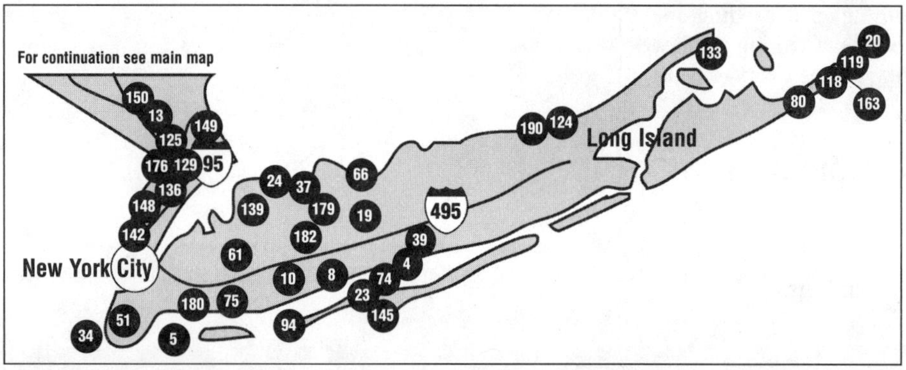

For continuation see main map
Long Island
New York City

106 Lodi Point SP F-6
107 Long Point on Lake Chautauqua SP G-1
108 Long Point SP - Finger Lakes F-6
109 Long Point SP - Thousand Islands B-8
110 Lorenzo SHS F-8
111 Macomb Reservation SP A-11
112 Margaret Lewis Norrie SP H-11
113 Mark Twain SP & Soaring Eagles Golf Course G-6
114 Mary Island SP C-7
115 Max V. Shaul SP G-10
116 Mine Kill SP G-10
117 Minnewaska SPPr I-11

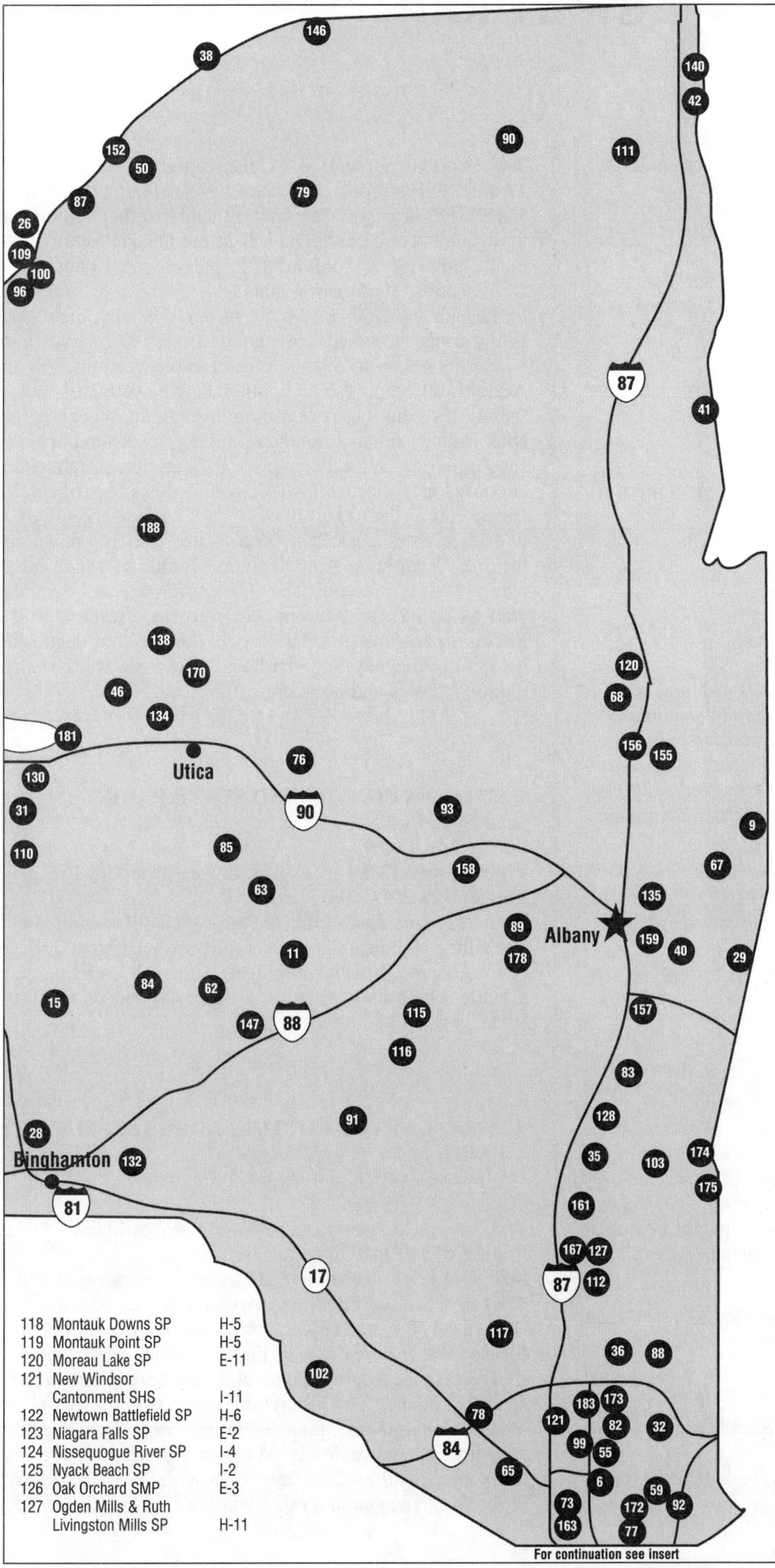

8 9 10 11 12 13 14

A B C D E F G H I J

128	Olana SHS	G-11
129	Old Croton Aqueduct SHP	I-2
130	Old Erie Canal SHP	E-8
131	Old Fort Niagara SHS	E-2
132	Oquaga Creek SP	H-8
133	Orient Beach SP	H-4
134	Oriskany Battlefield SHS	E-8
135	Peebles Island SP	F-12
136	Philipse Manor Hall SHS	I-2
137	Pinnacle SP & Golf Course	H-5
138	Pixley Falls SP	D-8
139	Planting Fields Arboretum SHP/Coe Hall Historic House Museum	I-2
140	Pointe Au Roche SP	A-12
141	Reservoir SP	E-2
142	Riverbank SP	I-1
143	Robert G. Wehle SP	C-7
144	Robert H. Treman SP	G-6
145	Robert Moses SP - Long Island	J-3
146	Robert Moses SP - Thousand Islands	A-9
147	Robert V. Ridell SP	G-9
148	Roberto Clemente SP	I-1
149	Rockefeller SPPr	I-2
150	Rockland Lake SP	H-1
151	Sackets Harbor Battlefield SHS	C-7
152	Saint Lawrence SP & Golf Course	A-8
153	Sampson SP	F-6
154	Sandy Island Beach SP	D-7
155	Saratoga Lake SMP	E-12
156	Saratoga Spa SP	E-11
157	Schodack Island SP	G-12
158	Schoharie Crossing SHS	F-10
159	Schuyler Mansion SHS	F-12
160	Selkirk Shores SP	D-7
161	Senate House SHS	H-11
162	Seneca Lake SP	F-6
163	Shadmoor SP	H-5
164	Silver Lake SP	F-4
165	Sonnenberg Gardens & Mansion SHP	F-5
166	Southwick Beach SP	D-7
167	Staatsburgh SHS	H-11
168	State Park at the Fair	E-7
169	Sterling Forest® SP	J-11
170	Steuben Memorial SHS	E-9
171	Stony Brook SP	G-4
172	Stony Point Battlefield SHS	J-11
173	Storm King SP	I-11
174	Taconic SP - Copake Falls Area	G-12
175	Taconic SP - Rudd Pond Area	H-12
176	Tallman Mountain SP	I-1
177	Taughannock Falls SP	F-6
178	Thompson's Lake SP	F-11
179	Trail View SP	I-2
180	Valley Stream SP	J-2
181	Verona Beach SP	E-8
182	Walt Whitman Birthplace SHS	I-2
183	Washington's Headquarters SHS	I-11
184	Waterson Point SP	B-7
185	Watkins Glen SP	G-6
186	Wellesley Island SP	B-7
187	Westcott Beach SP	C-7
188	Whetstone Gulf SP	D-8
189	Whirlpool SP	E-2
190	Wildwood SP	I-4
191	Wilson-Tuscarora SP	E-2
192	Woodlawn Beach SP	F-2

SHP	State Historic Park	
SHS	State Historic Site	
SMP	State Marine Park	
SP	State Park	
SPPr	State Park Preserve	

118	Montauk Downs SP	H-5
119	Montauk Point SP	H-5
120	Moreau Lake SP	E-11
121	New Windsor Cantonment SHS	I-11
122	Newtown Battlefield SP	H-6
123	Niagara Falls SP	E-2
124	Nissequogue River SP	I-4
125	Nyack Beach SP	I-2
126	Oak Orchard SMP	E-3
127	Ogden Mills & Ruth Livingston Mills SP	H-11

Utica

Albany

Binghamton

For continuation see insert

653

★3393★ New York State Office of Parks, Recreation & Historic Preservation

1 Empire State Plaza
Albany, NY 12238
(518) 474-0456 - Phone
(518) 486-1805 - Fax
(800) 456-2267 - Reservations
518-486-1899 - TDD
Web: www.nysparks.com
Oversees state parks, historic sites, and trails. Coordinates boating and snowmobiling safety programs.

★3394★ New York State Department of Environmental Conservation

625 Broadway
Albany, NY 12233
(518) 402-9401 - Phone
(518) 457-9016 - Fax
(800) 456-2267 - Campground Reservations
Web: www.dec.state.ny.us
Manages one million acres of land. Protects fish and wildlife resources; licenses fishing, hunting, and trapping; and oversees the enforcement of laws pertaining to environmental protection. Within the Adirondack and Catskill Forest Preserves, the department operates 52 campgrounds, maintains marked trails, and administers several day-use areas offering swimming, picnicking, fishing, and boat access.

★3395★ ALLAN H. TREMAN STATE MARINE PARK

c/o Robert H. Treman State Park
105 Enfield Falls Rd
Ithaca, NY 14850
Web: nysparks.state.ny.us/parks/info.asp?parkId=103
Phone: 607-273-3440
Size: 91 acres. **Location:** Off Route 89, north of Ithaca, at the southern end of Cayuga Lake's western shore. **Facilities:** Picnic tables (&), playing fields, marina, dockage (370 seasonal, 30 transient, and 30 dry boat slips), boat launch sites, showers (&). **Activities:** Boating, fishing (&), picnicking. **Special Features:** Park features one of New York's largest inland marinas, with access to the Barge Canal and Seneca Lake.

★3396★ ALLEGANY STATE PARK

2373 ASP, Rt 1, Suite 3
Salamanca, NY 14779
Web: nysparks.state.ny.us/parks/info.asp?parkId=91
Phone: 716-354-9121
Size: 64,800 acres. **Location:** Allegany includes two recreational areas: the Quaker area is off I-86/Route 17 (Southern Tier Expressway) at Exit 18; the Red House area is off Exits 19 and 20. **Facilities:** 424 campsites (including tent and trailer sites; &), 375 cabins (&; 150 are winterized), 3 group camps, 8 vacation rental cottages (7 & at the Quaker area), showers, picnic areas (&), pavilions (&), playgrounds, playing fields, tennis courts, food concessions (&), hiking trails, nature trail, bridle path, mountain bike trails, paved bike paths, cross-country skiing trails, groomed snowmobile trails (90 miles), beaches, boat launches, boat rentals, bike rentals, museums, gift shops. **Activities:** Camping, boating (including powerboats), canoeing, fishing (&), hunting (&), swimming, hiking, bicycling, horseback riding, tennis, mountain biking, cross-country skiing, snowmobiling, snowshoeing, ice fishing, bird watching, recreation and nature programs (&), scenic views (&). **Special Features:** Park is the largest in New York's state park system, with two developed areas: The Red House area is known for its historic Tudor-style Administration Building, which houses a natural history museum. The Quaker area features two lakes as well as an old Quaker store that has been restored and now houses a park museum. Exhibits in the museum document the history of Allegany State Park and orient visitors to the park's unique features and attractions.

★3397★ BATTLE ISLAND STATE PARK

2150 State Rt 48
Fulton, NY 13069
Web: nysparks.state.ny.us/parks/info.asp?parkId=15
Phone: 315-593-3408
Size: 235 acres. **Location:** On Route 48, 3 miles north of Fulton. **Facilities:** 18-hole golf course, food (&). **Activities:** Golf, cross-country skiing. **Special Features:** Park derives its name from a battle which took place on a nearby island on the Oswego River in the mid-1700s.

★3398★ BAYARD CUTTING ARBORETUM STATE PARK

PO Box 466
Oakdale, NY 11769
Web: nysparks.state.ny.us/parks/info.asp?parkId=43
Phone: 631-581-1002
Size: 690 acres. **Location:** Off Montauk Highway (Rt 27A, Exit 45E) in Oakdale. **Facilities:** Arboretum, nature trail (&), gift shop, food (&). **Activities:** Recreation programs. **Special Features:** Park features one of the most extensive collections of fir, spruce, pine, cypress, hemlock, and other conifers to be found on Long Island. The arboretum also has extensive plantings of dwarf evergreens, rhododendron, azaleas, hollies and oaks, wildflowers, and daffodils. The park's ponds and streams and many trees, shrubs, and flowers provide food and homes for birds, fox, raccoon, and other wildlife.

★3399★ BAYSWATER POINT STATE PARK

c/o Gantry Plaza State Park
50-50 2nd St
Long Island City, NY 11101
Web: nysparks.state.ny.us/parks/info.asp?parkId=27
Phone: 718-471-2212
Size: 21 acres. Location: Mott Avenue and Jamaica Bay, Queens. Facilities: Undeveloped. Activities: Fishing, hiking, nature study. Special Features: Park is located at the tip of a peninsula in the Rockaways that juts out into the Mott Basin on the eastern shore of Jamaica Bay. Its diverse terrain includes beachfront, wetland, and woodlands, which helps make it an ideal habitat for migrating and nesting birds. Park's goal is to preserve the existing natural systems.

★3400★ BEAR MOUNTAIN STATE PARK

c/o Palisades Interstate Park Commission
Bear Mountain, NY 10911
Web: nysparks.state.ny.us/parks/info.asp?parkId=55
Phone: 845-786-2701
Size: 5,067 acres. Location: Off Palisades Parkway, 45 miles north of New York City. Facilities: Lodging, restaurant, picnic areas (&), playground, playing fields (&), nature trail, hiking, biking, and cross-country skiing trail, ski jumps, swimming pool, small boat dockage (&), boat rentals, skating rink (&), zoo, museum/visitor center and gift shop (&), lookout point. Activities: Boating (no power boats), fishing, swimming, hiking, bicycling, cross-country skiing, ice skating. Special Features: Atop Bear Mountain, Perkins Memorial Tower affords views of the park, the Hudson highlands, and Harriman State Park (see separate entry). Lodging and fine dining are offered at historic Bear Mountain Inn. The park's merry-go-round features hand-painted scenes of the park and 42 hand-carved seats of native animals.

★3401★ BEAVER ISLAND STATE PARK

2136 W Oakfield Rd
Grand Island, NY 14072
Web: nysparks.state.ny.us/parks/info.asp?parkId=94
Phone: 716-773-3271
Size: 952 acres. Location: Off I-190, 9 miles north of Buffalo, on Grand Island. Facilities: Picnic areas, picnic pavilions (&), playgrounds, food concession, bike and nature trails, 18-hole golf course, disc golf course (18-hole), horseshoe pits, athletic fields, beach with bathhouse, 80-slip marina, historic home. Activities: Boating, fishing, swimming, bicycling, golf, cross-country skiing, snowmobiling, snowshoeing, sledding, ice fishing, hunting, recreation programs (&). Special Features: Park is located at the south end of Grand Island in the Niagara River and is considered one of the best beaches in the area. A historic home that was once President Grover Cleveland's summer home is located at the park. The Beaver Island Clubhouse has banquet and catering facilities.

★3402★ BELMONT LAKE STATE PARK

PO Box 247
Babylon, NY 11702
Web: nysparks.state.ny.us/parks/info.asp?parkId=159
Phone: 631-667-5055
Size: 463 acres. Location: Exit 38 off Southern State Parkway, north of Babylon, 42 miles from Manhattan. Facilities: Picnic areas and pavilions (&), playgrounds (&), playing fields, horseshoe and basketball courts, trails (including nature trail), food concession (&), boat rentals (&). Activities: Boating (no power boats), fishing, hiking, bicycling, horseback riding, recreation programs (&). Special Features: Park serves as headquarters of the Long Island Region.

★3403★ BENNINGTON BATTLEFIELD STATE HISTORIC SITE

c/o Grafton Lakes State Park
PO Box 163
Grafton, NY 12082
Web: www.nysparks.com/sites/info.asp?siteID=3
Phone: 518-686-7109; Fax: 518-279-1902
Size: 421 acres. Location: Off Route 67, between Walloomsac and Vermont state line. Facilities: Picnic area (&), game fields, trails, interpretive displays, scenic view. Activities: Hiking. Special Features: Site is the location of a Revolutionary War battle in which American militiamen defeated the British in 1777.

★3404★ BETHPAGE STATE PARK

Bethpage Pkwy
Farmingdale, NY 11735
Web: nysparks.state.ny.us/parks/info.asp?parkId=67
Phone: 516-249-0701
Size: 1,477 acres. Location: East on the Long Island Expressway (Route 495) to Exit 44S, then south on the Seaford/Oyster Bay Expressway (Rout 135) to Powell Avenue Exit 8 and east to the park. Facilities: 5 18-hole golf courses (&), driving range, pro shop, restaurant (&), picnic areas (&), playgrounds (&), playing fields, tennis courts, hiking and biking (&) trails, nature trail, bridle path, cross-country skiing trails, showers (&). Activities: Golf, tennis, hiking, bicycling, horseback riding, cross-country skiing, sledding, recreation programs. Special Features: Park is best known for its 5 world-class golf courses, including the Black Course, which hosted the US Open in 2002 and will again in 2009. Park also has a polo field where matches are played on Sundays from June through October.

★3405★ BETTY & WILBUR DAVIS STATE PARK

c/o Glimmerglass State Park
1527 County Hwy 31
Cooperstown, NY 13326
Web: nysparks.state.ny.us/parks/info.asp?parkId=179
Phone: 607-547-8662; Fax: 607-547-5465
Size: 199 acres. Location: In the town of Westford, near Cooperstown. Facilities: Picnic area, pavilion, hiking trails. Activities: Hiking, fishing (catch and release), hunting (by permit only), cross-country skiing, snowshoeing, snowmobiling. Special Features: Nearly two-thirds of the park is forest; the remainder is meadowlands and two ponds. The park has an extensive network of hiking trails, and its snowmobile trails connect to the state corridor trail system. Cooperstown, home of the National Baseball Hall of Fame, is a short drive away.

9. State Parks

★3406★ BIG SIX MILE CREEK MARINA STATE PARK

c/o Beaver Island State Park
2136 W Oakfield Rd
Grand Island, NY 14072
Web: nysparks.state.ny.us/parks/info.asp?parkId=40
Phone: 716-773-3271
Size: 19 acres. **Location:** Off the West River Parkway on Whitehaven, mid-way up the west shore of Grand Island. **Facilities:** Marina, dockage, boat launch. **Activities:** Boating, fishing. **Special Features:** Marina has 134 seasonal boat slips, with vacancies filled by a lottery every year. The park is open from May to November.

★3407★ BLAUVELT STATE PARK

c/o Palisades Interstate Park Commission
Bear Mountain, NY 10911
Web: nysparks.state.ny.us/parks/info.asp?parkId=53
Phone: 845-359-0544
Size: 633 acres. **Location:** On Greenbush Road in Nyack via Route 303 north. **Facilities:** Undeveloped. **Activities:** Hiking. **Special Features:** Hiking trails provide the only access to this forested green space in Rockland County and afford spectacular views of the Hudson Valley.

★3408★ BONAVISTA STATE PARK GOLF COURSE

7194 County Rd 132
Ovid, NY 14521
Web: nysparks.state.ny.us/parks/info.asp?parkId=30
Phone: 607-869-5482
Size: 235 acres. **Location:** From Geneva, take Route 96A south to Route 132. **Facilities:** 9-hole golf course, clubhouse, restaurant, snack bar, picnic areas. **Activities:** Golf, hiking, bow hunting (in season), cross-country skiing. **Special Features:** Park derives its name from the course's scenic view of Lake Seneca. The 9-hole course can be played twice from different tees for an 18-hole round. Park is open from April until November.

★3409★ BOWMAN LAKE STATE PARK

745 Bliven Sherman Rd
Oxford, NY 13830
Web: nysparks.state.ny.us/parks/info.asp?parkId=16
Phone: 607-334-2718
Size: 653 acres. **Location:** Off Route 220, 8 miles west of Oxford. **Facilities:** Tent and trailer campsites (&), showers (&), picnic areas (&), picnic pavilions, playground, food concession, self-guided nature trail, multi-use trails (8 miles), beach, boat launch, boat rentals, nature center. **Activities:** Camping, boating (no power boats), deer hunting (in season), fishing, swimming, hiking, bicycling, cross-country skiing, snowmobiling, bird watching, recreation programs. **Special Features:** Park features a sandy lakefront for swimmers and sunbathers. The lake is stocked with trout, and around the lake birdwatchers can spot as many as 103 different species of birds.

★3410★ BUCKHORN ISLAND STATE PARK

c/o Beaver Island State Park
2136 W Oakfield Rd
Grand Island, NY 14072
Web: nysparks.state.ny.us/parks/info.asp?parkId=21
Phone: 716-773-3271
Size: 895 acres. **Location:** Off I-190 at the north end of Grand Island. **Facilities:** Nature trail; no restroom facilities. **Activities:** Fishing, hiking, bicycling, cross-country skiing. **Special Features:** Park contains the last vestige of the once-vast marshlands and meadows that bordered the Niagara River. The park is classified as a preserve and is undergoing restoration to establish wetland cover and increase diversity of native flora and fauna.

★3411★ BURNHAM POINT STATE PARK

340765 NYS Rt 12E
Cape Vincent, NY 13618
Web: nysparks.state.ny.us/parks/info.asp?parkId=140
Phone: 315-654-2522
Size: 12 acres. **Location:** Off Route 12E, 4 miles east of Cape Vincent. **Facilities:** Tent and trailer campsites (&), showers (&), picnic areas and pavilions (&), playground, boat docks and launch site. **Activities:** Camping, boating (including power boats), fishing, waterfowl hunting (in season). **Special Features:** Park is northeast of Lake Ontario on the Saint Lawrence River. From the park, boaters can explore towns, islands, and historic sites for miles up and down the scenic river.

★3412★ BUTTERMILK FALLS STATE PARK

c/o Robert H. Tremin State Park
105 Enfield Falls Rd
Ithaca, NY 14850
Web: nysparks.state.ny.us/parks/info.asp?parkId=25
Phone: 607-273-3440
Size: 804 acres. **Location:** Off Route 13, south of Ithaca. **Facilities:** Campground with tent and trailer campsites, cabins, showers, picnic areas and pavilions, playground, playing fields, beach, hiking trails (6 miles), hiking trails, nature trail, scenic views (&&). **Activities:** Camping, boating (no power boats), fishing, swimming, hiking, deer hunting (bow only, in season), recreation and nature programs. **Special Features:** Park is named for the foaming cascade that's formed by Buttermilk Creek as it flows down the steep valley side toward Cayuga Lake. Park activities from July 4th through Labor Day include tours through Buttermilk gorge, and hiking trails wind along the gorge. A nature trail winds through Larch Meadows, a moist glen and wetland area that lies beyond the camping area in the lower portion of the park.

★3413★ CALEB SMITH STATE PARK PRESERVE

PO Box 963
Smithtown, NY 11787
Web: nysparks.state.ny.us/parks/info.asp?parkId=160
Phone: 631-265-1054
Size: 546 acres. **Location:** Off Jericho Turnpike 3 miles from Smithtown. **Facilities:** Hiking and nature trails (&), gift shop. **Activities:** Fly fishing, hiking, cross-country skiing. **Special Features:** Nestled in the midst of a suburb, the preserve's ponds,

streams, fields, and woods are a refuge for wildlife and a place for visitors to develop an appreciation of the natural world.

★3414★ CAMP HERO STATE PARK

50 S Fairview Ave
Montauk, NY 11954
Web: nysparks.state.ny.us/parks/info.asp?parkId=82
Phone: 631-668-3781
Size: 754 acres. **Location:** Route 27 (Sunrise Hwy) east to its terminus. **Facilities:** Picnic areas, beach, trails. **Activities:** Surf fishing, hiking, biking, horseback riding, cross-country skiing. **Special Features:** Park encompasses a diverse landscape that includes maritime forests, freshwater wetlands, ocean vistas, and bluffs rising from the beach. The park has an extensive trail system as well as excellent surf fishing available 24 hours a day (with permit). A former military base at the park is a registered National Historic Site.

★3415★ CANANDAIGUA LAKE STATE MARINE PARK

620 S Main St
Canandaigua, NY 14424
Web: nysparks.state.ny.us/parks/info.asp?parkId=4
Phone: 315-789-2331
Size: 15 acres. **Location:** South of US 20, near Canandaigua, at northern end of lake. **Facilities:** Boat launch. **Activities:** Boating (including power boats), fishing (&). **Special Features:** Park is a boat launch facility and provides fishing access to Canandaigua Lake.

★3416★ CANOE-PICNIC POINT STATE PARK

c/o Cedar Point State Park
36661 Cedar Point State Park Dr
Clayton, NY 13624
Web: nysparks.state.ny.us/parks/info.asp?parkId=118
Phone: 315-654-2522
Size: 70 acres. **Location:** Northeastern end of Grindstone Island, facing Eel Bay and the Canadian Channel; access by boat only. **Facilities:** Camping sites, cabins (&), showers, dockage, nature trail, picnic area (&), picnic gazebo. **Activities:** Camping, boating (including power boats), fishing, hiking, waterfowl hunting in season. **Special Features:** Park offers a quiet camping experience in a wooded setting. Fishing here is excellent.

★3417★ CAPTREE STATE PARK

c/o Long Island Regional Office
PO Box 247
Babylon, NY 11702
Web: nysparks.state.ny.us/parks/info.asp?parkId=151
Phone: 631-669-0449
Size: 340 acres. **Location:** Southern end of Robert Moses Causeway, at the eastern tip of Jones Beach Island. **Facilities:** Marina, boat launch sites, picnic tables, playground, food concession (&&). **Activities:** Fishing, recreation programs. **Special Features:** Park features a boat basin with open and charter boats available for fishing, as well as scuba diving, sightseeing, and excursion boats.

★3418★ CAUMSETT STATE HISTORIC PARK

25 Lloyd Harbor Rd
Huntington, NY 11743
Web: www.nysparks.com/sites/info.asp?siteID=4
Phone: 631-423-1770; **Fax:** 631-423-8645
Size: 1,520 acres. **Location:** On a peninsula extending into Long Island Sound. **Facilities:** Nature trails, bridle trails, cross-country skiing trails, hiking trails, bike trails, scenic views, historic house. **Activities:** Fishing, scuba diving, hiking, bicycling, horseback riding, cross-country skiing, guided tours. **Special Features:** Situated on a scenic peninsula extending into Long Island Sound, park lands include woodlands, meadows, salt marsh, and rocky shoreline. Park features an estate built in 1921 by Marshall Field III. The English-style estate was a private country club, hunting preserve, and home, complete with its own water and electrical supply and facilities for every sport except golf. Today, several of the park's buildings serve as headquarters for various environmental education groups.

★3419★ CAYUGA LAKE STATE PARK

2678 Lower Lake Rd
Seneca Falls, NY 13148
Web: nysparks.state.ny.us/parks/info.asp?parkId=9
Phone: 315-568-5163
Size: 141 acres. **Location:** Off Route 89, at the north end of Cayuga Lake, west shore. **Facilities:** Tent and trailer campsites (&), showers (&), cabins (&), vacation rental property, beach, picnic area (&), picnic pavilions, playground, playing fields, nature trail, boat launch. **Activities:** Camping, boating (including power boats), fishing (&), swimming, hiking, cross-country skiing, sledding, ice fishing. **Special Features:** An expansive view of Cayuga Lake is the scenic highlight of this park. The vacation rental property at the lake is located on Lower Lake Road, and the park provides lake rights to renters. A lakefront dock is also available for tenants.

★3420★ CEDAR ISLAND STATE PARK

c/o Keewaydin State Park
PO Box 247
Alexandria Bay, NY 13607
Web: nysparks.state.ny.us/parks/info.asp?parkId=141
Phone: 315-482-3331
Size: 10 acres. **Location:** On Cedar Island in Chippewa Bay near Hammond; access by boat only. **Facilities:** Campsites, dockage, picnic area with pavilion. **Activities:** Camping, boating (including powerboats), fishing, waterfowl hunting (in season). **Special Features:** Park encompasses half of the island and provides a quiet setting with lovely scenery.

★3421★ CEDAR POINT STATE PARK

36661 Cedar Point State Park Dr
Clayton, NY 13624
Web: nysparks.state.ny.us/parks/info.asp?parkId=126
Phone: 315-654-2522
Size: 48 acres. **Location:** On Route 12E, 6 miles west of Clayton. **Facilities:** Tent and trailer campsites (&), showers (&), picnic area with pavilions (&), playing fields, playground, beach

with bathhouse, marina, dockage, boat launch, boat rentals, fishing pier (&). **Activities:** Camping, boating (including power boats), fishing, swimming, waterfowl hunting in season, recreation programs. **Special Features:** One of New York's oldest state parks, the park features a sheltered sandy beach. From the overlook area, visitors can watch ocean-going freighters pass by. Park is open from early May through Columbus Day.

★3422★ **CHENANGO VALLEY STATE PARK**

153 State Park Rd
Chenango Forks, NY 13746
Web: nysparks.state.ny.us/parks/info.asp?parkId=5
Phone: 607-648-5251
Size: 1,137 acres. **Location:** Off Route 369, 13 miles north of Binghamton. **Facilities:** 216 tent and trailer campsites (&), showers (&), 24 cabins, picnic areas (&), picnic pavilions, playground, hiking trails, nature trail, biking trail, cross-country ski trails, 18-hole golf course, food concession, beach with bathhouse, boat rentals. **Activities:** Camping, boating (no power boats), fishing, swimming, hiking, bicycling, golf, cross-country skiing, ice skating, sledding, recreation programs (&). **Special Features:** Park includes two kettle lakes, Lily and Chenango, created at the end of the last Ice Age when the retreating glacier left behind huge chunks of buried ice which melted to form the lakes.

★3423★ **CHERRY PLAIN STATE PARK**

26 State Park Rd
PO Box 11
Cherry Plain, NY 12040
Web: nysparks.state.ny.us/parks/info.asp?parkId=115
Phone: 518-733-5400
Size: 175 acres. **Location:** 19 miles southeast of Grafton and 7 miles north of Stephentown, off NYS Rt 22 on CCC Dam Road. **Facilities:** 10 trailer campsites, 10 tent campsites, picnic area (&), picnic pavilions, multi-use trails, nature trail, bridle paths, beach with bathhouse, showers, comfort stations, playground, boat launch, boat rentals, food concession. **Activities:** Boating (no power boats), fishing, swimming, hiking, bicycling, horseback riding, cross-country skiing, snowmobiling, ice fishing, recreation programs, deer and small game hunting in season. **Special Features:** Park features a sandy beach on Black River Pond.

★3424★ **CHIMNEY BLUFFS STATE PARK**

7700 Garner Rd
Wolcott, NY 14590
Web: nysparks.state.ny.us/parks/info.asp?parkId=168
Phone: 315-947-5205
Size: 597 acres. **Location:** North on Bluff Road off Route 104. **Facilities:** Picnic areas, nature trails, restrooms, scenic views. **Activities:** Hiking, fishing, hunting, cross-country skiing, snowshoeing, snowmobiling. **Special Features:** Park's most outstanding feature is its dramatic landscape, where land and water have clashed to create massive earthen spires that can be viewed from above or along the Lake Ontario shore.

★3425★ **CHITTENANGO FALLS STATE PARK**

2300 Rathbun Rd
Cazenovia, NY 13035
Web: nysparks.state.ny.us/parks/info.asp?parkId=11
Phone: 315-655-9620
Size: 193 acres. **Location:** Off Route 13, 4 miles north of Cazenovia. **Facilities:** Picnic areas (&), picnic pavilions, playground, nature trail, showers (&), disk golf course. **Activities:** Fishing, hiking, picnicking. **Special Features:** A trail leads to the 167-foot falls, the park's main attraction. Visitors can view the falls from above, follow the trail into the gorge to a footbridge, and return to the top on the opposite side of the gorge.

★3426★ **CLARENCE FAHNESTOCK STATE PARK**

1498 Rt 301
Carmel, NY 10512
Web: nysparks.state.ny.us/parks/info.asp?parkId=129
Phone: 845-225-7207
Size: 16,172 acres. **Location:** Off Route 301, west of Taconic State Parkway or east of NYS Rt 9. **Facilities:** 80 tent campsites, RV camping area, restrooms and showers (&), picnic areas, picnic pavilions, hiking trails (70 miles), nature trail, hiking and bike trails, bridle path, groomed trails for cross-country skiing and snowshoeing, sledding area, beach, hand launch boat ramp, rowboat rentals, food (&). **Activities:** Camping (includng group camping), boating (no power boats), fishing, swimming, hiking, biking, horseback riding, hunting (with restrictions), cross-country skiing, snowshoeing, ice fishing, snowmobiling, sledding, recreation and nature programs, educational programs. **Special Features:** Park includes a large, sandy beach at Canopus Lake, groomed trails at Fahnestock Winter Park, and the Taconic Outdoor Education Center. The campground is formed along the park's natural rock ridges, providing alcoves of privacy for campers.

★3427★ **CLARK RESERVATION STATE PARK**

6105 E Seneca Tpke
Jamesville, NY 13078
Web: nysparks.state.ny.us/parks/info.asp?parkId=17
Phone: 315-492-1590
Size: 377 acres. **Location:** South of Syracuse, off Route 173. From Buffalo-Rochester or NYC-Albany, exit 34A off I-90. **Facilities:** Picnic areas (&), picnic pavilions, playground, hiking trails, nature trail, nature center, exhibits. **Activities:** Fishing, hiking, birdwatching, guided nature walks. **Special Features:** Park's natural features include rugged cliffs, rocky outcrops, woodlands, meadows, wetlands, and a glacial plunge basin lake in which the surface waters and bottom waters do not mix. The park's cliff trail has a ledge overlook 175 feet above the water.

★3428★ **CLAY PIT PONDS STATE PARK PRESERVE**

83 Nielsen Ave
Staten Island, NY 10309
Web: nysparks.state.ny.us/parks/info.asp?parkId=32
Phone: 718-967-1976
Size: 265 acres. **Location:** On Nielson Avenue, off Sharrotts Road, in the southwestern area of Staten Island. **Facilities:** Picnic tables and pavilions (&), hiking trails, nature trail, bridle

9. State Parks

path (5 miles). **Activities:** Hiking, horseback riding, educational programs. **Special Features:** Preserve contains a variety of unique habitats and is managed to retain its unique ecology while offering educational and recreational opportunities.

★3429★ CLERMONT STATE HISTORIC SITE

1 Clermont Ave
Germantown, NY 12526
Web: www.nysparks.com/sites/info.asp?siteID=5
Phone: 518-537-4240; **Fax:** 518-537-6240
Size: 589 acres. **Location:** On County Road 6, off Route 9G, 1 mile north of Tivoli. **Facilities:** Picnic area, hiking trail, bridle trail, nature trails, visitor center, interpretive exhibit, museum, scenic view. **Activities:** Guided tours, hiking, horseback riding, cross-country skiing, interpretive programs and demonstrations. **Special Features:** Site preserves the home of seven successive generations of New York's politically and socially prominent Livingston family. Robert R. Livingston, Jr. was Clermont's most notable resident. His accomplishments include drafting the Declaration of Independence, serving as the first U.S. Minister of Foreign Affairs, administering the oath of office to George Washington, negotiating the Louisiana Purchase, and developing steamboat technology with Robert Fulton. Designated a National Historic Landmark in 1973, Clermont is also an anchor in the Hudson River National Landmark District.

★3430★ CLINTON HOUSE STATE HISTORIC SITE

PO Box 88
549 Main St
Poughkeepsie, NY 12602
Web: nysparks.state.ny.us/sites/info.asp?siteID=1
Phone: 845-471-1630; **Fax:** 845-471-8777
Size: 1.1 acres. **Location:** At the corner of Main and North White Streets, in Poughkeepsie. **Facilities:** Historic site, gift shop. **Activities:** Educational services (by appointment only). **Special Features:** Built in 1765, the house was actively used from 1777-1783 when Poughkeepsie was the capital of New York. Named for the first governor of New York, the site houses archives and a library for local historical research.

★3431★ COLD SPRING HARBOR STATE PARK

c/o Caumsett State Historic Park
25 Lloyd Harbor Rd
Huntington, NY 11743
Web: nysparks.state.ny.us/parks/info.asp?parkId=85
Phone: 631-423-1770
Size: 45 acres. **Location:** On Route 25A in the village of Cold Spring Harbor. **Facilities:** Undeveloped. **Activities:** Hiking, bird watching, cross-country skiing, snowshoeing. **Special Features:** Park's hilly terrain includes mixed hardwood forests and thickets of wild mountain laurel. The area is a good place to observe spring and fall migrations of songbirds and is also home to great horned owls and redtailed hawks. The park serves as the northern trailhead of the Nassau Suffolk Greenbelt Trail.

★3432★ COLES CREEK STATE PARK

PO Box 442
Waddington, NY 13694
Web: nysparks.state.ny.us/parks/info.asp?parkId=156
Phone: 315-388-5636
Size: 1,800 acres. **Location:** Off Route 37, 4 miles east of Waddington. **Facilities:** Tent and trailer campsites (&), showers (&), picnic area (&), pavilion (&), playground, playing fields, swimming beach, boat launch, boat rentals, marina, dockage, food concession. **Activities:** Camping, hunting (with restrictions), boating, fishing, swimming, recreation programs (&). **Special Features:** Park is located on a sheltered bay on the south shore of Lake Saint Lawrence, upriver from the Robert Moses Power Dam, and is open from mid-May until after Columbus Day.

★3433★ CONNETQUOT RIVER STATE PARK PRESERVE

PO Box 505
Oakdale, NY 11769
Web: nysparks.state.ny.us/parks/info.asp?parkId=69
Phone: 631-581-1005
Size: 3,473 acres. **Location:** On the north side of Sunrise Highway, just west of Pond Road, in Oakdale. **Facilities:** Multi-use trails (50 miles), museum/visitor center, gift shop. **Activities:** Fishing (&), hiking, horseback riding, cross-country skiing, snowshoeing, nature programs. **Special Features:** Preserve maintains land and water for the protection and propagation of game birds, fish, and animals. Rare nesting birds, including osprey, are found here, as well as rare plants such as trailing arbutus and pyxie moss in their native habitats.

★3434★ CRAILO STATE HISTORIC SITE

9 1/2 Riverside Ave
Rensselaer, NY 12144
Web: www.nysparks.com/sites/info.asp?siteID=7
Phone: 518-463-8738
Size: 1 acre. **Location:** In Rensselaer, one and one-half blocks south of Routes 9 and 20. **Facilities:** Museum. **Activities:** Guided tours (including group tours, by appointment). **Special Features:** Museum depicts the lives of early Dutch inhabitants in the upper Hudson Valley through exhibits highlighting archeological finds from the Albany Fort Orange excavations, and through special programs and guided tours.

★3435★ CROWN POINT STATE HISTORIC SITE

739 Bridge Rd
Crown Point, NY 12928
Web: www.nysparks.com/sites/info.asp?siteID=8
Phone: 518-597-4666; **Fax:** 518-597-3666
Size: 380 acres. **Location:** 4 miles off Routes 9N/22 at Champlain Bridge, Crown Point. **Facilities:** Picnic area (&), hiking trail, bike trail, interpretive exhibits, visitor center, scenic views (&), cross-country skiing trails, educational programs, museum (&). **Activities:** Hiking, bicycling, cross-country skiing, guided and self-guided tours, living history demonstrations. **Special Features:** Site includes the ruins of Fort Saint Frederic (1734) and His Majesty's Fort of Crown Point (1759), one of the largest

fortifications in colonial America. Exhibits interpret the French, British, and American chapters of Crown Point's history, at a time when the British and the French both claimed the area.

★3436★ **CUMBERLAND BAY STATE PARK**
152 Cumberland Head Rd
Plattsburg, NY 12901
Web: nysparks.state.ny.us/parks/info.asp?parkId=127
Phone: 518-563-5240
Size: 350 acres. **Location:** North of Plattsburg on Route 314.
Facilities: 152 tent and trailer campsites (&), showers (&), picnic areas (&), pavilions, playground, playing fields, food (&), beach. **Activities:** Camping, swimming, picnicking. **Special Features:** Park is a day-use facility on the west shore of Lake Champlain, open from early May through Columbus Day. Cross country runners frequent the park in the fall.

★3437★ **DARIEN LAKES STATE PARK**
10289 Harlow Rd
Darien Center, NY 14040
Web: nysparks.state.ny.us/parks/info.asp?parkId=63
Phone: 585-547-9242
Size: 1,845 acres. **Location:** Off Route 77 (Allegany Road) on Harlow Road in Darien Center, 3 miles from Darien Lakes Amusement and Camping Resort. **Facilities:** 158 tent and trailer campsites (45 with electricity), heated comfort stations, showers (&), picnic areas, picnic pavilions (&), playgrounds, hiking and horseback riding trails, multi-use trails, beach, boat rentals, outdoor skating rink. **Activities:** Camping, deer and small game hunting (in season), fishing, swimming, hiking, bicycling, horseback riding, cross-country skiing, ice skating, snowmobiling, recreation programs. **Special Features:** Park's terrain is hilly with woodlands, ravines, streams, and 12-acre Harlow Lake.

★3438★ **DARWIN MARTIN HOUSE STATE HISTORIC SITE**
125 Jewett Pkwy
Buffalo, NY 14214
Web: nysparks.state.ny.us/sites/info.asp?siteID=35
Phone: 716-856-3858; **Fax:** 716-856-4009
Location: Thruway Exit 51 to Route 33, west to Route 198 to Parkside Ave, then right on Jewett Pkwy. **Facilities:** Historic site, gift shop. **Activities:** Guided tours (by reservation). **Special Features:** One of Frank Lloyd Wright's most impressive and successful "Prairie Houses," this residential complex was designed and built for self-made businessman Darwin Martin and his family in 1905. Martin House is currently undergoing a comprehensive restoration.

★3439★ **DE VEAUX WOODS STATE PARK**
c/o Niagara Frontier Region
PO Box 1132
Niagara Falls, NY 14303
Web: nysparks.state.ny.us/parks/info.asp?parkId=171
Phone: 716-284-4691
Size: 51 acres. **Location:** Findlay Exit to Lewiston off Robert Moses Parkway, 2 miles northwest of Niagara Falls. **Facilities:**

Playground, 2 ball diamonds, nature trail; restrooms available mid-April through late October. **Activities:** Hiking, biking, hunting, cross-country skiing. **Special Features:** A large meadow area at the park can be used for picnicking.

★3440★ **DELTA LAKE STATE PARK**
8797 State Rt 46
Rome, NY 13440
Web: nysparks.state.ny.us/parks/info.asp?parkId=18
Phone: 315-337-4670
Size: 400 acres. **Location:** Off Route 46, 6 miles north of Rome.
Facilities: 101 tent, trailer, or RV campsites (&), showers (&), food concession (&), picnic areas (&), picnic pavilions (&), playground, hiking and nature trails, beach, boat launch (seasonal), cross-country ski trails. **Activities:** Camping, boating (including power boating), fishing, swimming, hiking, bicycling, cross-country skiing, snowmobiling, ice fishing, recreation programs (&). **Special Features:** Park is located on a peninsula extending into Delta Reservoir. The terrain is wooded and generally flat.

★3441★ **DEVIL'S HOLE STATE PARK**
c/o Niagara Frontier Region
PO Box 1132
Niagara Falls, NY 14303
Web: nysparks.state.ny.us/parks/info.asp?parkId=28
Phone: 716-284-4691
Size: 42 acres. **Location:** Off Robert Moses Parkway, 1 mile north of Whirlpool State Park. **Facilities:** Picnic areas, hiking and nature trails. **Activities:** Fishing, hiking, cross-country skiing, snowshoeing. **Special Features:** A walkway leads down from the park along the turbulent Niagara River 300 feet into a wooded gorge and offers a close-up, spectacular view of the lower Whirlpool rapids.

★3442★ **DEWOLF POINT STATE PARK**
45920 County Rt 191
Fineview, NY 13640
Web: nysparks.state.ny.us/parks/info.asp?parkId=142
Phone: 315-482-2012
Size: 13 acres. **Location:** Off I-81 (Exit 51), 2 miles north of Alexandria Bay on Wellesley Island. **Facilities:** Tent and trailer campsites (&), showers (&), cabins (&), stone gazebo, picnic area, pavilions, boat launch, dockage. **Activities:** Camping, boating (including power boating), fishing. **Special Features:** Park is located on the Lake of the Isles in the Saint Lawrence River.

★3443★ **EARL W. BRYDGES ARTPARK STATE PARK**
450 S 4th St
Lewiston, NY 14092
Web: nysparks.state.ny.us/parks/info.asp?parkId=106
Phone: 716-754-9000
Size: 108 acres. **Location:** In Lewiston. **Facilities:** Picnic tables and pavilions (&), food (&), nature trails, performing arts theater (&). **Activities:** Fishing, hiking, cross-country skiing, cultural

programs (&). **Special Features:** Artpark is devoted to the visual and performing arts, including Broadway musicals as well as classical, jazz, and pop music concerts, art exhibits, and workshops and demonstrations. Tours of the park's geological and historic sites are offered as well.

★3444★ EEL WEIR STATE PARK

RD 3
Ogdensburg, NY 13669
Web: nysparks.state.ny.us/parks/info.asp?parkId=122
Phone: 315-393-1138
Size: 16 acres. **Location:** Off Route 812, 7 miles south of Ogdensburg. **Facilities:** 38 campsites (&), showers (&), picnic area (&), picnic pavilions, boat launch. **Activities:** Camping, canoeing, fishing. **Special Features:** Park is located on the Oswegatchie River, just two miles from Black Lake. Both waterways are known for excellent bass fishing and are ideal for canoes or rowboats.

★3445★ EMPIRE-FULTON FERRY STATE PARK

26 New Dock St
Brooklyn, NY 11201
Web: nysparks.state.ny.us/parks/info.asp?parkId=70
Phone: 718-858-4708
Size: 9 acres. **Location:** Along the East River in Brooklyn, between the Manhattan and Brooklyn Bridges. **Facilities:** Picnic tables. **Activities:** Picnicking, photography. **Special Features:** This waterfront park is a great place to view the lower Manhattan skyline. Bordering the park are Civil-War-era coffee and tobacco warehouses, evidence of the freight shipping business that once dominated Brooklyn's waterfront.

★3446★ EVANGOLA STATE PARK

10191 Old Lake Shore Rd
Irving, NY 14081
Web: nysparks.state.ny.us/parks/info.asp?parkId=101
Phone: 716-549-1802
Size: 733 acres. **Location:** Off Route 5, 27 miles south of Buffalo. **Facilities:** 80 campsites (&), picnic areas, picnic pavilions (&), playground, nature trail, food (&), beach, baseball and soccer fields, tennis and basketball courts. **Activities:** Camping, fishing, swimming, hiking, bicycling, tennis, cross-country skiing, snowmobiling, pheasant and small game hunting (during pheasant season). **Special Features:** Park's major attraction is its arc-shaped shoreline and natural sand beach on Lake Erie.

★3447★ FAIR HAVEN BEACH STATE PARK

Rt 104A, PO Box 16
Fair Haven, NY 13064
Web: nysparks.state.ny.us/parks/info.asp?parkId=34
Phone: 315-947-5205
Size: 1,121 acres. **Location:** On Lake Ontario, southwest of Oswego on Route 104A, 2 miles north of Fairhaven. **Facilities:** Campsites (&), showers (&), cabins (&; 8 are winterized), vacation rental cottages, picnic areas (&), picnic pavilions (&), playground, playing field(s), food, trails, beach, marina, dockage, boat launch, boat rentals (rowboats, paddleboats, canoes), scenic

views. **Activities:** Camping, boating, fishing, swimming, hiking, biking, cross-country skiing, snowshoeing, sledding, ice skating, snowmobiling, ice fishing, recreation programs, waterfowl hunting in season (designated areas only). **Special Features:** Park contains one of the finest public lakefronts in upstate New York, with high bluffs above sandy beaches and hilly woodlands. The campgrounds were ranked among the top 100 in the US in 2004.

★3448★ FILLMORE GLEN STATE PARK

1686 State Rt 38
Moravia, NY 13118
Web: nysparks.state.ny.us/parks/info.asp?parkId=35
Phone: 315-497-0130
Size: 941 acres. **Location:** On Route 38, 1 mile south of Moravia. **Facilities:** 60 tent and trailer campsites (&), showers, cabins, full-service rental cottage with boat dock, hiking trails, picnic area (&), picnic pavilions (&), playground, playing fields, stream-fed swimming pool. **Activities:** Camping, fishing, swimming, hiking, cross-country skiing, snowmobiling, recreation programs, deer hunting (in season). **Special Features:** Park is an oasis of cool, dense woods in a long and narrow gorge. Hiking trails lead to scenic views, including five waterfalls and unique geological formations.

★3449★ FORT MONTGOMERY STATE HISTORIC SITE

c/o Bear Mountain State Park
Bear Mountain, NY 10911
Web: www.nysparks.com/sites/info.asp?siteID=36
Phone: 845-786-2701; **Fax:** 845-786-5367
Size: 150 acres. **Location:** 1/2 mile north of Bear Mountain State Park, on Route 9W. **Activities:** Interpretive exhibits, self-guided audio tours, guided tours (by appointment), demonstrations. **Special Features:** Park preserves stone foundation and earthworks of Fort Montgomery, site of a fierce Revolutionary War battle for control of the Hudson River.

★3450★ FORT NIAGARA STATE PARK

Rt 18F
Youngstown, NY 14174
Web: www.nysparks.com/parks/info.asp?parkId=109
Phone: 716-745-7273
Size: 504 acres. **Location:** Off Route 18F or Robert Moses Parkway in Youngstown, 18 miles north of Niagara Falls. **Facilities:** Picnic areas (&), picnic pavilions (&), playgrounds, hiking trails, nature trail, food concession (&), swimming pools, waterslide, 2 boat launches, fish cleaning station, tennis courts, 18 soccer fields. **Activities:** Boating, swimming, fishing, waterfowl hunting (in season), hiking, bicycling, tennis, cross-country skiing, snowshoeing, sledding, recreation programs. **Special Features:** Park is adjacent to Old Fort Niagara State Historic Site (see separate entry) and provides access to both the Lower Niagara River and Lake Ontario.

★3451★ FORT ONTARIO STATE HISTORIC SITE

1 E 4th St
Oswego, NY 13126
Web: www.nysparks.com/sites/info.asp?siteID=9
Phone: 315-343-4711; **Fax:** 315-343-1430

Size: 36 acres. **Location:** Off Route 104 in Oswego. **Facilities:** Picnic area, visitor center/museum (&), interpretive exhibits, scenic views. **Activities:** Guided and self-guided tours, living history demonstrations. **Special Features:** Visitors can watch the guard unit reenact the activities of the troops in 1868-1869 at this star-shaped fortress. Exhibits and a furnished officers' quarters interpret its history from the French and Indian War through World War II.

★3452★ **FOUR MILE CREEK STATE PARK**
Lake Rd
Youngstown, NY 14174
Web: www.nysparks.com/parks/info.asp?parkId=110
Phone: 716-745-3802
Size: 248 acres. **Location:** 4 miles east of Youngstown via Route 18F or the Robert Moses Parkway. **Facilities:** 275 tent and trailer campsites (&; 131 sites have electricity), showers (&), hiking trails, picnic areas, playground, camp store, food. **Activities:** Camping, fishing, hiking, bicycling, recreation programs. **Special Features:** Four Mile Creek is a campground for use by campers and guests only, located just 15 minutes north of Niagara Falls. The marsh at the mouth of Four Mile Creek is home to many varieties of plants, animals, and birds, including the great blue heron.

★3453★ **FRANKLIN D. ROOSEVELT STATE PARK**
2957 Crompond Rd
Yorktown Heights, NY 10598
Web: www.nysparks.com/parks/info.asp?parkId=139
Phone: 914-245-4434
Size: 960 acres. **Location:** Off Taconic State Parkway, approximately 40 miles from New York City. **Facilities:** Picnic areas (&), picnic pavilions (&), food concession (&), trails, swimming pool, boat launch, boat rentals (rowboats and pedalboats), fishing pier (&), playing fields, disc golf course, playground. **Activities:** Boating (no power boats), canoeing or kayaking (with regional permit), fishing, swimming, hiking, bicycling, cross-country skiing, ice skating, snowmobiling, sledding, ice fishng, recreation programs. **Special Features:** Park includes one of the nation's largest swimming pools, which can accommodate as many as 4,000 people at one time.

★3454★ **GANONDAGAN STATE HISTORIC SITE**
1488 Victor-Bloomfield Rd
Victor, NY 14564
Web: www.nysparks.com/sites/info.asp?siteID=10
Phone: 585-924-5848
Size: 535 acres. **Location:** Southeast of Rochester in Victor. **Facilities:** Picnic area, interpretive trails, visitor center (&), gift shop, scenic views, gardens. **Activities:** Hiking, self-guided tours, group tours (2 weeks advance reservation required). **Special Features:** Site of a major 17th-century Seneca town and palisaded granary and the only New York state historic site dedicated to interpreting Native American life. Interpretive signs mark trails where visitors can learn about Iroquois customs and beliefs, about the significance of plant life to the Seneca, and about Fort Hill (the granary) and historic events that occurred

there. A replica of a traditional Seneca longhouse is open to the public.

★3455★ **GANTRY PLAZA STATE PARK**
50-50 2nd St
Long Island City, NY 11101
Web: www.nysparks.com/parks/info.asp?parkId=86
Phone: 718-786-6385
Size: 2.5 acres. **Location:** Along the East River at 50th Avenue, in front of the City Lights Building, Queens. **Facilities:** Picnic tables, playground, fishing pier with cleaning table, basketball and handball courts. **Activities:** Fishing, picnicking. **Special Features:** Park includes four restored piers, gardens, mist fountain, restored gantries, and a spectacular view of the midtown Manhattan skyline, including the Empire State Building and the United Nations. Park's location is also a good spot for viewing Macy's Fourth of July fireworks displays.

★3456★ **GILBERT LAKE STATE PARK**
18 CCC Rd
Laurens, NY 13796
Web: www.nysparks.com/parks/info.asp?parkId=19
Phone: 607-432-2114
Size: 1,584 acres. **Location:** Off County Route 12 northwest of Oneonta. **Facilities:** Tent and trailer campsites (&), cabins (&), showers (&), picnic areas (&), picnic pavilions, playgrounds, food concession (&), trails (12 miles), beach, boat launch, boat rentals, visitor center (&), disc golf course. **Activities:** Camping, boating (nonmotorized only), fishing, swimming, hiking, biking, cross-country skiing, snowshoeing, snowmobiling, recreation programs, deer hunting (bow only) in season. **Special Features:** Park's lake and three ponds lie in wooded, hilly terrain in the foothills of the Catskills.

★3457★ **GLIMMERGLASS STATE PARK**
1527 County Hwy 31
Cooperstown, NY 13326
Web: www.nysparks.com/parks/info.asp?parkId=22
Phone: 607-547-8662
Size: 593 acres. **Location:** 8 miles outside the village of Cooperstown, on County Road 31. **Facilities:** Campsites (&), showers, picnic areas (&), picnic pavilions, playground, food concession, trails, beach (&). **Activities:** Camping, fishing, swimming, hiking, biking, cross-country skiing, ice skating, ice fishing, snowmobiling, tubing, recreation and nature programs. **Special Features:** Park overlooks Otsego Lake, the "Glimmerglass" of James Fenimore Cooper's *Leatherstocking Tales*. The park's campgrounds were ranked among the top 100 in the US in 2005.

★3458★ **GOLDEN HILL STATE PARK**
9691 Lower Lake Rd
Barker, NY 14102
Web: www.nysparks.com/parks/info.asp?parkId=111
Phone: 716-795-3885
Size: 510 acres. **Location:** On Lower Lake Road, off Route 269, in Barker, via Route 18 or 104. **Facilities:** Tent and trailer

9. State Parks

campsites, showers (&), vacation rental, picnic area, picnic pavilion (&), playground, playing fields, hiking and nature trails, snowmobile trails (5 miles), boat launch. **Activities:** Camping, boating (including powerboats), fishing, hiking, biking, cross-country skiing, snowmobiling, small game and waterfowl hunting in season. **Special Features:** Thirty Mile Lighthouse, built in 1875, is part of the park. The lighthouse, which once provided family living quarters for keepers and their families, is available for vacation rental.

★3459★ GOOSEPOND MOUNTAIN STATE PARK
c/o Palisades Interstate Park Commission
Bear Mountain, NY 10911
Web: www.nysparks.com/parks/info.asp?parkId=56
Phone: 845-786-2701
Size: 1,558 acres. **Location:** Off Route 17M between Chester and Monroe. **Facilities:** Undeveloped. **Activities:** Hiking, horseback riding. **Special Features:** Park is almost completely wooded and is managed as open space.

★3460★ GOVERNOR ALFRED E. SMITH/SUNKEN
     MEADOW STATE PARK
PO Box 716
Kings Park, NY 11754
Web: www.nysparks.com/parks/info.asp?parkId=44
Phone: 631-269-4333
Size: 1,288 acres. **Location:** Route 25A and Sunken Meadow State Parkway in Kings Park. **Facilities:** Picnic area (&), food concession (&), multi-use trails (6 miles), golf courses (27 holes), driving range, putting green, beach (&), showers (&), playing fields, playground (&), boardwalk. **Activities:** Golf, fishing, swimming, windsurfing, canoeing, kayaking, hiking, biking, horseback riding, cross-country skiing, recreation programs. **Special Features:** Park fronts Long Island Sound, where three miles of beach meet tall bluffs at the western end of the shoreline. A manmade dam separates the park's brackish creek and marshes from the tidal flats.

★3461★ GRAFTON LAKES STATE PARK
61 N Long Pond Rd
Grafton, NY 12082
Web: www.nysparks.com/parks/info.asp?parkId=116
Phone: 518-279-1155
Size: 2,357 acres. **Location:** Off Route 2, 12 miles east of Troy. **Facilities:** Picnic areas and pavilions (&), multi-use trails (25 miles), nature center, food concession (&), swimming beach (&), boat launches (canoes, rowboats, sailboats), boat rentals, playground. **Activities:** Boating (electric motors only), canoeing, fishing (&), swimming, hiking, biking, horseback riding, cross-country skiing, snowmobiling, snowshoeing, ice skating, deer and small game hunting (in season), recreation programs, education programs. **Special Features:** Park is located on the forested mountain ridge between the Taconic and Hudson valleys. It includes five ponds (all with launch facilities) and the Shaver Pond Nature Center.

★3462★ GRANT COTTAGE STATE HISTORIC SITE
PO Box 2294
Wilton, NY 12831
Web: www.nysparks.com/sites/info.asp?siteID=11
Phone: 518-587-8277
Size: 1 acre. **Location:** On the summit of Mount McGregor. **Facilities:** Picnic area (&), scenic view, historic house, gift shop (&). **Activities:** Guided tours. **Special Features:** Here at the summit of Mount McGregor, Ulysses S. Grant, 18th President of the United States, died in 1885. The cottage and its furnishings remain essentially the same as during the Grant family's stay.

★3463★ GRASS POINT STATE PARK
42247 Grassy Point Rd
Alexandria Bay, NY 13607
Web: nysparks.state.ny.us/parks/info.asp?parkId=123
Phone: 315-686-4472
Size: 114 acres. **Location:** Off Route 12, 1 mile west of I-81 in Alexandria Bay. **Facilities:** Campgrounds (&), showers (&), vacation rental, picnic areas (&), picnic pavilions, playground, game area, swimming beach, marina with dockage and boat launch. **Activities:** Camping, boating (including powerboats), fishing, swimming, waterfowl hunting (in season). **Special Features:** Park is located on a point of land that projects into the American Channel of the Saint Lawrence River and offers some of the best fishing in the country. The Grass Point Cottage, located on the west side of the beach, is a full-service accommodation that's available for rent.

★3464★ GREEN LAKES STATE PARK
7900 Green Lakes Rd
Fayetteville, NY 13066
Web: www.nysparks.com/parks/info.asp?parkId=23
Phone: 315-637-6111
Size: 1,955 acres. **Location:** Off NYS 290, 10 miles east of Syracuse. **Facilities:** Campgrounds (&), showers (&), cabins (&), picnic areas (&), picnic pavilions (&), food concession, trails, 18-hole golf course, beach (&), boat rentals, playground (&). **Activities:** Camping, boating (no power boats), fishing, swimming, hiking, bicycling, golf, cross-country skiing, snowshoeing, recreation programs (&). **Special Features:** Among the park's outstanding features are two glacial lakes, known as meromictic lakes, where the surface and bottom waters do not mix during seasonal changes. The park's golf course was designed by Robert Trent Jones. The campgrounds were named among America's top 100 in 2004.

★3465★ HAMLIN BEACH STATE PARK
1 Camp Rd
Hamlin, NY 14464
Web: www.nysparks.com/parks/info.asp?parkId=6
Phone: 585-964-2462; **Fax:** 585-964-7821; **Toll Free:** 800-456-2267
Size: 1,287 acres. **Location:** Off Lake Ontario State Parkway, 25 miles west of Rochester. **Facilities:** 264 tent and trailer campsites (all with electricity), showers (&), picnic areas, picnic pavilions (&), playground, food concession, multi-use trails (10 miles), self-guided nature trail (1 mile), beach, hand launch

boat ramp, environmental education center. **Activities:** Camping (including group camping), boating (no power boats), fishing, swimming, hiking, bicycling, cross-country skiing, snowmobiling, recreation programs. **Special Features:** Park's most prominent feature is the bluff known as Devil's Nose, a familiar landmark for passing boats. The environmental education center is located at the east end of the park, in the Yanty Creek Marsh Area.

★3466★ HARRIET HOLLISTER SPENCER STATE RECREATION AREA

10820 Rt 36 S
Dansville, NY 14437
Web: www.nysparks.com/parks/info.asp?parkId=98
Phone: 585-335-8111
Size: 766 acres. **Location:** On Candice Hill Road, 6 miles south of Honeoye. **Facilities:** Picnic area, pavilion, trails. **Activities:** Hiking, biking, cross-country skiing, snowshoeing, snowmobiling, deer hunting in season. (Small game hunting is not permitted at any time.) **Special Features:** Land was deeded to state of New York in 1963 by Thomas G. Spencer as a memorial to his wife. Area offers beautiful views of the Honeoye Lake Valley.

★3467★ HARRIMAN STATE PARK

c/o Palisades Interstate Park Commission
Bear Mountain, NY 10911
Web: nysparks.state.ny.us/parks/info.asp?parkId=143
Phone: 845-786-2701
Size: 46,613 acres. **Location:** Off Palisades Parkway, 30 miles north of New York City. **Facilities:** Campgrounds (including tent and trailer sites), group camps (including Scout camping), comfort stations, showers, cabins, full-service cottages, picnic areas, playgrounds, playing fields, tennis courts, beaches, boat launch sites, boat rentals, trails, food concessions, museum/visitor center, gift shop, scenic views. **Activities:** Camping, boating, fishing, swimming, hiking, bicycling, horseback riding, ice fishing, cross-country skiing, snowmobiling. **Special Features:** Harriman is New York's second largest state park and includes 31 lakes and reservoirs, 200 miles of hiking trails, three beaches, two public camping areas, a network of group camps, miles of streams and scenic roads, lookout points, and numerous wildlife species. The park's major facilities include: Lakes Welch, Sebago, Tiorati, and Silver Mine, the Anthony Wayne Recreation Area, Sebago Cabins, and Beaver Pond Campgrounds. The largest of Harriman's beaches is at Lake Welch, a man-made lake in the wooded hills of the Ramapo Mountains.

★3468★ HECKSCHER STATE PARK

PO Box 160
East Islip, NY 11730
Web: www.nysparks.com/parks/info.asp?parkId=153
Phone: 631-581-2100
Size: 1,657 acres. **Location:** At the end of Heckscher State Parkway, in the East Islip/Great River Area in Suffolk County. **Facilities:** 69 campsites (vehicles must be under 11 feet high to enter campground), showers, picnic areas, picnic pavilions, playground, playing fields, food concession, multi-use trails (20 miles), nature trail, beach, swimming pool, boat launch ramp

(&&). **Activities:** Camping, boating, fishing, bay and pool swimming, hiking, bicycling, horseback riding, cross-country skiing, recreation and nature programs. **Special Features:** Located on Great South Bay, park attacts more than a million visitors a year. Its campgrounds were ranked among the top 100 in the US in 2005.

★3469★ HEMPSTEAD LAKE STATE PARK

West Hempstead, NY 11552
Web: www.nysparks.com/parks/info.asp?parkId=155
Phone: 516-766-1029
Size: 737 acres. **Location:** Exit 18 off Southern State Parkway in West Hempstead. **Facilities:** Picnic areas (&), picnic pavilions (&), food concession (&), hiking and biking trails, bridle trails, boat launch (cartop boats only), 20 tennis courts (&), basketball courts, playgrounds (&). **Activities:** Fishing, hiking, biking, horseback riding, tennis, cross-country skiing, ice skating, ice fishing, recreation programs (&). **Special Features:** Park features include three stocked ponds for fishing (catch and release only in Lake Hempstead) and a historic wooden carousel.

★3470★ HERKIMER HOME STATE HISTORIC SITE

200 State Rt 169
Little Falls, NY 13365
Web: www.nysparks.com/sites/info.asp?siteID=12
Phone: 315-823-0398; **Fax:** 315-823-0587
Size: 155 acres. **Location:** Off Route 169, east of Little Falls. **Facilities:** Picnic area, visitor center (&), historic house, scenic view (&), gardens, interpretive exhibits, hiking trail. **Activities:** Hiking, reenactments, living history demonstrations, guided tours. **Special Features:** Site preserves the historic Georgian-style mansion home of General Nicholas Herkimer, a Revolutionary War hero. The landscape, including the Herkimer family burial ground, is remarkably unchanged from that of the 18th century.

★3471★ HIGH TOR STATE PARK

c/o Palisades Interstate Park Commission
Bear Mountain, NY 10911
Web: www.nysparks.com/parks/info.asp?parkId=58
Phone: 845-634-8074
Size: 651 acres. **Location:** 2 miles east of Palisades Parkway Exit 13, on South Mountain Road. **Facilities:** Picnic area (&), food concession, hiking trails, swimming pool, showers. **Activities:** Swimming, hiking, picnicking. **Special Features:** Park is a day-use facility (open June to September) that affords great views of the Hudson River. The Long Path passes through the park just before the trail heads inland to the Catskills.

★3472★ HIGHLAND LAKES STATE PARK

c/o Palisades Interstate Park Commission
Bear Mountain, NY 10911
Web: www.nysparks.com/parks/info.asp?parkId=76
Phone: 845-786-2701
Size: 3,116 acres. **Location:** Off Route 211 near Middletown. **Facilities:** Undeveloped. **Activities:** Fishing, hiking, horseback

9. State Parks

riding (by permit). **Special Features:** Park includes an area for flying radio-controlled model airplanes.

★3473★ HIGLEY FLOW STATE PARK
442 Cold Brook Dr
Colton, NY 13625
Web: www.nysparks.com/parks/info.asp?parkId=144
Phone: 315-262-2880
Size: 1,115 acres. **Location:** Off Route 56, west of South Colton on Cold Brook Drive. **Facilities:** Campgrounds (&), showers (&), picnic areas (&), picnic pavilions (&), playground, multi-use trails, nature trail, beach, boat launch. **Activities:** Camping, canoeing, fishing, swimming, hiking, cross-country skiing, snowmobiling, snowshoeing, ice fishing, recreation programs deer hunting in season (south of Cold Brook Drive). **Special Features:** Park is situated on the Racquette River in the Adirondack foothills and the terrain is hilly and heavily wooded.

★3474★ HITHER HILLS STATE PARK
50 S Fairview Ave
Montauk, NY 11754
Web: www.nysparks.com/parks/info.asp?parkId=48
Phone: 631-668-2554
Size: 1,755 acres. **Location:** Sunrise Highway (Route 27) east from Manhattan (122 miles), in Montauk. **Facilities:** 168 campsites, showers, picnic areas, playground, playing fields, food concession, ocean beach, bridle paths, multi-use trails (&&). **Activities:** Camping, fishing, swimming, hiking, biking, horseback riding, hunting (big and small game, in season), recreation programs (&). **Special Features:** The unique ''walking dunes'' of Napeague Harbor are located on the eastern boundary of the park.

★3475★ HONEOYE LAKE MARINE PARK
6150 East Lake Rd
Honeoye, NY 14471
Web: www.nysparks.com/parks/info.asp?parkId=36
Phone: 585-335-8111
Size: 8.6 acres. **Location:** On East Lake Road, on the southeast side of the lake. **Facilities:** Boat launch facilities. **Activities:** Boating (including power boats), fishing (&), ice fishing. **Special Features:** Park is a boat launch site.

★3476★ HUDSON HIGHLANDS STATE PARK
Rt 9D
Beacon, NY 10512
Web: www.nysparks.com/parks/info.asp?parkId=130
Phone: 845-225-7207
Size: 6,251 acres. **Location:** Off Route 9D, 2 miles south of Beacon. **Facilities:** Undeveloped. **Activities:** Fishing, hunting (with restrictions), hiking, canoeing, kayaking. **Special Features:** Park's extensive hiking trail network includes a segment of the Appalachian National Scenic Trail (see separate entry in national trails section) and mountaintop views of the Hudson River and the Hudson Highland Range. The most well-known of the park's trails is 5.5-mile Breakneck Ridge, which rises

1,250 feet in just three-quarters of a mile. *Newsweek* rated it one of the top ten day hikes in the country.

★3477★ HUDSON RIVER ISLANDS STATE PARK
Schodack Island State Park
Schodack Landing, NY 12156
Web: www.nysparks.com/parks/info.asp?parkId=107
Phone: 518-732-0187; **Fax:** 518-732-0263
Size: 235 acres. **Location:** On the Hudson River, 1 mile south of Coxsackie Boat Launch Site and 4 miles north of Athens Boat Launch Site; access by boat only. **Facilities:** Campsites, picnic areas, nature trail, dockage. **Activities:** Transient camping, boating (including power boats), fishing, hiking, hunting. **Special Features:** Park facilities are concentrated on the islands of Gay's Point and Stockport Middle Ground, which are fragile communities with many rare and endangered plant and animal species. The park operates from Memorial Day to Columbus Day, and transient camping is permitted.

★3478★ HUNT'S POND STATE PARK
c/o Bowman Lake State Park
745 Bliven Sherman Rd
Oxford, NY 13830
Web: www.nysparks.com/parks/info.asp?parkId=1
Phone: 607-859-2249
Size: 235 acres. **Location:** Off Route 8, on Hunt's Pond Road near New Berlin. **Facilities:** 18 primitive campsites, picnic area (&), pavilions (&), boat launch (non-motorized boats only). **Activities:** Camping, boating (no power boats), fishing, deer hunting in season (restricted area). **Special Features:** Park is adjacent to New York Department of Environmental Conservation property, where land is available to park visitors for hiking, cross-country skiing, and snowmobiling.

★3479★ HYDE HALL STATE HISTORIC SITE
PO Box 721
Cooperstown, NY 13326
Web: www.nysparks.com/sites/info.asp?siteID=13
Phone: 607-547-5098; **Fax:** 607-547-8462
Size: 12 acres. **Location:** On the shore of Otsego Lake in Cooperstown, NY. **Facilities:** Picnic area, historic house, visitor center, museum (&), scenic views (&), gift shop, biking trail, hiking trail, interpretive exhibits. **Activities:** Guided tours, hiking, bicycling, cross-country skiing. **Special Features:** Believed to be the largest private home built in the U.S. during the time between the Revolutionary and Civil wars, this residence was built by George Clarke (1768-1835) in a style reminiscent of an English country estate. Site is located adjacent to Glimmerglass State Park.

★3480★ IRONDEQUOIT BAY STATE MARINE PARK
c/o Hamlin Beach State Park
1 Camp Rd
Hamlin, NY 14464
Web: www.nysparks.com/parks/info.asp?parkId=7
Phone: 585-964-2462
Size: 35 acres. **Location:** Off Culver Road, on Lake Ontario and

9. State Parks

Irondequoit Bay. **Facilities:** Boat launch. **Activities:** Boating (including power boats), fishing. **Special Features:** Facility is a launch site for small and power boats and provides fishing access to Lake Ontario. The park is operated by Monroe County Parks Department.

★3481★ JACQUES CARTIER STATE PARK

PO Box 380
Morristown, NY 13664
Web: www.nysparks.com/parks/info.asp?parkId=145
Phone: 315-375-6371
Size: 461 acres. **Location:** Off Route 12, 3 miles west of Morristown. **Facilities:** Tent and trailer campsites (&), showers (&), picnic areas (&), pavilions, playground, food concession (&), beach, dockage, boat launch, nature trail. **Activities:** Camping, hunting (with restrictions), boating (including powerboats), fishing, swimming, cross-country skiing. **Special Features:** Park's sandy swimming beach is located in a sheltered bay on the Saint Lawrence River. The park is open from mid-May through Columbus Day week-end.

★3482★ JAMES BAIRD STATE PARK

14 Maintenance Ln
Pleasant Valley, NY 12569
Web: www.nysparks.com/parks/info.asp?parkId=59
Phone: 845-452-1489
Size: 590 acres. **Location:** In the town of Pleasant Valley, midway between New York City and Albany. Off Taconic State Parkway, park is 1 mile north of the exit for NYS Route 55/Poughkeepsie. **Facilities:** 18-hole golf course, driving range, pro shop, clubhouse, snack bars, full-service restaurant (&), picnic areas (&), 2 picnic pavilions (&), sports complex, playground (&), nature center, multi-use trails (7 miles). **Activities:** Golf, tennis, hiking, biking, cross-country skiing, snowshoeing, recreation programs, nature programs. **Special Features:** Park land was donated to the state by James Baird, whose construction company built the Lincoln Memorial. The golf course was designed by Robert Trent Jones, and the par 5, 13th hole is among the most challenging in the Hudson Valley. The restaurant overlooking the golf course is open both to golfers and to the general public. The golf course is open from early April through mid-November; the park is open year round.

★3483★ JOHN BOYD THACHER STATE PARK

1 Hailes Cave Rd
Voorheesville, NY 12186
Web: www.nysparks.com/parks/info.asp?parkId=125
Phone: 518-872-1237; **Fax:** 518-872-9133
Size: 1,967 acres. **Location:** On Route 157, off Route 85, 15 miles southwest of Albany. **Facilities:** Picnic areas (&), 9 picnic pavilions (&), playgrounds, volleyball courts, ball fields, multi-use trails (12+ miles), nature trail, Olympic-size swimming pool, scenic views. **Activities:** Swimming, hiking, bicycling, cross-country skiing, snowmobiling, snowshoeing, hunting, recreation programs, interpretive programs. **Special Features:** Park is located along the Helderberg escarpment, one of the richest fossil-bearing formations in the world. Year-round interpretive programs at the park include guided tours of the Indian Ladder

Trail. Other programs are available at the Emma Treadwell Thacher Nature Center, which is located 2 miles from the park on Thompson Lake.

★3484★ JOHN BROWN FARM STATE HISTORIC SITE

2 John Brown Rd
Lake Placid, NY 12946
Web: www.nysparks.com/sites/info.asp?siteID=14
Phone: 518-523-3900
Size: 270 acres. **Location:** On John Brown Road, off Route 73, 2 miles south of Lake Placid. **Facilities:** Historic house, picnic ares, trails, scenic views. **Activities:** Guided and self-guided tours, reenactments, hiking, cross-country skiing. **Special Features:** Site preserves the home and grave of abolitionist John Brown. On October 16, 1859, Brown and his followers assaulted the US Arsenal at Harper's Ferry, planning to use the captured arms for the liberation of the slaves in the South. Brown was captured and tried, then hanged on December 2, 1859.

★3485★ JOHN BURROUGHS MEMORIAL STATE HISTORIC SITE

c/o Mine Kill State Park
PO Box 923, Rte 30
North Blenheim, NY 12131
Web: www.nysparks.com/sites/info.asp?siteID=15
Phone: 518-827-6111; **Fax:** 518-827-6782
Size: 3 acres. **Location:** 2.25 miles west of Route 30, north of Roxbury. **Facilities:** Picnic area, scenic view, trails, interpretive displays. **Activities:** Self-guided tours, hiking. **Special Features:** Surrounded by the Catskill Mountains, site includes the grave of famous literary naturalist John Burroughs.

★3486★ JOHN JAY HOMESTEAD STATE HISTORIC SITE

PO Box 832
Katonah, NY 10536
Web: www.nysparks.com/sites/info.asp?siteID=16
Phone: 914-232-5651; **Fax:** 914-232-8085
Size: 64 acres. **Location:** Off Route 22, south of Route 35, between Katonah and Bedford Village. **Facilities:** Picnic area, historic house and gardens, interpretive displays, scenic views, gift shop, trails. **Activities:** Guided and self-guided tours, hiking, horseback riding, educational programs. **Special Features:** Visitors can view furnishings, portraits, and memorabilia at the retirement home of this patriot, founding father, and first Chief Justice of the US Supreme Court. Site also includes an 1820s schoolhouse and an 1830s barn, which are open for touring.

★3487★ JOHNSON HALL STATE HISTORIC SITE

Hall Ave
Johnstown, NY 12095
Web: www.nysparks.com/sites/info.asp?siteID=17
Phone: 518-762-8712; **Fax:** 518-762-2330
Size: 19 acres. **Location:** On Hall Avenue in Johnstown. **Facilities:** Picnic area, historic house and garden, interpretive displays, visitor center (&), museum (&), gift shop (&). **Activities:** Guided

9. State Parks

tours, reenactments. **Special Features:** Grounds and scented herb garden surround the 1763 Mohawk Valley mansion of Sir William Johnson, Superintendent of Indian Affairs for the Northern colonies.

★**3488**★ **JONES BEACH STATE PARK**
PO Box 1000
Wantagh, NY 11793
Web: www.nysparks.com/parks/info.asp?parkId=46
Phone: 516-785-1600
Size: 2,413 acres. **Location:** 33 miles from Manhattan via Meadowbrook Parkway South and Wantagh Parkway south to the park. **Facilities:** Ocean beaches, 2 swimming pools, bathhouses, showers, marina, boat basin, 2-mile boardwalk, picnic tables, playground, food concession, miniature golf course, performing arts theater, museum/visitor center, gift shop (&&). **Activities:** Swimming, surf fishing, bicycling, golf, boating, recreation programs. **Special Features:** With more than six miles of Atlantic and bay beaches and a two-mile-long boardwalk, Jones Beach is Long Island's most popular state park destination. The park's Theodore Roosevelt Nature Center offers educational, hands-on exhibits for children, and a photo collection entitled ƒCastles In the Sand§ depicts the development of the Long Island State Park and parkway systems.

★**3489**★ **JOSEPH DAVIS STATE PARK**
4143 Lower River Rd
Lewiston, NY 14092
Web: www.nysparks.com/parks/info.asp?parkId=108
Phone: 716-754-4596
Size: 388 acres. **Location:** From Buffalo, take I-190 north to last exit (just before bridge into Canada), follow sign for Robert Moses-Fort Niagara and exit at Pletcher Road. **Facilities:** Picnic areas (&), picnic pavilions (&), playground, fishing dock, multi-use trails, nature trail, 27-hole disc golf course. **Activities:** Fishing, hiking, disc golf, cross-country skiing, snowmobiling, snowshoeing, hunting (with restrictions). **Special Features:** Park has generally flat terrain, with fields, woodland, and ponds. Visitors can catch a variety of fish from a dock on the lower Niagara River or largemouth bass from a pond near the park entrance.

★**3490**★ **KEEWAYDIN STATE PARK**
PO Box 247
46165 NYS Rt 12
Alexandria Bay, NY 13607
Web: www.nysparks.com/parks/info.asp?parkId=146
Phone: 315-482-3331
Size: 282 acres. **Location:** Off Route 12, 1 mile west of Alexandria Bay. **Facilities:** 48 campsites (&), showers (&), picnic areas (&), playground, swimming pool (&), marina, dockage, boat launch, boat rentals. **Activities:** Camping, boating (including power boats), fishing, swimming, cross-country skiing, ice fishing. **Special Features:** Park's terrain includes steep, rocky outcroppings along the shoreline which provide good vantage points for watching the ocean-going vessels on the Saint Lawrence River. The marina is open from mid-May through October; park is open year round.

★**3491**★ **KEUKA LAKE STATE PARK**
3370 Pepper Rd
Bluff Point, NY 14478
Web: www.nysparks.com/parks/info.asp?parkId=37
Phone: 315-536-3666
Size: 621 acres. **Location:** Off Route 54A, 6 miles west of Penn Yan, on the north end of the west branch of Keuka Lake. **Facilities:** 150 tent and trailer campsites (&), showers (&), picnic area (&) with pavilion, playground, hiking trails, swimming beach, boat launch ramp, docking space. **Activities:** Camping, boating (including power boats), fishing, hunting, swimming, hiking, cross-country skiing, snowmobiling. **Special Features:** Park is located in the heart of New York's wine country.

★**3492**★ **KNOX FARM STATE PARK**
437 Buffalo Rd
East Aurora, NY 14052
Web: nysparks.state.ny.us/parks/info.asp?parkId=89
Phone: 716-655-7200; **Fax:** 716-652-2207
Size: 633 acres. **Location:** Off I-90 to Exit 54 (Route 400), then from Route 400 to Jamison Road exit, to Route 16 (Seneca Street). **Facilities:** Nature trails, visitor center, exhibits. **Activities:** Hiking, biking, horseback riding, cross-country skiing, snowshoeing, interpretive programs. **Special Features:** Park is the former country estate of Buffalo's renowned Knox family. It is home to several species of farm animals and offers interpretive programs about the animals. The visitor center has exhibits of historical and natural interest.

★**3493**★ **KNOX'S HEADQUARTERS STATE HISTORIC SITE**
PO Box 207
Vails Gate, NY 12584
Web: www.nysparks.com/sites/info.asp?siteID=18
Phone: 845-561-5498
Size: 48 acres. **Location:** Off Route 94, in Vails Gate. **Facilities:** Picnic area, historic house and garden, interpretive displays, nature trail. **Activities:** Guided tours, reenactments, living history demonstrations, educational programs, hiking. **Special Features:** Site features the 18th-century stone house that John Ellison and his family shared with Revolutionary War heroes Generals Henry Knox, Horatio Gates, and Nathaniel Greene. Site also includes the ruins of the Ellison's grist mill.

★**3494**★ **KRING POINT STATE PARK**
25950 Kring Point Rd
Redwood, NY 13679
Web: www.nysparks.com/parks/info.asp?parkId=149
Phone: 315-482-2444
Size: 61 acres. **Location:** Off Route 12, 6 miles east of Alexandria Bay. **Facilities:** 100 campsites (&)), showers (&), cabins (&), picnic areas (&), picnic pavilions (&), playground, beach, boat docks, boat launch. **Activities:** Camping, boating (including power boats), fishing, swimming, cross-country skiing, waterfowl hunting (in season). **Special Features:** Park occupies a narrow peninsula, with its south shore facing Goose Bay and its north shore facing the Saint Lawrence River. Visitors can

see water and many of the 1,700 islands for which the region is named from anywhere in the park. The park is open from the last Friday in April to Columbus Day.

★3495★ LAKE ERIE STATE PARK
5905 Lake Rd
Brockton, NY 14716
Web: www.nysparks.com/parks/info.asp?parkId=96
Phone: 716-792-9214
Size: 355 acres. Location: 5 miles west of Dunkirk and 8.5 miles from Westfield, off Route 5. Facilities: 97 campsites, showers, 10 cabins, picnic areas with shelters, playground, food concession, multi-use trails, nature trail, beach. Activities: Camping, fishing, swimming, hiking, bicycling, cross-country skiing, snowmobiling, bird watching. Special Features: High bluffs overlooking Lake Erie afford breathtaking views. Park is recognized as an excellent place to locate rare migratory birds following the lake's edge. The park is open daily from May through October.

★3496★ LAKE SUPERIOR STATE PARK
c/o Sullivan County Dept of Public Works
Box 5012
Monticello, NY 12701
Web: www.nysparks.com/parks/info.asp?parkId=77
Phone: 845-794-3000
Size: 1,409 acres. Location: Take Route 17 to Route 17B to Route 55. Facilities: Picnic areas (&), pavilions, food concession, beaches, boat launches, boat rentals. Activities: Boating, fishing, swimming, picnicking, deer and turkey hunting in season. Special Features: Park is managed by Sullivan County under license from the Palisades Interstate Park Commission.

★3497★ LAKE TAGHKANIC STATE PARK
1528 Rt 82
Ancram, NY 12502
Web: www.nysparks.com/parks/info.asp?parkId=131
Phone: 518-851-3631; Fax: 518-851-3633
Size: 1,569 acres. Location: Adjacent to the Taconic State Parkway, 1 mile south of the Route 82 interchange. Facilities: Tent and trailer campsites, camping cabins (&), showers, 3 vacation rental cottages, picnic areas, picnic pavilions (&), playground, playing fields, food concession (&), multi-use trails (10 miles), 2 beaches, boat launch, boat rentals. Activities: Camping, boating (no power boats), fishing, swimming, hiking, bicycling, cross-country skiing, ice skating, snowmobiling, ice fishing, sledding, bow hunting for deer and turkey (in season), recreation programs. Special Features: Park is located alongside Lake Taghkanic in the rolling hills and lush forests of Columbia County. The campgrounds were ranked among the top 100 in the US in 2005.

★3498★ LAKESIDE BEACH STATE PARK
Rt 18
Waterport, NY 14571
Web: www.nysparks.com/parks/info.asp?parkId=8
Phone: 585-682-4888
Size: 744 acres. Location: Off Lake Ontario State Parkway, 10 miles north of Albion on Route 18 west. Facilities: 274 campsites, showers &), picnic areas, picnic pavilions (&), playground, playing fields, food concession, hiking and biking trails (4 miles), scenic views. Activities: Camping, lakefront fishing, hiking, biking, cross-country skiing, snowmobiling, waterfowl hunting (in season), recreation programs. Special Features: Park offers a panoramic view of Lake Ontario and surrounding farms and fruit orchards.

★3499★ LETCHWORTH STATE PARK
1 Letchworth State Park
Castile, NY 14427
Web: www.nysparks.com/parks/info.asp?parkId=12
Phone: 585-493-3600
Size: 14,428 acres. Location: 35 miles south of Rochester, along the Genesee River; Exit 7 off I-390. Facilities: Tent and trailer campsites (&)), showers (&), winterized cabins (&), vacation rental lodge, inn, restaurant (open to the public), conference center, picnic areas and pavilions (&), playground, hiking trails (66 miles), nature trail (&), trails for horseback riding, biking, cross-country skiing, and snowmobiling, swimming pool (&), visitor center/museum, gift shop. Activities: Camping, kayaking, whitewater rafting, hot air ballooning, fishing, swimming, hiking, bicycling, cross-country skiing, ice skating, snow tubing, snowmobiling, horse-drawn sleigh rides, nature, history, and performing arts programs, guided walks and tours, a summer lecture series. Deer and spring turkey hunting permitted in season. Special Features: Park is sometimes referred to as the "Grand Canyon of the East." Features include the Genesee River, which roars through the gorge over three major waterfalls between cliffs as high as 600 feet, scenic trails, and lush forests. The historic, completely restored Glen Iris Inn, a hotel built in 1914, offers overnight accommodations and is open to the public for meals.

★3500★ LODI POINT STATE MARINE PARK
c/o Sampson State Park
6096 Rt 96A
Romulus, NY 14541
Web: www.nysparks.com/parks/info.asp?parkId=38
Phone: 315-585-6392
Size: 12 acres. Location: On Lodi Point Road, off Route 414, 2 miles west of Lodi. Facilities: Picnic area, picnic pavilion (&), playground, marina, boat launch. Activities: Boating, fishing. Special Features: Park is located on the east shore of Seneca Lake, with modest accommodations for boaters and fishermen.

★3501★ LONG POINT STATE PARK - FINGER LAKES
2063 Lake Rd
Aurora, NY 13026
Web: www.nysparks.com/parks/info.asp?parkId=39
Phone: 315-497-0130
Size: 229 acres. Location: Off Route 90, 4 miles south of Aurora. Facilities: Vacation rental cottage, picnic area, beach with swimming area, boat launch facilities. Activities: Boating (including power boats), fishing (&), hunting (with restrictions).

Special Features: The vacation rental cottage at Long Point State Park is located on the shore of Cayuga Lake and includes a boat dock.

★3502★ **LONG POINT STATE PARK ON LAKE CHAUTAUQUA**
4459 Rt 430
Bemus Point, NY 14712
Web: www.nysparks.com/parks/info.asp?parkId=3
Phone: 716-386-2722
Size: 360 acres. **Location:** Off Route 17, on Route 430 west of Bemus Point. **Facilities:** Picnic area, picnic pavilions, playground, multi-use trails, nature trail, beach, marina, dockage, boat launch, food (&&). **Activities:** Boating (including power boating), fishing, swimming, hiking, bicycling, cross-country skiing, snowmobiling, ice fishing. **Special Features:** Park property includes peninsular waterfront and a large public marina with the most modern boat launch on Lake Chatauqua. The lake, at 1,308 feet above sea level, is one of the highest navigable bodies of water in North America. Its major attraction is fishing for muskellunge (muskie), which are native to the lake and noted for their size.

★3503★ **LONG POINT STATE PARK - THOUSAND ISLANDS**
7495 State Park Rd
Three Mile Bay, NY 13693
Web: www.nysparks.com/parks/info.asp?parkId=152
Phone: 315-649-5258
Size: 23 acres. **Location:** Off Route 12E, 8 miles west of Three Mile Bay. **Facilities:** Tent and trailer campsites, showers (&), picnic area, picnic pavilions, playground (&), dockage, boat launch, boat rentals. **Activities:** Camping, boating, fishing (&), waterfowl hunting (in season). **Special Features:** Park is situated on a peninsula facing Chaumont Bay on Lake Ontario and is almost completely surrounded by water. The bay provides excellent harbor for boats. The park is open from early May until Columbus Day.

★3504★ **LORENZO STATE HISTORIC SITE**
17 Rippleton Rd
Cazenovia, NY 13035
Web: www.nysparks.com/sites/info.asp?siteID=19
Phone: 315-655-3200; **Fax:** 315-655-4304
Size: 87 acres. **Location:** 1/4 mile south of US 20 in Cazenovia. **Facilities:** Picnic area (&), historic house and gardens, visitor center (&), interpretive displays, scenic views, gift shop (&). **Activities:** Guided tours, living history demonstrations, educational programs, cross-country skiing. **Special Features:** Site was established in 1807 as the neoclassical home of John Lincklaen, Holland Land Company agent and founder of the village of Cazenovia.

★3505★ **MACOMB RESERVATION STATE PARK**
201 Campsite Rd
Schuyler Falls, NY 12985
Web: www.nysparks.com/parks/info.asp?parkId=148
Phone: 518-643-9952
Size: 600 acres. **Location:** Off Route 22B, 2 miles west of Schuyler Falls. **Facilities:** Tent and trailer campsites (&), showers (&), picnic area (&), picnic shelters, nature trails, hiking trails, beach, playing fields, boat rentals, recreation programs, playground. **Activities:** Camping, boating (no power boats), fishing, swimming, hiking, cross-country skiing, snowmobiling, snowshoeing, recreation programs. **Special Features:** Macomb Reservation lies just outside the Adirondack Park along the Salmon River. The park is surrounded by state lands and has a wilderness atmosphere.

★3506★ **MARGARET LEWIS NORRIE STATE PARK**
Old Post Rd
PO Box 893
Staatsburg, NY 12580
Web: nysparks.state.ny.us/parks/info.asp?parkId=134
Phone: 845-889-4646; **Fax:** 845-889-8321
Size: 350 acres. **Location:** Off Route 9, 4 miles north of Hyde Park, adjoining Ogden Mills & Ruth Livingston Mills State Park (see separate entry). **Facilities:** 46 tent campsites, showers (&), 10 cabins, picnic area, food, hiking trails, bike trails, nature trails, ski trails, boat launch, marina with anchorage, playground, scenic views, environmental center. **Activities:** Camping, boating, fishing, hiking, bicycling, cross-country skiing, snowshoeing. **Special Features:** Park includes numerous trails with great views of the Hudson River, which runs directly along the park's western boundary.

★3507★ **MARK TWAIN STATE PARK & SOARING EAGLES GOLF COURSE**
201 Middle Rd
Horseheads, NY 14845
Web: www.nysparks.com/parks/info.asp?parkId=41
Phone: 607-739-0034
Size: 469 acres. **Location:** Route 17 to Route 14 exit (Watkins Glen), go 2 miles, turn right at Route 14, then left onto Ridge Road, go 1 block and turn left onto Middle Road. **Facilities:** 18-hole golf course, food, showers. **Activities:** Golf, bow hunting (in season), cross-country skiing. **Special Features:** Park is named for the great 19th-century author, who spent summers in the area. The park's Soaring Eagles Golf Course is one of the most scenic and challenging golf courses in the area. The course is dotted with kettle ponds, created by glacial retreat at the end of the last Ice Age.

★3508★ **MARY ISLAND STATE PARK**
c/o Cedar Point State Park
36661 Cedar Point State Park Dr
Clayton, NY 13624
Web: www.nysparks.com/parks/info.asp?parkId=150
Phone: 315-654-2522
Size: 13 acres. **Location:** East of Wellesley Island; access by boat only. **Facilities:** 12 tent campsites, boat moorage, picnic area, trails. **Activities:** Camping, boating, fishing, hiking. **Special Features:** Island is heavily wooded with steep rocky outcroppings, offering visitors seclusion and views of the Canadian shore and shipping channel.

9. State Parks

★3509★ **MAX V. SHAUL STATE PARK**
Rt 30, Box 23
Fultonham, NY 12071
Web: www.nysparks.com/parks/info.asp?parkId=135
Phone: 518-827-4711
Size: 70 acres. **Location:** Off Route 30, 6 miles south of Middleburgh. **Facilities:** 30 tent and trailer campsites (&), showers (&), picnic area (&), picnic pavilions, nature trail, hiking trail, playground, playfields. **Activities:** Camping, fishing, hiking, cross-country skiing, softball, basketball. **Special Features:** Park is a small, quiet campground with shady picnic grounds and fishing in Panther Creek. It is located near Mine Kill State Park, which offers additional recreation opportunities.

★3510★ **MINE KILL STATE PARK**
PO Box 923 Rt 30
North Blenheim, NY 12131
Web: www.nysparks.com/parks/info.asp?parkId=117
Phone: 518-827-6111; **Fax:** 518-827-6782
Size: 500 acres. **Location:** Off Route 30, 15 miles south of Middleburgh. **Facilities:** Picnic area (&), picnic pavilions, food (&), multi-use trails, swimming pool (&), wading pool, boat launch, playground, recreation programs (&). **Activities:** Boating, fishing, swimming, water-skiing, hiking, cross-country skiing, snowmobiling, snowshoeing, bow hunting (with restrictions), recreation programs. **Special Features:** Park overlooks the New York Power Authority's Blenheim-Gilboa Pumped Storage Project's lower reservoir and surrounding hills. The reservoir is stocked with rainbow trout, brown trout, bass, walleye, carp, and pan fish.

★3511★ **MINNEWASKA STATE PARK PRESERVE**
PO Box 893
New Paltz, NY 12561
Web: www.nysparks.com/parks/info.asp?parkId=78
Phone: 845-256-0579
Size: 20,104 acres. **Location:** Route 44/55 west from New Paltz. **Facilities:** Picnic area, food, beach (&), hiking trails, bridle path, bike path, ski trails, recreation programs. **Activities:** Hiking, bicycling, horseback riding, cross-country skiing, snowshoeing, swimming, canoeing, hunting (with restrictions), recreation programs. **Special Features:** Park is situated on the Shawangunk Mountain ridge that rises more than 2,000 feet above sea level. The terrain is rugged and rocky, and technical rock climbing is permitted.

★3512★ **MONTAUK DOWNS STATE PARK**
50 S Fairview Ave
Montauk, NY 11954
Web: www.nysparks.com/parks/info.asp?parkId=165
Phone: 631-668-3781
Size: 171 acres. **Location:** Off South Fairview Avenue in Montauk. **Facilities:** 18-hole golf course, driving range, tennis courts, food, swimming pool (&), showers (&), wading pool, playground. **Activities:** Swimming, tennis, golf, recreation programs (&). **Special Features:** The park's main attraction is its Robert Trent Jones-designed golf course.

★3513★ **MONTAUK POINT STATE PARK**
c/o Montauk Downs State Park
50 S Fairview Ave
Montauk, NY 11954
Web: www.nysparks.com/parks/info.asp?parkId=136
Phone: 631-668-3781
Size: 862 acres. **Location:** Off Route 27 in Montauk. **Facilities:** Picnic area (&), food (&), multi-use trails, playground. **Activities:** Fishing, hiking, cross-country skiing, hunting (with restrictions). **Special Features:** Located on the eastern tip of Long Island, park offers great surf fishing and a unique view — when the water is calm, visitors can see the "race" of converging tides from the Atlantic and Block Island Sound.

★3514★ **MOREAU LAKE STATE PARK**
605 Old Saratoga Rd
Gansevoort, NY 12831
Web: www.nysparks.com/parks/info.asp?parkId=119
Phone: 518-793-0511; **Fax:** 518-761-6843
Size: 4,184 acres. **Location:** 10 miles north of Saratoga Springs in the Adirondack Foothills. **Facilities:** Tent and trailer campsites, showers (&), cabins, vacation rental cottage, picnic area (&), picnic pavilion, museum, visitor center, recreation programs. **Activities:** Camping (including group camping), hunting (with restrictions), boating, fishing, swimming, hiking, bicycling, cross-country skiing, snowshoeing, recreation and nature programs. **Special Features:** Park's lake lies amid hardwood forests, pine stands, and rocky ridges, and its wooded campgrounds are quiet and secluded.

★3515★ **NEW WINDSOR CANTONMENT STATE HISTORIC SITE**
PO Box 207
Vails Gate, NY 12584
Web: www.nysparks.com/sites/info.asp?siteID=20
Phone: 845-561-1765
Size: 120 acres. **Location:** Along NY 300, 1 mile north of Vails Gate. **Facilities:** Picnic area (&), interpretive displays, visitor center, scenic view (&), hiking trail. **Activities:** Guided and self-guided tours, reenactments, living history demonstrations, educational programs, hiking. **Special Features:** Site is the location of the final encampment of George Washington's army. It was from here that cease-fire orders were issued on April 19, 1783, ending the eight-year War of Independence. The National Purple Heart Hall of Honor is located here also, and the site played a central role in the history of the Purple Heart.

★3516★ **NEWTOWN BATTLEFIELD STATE PARK**
451 Oneida Rd
Elmira, NY 14901
Web: www.nysparks.com/parks/info.asp?parkId=175
Phone: 607-732-6067
Size: 369 acres. **Location:** In the southern-tier area of the state, near Elmira. **Facilities:** Picnic area (&), picnic pavilions (&), scenic views, tent and trailer campsites (&), cabins, showers (&). **Activities:** Camping. **Special Features:** A granite monument, erected in 1912, commemorates the Battle of Newtown, one of the largest offensive campaigns of the American Revolution.

9. State Parks

★3517★ NIAGARA FALLS STATE PARK
PO Box 1132
Niagara Falls, NY 14303
Web: www.nysparks.com/parks/info.asp?parkId=113
Phone: 716-278-1796
Size: 435 acres. **Location:** Access via the Robert Moses Parkway into Niagara Falls. **Facilities:** Picnic area, food concession (&), nature trail, visitor center/museum, gift shop, observation tower. **Activities:** Fishing, hiking, bicycling, recreation programs (&). **Special Features:** Spectacular Niagara Falls is the centerpiece of this park, the oldest state park in the United States and one of the wonders of the world. Park's other attractions include Great Lakes Garden, Cave of the Winds, Maid of the Mist boat tours, panoramic view from the observation tower, Niagara Scenic Trolley tours, and Niagara Gorge Discovery Center, which chronicles the creation of the falls.

★3518★ NISSEQUOGUE RIVER STATE PARK
St Johnland Rd
PO Box 639
Kings Park, NY 11754
Web: www.nysparks.com/parks/info.asp?parkId=79
Phone: 631-269-4927
Size: 153 acres. **Location:** North shore of Long Island. **Facilities:** Trails, boat launch, boat rentals, play field, interpretive displays, visitor center/museum, marina, guided tours, bike rentals, conference room. **Activities:** Fishing, hiking, biking, boating (nonpowered only), bird watching, cross-country skiing, snowshoeing. **Special Features:** Tidal and fresh water wetlands and hardwood forests provide habitat for shore birds, reptiles, and amphibians. The Greenbelt Trail parallels the Nissequogue River, affording scenic views of the river and Long Island Sound from the top of the bluffs. A section of the park has been designated a State Bird Conservation Area.

★3519★ NYACK BEACH STATE PARK
PO Box 217
Congers, NY 10920
Web: www.nysparks.com/parks/info.asp?parkId=62
Phone: 845-268-3020
Size: 61 acres. **Location:** Route 9W to Broadway in Nyack. **Facilities:** Picnic area, trails, boat ramp. **Activities:** Canoeing, fishing, hiking, bicycling, cross-country skiing **Special Features:** Park is situated along the Hudson riverfront in Rockland County.

★3520★ OAK ORCHARD STATE MARINE PARK
c/o Lakeside Beach State Park
Rt 18
Waterport, NY 14571
Web: www.nysparks.com/parks/info.asp?parkId=13
Phone: 585-682-4888
Size: 81 acres. **Location:** Off Route 18 on Archibald Road in Waterport. **Facilities:** Picnic area, boat launch. **Activities:** Boating (including power boating), fishing. **Special Features:** Park is a boat launch facility on Lake Ontario.

★3521★ OGDEN MILLS & RUTH LIVINGSTON MILLS STATE PARK
Old Post Rd
PO Box 893
Staatsburg, NY 12580
Web: www.nysparks.com/parks/info.asp?parkId=133
Phone: 845-889-4646
Size: 744 acres. **Location:** Off Route 9, 4 miles north of Hyde Park. **Facilities:** Scenic views, food(&), multi-use trails (4 miles), 18-hole golf course, recreation programs. **Activities:** Fishing, hiking, bicycling, cross-country skiing, snowshoeing, sledding, golf, recreation programs. **Special Features:** Park is home to Dinsmore Golf Course, one of the oldest public golf courses in the country. Staatsburgh State Historic Site (see separate entry), an elegant country house located atop a grassy hill overlooking the Hudson River and the Catskill Mountains, is the park's centerpiece.

★3522★ OLANA STATE HISTORIC SITE
5720 Rt 9G
Hudson, NY 12534
Web: www.nysparks.com/sites/info.asp?siteID=21
Phone: 518-828-0135; **Fax:** 518-828-6742
Size: 763 acres. **Location:** Off Route 9G, 1 mile south of Rip Van Winkle Bridge. **Facilities:** Picnic area, historic house and gardens, educational programs (&), visitor center (&), gift shop, scenic view, hiking trail. **Activities:** Guided and self-guided tours, hiking, cross-country skiing. **Special Features:** Olana is the fanciful Persian-style home and picturesque landscape created by Frederic Edwin Church (1826-1900), one of the most renowned American artists of the Hudson River School. Site encompasses the house, farm, and entire 250-acre estate owned by Church.

★3523★ OLD CROTON AQUEDUCT STATE HISTORIC PARK
15 Walnut St
Dobbs Ferry, NY 10522
Web: www.nysparks.com/sites/info.asp?siteID=34
Phone: 914-693-5259; **Fax:** 914-674-8529
Size: 26-mile linear trail; 216 acres. **Location:** From Van Cortlandt Park at the Bronx County/City of Yonkers border to the Croton Dam in Cortlandt. **Activities:** Hiking, bicycling, horseback riding, cross-country skiing, snowshoeing, bird watching. **Special Features:** The Old Croton Aqueduct was New York city's first public water supply system, capable of carrying 100 million gallons of water a day. Construction of the Aqueduct and dam began in 1837, and today northern sections continue to supply water to the town of Ossining. In 1992, the Old Aqueduct was granted National Historic Landmark status, and a 22-mile segment was designated as part of the Hudson River Trail.

★3524★ OLD ERIE CANAL STATE HISTORIC PARK
RD 2 Andrus Rd
Kirkville, NY 13082
Web: nysparks.state.ny.us/sites/info.asp?siteID=31
Phone: 315-687-7821

Size: 1,065 acres. **Location:** Off I-90. **Facilities:** Picnic area, picnic pavilions, multi-use trails (36 miles), interpretive displays. **Activities:** Canoeing, fishing, hiking, bicycling, horseback riding, cross-country skiing, snowmobiling, carriage rides. **Special Features:** Park preserves a 36-mile stretch of the Old Erie Canal, designated a National Recreational Trail. The terrain is woodland and wetland, and several footbridges provide access to the canal towpath. Along the trail, visitors can see remnants of stone aqueducts, Chittenango Landing Canal Boat Museum, Erie Canal Village, and other historic sites.

★3525★ OLD FORT NIAGARA STATE HISTORIC SITE

PO Box 169
Youngstown, NY 14174
Web: www.nysparks.com/sites/info.asp?siteID=22
Phone: 716-745-7611; **Fax:** 716-745-9141
Size: 25 acres. **Location:** 18 miles north of Niagara Falls via Robert Moses Parkway. **Facilities:** Picnic area(&), historic building and garden, gift shop (&), scenic views. **Activities:** Guided tours, living history demonstrations, reenactments, education programs. **Special Features:** Fort's history spans more than 300 years, during which time it was occupied by three nations: France, Great Britain, and the United States. The French established the first post in 1679 and in 1726 built the impressive "French Castle," which still stands today. Visitors to the fort will see the oldest buildings in the Great Lakes region.

★3526★ OQUAGA CREEK STATE PARK

5995 County Rte 20
Bainbridge, NY 13733
Web: www.nysparks.com/parks/info.asp?parkId=2
Phone: 607-467-4160
Size: 1,385 acres. **Location:** Off Route 206, 11 miles south of Sidney. **Facilities:** 95 tent and trailer campsites, cottage, showers (&), picnic area, picnic pavilions (&), food, multi-use trails (6 miles), nature trail, beach, hand launch boat ramp, boat rentals, playground, recreation programs. **Activities:** Camping, hunting (with restrictions), boating (no power boats), fishing, swimming, hiking, bicycling, ice skating, cross-country skiing, sledding, snowshoeing, sledding, ice fishing, recreation and nature programs. **Special Features:** Park has a sand beach for swimmers, a lake for fishing, and rolling wooded hills that are ideal for sledding.

★3527★ ORIENT BEACH STATE PARK

PO Box 117
Orient, NY 11957
Web: www.nysparks.com/parks/info.asp?parkId=50
Phone: 631-323-2440
Size: 364 acres. **Location:** On North Country Road, off Route 25, in Orient. **Facilities:** Picnic area, picnic pavilions, food, hiking trails, nature trail, beach, showers, bike rentals, playground, playfields (&&). **Activities:** Fishing, swimming, hiking, bicycling, recreation programs (&). **Special Features:** Park features 45,000 feet of frontage on Gardiner's Bay and a rare maritime forest with red cedar, blackjack oak trees, and prickly pear cactus.

★3528★ ORISKANY BATTLEFIELD STATE HISTORIC SITE

7801 State Rt 69
Oriskany, NY 13424
Web: www.nysparks.com/sites/info.asp?siteID=23
Phone: 315-768-7224; **Fax:** 315-377-3081
Size: 83 acres. **Location:** Off Route 69, east of Rome. **Facilities:** Picnic area, visitor center and museum, interpretive displays, scenic view, trails. **Activities:** Guided and self-guided tours, reenactments, educational programs, hiking. **Special Features:** The Battle of Oriskany, fought here in 1777, has been described as one of the bloodiest of the War of Independence and is considered a significant turning point in the war.

★3529★ PEEBLES ISLAND STATE PARK

PO Box 219
Waterford, NY 12188
Web: nysparks.state.ny.us/parks/info.asp?parkId=120
Phone: 518-237-8643
Size: 190 acres. **Location:** 12 miles north of Albany at the confluence of the Hudson and Mohawk Rivers; access by Delaware Avenue in Cohoes. **Facilities:** Picnic areas and pavilions (&), trails, visitor center and gift shop (&). **Activities:** Fishing, hiking, cross-country skiing, snowshoeing. **Special Features:** Park's miles of paths offer spectacular views of the rivers and rapids.

★3530★ PHILIPSE MANOR HALL STATE HISTORIC SITE

PO Box 496
Yonkers, NY 10702
Web: www.nysparks.com/sites/info.asp?siteID=24
Phone: 914-965-4027; **Fax:** 914-965-6485
Size: 1.5 acres. **Location:** Warburton Avenue and Dock Street in Yonkers. **Facilities:** Historic site, interpretive exhibits. **Activities:** Group tours. **Special Features:** Elegant home of British loyalist Frederick Philipse III. After the start of the American Revolution, Philipse and his family fled to England, and the home was confiscated by the state and sold at auction. One of New York's finest examples of Georgian-style architecture, the house now serves as a museum of history, art, and architecture.

★3531★ PINNACLE STATE PARK & GOLF COURSE

1904 Pinnacle Rd
Addison, NY 14801
Web: nysparks.state.ny.us/parks/info.asp?parkId=99
Phone: 607-359-2767
Size: 681 acres. **Location:** Off Route 417, in Addison. **Facilities:** Picnic area, picnic pavilions (&), food (&), multi-use trails (11 miles), 9-hole golf course, scenic views. **Activities:** Golf, hunting (with restrictions), fishing, hiking, biking, ice fishing, cross-country skiing. **Special Features:** Park is known mainly for its challenging golf course, but it also offers other recreational opportunities as well as great views of the Canisteo River Valley, Harris Hill, and the village of Addison.

★3532★ PIXLEY FALLS STATE PARK
11430 State Rt 46
Boonville, NY 13309
Web: www.nysparks.com/parks/info.asp?parkId=20
Phone: 315-942-4713
Size: 375 acres. **Location:** Off Route 46, 6 miles south of Boonville. **Facilities:** 22 tent and trailer campsites, picnic area (&), picnic pavilions, nature trails, hiking trails. **Activities:** Camping, hunting (with restrictions), fishing, hiking, cross-country skiing. **Special Features:** Park features a 50-foot waterfall, trout streams, and steep, wooded hills. A cross-country ski trail runs along the Black River Canal.

★3533★ PLANTING FIELDS ARBORETUM STATE HISTORIC PARK/COE HALL HISTORIC HOUSE MUSEUM
PO Box 58
Oyster Bay, NY 11771
Web: www.nysparks.com/sites/info.asp?siteID=33
Phone: 516-922-9200; **Fax:** 516-922-8610
Size: 409 acres. **Location:** On Planting Fields Road in Oyster Bay. **Facilities:** Historic house and gardens, visitor center (&), gift shop, nature trails. **Activities:** Guided tours, self-guided tours, educational programs. **Special Features:** Site is the former Gold Coast estate of the WR Coe family. Its 400 acres of lawns, gardens, woodlands, and nature walks include two greenhouses, one of which has an extensive collection of camellias. Coe Hall, which is in the Tudor Revival style, is open for tours from April to September. In addition to the mansion, the site features a wide variety of gardens, specimen plantings, and charming outbuildings.

★3534★ POINT AU ROCHE STATE PARK
19 Camp Red Cloud Rd
Plattsburg, NY 12901
Web: www.nysparks.com/parks/info.asp?parkId=162
Phone: 518-563-0369
Size: 856 acres. **Location:** Off Route 9, 4 miles north of Plattsburg. **Facilities:** Picnic area (&), picnic pavilions (&), hiking trails, bike trails, nature trails, beach, boat launch, playfields, playground, showers (&). **Activities:** Boating, fishing, swimming, hiking, bicycling, cross-country skiing, ice fishing, recreation and nature programs. **Special Features:** Located on the northwestern shore of Lake Champlain, park is a mixture of open and forested areas, most of them natural and undeveloped, with a diversity of habitats ranging from forest to marsh to shoreline.

★3535★ RESERVOIR STATE PARK
c/o Niagara Frontier Region
PO Box 1132
Niagara Falls, NY 14303
Web: www.nysparks.com/parks/info.asp?parkId=112
Phone: 716-284-4691
Size: 132 acres. **Location:** At the intersection of Routes 31 and 265, 6 miles from the Falls. **Facilities:** Picnic area (&), picnic shelters, playground, trails, 3 tennis courts, 8 baseball diamonds,
2 basketball courts, roller hockey court, softball complex. **Activities:** Tennis, fishing, hiking, bicycling, cross-country skiing, snowmobiling, sledding, radio-controlled model airplane flying, kite flying, field sports. **Special Features:** Park is the most heavily used park in Niagara County.

★3536★ RIVERBANK STATE PARK
679 Riverside Dr
New York, NY 10031
Web: www.nysparks.com/parks/info.asp?parkId=75
Phone: 212-694-3600
Size: 28 acres. **Location:** West 145th Street and Riverside Drive in Manhattan. **Facilities:** Picnic areas (&), restaurant (&), indoor and outdoor swimming pools (&), outdoor amphitheater, indoor cultural theater (&), athletic complex with fitness room, running track, soccer/football field, 4 tennis courts, 4 basketball courts, 4 handball courts, softball field, indoor skating rink (&), 2 playgrounds (&), boat dockage, scenic views. **Activities:** Swimming, hiking, tennis, softball, basketball, handball, football, soccer, ice skating, roller skating, recreation and cultural programs. **Special Features:** The park's multi-level recreational facility rises 69 feet above the Hudson River and offers a wide variety of recreational, athletic, and arts experiences for all ages, interests, and abilities. In addition to outdoor recreation facilities, five major buildings house an Olympic-size swimming pool, covered skating rink, an 800-seat cultural theater, a 2,500-seat athletic complex, and a 150-seat restaurant.

★3537★ ROBERT G WEHLE STATE PARK
5502 Military Rd
Henderson, NY 13650
Web: www.nysparks.com/parks/info.asp?parkId=173
Phone: 315-938-5083
Size: 1,067 acres. **Location:** On Lake Ontario. **Facilities:** Picnic areas, hiking/mountain biking trails, vacation rental cottage. **Activities:** Hiking, biking. **Special Features:** Park was the former estate of Robert G. Wehle and has more than 17,000 feet of Lake Ontario shoreline. The residential compound on the property is available for rent Memorial Day week-end through Columbus Day. It includes the main house, guest quarters, tennis court, and formal gardens.

★3538★ ROBERT H. TREMAN STATE PARK
105 Enfield Falls Rd
Ithaca, NY 14850
Web: www.nysparks.com/parks/info.asp?parkId=104
Phone: 607-273-3440
Size: 1,076 acres. **Location:** Off Route 13, 5 miles south of Ithaca. **Facilities:** Tent and trailer campsites (&), showers (&), cabins (&), picnic area (&), picnic pavilions (&), hiking trails (9 miles), beach (&), playground, recreation programs. **Activities:** Camping, bow hunting for deer (in season), fishing, swimming, hiking, recreation programs. **Special Features:** Trails on either side of Enfield Glen offer views of 12 waterfalls, including 115-foot Lucifer Falls.

★3539★ ROBERT MOSES STATE PARK - LONG ISLAND

c/o Long Island Regional Office
PO Box 247
Babylon, NY 11702
Web: www.nysparks.com/parks/info.asp?parkId=45
Phone: 631-669-0449
Size: 875 acres. **Location:** 48 miles from Manhattan via Southern State Parkway. **Facilities:** Picnic area (&), food (&), beach (&), marina, showers, 18-hole pitch & putt golf course, playground. **Activities:** Boating, fishing, swimming, golf, recreation programs. **Special Features:** Park features five miles of ocean beach and a day-use boat basin that can accommodate 40 boats.

★3540★ ROBERT MOSES STATE PARK - THOUSAND ISLANDS

PO Box 548
Massena, NY 13662
Web: www.nysparks.com/parks/info.asp?parkId=157
Phone: 315-769-8663
Size: 2,322 acres. **Location:** Off Route 37, 3 miles north of Massena. **Facilities:** Tent and trailer campsites, showers, cabins (&), showers (&), picnic area (&), picnic pavilions (&), multi-use trails, beach, boat launch, boat rentals, marina, nature center, playfields, playground, tennis courts. **Activities:** Camping, boating, fishing, swimming, hiking, bicycling, cross-country skiing, snowmobiling, snowshoeing, recreation and nature programs. **Special Features:** Park is located partly on the mainland and partly on Barnhart island; park is reached through a tunnel under the Eisenhower Lock.

★3541★ ROBERT V. RIDDELL STATE PARK

c/o Gilbert Lake State Park
18 CCC Rd
Laurens, NY 13796
Web: www.nysparks.com/parks/info.asp?parkId=180
Phone: 607-432-2114
Size: 1,036 acres. **Location:** Off I-88, on Route 28, 20 miles from Cooperstown. **Facilities:** Hiking trails. **Activities:** Fishing, hiking, cross-country skiing, snowshoeing, birdwatching. **Special Features:** Park consists of forested woodlands located in the Susquehanna River Valley and offers a variety of passive recreational activities.

★3542★ ROBERTO CLEMENTE STATE PARK

W Tremont Ave & Mattewson Rd
Bronx, NY 10453
Web: nysparks.state.ny.us/parks/info.asp?parkId=33
Phone: 718-299-8750
Size: 22 acres. **Location:** Off West Tremont Avenue and Mattewson Road in the Bronx. **Facilities:** Picnic area (&), food (&), gymnasium (&), swimming pool (&), ballfields, playground (&). **Activities:** Swimming, bicycling, recreation programs, entertainment programs. **Special Features:** Park includes an entertainment pavilion for live music and dance performances, and a waterfront promenade along the Harlem River. It is named for the first Latino-American inducted into the Baseball Hall of Fame.

★3543★ ROCKEFELLER STATE PARK PRESERVE

PO Box 338
Tarrytown, NY 10591
Web: www.nysparks.com/parks/info.asp?parkId=60
Phone: 914-631-1470
Size: 1,569 acres. **Location:** Off Route 117 in Tarrytown. **Facilities:** Multi-use trails (&), bridle paths, visitor center, picnic area (&), recreation programs. **Activities:** Fishing, hiking, horseback riding, cross-country skiing, snowshoeing, sledding. **Special Features:** Preserve's most notable feature is its system of carriage roads, which wind throughout the park and cross wood and stone bridges, including the first triple arch bridge in America. The preserve is a favorite with birders and has been designated an Important Bird Area, with 180 species of birds recorded there.

★3544★ ROCKLAND LAKE STATE PARK

PO Box 217
Congers, NY 10920
Web: nysparks.state.ny.us/parks/info.asp?parkId=64
Phone: 845-268-3020
Size: 1,133 acres. **Location:** Off Route 9W, 24 miles north of New York City. **Facilities:** Picnic area (&), food (&), hiking trails, nature trail, fitness trail, bike trail, 2 swimming pools (&), 2 kiddie pools, 2 18-hole golf courses, hand launch boat ramp, boat rentals, tennis courts, playground (&). **Activities:** Boating (no power boats), fishing, ice fishing, swimming, hiking, bicycling, tennis, golf, cross-country skiing, sledding, recreation programs. **Special Features:** Park is located on a ridge of Hook Mountain above the west bank of the Hudson River.

★3545★ SACKETS HARBOR BATTLEFIELD STATE HISTORIC SITE

PO Box 27
505 W Washington St
Sackets Harbor, NY 13685
Web: nysparks.state.ny.us/sites/info.asp?siteID=25
Phone: 315-646-3634; **Fax:** 315-646-1203
Size: 31 acres. **Location:** 1 mile from Route 3, west of Sackets Harbor. **Facilities:** Picnic area (&), historic buildings and gardens, scenic views, interpretive displays, gift shop (&), visitor center/museum (&). **Activities:** Guided and self-guided tours, costumed interpreters. **Special Features:** During the war of 1812 Sackets Harbor was the center of American naval and military activity for the upper Saint Lawrence Valley and Lake Ontario. A British-Canadian force attempted to destroy the American shipyard there in an 1813 battle. After the war, the fleet was placed in storage and the battlefield reverted to farmlands.

★3546★ SAINT LAWRENCE STATE PARK GOLF COURSE

4955 State Hwy 37
Ogdensburg, NY 13669
Web: www.nysparks.com/parks/info.asp?parkId=163
Phone: 315-393-2286

Size: 318 acres. **Location:** Off Route 37, 5 miles west of Ogdensburg. **Facilities:** 9-hole golf course, showers, food concession (&), hiking trails. **Activities:** Golf, hiking, cross-country skiing, sledding, snowmobiling. **Special Features:** The golf course was designed to incorporate panoramic views of the Saint Lawrence River shipping channel and the Canadian shore. It is open from late April to Columbus Day.

★3547★ SAMPSON STATE PARK

6096 Rt 96A
Romulus, NY 14541
Web: www.nysparks.com/parks/info.asp?parkId=100
Phone: 315-585-6392
Size: 1,905 acres. **Location:** Off Route 96A, 11 miles south of Geneva. **Facilities:** 245 tent and trailer campsites with electricity, 64 campsites without electricity, showers (&), picnic area, picnic pavilions (&), food, nature trail, hiking trail, beach, marina with dockage, boat launch, playfields, playground, museum, tennis courts. **Activities:** Camping, hunting (with restrictions), boating, fishing, tennis, hiking, bicycling, cross-country skiing, snowshoeing, ice fishing, recreation programs. **Special Features:** Located on the east shore of Seneca Lake, the property was once a naval training station and later an Air Force base.

★3548★ SANDY ISLAND BEACH STATE PARK

3387 County Rte 15
Pulaski, NY 13142
Web: www.nysparks.com/parks/info.asp?parkId=166
Phone: 315-387-2657
Size: 13 acres. **Location:** County Rte 15, 8 miles from Sandy Creek. **Facilities:** Beach, picnic area (&), showers, viewing platforms. **Activities:** Swimming, fishing, hiking, canoeing, kayaking, bird watching. **Special Features:** Park is part of the Eastern Lake Ontario Dune and Wetland System, a 17-mile stretch extending from Richland to Lake Ontario. The dunes were formed by wind and wave motion of a giant inland sea that preceded Lake Ontario. The area is the only significant freshwater dune site in the northeastern United States.

★3549★ SARATOGA LAKE MARINE PARK

19 Roosevelt Dr
Saratoga Springs, NY 12866
Web: www.nysparks.com/parks/info.asp?parkId=121
Phone: 518-584-2000
Size: 3 acres. **Location:** Route 9P, east of Sarasota Springs. **Facilities:** Boat launch facilities. **Activities:** Boating. **Special Features:** Park has parking capacity for up to 100 boat trailers.

★3550★ SARATOGA SPA STATE PARK

19 Roosevelt Dr
Saratoga Springs, NY 12866
Web: www.nysparks.com/parks/info.asp?parkId=124
Phone: 518-584-2535
Size: 2,724 acres. **Location:** Exit 13N off Route 87 (Northway) in Saratoga Springs. **Facilities:** Picnic area (&), picnic pavilions (&), food, nature trail, ski trails (12 miles), swimming pool, showers, 2 golf courses, running courses, playground, performing arts center. **Activities:** Fishing, swimming, hiking, tennis, golf, bicycling, cross-country skiing, ice hockey, ice skating, recreation and cultural programs. **Special Features:** A National Historic Landmark, the park's many features include classical architecture, sloped lawns, covered arcades, shady streamside trails, and world-renowned mineral waters. The park is also noted for the Saratoga Performing Arts Center and the Spa Little Theater.

★3551★ SCHODACK ISLAND STATE PARK

1 Schodack Way
PO Box 7
Schodack Landing, NY 12156
Web: www.nysparks.com/parks/info.asp?parkId=87
Phone: 518-732-0187
Size: 1,052 acres. **Location:** Off Route 9J, south of Castleton-on-Hudson. **Facilities:** Picnic area (&), boat launch (&), multi-use trails (8 miles), interpretive signs, playfields. **Activities:** Hiking, bicycling, fishing, bird watching, cross-country skiing, snowshoeing, ice skating. **Special Features:** Nearly seven miles of Hudson River and Schodack Creek shoreline bound the park. A portion of the park is a designated Bird Conservation Area, home to bald eagles, cerulean warblers, and blue herons.

★3552★ SCHOHARIE CROSSING STATE HISTORIC SITE

PO Box 140
129 Schoharie St
Fort Hunter, NY 12069
Web: www.nysparks.com/sites/info.asp?siteID=33
Phone: 518-829-7516; **Fax:** 518-829-7491
Size: 240 acres. **Location:** Route 5S to Fort Hunter, then Main Street to Railroad Street. **Facilities:** Picnic area (&), visitor center, gift shop (&), hiking trails, bike trails, bridle trails, scenic view (&), interpretive displays. **Activities:** Guided and self-guided tours, hiking, bicycling, horseback riding, cross-country skiing, educational programs. **Special Features:** Site is dedicated to the preservation and interpretation of the Erie Canal as one of the 19th century's greatest commercial and engineering projects. Visitors can see structures dating from the three eras of the canal's development and walk along the original Erie Canal and the Enlarged Erie Canal.

★3553★ SCHUYLER MANSION STATE HISTORIC SITE

32 Catherine St
Albany, NY 12202
Web: nysparks.state.ny.us/sites/info.asp?siteID=27
Phone: 518-434-0834; **Fax:** 518-434-3821
Size: 3 acres. **Location:** On Catherine Street in Albany. **Facilities:** Historic house, visitor center (&), gift shop (&). **Activities:** Guided tours, educational programs. **Special Features:** Visitors can tour the hillside home of Philip Schuyler, the noted Revolutionary War general. Alexander Hamilton married one of Schuyler's daughters in this mansion.

★3554★ SELKIRK SHORES STATE PARK

7101 State Rt 3
Pulaski, NY 13142
Web: www.nysparks.com/parks/info.asp?parkId=24
Phone: 315-298-5737
Size: 980 acres. **Location:** Off Route 3, 3 miles west of Pulaski. **Facilities:** Tent and trailer campsites (&), showers (&), cabins (&), picnic area (&), picnic pavilions(&), food, multi-use trails, beach, boat launch, playground. **Activities:** Camping, boating, fishing, swimming, hiking, bicycling, cross-country skiing, snowmobiling, recreation programs. **Special Features:** Campground is located on a bluff above Lake Ontario, where visitors are often treated to picturesque sunsets.

★3555★ SENATE HOUSE STATE HISTORIC SITE

296 Fair St
Kingston, NY 12401
Web: www.nysparks.com/sites/info.asp?siteID=28
Phone: 845-338-2786; **Fax:** 845-334-8173
Size: 3 acres. **Location:** On Fair Street in Kingston. **Facilities:** Picnic area (&), historic home and gardens, visitor center/museum (&). **Activities:** Guided tours, re-enactments, educational programs. **Special Features:** Meeting place of New York's first senate in 1777. Among its treasures are major art works by John Vanderlyn and other members of the Vanderlyn family of Kingston, dating from the 1720s through the 1870s, and notable paintings by Ammi Phillips, Joseph Tubby, James Bard, and Thomas Sully.

★3556★ SENECA LAKE STATE PARK

1 Lakefront Dr
Geneva, NY 14456
Web: www.nysparks.com/parks/info.asp?parkId=97
Phone: 315-789-2331
Size: 141 acres. **Location:** Off Routes 5 and 20, 1 mile east of Geneva. **Facilities:** Picnic area, picnic pavilions (&), beach, showers (&), boat launch, 2 marinas with dockage (132 electric slips; 84 nonelectric slips), playfields, playground, trails. **Activities:** Boating, fishing, ice fishing, swimming, bicycling, hiking, cross-country skiing. **Special Features:** Park offers a ''sprayground'' with more than 100 water jets spontaneously spraying water for children.

★3557★ SHADMOOR STATE PARK

c/o Montauk Downs State Park
50 S Fairview Ave
Montauk, NY 11954
Web: www.nysparks.com/parks/info.asp?parkId=83
Phone: 631-668-3781
Size: 66 acres. **Location:** 1/2 mile east of Montauk Village at the corner of Route 27 and Seaside Ave. **Facilities:** Beach, trails. **Activities:** Hiking, biking, fishing, swimming. **Special Features:** Park has more than 2,400 feet of ocean beach accessed by two stairways. On site are two concrete bunkers, erected during World War II, that once housed artillery guns positioned to protect the coast from enemy invasion.

★3558★ SILVER LAKE STATE PARK

c/o Letchworth State Park
Castile, NY 14427
Web: www.nysparks.com/parks/info.asp?parkId=14
Phone: 585-493-3600
Size: 776 acres. **Location:** Off West Lake Road in Silver Springs. **Facilities:** Picnic area, trails, boat launch, scenic views. **Activities:** Boating, fishing, ice fishing, hunting (with restrictions), hiking, cross-country skiing, snowmobiling. **Special Features:** Park provides a boat launch facility, picnic facilities, and a comfort station.

★3559★ SONNENBERG GARDENS & MANSION
         STATE HISTORIC PARK

151 Charlotte St
Canandaigua, NY 14424
Web: www.nysparks.com/sites/info.asp?siteID=37
Phone: 585-394-4922
Size: 50 acres. **Location:** Off I-90 in Canandaigua. **Facilities:** Historic site, gardens, gift shop, interpretive displays, picnic area, bridle path, scenic view. **Activities:** Guided and self-guided tours, group tours, horseback riding. **Special Features:** New York's newest state historic park, site is one of the country's most extensively preserved country estates from the Victorian era. The Queen Anne-style mansion was built in 1887. The gardens were developed between 1902 and 1920 and reflect a variety of styles. Park is also home to the Finger Lakes Wine Center.

★3560★ SOUTHWICK BEACH STATE PARK

8119 Southwicks Pl
Woodville, NY 13650
Web: www.nysparks.com/parks/info.asp?parkId=154
Phone: 315-846-5338
Size: 464 acres. **Location:** Off Route 3, southwest of Watertown. **Facilities:** Tent and trailer campsites, showers (&), picnic area (&), food, multi-use trails, beach, playground, playfields. **Activities:** Camping, fishing, swimming, hiking, cross-country skiing, snowshoeing, recreation programs. **Special Features:** Park is located on Lake Ontario shore adjacent to the Lakeview Wildlife Management Area, an environmentally sensitive coastal sand dunes habitat.

★3561★ STAATSBURGH STATE HISTORIC SITE

Old Post Rd
PO Box 308
Staatsburg, NY 12580
Web: www.nysparks.com/sites/info.asp?siteID=2
Phone: 845-889-8851; **Fax:** 845-889-8321
Size: 1 acre. **Location:** Off NYS Route 9, midway between Hyde Park and Rhinebeck. **Facilities:** Picnic area (&), historic house, interpretive displays (&), scenic view, gift shop (&), hiking trail, bike trail. **Activities:** Guided tours, hiking, bicycling, cross-country skiing, educational programs. **Special Features:** Site is the country home of Ogden Mills and his wife, Ruth Livingston Mills. Mills Mansion is an elegant example of the great estates built by America's financial and industrial leaders during the Gilded Age. At its completion in 1896, the

mansion contained 65 rooms and 14 bathrooms, and its interior was lavishly decorated in the styles of 17th- and 18th-century France. The house has been restored to its original appearance.

★3562★ STATE PARK AT THE FAIR

581 State Fair Blvd
Syracuse, NY 13209
Web: nysparks.state.ny.us/parks/info.asp?parkId=174
Size: 0.7 acres. **Location:** Empire Expo Center (home of the state fair) is immediately adjacent to Route 690 just west of Syracuse. **Facilities:** Visitor center, gift shop, picnic tables, mini-golf course. **Activities:** Interpretive and recreational programs. **Special Features:** Park is the smallest within New York's state park system and is dedicated to providing information about the recreational and other opportunities available at the state's parks and historic sites.

★3563★ STERLING FOREST STATE PARK

116 Old Forge Rd
Tuxedo, NY 10987
Web: www.nysparks.com/parks/info.asp?parkId=81
Phone: 845-351-5907
Size: 18,215 acres. **Location:** On Route 17 just south of Route 17A in Tuxedo. **Facilities:** Visitor center, boat launch, bike trail, hiking trail, gift shop, museum/visitor center (&), scenic views. **Activities:** Hiking, fishing, hunting (with restrictions), biking, boating, ice fishing, snowshoeing, recreation programs. **Special Features:** Park is a nearly pristine natural refuge in the midst of one of the nation's most densely populated areas. The park's deep forest provides habitat for the black bear and rare species of invertebrates and plants, as well as a variety of hawks and songbirds.

★3564★ STEUBEN MEMORIAL STATE HISTORIC SITE

c/o Oriskany Battlefield SHS
7801 State Rt 69
Oriskany, NY 13424
Web: www.nysparks.com/sites/info.asp?siteID=6
Phone: 315-831-3737; **Fax:** 315-337-3081
Size: 64 acres. **Location:** Off Star Hill Road, 2.5 miles west of Routes 12 and 28, in Remsen. **Facilities:** Historic site, picnic area (&), scenic view (&), gift shop. **Activities:** Guided tours, reenactments, educational programs. **Special Features:** Site honors Baron Frederick William von Steuben, known as the "Drillmaster of the American Revolution," whose wartime services are recognized by some authorities as being second only to those of George Washington. A plain, large monument marks his grave.

★3565★ STONY BROOK STATE PARK

10820 Rt 36 S
Dansville, NY 14437
Web: www.nysparks.com/parks/info.asp?parkId=102
Phone: 585-335-8111
Size: 568 acres. **Location:** Off Route 36, 3 miles south of Dansville. **Facilities:** 125 tent and trailer campsites, showers, picnic area (&), picnic pavilions, food, multi-use trails, nature trail, beach, playground, tennis courts. **Activities:** Camping, swimming, hiking, tennis, cross-country skiing, bow hunting for deer in season, recreation programs. **Special Features:** Park's terrain comprises hilly woodlands, a deep gorge with rugged cliffs overlooking three waterfalls, and rock formations.

★3566★ STONY POINT BATTLEFIELD STATE HISTORIC SITE

PO Box 182
Stony Point, NY 10980
Web: nysparks.state.ny.us/sites/info.asp?siteID=29
Phone: 845-786-2521
Size: 87 acres. **Location:** Off Route 9W, 2.5 miles north of Stony Point. **Facilities:** Picnic area, visitor center, scenic view. **Activities:** Group tours, costumed interpreters, demonstrations, educational programs. **Special Features:** Site of American light infantry's daring midnight raid against this British post. Lighthouse is the oldest of 8 lighthouses that remain standing along the Hudson River. Visitors can enter the restored lighthouse for a panoramic view of the Hudson Valley.

★3567★ STORM KING STATE PARK

c/o Palisades Interstate Park Commission
Bear Mountain, NY 10911
Web: www.nysparks.com/parks/info.asp?parkId=65
Phone: 845-786-2701
Size: 1,971 acres. **Location:** Off Route 9W, south of Cornwall. **Facilities:** Undeveloped. **Activities:** Hiking, hunting (with restrictions). **Special Features:** Undisturbed green space with scenic views of the Catskills and Hudson Valley.

★3568★ TACONIC STATE PARK - COPAKE FALLS AREA

Rt 344
PO Box 100
Copake Falls, NY 12517
Web: www.nysparks.com/parks/info.asp?parkId=137
Phone: 518-329-3993
Size: 3,408 acres (Copake Falls Area); 6,054 acres (entire park). **Location:** East of Route 22 in Copake Falls. **Facilities:** 46 tent campsites, 24 tent platform sites, 36 trailer campsites, 3 cabin areas (&), showers, picnic area, hiking trails, ski and snowmobile trails (10 miles), beach, playground, museum, visitor center, recreation programs. **Activities:** Camping, hunting (with restrictions), fishing, swimming, hiking, bicycling, cross-country skiing, snowmobiling, snowshoeing, recreation and nature programs. **Special Features:** Park includes trails leading to Bash Bish Falls, just over the Massachusetts border, and Brace Mountain, the highest point in the county. Iron Works Museum features exhibits about the iron industry at the former site of Copake Iron Works, established in 1845.

★3569★ TACONIC STATE PARK - RUDD POND AREA

59 Rudd Pond Dr
Millerton, NY 12546
Web: www.nysparks.com/parks/info.asp?parkId=132
Phone: 518-789-3059

Size: 2,646 acres (Rudd Pond Area); 6,054 acres (entire park). **Location:** Off Route 22, 2 miles north of Millerton. **Facilities:** 15 tent and 26 tent platform campsites, showers, picnic area, hiking trail, beach, boat launch, boat rentals, playground. **Activities:** Camping, hunting (with restrictions), boating (no power boats), fishing, ice fishing, swimming, hiking, bicycling, ice skating. **Special Features:** Taconic Park is located along 11 miles of the Taconic Mountain Range, sharing a border with Massachusetts and Connecticut. Rudd Pond is one of the park's two developed areas (see also Taconic State Park — Copake Falls).

★3570★ **TALLMAN MOUNTAIN STATE PARK**
c/o Palisades Interstate Park Commission
Bear Mountain, NY 10911
Web: www.nysparks.com/parks/info.asp?parkId=66
Phone: 845-359-0544
Size: 687 acres. **Location:** Off Route 9W, 18 miles north of New York City. **Facilities:** Picnic area (&), hiking trails, bike trails, swimming pool (&), running track, playground, play fields, tennis courts, showers, scenic views. **Activities:** Fishing, swimming, hiking, bicycling, tennis, cross-country skiing. **Special Features:** Park is located on the eastern slope of the Palisades uplands, overlooking the Hudson River and Piermont Marsh. The ecologically significant marsh is part of the Hudson River National Estuarine Research Reserve.

★3571★ **TAUGHANNOCK FALLS STATE PARK**
2221 Taughannock Rd
Trumansburg, NY 14886
Web: www.nysparks.com/parks/info.asp?parkId=93
Phone: 607-387-6739
Size: 746 acres. **Location:** Off Route 89, 8 miles north of Ithaca. **Facilities:** Tent and trailer campsites (&), showers (&), cabins (&), picnic area (&), picnic pavilions (&), food, multi-use trails, nature trail, beach (&), boat launch, marina with anchorage, playfields, playground, scenic view. **Activities:** Camping, boating, fishing, swimming, hiking, cross-country skiing, ice skating, sledding, snowshoeing, bow hunting for deer (in season), recreation and nature programs. **Special Features:** At 215 feet, Taughannock Falls is one of the highest waterfalls in the eastern United States. Trails along the gorge and rim offer scenic views from above and below the falls.

★3572★ **THOMPSON'S LAKE STATE PARK**
68 Thompson's Lake Rd
East Berne, NY 12059
Web: www.nysparks.com/parks/info.asp?parkId=128
Phone: 518-872-1674; **Fax:** 518-872-9133
Size: 308 acres. **Location:** Off Route 157, 18 miles southwest of Albany. **Facilities:** 140 tent and trailer campsites, showers (&), picnic area (&), nature trail, ski trails, beach, hand launch boat ramp, boat rentals, volleyball court, playfield, playground, nature center. **Activities:** Camping, fishing, boating, swimming, hiking, cross-country skiing, ice fishing, snowshoeing, recreation and nature programs. **Special Features:** Park's natural features include a sandy beach, mixed hardwood and conifer forests, limestone outcroppings, and open fields.

★3573★ **TRAIL VIEW STATE PARK**
25 Lloyd Harbor Rd
Huntinton, NY 11743
Web: www.nysparks.com/parks/info.asp?parkId=90
Phone: 631-423-1770
Size: 7.4 mile linear park (454 acres). **Location:** Along the Nassau/Suffolk Greenbelt Trail, from Cold Spring Harbor State Park to the south shore of Nassau County. **Facilities:** Trails. **Activities:** Biking and hiking; horseback riding and cross-country skiing on a limited basis. **Special Features:** Park encompasses a variety of habitats and natural resources, including hardwood forests, marshes, and succession fields with elevations ranging from 60 to 300 feet. It lies along the Atlantic flyway, making it a favorite among birdwatchers, especially during spring and fall migrations.

★3574★ **VALLEY STREAM STATE PARK**
PO Box 670
Valley Stream, NY 11580
Web: www.nysparks.com/parks/info.asp?parkId=51
Phone: 516-825-4128
Size: 97 acres. **Location:** Off Southern State Parkway in Valley Stream. **Facilities:** Picnic area (&), picnic pavilions (&), nature trails, fitness trail, bike path, playfields, playground. **Activities:** Fishing, hiking, bicycling, cross-country skiing, volleyball, basketball, bocce ball, recreation programs. **Special Features:** Park features nature trails designed to give children the opportunity to explore the various habitats within the park.

★3575★ **VERONA BEACH STATE PARK**
PO Box 245
Verona Beach, NY 13162
Web: www.nysparks.com/parks/info.asp?parkId=26
Phone: 315-762-4463
Size: 1,735 acres. **Location:** Off Route 13, 7 miles northwest of Oneida. **Facilities:** Tent and trailer campsites, showers (&), picnic area (&), picnic pavilions (&), food, bridle trail, bike trail, hiking trail, nature trails, beach, playground. **Activities:** Camping, hunting (with restrictions), fishing, ice fishing, swimming, hiking, bicycling, horseback riding, cross-country skiing, snowmobiling, ice fishing. **Special Features:** Park is located on the eastern shore of Oneida Lake, and the lake, Black Creek, cattail marshes, and bottomland hardwood swamps give Verona Beach some of the most diverse aquatic habitats in the region.

★3576★ **WALT WHITMAN BIRTHPLACE STATE HISTORIC SITE**
246 Old Walt Whitman Rd
Huntington Station, NY 11746
Web: www.nysparks.com/sites/info.asp?siteID=30
Phone: 631-427-5240; **Fax:** 631-427-5247
Size: 1 acre. **Location:** Old Walt Whitman Road, off Route 110 in South Huntington. **Facilities:** Picnic area (&), historic house (&), visitor center, gift shop (&), hiking trail. **Activities:** Guided tours, educational programs, hiking. **Special Features:** The Long Island farmhouse where poet Walt Whitman was born was built by his father around 1819 and is now fully restored.

9. State Parks

Site houses historic 19th century furniture, including a schoolmaster's desk; the interpretive center at the site includes portraits, original letters, manuscripts, and artifacts.

★3577★ WASHINGTON'S HEADQUARTERS STATE HISTORIC SITE

PO Box 1783
Newburgh, NY 12551
Web: nysparks.state.ny.us/sites/info.asp?siteID=32
Phone: 845-562-1195
Size: 8.4 acres. **Location:** Corner of Liberty and Washington Streets in Newburgh. **Facilities:** Picnic area (&), historic house, museum (&), scenic views. **Activities:** Guided tours, educational programs. **Special Features:** Site is the farmhouse used by General George Washington as Continental Army headquarters and residence from April of 1782 until August of 1783. It is located about 12 miles north of the forts at West Point.

★3578★ WATERSON POINT STATE PARK

c/o Wellesley Island State Park
44927 Cross Island Rd
Fineview, NY 13640
Web: nysparks.state.ny.us/parks/info.asp?parkId=147
Phone: 315-482-2722
Size: 6 acres. **Location:** On Wellesley Island; access by boat only. **Facilities:** Picnic area, picnic shelters, boat docks. **Activities:** Boating, fishing. **Special Features:** Park is small and picturesque, with a century-old picnic gazebo.

★3579★ WATKINS GLEN STATE PARK

PO Box 304
Watkins Glen, NY 14891
Web: www.nysparks.com/parks/info.asp?parkId=105
Phone: 607-535-4511
Size: 776 acres. **Location:** In Watkins Glen, off Route 14. **Facilities:** Tent and trailer campsites, showers, picnic area (&), picnic pavilions, food, hiking trails, swimming pool (&), bathhouse, playground, gift shop. **Activities:** Camping, hunting, fishing, swimming, hiking, bicycling, cross-country skiing, recreation and nature programs, gorge tours. **Special Features:** The most famous of the Finger Lakes state parks, Watkins Glen is known for its scenic beauty. In the course of just two miles, the glen's stream descends 400 feet past 200-foot cliffs, generating 19 waterfalls along its way. The gorge trail winds under and behind waterfalls and through the spray of Cavern Cascade.

★3580★ WELLESLEY ISLAND STATE PARK

44927 Cross Island Rd
Fineview, NY 13640
Web: www.nysparks.com/parks/info.asp?parkId=164
Phone: 315-482-2722
Size: 2,636 acres. **Location:** Off Route 81 (Exit 51), 4 miles west of Alexandria Bay. **Facilities:** Tent and trailer campsites (&), group camp, cabins, cottages, showers, picnic area (&), pavilion, food, hiking trails, bike trail, nature trail (&), beach, boat launches, boat rentals, marina with dockage, 9-hole golf course, nature center, store, butterfly house, playground, playfield. **Activities:** Camping, hunting, boating, fishing, ice fishing, swimming, hiking, bicycling, cross-country skiing, snowmobiling, golf, recreation and nature programs. **Special Features:** Park features varied habitats including wooded wetlands, 3 miles of shoreline, and granite outcrops. The Minna Anthony Common Nature Center is an outdoor education center offering year-round exhibits, workshops, and special events.

★3581★ WESTCOTT BEACH STATE PARK

PO Box 339
Sackets Harbor, NY 13685
Web: www.nysparks.com/parks/info.asp?parkId=161
Phone: 315-646-2239
Size: 319 acres. **Location:** Off Route 3, 3 miles west of Sackets Harbor. **Facilities:** Tent and trailer campsites, showers, group camp (&), picnic area (&), picnic pavilions, food, multi-use trails, beach, bathhouse, marina with dockage, boat launch, playground (&), playfield. **Activities:** Camping, hunting (with restrictions), boating, fishing, swimming, hiking, cross-country skiing, snowshoeing, recreation programs. **Special Features:** Park is located on Lake Ontario in Henderson Bay. A small marina is adjacent to the beach to accommodate anglers interested in the lake's black bass fishing.

★3582★ WHETSTONE GULF STATE PARK

RD 2 Box 69
Lowville, NY 13367
Web: www.nysparks.com/parks/info.asp?parkId=42
Phone: 315-376-6630
Size: 2,100 acres. **Location:** Off Route 26, 6 miles south of Lowville. **Facilities:** 56 campsites (&; some with electrical hookups), showers (&), picnic area, picnic pavilions (&), multi-use trails, beach with bathhouse, boat launch, playground. **Activities:** Camping, hunting, fishing, swimming, hiking, canoeing, cross-country skiing, snowmobiling, snowshoeing. **Special Features:** Park is built in and around a three-mile-long gorge cut in the eastern edge of the Tug Hill Plateau. The gorge is one of the most spectacular scenic vistas east of the Rocky Mountains. Above the gorge is Whetstone Reservoir, stocked with tiger muskie and largemouth bass.

★3583★ WHIRLPOOL STATE PARK

c/o Niagara Frontier Region
PO Box 1132
Niagara Falls, NY 14303
Web: www.nysparks.com/parks/info.asp?parkId=29
Phone: 716-284-4691
Size: 109 acres. **Location:** Via Robert Moses Parkway, 2 miles northwest of Niagara Falls. **Facilities:** Picnic area, picnic pavilions (&), hiking trails, bike trails, playground. **Activities:** Fishing, hiking, bicycling, cross-country skiing, recreation programs. **Special Features:** The park's upper (street) level features many overlooks with spectacular views of the swirling rapids, the whirlpool, and the Niagara River Escarpment. The lower (river) level is accessible by hiking 300 feet down into the gorge. This level features nature trails and fishing access.

★3584★ WILDWOOD STATE PARK
PO Box 518
N Wading River Rd
Wading River, NY 11792
Web: www.nysparks.com/parks/info.asp?parkId=52
Phone: 631-929-4314
Size: 767 acres. **Location:** Off Route 46 in Wading River.
Facilities: Tent and trailer campsites, showers, picnic area, food, multi-use trails, beach, playfields, playground. **Activities:** Camping, fishing, swimming, hiking, bicycling, cross-country skiing, recreation programs. **Special Features:** Park features undeveloped hardwood forest that terminates on a high bluff overlooking Long Island Sound.

★3585★ WILSON-TUSCARORA STATE PARK
PO Box 324
3371 Lake Rd
Wilson, NY 14172
Web: www.nysparks.com/parks/info.asp?parkId=31
Phone: 716-751-6361
Size: 425 acres. **Location:** Off Route 18, 1 mile west of Wilson.
Facilities: Picnic area, picnic pavilions, food, multi-use trails, marina, boat launch, beach, bathhouse, playground. **Activities:** Boating (no power boats), fishing, hunting (with restrictions), hiking, cross-country skiing, snowmobiling, snowshoeing. **Special Features:** Park consists of mature woods, open meadows, and marshland, and provides scenic views of Lake Ontario and Tuscalora Bay.

★3586★ WOODLAWN BEACH STATE PARK
S 3585 Lake Shore Rd
Blasdell, NY 14219
Web: www.nysparks.com/parks/info.asp?parkId=47
Phone: 716-826-1930; **Fax:** 716-827-0293
Size: 107 acres. **Location:** Off Route 5 in Hamburg, south of Buffalo. **Facilities:** Beach, trails, food, playground. **Activities:** Swimming, windsurfing, hiking, recreation programs. **Special Features:** Park features a natural sand beach nearly a mile long and panoramic views of Lake Erie.

9. State Parks

North Carolina State Parks

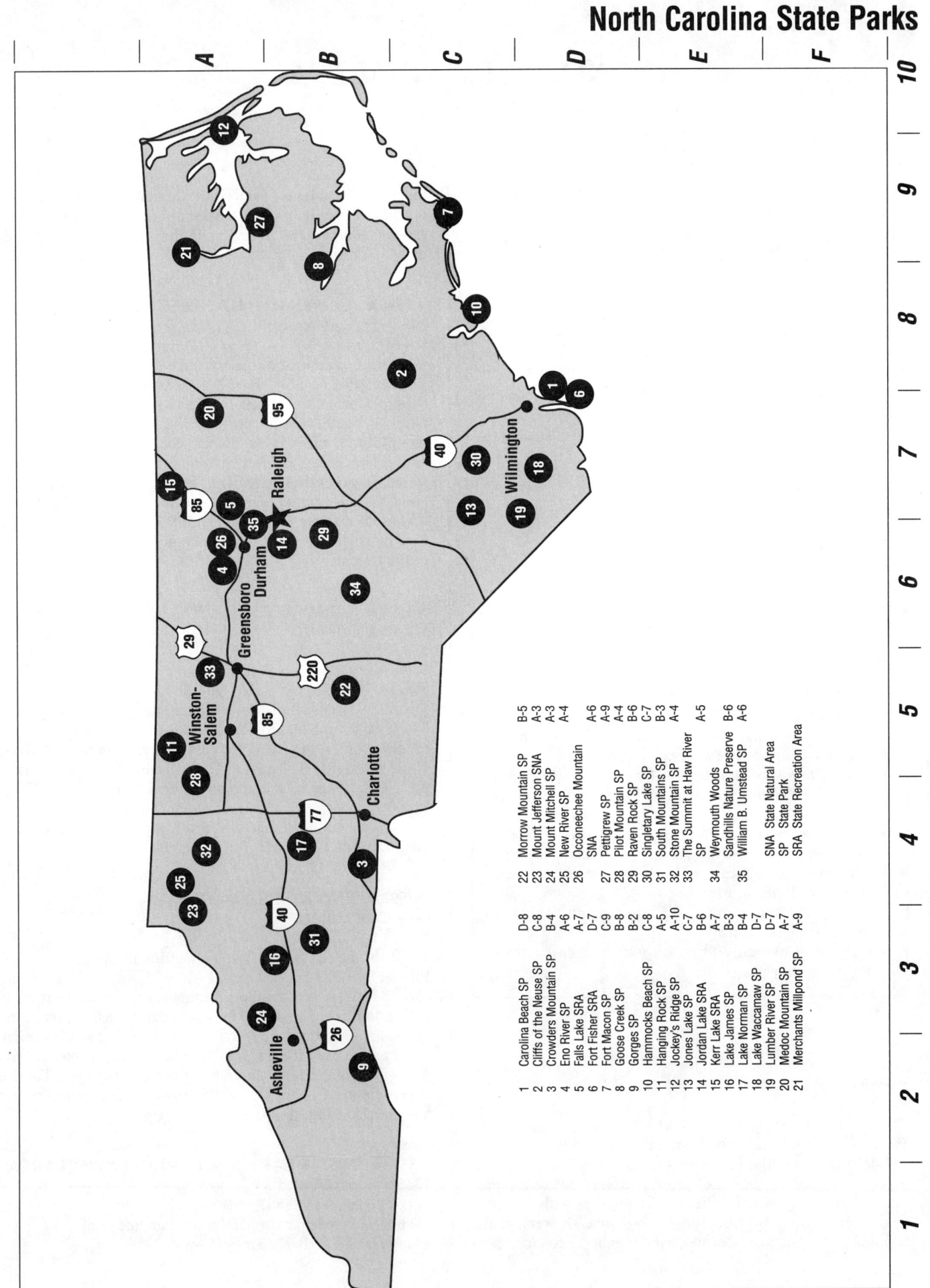

1	Carolina Beach SP	D-8	
2	Cliffs of the Neuse SP	C-8	
3	Crowders Mountain SP	B-4	
4	Eno River SP	A-6	
5	Falls Lake SRA	A-7	
6	Fort Fisher SRA	D-7	
7	Fort Macon SP	C-9	
8	Goose Creek SP	B-8	
9	Gorges SP	B-2	
10	Hammocks Beach SP	C-8	
11	Hanging Rock SP	A-5	
12	Jockey's Ridge SP	A-10	
13	Jones Lake SP	C-7	
14	Jordan Lake SRA	B-6	
15	Kerr Lake SRA	A-7	
16	Lake James SP	B-3	
17	Lake Norman SP	B-4	
18	Lake Waccamaw SP	D-7	
19	Lumber River SP	D-7	
20	Medoc Mountain SP	A-7	
21	Merchants Millpond SP	A-9	
22	Morrow Mountain SP	B-5	
23	Mount Jefferson SNA	A-3	
24	Mount Mitchell SP	A-4	
25	New River SP	A-6	
26	Occoneechee Mountain SNA	A-9	
27	Pettigrew SP	A-4	
28	Pilot Mountain SP	B-6	
29	Raven Rock SP	C-7	
30	Singletary Lake SP	B-3	
31	South Mountains SP	A-4	
32	Stone Mountain SP	A-5	
33	The Summit at Haw River SP	
34	Weymouth Woods	A-5	
35	William B. Umstead SP	A-6	

SNA State Natural Area
SP State Park
SRA State Recreation Area

NORTH CAROLINA

★3587★ North Carolina Division of Parks & Recreation
1615 Mail Service Center
Raleigh, NC 27699
(919) 733-4181 - Phone
(919) 733-4181 - Employment
Web: www.ncsparks.net
Administers the state's system of 33 parks and recreation areas, plus numerous natural sites, trails, lakes, and rivers totaling more than 160,000 acres. Oversees development of the Mountains-to-Sea Trail, which, when finished, will extend more than 900 miles, from Great Smoky Mountains National Park to the Outer Banks.

★3588★ North Carolina Wildlife Resources Commission
1751 Varsity Dr
Raleigh, NC 27606
(919) 707-0010
Web: www.ncwildlife.org
Manages land for game hunting. Supports habitat preservation for non-game animals, migratory birds, and endangered species. Enforces hunting, fishing, trapping regulations, issues licenses and boat registrations, and sponsors public education campaigns.

Key to campsite classification:

- **Campsites with hookups** — Drive-to site with electrical and water hookups, picnic table, grill. Water, restrooms, and shower facilities located nearby.
- **Campsite without hookups** — Drive-to site with picnic table, grill. Water, restrooms, and shower facilities located nearby.
- **Primitive (backpack and canoe) campsites** — Walk-to site with pit privies and fresh water available nearby.
- **Improved group camps** — Water, restrooms, and shower facilities nearby.
- **Primitive group camps** — Walk-to site with pit privies. Water available nearby.
- **Cabins** — Modestly furnished with kitchen facilities for up to six persons.

★3589★ CAROLINA BEACH STATE PARK
PO Box 475
Carolina Beach, NC 28428
Web: ils.unc.edu/parkproject/visit/cabe/home.html
Phone: 910-458-8206; **Fax:** 910-458-6350
Size: 420 acres (land area). **Location:** 10 miles south of Wilmington off Highway 421. **Facilities:** 83 campsites without hookups, 2 primitive group campsites, picnic area, showers, trails, boat ramp, marina, visitor center, exhibit hall, concession stand (open during summer). **Activities:** Camping, boating, river fishing, hiking, nature programs. **Special Features:** Coastal ecosystem includes Venus' flytrap and other species of insect-eating plants.

★3590★ CLIFFS OF THE NEUSE STATE PARK
345-A Park Entrance Rd
Seven Springs, NC 28578
Web: ils.unc.edu/parkproject/visit/clne/home.html
Phone: 919-778-6234; **Fax:** 919-778-7447
Size: 890 acres. **Location:** 14 miles southeast of Goldsboro off NC 111. **Facilities:** 35 campsites without hookups, 4 primitive group camps, picnic area, picnic shelter, trails, showers, bathhouse, boat rental, exhibit hall, concession stand (open during summer). **Activities:** Camping, boating, river fishing, swimming, hiking, nature programs. **Special Features:** Multicolored cliffs tower above the west bank of the historic Neuse River. Park includes museum depicting the geology and natural history of the region.

★3591★ CROWDERS MOUNTAIN STATE PARK
522 Park Office Ln
Kings Mountain, NC 28086
Web: www.crowdersmountain.com
Phone: 704-853-5375; **Fax:** 704-853-5391
Size: 5,094 acres. **Location:** 6 miles west of Gastonia off 29/74 on State Road 1125. **Facilities:** 10 primitive campsites, 6 primitive group camps, picnic area, picnic shelters, trails, canoe rental. **Activities:** Camping, lake fishing, canoeing, hiking, horseback riding, rock climbing, nature programs. **Special Features:** Crowders Mountain, at an elevation of 1,625 feet, is a registered natural heritage area that features sheer vertical cliffs ranging from 100 to 150 feet in height.

★3592★ ENO RIVER STATE PARK
6101 Cole Mill Rd
Durham, NC 27705
Web: ils.unc.edu/parkproject/visit/enri/home.html
Phone: 919-383-1686; **Fax:** 919-382-7378
Size: 3,901 acres. **Location:** 5 miles northwest of Durham off I-85. **Facilities:** 5 primitive backpack campsites, 1 group camp, picnic area, picnic shelter, trails, boat ramp (for non-motorized boats only). **Activities:** Camping, river rafting, canoeing, river fishing, hiking, nature programs. **Special Features:** The Eno River features Class I, II, and III rapids. Five river access areas are located within the park.

★3593★ FALLS LAKE STATE RECREATION AREA
13304 Creedmoor Rd
Wake Forest, NC 27587
Web: ils.unc.edu/parkproject/visit/fala/home.html
Phone: 919-676-1027; **Fax:** 919-676-2954

Size: 5,035 acres (land area). Location: 10 miles north of Raleigh on NC 50. Facilities: 300+ campsites (many with hookups), 18 group camps, showers, picnic areas, picnic shelters, trails, boat ramps, bathhouses, marina, concession. Activities: Camping, lake fishing, swimming, boating, hiking, bicycling, nature programs. Special Features: Privately-operated marina at Rolling View offers boat slips and mooring, equipment rental, supplies, and gasoline.

★3594★ FORT FISHER STATE RECREATION AREA

1000 Loggerhead Rd
Kure Beach, NC 28449
Web: ils.unc.edu/parkproject/visit/fofi/home.html
Phone: 910-458-5798; Fax: 910-458-5799
Size: 287 acres. Location: 5 miles south of Carolina Beach off Highway 421. Facilities: Trails, beach, bathhouse, visitor center, nature exhibits, concession stand (open during summer). Activities: Surf fishing, swimming, hiking, wildlife viewing. Licensed four-wheel drive vehicles may travel on the beach in designated areas. Special Features: Located on a barrier island between Cape Fear River and the Atlantic Ocean, this park supports a variety of maritime habitats including a nesting area for loggerhead sea turtles. Property includes Fort Fisher State Historic Site and Museum.

★3595★ FORT MACON STATE PARK

PO Box 127
Atlantic Beach, NC 28512
Web: ils.unc.edu/parkproject/visit/foma/home.html
Phone: 252-726-3775; Fax: 252-726-2497
Size: 389 acres. Location: 2 miles east of Atlantic Beach on NC 58. Facilities: Picnic area, picnic shelters, trails, bathhouse, exhibit hall, concession stand (open during summer). Activities: Surf fishing, swimming, hiking, fort tour, nature programs. Special Features: The restored fort, which guarded Beaufort Harbor during the Civil War, features Civil War era artifacts and a World War II barracks. Tours are available during the summer months and by appointment.

★3596★ GOOSE CREEK STATE PARK

2190 Camp Leach Rd
Washington, NC 27889
Web: ils.unc.edu/parkproject/visit/gocr/home.html
Phone: 252-923-2191; Fax: 252-923-0052
Size: 1,669 acres. Location: 10 miles east of Washington off US 264. Facilities: 12 primitive campsites, picnic area, picnic shelters, trails, boat ramp, visitor center, exhibit hall. Activities: Camping, boating, canoeing, sailing, river fishing, swimming, windsurfing, hiking, nature programs. Special Features: Park includes two marsh and swamp observation decks along the Pamlico River. Its visitor center includes interactive wetland exhibits.

★3597★ GORGES STATE PARK

PO Box 100
Sapphire, NC 28774
Web: ils.unc.edu/parkproject/visit/gorg/home.html
Phone: 828-966-9009

Size: 7,443 acres. Location: 45 miles southwest of Asheville at the South Carolina state line. Facilities: Primitive campsites, picnic areas, trails. Activities: Backpack camping, fishing, hiking, nature study, horseback riding, mountain biking. Special Features: Park features rugged river gorges, sheer rock walls, and waterfalls, as well as one of the greatest concentrations of rare and unique plant species in the eastern United States. It is located in a temperate rain forest and receives 80+ inches of rain per year.

★3598★ HAMMOCKS BEACH STATE PARK

1572 Hammock Beach Rd
Swansboro, NC 28584
Web: ils.unc.edu/parkproject/visit/habe/home.html
Phone: 910-326-4881; Fax: 910-326-2060
Size: 1,138 acres. Location: Bear Island; 4.5 miles west of Swansboro off NC 24 on State Road 1511. Accessible only by boat; park operates passenger ferry from Memorial Day through Labor Day. Facilities: 14 primitive campsites, 3 primitive group camps, picnic area, trails, canoe trail, bathhouse, concession stand (open during summer). Activities: Camping, boating, surf fishing, canoeing, kayaking, swimming, hiking, nature programs. Special Features: Undeveloped barrier island with dunes as tall as 60 feet. Park includes 3.5 miles of ocean beach, maritime forests, salt marshes, and tidal creeks.

★3599★ HANGING ROCK STATE PARK

PO Box 278
Danbury, NC 27016
Web: ils.unc.edu/parkproject/visit/haro/home.html
Phone: 336-593-8480; Fax: 336-593-9166
Size: 7,040 acres. Location: 4 miles northwest of Danbury off State Road 8. Facilities: 73 campsites without hookups, 8 primitive group camps, 6 cabins, picnic area, picnic shelters, trails, showers, bathhouse, boat ramps, boat rental, fishing pier, concession stand, visitor center, exhibit hall. Activities: Camping, boating, lake fishing, swimming, hiking, horseback riding, rock climbing, nature programs. Special Features: Observation tower atop Moore's Knob offers panoramic views. Rock climbing is permitted at Cook's Wall and Moore's Wall, a two-mile-long series of cliffs up to 400 feet in height.

★3600★ JOCKEY'S RIDGE STATE PARK

PO Box 592
Nags Head, NC 27959
Web: ils.unc.edu/parkproject/visit/jori/home.html
Phone: 252-441-7132; Fax: 252-441-8416
Size: 426 acres. Location: Off US 158 Bypass in Nags Head. Facilities: Picnic area, picnic shelters, trails, dune vehicle rental, visitor center, exhibit hall. Activities: Swimming, hiking, hang gliding, kite flying, nature programs. Special Features: Park includes the tallest natural sand dune system in the eastern U.S., a favorite spot for hang gliding. Shifting sand prevents construction of a traditional trail, but there is a 1.5-mile route marked with 14 stations.

9. State Parks

★3601★ JONES LAKE STATE PARK

4117 NC 242 Hwy
Elizabethtown, NC 28337
Web: ils.unc.edu/parkproject/visit/jone/home.html
Phone: 910-588-4550
Size: 1,669 acres (land area). Location: 4 miles north of Eliza-bethtown on NC 242. Facilities: 20 campsites without hookups, group camp, picnic area, picnic shelter, bathhouse, showers, trails, boat ramp, canoe and pedal boat rentals. Activities: Camping, boating, lake fishing, swimming, hiking, nature programs. Special Features: Jones Lake is one of the few remaining Carolina bay lakes.

★3602★ JORDAN LAKE STATE RECREATION AREA

280 State Park Rd
Apex, NC 27523
Web: ils.unc.edu/parkproject/visit/jord/home.html
Phone: 919-362-0586; Fax: 919-362-1621
Size: 3,916 acres (land area). Location: 21 miles southwest of Raleigh, off US 64. Facilities: 1000+ campsites (including 500+ with hookups), group RV campsites, picnic areas, picnic shelters, bathhouses, beaches, trails, boat ramps, boat rental, nearby marina (privately owned). Activities: Camping, boating, fishing, swimming, hiking, nature programs. Special Features: Largest summertime home of bald eagles in the area.

★3603★ KERR LAKE STATE RECREATION AREA

6254 Satterwhite Point Rd
Henderson, NC 27537
Web: www.ils.unc.edu/parkproject/visit/kela/home.html
Phone: 252-438-7791; Fax: 252-438-7582
Size: 3,002 acres (land area). Location: 11 miles north of Henderson off US 85 to State Road 1319. Facilities: Nearly 700 family campsites (in seven recreation areas), 2 group campsites, hookups, picnic areas, picnic shelters, trails, 2 privately-operated marinas, boat ramp, concession stands. Activities: Camping, boating, lake fishing, sailing, water-skiing, hiking, nature programs. Special Features: Kerr Lake features some of the best fishing holes in North Carolina. Recreation areas include Bullocksville, County Line, Henderson Point, Hibernia, Kimball Point, Nutbush Bridge, and Satterwhite Point.

★3604★ LAKE JAMES STATE PARK

PO Box 340
Nebo, NC 28761
Web: ils.unc.edu/parkproject/visit/laja/home.html
Phone: 828-652-5047; Fax: 828-659-8911
Size: 3,605 acres. Location: 5 miles northeast of Marion on Highway 126. Facilities: 20 primitive campsites, showers, picnic area, picnic shelter, trails, boat ramps, canoe rental, concession stand. Activities: Camping, boating, canoeing, lake fishing, swimming, hiking, nature programs. Special Features: Rolling hills at the base of Linville Gorge offer scenic vistas of the Black Mountains.

★3605★ LAKE NORMAN STATE PARK

159 Inland Sea Ln
Troutman, NC 28166
Web: ils.unc.edu/parkproject/visit/lano/home.html
Phone: 704-528-6350; Fax: 704-528-5623
Size: 1,679 acres (land area). Location: 10 miles south of Statesville on State Road 1330. Facilities: 33 campsites without hookups, group camp, picnic area, picnic shelter, trails, showers, bathhouse, boat ramp, boat rental, community building, concession stand. Activities: Camping, boating, lake fishing, swimming, hiking, mountain biking, nature programs. Special Features: Park features Lake Norman, the largest manmade lake in the state, offering excellent freshwater fishing. Game fish include crappie, bluegill, yellow perch, and striped, largemouth, and white bass.

★3606★ LAKE WACCAMAW STATE PARK

1866 State Park Dr
Lake Waccamaw, NC 28450
Web: ils.unc.edu/parkproject/visit/lawa/home.html
Phone: 910-646-4748; Fax: 910-646-4915
Size: 1,756 acres (land area). Location: 38 miles west of Wilmington and 12 miles east of Whiteville, off US 74/76. Facilities: 4 primitive group camps, picnic area, trails, boat ramps (near park), visitor center, exhibit hall. Activities: Camping, boating, lake fishing, hiking, nature programs. Special Features: Covering more than 9,000 acres and 14 miles of shoreline, Lake Waccamaw is home to a number of unique fish and mollusks found nowhere else on earth.

★3607★ LUMBER RIVER STATE PARK

2819 Princess Ann Rd
Orrum, NC 28369
Web: ils.unc.edu/parkproject/visit/luri/home.html
Phone: 910-628-9844; Fax: 910-628-8172
Size: 8,201 acres. Location: 12 miles east of Fairmont, off NC 130. Facilities: 9 primitive campsites, primitive group camp, 3 canoe campsites, picnic area, picnic shelter, trails, boat ramp. Activities: Camping, fishing, boating, canoeing, hiking, wildlife viewing. Special Features: Park encompasses a 115-mile stretch of the Lumber, a registered National Wild and Scenic River. A variety of natural communities unique to blackwater streams, such as a cypress gum swamp and pine savannas, offer the visitor an exceptional opportunity to view wildlife.

★3608★ MEDOC MOUNTAIN STATE PARK

1541 Medoc State Park Rd
Hollister, NC 27844
Web: ils.unc.edu/parkproject/visit/memo/home.html
Phone: 252-586-6588
Size: 2,385 acres. Location: 21 miles southwest of Roanoke Rapids off NC 561. Facilities: 34 campsites (12 with hookups), 3 improved group camps, picnic area, picnic shelter, trail, boat ramp. Activities: Camping, canoeing, river fishing, hiking, nature programs. Special Features: Medoc Mountain is not really a mountain but a granite ridge, the remains of an ancient mountain range formed by volcanic action during the Paleozoic Age, about 350 million years ago.

9. State Parks

★3609★ MERCHANTS MILLPOND STATE PARK
71 US Hwy 158E
Gatesville, NC 27938
Web: ils.unc.edu/parkproject/visit/memi/home.html
Phone: 252-357-1191; Fax: 252-357-0149
Size: 3,296 acres. Location: 6 miles northeast of Gatesville, accessible via US 158, NC 32 and NC 37. Facilities: 20 campsites with hookups, showers, 5 primitive campsites, 3 primitive group camps, 10 canoe campsites (including 3 group camps), picnic area, picnic shelter, trails, canoe rental, concession stand. Activities: Camping, canoeing, lake fishing, hiking, wildlife viewing, nature programs. Special Features: Massive cypress and gum trees covered with Spanish moss form a canopy over the dark, acid waters of the millpond, creating an ideal habitat for beavers, otters, and other wetland wildlife.

★3610★ MORROW MOUNTAIN STATE PARK
49104 Morrow Mountain Rd
Albemarle, NC 28001
Web: ils.unc.edu/parkproject/visit/momo/home.html
Phone: 704-982-4402; Fax: 704-982-5323
Size: 4,496 acres. Location: 6 miles east of Albemarle, accessible from NC highways 24/27, 73 and 740. Facilities: 106 campsites without hookups, showers, 4 primitive campsites, 6 improved group camps, 6 cabins, picnic area, picnic shelters, trails, bathhouse, boat ramp, boat rentals, visitor center, exhibit hall, concession stand. Activities: Camping, boating, canoeing, lake fishing, swimming, hiking, horseback riding, nature programs. Special Features: Located in the Uwharrie Mountains along the Pee Dee River and Lake Tillery, the park features the historic Kron House, residence and hospital of an early 19th-century physician.

★3611★ MOUNT JEFFERSON STATE NATURAL
   AREA
PO Box 48
Jefferson, NC 28640
Web: ils.unc.edu/parkproject/visit/moje/home.html
Phone: 336-246-9653; Fax: 336-246-3386
Size: 607 acres. Location: 1.5 miles south of Jefferson on US 221. Facilities: Picnic area, picnic shelter, trails. Activities: Nature programs, hiking. Special Features: Mount Jefferson has been designated a National Natural Landmark because of its unusual plant life. This high-altitude, deciduous forest includes one of the most diverse offerings of trees, shrubs, and wildflowers in the eastern United States. Visitors can hike the 0.3-mile Summit Trail to the top of 4,684-foot Mount Jefferson.

★3612★ MOUNT MITCHELL STATE PARK
2388 State Hwy 128
Burnsville, NC 28714
Web: ils.unc.edu/parkproject/visit/momi/home.html
Phone: 828-675-4611; Fax: 828-675-9655
Size: 1,878 acres. Location: 33 miles northeast of Asheville off the Blue Ridge Parkway (mile marker 355) on NC 128. Facilities: 9 primitive campsites, picnic area, picnic shelters, restaurant, trails, concession stand, visitor center, exhibit hall. Activities: Camping, hiking, hoserback riding (along the park

perimeter), nature programs. Special Features: An observation tower located on top of the highest peak east of the Mississippi (6,684 feet) and hiking trails offer spectacular views of the Blue Ridge Mountains. Park also includes the most extensive stand of Fraser fir remaining in the country.

★3613★ NEW RIVER STATE PARK
PO Box 48
Jefferson, NC 28640
Web: ils.unc.edu/parkproject/visit/neri/home.html
Phone: 336-982-2587; Fax: 336-982-3943
Size: 1,701 acres. Location: 8 miles southeast of Jefferson, off NC 88 on State Road 1590. Facilities: 32 primitive campsites, picnic area, picnic shelter, trails, 3 canoe access ramps. Activities: Camping, canoeing, river fishing, hiking, nature programs. Special Features: Park surrounds a 26-mile stretch of the south fork of New River, one of the oldest rivers in the world and designated both as a National Wild and Scenic River and an American Heritage River. Easy paddling and spectacular scenery make the New River a natural canoe trail.

★3614★ OCCONEECHEE MOUNTAIN STATE
   NATURAL AREA
c/o Eno River State Park
6101 Cole Mill Rd
Durham, NC 27705
Web: ils.unc.edu/parkproject/visit/ocmo/home.html
Phone: 919-383-1686
Size: 96 acres. Location: Northwest of Durham off I-85 Exit 164. Facilities: Trails. Activities: Hiking, fishing, interpretive programs. Special Features: Highest point of land (867 feet) in the area. Occoneechee Mountain is recognized as one of the most important natural areas in the Triangle, with habitats that support rare and significant species.

★3615★ PETTIGREW STATE PARK
2252 Lake Shore Rd
Creswell, NC 27928
Web: ils.unc.edu/parkproject/visit/pett/home.html
Phone: 252-797-4475; Fax: 252-797-7405
Size: 3,141 acres (includes Scuppernong River). Location: 7 miles south of Creswell, off US 64. Facilities: 13 campsites without hookups, 1 primitive group camp, showers, picnic area, picnic shelters, trails, boat ramp, fishing pier, exhibit hall (&, &). Activities: Camping, sailing, canoeing, windsurfing, waterskiing, lake fishing, hiking, bicycling, cultural history programs, nature programs. Special Features: Park features North Carolina's second largest natural lake, 16,600-acre Lake Phelps, known throughout the East for its bass fishing. Park is also home to the longest Indian dugout canoe in North Carolina and the second oldest in the nation, radiocarbon dated at 4,400 years.

★3616★ PILOT MOUNTAIN STATE PARK
1792 Pilot Knob Park Rd
Pinnacle, NC 27043
Web: ils.unc.edu/parkproject/visit/pimo/home.html
Phone: 336-325-2355; Fax: 336-325-2751

9. State Parks

Size: 3,651 acres. **Location:** 24 miles north of Winston-Salem off US 52. **Facilities:** 49 campsites without hookups, showers, 1 primitive group camp, 2 canoe campsites, picnic area, picnic shelters, canoe ramps, trails. **Activities:** Camping, river fishing, canoeing, hiking, horseback riding, rock climbing, cultural history programs, nature programs. **Special Features:** Pilot Mountain's prominent Big Pinnacle, with walls of bare rock and a rounded top covered by vegetation, rises 1,400 feet above the valley floor. The 165-mile Yadkin River Canoe Trail includes a two-mile portion of the Yadkin River that flows through the park and is one of the most scenic stretches along the river's course.

★3617★ RAVEN ROCK STATE PARK

3009 Raven Rock Rd
Lillington, NC 27546
Web: ils.unc.edu/parkproject/visit/raro/home.html
Phone: 910-893-4888; **Fax:** 910-814-2200
Size: 4,677 acres. **Location:** 9 miles west of Lillington and 20 miles east of Sanford on US 421. **Facilities:** 5 primitive campsites, 5 primitive group camps, 6 canoe campsites, picnic area, trails, concession stand. **Activities:** Camping, canoeing, river fishing, hiking, horseback riding, nature programs. **Special Features:** Raven Rock is a mile-long, 150-foot-high rock outcrop, which juts out at a 45-degree angle over the Cape Fear River. A portion of the 56-mile Cape Fear Canoe Trail runs through the park.

★3618★ SINGLETARY LAKE STATE PARK

6707 NC 53 Hwy E
Kelly, NC 28448
Web: ils.unc.edu/parkproject/visit/sila/home.html
Phone: 910-669-2928; **Fax:** 910-669-2034
Size: 649 acres (land area). **Location:** 10 miles southeast of Elizabethtown on NC 53. **Facilities:** 2 improved group campsites (including cabins and mess hall with kitchen facilities), trails, pier, exhibit hall. **Activities:** Camping, fishing, swimming, boating (10 hp or less), canoeing, hiking, nature programs. **Special Features:** Encompassing all the plant communities found in Carolina bays, park provides an ideal location to study Carolina bay ecosystems. It is located within the boundaries of Bladen Lakes State Forest.

★3619★ SOUTH MOUNTAINS STATE PARK

3001 South Mountains State Park Ave
Connelly Springs, NC 28612
Web: ils.unc.edu/parkproject/visit/somo/home.html
Phone: 828-433-4772; **Fax:** 828-433-4778
Size: 17,367 acres. **Location:** 20 miles south of Morganton on State Road 1904. **Facilities:** 20 primitive campsites, 11 family campsites, 15 equestrian campsites, picnic area, picnic shelter, trails. **Activities:** Camping, river fishing, hiking, horseback riding, mountain biking, nature programs. **Special Features:** Park includes a 1.5-mile loop trail along Jacob's Fork River to High Shoals Falls, an 80-foot waterfall.

★3620★ STONE MOUNTAIN STATE PARK

3042 Frank Pkwy
Roaring Gap, NC 28668
Web: ils.unc.edu/parkproject/visit/stmo/home.html
Phone: 336-957-8185; **Fax:** 336-957-3985
Size: 14,119 acres. **Location:** 7 miles southwest of Roaring Gap (off US 21) on State Road 1002 to the John P. Frank Parkway. **Facilities:** 90 family campsites (some with hookups), 6 primitive campsites, 4 primitive group camps, showers, picnic area, picnic shelters, trails, fishing piers, visitor center, historic exhibits, concession stand. **Activities:** Camping, river fishing, hiking, horseback riding, rock climbing, cultural history programs, nature programs. **Special Features:** One of the park's most spectacular features is Stone Mountain, a 600-foot granite dome that is part of a 25-square-mile pluton, an igneous rock formed beneath the earth's surface by molten lava.

★3621★ THE SUMMIT AT HAW RIVER STATE PARK

339 Conference Center Dr
Browns Summit, NC 27214
Web: ils.unc.edu/parkproject/TheSummit/
Phone: 336-342-6163; **Fax:** 336-342-0583
Size: 303 acres. **Location:** 3 miles northwest of Brown Summit off Spearman Road. **Facilities:** Motel-style cottages, retreat cottages, cabins, dining hall, outdoor amphitheater, picnic area, trails, boardwalk, gymnasium, athletic field, swimming pool, disc golf course, floating docks, swimming area. **Activities:** Swimming, hiking, boating. **Special Features:** The Haw River Program (HARP) specializes in outdoor environmental science programs ranging from half-day teambuilding sessions to 5-day/4-night overnight stays.

★3622★ WEYMOUTH WOODS SANDHILLS NATURE PRESERVE

1024 Fort Bragg Rd
Southern Pines, NC 28387
Web: ils.unc.edu/parkproject/visit/wewo/home.html
Phone: 910-692-2167; **Fax:** 910-692-8042
Size: 900 acres. **Location:** 2 miles southeast of Southern Pines, off US 1 on State Road 2074. **Facilities:** Trails, exhibit hall. **Activities:** Nature programs, hiking, horseback riding. **Special Features:** Park's nature center museum is dedicated to the study, interpretation, and protection of the threatened longleaf pine ecosystem, home to the endangered red-cockaded woodpecker.

★3623★ WILLIAM B. UMSTEAD STATE PARK

8801 Glenwood Ave
Raleigh, NC 27612
Web: ils.unc.edu/parkproject/visit/wium/home.html
Phone: 919-571-4170; **Fax:** 919-571-4161
Size: 5,579 acres. **Location:** 10 miles west of Raleigh on US 70 or 11 miles west of Raleigh on I-40. **Facilities:** 28 campsites without hookups, showers, 2 improved group camps (including cabins and mess hall with kitchen facilities), 3 primitive group camps, picnic area, picnic shelters, trails, boat rental, visitor

center, exhibit hall. **Activities:** Camping, boating, canoeing, fishing, swimming, hiking, horseback riding, mountain biking, nature programs. **Special Features:** Located between Raleigh and Durham in the midst of high-tech Research Triangle Park, the state park encompasses Piedmont Beech Natural Area, a 50-acre tract of centuries-old trees.

North Dakota State Parks

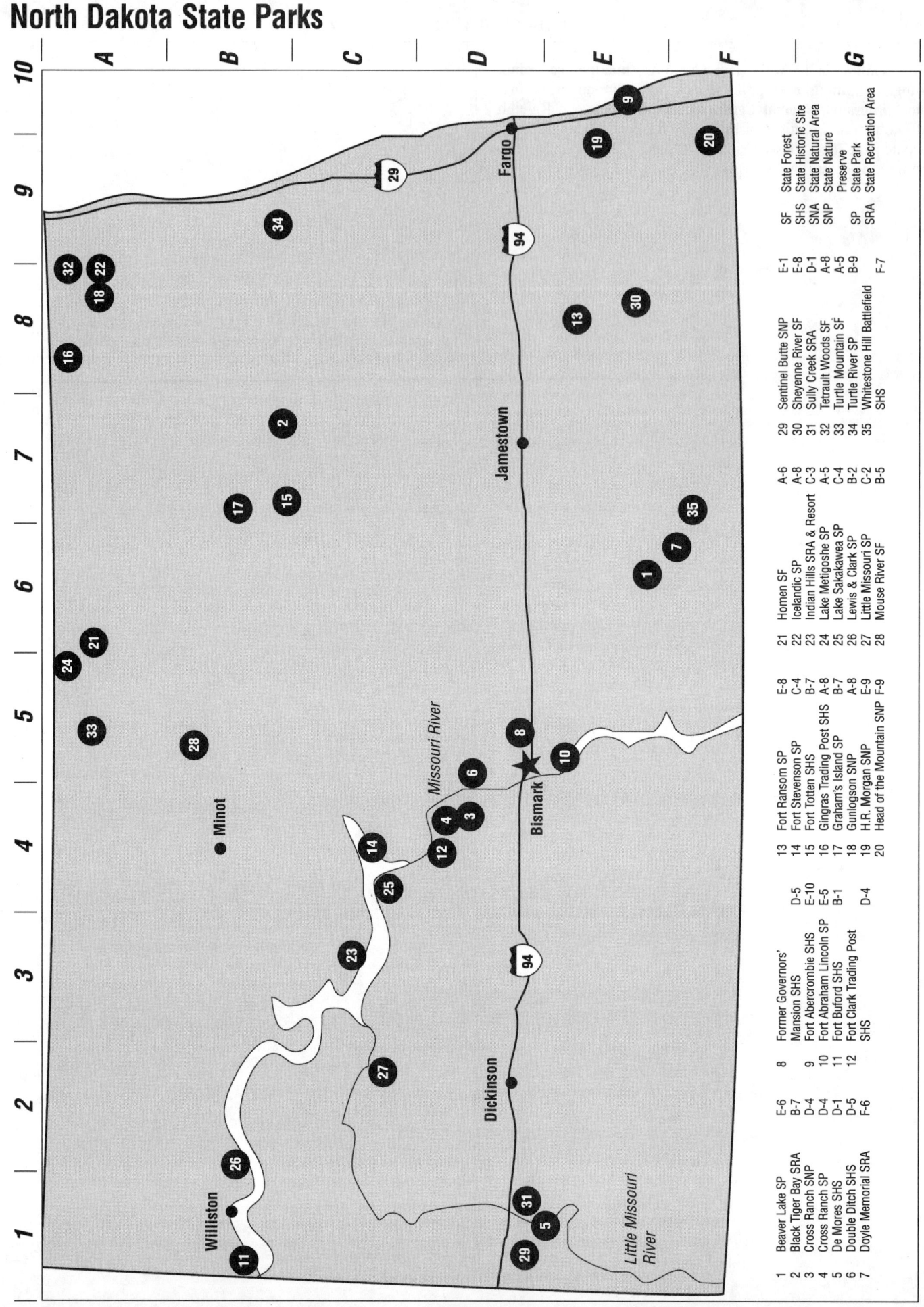

1	Beaver Lake SP	E-6	
2	Black Tiger Bay SRA	B-7	
3	Cross Ranch SNP	D-4	
4	Cross Ranch SP	D-4	
5	De Mores SHS	D-1	
6	Double Ditch SHS	D-5	
7	Doyle Memorial SRA	F-6	
8	Former Governors' Mansion SHS	D-5	
9	Fort Abercrombie SHS	E-10	
10	Fort Abraham Lincoln SP	E-5	
11	Fort Buford SHS	B-1	
12	Fort Clark Trading Post SHS	D-4	
13	Fort Ransom SP	E-8	
14	Fort Stevenson SP	C-4	
15	Fort Totten SHS	B-7	
16	Gingras Trading Post SHS	A-8	
17	Graham's Island SP	B-7	
18	Gunlogson SNP	A-8	
19	H.R. Morgan SNP	E-9	
20	Head of the Mountain SNP	F-9	
21	Homen SF	A-6	
22	Icelandic SP	A-8	
23	Indian Hills SRA & Resort	C-3	
24	Lake Metigoshe SP	A-5	
25	Lake Sakakawea SP	C-4	
26	Lewis & Clark SP	B-2	
27	Little Missouri SP	C-2	
28	Mouse River SF	B-5	
29	Sentinel Butte SNP	E-1	
30	Sheyenne River SF	E-8	
31	Sully Creek SRA	D-1	
32	Tetrault Woods SF	A-8	
33	Turtle Mountain SF	A-5	
34	Turtle River SP	B-9	
35	Whetstone Hill Battlefield SHS	F-7	

SF   State Forest
SHS   State Historic Site
SNA   State Natural Area
SNP   State Nature Preserve
SP   State Park
SRA   State Recreation Area

NORTH DAKOTA

★3624★ North Dakota Parks & Recreation Department

1600 E Century Ave, Suite 3
Bismarck, ND 58503
(701) 328-5357 - Phone
(701) 328-5363 - Fax
(800) 3666886 - TDD
(800) 807-4723 - Reservations (seasonal)
Web: www.ndparks.com
Maintains 18 parks. Most parks are open year round to provide winter recreation, including access to the department's 2,000-mile-long snowmobile trail system.

★3625★ North Dakota Forest Service

307 1st St E
Bottineau, ND 58318
(701) 228-5422 - Phone
(701) 228-5448 - Fax
Web: www.ndsu.nodak.edu/forestservice
Owns and manages approximately 13,278 acres of forest land in five designated state forests.

★3626★ North Dakota Game & Fish Department

100 N Bismarck Expy
Bismarck, ND 58501
(701) 328-6300 - Phone
(701) 328-6352 - Fax
Web: http://gf.nd.gov
Responsible for managing the state's native wildlife and fish species. Maintains state wildlife management areas, enforces state wildlife laws, and works with private landowners to preserve and recreate wildlife habitats. Administers hunting and fishing licenses.

★3627★ State Historical Society of North Dakota

North Dakota Heritage Center Bldg
612 E Boulevard Ave
Bismarck, ND 58505
(701) 328-2666 - Phone
(701) 328-3710 - Fax
Web: www.state.nd.us/hist
Preserves and protects 56 historic properties; listed in this chapter are the state's most significant sites.

Key to campsite classification:

- **Modern campsites** — Electrical and water hook-ups and modern comfort stations with flush toilets and hot showers.

- **Semi-modern campsites** — Depending on the park, site include either electrical hookups or modern comfort stations.
- **Primitive campsites** — Running water and vault toilets available nearby.

★3628★ BEAVER LAKE STATE PARK

3850 70th St SE
Wishek, ND 58495
Web: www.ndparks.com/Parks/blsp.htm
Phone: 701-452-2752
Size: 283 acres. **Location:** 17 miles southeast of Napoleon on the west shore of Beaver Lake. **Facilities:** 25 campsites with electrical hookups and showers, 2 camping cabins, picnic area, picnic shelters, boat ramp, hiking trails, swim beach, playground. **Activities:** Camping, hiking, boating, canoeing, fishing, swimming, water-skiing. **Special Features:** A stone cairn in the park commemorates the work accomplished by the Works Progress Administration (WPA) crews of the 1930s.

★3629★ BLACK TIGER BAY STATE RECREATION AREA

152 S Duncan Dr
Devils Lake, ND 58301
Web: www.ndparks.com/Parks/DLSP.htm
Phone: 701-766-4015
Location: 7 miles east of Devil's Lake (5 miles south, then 3 miles west). **Facilities:** Boat ramp, bait shop, parking, vault toilets. **Activities:** Boating, fishing. **Special Features:** Area is one of two state recreation areas on Devils Lake (see also Graham's Island State Recreation Area). Black Tiger Bay is used exclusively as a boat access area and has a parking area for boat trailers.

★3630★ CROSS RANCH STATE NATURE PRESERVE

c/o North Dakota Parks & Recreation Dept
1600 E Century Ave Suite 3
Bismarck, ND 58503
Web: www.ndparks.com/Nature/Preserves.htm
Phone: 701-328-5357
Size: 6,000 acres. **Location:** 20 miles north of Mandan, adjacent to Cross Ranch State Park (see separate entry). **Facilities:** Trails. **Activities:** Hiking, canoeing, birdwatching, wildlife viewing. **Special Features:** Located along one of the last undeveloped stretches of the Missouri River, the preserve contains the largest remaining tract of floodplain woodland on this stretch of the Missouri. Wildlife includes mule deer, white-tailed deer, badger, raccoon, and coyote, as well as bison, which were introduced

to the area in 1986. Among the many bird species found here are Baird's sparrow and Sprague's pipit, both rare. The preserve also includes more than 100 archeological sites.

★3631★ CROSS RANCH STATE PARK
1403 River Rd
Center, ND 58530
Web: www.ndparks.com/Parks/CRSP.htm
Phone: 701-794-3731; **Fax:** 701-794-3262
Size: 589 acres. **Location:** 12 miles southeast of Hensler. **Facilities:** 70 campsites (7 with electrical hookups), showers, backcountry hike-in campsites, 3 log cabins, picnic shelters, playground, hiking trails, boat ramp, canoe rentals, visitor center, amphitheater. **Activities:** Camping, boating, fishing, hiking, cross-country skiing. **Special Features:** Park is located along seven miles of the last free-flowing, undeveloped stretches of the Missouri River. The park's visitor center features exhibits and displays interpreting the once-mighty river and how man's alterations have affected it. An extensive trail system allows access to the adjacent Cross Ranch Nature Preserve (see separate entry) and its varied ecosystems.

★3632★ DE MORES STATE HISTORIC SITE
PO Box 106
Medora, ND 58645
Web: www.state.nd.us/hist/chateau/chateau.htm
Phone: 701-623-4355
Size: 128 acres. **Location:** In and near the town of Medora. **Facilities:** Visitor center, museum. **Special Features:** Site interprets the life of wealthy French aristocrat, the Marquis de Mores, who arrived in North Dakota in 1883. The historic site comprises 3 parts: The Chateau de Mores is the 26-room house the Marquis built for his wife, which is now a museum containing may of its original elegant furnishings and personal effects; Chimney Park is the site of what was once his meat-packing plant, where all that remains is its brick chimney; and de Mores Memorial Park in downtown Medora features a statue of the Marquis.

★3633★ DEVILS LAKE STATE PARKS
152 S Duncan Dr
Devil's Lake, ND 58301
Web: www.ndparks.com/Parks/DLSP.htm
Phone: 701-766-4015; **Fax:** 701-766-4311
Special Features: Devils Lake State Parks consist of two park and recreation areas in north central North Dakota on Devils Lake, the state's largest natural body of water. The two areas are Grahams Island and Black Tiger Bay (see separate entries).

★3634★ DOUBLE DITCH STATE HISTORIC SITE
c/o State Historical Society of North Dakota
612 E Boulevard Ave
Bismarck, ND 58505
Web: www.state.nd.us/hist/doubleditch/doubleditch.htm
Phone: 701-328-2666; **Fax:** 701-328-3710
Location: 7.5 miles north of Bismarck on ND Highway 1804. **Facilities:** Interpretive signs. **Special Features:** Overlooking the Missouri River, Double Ditch Indian Village was a large

earthlodge village inhabited by the Mandan people between about 1500 and 1781. The remains of earthlodges, midden mounds (trash heaps), and fortification ditches are clearly visible. The village was abandoned because of the smallpox epidemic that swept the interior of North America in 1780-81. By 1800, the Mandans had been reduced to as few as 1,200 individuals.

★3635★ DOYLE MEMORIAL STATE PARK
Wishek, ND 58495
Web: www.ndparks.com/Parks/DMSP.htm
Phone: 701-452-2351
Size: 21 acres. **Location:** 7 miles southeast of Wishek. **Facilities:** 6 modern campsites with electrical hookups, showers, picnic shelters, boat ramp, playground. **Activities:** Camping, fishing, boating. **Special Features:** This small prairie park, established in 1925, occupies a peninsula jutting into Green Lake in the rolling farmland of south central North Dakota. It is leased and operated by the city of Wishek.

★3636★ FORMER GOVERNORS' MANSION STATE HISTORIC SITE
612 E Boulevard Ave
Bismarck, ND 58505
Web: www.state.nd.us/hist/fgm/fgm.htm
Phone: 701-328-2666; **Fax:** 701-328-3710
Location: 320 East Avenue B in Bismarck. **Facilities:** Historic house. **Activities:** Video and guided tours (Wednesday-Sunday, May 16-September 15). **Special Features:** Site preserves a restored Victorian mansion that housed 21 chief executives of North Dakota between 1893 and 1960. Exhibits highlight how home furnishings and architectural styles changed through the years.

★3637★ FORT ABERCROMBIE STATE HISTORIC SITE
PO Box 148
Abercrombie, ND 58001
Web: www.state.nd.us/HIST/abercrombie/abercrombie.html
Phone: 701-553-8513
Location: .25 miles east of the town of Abercrombie, on Richland County Road 4. **Facilities:** Museum, park pavilion, recreational facilities (on the east edge of the town of Abercrombie); historic fort (further east). **Activities:** Informational markers, self-guided tours, brochures, museum exhibits and displays. **Special Features:** Fort Abercrombie was the first US military post established in what was to become North Dakota and served as the gateway to several major travel routes into the Dakota frontier from 1857 to 1878. It was also the only post in the area to be besieged by Dakota (Sioux) warriors for more than six weeks during the Dakota conflict of 1862. The fort today is an outdoor museum consisting of a reconstructed palisade, two reconstructed blockhouses, the original guardhouse, a reconstructed cannon bastion, and several "ghosted" buildings.

★3638★ FORT ABRAHAM LINCOLN STATE PARK

4480 Fort Lincoln Rd
Mandan, ND 58554
Web: www.ndparks.com/Parks/FLSP.htm
Phone: 701-667-6340; **Fax:** 701-667-6349
Size: 1,006 acres. **Location:** 7 miles south of Mandan on Highway 1806. **Facilities:** 95 modern campsites with electrical hookups, showers, sleeping cabins, picnic shelters, playground, hiking trails, historic buildings, visitor center. **Activities:** Camping, hiking, interpretive tours. **Special Features:** Rich in military and Indian history, Fort Abraham Lincoln was once an important infantry and cavalry post. It was from here that Lieutenant Colonel George Custer and the Seventh Cavalry rode out on their ill-fated expedition against the Sioux at the Little Big Horn. Portions of the military post, including the Custer House, have been reconstructed. Reconstructed earthlodges at the park's On-A-Slant Indian Village depict the lifestyle of the Mandan Indians, who occupied this site from about 1575-1781.

★3639★ FORT BUFORD STATE HISTORIC SITE

15349 39th Ln NW
Williston, ND 58801
Web: www.state.nd.us/hist/buford/buford.htm
Phone: 701-572-9034
Location: 25 miles southwest of Williston, just off Highway 23. **Facilities:** Historic fort and cemetery, museum/interpretive center, restrooms, picnic area, campground. **Activities:** Interpretive programs about the frontier military and Fort Buford's role in the history of Dakota Territory. **Special Features:** Fort Buford, built in 1866, was one of a number of military posts established to protect overland and river routes used by immigrants settling the West, but is best known as the location of Sitting Bull's surrender in 1881. Three of the fort's original buildings still stand: the stone powder magazine, wood-frame officers' quarters (in which the site's museum is located), and a wood-frame officer of the guard building.

★3640★ FORT CLARK TRADING POST STATE HISTORIC SITE

HC 2, Box 26
Center, ND 58530
Web: www.state.nd.us/HIST/ftClark/index.html
Phone: 701-794-8832
Location: 1.25 miles west of the town of Fort Clark in Mercer County. **Facilities:** Historic site, interpretive signs, picnic area, observation deck, modern restrooms. **Activities:** Self-guided tours (May 16-September 15). **Special Features:** Site protects the archeological remains of a large earthlodge village, cemetery, and two fur trade posts (Fort Clark Trading Post and Primeau's Post). Site is one of the most important archeological sites in the state because of its well-preserved record of the fur trade and because it was the scene of devastating smallpox and cholera epidemics that decimated most of the inhabitants of a Mandan and later an Arikara Indian village.

★3641★ FORT RANSOM STATE PARK

5981 Walt Hjelle Pkwy
Fort Ransom, ND 58033
Web: www.ndparks.com/Parks/FRSP.htm
Phone: 701-973-4331; **Fax:** 701-973-4151
Size: 887 acres. **Location:** 2 miles north of the town of Fort Ransom in southeastern North Dakota. **Facilities:** 30 campsites with electrical hookups, showers, picnic shelters, playground, trails, horse corrals, canoe and kayak rentals, group kitchen facilities, historic buildings, visitor center. **Activities:** Camping, canoeing, fishing, hiking, horseback riding, cross-country skiing, snowmobiling. **Special Features:** Park is located in the scenic Sheyenne River Valley on one of North Dakota's officially designated Scenic Byways and Backways. A short segment of the North Country National Scenic Trail winds through the park (see separate entry in national trails section). A farmstead within the park provides the setting for annual Sodbuster Days celebrations, with demonstrations and exhibits of early homesteading life.

★3642★ FORT STEVENSON STATE PARK

1252A 41st St NW
Garrison, ND 58540
Web: www.ndparks.com/Parks/fssp.htm
Phone: 701-337-5576; **Fax:** 701-337-5313
Size: 438 acres. **Location:** 3 miles south of Garrison. **Facilities:** 145 campsites, electrical hookups, sleeping cabins, camp store, picnic shelters, hiking trails, boat ramp, gas dock, boat and canoe rentals, arboretum, visitor center, meeting room.. **Activities:** Camping, boating, fishing, hiking. **Special Features:** Situated on the north shore of Lake Sakakawea, park is known as the walleye capital of North Dakota. Park also features a thriving prairie dog community.

★3643★ FORT TOTTEN STATE HISTORIC SITE

PO Box 224
Fort Totten, ND 58335
Web: www.state.nd.us/hist/totten/totten.htm
Phone: 701-766-4441
Location: Southeastern edge of the town of Fort Totten. **Facilities:** Visitor center, modern restrooms, 17 original buildings housing interpretive center, museum, gift shop. **Activities:** Tours (May 16-September 15; rest of year by appointment). **Special Features:** Fort was established in 1867 as a frontier military outpost to police the surrounding reservation and guard overland mail and transportation routes. The post was decommissioned in 1890 and became the property of the Bureau of Indian Affairs in 1891, serving as an Indian Boarding School until 1940. After independent tribal government was established, a community school operated in the buildings from 1940 to 1959.

★3644★ GINGRAS TRADING POST STATE HISTORIC SITE

RR 1, Box 55
Walhalla, ND 58202
Web: www.state.nd.us/HIST/gingras/index.html
Phone: 701-549-2775
Location: 1.25 miles northeast of Walhalla. **Facilities:** Restored historic buildings, interpretive panels and exhibits. **Activities:** Self-guided tours (May 16-September 15). **Special Features:** Site preserves the 1840s home and trading post of Métis legislator and prominent fur trader Antoine Blanc Gingras. (Métis, meaning ''mixed blood'' or ''mixed race,'' is a term used by

9. State Parks

people of combined Indian and European ancestry to describe themselves.) Gingras's hand-hewn oak log store and home, which have been restored to their original appearance, are among the few tangible remains of the fur trade in the Red River Valley.

★3645★ GRAHAM'S ISLAND STATE PARK

152 S Duncan Dr
Devils Lake, ND 58301
Web: www.ndparks.com/parks/DLSP.htm
Phone: 701-766-4015
Size: 1,122 acres. **Location:** 10 miles west of the town of Devil's Lake on Highway 19, then 6 miles south. **Facilities:** 107 modern campsites, electrical hookups, showers, sleeping cabins, picnic shelters, playground, group activities center, boat ramp, bait shop, hiking trails. **Activities:** Camping, boating, fishing, ice fishing, hiking, snowmobiling. **Special Features:** Park is one of two park/recreation areas that make up Devil's Lake State Parks. Grahams Island is the largest and most developed of the two sites.

★3646★ GUNLOGSON STATE NATURE PRESERVE

c/o North Dakota Parks & Recreation Dept
1600 E Century Ave Suite 3
Bismarck, ND 58503
Web: www.ndparks.com/Nature/Preserves.htm
Phone: 701-328-5357
Size: 200 acres. **Location:** 5 miles west of Cavalier on Highway 5, at Icelandic State Park. **Facilities:** Hiking and cross country ski trails (3 miles). **Activities:** Hiking, cross-country skiing, birdwatching. **Special Features:** Preserve is an island of intact habitat within an extensively modified landscape. Its significant features are its forest and wetland habitats and the plants and animals they support.

★3647★ HEAD OF THE MOUNTAIN STATE NATURE PRESERVE

c/o North Dakota Parks & Recreation Dept
1600 E Century Ave Suite 3
Bismarck, ND 58503
Web: www.ndparks.com/Nature/Preserves.htm
Phone: 701-328-5357
Size: 100 acres. **Location:** 9 miles southeast of Rutland. **Facilities:** Undeveloped. **Activities:** Hiking, cross-country skiing, birdwatching, other passive recreation. **Special Features:** Preserve is located at the edge of a steep escarpment, providing an overlook of the surrounding landscape. It contains a native prairie, ravine woodland, and an adjacent reservoir.

★3648★ HOMEN STATE FOREST

c/o North Dakota Forest Service
307 1st St E
Bottineau, ND 58318
Web: www.ndsu.nodak.edu/forestservice/stateforest/homen.htm
Phone: 701-228-5422; **Fax:** 701-228-5448
Size: 4,485 acres. **Location:** Recreation areas are 8 miles north of Bottineau. **Facilities:** Primitive campsites, drinking water,

picnic shelters, boat access to Pelican Lake, multi-use trails. **Activities:** Camping, fishing, hunting. **Special Features:** Forest is made up of dense forest, small lakes, and wetlands and contains Hartley-Boundary Primitive Area, Pelican-Sandy Lake Recreation Area, and public acces to Long Lake.

★3649★ HR MORGAN STATE NATURE PRESERVE

c/o North Dakota Parks & Recreation Dept
1600 E Century Ave Suite 3
Bismarck, ND 58503
Web: www.ndparks.com/Nature/Preserves.htm
Phone: 701-328-5357
Size: 40 acres. **Location:** 24 miles east-northeast of Lisbon in Ransom and Richland counties. **Facilities:** Developed hiking and horseback riding trail; camping permitted where posted (but no camping facilities provided). **Activities:** Hiking, horseback riding, birdwatching, other passive recreation. **Special Features:** This area of the Sheyenne River hardwood forest bottomland is home to several unique species of plants and birds.

★3650★ ICELANDIC STATE PARK

13571 Hwy 5
Cavalier, ND 58220
Web: www.ndparks.com/Parks/ISP.htm
Phone: 701-265-4561; **Fax:** 701-265-4443
Size: 912 acres. **Location:** 5 miles west of Cavalier on Highway 5, near the US-Canadian border. **Facilities:** 159 campsites with electrical hookups and modern camfort stations, showers, 3 sleeping cabins (seasonal), picnic areas, picnic shelter, playground, hiking trails, cross-country ski trails, swimming beach, boat ramp, fish dock, historic buildings, visitor center. **Activities:** Camping, boating, fishing, swimming, hiking, cross-country skiing. **Special Features:** Located on the north shore of Lake Renwick, the park offers not only recreational opportunities, but also a glimpse into North Dakota's heritage at the Pioneer Heritage Center. The Gunlogson State Nature Preserve (see separate entry), also located at the park, is a sanctuary for plants, birds, and wildlife.

★3651★ INDIAN HILLS STATE RECREATION AREA & RESORT

7302 14th St NW
Garrison, ND 58540
Web: www.ndparks.com/parks/Stevenson/IndianHills.htm
Phone: 701-743-4122
Size: 80 acres. **Location:** 31 miles west of Garrison. **Facilities:** Modern campsites with water and electric hookups available, primitive campsites, group campsites, showers, 4 cabins, 4 condominium units, lodge accommodations, picnic areas, full-service marina, camp store, fishing guide services, hiking trails. **Activities:** Camping, boating, fishing, hiking. **Special Features:** Resort is operated under lease to a private company.

★3652★ LAKE METIGOSHE STATE PARK

2 Lake Metigoshe State Park
Bottineau, ND 58318
Web: www.ndparks.com/Parks/LMSP.htm
Phone: 701-263-4651; **Fax:** 701-263-4648

Size: 1,551 acres. **Location:** 14 miles northeast of Bottineau, along the US-Canadian border. **Facilities:** 130 modern campsites, electrical hookups, showers, primitive campsites, rental cabins, group dormitories, kitchen and meeting facilities, picnic areas, picnic shelters, playground, boat ramp, canoe rentals, trails, ski and snowshoe rentals. **Activities:** Camping, boating, canoeing, fishing, hiking, cross-country skiing, ice skating, sledding, ice fishing, snowmobiling. **Special Features:** Nestled in the Turtle Mountains on the shores of Lake Metigoshe, this park is one of the most popular year-round vacation spots in North Dakota. Snowmobile trails within the park connect with more than 250 miles of groomed trails throughout the mountains. The Old Oak Trail, a National Recreation Trail, is located within park boundaries. Ecology, conservation, and outdoor recreation programs are offered at the park's Turtle Mountain Environmental Learning Center.

★3653★ LAKE SAKAKAWEA STATE PARK

PO Box 732
Riverdale, ND 58565
Web: www.ndparks.com/Parks/LSSP.htm
Phone: 701-487-3315; Fax: 701-487-3305
Size: 1,293 acres. **Location:** 1 mile north of Pick City, on the south shore of Lake Sakakawea adjacent to Garrison Dam. **Facilities:** 192 campsites, electrical hookups, showers, 2 sleeping cabins, picnic shelters, hiking trails, full-service marina with boat rentals, convenience store, fishing guide services, and boat and camper storage, 2 boat ramps, fish cleaning station. **Activities:** Camping, boating, fishing, hiking. **Special Features:** Lake Sakakawea is one of the three largest manmade reservoirs in the US, 178 miles long and with a surface area of about 368,000 acres. The park is the terminus of the North Country National Scenic Trail which, when completed, will stretch 3,200 miles from upstate New York to Lake Sakakawea State Park, where it joins the route of the Lewis and Clark National Historic Trail. The park and lake are named in honor of Sakakawea, the Shoshone woman who accompanied Lewis and Clark and the Corps of Discovery on their journey to find a waterway to the Pacific Ocean.

★3654★ LEWIS & CLARK STATE PARK

4904 119th Rd NW
Epping, ND 58843
Web: www.ndparks.com/Parks/LCSP.htm
Phone: 701-859-3071; Fax: 701-859-3001
Size: 490 acres. **Location:** 19 miles southeast of Williston on Highway 1804. **Facilities:** 80 campsites, electrical hookups, showers, sleeping cabins, picnic shelters, playground, hiking and cross-country ski trails, self-guided nature trail, boat ramp, concession. **Activities:** Camping, boating, fishing, hiking, cross-country skiing. **Special Features:** Located on one of the upper bays on Lake Sakakawea, park is named for the famous explorers, who camped near here in 1805.

★3655★ LITTLE MISSOURI STATE PARK

c/o Cross Ranch State Park
1403 River Rd
Center, ND 58530
Web: www.ndparks.com/Parks/Little_Mo/Home.htm
Phone: 701-974-3731

Size: 5,749 acres. **Location:** 17 miles north of Killdeer on Highway 22. **Facilities:** 30 campsites with electrical hookups, picnic shelters, hiking trails, horse trails (30 miles), corrals, horse rentals and guide service. **Activities:** Camping, hiking, horseback riding. **Special Features:** Park contains some of the most rugged and picturesque Badlands scenery in the state, most of which is accessible only on foot or horseback.

★3656★ MOUSE RIVER STATE FOREST

c/o North Dakota Forest Service
307 1st St E
Bottineau, ND 58318
Web: www.ndsu.nodak.edu/ndsu/lbakken/forest/stateforest/
    mouse_river.htm
Phone: 701-228-5422; Fax: 701-228-5448
Size: 259 acres total (2 parcels). **Location:** North of Towner, in McHenry County. **Facilities:** Undeveloped. **Activities:** Hiking, fishing, canoeing. **Special Features:** Forest consists of 2 parcels of land with different ecosystems — one parcel contains stunted aspen forests with sandy soils and the other is made up of mixed hardwoods along the Mouse River, also know as the Souris River.

★3657★ SENTINEL BUTTE STATE NATURE PRESERVE

c/o North Dakota Parks & Recreation Dept
1600 E Century Ave Suite 3
Bismarck, ND 58503
Web: www.ndparks.com/Nature/Preserves.htm
Phone: 701-328-5357
Size: 4 acres. **Location:** 3 miles south of the town of Sentinel Butte. **Facilities:** None. **Activities:** Hiking, birdwatching, other passive recreation. **Special Features:** Site protects fish fossils located on the northern plateau of the butte.

★3658★ SHEYENNE RIVER STATE FOREST

c/o North Dakota Forest Service
307 1st St E
Bottineau, ND 58318
Web: www.ndsu.nodak.edu/forestservice/stateforest/
    sheyenne_river.htm
Phone: 701-228-5422; Fax: 701-228-5448
Size: 509 acres. **Location:** 10 miles northwest of Lisbon on County Road 13 along the Sheyenne River Valley Scenic Byway/Backway. **Facilities:** Hiking trails, river access. **Activities:** Hiking, fishing, canoeing. **Special Features:** Forest encompasses part of the Sheyenne River flood plain, deep draws, and steep banks of the valley. Common forest species include oak, ash, elm, ironwood, and basswood.

★3659★ SULLY CREEK STATE RECREATION AREA

c/o Fort Abraham Lincoln State Park
4480 Fort Lincoln Rd
Mandan, ND 58554
Web: www.ndparks.com/parks/Little_Mo/Home.htm
Phone: 701-667-6340; Fax: 701-667-6349
Size: 80 acres. **Location:** 2.5 miles south of Medora on gravel

road. **Facilities:** 33 campsites, vault toilets, trails, corrals. **Activities:** Camping, canoeing, hiking, mountain biking, horseback riding. **Special Features:** Park is located in the heart of the North Dakota Badlands, with access for hikers, mountain bikers, and horseback riders to the 120-mile long Maah Daah Hey Trail, which traverses the Little Missouri National Grassland (see entry in national forests section).

★3660★ TETRAULT WOODS STATE FOREST
c/o North Dakota Forest Service
307 1st St E
Bottineau, ND 58318
Web: www.ndsu.nodak.edu/forestservice/stateforest/
tetrault_woods.htm
Phone: 701-228-5422; **Fax:** 701-228-5448
Size: 432 acres. **Location:** 0.5 miles south of Walhalla, on the west side of Highway 32. **Facilities:** Hiking trails, scenic overlook. **Activities:** Hiking. **Special Features:** Forest is located along the banks of the Pembina River and preserves part of the riparian forest typical of the area, including oak, ash, elm, birch, and aspen.

★3661★ TURTLE MOUNTAIN STATE FOREST
c/o North Dakota Forest Service
307 1st St E
Bottineau, ND 58318
Web: www.ndsu.nodak.edu/forestservice/stateforest/
turtle_mtn.htm
Phone: 701-228-5422; **Fax:** 701-228-5448
Size: 7,494 acres. **Location:** 8 miles north of Bottineau, off Highway 43. **Facilities:** Strawberry Lake: Primitive and equestrian campsites, drinking water, swimming beach, boat launch. Hahn's Bay: Primitive campsites, drinking water, fishing pier, boat launch to Lake Metigoshe, picnic shelters. Twisted Oaks: Picnic tables, vault toilets. All 3 locations provide trailhead access to an extensive trail system. **Activities:** Camping (primitive only), fishing, swimming, boating (electric motors only on Strawberry Lake), hiking, mountain biking, horseback riding, snowmobiling, cross-country skiing. **Special Features:** Forest extends from the foothills of the Turtle Mountains to the Canadian border and is the largest contiguous block of forested land in the state. Within its boundaries are Strawberry Lake Recreation Area, Hahn's Bay Recreation Area, and Twisted Oaks, a day use area.

★3662★ TURTLE RIVER STATE PARK
3084 Park Ave
Arvilla, ND 58214
Web: www.ndparks.com/Parks/TRSP.htm
Phone: 701-594-4445; **Fax:** 701-594-2556
Size: 784 acres. **Location:** 22 miles west of Grand Forks on Highway 2. **Facilities:** 125 campsites, electrical hookups, showers, rustic group cabins, kitchen and dining hall, picnic shelters, playground, park store, hiking trails, mountain bike trails, cross-country ski trails, sledding hill, heated warming house. **Activities:** Camping, fishing, hiking, mountain biking, cross-country skiing, snow sledding. **Special Features:** The Turtle River is located in a wooded valley, and the entire park is a nature

sanctuary, with an abundance of plant and animal life. Trails may be periodically closed due to safety concerns following heavy rain.

★3663★ WHITESTONE HILL BATTLEFIELD STATE HISTORIC SITE
RR 1, Box 125
Kulm, ND 58456
Web: www.state.nd.us/HIST/whitestone/index.html
Phone: 701-396-7731
Location: 23 miles southeast of Kulm, in Dickey County. **Facilities:** Historic site, museum, picnic area with shelter, horseshoe pits, pit toilets. Open May 16-September 15, Thursday-Monday. **Special Features:** Site marks the scene of the fiercest clash between Indians and white soldiers in North Dakota. On September 3, 1863, troops attacked a tipi camp as part of a military mission to punish participants of the Dakota Conflict of 1862. In the ensuing battle, military casualties were comparatively light, but hundreds of Indian men, women, and children died or were captured. The Indians also suffered the destruction of virtually all of their property, leaving them nearly destitute for the coming winter. Today the site includes a portion of the battlefield, with a monument honoring the Indian dead and another honoring the soldiers who died in the battle.

49	Middle Bass Island SP	A-3
50	Mohican SP	C-4
51	Mosquito Lake SP	B-7
52	Mount Gilead SP	C-4
53	Muskingum River SP	E-5
54	Nelson-Kennedy Ledges SP	B-6
55	Oak Point SP	A-4
56	Paint Creek SP	F-3
57	Pike Lake SP	F-3
58	Portage Lakes SP	C-5
59	Punderson SP	B-6
60	Pymatuning SP	A-7
61	Quail Hollow SP	C-6
62	Rocky Fork SP	F-3
63	Salt Fork SP	D-6
64	Scioto Trail SP	F-4
65	Shawnee SP	G-3
66	South Bass Island SP	A-3
67	Stonelick SP	F-2
68	Strouds Run SP	F-5
69	Sycamore SP	E-1
70	Tar Hollow SP	F-4
71	Tinkers Creek SP	B-6
72	Van Buren SP	B-2
73	West Branch SP	B-6
74	Wolf Run SP	E-6

1	A. W. Marion SP	E-4	18	East Fork SP	G-2				34	John Bryan SP	E-2
2	Adams Lake SP	G-3	19	East Harbor SP	A-4				35	Kelleys Island SP	A-4
3	Alum Creek SP	D-3	20	Findley SP	B-4				36	Kiser Lake SP	D-2
4	Barkcamp SP	D-6	21	Forked Run SP	F-5				37	Lake Alma SP	F-4
5	Beaver Creek SP	C-7	22	Geneva SP	A-6				38	Lake Hope SP	F-4
6	Blue Rock SP	E-5	23	Grand Lake Saint Marys SP	D-1				39	Lake Logan SP	F-4
7	Buck Creek SP	E-2	24	Great Seal SP	F-4				40	Lake Loramie SP	D-1
8	Buckeye Lake SP	E-4	25	Guilford Lake SP	C-6				41	Lake Milton SP	B-6
9	Burr Oak SP	E-5	26	Harrison Lake SP	A-1				42	Lake White SP	G-3
10	Caesar Creek SP	F-2	27	Headlands Beach SP	A-6				43	Little Miami Scenic SP	E-2
11	Catawaba Island SP	A-3	28	Hocking Hills SP	F-4				44	Madison Lake SP	E-3
12	Cleveland Lakefront SP	A-5	29	Hueston Woods SP	F-1				45	Malabar Farm SP	C-4
13	Cowan Lake SP	F-2	30	Independence Dam SP	B-1				46	Marblehead Lighthouse SP	B-4
14	Crane Creek SP	A-3	31	Indian Lake SP	D-2				47	Mary Jane Thurston SP	B-2
15	Deer Creek SP	E-3	32	Jackson Lake SP	G-4				48	Maumee Bay SP	A-3
16	Delaware SP	D-3	33	Jefferson Lake SP	D-7						
17	Dillon SP	D-5								SP	State Park	

OHIO

★3664★ Ohio Division of Parks & Recreation
1952 Belcher Dr, C-3
Columbus, OH 43224
(614) 265-6561 - Phone
(800) 282-7275 - Reservations
Web: www.ohiodnr.com/parks
Administers 74 state parks comprising more than 163,000 acres of land and water resources. Maintains more than 1,100 miles of trails.

★3665★ Ohio Division of Forestry
2045 Morse Rd, Bldg H-1
Columbus, OH 43229
(614) 265-6694 – Phone
(877) 247-8733
Web: www.ohiodnr.com/forestry
Manages 20 forests covering more than 185,000 acres. State forests include designated areas for camping, target practice, hunting, and fishing, and miles of trails for hiking, horseback riding, cross-country skiing, and ATV riding.

★3666★ Ohio Division of Wildlife
2045 Morse Rd, Bldg C
Columbus, OH 43229
(614) 265-6300
http://www.ohiodnr.com/wildlife
Manages fish and wildlife resources, including fish and wildlife management, information, education and law enforcement. Division has five wildlife districts, four fish and wildlife research stations, five fish hatcheries, and 80 wildlife areas.

Key to campsite classification:

- **Campsites** — Include picnic tables, fire rings, sanitary facilities, and drinking water. Laundries, flush toilets, electricity, and heated showers available at many parks.
- **Horsemen's campsites** — Primarily primitive camps accessible via bridle trails.
- **Rent-a-Camp** — Tent set up on a wooden platform with fire ring and picnic table under canopy, two cots with sleeping pads, camp light and camp stove.
- **Camper Cabins** — Wooden structure with the same equipment as rent-a-camp.
- **Rent-a-RV** — 29-foot travel trailer which sleeps 4 adults or 2 adults and 4 children. Parked at campsite with electrical, sewer, and water hookups. Each contains bath with shower, furnace, air conditioner, television, stereo, electrical outlets, and full kitchen.

- **Rent-a-Tepee** or **Yurt** — Round canvas structures on wooden platforms, with dome skylight. Come furnished with convertible futon beds and bunks, table and chairs, mini refrigerator or cooler, and internal electrical outlets. Each yurt has a sheltered picnic table and fire ring.

★3667★ A. W. MARION STATE PARK
c/o Deer Creek State Park
20635 Waterloo Rd
Mount Sterling, OH 43143
Web: www.ohiodnr.com/parks/parks/awmarion.htm
Phone: 740-869-3124
Size: 309 acres land; 145 acres water. **Location:** 4 miles northeast of Circleville, off State Route 22. **Facilities:** 58 campsites (29 with electricity), group camp, picnic areas, picnic shelters, hiking trails (6 miles), boat ramps, docks, boat rentals. **Activities:** Camping, boating (electric motors only), fishing, hiking, hunting, ice fishing, ice skating, sledding. **Special Features:** Park offers some of the finest fishing in central Ohio.

★3668★ ADAMS LAKE STATE PARK
c/o Shawnee State Park
4404 State Rt 125
Portsmouth, OH 45663
Web: www.ohiodnr.com/parks/parks/adams.htm
Phone: 740-858-6652
Size: 49 acres land; 47 acres water. **Location:** 36 miles west of Portsmouth, in the southeast corner of the state. **Facilities:** Picnic areas, picnic shelters, boat ramps, hiking trail. **Activities:** Fishing, boating (electric motors only), hiking. **Special Features:** Located between the foothills of the Appalachian Mountains and glaciated land in an area known as the Bluegrass Region, park has an abundance of plant species. This area was once inhabited by prehistoric and mound-building cultures; Serpent Mound is found north of the park.

★3669★ ALUM CREEK STATE PARK
3615 S Old State Rd
Delaware, OH 43015
Web: www.ohiodnr.com/parks/parks/alum.htm
Phone: 740-548-4631
Size: 4,630 acres land; 3,387 acres water. **Location:** 8 miles east of Delaware, in the center of the state. **Facilities:** 289 campsites with electricity, group camp, showers, flush toilets, 3 rent-a-RV units, 5 camper cabins, horseman's camp, picnic areas, hiking trails (9.5 miles), bridle trails (38 miles), bike trails (14 miles), swimming beach, food concession, marina, boat ramps, boat rentals, dog park. **Activities:** Camping, boating,

9. State Parks

canoeing, fishing, swimming, hiking, horseback riding, hunting, mountain biking, cross-country skiing, snowmobiling, ice skating, ice fishing, ice boating, sledding. **Special Features:** Alum Creek rests in the midst of agricultural till plains and river valleys. Cliffs of Ohio shale are found in many areas. The shale was formed as mud washed into the ancient sea which covered the area; the dark color of the rock is due to the mixture of carbonized plant material and mud that formed the shale.

★3670★ BARKCAMP STATE PARK
65330 Barkcamp Rd
Belmont, OH 43718
Web: www.ohiodnr.com/parks/parks/barkcamp.htm
Phone: 740-484-4064
Size: 1,005 acres land; 117 acres water. **Location:** 13 miles from St. Clairsville, in the southeast corner of the state. **Facilities:** 125 campsites with electricity (&), 3 rent-a-camp units, group camp, 2 camper cabins, horsemen's camp, showers, picnic areas, picnic shelters, hiking trails (4 miles), bridle trails (24 miles), swimming beach, boat ramp, docks (&). **Activities:** Camping, boating (electric motors only), fishing, swimming, hiking, horseback riding, hunting, snowmobiling, ice fishing, ice skating, cross-country skiing, ice boating, nature programs. **Special Features:** Park includes an antique barn built in the 1800s, a reconstructed log cabin, and other pioneer-era structures.

★3671★ BEAVER CREEK STATE PARK
12021 Echo Dell Rd
East Liverpool, OH 43920
Web: www.ohiodnr.com/parks/parks/beaverck.htm
Phone: 330-385-3091
Size: 2,722 acres land; 4 acres water. **Location:** 9 miles from East Liverpool, in the northeast corner of the state. **Facilities:** 53 campsites (without electricity), group camp, horseman's camp, 2 rent-a-tepee units, picnic areas, picnic shelter, hiking trails (16 miles), bridle trails (25 miles), bike trails, game courts. **Activities:** Camping, canoeing, fishing, hiking, horseback riding, mountain biking, hunting, sledding. **Special Features:** Pioneer Village and Gaston's Mill come to life during the annual Pioneer Craft Days held in the fall; the nature center houses natural history displays.

★3672★ BLUE ROCK STATE PARK
c/o Dillon State Park
5265 Dillon Hills Dr
Nashport, OH 43830
Web: www.ohiodnr.com/parks/parks/bluerock.htm
Phone: 740-453-4377
Size: 335 acres land; 15 acres water. **Location:** 16 miles southeast of Zanesville, in the southeast portion of the state. **Facilities:** 94 campsites (without electricity), 3 rent-a-camp units, 3 camper cabins, group camp, primitive camp, showers, picnic areas, picnic shelters, hiking trails (4 miles), swimming beach, boat ramp, game courts, playground. **Activities:** Camping, boating (electric motors only), canoeing, fishing, swimming, hiking, horseback riding, sledding, ice skating, ice fishing. **Special Features:** Park is surrounded by 4,573-acre Blue Rock State Forest.

★3673★ BUCK CREEK STATE PARK
1901 Buck Creek Ln
Springfield, OH 45502
Web: www.ohiodnr.com/parks/parks/buckck.htm
Phone: 937-322-5284
Size: 1,896 acres land; 2,120 acres water. **Location:** Off State Route 40, 5 miles from Springfield. **Facilities:** 101 campsites (89 with electricity), showers, flush toilets, 26 cottages, picnic areas, picnic shelters, hiking trails (7.5 miles), bike rentals, fishing pier (&), game courts, playground, swimming beach, food concession, marina, boat ramps, boat rentals. **Activities:** Camping, boating, fishing, swimming, hiking, hunting, cross-country skiing, snowmobiling, sledding, ice fishing. **Special Features:** Park's recreational facilities center on the 2,120-acre lake.

★3674★ BUCKEYE LAKE STATE PARK
2905 Liebs Island Rd
Millersport, OH 43046
Web: www.ohiodnr.com/parks/parks/buckeye.htm
Phone: 740-467-2690
Size: 176 acres land; 3,173 acres water. **Location:** 30 miles east of Columbus, in the central part of the state. **Facilities:** Picnic areas, picnic shelters, swimming beach, boat ramps, docks, boat rentals, dock. **Activities:** Boating, fishing, swimming, waterfowl hunting, snowmobiling, ice skating, cross-country skiing, ice fishing, ice boating. **Special Features:** A unique feature of Buckeye Lake is its floating island, actually a piece of ancient glacial bog which buoyed up as the water level rose. On this natural raft, designated as a state nature preserve, can be found some of the most unusual plant life in Ohio. Known as Cranberry Bog, the floating island is a nursery for such unique oddities as the tiny berries of its namesake, rare orchids, the tiny sundew, and the carnivorous pitcher plant. Access to Cranberry Bog is only by written permission from the Division of Natural Areas and Preserves.

★3675★ BURR OAK STATE PARK
5250 Beach Rd
Glouster, OH 45732
Web: www.ohiodnr.com/parks/parks/burroak.htm
Phone: 740-767-3570
Size: 2,593 acres land; 664 acres water. **Location:** 17 miles north of Athens, in the southeast corner of the state. **Facilities:** 100 campsites (without electricity), 13 primitive campsites, youth group camp, showers, flush toilets, 30 cottages, 60-room lodge, picnic areas, picnic shelters, restaurant, hiking trails (28 miles), swimming beach, food concession, marina, boat ramps, boat rentals, fuel dock, playground, nature center. **Activities:** Camping, boating (10 HP limit), fishing, swimming, hiking, hunting, sledding, ice skating, ice fishing, summer programs. **Special Features:** As one of Ohio's resort state parks, Burr Oak offers a wide array of overnight accommodations, blending modern conveniences with the wilderness spirit of the state.

★3676★ CAESAR CREEK STATE PARK
8570 E State Rt 73
Waynesville, OH 45068
Web: www.ohiodnr.com/parks/parks/caesarck.htm
Phone: 513-897-3055

Size: 3741 acres land; 2,830 acres water. **Location:** 24 miles from Dayton in the southwest corner of the state. **Facilities:** 28 campsites with electricity, rent-a-RV unit, showers, 3 cabins, horsemen's camp, group camp, flush toilets, showers, picnic areas, picnic shelters, hiking trails (43 miles), bridle trails (31 miles), bike trails (8 miles), swimming beach, concession, 5 boat ramps, docks, educational programs, playground, game courts. **Activities:** Camping, boating, fishing, swimming, hiking, horseback riding, mountain biking, ice skating, cross-country skiing, ice fishing, nature programs. **Special Features:** Park includes Pioneer Village, featuring 15 historic buildings depicting life in the early 1800s.

★**3677**★ **CATAWBA ISLAND STATE PARK**
4049 E Moores Dock Rd
Port Clinton, OH 43452
Web: www.ohiodnr.com/parks/parks/lakeerie.htm
Phone: 419-797-4530
Size: 18 acres. **Location:** 8 miles northeast of Port Clinton. **Facilities:** Picnic areas, picnic shelter, boat ramps, fishing pier. **Activities:** Boating, swimming, fishing. **Special Features:** Park is one of five state parks that make up the Lake Erie Islands State Parks. The other four are: Kelleys Island, Middle Bass Island, Oak Point, and South Bass Island state parks. Catawba Island serves as the headquarters for the group.

★**3678**★ **CLEVELAND LAKEFRONT STATE PARK**
8701 Lakeshore Blvd NE
Cleveland, OH 44108
Web: www.ohiodnr.com/parks/parks/clevelkf.htm
Phone: 216-881-8141
Size: 419 acres. **Location:** Downtown Cleveland. **Facilities:** Picnic areas, picnic shelters, swimming beaches, concession, 4 boat ramps, docks, boardwalk, fitness trail, bike trail (3 miles), fishing pier (&). **Activities:** Boating, fishing, swimming, sledding, ice fishing, ice boating, cross-country skiing. **Special Features:** Park features sand beaches along the Lake Erie shoreline, tree-lined picnic areas, and panoramic views.

★**3679**★ **COWAN LAKE STATE PARK**
1750 Osborn Rd
Wilmington, OH 45177
Web: www.ohiodnr.com/parks/parks/cowanlk.htm
Phone: 937-382-1096
Size: 1,075 acres land; 700 acres water. **Location:** 6 miles from Wilmington, in the southwest corner of the state. **Facilities:** 254 campsites (237 with electricity), 27 cottages, showers, flush toilets, picnic areas, picnic shelter, dance pavilion, hiking trails (4 miles), bike rentals, swimming beach, food concession, meeting rooms, marina, boat ramps, boat rentals, fuel dock. **Activities:** Camping, boating (10 HP limit), canoeing, fishing, swimming, hiking, hunting, sledding, cross-country skiing, educational programs. **Special Features:** Park lies near the Cincinnati Arch, an uplifting of bedrock that occurred during the Appalachian Mountains' building process. The erosion of this arch in the Cowan region exposes fossil-rich limestone. The limestone near Cowan and other parts of the exposed arch are some of the most famous fossil hunting fields in the world.

★**3680**★ **CRANE CREEK STATE PARK**
13531 W State Rt 2
Oak Harbor, OH 43449
Web: www.ohiodnr.com/parks/parks/cranecrk.htm
Phone: 419-836-7758
Size: 42 acres. **Location:** 16 miles from Toledo, in the north central part of the state. **Facilities:** Picnic areas, picnic shelter, boardwalk (&), swimming beach. **Activities:** Boating, fishing, swimming, hiking, hunting, snowmobiling, ice fishing. **Special Features:** The Crane Creek area was originally part of the Great Black Swamp, a flat plain 120 miles long and 30 to 40 miles wide. Drainage and lumbering nearly wiped out the swamp as it became an agricultural area. Today the park consists of beach and marshlands adjoining the Magee Marsh Wildlife Area and the Ottawa National Wildlife Refuge.

★**3681**★ **DEER CREEK STATE PARK**
20635 Waterloo Rd
Mount Sterling, OH 43143
Web: www.ohiodnr.com/parks/parks/deercrk.htm
Phone: 740-869-3124
Size: 2,337 acres land; 1,277 acres water. **Location:** 7 miles from Mount Sterling on State Route 207, in the center of the state. **Facilities:** 227 campsites with electricity, 5 rent-a-camp units, showers, flush toilets, rent-a-campsites, youth group camp, horseman's camp, 25 cottages, 110-room lodge, picnic areas, restaurant, hiking trails (9 miles), bridle trails (14 miles), bike trail (14 miles), bike rentals, fitness center, swimming beach, food concession, marina, boat ramps, boat rentals, fuel dock, 18-hole golf course, miniature golf, playground. **Activities:** Camping, boating, fishing, swimming, hiking, horseback riding, hunting, golf, snowmobiling, ice skating, cross-country skiing, ice fishing, nature programs. **Special Features:** This resort park is located in the heart of Ohio's agricultural country. On a long ridge that once overlooked Deer Creek and its valley, researchers have found evidence of an ancient Indian tribe's camp. Burial sites near the camp indicate it was inhabited over a period of time.

★**3682**★ **DELAWARE STATE PARK**
5202 US Hwy 23 N
Delaware, OH 43015
Web: www.ohiodnr.com/parks/parks/delaware.htm
Phone: 740-369-2761
Size: 1,686 acres land; 1,330 acres water. **Location:** Just outside Delaware, in the center of the state. **Facilities:** 211 campsites with electricity, 3 rent-a-yurts, showers, flush toilets, youth group camp, picnic areas, picnic shelter, hiking trails (7 miles), swimming beach, food concession, bike rentals, marina, boat ramps, boat rentals, fuel dock, game courts. **Activities:** Camping, boating, fishing, swimming, hiking, hunting, cross-country skiing, sledding, ice skating, ice fishing, nature programs. **Special Features:** Birdwatching is popular here, and many species of songbirds nest in the area. In the summer, visitors can explore Delaware's bluebird management trail.

★3683★ DILLON STATE PARK
5265 Dillon Hills Dr
Nashport, OH 43830
Web: www.ohiodnr.com/parks/parks/dillon.htm
Phone: 740-453-4377
Size: 2,285 acres land; 1,560 acres water. **Location:** Near Zanesville, in the southeast corner of the state. **Facilities:** 195 campsites (183 with electricity), teepee, showers, flush toilets, 29 cottages, picnic areas, picnic shelters, hiking trails (8 miles), bridle trails (15 miles), swimming beach, food concession, marina, boat ramps, boat rentals, fuel dock, game courts, playground, shooting range, laundry. **Activities:** Camping, boating, fishing, swimming, hiking, hunting, ice skating, sledding, trap shooting, horseback riding, summer programs. **Special Features:** Park is situated in an area of diverse natural features resulting from the unique properties of Black Hand Sandstone. Sand, eroded hundreds of millions of years ago, accumulated in a delta in the sea covering the region. This hard bedrock eroded to form sheer cliffs and supports a lush, hardwood forest.

★3684★ EAST FORK STATE PARK
3294 Elklick Rd
Bethel, OH 45106
Web: www.ohiodnr.com/parks/parks/eastfork.htm
Phone: 513-734-4323
Size: 3,294 acres land; 2,160 acres water. **Location:** 30 miles east of Cincinnati, in the southwest corner of the state. **Facilities:** 399 campsites with electricity, 4 cabins, showers, flush toilets, horseman's camp, picnic areas, picnic shelters, hiking trails (85 miles), bridle trails (55 miles), bike trails (5 miles), swimming beach, 6 boat ramps, game courts, playground, miniature golf, bike rentals. **Activities:** Camping, boating, fishing, swimming, hiking, horseback riding, hunting (nearby), mountain biking, sledding, ice skating, ice fishing. **Special Features:** Not far from the present park office, the "Old Bethel Church" dates from 1867. It occupies the site of a log church built around 1807. Some of the hand-hewn timbers secured with wooden pegs and hand-forged nails used to construct the church are still present in the existing church.

★3685★ EAST HARBOR STATE PARK
1169 N Buck Rd
Lakeside-Marblehead, OH 43440
Web: www.ohiodnr.com/parks/parks/eastharbor.htm
Phone: 419-734-4424
Size: 1,831 acres. **Location:** East of Port Clinton on Lake Erie, in the north central part of the state. **Facilities:** 570 campsites (365 with electricity), camper cabin, rent-a-RV units, group camp, showers, flush toilets, picnic areas, picnic shelters, hiking trails (10 miles), swimming beach, food concession, restaurant, marina, boat ramps, boat rentals, fuel dock, camp store (seasonal). **Activities:** Camping, boating, fishing, swimming, hiking, waterfowl hunting, cross-country skiing, snowmobiling, sledding, ice skating, ice fishing, ice boating. **Special Features:** Park offers the largest state park campground in Ohio. Remnants of Ohio's last great ice age can be seen at East Harbor in the form of glacial scratches carved in the bedrock. East Harbor also provides ample opportunity for bird watchers to study black-crowned night herons as well as resident and migratory waterfowl.

★3686★ FINDLEY STATE PARK
25381 State Rt 58
Wellington, OH 44090
Web: www.ohiodnr.com/parks/parks/findley.htm
Phone: 440-647-4490
Size: 838 acres land; 93 acres water. **Location:** 30 miles north of Mansfield, in the northeast corner of the state. **Facilities:** 272 campsites (without electricity), 2 camper cabins, group camp, showers, flush toilets, picnic areas, picnic shelter, hiking trails (10 miles), swimming beach, food concession, boat ramps, boat rentals, game courts, nature programs, playground. **Activities:** Camping, boating (electric motors only), fishing, swimming, hiking, waterfowl hunting, cross-country skiing, ice skating, ice fishing. **Special Features:** Park was once a state forest and is heavily wooded. One area of the park is set aside as a sanctuary for the Duke's skipper butterfly, an extremely rare insect.

★3687★ FORKED RUN STATE PARK
63300 State Rt 124
PO Box 127
Reedsville, OH 45772
Web: www.ohiodnr.com/parks/parks/forkedrn.htm
Phone: 740-378-6206
Size: 791 acres land; 102 acres water. **Location:** 34 miles southwest of Marietta, in the southeast corner of the state. **Facilities:** 151 campsites (86 with electricity), 3 camper cabins, group camp, showers, picnic areas, picnic shelters, hiking trails (4 miles), swimming beach, boat ramps (&), boat rentals, disc golf course, game courts, playgrounds. **Activities:** Camping, boating (10 HP limit), fishing, swimming, hiking, hunting, sledding. **Special Features:** Much of this area, now heavily forested, was once void of timber. Stands of oak, hickory, maple, and tuliptree cover deep ravines and hillsides.

★3688★ GENEVA STATE PARK
PO Box 429
4499 Pandanarum Rd
Geneva, OH 44041
Web: www.ohiodnr.com/parks/parks/geneva.htm
Phone: 440-466-8400
Size: 698 acres. **Location:** Off State Route 534, east of Cleveland. **Facilities:** 88 campsites with electricity, showers, flush toilets, 12 cedar cabins, 109-room lodge, picnic areas, picnic shelters, hiking trails (3 miles), swimming beach, marina, boat ramps, fuel dock, game courts, fish cleaning station. **Activities:** Camping, boating, fishing, swimming, hiking, hunting, cross-country skiing, ice fishing, snowmobiling. **Special Features:** Park is set on the shore of Lake Erie, a relatively shallow lake, and offers a natural beach, several areas of freshwater marsh, and mature woodlots.

★3689★ GRAND LAKE SAINT MARYS STATE PARK
834 Edgewater Dr
Saint Marys, OH 45885
Web: www.ohiodnr.com/parks/parks/grndlake.htm
Phone: 419-394-3611
Size: 591 acres land; 13,500 acres water. **Location:** 35 miles

southwest of Lima, in the northwest corner of the state. **Facilities:** 210 campsites (142 with electricity), 2 camper cabins, 2 cedar cabins, group camp, showers, flush toilets, picnic areas, picnic shelters, swimming beach, bike rentals, game courts, playground, marina, boat ramps, boat rentals, fuel dock, miniature golf. **Activities:** Camping, boating, fishing, swimming, bicycling, hunting, snowmobiling, ice fishing, cross-country skiing, naturalist programs (seasonal). **Special Features:** Grand Lake Saint Marys was constructed from 1837 to 1845 as a feeder reservoir for the Miami-Erie Canal system. Before Hoover Dam was built to create Nevada's Lake Mead, Grand Lake was the largest manmade lake in the world.

★3690★ GREAT SEAL STATE PARK

635 Rocky Rd
Chillicothe, OH 45601
Web: www.ohiodnr.com/parks/parks/grtseal.htm
Phone: 740-663-2125
Size: 1,862 acres land; 2 acres water. **Location:** An hour south of Columbus, in the southeast corner of the state. **Facilities:** 15 campsites (without electricity), horseman's camp, picnic areas, picnic shelters, hiking trails (5 miles), bike trails, bridle trails (17 miles), disc golf course, game courts, playground. **Activities:** Camping, hiking, horseback riding, hunting, cross-country skiing. **Special Features:** The history of the Shawnee nation and Ohio's early statehood is centered in the area's rugged hills, which are depicted on the Great Seal of the State of Ohio, from which the park gets its name.

★3691★ GUILFORD LAKE STATE PARK

6835 E Lake Rd
Lisbon, OH 44432
Web: www.ohiodnr.com/parks/parks/guilford.htm
Phone: 330-222-1712
Size: 93 acres land; 396 acres water. **Location:** In east central Ohio, 28 miles east of Canton. **Facilities:** 41 campsites with electricity, showers, flush toilets, picnic areas, picnic shelters, hiking trail (0.5 miles), swimming beach, fishing pier (&), boat ramps, docks, playground, game courts. **Activities:** Camping, boating (10 HP limit), fishing, swimming, hiking, ice fishing, ice skating. **Special Features:** The area surrounding Guilford Lake, before being impounded as a reservoir, was extremely swampy, indicating it may have been a remnant of a natural glacial lake.

★3692★ HARRISON LAKE STATE PARK

26246 Harrison Lake Rd
Fayette, OH 43521
Web: www.ohiodnr.com/parks/parks/harrison.htm
Phone: 419-237-2593
Size: 142 acres land; 105 acres water. **Location:** Northwest corner of the state, an hour from Toledo. **Facilities:** 175 campsites (150 with electricity), 2 rent-a-yurts, camper cabin, youth group camp, showers, flush toilets, picnic areas, picnic shelters, hiking trails (4 miles), swimming beach, boat ramps, nature center, bike rentals, game courts, playground. **Activities:** Camping, boating (electric motors only), canoeing, fishing, swimming,

hiking, biking, sledding, cross-country skiing, ice fishing. **Special Features:** Once a vast swampland, the area around the park was a tremendous barrier to western settlement. It wasn't until the development of soil drainage techniques in the 1850s that settlers began to move here and develop the area into one of Ohio's richest agricultural regions.

★3693★ HEADLANDS BEACH STATE PARK

c/o Cleveland Lakefront State Park
8701 Lakeshore Blvd NE
Cleveland, OH 44108
Web: www.ohiodnr.com/parks/parks/headlnds.htm
Phone: 216-881-8141
Size: 120 acres. **Location:** 27 miles from Cleveland, in the northeast corner of the state. **Facilities:** Picnic areas, picnic shelter, restrooms, swimming beach, food concession, playground. **Activities:** Boating, fishing, swimming, cross-country skiing, sledding. **Special Features:** Park's trademark is its mile-long natural beach, the largest in the state. The area is home to many plant species typically found only along the Atlantic Coast.

★3694★ HOCKING HILLS STATE PARK

19852 State Rt 664 S
Logan, OH 43138
Web: www.ohiodnr.com/parks/parks/hocking.htm
Phone: 740-385-6842
Size: 2,356 acres land; 17 acres water. **Location:** 1 hour southeast of Columbus, in the southeast part of the state. **Facilities:** 172 campsites (159 with electricity), 3 camper cabins, group camp, 40 cottages, showers, flush toilets, laundry, picnic areas, picnic shelters, restaurant, hiking trails (26 miles), swimming pool, camp store, playgrounds, game courts. **Activities:** Camping, fishing, swimming, hiking, ice fishing, nature programs. **Special Features:** Park features towering cliffs, waterfalls, gorges, and recess caves.

★3695★ HUESTON WOODS STATE PARK

6301 Park Office Rd
College Corner, OH 45003
Web: www.ohiodnr.com/parks/parks/huestonw.htm
Phone: 513-523-6347
Size: 2,936 acres land; 625 acres water. **Location:** In the southwest part of the state, 1 hour northwest of Cincinnati. **Facilities:** 488 campsites (252 with electricity), 3 camper cabins (&), 37 cottages, 96-room lodge, group camp, horsemen's camp, showers, flush toilets, picnic areas, restaurant, hiking trails (10 miles), bridle trails (18 miles), bike trails (12 miles), bike rentals, horse rentals, swimming beach, fishing pier (&), food concession, marina, boat ramps, boat rentals, fuel dock, 18-hole golf course, paintball field, target range, nature center, playground, game courts. **Activities:** Camping, boating (10 HP limit), fishing, swimming, hiking, mountain biking, horseback riding, golf, cross-country skiing, sledding, ice skating, ice fishing, ice boating, paintball, nature programs. **Special Features:** Park includes a year-round nature center which provides bird and flower walks, slide talks, and fossil hunts.

★3696★ **INDEPENDENCE DAM STATE PARK**
27722 State Rt 424
Defiance, OH 43512
Web: www.ohiodnr.com/parks/parks/indpndam.htm
Phone: 419-237-1503
Size: 591 acres. **Location:** 16 miles west of Bowling Green, in the northwest corner of the state. **Facilities:** Picnic areas, picnic shelters, hiking trails (3 miles), marina, boat ramp. **Activities:** Boating, canoeing, water-skiing, fishing, hiking, bicycling, cross-country skiing, sledding, ice skating. **Special Features:** Park is situated along the banks of the Maumee River, and nearby Maumee State Forest offers additional recreational opportunities.

★3697★ **INDIAN LAKE STATE PARK**
12774 State Rt 235 N
Lakeview, OH 43331
Web: www.ohiodnr.com/parks/parks/indianlk.htm
Phone: 937-843-2717
Size: 800 acres land; 5,800 acres water. **Location:** Off US 33 northwest of Bellefontaine; also accessible via State Route 233. **Facilities:** 441 campsites (416 with electricity), rent-an-RV, group camp, 20 boat camping spaces, 3 camper cabins, showers, flush toilets, laundry, picnic areas, picnic shelters, hiking trails (7 miles), 2 swimming beaches, boat ramps, docks, playgrounds, miniature golf course, game courts, bike rentals, boat rentals. **Activities:** Camping, boating, fishing, swimming, water-skiing, hiking, biking, hunting, cross-country skiing, snowmobiling, ice skating, ice fishing, ice boating, nature programs. **Special Features:** The region of Indian Lake was originally a cluster of natural lakes situated on the Miami River. The present, much larger lake lies along one of the country's major avian migration routes and is a resting stop for several species of birds.

★3698★ **JACKSON LAKE STATE PARK**
35 Tommy Been Rd
PO Box 174
Oak Hill, OH 45656
Web: www.ohiodnr.com/parks/parks/jacksonl.htm
Phone: 740-596-5253
Size: 107 acres land; 242 acres water. **Location:** 25 miles northeast of Portsmouth, in the southeast corner of the state. **Facilities:** 34 campsites with electricity, picnic areas, picnic shelters, swimming beach, boat ramps, game courts, playgrounds. **Activities:** Camping, boating (10 HP limit), fishing, swimming, sledding, ice fishing, ice skating. **Special Features:** Once the heart of the iron-producing region, the area still contains the remains of Jefferson Iron Furnace, one of the last iron-smelting furnaces to shut down. It its heyday, it supplied part of the metal necessary to adorn the iron-clad *Monitor*, the famous battleship of the Civil War.

★3699★ **JEFFERSON LAKE STATE PARK**
501 Township Rd 261A
Richmond, OH 43944
Web: www.ohiodnr.com/parks/parks/jefferso.htm
Phone: 740-765-4459

Size: 945 acres land; 17 acres water. **Location:** 10 miles northwest of Steubenville, in the east central part of the state. **Facilities:** 97 campsites (without electricity), picnic areas, picnic shelters, multi-use trails (18 miles), swimming beach, boat ramps, bathhouse, showers, game courts. **Activities:** Camping, boating (electric motors only), fishing, swimming, hiking, mountain biking, horseback riding, hunting, cross-country skiing, ice skating, ice fishing. **Special Features:** Nestled in oak and hickory wooded hills, Jefferson Lake is one of Ohio's quiet, out-of-the-way camping parks.

★3700★ **JOHN BRYAN STATE PARK**
3790 State Rt 370
Yellow Springs, OH 45387
Web: www.ohiodnr.com/parks/parks/jhnbryan.htm
Phone: 937-767-1274
Size: 752 acres. **Location:** 27 miles from Dayton, in the southwest part of the state. **Facilities:** 99 campsites (10 with electricity), group camp, rent-a-teepee, picnic areas, picnic shelters, hiking trails (9 miles), rock climbing area. **Activities:** Camping, fishing, hiking, cross-country skiing, sledding, bow hunting, rock climbing. **Special Features:** The history of the park is told in the rocks of the Little Miami River Gorge. Entering the area at Clifton at 980 feet above sea level, the Little Miami drops 130 feet through layer upon layer of bedrock. Each layer has its own characteristics: some are easily worn away by erosion, causing undercutting in the cliff face; more erosion-resistant dolomite or limestone rocks above are weakened by this undercutting and slump blocks fall away creating unusual rock formations. Waterfalls and cascades are common.

★3701★ **KELLEYS ISLAND STATE PARK**
c/o Catawba Island State Park
4049 E Moores Dock Rd
Port Clinton, OH 43452
Web: www.ohiodnr.com/parks/parks/lakeerie.htm
Phone: 419-797-4530
Size: 677 acres. **Location:** Lake Erie; accessible by ferry from Marblehead and Sandusky. **Facilities:** 127 campsites (82 with electricity), 2 rent-a-camp units, youth group camp, 2 rent-a-yurts, showers, flush toilets, picnic areas, picnic shelters, hiking trails (6 miles), swimming beach, boat ramps, game courts, playground. **Activities:** Camping, boating, fishing, swimming, hiking, hunting, ice fishing, ice skating, cross-country skiing. **Special Features:** Park's hiking trails lead to scenic vistas, historic sites, and two nature preserves that provide good locations for viewing wildlife.

★3702★ **KISER LAKE STATE PARK**
4889 N State Rt 235
Saint Paris, OH 43072
Web: www.ohiodnr.com/parks/parks/kisrlake.htm
Phone: 937-362-3822
Size: 531 acres land; 396 acres water. **Location:** An hour north of Dayton, in the southwest corner of the state. **Facilities:** 115 campsites (without electricity), group camp, camper cabin, picnic areas, picnic shelters, hiking trails (5 miles), swimming

beach, boat ramps, boat rentals, docks, game courts, playgrounds, nature center. **Activities:** Camping, boating (no motors permitted), sailing, fishing, swimming, scuba diving, hiking, hunting, ice skating, sledding, cross-country skiing, ice boating, ice fishing. **Special Features:** During the ice age, when ice edge remained stationary for a period of time, it created a linear ridge along its front, called a moraine. The Farmersville Moraine surrounds the lake on three sides, and contains boulders, some weighing several tons, carried from as far away as Canada. Called erratics, these boulders are a common sight at Kiser.

★3703★ LAKE ALMA STATE PARK

c/o Lake Hope State Park
27331 State Rt 278
McArthur, OH 45651
Web: www.ohiodnr.com/parks/parks/lakealma.htm
Phone: 740-384-4474
Size: 292 acres land; 60 acres water. **Location:** 34 miles southwest of Athens, in the southeast corner of the state. **Facilities:** 83 campsites (72 with electricity), camper cabin, group camp, picnic areas, picnic shelters, hiking trails (4 miles), paved bike path, swimming beaches, boat ramps, boat rentals, bike rentals, game courts, playground. **Activities:** Camping, boating (electric motors only), fishing, swimming, hiking, bicycling, sledding, ice skating, ice fishing, cross-country skiing. **Special Features:** Park is located in the Appalachian Highlands in the midst of some of Ohio's most rugged and scenic terrain.

★3704★ LAKE HOPE STATE PARK

27331 State Rt 278
McArthur, OH 45651
Web: www.ohiodnr.com/parks/parks/lakehope.htm
Phone: 740-596-5253
Size: 2983 acres land; 120 acres water. **Location:** 20 miles west of Athens in the southeast corner of the state. **Facilities:** 219 campsites (46 with electricity), 3 rent-a-camp units, camper cabins, youth group camp, 2 primitive campsites, group camp, 66 cottages, showers, picnic areas, picnic shelters, hiking trails (17 miles), bike trails (14 miles), restaurant, swimming beach, food concession, boat ramp, boat rentals, nature center, game courts, playgrounds. **Activities:** Camping, boating (electric motors only), canoeing, fishing, swimming, hiking, mountain biking, nature programs, ice fishing, cross-country skiing, ice skating, sledding. **Special Features:** Park lies entirely within the 26,824-acre Zaleski State Forest in the valley of Big Sandy Run. The yellow lady's slipper, one of the rarest and most showy orchids, blooms in secluded hollows of the park.

★3705★ LAKE LOGAN STATE PARK

20160 State Rd 664
Logan, OH 43138
Web: www.ohiodnr.com/parks/parks/lklogan.htm
Phone: 740-385-6842
Size: 318 acres land; 400 acres water. **Location:** 1 hour south of Columbus, in the southeast part of the state. **Facilities:** Picnic areas, hiking trails (4 miles), swimming beach, concession, boat ramps, boat rentals, docks. **Activities:** Boating (10 HP limit),

sailing, fishing, swimming, hiking, hunting, sledding, ice skating, ice fishing. **Special Features:** Lake Logan is one of the best fishing lakes in Ohio, with northern pike, bass, bluegill, crappie, catfish, and saugeye.

★3706★ LAKE LORAMIE STATE PARK

4401 Fort Loramie Swanders Rd
Minster, OH 45865
Web: www.ohiodnr.com/parks/parks/lkloramie.htm
Phone: 937-295-2011
Size: 407 acres land; 1,655 acres water. **Location:** 1 hour northwest of Dayton, in the northwest corner of the state. **Facilities:** 161 campsites with electricity, 4 rent-a-camp units, 3 group camps, showers, flush toilets, picnic areas, picnic shelters, hiking trails (8 miles), swimming beach, bike rentals, boat rentals, boat ramps, docks, playground. **Activities:** Camping, boating, fishing, swimming, hiking, biking, hunting, snowmobiling, sledding, cross-country skiing, ice boating, ice skating, ice fishing, nature programs. **Special Features:** Park's campground supports a colony of the unique bald cypress tree as well as a plantation of sweet gum dating back to the early 1950s. Wildflowers flourish in the forests and fields.

★3707★ LAKE MILTON STATE PARK

16801 Mahoning Ave
Lake Milton, OH 44429
Web: www.ohiodnr.com/parks/parks/lkmilton.htm
Phone: 330-654-4989
Size: 1,006 acres land; 1,685 acres water. **Location:** Off I-76 in Lake Milton, 17 miles west of Youngstown. **Facilities:** Picnic areas, picnic shelters, hiking trail (2 miles), showers, playground, game courts, swimming beach, marina, boat rentals, boat ramps, fuel dock, game courts. **Activities:** Boating, fishing, swimming, hiking, hunting, snowmobiling, cross-country skiing, ice fishing. **Special Features:** The lake's scenic shoreline provides a habitat for waterfowl and shorebirds. The south end of the lake offers boaters access to a section of the Mahoning River.

★3708★ LAKE WHITE STATE PARK

2767 State Rt 551
Waverly, OH 45690
Web: www.ohiodnr.com/parks/parks/lkwhitew.htm
Phone: 740-947-4059
Size: 92 acres land; 337 acres water. **Location:** 30 miles north of Portsmouth, in the southeast corner of the state. **Facilities:** 10 campsites (without electricity), picnic areas, picnic shelters, swimming beach, boat ramp. **Activities:** Camping, boating, water-skiing, fishing, swimming, ice skating, ice fishing, sledding. **Special Features:** Park is located in the Appalachian foothills near the Scioto River, and its sandstone outcroppings are coated with ferns, mosses, lichens, and fungi, including morel mushrooms. Part of the park includes the remains of the old Ohio and Erie Canal channel.

★3709★ LITTLE MIAMI SCENIC STATE PARK

c/o Caesar Creek State Park
8570 E State Rt 73
Waynesville, OH 45068
Web: www.ohiodnr.com/parks/parks/lilmiami.htm
Phone: 513-897-3055

Size: 50-mile linear park. **Location:** Along the Little Miami River from Green to Clermont Counties in the southwestern part of the state. **Facilities:** Multi-use paved trail, 3 staging areas (at Loveland, Morrow, and Corwin) with parking lots, restrooms, and trail access points (&&). **Activities:** Fishing, canoeing, rafting, hiking, bicycling, horseback riding, inline skating, cross-country skiing. **Special Features:** Located in the Little Miami River Valley, the park consists of nearly 50 miles of abandoned railroad right-of-way that was once part of the Penn Central railway system. The trail averages 66 feet in width and runs through four counties in southwestern Ohio. The park also offers access to the Little Miami River, one of Ohio's designated scenic rivers.

★3710★ MADISON LAKE STATE PARK

c/o Deer Creek State Park
20635 Waterloo Rd
Mount Sterling, OH 43143
Web: www.ohiodnr.com/parks/parks/madison.htm
Phone: 740-869-3124
Size: 80 acres land; 106 acres water. **Location:** 22 miles west of Columbus, in the center of the state. **Facilities:** Picnic areas, picnic shelters, hiking trail (0.5 mile), swimming beach, boat ramp, docks, game courts. **Activities:** Boating (electric motors only), sailing, canoeing, fishing, swimming, hunting. **Special Features:** Park lies within the vast Darby Plains of Ohio and features a lake formed by an impoundment on Deer Creek.

★3711★ MALABAR FARM STATE PARK

4050 Bromfield Rd
Lucas, OH 44843
Web: www.ohiodnr.com/parks/parks/malabar.htm
Phone: 419-892-2784; **Fax:** 419-892-3988
Size: 875 acres land; 3 acres water. **Location:** 1 hour northeast of Columbus, in the center of the state. **Facilities:** 15 campsites (without electricity), horsemen's camp, youth hostel, day-use lodge, picnic areas, restaurant, multi-use trails (12 miles). **Activities:** Camping, fishing, hiking, horseback riding, cross-country skiing, ice skating, sledding, guided tours, nature programs. **Special Features:** Malabar Farm was the dream of Louis Bromfield, Pulitzer Prize-winning author and dedicated conservationist who purchased 600 acres of worn-out farmland and, by applying wise conservation measures, made Malabar productive. Park offers daily tours of the 32-room "Big House" as well as special programs every month that include workshops on spinning, hearthside cooking, and other pioneer skills.

★3712★ MARBLEHEAD LIGHTHOUSE STATE PARK

c/o East Harbor State Park
1169 N Buck Rd
Lakeside-Marblehead, OH 43440
Web: www.ohiodnr.com/parks/parks/marblehead.htm
Phone: 419-734-4424
Size: 3 acres. **Location:** At the tip of a peninsula jutting into Lake Erie, east of Port Clinton. **Facilities:** Picnic areas, tours. **Activities:** Guided tours. **Special Features:** Park features Marblehead Lighthouse, the oldest lighthouse in continuous operation on the Great Lakes and one of Lake Erie's best-known and most-photographed landmarks. The grounds surrounding the lighthouse offer excellent views of Lake Erie, Sandusky Bay, Kelleys Island, and South Bass Island.

★3713★ MARY JANE THURSTON STATE PARK

1-466 State Rt 65
McClure, OH 43534
Web: www.ohiodnr.com/parks/parks/mjthrstn.htm
Phone: 419-832-7662
Size: 591 acres. **Location:** 12 miles west of Bowling Green, in the northwest part of the state. **Facilities:** 35 campsites (without electricity), 2 camper cabins, flush toilets, picnic areas, picnic shelters, day-use lodge (&), hiking trails (9 miles), bridle trails (6 miles), bike trails (6 miles), marina, 2 boat ramps, docks, playgrounds. **Activities:** Camping, hunting, boating, fishing, hiking, mountain biking, horseback riding, cross-country skiing, sledding, ice skating, ice fishing. **Special Features:** Situated along the historic Maumee River, this scenic park provides excellent stream fishing.

★3714★ MAUMEE BAY STATE PARK

1400 State Park Rd
Oregon, OH 43618
Web: www.ohiodnr.com/parks/parks/maumeebay.htm
Phone: 419-836-7758; **Fax:** 419-836-8711
Size: 1,336 acres. **Location:** 14 miles from Toledo in north central Ohio. **Facilities:** 252 campsites with electricity, 3 camper cabins, rent-a-yurt, showers, flush toilets, 120-room lodge, cottages, picnic areas, restaurant, hiking trails (10 miles), bike trails, boardwalk (&), swimming beach, food concession, swimming pool, docks, boat rentals, nature center, 18-hole golf course, playground, observation tower, observation blind, nature center, nature programs. **Activities:** Camping, boating (electric motors only), fishing, hiking, hunting, golf, cross-country skiing, snowmobiling, ice fishing, sledding. **Special Features:** Park provides visitors the rare opportunity to experience a largely unchanged coastal environment, including scenic meadows, wet woods, and marshes. Summer bird watchers may catch a glimpse of such unusual species as dickcissels, bobolinks, and western meadowlarks as well as bitterns and rails. Winter bird watchers may sight short-eared owls and marsh hawks.

★3715★ MIDDLE BASS ISLAND STATE PARK

c/o Catawba Island State Park
4049 E Moores Dock Rd
Port Clinton, OH 43452
Web: www.ohiodnr.com/parks/parks/middlebass.htm
Phone: 419-797-4530
Size: 124 acres. **Location:** On Lake Erie, accessible by boat only. **Facilities:** 21 primitive campsites, marina with 50 slips, half with electrical hookups. **Activities:** camping, boating. **Special Features:** Middle Bass is composed of limestone bedrock. The island's glacial past is evident in small scratches in the rock surface, known as glacial striations, carved by rocks embedded in the glacial ice. Stands of red cedar and the presence of underground caverns, both associated with limestone, are found here.

★3716★ MOHICAN STATE PARK

3116 State Rt 3
Loudonville, OH 44842
Web: www.ohiodnr.com/parks/parks/mohican.htm
Phone: 419-994-5125
Size: 1,110 acres. **Location:** Southwest of Loudonville, in the center of the state. **Facilities:** 186 campsites (153 with electricity), showers, flush toilets, group camp, 25 cottages, 96-room lodge, picnic areas, picnic shelters, restaurant, hiking trails (13 miles), bike trail (8.5 miles), bike rentals, game courts, meeting rooms, swimming pool, boat rentals. **Activities:** Camping, canoeing, fishing, swimming, hiking, biking, nature programs. **Special Features:** Wolf Creek/Pine Run Grist Mill is located in the park. Built in 1831, it originally stood north of Loudonville; it was dismanted, moved, and reconstructed at its present location in 1971. It features an overshot waterwheel that powers two millstones. Today the grist mill is being restored and operated as a working museum.

★3717★ MOSQUITO LAKE STATE PARK

1439 State Rt 305
Cortland, OH 44410
Web: www.ohiodnr.com/parks/parks/mosquito.htm
Phone: 330-637-2856
Size: 2,483 acres land; 4,000 acres water. **Location:** 26 miles northwest of Youngstown, in the northeast corner of the state. **Facilities:** 234 campsites (218 with electricity), showers, flush toilets, picnic areas, hiking trails (20 miles), bridle trails (20 miles), multi-use trails, swimming beach, marina, boat ramps, boat rentals, fuel dock, game courts, playground. **Activities:** Camping, boating, fishing, swimming, hiking, mountain biking, horseback riding, hunting, cross-country skiing, snowmobiling, ice skating, ice fishing, ice boating. **Special Features:** Mosquito Lake is one of the largest lakes in the state. This area has more cloudy days, cooler summer temperatures, and more winter snow cover than other areas of Ohio.

★3718★ MOUNT GILEAD STATE PARK

4119 State Rt 95
Mount Gilead, OH 43338
Web: www.ohiodnr.com/parks/parks/mtgilead.htm
Phone: 419-946-1961
Size: 181 acres land; 32 acres water. **Location:** In Morrow County near the center of the state. **Facilities:** 65 campsites (59 with electricity), 2 camper cabins, group camp, picnic areas, picnic shelters, hiking trails (6 miles), bridle trails, boat rentals, boat ramps, game courts, playground, amphitheater, gazebo. **Activities:** Camping, boating (electric motors only), canoeing, fishing, hiking, sledding, ice skating, ice fishing, cross-country skiing, horseback riding. **Special Features:** In the vicinity of Mount Gilead, three end moraines (linear ridges of glacial sediment deposited along the ice edge) converged and account for the rolling terrain seen there today. The first lake here was built in 1919 on the upper level of Sam's Creek. In 1930, a larger lake was completed below the first one on the same tributary of Whetstone Creek.

★3719★ MUSKINGUM RIVER STATE PARK

1390 Ellis Dam Rd
Zanesville, OH 43701
Web: www.ohiodnr.com/parks/parks/muskngmr.htm
Phone: 740-453-4377
Size: 120 acres. **Location:** On the Muskingum River, in the southeast corner of the state. **Facilities:** 20 campsites (without electricity), picnic areas, hiking trail (1 mile), boat ramps. **Activities:** Camping, boating, fishing, hiking. **Special Features:** Muskingum River Parkway features 10 manually-operated locks that are similar to those built throughout the United States before the 20th century.

★3720★ NELSON-KENNEDY LEDGES STATE PARK

c/o Punderson State Park
PO Box 338
Newberry, OH 44065
Web: www.ohiodnr.com/parks/parks/nelsonk.htm
Phone: 440-564-2279
Size: 167 acres. **Location:** Near Cleveland, in the northeast corner of the state. **Facilities:** Picnic areas, hiking trails (3 miles). **Activities:** Hiking, picnicking. **Special Features:** Park features interesting rock formations that are among the few outcrops in northern Ohio still exposed to view. The sandstone cliff formations are the result of erosion (wind, water freezing and thawing) that wore away at the softer rock layers. As these soft layers eroded, large blocks of rock called slump blocks fell away, leaving more resistant layers to form ledges above.

★3721★ OAK POINT STATE PARK

c/o Catawba Island State Park
4049 E Moores Dock Rd
Port Clinton, OH 43452
Web: www.ohiodnr.com/parks/parks/lakeerie.htm
Phone: 419-797-4530
Size: 1 acre. **Location:** On the northwestern tip of South Bass Island, just outside the village of Put-In-Bay. Accessible by boat only. **Facilities:** Picnic areas. **Activities:** Fishing, boating, ice fishing. **Special Features:** Park features overnight docking facilities on Lake Erie.

★3722★ PAINT CREEK STATE PARK

14265 US Hwy 50
Bainbridge, OH 45612
Web: www.ohiodnr.com/parks/parks/paintcrk.htm
Phone: 937-365-1401
Size: 5,652 acres land; 1,190 acres water. **Location:** 20 miles southwest of Chillicothe, in the southeast corner of the state. **Facilities:** 195 campsites with electricity, 2 camper cabins, horseman's camp, showers, flush toilets, laundry, picnic areas, picnic shelter, hiking trails (8 miles), bridle trails (25 miles), bike trails (14 miles), swimming beach, food concession, boat ramps, boat rentals, houseboat rentals, fuel dock, nature center, game courts. **Activities:** Camping, boating, fishing, swimming, hiking, horseback riding, mountain biking, hunting, cross-country skiing, sledding. **Special Features:** Located within the park, Paint Creek Pioneer Farm includes a log house, a collection of

9. State Parks

log buildings, livestock, gardens, and fields which represent a typical farm of the early 1800s.

★3723★ PIKE LAKE STATE PARK

1847 Pike Lake Rd
Bainbridge, OH 45612
Web: www.ohiodnr.com/parks/parks/pikelake.htm
Phone: 740-493-2212
Size: 587 acres land; 13 acres water. Location: 70 miles south of Columbus, in the southeast part of the state. Facilities: 80 campsites with electricity, group camp, 24 cottages, picnic areas, picnic shelter, hiking trails (6 miles), backpack trail (3 miles), bridle trails (nearby), swimming beach, food concession, boat rentals, game courts. Activities: Camping, boating (electric motors only), fishing, swimming, hiking, bird watching, sledding, ice fishing, ice skating. Special Features: A portion of the 1,300-mile Buckeye Trail passes through the park. Hunting is permitted in Pike State Forest, which surrounds the park.

★3724★ PORTAGE LAKES STATE PARK

5031 Manchester Rd
Akron, OH 44319
Web: www.ohiodnr.com/parks/parks/portage.htm
Phone: 330-644-2220; Fax: 330-644-7550
Size: 411 acres land; 2,034 acres water. Location: Between Akron and Canton, in the northeast corner of the state. Facilities: 74 campsites (without electricity), picnic areas, picnic shelters, hiking trails (5 miles), swimming beach, boat ramps, game courts. Activities: Camping, hunting, boating (400 HP limit), fishing, swimming, hiking, hunting, cross-country skiing, snowmobiling, ice fishing, ice skating. Special Features: Portage Lakes is named after the old Indian portage path that connected the Cuyahoga River flowing north to Lake Erie and the Tuscarawas River flowing south (through the Muskingum) to the Ohio River.

★3725★ PUNDERSON STATE PARK

PO Box 338
11755 Kinsman Rd
Newbury, OH 44065
Web: www.ohiodnr.com/parks/parks/punderson.htm
Phone: 440-564-2279
Size: 741 acres land; 150 acres water. Location: 25 miles east of Cleveland, in the northeast corner of the state. Facilities: 196 campsites with electricity, 4 rent-a-camp units, 3 rent-a-RV units, showers, flush toilets, 26 cottages, 31-room lodge, picnic areas, hiking trails (14 miles), swimming beach, boat ramps, boat rentals, docks, toboggan and ski rentals, restaurant, 18-hole golf course, nature center, game courts. Activities: Camping, boating (electric motors only), fishing, swimming, hiking, golf, cross-country skiing, snowmobiling, sledding, ice fishing. Special Features: Punderson Lake, which is one of the state's few natural lakes, is a kettle lake formed when a large block of ice broke off a glacier, creating a depression which filled with meltwater. It is the largest and deepest kettle lake in Ohio.

★3726★ PYMATUNING STATE PARK

PO Box 1000
Andover, OH 44003
Web: www.ohiodnr.com/parks/parks/pymatuning.htm
Phone: 440-293-6030
Size: 3,512 acres land; 1,407 acres water. Location: 1 hour east of Cleveland, in the northeast part of the state. Facilities: 352 campsites (331 with electricity), 3 rent-a-yurt units, showers, flush toilets, laundry, 58 cottages, picnic areas, picnic shelters, hiking trails (2 miles), swimming beach, food concession, boat ramps, boat rentals, playgrounds, game courts, nature center. Activities: Camping, boating (10 HP limit), fishing, swimming, hiking, hunting, cross-country skiing, ice skating, ice fishing, ice boating, nature programs. Special Features: Pymatuning is a state park in both Ohio and Pennsylvania (see separate entry in Pennsylvania state parks section). Pymatuning Lake is one of the finest walleye and muskellunge fishing lakes in the country.

★3727★ QUAIL HOLLOW STATE PARK

13340 Congress Lake Ave
Hartville, OH 44632
Web: www.ohiodnr.com/parks/parks/quailhlw.htm
Phone: 330-877-1528
Size: 701 acres land; 2 acres water. Location: Between Akron and Canton in the east central part of the state. Facilities: Group camp, picnic areas, hiking trails (19 miles), bike trail (2 miles), interpretive trail (&), visitor center, nature viewing site, herb garden, playground, volleyball court, ski rentals. Activities: Camping, hiking, mountain biking, cross-country skiing, sledding, ice skating, nature programs. Special Features: Quail Hollow is the 1920s-era family estate of railroad entrepreneur H.B. Stewart, featuring a 40-room manor house and grounds.

★3728★ ROCKY FORK STATE PARK

9800 N Shore Dr
Hillsboro, OH 45133
Web: www.ohiodnr.com/parks/parks/rockyfrk.htm
Phone: 937-393-4284
Size: 1,384 acres land; 2,080 acres water. Location: 1 hour southwest of Columbus in the southeast corner of the state. Facilities: 230 campsites (130 with electricity), group camp, showers, flush toilets, picnic areas, picnic shelters, hiking trails (2 miles), bike trail (2 miles), 2 swimming beaches, bathhouses, food concession, fishing pier (&), marina, boat ramps, boat rentals, fuel dock, restaurant, game courts, playground. Activities: Camping, boating, fishing, swimming, water-skiing, hiking, hunting, nature programs. Special Features: Especially popular with boating enthusiasts, Rocky Fork's lake offers excellent fishing for bass, muskellunge, and walleye. The park's other natural features include a scenic gorge, dolomite caves, and a wetlands preserve. A short trail near the campground leads to a bird observation station.

★3729★ SALT FORK STATE PARK

14755 Cadiz Rd
Lore City, OH 43755
Web: www.ohiodnr.com/parks/parks/saltfork.htm
Phone: 740-439-3521

Size: 17,229 acres land; 2,952 acres water. **Location:** 35 miles east of Zanesville, in the southeast corner of the state. **Facilities:** 212 campsites with electricity (&), 3 rent-a-camp units, group camp, horseman's camp, showers, flush toilets, 148-room lodge, 54 cottages, picnic areas (&), picnic shelters, restaurant, hiking trails (14 miles), bridle trails (36 miles), swimming beach, food concession, marina, boat ramps, boat rentals, fuel dock, 18-hole golf course, minature golf course, game courts, nature center. **Activities:** Camping, boating, fishing, swimming, hiking, horseback riding, hunting, golf, cross-country skiing, snowmobiling, sledding, ice skating, ice fishing, ice boating, nature programs. **Special Features:** Park features the Kennedy Stone House, built in 1837 from locally-quarried stone by an early resident. It is listed on the *National Register of Historic Places* and can be visited throughout the year.

★3730★ SCIOTO TRAIL STATE PARK

144 Lake Rd
Chillicothe, OH 45601
Web: www.ohiodnr.com/parks/parks/sciototr.htm
Phone: 740-663-2125
Size: 218 acres land; 30 acres water. **Location:** Off US 23, south of Chillicothe, on State Route 372. **Facilities:** 73 campsites (40 with electricity), 2 camper cabins, picnic areas, hiking trails (12 miles), boat ramp, wading beach, 2-acre playfield, nature center. **Activities:** Camping, boating (electric motors only), canoeing, fishing, hiking, hunting, cross-country skiing, sledding, ice skating, ice fishing. **Special Features:** Park's nature center is housed in the restored Old Log Church, a replica of the oldest Presbyterian church in the Northwest territory.

★3731★ SHAWNEE STATE PARK

4404 State Rt 125
West Portsmouth, OH 45663
Web: www.ohiodnr.com/parks/parks/shawnee.htm
Phone: 740-858-6652
Size: 1,095 acres land; 68 acres water. **Location:** Off State Route 125, northwest of Portsmouth. **Facilities:** 107 campsites (101 with electricity), rent-a-camp, 2 camper cabins, showers, flush toilets, laundry, 50-room lodge, 25 cottages, picnic areas, picnic shelters (&), restaurant, hiking trails (5 miles), bike rentals, swimming beach, food concession, marina, boat ramps, boat rentals, fuel dock, amphitheater, 18-hole golf course, miniature golf, game courts, playground. **Activities:** Camping, boating (electric motors only), fishing, swimming, hiking, golf, ice fishing, nature programs. **Special Features:** Located in the Appalachian foothills bordering the Ohio River, park is nestled in the 60,000-acre Shawnee State Forest. The state forest includes a multitude of trails, including a popular 50-mile backpack trail and 75 miles of bridle trails.

★3732★ SOUTH BASS ISLAND STATE PARK

c/o Catawba Island State Park
4049 E Moores Dock Rd
Port Clinton, OH 43452
Web: www.ohiodnr.com/parks/parks/lakeerie.htm
Phone: 419-797-4530
Size: 32 acres. **Location:** Lake Erie; accessible by ferry from Catawba and Port Clinton. **Facilities:** 135 campsites (10 with electricity), youth group camp, showers, picnic areas, picnic shelters, swimming beach, boat ramps, docks, boat/jetski rentals. **Activities:** Camping, boating, fishing, swimming, ice fishing, ice skating. **Special Features:** South Bass Island is one of five islands that comprise Lake Erie Islands State Park. South Bass has been famous as a summer resort for more than a century.

★3733★ STONELICK STATE PARK

2895 Lake Dr
Pleasant Plain, OH 45162
Web: www.ohiodnr.com/parks/parks/stonelck.htm
Phone: 513-734-4323
Size: 1,058 acres land; 200 acres water. **Location:** 22 miles from Cincinnati, in the southwest part of the state. **Facilities:** 114 campsites (108 with electricity), camper cabin, group camp, showers, flush toilets, picnic areas, picnic shelters, hiking and bike trails (7 miles), swimming beach, boat rentals, boat ramp, game courts, bike rental, playground, camp store, laundry. **Activities:** Camping, boating (electric motors only), fishing, swimming, hiking, hunting, mountain biking, cross-country skiing, sledding, ice skating, ice fishing, ice boating, nature programs. **Special Features:** Located in the rolling highlands of southwest Ohio, the park includes portions of uplifted bedrock with exposed fossils of trilobites, brachiopods, cephalopods, and other species, giving Stonelick one of the richest fossil records in the state.

★3734★ STROUDS RUN STATE PARK

c/o Burr Oak State Park
1022 Burr Oak Lodge Rd
Glouster, OH 45732
Web: www.ohiodnr.com/parks/parks/strouds.htm
Phone: 740-592-2302
Size: 2,606 acres land; 161 acres water. **Location:** 1 hour south of Columbus in the southeast corner of the state. **Facilities:** 75 campsites (without electricity), 3 rent-a-camp units, group camp, picnic areas, picnic shelters, hiking trails (16 miles), bridle trails (8 miles), swimming beach, boat ramp, boat rentals, game courts, playground. **Activities:** Camping, boating (10 HP limit), fishing, swimming, scuba diving, hiking, hunting, sledding, cross-country skiing. **Special Features:** Although untouched by the ice sheets that moved across portions of the state more than 12,000 years ago, the effects of the glaciers can be seen in the park's deep ravines and high hills.

★3735★ SYCAMORE STATE PARK

c/o Hueston Woods State Park
6301 Park Office Rd
College Corner, OH 45003
Web: www.ohiodnr.com/parks/parks/sycamore.htm
Phone: 513-523-6347
Size: 2,384 acres land; 5 acres water. **Location:** Just west of Dayton in the southwest part of the state. **Facilities:** Group camps (&), horsemen's campsite, picnic areas, picnic shelters, hiking trails (8 miles), bridle trails (15 miles), snowmobile trail (15 miles). **Activities:** Camping, canoeing, fishing, hiking, horseback riding, hunting, cross-country skiing, snowmobiling,

9. State Parks

sledding, ice skating, ice fishing, snowmobiling. **Special Features:** Ghost Hedge Nature Trail allows hikers to explore the Wolf Creek Valley; giant sycamore trees form a picturesque canopy over the trail.

★3736★ TAR HOLLOW STATE PARK

16396 Tar Hollow Rd
Laurelville, OH 43135
Web: www.ohiodnr.com/parks/parks/tarhollw.htm
Phone: 740-887-4818
Size: 604 acres land; 15 acres water. **Location:** 1 hour south of Columbus, in the southeast corner of the state. **Facilities:** 105 campsites (71 with electricity), showers, picnic areas, picnic shelters, hiking trails (24 miles), bridle trails (25 miles), backpack trails (21 miles), bike trails (3.5 miles), swimming beach, boat ramps, bike rentals, playground, miniature golf, nature center. **Activities:** Camping, boating (electric motors only), fishing, swimming, hiking, mountain biking, horseback riding, backpacking. **Special Features:** Surrounded by the rugged foothills of the Appalachian plateau, park and surrounding state forest are reminiscent of the wilderness that characterized the Ohio country in the days of the early settlers.

★3737★ TINKERS CREEK STATE PARK

c/o Punderson State Park
11755 Kinsman Rd
Newbury, OH 44065
Web: www.ohiodnr.com/parks/parks/tinkers.htm
Phone: 440-564-2279
Size: 355 acres land; 15 acres water. **Location:** 19 miles east of Akron, in the northeast part of the state. **Facilities:** Picnic areas, picnic shelters, hiking trail (3.5 miles), game courts, playground. **Activities:** Fishing, hiking, cross-country skiing, ice fishing. **Special Features:** The majority of the park is maintained in its original state as a swamp and marshland. The park is ideal for those who enjoy watching birds and animals in their natural habitat.

★3738★ VAN BUREN STATE PARK

c/o Mary Jane Thurston State Park
1-466 State Rt 65
McClure, OH 43534
Web: www.ohiodnr.com/parks/parks/vanburen.htm
Phone: 419-832-7662
Size: 251 acres land; 45 acres water. **Location:** 1 hour south of Toledo, in the northwest part of the state. **Facilities:** 65 campsites (without electricity), group camp, horsemen's camp, picnic areas, picnic shelters, hiking trails (10 miles), bridle trails (6 miles), nature center, amphitheater, playground, nature programs. **Activities:** Camping, boating (electric motors only), fishing, hiking, horseback riding, hunting, ice fishing, ice skating, cross-country skiing. **Special Features:** The area that is now the park was originally inhabited by the Shawnee Indians. Banished from their original homelands in southern Ohio, this was one of the last strongholds of the tribe before they finally departed for lands west of the state.

★3739★ WEST BRANCH STATE PARK

5708 Esworthy Rd
Ravenna, OH 44266
Web: www.ohiodnr.com/parks/parks/westbrnc.htm
Phone: 330-296-3239
Size: 5,379 acres land; 2,650 acres water. **Location:** 19 miles east of Akron, in the northeast part of the state. **Facilities:** 198 campsites (14 without electricity), group camp, horseman's camp, picnic areas, picnic shelters, hiking trails (41 miles), bridle trails (20 miles), bike trails (7 miles), swimming beach, food concession, marina, boat ramps, boat rentals, fuel dock, game courts, playground. **Activities:** Camping, boating, fishing, swimming, hiking, horseback riding, hunting, cross-country skiing, snowmobiling, ice boating, ice fishing, nature programs. **Special Features:** Park contains numerous bogs, created when kettle lakes formed by melting glacial blocks filled with sediment.

★3740★ WOLF RUN STATE PARK

16170 Wolf Run Rd
Caldwell, OH 43724
Web: www.ohiodnr.com/parks/parks/wolfrun.htm
Phone: 740-732-5035
Size: 1,118 acres land; 220 acres water. **Location:** Off State Route 821 at Belle Valley. **Facilities:** 138 campsites (71 with electricity), showers, youth group camp, picnic areas, picnic shelters, hiking trails (5.5 miles), swimming beach, boat ramps. **Activities:** Camping, boating (10 HP limit), fishing, swimming, hiking, hunting, sledding. **Special Features:** Park received its name from the Wolf family, the first to settle in the area.

Oklahoma State Parks

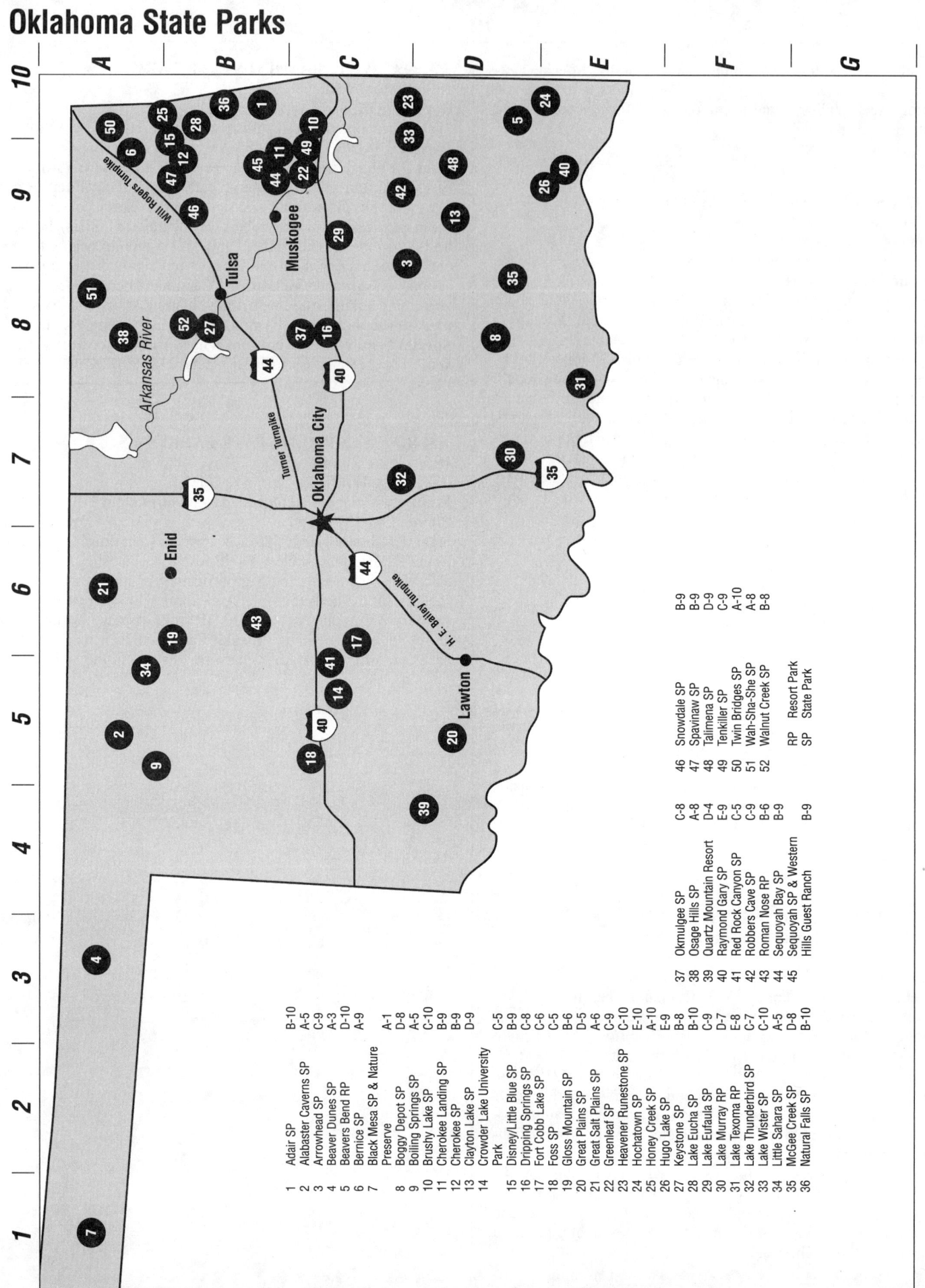

1	Adair SP	B-10	
2	Alabaster Caverns SP	A-5	
3	Arrowhead SP	C-9	
4	Beaver Dunes SP	A-3	
5	Beavers Bend RP	D-10	
6	Bernice SP	A-9	
7	Black Mesa SP & Nature		
	Preserve	A-1	
8	Boggy Depot SP	D-8	
9	Boiling Springs SP	A-5	
10	Brushy Lake SP	C-10	
11	Cherokee Landing SP	B-9	
12	Cherokee SP	B-9	
13	Clayton Lake SP	D-9	
14	Crowder Lake University		
	Park	C-5	
15	Disney/Little Blue SP	B-9	
16	Dripping Springs SP	C-8	
17	Fort Cobb Lake SP	C-6	
18	Foss SP	C-5	
19	Gloss Mountain SP	B-6	
20	Great Plains SP	D-5	
21	Great Salt Plains SP	A-6	
22	Greenleaf SP	C-9	
23	Heavener Runestone SP	C-10	
24	Hochatown SP	E-10	
25	Honey Creek SP	A-10	
26	Hugo Lake SP	E-9	
27	Keystone SP	B-8	
28	Lake Eucha SP	B-10	
29	Lake Eufaula SP	C-9	
30	Lake Murray RP	D-7	
31	Lake Texoma RP	E-8	
32	Lake Thunderbird SP	C-7	
33	Lake Wister SP	C-10	
34	Little Sahara SP	A-5	
35	McGee Creek SP	D-8	
36	Natural Falls SP	B-10	
37	Okmulgee SP	C-8	
38	Osage Hills SP	A-8	
39	Quartz Mountain Resort	D-4	
40	Raymond Gary SP	E-9	
41	Red Rock Canyon SP	C-5	
42	Robbers Cave SP	C-9	
43	Roman Nose RP	B-6	
44	Sequoyah Bay SP	B-9	
45	Sequoyah SP & Western		
	Hills Guest Ranch	B-9	
46	Snowdale SP	B-9	
47	Spavinaw SP	B-9	
48	Talimena SP	D-9	
49	Tenkiller SP	C-9	
50	Twin Bridges SP	A-10	
51	Wah-Sha-She SP	A-8	
52	Walnut Creek SP	B-8	
	RP	Resort Park	
	SP	State Park	

**★3741★ Oklahoma Tourism & Recreation Department
State Parks Division**
15 N Robinson Ave, Suite 210
Oklahoma City, OK 73102
(405) 521-3411 - Phone
(405) 521-2428 - Fax
(800) 654-8240 - Information & Reservations
Web: www.touroklahoma.com
Oversees more than 50 state parks including six resorts, each
of which was developed around a historical theme. Maintains
an extensive and varied trail system. Sponsors environmental
activities and educational programs for students and park visitors.

★3742★ Oklahoma Department of Wildlife Conservation
1801 N Lincoln Blvd
Oklahoma City, OK 73105
(405) 521-4660 - Phone
(405) 521-6535 - Fax
Web: www.wildlifedepartment.com
Manages wildlife management areas; administers hunting and
fishing licensing. Coordinates educational programs on wildlife
conservation and hunting safety.

★3743★ Oklahoma Historical Society
2401 N Laird Ave
Oklahoma City, OK 73105
(405) 522-5248
Web: www.ok-history.mus.ok.us
Operates 32 historical properties, which include archeological
sites, historic homes, battlegrounds, and museums.

Key to campsite classification:

- **Modern campsites** — Electricity, sewer, and water
  hookups, and table and grill at each site.
- **Semi-modern campsites** — Electricity hookup, table
  and grill at each site; water hookup either at the campsite
  or water available at every 2 to 3 campsites.
- **Primitive campsites** — No utility hookups. Many offer
  table and grill, and nearby drinking water and comfort
  station. Trailside campsites may include no facilities.
- **Teepee** and **Yurt units** — Equipped with lights and
  electrical outlets.

★3744★ ADAIR STATE PARK
Hwy 51 & Hwy 59
Stilwell, OK 74960
Web: www.oklahomaparks.com
Phone: 918-696-6613; **Fax:** 918-696-2908

Size: 25 acres. **Location:** Within the city limits of Stilwell just
off SH 51E. **Facilities:** 6 semi-modern campsites, 20 primitive
campsites, fishing pond, ball fields, boat rental, playground,
showers, picnic facilities. **Activities:** Camping, boating, fishing,
baseball, softball. **Special Features:** Park includes a 15-acre
pond.

★3745★ ALABASTER CAVERNS STATE PARK
Hwy 50 & Hwy 50-A
Freedom, OK 73842
Web: www.oklahomaparks.com
Phone: 580-621-3381; **Fax:** 580-621-3572
Size: 200 acres. **Location:** 6 miles south of Freedom on SH
50, then 0.5 miles east on Highway 50A. **Facilities:** 20 campsites
(semi-modern and primitive), comfort stations, showers, picnic
area, picnic shelter, trails, visitor center (&&). **Activities:** Camping, hiking, volleyball, spelunking, guided cave tours, interpretive programs. **Special Features:** The 0.75-mile-long underground cavern is the nation's largest gypsum cave open to guided
tours, offering visitors the opportunity to view massive boulders
of pink, white, and even rare black alabaster. From March to
September, park visitors may also explore five undeveloped
caves.

★3746★ ARROWHEAD STATE PARK
HC 67, Box 57
Canadian, OK 74425
Web: www.oklahomaparks.com
Phone: 918-339-2204; **Fax:** 918-339-7236
Size: 2,202 acres. **Location:** 4 miles east of Canadian off US
69, on State Park Road. **Facilities:** 214 campsites (modern,
semi-modern, and primitive), horsemen's camp, group camp,
showers, picnic area, group shelters, trails, beach and bathhouse,
marina, boat ramp, fishing dock, boat rentals, playgrounds, miniature golf, 18-hole golf course, gift shop, airplane landing strip
(&&). **Activities:** Camping, boating, fishing, swimming, water-
skiing, jet skiing, hiking, horseback riding, golf. **Special Features:** Park is located on the shores of 102,500-acre Lake Eufaula, Oklahoma's largest lake, which offers good fishing for
crappie, bass, catfish, and sunfish.

★3747★ BEAVER DUNES STATE PARK
PO Box 1190
Beaver, OK 73932
Web: www.oklahomaparks.com
Phone: 580-625-3373; **Fax:** 580-625-3525
Size: 520 acres. **Location:** 1 mile north of Beaver on US 270.
Facilities: 20 semi-modern campsites, 10 primitive campsites,
comfort stations, showers, picnic area, 2 group shelters, interpre-
tive trail, game courts, playground (&&). **Activities:** Camping,
fishing, hiking, volleyball, ORV riding. **Special Features:** Park

9. State Parks

features 300 acres of sand dunes set aside for dune buggies and other off-road vehicles.

★3748★ BEAVERS BEND RESORT PARK

PO Box 10
Broken Bow, OK 74728
Web: www.oklahomaparks.com
Phone: 580-494-6300; **Fax:** 580-494-6689
Size: 3,482 acres. **Location:** Off US 259, adjacent to Broken Bow Lake. **Facilities:** 393 campsites (modern, semi-modern, and primitive), 2 group camps, showers, 47 cabins, 40-room lodge, beach and bathhouse, boat ramps, boat rentals, 18-hole golf course, miniature golf course, restaurant, nature center, amphitheater, game courts, store (&&). **Activities:** Camping, boating, canoeing, water-skiing, fishing, swimming, scuba diving, hiking, backpacking, horseback riding, mountain biking, golf, tennis, archery, excursion train rides, interpretive programs. **Special Features:** Park straddles the banks of the Mountain Fork River where it begins flowing out of 14,000-acre Broken Bow Lake. The park's Forest Heritage Center and Museum houses historical documents, antique forestry tools, wood art, homestead memorabilia, and a research library with materials pertaining to forestry. Park trails include the 26-mile David L. Boren Trail. Eagle watches are held every November-February.

★3749★ BERNICE STATE PARK

901 State Park Rd
Grove, OK 74344
Web: www.oklahomaparks.com
Phone: 918-786-9447; **Fax:** 918-787-5634
Size: 88 acres. **Location:** 0.5 miles east of Bernice off SH 85A **Facilities:** 31 semi-modern campsites, 200 primitive campsites, showers, picnic areas, group shelter, 2 wildlife watch towers, boat ramp, swimming beach, walking and jogging path (&&). **Activities:** Camping, boating, fishing, swimming, water-skiing, scuba diving. **Special Features:** Park sits on the western shore of Grand Lake, which has 46,300 surface acres and 1,300 miles of shoreline. The lake is considered the best in the state for crappie and also offers excellent fishing opportunities for bass and catfish.

★3750★ BLACK MESA STATE PARK & NATURE PRESERVE

County Rd 325
Kenton, OK 73946
Web: www.oklahomaparks.com
Phone: 580-426-2222; **Fax:** 580-426-2405
Size: 349 acres. **Location:** 27 miles northwest of Boise City on County Road 325. **Facilities:** 34 semi-modern campsites, 30 primitive campsites, group camp, horsemen's camp, comfort station, showers, picnic area, group shelter, boat ramps, playground (&&). **Activities:** Camping, boating, fishing, ice fishing, hiking, mountain biking, horseback riding, birding, wildlife viewing. **Special Features:** Park is located on the extreme western edge of Oklahoma's panhandle, surrounding 159-acre Lake Carl Etling. Black Mesa Nature Preserve, 15 miles to the north, includes a 4.2-mile trail that leads to a monument marking the state's highest point (4,973 feet).

★3751★ BOGGY DEPOT STATE PARK

Hwy 7 & Park Access Ln
Atoka, OK 74525
Web: www.oklahomaparks.com
Phone: 580-889-5625; **Fax:** 580-889-8816
Size: 630 acres. **Location:** 11 miles west of Atoka on SH 7, then 4 miles south. **Facilities:** 6 modern campsites, 20 semi-modern campsites, 80 primitive campsites, showers, picnic area, 3 picnic shelters, nature trail, historical area, ballparks, playground. **Activities:** Camping, fishing, hiking. **Special Features:** Located along the old Texas Road between Fort Gibson and Fort Washita, Boggy Depot was a well established crossroads during the Civil War. Park includes a six-acre stocked fishing lake.

★3752★ BOILING SPRINGS STATE PARK

Rt 2, Box 299
Woodward, OK 73802
Web: www.oklahomaparks.com
Phone: 580-256-7664; **Fax:** 580-256-4338
Size: 820 acres. **Location:** 1 mile north of Woodward on SH 34, then 5 miles east on SH 34C. **Facilities:** 50 campsites (modern, semi-modern, and primitive), 2 group camps, 4 cabins, showers, picnic area, group shelters, trails, swimming pool and bathhouse, snack bar, gift shop (&&). **Activities:** Camping, fishing, swimming, hiking, mountain biking. **Special Features:** Park is named for the cool springs that "boil up" at 200 gallons per minute through the white sand of the North Canadian River. The last stand of Big Timber in western Oklahoma lies within park property.

★3753★ BRUSHY LAKE STATE PARK

Rt 3, Box 36
Sallisaw, OK 74955
Web: www.oklahomaparks.com
Phone: 918-775-6507; **Fax:** 918-775-0970
Size: 90 acres. **Location:** 8 miles north of Sallisaw on US 59. **Facilities:** 35 campsites (semi-modern and primitive), picnic area, group shelters, boat ramp, boat dock, playground. **Activities:** Camping, boating, fishing. **Special Features:** Located in the scenic wooded Cookson Hills, this eastern Oklahoma park features 300-acre Brushy Lake.

★3754★ CHEROKEE LANDING STATE PARK

Hwy 82 S
Park Hill, OK 74451
Web: www.oklahomaparks.com
Phone: 918-457-5716; **Fax:** 918-457-4871
Size: 146 acres. **Location:** 10 miles south of the junction of US 62 and US 82, south of Tahlequah. **Facilities:** 150 campsites (semi-modern and primitive), RV group camp, showers, picnic area, group shelters, boat ramp, fishing dock, beach, ballparks, playground (&&). **Activities:** Camping, boating, fishing, swimming, water-skiing, volleyball, interpretive programs. **Special Features:** In the early 1800s, after a devastating journey from Georgia over the Trail of Tears, the Cherokee Indians came to this area and built a nation. The park lies in the heart of Cherokee

Territory, on the north shore of 12,500-acre Lake Tenkiller, surrounded by thick pine forests.

★3755★ CHEROKEE STATE PARK

PO Box 220
Disney, OK 74340
Web: www.oklahomaparks.com
Phone: 918-435-8066; **Fax:** 918-435-4067
Size: 43 acres. **Location:** East of Langley to River Road, then 1 mile south. **Facilities:** 124 campsites (semi-modern and primitive), showers, picnic areas, group shelters, boat ramps, swimming beach, 9-hole golf course, playground. **Activities:** Camping, boating, sailing, fishing, swimming, water-skiing, jet skiing, scuba diving, golfing. **Special Features:** Park consists of three small parcels below Pensacola Dam, alongside 46,300-acre Grand Lake.

★3756★ CLAYTON LAKE STATE PARK

HC 60, Box 33-10
Clayton, OK 74536
Web: www.oklahomaparks.com
Phone: 918-569-7981; **Fax:** 918-569-7981
Size: 510 acres. **Location:** 5 miles south of Clayton on SH 271. **Facilities:** 26 semi-modern campsites, 33 primitive campsites, cabins, showers, picnic area, group shelters, swimming beach, boat ramp, playground (&&). **Activities:** Camping, boating, fishing, swimming. **Special Features:** 95-acre Clayton Lake is considered a hot spot for bass fishing.

★3757★ CROWDER LAKE UNIVERSITY PARK

RR 1, Box 186
Colony, OK 73031
Web: www.swosu.edu/academics/crowderlake/
Phone: 580-343-2443; **Fax:** 580-774-7059
Size: 10 acres. **Location:** 8 miles south of Weatherford on SH 54, 2 miles east and 1 mile south on County Road, and then 0.75 miles west on Park Road. **Facilities:** 7 semi-modern campsites, showers, picnic area, boat ramp, boat dock, fishing pier, ballparks, ropes course, rapelling tower, rock climbing wall, canoe rentals, interpretive nature trail (&&). **Activities:** Camping, boating, fishing, swimming, rock climbing. **Special Features:** Owned and operated by Southwestern Oklahoma State University, park is situated on the shores of 158-acre Crowder Lake, which has been designated a Trophy Bass Lake by the Oklahoma Department of Wildlife Conservation. In addition to excellent black and white bass, many game fish can be found in large numbers, including crappie, saugeye, blue gill, and channel catfish.

★3758★ DISNEY/LITTLE BLUE STATE PARK

c/o Cherokee State Park
PO Box 220
Disney, OK 74340
Web: www.oklahomaparks.com
Phone: 918-435-8066
Size: 32 acres. **Location:** 1 block east of Disney on SH 28, near the flood gates of Pensacola Dam. **Facilities:** 80 primitive campsites, picnic areas, group shelters, boat ramp, playground. **Activities:** Camping, boating, fishing, water-skiing. **Special Features:** Park has the only boat ramp on the east side of Pensacola Dam. The dam was built in 1940 and is believed to be the longest multiple-arch dam in the world.

★3759★ DRIPPING SPRINGS STATE PARK

16830 Dripping Springs Rd
Okmulgee, OK 74447
Web: www.oklahomaparks.com
Phone: 918-756-5971; **Fax:** 918-759-9933
Size: 1,075 acres. **Location:** West of Okmulgee, just south of Okmulgee State Park. **Facilities:** Semi-modern and primitive campsites, group camp, showers, picnic area, group shelters, boat ramp, fishing dock, swimming beach. **Activities:** Camping, boating, fishing, swimming. **Special Features:** Park is located just south of the dam on 1,050-acre Dripping Springs Lake, which was designated as Oklahoma's first "trophy bass lake."

★3760★ FORT COBB LAKE STATE PARK

1269 Copperhead Rd
Fort Cobb, OK 73038
Web: www.oklahomaparks.com
Phone: 405-643-2249; **Fax:** 405-643-5167
Size: 1,872 acres. **Location:** 7 miles north of the city of Fort Cobb. **Facilities:** 344 semi-modern campsites, 600+ primitive campsites, yurt rentals, showers, picnic area, picnic pavilions, trails, swimming beach, boat ramps, marina, fuel dock, enclosed fishing dock, boat rentals, tackle shop, community center (120-person capacity), 18-hole golf course, camp store, snack bar, playground (&&). **Activities:** Camping, boating, fishing, swimming, water-skiing, golf, birding. **Special Features:** Park features the pristine blue-green waters of Fort Cobb Lake, an excellent fishing and water sports lake with 4,100 surface acres and 45 miles of shoreline. Situated in the heart of the Plains Indians historic tribal lands, numerous museums and attractions in towns near the park offer visitors the opportunity to learn about the rich cultures of the Kiowa, Apache, Comanche, and Delaware tribes.

★3761★ FOSS STATE PARK

HC 66, Box 111
Foss, OK 73647
Web: www.oklahomaparks.com
Phone: 580-592-4433; **Fax:** 580-592-4701
Size: 1,749 acres. **Location:** 11 miles west of Clinton on Highway 73, then 2 miles north on SH 44. **Facilities:** 10 modern campsites, 59 semi-modern campsites, 50 primitive campsites, showers, picnic area, group shelters, trails, equestrian camp, swimming beach, marina, boat ramps, boat rentals, tackle shop, restaurant, snack bar, gift shop, playgrounds (&&). **Activities:** Camping, boating, fishing, swimming, water-skiing, hiking, mountain biking, horseback riding, hunting (seasonal), wildlife viewing, birding. **Special Features:** Park features several campgrounds around 8,800-acre Foss Lake, the largest lake in western Oklahoma. Washita National Wildlife Refuge (see entry in national refuges section), located adjacent to the park, provides wintering grounds for Canada geese and bald eagles.

9. State Parks

★3762★ GLOSS MOUNTAIN STATE PARK
PO Box 512
Fairview, OK 73737
Web: www.oklahomaparks.com
Phone: 580-227-2512; **Fax:** 580-227-2513
Location: 5 miles west of Orienta on Hwy 412. **Facilities:** Picnic area, public water supply, trail (&). **Activities:** Hiking, wildlife viewing. **Special Features:** Park includes a hiking trail to the top of Cathedral Mountain and across the mesa to view the valley floor and Lone Peak Mountain. At sunrise and sunset, the selenite crystal formations on Gloss Mountains shimmer like diamonds.

★3763★ GREAT PLAINS STATE PARK
Hwy 183 & County Rd
Mountain Park, OK 73552
Web: www.oklahomaparks.com
Phone: 580-569-2032; **Fax:** 580-569-2375
Size: 487 acres. **Location:** 2 miles north of Mountain Park on US 183, then 2 miles west on Access Road. **Facilities:** 14 modern campsites, 56 semi-modern campsites, 30 primitive campsites, showers, picnic area, group shelters, trails, swimming beach, boat ramp, tackle shop, playground, camp store (&&). **Activities:** Camping, boating, fishing, swimming, water-skiing, hiking, mountain biking. **Special Features:** Park is located on the west side of 6,400-acre Tom Sneed Lake, which offers excellent opportunities for catfish, crappie, and bass fishing.

★3764★ GREAT SALT PLAINS STATE PARK
Rt 1, Box 28
Jet, OK 73749
Web: www.oklahomaparks.com
Phone: 580-626-4731; **Fax:** 580-626-4730
Size: 840 acres. **Location:** 8 miles north of Jet on SH 38. **Facilities:** 64 semi-modern campsites, 106 primitive campsites, horsemen's camp, 6 cabins, showers, picnic areas, group picnic pavilions, trails (7+ miles), swimming beach, 4 boat ramps, community center, ball field (&&). **Activities:** Camping, boating, fishing, swimming, sailboarding, water-skiing, hiking, mountain biking, horseback riding, birding, rock hounding. **Special Features:** The Great Salt Plains is the only place in the world where visitors can dig for hourglass-shaped selenite crystals. Found just beneath the surface, the crystals are believed to be evidence that a prehistoric sea once covered this area. The park also features the 9,300-acre Great Salt Plains Lake, which is half as salty as the ocean and averages only about 4 feet of depth, but offers good fishing. The adjacent Salt Plains National Wildlife Refuge (see entry on the national refuges section) is home to golden and bald eagles and is a resting place for nearly 250 species of migratory birds.

★3765★ GREENLEAF STATE PARK
Rt 1, Box 119
Braggs, OK 74423
Web: www.oklahomaparks.com
Phone: 918-487-5196; **Fax:** 918-487-5406
Size: 565 acres. **Location:** 3 miles south of Braggs on SH 10A.
Facilities: 22 modern campsites, 64 semi-modern campsites, 94 primitive campsites, group camp, showers, 15 cabins, picnic areas, group picnic pavilions, trails, swimming beach, swimming pool (seasonal), marina, boat ramps, boat rentals, enclosed fishing dock, bicycle rentals, nature center, community building, snack bar, camp store, game courts, playfields, playgrounds (&&). **Activities:** Camping, boating, fishing, swimming, hiking, mountain biking, hunting (nearby), hayrides and campfire programs. **Special Features:** One of Oklahoma's first state parks, Greenleaf features rustic stone and log buildings typical of the public works projects of the 1930s. The 930-acre Lake Greenleaf is the park's centerpiece.

★3766★ HEAVENER RUNESTONE STATE PARK
18365 Runestone Rd
Heavener, OK 74937
Web: www.oklahomaparks.com
Phone: 918-653-2241; **Fax:** 918-653-3435
Size: 50 acres. **Location:** 2.5 miles northeast of Heavener, off US 59 and 270. **Facilities:** Picnic area, group shelters, trails, amphitheater, gift shop, playground. **Activities:** Hiking, educational programs. **Special Features:** The runestone stands 12 feet high, 10 feet wide, and 16 inches thick, and is located in a deep ravine where a 32-foot waterfall cascades down the cliff face. It is believed that the stone marks a land claim made more than 1,000 years ago by Scandinavian explorers.

★3767★ HOCHATOWN STATE PARK
c/o Beavers Bend State Park
PO Box 10
Broken Bow, OK 94728
Phone: 580-494-6452; **Fax:** 580-494-6453
Size: 1,713 acres. **Location:** 10 miles north of Broken Bow on US 259 and 2.5 miles east on Carson Creek Access Road. **Facilities:** 22 modern campsites, 29 semi-modern campsites, 180 primitive campsites, lodge, showers, picnic area, snack bar, 2 group shelters, trails, beach, marina, fuel dock, boat ramps, boat rentals, golf course (&&). **Activities:** Camping, boating, fishing, swimming, water-skiing, hiking, golf. **Special Features:** One of two state parks on Broken Bow Lake, Hochatown is located above the dam in an area of tall trees, clear water, and mountainous terrain.

★3768★ HONEY CREEK STATE PARK
901 State Park Rd
Grove, OK 74344
Web: www.oklahomaparks.com
Phone: 918-786-9447; **Fax:** 918-787-5634
Size: 30 acres. **Location:** South of Grove on State Park Road, off US 59. **Facilities:** 52 semi-modern campsites, 200+ primitive campsites, showers, picnic area, 2 group shelters, trails, swimming pool (seasonal), boat ramp, playground (&&). **Activities:** Camping, boating, fishing, swimming, water-skiing, scuba diving, hiking. **Special Features:** Park is situated on a hillside overlooking 46,300-acre Grand Lake.

★3769★ HUGO LAKE STATE PARK
PO Box 907
Hugo, OK 74743
Phone: 580-326-0303; **Fax:** 580-326-0505

Size: 289 acres. Location: 7 miles east of Hugo on US 70, then 2.5 miles north on Armadillo Road. Facilities: 10 primitive campsites, 26 cabins, picnic area, group shelter, hospitality and training center, trails, marina, boat and slip rentals, boat ramps, store (&&). Activities: Camping, boating, fishing, swimming, hiking, biking. Special Features: Formerly the property of the U.S. Army Corps of Engineers, park features Lake Hugo, which offers some of the best bass fishing in the state.

★3770★ KEYSTONE STATE PARK
1926 S Hwy 151
Sand Springs, OK 74063
Web: www.oklahomaparks.com
Phone: 918-865-4477; Fax: 918-865-2050
Size: 714 acres. Location: 10 miles west of Sand Springs on US 412, then 0.5 miles south on Keystone Dam Road (between US 64 & SH 51). Facilities: 40 modern campsites, 40 semi-modern campsites, 64 primitive campsites, 22 cabins, showers, picnic area, 5 group shelters, restaurant, trails, fitness trail, bicycle rentals, marina, fuel dock, boat ramps, boat rentals, enclosed fishing dock, camp store, snack bar, playground (&&). Activities: Camping, boating, sailing, windsurfing, fishing, swimming, water-skiing, hiking, wildlife viewing. Special Features: Surrounded by woods, high bluffs, and low rolling hills, the park's blue-green Keystone Reservoir features white sandy beaches and unusual sandstone outcrops. The lake, which encompasses 26,300 surface acres with 330 miles of shoreline, offers outstanding fishing for stripers, walleyes, catfish, white and black bass, and crappie. Eagles visit the park between October and March; an observation platform is located on the north end of the dam.

★3771★ LAKE EUCHA STATE PARK
PO Box 349
Hwy 59 S
Jay, OK 74346
Web: www.oklahomaparks.com
Phone: 918-253-8790
Size: 55 acres. Location: 5 miles south of Jay on US 59 and SH 10. Facilities: Picnic area, group shelter, swimming pool, bathhouse (&), game courts, trail. Activities: Boating, fishing, swimming. Special Features: Lake Eucha covers 2,860 surface acres and has 49 miles of shoreline. The entire park may be rented for private parties.

★3772★ LAKE EUFAULA STATE PARK
HC 60, Box 1340
Checotah, OK 74426
Web: www.touroklahoma.com/detail.asp?id=1+5U+7777
Phone: 918-689-5311
Size: 2,853 acres. Location: 14 miles southwest of Checotah off I-40 and SH 150. Facilities: 235 campsites (modern, semi-modern, and primitive), group camp, showers, picnic area, picnic shelter, trails, swimming beach, marina, indoor and outdoor fishing docks, boat rentals, boat ramps, horse stables, 18-hole golf course, visitor center, nature center, restaurant, camp store, gift shop, playgrounds (&&). Activities: Camping, boating, fishing, swimming, water-skiing, hiking, mountain biking, horseback riding, golf, interpretive programs. Special Features: Park

is located on a peninsula jutting into Oklahoma's largest lake, Lake Eufaula. The lake covers 102,400 acres, has 640 miles of shoreline, and offers more than 1,000 bays, inlets, and points. The park's marina is the state's largest indoor/outdoor fishing arena.

★3773★ LAKE MURRAY STATE PARK
18407 Scenic State Hwy 77
Ardmore, OK 73401
Web: www.oklahomaparks.com
Phone: 580-223-4044; Fax: 580-223-4052
Size: 12,496 acres. Location: 3 miles south of Ardmore on Highway 77. Facilities: 56 modern campsites, 205 semi-modern campsites, 190 primitive campsites, showers, 3 group camps, 50-room lodge, 81 cottages, picnic area, 6 group shelters, 7 meeting rooms, restaurant, hiking trails, BMX trail, equestrian trails, stables, beach, swimming pool and bathhouse, boat rentals, boat ramps, marina, enclosed fishing dock, bicycle rentals, 18-hole golf course, miniature golf, radio-controlled model airplane field, ballparks, airplane landing strip, nature center, camp store, game courts, ball field, game room, playground (&&). Activities: Camping, boating, fishing, swimming, scuba diving, water-skiing, jet skiing, hiking, motorcycling, bicycling, mountain biking, roller blading, horseback riding, tennis, golf, archery, interpretive programs. Special Features: Oklahoma's largest state park, Lake Murray is also the state's first resort park. Its lodge, built in 1949, was the first in the state system to offer modern, first-class facilities. The park also includes Tucker Tower Museum. Originally designed in the 1930s as a summer home for Oklahoma governors, the Tower now houses an impressive natural history collection. Park surrounds Lake Murray, a 5,728-acre lake with 150 miles of shoreline.

★3774★ LAKE TEXOMA STATE PARK
PO Box 248
Kingston, OK 73439
Web: www.oklahomaparks.com
Phone: 580-564-2566; Fax: 580-564-2262
Size: 1,882 acres. Location: 5 miles east of Kingston on US 70. Facilities: 517 campsites (modern, semi-modern, and primitive), RV rally group camp, showers, cottages, picnic area, group shelters, restaurant, trails, bicycle rentals, beach, swimming pool and bathhouse, boat rentals, boat ramps, marina, enclosed fishing dock, horse stables, nature center, fitness and recreation center, meeting rooms, 18-hole golf course, miniature golf, go-cart track, airplane landing strip, camp store, playground (&&). Activities: Camping, boating, fishing, swimming, water-skiing, hiking, bicycling, horseback riding, tennis, golf, archery, interpretive programs. Special Features: Park sits along a western shore of Lake Texoma, one of the largest manmade lakes in the world with more than 93,000 acres of water surface. The lake is famous for its striped bass fishing and hosts several nationally recognized fishing events.

★3775★ LAKE THUNDERBIRD STATE PARK
13101 Alameda Dr
Norman, OK 73026
Web: www.oklahomaparks.com
Phone: 405-360-3572; Fax: 405-366-8150

Size: 1,874 acres. **Location:** 13 miles east of Norman on Alameda Drive. **Facilities:** 447 campsites (semi-modern and primitive), 8 lake huts, showers, picnic area, group shelters, trails, horse stables, 2 swimming beaches, 2 marinas, boat ramps, fishing dock, boat rentals, miniature golf, game room, restaurant (seasonal), nature center, camp store, gift shop, playgrounds (&&). **Activities:** Camping, boating, fishing, swimming, water-skiing, hiking, mountain biking, horseback riding, archery, hunting (seasonal), interpretive programs. **Special Features:** Located on the edge of the largest metropolitan area in the state, Lake Thunderbird is a 6,000-acre reservoir with 86 miles of shoreline, offering fishermen great opportunities for bass, crappie, catfish, and saugeye. Rose rock, the official state rock of Oklahoma, can be found on park grounds. The unusual reddish-colored formation resembles a rose in full bloom and, although visitors are not permitted to keep rocks they find, souvenir samples may be purchased at the gift shop.

★3776★ LAKE WISTER STATE PARK

25567 US Hwy 270
Wister, OK 74966
Web: www.oklahomaparks.com
Phone: 918-655-7212; **Fax:** 918-655-7274
Size: 3,428 acres. **Location:** 2 miles south of Wister on US 270. **Facilities:** 16 modern campsites, 86 semi-modern campsites, 95 primitive campsites, group camp, 15 cabins, showers, picnic area, group shelters, trails, bicycle rentals, beach, swimming pool and bathhouse, boat rentals, boat ramp, nature center, restaurant, camp store, gift shop (&&). **Activities:** Camping, boating, fishing, swimming, water-skiing, hiking, mountain biking, hunting (nearby), wildlife viewing, interpretive programs. **Special Features:** Park is surrounded by the Ouachita National Forest and more than 33,000 acres of state wildlife management land, including a 2,000-acre waterfowl refuge. Lake Wister offers some of the finest fishing in Oklahoma.

★3777★ LITTLE SAHARA STATE PARK

101 Main St
Waynoka, OK 73860
Web: www.oklahomaparks.com
Phone: 580-824-1471; **Fax:** 580-824-1472
Size: 1,867 acres. **Location:** 4 miles south of Waynoka on US 281. **Facilities:** 100 campsites (semi-modern and primitive), group camp, showers, picnic area, 3 group shelters, concession stand (seasonal), off-road vehicle trails (&&). **Activities:** Camping, hiking, ORV driving. **Special Features:** Little Sahara sand dunes were formed 11,000 years ago and range from 25 to 75 feet in height. Park is a popular spot for all-terrain vehicles, dune buggies, and four-wheel drive vehicles.

★3778★ MCGEE CREEK STATE PARK

576-A S McGee Creek Dam Rd
Atoka, OK 74525
Web: www.oklahomaparks.com
Phone: 580-889-5822; **Fax:** 580-889-7868
Size: 2,600 acres. **Location:** 16 miles E of Atoka, then 3 miles north of Hwy 3. **Facilities:** 41 semi-modern campsites, 60 primitive campsites, 8 lake huts, showers, picnic area, group shelters, trails, boat ramps, fishing dock, swimming beach, playground (&&). **Activities:** Camping, boating, water-skiing, fishing, swimming, hiking, horseback riding, mountain biking, hunting (nearby), interpretive programs. **Special Features:** Park features 3,800-acre McGee Creek Reservoir. Thousands of acres of wildlife areas and natural scenic areas adjoin the park, offering more than 25 miles of trails and primitive trailside camps for hikers, bikers, horsemen, and river paddlers.

★3779★ NATURAL FALLS STATE PARK

Rt 4, Box 32
West Siloam Springs, OK 74338
Web: www.oklahomaparks.com
Phone: 918-422-5802; **Fax:** 918-422-0026
Size: 120 acres. **Location:** 6 miles west of West Siloam Springs on US 412. **Facilities:** 74 campsites (semi-modern and primitive), picnic area, group shelter, trail, reunion center, observation platform (&), playground. **Activities:** Camping, nature study, fishing (catch and release). **Special Features:** Located in the Ozark Highlands region of Oklahoma, the small park's terrain ranges from dry, rocky ridgetop to a dense fern-filled forest at the base of a 77-foot waterfall. The 1974 movie *Where the Red Fern Grows* was filmed here.

★3780★ OKMULGEE STATE PARK

16830 Dripping Springs Rd
Okmulgee, OK 74447
Web: www.oklahomaparks.com/parks.asp
Phone: 918-756-5971; **Fax:** 918-759-9933
Size: 1,075 acres. **Location:** I-40 Exit 240 (Hwy 75) north to Okmulgee, then 7 miles west on Hwy 56. **Facilities:** 297 campsites (semi-modern and primitive), showers, picnic area, 2 group shelters, trails, boat ramps, fishing dock, swimming areas, playgrounds (&&). **Activities:** Camping, boating, fishing, swimming, water-skiing, hiking. **Special Features:** Park is located on the shores of Okmulgee Lake and three miles from Dripping Springs State Park. The name Okmulgee comes from a Creek word meaning boiling or bubbling water, referring to a year-round spring found here. Okmulgee has been the capital of the Creek Nation since the Civil War.

★3781★ OSAGE HILLS STATE PARK

Hwy 60 W
Bartlesville, OK 74006
Web: www.oklahomaparks.com
Phone: 918-336-4141; **Fax:** 918-337-2176
Size: 1,199 acres. **Location:** 11 miles west of Bartlesville on Hwy 60 from Hwy 123. **Facilities:** 20 semi-modern campsites, 25 primitive campsites, group camp, 8 cabins, showers, picnic area, 2 picnic shelters, trails, swimming pool and bathhouse, boat rentals, game courts (&&). **Activities:** Camping, boating, fishing, swimming, hiking, mountain biking, tennis, volleyball. **Special Features:** Park is densely wooded, with winding roads, a deep forested canyon, scenic waterfalls, and an 18-acre lake providing excellent fishing opportunities. Water recreation is also available at Hulah Lake in Wah-Sha-She State Park (see separate entry), located about 30 miles north of the park.

★3782★ QUARTZ MOUNTAIN RESORT
22469 Lodge Rd
Lone Wolf, OK 73655
Web: www.quartzmountainresort.com
Phone: 580-563-2424; Fax: 580-563-2422
Size: 4,600 acres. Location: 10 miles south of Lone Wolf on SH 44 to SH 44A Junction, then 2 miles north. Facilities: 20 modern campsites, 100 semi-modern campsites, 99 primitive campsites, showers, group camp, 118-room lodge, 14 cabins, 64-bed dormitory, picnic area, 5 group shelters, trails, swimming pool (seasonal), beach and bathhouse, marina, boat ramps, paddleboat rental, off-road vehicle area (seasonal), nature center, performing arts center, outdoor amphitheater, 18-hole golf courses, restaurant, camp store, gift shop (&&). Activities: Camping, boating, fishing, swimming, water-skiing, hiking, rock climbing, motorcycling, tennis, volleyball, archery, golf, field sports, interpretive programs. Special Features: Located at southwestern edge of the Wichita Mountains, the park surrounds 6,260-acre Lake Altus-Lugert. It features the Quartz Mountain Resort Arts and Conference Center, a showplace of Southwestern art and design and a premier resort.

★3783★ RAYMOND GARY STATE PARK
HC 63 , Box 1450
Fort Towson, OK 74735
Web: www.oklahomaparks.com
Phone: 580-873-2307; Fax: 580-326-2305
Size: 64 acres. Location: 1.5 miles south of Fort Towson on US 70. Facilities: 10 modern campsites, 10 semi-modern campsites, 100 primitive campsites, showers, picnic area, 2 group shelters, boat ramp, fishing dock, swimming beach, playground (&&). Activities: Camping, boating, fishing, swimming. Special Features: Situated near the Texas border, park features 390-acre Raymond Gary Lake.

★3784★ RED ROCK CANYON STATE PARK
PO Box 502
Hinton, OK 73047
Web: www.oklahomaparks.com
Phone: 405-542-6344; Fax: 405-542-6342
Size: 310 acres. Location: 1 mile south of Hinton on US 281. Facilities: 52 semi-modern campsites, 32 primitive campsites, group camp, showers, picnic area, 5 group shelters, trails, swimming pool, historical landmark, snack bar, fishing pond, playground (&&). Activities: Camping, fishing, swimming, hiking, rock climbing, rappelling, volleyball. Special Features: The soft, deep red sandstone of Red Rock Canyon was formed 200 million years ago during the Permian era. Cheyenne Indians, who once roamed the area, used the canyons in winter as a refuge against the cold north wind. During the mid-1800s, the canyon was a favorite stop for wagon trains traveling from Arkansas to California. Today, the canyon floor supports an unusually wide variety of foliage, including sugar maples, trees not normally found this far west.

★3785★ ROBBERS CAVE STATE PARK
PO Box 9
Wilburton, OK 74578
Web: www.oklahomaparks.com
Phone: 918-465-2565; Fax: 918-465-5763

Size: 8,246 acres. Location: 5 miles north of Wilburton on SH 2. Facilities: 122 campsites (modern, semi-modern, and primitive), 2 group camps, horsemen's campground, showers, 26 cabins, 20-room lodge, picnic area, 4 group shelters, hiking trails (12 miles), bridle trails (50 miles), bicycle rentals, 3 lakes, beach, swimming pool and bathhouse, boat rentals, miniature golf, nature center, restaurant, amphitheater, ballparks, game courts, camp store, gift shop (&&). Activities: Camping, boating, fishing, swimming, hiking, bicycling, mountain biking, horseback riding, rock climbing, rappelling, interpretive programs, guided tours. Special Features: Robbers Cave has a long and colorful history. Outlaw legends began to spread during the Civil War, when deserters from both sides hid in the cave. After the war, gangs of robbers used it as a rendezvous point. Famous outlaws associated with the cave include the Younger Brothers, Frank and Jesse James, and outlaw queen Belle Star.

★3786★ ROMAN NOSE RESORT PARK
Rt 1, Box 2-2
Watonga, OK 73772
Web: www.oklahomaparks.com
Phone: 580-623-4215; Fax: 580-623-2190
Size: 840 acres. Location: 4 miles north of Watonga on SH 8, then 3 miles north on SH 8A. Facilities: 93 campsites (modern, semi-modern, and primitive), group camp, rent-a-tepee units, showers, 10 cottages, 47-room lodge, picnic area, 2 group shelters, restaurant, trails, swimming pool and bathhouse, boat rentals, boat ramp, meeting rooms, 18-hole golf course, archery range, horse stables, miniature golf, gift shop (&&). Activities: Camping, boating, fishing, swimming, hiking, bicycling, mountain biking, horseback riding, tennis, golf, volleyball, guided horseback tours, recreational and interpretive programs. Special Features: Set on a canyon bluff overlooking ancient mesas, Roman Nose is a scenic resort park which highlights the rich heritage and culture of Oklahoma's Cheyenne and Plains Indians. The park's Spring of Everlasting Waters is fed by subterranean rivers at the rate of 600 gallons per minute.

★3787★ SEQUOYAH BAY STATE PARK
6237 E 100th St N
Wagoner, OK 74467
Web: www.oklahomaparks.com
Phone: 918-683-0878; Fax: 918-687-6797
Size: 303 acres. Location: 5 miles south of Wagoner on SH 16, then 4 miles east on on 100th St N. Facilities: 77 semi-modern campsites, 110 primitive campsites, nature trail, RV group rally camp, showers, 5 cabins, picnic area, 4 group shelters, snack bar, beach, marina, fuel dock, boat rentals, enclosed fishing dock, swimming beach, bicycle rentals, ballparks, game courts, playgrounds (&&). Activities: Camping, boating, fishing, swimming, water-skiing, tennis, volleyball. Special Features: Park is situated in a oak-hickory woodland in eastern Oklahoma on the shores of 19,100-acre Fort Gibson Lake. The lake was named for the U.S. Army fort (established in 1824) where, for many Native Americans, the Trail of Tears ended. Today, the park strives to honor the cultures of the Five Civilized Tribes, outstanding individual Native Americans, and the memory of those who walked the trail.

9. State Parks

★3788★ **SEQUOYAH STATE PARK & WESTERN HILLS GUEST RANCH**

17131 Park 10
Wagoner, OK 74477
Web: www.oklahomaparks.com
Phone: 918-772-2046; **Fax:** 918-772-2030
Size: 2,200 acres (park). **Location:** 8 miles east of Wagoner on SH 51. **Facilities:** 425 campsites (modern, semi-modern, and primitive), group camp, showers, 54 cottages, lodge, 46-bed bunkhouse, 9 meeting rooms, picnic area, 5 group shelters, trails, fitness trail, swimming pool, swimming beach, marina, boat rentals, boat ramps, enclosed fishing docks, nature center, horse stables, 18-hole golf course, restaurant and saloon, game room, camp store, playground, airplane landing strip (&&). **Activities:** Camping, fishing, swimming, water-skiing, hiking, bicycling, mountain biking, horseback riding, tennis, archery, golf, volleyball, children's activity programs, stagecoach and covered wagon rides, interpretive programs. **Special Features:** One of Oklahoma's most scenic parks, Sequoyah sits on a wooded peninsula on 19,100-acre Fort Gibson Lake. Park encompasses a state waterfowl refuge and is well-known for its abundance of deer, wild turkey, fox, and other wildlife.

★3789★ **SNOWDALE STATE PARK**

PO Box 6
Salina, OK 74365
Web: www.oklahomaparks.com
Phone: 918-434-2651; **Fax:** 918-435-4067
Size: 15 acres. **Location:** 1 mile west of Salina on SH 20. **Facilities:** 84 campsites (semi-modern and primitive), picnic area, group shelter, swimming beach, boat ramp, playground (&&). **Activities:** Camping, boating, fishing, swimming, water-skiing, hiking, volleyball. **Special Features:** Park is adjacent to 12,000-acre Lake Hudson, the second in a chain of three lakes along the Grand River. Lake Hudson is considered one of the best bass lakes in Oklahoma and hosts several tournaments each year.

★3790★ **SPAVINAW STATE PARK**

Hwy 82 S
Spavinaw, OK 74366
Web: www.oklahomaparks.com
Phone: 918-589-2651; **Fax:** 918-435-4067
Size: 35 acres. **Location:** 0.75 miles south of Spavinaw via SH 20 at the SH 82 junction. **Facilities:** 86 campsites (semi-modern and primitive), showers, picnic area, group shelter, swimming beach, playground. **Activities:** Camping, boating, fishing, swimming. **Special Features:** Families with small children enjoy this park because of the shallow water in the swimming area of Spavinaw Creek. Nearby Spavinaw Wildlife Management Area allows hunting and hiking.

★3791★ **TALIMENA STATE PARK**

PO Box 318
Talihina, OK 74571
Web: www.oklahomaparks.com
Phone: 918-567-2052; **Fax:** 918-567-2052
Size: 20 acres. **Location:** 7 miles north of Talihina on US 271.

Facilities: 7 semi-modern campsites, 15 primitive campsites, showers, picnic area, group shelter, trails, playground. **Activities:** Camping, hiking, backpacking. **Special Features:** Talimena is the western terminus of the Ouachita National Recreation Trail, a 223-mile corridor which traverses the rugged peaks of the Ouachita Mountains into Arkansas through the Ouachita National Forest (see separate entry in National Forests and Grasslands section).

★3792★ **TENKILLER STATE PARK**

HCR 68, Box 1095
Vian, OK 74962
Web: www.oklahomaparks.com
Phone: 918-489-5643; **Fax:** 918-489-2111
Size: 1,190 acres. **Location:** 10 miles north of the Vian exit on SH 82. **Facilities:** 37 modern campsites, 50 semi-modern campsites, 150 primitive campsites, 39 cabins, 10 cottages, showers, picnic area, 4 group shelters, trails, restaurant, swimming pool and bathhouse, beaches, boat rentals, boat ramps, marina, enclosed fishing dock, kids fishing pond, nature center, community building, amphitheater, camp store, gift shop, playgrounds (&&). **Activities:** Camping, boating, fishing, swimming, scuba diving, water-skiing, hiking, mountain biking, birding, interpretive programs. **Special Features:** Park's main attraction is Lake Tenkiller, with 12,500 surface acres of clear water and 130 miles of shoreline. The scenic lake includes secluded coves, rocky banks, and limestone bluffs both above and below the water.

★3793★ **TWIN BRIDGES STATE PARK**

14801 Hwy 137 S
Fairland, OK 74343
Web: www.oklahomaparks.com
Phone: 918-540-2545; **Fax:** 918-540-2545
Size: 63 acres. **Location:** 6 miles east of Fairland at the junction of US 60 and SH 137. **Facilities:** 160 campsites (semi-modern and primitive), lake huts, showers, picnic area, 5 group shelters, canoe trail, boat ramp, enclosed fishing dock, playground (&&). **Activities:** Camping, boating, canoeing, fishing, swimming, volleyball. **Special Features:** Park sits at the confluence of the Neosho and Spring rivers, two of the main feeders of Grand Lake. Spring River's canoe trail is popular for float fishing.

★3794★ **WAH-SHA-SHE STATE PARK**

Hwy 10 W
Copan, OK 74022
Web: www.oklahomaparks.com
Phone: 918-336-4141; **Fax:** 918-337-2176
Size: 266 acres. **Location:** 15 miles north of Pawhuska on SH 99, then 10 miles east on SH 10; or from Hwy 75, 13 miles west on Hwy 10. **Facilities:** 46 semi-modern campsites, 112 primitive campsites, showers, picnic area, 3 group shelters, trail, swimming beach, boat ramp, boat dock (&&). **Activities:** Camping, boating, fishing, swimming, water-skiing, hunting (nearby). **Special Features:** Park is located on the east side of 3,600-acre Hulah Lake, just north of the dam. The name "Hulah" was derived from the Osage word for eagle, and wintering eagles are a common sight on the lake, January through mid-March.

★3795★ **WALNUT CREEK STATE PARK**
1926 State Hwy 151
Sand Springs, OK 74063
Web: www.oklahomaparks.com
Phone: 918-865-4991
Size: 1,429 acres. **Location:** Off the Cimarron Turnpike in Sand Springs, 13 miles east of the 209th Street exit. **Facilities:** 4 modern campsites, 68 semi-modern campsites, 100 primitive campsites, horsemen's camp, showers, picnic area, group shelters, trails (20+ miles), swimming beach, ball fields, playground (占占). **Activities:** Camping, boating, fishing, swimming, water-skiing, hiking, mountain biking, horseback riding. **Special Features:** Park is situated along 26,300-acre Lake Keystone, which offers good fishing for crappie, sand bass, and stripers. The park also offers one of the best equestrian trails in the Oklahoma State Park System.

Oregon State Parks

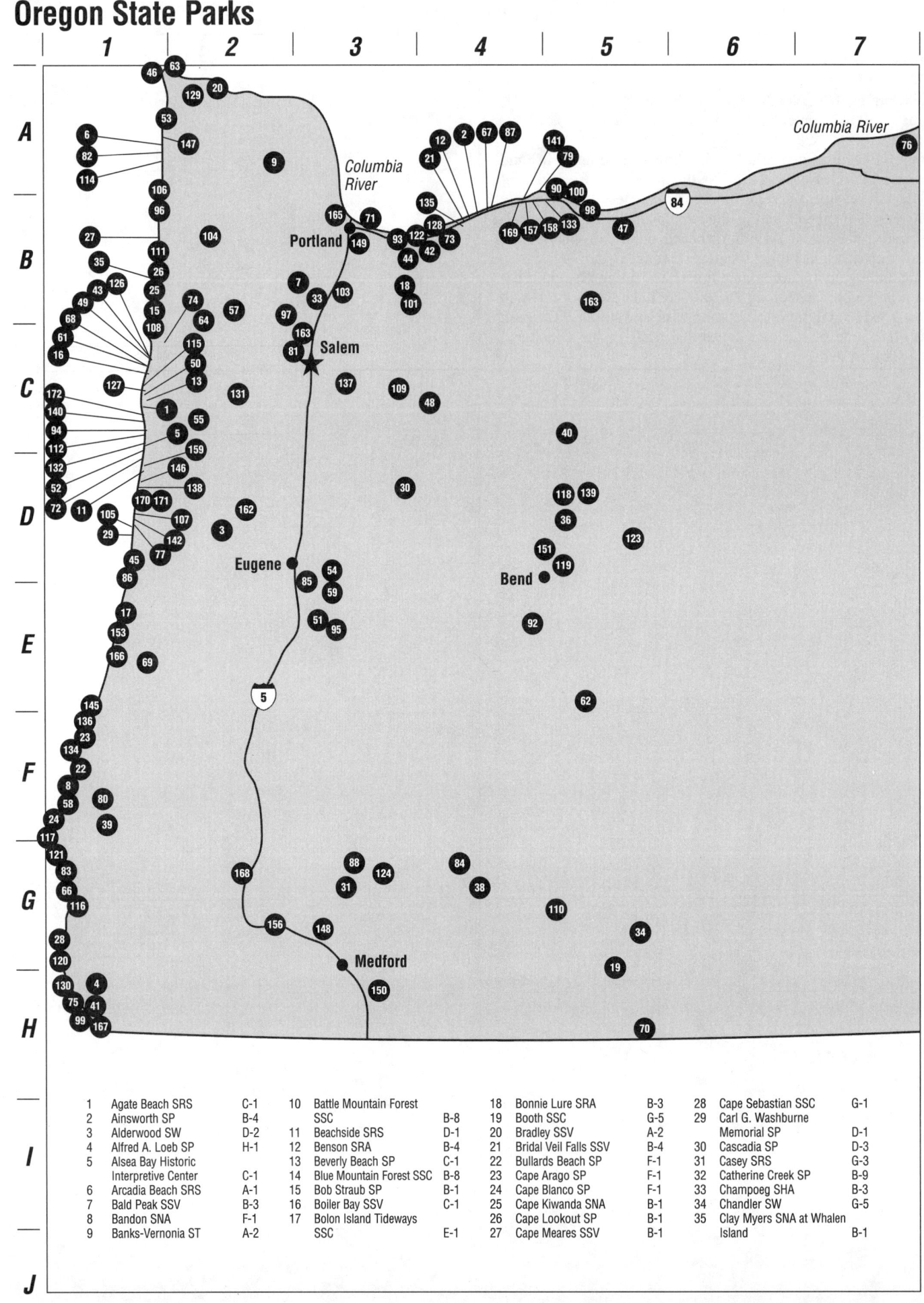

1	Agate Beach SRS	C-1	
2	Ainsworth SP	B-4	
3	Alderwood SW	D-2	
4	Alfred A. Loeb SP	H-1	
5	Alsea Bay Historic		
	Interpretive Center	C-1	
6	Arcadia Beach SRS	A-1	
7	Bald Peak SSV	B-3	
8	Bandon SNA	F-1	
9	Banks-Vernonia ST	A-2	
10	Battle Mountain Forest		
	SSC	B-8	
11	Beachside SRS	D-1	
12	Benson SRA	B-4	
13	Beverly Beach SP	C-1	
14	Blue Mountain Forest SSC	B-8	
15	Bob Straub SP	B-1	
16	Boiler Bay SSV	C-1	
17	Bolon Island Tideways		
	SSC	E-1	
18	Bonnie Lure SRA	B-3	
19	Booth SSC	G-5	
20	Bradley SSV	A-2	
21	Bridal Veil Falls SSV	B-4	
22	Bullards Beach SP	F-1	
23	Cape Arago SP	F-1	
24	Cape Blanco SP	F-1	
25	Cape Kiwanda SNA	B-1	
26	Cape Lookout SP	B-1	
27	Cape Meares SSV	B-1	
28	Cape Sebastian SSC	G-1	
29	Carl G. Washburne		
	Memorial SP	D-1	
30	Cascadia SP	D-3	
31	Casey SRS	G-3	
32	Catherine Creek SP	B-9	
33	Champoeg SHA	B-3	
34	Chandler SW	G-5	
35	Clay Myers SNA at Whalen		
	Island	B-1	

8	9	10	11	12	13	14

Pendleton

56	Emigrant Springs SHA	B-8
57	Erratic Rock SNS	B-2
58	Face Rock SSV	F-1
59	Fall Creek SRA	E-3
60	Farewell Bend SRA	D-10
61	Fogarty Creek SRA	C-1
62	Fort Rock SNA	E-5
63	Fort Stevens SP	A-2
64	Fort Yahmill SHA	B-2
65	Frenchglen Hotel SHS	F-8
66	Geisel Monument SHS	G-1
67	George W. Joseph SNA	B-4
68	Gleneden Beach SRS	C-1
69	Golden & Silver Falls SNA	E-1
70	Goose Lake SRA	H-5
71	Government Island SRA	B-3
72	Governor Patterson Memorial SRS	D-1
73	Guy W. Talbot SP	B-4
74	H. B. Van Duzer Forest SSC	C-1
75	Harris Beach SP	H-1
76	Hat Rock SP	A-7
77	Heceta Head Lighthouse SSV	D-1
78	Hilgard Junction SP	B-8
79	Historic Columbia River Highway ST	A-4
80	Hoffman Memorial SW	F-1
81	Holman SW	C-2
82	Hug Point SRS	A-1
83	Humbug Mountain SP	G-1
84	Jackson F. Kimball SRS	G-4
85	Jasper SRS	D-3
86	Jessie M. Honeyman Memorial SP	D-1
87	John B. Yeon SSC	B-4
88	Joseph H. Stewart SRA	G-3
89	Kam Wah Chung SHS	D-8
90	Koberg Beach SRS	A-5
91	Lake Owyhee SP	E-10
92	LaPine SP	E-4
93	Lewis & Clark SRS	B-3
94	Lost Creek SRS	C-1
95	Lowell SRS	E-3
96	Manhattan Beach SRS	B-1
97	Maud Williamson SRS	B-2
98	Mayer SP	B-5
99	McVay Rock SRS	H-1
100	Memaloose SP	A-5
101	Milo McIver SP	B-3
102	Minam SRA	A-9
103	Molalla River SP	B-3
104	Munson Creek Falls SNS	B-2
105	Muriel O. Ponsler Memorial SSV	D-1
106	Nehalem Bay SP	A-1
107	Neptune SSV	D-1
108	Neskowin Beach SRS	C-1
109	North Santiam SRA	C-3
110	OC&E Woods Line ST	G-5
111	Oceanside Beach SRS	B-1
112	Ona Beach SP	C-1
113	Ontario SRS	D-10
114	Oswald West SP	A-1
115	Otter Crest SSV	C-1
116	Otter Point SRS	G-1
117	Paradise Point SRS	F-1
118	Peter Skene Ogden SSV	D-5
119	Pilot Butte SSV	D-5
120	Pistol River SSV	G-1
121	Port Orford Heads SP	G-1
122	Portland Women's Forum SSV	B-3
123	Prineville Reservoir SP	D-5
124	Prospect SSV	G-3
125	Red Bridge SW	B-8
126	Roads End SRS	C-1

127	Rocky Creek SSV	C-1
128	Rooster Rock SP	B-4
129	Saddle Mountain SNA	A-2
130	Samuel H. Boardman SSC	H-1
131	Sarah Helmick SRS	C-2
132	Seal Rock SRS	C-1
133	Seneca Fouts Memorial SNA	B-5
134	Seven Devils SRS	F-1
135	Shepperd's Dell SNA	B-4
136	Shore Acres SP	F-1
137	Silver Falls SP	C-3
138	Smelt Sands SRS	D-1
139	Smith Rock SP	D-5
140	South Beach SP	C-1
141	Starvation Creek SP	B-4
142	Stonefield Beach SRS	D-1
143	Succor Creek SNA	E-10
144	Sumpter Valley Dredge SHA	C-9
145	Sunset Bay SP	E-1
146	Tokatee Klootchman SNS	D-1
147	Tolovana Beach SRS	A-1
148	Touvelle SRS	G-3
149	Tryon Creek SNA	B-3
150	Tub Springs SW	H-3
151	Tumalo SP	D-5
152	Ukiah-Dale Forest SSC	B-8
153	Umpqua Lighthouse SP	E-1
154	Unity Forest SSC	C-9
155	Unity Lake SRS	C-9
156	Valley of the Rogue SP	G-2
157	Viento SP	B-4
158	Vinzenz Lausmann Memorial SNA	B-4
159	W. B. Nelson SRS	D-1
160	Wallowa Lake Highway Forest SSC	A-9
161	Wallowa Lake SP	B-10
162	Washburne SW	D-2
163	White River Falls SP	B-5
164	Willamette Mission SP	C-3
165	Willamette Stone SHS	B-3
166	William M. Tugman SP	E-1
167	Winchuck SRS	H-1
168	Wolf Creek Inn SHS	G-2
169	Wygant SNA	B-4
170	Yachats Ocean Road SNS	D-1
171	Yachats SRA	D-1
172	Yaquina Bay SRS	C-1

SHA	State Heritage Area
SHS	State Heritage Site
SNA	State Natural Area
SNS	State Natural Site
SP	State Park
SRA	State Recreation Area
SRS	State Recreation Site
SSC	State Scenic Corridor
SSV	State Scenic Viewpoint
ST	State Trail
SW	State Wayside

36	Cline Falls SSV	D-5
37	Clyde Holliday SRS	D-8
38	Collier Memorial SP	G-4
39	Coquille Myrtle Grove SNS	F-1
40	Cove Palisades SP	C-5
41	Crissey Field SRS	H-1
42	Crown Point SSC	B-4
43	D River SRS	C-1
44	Dabney SRA	B-3
45	Darlingtonia SNS	D-1

46	Del Rey Beach SRS	A-1
47	Deschutes River SRA	B-5
48	Detroit Lake SRA	C-4
49	Devil's Lake SRA	C-1
50	Devil's Punchbowl SNA	C-1
51	Dexter SRS	E-3
52	Driftwood Beach SRS	C-1
53	Ecola SP	A-1
54	Elijah Bristow SP	D-3
55	Ellmaker SW	C-2

OREGON

★3796★ Oregon Parks & Recreation Department
725 Summer St NE Suite C
Salem, OR 97301
(503) 986-0707 - Phone
(503) 986-0794 - Fax
(800) 551-6949 - Toll-free
(503) 986-0654 - Employment
(877) 225-9803 - Volunteering (Toll-free, Oregon only)
Web: www.oregon.gov/oprd/parks
Owns 235 park properties totaling 101,905 acres. Manages and preserves Oregon's Pacific Ocean coastline, protects scenic river waterways, and oversees the recreational development of the Willamette River Greenway. Coordinates plans for a statewide trail system, administers the all-terrain vehicle program, and promotes beach safety education.

★3797★ Oregon Department of Fish & Wildlife
3406 Cherry Ave NE
Salem, OR 97303
(503) 947-6000
Web: www.dfw.state.or.us
Oversees 33 fish hatcheries and 16 wildlife management areas, including some with developed visitor facilities such as campgrounds, picnic areas, and restrooms. These areas offer hunting, fishing, hiking, and wildlife viewing opportunities.

Key to campsite classification:

- **Full hookup campsites** — Sewer, electricity, and water. Include paved parking area adjacent to site, picnic table, and camp stove or fire ring. Convenient access to hot showers and modern restrooms.
- **Electrical hookup campsites** — Same facilities as full-utility hookup campsites, but without sewer hookups.
- **Tent campsites** — No utilities; water at or near site. Include picnic tables, and fire rings or camp stoves. Convenient access to hot showers and modern restrooms.
- **Primitive campsites** — No utilities; one water source may serve multiple sites in natural, cleared setting; no paved parking at most sites. Showers may be available in another area of a campground.
- **Hiker/biker camps** — Most include a picnic table and fire ring with water nearby; many are in a common area shared by other hikers and bikers. Although hiker/biker areas are normally separated from the main campground, park facilities such as restrooms and showers are available.
- **Horse camps** — Primitive campsites with corrals and/or hitching rails.

- **Group camps** — Special tent camping areas designed to accommodate 25 or more people.
- Some parks also offer a limited number of **yurts, cabins, tepees,** and **covered wagons.** Accommodations in these enclosed structures vary, but most include beds and electricity.

★3798★ AGATE BEACH STATE RECREATION SITE
c/o Beverly Beach Management Unit
198 NE 123rd St
Newport, OR 97365
Web: www.oregonstateparks.org/park_212.php
Phone: 800-551-6949
Size: 18 acres. **Location:** Off US 101, 1 mile north of Newport. **Facilities:** Picnic area, beach access, restrooms. **Activities:** Fishing, clamming, surfing, beachcombing. **Special Features:** Site features an under-highway tunnel that leads to the beach and day-use area.

★3799★ AINSWORTH STATE PARK
c/o Columbia River Gorge Management Unit
PO Box 100
Corbett, OR 97019
Web: www.oregonstateparks.org/park_146.php
Phone: 800-551-6949
Size: 156 acres. **Location:** Off Historic Columbia River Highway, 18 miles east of Troutdale. **Facilities:** 45 full hookup campsites, 6 walk-in tent sites, showers, restrooms, picnic area, hiking trails, playground, amphitheater. **Activities:** Camping, hiking, interpretive programs. **Special Features:** Park is situated at the eastern end of historic Highway 30, an area with the world's greatest concentration of high waterfalls.

★3800★ ALDERWOOD STATE WAYSIDE
c/o Southern Willamette Management Unit
PO Box 511
Lowell, OR 97452
Web: www.oregonstateparks.org/park_80.php
Phone: 800-551-6949
Size: 76 acres. **Location:** Off OR 36, 15 miles southwest of Junction City. **Facilities:** Picnic area, restrooms. **Activities:** Fishing, hiking. **Special Features:** A forested tract with a trail to Long Tom River.

★3801★ ALFRED A. LOEB STATE PARK
c/o Harris Beach Management Unit
1655 Hwy 101 N
Brookings, OR 97415
Web: www.oregonstateparks.org/park_72.php
Phone: 800-551-6949

Size: 320 acres. **Location:** Off US 101, 10 miles northeast of Brookings on Chetco River. **Facilities:** 48 electrical hookup campsites, 3 cabins, showers, restrooms, picnic area. **Activities:** Camping, fishing, swimming, rafting, hiking, wildlife viewing. **Special Features:** The northernmost redwood stand in the U.S. can be reached by a .75-mile self-guided trail along the Chetco River, and the park itself lies in a grove of myrtlewood trees, many of which are well over 200 years old.

★3802★ ALSEA BAY HISTORIC INTERPRETIVE CENTER

c/o South Beach Management Unit
5580 S Coast Hwy
Newport, OR 97366
Web: www.oregonstateparks.org/park_202.php
Phone: 800-551-6949
Location: Off US 101 in Waldport. **Facilities:** Visitor center, restrooms. **Activities:** Interpretive programs, crabbing and clamming demonstrations (seasonal), whale watching, interpretive programs and events. **Special Features:** Constructed by the Oregon Department of Transportation as part of a bridge replacement project, the center depicts the history of transportation along the Oregon Coast from 1800 to the present. Exhibits focus on the historic Alsea Bay Bridge, completed in 1936, and its replacement, which opened in 1991.

★3803★ ARCADIA BEACH STATE RECREATION SITE

c/o Nehalem Bay Management Unit
9500 Sandpiper Lane - PO Box 366
Nehalem, OR 97131
Web: www.oregonstateparks.org/park_187.php
Phone: 800-551-6949
Size: 8 acres. **Location:** Off US 101, 3 miles south of Cannon Beach. **Facilities:** Picnic area, restrooms, beach access. **Activities:** Fishing, beachcombing. **Special Features:** A shady spot just off the highway a few feet from the Pacific Ocean.

★3804★ BALD PEAK STATE SCENIC VIEWPOINT

c/o Champoeg Management Unit
7679 Champoeg Rd NE
Saint Paul, OR 97137
Web: www.oregonstateparks.org/park_110.php
Phone: 800-551-6949
Size: 26 acres. **Location:** Off Hwy 219, 9 miles northwest of Newberg. **Facilities:** Picnic area, vault toilets, walking trail. **Activities:** Picnicking, walking. **Special Features:** Park features views of the Willamette Valley and, on a clear day, five snow-capped peaks in the Cascade range.

★3805★ BANDON STATE NATURAL AREA

c/o Bullards Beach Management Unit
PO Box 569
Bandon, OR 97411
Web: www.oregonstateparks.org/park_64.php
Phone: 800-551-6949
Size: 879 acres. **Location:** Off US 101, 5 miles south of Bandon

on Beach Loop Drive. **Facilities:** Picnic area, restrooms, beach access, hiking trail. **Activities:** Fishing, hiking, wildlife viewing. **Special Features:** Area includes three waysides with scenic views.

★3806★ BANKS-VERNONIA STATE TRAIL

24600 NW Bachona Rd
Buxton, OR 97109
Web: www.oregonstateparks.org/park_145.php
Phone: 800-551-6949
Size: 21-mile linear park, 475 acres. **Location:** Along OR 47 between Banks and Vernonia. **Facilities:** Multi-use trail (&), picnic area, restrooms (&). **Activities:** Fishing, hiking, bicycling, horseback riding, wildlife viewing. **Special Features:** Although located just 40 miles west of Portland, the trail area is very remote and has few amenities. The asphalt and gravel trail is 8 feet wide, paralleled by a 4-foot-wide horse trail. Converted from a historic railroad corridor, the trail features 12 bridges, two of which are 600 feet long and 80 feet high.

★3807★ BATTLE MOUNTAIN FOREST STATE SCENIC CORRIDOR

c/o Blue Mountain Management Unit
PO Box 85
Meacham, OR 97859
Web: www.oregonstateparks.org/park_238.php
Phone: 800-551-6949
Size: 420 acres. **Location:** Off US 395, 9 miles north of Ukiah. **Facilities:** Picnic area, restrooms, historic sites. **Activities:** Wildlife viewing. **Special Features:** Park protects a forest of ponderosa pine, larch, Douglas fir, and spruce, and provides prime habitat for all kinds of wildlife. The name commemorates one of the last battles between Native Americans and settlers in eastern Oregon.

★3808★ BEACHSIDE STATE RECREATION SITE

c/o South Beach Management Unit
5580 S Coast Hwy
Newport, OR 97366
Web: www.oregonstateparks.org/park_122.php
Phone: 800-551-6949
Size: 17 acres. **Location:** Off US 101, 4 miles south of Waldport. **Facilities:** 32 electrical hookup campsites, 42 tent campsites, 2 yurts, hiker/biker camp, showers, restrooms (&), picnic area, beach access. **Activities:** Camping, fishing, swimming, hiking, biking, wildlife viewing, kite flying, whale watching, nature programs. **Special Features:** Campsites are located just a few feet from a broad, sandy beach.

★3809★ BENSON STATE RECREATION AREA

c/o Columbia River Gorge Management Unit
PO Box 100
Corbett, OR 97019
Web: www.oregonstateparks.org/park_147.php
Phone: 800-551-6949
Size: 272 acres. **Location:** Off I-84 (eastbound access only from Exit 30), 30 miles east of Portland. **Facilities:** Picnic area, group

shelter, restrooms, disc golf course. **Activities:** Boating, fishing, swimming, disc golf. **Special Features:** Park features an annual Free Fishing Day (first weekend in June); anyone can bring a pole (or use provided equipment) to try and catch some of the thousands of rainbow trout with which the lake is stocked.

★3810★ BEVERLY BEACH STATE PARK
198 NE 123rd St
Newport, OR 97365
Web: www.oregonstateparks.org/park_227.php
Phone: 541-265-9278
Size: 130 acres. **Location:** Off US 101, 7 miles north of Newport. **Facilities:** 53 full hookup campsites, 75 electrical hookup campsites, 128 tent campsites, hiker/biker camp, group camps, 21 yurts, showers, restrooms (&), picnic area, beach access, nature trail, visitor center, playgrounds, meeting hall, nature programs, store. **Activities:** Camping, fishing, swimming, surfing, hiking, kite flying, wildlife viewing. **Special Features:** A walkway goes under the highway and leads to a long expanse of sandy beach. Interpretive signs along the creek explain salmon migration.

★3811★ BLUE MOUNTAIN FOREST STATE SCENIC CORRIDOR
c/o Blue Mountain Management Unit
PO Box 85
Meecham, OR 97859
Web: www.oregonstateparks.org/park_237.php
Phone: 800-551-6949
Size: 2,129 acres. **Location:** Off I-84, in the northeast corner of the state. **Activities:** Wildlife viewing. **Special Features:** Corridor lies along the Old Oregon Trail Highway and protects an area of mature evergreen forest.

★3812★ BOB STRAUB STATE PARK
c/o Cape Lookout Management Unit
13000 Whiskey Creek Rd W
Tillamook, OR 97141
Web: www.oregonstateparks.org/park_183.php
Phone: 800-551-6949
Size: 484 acres. **Location:** Off US 101, Pacific City. **Facilities:** Beach access, picnic area, restrooms (&). **Activities:** Fishing, wildlife viewing. **Special Features:** Situated on a sand spit where the Nestucca River empties into the sea.

★3813★ BOILER BAY STATE SCENIC VIEWPOINT
c/o Beverly Beach Management Unit
198 NE 123rd St
Newport, OR 97365
Web: www.oregonstateparks.org/park_213.php
Phone: 800-551-6949
Size: 33 acres. **Location:** Off US 101, 1 mile north of Depoe Bay. **Facilities:** Picnic area. **Activities:** Whale watching, bird watching, tide pool exploration. **Special Features:** Site is a steep, rocky bluff overlooking the ocean. It is one of the best places in Oregon to see ocean-going birds, including shearwaters, jaegers, albatrosses, grebes, oystercatchers, and murrelets.

At low tide you can see the boiler of J. Marhoffer, sunk by an explosion in 1910.

★3814★ BOLON ISLAND TIDEWAYS STATE SCENIC CORRIDOR
c/o Honeyman Management Unit
84505 Hwy 101 S
Florence, OR 97439
Web: www.oregonstateparks.org/park_114.php
Phone: 800-551-6949
Size: 11.5 acres. **Location:** Off US 101, 5 miles north of Reedsport. **Facilities:** Hiking trail, beach access. **Activities:** Fishing, hiking. **Special Features:** Site features a hiking trail with a scenic view of the Umpqua River.

★3815★ BONNIE LURE STATE RECREATION AREA
c/o Tryon Creek Management Unit
11321 SW Terwilliger Blvd
Portland, OR 97219
Web: www.oregonstateparks.org/park_140.php
Phone: 800-551-6949
Size: 94 acres. **Location:** Off Hwy 224, 6 miles north of Estacada. **Facilities:** Walking trail, restrooms. **Activities:** Fishing, swimming, hiking, wildlife viewing. **Special Features:** Remote and rustic area along Eagle Creek.

★3816★ BOOTH STATE SCENIC CORRIDOR
c/o LaPine Management Unit
15800 State Recreation Rd
La Pine, OR 97739
Web: www.oregonstateparks.org/park_52.php
Phone: 800-551-6949
Size: 318 acres. **Location:** Off OR 66, 12 miles west of Lakeview. **Facilities:** Picnic area, restrooms. **Special Features:** Quaking aspen offer a spectacular show of fall color.

★3817★ BRADLEY STATE SCENIC VIEWPOINT
c/o Fort Stevens Management Unit
100 Peter Iredale Rd
Hammond, OR 97121
Web: www.oregonstateparks.org/park_176.php
Phone: 800-551-6949
Size: 18 acres. **Location:** Off US 30, 22 miles east of Astoria. **Facilities:** Picnic area, restrooms, monument. **Special Features:** Overlooks the Columbia River from a Douglas fir forest.

★3818★ BRIDAL VEIL FALLS STATE SCENIC VIEWPOINT
c/o Columbia River Gorge Management Unit
PO Box 100
Corbett, OR 97019
Web: www.oregonstateparks.org/park_149.php
Phone: 800-551-6949
Size: 16 acres. **Location:** Off Historic Columbia River Highway, 15 miles east of Troutdale. **Facilities:** Picnic area, restrooms, interpretive displays, hiking trails. **Activities:** Hiking.

9. State Parks

Special Features: Scenic area features two short trails: the upper interpretive trail is paved and leads to a scenic overlook of the falls, while the lower trail takes a more rugged route to the base of the waterfalls.

★3819★ **BULLARDS BEACH STATE PARK**
PO Box 569
Bandon, OR 97411
Web: www.oregonstateparks.org/park_71.php
Phone: 541-347-2209
Size: 1,289 acres. **Location:** Off US 101, 2 miles north of Bandon. **Facilities:** 104 full hookup campsites, 81 electrical hookup campsites, 13 yurts, hiker/biker camp, horsemen's camp, showers, restrooms (&), picnic area, group picnic shelters, hiking trails, bridle trail (7 miles), beach access, boat ramp, lighthouses. **Activities:** Camping, boating, fishing, crabbing, hiking, biking, horseback riding, sightseeing, wildlife viewing. **Special Features:** Park features 4.5 miles of beach, views of the Coquille River, and a historic 1896 lighthouse. Across the river is Bandon Marsh National Wildlife Refuge (see entry in national wildlife refuges section).

★3820★ **CAPE ARAGO STATE PARK**
c/o Sunset Bay Management Unit
89814 Cape Arago Hwy
Coos Bay, OR 97420
Web: www.oregonstateparks.org/park_94.php
Phone: 541-888-3778
Size: 145 acres. **Location:** Off US 101, 14 miles southwest of Coos Bay. **Facilities:** Picnic area, group picnic shelter, restrooms, beach access, hiking trail. **Activities:** Fishing, hiking, tide pool exploration, beachcombing, whale watching, wildlife viewing. **Special Features:** Park features outstanding views of migrating whales and other marine mammals, as well as fishing boats and ships entering and leaving nearby Coos Bay.

★3821★ **CAPE BLANCO STATE PARK**
39745 S Hwy 101
Port Orford, OR 97465
Web: www.oregonstateparks.org/park_62.php
Phone: 541-332-6774
Size: 1,895 acres. **Location:** Off US 101, 9 miles north of Port Orford. **Facilities:** 53 electrical hookup campsites, hiker/biker camp, horsemen's camp, 4 cabins, group camp, picnic area, showers, restrooms, hiking trails, bridle trail, beach access, lighthouse, store, historic buildings. **Activities:** Camping, fishing, swimming, hiking, horseback riding, wildlife viewing, sightseeing. **Special Features:** Cape Blanco was the first lighthouse in the state outfitted with a first-order Fresnel lens in 1870. Lighthouse and historic home are open for tours April through October.

★3822★ **CAPE KIWANDA STATE NATURAL AREA**
c/o Cape Lookout Management Unit
13000 Whiskey Creek Rd W
Tillamook, OR 97141
Web: www.oregonstateparks.org/park_180.php
Phone: 800-551-6949
Size: 185 acres. **Location:** Off US 101, 1 mile north of Pacific City. **Facilities:** Beach access, boat ramp, interpretive events, picnic areas. **Activities:** Fishing, windsurfing, wildlife viewing, nature programs, boating, hang gliding, kite flying. **Special Features:** Cape Kiwanda is part of the Three Capes Scenic Route. It's the smallest of the three, but is one of the best places to experience spectacular wave action.

★3823★ **CAPE LOOKOUT STATE PARK**
13000 Whiskey Creek Rd W
Tillamook, OR 97141
Web: www.oregonstateparks.org/park_186.php
Phone: 503-842-4981
Size: 2,014 acres. **Location:** Off US 101, 12 miles southwest of Tillamook. **Facilities:** 38 full hookup campsites, electrical hookup campsite, 173 tent campsites, 3 deluxe cabins, 13 yurts, hiker/biker camp, showers, restrooms, picnic area, group picnic shelter, hiking trails, beach access, historical features. **Activities:** Camping, fishing, swimming, hiking, beachcombing, wildlife viewing, bird watching, interpretive programs. **Special Features:** Located on a sand spit between Netarts Bay and the ocean. Park is a good place to find glass floats.

★3824★ **CAPE MEARES STATE SCENIC VIEWPOINT**
c/o Cape Lookout Management Unit
13000 Whiskey Creek Rd W
Tillamook, OR 97141
Web: www.oregonstateparks.org/park_181.php
Phone: 800-551-6949
Size: 233 acres. **Location:** Off US 101, 10 miles west of Tillamook. **Facilities:** Picnic area, restrooms, historic site, hiking trails, store. **Activities:** Hiking, wildlife viewing, interpretive programs, whale watching. **Special Features:** Viewpoint is situated on a headland 200 feet above the ocean, along Three Capes Scenic Route. Site provides an excellent view of the largest colony of nesting common murres on the continent. Other features include an 1890s lighthouse and a mile-long walking trail that winds through a stand of old-growth spruce trees (including the uniquely shaped Octopus Tree).

★3825★ **CAPE SEBASTIAN STATE SCENIC CORRIDOR**
c/o Harris Beach Management Unit
1655 Hwy 101 N
Brookings, OR 97415
Web: www.oregonstateparks.org/park_73.php
Phone: 800-551-6949
Size: 1,400 acres. **Location:** Off US 101, 7 miles south of Gold Beach. **Facilities:** Beach access, restrooms, hiking trail. **Activities:** Hiking, wildlife viewing, sightseeing, whale watching, interpretive programs. **Special Features:** One of the most spectacular vista points on the Oregon Coast. On a clear day, visitors can see north to Humbug Mountain (43 miles) and south to Point Saint George, California (50 miles).

★3826★ CARL G. WASHBURNE MEMORIAL STATE PARK
9311 Hwy 101 N
Florence, OR 97439
Web: www.oregonstateparks.org/park_123.php
Phone: 541-547-3416
Size: 1,089 acres. Location: Off US 101, 14 miles north of Florence. Facilities: 56 full hookup campsites, 2 electrical sites, 7 tent campsites, 2 yurts, hiker/biker camp, showers, restrooms, picnic area, beach access, hiking trails, historic trails. Activities: Camping, fishing, swimming, hiking, biking, wildlife viewing, interpretive programs. Special Features: Park includes 5 miles of beach and features trails leading to tide pools and Heceta Head Lighthouse.

★3827★ CASCADIA STATE PARK
PO Box 736
Cascadia, OR 97329
Web: www.oregonstateparks.org/park_210.php
Phone: 541-367-6021
Size: 254 acres. Location: Off US 20, 14 miles east of Sweet Home. Facilities: 25 primitive campsites, 1 group camp, restrooms (&), picnic area, trails, playground, nature programs. Activities: Camping, fishing, swimming, hiking. Special Features: Located in the Cascade Range, the park includes a .75-mile trail to Soda Creek Falls and a riverside nature trail. Ruts from the historic Santiam Wagon Road, used as a military route in the 1800s, are still visible.

★3828★ CASEY STATE RECREATION SITE
c/o Joseph Stewart Management Unit
35251 Hwy 62
Trail, OR 97541
Web: www.oregonstateparks.org/park_28.php
Phone: 800-551-6949
Size: 80 acre. Location: Off OR 62, 29 miles northeast of Medford. Facilities: Picnic area, boat ramp. Activities: Boating, fishing. Special Features: Site provides fishing and rafting access to the Rogue River.

★3829★ CATHERINE CREEK STATE PARK
c/o Blue Mountain Management Unit
PO Box 85
Meacham, OR 97859
Web: www.oregonstateparks.org/park_17.php
Phone: 800-551-6949
Size: 168 acres. Location: Off OR 203, 8 miles southeast of Union. Facilities: 20 primitive campsites, restrooms, picnic area, hiking trails, interpretive displays. Activities: Camping, fishing, hiking, wildlife viewing. Special Features: Peaceful canyon setting in the western foothills of the Wallowa Mountains.

★3830★ CHAMPOEG STATE HERITAGE AREA
7679 Champoeg Rd NE
Saint Paul, OR 97137
Web: www.oregonstateparks.org/park_113.php
Phone: 503-678-1251

Size: 615 acres. Location: Off US 99W, 7 miles east of Newberg. Facilities: 12 full hookup campsites, 67 electrical hookup campsites, 6 tent campsites, 6 yurts, 6 cabins, RV group camp, showers, restrooms (&), picnic area, group picnic shelters, hiking and biking trails, fishing dock, nature/visitor center, amphitheater, museum, gift shop, disc golf course. Activities: Camping, boating, fishing, hiking, bicycling, interpretive and entertainment programs. Special Features: Site of a momentous meeting of French Prairie settlers on May 2, 1843, which led to the establishment of provisional government for the Oregon Country. Park is located along the Willamette River and includes a historic home, 1860s-style garden, and the Butteville Store founded in 1863.

★3831★ CHANDLER STATE WAYSIDE
c/o LaPine Management Unit
15800 State Recreation Rd
La Pine, OR 97739
Web: www.oregonstateparks.org/park_53.php
Phone: 800-551-6949
Size: 85 acres. Location: Off US 395, 16 miles north of Lakeview. Facilities: Picnic area, restrooms. Activities: Fishing. Special Features: Wooded area of ponderosa pine with access to Crooked Creek.

★3832★ CLAY MYERS STATE NATURAL AREA AT WHALEN ISLAND
c/o Cape Lookout Management Unit
13000 Whiskey Creek Rd W
Tillamook, OR 97141
Web: www.oregonstateparks.org/park_248.php
Phone: 800-551-6949
Size: 180 acres. Location: In the northwest corner of the state. Facilities: Walking trail. Activities: Hiking, fishing, bird watching. Special Features: Area is a virtually untouched coastal estuarine ecosystem, bounded by the Sand Creek estuary.

★3833★ CLINE FALLS STATE SCENIC VIEWPOINT
c/o Tumalo Management Unit
62976 OB Riley Rd
Bend, OR 97701
Web: www.oregonstateparks.org/park_38.php
Phone: 800-551-6949
Size: 9 acres. Location: Off OR 126, 4 miles west of Redmond. Facilities: Picnic area, restrooms. Activities: Fishing. Special Features: Park is located on the Deschutes River and provides fishing access to the river.

★3834★ CLYDE HOLLIDAY STATE RECREATION SITE
PO Box 10
Mount Vernon, OR 97865
Web: www.oregonstateparks.org/park_11.php
Phone: 541-932-4453
Size: 40 acres. Location: Off US 26, 8 miles west of John Day. Facilities: 31 electrical hookup campsites, 2 teepees, hiker/biker camp, showers, restrooms, picnic area, interpretive exhibits.

Activities: Camping, fishing, hiking, biking, wildlife watching, interpretive programs. **Special Features:** Park borders the John Day River and is surrounded on all sides by pristine wilderness areas. Visitors can see steelhead rush upriver to spawn.

★3835★ COLLIER MEMORIAL STATE PARK
46000 Hwy 97 N
Chiloquin, OR 97624
Web: www.oregonstateparks.org/park_228.php
Phone: 541-783-2471
Size: 537 acres. **Location:** Off US 97, 30 miles north of Klamath Falls. **Facilities:** 50 full hookup campsites, 18 tent campsites, showers, restrooms (&), laundry, picnic area, trails, day-use horse area, bridle trailhead, interpretive exhibits. **Activities:** Camping, fishing, hiking, horseback riding. **Special Features:** Park features an open-air logging museum and pioneer log cabin village. Rare and antique logging equipment dates to the 1800s.

★3836★ COQUILLE MYRTLE GROVE STATE NATURAL SITE
c/o Bullards Beach Management Unit
PO Box 569
Bandon, OR 97411
Web: www.oregonstateparks.org/park_65.php
Phone: 800-551-6949
Size: 7 acres. **Location:** Off OR 42, 14 miles south of Myrtle Point. **Facilities:** Picnic area, restrooms (&). **Activities:** Swimming, tubing. **Special Features:** Site features a secluded swimming hole and a stand of old Oregon myrtle trees.

★3837★ COVE PALISADES STATE PARK
7300 Jordan Rd
Culver, OR 97734
Web: www.oregonstateparks.org/park_32.php
Phone: 541-546-3412
Size: 4,402 acres. **Location:** Off US 97, 15 miles southwest of Madras. **Facilities:** 82 full hookup campsites, 91 electrical hookup campsites, 92 tent campsites, 3 group camps, cabins, showers, restrooms (&), picnic area, hiking trails (10 miles), fishing pier, marina, boat ramps, playgrounds, interpretive displays, historic displays, amphitheater, store. **Activities:** Camping, boating, fishing, swimming, hiking, interpretive programs. **Special Features:** Located in Oregon's high desert region beside Lake Billy Chinook, the park includes massive geological formations and colorful pinnacles.

★3838★ CRISSEY FIELD STATE RECREATION SITE
c/o Harris Beach Management Unit
1655 Hwy 101 N
Brookings, OR 97415
Web: www.oregonstateparks.org/park_74.php
Phone: 800-551-6949; **Toll Free:** 800-551-6949
Size: 40 acres. **Location:** Off Hwy 101, 5 miles south of Brookings. **Facilities:** Walking trails, historic features, beach access. **Activities:** Swimming, boating, fishing, birdwatching, wildlife viewing. **Special Features:** Crissey Field provides the first available beach access north of the California-Oregon border.

In World War II, it served as a coastal air strip and refueling station for reconnaissance flights searching for Japanese submarines. Remnants of the original bunkers can still be found. Harbor seals and California sea lions surf and feed in this mix of fresh and salt water.

★3839★ CROWN POINT STATE SCENIC CORRIDOR
c/o Columbia River Gorge Management Unit
PO Box 100
Corbett, OR 97019
Web: www.oregonstateparks.org/park_150.php
Phone: 800-551-6949
Size: 307 acres. **Location:** Off Historic Columbia River Highway, 11 miles east of Troutdale. **Facilities:** Visitor center, gift shop, picnic area, restrooms, interpretive exhibits, historic buildings. **Activities:** Sightseeing, interpretive tours. **Special Features:** Built in 1918, Vista House is an octagonal building with a copper roof, built at the summit of Crown Point and offering a spectacular panoramic view of Columbia Gorge.

★3840★ D RIVER STATE RECREATION SITE
c/o Beverly Beach Management Unit
198 NE 123rd St
Newport, OR 97365
Web: www.oregonstateparks.org/park_214.php
Phone: 800-551-6949
Size: 4 acres. **Location:** Off US 101 in Lincoln City. **Facilities:** Beach access, restrooms. **Activities:** Fishing, kite flying. **Special Features:** Site is named for the shortest river in the world, which flows a mere 120 feet from Devils Lake into the ocean. Park is also home to a pair of the world's largest kite festivals, which gives Lincoln City the title "Kite Capital of the World."

★3841★ DABNEY STATE RECREATION AREA
c/o Columbia River Gorge Management Unit
PO Box 100
Corbett, OR 97019
Web: www.oregonstateparks.org/park_151.php
Phone: 800-551-6949
Size: 135 acres. **Location:** Off Historic Columbia River Highway, 4 miles east of Troutdale. **Facilities:** Trail, picnic area, group shelter, restrooms, boat ramp, disc golf course. **Activities:** Boating, fishing, swimming, hiking, wildlife viewing, disc golf. **Special Features:** Area features a swimming hole on the Sandy River.

★3842★ DARLINGTONIA STATE NATURAL SITE
c/o Honeyman Management Unit
84505 Hwy 101 S
Florence, OR 97439
Web: www.oregonstateparks.org/park_115.php
Phone: 800-551-6949
Size: 18 acres. **Location:** Off US 101, 5 miles north of Florence. **Facilities:** Picnic area, restrooms, interpretive exhibits, walking trail. **Special Features:** Park features a boardwalk trail that traverses an unusual botanical area set aside to preserve the carnivorous cobra lily, the only carnivorous flora in the state.

9. State Parks

★3843★ DEL REY BEACH STATE RECREATION SITE

c/o Fort Stevens Management Unit
100 Peter Iredale Rd
Hammond, OR 97121
Web: www.oregonstateparks.org/park_177.php
Phone: 800-551-6949
Size: 19 acres. **Location:** Off US 101, 2 miles north of Gearhart. **Facilities:** Beach access. **Activities:** Kite flying. **Special Features:** Site is a good spot for flying kites and building sandcastles.

★3844★ DESCHUTES RIVER STATE RECREATION AREA

89600 Biggs-Rufus Hwy
Wasco, OR 97065
Web: www.oregonstateparks.org/park_37.php
Phone: 541-739-2322
Size: 783 acres. **Location:** Off I-84, 17 miles east of The Dalles. **Facilities:** 34 electrical hookup campsites, 25 primitive campsites, 4 group camps, restrooms, picnic area, hiking trails, bridle trail, bike trail, boat ramp, interpretive exhibits. **Activities:** Camping, boating, fishing, hiking, bicycling, horsebak riding, wildlife viewing. **Special Features:** Located where the Deschutes and Columbia rivers converge, the area offers boating access from the Heritage Landing day-use area across the river. Other features include an Oregon Trail interpretive shelter and access to a bridle trail and bike trail.

★3845★ DETROIT LAKE STATE RECREATION AREA

PO Box 549
Detroit, OR 97342
Web: www.oregonstateparks.org/park_93.php
Phone: 503-854-3346
Size: 104 acres. **Location:** Off OR 22, 50 miles east of Salem. **Facilities:** 106 full hookup campsites, 72 electrical hookup campsites, 133 tent campsites, showers, restrooms (&), picnic area, moorage docks, nature/visitor center, playgrounds, observation decks, amphitheater, store. **Activities:** Camping, boating, fishing, swimming, water-skiing, jet skiing, wildlife viewing. **Special Features:** Park features the 400-foot-deep Detroit Lake, created in 1953. Lake is nine miles long and has more than 32 miles of shoreline, with two swimming areas.

★3846★ DEVIL'S LAKE STATE RECREATION AREA

c/o Beverly Beach Management Unit
198 NE 123rd St
Newport, OR 97365
Web: www.oregonstateparks.org/park_216.php
Phone: 800-551-6949
Size: 109 acres. **Location:** Off US 101 in Lincoln City. **Facilities:** 28 full hookup campsites, 54 tent campsites, 10 yurts, hiker/biker camp, showers, restrooms, picnic area, fishing dock, boat ramp, boat slips. **Activities:** Camping, boating, kayak tours, fishing, swimming, water-skiing, jet skiing, wildlife viewing, nature programs. **Special Features:** Park is located just minutes from downtown Lincoln City; the lake is the center of summertime activity.

★3847★ DEVIL'S PUNCHBOWL STATE NATURAL AREA

c/o Beverly Beach Management Unit
198 NE 123rd St
Newport, OR 97365
Web: www.oregonstateparks.org/park_217.php
Phone: 800-551-6949
Size: 8 acres. **Location:** Off US 101, 8 miles north of Newport. **Facilities:** Picnic area, beach access, hiking trail. **Activities:** Hiking, tide pool exploration, whale watching. **Special Features:** During winter storms, the ocean churns, foams, and swirls into a hollow rock formation shaped like a huge punch bowl, probably created when the roof of a sea cave collapsed.

★3848★ DEXTER STATE RECREATION SITE

c/o Southern Willamette Management Unit
PO Box 511
Lowell, OR 97452
Web: www.oregonstateparks.org/park_244.php
Phone: 541-937-1173
Size: 94 acres. **Location:** Off Hwy 58, 16 miles east of Eugene. **Facilities:** Picnic area, boat ramp, walking trail, hiking trail, bridle trail, disc golf course, restrooms (&). **Activities:** Boating, fishing, hiking, horseback riding, swimming, disc golf. **Special Features:** Located on the western edge of Dexter Reservoir, this day-use recreation site provides water-based recreation as well as access to nearby Elijah Bristow State Park (see separate entry).

★3849★ DRIFTWOOD BEACH STATE RECREATION SITE

c/o South Beach Management Unit
5580 S Coast Hwy
Newport, OR 97366
Web: www.oregonstateparks.org/park_203.php
Phone: 800-551-6949
Size: 8 acres. **Location:** Off US 101, 3 miles north of Waldport. **Facilities:** Picnic area, beach access, restrooms. **Activities:** Fishing, beachcombing. **Special Features:** A wide, flat, sandy beach fronted by the Pacific Ocean.

★3850★ ECOLA STATE PARK

c/o Nehalem State Park
PO Box 366
Nehalem, OR 97131
Web: www.oregonstateparks.org/park_188.php
Phone: 503-436-2844
Size: 1,304 acres. **Location:** Off US 101, 2 miles north of Cannon Beach. **Facilities:** Primitive cabins, picnic area, group shelter, beach access, restrooms, hiking trails. **Activities:** Camping, fishing, hiking, surfing, wildlife viewing, whale watching. **Special Features:** Park is located near the end of the Lewis and Clark Trail. One of its first attractions was a beached whale: in 1806 Captain William Clark and twelve others climbed over

rocky headlands and fought their way through thick shrubs and trees to get to the whale. The Clatsop Loop Trail follows in the footsteps of Clark and his men.

★3851★ ELIJAH BRISTOW STATE PARK

c/o Southern Willamette Management Unit
PO Box 511
Lowell, OR 97452
Web: www.oregonstateparks.org/park_83.php
Phone: 800-551-6949
Size: 847 acres. **Location:** Off OR 58, 16 miles southeast of Eugene. **Facilities:** Picnic area, multi-use trails (12 miles), group shelter, viewing platform (&), boat ramp, restrooms. **Activities:** Fishing, hiking, bicycling, horseback riding. **Special Features:** Named for one of the first pioneer settlers in Lane County, the park sits along the Middle Fork of Willamette River, north of Dexter Reservoir. It features Channel Lake, a land-locked river channel that meanders through the park.

★3852★ ELLMAKER STATE WAYSIDE

c/o Beverly Beach Management Unit
198 NE 123rd St
Newport, OR 97365
Web: www.oregonstateparks.org/park_218.php
Phone: 800-551-6949
Size: 76 acres. **Location:** Off US 20, 31 miles east of Newport. **Facilities:** Picnic area, restrooms. **Special Features:** On the highway between Newport and Corvallis, this land serves as a highway rest stop and a tree preserve, with a combination of old fruit trees and a fir forest.

★3853★ EMIGRANT SPRINGS STATE HERITAGE AREA

c/o Blue Mountain Management Unit
PO Box 85
Meacham, OR 97859
Web: www.oregonstateparks.org/park_23.php
Phone: 800-551-6959
Size: 63 acres. **Location:** Off I-84, 26 miles southeast of Pendleton. **Facilities:** 8 full hookup campsites (&), 1 electric campsite, 15 tent campsites, horse camp, 8 cabins, showers, restrooms (&), picnic area, hiking trail, bridle trail, game court, amphitheater, interpretive exhibits. **Activities:** Camping, hiking, horseback riding, winter recreation, nature programs. **Special Features:** Park is located near the summit of the Blue Mountains on the route of the Oregon Trail, offering visitors a chance to explore a popular pioneer stopover, and features an Oregon Trail exhibit.

★3854★ ERRATIC ROCK STATE NATURAL SITE

c/o Willamette Mission Management Unit
10991 Wheatland Rd NE
Gervais, OR 97026
Web: www.oregonstateparks.org/park_135.php
Phone: 800-551-6949
Size: 4 acres. **Location:** Off OR 18, 6 miles east of Sheridan. **Facilities:** Trail, restrooms. **Special Features:** Carried here during an Ice Age around 20,000 years ago, this 40-ton rock is the largest glacial erratic found in the Willamette Valley. A trail leading to the rock offers an excellent view of Yamhill Valley vineyards.

★3855★ FACE ROCK STATE SCENIC VIEWPOINT

c/o Bullards Beach Management Unit
PO Box 569
Bandon, OR 97411
Web: www.oregonstateparks.org/park_66.php
Phone: 800-551-6949
Size: 15 acres. **Location:** Off US 101, 1 mile southwest of Bandon. **Facilities:** Picnic area, restrooms, trail, beach access. **Activities:** Fishing, beachcombing, tide pool exploration. **Special Features:** From the cliff overlooking the ocean, visitors can easily pick out the facial features of Face Rock.

★3856★ FALL CREEK STATE RECREATION AREA

c/o Southern Willamette Management Unit
PO Box 511
Lowell, OR 97452
Web: www.oregonstateparks.org/park_241.php
Phone: 541-937-1173
Size: 167 acres. **Location:** Off OR 58 north of Lowell; 27 miles southeast of Eugene. **Facilities:** 42 primitive campsites, 5 walk-in tent sites, group camp, picnic area, boat ramps, fishing pier (&), vault toilets. **Activities:** Camping, boating, fishing, swimming, interpretive programs. **Special Features:** Site is surrounded by day-use parks and a campground.

★3857★ FAREWELL BEND STATE RECREATION AREA

23751 Old Hwy 30
Huntington, OR 97907
Web: www.oregonstateparks.org/park_7.php
Phone: 541-869-2365
Size: 77 acres. **Location:** Off I-84, 25 miles northwest of Ontario. **Facilities:** 101 electrical hookup campsites (&), 30 tent campsites, hiker/biker camp, 2 cabins, tepees, covered wagons, 2 group camps, showers, restrooms (&), picnic area, boat ramp, fishing dock, fish cleaning station, game courts, interpretive exhibits, trails (&), amphitheater. **Activities:** Camping, boating, fishing, swimming, water-skiing, wildlife viewing. **Special Features:** Pioneers on the Oregon Trail took a final rest here before leaving the Snake River to travel inland.

★3858★ FOGARTY CREEK STATE RECREATION AREA

c/o Beverly Beach Management Unit
198 NE 123rd St
Newport, OR 97365
Web: www.oregonstateparks.org/park_220.php
Phone: 800-551-6949
Size: 165 acres. **Location:** Off US 101, 2 miles north of Depoe Bay. **Facilities:** Picnic area, beach access, restrooms, hiking trail. **Activities:** Fishing, hiking, tide pool exploration, beachcombing, bird watching. **Special Features:** Area features

a scenic ocean cove, a small creek, and a forest of Sitka spruce, western hemlock, and shore pine.

★3859★ FORT ROCK STATE NATURAL AREA

c/o LaPine Management Unit
15800 State Recreation Rd
La Pine, OR 97739
Web: www.oregonstateparks.org/park_40.php
Phone: 800-551-6949
Size: 210 acres. **Location:** Off OR 31, 2 miles northwest of Fort Rock. **Facilities:** Picnic area, trail. **Activities:** Hiking. **Special Features:** Park features an enormous near-circle of towering jagged rock walls rising out of the barren flatness of high desert. A National Natural Landmard, it's really an old tuff ring set in what was a shallow sea in prehistoric times. Sandals found in a nearby cave are the oldest ever discovered, dating back about 9,000 years.

★3860★ FORT STEVENS STATE PARK

100 Peter Iredale Rd
Hammond, OR 97121
Web: www.oregonstateparks.org/park_179.php
Phone: 503-861-1671
Size: 3,809 acres. **Location:** Off US 101, 10 miles west of Astoria. **Facilities:** 174 full hookup campsites, 302 electrical hookup campsites, 19 tent campsites, 15 yurts, hiker/biker camp, showers, restrooms (&), picnic area, picnic shelters, hiking trails, bike trail, bridle trail, beach access, boat ramp, wildlife observation platforms, interpretive exhibits, playgrounds, nature/visitor center, store, museum. **Activities:** Camping, boating, fishing, swimming, windsurfing, hiking, bicycling, horseback riding, wildlife viewing. **Special Features:** From the Civil War to the end of World War II, Fort Stevens was the primary military defense installation of the three-fort Harbor Defense System at the mouth of the Columbia River. Related sites at the park today include a historic shipwreck and a historic military area.

★3861★ FORT YAMHILL STATE HERITAGE AREA

c/o Willamette Mission Management Unit
10991 Wheatland Rd NE
Gervais, OR 97026
Web: www.oregonstateparks.org/park_254.php
Phone: 800-551-6949
Size: 94 acres. **Location:** Oregon 22, 1 mile north of Valley Junction. **Facilities:** Walking trail (&), interpretive exhibits, restrooms (&). **Activities:** Hiking. **Special Features:** Fort was built in the mid-1800s to regulate the eastern border of the Grand Ronde Agency Coastal Reservation. The fort served to ease tensions between settlers and natives, protect both populations, and control traffic between them. Exhibits and cultural restoration at the park are provided in partnership with the Confederated Tribes of the Grand Ronde.

★3862★ FRENCHGLEN HOTEL STATE HERITAGE SITE

c/o Clyde Holliday Management Unit
PO Box 10
Mount Vernon, OR 97865
Web: www.oregonstateparks.org/park_3.php
Phone: 800-551-6949

Size: 33 acres. **Location:** Off OR 205, 60 miles south of Burns. **Facilities:** Historic hotel, restrooms, interpretive exhibits. **Special Features:** This quaint hotel sits at the gateway to the Steens Mountains, offering rustic accommodations. Building has been preserved and is open during the summer.

★3863★ GEISEL MONUMENT STATE HERITAGE SITE

c/o Cape Blanco Management Unit
PO Box 1345
Port Orford, OR 97465
Web: www.oregonstateparks.org/park_55.php
Phone: 800-551-6949
Size: 3 acres. **Location:** Off US 101, 7 miles north of Gold Beach. **Facilities:** Picnic area, interpretive exhibits. **Special Features:** Site contains the grave of John Geisel and his sons, killed during a Rogue Indian War skirmish.

★3864★ GEORGE W. JOSEPH STATE NATURAL AREA

c/o Columbia River Gorge Management Unit
PO Box 100
Corbett, OR 97019
Web: www.oregonstateparks.org/park_153.php
Phone: 800-551-6949
Size: 150 acres. **Location:** Off Historic Columbia River Highway, 12 miles east of Troutdale. **Facilities:** Trails; largely undeveloped. **Activities:** Hiking. **Special Features:** Accessible only by trail from Latourell Falls and Guy Talbot State Park. Area is a dense forest where sword fern, moss, and lichens grow. Trail leads to the rarely visited upper Latourell Falls.

★3865★ GLENEDEN BEACH STATE RECREATION SITE

c/o Beverly Beach Management Unit
198 NE 123rd St
Newport, OR 97365
Web: www.oregonstateparks.org/park_221.php
Phone: 800-551-6949
Size: 17.5 acres. **Location:** Off US 101, 7 miles south of Lincoln City. **Facilities:** Picnic area, group shelter, beach access, restrooms. **Activities:** Fishing, surfing, beachcombing, wildlife observation. **Special Features:** A paved trail descends through forest to the sandy beach flanked by sandstone bluffs. Sea lions can be seen at the tip of Salishan Spit.

★3866★ GOLDEN & SILVER FALLS STATE NATURAL AREA

c/o Sunset Bay Management Unit
89814 Cape Arago Hwy
Coos Bay, OR 97420
Web: www.oregonstateparks.org/park_96.php
Phone: 541-888-3778
Size: 157 acres. **Location:** Off US 101, 24 miles northeast of Coos Bay. **Facilities:** Picnic area, hiking trails, restrooms. **Activities:** Fishing, hiking. **Special Features:** Park includes

two 100-foot-plus waterfalls and an old-growth forest with myrtlewood trees.

★3867★ GOOSE LAKE STATE RECREATION AREA

c/o LaPine Management Unit
15800 State Recreation Rd
La Pine, OR 97739
Web: www.oregonstateparks.org/park_1.php
Phone: 800-551-6949
Size: 64 acres. **Location:** Off US 395, 15 miles south of Lakeview. **Facilities:** 47 electrical hookup campsites, picnic area, showers, restrooms, boat ramp. **Activities:** Camping, boating, swimming, wildlife viewing. **Special Features:** Situated on a lake shared by Oregon and California, the park is home to many species of birds and other wildlife, including a large herd of mule deer.

★3868★ GOVERNMENT ISLAND STATE RECREATION AREA

c/o Columbia River Gorge Management Unit
PO Box 100
Corbett, OR 97019
Web: www.oregonstateparks.org/park_250.php
Phone: 800-551-6949
Size: 1,578 acres. **Location:** In the Columbia River, northeast of Portland; accessible by boat only. **Facilities:** Primitive campsites, 2 docks, floating tie-up, beach access, picnic areas. **Activities:** Camping, fishing, boating. **Special Features:** Area has 15 miles of shoreline. The interior of the island is a cattle ranch and contains protected natural areas. Entry to the interior is prohibited.

★3869★ GOVERNOR PATTERSON MEMORIAL STATE RECREATION SITE

c/o South Beach Management Unit
5580 S Coast Hwy
Newport, OR 97439
Web: www.oregonstateparks.org/park_117.php
Phone: 800-551-6949
Size: 10 acres. **Location:** Off US 101, 1 mile south of Waldport. **Facilities:** Picnic area, restrooms, beach access. **Activities:** Hiking, fishing, crabbing, beachcombing, wildlife observation, windsurfing, whale watching. **Special Features:** Park features miles of flat, sandy beach a short hike from mouth of the Alsea Bay, which provides recreational activities.

★3870★ GUY W. TALBOT STATE PARK

c/o Columbia River Gorge Management Unit
PO Box 100
Corbett, OR 97019
Web: www.oregonstateparks.org/park_154.php
Phone: 800-551-6949
Size: 378 acres. **Location:** Off Historic Columbia River Highway, 12 miles east of Troutdale. **Facilities:** Picnic area, group shelter, trail, restrooms, historic buildings. **Activities:** Hiking. **Special Features:** A short foot trail underneath the Historic

Columbia River Highway bridge leads to 250-foot Latourell Falls.

★3871★ H.B. VAN DUZER FOREST STATE SCENIC CORRIDOR

c/o Beverly Beach Management Unit
198 NE 123rd St
Newport, OR 97365
Web: www.oregonstateparks.org/park_222.php
Phone: 800-551-6949
Size: 1,527 acres. **Location:** Off OR 18, 15 miles east of Lincoln City. **Facilities:** Picnic area, restrooms. **Special Features:** Corridor protects some of coastal Oregon's finest examples of old forests of Douglas fir.

★3872★ HARRIS BEACH STATE PARK

1655 Hwy 101 N
Brookings, OR 97415
Web: www.oregonstateparks.org/park_79.php
Phone: 541-469-2021
Size: 174 acres. **Location:** Off US 101, north of Brookings. **Facilities:** 36 full hookup campsites(&), 50 electrical hookup campsites, 63 tent campsites, 6 yurts, hiker/biker camp, showers, restrooms (&), picnic area, beach access, walking trail. **Activities:** Camping, boating, fishing, swimming, hiking, interpretive tours. **Special Features:** Park boasts the largest island off the Oregon coast: Bird Island is a National Wildlife Sanctuary and breeding site for such rare birds at the tufted puffin.

★3873★ HAT ROCK STATE PARK

c/o Blue Mountain Management Unit
PO Box 85
Meacham, OR 97859
Web: www.oregonstateparks.org/park_19.php
Phone: 800-551-6959
Size: 756 acres. **Location:** Off US 730, 9 miles east of Umatilla on Columbia River. **Facilities:** Picnic area, picnic shelter, restrooms, boat ramp, hiking trail, game courts. **Activities:** Boating, fishing, swimming, water-skiing, jet skiing, hiking. **Special Features:** Park lies on the south shore of Lake Wallula behind McNary Dam on the Columbia River. Hat Rock was the first distinctive Oregon landmark passed by the Lewis and Clark expedition on its journey down the Columbia River.

★3874★ HECETA HEAD LIGHTHOUSE STATE SCENIC VIEWPOINT

c/o Washburne Management Unit
93111 Hwy 101 N
Florence, OR 97439
Web: www.oregonstateparks.org/park_124.php
Phone: 800-551-6949
Size: 549 acres. **Location:** Off US 101, 13 miles north of Florence. **Facilities:** Picnic area, beach access, restrooms, hiking trail, lighthouse, caves. **Activities:** Fishing, hiking, surfing, wildlife viewing, tidepool exploration, whale watching, interpretive tours. **Special Features:** Park is located in a cove at the mouth of Cape Creek. The 56-foot lighthouse is one of the most

photographed on the coast. The light was illuminated in 1894, and the automated beacon, which can be seen 21 miles from land, is the strongest light on the Oregon coast. Heceta House (built in 1893) is the asistant lighthouse keeper's house and offers bed and breakfast rentals and facilities for group events.

★3875★ HILGARD JUNCTION STATE PARK

c/o Blue Mountain Management Unit
PO Box 85
Meacham, OR 97859
Web: www.oregonstateparks.org/park_20.php
Phone: 800-551-6949
Size: 299 acres. Location: Off I-84, 8 miles west of La Grande. Facilities: 17 primitive campsites, restrooms, picnic area. Activities: Camping, hiking, fishing, wildlife viewing. Special Features: The Grande Ronde River flows through the park, offering access to whitewater rafting. Other highlights include bright fall foliage along the river, and a variety of wildlife.

★3876★ HISTORIC COLUMBIA RIVER HIGHWAY
    STATE TRAIL

c/o Columbia River Gorge Management Unit
PO Box 100
Corbett, OR 97019
Web: www.oregonstateparks.org/park_155.php
Phone: 800-551-6949
Size: 249 acres. Location: Trail is more than 10 miles made up of 2 disconnected paved ribbons along stretches of historic Highway 30. Facilities: Picnic areas, restrooms (&), vault toilets, interpretive displays, visitor center (at Hood River trailhead), paved trail (&), nature/visitor center, historic sites. Activities: Hiking, bicycling, wildlife viewing. Special Features: Following the route of the nation's oldest scenic highway, this road-to-trails project consists of two unconnected paved paths along abandoned portions of the highway. Trail leads through semi-arid terrain, past geologic formations that tell the story of the gorge's creation, into forest and lush greenery.

★3877★ HOFFMAN MEMORIAL STATE WAYSIDE

c/o Bullards Beach Management Unit
PO Box 569
Bandon, OR 97411
Web: www.oregonstateparks.org/park_67.php
Phone: 800-551-6949
Size: 4 acres. Location: Off OR 42, 3 miles south of Myrtle Point. Facilities: Picnic area, interpretive exhibit. Activities: Fishing, self-guided tour. Special Features: Wayside is a shaded glen canopied with old myrtlewood trees.

★3878★ HOLMAN STATE WAYSIDE

c/o Willamette Mission Management Unit
10991 Wheatland Rd NE
Gervais, OR 97026
Web: www.oregonstateparks.org/park_136.php
Phone: 800-551-6949
Size: 10 acres. Location: Off OR 22, 4 miles west of Salem.

Facilities: Picnic area, restrooms, bike trail. Activities: Bicycling. Special Features: Historically, the old territorial road of the 1850s passed through this wayside on the way to Dallas and points south. A spring on the property was used as a watering hole. The wayside is covered with a stand of fir trees overlooking the Willamette River.

★3879★ HUG POINT STATE RECREATION SITE

c/o Nehalem Bay Management Unit
9500 Sandpiper Lane - PO Box 366
Nehalem, OR 97131
Web: www.oregonstateparks.org/park_191.php
Phone: 800-551-6949
Size: 43 acres. Location: Off US 101, 5 miles south of Cannon Beach. Facilities: Picnic area, beach access, restrooms. Activities: Fishing. Special Features: Before the highway was built, stagecoaches traveled along the beach. Visitors can still see the ruts of the original trail north of the parking area. Site also includes two natural beachside caves and a view of Haystack Rock.

★3880★ HUMBUG MOUNTAIN STATE PARK

c/o Cape Blanco Management Unit
PO Box 1345
Port Orford, OR 97465
Web: www.oregonstateparks.org/park_56.php
Phone: 541-332-6774
Size: 1,842 acres. Location: Off US 101, 6 miles south of Port Orford. Facilities: 32 electrical hookup campsites, 62 tent campsites, hiker/biker camp, showers, restrooms, picnic area, beach access, hiking trail. Activities: Camping, fishing, hiking, windsurfing, scuba diving, interpretive programs. Special Features: Park is dominated by Humbug Mountain (1,756 feet) and surrounded by forested hills.

★3881★ JACKSON F. KIMBALL STATE
    RECREATION SITE

c/o Collier Memorial Management Unit
46000 Hwy 97 N
Chiloquin, OR 97624
Web: www.oregonstateparks.org/park_229.php
Phone: 800-551-6949
Size: 19.5 acres. Location: Off OR 232, 3 miles north of Fort Klamath. Facilities: 10 primitive campsites, picnic area, walking trail. Activities: Camping, hiking, wildlife viewing. Special Features: A pristine site located at the headwaters of the Wood River in the southern Cascade Range. A walking trail connects the campground to the site where clear spring water bubbles from a rocky hillside.

★3882★ JASPER STATE RECREATION SITE

c/o Southern Willamette Management Unit
PO Box 511
Lowell, OR 97452
Web: www.oregonstateparks.org/park_243.php
Phone: 541-937-1173
Size: 66 acres. Location: Off Hwy 58, 12 miles southeast of

Eugene. **Facilities:** Picnic areas, group picnic shelters, restrooms (♿), trails, playgrounds, play areas. **Activities:** Hiking, fishing, wildlife viewing. **Special Features:** Trails offer access to a riverbank shaded by giant cottonwoods and maple trees.

★3883★ **JESSIE M. HONEYMAN MEMORIAL STATE PARK**
c/o Honeyman Management Unit
84505 Hwy 101 S
Florence, OR 97439
Web: www.oregonstateparks.org/park_134.php
Phone: 800-551-6949
Size: 522 acres. **Location:** Off US 101, 3 miles south of Florence. **Facilities:** 44 full hookup campsites, 122 electrical hookup campsites, 193 tent campsites, 10 yurts, hiker/biker camp, 6 group camps, showers, restrooms, picnic area, nature trails, boat ramps, boat rentals, food concession, store, meeting hall, playground (♿♿). **Activities:** Camping, boating, fishing, swimming, water-skiing, windsurfing, hiking, ATV riding, dune buggy tours. **Special Features:** Park is the northern gateway to the Oregon Dunes National Recreation Area, featuring some of the continent's highest sand dunes. Park includes 3 freshwater lakes and direct 4-wheel access to the dunes.

★3884★ **JOHN B. YEON STATE SCENIC CORRIDOR**
c/o Columbia River Gorge Management Unit
PO Box 100
Corbett, OR 97019
Web: www.oregonstateparks.org/park_156.php
Phone: 800-551-6949
Size: 284 acres. **Location:** Off I-84, 40 miles east of Portland. **Facilities:** Trail, interpretive exhibit. **Activities:** Hiking, wildlife watching. **Special Features:** Trail leads to two secluded waters in the Columbia River Gorge: lower Elowah Ralls (289-foot drop) and McCord Creek.

★3885★ **JOSEPH H. STEWART STATE RECREATION AREA**
35251 Hwy 62
Trail, OR 97541
Web: www.oregonstateparks.org/park_30.php
Phone: 541-560-3334
Size: 910 acres. **Location:** Off OR 62, 35 miles northeast of Medford. **Facilities:** 151 electrical hookup campsites, 50 tent campsites, 2 group camps, showers, restrooms, picnic area, group shelters, hiking trails, bike trail, marina, boat ramp, boat rentals, game courts, playgrounds, beach access. **Activities:** Camping, boating, fishing, swimming, water-skiing, hiking, bicycling, interpretive programs. **Special Features:** Park is located beside Lost Creek Reservoir and is about 40 miles from Crater Lake National Park (see entry in national parks section), making it a good jumping-off point for exploration of southern Oregon.

★3886★ **KAM WAH CHUNG STATE HERITAGE SITE**
c/o Clyde Holliday Management Unit
PO Box 10
Mount Vernon, OR 97865
Web: www.oregonstateparks.org/park_8.php
Phone: 800-551-6949
Size: 0.4 acres. **Location:** Off US 26 in John Day. **Facilities:** Museum, interpretive center. **Activities:** Interpretive tours. **Special Features:** Museum preserves the history of the Chinese workforce in Oregon, with artifacts and displays that depict their everyday life. The museum is undergoing restoration and is expected to reopen mid- to late summer 2007.

★3887★ **KOBERG BEACH STATE RECREATION SITE**
c/o Columbia River Gorge Management Unit
PO Box 100
Corbett, OR 97019
Web: www.oregonstateparks.org/park_157.php
Phone: 800-551-6949
Size: 75 acres. **Location:** Off I-84 (westbound access only), 3 miles east of Hood River. **Facilities:** Picnic area, beach access, restrooms. **Activities:** Fishing, windsurfing. **Special Features:** Columbia River beach lies behind a large rock formation, screening it from the busy freeway.

★3888★ **LAKE OWYHEE STATE PARK**
c/o Farewell Bend Management Unit
23751 Old Hwy 30
Huntington, OR 97907
Web: www.oregonstateparks.org/park_14.php
Phone: 800-551-6949
Size: 730 acres. **Location:** Off OR 201, 33 miles southwest of Nyssa. **Facilities:** 58 electrical hookup campsites, 8 tent campsites, 25 primitive campsites, 2 tepees, showers, restrooms (♿), picnic area, boat ramps. **Activities:** Camping, boating, fishing, swimming, hiking, rock hounding. **Special Features:** Park lies next to a 53-mile-long lake formed by Owyhee Dam. A boat trip or canoe ride up the lake offers breathtaking views of the Owyhee Mountains. Wildlife living in the area include bighorn sheep, pronghorn antelope, golden eagles, coyotes, mule deer, wild horses, and (rarely) mountain lions. Park makes a good base camp to explore Oregon's badlands.

★3889★ **LAPINE STATE PARK**
15800 State Recreation Rd
La Pine, OR 97739
Web: www.oregonstateparks.org/park_41.php
Phone: 800-551-6949
Size: 2,333 acres. **Location:** Off US 97, 27 miles southwest of Bend. **Facilities:** 80 full hookup campsites, 48 electrical hookup campsites, 10 cabins, showers, restrooms, hiking trail (0.5 miles), picnic area, meeting hall. **Activities:** Camping, boating, fishing, swimming, hiking, bicycling. **Special Features:** Park is located in the vicinity of enormous lava fields, lava tubes, caves, and other remnants of past volcanic eruptions. It features the state's largest ponderosa pine, estimated to be 500 years old.

9, State Parks

★3890★ LEWIS & CLARK STATE RECREATION SITE

c/o Columbia River Gorge Management Unit
PO Box 100
Corbett, OR 97019
Web: www.oregonstateparks.org/park_159.php
Phone: 800-551-6949
Size: 54 acres. **Location:** Off I-84, 16 miles east of Portland. **Facilities:** Picnic area, restrooms, boat ramp, hiking trails, beach access, interpretive exhibit. **Activities:** Boating, fishing, swimming, rock climbing, hiking. **Special Features:** Located at the mouth of the Sandy River, the park is named for explorers Lewis and Clark who, on November 3, 1805, examined the Sandy River. A trail climbs the cliffs to Broughton's Bluff, which serves as a geologic boundary between the foothills of the Cascade Mountain Range and the Willamette Valley to the west.

★3891★ LOST CREEK STATE RECREATION SITE

c/o South Beach Management Unit
5580 S Coast Hwy
Newport, OR 97366
Web: www.oregonstateparks.org/park_205.php
Phone: 800-551-6949
Size: 34 acres. **Location:** On both sides of US 101, 7 miles south of Newport. **Facilities:** Picnic area, restrooms, beach access. **Activities:** Fishing, whale watching, beachcombing. **Special Features:** Park offers great beachcombing, whalewatching, and sunsets.

★3892★ LOWELL STATE RECREATION SITE

c/o Southern Willamette Management Unit
PO Box 511
Lowell, OR 97452
Web: www.oregonstateparks.org/park_242.php
Phone: 541-937-1173
Size: 55 acres. **Location:** Off OR 58 on Old Pengrà Road, 17 miles southeast of Eugene. **Facilities:** Picnic area, group picnic shelters, boat ramp, marina, restrooms (&), walking trail. **Activities:** Boating, fishing, swimming, hiking, wildlife observation. **Special Features:** Park is located on the northern bank of Dexter Reservoir.

★3893★ MANHATTAN BEACH STATE RECREATION SITE

c/o Nehalem Bay Management Unit
9500 Sandpiper Lane - PO Box 366
Nehalem, OR 97131
Web: www.oregonstateparks.org/park_193.php
Phone: 800-551-6949
Size: 41 acres. **Location:** Off US 101, 2 miles north of Rockaway Beach. **Facilities:** Picnic area, beach access. **Activities:** Fishing. **Special Features:** Site offers wind-protected picnic tables.

★3894★ MAUD WILLIAMSON STATE RECREATION SITE

c/o Willamette Mission Management Unit
10991 Wheatland Rd NE
Gervais, OR 97026
Web: www.oregonstateparks.org/park_137.php
Phone: 800-551-6949
Size: 24 acres. **Location:** Off OR 221, 12 miles north of Salem. **Facilities:** Picnic area, group shelter, restrooms, game courts, historic building. **Special Features:** Site once was Willamette Valley farmland and includes a historic farm house. Today, much of the land is covered by a stand of second-growth Douglas fir.

★3895★ MAYER STATE PARK

c/o Columbia River Gorge Management Unit
PO Box 100
Corbett, OR 97019
Web: www.oregonstateparks.org/park_161.php
Phone: 800-551-6949
Size: 637 acres. **Location:** Off I-84, 10 miles west of The Dalles. **Facilities:** Picnic area, beach access, boat ramp, restrooms. **Activities:** Boating, fishing, swimming, windsurfing. **Special Features:** Park affords an outstanding view of the eastern Columbia River Gorge from Rowena Crest. Springtime blooming wildflowers are one of the most stunning vistas in the area.

★3896★ MCVAY ROCK STATE RECREATION SITE

c/o Harris Beach Management Unit
1655 Hwy 101 N
Brookings, OR 97415
Web: www.oregonstateparks.org/park_75.php
Phone: 800-551-6949
Size: 19 acres. **Location:** Off US 101, 2.5 miles south of Brookings. **Facilities:** Beach access, restrooms, walking trail. **Activities:** Fishing, swimming, whale watching, beachcombing, wildlife watching. **Special Features:** Includes a large lawn area for blanket picnics. The site is on a bluff above the beach, which gives visitors a rare opportunity to see seabirds, catching updrafts from the ocean, flying at eye level.

★3897★ MEMALOOSE STATE PARK

PO Box 472
Mosier, OR 97040
Web: www.oregonstateparks.org/park_163.php
Phone: 541-478-3008
Size: 355 acres. **Location:** Off I-84 (westbound access only), 11 miles west of The Dalles. **Facilities:** 44 full hookup campsites, 66 tent campsites, showers, restrooms, playground. **Activities:** Camping, fishing, windsurfing, interpretive programs. **Special Features:** Park was named for an island in the Columbia River island used by Chinook Indians as a sacred burial ground.

★3898★ MILO MCIVER STATE PARK

24101 SE Entrance Rd
Estacada, OR 97023
Web: www.oregonstateparks.org/park_142.php
Phone: 503-630-7150

9. State Parks

Size: 952 acres. **Location:** Springwater Road, 4 miles west of Estacada. **Facilities:** 44 electrical hookup campsites, 9 primitive campsites, hiker/biker camp, 3 group camps, showers, restrooms (&), picnic area, group picnic shelters, hiking trails, bike trail, bridle trail, boat ramp, disc golf course, off-leash dog area. **Activities:** Camping, boating, fishing, rafting, hiking, bicycling, horseback riding, wildlife viewing, interpretive programs, disc golf. **Special Features:** River lovers can challenge the wild (and picturesque) Clackamas River with rafts, canoes, or kayaks. A civil War reenactment, with more than 300 actors, takes place every April.

★3899★ MINAM STATE RECREATION AREA
c/o Wallowa Lake Management Unit
72214 Marina Lane
Joseph, OR 97846
Web: www.oregonstateparks.org/park_26.php
Phone: 800-551-6949
Size: 602 acres. **Location:** Off OR 82, 15 miles northeast of Elgin. **Facilities:** 12 primitive campsites, restrooms, picnic area, boat ramp, walking trail. **Activities:** Camping, fishing, rafting, hiking, wildlife viewing. **Special Features:** The area is located in a steep, remote valley and features picturesque Wallowa River, noted for river rafting and steelhead fishing in the spring and fall. Abundant wildlife includes deer, bear, elk, and an occasional cougar.

★3900★ MOLALLA RIVER STATE PARK
c/o Willamette Mission Management Unit
7679 Champoeg Rd NE
Saint Paul, OR 97137
Web: www.oregonstateparks.org/park_111.php
Phone: 800-551-6949
Size: 567 acres. **Location:** 2 miles north of Canby. **Facilities:** Picnic area, hiking trail, restrooms, boat ramp. **Activities:** Boating, fishing, hiking, wildlife viewing, interpretive programs. **Special Features:** Park sits at the confluence of the Willamette, Molalla, and Pudding Rivers. The floodplains of these rivers provide important habitat for waterfowl, wading birds, deer, small mammals, reptiles, and amphibians. One of the largest blue heron rookeries in the Willamette Valley is located here.

★3901★ MUNSON CREEK FALLS STATE NATURAL
  SITE
c/o Cape Lookout Management Unit
13000 Whiskey Creek Rd W
Tillamook, OR 97141
Web: www.oregonstateparks.org/park_245.php
Phone: 800-551-6949
Size: 62 acres. **Location:** Hwy 101, 6 miles south of Tillamook. **Facilities:** Picnic area, hiking trail. **Activities:** Hiking, wildlife observation. **Special Features:** Site is home to ancient western red cedar and Sitka spruce and includes Munson Creek Falls, which, at 319-feet, is the tallest waterfall in the Coast Range and is an important salmon spawning ground.

★3902★ MURIEL O. PONSLER MEMORIAL STATE
  SCENIC VIEWPOINT
c/o Washburne Management Unit
93111 Hwy 101 N
Florence, OR 97439
Web: www.oregonstateparks.org/park_125.php
Phone: 800-551-6949
Size: 2 acres. **Location:** Off US 101, 16 miles north of Florence. **Facilities:** Picnic area, beach access. **Activities:** Fishing, windsurfing, whale watching, beachcombing. **Special Features:** Site includes almost five miles of sandy beach.

★3903★ NEHALEM BAY STATE PARK
9500 Sandpiper Lane
PO Box 366
Nehalem, OR 97131
Web: www.oregonstateparks.org/park_201.php
Phone: 503-368-5154
Size: 817 acres. **Location:** Off US 101, 3 miles south of Manzanita Junction. **Facilities:** 265 electrical hookup campsites, 18 yurts, hiker/biker camp, horsemen's camp, fly-in camp, showers, restrooms (&), picnic area, hiking trails, bike trail, bridle trail, beach access, meeting hall, interpretive exhibits, playground, amphitheater. **Activities:** Camping, boating, fishing, crabbing, swimming, hiking, bicycling, horseback riding, beachcombing, wildlife viewing, interpretive programs. **Special Features:** Park is located on a sandspit between the bay and ocean, with 6 miles of ocean beach frontage, and includes an airstrip with a designated campground for fly-in campers.

★3904★ NEPTUNE STATE SCENIC VIEWPOINT
c/o Washburne Management Unit
93111 Hwy 101 N
Florence, OR 97439
Web: www.oregonstateparks.org/park_126.php
Phone: 800-551-6949
Size: 302.5 acres. **Location:** Off US 101, 3 miles south of Yachats. **Facilities:** Picnic area, beach access, restrooms (&), hiking trail. **Activities:** Fishing, hiking, wildlife viewing, tide pool exploration, whale watching. **Special Features:** Site provides scenic views of the ocean and Cumming Creek and is a good place to watch for whales, sea lions, and an occasional deer. It's also a great place to look for agates.

★3905★ NESKOWIN BEACH STATE RECREATION
  SITE
c/o Beverly Beach Management Unit
198 NE 123rd St
Newport, OR 97365
Web: www.oregonstateparks.org/park_223.php
Phone: 800-551-6949
Size: 8 acres. **Location:** Off US 101 at Neskowin. **Facilities:** Beach access. **Activities:** Fishing. **Special Features:** Located near the Cascade Head bike trail, the site includes a long, pristine beach.

9, State Parks

★3906★ NORTH SANTIAM STATE RECREATION
  AREA
c/o Detroit Management Unit
PO Box 549
Detroit, OR 97342
Web: www.oregonstateparks.org/park_92.php
Phone: 800-551-6949
Size: 119.5 acres. Location: Off OR 22, 4 miles west of Mill
City. Facilities: Picnic area, restrooms, hiking trails, boat ramp.
Activities: Boating, fishing, hiking. Special Features: One of
the most beautiful riverfront sites in the Willamette Valley, the
area is also one of the finest steelhead fishing spots on the North
Santiam River.

★3907★ OC&E WOODS LINE STATE TRAIL
c/o Collier Memorial Management Unit
46000 Hwy 97 N
Chiloquin, OR 97624
Web: www.oregonstateparks.org/park_230.php
Phone: 800-551-6949
Size: 100-mile linear park. Location: From Klamath Falls, ex-
tending east to Bly and north to the Sycan Marsh in Fremont
National Forest (see separate entry in National Forests chapter).
Facilities: Multi-use trail. Activities: Hiking, mountain biking,
bicycling, inline skating, horseback riding, cross-country skiing,
wildlife viewing. Special Features: Rail-to-trail conversion
built on the old railbed of the Oregon, California and Eastern
Railroad (OC&E). The trail is paved for 8 miles (between the
Klamath Falls Trailhead and Highway 39) and the remainder
is rough, hard-packed rock. From Beatty to the Sycan Marsh, the
trail leads into Fremont National Forest, where winter snowfall is
consistent. A campground is available at Horse Glade Trailhead.

★3908★ OCEANSIDE BEACH STATE RECREATION
  SITE
c/o Cape Lookout Management Unit
13000 Whiskey Creek Rd W
Tillamook, OR 97141
Web: www.oregonstateparks.org/park_182.php
Phone: 800-551-6949
Size: 7 acres. Location: Off US 101, 11 miles west of Tillamook. Facilities: Beach access, picnic areas, restrooms. Activities: Fishing, surfing, wildlife watching, tide pool exploration,
kite flying, beachcombing. Special Features: Site offers good
agate hunting during the winter, when the sand is stripped away
by ocean currents.

★3909★ ONA BEACH STATE PARK
c/o South Beach Management Unit
5580 S Coast Hwy
Newport, OR 97366
Web: www.oregonstateparks.org/park_206.php
Phone: 800-551-6949
Size: 237 acres. Location: Off US 101, 8 miles south of Newport. Facilities: Picnic area, beach access. Activities: Boating,
fishing, swimming, beachcombing. Special Features: Park is
developed for extensive daytime shore use.

★3910★ ONTARIO STATE RECREATION SITE
c/o Farewell Bend Management Unit
23751 Old Hwy 30
Huntington, OR 97907
Web: www.oregonstateparks.org/park_4.php
Phone: 800-551-6949
Size: 35 acres. Location: Off I-84, 1 mile north of Ontario.
Facilities: Picnic area, boat ramp, restrooms, historic sites. Ac-
tivities: Boating, fishing, swimming, wildlife viewing. Special
Features: Situated on the west bank of the historic Snake River,
where blue heron, Canada geese, river otter, and muskrat can
be seen in the reeds and grass along the shore.

★3911★ OSWALD WEST STATE PARK
c/o Nehalem Bay State Park
PO Box 366
Nehalem, OR 97131
Web: www.oregonstateparks.org/park_195.php
Phone: 503-368-5154
Size: 2,484 acres. Location: Off US 101, 10 miles south of
Cannon Beach. Facilities: 30 walk-in campsites (wheelbarrows
provided), picnic area, restrooms, hiking trails, beach access.
Activities: Camping, fishing, swimming, surfing, windsurfing,
hiking. Special Features: Park includes several trails leading
through mature forest to the beach, which is located in a cove
that provides a sense of privacy.

★3912★ OTTER CREST STATE SCENIC VIEWPOINT
c/o Beverly Beach Management Unit
198 NE 123rd St
Newport, OR 97365
Web: www.oregonstateparks.org/park_224.php
Phone: 800-551-6949
Size: 1.5 acres. Location: Off US 101, 10 miles north of Newport. Activities: Whale watching, sightseeing. Special Features: From 500 feet above the ocean, the site overlooks a
crescent sweep of beach stretching to the south. A popular spot
for whale watching, it also affords a good view of the Devil's
Punchbowl area.

★3913★ OTTER POINT STATE RECREATION SITE
c/o Cape Blanco Management Unit
PO Box 1345
Port Orford, OR 97465
Web: www.oregonstateparks.org/park_58.php
Phone: 800-551-6949
Size: 85.5 acres. Location: Off US 101, 4 miles north of Gold
Beach. Facilities: Hiking trails, beach access. Activities: Hik-
ing, wildlife watching. Special Features: Trails lead to scenic
overlooks of pristine beaches and unusual offshore rock forma-
tions.

★3914★ PARADISE POINT STATE RECREATION
  SITE
c/o Cape Blanco Management Unit
PO Box 1345
Port Orford, OR 97465
Web: www.oregonstateparks.org/park_59.php
Phone: 800-551-6949

9. State Parks

Size: 12 acres. Location: Off US 101, north of Port Orford. Facilities: Beach access. Activities: Beachcombing, wildlife viewing. Special Features: Expansive coastal view encompasses the Oregon Coast from Port Orford Heads (in the south) to the Cape Blanco Lighthouse.

★3915★ PETER SKENE OGDEN STATE SCENIC VIEWPOINT

c/o Cove Palisades Management Unit
7300 Jordan Rd
Culver, OR 97734
Web: www.oregonstateparks.org/park_50.php
Phone: 800-551-6949
Size: 86 acres. Location: Off US 97, 9 miles north of Redmond. Facilities: Picnic area, restrooms. Special Features: Park is situated at the top of a canyon, offering views of vertical basalt cliffs and river canyons.

★3916★ PILOT BUTTE STATE SCENIC VIEWPOINT

c/o Tumalo Management Unit
62976 OB Riley Rd
Bend, OR 97701
Web: www.oregonstateparks.org/park_42.php
Phone: 800-551-6949
Size: 95 acres. Location: Off US 20 east of Bend. Facilities: Hiking trails, interpretive exhibit. Activities: Hiking. Special Features: Trails lead up and around an old cinder cone to its summit, affording panoramic views of the high desert to the south and east, and of the Cascade Range to the west and north. On a clear day, visitors can see Three Sisters, Mount Jefferson, Black Butte, and Mount Hood.

★3917★ PISTOL RIVER STATE SCENIC VIEWPOINT

c/o Harris Beach Management Unit
1655 Hwy 101 N
Brookings, OR 97415
Web: www.oregonstateparks.org/park_76.php
Phone: 800-551-6949
Size: 448 acres. Location: Off US 101, 11 miles south of Gold Beach. Facilities: Beach access, restrooms, bridle trail, hiking trail, picnic areas. Activities: Fishing, windsurfing, hiking, horseback riding, wildlife observation, interpretive programs. Special Features: Park is situated in a unique dune and river area. During the spring and summer months, the dunes grow larger and the river sometimes changes course, creating pothole ponds that attract waterfowl and shorebirds. Site has prime conditions for ocean windsurfing; the national championships have been held here several times.

★3918★ PORT ORFORD HEADS STATE PARK

c/o Cape Blanco Management Unit
PO Box 1345
Port Orford, OR 97465
Web: www.oregonstateparks.org/park_61.php
Phone: 800-551-6949
Size: 103 acres. Location: Off US 101 at Port Orford. Facilities: Picnic area, hiking trails, museum, nature/visitor center, historic sites, interpretive displays. Activities: Fishing, hiking, wildlife viewing. Special Features: Park includes a former U.S. Coast Guard lifeboat station constructed in 1934; a museum is now housed in the station. Trails afford spectacular views up and down the Pacific Coast.

★3919★ PORTLAND WOMEN'S FORUM STATE SCENIC VIEWPOINT

c/o Columbia River Gorge Management Unit
PO Box 100
Corbett, OR 97019
Web: www.oregonstateparks.org/park_164.php
Phone: 800-551-6949
Size: 7 acres. Location: Off Historic Columbia River Highway, 9 miles east of Troutdale. Activities: Sightseeing. Special Features: Breathtaking view of the Columbia River Gorge.

★3920★ PRINEVILLE RESERVOIR STATE PARK

19020 SE Parkland Dr
Prineville, OR 97754
Web: www.oregonstateparks.org/park_34.php
Phone: 541-447-4363
Size: 385 acres. Location: Off US 26, 14 miles southeast of Prineville. Facilities: 22 full hookup campsites, 52 electrical hookup campsites, 23 tent campsites, 5 cabins, showers, restrooms (&), picnic areas, boat ramps, boat moorage, amphitheater, hiking trail. Activities: Camping, boating, fishing, ice fishing, swimming, water-skiing, hiking, wildlife viewing, interpretive programs. Special Features: Park is a major destination area for rock hounds in the Northwest. Popular finds include agates, jasper, chalcedony, and petrified wood.

★3921★ PROSPECT STATE SCENIC VIEWPOINT

c/o Joseph Stewart Management Unit
35251 Hwy 62
Trail, OR 97541
Web: www.oregonstateparks.org/park_29.php
Phone: 800-551-6949
Size: 11 acres. Location: Off OR 62, 1 mile south of Prospect. Facilities: Picnic area, hiking trail. Activities: Hiking, wildlife viewing. Special Features: Site is a secluded forest with trails leading to Pearsony Falls, the Rogue River, and Mill Creek Falls.

★3922★ RED BRIDGE STATE WAYSIDE

c/o Blue Mountain Management Unit
PO Box 85
Meacham, OR 97859
Web: www.oregonstateparks.org/park_21.php
Phone: 800-551-6949
Size: 37 acres. Location: Off OR 244, 16 miles southwest of La Grande. Facilities: 20 primitive campsites, picnic area, restrooms. Activities: Camping, fishing. Special Features: Wayside sits along the banks of the Grande Ronde River in the heart of the Blue Mountains. Adjacent federal lands offer miles of hiking trails and big game hunting opportunities.

★3923★ **ROADS END STATE RECREATION SITE**
c/o Beverly Beach Management Unit
198 NE 123rd St
Newport, OR 97365
Web: www.oregonstateparks.org/park_225.php
Phone: 800-551-6949
Size: 5 acres. **Location:** Off US 101, 1 mile north of Lincoln City. **Facilities:** Picnic area, beach access. **Activities:** Fishing, windsurfing, wildlife observation. **Special Features:** Site features tidepools, islands, and a hidden cove.

★3924★ **ROCKY CREEK STATE SCENIC VIEWPOINT**
c/o Beverly Beach Management Unit
198 NE 123rd St
Newport, OR 97365
Web: www.oregonstateparks.org/park_253.php
Phone: 800-551-6949
Size: 58 acres. **Location:** Off Highway 101, north of Newport. **Facilities:** Picnic area, restrooms. **Activities:** Bird watching, whale watching. **Special Features:** Rocky Creek is an ocean-front park on a forested bluff overlooking the ocean. Offshore rocks provide spectacular wave action in storms and are nesting areas for birds and sea lions. The viewpoint is an official ''Whale Spoken Here'' site for watching migrating and resident gray whales.

★3925★ **ROOSTER ROCK STATE PARK**
PO Box 100
Corbett, OR 97019
Web: www.oregonstateparks.org/park_175.php
Phone: 503-695-2261
Size: 873 acres. **Location:** Off I-84, 22 miles east of Portland. **Facilities:** Picnic area, group shelter, restrooms, boat ramp, hiking trails, beach access, interpretive exhibits, 2 disc golf courses. **Activities:** Boating, fishing, swimming, windsurfing, hiking, bird watching, disc golf. **Special Features:** Park features 3 miles of sandy beaches along the Columbia River and a secluded nude beach. Boat ramp is located in the lagoon at the base of looming Rooster Rock.

★3926★ **SADDLE MOUNTAIN STATE NATURAL AREA**
c/o Nehalem Bay Management Unit
9500 Sandpiper Lane - PO Box 366
Nehalem, OR 97131
Web: www.oregonstateparks.org/park_197.php
Phone: 800-551-6949
Size: 3,072 acres. **Location:** Off US 26, 8 miles northeast of Necanicum Junction. **Facilities:** 10 primitive campsites, restrooms, picnic area, hiking trail. **Activities:** Camping, hiking. **Special Features:** Principal feature of park is Saddle Mountain, a double peak rising 3,283 feet and providing views of the Columbia River mouth as well as the Pacific Ocean shoreline. Park also features rare plants and wildflowers.

★3927★ **SAMUEL H. BOARDMAN STATE SCENIC CORRIDOR**
c/o Harris Beach Management Unit
1655 Hwy 101 N
Brookings, OR 97415
Web: www.oregonstateparks.org/park_77.php
Phone: 800-551-6949
Size: 1,471 acres. **Location:** Off US 101, 4 miles north of Brookings. **Facilities:** Picnic area, beach access, restrooms (&), hiking trail. **Activities:** Hiking, fishing, swimming, interpretive tours, boating. **Special Features:** The corridor is a 12-mile densely forested, linear park with a rugged, steep coastline interrupted by small sand beaches. It features 300-year-old Sitka spruce trees and a 27-mile segment of the Oregon Coast Trail.

★3928★ **SARAH HELMICK STATE RECREATION SITE**
c/o Willamette Mission Management Unit
10991 Wheatland Rd NE
Gervais, OR 97026
Web: www.oregonstateparks.org/park_138.php
Phone: 800-551-6949
Size: 80 acres. **Location:** Off US 99W, 6 miles south of Monmouth. **Facilities:** Picnic area, group shelter, walking trail, restrooms. **Activities:** Fishing, hiking. **Special Features:** Forested recreation area on the Luckiamute River provides lots of shade for picnicking and plenty of birds and native plant life to view along the trails.

★3929★ **SEAL ROCK STATE RECREATION SITE**
c/o South Beach Management Unit
5580 S Coast Hwy
Newport, OR 97366
Web: www.oregonstateparks.org/park_207.php
Phone: 800-551-6949
Size: 5 acres. **Location:** Off US 101, 10 miles south of Newport. **Facilities:** Picnic area, beach access, hiking trails, interpretive exhibit. **Activities:** Fishing, hiking, tide pool exploration, wildlife viewing. **Special Features:** Site includes large offshore basaltic rock formations, which provide habitat for seals, sea lions, sea birds, and other marine life.

★3930★ **SENECA FOUTS MEMORIAL STATE NATURAL AREA**
c/o Columbia River Gorge Management Unit
PO Box 100
Corbett, OR 97019
Web: www.oregonstateparks.org/park_167.php
Phone: 800-551-6949
Size: 425.5 acres. **Location:** Off I-84 (eastbound access only), 6 miles west of Hood River. **Facilities:** Hiking trail. **Activities:** Hiking. **Special Features:** The terrain is rocky and mountainous at Seneca Fouts, which is is the third leg of state parks joined together at Mitchell Point; the other two are Vinzenz Lausmann Memorial State Natural Area and Wygant State Natural Area (see separate entries).

★3931★ SEVEN DEVILS STATE RECREATION SITE
c/o Bullards Beach Management Unit
PO Box 569
Bandon, OR 97411
Web: www.oregonstateparks.org/park_69.php
Phone: 800-551-6949
Size: 54 acres. **Location:** Off US 101, 10 miles north of Bandon. **Facilities:** Picnic area, beach access. **Activities:** Fishing, beachcombing. **Special Features:** A jumping-off point for beach exploration. From here, visitors can travel several miles up and down the open beach to look for agates.

★3932★ SHEPPERD'S DELL STATE NATURAL AREA
c/o Columbia River Gorge Management Unit
PO Box 100
Corbett, OR 97019
Web: www.oregonstateparks.org/park_168.php
Phone: 800-551-6949
Size: 521 acres. **Location:** Off Historic Columbia River Highway, 14 miles east of Troutdale. **Facilities:** Trail. **Activities:** Hiking. **Special Features:** Short trail leads to a waterfall viewpoint and historic highway bridge.

★3933★ SHORE ACRES STATE PARK
c/o Sunset Bay Management Unit
89814 Cape Arago Hwy
Coos Bay, OR 97420
Web: www.oregonstateparks.org/park_97.php
Phone: 541-888-3778
Size: 745 acres. **Location:** Off US 101, 13 miles southwest of Coos Bay. **Facilities:** Picnic area, trails, beach access, observation shelter, gift shop, restrooms, gardens (&). **Activities:** Hiking, wildlife viewing. **Special Features:** Once the grand estate of pioneer timber baron Louis Simpson, Shore Acres features a formal garden, an oriental pond, and 2 rose gardens. A trail leads to a secluded ocean cove; the cliff's edge affords spectacular ocean vistas and views of migrating grey whales.

★3934★ SILVER FALLS STATE PARK
20024 Silver Falls Hwy SE
Sublimity, OR 97385
Web: www.oregonstateparks.org/park_211.php
Phone: 503-873-8681; **Fax:** 503-873-8925
Size: 9,064 acres. **Location:** Off OR 214, 26 miles east of Salem. **Facilities:** 52 electrical hookup campsites, 45 tent campsites, 14 cabins, horsemen's camp, group camps, showers, restrooms (&), picnic areas, group picnic shelters, day-use lodge, hiking trails, bridle trails, bike trail, meeting hall, interpretive exhibit, nature center, amphitheater, playgrounds, conference center, museum. **Activities:** Camping, fishing, swimming, hiking, bicycling, mountain biking, horseback riding, jogging, wildlife viewing, interpretive and entertainment programs. **Special Features:** Located in the western foothills of the Cascade Range, the park includes more than 25 miles of trails, featuring the nationally recognized Trail of Ten Falls, a 7-mile hike that passes 10 waterfalls ranging in height from 27 to 177 feet.

★3935★ SMELT SANDS STATE RECREATION SITE
c/o South Beach Management Unit
5580 S Coast Hwy
Newport, OR 97366
Web: www.oregonstateparks.org/park_128.php
Phone: 800-551-6949
Size: 9 acres. **Location:** Off US 101 in Yachats. **Facilities:** Beach access, picnic areas, hiking trails, interpretive exhibits, restrooms (&). **Activities:** Fishing, hiking, whale watching, tide-pool exploration. **Special Features:** Features the historic 804 Trail, a dramatic 3/4-mile walk along the ocean's edge. Site is also the traditional location of the annual run of smelt, small silver fish related to salmon.

★3936★ SMITH ROCK STATE PARK
9241 NE Crooked River Dr
Terrebonne, OR 97760
Web: www.oregonstateparks.org/park_51.php
Phone: 541-548-7501
Size: 651 acres. **Location:** Off US 97, 9 miles northeast of Redmond. **Facilities:** Walk-in bivouac camp, picnic area, hiking trails, interpretive exhibits, restrooms (&). **Activities:** Camping, fishing, hiking, mountain biking, rock climbing, wildlife viewing. **Special Features:** Recognized as having some of the most colorful and spectacular geological formations in Oregon, park is an international mecca for rock climbers. The park and surrounding federal land offer thousands of climbs, including more than than a thousand bolted routes, some of which are rated among the most difficult in the world.

★3937★ SOUTH BEACH STATE PARK
5580 S Coast Hwy
South Beach, OR 97366
Web: www.oregonstateparks.org/park_209.php
Phone: 541-867-4715
Size: 499 acres. **Location:** Off US 101, 2 miles south of Newport. **Facilities:** 228 electrical hookup campsites (&), 27 yurts (&), hiker/biker camp, 3 group camps, showers, restrooms (&), picnic area, nature trail, hiking trail, bike trail, beach access, meeting hall, game courts, nature/visitor center, gift shop. **Activities:** Camping, kayak tours, boating, fishing, crabbing, windsurfing, swimming, hiking, beachcombing, wildlife viewing. **Special Features:** Park offers easy access to miles of broad, sandy ocean beach, providing many recreational activities.

★3938★ STARVATION CREEK STATE PARK
c/o Columbia River Gorge Management Unit
PO Box 100
Corbett, OR 97019
Web: www.oregonstateparks.org/park_170.php
Phone: 503-695-2261
Size: 153 acres. **Location:** Off I-84 (eastbound access only), 10 miles west of Hood River. **Facilities:** Picnic area, restrooms (&), interpretive exhibit, hiking trails. **Activities:** Hiking, bird watching. **Special Features:** The waterfall here is one of few in this area of the gorge. Trails lead to adjacent U.S. Forest Service land and connect to the Mount Defiance and Starvation Ridge trails.

★3939★ STONEFIELD BEACH STATE RECREATION SITE

c/o Area 3 Field Office
84505 Hwy 101 S
Florence, OR 97439
Web: www.oregonstateparks.org/park_130.php
Phone: 541-997-5755
Size: 19 acres. **Location:** Off US 101, 6 miles south of Yachats and just south of Tenmile Creek. **Facilities:** Beach access. **Activities:** Fishing, whale watching. **Special Features:** Park offers a good vantage point from which to observe whales.

★3940★ SUCCOR CREEK STATE NATURAL AREA

c/o Farewell Bend Management Unit
23751 Old Hwy 30
Huntington, OR 97907
Web: www.oregonstateparks.org/park_13.php
Phone: 800-551-6949
Size: 2,202 acres. **Location:** Off OR 201, 30 miles south of Nyssa. **Facilities:** 16 walk-in campsites, 12 hike-in campsites, picnic area. **Activities:** Camping, hiking, wildlife viewing. **Special Features:** Area features colorful, rugged rock formations.

★3941★ SUMPTER VALLEY DREDGE STATE HERITAGE AREA

c/o Clyde Holliday Management Unit
PO Box 10
Mount Vernon, OR 97865
Web: www.oregonstateparks.org/park_239.php
Phone: 800-551-6949
Size: 84 acres. **Location:** Off OR 7, 30 miles west of Baker City. **Facilities:** Picnic area, historic site, interpretive exhibits, trails, restrooms. **Activities:** Interpretive programs, hiking, wildlife viewing. **Special Features:** Sumpter Valley's historic dredge is one of the largest and most accessible gold dredges in the U.S. and represents an important link to Oregon's pioneering past and development. Miles of tailings line the banks of the Powder River, a reminder of the prosperous but environmentally damaging years of mining.

★3942★ SUNSET BAY STATE PARK

c/o Sunset Bay Management Unit
89814 Cape Arago Hwy
Coos Bay, OR 97420
Web: www.oregonstateparks.org/park_100.php
Phone: 541-888-4902
Size: 395 acres. **Location:** Off US 101, 12 miles southwest of Coos Bay. **Facilities:** 29 full hookup campsites, 34 electrical hookup campsites, 66 tent campsites, 8 yurts, hiker/biker camp, 2 group camps, showers, restrooms (&), picnic area, group picnic shelter, hiking trails, beach access, nature programs. **Activities:** Camping, boating, fishing, swimming, hiking, beachcombing, wildlife viewing. **Special Features:** One of the most scenic parks on the Oregon coast, Sunset Bay features sandy beaches protected by towering sea cliffs. A network of hiking trails gives visitors a chance to experience a pristine coastal forest, seasonal wildflowers, and ocean vistas from atop the rugged cliffs and headlands.

★3943★ TOKATEE KLOOTCHMAN STATE NATURAL SITE

c/o Washburne Management Unit
93111 Hwy 101 N
Florence, OR 97439
Web: www.oregonstateparks.org/park_129.php
Phone: 800-551-6949
Size: 7 acres. **Location:** Off US 101, 16 miles north of Florence. **Activities:** Swimming, bird watching, wildlife viewing. **Special Features:** A good park for whale watching.

★3944★ TOLOVANA BEACH STATE RECREATION SITE

c/o Nehalem Bay Management Unit
9500 Sandpiper Lane - PO Box 366
Nehalem, OR 97131
Web: www.oregonstateparks.org/park_199.php
Phone: 800-551-6949
Size: 3 acres. **Location:** Off US 101, 1 mile south of Cannon Beach. **Facilities:** Picnic area, beach access. **Activities:** Fishing, tide pool exploration, wildlife watching. **Special Features:** Site features views of Haystack Rock.

★3945★ TOUVELLE STATE RECREATION SITE

c/o Valley of the Rogue Management Unit
3792 N River Rd
Gold Hill, OR 97525
Web: www.oregonstateparks.org/park_106.php
Phone: 800-551-6949
Size: 58 acres. **Location:** Off OR 62, 9 miles north of Medford. **Facilities:** Picnic area, group picnic shelter, boat ramp, restrooms (&), hiking trail. **Activities:** Boating, fishing, hiking, wildlife viewing. **Special Features:** Located on the bank of the Rogue River at the foot of geologically-prominent Table Rocks, this day-use site is adjacent to Denman Wildlife Refuge, a haven for local and migratory wildlife.

★3946★ TRYON CREEK STATE NATURAL AREA

11321 SW Terwilliger Blvd
Portland, OR 97219
Web: www.oregonstateparks.org/park_144.php
Phone: 503-636-9886
Size: 662 acres. **Location:** Off I-5, on Terwilliger Boulevard in southwest Portland. **Facilities:** Hiking trail, bike trail, bridle trails, nature center, gift shop, interpretive exhibit, restrooms (&), store. **Activities:** Hiking, bicycling, horseback riding, wildlife viewing, interpretive programs. **Special Features:** Located only minutes from downtown Portland, park's nature trails wind through a verdant ravine. Tryon Creek is one of the only streams in the metro area with a run of steelhead trout.

★3947★ TUB SPRINGS STATE WAYSIDE

c/o Valley of the Rogue Management Unit
3792 N River Rd
Gold Hill, OR 97525
Web: www.oregonstateparks.org/park_107.php
Phone: 800-551-6949

9. State Parks

Size: 40 acres. **Location:** Off OR 66, 18 miles east of Ashland. **Facilities:** Picnic area, walking trail, interpretive displays, restrooms. **Activities:** Hiking, wildlife watching. **Special Features:** Wayside features freshwater springs that flow into three rock tubs situated along the historic Applegate Trail wagon train stop.

★3948★ TUMALO STATE PARK

62976 OB Riley Rd
Bend, OR 97701
Web: www.oregonstateparks.org/park_45.php
Phone: 541-382-3586
Size: 327 acres. **Location:** Off US 20, 5 miles northwest of Bend. **Facilities:** 23 full hookup campsites, 54 tent campsites, 7 yurts, hiker/biker camp, 2 group camps, showers, restrooms (&), picnic areas, 2 group picnic shelters, playgrounds, hiking trail. **Activities:** Camping, fishing, swimming, hiking. **Special Features:** Situated along the Deschutes River, park offers opportunities for trout fishing, rafting, hiking and wildlife watching.

★3949★ UKIAH-DALE FOREST STATE SCENIC CORRIDOR

c/o Blue Mountain Management Unit
PO Box 85
Meacham, OR 97859
Web: www.oregonstateparks.org/park_22.php
Phone: 800-551-6949
Size: 6,007 acres. **Location:** Off US 395, 3 miles southwest of Ukiah. **Facilities:** 27 primitive campsites, restrooms. **Activities:** Camping, fishing. **Special Features:** Corridor is situated on Camas Creek above the North Fork of the John Day River. Springtime wildflower displays include camas, a traditionally important food source for Native Americans.

★3950★ UMPQUA LIGHTHOUSE STATE PARK

c/o Honeyman Management Unit
84505 Hwy 101 S
Florence, OR 97439
Web: www.oregonstateparks.org/park_121.php
Phone: 800-551-6949
Size: 450 acres. **Location:** Off US 101, 6 miles south of Reedsport. **Facilities:** 20 full hookup campsites, 24 tent campsites, 8 yurts, 2 cabins, showers, restrooms, picnic area, trail, boat ramp, beach access. **Activities:** Camping, boating (non-motorized), fishing, swimming, hiking. **Special Features:** Park is centered in the stretch of sand dunes protected by Oregon Dunes National Recreation Area, and includes access to freshwater Lake Marie.

★3951★ UNITY FOREST STATE SCENIC CORRIDOR

c/o Farewell Bend Management Unit
23751 Old Hwy 30
Huntington, OR 97907
Web: www.oregonstateparks.org/park_9.php
Phone: 800-551-6949
Size: 85 acres. **Location:** On US 26, 50 miles east of John Day. **Facilities:** Undeveloped. **Special Features:** Heavily forested corridor is home to a wide variety of wildlife. Elk, mule deer, antelope, cougar, bobcat, and black bear can be seen along this stretch of highway.

★3952★ UNITY LAKE STATE RECREATION SITE

c/o Clyde Holliday Management Unit
PO Box 10
Mount Vernon, OR 97865
Web: www.oregonstateparks.org/park_10.php
Phone: 800-551-6949
Size: 39 acres. **Location:** Off OR 245, 50 miles east of John Day. **Facilities:** 35 electrical hookup campsites, hiker/biker camp, showers, restrooms (&), picnic area, boat ramp, hiking trail. **Activities:** Camping, boating, fishing, swimming, water-skiing. **Special Features:** High desert park features cool grasses, which are in contrast to the sagebrush and cheatgrass of bordering lands; the smell of juniper lingers in the air.

★3953★ VALLEY OF THE ROGUE STATE PARK

3792 N River Rd
Gold Hill, OR 97525
Web: www.oregonstateparks.org/park_109.php
Phone: 541-582-1118
Size: 277 acres. **Location:** Off I-5, 12 miles east of Grants Pass on Rogue River. **Facilities:** 88 full hookup campsites, 59 electrical hookup campsites, 21 tent campsites, 6 yurts, 3 group camps, showers, restrooms (&), picnic area, group picnic shelters, boat ramp, meeting hall, interpretive trail, bike path, walking trail, outdoor amphitheater, playgrounds. **Activities:** Camping, boating, fishing, hiking, interpretive programs. **Special Features:** Park features 3 miles of shoreline on the Rogue River, offering opportunities for camping and recreation along the river made famous by novelist Zane Grey.

★3954★ VIENTO STATE PARK

PO Box 472
Mosier, OR 97040
Web: www.oregonstateparks.org/park_171.php
Phone: 541-374-8811
Size: 248 acres. **Location:** Off I-84, 8 miles west of Hood River. **Facilities:** 56 electrical hookup campsites, 18 tent campsites, showers, restrooms (&), picnic area, hiking trails, playgrounds. **Activities:** Camping, hiking, swimming, windsurfing, interpretive programs. **Special Features:** Park includes a day-use area with easy access to the Columbia River.

★3955★ VINZENZ LAUSMANN MEMORIAL STATE NATURAL AREA

c/o Columbia River Gorge Management Unit
PO Box 100
Corbett, OR 97019
Web: www.oregonstateparks.org/park_172.php
Phone: 800-551-6949
Size: 126 acres. **Location:** Off I-84, 7 miles west of Hood River. **Facilities:** Restrooms, trail. **Activities:** Hiking. **Special Features:** Lined with fir, alder and maple, which define the Columbia River Gorge in this area, park trail offers spectacular

9. State Parks

views of the gorge. Vinzenz Lausmann is one of three state parks joined together at Mitchell Point; the other two are Seneca Fouts Memorial State Natural Area and Wygant State Natural Area (see separate entries).

★3956★ W.B. NELSON STATE RECREATION SITE

c/o South Beach Management Unit
5580 S Coast Hwy
Newport, OR 97366
Web: www.oregonstateparks.org/park_131.php
Phone: 800-551-6949
Size: 2 acres. **Location:** Off OR 34, 1 mile east of Waldport. **Facilities:** Picnic area, fishing dock, restrooms. **Activities:** Fishing, swimming, wildlife viewing. **Special Features:** Site is adjacent to the Alsea River and features a freshwater lake and a scenic wetlands area.

★3957★ WALLOWA LAKE HIGHWAY FOREST STATE SCENIC CORRIDOR

c/o Wallowa Lake Management Unit
72214 Marina Ln
Joseph, OR 97846
Web: www.oregonstateparks.org/park_24.php
Phone: 541-432-4185
Size: 286 acres. **Location:** Off OR 82, 12 miles west of Enterprise. **Facilities:** Picnic area, restrooms. **Activities:** Fishing, wildlife viewing. **Special Features:** Corridor runs alongside the clear and cold Wallowa River. Popular with fly fishing enthusiasts, this part of the river can be waded in many locations.

★3958★ WALLOWA LAKE STATE PARK

72214 Marina Lane
Joseph, OR 97846
Web: www.oregonstateparks.org/park_27.php
Phone: 541-432-4185
Size: 166 acres. **Location:** Off OR 82, 6 miles south of Joseph. **Facilities:** 121 full hookup campsites, 89 tent campsites, 2 yurts, cabin, group camps, hiker/biker camp, showers, restrooms (&), picnic area, hiking trails, bridle trails, boat ramp, marina, boat slip rentals, miniature golf. **Activities:** Camping, boating, fishing, swimming, hiking, horseback riding, miniature golf, wildlife viewing, interpretive programs. **Special Features:** Campground is surrounded on three sides by 9,000-foot snow capped mountains and a large, clear lake. A tramway to the top of 8,200-foot Mt. Howard offers visitors views of Wallowa Lake and the Eagle Cap Wilderness.

★3959★ WASHBURNE STATE WAYSIDE

c/o Southern Willamette Management Unit
PO Box 511
Lowell, OR 97452
Web: www.oregonstateparks.org/park_87.php
Phone: 800-551-6949
Size: 37 acres. **Location:** Off US 99W, 4 miles northwest of Junction City. **Facilities:** Picnic area, restrooms, nature trail, interpretive exhibits. **Activities:** Hiking, wildlife watching. **Special Features:** Wayside markers relate the story of the Applegate

Trail, a historic route blazed in 1846 as a safer alternative to the better-known Oregon Trail.

★3960★ WHITE RIVER FALLS STATE PARK

c/o Deschutes River Management Unit
PO Box 2330
Wasco, OR 97065
Web: www.oregonstateparks.org/park_36.php
Phone: 800-551-6949
Size: 299 acres. **Location:** Off OR 216, 39 miles south of The Dalles. **Facilities:** Picnic area, hiking trail, restrooms. **Activities:** Fishing, hiking. **Special Features:** Park features an overlook of 90-foot White River Falls and the remnants of an old hydroelectric power plant.

★3961★ WILLAMETTE MISSION STATE PARK

10991 Wheatland Rd
Gervais, OR 97026
Web: www.oregonstateparks.org/park_139.php
Phone: 503-393-1172; **Fax:** 503-393-8863
Size: 1,686 acres. **Location:** On Wheatland Road, 8 miles north of Salem. **Facilities:** Picnic area, group picnic shelters, hiking trail, bike path, bridle trail, horse camp, boat ramp, boat rentals, restrooms (&), interpretive exhibit, game courts. **Activities:** Group camping, fishing, boating, hiking, bicycling, horseback riding, interpretive programs. **Special Features:** Park is the site of Jason Lee Methodist Mission (founded in 1834) and is listed on the *National Register of Historic Places*. It also includes the nation's largest known black cottonwood tree, about 250 years old.

★3962★ WILLAMETTE STONE STATE HERITAGE SITE

c/o Tryon Creek Management Unit
11321 SW Terwilliger Blvd
Portland, OR 97219
Web: www.oregonstateparks.org/park_246.php
Phone: 800-551-6949
Size: 2 acres. **Location:** On Skyline Boulevard, 4 miles west of Portland. **Facilities:** Historical marker, walking trail. **Special Features:** Monument marks Willamette Meridian, the point from which all Northwest township surveys were made.

★3963★ WILLIAM M. TUGMAN STATE PARK

72549 Hwy 101
Lakeside, OR 97449
Web: www.oregonstateparks.org/park_98.php
Phone: 800-551-6949
Size: 560 acres. **Location:** Off US 101, 8 miles south of Reedsport. **Facilities:** 94 electrical hookup campsites, 16 yurts, hiker/biker camp, showers, restrooms (&), picnic areas, group picnic shelter, bike trail, hiking trails, boat ramp, fishing pier (&). **Activities:** Camping, boating, fishing, swimming, hiking, biking, wildlife viewing. **Special Features:** Park features Eel Lake, which has a healthy population of largemouth bass, as well as crappie, rainbow trout, and steelhead and coho salmon.

9. State Parks

A trail around the south end of the lake allows hikers to explore the lake's many coves and inlets.

★3964★ WINCHUCK STATE RECREATION SITE
c/o Harris Beach Management Unit
1655 Hwy 101 N
Brookings, OR 97415
Web: www.oregonstateparks.org/park_78.php
Phone: 800-551-6949
Size: 7 acres. Location: Off US 101, 5 miles south of Brookings. Facilities: Beach access. Activities: Fishing, boating, swimming. Special Features: Site provides access to the Winchuck River and the beach.

★3965★ WOLF CREEK INN STATE HERITAGE SITE
PO Box 6
Wolf Creek, OR 97497
Web: www.oregonstateparks.org/park_108.php
Phone: 541-866-2474
Size: 12 acres. Location: Off I-5 (Exit 76), 20 miles north of Grants Pass. Special Features: Originally opened in the 1880s on the Oregon-California stagecoach road, Wolf Creek Inn is the oldest continuously operated hotel in the Pacific Northwest. Jack London completed his novel *Valley of the Moon here*.

★3966★ WYGANT STATE NATURAL AREA
c/o Columbia River Gorge Management Unit
PO Box 100
Corbett, OR 97019
Web: www.oregonstateparks.org/park_174.php
Phone: 800-551-6949
Size: 667 acres. Location: Off I-84, 7 miles west of Hood River. Facilities: Hiking trails. Activities: Hiking. Special Features: Wygant is one of three state parks joined together at Mitchell Point; the other two are Seneca Fouts Memorial State Natural Area and Vinzenz Lausmann Memorial State Natural Area (see separate entries). Area's trail strikes through a dense, hilly wilderness that was once the old Oregon Trail and later the Columbia River Highway.

★3967★ YACHATS OCEAN ROAD STATE NATURAL SITE
c/o South Beach Management Unit
5580 S Coast Hwy
Newport, OR 97366
Web: www.oregonstateparks.org/park_132.php
Phone: 800-551-6949
Size: 79 acres. Location: Off US 101, on the south side of the Yachats River in Yachats. Facilities: Picnic area, beach access. Activities: Beachcombing, whale watching, tidepool exploration. Special Features: The highway makes a one-mile loop, providing scenic views of Yachats Bay and the Pacific Ocean.

★3968★ YACHATS STATE RECREATION AREA
c/o South Beach Management Unit
5580 S Coast Hwy
Newport, OR 97366
Web: www.oregonstateparks.org/park_133.php
Phone: 800-551-6949
Size: 94 acres. Location: Off US 101 at Yachats. Facilities: Picnic area, beach access, interpretive exhibits, restrooms. Activities: Fishing, tide pool exploration, whale watching. Special Features: Recreation area is situated where the Yachats River meets the Pacific Ocean.

★3969★ YAQUINA BAY STATE RECREATION SITE
c/o South Beach Management Unit
5580 S Coast Hwy
Newport, OR 97366
Web: www.oregonstateparks.org/park_208.php
Phone: 800-551-6949
Size: 32 acres. Location: Off US 101 in Newport. Facilities: Picnic area, restrooms, beach access, museum, lighthouse, walking trail, historic buildings. Activities: Fishing, guided tours, hiking. Special Features: Park features a historic lighthouse, once used as a Coast Guard Lifeboat Station. Nearby attractions include the historic Newport bayfront, Hatfield Marine Science Center, and the Oregon Coast Aquarium.

9. State Parks

Pennsylvania State Parks

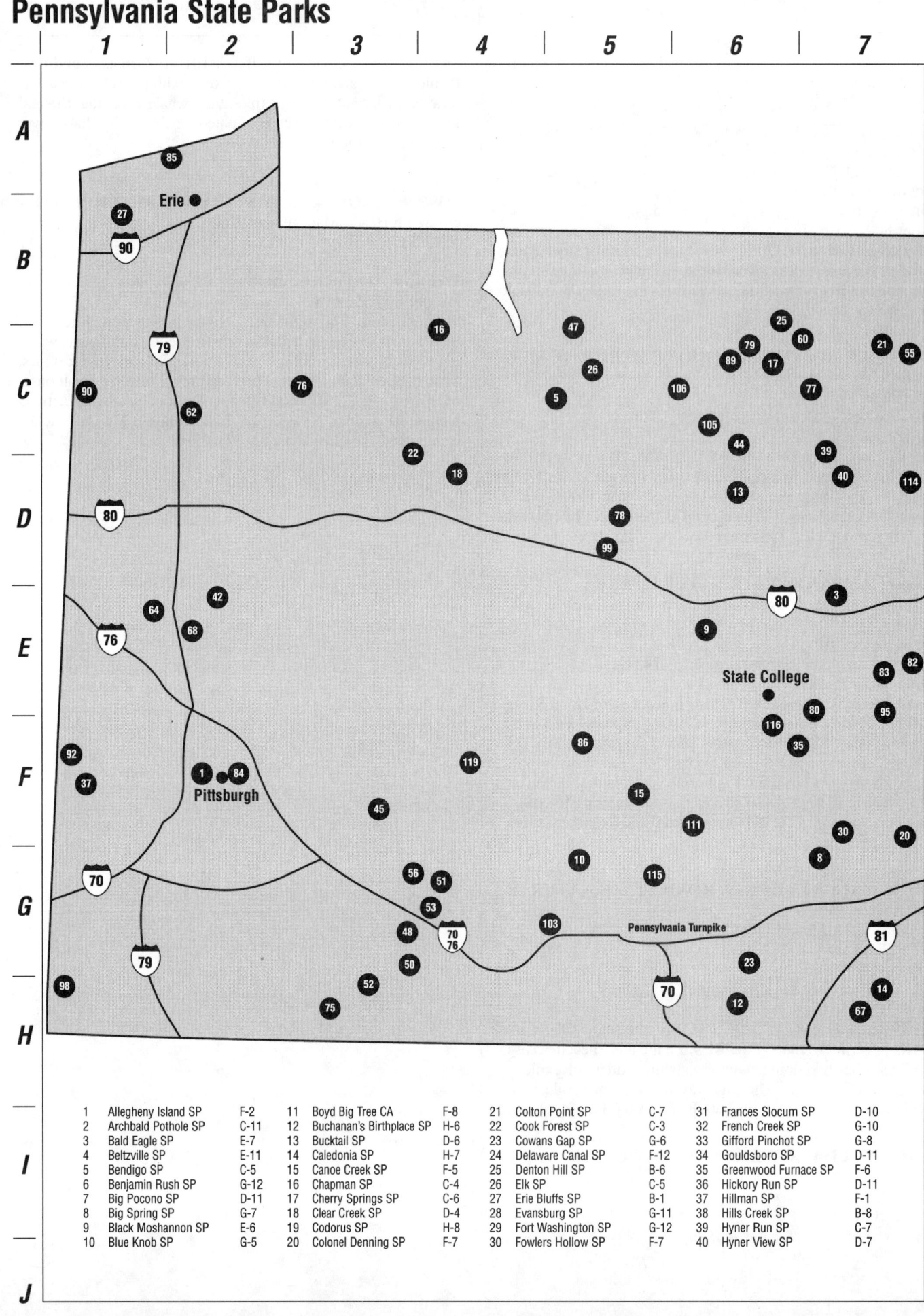

1	Allegheny Island SP	F-2	11	Boyd Big Tree CA	F-8	21	Colton Point SP	C-7	31	Frances Slocum SP	D-10
2	Archbald Pothole SP	C-11	12	Buchanan's Birthplace SP	H-6	22	Cook Forest SP	C-3	32	French Creek SP	G-10
3	Bald Eagle SP	E-7	13	Bucktail SP	D-6	23	Cowans Gap SP	G-6	33	Gifford Pinchot SP	G-8
4	Beltzville SP	E-11	14	Caledonia SP	H-7	24	Delaware Canal SP	F-12	34	Gouldsboro SP	D-11
5	Bendigo SP	C-5	15	Canoe Creek SP	F-5	25	Denton Hill SP	B-6	35	Greenwood Furnace SP	F-6
6	Benjamin Rush SP	G-12	16	Chapman SP	C-4	26	Elk SP	C-5	36	Hickory Run SP	D-11
7	Big Pocono SP	D-11	17	Cherry Springs SP	C-6	27	Erie Bluffs SP	B-1	37	Hillman SP	F-1
8	Big Spring SP	G-7	18	Clear Creek SP	D-4	28	Evansburg SP	G-11	38	Hills Creek SP	B-8
9	Black Moshannon SP	E-6	19	Codorus SP	H-8	29	Fort Washington SP	G-12	39	Hyner Run SP	C-7
10	Blue Knob SP	G-5	20	Colonel Denning SP	F-7	30	Fowlers Hollow SP	F-7	40	Hyner View SP	D-7

71	Neshaminy SP	G-12
72	Nockamixon SP	F-12
73	Nolde Forest EEC	F-10
74	Norristown Farm Park	G-12
75	Ohiopyle SP	H-3
76	Oil Creek SP	C-3
77	Ole Bull SP	C-7
78	Parker Dam SP	D-5
79	Patterson SP	C-6
80	Penn Roosevelt SP	E-7
81	Pine Grove Furnace SP	G-8
82	Poe Paddy SP	E-7
83	Poe Valley SP	E-7
84	Point SP	F-2
85	Presque Isle SP	A-2
86	Prince Gallitzin SP	F-5
87	Promised Land SP	D-12
88	Prompton SP	C-11
89	Prouty Place SP	C-6
90	Pymatuning SP	C-1
91	R. B. Winter SP	E-8
92	Raccoon Creek SP	F-1
93	Ralph Stover SP	F-12
94	Ravensburg SP	D-8
95	Reeds Gap SP	E-7
96	Ricketts Glen SP	D-9
97	Ridley Creek SP	G-11
98	Ryerson Station SP	H-1
99	S. B. Elliott SP	D-5
100	Salt Spring SP	B-10
101	Samuel S. Lewis SP	G-9
102	Sand Bridge SP	E-8
103	Shawnee SP	G-5
104	Shikellamy SP	E-8
105	Sinnemahoning SP	C-6
106	Sizerville SP	C-6
107	Susquehanna SP	D-8
108	Susquehannock SP	H-9
109	Swatara SP	F-9
110	Tobyhanna SP	D-11
111	Trough Creek SP	F-6
112	Tuscarora SP	E-10
113	Tyler SP	G-12
114	Upper Pine Bottom SP	D-7
115	Warriors Path SP	G-5
116	Whipple Dam SP	F-6
117	White Clay Creek Preserve	H-10
118	Worlds End SP	C-9
119	Yellow Creek SP	F-4

CA	Conservation Area
EEC	Environmental Education Center
SP	State Park

41	Jacobsburg EEC	E-12	51	Laurel Mountain SP	G-4	61	Marsh Creek SP	G-11
42	Jennings EEC	E-2	52	Laurel Ridge SP	H-3	62	Maurice K. Goddard SP	C-2
43	Joseph E. Ibberson CA	F-8	53	Laurel Summit SP	G-4	63	McCalls Dam SP	E-8
44	Kettle Creek SP	C-6	54	Lehigh Gorge SP	E-10	64	McConnell's Mill SP	E-1
45	Keystone SP	F-3	55	Leonard Harrison SP	C-7	65	Memorial Lake SP	F-9
46	Kings Gap EEC	G-8	56	Linn Run SP	G-3	66	Milton SP	E-8
47	Kinzua Bridge SP	C-5	57	Little Buffalo SP	F-8	67	Mont Alto SP	H-7
48	Kooser SP	G-3	58	Little Pine SP	C-8	68	Moraine SP	E-2
49	Lackawanna SP	C-11	59	Locust Lake SP	E-10	69	Mount Pisgah SP	B-9
50	Laurel Hill SP	G-3	60	Lyman Run SP	C-7	70	Nescopeck SP	E-11

PENNSYLVANIA

★3970★ **Pennsylvania Department of Conservation &
Natural Resources**
Bureau of State Parks
PO Box 8551
Harrisburg, PA 17105
(717) 787-6640 - Phone
(717) 783-8817 - Fax
(888) 537-7294 - TDD
(888) 727-2757 - Reservations
Web: www.dcnr.state.pa.us/stateparks
System includes 116 parks covering more than 292,000 acres,
featuring 56 major recreational lakes and more than 1,274 miles
of trails. Also supports environmental education programs for
communities and school groups, pre-school through college-
aged youth, through its four environmental education centers.

★3971★ **Pennsylvania Department of Conservation &
Natural Resources**
Bureau of Forestry
PO Box 8552
Harrisburg, PA 17105
(717) 787-2703 - Phone
(717) 783-5109 - Fax
(877) 766-6253 - Snow Conditions
Web: www.dcnr.state.pa.us/forestry
Manages 20 named forests comprising more than 2 million
acres. State forest lands offer primitive camping and thousands
of miles of trails for hiking, cross-country skiing, mountain
biking, snowmobiling, horseback riding, and ATV riding.

Key to campsite classification:

- **Class A campsites** — Nearby flush toilets and showers.
- **Class B campsites** — Non-flush toilets and drinking
  water.
- **Class A/B campsites** — Sites which are class A until
  sometime in October then become class B to the end
  of the season or until spring.
- **Camping cottages** — Sparsely furnished with wooden
  walls and floors, windows, electric lights and outlets.
  Sleep five.
- **Group camps** — For organized groups. Normally located in isolated areas of the park, sites have drinking
  water and pit or flush toilets.
- **Yurts** — Mongolian-style round tents on a wooden
  deck; contain cookstove, refrigerator, countertop, table,
  chairs, electric heat and outlets. Sleep four.
- **Rustic cabins** — Include refrigerator and gas or electric
  kitchen stove. Each has a fireplace, wood stove or gas
  heater for heat. No indoor plumbing. Sleep two to eight
  people.

- **Modern cabins** — Offer carpeting, electric heat, bedrooms, living room/dining room, modern bathroom, and
  kitchen. Two-bedroom model sleeps six, three-bedroom
  model sleeps eight.
- **Youth Hostels** — Dormitory-style accommodations
  with separate quarters for males and females, although
  some have reservable private rooms. Include kitchen
  facilities, linen rentals, and group accommodations. Historically, hostels attract budget-minded students but all
  age groups are welcome. Must be a member of Hostelling International (see entry in associations chapter)
  to use facilities.

★3972★ **ALLEGHENY ISLANDS STATE PARK**
c/o Region 2 Office
Prospect, PA 15834
Web: www.dcnr.state.pa.us/stateparks/parks/
alleghenyislands.aspx
Phone: 724-865-2131
Size: 43 acres. **Location:** In the Allegheny River above and
below Lock and Dam 3. Accessible by boat only. **Facilities:**
Undeveloped. **Activities:** Group camping by permit. **Special
Features:** Park consists of three alluvial islands in the middle
of the Allegheny River northeast of Pittsburgh.

★3973★ **ARCHBALD POTHOLE STATE PARK**
c/o Lackawanna State Park
Dalton, PA 18414
Web: www.dcnr.state.pa.us/stateparks/parks/
archbaldpothole.asp
Phone: 570-945-3239
Size: 150 acres. **Location:** 9 miles north of Scranton, off I-81,
in northeast Pennsylvania. **Facilities:** Hiking trail. **Activities:**
Hiking, hunting. **Special Features:** Park contains what is believed to be the world's largest glacial pothole—38 feet deep
and 42 feet across—which formed during the Wisconsin Ice
Age more than 15,000 years ago. It has a volume of 18,600
cubic feet, so could hold about 140,000 gallons.

★3974★ **BALD EAGLE STATE PARK**
149 Main Park Rd
Howard, PA 16841
Web: www.dcnr.state.pa.us/stateparks/parks/baldeagle.asp
Phone: 814-625-2775
Size: 5,900 acres. **Location:** Off PA 150, midway between
Milesburg and Lock Haven, via I-80. **Facilities:** 101 class A
campsites, 70 class B campsites, showers, flush toilets, picnic

area, picnic pavilions, snack bar, hiking trails (8 miles), swimming beach and bathhouse, boat rentals, 6 boat launch ramps, marina, moorage, store (within 5 miles), playfield, playground (&&). **Activities:** Camping, boating, fishing, swimming, water-skiing, hiking, hunting, cross-country skiing, ice boating, ice fishing, ice skating, sledding, snowmobiling, tobogganing, nature programs. **Special Features:** Bordered on the south and east by the beautiful and rugged Bald Eagle Mountains, and to the west and north by the beginning of the Allegheny Plateaus. Park features a butterfly trail.

★3975★ BELTZVILLE STATE PARK
2950 Pohopoco Dr
Lehighton, PA 18235
Web: www.dcnr.state.pa.us/stateparks/parks/beltzville.aspx
Phone: 610-377-0045
Size: 2,972 acres. **Location:** 5 miles east of Lehighton, just off US 209, in the central eastern portion of the state. **Facilities:** Picnic areas, picnic pavilions (&), restrooms, snack bar, hiking trails (15 miles), cross-sountry ski trails (9 miles), swimming beach, bathhouse, boat rentals, boat launch, moorage, interpretive center (&), amphitheater, playfield, playground (&). **Activities:** Boating, fishing, swimming, water skiing, hiking, hunting, cross-country skiing, ice boating, ice fishing, ice skating, nature programs. **Special Features:** Park features a covered bridge for pedestrian use. Originally built across Pohopoco Creek in 1841 and used by horse and buggy traffic, it was relocated to its present location at the suggestion of local residents.

★3976★ BENDIGO STATE PARK
533 State Park Rd
Johnsonburg, PA 15845
Web: www.dcnr.state.pa.us/stateparks/parks/bendigo.aspx
Phone: 814-965-2646
Size: 100 acres. **Location:** 4 miles northeast of Johnsonburg on SR 1004, in the central northern part of the state. **Facilities:** Picnic areas, picnic pavilions (&), swimming pool, playfield, game courts, restrooms (&). **Activities:** Swimming, picnicking. **Special Features:** Park is in a small valley surrounded by hills. Only 20 acres of the park is developed, half of which is shaded picnic area. The East Branch of the Clarion River flows through the park. Once polluted by mine acid drainage, the river is now healthy and offers good fishing for stocked trout.

★3977★ BENJAMIN RUSH STATE PARK
c/o Fort Washington State Park
Fort Washington, PA 19034
Web: www.dcnr.state.pa.us/stateparks/parks/
benjaminrush.aspx
Phone: 215-591-5250
Size: 276 acres. **Location:** In Philadelphia County, in the southeastern portion of the state. **Facilities:** Undeveloped. **Special Features:** A mixture of open fields and woodlots, this undeveloped park contains one of the world's largest community gardens.

★3978★ BIG POCONO STATE PARK
c/o Tobyhanna State Park
Tobyhanna, PA 18466
Web: www.dcnr.state.pa.us/stateparks/parks/bigpocono.aspx
Phone: 570-894-8336
Size: 1,306 acres. **Location:** Off PA 715 at Tannersville in the northeastern part of the state. **Facilities:** Picnic areas (&), snack bar, hiking trails (7 miles), bridle trails (3 miles), restrooms (&), scenic drive. **Activities:** Hiking, hunting, horseback riding. **Special Features:** Park consists of rugged terrain on the summit and slopes of Camelback Mountain. From the summit, visitors are afforded views of eastern Pennsylvania and portions of New Jersey and New York. A scenic drive encircles the mountaintop, allowing panoramic views in all directions.

★3979★ BIG SPRING STATE PARK
c/o Colonel Denning State Park
1599 Doubling Gap Rd
Newville, PA 17241
Web: www.dcnr.state.pa.us/stateparks/parks/bigspring.asp
Phone: 717-776-5272
Size: 45 acres. **Location:** 5 miles southwest of New Germantown, along PA 274. **Facilities:** Picnic areas, restrooms, hiking trail, snowmobile trailhead. **Activities:** Hiking, picnicking, snowmobiling. **Special Features:** Located on the side of Conococheague Mountain, park provides access to the hiking trail in Tuscarora State Forest. Park also serves as the trailhead for an extensive snowmobile trail system, providing parking, restrooms, and trail access. A short loop trail in Big Spring leads to a partially completed railroad tunnel, with historic interpretation at the trailhead.

★3980★ BLACK MOSHANNON STATE PARK
4216 Beaver Rd
Philipsburg, PA 16866
Web: www.dcnr.state.pa.us/stateparks/parks/
blackmoshannon.aspx
Phone: 814-342-5960
Size: 3,394 acres. **Location:** On PA 504, 9 miles east of Philipsburg, in the center of the state. **Facilities:** 80 class A campsites (most with electricity), group tent camp, flush toilets, showers, 6 modern cabins (&), 13 rustic cabins, picnic areas, picnic pavilions (&), snack bar, hiking trails (16 miles), snowmobile trailhead and trails (2 miles), bike trails, swimming beach, boat rentals, boat launches, boat mooring, park store, environmental programs. **Activities:** Camping, boating, fishing, swimming, hiking, hunting, mountain biking, cross-country skiing, ice boating, ice fishing, ice skating, snowmobiling, nature programs. **Special Features:** According to local tradition, American Indians called this watershed ''Moss-Hanne'' meaning moose stream, from which the park got its name. The ''black'' in the park name describes the tea-colored waters. The 250-acres Black Moshannon Lake is fed by clear springs and small streams which flow through the bogs all around. As the clear water flows through sphagnum moss and other wetland plants, it becomes colored by plant tannins.

★3981★ BLUE KNOB STATE PARK
124 Park Rd
Imler, PA 16655
Web: www.dcnr.state.pa.us/stateparks/parks/blueknob.aspx
Phone: 814-276-3576
Size: 6,128 acres. **Location:** On the northwestern tip of Bedford County, west of US 220 in the south central portion of the state. **Facilities:** Group cabin camp, 45 class A campsites (25 with electric hookups), picnic areas, picnic pavilions, hiking trails, bike trails, bridle trails, snowmobile trailhead and trails (8 miles), swimming pool, playground. **Activities:** Camping, hunting, fishing, swimming, hiking, mountain biking, horseback riding, hunting, cross-country and downhill skiing, snowmobiling, snow tubing, nature programs, bluegrass festival (annually). **Special Features:** Park is named after the dome-shaped Blue Knob, the second highest mountain in Pennsylvania at 3,146 feet. Situated on a spur of the Allegheny Front, Blue Knob offers panoramic views of Pennsylvania's scenic Ridge and Valley Province. The Blue Knob ski area, located within the park, offers some of the best downhill skiing in the state.

★3982★ BOYD BIG TREE CONSERVATION AREA
c/o Little Buffalo State Park
RR 2 Box 256A
Newport, PA 17074
Web: www.dcnr.state.pa.us/stateparks/parks/boydbigtree.aspx
Phone: 717-567-9255
Size: 914 acres. **Location:** On Blue Mountain in Middle Paxton and Lower Paxton townships in south central portion of the state. **Facilities:** Hiking trails (11 miles), cross-country ski trails. **Activities:** Hiking, cross-country skiing, hunting, interpretive programs. **Special Features:** Large trees of numerous species are scattered throughout the area, providing habitat for deep forest birds, especially warblers. A large field of butterfly weed blooms in late July and early August, attracting many butterflies.

★3983★ BUCHANAN'S BIRTHPLACE STATE PARK
c/o Cowans Gap State Park
6235 Aughwick Rd
Fort Loudon, PA 17224
Web: www.dcnr.state.pa.us/stateparks/parks/
    buchanansbirthplace.aspx
Phone: 717-485-3948
Size: 18 acres. **Location:** In the foothills of the Tuscarora Mountains on the western side of the Cumberland Valley, just south of US 30. **Facilities:** Picnic area, picnic pavilions (&), restrooms (&). **Activities:** Fishing. **Special Features:** Park is the birthplace of James Buchanan, 15th president of the United States and the only Pennsylvanian to occupy the office of president. The site of the cabin in which Buchanan was born is marked by a 25-foot-high stone pyramid, surrounded by tall conifers. A native trout stream, Buck Run, flows through the park.

★3984★ BUCKTAIL STATE PARK
c/o Region 1 Office
Emporium, PA 15834
Web: www.dcnr.state.pa.us/stateparks/parks/bucktail.aspx
Phone: 814-486-3365
Size: Approximately 75 miles. **Location:** Along Pennsylvania Route 120 from Emporium, through Renovo, to Lock Haven. **Special Features:** Park provides a 75-mile scenic drive through a narrow valley along PA Route 120. It stretches through a narrow valley called the Bucktail Trail, which is the old Sinnemahoning Trail used by American Indians on their way to and from the eastern continental divide.

★3985★ CALEDONIA STATE PARK
101 Pine Grove Rd
Fayetteville, PA 17222
Web: www.dcnr.state.pa.us/stateparks/parks/caledonia.aspx
Phone: 717-352-2161; **Fax:** 717-352-7026
Size: 1,125 acres. **Location:** Midway between Chambersburg and Gettysburg on US 30, in the central southern portion of the state. **Facilities:** 184 class A campsites (all with electricity), group tent camp, showers, flush toilets, 2 modern cabins, picnic areas, picnic pavilions, hiking trails (10 miles), swimming pool (&), historical center, store (within 5 miles), 18-hole golf course, playground. **Activities:** Camping, fishing, swimming, hiking, hunting, golf, nature programs. **Special Features:** Totem Pole Playhouse, a summer stock theater, offers performances during the summer months (call 717-352-2164 for more information). In addition, the Thaddeus Stevens Blacksmith Shop is a historical center.

★3986★ CANOE CREEK STATE PARK
RR 2, Box 560
Hollidaysburg, PA 16648
Web: www.dcnr.state.pa.us/stateparks/parks/canoecreek.aspx
Phone: 814-695-6807
Size: 958 acres. **Location:** 12 miles east of Altoona, in the center of the state. **Facilities:** 8 modern cabins, picnic area, picnic pavilions, hiking trails (8 miles), bridle trail, bike trail, beach, boat rentals, boat launch, boat mooring. **Activities:** Boating (electric motors only), fishing, swimming, hiking, bicycling, horseback riding, hunting, cross-country skiing, ice boating, ice fishing, ice skating, interpretive programs. **Special Features:** Park is the home of one of the largest nursery colonies of little brown bats in Pennsylvania. On summer evenings, thousands of bats can be seen exiting the old church sanctuary. A deep limestone mine is a hibernaculum (where animals hibernate) for more than 20,000 bats of six species. Geologic formations in and around the park are rich in limestone. The park has several old quarry operations.

★3987★ CHAPMAN STATE PARK
RR 2, Box 1610
Clarendon, PA 16313
Web: www.dcnr.state.pa.us/stateparks/parks/chapman.aspx
Phone: 814-723-0250
Size: 805 acres. **Location:** Just west of Clarendon, off US 6, in the northern part of the state. **Facilities:** 83 class B campsites (some with electricity), 3 cottages, yurts, group tent or trailer camp, picnic area, picnic pavilions, backpacking trailhead, hiking trails (12 miles), snowmobile trailhead and trail (2 miles), sledding slope, boat rentals, 2 boat launches, boat mooring,

playground, beach, snack bar, warming hut. **Activities:** Camping, boating (electric motors only), fishing, swimming, hiking, bicycling, hunting, cross-country skiing, ice fishing, snowmobiling, sledding, tobogganing, nature programs. **Special Features:** Park is in the midst of approximately 517,000 acres of state game lands and Allegheny National Forest (see separate entry in national forests section), and includes 68-acre Chapman Lake on the West Branch of Tionesta Creek.

★3988★ CHERRY SPRINGS STATE PARK

c/o Lyman Run State Park
454 Lyman Run Rd
Galeton, PA 16922
Web: www.dcnr.state.pa.us/stateparks/parks/
cherrysprings.aspx
Phone: 814-435-5010
Size: 48 acres. **Location:** Along PA 44 in Potter County, in the north central portion of the state. **Facilities:** 30 class B campsites, picnic area, picnic pavilions, bike trail, historic site. **Activities:** Camping, hiking, mountain biking, interpretive programs. **Special Features:** Park is named for the large stands of native black cherry trees it contains. For amateur astronomers, the park offers some of the darkest night skies in the state and a 360-degree view. An annual woodsmen's show in August features lumberjack contests in tree-felling, log rolling, chopping, and chainsaw events.

★3989★ CLEAR CREEK STATE PARK

38 Clear Creek State Park Rd
Sigel, PA 15860
Web: www.dcnr.state.pa.us/stateparks/parks/clearcreek.aspx
Phone: 814-752-2368
Size: 1,676 acres. **Location:** In the Clear Creek Valley from PA 949 to the Clarion River, in the northwestern part of the state. **Facilities:** 53 class B campsites (&), showers, pit toilets, 22 rustic cabins, 2 yurts, flush toilets, picnic area, picnic pavilions (&), hiking trails (25 miles), fitness trail, beach, hand launch boat ramp, playfield, playground, 9-hole disc golf course, sledding slope. **Activities:** Camping, canoeing, fishing, swimming, hiking, hunting, cross-country skiing, sledding, interpretive programs. **Special Features:** The Clarion River, a class C waterway, offers excellent canoeing, especially during the spring and fall. A 10-mile trip from Clear Creek to Cook Forest State Park (see separate entry) takes about 4.5 hours. Rental canoes are available from commercial sources outside the park.

★3990★ CODORUS STATE PARK

2600 Smith Station Rd
Hanover, PA 17331
Web: www.dcnr.state.pa.us/stateparks/parks/codorus.aspx
Phone: 717-637-2816; **Fax:** 717-637-4720
Size: 3,329 acres. **Location:** 3 miles southeast of Hanover, along PA 216. **Facilities:** 198 class A campsites (many with electricity, 8 &), showers, flush toilets, picnic area, picnic pavilions, snack bar, bike trails, hiking trails (5 miles), bridle trails (7 miles), snowmobile trails (6.5 miles), sledding slope (2.5 acres) , 36-hole disc golf course, swimming pool, bathhouse, boat rentals, boat launch, marina. **Activities:** Camping, boating

(20 HP limit), fishing, swimming, hiking, bicycling, mountain biking, horseback riding, hunting, cross-country skiing, ice boating, ice fishing, ice skating, snowmobiling, sledding, bird watching, interpretive programs. **Special Features:** Park includes 1,275-acre Lake Marburg, which has 26 miles of shoreline and good winds for sailing.

★3991★ COLONEL DENNING STATE PARK

1599 Doubling Gap Rd
Newville, PA 17241
Web: www.dcnr.state.pa.us/stateparks/parks/
coloneldenning.aspx
Phone: 717-776-5272
Size: 273 acres. **Location:** In Doubling Gap, north-central Cumberland County, in the south central portion of the state. **Facilities:** 52 class B campsites, pit toilets, picnic areas, picnic pavilions, snack bar, swimming beach, backpacking trailhead, hiking trails (18 miles), playground. **Activities:** Camping, fishing, swimming, hiking, hunting, cross-country skiing, ice skating, environmental education programs. **Special Features:** Park was named for Revolutionary War hero Colonel William Denning (1737-1830), who lived near Newville and invented a type of iron cannon used by the colonists during the Revolutionary War. He was never really a colonel, and it is uncertain when or who added the colonel to his name.

★3992★ COLTON POINT STATE PARK

c/o Leonard Harrison State Park
4797 Route 660
Wellsboro, PA 16901
Web: www.dcnr.state.pa.us/stateparks/parks/coltonpoint.aspx
Phone: 570-724-3061
Size: 368 acres. **Location:** 5 miles south of US 6 at Ansonia, in the north central part of the state. **Facilities:** 25 class B campsites, pit toilets, group tent camp, picnic area, picnic pavilions, hiking trails (4 miles), snowmobile trailhead and trail, playground. **Activities:** Camping, fishing, hiking, mountain biking, hunting, cross-country skiing, snowmobiling. **Special Features:** Park offers spectacular views of Pine Creek Gorge, Pennsylvania's ''Grand Canyon,'' which is scenic year round but especially so in early October. Hiking trails pass through very rugged terrain near many steep cliffs. The main trail, Turkey Path, descends one mile to the canyon floor.

★3993★ COOK FOREST STATE PARK

PO Box 120
Cooksburg, PA 16217
Web: www.dcnr.state.pa.us/stateparks/parks/cookforest.aspx
Phone: 814-744-8407
Size: 8,500 acres. **Location:** In northwestern Pennsylvania, off PA 36 north. **Facilities:** 226 class A campsites (some with electricity, 6 &), group tent camp, showers, flush and pit toilets, 23 rustic cabins, laundry, picnic areas (&), picnic pavilions, canoe launch, snack bar, swimming pool, hiking trails (29 miles), bike trail (11miles), bridle trails (4.5 miles), snowmobile trails (12 miles), craft center, playground, lookout tower, scenic overlook. **Activities:** Camping, canoeing, fishing, swimming, hiking,

9. State Parks

mountain biking, horseback riding, hunting, cross-country skiing, ice skating, snowmobiling, nature programs. **Special Features:** Park contains "Forest Cathedral," a significant stand of virgin white pine and hemlock timber which has been designated a National Natural Landmark.

★3994★ COWANS GAP STATE PARK

6235 Aughwick Rd
Fort Loudon, PA 17224
Web: www.dcnr.state.pa.us/stateparks/parks/cowansgap.aspx
Phone: 717-485-3948
Size: 1,085 acres. **Location:** Between Chambersburg and McConnellsburg, off PA 75 in the central southern portion of the state. **Facilities:** 224 class A campsites (some with electricity), group tent camp, showers, flush toilets, 10 rustic cabins, picnic areas, picnic pavilions, snack bar, hiking trails (10 miles), swimming beach, boat rentals, boat launch, boat mooring, fishing pier (&). **Activities:** Camping, boating (electric motors only), fishing, swimming, hiking, hunting, cross-country skiing, ice fishing, ice skating, nature programs. **Special Features:** Park's 42-acre Cowans Gap Lake has a 500-foot sand beach and excellent trout fishing.

★3995★ DELAWARE CANAL STATE PARK

11 Lodi Hill Rd
Upper Black Eddy, PA 18972
Web: www.dcnr.state.pa.us/stateparks/parks/
delawarecanal.aspx
Phone: 610-982-5560
Size: 60 miles as it follows the canal. **Location:** Park follows the Delaware River from Easton to Bristol, paralleled by PA Routes 611 and 32. **Facilities:** Picnic area, multi-use trails (60 miles), boat launch, visitor center. **Activities:** Boating (electric motors only), canoeing, fishing, hiking, nature and historic programs. **Special Features:** The Delaware Canal is the only remaining continuously intact remnant of the great towpath canals of the early and mid-19th century. Today, nearly all of its features remain as they were during its 100 years of commercial operation. A walk along the towpath is a trip back in history. Park contains the historic canal and towpath, shoreline, and 11 river islands.

★3996★ DENTON HILL STATE PARK

c/o Lyman Run
454 Lyman Run Rd
Galeton, PA 16922
Web: www.dcnr.state.pa.us/stateparks/parks/dentonhill.aspx
Phone: 814-435-2115
Size: 700 acres. **Location:** Off US 6 in Potter County in the central northern portion of the state. **Facilities:** 5 modern cabins, cross-country ski trails, chair lifts, downhill skiing facilities. **Activities:** Cross-country and downhill skiing, snowmobiling, snowboarding. **Special Features:** Located in the snow belt of northern Pennsylvania, this park offers great downhill skiing for beginners and experts. Ski facilities and cabins are operated by a private concessionaire.

★3997★ ELK STATE PARK

c/o Bendigo State Park
533 State Park Rd
Johnsonburg, PA 15845
Web: www.dcnr.state.pa.us/stateparks/parks/elk.aspx
Phone: 814-965-2646
Size: 3,192 acres. **Location:** 8 miles west of Wilcox in the north central portion of the state. **Facilities:** Picnic areas, boat launch. **Activities:** Boating, fishing, hunting, ice boating, ice fishing. **Special Features:** Park features 1,160-acre East Branch Lake. Elk State Forest (195,911 acres) lies adjacent to the park.

★3998★ ERIE BLUFFS STATE PARK

c/o Presque Isle State Park
301 Peninsula Dr Suite 1
Erie, PA 16505
Web: www.dcnr.state.pa.us/stateParks/parks/eriebluffs.aspx
Phone: 814-833-7424
Size: 540 acres. **Location:** 12 miles east of Erie, in the northwest corner of the state. **Facilities:** Undeveloped. **Special Features:** The state's newest Park, Erie Bluffs has one mile of shoreline, 90-foot bluffs overlooking Lake Erie, a world-class shallow stream fishery, old-growth forest, and significant archeological sites.

★3999★ EVANSBURG STATE PARK

851 May Hall Rd
Collegeville, PA 19426
Web: www.dcnr.state.pa.us/stateparks/parks/evansburg.aspx
Phone: 610-409-1150
Size: 3,349 acres. **Location:** In the southeastern portion of the state between Norristown and Collegeville. **Facilities:** Youth hostel, picnic area, picnic pavilions (&), hiking trails (6 miles), bike trail (5 miles), bridle trails (15 miles), cross-country skiing trails, fishing pier (&), 18-hole golf course, playfield, playground, visitor center/historic building. **Activities:** Fishing, hiking, mountain biking, horseback riding, hunting, golf, cross-country skiing, interpretive programs. **Special Features:** The Friedt Visitor Center is located in a home built by German Mennonites in the early 1700s. It includes historical material on the lives of the families who owned the home for 190 years. The root cellar, well, herb and sensory gardens add to the 18th century atmosphere.

★4000★ FORT WASHINGTON STATE PARK

500 Bethlehem Pike
Fort Washington, PA 19034
Web: www.dcnr.state.pa.us/stateparks/parks/
fortwashington.aspx
Phone: 215-591-5250
Size: 493 acres. **Location:** Between the towns of Fort Washington and Flourtown along the Bethlehem Pike, 2 miles from PA Turnpike Exit 26. **Facilities:** Group tent camp, pit toilets, picnic areas, picnic pavilions (&), hiking trails (3 miles), playfields, playground (&), wildlife observation deck (&), sledding slope, cross-country skiing trail, butterfly garden. **Activities:** Fishing, camping, hiking, cross-country skiing, sledding, tobogganing, bird watching, nature programs. **Special Features:** Park and the

community of Fort Washington take their name from the fort built here by American revolutionary soldiers in the fall of 1777. All 16 species of raptors that migrate on the east coast can be seen here. The "watch" begins September 1 and lasts through the end of October.

★4001★ FOWLERS HOLLOW STATE PARK

c/o Colonel Denning State Park
1599 Doubling Gap Rd
Newville, PA 17241
Web: www.dcnr.state.pa.us/stateparks/parks/
    fowlershollow.aspx
Phone: 717-776-5272
Size: 104 acres. **Location:** 7 miles south of Blain of PA 274. **Facilities:** 18 class A campsites, picnic area, picnic pavilions, backpacking trailhead, hiking trails (6 miles), snowmobile trailhead and trail (1 mile), cross-country skiing trail (2 miles). **Activities:** Camping, fishing, hiking, cross-country skiing, snowmobiling. **Special Features:** Park is located adjacent to Tuscarora State Forest. In the late 1800s, the picnic area of the park was the site of a sawmill that supplied lumber products to the forest industry.

★4002★ FRANCES SLOCUM STATE PARK

565 Mount Olivet Rd
Wyoming, PA 18644
Web: www.dcnr.state.pa.us/stateparks/parks/
    francesslocum.aspx
Phone: 570-696-3525
Size: 1,035 acres. **Location:** 10 miles from Wilkes-Barre off PA 309. **Facilities:** 100 class A campsites (some with electricity), group tent camp, showers, flush toilets, picnic areas, picnic pavilions, hiking trails (9 miles), snowmobile trails (7 miles), fishing pier (&), swimming pool, boat rentals, boat launch, mooring. **Activities:** Camping, boating (electric motors only), fishing, swimming, hiking, hunting, ice fishing, ice skating, snowmobiling, sledding, tobogganing, interpretive programs. **Special Features:** Park is named for Frances Slocum, a young Quaker girl who was kidnapped by a Lenni Lenape raiding party in 1778. She spent the rest of her life with the tribe, married twice, and had four children. She died in New Reserve, Indiana, in 1847 at the age of 74. Near Peru, Indiana, there is a state recreation area named for her (see Mississinewa Lake entry in Indiana State Parks section).

★4003★ FRENCH CREEK STATE PARK

843 Park Rd
Elverson, PA 19520
Web: www.dcnr.state.pa.us/stateparks/parks/frenchcreek.aspx
Phone: 610-582-9680
Size: 7,339 acres. **Location:** Off PA 345, south of Birdsboro, in the southeastern part of the state. **Facilities:** 201 class A campsites (50+ with electricity), 10 modern cabins, group tent camps, showers, pit and flush toilets, picnic areas, snack bar, hiking trails (30 miles), bridle trails, swimming pool, boat rentals, boat launch, 2 disc golf courses, amphitheater, orienteering course. **Activities:** Camping, boating (electric motors only), fishing, swimming, hiking, mountain biking, horseback riding,

hunting, orienteering, educational programs. **Special Features:** Park features a self-guiding orienteering course that allows visitors to follow a permanently marked course as an introduction to this Scandinavian sport. The game's objective is to find markers in the woods with the aid of a map and compass.

★4004★ GIFFORD PINCHOT STATE PARK

2200 Rosstown Rd
Lewisberry, PA 17339
Web: www.dcnr.state.pa.us/stateparks/parks/
    giffordpinchot.aspx
Phone: 717-432-5011
Size: 2,338 acres. **Location:** Along PA 177 between the towns of Rossville and Lewisberry in the southeastern portion of the state. **Facilities:** 339 class A campsites, group tent campsite, yurts, 3 cottages, 10 cabines, showers, flush toilets, picnic area, picnic pavilions (&), snack bar, hiking trails (18 miles), bridle trails, bike trails (3.5 miles), swimming beach, 3 boat launches, boat mooring, boat rentals, playfield, 18-hole disc golf course, amphitheater. **Activities:** Camping, boating (electric motors only), sailing, sailboarding, fishing, swimming, hiking, bicycling, horseback riding, hunting, disc golf, cross-country skiing, ice boating, ice fishing, ice skating, nature programs, boat tours. **Special Features:** Park consists of reverting farm fields and wooded hillsides, with 340-acre Pinchot Lake as its centerpiece.

★4005★ GOULDSBORO STATE PARK

c/o Tobyhanna State Park
PO Box 387
Tobyhanna, PA 18466
Web: www.dcnr.state.pa.us/stateparks/parks/gouldsboro.aspx
Phone: 570-894-8336
Size: 2,800 acres. **Location:** 0.5 miles south of the village of Gouldsboro on PA 507. **Facilities:** Picnic areas, picnic pavilion (&), hiking trails, swimming beach, fishing pier (&), boat launch, boat mooring. **Activities:** Boating (electric motors only), fishing, swimming, hiking, biking, hunting, cross-country skiing, ice fishing, snowmobiling. **Special Features:** Park includes the 250-acre Gouldsboro Lake and a rugged terrain that makes for challenging hiking.

★4006★ GREENWOOD FURNACE STATE PARK

15795 Greenwood Rd
Huntingdon, PA 16652
Web: www.dcnr.state.pa.us/stateparks/parks/
    greenwoodfurnace.aspx
Phone: 814-667-1800
Size: 423 acres. **Location:** On the western edge of an area of Central Pennsylvania known as the Seven Mountains, off PA 305. **Facilities:** 51 class A campsites (46 with electricity), showers, flush toilets, picnic area, picnic pavilions, snack bar, backpacking trailhead, hiking trails (approximately 20 miles), swimming beach, visitor center, gift shop, orienteering course, playfield, game courts, historic buildings. **Activities:** Camping, swimming, fishing, hiking, hunting, cross-country skiing, ice fishing, ice skating, snowmobiling, interpretive programs. **Special Features:** Greenwood Furnace was once a thriving iron-making village. Today, only a handful of its 127 buildings

remain. They include the blacksmith shop, which features displays on the history of the park and blacksmithing demonstrations in summer.

★4007★ HICKORY RUN STATE PARK

RR 1, Box 81
White Haven, PA 18661
Web: www.dcnr.state.pa.us/stateparks/parks/hickoryrun.aspx
Phone: 570-443-0400
Size: 15,500 acres. **Location:** In the western foothills of the Pocono Mountains, off PA 534. **Facilities:** 381 class A/B campsites, group tent camps, 2 group cabin camps, showers, pit and flush toilets, picnic area, picnic pavilion, snack bar, hiking trails (43 miles), cross-country skiing trails (13 miles), snowmobile trails (21 miles), swimming beach, disc golf course, fishing pier, amphitheater, camp store, playfield, playground. **Activities:** Camping, fishing, swimming, hiking, hunting, disc golf, cross-country skiing, ice fishing, ice skating, snowmobiling, sledding, tobogganing, nature and historical programs. **Special Features:** Located in the northeastern corner of the park is Boulder Field, a large area (400 feet by 1,800 feet) strewn with boulders, some as long as 25 feet. A National Natural Landmark, the site is flat and lacks vegetation, and has remained essentially unchanged for more than 20,000 years.

★4008★ HILLMAN STATE PARK

c/o Raccoon Creek State Park
3000 State Rt 18
Hookstown, PA 15050
Web: www.dcnr.state.pa.us/stateparks/parks/hillman.aspx
Phone: 724-899-2200
Size: More than 3,600 acres. **Location:** In the center of the state, near the western border. **Facilities:** Undeveloped. **Activities:** Hunting, hiking. **Special Features:** Park is managed for hunting by the Pennsylvania Game Commission.

★4009★ HILLS CREEK STATE PARK

111 Spillway Rd
Wellsboro, PA 16901
Web: www.dcnr.state.pa.us/stateparks/parks/hillscreek.aspx
Phone: 570-724-4246
Size: 407 acres. **Location:** Just north of US 6, midway between Wellsboro and Mansfield near the central northern border. **Facilities:** 102 class A campsites, 10 modern cabins, 3 cottages, yurts, group tent camp, showers, flush toilets, picnic areas, picnic pavilions, snack bar, hiking trails (5 miles), swimming beach, bathhouse, boat rentals, boat launches, boat mooring, fishing pier, nature center, amphitheater, playfield, playground. **Activities:** Camping, boating (electric motors only), fishing, swimming, hiking, ice fishing, ice skating, sledding, nature programs. **Special Features:** The focal point of the park is the 137-acre lake developed by impounding Hills Creek. The area now covered by water has been almost continually influenced by beavers and beaver dams, and beavers still abound in the area. The depth of the beaver marsh is as great as 20 feet deep.

★4010★ HYNER RUN STATE PARK

56 Hyner Park Rd
Hyner, PA 17738
Web: www.dcnr.state.pa.us/stateparks/parks/hynerrun.aspx
Phone: 570-923-6000
Size: 180 acres. **Location:** In Chapman Township, 6 miles east of Renovo, on PA 120. **Facilities:** 30 class B campsites, pit toilets, 1 modern cabin, picnic area, picnic pavilions, snack bar, backpacking trailhead, hiking trail, snowmobile trailhead and trail, swimming pool, playground. **Activities:** Camping, fishing, swimming, hiking, hunting, snowmobiling. **Special Features:** Park is entirely surrounded by the Sproul State Forest and serves as the eastern trailhead for the 50-mile Donut Hole Trail and the 64-mile Hyner Mountain Snowmobile Trail.

★4011★ HYNER VIEW STATE PARK

c/o Hyner Run State Park
56 Hyner Park Rd
Hyner, PA 17738
Web: www.dcnr.state.pa.us/stateparks/parks/hynerview.aspx
Phone: 570-923-6000
Size: 6 acres. **Location:** In Chapman Township, 6 miles east of Renovo on PA 120. **Facilities:** Picnic area, scenic vista. **Activities:** Hang gliding, picnicking. **Special Features:** Park features a scenic vista overlooking the west branch of the Susquehanna River and is a favorite spot for hang gliding.

★4012★ JACOBSBURG ENVIRONMENTAL
        EDUCATION CENTER

835 Jacobsburg Rd
Wind Gap, PA 18091
Web: www.dcnr.state.pa.us/stateparks/parks/jacobsburg.aspx
Phone: 610-746-2801
Size: 1,168 acres. **Location:** At the foot of blue Mountain, off PA 33, near Nazareth. **Facilities:** Picnic area, hiking trails (18.5 miles), bridle trails, historical center. **Activities:** Fishing, hiking, mountain biking, horseback riding, hunting, nature and historical programs. **Special Features:** Located at the foot of the Blue Mountain, the Environmental Education Center offers environmental education programs for school students and workshops and training sessions for educators. The center also supports ecological, archeological, and historical research. The Jacobsburg National Historic District lies almost entirely within the center's boundaries. The history of Jacobsburg centers on the Henry family and their small arms industry, an industry that played a key role in the Industrial Revolution.

★4013★ JENNINGS ENVIRONMENTAL EDUCATION
        CENTER

2951 Prospect Rd
Slippery Rock, PA 16057
Web: www.dcnr.state.pa.us/stateparks/parks/jennings.aspx
Phone: 724-794-6011
Size: 320 acres. **Location:** 12 miles north of Butler on PA 528, in the central western part of the state. **Facilities:** Hiking trails (5 miles). **Activities:** Hiking, nature programs. **Special Features:** A unique attraction at the Center is its prairie ecosystem, rare in Pennsylvania, with the well-known prairie flower, the

9. State Parks

blazing star. Visitors in late July to early August can see the prairie in full bloom.

★4014★ JOSEPH E. IBBERSON CONSERVATION AREA

c/o Little Buffalo State Park
1579 State Park Rd
Newport, PA 17074
Web: www.dcnr.state.pa.us/stateparks/parks/
  josepheibberson.aspx
Phone: 717-567-9255
Size: 350 acres. Location: Off PA 225 south of the village of Matamoras, on Hebron Road. Facilities: Hiking trails, cross-country skiing trails. Activities: Hiking, cross-country skiing, hunting (with restrictions), wildlife viewing, interpretive programs. Special Features: Straddling Peters Mountain, park is dominated by large hardwood trees. This large block of nearly unbroken forest is a haven for wildlife like forest warblers and other deep-woods animals.

★4015★ KETTLE CREEK STATE PARK

97 Kettle Creek Park Ln
Renovo, PA 17764
Web: www.dcnr.state.pa.us/stateparks/parks/kettlecreek.aspx
Phone: 570-923-6004
Size: 1,793 acres. Location: Along State Route 4001, 7 miles north of Westport and PA 120. Facilities: 71 class B campsites (50 with electricity), pit toilets, picnic areas, picnic pavilion, backpack trailhead, hiking trails (2 miles), bridle trails (22 miles), bike trail (5 miles), snowmobile trails, sledding slope, swimming beach, boat rentals, boat launch, boat mooring, playfields, playgrounds. Activities: Camping, boating (electric motors only), fishing, swimming, hiking, mountain biking, horseback riding, hunting, cross-country skiing, ice fishing, ice skating, snowmobiling, sledding, tobogganing, nature programs. Special Features: Park is surrounded by 278,000-acre Sproul State Forest, which allows park visitors access to many additional miles of trails.

★4016★ KEYSTONE STATE PARK

1150 Keystone Park Rd
Derry, PA 15627
Web: www.dcnr.state.pa.us/stateparks/parks/keystone.aspx
Phone: 724-668-2939
Size: 1,200 acres. Location: Just south of US 22, off Highway 981, near New Alexandria. Facilities: 100 class A campsites, showers, flush toilets, 11 modern cabins (1 ♿), picnic areas, picnic pavilions, snack bar, hiking trails (6 miles), bike trail (2 miles), swimming beach, fishing pier (♿), boat launch, boat mooring, visitor center. Activities: Camping, boating (electric motors only), fishing, swimming, hiking, bicycling, hunting, cross-country skiing, ice fishing, ice skating, sledding, snowshoeing, nature programs. Special Features: Park features 78-acre Keystone Lake, which was constructed by the Keystone Coal and Coke Company in the early 1900s. The coal company purchased the land from the McClelland family in 1909, and the original farmhouse remains in use in the park today.

★4017★ KINGS GAP ENVIRONMENTAL EDUCATION & TRAINING CENTER

500 Kings Gap Rd
Carlisle, PA 17015
Web: www.dcnr.state.pa.us/stateparks/parks/kingsgap.aspx
Phone: 717-486-5031
Size: 1,454 acres. Location: On South Mountain in Cumberland County. Facilities: Hiking trails (16 miles, ♿), orienteering course. Activities: Hiking, hunting, orienteering, nature programs. Special Features: Kings Gap sits astride South Mountain with a panoramic view of the Cumberland Valley. The center offers a wide variety of educational services to teach about nature and environmental issues, and helps students gain skills for appreciating and enjoying the outdoors. Kings Gap also functions as a training center for state government agencies.

★4018★ KINZUA BRIDGE STATE PARK

c/o Bendigo State Park
533 State Park Rd
Johnsonburg, PA 15845
Web: www.dcnr.state.pa.us/stateparks/parks/
  kinzuabridge.aspx
Phone: 814-965-2646
Size: 329 acres. Location: 4 miles north of US 6 at Mount Jewett in the central northern part of the state. Facilities: Picnic area, picnic pavilions, hiking trails, scenic overlook. Activities: Hiking, hunting. Special Features: When Kinzua Bridge was built in 1882, it was the highest railroad bridge in the world. In 1900 the entire structure was rebuilt to accommodate heavier trains. A tornado struck the bridge in July 2003, and 11 towers from the center of the bridge were torn from their bases. Although the park is open, areas surrounding the bridge are not open to hikers.

★4019★ KOOSER STATE PARK

943 Glades Pike
Somerset, PA 15501
Web: www.dcnr.state.pa.us/stateparks/parks/kooser.aspx
Phone: 814-445-8673
Size: 250 acres. Location: On PA 31 midway between the Donegal and Somerset Turnpike interchanges. Facilities: 47 class B campsites (14 with electricity, ♿), 9 rustic cabins, group tent camp, restrooms (♿), picnic area, picnic pavilion, snack bar, hiking trail, swimming beach. Activities: Camping, fishing, swimming, hiking, cross-country skiing, nature programs. Special Features: Kooser features a good trout stream running the full length of the park. Park design stresses rustic values in site and building materials: native stone, rough sawn and stained wood surfaces, log and timber.

★4020★ LACKAWANNA STATE PARK

RR 1, Box 230
Dalton, PA 18414
Web: www.dcnr.state.pa.us/stateparks/parks/lackawanna.aspx
Phone: 570-945-3239
Size: 1,411 acres. Location: 10 miles north of Scranton off I-81, in the northeastern corner of the state. Facilities: 61 class A campsites, 3 group tent camps, showers, flush toilets, picnic

area (&), picnic pavilion, snack bar, hiking trails (5 miles), bike trail (3.5 miles), bridle trail (3.5 miles), fishing pier (&), swimming pool, boat rentals, boat launches, boat mooring, amphitheater, playground, sledding slope. **Activities:** Camping, boating (electric motors only), canoeing, fishing, swimming, hiking, mountain biking, horseback riding, hunting, cross-country skiing, ice fishing, ice skating, sledding, tobogganing, interpretive programs. **Special Features:** Focal point of the park is 210-acre Lackawanna Lake. Lacka-wanna is an American Indian word meaning ''the meeting of two streams.''

★4021★ LAUREL HILL STATE PARK

1454 Laurel Hill Park Rd
Somerset, PA 15501
Web: www.dcnr.state.pa.us/stateparks/parks/laurelhill.aspx
Phone: 814-445-7725
Size: 3,935 acres. **Location:** In the southwestern corner of the state, off PA 31. **Facilities:** 264 class A campsites (149 with electricity), group tent camp, group cabin camp, 8 cottages, 5-bedroom lodge, showers, pit and flush toilets, picnic areas, picnic pavilions, snack bar, hiking trails (12 miles), snowmobile trailhead and trails (10 miles), swimming beach, boat rentals, 2 boat launches, boat mooring, visitor center, amphitheater, playfield, playground. **Activities:** Camping, boating (electric motors only), fishing, swimming, hiking, hunting, ice fishing, cross-country skiing, ice boating, snowmobiling, interpretive programs. **Special Features:** Laurel Hill Lake, at 63 acres, is the focal point of the park, which is surrounded by thousands of acres of pristine state park and state forest lands. A stand of old growth hemlocks lies along the Hemlock Trail.

★4022★ LAUREL MOUNTAIN STATE PARK

c/o Linn Run State Park
PO Box 50
Rector, PA 15677
Web: www.dcnr.state.pa.us/stateparks/parks/laurelmountain.aspx
Phone: 724-238-6623
Size: 493 acres. **Location:** 8 miles east of Ligonier US Route 30, in the southwestern corner of the state. **Facilities:** Ski and mountain board rentals, ski lift, lodge. **Activities:** Downhill and cross-country skiing, snowboarding, mountain boarding. **Special Features:** Park sits atop 3,000-foot Laurel Ridge, and features family-oriented downhill skiing and beautiful views. Opened in 1939, Laurel Mountain was one of the first ski areas in the state.

★4023★ LAUREL RIDGE STATE PARK

1117 Jim Mountain Rd
Rockwood, PA 15557
Web: www.dcnr.state.pa.us/stateparks/parks/laurelridge.aspx
Phone: 724-455-3744
Size: 13,625 acres. **Location:** Park stretches along the Laurel Mountain from the Youghiogheny River at Ohiopyle to the Conemaugh Gorge near Johnstown. **Facilities:** 8 backpacking camps (each with 5 Adirondack-type shelters), backpacking trailhead, hiking trails (70 miles), cross-country skiing trails (35 miles), snowmobile trails (70 miles). **Activities:** Camping,

hiking, hunting, cross-country skiing, snowmobiling. **Special Features:** The 70-mile Laurel Highlands Hiking Trail from Ohiopyle to near Johnstown is the main feature of the park. The trail traverses state parks, state forests, state game lands, other public lands, and private lands. The trail is open year round.

★4024★ LAUREL SUMMIT STATE PARK

c/o Linn Run State Park
PO Box 50
Rector, PA 15677
Web: www.dcnr.state.pa.us/stateparks/parks/laurelsummit.aspx
Phone: 724-238-6623
Size: 6 acres. **Location:** In the Laurel highlands, in the southwestern corner of the state. **Facilities:** Picnic area, picnic pavilion. **Activities:** Hiking, cross-country skiing, snowmobiling. **Special Features:** The area is 2,739 feet above sea level and is usually several degrees cooler than the surrounding towns.

★4025★ LEHIGH GORGE STATE PARK

RR 1, Box 81
White Haven, PA 18661
Web: www.dcnr.state.pa.us/stateparks/parks/lehighgorge.aspx
Phone: 570-443-0400
Size: 3,772 acres. **Location:** Park follows the Lehigh River from the outlet of the Francis E Walter Dam to the town of Jim Thorpe. **Facilities:** Hiking trails, bike trail (26 miles), snowmobile trails (15 miles). **Activities:** Whitewater boating (rafting, canoeing, and kayaking), fishing, hiking, bicycling, hunting, cross-country skiing, snowmobiling, interpretive programs. **Special Features:** The entire park is characterized by its deep gorge, steep walls, rock outcroppings, waterfalls, and thick vegetation. The major attraction of the park is whitewater boating. This section of the Lehigh River is Class III whitewater and is popular for rafting, kayaking, and canoeing.

★4026★ LEONARD HARRISON STATE PARK

4797 Route 660
Wellsboro, PA 16901
Web: www.dcnr.state.pa.us/stateparks/parks/leonardharrison.aspx
Phone: 570-724-3061
Size: 585 acres. **Location:** 10 miles west of Wellsboro off PA 660. **Facilities:** Rustic campsite (some with electricity), pit toilets, picnic area, picnic pavilion, snack bar, hiking trails (42 miles), bike trails, cross-country skiing trails, bridle trails (9 miles), scenic overlooks, interpretive center, playground, gift shop. **Activities:** Camping, fishing, hiking, bicycling, horseback riding, cross-country skiing, hunting, fall foliage viewing, nature programs. **Special Features:** Turkey Path Trail was constructed by the Youth Conservation Coprs in 1978. It features scenic vistas, waterfalls, and observations decks. Other trails offer ample opportunities for sightseeing. Park is on the edge of Pine Creek Gorge, called the Grand Canyon of Pennsylvania.

★4027★ LINN RUN STATE PARK

PO Box 50
Rector, PA 15677
Web: www.dcnr.state.pa.us/stateparks/parks/linnrun.aspx
Phone: 724-238-6623
Size: 612 acres. **Location:** East of Ligonier, off US 30 in the southwest corner of the state. **Facilities:** 9 rustic family cabins, showers, pit and flush toilets, picnic areas, picnic pavilion, snowmobile trailhead, hiking trails (6 miles), playground, **Activities:** Camping, fishing, hiking, hunting, horseback riding, snowmobiling. **Special Features:** Located in the heart of the Laurel Mountains, the park features an excellent trout stream with a scenic waterfall.

★4028★ LITTLE BUFFALO STATE PARK

1579 State Park Rd
Newport, PA 17074
Web: www.dcnr.state.pa.us/stateparks/parks/littlebuffalo.aspx
Phone: 717-567-9255
Size: 830 acres. **Location:** Off PA 322, in the south central part of the state. **Facilities:** 40 class A campsites (some with electricity), picnic areas, picnic pavilions, snack bar, hiking trails (7 miles), swimming pool, bathhouse, boat rentals, boat launches, boat mooring, historic structures, playfield, playgrounds. **Activities:** Boating (electric motors only), fishing, swimming, hiking, hunting, cross-country skiing, ice fishing, ice skating, sledding, nature and historical programs. **Special Features:** Park's historical features include a restored, operating grist mill, a covered bridge, an old farmhouse built on the site of a colonial-era tavern, and a narrow-gauge railroad track with one of the original railroad cars.

★4029★ LITTLE PINE STATE PARK

4205 Little Pine Creek Rd
Waterville, PA 17776
Web: www.dcnr.state.pa.us/stateparks/parks/littlepine.aspx
Phone: 570-753-6000
Size: 2,158 acres. **Location:** Off SR 4001 in the north central part of the state. **Facilities:** 104 class A campsites (some with electricity), 4 group tent camps, 3 cottages, flush toilets, picnic areas, picnic pavilions, hiking trails (13 miles), cross-country ski trail (5 miles), sledding slope, snowmobile trailhead and trails, swimming beach, boat rentals, boat launch, boat mooring, playfield, playground. **Activities:** Camping, boating (electric motors only), fishing, swimming, hiking, hunting, cross-country skiing, ice boating, ice fishing, snowmobiling, sledding, tobogganing, interpretive programs. **Special Features:** Park is located in one of the most beautiful mountain sections of Tiadaghton State Forest in the Appalachian Mountain Region. Many of the park's trails join the surrounding state forest trails, including more than 100 miles of groomed snowmobile trails in Tiadaghton State Forest.

★4030★ LOCUST LAKE STATE PARK

c/o Tuscarora State Park
687 Tuscarora Park Rd
Barnesville, PA 18214
Web: www.dcnr.state.pa.us/stateparks/parks/locustlake.aspx
Phone: 570-467-2404
Size: 1,089 acres. **Location:** In the central eastern part of the state, 7 miles north of Pottsville. **Facilities:** 282 class A campsites, showers, flush toilets, hiking trails (5 miles), bike trail, swimming beach, boat rentals, boat launch, amphitheater, camp store, playgrounds. **Activities:** Camping, boating (electric motors only), fishing, swimming, hiking, bicycling, hunting, ice fishing, ice skating, sledding, nature programs. **Special Features:** Park is adjacent to Weiser State Forest, with numerous miles of scenic state forest roads, trails, and scenic overlooks. Locust Lake sits between two campgrounds and is surrounded by forest.

★4031★ LYMAN RUN STATE PARK

454 Lyman Run Rd
Galeton, PA 16922
Web: www.dcnr.state.pa.us/stateparks/parks/lymanrun.aspx
Phone: 814-435-5010
Size: 595 acres. **Location:** 15 miles east of Coudersport and 7 miles west of Galeton. **Facilities:** 35 class B campsites (29 with electricity), pit toilets, picnic areas, picnic pavilion, snack bar, hiking trails (6 miles), snowmobile trailhead and trails, swimming beach, bathhouse, boat rentals, boat launch, boat mooring, playground, amphitheater. **Activities:** Camping, boating (electric motors only), fishing, swimming, hiking, mountain biking, hunting, ice fishing, ice skating, snowmobiling. **Special Features:** Lyman Run Trail merges with the Fish Trail, which is part of the Susquehannoc Trail system, an 85-mile loop trail covering some of the most rugged, mountainous terrain in north-central Pennsylvania.

★4032★ MARSH CREEK STATE PARK

675 Park Rd
Downingtown, PA 19335
Web: www.dcnr.state.pa.us/stateparks/parks/marshcreek.aspx
Phone: 610-458-5119
Size: 1,705 acres. **Location:** 2 miles west of the village of Eagle on PA 100, in the southeastern corner of the state. **Facilities:** Picnic areas, snack bar, hiking trails, bridle trails, swimming pool (&.), bathhouse, boat rentals, 2 boat launches, boat mooring. **Activities:** Boating (electric motors only), fishing, swimming, hiking, horseback riding, hunting, cross-country skiing, ice boating, ice fishing, ice skating, ice boating, sledding, tobogganing, bird watching. **Special Features:** With its 535-acre lake, Marsh Creek is especially popular with sailboaters who take advantage of the combination of good natural terrain and prevailing winds.

★4033★ MAURICE K. GODDARD STATE PARK

684 Lake Wilhelm Rd
Sandy Lake, PA 16145
Web: www.dcnr.state.pa.us/stateparks/parks/
mauricekgoddard.aspx
Phone: 724-253-4833
Size: 2,856 acres. **Location:** Just off I-79, in the northwest corner of the state. **Facilities:** Picnic areas, picnic pavilions, hiking trails (14 miles), bike trail (12 miles), snowmobile trails (12 miles), cross-country ski trails (8 miles), sledding hill (1 acre), boat rentals, boat launches, boat mooring, marina. **Activities:** Boating (20 HP limit), fishing, hiking, mountain biking,

hunting, cross-country skiing, ice boating, ice fishing, ice skating, snowmobiling, sledding, interpretive programs. **Special Features:** A major attraction of the park is 1,860-acre Lake Wilhelm. The lake, wetlands, old fields, and forests provide a diversity of habitats for wildlife, especially waterfowl, eagles, and osprey.

★4034★ MCCALLS DAM STATE PARK

c/o R.B. Winter State Park
17215 Buffalo Rd
Mifflinburg, PA 17844
Web: www.dcnr.state.pa.us/stateparks/parks/mccallsdam.aspx
Phone: 570-966-1455
Size: 8 acres. **Location:** On McCalls Dam State Forest Road, in the north central part of the state. **Facilities:** Group tent camp, pit toilets, picnic area. **Activities:** Camping, fishing, picnicking. **Special Features:** Park occupies the former site of a dam on White Deer Creek, which was built around 1850 to provide power to a sawmill and shingle mill operation.

★4035★ MCCONNELLS MILL STATE PARK

RR 2, Box 16
Portersville, PA 16051
Web: www.dcnr.state.pa.us/stateparks/parks/
  mcconnellsmill.aspx
Phone: 724-368-8091
Size: 2,546 acres. **Location:** 40 miles north of Pittsburgh, via I-79, in the central western portion of the state. **Facilities:** Picnic areas, hiking trails (11 miles), historical center, playfield, playground, scenic vistas. **Activities:** Whitewater boating (rafting, canoeing, and kayaking), fishing, hiking, hunting, rock climbing and rappelling, nature programs, guided tours of the restored gristmill. **Special Features:** Park features Slippery Rock Creek, a steep-sided gorge, and class II to IV river (depending on water level), Trail of Geology, and the Slippery Rock Gorge, designated a National Natural Landmark.

★4036★ MEMORIAL LAKE STATE PARK

RR 1, Box 7045
Grantville, PA 17028
Web: www.dcnr.state.pa.us/stateparks/parks/
  memoriallake.aspx
Phone: 717-865-6470
Size: 230 acres. **Location:** 30 miles east of Harrisburg, off I-81. **Facilities:** Picnic areas, picnic pavilions, hiking trails, fitness course, boat rentals, 2 boat launches, boat mooring, dock, playfields, playground. **Activities:** Boating (electric motors only), sailing, windsurfing, fishing, hiking, cross-country skiing, ice fishing, ice skating, bird watching. **Special Features:** Park is surrounded by Fort Indiantown Gap Military Reservation in East Hanover Township. The park is located near the southern base of Blue Mountain.

★4037★ MILTON STATE PARK

c/o Shikellamy State Park
Bridge Ave
Sunbury, PA 17801
Web: www.dcnr.state.pa.us/stateparks/parks/milton.aspx
Phone: 570-988-5557

Size: 82 acres. **Location:** Park is an island on the Susquehanna River, between the boroughs of Milton and West Milton. **Facilities:** Picnic areas, hiking trail (1 mile), boat launch, playfields, playground. **Activities:** Boating, fishing, hiking. **Special Features:** The southern part of the island is undeveloped and covered in a forest of predominantly silver maple, river birch, and sycamore. It provides a safe resting place for migrating songbirds and waterfowl.

★4038★ MONT ALTO STATE PARK

c/o Caledonia State Park
101 Pine Grove Rd
Fayetteville, PA 17222
Web: www.dcnr.state.pa.us/stateparks/parks/montalto.aspx
Phone: 717-352-2161; **Fax:** 717-352-7026
Size: 23 acres. **Location:** Park can be reached from Caledonia State Park off US 30. **Facilities:** Picnic areas, picnic pavilions, hiking trails, snowmobile trailhead, playfield, playground. **Activities:** Fishing, hiking, snowmobiling. **Special Features:** Adjacent to the park was the site of the Mont Alto Iron Furnace, built in 1807. It produced 2-3 tons of iron a day. It later became the Mont Alto Iron Company, and the Mont Alto Railroad, which brought visitors to the area. In 1875 Mont Alto Park was opened, and in 1902 it was acquired by the Commonwealth and became the first ''state forest park.''

★4039★ MORAINE STATE PARK

225 Pleasant Valley Rd
Portersville, PA 16051
Web: www.dcnr.state.pa.us/stateparks/parks/moraine.aspx
Phone: 724-368-8811
Size: 16,725 acres. **Location:** In central western Pennsylvania, near the crossroads of I-79 and I-80. **Facilities:** 2 group tent camps, 11 modern cabins, picnic areas, picnic pavilions, snack bar, hiking trails (29 miles), bike trails (7 miles), bridle trails (20 miles), snowmobile trails (20 miles), sledding area, bicycle rental, swimming beaches, boat rentals, boat launch, boat mooring, marina, 18-hole disc golf course, playfield, playground, auto tour route. **Activities:** Camping, boating (20 HP limit), windsurfing, fishing, swimming, hiking, bicycling, mountain biking, horseback riding, hunting, disc golf, cross-country skiing, ice boating, ice fishing, ice skating, snowmobiling, sledding, nature programs. **Special Features:** Park is in an area that has endured the effects of continental glaciers and massive mineral extraction. The park has been restored from prior coal mining and oil and gas practices and is an outstanding example of environmental engineering achievement.

★4040★ MOUNT PISGAH STATE PARK

RR 3, Box 362A
Troy, PA 16947
Web: www.dcnr.state.pa.us/stateparks/parks/mtpisgah.aspx
Phone: 570-297-2734
Size: 1,302 acres. **Location:** 2 miles north of US 6, midway between Troy and Towanda, at the base of Mount Pisgah (elevation 2,260 feet). **Facilities:** Picnic areas, picnic pavilions, snack

bar, hiking trails (10 miles), snowmobile trails (9 miles), swimming pool (&), bathhouse, boat rentals, boat launch, boat mooring, fishing pier, nature center, butterfly garden. **Activities:** Boating (electric motors only), fishing, swimming, hiking, hunting, cross-country skiing, ice boating, ice fishing, ice skating, snowmobiling, snowshoeing, sledding, fall foliage viewing, interpretive programs. **Special Features:** The parks sits at the base of Mount Pisgah along Mill Creek in the Endless Mountains region. A dam on Mill Creek forms Stephen Foster Lake, named after the famous composer and one-time local resident.

★4041★   **NESCOPECK STATE PARK**
c/o Hickory Run State Park
RR 1, Box 81
White Haven, PA 18661
Web: www.dcnr.state.pa.us/stateparks/parks/nescopeck.aspx
Phone: 570-443-0400
Size: 3,550 acres. **Location:** North of I-80, in the northeast corner of the state. **Facilities:** Undeveloped; trails (19 miles), pit toilets. **Activities:** Fishing, ice fishing, hunting, hiking, cross-country skiing, educational programs. **Special Features:** Park includes forested areas, a variety of wetlands, a small lake, and a high-quality trout stream.

★4042★   **NESHAMINY STATE PARK**
3401 State Rd
Bensalem, PA 19020
Web: www.dcnr.state.pa.us/stateparks/parks/neshaminy.aspx
Phone: 215-639-4538
Size: 330 acres. **Location:** Along the Delaware River in the extreme southeastern corner of the state. **Facilities:** Picnic areas (&), picnic pavilions (&), snack bar (&), hiking trails (4 miles), swimming pools, 2 boat launches, boat mooring, marina, theater (&). **Activities:** Boating, fishing, swimming, hiking. **Special Features:** Park includes Tidal Marsh Natural Area, a 71-acre freshwater intertidal zone along the shores of the Delaware River and Neshaminy Creek. It contains wetlands and unique plants.

★4043★   **NOCKAMIXON STATE PARK**
1542 Mountain View Dr
Quakertown, PA 18951
Web: www.dcnr.state.pa.us/stateparks/parks/nockamixon.aspx
Phone: 215-529-7300
Size: 5,283 acres. **Location:** On PA 563, in the southeastern corner of the state. **Facilities:** 10 modern cabins, youth hostel, picnic areas, snack bar, hiking trails (3 miles), bridle trails (20 miles), bike trail (3 miles), swimming pool, fishing pier, boat rentals, 4 boat launches, marina, environmental education center, scenic overlooks. **Activities:** Boating (20 HP limit), canoeing, windsurfing, fishing, swimming, hiking, bicycling, horseback riding, hunting, cross-country skiing, ice boating, ice fishing, ice skating, sledding, tobogganing, nature programs. **Special Features:** Tohickon Creek, Three Mile Run and Haycock Run feed the 1,450-acre Lake Nockamixon. Bucks County Department of Parks and Recreation operates the Weisel Youth Hostel in the northwest corner of the park.

★4044★   **NOLDE FOREST ENVIRONMENTAL EDUCATION CENTER**
2910 New Holland Rd
Reading, PA 19607
Web: www.dcnr.state.pa.us/stateparks/parks/noldeforest.aspx
Phone: 610-796-3699
Size: 665 acres. **Location:** On Route 625, 6 miles south of Reading. **Facilities:** Hiking trails, wildflower garden. **Activities:** Hiking, bird watching, educational programs. **Special Features:** Center provides a wide variety of programs for students, teachers, adult groups, civic groups, and individuals. Site includes Nolde mansion, located near the eastern park boundary, which houses offices for the center staff. Near the mansion is C.H. McConnell Environmental Education Hall, an indoor site for year-round activites.

★4045★   **NORRISTOWN FARM PARK**
2500 Upper Farm Rd
Norristown, PA 19403
Web: www.dcnr.state.pa.us/stateparks/parks/
norristownfarmpark.aspx
Phone: 610-270-0215
Size: 690 acres. **Location:** Off West Germantown Pike in Norristown, in the southwestern corner of the state. **Facilities:** Paved trail, picnic area, picnic pavilions. **Activities:** Fishing, hiking, bicycling, inline skating, skateboarding, snowshoeing, cross-country skiing, sledding, summer concerts. **Special Features:** A green oasis in a fast-growing suburban setting, the park offers miles of trails and fishing in Stony Creek. Operated by Montgomery County Department of Parks.

★4046★   **OHIOPYLE STATE PARK**
PO Box 105
Ohiopyle, PA 15470
Web: www.dcnr.state.pa.us/stateparks/parks/ohiopyle.aspx
Phone: 724-329-8591
Size: 19,052 acres. **Location:** Off PA 381, in the southwestern corner of the state. **Facilities:** 226 class A campsites, camping cottages, group tent camp, showers, flush toilets, picnic areas, picnic pavilions, snack bar, backpacking trailhead, hiking trails (79 miles), bike trails (40 miles), bridle trails (9 miles), snowmobile trailhead and trails (13 miles), cross-country ski trails (34 miles), sledding hill, waterslides, bicycle rentals, boat rentals, boat launch, amphitheater, playfield, playgrounds, scenic overlooks. **Activities:** Camping, hunting, whitewater boating (rafting, canoeing, and kayaking), fishing, hiking, bicycling, mountain biking, cross-country skiing, snowmobiling, sledding, tobogganing, nature programs. **Special Features:** More than 14 miles of the Youghiogheny River Gorge pass through the heart of the park. The ''Yough'' offers some of the best whitewater boating in the East as well as spectacular scenery. Park also has several waterfalls, and natural waterslides.

★4047★   **OIL CREEK STATE PARK**
305 State Park Rd
Oil City, PA 16301
Web: www.dcnr.state.pa.us/stateparks/parks/oilcreek.aspx
Phone: 814-676-5915

Size: 7,100 acres. **Location:** Off PA Route 8, one mile north of the borough of Rouseville, in the northwestern corner of the state. **Facilities:** Picnic areas (&), picnic pavilions, snack bar, hiking trails, bike trail, visitor/historical center. **Activities:** Canoeing, fishing, hiking, bicycling, hunting, cross-country skiing, interpretive programs. **Special Features:** Park's displays and programs identify oil boom towns, important oil well ruins, Indian oil pits, foundations, and cemeteries. Various sites feature an engine house, pumping jacks, stock tanks, oil derricks, and an oil barge. A train still travels through the valley and stops at the train station in Petroleum Centre, just as it did 100 years ago.

★4048★ OLE BULL STATE PARK

HCR 62, Box 9
Cross Fork, PA 17729
Web: www.dcnr.state.pa.us/stateparks/parks/olebull.aspx
Phone: 814-435-5000
Size: 132 acres. **Location:** Along PA 144, 18 miles south of Galeton, in the north central part of the state. **Facilities:** 81 class A campsites (45 with electricity), modern cabin, picnic areas, picnic pavilions, backpacking trailhead, hiking trails (2 miles), snowmobile trailhead, swimming beach, amphitheater, playgrounds. **Activities:** Camping, fishing, swimming, hiking, hunting, cross-country skiing, snowmobiling, snowshoeing, nature programs. **Special Features:** Park is named after Ole Bornemann Bull, the famous Norwegian violinist who toured the United States in the 1850s.

★4049★ PARKER DAM STATE PARK

28 Fairview Rd
Penfield, PA 15849
Web: www.dcnr.state.pa.us/stateparks/parks/parkerdam.aspx
Phone: 814-765-0630
Size: 968 acres. **Location:** Off PA 153 in the central portion of the state. **Facilities:** 110 class A campsites (80 with electricity), 16 rustic cabins, 3 group tent/trailer camps, showers, flush toilets, picnic areas, picnic pavilions, snack bar, hiking trails, backpacking trailhead, cross-country ski trails, snowmobile trailhead and trails, swimming beach, boat rentals, boat launch, amphitheater, playfield, playground. **Activities:** Camping, boating (electric motors only), fishing, swimming, hiking, bicycling, hunting, cross-country skiing, ice fishing, ice skating, snowmobiling, sledding, tobogganing, nature programs. **Special Features:** Located in the heart of Moshannon State Forest, the park is almost entirely wooded and offers picturesque areas of forest and swamp meadows, pine plantations, and mixed hardwood. For explorers, park offers the opportunity to walk through a tornado-ravaged woods or backpack into the 50,000-acre Quehanna Wilderness.

★4050★ PATTERSON STATE PARK

c/o Lyman Run State Park
454 Lyman Run Rd
Galeton, PA 16922
Web: www.dcnr.state.pa.us/stateparks/parks/patterson.aspx
Phone: 814-435-5010
Size: 10 acres. **Location:** 6.5 miles south of Sweden Valley on PA 44, in the north central part of the state. **Facilities:** Primitive campsites, picnic area, picnic pavilion, backpacking trailhead, mountain bike trail. **Activities:** Camping, hiking, mountain biking. **Special Features:** Park is surrounded by Susquehannock State Forest and provides access to ski and snowmobile trails. The 85-mile Susquehannock Trail passes through the park.

★4051★ PENN-ROOSEVELT STATE PARK

c/o Greenwood Furnace State Park
RR 2, Box 118
Huntingdon, PA 16652
Web: www.dcnr.state.pa.us/stateparks/parks/pennroosevelt.aspx
Phone: 814-667-1800
Size: 41 acres. **Location:** Off US 322, 0.5 mile east of Potters Mills, in the center of the state. **Facilities:** 18 rustic tent campsites, pit toilets, picnic areas, picnic pavilion, hiking trail. **Activities:** Camping, hiking, cross-country skiing, horseback riding, snowmobiling. **Special Features:** Located in an isolated area of the Seven Mountains region known locally as Stone Creek Kettle, the park is totally surrounded by Rothrock State Forest (80,000+ acres).

★4052★ PINE GROVE FURNACE STATE PARK

1100 Pine Grove Rd
Gardners, PA 17324
Web: www.dcnr.state.pa.us/stateparks/parks/pinegrovefurnace.aspx
Phone: 717-486-7174; **Fax:** 717-486-4961; **Toll Free:** 888-727-2757
Size: 696 acres. **Location:** Off PA 233 in southern Cumberland County. **Facilities:** 71 class B campsites (some with electricity), 6 group tent camps, 2 cabins, youth hostel, pit toilets, picnic areas (&), picnic pavilions, snack bar, backpacking trailhead, hiking trails (3 miles), swimming beaches, oat launch, boat mooring, interpretive center (&). **Activities:** Camping, boating (electric motors only), fishing, swimming, hiking, bicycling, hunting, cross-country skiing, ice fishing, ice skating, snowmobiling, nature and historical programs. **Special Features:** Park is on the site of Pine Grove Iron Furnace, which opened in 1764 and operated for over 100 years, manufacturing cast iron stoves, kettles, and military supplies. Buildings dating back to the charcoal and iron community still stand and include the ironmaster's mansion, clerk's office, stable, grist mill (now the Visitor Center), inn (now the park office), and several residences. A portion of the Appalachian National Scenic Trail (see entry in national trails section) passes through the park and the adjacent Michaux State Forest.

★4053★ POE PADDY STATE PARK

c/o Reeds Gap State Park
1405 New Lancaster Valley Rd
Milroy, PA 17063
Web: www.dcnr.state.pa.us/stateparks/parks/poepaddy.aspx
Phone: 717-667-3622
Size: 23 acres. **Location:** 4 miles east of Poe Valley State Park on Big Poe Road, in the center of the state. **Facilities:** 39 class B campsites, 2 group tent camps, pit toilets, picnic area, picnic

pavilions, snowmobile trails, hiking trail, playground. **Activities:** Camping, fishing, hiking, snowmobiling. **Special Features:** Site was once Poe Mills, a prosperous but short-lived lumbering town of the 1880s and 1890s. Park got its name from Poe Mountain to the east and Paddy Mountain to the west, which were once one long mountain. More than a million years of erosion by Penns Creek divided the mountain, creating the valley that cradles Poe Paddy State Park.

★4054★ POE VALLEY STATE PARK

c/o Reeds Gap State Park
1405 New Lancaster Valley Rd
Milroy, PA 17063
Web: www.dcnr.state.pa.us/stateparks/parks/poevalley.aspx
Phone: 814-349-2460
Size: 620 acres. **Location:** Of US 322, in the center of the state. **Facilities:** 79 class B campsites (14 with electric hookups), pit toilets, picnic area, picnic pavilions, snack bar, backpacking trailhead, hiking trails (3 miles), snowmobile trails, swimming beach, boat rentals, boat launches, boat mooring, nature center, playgrounds, amphitheater, scenic vistas. **Activities:** Camping, boating (electric motors only), fishing, swimming, hiking, hunting, cross-country skiing, ice fishing, ice skating, snowmobiling, nature programs. **Special Features:** Poe Valley's trail system connects to the extensive trail network of Bald Eagle State Forest, which includes a portion of the 189-mile Mid State Trail.

★4055★ POINT STATE PARK

101 Commonwealth Pl
Pittsburgh, PA 15222
Web: www.dcnr.state.pa.us/stateparks/parks/point.aspx
Phone: 412-471-0235
Size: 36 acres. **Location:** At the tip of Pittsburgh's "Golden Triangle," in the southwest corner of the state. **Facilities:** Paved walk promenades, fountain, stepped wall, inline skate route, bike paths, museum, historic buildings. **Activities:** Inline skating, bicycling, historical interpretation. **Special Features:** Located at the tip of Pittsburgh's Golden Triangle, park commemorates and preserves the strategic heritage of the area during the French and Indian War (1754-1763). The park is currently undergoing renovations and is expected to be completed by the end of 2007.

★4056★ PRESQUE ISLE STATE PARK

301 Peninsula Dr, Suite 1
Erie, PA 16505
Web: www.dcnr.state.pa.us/stateparks/parks/presqueisle.aspx
Phone: 814-833-7424; **Fax:** 814-833-0266
Size: 3,200 acres. **Location:** Peninsula on Lake Erie, reached by PA 832 or via boat. **Facilities:** Picnic areas (&), picnic pavilions, picnic shelters, snack bar, hiking trails (11 miles), swimming beaches (1 &), fishing piers (&), boat rentals, 4 boat launches, boat mooring, marina, visitor center, playfield, boat tours, interpretive center (&), nature shop. **Activities:** Boating, fishing, swimming, water-skiing, scuba diving, hunting, hiking, bicycling, inline skating, cross-country skiing, ice boating, ice fishing, ice skating, bird watching, interpretive programs. **Special Features:** Park is a sand spit jutting into Lake Erie and the only surf beach in Pennsylvania. A National Natural Landmark,

Presque Isle is a favorite spot for migrating birds. Because of its many unique habitats, the park contains a greater number of the state's endangered, threatened, and rare species than any other area of comparable size in the state.

★4057★ PRINCE GALLITZIN STATE PARK

966 Marina Rd
Patton, PA 16668
Web: www.dcnr.state.pa.us/stateparks/parks/princegallitzin.aspx
Phone: 814-674-1000
Size: 6,249 acres. **Location:** In northern Cambria County, park can be reached by PA Routes 36 and 53 and US 219. **Facilities:** 437 class A campsites (many with electricity, &), 10 modern cabins, group tent camp, showers, flush toilets, laundry, picnic areas, picnic pavilions, snack bar, hiking trails (9 miles), bridle trail, bike trails, snowmobile trails (20 miles), cross-country ski trails (7 miles), swimming beach, boat rentals, boat launch, boat mooring, marina, amphitheater, camp store, playground, scenic vistas. **Activities:** Camping, hunting, boating (20 HP limit), fishing, swimming, hiking, horseback riding, bicycling, cross-country skiing, ice boating, ice fishing, snowmobiling, environmental education programs. **Special Features:** Park features 1,600-acre Glendale Lake, which provides 26 miles of shoreline and is home to many species of fish, birds, and animals. Fields in the park are excellent for seeing butterflies.

★4058★ PROMISED LAND STATE PARK

RR 1, Box 96
Greentown, PA 18426
Web: www.dcnr.state.pa.us/stateparks/parks/promisedland.aspx
Phone: 570-676-3428
Size: 3,000 acres. **Location:** 10 miles north of Canadensis in Pike County, in the northeast corner of the state. **Facilities:** More than 900 campsites (many with electricity), 12 rustic cabins, showers, flush and pit toilets, picnic areas, picnic pavilions, snack bar, hiking trails (50 miles), bike trails, snowmobile trailhead and trail (23 miles), swimming beaches, boat rentals, boat launches, boat mooring, orienteering course, game court. **Activities:** Camping, hunting, boating (electric motors only), fishing, swimming, hiking, bicycling, cross-country skiing, ice fishing, ice skating, snowmobiling, interpretive programs. **Special Features:** Park is situated in the heart of the Poconos, 1,800 feet above sea level, surrounded by 12,464 acres of the Delaware State Forest and the Bruce Lake Natural Area. It features two lakes and several small streams.

★4059★ PROMPTON STATE PARK

c/o Lackawanna State Park
RR 1, Box 230
Dalton, PA 18414
Web: www.dcnr.state.pa.us/stateparks/parks/prompton.asp
Phone: 570-945-3239
Location: Off US 6, northeast of Scranton. **Facilities:** Undeveloped. **Special Features:** Park is located in Wayne County.

★4060★ PROUTY PLACE STATE PARK

c/o Lyman Run State Park
454 Lyman Run Rd
Galeton, PA 16922
Web: www.dcnr.state.pa.us/stateparks/parks/proutyplace.aspx
Phone: 814-435-5010
Size: 5 acres. **Location:** 5 miles southwest of PA Route 44 along Long Toe Road. **Special Features:** Park offers access to hunting, fishing, and hiking within surrounding Susquehannock State Forest land.

★4061★ PYMATUNING STATE PARK

2660 Williamsfield Rd
Jamestown, PA 16134
Web: www.dcnr.state.pa.us/stateparks/parks/pymatuning.aspx
Phone: 724-932-3141
Size: 21,122 acres. **Location:** Off US 322 in the northwest corner of the state. **Facilities:** More than 1,000 class A/B campsites (about half with electricity), group tent/trailer camp, 25 modern cabins (&), showers, flush and pit toilets, laundry, picnic areas (&), picnic pavilions, snack bar, swimming beaches, boat rentals, boat launch, boat mooring, marina, hiking trails (2 miles), snowmobile trails, amphitheater, playfield, playground, environmental programs. **Activities:** Camping, hunting, boating (10 HP limit), fishing, swimming, hiking, cross-country skiing, ice boating, ice fishing, snowmobiling, sledding, nature programs. **Special Features:** Park includes 17,088-acre Pymatuning Reservoir, a large manmade lake featuring a dam, spillway, fish hatchery, two causeways across the lake, and the Pennsylvania Game Commission Visitor Center and Waterfowl Museum. The spillway is one of the more popular spots for visitors because the fish being fed are so crowded that ducks appear to walk on the fishes' backs to compete for handouts.

★4062★ R. B. WINTER STATE PARK

17215 Buffalo Rd
Mifflinburg, PA 17844
Web: www.dcnr.state.pa.us/stateparks/parks/rbwinter.aspx
Phone: 570-966-1455
Size: 695 acres. **Location:** On PA 192, 18 miles west of Lewisburg, in the center of the state. **Facilities:** 59 class B campsites (some with electricity), modern cabin, 3 camping cottages (&), pit toilets, picnic areas, picnic pavilions, snack bar, hiking trails (6 miles), bike trails (48 miles), cross-country ski trails (5 miles), snowmobile trailhead and trails, swimming beach, amphitheater, playfield, playground, butterfly garden. **Activities:** Camping, hunting, fishing, swimming, hiking, mountain biking, cross-country skiing, ice fishing, ice skating, snowmobiling, nature programs. **Special Features:** Park is located within Bald Eagle State Forest. Its focal point is Halfway Lake, which is filled by spring-fed mountain streams and contained by a hand-laid, native sandstone dam. The park offers a variety of environmental education and interpretive programs on a year- round basis, including curriculum-based programs available to schools, youth organizations, and homeschool associations.

★4063★ RACCOON CREEK STATE PARK

3000 State Rt 18
Hookstown, PA 15050
Web: www.dcnr.state.pa.us/stateparks/parks/raccooncreek.aspx
Phone: 724-899-2200
Size: 7,572 acres. **Location:** 25 miles west of Pittsburgh via US 22 or 30. **Facilities:** 172 class A campsites (&), 10 modern cabins, cottage, 6 group tent camps, 3 group camps, recreation hall, showers, flush toilets, picnic areas, picnic pavilions, snack bar, hiking trails (44 miles), bike trails (17 miles), bridle trails (16 miles), cross-country ski trails, swimming beach, boat rentals, boat launch, boat mooring, playfield. **Activities:** Camping, boating (electric motors only), fishing, swimming, hiking, mountain biking, horseback riding, hunting, cross-country skiing, ice fishing, ice skating, sledding, nature programs. **Special Features:** Historic Frankfort Mineral Springs, site of a nationally known health spa during the 1800s, is located in the park. The area once attracted thousands of visitors who believed in the healing powers of the mineral water. The springs can currently be viewed from a scenic self-guiding trail that passes through the area. Park also includes Wildflower Reserve, a 314-acre area that contains one of the most diverse stands of wildflowers in western Pennsylvania. More than 500 species of plants have been identified.

★4064★ RALPH STOVER STATE PARK

c/o Delaware Canal State Park
11 Lodi Hill Rd
Upper Black Eddy, PA 18972
Web: www.dcnr.state.pa.us/stateparks/parks/ralphstover.aspx
Phone: 610-982-5560
Size: 45 acres. **Location:** 2 miles north of Point Pleasant on State Park Road and Stump Road, in the southeast corner of the state. **Facilities:** Picnic area, picnic pavilions, restrooms, hiking trails (1 mile), scenic vista. **Activities:** Whitewater boating (rafting and kayaking), fishing, hiking, rock climbing. **Special Features:** The High Rocks section of the park features an outstanding view of a horseshoe bend in Tohickon Creek and the surrounding forest. When high water conditions exist, Tohickon Creek offers a challenging course for closed-deck canoes and kayaks.

★4065★ RAVENSBURG STATE PARK

c/o R. B. Winter State Park
17215 Buffalo Rd
Mifflinburg, PA 17844
Web: www.dcnr.state.pa.us/stateparks/parks/ravensburg.aspx
Phone: 570-966-1455
Size: 78 acres. **Location:** In central Pennsylvania, on PA 880. **Facilities:** 21 campsites, showers, flush toilets, picnic areas, picnic pavilions, hiking trail (1 mile), playground. **Activities:** Camping, fishing, hiking. **Special Features:** The park's outstanding geologic feature is Castle Rocks, tall spires of sandstone created by selective erosion. Park is named for ravens that once roosted on the rock ledges at the southern end of the park.

★4066★ REEDS GAP STATE PARK

1405 New Lancaster Valley Rd
Milroy, PA 17063
Web: www.dcnr.state.pa.us/stateparks/parks/reedsgap.aspx
Phone: 717-667-3622
Size: 220 acres. **Location:** 7 miles from Milroy, off US 322.
Facilities: Tent campsites, showers, flush toilets, picnic areas, picnic pavilions, hiking trails (4 miles), swimming pools (&), bathhouse, snack bar, playground. **Activities:** Camping, fishing, swimming, hiking, hunting, cross-country skiing. **Special Features:** Reeds Gap is a natural water gap in Hightop, also called Thick Mountain. In the mid-1800s the park's namesakes set up a water-powered sawmill just inside the western boundary of the present park, and part of the water-storage dam is still visible along the Honey Creek Trail loop.

★4067★ RICKETTS GLEN STATE PARK

695 State Rt 487
Benton, PA 17814
Web: www.dcnr.state.pa.us/stateparks/parks/rickettsglen.aspx
Phone: 570-477-5675
Size: 13,050 acres. **Location:** 30 miles north of Bloomsburg on PA 487. **Facilities:** 120 class A campsites (6 &), 10 modern cabins, group tent camp, showers, flush toilets, picnic areas, snack bar, hiking trails (26 miles), bridle trails (9 miles), snowmobile trails, swimming beach, boat rentals, boat launches, boat mooring, amphitheater. **Activities:** Camping, boating (electric motors only), fishing, swimming, hiking, horseback riding, hunting, cross-country skiing, ice fishing, ice climbing, snowmobiling, snowshoeing, nature programs. **Special Features:** The Glens Natural Area, a registered National Natural Landmark, is the main scenic attraction in the park. It features 900-year-old trees, a series of trails, and the 94-foot Ganoga Falls, the highest of more than 20 named waterfalls in the park.

★4068★ RIDLEY CREEK STATE PARK

1023 Sycamore Mills Rd
Media, PA 19063
Web: www.dcnr.state.pa.us/stateparks/parks/ridleycreek.aspx
Phone: 610-892-3900
Size: 2,607 acres. **Location:** 16 miles from Philadelphia, off PA 3. **Facilities:** Group tent camp, picnic areas, picnic pavilions, mobile snack bar, fishing pier (&), hiking trails (12 miles), bridle trails (5 miles), paved multi-use trail (5 miles), sledding slope, playfields, playgrounds, gardens. **Activities:** Camping, fishing, hiking, bicycling, horseback riding, cross-country skiing, sledding, tobogganing, nature and historical programs. **Special Features:** Park includes Colonial Pennsylvania Plantation, a working farm and living museum that depicts life on a Delaware County Quaker farm prior to the American Revolution. Visitors can observe and participate in the making of farm tools, clothing, furniture, and colonial meals. Other colonial chores demonstrated include spinning, crop harvesting, butter churning, salting and smoking of meat, and food preservation.

★4069★ RYERSON STATION STATE PARK

361 Bristoria Rd
Wind Ridge, PA 15380
Web: www.dcnr.state.pa.us/stateparks/parks/ryersonstation.aspx
Phone: 724-428-4254
Size: 1,164 acres. **Location:** On both sides of Bristoria Rd, just off PA 21, in the extreme southwestern corner of the state. **Facilities:** 48 class B campsites (16 with electricity), group tent camp, 2 cottages, showers, pit toilets, picnic areas, picnic pavilions, snack bar, hiking trails (11 miles), snowmobile trails (6 miles), sledding slopes (5 acres), swimming pool (&), boat rentals, fishing pier, amphitheater, playfield, playground. **Activities:** Camping, boating (electric motors only), fishing, swimming, hiking, hunting, cross-country skiing, ice fishing, ice skating, snowmobiling, sledding, nature programs. **Special Features:** Park's name originated from nearby Fort Ryerson, which was constructed in 1792 at the order of the Virginia authorities to be used principally as a place of refuge from Indian raids.

★4070★ S. B. ELLIOTT STATE PARK

c/o Parker Dam State Park
28 Fairview Rd
Penfield, PA 15849
Web: www.dcnr.state.pa.us/stateparks/parks/sbelliott.aspx
Phone: 814-765-0630
Size: 318 acres. **Location:** 9 miles north of Clearfield, off PA Route 153. **Facilities:** 25 class B campsites (7 &), 6 rustic cabins, flush toilets, picnic areas, picnic pavilions, hiking trails (3 miles), cross-country skiing trails (4 miles), snowmobile trailhead, playfield. **Activities:** Camping, hunting, fishing, hiking, cross-country skiing. **Special Features:** Located near the midpoint of the state in the heart of the Moshannon State Forest, the park is densely wooded with typical second-growth mixed hardwood and oak timber and occasional swamp meadows.

★4071★ SALT SPRINGS STATE PARK

c/o Lackawanna State Park
RR 1, Box 230
Dalton, PA 18414
Web: www.dcnr.state.pa.us/stateparks/parks/saltsprings.aspx
Phone: 570-945-3239
Size: 405 acres. **Location:** Off Route 29, in the northeastern corner of the state. **Facilities:** Rustic tent campsites, cottages, restrooms, picnic pavilion, picnic area, hiking trail (8.5 miles), snowshoeing trails, cross-country skiing trails, sledding areas. **Activities:** Camping, fishing, hiking, hunting, cross-country skiing, sledding, snowshoeing, interpretive programs. **Special Features:** Park features old-growth hemlock trees, estimated to be between 500 and 600 years old, and the scenic waterfalls of Fall Brook.

★4072★ SAMUEL S. LEWIS STATE PARK

c/o Gifford Pinchot State Park
2200 Rosstown Rd
Lewisberry, PA 17339
Web: www.dcnr.state.pa.us/stateparks/parks/samuelslewis.aspx
Phone: 717-432-5011

Size: 85 acres. **Location:** 12 miles east of York on US 30, in the south central part of the state. **Facilities:** Picnic area, picnic pavilions, snack bar, hiking trails (1 mile), playfield, playground, arboretum. **Activities:** Hiking, picnicking, kite flying. **Special Features:** Park is located atop 885-foot-high Mount Pisgah, offering a panoramic view of the Susquehanna River Valley and the surrounding farmland. Coin-operated binoculars are available at the summit.

★4073★ SAND BRIDGE STATE PARK

c/o R. B. Winter State Park
RR 2, Box 314
Mifflinburg, PA 17844
Web: www.dcnr.state.pa.us/stateparks/parks/sandbridge.aspx
Phone: 570-966-1455
Size: 3 acres. **Location:** On PA 192, 15 miles west of Lewisburg. **Facilities:** Picnic area, picnic pavilion, restrooms. **Activities:** Fishing, picnicking. **Special Features:** Small, quaint park includes a fishing stream and lovely scenery, and is located adjacent to Bald Eagle State Forest.

★4074★ SHAWNEE STATE PARK

132 State Park Rd
Schellsburg, PA 15559
Web: www.dcnr.state.pa.us/stateparks/parks/shawnee.aspx
Phone: 814-733-4218
Size: 3,983 acres. **Location:** Along Route 30, 10 miles west of historic Bedford. **Facilities:** 293 class A campsites (65 with electricity, 2 &), group tent camp, lodge (&), showers, flush and pit toilets, picnic areas, picnic pavilions ·(&), snack bar, hiking trails (15 miles), snowmobile trails (11 miles), sledding area, bike trails (7.5 miles), fishing pier (&), swimming beach, boat rentals, 3 boat launches, boat mooring, dock (&), amphitheater, camp store, playfield. **Activities:** Camping, hunting, boating (electric motors only), fishing, swimming, hiking, mountain biking, ice fishing, ice skating, snowmobiling, sledding, tobogganing, nature programs. **Special Features:** Situated in Pennsylvania's scenic Ridge and Valley Province, the park's main focal point is 451-acre Shawnee Lake. Situated on an island in the middle of the park is a three-story house that offers year-round accommodations with panoramic views of Shawnee Lake and the surrounding countryside.

★4075★ SHIKELLAMY STATE PARK

Bridge Ave
Sunbury, PA 17801
Web: www.dcnr.state.pa.us/stateparks/parks/shikellamy.aspx
Phone: 570-988-5557
Size: 132 acres. **Location:** In both Union and Northumberland counties. Shikellamy Overlook is on US 11, near the town of Shamokin Dam; Shikellamy Marina is off PA 147. **Facilities:** Picnic areas, picnic pavilions, restaurant, snack bar, hiking trails (2 miles), bike trail (1 mile), bike rentals, boat rentals, boat launches, marina, playground, observation platform. **Activities:** Boating, water-skiing, fishing, hiking, bicycling. **Special Features:** Park was named in honor of the famous Iroquois Chief Shikellamy, who played a prominent role in the development of the Pennsylvania frontier in the early and middle 18th century.

The park consists of two distinct areas: a large marina that provides access to Lake Augusta; and, across the river from the marina, the overlook section with panoramic views of Packer's Island and the confluence of two branches of the Susquehanna River.

★4076★ SINNEMAHONING STATE PARK

8288 First Fork Rd
Austin, PA 16720
Web: www.dcnr.state.pa.us/stateparks/parks/sinnemahoning.aspx
Phone: 814-647-8401
Size: 1,910 acres. **Location:** 8 miles north on PA 872 from its junction with PA 120 in Sinnemahoning, in the north central portion of the state. **Facilities:** 35 class A campsites (some with electricity), modern cabin, showers, flush toilets, picnic areas, picnic pavilions, hiking trails (5 miles), snowmobile trailhead and trails (5 miles), boat launch, boat mooring, amphitheater, scenic vistas, playground. **Activities:** Camping, boating (electric motors only), fishing, swimming, hiking, hunting, ice fishing, snowmobiling, nature programs. **Special Features:** Situated in the midst of the Elk State Forest, the park offers an abundance of wildlife and includes feeding grounds of the American bald eagle.

★4077★ SIZERVILLE STATE PARK

199 E Cowley Run Rd
Emporium, PA 15834
Web: www.dcnr.state.pa.us/stateparks/parks/sizerville.aspx
Phone: 814-486-5605
Size: 386 acres. **Location:** 6 miles north of Emporium on PA Route 155. **Facilities:** 23 class A campsites (some with electricity), 5 walk-in campsites, showers, flush toilets, picnic areas, picnic pavilions, snack bar, hiking trails (5 miles), snowmobile trailhead and trails, swimming pool (&), amphitheater, playground, butterfly garden. **Activities:** Camping, fishing, swimming, hiking, hunting, snowmobiling, nature programs. **Special Features:** In spring and summer, woodland flowers, flowering trees, and mountain laurel blossom in profusion; in fall, mixed hardwoods provide flaming foliage.

★4078★ SUSQUEHANNA STATE PARK

c/o Shikellamy State Park
Bridge Ave
Sunbury, PA 17801
Web: www.dcnr.state.pa.us/stateparks/parks/susquehanna.aspx
Phone: 570-988-5557
Size: 20 acres. **Location:** On US 220 just south of Williamsport. **Facilities:** Picnic area, boat launch, snack bar. **Activities:** Boating, fishing, riverboat excursion. **Special Features:** Operated by the Williamsport Chamber of Commerce, the park's primary attraction is the recreational riverboat *Hiawatha*, a modern paddlewheeler.

★4079★ SUSQUEHANNOCK STATE PARK

1880 Park Dr
Drumore, PA 17518
Web: www.dcnr.state.pa.us/stateparks/parks/susquehannock.aspx
Phone: 717-432-5011

Size: 224 acres. **Location:** From PA Route 372 west of Buck, in the extreme southern part of the state. **Facilities:** Group tent camp, pit toilets, picnic areas, picnic pavilions (&), hiking trails (5 miles), bridle trails, softball fields, playground, scenic overlook (&). **Activities:** Camping, hiking, horseback riding, picnicking. **Special Features:** The old stone house near the park office is the Landis House, named for the last owner. It was built in 1850 and is an example of stone architecture and craftsmanship of the time. The exterior of the structure has been stabilized, but the interior is not safe for public use.

★4080★ SWATARA STATE PARK

c/o Memorial Lake State Park
RR 1, Box 7045
Grantville, PA 17028
Web: www.dcnr.state.pa.us/stateparks/parks/swatara.aspx
Phone: 717-865-6470
Size: 3,520 acres. **Location:** 14 miles north of Lebanon off I-81. **Facilities:** Undeveloped. Backpacking trailhead, trails. **Activities:** Boating (non-powered only), fishing, hiking, bicycling, horseback riding, hunting, cross-country skiing. **Special Features:** Geology of the park is predominately sedimentary rocks formed in a shallow ocean during the Middle Devonian Period of the Paleozoic Era, about 375 million years ago. An Upper Mahantango Formation that contains significant marine fossil beds is exposed at a site along Old State Road and provides opportunities for fossil collectors.

★4081★ TOBYHANNA STATE PARK

PO Box 387
Tobyhanna, PA 18466
Web: www.dcnr.state.pa.us/stateparks/parks/tobyhanna.aspx
Phone: 570-894-8336
Size: 5,440 acres. **Location:** 2 miles north of Tobyhanna on PA 423, in the northeastern corner of the state. **Facilities:** 140 class B campsites, group tent camp, pit toilets, picnic areas, picnic pavilion (&), snack bar, hiking trails (12 miles), snowmobile trailhead and trails (5.5 miles), swimming beach, boat rentals, boat launch, fishing pier (&), boat mooring, amphitheater, playfield, playground. **Activities:** Camping, boating (electric motors only), fishing, swimming, hiking, bicycling, hunting, cross-country skiing, ice fishing, ice skating, snowmobiling. **Special Features:** Park includes 170-acre Tobyhanna Lake. Tobyhanna is derived from an American Indian word meaning "a stream whose banks are fringed with alder."

★4082★ TROUGH CREEK STATE PARK

RR 1, Box 211
James Creek, PA 16657
Web: www.dcnr.state.pa.us/stateparks/parks/troughcreek.aspx
Phone: 814-658-3847
Size: 554 acres. **Location:** 16 miles south of Huntington, in the south central part of the state. **Facilities:** 32 class B campsites (all with electricity), lodge (&), pit toilets, picnic areas, picnic pavilions, hiking trails (12 miles), bike trail, snowmobile trailhead, amphitheater. **Activities:** Camping, fishing, hiking, biking, hunting, snowmobiling, nature programs. **Special Features:** Park is a gorge created as Great Trough Creek cuts through

Terrace Mountain and empties into Raystown Lake. Rugged trails lead to such natural wonders as Balanced Rock and Rainbow Falls.

★4083★ TUSCARORA STATE PARK

687 Tuscarora Park Rd
Barnesville, PA 18214
Web: www.dcnr.state.pa.us/stateparks/parks/tuscarora.aspx
Phone: 570-467-2404
Size: 1,618 acres. **Location:** South of Barnesville, on PA Route 54. **Facilities:** 6 camping cottages, picnic areas, snack bar, hiking trails (3 miles), swimming beach, bathhouse, boat rentals, boat launch, boat mooring. **Activities:** Boating (electric motors only), fishing, swimming, hiking, hunting, ice fishing, ice skating, sledding, nature programs. **Special Features:** Park is in the area known locally as "Locust Valley," which was spared the ravages of the coal mining that once was the dominant industry of the region.

★4084★ TYLER STATE PARK

101 Swamp Rd
Newtown, PA 18940
Web: www.dcnr.state.pa.us/stateparks/parks/tyler.aspx
Phone: 215-968-2021
Size: 1,711 acres. **Location:** Off I-95 in the extreme eastern part of the state, near Newtown. **Facilities:** Hostel, picnic areas (&), picnic groves (&), hiking trails (4 miles), bike trails (10 miles), bridle trails (9 miles), canoe rentals, boat launch, playfield, playgrounds, 27-hole disc golf course. **Activities:** Boating (electric motors only), fishing, hiking, bicycling, horseback riding, cross-country skiing, ice fishing, ice skating, sledding, tobogganing, nature programs. **Special Features:** The Spring Garden Mill, once an active grain and feed mill, is now leased to the Langhorne Players, a local theater group. Park also features the Schofield Ford Covered Bridge, built in 1874. The 166-foot, two-span bridge has been rebuilt and sits on its original stone abutments and center pier.

★4085★ UPPER PINE BOTTOM STATE PARK

c/o Little Pine State Park
4205 Little Pine Creek Rd
Waterville, PA 17776
Web: www.dcnr.state.pa.us/stateparks/parks/
   upperpinebottom.aspx
Phone: 570-753-6000
Size: Roadside park. **Location:** Along PA 44, west of Waterville. **Facilities:** Picnic area. **Activities:** Picnicking.. **Special Features:** Small park provides access to hiking, cross-country skiing, snowmobiling, and hunting in adjacent Tiadaghton State Forest.

★4086★ WARRIORS PATH STATE PARK

c/o Trough Creek State Park
RR 1, Box 211
James Creek, PA 16657
Web: www.dcnr.state.pa.us/stateparks/parks/warriorspath.aspx
Phone: 814-658-3847

9. State Parks

Size: 349 acres. **Location:** In Liberty Township, 2 miles south of the borough of Saxton, in the south central part of the state. **Facilities:** Picnic areas, picnic pavilions (&), hiking trails (3 miles), cross-country ski trails, boat launch, playfield. **Activities:** Boating, fishing, hiking, hunting, cross-country skiing. **Special Features:** Park is located on a finger of land bounded on three sides by the Raystown Branch of the Juniata River. It lies very near the famous path used by the Iroquois Indians in raids and wars with the Cherokees and other native tribes in southern Pennsylvania.

★4087★ WHIPPLE DAM STATE PARK

c/o Greenwood Furnace State Park
RR 2, Box 118
Huntingdon, PA 16652
Web: www.dcnr.state.pa.us/stateparks/parks/whippledam.aspx
Phone: 814-667-1800
Size: 256 acres. **Location:** 12 miles south of State College, in the center of the state. **Facilities:** Picnic areas, picnic pavilions, snack bar, hiking trails, snowmobile trails, swimming beach, boat launch, boat mooring, game court. **Activities:** Boating (electric motors only), canoeing, fishing, swimming, hiking, hunting, ice fishing, ice skating, cross-country skiing, snowmobiling. **Special Features:** Park area was purchased from the Iroquois Confederation in 1754. It eventually became part of the Monroe Iron Works; charcoal was produced for use in the iron furnace, and there is some evidence of iron ore mining. It was purchased in 1868 by Osgood Whipple, who built a dam and sawmill and for whom the park is named.

★4088★ WHITE CLAY CREEK PRESERVE

PO Box 172
Landenberg, PA 19350
Web: www.dcnr.state.pa.us/stateparks/parks/
   whiteclaycreek.aspx
Phone: 610-274-2900
Size: 1,255 acres. **Location:** 3 miles north of Newark, Delaware, off Rt 896. **Facilities:** Hiking trails (3 miles), bike trails, bridle trails (8 miles). **Activities:** Fishing, hiking, bicycling, horseback riding, cross-country skiing, hunting. **Special Features:** Points of historical interest in and around the preserve include the Yeatman Mill House, the hub of a prosperous milling and agricultural complex in the 18th and 19th centuries; the London Tract Baptist Meetinghouse, built in 1729; and the tri-state Pennsylvania, Delaware, Maryland, and Arc Corner monuments, marking points along the Mason-Dixon Line.

★4089★ WORLDS END STATE PARK

PO Box 62
Forksville, PA 18616
Web: www.dcnr.state.pa.us/stateparks/parks/worldsend.aspx
Phone: 570-924-3287
Size: 780 acres. **Location:** On PA 154, in the northeast corner of the state. **Facilities:** 70 class A campsites, 19 rustic cabins, 3 group tent camps, showers, pit toilets, group tent camp, picnic area (&), picnic pavilions, hiking trails (20 miles), snowmobile trailhead and trails (3 miles), cross-country ski trail (20 miles), snack bar, swimming beach, rock garden, scenic overlooks, amphitheater. **Activities:** Camping, whitewater boating (closed-deck canoes and kayaks), fishing, swimming, hiking, hunting, cross-country skiing, snowmobiling, nature programs. **Special Features:** Park is located in a narrow S-shaped valley of the Loyalsock Creek. Worlds End vista, at the junction of Pioneer Road Trail and Worlds End Trail, is the view that may have inspired the name of the park.

★4090★ YELLOW CREEK STATE PARK

170 Rt 259 Hwy
Penn Run, PA 15765
Web: www.dcnr.state.pa.us/stateparks/parks/yellowcreek.aspx
Phone: 724-357-7913
Size: 2,981 acres. **Location:** Along 422, in the southwest corner of the state. **Facilities:** Camping cottages, picnic areas, picnic pavilions, snack bar, hiking trails (5 miles), snowmobile trails (350 acres), swimming beach, bathhouse, boat rentals, boat launch, boat mooring, fishing pier (&), playground, sledding area, scenic overlook. **Activities:** Camping, boating (20 HP limit), fishing, swimming, hiking, hunting, cross-country skiing, ice boating, ice fishing, ice skating, snowshoeing, snowmobiling, sledding, tobogganing, nature programs. **Special Features:** Park is located along one of the first ''highways'' in the state, the Kittanning Path. This trail was used by the Delaware and Shawnee Indians and by early settlers.

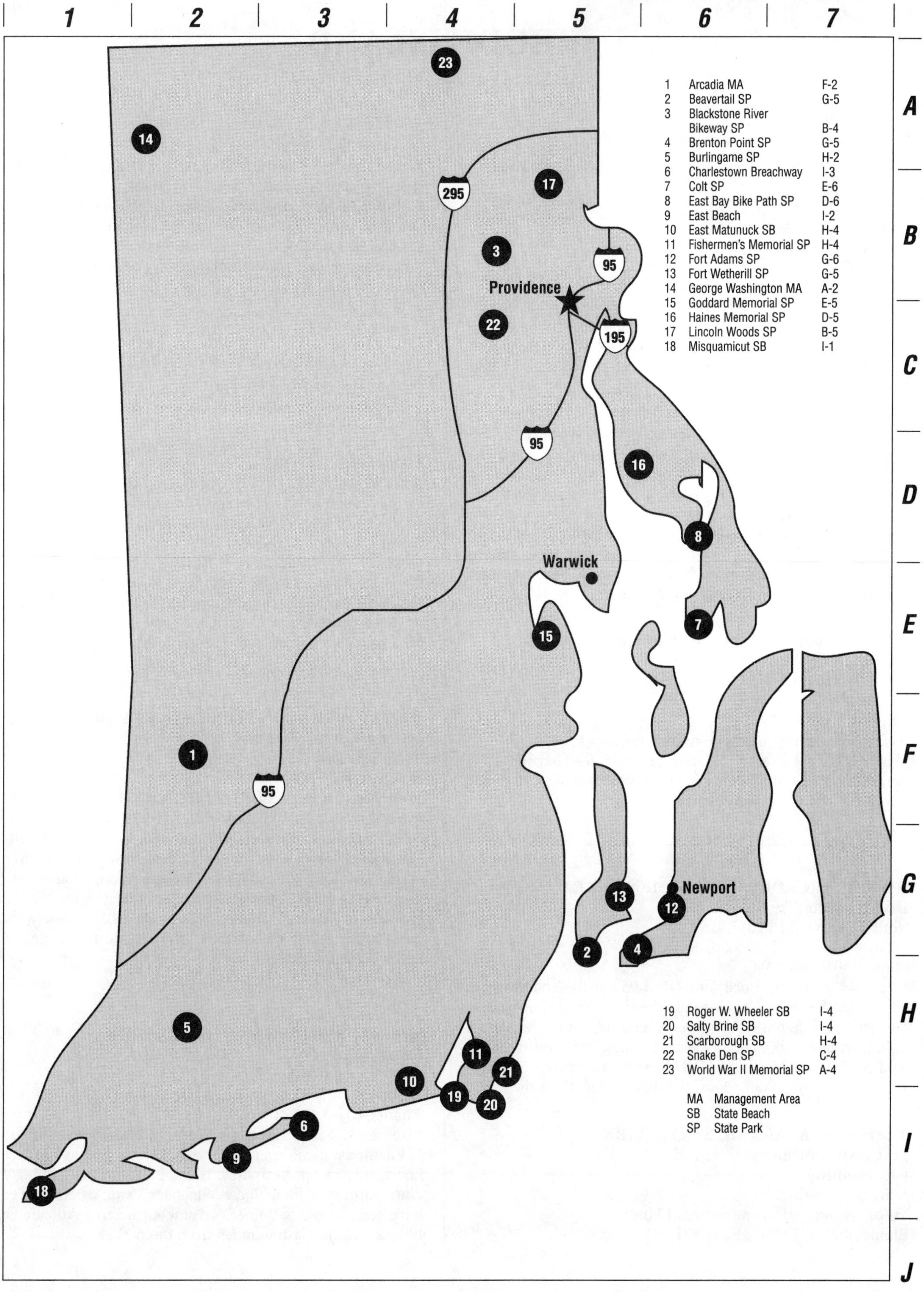

Rhode Island State Parks

1	Arcadia MA	F-2
2	Beavertail SP	G-5
3	Blackstone River Bikeway SP	B-4
4	Brenton Point SP	G-5
5	Burlingame SP	H-2
6	Charlestown Breachway	I-3
7	Colt SP	E-6
8	East Bay Bike Path SP	D-6
9	East Beach	I-2
10	East Matunuck SB	H-4
11	Fishermen's Memorial SP	H-4
12	Fort Adams SP	G-6
13	Fort Wetherill SP	G-5
14	George Washington MA	A-2
15	Goddard Memorial SP	E-5
16	Haines Memorial SP	D-5
17	Lincoln Woods SP	B-5
18	Misquamicut SB	I-1

19	Roger W. Wheeler SB	I-4
20	Salty Brine SB	I-4
21	Scarborough SB	H-4
22	Snake Den SP	C-4
23	World War II Memorial SP	A-4

MA	Management Area
SB	State Beach
SP	State Park

Providence

Warwick

Newport

RHODE ISLAND

★4091★ Rhode Island Division of Parks & Recreation
2321 Hartford Ave
Johnston, RI 02919
(401) 222-2632 - Phone
(401) 934-0610 - Fax
(401) 222-2774 - Employment
Web: www.riparks.com
Operates and maintains 19 parks, beaches, campgrounds, bicycle paths, a golf course, and many smaller parks and historical sites totaling approximately 14,000 acres. Oversees a comprehensive system of greenways and bike trails, with plans for more than 700 miles of interconnected trails.

★4092★ Rhode Island Division of Fish & Wildlife
4808 Tower Hill Rd
Wakefield, RI 02879
(401) 789-3094 - Phone
(401) 783-4460 - Fax
Web: www.dem.ri.gov/programs/bnatres/fishwild
Operates and manages 23 wildlife management areas totaling 45,000 acres, including more than 100 shore fishing areas and boat launching ramps throughout the state.

★4093★ Rhode Island Division of Forest Environment
1037 Hartford Pike
North Scituate, RI 02857
(401) 647-3367 - Phone
(401) 647-3590 - Fax
Web: www.dem.ri.gov/programs/bnatres/forest
Manages 40,000 acres of state-owned rural forestland, including limited recreational facilities at Arcadia Management Area and George Washington Management Area.

★4094★ ARCADIA MANAGEMENT AREA
1037 Hartford Pike
North Scituate, RI 02857
Web: www.riparks.com/arcadia.htm
Phone: 401-789-3094
Size: 14,000 acres. **Location:** Off I-95, in the southwestern portion of the state. **Facilities:** 3 camping areas, hiking trails, bike trails, bridle trails. **Activities:** Camping, hiking, horseback riding, mountain biking, canoeing, hunting (with restrictions), wildlife observation. **Special Features:** Rhode Island's 70-mile-long North-South Trail passes through the length of the area.

★4095★ BEAVERTAIL STATE PARK
c/o Goddard Memorial State Park
Beavertail Rd
Jamestown, RI 02835
Web: www.riparks.com/beaverta1.htm
Phone: 401-423-9941; **Fax:** 401-885-7720

Size: 153 acres. **Location:** South of Providence, off I-95. **Facilities:** Portable restrooms, scenic overlook. **Activities:** Fishing, hiking, naturalist programs (seasonal). **Special Features:** Beavertail is a premiere site for marine education. Tide pools are accessible for ecology or marine biology studies. Fault and associated gelogic features tell the story of ancient Rhode Island history.

★4096★ BLACKSTONE RIVER BIKEWAY
c/o Lincoln Woods State Park
2 Manchester Print Works Rd
Lincoln, RI 02865
Web: www.riparks.com/blacksto.htm
Phone: 401-723-7892
Size: 17-mile linear park (when completed). **Location:** Completed section is between Lonsdale and the George Washington Highway (Route 123). **Facilities:** Picnic area, restrooms (&), paved trail (&). **Activities:** Bicycling, jogging, roller blading, cross-country skiing. **Special Features:** Bikeway will run along the Blackstone Canal Towpath from Pawtucket through Woonsocket to the Massachusetts border. Route is slated to be part of the proposed East Coast Greenway, a series of connecting bike paths stretching from Florida to Maine.

★4097★ BRENTON POINT STATE PARK
c/o Fort Adams State Park
84 Adams Dr
Newport, RI 02840
Web: www.riparks.com/BRENTON.HTM
Phone: 401-847-2400; **Fax:** 401-841-9821
Size: 89 acres. **Location:** Off Route 138, in Newport. **Facilities:** Picnic area, concession, public gardens, restrooms, hiking trail, scenic overlooks. **Activities:** Fishing, hiking, naturalist programs (seasonal). **Special Features:** Located on the former grounds of one of Newport's grandest estates where Narragansett Bay meets the Atlantic, this parks offers commanding and spectacular views.

★4098★ BURLINGAME STATE PARK
Santuary Rd
Charlestown, RI 02813
Web: www.riparks.com/burlingastatepark.htm
Phone: 401-322-8910
Size: 2,672 acres. **Location:** North of Charlestown, off Route 1. **Facilities:** Picnic areas, picnic shelter, swimming beach, bathhouse, boat ramp. **Activities:** Boating, fishing, swimming. **Special Features:** Park includes Watchaug Pond, where bald eagles have been known to winter. Several outstanding Atlantic Ocean beaches are just a few miles from the park.

★4099★ CHARLESTOWN BREACHWAY

Charlestown Beach Rd
Charlestown, RI 02813
Web: www.riparks.com/charlesbreach.htm
Phone: 401-364-7000; Fax: 401-322-3083
Size: 62 acres. Location: South of Providence, off Route 1.
Facilities: 75 campsites, restrooms (&), boat ramp. Activities: Camping (no tents), boating, fishing, shellfishing, swimming. Special Features: The breachway is a prime spot for saltwater fishing and offers a panoramic view of Block Island Sound.

★4100★ COLT STATE PARK

Hope St
Bristol, RI 02809
Web: www.riparks.com/colt.htm
Phone: 401-253-7482; Fax: 401-253-6766
Size: 464 acres. Location: South of Providence on Route 114.
Facilities: Picnic areas, picnic shelter, fireplaces, bike trail, bridle trail, fitness trail, boat ramp (&), play fields, scenic overlook, restrooms (&), playgrounds, wedding chapel, gardens. Activities: Boating, fishing, hiking, bicycling, horseback riding, jogging, snowmobiling. Special Features: Western border of the park offers an open panorama onto Narragansett Bay. Park features 464 acres of groomed fruit trees, flowering bushes and manicured lawns, and the open-air Chapel-by-the-Sea.

★4101★ EAST BAY BIKE PATH

c/o Colt State Park
Hope St
Bristol, RI 02809
Web: www.riparks.com/eastbay.htm
Phone: 401-253-7482
Size: 14.5-mile linear park. Location: From Providence to Bristol along the abandoned railroad line. Facilities: Picnic areas, restrooms (&), paved trail (&). Activities: Bicycling, jogging, inline skating, cross-country skiing. Special Features: Path will eventually link with Blackstone River Bikeway (see separate entry). This rails-to-trails bikepath passes over bridges, through state parks, and along the shore of Narragansett Bay, affording riders the sights and smells of its coves and marshes.

★4102★ EAST BEACH

c/o Burlingame State Park
1 Burlingame State Park Rd
Charlestown, RI 02813
Web: www.riparks.com/eastbeach.htm
Phone: 401-322-0450; Fax: 401-322-3083
Size: 174 acres. Location: Off Route 1, in Charlestown. Facilities: 20 campsites (on barrier beach), portable toilets. Activities: Camping, boating, fishing, shellfishing, swimming, windsurfing. Special Features: A 3-mile-long barrier beach bordering Ninigret National Wildlife Refuge (see entry in national wildlife refuges section).

★4103★ EAST MATUNUCK STATE BEACH

950 Succotash Rd
South Kingstown, RI 02881
Web: www.riparks.com/eastmatunuck.htm
Phone: 401-789-8585
Size: 102 acres. Location: South of Providence on Route 1.
Facilities: Picnic area, pavilion, food concession, restrooms. Activities: Swimming. Special Features: Lifeguards are on duty during the summer months.

★4104★ FISHERMEN'S MEMORIAL STATE PARK

1011 Point Judith Rd
Narragansett, RI 02882
Web: www.riparks.com/fisherma.htm
Phone: 401-789-8374
Size: 91 acres. Location: South of Providence on Route 108.
Facilities: 182 campsites (40 with full hookups, 35 with no hookups), showers, restrooms, information center, playground, tennis courts, basketball courts, horseshoe pit. Activities: Camping, tennis, basketball, horseshoes. Special Features: Park offers a seaside village atmosphere where visitors find grass lawns, tree-lined paths, and activities for the whole family. Nearby are Scarborough, Roger Wheeler, and Salty Brine state beaches.

★4105★ FORT ADAMS STATE PARK

84 Adams Dr
Newport, RI 02840
Web: www.riparks.com/fortadams.htm
Phone: 401-847-2400; Fax: 401-841-9821
Size: 105 acres. Location: Off Route 138, at the mouth of the Newport Harbor. Facilities: Picnic areas, concessions, swimming beach, boat ramps, fishing piers, museum, sailing center, soccer fields, rugby field, showers, restrooms (&). Activities: Boating (sail and power boat), fishing, swimming, windsurfing, soccer, rugby, road races, summer concerts and festivals. Special Features: Other park facilities include: Sail Newport, a nonprofit community sailing facility offering sailboat instruction and rental to the general public, as well as regattas and other sailing events (for information call 401-849-6177); the Museum of Yachting, featuring displays of photographs, models, costumes, boats, and yachting memorabilia from the turn of the century (for information call 401-847-1018); and the Eisenhower House, a conference and seminar center overlooking Narragansett Bay (for information call 401-847-6740).

★4106★ FORT WETHERILL STATE PARK

c/o Goddard Memorial State Park
Ives Rd
Warwick, RI 02818
Web: www.riparks.com/fortweth.htm
Phone: 401-423-1771
Size: 62 acres. Location: South of Providence on Route 138.
Facilities: Picnic area, boat ramp, restrooms (seasonal), scenic overlooks. Activities: Boating, saltwater fishing, scuba diving, hiking. Special Features: Situated on 100-foot-high granite cliffs, park is a former coastal defense battery and training camp. Known for its spectacular view of Newport Harbor and the east passage of Narragansett Bay, park is a popular site for viewing tall ship events and America's Cup races. Exceptional scuba diving off the rocks of Fort Wetherill attracts divers from all over New England.

★4107★ GEORGE WASHINGTON MANAGEMENT AREA

2185 Putnam Pike
Gloucester, RI 02814
Phone: 401-568-2013
Size: 3,489 acres. **Location:** Off Route 44 in the towns of Burrillville and Gloucester. **Facilities:** Primitive tent and trailer campsites, 2 shelters, trails, picnic area, restrooms, boat ramp, beach. **Activities:** Camping, boating, swimming, fishing, hiking. **Special Features:** Management area is dominated by forest cover and contains two ponds and the Pulaski Wildlife Marsh.

★4108★ GODDARD MEMORIAL STATE PARK

1095 Ives Rd
Warwick, RI 02818
Web: www.riparks.com/goddard.htm
Phone: 401-884-2010; **Fax:** 401-885-7720
Size: 489 acres. **Location:** South of Providence off Route 4. **Facilities:** Picnic areas, concession stands, bridle trails, equestrian show area, swimming beach, bathhouse, beach picnic shelter, boat ramp, information center, 9-hole golf course, 11 game fields, performing arts center. **Activities:** Boating, fishing, swimming, windsurfing, hiking, horseback riding, road races, golf, ice skating, concerts and special events. **Special Features:** Once a private estate, the park includes 62 deciduous and 19 evergreen tree varieties, including red and white pine, Douglas fir, red and white oak, and larch. This tract has been described by the U.S. Forest Service as ''the finest example of private forestry in America.''

★4109★ HAINES MEMORIAL STATE PARK

c/o Colt State Park
Hope St
Bristol, RI 02809
Web: www.riparks.com/haines.htm
Phone: 401-433-3001; **Fax:** 401-253-6766
Size: 102 acres. **Location:** East of Providence on Veteran's Memorial Parkway. **Facilities:** Picnic areas, boat ramp (&), softball and baseball fields, restroom. **Activities:** Boating, fishing, picnicking. **Special Features:** East Bay Bike Path, from Providence to Bristol, passes through the park.

★4110★ LINCOLN WOODS STATE PARK

2 Manchester Print Works Rd
Lincoln, RI 02865
Web: www.riparks.com/lincoln.htm
Phone: 401-723-7892; **Fax:** 401-724-7951
Size: 627 acres. **Location:** Between Routes 146 and 123, near Providence. **Facilities:** Picnic areas and picnic shelters, concession stand, bridle trails, hiking trails, swimming beach, bathhouse, boat ramp, playfields, game fields, ice skating rink, showers, restrooms (&). **Activities:** Boating (with restrictions), fishing, swimming, hiking, horseback riding, snowmobiling, ice skating, road races. **Special Features:** Park is a popular getaway for northeastern Rhode Islanders and features a new stable and covered bridge.

★4111★ MISQUAMICUT STATE BEACH

c/o Burlingame State Park
1 Burlingame State Park Rd
Charlestown, RI 02813
Web: www.riparks.com/misquamicut.htm
Phone: 401-596-9097
Size: 152 acres. **Location:** Off Route 1, north of Westerly. **Facilities:** Picnic area, pavilion, beach, food concessions, showers, restrooms (&). **Activities:** Swimming. **Special Features:** A favorite surf beach among Rhode Island residents, Misquamicut is also a popular destination for visitors from Connecticut.

★4112★ ROGER W. WHEELER STATE BEACH

100 Sand Hill Cove Rd
Narragansett, RI 02882
Web: www.riparks.com/wheeler.htm
Phone: 401-789-3563
Size: 27 acres. **Location:** South of Providence off Route 108. **Facilities:** Picnic area, pavilion, beach, food concession, showers, restrooms (&), playground. **Activities:** Swimming, picnicking. **Special Features:** Beach is named in honor of Captain Roger W. Wheeler, who developed the Rhode Island State Life-Saving System.

★4113★ SALTY BRINE STATE BEACH

c/o Fishermen's Memorial State Park
1011 Point Judith Rd
Narragansett, RI 02882
Web: www.riparks.com/saltybrine.htm
Phone: 401-789-3563
Size: 1 acre. **Location:** Off Route 108 in Point Judith. **Facilities:** Restrooms, coastal exhibit, observation area, beach. **Activities:** Fishing, swimming. **Special Features:** During the Revolutionary War, British ships frequently sailed through the natural breachway and anchored here. The pier and surrounding area has long been used by fishermen and is a favorite spot for those who enjoy watching the boats come and go.

★4114★ SCARBOROUGH STATE BEACH

c/o Fishermen's Memorial State Park
1011 Point Judith Rd
Narragansett, RI 02882
Web: www.riparks.com/scarborough.htm
Phone: 401-789-2324
Size: 42 acres. **Location:** 35 miles south of Providence, off Route 108. **Facilities:** Picnic area, 2 pavilions, food concessions, showers, restrooms (&), gazebos, walkways with ocean view, park benches, observation tower. **Activities:** Swimming, beachcombing. **Special Features:** Rhode Island's most popular beach, it is made up of two parcels totalling 42 acres.

★4115★ SNAKE DEN STATE PARK

2321 Hartford Ave
Johnston, RI 02919
Web: www.riparks.com/snakeden.htm
Phone: 401-222-2632
Size: 1,000 acres. **Location:** From Providence, take I-295 north

9. State Parks

to Route 6. **Facilities:** Undeveloped. **Activities:** Hiking. **Special Features:** Park has self-guided walking trails and a working farm.

★4116★ **WORLD WAR II MEMORIAL STATE PARK**
c/o Lincoln Woods State Park
2 Manchester Print Works Rd
Lincoln, RI 02865
Web: www.riparks.com/worldwar.htm
Phone: 401-762-9717
Size: 14 acres. **Location:** North of Providence in Woonsocket. **Facilities:** Swimming beach, bathhouse, information office, 2 tennis courts, 2 volleyball courts, 2 horseshoe pits, playground, showers, restrooms, picnic area, pavilion, bandstand. **Activities:** Swimming, tennis, volleyball, horseshoes, shuffleboard, ice skating, concerts. **Special Features:** Park features a ''Monument of Peace'' honoring those who served in the Korean and Vietnam wars.

South Carolina State Parks

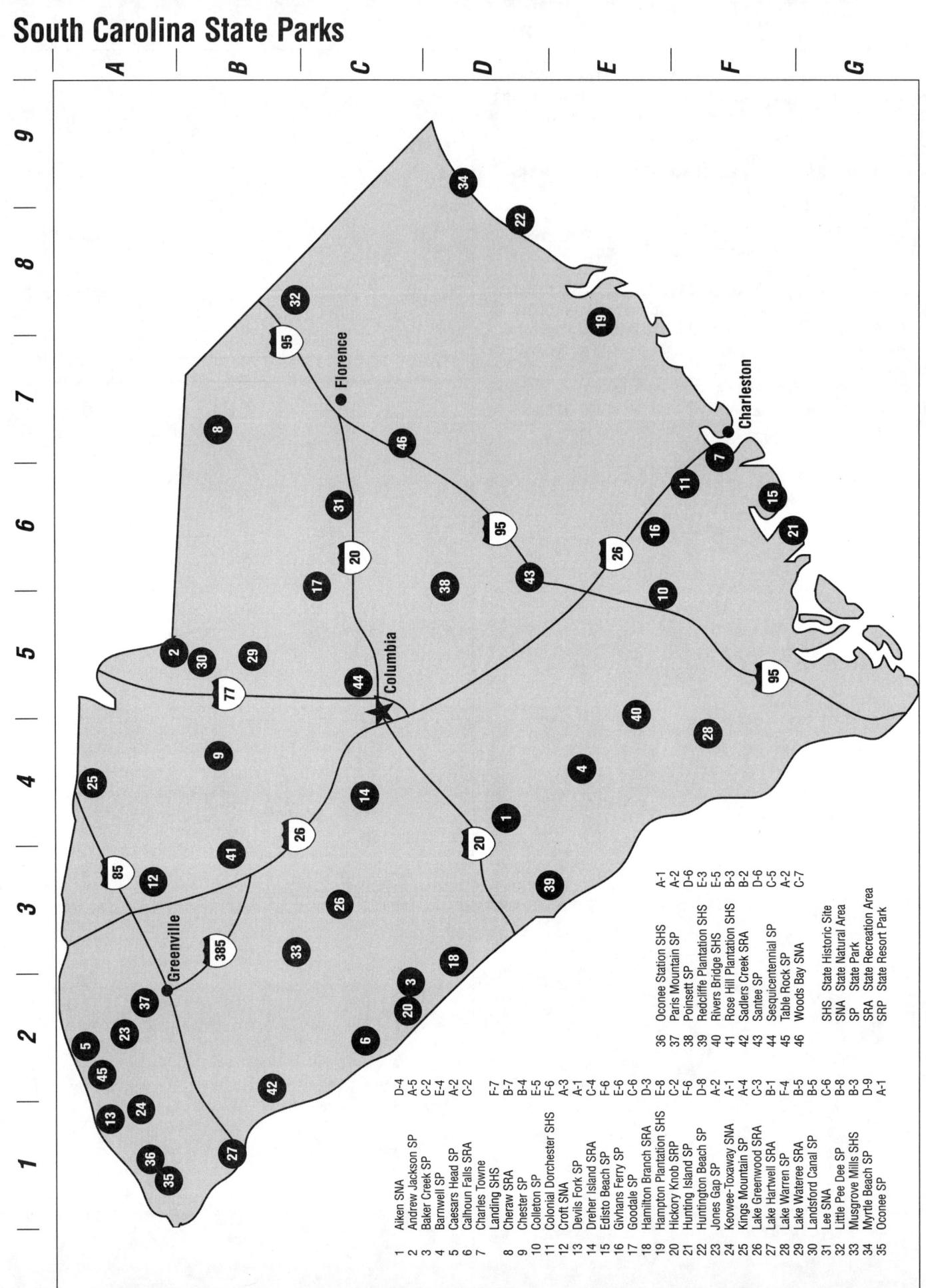

1	Aiken SNA	D-4
2	Andrew Jackson SP	A-5
3	Baker Creek SP	C-2
4	Barnwell SP	E-4
5	Caesars Head SP	A-2
6	Calhoun Falls SRA	C-2
7	Charles Towne	
	Landing SHS	F-7
8	Cheraw SRA	B-7
9	Chester SP	B-4
10	Colleton SP	E-5
11	Colonial Dorchester SHS	F-6
12	Croft SNA	A-3
13	Devils Fork SP	A-1
14	Dreher Island SRA	C-4
15	Edisto Beach SP	F-6
16	Givhans Ferry SP	E-6
17	Goodale SP	C-6
18	Hamilton Branch SRA	D-3
19	Hampton Plantation SHS	E-8
20	Hickory Knob SRP	C-2
21	Hunting Island SP	F-6
22	Huntington Beach SP	D-8
23	Jones Gap SP	A-2
24	Keowee-Toxaway SNA	A-1
25	Kings Mountain SP	A-4
26	Lake Greenwood SRA	C-3
27	Lake Hartwell SRA	B-1
28	Lake Warren SP	F-4
29	Lake Wateree SRA	B-5
30	Landsford Canal SP	B-5
31	Lee SNA	C-6
32	Little Pee Dee SP	B-8
33	Musgrove Mills SHS	B-3
34	Myrtle Beach SP	D-9
35	Oconee SP	A-1

36	Oconee Station SHS	A-1
37	Paris Mountain SP	A-2
38	Poinsett SP	D-6
39	Redcliffe Plantation SHS	E-3
40	Rivers Bridge SHS	E-5
41	Rose Hill Plantation SHS	B-3
42	Sadlers Creek SRA	B-2
43	Santee SP	D-6
44	Sesquicentennial SP	C-5
45	Table Rock SP	A-2
46	Woods Bay SNA	C-7

SHS	State Historic Site
SNA	State Natural Area
SP	State Park
SRA	State Recreation Area
SRP	State Resort Park

768

SOUTH CAROLINA

★4117★ **South Carolina State Park Service**
1205 Pendleton St
Columbia, SC 29201
(803) 734-0156 - Phone
(803) 734-1017 - Fax
(888) 224-9339- Toll-free
(803) 734-0156 Volunteering
Web: www.southcarolinaparks.com
Operates facilities and programs at 46 park properties and six historic properties, which together comprise more than 80,000 acres.

★4118★ **South Carolina Department of Natural Resources**
1000 Assembly St
Columbia, SC 29202
(803) 734-3886
Web: www.dnr.sc.gov
Administers boat registrations and hunting and fishing licensing. Offers safety education programs. Manages 39 wildlife management areas (which include 82,000 state-owned acres) and four regional hunt units covering more than 1.2 million acres.

★4119★ **South Carolina Forestry Commission**
5500 Broad River Rd
Columbia, SC 29212
(803) 896-8800 - Phone
(803) 798-8097 - Fax
Web: www.state.sc.us/forest
Protects forest resources through forest management practices, fire fighting and prevention, and educational services. Operates three state forests comprising approximately 72,000 acres. Recreation opportunities include horseback riding, mountain biking, off-highway vehicle riding, nature study, hunting, and target practice.

Key to campsite classification:

- **Campsites** — Most include water and electric hookups and picnic tables. Nearby are heated restroom facilities with hot showers. Each camping area has at least two sites reserved for disabled persons.
- **Cabins** — Furnished, heated, air-conditioned, supplied with linens and all necessary cookware and eating utensils. Cabin sizes vary, accommodating from 4 to 12 persons.

★4120★ **AIKEN STATE NATURAL AREA**
1145 State Park Rd
Windsor, SC 29856
Web: www.southcarolinaparks.com/park-finder/state-park/
1831.aspx
Phone: 803-649-2857
Size: 1,067 acres. **Location:** Off US 78, 32 miles from Augusta.
Facilities: 25 campsites, primitive group camp, picnic area, 3 picnic shelters, comfort station, hiking trails, canoe trail, lake beach, boat ramp, boat rentals, ballfield, playground. **Activities:** Camping, boating (non-motorized; no private boats), canoeing, fishing, swimming, hiking. **Special Features:** Four spring-fed lakes and the meandering South Edisto River make park popular with both fishermen and campers. This area is a combination of river swamp and dry sandhills, evidence of an era when the sea reached this far inland.

★4121★ **ANDREW JACKSON STATE PARK**
196 Andrew Jackson Park Rd
Lancaster, SC 29720
Web: www.southcarolinaparks.com/park-finder/state-park/
1797.aspx
Phone: 803-285-3344
Size: 360 acres. **Location:** On US 521, 9 miles north of Lancaster. **Facilities:** 25 campsites, primitive group camp, 2 picnic shelters, hiking trails, boat rentals, fishing pier (&), amphitheater, meeting house, playground, gift shop. **Activities:** Camping, boating (no private boats), fishing, hiking. **Special Features:** Created as a memorial to Andrew Jackson, seventh president of the United States, the park features a sculpture of young Jackson by Anna Hyatt Huntington and a replica of an 18th-century one-room schoolhouse.

★4122★ **BAKER CREEK STATE PARK**
Rt 1, Box 50
McCormick, SC 29835
Web: www.southcarolinaparks.com/park-finder/state-park/
1764.aspx
Phone: 864-443-2457
Size: 1,305 acres. **Location:** On US 378, 3 miles west of McCormick near the South Carolina-Georgia border. **Facilities:** 100 campsites, picnic area, primitive group camp, 2 picnic shelters, meeting pavilion, hiking trails, bike trails, lake beach, boat ramps, game courts, playground. **Activities:** Camping, boating, fishing, swimming (seasonal), mountain biking. **Special Features:** Park is located along the South Carolina Heritage Corridor, on Lake Thurmond.

★4123★ **BARNWELL STATE PARK**
223 State Park Rd
Blackville, SC 29817
Web: www.southcarolinaparks.com/park-finder/state-park/
1773.aspx
Phone: 803-284-2212

Size: 307 acres. **Location:** Off SC 3, 7 miles northeast of Barnwell. **Facilities:** 25 campsites, primitive group camp, 5 cabins, picnic area, 4 picnic shelters, interpretive trail, boat rentals, fishing pier, meeting facility, comfort station. **Activities:** Camping, boating (non-motorized; no private boats), fishing. **Special Features:** Located in the coastal plain, the park features two small lakes, good for largemouth bass, catfish, crappie, and bluegill fishing. The park was originally constructed by the Civilian Conservation Corps in the 1930s; examples of their work can be seen at the spillway, picnic shelters, and the lower lake.

★4124★ CAESARS HEAD STATE PARK

8155 Geer Hwy
Cleveland, SC 29635
Web: www.southcarolinaparks.com/park-finder/state-park/
1648.aspx
Phone: 864-836-6115; **Fax:** 864-836-3081
Size: 7,467 acres. **Location:** On US 276, 37 miles northwest of Greenville near the North Carolina border. **Facilities:** 24 primitive campsites, picnic area, picnic shelter, hiking trails (12 miles), visitor center, gift shop. **Activities:** Camping, fishing, hiking. **Special Features:** At 3,266 feet above sea level, Caesars Head affords panoramic views of the mountain country. This area of the Blue Ridge Escarpment ends in South Carolina with an abrupt drop of 2,000 feet to the foothills below, where the Piedmont region begins. The escarpment affords scenic vistas and waterfalls, and provides a protected environment for many rare and endangered plant and animal species.

★4125★ CALHOUN FALLS STATE RECREATION AREA

46 Maintenance Shop Rd
Calhoun Falls, SC 29628
Web: www.southcarolinaparks.com/park-finder/state-park/
1652.aspx
Phone: 864-447-8267; **Fax:** 864-447-8638
Size: 318 acres. **Location:** Near Calhoun Falls, off SC 81. **Facilities:** 86 campsites, 14 walk-in campsites, picnic areas, 2 picnic shelters, hiking trails, marina, boat ramps, boat rentals, fishing pier (&), lake beach, game courts, camp store (&), meeting facilities, playground, amphitheater, wildlife observation area. **Activities:** Camping, boating, fishing, hiking, tennis, swimming. **Special Features:** Located on 26,650-acre Lake Russell, one of South Carolina's most popular fishing lakes. The lake's coves support excellent fish habitats, offering anglers an abundance of bass, bluegill, crappie, catfish, and more.

★4126★ CHARLES TOWNE LANDING STATE HISTORIC SITE

1500 Old Towne Rd
Charleston, SC 29407
Web: www.southcarolinaparks.com/park-finder/state-park/
1575.aspx
Phone: 843-852-4200; **Fax:** 843-852-4205
Size: 664 acres. **Location:** West of the Ashley River, off SC 171, 3 miles northwest of Charleston. **Facilities:** Picnic area, picnic shelter, nature trails. **Activities:** Picnicking, historical

sites, hiking. **Special Features:** Site of the first English settlement (1670) in South Carolina, park features a natural habitat zoo, a replica of a 17th-century trading vessel, and an experimental crop garden. Site is listed on the *National Register of Historic Places*.

★4127★ CHERAW STATE PARK

100 State Park Rd
Cheraw, SC 29520
Web: www.southcarolinaparks.com/park-finder/state-park/
1554.aspx
Phone: 843-537-9656
Size: 7,361 acres. **Location:** 4 miles southwest of Cheraw, off US Highway 52. **Facilities:** 17 campsites, 2 group camps, horsemen's camp, 8 cabins, showers, 2 picnic shelters, hiking trail, bike trails, bridle trails, boat ramp, boat rentals, meeting building, 18-hole golf course, playground. **Activities:** Camping, boating (10 hp limit), fishing, hiking, biking, horseback riding **Special Features:** Originally developed in the 1930s by the Civilian Conservation Corps (CCC), park protects habitat for the threatened Red Cockaded woodpecker. A number of the buildings built by the CCC are still in use.

★4128★ CHESTER STATE PARK

759 State Park Dr
Chester, SC 29706
Web: www.southcarolinaparks.com/park-finder/state-park/
1564.aspx
Phone: 803-385-2680
Size: 523 acres. **Location:** On SC 72, 2 miles southwest of Chester. **Facilities:** 25 campsites, primitive group camp, picnic area, 3 picnic shelters, comfort station, hiking trails, boat rentals, archery range, meeting building, amphitheater, playground. **Activities:** Camping, boating, fishing, horseback riding, hiking, archery. **Special Features:** Park includes a 160-acre lake that offers excellent fishing opportunities. The lake is surrounded by a nature trail that winds through pine forest.

★4129★ COLLETON STATE PARK

147 Wayside Ln
Canadys, SC 29433
Web: www.southcarolinaparks.com/park-finder/state-park/
1876.aspx
Phone: 843-538-8206
Size: 35 acres. **Location:** On US 15, 11 miles north of Walterboro. **Facilities:** 25 campsites, primitive group camp, picnic area, 2 picnic shelters, hiking trail, canoe trail, boat ramp, playground. **Activities:** Camping, canoeing, kayaking, fishing, hiking. **Special Features:** The section of the Edisto River that passes through the park has been designated the state's first canoe and kayak trail. (The Edisto River is the world's longest free-flowing blackwater river.)

★4130★ COLONIAL DORCHESTER STATE HISTORIC SITE

300 State Park Rd
Summerville, SC 29485
Web: www.southcarolinaparks.com/park-finder/state-park/
725.aspx
Phone: 843-873-1740

Size: 325 acres. **Location:** On SC 642, 4 miles south of Summerville. **Facilities:** Picnic area, interpretive trail, interpretive exhibits, historic features. **Activities:** Historical programs. **Special Features:** This historic park is the site of a colonial village founded in 1697 and includes the brick bell tower of St. George's Anglican Church and a fort made of oyster-shell concrete. A small outdoor kiosk explains the history of Dorchester and the upper Ashley River area. Park visitors can observe on-going archeological excavations of the village.

★4131★ CROFT STATE NATURAL AREA

450 Croft State Park Rd
Spartanburg, SC 29302
Web: www.southcarolinaparks.com/park-finder/state-park/
1443.aspx
Phone: 864-585-1283
Size: 7,054 acres. **Location:** Off SC 56, 5 miles from Spartanburg. **Facilities:** 50 campsites, primitive group camp, comfort station, picnic area, 3 picnic shelters, hiking trails, bike trails, bridle trails, stable, equestrian show ring, boat rentals, boat ramp, playground. **Activities:** Camping, boating (no gas motors), fishing, horseback riding, hiking. **Special Features:** Once part of a World War II Army training camp known as Camp Croft, park includes remnants of a Native American soapstone quarry, registered as a Heritage Trust site.

★4132★ DEVILS FORK STATE PARK

161 Holcombe Cir
Salem, SC 29676
Web: www.southcarolinaparks.com/park-finder/state-park/
1355.aspx
Phone: 864-944-2639; **Fax:** 864-944-8777
Size: 622 acres. **Location:** Off SC 11, on Lake Jocassee. **Facilities:** 59 campsites with water and electric hookups, 25 walk-in tent campsites, boat-in backcountry campsites, 20 villas (&), 2 picnic shelters, hiking trails, boat ramps, camp store, gift shop, playground. **Activities:** Camping, boating, fishing, hiking. **Special Features:** Against a backdrop of the Blue Ridge Mountains, the park sits along the shore of Lake Jocassee, which offers excellent fishing for trout, smallmouth bass, bluegill, and black crappie.

★4133★ DREHER ISLAND STATE RECREATION
  AREA

3677 State Park Rd
Prosperity, SC 29127
Web: www.southcarolinaparks.com/park-finder/state-park/
1371.aspx
Phone: 803-364-4152; **Fax:** 803-364-0756
Size: 348 acres. **Location:** 30 miles northwest of Columbia; 12 miles off I-26, via Chapin exit 91. **Facilities:** 112 campsites, primitive group camp, 5 villas (&), picnic area, 14 picnic shelters, hiking trails, bike trail, lake beach, marina, boat ramps, fuel dock, tackle shop, meeting building (&), park store, playground. **Activities:** Camping, boating, fishing, swimming, hiking, biking. **Special Features:** Made up of three islands linked to the mainland by a causeway and two bridges, park is on 50,000-acre Lake Murray and includes 12 miles of shoreline.

★4134★ EDISTO BEACH STATE PARK

8377 State Cabin Rd
Edisto Island, SC 29438
Web: www.southcarolinaparks.com/park-finder/state-park/
1298.aspx
Phone: 843-869-2756; **Fax:** 843-869-4428
Size: 1,255 acres. **Location:** On SC 174, in the extreme eastern part of the state. **Facilities:** 111 campsites, 7 cabins, picnic area, 2 picnic shelters, interpretive trails, ocean beach, boat ramps, dock, fishing pier, nature center, gift shop, playground. **Activities:** Camping, boating, fishing, swimming, hiking, interpretive programs (seasonal). **Special Features:** Beachfront park contains some of the tallest palmetto trees in the state. Visitors can enjoy observing life in the salt marsh and combing the beach for seashells and fossils.

★4135★ GIVHANS FERRY STATE PARK

746 Givhans Ferry Rd
Ridgeville, SC 29472
Web: www.southcarolinaparks.com/park-finder/state-park/
1219.aspx
Phone: 843-873-0692
Size: 988 acres. **Location:** Off I-95, 35 miles from Charleston. **Facilities:** 25 campsites, primitive group camp, 4 cabins, restrooms with showers, picnic area, 2 picnic shelters, hiking trail, canoe trail, meeting building, comfort station. **Activities:** Camping, fishing, boating, hiking, interpretive programs. **Special Features:** Park sits on a high bluff overlooking the Edisto River, which is the longest free-flowing blackwater river on the continent. The Park is on the stretch known as the Edisto River Canoe and Kayak Trail. The park's riverbanks are protected as a Heritage Trust site because of several species of rare plants that live there.

★4136★ GOODALE STATE PARK

650 Park Rd
Camden, SC 29020
Web: www.southcarolinaparks.com/park-finder/state-park/
1199.aspx
Phone: 803-432-2772
Size: 763 acres. **Location:** Off I-95, in the north central portion of the state. **Facilities:** Picnic area, 2 picnic shelters, interpretive trail, boat rentals, meeting building (&), playground. **Activities:** Boating (no gas motors), fishing, hiking. **Special Features:** Park's lake, formerly a mill pond that dates back to Civil War days, features cypress trees and a variety of wildlife and plant life.

★4137★ HAMILTON BRANCH STATE RECREATION
  AREA

111 Campground Rd
Plum Branch, SC 29845
Web: www.southcarolinaparks.com/park-finder/state-park/
1188.aspx
Phone: 864-333-2223
Size: 731 acres. **Location:** Off I-20, near the western border of the state. **Facilities:** 140 campsites, primitive group camp, picnic

shelters, hiking trail, bike trails, boat ramps, playground. **Activities:** Camping, boating, fishing, hiking, mountain biking. **Special Features:** Area is located in the western Piedmont, on Strom Thurmond Lake. The park covers an entire peninsula, so most of its campsites are lakefront.

★4138★ HAMPTON PLANTATION STATE HISTORIC SITE

1950 Rutledge Rd
McClellanville, SC 29458
Web: www.southcarolinaparks.com/park-finder/state-park/ 1142.aspx
Phone: 843-546-9361; **Fax:** 843-527-4995
Size: 337 acres. **Location:** Off US 17, 16 miles southwest of Georgetown. **Facilities:** Picnic area, picnic shelter, hiking trails, historic home, gift shop. **Activities:** Guided tours. **Special Features:** In the 18th and 19th centuries, Hampton Plantation was a working rice plantation. Interpretive programming at the site focuses on the Lowcountry rice culture and plantation system.

★4139★ HICKORY KNOB STATE RESORT PARK

Rt 4, Box 199-B
McCormick, SC 29835
Web: www.southcarolinaparks.com/park-finder/state-park/ 1109.aspx
Phone: 864-391-2450; **Fax:** 864-391-5390
Size: 1,091 acres. **Location:** Off US 378, 8 miles west of McCormick, at the South Carolina-Georgia border. **Facilities:** 44 campsites, 18 cabins, 77-room lodge, restaurant, hiking trails, bike trails, boat rentals, boat ramps, docks, tackle shop, 18-hole golf course, swimming pool, archery range, skeet range, tennis court, meeting facilities, game courts, gift shop, playground. **Activities:** Camping, boating, fishing, archery, skeet shooting, golf, tennis, swimming. **Special Features:** In addition to its numerous amenities, South Carolina's only resort park also offers visitors the opportunity to stay in Guillebeau House, a restored French Huguenot style house. Park sits alongside 70,000-acre Strom Thurmond Lake.

★4140★ HUNTING ISLAND STATE PARK

2555 Sea Island Pkwy
Hunting Island, SC 29920
Web: www.southcarolinaparks.com/park-finder/state-park/ 1019.aspx
Phone: 843-838-2011; **Fax:** 843-838-4263
Size: 5,000 acres. **Location:** On US 21, in the southeastern portion of the state. **Facilities:** 173 campsites, 10 trail sites, 14 cabins (1 ♿), primitive group camp, picnic shelter, hiking trails, bridle trail, boardwalk trail, bike trails, ocean beach, boat ramp, fishing pier, nature center, gift shop, camp store, playground, lighthouse. **Activities:** Camping, boating, fishing, swimming, hiking, biking, horseback riding. **Special Features:** Park is a barrier island with one of the last remaining 19th-century lighthouses on the South Atlantic coast. The lighthouse and its complex are listed on the *National Register of Historic Places.*

★4141★ HUNTINGTON BEACH STATE PARK

16148 Ocean Hwy
Murrells Inlet, SC 29576
Web: www.southcarolinaparks.com/park-finder/state-park/ 1020.aspx
Phone: 843-237-4440; **Fax:** 843-237-3387
Size: 2,500 acres. **Location:** On US 17, 3 miles south of Murrells Inlet. **Facilities:** 131 campsites, primitive group camp, 6 walk-in tent sites, picnic area, 3 picnic shelters, boardwalk trails, hiking trails, ocean beach, historic house, education center, park store/gift shop. **Activities:** Camping, boating, fishing, swimming, hiking, birding, guided tours, interpretive programs. **Special Features:** Park has the best preserved beach on the Grand Strand and provides prime habitat for birds, making it one of the best birding sites along the East Coast. The park is also the site of ''Atalaya'' castle, a National Historic Landmark that was the winter home and studio of noted American sculptor Anna Hyatt Huntington.

★4142★ JONES GAP STATE PARK

303 Jones Gap Rd
Marietta, SC 29661
Web: www.southcarolinaparks.com/park-finder/state-park/ 962.aspx
Phone: 864-836-3647
Size: 3,346 acres. **Location:** Off US 276, 11 miles northwest of Marietta. **Facilities:** 24 trailside campsites, hiking trails, nature center, fish hatchery. **Activities:** Camping, hiking, backpacking, river fishing (artificial lures only), interpretive programs. **Special Features:** Park is located in one of South Carolina's most pristine wildernesses—the 10,000-acre Mountain Bridge Wilderness Area—and includes the Middle Saluda River, the state's first scenic river. Jones Gap offers access to the Foothills Trail; more than 400 species of flora, including rare and endangered plants and state record trees, are also found here.

★4143★ KEOWEE-TOXAWAY STATE NATURAL AREA

108 Residence Dr
Sunset, SC 29685
Web: www.southcarolinaparks.com/park-finder/state-park/ 972.aspx
Phone: 864-868-2605
Size: 1,000 acres. **Location:** On SC 11 at Lake Keowee, near the Georgia border. **Facilities:** 24 campsites, trailside campsites, cabin, 5 picnic shelters, interpretive trail, hiking trails, museum, gift shop, education center. **Activities:** Camping, fishing, boating, hiking, backpacking. **Special Features:** Park is located in an area of rock outcroppings and views of the Foothills and Blue Ridge Mountains. The history of South Carolina's Upper Cherokee Indians, who once lived in this area, is interpreted in the park museum.

★4144★ KINGS MOUNTAIN STATE PARK

1277 Park Rd
Blacksburg, SC 29702
Web: www.southcarolinaparks.com/park-finder/state-park/ 945.aspx
Phone: 803-222-3209; **Fax:** 803-222-6948

Size: 6,883 acres. **Location:** On SC 161, on the border with North Carolina. **Facilities:** 115 campsites, 10 tent sites, primitive group camps, 2 group camps, cabins, horsemen's camp, bathhouse, comfort stations, 5 picnic shelters, hiking trails, bridle trails, boat rentals, museum, camp store, laundry, playground, living history farm. **Activities:** Camping, boating (no private boats), canoeing, fishing, hiking, horseback riding, guided tours, interpretive programs. **Special Features:** Park is adjacent to Kings Mountain National Military Park (see separate entry in national parks section), a prominent Revolutionary War battle site. A living history farm at the park illustrates the lifestyle of early pioneers.

★4145★ LAKE GREENWOOD STATE RECREATION AREA
302 State Park Rd
Ninety Six, SC 29666
Web: www.southcarolinaparks.com/park-finder/state-park/ 926.aspx
Phone: 864-543-3535
Size: 914 acres. **Location:** On SC 702, 17 miles east of Greenwood. **Facilities:** 125 campsites, 5 tent sites, primitive group camp, 4 picnic shelters, hiking trails, boat ramps, fishing pier (&), playground, meeting building, education center. **Activities:** Camping, boating, fishing. **Special Features:** Park covers five peninsulas that provide 212 miles of shoreline. The park was built in 1938 by the Civilian Conservation Corps, and evidence of their craftsmanship can still be seen in two of the park's picnic shelters, the retaining wall at the lake, a boathouse, and a water fountain.

★4146★ LAKE HARTWELL STATE RECREATION AREA
19138-A S Hwy 11
Fair Play, SC 29643
Web: www.southcarolinaparks.com/park-finder/state-park/ 927.aspx
Phone: 864-972-3352
Size: 680 acres. **Location:** On SC 11 in Fair Play, near the South Carolina-Georgia border. **Facilities:** 117 campsites, 13 walk-in sites, picnic shelter (&), boat ramps, camp store, playground. **Activities:** Camping, boating, fishing. **Special Features:** Park includes 14 miles of shoreline on 56,000-acre Lake Hartwell.

★4147★ LAKE WARREN STATE PARK
1079 Lake Warren Rd
Hampton, SC 29924
Web: www.southcarolinaparks.com/park-finder/state-park/ 935.aspx
Phone: 803-943-5051; **Fax:** 803-943-4736
Size: 440 acres. **Location:** Off US 601, 5 miles southwest of Hampton. **Facilities:** Primitive group camp, 3 picnic shelters, interpretive trail, boat ramps, floating dock, meeting building (&), playground. **Activities:** Boating (10 HP limit), fishing, camping, hiking. **Special Features:** Park includes a 200-acre lake and large tracts of wetlands and woodlands that support a wide range of plant species and animals.

★4148★ LAKE WATEREE STATE RECREATION AREA
881 State Park Rd
Winnsboro, SC 29180
Web: www.southcarolinaparks.com/park-finder/state-park/ 936.aspx
Phone: 803-482-6401; **Fax:** 803-482-6126
Size: 238 acres. **Location:** 5 miles off US 21, in the north central portion of the state. **Facilities:** 72 campsites, restrooms with showers, picnic area, nature trails, boat ramps, tackle shop, playground. **Activities:** Camping, boating, fishing, hiking. **Special Features:** Lake Wateree is one of South Carolina's premier fishing lakes, with more than 13,700 surface acres. Wateree Dam was completed in 1919, making the lake one of the oldest reservoirs in the state.

★4149★ LANDSFORD CANAL STATE PARK
2051 Park Dr
Catawba, SC 29704
Web: www.southcarolinaparks.com/park-finder/state-park/ 916.aspx
Phone: 803-789-5800
Size: 244 acres. **Location:** Off US 21, 15 miles west of Lancaster. **Facilities:** Picnic shelter, hiking trails, canoe access point, education center, historic features, meeting building (&), playground. **Activities:** Canoeing, fishing, interpretive programs, hiking. **Special Features:** Landsford Canal, the best preserved of numerous 19th-century South Carolina river canals, is the uppermost of four canals built on the Catawba-Wateree river system between 1820 and 1835. The park includes the historic ruins of canal culverts, stone bridges, locks, a mill site, and a lockkeeper's house that contains interpretive exhibits on South Carolina's canal system.

★4150★ LEE STATE NATURAL AREA
487 Loop Rd
Bishopville, SC 29010
Web: www.southcarolinaparks.com/park-finder/state-park/ 891.aspx
Phone: 803-428-5307
Size: 2,839 acres. **Location:** 1 mile north of Exit 23 off I-20. **Facilities:** 25 campsites, primitive group camp, horsemen's camp, 2 picnic shelters, hiking trails, bridle trail, stable, playground, education center. **Activities:** Camping, canoeing, fishing, hiking, horseback riding, birding, interpretive programs. **Special Features:** Area serves as a gateway to the scenic Lynches River, a designated state scenic river. Diverse habitats include hardwood floodplain forest, artesian springs, a millpond, and sandhills.

★4151★ LITTLE PEE DEE STATE PARK
1298 State Park Rd
Dillon, SC 29536
Web: www.southcarolinaparks.com/park-finder/state-park/ 881.aspx
Phone: 843-774-8872
Size: 835 acres. **Location:** Off SC 57, 11 miles southeast of Dillon. **Facilities:** 50 campsites, primitive group camp, 2 picnic

shelters, comfort station, nature trail, lake beach, boat ramp, boat rentals, low ropes course, playground. **Activities:** Camping, boating, fishing, hiking, wildlife viewing. **Special Features:** Park includes 54-acre Lake Norton, the Little Pee Dee River, a small river swamp, and a tract of a Heritage Trust Site that includes a Carolina Bay.

★4152★ MUSGROVE MILL STATE HISTORIC SITE

398 State Park Rd
Clinton, SC 29325
Web: www.southcarolinaparks.com/park-finder/state-park/
3888.aspx
Phone: 864-938-0100
Size: 358 acres. **Location:** Off SC 56, in the northwestern portion of the state. **Facilities:** Interpretive center, trail. **Activities:** Interpretive walk. **Special Features:** The park and its interpretive center are a hub for the Cradle of Democracy project, which seeks to understand South Carolina's pivotal role in the creation of the nation. A Revolutionary War battle that took place here exemplified the ''hit and run'' tactics used by the Patriot militia fighting in the upcountry.

★4153★ MYRTLE BEACH STATE PARK

4401 S Kings Hwy
Myrtle Beach, SC 29575
Web: www.southcarolinaparks.com/park-finder/state-park/
795.aspx
Phone: 843-238-5325
Size: 312 acres. **Location:** On US 17, 4 miles south of Myrtle Beach, on the coast. **Facilities:** 302 campsites, 5 cabins, 2 apartments, overflow campsites, 7 picnic shelters, nature trail, bridle trail, ocean beach, fishing pier, boardwalk (♿), butterfly garden, education center, camp store, gift shop, playground, laundry. **Activities:** Camping, boating, fishing, swimming, horseback riding, hiking, birding, guided tours, interpretive programs. **Special Features:** Located in the heart of the Grand Strand, Myrtle Beach is one of the state's most popular public beaches and contains one of the last remaining stands of maritime forest on the northern coast of the state.

★4154★ OCONEE STATE PARK

624 State Park Rd
Mountain Rest, SC 29664
Web: www.southcarolinaparks.com/park-finder/state-park/
750.aspx
Phone: 864-638-5353; **Fax:** 864-638-8776
Size: 1,165 acres. **Location:** On SC 107, 12 miles northwest of Walhalla. **Facilities:** 155 campsites, 19 cabins (♿), primitive group camp, 4 picnic shelters, hiking trails, lake beach, boat rentals, comfort stations, museum, camp store, recreation building (♿), meeting rooms, laundry, playground. **Activities:** Camping, boating (no private boats), fishing, swimming, hiking, miniature golf (seasonal). **Special Features:** Situated on a plateau, this popular mountain park includes two small fishing lakes that include bass, bream, and catfish, as well as stocked trout during the winter months. Park is near the western terminus of the Foothills Trail.

★4155★ OCONEE STATION STATE HISTORIC SITE

500 Oconee Station Rd
Walhalla, SC 29691
Web: www.southcarolinaparks.com/park-finder/state-park/
1887.aspx
Phone: 864-638-0079
Size: 210 acres. **Location:** 2 miles off SC 11 in the extreme western tip of the state. **Facilities:** Interpretive trail, bike trail, historic features. **Activities:** Fishing, hiking, biking, interpretive programs. **Special Features:** Park contains two historic structures: a stone blockhouse (fort) constructed in 1792 and known as Oconee Station, and a two-story brick residence built in 1805 and known as the William Richards House. The site is listed on the *National Register of Historic Places.*

★4156★ PARIS MOUNTAIN STATE PARK

2401 State Park Rd
Greenville, SC 29609
Web: www.southcarolinaparks.com/park-finder/state-park/
722.aspx
Phone: 864-244-5565; **Toll Free:** 866-345-7275
Size: 1,540 acres. **Location:** Off US 25, 9 miles north of Greenville, near the northern border. **Facilities:** 39 campsites, primitive group camp, group lodge, 10 primitive cabins, 7 picnic shelters, hiking trails, bike trail, lake beach, boat rentals, meeting rooms, playground. **Activities:** Camping, boating (no private boats), fishing, hiking, mountain biking. **Special Features:** Paris Mountain is one of the oldest protected areas in the state, well known for its stands of old growth hardwood forests. Originally built in the 1930s by the Civilian Conservation Corps, many of the park's buildings feature the CCC's rustic style of architecture and stonework.

★4157★ POINSETT STATE PARK

6660 Poinsett Park Rd
Wedgefield, SC 29168
Web: www.southcarolinaparks.com/park-finder/state-park/
662.aspx
Phone: 803-494-8177
Size: 1,000 acres. **Location:** Off SC 261, near Wedgefield, in the north central part of the state. **Facilities:** 50 campsites, 4 cabins, primitive group camp, horsemen's camp, picnic area, 5 picnic shelters, hiking trails, bike trail, bridle trail, lake beach, boat rentals, comfort stations. **Activities:** Camping, boating, fishing, hiking, biking, horseback riding. **Special Features:** Located on the edge of the Wateree Swamp, this secluded park combines mountainous rolling terrain with moss-draped trees of the swampland. Some park trails lead into the adjacent Manchester State Forest and end at Mill Creek County Park.

★4158★ REDCLIFFE PLANTATION STATE HISTORIC SITE

181 Redcliffe Rd
Beech Island, SC 29842
Web: www.southcarolinaparks.com/park-finder/state-park/
2015.aspx
Phone: 803-827-1473
Size: 369 acres. **Location:** 14 miles off I-20, in the central part

of the western coast. **Facilities:** Hiking trail (2.5 miles), historic home, gift shop. **Activities:** Guided tours, fishing, interpretive programs. **Special Features:** Completed in 1859, Redcliffe was the home of South Carolina Governor James Henry Hammond and three generations of his descendants. It is listed on the *National Register of Historic Places*.

★4159★ RIVERS BRIDGE STATE HISTORIC SITE

325 State Park Rd
Ehrhardt, SC 29801
Web: www.southcarolinaparks.com/park-finder/state-park/566.aspx
Phone: 803-267-3675
Size: 390 acres. **Location:** 7 miles southwest of Ehrhardt and 13 miles east of Allendale off SC 641. **Facilities:** Picnic shelters, interpretive trail, historic features, meeting building. **Activities:** boating, hiking, interpretive programs. **Special Features:** Park is the site of one of the Confederacy's last stands against General William T. Sherman's sweep across the South. Rivers Bridge is on the *National Register of Historic Places* and is the only state historic site in South Carolina that commemorates the Civil War.

★4160★ ROSE HILL PLANTATION STATE HISTORIC SITE

2677 Sardis Rd
Union, SC 29379
Web: www.southcarolinaparks.com/park-finder/state-park/540.aspx
Phone: 864-427-5966
Size: 44 acres. **Location:** 10 miles from Union on Hwy 49, in the north central portion of the state. **Facilities:** Picnic shelter, nature trails, historic house. **Activities:** Interpretive programs, guided tours. **Special Features:** Site preserves the former home of South Carolina's "Secession Governor," William H. Gist. Tours of the house focus on plantation life from 1828-1860.

★4161★ SADLERS CREEK STATE RECREATION AREA

940 Sadlers Creek Rd
Anderson, SC 29626
Web: www.southcarolinaparks.com/park-finder/state-park/1888.aspx
Phone: 864-226-8950
Size: 395 acres. **Location:** Off SC 187, in the northwestern portion of the state. **Facilities:** 47 campsites, primitive group camp, 2 picnic shelters, hiking trails, bike trail, boat ramps, meeting buildings (&), playground. **Activities:** Camping, boating, fishing, hiking, biking. **Special Features:** Park sits on a peninsula jutting into 56,000-acre Lake Hartwell.

★4162★ SANTEE STATE PARK

251 State Park Rd
Santee, SC 29142
Web: www.southcarolinaparks.com/park-finder/state-park/535.aspx
Phone: 803-854-2408; **Fax:** 803-854-4834

Size: 2,500 acres. **Location:** Off SC 6, 1 mile west of Santee. **Facilities:** 158 campsites, 30 cabins (&), primitive group camp, laundry, 6 picnic shelters, hiking trails, bike trail, boat rentals, boat ramps, fishing pier (&), visitor center (&), tackle shop, meeting building, game courts, playground. **Activities:** Camping, boating, fishing, hiking, bicycling, tennis, interpretive programs. **Special Features:** Park is located on Lake Marion, one of two Santee Cooper lakes (the other is Lake Moultrie) created when more than 100,000 acres were flooded for electric power. The lake's flooded forest is across from the park.

★4163★ SESQUICENTENNIAL STATE PARK

9564 Two Notch Rd
Columbia, SC 29223
Web: www.southcarolinaparks.com/park-finder/state-park/469.aspx
Phone: 803-788-2706; **Fax:** 803-788-4414; **Toll Free:** 866-788-4414
Size: 1,419 acres. **Location:** 3 miles from I-20, in the north central portion of the state. **Facilities:** 87 campsites, primitive group camp, picnic area, 5 picnic shelters, hiking trails, bike trail, lake beach, boat rentals, nature center, retreat center, playground. **Activities:** Camping, boating (non-motorized; no private boats), fishing, swimming, hiking, biking. **Special Features:** Park is situated in the middle of the sandhills region and features a 30-acre lake surrounded by trails and picnic areas. A new feature of the park is a 2-acre fenced-in dog park where dogs can run off-leash.

★4164★ TABLE ROCK STATE PARK

158 E Ellison Ln
Pickens, SC 29671
Web: www.southcarolinaparks.com/park-finder/state-park/350.aspx
Phone: 864-878-9813; **Fax:** 864-878-9077
Size: 3,083 acres. **Location:** On SC 11, in the northwestern corner of the state. **Facilities:** 94 campsites, 6 trailside campsites, 3 primitive group camps, 14 cabins (&), comfort stations, 4 picnic shelters, hiking trails (14 miles), lake beach, boat rentals, boat ramp, fishing pier (&), camp store, meeting building, recreation center, playground. **Activities:** Camping, boating (non-motorized), fishing, swimming, hiking. **Special Features:** Table Rock Mountain provides a towering backdrop for this upcountry retreat at the edge of the Blue Ridge Escarpment. The entire park, including the mountain, is listed on the *National Register of Historic Places* and is also a South Carolina Heritage Trust Site.

★4165★ WOODS BAY STATE NATURAL AREA

11020 Woods Bay Rd
Olanta, SC 29114
Web: www.southcarolinaparks.com/park-finder/state-park/216.aspx
Phone: 843-659-4445
Size: 1,540 acres. **Location:** On Hwy 50, in the northeastern

portion of the state. **Facilities:** Picnic shelter, nature trail, canoe trail, canoe rentals, nature center (&). **Activities:** Canoeing, fishing, hiking, interpretive programs. **Special Features:** Visitors can observe a variety of plant and animal life from a boardwalk trail that passes through the dense swamp of the park's Carolina Bay. Park is a Heritage Trust site.

South Dakota State Parks

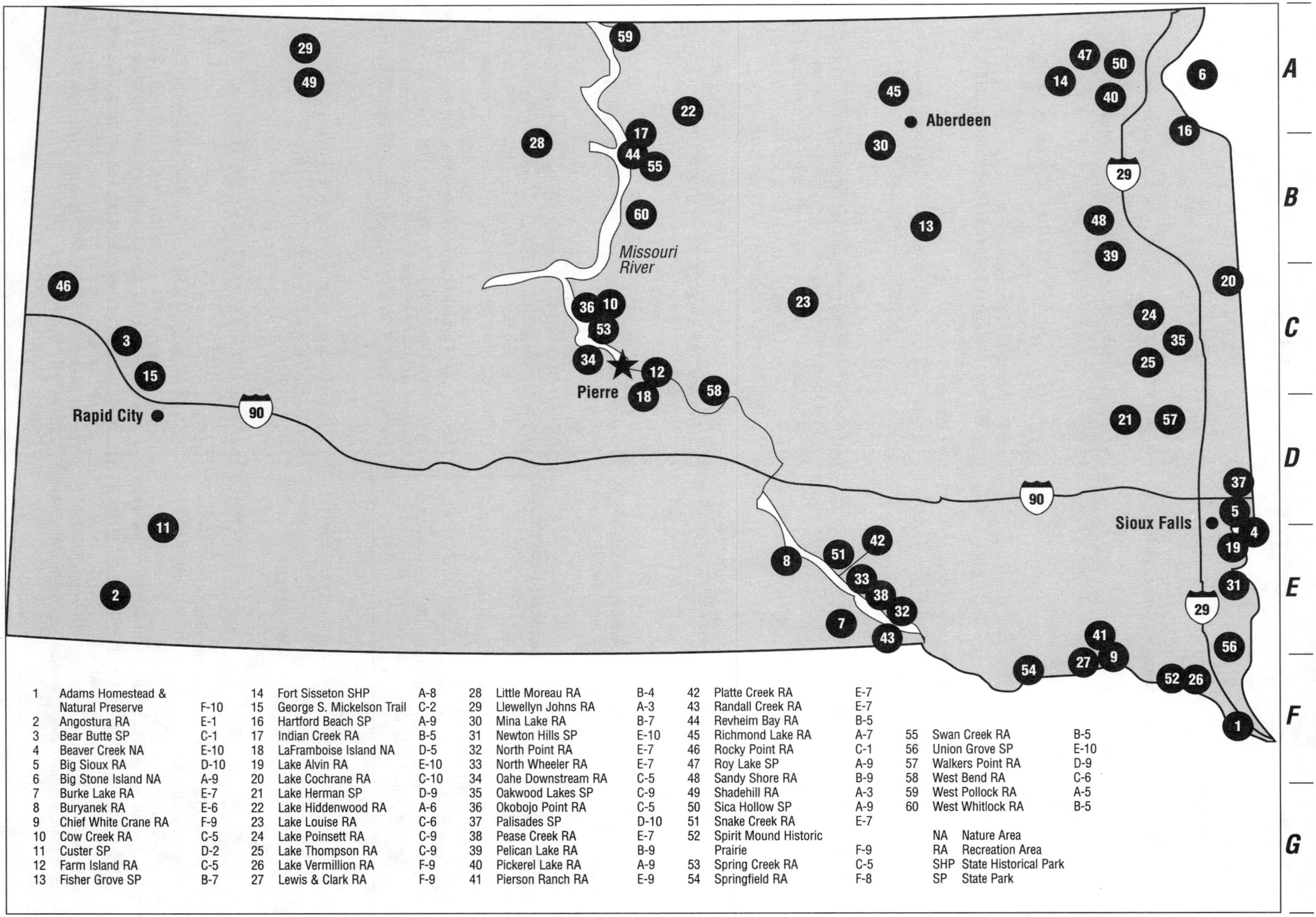

Map labels: Aberdeen · Sioux Falls · Pierre · Rapid City · Missouri River

Interstate/highway markers: 90, 29

Legend

#	Park	Grid
1	Adams Homestead & Natural Preserve	F-10
2	Angostura RA	E-1
3	Bear Butte SP	C-1
4	Beaver Creek NA	E-10
5	Big Sioux RA	D-10
6	Big Stone Island NA	A-9
7	Burke Lake RA	E-7
8	Buryanek RA	E-6
9	Chief White Crane RA	F-9
10	Cow Creek RA	C-5
11	Custer SP	D-2
12	Farm Island RA	C-5
13	Fisher Grove SP	B-7
14	Fort Sisseton SHP	A-8
15	George S. Mickelson Trail	C-2
16	Hartford Beach SP	B-5
17	Indian Creek RA	D-5
18	LaFramboise Island NA	E-10
19	Lake Alvin RA	E-10
20	Lake Cochrane RA	C-10
21	Lake Herman SP	D-9
22	Lake Hiddenwood RA	A-6
23	Lake Louise RA	C-6
24	Lake Poinsett RA	C-9
25	Lake Thompson RA	C-9
26	Lake Vermillion RA	C-5
27	Lewis & Clark RA	B-7
28	Little Moreau RA	B-4
29	Llewellyn Johns RA	A-3
30	Mina Lake RA	B-7
31	Newton Hills SP	E-10
32	North Point RA	E-7
33	North Wheeler RA	C-5
34	Oahe Downstream RA	C-9
35	Oakwood Lakes SP	C-5
36	Okobojo Point RA	D-10
37	Palisades SP	A-6
38	Pease Creek RA	C-6
39	Pelican Lake RA	C-9
40	Pickerel Lake RA	F-9
41	Pierson Ranch RA	F-9
42	Platte Creek RA	B-4
43	Randall Creek RA	A-3
44	Revheim Bay RA	B-7
45	Richmond Lake RA	E-10
46	Rocky Point RA	E-7
47	Roy Lake SP	C-5
48	Sandy Shore RA	C-9
49	Shadehill RA	B-9
50	Sica Hollow SP	A-3
51	Snake Creek RA	A-9
52	Spirit Mound Historic Prairie	D-10
53	Spring Creek RA	E-7
54	Springfield RA	F-9
55	Swan Creek RA	B-5
56	Union Grove SP	E-10
57	Walkers Point RA	D-9
58	West Bend RA	C-6
59	West Pollock RA	A-5
60	West Whitlock RA	B-5

NA	Nature Area
RA	Recreation Area
SHP	State Historical Park
SP	State Park

SOUTH DAKOTA

★4166★ South Dakota Department of Game, Fish & Parks
Division of Parks & Recreation
523 E Capitol Ave
Pierre, SD 57501
(605) 773-3391 - Phone
(605) 773-6245 - Fax
(800) 710-2267 - Reservations
(605) 773-3930 - Volunteering
Web: www.sdgfp.info
Oversees some 60 properties, including state parks, recreation areas, nature areas, trails, and a historic prairie. Of the system's 91,500 acres, Custer State Park accounts for 71,000 acres, or nearly 80 percent of the total. The division also manages more than 800 miles of groomed snowmobile trails, including the Black Hills region system with 342 miles of trails.

★4167★ South Dakota Department of Game, Fish & Parks
Division of Wildlife
523 E Capitol Ave
Pierre, SD 57501
(605) 773-3485 - Phone
(605) 773-6245 - Fax
Web: www.sdgfp.info/wildlife
Manages wildlife and fish species and maintains their habitats. Provides access to hunting and fishing areas, issues licenses, and offers educational programs.

Key to campsite classification:

- **Modern campsites** — Generally, comfort stations with hot showers are nearby.
- **Basic campsites** — Vault toilets nearby.
- **Horsemen's camp** — Facilities vary, but include corrals and parking for trailers.

★4168★ ADAMS HOMESTEAD & NATURE PRESERVE
272 Westshore Dr
McCook Lake, SD 57049
Web: www.sdgfp.info/parks/regions/heartland/
adamshomestead.htm
Phone: 605-232-0873
Size: 1,500 acres. **Location:** 2 miles west and 0.5 miles south of I-29 (McCook exit). **Facilities:** Visitor center, picnic areas, picnic shelter (&), hiking trails, historic sites, interpretive exhibits, wildlife viewing blinds. **Activities:** Hiking, mountain biking, wildlife viewing, guided tours. **Special Features:** Established

in 1872 by Stephen Searls Adams, the homestead includes the Adams family farmhouse, a country school, and church. The house contains many of the original furnishings.

★4169★ ANGOSTURA RECREATION AREA
13157 N Angostura Rd
Hot Springs, SD 57747
Web: www.sdgfp.info/parks/regions/SouthernHills/
Angostura.htm
Phone: 605-745-6996
Size: 1,125 acres. **Location:** 10 miles southeast of Hot Springs off US 18. **Facilities:** 168 modern campsites (146 with electricity), 8 cabins (6 &), picnic areas, picnic shelters (&), concession and food service, hiking trails, swimming beach, disc golf course, boat ramps, marinas, playground, game courts, playfield. **Activities:** Camping, boating, canoeing, fishing, swimming, water-skiing, hiking, interpretive program. **Special Features:** Park is located on the shores of a 5,000-acre reservoir, which offers 36 miles of shoreline and sandy beaches.

★4170★ BEAR BUTTE STATE PARK
Box 688
E Hwy 79
Sturgis, SD 57785
Web: www.sdgfp.info/parks/regions/northernhills/
bearbutte.htm
Phone: 605-347-5240
Size: 1,935 acres. **Location:** 6 miles northeast of Sturgis off SD 79. **Facilities:** 16 basic campsites, horsemen's campsite, picnic areas, picnic shelter, hiking trails, bridle trails, fishing dock (&), historic site, education center, playground. **Activities:** Camping, boating, hiking, horseback riding, fishing, interpretive programs. **Special Features:** Mato Paha, or Bear Mountain, is the Lakota name given to this site. The mountain is sacred to many American Indian tribes, who come here to hold religious ceremonies. A small bison herd roams the base of the mountain.

★4171★ BEAVER CREEK NATURE AREA
c/o Palisades State Park
25495 485th Ave
Garretson, SD 57030
Web: www.sdgfp.info/Parks/Regions/Heartland/
BeaverCreek.htm
Phone: 605-594-3824
Size: 165 acres. **Location:** 5 miles southeast of Brandon, off I-90. **Facilities:** Picnic shelters (&), hiking trails, historic site. **Activities:** Hiking, educational programs. **Special Features:** Named for the numerous beavers found along the spring-fed stream, this area showcases woodland slopes, native prairie, and creek bottom habitats and features an original 1870s homestead cabin.

★4172★ BIG SIOUX RECREATION AREA

c/o Palisades State Park
25495 485th Ave
Garretson, SD 57030
Web: www.sdgfp.info/parks/regions/heartland/bigsioux.htm
Phone: 605-594-3824
Size: 430 acres. **Location:** 4 miles southwest of Brandon off I-90. **Facilities:** 50 campsites (43 with electrical hookups, 1 ♿), 2 cabins, picnic areas, picnic shelter (♿), hiking trails, bridle trails, historic site, canoe ramp, playground, archery range, volleyball court, warming house. **Activities:** Camping, canoeing, fishing, hiking, biking, archery, disc golf, cross-country skiing, snowmobiling, interpretive programs. **Special Features:** A log house and storm cellar on the park grounds mark the original Ole Bergerson homestead.

★4173★ BIG STONE ISLAND NATURE AREA

c/o Hartford Beach State Park
RR 1 Box 50
Corona, SD 57227
Web: www.sdgfp.info/parks/regions/GlacialLakes/
 BigStone.htm
Phone: 605-432-6374
Size: 100 acres. **Location:** Big Stone Lake, accessible only by boat in the summer or by crossing the ice in winter. **Facilities:** Undeveloped. **Activities:** Boating, canoeing, fishing, hiking. **Special Features:** In the 1800s and early 1900s, resort hotels dotted the shore, and in the 1940s military aircraft practiced landing and take offs from a runway on the island in preparation for war in the Pacific. Today the island is only accessible by boat.

★4174★ BURKE LAKE RECREATION AREA

c/o Snake Creek Recreation Area
35316 SD Hwy 44
Platte, SD 57369
Web: www.sdgfp.info/Parks/Regions/Heartland/
 BurkeLake.htm
Phone: 605-337-2587
Size: 206 acres. **Location:** 2 miles east of Burke off US 18. **Facilities:** 16 basic campsites, picnic areas, picnic shelters, fishing dock (♿), hiking trail. **Activities:** Camping, boating, canoeing, fishing, hiking. **Special Features:** Area's 25-acre lake averages only eight feet in depth.

★4175★ BURYANEK RECREATION AREA

c/o Snake Creek Recreation Area
35316 SD Hwy 44
Platte, SD 57369
Web: www.sdgfp.info/Parks/Regions/Heartland/Buryanek.htm
Phone: 605-337-2587
Size: 166 acres. **Location:** 20 miles northwest of Platte off SD 44. **Facilities:** 44 modern campsites (41 with electricity), 2 cabins (♿), swimming beach, picnic shelter, picnic areas, boat ramp, fish cleaning station, playground. **Activities:** Camping, boating, canoeing, fishing, swimming. **Special Features:** An interpretive sign near the park tells the story of Private George Shannon, a member of the Lewis and Clark Expedition who was lost here for nearly two weeks. When he was found, he learned that the expedition had been downstream from him the entire time.

★4176★ CHIEF WHITE CRANE RECREATION AREA

c/o Lewis & Clark Recreation Area
43349 SD Hwy 52
Yankton, SD 57442
Web: www.sdgfp.info/Parks/Regions/LewisClark/
 ChiefWhiteCrane.htm
Phone: 605-668-2985
Size: 186 acres. **Location:** 5 miles west of Yankton off SD 52. **Facilities:** 146 modern campsites (144 with electricity, 2 ♿), 10 cabins (♿), picnic shelter, picnic areas, boat ramps, fish cleaning station, game courts, playground. **Activities:** Camping, boating, fishing, biking, hiking, cross-country skiing, bird watching. **Special Features:** Park was named for Chief White Crane, who met with Lewis and Clark in this area in 1804. The park's large cottonwood trees provide shade for campers as well as a place for bald eagles to roost in winter.

★4177★ COW CREEK RECREATION AREA

20439 Marina Loop Rd
Ft Pierre, SD 57532
Web: www.sdgfp.info/parks/regions/OaheSharpe/
 CowCreek.htm
Phone: 605-223-7722
Size: 257 acres. **Location:** 15 miles northwest of Pierre off SD 1804 **Facilities:** 40 modern campsites (30 with electricity), picnic shelter, boat ramp, fish cleaning station. **Activities:** Camping, boating, sailing, fishing, swimming, waterskiing, diving. **Special Features:** Situated along the shore of Lake Oahe, with more than 2,000 miles of shoreline.

★4178★ CUSTER STATE PARK

13329 US Hwy 16A
Custer, SD 57730
Web: www.sdgfp.info/parks/Regions/Custer
Phone: 605-255-4515; **Fax:** 605-255-4460.
Size: 71,000 acres. **Location:** 5 miles east of Custer off US 16A. **Facilities:** 323 campsites, horsemen's camp, picnic areas, picnic shelter, hiking trails, bridle trails, fishing dock, historic site, 2 visitor centers, theater playhouse, playground, volksmarch. **Activities:** Camping, boating, canoeing, fishing, swimming, hiking, mountain biking, horseback riding, cross-country skiing, snowmobiling, ice fishing, rock climbing, interpretive programs. **Special Features:** Park is located in the Black Hills and has spectacular terrain. One of the scenic drives in the area is Needles Highway (SD 87), which passes towering rock formations and goes through narrow tunnels. At the end of one tunnel stands the Needles Eye, a granite spire with a slit only 3 to 4 feet wide but reaching 30 to 40 feet in the air. There are four resorts at the park, each with its own personality and activities.

★4179★ FARM ISLAND RECREATION AREA

1301 Farm Island Rd
Pierre, SD 57501
Web: www.sdgfp.info/Parks/Regions/OaheSharpe/
 FarmIsland.htm
Phone: 605-773-2885

Size: 1,800 acres. **Location:** 4 miles east of Pierre off SD 34. **Facilities:** 90 modern campsites (76 with electrical hookups, 1 &), 2 cabins, picnic areas, picnic shelters (&), comfort stations with showers, hiking trails, boat ramps, boat rentals, fishing dock (&), beach, fish cleaning station, historic site, visitor center, amphitheater, playgrounds, warming house. **Activities:** Camping, boating, canoeing, fishing, archery, swimming, water-skiing, hiking, biking, cross-country skiing, sledding, disc golf, interpretive programs. **Special Features:** The park is located on the Missouri River and includes an island nature area, which provides an outdoor classroom for visitors. Ties to the Lewis and Clark expedition are detailed in the Lewis and Clark Family Center.

★4180★ FISHER GROVE STATE PARK

c/o Lake Louise Recreation Area
35250 191st St
Miller, SD 57362
Web: www.sdgfp.info/Parks/Regions/GlacialLakes/
fishergrove.htm
Phone: 605-853-2533
Size: 277 acres. **Location:** 7 miles east of Redfield off US 212. **Facilities:** 28 modern campsites (22 with electrical hookups), picnic areas, picnic shelter, hiking trails, boat launch, historic site, playground, warming house. **Activities:** Camping, boating, canoeing, fishing, hiking, interpretive program. **Special Features:** Park is named after Frank I. Fisher, the first permanent European settler in the county, who lived at this site. The Watertown-to-Pierre stage line crossed the river here on American Indians' traditional rock river crossing, and a hotel for tourists was located at the site.

★4181★ FORT SISSETON STATE HISTORICAL
PARK

c/o Roy Lake State Park
11545 434th Ave
Lake City, SD 57247
Web: www.sdgfp.info/Parks/Regions/GlacialLakes/
fortsisseton.htm
Phone: 605-448-5474
Size: 125 acres. **Location:** 10 miles southwest of Lake City off SD 10. **Facilities:** 14 modern campsites (10 with electrical hookups), 3 cabins, 2 tipis, picnic areas, picnic shelter (&), hiking trails, bridle trail, boat rentals, historic site, visitor center, museum, gift shop. **Activities:** Camping, boating, fishing, hiking, horseback riding, interpretive programs. **Special Features:** Originally established in 1864 to provide military protection for the Minnesota frontier, Fort Sisseton is one of the best preserved prairie forts in the nation. The officers' quarters, stone barracks, powder magazine, guard house and other buildings remain. Guided tours by costumed soldiers are available.

★4182★ GEORGE S. MICKELSON TRAIL

c/o Black Hills Trails Office
HC 37 Box 604
Lead, SD 57754
Web: www.sdgfp.info/parks/regions/northernhills/
mickelsontrail
Phone: 605-584-3896

Size: 114 miles. **Location:** Between Deadwood and Edgemont. **Facilities:** Paved trail, toilets, drinking water. **Activities:** Hiking, bicycling, jogging, horseback riding, snowmobiling (18 miles, between Deadwood and DuMont only). **Special Features:** Trail winds through some of the most beautiful areas in the Black Hills, passing over more than 100 bridges, through 4 hardrock tunnels, and past old mining and mill sites. Located just east of the trail, north of Custer, is Crazy Horse Memorial.

★4183★ HARTFORD BEACH STATE PARK

RR 1, Box 50
Corona, SD 57227
Web: www.sdgfp.info/parks/regions/glaciallakes/
hartfordbeach.htm
Phone: 605-432-6374
Size: 331 acres. **Location:** 15 miles north of Milbank off SD 15. **Facilities:** 49 modern campsites (36 with electrical hookups, 1 &, 6 tent only), cabin, showers, picnic areas, picnic shelter, hiking trails, boat ramp, fishing dock (&), fish cleaning station, historic site, game courts, 9-hole disc golf course, playground, amphitheater, warming house. **Activities:** Camping, boating, canoeing, fishing, swimming, hiking, interpretive programs. **Special Features:** Park's hiking trails take visitors past scenic overlooks and historic sites, including burial mounds and a prehistoric village site. Interpretive trail guidebooks are available.

★4184★ INDIAN CREEK RECREATION AREA

12905 288th Ave
Mobridge, SD 57601
Web: www.sdgfp.info/parks/regions/oahesharpe/
indiancreek.htm
Phone: 605-845-7112
Size: 187 acres. **Location:** 2 miles southeast of Mobridge off US 12. **Facilities:** 124 modern campsites (all with electricity, 1 &), 2 cabins (&), picnic shelters, picnic areas, boat ramps, fishing dock, fish cleaning station, playground, land navigation courses. **Activities:** Camping, boating, fishing, swimming, hiking, biking. **Special Features:** Park has three land navigation courses that lead visitors to several stations located throughout the park using a compass or global positioning systems unit. GPS units with instruction manuals are available for checkout at the park office.

★4185★ LAFRAMBOISE ISLAND NATURE AREA

c/o Farm Island Recreation Area
1301 Farm Island Rd
Pierre, SD 57501
Web: www.sdgfp.info/parks/regions/oahesharpe/
laframboiseisland.htm
Phone: 605-773-2885
Size: 555 acres. **Location:** Southwest side of Pierre. **Facilities:** Picnic shelter, hiking trails, bike trails, cross-country skiing trails. **Activities:** Hiking, bicycling, cross-country skiing, snowshoeing, wildlife watching. **Special Features:** More than seven miles of trails wind through this sand bar island, where visitors can view a variety of birds and wildlife.

★4186★ **LAKE ALVIN RECREATION AREA**
c/o Newton Hills State Park
28771 482nd Ave
Canton, SD 57013
Web: www.sdgfp.info/parks/regions/heartland/lakealvin.htm
Phone: 605-987-2263
Size: 59 acres. **Location:** 4 miles east and 1 mile north of Harrisburg. **Facilities:** Picnic shelter (&), picnic area, swimming beach, fishing pier (&). **Activities:** Boating, canoeing, fishing, swimming. **Special Features:** Park is best known for its beach facilities and excellent fishing.

★4187★ **LAKE COCHRANE RECREATION AREA**
c/o Pelican Lake Recreation Area
400 W Kemp
Watertown, SD 57201
Web: www.sdgfp.info/parks/regions/glaciallakes/
    lakecochrane.htm
Phone: 605-882-5200
Size: 88 acres. **Location:** 10 miles east of Clear Lake off SD 22. **Facilities:** 30 modern campsites with electricity (1 &), cabins (&), picnic area, picnic shelter, playground, swimming beach, bathhouse. **Activities:** Camping, boating, canoeing, fishing, swimming. **Special Features:** Lake Cochrane is a spring-fed lake that retains a clear, natural quality most of the year.

★4188★ **LAKE HERMAN STATE PARK**
23409 State Park Dr
Madison, SD 57042
Web: www.sdgfp.info/parks/regions/heartland/
    lakeherman.htm
Phone: 605-256-5003
Size: 227 acres. **Location:** 2 miles west of Madison off SD 34. **Facilities:** 70 modern campsites (1 &), 2 tent campsites, 2 cabins, picnic areas, picnic shelter, comfort station, hiking trails, swimming beach, bathhouse, boat ramp, boat rentals, fishing dock (&), historical site, playground, amphitheater, 9-hole disc golf course. **Activities:** Camping, fishing, swimming, water skiing, boating, canoeing, sailing, hiking, cross-country skiing, interpretive programs. **Special Features:** Melting glacial ice formed this 1,350-acre lake thousands of years ago.

★4189★ **LAKE HIDDENWOOD RECREATION AREA**
c/o West Whitlock Recreation Area
16157A W Whitlock Rd
Gettysburg, SD 57442
Web: www.sdgfp.info/parks/regions/oahesharpe/
    lakehiddenwood.htm
Phone: 605-765-9410
Size: 332 acres. **Location:** 2 miles east and 3 miles north of Selby, off US 12-83. **Facilities:** 14 basic campsites (7 with electrical hookups), picnic shelter (&), swimming beach, hiking trails, boat ramp. **Activities:** Camping, boating, fishing, swimming, hiking. **Special Features:** Lake Hiddenwood derives its name from its location. Situated in a small, wooded bowl, the park is hidden from the view of travelers.

★4190★ **LAKE LOUISE RECREATION AREA**
35250 191st St
Miller, SD 57362
Web: www.sdgfp.info/parks/regions/glaciallakes/
    lakelouise.htm
Phone: 605-853-2533
Size: 320 acres. **Location:** 14 miles northwest of Miller off US 14. **Facilities:** 39 modern campsites (29 with electrical hookups), cabins (&), picnic areas, picnic shelters (&), hiking trails, swimming beach, bathhouse, boat ramp, fishing dock (&), fish cleaning station, playground. **Activities:** Camping, boating, canoeing, fishing, hunting, swimming, hiking. **Special Features:** Lake Louise was formed when the south fork of Wolf Creek was dammed. Water depth in the 164-acre lake averages 9 feet.

★4191★ **LAKE POINSETT RECREATION AREA**
46109 202nd St
Bruce, SD 57220
Web: www.state.sd.us/gfp/sdparks/poinsett/poinsett.htm
Phone: 605-627-5441
Size: 196 acres. **Location:** 12 miles north and 2 miles east of Arlington, off US 81. **Facilities:** 151 modern campsites (89 with electrical hookups), camping cabin, comfort station with showers, picnic areas, hiking trail, swimming beach, boat launch, fishing dock, playground (&&). **Activities:** Camping, boating, canoeing, fishing, swimming, water-skiing, jet skiing, hiking, cross-country skiing, junior naturalist program, interpretive programs. **Special Features:** Lake Poinsett is one of the largest lakes in the state and was named after Secretary of War Joel Poinsett, who was instrumental in promoting the expedition that first explored this region.

★4192★ **LAKE THOMPSON RECREATION AREA**
21176 Flood Club Rd
Lake Preston, SD 57249
Web: www.sdgfp.info/Parks/Regions/GlacialLakes/
    lakethompson.htm
Phone: 605-847-4893
Size: 416 acres. **Location:** 6 miles southwest of Preston off US 14. **Facilities:** 103 modern campsites (97 with electrical hookups,1 &), 4 cabins (&), comfort stations with showers, 5-bedroom rental lodge, boat ramps, hiking trail, game courts, ski beach, swimming beach, fish cleaning station, playground. **Activities:** Camping, boating, fishing, swimming, water skiing, hiking. **Special Features:** Originally called Dry Woods Lake by American Indians, the lake was renamed for Secretary of the Interior Jacob Thompson. It is mentioned as one of the Twin Lakes in many of Laura Ingalls Wilder's books. In the 1930s the lake was completely dry and used for pasture. In the 1980s, heavy rains and snowmelt filled it to a depth of 20 feet, and it now covers 18,000 acres.

★4193★ **LAKE VERMILLION RECREATION AREA**
26140 451st Ave
Canistota, SD 57012
Web: www.sdgfp.info/Parks/Regions/heartland/
    lakevermillion.htm
Phone: 605-296-3643

9. State Parks

Size: 267 acres. **Location:** 5 miles south of I-90 at Montrose Exit. **Facilities:** 66 modern campsites (62 with electrical hookups, 1 &), 2 cabins, picnic areas, picnic shelter (&), hiking trail, swimming beach, ski beach, boat ramp, fishing dock (&), fish cleaning station, game courts, playground. **Activities:** Camping, boating, canoeing, fishing, swimming, water-skiing, hiking. **Special Features:** Lake was created by impounding waters from the east fork of the Vermillion River in 1958. Some say the river it got its name from the outcropping of red quartzite along its bank.

★4194★ **LEWIS & CLARK RECREATION AREA**
43349 SD Hwy 52
Yankton, SD 57078
Web: www.sdgfp.info/Parks/Regions/LewisClark/
    LewisClark.htm
Phone: 605-668-2985
Size: 928 acres. **Location:** 4 miles west of Yankton off SD 52. **Facilities:** 374 modern campsites, comfort station with showers, horsemen's camp, cabins (some &), 24-unit lodge, picnic areas, picnic shelters, hiking trails, bridle trails, nature trails, bike trails, swimming beach, ski beach, swimming pool, marina, boat ramps, boat rentals, fishing dock, fish cleaning station, archery range, disc golf course, playground. **Activities:** Camping, boating, fishing, swimming, water-skiing, hiking, bicycling, horseback riding, archery, disc golf. **Special Features:** Located on the shores of Lewis and Clark Lake on the Missouri River, this is one of the state park system's most popular parks. It offers the state parks' only Rent-A Camper, a 24-foot trailer with microwave and TV/VCR.

★4195★ **LITTLE MOREAU RECREATION AREA**
c/o Shadehill Recreation Area
19150 Summerville Box 63
Shadehill, SD 57653
Web: www.sdgfp.info/Parks/Regions/OaheSharpe/
    LittleMoreau.htm
Phone: 605-374-5114
Size: 160 acres. **Location:** 6 miles south of Timber Lake off SD 20. **Facilities:** 5 campsites, picnic areas, picnic shelter, boat ramp, swimming beach, playfields. **Activities:** Camping, boating, canoeing, swimming. **Special Features:** The sheltered watersheds of the Moreau and Little Moreau Rivers (originally Big Owl and Little Owl) provided traditional winter campgrounds for the Cheyenne and later for the Minneconjou and Two Kettle bands of Teton Sioux. During the late 1870s through 1890s, cattle barons from southern states grazed thousands of cattle on the rich grassland here.

★4196★ **LLEWELLYN JOHNS RECREATION AREA**
c/o Shadehill Recreation Area
19150 Summerville Box 63
Shadehill, SD 57653
Web: www.sdgfp.info/Parks/Regions/northernhills/
    llewellynjohns.htm
Phone: 605-374-5114
Size: 114 acres. **Location:** 12 miles south of Lemmon off SD 73. **Facilities:** 10 basic campsites with electrical hookups, picnic shelter, playground. **Activities:** Camping, picnicking. **Special Features:** Many historic figures have crossed through this area, including Hugh Glass and Custer's 1874 expedition. Glass was attacked by a grizzly bear here, which is documented in the novel Lord Grizzly.

★4197★ **MINA LAKE RECREATION AREA**
c/o Richmond Lake Recreation Area
37908 Youth Camp Rd
Aberdeen, SD 57401
Web: www.sdgfp.info/Parks/Regions/glaciallakes/
    minalake.htm
Phone: 605-626-3488
Size: 300 acres. **Location:** 11 miles west of Aberdeen off US 12. **Facilities:** 37 modern campsites (36 with electrical hookups, 1 &), cabin (&), lodge, picnic areas, picnic shelter, hiking trail (&), swimming beach, boat ramp, fishing dock (&), game courts, playground. **Activities:** Camping, boating, canoeing, fishing, swimming, hiking. **Special Features:** Mina was one of the first man-made lakes in northeast South Dakota. In 1934 the Mina Dam was completed and the lake was named Shake Maza, a Lakota word for "shaped like a horseshoe." The name didn't catch on, and it was later renamed in honor of a railroad president's daughter.

★4198★ **NEWTON HILLS STATE PARK**
28767 482nd Ave
Canton, SD 57013
Web: www.sdgfp.info/Parks/Regions/heartland/
    newtonhills.htm
Phone: 605-987-2263
Size: 948 acres. **Location:** 6 miles south of Canton off County 135. **Facilities:** 118 modern campsites (108 with electrical hookups, 1 &), horsemen's camp, 7 cabins, comfort stations with showers, picnic areas (&), picnic shelters, hiking trails, bridle trails, swimming beach, boat ramp, historic site, amphitheater, observation tower, volleyball court, playground. **Activities:** Camping, boating (with restrictions), fishing, swimming, hiking, biking, horseback riding. **Special Features:** Park is located at the southern tip of a geological feature called Coteau des Prairies (Hills of the Prairies). The rich glacial soils support an abundance of plant and animal life, including more than 200 species of birds that visit the park during the year.

★4199★ **NORTH POINT RECREATION AREA**
38180 297th St
Lake Andes, SD 57356
Web: www.sdgfp.info/Parks/Regions/LewisClark/
    NorthPoint.htm
Phone: 605-487-7046
Size: 1,055 acres. **Location:** 1 mile northwest of Pickstown off US 281. **Facilities:** 111 modern campsites with electricity (1 &), 6 cabins (2 &), picnic shelter (&), picnic areas, hiking trail, bike trail, boat ramps, swimming beach, fish cleaning station, playground, rifle range, trap shooting range. **Activities:** Camping, boating, fishing, swimming, water skiing, hiking, biking, target shooting. **Special Features:** Park is located on the shores of the Missouri and provides a spectacular view of the river.

9. State Parks

Lewis and Clark came up the river in 1804 and saw their first prairie dogs in this area, which they called "barking squirrels."

★4200★ NORTH WHEELER RECREATION AREA

c/o North Point Recreation Area
38180 297th St
Lake Andes, SD 57356
Web: www.sdgfp.info/Parks/Regions/LewisClark/
   northwheeler.htm
Phone: 605-487-7046
Size: 156 acres. Location: 16 miles south of Platte off SD 1804. Facilities: 22 campsites (15 with electrical hookups), boat ramps, fish cleaning table. Activities: Camping, boating, fishing. Special Features: Small, quiet park with lake access between Pease and Platte Creeks.

★4201★ OAHE DOWNSTREAM RECREATION AREA

20439 Marina Loop Rd
Fort Pierre, SD 57532
Web: www.sdgfp.info/Parks/Regions/oahesharpe/
   oahedownstream.htm
Phone: 605-223-7722
Size: 933 acres. Location: 5 miles north of Fort Pierre off SD 1806. Facilities: 205 modern campsites (all with electricity, 3 &), 4 cabins (&), picnic shelters, picnic areas, comfort stations, boat ramps, marina, restaurant, amphitheater, playground, archery range, 9-hole disc golf course, hiking trail, swimming beach, fish cleaning station.. Activities: Camping, boating, fishing, bird watching, disc golf, hiking, biking, target shooting, cross-country skiing. Special Features: Engineers began building Oahe Dam in 1948 and started generating electricity in 1962. It is one of the largest constructed reservoirs in the United States, measuring 231 miles and connecting the capital cities of South and North Dakota.

★4202★ OAKWOOD LAKES STATE PARK

46109 202nd St
Bruce, SD 57220
Web: www.state.sd.us/gfp/sdparks/oakwood/oakwood.htm
Phone: 605-627-5441
Size: 293 acres. Location: 7 miles north and 3 miles west of Volga, off US 14. Facilities: 69 modern campsites (64 with electrical hookups), horsemen's camp, 2 camping cabins, 2 group camps, picnic areas, comfort station with showers, picnic shelter, hiking and bridle trails, swimming beach and bathhouse, boat launch, fishing dock, historic site, visitor center, playground (&&). Activities: Camping, boating, canoeing, fishing, swimming, water-skiing, hiking, horseback riding, cross-country skiing, snowmobiling, snowshoeing, ice fishing, junior naturalist program, interpretive programs. Special Features: Situated in the midst of eight scenic glacial lakes, the area was once used as camp and annual gathering spot for Native American tribes. Park includes an 1860s log cabin.

★4203★ OKOBOJO POINT RECREATION AREA

c/o Oahe Downstream Rd
20439 Marina Loop Rd
Fort Pierre, SD 57532
Web: www.sdgfp.info/Parks/Regions/oahesharpe/
   okobojopoint.htm
Phone: 605-223-7722
Size: 135 acres. Location: 17 miles northwest of Pierre off SD 1804. Facilities: 15 modern campsites (all non-electric), group camping loops, showers, picnic shelters, picnic areas, boat ramps. Activities: Camping, boating, fishing, swimming, water-skiing, diving, hiking, biking. Special Features: Located on the shore of Lake Oahe, with more than 2,000 miles of shoreline. Park is along the Lewis and Clark Trail.

★4204★ PALISADES STATE PARK

25495 485th Ave
Garretson, SD 57030
Web: www.sdgfp.info/parks/regions/heartland/palisades.htm
Phone: 605-594-3824; Fax: 605-594-2369; Toll Free: 800-710-2267
Size: 157 acres. Location: 10 miles north of I-90. Facilities: 35 modern campsites (16 with electrical hookups, 1 &), 5 cabins (1 &), comfort station (&), picnic areas, picnic shelter (&), hiking trails, historic site, volleyball court, playground, amphitheater. Activities: Camping, canoeing, fishing, hiking, rock climbing. Special Features: The beautiful formations of Sioux quartzite found in the park were carved out by Split Rock Creek over millions of years. The vertical cliffs offer spectacular scenery and challenging rock climbing opportunities.

★4205★ PEASE CREEK RECREATION AREA

c/o Snake Creek Recreation Area
35316 SD Hwy 44
Platte, SD 57369
Web: www.sdgfp.info/parks/regions/lewisclark/
   peasecreek.htm
Phone: 605-337-2587
Size: Almost 600 acres. Location: 9 miles south of Geddes off SD 1804. Facilities: 23 campsites (all with electricity), horsemen's camp, picnic shelter, hiking trails, bike trails, bridle trails, fish cleaning station, boat ramp. Activities: Camping, boating, fishing, hiking, biking, horseback riding. Special Features: The park's hilly, wooded terrain makes the trails challenging, whether on foot or mountain bike.

★4206★ PELICAN LAKE RECREATION AREA

400 W Kemp
Watertown, SD 57201
Web: www.sdgfp.info/Parks/Regions/GlacialLakes/
   PelicanLake.htm
Phone: 605-882-5200
Size: 152 acres. Location: 9 miles southwest of Watertown off US 212. Facilities: 46 campsites with electrical hookups (1 &), horsemen's camp, 2 cabins (1 &), comfort station with showers, picnic areas, picnic shelter (&), hiking trails, bridle trails, swimming beach, boat launch, observation tower, warming house.

Activities: Camping, boating, canoeing, hunting, fishing, swimming, hiking, horseback riding, cross-country skiing, snowshoeing, ice fishing. **Special Features:** White pelicans frequent the lake; they were so numerous when the region was first settled that the lake was named in their honor.

★4207★ **PICKEREL LAKE RECREATION AREA**
12980 446th Ave
Grenville, SD 57239
Web: www.sdgfp.info/Parks/Regions/GlacialLakes/
   pickerellake.htm
Phone: 605-882-5200
Size: 368 acres. **Location:** 10 miles north of Waubay off US 12. **Facilities:** 77 modern campsites (69 with electrical hookups, 1 &), 2 cabins, comfort station with showers, picnic areas, picnic shelter (&), hiking trails, boat ramp, swimming beach, fish cleaning station, playground, game courts. **Activities:** Camping, boating, canoeing, fishing, swimming, hiking, bird watching. **Special Features:** Noted for its cool, spring-fed waters, 955-acre Pickerel Lake is one of the deepest natural lakes in the state and is located in the heart of South Dakota's glacial lakes region.

★4208★ **PIERSON RANCH RECREATION AREA**
c/o Lewis & Clark Recreation Area
43349 SD Hwy 52
Yankton, SD 57442
Web: www.sdgfp.info/Parks/Regions/LewisClark/
   PiersonRanch.htm
Phone: 605-668-2985
Size: 60 acres. **Location:** 4 miles southwest of Yankton off SD Hwy 52. **Facilities:** 67 modern campsites with electricity (1 &), 2 cabins (1 &), picnic shelters (&), picnic area, hiking trail, bike trail, game courts, playground. **Activities:** Camping, hiking, bicycling, fishing. **Special Features:** Opened in 1959, Pierson Ranch is the oldest campground in the area and is located between two other recreation areas, Chief White Crane and Lewis and Clark.

★4209★ **PLATTE CREEK RECREATION AREA**
c/o Snake Creek Recreation Area
35316 SD Hwy 44
Platte, SD 57369
Web: www.sdgfp.info/Parks/Regions/heartland/
   plattecreek.htm
Phone: 605-337-2587
Size: 252 acres. **Location:** 8 miles west and 10 miles south of Platte, off SD 44. **Facilities:** 54 modern campsites (39 with electrical hookups, 1 &), comfort station with showers, boat launch, fish cleaning station. **Activities:** Camping, boating, fishing. **Special Features:** The 107-mile long lake is surrounded by 540 miles of shoreline, some featuring the ''burning bluffs,'' which are created by oil-bearing shale. Lightning strikes or chemical reactions ignite the shale, which may then smoke for years.

★4210★ **RANDALL CREEK RECREATION AREA**
38180 297th St
Lake Andes, SD 57356
Web: www.sdgfp.info/parks/regions/lewisclark/
   randallcreek.htm
Phone: 605-487-7046
Size: 184 acres. **Location:** 1 miles west of Pickstown off US 281. **Facilities:** 132 modern campsites with electricity (3 &), 4 cabins (2 &), picnic shelters (&), picnic areas, boat ramp, playground. 9-hole disc golf course, fish cleaning station. **Activities:** Camping, boating, canoeing, kayaking, fishing, bird watching, cross-country skiing. **Special Features:** Randall Creek is located on the banks of the Missouri River, immediately downstream from Fort Randall Dam. It is one of the parks in the state that allow visitors an opportunity to see bald eagles.

★4211★ **REVHEIM BAY RECREATION AREA**
c/o Indian Creek Recreation Area
12905 288th Ave
Mobridge, SD 57601
Web: www.sdgfp.info/parks/Regions/oahesharpe/
   revheimbay.htm
Phone: 605-845-7112
Size: 296 acres. **Location:** 1 mile southeast of Mobridge off US Hwy 12. **Facilities:** Picnic shelters, hiking trail, game courts, playground, swimming beach. **Activities:** Hiking, swimming, archery, fishing. **Special Features:** Park's 1.75 miles of hiking trail provide opportunities for wildlife viewing.

★4212★ **RICHMOND LAKE RECREATION AREA**
37908 Youth Camp Rd
Aberdeen, SD 57401
Web: www.sdgfp.info/parks/regions/glaciallakes/
   richmondlake.htm
Phone: 605-626-3488
Size: 349 acres. **Location:** 10 miles northwest of Aberdeen off US 281. **Facilities:** 24 modern campsites (23 with electrical hookups, 1 &), showers, cabin (&), picnic shelter, hiking trails, bridle trails, swimming beach, boat launch, fishing dock (&), playground, warming house, 18-hole disc golf course, game courts. **Activities:** Camping, fishing, swimming, boating, hiking, biking, horseback riding, cross-country skiing, snow sledding and tobogganing. **Special Features:** Park comprises three separate units, each offering its own form of outdoor recreation.

★4213★ **ROCKY POINT RECREATION AREA**
c/o Black Hills Trails
11361 Nevada Gulch Rd
Lead, SD 57754
Web: www.sdgfp.info/parks/Regions/northernhills/
   rockypoint.htm
Phone: 605-584-3896
Size: 350 acres. **Location:** 8 miles east of Belle Fourche off SD 212. **Facilities:** 61 campsites (50 with electrical hookups, 3 &), comfort station with showers (&), picnic area, picnic shelter, boat ramps, fish cleaning station, playground. **Activities:** Camping, boating, fishing, picnicking. **Special Features:**

Opened in 2006, Rocky Point sits on the 8,000-acre Belle Fourche Reservoir, which was created in 1911 when the Orman Dam was constructed. At the time of its completion, Orman Dam was the largest earthen dam in the world.

★4214★ ROY LAKE STATE PARK

11545 Northside Dr
Lake City, SD 57247
Web: www.sdgfp.info/parks/regions/glaciallakes/roylake.htm
Phone: 605-448-5701
Size: 560 acres. **Location:** 3 miles southwest of Lake City off SD 10. **Facilities:** 102 modern campsites (88 with electrical hookups, 1 ♿), comfort station with showers, resort with rental cabins and restaurant, picnic shelters (♿), concession and food service, hiking trails, swimming beach, boat ramp, boat rentals, fish-cleaning station, fish dock (♿), playgrounds, warming house, amphitheater, interpretive displays, 9-hole disc golf course. **Activities:** Camping, boating, canoeing, fishing, swimming, water skiing, hiking, cross-country skiing, disc golf, interpretive programs. **Special Features:** The earliest known inhabitants of Roy Lake were members of the Woodland Culture, who built large burial mounds. Artifacts dating between 900 and 1300 A.D. have been found near the park. The Roy (Roi) family has been credited with building the area's first white settlement.

★4215★ SANDY SHORE RECREATION AREA

c/o South Dakota Dept of Game Fish & Parks
400 W Kemp Ave
Watertown, SD 57201
Web: www.sdgfp.info/parks/Regions/GlacialLakes/SandyShore.htm
Phone: 605-882-5200
Size: 19 acres. **Location:** 5 miles west of Watertown off US 212. **Facilities:** 20 modern campsites (12 with electrical hookups), comfort station, picnic area, picnic shelter (♿), swimming beach, boat launch, playground, 9-hole disc golf course. **Activities:** Camping, boating, fishing, swimming. **Special Features:** On the banks of Lake Kampeska, Sandy Shore offers a long sandy beach. The lake is a glacial lake and is known for its clear water.

★4216★ SHADEHILL RECREATION AREA

19150 Summerville Rd Box 63
Shadehill, SD 57653
Web: www.sdgfp.info/parks/Regions/northernhills/shadehill.htm
Phone: 605-374-5114
Size: 2,150 acres. **Location:** 14 miles south of Lemmon off SD 73. **Facilities:** 52 modern campsites with electrical hookups (2 ♿), 3 cabins (♿), lodge, comfort station with showers, picnic areas, picnic shelters, bridle trails, swimming beach, boat ramps, fish-cleaning station, historic site, interpretive displays, playgrounds. **Activities:** Camping, boating, canoeing, fishing, swimming, horseback riding, hunting, interpretive programs. **Special Features:** Shadehill Reservoir is one of South Dakota's few large lakes, with more than 5,000 surface acres of water.

★4217★ SICA HOLLOW STATE PARK

c/o Roy Lake State Park
11545 Northside Dr
Lake City, SD 57247
Web: www.sdgfp.info/parks/Regions/glaciallakes/sicahollow.htm
Phone: 605-448-5701
Size: 900 acres. **Location:** 15 miles northwest of Sisseton off SD 10. **Facilities:** 12 campsites, horsemen's camp, picnic areas, hiking trails, bike trails, bridle trails, historic site. **Activities:** Camping, hiking, biking, horseback riding, cross-country skiing, interpretive programs. **Special Features:** The hills in Sica Hollow were the subject of many legends, and the Hollow's first Indian visitors named it ''Sica,'' which means evil or bad. Along the Trail of the Spirits, a National Recreation Trail, are gurgling reddish bogs, swamp gas and stumps that glow in the dark, and small waterfalls that are heard echoing as trapped air escapes.

★4218★ SNAKE CREEK RECREATION AREA

35316 SD Hwy 44
Platte, SD 57369
Web: www.sdgfp.info/parks/Regions/heartland/snakecreek.htm
Phone: 605-337-2587
Size: 695 acres. **Location:** 14 miles west of Platte off SD 44. **Facilities:** 115 modern campsites (111 with electrical hookups, 1 ♿), 9 cabins (4 ♿), picnic shelter, marina, concession and food service, hiking trails, swimming beach, boat ramps, volleyball court, playground. **Activities:** Camping, boating, fishing, swimming, hiking, bird watching. **Special Features:** Scenic bluffs along the Missouri River form a backdrop for this area that played an important role in steamboat traffic from 1830 until the 1880s.

★4219★ SPIRIT MOUND HISTORIC PRAIRIE

c/o Newton Hills State Park
28771 482nd Ave
Canton, SD 57013
Web: www.sdgfp.info/parks/Regions/Heartland/SpiritMound.htm
Phone: 605-987-2263
Size: 320 acres. **Location:** 5 miles north of Vermillion off SD 19. **Facilities:** Interpretive trail (♿), picnic areas, vault toilet. **Activities:** Hiking, picnicking. **Special Features:** Spirit Mound was one of the sites noted in the Lewis and Clark journals. Describing the view from mound's summit, Clark called the expansive treeless plain ''most butifull.''

★4220★ SPRING CREEK RECREATION AREA

c/o Oahe Downstream Recreation Area
20439 Marina Loop Rd
Fort Pierre, SD 57532
Web: www.sdgfp.info/parks/Regions/oahesharpe/springcreek.htm
Phone: 605-223-7722
Size: 149 acres. **Location:** 15 miles northwest of Pierre off SD 1804. **Facilities:** Access to the Oahe Reservoir. **Activities:** Boating, sailing, water skiing, diving, fishing. **Special Features:**

Lake Oahe Reservoir provides more than 2,000 miles of shoreline.

★4221★ SPRINGFIELD RECREATION AREA

c/o Lewis & Clark Recreation Area
43349 SD Hwy 52
Yankton, SD 57078
Web: www.sdgfp.info/parks/Regions/LewisClark/
Springfield.htm
Phone: 605-668-2985
Size: 24 acres. **Location:** 1 mile east of Springfield off SD 37. **Facilities:** 21 basic campsites (20 with electrical hookups), 2 cabins, comfort station, picnic shelter, boat ramp, fishing dock (&), fish cleaning station, hiking trail, bike trail, playground. **Activities:** Camping, boating, canoeing, fishing, swimming, hiking, biking. **Special Features:** Nestled along the shore of the Missouri River, Springfield is also along the Lewis & Clark Trail.

★4222★ SWAN CREEK RECREATION AREA

c/o West Whitlock Recreation Area
16157A West Whitlock Rd
Gettysburg, SD 57442
Web: www.sdgfp.info/parks/Regions/oahesharpe/
swancreek.htm
Phone: 605-765-9410
Size: 106 acres. **Location:** 9 miles west of Akaska off US 83. **Facilities:** 23 modern campsites with electrical hookups (2 &), comfort stations, fish cleaning station, boat ramps. **Activities:** Camping, boating, fishing. **Special Features:** Located on rolling prairie bluffs, Swan Creek has two campgrounds and two boat ramps offering access to Lake Oahe.

★4223★ UNION GROVE STATE PARK

c/o Newton Hills State Park
28771 482nd Ave
Canton, SD 57013
Web: www.sdgfp.info/parks/Regions/heartland/
uniongrove.htm
Phone: 605-987-2263
Size: 499 acres. **Location:** 11 miles south of Beresford off I-29. **Facilities:** 25 modern campsites (17 with electrical hookups), showers, horsemen's camp, picnic areas, picnic shelters, hiking trails, bridle trails, playground. **Activities:** Camping, hiking, biking, horseback riding, cross-country skiing. **Special Features:** Horseback riding is a major attraction of this park, which has 150 acres available for riding.

★4224★ WALKERS POINT RECREATION AREA

23409 State Park Dr
Madison, SD 57042
Web: www.sdgfp.info/parks/Regions/heartland/
walkerspoint.htm
Phone: 605-256-5003
Size: 41 acres. **Location:** 9 miles southeast of Madison off SD 19. **Facilities:** 43 modern campsites (42 with electrical hookups, 1 &), 2 cabins (1 &), comfort station with showers, picnic shelter

(&), boat ramp, boat rentals, fish cleaning station, fishing dock, playground, ski beach. **Activities:** Camping, boating, canoeing, fishing, water skiing. **Special Features:** Located on 2,800-acre Lake Madison.

★4225★ WEST BEND RECREATION AREA

c/o Farm Island Recreation Area
1301 Farm Island Rd
Pierre, SD 57501
Web: www.sdgfp.info/parks/Regions/oahesharpe/
westbend.htm
Phone: 605-773-2885
Size: 154 acres. **Location:** 35 miles southeast of Pierre, off SD 34. **Facilities:** 126 modern campsites (110 with electrical hookups), 4 cabins, comfort station with showers, picnic shelters (&), swimming beach, marina, fish cleaning station, boat ramp, playground. **Activities:** Camping, boating, fishing, swimming. **Special Features:** The West Bend Recreation Area is one of the South Dakota parks along the Lewis and Clark Trail. It has a protected marina that makes boat launching convenient regardless of wind direction.

★4226★ WEST POLLOCK RECREATION AREA

c/o Indian Creek Recreation Area
12905 288th Ave
Mobridge, SD 57601
Web: www.sdgfp.info/parks/Regions/oahesharpe/
westpollock.htm
Phone: 605-845-7112
Size: 243 acres. **Location:** 3 miles southwest of Pollock off SD 1804. **Facilities:** 29 modern campsites with electricity, boat ramp. **Activities:** Camping, boating, fishing. **Special Features:** The town of Pollock and the recreation area are both named after a pioneer lay minister and respected citizen of the area, R.Y. Pollock. Area is one of the South Dakota parks along the Lewis and Clark Trail.

★4227★ WEST WHITLOCK RECREATION AREA

16157A West Whitlock Rd
Gettysburg, SD 57442
Web: www.sdgfp.info/parks/Regions/oahesharpe/
westwhitlock.htm
Phone: 605-765-9410
Size: 260 acres. **Location:** 18 miles west of Gettysburg off US 212. **Facilities:** 100 modern campsites (87 with electrical hookups, 1 &), 2 cabins, comfort stations with showers, picnic areas, picnic shelter, hiking trails, ski beach, swimming beach, boat, fish cleaning station, historic site, playground. **Activities:** Camping, boating, fishing, swimming, water-skiing, diving, hiking, biking, cross-country skiing. **Special Features:** The replica of an Arikara earth lodge found in the park is a reminder of the many lodges that the Lewis and Clark expedition saw as they traveled this area. Each lodge, made of cottonwood logs, willow branches, and grass, could house up to 20 people.

Tennessee State Parks

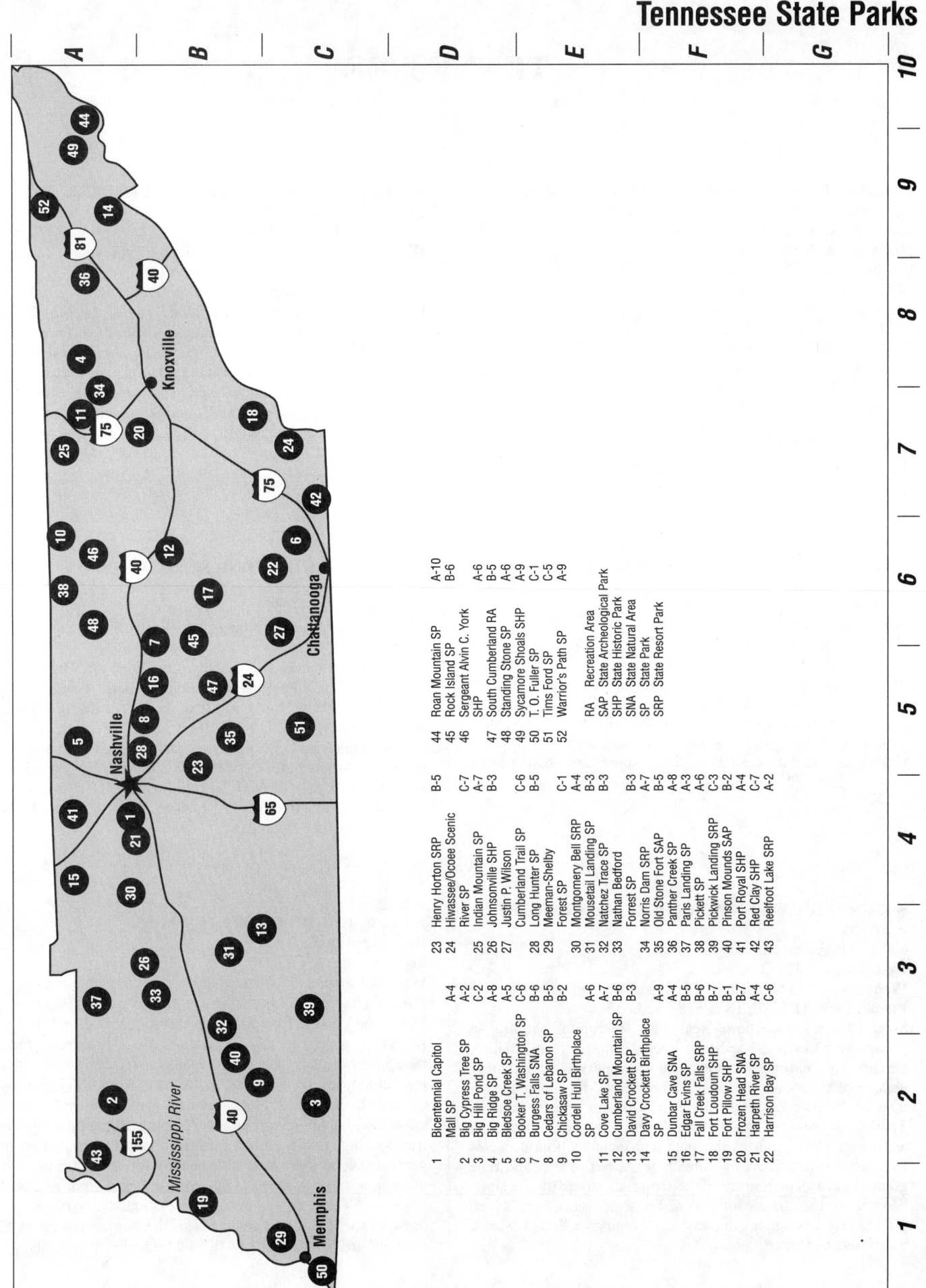

1	Bicentennial Capitol Mall SP		23	Henry Horton SRP	B-5	44	Roan Mountain SP	A-10
2	Big Cypress Tree SP	A-4	24	Hiwassee/Ocoee Scenic River SP	C-7	45	Rock Island SP	B-6
3	Big Hill Pond SP	A-2	25	Indian Mountain SP	A-7	46	Sergeant Alvin C. York SHP	A-6
4	Big Ridge SP	C-2	26	Johnsonville SHP	B-3	47	South Cumberland RA	B-5
5	Bledsoe Creek SP	A-8	27	Justin P. Wilson		48	Standing Stone SP	A-6
6	Booker T. Washington SP	A-5		Cumberland Trail SP	C-6	49	Sycamore Shoals SHP	A-9
7	Burgess Falls SNA	C-6	28	Long Hunter SP	B-5	50	T. O. Fuller SP	C-1
8	Cedars of Lebanon SP	B-6	29	Meeman-Shelby		51	Tims Ford SP	C-5
10	Cordell Hull Birthplace	B-5		Forest SP	C-1	52	Warrior's Path SP	A-9
	SP	B-2	30	Montgomery Bell SRP	A-4			
11	Cove Lake SP	A-6	31	Mousetail Landing SP	B-3	RA	Recreation Area	
12	Cumberland Mountain SP	A-7	32	Natchez Trace SP	B-3	SAP	State Archeological Park	
13	David Crockett SP	B-6	33	Nathan Bedford		SHP	State Historic Park	
14	Davy Crockett Birthplace	B-3		Forrest SP	B-3	SNA	State Natural Area	
	SP	A-9	34	Norris Dam SRP	A-7	SP	State Park	
15	Dunbar Cave SNA	A-4	35	Old Stone Fort SAP	B-5	SRP	State Resort Park	
16	Edgar Evins SP	B-5	36	Panther Creek SP	A-8			
17	Fall Creek Falls SRP	B-6	37	Paris Landing SP	A-3			
18	Fort Loudoun SHP	B-7	38	Pickett SP	A-6			
19	Fort Pillow SHP	B-1	39	Pickwick Landing SRP	C-3			
20	Frozen Head SNA	B-7	40	Pinson Mounds SAP	B-2			
21	Harpeth River SP	A-4	41	Port Royal SHP	A-4			
22	Harrison Bay SP	C-6	42	Red Clay SHP	C-7			
			43	Reelfoot Lake SRP	A-2			

787

★4228★ **Tennessee Department of Environment & Conservation**
State Parks Division
401 Church St, 7th Fl
Nashville, TN 37243
(615) 532-0001 - Phone
(615) 532-0732 - Fax
(888) 867-2757 - Toll-free
(615) 532-0027 - Employment
Web: state.tn.us/environment/parks
Oversees 54 state parks, comprising nearly 150,000 acres, which include historic, recreation, and natural areas. Maintains seven resort inns, eleven golf courses, five marinas, and nearly 900 miles of trails. Reservations may be made for cabins and resort lodging, but all campsites are available on a first-come, first-served basis only.

★4229★ **Tennessee Wildlife Resources Agency**
Ellington Agricultural Center
PO Box 40747
Nashville, TN 37204
(615) 781-6500
Web: www.state.tn.us/twra
Manages and preserves the state's forests and waters for the protection of game and non-game wildlife. Offers educational and safety programs for boaters and young hunters. Administers hunting and fishing licenses, provides public access boat ramps and docks, and enforces the hunting, fishing, and boating laws.

★4230★ **BICENTENNIAL CAPITOL MALL STATE PARK**
600 James Robertson Pkwy
Nashville, TN 37243
Web: www.state.tn.us/environment/parks/bicenmal
Phone: 615-741-5280; **Fax:** 615-532-0653
Size: 19 acres. **Location:** Near the state capitol building in downtown Nashville. **Facilities:** Visitor center, gift shop, snack bar. **Special Features:** A monument to Tennessee's 200th anniversary of statehood, the mall features a 200-foot-long granite map of the state; 31 vertical water fountains, one for each of Tennessee's main rivers; Walkway of the Counties, a historical and geographical tour of the state that includes time capsules for each county; Court of Three Stars, a red, white, and blue granite plaza depicting the three major divisions of the state; 95 carillons (bells), one for each of Tennessee's counties, which play hourly throughout the day and evening; a World War II memorial; and more.

★4231★ **BIG CYPRESS TREE STATE PARK**
295 Big Cypress Rd
Greenfield, TN 38230
Web: state.tn.us/environment/parks/BigCypress
Phone: 731-235-2700
Size: 27 acres within Big Cypress Tree State Natural Area.
Location: Off US 45E in the flood plain of the Middle Fork of the Obion River in west Tennessee. **Facilities:** Picnic areas, playground, nature trail (&), playfield. **Activities:** Hiking, guided nature tours (by appointment). **Special Features:** The area is named for a champion bald cypress tree. Once the largest and oldest bald cypress in the United States and the largest tree of any species east of the Mississippi River, the tree was killed in 1976 when a lightning bolt struck it. Park is located within 330-acre Big Cypress Tree State Natural Area.

★4232★ **BIG HILL POND STATE PARK**
984 John Howell Rd
Pocahontas, TN 38061
Web: state.tn.us/environment/parks/BigHillPond
Phone: 731-645-7967
Size: Approximately 5,000 acres. **Location:** Off Highway 57, south of Selmer. **Facilities:** 4 camp shelters, 4 scout camps, picnic areas, hiking trails, bridle trails, bike trails, boat launch, boardwalk, playground. **Activities:** Camping, boating, canoeing, fishing, hiking, backpacking, horseback riding, mountain biking, hunting (restricted areas). **Special Features:** Park has a boardwalk trail that goes through Dismal Swamp (0.8 of a mile) and a 70-foot observation tower that offers views of Travis McNatt Lake and Dismal Swamp.

★4233★ **BIG RIDGE STATE PARK**
1015 Big Ridge Rd
Maynardville, TN 37807
Web: www.state.tn.us/environment/parks/bigridge
Phone: 865-992-5523
Size: 3,687 acres. **Location:** On the southern shore of Norris Reservoir, approximately 25 miles north of Knoxville. **Facilities:** 50 campsites, group camp, backcountry campsites, 19 cabins, bathhouses, picnic areas, snack bar, hiking trails, boat rentals, boat launch, dock, recreation hall, game courts, playground, gift shop, laundry. **Activities:** Camping, swimming, boating, water-skiing, fishing, hiking, biking, tennis, interpretive programs. **Special Features:** This heavily forested park lies along the southern shore of the Tennessee Valley Authority's Norris Reservoir. The park was one of five demonstration parks developed by the TVA, and remnants of the homes and farms that existed here before that can still be seen along the trails.

9. State Parks

★4234★ BLEDSOE CREEK STATE PARK
400 Zeiglers Fort Rd
Gallatin, TN 37066
Web: state.tn.us/environment/parks/bledsoecreek
Phone: 615-452-3706
Size: 164 acres. **Location:** Off TN 25 and Route 2, on the Bledsoe Creek embayment of Old Hickory Lake in Sumner County. **Facilities:** 26 campsites with electrical hookups, showers, restrooms, picnic area, hiking trails (&), boat ramps, playground, game courts, playfield. **Activities:** Camping, boating, fishing, hiking. **Special Features:** Environmental programs are available from park rangers year round with advance notice.

★4235★ BOOKER T. WASHINGTON STATE PARK
5801 Champion Rd
Chattanooga, TN 37416
Web: www.state.tn.us/environment/parks/bookertwashington
Phone: 423-894-4955; **Fax:** 423-855-7879
Size: 353 acres. **Location:** Off TN 58 and Route 2, on the shores of Chickamauga Lake. **Facilities:** Group lodge, 16 cabins, picnic areas, hiking trails, swimming pool, boat ramps, playfields, playgrounds, game courts. **Activities:** Camping, boating, water-skiing, fishing, swimming, hiking. **Special Features:** Park was named to honor Booker Taliaferro Washington, a prominent writer, thinker, and educator who is most widely remembered for his many years as president of the Tuskegee Institute, a historically black institution of higher education.

★4236★ BURGESS FALLS STATE NATURAL AREA
4000 Burgess Falls Dr
Sparta, TN 38583
Web: www.state.tn.us/environment/parks/burgessfalls
Phone: 931-432-5312
Size: 154 acres. **Location:** Off State Route 135, in middle Tennessee. **Facilities:** Picnic area, hiking trails, playground, butterfly garden, interpretive programs. **Activities:** Fishing, boating (with restrictions), hiking, guided tours. **Special Features:** The Falling Water River drops 250 feet, providing numerous waterfalls and scenic overlooks. The main trail loop passes four waterfalls, ranging from 20-foot cascades to 136-foot falls. A large Native Butterfly Garden is located adjacent to the upper parking lot.

★4237★ CEDARS OF LEBANON STATE PARK
328 Cedar Forest Rd
Lebanon, TN 37087
Web: state.tn.us/environment/parks/cedars
Phone: 615-443-2769; **Fax:** 615-443-2793
Size: 900 acres. **Location:** 31 miles east of Nashville on US 231. **Facilities:** 117 campsites, 9 cabins, group lodge, 3 bathhouses, picnic areas, picnic shelters, snack bar, hiking trails (8 miles), bridle trails (12 miles), horse rentals, stable, swimming pool, visitor center, recreation building, meeting hall, nature center, stables, camp store, playground, game courts, disc golf course, tennis courts, laundromat. **Activities:** Camping, swimming, hiking, horseback riding, tennis, basketball. **Special Features:** Park is named for the dense cedar forests that existed in the Biblical land of Lebanon. During the early 1800s, settlers in the area

mistook the juniper forests they found there for cedar and named it accordingly.

★4238★ CHICKASAW STATE PARK
20 Cabin Ln
Henderson, TN 38340
Web: www.state.tn.us/environment/parks/chickasaw
Phone: 731-989-5141
Size: 14,384 acres (includes state forest acreage). **Location:** 18 miles south of Jackson, on Highway 100. **Facilities:** 113 campsites (84 with electrical hookups), group camp, wrangler camp, 13 cabins, group lodge, bathhouses, picnic areas, restaurant, snack bar, hiking trails, bike trails, bridle trail, beach, archery ranges, boat rentals, stables, horse rentals, meeting rooms, game courts, playground, playfield. **Activities:** Camping, boating, fishing, swimming, hiking, biking, horseback riding, tennis, basketball. **Special Features:** Park is situated on some of the highest terrain in west Tennessee. Of the area's 14,384 acres of timerland, 1,280 are used for recreation, the remainder is state forest.

★4239★ CORDELL HULL BIRTHPLACE STATE PARK
1300 Cordell Hull Memorial Dr
Byrdstown, TN 38549
Web: www.state.tn.us/environment/parks/cordellhull
Phone: 931-864-3247; **Fax:** 931-864-6389
Size: 45 acres. **Location:** West of Byrdstown, on State Route 325, near the Kentucky border. **Facilities:** Activity center, historic site, museum, picnic area. **Special Features:** Hull served as Secretary of State under President Franklin D. Roosevelt between 1933 and 1944. In 1945, he was awarded the Nobel Prize for Peace. Park consists of a representation of Hull's log cabin birthplace and museum with documents and artifacts, including his Nobel Peace Prize.

★4240★ COVE LAKE STATE PARK
110 Cove Lake Ln
Caryville, TN 37714
Web: www.state.tn.us/environment/parks/covelake
Phone: 423-566-9701; **Fax:** 423-566-9717
Size: 673 acres. **Location:** In Caryville, on the eastern edge of the Cumberland Mountains. **Facilities:** 100 campsites with water and electricity hookups (&), bathhouses, picnic areas, day-use pavilion, restaurant, hiking trail, bike trail, boat rentals, recreation building, game courts, swimming pool (&), playgrounds. **Activities:** Camping, boating, fishing, swimming, hiking, bicycling, tennis. **Special Features:** During the winter months, the park serves as the feeding ground for several hundred Canada geese.

★4241★ CUMBERLAND MOUNTAIN STATE PARK
24 Office Dr
Crossville, TN 38555
Web: www.state.tn.us/environment/parks/CumberlandMtn
Phone: 931-484-6138
Size: 1,720 acres. **Location:** US 127 off I-40 near Nashville.

Facilities: 147 campsites, bathhouse, meeting room, hiking trails, picnic area, restaurant, boat rentals, dock, swimming pool, game courts, playfield, playground, 18-hole golf course. **Activities:** Camping, boating, fishing, swimming, hiking, tennis, golf, interpretive programs. **Special Features:** Cumberland Mountain is situated on the Cumberland Plateau, said to be the largest timbered plateau in America, which extends from western New York to central Alabama. Park features Bear Trace, a challenging Jack Nicklaus-designed championship golf course in a scenic setting of flowing streams, clustered pines, and elevation changes. The signature seventh hole features a blind tee shot and a protected green surrounded by sand traps and layered flagstone.

★4242★ **DAVID CROCKETT STATE PARK**
PO Box 398
1400 W Gaines
Lawrenceburg, TN 38464
Web: state.tn.us/environment/parks/davidcrockettsp
Phone: 931-762-9408; **Fax:** 931-766-0047
Size: 1,100 acres. **Location:** Off US 64, on the banks of Shoal Creek, 1/2 mile west of Lawrenceburg. **Facilities:** 107 campsites with water and electricity hookups, picnic areas, restaurant, hiking trails, paved bike trails, swimming pool, boat rentals, museum, recreation building, restaurant, game courts, playground, playfield. **Activities:** Camping, boating, fishing, swimming, hiking, bicycling, archery, tennis, interpretive programs (seasonal). **Special Features:** Located on the site where Crockett once operated a powder mill, grist mill, and distillery, the park features 40-acre Lindsey Lake, which offers year-round fishing for bass, crappie, bluegill, and catfish.

★4243★ **DAVY CROCKETT BIRTHPLACE STATE PARK**
1245 Davy Crockett Park Rd
Limestone, TN 37681
Web: state.tn.us/environment/parks/davycrockettshp
Phone: 423-257-2167; **Fax:** 423-257-2430
Size: 105 acres. **Location:** Southwest of Johnson City, just off US 11E. **Facilities:** 88 campsites with water and electricity hookups, picnic area, hiking trails, boat ramp, historical site, museum, gift shop, swimming pool, playground, playfield. **Activities:** Camping, canoeing, swimming, fishing. **Special Features:** This historic area is maintained as a memorial to Davy Crockett, with a limestone marker on the spot where Crockett was born and a replica of the cabin in which he was born.

★4244★ **DUNBAR CAVE STATE NATURAL AREA**
401 Old Dunbar Cave Rd
Clarksville, TN 37043
Web: www.state.tn.us/environment/parks/dunbarcave
Phone: 931-648-5526
Size: 110 acres. **Location:** 1 1/2 miles northeast of Clarksville off I-24. **Facilities:** Picnic areas, hiking trails, visitor center. **Activities:** Fishing, spelunking, cave tours (reservations required), interpretive programs. **Special Features:** Dunbar Cave is the most prominent of the many caves and sinkholes found in this area. Excavations have revealed that the cave has been occupied by man for thousands of years due to its constant flowing stream and natural air conditioning. In the roomy mouth of the cave, square dances, radio shows, and big band concerts were once held.

★4245★ **EDGAR EVINS STATE PARK**
1630 Edgar Evins State Park Rd
Silver Point, TN 38582
Web: www.state.tn.us/environment/parks/edgarevins
Phone: 931-858-2446
Size: Approximately 6,000 acres. **Location:** 60 miles east of Nashville on Hwy 96. **Facilities:** 60 campsites with electricity, 34 cabins, bathhouses, picnic areas, picnic shelters, hiking trails, marina, boat rentals, boat ramps, visitor center, restaurant, playgrounds, swimming pool. **Activities:** Camping, boating, fishing, swimming, water-skiing, hiking. **Special Features:** Located on the shores of Center Hill Reservoir in the rolling hills of central Tennessee. The park was named to honor James Edgar Evins, a former state senator who was instrumental in the development of Center Hill Dam and Reservoir.

★4246★ **FALL CREEK FALLS STATE RESORT PARK**
2009 Village Camp Rd
Rt 3 Box 300
Pikeville, TN 37367
Web: www.state.tn.us/environment/parks/fallcreekfalls
Phone: 423-881-5298
Size: 19,500 acres. **Location:** Off TN 30, west of Pikeville. **Facilities:** 228 campsites with electricity, 144-room inn, 30 cabins, group lodges, group camps, bathhouses, picnic areas, restaurant, hiking trails, bike trails, swimming pool, boat rentals, boat launch, boat cruise, visitor center, conference center, gift shop, 18-hole golf course, game courts, playfields, playground. **Activities:** Camping, boating, canoeing, fishing, swimming, hiking, backpacking, mountain biking, golf, tennis, rock climbing, interpretive programs. **Special Features:** Tennessee's largest state park offers some of the most spectacular scenery in the state, including cascading waterfalls, deep chasms and gorges, virgin timber, and the striking Fall Creek Falls, plunging 256 feet into a shaded pool.

★4247★ **FORT LOUDOUN STATE HISTORIC PARK**
338 Fort Loudoun Rd
Vonore, TN 37885
Web: www.state.tn.us/environment/parks/fortloudoun
Phone: 423-884-6217
Size: 1,200 acres. **Location:** Off US 411 to TN 360. **Facilities:** Picnic areas, hiking trails, visitor center, museum. **Activities:** Boating, canoeing, water-skiing, fishing, swimming, hiking, living history demonstrations. **Special Features:** Site of one of the earliest fortifications on the western frontier, built by British soldiers in 1756. Today a reconstruction of the fort overlooks the Tellico Reservoir and the Appalachian Mountains.

★4248★ FORT PILLOW STATE HISTORIC PARK
3122 Park Rd
Henning, TN 38041
Web: www.state.tn.us/environment/parks/fortpillow
Phone: 731-738-5581; **Fax:** 731-738-9117
Size: 1,642 acres. **Location:** Off TN 87, on the Chickasaw Bluffs overlooking the Mississippi River. **Facilities:** 38 campsites, primitive campsites, picnic areas, pavilions, hiking trails (15 miles), boat ramp, museum, game courts, playground. **Activities:** Camping, boating, canoeing, fishing, hiking, backpacking. **Special Features:** In 1861, the Confederates built an extensive fortification here and named it for one of their generals, Gideon J. Pillow. Remains of the earthworks of this structure are still present.

★4249★ FROZEN HEAD STATE NATURAL AREA
964 Flat Fork Rd
Wartburg, TN 37887
Web: www.state.tn.us/environment/parks/frozenhead
Phone: 423-346-3318; **Fax:** 423-346-6629
Size: 11,876 acres. **Location:** In the Cumberland Mountains of eastern Tennessee near Wartburg. **Facilities:** 19 tent-only campsites, 11 backcountry campsites, bathhouse, picnic areas, picnic shelters, hiking trails, bridle trails, game courts, playground. **Activities:** Camping, fishing, hiking, backpacking, horseback riding. **Special Features:** This wild, scenic, and natural area is named for one of the highest peaks in the Cumberland Mountains, the top of which is often shrouded in ice and snow. A creek running through the area is stocked with trout for fly fishing.

★4250★ HARPETH RIVER STATE PARK
Hwy 70
Kingston Springs, TN 37887
Web: www.state.tn.us/environment/parks/harpethriver
Phone: 615-797-6096
Size: 450 acres. **Location:** Off Highway 70, 20 miles west of Nashville. **Facilities:** Picnic areas, hiking trails, boat launches. **Activities:** Canoeing, fishing, hiking, backpacking, interpretive tours. **Special Features:** Linear park along the Harpeth River offers natural, cultural and recreational areas rich in historic significance and natural beauty.

★4251★ HARRISON BAY STATE PARK
8411 Harrison Bay Rd
Harrison, TN 37341
Web: www.state.tn.us/environment/parks/harrisonbay
Phone: 423-344-6214
Size: 1,200 acres. **Location:** Off TN 58, 5 miles west of Cleveland. **Facilities:** 149 campsites (including 29 tent only sites), group camp, bathhouses, picnic areas, hiking trails, swimming pool, marina, boat launch, 18-hole golf course, game courts, playfield, playground, meeting room. **Activities:** Camping, boating, fishing, swimming, hiking, tennis, golf. **Special Features:** Originally developed as a TVA recreation demonstration area in the 1930s, park has about 40 miles of Chickamauga Lake shoreline. The park's name is derived from a large bay at the main channel of the Tennessee River that covers the old town

of Harrison, which was also the last Cherokee Campground. The campground consisted of three villages that were ruled by one of the last great Cherokee Chieftains, Chief Joe Vann.

★4252★ HENRY HORTON STATE RESORT PARK
4358 Nashville Hwy
Chapel Hill, TN 37034
Web: www.state.tn.us/environment/parks/henryhorton
Phone: 931-364-2222
Size: 1,140 acres. **Location:** Off US 31A, in middle Tennessee. **Facilities:** 75 campsites (including 21 tent only sites), primitive camping, 7 cabins, 72-room inn, group lodge, picnic areas, pavilions, hiking trails, restaurant, conference center, meeting rooms, swimming pool, bathhouse, shooting range, 18-hole golf course, game courts, playfield, playground, gift shop. **Activities:** Camping, canoeing, fishing, swimming, hiking, golf, tennis, archery, recreational programs. **Special Features:** Park is located along the Duck River, on the former estate of the 36th governor of Tennessee, Henry H. Horton. A favorite of target enthusiasts, park features trap, skeet, Crazy Quail, and 5-stand shooting.

★4253★ HIWASSEE/OCOEE SCENIC RIVER STATE PARK
PO Box 5
Delano, TN 37325
Web: www.state.tn.us/environment/parks/hiwasseeriver
Phone: 615-263-4133
Size: 76 acres. **Location:** On Spring Creek Road at US Highway 411. **Facilities:** 43 campsites, primitive campsites, picnic area, hiking trails, bridle trails, boat ramp. **Activities:** Camping, boating, whitewater rafting and canoeing, fishing, hiking, horseback riding. **Special Features:** The Ocoee River is one of the premier whitewater rivers in the southeastern United States and includes Class III, IV, and V rapids.

★4254★ INDIAN MOUNTAIN STATE PARK
143 State Park Cir
Jellico, TN 37762
Web: www.state.tn.us/environment/parks/indianmountain
Phone: 423-784-7958
Size: 200 acres. **Location:** Between the city limits of Jellico and the Kentucky state line, off I-75. **Facilities:** 49 campsites with water and electricity hookups, picnic areas, picnic shelters, hiking trails, swimming pool, boat rentals, boat launch. **Activities:** Camping, boating, fishing, swimming, hiking. **Special Features:** Developed on reclaimed strip-mined land, the park features several ponds which offer fishing for bass, crappie, and catfish.

★4255★ JOHNSONVILLE STATE HISTORIC PARK
Rt 1, Box 374
New Johnsonville, TN 37134
Web: www.state.tn.us/environment/parks/johnsonville
Phone: 931-535-2789; **Fax:** 931-535-3776
Size: 600 acres. **Location:** On the eastern side of Kentucky Lake, off Hwy 70. **Facilities:** Picnic area, pavilions, hiking

9. State Parks

trails, historic site, game courts, playground. **Activities:** Fishing, hiking, interpretive programs. **Special Features:** Park is located on the eastern side of Kentucky Lake overlooking the site of the Battle of Johnsonville. Cavalry forces under Lt. Gen. Nathan Bedford Forrest sank four federal gunboats downstream and destroyed a Union Army supply depot at Johnsonville. Park preserves four of the original breastworks.

★4256★ JUSTIN P. WILSON CUMBERLAND TRAIL STATE PARK

220 Park Rd
Caryville, TN 38555
Web: www.state.tn.us/environment/parks/cumberlandtrail
Phone: 423-566-2229; **Fax:** 423-566-2290
Size: 300-mile linear park. **Location:** From the Cumberland Gap National Historic Park on the Tennessee-Virginia-Kentucky border, to Signal Point near Chattanooga. **Facilities:** Hiking path. **Activities:** Hiking. **Special Features:** On completion, the trail will be 300 miles, cutting through 11 counties. 150 miles of the trail are now open for exploration, winding through the Cumberland Mountains that once rose as high as the Rockies.

★4257★ LONG HUNTER STATE PARK

2910 Hobson Pike
Hermitage, TN 37076
Web: www.state.tn.us/environment/parks/longhunter
Phone: 615-855-2422
Size: 2,315 acres. **Location:** Just east of Nashville, off I-40, Exit 226-A. **Facilities:** Group camp, picnic shelters, hiking trails, boat rentals, boat ramps, meeting facility, gift shop, game courts, playground. **Activities:** Boating, canoeing, sailing, fishing, water-skiing, swimming, hiking, backpacking. **Special Features:** Located beside 14,000-acre J Percy Priest Lake, the park's trails follow the shore of the lake to bluff overlooks and through hardwood forest and cedar thickets.

★4258★ MEEMAN-SHELBY FOREST STATE PARK

910 Riddick Rd
Millington, TN 38053
Web: www.state.tn.us/environment/parks/meemanshelby
Phone: 901-876-5215; **Fax:** 901-876-3217; **Toll Free:** 800-471-5293
Size: 13,467 acres. **Location:** North of Memphis, off I-40. **Facilities:** 49 campsites with water and electricity hookups, group camps (&), 6 cabins (1 &), bathhouse, picnic areas, picnic shelters, hiking trails, bike trails, swimming pool (&), 2 lakes, boat rentals, boat ramp, visitor center, nature center. **Activities:** Camping, boating, fishing, swimming, hiking, bicycling. **Special Features:** Bordering the Mississippi River, two-thirds of the park is bottomland hardwood forests of large oak, cypress, and tupelo. The park also contains two lakes, many miles of trails, and the Meeman Museum and Nature Center.

★4259★ MONTGOMERY BELL STATE RESORT PARK

1020 Jackson Hill Rd
Burns, TN 37029
Web: www.state.tn.us/environment/parks/montgomerybell
Phone: 615-797-9052

Size: 3,782 acres. **Location:** 7 miles east of Dickson, in middle Tennessee. **Facilities:** Campsites with electricity hookups, group camp, 8 cabins, bathhouses, 120-room inn, picnic areas, hiking trails, bike trails, boat ramps, convention center, meeting rooms, restaurant, gift shop, snack bar, camp store, 18-hole golf course, game courts, playfield, playground, beach. **Activities:** Camping, boating, canoeing, fishing, swimming, hiking, biking, archery, tennis, interpretive programs. **Special Features:** Located within the park area was Laurel Furnace, the iron manufacturing operation of early Tennessee industrialist Montgomery Bell. The site of the first Cumberland Presbyterian Church is also located at the park.

★4260★ MOUSETAIL LANDING STATE PARK

Rt 3, Box 280B
Linden, TN 37096
Web: www.state.tn.us/environment/parks/mousetaillanding
Phone: 731-847-0841
Size: 1,247 acres. **Location:** Beside the Tennessee River, north of US 412, in the western valley. **Facilities:** 24 campsites (19 with water and electricity hookups), backcountry campsites, picnic areas, pavilion, hiking trail, bike path, boat launch, fishing pier, beach, visitor center, archery range, game courts, playground. **Activities:** Camping, boating, fishing, water-skiing, swimming, hiking, interpretive programs. **Special Features:** Tradition has it that Mousetail Landing got its name during the Civil War period when one of the area's tanning companies caught fire. The exodus of mice fleeing the burning building was so profuse that the area became known as Mousetail Landing.

★4261★ NATCHEZ TRACE STATE PARK

24845 Natchez Trace Rd
Wildersville, TN 38388
Web: www.state.tn.us/environment/parks/natcheztrace
Phone: 731-968-3742
Size: 48,000 acres (includes state forest acreage). **Location:** 35 miles east of Jackson off I-40 between Nashville and Memphis. **Facilities:** 190 campsites with full hookups, 20 tent campsites, wranglers camp, backcounty campsites, group camp (&), cabins, villas, 47-room inn, picnic areas, bathhouses, hiking trails, beach, boat launch, boat rentals, stables, horse rentals, archery range, shooting range, visitor center, restaurant, gift shop, camp store, game courts, playground. **Activities:** Camping, boating, swimming, fishing, hiking, backpacking, horseback riding, tennis, basketball, interpretive programs. **Special Features:** Park is named for the famous ''Natchez to Nashville'' highway, an important wilderness road during the early 18th and early 19th centuries.

★4262★ NATHAN BEDFORD FORREST STATE PARK

1825 Pilot Knob Rd
Eva, TN 38333
Web: www.state.tn.us/environment/parks/nbforrest
Phone: 731-584-6356; **Fax:** 731-584-1841
Size: 2,587 acres. **Location:** 15 miles north of I-40 on US Highway 641. **Facilities:** 53 campsites (including 15 tent only

9. State Parks

sites), backcountry campsites, group lodge, picnic areas, pavilions, hiking trails, boat ramps, museum, gift shop, game courts, playfield, playgrounds, interpretive center. **Activities:** Camping, boating, water-skiing, swimming, fishing, hiking, interpretive programs. **Special Features:** Park marks the site of the Civil War Battle of Johnsonville, where Confederate forces under General Nathan Bedford Forrest destroyed a Union supply depot. Pilot Knob, named for its use as a landmark by riverboat pilots, offers a spectacular view of the lake and is home of the Tennessee River Folklife Center.

★4263★ NORRIS DAM STATE RESORT PARK
125 Village Green Cir
Lake City, TN 37769
Web: www.state.tn.us/environment/parks/norrisdam
Phone: 865-426-7461
Size: 4,038 acres. **Location:** Off US 441 on Norris Lake, 20 miles northwest of Knoxville. **Facilities:** 75 campsites with water and electricity hookups (&), 29 cabins (&), bathhouses, laundromat, picnic areas, hiking trails, swimming pool, marina, boat rentals, boat launch, museum, recreation building, gift shop, game courts, playgrounds. **Activities:** Camping, boating, canoeing, fishing, swimming, hiking, tennis, recreation and interpretive programs (seasonal). **Special Features:** Park is located at the site of the massive Norris Dam, which was begun in 1933 as the first Tennessee Valley Authority project. Lenoir Museum Cultural Complex features the Lenoir Pioneer Museum, an 18th century Rice Grist Mill and Crosby Threshing Barn.

★4264★ OLD STONE FORT STATE ARCHAEOLOGICAL PARK
732 Stone Fort Dr
Manchester, TN 37355
Web: www.state.tn.us/environment/parks/oldstonefort
Phone: 931-723-5073
Size: 760 acres. **Location:** Off US Highway 41 in Manchester, 1.5 miles off I-24. **Facilities:** 51 campsites with water and electricity hookups (&), primitive campsites, showers, picnic areas, hiking trails, boat launch, historic site, 9-hole golf course. **Activities:** Camping, fishing, hiking, golf, interpretive programs. **Special Features:** The Old Stone Fort is a 2,000-year-old Native American ceremonial site. It consists of mounds and walls which combine with cliffs and rivers to form an enclosure measuring 1.25 miles around. The 50 enclosed acres appear to have served as a central ceremonial gathering place for some 500 years.

★4265★ PANTHER CREEK STATE PARK
2010 Panther Creek Park Rd
Morristown, TN 37814
Web: www.state.tn.us/environment/parks/panthercreek
Phone: 423-587-7046; **Fax:** 423-587-7047
Size: 1,435 acres. **Location:** Off US 11E and Route 1, 6 miles west of Morristown, on Cherokee Lake. **Facilities:** 50 campsites with water and electricity hookups, laundromat, bathhouses, picnic areas, pavilions, hiking trails, bridle trails, bike trails, swimming pool, game courts, playfield, playgrounds. **Activities:**

Camping, fishing, canoeing, swimming, hiking, mountain biking, horseback riding, tennis. **Special Features:** Park is located on the shores of the Cherokee Reservoir, an impoundment of the Holston River. Legend has it that Panther Creek and Panther Springs, which is located about 1.5 miles southeast of the park, received their names from the claim of a Virginia man who shot a panther that fell into the spring.

★4266★ PARIS LANDING STATE PARK
16055 Hwy 79N
Buchanan, TN 38222
Web: www.state.tn.us/environment/parks/parislanding
Phone: 731-641-4465
Size: 841 acres. **Location:** 18 miles east of Paris on US Hwy 79. **Facilities:** 44 campsites with water and electricity hookups (&), bathhouses, 130-room inn, 10 cabins (&), conference facility, restaurant, picnic areas, picnic shelter, hiking trail (2 miles), swimming pool (&), beach, marina, boat ramp, amphitheater, 18-hole golf course, game courts, playground, gift shop. **Activities:** Camping, boating, fishing, swimming, water-skiing, hiking, musical programs. **Special Features:** Park is named for a steamboat and freight landing on the Tennessee River, dating back to the mid-1800s. From here supplies were transported to surrounding towns and communities by ox cart.

★4267★ PICKETT STATE PARK
4605 Pickett Park Hwy
Jamestown, TN 38556
Web: www.state.tn.us/environment/parks/pickett
Phone: 931-879-5821
Size: 17,372 acres. **Location:** From I-40 (Crossville exit), north on Highway 127 for 46 miles, then 12 miles east on Highway 154. **Facilities:** 40 campsites (20 with water and electricity hookups, &), group camp (&), 15 cabins (&), backcountry camping, bathhouse, picnic areas, picnic shelters, hiking trails, beach, boat rentals, stable. **Activities:** Camping, boating, fishing, swimming, hiking, horseback riding. **Special Features:** Situated in a remote section of the upper Cumberland Mountains, Pickett State Park possesses a combination of scenic, botanical, and geological wonders found nowhere else in Tennessee. Features include unusual rock formations, natural bridges, numerous caves, and remains of ancient Indian occupation.

★4268★ PICKWICK LANDING STATE RESORT PARK
PO Box 15
Pickwick Dam, TN 38365
Web: www.state.tn.us/environment/parks/pickwicklanding
Phone: 731-689-3129
Size: 1,392 acres. **Location:** Off TN Highway 57 at Pickwick Dam. **Facilities:** 48 campsites, cabins, 119-room inn, picnic areas (&), picnic shelters, marina, boat ramps, boat rentals, fishing piers, beaches, restaurant, conference center, 18-hole golf course, gift shop, playground. **Activities:** Camping, boating, fishing, swimming, golf. **Special Features:** Pickwick Landing was a riverboat stop dating from the 1840s. During the Great Depression, the site was chosen for one of the Tennessee Valley

Authority's dams on the Tennessee River. Today Pickwick Landing is one of the most visited parks in the system.

★4269★ PINSON MOUNDS STATE ARCHAEOLOGICAL PARK

460 Ozier Rd
Pinson, TN 38366
Web: www.state.tn.us/environment/parks/pinsonmounds
Phone: 731-988-5614
Size: Almost 1200 acres. **Location:** Off US 45, 5 miles south of Jackson. **Facilities:** Group camp, showers, picnic areas, picnic shelters, hiking trails, museum, gift shop, historic area. **Activities:** Camping, hiking, interpretive programs. **Special Features:** The grouping known as Pinson Mounds consists of at least 15 earthen mounds (including the second tallest ceremonial mound in the United States), a geometric enclosure, habitation areas, and related earthworks. A number of cremation and activity areas have been found nearby. Fieldwork is normally conducted in the summer, and visitors are welcome to watch the archeologists at work.

★4270★ PORT ROYAL STATE HISTORIC PARK

3300 Old Clarksville Hwy
Adams, TN 37010
Web: www.state.tn.us/environment/parks/portroyal
Phone: 931-648-5526
Size: 26 acres. **Location:** 12 miles southeast of downtown Clarksville, Tennessee, off Hwy. 76. **Facilities:** Picnic areas, hiking trails. **Activities:** Hiking, picnicking, sightseeing. **Special Features:** Site of one of Tennessee's earliest communities and trading centers, the park is an official site on the Trail of Tears National Historic Trail. The covered bridge is a reconstruction of an earlier bridge, whose remains were washed away in the flood of 1866. The present concrete and steel bridge was built in 1955.

★4271★ RADNOR LAKE STATE PARK

1160 Otter Creek Rd
Nashville, TN 37220
Web: www.state.tn.us/environment/parks/RadnorLake
Phone: 615-373-3467
Size: 1,130 acres. **Location:** In the Overton Hills, south of metropolitan Nashville, in the community of Oak Hill. **Facilities:** Hiking trails. **Activities:** Hiking, wildlife viewing, interpretive programs. **Special Features:** Park is one of the largest pockets of wilderness in the US in close proximity to a major city, providing scenic, biological, geological, and passive recreational opportunities not usually found in metropolitan areas of Nashville's size. The park is managed as a nature sanctuary, and its trails can be used only for hiking and wildlife observation.

★4272★ RED CLAY STATE HISTORIC PARK

1140 Red Clay Park Rd
Cleveland, TN 37311
Web: www.state.tn.us/environment/parks/redclay
Phone: 423-478-0339
Size: 263 acres. **Location:** Off I-75, just east of Chattanooga.

Facilities: Picnic areas, hiking trails, amphitheater. **Activities:** Hiking, interpretive programs. **Special Features:** Park contains a natural landmark, Blue Hole Spring, which rises from beneath a limestone ledge to form a deep pool that flows into Mill Creek. The spring was used by the Cherokee for their water supply during council meetings.

★4273★ REELFOOT LAKE STATE PARK

3120 SR 213
Tiptonville, TN 38079
Web: www.state.tn.us/environment/parks/reelfootlake
Phone: 731-253-7756
Size: 338 acres. **Location:** Off TN 21, 15 miles southwest of Union City in the northwest corner of the state. **Facilities:** 100 campsites with water and electricity hookups, 20-room inn, picnic areas, picnic shelters, hiking trails, fishing piers, visitor center, auditorium, game courts, playgrounds. **Activities:** Camping, boating, canoeing, fishing, swimming, tennis, boat and canoe tours, interpretive programs. **Special Features:** Reelfoot Lake is one of the greatest hunting and fishing preserves in the U.S. It is also a favorite wintering ground for the American bald eagle, and guided tours to view the majestic birds are offered during the winter months.

★4274★ ROAN MOUNTAIN STATE PARK

1015 Hwy 143
Roan Mountain, TN 37687
Web: www.state.tn.us/environment/parks/roanmtn
Phone: 423-772-0190
Size: 2,006 acres. **Location:** Off TN 143, 16 miles south of Elizabethton. **Facilities:** 107 campsites (including 20 tent only sites), group camp, 30 cabins, picnic areas, pavilions, hiking trails, swimming pool, game courts, playfield, playgrounds, conference center. **Activities:** Camping, fishing, swimming, hiking, backpacking, tennis, interpretive programs. **Special Features:** Park is situated at the base of Roan Mountain (6,285 feet). Atop the mountain is a 600-acre natural rhododendron garden, which blooms with pink and purple blossoms during the summer. The 2,144-mile Appalachian Trail (see entry in national trails section) crosses Roan Mountain in the adjoining Cherokee National Forest (see entry in national forests section).

★4275★ ROCK ISLAND STATE PARK

82 Beach Rd
Rock Island, TN 38581
Web: www.state.tn.us/environment/parks/rockisland
Phone: 931-686-2471
Size: 883 acres. **Location:** At the upper end of Center Hill Lake, at the confluence of the Collins and Caney Fork Rivers. **Facilities:** 60 campsites with water and electricity hookups, 10 cabins (&), picnic areas, pavilions, hiking trails, beach, boat ramp, game courts, playground. **Activities:** Camping, boating, canoeing, fishing, swimming, water skiing, hiking, tennis, interpretive programs. **Special Features:** Park is dominated by the Great Falls of the Caney Fork River, a limestone gorge with scenic overlooks, waterfalls, and deep pools for fishing, rock-hopping, and exploring.

9. State Parks

★4276★ SERGEANT ALVIN C. YORK STATE HISTORIC PARK

General Delivery
Hwy 127
Pall Mall, TN 38577
Web: www.state.tn.us/environment/parks/sgtyork
Phone: 931-879-9406
Size: 343 acres. **Location:** In Pall Mall, on US Highway 127.
Facilities: Historic buildings, picnic areas, picnic shelters. **Special Features:** Park pays tribute to Sgt. Alvin C. York, the backwoods marksman from the mountains of Tennessee who became one of the most decorated soldiers of World War I. York's fame rose from his legendary exploits in the Argonne Forest in France when he found himself alone opposing a German machine gun unit. When the battle was over, York and six comrades had 132 German prisoners. Site includes the York family farm and the grist mill he operated on the banks of the Wolf River.

★4277★ SOUTH CUMBERLAND RECREATION AREA

Rt 1, Box 2196
Monteagle, TN 37356
Web: state.tn.us/environment/parks/southcumberland
Phone: 931-692-3887
Size: 16,000 acres. **Location:** Exit 134 off I-24 in Monteagle.
Facilities: Backcountry campsites, picnic areas (&), pavilion, hiking trails, visitor center, museum, game courts, playfield.
Activities: Camping, hiking, backpacking, tennis, guided hikes, interpretive programs. **Special Features:** The South Cumberland is composed of ten separate areas in four counties. Almost all of the park lies atop the Cumberland Plateau.

★4278★ STANDING STONE STATE PARK

1674 Standing Stone Park Hwy
Hilham, TN 38568
Web: www.state.tn.us/environment/parks/standstn
Phone: 931-823-6347
Size: Nearly 11,000 acres. **Location:** Off TN 52, on the Cumberland Plateau of north-central Tennessee. **Facilities:** 36 campsites, cabins, 4 group lodges, bathhouses, laundry, picnic areas, picnic pavilions, hiking trails, swimming pool, boat rentals, meeting room, recreation building, game courts, snack bar. **Activities:** Camping, boating, fishing, swimming, hiking, tennis.
Special Features: Park takes its name from an 8-foot-tall rock standing upright on a sandstone ledge, which is said to have marked a boundary between two separate native tribes. When the rock fell, a portion of it was placed on an improvised monument to preserve it. The stone is still preserved in Monterey, Tennessee.

★4279★ SYCAMORE SHOALS STATE HISTORIC PARK

1651 W Elk Ave
Elizabethton, TN 37643
Web: www.state.tn.us/environment/parks/sycamoreshoals
Phone: 423-543-5808; **Fax:** 423-543-0078
Size: 75 acres. **Location:** Off US 321 in Elizabethton. **Facilities:**
Picnic areas, hiking trails, visitor center, historic park. **Activities:** Picnicking, hiking. **Special Features:** Sycamore Shoals is the site of the first permanent settlement outside the 13 original colonies.

★4280★ T. O. FULLER STATE PARK

1500 Mitchell Rd
Memphis, TN 38109
Web: www.state.tn.us/environment/parks/tofuller
Phone: 901-543-7581; **Fax:** 901-785-8485
Size: 1,138 acres. **Location:** 11 miles south of downtown Memphis, on Mitchell Road west of US 61. **Facilities:** 45 campsites, bathhouse, pavilions, picnic areas, hiking trails, swimming pool, 18-hole golf course, game courts, playfield, playground. **Activities:** Camping, swimming, hiking, tennis, golf. **Special Features:** Within the boundaries of this park is the historic Chucalissa Village, operated by the University of Memphis. Choctaw guides and native craftsmen show how the area's early residents lived. The village contains native houses, a historic Indian temple, a covered excavation, and a museum.

★4281★ TIMS FORD STATE PARK

570 Tims Ford Dr
Winchester, TN 37398
Web: www.state.tn.us/environment/parks/timsford
Phone: 931-962-1183
Size: 1,895 acres. **Location:** On Tims Ford Lake just west of Winchester, in southern middle Tennessee. **Facilities:** 50 campsites (&), 20 cabins (&), picnic areas, pavilions, hiking trails, bike trails, swimming pool (&), marina, bait shop, boat rentals, boat ramp, 18-hole golf course, disc golf course, restaurant, snack bar, visitor center, recreation building, game courts, playfield, playground. **Activities:** Camping, boating, fishing, swimming, hiking, bicycling, tennis, golf, interpretive programs.
Special Features: Archeological excavations have uncovered numerous artifacts and occupational sites, indicating that man had occupied the area as much as 10,000 to 12,000 years ago.

★4282★ WARRIORS' PATH STATE PARK

PO Box 5026
Kingsport, TN 37663
Web: www.state.tn.us/environment/parks/warriorspath
Phone: 423-239-8531; **Fax:** 423-239-4982
Size: 905 acres. **Location:** Off Route 36, on the shores of Fort Patrick Henry Lake. **Facilities:** 135 campsites (94 with water and electricity hookups), bathhouse, picnic areas, pavilions, hiking trails (&), bike trails, bridle trails, swimming pool, marina, bait shop, boat rentals, boat launch, stables, horse rentals, 18-hole golf course, disc golf course, game courts, playfield, playground. **Activities:** Camping, boating, canoeing, fishing, swimming, water-skiing, hiking, bicycling, mountain biking, horseback riding, golf, tennis. **Special Features:** Named for its proximity to the ancient war and trading path used by the Cherokee, the park is situated on the shores of the Tennessee Valley Authority's Patrick Henry Reservoir on the Holston River.

9. State Parks

Texas State Parks

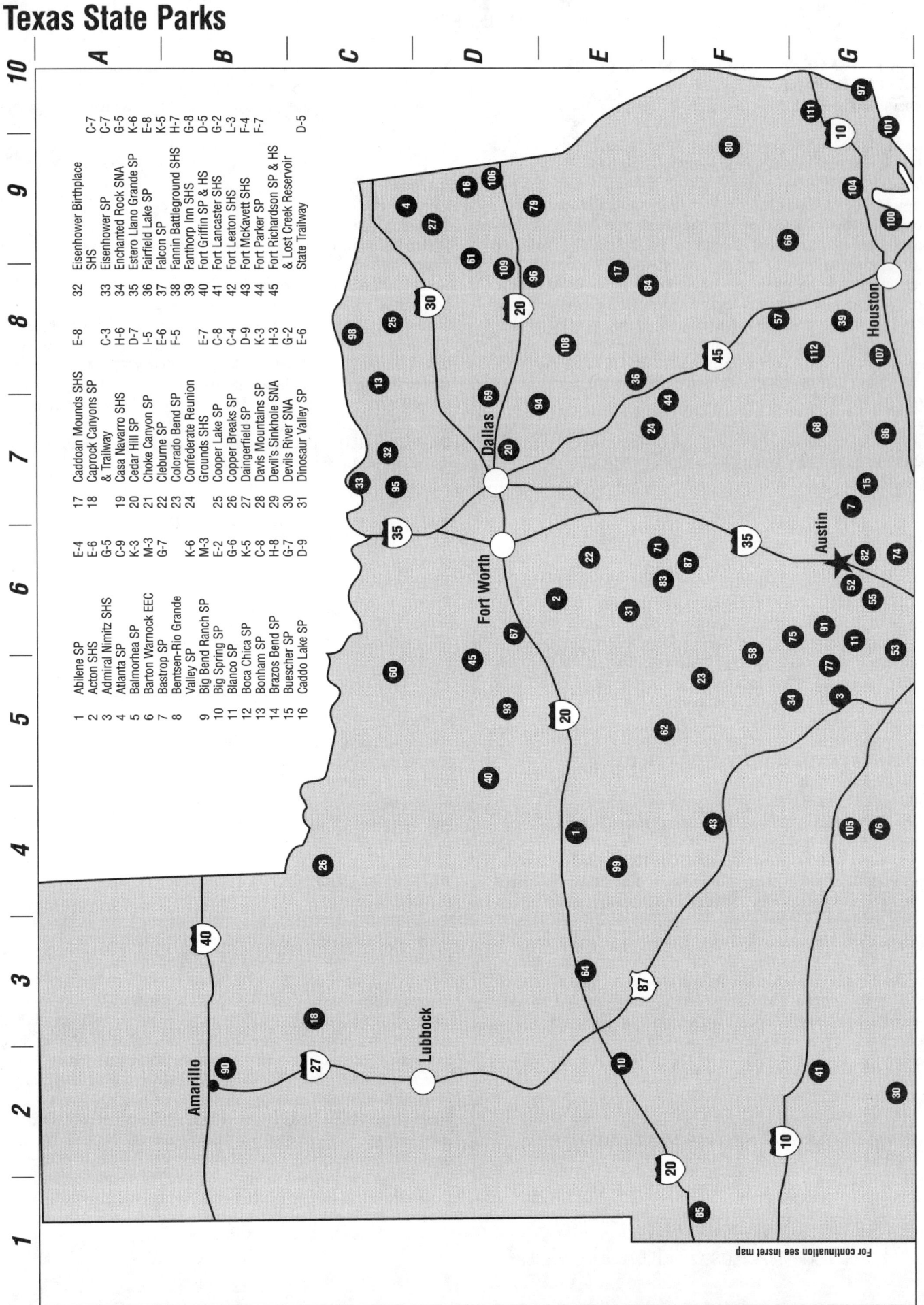

1	Abilene SP	E-4
2	Acton SHS	E-6
3	Admiral Nimitz SHS	G-5
4	Atlanta SP	C-9
5	Balmorhea SP	K-3
6	Barton Warnock EEC	M-3
7	Bastrop SP	G-7
8	Bentsen-Rio Grande Valley SP	K-6
9	Big Bend Ranch SP	M-3
10	Big Spring SP	E-2
11	Blanco SP	G-6
12	Boca Chica SP	K-5
13	Bonham SP	C-8
14	Brazos Bend SP	H-8
15	Buescher SP	G-7
16	Caddo Lake SP	D-9

17	Caddoan Mounds SHS	E-8
18	Caprock Canyons SP & Trailway	C-3
19	Casa Navarro SHS	H-6
20	Cedar Hill SP	D-7
21	Choke Canyon SP	I-5
22	Cleburne SP	E-6
23	Colorado Bend SP	F-5
24	Confederate Reunion Grounds SHS	E-7
25	Cooper Lake SP	C-8
26	Copper Breaks SP	C-4
27	Daingerfield SP	D-9
28	Davis Mountains SP	K-3
29	Devil's Sinkhole SNA	H-3
30	Devils River SNA	G-2
31	Dinosaur Valley SP	E-6

32	Eisenhower Birthplace SHS	C-7
33	Eisenhower SP	C-7
34	Enchanted Rock SNA	G-5
35	Estero Llano Grande SP	K-6
36	Fairfield Lake SP	E-8
37	Falcon SP	K-5
38	Fannin Battleground SHS	H-7
39	Fanthorp Inn SHS	G-8
40	Fort Griffin SP & HS	D-5
41	Fort Lancaster SHS	G-2
42	Fort Leaton SHS	L-3
43	Fort McKavett SHS	F-4
44	Fort Parker SP	F-7
45	Fort Richardson SP & HS & Lost Creek Reservoir State Trailway	D-5

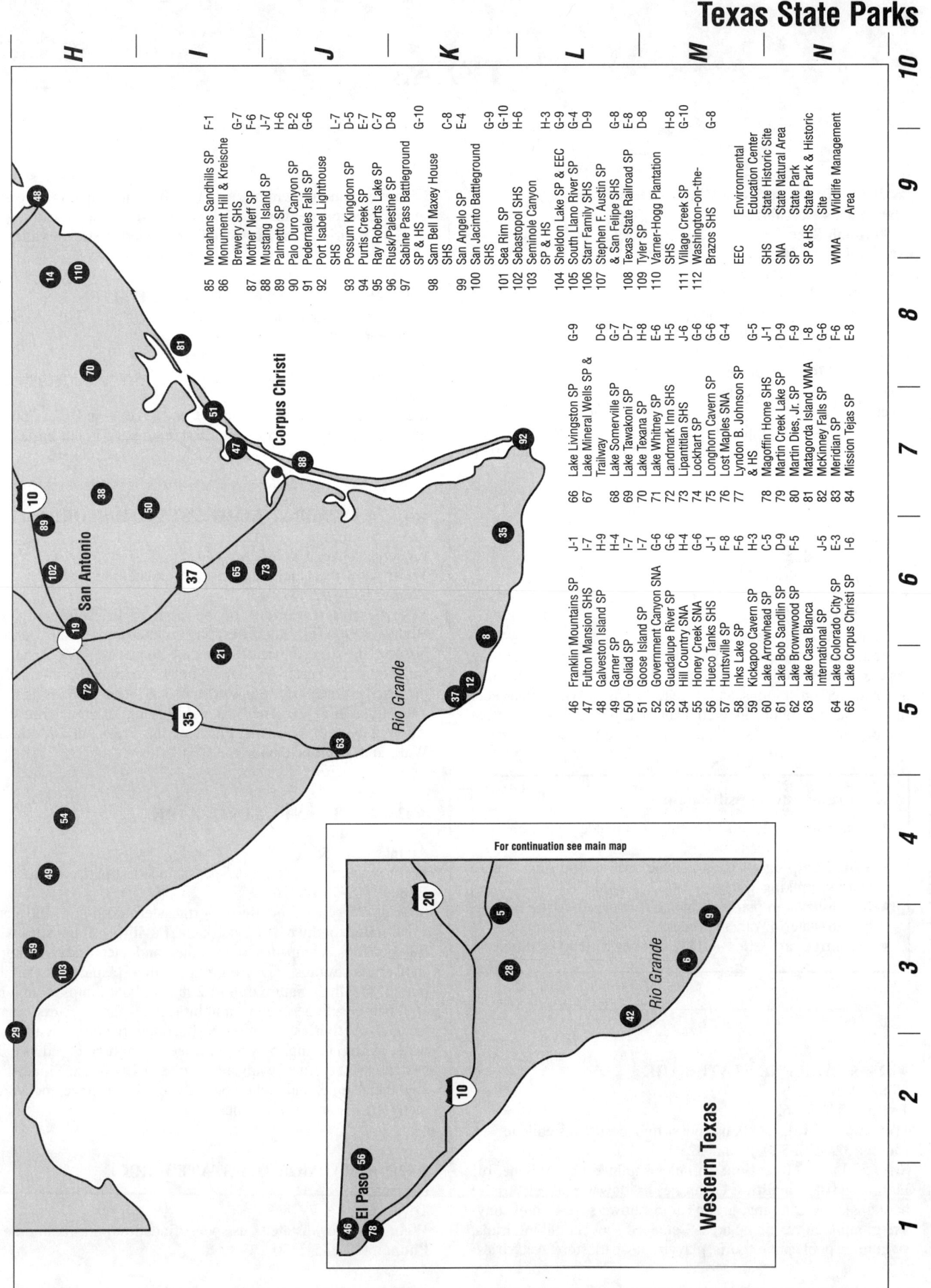

Western Texas

For continuation see main map

San Antonio

Corpus Christi

El Paso

Rio Grande

Rio Grande

46	Franklin Mountains SP	J-1
47	Fulton Mansion SHS	I-7
48	Galveston Island SP	H-9
49	Garner SP	I-7
50	Goliad SP	I-7
51	Goose Island SP	I-7
52	Government Canyon SNA	G-6
53	Guadalupe River SP	G-6
54	Hill Country SNA	H-4
55	Honey Creek SNA	G-6
56	Hueco Tanks SHS	J-1
57	Huntsville SP	F-8
58	Inks Lake SP	F-6
59	Kickapoo Cavern SP	H-3
60	Lake Arrowhead SP	C-5
61	Lake Bob Sandlin SP	D-9
62	Lake Brownwood SP	F-5
63	Lake Casa Blanca	
	International SP	J-5
64	Lake Colorado City SP	E-3
65	Lake Corpus Christi SP	I-6

66	Lake Livingston SP	G-9
67	Lake Mineral Wells SP &	
	Trailway	D-6
68	Lake Somerville SP	G-7
69	Lake Tawakoni SP	D-7
70	Lake Texana SP	H-8
71	Lake Whitney SP	E-6
72	Landmark Inn SHS	H-5
73	Lipantitlan SHS	J-6
74	Lockhart SP	G-6
75	Longhorn Cavern SP	G-6
76	Lost Maples SNA	G-4
77	Lyndon B. Johnson SP	
	& HS	G-5
78	Magoffin Home SHS	J-1
79	Martin Creek Lake SP	D-9
80	Martin Dies, Jr. SP	F-9
81	Matagorda Island WMA	I-8
82	McKinney Falls SP	G-6
83	Meridian SP	F-6
84	Mission Tejas SP	E-8

85	Monahans Sandhills SP	F-1
86	Monument Hill & Kreische	
	Brewery SHS	G-7
87	Mother Neff SP	F-6
88	Mustang Island SP	J-7
89	Palmetto SP	H-6
90	Palo Duro Canyon SP	B-2
91	Pedernales Falls SP	G-6
92	Port Isabel Lighthouse	
	SHS	L-7
93	Possum Kingdom SP	D-5
94	Purtis Creek SP	E-7
95	Ray Roberts Lake SP	C-7
96	Rusk/Palestine SP	D-8
97	Sabine Pass Battleground	
	SP & HS	G-10
98	Sam Bell Maxey House	
	SHS	C-8
99	San Angelo SP	E-4
100	San Jacinto Battleground	
	SHS	G-9
101	Sea Rim SP	G-10
102	Sebastopol SHS	H-6
103	Seminole Canyon	
	SP & HS	H-3
104	Sheldon Lake SP & EEC	G-9
105	South Llano River SP	G-4
106	Starr Family SHS	D-9
107	Stephen F. Austin SP	
	& San Felipe SHS	G-8
108	Texas State Railroad SP	E-8
109	Tyler SP	D-8
110	Varner-Hogg Plantation	
	SHS	H-8
111	Village Creek SP	G-10
112	Washington-on-the-	
	Brazos SHS	G-8

EEC	Environmental Education Center
SHS	State Historic Site
SNA	State Natural Area
SP	State Park
SP & HS	State Park & Historic Site
WMA	Wildlife Management Area

TEXAS

★4283★ **Texas Parks & Wildlife Department**
State Parks Division
4200 Smith School Rd
Austin, TX 78744
(512) 389-4800 - Phone
(512) 389-4436 - Fax
(512) 389-8900 - Reservations
(800) 792-1112 - Toll-free
(512) 389-4954 - Employment
(512) 389-4746- Volunteering
Web: www.tpwd.state.tx.us/park
Oversees 122 state properties comprising more than 600,000 acres of land. Park units include more than 30 historic sites, four state trails, seven natural areas, and an international park near the Mexico border.

★4284★ **Texas Parks & Wildlife Department**
Wildlife Division
4200 Smith School Rd
Austin, TX 78744
(512) 389-8092
Web: www.tpwd.state.tx.us
Operates and manages 51 wildlife management areas totaling approximately 750,000 acres for wildlife research, wildlife management demonstrations, and recreational uses. Works to protect rare, threatened, or endangered plants and animals, and sensitive ecological habitats on state parks lands and private property.

Key to campsite classification:

- **Campsites with full hookups** — Include water, electricity, and sewer hookups.
- **Tent Camping** — Include table, grill or fire ring, and nearby drinking water.
- **Developed campsites** — Include table, grill or fire ring, but no water or other utilities.
- **Primitive campsites** — Hike-in sites with no facilities.

★4285★ **ABILENE STATE PARK**
150 Park Rd 32
Tuscola, TX 79562
Web: www.tpwd.state.tx.us/spdest/findadest/parks/abilene
Phone: 325-572-3204; **Fax:** 325-572-3008
Size: 529 acres. **Location:** 16 miles southwest of Abilene, off Farm Road 89. **Facilities:** Campsites (with water and electricity hookups), tent camping, group camp, showers, restrooms, day-use group facility, picnic areas, screened shelters, hiking trails, swimming pool, game courts, playground, park store. **Activities:**

Camping, fishing, swimming, hiking, bicycling, interpretive programs. **Special Features:** Park is located in a semi-arid region of short prairie grass, brushland, and wooded stream valley.

★4286★ **ACTON STATE HISTORIC SITE**
c/o Cleburne State Park
5800 Park Rd 21
Cleburne, TX 76031
Web: www.tpwd.state.tx.us/spdest/findadest/parks/acton/
Phone: 817-645-4215
Size: .01 acres. **Location:** North Central Texas in Hood County. **Special Features:** Texas' smallest state park is the burial site of Elizabeth Crockett, second wife of Davy Crockett.

★4287★ **ADMIRAL NIMITZ STATE HISTORIC SITE**
328 E Main St
Fredericksburg, TX 78624
Web: www.thc.state.tx.us/museums/musnimitz.html
Phone: 830-997-4379
Size: 9 acres. **Location:** In the town of Fredericksburg, off Highway 290 West. **Facilities:** Nature/interpretive trails, garden, historic structure, museum. **Special Features:** Park is named for Admiral Chester William Nimitz, commander-in-chief of the Pacific forces during World War II. The grounds include the Garden of Peace, The National Museum of the Pacific War, Admiral Nimitz Museum, Plaza of the Presidents, Memorial Wall, and Walk of Honor.

★4288★ **ATLANTA STATE PARK**
927 Park Rd 42
Atlanta, TX 75551
Web: www.tpwd.state.tx.us/spdest/findadest/parks/atlanta
Phone: 903-796-6476
Size: 1,475 acres. **Location:** Northeastern portion of the state, a few miles southwest of Texarkana. **Facilities:** Campsites with full hookups, campsites with water and electricity hookups, showers, restrooms, day-use group facility, picnic areas, hiking trails (3.8 miles), nature trail (1.2 miles), boat ramps, boat rentals, fish-cleaning shelter, amphitheater, game courts, playground. **Activities:** Camping, boating, fishing, swimming, water-skiing, hiking, bicycling. **Special Features:** Caddo Indians, the most culturally advanced tribe in Texas, once made this area their home, and archeological excavations have uncovered many graves and artifacts here.

★4289★ **BALMORHEA STATE PARK**
PO Box 15
Toyahvale, TX 79786
Web: www.tpwd.state.tx.us/spdest/findadest/parks/balmorhea
Phone: 432-375-2370

9. State Parks

Size: 46 acres. Location: In the foothills of the Davis Mountains southwest of Balmorhea in the midwestern portion of the state. Facilities: Campsites with water and electrical hookups, tent camping, showers, restrooms, motel, picnic areas, food concession, swimming pool, bathhouse, recreation hall, playground. Activities: Camping, swimming, scuba diving, snorkeling. Special Features: The waters of San Solomon Springs form the world's largest spring-fed swimming pool. With a capacity of more than 3.5 million gallons, the pool offers a unique setting for divers to observe the variety of aquatic life found in its clear waters.

★4290★ BARTON WARNOCK ENVIRONMENTAL EDUCATION CENTER
HC 70, Box 375
Terlingua, TX 79852
Web: www.tpwd.state.tx.us/spdest/findadest/parks/
   barton_warnock
Phone: 432-424-3327
Size: 100 acres. Location: Extreme mid-western portion of the state, 1 mile east of Lajitas. Facilities: Interpretive center, book store, gift shop, auditorium, botanical garden with self-guided trail. Special Features: Originally created in 1982 as the Lajitas Museum Desert Gardens, the land was purchased by Texas Parks and Wildlife, who renamed it after Dr. Barton Warnock, a well-respected botanist who specialized in the study of the region. The Center interprets 570 million years of geological history and the five biological landscapes of the Chihuahuan Desert, better known to west Texas travelers as the Big Bend area. The renovated Center is the result of an international partnership of state and national park experts in Texas and the Mexican states of Coahuila and Chihuahua, and it serves as the eastern entrance gateway to Big Bend Ranch State Park.

★4291★ BASTROP STATE PARK
PO Box 518
Bastrop, TX 78602
Web: www.tpwd.state.tx.us/spdest/findadest/parks/bastrop
Phone: 512-321-2101
Size: 5,926 acres. Location: Approximately 30 miles southeast of Austin. Facilities: Campsites with water and electricity hookups, tent camping, primitive campsites, group camp, showers, restrooms, rustic cabins, day-use group facility, picnic areas, hiking trails, swimming pool, 18-hole golf course, park store, playground, auto tour route. Activities: Camping, fishing, canoeing, swimming, hiking, backpacking, bicycling, golf. Special Features: Park is the site of the "Lost Pines," an isolated timbered region of loblolly pine and hardwoods. This woodland is separated from the main body of East Texas Pines by approximately 100 miles of post oak woodlands.

★4292★ BENTSEN-RIO GRANDE VALLEY STATE PARK
2800 Bensen Palm Dr
Mission, TX 78572
Web: www.worldbirdingcenter.org/sites/mission/
Phone: 956-585-1107; Fax: 956-585-3448
Size: 760 acres. Location: Along the Rio Grande River, 5 miles southwest of Mission. Facilities: Campsites with full hookups, primitive campsites, youth group camp, showers, restrooms, picnic areas, day-use group facility, hiking trails, interpretive trails, boat ramp, bird observation blinds, game courts, playground (&&). Activities: Camping, boating, fishing, hiking, backpacking, bicycling, birding, interpretive programs. Special Features: Park is headquarters of the World Birding Center and is known as a treasure trove of birds found nowhere else in the US except deepest South Texas. Found here also are so-called "Mexican vagrants," which are birds rarely seen on this side of the Rio Grande.

★4293★ BIG BEND RANCH STATE PARK
PO Box 2319
Presidio, TX 79845
Web: www.tpwd.state.tx.us/spdest/findadest/parks/
   big_bend_ranch/
Phone: 432-229-3416
Size: 299,008 acres. Location: Western portion of the state, along the Rio Grande from southeast of Presidio to near Lajitas. Facilities: Primitive campsites, group camps, picnic areas, OHV trails, hiking trails, bridle trails, bike trails, bike rentals. Activities: Camping, fishing, rafting, canoeing, swimming, hiking, biking, backpacking, OHV riding, interpretive programs. Special Features: Embracing some of the most remote and rugged terrain in the Southwest, the park encompasses two mountain ranges containing ancient extinct volcanoes, precipitous canyons, and waterfalls. The park is home to a tremendous diversity of animal and plant species, including 14 species of bats, several species of hummingbirds, and at least 11 other rare plants and animals, including Hinckley oaks and mountain lions. The park also maintains a small herd of Texas longhorn cattle, a remnant of the property's ranching heritage.

★4294★ BIG SPRING STATE PARK
1 Scenic Dr
Big Spring, TX 79720
Web: www.tpwd.state.tx.us/spdest/findadest/parks/big_spring/
Phone: 432-263-4931
Size: 382 acres. Location: 100 miles west of Abilene, at the southern tip of the High Plains caprock escarpment, within the city limits of Big Spring. Facilities: 8 developed campsites, group camp, picnic areas, group pavilion, day-use group facility, nature trail (&), scenic drive, interpretive center, park store, playground, restrooms. Activities: Camping, hiking, biking, nature study. Special Features: Interpretive center includes an Indian artifact display and assorted fossils found in the area.

★4295★ BLANCO STATE PARK
PO Box 493
Blanco, TX 78606
Web: www.tpwd.state.tx.us/spdest/findadest/parks/blanco/
Phone: 830-833-4333
Size: 105 acres. Location: Off Highway 281, southwest of Blanco. Facilities: Campsites with full hookups, campsites with water and electricity hookups, showers, restrooms, day-use group facility, picnic areas, screened shelters, hiking trails, park

store, playgrounds. **Activities:** Camping, boating, fishing, swimming, hiking. **Special Features:** A natural spring has made this area an attractive campsite since the time of early explorers and settlers.

★4296★ **BONHAM STATE PARK**
1363 State Park 24
Bonham, TX 75418
Web: www.tpwd.state.tx.us/spdest/findadest/parks/bonham
Phone: 903-583-5022
Size: 261 acres. **Location:** In Fannin County, northeast of Dallas. **Facilities:** Campsites with water and electricity hookups, tent camping, group camp, showers, restrooms, day-use group facility, picnic areas, hiking trail, bike trail, boat ramps, dock, fishing pier, park store, playground. **Activities:** Camping, boating (5 mph speed limit), fishing, swimming, hiking, mountain biking. **Special Features:** Lake Bonham is a manmade 65-acre lake in the midst of rolling prairies and woodlands.

★4297★ **BRAZOS BEND STATE PARK**
21901 FM 762
Needville, TX 77461
Web: www.tpwd.state.tx.us/spdest/findadest/parks/brazos_bend/
Phone: 409-553-5101
Size: Approximately 5,000 acres. **Location:** 28 miles southwest of Houston. **Facilities:** Campsites with water and electricity hookups, primitive horseman's camp, showers, restrooms, day-use group facility, picnic areas, screened shelters, hiking trails, bike trails, interpretive center, observatory, aquarium, observation tower, fishing pier, park store, playground. **Activities:** Camping, fishing, hiking, bicycling, horseback riding, interpretive programs, astronomy programs. **Special Features:** Archeological materials show that prehistoric people visited this area, possibly as early as 300 BC; in early historical times, the Capoque band of the Karankawa Indians roamed between the mouth of the Brazos River and Galveston Bay and may have traveled inland as far as Brazos Bend.

★4298★ **BUESCHER STATE PARK**
PO Box 75
Smithville, TX 78957
Web: www.tpwd.state.tx.us/spdest/findadest/parks/buescher
Phone: 512-237-2241
Size: 1,017 acres. **Location:** 2 miles north of Smithville off State Highway 71, 0.5 miles north of Farm Road 153. **Facilities:** Campsites with water and electricity hookups, group camp, cabins, showers, restrooms, picnic areas, screened shelters, hiking trails, auto tour route, park store, recreational hall. **Activities:** Camping, boating (no motors), fishing, swimming, hiking, bicycling. **Special Features:** A scenic park road connects this park with Bastrop State Park and travels through a part of the lost pines, a remnant of what is thought to have been an extensive pine-oak forest covering much of central Texas during the Ice Age. The steep, hilly 12-mile paved road is ideal for biking, but only by experienced cyclists.

★4299★ **CADDO LAKE STATE PARK**
245 Park Rd 2
Karnack, TX 75661
Web: www.tpwd.state.tx.us/spdest/findadest/parks/caddo_lake/
Phone: 903-679-3351
Size: 484 acres. **Location:** 15 miles northeast of Marshall on Highway 43, then east 1 mile on Farm Road 2198 to Park Road 2. **Facilities:** Campsites with full hookups, campsites with water and electricity hookups, group camp, cabins, showers, restrooms, day-use group facility, picnic areas, screened shelter, interpretive center, hiking trails, nature trails, boat ramp, boat rentals, fishing pier, park store, playground, concession, recreation hall, amphitheater. **Activities:** Camping, boating, fishing, swimming, water-skiing, hiking, bicycling, boat tours. **Special Features:** This lake was the only natural lake in Texas until it was artificially dammed in the early 1900s. The lake is a maze of sloughs, ponds, and bayous with cypress groves.

★4300★ **CADDOAN MOUNDS STATE HISTORIC SITE**
1649 S Hwy 21 W
Alto, TX 75925
Web: www.tpwd.state.tx.us/spdest/findadest/parks/caddoan_mounds
Phone: 936-858-3218
Size: 94 acres. **Location:** 6 miles southwest of Alto on State Highway 21, in the northeastern portion of the state. **Facilities:** Interpretive center, interpretive trails, archeological experiment exhibit, park store. **Special Features:** Site of the park was the home of Mound Builders of Caddoan origin who lived in the region for 500 years beginning about AD 800. Park offers exhibits and interpretive trails through its reconstructed sites of Caddo dwellings and ceremonial areas, including 2 temple mounds, a burial mound, and a village area.

★4301★ **CAPROCK CANYONS STATE PARK & TRAILWAY**
PO Box 204
Quitaque, TX 79255
Web: www.tpwd.state.tx.us/spdest/findadest/parks/caprock_canyons/
Phone: 806-455-1492
Size: 15,314 acres. **Location:** In the southern portion of the panhandle, 100 miles southeast of Amarillo. **Facilities:** Developed tent campsites, campsites with water and electricity hookups, primitive campsites, horsemen's camp, group camp, showers, restrooms, picnic areas, hiking trails, bike trails, bridle trails, horse rentals, boat ramp, boat rentals (seasonal), fishing pier, interpretive center, amphitheater, park store, playground, scenic overlook. **Activities:** Camping, boating, fishing, swimming, hiking, backpacking, bicycling, mountain biking, horseback riding, rock climbing. **Special Features:** Park includes the Trailway, a 64-mile rail-to-trail conversion that traverses three counties, crosses 46 bridges, and runs through Clarity Tunnel, one of the last active railroad tunnels in Texas.

★4302★ CASA NAVARRO STATE HISTORIC SITE
228 S Laredo St
San Antonio, TX 78207
Web: www.tpwd.state.tx.us/spdest/findadest/parks/
casa_navarro/
Phone: 210-226-4801; **Fax:** 210-226-4801
Size: 0.6 acres. **Location:** At the corner of South Laredo and West Nueva streets in downtown San Antonio. **Facilities:** Historic structures, exhibits, restrooms. **Activities:** Guided tours, demonstrations. **Special Features:** Site is the restored home of Tejano patriot Jose Antonio Navarro, a leading advocate of Tejano rights. The home is furnished with period antiques and is the only historic site in San Antonio dedicated to the interpretation of the Mexican history and heritage of Texas.

★4303★ CEDAR HILL STATE PARK
1570 FM 1382
Cedar Hill, TX 75104
Web: www.tpwd.state.tx.us/spdest/findadest/parks/cedar_hill/
Phone: 972-291-3900
Size: 1,826 acres. **Location:** In the cedar-covered hills of southwest Dallas County, 10 miles southwest of Dallas. **Facilities:** Campsites with water and electricity hookups, 30 primitive campsites, showers, restrooms, day-use group facility, picnic areas, boat ramps, beach, playgrounds, hiking trails, bike trails, fish cleaning station **Activities:** Camping, boating, fishing, swimming, mountain biking, birding. **Special Features:** Park is an urban nature preserve located on the 7,500-acre Joe Pool Reservoir, with 100 miles of shoreline. Remnants of the Penn Farm remain intact within the park, and the Penn Farm Agricultural History Center offers a glimpse into agrarian history.

★4304★ CHOKE CANYON STATE PARK
PO Box 2
Calliham, TX 78007
Web: www.tpwd.state.tx.us/spdest/findadest/parks/
choke_canyon/
Phone: 361-786-3868
Size: 1,485 acres, in two units. **Location:** Park comprises two main units alongside Choke Canyon Reservoir: The Calliham Unit is 12 miles west of Three Rivers on Highway 72; the South Shore Unit is 4 miles west of Three Rivers on Highway 72. **Facilities:** Campsites with water and electricity hookups, tent camping, primitive campsites, group camp, horsemen's camp, showers, restrooms, day-use group facilities, picnic areas, screened shelters, hiking trails, boat ramp, playfields, fishing piers, fish-cleaning stations, amphitheater, gymnasium, game courts, playgrounds, recreation hall. **Activities:** Camping, boating, fishing, swimming, backpacking, mountain biking, hunting (with restrictions), birding, interpretive programs. **Special Features:** Paleo Indians crossed the Frio River Valley more than 10,000 years ago following game such as bison and mammoth. Later, after the large game had disappeared, nomadic hunters and gatherers associated with the Archaic culture camped near the river making tools, building fires, processing and gathering food. Numerous Archaic sites in the Choke Canyon have been recorded.

★4305★ CLEBURNE STATE PARK
5800 Park Rd 21
Cleburne, TX 76031
Web: www.tpwd.state.tx.us/spdest/findadest/parks/cleburne
Phone: 817-645-4215
Size: 528 acres. **Location:** Southwest of Fort Worth, in north central Texas. **Facilities:** Campsites with full hookups, campsites with water and electricity hookups, group camp, showers, restrooms, day-use group facility, picnic areas, screened shelters, hiking trail, nature trail, boat ramp, amphitheater, playground. **Activities:** Camping, boating (5 mph speed limit), canoeing, fishing, swimming, hiking, mountain biking. **Special Features:** Park was developed in the 1930s by the Civilian Conservation Corps, who built a small earthen dam to impound the park's 116-acre lake with a masonry, three-level spillway. They then cleared a three-mile-long scenic roadway around the lake.

★4306★ COLORADO BEND STATE PARK
Box 118
Bend, TX 76824
Web: www.tpwd.state.tx.us/spdest/findadest/parks/
colorado_bend
Phone: 325-628-3240
Size: 5,328 acres. **Location:** West of Lampasas, in the center of the state. **Facilities:** Drive-up campsites, riverside tent sites, primitive backpack camping areas, restrooms, picnic area, hiking trails, bike trails, boat ramp, fish-cleaning station, park store. **Activities:** Camping, fishing, swimming, hiking, backpacking, mountain biking, spelunking, birding, hunting (with restrictions), guided tours. **Special Features:** Rangers offer tours to Gorman Falls and guided tours (both walking and crawling) of wild caves. Due to hazardous conditions, all caves in the park are closed except through guided tours, and reservations are recommended.

★4307★ CONFEDERATE REUNION GROUNDS
STATE HISTORIC SITE
c/o Fort Parker State Park
194 Park Rd 28
Mexia, TX 76667
Web: www.tpwd.state.tx.us/spdest/findadest/parks/
confederate_reunion_grounds
Phone: 254-562-5751
Size: 77 acres. **Location:** Northeastern portion of the state, 6 miles south of Mexia. **Facilities:** Day-use group facility, picnic areas, pavilion, hiking trail, historic structures, playground, restrooms, boat rentals. **Activities:** Fishing, canoeing, swimming, hiking, backpacking, birding. **Special Features:** Park evolved from an encampment where annual reunions were held by Confederate veterans of the Civil War. Historical attractions include the 1872 Heritage House, an 1893 dance pavilion, and a Civil War vintage cannon.

★4308★ COOPER LAKE STATE PARK
1664 Farm Rd 1529 S
Cooper, TX 75432
Web: www.tpwd.state.tx.us/spdest/findadest/parks/
cooper_lake
Phone: 903-395-3100

Size: 3,026 acres in two units: Doctors Creek Unit - 715.5 acres; South Sulphur Unit - 2,310.5 acres. **Location:** Located in northern Hopkins County, in the northeast part of the state. **Facilities:** Campsites with water and electricity hookups, tent camping, horseman's camp, cabins, restrooms, showers, picnic areas, picnic shelters, screened shelters, hiking trails, bike trails, bridle trails, beaches, boat ramps, fishing piers, fish cleaning station, playgrounds, game court, amphitheater. **Activities:** Camping, fishing, boating, water-skiing, swimming, hiking, mountain biking, horseback riding, birding, nature study, interpretive programs, guided tours. **Special Features:** Park is located in two counties on land owned by the US Army Corps of Engineers and is operated through a lease agreement. The lake, which was completed in 1991, covers about 19,000 acres and is surrounded by thousands of acres devoted to parks and wildlife management.

★4309★ COPPER BREAKS STATE PARK
777 Park Rd 62
Quanah, TX 79252
Web: www.tpwd.state.tx.us/spdest/findadest/parks/
copper_breaks
Phone: 940-839-4331
Size: 1,899 acres. **Location:** 12 miles south of Quanah, near the panhandle. **Facilities:** Campsites with water and electricity hookups, tent camping, horsemen's camp, primitive campsites, group camp, showers, restrooms, day-use group facility, picnic areas, hiking trails, bike trails, bridle trails, nature trail, boat ramp, dock, fishing pier, interpretive center, amphitheater, park store, game courts, playground. **Activities:** Camping, boating, fishing, swimming, hiking, horseback riding, mountain biking, kite flying, interpretive programs. **Special Features:** Park features natural and historical exhibits, and a portion of the state's official Texas longhorn herd is maintained at the park.

★4310★ DAINGERFIELD STATE PARK
455 Park Rd 17
Daingerfield, TX 75638
Web: www.tpwd.state.tx.us/spdest/findadest/parks/
daingerfield
Phone: 903-645-2921
Size: 507 acres. **Location:** Southwest of Texarkana, near the Oklahoma border. **Facilities:** Campsites with full hookups, campsites with water and electricity hookups, tent camping, group camp, cabins, showers, restrooms, picnic areas, day-use group facility, hiking trails, boat ramp, boat rentals (seasonal), dock, fishing pier, fish cleaning station, amphitheater, park store, playground. **Activities:** Camping, boating, canoeing, fishing, swimming, hiking. **Special Features:** Although northwest Texas is primarily known for evergreen pines, each autumn the park's sweetgum, oak, and maple trees produce showy shades of red and gold. In springtime, the rolling hills burst into bloom with dogwoods, redbuds, and wisteria vines.

★4311★ DAVIS MOUNTAINS STATE PARK
PO Box 1458
Fort Davis, TX 79734
Web: www.tpwd.state.tx.us/spdest/findadest/parks/
davis_mountains
Phone: 432-426-3337

Size: 2,709 acres. **Location:** 4 miles northwest of Fort Davis, via State Highway 118. **Facilities:** Campsites with full hookups, campsites with water and electricity hookups, tent camping, primitive campsites, showers, restrooms, 39-room lodge (with swimming pool and restaurant), day-use group facility, picnic areas, hiking trails, amphitheater, interpretive center, park store, playground. **Activities:** Camping, hiking, backpacking, hunting (with restrictions), nature study, interpretive programs. **Special Features:** Skyline Drive, the highest road in Texas, is a 74-mile scenic loop drive that winds to the park's highest ridges and provides a breathtaking view of the park and the highest peaks of the Davis Mountains. Two scenic overlooks are almost 6,000 feet above sea level. Thirteen miles west of the park on the scenic loop, travelers may tour McDonald Observatory, operated by the University of Texas. Park includes Indian Lodge, constructed in the 1930s by the Civilian Conservation Corps (CCC) and featuring original interiors and furnishings.

★4312★ DEVILS RIVER STATE NATURAL AREA
HC 01, Box 513
Del Rio, TX 78840
Web: www.tpwd.state.tx.us/spdest/findadest/parks/
devils_river
Phone: 830-395-2133
Size: 19,989 acres. **Location:** 45 miles north of Del Rio Road and 22 miles off US 277. **Facilities:** Primitive campsites, group camp (with bunkhouses, dining hall with kitchen, and conference room), hiking trails, bike trails, hand launch boat ramp, restrooms, showers. **Activities:** Backpacking, camping, canoeing, hiking, mountain biking, nature study, guided canyon tours. **Special Features:** The natural area is large and remote, with access to the river by hiking, biking, or park tour only; no vehicle access is permitted. The river is wild and rugged with long, deep pools, wide shallow areas, and deep turbulent rapids. Visitation of archeological pictograph sites is permitted on a pre-approved basis only.

★4313★ DEVIL'S SINKHOLE STATE NATURAL AREA
PO Box 678
Rocksprings, TX 78880
Web: www.tpwd.state.tx.us/spdest/findadest/parks/
devils_sinkhole
Phone: 830-683-3762
Size: 1,860 acres. **Location:** 6 miles northeast of Rocksprings in the southwestern portion of the state. Access to the area may be obtained only by contacting Devil's Sinkhole Society (830-683-2287) to prearrange a tour. **Facilities:** Picnic sites, chemical toilet, trail (&). **Special Features:** Devil's Sinkhole is a vertical cavern with an opening measuring approximately 40 feet by 60 feet and a drop of about 140 feet to the main cavern below. Inside the cavern, freshwater lakes support two crustacean species found only here. Between March and October, evening visitors may witness a large seasonal population of Brazilian freetail bats emerge from the cave to forage.

★4314★ DINOSAUR VALLEY STATE PARK

PO Box 396
Glen Rose, TX 76043
Web: www.tpwd.state.tx.us/spdest/findadest/parks/
dinosaur_valley
Phone: 254-897-4588
Size: 1,525 acres. Location: 4 miles west of Glen Rose on Farm Road 205, in the north central part of the state. Facilities: Campsites with water and electricity hookups, primitive campsites, showers, restrooms, day-use group facility, picnic areas, hiking trails, nature trail, bridle trails, bike trails, interpretive center (&), amphitheater, park store, playground. Activities: Camping, fishing, swimming, hiking, horseback riding, mountain biking. Special Features: Eastward-dipping limestones, sandstones, and mudstones, deposited from approximately 113 million years ago along the shorelines of an ancient sea, form the geological setting for the park area. The park contains some of the best-preserved dinosaur tracks in the world. The tracks are preserved in the riverbed, so visitors should call ahead to check on river conditions.

★4315★ EISENHOWER BIRTHPLACE STATE HISTORIC SITE

609 S Lamar Ave
Denison, TX 75021
Web: www.tpwd.state.tx.us/spdest/findadest/parks/
eisenhower_birthplace
Phone: 903-465-8908
Size: 6 acres. Location: In Grayson County, in the city of Denison. Facilities: Visitor's center, covered pavilion, restrooms, education building, hiking trails. Activities: Hiking, guided tours. Special Features: Dwight David Eisenhower, five-star general of the Army and two-term president of the United States, was born in a modest two-story frame house in Denison, Texas. The restored house and surrounding property were deeded to the State Park Board in 1958. The home's furnishings are representative of the 1890s.

★4316★ EISENHOWER STATE PARK

50 Park Rd 20
Denison, TX 75020
Web: www.tpwd.state.tx.us/spdest/findadest/parks/eisenhower
Phone: 903-465-1956
Size: 423 acres. Location: 5 miles northwest of Denison, near the Oklahoma border. Facilities: Campsites with full hookups, campsites with water and electricity hookups, tent camping, group camp, showers, restrooms, picnic area, screened shelters, day-use group facility, hiking trails, bike trail, ATV area, marina, boat ramp, docks, fishing pier, fish cleaning facility, amphitheater, park store, playgrounds, recreation hall. Activities: Camping, boating, fishing, swimming, water-skiing, hiking, mountain biking, ATV riding, interpretive programs. Special Features: Park is named for the 34th President of the United States, Dwight D. Eisenhower, who was born nearby (see separate entry on Eisenhower Birthplace State Historic Site). The park is situated on the shores of Lake Texoma, and a privately operated, full-service marina is located in the park.

★4317★ ENCHANTED ROCK STATE NATURAL AREA

16710 Ranch Rd 965
Fredericksburg, TX 78624
Web: www.tpwd.state.tx.us/spdest/findadest/parks/
enchanted_rock
Phone: 325-247-3903
Size: 1,644 acres. Location: 28 miles north of Fredericksburg on Ranch Road, in the central part of the state. Facilities: Tent camping, primitive campsites, showers, restrooms, day-use group facility, picnic areas, interpretive center, hiking trails, interpretive center, park store, playground. Activities: Camping, hiking, backpacking, rock climbing, hunting (with restrictions). Special Features: The rock is a huge pink granite exfoliation dome that rises 425 feet above ground, 1,825 feet above sea level, and covers 640 acres. It is one of the largest batholiths (an underground rock formation uncovered by erosion) in the United States. Tonkawa Indians believed ghost fires flickered at the top, and they heard creaking and groaning coming from the rock, which geologists say resulted from the rock's heating by day and contracting in the cool night.

★4318★ ESTERO LLANO GRANDE STATE PARK

3301 S International Blvd
Weslaco, TX 78596
Web: www.worldbirdingcenter.org/sites/weslaco
Phone: 956-565-3919
Size: 176 acres. Location: In the southeastern portion of the state, near the Mexico border. Facilities: Visitor center, viewing deck, boardwalk, trails, butterfly garden, meeting room. Activities: Wildlife observation, hiking. Special Features: At the geographic center of the World Birding Center network, the park attracts a wide variety of South Texas wildlife with its varied landscape of shallow lake, woodlands, and thorn forest.

★4319★ FAIRFIELD LAKE STATE PARK

123 State Park Rd 64
Fairfield, TX 75840
Web: www.tpwd.state.tx.us/spdest/findadest/parks/
fairfield_lake
Phone: 214-389-4514
Size: 1,460 acres. Location: In the northeastern portion fo the state, 6 miles northeast of Fairfield. Facilities: Campsites with water and electricity hookups, tent camping, primitive campsite, showers, restrooms, day-use group facility, picnic areas, hiking trails, bridle trails, bike trails, boat ramps, fishing pier, fish cleaning shelter, beach, amphitheater, park store, playground. Activities: Camping, boating, fishing, swimming, water-skiing, jet skiing, hiking, backpacking, mountain biking, horseback riding. Special Features: Park is situated on the southern end of 2,400-acre Fairfield Lake and is the wintering home of a population of bald eagles.

★4320★ FALCON STATE PARK

PO Box 2
Falcon Heights, TX 78545
Web: www.tpwd.state.tx.us/spdest/findadest/parks/falcon
Phone: 956-848-5327

9. State Parks

Size: 573 acres. **Location:** 15 miles north of Roma in the extreme southern portion of the state. **Facilities:** Campsites with full hookups, campsites with water and electricity hookups, showers, restrooms, picnic areas, screened shelters, nature trail, hiking trail, bike trail, boat ramps, park store, playground, fish cleaning shelter, recreation hall. **Activities:** Camping, boating, fishing, swimming, water-skiing, mountain biking, birding. **Special Features:** Falcon Lake offers excellent fishing for black and white bass, catfish, and stripers. The area is also a good spot to see many varieties of birds, including tropical species at the northwesternmost fringe of their range.

★4321★ FANNIN BATTLEGROUND STATE HISTORIC SITE

c/o Goliad State Park
108 Park Rd 6
Goliad, TX 77963
Web: www.tpwd.state.tx.us/spdest/findadest/parks/fannin
Phone: 361-645-3405
Size: 14 acres. **Location:** 9 miles east of Goliad on US 59, in the southeastern part of the state. **Facilities:** Day-use group facility, picnic areas, interpretive center, playground, restroom. **Special Features:** On March 20, 1836, at this site, Colonel J.W. Fannin surrendered himself and 284 of his men to Mexican General Jose Urrea after the Battle of Coleto. Seven days after the capture, 342 men, including Fannin, his troops, and other men captured in the area, were executed.

★4322★ FANTHORP INN STATE HISTORIC SITE

PO Box 296
Anderson, TX 77830
Web: www.tpwd.state.tx.us/spdest/findadest/parks/fanthorp_inn
Phone: 936-873-2633
Size: 1 acre. **Location:** 30 miles southeast of Bryan/College Station in the central eastern portion of the state. **Facilities:** Historic tours, stagecoach rides. **Activities:** Guided tours. **Special Features:** Fanthorp Inn is a double-pen, cedar log, dogtrot house, built in 1834 by an English immigrant, Henry Fanthorp, when Texas was part of Mexico. Fanthorp built his house beside the road that crossed his land, thus bringing travelers right to his door. Over time, Fanthorp's became a well-known stopping place for both travelers and the community. After the land was purchased by the state from a descendant, ten years were spent researching and restoring the Inn to its 1850 appearance. Today it provides an authentic look at a nineteenth-century Texas stagecoach stop and family home.

★4323★ FORT GRIFFIN STATE PARK & HISTORIC SITE

1701 N US Hwy 283
Albany, TX 76430
Web: www.tpwd.state.tx.us/spdest/findadest/parks/fort_griffin
Phone: 325-762-3592
Size: 506 acres. **Location:** 15 miles north of Albany on US 283. **Facilities:** Campsites with full hookups, tent camping, primitive camping, horsemen's camp, group camp, showers, restrooms, day-use group facility, picnic areas, hiking trails, nature trails, historic structure, interpretive center, amphitheater, playgrounds, game courts, ballfield, park store. **Activities:** Camping, fishing, hiking, nature study, historical interpretive programs. **Special Features:** Park includes the ruins of the fort buildings, including a hand-dug well, mess hall, ghost building, barracks, library, rock chimney, store, administration building, cistern, hospital, and officers' quarters. A portion of the official Texas longhorn cattle herd resides here.

★4324★ FORT LANCASTER STATE HISTORIC SITE

PO Box 306
Sheffield, TX 79781
Web: www.tpwd.state.tx.us/spdest/findadest/parks/fort_lancaster
Phone: 432-836-4391
Size: 82 acres. **Location:** 8 miles east of Sheffield on US 290 (a scenic loop off I-10). Take Exit 343 and follow US 290 to park. **Facilities:** Nature trail, historic structure, interpretive center, park store, restrooms. **Activities:** Nature study, historical interpretation. **Special Features:** Fort Lancaster is one of five historic Texas forts designated as State Historic Sites. (The others are Fort Griffin, Fort Leaton, Fort McKavett, and Fort Richardson.) It was originally established in 1855 to protect the route between San Antonio and El Paso. When Texas joined the Confederacy in 1861, the fort was officially abandoned. Park features site tours and exhibits on history, natural history, and archeology.

★4325★ FORT LEATON STATE HISTORIC SITE

PO Box 2319
Presidio, TX 79845
Web: www.tpwd.state.tx.us/spdest/findadest/parks/fort_leaton
Phone: 432-229-3413
Size: 23 acres. **Location:** 4 miles southeast of Presidio in the western portion of the state. **Facilities:** Picnic areas, historic structure, interpretive center, park store, restrooms. **Activities:** Guided tours. **Special Features:** Fort Leaton was built in 1848 as a trading post and dominated border trade with the Apache and Comanche Indians. The park offers guided tours and exhibits on 15th century history, natural history, and the archeology of the area.

★4326★ FORT MCKAVETT STATE HISTORIC SITE

PO Box 68
Fort McKavett, TX 76841
Web: www.tpwd.state.tx.us/spdest/findadest/parks/fort_mckavett
Phone: 325-396-2358
Size: 80 acres. **Location:** 23 miles west of Menard, in the central portion of the state. **Facilities:** Picnic areas, nature trail, historic structure, park store, restrooms. **Special Features:** Fort McKavett is one of five historic Texas forts designated as State Historic Sites. (The others are Fort Griffin, Fort Lancaster, Fort Leaton, and Fort Richardson.) Built in 1852, the fort was part of a new line of military posts stretching from the Rio Grande to the Red River. The site now consists of 25 restored buildings (including officers' quarters, barracks, hospital, school house, and post headquarters) and the ruins of numerous others. Interpretive

exhibits trace the history of the area, emphasizing military history, the post-military community, and historic archeology.

★4327★ FORT PARKER STATE PARK

194 Park Rd 28
Mexia, TX 76667
Web: www.tpwd.state.tx.us/spdest/findadest/parks/fort_parker
Phone: 254-562-5751
Size: 1,459 acres. **Location:** 6 miles southeast of Mexia, off State Highway 14. **Facilities:** Campsites with water and electricity hookups, group camp, showers, restrooms, day-use group facility, picnic areas, screened shelters, hiking trails, nature trails, bike trails, boat ramp, dockboat rentals (seasonal), fishing pier, fish cleaning station, park store, playground, recreational hall, ball field. **Activities:** Camping, boating, canoeing, fishing, swimming, hiking, mountain biking. **Special Features:** Park was named for Fort Parker, a nearby historic settlement established in 1833 that was the site of a Comanche Indian raid during which Cynthia Ann Parker was captured. During captivity, she became the mother of the last great Comanche chief, Quanah Parker. The parklands encompass the historic town of Springfield, which became a ghost town in the late 1800s. Only the cemetery remains and is the last resting place of many East Texas pioneers.

★4328★ FORT RICHARDSON STATE PARK HISTORIC SITE & LOST CREEK RESERVOIR STATE TRAILWAY

228 State Park Rd 61
Jacksboro, TX 76458
Web: www.tpwd.state.tx.us/spdest/findadest/parks/fort_richardson
Phone: 817-567-3506
Size: 454 acres. **Location:** In Jack County, on the south side of the city of Jacksboro, on US 281 South. **Facilities:** Campsites with water and electricity hookups, tent camping, showers, restrooms, day-use group facility, picnic areas, screened shelters, hiking trail, bike trail, bridle trail, interpretive trail, beach, historic structure, interpretive center, exhibits, park store, playground. **Activities:** Camping, fishing, hiking, swimming, horseback riding, guided tours. **Special Features:** Fort Richardson is the northernmost of five historic Texas forts designated as State Historic Sites. (The others are Fort Griffin, Fort Lancaster, Fort Leaton, and Fort McKavett.) Established in 1867 after the Civil War, the fort was used as a military installation until 1878. Several of the original buildings are preserved, and interpretive exhibits describe the history of the fort. The 10-mile trailway runs adjacent to Fort Richardson and along Lost Creek.

★4329★ FRANKLIN MOUNTAINS STATE PARK

1331 McKelligon Canyon Rd
El Paso, TX 79930
Web: www.tpwd.state.tx.us/spdest/findadest/parks/franklin
Phone: 915-566-6441
Size: 24,247 acres. **Location:** Within the city limits of El Paso. **Facilities:** Primitive campsites, picnic areas, hiking trails, park store, amphitheater, restrooms (&). **Activities:** Camping, hiking, backpacking, mountain biking, horseback riding, rock climbing,

interpretive tours. **Special Features:** Franklin Mountains State Park is both the largest state park in Texas and the largest urban wilderness park in the nation. The Franklin Mountains are the northern ramparts of the Paso del Norte (Pass of the North), leading from Mexico into the United States. Native American groups made the area home, using the plant and animal resources for more than 12,000 years; they left their marks on the rocks—colorful pictographs on boulders and in rock shelters, and deep mortar pits used to grind seeds in rock outcrops.

★4330★ FULTON MANSION STATE HISTORIC SITE

PO Box 1859
Fulton, TX 78358
Web: www.tpwd.state.tx.us/spdest/findadest/parks/fulton_mansion
Phone: 361-729-0386
Size: 2 acres. **Location:** Southeastern portion of the state, in Fulton. **Facilities:** Picnic area, historic structure, interpretive center, park store, restrooms (&&). **Special Features:** Built in the mid-1870s, the mansion features the French Second Empire style of architecture and is one of the few surviving examples of a high-style Victorian suburban villa in Texas. As the home of entrepreneur, engineer, inventor, and rancher George Ware Fulton and his wife Harriet, it is a visible reminder of the heyday of the cattle barons of South Texas.

★4331★ GALVESTON ISLAND STATE PARK

14901 FM 3005
Galveston, TX 77554
Web: www.tpwd.state.tx.us/spdest/findadest/parks/galveston
Phone: 409-737-1222
Size: 2,013 acres. **Location:** 6 miles southwest of the Galveston City seawall on Farm Road 3005. **Facilities:** Campsites with water and electricity hookups, group camp, showers, restrooms, boat ramp, day-use group facility, picnic areas, screened shelters, beach, hiking trails, nature trail, interpretive center, park store, amphitheater. **Activities:** Camping, fishing, swimming, mountain biking, hiking, birding. **Special Features:** In 1998 Tropical Storm Frances destroyed the park's sand dunes, which serve as the only protection the park has for its facilities. A project was implemented to rebuild the dunes through the use of Christmas trees. The great storm of 1900 devastated the island, killing 5,000-10,000 people, and prompted the construction of the seawall that protects the northern half of the island.

★4332★ GARNER STATE PARK

HCR 70, Box 599
Concan, TX 78838
Web: www.tpwd.state.tx.us/spdest/findadest/parks/garner
Phone: 830-232-6132
Size: 1,420 acres. **Location:** 31 miles north of Uvalde and 7 miles north of Concan on US 83. **Facilities:** Campsites with water and electricity hookups, tent camping, showers, restrooms, group camp, cabins, day-use group facility, picnic areas, screened shelters, hiking trails, bike path, boat rentals, food concession, miniature golf course, park store, playground, game courts, laundry, grocery. **Activities:** Camping, fishing, canoeing,

swimming, tubing, hiking, bicycling, interpretive and entertainment programs. **Special Features:** Deep canyons, crystal-clear streams, high mesas and carved limestone cliffs are some of the geologic features of this park. The rock formations are early Cretaceous in age, deposited over millions of years in warm, shallow seas that once covered Texas. The Glen Rose Formation, a collection of limestone, shale, marl and siltstone beds was deposited along the shifting margins of the sea where dinosaurs roamed in great numbers, leaving their footprints in the sands.

★4333★ GOLIAD STATE PARK

108 Park Rd 6
Goliad, TX 77963
Web: www.tpwd.state.tx.us/spdest/findadest/parks/
goliad_and_mission_espiritu_santo
Phone: 361-645-3405
Size: 188 acres. **Location:** 0.25 miles south of Goliad on US 183. **Facilities:** Campsites with full hookups, campsites with water and electricity hookups, primitive campsites, showers, restrooms, day-use group facility, picnic areas, screened shelters, hiking trails, historic structures, park store, playground, amphitheater. **Activities:** Camping, fishing, hiking, swimming, boating, guided tours. **Special Features:** Located at the park is the Franciscan Mission Espiritu Santo, which was the home of the largest ranching operation in Texas in the 18th century. Visitors can tour the church and view exhibits that explore the history and daily life of the missionaries and Indian converts, including artifacts.

★4334★ GOOSE ISLAND STATE PARK

202 S Palmetto St
Rockport, TX 78382
Web: www.tpwd.state.tx.us/spdest/findadest/parks/
goose_island
Phone: 361-729-2858
Size: 321 acres. **Location:** 10 miles north of Rockport off State Highway 35. **Facilities:** Campsites with water and electricity hookups, tent camping, showers, restrooms, day-use group facility, picnic areas, boat ramp, fishing pier (&), fish cleaning stations, park store, playgrounds, recreation hall. **Activities:** Camping, boating, fishing, birding, interpretive programs. **Special Features:** Located within park property is ''Big Tree,'' the State Champion Coastal Live Oak, estimated to be more than 1,000 years old. The tree has a circumference of 35 feet, is 44 feet in height, and has a crown spread of 90 feet. Located directly across St. Charles Bay from the park are the wintering grounds for rare and endangered whooping cranes in the Aransas National Wildlife Refuge (see entry in national wildlife refuges section).

★4335★ GOVERNMENT CANYON STATE NATURAL AREA

12861 Galm Rd
San Antonio, TX 78254
Web: www.tpwd.state.tx.us/spdest/findadest/parks/
government_canyon
Phone: 210-688-9055
Size: 8,622 acres. **Location:** Just outside San Antonio, in Bexar County. **Facilities:** Exhibit hall, park store, day-use group facility, picnic areas, restrooms, hiking trails. **Activities:** Interpretive programs, hiking, nature study. **Special Features:** Park opened to the public on October 15, 2005, and some areas and facilities are still being developed.

★4336★ GUADALUPE RIVER STATE PARK

3350 Park Rd 31
Spring Branch, TX 78070
Web: www.tpwd.state.tx.us/spdest/findadest/parks/
guadalupe_river
Phone: 830-438-2656
Size: 1,939 acres. **Location:** 30 miles north of San Antonio at the north end of Park Road 31. **Facilities:** Campsites with water and electricity hookups, tent camping, showers, restrooms, picnic areas, hiking trails, bike trails, bridle trails, park store, playgrounds, amphitheater. **Activities:** Camping, canoeing, tubing, fishing, swimming, hiking, mountain biking, horseback riding. **Special Features:** The Guadalupe River, with banks lined by huge bald cypress trees, is the park's most outstanding natural feature.

★4337★ HILL COUNTRY STATE NATURAL AREA

10600 Bandera Creek Rd
Bandera, TX 78003
Web: www.tpwd.state.tx.us/spdest/findadest/parks/
hill_country
Phone: 830-796-4413
Size: 5,370 acres. **Location:** 45 miles northwest of San Antonio. **Facilities:** Primitive campsites, horsemen's camp, group camp, group lodge, multi-use trails, swimming areas, scenic overlook. **Activities:** Camping, hiking, backpacking, bicycling, horseback riding, mountain biking, fishing. **Special Features:** Area features a scenic setting of rocky hills, flowing springs, oak groves, grasslands, and canyons. The West Verde Creek has several spring-fed streams, and tanks in the park provide several swimming holes, with limited fishing for catfish, perch, and largemouth bass.

★4338★ HONEY CREEK STATE NATURAL AREA

c/o Guadalupe River State Park
3350 Park Rd 31
Spring Branch, TX 78070
Web: www.tpwd.state.tx.us/spdest/findadest/parks/
honey_creek
Phone: 210-438-2656
Size: 2,294 acres. **Location:** In Guadalupe River State Park, 30 miles north of San Antonio. **Facilities:** Nature/interpretive trails (2 miles). **Activities:** Guided nature hikes, wildlife viewing, nature study. **Special Features:** Entry into Honey Creek is by guided tour only. The area encompasses unusually diverse vegetation and geographical features which give rise to a varied and abundant wildlife.

★4339★ HUECO TANKS STATE HISTORIC SITE

6900 Hueco Tanks Rd No 1
El Paso, TX 79938
Web: www.tpwd.state.tx.us/spdest/findadest/parks/
hueco_tanks
Phone: 915-857-1135; **Fax:** 915-857-3628

Size: 860 acres. **Location:** 32 miles northeast of El Paso on Ranch Road 2775. **Facilities:** Campsites with water and electricity hookups, tent camping, showers, restrooms, picnic areas, day-use group facility, hiking trails, nature/interpretive trails, historic structure, interpretive center, amphitheater, park store. **Activities:** Camping, hiking, biking, rock climbing, guided tours, interpretive programs. **Special Features:** For centuries, Hueco Tanks has been a well-known landmark in this arid region of western Texas. Desert dwellers and travelers have long made use of the supply of rainwater trapped in the natural basins (*huecos*) among the rocks. The park also features caves and rock formations with pictographs, most notably more than 200 face designs or "masks" left by the prehistoric Jornada Mogollon culture. To protect the park's natural and cultural resources, visitation is limited.

★4340★ HUNTSVILLE STATE PARK

PO Box 508
Huntsville, TX 77342
Web: www.tpwd.state.tx.us/spdest/findadest/parks/huntsville
Phone: 936-295-5644
Size: 2,083 acres. **Location:** Off I-45, 6 miles south of Huntsville, take Exit 109 to Park Road 40. **Facilities:** Campsites with water and electricity hookups, tent camping, showers, restrooms, day-use group facility, picnic areas, screened shelters, hiking trails, nature trail, bike trails, boat ramp, docks, boat rentals, fishing pier, fish cleaning stations, interpretive center, park store, playground. **Activities:** Camping, boating (5 mph speed limit), canoeing, fishing, swimming, hiking, bicycling, mountain biking, horseback riding, hunting (with restrictions). **Special Features:** Park adjoins Sam Houston National Forest (see entry in national forests section) and consists of woodlands dominated by loblolly and shortleaf pines typical of east Texas. Park includes Lake Raven, a 210-acre impoundment fed by three major creeks, which offers fishing for crappie, perch, catfish, and bass.

★4341★ INKS LAKE STATE PARK

3630 Park Rd 4 W
Burnet, TX 78611
Web: www.tpwd.state.tx.us/spdest/findadest/parks/inks
Phone: 512-793-2223
Size: 1,201 acres. **Location:** 9 miles west of Burnet on Hwy 29, in the central portion of the state. **Facilities:** Campsites with water and electricity hookups, tent camping, primitive campsites, group camp, limited use cabins, showers, restrooms, day-use group facility, picnic areas, hiking trails, beach, boat ramp, fishing piers, boat rentals, 9-hole golf course, amphitheater, park store, playgrounds. **Activities:** Camping, hiking, boating, canoeing, fishing, swimming, water-skiing, scuba diving, golf, interpretive programs. **Special Features:** Located along the Colorado River in central Texas, Inks Lake is one in a chain of seven lakes. It is a constant-level lake, unaffected by drought conditions, and is surrounded by granite hills.

★4342★ KICKAPOO CAVERN STATE PARK

PO Box 705
Brackettville, TX 78832
Web: www.tpwd.state.tx.us/spdest/findadest/parks/kickapoo_cavern
Phone: 830-563-2342

Size: 6,368 acres. **Location:** 40 miles west of Uvalde on US 90. Access by reservation only. **Facilities:** Undeveloped. **Activities:** Wildlife viewing, guided cave tours. **Special Features:** Vistors must call the park to make advance arrangements. The caverns include 15 known caves, two of which are large enough to be significant. Between mid-March and the end of October, some caves serve as a migratory stopover for large numbers of Brazilian freetail bats.

★4343★ LAKE ARROWHEAD STATE PARK

229 Park Rd 63
Wichita Falls, TX 76310
Web: www.tpwd.state.tx.us/spdest/findadest/parks/lake_arrowhead
Phone: 940-528-2211
Size: 524 acres. **Location:** 14 miles southeast of Wichita Falls on Farm Road 1954. **Facilities:** Campsites with water and electricity hookups, tent camping, horsemen's campsites, primitive camp, showers, restrooms, day-use group facility, picnic areas, nature trails, bridle trails, boat ramps, dock, boat rentals, fishing pier, fish cleaning station, park store, disc golf course, playground. **Activities:** Camping, boating, fishing, swimming, water-skiing, horseback riding, hiking, disc golf, birding. **Special Features:** Lake Arrowhead covers 16,200 surface acres with 106 miles of shoreline. Built primarily as a water supply source for the city of Wichita Falls, the lake is also a major recreational site for the area.

★4344★ LAKE BOB SANDLIN STATE PARK

341 State Park Rd 2117
Pittsburg, TX 75686
Web: www.tpwd.state.tx.us/spdest/findadest/parks/lake_bob_sandlin
Phone: 903-572-5531
Size: 640 acres. **Location:** On the north side of Lake Bob Sandlin, southeast of Mount Pleasant, in the northeastern part of the state **Facilities:** Campsites with water and electricity hookups, primitive campsites, limited use cabins, showers, restrooms, day-use group facility, picnic areas, screened shelters, hiking trails, bike trails, boat ramp, fishing pier, fish cleaning station, park store, playground. **Activities:** Camping, boating, fishing, swimming, water-skiing, hiking, mountain biking, inline skating, interpretive programs. **Special Features:** There is evidence of prehistoric Caddoan people who occupied East Texas from 200 BC to 1700. The French and Spanish periodically occupied the area, as did various Indian tribes. By 1841 Fort Sherman, a wooden stockade whose site is believed to be in or near the park, was established; its cemetery is located in the park.

★4345★ LAKE BROWNWOOD STATE PARK

200 Highway Park Rd 15
Lake Brownwood, TX 76801
Web: www.tpwd.state.tx.us/spdest/findadest/parks/lake_brownwood
Phone: 325-784-5223
Size: 537 acres. **Location:** 16 miles northwest of Brownwood

on Park Rd 15. **Facilities:** Campsites with full hookups, campsites with water and electricity hookups, tent camping, group camp, showers, restrooms, cabins, picnic areas, screened shelters, hiking trails, boat ramps, docks, fishing piers, park store, ball field. **Activities:** Camping, boating, fishing, swimming, water-skiing, jet skiing, hiking. **Special Features:** Park is situated on Lake Brownwood, a 7,300-acre reservoir created by damming Pecan Bayou, a tributary of the Colorado River. Many structures in use today were constructed in the 1930s by the Civilian Conservation Corps (CCC) from timber and native rock found in the park.

★4346★ LAKE CASA BLANCA INTERNATIONAL STATE PARK

5102 Bob Bullock Loop
Laredo, TX 78044
Web: www.tpwd.state.tx.us/spdest/findadest/parks/
    lake_casa_blanca
Phone: 956-725-3826
Size: 371 acres. **Location:** 1 mile east of Laredo off TX 59 on Lake Casa Blanca Road. **Facilities:** Campsites with water and electricity hookups, tent camping, showers, restrooms, group camp, day-use group facility, picnic areas, bike trails, boat ramp, park store, game courts, playfield, playgrounds, amphitheater, park store, playground, ballfield, amphitheater. **Activities:** Camping, boating, fishing, swimming, mountain biking, birding. **Special Features:** The 1,656-acre lake is among the state's best for largemouth bass fishing and is also an excellent spot for birding and wildlife watching.

★4347★ LAKE COLORADO CITY STATE PARK

4582 FM 2836
Colorado City, TX 79512
Web: www.tpwd.state.tx.us/spdest/findadest/parks/
    lake_colorado_city
Phone: 325-728-3931
Size: 500 acres. **Location:** 11 miles southwest of Colorado City, on Farm Road 2836. **Facilities:** Campsites with water and electricity hookups, tent camping, showers, restrooms, group camp, day-use group facility, picnic areas, boat ramp, fishing piers, playgrounds. **Activities:** Camping, boating, fishing, swimming, water-skiing, jet skiing, birding. **Special Features:** Lake Colorado City was built in 1949 on Morgan Creek, a tributary of the Colorado River, by Texas Electric Service Company and contains more than 5 miles of shoreline. Park is home to part of the Texas Longhorn herd.

★4348★ LAKE CORPUS CHRISTI STATE PARK

Box 1167
Mathis, TX 78368
Web: www.tpwd.state.tx.us/spdest/findadest/parks/
    lake_corpus_christi
Phone: 361-547-2635
Size: 14,112 acres. **Location:** 35 miles northwest of Corpus Christi on Farm Road 1068. **Facilities:** Campsites with water and electricity hookups, tent camping, showers, restrooms, day-use group facility, picnic areas, screened shelters, boat ramp, boat rentals, fishing piers, fish cleaning facilities, playground,

scenic overlook. **Activities:** Camping, boating, fishing, swimming, water-skiing, birding, bicycling, hiking. **Special Features:** Many of the park's facilities were built by the Civilian Conservation Corp during the 1930s. CCC buildings included a bathhouse, park residence, and a refectory, but only the refectory remains. It was built of cast blocks of local caliche.

★4349★ LAKE LIVINGSTON STATE PARK

300 Park Rd 65
Livingston, TX 77351
Web: www.tpwd.state.tx.us/spdest/findadest/parks/
    lake_livingston
Phone: 936-365-2201
Size: 636 acres. **Location:** 75 miles north of Houston on Park Road 65. **Facilities:** Campsites with water and electricity hookups, campsites with full hookups, tent camping, showers, restrooms, group camp, day-use group facility, picnic areas, screened shelters (&), hiking trails, nature trails, bike trails, bridle trails, swimming pool, bathhouse (seasonal), horse rentals, boat ramp, dock, fishing pier, fish cleaning stations, park store (seasonal), observation tower, playground, amphitheater, recreation hall. **Activities:** Camping, boating, fishing, swimming, hiking, bicycling, mountain biking, horseback riding. **Special Features:** Park is located near the ghost town of Swartout. In the 1830s and 1840s, the town was a thriving steamboat landing on the Trinity River.

★4350★ LAKE MINERAL WELLS STATE PARK & TRAILWAY

100 Park Rd 71
Mineral Wells, TX 76067
Web: www.tpwd.state.tx.us/spdest/findadest/parks/
    lake_mineral_wells
Phone: 940-328-1171
Size: 3,283 acres. **Location:** 4 miles east of Mineral Wells on US 180. **Facilities:** Campsites with water and electricity hookups, tent camping, horsemen's camp, primitive campsites, showers, restrooms (&), day-use group facility, picnic areas, screened shelters, hiking trails, nature trails, bike trail, bridle trail, beach, boat ramp, boat rentals, fishing piers (&), playground, park store, amphitheater. **Activities:** Camping, boating, fishing, swimming, hiking, backpacking, mountain biking, horseback riding, rock climbing. **Special Features:** Park is located along Rock Creek, a large tributary of the Brazos River, and encompasses its namesake 646-acre lake. Lake Mineral Wells Trailway is a converted railroad track that begins northwest of Weatherford and travels 20 miles westward to the downtown district of Mineral Wells. It passes over 16 bridges, including the trailway's 500-foot signature bridge adorned with 104 Lone Stars.

★4351★ LAKE SOMERVILLE STATE PARK

14222 Park Rd 57
Somerville, TX 77879
Web: www.tpwd.state.tx.us/spdest/findadest/parks/
    lake_somerville
Phone: 979-535-7763
Size: 5,970 acres. **Location:** Park comprises two main units: Birch Creek Unit is in Burleson County on the north shore of

the reservoir; Nails Creek Unit is in Lee County on the south shore, near the west end of the reservoir. **Facilities:** Campsites with water and electricity hookups, tent camping, horsemen's campsites, primitive campsites, showers, restrooms (&), day-use group facility, picnic areas, screened shelters, multi-use trails (&), boat ramps, dock, fishing pier, fish cleaning station, game courts, playgrounds, park store. **Activities:** Camping, boating, fishing, swimming, water-skiing, hiking, mountain biking, horseback riding, birding, hunting (with restrictions). **Special Features:** The park features 11,630-acre Lake Somerville, which includes 85 miles of shoreline. The two main units of the park are connected by the 13-mile Somerville Trailway.

★4352★ LAKE TAWAKONI STATE PARK
c/o Purtis Creek State Park
10822 FM 2475
Wills Point 75169, TX 75124
Web: www.tpwd.state.tx.us/spdest/findadest/parks/
lake_tawakoni
Phone: 903-560-7123
Size: 376 acres. **Location:** From Wills Point, 6 miles north on Highway 47, then left on County Road 2475 for 4 miles. **Facilities:** Campsites with water and electricity hookups, group camp, restrooms, showers, picnic areas, hiking trails, bike trails, beach, boat ramp. **Activities:** Camping, boating, swimming, fishing, hiking, biking. **Special Features:** Park is located beside Lake Tawakoni, a 36,700-acre reservoir on the headwaters of the Sabine River. The terrain consists mostly of upland regrowth with post oak woodlands and includes a small tract of tallgrass prairie.

★4353★ LAKE TEXANA STATE PARK
46 Park Rd 1
Edna, TX 77957
Web: www.tpwd.state.tx.us/spdest/findadest/parks/
lake_texana
Phone: 361-782-5718
Size: 575 acres. **Location:** 6.5 miles east of Edna on State Highway 111, halfway between Houston and Corpus Christi. **Facilities:** Campsites with water and electricity hookups, tent camping, restrooms, showers, picnic areas, nature trail, hiking trail, nature center, amphitheater, boat ramp, fishing piers (&), park store, playground, boat rentals. **Activities:** Camping, boating, water-skiing, jet skiing, sailing, canoeing, fishing, swimming, hiking, birding, interpretive programs. **Special Features:** Park is located on Lake Texana, which has 11,000 surface acres and 125 miles of shoreline.

★4354★ LAKE WHITNEY STATE PARK
PO Box 1175
Whitney, TX 76692
Web: www.tpwd.state.tx.us/spdest/findadest/parks/
lake_whitney
Phone: 254-694-3793
Size: 955 acres. **Location:** 3 miles west of Whitney on Farm Road 1244, on the shore of Lake Whitney. **Facilities:** Campsites with water and electricity hookups, tent camping, showers, restrooms, group camp, day-use group facility, picnic areas, screened shelters, hiking trail, multi-use trail, airplane landing strip, boat ramp, fish cleaning station, park store, playground, recreation hall. **Activities:** Camping, boating, fishing, swimming, water-skiing, scuba diving, hiking, mountain biking, hunting (with restrictions), birding. **Special Features:** Park is located on 1,281-acre Lake Whitney, near ruins of Towash, an early Texas settlement that was inundated by the lake.

★4355★ LANDMARK INN STATE HISTORIC SITE
402 E Florence St
Castroville, TX 78009
Web: www.tpwd.state.tx.us/spdest/findadest/parks/
landmark_inn
Phone: 830-931-2133
Size: 4.5 acres. **Location:** South central Texas, about 20 minutes from the San Antonio Riverwalk. **Facilities:** 10-room inn, nature trails, historic structure, interpretive center, restrooms. **Activities:** Bicycling, interpretive and historical programs. **Special Features:** The Landmark Inn, built in 1849, is a bed and breakfast that has provided accommodations for travelers for more than a century. A small museum is located in a wing of the inn, with exhibits on early Castroville.

★4356★ LIPANTITLAN STATE HISTORIC SITE
c/o Lake Corpus Christi State Park
PO Box 1167
Mathis, TX 78368
Web: www.tpwd.state.tx.us/spdest/findadest/parks/lipantitlan
Phone: 361-547-2635
Size: 5 acres. **Location:** 9 miles east of Orange Grove, off TX 359. **Facilities:** Picnic area, historical site. **Special Features:** Mexican forces constructed a wood picket fort near this area around 1831 in anticipation of trouble with Anglo immigrants. In 1835 the fort was surrendered without a shot being fired.

★4357★ LOCKHART STATE PARK
4179 State Park Rd
Lockhart, TX 78644
Web: www.tpwd.state.tx.us/spdest/findadest/parks/lockhart
Phone: 512-398-3479
Size: 264 acres. **Location:** Off Farm Road 20, southwest of Lockhart. **Facilities:** Campsites with full hookups, campsites with water and electricity hookups, restrooms, showers, day-use group facility, picnic areas, swimming pool, 9-hole golf course, hiking trail, park store, playground. **Activities:** Camping, fishing, swimming, hiking, golf, nature study. **Special Features:** Park offers the only staff-operated golf course in the Texas park system.

★4358★ LONGHORN CAVERN STATE PARK
PO Box 732
Burnet, TX 78611
Web: www.tpwd.state.tx.us/spdest/findadest/parks/
longhorn_cavern
Phone: 830-598-2283
Size: 646 acres. **Location:** 6 miles west and 6 miles south of Burnet on Park Road 4, in the central portion of the state.

Facilities: Interpretive center, historic site, picnic areas, restrooms, hiking trails, snack bar, park store. **Activities:** Daily cavern tours, hiking, hunting (with restrictions). **Special Features:** The cave was formed when the ground levels of water began to drop. As this downward movement occurred, the water began to dissolve the limestone. This downward drainage continued until great underground stream beds were cut out of solid rock. This unusual combination of dissolving and cutting by water makes Longhorn Cavern one of the most unique caves in the world.

★4359★ LOST MAPLES STATE NATURAL AREA

37221 FM 187
Vanderpool, TX 78885
Web: www.tpwd.state.tx.us/spdest/findadest/parks/
lost_maples
Phone: 830-966-3413
Size: 2,174 acres. **Location:** On the Sabinal River, 5 miles north of Vanderpool on Farm Road 187. **Facilities:** Campsites with water and electricity hookups, primitive capsites, showers, restrooms (&), picnic areas (&), hiking trails, nature trails, park store. **Activities:** Camping, fishing, swimming, hiking, backpacking, birding. **Special Features:** Bigtooth maples, or canyon maples, are the outstanding feature of the park. During the fall (generally the last two weeks of October through the first two weeks of November), displays of red, yellow, and orange foliage attract a number of visitors to the park, especially on weekends. Park was designated a National Natural Landmark in 1980.

★4360★ LYNDON B. JOHNSON STATE PARK & HISTORIC SITE

PO Box 238
Stonewall, TX 78671
Web: www.tpwd.state.tx.us/spdest/findadest/parks/
lyndon_b_johnson
Phone: 830-644-2252
Size: 718 acres. **Location:** 2 miles east of Stonewall on US Hwy 290, in the central portion of the state. **Facilities:** Day-use group facility, picnic areas, hiking trails, nature/interpretive trails, swimming pool, historic structure, exhibits, amphitheater, auditorium, tennis courts, ball field, playground, restrooms, park store. **Activities:** Fishing, swimming, hiking, interpretive programs. **Special Features:** Park's visitor center contains memorabilia from President Johnson's boyhood, as well as pictures from the presidential years and photos of famous guests at the nearby LBJ Ranch.

★4361★ MAGOFFIN HOME STATE HISTORIC SITE

1120 Magoffin Ave
El Paso, TX 79901
Web: www.tpwd.state.tx.us/spdest/findadest/parks/
magoffin_home/
Phone: 915-533-5147
Size: 1.5 acres. **Location:** In the city of El Paso on Magoffin Avenue. **Facilities:** Historic structure, interpretive center, restrooms (&&). **Activities:** Guided tours. **Special Features:** The Magoffin Home, built in 1875 by pioneer El Pasoan Joseph Magoffin, displays a regional architectural style developed in the Southwest. The home is filled with many original family furnishings, including a Victorian-style parlor with a distinctly Mexican influence. One of the bedrooms is furnished with a 13-foot-tall, half canopy bed and four matching pieces purchased at the 1884 New Orleans World's Fair.

★4362★ MARTIN CREEK LAKE STATE PARK

9515 CR 2181D
Tatum, TX 75691
Web: www.tpwd.state.tx.us/spdest/findadest/parks/
martin_creek
Phone: 903-836-4336
Size: 287 acres. **Location:** 20 miles southeast of Longview in the northeastern portion of the state. **Facilities:** Campsites with water and electricity hookups, primitive campsites, 2 cottages, showers, restrooms, day-use group facility, picnic areas, screened shelters, hiking trails, bike trails, boat ramp, fishing pier, park store, playground, amphitheater. **Activities:** Camping, boating, fishing, swimming, water-skiing, hiking, mountain biking, interpretive programs. **Special Features:** Martin Creek Lake was constructed to provide cooling water for a lignite-fired, electric power generation plant. The park area was deeded to the state by the Texas Utilities Generating Company in 1976.

★4363★ MARTIN DIES, JR. STATE PARK

RR 4, Box 274
Jasper, TX 75951
Web: www.tpwd.state.tx.us/spdest/findadest/parks/
martin_dies_jr
Phone: 409-384-5231
Size: 705 acres. **Location:** In the extreme eastern portion of the state, 15 miles east from Woodville on US 190. **Facilities:** Campsites with water and electricity hookups, tent camping, limited use cabin, showers, restrooms, day-use group facility (&), picnic areas, screened shelters, nature trails, hiking trails, bike trails, fishing piers (&), fish cleaning stations, boat ramps, park store, amphitheater, nature center, playgrounds. **Activities:** Camping, boating, fishing, swimming, hiking, mountain biking, birding, interpretive programs. **Special Features:** Park is located alongside 15,000-acre B.A. Steinhagen Reservoir in the heavily forested area known as the "East Texas Piney Woods."

★4364★ MATAGORDA ISLAND WILDLIFE MANAGEMENT AREA

1700 7th St
Bay City, TX 77414
Web: www.tpwd.state.tx.us/huntwild/hunt/wma/find_a_wma/
list/?id=48
Phone: 979-244-6824
Size: 56,688 acres. **Location:** Offshore barrier island, 11 water miles from Port O'Connor. **Facilities:** Primitive camp, picnic areas, beach, hiking trails. **Activities:** Camping, boating, fishing, swimming, hiking, bicycling, beachcombing, nature study, hunting (with restrictions), guided hikes. **Special Features:** The island, which protects the mainland from the tidal and wave action of the open Gulf, is a haven for wildlife. Nineteen species on state or federal endangered lists live here, including the

whooping crane, Alpomado falcon, and brown pelican. A lighthouse dating from 1852 still stands at the north end of the island.

★4365★ MCKINNEY FALLS STATE PARK
5808 McKinney Falls Pkwy
Austin, TX 78744
Web: www.tpwd.state.tx.us/spdest/findadest/parks/
mckinney_falls
Phone: 512-243-1643; Fax: 512-243-0536
Size: 744 acres. Location: 13 miles southeast of Austin off US 183. Facilities: Campsites with water and electricity hookups, tent camping, showers, restrooms, shelter with bunk beds, picnic areas, screened shelters, historic structure, interpretive center, hiking trails, nature trails, bike trails, amphitheater, playground, park store. Activities: Camping, fishing, swimming, hiking, bicycling. Special Features: Park is named for Thomas F. McKinney (1801-1873), one of Stephen F. Austin's original colonists. McKinney became a prominent breeder of race horses, with his own stable and private track. Preserved in the park are the ruins of his trainer's cabin and the stabilized ruins of his own homestead dating to the mid-1800s.

★4366★ MERIDIAN STATE PARK
173 Park Rd 7
Meridian, TX 76665
Web: www.tpwd.state.tx.us/spdest/findadest/parks/meridian
Phone: 254-435-2536
Size: 505 acres. Location: 3 miles southwest of Meridian off State Highway 22. Facilities: Campsites with water and electricity hookups, tent camping, showers, restrooms, group camp, picnic areas, screened shelters, hiking trails (&), nature trails, boat ramp. Activities: Camping, boating, fishing, swimming, hiking, bicycling. Special Features: The hiking trail encircling Lake Meridian features limestone outcroppings with fossils, a scenic overlook, and aquatic vegetation. A variety of wildlife and birds inhabit the park, including the endangered golden-cheeked warbler.

★4367★ MISSION TEJAS STATE PARK
RR 2, Box 108
Grapeland, TX 75844
Web: www.tpwd.state.tx.us/spdest/findadest/parks/
mission_tejas
Phone: 936-687-2394
Size: 363 acres. Location: 22 miles northeast of Crockett in the northeastern part of the state. Facilities: Campsites with full hookups, campsites with water and electricity hookups, tent camping, showers, restrooms, group camp, day-use group facility, picnic areas, hiking trails, historic structures, park store, amphitheater, playground. Activities: Camping, fishing, hiking. Special Features: Park was built as a commemorative representation of Mission San Francisco de los Tejas, the first Spanish mission in the province of Texas. In the park also is the Rice Family Log Home, which was constructed betweeen 1828 and 1838 and served as a stopover for travelers on the Old San Antonio Road across pioneer Texas.

★4368★ MONAHANS SANDHILLS STATE PARK
PO Box 1738
Monahans, TX 79756
Web: www.tpwd.state.tx.us/spdest/findadest/parks/
monahans_sandhills
Phone: 432-943-2092
Size: 3,840 acres. Location: 6 miles northeast of Monahans off I-20, in the midwestern portion of the state. Facilities: Campsites with water and electrical hookups, tent camping, showers, restrooms, day-use group facility, picnic areas, nature trails, bridle trails, interpretive center, park store, equestrian area. Activities: Camping, hiking, horseback riding, sand sledding. Special Features: Park encompasses a small portion of the sand dune field that extends 200 miles from south of Monahans westward and north into New Mexico. Most of the dunes are stabilized by vegetation, but the park is one area where many dunes are still active. Active dunes grow and change shape in response to seasonal prevailing winds. The park's Dunagan Visitor Center features hands-on exhibits on the botanical, archeological, historical, and geological features of the area.

★4369★ MONUMENT HILL & KREISCHE BREWERY STATE HISTORIC SITES
414 State Loop 92
La Grange, TX 78945
Web: www.tpwd.state.tx.us/spdest/findadest/parks/
monument_hill_and_kreische_brewery
Phone: 979-968-5658
Size: 40 acres. Location: 1 miles southwest of La Grange on US 77. Facilities: Interpretive center, picnic areas, restrooms, interpretive exhibits, historic structures, playground, park store. Activities: Guided tours. Special Features: Monument Hill State Historic Site and Kreische Brewery State Historic Site are administered as a single operational unit and include a monument commemorating events of the war between Mexico and Texas in the 1840s, and the Kreische home, brewery, and other outbuildings.

★4370★ MOTHER NEFF STATE PARK
1680 Texas 236 Hwy
Moody, TX 76557
Web: www.tpwd.state.tx.us/spdest/findadest/parks/
mother_neff
Phone: 254-853-2389
Size: 259 acres. Location: 6 miles west of Moody on State Highway 236. Facilities: Campsites with water and electricity hookups, tent camping, showers, restrooms, group camp (&), day-use group facility (&), picnic areas, hiking trail (1.5 miles), playfield, playground, scenic areas. Activities: Camping, fishing, hiking, interpretive programs. Special Features: The oldest state park in Texas was named for Isabella Eleanor (Mother) Neff, who donated six acres of land along the Leon River to the state of Texas in 1916. Her son was Texas governor Pat M. Neff, who served from 1921 to 1925.

9. State Parks

★4371★ MUSTANG ISLAND STATE PARK
17047 State Hwy 361
Port Aransas, TX 78373
Web: www.tpwd.state.tx.us/spdest/findadest/parks/
  mustang_island
Phone: 361-749-5246; **Fax:** 361-749-6455
Size: 3,954 acres. **Location:** Southeast from Corpus Christi to Padre Island, then north on Park Road 53. **Facilities:** Campsites with water and electricity hookups, primitive campsites, showers, restrooms, picnic areas, beach, park store. **Activities:** Camping, fishing, swimming, hiking, mountain biking, birding, interpretive programs (by appointment). **Special Features:** Mustang Island is a coastal barrier island with a unique and complicated ecosystem dependent upon sand dunes. The earliest known inhabitants of Mustang Island were Karankawa Indians, known for their fierceness and cannibalism. The island was first named "Wild Horse Island," then "Mustang," for the wild horses brought to the island by Spaniards in the 1800s.

★4372★ PALMETTO STATE PARK
78 Park Rd 11 S
Gonzales, TX 78629
Web: www.tpwd.state.tx.us/spdest/findadest/parks/palmetto
Phone: 830-672-3266
Size: 270 acres. **Location:** 6 miles southeast of Luling on US 183. **Facilities:** 41 campsites (18 with water and electric hookups, 1 with full hookup), group camp, showers, restrooms, day-use group facility, picnic areas, hiking trails, nature trails, fishing pier, boat rentals, interpretive programs, park store, playgrounds, scenic overlook. **Activities:** Camping, canoeing, fishing, swimming, tubing, hiking, birding. **Special Features:** Park is in an unusual botanical area that resembles the tropics more than Central Texas, and the park is named for a stand of dwarf palmetto plants usually found only in eastern and southeastern Texas.

★4373★ PALO DURO CANYON STATE PARK
11450 Park Rd 5
Canyon, TX 79015
Web: www.tpwd.state.tx.us/spdest/findadest/parks/palo_duro
Phone: 806-488-2227; **Fax:** 806-488-2729
Size: 16,402 acres. **Location:** South of Amarillo in the Texas Panhandle. **Facilities:** Campsites with water and electricity hookups, tent camping, showers, restrooms, primitive campsites, cabins, picnic areas, multi-use trails, horse rentals, interpretive center, visitor center, amphitheater, park store, restaurant, playground. **Activities:** Camping, fishing, hiking, mountain biking, horseback riding, guided tours, interpretive programs. **Special Features:** Canyon is approximately 120 miles long, 20 miles wide, and 800 feet deep and was formed primarily by water erosion from the Prairie Dog Town Fork of the Red River.

★4374★ PEDERNALES FALLS STATE PARK
2585 Park Rd 6026
Johnson City, TX 78636
Web: www.tpwd.state.tx.us/spdest/findadest/parks/
  pedernales_falls
Phone: 830-868-7304

Size: 5,212 acres. **Location:** 32 miles west of Austin on US 290. **Facilities:** Campsites with water and electricity hookups, primitive campsites, group camp, showers, restrooms, picnic areas, hiking trails, nature trail, bike trails, bridle trails, park store. **Activities:** Camping, fishing, swimming, tubing, hiking, mountain biking, horseback riding, interpretive programs. **Special Features:** Pedernales Falls is the park's main attraction, formed by a series of tilted "stair steps" of layered limestone, descending about 50 feet over a distance of 3,000 feet. An overlook at the northern end of the park affords a scenic view of the falls.

★4375★ PORT ISABEL LIGHTHOUSE STATE HISTORIC SITE
421 E Queen Isabella Blvd
Port Isabel, TX 78578
Web: www.tpwd.state.tx.us/spdest/findadest/parks/
  port_isabel_lighthouse
Phone: 956-943-2262
Size: 1 acre. **Location:** In the city of Port Isabel on TX 100. **Facilities:** Historic site, picnic area, restrooms (&). **Special Features:** Located at the southern tip of the Texas Gulf Coast, the lighthouse was built in 1852. Of 16 lighthouses constructed along the Texas coast, Port Isabel Lighthouse is the only one now open to the public.

★4376★ POSSUM KINGDOM STATE PARK
PO Box 70
Caddo, TX 76429
Web: www.tpwd.state.tx.us/spdest/findadest/parks/
  possum_kingdom
Phone: 940-549-1803
Size: 1,529 acres. **Location:** West of Mineral Wells, in the northern portion of the state. **Facilities:** Campsites with water and electricity hookups, tent camping, primitive campsites, cabins, showers, restrooms, picnic areas, hiking trail, boat ramp, boat rentals, fuel dock, fishing pier, fish cleaning station, playgrounds. **Activities:** Camping, boating, fishing, swimming, water-skiing, hiking, biking. **Special Features:** Park is located in the rugged canyon country of the Palo Pinto Mountains and Brazos River Valley, adjacent to 20,000-acre Possum Kingdom Lake.

★4377★ PURTIS CREEK STATE PARK
14225 FM 316
Eustace, TX 75124
Web: www.tpwd.state.tx.us/spdest/findadest/parks/
  purtis_creek
Phone: 903-425-2332
Size: 1,582 acres. **Location:** 65 miles east of the Dallas/Fort Worth area, on Farm Road 316. **Facilities:** Campsites with water and electricity hookups, tent camping, primitive campsites, showers, restrooms, day-use group facility, picnic areas, hiking trails, boat ramp, docks, boat rentals, fishing piers, fish cleaning stations, swimming area, park store, playground, amphitheater. **Activities:** Camping, boating (with restrictions), fishing, hiking, swimming, interpretive programs (seasonal). **Special Features:** The park's unique 355-acre lake was designed specifically for

9. State Parks

fishing; large catfish, crappie, and largemouth bass are plentiful, although bass fishing is "catch and release" only. Due to the small size of the lake, no more than 50 boats are permitted on the lake at any time.

★4378★ RAY ROBERTS LAKE STATE PARK
100 PW 4137
Pilot Point, TX 76258
Web: www.tpwd.state.tx.us/spdest/findadest/parks/ray_roberts_lake
Phone: 940-686-2148
Size: 5,849 acres. Location: Park consists of two main units around Ray Roberts Lake: The Isle du Bois Unit is located on Farm Road 455, 10 miles east of I-35 on the south side of the lake; the Johnson Branch Unit is located on Farm Road 3002, 7 miles east of I-35, on the north side of the lake. Facilities: Campsites with water and electricity hookups, tent camping, primitive campsites, horsemen's camp, group camp, showers, restrooms, lodge, picnic areas, day-use group facilities, hiking trails, bike trails, bridle trails, beaches, marina, boat ramps, boat rentals, fishing piers, restaurant, park store, playgrounds. Activities: Camping, boating, canoeing, fishing, swimming, hiking, bicycling, mountain biking, horseback riding, inline skating. Special Features: Situated along the shores of a 30,000-acre reservoir, the park complex consists of two state park units, six satellite parks, wildlife management units, wetlands, waterfowl sanctuaries, and the 20-mile Ray Roberts Lake/Lake Lewisville Greenbelt Corridor.

★4379★ RUSK/PALESTINE STATE PARK
RR 4, Box 431
Rusk, TX 75785
Web: www.tpwd.state.tx.us/spdest/findadest/parks/rusk_and_palestine
Phone: 903-683-5126
Size: 136 acres. Location: The Rusk Unit is located 3 miles west of Rusk on Highway 84; the Palestine Unit is located 6 miles east of Palestine. Facilities: Campsites with full hookups, campsites with water and electricity hookups, tent camping, showers, restrooms, day-use group facility, picnic areas, nature trail, 15-acre lake, fishing pier, park store, playgrounds. Activities: Camping, fishing, tennis, train excursion rides. Special Features: Unique in the Texas park system, Rusk/Palestine State Park consists of two separate units connected by the historic Texas State Railroad. Train rides covering the 26-mile journey are offered on a regular basis from both locations.

★4380★ SABINE PASS BATTLEGROUND STATE PARK & HISTORIC SITE
c/o Sea Rim State Park
PO Box 1066
Sabine Pass, TX 77655
Web: www.tpwd.state.tx.us/spdest/findadest/parks/sabine_pass_battleground
Phone: 409-971-2559
Size: 57 acres. Location: 1.5 miles south of Sabine Pass on Dowling Road on the eastern border of the state. Facilities: Campsites with water and electricity hookups, primitive campsites, picnic areas, walking trail, boat ramp (&), historical monument, interpretive exhibit. Activities: Camping, boating, fishing, crabbing, hiking. Special Features: Park includes a monument in memory of Lieutenant Richard W. Dowling and his men, defenders of Sabine Pass for the Confederacy during the Civil War. Also located in the park are four concrete ammunition bunkers which were built during World War II.

★4381★ SAM BELL MAXEY HOUSE STATE HISTORIC SITE
812 S Church St
Paris, TX 75460
Web: www.tpwd.state.tx.us/spdest/findadest/parks/sam_bell_maxey_house
Phone: 903-785-5716
Size: 0.4 acres. Location: In Paris, near the northern border of the state. Facilities: Historic structure, museum, park store, restrooms. Special Features: Built in 1867 in the High Victorian Italianate style, the two-story Maxey House was home to ex-Confederate general and later United States senator Sam Bell Maxey. Members of the Maxey family lived in the house until 1966.

★4382★ SAN ANGELO STATE PARK
3900 - 2 Mercedes
San Angelo, TX 76901
Web: www.tpwd.state.tx.us/spdest/findadest/parks/san_angelo
Phone: 325-949-4757
Size: 7,677 acres. Location: Adjacent to the city of San Angelo, on the shore of the OC Fisher Reservoir, in the central portion of the state. Facilities: Campsites with water and electricity hookups, primitive campsites, horsemen's camp, group camps, cabins, showers, restrooms, day-use group facility, picnic areas, multi-use trails, boat ramps, docks, fishing piers, park store. Activities: Camping, boating, fishing, swimming, hiking, backpacking, horseback riding, mountain biking, birding, hunting (with restrictions), guided hikes (by request). Special Features: Park is located on the shores of O.C. Fisher Reservoir, which was constructed in 1952 for flood control on the North Concho River. The name "Concho" (meaning "shell" in Spanish) comes from the freshwater mussels that inhabit the area's rivers and streams and produce iridescent gems.

★4383★ SAN JACINTO BATTLEGROUND STATE HISTORIC SITE
3527 Battleground Rd
La Porte, TX 77571
Web: www.tpwd.state.tx.us/spdest/findadest/parks/san_jacinto_battleground
Phone: 281-479-2431; Fax: 281-479-5618
Size: 1,200 acres. Location: 22 miles east of downtown Houston off Highway 225 East, then north on Highway 134. Facilities: Day-use group facility, picnic areas, interpretive trails, historic structure, museum, park store, amphitheater, restrooms (&). Activities: Guided tours. Special Features: Dedicated in April of 1939, the San Jacinto Monument commemorates the famous battle between the Texan and Mexican armies on April 21, 1836,

which won independence for Texas. The San Jacinto Museum of History, housed in the base of the monument, interprets four centuries of Texas history. Park is also the temporary berth of the historic Battleship Texas, last of the World War I-era dreadnoughts and the only surviving combat ship to have served in both World Wars I and II.

★4384★ SEA RIM STATE PARK

PO Box 356
Sabine Pass, TX 77655
Web: www.tpwd.state.tx.us/spdest/findadest/parks/sea_rim
Phone: 409-971-2559
Size: 4,141 acres. **Location:** On State Highway 87 in the extreme southeast corner of the Texas coast near Louisiana. **Facilities:** Campsites with water and electricity hookups, tent camping, primitive campsite, showers, restrooms, picnic areas, nature trail (&), beach, boat ramp, boat rentals, observation decks, interpretive center. **Activities:** Camping, boating, canoeing, fishing, swimming, waterfowl hunting (in season), airboat tours. **Special Features:** Park includes a 5.2-mile Gulf of Mexico coastline and features both sandy beach for recreation and the biologically significant zone where salt tidal marshlands meet Gulf waters.

★4385★ SEBASTOPOL STATE HISTORIC SITE

PO Box 900
Seguin, TX 78156
Web: www.tpwd.state.tx.us/spdest/findadest/parks/sebastopol
Phone: 830-379-4833
Size: 2 acres. **Location:** In the city of Seguin; 34 miles east of San Antonio. **Facilities:** Historic structure, interpretive center, park store. **Special Features:** Sebastopol House, an unusual split-level, T-shaped home in the Greek Revival style, was built around 1856 using a unique ''limecrete'' construction technique. Restored to its 1880s appearance, the house includes family furnishings depicting the tastes of middle-class families of the late 19th century. Exhibits explain the original construction, the restoration process, and the history of the house and its inhabitants.

★4386★ SEMINOLE CANYON STATE PARK & HISTORIC SITE

PO Box 820
Comstock, TX 78837
Web: www.tpwd.state.tx.us/spdest/findadest/parks/seminole_canyon
Phone: 432-292-4464
Size: 2,173 acres. **Location:** 45 miles west of Del Rio, near the confluence of the Rio Grande with the Pecos River. **Facilities:** Campsites with water and electricity hookups, tent camping, showers, restrooms (&), picnic areas, multi-use trails, interpretive trail, interpretive center, scenic overlook, park store. **Activities:** Camping, hiking, mountain biking, hunting (with restrictions), guided tours. **Special Features:** Fate Bell cave, located in the canyon, contains some of North America's oldest pictographs. Guided tours allow visitors to see examples of ancient Native American rock art at several different sites in the canyon.

★4387★ SHELDON LAKE STATE PARK & ENVIRONMENTAL LEARNING CENTER

15315 Beaumont Hwy at Park Rd 138
Houston, TX 77049
Web: www.tpwd.state.tx.us/spdest/findadest/parks/sheldon_lake
Phone: 281-456-2800
Size: 2,800 acres. **Location:** 15 miles east of Houston, just north of Highway 90. **Facilities:** Picnic areas, hiking trails, fishing piers, boat ramp, naturalist programs. **Activities:** Fishing, canoeing, birding, nature study, interpretive programs. **Special Features:** Sheldon Reservoir is located on Carpenter's Bayou, a tributary of Buffalo Bayou, and contains the last remaining freshwater marsh habitat within the city limits of the greater Houston area.

★4388★ SOUTH LLANO RIVER STATE PARK

HC 15, Box 224
Junction, TX 76849
Web: www.tpwd.state.tx.us/spdest/findadest/parks/south_llano_river
Phone: 325-446-3994
Size: 2,657 acres (includes wildlife management area acreage). **Location:** 5 miles south of Junction, off Highway 377 on Park Road 73. **Facilities:** Campsites with water and electricity hookups, tent camping, primitive campsites, showers, restrooms, picnic areas, multi-use trails (4 miles), hiking trails (16 miles), beach, historic structure, park store. **Activities:** Camping, canoeing, fishing, swimming, tubing, hiking, mountain biking, hunting (with restrictions). **Special Features:** The park includes two miles of river frontage and adjoins a 2,000-acre wildlife management area, which is one of the largest and oldest wild turkey roosts in the state. Turkeys may be viewed from observation blinds or, sometimes, visiting picnic areas for leftovers. From October through March the roost area is closed to the public, but campgrounds remain open and the river is accessible.

★4389★ STARR FAMILY STATE HISTORIC SITE

407 W Travis St
Marshall, TX 75670
Web: www.tpwd.state.tx.us/spdest/findadest/parks/starr_family
Phone: 903-935-3044
Size: 3 acres. **Location:** In Marshall, in the northeastern portion of the state. **Facilities:** Historic structure, interpretive center, park store. **Activities:** Guided and self-guided tours. **Special Features:** Park interprets the 150-year history of the Starr family in Texas. The centerpiece is Maplecroft, a two-story, wood-sided house built in 1870. Expanded and altered during the years the family occupied it, the house and its furnishings reflect the development of Texas through four generations of Starrs.

★4390★ STEPHEN F. AUSTIN STATE PARK & SAN FELIPE STATE HISTORIC SITE

PO Box 125
San Felipe, TX 77473
Web: www.tpwd.state.tx.us/spdest/findadest/parks/stephen_f_austin_and_san_felipe
Phone: 979-885-3613

Size: 663 acres. **Location:** In the historic township of San Felipe, near Houston. **Facilities:** Campsites with full hookups, tent camping, showers, restrooms, day-use group facility, picnic areas, screened shelters, hiking trails, nature trail, swimming pool, museum, 18-hole golf course, park store, playground. **Activities:** Camping, fishing, swimming, hiking, 18-hole golf course, guided tours, interpretive programs. **Special Features:** San Felipe was the home of Stephen Austin, the ''Father of Texas,'' and other famous early Texans, and it was here that Austin brought the first 297 families to colonize Texas under a contract with the Mexican Government. The 12 acres of the park that were the site of San Felipe have been set aside in honor of the area's past.

★4391★ **TEXAS STATE RAILROAD STATE PARK**
PO Box 39
Rusk, TX 75785
Web: www.tpwd.state.tx.us/spdest/findadest/parks/
texas_state_railroad
Phone: 903-683-2561
Size: 499 acres. **Location:** In Anderson and Cherokee counties between the cities of Rusk and Palestine, adjacent to US 84. **Facilities:** This park connects the two units of Rusk/Palestine State Park (see separate entry). **Activities:** Visitors can enjoy a 26-mile train ride between Rusk and Palestine depots. Special train runs are provided during the operating season in addition to the normal schedule. Film presentations on the railroad's history are presented at a small theater at the Rusk station. **Special Features:** Construction of the Texas State Railroad was begun in 1893 by the state prison system as a plant facility of the penitentiary, to serve an iron furnace and other industries. Most of the railroad line was given to the Texas Parks and Wildlife Department in 1971 for creation of a state historical park dedicated to the preservation of steam locomotives and railroading's golden age.

★4392★ **TYLER STATE PARK**
789 Park Rd 16
Tyler, TX 75706
Web: www.tpwd.state.tx.us/spdest/findadest/parks/tyler
Phone: 903-597-5338
Size: 986 acres. **Location:** 2 miles north of I-20 on Farm Road 14, north of Tyler. **Facilities:** Campsites with full hookups, campsites with water and electricity hookups, tent camping, group camp, showers, restrooms, day-use group facility, screened shelters, picnic areas, hiking trails, bike trails, boat ramp, boat rentals, fishing pier, amphitheater, park store, playground. **Activities:** Camping, boating (5 mph speed limit), fishing, swimming, hiking, mountain biking. **Special Features:** Park includes a 64-acre lake with good fishing for crappie, perch, catfish, and bass.

★4393★ **VARNER-HOGG PLANTATION STATE HISTORIC SITE**
PO Box 696
West Columbia, TX 77486
Web: www.tpwd.state.tx.us/spdest/findadest/parks/
varner_hogg_plantation
Phone: 979-345-4656

Size: 66 acres. **Location:** 50 miles south of Houston, near the Gulf Coast border. **Facilities:** Picnic areas, interpretive trail, historic structure, museum, park store. **Activities:** Picnicking, guided tours. **Special Features:** The two-story Colonial Revival mansion at the park has survived several epochs of Texas history. Originally built as the home of the Pattons, an antebellum cotton and sugar plantation family, the house saw several changes of ownership following the Civil War. In 1901, James Stephen Hogg, one of Texas's most famous governors, acquired the property. The Hogg family remodeled the house extensively, and vestiges of the plantation period disappeared, with the exception of foundation ruins of the sugar mill and several slave cabins. The mansion now houses an extensive collection of historic furnishings.

★4394★ **VILLAGE CREEK STATE PARK**
PO Box 8565
Lumberton, TX 77657
Web: www.tpwd.state.tx.us/spdest/findadest/parks/
village_creek
Phone: 409-755-7322
Size: 1,090 acres. **Location:** 10 miles north of Beaumont, near the Gulf Coast border. **Facilities:** Campsites with water and electricity hookups, tent camping, cabin, group camp, showers, restrooms (&), day-use group facility, picnic areas, hiking trails, interpretive trails, bike trail, park store, playground. **Activities:** Camping, canoeing, swimming, fishing, hiking, mountain biking, wildlife viewing, birding, interpretive programs. **Special Features:** Village Creek is a free-flowing stream that rises near the Alabama-Coushatta Indian Reservation and meanders to a junction with the Neches River. It is a popular flat-water canoe stream in what remains of the Old Texas Big Thicket, a ''rain forest'' of cypress swamps and blackwater sloughs in the flood plain of the Neches River.

★4395★ **WASHINGTON-ON-THE-BRAZOS STATE HISTORIC SITE**
PO Box 305
Washington, TX 77880
Web: www.tpwd.state.tx.us/spdest/findadest/parks/
washington_on_the_brazos
Phone: 936-878-2214
Size: 294 acres. **Location:** 20 miles northeast of Brenham off State Highway 105. **Facilities:** Visitor center, day-use group facility, picnic areas, hiking trails, historic structure, museum, amphitheater, conference center, restaurant, gift shop, playground. **Activities:** Hiking, guided tours, living history demonstrations. **Special Features:** Washington-on-the-Brazos was the site of the signing of the Texas Declaration of Independence on March 2, 1836. The Star of the Republic Museum, Independence Hall, and the Barrington Living History Farm provide park visitors with insight into the lives and times of the men who fought and won Texas' independence from Mexico.

Utah State Parks

	1	2	3	4	5	6	7

1	Anasazi SP Museum	G-4
2	Antelope Island SP	B-2
3	Bear Lake SP	A-4
4	Camp Floyd/Stagecoach Inn SP & Museum	C-3
5	Coral Pink Sand Dunes SP	H-2
6	Dead Horse Point SP	F-6
7	Deer Creek SP	C-3
8	East Canyon SP	B-3
9	Edge of the Cedars SP Museum	G-6
10	Escalante SP	G-3
11	Flight Park SRA	C-3
12	Fremont Indian SP & Museum	F-3
13	Goblin Valley SP	F-5
14	Goosenecks SP	H-6
15	Great Salt Lake SP	B-3
16	Green River SP	E-5
17	Gunlock SP	H-1
18	Historic Union Pacific Rail Trail SP	C-3
19	Huntington SP	D-4
20	Hyrum SP	A-3
21	Iron Mission SP	G-2
22	Jordanelle SP	C-4
23	Kodachrome Basin SP	G-3
24	Millsite SP	E-4
25	Otter Creek SP	F-3
26	Palisade SP	E-3
27	Piute SP	F-3
28	Quail Creek SP	H-1
29	Red Fleet SP	C-6
30	Rockport SP	B-4
31	Sand Hollow SP	H-1
32	Scofield SP	D-4
33	Snow Canyon SP	H-1
34	Starvation SP	C-5
35	Steinaker SP	C-6
36	Territorial Statehouse SP	E-3
37	Utah Field House of Natural History SP	C-6
38	Utah Lake SP	C-3
39	Wasatch Mountain SP	C-3
40	Willard Bay SP	B-3
41	Yuba SP	E-3
SP	State Park	
SRA	State Recreation Area	

816

★4396★ Utah Department of Natural Resources
Division of Parks & Recreation
1594 W North Temple, Suite 116
PO Box 146001
Salt Lake City, UT 841169
(801) 538-7220 - Phone
(801) 538-7378 - Fax
(800) 322-3770 – Toll-free Reservations
(801) 538-3025 - Employment
Web: www.stateparks.utah.gov
Manages and maintains some 42 properties which include heritage, scenic, and recreation parks. Administers off-highway vehicle programs including education, trail maintenance, law enforcement, and search and rescue. Promotes boating safety and education programs.

★4397★ Utah Department of Natural Resources
Division of Wildlife Resources
1594 W North Temple, Suite 2110
PO Box 146301
Salt Lake City, UT 84114
(801) 538-4700 - Phone
(801) 538-4745 - Fax
(877) 592-5169 - Toll-free Information
Web: www.wildlife.utah.gov
Maintains 30 wildlife management areas and 10 fish hatcheries. Develops wildlife education programs, promotes hunter safety training, and regulates hunting, fishing, and trapping licensing.

★4398★ ANASAZI STATE PARK MUSEUM
460 N Hwy 12
Boulder, UT 84716
Web: www.stateparks.utah.gov/park/index.php?id=ANSP
Phone: 435-335-7308
Size: 6 acres. **Elevation:** 6,700 feet. **Location:** Near the city limits of Boulder on State Route 12. **Facilities:** Picnic areas, museum, historic site, modern restrooms (&). **Special Features:** This ancient Indian village was one of the largest Anasazi communities west of the Colorado River. The site is believed to have been occupied from A.D. 1050 to 1200. The village remains largely unexcavated, but many artifacts have been uncovered and are on display in the museum.

★4399★ ANTELOPE ISLAND STATE PARK
4528 West 1700 South
Syracuse, UT 84075
Web: www.stateparks.utah.gov/park/index.php?id=AISP
Phone: 801-652-2043
Size: 28,022 acres. **Elevation:** 4,200 feet. **Location:** In Great Salt Lake, accessible by causeway. **Facilities:** 26 campsites (2 &), showers, modern restrooms (&), picnic areas, group pavilion, trails, swimming beach, horse rentals, food concession, gift shop, visitor center. **Activities:** Camping, boating, swimming, hiking, mountain biking, horseback riding, wildlife observation, snowshoeing. **Special Features:** Antelope Island is the largest island in the Great Salt Lake and the largest state park in Utah. It is the undisturbed home of bison, antelope, mule deer, coyotes, bobcats, upland game birds, and waterfowl.

★4400★ BEAR LAKE STATE PARK
PO Box 184
Garden City, UT 84028
Web: www.stateparks.utah.gov/park/index.php?id=BLSP
Phone: 435-946-3343
Size: 906 acres. **Elevation:** 5,900 feet. **Location:** In the Rocky Mountains on the Utah-Idaho border, on Hwy 89. **Facilities:** 178 campsites, 6 primitive campgrounds at Eastside unit, group camps, cabins, showers, modern restrooms (&), vault toilets, picnic areas, group pavilion, food concession, visitor center, swimming beach, marina, boat launch, boat rentals. **Activities:** Camping, boating, sailing, fishing, swimming, water-skiing, scuba diving, winter camping, ice fishing, bicycling. **Special Features:** Bear Lake is a natural lake, 20 miles long, 8 miles wide, 200 feet deep, and covering 112 square miles. Its unique aqua-blue color is the result of calcium carbonates suspended in the lake. Cisco Beach, on Bear Lake's east side, is famous for mid-winter fishing for the 7-inch Bonneville Cisco. For a week in January, swarms of the little fish come close to the shore to spawn. Additionally, Cisco Beach's rocky bottom and steep drop-off close to shore make it a favorite of divers. Two designated diving areas have wooden walkways to assist divers and their gear into the water.

★4401★ CAMP FLOYD/STAGECOACH INN STATE
PARK & MUSEUM
18035 W 1540 North
Fairfield, UT 84013
Web: www.stateparks.utah.gov/park/index.php?id=CFSP
Phone: 801-768-8932
Size: 40 acres. **Elevation:** 4,900 feet. **Location:** 25 miles southwest of Lehi on SR 73. **Facilities:** Picnic areas, group pavilion, visitor center, historic site, modern restrooms. **Activities:** Picnicking, educational programs. **Special Features:** This former military post quartered the largest troop concentration in the United States from 1858 to 1861. About 400 buildings housed the 3,500 troops sent west to suppress the assumed Mormon rebellion. The troops returned to the East in 1861 for Civil War duty. Only the commissary building (which serves as Camp Floyd Museum) and a cemetery remain as evidence of Camp Floyd. Nearby Stagecoach Inn was an overnight stop on the historic overland stage and Pony Express route.

9. State Parks

★4402★ CORAL PINK SAND DUNES STATE PARK

PO Box 95
Kanab, UT 84741
Web: www.stateparks.utah.gov/park/index.php?id=CPSP
Phone: 435-648-2800
Size: Nearly 4,000 acres. **Elevation:** 6,000 feet. **Location:** 22 miles northwest of Kanab off US 89. **Facilities:** 22 campsites, showers, modern restrooms, picnic areas, hiking trails, interpretive trails, OHV trails, equestrian trails. **Activities:** Camping, OHV riding, hiking, horseback riding, wildlife observation. **Special Features:** Park sits among rust-colored sand dunes which change shape and position with the prevailing winds.

★4403★ DEAD HORSE POINT STATE PARK

PO Box 609
Moab, UT 84532
Web: www.stateparks.utah.gov/park/index.php?id=DHSP
Phone: 435-259-2614
Size: 5,362 acres. **Elevation:** 5,900 feet. **Location:** 9 miles northwest of Moab on US 191. **Facilities:** Campsites (&), modern restrooms, picnic areas, trails, visitor center, bike trails, hiking trails (&), interpretive trails. **Activities:** Camping, bicycling, guided walks, wildlife observation, interpretive programs (seasonal), mountain biking and OHV riding (nearby). **Special Features:** Considered Utah's most scenic park, Dead Horse Point sits high on a desert plateau with a breathtaking, panoramic view of the sculptured pinnacles and buttes of Canyonlands National Park (see separate entry in national parks section) and the Colorado River.

★4404★ DEER CREEK STATE PARK

PO Box 257
Midway, UT 84049
Web: www.stateparks.utah.gov/park/index.php?id=DCSP
Phone: 435-654-0171
Size: 2,626 acres. **Elevation:** 5,400 feet. **Location:** 10 miles south of Heber, in the southwest corner of Heber Valley. **Facilities:** 74 campsites, group camp, showers, modern restrooms (&), picnic areas, food concession, boat rentals, boat ramp, hiking trails, bridle trails, bike trails. **Activities:** Camping, boating, sailing, windsurfing, fishing, swimming, hiking, biking, horseback riding. **Special Features:** Deer Creek Reservoir is a main feature of the park, offering 18 miles of shoreline.

★4405★ EAST CANYON STATE PARK

5535 S Hwy 66
Morgan, UT 84050
Web: www.stateparks.utah.gov/park/index.php?id=ECSP
Phone: 801-829-6866
Size: 680 acres. **Elevation:** 5,700 feet. **Location:** 12 miles south of Morgan on State Route 65, in the mountains northeast of Salt Lake City. **Facilities:** Campsites, group camp, showers, modern restrooms (&), picnic areas, food concession, boat rentals, boat launch, boat slips, hiking trails, bike trails, bridle trails. **Activities:** Camping (&), boating, fishing, swimming, hiking, biking, horseback riding, wildlife observation. **Special Features:** East Canyon and the surrounding area are rich in pioneer history. The Donner Party passed through in 1846; a year later Mormon pioneers, including Brigham Young, passed this way.

★4406★ EDGE OF THE CEDARS STATE PARK MUSEUM

660 West 400 North
Blanding, UT 84511
Web: www.stateparks.utah.gov/park_pages/edge.htm
Phone: 435-678-2238
Size: 16 acres. **Elevation:** 6,200 feet. **Location:** Within the city limits of Blanding. **Facilities:** Picnic area, interpretive trail, historic site, museum, modern restrooms (&), trails, visitor center. **Special Features:** Remains of an Anasazi pueblo with its ceremonial kivas, built between A.D. 700 and 1220, are testaments to the ancient civilization that once flourished in southeastern Utah. Museum houses an excellent collection of Anasazi artifacts and pottery, as well as the only known Anasazi metal artifacts in Utah.

★4407★ ESCALANTE STATE PARK

710 N Reservoir Rd
Escalante, UT 84726
Web: www.stateparks.utah.gov/park/about.php?id=ESSP
Phone: 435-826-4466
Size: 1,784 acres. **Elevation:** 5,800 feet. **Location:** 1 mile west of Escalante on State Route 12. **Facilities:** 22 campsites, group camp, showers, modern restrooms, picnic shelters, hiking trail, interpretive trail, visitor center (&), boat ramp. **Activities:** Camping, boating, sailing, fishing, ice fishing, swimming, mountain biking. **Special Features:** Park features colorful deposits of mineralized wood and fossilized dinosaur bones, as well as 1,000-year-old village remnants and petroglyphs of the Fremont Indians.

★4408★ FLIGHT PARK STATE RECREATION AREA

121100 North E Frontage Rd
Lehi, UT 84020
Web: www.stateparks.utah.gov/park/index.php?id=FLSP
Phone: 801-533-5127
Location: Off I-15, in Lehi. **Facilities:** Picnic areas, vault toilets. **Special Features:** Utah State Parks and Recreation and the Utah Hang Gliding and Paragliding Association partner to preserve this recreation area, which is an excellent site for teaching and gathering experience for flyers of all levels. It is known worldwide as one of the best training sites for both paragliding and hang gliding.

★4409★ FREMONT INDIAN STATE PARK & MUSEUM

11550 W Clear Creek Canyon Rd
Sevier, UT 84766
Web: www.stateparks.utah.gov/park/index.php?id=FISP
Phone: 435-527-4631
Size: 889 acres. **Elevation:** 5,900 feet. **Location:** 21 miles southwest of Richfield on I-70. **Facilities:** 31 campsites (&), modern restrooms (&), picnic areas, hiking trails, bike trails,

9. State Parks

OHV trails, interpretive trails, visitor center and museum, historic site. **Activities:** Camping, fishing, hiking, mountain biking, sightseeing, wildlife observation. **Special Features:** A thousand years ago, the valleys along what is now I-70 were home to the largest community of Fremont Indians ever discovered. Their rock art and structures are still visible in the canyons of Fremont Indian State Park. The museum contains artifacts, exhibits, and a film that reveal the lives of these Indians.

★4410★ GOBLIN VALLEY STATE PARK

PO Box 637
Green River, UT 84525
Web: www.stateparks.utah.gov/park/index.php?id=GVSP
Phone: 435-564-3633; **Fax:** 435-564-3223
Size: 3,654 acres. **Elevation:** 5,100 feet. **Location:** Between Green River and Hanksville, off SR 24. **Facilities:** 24 campsites, group camp, showers, modern restrooms (占), vault toilets, picnic areas, observation shelter, visitor center, museum, hiking trails. **Activities:** Camping, hiking, mountain biking. **Special Features:** Park is the site of intricately eroded rock formations that create an atmosphere of unearthly scenery. Exposed cliffs reveal parallel layers of rock bared by erosion. Because of the uneven hardness of sandstone, some areas resist erosion better than others. The softer material is removed by wind and water, leaving thousands of unique geologic ''goblins.''

★4411★ GOOSENECKS STATE PARK

c/o Edge of Cedars State Park
660 West 400 North
Blanding, UT 84511
Web: www.stateparks.utah.gov/park/index.php?id=GNSP
Phone: 435-678-2238
Size: 10 acres. **Elevation:** 5,000 feet. **Location:** 10 miles north of Mexican Hat on SR 316. **Facilities:** 4 primitive campsites, group camp, vault toilets, picnic areas. No drinking water. **Activities:** Camping, picnicking. **Special Features:** Located on a plateau overlooking the Great Goosenecks of the San Juan River, the park provides a view of the river's twists and turns 1,000 feet below, in one of the most striking examples of an entrenched meander in North America.

★4412★ GREAT SALT LAKE STATE MARINA

PO Box 16658
Salt Lake City, UT 84116
Web: www.stateparks.utah.gov/park/index.php?id=GSSP
Phone: 801-250-1898
Size: 3,115 acres. **Elevation:** 4,200 feet. **Location:** 16 miles west of Salt Lake City on I-80. **Facilities:** Picnic areas, concession, marina, showers, modern restrooms, vault toilets, historic site. **Activities:** Boating, sailing, picnicking, swimming, wildlife observation. **Special Features:** A remnant of ancient Lake Bonneville, the Great Salt Lake covers more than 2,000 square miles and is two to seven times saltier than the ocean. The lake attracts more than 250 species of birds, and is a major stop for millions of migratory birds.

★4413★ GREEN RIVER STATE PARK

PO Box 637
Green River, UT 84525
Web: www.stateparks.utah.gov/park/index.php?id=GRSP
Phone: 435-564-3633
Size: 52 acres. **Elevation:** 4,050 feet. **Location:** Within the city limits of Green River, just off I-70. **Facilities:** 40 campsites, group camp, showers, modern restrooms (占), picnic areas, 9-hole golf course. **Activities:** Camping, boating, kayaking, rafting, fishing, swimming, golfing. **Special Features:** Green River State Park is the put-in point for the 186-mile float through Labyrinth and Stillwater Canyons. This section of the river is rated for beginners and intermediate boaters.

★4414★ GUNLOCK STATE PARK

4405 W 3600 S
Hurricane, UT 84737
Web: www.stateparks.utah.gov/park/index.php?id=GLSP
Phone: 435-680-0715
Size: 600 acres. **Elevation:** 3,600 feet. **Location:** 15 miles northwest of Saint George. **Facilities:** Primitive campsites, picnic area, boat launches, vault toilets. **Activities:** Camping, boating, fishing, swimming. **Special Features:** Park features a 240-acre manmade lake in scenic red rock country. A mild climate makes this a year-round destination.

★4415★ HISTORIC UNION PACIFIC RAIL TRAIL STATE PARK

PO Box 754
Park City, UT 84060
Web: www.stateparks.utah.gov/park/index.php?id=RTSP
Phone: 435-649-6839
Size: 450 acres. **Elevation:** 6,000 feet. **Location:** From Park City through Wanship and Coalville to Echo Reservoir. **Facilities:** Crushed gravel trail, picnic area, vault toilets, historic sites. **Activities:** Hiking, mountain biking, horseback riding, jogging, cross-country skiing, wildlife viewing. **Special Features:** The 28-mile rail trail begins (or ends) in Park City and follows Interstate 80 through Wanship and Coalville to Echo Reservoir.

★4416★ HUNTINGTON STATE PARK

PO Box 1343
Huntington, UT 84528
Web: www.stateparks.utah.gov/park/index.php?id=HNSP
Phone: 435-687-2491
Size: 111 acres. **Elevation:** 5,800 feet. **Location:** 2 miles northwest of Huntington on State Route 10. **Facilities:** 22 campsites (1 占), showers, modern restrooms (占), picnic areas, group pavilion, swimming beach, boat ramp. **Activities:** Camping, boating, canoeing, sailing, fishing, swimming, water skiing. **Special Features:** Cinnamon-colored buttes provide a backdrop for the park, which sits on a 200-acre reservoir.

★4417★ HYRUM STATE PARK

405 West 300 South
Hyrum, UT 84319
Web: www.stateparks.utah.gov/park/index.php?id=HLSP
Phone: 435-245-6866

9. State Parks

Size: 264 acres. **Elevation:** 4,700 feet. **Location:** Within the city limits of Hyrum. **Facilities:** 26 campsites, group camp, modern restrooms (&), showers, vault toilets, picnic areas. **Activities:** Camping, boating, fishing, swimming, water-skiing. **Special Features:** Mormon settlers founded the area of Hyrum, which is located in Cache Valley, and Hyrum is named after the brother of the founder of the Mormon Church.

★4418★ IRON MISSION STATE PARK

635 N Main St
Cedar City, UT 84720
Web: www.stateparks.utah.gov/park/index.php?id=IMSP
Phone: 435-586-9290
Size: 11 acres. **Elevation:** 5,800 feet. **Location:** Within the city limits of Cedar City. **Facilities:** Museum, historic site. **Special Features:** The Iron Mission Museum tells the story of development in Iron County. Modern development began in the 1850s when Brigham Young sent young Mormon missionaries here to mine iron. Museum displays include horse-drawn vehicles used from 1850 to 1920 and a small collection of Indian and pioneer artifacts.

★4419★ JORDANELLE STATE PARK

SR 319 515 Box 4
Heber City, UT 84032
Web: www.stateparks.utah.gov/park/index.php?id=JDSP
Phone: 435-649-9540
Size: 4,000 acres. **Elevation:** 6,166 feet. **Location:** Includes 2 units: Hailstone, on the west shore of Jordanelle Reservoir just off Highway 40; and Rock Cliff, on the southeast corner of the Reservoir, on State Route 32. **Facilities:** 184 campsites, group camp, utility hookups, showers, modern restrooms (&), laundry, picnic areas, bike trails, bridle trails, hiking trails, OHV trails, boardwalk, swimming beach, boat rentals, boat ramp, marina, visitor center, nature center. **Activities:** Camping, boating, sailing, kayaking, fishing, swimming, hiking, mountain biking. **Special Features:** Park is located in a picturesque mountain setting near the Wasatch Front. The Hailstone campground is fully developed with many amenities, while Cliff Rock is more primitive.

★4420★ KODACHROME BASIN STATE PARK

PO Box 238
Cannonville, UT 84718
Web: www.stateparks.utah.gov/park/index.php?id=KDSP
Phone: 435-679-8562
Size: 4,000 acres. **Elevation:** 5,800 feet. **Location:** 9 miles south of State Route 12 near Cannonville. **Facilities:** 24 campsites, group camp, cabins, shower, modern restrooms (&), concessions, picnic areas, bike trails, bridle trails, hiking trails, visitor center, museum. **Activities:** Camping, hiking, mountain biking, horseback riding. **Special Features:** Geologists believe the park was once similar to Yellowstone, with hot springs and geysers, which eventually filled up with sediment and solidified. Through time, the Entrada sandstone surrounding the solidified geysers eroded, leaving large sand pipes; 67, ranging from two to 52 meters have been identified in the park.

★4421★ MILLSITE STATE PARK

c/o Huntington State Park
PO Box 1343
Huntington, UT 84528
Web: www.stateparks.utah.gov/park/index.php?id=MSSP
Phone: 435-687-2491
Size: 638 acres. **Elevation:** 6,100 feet. **Location:** 4 miles west of Highway 10 near Ferron. **Facilities:** 20 campsites, showers, modern restrooms (&), vault toilets, picnic areas, 2 group pavilions, boat ramp, bike trails, hiking trails, bridle trails. **Activities:** Camping, boating, sailing, fishing, ice fishing, swimming, mountain biking, horseback riding. **Special Features:** Park is on 435-acre Millsite Reservoir. Before the present dam was built, there was a dam at the site to service a flourmill, from which the reservoir took its name.

★4422★ OTTER CREEK STATE PARK

PO Box 43
Antimony, UT 84712
Web: www.stateparks.utah.gov/park/index.php?id=OCSP
Phone: 435-624-3268
Size: 80 acres. **Elevation:** 6,400 feet. **Location:** 4 miles northwest of Antimony on State Route 22. **Facilities:** 61 campsites, showers, modern restrooms (&), picnic areas, interpretive trails, boat ramp, boat dock. **Activities:** Camping, boating, sailing, fishing, ice fishing, swimming. **Special Features:** The 3,120-acre Otter Creek Reservoir produces fish in record-breaking sizes. Spring and fall brings many bird species through the park as they journey along the Pacific Migratory Bird Flyway.

★4423★ PALISADE STATE PARK

2200 E Palisade Rd
Sterling, UT 84665
Web: www.stateparks.utah.gov/park/index.php?id=PSSP
Phone: 435-835-7275
Size: 65 acres. **Elevation:** 5,800 feet. **Location:** 2 miles east of Sterling and 5 miles south of Manti, in central Utah. **Facilities:** 55 campsites, group camp, showers, modern restrooms (&), picnic areas, group pavilion, food concession, boat rentals, boat ramp, swimming beach, 18-hole golf course, pro shop. **Activities:** Camping, boating, canoeing, sailing, fishing, ice fishing, swimming, hiking, golf. **Special Features:** Park features 70-acre Palisade Reservoir. Just outside the park, Six-Mile Canyon offers excellent off-highway vehicle riding. Park's golf course has some of the best putting greens in the state.

★4424★ PIUTE STATE PARK

c/o Otter Creek State Park
PO Box 43
Antimony, UT 84712
Web: www.stateparks.utah.gov/park/index.php?id=PISP
Phone: 435-624-3268
Size: 40 acres. **Elevation:** 5,900 feet. **Location:** 12 miles south of Marysvale, just off US 89. **Facilities:** Primitive campsites, vault toilets, picnic area, boat launch. **Activities:** Camping, boating, fishing, swimming. **Special Features:** This primitive park is situated on the cliffs of the Sevier Plateau. The reservoir is a good place to catch rainbow, cutthroat, and brown trout.

★4425★ QUAIL CREEK STATE PARK
PO Box 1943
Saint George, UT 84771
Web: www.stateparks.utah.gov/park/about.php?id=QCSP
Phone: 435-879-2378
Size: 600 acres. Elevation: 3,300 feet. Location: 3 miles east of the I-15 Hurricane Exit on State Route 9, 14 miles northeast of Saint George. Facilities: 23 campsites (2 ♿), group camp, modern restrooms (♿), showers, picnic areas, group pavilions. Activities: Camping, boating, kayaking, sailing, fishing, swimming. Special Features: Boasting some of the warmest waters in the state and a mild winter climate, Quail Creek Reservoir lures boaters and anglers year round.

★4426★ RED FLEET STATE PARK
8750 N Hwy 191
Vernal, UT 84078
Web: www.stateparks.utah.gov/park/index.php?id=RFSP
Phone: 435-789-4432
Size: 1,963 acres. Elevation: 5,500 feet. Location: 13 miles north of Vernal, just off Highway 191. Facilities: 38 campsites, modern restrooms, picnic areas, swimming beach, hiking trails, boat ramp. Activities: Camping, boating, swimming, fishing, ice fishing. Special Features: Park is named for the red sandstone formations found on the north side of the reservoir that resemble a fleet of ships. A 2.5-mile trail loop leads to 200-million-year-old dinosaur tracks.

★4427★ ROCKPORT STATE PARK
9040 N State Hwy 302
Peoa, UT 84061
Web: www.stateparks.utah.gov/park/index.php?id=RPSP
Phone: 801-336-2241
Size: 770 acres. Elevation: 6,000 feet. Location: 45 miles east of Salt Lake City, on Hwy 32. Facilities: Campsites (♿), cabin rentals, group camp, showers, modern restrooms (♿), vault toilets, picnic areas, boat ramp, boat rentals, food service Activities: Camping, boating, fishing, swimming, water-skiing, ice fishing, wildlife observation. Special Features: Rockport Reservoir is a prime water recreation site.

★4428★ SAND HOLLOW STATE PARK
4405 W 3600 S
Hurricane, UT 84737
Web: www.stateparks.utah.gov/park/index.php?id=SHSP
Phone: 435-680-0715
Size: 20,000 acres. Elevation: 3,000 feet. Location: 15 miles east of St. George, 7 miles east of the I-15 Hurricane Exit. Facilities: 50 campsites (♿), group camp, picnic area, vault toilets, modern restrooms, boat ramp, bike trails, hiking trails, bridle trails, OHV trails. Activities: Camping, boating, fishing, swimming, OHV riding, hiking, biking, horseback riding. Special Features: Utah's newest state park features a red sandstone landscape and warm blue waters.

★4429★ SCOFIELD STATE PARK
1343 Huntington
Price, UT 84528
Web: www.stateparks.utah.gov/park/index.php?id=SFSP
Phone: 435-448-9449
Size: 418 acres. Elevation: 7,600 feet. Location: On State Route 96, 13 miles off US 6, in the Manti-LaSal Mountains of the Wasatch Plateau. Facilities: 74 campsites, group camp, showers, modern restrooms (♿), vault toilets, picnic areas, group pavilion, boat ramp. Activities: Camping, boating, fishing, ice fishing, swimming, cross-country skiing, snowmobiling. Special Features: Park is situated high in the Manti-LaSal Mountains. The 2,800-acre lake offers water recreation in the summer, and in winter it's one of the best places to ice fish for rainbow and cutthroat trout.

★4430★ SNOW CANYON STATE PARK
1002 Snow Canyon Dr
Ivins, UT 84738
Web: www.stateparks.utah.gov/park/index.php?id=SNSP
Phone: 435-628-2255
Size: 7,100 acres. Elevation: 4,875 feet. Location: 8 miles north of Saint George on Hwy 18. Facilities: 29 campsites, group camp, electrical hookups, showers, modern restrooms (♿), picnic areas, group pavilion, hiking trails, bike trails, bridle trails, visitor center. Activities: Camping, hiking, mountain biking, horseback riding, rock climbing, wildlife observation. Special Features: A remote desert park in southern Utah, Snow Canyon's spectacular landscape includes a rugged mix of red rock, black lava rock, and serpentine sandy washes. The canyon is named for Mormon pioneers Lorenzo and Erastus Snow—not for its winters, which are usually quite mild.

★4431★ STARVATION STATE PARK
PO Box 584
Duchesne, UT 84021
Web: www.stateparks.utah.gov/park/index.php?id=SVSP
Phone: 435-738-2326
Size: 3,500 acres. Elevation: 5,700 feet. Location: 4 miles northwest of Duchesne, just off Highway 40. Facilities: 54 campsites, group camp, showers, modern restrooms (♿), picnic areas, group pavilion, swimming beach, boat ramp. Activities: Camping, boating, sailing, kayaking, fishing, swimming, ice fishing. Special Features: One legend has it that a group of mountain men caught in winter snows survived by stealing a cache of food from local Indians, and the Indians starved. Another version is that the Indians stole the trappers' cache of food and left the trappers to starve. It's unlikely that either tale bears reference to the naming of the Starvation dam and reservoir. The name more likely derived from the fact that settlers in this area endured tremendous hardship, so they nicknamed the area "Starvation."

★4432★ STEINAKER STATE PARK
4335 N Hwy 191
Vernal, UT 84078
Web: www.stateparks.utah.gov/park/index.php?id=STSP
Phone: 435-789-4432

Size: 2,283 acres. Elevation: 5,500 feet. Location: 7 miles north of Vernal, just off State Highway 191. Facilities: 29 campsites, group camp, modern restrooms (&), picnic areas, group pavilions, swimming beach, boat ramp. Activities: Camping, boating, fishing, swimming, water-skiing, ice fishing. Special Features: In addition to its water recreation attractions, park is a popular base for exploring nearby Dinosaurland or Flaming Gorge National Recreation Area. Park is also a site where relics once found in ancient seas such as oysters, clams, and other shellfish can be found.

★4433★ TERRITORIAL STATEHOUSE STATE PARK

50 W Capitol Ave
Fillmore, UT 84631
Web: www.stateparks.utah.gov/park/index.php?id=TESP
Phone: 435-743-5316
Size: 3 acres. Elevation: 5,100 feet. Location: Within the city limits of Fillmore, off the I-15 business loop. Facilities: Picnic area, group pavilion, garden, museum, store, auditorium, historic site. Special Features: Utah's oldest existing governmental building is the Territorial Statehouse in Fillmore. In anticipation of Utah's statehood, Brigham Young directed construction of the building to house the state's capitol, but only the south wing was ever completed. The existing portion was finished in time for the 1855 meeting of the territorial legislature, which was the only full session held in the old statehouse. In 1858, the seat of government was returned to Salt Lake City. The Territorial Statehouse was reopened as a museum in 1930 and houses a pioneer collection, as well as items from the late 19th and early 20th centuries.

★4434★ UTAH FIELD HOUSE OF NATURAL HISTORY STATE PARK

496 E Main St
Vernal, UT 84078
Web: www.stateparks.utah.gov/park/index.php?id=UFSP
Phone: 435-789-3799
Size: 2 acres. Elevation: 5,300 feet. Location: Within the city limits of Vernal. Facilities: Picnic area, museum, modern restrooms. Special Features: A museum and a dinosaur garden are the featured attractions of the park. The museum houses ancient fossil skeletal reproductions, archeological and geological exhibits, fluorescent minerals, and other natural history aspects of the Uinta Basin. The dinosaur garden features 17 life-size replicas of prehistoric animals in natural settings.

★4435★ UTAH LAKE STATE PARK

4400 W Center St
Provo, UT 84601
Web: www.stateparks.utah.gov/park/index.php?id=ULSP
Phone: 801-375-0731; Fax: 801-373-4215
Size: 308 acres. Elevation: 4,500 feet. Location: 3 miles west of Provo, just off I-15. Facilities: 55 campsites, group camp, showers, modern restrooms (&), picnic areas, group pavilion, swimming beach, boat ramps, 30-acre sheltered marina, boat rentals, fishing pier (&), food service, visitor center. Activities: Camping, boating, canoeing, sailing, kayaking, fishing, ice fishing, swimming. Special Features: Park features Utah's largest freshwater lake, a 96,600-acre body of water. It is very shallow, averaging about 9 feet in depth.

★4436★ WASATCH MOUNTAIN STATE PARK

PO Box 10
Midway, UT 84049
Web: www.stateparks.utah.gov/park/index.php?id=WMSP
Phone: 435-654-1791
Size: 21,592 acres. Elevation: 6,000 feet. Location: 2 miles northwest of Midway, in the Heber Valley. Facilities: 139 campsites, utility hookups, showers, modern restrooms (&), chalet, picnic areas, 2 group pavilions, bike trails, hiking trails, bridle trails, OHV trails, visitor center, golf courses, amphitheater. Activities: Camping, hiking, mountain biking, horseback riding, hunting (in season), golf, OHV riding, cross-country skiing, snowshoeing, snowmobiling. Special Features: Wasatch Mountain is Utah's second largest and most developed state park and offers a number of summer and winter recreational opportunities. The Soldier Hollow area of the park was the site of biathalon and cross-country events of the 2002 Winter Olympic Games.

★4437★ WILLARD BAY STATE PARK

900 West 650 North #A
Willard, UT 84340
Web: www.stateparks.utah.gov/park/index.php?id=WBSP
Phone: 435-734-9494; Fax: 435-734-2659
Size: 2,673 acres. Elevation: 4,200 feet. Location: North Marina is 15 miles north of Ogden off I-15; South Marina is 8 miles north of Ogden. Facilities: 101 campsites (in north marina area and south marina area. &), group camp, showers, modern restrooms (&), picnic areas, group pavilion, food concession, swimming beaches, boat ramps, boat slip rentals, interpretive trail. Activities: Camping, boating, canoeing, sailing, fishing, swimming, water-skiing, ice fishing, bird watching. Special Features: Willard Bay is a freshwater reservoir in the the Great Salt Lake floodplain of northern Utah. An earth-filled dike makes up the 20-mile enclosures. The park consists of two marinas next to the bay.

★4438★ YUBA STATE PARK

PO Box 159
Levan, UT 84639
Web: www.stateparks.utah.gov/park/index.php?id=YLSP
Phone: 435-758-2611
Size: 629 acres. Elevation: 5,500 feet. Location: 25 miles south of Nephi, just off I-15. Facilities: 89 campsites, group camp, modern restrooms (&), vault toilets, picnic areas, group pavilion, swimming beach, boat ramps. Activities: Camping, boating, fishing, swimming, mountain biking. Special Features: Park features warm water and sandy beaches on Yuba Reservoir.

9. State Parks

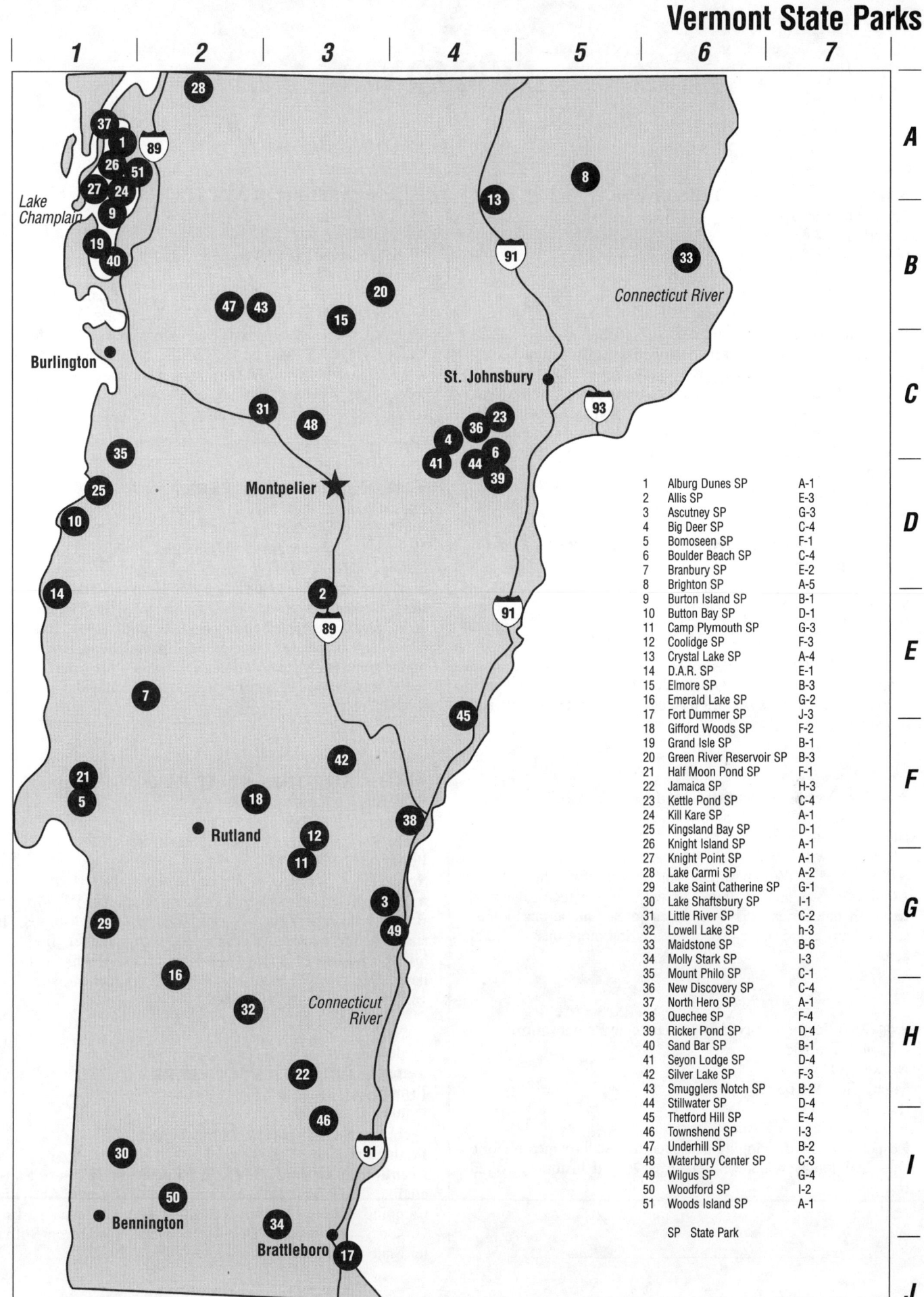

Vermont State Parks

1	Alburg Dunes SP	A-1
2	Allis SP	E-3
3	Ascutney SP	G-3
4	Big Deer SP	C-4
5	Bomoseen SP	F-1
6	Boulder Beach SP	C-4
7	Branbury SP	E-2
8	Brighton SP	A-5
9	Burton Island SP	B-1
10	Button Bay SP	D-1
11	Camp Plymouth SP	G-3
12	Coolidge SP	F-3
13	Crystal Lake SP	A-4
14	D.A.R. SP	E-1
15	Elmore SP	B-3
16	Emerald Lake SP	G-2
17	Fort Dummer SP	J-3
18	Gifford Woods SP	F-2
19	Grand Isle SP	B-1
20	Green River Reservoir SP	B-3
21	Half Moon Pond SP	F-1
22	Jamaica SP	H-3
23	Kettle Pond SP	C-4
24	Kill Kare SP	A-1
25	Kingsland Bay SP	D-1
26	Knight Island SP	A-1
27	Knight Point SP	A-1
28	Lake Carmi SP	A-2
29	Lake Saint Catherine SP	G-1
30	Lake Shaftsbury SP	I-1
31	Little River SP	C-2
32	Lowell Lake SP	h-3
33	Maidstone SP	B-6
34	Molly Stark SP	I-3
35	Mount Philo SP	C-1
36	New Discovery SP	C-4
37	North Hero SP	A-1
38	Quechee SP	F-4
39	Ricker Pond SP	D-4
40	Sand Bar SP	B-1
41	Seyon Lodge SP	D-4
42	Silver Lake SP	F-3
43	Smugglers Notch SP	B-2
44	Stillwater SP	D-4
45	Thetford Hill SP	E-4
46	Townshend SP	I-3
47	Underhill SP	B-2
48	Waterbury Center SP	C-3
49	Wilgus SP	G-4
50	Woodford SP	I-2
51	Woods Island SP	A-1

SP   State Park

VERMONT

★4439★ Vermont State Parks Division
103 S Main St
Waterbury, VT 05671
(802) 241-3655 - Phone
(802) 244-1481 - Fax
(888) 409-7579 - Toll-free Reservations
(800) 640-1657 - Employment
Web: www.vtstateparks.com
In order to provide outdoor recreation in the most natural setting possible, the state's system of 50 parks offers few amenities. Although most are closed to camping during much of the year, visitors are encouraged to use parks for daytime activities, including traditional winter pursuits such as cross-county and downhill skiing, snowboarding, ice fishing, skating, snowshoeing, and snow sledding.

★4440★ Vermont Departments of Forests, Parks & Recreation
103 S Main St
Waterbury, VT 05671
(802) 241-3678
(802) 244-1481 - Fax
Web: http://www.vtfpr.org
Manages 38 state forests which, along with state parks lands, account for more than 4 million acres. Also maintains trails and forest roads.

★4441★ Vermont Department of Fish & Wildlife
103 S Main St
Bldg 10 South
Waterbury, VT 05671
(802) 241-3700 *Web:* www.anr.state.vt.us/fw/fwhome
Administers 33 natural areas, 85 wildlife management areas, five fish hatcheries, 151 boat access areas, numerous ponds, stream banks, and other properties totaling more than 133,000 acres.

★4442★ Vermont Division for Historic Preservation
National Life Bldg
Drawer 2O
Montpelier, VT 05620
(802) 828-3211
Web: www.historicvermont.org
Responsible for developing and operating state-owned historic sites, including an underwater preserve and historic covered bridges.

★4443★ ALBURG DUNES STATE PARK
151 Coon Point Rd
Alburg, VT 05440
Web: www.vtstateparks.com/htm/alburg.cfm
Phone: 802-796-4170
Size: 625 acres. **Location:** In the Lakes Champlain area of northwestern Vermont on VT 128. **Facilities:** Walking trail, bike trail, picnic area. **Activities:** Hiking, biking, wildlife observation. **Special Features:** One of the state's rare examples of a sand dune community. The area also contains wetlands, a spruce bog, a good swimming beach, and the largest deer wintering area in Grand Isle County.

★4444★ ALLIS STATE PARK
284 Allis State Park Rd
Randolph, VT 05060
Web: www.vtstateparks.com/htm/allis.cfm
Phone: 802-276-3175
Size: 486 acres. **Location:** 12 miles north of Randolph. **Facilities:** 26 campsites (8 with lean-tos), showers, flush toilets, picnic areas, picnic shelters, fireplaces, observation tower. **Activities:** Camping, sightseeing, picnicking. **Special Features:** Located on the summit of Bear Mountain, the park's fire tower provides outstanding views of central Vermont's farmland, forests, and mountains.

★4445★ ASCUTNEY STATE PARK
1826 Black Mountain Rd
Windsor, VT 05089
Web: www.vtstateparks.com/htm/ascutney.cfm
Phone: 802-674-2060
Size: About 2,000 acres. **Location:** From I-91 (Exit 8), go 2 miles north on US 5, then 1 mile northwest on VT 44A from Brownsville. **Facilities:** 49 campsites (10 with lean-tos), hot showers, flush toilets, picnic areas, picnic shelter, fireplaces, hiking trail, observation tower. **Activities:** Camping, hiking, hangliding. **Special Features:** Park offers excellent views from various points along its trails.

★4446★ BIG DEER STATE PARK
1467 Boulder Beach Rd
Groton, VT 05046
Web: www.vtstateparks.com/htm/bigdeer.cfm
Phone: 802-584-3822
Location: In Groton, off VT 232. **Facilities:** 28 campsites (including 5 lean-tos), hot showers, restrooms, trails. **Activities:** Camping, hiking. **Special Features:** One of seven parks in Groton State Forest, Big Deer serves overflow visitors at Stillwater State Park.

★4447★ BOMOSEEN STATE PARK

22 Cedar Mountain Rd
Fair Haven, VT 05743
Web: www.vtstateparks.com/htm/bomoseen.cfm
Phone: 802-265-4242
Size: 2,878 acres. **Location:** In the Taconic Mountains on the shores of Lake Bomoseen. **Facilities:** 66 campsites (10 with lean-tos), hot showers, flush toilets, picnic areas, picnic shelter, beach, snack bar, hiking trails, boat rentals. **Activities:** Camping, boating, fishing, swimming, hiking. **Special Features:** Park is located in the Taconic Mountains, on the shores of Vermont's largest lake wholly within the state. This is the slate-producing region of Vermont, and the park has several quarry holes and their adjacent colorful slate rubble piles.

★4448★ BOULDER BEACH STATE PARK

2278 Boulder Beach Rd
Groton, VT 05046
Web: www.vtstateparks.com/htm/boulder.cfm
Phone: 802-584-3823
Size: 25 acres. **Location:** In Groton, off VT 232. **Facilities:** Picnic areas, snack bar, hand launch boat ramp, restrooms, beach, play area. **Activities:** Boating, swimming, winter sports. **Special Features:** Located in Groton State Forest, park includes 200 feet of beach and a swimming area.

★4449★ BRANBURY STATE PARK

3570 Lake Dunmore Rd
Rt 53
Brandon, VT 05733
Web: www.vtstateparks.com/htm/branbury.cfm
Phone: 802-247-5925
Size: 69 acres. **Location:** On the eastern shore of Lake Dunmore, at the base of Mount Moosalamoo, off Highway 53. **Facilities:** 45 campsites (6 with lean-tos), hot showers, flush toilets, picnic areas, boat and canoe rentals, hiking trails, beach. **Activities:** Camping, boating, fishing, swimming, hiking. **Special Features:** Park contains a network of trails leading to scenic vistas, caves, waterfalls, and mountain lakes.

★4450★ BRIGHTON STATE PARK

102 State Park Rd
Island Pond, VT 05846
Web: www.vtstateparks.com/htm/brighton.cfm
Phone: 802-723-4360
Size: 152 acres. **Location:** In Island Pond, on Highway 105. **Facilities:** 84 campsites (21 with lean-tos), 5 cabins, hot showers, flush toilets, picnic areas, fireplace, hiking trails, boat rentals, beach, nature museum, amphitheater, play area. **Activities:** Camping, boating, fishing, swimming, hiking. **Special Features:** Park's main attraction is its wilderness—mountains with tree-covered slopes, clear lakes, and fast running rivers and streams. The land east of Island Pond is virtually without paved roads or towns, but numerous logging roads lead into the deeper reaches of the area.

★4451★ BURTON ISLAND STATE PARK

Box 123
Saint Albans Bay, VT 05481
Web: www.vtstateparks.com/htm/burton.cfm
Phone: 802-524-6353
Size: 253 acres. **Location:** Off the southwestern tip of St Albans Point in Lake Champlain's ''inland sea.'' Park is accessible only by boat. Ferry departs from Kill Kare State Park. **Facilities:** 43 campsites (26 with lean-tos), hot showers, flush toilets, picnic areas, snack bar, 100-slip marina with power hookups, boat and canoe rentals, park store, nature center. **Activities:** Camping, boating, fishing, swimming, hiking. **Special Features:** A farm in the 1840s through the early 1900s, old fence lines, stone piles, rusted farm implements and the foundation of an old barn can still be seen.

★4452★ BUTTON BAY STATE PARK

5 Button Bay State Park Rd
Vergennes, VT 05491
Web: www.vtstateparks.com/htm/buttonbay.cfm
Phone: 802-475-2377
Size: 253 acres. **Location:** On a bluff in Ferrisburgh along the 130-mile long Lake Champlain. **Facilities:** 73 campsites (13 with lean-tos), group camp, hot showers, flush toilets, picnic areas, picnic shelter, nature center, swimming pool, play area, boat rentals. **Activities:** Camping, boating, fishing, swimming. **Special Features:** Park is named for the button-like concretions found along the shoreline, formed by clay deposits.

★4453★ CAMP PLYMOUTH STATE PARK

2008 Scout Camp Rd
Ludlow, VT 05149
Web: www.vtstateparks.com/htm/plymouth.cfm
Phone: 802-228-2025
Size: 295 acres. **Location:** Off Rt 100 in Plymouth, on the east side of Echo Lake. **Facilities:** Group camp (including 6 lean-tos), 4 cottages (with gas heat and bathroom), picnic shelters (one with kitchen), play area, hiking trails, swimming beach, concession, boat rentals. **Activities:** Camping, boating, fishing, hunting, swimming, hiking, horseshoes, gold panning. **Special Features:** Located along the banks of Buffalo Brook, once known as ''Gold Brook,'' where gold was discovered in 1855. Mining operations continued for 30 years; today's park visitors still pan for gold.

★4454★ COOLIDGE STATE PARK

855 Coolidge State Park Rd
Plymouth, VT 05056
Web: www.vtstateparks.com/htm/coolidge.cfm
Phone: 802-672-3612
Size: 500 acres. **Location:** 2 miles north of Plymouth on 100A. **Facilities:** 60 campsites (35 with lean-tos),hot showers, flush toilets, picnic area, picnic shelters, hiking trails, play area. **Activities:** Camping, hiking, gold panning. **Special Features:** Park is the developed recreation centerpiece of the 21,500 acre Calvin Coolidge State Forest, the largest state-owned land holding in central Vermont. Nearby is the village of Plymouth Notch, the

birthplace of Calvin Coolidge, 30th president of the United States.

★4455★ CRYSTAL LAKE STATE PARK
96 Bellwater Ave
Barton, VT 05822
Web: www.vtstateparks.com/htm/crystal.cfm
Phone: 802-525-6205
Size: 16 acres. **Location:** At the north end of Crystal Lake in Barton Village. **Facilities:** Cottage (furnished, with electricity and bathroom), picnic area, snack bar, play areas, swimming beach, bathhouse, boat rentals, restrooms. **Activities:** Boating, fishing, swimming. **Special Features:** Crystal Lake is a glacial lake situated among roughhewn mountain sides. Approximately three miles long and about one mile wide, it is known to be more than 100 feet deep in places. The park's beach house was built from granite quarried beside the lake.

★4456★ D.A.R. STATE PARK
6750 VT Rt 17 W
Addison, VT 05491
Web: www.vtstateparks.com/htm/dar.cfm
Phone: 802-759-2354
Size: 95 acres. **Location:** On the shores of Lake Champlain, 6 miles from Vergennes. **Facilities:** 70 campsites (24 with lean-tos), hot showers, flush toilets, picnic area, picnic shelter. **Activities:** Camping, boating, sailing, swimming, fishing. **Special Features:** Park lands were donated by the Daughters of the American Revolution in 1955. Much of the park was once open farm and pasture land. Stone foundations of the homes of the first English settlers (circa 1765) can be seen today around the picnic area.

★4457★ ELMORE STATE PARK
856 VT Rt 12
Lake Elmore, VT 05657
Web: www.vtstateparks.com/htm/elmore.cfm
Phone: 802-888-2982
Size: More than 700 acres. **Location:** In Elmore, in northeastern Vermont. **Facilities:** 60 campsites (15 with lean-tos, 3 &), bathhouse (&), picnic areas, picnic shelter, fireplaces, snack bar, boat and canoe rentals, hiking trails, beach, observation tower. **Activities:** Camping, boating, canoeing, swimming, hiking. **Special Features:** A fire tower sits atop Elmore Mountain (2,608 feet), and affords a 360-degree view of the surrounding area.

★4458★ EMERALD LAKE STATE PARK
65 Emerald Lake Ln
East Dorset, VT 05253
Web: www.vtstateparks.com/htm/emerald.cfm
Phone: 802-362-1655
Size: 430 acres. **Location:** In North Dorset, on US 7. **Facilities:** 105 campsites (36 with lean-tos; &), hot showers (&), flush toilets (&), picnic areas (&), picnic shelter, snack bar, hiking trails, boat and canoe rentals. **Activities:** Camping, boating (no motors), canoeing, fishing, swimming, hiking. **Special Features:** Property was once a productive marble quarry. It also

operated as a farm and summer retreat before becoming a state park.

★4459★ FORT DUMMER STATE PARK
517 Old Guilford Rd
Brattleboro, VT 05301
Web: www.vtstateparks.com/htm/fortdummer.cfm
Phone: 802-254-2610
Size: 217 acres. **Location:** In the Connecticut River Valley, just outside of Brattleboro. **Facilities:** 61 campsites (10 with lean-tos), hot showers, flush toilets, picnic area, hiking trails. **Activities:** Camping, hiking. **Special Features:** Park was named for Fort Dummer, the first permanent English settlement in Vermont. The remains of the fort lie underwater, flooded when the Vernon Dam was built on the Connecticut River in 1908.

★4460★ GIFFORD WOODS STATE PARK
34 Gifford Woods
Killington, VT 05751
Web: www.vtstateparks.com/htm/gifford.cfm
Phone: 802-775-5354
Size: 115 acres. **Location:** In the shadows of Killington and Pico Mountains off Rt 100. **Facilities:** 48 campsites (21 with lean-tos), 4 cabins, hot showers, flush toilets, picnic area, play area, hiking trails. **Activities:** Camping, hiking. **Special Features:** Popular fall foliage destination. A portion of the Appalachian National Scenic Trail passes directly through the park (see separate entry in national trails section).

★4461★ GRAND ISLE STATE PARK
36 East Shore S
Grand Isle, VT 05458
Web: www.vtstateparks.com/htm/grandisle.cfm
Phone: 802-372-4300
Size: 226 acres. **Location:** On the east shore of Grand Isle, the largest island in Lake Champlain. **Facilities:** 153 campsites (36 with lean-tos), 4 cabins, hot showers, flush toilets, picnic areas, boat rentals, boat ramp, nature center, activity center, game courts, play area. **Activities:** Camping, boating, kayaking, fishing, swimming, nature walk, nature programs. **Special Features:** Park is located on the largest island on Lake Champlain, Grand Isle, which is about 14 miles long and three miles wide. It is also known as South Hero.

★4462★ GREEN RIVER RESERVOIR STATE PARK
29 Sunset Drive Suite 1
Morrisville, VT 05661
Web: www.vtstateparks.com/htm/grriver.cfm
Phone: 802-888-1349
Size: 5,113 acres. **Location:** Northeast of Hyde Park, at the southern end of the reservoir off Green River Dam Road. **Facilities:** 28 campsites, 1 group camp. **Activities:** Camping, boating, swimming. **Special Features:** The park's 653-acre reservoir has one of the longest stretches of undeveloped shoreline (nearly 19 miles) in Vermont. The reservoir is a designated ''quiet'' lake: gas-powered boats, personal watercraft, and floatplanes are prohibited.

9. State Parks

★4463★ **HALF MOON POND STATE PARK**
1621 Black Pond Rd
Fair Haven, VT 05743
Web: www.vtstateparks.com/htm/halfmoon.cfm
Phone: 802-273-2848
Size: 50 acres. Location: Between Fair Haven and Rutland on Rt 4. Facilities: 69 campsites (10 with lean-tos), 5 cabins, hot showers, flush toilets, play area, hiking trails. Activities: Camping, boating (no motors), canoeing, swimming, hiking. Special Features: Located in Bomoseen State Forest, the park is set in dense woods in a small sheltered basin surrounding Half Moon Pond.

★4464★ **JAMAICA STATE PARK**
285 Salmon Hole Ln
Jamaica, VT 05343
Web: www.vtstateparks.com/htm/jamaica.cfm
Phone: 802-874-4600
Size: 772 acres. Location: From Jamaica, 0.5 miles north on town road from center of village. Facilities: 61 campsites (18 with lean-tos), hot showers, flush toilets, picnic areas, picnic shelter, swimming hole, hiking trail, nature center. Activities: Camping, canoeing, kayaking, river rafting, fishing, hiking. Special Features: Every spring and fall, water is released into the West River from Ball Mountain Dam, attracting kayakers and canoeists from all over New England.

★4465★ **KETTLE POND STATE PARK**
4239 VT Rd 232
Marshfield, VT 05658
Web: www.vtstateparks.com/htm/kettlepond.cfm
Phone: 802-426-3042
Size: 20 acres. Location: 2 miles west of Groton, on VT 232. Facilities: 5 group camps with 26 with lean-tos, 6 remote campsites, pit toilets, drinking water, swimming area, multi-use trails, hiking trails. Activities: Camping, swimming, hiking. Special Features: Located within Groton State Forest, with access to miles of trails.

★4466★ **KILL KARE STATE PARK**
c/o Burton Island State Park
Box 123
Saint Albans Bay, VT 05481
Web: www.vtstateparks.com/htm/killkare.cfm
Phone: 802-524-6021
Size: 17 acres. Location: On the southwestern tip of Saint Albans Point, a 3-mile peninsula in Saint Albans Bay. Facilities: Picnic area (&), picnic shelter, snack bar, swimming beach, boat rentals, boat ramp, bathhouse. Activities: Boating, swimming, picnicking. Special Features: Property used to be a summer resort, then a summer camp for boys, before becoming a state park. The 3-story building in the center of the park was built in the 1870s as the resort hotel.

★4467★ **KINGSLAND BAY STATE PARK**
787 Kingsland Bay State Park Rd
Ferrisburgh, VT 05456
Web: www.vtstateparks.com/htm/kingsland.cfm
Phone: 802-877-3445
Size: 264 acres. Location: Just south of McDonough Natural Area, along the shores of Lake Champlain. Facilities: Picnic area (&), picnic shelter, trails, restrooms (&). Activities: Fishing, boating, sailing, swimming, hiking. Special Features: Much of the park's land along the shores of Lake Champlain remains a natural area. Park includes historic Hawley House, dating from 1790.

★4468★ **KNIGHT ISLAND STATE PARK**
c/o Burton Island State Park
Box 123
Saint Albans Bay, VT 05481
Web: www.vtstateparks.com/htm/knightisland.cfm
Phone: 802-524-6353
Size: 185 acres. Location: On Lake Champlain, off North Hero, accessible only by boat. Ferry service available by advance arrangement. Facilities: 7 primitive campsites, perimeter trail system. No toilets or potable water. Activities: Camping, boating, hiking. Special Features: The island was farmed historically, then was uninhabited for many years. It was a privately owned primitive campground through the 1980s. Land management activities are those which will keep the island unique and unspoiled.

★4469★ **KNIGHT POINT STATE PARK**
44 Knight Point Rd
North Hero, VT 05474
Web: www.vtstateparks.com/htm/knightpoint.cfm
Phone: 802-372-8389
Size: 54 acres. Location: On Lake Champlain, 3 miles south of North Hero Village. Facilities: Picnic area (&), picnic shelter, swimming beach, boat rentals, restrooms (&). Activities: Boating, fishing, swimming, hiking. Special Features: Park is home to the Island Center for Arts and Recreation, and Hermann's Royal Lipizzan Stallions summer here. Performances are held weekly. When the horses are not performing, park guests are welcome to watch them train in the arena.

★4470★ **LAKE CARMI STATE PARK**
460 Marsh Farm Rd
Enosburg Falls, VT 05450
Web: www.vtstateparks.com/htm/carmi.cfm
Phone: 802-933-8383
Size: 482 acres. Location: From Enosburg Falls, go 3 miles west on Highway 105, then 3 miles north on VT 236. Facilities: 175 campsites (35 with lean-tos), hot showers, 2 cabins, picnic areas, beach, snack bar, boat rentals. Activities: Camping, boating, fishing, swimming. Special Features: Most of Vermont's largest peat bog (140 acres) lies within Lake Carmi State Park and is a designated State Natural Area. High ground on which camping area "B" is built would be an island if not for the bog.

★4471★ **LAKE SAINT CATHERINE STATE PARK**
3034 VT Rt 30 S
Poultney, VT 05764
Web: www.vtstateparks.com/htm/catherine.cfm
Phone: 802-287-9158

9. State Parks

Size: 128 acres. **Location:** From Poultney, go 3 miles south on Highway 30. **Facilities:** 61 campsites (10 with lean-tos; &), no hookups, hot showers (&), flush toilets (&), picnic areas (&), fireplaces, nature trail, boat rentals, boat ramp. **Activities:** Camping, boating, fishing, swimming, hiking, nature programs, winter sports. **Special Features:** This area is known for its past slate quarrying operations, and remains of slate mills, quarries, and rubble piles are still visible.

★4472★ LAKE SHAFTSBURY STATE PARK

262 Shaftsbury State Park Rd
Shaftsbury, VT 05262
Web: www.vtstateparks.com/htm/shaftsbury.cfm
Phone: 802-375-9978
Size: 84 acres. **Location:** Southwestern Vermont, 10 miles north of Bennington. **Facilities:** Group campground (with 15 lean-tos), cottage, restrooms (&), picnic area (&), picnic shelter, snack bar, swimming beach, bathhouse, play area, boat and canoe rentals, nature trail. **Activities:** Camping, boating, canoeing, fishing, swimming, nature walks. **Special Features:** Park surrounds a small, picturesque lake and is a popular outdoor destination in southwestern Vermont.

★4473★ LITTLE RIVER STATE PARK

3444 Little River Rd
Waterbury, VT 05676
Web: www.vtstateparks.com/htm/littleriver.cfm
Phone: 802-244-7103
Size: 12,000 acres. **Location:** 30 miles south of Burlington, off I-89. **Facilities:** 101 campsites (20 with lean-tos, &), hot showers, flush toilets (&), picnic areas, swimming beaches, hiking trails, boat rentals, boat ramp, play areas, ballfield, nature museum. **Activities:** Camping, boating, fishing, swimming, nature programs. **Special Features:** At one time, a settlement of 50 or so families lived in this area. Old cemeteries, a sawmill, old roads, bridges, and many cellar holes can still be found.

★4474★ LOWELL LAKE STATE PARK

1756 Little Pond Rd
Londonderry, VT 05148
Web: www.vtstateparks.com/htm/lowell.cfm
Phone: 802-824-4035
Size: 361 acres of land and 100-acre lake. **Location:** 3 miles east of Londonderry. **Facilities:** Hiking trail, hand boat launch. **Activities:** Boating, swimming, hiking, nature study, snowmobiling. **Special Features:** Park features a large, secluded lake with nearly a mile of shoreline, as well as a Revolutionary War-era cemetery.

★4475★ MAIDSTONE STATE PARK

Rt 1, Box 388
Guildhall, VT 05905
Web: www.vtstateparks.com/htm/maidstone.cfm
Phone: 802-676-3930
Size: 469 acres. **Location:** Northeast portion of the state, off

State Forest Highway. **Facilities:** 82 campsites (37 with lean-tos), hot showers, flush toilets, picnic areas, picnic shelter, swimming beach, trails. **Activities:** Camping, fishing, swimming, hiking. **Special Features:** Maidstone Lake is one of the few places in the state where loons have reared their young in recent years. Once common in Vermont, the loon is now considered a threatened species (though no longer on the endangered species list).

★4476★ MOLLY STARK STATE PARK

705 Rt 9 E
Wilmington, VT 05363
Web: www.vtstateparks.com/htm/mollystark.cfm
Phone: 802-464-5460
Size: 150 acres. **Location:** 15 miles west of Brattleboro on VT 9. **Facilities:** 34 campsites (11 with lean-tos), showers, play area, picnic areas, picnic shelter, hiking trail, observation tower. **Activities:** Camping, fishing, hiking. **Special Features:** Park is named after the wife of Revolutionary War General John Stark and is especially popular during the fall foliage season. The park features open lawn areas, woods, and Mount Olga to the east, where an old fire tower provides spectacular views.

★4477★ MOUNT PHILO STATE PARK

5425 Mt Philo Rd
Charlotte, VT 05445
Web: www.vtstateparks.com/htm/philo.cfm
Phone: 802-425-2390
Size: 168 acres. **Location:** 6 miles north of the junction of Highway 22A and US 7, then 1 mile east on local road. **Facilities:** 10 campsites (3 with lean-tos), hot showers, flush toilets, picnic areas, picnic shelter, hiking trails. **Activities:** Camping, hiking. **Special Features:** Located atop Mount Philo, the park overlooks the Lake Champlain Valley and the Adirondack Mountains of New York. A narrow, steep road (not recommended for trailers) provides visitors access to the top of the mountain. This is Vermont's oldest state park, created in 1924.

★4478★ NEW DISCOVERY STATE PARK

4239 VT Rt 232
Marshfield, VT 05658
Web: www.vtstateparks.com/htm/newdiscovery.cfm
Phone: 802-426-3042
Size: 20 acres. **Location:** 2 miles west of Groton on VT 232. **Facilities:** 61 campsites (14 with lean-tos 3 &), 5 remote campsites, horse camps, restrooms, hot showers, picnic shelter, hiking trails, play area, horseshoe pits. **Activities:** Camping, hiking. **Special Features:** One of seven state park campgrounds located in Groton State Forest.

★4479★ NORTH HERO STATE PARK

3803 Lakeview Dr
North Hero, VT 05474
Web: www.vtstateparks.com/htm/northhero.cfm
Phone: 802-372-8727
Size: 399 acres. **Location:** On the northern tip of Lake Champlain's North Hero Island. **Facilities:** 117 campsites (18 with

lean-tos; &), group camp, hot showers (&), flush toilets (&), picnic areas, hiking trails, swimming beach, boat rentals, boat ramp, playground. **Activities:** Camping, boating, swimming, hiking. **Special Features:** Although much of the property was farmed and pastured before becoming a park, the old fields are in the process of reverting back to forest. Thick woods surrounding the campground make an ideal habitat for wildlife, and white-tailed deer are common.

★4480★ QUECHEE STATE PARK

764 Dewey Mills Rd
White River Junction, VT 05001
Web: www.vtstateparks.com/htm/quechee.cfm
Phone: 802-295-2990
Size: 611 acres. **Location:** In Quechee, off US 4. **Facilities:** 47 campsites (7 with lean-tos, &), hot showers, flush toilets, picnic areas, play area, hiking trail. **Activities:** Camping, hiking. **Special Features:** Park occupies the site of an old wool mill. Remains of the mill and an old dam can still be seen at the head of the gorge. The park's campground was the mill's recreation area, and the current toilet building contained a skeet range, baseball field, and picnic area. All that remains of this facility are a few foundations of the fireplaces and millions of broken clay pigeons.

★4481★ RICKER POND STATE PARK

18 Ricker Pond Camp Ground Rd
Groton, VT 05046
Web: www.vtstateparks.com/htm/ricker.cfm
Phone: 802-584-3821
Size: 39 acres. **Location:** Northeastern portion of the state, 2 miles west of Groton. **Facilities:** 50 campsites (23 with lean-tos), 5 cabins, cottage, hot showers, flush toilets, picnic areas, canoe and kayak rentals, boat ramp, beach, hiking trails, nature center. **Activities:** Camping, boating, fishing, swimming, winter sports. **Special Features:** One of seven state park campgrounds located in Groton State Forest.

★4482★ SAND BAR STATE PARK

1215 US Rt 2
Milton, VT 05468
Web: www.vtstateparks.com/htm/sandbar.cfm
Phone: 802-893-2825
Size: 15 acres. **Location:** Northwest portion of the state between South Hero Island and the town of Milton on the mainland. **Facilities:** Picnic areas (&), snack bar, swimming beach, bathhouse, boat rentals, restrooms (&), play area. **Activities:** Boating, canoeing, kayaking, swimming. **Special Features:** Park takes its name from a natural sandbar between South Hero Island and the Vermont mainland. Over tens of thousands of years, sediment washing downstream from the Lamoille River sank to the bottom where the river emptied into the lake, eventually creating a marshland south and east of the park, and a sandbar to the west.

★4483★ SEYON LODGE STATE PARK

400 Seyon Park Rd
Groton, VT 05046
Web: www.vtstateparks.com/htm/seyon.cfm
Phone: 802-584-3829
Size: 20 acres. **Location:** Northeastern area of state. **Facilities:** Lodge, dining hall, group meeting rooms, boat rentals. **Activities:** Fishing, boating, hiking, wildlife observation. **Special Features:** The park's rustic lodge is located in 27,000-acre Groton State Forest, and fly fishing for brook trout on Noyes Pond is considered among the best in the state.

★4484★ SILVER LAKE STATE PARK

214 North Rd
Bethel, VT 05032
Web: www.vtstateparks.com/htm/silver.cfm
Phone: 802-234-9451
Size: 34 acres. **Location:** From Barnard, go 0.25 miles north on Town Road. **Facilities:** 47 campsites (7 with lean-tos), hot showers, flush toilets, picnic areas, picnic shelter, snack bar, boat and canoe rentals, play area. **Activities:** Camping, boating, canoeing, fishing, swimming, ice skating, ice fishing. **Special Features:** Silver Lake supports a good fishery of northern pike, perch, bass, and other warm water species. During the winter months when the park is closed, the lake is a popular spot for ice skating and ice fishing.

★4485★ SMUGGLERS NOTCH STATE PARK

6443 Mountain Rd
Stowe, VT 05672
Web: www.vtstateparks.com/htm/smugglers.cfm
Phone: 802-253-4014
Size: 25 acres. **Location:** 10 miles northwest of Stowe, Highway 108. **Facilities:** 34 campsites (14 with lean-tos), 15 walk-in campsites (3 lean-tos), hot showers, picnic areas, hiking trails. **Activities:** Camping, hiking. **Special Features:** Smugglers Notch is a narrow pass through the mountain with 1,000-foot cliffs on both sides. In 1807, when an embargo forbade trade with Great Britain and Canada, Vermonters continued to trade illegally with Canada, herding cattle and carrying other goods through the Notch. Later, fugitive slaves used the Notch as an escape route. During Prohibition in the 1920s, liquor was smuggled in from Canada.

★4486★ STILLWATER STATE PARK

445 Stillwater Rd
Groton, VT 05046
Web: www.vtstateparks.com/htm/stillwater.cfm
Phone: 802-584-3822
Size: 42 acres. **Location:** East central Vermont, near Groton. **Facilities:** 79 campsites (17 with lean-tos), hot showers, flush toilets, picnic areas, swimming beach, play area, hiking trails, boat rentals, boat ramp, nature center. **Activities:** Camping, boating, fishing, nature programs, hiking, swimming. **Special Features:** One of seven state park campgrounds in Groton State Forest.

★4487★ THETFORD HILL STATE PARK

622 Academy Rd
Thetford, VT 05074
Web: www.vtstateparks.com/htm/thetford.cfm
Phone: 802-785-2266
Size: 262 acres. **Location:** From I-91 (Exit 4), go 1 mile north on VT 113A to Thetford Hill, then south 1.5 miles on Academy Road. **Facilities:** 16 campsites (2 with lean-tos), restrooms (&), hot showers, picnic area, fireplaces, hiking trails. **Activities:** Camping, hiking, cross-country skiing. **Special Features:** This quiet, secluded park is known for the world class trail system used for running and cross-country skiing.

★4488★ TOWNSHEND STATE PARK

2755 State Forest Rd
Townshend, VT 05353
Web: www.vtstateparks.com/htm/townshend.cfm
Phone: 802-365-7500
Size: Approximately 40 acres, inside the Townshend State Forest. **Location:** Located at the foot of Bald Mountain on a bend of the West River. **Facilities:** 34 campsites (4 with lean-tos), showers, picnic shelter, fireplace, hiking trails. **Activities:** Camping, hiking. **Special Features:** From the campground, a hiking trail leads up the mountain, climbing vertically 1,100 feet. Waterfalls, chutes, and pools can be seen along the trail, and, at the summit, spectacular views to the north, east, and south.

★4489★ UNDERHILL STATE PARK

PO Box 249
Underhill Center, VT 05490
Web: www.vtstateparks.com/htm/underhill.cfm
Phone: 802-899-3022
Size: 150 acres. **Location:** On the headwaters of Brown's River, on the west slope of Mount Mansfield. **Facilities:** 26 campsites (15 with lean-tos), group camp, flush toilets, picnic areas, picnic shelter, hiking trails. **Activities:** Camping, hiking. **Special Features:** Park's elevation and exposure to harsh climate conditions have resulted in the growth of low, stunted plants along the mountain's ridge that are rare in New England and more typical of plant types found on the Arctic tundra 1,000 miles to the north.

★4490★ WATERBURY CENTER STATE PARK

177 Reservoir Rd
Waterbury Center, VT 05677
Web: www.vtstateparks.com/htm/waterbury.cfm
Phone: 802-244-1226
Size: 90 acres. **Location:** On the easterly trivium of Waterbury Reservoir, 0.25 mile off Rt 100. **Facilities:** Picnic areas, boat launch, boat rentals, swimming beach, concession, restrooms. **Activities:** Boating, swimming. **Special Features:** Park is located in Mount Mansfield State Forest on a peninsula that juts into Waterbury Reservoir.

★4491★ WILGUS STATE PARK

Box 196
Ascutney, VT 05030
Web: www.vtstateparks.com/htm/wilgus.cfm
Phone: 802-674-5422
Size: 89 acres. **Location:** Southeastern Vermont along the shores of the Connecticut River. **Facilities:** 25 campsites (6 with lean-tos), group camp with 3 lean-tos, 2 cabins, hot showers, picnic areas, picnic shelter, fireplaces, hiking trails, canoe rentals. **Activities:** Camping, boating, canoeing, hiking. **Special Features:** Park is located on a scenic stretch of the Connecticut River, and the Pinnacle Trail hike provides vistas of the Connecticut River Valley.

★4492★ WOODFORD STATE PARK

142 State Park Rd
Bennington, VT 05201
Web: www.vtstateparks.com/htm/woodford.cfm
Phone: 802-447-7169
Size: 398 acres. **Location:** 10 miles east of Bennington on Highway 9. **Facilities:** 103 campsites (20 with lean-tos), hot showers, flush toilets, beach, picnic areas, hiking trails, boat and canoe rentals. **Activities:** Camping, boating, canoeing, hiking, cross-country skiing. **Special Features:** Located on a mountain plateau surrounding Adams Reservoir. At 2,400 feet, this is the highest of all Vermont's state parks.

★4493★ WOODS ISLAND STATE PARK

c/o Burton Island State Park
Box 123
Saint Albans Bay, VT 05481
Web: www.vtstateparks.com/htm/woodsisland.cfm
Phone: 802-524-6353
Size: 125 acres. **Location:** On Lake Champlain, 2 miles north of Burton Island and Kamp Kill Kare State Parks. Accessible only by boat; no scheduled ferry service. **Facilities:** 5 primitive campsites, perimeter trail system. **Activities:** Camping, nature study, hiking. **Special Features:** Park is one of three neighboring island parks in Lake Champlain's ''inland sea.'' Park management is aimed at preserving the primitive character of the island. The five campsites have minimal sanitary facilities and there is no potable water.

9. State Parks

Virginia State Parks map showing numbered park locations with grid coordinates.

1	Bear Creek Lake SP	C-7
2	Belle Isle SP	C-9
3	Bethel Beach NAP	C-9
4	Breaks Interstate Park	D-2
5	Bush Mill Stream NAP	C-9
6	Caledon NA	B-8
7	Chippokes Plantation SP	D-8
8	Claytor Lake SP	D-4
9	Clinch Mountain WMA	D-2
10	Douthat SP	C-5
11	Fairy Stone SP	D-5
12	False Cape SP	D-9
13	First Landing SP & NA	D-9

14	George Washington's Grist Mill HSP	A-8
15	Goshen Pass NAP	C-5
16	Grayson Highlands SP	D-3
17	Holliday Lake SP	C-6
18	Hungry Mother SP	D-3
19	James River SP	C-6
20	Kiptopeke SP	D-9
21	Lake Anna SP	C-7
22	Leesylvania SP	B-8
23	Mason Neck SP	B-8
24	Natural Tunnel SP	D-1
25	New River Trail SP	D-4

26	Occoneechee SP	D-6
27	Pocahontas SP	C-7
28	Raymond R. "Andy" Guest Jr. Shenandoah River SP	A-7
29	Sailor's Creek Battlefield SP	D-7
30	Shot Tower HSP	D-4
31	Sky Meadows SP	A-7
32	Smith Mountain Lake SP	D-5
33	Southwest Virginia Museum HSP	D-2
34	Staunton River Battlefield SP	D-6

35	Staunton River SP	D-6
36	Twin Lakes SP	D-6
37	Westmoreland SP	B-8
38	Wilderness Road SP	D-1
39	York River SP	C-8

HSP	Historical State Park
NA	Natural Area
NAP	Natural Area Preserve
SP	State Park
WMA	Wildlife Management Area

VIRGINIA

★4494★ Virginia Division of State Parks
203 Governor St, Suite 213
Richmond, VA 23219
(804) 786-1712 - Phone
(804) 786-9294 - Fax
(800) 933-7275 - Toll-free
(703) 583-5497 - Volunteering
Web: www.dcr.state.va.us/parks
Oversees more than 70 state parks and natural areas totaling about 100,000 acres. Maintains nearly 500 miles of trails and provides boating and fishing access to lakes, rivers, the Chesapeake Bay, and the Atlantic Ocean. Sponsors natural and cultural history education programs and outdoor skills classes.

★4495★ Virginia Department of Forestry
900 Natural Resources Dr, Suite 800
Charlottesville, VA, 22903
(804) 977-6555 - Phone
(804) 296-2369 - Fax
Web: www.dof.virginia.gov
Manages 17 state forests and other state lands totaling about 50,000 acres. Valued primarily for their timber, research, wildlife, and biodiversity resources, state forest lands also offer recreational opportunities including hunting, hiking, wildlife observation, and trailside primitive camping.

★4496★ Virginia Department of Game & Inland Fisheries
4010 W Broad St
Richmond, VA 23230
(804) 367-1000 - Phone
(804) 367-9147 - Fax
Web: www.dgif.state.va.us
Maintains 30 wildlife management areas and numerous lakes, conducts educational and safety programs, administers hunting, fishing, and boating licensing. Developing a statewide system of trails for bird and wildlife observation.

Key to campsite classification:

- **Campsites** — Accommodate 1 tent, trailer, and/or motor vehicle and a maximum of 6 people. Each site includes table and grill with bathhouses located nearby.
- **Group campsites** — Include a minimum of 3 sites, each site can accommodate up to 6 people. Each site includes table and grill with bathhouses located nearby.
- **Primitive campsites** — Generally have fire grills, picnic tables, pit toilets, and non-potable water.

- **Cabins** — May be log, wood, or cinderblock construction. Include fireplaces or wood stoves and air conditioning. Most include furnished kitchen and bathroom, complete with appliances, cookware and tableware, bedding, and linens.

★4497★ BEAR CREEK LAKE STATE PARK
22 Bear Creek Lake Rd
Cumberland, VA 23040
Web: www.dcr.state.va.us/parks/bearcreek.htm
Phone: 804-492-4410
Size: 326 acres. **Location:** 4.5 miles northwest of Cumberland. **Facilities:** 53 campsites (29 with water and electrical hookups), 12 cabins, picnic area, picnic shelter, snack bar, multi-use trails (14 miles), swimming beach and bathhouse, fishing pier, boat launch, boat rentals, archery range. **Activities:** Camping, boating, fishing, swimming, hiking, mountain biking, horseback riding, interpretive programs. **Special Features:** Located in the heart of Cumberland State Forest, the park's 40-acre lake supports healthy populations of largemouth bass, crappie, bream, and channel catfish.

★4498★ BELLE ISLE STATE PARK
1632 Belle Isle Rd
Lancaster, VA 22503
Web: www.dcr.state.va.us/parks/bellisle.htm
Phone: 804-462-5030
Size: 733 acres. **Location:** In the rural northern neck of Virginia. **Facilities:** 28 campsites, lodging in historic houses, picnic shelters, trails, boat launch, bicycle rentals, boat rentals, docks, tackle shop, fishing pier, snack bar, restrooms, playground, observation deck, hiking trails, bike trails, bridle trails. **Activities:** Camping, fishing, boating, windsurfing, guided canoe trips, hiking biking, horseback riding, **Special Features:** Park includes seven miles of frontage on the north shore of the Rappahannock, and borders Deep and Mulberry creeks. It features diverse tidal and non-tidal wetlands, lowland marshes, tidal coves, and upland forests.

★4499★ BETHEL BEACH NATURAL AREA PRESERVE
217 Governor St
Richmond, VA 23219
Web: www.dcr.virginia.gov/dnh/bethel.htm
Phone: 804-225-2303
Size: 83 acres. **Location:** On the western shore of the Chesapeake Bay. **Activities:** Bird watching, photography. **Special Features:** A globally rare coastal insect, rare colonial and marsh

9. State Parks

nesting birds, and a rare beach plant are protected in this preserve.

★4500★ BREAKS INTERSTATE PARK

PO Box 100
Breaks, VA 24607
Web: www.parks.ky.gov/stateparks/bi
Phone: 800-982-5122
Size: 4,500 acres. **Location:** Park sits astride the state line shared by both Kentucky and Virginia. It is located 8 miles north of Haysi, Virginia, and 7 miles east of Elkhorn, Kentucky, on KY-VA 80. **Facilities:** Lodge with 82 rooms and 1 suite (seasonal), cottages (year-round), restaurant (seasonal), convention center (seasonal), 122 campsites with utilities, showers, and restrooms (seasonal), picnic area, picnic shelters, hiking trails (12 miles), bike trails (2 miles), riding stables and trails, Olympic-sized swimming pool, concession stand, boat dock, pedal boat rental, visitor/interpretive center (seasonal), amphitheater, gift shop (seasonal). **Activities:** Camping, boating (electric motors only), whitewater rafting, fishing, swimming, hiking, mountain biking, horseback riding, interpretive programs. **Special Features:** Often referred to as "The Grand Canyon of the South," Breaks Canyon, the deepest gorge east of the Mississippi River, is 5 miles long, 1,600 feet deep, and 250 million years old. The gorge was carved by the Russell Fork River, a tributary of the Big Sandy. The park is operated by a separate commission comprising members from both Virginia and Kentucky.

★4501★ BUSH MILL STREAM NATURAL AREA PRESERVE

Rt 642
Heathsville, VA 22473
Web: www.dcr.virginia.gov/dnh/bushmill.htm
Phone: 804-684-7577
Size: 103 acres. **Facilities:** Trails, boardwalk, viewing platform, interpretive signs. **Activities:** Hiking, wildlife observation. **Special Features:** This remote reach of stream and river is an excellent example of a habitat that once was abundant in the Chesapeake Bay drainage. Several ancient oaks and large mountain laurel remain in the mostly second-growth forest.

★4502★ CALEDON NATURAL AREA

11617 Caledon Rd
King George, VA 22485
Web: www.dcr.state.va.us/parks/caledon.htm
Phone: 540-663-3861
Size: 2,579 acres. **Location:** 23 miles east of Fredericksburg on Route 218. **Facilities:** Picnic shelters, hiking trails, visitor center, restrooms, environmental education center. **Activities:** Hiking, interpretive programs. **Special Features:** Overlooking the banks of the Potomac, Caledon Natural Area is summer home to one of the largest concentrations of American bald eagles on the East Coast. Though access to the forests and marshes is restricted, limited tours into the eagle area are offered seasonally (mid-June to September).

★4503★ CHIPPOKES PLANTATION STATE PARK

695 Chippokes Park Rd
Surry, VA 23883
Web: www.dcr.state.va.us/parks/chippoke.htm
Phone: 757-294-3625
Size: 1,683 acres. **Location:** Take State Route 10 east to Route 634, then follow Route 634 to park entrance. **Facilities:** 37 campsites (all with water and electric hookups, 1 ♿), 3 cabins, 4 group camps, bathhouse (♿), picnic area, picnic shelter, snack bar, hiking trail, bicycle trail (3.5 miles), auto tour route, swimming pool, visitor center, garden, museum. **Activities:** Camping, fishing, swimming, hiking, bicycling, horseback riding, guided tours (seasonal), interpretive programs, hunting (by reservation). **Special Features:** A working farm for over 360 years, the park includes an antebellum mansion, gardens, and the Farm and Forestry Museum, with a collection of antique farm and forestry equipment. During the Christmas season, the mansion is decked in Victorian period decorations.

★4504★ CLAYTOR LAKE STATE PARK

6620 Ben H Boden Dr
Dublin, VA 24084
Web: www.dcr.state.va.us/parks/claytor.htm
Phone: 540-643-2500
Size: 472 acres. **Location:** Southwestern portion of state, off I-81. **Facilities:** 110 campsites, 16 cabins, picnic area, 7 picnic shelters, gazebo, showers, toilets, snack bar, hiking trails (3 miles), swimming beach, bathhouse, fishing pier, boat launch, boat rentals, marina, gazebo, environmental education center, visitor center (seasonal). **Activities:** Camping, boating, fishing, swimming, hiking, bicycling, interpretive programs (seasonal). **Special Features:** Park includes 3 miles of shoreline on 4,500-acre Claytor Lake. The visitor center, located in the historic Howe House, features interactive, hands-on exhibits.

★4505★ CLINCH MOUNTAIN WILDLIFE MANAGEMENT AREA

2387 Tumbling Creek Rd
Saltville, VA 24370
Web: www.dgif.state.va.us/hunting/wma/
    clinch_mountain.html
Phone: 276-783-3422
Size: 25,477 acres. **Location:** Near Saltville, off I-81, in the southwest highlands. **Facilities:** Primitive campsites, hiking trails, 2 boat launches, archery shooting range. **Activities:** Camping, boating, fishing, hiking, horseback riding, hunting. **Special Features:** Area is dominated by mountains rising steeply from narrow valley floors. Due to difference in elevation, ranging from 1,600 feet to 4,700 feet on top of Beartown Mountain, a unique forest has developed: tree species from both southern and northern forests are found.

★4506★ DOUTHAT STATE PARK

Rt 1, Box 212
Millboro, VA 24460
Web: www.dcr.state.va.us/parks/douthat.htm
Phone: 540-862-8100

Size: 4,493 acres. **Location:** Near Clifton Forge in the Allegheny Mountains. **Facilities:** 74 campsites (55 with electric and water hookups), group camp, 32 cabins, 2 lodges, picnic shelters, restaurant, snack bar, hiking trails (40+ miles), bike trails, self-guiding trail, swimming beach, bathhouse, boat launch, boat rentals, bicycle rentals, camp store, gift shop, amphitheater. **Activities:** Camping, boating, fishing, swimming, hiking, mountain biking, hunting, interpretive programs. **Special Features:** Created in 1936, Douthat was one of Virginia's six original state parks. It is on the National Register of Historic Places.

★4507★ FAIRY STONE STATE PARK

967 Fairystone Lake Dr
Stuart, VA 24171
Web: www.dcr.state.va.us/parks/fairyst.htm
Phone: 276-930-2424
Size: 4,868 acres. **Location:** In the foothills of the Blue Ridge Mountains, off Rt. 57. **Facilities:** 51 campsites (all with electric and water), 4 backcountry campsites, 6 group campsites, 24 cabins (15 ♿), 5-bedroom lodge (♿), picnic area, picnic shelters (♿), multi-use trails (9 miles), swimming beach, bathhouse, fishing pier, boat launch, boat rentals, snack bar, visitor center. **Activities:** Camping, boating (electric motors only), fishing, swimming, hiking, mountain biking, horseback riding, hunting, interpretive programs (seasonal). **Special Features:** The largest of the six original Virginia state parks, this park is home to mysterious "fairy stones." Fairy stones are brown staurolite, a combination of silica, iron, and aluminum, which form into the shape of a cross.

★4508★ FALSE CAPE STATE PARK

4001 Sandpiper Rd
Virginia Beach, VA 23456
Web: www.dcr.state.va.us/parks/falscape.htm
Phone: 757-426-7128; **Fax:** 757-426-0055
Size: 4,321 acres. **Location:** Southwest of Virginia Beach. Access is through the Back Bay National Wildlife Refuge (see separate entry in national wildlife refuges chapter). No vehicular access; accessible by foot, bicycle, or boat. **Facilities:** 4 primitive campgrounds, pit toilets, hiking trails, bicycle trails, self-guiding trail, 5.9-mile beach, environmental education center. **Activities:** Camping, boating, fishing, hiking, bicycling, interpretive programs. **Special Features:** Park is a mile-wide barrier spit between Back Bay and the Atlantic Ocean. In the 1800s, it gained a reputation as a ship's graveyard because its land mass resembled Cape Henry, luring boats into shallow waters. This is how it got its name.

★4509★ FIRST LANDING STATE PARK

2500 Shore Dr
Virginia Beach, VA 23451
Web: www.dcr.state.va.us/parks/1stland.htm
Phone: 757-412-2300
Size: 2,888 acres. **Location:** On US 60 at Cape Henry in Virginia Beach. **Facilities:** 218 campsites (109 with electricity and water), 20 cabins, showers, picnic area, picnic shelter, hiking trails (19 miles), self-guiding trails, bicycle trails, bicycle rentals, boat rentals, boat launch, environmental education center, camp store. **Activities:** Camping, boating, fishing, crabbing, swimming, hiking, bicycling, interpretive programs. **Special Features:** In 1965 the park's natural area was included in the *National Register of Natural Landmarks* because of its distinction as the northernmost location on the East Coast where subtropical and temperate plants grow and thrive together.

★4510★ GEORGE WASHINGTON'S GRIST MILL HISTORICAL STATE PARK

PO Box 110
Mount Vernon, VA 22121
Web: www.dcr.state.va.us/parks/georgewa.htm
Phone: 703-780-2000
Location: On Mount Vernon Memorial Highway (Route 235), 0.25 miles south from US 1, or 3 miles west of the Mount Vernon Estate. **Facilities:** Historic sites, shop. **Activities:** Interpretive programs (seasonal). **Special Features:** The present grist mill is a reconstruction of the mill George Washington built and operated for almost three decades. Replicas of machinery are on display, and exhibits explain how the mill operated. Visitors can watch the water-powered wheel grind grain into flour just as it did 200 years ago.

★4511★ GOSHEN PASS NATURAL AREA PRESERVE

c/o Virginia Department of Conservation & Recreation -
   Natural Heritage Program
217 Governor St
Richmond, VA 23219
Phone: 540-265-5278
Size: 936 acres. **Location:** In Rockbridge County, 10 miles north of Lexington. **Facilities:** Hiking trail. **Activities:** Hiking, birding, wildlife viewing. **Special Features:** The narrow deep-sided gorge in Goshen Pass is the result of the Maury River's cutting action through erosion-resitant rocks that comprise the adjacent Little North, Forge, and Hogback mountains. The preserve's hiking trail links to trails in the Goshen-Little North Mountain Wildlife Management Area.

★4512★ GRAYSON HIGHLANDS STATE PARK

829 Grayson Highland Ln
Mouth of Wilson, VA 24363
Web: www.dcr.state.va.us/parks/graysonh.htm
Phone: 276-579-7092
Size: 4,822 acres. **Location:** Midway between Independence and Damascus on US 58. **Facilities:** 75 campsites (43 with water and electric hookups), 23 horsemen's campsites, group campsite, picnic area, picnic shelters, hiking trails, ski trails, biking trails, bridle trails, 67 horse stalls, visitor center with crafts shop. **Activities:** Camping, fishing, hiking, mountain biking, horseback riding, rock climbing, cross-country skiing, interpretive programs, outdoor skills workshops. **Special Features:** Located near Mount Rogers, the state's highest mountain peak, Grayson Highlands offers some of the state's most scenic alpine vistas and provides access to the Appalachian National Scenic Trail (see separate entry in national trails section) and trails in the surrounding Jefferson National Forest (see separate entry in national forests section).

★4513★ HOLLIDAY LAKE STATE PARK

Rt 2, Box 622
Appomattox, VA 24522
Web: www.dcr.state.va.us/parks/holliday.htm
Phone: 434-248-6308
Size: 250 acres. **Location:** Accessible via State Route 24 (between Appomattox and US 60), and Routes 626 and 692. **Facilities:** 30 campsites (all with water and electric hookups), lodge, showers, toilets, picnic area, picnic shelters, snack bar, hiking trails, aquatic trail, swimming beach and bathhouse, boat launch, boat rentals, visitor center, playground. **Activities:** Camping, boating (electric motors only), fishing, swimming, hiking, mountain biking, horseback riding, interpretive programs. **Special Features:** Park features 150-acre Holliday Lake, which is good for fishing. The area encompassing the park was cleared in the 1800s for farmland, then bought back by the government to return it to its hardwood forest state. Traces of family cemeteries can still be found in the area.

★4514★ HUNGRY MOTHER STATE PARK

2854 Park Blvd
Marion, VA 24354
Web: www.dcr.state.va.us/parks/hungrymo.htm
Phone: 276-781-7400
Size: 2,215 acres. **Location:** Southwestern Virginia, off I-81. **Facilities:** 43 campsites (32 with water and electric hookups), 20 cabins, 6-bedroom lodge, showers, toilets, picnic area, 3 picnic shelters, hiking trails, bicycle trails, swimming beach, bathhouse, boat launch, boat rentals, fishing pier, conference center (with meeting rooms, cabins, a swimming pool, sports complex, and picnic area), visitor center, amphitheater, restaurant, snack bar, gift shop, playground. **Activities:** Camping, boating (electric motors only), fishing, swimming, hiking, mountain biking, interpretive programs. **Special Features:** Park is named for a legend that a mother and her child, abducted by Native Americans, later escaped and wandered through the wilderness eating berries. The mother collapsed, her child ran for help and when found could only utter the words ''hungry mother.'' The site where her body was found is known as Molly's Knob.

★4515★ JAMES RIVER STATE PARK

Rt 1, Box 787
Gladstone, VA 24553
Web: www.dcr.state.va.us/parks/jamesriv.htm
Phone: 434-933-4355
Size: 1,500 acres. **Location:** From Route 60 west, turn right on Route 605 at the James River Bridge. Go 7 miles and turn left at Route 606. **Facilities:** 27 primitive campsites, canoe camp, horsemen's camp, picnic areas, picnic shelters, multi-use trails (20 miles), boat launches, fishing pier, toilets (&&). **Activities:** Camping, boating, canoeing, freshwater fishing, hiking, mountain biking, horseback riding, hunting, interpretive programs. **Special Features:** One of Virginia's newest state parks, James River includes three fishing ponds and three miles of shoreline along its namesake river.

★4516★ KIPTOPEKE STATE PARK

3540 Kiptopeke Dr
Cape Charles, VA 23310
Web: www.dcr.state.va.us/parks/kiptopek.htm
Phone: 757-331-2267
Size: 540 acres. **Location:** Eastern shore of Virginia, on State Route 704. **Facilities:** 147 campsites (32 with full hookups, 54 with water and electric, 2 &), group campsites, 5 lodges, RV trailer rentals, showers, toilets, picnic shelters, hiking trails, bicycle trails, swimming beach, bathhouse (&), laundry, boat launch, lighted fishing pier, camp store, observatory, environmental education center. **Activities:** Camping, boating, fishing, swimming, hiking, bicycling, interpretive programs. **Special Features:** Kiptopeke has been the site of bird population studies since 1963. It features a raptor research area where birds of prey are observed and banded. Kiptopeke hawk observatory is among the top 15 nationwide.

★4517★ LAKE ANNA STATE PARK

6800 Lawyers Rd
Spotsylvania, VA 22553
Web: www.dcr.state.va.us/parks/lakeanna.htm
Phone: 540-854-5503
Size: 2,058 acres. **Location:** From State Route 208, take Route 601 north 3 miles. **Facilities:** Picnic area, 2 picnic shelters, snack bar, hiking trails, self-guiding trails, swimming beach and bathhouse, boat launch, visitor center, environmental education pavilion, showers, toilets, playground (&&). **Activities:** Boating, freshwater fishing, swimming, hiking, boat tours, interpretive programs, gold panning. **Special Features:** Visitor center exhibits trace the history of gold mining in the area and highlight the natural features of the park.

★4518★ LEESYLVANIA STATE PARK

2001 Daniel K Ludwig Dr
Woodbridge, VA 22191
Web: www.dcr.state.va.us/parks/leesylva.htm
Phone: 703-730-8205
Size: 508 acres. **Location:** Approximately 25 miles from Washington, D.C. on US Route 1. **Facilities:** Group camp, picnic area, picnic shelter, hiking trails, boat launch, fishing pier, camp store, showers, toilets, amphitheater, playground, visitor center, gift shop. **Activities:** Camping, boating, fishing, hiking, interpretive programs. **Special Features:** Listed on the *National Register of Historic Landmarks*, Leesylvania was the home of the famous Lee family. Henry Lee III (Light Horse Harry), a cavalry colonel during the American Revolution, governor of Virginia (1791-1794), and father of Robert E. Lee, was one of eight children born here. The family gravesite is still on the property.

★4519★ MASON NECK STATE PARK

7301 High Point Rd
Lorton, VA 22079
Web: www.dcr.state.va.us/parks/masonnec.htm
Phone: 703-550-0960
Size: 1,814 acres. **Location:** In southern Fairfax County, about 20 miles from Washington, D.C., on Route 242. **Facilities:** Picnic shelter, hiking trails (&), biking trails, self-guiding trails,

hand launch boat ramp, boat rentals, bike rentals, playground (&), restrooms (&), visitor center, environmental education center. **Activities:** Fishing, hiking, biking, hunting (with restrictions), bird watching, interpretive programs. **Special Features:** Mason Neck is situated on a peninsula formed by Pohick Bay on the north, Belmont Bay on the south, and the Potomac River on the east. It is the site of an active heron rookery and also attracts several other migrating and non-migrating species of birds, including whistling swans and bald eagles.

★4520★ NATURAL TUNNEL STATE PARK
Rt 3, Box 250
Duffield, VA 24244
Web: www.dcr.state.va.us/parks/naturalt.htm
Phone: 276-940-2674
Size: 850 acres. **Location:** 13 miles north of Gate City on Route 871. **Facilities:** 23 campsites (18 with water and electric hookups, &), group campsite, showers, toilets, picnic area, picnic shelters, snack bar, hiking trails, biking trails, bicycle rentals, self-guiding trails, boardwalk, swimming pool (&), bathhouse, visitor center, gift shop, environmental education center, amphitheater. **Activities:** Camping, fishing, swimming, hiking, biking, interpretive programs, guided canoe trips, cave tours, naturalist programs. **Special Features:** Over 850 feet long and 100 feet high, Natural Tunnel was carved through a limestone ridge over thousands of centuries. Park features a chairlift to view the naturally formed tunnel (operating seasonally). Walls of the tunnel show evidence of prehistoric life, and many fossils can be found in the creek bed and on tunnel walls.

★4521★ NEW RIVER TRAIL STATE PARK
176 Orphanage Dr
Foster Falls, VA 24360
Web: www.dcr.state.va.us/parks/newriver.htm
Phone: 276-699-6778
Size: 57-mile linear trail comprising 765 acres. **Location:** In southwestern Virginia, parallelling the New River. **Facilities:** 29 campsites, 3 horse camps, 9 group camps, picnic areas, picnic shelter, hiking trail (&), biking trail, bridle trail, hand launch boat ramp, boat rentals, horse rentals, visitor center, toilets (&), livery, playground. **Activities:** Camping, fishing, tubing, canoeing, hiking, bicycling, horseback riding, interpretive programs. **Special Features:** The park follows an abandoned railroad right-of-way, running parallel to the scenic and historic New River for 39 miles. Other points of interest include two tunnels, three major bridges and nearly 30 smaller bridges and trestles, and a shot tower used more than 150 years ago to make ammunition.

★4522★ OCCONEECHEE STATE PARK
1192 Occoneechee Park Rd
Clarksville, VA 23927
Web: www.dcr.state.va.us/parks/occoneec.htm
Phone: 434-374-2210
Size: 2,698 acres. **Location:** 1 mile east of Clarksville on US 58, near the US 15 intersection. **Facilities:** 88 campsites (34 with water and electric hookups), 2 lodges, 13 cabins, showers, pit toilets, picnic area, picnic shelters, hiking trails, bike trails, bridle trails, bicycle rentals, boat rentals, boat launch, visitor center, playground. **Activities:** Camping, boating, fishing, hiking, biking, horseback riding, hunting (with restrictions), interpretive programs. **Special Features:** Trails allow visitors to experience the history of the Occoneechee Indians and plantation life in the 1800s. In 1839 a mansion with terraced gardens was built on this site. The mansion was destroyed by fire 1898, but the landscaping of the garden can still be seen in the park today.

★4523★ POCAHONTAS STATE PARK
10301 State Park Rd
Chesterfield, VA 23802
Web: www.dcr.state.va.us/parks/pocahont.htm
Phone: 804-796-4255; **Fax:** 804-796-4004; **Toll Free:** 800-933-7275
Size: 7,625 acres. **Location:** 20 miles south of Richmond. Take I-95 to Exit 61, then go west on Route 10 to Route 655, Beach Road. **Facilities:** 119 campsites (all with water and electric hookups), 5 popup camper sites, group campsites, group bunkhouses, showers, toilets, picnic area, 7 picnic shelters, snack bar, hiking trails, bridle trails (9 miles), bicycle trail (5 miles), bicycle rentals, large swimming pool, boat launch, boat rentals, museum, gift shop, amphitheater. **Activities:** Camping, boating, fishing, swimming, hiking, horseback riding, bicycling, hunting (with restrictions), interpretive programs. **Special Features:** Located just 20 miles from downtown Richmond, Pocahontas is one of Virginia's most popular states park and includes 150-acre Swift Creek Lake and 24-acre Beaver Lake. The Civilian Conservation Corps Museum at the park displays historic photographics, artifacts, and personal mementos in an original building outfitted with modern conveniences.

★4524★ RAYMOND R. "ANDY" GUEST JR. SHENANDOAH RIVER STATE PARK
PO Box 235
Daughter of Stars Dr
Bentonville, VA 22610
Web: www.dcr.state.va.us/parks/andygues.htm
Phone: 540-622-6840; **Fax:** 540-622-6841
Size: 1,604 acres. **Location:** Just off US 340 between Front Royal and Luray. **Facilities:** 10 primitive campsites (&), primitive group camp, bathhouse, picnic shelters (&), multi-use trails (13 miles), hand launch boat ramp, information kiosk, restrooms. **Activities:** Fishing, canoeing, rafting, swimming, hiking, mountain biking. **Special Features:** Park includes 5.6 miles of river frontage along the south fork of the Shenandoah River. The mountainous terrain is mostly wooded and features steep slopes with scenic vistas of Massanutten Mountain to the west and Shenandoah National Park (see separate entry in national parks section) to the east.

★4525★ SAILOR'S CREEK BATTLEFIELD STATE PARK
788 Twin Lakes Rd
Green Bay, VA 23942
Web: www.dcr.state.va.us/parks/sailorcr.htm
Phone: 434-392-3435
Size: 321 acres. **Location:** 5 miles east of Farmville, Virginia on Rt 617. **Facilities:** Picnic areas, nature programs, historical

programs. **Activities:** Interpretive programs. **Special Features:** Site of the last major battle in the Civil War in Virginia. General Lee surrendered at Appomattox 72 hours after this battle, in which he had lost more than half his army. Park is site of the Overton-Hillsman House, a handmade colonial structure that served as a federal field hospital to the wounded of both the northern and southern commands. Bloodstains remain on the floor today. The Hillsman House is open to the public June through August, and by request at other times.

★4526★ **SHOT TOWER HISTORICAL STATE PARK**
Rt 1 Box 81X
Austinville, VA 24312
Web: www.dcr.state.va.us/parks//shottowr.htm
Phone: 276-699-6778
Size: 254 acres. **Location:** Southwestern Virginia. Park stands at the midway point of New River Trail State Park (see separate entry). **Facilities:** Picnic area, hiking trail, visitor center, restrooms. **Activities:** Hiking, guided tours (seasonal), interpretive programs. **Special Features:** Overlooking the New River, Shot Tower was built more than 150 years ago to make ammunition for the firearms of early settlers.

★4527★ **SKY MEADOWS STATE PARK**
11012 Edmonds Ln
Delaplane, VA 20144
Web: www.dcr.state.va.us/parks/skymeado.htm
Phone: 540-592-3556
Size: 1,862 acres. **Location:** 2 miles south of Paris on Route 17 South. **Facilities:** 12 primitive hike-in campsites, group campsite, toilets, picnic shelters, hiking trails, bridle trails, playground, visitor center, gift shop. **Activities:** Camping, fishing, hiking, horseback riding, naturalist programs, historical programs, historical tours. **Special Features:** Historic Mount Bleak House, furnished as a middle-class farmhouse circa 1860, serves as the park's visitor center. Park provides an access point to the Appalachian National Scenic Trail (see entry in national trails section).

★4528★ **SMITH MOUNTAIN LAKE STATE PARK**
1235 State Park Rd
Huddleston, VA 24104
Web: www.dcr.state.va.us/parks/smithmtn.htm
Phone: 540-297-6066
Size: 1,248 acres. **Location:** 40 miles from Lynchburg on the north shore of Smith Mountain Lake. **Facilities:** 50 campsites (24 with water and electric hookups), 20 cabins (&), restrooms, picnic area, picnic shelter, hiking trails, boat launch, dock, boat rentals, fishing pier (&), swimming beach, bathhouse (&), snack bar, visitor center, amphitheater, playground (&), gift shop. **Activities:** Camping, boating, hiking, fishing, swimming, hunting (by reservation), interpretive programs. **Special Features:** Located on the second largest freshwater lake in the state, the park is a favorite destination for water enthusiasts. Smith Mountain Lake was created in 1960 when Appalachian Power built a dam on the Roanoke River in Smith Mountain Gap.

★4529★ **SOUTHWEST VIRGINIA MUSEUM HISTORICAL STATE PARK**
10 W 1st St
Big Stone Gap, VA 24219
Web: www.dcr.state.va.us/parks/swvamus.htm
Phone: 276-523-1322
Size: 1 acre. **Location:** 35 miles northwest of Kingsport, Tennessee in the Appalachian Mountains. **Facilities:** Picnic areas, self-guiding trail, visitor center, gift shop. **Activities:** Interpretive programs. **Special Features:** Museum contains exhibits chronicling the exploration and development of the town and surrounding area during the 1890s coal boom. The four-story mansion was started as a neighborhood attraction by Congressman C. Bascom Slemp. It was opened as a state museum in 1948.

★4530★ **STAUNTON RIVER BATTLEFIELD STATE PARK**
1035 Fort Hill Tr
Randolph, VA 23962
Web: www.dcr.state.va.us/parks/srbbsp.htm
Phone: 434-454-4312
Size: 300 acres. **Location:** 18 miles east of South Boston, off VA 92. **Facilities:** Picnic area, picnic shelter (&), hiking trails, bike trails, self guided trails, visitor center, environmental education center. **Activities:** Hiking, bicycling, interpretive programs, historical reenactments. **Special Features:** On June 25th, 1864, a battle between Confederate troops, led by Captain Benjamin L. Farinholt, and Union troops, led by Colonel R. M. West, took place here. Visitor Center contains displays detailing this history, as well as exhibits on electric energy.

★4531★ **STAUNTON RIVER STATE PARK**
1170 Staunton Tr
Scottsburg, VA 24589
Web: www.dcr.state.va.us/parks/staunton.htm
Phone: 434-572-4623
Size: 1,597 acres. **Location:** 18 miles east of South Boston on Route 344. **Facilities:** 48 campsites (34 with water and electric hookups), 7 cabins, picnic area, picnic shelters, snack bar, hiking trails, self-guiding trails, swimming pool, bathhouse (&), boat launch (&), game courts, amphitheater. **Activities:** Camping, boating, fishing, swimming, hiking, mountain biking, horseback riding, tennis, interpretive programs. **Special Features:** Six wooded trails offer miles of hiking along the Dan and Staunton Rivers as well as Buggs Island Lake, the state's largest lake.

★4532★ **TWIN LAKES STATE PARK**
788 Twin Lakes Rd
Green Bay, VA 23942
Web: www.dcr.state.va.us/parks/twinlake.htm
Phone: 434-392-3435
Size: 495 acres. **Location:** Virginia's Piedmont region, near Farmville, on Route 629. **Facilities:** 34 campsites (30 with water and electric), 16 group campsites, 7 cabins, lodge, bathhouse, picnic area, 2 picnic shelters (&), snack bar (&), hiking trails, swimming beach, boat launch, boat rentals, conference center (&). **Activities:** Camping, boating, fishing, swimming, hiking,

9. State Parks

bicycling, interpretive programs. **Special Features:** Park property was initially bought from struggling farmers by the federal government during the Great Depression. Two parks, Goodwin Lake and Prince Edward Lake, were founded in 1939 and until the early 1960s were run as two racially segregated parks. The parks merged in 1976 and became Twin Lakes State Park in 1986.

★4533★ WESTMORELAND STATE PARK
1650 State Park Rd
Montross, VA 22520
Web: www.dcr.state.va.us/parks/westmore.htm
Phone: 804-493-8821
Size: 1,299 acres. **Location:** 6 miles northwest of Montross, just off State Route 3. **Facilities:** 133 campsites (42 with water and electric hookups), 4 group campsites, 26 cabins (2 &), 5-bedroom lodge, bathhouse, picnic area, picnic shelters, snack bar, hiking trails, self-guiding trails, swimming pool (&), boat launch, boat rentals, fishing pier, visitor center, camp store, playground (&). **Activities:** Camping, boating, canoeing, fishing, swimming, hiking, kayaking tours, interpretive programs. **Special Features:** Built in the 1930s by the Civilian Conservation Corps, most of the roads and trails found in the park were originally dug by hand. The park is minutes away from the birthplaces of George Washington and Robert E. Lee.

★4534★ WILDERNESS ROAD STATE PARK
Rt 2, Box 115
Ewing, VA 24248
Web: www.dcr.state.va.us/parks/wildroad.htm
Phone: 276-445-3065
Size: 200 acres. **Location:** 5 miles west of Ewing, off US 58. **Facilities:** Primitive group campsites, picnic area, picnic shelters, trails, bike rentals, historic home, visitor center, snack bar, restrooms. **Activities:** Camping, hiking, bicycling, horseback riding, interpretive programs. **Special Features:** Park is located in the valley where Daniel Boone carved out the famous Wilderness Road in 1775. By 1800, more than 300,000 settlers had traveled the road westward through Cumberland Gap into Kentucky and the Midwest. Park will eventually include a reproduction pioneer station and fort house depicting lifestyles of the late 1700s during America's westward expansion.

★4535★ YORK RIVER STATE PARK
5526 Riverview Rd
Williamsburg, VA 23188
Web: www.dcr.state.va.us/parks/yorkrive.htm
Phone: 757-566-3036
Size: 2,550 acres. **Location:** 11 miles west of Williamsburg, on Route 606. **Facilities:** Picnic area, picnic shelters, hiking trails, bike trails, bridle trails, self-guiding trails (&), boat launch, boat rentals, bike rentals, visitor center, toilets, amphitheater (&), playground. **Activities:** Boating, fishing, hiking, mountain biking, horseback riding, guided canoe trips, interpretive programs. **Special Features:** Park is known for its rare and delicate estuarine environment, where fresh and salt water meet to create a habitat rich in marine and plant life. Croaker Landing, found

within the park, is an archeological site included in the *National Register of Historic Places.*

Washington State Parks

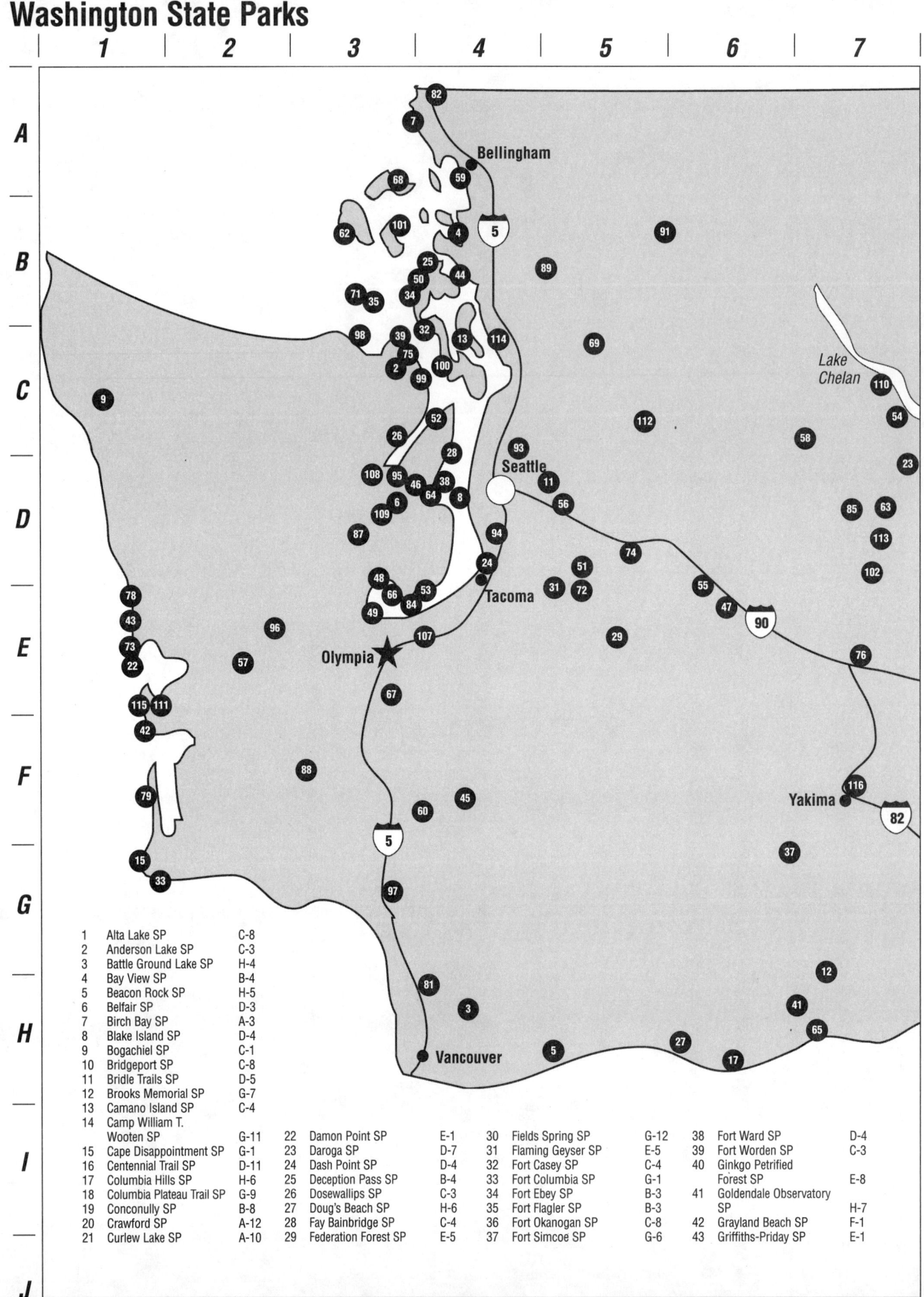

1	Alta Lake SP	C-8	
2	Anderson Lake SP	C-3	
3	Battle Ground Lake SP	H-4	
4	Bay View SP	B-4	
5	Beacon Rock SP	H-5	
6	Belfair SP	D-3	
7	Birch Bay SP	A-3	
8	Blake Island SP	D-4	
9	Bogachiel SP	C-1	
10	Bridgeport SP	C-8	
11	Bridle Trails SP	D-5	
12	Brooks Memorial SP	G-7	
13	Camano Island SP	C-4	
14	Camp William T. Wooten SP	G-11	
15	Cape Disappointment SP	G-1	
16	Centennial Trail SP	D-11	
17	Columbia Hills SP	H-6	
18	Columbia Plateau Trail SP	G-9	
19	Conconully SP	B-8	
20	Crawford SP	A-12	
21	Curlew Lake SP	A-10	

22	Damon Point SP	E-1
23	Daroga SP	D-7
24	Dash Point SP	D-4
25	Deception Pass SP	B-4
26	Dosewallips SP	C-3
27	Doug's Beach SP	H-6
28	Fay Bainbridge SP	C-4
29	Federation Forest SP	E-5

30	Fields Spring SP	G-12
31	Flaming Geyser SP	E-5
32	Fort Casey SP	C-4
33	Fort Columbia SP	G-1
34	Fort Ebey SP	B-3
35	Fort Flagler SP	B-3
36	Fort Okanogan SP	C-8
37	Fort Simcoe SP	G-6

38	Fort Ward SP	D-4
39	Fort Worden SP	C-3
40	Ginkgo Petrified Forest SP	E-8
41	Goldendale Observatory SP	H-7
42	Grayland Beach SP	F-1
43	Griffiths-Priday SP	E-1

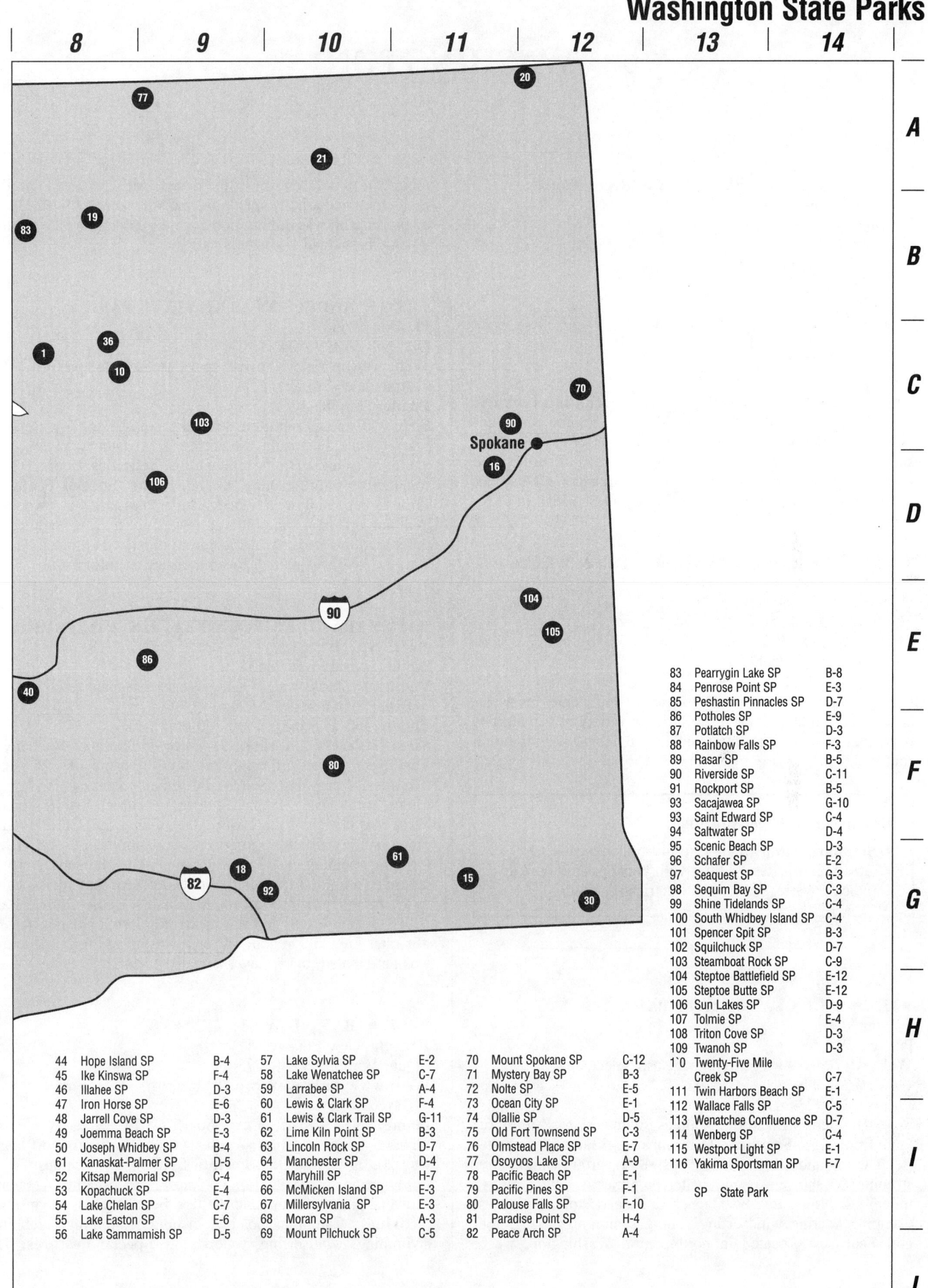

| | 8 | 9 | 10 | 11 | 12 | 13 | 14 |

A

B

C

Spokane

D

E

F

G

H

I

J

WASHINGTON

★4536★ Washington State Parks & Recreation Commission
PO Box 42650
Olympia, WA 98504
(360) 902-8500 - Phone
(360) 753-1594 - Fax
(360) 664-3133 - TDD
(888) 226-7688 - Toll-free Reservations
(360) 902-8565 - Employment
(360) 902-8583 - Volunteering
Web: www.parks.wa.gov
Operates 115 developed state parks and several small satellite properties, totaling more than 260,000 acres. Several parks provide winter camping sites and groomed trails for cross-country skiing, snowmobiles, and other winter activities. There is also an extensive system of underwater dive parks along the shores of Puget Sound, Strait of Juan De Fuca, and San Juan Islands.

★4537★ Washington Department of Fish & Wildlife
600 Capitol Way N
Olympia, WA 98501
(360) 902-2200 - Phone
(360) 902-2230 - Fax
(360) 902-2207 - TDD
Web: www.wdfw.wa.gov
Maintains more than 65 wildlife areas and numerous water access sites on 800,000 acres, offering a variety of recreational opportunities as well as important animal habitat and migration routes.

Key to campsite classification:

- **Standard campsites** — No utility hookups.
- **Utility campsites** — Sites with hookups; full hookups indicate water, sewer, and electrical hookups.

★4538★ ALTA LAKE STATE PARK
40 Star Rt
Pateros, WA 98846
Web: www.parks.wa.gov/parkpage.asp?selectedpark=
Alta%20Lake
Phone: 509-923-2473
Size: 181 acres. **Location:** 4 miles southwest of Pateros off State Route 153. **Facilities:** 168 campsites, 32 utility campsites (with water and electrical hookups; 1 &), group camp, 4 restrooms (&), showers, picnic shelter, picnic areas, hiking trails (2 miles), swimming area, boat launch, dock, park store. **Activities:** Camping, boating, windsurfing, fishing, swimming, hiking. **Special Features:** Located in north-central Washington, where

mountain pine forests meet the desert. Alta Lake is about two miles long and a half-mile wide, and was named by Mr Heinz, a jeweler who was mining in the area. Finding the lake without a name he named it after his daughter.

★4539★ ANDERSON LAKE STATE PARK
PO Box 42650
Olympia, WA 98504
Web: www.parks.wa.gov/parkpage.asp?selectedpark=
Anderson%20Lake
Phone: 360-385-1259
Size: 410 acres. **Location:** 8 miles south of Port Townsend on the Olympic Peninsula. **Facilities:** Boat launch, picnic area, vault toilets, hiking trails, biking trails. **Activities:** Boating (electric motors only), fishing, hiking, biking. **Special Features:** Prior to becoming a state park, Anderson Lake was owned by William F. Anderson, although it was not named for him. He purchased the property in 1947 from unrelated Amanda Anderson; the lake was named for one of her ancestors.

★4540★ BATTLE GROUND LAKE STATE PARK
18002 NE 249th St
Battle Ground, WA 98604
Web: www.parks.wa.gov/parkpage.asp?selectedpark=
Battle%20Ground%20Lake
Phone: 360-687-4621; **Fax:** 360-666-8158
Size: 280 acres. **Location:** 21 miles northeast of Vancouver. **Facilities:** 25 standard campsites, 6 utility campsites, 15 primitive sites, 4 camping shelters, horseman's camp, 4 cabins, pit toilets, bathhouse, 3 kitchen shelters (1 with electricity), picnic sites, boat launch, dock, boat rentals, hiking trails, bridle trails, playground, ballfields, game courts, camp store. **Activities:** Camping, boating, fishing, swimming, hiking, horseback riding, naturalist programs (seasonal). **Special Features:** Park is located in the foothills of the Cascade Mountains. Battle Ground Lake is of volcanic origin and is considered to be a smaller version of Crater Lake in Oregon. The area was named for a battle that was anticipated, but it never actually occurred.

★4541★ BAY VIEW STATE PARK
1093 Bayview Edison Rd
Mount Vernon, WA 98273
Web: www.parks.wa.gov/parkpage.asp?selectedpark=
Bay%20View
Phone: 360-757-0227; **Fax:** 360-757-1029
Size: 25 acres. **Location:** 7 miles west of Burlington, off Highway 20, on Padilla Bay. **Facilities:** 46 standard campsites, 30 utility campsites (with full hookups), group camp, 4 cabins, showers, picnic sites, picnic shelters, beach access, playground. **Activities:** Camping, boating, fishing, clamming, crabbing, swimming, windsurfing, waterskiing. **Special Features:** The

park offers views of the San Juan Islands fronting Padilla Bay, one of 15 existing national marine estuaries. On clear days, park users can see the Olympic Mountains to the west and Mount Ranier to the south.

★4542★ BEACON ROCK STATE PARK

34841 State Rd 14
Skamania, WA 98648
Web: www.parks.wa.gov/parkpage.asp?selectedpark=
   Beacon%20Rock
Phone: 509-427-8265; Fax: 509-427-3242
Size: 4,650 acres. Location: 35 miles east of Vancouver on State Route 14. Facilities: 29 standard campsites, group camp, 2 camp shelters, showers, picnic shelter, 2 kitchen shelters with electricity, hiking trails (9 miles), bike trails (13 miles), bridle trails (13 miles), beach access, boat launch, dock. Activities: Camping (including winter camping), boating, fishing, hiking, rock climbing, horseback riding, mountain biking. Special Features: Beacon Rock is the core of an ancient volcano. The ice-age floods through the Columbia River Gorge eroded the softer material away, leaving this unique geological structure standing by itself. Visitors can hike to the top of this massive rock formation, the world's second largest monolith, and view the Columbia River Gorge.

★4543★ BELFAIR STATE PARK

410 NE Beck Rd
Belfair, WA 98528
Web: www.parks.wa.gov/parkpage.asp?selectedpark=Belfair
Phone: 360-275-0668; Fax: 360-275-8734
Size: 63 acres. Location: 3 miles west of Belfair on State Route 300. Facilities: 137 standard campsites, 47 utility campsites (with full hookups), primitive campsite, bathhouse (&), picnic shelter, picnic areas, kitchen shelter, ballfield, game courts, playground. Activities: Camping, boating, fishing, swimming, beachcombing, kite flying, crabbing. Special Features: The swimming beach is in an enclosed manmade saltwater basin, controlled by a tide gate.

★4544★ BIRCH BAY STATE PARK

5105 Helwig Rd
Blaine, WA 98230
Web: www.parks.wa.gov/parkpage.asp?selectedpark=
   Birch%20Bay
Phone: 360-371-2800; Fax: 360-371-0455
Size: 194 acres. Location: 10 miles south of Blaine near the Canadian border. Facilities: 147 standard campsites, 20 utility sites, 2 group camps (5 with hookups), primitive group camp, bathhouse, kitchen shelter (with electricity), picnic shelters, picnic areas, trails, amphitheater, game courts. Activities: Camping, fishing, hiking, clamming, crabbing, bird watching, beachcombing. Special Features: Park has both freshwater and saltwater shorelines and offers panoramic views of the Cascade Mountains and the Canadian Gulf Islands.

★4545★ BLAKE ISLAND STATE PARK

PO Box 277
Manchester, WA 98353
Web: www.parks.wa.gov/parkpage.asp?selectedpark=
   Blake%20Island
Phone: 360-731-8330
Size: 476 acres. Location: In Puget Sound, 3 miles west of Seattle; accessible by boat only. Facilities: 51 primitive campsites, showers, group camp, primitive camp sites, picnic shelter, concession, snack bar (seasonal), hiking trail, biking trail, beach access, ball fields, game courts, boat moorage. Activities: Camping (including winter camping), fishing, hiking, scuba diving, clamming, crabbing, bird watching. Special Features: Tillicum Village, a concession on the island, offers Indian-style salmon dinners and Northwest Indian dancing.

★4546★ BOGACHIEL STATE PARK

185983 Hwy 101
Forks, WA 98331
Web: www.parks.wa.gov/parkpage.asp?selectedpark=
   Bogachiel
Phone: 360-374-6356
Size: 123 acres. Location: Northwest tip of state, 6 miles south of Forks. Facilities: 36 standard campsites, 6 utility campsites, group camp, bathhouse (&), picnic area. Activities: Camping (including winter camping), hiking, birdwatching. Special Features: Park is located on the tip of the Hoh Rainforest. Lush rainforest terrain is formed from the dense rainfall (140-160 inches per year) that occurs in this region.

★4547★ BRIDGEPORT STATE PARK

c/o Alta Lake State Park
40 Star Rt
Pateros, WA 98846
Web: www.parks.wa.gov/parkpage.asp?selectedpark=
   Bridgeport
Phone: 509-923-2473
Size: 748 acres. Location: 3 miles northeast of Bridgeport, off Highway 17, beside Lake Rufus Woods. Facilities: 14 standard campsites, 20 utility campsites, group camp, showers, picnic area, swimming area, boat launches, dock, 9-hole golf course, hiking trail. Activities: Camping, boating, fishing, swimming, water-skiing, windsurfing, golfing, hiking. Special Features: Park provides 18 acres of lawn and some shade in the midst of a desert terrain. ''Haystacks,'' unusual volcanic formations which resemble their name, are the park's most striking feature.

★4548★ BRIDLE TRAILS STATE PARK

c/o Lake Sammamish State Park
20606 SE 56th St
Issaquah, WA 98027
Web: www.parks.wa.gov/parkpage.asp?selectedpark=
   Bridle%20Trails
Phone: 425-455-7010
Size: 482 acres. Location: 3 miles northeast of Bellevue, off Exit 17 from I-405. Facilities: Hiking and bridle trails (28 miles), horse show arena (open to the public). Activities: Hiking, horseback riding. Special Features: Well-maintained horse

trails in a forest environment make this park a favorite among equestrians.

★4549★ BROOKS MEMORIAL STATE PARK
2465 Hwy 97
Goldendale, WA 98620
Web: www.parks.wa.gov/parkpage.asp?selectedpark=
Brooks%20Memorial
Phone: 509-773-4611
Size: 700 acres. **Location:** 13 miles north of Goldendale on Highway 97. **Facilities:** 22 standard campsites, 23 utility campsites, group camp, showers, 2 kitchen shelters with electricity, hiking trails, bike trails, game courts, ball fields, environmental learning center. **Activities:** Camping, fishing, hiking, biking, cross-country skiing, snowshoeing, naturalist programs. **Special Features:** Trails lead along the Little Klickitat River and through Ponderosa and Oregon Pine forests. At the top are open meadows with a panoramic view of Mount Hood.

★4550★ CAMANO ISLAND STATE PARK
2269 S Lowell Point Rd
Stanwood, WA 98292
Web: www.parks.wa.gov/parkpage.asp?selectedpark=
Camano%20Island
Phone: 360-387-3031
Size: 134 acres. **Location:** 14 miles southwest of Stanwood, off I-5 (Exit 212). **Facilities:** 88 standard campsites, group camp, picnic shelter, shelter, hiking trail, bike trail, ball fields, beach access, boat launch, amphitheater. **Activities:** Camping, boating, fishing, clamming, crabbing, swimming, windsurfing, water skiing, scuba diving, hiking, biking, bird watching. **Special Features:** During the last ice age, the area was covered by an ice sheet approximately one mile thick. The glacier carved the shape of the island with its high ''feeder banks'' that helped build the beaches.

★4551★ CAPE DISAPPOINTMENT STATE PARK
PO Box 488
Ilwaco, WA 98624
Web: www.parks.wa.gov/parkpage.asp?selectedpark=
Cape%20Disappointment
Phone: 360-642-3078
Size: 1,882 acres. **Location:** 2.5 miles southwest of Ilwaco. **Facilities:** 152 standard campsites, 83 utility campsites, 5 primitive campsites, cabins and yurts, showers (4 &), picnic areas, comfort stations, 2 boat launch, dock, interpretive center, hiking trails, 27 miles of ocean beach, 2 lighthouses, amphitheater, museum, game courts, ball fields, park store. **Activities:** Camping, boating, fishing, clamming, crabbing, hiking, beachcombing. **Special Features:** The Cape Disappointment Lighthouse was constructed in 1856 to warn seamen of the treacherous river bar known as the ''graveyard of the Pacific.'' It is the oldest functioning lighthouse on the West Coast.

★4552★ CENTENNIAL TRAIL STATE PARK
c/o Riverside State Park
9711 W Charles Rd
Nine Mile Falls, WA 99206
Web: www.parks.wa.gov/parkpage.asp?selectedpark=
Centennial%20Trail
Phone: 509-456-5065
Size: 372 acres. **Location:** Along the Spokane River, between Nine Mile Falls, WA, and the Idaho state border. **Facilities:** Paved trail (&), bike trail, kitchen shelter (with electric), picnic areas. **Activities:** Hiking, jogging, bicycling, in-line skating, horseback riding (some sections), fishing, swimming, cross-country skiing, snowshoeing. **Special Features:** Several interpretive signs mark the trail for spots of historic and archeological interest. As most significant sites are still unmarked, more signage is planned for the future. Jointly managed by Washington State Parks, Spokane County, and the cities of Spokane and Liberty Lake.

★4553★ COLUMBIA HILLS STATE PARK
PO Box 426
Dallesport, WA 98617
Web: www.parks.wa.gov/parkpage.asp?selectedpark=
Columbia%20Hills
Phone: 509-767-1159
Size: 3,338 acres. **Location:** On the Columbia River on the state's southern border. **Facilities:** 12 standard campsites, 2 primitive campsites, picnic areas, beach access, 2 boat launches, hiking trails, game courts. **Activities:** Camping, boating, fishing, rock climbing, hiking, swimming, windsurfing. **Special Features:** Site of some of the oldest pictographs in the northwest and one of the largest burial grounds of Native Americans in the area.

★4554★ COLUMBIA PLATEAU TRAIL STATE PARK
100 SW Main St
Washtucna, WA 99371
Web: www.parks.wa.gov/parkpage.asp?selectedpark=
Columbia+Plateau+Trail
Phone: 509-235-4696
Size: 4,109 acres. **Location:** In the east central part of the state, between Cheney and East Pasco. **Facilities:** Trail (& in places), mile markers, interpretive signs, restrooms (&), picnic areas (&). **Activities:** Hiking, jogging, bicycling, horseback riding, nature viewing, cross-country skiing, snowshoeing. **Special Features:** Park is a 130-mile-long rail-bed trail that traces the 1908 path of the Spokane, Portland, and Seattle Railroad. Twenty-three miles of the trail between Lincoln County and Cheney are developed and open for public use.

★4555★ CONCONULLY STATE PARK
PO Box 95
Conconully, WA 98819
Web: www.parks.wa.gov/parkpage.asp?selectedpark=
Conconully
Phone: 509-826-7408
Size: 81 acres. **Location:** North-central part of the state, 22 miles northwest of Omak on Highway 97. **Facilities:** 82 tent

spaces, 4 restrooms (1 ♿), 4 showers (1 ♿), kitchen shelter (with electricity), nature trail, bike trail, 2 boat launch ramps, dock, horseshoe pits. **Activities:** Camping, boating, fishing, hiking, mountain biking, personal watercraft, water-skiing, wildlife viewing, cross-country skiing, dog sledding, snowmobiling, snowshoeing. **Special Features:** Conconully was a silver-mining town that was washed away by a flood in 1894. An early schoolhouse and a replica of the town's first courthouse are still in place on park grounds.

★4556★ CRAWFORD STATE PARK

c/o Mount Spokane State Park
N 26107 Mt Spokane Park Dr
Mead, WA 99021
Web: www.parks.wa.gov/parkpage.asp?selectedpark=
    Crawford
Phone: 509-446-4065
Size: 49 acres. **Location:** 11 miles northwest of Metaline Falls, in the extreme northeastern corner of the state. **Facilities:** Picnic tables, picnic shelters, kitchen shelter. **Activities:** Guided cave tours, offered daily during the summer. **Special Features:** Park features Gardner Cave, the third longest limestone cave in the state.

★4557★ CURLEW LAKE STATE PARK

974 Curlew Lake State Park Rd
Republic, WA 99166
Web: www.parks.wa.gov/parkpage.asp?selectedpark=
    Curlew%20Lake
Phone: 509-775-3592
Size: 123 acres. **Location:** 8 miles north of Republic in northeastern portion of state. **Facilities:** 57 standard campsites, 25 utility campsites, 2 primitive campsites, showers, picnic areas, beach access, boat launch, dock, hiking trails, bike trails, amphitheater. **Activities:** Camping, boating, fishing, hiking, biking, water-skiing, swimming. **Special Features:** An area of the park was once a summer camp for some of the regional Indian tribes. In one section an indigenous pestle was found; in another, discarded shells of freshwater clams lie close by an ancient fire ring.

★4558★ DAMON POINT STATE PARK

c/o Ocean City State Park
148 State Rt 115
Hoquiam, WA 98550
Web: www.parks.wa.gov/parkpage.asp?selectedpark=
    Damon%20Point
Phone: 360-289-3553
Size: 61 acres. **Location:** At the southeastern tip of the Ocean Shores Peninsula, 25 miles from Hoquiam. **Facilities:** 5 picnic sites, trail. **Activities:** Boating, fishing, clamming, crabbing, beachcombing, rock collecting, wildlife observation. **Special Features:** Park is an excellent example of accreted land. (Accretion is the opposite of erosion and occurs when sand accumulates over the years, forming land where there was none.)

★4559★ DAROGA STATE PARK

1 S Daroga Park Rd
Orondo, WA 98843
Web: www.parks.wa.gov/parkpage.asp?selectedpark=Daroga
Phone: 509-664-6380
Size: 90 acres. **Location:** 18 miles north of Wenatchee on the east side of the Columbia River. **Facilities:** 28 utility campsites, 17 primitive campsites, 2 group camps, 12 showers (6 ♿), kitchen shelter (with water and electric), picnic areas, swimming area, boat launch, docks, playfields. **Activities:** Camping, boating, fishing, swimming, water-skiing, golf, wildlife observation. **Special Features:** Park is located along 1.5 miles of Columbia River shoreline on the elevated edge of the desert "scablands." Nationally recognized Desert Canyon Golf Course is just two miles away.

★4560★ DASH POINT STATE PARK

5700 SW Dash Point Rd
Federal Way, WA 98023
Web: www.parks.wa.gov/parkpage.asp?selectedpark=
    Dash%20Point
Phone: 253-661-4955; **Fax:** 253-661-4995; **Toll Free:** 888-226-7688
Size: 398 acres. **Location:** On the west side of Federal Way, near Seattle. **Facilities:** 114 standard campsites, 27 utility campsites, group camp, showers, picnic shelters, picnic areas, hiking and biking trails (11 miles), beach access, amphitheater. **Activities:** Camping, boating, fishing, hiking, biking, beachcombing, windsurfing, swimming, interpretive programs, wildlife observation. **Special Features:** Park features 3,301 feet of saltwater shoreline and provides unobstructed views of Puget Sound and excellent opportunities for sea-life study.

★4561★ DECEPTION PASS STATE PARK

41229 State Rt 20
Oak Harbor, WA 98277
Web: www.parks.wa.gov/parkpage.asp?selectedpark=
    Deception%20Pass
Phone: 360-675-2417; **Fax:** 360-675-8991
Size: 4,134 acres. **Location:** 9 miles north of Oak Harbor on Whidbey Island in Puget Sound. **Facilities:** 167 standard campsites, 143 utility campsites, 5 primitive campsites, 3 group camps, 6 showers (4 ♿), picnic areas, picnic shelters, 10 kitchen shelters (4 with electricity), hiking trails (38 miles), horse trails (6 miles), freshwater and saltwater shoreline, swimming area, boat rentals, boat launch, dock, moorage, 2 amphitheaters, museum, environmental learning center, concessions, park store, game courts, observation deck. **Activities:** Camping, boating, fishing, swimming, windsurfing, white-water kayaking, scuba diving, clamming, crabbing, hiking, biking, horseback riding. **Special Features:** During his Northwest coastal explorations, Captain Vancouver realized he'd mistaken an island for a peninsula, so he named the island Whidbey and the inlet in which he was anchored Deception Pass, to commemorate the error. His assistant, Joseph Whidbey, was at his side when he made the mistake, and the island was named in his honor.

★4562★ DOSEWALLIPS STATE PARK
PO Drawer K
Brinnon, WA 98320
Web: www.parks.wa.gov/parkpage.asp?selectedpark=
Dosewallips
Phone: 360-796-4415
Size: 425 acres. **Location:** On the shore Hood Canal on the state's western side. **Facilities:** 100 standard campsites, 40 utility campsites, group camp, 4 primitive campsites, 2 showers (1 &), kitchen shelter, picnic shelters, hiking trail, bike trail, amphitheater, game courts, boat ramp. **Activities:** Camping, boating, fishing, clamming, crabbing, wildlife watching, hking, biking, swimming, scuba diving, beachcombing, mushrooming. **Special Features:** Old rail beds can be found at the park where logs were hauled from the mountains down to the water before being floated to ships and mills around Puget Sound.

★4563★ DOUG'S BEACH STATE PARK
c/o Maryhill State Park
50 Hwy 97
Goldendale, WA 98620
Web: www.parks.wa.gov/parkpage.asp?selectedpark=
Doug%27s%20Beach
Phone: 509-773-5007
Size: 400 acres. **Location:** 7 miles west of Horsethief Lake State Park (see separate entry), near Lyle, on State Route 14. **Facilities:** Picnic areas, portable toilets. **Activities:** Fishing, windsurfing. **Special Features:** This undeveloped day-use park on the Columbia River is one of the premier windsurfing sites in the Columbia Gorge and is rated for advanced sailors.

★4564★ FAY BAINBRIDGE STATE PARK
15446 Sunrise Dr NE
Bainbridge Island, WA 98110
Web: www.parks.wa.gov/parkpage.asp?selectedpark=
Fay%20Bainbridge
Phone: 206-842-3931
Size: 17 acres. **Location:** At the northeastern end of Bainbridge Island. **Facilities:** 26 utility campsites (with water), 10 primitive campsites, showers, 2 kitchen shelters (with electricity), picnic shelters, picnic areas, beach access, boat launch, moorage, game courts. **Activities:** Camping, boating, fishing, clamming, crabbing, swimming, waterskiing, scuba diving. **Special Features:** Park offers scenic views of Puget Sound, the Cascade Range, and the Seattle metropolitan area.

★4565★ FEDERATION FOREST STATE PARK
49201 Enumclaw-Chinook Pass Rd
Enumclaw, WA 98022
Web: www.parks.wa.gov/parkpage.asp?selectedpark=
Federation%20Forest
Phone: 360-663-2207
Size: 619 acres. **Location:** 18 miles southeast of Enumclaw, off Highway 410, on the banks of the White River. **Facilities:** Picnic shelter, picnic areas, hiking trails, nature trails, interpretive center, gift shop, amphitheater. **Activities:** Fishing, hiking, interpretive programs. **Special Features:** Gardens in front of

the park's interpretive center highlight plants from six of the nine biosystems in the state of Washington.

★4566★ FIELDS SPRING STATE PARK
PO Box 37
Anatone, WA 99401
Web: www.parks.wa.gov/parkpage.asp?selectedpark=
Fields%20Spring
Phone: 509-256-3332
Size: 792 acres. **Location:** In the Blue Mountains on the southeastern tip of the state, 30 miles south of Clarkston. **Facilities:** 20 standard campsites, 2 teepees, showers, picnic shelter, 2 kitchen shelters (with electricity), picnic areas, hiking trails, bike trails, game courts, ball fields, 2 environmental learning centers (group rental facilities). **Activities:** Camping, hiking, biking, hang gliding, cross-country skiing, snowshoeing, bird watching. **Special Features:** A one-mile hike up 4,500-foot Puffer Butte affords views of Idaho, Oregon, Washington, Wallowa Mountains, and Grande Ronde and Snake River basins. Park features more than 150 species of wildflowers.

★4567★ FLAMING GEYSER STATE PARK
23700 SE Flaming Geyser Rd
Auburn, WA 98092
Web: www.parks.wa.gov/parkpage.asp?selectedpark=
Flaming%20Geyser
Phone: 253-931-3930
Size: 480 acres. **Location:** 2.5 miles south of Black Diamond and 8 miles north of Enumclaw. **Facilities:** Picnic areas and shelters, 6 kitchen shelters, horseshoe pits, volleyball courts, hiking trails, bike trails, horse trails, game courts, ball fields, model airplane flying area. **Activities:** Kayaking, fishing, river rafting, tube floating, swimming, bird watching, interpretive walks, hiking, biking, model airplane flying. **Special Features:** Flaming Geyser derives its name from the seepage of methane gas from an old test core bored into the rock where coal was once mined. When ignited, the gas creates a small torch flame in a rock pit. Area is part of Green River Gorge State Park conservation area.

★4568★ FORT CASEY STATE PARK
1280 S Fort Casey Rd
Coupeville, WA 98239
Web: www.parks.wa.gov/parkpage.asp?selectedpark=
Fort%20Casey
Phone: 360-678-4519
Size: 467 acres. **Location:** 3 miles south of Coupeville, on Whidbey Island. **Facilities:** 35 standard campsites, shower, picnic areas, hiking trails, boat launches, interpretive center, lighthouse, amphitheater. **Activities:** Camping, boating, fishing, scuba diving, beachcombing, hiking, kite flying, remote controlled glider flying. **Special Features:** Park features a lighthouse and sweeping views of Admiralty Inlet and the Strait of Juan de Fuca, and a coast artillery post has two historic guns on display. The Admiralty Head Lighthouse at Fort Casey serves both as a historic landmark and as interpretive center.

9. State Parks

★4569★ FORT COLUMBIA STATE PARK

PO Box 488
Chinook, WA 98614
Web: www.parks.wa.gov/parkpage.asp?selectedpark=
Fort%20Columbia
Phone: 360-642-3078
Size: 593 acres. Location: 2 miles southeast of Chinook on Highway 101. Facilities: Picnic areas, hiking trails, museum, observation stations, interpretive centers, historic features. Activities: Hiking, sightseeing. Special Features: Fort Columbia was built to support the defenses of the Columbia River and is one of the few intact coastal defense sites in the U.S. It was constructed on the Chinook Point promontory because of the unobstructed view. Declared surplus after World War II, it was transferred to the state and has been a state park ever since. Twelve historic wood-frame buildings still stand on the site.

★4570★ FORT EBEY STATE PARK

395 N Fort Ebey Rd
Coupeville, WA 98239
Web: www.parks.wa.gov/parkpage.asp?selectedpark=
Fort%20Ebey
Phone: 360-678-4636
Size: 645 acres. Location: 8 miles south of Oak Harbor, off Highway 20. Facilities: 40 standard campsites, 10 utility campsites, 2 showers (1 ♿), group camp, picnic areas, picnic shelters, hiking trails, bike trails, ball fields, game courts, historic features. Activities: Camping, fishing, hiking, biking, paragliding, surfing, beachcombing. Special Features: The area around the park is known for its ''kettles,'' large depressions left in the earth by receding glaciers 15,000 years ago. Park stands on the site of a World War II gun battery, which had two six-inch guns in place during the war. Concrete bunkers are available for exploration.

★4571★ FORT FLAGLER STATE PARK

10541 Flagler Rd
Nordland, WA 98358
Web: www.parks.wa.gov/parkpage.asp?selectedpark=
Fort%20Flagler
Phone: 360-385-1259
Size: 784 acres. Location: On Marrowstone Island, 8 miles northeast of Hadlock. Facilities: 101 standard campsites, 14 utility campsites, 2 primitive campsites, 8 showers (4 ♿), picnic shelter, picnic areas, kitchen shelter, hiking trails, bike trails, park store, beach access, boat launch, dock, moorage, museum, environmental learning center. Activities: Camping, hiking, biking, swimming, water skiing, boating, fishing, clamming, crabbing. Special Features: Park is situated on a high bluff overlooking Puget Sound, with views of the Olympic and Cascade Mountains. The park is surrounded on three sides by more than 19,000 feet of saltwater shoreline.

★4572★ FORT OKANOGAN STATE PARK

c/o Alta Lake State Park
40 Star Rt
Pateros, WA 98846
Web: www.parks.wa.gov/parkpage.asp?selectedpark=
Fort%20Okanogan
Phone: 509-923-2473

Size: 45 acres. Location: Located 4 miles northeast of Brewster, on a bluff overlooking the Columbia River. Facilities: Picnic shelter, picnic area, restroom (♿), interpretive center, museum. Special Features: Park's interpretive center provides displays and information on one of the first settlements in Washington and the fur-trapping history of the area.

★4573★ FORT SIMCOE STATE PARK

5150 Fort Simcoe Rd
White Swan, WA 98952
Web: www.parks.wa.gov/parkpage.asp?selectedpark=
Fort%20Simcoe
Phone: 509-874-2372
Size: 200 acres. Location: 30 miles west of Toppenish on Highway 220. Facilities: Picnic shelter, interpretive center, hiking trail, historical sites, museum, game courts, ball fields. Activities: Hiking, sightseeing, wildlife observation. Special Features: Fort Simcoe was an 1850s-era military installation established to keep peace between the settlers and the Indians. Five original buildings are still standing at the fort; various others have been recreated. Some of the buildings are open to the public.

★4574★ FORT WARD STATE PARK

c/o Fay Bainbridge State Park
15446 Sunrise Dr NE
Bainbridge Island, WA 98118
Web: www.parks.wa.gov/parkpage.asp?selectedpark=
Fort%20Ward
Phone: 206-842-3931
Size: 137 acres. Location: Southwest of Winslow on Bainbridge Island, 6 miles from Winslow Ferry. Facilities: Picnic area, underwater park, boat launch, hiking trail. Activities: Boating, fishing, hiking, crabbing, water skiing, scuba diving, beachcombing, windsurfing. Special Features: Fort was built by the U.S. Army Corps of Engineers at the turn of the century to protect the entrance to the Bremerton Naval Shipyard. Two gun batteries are located in the park.

★4575★ FORT WORDEN STATE PARK

200 Battery Way
Port Townsend, WA 98368
Web: www.parks.wa.gov/parkpage.asp?selectedpark=
Fort%20Worden
Phone: 360-385-4730
Size: 433 acres. Location: At the northern limits of Port Townsend. Facilities: 50 utility campsites, 30 standard campsites, picnic areas, housing and conference facilities, snack bar, beach access, boat launch, dock, 9 mooring buoys, hiking trails (12 miles; 5 miles ♿), bike trails (12 miles), amphitheater, ball fields, game courts, museum. Activities: Camping, fishing, boating, scuba diving, hiking, biking, swimming, water skiing, crabbing, kite flying, tennis. Special Features: Park houses the Port Townsend Marine Science Center (featuring saltwater aquariums, touch pools, and exhibits) and the 248th Coast Artillery Museum, both operated by private organizations.

9. State Parks

★4576★ GINKGO PETRIFIED FOREST STATE PARK
PO Box 1203
Vantage, WA 98950
Web: www.parks.wa.gov/alpha.asp
Phone: 509-856-2700
Size: 7,470 acres. **Location:** 29 miles east of Ellensburg, on the Columbia River. **Facilities:** 50 utility campsites, picnic sites, shoreline, boat launch, museum, gift shop, interpretive center, hiking trails. **Activities:** Camping, boating, fishing, swimming, water-skiing, hiking. **Special Features:** Park was set aside as a historic preserve when remains of a fossil forest were unearthed during construction in the 1930s. Petrified wood from many different trees is common, but specimens of petrified Ginkgo are rare. Park is a National Natural Landmark, and is regarded as one of the most unusual fossil forests in the world.

★4577★ GOLDENDALE OBSERVATORY STATE PARK
1602 Observatory Dr
Goldendale, WA 98620
Web: www.parks.wa.gov/parkpage.asp?selectedpark=
Goldendale%20Observatory
Phone: 509-773-3141
Size: 5 acres. **Location:** 1 mile north of Goldendale. **Facilities:** Interpretive center, amphitheater, picnic area. **Activities:** Hands-on observing through telescopes, lectures, tours, special programs. **Special Features:** The interpretive center houses the nation's largest public telescope, a 24.5-inch reflecting telescope.

★4578★ GRAYLAND BEACH STATE PARK
c/o Twin Harbors State Park
Hwy 105
Westport, WA 98595
Web: www.parks.wa.gov/parkpage.asp?selectedpark=
Grayland%20Beach
Phone: 360-268-9717
Size: 412 acres. **Location:** On the western coast of the state, 5 miles south of Westport. **Facilities:** 60 utility campsites, 4 standard campites, 3 primitive campsites, 10 yurts, 8 showers, interpretive trail. **Activities:** Camping, hiking, fishing, clamming, crabbing, beachcombing, kite flying. **Special Features:** Grayland received its name from Captain Robert Gray, the American explorer who, in 1792, discovered the harbors now named for him.

★4579★ GRIFFITHS-PRIDAY OCEAN STATE PARK
PO Box 42650
Olympia, WA 98504
Web: www.parks.wa.gov/parkpage.asp?selectedpark=
Griffiths%2DPriday
Phone: 360-902-8500
Size: 364 acres. **Location:** 21 miles northwest of Hoquiam, Washington, on the coast of the Pacific Ocean. **Facilities:** Picnic area, kitchen shelter (with electricity), beach access, play area, rest rooms. **Activities:** Fishing, clamming, horseback riding, bird watching, beachcombing, mountain biking. **Special Features:** Encompassing the area from the beach through the dunes to the Copalis River, this park contains both saltwater and freshwater shoreline. Included is Copalis Spit Natural Area, a designated wildlife refuge.

★4580★ HOPE ISLAND STATE PARK
c/o Jarrell Cove State Park
E 391 Wingert Rd
Shelton, WA 98584
Web: www.parks.wa.gov/parkpage.asp?selectedpark=
Hope+Island+%28Mason%29
Phone: 360-426-9226
Size: 106 acres. **Location:** Between Steamboat Island and the southwestern end of Squaxin Island; accessible by boat only. **Facilities:** Cabin, pit toilet, picnic area, trail, mooring buoys. **Activities:** Fishing, clamming, beachcombing. **Special Features:** Day-use park includes a historical heritage orchard.

★4581★ IKE KINSWA STATE PARK
873 SR 122
Silver Creek, WA 98585
Web: www.parks.wa.gov/parkpage.asp?selectedpark=
Ike%20Kinswa
Phone: 360-983-3402
Size: 454 acres. **Location:** On Mayfield Lake, off Highway 12. **Facilities:** 62 standard campsites, 41 utility campsites, showers, picnic areas, play area, game courts, swimming beach, boat launches, dock, hiking trails, bike trails. **Activities:** Camping, boating, fishing, swimming, water-skiing, hiking, biking, wind surfing. **Special Features:** Park was renamed in 1971 to honor Native American Ike Kinswa, both as an individual and as a representative of the original inhabitants of the area, the Cowlitz Indians.

★4582★ ILLAHEE STATE PARK
3540 Bahia Vista
Bremerton, WA 98310
Web: www.parks.wa.gov/parkpage.asp?selectedpark=Illahee
Phone: 360-478-6460
Size: 75 acres. **Location:** 3 miles northeast of Bremerton, on the Kitsap Peninsula. **Facilities:** 62 standard campsites, 41 utility campsites, showers, picnic areas, play area, game courts, swimming beach, boat launches, dock, hiking trails, bike trails. **Activities:** Camping, boating, fishing, clamming, crabbing, oyster gathering, swimming, water-skiing, beachcombing. **Special Features:** The park features a veterans' war memorial and the last stand of old-growth timber in Kitsap County. One of the largest yew trees in the nation grows here.

★4583★ IRON HORSE STATE PARK
c/o Ginkgo Petrified Forest State Park
PO Box 1203
Vantage, WA 98950
Web: www.parks.wa.gov/parkpage.asp?selectedpark=
Iron%20Horse%20Trail
Phone: 509-856-2700
Size: 1,612 acres. **Location:** In Easton, off I-90. **Facilities:** Trail (110 miles), 4 campgrounds, vault toilets, picnic area.

9. State Parks

Activities: Fishing, hiking, horseback riding, bicycling, rock climbing, cross-country skiing, dog sledding, snowmobiling. **Special Features:** Park was once part of the path of the Chicago-Milwaukee-St Paul-Pacific Railroad. More than 100 miles of trail extends from Cedar Falls to the Columbia River. It passes over 30 trestles and through 4 tunnels, one of which is 2.3 miles long. Along its course, the trail descends from 3,100 feet to 1,500 feet, but the grade does not exceed 2 percent. Also known as the John Wayne Pioneer Trail.

★4584★ JARRELL COVE STATE PARK

E 391 Wingert Rd
Shelton, WA 98584
Web: www.parks.wa.gov/parkpage.asp?selectedpark=
    Jarrell%20Cove
Phone: 360-426-9226
Size: 43 acres. **Location:** At the northwest end of Harstine Island, in south Puget Sound. **Facilities:** 22 tent sites (1 ♿), group camp, picnic sites, shower, 2 picnic shelters, 2 kitchen shelters, dock, moorage piers, hiking trail, bike trail, ball field. **Activities:** Camping, hiking, biking, boating, fishing, clamming, crabbing, swimming, water skiing, scuba diving, beachcombing. **Special Features:** Forested island is accessible by both road and bridge and is off the beaten path. Most visitors arrive by boat.

★4585★ JOEMMA BEACH STATE PARK

PO Box 898
Lakebay, WA 98349
Web: www.parks.wa.gov/parkpage.asp?selectedpark=
    Joemma%20Beach
Phone: 253-884-1944
Size: 122 acres. **Location:** 28 miles southwest of Tacoma, Washington. **Facilities:** 19 campsites, 2 canoe trail campsites, 3 primitive campsites, picnic areas, picnic shelter, trails, vault toilets, boat launch. **Activities:** Camping, boating, canoeing, kayaking, fishing, clamming, crabbing, water skiing, beachcombing. **Special Features:** Park features 3,000 feet of saltwater frontage on southeastern Key Peninsula.

★4586★ JOSEPH WHIDBEY STATE PARK

PO Box 42650
Olympia, WA 89504
Web: www.parks.wa.gov/parkpage.asp?selectedpark=
    Joseph%20Whidbey
Phone: 360-902-8500
Size: 112 acres. **Location:** 3 miles west of Oak Harbor on Swantown Road. **Facilities:** 1 canoe trail campsite, beach access, kitchen shelter, picnic area, picnic shelter, hiking trails (♿), bike trail, ball fields. **Activities:** Canoeing, hiking, beachcombing. **Special Features:** Park features one mile of sandy beach on Puget Sound.

★4587★ KANASKAT-PALMER STATE PARK

32101 Kanaskat-Cumberland Rd
Ravensdale, WA 98051
Web: www.parks.wa.gov/parkpage.asp?selectedpark=
    Kanaskat%2DPalmer
Phone: 360-886-0148
Size: 320 acres. **Location:** 11 miles northeast of Enumclaw on the Green River. **Facilities:** 31 standard campsites, 19 utility campsites, group camp (2 sleep shelters), 6 showers (4 ♿), picnic shelters, picnic area, kitchen shelter (with electricity), beach access, hiking trail. **Activities:** Camping, fishing, hiking, mountain biking, swimming, kayaking, river rafting. **Special Features:** Park has two miles of shoreline on the Green River. River rafting and kayaking down the Green River Gorge is available, but is for expert-level enthusiasts only.

★4588★ KITSAP MEMORIAL STATE PARK

202 NE Park St
Poulsbo, WA 98370
Web: www.parks.wa.gov/parkpage.asp?selectedpark=
    Kitsap%20Memorial
Phone: 360-779-3205
Size: 58 acres. **Location:** 4 miles south of Hood Canal Bridge. **Facilities:** 28 standard campsites, 18 utility campsites, cabin, shower, picnic shelter, picnic area, kitchen shelter (with electricity), beach access, moorage, soccer field, volleyball court, hiking trail. **Activities:** Camping, boating, fishing, clamming, crabbing, oyster gathering, hiking, swimming, scuba diving. **Special Features:** Park features a log hall that sits atop a wooded bluff, providing spectacular views of Hood Canal and the snowcapped Olympic Mountains.

★4589★ KOPACHUCK STATE PARK

11101 56th St NW
Gig Harbor, WA 98335
Web: www.parks.wa.gov/parkpage.asp?selectedpark=
    Kopachuck
Phone: 253-265-3606
Size: 109 acres. **Location:** 5 miles west of Gig Harbor on Puget Sound. **Facilities:** 41 standard campsites, 2 primitive campsites, showers, picnic shelter, picnic areas, 4 kitchen shelters (with electricity), beach access, hiking trail. **Activities:** Camping, fishing, clamming (year round), crabbing, hiking, boating, swimming, water skiing, scuba diving, beachcombing, bird watching, naturalist programs (seasonal). **Special Features:** The park provides numerous trails, some with views of Henderson Bay and the Olympic Mountains.

★4590★ LAKE CHELAN STATE PARK

7544 S Lakeshore Dr
Chelan, WA 98816
Web: www.parks.wa.gov/parkpage.asp?selectedpark=
    Lake%20Chelan
Phone: 509-687-3710
Size: 127 acres. **Location:** 9 miles west of Chelan. **Facilities:** 109 standard campsites, 35 utility campsites, 5 showers, kitchen shelter, picnic areas, playground, beach access, boat launch, dock, water ski floats. **Activities:** Camping, boating, fishing, swimming, water-skiing, windsurfing. **Special Features:** The lake was carved by two competing glaciers, the Chelan Glacier and the continental ice sheet. Their back-and-forth movement created the broad lower lake and narrow upper lake.

9. State Parks

★4591★ LAKE EASTON STATE PARK
PO Box 26
Easton, WA 98925
Web: www.parks.wa.gov/parkpage.asp?selectedpark=
Lake%20Easton
Phone: 509-656-2230
Size: 516 acres. **Location:** 15 miles east of Snoqualmie Pass, Washington. **Facilities:** 95 standard campsites, 45 utility campsites, 8 group camps, 4 restrooms (3 &), 4 showers (2 &), picnic area, hiking trails, bike trails, playground, boat launch, dock, game courts, amphitheater. **Activities:** Camping, boating, fishing, swimming, hiking, biking, cross-country skiing, snowmobiling, dog sledding, interpretive programs (seasonal). **Special Features:** Park is on the Yakima River and Lake Easton, with 24,000 feet of lakeshore access.

★4592★ LAKE SAMMAMISH STATE PARK
20606 SE 56th St
Issaquah, WA 98027
Web: www.parks.wa.gov/parkpage.asp?selectedpark=
Lake%20Sammamish
Phone: 425-455-7010
Size: 512 acres. **Location:** On the south end of Lake Sammamish, bordering the city of Issaquah. **Facilities:** Picnic area and picnic shelter, kitchen shelters (with electricity), bathhouses, boat rentals, swimming area, boat launch, dock, ball fields, hiking trails, bike trails. **Activities:** Boating, kayaking, fishing, hiking, biking, swimming, water-skiing, bird watching. **Special Features:** Park includes diverse natural wetlands, a great blue heron rookery, and the salmon-bearing Issaquah Creek, as well as one of the largest freshwater beaches in the Seattle area.

★4593★ LAKE SYLVIA STATE PARK
PO Box 701
Montesano, WA 98563
Web: www.parks.wa.gov/parkpage.asp?selectedpark=
Lake%20Sylvia
Phone: 360-249-3621
Size: 233 acres. **Location:** 1 mile north of Montesano off Highway 12. **Facilities:** 35 standard campsites, 2 primitive campsites, group camp, 6 showers (4 &), picnic areas, picnic shelter, kitchen shelter, swimming area, boat launch, hiking trail (&), **Activities:** Camping, boating, fishing, swimming, hiking, mountain biking, bird watching. **Special Features:** Park is located at an old logging camp and has interesting displays of old logging gear and curiosities.

★4594★ LAKE WENATCHEE STATE PARK
21588 A Hwy 207
Leavenworth, WA 98826
Web: www.parks.wa.gov/parkpage.asp?selectedpark=
Lake%20Wenatchee
Phone: 509-763-3101
Size: 489 acres. **Location:** 18 miles northwest of Leavenworth on Highway 207. **Facilities:** 155 standard campsites, 42 utility campsites, group camp, 2 accessible campsites, 7 restrooms, 16 showers, picnic areas, kitchen shelters, concession, bridle trails, horse rentals, stable, shoreline, boat launch, dock, sledding hills, cross-country ski trails, snowshoe trails, hiking trails, bike trails, amphitheater. **Activities:** Camping, kayaking, canoeing, fishing, hiking, biking, swimming, beachcombing, wind surfing, water skiing, whitewater kayaking, rock climbing, horseback riding, cross-country skiing, snowmobiling, dog sledding, snowmobiling, ice climbing. **Special Features:** Park features 12,623 feet of waterfront on glacier-fed Lake Wenatchee and the Wenatchee River. It is bisected by the river, creating two distinct areas—South Park, with recreation areas, and North Park, a less developed, forested section.

★4595★ LARRABEE STATE PARK
245 Chuckanut Dr
Bellingham, WA 98226
Web: www.parks.wa.gov/parkpage.asp?selectedpark=Larrabee
Phone: 360-676-2093
Size: 2,683 acres. **Location:** 6 miles south of Bellingham, on Samish Bay in Puget Sound. **Facilities:** 51 standard campsites, 26 utility campsites, 8 primitive campsites, group camp, 8 showers (&), 2 picnic shelters (with electricity), picnic area, beach access, boat launch, hiking trail, bike trail, amphitheater. **Activities:** Camping, boating, fishing, clamming, crabbing, hiking, biking, scuba diving, beachcombing, windsurfing, birdwatching. **Special Features:** Park includes two freshwater lakes, coves and tidelands, and 15 miles of foot trails, including two trails to mountain lakes.

★4596★ LEWIS & CLARK STATE PARK
4583 Jackson Hwy
Winlock, WA 98596
Web: www.parks.wa.gov/parkpage.asp?selectedpark=
Lewis%20%26%20Clark
Phone: 360-864-2643
Size: 621 acres. **Location:** 12 miles southeast of Chehalis. **Facilities:** 25 standard campsites, 2 group camps, lodge, 2 showers, picnic areas, 2 kitchen shelters (with electricity), horse trail (5 miles), hiking trails (8 miles), amphitheater, game courts, environmental learning center. **Activities:** Camping, hiking, horseback riding. **Special Features:** Park contains one of the Pacific Northwest's last stands of lowland old growth forest, and a great view of the crater of Mount Saint Helens. A self-guided half-mile interpretive trail features information on the forest.

★4597★ LEWIS & CLARK TRAIL STATE PARK
36149 Hwy 12
Dayton, WA 99328
Web: www.parks.wa.gov/alpha.asp
Phone: 509-337-6457
Size: 37 acres. **Location:** 25 miles northeast of Walla Walla in the southeast corner of state. **Facilities:** 24 standard campsites, 17 primitive campsites, 2 group camps, 2 showers, picnic shelter, kitchen shelter (with electricity), beach access, amphitheater, ball fields, hiking trails. **Activities:** Camping, fishing, hiking, swimming, tubing, cross-country skiing, snowshoeing, campfire programs (seasonal), living history demonstrations. **Special Features:** The day-use area restroom was constructed in 1934 from 10,000 stones acquired from the Touchet River.

9. State Parks

★4598★ **LIME KILN POINT STATE PARK**
1567 Westside Rd
Friday Harbor, WA 98250
Web: www.parks.wa.gov/parkpage.asp?selectedpark=
Lime%20Kiln%20Point
Phone: 360-378-2044
Size: 36 acres. **Location:** West end of San Juan Island on east bank of the Columbia River. **Facilities:** 12 picnic areas (1 &), restrooms, trails, lighthouse, guided tours. **Activities:** Whale watching, hiking, fishing, scuba diving, naturalist programs (seasonal), beachcombing. **Special Features:** Whales and other sea mammals can be sighted from viewing platforms.

★4599★ **LINCOLN ROCK STATE PARK**
13253 State Rt 2
East Wenatchee, WA 98802
Web: www.parks.wa.gov/parkpage.asp?selectedpark=
Lincoln%20Rock
Phone: 509-884-8702
Size: 80 acres. **Location:** 7 miles north of Wenatchee on Highway 2. **Facilities:** 27 standard campsites, 67 utility campsites, 3 kitchen shelters (with electricity), 14 showers (3 &), picnic area, picnic shelters, hiking trail, bike trail, swimming area, boat launch, dock, moorage, tennis courts, ball fields, amphitheater, playground. **Activities:** Camping, boating, fishing, swimming, water-skiing, hiking, biking, paragliding. **Special Features:** Park is named for a prominent geological feature said to look like a profile of Abraham Lincoln.

★4600★ **MANCHESTER STATE PARK**
PO Box 338
Manchester, WA 98353
Web: www.parks.wa.gov/parkpage.asp?selectedpark=
Manchester
Phone: 360-871-4065
Size: 111 acres. **Location:** 6 miles east of Port Orchard. **Facilities:** 35 standard campsites, 15 utility campsites, 3 hiker campsites, group camp, 2 showers, 3 picnic shelters, picnic area, shoreline, hiking trail, ball field. **Activities:** Camping, boating, fishing, scuba diving, hiking. **Special Features:** Park was originally constructed as a US Coast Guard Artillery harbor installation for the defense of Bremerton. One of the park's picnic shelters was originally a torpedo warehouse built in 1901, and the small concrete building to its east was originally used as a mining casement, then for coal storage. A gun battery also remains. All three structures are on the register of National Historical Monuments.

★4601★ **MARYHILL STATE PARK**
50 Hwy 97
Goldendale, WA 98620
Web: www.parks.wa.gov/parkpage.asp?selectedpark=Maryhill
Phone: 509-773-5007
Size: 99 acres. **Location:** 12 miles south of Goldendale on State Route 97. **Facilities:** 50 utility campsites, 2 standard campsites, group camp, 10 showers (2 &), 2 kitchen shelters, beach access, boat launch, dock. **Activities:** Camping, boating, fishing, hiking, beachcombing, swimming, windsurfing, water-skiing (on the Columbia River). **Special Features:** Just one mile away is a full-scale model of Stonehenge, open to the public.

★4602★ **MCMICKEN ISLAND STATE PARK**
c/o Jarrell Cove State Park
E 391 Wingert Rd
Shelton, WA 98584
Phone: 360-426-9226
Size: 11.5 acres. **Location:** East of Harstene Island; accessible by boat only. **Facilities:** Beach access, 5 mooring buoys. **Activities:** Fishing, hiking, clamming, kayaking. **Special Features:** One of five satellite parks administered by Jarrell Cove State Park, McMicken is a small island with 1,661 feet of saltwater shoreline.

★4603★ **MILLERSYLVANIA STATE PARK**
12245 Tilley Rd S
Olympia, WA 98512
Web: www.parks.wa.gov/parkpage.asp?selectedpark=
Millersylvania
Phone: 360-753-1519; **Fax:** 360-664-2180
Size: 842 acres. **Location:** 10 miles south of Olympia. **Facilities:** 120 standard campsites, 48 utility campsites, group campsite, 19 cabins, cottage, 8 showers (2 &), picnic area, picnic shelter, 4 kitchen shelters (with electricity), boat launch, hiking trails, bike trails, exercise trail, environmental learning center, boat rentals, amphitheater. **Activities:** Camping, boating, fishing, swimming, hiking, biking. **Special Features:** Historic Millersylvania was constructed almost entirely by hand by the Civilian Conservation Corps in 1935. Relics of a narrow-gauge railroad and several skid roads used in the 1800s by the logging industry remain on park grounds.

★4604★ **MORAN STATE PARK**
3572 Olga Rd
Eastsound, WA 98245
Web: www.parks.wa.gov/parkpage.asp?selectedpark=Moran
Phone: 360-376-2326
Size: 5,252 acres. **Location:** On Orcas Island near Eastsound; accessible by ferry. **Facilities:** 151 standard campsites, 15 primitive campsites, 10 showers (2 &), picnic shelter, picnic area, kitchen shelter (with electricity), beach access, boat rentals, boat launch, environmental learning center, hiking trails, bike trails, horse trails. **Activities:** Camping, swimming, hiking, biking, horseback riding, boating, fishing, interpretive programs. **Special Features:** Visitors can view Vancouver (British Columbia), Mount Baker, and San Juan Islands from a stone observation tower atop Mount Constitution. The tower was built by the Civilian Conservation Corps in 1936.

★4605★ **MOUNT PILCHUCK STATE PARK**
c/o Wenburg State Park
15430 E Lake Goodwin Rd
Stanwood, WA 98292
Web: www.parks.wa.gov/mtpilchuck.asp
Phone: 360-652-7417
Size: 1,893 acres. **Location:** 8 miles east of Granite Falls off

I-5. **Facilities:** Trails, picnic area. **Activities:** Fishing, hiking, mountain climbing, snowshoeing, bird watching, rock climbing. **Special Features:** A 3-mile trail leads to an old fire lookout at the summit of Mount Pilchuck (5,324 feet). The trail begins at 3,100 feet above sea level and winds through old growth forest to alpine heather and large rocks. At the top is a panoramic view of the Cascades, Olympics, and Puget Sound.

★4606★ MOUNT SPOKANE STATE PARK

N 26107 Mt Spokane Park Rd
Mead, WA 90021
Web: www.parks.wa.gov/parkpage.asp?selectedpark=
    Mount%20Spokane
Phone: 509-238-4258; **Fax:** 509-238-6845
Size: 13,919 acres. **Location:** 25 miles northeast of Spokane. **Facilities:** 12 standard campsites, group camp, kitchen shelter, concession-operated ski resort and restaurant, picnic shelter, bridle trails, hiking trails (100 miles), bike trails (90 miles), ski trails. **Activities:** Camping, hiking, bicycling, mountain biking, horseback riding, interpretive programs, cross-country skiing, downhill skiing, snowmobiling, dog sledding, snowshoeing. **Special Features:** Forested park features stands of old-growth timber and granite rock outcroppings. In winter, the park receives 300 inches of snow, making it a popular destination for winter sports enthusiasts.

★4607★ MYSTERY BAY STATE PARK

PO Box 42650
Olympia, WA 98504
Web: www.parks.wa.gov/parkpage.asp?selectedpark=
    Mystery%20Bay
Phone: 360-902-8500
Size: 10 acres. **Location:** On the west side of Marrowstone Island off the Olympic Peninsula. **Facilities:** Picnic area, kitchen shelter, boat launch, moorage, shoreline. **Activities:** Boating, clamming, crabbing, scuba diving, beachcombing. **Special Features:** This park offers a protected harbor and 685 feet of shoreline on Mystery Bay, as well as a great view of the Olympic Mountains.

★4608★ NOLTE STATE PARK

36921 Veazie Cumberland Rd
Enumclaw, WA 98022
Web: www.parks.wa.gov/parkpage.asp?selectedpark=Nolte
Phone: 360-825-4646
Size: 117 acres. **Location:** North of Enumclaw at the western edge of the Cascade Mountains. **Facilities:** Picnic area, picnic shelter, 2 kitchen shelters, swimming area, hiking trail, bike trail, ball field. **Activities:** Boating, fishing, swimming, hiking, biking. **Special Features:** Covered with forests and water, park features 7,174 feet of freshwater shoreline on Deep Lake in the Green River Gorge.

★4609★ OCEAN CITY STATE PARK

148 State Rt 115
Hoquiam, WA 98550
Web: www.parks.wa.gov/parkpage.asp?selectedpark=
    Ocean%20City
Phone: 360-289-3553

Size: 170 acres. **Location:** 2 miles north of Ocean Shores on Highway 115. **Facilities:** 149 standard campsites, 29 utility campsites, 2 group campsites, picnic shelters, picnic areas, beach access, amphitheater, ball fields. **Activities:** Camping, fishing, clamming, crabbing, swimming, scuba diving, beachcombing, surfing, kite flying. **Special Features:** Native American artifacts, including cooking, hunting, fishing, and clothing items found in the area are on display at the Ocean Shores Interpretive Center. Beachcombers occasionally find glass floats on the shore, washed in from Japanese and Russian fishing boats.

★4610★ OLALLIE STATE PARK

c/o Lake Sammamish State Park
20606 SE 56th St
Issaquah, WA 98027
Web: www.parks.wa.gov/parkpage.asp?selectedpark=Olallie
Phone: 360-455-7010
Size: 539 acres. **Location:** 4 miles east of North Bend, on I-90. **Facilities:** Interpretive trail, picnic areas, play field, hiking trails. **Activities:** Hiking, fishing, mountain biking, rock climbing. **Special Features:** Park features two waterfalls, Weeks Falls and 100-foot Twin Falls, that are connected by an 80-foot bridge. The falls are particularly spectacular in winter, when the water volume increases dramatically.

★4611★ OLD FORT TOWNSEND STATE PARK

1370 Old Fort Townsend Rd
Port Townsend, WA 98368
Web: www.parks.wa.gov/parkpage.asp?selectedpark=
    Old%20Fort%20Townsend
Phone: 360-385-3595
Size: 367 acres. **Location:** 4 miles south of Port Townsend, on the Olympic Peninsula. **Facilities:** 40 standard campsites, group camp, shower, picnic shelters, picnic areas, beach access, ball field, hiking trails, playground. **Activities:** Camping, fishing, crabbing, hiking, bicycling, scuba diving. **Special Features:** Park consists of just over a third of the original Fort Townsend built in 1856 by the U.S. Army for the protection of settlers. A trail highlights historical information.

★4612★ OLMSTEAD PLACE STATE PARK

921 N Ferguson Rd
Ellensburg, WA 98926
Web: www.parks.wa.gov/parkpage.asp?selectedpark=
    Olmstead%20Place
Phone: 509-925-1943
Size: 217 acres. **Location:** 4 miles east of Ellensburg in the center of the state. **Facilities:** Picnic area, trails, museum, working pioneer farm, guided tours. **Activities:** Hiking, fishing, interpretive activities, cross-country skiing, snowshoeing. **Special Features:** Olmstead Place is one of the first homesteads in the Kittitas Valley. The original 1875 log cabin and 1908 farmhouse (with the family's furnishings intact) are still standing, as are most of the outbuildings. Guided tours are available.

★4613★ OSOYOOS LAKE STATE PARK
2207 Juniper
Oroville, WA 98844
Web: www.parks.wa.gov/parkpage.asp?selectedpark=
Osoyoos%20Lake
Phone: 509-476-3321
Size: 47 acres. **Location:** Just north of Oroville near the Canadian border. **Facilities:** 86 standard campsites, 2 showers, 2 restrooms (1 &), picnic area, kitchen shelter, swimming area, 2 boat launches, dock, moorage, ball field, park store. **Activities:** Camping, boating, fishing, swimming, water-skiing, snow sledding, ice fishing, ice skating. **Special Features:** 14-mile-long Osoyoos Lake is formed by the Okanogan River widening south of the Canadian Rockies. The park has expansive lawns leading to the sandy shore of the lake. Willow trees provide shade.

★4614★ PACIFIC BEACH STATE PARK
c/o Ocean City State Park
148 State Rt 115
Hoquiam, WA 98550
Web: www.parks.wa.gov/parkpage.asp?selectedpark=
Pacific%20Beach
Phone: 360-289-3553
Size: 10 acres. **Location:** 15 miles north of Ocean Shores on Highway 109. **Facilities:** 32 standard campsites, 32 utility campsites, 2 showers (1 &), picnic area, beach access. **Activities:** Camping, fishing, clamming, swimming, beachcombing, kite flying. **Special Features:** Park features 2,300 feet of sandy ocean shoreline.

★4615★ PACIFIC PINES STATE PARK
c/o Fort Canby State Park
PO Box 488
Ilwaco, WA 98624
Web: www.parks.wa.gov/parkpage.asp?selectedpark=
Pacific%20Pines
Phone: 360-642-3078
Size: 11 acres. **Location:** 1 mile north of Ocean Park on the Pacific shore. **Facilities:** 15 picnic sites, beach access, wind breaks, ball fields. **Activities:** Fishing, clamming, crabbing, beachcombing. **Special Features:** Park was at one time a proposed development under private ownership. The park was created to establish permanent public access to the beach.

★4616★ PALOUSE FALLS STATE PARK
10152 SR 127
Pomeroy, WA 99347
Web: www.parks.wa.gov/parkpage.asp?selectedpark=
Palouse%20Falls
Phone: 509-549-3551
Size: 105 acres. **Location:** 23 miles southeast of Washtucna, Washington in the southeast portion of the state. **Facilities:** 10 primitive campsites, 2 restrooms (&), picnic area, picnic shelter, hiking trail (&), observation shelter, historical displays. **Activities:** Camping, hiking. **Special Features:** Park offers a dramatic view of a waterfall which drops from a height of 200 feet. A quarter-mile wheelchair-accessible trail leads to an observation deck overlooking the waterfall.

★4617★ PARADISE POINT STATE PARK
Rt 1, Box 33914
Ridgefield, WA 98642
Web: www.parks.wa.gov/parkpage.asp?selectedpark=
Paradise%20Point
Phone: 360-263-2350
Size: 86 acres. **Location:** 6 miles south of Woodland on the southwestern side of the state. **Facilities:** 58 standard campsites, 20 utility campsites, 9 primitive campsites, 4 showers (2 &), beach access, boat launch, hiking trails, amphitheater. **Activities:** Camping, fishing, boating, hiking, swimming. **Special Features:** Park features 6,180 feet of freshwater shoreline and a small apple orchard.

★4618★ PEACE ARCH STATE PARK
PO Box 87
Blaine, WA 98230
Web: www.parks.wa.gov/parkpage.asp?selectedpark=
Peace%20Arch
Phone: 360-332-8221
Size: 20 acres. **Location:** In Blaine, 21 miles north of Bellingham. **Facilities:** Picnic area, picnic shelters, landscaped gardens, hiking trail. **Activities:** Interpretive programs, bird watching, hiking. **Special Features:** Park commemorates treaties and agreements arising from the War of 1812 that provide for an unguarded US/Canadian border from the Strait of Juan de Fuca to the Bay of Fundy. The 67-foot Peace Arch is jointly maintained by both countries.

★4619★ PEARRYGIN LAKE STATE PARK
861 Bear Creek Rd
Winthrop, WA 98862
Web: www.parks.wa.gov/parkpage.asp?selectedpark=
Pearrygin%20Lake
Phone: 509-996-2370
Size: 696 acres. **Location:** 4 miles northeast of Winthrop in north central Washington. **Facilities:** 92 standard campsites, 71 utility campsites (with full hookups), 2 primitive campsites, 2 group camps, 2 cabins, 6 showers (2 &), picnic areas, sandy beach, boat launch, dock, campfire programs (seasonal). **Activities:** Camping, boating, fishing, swimming, water skiing, cross-country skiing, snowshoeing, snowmobiling. **Special Features:** Park is filled with colorful wildflowers in spring and summer, and red-winged and yellow-headed blackbirds and marmots add to the display of color.

★4620★ PENROSE POINT STATE PARK
321 158th KPS
Lakebay, WA 98349
Web: www.parks.wa.gov/parkpage.asp?selectedpark=
Penrose%20Point
Phone: 253-884-2514
Size: 152 acres. **Location:** 16 miles southwest of Purdy, on the western side of the state. **Facilities:** 82 standard campsites, group camp, 2 showers, 2 picnic shelters, beach access, hiking trails, bike trails, interpretive trail, 8 mooring buoys, dock. **Activities:** Camping, boating, fishing, swimming, water skiing, beachcombing, mountain biking, clamming, crabbing, oyster

9. State Parks

gathering. **Special Features:** A self-guided interpretive trail in the park's day-use area was built by Eagle Scouts in 1982. The trail extends for about 1,000 feet.

★4621★ PESHASTIN PINNACLES STATE PARK

c/o Wenatchee Confluence State Park
333 Olds Station Rd
Wenatchee, WA 98801
Web: www.parks.wa.gov/parkpage.asp?selectedpark= Peshastin%20Pinnacles
Phone: 509-664-6373
Size: 34 acres. **Location:** 14 miles west of Wenatchee, in the foothills of the Cascade Mountains. **Facilities:** Picnic area, hiking trail. **Activities:** Hiking, rock climbing. **Special Features:** Park features a group of sandstone slabs and spires called "the pinnacles." Climbable spires reach 200 feet into the air. Rocks and trails provide views of surrounding orchards, the Enchantment Mountain Range, and the Wenatchee River Valley.

★4622★ POTHOLES STATE PARK

6762 Hwy 262 E
Othello, WA 99344
Web: www.parks.wa.gov/parkpage.asp?selectedpark=Potholes
Phone: 509-346-2759
Size: 640 acres. **Location:** 17 miles southwest of Moses Lake, just east of the Cascades. **Facilities:** 61 standard campsites, 60 utility campsites, group camp, 4 showers (2 &), picnic shelters, hiking trails, beach, boat ramps, dock, ball fields. **Activities:** Boating, camping, fishing, hiking, swimming, water-skiing, white-water kayaking. **Special Features:** Potholes Reservoir (also called O'Sullivan Reservoir) was formed as a result of two major events. First, huge depressions were made in the earth during the Pleistocene flooding. Then, during the 1950s, those depressions were filled with water (making "pothole" lakes) when the water table rose with the creation of O'Sullivan Dam.

★4623★ POTLATCH STATE PARK

PO Box 1051
Hoodsport, WA 98548
Web: www.parks.wa.gov/parkpage.asp?selectedpark=Potlatch
Phone: 360-877-5361
Size: 57 acres. **Location:** 12 miles north of Shelton on Highway 101. **Facilities:** 17 standard campsites, 18 utility campsites, 2 primitive campsites, 2 showers, picnic shelter, picnic area, beach access, hiking trail, bike trail, amphitheater, mooring buoys. **Activities:** Camping, boating, fishing, scuba diving, wind surfing, crabbing, clamming, hiking, biking, beachcombing, kite flying. **Special Features:** Sunny days and low tides attract many to Potlatch to harvest oysters, dig for clams, or catch crab and fish. Scuba divers favor the area for its easy descent, and kayaking is popular here as well.

★4624★ RAINBOW FALLS STATE PARK

4008 State Hwy 6
Chehalis, WA 98532
Web: www.parks.wa.gov/parkpage.asp?selectedpark= Rainbow%20Falls
Phone: 360-291-3767; **Fax:** 360-291-3377

Size: 139 acres. **Location:** 17 miles west of Chehalis on Highway 6. **Facilities:** 39 standard campsites, group camp, 3 hiker campsites, 3 horseman's campsites, 2 showers, kitchen shelter (with electricity), picnic area, hiking trails, bike trails, horse trails, playfield, garden. **Activities:** Camping, fishing, hiking, horseback riding, swimming, kayaking, wildlife viewing. **Special Features:** Constructed in 1935 in the heart of old-growth forest, this wooded park is known for its rainbow-crowned waterfall, which gives the park its name. Park also features a garden with 40 varieties of fuschia.

★4625★ RASAR STATE PARK

38730 Cape Horn Rd
Concrete, WA 98237
Web: www.parks.wa.gov/parkpage.asp?selectedpark=Rasar
Phone: 360-826-3942
Size: 169 acres. **Location:** 19 miles east of Burlington on State Road 20. **Facilities:** 18 standard campsites, 20 utility campsites, 3 group camps, kitchen shelter (with electricity), picnic sites, hiking trails, amphitheater, playground. **Activities:** Camping, hiking, fishing. **Special Features:** Park features 4,000 feet of freshwater shoreline. Eagle watching opportunities are excellent in fall and early winter.

★4626★ RIVERSIDE STATE PARK

9711 W Charles Rd
Nine Mile Falls, WA 99206
Web: www.parks.wa.gov/parkpage.asp?selectedpark= Riverside
Phone: 509-456-5064
Size: 10,000 acres. **Location:** Northwest of Spokane, on the Spokane and Little Spokane Rivers. **Facilities:** 101 standard campsites, 2 primitive campsites, 2 group camping areas, picnic areas, 3 picnic shelters with kitchens, interpretive center, comfort stations, vault toilets, 9 historic buildings, trails, pedestrian suspension bridge, boat launch. **Activities:** Camping, boating, fishing, hiking, horseback riding, motorcycle and ATV riding, snowmobiling, cross-country skiing, bird watching. **Special Features:** The building that today houses Spokane House Interpretive Center was originally a trading post established in 1810. Exhibits illustrate the fur trade that took place in the area. A lava formation commonly referred to as "Bowl and Pitcher" is located in the park river.

★4627★ ROCKPORT STATE PARK

51905 State Rt 20
Rockport, WA 98283
Web: www.parks.wa.gov/parkpage.asp?selectedpark= Rockport
Phone: 360-853-8461
Size: 670 acres. **Location:** 8 miles east of Concrete, Washington, in the northwest portion of the state. **Facilities:** 8 standard campsites, 50 utility campsites, 4 primitive campsites, group camp, 4 showers, picnic shelter, kitchen shelter, hiking trails (5 miles). **Activities:** Camping, fishing, hiking, whitewater kayaking, rafting. **Special Features:** Park has more than 600 acres of old-growth timber and an ecosystem that has never been

9. State Parks

disrupted. Some of the park's Douglas firs stand as tall as 250 feet.

★4628★ SACAJAWEA STATE PARK
2503 Sacajawea Park Rd
Pasco, WA 99301
Web: www.parks.wa.gov/parkpage.asp?selectedpark=
Sacajawea
Phone: 509-545-2361
Size: 284 acres. Location: 5 miles southeast of Pasco, at the confluence of the Snake and Columbia Rivers. Facilities: Picnic area, 2 kitchen shelters (1 with electricity), beach access, boat launches, dock, moorage, hiking trail, game courts, ball field, playground. Activities: Boating, fishing, hiking, swimming, water skiing, guided tours. Special Features: Newly expanded interpretive center features exhibits on the Lewis and Clark Expedition through the experiences of Sacajawea, the Shoshone Indian woman who accompanied the expedition. The park is located on one of the expedition's campsites, used by Lewis and Clark from October 16-18, 1805.

★4629★ SAINT EDWARD STATE PARK
14445 Juanita Dr NE
Kenmore, WA 98028
Web: www.parks.wa.gov/parkpage.asp?selectedpark=
Saint%20Edward
Phone: 425-823-2992
Size: 316 acres. Location: On the northeastern shoreline of Lake Washington, in Kenmore. Facilities: Picnic areas, hiking trails, horse trails (Holmes Point area), beach access, swimming pool, playground. Activities: Fishing, hiking, boating, swimming, water skiing, mountain biking, horseback riding. Special Features: Once a Catholic seminary, the park's history is reflected in its grounds and architecture. The undeveloped waterfront (the last along Lake Washington's shore) provides opportunities for nature study.

★4630★ SALTWATER STATE PARK
25205 8th Pl S
Des Moines, WA 98198
Web: www.parks.wa.gov/parkpage.asp?selectedpark=
Saltwater
Phone: 253-661-4956
Size: 88 acres. Location: 2 miles south of Des Moines on Highway 509. Facilities: 50 standard campsites, group camp, 2 showers (&), picnic area, 2 kitchen shelters, hiking trail, bike trail, beach access, ball fields, educational programs, artificial reef. Activities: Camping, hiking, biking, scuba diving, fishing. Special Features: Park dedication in 1926 included a peace effort to stop bad feelings between the cities of Tacoma and Seattle. The Park is located halfway between the two cities, and a hatchet is symbolically buried under a rock somewhere in the park.

★4631★ SCENIC BEACH STATE PARK
PO Box 7
Seabeck, WA 98380
Web: www.parks.wa.gov/parkpage.asp?selectedpark=
Scenic%20Beach
Phone: 360-830-5079

Size: 88 acres. Location: 9 miles southwest of Silverdale, on Hood Canal. Facilities: 52 standard campsites, group camp, kitchen shelter (with electricity), picnic shelter, picnic area, beach access, garden, gazebo, accessible paths, ball fields. Activities: Camping, hiking, bicycling, boating, swimming, water skiing, wind surfing, beachcombing, fishing, scuba diving, crabbing, oyster gathering (in season). Special Features: Park is known for its wild, native rhododendrons and clear-day views of Hood Canal and the Olympic Mountains.

★4632★ SCHAFER STATE PARK
W 1365 Schafer Park Rd
Elma, WA 98541
Web: www.parks.wa.gov/parkpage.asp?selectedpark=Schafer
Phone: 360-482-3852
Size: 119 acres. Location: 12 miles north of Elma on the east fork of Satsop River. Facilities: 43 standard campsites, 6 utility campsites, 2 group camps, 2 bicycle camping sites, shower, 2 picnic shelters, playground, beach access, hiking trail. Activities: Camping, fishing, hiking, swimming, bird watching. Special Features: Park offers abundant fishing as well as swimming and wading in the river's shallow water. Buildings are constructed from native stone.

★4633★ SEAQUEST STATE PARK
Box 3030 Spirit Lake Hwy
Castle Rock, WA 98611
Web: www.parks.wa.gov/parkpage.asp?selectedpark=Seaquest
Phone: 360-274-8633
Size: 475 acres. Location: 6 miles east of Castle Rock, on Silver Lake. Facilities: 55 standard campsites, 33 utility campsites, 6 showers (4 &), picnic areas, kitchen shelter (with electricity), hiking trails (8 miles, 1 mile &), ball fields, playground. Activities: Camping, fishing, hiking. Special Features: Park is located along the banks of Silver Lake, formed when a previous eruption of Mount Saint Helens permanently dammed Silver Creek. Silver Lake is only ten feet deep. Mount Saint Helens is the park's main attraction, and the interpretive center at the park details the history and geology of the volcano.

★4634★ SEQUIM BAY STATE PARK
269035 Hwy 101
Sequim, WA 98382
Web: www.parks.wa.gov/parkpage.asp?selectedpark=
Sequim%20Bay
Phone: 360-683-4235
Size: 92 acres. Location: 3 miles southeast of Sequim on Highway 101. Facilities: 60 standard campsites, 16 utility campsites (with full hookups), group camp, 3 showers (2 &), picnic shelter, picnic area, 2 kitchen shelters, beach access, boat launch, moorage, tennis court, ball fields, hiking trail, environmental learning center, amphitheater. Activities: Camping, boating, hiking, fishing, swimming, clamming, crabbing, beachcombing, nature study, bird watching, snowshoeing. Special Features: Sequim is a Native American word for "quiet waters". Two natural overlapping sandbars protect the bay waters from the rough waves and currents of the Strait of Juan de Fuca. These same

sandbars also protected the area from discovery by the first three expeditions that ventured into the Puget Sound.

★4635★ SHINE TIDELANDS STATE PARK

202 NE Park St
Poulsbo, WA 98370
Web: www.parks.wa.gov/parkpage.asp?selectedpark=
   Shine%20Tidelands
Phone: 360-779-3205
Size: 13 acres. **Location:** 7 miles south of Port Ludlow. **Facilities:** Picnic area, beach access. **Activities:** Fishing, clamming, crabbing, windsurfing, kayaking, beachcombing. **Special Features:** Park has 5,000 feet of tideland along Bywater Bay, although at high tide there is little beach available.

★4636★ SOUTH WHIDBEY ISLAND STATE PARK

4128 S Smugglers Cove Rd
Freeland, WA 98249
Web: www.parks.wa.gov/parkpage.asp?selectedpark=
   South%20Whidbey
Phone: 360-331-4559
Size: 347 acres. **Location:** Whidbey Island, 7 miles north of Freeland. **Facilities:** 46 standard campsites, 8 utility campsites, group camp, 4 showers, kitchen shelter, picnic shelter, picnic area, hiking trails, beach access, amphitheater. **Activities:** Camping, fishing, clamming, crabbing, hiking, beachcombing. **Special Features:** The park features 4,500 feet of saltwater shoreline, old-growth forest, and views of Puget Sound and the Olympic Mountains.

★4637★ SPENCER SPIT STATE PARK

521-A Bakerview Rd
Lopez Island, WA 98261
Web: www.parks.wa.gov/parkpage.asp?selectedpark=
   Spencer%20Spit
Phone: 360-468-3176
Size: 138 acres. **Location:** On the east side of Lopez Island; accessible by ferry. **Facilities:** 37 standard campsites, 7 hiker campsites, 2 group camps, 2 kitchen shelters, picnic shelter, picnic area, hiking trail, mooring buoys, beach access. **Activities:** Camping, boating, fishing, clamming, crabbing, hiking, swimming, scuba diving, beachcombing, bird watching. **Special Features:** Park is named for the lagoon-enclosing sandspit on which it is situated.

★4638★ SQUILCHUCK STATE PARK

c/o Wenatchee Confluence State Park
333 Olds Station Rd
Wenatchee, WA 98801
Web: www.parks.wa.gov/parkpage.asp?selectedpark=
   Squilchuck
Phone: 509-664-6373
Size: 288 acres. **Location:** 9 miles southwest of Wenatchee on Squilchuck Road. **Facilities:** 20 standard campsites, group camp, lodge, picnic area, hiking trails, bike trails, ski trails. **Activities:** Camping, hiking, cross-country skiing, snow sledding, snowshoeing, inner tubing. **Special Features:** Situated at

an elevation of 4,000 feet, the park gets plenty of snow and is a popular site for winter sports.

★4639★ STEAMBOAT ROCK STATE PARK

PO Box 370
Electric City, WA 99123
Web: www.parks.wa.gov/parkpage.asp?selectedpark=
   Steamboat%20Rock
Phone: 509-633-1304
Size: 3,522 acres. **Location:** 16 miles north of Coulee City, Washington. **Facilities:** 26 standard campsites, 100 utility campsites, 12 primitive campsites, 6 showers (4 &), hiking trails (13 miles), bike trails, horse trails, beach access, 7 boat launches, dock, ball field. **Activities:** Camping, boating, fishing, swimming, water-skiing, cross-country skiing, horseback riding, rock climbing, ice climbing, hiking, biking, bird watching. **Special Features:** Steamboat Rock is a butte that rises 800 feet above Banks Lake and has a surface area of 600 acres. This columnar basalt rock, which dominates the park, has long been used as a natural landmark, first by nomadic native tribes, later by pioneers, and today by military aircraft pilots on training missions.

★4640★ STEPTOE BATTLEFIELD STATE PARK

c/o Central Ferry State Park
10152 State Hwy 127
Pomeroy, WA 99347
Web: www.parks.wa.gov/parkpage.asp?selectedpark=
   Steptoe+Battlefield
Phone: 509-549-3551
Size: 4 acres. **Location:** On the outskirts of Rosalia in the central eastern portion of the state. **Activities:** Interpretive activities, wildlife observation. **Special Features:** Park marks the authentic site of Steptoe Battlefield, where the last defeat of the U.S. Army by Native Americans in the Pacific Northwest occurred. A 25-foot granite memorial marks the site of the battle.

★4641★ STEPTOE BUTTE STATE PARK

c/o Central Ferry State Park
10152 State Hwy 127
Pomeroy, WA 99347
Web: www.parks.wa.gov/parkpage.asp?selectedpark=
   Steptoe%20Butte
Phone: 509-549-3551
Size: 150 acres. **Location:** 12 miles north of Colfax. **Facilities:** Picnic areas, interpretive signs. **Activities:** Historical and natural interpretation, sightseeing. **Special Features:** Steptoe Butte is a 3,612-foot-tall thimble-shaped quartzite butte which looms over the surrounding flatlands. Native Americans called the butte the "power mountain". It was believed that a journey to the butte bestowed a gift of power from the mountain's guardian spirit.

★4642★ SUN LAKES STATE PARK

34875 Park Lane Rd NE
Coulee City, WA 99115
Web: www.parks.wa.gov/parkpage.asp?selectedpark=
   Sun%20Lakes
Phone: 509-632-5583

Size: 4,027 acres. **Location:** 7 miles southwest of Coulee City on Highway 17. **Facilities:** 152 standard campsites, 39 utility campsites, group camp, 12 showers, picnic area, concession, hiking trails (15 miles), bridle trails, horse rentals, swimming area, boat rentals, 2 boat launches, dock, 9-hole golf course, miniature golf, laundromat, museum, environmental learning center. **Activities:** Camping, boating, fishing, hiking, swimming, water skiing, horseback riding, golf. **Special Features:** Dry Falls, a gigantic dried-up waterfall and one of the world's natural wonders, is located in the park. Dry Falls was carved by ice-age floods and is now a stark cliff 400 feet high and 3.5 miles wide. At its peak, it was ten times the size of Niagara Falls.

★4643★ TOLMIE STATE PARK

7730 61st Ave NE
Olympia, WA 98506
Web: www.parks.wa.gov/parkpage.asp?selectedpark=Tolmie
Phone: 360-456-6464
Size: 105 acres. **Location:** 8 miles northeast of Olympia on Johnson Point. **Facilities:** Picnic shelter, picnic area, 2 kitchen shelters (with electricity), 5 mooring buoys, underwater park, hiking trail, beach access. **Activities:** Fishing, clamming, crabbing, boating, scuba diving, swimming, hiking. **Special Features:** Park includes an underwater park built by scuba divers.

★4644★ TRITON COVE STATE PARK

c/o Dosewallips State Park
PO Drawer K
Brinnon, WA 98320
Web: www.parks.wa.gov/parkpage.asp?selectedpark=Triton%20Cove
Phone: 360-796-4415
Size: 29 acres. **Location:** On the Olympic Peninsula, 6 miles south of Brinnon. **Facilities:** 6 picnic sites, shoreline, boat launch (&), moorage dock. **Activities:** Boating, fishing, crabbing, oyster collecting, scuba diving, bird watching. **Special Features:** Park features 555 feet of saltwater shoreline on Hood Canal.

★4645★ TWANOH STATE PARK

12190 E Hwy 106
Union, WA 98592
Web: www.parks.wa.gov/parkpage.asp?selectedpark=Twanoh
Phone: 360-275-2222
Size: 182 acres. **Location:** 8 miles west of Belfair on Highway 106. **Facilities:** 25 standard campsites, 22 utility campsites, group camp, shower, picnic areas, 2 kitchen shelters (with electricity), hiking trails, swimming area, boat launch, dock, moorage, ball field, horseshoe pit. **Activities:** Camping, boating, fishing, crabbing, oyster gathering, hiking, beachcombing, swimming, water-skiing. **Special Features:** Soil in the park is "glacial till," an unlayered sediment which was deposited by glaciers over most of western Washington. The park is on Hood Canal, which is a canal in name only—it is actually a "fjord," a long narrow body of water open to the ocean and bordered at one end by steep cliffs or hills.

★4646★ TWENTY-FIVE MILE CREEK STATE PARK

20530 S Lakeshore Dr
Chelan, WA 98816
Web: www.parks.wa.gov/parkpage.asp?selectedpark=Twenty%2DFive%20Mile%20Creek
Phone: 509-687-3710
Size: 235 acres. **Location:** 19.5 miles north of Chelan. **Facilities:** 46 standard campsites, 21 utility sites, group camp, 6 showers (2 &), picnic area, park store, fishing pier, marina, 2 boat launches. **Activities:** Camping, boating, fishing, hiking, swimming, water skiing, scuba diving, mountain biking. **Special Features:** Park is on the forested south shore of Lake Chelan and separates the mountains from the lake. The lake was carved by two competing glacers—the Chelan and the continental ice sheet. Their back-and-forth movement created the broad lower lake and narrow upper lake.

★4647★ TWIN HARBORS BEACH STATE PARK

Hwy 105
Westport, WA 98595
Web: www.parks.wa.gov/parkpage.asp?selectedpark=Twin%20Harbors
Phone: 360-268-9717
Size: 172 acres. **Location:** 3 miles south of Westport on Highway 105. **Facilities:** 250 standard campsites, 49 utility campsites, group camp, 16 showers (2 &), picnic area, kitchen shelter (with electricity), beach access. **Activities:** Camping, fishing, clamming, beachcombing, kite flying. **Special Features:** Park is on the Pacific coast, and beach activities predominate.

★4648★ WALLACE FALLS STATE PARK

PO Box 106
Gold Bar, WA 98251
Web: www.parks.wa.gov/parkpage.asp?selectedpark=Wallace%20Falls
Phone: 360-793-0420
Size: 4,375 acres. **Location:** 2 miles northeast of Goldbar. **Facilities:** 7 primitive campsites, picnic shelter, picnic area, 2 kitchen shelters, hiking trails, bike trails. **Activities:** Camping, hiking, biking, fishing, mountain biking, rock climbing, swimming, kayaking, boating. **Special Features:** Park contains numerous waterfalls, three back-country lakes, and a river. Wallace Falls drops from a height of 265 feet.

★4649★ WENATCHEE CONFLUENCE STATE PARK

333 Olds Station Rd
Wenatchee, WA 98801
Web: www.parks.wa.gov/parkpage.asp?selectedpark=Wenatchee%20Confluence
Phone: 509-664-6373
Size: 197 acres. **Location:** At the north end of Wenatchee at the confluence of Wenatchee and Columbia Rivers. **Facilities:** 8 standard campsites, 51 utility campsites, group camp, 6 restrooms (&), 16 showers (8 &), picnic sites, picnic shelter, kitchen shelter (with electricity), nature trail, paved trail, swimming beach, boat ramp, interpretive displays, tennis court, game courts, ball fields, playfield. **Activities:** Camping, boating, fishing, swimming, hiking, bicycling, field games, bird watching.

Special Features: Name refers to the location where the mouth of the Wenatchee River joins the Columbia River. Land within the park is separated into two sections. The northern site is classified a recreation area, and the southern site is a designated natural wetland area.

★4650★ WENBERG STATE PARK
15430 E Lake Goodwin Rd
Stanwood, WA 98292
Web: www.parks.wa.gov/parkpage.asp?selectedpark=
Wenberg
Phone: 360-652-7417
Size: 46 acres. **Location:** 18 miles northwest of Everett on Lake Goodwin. **Facilities:** 65 standard campsites, 10 utility campsites (with water and electrical hookups), 3 primitive campsites, picnic shelter, concession, swimming area, boat launch. **Activities:** Camping, boating, fishing, swimming. **Special Features:** The park is located on the banks of Lake Goodwin, renowned for cutthroat and rainbow trout fishing.

★4651★ WESTPORT LIGHT STATE PARK
PO Box 42650
Olympia, WA 98504
Web: www.parks.wa.gov/parkpage.asp?selectedpark=
Westport%20Light
Phone: 360-268-9717
Size: 212 acres. **Location:** 22 miles southwest of Aberdeen on the Pacific Ocean. **Facilities:** Picnic sites, beach access (&), hiking trail, boardwalk (&). **Activities:** Fishing, hiking, beachcombing. **Special Features:** Park is named for the historical (1898) lighthouse located on Coast Guard land adjacent to the park.

★4652★ YAKIMA SPORTSMAN STATE PARK
904 Keys Rd
Yakima, WA 98901
Web: www.parks.wa.gov/parkpage.asp?selectedpark=
Yakima%20Sportsman
Phone: 509-575-2774
Size: 247 acres. **Location:** 3 miles southeast of Yakima off I-82. **Facilities:** 30 standard campsites, 37 utility campsites, 4 showers (&), picnic area, picnic shelters, kitchen shelter (with electricity), hiking trail, guided nature walks. **Activities:** Camping, fishing, bird watching, hiking. **Special Features:** Stocked ponds in the park are set aside for children's fishing only. Adults may fish the Yakima River. Old clay-pigeon traps may still be found in the park, remnants from the Yakima Sportsman Club, which created the park in 1940.

9. State Parks

West Virginia State Parks

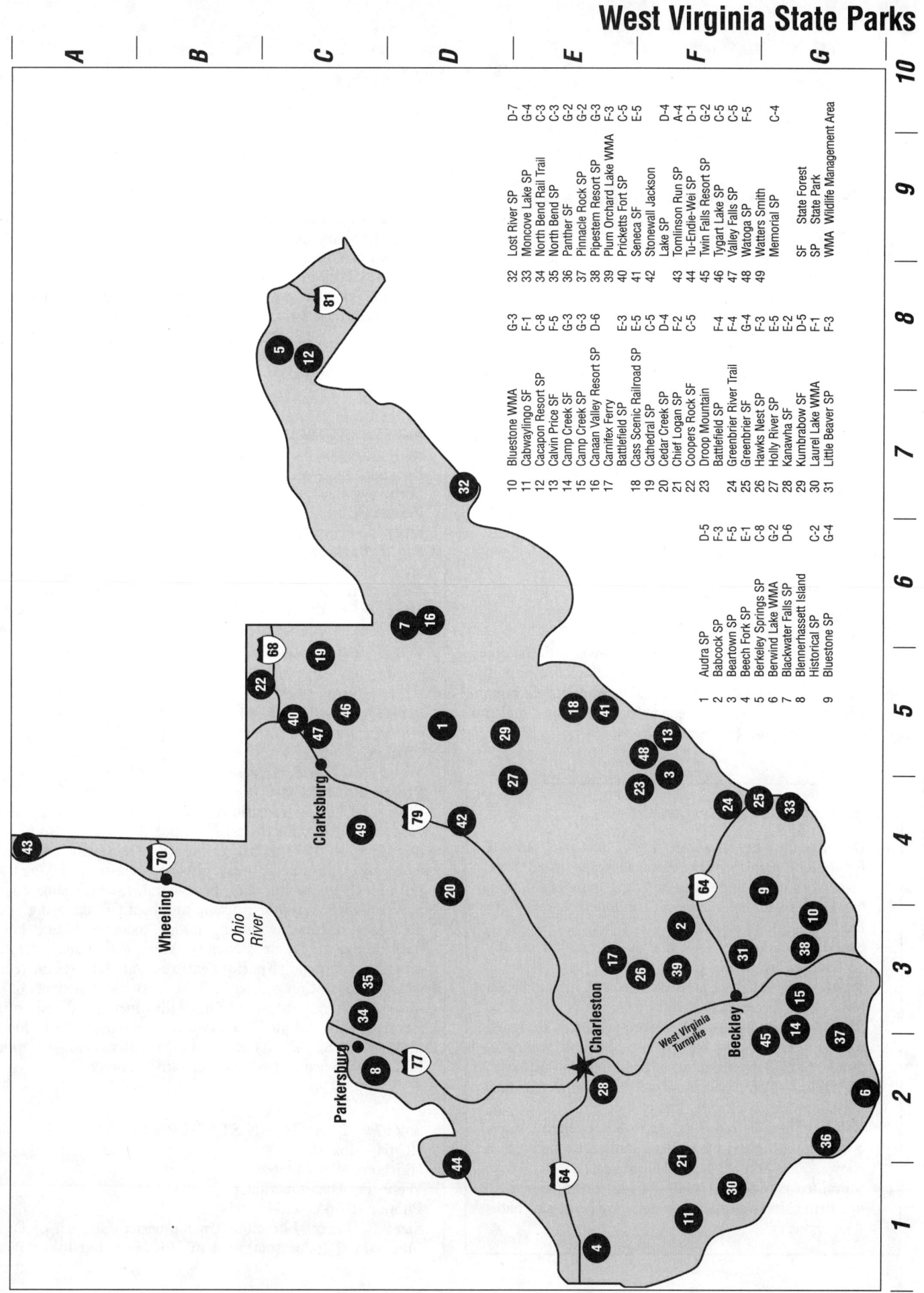

10	Bluestone WMA	G-3
11	Cabwaylingo SF	F-1
12	Cacapon Resort SP	C-8
13	Calvin Price SF	F-5
14	Camp Creek SF	G-3
15	Camp Creek SP	G-3
16	Canaan Valley Resort SP	D-6
17	Carnifex Ferry	
	Battlefield SP	E-3
18	Cass Scenic Railroad SP	E-5
19	Cathedral SP	C-5
20	Cedar Creek SP	D-4
21	Chief Logan SP	F-2
22	Coopers Rock SF	C-5
23	Droop Mountain	
	Battlefield SP	F-4
24	Greenbrier River Trail	F-4
25	Greenbrier SF	G-4
26	Hawks Nest SP	F-3
27	Holly River SP	E-5
28	Kanawha SF	E-2
29	Kumbrabow SF	D-5
30	Laurel Lake WMA	F-1
31	Little Beaver SP	F-3

32	Lost River SP	D-7
33	Moncove Lake SP	G-4
34	North Bend Rail Trail	C-3
35	North Bend SP	C-3
36	Panther SF	G-2
37	Pinnacle Rock SP	G-2
38	Pipestem Resort SP	F-3
39	Plum Orchard Lake WMA	F-3
40	Pricketts Fort SP	C-5
41	Seneca SF	E-5
42	Stonewall Jackson	
	Lake SP	D-4
43	Tomlinson Run SP	A-4
44	Tu-Endie-Wei SP	D-1
45	Twin Falls Resort SP	G-2
46	Tygart Lake SP	C-5
47	Valley Falls SP	C-5
48	Watoga SP	F-5
49	Watters Smith	
	Memorial SP	C-4
SF	State Forest	
SP	State Park	
WMA	Wildlife Management Area	

1	Audra SP	D-5
2	Babcock SP	F-3
3	Beartown SP	F-5
4	Beech Fork SP	E-1
5	Berkeley Springs SP	C-8
6	Berwind Lake WMA	G-2
7	Blackwater Falls SP	D-6
8	Blennerhassett Island	
	Historical SP	C-2
9	Bluestone SP	G-4

★4653★ West Virginia Division of Natural Resources Parks & Forests

State Capitol Complex, Bldg 3
1900 Kanawha Blvd E
Charleston, WV 25305
(304) 558-2764 - Phone
(304) 558-0077 - Fax
(800) 225-5982 - Toll-free
Web: www.wvparks.com

System consists of 35 parks (including historical sites and resorts), 9 forests, and 2 trails totaling more than 80,000 acres. Also operates campgrounds in four wildlife management areas.

★4654★ West Virginia Division of Natural Resources Wildlife Resources Section

State Capitol Complex, Bldg 3
1900 Kanawha Blvd
Charleston, WV 25305
(304) 558-2771
Web: www.wvdnr.gov/wildlife/wdpintro.shtm

Manages 58 named wildlife management areas with the objective of maintaining fish and wildlife populations and providing opportunities for recreation and research. Administers hunting and fishing licenses, conducts educational programs, and promotes non-game wildlife observation.

Key to campsite classification:

- **Deluxe campsites** — Outdoor grill, tent pad, pull-off for trailers, picnic table, electric hookups on all sites, some with water and sewer hookups, dumping station, bathhouses with hot showers, flush toilets, and laundry facilities.
- **Standard campsites** — Same as deluxe, but usually no hookups available.
- **Rustic campsites** — Improved sites with limited facilities, well water, and pit toilets.
- **Primitive campsites** — Undeveloped areas designed for use primarily by backpackers, hunters, and fishermen. Some have basic water and sanitation facilities.
- **Cottages** — Completely furnished and equipped including tableware, cookware, linens, etc.
- **Deluxe cabins** — Wood-paneled walls, open fireplaces, complete kitchens with modern appliances, baths with showers, and forced air or electric heat.
- **Standard cabins** — Usually of log construction with open fireplaces, modern equipped kitchens, and baths with showers.

- **Economy cabins** — One room with combination kitchen/bedroom. Built-in double bunks, small bath with shower.
- **Rustic cabins** — Equipped with gas lamps, wood-burning kitchen stoves, fireplaces, and gas refrigerators. Water and sanitary facilities are nearby.

★4655★ AUDRA STATE PARK

Rt 4, Box 564
Buckhannon, WV 26201
Web: www.audrastatepark.com
Phone: 304-457-1162

Size: 355 acres. **Location:** 6 miles east of US 119 and 15 miles east of Buckhannon. **Facilities:** 65 standard campsites, picnic areas, snack bar, hiking trails, game courts, playground, boardwalk. **Activities:** Camping, fishing, swimming, hiking, kayaking. **Special Features:** Heavily wooded riverside park features natural beauty as well as a touch of history. The spillway of a gristmill used in the early 1900s can still be seen today.

★4656★ BABCOCK STATE PARK

HC 35, Box 150
Clifftop, WV 25831
Web: www.babcocksp.com
Phone: 304-438-3004

Size: 4,127 acres. **Location:** Off US 60 on WV 41, 2 miles south of Clifftop. **Facilities:** 52 standard campsites (some with electricity, 4 &), 2 deluxe cabins (&), 18 standard cabins, 8 economy cabins, picnic areas, gift shop (seasonal), hiking trails (20 miles), swimming pool, boat rental, marina, game courts, playgrounds. **Activities:** Camping, boating, canoeing, paddleboating, fishing, swimming, hiking, mountain biking, horseback riding, tennis, cross-country skiing, nature and recreation programs (seasonal). **Special Features:** Park features the reconstructed Glade Creek Grist Mill, built from components of old mills throughout the state. This fully operational mill offers freshly ground cornmeal, buckwheat, and whole wheat flour to park guests. Site is adjacent to the New River Gorge National Forest in the heart of whitewater rafting country.

★4657★ BEARTOWN STATE PARK

HC 64, Box 189
Hillsboro, WV 24946
Web: www.beartownstatepark.com
Phone: 304-653-4254

Size: 107 acres. **Location:** On the eastern summit of Droop Mountain, 7 miles southwest of Hillsboro. **Facilities:** Picnic areas, boardwalk trail (&), hiking trails. **Activities:** Hiking. **Special Features:** This wild and remote hilltop park contains unusual rock formations, huge boulders, overhanging cliffs, and deep crevasses in a dense forest. Pocketing the face of the cliffs are hundreds of eroded pits, ranging from the size of marbles to others large enough to hold two grown men.

★4658★ BEECH FORK STATE PARK
5601 Long Branch Rd
Barboursville, WV 25504
Web: www.beechforksp.com
Phone: 304-528-5794
Size: 3,144 acres. **Location:** 12 miles south of Huntington. **Facilities:** 275 deluxe campsites (49 with full hookups), 6 deluxe cottages, picnic areas, picnic shelter, snack bar, hiking trails, fitness trail, bathhouses, swimming pool, boat ramp, visitor center, game courts, game room, camp store. **Activities:** Camping, boating, fishing, hiking, mountain biking, tennis, nature and recreation programs (seasonal). **Special Features:** Spring wildflowers are a common sight to hikers, as is an abundance of wildlife, including an occasional black bear.

★4659★ BERKELEY SPRINGS STATE PARK
121 S Washington St
Berkeley Springs, WV 25411
Web: www.berkeleyspringssp.com
Phone: 304-258-2711
Size: 4 acres. **Location:** Eastern panhandle of West Virginia, off I-81. **Facilities:** Museum, historic site, gift shop, mineral water and roman baths, swimming pool, exercise/fitness room. **Activities:** Swimming, massages, and heat treatments. **Special Features:** Berkeley Springs has served as a health spa since pre-colonial times. The mineral waters that flow from the spring in the park maintain a constant temperature of 74.3 degrees Fahrenheit and provide the medium for various baths, treatments, and health services.The springs discharge from five principle sources and numerous lesser ones, approximately 2,000 gallons of water per minute.

★4660★ BERWIND LAKE WILDLIFE MANAGEMENT AREA
Rt 16, Box 38
Warriormine, WV 24894
Web: www.berwindlake.com
Phone: 304-875-2577
Size: 18,000 acres. **Location:** 12 miles south of Welch on WV 16. **Facilities:** 2 standard campsites (both with electric), 6 rustic campsites, 1 accessible campsite, picnic areas, picnic shelters, swimming pool, fishing pier (&), boat launch, hiking trails, scenic overlook. **Activities:** Camping, swimming, hiking, fishing, hunting, boating (electric motors only), sightseeing. **Special Features:** Elevations range from 1,642 feet to 2,628 feet and the majority of the area is heavily forested. Most of the open land is located around 20-acre Berwind Lake.

★4661★ BLACKWATER FALLS STATE PARK
PO Drawer 490
Davis, WV 26260
Web: www.blackwaterfalls.com
Phone: 304-259-5216
Size: 1,688 acres. **Location:** 2 miles southwest of Davis off WV 32. **Facilities:** 65 standard campsites (30 with electrical hookups), 26 deluxe cabins, 54-room lodge (with restaurant, game room, and swimming pool), picnic areas, picnic shelter, snack bar, hiking trails (20+ miles), swimming beach, bathhouses, boat rentals, ski trails (10+ miles), toboggan run, warming hut, game courts, playgrounds, nature center, scenic vistas, gift shops. **Activities:** Camping, boating, swimming, hiking, horseback riding, fishing, cross-country skiing, sledding, tennis, nature and recreation programs (year round). **Special Features:** Several vantage points on the edge of the gorge offer panoramic views of Blackwater River's spectacular waterfalls. The name blackwater refers to the amber-colored waters, which are a result of tannic acid from fallen hemlock and red spruce needles.

★4662★ BLENNERHASSETT ISLAND HISTORICAL STATE PARK
137 Juliana St
Parkersburg, WV 26101
Web: www.blennerhassettislandstatepark.com
Phone: 304-420-4800
Size: 500 acres. **Location:** In the Ohio River, 2 miles west of Parkersburg. **Facilities:** Picnic areas, picnic shelter, snack bar, hiking trails, museum, historic site, gift shop. **Activities:** Fishing, hiking, bicycling, crafts demonstrations, horse-drawn wagon rides, excursion boat rides, guided tours. **Special Features:** This island in the Ohio River is the site where Blennerhassett and Aaron Burr allegedly plotted in 1806 to establish an empire in the southwest. A reconstructed mansion replaces the one originally built by Harman Blennerhassett in 1798 and destroyed by fire in 1811.

★4663★ BLUESTONE STATE PARK
HC 78, Box 3
Hinton, WV 25951
Web: www.bluestonesp.com
Phone: 304-466-2805
Size: More than 2,100 acres. **Location:** 5 miles south of Hinton, off WV 20. **Facilities:** 32 standard campsites (22 with electrical hookups), 44 rustic campsites, 26 deluxe cabins, 39 primitive campsites, picnic areas, hiking trails, swimming pool, bathhouses, boat rentals, boat ramp, game courts. **Activities:** Camping, boating, fishing, swimming, hiking, nature and recreation programs (seasonal). **Special Features:** Park sits alongside 2,000-acre Bluestone Lake, West Virginia's third largest body of water. Bluestone National Wild and Scenic River flows into Bluestone Lake within the park's boundaries.

★4664★ BLUESTONE WILDLIFE MANAGEMENT AREA
HC 65
Indian Mills, WV 24935
Web: www.bluestonewma.com
Phone: 340-466-3398

Size: 17, 632 acres. **Location:** Southern part of the state, off WV 20. **Facilities:** 315 primitive campsites, picnic areas, hiking trails, horse trails, stable, rustic recreation building. **Activities:** Camping, hiking, horseback riding, boating, fishing, hunting. **Special Features:** Adjacent to Bluestone Lake, the state's third largest body of water (see separate entry for Bluestone State Park).

★4665★ **CABWAYLINGO STATE FOREST**
Rt 1, Box 85
Dunlow, WV 25511
Web: www.cabwaylingo.com
Phone: 304-385-4255
Size: 8,123 acres. **Location:** 42 miles south of Huntington on US 152. **Facilities:** 20 rustic campsites (some with water and electrical hookups), 11 standard campsites (6 with electrical hookups), 14 standard cabins, group camp, showers, picnic areas, hiking trails, swimming pool, bathhouse, game courts, playground. **Activities:** Camping, fishing, swimming, hiking, hunting (in season). **Special Features:** Forest is named for the four counties it serves: CABell, WAYne, LINcoln, and MinGO.

★4666★ **CACAPON RESORT STATE PARK**
Rt 1, Box 230
Berkeley Springs, WV 25411
Web: www.cacaponresort.com
Phone: 304-258-1022
Size: More than 6,000 acres. **Location:** 105 miles from Washington, DC. **Facilities:** 13 modern cabins, 12 standard cabins, 12-room inn (&), 48-room lodge with conference rooms and restaurant, economy cabins, picnic areas, picnic shelters, hiking trails, swimming beach, boat rentals, game courts, 18-hole golf course, playground, gift shop. **Activities:** Boating, fishing, swimming, hiking, horseback riding, tennis, golf, nature and recreation programs. **Special Features:** Cacapon is a derivative of a Shawnee word meaning "medicine waters" and refers to the area's renowned medicinal waters, which have been acclaimed through history for their healing powers. These waters come to the surface approximately ten miles from Cacapon at nearby Berkeley Springs State Park (see separate entry in this section).

★4667★ **CALVIN PRICE STATE FOREST**
c/o Watoga State Park
HC 82 Box 252
Marlinton, WV 24954
Web: www.wvforestry.com/calvinpricestateforest.cfm
Phone: 304-799-4087
Size: 9,482 acres. **Location:** 9 miles south from WV 39 at Huntersville; adjacent to Watoga State Park. **Facilities:** Primitive campsites. **Activities:** Camping, fishing, hunting (in season). **Special Features:** Forest is named for one of the state's most famous newspapermen, who was a leading proponent of the purchase and designation of this area as a state forest.

★4668★ **CAMP CREEK STATE FOREST**
c/o Camp Creek State Park
PO Box 119
Camp Creek, WV 25820
Web: www.wvforestry.com/campcreekstateforest.cfm
Phone: 304-425-9481

Size: 5,269 acres. **Location:** 16 miles north of Princeton. **Facilities:** Hiking trails, mountain biking trails, horse trails. **Activities:** Fishing, hiking, hunting (in season), horseback riding, mountain biking. **Special Features:** Camp Creek, from which the forest derives its name, is one of the best trout streams in the mountains of southeastern West Virginia.

★4669★ **CAMP CREEK STATE PARK**
PO Box 119
Camp Creek, WV 25820
Web: www.campcreekstatepark.com
Phone: 304-425-9481
Size: 550 acres. **Location:** 16 miles north of Princeton. **Facilities:** 26 standard campsites (all with electrical hookups), 14 rustic campsites, horseman's camp, picnic areas, picnic shelters, hiking trails, mountain bike trails, horse trails (35 miles), game courts, playgrounds. **Activities:** Camping, fishing, hiking, mountain biking, horseback riding. **Special Features:** Park is located within the boundaries of Camp Creek State Forest (see separate entry).

★4670★ **CANAAN VALLEY RESORT STATE PARK**
HC 70, Box 330
Davis, WV 26260
Web: www.canaanresort.com
Phone: 304-866-4121
Size: 6,015 acres. **Location:** 10 miles south of Davis on WV 32. **Facilities:** 34 deluxe campsites (with full hookups), 23 cottages, 250-room lodge with convention center, restaurant, fitness room, sauna, swimming pools and bathhouses, snack bar, hiking trails, 18-hole golf course, game courts, playgrounds, gift shop (&&). **Activities:** Camping, fishing, swimming, hiking, bicycling, golf, miniature golf, tennis, cross-country and downhill skiing, ice skating, sledding, snowboarding, geocaching, nature and recreation programs. **Special Features:** Located in a mountain valley 3,300 feet above sea level, Canaan is one of West Virginia's finest year-round recreation and resort areas.

★4671★ **CARNIFEX FERRY BATTLEFIELD STATE PARK**
Rt 2, Box 435
Summersville, WV 26651
Web: www.carnifexferrybattlefieldstatepark.com
Phone: 304-872-0825
Size: 156 acres. **Location:** Off Route 129, 10 miles south of Summersville, on Route 19. **Facilities:** Picnic areas (&), picnic shelters, snack bar, hiking trails, museum, historic site, game courts, playground. **Activities:** Hiking, living history demonstrations. **Special Features:** On September 10, 1861 Union troops led by Brigadier General William S. Rosecrans forced Confederate troops to retreat from an entrenched position overlooking Carnifex Ferry. The Confederates' failure to regain control of the Kanawha Valley allowed the movement for West Virginia statehood to proceed.

★4672★ CASS SCENIC RAILROAD STATE PARK

PO Box 107
Cass, WV 24927
Web: www.cassrailroad.com
Phone: 304-456-4300
Size: 1,089 acres. **Location:** Eastern West Virginia on Route 28/92 in Pocahontas County between Dunmore and Greenbank. **Facilities:** Standard cottages, 3 cabooses for overnight rental, 1 rustic cabin, picnic areas, restaurant, museum, historical site. **Activities:** Excursion train rides, sightseeing, camping. **Special Features:** Park preserves an authentic remnant of what was a major logging train route. The track climbs from the old lumber town of Cass to the summit of Bald Knob, the second highest peak in the state. Powered by steam locomotives once used to haul logs, today the train takes passengers past breathtaking views of mountain scenery.

★4673★ CATHEDRAL STATE PARK

Rt 1, Box 370
Aurora, WV 26705
Web: www.cathedralstatepark.com
Phone: 304-735-3771
Size: 133 acres. **Location:** On US 50, 0.5 miles east of Aurora. **Facilities:** Picnic areas (&), picnic shelters, hiking trails, ski trails. **Activities:** Hiking, cross-country skiing, downhill skiing. **Special Features:** The forest is West Virginia's last remaining stand of virgin hemlock and hardwoods, declared a Natural Historical Landmark in 1966.

★4674★ CEDAR CREEK STATE PARK

2947 Cedar Creek Rd
Glenville, WV 26351
Web: www.cedarcreeksp.com
Phone: 304-462-7158
Size: 2,483 acres. **Location:** 3 miles southwest of Glenville on US 33, 6 miles south of WV 31. **Facilities:** 57 standard campsites (336 with electrical hookups), group camp (10 sites), picnic areas, picnic shelters (&), laundry, snack bar, hiking trails (14 miles), swimming pool, bathhouse, boat rentals, game courts, playgrounds, camp store. **Activities:** Camping, boating, fishing, swimming, hiking, bicycling, tennis, miniature golf, guided tours (seasonal), nature and recreation programs (seasonal). **Special Features:** Park features a reconstructed one-room schoolhouse, complete with authentic desks, inkwells, and a potbellied stove. A historic log building on-site has been restored to house the park headquarters.

★4675★ CHIEF LOGAN STATE PARK

General Delivery
Logan, WV 25601
Web: www.chiefloganstatepark.com
Phone: 304-792-7125
Size: 4,000 acres. **Location:** 4 miles north of Logan, off US 119 and WV 10. **Facilities:** 14 deluxe campsites, 11 standard campsites, bathhouse, picnic areas, picnic shelters, restaurant, hiking trails (18 miles), stable, swimming pool, wildlife center, museum, amphitheater, game courts, playground. **Activities:** Camping, fishing, swimming, hiking, mountain biking, horseback riding, tennis, miniature golf. **Special Features:** Park's many attractions include outdoor dramas, historical re-creations, wildflower hikes, and a small wildlife exhibit with live wild boar, bobcat, barred owls, hawk, and native reptiles.

★4676★ COOPERS ROCK STATE FOREST

Rt 1, Box 270
Bruceton Mills, WV 26525
Web: www.coopersrockstateforest.com
Phone: 304-594-1561
Size: 12,713 acres. **Location:** 13 miles east of Morgantown. **Facilities:** 25 standard campsites, picnic areas, picnic shelters, overlooks, hiking and biking trails (50 miles), historic site, playgrounds. **Activities:** Camping, fishing, hiking, hunting (in season), rock climbing, sightseeing. **Special Features:** During the Depression, the Civilian Conservation Corps built numerous structures in the forest. Eleven of these structures, including the rustic picnic shelters near the overlook, have been included in the National Register of Historic Places. The park features bands of rockcliffs lining the Cheat River Gorge and provide many overlooks, the centerpiece being the main overlook which furnishes a panorama of the gorge and distant horizons.

★4677★ DROOP MOUNTAIN BATTLEFIELD STATE PARK

HC 64, Box 189
Hillsboro, WV 24946
Web: www.droopmountainbattlefield.com
Phone: 304-653-4254
Size: 287 acres. **Location:** Off I-64 27 miles north of Lewisburg. **Facilities:** Picnic areas, shelters, hiking trails, museum, observation tower, historic site, playgrounds. **Activities:** Hiking, living history demonstrations. **Special Features:** On November 6, 1863, the last significant Civil War engagement in West Virginia occurred on this high mountain plateau overlooking Greenbrier Valley. Part of the battlefield is restored and marked for visitors, and a small museum contains Civil War artifacts.

★4678★ GREENBRIER RIVER TRAIL

c/o Watoga State Park
HC 82 Box 252
Marlinton, WV 24954
Web: www.greenbrierriverrailtrail.com
Phone: 304-799-4087
Size: 76 miles. **Location:** 1.5 miles from Caldwell; northern access from south end of Cass Scenic Railroad State Park (see separate entry). **Facilities:** Packed gravel trail. **Activities:** Hiking, bicycling, mountain biking, horseback riding, cross-country skiing. Trail also provides access to river for fishermen and canoeists. **Special Features:** A former Chesapeake and Ohio Railroad line, the 77-mile trail runs from North Caldwell to Cass. It passes through numerous small towns, over 35 bridges, and through 2 tunnels. Throughout much of its length, the trail runs adjacent to Greenbrier River and is surrounded by peaks of the Allegheny Mountains. The surface is mostly hard-packed gravel; fat bicycle and wheelchair tires are recommended. Motorized vehicles are not permitted.

★4679★ GREENBRIER STATE FOREST

HC 30, Box 154
Caldwell, WV 24925
Web: www.greenbriersf.com
Phone: 304-536-1944
Size: 5,130 acres. **Location:** Southeastern corner of the state, near the Virginia border. **Facilities:** 16 standard campsites (all with electrical hookups), 12 standard cabins, bathhouse, picnic areas, snack bar, hiking trails, biking trail, swimming pool, playgrounds, game courts, archery and rifle range. **Activities:** Camping, swimming, hiking, hunting (in season), mountain biking, fishing, nature and recreation programs (seasonal), historical reenactments **Special Features:** Magnificent views of the surrounding countryside are afforded by the forest's 3,200-foot-high Kate's Mountain.

★4680★ HAWKS NEST STATE PARK

PO Box 857
Ansted, WV 25812
Web: www.hawksnestsp.com
Phone: 304-658-5212
Size: 276 acres. **Location:** 8 miles west of US 19 on Route 60. **Facilities:** 31-room lodge, picnic areas, restaurant, hiking trails, swimming pool, bike rentals, golf course, gift shop, aerial tramway. **Activities:** Boating, swimming, hiking, bicycling, tennis, whitewater rafting, jetboat rides, nature and recreation program (seasonal). **Special Features:** Park offers spectacular views of the New River Gorge and includes an aerial tramway that links the lodge with the marina and boat dock on the lake below. Above and beyond the lake, the narrow canyon and rushing waters of the New River create one of the most challenging whitewater rafting experiences in the nation.

★4681★ HOLLY RIVER STATE PARK

PO Box 70
Hacker Valley, WV 26222
Web: www.hollyriver.com
Phone: 304-493-6353
Size: 8,101 acres. **Location:** 20 miles north of Webster Springs on WV 20. **Facilities:** 88 campsites (all with electrical hookups), 9 standard cabins, picnic areas, restaurant (open seasonally), hiking trails, swimming pool, bathhouses, laundry, game courts, playgrounds, gift shop, camp store. **Activities:** Camping, fishing, swimming, hiking, overnight backpacking, tennis, nature and recreation programs (seasonal). **Special Features:** Hiking trails through deep woodlands to secluded waterfalls and a brisk climb to scenic 2,480-foot Potato Knob are among the park's special natural attractions.

★4682★ KANAWHA STATE FOREST

Rt 2, Box 285
Charleston, WV 25314
Web: www.kanawhastateforest.com
Phone: 304-558-3500
Size: 9,300 acres. **Location:** 7 miles south of Charleston, off WV 214. **Facilities:** 46 standard campsites (25 with electrical hookups), picnic areas, snack bar, hiking trails, ski trails, braille trail, swimming pool, 2 bathhouses, playgrounds, shooting range. **Activities:** Camping, swimming, hiking, mountain biking, hunting and fishing (in season), cross-country skiing, bird watching. **Special Features:** Its close proximity to Charleston and the heavily populated Kanawha Valley has made this park a popular picnicking and recreational area. Park features the Spotted Salamander Trail, a paved, level trail with interpretive signs designed for blind and wheelchair-bound visitors.

★4683★ KUMBRABOW STATE FOREST

PO Box 65
Huttonsville, WV 26273
Web: www.kumbrabow.com
Phone: 304-335-2219
Size: 9,474 acres. **Location:** 24 miles south of Elkins, off US 219. **Facilities:** 13 rustic campsites, 5 rustic cabins, bathhouse, laundry, picnic areas, hiking trails, ski trails, playground. **Activities:** Camping, fishing, hiking, hunting (in season), cross-country skiing. **Special Features:** Kumbrabow is a showcase for stands of black cherry and red spruce. Diverse habitat has made black bear and bobcat sightings common, while mountain laurel and rhododendron are abundant and surround the majority of several pristine streams.

★4684★ LAUREL LAKE WILDLIFE MANAGEMENT AREA

HC 70, Box 626
Lenore, WV 25676
Web: www.laurellakewma.com
Phone: 304-475-2823
Size: 12,851 acres. **Location:** 7 miles east of Lenore, in the southwest corner of the state. **Facilities:** Picnic areas, picnic shelters, rental paddleboats, hiking trails, swimming pool, playgrounds. **Activities:** Swimming, hiking, hunting, boating, fishing. **Special Features:** Area's slopes are steep and its ridges and valleys narrow. Dogwood and rhododendron, the state flower, are common. The forest surrounding the lake is full of predators such as fox, owl, and raptors.

★4685★ LITTLE BEAVER STATE PARK

1402 Grandview Rd
Beaver, WV 25813
Web: www.littlebeaverstatepark.com
Phone: 304-763-2494
Size: 562 acres. **Location:** Raleigh County in southern West Virginia on WV 307. **Facilities:** Picnic areas, hiking trails, bike trails, boat rentals, boat dock, swimming beach, playground. **Activities:** Boating, fishing, swimming, hiking, mountain biking. **Special Features:** Park's 18-acre lake includes 300 feet of shoreline.

★4686★ LOST RIVER STATE PARK

321 Park Dr
Mathias, WV 26812
Web: www.lostriversp.com
Phone: 304-897-5372
Size: 3,712 acres. **Location:** 10 miles north of Virginia state line, off WV 259. **Facilities:** 11 deluxe cabins, 15 standard

9. State Parks

cabins, picnic areas, pavilions, restaurant, snack bar, hiking trails, bridle trail, mountain bike trail, swimming pool, stables, recreation building, game courts, playgrounds. **Activities:** Swimming, hiking, mountain biking, horseback riding, tennis, nature and recreation programs (seasonal). **Special Features:** Abundant wildlife is a prominent characteristic of mountainous Lost River. Scenic overlooks at ''Cranny Crow'' provide commanding views of the park and surrounding highlands of eastern West Virginia. Historically, the park is significant as having belonged to the famous Lee family of Virginia, who used it as a summer retreat in the early 1800s. A cabin from that era has been restored as a museum.

★4687★ MONCOVE LAKE STATE PARK

Rt 4 , Box 73-A
Gap Mills, WV 24941
Web: www.moncovelakestatepark.com
Phone: 304-772-3450
Size: 250 acres. **Location:** 6 miles east of Union on WV Route 3, then north for 6 miles. **Facilities:** 48 standard campsites (25 with electrical hookups), picnic areas, picnic shelters, hiking trails, swimming pool, bathhouses, fishing pier, boat rentals, boat ramp, game courts, playgrounds. **Activities:** Camping, boating (5 HP limit), fishing, hunting, swimming, hiking. **Special Features:** The area in and around Moncove Lake is a birding hot spot due to nearby Peter's Mountain and the ridge-and-valley section of the Appalachian Mountains. These ridges act as funnels for birds migrating in the fall and present excellent chances to glimpse birds that are considered rare or unusual for this region. More than 160 species of birds have been sighted in and around the area surrounding the lake.

★4688★ NORTH BEND RAIL TRAIL

c/o North Bend State Park
Rt 1 Box 221
Cairo, WV 26337
Web: www.wvparks.com/northbendrailtrail
Phone: 304-643-2931
Size: 72-mile trail. **Location:** From Parkersburg to Wolf Summit. **Facilities:** Packed gravel trail. **Activities:** Hiking, bicycling, horseback riding. **Special Features:** Trail is accessed from North Bend State Park (see separate entry), passing through 13 tunnels and crossing 36 bridges. On an abandoned spur of the CSX railroad system, the trail is part of the 5,500-mile, coast-to-coast American Discovery Trail.

★4689★ NORTH BEND STATE PARK

Rt 1, Box 221
Cairo, WV 26337
Web: www.northbendsp.com
Phone: 304-643-2931
Size: 1,400 acres. **Location:** Northwestern West Virginia, off WV 31. **Facilities:** 49 standard campsites (26 with electrical hookups), 9 deluxe cabins, 29-room lodge with restaurant and meeting rooms, picnic areas, hiking trails, horse-drawn carriage rides, fishing pier (&), boat and bike rentals, swimming pool, bathhouse, amphitheater, game courts, playground, gift shops.
Activities: Camping, fishing, swimming, hiking, bicycling,

horseback riding, tennis, nature and recreation programs. **Special Features:** Named for the horseshoe curve of the North Fork of Hughes River, the park is western West Virginia's major year-round park.

★4690★ PANTHER STATE FOREST

Box 287
Panther, WV 24872
Web: www.pantherstateforest.com
Phone: 304-938-2252
Size: 7,810 acres. **Location:** In the rugged mountains near the southern border of West Virginia, Virginia, and Kentucky, off Route 52. **Facilities:** 6 rustic campsites (with electrical hookups), group camp (with barracks, kitchen, and dining room), picnic areas, scenic overlooks, hiking trails, swimming pool, game court, playground. **Activities:** Camping, swimming, fishing, hiking, hunting (in season). **Special Features:** Park is heavily wooded, surrounded by mountains, and features a 4-mile section of Panther Creek, which is stocked with trout. A 2,830-acre wildlife management area connects to the park.

★4691★ PINNACLE ROCK STATE PARK

PO Box 1
Bramwell, WV 24715
Web: www.pinnaclerockstatepark.com
Phone: 304-248-8565
Size: Nearly 400 acres. **Location:** Near Bramwell on US 52. **Facilities:** Picnic area, picnic shelters, hiking trail, fishing pier, scenic overlook. **Activities:** Hiking, fishing, sightseeing. **Special Features:** Pinnacle Rock is an unusual sandstone formation reaching 3,100 feet above sea level.

★4692★ PIPESTEM RESORT STATE PARK

PO Box 150
Pipestem, WV 25979
Web: www.pipestemresort.com
Phone: 304-466-1800; **Fax:** 304-466-2803
Size: 4,023 acres. **Location:** Southeastern part of the state, 14 miles north of Princeton. **Facilities:** 31 deluxe campsites, 19 standard campsites, 32 rustic campsites, 26 cottages, 113-room lodge, 30-room lodge, conference rooms, picnic areas, trails, 2 swimming pools, bathhouse, 2 golf courses, stables, pro shop, tennis courts, gift shops, aerial tram, observation tower, overlooks, nature center, recreation center, visitor center, ampitheater, restaurant, snack bar, laundry, store, game courts, playground. **Activities:** Camping, boating, canoeing, fishing, hiking, bicycling, horseshoe, archery, swimming, horseback riding, cross-country skiing, sports, nature and recreation programs (year round). **Special Features:** Park's features include an aerial tramway with enclosed cars that carry passengers on a six-minute, 3,600-foot ride over Bluestone River Gorge; and an amphitheater, nestled in a natural bowl of the forested hills, site of summer weekend entertainment programs.

★4693★ PLUM ORCHARD LAKE WILDLIFE
MANAGEMENT AREA

Rt 1, Box 186
Scarbro, WV 25917
Web: www.plumorchardlakewma.com
Phone: 305-469-9905

Size: 3,201 acres. **Location:** In Fayette County, near Pax. **Facilities:** 38 primitive campsites, boat launches, rowboat rentals, rifle range. **Activities:** Camping, boating, fishing, hunting. **Special Features:** The lake is nestled between Haystack and Packs Mountains on Plum Orchard Creek. These mountains rise 700 to 900 feet above the lake (elevation 1,765 feet). Most of the area is forested in hickory and stands of mature red, white, and chestnut oaks.

★4694★ PRICKETTS FORT STATE PARK

Rt 3
Fairmont, WV 26554
Web: www.prickettsfortstatepark.com
Phone: 304-363-3030
Size: 188 acres. **Location:** North of Fairmont, 2 miles from I-79. **Facilities:** Picnic areas, interpretive trail, hiking trail, boat ramp, fishing pier, museum, historic site, gift shop, amphitheater (&&). **Activities:** Boating (access to the Monongahela River), fishing, hiking, mountain biking, living history demonstrations, programs and events (seasonal). **Special Features:** On the site of one of the state's early frontier forts, the park features a reconstructed fort built to resemble the 1774 original. Within the fort compound are 16 cabins, a meeting hall, and a storehouse. Park staff demonstrate authentic pioneer crafts, including blacksmithing, weaving, and spinning.

★4695★ SENECA STATE FOREST

Rt 1, Box 140
Dunmore, WV 24934
Web: www.senecastateforest.com
Phone: 304-799-6213
Size: 11,684 acres. **Location:** 4 miles south of Dunmore on WV 28. **Facilities:** 10 rustic campsites (1 &), 8 rustic cabins, showers (nearby, 1 &), laundry, picnic areas, hiking trails, bike trails, fishing pier (&), boat rentals, playgrounds, game courts. **Activities:** Camping, hunting (in season), boating, swimming, fishing, hiking, mountain biking, horseback riding. **Special Features:** The oldest of West Virginia's state forests, Seneca borders the Greenbrier River in Pocahontas County and contains 4-acre Seneca Lake. Both are named for the Indian tribe that once roamed the area.

★4696★ STONEWALL JACKSON LAKE STATE PARK

149 State Park Trail
Roanoke, WV 26447
Phone: 304-269-0523
Size: More than 1,800 acres. **Location:** Exit 91 off I-79, then 2 miles south. **Facilities:** 40 deluxe campsites, houseboat rental, 4 deluxe cottages, picnic areas, recreation building with kitchen, 198-room lodge with restaurant, lounge, and conference facilities, snack bar, hiking trails, boat ramp, marina, fishing pier, 18-hole golf course, gift shop. **Activities:** Camping, boating, fishing, hiking, bicycling. **Special Features:** The 2,650-acre lake is the recreational focus of the park, offering some of the best fishing in the state. Numerous abandoned roads crisscross the adjacent Wildlife Management Area, offering miles of hiking and biking opportunities.

★4697★ TOMLINSON RUN STATE PARK

PO Box 97
New Manchester, WV 26056
Web: www.tomlinsonrunsp.com
Phone: 304-564-3651
Size: 1,398 acres. **Location:** In West Virginia's northern panhandle, 19 miles north of Weirton on WV Rt. 2; accessible via WV 8 north. **Facilities:** 54 standard campsites (39 with electrical hookups), rustic campsites, group camp (11 cabins), 4 yurt rentals, picnic areas, picnic shelters, hiking trails, swimming pool with slide, snack bar, bathhouse, shower, laundry, boat rentals, game courts, playgrounds, gift shop. **Activities:** Camping, boating, fishing, swimming, hiking, tennis, miniature golf, nature and recreation programs (seasonal). **Special Features:** Located at the extreme tip of the state's northern panhandle, Tomlinson Run offers a wide range of recreational opportunities to local and out-of-state visitors. The park extends along the stream from which it gets its name to within a mile of the Ohio River. More than 33 acres of water, in the form of various ponds and streams, afford excellent fishing opportunities for bass, bluegill, and trout.

★4698★ TU-ENDIE-WEI STATE PARK

PO Box 486
Point Pleasant, WV 25550
Web: www.tu-endie-weistatepark.com
Phone: 304-675-0869
Size: 4 acres. **Location:** West central West Virginia, at the confluence of the Ohio and Kanawha rivers. **Facilities:** Museum (operated by the Daughters of the American Revolution), historic site. **Special Features:** Park's monument commemorates the frontiersmen who fought and died here in a battle with the forces of Chief Cornstalk on October 10, 1774. The name ''Tu-Endie-Wei'' is a Wyandotte word meaning ''point between two waters.''

★4699★ TWIN FALLS RESORT STATE PARK

PO Box 1023
Mullens, WV 25882
Web: www.twinfallsresort.com
Phone: 304-294-4000
Size: 3,776 acres. **Location:** 27 miles southeast of Beckley in the southern portion of the state. **Facilities:** 25 deluxe campsites, 25 standard campsites, 13 cottages, 20-room lodge with restaurant and conference rooms, picnic areas, snack bar, hiking trails, swimming pool, bathhouses, nature center, museum, historical site, 18-hole golf course, game courts, playgrounds, camp store, gift shop, amphitheater. **Activities:** Camping, swimming, hiking, golf, tennis, nature and recreation programs (year round). **Special Features:** Pioneer Farm is a living history farm that depicts the life and times of early settlers in the Twin Falls area around the 1830s.

★4700★ TYGART LAKE STATE PARK

Rt 1, Box 260
Grafton, WV 26354
Web: www.tygartlake.com
Phone: 304-265-6144

9. State Parks

Size: 2,134 acres. **Location:** 5 miles south of Grafton, off I-79. **Facilities:** 40 standard campsites (14 with electrical hookups), 11 deluxe cabins, 20-room lodge and restaurant, picnic areas, hiking trails, swimming beach, boat rentals, boat ramp, marina, playgrounds, gift shops. **Activities:** Camping, boating, fishing, swimming, water-skiing, scuba diving, jet skiing, hiking, nature and recreation programs (seasonal). **Special Features:** Park sits alongside 10-mile long, 1,750-acre Tygart Lake, and the 17-room park lodge overlooks the water. Dinner theater programs are scheduled at the lodge restaurant throughout the year.

★4701★ VALLEY FALLS STATE PARK
Rt 6, Box 244
Fairmont, WV 26273
Web: www.valleyfallsstatepark.com
Phone: 304-367-2719
Size: 1,145 acres. **Location:** Near Fairmont, off I-79. **Facilities:** Picnic areas, hiking trails (18 miles), playground, game courts, restrooms. **Activities:** Fishing, whitewater rafting, hiking, sightseeing. **Special Features:** Once the site of a lumber and grist mill community, park features a spectacular series of foaming falls created by the rushing Tygart Valley River.

★4702★ WATOGA STATE PARK
HC 82, Box 252
Marlinton, WV 24954
Web: www.watoga.com
Phone: 304-799-4087
Size: 10,100 acres. **Location:** Off US 219 at Hillsboro. **Facilities:** 88 standard campsites (50 with electrical hookups), 12 primitive campsites, 10 deluxe cabins, 24 standard cabins, picnic areas, restaurant (seasonal), trails, swimming pool, bathhouses, boat rentals, stables, arboretum, recreation building, lookout tower, game courts, playgrounds, museum, camp store, gift shop. **Activities:** Camping, boating, fishing, swimming, hiking, horseback riding, tennis, cross-country skiing, nature and recreation program (seasonal). **Special Features:** West Virginia's largest state park, Watoga is located in the Appalachian highlands along the state's eastern border. The park's unusual name is derived from the Cherokee word "watauga," which means "the river of islands."

★4703★ WATTERS SMITH MEMORIAL STATE PARK
PO Box 296
Lost Creek, WV 26385
Web: www.watterssmithstatepark.com
Phone: 304-745-3081
Size: 532 acres. **Location:** North central part of the state, off I-79. **Facilities:** Picnic areas, snack bar, hiking trails, biking trails, swimming pool, museums, historic site, activity building with meeting rooms, stables, game courts, playgrounds, gift shop. **Activities:** Swimming, hiking, biking, horseback riding, guided tours (seasonal). **Special Features:** The heritage of early West Virginia is preserved in this pioneer homestead restoration, which includes a museum with early farm artifacts, a restored log cabin, and the 1876 Smith family home, which has been restored as a museum.

Wisconsin State Parks

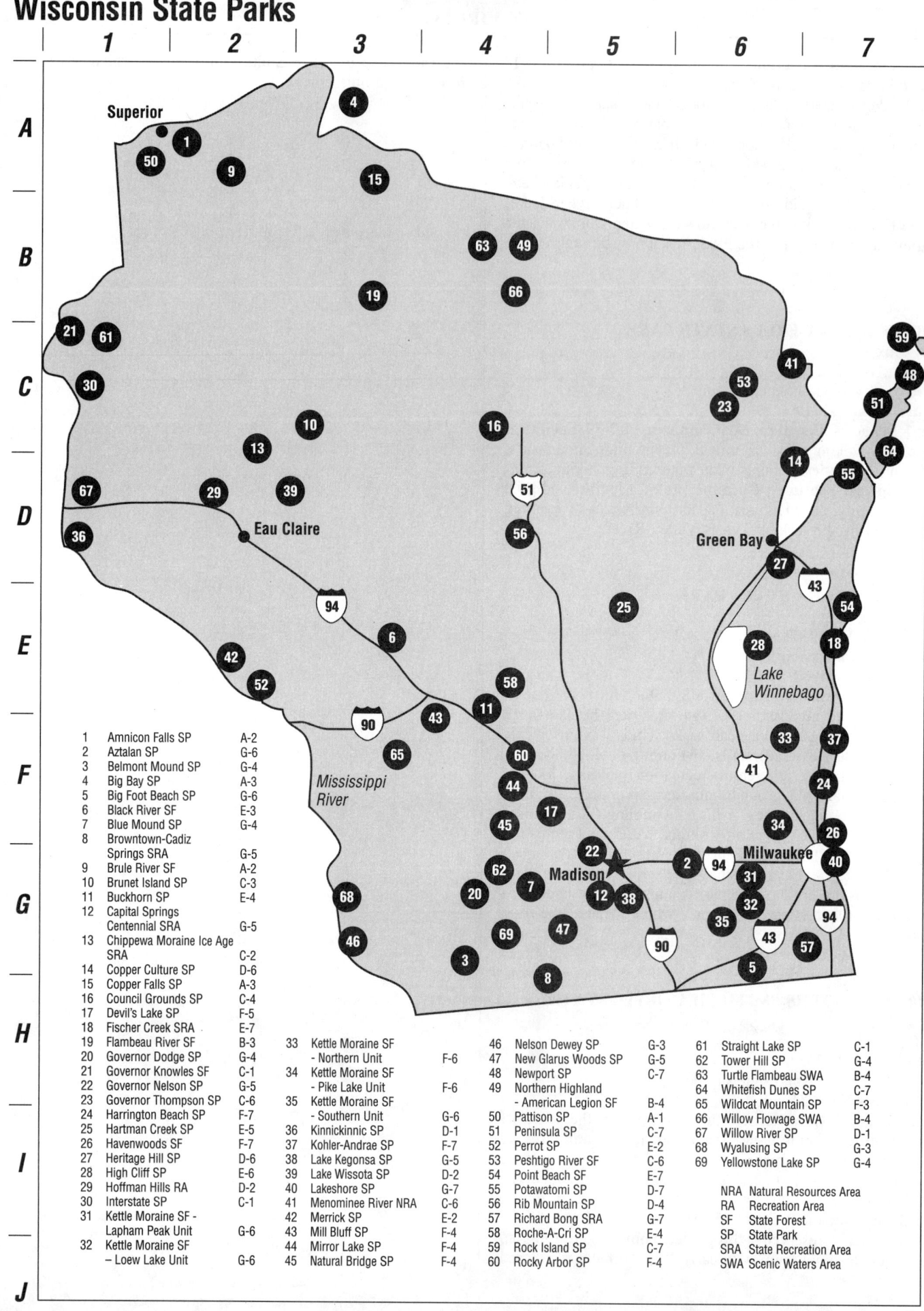

Superior

Eau Claire

Green Bay

Madison

Milwaukee

Lake Winnebago

Mississippi River

1	Amnicon Falls SP	A-2
2	Aztalan SP	G-6
3	Belmont Mound SP	G-4
4	Big Bay SP	A-3
5	Big Foot Beach SP	G-6
6	Black River SF	E-3
7	Blue Mound SP	G-4
8	Browntown-Cadiz Springs SRA	G-5
9	Brule River SF	A-2
10	Brunet Island SP	C-3
11	Buckhorn SP	E-4
12	Capital Springs Centennial SRA	G-5
13	Chippewa Moraine Ice Age SRA	C-2
14	Copper Culture SP	D-6
15	Copper Falls SP	A-3
16	Council Grounds SP	C-4
17	Devil's Lake SP	F-5
18	Fischer Creek SRA	E-7
19	Flambeau River SF	B-3
20	Governor Dodge SP	G-4
21	Governor Knowles SF	C-1
22	Governor Nelson SP	G-5
23	Governor Thompson SP	C-6
24	Harrington Beach SP	F-7
25	Hartman Creek SP	E-5
26	Havenwoods SF	F-7
27	Heritage Hill SP	D-6
28	High Cliff SP	E-6
29	Hoffman Hills RA	D-2
30	Interstate SP	C-1
31	Kettle Moraine SF - Lapham Peak Unit	G-6
32	Kettle Moraine SF – Loew Lake Unit	G-6

33	Kettle Moraine SF - Northern Unit	F-6
34	Kettle Moraine SF - Pike Lake Unit	F-6
35	Kettle Moraine SF - Southern Unit	G-6
36	Kinnickinnic SP	D-1
37	Kohler-Andrae SP	F-7
38	Lake Kegonsa SP	G-5
39	Lake Wissota SP	D-2
40	Lakeshore SP	G-7
41	Menominee River NRA	C-6
42	Merrick SP	E-2
43	Mill Bluff SP	F-4
44	Mirror Lake SP	F-4
45	Natural Bridge SP	F-4

46	Nelson Dewey SP	G-3
47	New Glarus Woods SP	G-5
48	Newport SP	C-7
49	Northern Highland - American Legion SF	B-4
50	Pattison SP	A-1
51	Peninsula SP	C-7
52	Perrot SP	E-2
53	Peshtigo River SF	C-6
54	Point Beach SF	E-7
55	Potawatomi SP	D-7
56	Rib Mountain SP	D-4
57	Richard Bong SRA	G-7
58	Roche-A-Cri SP	E-4
59	Rock Island SP	C-7
60	Rocky Arbor SP	F-4

61	Straight Lake SP	C-1
62	Tower Hill SP	G-4
63	Turtle Flambeau SWA	B-4
64	Whitefish Dunes SP	C-7
65	Wildcat Mountain SP	F-3
66	Willow Flowage SWA	B-4
67	Willow River SP	D-1
68	Wyalusing SP	G-3
69	Yellowstone Lake SP	G-4

NRA	Natural Resources Area
RA	Recreation Area
SF	State Forest
SP	State Park
SRA	State Recreation Area
SWA	Scenic Waters Area

WISCONSIN

★4704★ Wisconsin Department of Natural Resources
Bureau of Parks & Recreation
PO Box 7921
Madison, WI 53707
(608) 266-2181 - Phone
(608) 261-4380 - Fax
(888) 947-2757 - Reservations
(608) 267-7424 - Employment Information
(608) 264-7617 – Volunteering
Web: www.dnr.state.wi.us/org/land/parks
System includes more than 50 parks, eight forests, and five recreation areas, encompassing nearly 130,000 acres. Maintains an extensive trail system, totaling more than 1,000 miles, which includes 25 named trails. Designated trails require a pass for biking, horseback riding, or cross-country skiing.

★4705★ Wisconsin Historical Society
816 State St
Madison, WI 53706
(608) 264-6400 - Phone
(608) 264-6433 - Fax
Web: www.wisconsinhistory.org
Maintains a research facility in Madison. Owns and operates a statewide system of nine historic sites. Offers preservation services and educational programs.

★4706★ AMNICON FALLS STATE PARK
6294 S State Rd 35
Superior, WI 54880
Web: www.dnr.state.wi.us/ORG/land/parks/specific/amnicon
Phone: 715-398-3000
Size: 825 acres. **Location:** 8 miles east of Superior on Highway 2. **Facilities:** 36 campsites (some &), picnic areas, hiking trails (1.8 mile), nature trail (0.8 miles), playground. **Activities:** Camping, fishing, hiking, swimming, bicycling. **Special Features:** Park features a series of waterfalls and rapids along the Amnicon River and a covered foot bridge over the river.

★4707★ AZTALAN STATE PARK
1213 S Main St
Lake Mills, WI 53551
Web: www.dnr.state.wi.us/ORG/land/parks/specific/aztalan
Phone: 920-648-8774; **Fax:** 920-648-5166
Size: 172 acres. **Location:** South of I-94 near Lake Mills. **Facilities:** Picnic area, hiking trails (2 miles), nature trails (2 miles), historical features. **Activities:** Canoeing, fishing, hiking, interpretive tour. **Special Features:** Park preserves an important archeological site at the location of a 12th-century Indian village.

The people who settled Aztalan built large, flat-topped pyramidal mounds and a stockade around their village. Portions of the stockade and two mounds have been reconstructed in the park.

★4708★ BELMONT MOUND STATE PARK
c/o Yellowstone Lake State Park
7896 Lake Rd
Blanchardville, WI 53516
Phone: 608-523-4427
Size: 78 acres. **Location:** 2.5 miles northwest of Belmont off County Hwy G. **Facilities:** Picnic area, playground, observation tower. **Special Features:** This 400-foot mound is an outlier of the Niagara dolomite escarpment. From the park's 64-foot observation tower, visitors can see for miles in all directions. Belmont Lions Club operates and maintains this state park property.

★4709★ BIG BAY STATE PARK
Box 589
Bayfield, WI 54814
Web: www.dnr.state.wi.us/ORG/land/parks/specific/bigbay
Phone: 715-747-6425
Size: 2,350 acres. **Location:** On Madeline Island, off the northern tip of Wisconsin, on Lake Superior. **Facilities:** 60 campsites, showers, indoor group camp, picnic areas, hiking trails (9 miles), nature trails, ski trails, swimming beach, scenic view. **Activities:** Camping (including winter camping), boating, canoeing, fishing, hunting (with restrictions), swimming, hiking, cross-country skiing, snowshoeing, birdwatching, naturalist programs (seasonal). **Special Features:** Park features picturesque sandstone bluffs and caves where Lake Superior meets the shoreline.

★4710★ BIG FOOT BEACH STATE PARK
1452 Hwy H
Lake Geneva, WI 53147
Web: www.dnr.state.wi.us/org/land/parks/specific/bigfoot
Phone: 262-248-2528
Size: 271 acres. **Location:** On the shore of Lake Geneva. **Facilities:** 100 campsites, showers, picnic areas, hiking trails (5.5 miles), nature trails, shoreline, volleyball court, horseshoe pit. **Activities:** Camping, boating, fishing, swimming, hiking, cross-country skiing. **Special Features:** Located in a resort and recreation area on the shore of Lake Geneva, this park features a 2,200-foot sandy beach.

★4711★ BLACK RIVER STATE FOREST
910 Hwy 54 E
Black River Falls, WI 54615
Web: www.dnr.state.wi.us/org/land/Forestry/StateForests/SF-BlackRiver
Phone: 715-284-4103

Size: About 68,000 acres. **Location:** In Jackson County off I-94. **Facilities:** 100+ campsites (6 with electrical hookups), picnic area, enclosed day-use shelter, scenic view, observation tower, shoreline, boat launch, backpack and hiking trails, nature trails, mountain bike trails, snowmobile and ski trails. **Activities:** Camping (including winter camping), boating, canoeing, fishing, swimming, horseback riding, hiking, backpacking, mountain biking, ATV riding, hunting, cross-country skiing, snowmobiling. **Special Features:** Forest lies at the edge of the glaciated central plains, east of the "driftless" area of Wisconsin. Hiking to the top of Castle Mound provides views of the former bed of glacial Lake Wisconsin, as well as the unglaciated buttes, sandstone hills, and castellated bluffs that dot the landscape.

★4712★ BLUE MOUND STATE PARK

Box 98
Blue Mounds, WI 53517
Web: www.dnr.state.wi.us/org/land/parks/specific/bluemound
Phone: 608-437-5711
Size: 1,153 acres. **Location:** 25 miles west of Madison. **Facilities:** 78 campsites (14 with electrical hookups, 2 accessible), showers, picnic area, concessions, hiking trails, nature trails, mountain bike trails (6 miles), ski trails (10+ miles), swimming pool, playground, nature center, observation towers. **Activities:** Camping (including winter camping), swimming, hiking, bicycling, cross-country skiing, snowmobiling, sledding, snowshoeing, naturalist programs (seasonal). **Special Features:** Located at the highest point in southern Wisconsin, the park offers panoramic views of the surrounding area. Two 40-foot observation towers are equipped with landmark locators, which help pinpoint various cities and geologic features.

★4713★ BROWNTOWN-CADIZ SPRINGS STATE RECREATION AREA

PO Box 805
New Glarus, WI 53574
Web: www.dnr.state.wi.us/org/land/parks/specific/browntown
Phone: 608-966-3777
Size: 695 acres. **Location:** Green County in southwest Wisconsin. **Facilities:** Picnic area, shoreline, boat launch, hiking trails, nature trail, playground, fishing pier (&). **Activities:** Boating, canoeing, fishing, swimming, hiking, cross-country skiing. **Special Features:** Browntown-Cadiz Springs includes two spring-fed lakes totalling 95 acres, and a 600-acre wildlife area.

★4714★ BRULE RIVER STATE FOREST

6250 S Ranger Rd
Brule, WI 54820
Web: www.dnr.state.wi.us/org/land/Forestry/StateForests/SF-Brule
Phone: 715-372-5678; **Fax:** 715-372-4836
Size: 41,000 acres. **Location:** 1 mile west of Brule on US 2, then 1 mile south on Ranger Road. **Facilities:** 70 camp units, backpack campsites, picnic area, hiking trails (7 miles), nature trails, mountain bike trails (14 miles), snowmobile trails (26 miles), ski trails (16.5 miles), boat launch, shoreline. **Activities:** Camping (including winter camping), boating, canoeing, whitewater rafting, fishing, hunting, archery, hiking, backpacking, horseback riding, mountain biking, cross-country skiing, snowmobiling. **Special Features:** Forest encompasses the entire length of the Brule River, which drops 328 feet from its headwaters to the shore of Lake Superior.

★4715★ BRUNET ISLAND STATE PARK

Rt 2, Box 158
Cornell, WI 54732
Web: www.dnr.state.wi.us/org/land/parks/specific/brunetisland
Phone: 715-239-6888
Size: More than 1,200 acres. **Location:** Off WI Route 23, 1 mile northwest of Cornell. **Facilities:** 69 campsites (24 with electrical hookups, some &), showers, picnic areas, hiking trails (8 miles), nature trails (0.8 miles), ski trails (5 miles), shoreline, fishing pier, playground, boat launch. **Activities:** Camping, boating, canoeing, fishing, swimming, hiking, biking, cross-country skiing, snowshoeing, ice fishing. **Special Features:** Framed by the Chippewa and Fisher rivers, this island park features quiet bays and lagoons.

★4716★ BUCKHORN STATE PARK

W8450 Buckhorn Park Ave
Necedah, WI 54646
Web: www.dnr.state.wi.us/org/land/parks/specific/buckhorn
Phone: 608-565-2789
Size: 2,500 acres. **Location:** 11 miles north of Mauston. **Facilities:** 24 cart-in campsites, 11 drive-in campsites, outdoor group camp, 42 backpack campsites, cabin (& only), picnic areas, hiking and nature trails, snowmobile trails, ski trails, shoreline, canoe trail, boat launch, fishing pier (&). **Activities:** Camping, boating, canoeing, fishing, swimming, water-skiing, hiking, backpacking, hunting, cross-country skiing, snowmobiling, naturalist programs (seasonal). **Special Features:** A favorite of hunters, hikers, and nature lovers, the park features a wheelchair-accessible wildlife blind and fishing pier.

★4717★ CAPITAL SPRINGS CENTENNIAL STATE RECREATION AREA

3101 Lake Farm Rd
Madison, WI 53711
Web: www.dnr.state.wi.us/org/land/parks/specific/capsprings
Phone: 608-224-3606
Size: 3,000 acres. **Location:** Just south of Madison. **Facilities:** 54 campsites for tent or vehicle (39 with electrical hookups), hiking trails, skiing trails, picnic area with shelter, boat launch. **Activities:** Camping, hiking, bicycling, fishing, wildlife watching. **Special Features:** The park protects more than 0.75 miles of undeveloped shoreline on Lake Waubesa and is located at the hub of several state trails. Nine miles of the Capital City State Trail run through the park.

★4718★ CHIPPEWA MORAINE ICE AGE STATE RECREATION AREA

13394 County Hwy M
New Auburn, WI 54757
Web: www.dnr.state.wi.us/org/land/parks/specific/chipmoraine
Phone: 715-967-2800; **Fax:** 715-967-2801

9. State Parks

Size: 3,063 acres. **Location:** 7 miles west of New Auburn on County Road M. **Facilities:** Picnic areas (&), hiking trails, nature trails, primitive campsite, boat launch, interpretive center, scenic vista. **Activities:** Boating, fishing, hiking, snowshoeing, bird watching, naturalist programs. **Special Features:** The Ice Age National Scenic Trail, a 1,000-mile trail located entirely within Wisconsin, passes through park (see separate entry in national trails section). Interpretive center sits atop a hill that was once a glacial lake bottom. Park is part of the Ice Age National Scientific Reserve.

★4719★ COPPER CULTURE STATE PARK

N10008 Paust Ln
Crivitz, WI 54114
Phone: 715-757-3979
Size: 48 acres. **Location:** Off US Highway 41, in Oconto. **Facilities:** Picnic area, interpretive center, museum. **Activities:** Fishing (in the Oconto River). **Special Features:** Park features an Indian burial ground from the Copper Culture, about 6,000 years ago. It is the oldest cemetery site in Wisconsin. Also features a 15-acre shortgrass prairie.

★4720★ COPPER FALLS STATE PARK

36764 Copper Falls Rd
Mellen, WI 54546
Web: www.dnr.state.wi.us/org/land/parks/specific/copperfalls
Phone: 715-274-5123
Size: 2,700 acres. **Location:** North of Mellen in Ashland County. **Facilities:** 54 campsites (13 with electrical hookups), showers, outdoor group camp, backpack campsite, rustic cabin (& only), picnic areas, concessions, hiking trails (8 miles), nature trails (2 miles), mountain bike trails (8 miles), ski trails (8 miles), shoreline, boat launch, scenic vista. **Activities:** Camping (including winter camping), boating, canoeing, fishing, swimming, hiking, mountain biking, backpacking, cross-country skiing, snowshoeing. **Special Features:** Scenic park includes canyons, streams, and waterfalls. The North Country National Scenic Trail runs almost the entire length of the park (see separate entry in national trails section.)

★4721★ COUNCIL GROUNDS STATE PARK

N1895 Council Grounds Dr
Merrill, WI 54452
Phone: 715-536-8773
Size: 502 acres. **Location:** Along the Wisconsin River, 1 mile northwest of Merrill. **Facilities:** 55 campsites (some with electrical hookups), showers, picnic areas, enclosed day-use shelter, concessions, hiking trails, nature trail, paved bicycle trails (4 miles), mountain bike trails (3 miles), ski trails (5 miles), fitness trail, shoreline, boat launch, nature center. **Activities:** Camping, boating, canoeing, fishing, swimming, water-skiing, hiking, bicycling, mountain biking, cross-country skiing, interpretive programs (seasonal). **Special Features:** Located along the beautiful Wisconsin River, the park is a favorite of water enthusiasts.

★4722★ DEVIL'S LAKE STATE PARK

S5975 Park Rd
Baraboo, WI 53913
Web: www.dnr.state.wi.us/org/land/parks/specific/devilslake
Phone: 608-356-8301; **Fax:** 608-356-4281
Size: 9,117 acres. **Location:** 2 miles south of Baraboo. **Facilities:** 535 campsites (117 with electrical hookups), showers, picnic areas, enclosed day-use shelter, concessions, hiking trails (30 miles), nature trails, mountain bike trails (8 miles), ski trails (17 miles), nature center, scenic vista, shoreline, boat launch, amphitheater. **Activities:** Camping (including winter camping), boating, canoeing, fishing, swimming, scuba diving, hiking, mountain biking, rock climbing, cross-country skiing, snowshoeing, dogsledding, naturalist programs. **Special Features:** Park is designated an Ice Age Unit of the Ice Age National Scientific Reserve. It features 500-foot bluffs flanking a 360-acre lake. (See also listing of Ice Age National Scenic Trail in national trails section.)

★4723★ FISCHER CREEK STATE RECREATION AREA

4319 Expo Dr
Manitowoc, WI 54220
Phone: 920-683-4185
Size: 123 acres. **Location:** Off Highway U, just south of Manitowoc. **Facilities:** Nature trail (1 mile). **Activities:** Boating, fishing, hiking. **Special Features:** Includes nearly a mile of Lake Michigan shoreline, as well as scenic wooded bluffs, grasslands, and wetlands.

★4724★ FLAMBEAU RIVER STATE FOREST

W1613 County Rd
Winter, WI 54896
Web: www.dnr.state.wi.us/org/land/Forestry/StateForests/SF-Flambeau
Phone: 715-332-5271
Size: 90,147 acres. **Location:** North central Wisconsin. **Facilities:** 60 campsites, 35 canoe campsites, picnic areas, hiking trails, nature trails, bridle trails, mountain bike trails, snowmobile trails, ski trails, shoreline, boat launch. **Activities:** Camping (including winter camping), boating, canoeing, whitewater rafting, fishing, hunting, swimming, hiking, backpacking, mountain biking, ATV riding, cross-country skiing, snowmobiling. **Special Features:** One of the best whitewater rivers in the midwest, the Flambeau River flows 75 miles through this state forest.

★4725★ GOVERNOR DODGE STATE PARK

4175 Hwy 23
Dodgeville, WI 53533
Web: www.dnr.state.wi.us/org/land/parks/specific/govdodge
Phone: 608-935-2315
Size: 5,270 acres. **Location:** 3 miles north of Dodgeville on WI 23. **Facilities:** 269 campsites (80 with electrical hookups), showers, 8 group camps, 6 backpack campsites, 11 horsemen's campsites, picnic areas, concessions, hiking trails, nature trails, bridle trails, mountain bike trails, snowmobile trails, ski trails, nature center, scenic vista, shoreline, boat launch. **Activities:** Camping (including winter camping), boating (electric motors

9. State Parks

only), canoeing, fishing, ice fishing, hunting, swimming, hiking, bicycling, horseback riding, cross-country skiing, snowmobiling, ice skating, sledding, naturalist programs (seasonal). **Special Features:** In 1958 a dam was constructed across Mill Creek and Cox Hollow Lake was created. A second dam was built in 1966, forming Twin Valley Lake. These two lakes are just some of the scenic points of this park, which also features steep hills, bluffs, deep valleys, and a waterfall.

★4726★ GOVERNOR KNOWLES STATE FOREST

325 SR 70
Grantsburg, WI 54840
Web: www.dnr.state.wi.us/org/land/Forestry/stateforests/SF-Knowles
Phone: 715-463-2897
Size: 32,500 acres, of which 19,753 acres are state-owned. **Location:** Along the St. Croix River in northwestern Wisconsin. **Facilities:** 31 campsites (2 accessible), backpack camp, picnic areas, hiking trails, nature trails, bridle trails, snowmobile trails, ski trails, viewing sites. **Activities:** Camping, boating, canoeing, swimming, fishing, ice fishing, hiking, bicycling, horseback riding, cross-country skiing, snowmobiling, tobogganing, snowshoeing, hunting. **Special Features:** Forest preserves a wilderness area along the Saint Croix River. Six designated State Natural Areas within the forest preserve unique biotic communities.

★4727★ GOVERNOR NELSON STATE PARK

5140 County Hwy M
Waunakee, WI 53597
Web: www.dnr.state.wi.us/org/land/parks
Phone: 608-831-3005; **Fax:** 608-831-4071
Size: 422 acres. **Location:** On Lake Mendota. **Facilities:** Picnic areas, hiking and ski trails (11 miles), concessions, shoreline, showers, boat launch, scenic vista (&&). **Activities:** Boating, canoeing, fishing, ice fishing, swimming, hiking, cross-country skiing, naturalist programs (seasonal). **Special Features:** Located on Lake Mendota, within sight of the state capitol building. Park includes several effigy mounds, the most striking being a 358-foot panther-shaped mound.

★4728★ GOVERNOR THOMPSON STATE PARK

N 10008 Paust Ln
Crivitz, WI 54115
Web: www.dnr.state.wi.us/org/land/parks/specific/govthompson
Phone: 715-757-3979; **Fax:** 715-757-3779
Size: 2,600 acres. **Location:** 13 miles northwest of Crivitz in Marinette County. **Facilities:** Primitive boat launch, hiking trails. **Activities:** Non-motorized boating, hiking, berry picking, wildlife observation, hunting, swimming. **Special Features:** Site protects 5,300 feet of shoreline on Wood and Huber lakes as well as Handsaw Creek and Woods Outlet, both excellent brook and brown trout waters.

★4729★ HARRINGTON BEACH STATE PARK

531 Hwy D
Belgium, WI 53004
Web: www.dnr.state.wi.us/org/land/parks/specific/harrington
Phone: 262-285-3015
Size: 636 acres. **Location:** Off I-43, 35 miles north of Milwaukee. **Facilities:** Picnic areas, shelters, shoreline, hiking trail, bridle trail, ski trail. **Activities:** Fishing, swimming, scuba diving, hiking, bicycling, mountain biking, horseback riding, cross-country skiing, naturalist programs (seasonal). **Special Features:** On the site of a former limestone quarry, park features a serene lake as well as a mile-long stretch of Lake Michigan shoreline.

★4730★ HARTMAN CREEK STATE PARK

N2480 Hartman Creek Rd
Waupaca, WI 54981
Web: www.dnr.state.wi.us/org/land/parks/specific/hartman
Phone: 715-258-2372
Size: 1,417 acres. **Location:** 6 miles west of Waupaca on WI 54. **Facilities:** 101 campsites, 5 group camps, showers, picnic areas, hiking trails (10 miles), bridle trails (7 miles), mountain bike trails (5 miles), ski trails (8 miles), scenic vista, shoreline, amphitheater. **Activities:** Camping (including winter camping), canoeing, kayaking, fishing, swimming, hiking, bicycling, mountain biking, horseback riding, cross-country skiing, snowmobiling, naturalist programs (seasonal). **Special Features:** Located on the beautiful Chain O'Lakes, park features the Hellestad House log cabin.

★4731★ HAVENWOODS STATE FOREST

6141 N Hopkins St
Milwaukee, WI 53209
Web: www.dnr.state.wi.us/org/land/parks/specific/havenwoods
Phone: 414-527-0232; **Fax:** 414-527-0761
Size: 237 acres. **Location:** One block west of Sherman and Douglas in Milwaukee. **Facilities:** Picnic area, hiking, nature and ski trails (6+ miles, some &), arboretum, environmental awareness center. **Activities:** Hiking, biking, cross-country skiing, naturalist programs, educational programs (for school and youth groups). **Special Features:** Forest is an open, green space within the City of Milwaukee, providing environmental education and recreation opportunities and maintaining natural habitat in the urban environment.

★4732★ HERITAGE HILL STATE PARK

2640 S Webster Ave
Green Bay, WI 54301
Web: www.heritagehillgb.org
Phone: 920-448-5150
Size: 54 acres. **Location:** On Webster Street just north of WI 172, 2 miles south of Green Bay. **Facilities:** Historical buildings, visitor center, gift shop. **Activities:** Sightseeing, educational programs. **Special Features:** Heritage Hill is a living history museum, featuring 25 structures from northeastern Wisconsin's past, placed into historical settings and containing an extensive collection of artifacts.

9. State Parks

★4733★ HIGH CLIFF STATE PARK

N7630 State Park Rd
Sherwood, WI 54169
Web: www.dnr.state.wi.us/org/land/parks/specific/highcliff
Phone: 920-989-1106
Size: 1,147 acres. **Location:** 9 miles east of Menasha. **Facilities:** 112 campsites (32 with electrical hookups, 2 ♿), cabin (♿), showers, 8 group sites, picnic areas, enclosed day-use shelter, hiking trails, nature trails, bridle trails, mountain bike trails, marina, boat launch, nature center, museum, scenic vista, observation tower, ball fields, playground. **Activities:** Camping boating, fishing, swimming, water-skiing, horseback riding, mountain biking, cross-country skiing, snowmobiling, interpretive programs (seasonal). **Special Features:** Park rests on limestone cliffs overlooking 215-square-mile Lake Winnebago. Park's museum features exhibits on effigy mound builders, lime kiln and quarry operations, and glaciers.

★4734★ HOFFMAN HILLS RECREATION AREA

921 Brickyard Rd
Menomonie, WI 54751
Web: www.dnr.state.wi.us/org/land/parks/specific/
   hoffmanhills
Phone: 715-232-1242
Size: 707 acres. **Location:** 10 miles northeast of Menomonie. **Facilities:** Outdoor group camp, picnic areas, hiking and ski trails (9 miles), nature trails (2 miles), observation tower. **Activities:** Camping, hiking, berry, nut, and mushroom picking, cross-country skiing, sledding, snowshoeing, wildlife watching, hunting. **Special Features:** Park's 60-foot observation tower affords sweeping views of rugged hill country, wetlands, and restored prairie.

★4735★ INTERSTATE STATE PARK

PO Box 703
Saint Croix Falls, WI 54024
Web: www.dnr.state.wi.us/org/land/parks/specific/interstate
Phone: 715-483-3747
Size: 1,377 acres. **Location:** Just south of Saint Croix Falls on WI 35. **Facilities:** 85 campsites, showers, outdoor group camp, picnic areas, hiking trails (9 miles), snowshoe trails, interpretive center, scenic vista, shoreline, boat launch, fishing pier, amphitheater. **Activities:** Camping, boating, canoeing, fishing, swimming, hiking, cross-country skiing, naturalist programs. **Special Features:** A deep gorge called the "Dalles of the Saint Croix" is a scenic feature of Wisconsin's oldest state park. Frost action and weathering over the years formed interesting rock features here. As part of the Ice Age National Scientific Reserve, the Ice Age Interpretive Center features photographs, murals, and other information about the great glaciers. (See also listing of Ice Age National Scenic Trail in national trails section.)

★4736★ KETTLE MORAINE STATE FOREST - LAPHAM PEAK UNIT

W329 N846 County Hwy C
Delafield, WI 53018
Web: www.dnr.state.wi.us/org/land/parks/specific/lapham
Phone: 262-646-3025
Size: More than 1,000 acres. **Location:** 25 miles west of Milwaukee. **Facilities:** Backpack campsites, picnic area, enclosed day-use shelter, butterfly garden, hiking trails (21 miles), bridle trails (5 miles), mountain bike trails (5 miles), ski trails (17 miles), observation tower. **Activities:** Camping (including winter camping), hiking, horseback riding, mountain biking, inline skating, cross-country skiing, naturalist programs (seasonal). **Special Features:** The Kettle Moraine and Lapham Peak were formed 10,000 years ago when a glacier covered much of Wisconsin. A 45-foot lookout tower offers excellent view of the hills and meadows.

★4737★ KETTLE MORAINE STATE FOREST - LOEW LAKE UNIT

c/o Pike Lake Unit
3544 Kettle Moraine Rd
Hartland, WI 53027
Phone: 262-670-3400
Size: 1,170 acres. **Location:** Washington County, near the intersection of county highways K and Q. **Facilities:** Trails (3 miles). **Activities:** Hiking, hunting, horseback riding. **Special Features:** Park's picturesque valley includes the east branch of the Oconomowoc River and 23-acre Loew Lake. The Ice Age National Scenic Trail (see entry in national trails section) passes through the park on the west side of the river.

★4738★ KETTLE MORAINE STATE FOREST - NORTHERN UNIT

N1765 Hwy G
Campbellsport, WI 53010
Web: www.dnr.state.wi.us/org/land/parks/specific/kmn
Phone: 262-626-2116
Size: Almost 30,000 acres. **Location:** 7 miles north of Kewaskum on County Highway G. **Facilities:** More than 300 campsites (49 with electrical hookups), showers, playground, outdoor group camp, backpack campsites, horsemen's camp, picnic areas, enclosed day-use shelter, concessions, multi-use trails (132 miles), visitor center, scenic vista, auto tour, boat launch. **Activities:** Camping (including winter camping), boating, canoeing, fishing, hunting, swimming, hiking, backpacking, mountain biking, horseback riding, cross-country skiing, snowmobiling, snowshoeing, naturalist programs. **Special Features:** Forest features several kames, which are irregularly shaped hills or mounds composed chiefly of poorly sorted sand and gravel deposited by a sub-glacial stream. Dundee Kame (aka White Kame) is known throughout the world by geology students because of its near-perfect form. The Kame field offers visitors a chance to experience the rock, rubble, and gravel insides of a kame up close.

★4739★ KETTLE MORAINE STATE FOREST - PIKE LAKE UNIT

3544 Kettle Moraine Rd
Hartford, WI 53027
Web: www.dnr.state.wi.us/org/land/parks/specific/pikelake
Phone: 262-670-3400
Size: 678 acres. **Location:** 25 miles north of Milwaukee. **Facilities:** 32 campsites (1 with electric, ♿), showers, picnic areas,

shoreline, hiking trails, nature trail, bike trail. **Activities:** Camping, fishing, swimming, hiking, bicycling, cross-country skiing, snowmobiling, naturalist programs (seasonal). **Special Features:** Powder Hill, a 1,350-foot glacial kame, offers panoramic views of the park's unique glacial topography. The Ice Age National Scenic Trail passes through the park (see separate entry in national trails section).

★4740★ KETTLE MORAINE STATE FOREST - SOUTHERN UNIT

S91 W39091 Hwy 59
Eagle, WI 53119
Web: www.dnr.state.wi.us/org/land/parks/specific/kms
Phone: 262-594-6201
Size: More than 20,000 acres. **Location:** 3 miles west of Eagle on WI 59. **Facilities:** 3 family campsites, showers, cabin (& only), 2 group camps, backpack campsites, horsemen's camp, picnic areas, , multi-use trails (160 miles), boat launches, fishing pier (&), visitor center, scenic vista, auditorium. **Activities:** Camping (including winter camping), boating, canoeing, fishing, hunting, trapping, swimming, hiking, backpacking, mountain biking, horseback riding, cross-country skiing, snowmobiling, naturalist programs. **Special Features:** Forest features Old World Wisconsin, considered America's largest outdoor museum of rural life, with displays such as ethnic farmsteads, furnished houses, rural outbuildings, and crossroads villages.

★4741★ KINNICKINNIC STATE PARK

W11983 820th Ave
River Falls, WI 54022
Phone: 715-425-1129
Size: 1,242 acres. **Location:** Western Wisconsin at the confluence of the Lower St Croix and Kinnickinnic Rivers. **Facilities:** Picnic areas (&), boat-in campsites, hiking and ski trails, scenic vista, visitor station. **Activities:** Camping, boating, canoeing, fishing, ice fishing, swimming, hiking, sledding, cross-country skiing. **Special Features:** Park is located on the banks of the Kinnickinnic, a cold-water trout stream that forms a large sandy delta where it flows into the Saint Croix River.

★4742★ KOHLER-ANDRAE STATE PARK

1020 Beach Park Ln
Sheboygan, WI 53081
Web: www.dnr.state.wi.us/org/land/parks/specific/ka
Phone: 920-451-4080
Size: Approximately 1,000 acres. **Location:** 2 miles south of Sheboygan. **Facilities:** 105 campsites (49 with electrical hookups), showers, 2 group camps, picnic areas, concession, hiking trails, nature trails, bridle trails, mountain bike trails, ski trails, nature center, scenic vista, shoreline, auditorium. **Activities:** Camping (including winter camping), fishing, swimming, hiking, mountain biking, horseback riding, cross-country skiing, candlelight skiing, snowshoeing, sledding, naturalist programs (seasonal). **Special Features:** Park is one of the last natural preserves along the Lake Michigan shore and includes two miles of beach and sand dunes.

★4743★ LAKE KEGONSA STATE PARK

2405 Door Creek Rd
Stoughton, WI 53589
Web: www.dnr.state.wi.us/org/land/parks/
Phone: 608-873-9695; **Fax:** 608-873-0674
Size: 342 acres. **Location:** 4 miles north of Stoughton in southern Wisconsin. **Facilities:** 80 campsites (2 with electrical hookup, &), group camp (3 sites), showers, picnic areas, shelters, boat launch, fishing pier, hiking trails (5 miles), ski trails (6 miles), nature trail, 2 playgrounds, sledding hill. **Activities:** Camping, boating, canoeing, sailing, fishing, ice fishing, swimming, water-skiing, hiking, cross-country skiing, sledding, naturalist programs (seasonal). **Special Features:** Park was once inhabited by ancient Effigy Mound Builders, and evidence of their efforts is still visible along the White Oak Nature Trail.

★4744★ LAKE WISSOTA STATE PARK

18127 County Hwy 'O'
Chippewa Falls, WI 54729
Web: www.dnr.state.wi.us/org/land/parks/specific/lakewissota
Phone: 715-382-4574; **Fax:** 715-382-5187
Size: 1,062 acres. **Location:** 5 miles east of Chippewa Falls. **Facilities:** 81 campsites (17 with electrical hookups, 2 &), showers, outdoor group camp (80 sites), picnic areas, shelter, hiking trails (18 miles), bridle trails (7 miles), mountain bike trails (11 miles), snowmobile trails (5 miles), ski trails (7 miles), snowshoeing trails (10 miles), ballfield, nature center, amphitheater, scenic vista, boat launch. **Activities:** Camping, boating, canoeing, fishing, ice fishing, swimming, water-skiing, hiking, bicycling, horseback riding, cross-country skiing, snowmobiling, snowshoeing, naturalist programs (seasonal). **Special Features:** The 6,300-acre lake attracts anglers seeking walleyes, muskies, and bass. A permanent fishing pier provides easy access for anglers with disabilities.

★4745★ LAKESHORE STATE PARK

2300 N Martin Luther King Jr Dr
Milwaukee, WI 53212
Web: www.dnr.state.wi.us/org/land/parks/specific/lakeshore
Phone: 414-263-8570
Size: 22 acres. **Location:** Along Lake Michigan on Milwaukee's lakefront. **Facilities:** Undeveloped; currently closed to the public. **Special Features:** Park will connect the Hank Aaron State Trail, the Oak Leaf Trail, and Milwaukee's recreational lakefront resources.

★4746★ MENOMINEE RIVER NATURAL RESOURCES AREA

PO Box 199
Wausaukee, WI 54177
Web: www.dnr.state.wi.us/org/land/facilities/menominee
Phone: 715-856-9160
Size: 1,962 acres. **Location:** On the Wisconsin side of the Menominee River, east of Pembine. **Facilities:** Primitive campsites, 2 canoe campsites, canoe launch, hiking trails, scenic vistas. **Activities:** Canoeing, hiking, camping, sightseeing, hunting, trapping, fishing, berry picking. **Special Features:** Area is a river corridor of towering pines, granite rock outcrops, and

9. State Parks

falls in northeast Wisconsin next to the Michigan border. Developed areas of the park are rustic, and the property is generally intended for quiet use, with limited vehicular access.

★4747★ MERRICK STATE PARK

PO Box 127
Fountain City, WI 54629
Phone: 608-687-4936
Size: 320 acres. **Location:** Off WI Highway 31, north of Fountain City. **Facilities:** 69 campsites (22 with electrical hookups), showers, outdoor group camp, picnic areas, hiking trails (3 miles), ski trails (3 miles), nature center, scenic vista, boat launch. **Activities:** Camping, boating, canoeing, fishing, swimming, water-skiing, hiking, cross-country skiing, naturalist programs (seasonal). **Special Features:** Located between 500-foot bluffs and the Mississippi River. The park's marshy backwaters are home for egrets, herons, muskrats, and otter.

★4748★ MILL BLUFF STATE PARK

PO Box 99
Ontario, WI 54651
Phone: 608-427-6692
Size: 1,258 acres. **Location:** 2 miles northwest of I-90 (Camp Douglas Exit) on US 12/16. **Facilities:** 21 campsites (6 with electrical hookups, 3 ♿), picnic areas (2 ♿), hiking trails (2 miles), nature trail, bike trail, scenic vista. **Activities:** Camping, swimming, hiking, biking, naturalist programs (seasonal). **Special Features:** Park is a designated Ice Age Unit of the Ice Age National Scientific Reserve. It features picturesque rock formations, mesas, buttes, and pinnacles. (See also listing of Ice Age National Scenic Trail in national trails section.)

★4749★ MIRROR LAKE STATE PARK

E10320 Fern Dell Rd
Baraboo, WI 53913
Phone: 608-254-2333
Size: 2,050 acres. **Location:** 3 miles from Wisconsin Dells. **Facilities:** 147 campsites (30 with electrical hookups), showers, cabin (♿ only), 7 group camps, picnic areas, hiking trails (20 miles), mountain bike trails (10 miles), ski trails (20 miles), canoe trail., playground, vollyeball court, concessions, bike and canoe rentals, boat launch. **Activities:** Camping (including winter camping), boating, canoeing, fishing, swimming, hiking, mountain biking, cross-country skiing, naturalist programs (seasonal). **Special Features:** The sandstone gorge that surrounds 137-acre Mirror Lake is the result of meltwater chiseling through the landscape 10,000 years ago. Etched ripples mark the stone.

★4750★ NATURAL BRIDGE STATE PARK

c/o Devil's Lake State Park
S5975 Park Rd
Baraboo, WI 53913
Phone: 608-356-8301
Size: 530 acres. **Location:** 16 miles south of Baraboo. **Facilities:** Picnic areas, hiking trail (4 miles), nature trail (1 mile). **Activities:** Hiking, sightseeing, snowmobiling. **Special Features:** Park features a natural sandstone arch and a rock shelter used by prehistoric people 11,000 years ago, at the end of the last Ice Age.

★4751★ NELSON DEWEY STATE PARK

Box 658
Cassville, WI 53806
Phone: 608-725-5374
Size: 756 acres. **Location:** Southwest Wisconsin, along the banks of the Mississippi River. **Facilities:** 40 campsites (some with electrical hookups), showers, group camp, 2 walk-in camps, picnic areas, hiking trails,scenic vista. **Activities:** Camping (including winter camping), hiking, mountain biking. **Special Features:** Park features Stonefield, home of Wisconsin's first governor, Nelson Dewey, and Stonefield Village, a reconstructed 1890s village.

★4752★ NEW GLARUS WOODS STATE PARK

W5446 County Hwy NN
New Glarus, WI 53574
Web: www.dnr.state.wi.us/org/land/parks/specific/ngwoods
Phone: 608-527-2335
Size: 411 acres. **Location:** Along Highway 39/69, south of New Glarus. **Facilities:** 32 campsites, 6 group camps, picnic area, hiking trails (7 miles), playground. **Activities:** Camping (including winter camping), hiking, backpacking, biking, snowshoeing, snowmobiling, wildlife observation, naturalist programs (seasonal), hunting, picking of edible fruits, nuts, asparagus and mushrooms. **Special Features:** Located near the Sugar River Trail, park features quiet campsites in an undisturbed woodland. The space that is now the group campground was originally logged to build a sawmill that today houses the administrative office. The lumber milled there was made into barrels to ship Limburger cheese on a railroad line that would later become the Sugar River State Trail. Hilly terrain kept much of the park from being logged, leaving many trees untouched; some are more than 250 years old.

★4753★ NEWPORT STATE PARK

475 County Rd NP
Ellison Bay, WI 54210
Web: www.dnr.state.wi.us/org/land/parks/specific/newport
Phone: 920-854-2500; **Fax:** 920-854-1914
Size: 2,373 acres. **Location:** Northeast Wisconsin at the tip of Door Peninsula. **Facilities:** 16 campsites, backpack campsites, picnic areas, multi-use trails (38 miles), interpretive center. **Activities:** Camping (including winter camping), canoeing, fishing, swimming, hiking, mountain biking, cross-country skiing, naturalist programs (seasonal). **Special Features:** This semi-wilderness area includes 11 miles of Lake Michigan shoreline.

★4754★ NORTHERN HIGHLAND - AMERICAN LEGION STATE FOREST

4125 County Hwy M
Boulder Junction, WI 54512
Web: www.dnr.state.wi.us/org/land/Forestry/StateForests/sf-nh-al
Phone: 715-385-2727

9. State Parks

Size: More than 225,000 acres. **Location:** Vilas, Oneida, and Iron counties in northern Wisconsin. **Facilities:** More than 900 campsites (including a group camp, backpack campsites, and family campground), picnic areas, hiking trails (18 miles), nature trails (7 miles), mountain bike trails (32 miles), snowmobile trails (400 miles), ski trails (70 miles), nature center, scenic vistas, shoreline, boat launches. **Activities:** Camping (including winter camping), boating, canoeing, fishing, horseback riding, swimming, hiking, backpacking, mountain biking, hunting, cross-country skiing, snowmobiling, snowshoeing, skijoring, naturalist programs. **Special Features:** The largest of Wisconsin's state forests has one of the highest concentrations of lakes in the world and offers ''wild land'' recreation for those seeking a pristine and quiet backcountry experience.

★4755★ PATTISON STATE PARK

6294 S State Rd 35
Superior, WI 54880
Web: www.dnr.state.wi.us/org/land/parks/specific/pattison
Phone: 715-399-3111
Size: 1,436 acres. **Location:** 13 miles south of Superior on State Road 35. **Facilities:** 59 campsites (18 with electrical hookups, 1 &), showers, backpack campsites, picnic areas, enclosed day-use shelter, hiking trails (9 miles), ski trails (4 miles), playground, volleyball court, nature center, scenic vista, shoreline. **Activities:** Camping (including winter camping), boating, canoeing, fishing, swimming, hiking, backpacking, cross-country skiing, naturalist programs. **Special Features:** One of the state's outstanding scenic features is the 165-foot-high Big Manitou Falls, the highest falls in Wisconsin and fourth-highest falls east of the Rockies. Park also features a steep-walled gorge of dark basalt carved by the Black River.

★4756★ PENINSULA STATE PARK

PO Box 218
Fish Creek, WI 54212
Web: www.dnr.state.wi.us/org/land/parks/specific/peninsula
Phone: 920-868-3258
Size: 3,776 acres. **Location:** Northeast of Fish Creek on WI 42 in Door County. **Facilities:** 472 campsites (101 with electrical hookups), showers, outdoor group camp (50 sites), picnic areas, enclosed day-use shelter, concessions, hiking trails (20 miles), mountain bike trails (9 miles), snowmobile trails (17 miles), ski trails (16 miles), playground, volleyball court, tennis court, nature center, scenic vistas, observation tower, boat launch, 18-hole golf course, outdoor amphitheater. **Activities:** Camping (including winter camping), boating, canoeing, fishing, swimming, hiking, mountain biking, tennis, volleyball, in-line skating, cross-country skiing, snowmobiling, sledding, snowshoeing, naturalist programs. **Special Features:** Located on a peninsula jutting into Green Bay, the park's bluffs afford views of passing ships and nearby islands. Features include a lighthouse built in 1868 and bays fringed by sand and cobblestone.

★4757★ PERROT STATE PARK

Rt 1, Box 407
Trempealeau, WI 54661
Phone: 608-534-6409

Size: 1,400 acres. **Location:** Near the confluence of the Trempealeau and Mississippi Rivers in southwest Wisconsin. **Facilities:** 95 campsites (44 with electrical hookups), showers, outdoor group camp (50 sites), picnic areas, hiking trails (13 miles), mountain bike trails, ski trails, nature center, scenic vista, boat launch. **Activities:** Camping, boating, canoeing, fishing, hiking, mountain biking, cross-country skiing, naturalist programs (seasonal). **Special Features:** Early inhabitants include the ancient Indian cultures of archaic, early woodland and effigy mound builders. Mounds from the Hopewell culture have been identified.

★4758★ PESHTIGO RIVER STATE FOREST

N 10008 Paust Ln
Crivitz, WI 54114
Web: www.dnr.state.wi.us/org/land/Forestry/StateForests/
meet.htm#Peshtigo
Phone: 715-757-3965
Size: Two parcels totaling approximately 9,200 acres. **Location:** 20 miles northwest of Crivitz. **Activities:** Hiking, fishing, boating, canoeing, hunting, snowmobiling, cross-country skiing. **Special Features:** Undeveloped forest along 70 miles of Peshtigo River in Marinette County. A section of the forest is adjacent to the new Governor Thompson State Park (see separate entry).

★4759★ POINT BEACH STATE FOREST

9400 County Hwy 'O'
Two Rivers, WI 54241
Web: www.dnr.state.wi.us/org/land/parks/specific/pointbeach
Phone: 920-794-7480
Size: 2,903 acres. **Location:** 4 miles north of Two Rivers on County Highway O. **Facilities:** 127 campsites (70 with electrical hookups), showers, indoor group camp, outdoor group camp, picnic areas, concessions, hiking trails (11 miles), mountain bike trails (4 miles), ski trails (11 miles), snowmobile trails (3 miles), nature center. **Activities:** Camping (including winter camping), fishing, hunting, swimming, hiking, mountain biking, cross-country skiing, naturalist program (seasonal). **Special Features:** A major feature is Rawley Point and the lighthouse which has been operated by the US Coast Guard since 1853. It is the largest and brightest on the Great Lakes, boasting a 2-million candlepower lamp.

★4760★ POTAWATOMI STATE PARK

3740 County PD
Sturgeon Bay, WI 54235
Web: www.dnr.state.wi.us/org/land/parks/specific/Potawatomi
Phone: 920-746-2890
Size: 1,225 acres. **Location:** 1 mile northwest of Sturgeon Bay on Park Drive. **Facilities:** 123 campsites (25 with electrical hookups), cabin (& only), showers, picnic areas, hiking trails (9 miles), mountain bike trails (8 miles), snowmobile trails (9 miles), ski trails (8 miles), sledding hill, concessions, nature center, scenic vista, observation tower, boat launch. **Activities:** Camping (including winter camping), boating, canoeing, kayaking, fishing, water-skiing, scuba diving, hiking, mountain biking, cross-country skiing, snowmobiling, naturalist programs

(seasonal). **Special Features:** On a clear day, views from the 75-foot observation tower can reach 16 miles across Green Bay.

★4761★ RIB MOUNTAIN STATE PARK

5301 Rib Mountain Dr
Wausau, WI 54401
Phone: 715-842-2522
Size: 1,480 acres. **Location:** 3 miles southwest of Wausau on US 51. **Facilities:** 30 campsites, showers, picnic area, enclosed day-use shelter, concessions, hiking trails (13 miles), accessible trails (8 miles), snowmobile trails (10 miles), snowshoe trails (8 miles), playground, scenic vistas, observation tower, outdoor amphitheater. **Activities:** Camping, hiking, snowshoeing, downhill skiing, hunting, naturalist programs (seasonal). **Special Features:** One of the oldest geological formations on earth, this billion-year-old hill was long thought to be the highest point in Wisconsin. (It is actually the third-highest point.) The top of the 60-foot observation tower is 700 feet above the surrounding plain.

★4762★ RICHARD BONG STATE RECREATION AREA

26313 Burlington Rd
Kansasville, WI 53139
Web: www.dnr.state.wi.us/org/land/parks/specific/bong
Phone: 262-878-5600; **Fax:** 262-878-5615
Size: 4,515 acres. **Location:** 8 miles southeast of Burlington, Wisconsin. **Facilities:** 217 campsites (54 with electrical hookups), 6 group camps, showers, picnic area, hiking trails (16 miles), nature trails (2 miles), bridle trails (13 miles), mountain bike trails (10 miles), snowmobile trails (12 miles), ski trails (15 miles), snowshoeing trails (10 miles), ATV trails (7 miles), shoreline, nature center, auditorium, boat launch, volleyball nets, ballfield, horsehoe pits, fishing pier (&). **Activities:** Camping (including winter camping), canoeing, fishing, swimming, hiking, mountain biking, horseback riding, motorcycling, hunting, ATV riding, cross-country skiing, snowmobiling, year-round naturalist programs, hang gliding, hot-air ballooning, model airplane flying. **Special Features:** Property was originally cleared to become a military base, but was later converted to open parkland. It was the state's first recreation area.

★4763★ ROCHE-A-CRI STATE PARK

1767 Hwy 13
Friendship, WI 53934
Web: www.dnr.state.wi.us/org/land/parks/specific/roche-a-cri
Phone: 608-339-6881
Size: 605 acres. **Location:** 1.5 miles north of Friendship on WI 13. **Facilities:** 41 rustic campsites, picnic areas, hiking trails (5 miles), nature trail, scenic vista, playgrounds, volleyball courts, horseshoe pits. **Activities:** Camping, hiking, fishing, sightseeing, naturalist programs (seasonal). **Special Features:** The French name which means ''crevice in the rock'' refers to the 300-foot-high outcrop of rock that is the central feature of this small park. A 303-step staircase leads to the top of the outcrop, which has Native American petrglyphs and pictographs.

★4764★ ROCK ISLAND STATE PARK

Rt 1, Box 118A
Washington Island, WI 54246
Web: www.dnr.state.wi.us/org/land/parks/specific/rockisland
Phone: 920-847-2235
Size: 912 acres. **Location:** Tip of Door County Peninsula. **Facilities:** 40 campsites, picnic areas, hiking trails (10 miles), nature trail (1 mile), nature center, scenic vista, shoreline, boat launch. **Activities:** Camping, boating, canoeing, fishing, swimming, hiking, backpacking, naturalist programs (seasonal). **Special Features:** Ferryboat transportation is seasonally available to this primitive Lake Michigan island. Stone buildings, built by a wealthy inventor who owned the island between 1910 and 1930, house interpretive exhibits.

★4765★ ROCKY ARBOR STATE PARK

c/o Mirror Lake State Park
E10320 Fern Dell Rd
Baraboo, WI 53913
Phone: 608-254-8001
Size: 225 acres. **Location:** 1.5 miles from Wisconsin Dells. **Facilities:** 89 campsites (17 with electrical hookups, 2 &), nature trail, playground. **Activities:** Camping, hiking, raspberry picking. **Special Features:** Park features a sandstone gorge believed to be 500 million years old. Picturesque rock walls, ledges, and formations dominate the park.

★4766★ STRAIGHT LAKE STATE PARK

PO Box 703
Saint Croix Falls, WI 74024
Web: www.dnr.state.wi.us/org/land/parks/specific/straightlake
Phone: 715-483-3747
Size: 2,780 acres. **Location:** Northwestern Wisconsin near Luck. **Activities:** Canoeing, kayaking, rowboating. **Special Features:** Dedicated in 2005, acquisition of this land completes the largest missing gap in the Ice Age National Scenic Trail system in Western Wisconsin. Park contains an 850-acre block of mature forest with some trees approaching 100 years old, and it has been named an important bird area.

★4767★ TOWER HILL STATE PARK

5808 County Rd C
Spring Green, WI 53588
Phone: 608-588-2116
Size: 77 acres. **Location:** 3.5 miles southeast of Spring Green on County Road C, east of WI 23. **Facilities:** 15 campsites, picnic area, shelter, hiking trails, scenic vista. **Activities:** Camping, boating, canoeing, fishing, hiking. **Special Features:** Visitors can hike to the unique shot tower and melting house to view a film and displays on lead shot manufacturing in the 1800s.

★4768★ TURTLE FLAMBEAU SCENIC WATERS AREA

3291 State House Cir
Mercer, WI 54547
Phone: 715-476-2240

9. State Parks

Location: Southwest of Mercer in Iron County. **Facilities:** 60 campsites, trails, auto tour, 6 boat launches. **Activities:** Camping, hiking, boating, canoeing, birdwatching, hiking, hunting. **Special Features:** The Turtle-Flambeau Flowage has the highest density of bald eagle, osprey, and common loon breeding pairs in Wisconsin.

★4769★ WHITEFISH DUNES STATE PARK

3275 County Hwy WD
Sturgeon Bay, WI 54235
Web: www.dnr.state.wi.us/org/land/parks/specific/whitefish
Phone: 920-823-2400

Size: 865 acres. **Location:** 10 miles northeast of Sturgeon Bay on Clark Lake Road. **Facilities:** Picnic area (&), hiking trails (15 miles), bicycle trail, nature trail (1 mile, &), ski trails (8 miles), beach (&), concessions, nature center, scenic vistas. **Activities:** Fishing, swimming, hiking, biking, cross-country skiing, naturalist programs (seasonal). **Special Features:** Park offers an unusual combination of natural features, including the rugged Lake Michigan shoreline, a dense upland forest, shoreline on an interior lake, a winding creek with associated wetlands, and the highest sand dunes in Wisconsin.

★4770★ WILDCAT MOUNTAIN STATE PARK

E13660 SR 33, Box 99
Ontario, WI 54651
Web: www.dnr.state.wi.us/org/land/parks/specific/wildcat
Phone: 608-337-4775

Size: 3,603 acres. **Location:** 2 miles east of Ontario on WI 33. **Facilities:** 30 campsites, 3 group camps, 24 equestrian campsites, showers, picnic areas, hiking trails (26 miles), nature trails (1 mile), bridle trails (15 miles), ski trails (7 miles), snowshoe trails (18 miles), nature center, scenic vista, boat launch, canoe rentals. **Activities:** Camping, canoeing, fishing, hiking, horseback riding, cross-country skiing, naturalist programs (seasonal). **Special Features:** The Kickapoo River's erosion has created beautiful vertical or nearly vertical sandstone cliffs along the river. Some of these cliffs are large enough to create an isolated humid environment capable of supporting rare plants.

★4771★ WILLOW FLOWAGE SCENIC WATERS AREA

8770 Hwy 7
Woodruff, WI 54568
Phone: 715-356-5211

Size: 17,000 acres. **Location:** 12 miles from Tomahawk. **Facilities:** Boat landings, shoreline, 55 rustic campsites. **Activities:** Camping, boating, canoeing, fishing, hiking. **Special Features:** Described as "almost Canada," this flowage has a wild flavor, with more than 73 miles of shoreline and 106 islands.

★4772★ WILLOW RIVER STATE PARK

1034 County Hwy A
Hudson, WI 54016
Web: www.dnr.state.wi.us/org/land/parks/specific/willowriver
Phone: 715-386-5931; **Fax:** 715-386-0431
Size: 2,891 acres. **Location:** 5 miles northeast of Hudson on County Highway A. **Facilities:** 72 campsites (18 with electrical hookups. 1 &), showers, outdoor group camp, picnic areas, hiking trails (13 miles), nature trails (0.6 miles), ski trails (9 miles), sandy beach shoreline, boat launch, nature center, scenic vista. **Activities:** Camping (including winter camping), boating, canoeing, fishing, swimming, hiking, backpacking, cross-country skiing, dog sledding, snowshoeing, sledding, ice fishing, naturalist programs (seasonal). **Special Features:** Park's rolling countryside features two dams, three lakes, a trout stream, remnants of prairie land, and scenic views of historic Willow Falls and the Willow River Gorge.

★4773★ WYALUSING STATE PARK

13081 State Park Ln
Bagley, WI 53801
Web: www.dnr.state.wi.us/org/land/parks/specific/wyalusing
Phone: 608-996-2261; **Fax:** 608-996-2410

Size: 2,628 acres. **Location:** Southwest Wisconsin, in rural Grant County. **Facilities:** 109 campsites (34 with electrical hookups), showers, dormitory lodge (108 beds), outdoor group camp, picnic areas, concessions, hiking trails (22 miles), nature trail (2 miles), mountain bike trail (8 miles), ski trails (7 miles), accessible trail (.8 mile), nature center, scenic vista, boat launch. **Activities:** Camping (including winter camping), boating, canoeing, fishing, hiking, bicycling, cross-country skiing, naturalist programs (seasonal). **Special Features:** Park sits on a bluff 500 feet above the confluence of the Wisconsin and Mississippi rivers. Wyalusing is one of Wisconsin's oldest parks and features Indian burial grounds, an interpretive center, and four historical markers.

★4774★ YELLOWSTONE LAKE STATE PARK

8495 Lake Rd
Blanchardville, WI 53516
Web: www.dnr.state.wi.us/org/land/parks/specific/
yellowstone/index.html
Phone: 608-523-4427

Size: 968 acres. **Location:** 7 miles southwest of Blanchardville on County Highway F. **Facilities:** 128 campsites (36 with electrical hookups), showers, 6 group camps (4 with electrical hookups), picnic areas, concessions, hiking trails (10 miles), mountain bike trails (3 miles), snowmobile trails (3 miles), ski trails (5 miles), scenic vista, shoreline, boat launch. **Activities:** Camping (including winter camping), boating, canoeing, fishing, swimming, water-skiing, hiking, cross-country skiing, snowmobiling, naturalist programs (seasonal). **Special Features:** Park is home to more than 4,000 brown bats that roost in 31 bat houses throughout the park. Because each bat can eat up to 600 mosquitoes an hour, they have nearly eliminated the park's mosquito population.

9. State Parks

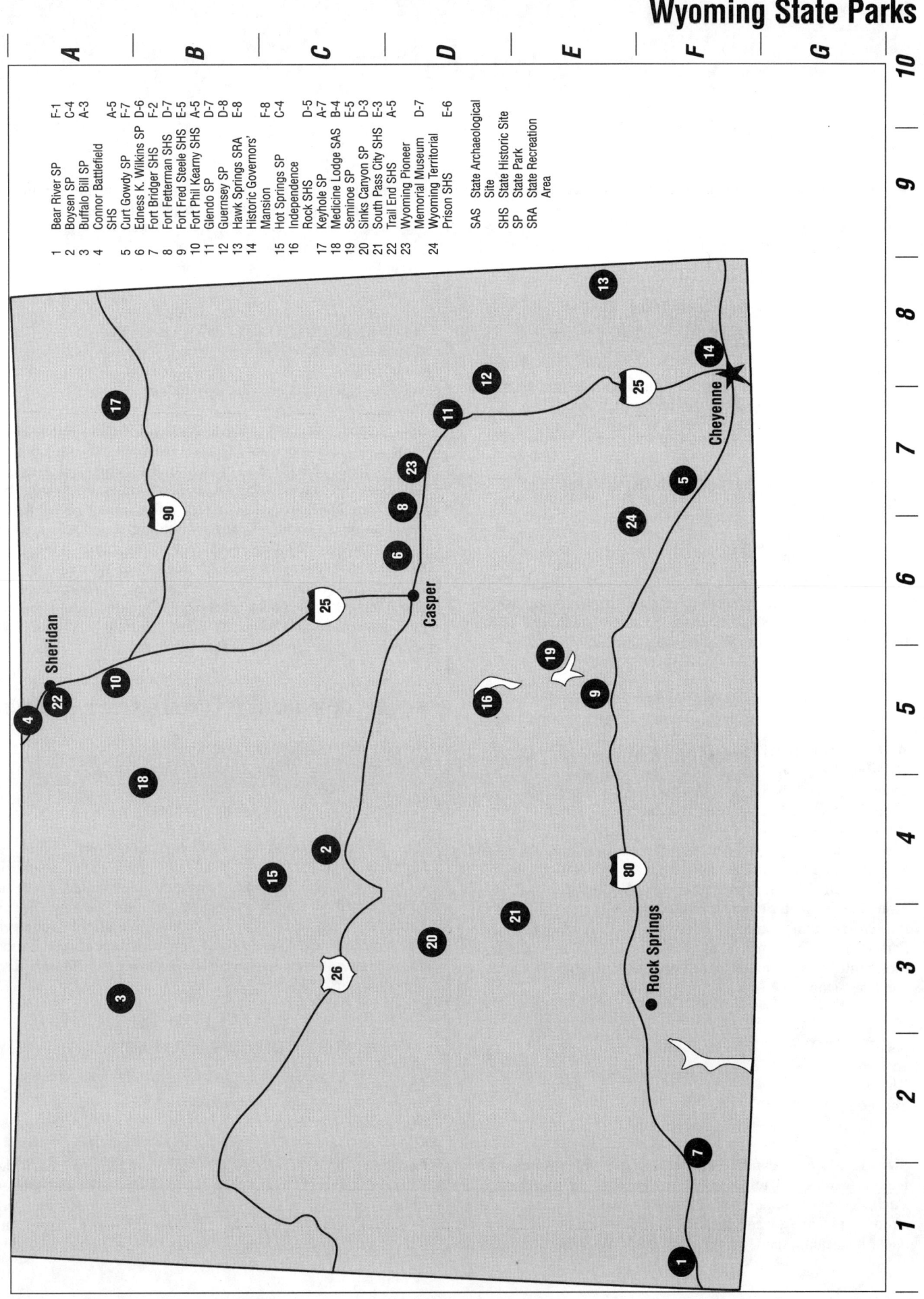

Wyoming State Parks

1	Bear River SP	F-1
2	Boysen SP	C-4
3	Buffalo Bill SP	A-3
4	Connor Battlefield SHS	A-5
5	Curt Gowdy SP	F-7
6	Edness K. Wilkins SP	D-6
7	Fort Bridger SHS	F-2
8	Fort Fetterman SHS	D-7
9	Fort Fred Steele SHS	E-5
10	Fort Phil Kearny SHS	A-5
11	Glendo SP	D-7
12	Guernsey SP	D-8
13	Hawk Springs SRA	E-8
14	Historic Governors' Mansion	F-8
15	Hot Springs SP	C-4
16	Independence Rock SHS	D-5
17	Keyhole SP	A-7
18	Medicine Lodge SAS	B-4
19	Seminoe SP	E-5
20	Sinks Canyon SP	D-3
21	South Pass City SHS	E-3
22	Trail End SHS	A-5
23	Wyoming Pioneer Memorial Museum	D-7
24	Wyoming Territorial Prison SHS	E-6

SAS State Archaeological Site
SHS State Historic Site
SP   State Park
SRA State Recreation Area

Sheridan

Casper

Rock Springs

Cheyenne

WYOMING

★4775★ Wyoming Division of State Parks & Historic Sites

2301 Central Ave
Cheyenne, WY 82002
(307) 777-5598 - Phone
(307) 777-6472 - Fax
(877) 996-7275 - Toll-free Reservations
(307) 777-7188 - Employment
(307) 777-7010 - Volunteering
Web: wyoparks.state.wy.us
Operates 12 state parks, 11 historic and archeological sites, and a recreation area, which together encompass more than 94,000 acres. Maintains some 2,000 miles snowmobile trails.

★4776★ Wyoming Game & Fish Department

5400 Bishop Blvd
Cheyenne, WY 82006
(307) 777-4600 - Phone
(307) 777-4610 - Fax
Web: gf.state.wy.us
Manages and protects wildlife species and their habitats. Administers hunting and fishing licenses, promotes safety and education programs, sponsors wildlife watching activities.

★4777★ BEAR RIVER STATE PARK

601 Bear River Dr
Evanston, WY 82930
Web: wyoparks.state.wy.us/brslide.htm
Phone: 307-789-6547
Size: 280 acres. **Location:** Along I-80 near Evanston. **Facilities:** Visitor center, picnic area and shelters, restrooms, trails (1.2 miles paved, 1.7 miles packed gravel), Volksmarch trail, playground (&&). **Activities:** Fishing, hiking, bicycling, inline skating, cross-country skiing, wildlife viewing. **Special Features:** Park is home to a small herd of bison and elk. Site includes a travel information center that offers travelers on I-80 a convenient rest stop.

★4778★ BOYSEN STATE PARK

15 Ash
Boysen Rt
Shoshoni, WY 82649
Web: wyoparks.state.wy.us/boslide.htm
Phone: 307-876-2796
Size: 15,145 acres land; 19,560 acres water. **Elevation:** 4,820 feet. **Location:** 13 miles north of Shoshoni on Highway 20. **Facilities:** 11 campgrounds, tent and trailer campsites, restrooms, picnic area and shelters, trails, swimming beach, boat dock, boat ramp, dam, playground (&&). **Activities:** Camping,

boating, fishing, swimming, water-skiing, windsurfing, hunting (with restrictions), ice fishing. **Special Features:** The original dam was built by Asmus Boysen in 1908; parts of it can still be seen adjacent to the tunnels in the Lower Wind River campground.

★4779★ BUFFALO BILL STATE PARK

47 Lakeside Rd
Cody, WY 82414
Web: wyoparks.state.wy.us/buffalo.htm
Phone: 307-587-9227
Size: Approximately 3,500 acres land, 8,150 acres water. **Elevation:** 5,400 feet. **Location:** 6 miles west of Cody, on US Highway 14-16-20. **Facilities:** Tent and trailer campsites, restrooms, day-use lodge, picnic area and shelters, trails, boat ramp, boat dock, dam, ballfields, playground, visitor center (&&). **Activities:** Camping, boating, fishing, swimming, water-skiing, windsurfing, hiking, bicycling, wildlife viewing. **Special Features:** Majestic mountains dominate the scenery of Wyoming's northernmost park, which serves as a gateway to Yellowstone National Park (see separate entry in the national parks section). Park was named for Colonel William ''Buffalo Bill'' Cody, who owned much of this land before the reservoir was constructed.

★4780★ CONNOR BATTLEFIELD STATE HISTORIC SITE

c/o Fort Kearny State Historic Site
PO Box 520
Story, WY 82842
Web: wyoparks.state.wy.us/coslide.htm
Phone: 307-684-7629
Size: 26 acres. **Elevation:** 3,745 feet. **Location:** 2 blocks off Highway 14 in Ranchester, near the Tongue River. **Facilities:** 20 camping and picnic sites, restrooms, playground, horseshoe pits. **Activities:** Camping, fishing, wildlife viewing. **Special Features:** Park surrounds the Connor Battlefield Monument, which memorializes the Battle of Tongue River between General P.E. Connor and an Arapaho village during the Powder River Expedition in 1865.

★4781★ CURT GOWDY STATE PARK

1319 Hynds Lodge Rd
Cheyenne, WY 82009
Web: wyoparks.state.wy.us/curt.htm
Phone: 307-632-7946
Size: 1,635 acres land, 325 acres water. **Elevation:** 7,500 feet. **Location:** Halfway between Cheyenne and Laramie. **Facilities:** 150 tent and trailer campsites, lodge, picnic area and shelters, summer concessions, trails (6.2 miles), Volksmarch trail, boat dock, boat ramp, fishing pier, dam, amphitheater, playgrounds (&&). **Activities:** Camping, boating, fishing, horseback riding,

hiking, archery. **Special Features:** Park, named after the famous sports broadcaster, features two reservoirs and an undeveloped area for hikers to explore the forest.

★4782★ **EDNESS K. WILKINS STATE PARK**
PO Box 1596
Evansville, WY 82636
Web: wyoparks.state.wy.us/ewslide.htm
Phone: 307-577-5150
Size: 315 acres. **Location:** 6 miles east of Casper, off I-25. **Facilities:** Picnic area and shelters, trail (2.8 miles paved), volleyball court, swimming beach, fishing pier, boat ramp, playgrounds, restrooms (&&). **Activities:** Boating, rafting, fishing, swimming, hiking, bicycling. **Special Features:** Located at the site of an old rock quarry on the North Platte River, the reclaimed park land provides habitat for a variety of wildlife, including more than 200 species of birds.

★4783★ **FORT BRIDGER STATE HISTORIC SITE**
PO Box 35
Fort Bridger, WY 82933
Web: wyoparks.state.wy.us/fbslide.htm
Phone: 307-782-3842
Size: 38 acres. **Elevation:** 6,675 feet. **Location:** Near Black's Fork on the Green River, 3 miles off I-80. **Facilities:** Picnic area, historical trail, Volksmarch trail, visitor center, museum, gift shop, restrooms (&&). **Activities:** Self-guiding tours, interpretive programs. **Special Features:** Mountain man Jim Bridger chose this site for his post in 1843, and in 1858 it became a major military installation that was vital to the Pony Express and Overland Stage routes. Structures in the fort have been restored.

★4784★ **FORT FETTERMAN STATE HISTORIC SITE**
752 Hwy 93
Douglas, WY 82633
Web: wyoparks.state.wy.us/ffslide.htm
Phone: 307-684-7629
Size: 62 acres. **Location:** Near Douglas, off I-25. **Facilities:** Picnic area and shelter, visitor center, historic trail (&), campsites, restrooms. **Activities:** Guided tours (with prior arrangements), interpretive walks, camping. **Special Features:** Fort was regarded as an often-dangerous hardship post in the years following the Civil War. As an outpost of civilization on the western frontier, the fort represented protection and a haven to travelers.

★4785★ **FORT FRED STEELE STATE HISTORIC SITE**
c/o Seminoe State Park
Box 30 HCR 67
Sinclair, WY 82334
Web: wyoparks.state.wy.us/fsslide.htm
Phone: 307-320-3013
Size: 152 acres. **Location:** On the North Platte River, east of Rawlins, off I-80. **Facilities:** Historic features. **Activities:** Fishing, sightseeing. **Special Features:** Fort Fred Steele was established June 30, 1868 and occupied until August 7, 1886 by soldiers who were sent by the U.S. government to guard the railroad against attack. For many years, its served as a center for the sheep industry. Remnants of the company town called the Carbon Timber Company remain on the east side of the river.

★4786★ **FORT PHIL KEARNY STATE HISTORIC SITE**
PO Box 520
Story, WY 82842
Web: wyoparks.state.wy.us/fkslide.htm
Phone: 307-684-7629
Size: 19 acres. **Location:** 20 miles south of Sheridan on I-90. **Facilities:** Picnic areas, restrooms, historical trails, museum, visitor center. **Activities:** Self-guiding tours of the fort grounds and fight sites. **Special Features:** During its two year existence, Fort Phil Kearny was the focal point of a violent war between the U.S. Army and the Sioux, Cheyenne, and Arapaho Indians opposed to intrusions into the last great hunting grounds on the Northern Plains.

★4787★ **GLENDO STATE PARK**
PO Box 398
Glendo, WY 82213
Web: wyoparks.state.wy.us/glslide.htm
Phone: 307-735-4433
Size: 9,930 acres land; 12,550 acres water. **Elevation:** 4,718 feet. **Location:** Just outside the town of Glendo, off I-25. **Facilities:** More than 400 tent and trailer campsites, restrooms, picnic area and shelter, trails (4 miles &), swimming beach, boat ramp, boat dock, marina, dam (&), playground. **Activities:** Camping, boating, fishing, swimming, water-skiing, windsurfing, hiking. **Special Features:** Visitors may find tepee rings and other traces from times when Arapaho, Cheyenne, Oglala, and Brule Indians called this territory home.

★4788★ **GUERNSEY STATE PARK**
PO Box 429
Guernsey, WY 82214
Web: wyoparks.state.wy.us/guslide.htm
Phone: 307-836-2334
Size: 6,227 acres land, 2,375 acres water. **Elevation:** 4,420 feet. **Location:** Off Highway 26, just outside the town of Guernsey. **Facilities:** 142 tent and trailer campsites, restrooms, picnic area and shelter, hiking trails, Volksmarch trail, historic trail, swimming beaches, volleyball court, horshoe pits, playground, boat dock, boat ramp, dam, visitor center, museum. **Activities:** Camping, boating, swimming, water-skiing, hiking, hunting (with restrictions). **Special Features:** Guernsey features one of the best collections of historic 1930s Civilian Conservation Corps structures in the west. The CCC's rock and log buildings, including the Castle, Brimmer Point, and the museum, can be seen throughout the park. Other CCC projects included trails, roads, and bridges. Located two miles south of Guernsey is Register Cliff, where thousands of pioneers traveling the Oregon Trail carved their names in the sandstone cliff.

9. State Parks

★4789★ HAWK SPRINGS STATE RECREATION AREA
c/o Guernsey State Park
PO Box 429
Guernsey, WY 82214
Web: wyoparks.state.wy.us/hwslide.htm
Phone: 307-836-2334
Size: 50 acres land; 1,950 acres water. **Elevation:** 4,400 feet. **Location:** In the southeastern corner of the state on Highway 85, 40 miles south of Torrington. **Facilities:** Tent and trailer campsites, restrooms, picnic area, beach area, boat ramp, boat dock, dam, playground (&). **Activities:** Camping, boating, fishing, ice fishing, swimming, birdwatching, hunting (with restrictions). **Special Features:** Hawk Springs reservoir supports healthy populations of walleye, channel catfish, perch, and black crappie. The reeds at the south end of the lake provide a rookery for blue herons.

★4790★ HISTORIC GOVERNORS' MANSION
300 E 21st St
Cheyenne, WY 82009
Web: wyoparks.state.wy.us/hgmslide.htm
Phone: 307-777-7878
Location: On East 21st Street in Cheyenne. **Facilities:** Museum (&), restrooms (&). **Activities:** Guided tours. **Special Features:** Completed in 1904, mansion is a fine example of Colonial Revival-style architecture. It served as home to Wyoming's governors until 1976, when it became a historic house/museum. Guided tours and a video provide interpretive information about Wyoming's first families and details of the mansion's interior design.

★4791★ HOT SPRINGS STATE PARK
220 Park St
Thermopolis, WY 82443
Web: wyoparks.state.wy.us/hsslide.htm
Phone: 307-864-2176
Size: 1,039 acres. **Location:** In Thermopolis. **Facilities:** Picnic area and shelters, trails (6.2 miles), Volksmarch trail, swimming pool, boat ramp, visitor center, suspension bridge, restrooms. **Activities:** Boating, fishing, bathing, wildlife observation. **Special Features:** Visitors can soak in the park's indoor and outdoor hot mineral water pools, the largest natural mineral hot springs in the world and believed by some to possess healing qualities. Other features include extraordinary summer flower gardens, the state's official bison herd, and unusual travertine formations. Tours of Legend Rock State Petroglyph Site, located about 30 minutes northwest, may be arranged through the park's office staff.

★4792★ INDEPENDENCE ROCK STATE HISTORIC SITE
PO Box 1596
Evansville, WY 82636
Web: wyoparks.state.wy.us/irslide.htm
Phone: 307-577-5150
Size: 197 acres. **Location:** On Highway 220 southwest of Casper. **Facilities:** Picnic area and shelters, visitor center, restrooms (&). **Activities:** Camping (by permit only). **Special Features:** A well-known landmark along the Oregon Trail, this large dome-shaped rock was a favorite resting spot for travelers. More than 5,000 names of early emigrants are carved into the granite boulder.

★4793★ KEYHOLE STATE PARK
353 McKean Rd
Moorcroft, WY 82721
Web: wyoparks.state.wy.us/keslide.htm
Phone: 307-756-3596
Size: 6,256 acres land; 9,418 acres water. **Elevation:** 4,100 feet. **Location:** On the western edge of the Black Hills between Sundance and Moorcroft, within sight of Devil's Tower. Access is via Pine Ridge Road, 8 miles off I-90. **Facilities:** 170 tent and trailer campsites, restrooms, picnic area and shelters, Volksmarch trail, swimming beach, boat ramp, boat dock, marina, motel, dam, playground (&). **Activities:** Camping, boating, fishing, swimming, water-skiing, snowmobiling, bird watching, hunting (with restrictions). **Special Features:** Nearly 225 species of birds can be observed in and around the park. During the summer, the most abundant species include the white pelican, osprey, common yellowthroat, and Savannah sparrow. Winter birds include bald eagles, red and white-breasted nuthatches, and red crossbills. A bird checklist is usually available from the park office.

★4794★ MEDICINE LODGE STATE ARCHAEOLOGICAL SITE
PO Box 62
Hyattville, WY 82428
Web: wyoparks.state.wy.us/mlslide.htm
Phone: 307-469-2234
Size: 200 acres. **Elevation:** 4,800 feet. **Location:** 6 miles northeast of Hyattville, off Highway 31, along the western slope of the Big Horn Mountains. **Facilities:** 25 tent and trailer campsites, restrooms (&), picnic area, nature trail, visitor center, fishing pier, historic features, playground. **Activities:** Camping, fishing (&), hunting (with restrictions), wildlife observation, hiking, mountain biking, rock hunting. **Special Features:** An important archeological site, Medicine Lodge features prehistoric petroglyphs and pictographs on red sandstone cliffs. Archeologists have uncovered a human habitation site that had been occupied for more than 10,000 years. Because the archeological site is located in a Wyoming Game and Fish Wildlife Habitat Management Unit, visitors are often afforded a close look at deer and elk, along with other wildlife.

★4795★ SEMINOE STATE PARK
Box 30 HCR 67
Sinclair, WY 82334
Web: wyoparks.state.wy.us/seslide.htm
Phone: 307-320-3013
Size: 1,450 acres land, 20,191 acres water. **Elevation:** 6,500 feet. **Location:** 34 miles north of Sinclair on Country Road 351, near Rawlins. **Facilities:** 61 tent and trailer campsites, restrooms (&), picnic area and shelters, swimming beaches, boat ramp,

9. State Parks

dam, playgrounds. **Activities:** Camping, boating, fishing, swimming, wildlife observation. **Special Features:** Wildlife enthusiasts can view bighorn sheep, deer, antelope, and prairie dog. Twelve miles north of the park is Wyoming's "Miracle Mile," a prime fishing stretch of the North Platte River.

★4796★ SINKS CANYON STATE PARK

3079 Sinks Canyon Rd
Lander, WY 82520
Web: wyoparks.state.wy.us/scslide.htm
Phone: 307-332-3077
Size: 600 acres. **Elevation:** 5,357 feet. **Location:** 6 miles southeast of Lander on Highway 131. **Facilities:** 30 tent and trailer campsites, restrooms, picnic areas and shelters, fishing pier, hiking trails (5 miles), Volksmarch trail, nature trail, visitor center, playground. **Activities:** Camping, fishing, hiking, rock climbing, wildlife viewing, interpretive programs. **Special Features:** Park features a geologic phenomenon in which the Popo Agie River vanishes into a large cavern (the Sinks), only to reappear in a trout-filled pool (the Rise) about one-half mile down the canyon.

★4797★ SOUTH PASS CITY STATE HISTORIC SITE

125 South Pass Main
South Pass City, WY 82520
Web: wyoparks.state.wy.us/spcslide.htm
Phone: 307-332-3684
Size: 39 acres. **Location:** 32 miles south and west of Lander, off Highway 28. **Facilities:** Picnic area (&), hiking trail (3 miles), Volksmarch trail, museum, visitor center, gift shop (&), restrooms. **Activities:** Fishing, hiking, living history demonstrations, interpretive programs (seasonal). **Special Features:** This once-thriving gold camp was also the birthplace of women's rights in Wyoming and home of the first woman judge in America, Esther Hobart Morris. One of the most authentic historic sites in existence, 30 original buildings have been restored and furnished, including the school house, the general store, the hotel, and two saloons. Thirty thousand artifacts are housed in the buildings, of which approximately 90 percent are authentic to the site.

★4798★ TRAIL END STATE HISTORIC SITE

400 Clarendon Ave
Sheridan, WY 82801
Web: www.trailend.org
Phone: 307-674-4589; **Fax:** 307-672-1720
Size: 3.8 acres. **Location:** In Sheridan on I-90. **Facilities:** Trail, mansion, carriage house, gardens (&&). **Activities:** Self-guided tours, guided tours by appointment. **Special Features:** Elegant Flemish-style mansion was built in 1913 by John B. Kendrick, who served as both governor and U.S. senator for Wyoming. The home periodically displays temporary whole-house exhibits which show how global events (such as World War I) affected the everyday lives of small-town Americans. The grounds contain several hundred trees and shrubs indigenous to Wyoming and also feature an unusual collection of non-native species planted by the Kendricks.

★4799★ WYOMING PIONEER MEMORIAL MUSEUM

PO Box 911
Douglas, WY 82633
Phone: 307-358-9288
Location: On the Wyoming State Fairgrounds in Douglas. **Facilities:** Museum, visitor center, historic structures. **Activities:** Historical interpretation, sightseeing. **Special Features:** Museum collects, preserves, interprets, and displays historical and cultural materials related to westward expansion. Displays cover the West in general but with focus particularly on Wyoming pioneers.

★4800★ WYOMING TERRITORIAL PRISON STATE HISTORIC SITE

975 Snowy Range Rd
Laramie, WY 82070
Web: www.wyoprisonpark.org
Phone: 307-746-6161
Size: 190 acres. **Location:** Off I-80, in Laramie. **Facilities:** Picnic area, restrooms, playground, museums, dinner theater, gift shop. **Activities:** Self guided tours, interpretive programs, entertainment programs. **Special Features:** Park includes the restored Wyoming Territorial Prison, the National U.S. Marshals Museum, Frontier Town, Ranchland (depicting daily life on a western ranch), the Union Pacific Survey Camp, a tepee campground, and other restored historic structures. The park is a state historic site independently operated by the non-profit Wyoming Territorial Prison Corp.

9. State Parks

10. URBAN PARKS

This section provides information on some of the largest, most frequently visited, and important parks for more than 60 of the largest metropolitan areas in the United States. Parks for Washington, D.C. fall under the jurisdiction of the National Park Service and therefore are listed in the ''US National Parks'' section. Listings here are arranged alphabetically by city and then by park name.

ALBUQUERQUE

★4801★ ELENA GALLEGOS PICNIC AREA AND ALBERT G. SIMMS PARK

7100 Tramway Blvd. NE
Albuquerque, NM 87122
Web: www.cabq.gov/parks/
Phone: 505-452-5200
Size: 640 acres. **Location:** Northeast of Alburquerque, north of US-40 on Tramway Blvd. **Facilities:** Picnic shelters, multiuse trails. **Activities:** Hiking, mountain biking, and equestrian activities.

ANCHORAGE

★4802★ KINCAID PARK

9401 Raspberry Rd
Anchorage, AK 99502
Phone: 907-343-6397
Size: 1,400 acres. **Location:** At the west end of Raspberry Road in Anchorage. **Facilities:** Outdoor center, 25-30 miles of groomed ski trails (some lighted), archery target range, disc golf course, ball fields. **Activities:** Biking, hiking, walking, running, cross-country skiing, canoeing, kayaking, archery. **Special Features:** Situated among rolling, forested hills, park offers a spectacular view of Mount Susitna across Cook Inlet, Fire Island to the southwest, and both Mount Denali and Mount Foraker to the North. Park has hosted a number of major events, including national level competitions for the selection of the U.S. Olympic Teams for cross-country skiing, as well as other local and national skiing competitions. Park marks one end of the Tony Knowles Coastal Trail.

ARLINGTON

★4803★ RIVER LEGACY PARKS

701 NW Green Oaks Blvd
Arlington, TX 76006
Web: www.ci.arlington.tx.us/park/
Phone: 817-860-6752

Size: 1,300 acres. **Location:** North Arlington, along the banks of the Trinity River. **Facilities:** Paved trails (eight miles), Legacy Pavilion, picnic areas, playground. **Activities:** Hiking, jogging, biking, birdwatching. **Special Features:** The park houses the River Legacy Living Science Center, which provides a variety of educational programs for children and other citizens of the greater Arlington area.

ATLANTA

★4804★ CENTENNIAL OLYMPIC PARK

265 Park Ave W NW
Atlanta, GA 30313
Web: www.centennialpark.com
Phone: 404-222-7275; **Fax:** 404-223-4499
Size: 21 acres. **Location:** Downtown Atlanta off Marietta St. **Facilities:** Picnic areas, visitor center, amphitheater, playground, water garden. **Activities:** Recreation and cultural programs. **Special Features:** Park's Fountain of Rings, designed in the form of the Olympic symbol of five interconnecting rings, is the world's largest interactive fountain. The fountain measures 82 feet in length and uses 251 water jets, 400 fog jets, and 487 lights. Fountain motion and lights are programmed to synchronize with music that plays four times daily.

★4805★ CHASTAIN MEMORIAL PARK

135 W Wieuca Rd NW
Atlanta, GA 30342
Phone: 404-817-6744
Size: 158 acres. **Location:** At Powers Ferry and West Wieuca roads in northwest Atlanta. **Facilities:** Picnic areas with shelters, pond, swimming pool, amphitheater, playground, sports courts, ball fields, horse stables (for groups of disabled and disadvantaged persons), 18-hole golf course, arts center, rec center with weightroom facility. **Activities:** Hiking, biking, swimming, horseback riding, golf, basketball, tennis, football, soccer, baseball, softball. **Special Features:** Park's stone grills, wooden pavilions, and walking trails were built in the late 1930s by Works Progress Administration. Chastain's amphitheater hosts jazz, rock, and pop concerts during the summer.

★4806★ GRANT PARK

537 Park Ave SE
Atlanta, GA 30312
Phone: 404-624-0697; **Fax:** 404-624-0823
Size: 131 acres. **Location:** In Southeast Atlanta; bordered by Boulevard on the east, Atlanta Ave on the south, Cherokee Ave on the west, Sydney St on the north and Park Ave on the northeast. **Facilities:** Picnic areas with pavilions, gazebo, recreation center, swimming pool, zoo, playgrounds, sports courts,

ball fields. **Activities:** Swimming, tennis, basketball, baseball, softball, soccer. **Special Features:** Atlanta's oldest and most popular park hosts 2 million visitors each year. Its features include Atlanta Cyclorama, an immense painting-in-the-round of the 1864 Civil War Battle of Atlanta, completed in 1885; and Zoo Atlanta, established in 1889, one of the ten oldest continuously operated zoos in the United States.

★4807★ PIEDMONT PARK

400 Park Dr NE
Atlanta, GA 30306
Web: www.piedmontpark.org
Phone: 404-875-7275; **Fax:** 404-875-0530
Size: 185 acres. **Location:** Two miles northeast of downtown; enter on Park Drive off Monroe Drive. **Facilities:** Picnic areas with pavilions, gazebo, bathhouse, lake with fishing pier and dock, swimming pools, trails, botanical garden, stage, playground, ball fields, sports courts, leash-free dog area, visitor center. **Activities:** Fishing, swimming, tennis, baseball, softball, volleyball, soccer, running, recreation and environmental programs. **Special Features:** A part of Piedmont Park's acreage is occupied by Atlanta Botanical Garden which features tropical, desert, and endangered plants from around the world. Guided tours of the park are offered by volunteers from Piedmont Park Conservancy on Saturday mornings, April through October. In November 2006 the park completed a two-year, $1.8 million renovation of its field complex. New features included in the renovation included new softball and soccer fields, regulation-size sand volleyball courts, and a running track.

AUSTIN

★4808★ EMMA LONG METROPOLITAN PARK

1706 City Park Rd
Austin, TX 78730
Phone: 512-346-1831; **Fax:** 512-343-1896
Size: 1,147 acres. **Location:** West of downtown on City Park Road. **Facilities:** Campsites (66), bathhouse, wading pool, picnic areas, lake (Lake Austin), boat ramps, hiking trail (2.5 miles), motorcycle trail (6.5 miles), sports field, sports courts. **Activities:** Camping, boating, fishing, swimming, hiking, bicycling, mountain biking, off-road motorcycle riding, archery, baseball, volleyball. **Special Features:** Oldest city park in Austin, and only Austin park to offer overnight camping.

★4809★ TOWN LAKE METROPOLITAN PARK

920 West Riverside Trail
(Auditorium Shores Unit)
Austin, TX 78704
Web: www.ci.austin.tx.us/parks/parks.htm
Phone: 512-974-6700
Size: 509 acres. **Location:** Along the banks of the Colorado River from the Tom Miller Dam to the Longhorn Dam. **Facilities:** Picnic areas, boat ramp, pool, trails (10 miles), amphitheater, sports fields. **Activities:** Canoeing, rowing, swimming, hiking, mountain biking, bicycling, baseball, football, soccer, rugby, volleyball. **Special Features:** Town Lake Metropolitan Park is comprised of 10 discrete units/branches along the banks of the Colorado Rivers. The Auditorium Shores unit is the most visited of the branches; its terraced amphitheater is the home of the Summer Concert Series and the Austin Symphony Independence Day Concert.

★4810★ WALTER E. LONG METROPOLITAN PARK

6614 Blue Bluff Rd
Austin, TX 78704
Phone: 512-926-5230
Size: 3,802 acres. **Location:** East of downtown on Blue Bluff Road. **Facilities:** Picnic areas with pavilions, lake, boat ramps, trails, sports courts. **Activities:** Fishing, swimming, water-skiing, hiking, volleyball. **Special Features:** Park houses the Indiangrass Wildlife Sanctuary, a 200-acre nature preserve. Access to preserve is limited and tours are by appointment only.

★4811★ ZILKER METROPOLITAN PARK

2201 Barton Springs Rd
Austin, TX 78746
Web: www.ci.austin.tx.us/zilker
Phone: 512-472-4914; **Fax:** 512-472-1267
Size: 355 acres. **Location:** On Barton Springs Road off Highway 1. **Facilities:** Picnic areas with pavilions, swimming and wading pools, trails, botanical garden, nature preserve, theater, sports fields, sports courts, miniature train, fishing pier, disc golf course, playground, recreation center, (&&). **Activities:** Swimming, fishing, canoeing, hiking, bicycling, baseball, football, rugby, soccer, volleyball, train rides. **Special Features:** Park houses Zilker Botanical Garden, which includes the Taniguchi Oriental Garden and the Austin Area Garden Center. Also home to the Barton Springs Pool, a natural spring-fed pool with a year-round average temperature of 68 degrees. The Zilker Hillside Theatre hosts concerts and is the site of the Zilker Summer Musical and Shakespeare in the Park. On the south end of the park is the Umlauf Sculpture Garden and Museum, home of the collection of work by sculptor Charles Umlauf.

BALTIMORE

★4812★ DRUID HILL PARK

3100 Swann Dr
Baltimore, MD 21217
Phone: 410-396-7900; **Fax:** 410-396-7038
Size: 649 acres. **Location:** Off I-83, Exit 7. **Facilities:** Picnic area, pools, trails, city farm, conservatory, historical site, playground, sports courts, ball fields, scenic viewpoints. **Activities:** Swimming, hiking, bicycling, tennis, basketball, football, soccer, baseball, softball. **Special Features:** Park features several historic structures including Orem's Way Station (1864), entrance gates at Madison Avenue (1867-68), Chinese Pagoda (1865), and the Conservatory (1888). Baltimore Zoo is located here; its 180-acre wooded setting is home to more than 2,000 exotic mammals, birds, and reptiles.

★4813★ GWYNN'S FALLS PARK & LEAKIN PARK
4921 Windsor Mill Rd
Baltimore, MD 21207
Web: www.ci.baltimore.md.us/government/recnparks/
parks.htm
Phone: 410-396-7900; **Fax:** 410-396-7945
Size: 1,200 acres. **Location:** West Baltimore, bounded to the north by Windsor Mill Road and to the south by Wilkens Avenue. **Facilities:** Picnic areas, recreation center, trails, city farm, nature center, historical site, playground, sports courts, ball fields, historic sites. **Activities:** Fishing, hiking, bicycling, tennis, basketball, football, soccer, baseball, softball. **Special Features:** Gwynn's Falls Trail is a new hiking trail that is under development. When completed, the trail will span nearly 15 miles from Franklintown Road at Winans Meadow to the Middle Branch of Patapsco River. The Gwynn's Falls Trail has been designated as part of the East Coast Greenway and the Chesapeake Bay Gateways Network.

BERKELEY

★4814★ TILDEN PARK
Wildcat Canyon Road
Berkeley, CA 94703
Web: www.ebparks.org
Phone: 510-562-7275
Size: 2,077 acres. **Location:** East Bay area of Berkeley, with entrances off Wildcat Canyon Road and Grizzly Peak Boulevard. **Facilities:** Picnic areas, swimming beach with lifeguards, equestrian camping facilities, 18-hole golf course with driving range and pro shop, 10-acre botanical garden, educational farm, hiking and biking trails. **Activities:** Camping, swimming, fishing, horseback riding and equestrian camping, golfing, hiking, bicycling. **Special Features:** The park includes an antique carousel, a scaled-down steam train that offers rides along one of the park's scenic ridges, and the Brazil Building, which contains the interior from the Brazilian exhibit at the 1939 World's Fair.

BIRMINGHAM

★4815★ GEORGE WARD PARK
331 16th Ave S.
Birmingham, AL 35205
Phone: 205-332-9958
Size: 111 acres. **Location:** South of downtown at 16th Ave and 14th St South. **Facilities:** Picnic areas, playground, ball fields, sports courts, disc golf course. **Activities:** Softball, tennis, disc golf. **Special Features:** Park's disc golf course was created on a old "ball" golf course.

BOSTON

★4816★ BOSTON COMMON
Tremont Beacon Charles & Boylston Sts
Boston, MA 02118
Web: www.ci.boston.ma.us/freedomtrail/bostoncommon.asp
Phone: 617-635-4505; **Fax:** 617-635-7414
Size: 50 acres. **Location:** In Back Bay/Beacon Hill. **Facilities:** Pavilions, monuments, playground, "tot lot", spray fountain, pond, ball fields, tennis courts, historic cemetery. **Activities:** Self-guided walks, tennis, softball, crickett, ice skating. **Special Features:** Boston Common was founded in 1634 to provide pasturage, a military training field, and other shared needs for the town, based upon the English concept of public land. Park marks the start of the Freedom Trail, a well-marked, three-mile walking tour of Boston that links 16 sites of historical interest. The Commons also has a longstanding tradition as a place where demonstrators can exercise their right to freedom of speech. Designated a National Historic Landmark, the park is part of the Emerald Necklace, a continuous line of parks that stretch from the Boston Common to Franklin Park.

★4817★ FRANKLIN PARK
1 Franklin Park Dr
Boston, MA 02121
Phone: 617-635-4505; **Fax:** 617-287-8313
Size: 527 acres. **Location:** Surrounded by Jamaica Plain, Roxbury, Roslindale, and Dorchester. **Facilities:** Paths, zoo, playgrounds including "tot lot", sports fields, sports courts, ball fields, 18-hole golf course. **Activities:** Bicycling, golf, tennis, baseball, softball, football, rugby, lacrosse, soccer. **Special Features:** Designed by Frederick Law Olmsted, the park is the "pendant" of Boston's Emerald Necklace chain of public spaces and the largest greenspace in the city. The park is also home to the 72-acre Franklin Park Zoo, established in 1911.

★4818★ PUBLIC GARDEN
Charles Boylestown Arlington & Beacon Sts
Boston, MA 02118
Phone: 617-635-4505
Size: 24 acres. **Location:** Adjacent to Boston Common in Back Bay/Beacon Hill. **Facilities:** Pathways, gardens. **Activities:** Jogging, walking. **Special Features:** Oldest public botanical garden in the United States. Ornamental foliage, serpentine paths, fountains, sculptures, and planting beds surround a central lagoon where Boston's famed swan boat rides are available during the spring and summer. Designated a National Historic Landmark.

BUFFALO

★4819★ CAZENOVIA PARK
Cazenovia Parkway
Buffalo, NY 14210
Phone: 716-884-9660
Size: 191 acres. **Location:** South of downtown at Cazenovia and Abbott streets. **Facilities:** Picnic areas with pavilions, concessions, swimming and wading pool, visitor center, playground with "tot lot," sports fields, sports courts, ball fields, 9-hole golf course, running track, indoor skating rink, hockey rink. **Activities:** Canoeing, golf, tennis, baseball, softball, basketball, bowling, football, soccer, roller hockey, ice skating. **Special Features:** Cazenovia Creek, which runs through the park, offers a good launch site for canoe trips to the Buffalo River.

★4820★ DELAWARE PARK

Parkside & Elmwood Ave
Buffalo, NY 14214
Phone: 716-884-9660
Size: 350 acres. **Location:** North of downtown at the Scajaquada Expy and Parkside St. **Facilities:** Picnic areas with shelters, concessions, lake, visitor center, playground, sports courts, ball fields, running track, 18-hole golf course, zoo. **Activities:** Paddleboating, golf, tennis, baseball, basketball, bowling, rugby, soccer, jogging, roller blading, sledding, cultural programs. **Special Features:** One of six Buffalo city parks designed by Frederick Law Olmsted. Park includes Buffalo Zoo, 42-acre Hoyt Lake, and a Japanese garden and hosts Shakespeare in the Park outdoor summer theater. Adjacent to the park are the Albright Knox Museum and the Buffalo and Erie County Historical Society Museum.

CHARLESTON

★4821★ JAMES ISLAND COUNTY PARK

871 Riverland Dr
Charleston, SC 29412
Web: www.ccprc.com
Phone: 843-795-7275
Size: 643 acres. **Location:** West of Centerville off Camp Road. **Facilities:** Picnic areas, off-leash dog area, climbing wall, vacation cottages, modern campground, playground, seasonal Splash Zone Waterpark. **Activities:** Fishing and crabbing, kayaking, swimming, climbing, bicycling.

★4822★ NORTH CHARLESTON WANNAMAKER COUNTY PARK

8888 University Blvd
North Charleston, SC 29406
Web: www.ccprc.com
Phone: 843-572-7275
Size: 1,015 acres. **Location:** Located in North Charleston, the park is bordered by the Goose Creek Reservoir to the north, Highway 78 to the west and Highway 52 to the east. **Facilities:** Picnic shelters, two playgrounds, paved trails, seasonal water play area, bicycle and kayak rentals. **Activities:** Hiking, bicycling, skating, swimming, kayaking.

CHARLOTTE

★4823★ FREEDOM PARK

1900 East Blvd
Charlotte, NC 28203
Phone: 704-336-3375
Size: 98 acres. **Location:** South of downtown near where East Blvd. meets Kings Dr. **Facilities:** Picnic areas with shelters, concessions, trails, 7-acre lake, deck, amphitheater, playground, trails, ball fields, sports courts, sports fields. **Activities:** Fishing, hiking, bicycling, baseball, softball, tennis, soccer, basketball, volleyball, badminton, roller blading, cultural programs. **Special Features:** Freedom Park hosts "Festival in the Park" every September; the arts and crafts festival first began in 1965 and is one of Charlotte's longest running traditions.

★4824★ LATTA PLANTATION NATURE CENTER AND PRESERVE

6211 Sample Road
Huntersville, NC 28078
Web: www.charmeck.org/Departments/Park+and+Rec/ Home.atm
Phone: 704-875-2312; **Fax:** 704-875-1724
Size: 1,343 acres. **Location:** Twelve miles north of Charlotte. **Facilities:** Picnic areas, concessions, lake, beach area, boat dock, boat rentals, trails, visitor center, historic plantation, equestrian center, playground, sports area. **Activities:** Canoeing, kayaking, fishing, hiking, horseback riding, volleyball. **Special Features:** The marquee historical attraction at the park is the 1800 Catawba River Plantation, the restored home of park namesake James Latta. The park also houses the Carolina Raptor Center, a facility for injured or orphaned birds of prey.

★4825★ MCALPINE CREEK COMMUNITY PARK

8711 Monroe Rd
Charlotte, NC 28212
Phone: 704-568-4044; **Fax:** 704-535-5454
Size: 462 acres. **Location:** Southeast of downtown off Monroe Rd. **Facilities:** Picnic areas, 3-acre lake, trails, boardwalk, concessions, gazebo, fish pier, off-leash dog area, sports fields. **Activities:** Fishing, hiking, bicycling, soccer, horseshoes. **Special Features:** McAlpine Creek Greenway was the first of its kind in the western piedmont of North Carolina when it was built in 1978. It connects to James Boyce Park to form a 5K cross-county course.

★4826★ MCDOWELL NATURE PRESERVE

15222 York Rd
Charlotte, NC 28278
Phone: 704-588-5224; **Fax:** 704-588-5226
Size: 1,108 acres. **Location:** Southwestern Mecklenburg County off Highway 49 (York Rd.). **Facilities:** Campsites (58), picnic areas with shelters, concessions, lake, beach area, deck, boat launch, boat rentals, trail (7 miles, &), nature center with gift shop, amphitheater, playground. **Activities:** Camping, boating, fishing, swimming, hiking, bicycling, environmental education programs. **Special Features:** Composed of forested, rolling terrain along the banks of Lake Wylie, the preserve is the oldest in Mecklenburg County. It protects habitat for 119 species of birds, 21 species of mammals, 21 species of reptiles, and 14 species of amphibians. Endangered and threatened plant species grow in the preserve's Piedmont Prairie restoration sites.

★4827★ REEDY CREEK PARK & NATURE PRESERVE

2900 Rocky River Rd
Charlotte, NC 28215
Phone: 704-598-8857; **Fax:** 704-599-1770
Size: 826 acres (includes 710-acre nature preserve). **Location:** About 10 miles northeast of downtown, off E Harris Blvd.

Facilities: Picnic areas with shelters, trails (10 miles), nature center, sports courts, ball fields, sports fields, 18-hole disc golf course, concessions, historic sites, playground. **Activities:** Fishing, hiking, bicycling, basketball, baseball, softball, soccer, volleyball, wildlife viewing. **Special Features:** Park's trails offer visitors the opportunity to explore a variety of terrains while enjoying scenic views of forests, fields, streams, and three small lakes. One of the most popular routes leads to the ruins of the Robinson Rock House, built around 1790.

CHICAGO

★4828★ BURNHAM PARK
425 E Mcfetridge Dr
Chicago, IL 60605
Web: www.chicagoparkdistrict.com
Phone: 773-256-0949
Size: 598 acres. **Location:** Lake Michigan lakefront, south from downtown between 25th and 59th streets. **Facilities:** Boat launches, swimming beach, walking trails, playgrounds, ball fields, sports courts, stadium. **Activities:** Boating, bicycling, horseback riding, baseball, basketball, football, soccer, volleyball, tennis, roller blading, hiking. **Special Features:** Site of Chicago's second World's Fair in 1933. A sanctuary for migratory birds is currently under construction on top of the McCormick Place's underground parking garage. It will include viewing platforms, a water feature, five acres of short prairie grass, and hundreds of native trees and shrubs.

★4829★ JACKSON PARK
6401 S Stony Island Ave
Chicago, IL 60637
Phone: 773-256-0903; **Fax:** 773-256-0902
Size: 600 acres. **Location:** South Lake Michigan lakefront between 56th and 67th Sts. **Facilities:** Picnic area, boat launches, beaches, running track, paths, playgrounds, sports courts, fitness center, meeting rooms, 18-hole golf course and driving range. **Activities:** Boating, fishing, swimming, bicycling, horseback riding, golf, tennis, basketball, football, soccer, softball, cross-country skiing, recreation programs. **Special Features:** The park was first created to host the 1890 World's Columbian Exposition. Today, one of the most notable buildings from that historic World's Fair—the Fine Arts Palace—is the home of Chicago's Museum of Science and Industry. Other features in the park include a beach house with an interactive play fountain (at 63rd St.) and Wooded Island, which contains a nature sanctuary and Japanese garden. Immediately north of the park is famous Promontory Point, and to the south is the South Shore Cultural Center.

★4830★ LINCOLN PARK
2045 Lincoln Park W
Chicago, IL 60610
Web: www.chicagoparkdistrict.com
Phone: 312-742-7726; **Fax:** 312-742-7790
Size: 1,208 acres. **Location:** Lake Michigan lakefront north of downtown. **Facilities:** Picnic areas, boat launches, beaches, paths, theater, miniature golf course, playgrounds, ball fields, gymnasium, zoo, botanical garden. **Activities:** Boating, fishing, swimming, bicycling, golf, tennis, archery, baseball, basketball, football, soccer, volleyball, roller blading, cross-country skiing, ice skating. **Special Features:** Chicago's largest city park, Lincoln Park is known for its statuary. A memorial to Ulysses S. Grant, created in 1891 by Louis Rebisso, overlooks Cannon Drive at the south end of the zoo. A standing Abraham Lincoln (1887), by Augustus Saint-Gaudens, can be seen behind the Chicago Historical Society. Other statues include a tribute to Eugene Field (1922), Chicago Daily News columnist; William Shakespeare (1894); and Hans Christian Andersen (1896). The park is also home to the Lincoln Park Zoo, the Lincoln Park Conservatory, and the Lincoln Park Cultural Center.

CINCINNATI

★4831★ AULT PARK
3600 Observatory Ave
Cincinnati, OH 45208
Web: www.cincinnati-oh.gov/cityparks
Phone: 513-321-8439; **Fax:** 513-861-8669
Size: 224 acres. **Location:** North of Cincinnati Municipal Airport (Lunken Field), at the end of Observatory Avenue. **Facilities:** Picnic areas, nature trails, lookout point, gardens, historic sites, playground, athletic fields. **Activities:** Hiking, recreational sports. **Special Features:** Park features Ault Park Pavilion, said to be the grandest of all Cincinnati's park buildings. Built in Italian Renaissance style, the building was first opened to the public on May 30, 1930.

★4832★ CENTRAL RIVERFRONT - SAWYER POINT
801 E Pete Rose Way
Cincinnati, OH 45202
Web: www.cincinnati-oh.gov/parks
Phone: 513-352-6180; **Fax:** 513-352-6311
Size: Mile-long linear park. **Location:** Intersection of Eggleston Avenue and East Pete Rose Way, just south of downtown Cincinnati on the shore of the Ohio River. **Facilities:** Picnic areas, paths, sand volleyball courts, outdoor tennis courts, playground, outdoor skating rink, performance pavilion. **Activities:** Skating, tennis, jogging and bicycling, sand volleyball.

★4833★ EDEN PARK
950 Eden Park Dr
Cincinnati, OH 45202
Phone: 513-352-4080; **Fax:** 513-352-4096
Size: 186 acres. **Location:** Between I-71 and the Ohio River, five minutes east of downtown. **Facilities:** Picnic areas, trails, lakes, gardens, conservatory, art museum, planetarium, bandstand, theater, historic structures and exhibits, playground. **Activities:** Hiking, rock climbing, ice skating. **Special Features:** Park is home to one of Cincinnati's most familiar landmarks, the Spring House Gazebo, built in 1904 to cover a natural spring once thought to have medicinal qualities. Cincinnati Art Museum, Playhouse in the Park, Murray Seasongood Pavilion, and the Irwin M. Krohn Conservatory are also housed on park property.

★4834★ MOUNT AIRY FOREST & ARBORETUM
5083 Colerain Ave
Cincinnati, OH 45223
Web: www.cinci-parks.org/parks
Phone: 513-352-4080; **Fax:** 513-352-4096
Size: 1,470 acres. **Location:** Between Colerain Avenue and West Fork Road, 10 minutes west of downtown. **Facilities:** Group campgrounds, 3 lodges, picnic areas with shelters, concessions, hiking trails (14 miles), bridle trails (16 miles), arboretum, historic areas, off-leash dog area, ballfields, playground. **Activities:** Group camping, hiking, bicycling, horseback riding, softball, baseball, cross-country skiing, day camp. **Special Features:** Cincinnati's largest park, Mount Airy was the site of the first municipal reforestation project in the U.S. Park features Trail of the Explorers, a 10-mile hiking trail that winds through historic areas of the forest and was named for the French-Canadian explorers who pioneered much of the Midwest.

CLEVELAND

★4835★ BRECKSVILLE RESERVATION
Brecksville Road
Brecksville, OH 44141
Web: www.clemetparks.com
Phone: 216-635-3200
Size: 3,090 acres. **Location:** 10 miles south of downtown at Chippewa Creek Dr. and Valley Pkwy. **Facilities:** Picnic areas with shelters, concessions, trails (including a fitness trail), nature center, 18-hole golf course, stables, ball fields, playgrounds, geocache site. **Activities:** Hiking, horseback riding, golf, cross-country skiing, sledding. **Special Features:** Adjacent to the Cuyahoga Valley National Recreation Area. Cut by seven separate valleys, the reservation offers many scenic attractions including Chippewa Creek, which runs through a deep gorge, and Deer Lick Cave, a rock overhang composed of erosion-resistant Berea sandstone. The reservation's trails comprise part of Ohio's Buckeye Trail and Cuyahoga Valley Trail.

★4836★ HINCKLEY RESERVATION
Bellus Road
Hinckley, OH 44233
Web: www.clemetparks.com
Phone: 216-635-3200; **Fax:** 216-635-3286
Size: 2,275 acres. **Location:** About 20 miles southwest of downtown Cleveland, off State Route 606 about a mile south of the junction with Route 303. **Facilities:** Picnic areas with shelters, concessions, trails, lake, boat launch, pier, swimming pool (open seasonally), ball fields, sports courts, historic sites, geocache site. **Activities:** Boating, fishing, swimming, hiking, bicycling, horseback riding, basketball, volleyball, ice skating, ice fishing, sledding. **Special Features:** Annual park highlights include a March ''return of the buzzards,'' in which celebrations are carried out to welcome the returning migratory birds from their wintering grounds in Florida.

★4837★ LAKEWOOD PARK
14532 Lake Ave
Cleveland, OH 44107
Phone: 216-529-4474

Size: 31 acres. **Location:** West of downtown in Lakewood, at Lake and Belle Ave. **Facilities:** Picnic areas with shelters, meeting pavilion, outdoor swimming pool, zero-entry wading pool, bandshell, sport courts, ball fields, sports fields, playground, historic sites. **Activities:** Tennis, volleyball, basketball, soccer, baseball, softball, ice skating. **Special Features:** Park houses Lakewood's oldest stone house, aptly named Old Stone House. Free Sunday-evening concerts are offered in the park's bandshell during the summer months.

★4838★ MILL STREAM RUN RESERVATION
Albion Road
Strongsville, OH 44136
Web: www.clemetparks.com
Phone: 440-635-3200
Size: 2,307 acres. **Location:** Acreage is spread across Berea, Middleburg Heights, North Royalton, and Strongsville. **Facilities:** Hiking trails, picnic areas, toboggan runs. **Activities:** Hiking, tobogganing, sledding, fishing.

★4839★ ROCKY RIVER RESERVATION
c/o Cleveland Metroparks
4101 Fulton Pkwy
Cleveland, OH 44144
Phone: 216-351-6300
Size: 3,432 acres. **Location:** West and southwest of downtown. Straddles the Rocky River from Bagley Rd. in Berea north to Detroit Rd. near the Lake Erie shore. **Facilities:** Picnic areas, boat launch, trails, nature center, ball fields, 18-hole golf course, playgrounds, museum. **Activities:** Boating, fishing, hiking, horseback riding, golf, horseshoes, skating, cross-country skiing, ice skating, ice fishing, sledding. **Special Features:** Although surrounded by Cleveland suburbs, park lands comprise a tree-lined river valley that gives visitors a wilderness experience. Park houses the Frostville Museum of Nineteenth Century Americana (Olmsted Falls).

COLORADO SPRINGS

★4840★ GARDEN OF THE GODS PARK
1805 N 30th St
Colorado Springs, CO 80904
Web: www.gardenofgods.com
Phone: 719-219-0108; **Fax:** 719-634-0094
Size: 1,391 acres. **Location:** Main park entrance is 5 miles northeast of downtown on 30th St. **Facilities:** Picnic areas, concessions, visitor center with gift shop, trails, gardens, arboretum, historic site. **Activities:** Hiking, horseback riding, rock climbing, guided walks, mountain biking, interpretive programs. **Special Features:** Park features 20 major rock formations, including Balanced Rock, Steamboat Rock, Three Graces, and Kissing Camels. It also is home to historic Rock Ledge Ranch, a 19th-century homestead and ranch.

★4841★ NORTH CHEYENNE CAñON PARK

2110 North Cheyenne Cañon Road
Colorado Springs, CO 80906
Web: www.springsgov.com
Phone: 719-385-6086
Size: 1,600 acres. **Location:** W. Cheyenne Blvd. and Evan Ave. **Facilities:** Picnic areas, rock climbing demonstration area, 56 miles of trails for hiking and equestrian activity. **Activities:** Hiking, horseback riding, rock climbing. **Special Features:** White Fir Botanical Reserve and Starsmore Discovery Center.

★4842★ PALMER PARK

3650 Maizeland Rd
Colorado Springs, CO 80909
Phone: 719-385-5941; **Fax:** 719-578-6934
Size: 740 acres. **Location:** 5 miles northeast of downtown on Maizeland Road. **Facilities:** Picnic areas with shelters, stables, hiking and equestrian trails (25 miles), sports courts, ballfields, sports fields, arboretum, dog-run area, wilderness area, playground, scenic overlook. **Activities:** Hiking, mountain biking, horseback riding, baseball, softball, soccer, football, volleyball, bird watching, rock hounding. **Special Features:** Park's spectacular rock formations are the result of geological activity that took place approximately 60 million years ago. Semi-precious rocks and minerals common in the Rocky Mountains, such as quartz, topaz, and jasper, may be found in the park.

★4843★ RED ROCK CANYON OPEN SPACE

3615 W. High St
Colorado Springs, CO 80904
Web: www.springsgov.com
Phone: 719-385-5941
Size: 786 acres. **Location:** Ridge Road and Highway 24. **Facilities:** Hiking trails, including an off-leash dog trail area. **Activities:** Hiking trails.

COLUMBUS

★4844★ GRIGGS RESERVOIR PARK

2933 Riverside Dr
Columbus, OH 43221
Web: www.recparks.columbus.gov
Phone: 614-645-3300; **Fax:** 614-645-8839
Size: 521 acres. **Location:** Northwest of downtown on Riverside Drive. **Facilities:** Campgrounds, picnic area, bike path, garden, playground, disc golf course, boat ramps, amphitheater. **Activities:** Camping, boating, water-skiing, fishing, bicycling, sledding, sledding. **Special Features:** Covering 365 acres with 15 miles of shoreline, Griggs Reservoir is located in a scenic limestone valley with densely treed banks. A nationally recognized spot for rowing and water-skiing competitions, the park hosts such annual events as the Governor's Cup Ohio High School Rowing Championships, Jack Speakmon Regatta, and Mid-America Collegiate Rowing Championships.

★4845★ HOOVER RESERVOIR PARK

7701 Sunbury Rd
Columbus, OH 43081
Web: www.recparks.columbus.gov
Phone: 614-645-3300; **Fax:** 614-645-8839
Size: 4,705 acres. **Location:** 12 miles northeast of downtown on Sunbury Rd. in Westerville. **Facilities:** Picnic area, playground, marina, boat ramps, disc golf course, golf course, walking trails, athletic fields. **Activities:** Boating, fishing, water-skiing, golf, disc golf, hiking, rugby, cricket, soccer, bird watching. **Special Features:** Hoover Reservoir is a 3,272-acre, 8-mile-long impoundment of the Big Walnut River, and is the main water supply for Columbus. One of the park's more unusual attractions is a high ropes adventure course (available for use by reservation).

★4846★ WHETSTONE PARK

3923 N High St
Columbus, OH 43214
Web: www.recparks.columbus.gov
Phone: 614-645-3350; **Fax:** 614-645-3384
Size: 136 acres. **Location:** Along the Olentangy River between Henderson Rd and N. Broadway, northeast of downtown. **Facilities:** Picnic areas, shelters, paths, playground, sports courts, ball fields, recreation center. **Activities:** Fishing, hiking, bicycling, tennis, softball, baseball, soccer, basketball. **Special Features:** Park grounds include the Park of Roses, one of the nation's largest municipal rose gardens with more than 10,500 rose bushes and more than 340 varieties of roses. Peak season is mid-June through early September.

DALLAS

★4847★ BACHMAN LAKE PARK

3500 W. Northwest Hwy
Dallas, TX 75220
Phone: 214-671-4100; **Fax:** 214-670-3205
Size: 206 acres. **Location:** Six miles from downtown, off Northwest Highway, just north of Love Field. **Facilities:** Picnic areas, paddleboat rentals, lake, pools, trails, playgrounds. **Activities:** Boating, swimming, hiking, bicycling.

★4848★ FAIR PARK

1300 Robert B Cullum Blvd
Dallas, TX 75315
Web: www.fairpark.org
Phone: 214-670-8400
Size: 277 acres. **Location:** Five minutes east of downtown Dallas. **Facilities:** Picnic areas, lagoon, gardens. **Activities:** Skateboarding, roller blading, walking. **Special Features:** Home of the annual State Fair of Texas, Fair Park houses a wide assortment of attractions including the African American Museum, the Dallas Aquarium, the Museum of the American Railroad, the museum of Nature and Science, Texas Discovery Gardens, the Women's Museum, and a music hall that features major ballet, opera, and theatre productions.

★4849★ KIEST PARK

3080 S Hampton Rd
Dallas, TX 75232
Phone: 214-670-1918; **Fax:** 214-670-1975
Size: 264 acres. **Location:** In the Oak Cliff area. **Facilities:** Picnic areas, pool, trails, gymnasium, playgrounds, sports areas. **Activities:** Swimming, hiking, bicycling, tennis, baseball, basketball, football, soccer, volleyball. **Special Features:** Kiest Park recently opened a deluxe softball complex that includes six regulation fields with lighting.

★4850★ WHITE ROCK LAKE PARK

8300 Garland Rd
Dallas, TX 75238
Phone: 214-670-8885
Size: 2,115 acres. **Location:** On East Lawther Drive. **Facilities:** Picnic areas, paddleboat rentals, lake, trails, Dallas Arboretum and Botanical Garden, arts center, playgrounds, sports areas. **Activities:** Boating, hiking, bicycling, tennis, football, softball. **Special Features:** The Dallas Arboretum and Botanical Garden (327-8263), features 66 landscaped acres of towering trees, fragrant gardens, lush lawns, fountains, sculptures, and two historic mansions.

DENVER

★4851★ CITY PARK

York St & 17th Ave
Denver, CO 80202
Web: www.denvergov.org/parks/
Phone: 303-964-2522; **Fax:** 303-964-1321
Size: 314 acres. **Location:** East of downtown; bordered by 26th Avenue, 17th Avenue, Josephine Street, and Colorado Boulevard. **Facilities:** Picnic areas, concessions, lakes, trails, flower gardens, historical monuments, pavilion and bandshell, zoo, playground, golf course, sports areas. **Activities:** Paddleboating, fishing, bicycling, golf, tennis, baseball, field hockey, football, soccer. **Special Features:** Houses Denver Museum of Natural History, the fourth largest natural history museum in the country, featuring world-renowned wildlife exhibits, gems and minerals, dinosaurs, an IMAX Theater, and a planetarium. Also houses the 76-acre Denver Zoo, which features more than 1,700 animals.

★4852★ WASHINGTON PARK

Louisiana Ave & S. Downing St
Denver, CO 80202
Web: www.denvergov.org/parks/
Phone: 303-964-2522; **Fax:** 303-964-1321
Size: 165 acres. **Location:** Bordered by Virginia, Louisiana, Downing, and Franklin. **Facilities:** Picnic areas, concessions, pavilion, lakes, fishing pond, indoor pool, fitness trail, jogging path, flower gardens, playgrounds, sports areas. **Activities:** Boating, fishing, swimming, bicycling, tennis, horseshoes, lawn bowling, soccer, volleyball. **Special Features:** The park features two major botanical gardens that are well-known throughout the state.

DETROIT

★4853★ BELLE ISLE PARK

E Grand Blvd & Jefferson Ave
Detroit, MI 48207
Web: www.ci.detroit.mi.us/recreation/
Phone: 313-852-4075; **Fax:** 313-852-4074
Size: 983 acres. **Location:** Located five minutes from downtown business district on an island in the Detroit River. Accessible by bridge. **Facilities:** Canoe rentals, trails, conservatory, gardens, nature center, amphitheater, aquarium, casino, marine museum, fishing piers, swimming beach, nine-hole golf course and driving range, playgrounds, sports areas (including 10 lighted tennis courts and cinder running track). **Activities:** Canoeing, fishing, hiking, bicycling, swimming, golf, basketball, football, soccer, ice skating, handball, racquetball, tennis. **Special Features:** The park, which features five miles of shoreline, was designed by renowned landscape architect Frederick Law Olmsted.

★4854★ KENSINGTON METROPARK

2240 W. Buno Road
Milford, MI 483804410
Web: www.metroparks.com
Phone: 248-685-1561
Size: 4,481 acres. **Location:** Northwest corner of metropolitan Detroit, off I-96. **Facilities:** Boat launch, trails (including eight-mile paved trail), swimming beaches and bathhouses, 24-hole disc golf course, 18-hole golf course, group camping sites, ice rink, picnic areas, sledding/toboggan runs. **Activities:** Sailing, kayaking, birdwatching, hiking, rollerblading, bicycling, cross-country skiing, disc golf, swimming, fishing, golf, camping, horseback riding, ice skating, hockey, sledding. **Special Features:** Kensington is the largest of nine metroparks strung around metropolitan Detroit. Other attractions at the park include a Farm Learning Center and a nature center.

★4855★ RIVER ROUGE PARK

22000 Joy Rd
Detroit, MI 48239
Web: www.rougeriver.com
Phone: 313-224-1100; **Fax:** 313-852-4624
Size: 1,181 acres. **Location:** At West Warren and Outer Drive on the west side. **Facilities:** Picnic areas, pools, trails, nature study area, playgrounds, sports areas (including 14 regulation-size softball fields), 18-hole golf course. **Activities:** Swimming, bicycling, golf, tennis, basketball, football, soccer, softball, sledding.

EL PASO

★4856★ BLACKIE CHESHER PARK

1100 N Zaragoza Rd
El Paso, TX 79907
Web: www.ci.el-paso.tx.us/parks
Phone: 915-541-4331
Size: 157 acres. **Location:** On North Zaragoza Road on El

Paso's east side. **Facilities:** Picnic area, trail, sports areas. **Activities:** Baseball, basketball.

★4857★ **SKYLINE PARK**
5050 Yvette Ave
El Paso, TX 79924
Web: www.ci.el-paso.tx.us/parks
Phone: 915-541-4331; **Fax:** 915-541-4355
Size: 176 acres. **Location:** In northeast El Paso. **Facilities:** Playground, sports areas. **Activities:** Tennis, baseball, basketball, soccer.

FORT WORTH

★4858★ **FOREST PARK**
1500 Colonial Pkwy
Fort Worth, TX 76110
Phone: 817-336-3328; **Fax:** 817-871-5724
Size: 233 acres. **Location:** Colonial Parkway and University Drive. **Facilities:** Group shelters, pools, log cabin village, zoo, botanic garden, miniature train, playground, multi-use trails, sports areas. **Activities:** Swimming, camping, hiking, bicycling, soccer. **Special Features:** The Fort Worth Zoo (817-759-7555) is located within the park boundaries. The zoo is open daily, 10 am-5 pm. The park also maintains a miniature train that offers visitors a five-mile circuit of the park.

★4859★ **FORT WORTH NATURE CENTER & REFUGE**
9601 Fossil Ridge Rd
Fort Worth, TX 76135
Web: www.fortworthgov.org
Phone: 817-237-1111; **Fax:** 817-237-0653
Size: 3,671 acres. **Location:** 10 miles from downtown Fort Worth, off Highway 199. **Facilities:** Visitor center, 25 miles of hiking and nature trails, exhibits, nature programs. **Activities:** Hiking, bicycling (on paved roads), guided tours. **Special Features:** Largest city-owned nature center in the United States. Riverbottom and crosstimbers forests, prairie, and marshland provide habitat for native flora and fauna including a herd of buffalo.

★4860★ **GATEWAY PARK**
750 N Beach St
Fort Worth, TX 76111
Phone: 817-871-5700; **Fax:** 817-335-1103
Size: 504 acres. **Location:** East of downtown Fort Worth along the banks of the Trinity River. **Facilities:** Picnic areas, hard surface trails, sports areas. **Activities:** Bicycling, football, soccer, softball. **Special Features:** Home of Fort Woof, the city's first off-leash dog park. Fort Worth authorities have announced plans to consider a significant expansion of the park's acreage and recreational offerings.

★4861★ **TRINITY PARK**
2401 University Dr
Fort Worth, TX 76107
Phone: 817-871-5700; **Fax:** 817-871-5724
Size: 117 acres. **Location:** North University Drive and I-30. **Facilities:** Pavilion, river access, trails, gardens, playground. **Activities:** Hiking, bicycling. **Special Features:** Park is home to the Fort Worth Botanic Garden, which features more than 2,500 native and exotic plant species in gardens and natural settings.

FRESNO

★4862★ **REGIONAL SPORTS PARK**
1707 W. Jensen
Fresno, CA 93706
Web: www.fresno.gov
Phone: 559-621-6720
Size: 110 acres. **Location:** Jensen and West streets. **Facilities:** Nine soccer/football fields (two of championship size), 6 baseball fields, picnic areas, children's playground. **Activities:** Baseball, softball, soccer.

★4863★ **ROEDING REGIONAL PARK**
2326 Fresno St
Fresno, CA 93721
Web: www2.fresno.gov/parks-rec/
Phone: 559-621-2900; **Fax:** 559-498-1588
Size: 159 acres. **Location:** East of Highway 99 between Olive and Belmont avenues. **Facilities:** Picnic areas, concessions, lake, boat rentals (paddleboats, motor boats, rowboats), Japanese American Memorial, gardens, amusement rides, Rotary Storyland and Playland, fitness course, playground, tennis courts, sports areas. **Activities:** Boating, tennis, football, soccer, handball, volleyball. **Special Features:** Park is home to the Chaffee Zoological Gardens (209-498-2671) and the Rotary Storyland and Playland (209-486-2124), a play area and amusement park for children.

★4864★ **WOODWARD REGIONAL PARK**
7775 Friant Rd
Fresno, CA 93720
Web: www2.fresno.gov/parks-rec/
Phone: 559-621-2900; **Fax:** 559-498-1588
Size: 300 acres. **Location:** Northeast Fresno along the San Joaquin River, between Highway 41 and Friant Road. **Facilities:** Picnic areas, amphitheater, lake, trails, fitness course, bird sanctuary, Japanese garden, sports area. **Activities:** Bicycling, walking, birdwatching, golf. **Special Features:** The bird sanctuary in the park's southeast corner provides cover for a wide variety of wildfowl.

HARTFORD

★4865★ **BUSHNELL PARK**
Elm and Trinity Sts
Hartford, CT 06103
Web: www.bushnellpark.org
Phone: 860-246-7739

Size: 41 acres. **Location:** Trinity and Elm Streets, downtown Hartford. **Facilities:** Walking trails, restored 1914 carousel, Pump House Gallery. **Activities:** Walking, picnicking. **Special Features:** The first municipal park in the nation to be conceived, built, and paid for by citizens through a popular vote. Attracts an estimated one million visitors annually.

HONOLULU

★4866★ ALA MOANA REGIONAL PARK

1201 Ala Moana Blvd
Honolulu, HI 96814
Phone: 808-692-5585; **Fax:** 808-692-5131
Size: 119 acres. **Location:** On the southern shore of Oahu between Ward Ave. and Queen St. **Facilities:** Picnic areas, beach, bathhouses. **Activities:** Swimming, surfing.

★4867★ KAPIOLANI REGIONAL PARK

2805 Monsarrat Ave
Honolulu, HI 96815
Phone: 808-971-2510; **Fax:** 808-692-5131
Size: 175 acres. **Location:** Located at the Diamond Head end of Waikiki. **Facilities:** Campsites, picnic areas. **Activities:** Camping (by permit), volleyball, fishing, swimming, snorkeling/scuba diving, surfing. **Special Features:** The largest and oldest public park in Hawaii, it hosts the world famous Honolulu Marathon. Adjacent to Waikaki Aquarium and Honolulu Zoo.

HOUSTON

★4868★ BEAR CREEK PIONEERS PARK

3535 War Memorial Dr
Houston, TX 77084
Web: www.pct3.hctx.net/PBearCreek
Phone: 281-496-2177
Size: 3,080 acres. **Location:** Western outskirts of Houston, just east of US-10 and south of Highway 6. **Facilities:** Equestrian and nature trails, 19 lighted baseball/softball fields, 16 horseshoe courts, pavilions and picnic areas, playgrounds, rodeo arena, soccer fields, and tennis courts. The park also houses three 18-hole golf courses and a small zoo and aviary. **Activities:** Hiking, horseback riding, soccer, baseball, softball, tennis, golf.

★4869★ CULLEN PARK

19008 Saums Rd
Houston, TX 77084
Phone: 281-578-0693
Size: 10,532 acres. **Location:** On Saums Road off I-10 West and Barker-Cypress. **Facilities:** Picnic areas, trails, bicycle arena, bike rentals, athletic fields. **Activities:** Bicycling, inline skating, soccer, softball. **Special Features:** Home to the Alkek Velodrome, an Olympic-standard bicycle arena that is one of just 19 such facilities in the United States.

★4870★ GEORGE BUSH PARK

16756 Westheimer Parkway
Houston, TX 77082
Web: www.pct3.hctx.net/PGeorge
Phone: 281-496-2177
Size: 7,800 acres. **Location:** Westheimer Parkway, adjacent to Barker Reservoir. **Facilities:** Picnic areas and pavilions, shooting range, sports fields, dedicated areas for equestrian activities and biking, model airplane field, playgrounds, and ponds. Also maintains the Millie Bush Bark Park, a 15-acre park that includes three small lakes. **Activities:** Picnicking, fishing, target shooting, hiking and biking, horseback riding, model airplane operation, soccer and baseball. **Special Features:** Originally called Cullen-Barker Park, but the name was changed to honor President George H.W. Bush and to minimize confusion with nearby Cullen Park.

★4871★ HERMANN PARK

6001 Fannin St
Houston, TX 77030
Web: www.houstontx.gov/parks/
Phone: 713-284-8555; **Fax:** 713-284-8550
Size: 401 acres. **Location:** At the intersection of Main Street and Montrose Blvd. **Facilities:** Picnic areas, jogging trails, historic structures, aquarium, miniature train, water playground, golf course. **Activities:** Boating, bicycling, golf, jogging. **Special Features:** Tourist attractions within the park include the Houston Zoological Gardens, Houston Zoo, Miller Outdoor Theatre, Houston Museum of Natural Science, and Japanese Garden.

★4872★ MEMORIAL PARK

6501 Memorial Dr
Houston, TX 77024
Web: www.houstontx.gov/parks/
Phone: 713-845-1000
Size: 1,431 acres. **Location:** Near the I-10 and I-610 West Loop intersection. **Facilities:** Picnic areas, trails, athletic fields. **Activities:** Hiking, bicycling, jogging, golf, tennis, softball. **Special Features:** Houses the Houston Arboretum and Nature Center (713-681-8433), a 155-acre preserve with more than five miles of self-guided trails that introduce visitors to a pine and mixed hardwood forest, a re-created Gulf Coast prairie, ponds, and a native wildflower garden. Also home to the George and Barbara Bush Presidential Grove, a tranquil area comprising more than 54 native Texas trees of seven different species.

INDIANAPOLIS

★4873★ EAGLE CREEK PARK

7840 W 56th St
Indianapolis, IN 46254
Web: www.indygov.org/eGov/City/DPR/Parks/home.htm
Phone: 317-327-7110; **Fax:** 317-327-7122
Size: 5,290 acres. **Location:** Northwest of downtown Indianapolis. **Facilities:** Picnic areas, outdoor theater, 1360-acre reservoir, marina, boat rentals, trails, fitness course, archery/pistol range,

27-hole golf course, nature center, playground, dog park. **Activities:** Canoeing, kayaking, sailing, windsurfing, fishing, swimming, bird-watching, hiking, bicycling, golf, cross-country skiing, ice skating, environmental education program.

★4874★ GARFIELD PARK

2345 Pagoda Dr
Indianapolis, IN 46203
Web: www.eGov/City/DPR/Parks/home.htm
Phone: 317-327-7220; **Fax:** 317-327-7235
Size: 123 acres. **Location:** Central Indianapolis. **Facilities:** Picnic shelter, Burrello Family Center, horseshoe pits, pool, playground, pagoda, sunken gardens, conservatory, weight room, athletic fields. **Activities:** Swimming, tennis, basketball, football, softball, horseshoes, sledding. **Special Features:** Established in 1881, Garfield is the oldest park in Indianapolis. Other park attractions include the MacAllister Center for the Performing Arts.

JACKSONVILLE

★4875★ HUGUENOT MEMORIAL PARK

10980 Heckscher Dr
Jacksonville, FL 32226
Web: www.coj.net/Departments/Parks+and+Recreation/
Phone: 904-251-3335; **Fax:** 904-251-3019
Size: 295 acres. **Location:** On the ocean just past the Mayport Ferry. **Facilities:** Shelters, camping, lake, boat launch, beach area, salt water fishing areas, bird observation tower, sports areas. **Activities:** Boating, camping, swimming, fishing, bird-watching, volleyball.

★4876★ KATHRYN ABBEY HANNA PARK

500 Wonderwood Dr
Jacksonville, FL 32233
Web: www.coj.net/Departments/Parks+and+Recreation/
Phone: 904-249-4700; **Fax:** 904-247-8688
Size: 450 acres. **Location:** Near Mayport, on the shore of the Atlantic Ocean. **Facilities:** Campgrounds, picnic areas, beach, children's water playground, trails, shelters, 60-acre freshwater lake . **Activities:** Camping, fishing, swimming, hiking, bicycling, sailing, surfing, kayaking, canoeing.

★4877★ POPE DUVAL PARK

13500 W Beaver St
Jacksonville, FL 32220
Web: www.coj.net/Departments/Parks+and+Recreation/
Phone: 904-630-3500
Size: 383 acres. **Location:** Off Beaver Street. **Facilities:** Trails, fishing ponds, nature trails, boardwalk, picnic areas, community building. **Activities:** Hiking, bicycling, fishing.

KANSAS CITY

★4878★ FLEMING PARK

22807 Woods Chapel Rd
Jackson County Parks & Recreation
Blue Springs, MO 64015
Web: www.jacksongov.org
Phone: 816-503-4800; **Fax:** 816-795-1234
Size: 7,890 acres. **Location:** South of Kansas City. Two miles east of I-470/291 on Woods Chapel Rd. **Facilities:** Campgrounds (seasonal), marinas (two), boat ramps, fishing dock, beach, picnic areas, shelter houses, boat rentals, nature trails, wildlife exhibit, historic village, model airplane field. **Activities:** Camping, sailboating, fishing, model airplane competitions. **Special Features:** The park is home to the Kemper Outdoor Education Center, which provides a range of educational programs for area residents.

★4879★ LONGVIEW LAKE PARK

22807 Woods Chapel Rd
Blue Springs, MO 64105
Web: www.jacksongov.org
Phone: 816-503-4800; **Fax:** 816-795-1234
Size: 4,852 acres. **Location:** Take I-470 to 109th St. and go south on Raytown Rd. **Facilities:** Marina, fishing ponds, beach, campground, picnic shelter, boat rental, bike trail (6 miles), golf course, horse park, model airplane field. **Activities:** Camping, boating, swimming, fishing, bicycling, golf.

★4880★ RICHARD L. BERKLEY RIVERFRONT PARK

Grand Ave Viad
Kansas City, MO 64106
Web: www.berkleyriverfrontpark.org
Phone: 816-221-0636
Size: 955 acres. **Location:** Southern bank of the Missouri River, just west of US-29/US-35. **Facilities:** Lighted walkway, rental facilities for special events. **Activities:** Jogging, bicycling. **Special Features:** The park neighbors several downtown attractions, including the River Market, the Isle of Capri Casino, the Steamboat Arabia Museum, and various restaurants and galleries.

★4881★ ROBERT H. HODGE PARK

7000 NE Barry Rd
Kansas City, MO 64156
Web: www.kcmo.org/parks.nsf/web/hodgepark
Phone: 816-792-2655
Size: 811 acres. **Location:** On Northeast Barry Road in northeastern Kansas City. **Facilities:** Picnic areas and picnic shelters, ampitheatre, lakes, wildlife exhibit, 18-hole golf course, historic Shoal Creek, sports areas. **Activities:** Golf, softball. **Special Features:** Park houses Shoal Creek Living History Museum, a reconstructed village of 19th century buildings including a church, general store, schoolhouse, farm buildings, and residences.

★4882★ SWOPE PARK

Swope Pkwy & Meyer Blvd
Kansas City, MO 64132
Web: www.kcmo.org/parks.nsf/web/swopepark
Phone: 816-513-7500; **Fax:** 816-513-7719
Size: 1,769 acres. **Location:** Meyer Blvd. and Swope Parkway in southeastern Kansas City. **Facilities:** Picnic areas and picnic shelters, golf course, swimming pool, outdoor theater, band pavilion, greenhouses, zoo, playgrounds, sports areas, horseback riding academy. **Activities:** Fishing, swimming, hiking, bicycling, horseback riding, golf, disc golf, tennis, archery, baseball, basketball, football, rugby, soccer, summer day camp. **Special Features:** Park houses the Kansas City Zoo, Kansas City Zoological Gardens, and the Lakeside Nature Center. In August, the park hosts the annual Ethnic Enrichment Festival, which features food, crafts, dance, and music from the cultures of more than 30 ethnic groups.

LITTLE ROCK

★4883★ BURNS PARK

Interstate 40
North Little Rock, AK 72118
Web: www.arkansasstateparks.com
Phone: 501-753-7307
Size: 1,575 acres. **Location:** Located on the west side of North Little Rock, bisected by I-40. **Facilities:** 38 tent and RV campsites, picnic areas and pavilions, lighted fields for a wide variety of sports, 18-hole disc golf course, BMX track, indoor handball, racquetball, and wallyball courts, paved walking and bicycling trail, Burns Park Equestrian Trail. **Activities:** hiking, softball, basketball, miniature golf, bocce ball, BMX biking, disc golf, soccer, camping, horseback riding, tennis, racquetball, handball, golf. **Special Features:** The park includes Funland, a five-acre area for children that includes old-fashioned carnival rides and a miniature train.

LONG BEACH

★4884★ EL DORADO EAST REGIONAL PARK

7550 E Spring St
Long Beach, CA 90815
Web: www.longbeach.gov/park/facilities/parks/
el_dorado_regional_park.asp
Phone: 562-570-1771; **Fax:** 562-570-1134
Size: 401 acres. **Location:** East Long Beach between Carson Street in the North, the 605 Freeway in the East, Stearns Avenue in the South, and Studebaker Road in the West. **Facilities:** Campsites, picnic areas, radio-controlled glider flying and sailboat sailing areas, archery range, concessions, paddleboat rentals, lake, path, bicycle trails, nature center, playground, miniature train, athletic fields and courts. **Activities:** Boating, fishing, bicycling, archery, model craft operation. **Special Features:** Houses the El Dorado Nature Center, an 85-acre wildlife refuge and nature preserve, which displays foxes, weasels, turtles, and hawks.

★4885★ EL DORADO PARK WEST

2800 Studebaker Rd
Long Beach, CA 90815
Web: www.longbeach.gov/park/facilities/parks/
el_dorado_park_west.asp
Phone: 562-570-3225; **Fax:** 562-570-3163
Size: 304 acres. **Location:** Take I-605 south to Spring Street, then west to Studebaker Road. **Facilities:** Picnic areas, duck pond, playgrounds, community center, 18-hole golf course, skate park, athletic fields and courts, disc golf course. **Activities:** Golf, tennis, basketball, volleyball, soccer, softball, roller hockey, disc golf, skateboarding, roller blading. **Special Features:** Golf course is the site of the Long Beach Open.

★4886★ RECREATION PARK

4900 E 7th St
Long Beach, CA 90804
Web: www.longbeach.gov/park/facilities/parks/
recreation_park.asp
Phone: 562-570-1670; **Fax:** 562-570-3109
Size: 211 acres. **Location:** On Federation off of 7th Street. **Facilities:** Picnic areas, Billie Jean King Tennis Center, 18-hole and 9-hole golf courses, lawn bowling green, casting pond, gardens, dog park, playground, community center, sports areas. **Activities:** Fishing, golf, tennis, lawn bowling, baseball. **Special Features:** Houses the Sochi Friendship Grove, recognizing the city of Long Beach's friendship with Sochi, its sister city in Russia.

LOS ANGELES

★4887★ ELYSIAN PARK

835 Academy Rd
Los Angeles, CA 90012
Web: www.laparks.org
Phone: 213-485-5054; **Fax:** 323-221-4695
Size: 585 acres. **Location:** North Broadway, Park Drive, Riverside Drive, Valley View, and Casanova streets. **Facilities:** Picnic areas, trails, arboretum, playground, sports areas. **Activities:** Hiking, jogging, horseshoes, tennis, baseball, basketball. **Special Features:** In 1769 Spanish explorers entered Los Angeles for the first time by crossing the bluff in Elysian Park overhanging the Los Angeles River, about where the Broadway Bridge is today.

★4888★ GRIFFITH PARK

4730 Crystal Springs Dr
Los Angeles, CA 90027
Web: www.laparks.org
Phone: 323-913-4688; **Fax:** 323-644-6204
Size: 4,107 acres. **Location:** Bordered by the Los Angeles River, Riverside Drive, Western Avenue, Los Feliz Boulevard, and the Golden State Freeway. **Facilities:** Picnic areas, concessions, riding and hiking trails, Japanese garden park, Greek theater, athletic fields and courts (including four golf courses). **Activities:** Hiking, jogging, bicycling, horseback riding, train rides,

golf, tennis, horseshoes. **Special Features:** Park attractions include the Griffith Observatory and Planetarium; Travel Town, an outdoor transportation museum specializing in pre-World War II railroad equipment; the Autry Museum of Western Heritage; the Greek Theatre; and the Los Angeles Zoo, which is home to more than 2,000 rare and exotic mammals, birds, and reptiles.

★4889★ O'MELVENY PARK
17300 Sesnon Blvd
Granada Hills, CA 91344
Web: www.laparks.org
Phone: 818-349-7341
Size: 672 acres. **Location:** At the north end of the San Fernando Valley in the Santa Susana Mountains. **Facilities:** Picnic area, trails. **Activities:** Hiking. **Special Features:** Park includes trail from Bee Canyon to the 2,771-foot Mission Point, which provides a view of the Southland.

★4890★ SEPULVEDA BASIN RECREATION AREA
17017 Burbank Boulevard
Encino, CA 91316
Web: www.laparks.org
Phone: 818-756-8060
Size: 2,030 acres. **Location:** North of downtown Los Angeles, west of US-405. **Facilities:** Picnic areas and pavilions, golf courses, model airplane field, cricket fields, archery range. **Activities:** Archery, bicycling, cricket, model airplane operation, off leash dog walking, hiking. **Special Features:** The Recreation Area includes several discrete attractions in their own right, including three eighteen-hole golf courses (Encino, Balboa, and Woodley Lakes), the Sepulveda Garden Center, Lake Balboa/Anthony C. Beilenson Park, and the 225-acre Sepulveda Basin Wildlife Reserve.

LOUISVILLE

★4891★ CHEROKEE PARK
745 Cochran Hill Rd
Louisville, KY 40206
Web: www.louisvilleky.gov/MetroParks/
Phone: 502-456-8100; **Fax:** 502-456-3269
Size: 409 acres. **Location:** In eastern Louisville off the Eastern Parkway. **Facilities:** Picnic areas, lake, bridle path, pavilions, bird sanctuary, historic structures, playgrounds, tennis courts, 9-hole golf course, archery range, horse shoe pits, mountain biking trails, other sports areas. **Activities:** Fishing, bicycling, horseback riding, golf, archery, basketball, softball. **Special Features:** Most visited park in Louisville. Designed by Frederick Law Olmsted, noted landscape architect. Linked by parkways to Iroquois and Shawnee parks.

★4892★ IROQUOIS PARK
2120 Rundill Rd
Louisville, KY 40214
Web: www.louisvilleky.gov/MetroParks/
Phone: 502-456-8100; **Fax:** 502-456-3269

Size: 739 acres. **Location:** In South Louisville at Taylor Blvd. and Southern Parkway. **Facilities:** Picnic areas, trails, bridle paths, amphitheater, playground, sports areas, archery range, golf course, disc golf course. **Activities:** Hiking, bicycling, horseback riding, fishing, golf, tennis, basketball, archery, disc golf, volleyball. **Special Features:** Rustic woodland park dominated by Iroquois Hill, a "knob" rising 260 feet above the alluvial plain that spreads to the north. Linked by parkways to Cherokee and Shawnee parks.

★4893★ JEFFERSON MEMORIAL FOREST
11311 Mitchell Hill Rd
Fairdale, KY 40118
Web: www.memorialforest.com
Phone: 502-368-5404; **Fax:** 502-368-6517
Size: 6,057 acres. **Location:** Jefferson County off the Gene Snyder Freeway (I-265) and I-65, 20 minutes from downtown Louisville. **Facilities:** Hiking trails (30 miles), campgrounds, picnic shelters, handicapped-accessible fishing dock, conference center, playgrounds, alpine tower, gift shop. **Activities:** Hiking, camping, fishing, horseback riding, volleyball. **Special Features:** Touted as the nation's largest municipal urban forest, Jefferson Memorial Forest includes several discrete usage areas, including the Tom Wallace Recreation Area, the Paul Yost Recreation Area, and the Horine Conference Center and Reservation.

★4894★ SENECA PARK
3151 Pee Wee Reese Rd
Louisville, KY 40207
Web: www.louisvilleky.gov/MetroParks/
Phone: 502-458-9298
Size: 333 acres. **Location:** Six miles east of downtown Louisville off US-64. **Facilities:** Tennis courts, 18-hole golf course, volleyball courts, soccer and softball fields, field hockey grounds, cross-country trail (3.1 miles), basketball courts, playground, picnic facilities, and equestrian trails. **Activities:** Basketball, softball, soccer, field hockey, horseback riding, tennis, volleyball.

★4895★ SHAWNEE PARK
460 N Western Pkwy
Louisville, KY 40233
Phone: 502-456-8100; **Fax:** 502-456-8168
Size: 181 acres. **Location:** In western Louisville off the Southwestern Parkway. **Facilities:** Picnic areas, lily pond, pavilions, bandstand, playgrounds, sports areas. **Activities:** Golf, tennis, basketball, soccer, softball. **Special Features:** Low-lying riverfront park with a sweeping view of the Ohio River. Linked by parkways to Cherokee and Iroquois parks.

MEMPHIS

★4896★ AUDUBON PARK
4145 Southern Ave
Memphis, TN 38117
Phone: 901-683-6941

Size: 373 acres. **Location:** In East Memphis, Park Avenue at Goodlett. **Facilities:** Picnic areas, trails, theater, tennis center, sports areas. **Activities:** Fishing, golf, tennis, soccer. **Special Features:** Houses the 96-acre Memphis Botanic Gardens, which includes Japanese, sensory, sculpture, and day lily gardens. The W.C. Paul Arboretum is also part of the Gardens.

★4897★ MARTIN LUTHER KING-RIVERSIDE PARK

South Parkway at Riverside
Memphis, TN 38112
Phone: 901-454-5200
Size: 379 acres. **Location:** South Parkway at Riverside. **Facilities:** Picnic areas, marina, boat ramp, nature trail, 9-hole golf course, sports areas. **Activities:** Fishing, golf, tennis.

★4898★ OVERTON PARK

2080 Poplar Ave
Memphis, TN 38112
Phone: 901-576-4200; **Fax:** 901-579-4275
Size: 342 acres. **Location:** Downtown Memphis. **Facilities:** Picnic areas, fitness trail, nature trail, theater, art museum, zoo, playground, sports areas. **Activities:** Bicycling, golf, soccer, softball, tennis. **Special Features:** Houses Memphis College of Art and Memphis Brooks Museum of Art, Tennessee's oldest and largest museum of fine and decorative arts. Also houses the 70-acre Memphis Zoo and Aquarium, home to more than 2,800 animals representing 400 species.

★4899★ SHELBY FARMS PARK

500 Pine Lake Dr
Memphis, TN 38134
Web: www.shelbycountytn.gov
Phone: 901-382-2249
Size: 4,500 acres. **Location:** On Pine Lake Drive in Memphis. **Facilities:** Pavilions and picnic areas, outdoor amphitheatre, riding stables, jogging and biking trails. **Activities:** Hiking, jogging, mountain biking, kayaking and canoeing, fishing, bird-watching, horseback riding. **Special Features:** Distinct areas within the park include the 1,000-acre Lucius Burch Natural Area and two large lakes (Patriot Lake and Pine Lake).

MIAMI

★4900★ AMELIA EARHART PARK

401 East 65th St
Miami, FL 33013
Web: www.miamidade.gov/parks/
Phone: 305-685-8369
Size: 515 acres. **Location:** Off Gratigny Parkway in Hialeah. **Facilities:** Five lakes, swimming beach, paved trails, dog park. **Activities:** Fishing, canoeing, sailing, swimming, dog walking. **Special Features:** The park grounds also include the Bill Graham Farm Village, a working replica of an early twentieth century Florida farm.

★4901★ CRANDON PARK

4000 Crandon Blvd
Key Biscayne, FL 33149
Web: www.miamidade.gov/parks/
Phone: 305-361-5421; **Fax:** 305-365-3002
Size: 899 acres. **Location:** On Key Biscayne, just south of Miami. **Facilities:** Group shelters, picnic tables, trails, beach, boardwalk, boat ramps, marina, kayak rentals, cabana rentals, tennis center, golf course, running track, fishing pier, baseball diamonds, soccer fields, playground, food concessions, recreation center. **Activities:** Swimming, hiking, bicycling, golf, tennis, jogging, boating, kayaking. **Special Features:** Park is located next to The Links at Key Biscayne, one of the finest 18-hole municipal golf courses in the state. Park offerings include guided tours through the Bear Cut Nature Preserve.

★4902★ GREYNOLDS PARK

17530 W Dixie Hwy
North Miami Beach, FL 33160
Web: www.miamidade.gov/parks/
Phone: 305-945-3425; **Fax:** 305-945-3428
Size: 249 acres. **Location:** Entrance is at 22nd Ave. and NE 186th St. in North Miami Beach. **Facilities:** Campground (reserved for groups), picnic shelters, fishing pier (adjoining park), canoe rentals, trails, playground, physical fitness course, 9-hole golf course, food concessions. **Activities:** Camping, bicycling, golf, jogging, fishing, paddleboating and canoeing, bird-watching, group naturalist tours. **Special Features:** One of Dade County's oldest parks, Greynolds includes one of three South Florida bird sanctuaries recognized by the National Audubon Society. It is also the site of the Greynolds Park Love-In, an annual celebration of the music and lifestyle of the 1960s

MILWAUKEE

★4903★ BROWN DEER PARK

7835 N Green Bay Rd
Milwaukee, WI 53209
Web: www.county.milwaukee.gov
Phone: 414-352-7502; **Fax:** 414-352-1279
Size: 363 acres. **Location:** Northwestern Milwaukee off Range Line Road. **Facilities:** Picnic areas, bicycle track, sports areas. **Activities:** Bicycling, golf, archery, football, soccer, softball, cross-country skiing, ice skating, sledding. **Special Features:** Includes section of the Oak Leaf Recreational Trail.

★4904★ LINCOLN PARK

1301 W Hampton Ave
Milwaukee, WI 53209
Web: www.county.milwaukee.gov
Phone: 414-332-1350; **Fax:** 414-332-2260
Size: 313 acres. **Location:** Northeastern Milwaukee. **Facilities:** Picnic areas, pool, water slides, canoe launch, sports areas. **Activities:** Canoeing, fishing, swimming, golf, archery, baseball, football, soccer.

10. Urban Parks

★4905★ **WHITNALL PARK**
5879 S 92nd St
Hales Corners, WI 53130
Web: www.county.milwaukee.gov
Phone: 414-425-7931
Size: 625 acres. **Location:** South of Milwaukee. **Facilities:** Picnic areas, trails, bridle path, gardens, nature center, lodge, sports areas. **Activities:** Group camping, horseback riding, golf, archery, soccer, softball, volleyball, cross-country skiing, ice skating. **Special Features:** Houses the Boerner Botanical Gardens. Open daily April through October, 8 am to sunset.

MINNEAPOLIS

★4906★ **LAKE CALHOUN**
300 Calhoun Parkway
Minneapolis, MN 55408
Web: www.minneapolisparks.org
Phone: 612-230-6400
Size: 520 acres. **Location:** Western Minneapolis. **Facilities:** Lake, beaches (3), boat dock, fishing docks (2), 3.2-mile trail, athletic fields. **Activities:** Canoeing, kayaking, sailing, swimming, windsurfing, fishing, volleyball, soccer, softball, in-line skating, biking, jogging. **Special Features:** Part of Minneapolis's well-known ''Chain of Lakes.''

★4907★ **LAKE HARRIET**
200 Grain Exchange
400 S 4th St, Minneapolis Park & Recreation Board
Minneapolis, MN 55415
Web: www.minneapolisparks.org
Phone: 612-661-4875
Size: 402 acres. **Location:** 50th Street and Penn Avenue. **Facilities:** Lake, beach, boat dock, boat rentals, garden, bandstand. **Activities:** Sailing, fishing, swimming, windsurfing, bicycling, plays and concerts (summer).

★4908★ **THEODORE WIRTH PARK**
1339 Theodore Wirth Pkwy
Minneapolis, MN 55411
Web: www.minneapolisparks.org
Phone: 763-522-4584; **Fax:** 612-230-6500
Size: 787 acres. **Location:** At the intersection of Glenwood and Washburn avenues. **Facilities:** Picnic areas, trails, tamarack bog, gardens, bird sanctuary, sports areas. **Activities:** Hiking, golf, mountain biking. **Special Features:** Park houses the Eloise Butler Gardens, the oldest public wildflower gardens in the nation. The woodland, bog, and prairie areas provide visitors with seasonal displays of native wildflowers. Tours offered.

NASHVILLE

★4909★ **CENTENNIAL PARK**
West End Ave-between 25th & 28th Aves
Nashville, TN 37201
Web: www.nashville.gov/parks/
Phone: 615-862-8400; **Fax:** 615-880-2265

Size: 500 acres. **Location:** Two miles west of downtown Nashville. **Facilities:** Picnic sites, lake, paddleboat rentals, pool, historic monuments, art museum, bandshell, tennis center, Sportsplex. **Activities:** Boating, swimming, tennis, volleyball, ice skating. **Special Features:** Home of the only full-scale reproduction of the world-famous Parthenon. Structure houses an art museum and the Athena Parthenos (statue of Athena), the tallest indoor sculpture in the western world.

★4910★ **EDWIN WARNER PARK**
Centennial Park Ofc
Metropolitan Board of Parks & Recreation
Nashville, TN 37201
Web: www.nashville.gov/parks/warner.htm
Phone: 615-862-8400
Size: 2684 acres (combined with Percy Warner Park). **Location:** Nine miles from downtown, south of Old Hickory Boulevard. Adjoins Percy Warner Park. **Facilities:** Picnic sites, hiking and bridle trails, nature center, sports areas. **Activities:** Hiking, horseback riding, softball.

★4911★ **PERCY WARNER PARK**
2500 Old Hickory Blvd
Nashville, TN 37201
Web: www.nashville.gov/parks/warner.htm
Phone: 615-862-8400; **Fax:** 615-356-7737
Size: 2,684 acres (combined with Edwin Warner Park). **Location:** Nine miles from downtown, at Old Hickory Boulevard and Chickering Lane. Adjoins Edwin Warner Park. **Facilities:** Hiking and bridle trails, 2 golf courses. **Activities:** Hiking, horseback riding, golf. **Special Features:** Hosts the Iroquois Steeplechase (annually in spring), the oldest continuously-run amateur steeplechase in the United States.

NEW ORLEANS

★4912★ **AUDUBON PARK**
6500 Magazine St
New Orleans, LA 70118
Web: ani.convio.net
Phone: 504-581-4629; **Fax:** 504-212-5157; **Toll Free:** 800-774-7394
Size: 400 acres. **Location:** Six miles from downtown. Bordered by Saint Charles Avenue, Exposition Boulevard, the Mississippi River, and Walnut Street. **Facilities:** Concessions, sports areas, jogging and bridle trails. **Activities:** Golf, tennis, jogging, horseback riding, cycling, in-line skating. **Special Features:** Park is home to the Audubon Zoological Gardens, established in 1884, which houses 1,800 animals. Includes a wild bird rehabilitation program.

★4913★ **CITY PARK**
1 Palm Dr
New Orleans, LA 70124
Web: www.neworleanscitypark.com
Phone: 504-482-4888; **Fax:** 504-483-9412

10. Urban Parks

Size: 1,460 acres. **Location:** Bordered by City Park Avenue, Carrollton Avenue, Wisner Boulevard, Robert E. Lee Boulevard, Marconi Drive, and Orleans Avenue. **Facilities:** Picnic areas, concessions, lake, boat rentals, botanical gardens, New Orleans Museum of Art, carousel, child educational programs, sports areas. **Activities:** Boating, fishing, horseback riding, golf, tennis, football, softball, rugby. **Special Features:** Repairs and renovations from Hurricane Katrina are ongoing, but many of the park's attractions and special events have reopened. The park's annual "Celebration in the Oaks" holiday light exhibit, for example, returned in 2006.

NEW YORK

★4914★ CENTRAL PARK

830 5th Ave
New York, NY 10021
Web: www.centralparknyc.org
Phone: 212-360-8111; **Fax:** 212-830-7860
Size: 250 acres. **Location:** Visitor center is located at mid-park, at 65th street. Enter the park at 60th Street and Fifth Avenue and walk north. **Facilities:** Concessions, visitor center, pools, lakes, rowboat rentals, trails, gardens (Conservatory Garden and Shakespeare Garden), science and education center, historic structures and exhibits (including statues of William Shakespeare and Christopher Columbus), zoo, playground, climbing walls (indoor and outdoor), athletic fields. **Activities:** Boating, fishing, swimming, hiking, bicycling, jogging, rollerblading, horseback riding, guided walking tours (&), miniature golf, tennis, baseball, softball, basketball, football, soccer, wall climbing, handball, law bowling, croquet, ice skating, cross-country skiing. **Special Features:** America's most famous urban park. Central Park includes Strawberry Fields, a tear-drop shaped landscape dedicated to the memory of John Lennon. This landscape has become home to the "international garden of peace" since the introduction of 161 plant species to this area. Park also features the Central Park Wildlife Center, home to 450 different species of animals. In the summer, the park hosts the New York Shakespeare Festival and SummerStage, a performing arts festival. Performances are free, but the Shakespeare Festival productions require tickets.

★4915★ FLUSHING MEADOWS CORONA PARK

11101 Corona Ave
Flushing, NY 11368
Web: www.nycgovparks.org
Phone: 718-760-6565
Size: 1,255 acres. **Location:** Queens. **Facilities:** The park's large offerings of athletic fields is supplemented by a playground, picnic areas, and paved walking trails. **Activities:** Soccer and other field sports, ice skating, miniature golf. **Special Features:** Other attractions within the park include Shea Stadium, the USTA National Tennis Center, the New York Hall of Science, the Queens Museum of Art, Queens Wildlife Conservation Center, Queens Botanical Garden, and the World's Fair Ice Skating Rink.

★4916★ PELHAM BAY PARK

Bruckner Blvd & Middletown & Shore Rds
Bronx, NY 10464
Web: www.nycgovparks.org
Phone: 718-430-1890; **Fax:** 718-430-1893
Size: 2,764 acres. **Location:** Northeast Bronx, off the New England Thruway and the Hutchinson River Parkway. **Facilities:** Visitor center, picnic areas, beach, trails, bridle path, stable, exercise areas, historic sites, wildlife refuge, environmental center, sports areas, playgrounds. **Activities:** Boating, fishing, swimming, hiking, running, horseback riding, golf, tennis, baseball, basketball, football, soccer. **Special Features:** The city's largest park, it's most popular feature is Orchard Beach, a 115-acre, 1.1-mile long area on Long Island Sound that includes a sandy beach, a promenade, a central pavilion and food court, a games area, and two picnic areas.

★4917★ PROSPECT PARK

95 Prospect Park West
Brooklyn, NY 11215
Web: www.prospectpark.org
Phone: 718-965-8951
Size: 585 acres. **Location:** Parkside and Ocean Avenues. **Facilities:** Outdoor sports facilities, trails (for biking, running, and horseback riding), Audubon Center, Prospect Park Zoo, 90-acre Long Meadow, Wollman Rink, and a 1912 carousel. **Activities:** Ice skating, pedal boating, tennis, hiking, bird-watching, roller blading, bicycling, fishing, horseback riding, baseball, football, roadracing, soccer, volleyball. **Special Features:** Designed by famed landscape architects Frederick Law Olmsted and Calvert Vaux. Attractions include the Grand Army Plaza, Brooklyn's only zoo, and outdoor concerts.

★4918★ RIVERSIDE PARK

16 W 61st St, 6th Fl
New York, NY 10023
Web: www.nycgovparks.org
Phone: 212-408-0264
Size: 316 acres. **Location:** Stretches for four miles from 72nd to 158th streets. **Facilities:** Waterfront marina (110 slips), paths, gardens, theater, historic monuments (including General Grant National Memorial; see separate entry in national parks section), bird sanctuary, viewing pavilion, athletic fields and courts, playgrounds. **Activities:** Kayaking, sailing, boating, fishing, bicycling, tennis, roller skating, basketball, handball, soccer, softball, volleyball, sledding, chess. **Special Features:** A walking and bicycling path, Riverside Walk, runs the full length of Riverside Park waterfront and is the longest section of a planned path encircling Manhattan. It also serves as a link on the Washington DC- Boston and Hudson River greenways. Each summer, the park hosts the Riverside Arts Festival, featuring music, jazz, dance, and art exhibits from around the world.

★4919★ THE GREENBELT

700 Rockland Ave
Staten Island, NY 10314
Web: www.nycgovparks.org
Phone: 718-351-3450

10. Urban Parks

Size: 2,800 acres. **Location:** Corridor of parks and natural areas running through the heart of Staten Island. **Activities:** Jogging, golf, softball, soccer, fishing, tennis, archery, hiking. **Special Features:** Attractions within The Greenbelt include the High Rock Environmental Center (at High Rock Park); the William T. Davis Wildlife Refuge (the first wildlife and bird sanctuary founded in New York City); La Tourette Park, which offers golf, ballfields, a driving range, and a model airplane field; Willowbrook Park, which has a historic children's carousel and maintains facilities for tennis, archery, fishing, and other recreational activities; and natural areas including Deer Park, Buck's Hollow, Bloodroot Valley, Reed's Basket Willow Swamp, Egbertville Ravine, and Amundson Trailway.

★4920★ VAN CORTLANDT PARK
Broadway & W 242nd St
Bronx, NY 10463
Web: www.nycgovparks.org
Phone: 718-430-1890; **Fax:** 718-430-1893
Size: 1,146 acres. **Location:** Northwestern Bronx. **Facilities:** Visitor center, lake, swimming pool, nature trails, bridle path, aqueduct trail, cross-country course, stable, historic site, Memorial and Constitution Groves, sports areas, playgrounds. **Activities:** Fishing, swimming, hiking, running, horseback riding, golf, tennis, baseball, football, soccer, bird-watching. **Special Features:** Park includes Van Cortlandt Mansion and Museum, the Bronx's oldest building, built in 1748. Rooms are furnished as they were in the 18th and 19th centuries. An abandoned railroad track, the first rail to link the city with Boston, passes through the park and serves as a nature trail.

NEWARK

★4921★ BRANCH BROOK PARK
Park Ave and Lake St
Newark, NJ 07014
Web: www.essex-countynj.org
Phone: 973-268-3500; **Fax:** 973-481-5302
Size: 360 acres. **Location:** Off Lake Street in Newark. **Facilities:** 23-acre lake, path, playgrounds, sports areas. **Activities:** Fishing, tennis, baseball, football, softball. **Special Features:** The park, which features a regionally famous cherry tree collection, was the first county park opened for public use in the United States. It was designed by Frederick Law Olmsted and John Charles Olmsted.

★4922★ EAGLE ROCK RESERVATION
Eagle Rock & Prospect Aves
West Orange, NJ 07052
Web: www.essex-countynj.org
Phone: 973-268-3500; **Fax:** 973-268-3546
Size: 408 acres. **Location:** In West Orange. **Facilities:** Picnic areas, hiking trails, bridle trails, wildlife preserve, lookout points, sports areas. **Activities:** Hiking, horse-drawn carriage rides, horseback riding, softball. **Special Features:** The park, which offers an unrivaled view of the Manhattan skyline, was designed by Frederick Law Olmsted and John Charles Olmsted.

★4923★ SOUTH MOUNTAIN RESERVATION
South Orange Ave and Cherry Lane
West Orange, NJ 07052
Web: www.essex-countynj.org
Phone: 973-731-3828; **Fax:** 973-325-9704
Size: 2,047 acres. **Location:** In South Orange, northwest of Newark. **Facilities:** Picnic areas, ponds, hiking and bridle trails (19 miles total), lookout points, wildlife preserve, arena, zoo, sports areas. **Activities:** Fishing, hiking, bicycling, horseback riding, archery, softball, indoor ice skating. **Special Features:** Portions of the park was designed by famed landscape architects Frederick Law Olmsted and John Charles Olmsted. The park is home to the Turtle Back Zoo, which features more than 200 species of animals.

★4924★ WEST ESSEX PARK
Eagle Rock Ave and Passaic River
Newark, NJ 07104
Web: www.essex-countynj.org
Phone: 973-268-3500
Size: 1,361 acres. **Location:** In Livingston, along the Passaic River in western Essex County. **Facilities:** Campsites, golf driving range, picnic area, wetlands, trails, wildlife preserves, nature study area. **Activities:** Camping, boating, canoeing, fishing, hiking. **Special Features:** Primarily a wetlands reserve, the park is a favorite destination for bird watchers.

OAKLAND

★4925★ JOAQUIN MILLER PARK
3590 Sanborn Dr
Oakland, CA 94602
Web: www.oaklandnet.com
Phone: 510-238-3481; **Fax:** 510-482-7850
Size: 513 acres. **Location:** Just east of Highway 13. **Facilities:** Picnic areas, hiking and mountain biking trails, horse arena, playground, theater. **Activities:** Hiking, horseback riding, mountain biking. **Special Features:** Park houses Joaquin Miller's original home, built in 1889 and classified as a Registered National Monument.

★4926★ LAKESIDE PARK
Grand Ave & Bellevue Ave
Oakland, CA 94612
Web: www.oaklandnet.com
Phone: 510-238-3191; **Fax:** 510-637-0379
Size: 122 acres. **Location:** Off Grand Avenue, just minutes from downtown Oakland. **Facilities:** Lake, gardens, garden center, trails, wild bird sanctuary, bandstand, children's theme park. **Activities:** Lawn bowling, jogging, bicycling.

OKLAHOMA CITY

★4927★ EARLYWINE PARK
3033 SW 119th St
Oklahoma City, OK 73170
Phone: 405-297-2211; **Fax:** 405-297-3657

Size: 453 acres. **Location:** Southwest 119th Street and May Avenue. **Facilities:** Picnic sites, jogging trail, playground, sports areas (including golf course), aquatic center (405-692-6050). **Activities:** Golf, tennis, soccer, softball, swimming.

★4928★ LAKE HEFNER PARK
201 Channing Sq, Suite B-1
Parks & Recreation Dept
Oklahoma City, OK 73102
Phone: 405-297-2211
Size: 4,000 acres (including 2,500-acre lake). **Location:** In northwestern Oklahoma City between Lake Hefner Parkway and MacArthur. **Facilities:** Picnic sites, marina and boat ramps, sailboat rentals, trails, playground, sports areas (including golf course). **Activities:** Boating, sailing, fishing, bicycling, jogging, golf, baseball, soccer. **Special Features:** Sailboat races are held from April through October.

★4929★ LAKE OVERHOLSER
1600 E Overholser Dr
Oklahoma City, OK 73102
Phone: 405-297-2211; **Fax:** 405-297-3657
Size: 2,800 acres (including 1,500-acre lake). **Location:** In northwestern Oklahoma City on Overholser Drive. **Facilities:** Picnic sites, boat ramps, fishing pier, trails, sports areas. **Activities:** Boating, fishing, jetskiing, tennis, soccer. **Special Features:** Park houses a wildlife refuge.

★4930★ TROSPER PARK
SE 29th St & Eastern Ave
Oklahoma City, OK 73102
Phone: 405-297-2211; **Fax:** 405-297-3657
Size: 640 acres. **Location:** Southeast 25th Street and Eastern Avenue. **Facilities:** Picnic sites, playground, sports areas (including golf course). **Activities:** Golf, tennis, archery, softball.

OMAHA

★4931★ GLENN CUNNINGHAM LAKE
8660 Cunningham Lake Rd
Omaha, NE 68114
Web: www.ci.omaha.ne.us/parks/
Phone: 402-444-4628
Size: 1,439 acres. **Location:** North central Omaha on Lake Cunningham Road via I-680 North. **Facilities:** Campsites, picnic area, lake, bike paths, hiking paths, bridle trails, playground. **Activities:** Camping, boating, fishing, hiking, bicycling, horseback riding.

★4932★ LEVI CARTER PARK
809 Carter Lake Shore Dr
Omaha, NE 68110
Web: www.ci.omaha.ne.us/parks/
Phone: 402-444-5900
Size: 520 acres. **Location:** In northeastern Omaha on Carter Lake Shore Drive. **Facilities:** Picnic area, pavilion, lagoon, bike paths, playground, sports areas. **Activities:** Boating, fishing, water-skiing, bicycling, basketball, soccer, softball.

★4933★ NP DODGE MEMORIAL PARK
11001 John J. Pershing Dr.
Omaha, NE 68112
Web: www.ci.omaha.ne.us/parks/
Phone: 402-444-5900
Size: 445 acres. **Location:** In northern Omaha on John J. Pershing Drive. **Facilities:** Campsites, playground, picnic area, pavilion, athletic fields (including eight soccer fields). **Activities:** Camping, boating, fishing, tennis, football, soccer, softball, horseshoes.

★4934★ STANDING BEAR LAKE
6404 North 132nd St
Omaha, NE 68164
Web: www. ci.omaha.ne.us/parks/
Phone: 402-444-5900
Size: 685 acres. **Location:** North side of Omaha. **Facilities:** Playground, picnic areas, shelters, lake, remote control airplane flying field. **Activities:** Fishing, boating, hiking, bicycling, roller blading.

★4935★ TRANQUILITY PARK
12222 West Maple Road
Omaha, NE 68164
Web: www. ci.omaha.ne.us/parks/
Phone: 402-444-5900
Size: 340 acres. **Location:** On West Maple Road in Omaha. **Facilities:** Playground, picnic shelters, indoor ice rink, and athletic fields, including 17 soccer fields, 8 baseball fields, and 24 tennis courts. **Activities:** Ice skating, tennis, soccer, baseball, softball.

★4936★ ZORINSKY LAKE PARK
156th and F Sts
Omaha, NE 68112
Web: www. ci.omaha.ne.us/parks/
Phone: 402-444-5900
Size: 1,023 acres. **Facilities:** Picnic areas, shelters, trails, playgrounds, athletic fields. **Activities:** Fishing, boating, hiking, baseball, football, soccer.

PHILADELPHIA

★4937★ COBBS CREEK PARK
6400 Market St
Upper Darby, PA 19082
Web: www.fairmountpark.org
Size: 786 acres. **Location:** Located due west from downtown Philadelphia. **Facilities:** Golf course, ice skating rink, recreational center and track, hiking trails. **Activities:** Ice skating, hiking, golf. **Special Features:** Attractions include the Cobbs

Creek Community Environmental Education Center, which features several science and urban ecology programs.

★4938★ FAIRMOUNT PARK, EAST AND WEST

4321 North Concourse Dr
Philadelphia, PA 19131
Web: www.fairmountpark.org
Phone: 215-683-0200
Size: Largest park in Philadelphia's 9,200-acre park system. **Location:** Located from the mouth of the Wissahickon Creek, south to Center City. The dividing line between East and West Fairmount Parks is the Schuylkill River. **Facilities:** Picnic areas, paved and unpaved trails, tennis and basketball courts, playing fields. **Activities:** Recreational options include cycling, walking, roller blading, hiking and horseback riding, tennis, basketball, soccer, and softball. **Special Features:** East Fairmount Park houses the Academy of Natural Sciences, the Fairmount Water Works, Boathouse Row, and the Philadelphia Museum of Art, and an assortment of historic homes and buildings. Attractions in the West unit include the Mann Center for the Performing Arts, the Horticulture Center, the Japanese House and Garden, the Philadelphia Zoo, and several historic mansions.

★4939★ FRANKLIN DELANO ROOSEVELT PARK

1800 Pattison Ave
Philadelphia, PA 19145
Web: www.fairmountpark.org
Phone: 215-683-0200
Size: 348 acres. **Location:** South Philadelphia. **Facilities:** Skate park, sport fields, golf course, tennis courts. **Activities:** Golf, tennis, rugby, baseball, softball, birdwatching, skateboarding, roller blading. **Special Features:** FDR Skate Park is a nationally known destination for skateboarding and roller blading enthusiasts. Other attractions in the park include the American Swedish Historical Museum and a series of ponds and tidal marshes that are home to numerous bird species.

INDEPENDENCE NATIONAL HISTORICAL PARK

(See US National Parks chapter for descriptive information.)

★4940★ NEWPORT NEWS PARK

13564 Jefferson Ave
Newport News, VA 23603
Web: www.nnparks.com
Phone: 757-888-3333; **Fax:** 757-888-3333; **Toll Free:** 800-203-8322
Size: 8,000 acres. **Location:** Midway between Richmond and Virginia Beach off I-64 (exit 250B). **Facilities:** Modern campground with 188 sites, more than 30 miles of paved and dirt trails for jogging, bicycling, and mountain biking, arboretum, playgrounds, picnic shelters, 30-acre model airplane flying field, archery range, two 18-hole golf courses, 18-hole disc golf course. **Activities:** Camping, boating, canoeing, fishing, hiking, jogging, biking, model airplane flying, mountain biking, disc golf, golf, archery. **Special Features:** Annual events at the park include the Newport News Children's Festival of Friends (first

Saturday in May) and the Newport News Fall Festival of Folklife (first weekend in October).

★4941★ PENNYPACK PARK

8550 Verree Rd
Philadelphia, PA 19111
Web: www.fairmountpark.org/
Phone: 215-683-0200; **Fax:** 215-878-9859
Size: 1,395 acres. **Location:** Stretches nine miles northwest from the Delaware River to where Philadelphia meets the border of Montgomery County. **Facilities:** Picnic areas, paved and unpaved trails. **Activities:** Horseback riding, mountain biking, soccer, softball, roller blading, jogging. **Special Features:** Part of the city's Fairmount Park system. Points of interest in Pennypack include the Fox Chase Farm, Pennypack Bandshell, and Pennypack Environmental Center.

★4942★ TACONY CREEK PARK

5653 Rising Sun Ave
Philadelphia, PA 19120
Web: www.fairmountpark.org
Phone: 215-683-0200
Size: 302 acres. **Location:** Between Cheltenham Township and Frankfort Creek. **Activities:** Hiking, birdwatching. **Special Features:** The park is adjacent to the Juniata Golf Course.

★4943★ WISSAHICKON VALLEY PARK

300 Northwestern Ave
Philadelphia, PA 19118
Web: www.fairmountpark.org
Phone: 215-685-9285; **Fax:** 215-685-9268
Size: 1,400 acres. **Location:** Northwestern Philadelphia. **Facilities:** Hiking trails, stocked stream, bridle trails and riding rings (and stables), picnic areas. **Activities:** Hiking, fishing, horseback riding. **Special Features:** Special attractions include Wissahickon Environmental Center, several historic mansions and homes, and Historic RittenhouseTown.

PHOENIX

★4944★ PAPAGO PARK

625 N Galvin Pkwy
Phoenix, AZ 85008
Web: phoenix.gov/parks/
Phone: 602-256-3220; **Fax:** 602-495-5561
Size: 1,496 acres (1,200 in Phoenix and 296 in Tempe). **Location:** At Van Buren Street and Galvin Parkway. From Phoenix, go east on Van Buren Street past 44th Street; from Scottsdale, go south on Scottsdale Road, west on McDowell Road, south on 64th Street; from Tempe, go north on Mill Avenue to the Salt River. **Facilities:** Picnic areas, trails, fishing lagoons, archery range, 1.7-mile exercise course, orienteering course, historical sites, zoo, botanical garden, fire museum, golf course, amphitheater, playground, sports areas. **Activities:** Fishing, hiking, archery, orienteering, bicycling, horseback riding, golf, softball. **Special Features:** The Papago Trail takes visitors through

the heart of the Phoenix metropolitan area. Heritage, Environmental, Recreation, and Entertainment trails take visitors to attractions and points of interest in Phoenix, Scottsdale, and Tempe.

★4945★   PHOENIX MOUNTAINS PRESERVE
10409 S Central Ave
Phoenix, AZ 85040
Web: www.phoenixmountains.org
Phone: 602-495-0222; **Fax:** 602-534-6330
Size: 7,000 acres. **Location:** North of downtown. **Facilities:** Picnic areas, 50 miles of trails. **Activities:** Hiking, bicycling, horseback riding. **Special Features:** Preserve includes Squaw Peak, North Mountain, Dreamy Draw, Shaw Butte, Lookout Mountain, and Shadow Mountain.

★4946★   REACH 11 RECREATION AREA
19224 N. Tatum Blvd
Phoenix, AZ 85024
Web: phoenix.gov/PARKS/
Phone: 602-534-9995
Size: 1,500 acres. **Location:** North of the Central Arizona Project canal between Cave Creek Road and Scottsdale Road. **Facilities:** Equestrian center, hiking and riding trails, picnic area. **Activities:** Horseback riding, hiking, bird watching. **Special Features:** Park activity centers around the Arizona Horse Lovers Park, a 90-acre equestrian facility that includes four lighted arenas, bridle trails, and facilities for equestrian and livestock care.

★4947★   SOUTH MOUNTAIN PARK/PRESERVE
10919 S Central Ave
Phoenix, AZ 85040
Web: phoenix.gov/PARKS/
Phone: 602-495-0222; **Fax:** 602-495-0212
Size: 16,500 acres. **Location:** On South Central Avenue, south of downtown. **Facilities:** Picnic areas, ramadas (with kitchen), dance platforms, 51 miles of trails, lookout point. **Activities:** Hiking, bicycling, horseback riding. **Special Features:** This park, the nation's largest municipal park, encompasses a vast rugged mountain range. Features include petroglyphs (ancient Indian rock inscriptions), historic and archeological sites, a mining camp, and a Depression-era work camp. The park is also home to the South Mountain Environmental Education Center (602-534-6324).

PITTSBURGH

★4948★   FRICK PARK
S Braddock & Forbes Aves
Pittsburgh, PA 15221
Web: www.city.pittsburgh.pa.us/parks/
Phone: 412-422-6550; **Fax:** 412-422-6407
Size: 600 acres. **Location:** East of downtown in Pittsburgh's Squirrel Hill South neighborhood. Park office is located on English Lane off Beechwood Boulevard. **Facilities:** Picnic shelters, playground, trails, fitness course, nature center, sports areas. **Activities:** Hiking, tennis, lawn bowling, baseball, basketball, football, soccer. **Special Features:** Attractions include the Frick Art and Historical Center (412-371-0600) and the Frick Environmental Center (412-422-6538).

★4949★   HIGHLAND PARK
Highland Ave at Bunker Hill
Pittsburgh, PA 15206
Web: www.city.pittsburgh.pa.us/parks/
Phone: 412-665-3632; **Fax:** 412-665-3633
Size: 475 acres. **Location:** East of downtown in Pittsburgh's Highland Park neighborhood. Park office is at the corner of Heberton and Grafton Streets. **Facilities:** Picnic shelters, swimming pool, lake, trails, fitness course, playgrounds, sports areas. **Activities:** Fishing, swimming, hiking, bicycling, tennis, baseball, basketball, football, soccer, volleyball. **Special Features:** Park houses the Pittsburgh Zoo (established in 1898), featuring more than 6,300 animals in natural habitat exhibits, including a tropical rain forest complex.

★4950★   RIVERVIEW PARK
Riverview Dr
Pittsburgh, PA 15214
Web: www.city.pittsburgh.pa.us/parks/
Phone: 412-323-7209; **Fax:** 412-323-7222
Size: 490 acres. **Location:** Located in city's Perry North neighborhood. Park entrance is on Riverview Avenue off Perrysville Avenue. **Facilities:** Picnic shelters, swimming pool, trails, fitness course, playgrounds, sports areas. **Activities:** Swimming, hiking, tennis, baseball, basketball, football, soccer, volleyball. **Special Features:** Park houses the Allegheny Observatory.

★4951★   SCHENLEY PARK
Forbes Ave & Schenley Dr
Pittsburgh, PA 15213
Web: www.city.pittsburgh.pa.us/parks/
Phone: 412-622-6904; **Fax:** 412-622-1280
Size: 525 acres. **Location:** East of downtown in city's Squirrel Hill South neighborhood. Office is located behind Phipps Conservatory off Frank Curto Drive. **Facilities:** Picnic shelters, visitor center, swimming pool, lake, trails, fitness course, gardens, ice rink, playgrounds, sports areas. **Activities:** Fishing, swimming, hiking, bicycling, golf, tennis, baseball, football, soccer, volleyball, ice skating, cross-country skiing. **Special Features:** The Carnegie Museum of Natural History, one of the area's most popular attractions, is located on the edge of the park.

PORTLAND

★4952★   FOREST PARK
NW 29th Ave and Upshur St to Newberry Rd
Portland, OR 97210
Web: www.portlandonline.com/parks/
Phone: 503-823-4492; **Fax:** 503-823-4213

Size: 5,150 acres. **Location:** In northwestern Portland on the northeastern face of Tualatin Mountain. **Facilities:** Trail system totals 40 miles, including the 30-mile Wildwood Trail. **Activities:** Hiking, bicycling, mountain biking, horseback riding. **Special Features:** The nation's largest forested park within a city's limits.

★4953★ POWELL BUTTE NATURE PARK
16160 SE Powell Blvd
Portland, OR 97236
Web: www.portlandparks.org/Parks/
Phone: 503-823-7529; **Fax:** 503-823-5297
Size: 608 acres. **Location:** In southeastern Portland. **Facilities:** Trails. **Activities:** Hiking, mountain biking, horseback riding. **Special Features:** Built on the site of an extinct volcano, the park offers an outstanding view of the Cascade Mountains.

★4954★ WASHINGTON PARK
SW Park Place
Portland, OR 97210
Web: www.portlandonline.com/parks/
Phone: 503-823-7529; **Fax:** 503-823-2515
Size: 130 acres. **Location:** Southwestern Portland. **Facilities:** Picnic areas, trails, arboretum, archery range, playground, Japanese gardens, rose garden, forestry center, zoo, athletic fields. **Activities:** Hiking, tennis, soccer, golf, archery. **Special Features:** Attractions within the park include the Hoyt Arboretum, containing the largest collection of conifers in the United States; the Oregon Zoo, featuring more than 200 species of birds, mammals, reptiles, and amphibians (including 21 endangered species); the International Rose Test Garden; the Portland Japanese Garden; the World Forestry Center; the Portland Children's Museum; and the Washington Park and Zoo Railway, which offers regularly scheduled trips on replicas of 19th century steam-powered trains and 1950s-era streamliners.

ROANOKE

★4955★ CARVINS COVE NATURAL RESERVE
210 Reserve Ave SW
Roanoke, VA 24016
Web: www. roanokeva.gov
Phone: 540-853-2236; **Fax:** 540-853-1287
Size: 12,700 acres. **Location:** Eight miles from downtown Roanoke. **Facilities:** Boat dock facilities, including picnic area and boat rentals, hiking and equestrian trails. **Activities:** Hiking, horseback riding, mountain biking, boating and fishing. **Special Features:** The Appalachian Trail follows one of the Reserve's northwest ridgelines.

SACRAMENTO

★4956★ DEL PASO PARK
3565 Auburn Blvd
Sacramento, CA 95814
Web: www.cityofsacramento.org/parks/
Phone: 916-264-5200; **Fax:** 916-454-3956

Size: 352 acres. **Location:** At Business 80 and Watt Avenue, south of I-80. **Facilities:** Picnic area, bridle trails, nature trail, amphitheater, sports areas (including 3 golf courses). **Activities:** Hiking, horseback riding, trap shooting, golf, baseball, softball. **Special Features:** Park features include the Sacramento Science and Space Center branch of the city's Discovery Museum.

★4957★ WILLIAM LAND PARK
4000 S Land Park Dr
Sacramento, CA 95814
Web: www.cityofsacramento.org/parks/
Phone: 916-264-5200; **Fax:** 916-264-7643
Size: 236 acres. **Location:** Sutterville Road and South Land Park Drive. **Facilities:** Picnic areas, concessions, lakes, amphitheater, amusement rides, Fairytale Town (children's theme park), playground, sports areas. **Activities:** Golf, baseball, soccer. **Special Features:** Park is home to the 15-acre Sacramento Zoo, featuring more than 400 mammals, birds, and reptiles.

SAINT LOUIS

★4958★ CARONDELET PARK
S Grand Blvd & Loughborough Ave
Saint Louis, MO 63110
Web: stlouis.missouri.org/citygov/parks/
Phone: 314-289-5300
Size: 180 acres. **Location:** South Grand Boulevard and Loughborough Avenue. **Facilities:** Picnic areas, lakes (2), boat house, bike paths, pavilion, music stand, playgrounds, sports areas. **Activities:** Fishing, bicycling, horse shoes, tennis, baseball, soccer. **Special Features:** Park contains a collection of sinkholes caused by the collapse of slowly dissolving limestone-formed underground chambers. The park's two lakes were formed as a result of the enlargement of a series of sinkholes.

★4959★ FOREST PARK
Kingshighway & Lindell Blvd
Saint Louis, MO 63110
Web: stlouis.missouri.org/citygov/parks/forestpark/
Phone: 314-289-5300
Size: 1,293 acres. **Location:** Kingshighway and Lindell Boulevard. **Facilities:** Picnic areas, concessions, lakes, boat and bicycle rentals, bike trails, gardens, historical monuments and exhibits, art museum, science center, theater, zoo, skating rink, playgrounds, golf course, athletic fields and courts. **Activities:** Boating, fishing, bicycling, golf, tennis, baseball, softball, rugby, soccer, ice skating. **Special Features:** Special attractions include the St. Louis Art Museum, St. Louis Science Center, Muny Opera, Missouri Historical Society, and regionally famous Jewel Box, a botanical garden/architectural landmark in the art deco style. The park also hosts annual wine festivals, balloon races, and Shakespeare festivals.

★4960★ TOWER GROVE PARK
4256 Magnolia Ave
Saint Louis, MO 63110
Web: www.towergrovepark.org
Phone: 314-771-2679; **Fax:** 314-771-6686

Size: 289 acres. **Location:** South side of St. Louis, bounded by Grand Boulevard (east), Magnolia Avenue (north), Kingshighway Boulevard (west), and Arsenal Street (south). **Facilities:** Pavilion and picnic areas, ball fields, tennis courts, playground, and wading pool. **Activities:** Hiking, birding, carriage rides, tennis, and other recreational activities. **Special Features:** Founded in 1868 by Henry Shaw, the park features Victorian pavilions and sculptures, as well as live music at its Music Stand and Piper Palm House.

★4961★ WILLMORE PARK
Hampton and Jamieson Aves
St. Louis, MO 63109
Web: stlouis.missouri.org/citygov/parks/
Phone: 314-289-5389
Size: 105 acres. **Location:** Southwest St. Louis, at Hampton and Jamieson Avenues. **Facilities:** Lighted athletic fields, picnic shelters, trails, dog park, playgrounds, stocked lakes. **Activities:** Fishing, bicycling, soccer, baseball and softball, tennis, jogging.

SAINT PAUL

★4962★ COMO PARK
1225 Estabrook Dr
Saint Paul, MN 55103
Web: www.ci.stpaul.mn.us/depts/parks
Phone: 651-632-5111; **Fax:** 651-632-5115
Size: 450 acres. **Location:** Hamline Avenue and Midway Parkway in north-central Saint Paul. Take I-94 to the North Lexington Parkway, then turn north. **Facilities:** Picnic areas, concessions, pavilion, pool, lake, boat launch, paddleboat rentals, trails, conservatory, Japanese garden, zoo, amusement rides, pony rides, playground, 18-hole golf course, miniature golf course, sports areas. **Activities:** Boating (electric trolling motors), fishing, swimming, bicycling, golf, tennis, softball. **Special Features:** Park was named after a lake in northern Italy on the Italian-Swiss border, an area famous for its beautiful lakes and forests. Park houses the Como Zoo, established in 1887.

★4963★ HARRIET ISLAND REGIONAL PARK
Plato Ave & Waubasha St
Saint Paul, MN 55102
Web: www.stpaul.gov/depts/parks/
Phone: 612-632-5111; **Fax:** 612-632-5115
Size: 510 acres. **Location:** Downtown Saint Paul, at Wabasha and Water streets, along the Mississippi River. **Facilities:** Picnic areas, pavilion, trail network, boat launch, playground, sports area. **Activities:** Fishing, softball, jogging, hiking. **Special Features:** Park hosts many large concerts and festivals, and private companies offer tours of the Mississippi River from the shores of the park.

★4964★ HIDDEN FALLS PARK
1313 Hidden Falls Dr
Saint Paul, MN 55116
Web: www.stpaul.gov/depts/parks/
Phone: 651-635-5111; **Fax:** 651-632-5115
Size: 736 acres (with Crosby Farms Nature Area). **Location:** On Mississippi River Boulevard between the Ford Parkway and West 7th Street bridges. **Facilities:** Picnic area, pavilion, lakes, marina, boat launch, bicycling trails, self-guided nature trail (&), nature center, playground, sports areas. **Activities:** Fishing, bicycling, golf. **Special Features:** Fishing available in either of the park's two lakes or the Mississippi River. Boating service offered at the 140-acre slip marina on the Mississippi River. The park is adjacent to the Crosby Farm Nature Area, and the two areas are sometimes referred to as a single entity. In addition, Fort Snelling State Park lies directly opposite Hidden Falls on the other side of the Mississippi River.

SAN ANTONIO

★4965★ BRACKENRIDGE PARK
3700 N Saint Mary's St
San Antonio, TX 78209
Web: www.sanantonio.gov/sapar/
Phone: 210-736-9534
Size: 343 acres. **Location:** Two miles north of downtown at 3910 North Saint Marys Street. **Facilities:** Picnic areas, pavilions, bridle trails, museum, botanical gardens, theater, zoo, miniature railway, sky rides, antique carousel, playgrounds, Swiss skyrides, 18-hole golf course, athletic fields. **Activities:** Paddleboating, horseback riding, hiking, jogging, train rides, golf, polo, football, softball. **Special Features:** Park features a miniature railroad containing replicas of the 1863 Central Pacific Huntington steam locomotive. Other attractions include the San Antonio Zoo and Aquarium (210-734-7184), Japanese Tea Gardens, and Sunken Garden Theatre (outdoor).

★4966★ EMILIE & ALBERT FRIEDRICH PARK
21395 Milsa St
San Antonio, TX 78283
Web: www.sanaturalareas.org/
Phone: 210-564-6400
Size: 600 acres. **Location:** Northwest Bexar County. **Facilities:** Hiking, bicycling, and nature trails. **Activities:** Hiking, bicycling, bird-watching. **Special Features:** Also known as Friedrich Wilderness Park.

★4967★ W W MCALLISTER PARK
13102 Jones-Maltsberger
San Antonio, TX 78247
Web: www.sanantonio.gov/sapar/
Phone: 210-207-8480
Size: 996 acres. **Location:** On Jones-Maltsberger. **Facilities:** Campsites, picnic areas, pavilions, hiking trails, biking trails, nature trails, garden, playgrounds, athletic fields (including 8 baseball fields). **Activities:** Camping, hiking, bicycling, baseball.

10. Urban Parks

SAN DIEGO

★4968★ BALBOA PARK
1549 El Prado
Suite 1
San Diego, CA 92101
Web: www.balboapark.org
Phone: 619-239-0512; **Fax:** 619-525-2254
Size: 1,172 acres. **Location:** Downtown San Diego. **Facilities:** Picnic areas, restaurants and concessions, visitor center, pool, botanical gardens, art galleries, playgrounds, athletic fields, municipal gymnasium, tennis club, golf complex, activity center (badminton, table tennis, volleyball, and other sports activities). **Activities:** Hiking, biking, swimming, bicycling, golf, tennis, lawn bowling, archery, baseball, basketball, soccer, guided tours. **Special Features:** Other popular park attractions include the San Diego Zoo (619-231-1515); Museum of Photographic Arts; Museum of San Diego History; San Diego Museum of Art; San Diego Natural History Museum; Centro Cultural de la Raza, a museum of Mexican, Indigenous, Chicano, and Latino art and culture; Japanese Friendship Garden; Marston House, an Arts and Crafts style museum; Mingei International Museum, a center of world folk art; Rueben H. Fleet Science Center; San Diego Air and Space Museum; San Diego Automotive Museum; San Diego Hall of Champions Sports Museum; San Diego Museum of Man, an anthropological museum; San Diego Model Railroad Museum; Timken Museum of Art, Veterans Museum and Memorial Center; and World Beat Center, a museum of art, music, and culture of African and other indigenous peoples.

★4969★ BLACK MOUNTAIN OPEN SPACE PARK
12115A Black Mountain Road
San Diego, CA 92129
Web: www.sandiego.gov/park-and-recreation/
Phone: 858-538-8082
Size: 2,352 acres. **Location:** Northern San Diego, situated between Camino Del Sur to the west, Penasquitos Drive to the east, Lusardi Creek to the north, and Carmel Mountain Road to the south. **Facilities:** Multi-use trail network. **Activities:** Hiking, mountain biking, equestrian.

★4970★ LOS PENASQUITOS CANYON PRESERVE
Mercy Rd-W Black Mountain Rd
San Diego, CA 92129
Web: www.sandiego.gov/park-and-recreation/
Phone: 858-484-7504
Size: 4,000 acres. **Location:** Between Rancho Penasquitos and Sorrento Hills to north and Mira Mesa to south. **Facilities:** Trails, historical adobes. **Activities:** Hiking, horseback riding, mountain biking. **Special Features:** Los Penasquitos Canyon Trail, an old ranch road, travels the six-mile length of the canyon and affords views of a eucalyptus grove, grassland, and a waterfall.

★4971★ MISSION BAY PARK
I-5 & Sea World Dr
San Diego, CA 92107
Web: aboutmissionbay.com
Phone: 619-235-1169
Size: 4,235 acres. **Location:** Northwest of downtown. **Facilities:** Picnic areas, playground, lake, beaches (19 miles with eight swimming areas), boat rentals. **Activities:** Boating, fishing, swimming, water-skiing, wind surfing, bicycling, volleyball, jogging. **Special Features:** Home to Sea World of California, featuring shows, exhibits, and attractions. Also includes youth campground on Fiesta Island and several small wildlife preserves.

★4972★ MISSION TRAILS REGIONAL PARK
1 Father Junipero Serra Trail
San Diego, CA 92119
Web: www.mtrp.org
Phone: 619-668-3281; **Fax:** 619-668-3282
Size: 5,900 acres. **Location:** Eight miles northeast of downtown. **Facilities:** Campsites, lake, trails, equestrian facilities, sports areas. **Activities:** Camping, hiking, rock climbing, horseback riding, golf.

SAN FRANCISCO

★4973★ GOLDEN GATE PARK
501 Stanyan St
San Francisco, CA 94117
Web: www.nps.gov/goga/
Phone: 415-831-2700; **Fax:** 415-668-3330
Size: 1,017 acres. **Location:** From Highway 101 or Highway 80, follow signs ''to Golden Gate Bridge,'' take the Fell Street Exit, head west into park. From Highway 1, follow signs to 19th Ave., turn right on Martin Luther King Jr. Dr. into the park. **Facilities:** Picnic areas, concessions, 11 lakes, waterfalls, boat rentals (pedal boats, electric boats, row boats), bike paths, bridle paths, two 18-hole disc golf courses, historical guided walking tours, historic monuments, museums, California Academy of Sciences (aquarium, planetarium, natural sciences exhibits), conservatory, gardens (including Shakespeare Garden and Japanese Tea Garden), carousel, playground, athletic fields. **Activities:** Boating, bicycling, horseback riding, golf, tennis, archery, baseball, basketball, football, soccer, disc golf, swing dancing, lawn bowling. **Special Features:** Park is home to the Asian Art Museum, the largest museum outside of Asia devoted exclusively to Asian art. The collections represent the greatest effort in the Western world to collect, display, and study the fine arts of more than 40 Asian countries. Collection includes the oldest-known dated Chinese Buddha image (AD 338). Other park attractions include the Strybing Arboretum and Botanical Gardens.

★4974★ JOHN MCLAREN PARK
Mansell St and Shelley Dr
San Francisco, CA 94117
Web: www.jennalex.com/projects/fomp/homepage/
Phone: 415-831-2700
Size: 317 acres. **Location:** Southeast part of the city, in Visitacion Valley. **Facilities:** Picnic areas, pool, hiking trails (7 miles), amphitheater, playgrounds, sports areas. **Activities:** Swimming, hiking, bicycling, tennis, basketball, softball, soccer. **Special**

Features: Park includes Jerry Garcia Amphitheatre (415-831-5500).

★4975★ LAKE MERCED
Skyline & Lake Merced Blvd
San Francisco, CA 94132
Phone: 415-831-2700; **Fax:** 415-221-8034
Size: 700 acres. **Location:** Skyline Boulevard at the Great Highway. **Facilities:** Concessions, 368-acre lake, boat rentals (row boats, paddleboats, sailboats, canoes), sports areas. **Activities:** Boating, fishing, wind surfing, bicycling, golf. **Special Features:** Lake is one of the most productive birding areas in the San Francisco area. North Lake at Lake Merced has been designated a trophy trout lake.

SAN JOSE

★4976★ ALUM ROCK PARK
15350 Penitencia Creek Rd
San Jose, CA 95127
Web: www.sjparks.org/
Phone: 408-259-5477; **Fax:** 408-277-3241
Size: 700 acres. **Location:** Park entrance is in Alum Rock Canyon in the foothills of the Diablo Range, at Penitencia Creek Rd. **Facilities:** Picnic areas, visitor center, hiking trails, bridle trails, mineral springs, lookout areas, Youth Science Institute (408-258-4322), playground. **Activities:** Hiking, bicycling, horseback riding. **Special Features:** The east-west canyon of San Jose's oldest and largest park contains many delicate plant and animal communities. Hikers can see black-tailed deer, bush rabbits, quail, and, on rare occasions, the elusive bobcat.

★4977★ ANDERSON LAKE COUNTY PARK
19245 Malaguerra Ave
Morgan Hill, CA 95037
Web: www.parkhere.org
Phone: 408-779-3634
Size: 3,109 acres. **Location:** About 15 miles south of San Jose just east of Highway 101. **Facilities:** Boat ramp facilities, paved and unpaved trails for hiking, biking, and horseback riding, picnic area. **Activities:** Power boating and jet-skiing, fishing, hiking, bicycling, rollerblading, equestrian activities. **Special Features:** The park's main attraction is Anderson Reservoir, a seven-mile long (1,250 acres of surface area) lake that supports a wide range of sportfish.

★4978★ KELLEY PARK
1300 Senter Rd
San Jose, CA 95112
Phone: 408-277-5254; **Fax:** 408-297-0778
Size: 156 acres. **Location:** Downtown San Jose near I-280 and the 101 Interchange, between Story Road and Phelan Avenue. **Facilities:** Picnic areas, bike paths, amphitheater, historical museum. **Activities:** Bicycling. **Special Features:** Park's main attraction is Happy Hollow Park and Zoo (408-277-3000). Other attractions include the Japanese Friendship Garden, modeled

after the Korakuen Gardens in San Jose's sister city, Okayama, Japan.

★4979★ LAKE CUNNINGHAM REGIONAL PARK
2305 S White Rd
San Jose, CA 95148
Web: www.lakecunningham.org
Phone: 408-277-4319; **Fax:** 408-238-1176
Size: 200 acres. **Location:** East of Highway 101. Bordered by the Capitol Expressway, Tully Road, White Road, and Cunningham Avenue. **Facilities:** Picnic areas, 50-acre lake, boat launch, water slides, boat rental (canoes, pedal boats, row boats, sailboats), bike paths, concessions, pavilion sports areas. **Activities:** Boating, fishing, swimming, windsurfing, bicycling, volleyball. **Special Features:** Park includes the Raging Waters theme park, a 23-acre water park that includes water slides, a Polynesian lagoon, and a beach.

SCOTTSDALE

★4980★ MCDOWELL SONORAN PRESERVE
7506 E. Indian School Road
Scottsdale, AZ 85251
Web: www.scottsdaleaz.gov/preserve
Phone: 480-312-7013
Size: 11, 559 acres. **Location:** East of Thompson Peak Parkway, north of Bell Road. **Facilities:** Undeveloped wilderness area. **Activities:** Hiking, horseback riding, rock climbing, mountain biking. **Special Features:** Planned expansion of the preserve will eventually encompass more than 36,000 acres. Multiple access areas are being planned for future use.

SEATTLE

★4981★ DISCOVERY PARK
3801 W Government Way
Seattle, WA 98199
Web: www.seattle.gov/parks/environment/
  discovparkindex.htm
Phone: 206-386-4236; **Fax:** 206-684-0195
Size: 534 acres. **Location:** Magnolia Bluff overlooking Puget Sound. **Facilities:** Visitor center, playground, trails (12 miles), nature programs. **Activities:** Hiking. **Special Features:** Largest city park in Seattle.

★4982★ GREEN LAKE PARK
7201 E Green Lake Dr North
Seattle, WA 98115
Web: www.seattle.gov/parks/parkspaces/greenlak.htm
Phone: 206-684-4075
Size: 324 acres. **Location:** Latona Avenue Northeast and East Green Lake Drive North. **Facilities:** Picnic areas, boathouse, pools, 2.8 mile path, pitch 'n putt, theater, sports areas. **Activities:** Canoeing, swimming, bicycling, tennis, softball, running, walking, skating.

★4983★ SEWARD PARK
5902 Lake Washington Blvd S
Seattle, WA 98118
Web: www.seattle.gov/parks/parkspaces/sewardpark.htm
Phone: 206-684-4396
Size: 300 acres. Location: Washington Boulevard South and South Juneau. Facilities: Picnic areas, native plant garden, lake, paths, amphitheater, art studio, playground, fish hatchery, sports areas. Activities: Swimming, hiking, bicycling, tennis, bird-watching tours. Special Features: Park features include Seattle's Environmental Learning Center (206-684-4396).

★4984★ WARREN G. MAGNUSON PARK
7400 Sand Point Way NE
Seattle, WA 98115
Web: www.seattle.gov/parks/Magnuson/
Phone: 206-684-4946
Size: 350 acres. Location: On Lake Washington in northeastern Seattle. Facilities: Boat launch areas (both motorized and non-motorized), beaches, biking and walking trails, playground, tennis courts (indoor and outdoor), basketball courts, dog off-leash areas, recreational fields. Activities: Boating, swimming, windsurfing, kayaking, biking, basketball, tennis, softball. Special Features: Park is located at the site of a former naval facilities, and some of the buildings—including a former brig—are available for special event rental.

TOLEDO

★4985★ OAK OPENINGS PRESERVE METROPARK
4139 Girdham Rd
Swanton, OH 43558
Web: www.metroparkstoledo.com/metroparks/
Phone: 419-407-9700; Fax: 419-407-9785
Size: 3,668 acres. Location: In western Lucas County, two miles west of Toledo Express Airport. Facilities: Group campsites (primitive), picnic areas, lakes, trails (50 miles), lodge, playground. Activities: Group camping, fishing, hiking, bicycling, horseback riding, cross-country skiing, ice skating. Special Features: Nearly one-third of Ohio's endangered plant species, as well as endangered insects, can be found within the park's boundaries.

★4986★ PEARSON METROPARK
4600 Starr Ave
Oregon, OH 43616
Web: www.metroparkstoledo.com/metroparks/
Phone: 419-407-9714; Fax: 419-407-9785
Size: 320 acres. Location: In Oregon (east of Toledo), between Starr and Navarre avenues. Facilities: Picnic areas, concessions, lake, pedalboat rentals, trails, nature center, exhibits, playground, sports equipment. Activities: Boating, hiking, bicycling, tennis, soccer, softball, cross-country skiing, ice skating. Special Features: Park's natural area is largely swamp woodland. It was once part of the Black Swamp, a nearly impassible barrier to early travel and settlement in the area.

★4987★ SECOR METROPARK
10001 W Central Ave
Berkey, OH 43504
Web: www.metroparkstoledo.com/metroparks/
Phone: 419-407-9756; Fax: 419-407-9785
Size: 600 acres. Location: Six miles west of US-23/I-475. Facilities: Picnic areas, trails (&), arboretum, amphitheater, playground. Activities: Hiking, bicycling, cross-country skiing. Special Features: Park's Nature Discovery Center features the Window on Wildlife, a protected, natural setting attracting wildlife to within a few feet of visitors. Other attractions include the National Center for Nature Photography.

★4988★ SWAN CREEK PRESERVE METROPARK
4659 Airport Hwy
Toledo, OH 43615
Web: www.metroparkstoledo.com/metroparks/
Phone: 419-407-9758; Fax: 419-407-9785
Size: 417 acres. Location: In southern Toledo between Eastgate and Byrne roads. Facilities: Picnic areas, trails (&), nature center, playground. Activities: Hiking, bicycling, cross-country skiing. Special Features: Wildflowers abound in the spring.

★4989★ WILDWOOD PRESERVE METROPARK
5100 W Central Ave
Toledo Metroparks
Toledo, OH 43615
Web: www.metroparkstoledo.com
Phone: 419-535-3050; Fax: 419-407-9785
Size: 460 acres. Location: Bordered by Central Avenue, Holland-Sylvania Road, I- 475, and Corey Road. Facilities: Picnic areas, visitor center, trails (&), garden, nature art exhibits, playground. Activities: Hiking, bicycling, cross-country skiing. Special Features: Park houses the Manor House, an example of an 18th-century Georgian Colonial estate. Open for tours Wednesday through Sunday, 12 noon-5 pm.

TUCSON

★4990★ GENE C REID REGIONAL PARK
900 S Randolph Way
City of Tucson Parks & Recreation Dept
Tucson, AZ 85716
Web: www.cityoftucson.org/parksmap/
Phone: 520-791-4870
Size: 431 acres. Location: East 22nd Street and South Country Club Road. Facilities: Picnic areas, lake, paddleboat rentals, path, rose gardens (&), outdoor performance center (&), zoo (&), playground, two 18-hole golf courses, athletic fields. Activities: Boating, fishing, bicycling, golf, tennis, baseball, football, soccer, horseshoes. Special Features: Home of the 17-acre Reid Park Zoo (520-791-3204), featuring 400 animals in natural settings.

★4991★ JOHN F KENNEDY REGIONAL PARK
3700 S Mission Rd
Tucson, AZ 85713
Web: www.cityoftucson.org/parksmap/
Phone: 602-791-4863
Size: 168 acres. **Location:** Southwestern Tucson at Ajo Way and Mission Road. **Facilities:** Picnic areas (&), swimming pool (&), lake, amphitheater, playground, sports areas. **Activities:** Boating, fishing, swimming, tennis, soccer, softball, volleyball.

★4992★ TUCSON MOUNTAIN PARK
Ajo Way & Kinney Rd
Tucson, AZ 85713
Web: www.pima.gov/nrpr/places/parkpgs/tucs_mtpk/
Phone: 520-740-2690
Size: 16,967 acres. **Location:** West of Tucson. **Facilities:** Campsites, recreational vehicle hookups, picnic areas, trails, playground, first-aid. **Activities:** Camping, hiking, bicycling, horseback riding, archery and rifle/pistol ranges. **Special Features:** Park is home to the Arizona-Sonora Desert Museum (520-883-2702), an internationally renowned living museum with more than 200 species of animals and 1,200 plant species native to the Sonoran Desert. Also houses Old Tucson Studios, a famous movie location and Western theme park featuring stunts, live shows, games, rides, and museums.

TULSA

★4993★ MOHAWK PARK
5701 E 36th St North
Tulsa, OK 74115
Web: www.cityoftulsa.org/Recreation/Parks/
Phone: 918-596-7877; **Fax:** 918-596-7249
Size: 2,806 acres. **Location:** Enter on 36th Street North, just east of Sheridan Road. **Facilities:** Shelters, concessions, visitor center, equestrian trails, nature trail, lakes, rodeo arena, nature center, zoo, playgrounds, sports areas. **Activities:** Fishing, hiking, bicycling, horseback riding, golf, polo, bird-watching, guided tours. **Special Features:** Tulsa Zoo and Living Museum (918-669-6600) is an accredited living history museum with an award-winning chimpanzee exhibit.

★4994★ RIVER PARKS
River Parks Authority
Riverside Dr-betw 11th & 101st Sts
Tulsa, OK 74127
Web: www.riverparks.org
Phone: 918-596-2001; **Fax:** 918-596-2004
Size: 800 acres. **Location:** Riverside Drive from 7th Street to 81st Street. Linear park lies along both sides of the Arkansas River from downtown Tulsa to the south end of the city. **Facilities:** Picnic areas, concessions, boat ramp, 20 miles of multi-use paved asphalt trails, amphitheater, nature conservatory, playgrounds, sports areas. **Activities:** Rowing, kayaking, fishing, hiking, horseback riding, bicycling, disc golf, rugby, bird-watching. **Special Features:** Park includes a Least Tern preserve and nesting area and a Bald Eagle nesting area. Also includes the

Turkey Mountain Urban Wilderness Area, the only area of the park where horseback riding is permitted. The park is adjacent to the city's River SkatePark.

VIRGINIA BEACH

★4995★ MOUNT TRASHMORE PARK
310 Edwin Dr
Virginia Beach, VA 23462
Web: www.vbgov.com/parks
Phone: 757-473-5237; **Fax:** 757-473-5047
Size: 164 acres. **Location:** Between Route 44 and Independence Boulevard. **Facilities:** Picnic areas, concessions, visitor center, lakes, playground, skate park, athletic fields. **Activities:** Swimming, tennis, basketball, volleyball, skateboarding. **Special Features:** Park includes city's own manmade mountain.

WICHITA

★4996★ RIVERSIDE PARKS
455 North Main St
Wichita, KS 67202
Web: www.wichitagov.org/CityOffices/Park
Phone: 316-268-4361; **Fax:** 316-268-4447
Size: 118 acres in three parks. **Location:** Located along the Arkansas River, at 551 South Central St. (South unit), 720 Nims St. (Central unit), and 1029 North Bitting (North Unit). **Facilities:** Picnic areas, playgrounds, boat ramp (at Central unit). **Activities:** Boating, tennis, handball. **Special Features:** The Kansas Wildlife Exhibit is located in the Central unit, the largest of the three parks in the Riverside system at 58 acres.

★4997★ WATSON PARK
3055 S Old Lawrence Rd
Wichita, KS 67217
Web: www.wichitagov.org/CityOffices/Park
Phone: 316-529-9940; **Fax:** 316-268-4447
Size: 119 acres. **Location:** West of Broadway on Carp Street. **Facilities:** Picnic areas, concessions, paddleboat rides, wooden sculptures (Wizard of Oz characters), miniature golf course. **Activities:** Boating, fishing, hay rides, pony rides, train rides.

10. Urban Parks

11. PARK- AND CONSERVATION-RELATED ORGANIZATIONS

★4998★ ACCESS FUND
PO Box 17010
Boulder, CO 80308
Web: www.accessfund.org
Phone: 303-545-6772; **Fax:** 303-545-6774; **Toll Free:** 888-863-6237
Dedicated to keeping climbing areas open and to conserving the climbing environment. Promotes political activism and local stewardship of climbing resources. Works with land management agencies, environmental organizations, climbing groups, outdoor businesses and guide services on conservation projects, land acquisitions, and climbing policy. **Established:** 1989. **Members:** 15,000+. **Dues:** $50/year. **Publications:** *Vertical Times* (bimonthly); free to members.

★4999★ ADIRONDACK COUNCIL
103 Hand Ave, Suite 3
Elizabethtown, NY 12932
Web: www.adirondackcouncil.org
Phone: 518-873-2240; **Fax:** 518-873-6675; **Toll Free:** 877-873-2240
Dedicated to protecting and preserving the Adirondack Park's wild and open-space resources. **Established:** 1975. **Members:** 18,000. **Dues:** $35/year. **Publications:** *Adirondack Council Newsletter* (quarterly); free to members. *State of the Park Report* (annually); free to members.

★5000★ ADIRONDACK MOUNTAIN CLUB
814 Goggins Rd
Lake George, NY 12845
Web: www.adk.org
Phone: 518-668-4447; **Fax:** 518-668-3746; **Toll Free:** 800-395-8080
Dedicated to the protection and responsible recreational use of the New York State Forest Preserve, parks and other wild lands and waters. Promotes a balanced approach to outdoor recreation and natural resource conservation and a committment to public service and stewardship. **Established:** 1932. **Members:** 30,000. **Dues:** $45/year. **Publications:** *Adirondack* (bimonthly); free to members.

★5001★ ADVENTURE CYCLING ASSOCIATION
150 E Pine St
PO Box 8308
Missoula, MT 59807
Web: www.adventurecycling.org
Phone: 406-721-1776; **Fax:** 406-721-8754; **Toll Free:** 800-755-2453
Dedicated to bicycle travel. Seeks to inspire people of all ages to travel by bicycle, and explore the landscape and history of America for fitness, fun, and self-discovery. Provides information about bicycle touring routes and organizes trips. **Established:** 1973 as Bikecentennial. **Members:** 42,000. **Dues:** $33/year. **Publications:** *Adventure Cyclist* (9x/year); free to members. *The Cyclists' Yellow Pages* (annual); free to members.

★5002★ ALASKA WILDERNESS LEAGUE
122 C St NW, Suite 240
Washington, DC 20001
Web: www.alaskawild.org
Phone: 202-544-5205; **Fax:** 202-544-5197
An alliance of environmental, civic, and Native organizations. Works in Washington D.C. to protect and defend the Arctic National Wildlife Refuge, Alaska's forests, and other wilderness lands in Alaska. Coordinates educational programs and monitors legislation to assure lasting protection of these lands. Comprises more than 107 international, national, regional, state, and local organizations. **Established:** 1993. **Members:** 107 (donors). **Dues:** $25/year. **Publications:** *Alaska Wilderness League News* (bimonthly).

★5003★ ALASKA WILDLIFE ALLIANCE
PO Box 202022
Anchorage, AK 99520
Web: www.akwildlife.org
Phone: 907-277-0897; **Fax:** 907-277-7423
Nonprofit wildlife conservation organization with the mission of protecting Alaska's natural wildlife. **Established:** 1978. **Members:** 5,000 **Dues:** $35/year. **Publications:** *Echoes* (2x/year); free to members.

★5004★ ALBERTA COMMUNITY DEVELOPMENT DEPARTMENT
Parks & Protected Areas Division
9820 106th St, 2nd Fl
Edmonton,
Web: www.cd.gov.ab.ca/enjoying_alberta/parks/planning/gateway
Phone: 780-427-9383; **Fax:** 780-427-5980; **Toll Free:** 866-427-3582
Government office that oversees Alberta's system of provincial parks and protected areas. Covering 27,500 square kms. and including more than 500 sites, the network includes provincial parks, ecological reserves, wilderness areas, wildland parks, natural areas, and provincial recreation areas.

★5005★ ALBERTA FISH & GAME ASSOCIATION (AFGA)

6924 104th St
Edmonton,
Web: www.afga.org
Phone: 780-437-2342; Fax: 780-438-6872
Through education, lobbying, and programs, promotes the conservation and utilization of fish and wildlife resources by protecting and enhancing habitat. Established: 1908. Members: 15,000. Dues: $25/year. Publications: *Outdoor Edge* (6x/year); free to members.

★5006★ ALOUETTE RIVER MANAGEMENT SOCIETY (ARMS)

PO Box 21117
Maple Ridge,
Phone: 604-467-6401; Fax: 604-467-6478
Committed to the protection and enhancement of the Alouette River watershed through advocacy, education, and coordination. Involved in almost all aspects of watershed stewardship, including inventory and monitoring, habitat restoration, and lobbying for the protection of aquatic habitat. Established: 1993. Members: 300. Dues: Donations accepted.

★5007★ AMERICA THE BEAUTIFUL FUND (ABF)

1730 K St NW, Suite 1002
Washington, DC 20006
Web: www.america-the-beautiful.org
Phone: 202-638-1649; Fax: 202-638-2175; Toll Free: 800-522-3557
Develops and assists volunteer projects to save the natural and man-made environment. Operates as a clearinghouse of ideas for community projects. Established: 1965. Publications: *Better Times* (quarterly); free to members. *Green Earth Guide* (annually); $5 for members and $15 for nonmembers.

★5008★ AMERICAN ASSOCIATION FOR LEISURE & RECREATION (AALR)

1900 Association Dr
Reston, VA 20191
Web: www.aahperd.org/aapar/
Phone: 703-476-3400; Fax: 703-476-9527; Toll Free: 800-213-7193
Organization dedicated to enhancing quality of life by promoting creative and active lifestyles through meaningful physical activity, recreation and fitness experiences across the lifespan with particular focus on community-based programs. Established: 2005. Members: 8,000. Dues: $125/year. Publications: *Par for Life* (newsletter); free to members.

★5009★ AMERICAN ASSOCIATION FOR STATE & LOCAL HISTORY (AASLH)

1717 Church St
Nashville, TN 37203
Web: www.aaslh.org
Phone: 615-320-3203; Fax: 615-327-9013
Professional organization of individuals and institutions working

to preserve and promote history. Provides information and training to members. Conducts workshops and seminars. Established: 1940. Members: 6,500. Dues: $60/year. Publications: *History News* (quarterly); free to members. *Dispatch* (monthly); free to members.

★5010★ AMERICAN BIRD CONSERVANCY (ABC)

PO Box 249
The Plains, VA 20198
Web: www.abcbirds.org
Phone: 540-253-5780; Fax: 540-253-5782; Toll Free: 888-247-3624
Protects and conserves wild birds and their habitats throughout the Americas. Dedicated to overcoming the greatest threats facing birds: a growing human population, the use of pesticides, and the introduction of destructive species including domestic cats. Established: 1922. Members: 7,000. Dues: $40/year. Publications: *Bird Conservation* magazine (3x/year). *Bird Calls* newsletter (3x/year); free to members.

★5011★ AMERICAN CANOE ASSOCIATION (ACA)

7432 Alban Station Blvd, Suite B-232
Springfield, VA 22150
Web: www.americancanoe.org
Phone: 703-451-0141; Fax: 703-451-2245; Toll Free: 800-929-5162
Promotes canoeing, kayaking, and rafting as wholesome lifetime recreational activities. Sponsors paddling events, works for environmental and paddlers' rights protection, and provides safety education and instructor certification. Established: 1880. Members: 45,000. Dues: $40/year. Publications: *Paddler* magazine (bimonthly); free to members. *ACA News* (monthly); free to members.

★5012★ AMERICAN CAVE CONSERVATION ASSOCIATION

119 E Main St
PO Box 409
Horse Cave, KY 42749
Web: www.cavern.org/acca/accahome.html
Phone: 270-786-1466; Fax: 270-786-1467
Promotes the conservation of caves and karstlands and their resources across America and across the world. Seeks to increase public awareness of the value of caves. Offers educational and training programs for cave owners and managers, and maintains an extensive library of information on cave management and conservation. Established: 1978. Members: 600. Dues: $25/year. Publications: *American Caves* (periodic); free to members.

★5013★ AMERICAN CONSERVATION ASSOCIATION

30 Rockefeller Plaza, 56th Fl
New York, NY 10112
Phone: 212-649-5819; Fax: 212-649-5729
Private foundation. Funds programs designed to advance knowledge and understanding of conservation, to preserve the beauty

of the landscape and the natural features in areas of the U.S. and Latin America, and to educate the public in the proper use of such areas. **Established:** 1958. **Members:** Nonmembership organization.

★5014★ AMERICAN FARMLAND TRUST (AFT)
1200 18th St NW, Suite 800
Washington, DC 20036
Web: www.farmland.org
Phone: 202-331-7300; **Fax:** 202-659-8339; **Toll Free:** 800-431-1499
Works to safeguard productive farmlands by promoting environmental-friendly practices. **Established:** 1980. **Members:** 25,000 **Dues:** $25/year. **Publications:** *American Farmland* (monthly); free to members.

★5015★ AMERICAN FORESTS
734 15th St NW Suite 800
PO Box 2000
Washington, DC 20013
Web: www.americanforests.org
Phone: 202-737-1944; **Fax:** 202-737-2457; **Toll Free:** 800-368-5748
Focuses on assisting communities in planning and implementing tree and forest actions to restore and maintain healthy ecosystems and communities. Also works with community-based forestry partners in both urban and rural areas to help them participate in national forest policy discussions. Since 1990, the American Forests' Global ReLeaf campaign has been planting native trees in rural and urban ecosystem restoration projects across the United States and around the world. **Established:** 1875. **Members:** 20,000. **Dues:** $25/year. **Publications:** *American Forests* (quarterly); free to members.

★5016★ AMERICAN HIKING SOCIETY (AHS)
1422 Fenwick Ln
Silver Spring, MD 20910
Web: www.americanhiking.org
Phone: 301-565-6704; **Fax:** 301-565-6714; **Toll Free:** 800-972-8608
Dedicated to preserving and expanding public and private trails and protecting the interest of hikers. Educates the public on the benefits of hiking and trails. Maintains a public information service. Sponsors volunteer trips to build and maintain trails. **Established:** 1976. **Members:** 5,000. **Dues:** $30/year. **Publications:** *American Hiker* magazine (quarterly); free to members.

★5017★ AMERICAN HISTORICAL ASSOCIATION (AHA)
400 A St SE
Washington, DC 20003
Web: www.historians.org
Phone: 202-544-2422; **Fax:** 202-544-8307
Promotes historical studies, the collection and preservation of historical documents and artifacts, and the circulation of historical research. Addresses the professional concerns of historians and educators and provides resources to ensure the proliferation of historical knowledge. **Established:** 1884. **Members:** 15,000. **Dues:** $37/year. **Publications:** Perspectives (monthly); free to members. The American Historical Review (5x/year); free to members.

★5018★ AMERICAN LANDS ALLIANCE
726 7th St SE
Washington, DC 20002
Web: www.americanlands.org
Phone: 202-547-9400; **Fax:** 202-547-9213
Seeks to educate the public on the value of protecting ancient forest ecosystems nationwide. **Established:** 1991. **Members:** 2,000. **Dues:** $25/year.

★5019★ AMERICAN LITTORAL SOCIETY (ALS)
Sandy Hook, Bldg 18
Highlands, NJ 07732
Web: www.littoralsociety.org
Phone: 732-291-0055; **Fax:** 732-291-3551
Naturalists interested in the enjoyment, study, and conservation of coastal environments. Promotes the protection of coastal beaches, wetlands, rivers, and estuaries. Conducts coastal field trips. Maintains chapters serving the Northeast, Mid-Atlantic, and Southern regions. **Established:** 1961. **Members:** 5,000 **Dues:** $35/year **Publications:** *Underwater Naturalist* (periodically); free to members. *Coastal Reporter* (quarterly); free to members.

★5020★ AMERICAN PARK & RECREATION SOCIETY (APRS)
c/o National Recreation & Park Association
22377 Belmont Ridge Rd
Ashburn, VA 20148
Web: www.nrpa.org/aprs
Phone: 703-858-4731; **Fax:** 703-858-0794; **Toll Free:** 800-626-6772
Park, recreation, and leisure service professionals who represent park and/or recreation interests in government, private agencies, and commercial organizations. Branch of the National Recreation & Park Assn (see separate entry for description). **Established:** 1965. **Members:** 7,000. **Publications:** Keeping You Current e-newsletter (monthly); free to members.

★5021★ AMERICAN PUBLIC INFORMATION ON THE ENVIRONMENT (AMERICAN PIE)
316 Oak St
PO Box 676
Northfield, MN 55057
Web: www.americanpie.org
Phone: 507-645-5613; **Fax:** 507-645-5724; **Toll Free:** 800-320-2743
Dedicated to developing and administering action programs that help build a more informed, environmentally responsible, activist citizenry in the United States. **Established:** 1993. **Members:** 1000. **Dues:** $25/year. **Publications:** *Fresh Tracks* (quarterly); free to members.

★5022★ AMERICAN RIVERS

1101 14th St NW, Suite 1400
Washington, DC 20005
Web: www.americanrivers.org
Phone: 202-347-7550; **Fax:** 202-347-9240; **Toll Free:** 877-347-7550
Dedicated to protecting and restoring America's river systems and to fostering a river stewardship ethic in the United States. **Established:** 1973. **Members:** 40,000. **Dues:** $25/year. **Publications:** *American Rivers* (quarterly); free to members.

★5023★ AMERICAN SHORE & BEACH
    PRESERVATION ASSOCIATION (ASBPA)

5460 Beaujolais Ln
Fort Myers, FL 33919
Web: www.asbpa.org
Phone: 239-489-2616; **Fax:** 239-489-9917
Dedicated to the protection and proper utilization of the shores of oceans, lakes, and rivers. Promotes the importance of the shorefronts for health and well-being and for the opportunity they provide for necessary rest and recreation. **Established:** 1926. **Members:** 1000. **Dues:** $100/year. **Publications:** *Shore & Beach* (quarterly) and *Coastal Voice* e-newsletter (monthly), both free to members.

★5024★ AMERICAN TRAILS

PO Box 491797
Redding, CA 96049
Web: www.americantrails.org
Phone: 530-547-2060; **Fax:** 530-547-2035
Works to promote, stimulate, and develop a better understanding and respect for all types of trails, including hiking, bicycling, mountain biking, horseback riding, water trails, snowshoeing, cross-country skiing, trail motorcycling, ATVs, snowmobiling and four-wheeling. Coordinates local, state, and national trails organizations and provides a forum for the exchange of technical information. Seeks to establish a network of trails and greenways across America for recreational and educational use by the public. **Established:** 1988. **Members:** 500. **Dues:** $25/year. **Publications:** *American Trails Magazine* (3x/year); free to members.

★5025★ AMERICAN WHITEWATER (AW)

PO Box 1540
Cullowhee, NC 28723
Web: www.americanwhitewater.org
Phone: 828-586-1930; **Fax:** 828-586-2840; **Toll Free:** 866-262-8429
Seeks to conserve and restore America's whitewater resources and to enhance opportunities to enjoy them safely. Organizes events to raise funds for river conservation. Maintains a national inventory of whitewater rivers, monitors threats to those rivers, provides technical advice to local groups, works with government agencies, and, when necessary, takes legal action to prevent river abuse. **Established:** 1954. **Members:** 6,700. **Dues:** $25/year. **Publications:** *American Whitewater* (bimonthly); free to members, $25/year to nonmembers.

★5026★ AMERICAN WILDLANDS

321 East Main St, Suite 418
Bozeman, MT 59715
Web: www.wildlands.org
Phone: 406-586-8175; **Fax:** 406-586-8242
Promotes the protection, restoration and connectivity of the wild landscapes and the mountain-fed waters of the U.S. Northern Rocky Mountain region. **Established:** 1977. **Members:** 500 **Dues:** $40/year. **Publications:** *On the Wild Side* (quarterly); free to members.

★5027★ ANIMAL ALLIANCE OF CANADA

221 Broadview Ave, Suite 101
Toronto,
Web: www.animalalliance.ca
Phone: 416-462-9541; **Fax:** 416-462-9647
Committed to the protection of all animals and the promotion of a harmonious relationship among people, animals, and the environment. Works to protect animals and the environment with local, national, and international educational and legislative advocacy initiatives. **Established:** 1990. **Members:** 20,000. **Dues:** $25/year. **Publications:** *Take Action* (2x/year); free to members.

★5028★ APPALACHIAN LONG DISTANCE HIKERS
    ASSOCIATION

10 Benning St
PMB 224
West Lebanon, NH 03054
Web: www.aldha.org
Sponsors the annual Gathering of Long Distance Hikers and work trips on the Appalachian National Scenic Trail (see separate entry in national trails section). **Established:** 1983. **Members:** 1500. **Dues:** $10/year. **Publications:** *The Long Distance Hiker* (quarterly); free to members.

★5029★ APPALACHIAN MOUNTAIN CLUB (AMC)

5 Joy St
Boston, MA 02108
Web: www.outdoors.org
Phone: 617-523-0655; **Fax:** 617-523-0722; **Toll Free:** 800-262-4455
Dedicated to protecting the natural resources of the northeast by conducting research on mountain ecology and backcountry use, developing policies for land management, and guiding environmental legislation. Maintains more than 1,500 miles of trails throughout the Northeast, including nearly 350 miles of the Appalachian Trail in five states. Provides overnight shelters to hikers. Maintains 12 regional chapters. **Established:** 1876. **Members:** 90,000. **Dues:** $40/year. **Publications:** *AMC Outdoors* (10x/year); free to members. *Appalachia Journal* (biannually); $15 for a one-year subscription.

★5030★ APPALACHIAN TRAIL CONFERENCE
    (ATC)

799 Washington St
PO Box 807
Harpers Ferry, WV 25425
Web: www.appalachiantrail.org
Phone: 304-535-6331; **Fax:** 304-535-2667

Protects, maintains, and manages the 2,175-mile Appalachian National Scenic Trail, a 250,000-acre greenway extending from Maine to Georgia. (See separate entry in national trails section.) Publishes guidebooks and maps for the Trail. **Established:** 1925. **Members:** 40,000 **Dues:** $30/year. **Publications:** *AT Journeys* (6x/year); free to members. *The Register* (4x/year) online newsletter; free to agency partners and individuals who manage a section of the Trail.

★5031★ ARCHAEOLOGICAL CONSERVANCY

5301 Central Ave NE, Suite 902
Albuquerque, NM 87108
Web: www.americanarchaeology.com/aaabout.html
Phone: 505-266-1540; **Fax:** 505-266-0311
Dedicated to preserving significant archeological sites in North America. The Conservancy has acquired more than 325 endangered archaeological sites in 39 states across the U.S. Operates regional offices in California, Ohio, Mississippi, and Maryland. **Established:** 1980. **Members:** 23,000. **Dues:** $25/year. **Publications:** *American Archaeology* (quarterly); free to members.

★5032★ ASSOCIATION OF CONSERVATION ENGINEERS (ACE)

Missouri Department of Conservation
PO Box 180
Jefferson City, MO 65102
Web: conservationengineers.org
Phone: 573-522-4115
Engineers and allied personnel employed by conservation and recreation agencies and consultants who share an interest in the areas of fish and wildlife, parks, forests, and related fields. Shares information, techniques, and designs while working to conserve and improve our national heritage and enhance our natural resources. **Established:** 1961. **Members:** 300. **Dues:** $25/year. **Publications:** *ACE Resources* (3x/year); free to members.

★5033★ ASSOCIATION FOR CONSERVATION INFORMATION (ACI)

c/o Fish Game & Wildlfe Div
PO Box 400
Trenton, NJ 08625
Web: www.aci-net.org
Phone: 609-984-0837
Trains members to provide natural resource, environmental, and wildlife information and education to the public and provides forums for the exchange of information. Members are information and education agencies, organizations, and professionals involved in wildlife, conservation, parks, or natural resources. **Established:** 1938. **Members:** Includes 60 government agencies & private organizations, as well as individual members. **Dues:** $25/year. **Publications:** *The Balance Wheel* (quarterly); free to members.

★5034★ ASSOCIATION FOR THE PRESERVATION OF VIRGINIA ANTIQUITIES (APVA)

204 W Franklin St
Richmond, VA 23220
Web: www.apva.org
Phone: 804-648-1889; **Fax:** 804-775-0802
Dedicated to preserving and promoting Virginia's historic structures, landscapes, collections, communities and archaeological sites. Conducts lectures and workshops at its sites. Members receive free admission to APVA properties open to the public. **Established:** 1889. **Members:** 4,000. **Dues:** $40/year. **Publications:** *Preservation Virginia Journal* (biannually); free to members.

★5035★ ASSOCIATION OF STATE WETLAND MANAGERS

2 Basin Rd
Windham, ME 04062
Web: www.aswm.org
Phone: 207-892-3399; **Fax:** 207-892-3089
Seeks to promote and enhance protection and management of wetlands resources and to better apply science to such management efforts. **Dues:** $60/year. **Publications:** *Wetlands News* (quarterly); free to members.

★5036★ ATLANTIC SALMON FEDERATION (ASF)

PO Box 5200
Saint Andrews,
Web: www.asf.ca
Phone: 506-529-1033; **Fax:** 506-529-4438; **Toll Free:** 800-565-5666
Promotes the conservation and sensible management of the wild Atlantic salmon and its environment. Efforts include preventing the extinction of salmon and restoring depleted populations. Promotes public awareness and workshops to educate individuals about the importance of healthy rivers and salmon populations. **Established:** 1948. **Dues:** $40/year. **Publications:** *Atlantic Salmon Journal* (quarterly); free to members.

★5037★ AUDUBON NATURALIST SOCIETY

8940 Jones Mill Rd
Chevy Chase, MD 20815
Web: www.audubonnaturalist.org
Phone: 301-652-9188; **Fax:** 301-951-7179
Seeks to increase environmental awareness and understanding, promote conservation of biodiversity, and protecting wildlife habitat, focusing its efforts in the mid-Atlantic region. Promotes numerous education and conservation programs and maintains three wildlife sanctuaries. **Established:** 1897. **Members:** 10,000. **Dues:** $40/year. **Publications:** *Audubon Naturalist News* (6x/year); free to members.

★5038★ BACK COUNTRY HORSEMEN OF AMERICA (BCHA)

PO Box 1367
Graham, WA 98338
Web: www.backcountryhorse.com
Phone: 360-832-2461; **Fax:** 360-832-2471; **Toll Free:** 888-893-5161
Nonprofit corporation made up of state organizations, affiliates, and at large members concerned with promoting the common sense use and responsible enjoyment of horseback riding in America's backcountry and wilderness areas. Works to insure

that public lands remain open for recreational stock use; assists government agencies in maintenance of backcountry lands. BCHA also educates and encourages wise use of backcountry resources by horsemen and the general public. **Established:** 1973. **Members:** 16,000. **Dues:** $30/year. **Publications:** *BCHA Newsletter* (quarterly); free to members and $15/year for non-members.

★5039★ BAT CONSERVATION INTERNATIONAL (BCI)

PO Box 162603
Austin, TX 78716
Web: www.batcon.org
Phone: 512-327-9721; **Fax:** 512-327-9724; **Toll Free:** 800-538-2287
Dedicated to preserving the earth's biodiversity by protecting and restoring bats and their habitats worldwide. Works to advance scientific knowledge about the ecosystem that sustains various bat species and to educate the public about bats and their habitats. **Established:** 1982. **Members:** 14,000. **Dues:** $35/year. **Publications:** Bats Magazine (quarterly); free to members.

★5040★ BEYOND PESTICIDES

701 'E' St SE, Suite 200
Washington, DC 20003
Web: www.beyondpesticides.org
Phone: 202-543-5450; **Fax:** 202-543-4791
Provides the public with information on pesticides and alternatives to their use. Encourages individuals to protect themselves and the environment from the potentially harmful health and environmental effects associated with the use and misuse of pesticides. **Established:** 1981. **Dues:** $25/year. **Publications:** *Pesticides and You* (quarterly); free to members.

★5041★ BIG BEND NATURAL HISTORY ASSOCIATION

PO Box 196
Big Bend National Park, TX 79834
Web: www.bigbendbookstore.org
Phone: 432-477-2236; **Fax:** 432-477-2234
Seeks to educate the public and increase their understanding and appreciation of the Big Bend Area and what it represents in terms of historical and natural heritage. (See separate entry on Big Bend National Park in national parks section.) **Established:** 1956. **Members:** 570. **Dues:** $50/year. **Publications:** *Big Bend Paisano* (periodically); free to members.

★5042★ BIRD STUDIES CANADA

PO Box 160
Port Rowan,
Web: www.bsc-eoc.org
Phone: 519-586-3531; **Fax:** 519-586-3532; **Toll Free:** 888-448-2473
Dedicated to advancing the understanding, appreciation, and conservation of wild birds and their habitats, in Canada and elsewhere, through studies that engage the skills, enthusiasm,

and support of its members, volunteers, staff, and the interested public. **Established:** 1998. **Members:** 6,000. **Dues:** $25/year. **Publications:** *Birdwatch Canada* (3x/year); free to members.

★5043★ BRITISH COLUMBIA CONSERVATION FOUNDATION (BCCF)

17564 56A Ave, Suite 206
Surrey,
Web: www.bccf.com
Phone: 604-576-1433; **Fax:** 604-576-1482
Dedicated to the conservation and stewardship of British Columbia's ecosystems and species. Works both independently and with partners to undertake projects in fish and wildlife habitat inventories, research, enhancement, restoration, resource stewardship, and environmental education. Pursues scientific investigation, cooperation, and education to help conserve fish, wildlife, and habitat. **Established:** 1969. **Members:** Nonmembership organization. **Dues:** Donations accepted.

★5044★ BRITISH COLUMBIA WATER, LAND & AIR MINISTRY

Parks & Protected Areas Branch
PO Box 9398
Stn Prov Gov
Victoria,
Web: wlapwww.gov.bc.ca/bcparks
Phone: 250-387-4339; **Fax:** 250-387-5757
Responsible for the designation, management and conservation of British Columbia's system of parks, recreation areas, and ecological reserves. Currently comprised of more than 675 sites, the system encompasses 10.8 million hectares, equal to 11.4 percent of the province's land base, and attracts 24 million visitors a year.

★5045★ BRITISH COLUMBIA WILDLIFE FEDERATION (BCWF)

19292 60th Ave, Suite 303
Surrey,
Web: www.bcwf.bc.ca
Phone: 604-533-2293; **Fax:** 604-533-1592; **Toll Free:** 800-533-2293
Dedicated to ensuring the sound, long-term management of British Columbia's fish, wildlife, park, and outdoor recreational resources. Focuses on coordinating voluntary agencies, societies, clubs, and individuals interested in that objective; and developing and supporting a comprehensive educational program to make all British Columbians aware of the value of the province's fish, wildlife, park, and outdoor recreational resources. **Established:** 1969. **Members:** 31,000 individuals and groups. **Dues:** $30/year. **Publications:** *Outdoor Edge* (bimonthly); free to members.

★5046★ BUREAU OF LAND MANAGEMENT (BLM)

Office of Public Affairs
1849 C St NW - Rm 406-LS
Washington, DC 20240
Web: www.blm.gov
Phone: 202-452-5125; **Fax:** 202-452-5124

Manages 258 million acres of federal land —about one-eighth of the land in the United States — and approximately 700 million acres of subsurface mineral resources ''to sustain the health, diversity and productivity of the public lands for the use and enjoyment of present and future generations.'' Most of the lands the BLM manages are located in 12 western states, including Alaska, and comprise grasslands, forests, high mountains, arctic tundra, and deserts. The lands are managed for a wide variety of uses including energy, minerals, timber, forage, wild horse and burro populations, fish and wildlife habitat, wilderness areas, as well as the protection of archaeological, paleontological, and historical sites. **Established:** 1946. **Publications:** Numerous brochures, reports, and pamphlets, including *Public Land Statistics*, and *Public Rewards from Public Lands*.

BUREAU OF LAND MANAGEMENT (BLM)
Alaska State Office
222 W 7th Ave, Suite 13
Anchorage, AK 99513
Web: www.blm.gov/ak
Phone: 907-271-5960; **Fax:** 907-271-3684

BUREAU OF LAND MANAGEMENT (BLM)
Arizona State Office
One North Central Avenue, Suite 800
Phoenix, AZ 85004
Web: www.blm.gov/az/
Phone: 602-417-9200; **Fax:** 602-417-9556

BUREAU OF LAND MANAGEMENT (BLM)
California State Office
2800 Cottage Way, Suite W-1834
Sacramento, CA 95825
Web: www.blm.gov/ca/
Phone: 916-978-4400; **Fax:** 916-978-4416

BUREAU OF LAND MANAGEMENT (BLM)
Colorado State Office
2850 Youngfield St
Lakewood, CO 80215
Web: www.co.blm.gov
Phone: 303-239-3600; **Fax:** 303-239-3933

BUREAU OF LAND MANAGEMENT (BLM)
Eastern States Office
7450 Boston Blvd
Springfield, VA 22153
Web: www.es.blm.gov
Phone: 703-440-1600; **Fax:** 703-440-1599

BUREAU OF LAND MANAGEMENT (BLM)
Idaho State Office
1387 S Vinnell Way
Boise, ID 83709
Web: www.id.blm.gov
Phone: 208-373-4000; **Fax:** 208-373-3904

BUREAU OF LAND MANAGEMENT (BLM)
Montana State Office
5001 Southgate Dr
Billings, MT 59101
Web: www.mt.blm.gov
Phone: 406-896-5000; **Fax:** 406-896-5298

BUREAU OF LAND MANAGEMENT (BLM)
National Science & Technology Center
PO Box 25047
Denver Federal Center, Bldg 50
Denver, CO 80225
Web: www.blm.gov/nstc/
Phone: 303-236-6454; **Fax:** 303-236-6450

BUREAU OF LAND MANAGEMENT (BLM)
Nevada State Office
1340 Financial Blvd
Reno, NV 89502
Web: www.nv.blm.gov
Phone: 775-861-6400; **Fax:** 775-861-6606

BUREAU OF LAND MANAGEMENT (BLM)
New Mexico State Office
1474 Rodeo Rd
PO Box 27115
Santa Fe, NM 87502
Web: www.nm.blm.gov
Phone: 505-438-7400; **Fax:** 505-438-7435

BUREAU OF LAND MANAGEMENT (BLM)
Oregon-Washington State Office
333 SW 1st Ave
Portland, OR 97204
Web: www.blm.gov/or/
Phone: 503-808-6002; **Fax:** 503-808-6308

BUREAU OF LAND MANAGEMENT (BLM)
Utah State Office
440 West 200 South, Suite 500
Salt Lake City, UT 84145
Web: www.ut.blm.gov
Phone: 801-539-4001; **Fax:** 801-539-4013

BUREAU OF LAND MANAGEMENT (BLM)
Wyoming State Office
5353 Yellowstone Rd
Cheyenne, WY 82003
Web: www.wy.blm.gov
Phone: 307-775-6256; **Fax:** 307-775-6129

★5047★ BUREAU OF RECLAMATION
US Dept of the Interior
1849 C St NW
Washington, DC 20240
Web: www.usbr.gov
Phone: 202-513-0501; **Fax:** 202-513-0314
Responsible for managing water resources in the western U.S. The Bureau has constructed more than 600 dams, canals and reservoirs in seventeen western states, including Hoover Dam on the Colorado River and Grand Coulee on the Columbia River. Recreation areas (numbering more than 300) at the Bureau's water management sites are operated in cooperation with federal and state agencies and local governments. **Established:** 1902. **Publications:** Various brochures, pamphlets, books, reports, fact sheets, and maps. For a publications list, write to: Department of the Interior, Bureau of Reclamation, PO Box 25007, Denver, CO 80225; or call 303-445-2072.

BUREAU OF RECLAMATION
Great Plains Region
PO Box 36900
Billings, MT 59107
Web: www.usbr.gov/gp
Phone: 406-247-7600; **Fax:** 406-247-7793

BUREAU OF RECLAMATION
Lower Colorado Region
PO Box 61470
Boulder City, NV 89006
Web: www.usbr.gov/lc/region
Phone: 702-293-8000; **Fax:** 702-293-8766

BUREAU OF RECLAMATION
Mid-Pacific Region
2800 Cottage Way
Sacramento, CA 95825
Web: www.usbr.gov/mp
Phone: 916-978-5100; **Fax:** 916-978-5114

BUREAU OF RECLAMATION
Pacific Northwest Region
1150 N Curtis Rd, Suite 100
Boise, ID 83706
Web: www.usbr.gov/pn
Phone: 208-378-5012; **Fax:** 208-378-5019

BUREAU OF RECLAMATION
Upper Colorado Region
125 S State St, Rm 6107
Salt Lake City, UT 84138
Web: www.usbr.gov/uc
Phone: 801-524-3600; **Fax:** 801-524-5499

★5048★ CALIFORNIA PARK & RECREATION SOCIETY (CPRS)
7971 Freeport Blvd
Sacramento, CA 95832
Web: www.cprs.org
Phone: 916-665-2777; **Fax:** 916-665-9149
Professional and public-interest organization dedicated to providing the leadership to advance the positive impact and value of the park and recreation profession. **Established:** 1946. **Members:** 4,000. **Dues:** $53-140/year. **Publications:** *California Parks and Recreation* (quarterly) and *Job Line & News from CPRS* (monthly); free to members.

★5049★ CALIFORNIA STATE PARKS FOUNDATION
800 College Ave
PO Box 548
Kentfield, CA 94914
Web: www.calparks.org
Phone: 415-258-9975; **Fax:** 415-258-9930
Raises funds for the protection, preservation, and enhancement of California's state parks. Park projects include renovation of historic buildings, construction of trails and facilities, restoration of native species, and educational programs. **Established:** 1969. **Members:** 75,000. **Dues:** $40/year. **Publications:** *California Parklands* newsletter (quarterly); free to members.

★5050★ CAMPING WOMEN
PO Box 13261
Sacramento, CA 95813
Web: www.campingwomen.org
Provides camping opportunities for women to join together to learn new skills, develop their potential, and enjoy the outdoors. Sponsors camping events for women. **Established:** 1977. **Members:** 2,000. **Dues:** $25/year. **Publications:** *Camping Women Trails* (monthly); free to members.

★5051★ CANADIAN HERITAGE RIVERS SYSTEM (CHRS)
c/o Parks Canada
Ottawa,
Web: www.chrs.ca
Phone: 819-994-2913; **Fax:** 819-997-0835
Established by federal, provincial, and territorial governments to conserve and protect the best examples of Canada's river heritage, to give them national recognition, and to encourage the public to enjoy and appreciate them. Today, there are 39 Heritage Rivers across Canada, and more are being added to the system each year. **Established:** 1984. **Members:** 15 (appointed by government). **Publications:** *Heritage Riverscapes Newsletter* (annually); free. *The Canadian Heritage Rivers System Annual Report* (annually); free.

★5052★ CANADIAN PARKS & RECREATION ASSOCIATION (CPRA)
2197 Riverside Dr, Suite 404
Ottawa,
Web: www.cpra.ca
Phone: 613-523-5315; **Fax:** 613-523-1182

Dedicated to the enhancement of quality community leisure services, lifestyles, and environment for all Canadians through the efforts of its members and allies in advocacy, education, information sharing, policy development, and national initiatives. **Established:** 1945. **Members:** 3,600. **Dues:** $500/year (commercial memberships only). **Publications:** *Parks & Recreation Canada* (6x/year); free to members.

★5053★ CANADIAN PARKS & WILDERNESS SOCIETY (CPAWS)

250 City Center Ave, Suite 506
Ottawa,
Web: www.cpaws.org
Phone: 613-569-7226; **Fax:** 613-569-7098; **Toll Free:** 800-333-9453
Dedicated to protecting Canada's wild ecosystems in parks, wilderness, and similar natural areas and preserving the full diversity of habitats and their species. Promotes awareness and understanding of ecological principles and the inherent values of wilderness through education, appreciation, and experience. CPAWS has played a significant role in saving more than 40 million acres of Canadian wilderness. **Established:** 1963. **Members:** 20,000. **Dues:** $35/year. **Publications:** *The Wilderness Activist* (2x/year); free to members.

★5054★ CANADIAN PEREGRINE FOUNDATION

250 Merton St, Suite 404
Toronto,
Web: www.peregrine-foundation.ca
Phone: 416-481-1233; **Fax:** 416-481-7158; **Toll Free:** 888-709-3944
Works to facilitate the recovery of Canada's endangered and threatened raptor species. Committed to raising public awareness of environmental issues affecting Canada's endangered and threatened species, and to providing support to projects involving the recovery, restoration, and rehabilitation of Canada's endangered and threatened raptor species. **Established:** 1997. **Dues:** $30/year. **Publications:** *Talon Tales* (quarterly); free to members.

★5055★ CANADIAN WATER RESOURCES ASSOCIATION (CWRA)

280 Albert St, Suite 900
Ottawa,
Web: www.cwra.org
Phone: 613-237-9363; **Fax:** 613-594-5190
Dedicated to stimulating public awareness and understanding of Canada's water resources, encouraging individuals to recognize the importance of water as a valued resource, and to provide a forum for the exchange of information and opinions. Branch organizations are located in eight provinces. **Established:** 1947. **Members:** 800. **Dues:** $90/year. **Publications:** *Water News* (quarterly); free to members.

★5056★ CANADIAN WILDLIFE FEDERATION (CWF)

350 Michael Cowpland Dr
Kanata,
Web: www.cwf-fcf.org
Phone: 613-599-9594; **Fax:** 613-599-4428; **Toll Free:** 800-563-9453

Dedicated to fostering awareness and enjoyment of our natural world. Objectives include promoting the sustainable use of our natural resources, encouraging an understanding of the impact of human activities on the environment, conducting and sponsoring research relating to wildlife and the environment, recommending legislative changes to protect wildlife and its habitats, and cooperating with organizations and government agencies with similar objectives. **Established:** 1962. **Members:** 300,000. **Dues:** $25/year. **Publications:** *Wild* (8x/year); free to members. *Canadian Wildlife* (5x/year); free to members.

★5057★ CENTER FOR PLANT CONSERVATION (CPC)

4344 Shaw Blvd
Saint Louis, MO 63110
Web: www.centerforplantconservation.org
Phone: 314-577-9450; **Fax:** 314-577-9465
National network of 33 botanical institutions dedicated to the conservation of threatened and endangered plants of the United States through research, education, and the development of the National Collection of Endangered Plants, which maintains almost 600 of the country's rarest plants. **Established:** 1984. **Publications:** *Plant Conservation Newsletter* (biannually); free to members. Other publications are available via the web site or by calling the CPC National Office.

★5058★ CHARLES A & ANNE MORROW LINDBERGH FOUNDATION

2150 3rd Ave N, Suite 310
Anoka, MN 55303
Web: www.lindberghfoundation.org
Phone: 763-576-1596; **Fax:** 763-576-1664
Works to honor the legacy of Charles and Anne Morrow Lindbergh and further their vision of seeking a balance between technological advancement and environmental preservation. **Established:** 1977. **Members:** 1,400. **Dues:** $35/year. **Publications:** *Foundation Newsletter* (3x/year); free to members and nonmembers.

★5059★ CIVIL WAR PRESERVATION TRUST (CWPT)

1331 H St NW, Suite 1001
Washington, DC 20005
Web: www.civilwar.org
Phone: 202-367-1861; **Fax:** 202-367-1865; **Toll Free:** 888-606-1400
Dedicated to preserving endangered Civil War battlefields. Conducts heritage tours, educational activities and historical reenactment programs to inform Americans about the significance of the Civil War in their nation's history. **Established:** 1999, through the merger of the Association for the Preservation of Civil War Sites (1987) with the Civil War Trust (1991). **Members:** 70,000. **Dues:** $35/year. **Publications:** *Hallowed Ground* (quarterly); free to members.

★5060★ CLEAN NOVA SCOTIA
126 Portland St
Dartmouth,
Web: www.clean.ns.ca
Phone: 902-420-3474; **Fax:** 902-424-5334; **Toll Free:** 800-665-5377
Dedicated to working with others to secure a sustainable, environmentally healthy society for future generations to enjoy. Encourages all Nova Scotians to make positive decisions about the environment and offers environmental programs province-wide. **Established:** 1987. **Members:** 500 individuals, groups, and corporations. **Dues:** $25/year. **Publications:** *ReNews* (3x/year); free to members.

★5061★ CLEAN WATER ACTION
4455 Connecticut Ave NW, Suite A-300
Washington, DC 20008
Web: www.cleanwateraction.org
Phone: 202-895-0420; **Fax:** 202-895-0438; **Toll Free:** 800-709-2837
National citizens' organization working for clean, safe, and affordable water, prevention of health-threatening pollution, creation of environmentally safe jobs and businesses, and empowerment of people to make democracy work. **Established:** 1972. **Members:** 700,000.

★5062★ CLEAN WATER FUND (CWF)
4455 Connecticut Ave NW, Suite A300-16
Washington, DC 20008
Web: www.cleanwaterfund.org
Phone: 202-895-0432; **Fax:** 202-895-0438; **Toll Free:** 800-709-2837
Research and educational organization dedicated to improving environmental conditions for present and future generations. Work is concerned with achieving cleaner and safer water, cleaner air, and protection from toxic pollution in homes, neighborhoods, and workplaces. Clean Water Fund's programs build on and complement those of the affiliated Clean Water Action organization. **Established:** 1978.

★5063★ CO-OP AMERICA
1612 K St NW, Suite 600
Washington, DC 20006
Web: www.coopamerica.org
Phone: 202-872-5307; **Fax:** 202-331-8166; **Toll Free:** 800-584-7336
Provides the economic strategies, organizing power and practical tools for businesses and individuals to address today's social and environmental problems. Encourages consumers to buy products and services from businesses that create jobs, care about their communities, engage in fair trade, and protect our environment. **Established:** 1982. **Members:** 2,500 businesses and 65,000 individuals. **Dues:** $20/year. **Publications:** *Co-op America Quarterly* (quarterly); free to members. *National Green Pages* (annually); free to members and $6.95 for nonmembers. *Financial Planning Handbook* (annually); free to members and $11.95 for nonmembers. *Real Money* (bimonthly); newsletter. Also publishes occasional consumer guides.

★5064★ COASTAL CONSERVATION ASSOCIATION (CCA)
6919 Portwest Dr, Suite 100
Houston, TX 77024
Web: www.joincca.org
Phone: 713-626-4234; **Fax:** 713-626-5852; **Toll Free:** 800-201-3474
Dedicated to the conservation and preservation of marine resources and to preventing the depletion and destruction of coastal waters. Members include recreational saltwater anglers and other outdoor sports enthusiasts who seek to address coastal conservation issues at the state and national level. **Established:** 1977. **Members:** 90,000. **Dues:** $25/year ($10/year for members under age 17). **Publications:** *Tide* (bimonthly); free to members. *Change of Tides*; $45; *The Rising Tide* (quarterly); free to youth members.

★5065★ COLORADO ENVIRONMENTAL COALITION
1536 Wynkoop St, Suite 5C
Denver, CO 80202
Web: www.ourcolorado.org
Phone: 303-534-7066; **Fax:** 303-534-7063
State-based citizens' group committed to protecting Colorado's unique natural heritage. Builds and mobilizes citizen campaigns that work to safeguard the state's wild lands, wildlife, and quality of life. Seeks to protect Colorado's land and water from environmentally damaging activities including mining, logging, road construction, and dam building. **Established:** 1965. **Members:** 3,800 individuals, 93 organizations. **Dues:** $30/year. **Publications:** *Colorado Environment Report* (quarterly); free to members.

★5066★ COLORADO WILDLIFE FEDERATION
4045 Wadsworth Blvd, Suite 20
Wheat Ridge, CO 80033
Web: www.coloradowildlife.org
Phone: 303-987-0400; **Fax:** 303-987-0200
Promotes the conservation, sound management, and sustainable use of Colorado's wildlife and wildlife habitat through education and advocacy. Dedicated to conserving Colorado's natural resources and wildlife heritage for fishing, hunting, and wildlife viewing. **Established:** 1953. **Members:** 5,000. **Dues:** $35/year ($15/year for students). **Publications:** *Colorado Wildlife* (bimonthly); free to members.

★5067★ CONSERVATION COUNCIL OF NEW BRUNSWICK (CCNB)
180 Saint John St
Fredericton,
Web: www.conservationcouncil.ca
Phone: 506-458-8747; **Fax:** 506-458-1047
Supports environmental protection in New Brunswick and surrounding Maritime provinces by safeguarding land, air, and water. Develops and promotes solutions to pollution and resource destruction through research and education. **Established:** 1969. **Members:** 600 members. **Dues:** $25/year ($10/year for

students/seniors/low income). **Publications:** *EcoAlert* (quarterly); free to members.

★5068★ CONSERVATION FUND
1655 N Fort Myer Dr, Suite 1300
Arlington, VA 222092156
Web: www.conservationfund.org
Phone: 703-525-6300; **Fax:** 703-525-4610
Non-membership, non-advocacy, nonprofit organization. Solicits funds and awards grants to conservation projects across the U.S. Creates partnerships with other organizations to help protect and conserve open space, parkland, historic sites, wetlands, and wildlife. Projects include developing greenways networks, Civil War battlefield preservation, and leadership training for land conservation professionals. Maintains offices throughout the U.S. **Established:** 1985. **Members:** Nonmembership organization. **Publications:** *Common Ground* (quarterly). Occasional other reports on land conservation and sustainable development issues.

★5069★ CONSERVATION INTERNATIONAL (CI)
2011 Crystal Drive, Suite 500
Arlington, VA 22202
Web: www.conservation.org
Phone: 703-341-2400; **Toll Free:** 800-406-2306
Dedicated to saving endangered rain forests and other ecosystems worldwide and the animals and plants that rely on these habitats. Provides financial and technical support to local communities, private organizations, and government agencies in developing countries to help build sustainable economies while protecting rain forest ecosystems. **Established:** 1987. **Members:** 10,000. **Dues:** $35/year. **Publications:** *CI Frontlines* (quarterly); free to members.

★5070★ CONSERVATION TREATY SUPPORT FUND (CTSF)
3705 Cardiff Rd
Chevy Chase, MD 20815
Web: www.conservationtreaty.org
Phone: 301-654-3150; **Fax:** 301-652-6390; **Toll Free:** 800-654-3150
Promotes awareness and understanding of conservation treaties and their goals and seeks to enhance public support, compliance, and funding. Specifically uses education programs and grants to encourage compliance with the *Convention on International Trade in Endangered Species of Wild Fauna and Flora*, known as CITES, as well as other international treaties and conventions that address environmental conservation and pollution problems. **Established:** 1986. **Members:** Nonmembership organization. **Publications:** Educational books, posters, and pamphlets including *CITES Endangered Species Book*; $5.00, for elementary school audiences.

★5071★ CONTINENTAL DIVIDE TRAIL SOCIETY
3704 N Charles St, Suite 601
Baltimore, MD 21218
Web: www.cdtsociety.org
Phone: 410-235-9610; **Fax:** 410-243-1960

Mission is to help in the planning, development, and maintenance of the 3,000-mile Continental Divide National Scenic Trail. Located in close proximity to the continental divide, the trail starts 14 miles north of the US-Canadian border in Waterton, Alberta, and extends southward through Montana, Idaho, Wyoming, Colorado, and New Mexico to Mexico. **Established:** 1978. **Members:** 250. **Dues:** $10/year. **Publications:** *DIVIDEnds* (semiannually); free to members and $7.50/year for nonmembers.

★5072★ CORPORATION FOR JEFFERSON'S POPLAR FOREST
PO Box 419
Forest, VA 245510419
Web: www.poplarforest.org
Phone: 434-525-1806; **Fax:** 434-525-7252
Dedicated to preserving, restoring, maintaining, and operating Poplar Forest, Thomas Jefferson's plantation retreat. **Established:** 1984. **Members:** Nonmembership organization.

★5073★ COUNCIL OF CANADIANS
170 Laurier Ave W, Suite 700
Ottawa,
Web: www.canadians.org
Phone: 613-233-2773; **Fax:** 613-233-6776; **Toll Free:** 800-387-7177
Citizens' organization committed to safeguarding social programs, promoting economic justice, renewing democracy, asserting Canadian sovereignty, advancing alternatives to corporate-style free trade, and preserving the environment. **Established:** 1985. **Members:** 100,000. **Dues:** $45/year. **Publications:** *Canadian Perspectives* (quarterly); free to members.

★5074★ COUSTEAU SOCIETY
710 Settlers Landing Rd
Hampton, VA 23669
Web: www.cousteausociety.org
Phone: 757-722-9300; **Fax:** 757-722-8185; **Toll Free:** 800-441-4395
Dedicated to protecting and improving the quality of life for present and future generations by educating the public about the fragile state of water on our planet. Undertakes expeditions exploring and filming natural systems to increase environmental awareness and knowledge. **Established:** 1973. **Members:** 60,000. **Dues:** $30/year; $40/year for families. **Publications:** *Calypso Log* (quarterly); free to members. *Cousteau Kids* (bimonthly); free to members who join at the family level or $20/year with a young people's membership.

★5075★ DEFENDERS OF WILDLIFE
1130 17th St NW
Washington, DC 20036
Web: www.defenders.org
Phone: 202-682-9400; **Fax:** 202-682-1331; **Toll Free:** 800-989-8981
Dedicated to the protection of all native wild animals and plants

in their natural communities. Works to protect endangered species and advocates new approaches to wildlife conservation that will help keep species from becoming endangered. Programs focus on the accelerating rate of extinction of species and the associated loss of biological diversity, and habitat alteration and destruction. Educates on how and where to watch wildlife. **Established:** 1947. **Members:** 80,000. **Dues:** $15/year. **Publications:** *Defenders* (bimonthly); free to members.

★5076★ DELTA WATERFOWL FOUNDATION
P.O. Box 3128
Bismarck, ND 58501
Web: www.deltawaterfowl.org
Phone: 701-222-8857; **Fax:** 701-223-4645; **Toll Free:** 888-987-3695
Seeks to secure the future of waterfowl hunting. Promotes educational research, wise management practices, and leadership development for scientists, resource managers, hunters, conservationists and the public with regard to waterfowl habitat preservation and science. **Established:** 1911. **Members:** 40,000. **Dues:** $25/year; $15/year for ages 17 and under. **Publications:** *Delta Waterfowl Report* (quarterly); free to members.

★5077★ DUCKS UNLIMITED INC
1 Waterfowl Way
Memphis, TN 38120
Web: www.ducks.org
Phone: 901-758-3825; **Fax:** 901-758-3850; **Toll Free:** 800-453-8257
Dedicated to conservation, restoration, and management of wetlands and other habitat for North American waterfowl. **Established:** 1937. **Dues:** $25/year. **Publications:** *Ducks Unlimited* (bimonthly); free to members.

★5078★ EARTH ISLAND INSTITUTE
300 Broadway, Suite 28
San Francisco, CA 941333312
Web: www.earthisland.org
Phone: 415-788-3666; **Fax:** 415-788-7324
Develops innovative projects for the conservation, preservation, and restoration of the global environment. Provides support to creative individuals for their work on ecologically linked issues. Projects include the John Muir Project, International Marine Mammal Project, Brower Fund, Reef Protection International, Global Service Corps, and the Campaign to Safeguard America's Waters. **Established:** 1982. **Members:** 7,500. **Dues:** $25/year; $15/year for students and low-income members. **Publications:** *Earth Island Journal* (quarterly); free to members, $15/year for nonmembers.

★5079★ EARTHJUSTICE
426 17th St, 6th Fl
Oakland, CA 94612
Web: www.earthjustice.org
Phone: 510-550-6700; **Fax:** 510-550-6740; **Toll Free:** 800-584-6460
Independent, nonprofit environmental law firm representing —

without charge — hundreds of public interest clients. Mission is to work through the courts to safeguard public lands, national forests, parks, and wilderness areas; to reduce air and water pollution; to prevent toxic contamination; and to preserve endangered species and wildlife habitat. Runs an environmental law clinic at Stanford University, training students in public interest environmental law. **Established:** 1971 as the Sierra Club Legal Defense Fund. **Members:** 135,000. **Publications:** *In Brief* (quarterly); free to supporters.

★5080★ EARTHWATCH INSTITUTE
3 Clock Tower Pl Suite 100
PO Box 75
Maynard, MA 01754
Web: www.earthwatch.org
Phone: 978-461-0081; **Fax:** 978-461-2332; **Toll Free:** 800-776-0188
Promotes sustainable conservation of our natural resources and cultural heritage by creating partnerships between field scientists and the general public. Recruits some 4,000 paying volunteers each year to help scientists on their field research expeditions worldwide; student and teacher fellowships offered. In addition to U.S. headquarters, maintains offices in Oxford, England, Melbourne, Australia, and Tokyo, Japan. **Established:** 1971. **Members:** 25,000. **Dues:** $30/year. **Publications:** *Earthwatch Journal* (3 times a year); free to members. Also publishes *Off the Beaten Path*, a free monthly e-newsletter.

★5081★ ENDANGERED SPECIES COALITION (ESC)
PO Box 65195
Washington, DC 20035
Web: www.stopextinction.org
A coalition of 440 environmental, conservation, religious, scientific, humane, sporting, and business groups. Defends the Endangered Species Act by working to increase funding for endangered species protection and monitoring federal legislation for anti-environmental riders. Also works with regional organizations on issues affecting species survival and recovery. **Established:** 1981. **Publications:** *Activist Updates* (biweekly); free to members.

★5082★ ENVIRONMENT CANADA
70 Cremazie St
Gatineau,
Web: www.ec.gc.ca
Phone: 819-997-2800; **Fax:** 819-994-1412; **Toll Free:** 800-668-6767
National agency charged with preserving and improving the quality of the natural environment, including water, air and soil. Works to help people make responsible decisions about the environment. Aids in protecting more than 400 species of internationally shared migratory birds, 11 million hectares of habitat, and 340 plant and animal species facing extinction. Funds more than 560 community action projects in support of the protection of Canada's natural heritage.

★5083★ ENVIRONMENT MICHIGAN
103 East Liberty, Suite 202
Ann Arbor, MI 48104
Web: www.environmentmichigan.org
Phone: 734-662-9797; Fax: 734-662-8393
Statewide, citizen-based environmental advocacy and research organization dedicated to preserving and protecting Michigan's natural heritage and resources. Members: 10,000. Dues: $25/year.

★5084★ ENVIRONMENTAL DEFENSE
257 Park Ave S
New York, NY 10010
Web: www.environmentaldefense.org
Phone: 212-505-2100; Fax: 212-505-2375; Toll Free: 800-505-0703
Links science, economics, and law to create solutions to environmental problems. Goals include stabilizing the earth's climate, safeguarding the world's oceans, protecting human health, and defending and restoring biodiversity. Maintains regional offices throughout the United States. Established: 1967. Members: 500,000. Dues: $25/year. Publications: Solutions (bimonthly); free. Wide variety of other print and online materials.

★5085★ ENVIRONMENTAL GRANTMAKERS
ASSOCIATION (EGA)
437 Madison Ave, 37th Fl
New York, NY 10022
Web: www.ega.org
Phone: 212-812-4260; Fax: 212-812-4299
Mission is to help member organizations become more effective environmental grantmakers through information sharing, collaboration and networking. Established: 1987. Members: More than 250 foundations from North America and around the world.

★5086★ ENVIRONMENTAL INFORMATION
ASSOCIATION (EIA)
6935 Wisconsin Ave, Suite 306
Chevy Chase, MD 208156112
Web: www.eia-usa.org
Phone: 301-961-4999; Fax: 301-961-3094; Toll Free: 888-343-4342
Disseminates information about the abatement of asbestos and lead-based paint, safety and health issues, analytical issues, and environmental site assessments. Dedicated to providing environmental information to individuals, members, and industry. Dues: $105/year; $35/year for students; $400/year for organizations.

★5087★ ENVIRONMENTAL PROTECTION AGENCY
(EPA)
1200 Pennsylvania Ave NW
Ariel Rios Bldg
Washington, DC 20460
Web: www.epa.gov
Phone: 202-564-4700
EPA's mission is to protect human health and to safeguard the natural environment - air, water, and land - upon which life depends. Provides leadership in environmental science, research, education and assessment. Works with other federal agencies, state and local governments, and Indian tribes to develop and enforce regulations under existing environmental laws. EPA also works with industries in voluntary pollution prevention programs and energy conservation efforts. Established: 1970.

★5088★ ENVIRONMENTAL PROTECTION
INFORMATION CENTER (EPIC)
351 Sprowl Creek Rd
PO Box 397
Garberville, CA 95542
Web: www.wildcalifornia.org
Phone: 707-923-2931; Fax: 707-923-4210
Strives to preserve the coastal low-elevation ancient forests of northern California through public education, citizen advocacy, and litigation. Also functions as a resource center for environmental activists. Established: 1977. Dues: $35/year.

★5089★ ENVIRONMENTAL TRAVELING
COMPANIONS (ETC)
Fort Mason Ctr, Building C
San Francisco, CA 94123
Web: www.etctrips.org
Phone: 415-474-7662; Fax: 415-474-3919
Volunteer-based organization that provides wilderness experiences for disadvantaged youth and people of all ages with physical, emotional, or developmental disabilities. ETC sea kayaking, rafting, and cross-country ski trips enable participants to access the wilderness, gain environmental awareness, and share adventure. Established: 1971. Dues: $30/year for participants. Donations also accepted. Publications: ETC Newsletter (annual); free to members.

★5090★ ESCAPEES RV CLUB
100 Rainbow Dr
Livingston, TX 77351
Web: www.escapees.com
Phone: 936-327-8873; Fax: 936-327-4388; Toll Free: 888-757-2582
Provides a support network for people who travel or live for extended periods in motor homes and travel trailers. Benefits to members include low-cost campground parking, mail and message service, RV insurance, and discounts on emergency road service. Maintains CARE Center (Continuing Assistance for Retired Escapees). Sponsors educational programs. Maintains 34 chapters in the U.S., Canada, and Mexico. Established: 1978. Members: 34,000. Dues: $60/year (plus a one-time enrollment fee of $10). Publications: Escapees Magazine (bimonthly); free to members. Also publishes an annual complimentary membership directory.

★5091★ FAMILY CAMPERS & RVERS (FCRV)
4804 Transit Rd, Bldg 2
Depew, NY 14043
Web: www.fcrv.org
Phone: 716-668-6242; Toll Free: 800-245-9755

Family-oriented camping organization dedicated to promoting and enhancing the enjoyment and experience of recreational group camping and RVing. Concerned with conservation and preserving the outdoors. Sponsors a Summer Rally (Campvention) and a Winter Retiree Rally. Originally founded as the National Campers and Hikers Association (NCHA). **Established: 1949. Members: 20,000. Dues: $25/year. Publications:** *Camping Today* (10x/year); free to members.

★5092★ **FAMILY MOTOR COACH ASSOCIATION (FMCA)**
8291 Clough Pike
Cincinnati, OH 45244
Web: www.fmca.com
Phone: 513-474-3622; **Fax:** 513-474-2332; **Toll Free:** 800-543-3622
Organizes social activities, exchanges information, and provides benefits to members. Membership is made up of families who own, use, or live in motor homes, and those in the RV industry including recreational vehicle dealers, manufacturers, and component suppliers. **Established: 1963. Members: 120,000. Dues:** $35/year (plus a one-time fee of $10). **Publications:** *Family Motor Coaching* (monthly); free to members and $30/year for nonmembers.

★5093★ **FEDERATION OF WESTERN OUTDOOR CLUBS**
PO Box 129
Selma, OR 97538
Web: www.federationofwesternoutdoorclubs.org
Coalition of conservation organizations. Promotes the proper use and protection of scenic, wilderness, and outdoor recreation resources in western states. Seeks to secure wilderness in state and national public lands and to acquire land for wildlife refuges. **Established: 1932. Members:** 50 groups with a combined membership of 500,000. **Dues:** $10/year. **Publications:** *Outdoors West* (semiannually); free to members.

★5094★ **FLORIDA TRAIL ASSOCIATION (FTA)**
5415 SW 13th St
Gainesville, FL 32608
Web: www.floridatrail.org
Phone: 352-378-8823; **Fax:** 352-378-4550; **Toll Free:** 877-445-3352
Builds, maintains, protects, and promotes the 1,400-mile Florida Trail, one of eight nationally designated scenic hiking trails in the country. (See also entry on Florida National Scenic Trail in national trails section.) **Established: 1964. Members: 5,000.. Dues:** $25/year ($30/year for families). **Publications:** *Footprint* (bimonthly); free to members.

★5095★ **FLORIDA WILDLIFE FEDERATION**
PO Box 6870
Tallahassee, FL 32314
Web: www.fwfonline.org
Phone: 850-656-7113; **Fax:** 850-942-4431; **Toll Free:** 800-656-3014

Private, nonprofit citizens' conservation organization with an interest in preserving, managing, and improving Florida's fish, wildlife, soil, water, and plant life. Through education and political action, promotes conservation, restoration, sound management, and wise and ethical use of Florida's natural resources. Affiliated with National Wildlife Federation. **Established: 1937. Members: 40,000. Dues:** $25/year ($15/year for students; $35/year for families). **Publications:** *Florida Fish and Wildlife News* (monthly); free to members.

★5096★ **FOREST GUILD**
PO Box 519
Santa Fe, NM 87504
Web: forestguild.org
Phone: 505-983-8992; **Fax:** 505-986-0798
Dedicated to protecting the integrity of the forest ecosystem, fostering productive relationships between human and natural communities, and improving the lives of people in rural communities. Provides resource protection strategies to environmental organizations, rural communities, and public agencies. Operates a training and forest products marketing center. **Established: 1984. Dues:** $20-99/year (supporting member); $15/year for students. **Publications:** Publishes a variety of papers and research reports.

★5097★ **FOREST HISTORY SOCIETY**
701 William Vickers Ave
Durham, NC 277013162
Web: www.foresthistory.org
Phone: 919-682-9319; **Fax:** 919-682-2349
Society identifies, collects, preserves, interprets, and disseminates information on the history of interactions between people, forests, and their related resources. Provides a historical perspective on the range of human interaction with forests over time. **Established: 1946. Members: 1,800. Dues:** $55/year. **Publications:** *Environmental History* (quarterly); free to members. *Forest History Today* (quarterly); free. Organization also publishes a range of other forest- and environment-related publications.

★5098★ **FOREST SERVICE EMPLOYEES FOR ENVIRONMENTAL ETHICS (FSEEE)**
PO Box 11615
Eugene, OR 97440
Web: www.fseee.org
Phone: 541-484-2692; **Fax:** 541-484-3004
Present, former, and retired Forest Service employees working with concerned citizens to forge a socially and environmentally responsible land management philosophy within the U.S. Forest Service. Encourages an institutional value system based on ecologically and economically sustainable land ethic. **Established: 1989. Members: 10,400. Dues:** $35/year. **Publications:** *Forest Magazine* (quarterly); free to members, $35 annual subscription for nonmembers.

★5099★ **FRIENDS OF THE EARTH**
1717 Massachusetts Ave NW, Suite 600
Washington, DC 20036
Web: www.foe.org
Phone: 202-783-7400; **Fax:** 202-783-0444; **Toll Free:** 877-843-8687

11. Park- and Conservation-Related Organizations

Dedicated to protecting the planet and safeguarding health and safety. Focuses on eliminating environmental hazards that threaten people's lives, such as the dangerous use of pesticides. Helps challenge environmental policies that directly threaten people living in poor communities. Provides technical assistance, activist training, and guidance on political organizing. Divisions of FOE include Bluewater Network, which wages campaigns to combat global warming, air and water pollution, and abuse of public lands. Member groups of Friends of the Earth International exist in 70 countries **Established:** 1969. **Members:** 30,000 in United States (two million in 70 countries). **Dues:** $35/year. **Publications:** *Friends of the Earth Newsmagazine* (quarterly); free to members.

★5100★ FRIENDS OF THE EARTH CANADA

260 Saint Patrick St, Suite 300
Ottawa,
Web: www.foecanada.org
Phone: 613-241-0085; **Fax:** 613-241-7998; **Toll Free:** 888-385-4444
Acts as Canada's national voice for the environment. Uses research, education, and advocacy to inspire the renewal of local communities and the earth. **Established:** 1978. **Members:** 10,000. **Dues:** $25/year.

★5101★ FRIENDS OF THE EVERGLADES

7800 Red Rd, Suite 215K
South Miami, FL 33143
Web: www.everglades.org
Phone: 305-669-0858; **Fax:** 305-669-4108
Works for the protection and restoration of Everglades National Park in Florida (see separate entry in national parks section). Monitors the implementation and enforcement of regulations designed to protect environments of Florida. Works to protect endangered species. Offers free public information services on environmental issues. **Established:** 1969. **Members:** 4,000. **Dues:** $25/year ($50/year for families). Young Friends memberships are $1/year for individuals and $15/year for classrooms. **Publications:** *Everglades Reporter* (quarterly); free to members.

★5102★ FRIENDS OF FORT MCHENRY

802 S Caroline St
Baltimore, MD 21231
Web: www.friendsoffortmchenry.org
Phone: 410-396-3453
Raises funds to restore and renovate Fort McHenry National Monument and Historic Shrine (see separate entry in national parks section), site of the War of 1812 Battle of Baltimore that inspired Francis Scott Key to write the Star-Spangled Banner. Works to continue research and to develop and preserve interpretive education programs offered to school children and visitors. **Established:** 1984. **Members:** 250. **Dues:** $35/year ($25/year for students, $65/year for families). **Publications:** Quarterly newsletter.

★5103★ FRIENDS OF THE RIVER

915 20th St
Sacramento, CA 95814
Web: www.friendsoftheriver.org
Phone: 916-442-3155; **Fax:** 916-442-3396; **Toll Free:** 888-464-2477
Preserves, protects, and restores California's rivers, streams, and their watersheds through public education, citizen activist training, and expert advocacy to influence public policy. Priorities include changing current water policies and promoting rivers and streams for federal protection through the Wild and Scenic River program. **Established:** 1973. **Members:** 6,000. **Dues:** $35/year. **Publications:** *Headwaters* (quarterly); free to members.

★5104★ FUND FOR ANIMALS

200 W 57th St
New York, NY 10019
Web: www.fundforanimals.org
Phone: 212-246-2096; **Fax:** 212-246-2633; **Toll Free:** 888-405-3863
National animal welfare society concerned with the protection of all animals, wild and domestic. Opposes sport hunting and commercial trapping; operates animal sanctuaries in Texas and California. In 2005 The Fund for Animals and the Humane Society of the United States formed the Humane Society Legislative Fund to push for legislation protecting animals in Congress and all 50 states. **Established:** 1967. **Dues:** $10/year. **Publications:** *Newsletter* (quarterly); free to donors.

★5105★ GEORGE WRIGHT SOCIETY

PO Box 65
Hancock, MI 49930
Web: www.georgewright.org
Phone: 906-487-9722; **Fax:** 906-487-9405
Association of researchers, managers, administrators, educators, and other professionals who work on behalf of the scientific and heritage values of protected areas by promoting research, resource management, and public education. **Established:** 1980. **Members:** 700. **Dues:** $45/year. **Publications:** *The George Wright Forum* (quarterly journal).

★5106★ GOOD SAM RECREATIONAL VEHICLE CLUB

PO Box 6888
Englewood, CO 80155
Web: www.goodsamclub.com
; **Fax:** 303-728-7306; **Toll Free:** 800-234-3450
Individuals interested in the recreational vehicle (RV) lifestyle. Benefits to members include emergency road service, insurance plans, travel services, and discounts at RV parks across North America. Maintains 2,300 local chapters. **Established:** 1966. **Members:** 1 million. **Dues:** $19/year. **Publications:** *Highways* (11x/year); free to members.

11. Park- and Conservation-Related Organizations

★5107★ GRAND CANYON TRUST

2601 N Fort Valley Rd
Flagstaff, AZ 86001
Web: www.grandcanyontrust.org
Phone: 928-774-7488; **Fax:** 928-774-7570; **Toll Free:** 888-428-5550
Strives to protect and restore the spectacular canyon country of the Colorado Plateau. **Established:** 1985. **Members:** 5,000. **Dues:** Donations accepted. **Publications:** *Colorado Plateau Advocate* (2x a year); free to members. Also publishes various reports and studies.

★5108★ GREAT BEAR FOUNDATION

802 E Front St
PO Box 9383
Missoula, MT 59807
Web: www.greatbear.org
Phone: 406-829-9378; **Fax:** 406-829-9379
Promotes conservation of wild bears and their natural habitat worldwide. Funds litigation in defense of bears and their habitats, holds government agencies accountable for land management decisions that affect bear populations, and supports advocacy, conservation, education, and scientific research on bears throughout the world. **Established:** 1982. **Members:** 1,000. **Dues:** $30/year ($20/year for students and seniors). **Publications:** *Bear News* (quarterly); free to members.

★5109★ GREAT LAKES UNITED (GLU)

Buffalo State College Cassety Hall
1300 Elmwood Ave
Buffalo, NY 14222
Web: www.glu.org
Phone: 716-886-0142; **Fax:** 716-886-0303; **Toll Free:** 800-846-0142
International coalition of environmental and outdoor sports organizations and individuals dedicated to preserving and restoring the Great Lakes-St. Lawrence River ecosystem. Develops and promotes effective policy initiatives, carries out education programs, and promotes citizen action and grassroots leadership. **Established:** 1982. **Members:** 170 organizations and 800 individuals. **Dues:** $35/year (individual membership). **Publications:** *GLU Newsletter* (quarterly); free to members.

★5110★ GREATER YELLOWSTONE COALITION (GYC)

13 S Willson Ave, Suite 2
PO Box 1874
Bozeman, MT 59715
Web: www.greateryellowstone.org
Phone: 406-586-1593; **Fax:** 406-556-2839; **Toll Free:** 800-775-1834
Dedicated to protecting and preserving the Greater Yellowstone ecosystem, the area including and surrounding Yellowstone and Grand Teton national parks in Wyoming, Idaho, and Montana. (see separate entries in national parks section). **Established:** 1983. **Members:** 13,000. **Dues:** $35/year. **Publications:** *Greater Yellowstone Report* (quarterly); free to members and

free online. Also publishes a wide range of other reports and studies on the Greater Yellowstone region.

★5111★ GREENPEACE CANADA

250 Dundas St W, Suite 605
Toronto,
Web: www.greenpeace.ca
Phone: 416-597-8408; **Fax:** 416-597-8422; **Toll Free:** 800-320-7183
Dedicated to ensuring the ability of the earth to nurture life in all its diversity. Greenpeace seeks to protect biodiversity in all its forms; promote peace, global disarmament, and nonviolence; prevent pollution and abuse of the earth's oceans, lands, and fresh water; and to end all nuclear threats. **Established:** 1971. **Members:** 73,000. **Dues:** Donations accepted.

★5112★ GREENPEACE USA

702 H St NW, Suite 300
Washington, DC 20001
Web: www.greenpeace.org
Phone: 202-462-1177; **Fax:** 202-462-4507; **Toll Free:** 800-326-0959
Dedicated to preserving the earth and the environment through direct nonviolent action. Works to protect the environment from nuclear and toxic pollution, to stop the threat of nuclear power and the production of nuclear weapons, to stop the threat of global warming, and to halt the slaughter of whales, dolphins, seals, and other endangered animals. **Established:** 1971. **Members:** 250,000. **Dues:** $30/year. **Publications:** *Greenpeace* (quarterly); free to members.

★5113★ GROUND WATER PROTECTION COUNCIL (GWPC)

13308 N MacArthur Blvd
Oklahoma City, OK 73142
Web: www.gwpc.org
Phone: 405-516-4972; **Fax:** 405-516-4973
National association of agencies, professionals, and corporations involved in ground water protection and underground disposal of drilling byproducts and other materials. Promotes the protection and conservation of ground water resources, recognizing ground water as a critical component of the ecosystem. **Established:** 1983. **Members:** 2,000. **Publications:** *Groundwater Communique. Groundwater Report to the Nation 2007.*

★5114★ HAWK MOUNTAIN SANCTUARY ASSOCIATION

1700 Hawk Mountain Rd
Kempton, PA 19529
Web: www.hawkmountain.org
Phone: 610-756-6961; **Fax:** 610-756-4468
Dedicated to the conservation of birds of prey and the central Appalachian environment through programs in education, research, and monitoring. Operates a visitor center and provides support for activities at the Hawk Mountain Sanctuary, founded in 1934 as the world's first sanctuary to protect birds of prey. **Established:** 1938. **Members:** 9,000. **Dues:** $35/year ($40/year

for families). **Publications:** *Hawk Mountain News* (biannually); free to members.

★5115★ **HELLS CANYON PRESERVATION COUNCIL**
105 Fir St Suite 327
PO Box 2768
La Grande, OR 97850
Web: www.hellscanyon.org
Phone: 541-963-3950; **Fax:** 541-963-0584
Works to protect and restore the Hells Canyon-Wallowa-Blue Mountain ecosystem in western Oregon and eastern Idaho. Goal is to achieve permanent federal protection for Hells Canyon and Blue Mountain. **Established:** 1965. **Members:** 2,400. **Dues:** $35/year. **Publications:** *Hells Canyon Falcon* (quarterly); free to members.

★5116★ **HERITAGE CANADA FOUNDATION**
5 Blackburn Ave
Ottawa,
Web: www.heritagecanada.org
Phone: 613-237-1066; **Fax:** 613-237-5987
Dedicated to the preservation and demonstration of the nationally significant historic, architectural, natural, and scenic heritage of Canada. Efforts directed to fostering and encouraging the understanding, promotion, and sustainable evolution of Canada's cultural landscape. **Established:** 1973. **Members:** 2,000 individuals and organizations. **Dues:** $35/year ($25/year for students). **Publications:** *Heritage Magazine* (quarterly); free to members.

★5117★ **HISTORIC NEW ENGLAND**
141 Cambridge St
Boston, MA 02114
Web: www.historicnewengland.org
Phone: 617-227-3956; **Fax:** 617-227-9204
Dedicated to protecting New England's cultural and architectural heritage. Operates 36 historic house museums in five New England states. Studies and interprets New England's daily life, architecture, and decorative arts between the mid-17th and 20th centuries. Maintains archives and a conservation center; conducts educational programs and leads historic tours. Also sponsors a helpline for homeowners' questions about preserving and maintaining their old houses. **Established:** 1910. **Members:** 3,000. **Dues:** $35/year. **Publications:** *Historic New England* (quarterly); free to members.

★5118★ **HOSTELLING INTERNATIONAL-AMERICAN YOUTH HOSTELS (HI-AYH)**
8401 Colesville Rd, Suite 600
Silver Spring, MD 20910
Web: www.hiusa.org
Phone: 301-495-1240; **Fax:** 301-495-6697
Promotes international understanding through its 80 low-cost, dormitory style youth hostels throughout the United States and through educational, cultural, and recreational travel programs. A member of the International Youth Hostel Federation, which operates nearly 4,000 hostels in 60 countries. **Established:** 1934. **Members:** 3 million Hostelling International members worldwide. **Dues:** $28/year for members age 18-54 (membership is free to youth under age 18 and $18/year for members over age 54). **Publications:** *USA Hostel Directory*; free to members and $3 for nonmembers.

★5119★ **ICE AGE PARK & TRAIL FOUNDATION**
306 East Wilson St, Lower Level
Madison, WI 53703
Web: www.iceagetrail.org
Phone: 608-663-8278; **Fax:** 608-663-1283; **Toll Free:** 800-227-0046
Works to protect, promote, build, and maintain the many segments of the Ice Age Trail - a 1000-mile national and state scenic trail located entirely in Wisconsin (see separate entry in national trails chapter). Sponsors hikes along the trail. **Established:** 1958. **Members:** 3,235. **Dues:** $30/year ($20 for students/seniors). **Publications:** *Mammoth Trails* (quarterly); free to members.

★5120★ **IDAHO CONSERVATION LEAGUE**
PO Box 844
Boise, ID 83701
Web: www.wildidaho.org
Phone: 208-345-6933; **Fax:** 208-344-0344; **Toll Free:** 877-645-6933
Seeks to preserve wild Idaho for future generations through citizen action, public education, and professional advocacy. **Established:** 1973. **Dues:** $30/year. **Publications:** *The Idaho Conservationist* (quarterly); free to members.

★5121★ **ILLINOIS ASSOCIATION OF PARK DISTRICTS (IAPD)**
211 E Monroe St
Springfield, IL 627011186
Web: ilparks.org
Phone: 217-523-4554; **Fax:** 217-523-4273
Park, forest, and conservation districts and recreation agencies dedicated to the conservation of natural and human resources, and the preservation of Illinois' environment. Provides legal assistance, conducts research, holds seminars, and raises public awareness to create favorable attitudes about parks, recreation, and conservation. **Established:** 1928. **Members:** $125/year. **Publications:** *Illinois Parks and Recreation Magazine* (bimonthly). *Membership Directory and Buyers' Guide* (annually).

★5122★ **ILLINOIS WILDLIFE FEDERATION**
2216 Troy Rd, Suite 294
Edwardsville, IL 62025
Web: www.illinoiswildlife.org
Devoted to advancing the cause of state conservation in all areas, including outdoor recreation, natural resources management, environmental education, enhancement of fish and wildlife populations, and prevention of environmental degradation. **Established:** 1946. **Dues:** $15/year. **Publications:** *Illinois Wildlife* (bimonthly); free to members.

★5123★ INTERNATIONAL ASSOCIATION OF FISH & WILDLIFE AGENCIES (IAFWA)
444 N Capitol St NW, Suite 725
Washington, DC 20001
Web: www.iafwa.org
Phone: 202-624-7890; **Fax:** 202-624-7891
Agencies, organizations, and individuals engaged in the conservation of fish and wildlife resources in the United States, Canada, and Mexico. Works to cultivate friendly relations and mutual understanding among officials engaged in natural resources conservation. Encourages rational management of fish and wildlife resources. Promotes public understanding and appreciation of the importance of conserving natural resources. **Established:** 1902. **Members:** 350. **Dues:** $25/year. **Publications:** *Fish and Wildlife Focus* (bimonthly); free online newsletter.

★5124★ INTERNATIONAL ASSOCIATION OF WILDLAND FIRE (IAWF)
PO Box 261
Hot Springs, SD 577470261
Web: www.iawfonline.org
Phone: 605-890-2348
Nonprofit association of the global wildland fire professionals; facilitates communication and provides leadership for the wildland fire community. Maintains library of literature on wildland fire. **Established:** 1991. **Members:** 1,200. **Dues:** $60/year for individuals ($25/year for students); beginning rate of $75/year for organizations/corporations. **Publications:** *Wildfire Magazine* (bimonthly); free to members and $52 for nonmembers. *International Journal of Wildland Fire* (bimonthly); $100 for members and $150 for nonmembers. Also publishes a range of other studies and reports.

★5125★ INTERNATIONAL FUND FOR ANIMAL WELFARE (IFAW)
411 Main St
PO Box 193
Yarmouth Port, MA 02675
Web: www.ifaw.org
Phone: 508-744-2000; **Fax:** 508-744-2009; **Toll Free:** 800-932-4329
Works to improve the welfare of wild and domestic animals throughout the world by reducing commercial exploitation of animals, protecting wildlife habitats, and assisting animals in distress. Seeks to motivate the public to prevent cruelty to animals and to promote animal welfare and conservation policies that advance the well-being of both animals and people. **Established:** 1969. **Dues:** Donations accepted. **Publications:** *IFAW Newsletter* (quarterly); free to members and free online. Also publishes a wide range of other reports.

★5126★ INTERNATIONAL MOUNTAIN BICYCLING ASSOCIATION (IMBA)
207 Canyon Blvd Suite 301
PO Box 7578
Boulder, CO 80306
Web: www.imba.com
Phone: 303-545-9011; **Fax:** 303-545-9026; **Toll Free:** 888-442-4622
Works to keep trails open for mountain bikes by encouraging responsible riding, supporting volunteer trail work, and promoting cooperation among trail users. **Established:** 1988. **Members:** 32,000. **Dues:** $25/year ($75/year for families). **Publications:** *IMBA Trail News* (bimonthly); free to members.

★5127★ INTERNATIONAL SOCIETY FOR THE PROTECTION OF MUSTANGS & BURROS (ISPMB)
PO Box 55
Lantry, SD 57636
Web: www.ispmb.org
Phone: 605-964-6866; **Fax:** 605-365-6991
Seeks to protect wild horses and burros by encouraging enforcement of existing protective laws and assisting in the development of new laws to protect wild horses and burros and their habitat. Sponsors educational programs to increase appreciation and understanding. Fosters cooperative efforts with government agencies for the benefit of wild horses and burros. **Established:** 1960. **Members:** 1,000. **Dues:** $35/year ($15/year for youth, $25/year for seniors). **Publications:** *Wild Horse and Burro Diary*; free to members, $35/year for nonmembers.

★5128★ INTERNATIONAL SOCIETY OF TROPICAL FORESTERS (ISTF)
5400 Grosvenor Ln
Bethesda, MD 20814
Web: www.istf-bethesda.org
Phone: 301-897-8720; **Fax:** 301-897-3690; **Toll Free:** 866-897-8720
Transfers technology and science information to those concerned with the effective management, ecological protection, and sustainable use of tropical forests. Plans conferences, workshops, and symposia in cooperation with other conservation and natural resource organizations. **Established:** 1950. **Dues:** $25/year ($10/year for students). **Publications:** *ISTF News* (English-language quarterly); free to members. *ISTF Noticias* (Spanish-language quarterly); free to members.

★5129★ INTERNATIONAL WILDLIFE COALITION (IWC)
70 E Falmouth Hwy
East Falmouth, MA 02536
Web: www.iwc.org
Phone: 508-457-1898; **Fax:** 508-457-1898
Works to protect wildlife and wildlife habitats. Dedicated to returning stranded whales and dolphins to the water, studying whales at sea, providing emergency care to marine mammals, and protecting the ocean environment. Conducts a Whale Adoption Program. The International Wildlife Coalition is legally constituted in four countries: the United States, Canada, the United Kingdom, and Brazil. **Established:** 1984.

★5130★ ISLAND NATURE TRUST
PO Box 265
Charlottetown,
Web: www.peisland.com/nature
Phone: 902-566-9150; **Fax:** 902-628-6331

Dedicated to the protection and management of natural areas on Prince Edward Island. Focuses on acquiring lands and waterways in order to protect plants and animals, and developing management plans designed to maintain and enhance the well-being of life systems under the care of the Trust. **Established:** 1979. **Members:** 400. **Dues:** $10/year ($15/year family). **Publications:** *Update* (quarterly); free.

★5131★ **IZAAK WALTON LEAGUE OF AMERICA (IWLA)**
707 Conservation Ln
Gaithersburg, MD 20878
Web: www.iwla.org
Phone: 301-548-0150; **Fax:** 301-548-0146; **Toll Free:** 800-453-5463
Dedicated to protecting and enjoying the nation's soil, air, woods, waters, and wildlife. Promotes citizen involvement in environmental protection and educates the public about natural resource threats. Maintains specific programs devoted to wilderness, sustainability, agriculture, clean water, and outdoor ethics. 300 chapters nationwide. **Established:** 1922. **Members:** 50,000. **Dues:** $36/year ($54/year for families). **Publications:** *Outdoor America* (quarterly); free to members.

★5132★ **LAND TRUST ALLIANCE (LTA)**
1331 H St NW, Suite 400
Washington, DC 200054734
Web: www.lta.org
Phone: 202-638-4725; **Fax:** 202-638-4730
Promotes voluntary land conservation and protects important land resources for public benefit. Ensures that land trusts have the information, skills, and resources they need to save land. **Established:** 1982. **Members:** 1,300. **Dues:** $35/year. **Publications:** *Exchange* (quarterly); free to members. *Landscape* (quarterly); free to members and $35 for nonmembers.

★5133★ **LEAGUE OF CONSERVATION VOTERS**
1920 L St NW, Suite 800
Washington, DC 20036
Web: www.lcv.org
Phone: 202-785-8683; **Fax:** 202-835-0491
Works to influence the U.S. Congress to be more supportive of environmental issues. Monitors and reports on the environmental voting records of members of Congress. **Established:** 1970. **Dues:** $25/year (full membership); $10/year (basic membership). **Publications:** *National Environmental Scorecard* (annually); free to members. *LCV Newsletter* (quarterly); free to members.

★5134★ **LEAGUE TO SAVE LAKE TAHOE**
955 Emerald Bay Rd
South Lake Tahoe, CA 96150
Web: www.keeptahoeblue.org
Phone: 530-541-5388; **Fax:** 530-541-5454
Dedicated to the protection and restoration of Lake Tahoe and its surrounding basin. **Established:** 1957. **Members:** 4,000.

Dues: $50/year. **Publications:** *Keep Tahoe Blue News* (quarterly); free to members and free online.

★5135★ **LEAVE NO TRACE CENTER FOR OUTDOOR ETHICS INC**
PO Box 997
Boulder, CO 80306
Web: www.lnt.org
Phone: 303-442-8222; **Fax:** 303-442-8217; **Toll Free:** 800-332-4100
National, non-profit organization dedicated to promoting and inspiring responsible outdoor recreation through education, research and partnerships. **Established:** 1994. **Dues:** $35/year. **Publications:** *Tracker* (quarterly newsletter).

★5136★ **LEWIS & CLARK TRAIL HERITAGE FOUNDATION**
PO Box 3434
600 Central Ave., Suite 327
Great Falls, MT 59403
Web: www.lewisandclark.org
Phone: 406-454-1234; **Fax:** 406-771-9237; **Toll Free:** 888-701-3434
Promotes public appreciation of the contributions made to America's heritage by the Lewis and Clark expedition of 1804-1806, and to preserving the Lewis and Clark experience. Supports the 3,700-mile Lewis and Clark National Historic Trail (see separate entry in national trails section), which runs from Wood River, Illinois along the Missouri River to the Pacific Ocean. Provides assistance, including modest monetary grants, to groups or organizations along the trail wishing to interpret an aspect of the Lewis and Clark story. Supports scholarship, research, and encourages historical accuracy in the popular media. **Established:** 1969. **Members:** 3,500. **Dues:** $49/year ($30/year for students). **Publications:** *The Orderly Report* (quarterly); free to members.

★5137★ **LONERS ON WHEELS (LOW)**
1795 O'Kelley Rd SE
Deming, NM 88030
Web: www.lonersonwheels.com
Phone: 505-546-4058; **Fax:** 505-546-6542
Social organization for singles who are interested in travel, the outdoors, camping, and/or the recreational vehicle (RV) lifestyle. Plans camping trips, rallies, and other activities for members. Includes 10 regional groups and 58 local groups. Owns its own RV park in Deming, New Mexico. **Established:** 1969. **Members:** 2,800. **Dues:** $45 per year (plus a one-time fee of $5). **Publications:** *Loners on Wheels Newsletter* (monthly); free to members. *Directory* (annual); members: $5.

★5138★ **MANITOBA NATURALISTS SOCIETY (MNS)**
63 Albert St, Suite 401
Winnipeg,
Web: www.manitobanature.ca
Phone: 204-943-9029
Dedicated to preserving the natural environment by fostering

public awareness and appreciation. Sponsors field trips, educational programs, and recreational activities (such as canoeing, snowshoeing, and cross-country skiing outings). Brings together Manitobans who share concern for the well-being of the province's natural areas and wildlife. **Established:** 1920. **Members:** 1,300. **Dues:** $40/year ($20/year for students, $35/year for seniors, $55 for families). **Publications:** *MNS Bulletin* (10x/year); free to members and online.

★5139★ **MICHIGAN UNITED CONSERVATION CLUBS (MUCC)**
PO Box 30235
Lansing, MI 48909
Web: www.mucc.org
Phone: 517-371-1041; **Fax:** 517-371-1505; **Toll Free:** 800-777-6720
Dedicated to protecting Michigan's outdoor heritage through the conservation of natural resources and by promoting the right of all citizens to enjoy Michigan's outdoor recreational offerings. **Established:** 1937. **Members:** 100,000. **Dues:** $25/year. **Publications:** *Michigan Out-of-Doors* (monthly); free to members and $25/year for non-members.

★5140★ **MIDWEST ASSOCIATION OF FISH & WILDLIFE AGENCIES**
Wisconsin Department of Natural Resources
107 Sutliff Ave
Rhinelander, WI 54501
Web: mafwa.iafwa.org
Phone: 715-365-8924; **Fax:** 715-365-8932
Fish and game commissioners and directors throughout midwestern states and three Canadian provinces. Gathers and disseminates information, exchanges ideas, and cooperates in all matters of administration and investigation pertinent to the protection, preservation, restoration, and management of fish and wildlife in the Midwest. **Established:** 1934. **Members:** 17. **Dues:** $300/year per state; $100/year per province.

★5141★ **MISSION: WOLF**
PO Box 211
Silver Cliff, CO 81252
Web: www.missionwolf.com
Phone: 719-859-2157
A non-profit educational facility and refuge for captive-born wolves and wolf-dog hybrids. Goal is to educate the public that wolves and wolf-dogs do not make suitable pets. Supports wild wolf recovery and habitat preservation. Offers tours of the refuge and traveling educational programs. **Established:** 1988.

★5142★ **MONTANA WILDERNESS ASSOCIATION (MWA)**
324 Fuller St
PO Box 635
Helena, MT 59624
Web: www.wildmontana.org
Phone: 406-443-7350; **Fax:** 406-443-0750

Protects and preserves Montana's remaining wildlands and naturally functioning ecosystems. MWA has seven active chapters across the state which offer educational programs and organize conservation efforts. MWA also has field organizers who work closely with the chapters and communities to develop grassroots support for important conservation issues and campaigns. Sponsors annual Wilderness Walks program to introduce hikers to the great diversity of wildlands in Montana. **Established:** 1958. **Members:** 5,000. **Dues:** $20/year. **Publications:** *Wild Montana* (quarterly); free to members and online.

★5143★ **MORMON TRAILS ASSOCIATION**
4681 W Villa View Dr, Unit C
West Valley City, UT 84120
Web: www.mormontrails.org
Phone: 801-538-6983
Dedicated to promoting communication among private and public agencies and individuals having interests relating to the Mormon Pioneer National Historic Trail (see separate entry in national trails section). Identifies and preserves Mormon historical sites, including trails and locations where historical events occurred. Sponsors four lecture meetings a year, with speakers on Mormon Trail history, locations, events, and journals. Assists in the development of the trail as administered by the National Park Service and promotes interest in the Trail. **Established:** 1991. **Members:** 650. **Dues:** $10/year. **Publications:** *Mormon Pioneer Trail Guide*; $6.

★5144★ **MOUNT RUSHMORE NATIONAL MEMORIAL SOCIETY**
825 Saint Joseph St Suite 300
PO Box 1524
Rapid City, SD 57709
Web: www.mountrushmoresociety.com
Phone: 605-341-8883; **Fax:** 605-341-8883
Cooperates with the National Park Service in supporting plans for preservation and improvements of Mount Rushmore and its visitor facilities. Promotes and assists in the historical, artistic, scientific, educational, and interpretive activities of Mount Rushmore. (See separate entry on Mount Rushmore National Memorial in national parks chapter.) **Established:** 1930. **Members:** 300. **Dues:** $500/lifetime membership ($700/lifetime membership for couples). **Publications:** *Newsletter* (quarterly); free online.

★5145★ **MOUNTAIN LION FOUNDATION**
PO Box 1896
Sacramento, CA 95812
Web: www.mountainlion.org
Phone: 916-442-2666; **Fax:** 916-442-2871; **Toll Free:** 800-319-7621
A conservation and education organization dedicated to protecting the mountain lion and its habitat in California and across the West. Seeks to preserve the cougar as a viable species — via habitat conservation, research, livestock protection, management, and education — in the hope that the cougars' success will assure the survival of other species. **Established:** 1986.

Members: 35,000. **Dues:** $35/year. **Publications:** *MLF Review* (quarterly); free to members.

★5146★ NATIONAL ALLIANCE OF PRESERVATION COMMISSIONS
325 S Lumpkin St
Founders Garden House
Athens, GA 30602
Web: www.uga.edu/sed/pso/programs/napc/napc.htm
Phone: 706-542-4731; **Fax:** 706-583-0320
National network of local preservation, historic district, and landmark commissions and boards of architectural review. Seeks to build strong local historic preservation programs throughout the United States through education, advocacy, and training. Also supports protection of historic districts and landmarks through local legislation. Maintains an information resource center. **Established:** 1983. **Members:** 600. **Dues:** $35/year for commissions with a budget under $500 or local nonprofit organizations. Sliding scale of dues for larger commissions, nonprofit organizations, and communities. **Publications:** *The Alliance Review* (bimonthly); free to members.

★5147★ NATIONAL ARBOR DAY FOUNDATION
100 Arbor Ave
Nebraska City, NE 68410
Web: www.arborday.org
Phone: 402-474-5655; **Fax:** 402-474-0820; **Toll Free:** 888-448-7337
Nonprofit education organization dedicated to tree planting and environmental stewardship. Encourages the celebration of Arbor Day, a tree planting event held annually across the United States. Each year the Foundation distributes millions of trees, fosters tree-care education, and works to help reforest fire-ravaged national forests lands. **Established:** 1972. **Members:** 800,000. **Dues:** $15/year (introductory membership). **Publications:** *Arbor Day* (bimonthly); free to members. *The Tree Book*; free to members.

★5148★ NATIONAL ASSOCIATION OF CONSERVATION DISTRICTS (NACD)
509 Capitol Ct NE
Washington, DC 20002
Web: www.nacdnet.org
Phone: 202-547-6223; **Fax:** 202-547-6450
National voice for America's 3,000 local conservation districts. Serves member districts in conservation, development, and prudent use of natural resources. Works to increase awareness of the critical need for conservation of soil and water resources. **Established:** 1946. **Members:** 3,000 conservation districts. **Dues:** $35/year. **Publications:** *NACD News & Views* (bimonthly); free to members.

★5149★ NATIONAL ASSOCIATION OF COUNTY PARK & RECREATION OFFICIALS (NACPRO)
22377 Belmont Ridge Rd
Ashburn, VA 20148
Web: www.nacpro.org
Phone: 703-858-0784; **Fax:** 703-858-0794

Advocate for parks, recreational facilities, and environmental conservation efforts that enhance the quality of life for communities across the country. **Established:** 1964. **Members:** 22,000. **Dues:** $55/year for citizens; $130/year for professionals. Discounted memberships available to seniors and students.

★5150★ NATIONAL ASSOCIATION FOR OLMSTED PARKS
1111 16th St NW, Suite 310
Washington, DC 20036
Web: www.olmsted.org
Phone: 202-223-9113; **Fax:** 202-223-9112; **Toll Free:** 866-666-6905
Coalition of park advocates, landscape architects, planners, historians, conservationists, and civic leaders committed to preserving the landscape heritage of Frederick Law Olmstead, the original landscape architect. Olmsted designed more than 100 public park grounds, including Central Park in New York City, as well as some 200 private estates, 50 residential communities, and 40 academic campuses. NAOP offers support, advice, and information for the preservation of Olmsted's historic landscapes. **Established:** 1980. **Members:** 350. **Dues:** $35/year. **Publications:** *Field Notes* (quarterly); free to members.

★5151★ NATIONAL ASSOCIATION OF STATE FORESTERS (NASF)
444 N Capitol St NW, Suite 540
Washington, DC 20001
Web: www.stateforesters.org
Phone: 202-624-5415; **Fax:** 202-624-5407
Represents the directors of the forestry agencies of the 50 states, eight U.S. territories, and the District of Columbia. Promotes cooperation among the states and territories and develops and promotes legislation, programs, and activities that will advance forest stewardship and use of forest resources. **Established:** 1920. **Members:** 59 (directors from all 50 states and 9 territories).

★5152★ NATIONAL ASSOCIATION OF STATE OUTDOOR RECREATION LIAISON OFFICERS (NASORLO)
3116 Woodbrook Pl
Boise, ID 83706
Phone: 208-384-5421
Organization of state officials working together for quality recreation through administration of the Land and Water Conservation Fund. Seeks to improve practices, programs, and management of outdoor recreation. **Established:** 1967. **Members:** 59 (officials from 50 states and 9 territories).

★5153★ NATIONAL ASSOCIATION OF STATE PARK DIRECTORS (NASPD)
8829 Woodyhill Rd
Raleigh, NC 27613
Web: naspd.org
Phone: 919-676-8365
Seeks to promote and advance the state park systems of Ameirca.

Mission is to provide a common forum for the exchange of information about state park programs; to present a united position on issues affecting state park programs; and to encourage the development of leadership in the administration of state park programs. **Established:** 1962. **Members:** 50. **Publications:** Annual research reports and statistical abstracts.

★5154★ NATIONAL AUDUBON SOCIETY (NAS)
700 Broadway
New York, NY 10003
Web: www.audubon.org
Phone: 212-979-3000; **Fax:** 212-979-3188
Coordinates the efforts of scientists, activists, lobbyists, educators, and naturalists into a program of environmental effectiveness. Fights for the protection of wildlife and its habitat, forests, and endangered species. Sponsors Audubon Adventures, a program aimed at teaching children environmental awareness. Maintains an activist network for members who pledge to contact their congressperson on environmental issues. **Established:** 1905. **Members:** 550,000. **Dues:** $20/year. **Publications:** *Audubon* (bimonthly); free to members, $20/year for nonmembers.

★5155★ NATIONAL CAVES ASSOCIATION
PO Box 280
Park City, KY 42160
Web: www.cavern.com
Phone: 270-749-2228; **Fax:** 270-749-2428; **Toll Free:** 866-552-2837
Organization of publicly and privately owned cave and caverns developed for public visitation. Members conform to standards of operation and offer regularly scheduled tours. Affiliated with American Cave Conservation Association (see separate entry). **Established:** 1965. **Dues:** $300-700/year. **Publications:** *NCA Cave Talk* (quarterly); free to members. *Caves & Caverns Directory* (annually); free.

★5156★ NATIONAL CENTER FOR RECREATION & CONSERVATION
c/o National Park Service
1201 Eye St NW 9th Fl
Washington, DC 20005
Web: www.nps.gov/ncrc
Phone: 202-354-6900; **Fax:** 202-371-5179
Serves as the National Park Service's focal point for working with a variety of public and private partners in providing close-to-home recreation opportunities throughout the nation. Provides leadership and support for nationally designated scenic and historic trails. The Center accomplishes its mission through an array of technical and financial assistance programs, advocacy, and interagency coordination. Programs include Rivers, Trails & Conservation Assistance Program, Land and Water Conservation Fund Program, National Trails System, Urban Park and Recreation Recovery Program, Federal Lands to Parks Program, and Partnership for Wild and Scenic Rivers.

★5157★ NATIONAL CONFERENCE OF STATE HISTORIC PRESERVATION OFFICERS
444 N Capitol St NW, Suite 342
Washington, DC 200011512
Web: www.ncshpo.org
Phone: 202-624-5465; **Fax:** 202-624-5419
National voice for historic preservation officers in each of the states, territories, and the District of Columbia. Acts as a forum for the exchange of information and techniques pertaining to the administration of state and federal historic and cultural preservation programs. Assists in researching and developing historic preservation programs. Works to increase public support for historic preservation. **Established:** 1969. **Members:** 59 (officers from 50 states and 9 territories). **Publications:** *NCSHPO News* (quarterly); free to members.

★5158★ NATIONAL FISH & WILDLIFE FOUNDATION
1120 Connecticut Ave NW, Suite 900
Washington, DC 20036
Web: www.nfwf.org
Phone: 202-857-0166; **Fax:** 202-857-0162
Conserves healthy populations of fish, wildlife and plants, on land and in the sea, by awarding matching grants to projects benefiting conservation education, habitat protection and restoration, and natural resource management. **Established:** 1984.

★5159★ NATIONAL FOREST FOUNDATION
27 Fort Missoula Rd, Bldg 27 Suite 3
Missoula, MT 59804
Web: www.natlforests.org
Phone: 406-542-2805; **Fax:** 406-542-2810; **Toll Free:** 866-733-4633
Engage in community-based and national programs that promote the health and public enjoyment of the National Forest System and administers private gifts of funds and land for the benefit of the National Forests. **Established:** 1990. **Members:** 160 partner organizations. **Dues:** $25/year. **Publications:** *Mosaic* (newsletter) and annual report.

★5160★ NATIONAL FOREST RECREATION ASSOCIATION (NFRA)
PO Box 488
Woodlake, CA 93286
Web: www.nfra.org
Phone: 559-564-2365; **Fax:** 559-564-2048
Represents and serves as an advocate for businesses offering recreational opportunities on federal lands and waters. **Established:** 1948. **Members:** 70 full members. **Dues:** $250/year (sliding scale depending on revenue and category of membership). **Publications:** *National Forest Recreation Association Newsletter* (quarterly); free online.

NATIONAL HERITAGE AREAS PROGRAM
(See Section 7 of this directory for information on the National Heritage Areas Program and descriptive listings of the heritage areas.)

NATIONAL MARINE SANCTUARIES PROGRAM
(See Section 6 of this directory for information on the National Marine Sanctuaries Program and descriptive listings of the national marine sanctuarie

★5161★ NATIONAL MARINE SANCTUARY FOUNDATION
8601 Georgia Ave, Suite 501
Silver Spring, MD 20910
Web: www.nmsfocean.org
Phone: 301-608-3040; **Fax:** 301-608-3044
Non-profit organization that assists the federally managed National Marine Sanctuary Program with education and outreach programs designed to preserve, protect and promote opportunities for public interaction with the nation's marine sanctuaries. **Dues:** $50-250 (Friend level of membership). **Publications:** Sanctuary Watch (quarterly newsletter, free to members), Encyclopedia of the National Marine Sanctuaries (online guide), New Ocean Users Handbook (online guide).

★5162★ NATIONAL PARK FOUNDATION (NPF)
11 Dupont Cir NW, Suite 600
Washington, DC 20036
Web: www.nationalparks.org
Phone: 202-238-4200; **Fax:** 202-234-3103
The official, private foundation of the National Park Service. Donations of money, land, buildings, and artifacts are channeled by the foundation into national parks to support education and preservation programs. **Established:** 1967. **Publications:** Newsletter (3x/year); free.

NATIONAL PARK SERVICE
(See Section 1 of this directory for information on the National Park Service and descriptive listings of all the national parks and affiliated areas.)

★5163★ NATIONAL PARK SERVICE RESERVATION CENTER
12501 Willowbrook Rd
Cumberland, MD 21502
Web: reservations.nps.gov
Phone: 800-365-2267; **Fax:** 301-784-9079

★5164★ NATIONAL PARK TRUST (NPT)
51 Monroe St, Suite 110
Rockville, MD 20850
Web: www.parktrust.org
Phone: 301-279-7275; **Fax:** 301-279-7211
Seeks to preserve the integrity of America's natural, historic, and cultural resources. Secures privately owned land in and around existing parks and acquires land to create new parks. **Established:** 1983. **Dues:** Donations accepted **Publications:** National Park Trust News; (3x/yr) free to members.

★5165★ NATIONAL PARKS CONSERVATION ASSOCIATION (NPCA)
1300 19th St NW, Suite 300
Washington, DC 20036
Web: www.npca.org
Phone: 202-223-6722; **Fax:** 202-659-0650; **Toll Free:** 800-628-7275
Membership organization dedicated to preserving and protecting the national parks while instilling an appreciation and understanding of all parklands. Major programs areas include park resource protection, visitor experience, park funding and management, and public advocacy. Maintains eight regional offices across the country. **Established:** 1919. **Members:** 300,000. **Dues:** $15/year. **Publications:** National Parks (quarterly); free to members.

★5166★ NATIONAL PONY EXPRESS ASSOCIATION
PO Box 236
Pollock Pines, CA 95726
Dedicated to the preservation of the Pony Express National Historic Trail (see separate entry in national trails section) and to recognizing the history of the Pony Express (1860-1861) as a significant episode in the development of the American West. A reenactment of the 1,966-mile trip is held annually in June. Maintains eight state divisions (California, Colorado, Kansas, Missouri, Nebraska, Nevada, Utah, and Wyoming). **Established:** 1978. **Members:** 800. **Dues:** $10/year (national) plus state dues. **Publications:** California division of association publishes regular online newsletter.

★5167★ NATIONAL RECREATION & PARK ASSOCIATION (NPRA)
22377 Belmont Ridge Rd
Ashburn, VA 20148
Web: www.nrpa.org
Phone: 703-858-0784; **Fax:** 703-858-0794; **Toll Free:** 800-626-6772
Promotes the importance of parks, recreation, and leisure services. Provides professional development opportunities to individuals who work in parks and leisure services. Holds an annual Congress which gathers professionals in the field to discuss products, ideas, and activities that pertain to the preservation of parks and improving recreational activities throughout the country. NRPA consists of ten branches/sections and maintains regional offices in California, Colorado, Connecticut, Illinois, and Georgia. **Established:** 1965. **Members:** 23,000. **Dues:** $35/year. **Publications:** Parks & Recreation (monthly); free to members and $36/year for nonmembers. Journal of Leisure Research (quarterly); $40 for members, $55 for nonmembers. Also publishes an electronic newsletter for members.

★5168★ NATIONAL RECREATION RESERVATION SERVICE

PO Box 140
Ballston Spa, NY 12020
Web: www.recreation.gov
; **Toll Free:** 877-444-6777
Public reservation service for cabins, campsites, and day-use facilities at Forest Service, Army Corps of Engineers, National Park Service, Bureau of Land Management, and Bureau of Reclamation outdoor recreation facilities. Provides reservation options for 45,000 facilities at 1,700 locations across the United States. Also integrating facilities of the National Park Service into the reservation service.

★5169★ NATIONAL RECREATIONAL VEHICLE OWNERS CLUB (NRVOC)

PO Box 520
Jack's Branch Road
Gonzalez, FL 32560
Web: www.nrvoc.com
; **Toll Free:** 800-281-9186
Provides information to those who own or use recreational vehicles (RVs). Seeks to introduce others to the RV lifestyle and provide resource to RV-related businesses. **Established:** 1983. **Members:** 38,000. **Dues:** $29/year. **Publications:** *The Recreation Advisor* (periodic); free to members. *On the Line UPDate* (annually); free to commercial members.

★5170★ NATIONAL REGISTER OF HISTORIC PLACES

c/o National Park Service
1201 Eye St NW 8th Fl
Washington, DC 20005
Web: www.cr.nps.gov/nr
Phone: 202-354-2213
The National Historic Preservation Act of 1966 authorized the National Register to coordinate and support public and private efforts to identify, evaluate, and protect our historical and cultural resources. Properties listed in the Register include districts, sites, buildings, structures, and objects that are significant in American history, architecture, archeology, engineering, and culture. Maintained by the National Park Service, the *National Register of Historic Places* is the nation's official list of historic properties worth preserving. Approximate 80,000 historic buildings, structures, sites, objects, and districts have been listed on the National Register, including 2,400 National Historic Landmarks. **Publications:** Wide range of publications on historic places and landmarks across the United States.

NATIONAL SCENIC BYWAYS PROGRAM

(See Section 8 of this directory for information on the National Scenic Byways Program and descriptive listings of the national byways.)

★5171★ NATIONAL SOCIETY FOR PARK RESOURCES (NSPR)

c/o National Recreation & Park Assn
22377 Belmont Ridge Rd
Ashburn, VA 20148
Phone: 703-858-0784; **Fax:** 703-858-0794; **Toll Free:** 800-626-6772

Park, forest, and natural resource professionals concerned with planning, maintaining, interpreting, and administering national, historic, and cultural resources. A branch of the National Park & Recreation Association. **Established:** 1971. **Members:** 1,000. **Publications:** *Parks and Recreation* (monthly); free to members and $36/year for nonmembers.

NATIONAL TRAILS SYSTEM

(See Section 5 of this directory for descriptive information on the national scenic and historic trails that comprise the National Trails System.)

★5172★ NATIONAL TRUST FOR HISTORIC PRESERVATION

1785 Massachusetts Ave NW
Washington, DC 20036
Web: www.nationaltrust.org
Phone: 202-588-6000; **Fax:** 202-588-6038; **Toll Free:** 800-944-6847
Committed to fostering an appreciation of America's cultural heritage and to preserving America's historic environments through education, grant and loan programs, preservation assistance, advocacy, and litigation. Maintains six regional offices and 28 historic sites across the country. **Established:** 1949. **Members:** 270,000. **Dues:** $20/year ($30/year for families). **Publications:** *Preservation* (bimonthly); free to members.

★5173★ NATIONAL WILDLIFE FEDERATION (NWF)

11100 Wildlife Center Dr
Reston, VA 20190
Web: www.nwf.org
Phone: 703-438-6000; **Fax:** 703-438-3570; **Toll Free:** 800-822-9919
Seeks to educate, inspire, and assist individuals and organizations of diverse cultures to conserve wildlife and other natural resources and to protect the earth's environment to achieve a peaceful, equitable, and sustainable future. **Established:** 1936. **Members:** 4 million. **Dues:** $30/year. **Publications:** *National Wildlife* (bimonthly); free to members. Also publishes three children's magazines: *Your Big Back Yard* (monthly); $20/year. *Ranger Rick* (monthly); $20/year. *Wild Animal Baby* (10x a year); $20/year.

★5174★ NATIONAL WILDLIFE REFUGE ASSOCIATION (NWRA)

1901 Pennsylvania Ave, Suite 407
Washington, DC 20006
Web: www.refugenet.org
Phone: 202-333-9075; **Fax:** 202-333-9077; **Toll Free:** 877-396-6972
Dedicated to the protection and expansion of the National Wildlife Refuge System. Monitors legislation affecting wildlife refuges. Conducts education and information programs on the system. (See Section 4 of this directory for information on the U.S. Fish and Wildlife Service and descriptive listings of the national wildlife refuges.) **Established:** 1975. **Members:** 1,650 paying

members (9,500 with free membership). **Dues:** $25/year. **Publications:** *Blue Goose Flyer* (quarterly); free to members.

★5175★ NATIVE AMERICAN RIGHTS FUND (NARF)
1506 Broadway St
Boulder, CO 80302
Web: www.narf.org
Phone: 303-447-8760; **Fax:** 303-443-7776
Dedicated to preserving tribal existence and protecting tribal natural resources. Promotes human rights and educates the public about Indian rights, laws, and issues. Provides legal representation and technical assistance to Indian tribes, organizations, and individuals nationwide. NARF also maintains a law library that offers reference and research assistance to the public. **Established:** 1970. **Dues:** $25/year. **Publications:** *JUSTICE Newsletter* (biannually); free. *NARF Legal Review* (biannually); free.

★5176★ NATURAL AREAS ASSOCIATION (NAA)
PO Box 1504
Bend, OR 97709
Web: www.naturalarea.org
Phone: 541-317-0199; **Fax:** 541-317-0140
Dedicated to the preservation of natural diversity. Works to inform, unite, and support persons engaged in identifying, protecting, managing, and studying natural areas and biological diversity. **Established:** 1978. **Members:** 2,000. **Dues:** $40/year ($20/year for students, $25/year for seniors); varying corporate/institutional rates. **Publications:** *Natural Areas Journal* (quarterly); free to members. *Natural Areas News* (quarterly); free to members.

★5177★ NATURAL RESOURCES COUNCIL OF AMERICA (NRCA)
1616 P St, Suite 340
Washington, DC 20036
Web: www.naturalresourcescouncil.org
Phone: 202-232-6531
More than 85 national and regional organizations concerned with conservation and sound management of the nation's natural resources. Promotes the adoption of public policies to further protect the environment. **Established:** 1946. **Members:** 85 organizations and 100 individuals. **Dues:** Organization dues based on operating budget; $125/year for individuals. **Publications:** *NRCA News* (bimonthly); free to members.

★5178★ NATURAL RESOURCES DEFENSE COUNCIL (NRDC)
40 W 20th St
New York, NY 10011
Web: www.nrdc.org
Phone: 212-727-2700; **Fax:** 212-727-1773
Seeks to preserve air, water, and land and to protect public health through litigation, advocacy, and research. Maintains regional offices in Los Angeles, San Francisco, and Washington, DC. **Established:** 1970. **Members:** 1.2 million members and online activists. **Dues:** $10/year. **Publications:** *Nature's Voice* (bimonthly); free online. *OnEarth* (quarterly); free online.

★5179★ NATURE CANADA
85 Albert St, Suite 900
Ottawa,
Web: www.naturecanada.ca
Phone: 613-562-3447; **Fax:** 613-562-3371; **Toll Free:** 800-267-4088
Committed to protecting nature, its diversity, and the processes that sustain it. Promotes a healthy interaction between humans and the natural environment and encourages individuals to be environmentally responsible in everyday life. **Established:** 1939. **Members:** 40,000. **Dues:** $35/year. **Publications:** *Nature Canada* (2x/year); free to members. *Nature Matters* (5x/year); free to members. *Nature in your Backyard* (special edition magazine); free to members. *Grass n' Roots (annually); free to members.*

★5180★ NATURE CONSERVANCY
4245 N Fairfax Dr, Suite 100
Arlington, VA 22203
Web: nature.org
Phone: 703-841-5300; **Fax:** 703-841-1283; **Toll Free:** 800-628-6860
Dedicated to protecting land where endangered species and threatened ecosystems exist. Purchases land to provide protected habitat for endangered plants and animals and negotiates sustainable land use practices with private and corporate landowners. Maintains operations in all 50 states and 30 countries. **Established:** 1951. **Members:** 1,000,000. **Dues:** $25/year. **Publications:** *Nature Conservancy* (quarterly); available to members ($50 level). *Landmarks* (quarterly); available to members ($25 level).

★5181★ NATURE CONSERVANCY OF CANADA
110 Eglinton Ave W, Suite 400
Toronto,
Web: www.natureconservancy.ca
Phone: 416-932-3202; **Fax:** 416-932-3208; **Toll Free:** 800-465-0029
Works to protect Canada's threatened natural habitats. Since its establishment, the Conservancy has secured more than 1.9 million acres of woodlands, seashores, wetlands, prairies, and other natural places. **Established:** 1962. **Members:** 35,000. **Dues:** $10/year. **Publications:** *The Ark* (3x a year); free to members.

★5182★ NATURE SASKATCHEWAN
206-1860 Lorne St, Suite 206
Regina,
Web: www.naturesask.ca
Phone: 306-780-9273; **Fax:** 306-780-9263; **Toll Free:** 800-667-4668
Dedicated to protecting and preserving natural ecosystems and their biodiversity in the province of Saskatchewan. Promotes appreciation and understanding of the environment through education, conservation, and research. Owns and maintains six nature sanctuaries. **Established:** 1949. **Members:** 1,400. **Dues:** $25/year ($30/year for families, $15/year for students, $20/year for seniors). **Publications:** *Nature Views* (quarterly); free to

members. *Blue Jay Journal* (quarterly); $25 for annual subscription.

★5183★ NEW BRUNSWICK TOURISM & PARKS DEPARTMENT

PO Box 6000
Fredericton,
Web: www.gnb.ca/0397/index-e.asp
Phone: 506-462-5924; **Fax:** 506-457-4984
Oversees New Brunswick's parks and tourism activities, including its nine provincial parks. Offers travel planners, guides, and maps.

★5184★ NEW ENGLAND WILD FLOWER SOCIETY

180 Hemenway Rd
Framingham, MA 01701
Web: www.newfs.org
Phone: 508-877-7630
Promotes the conservation of temperate North American plants through horticulture, education, research, habitat preservation, and conservation advocacy. Owns and operates Garden in the Woods, a 45-acre botanical garden. Coordinates the New England Plant Conservation Program, one of the first regional conservation networks in the United States. **Established:** 1900. **Members:** 3,500. **Dues:** $42/year ($58/year for families). **Publications:** *Conservation Notes*.

★5185★ NEWFOUNDLAND & LABRADOR TOURISM, CULTURE & RECREATION DEPARTMENT

PO Box 8700
St. Johns, NL
Web: www.tcr.gov.nl.ca/ter/
Phone: 709-635-4520; **Fax:** 709-635-4541; **Toll Free:** 800-563-6353
Oversees 14 provincial parks and 18 wilderness and ecological reserves in Newfoundland and Labrador. Mission includes preservation of natural heritage and promotion of outdoor recreation and tourism.

★5186★ NORTH AMERICAN FAMILY CAMPERS ASSOCIATION

PO Box 318
Lunenburg, MA 01462
Web: www.nafca.org
Plans family-oriented camping trips and provides services and benefits to members. Conducts conservation and legislative action programs. Includes local groups all over the New England region. **Established:** 1957. **Dues:** $23/year. **Publications:** *Campfire Chatter* (monthly); free to members.

★5187★ NORTH COUNTRY TRAIL ASSOCIATION

229 E. Main St
Lowell, MI 49331
Web: www.northcountrytrail.org
Phone: 616-897-5987; **Fax:** 616-897-6605; **Toll Free:** 888-454-3628

Directs and coordinates the development, maintenance, and promotion of the North Country National Scenic Trail (see separate listing in national trails section), which will extend more than 4,000 miles upon completion. Conceived in the mid-1960s, this trail links New York's Adirondack Mountains with the Missouri River in North Dakota. Today more than 1,600 miles of the trail are open for public use. **Established:** 1980. **Members:** 3,000. **Dues:** $30/year ($10/year for students). **Publications:** *North Star* (quarterly); free to members.

★5188★ NORTHWEST TERRITORIES RESOURCES, WILDLIFE & ECONOMIC DEVELOPMENT

Department of Industry, Tourism and Investment
PO Box 1320
Yellowknife,
Web: www.iti..nt.ca
Phone: 867-920-8974; **Fax:** 867-873-0163
Oversees 43 parks in the Northwest Territories. Responsibilities include developing, operating and maintaining parks, visitor centers, and interpretive displays.

★5189★ NOVA SCOTIA NATURAL RESOURCES DEPARTMENT

Parks & Recreation Division
McElmonds Pond
Onslow Hwy
Belmont,
Web: www.gov.ns.ca/natr/parks/
Phone: 902-662-3030; **Fax:** 902-662-2160
Oversees Nova Scotia's 120 provincial parks. Responsibilities include planning for parks, trails, and outdoor recreational opportunities; evaluating parkland acquisition options and negotiating private land stewardship agreements; and converting abandoned railways into trail systems.

★5190★ NUNAVUT PARKS

Department of Environment
PO Box 1000
Station 1340
Iqaluit,
Web: www.nunavutparks.com
Phone: 867-975-5900; **Fax:** 867-975-5981
Following the establishment of the Territory of Nunavut in 1999, Nunavut Parks was commissioned to develop the territorial park system in order to protect natural areas and to celebrate the area's natural and cultural heritage, including its communities, diverse landscape, abundant wildlife, and rich history.

★5191★ OCEAN CONSERVANCY

2029 K St NW
Washington, DC 20006
Web: www.oceanconservancy.org
Phone: 202-429-5609; **Toll Free:** 800-519-1541
Dedicated to worldwide protection of marine wildlife and their habitats and to conservation of coastal oceans and ocean resources. Supports major international efforts to protect wildlife species threatened by international trade. Maintains 9 regional

offices around the country. **Established:** 1972. **Members:** 500,000 members and volunteers. **Dues:** $25/year. **Publications:** *Blue Planet* (quarterly); free to members.

★5192★ OCEAN FUTURES SOCIETY

325 Chapala St
Santa Barbara, CA 93101
Web: www.oceanfutures.org
Phone: 805-899-8899; **Fax:** 805-899-8898
Dedicated to exploring the global ocean, inspiring and educating people throughout the world to act responsibly for its protection, documenting the critical connection between humanity and nature, and celebrating the ocean's importance to the survival of all life on our planet. **Established:** 1999 by the merger of the Jean-Michel Cousteau Institute and the Free Willy Keiko Foundation. **Dues:** Membership is free; donations are appreciated. **Publications:** *Jean-Michael Cousteau Dispatch* (online monthly); free to members.

**★5193★ ONTARIO NATURAL RESOURCES
MINISTRY**

Ontario Parks
300 Water St 6th Fl
PO Box 7000
Peterborough,
Web: www.ontarioparks.com
Phone: 705-755-2000; **Fax:** 705-755-1677; **Toll Free:** 800-667-1940
Administers, maintains, and protects Ontario's 108 provincial parks. Agency mandate is to ensure than Ontario's provincial park system protects significant natural, cultural, and recreational environments, while providing opportunities for visitors to participate in recreational activities.

★5194★ ONTARIO NATURE (FON)

355 Lesmill Rd
Don Mills,
Web: www.ontarionature.org
Phone: 416-444-8419; **Fax:** 416-444-9866
Dedicated to protecting and conserving Ontario's natural heritage through education, scientific research, public policy, and nature protection programs. Champions woodlands, wetlands, and wildlife and preserves essential habitat through its own system of nature reserves. **Established:** 1931. **Members:** 15,000 individuals and 100 member groups. **Dues:** $40/year. **Publications:** *Seasons* (quarterly); free to members.

★5195★ OPEN SPACE INSTITUTE (OSI)

1350 Broadway, Suite 201
New York, NY 10018
Web: www.osiny.org
Phone: 212-290-8200; **Fax:** 212-244-3441
Concerned with protecting land for public benefit, providing public access to resources, protecting open space for public use, and protecting important landscapes. Focus is on New York, with large preserves in the Husdon Valley, the Catskills, and the Shawangunk Mountains. **Established:** 1974. **Members:**

Nonmembership organization. **Dues:** Donations welcome. **Publications:** *Open Space* (biannual); free online.

**★5196★ OREGON-CALIFORNIA TRAILS
ASSOCIATION**

PO Box 1019
Independence, MO 64051
Web: www.octa-trails.org
Phone: 816-252-2276; **Fax:** 816-836-0989; **Toll Free:** 888-811-6282
Dedicated to the preservation, appreciation, and enjoyment of all the trans-Mississippi migration trails to the West. Encourages study of the trails through publications and educational programs. Maintains a research library. Includes 11 regional chapters. **Established:** 1982. **Members:** 1,800. **Dues:** $45/year ($20/year for students; $60/year for families). Sliding scale of corporation/institutional membership rates. **Publications:** *Overland Journal* (quarterly); free to members. *News From the Plains* (quarterly); free to members.

★5197★ OUTWARD BOUND USA

100 Mystery Point Rd
Garrison, NY 10524
Web: www.outwardbound.org
Phone: 845-424-4000; **Fax:** 845-424-4121; **Toll Free:** 800-243-8520
Operates 5 wilderness schools and 2 urban centers that are designed to inspire self-esteem, self-reliance, concern for others, and environmental awareness and stewardship. **Established:** 1961. **Members:** Nonmembership organization. **Dues:** Donations accepted. **Publications:** *True North* (biannually); available in print and online.

**★5198★ OVERMOUNTAIN VICTORY TRAIL
ASSOCIATION**

PO Box 242421
Charlotte, NC 28224
Web: www.ovta.org
Phone: 865-933-0883
Develops, protects, and promotes the 300-mile Overmountain Victory National Historic Trail (see separate listing in national trails section). This trail traces the route of patriots across the Appalachians to the Piedmont Region of the Carolinas where they defeated British troops at the Battle of Kings Mountain, setting in motion events that led to the British surrender at Yorktown and the end of the Revolutionary War. Sponsors annual reenactment and provides education on colonial life and the American Revolution. **Established:** 1975. **Members:** 240. **Dues:** $30/year ($40/year for families; $500 lifetime membership).

★5199★ OZARK SOCIETY

PO Box 2914
Little Rock, AR 72203
Web: www.ozarksociety.net
Dedicated to the preservation of wild and scenic rivers, wilderness, and unique natural areas. Primary focus is the Ozark-Ouachita mountain region. Sponsors hiking and boating trips.

Established: 1962. **Members:** 1,600. **Dues:** $15/year. **Publications:** *Park & Paddle* (periodically); free to members.

★5200★ PACIFIC CREST TRAIL ASSOCIATION (PCTA)
5325 Elkhorn Blvd
PMB 256
Sacramento, CA 95842
Web: www.pcta.org
Phone: 916-349-2109; **Fax:** 916-349-1268; **Toll Free:** 888-728-7245
Protects, promotes, and maintains the Pacific Crest National Scenic Trail (see separate listing in national trails section), a 2,650-mile trail from Mexico to Canada. Educates the public and provides information about travel on the trail. Publishes guidebooks and conducts volunteer vacation programs. **Established:** 1977. **Members:** 6,000. **Dues:** $25/year. **Publications:** *Pacific Crest Trail Communicator* (bimonthly); free to members.

★5201★ PACIFIC RIVERS COUNCIL (PRC)
540 Oak St, Suite E
Eugene, OR 97441
Web: www.pacrivers.org
Phone: 541-345-0119; **Fax:** 541-345-0710
River conservation organization dedicated to protecting and restoring our nation's rivers, their watersheds, and native aquatic species. **Established:** 1987. **Dues:** $25/year. **Publications:** *Freeflow* (quarterly); free to members.

PARKS CANADA
(See Section 2 of this directory for descriptive information on Canadian National Parks.)

★5202★ PENNSYLVANIA FORESTRY ASSOCIATION
56 E Main St
Mechanicsburg, PA 17055
Web: pfa.cas.psu.edu
Phone: 717-766-5371; **Toll Free:** 800-835-8065
Dedicated to good forest management and responsible stewardship of all forest resources for the citizens of Pennsylvania. Seeks to increase widespread public support for all forest values, including timber, water, wildlife, minerals, recreation, and aesthetics. **Established:** 1886. **Dues:** $25/year ($15/year for students, $30/year for families). **Publications:** *Pennsylvania Forests* (quarterly); free to members.

★5203★ PRAIRIE CLUB
110 E Schiller, Suite 302
Elmhurst, IL 60126
Web: www.prairieclub.org
Phone: 630-516-1277; **Fax:** 630-516-1278
Social club and nonprofit conservation organization. Sponsors activities for the enjoyment of nature and recreation; undertakes environment restoration projects in and around the Chicago area. **Established:** 1908. **Members:** 800. **Dues:** $100/year (plus a

one-time $50 entrance fee). **Publications:** *Bulletin* (bimonthly); free to members and $15/year for nonmembers.

★5204★ PREDATOR CONSERVATION ALLIANCE
PO Box 6733
Bozeman, MT 59771
Web: www.predatorconservation.org
Phone: 406-587-3389; **Fax:** 406-587-3178
Dedicated to conserving, protecting, and restoring native predators and their habitats in the Northern Rockies and Northern Plains. Also works to increase public awareness of the important ecological role predators play. **Established:** 1991. **Members:** 1,600. **Dues:** $35/year. **Publications:** *The Home Range* newletter (quarterly); free to members. *Wild Guardian* (quarterly).

★5205★ PRESERVATION ACTION
401 F Street NW, Suite 324
Washington, DC 20001
Web: www.preservationaction.org
Phone: 202-637-7873; **Fax:** 202-637-6874
Advocates federal legislation to foster historic preservation at the local, state, and national levels. Dedicated to making historic preservation a national priority, participating in political development, and creating an environment to support the preservation initiatives of others. **Established:** 1974. **Members:** 500. **Dues:** $55/year ($25/year for students). **Publications:** *PA Newsletter* (quarterly); free to members.

★5206★ PRINCE EDWARD ISLAND TOURISM DEPARTMENT
Parks & Recreation Division
PO Box 2000
Charlottetown,
Web: www.gov.pe.ca/visitorsguide/index.php3
Phone: 902-368-4404; **Fax:** 902-368-4438; **Toll Free:** 800-463-4734
Manages Prince Edwards Island's network of 25 provincial parks (11 with campgrounds and 14 day-use only) and heritage sites.

★5207★ PROJECT FOR PUBLIC SPACES
700 Broadway, 4th Fl
New York, NY 10003
Web: www.pps.org
Phone: 212-620-5660; **Fax:** 212-620-3821
Seeks to improve the use, design, and management of public places (plazas, parks, libraries, public markets, transportation facilities, etc.) for betterment of communities. Conducts on-site observational analysis to evaluate the needs, perceptions, and preferences of uscrs. Offers workshops and training seminars to designers, government agencies, and other institutions. **Established:** 1975. **Members:** Nonmembership organization. **Publications:** Publishes wide variety of publications on design and management of public places.

★5208★ PUBLIC LANDS FOUNDATION (PLF)
PO Box 7226
Arlington, VA 22207
Web: www.publicland.org
Phone: 703-790-1988; **Fax:** 703-821-3490
Monitors federal lands administered by the Bureau of Land Management and advocates for the ecological stability of those lands. (See separate entry in this section for information on the Bureau of Land Management and a list of its state offices.) **Established:** 1987. **Dues:** $25/year. **Publications:** *Public Lands Monitor* (quarterly); free to members and $10/year for non-members.

★5209★ QUEBEC MINISTRY OF WILDLIFE AND PARKS
Parcs Quebec
2640 Boulevard Laurier, Suite 250
Quebec,
Web: www.sepaq.com
Phone: 418-890-6527; **Fax:** 418-528-6025; **Toll Free:** 800-665-6527
Sepaq is the government agency responsible for operating and maintaining Quebec's provincial parks system, which includes 22 parks, 15 wildlife reserves, and 9 resort parks.

★5210★ RAILS-TO-TRAILS CONSERVANCY (RTC)
1100 17th St NW, 10th Fl
Washington, DC 20036
Web: www.railtrails.org
Phone: 202-331-9696
Seeks to convert abandoned rail corridors and connecting open space into a nationwide network of public trails. Carries out programs of technical assistance, public education, and advocacy. To date, has established 13,600 miles of rail-trails nationwide. **Established:** 1986. **Members:** 100,000. **Dues:** $18/year. **Publications:** *Rails-to-Trails* (quarterly); free to members.

★5211★ RAINFOREST ACTION NETWORK (RAN)
221 Pine St, Fifth Floor
San Francisco, CA 94104
Web: www.ran.org
Phone: 415-398-4404; **Fax:** 415-398-2732; **Toll Free:** 800-989-7246
Works to protect tropical rainforests and humans living in and around those forests through education, grassroots organizing, and non-violent direct action. **Established:** 1985. **Dues:** $35/year. **Publications:** *World Rainforest Report* (quarterly); free to members.

★5212★ RECREATION.GOV
Dept of the Interior MS 5258 MIB
1849 C St NW
Washington, DC 20240
Web: www.recreation.gov
Phone: 202-208-3171
A U.S. federal government web site with a searchable database that provides information about all federal recreation areas. A joint project of the Department of Agriculture's Forest Service; the Department of the Interior's National Park Service, Bureau of Land Management, U.S. Fish and Wildlife Service, U.S. Geological Survey, and Bureau of Reclamation; the U.S. Army Corps of Engineers; the Department of Transportation's Federal Highway Administration; and the Tennessee Valley Authority.

★5213★ RENEWABLE NATURAL RESOURCES FOUNDATION (RNRF)
5430 Grosvenor Ln
Bethesda, MD 20814
Web: www.rnrf.org
Phone: 301-493-9101; **Fax:** 301-493-6148
A consortium of professional, scientific, and educational organizations concerned with renewable natural resources. Advances sciences and education; promotes the application of sound, scientific practices; fosters cooperation among professionals. Has established a Renewable Natural Resources Center. **Established:** 1972. **Members:** 14 organizations. **Publications:** *Renewable Resources Journal* (quarterly); $25/year.

★5214★ RIVER MANAGEMENT SOCIETY
200 Pattee Canyon Dr
PO Box 9048
Missoula, MT 59807
Web: www.river-management.org
Phone: 406-549-0514; **Fax:** 406-542-6208
Works to protect and conserve river resources. Develops and promotes professional river management techniques, influences public policy on river management issues, educates lawmakers and the public, serves as a forum for information sharing, and promotes and encourages professional development opportunities for members. Includes seven regional chapters. **Established:** 1996. **Members:** 670. **Dues:** $25/year ($20/year for students, $40/year for professionals). **Publications:** *River Information Digest* (quarterly); free to members.

★5215★ RUFFED GROUSE SOCIETY (RGS)
451 McCormick Rd
Coraopolis, PA 15108
Web: www.ruffedgrousesociety.org
Phone: 412-262-4044; **Fax:** 412-262-9207; **Toll Free:** 888-564-6747
Dedicated to increasing the numbers of ruffed grouse, American woodcock, and other forest wildlife through habitat conservation, management, and improvement projects. Maintains 130 chapters across North America. **Established:** 1961. **Members:** 20,000. **Dues:** $25/year ($10/year for students). **Publications:** *Ruffed Grouse Society* (quarterly); free to members.

★5216★ RVING WOMEN
PO Box 1940
Apache Junction, AZ 85217
Web: www.rvingwomen.org
Phone: 480-671-6226; **Fax:** 480-671-6230; **Toll Free:** 888-557-8464
A support organization for women RVers (RV ownership not

required for membership). Provides women with education, training, and a means of networking for traveling and camping. A member traveling in the United States and portions of Canada and Mexico can call other members for information and support. Sponsors rallies, caravans, and classes. **Established:** 1991. **Members:** 2,500. **Dues:** $55/year (plus a one-time processing fee of $10). **Publications:** *RVing Women* (bimonthly); free to members.

★5217★ SANTA FE TRAIL ASSOCIATION
c/o Santa Fe Trail Ctr
1349 K-156 Hwy
Larned, KS 67550
Web: www.santafetrail.org
Phone: 620-285-2054
Promotes public awareness of and appreciation for the Santa Fe National Historic Trail, a 1,203-mile route from central Missouri to Santa Fe, New Mexico. (See separate entry in national trails section.) **Established:** 1986. **Members:** 800. **Dues:** $25/year ($15/year for students). **Publications:** *Wagon Tracks* (quarterly); free to members.

**★5218★ SASKATCHEWAN ENVIRONMENT
DEPARTMENT**
Provincial Parks Branch
3211 Albert St
Regina,
Web: www.se.gov.sk.ca/saskparks
Phone: 306-787-2700; **Fax:** 306-787-7000; **Toll Free:** 800-208-7070
Manages Saskatchewan's provincial parks system, which includes 34 provincial parks and 162 other designated parks. The provincial parks are classified as wilderness parks, recreation parks, natural environment parks, and historic parks.

**★5219★ SASKATCHEWAN ENVIRONMENTAL
SOCIETY (SES)**
PO Box 1372
Saskatoon,
Web: www.environmentalsociety.ca
Phone: 306-665-1915; **Fax:** 306-665-2128
Dedicated to maintaining the integrity of Saskatchewan's forests, farmlands, and natural prairie landscapes; protecting the atmosphere; promoting energy conservation and development of renewable resources; building sustainable communities and responsible waste management; and enhancing water quality of lakes and rivers. **Established:** 1970. **Members:** 350. **Dues:** $30/year. **Publications:** *Newsletter* (bimonthly); free to members in print or online.

★5220★ SAVE AMERICA'S FORESTS
4 Library Ct SE
Washington, DC 20003
Web: www.saveamericasforests.org
Phone: 202-544-9219; **Fax:** 202-544-7462
Dedicated to protecting and restoring wild and natural forests in the United States and around the world. Works to create comprehensive solutions to the problems of waste, destruction, and pollution, with a particular focus on ending the industry logging practice known as ''clearcutting.'' **Established:** 1990. **Members:** 550 groups and 1,600 individuals. **Dues:** $25/year. **Publications:** *DC Update* (quarterly), free to members.

★5221★ SAVE THE MANATEE CLUB (SMC)
500 N Maitland Ave
Maitland, FL 32751
Web: www.savethemanatee.org
Phone: 407-539-0990; **Fax:** 407-539-0871; **Toll Free:** 800-432-5646
Dedicated to saving and protecting the endangered West Indian manatee. Promotes public awareness and education on safeguarding the manatee and its habitat. Raises funds to protect manatees and their habitat. Conducts the Adopt-A-Manatee program. **Established:** 1981. **Dues:** $25/year. **Publications:** *The Manatee Zone* (quarterly); free to members.

★5222★ SAVE-THE-REDWOODS LEAGUE
114 Sansome St, Rm 1200
San Francisco, CA 94104
Web: www.savetheredwoods.org
Phone: 415-362-2352; **Fax:** 415-362-7017; **Toll Free:** 888-836-0005
Dedicated to acquiring and protecting California's ancient forests. Helped to establish the Redwood park system and works on expanding permanent protection of forest lands. Six out of every ten acres of California redwoods currently protected were saved through the work of the League. **Established:** 1918. **Members:** 50,000. **Dues:** $19/year. **Publications:** *Bulletin* (biannually); free to members.

★5223★ SCENIC AMERICA
1634 'I' St NW, Suite 510
Washington, DC 20006
Web: www.scenic.org
Phone: 202-638-0550; **Fax:** 202-638-3171
Dedicated to preserving and enhancing the natural beauty and distinctive character of America's communities and countryside. Works with citizens and elected officials to reduce billboard blight, maintain the scenic nature of highways and byways, and promote scenic conservation easements and community design guidelines. **Established:** 1978. **Members:** 6,500. **Dues:** $25/year. **Publications:** *Viewpoints* (3x/year); free to members.

**★5224★ SHENANDOAH NATIONAL PARK
ASSOCIATION**
3655 US Hwy 211 E
Luray, VA 22835
Web: www.snpbooks.org
Phone: 540-999-3582; **Fax:** 540-999-3583
Supports the scientific, educational, and historical activities of Shenandoah National Park in Virginia (see separate entry in national parks section). Dedicated to increasing public understanding, appreciation, and stewardship of the park and to provide interpretive educational materials, financial support, and

services in resource education. **Established:** 1950. **Members:** 1,000. **Dues:** $20/year ($8/year for students, $25/year for families). **Publications:** *Shenandoah Overlook* (annual); free to members and park visitors. *The Trillium* (bimonthly); free to members.

★5225★ SIERRA CLUB
85 2nd St, 2nd Fl
San Francisco, CA 94105
Web: www.sierraclub.org
Phone: 415-977-5500; **Fax:** 415-977-5799
Dedicated to exploring, enjoying, and protecting the earth's wildlands and to practicing and promoting the responsible use of the earth's resources. Maintains chapters and regional groups across the United States. Also offers support and cooperation with similar volunteer organizations around the world. **Established:** 1892. **Members:** 750,000. **Dues:** $25/year. **Publications:** *Sierra* (bimonthly); free to members and $15/year for nonmembers. *The Planet* (bimonthly); free to members and online.

★5226★ SIERRA CLUB OF CANADA
1 Nicholas St, Suite 412
Ottawa,
Web: www.sierraclub.ca
Phone: 613-241-4611; **Fax:** 613-241-2292; **Toll Free:** 888-810-4204
Concerned with protecting the integrity of global ecosystems. Focuses on five threats: loss of animal and plant species, deterioration of the planet's oceans and atmosphere, the growing presence of toxic chemicals in living things, destruction of wilderness areas, and population growth and over-consumption. **Established:** 1969. **Members:** 7,000 members and supporters. **Dues:** $40/year ($20/year for students/seniors). **Publications:** *SCAN* (quarterly); free to members and online. *Greenze Gazette* (monthly); free electronic newsletter.

★5227★ SIERRA LEGAL DEFENSE FUND
131 Water St, Suite 214
Vancouver,
Web: www.sierralegal.org
Phone: 604-685-5618; **Fax:** 604-685-7813; **Toll Free:** 800-926-7744
Provides free legal services to Canadian conservation groups and concerned citizens; works co-operatively with conservation groups and concerned citizens in solving environmental issues. **Established:** 1990. **Members:** 30,000. **Dues:** $25/year. **Publications:** *Sierra Legal Newsletter* (quarterly); free online for both members and nonmembers.

★5228★ SOCIETY FOR AMERICAN ARCHAEOLOGY (SAA)
900 2nd St NE, Suite 12
Washington, DC 20002
Web: www.saa.org
Phone: 202-789-8200; **Fax:** 202-789-0284
Dedicated to the research, interpretation, and protection of the archaeological heritage of the Americas. Seeks to advance knowledge and enhance awareness of the past to all segments of society, including governments, educators, and indigenous peoples. **Established:** 1934. **Members:** 6,600. **Dues:** $45/year. **Publications:** *American Antiquity* (quarterly); free to members and $28/year for nonmembers.

★5229★ SOCIETY OF ARCHITECTURAL HISTORIANS (SAH)
1365 N Astor St
Chicago, IL 60610
Web: www.sah.org
Phone: 312-573-1365; **Fax:** 312-573-1141
Encourages scholarly research and promotes preservation of architecture as an integral part of historical and cultural heritage. Works to advance knowledge and understanding of the history of architecture, design, landscape, and urbanism worldwide. **Established:** 1940. **Dues:** $95/year. **Publications:** *Journal of the Society of Architectural Historians* (quarterly); free to members. *Newsletter* (bimonthly); free to members.

★5230★ SOCIETY FOR ECOLOGICAL RESTORATION INTERNATIONAL (SER)
285 W 18th St, Suite 1
Tucson, AZ 85701
Web: www.ser.org
Phone: 520-622-5485; **Fax:** 520-622-5491
Interested in the repair and ecologically sensitive management of ecosystems. Facilitates communication among restorationists, encourages research into restoration, promotes awareness of the value of restoration, and contributes to public policy discussions related to restoration. **Established:** 1987. **Members:** 2,300. **Dues:** $45/year for full membership ($125/year for professionals). **Publications:** *Restoration Ecology* (quarterly); free to members. *Ecological Restoration* (quarterly); free to members. *SER News* (quarterly); free to members.

★5231★ SOCIETY OF PARK & RECREATION EDUCATORS (SPRE)
c/o National Recreation & Park Assn
22377 Belmont Ridge Rd
Ashburn, VA 20148
Web: www.nrpa.org
Phone: 703-858-0784; **Fax:** 703-858-0794; **Toll Free:** 800-626-6772
Provide a forum for interaction among recreation and park professionals who work in educational settings. Branch of the National Recreation & Park Association (NRPA). **Established:** 1966. **Members:** 700. **Dues:** $35/year. **Publications:** *SPRE News* (quarterly); free to members. *SCHOLE* (annually). Other NRPA publications also available.

★5232★ SOCIETY PROMOTING ENVIRONMENTAL CONSERVATION (SPEC)
2150 Maple St
Vancouver,
Web: www.spec.bc.ca
Phone: 604-736-7732; **Fax:** 604-736-7115

Dedicated to protecting the ecosystems of British Columbia and creating livable, sustainable communities, especially in the Lower Mainland and Georgia Basin. Uses education programs, publications, and research and media presentations to raise public awareness and to promote responsible action from business and industry. **Established:** 1969. **Dues:** $20/year. **Publications:** *The Spectrum* (quarterly); electronic newsletter free to members.

★5233★ SOCIETY FOR THE PROTECTION OF NEW HAMPSHIRE FORESTS

54 Portsmouth St
Concord, NH 03301
Web: www.spnhf.org
Phone: 603-224-9945; **Fax:** 603-228-0423
Dedicated to protecting New Hampshire's natural beauty through land protection and management, education, and advocacy. **Established:** 1901. **Members:** 10,000. **Dues:** $35/year. **Publications:** *Forest Notes* (quarterly); free to members.

★5234★ SOIL & WATER CONSERVATION SOCIETY (SWCS)

945 SW Ankeny Rd
Ankeny, IA 50021
Web: www.swcs.org
Phone: 515-289-2331; **Fax:** 515-289-1227
Scientific and educational advocate for conservation professionals and science-based natural resource management policies. Fosters policies based on long-term sustainability of soil, water, and other natural resources and recognition of the interdependence of people and the environment. 75 chapters in North America. **Established:** 1943. **Members:** 7,000. **Dues:** Varying corporate, organizational, and individual membership levels. **Publications:** *Conservogram* (monthly); free to members. *Journal of Soil and Water Conservation* (bimonthly); free to members. *Conservation Voices* (bimonthly); free to members.

★5235★ SOUTHERN UTAH WILDERNESS ALLIANCE (SUWA)

425 East 100 South
Salt Lake City, UT 84111
Web: www.suwa.org
Phone: 801-486-3161
Promotes local and national recognition of southern Utah's unique canyon country through research and public education; supports initiatives to permanently protect the Colorado Plateau and builds national support for such initiatives; provides leadership within the conservation movement through advocacy for wilderness preservation. **Established:** 1986. **Members:** 13,000. **Dues:** $30/year. **Publications:** *Redrock Wilderness* (quarterly); free to members.

★5236★ SPECIAL MILITARY ACTIVE RETIRED TRAVEL CLUB (SMART)

600 University Office Blvd, Suite 1A
Pensacola, FL 32504
Web: www.smartrving.net
Phone: 850-478-1986; **Toll Free:** 800-354-7681

Provides comradeship and information to active and retired members of the U.S. Armed Forces and Uniformed Services interested in the recreational vehicle (RV) lifestyle. Assists military installations with the improvement and expansion of their campgrounds. **Established:** 1982. **Dues:** $35/year regular membership (other membership levels available). **Publications:** *Traveler* (quarterly); free to members.

★5237★ STATUE OF LIBERTY-ELLIS ISLAND FOUNDATION

292 Madison Ave
New York, NY 10017
Web: www.statueofliberty.org
Phone: 212-561-4588
Dedicated to restoring and preserving the Statue of Liberty and Ellis Island; promotes public understanding of both monuments. (See separate entry on Statue of Liberty National Monument in national parks chapter.) Established the Ellis Island Immigration Museum, which recounts the story of the former immigration station, and the American Family Immigration History Center (AFIHC), which makes archived Ellis Island immigrant arrival records available to families and genealogical researchers. **Established:** 1982. **Dues:** $45/year.

★5238★ STUDENT CONSERVATION ASSOCIATION (SCA)

689 River Rd
PO Box 550
Charlestown, NH 03603
Web: www.thesca.org
Phone: 603-543-1700; **Fax:** 603-543-1828; **Toll Free:** 888-722-9675
Provides outdoor service opportunities for high school students and expense-paid internships for college students and other adults to assist with conservation projects in national parks, wilderness areas, and other sites nationwide. **Established:** 1957. **Members:** 3,000 annual members and 50,000 alumni. **Dues:** Donations accepted. **Publications:** *e-Volunteer* (quarterly); electronic newsletter, free to members.

★5239★ SURRATT SOCIETY

PO Box 427
Clinton, MD 20735
Web: www.surratt.org/su_scty.html
Phone: 301-868-1121; **Fax:** 301-868-8177
Dedicated to the preservation and interpretation of historic Surratt House. Assists the Maryland Park and Planning Commission in the preservation and interpretation of the Surratt House and Tavern. Encourages ongoing research into the role that this site played in the story surrounding the assassination of Abraham Lincoln and into 19th century culture. **Established:** 1975. **Members:** 1,200. **Dues:** $7/year. **Publications:** *Surratt Courier* (monthly); free to members.

★5240★ TALL TIMBERS

13093 Henry Beadel Dr
Tallahassee, FL 32312
Web: www.talltimbers.org
Phone: 850-893-4153; **Fax:** 850-893-6470

Fosters exemplary land stewardship through research, conservation, and education. Focuses on the ecology of fire and natural resource management, including bobwhite quail and other wildlife in the southeastern coastal plain. Dedicated to helping protect the distinctive Red Hills landscape of south Georgia and north Florida and its traditional land uses. Education program transfers research and conservation information for resource management. **Established:** 1958. **Members:** 2,000. **Dues:** $65/year. **Publications:** *Quail Call* (biannually); free to members. *Tall Timbers Annual Report* (annually); free to members at the Contributing Level.

★5241★ TENNESSEE VALLEY AUTHORITY (TVA)
400 W Summit Hill Dr
Knoxville, TN 37902
Web: www.tva.gov
Phone: 865-632-2101
TVA manages the Tennessee River — the nation's fifth largest river system — for power generation, flood control, navigation, water quality, and recreation (including campgrounds, day-use areas, boat-launching facilities, and other outdoor amenities). Supplies electricity and develops economic and environmental resources in Tennessee and parts of Alabama, Georgia, Kentucky, Mississippi, North Carolina, and Virginia. **Established:** 1933 (by Congress).

★5242★ THE MOUNTAINEERS
300 3rd Ave W
Seattle, WA 98119
Web: www.mountaineers.org
Phone: 206-284-6310; **Fax:** 206-284-4977
Explores, studies, preserves, and enjoys the mountains, forests, and watercourses of the northwestern United States. Conducts activities such as hiking, climbing, and bicycling trips for members. **Established:** 1906. **Members:** 11,000. **Dues:** $73/year ($130/year for families). **Publications:** *The Mountaineer* (monthly); free to members and $15/year for nonmembers. Publishes a wide range of books on conservation, outdoor activities, and natural history in Pacific Northwest.

★5243★ THORNE ECOLOGICAL INSTITUTE
PO Box 19107
Boulder, CO 80308
Web: www.thorne-eco.org
Phone: 303-499-3647; **Fax:** 720-565-3873
Offers hands-on environmental education for young people in the eastern Rockies area of Colorado. Sponsors Project BEAR programs (Building Environmental Awareness and Respect) in public and private schools and education programs at Thorne Natural Science School. **Established:** 1954. **Publications:** *Newsletter* (biannually); free to members.

★5244★ THORNTON W BURGESS SOCIETY
6 Discovery Hill Rd
East Sandwich, MA 02537
Web: www.thorntonburgess.org
Phone: 508-888-6870; **Fax:** 508-888-1919

Educational organization dedicated to honoring the memory of Thornton W. Burgess, pioneer conservationist, children's author, and creator of Peter Rabbit. Seeks to "to inspire reverence for wildlife and concern for the natural environment." Operates the Thornton W. Burgess Museum and the Green Briar Nature Center. **Established:** 1976. **Members:** 2,000. **Dues:** $25/year. **Publications:** *The Briar Patch Observer* (annually); free to members and online.

★5245★ TIGER FOUNDATION
999 W Hastings St, Suite 1780
Vancouver,
Web: www.tigerfdn.ca
Dedicated to the preservation of wild tigers. Focuses on habitat preservation initiatives, community development programs, anti-poaching patrols, park ranger training, and tiger ecology research. **Established:** 1996. **Dues:** Donations accepted.

★5246★ TONGASS CONSERVATION SOCIETY (TCS)
PO Box 23377
Ketchikan, AK 99901
Web: www.tongassconservation.org
Phone: 907-225-3275
Dedicated to preserving the biodiversity of the many island forests of the Tongass in southeastern Alaska through protection of habitat from the pressures of industrial exploitation. **Established:** 1960s. **Dues:** $25/year ($35/year for families, $15/year for students/seniors).

★5247★ TREES FOR TOMORROW (TFT)
519 Sheridan St
PO Box 609
Eagle River, WI 54521
Web: www.treesfortomorrow.com
Phone: 715-479-6456; **Fax:** 715-479-2318; **Toll Free:** 800-838-9472
Nonprofit natural resource specialty school for elementary, middle school, and high school students in Wisconsin, upper Michigan, and northern Illinois. Offers field studies and classroom presentations to teach conservation values and demonstrate the benefits of resource management. **Established:** 1944. **Members:** 400. **Dues:** $25/year. **Publications:** *Northbound* (monthly); free to members. *Tree Tips* (biweekly); free online to members.

★5248★ TROUT UNLIMITED (TU)
1300 N 17th St, Suite 500
Arlington, VA 22209
Web: www.tu.org
Phone: 703-522-0200; **Fax:** 703-284-9400; **Toll Free:** 800-834-2419
Dedicated to preserving and protecting North America's trout and salmon fisheries and their watersheds. Relies on a network of volunteers at the local, state, and national levels to restore natural resources. **Established:** 1959. **Members:** 152,000. **Dues:** $35/year ($20/year for students/seniors). **Publications:** *TROUT* (quarterly); free to members.

★5249★ TRUST FOR PUBLIC LAND (TPL)
116 New Montgomery St, 4th Fl
San Francisco, CA 94105
Web: www.tpl.org
Phone: 415-495-4014; **Fax:** 415-495-4103; **Toll Free:** 800-714-5263
Dedicated to protecting land as a living resource for present and future generations. Helps communities, public agencies, and nonprofit organizations acquire and protect open space. Maintains regional offices in Boston, Minneapolis, New York, Santa Fe, Seattle, and Tallahassee. **Established:** 1972. **Members:** Nonmembership organization. **Dues:** Donations accepted. **Publications:** *Land and People* (quarterly); free.

★5250★ UNION OF CONCERNED SCIENTISTS (UCS)
2 Brattle Sq, 6th Fl
Cambridge, MA 02238
Web: www.ucsusa.org
Phone: 617-547-5552; **Fax:** 617-864-9405; **Toll Free:** 800-664-8276
National partnership of scientists and citizens. Combines scientific research with citizen advocacy to work for a cleaner, healthier environment and a better world. **Established:** 1969. **Members:** 75,000. **Dues:** $25/year. **Publications:** *Catalyst* (biannually); free to members. *Earthwise* (quarterly); free to members.

★5251★ UPPER MISSISSIPPI RIVER
CONSERVATION COMMITTEE (UMRCC)
555 Lester Ave
Onalaska, WI 54650
Web: www.mississippi-river.com/umrcc
Phone: 608-783-8432
Natural resource biologists, resource managers, and administrators concerned with the preservation and development of the Upper Mississippi River. Promotes responsible use of the natural and recreational resources of the river and formulates policies, plans, and programs for conducting cooperative studies. **Established:** 1943. **Members:** 200. **Publications:** *UMRCC Newsletter* (quarterly); free to members.

★5252★ US ARMY CORPS OF ENGINEERS
441 G St NW
Washington, DC 20314
Web: www.usace.army.mil
Phone: 202-272-0011; **Fax:** 202-272-1803
Manages more than 11.5 million acres of land and water for natural resources and public recreation benefits. The Corps is the nation's largest provider of outdoor recreation, operating more than 2,500 recreation areas and leasing an additional 1,800 sites to state and local parks departments and to private interests. The Corps hosts about 360 million visits a year at its lakes, beaches and other areas, and estimates that 25 million Americans visit a Corps project at least once a year. Recreation sites are managed to promote the responsible use of public lands while conserving the natural environment. Includes 34,600 civilians and 650 Army members. **Established:** 1944.

★5253★ US COMMITTEE OF THE INTERNATIONAL
COUNCIL ON MONUMENTS & SITES (US/ICOMOS
National Building Museum
401 F St NW Rm 331
Washington, DC 20001
Web: www.icomos.org/usicomos
Phone: 202-842-1866; **Fax:** 202-842-1866
Promotes the study and conservation of historic buildings, districts, and sites and encourages the exchange of information between preservationists in the United States and abroad. US/ICOMOS membership includes professionals, practitioners, supporters, and organizations committed to the protection, preservation, and conservation of the world's cultural heritage. **Established:** 1965. **Members:** 700. **Dues:** $80/year ($30/year for students). **Publications:** *US/ICOMOS Newsletter* (quarterly); free to members and online. *US/ICOMOS Scientific Journal* (annually); free to members.

US FISH AND WILDLIFE SERVICE
(See Section 4 of this directory for information on the U.S. Fish and Wildlife Service and descriptive listings of the national wildlife refuges.)

US FOREST SERVICE
(See Section 3 of this directory for information on the USDA Forest Service and descriptive listings of the national forests.)

★5254★ US ORIENTEERING FEDERATION
PO Box 1444
Forest Park, GA 30298
Web: www.us.orienteering.org
Phone: 404-363-2110
Promotes orienteering as an activity for recreation, education, personal development, and environmental awareness. Helps improve competitive performances of U.S. orienteering athletes. **Established:** 1971. **Members:** 55 organizations and 1400 individuals and families. **Dues:** $30/year ($15/year for students). **Publications:** *Orienteering North America* (8x/year); free to members.

★5255★ US PUBLIC INTEREST RESEARCH GROUP
(US PIRG)
218 D St SE
Washington, DC 20003
Web: www.uspirg.org
Phone: 202-546-9707; **Fax:** 202-546-2461
National lobbying office for state-based public interest research groups (PIRGs) across the country. The 25 state PIRGs are independent, non-profit, non-partisan public interest advocacy organizations. Promotes research, education, and advocacy in public interest areas such as clean water, clean air, consumer protection, privacy rights, and toxins reduction. **Established:** 1983. **Dues:** $15/year.

★5256★ USDA FOREST SERVICE

(See Section 3 of this directory for information on the USDA Forest Service and descriptive listings of the national forests.)

★5257★ VANCOUVER NATURAL HISTORY SOCIETY (VNHS)

PO Box 3021
Vancouver,
Web: www.naturalhistory.bc.ca/VNHS
Phone: 604-737-3074
Committed to promoting the enjoyment of nature, encouraging the wise use and conservation of natural resources, and protecting endangered species and ecosystems. **Established:** 1918. **Dues:** $40/year (lower rates for students). **Publications:** *Discovery* (2x/year); free to members. *Vancouver Naturalist* (quarterly); free newsletter.

★5258★ VOLUNTEER.GOV/GOV

736 Jackson Place
Washington, DC 20002
Web: www.volunteer.gov/gov
; **Toll Free:** 877-872-2677
One-stop, web-based portal that connects people with volunteering opportunities in federal agencies. Participating agencies include the Bureau of Land Management, National Park Service, U.S. Fish and Wildlife Service, Natural Resources Conservation Service, U.S. Geological Survey, U.S. Department of Veterans Affairs, U.S. Army Corps of Engineers, and USA Freedom Corps. **Established:** 2002.

★5259★ WALDEN WOODS PROJECT

44 Baker Farm Rd
Lincoln, MA 01773
Web: www.walden.org
Phone: 781-259-4700; **Fax:** 781-259-4710; **Toll Free:** 800-554-3569
Dedicated to protecting the land of ecological and historic significance surrounding Walden Pond, the famed retreat of author/philosopher Henry D. Thoreau. Supports the Thoreau Institute and its educational initiatives related to the study of the environment and the humanities. **Established:** 1990. **Dues:** Donations accepted.

★5260★ WASHINGTON ENVIRONMENTAL COUNCIL (WEC)

615 2nd Ave, Suite 380
Seattle, WA 98104
Web: www.wecprotects.org
Phone: 206-622-8103; **Fax:** 206-622-8113
Works to protect, restore, and preserve the environment of Washington state. Advocates for the environment at the state legislature, develops environmental policy, educates and involves the public, and takes legal action in order to protect the forests and wildlife, water and fish, open spaces, and quality of life for future generations. **Established:** 1967. **Members:** 3,500. **Dues:** $30/year ($40/year for families, $20/year for students/

seniors). **Publications:** *Washington Environmental Council* (quarterly); free to members.

★5261★ WASHINGTON TRAILS ASSOCIATION (WTA)

2019 3rd Ave, Suite 100
Seattle, WA 98121
Web: www.wta.org
Phone: 206-625-1367; **Fax:** 206-625-9249
Works to protect and enhance Washington's trail system. Provides conservation education and information about recreational opportunities. Works to increase public funding for trail construction and maintenance on public lands, and to promote the interest of hikers and other trail users. Sponsors more than 400 volunteer trail maintenance work parties each year. **Established:** 1966. **Members:** 6,300. **Dues:** $35/year. **Publications:** *Washington Trails Magazine* (monthly); free to members.

★5262★ WATER ENVIRONMENT FEDERATION (WEF)

601 Wythe St
Alexandria, VA 22314
Web: www.wef.org
Phone: 703-684-2400; **Fax:** 703-684-2492; **Toll Free:** 800-666-0206
Educational and technical organization dedicated to the preservation and enhancement of the global water environment. **Established:** 1928. **Members:** 40,000. **Dues:** $75/year (plus Membership Association dues). **Publications:** *WEF Highlights* (quarterly); free to members. Choice of one of the following is also free to members: *Water Environment and Technology* (monthly), or *Water Environment Research* (monthly).

★5263★ WESTERN CANADA WILDERNESS COMMITTEE (WCWC)

227 Abbott St
Vancouver,
Web: www.wildernesscommittee.org
Phone: 604-683-8220; **Fax:** 604-683-8229; **Toll Free:** 800-661-9453
Works for the preservation of Canadian and international wilderness through research and grassroots education. **Established:** 1980. **Members:** 40,000. **Dues:** $35/year. **Publications:** Regular educational and campaign reports.

★5264★ WESTERN NATIONAL PARKS ASSOCIATION (WNPA)

12880 N Vistoso Village Dr
Tucson, AZ 85755
Web: www.wnpa.org
Phone: 520-622-1999; **Fax:** 520-623-9519
Authorized by Congress to promote the educational and scientific activities of the National Park Service and to enhance visitor understanding of national parks in the western United States. Operates bookstores at 65 national park sites that offer trail guides, maps, and other interpretive literature. Also maintains an

online bookstore. **Established:** 1938 as Southwest Monuments Association. **Members:** 900. **Dues:** $25/year.

★5265★ **WILDERNESS INQUIRY (WI)**
808 14th Ave SE
Minneapolis, MN 55414
Web: www.wildernessinquiry.org
Phone: 612-676-9400; **Fax:** 612-676-9401; **Toll Free:** 800-728-0719
Seeks to provide experiences in nature that integrate people from diverse backgrounds. Conducts multi-day wilderness adventures and a variety of activities, including community events, research, training, equipment design, trail and facility assessments, and policy development. **Established:** 1978. **Dues:** Donations accepted.

★5266★ **WILDERNESS SOCIETY**
1615 M St NW
Washington, DC 20036
Web: www.wilderness.org
Phone: 202-833-2300; **Fax:** 202-429-3958; **Toll Free:** 800-843-8443
Works to protect America's wilderness and to develop a nationwide network of wildlands through public education, scientific analysis, and advocacy. Maintains regional offices in Anchorage, Atlanta, Boston, Boise, Bozeman, Denver, San Francisco, and Seattle. **Established:** 1935. **Dues:** $30/year. **Publications:** *Wilderness* (annually); free to members. Also publishes a range of campaign and educational reports.

★5267★ **WILDLIFE CONSERVATION SOCIETY (WCS)**
2300 Southern Blvd
Bronx, NY 10460
Web: www.wcs.org
Phone: 718-220-5100; **Fax:** 718-220-2685; **Toll Free:** 800-234-5128
Dedicated to protecting and promoting a world rich in wildlife and wilderness. Operates the nation's largest system of urban wildlife parks: Bronx Zoo, New York Aquarium, Central Park Zoo, Queens Zoo, and Prospect Park Zoo. Developed and sponsors environmental education programs and conservation programs in over 50 countries. **Established:** 1895. **Members:** 105,000. **Dues:** $75/year ($60/year for seniors). **Publications:** *Wildlife Conservation* (bimonthly); free to members.

★5268★ **WILDLIFE FOREVER**
2700 Freeway Blvd, Suite 1000
Brooklyn Center, MN 55430
Web: www.wildlifeforever.org
Phone: 763-253-0222; **Fax:** 763-560-9961
Dedicated to preserving America's natural wildlife heritage through the preservation, conservation, and management of habitats, plant life, and wildlife. **Established:** 1987. **Members:** 40,000. **Dues:** $25/year. **Publications:** *Cry of the Wild!* (quarterly); free to members.

★5269★ **WILDLIFE HABITAT COUNCIL (WHC)**
8737 Colesville Rd, Suite 800
Silver Spring, MD 20910
Web: www.wildlifehc.org
Phone: 301-588-8994; **Fax:** 301-588-4629
Corporations, conservation groups, and individuals supporting the greater use of undeveloped corporate lands for increasing animal and plant populations. **Established:** 1988. **Members:** 109. **Dues:** $25/year. **Publications:** *WIN: Wildlife in the News* (quarterly); members: $10. Nonmembers: $25.

★5270★ **WILDLIFE MANAGEMENT INSTITUTE (WMI)**
1146 19th St NW, Suite 700
Washington, DC 20036
Web: www.wildlifemanagementinstitute.org
Phone: 202-371-1808; **Fax:** 202-408-5059
Private, nonprofit, organization committed to the conservation, enhancement, and sound management of North America's wildlife and other natural resources. **Established:** 1911. **Dues:** $35/year general membership (different rates for professionals, students, institutions). **Publications:** *Outdoor News Bulletin* (monthly); free to members.

★5271★ **WILDLIFE SOCIETY**
5410 Grosvenor Ln, Suite 200
Bethesda, MD 20814
Web: www.wildlife.org
Phone: 301-897-9770; **Fax:** 301-530-2471
Seeks to enhance capabilities and achievements of wildlife professionals in conserving diversity, sustaining productivity, and ensuring responsible use of wildlife resources. Seeks to increase awareness and appreciation of wildlife values. **Established:** 1937. **Members:** 7,500. **Dues:** $64/year ($32/year for students and seniors). **Publications:** *Journal of Wildlife Management* (8x a year); $40/year for members online, $60/year for members in print and online. *Wildlife Professional* (quartery); free to members.

★5272★ **WORLD FORESTRY CENTER (WFC)**
4033 SW Canyon Rd
Portland, OR 97221
Web: www.worldforestry.org
Phone: 503-228-1367; **Fax:** 503-228-4608
Aims to increase understanding of the importance of well-managed forests and forest resources. Promotes the benefits of conservation through publications, educational programs, and exhibits. Operates the Forest Discovery Center museum, The World Forest Institute, and two demonstration forests. **Established:** 1964. **Members:** 3,000. **Dues:** $35/year. **Publications:** *Forest Perspectives* (quarterly); free to members and $25/year for nonmembers. *Branching Out* (quarterly); free to members.

★5273★ **WORLD RESOURCES INSTITUTE (WRI)**
10 G St NE, Suite 800
Washington, DC 20002
Web: www.wri.org
Phone: 202-729-7600; **Fax:** 202-729-7610

Environmental research and policy organization that creates solutions to protect the planet and improve people's lives. Works to reverse degradation of ecosystems, halt changes to Earth's climate, increase access to environmental information, and create economic opportunities for the world's poor. **Established:** 1982. **Dues:** Donations accepted. **Publications:** *WRI Digest* (monthly); subscription e-newsletter. Also publishes a wide range of scholarly reports and books on various environmental topics.

★5274★ WORLD WILDLIFE FUND (WWF)
1250 24th St NW, Suite 500
Washington, DC 20037
Web: www.worldwildlife.org
Phone: 202-293-4800; **Fax:** 202-293-9211; **Toll Free:** 800-225-5993
Largest privately supported international conservation organization in the world, dedicated to protecting the world's wildlife and wildlands. Directs conservation efforts toward three global goals: protecting endangered spaces, saving endangered species, and addressing global threats. WWF has invested in more than 13,100 projects in 157 countries and helped establish nearly 450 national parks and reserves worldwide. **Established:** 1961. **Members:** 1,200,000 **Dues:** $15/year. **Publications:** *Focus* (bimonthly); free to members.

★5275★ WORLD WILDLIFE FUND CANADA
245 Eglinton Ave E, Suite 410
Toronto,
Web: www.wwf.ca
Phone: 416-489-8800; **Fax:** 416-489-3611; **Toll Free:** 800-267-2632
Dedicated to saving life on Earth through the conservation of nature and ecological processes. Since its founding, WWF has effectively safeguarded hundreds of species and millions of acres of wildlife habitat. WWF's ultimate goal is to stop, and eventually reverse, the accelerating degradation of our planet's natural environment and to help build a future in which humans live in harmony with nature. **Established:** 1967. **Members:** 50,000. **Dues:** $25/year.

★5276★ YOSEMITE ASSOCIATION (YA)
5020 El Portal Rd
PO Box 230
El Portal, CA 95318
Web: www.yosemite.org
Phone: 209-379-2646; **Fax:** 209-379-2486
Supports Yosemite National Park through visitor services, publications, and membership activities. Provides financial support to the National Park Service. Publishes literature, brochures, and maps about the park and offers outdoor courses and trips. (See separate entry on Yosemite National Park in national parks chapter.) **Established:** 1921. **Members:** 7,000. **Dues:** $35/year. **Publications:** *Yosemite* (quarterly); free to members. *Yosemite Meditations*; free to members and $9.95 for nonmembers.

★5277★ YUKON ENVIRONMENT DEPARTMENT - PARKS BRANCH
PO Box 7203, MC V4
Whitehorse,
Web: www.environmentyukon.gov.yk.ca/parks
Phone: 867-667-5652; **Fax:** 867-393-6213
Maintains a system of parks, including natural environment parks, ecological reserves, wilderness preserves, and campgrounds throughout the Yukon Territory.

★5278★ ZOOCHECK CANADA
2646 St. Clair Ave E
Toronto,
Web: www.zoocheck.com
Phone: 416-285-1744; **Fax:** 416-285-4670
National animal protection charity established to protect wildlife in captivity in Canada. Supports mandatory licensing of zoos and wildlife displays, the closure of substandard facilities, and ending the use of native and exotic wild animals in circuses, novelty acts, and the pet trade. **Established:** 1984. **Members:** Nonmembership organization. **Dues:** Donations accepted.

The Classification Index is an alphabetical listing of all parks, subdivided by type of park (see table below). Reference is to *entry number* rather than page number. Two-letter state codes appear parenthetically after each listing.

For a complete A-Z alphabetical listing of all entries included in the directory, see the Master Index beginning on page 1057. For listings in a state-by-state arrangement, see the Geographic Index beginning on page 1011.

*Numbers cited after listings are **entry numbers** rather than page numbers.*

10. Classification Index

National Grasslands

National Heritage Areas

National Historic Sites

*Numbers cited after listings are **entry numbers** rather than page numbers.*

National Historic Trails

National Historical Parks

*Numbers cited after listings are **entry numbers** rather than page numbers.*

*Numbers cited after listings are **entry numbers** rather than page numbers.*

10. Classification Index

National Monuments

National Parks (Canada)

*Numbers cited after listings are **entry numbers** rather than page numbers.*

*Numbers cited after listings are **entry numbers** rather than page numbers.*

10. Classification Index

*Numbers cited after listings are **entry numbers** rather than page numbers.*

National Scenic Trails

National Seashores

National Wild and Scenic Rivers

National Wildlife Refuges

*Numbers cited after listings are **entry numbers** rather than page numbers.*

*Numbers cited after listings are **entry numbers** rather than page numbers.*

10. Classification Index

*Numbers cited after listings are **entry numbers** rather than page numbers.*

*Numbers cited after listings are **entry numbers** rather than page numbers.*

10. Classification Index

Parks and Conservation-Related Organizations - Canada

Parks and Conservation-Related Organizations - US

*Numbers cited after listings are **entry numbers** rather than page numbers.*

State Agencies

*Numbers cited after listings are **entry numbers** rather than page numbers.*

State Archeological Parks

State Beaches

10. Classification Index

*Numbers cited after listings are **entry numbers** rather than page numbers.*

State Conservation Areas and Conservation Parks

State Fish and Wildlife Areas

State Forests

*Numbers cited after listings are **entry numbers** rather than page numbers.*

*Numbers cited after listings are **entry numbers** rather than page numbers.*

*Numbers cited after listings are **entry numbers** rather than page numbers.*

State Historical Parks

10. Classification Index

State Marine and Underwater Parks

*Numbers cited after listings are **entry numbers** rather than page numbers.*

Sea Lion Cove State Marine Park (AK)..................... 1396
Security Bay State Marine Park (AK) 1397
Shelter Island State Marine Park (AK)...................... 1399
Shoup Bay State Marine Park (AK) 1400
South Esther Island State Marine Park (AK)................. 1402
Sullivan Island State Marine Park (AK)..................... 1405
Sunny Cove State Marine Park (AK) 1407
Surprise Cove State Marine Park (AK) 1408
Taku Harbor State Marine Park (AK) 1409
Thom's Place State Marine Park (AK)....................... 1410
Thumb Cove State Marine Park (AK) 1411
Treman (Allan H.) State Marine Park (NY) 3395
Ziegler Cove State Marine Park (AK) 1421

State Memorial Parks and Commemorative Areas

Babler (Dr. Edmund A.) Memorial State Park (MO)......... 2994
Brooks Memorial State Park (WA).......................... 4549
Carl G. Washburne Memorial State Park (OR).............. 3826
Caswell Memorial State Park (CA).......................... 1556
Chicopee Memorial State Park (MA)........................ 2676
Collier Memorial State Park (OR) 3835
Dolliver Memorial State Park (IA) 2381
Donner Memorial State Park (CA) 1574
Doyle Memorial State Park (ND) 3635
Dr. Edmund A Babler Memorial State Park (MO)........... 2994
Fishermen's Memorial State Park (RI)...................... 4104
George Wyth Memorial State Park (IA) 2388
Goddard Memorial State Park (RI).......................... 4108
Golden Memorial State Park (MS) 2955
Haines Memorial State Park (RI)........................... 4109
Hannah Duston Memorial (NH) 3254
Harkness Memorial State Park (CT) 1838
Honeyman (Jessie M.) Memorial State Park (OR)........... 3883
Hyde Memorial State Park (NM) 3372
Jessie M. Honeyman Memorial State Park (OR)............. 3883
Kitsap Memorial State Park (WA) 4588
Lee (Oliver) Memorial State Park (NM) 3380
McArthur-Burney Falls Memorial State Park (CA) 1649
Memorial Lake State Park (PA) 4036
Oliver Lee Memorial State Park (NM)...................... 3380
Pilgrim Memorial (Plymouth Rock) State Park (MA)........ 2736
Plymouth Rock (Pilgrim Memorial State Park) (MA)........ 2736
Putnam Memorial State Park (CT) 1860
Rock Bridge Memorial State Park (MO).................... 3036
TH Stone Memorial Saint Joseph Peninsula State Park (FL)... 2032
Vietnam Veterans Memorial State Park (NM) 3391
Washburne (Carl G.) Memorial State Park (OR) 3826
Watters Smith Memorial State Park (WV) 4703
Whitewater Memorial State Park (IN) 2366
World War II Memorial State Park (RI) 4116
Wyth (George) Memorial State Park (IA) 2388

State Monuments

Beckley Furnace Industrial Monument (CT)................. 1817
Diamond Head State Monument (HI)....................... 2119
Halekii-Pihana Heiau State Monument (HI) 2121
Hearst San Simeon State Historical Monument (CA) 1603
Iao Valley State Monument (HI)........................... 2125
Iolani Palace State Monument (HI)......................... 2126
Kohala Historical Sites State Monument (HI).............. 2136
Kukaniloko Birthstones State Monument (HI) 2138
Lava Tree State Monument (HI)........................... 2141
Myles Standish Monument State Reservation (MA) 2726

Puu o Mahuka Heiau State Monument (HI) 2155
Royal Mausoleum State Monument (HI).................... 2157
Standish (Myles) Monument State Reservation (MA)........ 2726
Ulupo Heiau State Monument (HI)......................... 2160

State Museums

Arkansas Museum of Natural Resources (AR) 1454
Arkansas Post Museum (AR)............................... 1455
California State Capitol Museum (CA) 1542
California State Indian Museum (CA) 1543
California State Mining & Mineral Museum (CA).......... 1544
California State Railroad Museum (CA) 1545
Dahlonega Gold Museum State Historic Site (GA) 2058
Jefferson Landing State Historic Site & Missouri State
    Museum (MO)....................................... 3011
Plantation Agriculture Museum (AR)....................... 1494
Southwest Virginia Museum Historical State Park (VA)....... 4529
Wyoming Pioneer Memorial Museum (WY)................. 4799

State Natural Areas

Aiken State Natural Area (SC) 4120
Bandon State Natural Area (OR).......................... 3805
Beaver Creek Nature Area (SD) 4171
Big Stone Island Nature Area (SD) 4173
Burgess Falls State Natural Area (TN)...................... 4236
Cache River State Natural Area (IL) 2208
Caledon Natural Area (VA)................................ 4502
Cape Kiwanda State Natural Area (OR) 3822
Chesterfield Gorge Natural Area (NH)...................... 3234
Clark Creek Natural Area (MS) 2951
Clay Myers State Natural Area at Whalen Island (OR)....... 3832
Coquille Myrtle Grove State Natural Site (OR)............. 3836
Cossatot River State Park-Natural Area (AR) 1459
Croft State Natural Area (SC) 4131
Darlingtonia State Natural Site (OR) 3842
Devil's Punchbowl State Natural Area (OR) 3847
Devils River State Natural Area (TX) 4312
Devil's Sinkhole State Natural Area (TX) 4313
Dunbar Cave State Natural Area (TN) 4244
Enchanted Rock State Natural Area (TX) 4317
Erratic Rock State Natural Site (OR) 3854
Fort Rock State Natural Area (OR) 3859
Franklin Creek State Natural Area (IL) 2229
Frozen Head State Natural Area (TN) 4249
Fults Hill Prairie & Kidd Lake State Natural Areas (IL) 2230
George W. Joseph State Natural Area (OR) 3864
Golden & Silver Falls State Natural Area (OR).............. 3866
Goose Lake Prairie State Natural Area (IL) 2234
Government Canyon State Natural Area (TX) 4335
Harry "Babe" Woodyard State Natural Area (IL)........... 2237
Hill Country State Natural Area (TX) 4337
Honey Creek State Natural Area (TX)...................... 4338
Illinois Caverns State Natural Area (IL) 2247
Joseph (George W.) State Natural Area (OR) 3864
Keowee-Toxaway State Natural Area (SC).................. 4143
Kidd Lake (& Fults Hill Prairie) State Natural Areas (IL).... 2230
LaFramboise Island Nature Area (SD)...................... 4185
Lausmann (Vinzenz) Memorial State Natural Area (OR) 3955
Lee State Natural Area (SC) 4150
Lost Maples State Natural Area (TX)...................... 4359
Madison Boulder Natural Area (NH) 3260
Menominee River Natural Resources Area (WI) 4746
Morgan Run Natural Environment Area (MD).............. 2630

*Numbers cited after listings are **entry numbers** rather than page numbers.*

State Parks

*Numbers cited after listings are **entry numbers** rather than page numbers.*

*Numbers cited after listings are **entry numbers** rather than page numbers.*

*Numbers cited after listings are **entry numbers** rather than page numbers.*

*Numbers cited after listings are **entry numbers** rather than page numbers.*

*Numbers cited after listings are **entry numbers** rather than page numbers.*

*Numbers cited after listings are **entry numbers** rather than page numbers.*

*Numbers cited after listings are **entry numbers** rather than page numbers.*

*Numbers cited after listings are **entry numbers** rather than page numbers.*

*Numbers cited after listings are **entry numbers** rather than page numbers.*

*Numbers cited after listings are **entry numbers** rather than page numbers.*

*Numbers cited after listings are **entry numbers** rather than page numbers.*

*Numbers cited after listings are **entry numbers** rather than page numbers.*

*Numbers cited after listings are **entry numbers** rather than page numbers.*

*Numbers cited after listings are **entry numbers** rather than page numbers.*

*Numbers cited after listings are **entry numbers** rather than page numbers.*

*Numbers cited after listings are **entry numbers** rather than page numbers.*

*Numbers cited after listings are **entry numbers** rather than page numbers.*

Wilmington State Parks (DE) 1894
Wilson (Justin P.) Cumberland Trail State Park (TN) 4256
Wilson State Park (KS) 2457
Wilson State Park (MI) 2870
Wilson-Tuscarora State Park (NY) 3585
Winchester Lake State Park (ID) 2195
Wind Creek State Park (AL) 1299
Windley Key Fossil Reef Geological State Park (FL) 2044
Winslow State Park (NH) 3290
Winter (R. B.) State Park (PA) 4062
Withrow Springs State Park (AR) 1503
WJ Hayes State Park (MI) 2871
Wolf Creek State Park (IL) 2325
Wolf Run State Park (OH) 3740
Wolfe's Neck Woods State Park (ME) 2601
Wompatuck State Park (MA) 2766
Wood-Tikchik State Park (AK) 1418
Woodford State Park (VT) 4492
Woodlawn Beach State Park (NY) 3586
Woods Island State Park (VT) 4493
Woolly Hollow State Park (AR) 1504
Worlds End State Park (PA) 4089
Wyalusing State Park (WI) 4773
Wye Oak State Park (MD) 2659
Yakima Sportsman State Park (WA) 4652
Yampa River State Park (CO) 1813
Yatesville Lake State Park (KY) 2511
Ybor City Museum State Park (FL) 2045
Yellow Bay State Park (MT) 3110
Yellow Bluff Fort Historic State Park (FL) 2046
Yellow Creek State Park (PA) 4090
Yellowstone Lake State Park (WI) 4774
York River State Park (VA) 4535
Young State Park (MI) 2873
Yuba State Park (UT) 4438
Yulee Sugar Mill Ruins Historic State Park (FL) 2048
Zippel Bay State Park (MN) 2948

State Parks (Miscellaneous)

Ahukini State Recreation Pier (HI) 2116
Allagash Wilderness Waterway (ME) 2553
Alsea Bay Historic Interpretive Center (OR) 3802
Barton Warnock Environmental Education Center (TX) 4290
Blackstone River Bikeway (RI) 4096
Breaks Interstate Park (VA) 2465
Breaks Interstate Park (VA) 4500
Burleigh H. Murray Ranch (CA) 1537
Cedar Rock (IA) 2379
Charlestown Breachway (RI) 4099
Choptank River Fishing Piers (MD) 2610
Daniel Webster Birthplace (NH) 3238
Deer Mountain Campground (NH) 3239
Delta Meadows (CA) 1570
Dunn's Creek (FL) 1935
East Bay Bike Path (RI) 4101
Endicott Rock (NH) 3244
Farley (Senator Frank S.) State Marina (NJ) 3338
Forked River State Marina (NJ) 3310
Fortescu State Marina (NJ) 3312
Great Salt Lake State Marina (UT) 4412
Hearst Castle (CA) 1603
Hermitage (The) (NJ) 3345
Historic Governors' Mansion (WY) 4790
Holbrook Island Sanctuary (ME) 2577
Indio Hills Palms (CA) 1614

Jacobsburg Environmental Education Center (PA) 4012
Jennings Environmental Education Center (PA) 4013
John Marsh Home (CA) 1618
Kakaako Waterfront Park (HI) 2129
Kewalo Basin (HI) 2135
Kings Gap Environmental Education & Training Center (PA) . . 4017
Leonardo State Marina (NJ) 3323
Liberty Landing State Marina (NJ) 3324
Marsh (John) Home (CA) 1618
Murray (Burleigh H.) Ranch (CA) 1537
Nolde Forest Environmental Education Center (PA) 4044
Norristown Farm Park (PA) 4045
Orman House (FL) 2005
Point Lobos Ranch (CA) 1691
Point Montara Light Station (CA) 1693
Quabbin Reservoir Watershed (MA) 2739
Roger Pryor Pioneer Backcountry (MO) 3037
Schooner Ernestina (MA) 2747
Senator Frank S. Farley State Marina (NJ) 3338
Sideling Hill Exhibit Center (MD) 2649
Somers Cove Marina (MD) 2652
Spirit Mound Historic Prairie (SD) 4219
Verdugo Mountains (CA) 1756
Waimea State Recreation Pier (HI) 2169
Ward Creek (CA) 1757
Warnock (Barton) Environmental Education Center (TX) 4290

State Preserves

Adams Homestead & Nature Preserve (SD) 4168
Alaska Chilkat Bald Eagle Preserve (AK) 1305
Allen David Broussard Catfish Creek Preserve State
   Park (FL) 1900
Anclote Key Preserve State Park (FL) 1903
Bethel Beach Natural Area Preserve (VA) 4499
Black Mesa State Park & Nature Preserve (OK) 3750
Bush Mill Stream Natural Area Preserve (VA) 4501
Caleb Smith State Park Preserve (NY) 3413
Charlotte Harbor Preserve State Park (FL) 1920
Chilkat Bald Eagle Preserve (AK) 1305
Clay Pit Ponds State Park Preserve (NY) 3428
Connetquot River State Park Preserve (NY) 3433
Cross Ranch State Nature Preserve (ND) 3630
Crystal River Preserve State Park (FL) 1924
Estero Bay Preserve State Park (FL) 1940
Fakahatchee Strand Preserve State Park (FL) 1941
Fort Atkinson State Preserve (IA) 2385
Goshen Pass Natural Area Preserve (VA) 4511
Gunlogson State Nature Preserve (ND) 3646
Head of the Mountain State Nature Preserve (ND) 3647
HR Morgan State Nature Preserve (ND) 3649
Kissimmee Prairie Preserve State Park (FL) 1975
Lower Wekiva River Preserve State Park (FL) 1991
Minnewaska State Park Preserve (NY) 3511
Morgan (H. R.) State Nature Preserve (ND) 3649
Paynes Prairie Preserve State Park (FL) 2008
Pumpkin Hill Creek Preserve State Park (FL) 2012
River Rise Preserve State Park (FL) 2015
Rockefeller State Park Preserve (NY) 3543
Saint Lucie Inlet Preserve State Park (FL) 2018
Saint Sebastian River Preserve State Park (FL) 2019
San Felasco Hammock Preserve State Park (FL) 2020
Sandhills Nature Preserve (NC) 3622
Savannas Preserve State Park (FL) 2023
Seabranch Preserve State Park (FL) 2024
Sentinel Butte State Nature Preserve (ND) 3657

*Numbers cited after listings are **entry numbers** rather than page numbers.*

State Recreation Areas and Sites

*Numbers cited after listings are **entry numbers** rather than page numbers.*

*Numbers cited after listings are **entry numbers** rather than page numbers.*

State Reserves and Reservations

*Numbers cited after listings are **entry numbers** rather than page numbers.*

State Resort Parks

State Resources Management Areas

State Scenic Corridors and Viewpoints

State Trails

*Numbers cited after listings are **entry numbers** rather than page numbers.*

State Waysides

Urban Parks

*Numbers cited after listings are **entry numbers** rather than page numbers.*

US Government Agencies

*Numbers cited after listings are **entry numbers** rather than page numbers.*

10. Classification Index

13. SPECIAL FEATURES INDEX

The Special Features Index is an alphabetical listing of geographic and historical references described in the text portion of the park listings, such as references to a particular battle, a fort, a historical personage, a mountain peak, etc. Features are listed alphabetically, and then further subdivided by state; reference is to *entry number,* not page number.

*Numbers cited after listings are **entry numbers** rather than page numbers.*

*Numbers cited after listings are **entry numbers** rather than page numbers.*

*Numbers cited after listings are **entry numbers** rather than page numbers.*

*Numbers cited after listings are **entry numbers** rather than page numbers.*

*Numbers cited after listings are **entry numbers** rather than page numbers.*

*Numbers cited after listings are **entry numbers** rather than page numbers.*

*Numbers cited after listings are **entry numbers** rather than page numbers.*

*Numbers cited after listings are **entry numbers** rather than page numbers.*

*Numbers cited after listings are **entry numbers** rather than page numbers.*

*Numbers cited after listings are **entry numbers** rather than page numbers.*

*Numbers cited after listings are **entry numbers** rather than page numbers.*

*Numbers cited after listings are **entry numbers** rather than page numbers.*

*Numbers cited after listings are **entry numbers** rather than page numbers.*

*Numbers cited after listings are **entry numbers** rather than page numbers.*

11. Special Features Index

*Numbers cited after listings are **entry numbers** rather than page numbers.*

14. GEOGRAPHIC INDEX

The Geographic Index includes state-by-state listing of all the parks, forests, refuges, historic sites, and other properties, agencies, and organizations listed in the main body of the directory. Citations followed by a star (★) refer to parks, forests, or trails that are located under more than one state. For example, the Appalachian National Scenic Trail, which extends from Maine to Georgia, is listed in the index under 14 different states. Listings for U.S. Territories (American Samoa, Virgin Islands) are included alphabetically among the state listings. Canadian national parks are arranged by province and appear at the end of the U.S. state listings.

For a complete A-Z alphabetical listing of all entries included in the directory, see the Master Index beginning on page 1057. For listings arranged by park unit, see the Classification Index beginning on page 949.

*Numbers cited after listings are **entry numbers** rather than page numbers.*

12. Geographic Index

*Numbers cited after listings are **entry numbers** rather than page numbers.*

*Numbers cited after listings are **entry numbers** rather than page numbers.*

California

*Numbers cited after listings are **entry numbers** rather than page numbers.*

*Numbers cited after listings are **entry numbers** rather than page numbers.*

*Numbers cited after listings are **entry numbers** rather than page numbers.*

12. Geographic Index

Colorado

*Numbers cited after listings are **entry numbers** rather than page numbers.*

Connecticut

*Numbers cited after listings are **entry numbers** rather than page numbers.*

*Numbers cited after listings are **entry numbers** rather than page numbers.*

12. Geographic Index

*Numbers cited after listings are **entry numbers** rather than page numbers.*

12. Geographic Index

Georgia

*Numbers cited after listings are **entry numbers** rather than page numbers.*

*Numbers cited after listings are **entry numbers** rather than page numbers.*

12. Geographic Index

*Numbers cited after listings are **entry numbers** rather than page numbers.*

*Numbers cited after listings are **entry numbers** rather than page numbers.*

Kansas

Kentucky

*Numbers cited after listings are **entry numbers** rather than page numbers.*

12. Geographic Index

Louisiana

Maine

*Numbers cited after listings are **entry numbers** rather than page numbers.*

Maryland

*Numbers cited after listings are **entry numbers** rather than page numbers.*

12. Geographic Index

Numbers cited after listings are **entry numbers** rather than page numbers.

1029

Michigan

*Numbers cited after listings are **entry numbers** rather than page numbers.*

Minnesota

*Numbers cited after listings are **entry numbers** rather than page numbers.*

Mississippi

*Numbers cited after listings are **entry numbers** rather than page numbers.*

Missouri

*Numbers cited after listings are **entry numbers** rather than page numbers.*

Montana

Nebraska

*Numbers cited after listings are **entry numbers** rather than page numbers.*

12. Geographic Index

Nevada

*Numbers cited after listings are **entry numbers** rather than page numbers.*

*Numbers cited after listings are **entry numbers** rather than page numbers.*

12. Geographic Index

New Mexico

*Numbers cited after listings are **entry numbers** rather than page numbers.*

New York

*Numbers cited after listings are **entry numbers** rather than page numbers.*

*Numbers cited after listings are **entry numbers** rather than page numbers.*

*Numbers cited after listings are **entry numbers** rather than page numbers.*

*Numbers cited after listings are **entry numbers** rather than page numbers.*

Oklahoma

*Numbers cited after listings are **entry numbers** rather than page numbers.*

*Numbers cited after listings are **entry numbers** rather than page numbers.*

*Numbers cited after listings are **entry numbers** rather than page numbers.*

Pennsylvania

*Numbers cited after listings are **entry numbers** rather than page numbers.*

Puerto Rico

Rhode Island

*Numbers cited after listings are **entry numbers** rather than page numbers.*

12. Geographic Index

*Numbers cited after listings are **entry numbers** rather than page numbers.*

Tennessee

*Numbers cited after listings are **entry numbers** rather than page numbers.*

12. Geographic Index

*Numbers cited after listings are **entry numbers** rather than page numbers.*

Utah

*Numbers cited after listings are **entry numbers** rather than page numbers.*

12. Geographic Index

Vermont

Virgin Islands

Virginia

*Numbers cited after listings are **entry numbers** rather than page numbers.*

*Numbers cited after listings are **entry numbers** rather than page numbers.*

*Numbers cited after listings are **entry numbers** rather than page numbers.*

*Numbers cited after listings are **entry numbers** rather than page numbers.*

Wyoming

CANADA

Alberta

British Columbia

*Numbers cited after listings are **entry numbers** rather than page numbers.*

*Numbers cited after listings are **entry numbers** rather than page numbers.*

15. MASTER INDEX

The Master Index is an alphabetical listing of all the parks, forests, refuges, trails, byways, and organizations described in the directory. Reference is to *entry number* rather than page number. Two-letter state or province codes appear parenthetically after each listing.

To see listings arranged by type of park unit, refer to the Classification Index beginning on page 949. For listings in a state-by-state arrangement, see the Geographic Index beginning on page 1011.

*Numbers cited after listings are **entry numbers** rather than page numbers.*

*Numbers cited after listings are **entry numbers** rather than page numbers.*

*Numbers cited after listings are **entry numbers** rather than page numbers.*

*Numbers cited after listings are **entry numbers** rather than page numbers.*

13. Master Index

*Numbers cited after listings are **entry numbers** rather than page numbers.*

C

*Numbers cited after listings are **entry numbers** rather than page numbers.*

*Numbers cited after listings are **entry numbers** rather than page numbers.*

*Numbers cited after listings are **entry numbers** rather than page numbers.*

*Numbers cited after listings are **entry numbers** rather than page numbers.*

*Numbers cited after listings are **entry numbers** rather than page numbers.*

*Numbers cited after listings are **entry numbers** rather than page numbers.*

*Numbers cited after listings are **entry numbers** rather than page numbers.*

13. Master Index

*Numbers cited after listings are **entry numbers** rather than page numbers.*

*Numbers cited after listings are **entry numbers** rather than page numbers.*

G

*Numbers cited after listings are **entry numbers** rather than page numbers.*

*Numbers cited after listings are **entry numbers** rather than page numbers.*

H

*Numbers cited after listings are **entry numbers** rather than page numbers.*

*Numbers cited after listings are **entry numbers** rather than page numbers.*

13. Master Index

I

*Numbers cited after listings are **entry numbers** rather than page numbers.*

*Numbers cited after listings are **entry numbers** rather than page numbers.*

*Numbers cited after listings are **entry numbers** rather than page numbers.*

*Numbers cited after listings are **entry numbers** rather than page numbers.*

13. Master Index

13. Master Index

*Numbers cited after listings are **entry numbers** rather than page numbers.*

*Numbers cited after listings are **entry numbers** rather than page numbers.*

*Numbers cited after listings are **entry numbers** rather than page numbers.*

*Numbers cited after listings are **entry numbers** rather than page numbers.*

13. Master Index

*Numbers cited after listings are **entry numbers** rather than page numbers.*

*Numbers cited after listings are **entry numbers** rather than page numbers.*

*Numbers cited after listings are **entry numbers** rather than page numbers.*

*Numbers cited after listings are **entry numbers** rather than page numbers.*

*Numbers cited after listings are **entry numbers** rather than page numbers.*

*Numbers cited after listings are **entry numbers** rather than page numbers.*

Q

*Numbers cited after listings are **entry numbers** rather than page numbers.*

*Numbers cited after listings are **entry numbers** rather than page numbers.*

13. Master Index

S

*Numbers cited after listings are **entry numbers** rather than page numbers.*

*Numbers cited after listings are **entry numbers** rather than page numbers.*

13. Master Index

*Numbers cited after listings are **entry numbers** rather than page numbers.*

*Numbers cited after listings are **entry numbers** rather than page numbers.*

Master Index

13. Master Index

13. Master Index

*Numbers cited after listings are **entry numbers** rather than page numbers.*

*Numbers cited after listings are **entry numbers** rather than page numbers.*

U

*Numbers cited after listings are **entry numbers** rather than page numbers.*

*Numbers cited after listings are **entry numbers** rather than page numbers.*

*Numbers cited after listings are **entry numbers** rather than page numbers.*

*Numbers cited after listings are **entry numbers** rather than page numbers.*

Y

Z

*Numbers cited after listings are **entry numbers** rather than page numbers.*

Notes

Notes